13.50

THE ABINGDON BIBLE COMMENTARY

Edited by

FREDERICK CARL EISELEN
President and Professor of Old Testament Interpretation
Garrett Biblical Institute

EDWIN LEWIS
Professor of Systematic Theology in the College of Theology of
Drew University

and

DAVID G. DOWNEY
General Editor of the Abingdon Texts

A DOUBLEDAY — GALILEE BOOK

DOUBLEDAY & COMPANY, INC.
GARDEN CITY, NEW YORK

Copyright, 1929, by
The Abingdon Press, Inc.

Copyright renewal 1957 by Abingdon Press

All rights reserved, including that of translation
into foreign languages, including the Scandinavian.
This reprint edition is by permission of
The Abingdon Press, Inc.

ISBN: 0-385-14877-1

Printed in the United States of America

FOREWORD

THE ABINGDON BIBLE COMMENTARY utilizes the rich treasures of present-day biblical scholarship for practical and evangelical purposes. THE COMMENTARY will be found to be characterized by sound but unobtrusive scholarship, evangelical sympathy, social idealism, religious vitality, and directness and simplicity of expression. Many questions concerning the Scriptures which were once hotly debated are now generally regarded as settled. THE COMMENTARY is written from the standpoint of these accepted results while at the same time due attention is given to the processes by which they have been attained, and to all other matters necessary to adequate exposition and interpretation. While the elucidation of the religious and ethical significance of the Bible is the prime consideration, this is possible only as there is scholarly investigation of certain preliminary questions.

That there is need for such a volume is undeniable. The continuous advance in scientific discovery, in philosophic ideals, and in the social application of these discoveries and ideals necessitates a new appraisal and a restatement of religious truth. Within the limits of the distinctive emphases of historical Christianity, the scholars who have contributed to the making of this COMMENTARY have been allowed full freedom of expression. Devout and earnest thinkers of the earlier days met the attacks made upon Christianity by using the intellectual method and weaponry fit for that time. They spoke and wrote an understandable language, a language in harmony with the social, scientific, and philosophic knowledge of the age. The Church is permanently in the debt of such men. But knowledge has increased, vision is vastly widened, the material universe is immeasurably expanded, and life itself has become inconceivably complex. These new material and intellectual expansions and conceptions are providing the enemies of the faith with new weapons for their attack. They must be met on their own ground, with a weaponry and a method suited to the time. THE COMMENTARY has been prepared to help those who are interested in this vital problem of strengthening the appeal of the Christian religion by making clearer and more intelligible its essential message concerning God and man.

An examination of the list of contributors will show that no effort has been spared to make the COMMENTARY an expression of the ripest and most reverent biblical scholarship of the English-speaking world. The United States, Canada, England, Scotland, Wales, Australia, and India have been laid under tribute in the purpose to secure the persons whose spirit and training fitted them for the specific tasks assigned. A study of the general articles and of the individual commentaries will show how well we have succeeded in our purpose. Thoughtful pastors, intelligent laymen, and teachers in Sunday and Week-Day Schools of Religious Education will find in the wealth of material contained in this volume an invaluable aid to their preaching and teaching.

DAVID G. DOWNEY.

CONTRIBUTORS

Herbert T. Andrews, D.D.
Late Professor of New Testament Exegesis and Criticism, Hackney and New College, London.
Hebrews.

J. Vernon Bartlet, M.A., D.D.
Professor of Church History, Mansfield College, Oxford.
The Life and Work of Paul.

George Herbert Box, M.A., D.D.
Davidson Professor of Old Testament Studies, University of London; Fellow of King's College, London; Honorary Canon of St. Albans.
The Historical and Religious Backgrounds of the Early Christian Movement.

Ernest Ward Burch, S.T.B., Ph.D.
Associate Professor of New Testament Interpretation, Garrett Biblical Institute, Evanston, Illinois.
The Structure of the Synoptic Gospels. Acts.

Henry J. Cadbury, Ph.D.
Professor of Biblical Literature, Bryn Mawr College, Bryn Mawr, Pennsylvania.
The Language of the New Testament.

S. Parkes Cadman, S.T.D., L.H.D., LL.D.
Minister of the Central Congregational Church, Brooklyn, New York; Ex-President of the Federal Council of the Churches of Christ in America.
The Use of the Bible in Preaching.

Shirley Jackson Case, Ph.D., D.D.
Professor of Early Church History, and Chairman of the Department of Church History, Divinity School of the University of Chicago.
Second Peter. Jude.

Frank Bertram Clogg, M.A., B.D.
Professor of New Testament Language and Literature, Wesleyan Theological College, Richmond, Surrey, England.
Revelation.

Earle B. Cross, Ph.D.
Hoyt Professor of the Hebrew Language and Literature, Rochester Theological Seminary, Rochester, New York.
Proverbs.

J. Newton Davies, B.D., S.T.D.
Professor of the Greek New Testament, College of Theology, Drew University, Madison, New Jersey.
Matthew. Mark.

Charles Harold Dodd, M.A.
University Lecturer in New Testament Studies, and Grinfield Lecturer on the Septuagint, University of Oxford; Yates Professor of New Testament Greek and Exegesis, Mansfield College, Oxford.
Ephesians. Colossians. Philemon.

John Dow, M.A., D.D.
Professor of New Testament Literature and Exegesis, Emmanuel College (United Church of Canada), Toronto.
Galatians.

David G. Downey, Litt.D., LL.D.
General Editor of The Abingdon Texts.
Foreword.

G. R. Driver, M.A., M.C.
Fellow, Classical Tutor, and Librarian of Magdalen College; Lecturer in Semitic Philology, Oxford.
The Formation of the Old Testament.

BURTON SCOTT EASTON, Ph.D., S.T.D.
Professor of the Interpretation and Literature of the New Testament, General Theological Seminary, New York.
First, Second, and Third John.

FREDERICK CARL EISELEN, Ph.D., D.D, LL.D.
President and Professor of Old Testament Interpretation, Garrett Biblical Institute, Evanston, Illinois.
The Bible—A Library of Religion. The Pentateuch—Its Origin and Development.

J. ALEXANDER FINDLAY, M.A.
Professor of New Testament Language and Literature, Didsbury Wesleyan Theological College, Manchester, England.
Luke.

LESLIE E. FULLER, Ph.D., D.D.
Professor of Old Testament Interpretation, Garrett Biblical Institute, Evanston, Illinois; Chairman of the Department of History and Literature of Religions, Northwestern University, Evanston, Illinois.
Bible Manners and Customs. The Literature of the Intertestamental Period. The Religious Development of the Intertestamental Period.

ALFRED ERNEST GARVIE, M.A., D.D.
Principal of Hackney and New College (Divinity School of the University of London).
John.

ALEX. R. GORDON, D.Litt., D.D.
Professor of Hebrew, McGill University; Professor of Old Testament Literature and Exegesis, United Theological College, Montreal, Canada.
The Prophetic Literature of the Old Testament. The Poetic and Wisdom Literature of the Old Testament.

WILLIAM CREIGHTON GRAHAM, Ph.D., D.D.
Professor of Old Testament, University of Chicago.
Ruth. Jonah. Nahum. Zephaniah.

WILBERT FRANCIS HOWARD, M.A., B.D.
Professor of New Testament Language and Literature, Handsworth Wesleyan Theological College, Birmingham, England.
First and Second Corinthians.

W. G. JORDAN, D.D.
Emeritus Professor of Old Testament Criticism, Queen's Theological College (United Church of Canada); Professor of Hebrew Literature, Queen's University, Kingston, Canada.
The Old Testament and Science. The Legal and Historical Literature of the Old Testament. Lamentations.

ALBERT CORNELIUS KNUDSON, Ph.D., Theol.D., LL.D.
Dean and Professor of Systematic Theology, Boston University School of Theology.
The Old Testament Conception of God.

ELMER ARCHIBALD LESLIE, S.T.D., Ph.D.
Professor of Hebrew and Old Testament Literature, Boston University School of Theology.
The Chronology of the Old Testament. Psalms I—LXXII.

EDWIN LEWIS, Th.D., D.D.
Professor of Systematic Theology, College of Theology, Drew University, Madison, New Jersey.
The Miracles of the New Testament. The New Testament and Christian Doctrine.

LINDSAY B. LONGACRE, B.D., Ph.D.
Professor of Old Testament Literature and Religion, Iliff School of Theology, Denver, Colorado.
The Bible as Literature. Numbers. Joshua.

WILLIAM FREDERICK LOFTHOUSE, M.A., D.D.
Principal and Theological Professor, Handsworth Wesleyan Theological College, Birmingham, England.
Job.

WILLIAM J. LOWSTUTER, Ph.D., D.D.
Professor of New Testament Literature and Interpretation, Boston University School of Theology.
First and Second Timothy. Titus.

FRANCIS JOHN MCCONNELL, Ph.D., S.T.D., LL.D.
Bishop of the Methodist Episcopal Church.
The Christian Approach to the Study of the Scriptures.

CHESTER C. MCCOWN, Ph.D., D.D.
Professor of New Testament Literature and Interpretation, Pacific School of Religion, Berkeley, California.
First and Second Thessalonians.

JOHN EDGAR MCFADYEN, M.A., D.D.
Professor of Old Testament Language, Literature, and Theology, United Free Church College, Glasgow.
Israel's Messianic Hope. Micah. Habakkuk. Haggai. Zechariah. Malachi.

JOSEPH F. MCFADYEN, M.A., D.D.
Hislop College (United Free Church of Scotland), Nagpur, C. P., India; Formerly Professor of New Testament Literature and Criticism, Queen's Theological College, Kingston, Ontario.
The Life of Jesus Christ.

JOHN FLETCHER MCLAUGHLIN, B.D., D.D.
Dean and Professor of Old Testament Exegesis and Literature, Faculty of Theology; Professor of Oriental Languages and Literature, Faculty of Arts, Victoria University, Toronto.
Exodus.

HENRY H. MEYER, Ph.D., Th.D.
Editor of Church School Publications for the Methodist Episcopal Church.
The Place of the Bible in Religious Education.

NATHANIEL MICKLEM, M.A.
Professor of New Testament Literature and Criticism, Queen's Theological College (United Church of Canada), Kingston, Ontario; formerly Professor of Old Testament Literature and Religion, The Selly Oak Colleges, Birmingham, England.
First and Second Samuel.

JAMES MOFFATT, D.Litt., D.D.
Washburn Professor of Church History, Union Theological Seminary, New York.
The Formation of the New Testament.

CHRISTOPHER R. NORTH, M.A.
Professor of Old Testament Languages and Literature, Handsworth Wesleyan Theological College, Birmingham, England.
The Old Testament in the Light of Archæology. The Old Testament and Criticism. Leviticus.

W. O. E. OESTERLEY, M.A., D.D.
Rector of the Church of St. Mary Aldermary, London; Examining Chaplain to the Lord Bishop of London; Professor of Hebrew and Old Testament Exegesis, King's College, University of London.
Judges.

ISMAR J. PERITZ, Ph.D., Litt.D.
Professor of Biblical Languages and Literatures, and Willard Ives Professor of the English Bible, Syracuse University, Syracuse, New York.
The Chronology of the New Testament.

ROBERT HENRY PFEIFFER, S.T.M., Ph.D.
Associate Professor of Biblical and Cognate Languages, Boston University School of Theology; Instructor in Semitic Languages, Harvard University.
Esther. Song of Songs.

IRA MAURICE PRICE, Ph.D., LL.D.
Professor Emeritus of Semitic Languages and Literatures, University of Chicago.
The Transmission of the Old Testament.

FREDERICK J. RAE, M.A.
Director of Religious Education, Training Center for Students, Aberdeen, Scotland.
How to Study the Bible.

HARRIS FRANKLIN RALL, Ph.D., D.D.
Professor of Systematic Theology, Garrett Biblical Institute, Evanston, Illinois.
The Teaching of Jesus.

ARCHIBALD THOMAS ROBERTSON, D.D., LL.D., Litt.D.
Professor of New Testament Interpretation, Southern Baptist Theological Seminary, Louisville, Kentucky.
The Transmission of the New Testament.

James Alex. Robertson, M.A., D.D.
Professor of New Testament Language, Literature, and Theology, United Free Church College, Aberdeen, Scotland.
Philippians.

Benjamin Willard Robinson, Ph.D.
Professor of New Testament Interpretation, The Chicago (Congregational) Theological Seminary.
First Peter.

George Livingston Robinson, Ph.D., D.D., LL.D.
Professor of Biblical Literature and the English Bible, McCormick Theological Seminary, Chicago.
Ecclesiastes.

H. Wheeler Robinson, M.A., D.D.
Principal of the Regent's Park (Baptist) College, London.
The Religion of Israel. Amos. Hosea.

Theodore H. Robinson, M.A., D.D.
Professor of Semitic Languages, University College of South Wales and Monmouthshire (University of Wales).
The History of the Hebrew and Jewish People. Genesis.

Robert William Rogers, Ph.D., S.T.D., D.Litt. (Oxford).
Professor of Hebrew and Old Testament Exegesis, College of Theology, Drew University, Madison, New Jersey; Professor of Ancient Oriental Literature, Princeton University.
Ezra-Nehemiah. Isaiah.

Charles Anderson Scott, M.A., D.D.
Dunn Professor of New Testament, Westminster College, Cambridge.
Romans.

D. Russell Scott, M.A., Ph.D.
Professor of Biblical Languages, Criticism and Exegesis, Scottish Congregational College, Edinburgh.
Deuteronomy.

Ernest Findlay Scott, D.D., LL.D.
Professor of New Testament Criticism, Union Theological Seminary, New York.
The New Testament and Criticism.

W. A. Shelton, M.A., D.D., F.R.G.S.
Professor of Old Testament and Hebrew, Emory University, Atlanta, Georgia.
Psalms LXXIII—CL.

David Capell Simpson, M.A., D.D.
Oriel Professor of the Interpretation of Holy Scripture, University of Oxford; Fellow of Oriel College, Oxford; Canon of Rochester Cathedral, Kent, England.
First and Second Kings. First and Second Chronicles.

Charles Fremont Sitterly, S.T.D., Ph.D.
Professor of Biblical Literature, College of Theology, Drew University, Madison, New Jersey.
Time, Money, Weights and Measurements.

Edward H. Sugden, M.A., Litt.D.
Master of Queen's College, University of Melbourne, Australia.
James.

Wilbur F. Tillett, S.T.D., LL.D.
Professor of Christian Doctrine and Dean Emeritus of the Theological Faculty, Vanderbilt University, Nashville, Tennessee.
The Divine Element in the Bible.

Edwin Edgar Voigt, M.A., Ph.D.
Assistant Professor of Old Testament Interpretation, Garrett Biblical Institute, Evanston, Illinois.
The Land of Palestine.

W. Lansdell Wardle, M.A., D.D.
Principal and Professor of Hebrew, Hartley Primitive Methodist College, Manchester; Lecturer in Biblical Exegesis and Old Testament Criticism, University of Manchester, England.
Ezekiel.

W. Gladstone Watson, D.D.
Professor of Hebrew and Old Testament Exegesis, Pine Hill Divinity Hall, Halifax, Nova Scotia.
Joel. Obadiah.

Adam C. Welch, D.D., Th.D.
Professor of Hebrew and Old Testament Literature, New College, Edinburgh.
Jeremiah.

Laura H. Wild, B.A., B.D.
Professor of Biblical Literature, Mount Holyoke College, South Hadley, Massachusetts.
English Translations of the Bible.

Herbert L. Willett, M.A., Ph.D.
Professor of Old Testament and Semitic Languages, University of Chicago.
Daniel.

Herbert G. Wood, M.A.
Professor of New Testament and Church History, The Selly Oak Colleges; Director of Studies, Woodbroke, Selly Oak, Birmingham, England.
The Parables of Jesus.

TABLE OF CONTENTS

I. Articles on the Bible as a Whole

II. Articles on the Old Testament

III. Commentary on the Books of the Old Testament

IV. Articles on the New Testament

V. Commentary on the Books of the New Testament

VI. INDEX

EXPLANATIONS, ETC.

The idea of a Commentary such as this was originally suggested to The Abingdon Press by Dr. David G. Downey, for many years past the General Editor of the Abingdon Texts. While the more technical editorial work has naturally been done by Doctor Eiselen and myself, Doctor Downey shared with us in reading the manuscripts as they were received; we have been in constant touch with him during the three years in which the Commentary has been in preparation; he has freely given us the benefit of his wide experience and sound judgment; and for these reasons we have felt it to be only proper that his name should appear on the title-page with our own.

In arranging with the contributors, the editors reserved the right of making such revision of manuscripts as seemed necessary to secure the aims of the Commentary. For the most part, this revision has been confined to eliminations, additions, re-casting sentences, harmonizing or calling attention to differences, and rearranging material. Where in a given case anything more serious than this was required, the changes were made in consultation with the contributor. The contributor is responsible for the accuracy of references to general literature, including quotations, although, as a matter of fact, the editors have verified a great many of these. Editorial notes are nowhere indicated: the editors have preferred to remain as much in the background as possible.

The original plan called for the editorial work on the Old Testament and relevant articles being done by Doctor Eiselen, and the editorial work on the New Testament and relevant articles being done by myself. A very little experience, however, showed that such a division was not feasible, and we have therefore worked alike on the entire Commentary. There were, however, certain mechanical features of the work for which I assumed the additional responsibility. These included the verification of all the Scripture references (except the references to the Pseudepigrapha); all the editorial proof-reading (except that Doctor Eiselen went over the first galley-slips after I had passed them); the task of seeing the Commentary through the press; the insertion of the cross-references; and the preparation of the index. Every care has been taken to secure accuracy and consistency, but it is too much to hope that errors of various sorts have not crept in. Those will be most charitable in regard to such errors who have had some experience of the difficulties of work of this kind. Inconsistencies, however, in the transliteration and accenting of Hebrew words and in the spelling of certain Assyrian, Babylonian, and Egyptian names, are due to the preferences of the different authors.

We have worked consistently with the needs of "the average man" in view. This principle has determined many of the features of the Commentary. The keynote is *simplicity*, without, it is hoped, any sacrifice of scholarship. We have excluded all Hebrew and Greek words. Where an author felt he needed to use these, they have been transliterated. Abbreviations have been reduced to the minimum. The exegesis is based primarily on paragraphs, not on single words and clauses. The sense or the theme of the paragraph is printed in a black-type heading. Words or phrases taken directly from the Scripture under consideration are in general printed in italics, especially where they are being commented on or explained. Whenever possible, critical notes are kept together. Although the contributors were requested to have before them the English Revised Version, reference is made to important variations from the American Standard Version, especially as noted in marginal readings, so that the Commentary will be equally available with any of the English translations. In many cases new translations are suggested by contributors, and free use has been made of paraphrase, especially in certain New Testament Epistles. Chapter breaks are plainly indicated. To do this cost us considerable space, but we felt that this was justified in the greater ease of reference thereby secured.

The cross-references are by no means exhaustive, but they total many hundreds. Their insertion, of course, had to wait until the entire Commentary was in page form and folioed. This fact sometimes made insertion difficult, which accounts for some slight irregularities in the method of reference. In addition to the cross-references by page-numbers, very free use has been made of Scripture references. The student will find these of great value. This is especially true in the case of the synoptic Gospels, where I have endeavored to indicate all the parallels and many of the resemblances to a given passage, so as to make the discussions, wherever found, at once available. In many cases the word "note" or "notes" follows a reference, but the absence of this word is not to be taken as implying that the reference is not important. To indicate every important reference was soon found to be not feasible.

The preparation of the index proved to be an exceedingly heavy task. It was at first thought that an index limited to the special articles and the introductions to the separate books would be sufficient, but eventually I felt it wise to index the entire Commentary. While I personally listed every reference in the index, I was assisted in the alphabetical arrangement by the Reverend C. A. Whitemarsh, M.A., B.D., of Rye, New York, a graduate student of Drew University, and in other ways by my daughter, Miss Velva Lewis, M.A., and I desire to acknowledge their invaluable services. The thanks of the editors are also due to the contributors for the promptness and sympathetic understanding with which they did their work, to various publishers for permission to use quotations, and to the manufacturing staff of The Abingdon Press for their patience and skill. Here, as so often, the least heeded workman is the most indispensable.

EDWIN LEWIS.

ABBREVIATIONS, ETC.

Books of the Old Testament: Gen., Ex., Lev., Num., Deut., Josh., Judg., Ruth, Sam., Kings, Chr., Ezra, Neh., Esth., Job, Psa. (singular and plural), Prov., Eccl., Songs, Isa., Jer., Lam., Ezek., Dan., Hos., Joel, Amos, Obad., Jonah, Mic., Nah., Hab., Zeph., Hag., Zech., Mal.

Books of the New Testament: Mt., Mk., Lk., Jn., Acts, Rom., Cor., Gal., Eph., Phil., Col., Thess., Tim., Tit., Philm., Heb., Jas., Pet., John, Jude, Rev.

Books of the Apocrypha: Spelled in full except occasionally Ecclus. for Ecclesiasticus, and Macc. for Maccabees.

A.D., anno Domini.
A.V., authorized version.
A.S.V., American standard version.
B.C., before Christ.
cf., compare.
ch., chapter.
edit., edition.
e.g., for example.
Eng. trans., English translation.
f., following verse(s) or page(s). (The plural ff. has not been used.)
intro., introduction.
LXX, Septuagint.
mg., margin.
MS., MSS., manuscript, manuscripts.
N.T., New Testament.
O.T., Old Testament.
p., pp., page, pages.
R.V., or E.R.V., English revised version.
v., vv., verse, verses.
ad loc., at the place.
cir., about (with dates).
ibid., same place.
op. cit., cited above.

A few other abbreviations, such as C.C., for Schaff's *Creeds of Christendom*, and C.H., for John's *Code of Hammurabi*, are explained where they are used.

Superior figures are used to indicate verses when the chapters are given, thus: Deut. 8^{10} Rom. $12^{3, 6-8, 10}$. In a reference to the same book or chapter, the book or chapter is not repeated. Thus 12^{10} occurring in Judges means Judges 12^{10}. In the same way, in a reference to the same chapter, the chapter is not given, but the verse number is preceded by v. or vv., thus: v. 16, vv. 23–28. Where the verse number is followed by a, b, c, thus, v. 8a, v. 12b, v. 24c, the reference is to the first, second, or third clause of the verse, as the case may be. Where page-numbers are followed by a or b, whether in cross-references or in the index, the first or second column of the page is intended: thus p. 294a means the first or left-hand column of page 294; p. 863b means the second or right-hand column of page 863.

I. ARTICLES
THE BIBLE AS A WHOLE

HOW TO STUDY THE BIBLE

THE BIBLE—A LIBRARY OF RELIGION

THE BIBLE AS LITERATURE

THE DIVINE ELEMENT IN THE BIBLE

THE CHRISTIAN APPROACH TO THE STUDY OF THE SCRIPTURES

THE USE OF THE BIBLE IN PREACHING

THE PLACE OF THE BIBLE IN RELIGIOUS EDUCATION

THE LAND OF PALESTINE

HISTORY OF THE HEBREW AND JEWISH PEOPLE

BIBLE MANNERS AND CUSTOMS

TIME, MONEY, WEIGHTS, AND MEASUREMENTS

ENGLISH TRANSLATIONS OF THE BIBLE

HOW TO STUDY THE BIBLE

By Professor F. J. Rae

I. General

Motives to Bible Study. The motives which may induce anyone to study the Bible are of various kinds. You may wish to know the Bible as a great *literature*. After all, it is one of the two great literatures on which our civilization is founded. The other is the Greek—Greek philosophy, Greek drama, Greek poetry, Greek history. It is obvious that no one is educated in a real sense who is ignorant of either of these great literatures. And, of course, when one realizes the historical place of the Bible in human culture one will desire to read it for pleasure, for the uplift and the joy of beautiful and noble things. Job, the songs of Israel, Ruth, Hosea—these are wonderful books merely as the productions of the human spirit.

But there is another motive—just because the Bible is not merely literature. It is claimed to be, and is, one of the great *religious books* of the world. Indeed, it is *the* religious book of humanity, and therefore we may wish to study it for what it reveals of God and truth. Its books take on a different aspect in the light of this truth, and our motive will carry us further and demand a great deal more from us if we wish really to get into the heart of the Bible.

Necessity of Understanding What the Bible Is. It is obvious, then, that we must begin our study with some general idea of what the Bible is. It is nonsense to say we must go to it with *no* preconceived ideas. What intelligent person is there without any ideas about the Bible? What we must not do is to force upon the Bible any theories of its origin or value that foreclose any important issues. And, positively, what we must do is to begin with the truths about the Bible that are on the surface, that can be gathered from the most casual acquaintance with it.

For it is clear that the Bible contains the history and the literature of a people, a history and a literature that are wholly religious because they profess to reveal the nature and will of God for man. But note, it is primarily a history and a religion for the time contemporary with the writing of any given book of the Bible. Whatever you may think of the question of revelation, at any rate you must realize that the Bible embodies a religion. There may be something beyond that, but there is that. Therefore every book in the Bible has a reference, first of all, to its own time. It has a *religious* value. Whether it has a revelation value is another question. But its religious value is first of all its value for its own time. The book of Job, e.g., is a drama in which the question of suffering is discussed. Now, that may have a reference to us, but at any rate it has a clear reference to the time when it was written, when this question of suffering had arisen and pressed for an answer. It was an answer for that period. In the same way Paul wrote his letters, not to form part of a "Bible" but simply and solely to deal with matters that had arisen in the churches in which he had a special interest. Whatever other value these letters have for us, they were primarily simply letters like our own, dealing with the problems of the churches to which they were written and giving Paul's message to *them*. We must grasp this fact firmly because it contains guidance of an essential kind for our method of study. Whatever the Bible has to say to us, it had something first of all to say to its own time, and its message to us can only come to us through its message to its own age. This does not mean that there are two truths in the Bible, one for that age and another for this, but that if there is any truth for us in the Bible, it is because the truth which was true for that time is *true for all time*. The truth about God, e.g., which a prophet gave to his own day for its own problems is an eternal truth, valid for our problems.

And this is the other thing that we find in the Bible, just *this meaning for us to-day*. The Bible professes to give a message for all time. Its religion is also a revelation. Its experiences are experiences of a God who is ready to do the same things for us as he did for Abraham, Jacob, David, and Paul. That is what the Bible says to us. And so we learn at least this much to begin with—that we must seek the truth in the Bible in its own environment. We must find what a book, or a paragraph, or an incident or a saying meant then and for the people who were to read it or who heard it. And only when we have found that can we begin to come at the significance of that book, or paragraph, or incident, or saying for us and our day and our problems and needs.

General Principles of Bible Study. The

implications of these general statements, the guidance they give us about study, will be developed in the discussions below on O.T. and N.T. study. But before applying them in detail, we may gather some broad lessons of a very general kind.

1. One is that *we must be honest with the Bible* when we study it. We must try to find out what it means, and not what we may make it mean. Preachers are the greatest sinners in this matter. If a text can be twisted into a bizarre sense, it is sometimes taken as the theme of a "clever" discourse. The most amazing meanings are got out of harmless verses in the Psalms or Proverbs or Epistles, meanings that would have surprised David or Paul beyond measure. One of the worst sins against honest interpretation is the vice of "spiritualizing" scripture. By this method we can make anything of scripture, and we might as well be dealing with the Iliad or with Thucydides. We are not interpreting the Bible but imposing on it ideas which may or may not be true and useful but are certainly not where we claim to find them. If we are to study the Bible at all, we must find what is there, what the writer meant to say. We may then apply that truth, if we wish, all round, but let us not confuse our inferences with the original truth of the passage. This habit of spiritualizing has been employed specially in the interpretation of the parables of our Lord. Speakers and writers have discoursed on the spiritual significance of this or that detail in the parable. What do the two pence given by the good Samaritan to the innkeeper stand for? Is it, as some have claimed, for the two sacraments? What does the inn stand for? For the church? Nothing is more really injurious to the Bible than this kind of thing. A parable was spoken to enforce one truth and one truth only. And the details in it are just scenery or dressing meant to give reality and vividness to the tale with no meaning whatever beyond that. The truth in the parable of the good Samaritan is that our neighbor is the man who needs us. We may *apply* that to our own day and its social problems in any legitimate manner. But the parable has one truth only, and the two pence and the inn and the oil and wine and the ass are all part of the story and nothing else. (See art., *Parables of Jesus*, p. 914b.) This rule, that we must seek only the real meaning of any passage in the Bible, the historical and actual meaning, is vital to any study of it.

2. In this connection it may be well to say that an excellent method of reaching the meaning and message of the Bible is to *read a book or section at a sitting.* This is not done nearly often enough even by those whose duty it is to expound the Word. Almost any book in the Bible can be read through in an hour or two. And there are advantages in doing this. One is the pleasure that a piece of good literature gives. You cannot receive this by the piecemeal method of careful and measured study of a few verses or a chapter a day. That method has its own place. But the other is of extreme value. Take the book of Job for example. Never mind the details of exegesis for this time. Take it as a drama written to discuss the question of suffering, and read it through in the Revised Version, or in any good translation that does justice to its poetical form. You will then realize what a great book it is. You will grasp the argument, you will see the skillful delineation of character, you will receive the general impression of its message. And you will enjoy it as you never enjoyed the Bible before. Or take a quite different book, the memoirs of Nehemiah. What a wonderful piece of autobiography that is! There is a perfect picture of the condition of the returned exiles and the difficulties of their situation. And there is a naïve self-delineation by a man who was a saint and a soldier and an administrator and a *man.* This is one way to study the Bible for pleasure and also at the same time to absorb its big messages, its broad principles, and its contributions to the solution of life's problems.

3. And this leads me to another broad generalization, that you ought to *study the Bible in a proper edition.* I refer not so much to the translation as to the form of the Bible. Let me give one or two simple examples of my meaning. A great deal of the O.T. is poetry, but you would never gather that from our "Authorized Version." Much of Isaiah is poetical in form, but it is printed as prose. Job is poetical in form, but it is printed as prose. Even the Psalms are printed as prose. The Revised Version corrects this, and therefore we should, for study, use this version. Again, our older version breaks up the Bible into chapters and verses. But there are no chapters and no verses in the original. There never were any in any version until the thirteenth century. One evil effect of this splitting up of the Bible is to give it an artificial and unreal appearance. It is not like any other book. No other book is divided up into verses. And neither is the Bible itself. It is only an artificial division of the translation that is so treated. No doubt the chapters and verses are useful now for reference, and they are retained in all translations in the margin for that purpose. But when we

study the Bible, if we are confined to the English translation, it should be in a form which reproduces the original. And I would therefore strongly recommend the student to possess a modern translation like Moffatt's, or (in the N.T.) Weymouth's, Goodspeed's, *The Twentieth Century N.T.*, Ballantine's *Riverside N.T.*, or Montgomery's *Centenary Translation of the N.T.* Moffatt's O.T. has some grave faults. But it is literal and scholarly and takes you near the original. And there is one great advantage in using such a modern translation. It is often the best kind of commentary; indeed, that is its chief value. It gives you a translation of a word or passage which throws an entirely new light on what you are reading.

4. One thing more I would say before going into the matter in detail. This way of studying the Bible is very exacting. It will take *a great deal of time and pains.* But is it not worth it? If you study Shakespeare thoroughly, so as to get to know him, it means prolonged labor. And is it not worth while giving time and work to the greatest literature in the world, especially if that contains the secret of peace and happiness for yourself and others? You cannot know the Bible easily. You cannot possess its secret or learn its message or receive its gift without hard work. And therefore I make no apology for asking a great deal from those who would study the Bible seriously.

II. The Old Testament

Ascertaining the Background. For the study of the Bible the first and most important essential is a knowledge of the *Background*, and this is specially important for the O.T. The background of any passage or incident includes four things: (1) History, (2) Geography, (3) Religious Development, and (4) Context. What help do these give us for our study?

1. *History.* To understand any book of the Bible you must be able to place it in its historical setting. And you have to make clear to your mind a mental "map" of the periods into which the history in the O.T. is divided. You will find these described in the appropriate article in this book. (*History of Hebrew People*, pp. 60–72.) But they may be mentioned here for the sake of illustration. The *first period* (Gen. 1 to 11) is the Prehistoric, that of tradition and legend. The *second* is the Patriarchal (the fathers of the nation). The *third* is the Mosaic, when the nation was created at the Exodus, and received the truth that Jehovah was her God. The *fourth* is the Conquest of Canaan, Israel's heroic age. The *fifth* was the early kingdom, when, under David and Solomon, the nation was at its highest point of prosperity and came in contact with other peoples. The *sixth* was the Disruption of the Nation, and the beginning of the Northern Kingdom—the period of the great prophets. The *seventh* was the Exile. The *eighth* was the Restoration. Now, when you have set this scheme before your eyes see how it helps in our study. A few illustrations will suffice. The book of Proverbs is intelligible when you know it was the product (largely) of the fifth period, when a broader way of looking at life came into Israel from its wider contact with foreign peoples, a universal way of thinking instead of a Jewish. Again, you can understand Deborah's fierce song only if you set it in its place in a period of moral anarchy when the nation was already coming to some kind of unity. It is in this period, again, when the raw and immature people came in contact with the sensuous worship of the Canaanites, that idolatry, which was ever afterward Israel's peculiar weakness, began. Then, again, you can understand the whole history and nature of prophecy when you see how it began in the time of Samuel, its founder, for it began in a great revival movement which was also patriotic and national. Then you cannot read Isaiah or Jeremiah without seeing the political situation in the sixth period. A knowledge of even the broad facts of this period makes the whole message of the prophet intelligible and interesting. The same thing is true of Amos and Hosea. You find them at once alive when you see the social and religious condition of Israel in this same period, the extremes of riches and poverty, and the ritualistic and formal religiousness that passed for religion. And, finally, it is hopeless to try to understand Job or the second part of Isaiah or Ezekiel, or many of the psalms, without a clear vision of the Exile period, and the questions it raised. These are only pointers. But if I were advising anyone about Bible reading with special reference to the O.T., I should say with emphasis, "Begin by mapping out the periods, and place the books in their historical setting before you attempt to read them." (An excellent little book which will give you all you want is F. K. Sanders, *O.T. History.*)

2. *Geography.* The geographical background is not so essential, but it is an immense help. In the case of Israel more than in almost any other people the facts of geography determined the lines of history and even of religion. Why was it that most of the great battles in Israel's story were fought in the

Plain of Esdraelon? Why was idolatry so deadly and persistent an evil in Israel's life? Why did Judah last so much longer than the Northern Kingdom? Why was Israel split up into twelve tribes? Why was it so difficult to make Israel a unity? What was there in their geographical environment that affected the character and message of Amos and John the Baptist? Why were the Jews so enduring a race? All these questions are answered in part by the geography of Palestine. And far more than these. When you have formed a picture of the land and bring this to the study of the Bible, you find it throwing light on all sorts of incidents and features of the text. It explains our Lord's parable of the two hearers in Mt. 7. It explains the incident of David and Goliath. It shows why there were so many caves in Palestine. It makes the parable of the good Samaritan a new story. And therefore I strongly advise the student of the Bible to spend some of his time in the study of some first-rate work on this subject. By far the best is Sir George Adam Smith's *Historical Geography of the Holy Land.* It is not too much to say that this book is more fascinating than a novel, and that, once you have read it, you will possess an outfit for the understanding of scripture which you can get nowhere else. The insight it imparts is a lifelong and precious possession.

3. *Religious Development.* One of the greatest services which criticism has rendered to the true understanding of the Scriptures has been its emphasis on the great truth of the progressiveness of revelation. The older idea of revelation was that it was something complete, given as a whole, with no progress, but all on the same level. It was as mature at the beginning as at the end. You might, e.g., find the Trinity in Genesis as likely as in 2 Corinthians. To-day, however, this conception is impossible. We see that revelation is a growth. It is a growth, not because there is anything imperfect in the Revealer, but because our human capacity grows. God can only reveal to one age what it is capable of taking in. And when we read the Bible we find that the truth God revealed, both about himself and about our duty, came by degrees, becoming always clearer and fuller and more mature. We can trace the stages, from primitive ideas about God (such as his repenting, walking, breathing, and the like), on through the conception of Jehovah as a national God, to the proclamation of monotheism by the great prophets, and especially the declaration in Jeremiah and Ezekiel that God has an interest in the individual, and, finally, to the revelation of God's Fatherhood in Christ. But the main fact for the student of the Bible is the progress in the revelation of God's *love.* The earlier thought of God in Israel was that of a severe, righteous, and even arbitrary God. It was only gradually the people were able to grasp anything higher. And it is this primitive conception of an arbitrary and harsh God that accounts for many incidents in the early history that used to cause perplexity to readers of the Bible. When we are told, e.g., that God ordered the extermination of the Canaanites—men, women and children; when we read that Uzzah was killed by God for putting out his hand to steady the ark; when Samuel hews Agag in pieces "before the Lord," we find it difficult to reconcile this conception of God with the teaching of our Lord about him. In the same way we cannot understand how the writers of some of the psalms (e.g., Psa. 109) can invoke such dreadful curses on their enemies, or why the prophetess of God, Deborah, should in her great song gloat over a horrible crime. But these difficulties are removed when we grasp the truth that revelation is a growth, that God could only reveal his truth by degrees "as they were able to bear it." This truth disposes of most of the difficulties that puzzle and disturb a reader of the Bible. In fact, the difficulties do not arise at all if you come to the Bible with this key. We realize, e.g., that God did not order the extermination of the Canaanites, but that Israel imagined this to be her duty and attributed it to God. We do not believe that God destroyed Uzzah for a perfectly innocent and natural action. That was the writer's interpretation because he knew no better. We must constantly distinguish in the Bible between fact and interpretation. Uzzah's death was a *fact,* the writer's view of its cause was an *interpretation.* And the interpretation was wrong because the writer lived at an imperfect stage of revelation. Take this key in your hand as you study your Bible, and you will find that it opens many doors. And, remember, this truth in no way lessens the authority of the Bible. It is not the God who is revealing himself that grows or changes, but the capacities of men to grasp what he is ready to impart. (See art., *O.T. Conception of God,* pp. 158–9.)

4. *Context.* The context of any passage or incident is part of its background, and may be dealt with here. The broader context is, of course, the circumstances in which a book was written or a song was sung or a message was spoken or an incident happened. Take an example of each. Deborah's song in Judg.

5 is illuminated when you see the historical situation behind it: the summoning of the tribes, the slackness or cowardice of some, the heroism and willingness of others, the scene of the battle in the plain of Esdraelon, the position of the river Kishon, the terrible storm that made victory easy for the tribes; and, finally, the rough and primitive moral condition of the time. Or take Psa. 121. It belongs to a little group of songs, 120 to 134, which were pilgrim songs, composed for those who were going up to the feasts at Jerusalem. How vivid Psa. 121 is when you imagine the pilgrims singing it as they came in sight of Jerusalem on its hill, with all that that moving sight meant in the history of the past. Or, again, take Isa. 30. Take your map and look for Assyria, and then for Egypt, and you will see that Palestine is on the road between them. Then realize that these two powers were struggling for mastery in the world, and you will see the problem for Judah at the time. Should she support Assyria or Egypt? That is the situation behind Isa. 30. There are endless examples of this. The broader context of a book or a passage can never be ignored if you wish to understand it.

But there is *a narrower context* which is just as important. A single example of this will suffice. You may read a passage from Job, and imagine that you are receiving truth from the Word of God. But, if you paid careful attention, you would find that the passage is from a speech by Bildad, one of Job's false friends, who is represented as expressing a traditional and exploded view of sufferings. It is this view that the book rejects, and Bildad's words are therefore not part of the Word of God at all, any more than Satan's at the temptation of Jesus. This narrower context is not so vital in the O.T. as it is in the N.T., but it has its importance, and it is often essential in a prophecy or psalm to examine in what connection the utterance is found.

The Help of Criticism. So much for the background which must be known to a real student of the Scriptures. A second point of importance is the light criticism throws on the Bible. It is sometimes imagined that criticism is hostile to the Bible. That is an absurd misconception. It would be as true to say that criticism is hostile to Shakespeare because it examines his plays, and dates them, and analyzes them. The idea that criticism is hostile is due to the fact that it upsets some of our preconceived notions. It asserts, e.g., that Proverbs is not by Solomon, that David wrote very few of the psalms, that the Song of Songs is not a religious writing, that Isaiah did not write chs. 40 to 66 of his book, that Ecclesiastes is a very late production, that Jonah is an allegory and also very late, that Moses did not write the Pentateuch. These are all conclusions of criticism, but there is nothing in them to alarm us or to affect our faith in the Bible. Criticism is in reality a helpful friend to the Bible student. (See art., *O.T. and Criticism*, pp. 129–133.) Above all, it helps in this—that it has placed the books of the Bible in their proper order, and in their proper setting. Let us take one example only, to show how much help comes to the student for his Bible reading from criticism. The critic takes up Isaiah. He sees a mention of Cyrus. But he knows that Cyrus was not born for more than a hundred years after Isaiah's time. He concludes, therefore, that this part of Isaiah was written after Cyrus was born, and could not be by Isaiah himself. Then he examines further and finds that the situation behind the passage is the situation of the late Exile. Further, he sees that in other passages in this half of Isaiah the question of suffering is raised, and a wonderful answer given to it (Isa. 53). He finds also that all this part of Isaiah differs from the first part in style and language. And he places Isa. 40–66 in the time of the Exile or later. That at once makes it intelligible and natural (see intro. to Isaiah).

What criticism has done for the reader of the Bible, then, is to place the books of the O.T. in their environment, and to restore for some the order in which they were written. And the advantages of this are two. *First,* it enables the student to *see the Bible as a whole.* In spite of its being a library, the Bible is one book. It is a unity. And you see that clearly when you read it as a whole. If I were writing for one who had never seen a Bible before, I should advise him to read the Bible, first of all, without any commentaries and without paying any heed to details. I should say something like this: Read the narrative parts of the Pentateuch (the first five books of the Bible); then Joshua and Judges, to see Israel in the making; then the historical books, Samuel and Kings. When you come to David read the Psalms along with the history, because David was at least the fountainhead of the sacred song of Israel. When you come to Solomon read Proverbs, because Solomon was the first of the wise men (see p. 454a) and the way of thinking about life which we find in Proverbs began with Solomon's age. Then, later, when you come to the eighth century read Amos, Hosea, and Isaiah, alongside the history, and you will value both the history and prophecy. Then when you come to the events leading up to the great Exile read Jeremiah. He will make everything clear. For the Exile read Ezekiel, Isaiah 40–55, Job, the Psalms. Then go on to the Return from the Exile, and read Ezra and Nehemiah, and with them the later prophets, Haggai, Zechariah, Isaiah 56–66, Malachi, and Joel. At the same time read the law portions of the Pentateuch, which received their final form either from Ezra or in his time. Finally, read Jonah, which is one of the greatest books in the O.T. for its splendid universalism; and Daniel, the latest book in the O.T., and the example of a kind of literature which sprung up and flourished in the period between the O.T. and N.T. (see art., *Literature of Intertestamental Period*, pp. 187–8; also art., *Backgrounds*, p. 843–7). This, then, is the first thing to do in order to understand the Bible; read it through in the order which a wise and sane criticism shows to be the chronological order. You will thus see the Bible as a whole and understand the lines on which its history ran.

But, *secondly*, another advantage of having the books arranged properly is that *you see the real line of religious development in Israel.* This makes a great difference in more ways than one. According to the older view, the religion of Israel was originally one of law, and obedience to law; prophecy came in afterward as an addition. According to the view which criticism implies, the foundation of Israel's religion was purely spiritual. It was a fellowship between God and his people. The Law was a much later thing, it was the arresting of the spiritual element. (See art., *Religion of Israel*, pp. 169f.; cf. p. 146.) The elaborate laws of the Pentateuch were the result of a process in which religion was ceasing to be the free gracious communion of the soul with God and becoming simply obedience to precepts. So that the gracious element of spiritual life was the fundamental and characteristic feature of Israel's religion. The Law was a descent to externalism. This is really in substance Paul's view (Gal. 3), and criticism confirms it. But that is not the only way in which the arrangement of the O.T. literature shows us the religious development. It also enables us to follow the stages of that development. We can see the simplicity of the primitive conception of God giving way to a broader conception under Moses, who gave Israel its national faith. We can see this struggling for the mastery through the succeeding ages (e.g., under Elijah). We can see it broadening out in the utterances of the great prophets into pure monotheism. We can see this being made a practical faith in the individualism of Jeremiah. These are among the advantages that come to us from a sane and healthy critical treatment of the O.T.

Methods of Study. Having thus, as it were, erected the scaffolding, let us now try to complete the building by filling it with some content.

1. *For General Study.* Take a notebook, and make your general scheme of the history in periods and then place the books of the O.T. in their proper environment. You have already achieved a priceless and perfectly essential knowledge of the Bible. Take each period in turn and read over all the books belonging to this period. You will thus gain a knowledge of the conditions of the people at each stage and of the divine revelation that came to each as well as the contribution which each writer made to his day and to the growth of religious experience. Then take the literature, book by book. Let us take as examples Isaiah and Job. You now know something of Isaiah's day. But you can learn a great deal more if you begin to study him carefully. Set down in your notebook the following points: Foreign Policy, Social Conditions, the Messiah, the prophet himself, and finally the great promises of God. Now read over the book for what you can gather on all these points. When you have done that, you will *possess* Isaiah, you will have learned his message, you will know about the world of his day, about what Israel was like at that time, about the prophet's own personality and religious history. You can check your conclusions by reading any standard work on Isaiah, like Sir George Adam Smith's (in the *Expositor's Bible*). But you have no need to be dependent on any one. Your own study will be of far more value than that of anyone else. Again, take Job, in a good translation (Moffatt or R.V. or anyone that prints it as it was written). Read it over without any help. You find it has three parts, a prose prologue, a prose epilogue and between these the drama in poetry. You find the drama is constructed as a debate in three rounds with Elihu intervening and the debate wound up by the Almighty. Well, having gained this general knowledge, and a fair acquaintance with the theme, you begin to study the book seriously. Set down what you understand each debater to say at each stage of the discussion, what contribution he makes to the general subject, and what in each case Job says in reply. Finally, set down what you gather that the Almighty says, and what you think the significance of this is. All this is quite general and apart from commentaries. But in this way you will find what the real

meaning of the book is, and what its particular message is about the great question of suffering. This method is, as I said, entirely directed to gaining a broad insight into the purpose and bearing and contents of the books of the O.T.

2. *Topical Study.* There is another method which will amply repay the student of the Bible, supplementary and following on the previous one, and that is the topical. The simplest example is the book of Proverbs. This book, if you read it straight on, is "fine, confused feeding." But if you adopt the topical method, it at once gains in interest. Gather together all this wise book says about Education, the Issues of Sin, Wealth, the Tongue, Honesty, Friendship, Work and Idleness, Wine, the Fool, Woman. It is surprising how rich the book is in suggestive thoughts on all these (and other) topics. The advantage of this method is that you discover what the Wise Men of Israel taught about life in its various aspects in the early period of "Wisdom," before the clouds and disasters of the later age arrived.

But there is a wider application of this method which is well worth pursuing. Take a great subject like the "Idea of God," and follow it through the O.T. (see p. 158). Read the early literature to find out what the Patriarchs thought of God. Read the earlier portions of Exodus to find what Moses taught Israel about God. Read the development of this in the historical books, and then follow this idea through the prophets chronologically—the dawn of the great truth of monotheism, up to the wonderful teaching of Jeremiah on God's individual care. Or take another great reality of the O.T., "The Spirit of God." This is one of the most fascinating topics in the Bible. Do not carry back your N.T. conception, but gather together all that is said about the Spirit in the O.T., and you will be impressed with the magnificence of the conception of a living God, active in all the life of man and behind all his achievements. Or, again, take the conception of "Nature." Had the Hebrews any sense of the beauty of nature, at least in the modern way? Well, find out by setting down all that is said of it in the Psalms and prophets, in Genesis and Kings. Or, again, take the conception of "Divine Salvation," and its conditions, its meaning, its promises. God is everywhere a Saviour in the O.T. What is the salvation he offers? and the greater salvation he promises? Is it individual or only national? Was there any growth in the idea of it? Set it all down. Finally, take the idea of the "Messiah" (see p. 181). In what ways and to what extent do you find Christ in the O.T.? I do not suggest that the writers already knew of the historic Jesus Christ. But if you believe that God is behind all this process of history working toward a consummation (and I assume that your general study would lead you to that conclusion), he would naturally be preparing for the advent of his Son. How far do you find that? and in what ways? Set it down. What kind of hope of a Deliverer had the Hebrews? In the historical books, in Isaiah, in the Psalms, in Ezekiel, in Daniel? When you have set it down you will discover to your surprise one tremendous thing about the Bible, namely, that Christ is at the center of it, with one hand on the O.T. and the other on the N.T. And you will perceive how really and vitally Christ was in the O.T. from beginning to end. This subject is endless, but I have sufficiently suggested the method. (See H. Wheeler Robinson, *Religious Ideas of the O.T.;* Burney, *The Gospel in the O.T.;* also arts. on p. 175 and p. 177.)

3. *Study of Special Books.* But you will want after all this to study special books. You will want (either for yourself or for teaching) to go through a book verse by verse, or, indeed, to study a single verse. Well, to understand almost any verse in the Bible fully we need (1) its nearer context, what goes before and what follows; (2) the course of thought in which the context occurs; (3) the circumstances in which it was written; (4) the bigger context of history in which the book is to be placed; and very often, (5) the personality and history of the writer. That is why the detailed study is most wisely begun the other way. When you have satisfied yourself as to the circumstances in which a book was written, then you can read it over rapidly several times. Not once only, because each reading would give you something new. Then take it paragraph by paragraph (not chapter by chapter) without any commentary, and then verse by verse. The *detailed* reading needs a commentary to explain the meanings of the words used and the customs alluded to and any reference that a reader who is not an expert would not understand. There is hardly any book in the Bible that we can possess fully without the help of an expert in detail, just because the life of the East is so different from ours. There are, indeed, many words and phrases which are best explained by scripture itself, i.e., by the usage of these words in other connections. And here it is necessary to have a good concordance. Cruden is rather out of date. He has been surpassed by Young, and Young's *Analytical Concordance* or Strong's *Exhaustive Concord-*

ance should be at the student's elbow. Take such a word as "righteousness," e.g., in the O.T. We might, on general principles, interpret it to mean "uprightness." But in the O.T. the word has a far richer and a more genial meaning, as the passages in which it occurs soon show. The examination of the immediate context, along with a study of parallel examples of the same word or phrase, will usually determine the meaning for us. But often a good commentary, like the present one, will shed a flood of light on a word or a verse by revealing facts which we could not by our own study have discovered. Only, two warnings may be given here as to the use of books: As to commentaries, remember they are invaluable if rightly used. But if you use them to save you trouble and independent study, they become a hindrance. Your best study is what you do yourself, and its treasures are what you discover for yourself. Use a commentary after you have done your own work, and to settle a vexed question, and to solve difficulties. But do not seek for ready-made knowledge too easily. And as to the concordance, there is a special danger. No concordance gives the date at which the passages it cites were written. And you must remember in using it that revelation was a growth, and that a word written early in the history may have a different signification from what it would have later. The Bible is not all on the same level either of inspiration or truth, and this has to be remembered. (See art., *The Divine Element in the Bible*, p. 26.) And in using words or passages to determine certain truths we must recognize their source and authorship. A sentiment uttered by a noninspired person or uttered at an early stage of revelation may not be an authority for our knowledge of God or his will. Use your concordance then, by all means, but use it with judgment.

III. The New Testament

A great deal of what has been written above about the study of the O.T. applies in general terms to the N.T. But it has in some ways a different application, and therefore some particular guidance may be given in several directions.

The Background. As in the O.T., so here, a knowledge of the background is an indispensable condition to adequate Bible study.

1. *Historical Conditions.* Anyone coming to the N.T. directly from a reading of the O.T. might naturally expect to find the Jewish people very much what they were when he left them in the time of Ezra. But that turns out to be a mistaken impression. If four hundred years of American or English history, dating from to-day backward, were a complete blank, we could not in the least understand the America or England of to-day. And four hundred years elapsed between Ezra and Christ. So that we need to learn something of what occurred during that interval in order to understand the situation into which Christ was born. Consult the article on *Backgrounds* (pp. 839-52), and you will find three events which throw a flood of light on the Gospels: (1) One is *the dominance of the Law.* Jewish religion was radically changed after Ezra's time. It was largely a religion of obedience to law (see intro. to the books of Ezra-Nehemiah). And this Law had two sides, the ceremonial and the moral. The priest regulated the former, and was therefore the powerful, ruling influence henceforth. The scribe, or lawyer, directed the latter, and, because he interpreted the meaning and application of the Law, on its moral side, to conduct, he became the teacher of the people. The scribes built up a great edifice of regulations based on the Law until these became an intolerable burden. And it was this edifice Jesus swept away, when he came with a religion of the spirit and of liberty. The priest and the scribe, then, were the two powers in the life of the people during this period. (2) The second event was the attempt of the Greek kings, successors of Alexander the Great, who ruled Palestine during part of this period, to *force Greek culture on the Jews.* Greek culture was called Hellenism, and included art, idolatry, philosophy, and the worship of beauty. The attempt to force this culture on the Jews split the people into two camps. Some were willing to adopt these worldly customs. They were the aristocrats, the priestly section. The other refused it. This was the "pious" section, strict and faithful to the religion of their fathers. This event led to the famous Maccabean rebellion, and in the end to the formation of two parties who ultimately became the Sadducees and the Pharisees. The Sadducees were aristocratic, priestly, worldly, and latitudinarian. The Pharisees were the pious, strict, faithful, patriotic party. At its beginning, therefore, this Pharisaic party was orthodox and intensely spiritual, but, like many other parties that have originated in a spiritual movement, by the time of Christ it had degenerated and its religion had become largely one of form. (3) The third event was the appearance of the *Apocalyptic Literature.* This kind of literature always appears in a time of darkness and despair, when no hope of salvation is to be found in human agencies, and deliverance is

to be seen only in a special divine intervention of a cataclysmic nature which will destroy the enemies of God and establish his kingdom securely on the earth. And so during this period a great literature of hope appeared with its vision of the other world, and its proclamation of a great divine deliverance through a Messiah or "anointed" instrument. (See art., *Literature of Intertestamental Period*, p. 187; cf. introduction to Daniel.) This hope of a Messiah who was to be a national hero and set the people free from the yoke of Rome was very strong when Jesus appeared. Now, these three events explain the situation as we find it in the Gospels, and need to be carefully studied. The priesthood and its influence, the scribes with the Pharisees, the intense nationalistic, Messianic hope, the expectation of a sudden, violent end to things as they were, the burden of the legal traditions, all are explained in this way.

2. *Political Conditions.* But we need to understand also how the world of Jesus and of Paul was governed in order to read the Gospels, and Acts and the Epistles intelligently. Rome governed her empire in three ways: (1) Through native princes (as Britain governs some Indian provinces) who paid tribute to Rome and taxed their domain themselves. They enjoyed a large measure of freedom and local self-government. Galilee was governed in this way under the Herods. (2) Directly by Roman governors. This was done in the case of "difficult" provinces, where the people were apt to get out of hand. Judæa was one of these. The Jews in Judæa were narrow, fanatical, and rebellious. And so Rome governed Judæa directly, and among the Roman governors were Pilate, Felix, and Festus. Even in these provinces there was a good deal of freedom and the Jews had a series of courts, of which the chief was the Sanhedrin at Jerusalem. But Rome did not allow subject races to put anyone to death. Capital punishment was reserved to the Roman governor. That is why the Sanhedrin, though it condemned Jesus, could not execute him. He had to be tried and condemned by Pilate. (3) The third method was by settlements of ex-service men called "colonies," settled throughout the empire, and given a large amount of self-government. They were little bits of Rome through the world.

But the main thing to realize is the principle on which Rome governed. It was that of toleration. Every creed was protected in the empire. Religious questions were rarely interfered with by Roman governors. This explains the fact that Paul was everywhere protected by Roman governors against the Jews when they realized that the question was one of religion (cf. the scene before Gallio, Acts 18[12-17]). It also explains why the Jews when they brought Jesus before Pilate did not accuse him of blasphemy (the charge on which they had condemned him) but had to trump up a political charge, namely, treason. These are examples of the way in which the political background throws light on the Gospel and apostolic narratives.

3. *Religious Conditions.* I have pointed out the main features of the religious situation—Judaism as a religion of law, the materialistic nature of its religious hopes, the parties into which its history had split up the Jewish Church (Sadducees and priests, scribes and Pharisees). But it must be remembered that the piety of the Jews had not altogether degenerated. There was still a leaven of real spiritual life and hope. There was, as always, a remnant. We see this in the Gospels in people like John the Baptist's parents, in Simeon and Anna, in Nicodemus and Joseph of Arimathæa, and in the first disciples.

But, apart from Jewish religion, we ought to keep in mind so-called *pagan religion*, for we often meet it in the N.T. (1) There was the old *polytheism* prevalent in rural districts and still a vital faith. We find it in Paul's visit to Lystra (Acts 14[8-18]). (2) This simple belief, however, was no longer held by the educated. In its place many cultivated men tried to sustain their souls on *philosophy*. The Stoics and the Epicureans were the principal philosophic sects. And these we meet on Paul's visit to Athens (Acts 17[16f.]). (3) But in a time like that, a time of religious decline, with the old religion gone and no new one come, *superstition* is always rife. The world of Paul's day was full of it—spiritualism, fortune-telling, necromancy. Rich men had their private astrologers, and poor men had recourse to magicians. We meet this often in the N.T., e.g., Simon Magus, the girl "medium" in Philippi, the sorcerer Elymas in Cyprus. All these forms of pagan religion Paul had to meet. (4) A fourth we hardly meet except in Revelation, the *worship of the emperor*. This was the official religion. The emperor was regarded as the embodiment of authority and was rendered divine honors. This is the superstition that is spoken of so strongly in Revelation (see intro. to that book). It became the instrument of persecution against the Christians later. But with that we have nothing to do here.

4. *Geography.* The help of geography here is as great as in the case of the O.T. Let me take one or two examples to show how the map illuminates the study of the N.T. Take

a map of the Roman world, such as is supplied in this Commentary. Look at it. Now lay your finger on the places Paul evangelized. Antioch, Ephesus, Philippi, Corinth, Athens, Rome—these are the "strategic points" of the ancient world, i.e., the places from which whole districts could be influenced, key-places. Paul had the strategic genius, the kind of genius a great general has. You can see that he laid hold for Christ of just the places from which the world could be won. Again take the map of Palestine and its surroundings. In your study of the life of Jesus you find he retired from time to time out of Palestine proper in order to find quiet for the training of his apostles. Look where he went, to Phœnicia in the north, beyond the lake to the east, to Decapolis, a Greek region with a predominant Gentile population. Then study the larger map of the lake and see the region of Christ's ministry, how Capernaum, its center, was a kind of focus of life and business, how predominant the fishing industry was, how busy a place the lakeside was at that time and how full of life. Then look at Judæa, so high up on its plateau, with a climate different from Galilee. You understand its isolation, the narrow fanaticism of its people, and you understand why Jesus was crucified *there* and not in Galilee. These are only indications of the ways in which a study of the land opens up and explains the N.T. at a hundred points. Never study the Bible, O.T. or N.T., without a map at your hand.

The Study of the Gospels. When we come to the N.T. itself, we naturally wish to get a clear view of the ministry of our Lord. We can do this largely for ourselves. But we need some help at certain points. We need, e.g., to know something of the way in which the Gospels were written. It will be useful to read the article on this subject (p. 867). Here the matter is referred to for its guidance about study. One help we shall receive will be confidence in the trustworthiness of the gospel narrative. If Mark was written from the reminiscences of Peter, we have Peter's authority behind it. If Matthew and Luke were written with Mark before them and from other sources, we are pretty sure much of the supplementary material is as old as Mark. John is more an interpretation than a record and is much later. The best way to study the life of Jesus, then, is to take Mark as the basis, and go by it (as is done, e.g., in the art. in this Commentary on *The Life of Jesus*, p. 891). Go over it repeatedly until you master its outlines. You will then see the salient outstanding points, the crucial landmarks, and all the minor incidents will group themselves round these. Do not trouble to be too chronological. Some recent writers (Rawlinson on Mark, and Middleton Murry) deny that a chronological scheme of the ministry can be made. But you will find that this is wrong. Your independent study will show you that the big points are fixed and clear, and certain incidents lead up to these, and others lead away from them. So there is a *general* chronology, but do not worry about putting in every incident into a framework. These detailed frameworks are generally artificial and useless. In a great many cases it does not matter where and when an incident took place. But it will be a safe proceeding to take Mark's order as a basis, and fit in the events and discourses from the other Gospels in the big sector of the ministry where you feel they belong. It will be useful to have a reliable *Life of Christ* to fall back on. One of the best of the smaller books is Professor Stalker's. When you have the general run of the ministry clear in your mind, and the geography of it also, you can then begin the study of each phase. Take the early years of Jesus, and consider what you can discover of the influences that molded his thoughts—the education of a Jewish boy; the piety of such a home as his; how far he was affected by the Apocalyptic hope of his day; what the incident of his being found in the Temple, and his remark to his mother at twelve years of age, implied as to his thought of himself; the influence of Nazareth and what could be seen from there. A book like Sir William Ramsay's *The Education of Christ* throws a flood of light on all this. Then go on to the Baptism where he received his chief impulse for his ministry. What happened there? Why did he go to be baptized? His relation to the Baptist? The significance of the Divine Voice? And a great deal more. Then the temptation, the most critical point in all his ministry. Everything came out of it. *What* came out of it? What did he reject at that time? What was the real temptation and how often did this recur later? Then the Galilæan period with all its fascinating topics—the calling of disciples, the wonderful works, the parables, the friendship with outcasts, the periodical retirements. Then the crisis at Cæsarea Philippi, a great watershed. Then the later period of increasing gloom, going to Jerusalem. Then the last dark period culminating in the Passion. Finally the blaze of light at the Resurrection. In the present Commentary you will find all the help you need, but go to the Gospels for yourselves first, and study them first and always. You will get far more knowledge of Christ that way than merely by reading what other men say of him. Take a notebook, and, after reading the Gospel record over and over, put down your own thoughts on each stage; and then, when you go over it in detail, have your thoughts on each incident. Afterward read what the experts have to say and correct your own conclusions where they are clearly wrong. But see with your own eyes first and always.

The Study of the Epistles. The letters of Paul are the most important and may be taken as typical for study. The first thing to do is to get a clear view of Paul's life and work. This is found in Acts, but not in Acts alone, for there is a great deal of valuable information in the letters, especially in Galatians, and 1 and 2 Corinthians. The best way to study the apostolic period, it seems to me, is to take the book of Acts as a basis and (with a good map) to scheme it out. Then read at each point the letter that was addressed to each church. After the first missionary journey read the Galatian letter. After the story of what happened at Philippi read the Philippian letter, and so on. That is the best way for a first reading, because the letter is illuminated by the conditions in the church, and it also illuminates these. But on a second reading it is well to try to place the letter at the point of time when it was written because the letters reveal a great deal of the writer's life at the time. If Philippians was written during the Roman imprisonment, we have a picture of Paul the prisoner and of his thoughts and experiences in the Roman period. When you have read the Acts and letters in these two ways you will have learned all there is to know of Paul's outward life and of his inner experience. You will need some help at certain points. There is, e.g., a great deal of information available as to the conditions prevailing in the Roman Empire, as to the places Paul visited, and as to some difficult problems which arise as you study Acts and the letters side by side. You will find this help in the appropriate articles (see art., *Life and Work of Paul*, p. 931; also the discussions on pp. 1169 and 1207). And if you need more, you can find it in Stalker's *Life of Paul*, or in Foakes-Jackson's admirable *Life of St. Paul*, or in T. R. Glover's *Paul of Tarsus*.

Topical Study. All that has been said refers to the historical study of the N.T. But there is another, and very profitable way of studying it, and that is according to subjects. You will soon find, to your surprise, that there is no "system" in the N.T. The Lord Jesus had none. Paul had none. Paul was not a theologian, and there is no such thing as "Paulinism" in the letters. (What is meant by this is that Paul did not have a ready-made and complete system of thought which he sought to propagate through his letters.) But both Christ and Paul had a great message, and this message is embodied in great thoughts or ideas. These are a wonderfully fruitful subject of study. Take, e.g., the Lord's message about God, or his idea of man, or his thought of "salvation," or his teaching about the cross, or the kingdom of God, or love. Take the Gospels, and write down as you come to them his leading thoughts. Give each a page, and enter under the title all the passages where the word or idea appears. And then consider all he says about it. That will give you a series of fascinating lessons or sermons. And it will reveal much of the mind of the Lord. Do the same with Paul. Go over the letters and note, e.g., the characteristics of Paul himself, his prayerfulness, his intense sympathy, his capacity for friendship, his natural courtesy, his power of anger, his chivalry, and so on. You will learn in this way more about Paul than any book can tell you. Then take his ruling ideas. What is it to be "in Christ"? What does Paul teach on faith? on justification? on the atonement? on Christ's risen life? on the Law? on baptism? on the Spirit? on the flesh? on woman? on the future life? on the Godhead of Christ? Again, I say, you will probably learn more about Paul's message and his characteristic thoughts by such independent studies than by reading many books about Paul. Arrange the letters in the order in which they were written (see the art. on p. 879), and carefully trace what the apostle says on each point through the letters. You will see, for one thing, whether his thought developed at all, whether it altered in emphasis or content. On the Second Coming of Christ, e.g., you will probably find a gradual change. But you will find another thing—how as time went on different topics filled the apostle's mind. He began to lay stress on different things, partly because he found different conditions prevailing and partly because he was growing and living, and different things interested him. At any rate, this topical study is endless and endlessly interesting and revealing. Remember that the body of literature you have to study is very small. The whole of the letters contain not much more than forty thousand words, about four times as much as this article. So the study is not too vast. But it is the study of a part of the master book of the world and is well worth a little trouble.

Particular Passages. All that has been said bears on the study of any particular "text." You cannot understand a saying of Paul's unless you grasp the argument in which it occurs. But you cannot grasp this unless you know the meaning and drift of the whole letter. And for this you must know the circumstances in which it was written, and something of the conditions and the state of mind in which the writer penned it. All this is not so necessary in the Gospels, though even there it is often helpful. But it is absolutely essential in the case of the letters. And that is why the general study of background and conditions on which so much stress has been laid is so important. The whole of the general study throws light always and lavishly on the most insignificant of incidents and sayings. When Paul writes to the Philippians, "Our citizenship is in heaven" (3[20] R.V.), or, as Moffatt brilliantly renders it, "We are a colony of heaven," the words start out with a perfectly lovely meaning when you recall that Philippi was a Roman "colony," a settlement of Roman citizens among an alien race, one of the forms of Roman government (see p. 1238). We, in this world, are a "colony" of heaven (cf. Heb. 13[14]). That is an example of how the background illuminates a Scripture passage. And it is only one out of hundreds. So that detailed study must be done always with a view to the larger study, which alone makes the Bible intelligible, and which makes it the most fascinating and wonderful book in the world.

Literature: F. J. Rae, *How to Teach the O.T.* and *How to Teach the N.T.;* McFadyen, *The Approach to the N.T.;* Laura H. Wild, *A Literary Guide to the Bible;* W. N. Clark, *Sixty Years With the Bible;* Sanders, *Outlines for the Study of Biblical History and Literature;* Barclay and Eiselen, *The Worker and His Bible.* See also "Literature" cited on pp. 18, 25, 31, 38 and 44.

THE BIBLE—A LIBRARY OF RELIGION

By President F. C. EISELEN

The Bible a Collection of Books. The word "Bible," derived from the Greek, is the plural form *biblia* of a singular noun *biblion*, which has the meaning "little book"; *biblia*, therefore, is literally "little books." In Latin, which took the word over from the Greek, it came to be regarded as a singular noun, having the same form, meaning "book." As a singular it was early adopted into the language of the Western church, and as such it is used even now in modern European languages: the Bible—the Book. This use of the noun as a singular is responsible for much misapprehension, because the Bible can never be rightly appreciated unless it is borne in mind that it is not so much one book as a library consisting of many books, written by different authors at different times, in different places, from different points of view, and reflecting different stages of religious, moral, social, and political development. Altogether there are sixty-six separate writings in the collection as found in modern English translations.

There are two great divisions in the Bible used by Christians, called respectively the "Old Testament" and the "New Testament," the former containing thirty-nine books, the latter twenty-seven. The designation "Testament" is somewhat misleading; a more accurate rendering would be "Covenant." Indeed, some of the early church Fathers speak of "the divine Scriptures, the so-called Old and New Covenants." The O.T. includes books reflecting the religious life and experience of the Hebrews which originated during the period when the national covenant between Jehovah and the people of Israel, believed to have been mediated through Moses, was held to be in force. Similarly the N.T. contains books reflecting the early Christian movement, interpreted as marking the establishment of a new and universal covenant between God and men through Jesus Christ.

Contents of English Old Testament. The thirty-nine books of the O.T. are named below, arranged in a fourfold grouping, which, with some modifications, has been recognized for many centuries—since the Greek translation known as the Septuagint was made, before the opening of the Christian era.

I. *Law*: Genesis, Exodus, Leviticus, Numbers, Deuteronomy—5 books.

II. *History*: Joshua, Judges, Ruth, First and Second Samuel, First and Second Kings, First and Second Chronicles, Ezra, Nehemiah, Esther—12 books.

III. *Poetry*: Job, Psalms, Proverbs, Ecclesiastes, Song of Songs—5 books.

IV. *Prophecy*:
(1) The Major Prophets: Isaiah, Jeremiah, Lamentations, Ezekiel, Daniel—5 books. (2) The Minor Prophets: Hosea, Joel, Amos, Obadiah, Jonah, Micah, Nahum, Habakkuk, Zephaniah, Haggai, Zechariah, Malachi—12 books (total 17).

Contents of the English New Testament. The twenty-seven books of the N.T. may be arranged in three groups:

I. *Historical*: The four Gospels—Matthew, Mark, Luke, John; the Acts—5 books.

II. *Epistles or Doctrinal*: Romans, First and Second Corinthians, Galatians, Ephesians, Philippians, Colossians, First and Second Thessalonians, First and Second Timothy, Titus, Philemon, Hebrews, James, First and Second Peter, First, Second and Third John, Jude—21 books.

III. *Apocalyptic*: Revelation.

A Religious Library. The Bible contains sublime specimens of history, law, poetry, oratory—indeed, of almost every kind of literature known outside of the Bible. But it is well to keep in mind that the books in the Bible were not written or collected primarily as specimens of these various forms of literature but to record and interpret divine revelations. In describing the significance of the O.T. period the writer of the Epistle to the Hebrews says, among other things, that God spake "in divers manners" (Heb. 1^1). Though these words were spoken originally of the O.T. period, they are equally true of the period which gave rise to the individual N.T. books and the N.T. collection as a whole, as also of the whole course of human history.

Manifold Divine Revelations. God reveals himself, and always has revealed himself, in nature:

The heavens declare the glory of God;
And the firmament showeth his handiwork;
Day unto day uttereth speech,
And night unto night showeth knowledge
(Psa. $19^{1,2}$).

God reveals himself in the events of history, be it the history of individuals or of nations. Sometimes the voice may be almost inaudible; at other times it sounds like the roar of thunder; but always, recognized or unrecognized, God is working out his eternal purpose, slowly it may be because of man's stubbornness, but nevertheless steadily, because in the end the divine goodness cannot fail. Again, to many devout persons God speaks very distinctly through the outward acts of worship. To thousands of earnest seekers after God these forms and ceremonies are means of blessing and grace through which the divine comes into contact with the mind and conscience. Experience, moreover, shows that God, in his attempt to reach the human soul, may dispense with all external means; he may and does reveal himself by working directly in and upon the mind and spirit of the individual. Once more, God selects certain persons especially well qualified to hear his voice. These he commissions to declare him and his will to the people. The belief in this method of revelation is the philosophic basis for the offices of the modern preacher and religious teacher. In a real sense the revelation of God in and through Jesus belongs here, for in him, as he lives his life among men, God manifests himself more fully than ever before or since.

These are at least some of the ways in which God reveals himself to-day, and these are some of the ways in which God made himself known during the O.T. and N.T. periods; then, as now, he revealed himself in nature, in the events of history, in the ritual, by direct impressions; and at times he selected persons to whom he might make himself known in all these various ways, persons who had sufficient spiritual insight to appreciate and interpret these divine manifestations, and ability to transmit the discovered truth to others. Then, in the fullness of time, he made himself known in unique and supreme fashion through Jesus the Christ (Gal. 4[4] Eph. 1[10]).

Different Types of Old Testament Literature. The Bible contains records and interpretations of these manifold divine revelations. It is only natural, however, that when attempts were made to record or interpret these manifestations of God, different kinds of literature had to be used in order to express most intelligently and forcefully the truth or truths the author sought to impress upon his readers. In other words, the various types of literature are not the result of arbitrary selection; they are the natural outgrowth of the manifold character of divine revelation. In the O.T. five kinds of literature may be distinguished: the prophetic, the wisdom, the devotional, the legal or priestly, and the historical. In their production four classes of religious workers, who observed, interpreted, and mediated the divine revelations, were active, namely, the prophets, the wise men, the priests (Jer. 18[18]), and the sweet singers of Israel, the psalmists. In the N.T. the first five books may be regarded as in a general sense historical, while practically all the others resemble in general character and purpose the prophetic, and in one instance the apocalyptic, literature.

Prophetic Literature of the Old Testament. Prophetic literature owes its origin to prophetic activity. The prophets towered above their contemporaries in purity of character, strength of intellect, sincerity of purpose, intimacy of communion with God, and ensuing depth of spiritual insight. As a result of these intellectual, moral, and spiritual qualifications, they were able to apprehend and appreciate truth hidden from the eyes and minds of those who did not live in the same intimate fellowship with their God. Their deep insight into the character of God enabled them to appreciate the divine ideals of righteousness, and they sought, with flaming enthusiasm, to impress upon their less enlightened contemporaries the truth burning in their own hearts. In carrying out this purpose they became patient and painstaking teachers of religious truth, bold and fearless preachers of right living, sane and courageous reformers of social abuses, idealistic and tactful statesmen, seeking to establish a world order in harmony with the eternal purpose of God. No records have been preserved of the utterances of the earliest prophets; but when, with the general advance in culture, reading and writing became more general, the prophets, anxious to reach a wider circle and to preserve their messages for more responsive ears, began to put their messages in writing; and to this new development we owe the sublime specimens of prophetic literature in the O.T.

Wisdom Literature of the Old Testament. The ancient prophet with his direct appeal to the human conscience resembles the modern preacher. The ancient wise man, who, like the ancient prophet or the modern preacher, had as his chief objective the interpretation of the divine will to his contemporaries, resembles, in the methods used, the modern religious teacher. While his ultimate aim was to influence life and conduct, he addressed himself primarily to the common sense of the hearer through counsel and argument, instead of presenting his appeal as directly inspired by Jehovah, hoping that the effects of this appeal would show themselves in transformed conduct. Nothing escaped the observation of these wise men; and from beginning to end they sought to teach the important truth that religion and the daily life are inseparable. The book of Proverbs is a collection of such wise sayings coming from various periods of Hebrew and Jewish history. From giving simple practical precepts, the wise men advanced to speculation in the attempt to assist their contemporaries in the solution of some of the intellectual problems which presented obstacles to vital religious faith. The books of Job and Ecclesiastes bear witness that the problems the wise men sought to solve were no mean problems.

Devotional Literature of the Old Testament. In a sense the entire O.T. is devotional. It is the outgrowth of a spirit of intense devotion to Jehovah, and many portions of it have helped in all ages to nurture the devotional spirit and attitude of its readers. In this connection, however, the term is used of those poetic compositions, found in many parts of the book, which are the expressions of the religious experience and emotions of the authors inspired and fostered by intimate fellowship with Jehovah. The book of Psalms is the chief representative of this literature. It has been suggestively characterized by Johannes Arndt in these words: "What the heart is in man that is the psalter in the Bible." The Psalms contain in the form of sacred lyrics the outpourings of devout souls—prophets, priests, wise men, kings, and peasants—who came into the very presence of God, held communion with him, and were privileged to hear the sweet sound of his voice. No other literary compositions lift the devout reader into such an atmosphere of religious thought and emotion. And because these lyrics reflect personal experiences, they may be used even to-day to express the joy, sorrow, hope, fear, anticipation, and similar emotions of persons who live on a plane that may be higher than that on which the original authors moved.

Legal Literature of the Old Testament. The legal literature of the O.T. differs from the other in that it does not form separate books, but is embodied in other writings, principally the books of Exodus, Leviticus, Numbers, and Deuteronomy All the representatives of Jehovah—prophets, priests, and wise men—were thought competent to make known the *Law* of Jehovah, i.e., his will and purpose. However, the O.T. makes it clear that at a comparatively early period the giving of the Law, or the determination of the will and purpose of Jehovah, came to be looked upon as the peculiar duty of the priests. Indeed, during the earliest period this seems to have been their chief duty. Subsequently, and during the greater part of the national life of Israel, their principal responsibility was the care of the sanctuary and the performance of the ceremonial rites. But even then they continued to administer the "Law of Jehovah," consisting not only of ceremonial regulations but also of moral and judicial precepts and directions. For generations these laws were transmitted orally or were only partially committed to writing; but when changed circumstances made it desirable to codify the whole legal system and put it in writing, the priests were most active in meeting the need. Thus, while it cannot be doubted that other representatives of Jehovah helped to formulate laws, the legal literature embodied in the O.T. reached its final form under priestly direction and influence.

Historical Literature of the Old Testament. The historical literature of the O.T. gives interpretations of the movements of God in the history of Israel and of the nations with which the authors were familiar. It owes its origin in part to prophetic, in part to priestly activity. As has been pointed out, the prophet was a representative of Jehovah, whose business it was to make known the divine will to his own day and generation. Sometimes he looked into the future, and by doing so sought to give emphasis to a truth he was trying to express concerning the present. At other times he found inspiration in the past. Frequently the people failed to understand the real significance of events in their own history and thus missed the religious truths they might otherwise have drawn from them. If these lessons were not to be lost, some one must serve as an interpreter; and who would be better qualified than the prophet to furnish the right interpretation? Sometimes he embodied these interpretations in his discourses; but the demand for a religious interpretation of the entire course of events made the prophet in a sense a historian, not for the purpose simply of recording events but of interpreting them at the same time on the basis of his faith in Jehovah. To these prophet-historians we owe a large part of the historical literature.

But not all O.T. history comes from the prophets. As already indicated, the legal and ceremonial literature may be traced to priestly activity. Now, in connection with the recording of the laws, customs, institutions, and ceremonial requirements, the origin of these laws and institutions became a matter of importance. This interest and the demand arising from it led the priests also to become historians; and to these priestly writers we are indebted for not a small part of O.T. history.

Types of New Testament Literature. The types of literature in the N.T. are similar to those in the O.T. All its writings center around Jesus the Christ, and in one way or another they all seek to interpret the supreme revelation of God through him. Jesus was a historical Person. His life, activity, and teaching were matters of history. The Gospels, whose primary purpose is to record and interpret the life and activity of Jesus, are in the nature of *historical*, or possibly better, *biographical* sketches. The work of establishing the kingdom of God begun by Jesus was continued by his disciples and assumed organized form through the establishment of numerous churches. The progress of these events, especially in Syria, Asia Minor, Greece, and Italy, is recorded in another historical book, the Acts of the Apostles.

Every new movement gives rise to problems and perplexities. Christianity was no exception. Very soon troublesome questions began to disturb the newly organized churches. Individuals failed to grasp the true significance of the new teaching; corruption and schisms threatened to disrupt the believers. In these extremities the leaders in the new faith were appealed to for guidance and inspiration. Since they could not visit all the places from which requests for counsel came, they frequently sent their advice in the form of letters, which has given rise to the extensive *epistolary* literature in the N.T. This sets forth the doctrines of the new movement, seeks to assist in the proper administration of local churches, and gives counsel in the matter of personal and official conduct on the part of church leaders. In its general aims, if not in form and details, this literature resembles the prophetic books of the O.T.

The closing book, Revelation, is the only one of its kind in the N.T. It has its counterparts in the O.T. in the book of Daniel, portions of Isaiah, Ezekiel, and Zechariah, and less extensive sections elsewhere. It belongs to what is known commonly as *apocalyptic* literature, developed on the basis of the prophetic hope concerning the future (see p. 189). Like the prophet, the apocalyptic writer seeks to interpret God, his will, his purpose, and the nature and laws of his kingdom. But there is this fundamental difference (among others) between the two: "Prophecy still believes that this world is God's world, and that in this world his truth and justice will yet be justified. Hence the prophet addresses himself chiefly to the present and its concerns, and when he addresses himself to the future his prophecies spring naturally from the present, and the future which he predicts is regarded as in organic connection with it. The apocalyptic writer, on the other hand, almost wholly despairs of the present; his main interests are supramundane." As a result the apocalyptic literature dwells more especially upon the triumph of the kingdom of God in the coming age; hence the name "Apocalyptic," i.e., the literature that "makes known what is hidden" from the eyes of common men. The book of Revelation is the outgrowth of the early Christian persecutions, and its objective is the encouragement of the distressed and suffering Christians by the assurance of the ultimate triumph of the kingdom of God.

Literature: Eiselen, *The Christian View of the O.T.;* Willett, *Our Bible;* Kent, *The Origin and Permanent Value of the O.T.;* Peake, *The Bible: Its Origin, Its Significance, Its Abiding Worth.*

THE BIBLE AS LITERATURE

By Professor LINDSAY B. LONGACRE

Interpretation and Literary Form. Among the many reasons for regarding the Bible as "different from other books" is the quite obvious fact that it *looks* different. One opens it at random and finds a formal arrangement of chapters and verses not found in other books, and this difference in form easily suggests a difference in fact. The consequence has been that the chapters, which developed out of sections suitable for public reading, have become more important than the complete books; while the verse divisions, instead of being solely a practical expedient for ready reference—which they are—have come to be regarded as part and parcel of the inspired Scripture itself—which they most certainly are not. The original writers knew nothing of chapters and verses, and not until one is set free from the temptation to regard the Bible as a collection of these arbitrary fragments is he prepared to see it and to read it as it really is.

Imagine, e.g., Tennyson's "Idyls of the King" printed as prose, divided up into "verses," with the verse divisions often breaking the original lines as well as the original stanzas, then imagine these "verses" to be grouped into "chapters" that paid no regard to the original sections of Tennyson's poems. Finally, place this curious document in the hands of an earnest reader that he may read it for the good of his soul, but tell him nothing about Tennyson, or the occasion of the poems, or even that they are poems. Yet something similar to this has happened to the Bible. In spite of its luxuriant literary variety, distinctions even between prose and poetry, to say nothing of finer distinctions within these fields, are hopelessly obscured by the familiar custom of printing everything as though it were solid prose. This is to some extent corrected in the Revised Version by the use of paragraphs for prose and the use of lines for some of the poetry. But even this improvement is carried through with such reserve that the Bible is still left far behind any modern book in the use of printing devices appropriate to form and sense. And there are many who look askance even at the Revised Version, preferring the familiar, though in this respect misleading, Authorized Version. The fact that this is done in all good conscience does not defend the reader from the erroneous conclusions he so easily draws as to the meaning of what he reads.

Language and Literature. When reference is made to the Bible as literature, attention is directed to the medium through which the writers of the Bible convey their thoughts to others. That medium is language; not painting, or music, or mathematics, but speech. The art of speech, first oral, then written, is one of the most wonderful achievements of the human spirit, and some would freely call it the most wonderful of all. It is the chief means by which the ideas and inspirations, the hopes and fears, the plans and purposes, the discoveries and attainments, of one person may be passed on to others; not only to contemporaries, but to those who live long afterward in later and distant generations. After thousands of years of use and elaboration this marvelous instrument, language, is now seen to have well-defined forms which, in turn, are recognized as carrying with them their own definite laws of use and interpretation.

There are at least two reasons why the literary aspects of the biblical writings have been overlooked. The first of these is the fact that the Bible is, above all else, a religious book, and that it is studied almost exclusively for religious purposes. Indeed, it is sometimes felt that the religious values of the Bible are so predominant that to turn aside from them to a consideration of its historical or literary aspects is to turn away from its true purpose and to ignore its true character. The other reason is the fact that so many people pay no attention to any language, not even their own. If they can carry on a conversation in a way that does not invite any embarrassing criticism, ridicule, or misunderstanding, they are content as far as the language itself is concerned. Ignorant of the history of language, they are uninterested in its inherent power and insensitive to its intrinsic beauty. Both the literary and non-literary students of the Bible, however, are at one in their desire to discover what the Bible means. The difference between them is that the former try to take account of the laws of language in their bearing upon interpretation. Language is a wonderful instrument but, like all instruments, its use must be understood and to some extent mastered before one can be sure that it will not wound the hand that holds it. It is part of the divine order that human speech should play a large part in the communication of the divine will; and it is therefore not optional but essential that any reverent search for the meaning of the Scriptures be based upon the principles according to which speech serves its universal purposes. The literary study of the Bible, then, may be described as *a study of the characteristic forms and methods by means of which the Bible messages are expressed in language.*

Literary Differences. A convenient illustration of literary differences may be found in Judges 4 and 5. These two chapters give two accounts of the same event, namely, a battle between the Hebrews and the Canaanites. One of these accounts is in prose and the other in poetry. Here two literary methods stand side by side demanding a recognition of their contrasts in form and spirit if either is to be correctly interpreted. As soon as the distinction between the literary methods is recognized one is aware of the straightforward literal narrative method of the prose, and of the imaginative far-flung passion of the poetry. The former is a record of facts; the latter is an expression of feeling. One is barren of all figures of speech; the other is brimming over with them. If the facts of the narrative be taken as figures of speech, and the figures of speech in the poem be taken as literal facts, confusion at once results and interpretation becomes impossible. The question is not whether one account be nearer the truth than the other; but, rather, how did the event impress the two writers, and what (literary) means did these writers use to convey the truth they saw? Both passages were evidently written after the victory had become a fact, and were written in the glow of that victory. The prose account deals with the fact and the poem with the glow.

Similarly, when Jotham tells a fable or Samson propounds a riddle, it is clear that these are to be taken, not as scientific statements of abstract truth but as fable and riddle respectively. Unless such well-defined literary forms be recognized they cannot be understood. Those to whom the rich field of literature is an undesired or undiscovered country may well feel impatient or scornful of this sort of study; and their feeling would be in a measure justified were the study designed to exploit the Bible as a textbook of literature and nothing else. But the vital factor in the case is the bearing of literary form upon interpretation. Until one knows, for instance, whether the passage he is dealing with is a bit of daring poetical imagery or a statement of scientific fact his interpretation will be, to say the least, precarious. Whether a particular passage is literal or figurative is thus seen to be primarily and fundamentally a literary question. Other factors are involved, of course, but the bearing of these cannot be taken adequately into account until the literary form and character of the passage be clearly established. If for any reason this be impossible, the passage will then necessarily remain to that extent obscure; for neither scholarship nor piety can reliably interpret a passage whose literary character remains ambiguous or unknown.

Types of Literature. A further justification of the literary approach to the biblical writings appears in the fact that they were written, circulated, copied, and preserved as literature before they were regarded, and finally isolated, as Scripture. The making of the Bible was by no means the same thing as the first writing of the different books of which it is now composed. The winnowing and selecting of these particular books and booklets from the much larger body of writings existing at that time was a process that could operate only after these writings had established themselves as literature. They had proved themselves worth preserving by actually being preserved. The writing of the books, in the first place, was one process, while their selection and exaltation into a sacred canon was a very different and much later process. (See arts., *Formation of O.T.*, pp. 91–8; *Formation of N.T.*, pp. 853–9.)

It is not to be supposed that for the biblical author the literary product was an end in itself. It sprang from his desire to share with his fellows his feelings of joy or sorrow, to impart to them his knowledge, or to influence their conduct by praise or blame. To him the modern idea of writing a best seller would have been inconceivable. These writings are great literature because they are greatly felt and greatly uttered. And had it not been for their survival as writings, that is, as literature, they would have disappeared before they could have been gathered into the later collection now known as the Bible. To approach them as works of literature is simply to retrace the divine order according to which they first appeared.

In recent years there has been much study in this field. The biblical material has been examined and classified so that one no longer need lack information on this aspect of the sacred writings. While the various outlines and analyses differ in arrangement and in detail, they all agree in their acceptance of the literary principle of approach. The aim of the outline that follows is not to give a mechanically complete classification of all the biblical material, distributing every chapter and verse into appropriate departments. Even if this were desirable, it would involve much duplication, for a great many passages represent in themselves several different types of literature, and they would then have to be repeated under each type. It has seemed better to indicate the more obvious types, distinguishing them on the basis of their spirit, aim, and content, as well as on that of external form.

1. Pre-Biblical Fragments and Quotations. The mention of the "Book of Jashar" (Josh. 10^{13} 2 Sam. 1^{18}), and the "Book of the Wars of Jehovah" (Num. 21^{14}), as sources for the quotations taken from them, shows clearly that at some time previous to the writing of the present biblical books, collections of songs and sayings were current among the Hebrews. (See art., *The Poetic and Wisdom Literature*, p. 155b.) Even if these two collections had been the only ones, they are sufficient to show that there existed a body of literary material of much greater extent than a casual reading of the Bible might at first indicate. This fact is confirmed by the presence of many other quotations, the sources of which are not named, but which were evidently known and treasured by those responsible for the biblical books in their present form. They are almost without exception in poetical form, but beyond this similarity they vary greatly in extent and character. Some are mere fragments, e.g., Gen. $4^{23f.}$ 9^{25-27} Num. $21^{14, 15, 17, 18}$. Others are full-fledged poems, evidently quoted in their entirety, as Deut. $33^{2f.}$ Judg. $5^{2f.}$ 2 Sam. 1^{19-27}. All, however, are early songs or sayings of a popular character, some personal, some national. Well known in the days of the biblical writers, they seem to have been incorporated in the biblical books in order to illustrate and to brighten the narratives in which they now appear. They certainly do this; and the Bible reader needs only to observe their personal, or patriotic, pre-biblical character.

2. Prose Narrative. The term serves to indicate one of the most conspicuous and characteristic types of the biblical writings. It is so vivid, so concise, and so direct that it is easily taken for an immediate transcript of conversations and events reported on the spot. In this light one is inclined to accept them unreservedly as history, in the sense in which that word is commonly used. Further reading, however, reveals a character in these narratives quite different from that of modern scientific history, and much closer to what might be called, in a strictly literary sense, tale or story.

Story and history are two literary forms distinguished on the basis of their method and purpose. Story and history, in this literary sense, may deal with the same subject, and both may be equally true to fact. But the story will be told in a way that will appeal to the emotions and the imagination, personal and unimportant details will be included, the experiences and fates of individuals will be placed in the foreground, and the whole passage will be designed to arouse an emotional response in the hearer. History, on the contrary, will disregard personal items and individual experiences except where these are vital to the main theme, and will deal with more general material in a large way designed to provide an impersonal record. The story arouses interest while the history supplies information. The story-teller has his eye on his audience while the historian has his eye on the fact he reports. There is not in the Bible any large amount of strictly historical writing in this sense. Much historical material is there but it is presented for other than historical purposes. For instance, the books of Kings might be thought of as historical books. Yet, while they contain much historical material, they offer themselves as an interpretation rather than as a record, and point out the moral of the history rather than an uncolored view of the events; hence, in the Jewish canon the books are designated, not as historical, but as prophetic writings. The writers state explicitly that if one should desire a complete record, he may turn to the sources named for the purpose. An illustration on a miniature scale of history and story, as these occur in the Bible, may be seen in Judg. 1^{4-7}, in which vv. 4 and 5 illustrate the general and unemotional method of reporting an event as it might be done by a historian, while vv. 6 and 7, which obviously deal with the same events, pursue the individual and emotional method of enlisting the hearer's response characteristic of the story-teller.

Stories will naturally differ in subject and purpose. Some will preserve ancient traditions that explain names of persons and places, curious customs, and striking objects. These can usually be identified by the way they close with an explanatory statement, as, for instance, "therefore the name of the city (or person) was called ———," or "therefore the children of Israel eat not of the sinew which shrank." Others, telling about famous men and their exploits, will tempt one to regard them as biographies until it is seen that they too are intended much more to arouse enthusiasm for their heroes than to offer an accurate record of their respective careers. The difference between story and biography is closely parallel to the difference between story and history. Story, biography, and history, however, all have in common that rich, free-flowing, imaginative, pictorial, yet concise quality that has made the biblical narratives, wherever the Bible is known, conspicuous for their simplicity, their beauty, and their power. (See art., *Historical and Legal Literature*, p. 148.)

3. Drama and Dramatic Prose. When applied to the book of Job, which is the outstanding example of formal drama in the Bible, the use of the term needs no explanation. But the recognition of the dramatic form as a literary method has such a vital bearing on the interpretation of much of the Bible that unless the student recognizes it and understands its significance he may easily be misled in his study. By the term "dramatic" is meant a literary method which, instead of describing persons and events to a reader who was not there, presents them as though the reader were hearing and seeing them for himself. The writer of the opening verses of the book of Judges, e.g., looking back upon Israel's conquest of Canaan, might have written: "The tribes of Judah and Simeon were the first to advance into the new and hostile territory. They did this believing it to be the divine will." Instead of this, he dramatizes the event, letting the reader view the action and hear the speakers for himself. The children of Israel, Judah, and Simeon are personified, and then portrayed as individuals inquiring of Jehovah and consulting with each other. The two (personified) individuals then go out on their campaign, exactly as they would had the word "exeunt" stood at the end of a scene in a drama. When a poet wishes to portray the overthrow and humiliation of some detested tyrant, he can dramatize the whole situation by imagining the descent of the oppressor to the abode of the dead and even supply the exact words with which the newcomer is greeted by the shades already there (Isa. $14^{9, 10, 15-17}$). In the very nature of the case these words must be the poet's own. He could not have overheard a conversation that was still unspoken.

This dramatic method is in evidence from Genesis to Revelation. It is employed in the Bible far more extensively than in the works of European and Western writers. It is used for the simplest matter of fact and for the sublimest flights of prophetic imagery. If the prose narrative described (in paragraph 2) above is the typical literary form characteristic of much of the Bible, this dramatic method of portrayal is the typical literary means by which these biblical writers achieve some of their profoundest and most impressive results. It is to be emphasized, however, that this is a form or method of presenting what a writer wishes to say, and the form is not to be identified or confused with the message itself. The latter lies back of the words and is the idea the writer desires to convey; it is his *meaning*. This may be expressed in a great variety of literary forms, and the particular form chosen must be recognized as but the verbal clothing of the thought. It is just here that this dramatic method is so often misleading to a Western reader. He is accustomed to accept printed statements as though they were always to be received as literal matters of fact. In the Bible he meets a dramatic method which necessarily presents its message with an appearance of unqualified directness, and he leaps to the conclusion that what he is reading is a verbatim report of an actual occurrence. But in the nature of the case the writer himself does not appear. He stands aside and lets the story tell itself. His persons (or personifications) with their words and deeds are presented so naturally that at first it is not realized that these personifications, actions, and conversations are the work of the writer. A moment's reflection, however, shows that the sayings and speeches which seem to come so easily from the persons (or personifications) are the words of the writer rather than any literal reproduction of what actually was said. This is obviously the case in the brief passage in Judg. 1^{1-3} referred to above, where the speakers, Israel, Judah, and Simeon, are personifications, and the words they are represented as speaking are the writer's own. What is not so obvious is that this must also apply to the words attributed to Jehovah. Just as the words of Israel represent the writer's thought of Israel's purpose, so the words of Jehovah represent the writer's thought of Jehovah's purpose. This is demanded and established by the dramatic form in which the writer has chosen to say what he has to say.

This dramatic method, then, is (or should be) a constant reminder to the reader of the Bible that when he meets words placed in the mouth of personified nations; of the sea (Job 28^{14}); of a tyrant (Isa. 14^{13}); of a "voice" (Isa. 40^{3-6}); or even of Jehovah, he should consider carefully whether they are to be regarded as words actually and audibly spoken or whether they are not the author's words dramatically imagined. In either case, but especially the latter, they represent the idea the author wishes to convey. They are part of his way of showing what he believed to be the thoughts and purposes, the moods and motives, of the characters he portrays; and they are to be recognized as such under penalty of utterly misunderstanding his thought and purpose. For him this dramatic narrative is just as much his own as if he had set it all out in simple straightforward narrative style.

4. Poems. If one knows only the current Authorized Version, it would hardly occur to him that the Bible contained any poetry at all. It has so long been the custom everywhere else to print poetry in lines that where this arrangement does not appear the passage is assumed to be in prose. Since the year 1753, however, when Robert Lowth, Bishop of London, published his lectures on *The Sacred Poetry of the Hebrews*, the highly poetical character of the Bible has been increasingly recognized and studied.

The difference between the strictly prose view of the Bible and the more accurate prose-and-poetry view may be seen by comparing an ordinary copy of the Authorized Version with the same version as printed in the Paragraph Bible, or else with a modern translation like Moffatt's. In one case the whole Bible seems to consist of a series of brief prose propositions (verses), while in the other it is seen to consist of a rich variety of prose and poetry arranged in sections corresponding to sense and subject. Even then the Bible poetry lacks the accent, measure, and rime usually associated with poetry today. One reason for this is the extreme difficulty of carrying over these features from one language to another in any translation. The other is that these elements are largely lacking in biblical poetry. The biblical form corresponds more nearly to a combination (if such a thing could be) of blank verse and the modern so-called free verse. The lines are not rigidly limited in the number of their syllables, and rime is rare. The poetical character is determined partly by the vivid imaginative language and ideas, and partly by the regularity with which the successive sentences or parts of sentences fall into natural lines of approximately the same length. While these characteristics give to biblical poetry great freedom and flexibility of both form and expression, they also permit a translation that can keep closely to the sense of the original, while preserving a very close approximation to its exact form. Several varieties of biblical poetry may be distinguished but they all spring from the principles just mentioned.

It might seem that while these characteristics appear in the Hebrew poetry of the O.T., the case would be different in the Greek of the N.T. One recalls the classic Greek poetry with its exact systems of lines and quantities and he might expect to find the poetical passages in the N.T. conforming to the classic style. This, however, is not the case. For while the language of the N.T. is Greek, the thought, feeling, and literary methods are all Hebrew in spirit and form.

The book of Psalms is, of course, the supreme treasure house of biblical poems, but Job, Proverbs (cf. 7 below), Songs, and Lamentations are all in poetry. Outside these poetical books there are single poems of great beauty and importance. Some have been referred to under paragraph 1. Others are: Deut. 32^{1-43} 1 Sam. 2^{1-10} 2 Sam. 23^{1-7} Isa. 38^{10-20} Jonah 2^{2-9} Hab. 3^{2-19} Lk. $1^{46-55, 68-79}$, 2^{29-32}. These poems were not composed by the writers of the books in which they now stand, and are not offered as such. Their beauty and frequency tempt one to speculate upon the wealth of poetry the biblical writers must have had to choose from; and, in view of the place the Hebrew nation holds in the history of religion, tempt one further to speculate on the relation that exists between religion and poetry. These poems are all complete in themselves. The poetical passages which constitute large sections of prophetic and apostolic visions and apocalypses are not included. Their content and purpose place them, rather, under paragraph 6 below. As a matter of fact, the biblical writers, especially in their more exalted passages, step easily from prose to poetry, and the biblical language is friendly to such transitions—so friendly, in fact, that it is sometimes difficult to draw the line and to say, "Here the prose ends and the poetry begins." But no such question arises in connection with the poems referred to in this division. They are real poems, and, as in the case of the dramatic type of biblical literature, the reader must permit the literary form to guide him in his understanding of what he reads.

The poet must be allowed to say things in his own way, and often he deals with feelings and aspirations that "break through language and escape." Like Jacob, he wrestles with an angel. He must be read with spiritual sympathy and co-operation. His single words can neither be pressed into etymological niceties nor his separate statements be taken as theological formulæ. The biblical poet is a spiritual pioneer venturing into spiritual territory that he is the first to discover. He is a creative spirit building structures of fervent feeling and passionate prayer that ever after become the refuge, the Holy City, of those whose souls cry out "for God, for the living God." To interpret his words in any other way than as the exalted poetry that they are is to ignore the methods of that Divine Spirit who chooses, above all others, poets through whom to beckon men onward and upward. Where poems occur in the Bible, therefore, they should be read, not as theology, but as the free outpouring of an inspired soul who, under God, thus voices the joys and sorrows, the triumphs and defeats, of those who would otherwise remain inarticulate. More than in any other type of biblical literature, the poems not only speak *to men* but *for men.* As someone has said, "Poetry is the emotion of life made audible," and when this emotion, as in the Bible, is primarily religious, it is easy to understand why the poems in which it comes to utterance should be appropriated by all sorts and conditions of men throughout the ages as the perfect expression of their own deepest feelings and noblest aspirations. (See art., *Poetic and Wisdom Literature,* p. 154.)

5. Exhortation and Direct Appeal. In view of the general acceptance of the Bible as a book of religious guidance it is surprising that this type of literature does not appear in larger measure than is actually the case. One might expect that the Bible would be predominantly a book of explicit advice, warning, or correction; yet this type of literature while sufficiently abundant by no means exceeds in extent the types already noted. Where it occurs it is recognized by its aim, content, and method. It aims to stir the will rather than to inform the mind. It is often dramatic, often poetical, and always direct and urgent. It consists characteristically of rebuke, correction, warning; but these are only contributory to the main purpose of effecting in the hearers a change of action and attitude. The appeals are not easy generalities nor are they intended to develop what might be called an abstract piety. They deal with conditions of the speaker's own time, and are addressed to people, many of whom would know the speaker personally. They are, in fact, to be thought of in most cases as speeches, and much less frequently as documents. They are, in this sense, orations, but they belong to a very definite type of oratory. Oratory in the sense of "making a speech" is the last thing these men would have attempted. They were impassioned pleaders; and if they used the form of public address, it was because they had something they felt the public must hear.

Naturally, the books of the prophets are full of this type of appeal. It is one of the outstanding characteristics of the prophet, and he is always more a speaker than a writer. The Gospels are almost throughout of this type, especially the words of Jesus. The Sermon on the Mount, the Beatitudes, the parables, and many other words, whatever literary form they may assume, are above all else the strong, direct language of exhortation and appeal. In the use of this method Jesus takes his place with the prophets, and the Gospels themselves indicate that this was the place given him by the people of his own day. (See art., *Prophetic Literature,* p. 151). The hortatory sections found near the close of so many of the N.T. Epistles are of this same urgent immediate spirit even if, in the necessities of the case, they had to be written instead of spoken; and they are to be regarded as belonging to this same literary type.

6. Visions and Apocalypses. This type of literature is probably the most remote of all the biblical types from the various forms of literature generally familiar to Western readers. Here drama, poetry, and exhortation are combined to set forth ideas so novel, so strange, and apparently so unrelated to life, as life is thought of to-day, that these passages are either passed over as unintelligible or, at the other extreme, are treated as divine enigmas whose solution reveals a panorama of world history, a key to the meaning of current events, and a sure prediction of things to come. According to 1 Sam. 9[9] the prophet is a spiritual descendant of the seer, the one who sees; and what he sees when he looks into the future, or when he looks deeply into the meaning of the events of his own day, is appropriately termed a vision. In the case of the earlier prophets the visions came spontaneously and were comparatively simple in form and content (cf. Amos 7–9; Isa. 6). But with the later prophets the visions become more and more elaborate. In many cases they are so highly developed that it seems more reasonable to suppose that they are waking visions; the prophet adopting this special literary form as the one most suitable for messages of a special kind.

From these it is but a short step to the apocalypse. The word "apocalypse" (literally, "revelation," "uncovering") is applied to those passages which relate in the form of visions what the seer had seen when he believed himself to be witnessing a sort of panoramic, descriptive explanation of present and future events. These visions have for their background the courts of heaven, and the seer feels himself to be immediately in the Divine Presence. Indeed, a description of the celestial setting usually constitutes a part of the apocalypse. In view of what was said above in paragraph 3 it is easy to recognize in these apocalypses not photographs of reality but attempted portrayals of facts and forces which the seer hardly knows how to describe. He is dealing with a realm which is "not only unseen by man but is in its nature invisible" (Porter, *Messages of the Apocalyptists*, p. 40).

Here, again, form and meaning must be distinguished. The language is evidently figurative and symbolic, and this kind of language is highly attractive to many. But whatever literary form the writer adopts or however numerous and startling the pictures he paints, it must be remembered, (1) that the worth of a message depends upon the faith it reflects and the duty it enforces; and (2) that the faith and the duty are those (*a*) of the age in which the seer himself lived, and (*b*) of the situations which he and his fellow believers had then and there to face. While the book of Daniel in the O.T. and Revelation in the N.T. are the most conspicuous works of this type, briefer apocalypses appear in nearly all the books of the O.T. prophets, while in the N.T., apocalyptic passages occur in the Gospels and in some of the letters as well as in Revelation. In them all, the two principles just mentioned offer the basis of interpretation; and while other principles are involved, these are sufficient for the first approach to this striking type of biblical literature. (See art., *Literature of Intertestamental Period*, p. 187; also art., *Backgrounds*, p. 843.)

There remain a few types which do not call for any extended description yet which are sufficiently characteristic to deserve separate classification.

7. Didactic Literature. As the word implies, this material is dominated by the desire to counsel and instruct. Representative examples are the book of Proverbs; some of the psalms, such as 1, 32, 50, 78, 105, 119; and, in the N.T., many passages in the letters, and the whole letter of James.

8. Letters. Although a few examples of this type appear in the O.T., they are chiefly in the N.T. They vary in size and content from the brief, intimate, and personal note to Philemon, to the elaborate argumentative document "to the Romans." Nearly all, however, are letters in the commonly accepted sense of the term, only a few of the Pastoral Epistles approaching the form of pamphlets intended for an indefinite public.

9. Legal Literature. Down to the present day the orthodox Jews regard the laws of the O.T. as far and away the most important part of all their Scripture. Christian teaching has moved away from the Jewish system, yet the laws which occupy so large a part of the Pentateuch lie at the foundation of the Judaism into which Jesus was born, and constitute a highly important and characteristic type of O.T. literature. (See art., *Historical and Legal Literature*, p. 145.)

10. Statistical Summaries. These too are found chiefly in the O.T. and are represented in the summaries of the reigns of kings (cf. 1 Sam. 14:47-52 2 Sam. 8). But here belong also the numerous genealogies occurring at intervals from Genesis to 2 Chronicles, and even in the opening chapters of Matthew and Luke.

It is not to be supposed that all these types of biblical literature exist so independently and characteristically that all the material can be mechanically classified and pigeonholed. This would not be possible under any scheme of classification. The various forms grow naturally out of the writer's aim and method. In order to express himself intelligibly he had to take language as he found it, saying what he had to say in the literary forms determined (1) by the habits of thought and expression native to himself and his people, and (2) by the results he desired to achieve. In order to discover his purpose and to recover his message, it is necessary to retrace the path his words have traveled, working back through the language and its various forms to the ideas and purposes which, though we might state them in very different fashion, the ancient writer could state only in those forms which were as native to him as his food, his clothes, and his habits of life.

The vital messages of the past, insofar as they have come down through the medium of language, are recoverable only in the degree to which they can be discerned within the literary forms in which they were delivered. And unless these forms be recognized for what they are, both in themselves and in their function, the reader is in constant and imminent danger of mistaking form for substance.

Literature: Bewer, *Literature of the O.T.;* Fowler, *History of the Literature of Ancient Israel;* Genung, *Guidebook to the Biblical Literature;* Moffatt, *The Bible, a New Translation;* Moulton, *Modern Reader's Bible;* Muilenburg, *Specimens of Biblical Literature;* Wild, *Literary Guide to the Bible.*

THE DIVINE ELEMENT IN THE BIBLE

By Professor WILBUR F. TILLETT

The Approach to the Question. In pointing out some of the reasons why the great body of Christian believers have long regarded the Bible as a sacred book, possessed of a divine element, it is the writer's purpose to indicate and emphasize those considerations which may be expected to appeal most strongly to intelligent and devout minds in the day in which we now live. The pendulum of human thought and faith is not static but is in perpetual motion, and in the fact that it swings, swings to and from extremes, lies the secret of progress in seeking and finding truth. The history of religious and philosophical thought is a study in mental reactions. If one generation, in its study of the reasons for believing the Christian religion to be divine, states and stresses to the point of exaggeration what have been called the "external arguments" among the evidences of Christianity, it is sure to be followed by a generation that will seek and find most satisfaction in what are called the "internal evidences." We seem now to be living in such a time as this. We should, therefore, pursue that method in our study of the divine element in the Bible which seems to make for our day and generation the best approach to the subject and the strongest appeal to devout Bible students who, while reading the Bible reverently, interpret it rationally. Only as we do this can the Bible continue to hold its place.

A Book both Human and Divine. The Christian religion can be best understood and interpreted by considering its relation to three things: first, a Person, Christ; second, an organized institution, the church; and third, a book, the Bible. It is not uncommon to refer to and characterize Christ as a divine-human Person, the church as a divine-human institution, and the Bible as a divine-human book. It is important that we have a true conception of the sense and degree in which each of these three things is divine and in what sense human, and how they are related to each other. Misconceptions here lead not only to misinterpretations but to erroneous and hurtful views as to that which we may call divine in the realm of literature.

To see in the Bible nothing more than a collection of ordinary human contributions to religious literature would be, in the judgment of those who know it best and prize it most, to fail to see in it that which is its highest and noblest characteristic, namely, a message of God to the human soul—a message of highest moral and spiritual value not to the people of past ages only but to all generations of men in all ages. To read this book, on the other hand, as if it were, because of its divine inspiration, placed and poised above all human limitations and imperfections, as if it were divinely dictated and there were something so magical and divine in the manner of its writing as to make it improper to subject it to the canons of literary criticism—this would be not only to depreciate its value as literature, but would result in embarrassing the reader with literary and moral difficulties which, though altogether inexplicable on this theory, would disappear at once if its genuinely human element and character should be recognized as no less real than the divine. To read it as something combining in a unique way the human and divine, as a book in one aspect thoroughly human and in another aspect divine, as a book in which God is speaking to men in and through men, is to increase its value as human literature without in any way discrediting its significance as a divine message and as a book of unequaled moral and spiritual value to the human race for all time.

The Sphere of Trustworthiness. The church, although it is a divine-human institution, is now and always has been subject to errors and imperfections, both intellectual and moral, such as belong in varying degrees to all things human. This is at least the Protestant view of the church. The claim of Roman Catholics, however, is that the church (i.e., their church) is so guided and dominated by the divine Spirit as to make it inerrant and infallible. But Protestants, in affirming the errancy and fallibility of the church both as to its teachings and its practice, do not thereby give up the claim that it is, in some true and genuine sense, a divine institution through which God now works and has always worked for the salvation of the world. The faultlessness and infallibility which Roman Catholics claim for the church, Protestants claim only for Christ, the Head of the church. Christ was truly inerrant and faultless, but freedom from error cannot be claimed for his church.

Shall we say, now, that the Bible is inerrant, made inerrant by virtue of its divine inspiration, or that, being a product of the church, it is, like the church, subject to human limitations that may involve errors? If the latter be the case, we may carry the analogy still further and say that as the church, although it be subject to error both intellectual and moral, is nevertheless a divine institution and agency through which God works, so the Bible, a product of the church, even if it should be found to contain errors and imperfections such as are characteristic of all things human, may nevertheless be a divinely inspired book, a book abounding in moral and spiritual truth in and through which God reveals his mind and will to men. To say that Christians get their God and their church from their Bible is a statement full of confusion and error. On the contrary, God and the church come first. It is from God and the church that we get our Bible; and only by recognizing this fact are we prepared to understand and interpret it correctly.

To say that we believe in the Bible because we believe in God, rather than in God because we believe in the Bible, is to state a self-evident truth. God comes first, then the Bible later. God was believed in before there was any Bible at all. God makes the Bible to be what it is, gives it all its moral and spiritual value. Unless God had existed in the faith and experience of men before there was any Bible, there would have been no Bible. In like manner we believe in the N.T. because we believe in Christ. Christ comes first, the N.T. later. Christ existed and was believed in, and had thousands of followers, long before there was any N.T. The Christian church existed for a long time before there was any N.T. The N.T. did not make the church; it is more nearly correct to say that the church made the N.T. (see art., *Formation of the N.T.*, p. 858b; art., *The N.T. and Christian Doctrine*, pp. 946–8).

Nevertheless, while it is true that faith in God, both logically and chronologically, precedes faith in the Bible, it is also true that the Bible, because of the high and true conception of God and the many testimonies to God which it contains, is an aid and guide to our faith in and knowledge of God so invaluable as to warrant the claim that it is practically indispensable to the religious education and spiritual illumination of the world. It is indispensable, not only for correcting misconceptions but for clarifying, confirming, re-enforcing, and preserving the faith of those whose conceptions are true. To serve this purpose it must be a trustworthy book; but for a book to be a trustworthy and altogether safe and helpful guidebook in the realm of religion does not require that it shall be inerrant in all matters. In matters of science, for example, the biblical records simply reflect the views that prevailed at the time the records were made. To claim that its statements involving matters of science, chronology, archæology, and the like, are to be received as infallible and authoritative, is to subject the Bible to criticism and discredit that would be unjust. The purpose of the Bible is to furnish information and guidance, not in those realms of human research and knowledge, but in matters of religious, moral, and spiritual truth. (See the articles on the O.T. in relation to archæology, science, etc., pp. 114–133.)

The Claim of Verbal Inspiration. No other word applied by Christian theologians to the Bible is so suggestive of a divine element in it as the word "inspiration." This term does not mean exactly the same thing to all who use it. But whatever variations may be found in the use of the term, we may say that to all who use it intelligently it means that quality which the Bible, taken in its entirety, possesses by virtue of which it is a safe and trustworthy book of information concerning God, and man's relation to God's will so far as it has been revealed or may be known. How the biblical writers were inspired and how the Bible came to possess that high moral and spiritual value that has led to its being designated as an inspired book, may be and is a point about which there are more or less serious differences of opinion; but the fact that it does, when rightly interpreted, possess the highest moral and spiritual value as a trustworthy book about God and divine things is a point upon which all believers in the Scriptures are practically agreed.

From this point of agreement between those who hold different views of biblical inspiration in the Bible we may calmly consider the character and merits of the two views. Those who hold the view commonly designated as plenary and verbal inspiration claim that the biblical writers were divinely secured against any and all mistakes by virtue of their divine inspiration, and affirm, further, that that which constitutes the Bible a divine book is the fact that the Holy Spirit so dominated and guided the minds and pens of those who wrote as to make their writings free from mistakes of any and all kinds, whether it be mistakes of history or chronology or botany or biology or astronomy, or mistakes as to moral and spiritual truth pertaining to God and man, in time or eternity. According to this view of biblical inspiration, whatever the Bible says must be true because it is God's own Word; what it says is what God says.

This traditional method of setting forth the divine element in the Bible is still acceptable to many Bible students and makes to them the strongest appeal in the way of furnishing a divine credential. But an increasing number of modern-minded Christian believers and Bible students find a different approach to the divine-human book more satisfying and a different statement of the divine element in it more intelligible and convincing.

The Real Evidence of Inspiration. The Bible begins with God, continues with God, and ends with God in a sense and to an extent that is true of no other book in the literature of the world. To affirm that the Divine Presence is immanent in the sacred Scriptures does not mean, however, that the divine is not also here and there transcendently manifest in different portions of the Bible. From the earliest beginnings of a literature among the people whose thoughts of God and relations to God are recorded in the O.T., to the revelations of God made in and through Christ, as these are found, e.g., in the writings of John, the last of the inspired writers, there is a long but ever ascending pathway trodden by devout seekers after God. The one thing that characterizes these pilgrims always and everywhere is their consciousness of God, a consciousness of him that reveals sometimes their conformity and sometimes their disconformity to his will. This characteristic of the biblical literature would, in itself alone, call for and fully justify our recognition of a divine element in the Bible. The divine element in the Bible means this, but it means much more.

To most of those who in our day study and reverence the Bible, the divinest credential which these sacred writings furnish is found in their contents, the moral and spiritual truths of which need no miraculous attestations to make them carry the message of God to the souls of men. E.g., the twenty-third, forty-sixth, ninety-first, and one hundred and third psalms, the forty-second and fifty-third chapters of Isaiah, the Sermon on the Mount, the thirteenth chapter of First Corinthians, and hundreds of other chapters of like worth and meaning, are self-evidencing as to their divine inspiration. The dogma of verbal inspiration and biblical inerrancy and the "external arguments" drawn from miracles and predictive prophecy once occupied the foreground in apologetics. If these appeals were effective in making a former generation hear and heed the voice of God in the Scriptures, they served a good purpose, but their real value did not consist in any abnormal and preternatural and spectacular revelation or exhibition which they furnished of God's power, but in their causing men to hear and heed the word of God that bade them give up their sins, lead righteous lives, and love and serve their fellow men. This moral and spiritual truth in the Bible that makes it speak to the head and heart and conscience with the voice of God—that is the element in it which men of to-day recognize as divine, whether they heed it or not; and we can but feel that this always has been the divinest thing in the Word of God, whether that Word was spoken or written, and whether it was accompanied by miraculous attestations or not.

Interpreting the Whole through Christ. In order to discover this high moral and spiritual quality in these different types of literature, it is not essential that we have accurate knowledge concerning their date and authorship. It is not easy to account for the presence in these ancient documents of so much that is to this day morally edifying and inspiring, and deny the presence there of what we call, and properly so, the divine in the literature.

If, now, in the O.T. Scriptures there is recognizable an element worthy to be designated as divine, for a much stronger reason can we claim that a divine element is present and discernible in the N.T. In the matter of revealing the divine, the N.T. is, in comparison with the O.T., as the sunlight is to moonlight, as the daylight whose spiritual brightness comes from Christ is to the dim but increasing light of the O.T. dawn. The O.T., being a progressive revelation—or, rather, being the faithful record of a people whose progressive religious experience moved ever forward from lower to higher and truer conceptions of God—must needs be read and interpreted not only with religious sympathy but with wise discernment and discrimination, or its naïve simplicity and frank fidelity to facts will be improperly regarded as a divine approving of whatever is recorded concerning the beliefs and deeds of the men and women who appear in the narrative—which is by no means always true. The biblical corrective of what is imperfect and erroneous in these early ethical ideals and beliefs and the completion of whatever in them is good and true are to be obtained from the N.T. Here it is that we find not only that which satisfies us but that which inspires us to be and do our best. When I read the N.T., especially the four Gospels, my head and my heart and my conscience, all alike, respond to its moral appeal, and I rise from each lesson read rebuked if I am doing that which I know to be wrong, but re-enforced and reassured if I am doing that which is right. I find myself at my best when I am in accord with its teachings. In the spiritual reaction that comes to me thus from the reading of this book, I find satisfying evidence that in it God is speaking to me.

In reading the N.T., especially the four Gospels, we are so filled with a sense of the very presence of God whose Fatherhood and lovableness Christ reveals to us—reveals, not merely by what he says, but by what he himself is and does—that we feel profoundly the truth of Christ's declaration that he that hath seen the Son hath seen the Father. He that sees Christ, not the physical but the ethical and spiritual Christ, sees what we Christians mean by the word "divine." There is no other definition of the divine that is so rational and convincing to the intellect and so satisfying to the heart as the sight and the sense of that transcendent ethical and spiritual personal reality in Christ that differentiates him from other men. And no man can read the N.T. with an open and discerning mind, being ever as he reads in the presence of Christ, without realizing that there is a something in this book not found in other books, something so hostile to and corrective of anything and everything that is wrong in thought, spirit, word, or deed; something so appealing and insistent and potent in behalf of virtue, holiness, brotherly love, and whatsoever else is Christlike and Godlike, that the book, however human it may be, is possessed of a quality that may well be designated as divine.

Man's Progressive Apprehension of God. Whatever theory of inspiration makes God most perfect and his revealed will most rational and morally self-consistent must be the true view. No view of inspiration, no matter how divine it may make the Bible to be, can be accepted as true if it should make God less than perfect in his words and works and ways. However different and conflicting may be the conceptions of God reflected in certain portions of the Pentateuch, the book of Judges and the imprecatory psalms, on the one hand, and in the four Gospels on the other, we must not think that God himself was anywise different, was any less holy and just, wise and loving, in ancient days than he was in the time of Christ, or than he, as interpreted to us by Christ, is to our faith now. The difference is not in God, but in the variant, conflicting and changing views of God reflected in the different periods of biblical history and literature. The view of God's nature and character that is absolutely correct—the conception of God as a Being who is always essentially and absolutely perfect—is that which we find in the teachings of Christ and the Apostles as recorded in the N.T.

No view of biblical inspiration can be true that is inconsistent with this fundamental fact of the Christian faith—the absolute perfection of God in all that he does and says and approves. Accepting the interpretation and revelation of God given in and through Christ as the true conception, we may say that there is in the O.T. Scriptures an increasing ethicizing of the idea of God (see pp. 161–3). It is unthinkable that Christ should attribute to God some of the things which he is represented in the earliest period of O.T. history as doing, or commanding, or approving. To write thus of the O.T. is not to discredit it, but simply to explain how, when it is rightly interpreted as a record of the changing and progressive conceptions of God entertained by the people, it is entirely reconcilable with the later, fuller, perfect, and final revelation of Christ preserved in the N.T. While Christ treated the O.T. reverently as the divinely inspired Word of God, he yet not only pronounced erroneous some of the things which were "said by them of old time," but corrected them. If among the things Christ said and did any one thing may be said to be of highest moral and spiritual value, we are perhaps justified in saying that it was his interpretation and revelation of God in such terms of Fatherhood and love as made the Divine Being lovable and brought him near to us. The divinest thing in the Bible, we repeat, is its testimony to the holiness and lovableness of God. Christ showed us—and as the ever-living Christ he continues to show men—God as the loving heavenly Father; and that, and that alone, sufficeth to satisfy the minds and hearts of men.

Meaning and Method of Revelation. In speaking of the Scriptures as a divine revelation of God, there is a possibility of conveying a false impression as to what is meant. The term "revelation" expresses an important truth if properly used, but it is capable of being interpreted in an utterly misleading manner—and it is to be feared that some people so misinterpret it. It must not be interpreted as meaning that God, having prepared a book of divine revelations in some preternatural manner, sent it to men accompanied by miraculous attestations and divine credentials, in order to invest it with divine authority, without which miraculous attestations it would be without authority. God's "revelations" are nothing more nor less than communications of truth in and to and through believing and holy men, men who came to know him personally and vitally in an experience that was at once genuine and normal, and no less divine because it was normal.

If divine revelations were received in a normal way, and were recorded by the recipients in a normal way, with no supernatural accompaniments, they would still be divine revelations. Instead of calling the Bible a divine revelation, it would be more accurate to think of it as a trustworthy record of revelations which God has made from time to time to devout and holy men in and through experiences, which were none the less real and divine if they were normal and natural, than if they were abnormal and supernatural. In this sense we might say that the Bible, instead of being itself God's primary and original revelation, is, rather, the result of revelation. It is God's revelations to men that have made the Bible to be what it is, not the Bible that made the revelations. The revelations came before the Bible came. Nevertheless, having made this true and important distinction, it is proper to add that a book which collects and preserves in a trustworthy record the revelations which God has made to and in and through patriarchs and prophets and poets and psalmists and wise men and apostles, from age to age, all culminating in his revelation to and in and through Christ, may well be designated in its entirety as a book of divine revelation.

All this goes to show that, unless the divineness of the revelation is found in and evidenced by its contents and is discerned in the character of the truth communicated, no supernatural accompaniments attending its communication to men could suffice to make it divine. It may be a matter of much interest to seek and to discover the manner in which the word of the Lord came to patriarchs and psalmists and prophets and apostles—whether in a normal and natural manner, i.e., under normal psychological conditions, or in an abnormal and supernatural manner—but it would be a great mistake to make the divineness of the word revealed depend on the miraculousness of the manner of its communication to men. To make the divineness of the Ten Commandments depend in any degree upon the miraculous accompaniments of their first promulgation to the children of Israel as described in the book of Exodus rather than upon the moral contents and spiritual value of the commandments themselves, would be to misplace utterly the real and true ground of faith in their divineness.

It may be that modern Christian thinkers make too little of the miraculous physical accompaniments which are described as attending many divine revelations that were given to elect and holy men from age to age in the course of Bible history. On the other hand, they certainly are not open to the charge of minimizing or obscuring that divine element in the Scriptures which is found in the moral and spiritual truth which they contain, and in the moral and spiritual influence which they have on the character and destiny of men and nations.

Confirmation in Experience. No definition which we may give to the Bible and no claim, however high, which we may make for it, can give it divine authority. Only divine truth can give the Bible divine authority. What we need to be concerned about is not so much authority for the truth as truth for authority. No dogmatic definition of biblical inspiration in terms of divine infallibility can invest the Bible with inerrancy, unless it be really inerrant. It is only as the Bible contains the truth—the truth about God and man, the truth as it is in Jesus—that it can claim for itself a divine element, imparting to it divine authority. Let us not, then, look for the "divine" in the Bible as if it were a subtle, magic, mystic, preternatural or supernatural something in the origination or composition of it, that removes it from the province of literary criticism and from amenability to all the tests of truth to which other books are subjected. There is, indeed, a divine quality in it that distinguishes it in the literature of the world, that makes it not merely *primus inter pares* among the world's books of religion; it is that, but it is much more. (See art., *The Bible—a Library of Religion*, pp. 15–18.) And that divine quality which raises it above all other books is its self-evidencing truth about the heavenly Father and the divine-human Christ and the Spirit that keeps alive in men the sense of God and the truth that makes men free—free from superstition as well as from sin. The book that has in it the most truth about God and man, about salvation from sin and the life eternal, will always be the "Holy Bible" to all who reverently read it, however much they may fail to heed it.

It is here, then, that our claim for a divine element in the Bible must find supreme justification and permanent ground of acceptance: Is the Bible revelation of God confirmed by our own personal experience with God? Do we find ourselves at our best morally when our lives are most in accord with what the God of the Bible commands and approves? We can but answer these questions in the affirmative; and in so doing we ratify and confirm the truth of our Bible as having that revelation concerning God which alone can satisfy the enlightened conscience of normal religious and reasonable men. The devotees of non-Christian religions, it is true, from the fetish-worshiper of Africa to the Arab who makes a fetish of his Koran, all find varying degrees of satisfaction in the symbols of their religion. But this fact cannot nullify or weaken the force of our conviction that intelligent and truth-seeking men in all countries and in all ages will ever find in the Scriptures of the Christian religion moral and spiritual truth not only unequaled anywhere else, but so satisfying to their heads and hearts, and so potent and efficient in meeting their moral and religious needs, that it is no exaggeration to say that, however genuinely human the Bible is, it is also possessed of a life-giving and inspiring quality which may be truly called divine. This is at once the purpose and the abiding proof of the divine inspiration which Paul claims for it, and on the reasonableness and truth of this claim we can let the question of its divine inspiration rest. "Every scripture inspired of God is also profitable for teaching, for reproof. for correction, for instruction which is in righteousness: that the man of God may be complete, furnished completely unto every good work" (2 Tim. 3[16, 17]).

Literature: Peake, *The Bible: Its Origin, Its Significance and Its Abiding Worth;* Kent, *The Origin and Permanent Value of the O.T.;* Moffatt, *The Approach to the N.T.;* Watson, *God's Message to the Human Soul; The Use of the Bible in the Light of the New Knowledge;* Clarke, *Sixty Years with the Bible; The Use of the Scriptures in Theology;* Aytoun, *God in the O.T.;* Fosdick, *The Modern Use of the Bible;* McConnell, *Understanding the Scriptures;* Gore, *The Doctrine of the Infallible Book.*

Writings by the author of this article: *The Paths That Lead to God*, chs. x, xi, and xii; *Providence, Prayer, and Power*, chs. ii and x.

THE CHRISTIAN APPROACH TO THE STUDY OF THE SCRIPTURES

By Bishop FRANCIS J. McCONNELL

The Historical Approach. The first requisite in the Christian's use of the Scriptures is an honest intent to find out what the Scriptures meant to the people who first read them. We have moved pretty well away from the notion that the biblical writers had in mind the long future in composing their books. If they had thus written for the after-ages, their own periods would not have understood them, and the writings would thus have failed of any immediate purpose. Set forth, however, to meet an urgent current need, the Scriptures can at least be made intelligible for all time. There must be, though, the resolute purpose to discover what the utterances meant for the day in which they appeared. Here is the Christian sanction for all manner of earnest scientific investigation of whatever sort—historical, archæological, linguistic. To get a sound meaning for the readers of a later time we must first know the meaning intended for the first readers. It may well be that the Scripture writers wrote more profoundly than they knew, but we must start with their first meanings.

Perhaps it would be better to say that we must know, first of all, not so much what the first readers understood the Scriptures to mean as what the writers intended to say. In other words, we must ask as to the purpose of the various books. The school of biblical study associated with the name of Baur and his followers rendered lasting service in bringing out into the light the part played by "tendency" in the creation of certain N.T. documents. It is true that the Baur group were themselves so much under the influence of the Hegelian doctrine of thesis, antithesis, and synthesis that they allowed themselves unwarrantable liberties in dating and classifying N.T. material; but the fact that they had a wrong formula should not break the force of their having seized upon a true principle, namely, that the N.T. writers wrote on the basis of assumptions and presuppositions and out of theological tempers and in religious and social atmospheres. It is our duty to take account of all such factors, imponderable and elusive as they often are. There can be no doubt—though this applies especially to the O.T.—that passages having to do with Israel's history have been rewritten, or at least re-edited, more than once, from differing if not from opposing points of view; as, for example, in the treatment of the establishment of the monarchy by Samuel. Any reasonable interpretation of a Scripture passage must ask persistently as to what the author was trying to do. For practical, and especially for homiletic purposes, it is permissible for a reader of the Bible to resort to any use of Scripture he pleases, provided that he makes clear that the use is his own and not that warranted by the meaning of the text itself. The best course here is to tell what the passage means and then to avow frankly the purpose to use it without reference to that meaning. (See art., *How to Study the Bible*, pp. 5–8.)

Assumptions in Bible Study. Here a note of warning is necessary, due to the presence of assumption in our own thinking. Let us not forget that we never approach the study of the Scriptures, or of any other theme of human thought, utterly stripped of assumptions. Every student has some form of philosophy, a philosophy often all the more effective because its workings are not suspected or are not subjected to any close scrutiny. It requires only the slightest acquaintance with present-day biblical study to realize the extent to which the assumptions of the various schools determine the reading of the meanings of the documents. Schweitzer, in his *Quest of the Historical Jesus*, has told us of the course of interpretation as to N.T. miracles, particularly those recorded in the Gospels. At first students took such narratives as literal descriptions of fact. Then scholars of the Paulus type saw in them occurrences described as miraculous but which were, after all, capable of natural explanation. Next came those who saw the miracles as expressions of a myth-forming tendency. After Jesus had been done away with altogether by the seekers of myths, he was restored to the world of fact by the apocalyptic school. Now, here are four different sets of assumptions in N.T. investigation, with possibilities of all degrees of combination and interrelation;—and out of the assumptions the various types of thinkers can discover what the back-lying presupposition calls for. A determined believer in the miraculous once declared that if there had been no miracles in the Bible, we should have been compelled to put some there. The holder of a well-known type of scientific attitude toward natural law will cast miracle out of the Scriptures at whatever cost. The believers in the myth-forming factor in N.T. history have repeatedly hailed with rapture first one book about Jesus and then another which rules out Jesus as historic altogether. The adherents of the apocalyptic view have emptied much of the teaching of Jesus of its significance by their doctrine of an "interimsethik." All these schools are alike in their willingness practically to cut out of the gospel, if need be, any passage which cannot be fitted into the demands of their several theories.

Now, it would be folly to protest against the use of assumption. William James used to say that an investigator who approaches a field just "staring about" without any assumptions whatever is the "veriest duffer." We must have assumptions, and since we must, it seems clearly to be the part of intellectual honesty to admit that we hold assumptions—to recognize the assumptions—to make the most that is possible of them in some situations, and to be on our guard against them in others. Inasmuch as the fundamental battles over the Bible are in the end fought out on the basis of the assumptions, it is well for any biblical student to get his assumptions out into the fullest light. Coming back now to the point of view of the biblical writers, we find everywhere to-day the virtual admission that the Bible was written out of a religious purpose. It is a book of religion. It deals with views of the world and of man and of history, but always from the religious point of view. A good deal of unnecessary debate might have been spared if this primary aim of the biblical writers had been kept in full sight.

The Bible a Book of Religion. Still, this emphasis on the religious aim of the biblical writers is often set forth in a fashion that is not quite fair. We are asked to think of the biblical writers as so concerned about the religious aim that all other matters were indifferent to them. They have now and again been pictured as laboring somewhat after the manner of a present-day preacher—utilizing whatever material came to hand with a spiritual purpose. Just as a preacher to-day might use illustrations from current science or from history or biography, so the biblical writers took their material wherever they found it, thinking always of the main purpose of spiritual instruction. Thus we are told that this essential spiritual purpose gives us the key to the distinction between the permanent and the passing in the Scriptures. The oldtime writers would not have been disturbed, we are told, if they had discovered that their ideas of nature and history were mistaken, provided only that their central aim had been granted and their chief contention conceded.

The fundamental truth here no one can gainsay, but this way of putting it is open to question. The biblical writers took their ideas of the world and of history more seriously than this analogy between them and the modern preacher would imply. They were not searching merely for illustrations to be employed with an immediate, workaday practical intent. No book of religion, indeed, has ever come more directly out of life and has struck more definitely back into life than has the Bible, but it is more than a set of utterances for practical living. It is an attempt to construct, or to reconstruct, the thought of the world and of history with a religious aim, for the sake of the satisfaction of the religious nature. To be sure, such a religious view would be in the completest degree practical, but not practical as the interpretation I am discussing assumes. The biblical writers thought they had the truth in the first chapters of Genesis and in their narratives of the early history of Israel. We know to-day that the contribution which they made to the interpretation of the course of nature and of human history lies in the difference between their handling of materials common to them and, let us say, to peoples like the Babylonians, and the handling of the same material by those other peoples; but we can hardly understand the biblical authors if we do not think of them as taking the material on which they worked very seriously.

Moreover, the distinction between the religious aim in the use of materials and the materials themselves is not always so easy to apply as we often imagine. At the time when some parts of the Bible were written much more was conceived of as belonging to the sphere of religious duty than is usual with us to-day. We have to-day to look abroad to the Oriental peoples—like those of India—to get a hint as to the completeness with which religious significance entered into all phases of men's activity at the time the biblical writings began to take shape. It will not do merely to say that the Bible was written with a religious aim, for at the period when some at least of the Bible was written almost everything in that ancient world was done with a religious aim. The just condemnation of the peoples outside of Judaism in the old day—and of non-Christendom to-day for that matter—cannot be that such peoples have not been religious, or that they have not taken their religion seriously. Such peoples have carried religion into the last and least details of their daily lives. We have only to consider the extent to which the practice of human sacrifice has prevailed among so-called heathen peoples to realize that non-Christian peoples have taken their religion seriously. (See art., *The Bible—a Library of Religion*, p. 15.)

The Ethical Note in Biblical Religion. The statement then that the biblical writers work with a religious motive is not enough. We must consider the type of religion. Here we find at once that the religion of the scriptural writers moves from the start in the direction of the higher ethical insights. The difference between Judaism and Christianity on the one side, and the rest of the religions on the other side, is not so much in the sense of "rightness" as in the directions toward which that sense points. Religion in the Scriptures is increasingly conceived of as moving toward the moral ideal, thought of in such a way as to be stated in terms of the highest and best for human life. What this highest and best was depended more and more upon the direct insights of prophetically minded leaders, the insights in the end being accepted as part of the common thought. When Micah asked Israel if the Lord really required the first-born in sacrifice, he relied upon the direct question itself to prompt its own answer. The question presupposes enough moral insight on the part of the people to render the question intelligible and pertinent. The religious progress of Israel is a moral progress, the morality being conceived of as the realization of the highest and best in human life.

An even more distinctive feature of Hebrew religion was the inexorability with which the biblical writers made moral obligations which they pronounced binding upon men binding also upon God. We have here no need to consider the steps by which the biblical authors seized the moral nature of God, except to say that those authors no sooner thought of a moral principle as binding for man than they likewise conceived of it as inescapable for God. The challenge put upon the lips of Abraham: "Shall not the Judge of all the earth do right?" (Gen. 18[25]) is a characteristic and complete phrasing of the biblical attitude toward God. We seldom find traces in Scripture of the notion that God can do whatever he pleases—a peculiarity remarkable from the fact that Oriental gods, conceived after the likeness of Oriental despots, could do as they pleased. By the time the scriptural development has reached the period of the book of Job there is indeed a facing of questions in God's dealing with men which are insoluble. Job finds no direct answer to his questions whatsoever, but he stands upon his right to ask the questions and upon the obligation of God to deal with the questions himself, even though he will not give a direct answer. Job is satisfied when God himself replies to the challenge, even though the reply is a virtual refusal to give such an answer as Job sought. In Job's thought there might be innumerable reasons why God should decline to answer a man's question, but no reason at all why God should refuse to hearken to the question. The book of Job closes with confidence in God as accepting the moral obligations binding upon the Ruler of the universe.

The Prophetic and the Institutional Emphasis. There is, then, a double movement in the biblical revelation. The writers no sooner find a moral ideal which they conceive of as holding good for men than they make the same ideal hold good for God; and they no sooner get a deeper insight into the moral nature of God than they make the same insight hold good for the nature of man. We are all the time dealing with movement in terms of unfolding moral life. When, however, we are dealing with life, we have to do not with life in the abstract, but with actual human beings; and such human beings, united though they may be in fundamental spiritual aims, may show most diverse tendencies. For the purpose of this article we may look at two such tendencies —that which we may call the *Prophetic*, which seeks to follow the living insight into the spiritual ideal out to its implications; and the *Institutional*, which seeks to codify the moral gains of successive generations into actual statute. Each of these tendencies springs from deep sources in human nature, and each is entitled to consideration in our search for a true method by which to make the most of the biblical revelation.

The laws of Israel came from a variety of origins. They were in part the socially sanctioned ancient customs of a people, some of them selected out of the mass of primitive customs by the good moral sense of the Jewish community, some kept for what might be called their "survival value," such as those enjoining cleanliness and care in dealing with disease, some of indifferent moral significance, probably preserved because of traditions associated with them. Above all, there were the enactments which came out of the insights of prophets like Moses in the earlier and Amos in the later time. If our historical judgment in the consideration of ancient documents is not utterly deceived, Deuteronomy is a deliberate attempt to fasten down into institutional legal expression the teaching of some of the nobler prophets concerning man's true place and conduct in the world. (See intro. to Deuteronomy, and notes on Ex. 20–23 and 2 Kings 22, 23.)

Between the prophetic and the institutional

types of mind there is almost inevitable conflict. I say "almost" because somewhat of the conflict might be avoided if we were to pursue a plan like that suggested concerning assumptions in a paragraph above. If we could recognize and admit and discount our own prophetic or institutional tendency we might hasten the day when both tendencies will work together in the treatment of Scripture more harmoniously than ever in the past. Inevitably the prophetic mind lays stress on the ideal; inevitably the institutionalist puts the weight on the realistic. Temperamentally it is hard for the two types to sympathize with each other, though each at times works indispensably for religious progress. In a social plight such as Amos witnessed his word is the only one worth listening to. Before the need of saving anything spiritual out of the deluge of Babylonianism, in which the Israel of some three centuries later was weltering, the institutionalism of Ezekiel and even of Ezra was the path to salvation.

Of both the prophetic and the institutional types of temper it must be said that they were dealing with actual situations immediately confronting them. The institutionalist was not on the one hand looking backward or the prophet looking forward. Both were studying facts as they saw them, and trying to deal with the facts in the concrete. Both were very much men of their times, and spoke the language of their times. The picture of the prophet as a dreamy-eyed gazer on abstract truth is as much mistaken as that of the institutionalist as a defender of the days that were gone. Sometimes it was the prophet who looked backward; sometimes it was the realist who looked ahead. Sometimes the prophet proposed remedies utterly impossible. Sometimes the realist made the institution work only too well. (See intro. to Ezra-Nehemiah, pp. 454f.; also art., *Prophetic Literature*, pp. 150f.)

Jesus a Realist and an Idealist. The difference between the two types comes to its superlative climax in the career of Jesus. Jesus was both a realist and an idealist. He saw the needs of the times as they were. He saw that if the human and divine ideal of the law and the prophets had been held fast Israel would not have found herself in the clutches of an institutionalized system which had been built up around the letter to the death of the spirit. Against a conception of religion which had been institutionalized almost to death Jesus waged war. There is a good deal of misunderstanding as to the forces which actually brought Jesus to his death. He has been set before us as a teacher of rather abstract truth, misunderstood and persecuted, and finally killed because he was misunderstood. In fact, he was understood only too well. In the sense of not foreseeing the long consequences of their hostility to Jesus the institutionalists were indeed blind, but they were altogether open-eyed as to the immediate results of that hostility. They planned for and succeeded in keeping the Temple interests in their own hands. If they had not caught and killed Jesus just when they did a revolution—confined to the Temple itself but nevertheless potent there—might have swept them out of power and have put a group of prophetically minded leaders in their places. Those who to-day tell us that the concern of Jesus was merely for the individual soul forget that if individuals as such, rather than the vested religious interests of his time, had been the chief aim of Jesus, he might have gone on preaching for fifty years without serious disturbance. Even if he had been driven out of Galilee and Judæa, he could have devoted himself to an itinerant ministry to the Gentiles. Of course Jesus had to seek his results through individuals, but he aimed to purify institutionalism by holding before the people the prophetic ideal as over against an institutionalism which had become mechanical, political, and secular. In reflecting upon the career of Jesus we must not forget that the best of reasons, from the realistic point of view, could be given against following his prophetic idealism *at the time*. Few realists ever object to the ideal in itself. Their count is always against the untimeliness of the ideal. The realists, like Caiaphas, were confronted with what seemed the immediate duty of saving the institution of which they were a part. They would probably have admitted many of the evils of the institution, and would have admitted also the validity of the ideals of Jesus. Their objection was to putting those ideals into effect in a realistic situation which would not have stood the strain. These things are said because the conflict between the idealistic and the realistic goes on to-day and at all times. It may diminish the acuteness of the struggle itself to say that both idealistic and realistic points of view may be marked by complete sincerity, to recognize the importance of both attitudes for the full statement of truth, and to seek for all possible Christian charity on the part of differing tempers and temperaments toward one another.

Jesus the Fulfillment of Biblical Ideals. We see in Jesus the fulfillment of the ideals toward which all scriptural thought moves. The highest human ideals find embodiment in him and in him the same ideals are taught and seen as holding good for God. It would seem then that the adequate treatment of the theme of this article would be just to ask as to the attitude of Jesus toward the Scriptures of his time. This, indeed, would be a correct answer, provided we patiently set ourselves not so much to a swift, compendious statement, but tried to follow out the just implications of the answer. The summary statement is that Jesus sought in the Scriptures for the spirit that giveth life rather than for the letter that killeth. Now, this can be so put as to imply that Jesus had no place for the institutionalized religion of his time—and this would be far from the truth. Faulty as was the religion of the day of Jesus, that religion in its organized form served through the experience at the Temple to re-enforce in the boy Jesus a consciousness of his high destiny and largely shaped the mold of his thinking throughout his after career. The Temple itself was always a magnet which attracted his steps and his thought. His aim was not to overthrow the Temple worship, but to fill it with a new spirit. He saw in the Temple the outcome and expression of necessarily realistic tendencies arising out of the regular, official interpretation of the sacred books of the Jews; and his intention was not to destroy the institutionalism but to fulfill it. With that purpose he read the Law and the Prophets to seize their spirit and to discover their direction, and to follow that spirit and direction whithersoever they might lead. To love God with the whole heart and the neighbor as oneself was the purpose and goal of the scriptural movement. Wherever institutionalism, in the form of church, or creed, or law, or book, forgot that main aim and sought to become an end in itself and not an instrument, he set it aside. Nothing is more truly indicative of the attitude of Jesus than the pronouncement that the Sabbath was made for man and not man for the Sabbath.

Jesus as a Criterion of Biblical Revelation. Now, all this gives us a clue as to the way we are to use the example of Jesus in the study of the biblical revelation. The spirit of Jesus himself is always discernible in what he says and does. We know how he feels toward man and God. We see in him the revelation of God himself. We are to judge the revelations in the Bible by their varying measures of likeness to the spirit of Jesus. In the light of that spirit we are to discover our duty in the application of Christian truth to the problems of our own time.

Here again we have to be on our guard against the notion that Jesus was a teacher of abstract truth. Jesus spoke concretely and dealt with actual situations. Even in the fourth Gospel, where the utterances of Jesus are more general than in the Synoptics, they take their coloring from the detailed settings in which they are framed. We can hardly say that the words of Jesus can be packed into a formal system, except as the characteristic of their all-revealing one spirit bestows on them a genuine unity. Those who tell us that the method of Jesus was to announce a principle, and then leave the principle to work its own way to the overthrow of evil and the establishment of good, are not the soundest of interpreters. Jesus dealt with particular evils, especially those that had grown up around the Temple. In fighting those evils he did indeed act on principles and assumptions—and the principles and assumptions have implications and suggestions valid for us of to-day. When we have perceived the implications we have ourselves to put them into force in the concrete. They will not put themselves into effect.

As Jesus did not utter abstract truth on the one hand, neither did he promulgate formal rules on the other. He set forth a spirit and acted on assumptions everlastingly valid, but he issued no formulas good for all time. Every now and again some devout follower of Jesus declares that a sufficient guide to practice in all moral situations is to ask what Jesus would do. The measure of worth here lies in the fact that asking such a question is fitted to recall the mind of the questioner to the need of a thoroughgoing sincerity and the indispensability of a right spirit. Beyond this the question is of little avail. The determination to be loyal to the spirit of Jesus may conceivably lead to a bondage to the letter of Jesus which militates against the spirit.

For example, take the attempt to make the words of Jesus into a basis for economic procedure to-day. Modern economics might well set before itself the emphasis on human values which marked all the work of Jesus. Indeed, economics is being recast and rewritten from the point of view of human meanings. In so far the teachings of Jesus may be the best of foundations for modern social study, but the moment we advance to detailed considerations as to how the human values are to be guarded, the only light we get from Jesus is to remember that if Jesus were in our place he would do whatever we ought to do—but what we ought to do is the rub. Modern economics turns around modern capitalism. Institutionalized capitalism as we have to deal with it did not exist in the age of Jesus. There were the haves and the have-nots, the greedy and those envious of the rich who had a chance to be greedy. Jesus spoke more often and more pointedly about the temptations of wealth than about any other temptations. All this has to be held steadily in view in our dealing with wealth, but it does not solve specific problems—such, for illustration, as the ethics of charging and receiving interest in present-day capitalistic enterprises. So with scores of other current social difficulties.

We have here a glimpse of Paul's wisdom in meeting the crises which repeatedly came upon him in the creation and care of the apostolic churches. Paul sought most earnestly to discover the spirit of Jesus as a guide in his dealing with his churches, and he sought that spirit by patient inquiry into the actual career of Jesus on earth. It soon became apparent, however, that Paul could not thus find detailed guidance. The problems that confronted him were altogether different from any that Jesus actually solved. To begin with, the total environment was different from that of Jesus, as being Gentile rather than Jewish. The few excursions that Jesus made into Gentile territory threw no light on the duty of an apostle working all his days among the Gentiles, and working too on a different task from that of training the Twelve. So that there may be a very practical phase of significance in the word of Paul that he was determined no longer to know Christ after the flesh. Perhaps it was highly providential that Paul knew so little of the historic Jesus. Perhaps if he had known more of the actual history he might have so tried to repeat details of Jesus' actual procedure as to have lost the Christ-spirit. As it was, the spirit of Christ meant more to Paul with the passing of every day. The meaning of Christ deepened with continued reflection—a reflection which itself kept Paul from any slavish imitation. Christ was not before Paul as a pattern to be imitated, but as a Person whose thought and spirit were to be breathed in as one breathes in a personal atmosphere. If we were to define inspiration at all, the definition would have to be in terms of personal influence and atmosphere—and influences and atmospheres defy definition.

The Gospel of Jesus and the Gospel About Jesus. This reference to Paul suggests to us a current debate which we may appropriately use for illustration. We have heard much of late concerning the "gospel of Jesus" and the "gospel about Jesus." Those who talk about the religion of Jesus seem to desire a strictly critical examination of the scriptural materials to determine the actual facts of the life of Jesus, to determine just what he did and said and thought and how he lived, with the purpose of finding light on practical religious problems of to-day. Such study often professes to seek for the spirit of Jesus, that men may be taught to reproduce that spirit in their lives. The aim seems sound as thus stated. The stricter the scientific examination becomes, however, the more positively the student is likely to affirm that the ideas of Jesus were just theology after all, and then we have left what is called the spirit of Jesus. So it comes to pass that we behold moral phenomena like that of a great Hindu of to-day who avows that he seeks to live in the spirit of Jesus while nevertheless yielding to none in his own reverence for the sacred cow. Then a final step is taken by the more severely scientific—those who find the recorded facts about Jesus so meager that they dismiss him as historical altogether.

On the other side are those who declare that the essential is the gospel about Jesus. They tell us that from the beginning the believers in Jesus began to put larger and larger interpretations upon his life, insisting that in him we have the revelation of the divine, the manifestation of the spirit in which the universe itself is carried on. Hence the terms "virgin-born," "pre-existent," "Son of God," and the like. They point to the entire course of the history of the church as a warrant for putting on the character of Jesus the largest interpretation that the facts will warrant. What we need to know is not merely the significance of Christ for man but his significance for God as well. Or, rather, we are told, we cannot make the most of Christ for men unless we can make the most of him for God.

This aim too, as thus stated, seems sound. Nevertheless, those who so move in the direction of placing the largest interpretation upon Christ in their teaching about him may end as do the minutely specialized scientific—they may practically do away with the historic Christ altogether, or so ignore the historical facts as to reduce them to virtual insignificance. Then we are told that it is of no consequence how the Christ-idea of God arose in the course of human history; the idea is now here and we are to make the most of it for men and for humanity.

It is clear after a little reflection that we need both the gospel of Jesus and the gospel about Jesus. Either view taken by itself and pushed to extremes—and the religious temper tends to extremes—in the end is likely to do away with Jesus altogether. Here again we may profitably study the writings of Paul. Paul went further than any other Christian of his time—perhaps of all time—in putting upon the Christ-life the weightiest possible interpretation. Paul has an elaborately developed gospel about Christ. Nevertheless, it is evident that Paul always kept in mind the fundamental traits of Jesus as those had been described to him by the disciples. If we pick out of Paul's epistles passages like Phil. 2:5-11, which set out the self-sacrifice of the Divine Son of God, we find in them poetical or theological phrasings of the type of spirit which the historical Jesus is represented in the Gospels as manifesting. We might collect all the utterances of Paul about Jesus into a Pauline biography of Jesus and not find the Pauline statement out of harmony with the portraits given in the Gospels.

All of this leads to a word of summing up. In the study of the Scriptures we need the play and interplay of two types of activity. We need the most realistic search for the facts, and the most realistic handling of the facts of institutionalized religious utterance as embodied in the Scripture. On this basis of fact we need to erect the loftiest possible superstructure of idealistic interpretation—the ideals conceived of as pointing upward toward the highest and best in man and God.

Literature: W. N. Clarke, *Sixty Years with the Bible;* Eiselen, *The Christian View of the O.T.;* J. Morgan Jones, *The N.T. in Modern Education;* F. J. McConnell, *Understanding the Scriptures;* McFadyen, *The Approach to the O.T.;* Moffatt, *The Approach to the N.T.;* Thistleton Mark, *The Appeal of the Bible Today.* See also "Literature" under the articles, "The Bible a Library of Religion" and "The Divine Element in the Bible," in the present volume.

THE USE OF THE BIBLE IN PREACHING

By the Reverend S. PARKES CADMAN

The Diversity of the Scriptures. The Bible is a select literature of divinely inspired human experiences. It has survived centuries of mutation because of its permanent spiritual values. It is the product of a revelatory process covering many ages and enriched by individuals of diversified temperaments and conditions. Among them were princes and peasants, statesmen and poets, artisans and shepherds, prophets and annalists from various walks of life and appearing in different periods of time. All the sixty-six books of this sacred library deal in the main with the ways of God toward man. They describe with vivid realism the supreme issue of man's thought and imagination; his vital contacts with his Creator, and his obligations to the redemptive purpose of Deity manifested in Christ Jesus. Hence the Bible is pre-eminently the book of religion, the most complete record extant of the progressive self-disclosure of God adapted to the advancing intelligence and morality of his offspring. Its communications were determined by man's recipient ability; his spiritual evolution is indicated by its ascensive truth and illumination. It has been the companion of every human fate, journeying with the race out of the miry clay of its beginnings forward to the Delectable Heights of the incarnation and its evangel. Consequently, some human lesions and limitations are found in Holy Scripture. Indeed, it is the more divine because of its humanness, and its entire content is justified by the purpose of grace unto salvation pervading the Book, and culminating in Jesus Christ.

Its literary forms embrace legends, myths, folklore, fables, and parables; lyrical poetry, drama, idyls and hymns; letters, memoirs, maxims, philosophical observations, predictions, apocalypses, and homilies. Their general viewpoint is practical rather than theoretical. The biblical writers were not purists subservient to grammatical and linguistic canons. They spoke of things as they saw them in the light of the eternal verities. The literalist who interprets their words according to the rigid rules of a static theory fails to recognize the differences between prose and poetry, history and romance; between the picture thinking of the East and the conceptive thinking of the West; between the exalted visions of mysticism and the logical analyses of rationalism. (See art., *The Bible as Literature*, p. 19.)

The Unity of the Scriptures. Notwithstanding the Bible's marked dissimilarities, however, it has an underlying unity which demands that what is essential shall be distinguished from what is incidental. Its ancient formulations of truth and righteousness are applicable to our own generation and its problems. Things new and old in these treasuries of God are at the disposal of their wise stewards. The Book portrays a historic unveiling of the divine mind through human experiences which are reproducible in believers of every subsequent age. Their consciousness of the pardoning presence and peace of the Everlasting Father confirms the witness of the Bible to these certitudes of the soul.

A Progressive Revelation. The progressive nature of the biblical revelation is seen in the O.T. conception of God. (See art., *The O.T. Conception of God*, p. 158.) A similar development is seen within the more limited compass of the N.T., which covered a very brief period of time as compared with the centuries covered by the O.T. The testimony to Christ as Lord because Redeemer of the world is outspoken and unanimous from Matthew to the Apocalypse. Nevertheless, an ever-increasing evaluation and exaltation of our blessed Lord is discernible throughout the literature of the apostolic church. The law of development which Cardinal Newman set forth in his *Essay on Christian Doctrine* operated during the near interval after our Lord's resurrection. The enriched experience of early believers, the expansion of their religion throughout the Græco-Roman Empire, and its contact with the pagan culture which was still formidable though decadent, induced the N.T. church to interpret the person and mission of Christ with ever-widening fullness. True, it is the same Jesus of faith and fealty "who wrought with human hands the creed of creeds." But how much more fundamental is the apprehension of Romans than Thessalonians, of Ephesians than Corinthians, of Colossians than Galatians, of Hebrews than the Epistle of James, of the Gospel of John than the synoptic Gospels. As our appreciation of Israel's monotheism is heightened by the knowledge of the chaos preceding its declaration, so is our reverence for Christ intensified when we survey the ascensive confessions of his first disciples, as given in the chronological order of the N.T.

A Manual of Religious Devotion. The Bible is the unequaled manual of religious devotion. Other sacred literatures have their inspirational moods and nearly all chronicle some spiritual experiences which men will not willingly let die. But none compares with this Book of Books for its pledges of communion with God, its mystical loveliness, its precepts of righteousness, its programs for the spiritual life of the individual, the community, and the nation. Nor is it content merely to post those programs. The means for their fulfillment in godliness of deed and conversation are set out in detail. Legalism, sacramentarianism, and simple trust are in turn related to the divine prerogatives of forgiveness and restoration. Man and his immortal destiny are here so variously emphasized that the things of the Spirit become paramount for him. The Book's unsurpassed and lasting value is established by its devotional features alone.

The Need of Rational Interpretation. Life's pressing problems receive no uniform solutions in Holy Writ. Nor do its earlier answers to man's most insurgent questions always anticipate the prefect revelation of Christ. He is the light of all Scripture. Its contents should, therefore, be judged by his teachings, and wherein they fall below the level of those teachings they are either preparatory or negligible. Those who insist that the truth of the atonement is found in the Levitical ritual, or that the Pauline ideal of universal redemption is contained in Hebrew prophecy, or that the depth and intensity of the life which is hid with Christ in God have been plumbed by the Psalms, do violence to the essential meanings of the Book. Such inversions arise out of an excessive introspection blind to variant conditions, changing conceptions, progressive methods of religious thinking, and to the supremacy of Christ's message to mankind. The fact that they are intended to promote esteem for the Bible as a whole does not annul the mischief of these forced interpretations when they are made to do duty in the place of scientific exegesis. Yet it speaks with persuasive authority on all matters pertaining to man's highest welfare. And what it has to say is couched in terms of sympathy and insight as well as firmness and finality.

The Basis of Successful Preaching. For these reasons the Bible is the basis of successful preaching. It magnifies Christ as the vital source of that knowledge of God in which stands our eternal life and freedom. It directly relates the Christian minister of every age with his Lord. It assures him that his spiritual genealogy does not derive from Homer, Dante, Shakespeare, Milton, Goethe, or any other literary celebrities, but from the prophets of the O.T. and the apostles and confessors of the N.T. His chief business, then, is to explore the vast hinterlands of Holy Scripture, and make himself familiar with its fertile fields in order that he may bring their healing produce to his fellow believers. Every resource of ancient and modern learning should be drawn upon to expound its characteristic truths. Nor can he ignore the verification of these truths in his own experience. What he has felt in his soul's intercourse with the Book and its Author predicates his effective utterance in the pulpit. The internal conflicts and external obstacles which evoked the tremendous climaxes of the men of the Bible must be envisaged by him. Their confidence concerning God, assurance of things unseen, visions of everlasting righteousness, insistence upon human rectitude, and endurance of persecution were not the achievements of groundlings conformed to the fashion of this world. They were the gains of God-intoxicated spirits won in defiance of earthly custom and rule. We who follow with unequal steps should not the less but the more keep in sight these paladins of the Almighty.

Open-Mindedness and Biblical Preaching. Open-mindedness is a requisite for biblical preaching. It is sanctioned by our Lord's query addressed to one who was supposed to be well versed in the Scriptures, "How readest thou?" (Lk. 10[26].) This man had read to little purpose so far as the marrow of the Word was concerned or he could not have failed to apply the inclusive truth of love to God and service to man. Many of his contemporaries were equally at fault because of their rage for current orthodoxy. Had the Pharisees understood the story of David, they would have refrained from criticism of the disciples who plucked the ears of corn on the Sabbath Day (Mt. 12[1f.]). Had the Sadducees meditated intelligently upon the words, "I am the God of Abraham, of Isaac, and of Jacob," they might have correctly interpreted the doctrine of the future life (Mt. 22[23f.]). Had the religious leaders of Jerusalem read historically this prophecy, "The stone which the builders rejected, the same was made the head of the corner," they might have viewed the Messianic claims of Jesus in a different light (Mk. 12[10f.]). To be sure, these official coteries studied the O.T., but their mental reservations and prejudices disqualified them for its explanation. Its transcendencies were obscured for them by their willful limitations. The Scriptures' majestic verities were in their right hand, yet they did not know it. When interrogated they became irrelevant or dogmatic, stressing trivialities, "straining out the gnat and swallowing the camel," while the issues of justice and goodness were overlooked (Mt. 23[23f.]).

The Example of Our Lord. Our Lord quoted the O.T. with the freedom of perfect knowledge actuated by profound reverence. He showed fealty to the spirit rather than the letter of its prophets and psalmists. His censure fell upon those professionals who either could not or would not differentiate between the substance and the form of its contents. Their bewildering notions about its relative values obscured its redemptive righteousness. Paul, likewise, and other authors of apostolic literature, felt the same freedom toward the O.T., and none of them more so than the unknown writer of the Epistle to the Hebrews. The comprehensiveness of this Epistle exemplifies an organic method which every preacher can well afford to practice.

Again, our Lord quoted the text of the O.T. with reference to the context. His favorite phrase, "Again, it is written," signified his habit of comparing Scripture with Scripture and correcting when necessary by the comparison (Mt. 4[1f.]). He repudiated by inference the resort to the Bible as an arsenal of proof texts, to be seized without regard to their surroundings or moral and religious value, and used in confirmation of creedal statements, or as weapons for theological warfare. Some belated preachers are still addicted to this abuse of Holy Writ, with the result that numerous vagaries have obtained seeming support from the Bible. Indeed, there is scarcely a theological error, an ethical perversion, or an ecclesiastical misdemeanor for which the intellectual vice of quoting "proof texts" is not in part responsible. It is rooted in a theory of verbal inspiration which the Bible nowhere claims for itself. Literalists sound the alarm that the Scriptures are jeopardized by the scholarship which has elucidated their teachings afresh, and placed their light upon a golden candlestick of devout and constructive learning. What has really happened is that certain dogmatic presuppositions about the Bible have suffered a shock which shows them to be without foundation.

The Question of Authority. It is here pertinent to discuss the Bible's relation to religious authority. Roman Catholicism regards Christianity as a dogmatic and devotional system, promulgated by the church as the custodian of apostolic grace and tradition. Protestantism also reckons with the historic continuity of the faith and with what that continuity involves. But it insists upon the Christian's privileges to submit the greatest experiences of the past to his vital experience of the present, in accordance with the witness of the indwelling Spirit of Truth and Holiness, and the requirements of advancing knowledge. The exercise of this privilege, which belongs to the individual priesthood of the believer, has frequently exposed Protestantism to the perils of subjectivism. But it has also maintained that freedom of the spirit which is the inheritance of the sons of God and an essential part of the good in everything. A reliable safeguard for the preacher against the fancies of unregulated interpretation is the *consensus fidelium*—the collective judgment of Christian fellowship. It has not always functioned, because it was overridden by some expositors who were supposedly complete in themselves. Nevertheless, extravagances and obsessions cannot hide the truth that religious liberty guarantees research and welcomes verification without the handicap of *ex cathedra* pronouncements.

How, then, should the preacher view the authority of the Bible? Does it not inhere in the appeal which the Book makes because it adequately reckons with all the facts involved in the case? It imposes its mandates not as official edicts but as self-evident verities and practical suggestions, illuminated by God's gradual self-disclosure perfected in Christ. At any rate, this was the test applied by the third Council of Carthage in 397 A.D., which had to decide what Christian writings of apostolic origin should have biblical authority. In brief, the intrinsic values of these writings were the determinant of their admission, the same condition which had dominated the Jewish Synod of Jamnia, about 90 A.D., in establishing the canon of the O.T. (See art., *Christian Approach to the Bible*, p. 36.)

The principle of the believer's responsibility for biblical interpretation by spiritual discernment was never withdrawn from the church. It was advocated by the first Protestant reformers, neglected by the majority of their successors, conserved by an enlightened few, and revived in the early Victorian age in the interests of the historical methods of interpretation. We well understand that our Christian culture does not depend on an indiscriminate allegiance to what has been handed down. Yet tradition ought to be recognized so long as personal experience and the results of sound learning are conjoined with it. (See art., *N.T. and Christian Doctrine*, pp. 948–9.)

The Use of Scholarship. In thus using the Bible, the preacher should be characterized by honesty, accuracy, clarity of mind, and charity of spirit. Much weakness in preaching arises from the separation of intellectual ability from spiritual insight, of scientific appraisal from evangelistic appreciation, of the qualities of scholarship from a fervent zeal. It is not to be expected that the average preoccupied pastor shall become a first-rate biblical scholar, but he must know and incorporate into his sermons the best results of biblical scholarship. They forewarn him against the pitfalls of literalism, relieve him of countless embarrassments due to the contrasts between the earlier and later Scriptures, and conduct him to the bracing religious climate of their altitudes. (See art., *N.T. and Criticism,* p. 885.)

The well-poised minister will not be unduly disturbed by the contradictions and inconsistencies of Holy Writ, many of which enhance its charm and intensify the impression of its indestructible unity. Human limitations account for the former; the divine initiative behind them accounts for the latter qualities. The cranny through which the Eternal Will poured its radiance was narrow enough, as all must admit, in view of the oceanic extent of that Will. But the wonders of grace that followed its transmission justify the human element in the Book. It magnifies the protracted forbearance of God and shows that his delight is with the children of men.

The critical examination of the Bible is secondary for the minister's use until he passes beyond its stages to a candid estimate of the Book's religious values. Then what he has recruited beforehand becomes a formidable array. Imagination, which is to the pulpit what the eyes are to the body, flourishes in sound exegesis and falters on its opposite. Eaglelike pinions for the sermon's flights are obtained from what the preacher knows by verification and experience. Behind the onward thrust of his discourse is the barrage of organized knowledge. Ahead of it are the heights triumphantly scaled by a rational faith. Instead of sheltering in the vulnerable trenches of literalism the instructed advocate of Christianity seeks a profounder consciousness of the realities which his reasoned beliefs assure. He wastes no energies on a forced reconciliation between the Song of Songs and the Epistle to the Ephesians, or between the cosmogonies of Genesis and those of modern science. His audience is brought without irritating delays into the presence of the Eternal. The prophets and apostles who spoke *for God* as well as *from* him are introduced, and what they have to say is corroborated by the response it evokes.

Biblical Preaching Secures Diversity of Themes. In an age when the gulf between knowledge and ignorance of the Bible is widening, its real character and aims should be the themes of a teaching ministry. The stream of sorrow which is always falling darkly through the shadows of the world; the perplexities, woes and sins of men; the satiety which robs them of zest for existence, alike admonish the servant of the Most High that he must begin and end with the Book. The very splendor of our material civilization threatens its spiritual underpinning. Its inward resistance is not equal to the outward pressure it is called upon to sustain. This widespread condition cannot be remedied by dissertations upon literary, ethical, and social themes offered independently of the divine Word. It is as true now as when Macaulay said it nearly a century ago, that in passing from a people which knows and loves the Bible to one that does neither we pass from a higher to a lower stage of civilization. The practical application of its melioristic passages constitutes the life blood of individuals and commonwealths.

The concentration here advised is not liable to monotony. Every condition of human life and temperament is amply provided for in Scripture. The informed mind, the disciplined imagination, and the religious impulse of the pastor enable him to choose from its harmonious truth whatever feeds his flock. He escapes the snare of sameness so long as he cultivates the many-sidedness of the Book. Textual sermons persist, not because they are a homiletical convention, but by reason of the background and the spiritual suggestiveness a well-chosen text affords. The manifold aspects of truth in a single biblical passage open up much profitable moralizing and enrich the hearer's religious experience. The text binds the preacher to its author, to the God who inspired it, and to the countless souls it has blessed. The gifts of faith, hope, and love are ours in these memorable transcripts from prophetic hearts which beat again in earnest preaching.

Types of Biblical Preaching. Preaching may be expository, doctrinal, historical, biographical, pastoral, ethical, and evangelistic, and all may be given a biblical basis.

Expository preaching applies the message of words, phrases, chapters, and even books to present necessities. The poetic sense, practical sagacity, thirst for spiritualities and knowledge of literature of the expository preacher are so many servants of his purpose. He finds openings for his talents in the lyrics of the Psalter, Isaiah's theophanies, Jeremiah's deep insights, Ezekiel's visions; in the ethical deliverances of the lesser prophets; in the parables of the Master, the dialectics of Paul, and the mysticism of John.

Doctrinal preaching packs Christian truth in concise formulas. Its neglect in recent days is chargeable with much loose thinking and vaporous speech. The ordered presentation of positive beliefs is the best antidote known to men for the numerous current fallacies, not to say caricatures, relative to religion. One does not have to remark that this kind of preaching has no necessary connection with controversial mannerisms or negative assertions. It makes an intelligent use of philosophy, science, and comparative religions to illustrate the superior virtues of Christianity, and does justice to those mighty spirits of other days who by means of doctrinal preaching successfully defended Christianity against the onslaughts of its antagonists.

Historical preaching reviews our racial developments in the light of Heaven's guidance, and expatiates upon the interventions of that Power, not ourselves, which makes for righteousness. It warrants the assertion that a redeeming Providence presides over the rise and fall of civilizations. Beyond them all is the fair City of God, beloved and longed for, the goal of seers and saints from the time of the prophets to the present hour.

Biographical preaching analyzes the traits of human nature so strikingly depicted in the portrait galleries of the Bible. Here are the wise man and the fool, the patriot and the traitor, the saint and the sinner, the philanthropist and the cynic, the generous and the selfish man. All were of like passions with us. Some were molded by supernal influences for good, others yielded to their baser selves. A study of psychology and the reading of general biography forfend the preacher of this school against intellectual sophistries and keep him in touch with his fellow men. He calls their attention to "the great cloud of witnesses" who watch their progress heavenward, and also to those backsliders who having made shipwreck of faith are beacon lights of warning. The spiritual achievements of biblical characters and of those who emulated their example are fertile sources of his edification of believers.

Pastoral preaching exalts the privileges of fellowship. But it does not spend so much time coddling the saints that it has none left to catch sinners, nor does it cater to pharisaical complacency any more than to worldly corruption. It invigorates faith, rebukes lukewarmness, chides waywardness, and chastises hypocrisy or defiant wickedness. It feeds the flock of God and labors for those compacts of peace with justice which extend his fold. Its emphasis is laid upon the Fatherhood of God and the brotherhood of man, to be realized by conformity to Christ as Saviour and Lord.

Ethical preaching is eager about the conduct which is religion's convincing side for the world. The study of sociology and of comparative ethics helps the preacher to expound the great utterances of the Prophets, Gospels and Epistles on this important issue. Such preaching is inseparably related to the individual, the family, the nation, and mankind. Industry, politics, recreation, and kindred social pursuits are within its jurisdiction. The theme is susceptible to flabby sentimentalism, to platitudes, to inaccurate generalization and to the perversions of casuistry. But no type of preaching is more profitable provided it is equipped with lucid thinking and courageous faith.

Evangelistic preaching lays an urgent demand on the conscience and heart of its hearers for unconditional surrender to Christ. It presents life's alternatives and the penances and the praises of the "new creation" in him. Satisfaction of the human quest for God, deliverance from the burden and guilt of sin, and consciousness of the divine indwelling are essentials of the evangelical message. It has had a glorious history for the past twenty centuries during which the church repeatedly returned to it after seasons of scepticism and sterility. Its vision of sin's vileness and consequences and its passionate urgency for an immediate response to the appeal of the Cross were never more needed than now.

The Preacher and His Scripture Lesson. The public reading of the Bible should not be undertaken without a previous rehearsal of the selected lesson. One of the purposes of this reading is that it shall make divine worship far more effective and reverent than it is.

Read the Bible; do not mutilate it by a false manner of mouthing its predictions, exhortations, and advices. Young preachers may well consult the lectionaries of the Anglican and Lutheran Churches. *A Book of Old Testament Readings*, by Professor Robert W. Rogers, selections made by a master in the Scriptures, should also be kept on hand. These volumes may largely dictate our selection of the lessons for the day.

The Secret of the Great Preachers. The pulpit princes who have molded the destinies of nations were preachers of the Bible. Their conviction of its supremacy and truth induced in them the ministry worthy of their embassage. Think of Chrysostom, Augustine, the three Gregorics, Francis of Assisi, Savonarola, Wyclif, Wesley, Edwards, Whitefield; of Chalmers, Robertson of Brighton, Cardinal

Newman, Bishop Simpson, Liddon, Beecher and Brooks; of Behrends, Maclaren, Whyte, Watkinson, Bishop Galloway, Horne and Jowett; of many others, some of whom are fallen asleep, while others remain with us. They made the Bible the source of their authoritative preaching. From it they traversed the realms of history, literature, art, science, philosophy, but never to find a substitute for the Book. And they always came back to it laden with material for its illustration. They teach us that every method of preaching is legitimate which focuses attention upon the Bible in the light of Christ's life and teaching. By its aid they looked into his face and knew that he, and he alone, was and is the Word of the Living God, the Way, the Truth, the Life, and that in his will is man's eternal peace.

Literature: Gilbert, *Interpretation of the Bible;* Moulton, *The Literary Study of the Bible;* Malden, *Problems of the New Testament Today;* Peake (Editor), *The People and the Book;* Coffin, *What to Preach;* McConnell, *Understanding the Scriptures;* Cadman, *Ambassadors of God;* Fosdick, *The Modern Use of the Bible.*

THE PLACE OF THE BIBLE IN RELIGIOUS EDUCATION

By Dr. HENRY H. MEYER

The history of civilization reveals a gradual substitution of record for memory, i.e., of written scroll and printed book for oral tradition. Writing first made possible the permanent preservation and distant communication of experience. Later, the invention of printing made possible a wider distribution of multiplied records of the same experience. In morals and religion, as in other realms of human experience, progress is due largely to the preservation and communication from generation to generation of measurably dependable records of past experience. Such records constitute a permanent and indispensable part of the subject matter of religious education.

Religious Instruction Among the Hebrews. The early Christian records of the N.T., and the earlier Hebrew Scriptures as well, were produced from a sense of obligation to pass on to others the religious knowledge gained by the writers as a matter of personal insight and experience. The various writings of both the O.T. and the N.T. were produced in response to the need for religious inspiration and guidance. These books of the Bible for the most part were written for purposes of religious instruction. This was true, e.g., of the Torah or Law preserved in part in the Pentateuch. Concerning this Law, the children of Israel were exhorted:

"And these words, which I command thee this day, shall be upon thy heart: and thou shalt teach them diligently unto thy children, and shalt talk of them when thou sittest in thine house, and when thou walkest by the way, and when thou liest down, and when thou risest up. And thou shalt bind them for a sign upon thine hand, and they shall be for frontlets between thine eyes. And thou shalt write them upon the door-posts of thy house, and upon thy gates" (Deut. 6[6-9]).

The same is true of the writings of the earlier seers and wise men of Israel, who sought diligently to draw within the circle of their influence the youth who most needed instruction.

"Hear, my sons, the instruction of a father,
And attend to know understanding:
For I give you good doctrine;
Forsake ye not my law.
For I was a son unto my father,
Tender and only beloved in the sight of my mother.
And he taught me, and said unto me:
Let thine heart retain my words;
Keep my commandments, and live:
Get wisdom, get understanding;
Forget it not, neither decline from the words of my mouth:
Forsake her not, and she shall preserve thee;
Love her, and she will keep thee.
Wisdom is the principal thing; therefore get wisdom:
Yea, with all thou hast gotten get understanding.
Exalt her, and she shall promote thee:
She will bring thee to honor, when thou dost embrace her.
She will give to thine head a chaplet of grace:
A crown of beauty shall she deliver to thee" (Prov. 4[1-9]).

At the same time these ancient teachers of Israel reminded the parents of the importance and advantage of religious instruction:

"Bring up a child in the way he should go,
And even when he is old he will not depart from it."

The stirring messages of the great prophets, Amos, Hosea, Isaiah, Jeremiah, gave expression to religious insight and experience of their own, and appealed in the name of Jehovah for righteousness, justice, mercy, and obedience to the voice and the law of Jehovah.

As a matter of fact, however, the books of the O.T. actually represent only the sifted treasures of a larger Jewish teaching literature, parts of which did not survive the successive periods of religious persecution and decline, such as those which followed the final downfall of the Hebrew kingdom.

Dependence of Christianity on the Written Record. Isolated fragments of literary treasures of the first Christian centuries, in addition to the writings of the N.T., have been discovered in ancient rubbish heaps and scattered libraries in Bible lands. Such were the early Christian Psalter, discovered in 1909 by Professor Rendel Harris; the "Didache" or "Teachings of the Twelve Apostles," the "Apostolic Constitutions" preserved in the archives of the Church of the Holy Sepulcher at Jerusalem, and the "Pædagogus" of Clement of Alexandria, dating from the close of the second century, none of which was included in the canon of the N.T. itself.

Christianity, as "the Jesus way" of thinking and living, has been perpetuated and reinterpreted again and again during two thousand years, because there existed dependable records of the life, experience, and teachings of Jesus. As an organized fellowship of believers, with its creeds, rituals, ministry, and diversified forms of administration, Christianity has developed because to the original record of the work and words of Jesus each succeeding generation has given its own interpretation in the light of its own religious experience.

Jesus himself left no written account of his life or his teachings. His immediate followers, however, strove diligently to produce and preserve a record of both. They sought, moreover, to communicate to others, in writing, their own experiences in relation to Christ. In these earliest apostolic writings, the Gospels and the Epistles, there is already a marked element of interpretation as well as of record. The N.T. writings, therefore, constitute the beginning, or, as it were, the first installment of the teaching literature of historical Christianity. In this teaching literature of Christianity, now grown to almost immeasurable proportions, are preserved both its original message and the progressive interpretation of that message.

There is an interesting passage in Paul's second letter to Timothy (3^{16}), which suggests that the great apostle, while doubtless conscious of the promptings of the Holy Spirit in writing as he did to Timothy and others, was not unaware of the literary activities of his contemporaries, and that he believed that the Spirit of God was a silent partner in the production of many of these first Christian records, Gospels, hymn books, sermons, and letters. After reminding Timothy that the sacred writings of the O.T. which he has known from his youth were indeed intended to make him wise unto salvation, the apostle declares in fact that not only these sacred O.T. writings, but "every scripture inspired of God," i.e., every writing with the production of which the Divine Spirit has anything to do, "is also profitable for teaching" and for "instruction in righteousness," as well as for "reproof and correction," the negative factors in the same teaching process (2 Tim. 3^{15-17}). It is as though Paul would say, "The writings of the Hebrew wise men, lawgivers, and prophets are still our textbooks of religion, but even now there is in preparation a new teaching literature for the better and more perfect instruction in the Christian way."

Jesus himself emphasized the teaching value of his precepts and life example in his final exhortation to his disciples that they "teach all nations the things that he," by word and example, "had commanded them" (Mt. 28^{20}). During the centuries since the completion of the N.T., the Bible has been translated into practically all of the languages and dialects of the world. It has been distributed to the ends of the earth, in the interest of a world-wide program of Christian education, and with the definite purpose that it should serve as the textbook *par excellence* of the Christian way of life.

But to this first authentic collection of Christian writings there were added, during the centuries, the writings of the early Christian Fathers, of the mediæval saints, the leaders of the Reformation and subsequent periods of church history, all of which, like the writings of the O.T. and the N.T., were intended primarily for purposes of religious teaching. This is true also of the formulated creeds of the church, the decrees of the church councils, and, in particular, of the homilies, breviaries, and catechisms that appeared in great numbers during the centuries following the Reformation. During recent years, especially, the multiplication of textbooks and periodical literature for use in religious instruction has been one of the outstanding developments in the work of the Christian Church. Until recently, however, all of this teaching material has been based more or less directly on the Bible itself, and was intended to interpret and apply the teachings of the Bible to daily life.

The Varying Emphases in the History of Christian Education. In actual teaching content, Christian education in the beginning, i.e., in the period immediately following the death of Jesus, was Christ-centered. Since that earliest period of vivid, inspiring, mouth-to-mouth tradition regarding the actual precepts and example of Jesus, Christian education has been consecutively church-centered, book-centered, creed-centered, and conduct-centered. During more recent years, under the influence of a rapidly developing educational psychology, it has become pupil-centered, or better still, experience-centered. In each of these successive historic emphases in Christian education there have been elements of truth and value. None has excluded entirely the others.

(1) *In the Early Church: Conduct and Faith.* The religious instruction of the early catechumenate had a twofold emphasis, conduct

and faith in Christ. Inquirers (*audientes*) were instructed regarding the two ways: the way of life and the way of death. The way of life was the way of virtue, honesty, temperance, chastity, industry and service. It was the Jesus way. Christ himself was the great instructor (*Paedagogus*). He was the point of reference, the touchstone, the standard of measurement for faith as he was for conduct. Hence, faith in him as the great teacher and revealer of the Father, as example and Saviour, was the second essential to discipleship. *Audientes* gave evidence of their sincerity by becoming *genuflectentes* (knee-benders), believers in and worshipers of the Christ. After that they were instructed in the particular tenets and practices of the new way, the Christian mysteries, until their understanding and proficiency as learners of the Christian way entitled them to consideration as *competentes*, candidates in waiting under final instruction for admission to the Christian fraternity. Once within the close-drawn circle, the educative process was continued through the fellowship of the sacrament of the Common Meal, the coming together for worship and mutual testimony and exhortation, the reading of letters to and from individuals and churches, and later, of the first fragmentary Gospel records of the words and works of Jesus. The entire instruction, however, centered in Christ. His way of living, his example, his teaching, the meaning and value of his life, his suffering and his final triumph—these were the subject matter and the goal of Christian teaching. It was a glorious, heroic period of initial enthusiasm and daring, with persecution and martyrdom for many. It was a fellowship of the mystic sign and secret meeting place. Life and teachings were Christ-centered.

(2) *In the Mediæval Period: Obedience to the Church.* Then, suddenly, the church emerged from the catacombs triumphant, powerful, mightier than the state that had tried to crush it. Its organization was strengthened—its administration centralized. Rules and interpretation of the church superseded the simple example of the Jesus way of life. Christ was subordinated to an earthly vicegerent. The organized church assumed absolute control over body and soul, over conduct and thinking of the people. Education became education by and for the church. Military service and other non-Christian practices that once were anathema were sanctioned by the church now in league with the empire and the self-appointed final interpreter and arbiter of the Christian tradition and faith. The light of the Word was hid under a bushel. Tapers burned or dimly smoldered like pagan incense under the domes of great cathedrals. All through the Middle Ages the church commanded obedience to itself as the authoritative divine agent in human affairs. Yet there was effective teaching by and for the organization. It was the teaching of the confessional and of the altar, of ritual and ceremony, pilgrimage and pageantry, feasts and festivals. Christian education during the Middle Ages was church-centered. In the Roman Catholic Church and to a lesser extent in the Protestant Episcopal Church, education has retained this church-centered emphasis to the present day.

(3) *In Protestantism: The Bible and Dogma.* The Protestant Reformation substituted for the authority of the church the authority of the printed book, the rediscovered unchained Bible, the divinely inspired Word of God. Sermons and Bible expositions were substituted for the mass and for the rich ceremonial of the altar. Catechetical instruction based on the Bible as interpreted by the Reformation leaders took the place of the secret confessional. Popular education became the watchword. The free elementary school was born. Textbooks of religious education multiplied. The Bible itself was made accessible to the people in the vernacular. Christian education was book-centered, and, in the spirit if not in universal practice, Bible-centered.

But with the Reformation and its catechism came emphasis upon the doctrinal differences of major and minor Protestant groups. The Reformation, born in protest, gave rise to denominationalism, with its rivalry of interpretations of the printed Word, and with its diversity of administrations. The Christian school became a denominational institution. Christian education was centered in creeds and doctrines and so remained, for the most part, until the discovery of the greater importance of the child and the subsequent triumph of the psychological movement in education, and until the equally important change to the scientific and historical method of Bible study and interpretation.

With the advance in scientific knowledge, including this better understanding of the nature and contents of the Bible and a better psychological insight into child nature and the laws of human development, a marked change has come, both in the subject matter and the method of religious education. This change has affected vitally both the place and the use of the Bible, if not its importance, in the teaching work of the church. Fundamental to a right estimate of the importance and place of the Bible in modern religious education, therefore, is an understanding of the learning process and of the teaching objectives in terms of Christian character as these are conceived in the best theory and practice of to-day.

The Learning Process and the Character of the Bible. We have a new understanding of the learning process, and a new understanding of the character of the Bible. The problem is to relate these together.

(1) *Aims of Modern Religious Education.* Modern education, regarded as a purposeful activity of organized society, has as its objectives the interpretation, control, and enrichment of human experience. It seeks among other things to transmit to each succeeding generation the accumulated social, intellectual, and spiritual (moral and religious) heritage of the race. More particularly, it seeks the physical, mental, and moral development of persons through their intelligently directed participation with other persons in the progressive mastery and improvement of their common social and spiritual heritage by the discovery of new truth and the progressive reconstruction of human society. It results in the acquisition of the symbols and techniques of civilization, languages, arts, and sciences, and is reflected in improved attitudes, powers of appreciation and skills in actual individual and group living. Man learns to do by doing. He learns to live by living. Learning begins in life situations that stimulate interest and call forth responses. It results from purposeful activities carried through to successful outcomes in the solving of problems and the completion of individual and group enterprises. What formal education seeks to do, and the only thing which it really can do, is to facilitate and expedite the process of learning by controlling and manipulating the environment in which that process takes place, and by doing this in such a way that interesting and worthwhile problems and enterprises will emerge naturally and in a sequence advantageous to the uninterrupted growth and development of the learner.

(2) *Pupil-Centered and Society-Centered.* In harmony with this conception of the learning process, Christian religious education undertakes to stimulate and guide the developing religious experience of the individual and group with a view to a progressive realization of the Christian way of life in human society. Like all education, it is pupil-centered and society-centered. Its contents and its methods, the subject matter, the materials and forms of activity which it employs are determined at every stage of the process by the religious status, i.e., the stage of religious development, and by the consequent immediate religious needs of the persons and the community of persons to whom it ministers. In religious education, therefore, the determining factor is not the subject matter of instruction but, rather, the nature and need of the pupil. In relation to the Bible the pertinent question is not how to get successive portions of its contents, considered as subject matter, over into the knowledge equipment of the pupil. (Cf., however, the art., *How to Study the Bible,* pp. 8–10.) It is, rather, the question of where the human religious experiences reflected in this or that portion of the Bible fit into the growing knowledge and experience of the pupil. So stated, the problem of the religious educator becomes one of the selective and graded use of biblical materials in his total program of nurture and training.

(3) *The Modern View of the Bible.* But the selection and use of biblical materials for purposes of religious education raises the further problem of a correct understanding of the character and contents of the Bible regarded as the most important and, for Christian education, indispensable source book of religious experience and progress. (See art., *The Bible—a Library of Religion,* p. 15.) Present-day practice in religious education takes into account the historical origins, literary forms, and gradual growth of the Scriptures. The Bible is not a book of magic or of science but a collection of divine-human records of divine-human experience, written in terms of the thought and the forms of expression of the people of their own day. It reflects man's faltering but successful search for God and his gradual and often imperfect solution of the problems of individual and group conduct in the light of his discovery of God. The Bible is composed of many separate documents by many different authors, written many centuries apart, in widely separated places. Some of these documents have come down to us substantially in their original form. Others, like the total collection itself, are the composite product of various writers, skillfully woven together by successive editors, with a view to meeting immediate and changing needs for moral and religious guidance. The writings of the O.T. and N.T. are, therefore, necessarily of decidedly unequal value as aids to Christian experience to-day, and they retain their highest values only as the problems that their educational use presents are recognized and frankly faced in the light of the fuller knowledge of the character and purposes of God revealed in Christ, and in the light also of the known laws of character development in the individual.

The religious-political traditions and history of the Hebrews as set forth in the writings of the O.T. extend over many centuries from Abraham to the time of Christ. Rearranged in accordance with the chronological order of their production, these writings reveal successive periods of social progress, with successively higher levels of moral and religious understanding. The conception which the Hebrews had of God and their ideals of worship, of law and of right moral conduct were different at different periods of their history. When considered chronologically they reflect clearly the successive stages of their social and religious development. (See art., *Religion of Israel*, pp. 165f.; cf. p. 159b.)

Compared with the highest religious conceptions and ideals of the O.T., those of the N.T. based on and including the teachings and life example of Jesus furnish the culmination of all religious inspiration and guidance to be found in the combined writings of the two Testaments. For Christian life and conduct, therefore, the N.T. is more important than the O.T. Of the N.T. writings, in turn, the synoptic Gospels which record the words and works of Jesus would seem to be more important than the writings that give the interpretations which Peter and John and James and Paul and others placed on what Jesus said and did. Christian education undertakes the cultivation of intelligent Christian attitudes and conduct in individuals and groups. The inclusion of any given passage of the Bible in the curriculum of Christian education can be justified only as it can be shown that the moral and religious experience which the passage reflects is adapted to promote growth toward mature Christian character, and further, that it is especially adapted to promote such growth at a specific period of the religious development of the individual. (Cf. Myers, *The O.T. in the Sunday School*, p. 45.) There must be, in other words, reason for selecting the passage for the religious instruction of some particular age group or grade in the church school. Further, it must be shown that the particular passage in question presents this phase of experience in educationally usable and advantageous form. Used in this way the portrayals of religious experience and the record of spiritual insight and growth contained in the Bible may be made to enrich the life experiences of the pupil through definite mental activity, i.e., through intellectual contemplation of classic examples of typical human experiences such as the problems and projects of the pupil's immediate environment do not provide.

The Graded Use of Biblical Materials in Modern Religious Education. What are known as "graded" lessons conform to the sound principle that the lesson material must be adapted to the needs and capacities of the pupil.

(1) *Extensive Use of Bible Material in Modern Graded Lessons.* Far from lessening the amount of biblical material used effectively in the religious training of youth, the rigorous restriction and adaptation of this material in accordance with recognized educational principles of selection and gradation makes possible the more profitable use of a wider range and a greater total amount of biblical material, while allowing place in the total curriculum for that rich variety of other materials demanded for the full and symmetrical development of Christian character. Just as the pre-eminence of Jesus as a teacher has not been lessened by the subjection of his precepts and example to the test of modern pedagogical principles, so the importance of the Bible as the one indispensable source book of Christian religious instruction has not suffered from the practice of testing the teaching values of all biblical materials by the same rigorous demands of psychological insight and pedagogical procedure. This is brought out clearly by a comparison of the use of the Bible in the International Graded Lessons which constitute the standard curriculum for modern church schools in America, with its more limited haphazard use in the older system of the Uniform Lessons. In the fifty-four years from the beginning of the Uniform Lessons in 1872 to the close of the cycle ending with 1925, less than forty per cent of the material contained in the Bible was assigned for study. In other words, sixty per cent of the Bible was not used. In the International Graded Lessons covering the work of the Primary, Junior, Intermediate and Senior grades, on the contrary, sixty-two per cent of the Bible is assigned for study and less than thirty-eight per cent is left unused as lesson material. Graded lessons teach more of the Bible than uniform lessons because graded lessons undertake to teach to children in the various grades only those portions of the Bible which they can understand and which are best suited to further their moral and religious development. Freed from the limitations of the principle of uniformity and not compelled to seek biblical passages that may serve as lesson material for young and old at the same time, the graded curriculum can effectively use more difficult passages of the Bible as well as its simpler portions, and can use these in such fashion as most helpfully to meet the moral and religious needs and promote the moral and religious growth of various age groups and classes in the church school.

(2) *Adapting the Material to the Pupil.* One of the results of this selective and graded use of Bible materials in the modern church school has been the compilation of various lists of biblical materials for use with various age

groups. Examples of such compilations used extensively in the preparation of curricula of religious instruction, progressive Bible readers and other religious literature for children, are the "Basic List of Biblical Material" for primary grades (ages 6, 7, 8) and for junior grades (ages 9, 10, 11), prepared by the British Lessons Council in co-operation with the International Sunday School Lesson Committee of the United States and Canada.

Although in the nature of the case there can be no absolute agreement with regard to the teaching values of any given narrative or portion of the Bible for any particular age group, it is reasonable to expect that the two basic lists of biblical material just mentioned will, to a large extent, furnish the actual biblical material used in English-speaking countries in the religious training of children under thirteen years of age. The lists were originally released for use in the Church-school cycle of the Departmental (British) and Group-Graded (American) Lessons for 1929–31. In the explanatory statement accompanying the printed lists it is pointed out that "each of these bodies, and any other bodies who may use these lists, should be left free to omit or to add material, so that the selection of each may be as nearly adapted as possible to meet the needs of its own constituency and its own situation; . . . no extra-biblical material is suggested in these lists, because, in this material especially, adaptation to local conditions is essential, and there cannot be the same measure of common use as of the biblical."

The Group-Graded Lessons, for which these lists furnish the basic material, are prepared in accordance with the following statements of aim: "The *Primary age-group* includes children of the ages 6, 7, and 8, or who are in the public-school grades 1, 2, and 3. The Primary Group Lessons aim: 1. To help Primary children to think of God as the heavenly Father, and of all the world as dependent upon his love and care; and to lead them to express their love and gratitude to him in simple acts of worship and in deeds of good will and helpfulness to others. 2. To help them to know what God wants them to do, and to understand the happiness of right conduct and the hurtfulness of wrong. 3. To acquaint them with Jesus as the Son of God and the Friend and Helper of all God's children. The *Junior age-group* includes children of the ages 9, 10, 11, or who are in the public-school grades 4, 5, and 6. The Junior Group Lessons aim: 1. To bring these children into their heritage of Christian ideals and habits of life, and to help them meet their own problems and opportunities in the light of these ideals and in ways that lead to the establishment of these habits. 2. To train them to read and use the Bible for themselves, and help them to begin to appreciate its value as an inspiration and guide for daily living. 3. To present Jesus Christ and his teaching to them so concretely that he will command their allegiance and enlist their loyal service."

The gradual revision of the basic lists of biblical material in the light of their progressive use, as well as deviation from them in actual practice, is assumed by those responsible for their preparation. The arrangement of the materials is according to the order of their appearance in the Bible, not according to their use, which is determined by the sequence of teaching aims and project activities in the individual denominational or other courses of study.

In more closely graded curricula provision is made for the use of a larger amount and a wider range of biblical materials together with materials from nature study, home and community interests and needs, world friendship and service projects. With young people and adults, and to a lesser extent with older boys and girls, use is made of connected portions of the Bible based on the interests of the pupils and on the value both of the human experience reflected in the biblical record to the developing religious life of the pupils and of the value to them of an understanding of the historical and literary sources of the Christian faith. With older pupils the study of the Bible itself becomes a project enterprise as the student consciously seeks to acquaint himself with the historical origins of Christianity. In all of these graded curricula of religious education large place is given to the connected study of the biblical records of human religious experience with their portrayal of struggle and growth toward a fuller knowledge and experience of the truth as it is in Jesus Christ.

(3) *Week-day Religious Education.* While the books used in this phase of religious education draw freely upon general literature, biography, nature, and life, they never for a moment forget that their basic purpose is *to teach religion*, and their subject-matter is therefore of necessity rich in biblical material. The stories, the history, the narratives and precepts of the Bible are constantly and freely used in deepening the spiritual values and in emphasizing the application of Christian ideals to daily living.

The Assured Permanence of the Bible in Religious Education. The miracle of the preservation of these ancient Jewish-Christian records is accounted for by their intrinsic interest and value to men of each succeeding age in their search for God and in their efforts to regulate personal and group conduct in accordance with their deepest insight into truth and right. It is, moreover, this same continuing helpfulness that makes these records, rightly understood and used, indispensable in the work of religious education even to-day. Wherever Christian character is highly developed in an individual or group, there it will be found that selected portions of the Bible, especially the life and teachings of Jesus, have exercised a determining influence in the religious development of the individual or group, either preceptually as subject matter of instruction, or vicariously through the exemplary Christian life of parents and teachers. As a source book and record of religious experience the Bible will always have a place in religious education commensurate with its influence in the development of Christian character in the individual and the progressive transformation of human society. Nor can we conceive of the extension of Christianity apart from the extension of a knowledge of the literary source materials of the Christian faith. The place and use of these materials in the program of religious education will be in harmony with an increasingly accurate understanding of their exact character and contents and with an understanding also of the learning process and the laws of character development in the individual.

Literature: Betts, *New Program of Religious Education;* Laufer, *The Bible: Story and Content;* Fiske, *Jesus' Ideals of Living;* Kent, *Great Teachers of Judaism and Christianity;* A. J. W. Myers, *The O.T. in the Sunday School;* Knudson, *Religious Teaching of the O.T.;* Lotz, *Current Week-day Religious Education.* See also titles under "Literature" appended to such other general articles in this Commentary as "How to Study the Bible," "The Bible a Library of Religion," and "The Christian Approach to the Scriptures."

THE LAND OF PALESTINE

By Professor EDWIN E. VOIGT

Name. The most common O.T. designation for the Holy Land is the land of Canaan. Literally the word *canaan* means "lowland;" and in the beginning the Canaanites were the inhabitants of the lowlands. In time they became masters of the hill country also, and then the entire land became known as the land of the Canaanites. In the O.T. this is commonly taken to refer to the territory west of the Jordan River (cf. Gen. 11^{31} 12^{5} Ex. 6^{4} 16^{35} Lev. 14^{34} Num. 34^{2} Judg. $3^{1f.}$, etc.). Sometimes, however, the designation—land of Canaan—seems to have been applied only to the southern part of the land (Gen. $13^{1, 12}$), and on occasion to the northern part (Judg. $4^{2, 7, 23f.}$ 5^{19}). Once the territory east of the Jordan is included in the term (Gen. 50^{11}), and in one instance the land of Canaan is equated with the land of the Philistines (Zeph. 2^{5}). It is perhaps through the Philistines, who invaded the land of Canaan and subsequently settled on one of the important trade routes of the ancient world, that modern parlance knows this land as Palestine, which name is almost identical with one of the early Greek transliterations of Philistia. Herodotus (2^{104}, 7^{89}), as far as we know, was the first to apply this term to all of Canaan. Josephus (*Antiquities*, bk. i, ch. 6) and the Latin historians followed the same custom, and thus by the beginning of the Christian era the older term had fallen into disuse, and Western Europe adopted "Palestine" as the name for the home land of the Hebrew people.

Location and Extent. Geographically, Palestine is located in the southwestern corner of the continent of Asia, and its shores are washed by the waters of the southeastern corner of the Mediterranean Sea. Historically, of course, its size varied with the political fortunes of its people, but the average northerly and southerly extent of its territory was perhaps about one hundred and fifty miles. From the Mediterranean it extended inland to the desert, an average distance of less than seventy-five miles. Thus Palestine occupied a small stretch of land approximately one hundred and fifty miles long and fifty miles wide, the widest part being at the southern end, tapering toward the north; at no time did it include more than ten thousand square miles.

However small and insignificant in size Palestine may have been, it was nevertheless very strategically located. In the Oriental world, before Europe developed, the great centers of civilization were in the Nile basin and in the Tigris-Euphrates Valley, and Palestine lay on the only feasible overland route between these centers. For east of it lay the uncrossable Arabian Desert, and trade and commerce between East and West followed the Mediterranean coast. Also, with the development of Phœnician shipping in the Mediterranean the spices of Arabia were a commodity much in demand. One of the caravan routes to the sea from the interior of Arabia crossed northern Palestine. Consequently, this little land, hardly bigger than a large American county, was on or, indeed, was one of the crossroads of the ancient world.

The political importance of this strip of land was early recognized, for by the middle of the second millennium B.C. the Egyptian emperors had taken steps to fortify it against invasion, both from the east and from the north. The uncivilized Bedouin, called *Habiru* in the Tel-el-Amarna letters, were pushing into the land from the eastern desert; therefore a line of fortifications extending north and south was erected in strategic places in the inland to protect the flanks of the trade routes. Further, since the route between the East and the West had to pass through this narrow place, in time of war the nation that had possession of this bottle-neck, as it were, had a distinct military advantage. As a result, fenced cities were placed across Palestine for protection against an aggressor coming down or up the coast. The military significance of this location was largely responsible for much of the woe that befell the inhabitants of the land during the centuries, for East and West periodically came into armed conflict, and this narrow pass between the East and the West was repeatedly overrun and devastated, because it was impossible for the Palestinians in such a time to maintain neutrality. Thus we see that Israel occupied a location which, far from being in a remote corner, was actually in the center of the ancient world. The expression coined by Sir George Adam Smith (*Historical Geography of the Holy Land*, p. 6) that "Palestine was the bridge of Asia," admirably expresses the strategic importance of its location.

Geology. The geological history of Palestine is exceedingly interesting. Underlying the country is a bed of granite. Above this bed, coming from the Cretaceous Age, are several strata of limestone, sandstone, and chalk. The lowest of these is a beautiful white limestone, the choicest of building material, and therefore called *meliche*, that is royal stone. It is fairly soft for quarrying, but when exposed to the atmosphere becomes very hard and durable. It is thought that Solomon built his Temple from this type of stone, and at the present time under the northeast corner of Jerusalem is an extensive cave, called "Solomon's Quarries," where such stone was quarried in ancient times. Above the *meliche* are two further strata of limestone: *mize Jehudi*, the Arabs call the lower layer, and *mize Ahmar*, the upper. The *Jehudi* is a gray limestone, streaked with flint, and very difficult to quarry. It is, however, because of its accessibility, more commonly used for building than the *meliche*. The *Ahmar* is a rose-colored limestone, not as hard as the *Jehudi*, and perhaps the most common stone used for building in modern Palestine. West of Jerusalem in the ancient Valley of Rephaim is a very fine quarry of *Ahmar*. Above these are various strata of sandstone, covered by softer layers of limestone of dolomitic and nummulitic character. Above all these are traces of marl, but the action of nature has for the most part corroded these upper chalky strata and washed them down the valleys.

What thus seems to be a very simple geologic structure, was in later periods infinitely complicated by a series of cosmic cataclysms, whereby these strata were tilted, broken apart, and generally jumbled together. It is very likely that in the Pliocene age a great break, extending north and south, occurred in the earth's crust. This break can first be detected in northern Syria, where it formed the valley in which the Orontes River flows. It extends southward through the eastern part of Palestine, forming the Jordan valley, and still farther to the south, probably forming the Wadi Arabah, the Gulf of Akaba, and even some of the "finger" lakes of east-central Africa.

During the Pleistocene or Glacial Age the glaciers came as far south as the Lebanon Mountains of Syria. To the south of the glacier there was very heavy rainfall, causing the deep water-courses in the highlands of western Palestine. In this age there seem to have been alternate periods of rain and drought, and in the second dry period, which corresponds to the Paleolithic period of human culture, the first traces of man are found in Palestine.

Later still, in the Mesolithic period, the last geologic cataclysm took place, forming the Dead Sea. This cataclysm seems not to have been in the nature of a volcanic eruption. Rather, the earth subsided, and thus formed that rift, which is more than a half mile below sea level, and in the bottom of which the lowest salt sea lies.

However, during the process of time volcanic action did play a part in the formation of the contour of present Palestine. Especially is this true in the northeastern part, where innumerable extinct volcanoes are scattered all through the district east of the Sea of Galilee. Their impress on the terrain of this section may be seen in the extensive lava fields, in the diorite and other volcanic rocks that help to make up the mountains east of the Sea of Galilee, and farther inland in the decomposed lava and volcanic ash from which the plains derive a large part of their fertility. Consequently, during many centuries Palestine lay within the range of an active volcanic region and experienced the usual eruptions, upheavals, and earthquakes that go with such a region, and that were nature's processes in bringing about the character of its present surface.

Geographical Divisions. In the physical features of Palestine one finds about all the variety that the earth has to offer. On the west is a coastal plain which varies in width from a few yards to fifteen miles, made up of swamps, rolling sand dunes, and rich, fertile soil. Back of this plain is a rugged mountain range, never over thirty miles wide, sloping sharply both to east and west, and attaining a maximum altitude of thirty-five hundred feet. On the east it descends into the Jordan Valley, which lies considerably below sea level, and which takes its name from the river that meanders southward over its floor. The greatest width of the Jordan Valley is less than fifteen miles, and on its east it is fringed by a highland plateau, somewhat higher than the western highlands and now generally known as Trans-Jordania, which extends back into the hinterland until it is lost in the Arabian Desert. Thus, within the space of a few miles one can visit fertile valleys, wild mountain gorges, depressions that are below sea level, or sandy steppes. (See end of Commentary for maps.)

1. The Coastal Plains. Partly because of location, and partly for historical reasons, the Coastal Plain of Palestine may be divided into three subdivisions

(1) The Plain of Acre. The northwest

neighbor of biblical Palestine was Phœnicia, and the Plain of Tyre was joined on the south by the Plain of Acre, which received its name from its principal city and seaport, known as Accho in ancient times. The northern width of the plain is about three miles; it gradually widens toward the south until it is about ten miles wide. Its southern base is formed by Mount Carmel, which completely separates it from the rest of the Coastal Plain. Along the seashore are a fringe of sand hills, and back of them is more or less swampy land. The whole plain rises very little above sea level, and wherever possible it is extensively cultivated. In Bible times it must have been of considerable importance, for it is dotted with "tells," the ruins of ancient cities. Some of them show signs of having been heavily fortified with huge walls for protection against foreign aggression. Two rivers flow across the plain into the Mediterranean Sea. The first is the Belis, which flows past the city of Acre, and on the banks of which, so Pliny narrates, the Phœnicians first learned to make glass. Along the southern base of the plain flows the Kishon. Although it is the larger of the two, it is little more than a brook during most of the year; yet at times it becomes a raging river, as on that memorable occasion when the chariots of Sisera, the Canaanite, became embogged in the mire, and the hosts of Israel, led by Deborah and Barak, gained a long-remembered victory (Judg. 4, 5).

(2) The Plain of Sharon. Mount Carmel forms the northern apex of a narrow coast plain, extending southward forty or fifty miles, which was known in the O.T. as the Plain of Sharon. Its northern width is less than a mile, but it gradually extends away from the seacoast until it reaches a maximum width of less than fifteen miles. The northern part of Sharon is perhaps the most fertile tract in Palestine. In the springtime while the growing grain is still green it is indeed a beautiful garden, and everywhere wild flowers blossom profusely; one of these, the Rose of Sharon, was an O.T. byword for beauty and comeliness. In ancient times the city of Dor, on the sea in the northern part of the plain, was its most important city. At a later time, about five miles south of the site of Dor, Herod the Great built a new seaport, created a beautiful harbor along the unbroken shoreline, the ruins of which are still *in situ*, and under the procurators it became the main seaport and capital of Palestine. This was Cæsarea, and it was here that Paul languished in prison for two years (Acts 24[27]).

(3) The Plain of Philistia. Continuing the Plain of Sharon, and beginning approximately with the region back of modern Jaffa, is the Philistine plain. As it continues toward the south it becomes somewhat wider, and eventually merges into the desert which separates Palestine from Egypt. The southern border of the Plain of Philistia is traditionally a water-course, dry most of the year, called the River of Egypt (Num. 34[5]), and now known as Wadi el-Arish. Near its mouth on the north side is the site of ancient Raphia, made famous as the historic place where East and West met in more than one memorable contest of arms. The Philistine plain is a rolling expanse, and though much more sandy than Sharon it is extensively cultivated. Its name comes from the Philistine people, who settled there perhaps in the beginning of the twelfth century B.C. and fortified five strongholds (Askelon, Ashdod, Ekron, Gath, and Gaza). The princes of these five cities formed a confederacy, and in the O.T. are frequently referred to as the "Five Princes of the Philistines" (1 Sam. 6[16, 18]).

(4) The Shephelah. Just to the east of Philistia is a region made up of low, rounded hills not over a few hundred feet high. Properly, these hills are not a part of the Central Highlands, but are a fringe of foothills on the border of Philistia, and were first properly identified by Sir George Adam Smith as the region which the O.T. refers to as the Shephelah.

2. The Western Highlands. North of the Shephelah the Coastal Plains gradually slope upward until they come to an abrupt line of hills which form the western border of the mountain range that runs the length of Palestine. This range is in reality the southern continuation of the Lebanon Mountains of Syria, and is the backbone and watershed of the land of Canaan. It has several natural divisions.

(1) The Highlands of Galilee. The southern portion of the Lebanons loses much of its ruggedness to form a region with rounded contours and promiscuous hillocks among which nestle many small picturesque valleys. This is Galilee, a word which literally means "circuit," or "district," and in the O.T. is generally designated as the District of Naphtali. The highest portion of Galilee is in the north, where one mountain rises to an altitude of nearly four thousand feet. Southward the altitude appreciably drops, leaving many open spaces which are carefully cultivated. Thus the country is open, not easily or naturally fortified, accessible from all sides, and consequently in its history the harbor of many kinds of peoples. It is, therefore, well named,

"Galilee of the Nations" (Isa. 9[1]; cf. mg.). Not until N.T. times does it figure largely in Bible history.

(2) The Plains of Esdraelon and Jezreel. The plains of Esdraelon and Jezreel lie just to the south of Galilee and cause it to be completely cut off from the rest of the Western Highlands to the south. The Plain of Esdraelon slopes toward the northwest to the Mediterranean, and lies on both sides of the upper part of the Kishon. It is not much more than fifteen miles long, and never more than eight wide, and is separated in its lower end from the Plain of Acre by the narrows formed by the close approach of the southwest cliffs of the Galilæan hills to Mount Carmel. From an agricultural point of view this plain has always been important, for it is of sufficient extent and fertility to be the granary for the entire region.

On the east of the divide is the Plain of Jezreel. It is the eastern continuation of Esdraelon, although it is considerably narrower. In the history of the Northern Kingdom this plain has many historic associations, and from it comes the famous proverb, "His driving is like the driving of Jehu the son of Nimshi" (2 Kings 9[20]).

In ancient times these two plains formed, and even at present constitute the most used pass across Palestine. The route from Egypt to Damascus followed the seacoast to Carmel, and then across to the eastern highlands by the way of Esdraelon and Jezreel. At the eastern end of Jezreel, to protect the trade route and to defend the interior from the marauding nomads of the desert, stood a mighty fortress, Beth-Shean (Roman, Scythopolis) which served Palestine in this capacity for over four millenniums. Some of its ancient glories are being revealed by the excavations now in progress.

(3) Mount Carmel. On the southwest edge of the Plain of Esdraelon Mount Carmel, or the Carmel range, rises abruptly to a height of one to two thousand feet, and extends toward the southeast until it joins the highlands of Samaria. The western end of Carmel juts clear into the Mediterranean, and is so steep and rugged that it is altogether impassable. Consequently, the passes over Mount Carmel extended between the Plains of Sharon and Esdraelon rather than between Sharon and Acre. The water-courses, or *wadis* in Arabic, flow from Carmel down into the Kishon. The first is near the lower end of the Plain of Esdraelon, and is the pass that was most commonly used across the range in travel up and down the coast. At the north end of this pass stands the very important fortified city Megiddo on an almost inaccessible cliff; during the centuries it has acted as a sentinel over the pass. Farther inland another wadi cuts through the mountain to form another pass, which was, however, not used to the extent of the first. It also was protected at its northern end by a fenced city, which in the ancient records was called Ta'anach. Just at the point where the Carmel range joins the Central Highland, there is a little open space, which is really a continuation of Esdraelón, but which is known as the Plain of Dothan. It is only a few square miles in extent, and lies quietly among the mountains that rise steeply from its sides. In certain times of the year this is probably the most beautiful little haven in all Palestine. It is frequently mentioned in the O.T., and is important as the north opening of the third and most inland pass over Carmel, the most commonly used pass of the trade route between Egypt and Damascus.

(4) The Mountainous Region of Samaria. In pre-exilic times this region was commonly designated as Ephraim, or Mount Ephraim (Josh. 17[15] 20[7] Judg. 2[9] 4[5] Hos. 5[3] Isa. 7[2], etc.). After the restoration the Jews fell into the habit of calling the entire region "Samaria," after the name of its principal city and center of culture. In general, the contour of Samaria is exceedingly broken and deeply cut with steep V-shaped water-courses, or wadis, which are dry for the most part, but which during the rains frequently become raging torrents. The contrast between this region and Galilee is very marked. There are few open places in Samaria larger than a very few acres in extent. The agriculture and horticulture are carried on under great handicaps on the terraced hillsides and in the small open plots that occur here and there among the hills. On account of this broken character these highlands are not easily accessible and the approach to the interior has traditionally been along several of the deepest wadis that extend into the heart of the mountain district. The northern approach from the east is up a deep gorge, which is now called Wadi Far'ah, and it enters the highlands to the northeast of the city of Samaria. Several miles south of this is an opening from the west, at the present time called Wadi Deir Balaat, which comes up into the region of ancient Shiloh. Undoubtedly, the Philistines came up this pass to fight against Israel at the time when the sons of Eli lost their lives and the ark of the Lord was captured (1 Sam. 4[1-11]). About five miles to the south is another pass on the eastern slope. The lower portion of this cut is the Wadi Qelt, and its northern tributary, the Wadi es-Sweinit. This is usually taken

to be the Valley of Achor (Josh. 7:24 Hos. 2:15). This would then be the pass which Joshua and the Israelites ascended in the conquest of Canaan. The old fortress Ai is on the upper edge of the wadi, and farther inland lie Bethel, Ramah, and other notable places connected with the conquest of the land. The Wadi Qelt has also a southern tributary, known as the Wadi Ruwabi, in which are the remains of an old Roman road, and in which must have been the ancient descent from Jerusalem to Jericho. The modern road to Jericho is a few miles to the south. The district of Samaria reaches its highest point a little to the north of Bethel, where the peak, Baal Hazor, attains an altitude of more than thirty-three hundred feet. The second highest point is just to the north of Shechem, Mount Ebal, which is over three thousand feet high.

(5) The Highlands of Judæa. The mountain districts south of Esdraelon and Jezreel are without natural break, and consequently it never has been certain just at what point lay the boundary between Samaria and Judæa. From the O.T. it is clear that it was not far north of Jerusalem. On the eastern slope possibly it was along the Wadis Ruwabi and Qelt. On the opposite side of the watershed, it is commonly taken to be the Valley of Aijalon (cf. Kent, *Biblical Geography and History*, p. 40). This valley, sometimes broadening out sufficiently to make fine and productive tracts, rises in the region of Gibeon, descends past Beth-Horon, and breaks through the highlands northeast of Jaffa. It is the scene of the famous battle between Joshua and the five Canaanite kings narrated in Josh. 10, and a southern branch of this valley was used as the pass from Jerusalem to Joppa. About ten miles south is another natural opening on the western slope, the Valley of Sorek. The upper portion of this wadi is a narrow, wild, and precipitous gorge, but its lower portions become wider and are utilized for agriculture. On its south edge Beth-Shemesh stood; so the kine drew the ark of covenant up this valley (1 Sam. 6:12). On the opposite side of the valley is the site of Zorah, the home of Samson's parents (Judg. 13:2). Delilah is said to have lived in the Valley of Sorek (Judg. 16:4), and it is altogether a likely place for the scene of Samson's exploits against the Philistines. At the present time this is the pass used as the railway approach to Jerusalem. On the opposite side of the divide two wadis, known in the Bible as the Brook Kidron and the Valley of the Son of Hinnom, lie to the east and west of Jerusalem, and unite just south of the city to form the Valley of Jehoshaphat which descends southeastward into the Dead Sea. Five miles south of Jerusalem, to the west of Bethlehem, is another pass to the Philistine plain, the O.T. Vale of Elah. The Philistines used this ascent in one of their campaigns against Saul, and tradition designates it as the locality where David vanquished Goliath (1 Sam. 17:2). Finally, about ten miles farther south is another pass on the western slope, now called Wadi el-Afrang. It cuts into the highlands to the west of Hebron, and is very likely the Valley of Zephathah, where Asa came into conflict with an invading Ethiopian army (2 Chr. 14:10). Traditionally, this is the valley which Philip descended after he baptized the eunuch (Acts 9:26-40). Thus, as in Samaria, Judæa is mostly a highland country of rocks and crags. It has no real valleys, but only little open pockets and flat places. These and the terraced hillsides are, of course, carefully cultivated. It is a picturesque country, even though not especially fertile. In the northern part the altitude of Judæa is about twenty-five hundred feet, and the general slope is upward as far as the region of Hebron, where Judæa reaches its highest point, a little over three thousand feet above sea level.

(6) The Negeb. South of Hebron the highlands slope downward, the contour is not so rugged, the wadis are not so deep, and the hills round off and gradually merge into the desert south of Palestine. This region, sparsely settled, little cultivated, and largely the home of Bedouin, is called in the O.T. the *Negeb*, that is, the dry region.

3. The Jordan Valley. At a varying distance of forty to fifty miles inland from the Mediterranean Sea is a deep fault in the earth's crust, extending in a northerly and southerly direction, and known as the Jordan Valley, or the *Ghôr*, in modern parlance. Generally, references to this gorge are made, not to the chasm as a whole, but to its several natural divisions.

(1) The Upper Jordan. In the extreme northern part of Palestine, under the shadows of famous Mount Hermon, and in the region of modern Banias (very likely the N.T. Cæsarea Philippi) are a group of springs which drain into a papyrus swamp. This swamp in turn is drained into a little lake four or five miles long and two or three miles wide. This is Lake Huleh, which in the Bible is referred to as the Waters of Merom (Josh. 11:5, 7). Lake Huleh is seven feet above sea level, and lies in the valley which is little wider than the lake. South of Huleh the valley becomes narrower and descends rapidly,

so that in a distance of less than fifteen miles the Jordan River, which flows from the lake, makes a descent of nearly seven hundred feet. For that reason the river is named the Jordan, that is, "the descender."

(2) At a point where the Jordan is six hundred and eighty-two feet below sea level it flows into the Sea of Galilee, called the Sea of Chinnereth in the O.T. and sometimes in the N.T., and the Sea of Tiberias in the N.T. and Talmud. The Sea of Galilee is pear-shaped, pointing to the south, and is about twelve miles long and eight wide at the widest place. It is closely hemmed in by mountains on both the east and west sides, which rise from its very shore to a height of a thousand or fifteen hundred feet. The water is fresh. Set among the hills, the lake, with its deep-blue color, makes a scene of rare beauty.

(3) The Jordan River. From the southwest end of the Sea of Galilee the Jordan River proper starts its downward course through a valley which varies from six hundred to one thousand feet below sea level, and which having a width of five to twelve miles is flanked on either side by steep cliffs. The descent is not so rapid through this part of the Jordan Valley, and the river meanders back and forth across the bottom of the valley, so that in an actual distance of about sixty-five miles the length of the river is over two hundred miles. In this distance it descends six hundred and ten feet, sometimes sluggishly, and sometimes over sharp rapids. In the course of time the Jordan and its tributaries have inundated its flood plain with a very rich alluvial soil, which has always been under cultivation.

(4) The Dead Sea. Almost directly east of Jerusalem, down in the bottom of the Jordan Valley, the Jordan empties into the Dead Sea. The Dead Sea is also known as the Salt Sea (Gen. 14³), as the Sea of the Wilderness (Deut. 3¹⁷), as the Eastern Sea (Ezek. 47¹⁸), and among modern Arabs as the *Bahr Lût* (Sea of Lot). It is twelve hundred and ninety-two feet below sea level, and forms the end of the chain of lakes and rivers that flow southward through the Jordan Valley; in the process of time it has received millions of tons of mineral-laden water, the water of which evaporated, leaving the mineral behind. Consequently, the Dead Sea has the highest specific gravity (varying from 1.021 to 1.256) of any body of water on earth, and contains about twenty-five per cent of minerals in solution, one half of which is sodium chloride. The water is very bitter to the taste and irritating to the skin, due to the chloride of magnesium; and it is very oily to the touch, due to the chloride of calcium. Normal life, therefore, does not exist in it, and only a very few low-grade species of animal life can be found on its salt soaked shores. As to size, the Dead Sea is nearly fifty miles in length, and at the widest place measures about ten miles. Its deepest point is near the northeast corner, where the full depth has never been ascertained, but is over twelve hundred and fifty feet. About two thirds of the length of the sea from its north shore a promontory thrusts out from the east shore and reaches more than half way across. The Arabs call it *el-Lisan*, "the Tongue." To the south of *el-Lisan* the water is comparatively shallow, and reaches a depth of less than fifty feet. The elder dwellers of the region tell that fifty or seventy-five years ago it was possible to ford from *el-Lisan* to the western shore, but in recent years that has been abandoned with the slight rise in water level. With the exception of *el-Lisan* and the opposite side, the sea has practically no shore on the east and west sides, and the mountains rise precipitously from its very edge. Thus, this body of water is really a pocket of the Jordan Valley, deeper than the rest of the valley, which has been filled with water, flooding the valley from edge to edge.

(5) The Wadi Arabah. As a matter of fact, the Jordan Valley continues south beyond the Dead Sea, although it no longer bears the same name, but is called *Wadi Arabah*. It is about the same width as the valley farther north, and finally beyond the desert makes a junction with the Gulf of Akaba. Its northern part, next to the Dead Sea, shows signs of once having been covered by an extensive oil flow, which killed the trees, and then preserved their stumps in the asphalt for centuries. Although there are very few inhabitants in this region at the present time, it has indications of once existent civilizations. The most picturesque survival is the ruin of Petra, whose remains from the Roman period are to be seen in the wonderful cuttings in the multicolored strata of the cliffs on the east side of the *Ghôr*.

4. **Trans-Jordania.** Palestine proper has always stopped at the Jordan Valley. Even in ancient times the occupation of the territory east of the Jordan by the Israelitish and Jewish monarchies was ever more or less partial. This was largely due to the fact that the eastern table-land merges into the desert, and has been populated by a semi-nomadic people, who, although having more or less definite tribal districts, still could vanish into the desert, and over whom therefore it was

hard to establish authority. So also to-day, the English mandate over Palestine extends only to the Jordan, and in Trans-Jordania the British Commonwealth of Nations has only an "adviser." This region is traditionally subdivided into four districts.

(1) The Jaulan. The territory to the north and east of the Sea of Galilee is at present known as the Jaulan. Its southern border is the ancient River Yarmuk, which cuts a deep gorge in the eastern highland and flows into the Jordan just south of the Sea of Galilee. The Jaulan is a volcanic region with many extinct craters especially in its western part. In the west wadis cut through its extensive lava beds. To the east the features are more even, and the volcanic loam becomes good for agriculture. Its altitude is slightly above that of Galilee.

(2) The Hauran. The Jaulan slopes upward toward the east, and southeastern Jaulan becomes the Hauran, which is a high, well-watered plateau, having an excellent volcanic loam for soil. It is the granary of Syria. The eastern border of the Hauran ends in the Druze Mountains, which is the present home of the Druzes, with whom the French mandate of Syria has had so much difficulty in recent times. These two divisions of Trans-Jordania, the Jaulan and the Hauran, probably correspond to O.T. Bashan, which was famous for its oaks (Isa. 2^{13} Ezek. 27^{6} Zech. 11^{2}), its pastures (Mic. 7^{14}), and its well-fed cattle and herds (Deut. 32^{14} Amos 4^{1} Psa. 22^{12}). Such allusions to this ancient territory fit it well even to-day.

(3) Gilead. South of the Yarmuk, and extending as far as the Wadi Heshban east of the north end of the Dead Sea, is Gilead. This region is not volcanic as the Jaulan, and has a rock formation much like that of the highlands of Samaria. It is not as extensively cultivated as the districts to the north, but its rolling plateaus yield very well to a rude order of cultivation, such as is carried on by the semi-sedentary population, which depends for livelihood as much upon the grazing lands as on agriculture. One deep wadi cuts through the south central part of Gilead, the River Jabbok. It drains the central and southern part of Gilead, and extends in a large inland curve around to the south. Within this curve is the outstanding mountain of Gilead, Jebel Osha, which is over thirty-five hundred feet high, and is venerated as the burial place of the prophet Hosea. The vegetation of southern Gilead becomes more scarce, and the region takes on more of the brownish deadness of the Dead Sea district.

(4) The Hills of Moab. South of the Wadi Heshban and extending the full length on the east of the Dead Sea lies the territory that was ancient Moab. Moab, like Gilead, is a large rolling plateau with fine stretches of soil. However, its appearance is arid, for there is insufficient moisture to procure the full benefit of the soil. Several deep wadis cut precipitous gorges in this plateau. The Wadi Zerka Ma'in enters the Dead Sea near the northern border of Moab. Near its mouth a fine hot spring bubbles out of the rock and flows into the sea. The ancient name for this spring was Callirhoë, and, according to tradition, Herod the Great came here to seek relief during his last illness. About ten miles south is the Wadi el-Mojib, the biblical Arnon River. For the most of the year it is a little stream one can leap across, but in the course of time it has cut a canyon into the hills that in the interior is over three thousand feet deep. At its point of entrance into the Dead Sea it is only a few hundred yards wide, with perfectly perpendicular sides, and in the beautiful strata of rock makes the most picturesque gorge in Palestine. Back of el-Lisan a third deep wadi descends into the Dead Sea. It is now called the Wadi el-Kerak, and possibly gets its name by corruption from ancient Kir Moab (Isa. 15^{1}), the ruins of which lie up in the hills on the edge of its canyon. The general altitude of Moab is somewhat more than that of Judæa, the maximum peaks towering up about four thousand feet above sea level, and five thousand feet above the Dead Sea. South of el-Kerak the plateau of Moab becomes more rugged, and passes into the wild and jagged crags of Mount Seir southeast of the Dead Sea, the mountain fastness of ancient Edom.

Climate and Rainfall. Palestine, being within 31 and 33 north latitude, has a semi-tropical climate. This location corresponds with that of the southern end of California and northern Lower California. It is still within the zone of the westerly winds, and therein is the saving feature of Palestinian climate, for the winds, coming in from the Mediterranean, bring moisture in the winter and cooling breezes in the summer. In the winter the temperature rarely falls below freezing; in the summer the hottest days frequently have a temperature of over 100° F. The atmosphere is clear, however, and the radiation rapid; so that in the hills, especially, as soon as the sun goes down, the temperature falls rapidly and the evening and night become cool, and frequently chilly. But when the wind comes from the east or southeast, Palestine suffers, for this wind comes from the desert (the Arabs call it the *sirocco*), and is totally devoid of water moisture; whatever green vegetation is left in the hills seems to dry up in a day.

The Jordan Valley is considerably hotter than the hill country, for it lies back of the hills and is cut off from the Mediterranean breezes. Consequently, the heat of the valley becomes terrific, and the Sea of Galilee and the Dead Sea to a large degree become steaming caldrons. It is estimated that close to six million tons of water pour into the Dead Sea daily, and yet the level of the sea from year to year remains constant. Accordingly, the evaporation is equal to the inflow, and in summer days one can see the vapor rising in clouds.

During the winter Palestine has its rainy season. Commencing with September the heat of the summer lessens perceptibly, and by the end of the month the first light rains commence to fall. They increase in quantity, until by December the rainy season is in full swing. The heaviest rains fall in December, January, and February. The winds come over and through the western hills, which cool and condense the moisture-laden air, and heavy rains follow, often for a week or ten days at a stretch. Everything then becomes damp and clammy, and although the temperature is above freezing, yet the stone houses, mostly unheated save by oil burners, become so damp and cold that a traveler chills through and through. Occasionally it is cold enough for snow, and sometimes a storm becomes a fierce blizzard, blowing huge snow banks about the nooks and crannies of the hills and towns. However, within a few days after the end of the storm the snow has all melted and disappeared.

By March the rains become lighter, more days of sunshine appear, and everything becomes warmer. Little rain falls after the last of April. The rains in March and April are known as the "latter rains" (Amos 4[7]), and though they never bring more than a few inches of moisture, they are extremely important to agriculture. The total rainfall averages between twenty and twenty-four inches, and falls during the five winter months. In modern times, as well as earlier, the rainfall frequently is less, and then days of famine ensue (cf. Gen. 42; 1 Kings 17).

Occupations. Palestine has no mineral wealth. A rude kind of salt industry has always been carried on in the Dead Sea region, and is the most extensive effort in mineral industry. Some prospects of oil exist in the South, but no successful drillings have yet been made.

Agriculture has always been one of the most staple industries of the land. The largest difficulty to overcome has been the uncertainty of sufficient moisture. Some irrigation has been practiced from ancient times, but in the hills there is no reservoir to tap. The ruins of many ancient cisterns are scattered about, so that it is likely that some effort was made in Bible times to provide for irrigation of a sort in this way. The fertility of Palestine is great enough for fine agriculture, and in recent years barren hilltops have been transformed, with water supply and care, into veritable gardens. Every available spot is cultivated, the hillsides are terraced, and in a favorable year yield a fair return. The small grains are the most common product—wheat, barley, rye, sesame, etc., are extensively grown at present as they were in Bible times. Recently, the cultivation of all the varieties of modern vegetables has been successfully introduced.

Fruit-growing also has been a staple occupation of Palestine. In the valleys and on the terraced hillsides the fig, grape, sycamore, fruit palm, and olive have been grown since antiquity. In modern times other fruits have been introduced, as the orange, lemon, lime, apricot, and various varieties of nuts, etc., and are now extensively cultivated in parts of the Coastal Plains and the Jordan Valley. The oranges of Jaffa are known throughout Europe.

Herding, finally, must be mentioned. Even though a Palestinian has a little plot of ground, in which he and his family carefully nurture the trees, vines, or grain, yet he also has his herd of sheep and goats, which one of the younger members of the family herds on the uncultivated hills and along the roadways. These herds are very important, for from them the owners get their milk (both sweet and sour are used) and cheese, and out of the wool they have always made their own clothes. Cattle raising never was important in western Palestine.

Literature: G. A. Smith, *Historical Geography of the Holy Land;* Kent, *Biblical Geography and History;* Barton, *Description of the Geography of Palestine;* K. Baedeker, *Palestine and Syria;* Thomson, *The Land and the Book;* Ed. Robinson, *Researches; Later Researches;* Price, *The Monuments and the O.T.;* Rena L. Crosby, *Geography of Bible Lands;* Palestine Exploration Fund, *Maps of Western Palestine;* Kent and Madsen, *Topographical and Historical Maps and Chronological Chart for Bible Students* (used in this Commentary).

HISTORY OF THE HEBREW AND JEWISH PEOPLE

BY PROFESSOR THEODORE H. ROBINSON

Pre-Hebrew History of Palestine. "Thy birth and thy nativity is of the land of the Canaanite; the Amorite was thy father, and thy mother was an Hittite." So runs Ezekiel's judgment (Ezek. 16[3]) on the racial pedigree of Israel, and his testimony is supported by practically all that we know of the origins of the people. Palestine has throughout its history been a battleground of nations, and not a few of the invaders have settled down on the soil, mingling their blood with that of their predecessors, and producing one of the most mixed of the world's races. To those primitive neolithic tribes to whom the Hebrews gave the general name of Rephaim ("Ghosts"; Gen. 14[5] Deut. 3[11, 13]), there succeeded in turn the Semitic stratum known as the Amorites (Gen. 14[7]; cf. 15[21]), the Hittites (Gen. 23[3]), the Hebrews and the Philistines (Judg. 3[31]), each playing its part and leaving its mark on the resultant nation.

In the earliest times Palestine was a savage "no man's land," lying between the two great centers of early civilization in Mesopotamia and Egypt. The country must have been gradually settled by immigrants from the wilderness, for at the beginning of the second millennium B.C. it was a populous country, with a developed agricultural and city life in its more habitable portions. At this period it seems that Mesopotamian influence was dominant, and made itself felt in the traditions and legends of the people. The fifteenth century B.C. is marked by the great Egyptian conquest of Thothmes III, and the land remained nominally subject to the African power till the coming of the Philistines and the establishment of the Israelite monarchy. But the authority of Egypt was intermittent, save at such points as Beth-Shean (in the Valley of Jezreel), where, as at other fortified posts, archæological research shows that Egyptian occupation was practically continuous. With the decay of the eighteenth dynasty under Amenhotep III and Ikhnaton (about 1400–1358 B.C.), Palestine fell largely under the control of the rising empire of the Hittites, a non-Semitic people of Asia Minor, whose outposts were to be found in Judæan territory as far back as the beginning of the second millennium B.C., if we may trust the historicity of the narrative in Gen. 23. The revival of Egypt under the early kings of the nineteenth dynasty re-established her dominion, at least as far as the Lebanon, but by the beginning of the eleventh century the impulse had waned, and Egypt was once more fighting for her own existence. The last remains of the old Ægean civilization, expelled from Asia Minor and from Crete by the invading barbarians later called the Greeks, tried to find fresh homes to the south, and though they failed to conquer Egypt, yet their march by land settled them on the southern coasts of Palestine, where they formed the confederacy known to history as that of the Philistines (Amos 9[7]). During the eleventh century they spread inland, and destroyed the last relics of Egyptian occupation in the fertile plains—Beth-Shean, for instance, was occupied by them—and they were prevented from establishing a new empire in Palestine only by the rise of a native power which, for the first time in history, succeeded in uniting the whole country under an independent government.

Hebrew Origins. In view of the varied fortunes of the country and of the mingling of different races, it is curious to observe that the early traditions of the people who established that government are not those of any of the nations and empires we have mentioned, but are derived from a group of invaders from the wilderness whose immigrations have not been definitely dated (Gen. 12f., Josh. 24). These were the Hebrews, and though their contribution to the actual blood of the people may have been small, in all else they proved to be the dominant influence. When studying, therefore, the history of Israel, it is with the story and traditions of these newcomers that we have to deal, interpreting as best we may records which are universally admitted to be centuries younger than the events to which they refer (see art., *Pentateuch*, p. 138). Let us see what the traditions preserved in the book of Genesis have to tell us.

Round the inner or desert rim of the fertile crescent there have ranged throughout the historic period groups of wandering tribes, partly hunting and robber clans, partly given to pastoral occupations and forming, in ancient times, the group known to us as Aramæans (Gen. 24[10] mg.). While the settled life of agriculture and commerce, of the farm and of the city, is impossible to such a social order, people tend to group themselves in the neighborhood of some center of the more complicated civilization, with which they certainly have commercial relations, and possibly form also some loose political association. They can live, it is true, on the produce of their flocks and by hunting, but they often (as in Arabia to-day) keep in touch with the city life and secure the products of the field and of the factory by bartering their own property. The official history of the Hebrews begins with such a tribe domiciled in the neighborhood of Ur, in the far south of Mesopotamia. About the end of the third millennium B.C., a group of them moved northward, under the leadership of a chief named Terah (Gen. 11[31]). This migration may have been due to some political convulsion in southern Mesopotamia, which affected the status of Ur and its commercial position. It was perhaps the shifting of the center of power from the Mesopotamian cities to the Elamite tribes which made Ur an undesirable district, and this would place the first movement somewhere between 2300 and 2000 B.C. Be that as it may, the migration took place, and the wandering people halted for a time in the neighborhood of Haran, in the north of the fertile crescent. It is worth noting (whatever be the exact significance of the fact) that both Ur and Haran were early centers of the worship of the ancient Semitic Moon-god, Sin, whose name probably meets us again in Sinai.

Portions of the tribes still continued to move westward and southward. Some, finding arable land in the country between the Euphrates valley and the more fertile western hill country, settled down, founding cities of which the best known is Damascus. Another group, led by Abram, a "son" (the word "son" is often used simply in the sense of a descendant) of Terah, continued their slow march till they entered Palestine proper, then a country of isolated city states (Gen. 12[5, 6]). For some generations the wanderings continued, sometimes to the west of the Jordan and sometimes to the east, and ranging from the region of Damascus (or even further east) to the borders of Egypt. Once we have an account of direct contact between Egypt and these pastoral nomads (Gen. 12[10-20]) and several of the narratives describe the dealings of the Hebrew patriarchs with the settled inhabitans of Canaan (Gen. 20, 23, 26, 34, 38), while the stories of Jacob bring the ancestors of Israel into touch with both the Aramæans to the northwest and the Edomites to the south (Gen. 28–33).

The Hebrews in Egypt; the Exodus. The Joseph stories (Gen. 37f.) form a transition to the next stage, and explain how the early Hebrews came under Egyptian domination. There are suggestions, even in the book of Genesis, of tribes which never passed south of Canaan; Judah in ch. 38 seems to be domiciled permanently in the land. But it is clear that some, at least, found their way into Goshen, the northeastern borderland of Egypt, and were there reduced to serfdom by the Egyptians (Gen. 46[28] 47[1-12]). The date of these events is uncertain, though it seems probable that the entry into Egypt took place during the period known as the Hyksos empire (roughly eighteenth and seventeenth centuries B.C.), when a Semitic wave of invasion had overrun the country. There are, indeed, scholars who believe that the Hyksos were practically the Israelites, and that the story of the Exodus is the account of their expulsion given from their own point of view. This, however, is a conjecture which has little to support it, though, naturally, there is no direct evidence against it.

It is with the departure from Egypt (Ex. 12) that the history of Israel proper begins. The date is a matter of uncertainty, and opinions vary between the early sixteenth century and the middle of the thirteenth. If the statement in Ex. 1[11] be accepted as historically accurate, the Pharaoh of the oppression must have been Rameses II, and the Pharaoh of the Exodus his son Merneptah. The difficulty in accepting this date lies in the mention of Israel in an inscription of the latter king. The people are included in a list of Palestinian tribes defeated and destroyed by the Egyptian king, and the language of the inscription makes it clear that Israel was already settled in southern Palestine. It is, therefore, not impossible, though improbable, that the mention of Pithom and Raamses in Ex. 1[11] is due to an erroneous insertion in the original text, and that the Exodus itself is to be dated much earlier—possibly two hundred years before the time of Merneptah. Other details too must be left unsettled. We do not know the proportion of the later Israel that participated in the Exodus. As we have seen, there is reason to doubt whether Judah ever was in Egypt, and there is direct evidence that the tribe of Asher was domiciled in northern Palestine at an early date. We cannot be certain about the census figures supplied to us in Exodus (see comments there); the transmission of numbers is notoriously precarious, and a total of about two million people all told seems impossible, whether we consider the movements of the Israelites, the Exodus itself, or the water supply at the oases where they encamped after leaving Egypt. (For a brief discussion of the date of the Exodus see Eiselen, *The Christian View of the O.T.*, pp. 128, 129 and references there.)

The Person and Work of Moses. Certain facts, however, are beyond dispute. The enormous influence that events connected with the Exodus had on the later thought of the people makes doubt as to its historicity impossible. The first of these is the personality of Moses himself. He bears an Egyptian name, found as one element in the names of several of the kings of the eighteenth dynasty. Hebrew tradition stated that, though an Israelite by birth (Ex. 2[2]), he had been brought up at the Egyptian court (Ex. 2[3-10]), and had then spent many years in exile among the nomad tribe of Midian (Ex. 2[15-25]) with whom later Israel believed itself to be akin. Here he had an experience of direct divine revelation (Ex. 3–7), and returned to Egypt to bring his people out, to celebrate a festival to the God who had appeared to him. The departure was heralded by a series of calamities which befell the Egyptians (Ex. 8–12), and the actual flight was attended by a disaster which overtook an armed force sent in pursuit of the fugitives, numbers of them being drowned in an effort to follow the Israelites in their passage across the Red Sea—probably the northern end of the Gulf of Suez (Ex. 14[21-31]). This event made a profound impression on Israel, and men looked back on it throughout the whole of the people's history as the first and greatest manifestation of the national God's power.

The escape from Egypt, however, was but a preliminary to the great work of Moses. To him fell the task of binding together into a single political unit the various tribes, who, it seems, had hitherto maintained a real independence, though they had recognized a kinship of blood. The only force that could have achieved this (as Mohammed found nearly two thousand years later) was that of a new religion, and it was a new religion that Moses had to offer his people. What the earlier cults had been we do not know, but we may guess that each tribe had maintained its own worship and its own tribal deity—possibly its eponymous ancestor. In Midian, Moses had met a God whose name, at least, was previously unknown to any of the tribes, and it was to the mountain sacred to this God, known as Jehovah (a more accurate form of the name is probably *Yahweh*), that he led the people (Ex. 19[1, 2]). The site is variously placed at Sinai, apparently not far from Kadesh Barnea, between Egypt and Palestine, and at Horeb, which, it is conjectured, lay to the northeast of the Gulf of Akabah. (The tradition which places the scene at *Jebel Musa* in the Sinai peninsula cannot be traced further back than the sixth century A.D.). The traditions of northern Israel seem to have favored the latter locality, those of southern Israel the former. But, whatever be the exact position, and whatever may have been the earlier religious situation, the main historical fact stands out: by a solemn covenant Israel and Jehovah adopted one another. He became their God, and they became his people (Ex. 19[3-6]).

It is impossible to exaggerate the importance of this event. In the ancient world religion and politics could not be separated from one another. The god was a member of the tribe which worshiped him, and was always held to be its real leader, whether in peace or in war. This was true of all the peoples among whom Israel moved, but in this instance there was the special feature that the union of God and people was not a natural or inevitable association. On the contrary, it was the result of a deliberate act of choice on the part of Jehovah, who could thus dictate his own terms, and of an equally deliberate acceptance on the part of Israel, who thus bound herself to observe those terms. Other tribes too were connected with their deities by ties of local habitation; though Jehovah might have his proper home in the place where Israel had first met him, he could yet go with them, and take up his residence wherever they should make their home. Above all, this covenant relation with their God gave the Israelite tribes a sense of unity among themselves, and served to distinguish them from all others whom they met. Their acceptance of him was at once a domestic bond and an external barrier, consecrating them to one another, as well as to the object of their worship. The whole of the later history of Israel, political as well as religious, is based on the fundamental act of union achieved by Moses. (See also art., *Religion of Israel*, p. 166.)

Conquest of Canaan. The new people did not immediately take possession of the land which was to be theirs. An attempt was made to conquer the country from the south, but it failed, and the nomad life was continued for a period which the biblical narratives set at roughly forty years. (These wanderings are described in the book of Numbers.) It seems that Israel wandered over the arid pasture lands to the south of Palestine for the greater part of this time, and then moved eastward, making their definite attack across the Jordan. The country to the east of Jordan was first conquered, and was occupied by those elements in Israel whose wealth in cattle induced them to continue the pastoral life (Num. 32). The remainder pressed across the Jordan, and began to establish themselves on the west of the river (Josh. 1–3).

Light has been thrown on the Israelite invasions of Palestine by the discovery of the Tel-el-Amarna tablets, containing parts of the correspondence which passed between the Egyptian governors and vassal princes of Palestine, and the courts of Amenhotep III and his son Ikhnaton (Amenhotep IV). In addition to other troubles, loyal representatives of the Egyptian power are worried by inroads from desert tribes, who are usually called by a name written in ideographic characters whose phonetic equivalent would be ŠA-GAZ, but in the correspondence coming from Jerusalem are designated *Khabiru.* Such attacks must have taken place whenever the power holding Palestine was weak (we hear of them again in the story of early Israel), but the latter name has led a number of scholars to identify these invaders with the Hebrews. If this opinion is correct—and it appears to be gaining ground—then we have an interesting picture of the conquest from the Palestinian point of view. In the literature of Israel we have two presentations. One describes the conquest as complete, and comparatively sudden, being carried through under the leadership of a single commander, Joshua. The whole is accomplished in less than seven years after the first entry into the country, and the land is then formally divided among the twelve tribes, the Canaanites being exterminated (Josh. 4–10). The other account—earlier and intrinsically more probable—thinks of the conquest as a long, slow process, occupying generations, and sometimes leaving the settled Israelites in subordination to their predecessors (Judg. 1 and scattered passages in Joshua). In support of this presentation of the facts, we learn that Shechem did not pass into Israelite control till the time of Abimelech, that Jerusalem was first captured by David, and that Gezer was not occupied by Israel before the age of Solomon. The actual conquest, then, must be held to have lasted through the period covered by the books of Joshua and Judges. (See further, Eiselen, *The Prophetic Books of the O.T.*, vol. i, pp. 29–34.)

In attempting to overthrow and dispossess the Amorites and Canaanites, Israel was attacking a people on a higher level of civilization, with greater resources in material and in military art. The result was that the first settlements made by the invaders were located in the hills, and in the poorer parts of the land. Jericho fell at the first assault (Josh. 6; the fact of its destruction at this period is attested by archæology as well as by the biblical record), but for some generations the invaders made good their footing only in three districts. In the south they held Hebron and the surrounding country, and it is interesting to note that the heroes of the early days do not strictly belong to Israel at all but to the tribe known as Kenites, who seem to have been loosely attached to Judah. In the center there were settlements about Bethel, the Bethhorons, and northward in the hills of Ephraim and Manasseh, while to the far north a group of tribes found a home among the southern spurs of the Lebanon range and about the Lake of Huleh. The fortresses of Gezer and Jerusalem served as a barrier between the southern and the central settlements, while the latter were cut off from their brethren in the north by the great chain of strong cities that ran across the plain of Esdraelon from Megiddo to Beth-Shean.

A vivid picture of Israel during this period is drawn for us in the book of Judges. The Israelite settlements have little organization, though local leaders rise from time to time at the call of patriotism and of religion to relieve their immediate neighbors from the stress of their enemies. Only once is a serious attempt made to found a royal dynasty, and that is when the sons of Gideon seek to exercise authority over Shechem (Judg. 9). Abimelech, after destroying his half-brothers, achieves a local and temporary conquest; he is himself of mixed blood, and his story suggests that the ultimate unification of the land was achieved more by gradual intermingling with the older population than by their extermination.

Apart from Abimelech, Israelite forces only once face a Canaanite enemy, Sisera of Harosheth (Judg. 4, 5). His name has an Egyptian sound, and he may have owed nominal allegiance to the court of Thebes. The other adversaries are all invaders from without, and the Israelite heroes were fighting the battle of the Canaanites as much as that of their own people. This was especially true of the last and most serious struggle of the age, that in which the whole country was threatened by the invading Philistines (Judg. 13[1] 1 Sam. 4, 13, etc.). The tribe that lay nearest to their settlements on the coast, Dan, after a heroic resistance of which we get glimpses in the story of Samson, was compelled to migrate and find a fresh home in the far north (Judg. 17, 18), and the newcomers pressed further inland. So successful were they that there was at least the possibility that they would establish themselves firmly over the whole country, and that the power expelled from the north and west would rise again on Palestinian soil. (For the biblical accounts of this early period see the books of Joshua and Judges, and consult the commentaries on these books in this volume, especially the introductions.)

The United Monarchy. The failure of the Philistines to build up a new empire was due to the formation of a unified state in Palestine under Hebrew leadership. External pressure compelled the whole country to unite under the centralized government of Saul, whose election is in one narrative represented as an act of defection from Jehovah, in another (generally recognized as the earlier) as of divine appointment to save Israel from her enemies. (See further, Eiselen, *The Prophetic Books of the O.T.*, vol. i, pp. 68f.) The king himself belonged to that class of inspired ecstatics known as *Nebhîîm*, or "prophets" (1 Sam. 10^{9-13}), men who from time to time passed under the control of their God, and spoke and acted as his spirit impelled them. His first exploit, performed under the influence of the ecstasy, was the rescue of the east-Jordan city of Jabesh from an army of Ammonites (1 Sam. 11^{1-11}), but the great struggles of his life were those in which he met the Philistines. Saul united all Israel, probably including many of the Canaanites, against the invader from the west, and for a time succeeded in checking their advance.

The difficulties of his position in the long run proved too great for Saul. He had the foreign enemies of his people to fight, there were signs of disaffection within his own people, and his temperament was unsuited to the work which lay before him. The division in Israel which drove the young David into exile had its roots in Saul's own jealousy of a greater warrior than himself (1 Sam. 18^{10-16}), while that very ecstatic power which roused and inspired him in his earlier days, enabling him to do great and startling feats, unfitted him for the drudgery of organization and the slow toil of consolidating what he and his had won.

The real unity of the land begins with David. The romantic story of his early days (1 Sam. 16f.) is familiar to every one, and it is clear that he had exceptional opportunities. He had connections even with the Philistines, and it is possible that under the narrative which we actually have before us there lies a division among these enemies of Israel. Certainly, to the end of his days David enjoyed the friendship of Philistines, and from them drew his private bodyguard (2 Sam. 8^{18}; "Pelethites" here is regarded as meaning Philistines). The catastrophe of Mount Gilboa confined the house of Saul mainly to the east of Jordan, and the death of Ishbosheth left David without a rival in his own land. The capture of Jerusalem, which seems to have had Philistine affinities, marks the point at which the Israelite monarchy was really established, and David showed political genius by making it his capital (2 Sam. 5^{6-12}). It was not only a symbol of his prowess, but it was neutral ground between the two great divisions of Israel, the north and the south. David himself had that personal charm which distinguished Saul in his early days, and commanded the devoted enthusiasm of his people. At the same time he had those more solid qualities for lack of which his predecessor had failed, and was thus able to build up a great kingdom. His wars resulted in almost uniform success; he strengthened the frontiers of his realm on every side, and though he does not seem to have attempted a conquest of the Philistine cities, he kept them well within their own limits. His realm was carefully and thoroughly organized both for peace and for war, and even the domestic rebellion which he suffered in his later years (2 Sam. 15f.) failed to end his power. There were, it is true, dark passages in his life, but his sins were those of a strong elemental nature, and his moral character must be judged against the background of his age. Estimated on any fair standard, David stands out as one of the greatest and one of the noblest among the heroes of the ancient world. (See in the present volume the commentary on 1 and 2 Samuel, and cf. Kings and Chronicles.)

David's real greatness is best seen when we compare the kingdom of Saul—even at its best—with that of Solomon (1 Kings 3–11). His splendor has become proverbial; under him Israel reached its greatest wealth and its widest extent. Yet only one acquisition is ascribed to his reign, the city of Gezer, which was captured by an Egyptian king and given to Solomon as part of the dowry of the Egyptian princess whom he married. The king in question is not named, but was probably one of the last kings of the twenty-first dynasty, perhaps Siamon. It is to the time of Solomon that most of the great buildings of Jerusalem and of other cities were attributed. Nevertheless, his reign marked a serious decline. His magnificence was costly and his rule was oppressive. His commercial gains—and Solomon was a great trader—were inadequate for his expenditures, and the burdens laid upon his people, both in unpaid services and in taxation, were ruinous to the agricultural population. The spirit of revolt was more than once in evidence, and one of the rebels, Jeroboam by name, took refuge in Egypt. Here, it seems, a revolution had taken place, and a Lybian dynasty (the twenty-second) was now on the throne. Jeroboam was welcomed and maintained, and though Solomon himself was too strong to be attacked with impunity, Egypt was ready to take advantage of any weakness of his successors.

Division of the Kingdom. The opportunity

came on the death of Solomon. In political theory, as in other respects, the dominant influence in Israel was the traditional outlook of the Aramæan invaders rather than that of the settled communities among whom they made their new home, and they carried into their view of the organized state a democratic feeling which was unique, so far as we know, in the ancient East. We have from time to time indications of a "covenant" made at a king's accession, an agreement to which there were three parties, the sovereign, the people, and the national God. It is not impossible that every new monarch (Jehoiakim may have been an exception, but he was imposed on Judah by a foreign power) had to grant this "charter" as a condition of his acceptance by the people, and that, if they so wished, they could demand a modification of its terms. Certainly, such a right was exercised on the death of Solomon, and his son, Rehoboam, was faced with a popular claim for milder terms than those given in the past, and on his refusal to grant them lost almost all his dominions (1 Kings 12). The rebels sent for Jeroboam and made him king over northern Israel; possibly the royal bodyguard was sufficient to overawe Jerusalem and the country south of the city. Attempts were made to recover the allegiance of the rebels by force of arms, and, apparently, met with temporary success. But Jeroboam could rely on the support of Egypt, and any gains that Rehoboam may have made were more than neutralized by an invasion of Sheshonk, the first king of the twenty-second dynasty. He ravaged the country as far north as Samaria, and laid Rehoboam under tribute, which could be paid only by surrendering the treasures of the royal house and of the Temple (1 Kings 14[25-28]). The Chronicler's statement (2 Chr. 12[9]) that he captured Jerusalem itself is not borne out by the record in Kings, or by Sheshonk's own account of the expedition, and we may assume that, like Sennacherib two hundred years later, Sheshonk found that he could get all he wanted without the risk and loss involved in a serious siege of Jerusalem. Jeroboam was able to consolidate his kingdom, and probably found the organization of David still available for his own purposes. The most important of his changes was the establishment of the ancient sanctuaries of Dan and Bethel as the official centers of worship, to counteract the influence of Jerusalem, where the most sacred of all Israelite religious emblems, the ark, had been deposited by David (1 Kings 12[26-33]).

Throughout the next century the weakness of the great powers of Egypt and Mesopotamia left Palestine comparatively free from foreign interference. The records that have come down to us are scanty, and deal mainly with internal affairs. In the Northern Kingdom there were repeated changes of dynasty, with a corresponding political weakness, only relieved with the accession of Omri, one of the most powerful of the Israelite kings. In the south the people remained faithful to the house of David, and the country was poorer and weaker than the sister monarchy. There was jealousy between the two, occasionally breaking out into open war, in which the advantage normally lay with the north, and we have to think of the south as being at best a subordinate ally in times of peace. Twice only is a foreign enemy mentioned; Asa of Judah calls in the king of Damascus to help him against Baasha of Israel, and at the time when Omri succeeds to the throne the Israelite armies are besieging the Philistine city of Gibbethon. We gather also from a note referring to a later time that Edom was nominally subject to Judah (1 Kings 14–16).

From Omri to Jeroboam II. It is with the accession of Omri that there are positive movements in the history of the two kingdoms. The new dynasty looks out beyond its own narrow borders, and both to the northwest and to the southeast advance is made. A royal marriage cements a peaceful alliance with Phœnicia, and Moab is reduced to a subordinate position. At the same time there is practically continuous desultory warfare between Israel and Damascus, and with the greater pretensions of the Hebrew monarchy this becomes more serious. Though the records claim occasional victories for Ahab, son of Omri, and for his successors, it is clear that the balance of advantage lay with the Syrians until nearly the middle of the eighth century.

Curiously enough, the most striking event in the political history of Israel during the ninth century has not been included in the biblical records as they have come down to us, though it cannot to-day pass without mention, if only because it illustrates at once the strength of Israel and the yet greater superiority of Damascus. It was in 853 B.C., that Palestine once more became an object of importance to one of the great world powers, and from that date onward, her history is largely conditioned by that of Egypt and Mesopotamia. The southern power, it is true, still maintained that policy of isolation which alone was possible to a weak dynasty like the twenty-second, but Assyria was entering on that career of western conquest which ceased only with the final overthrow of her empire and the destruction of her capital.

We learn from the records of Shalmaneser III that in 853 B.C. he marched westward, but was met at Karkar by a combined force under Benhadad of Damascus. The troops at his disposal included contingents from many of the western states, and, next to that of Damascus itself, the most important is that of Ahab. The Assyrian claims a great victory, but he took no cities and returned to his own country—a step which, for an Assyrian king, was tantamount to a confession of defeat. As against this successful action must be set the revolt of Moab, which was attacked, but not reconquered, by Ahab's son, Jehoram. A description of the revolt, given by Mesha, king of Moab, is still extant, and it seems probable that for a time the territory east of the Jordan was practically divided between Damascus and Moab. (See notes on 2 Kings 3.)

After the death of Ahab internal politics had an important effect on the course of events. The alliance with Tyre, wise as it may have seemed to Omri and his son, gave double offense to that conservative element in Israel which clung to the old Hebrew tradition and still tried to maintain the religious and constitutional theories of the Aramæan invaders. Jezebel, the imported queen, brought with her the worship of the Tyrian god Melkart ("Baal") and thus challenged the sole supremacy of Jehovah. She also brought with her the normal theory of Oriental monarchy, which saw in kingship an absolute despotism, and in the king a ruler whose will might be neither disobeyed nor disputed. The opposition found its first champion in Elijah, who stood at once for the purity of the worship of Jehovah and for the liberty of the subject as against the new pretensions of the crown. He himself was content with attacking the evil as a foreign excrescence on the social and religious life of Israel, but his attitude was carried still further by the prophets who succeeded him, as well as by such conservative groups as the Rechabites. These men were not lacking in patriotism, as so many of the stories dealing with Elisha show, but they believed that the best interests of their country would be served by maintaining the old worship and the ancient ways. When, at length, it became clear that the house of Omri was and ever would be definitely against them, they found a leader in a certain Jehu, who overthrew the reigning dynasty with horrible and indiscriminate slaughter, and established himself on the throne. His first step seems to have been to break with the Syrians, and Shalmaneser's next invasion of the west found Damascus alone prepared to resist him, while Jehu paid tribute, probably as the price of Assyrian support (841 B.C.; see further for this entire period commentary on 1 Kings 17–2 Kings 10).

These events in the north were not without their repercussions on the southern kingdom. Jehoshaphat had been in close alliance with Ahab, probably as a subordinate, and his son Jehoram had married Athaliah, the daughter of Ahab. At the moment when the revolt of Jehu took place Ahaziah, son of Jehoram, was paying a complimentary visit to Jehoram of Israel, and shared his fate. Athaliah immediately tried to secure the throne for herself, and put to death all members of the royal family of Judah whom she could find. One, the infant Joash, escaped, saved by the devotion of his aunt and by the care of the priest Jehoiada. Six years later the latter organized a revolution in Jerusalem, slew Athaliah, and placed the child Joash on the throne (2 Kings 11, 12), thus restoring the dynasty of David, which retained its position for another two centuries and a half (835–585 B.C.).

The death of Shalmaneser III left Assyria comparatively weak, and the Palestinian states fell into the old border warfare again. Details of the history of both kingdoms (apart from the names of the kings) are hardly to be obtained from any source, but we hear of the oppression of northern Israel by Hazael of Damascus, and of the subjugation of Edom by Amaziah of Judah, son of Joash. There is also a reference to war between north and south in the latter reign, probably representing an attempt by Amaziah to assert his independence. Our knowledge becomes fuller only with the reign of the great-grandson of Jehu, Jeroboam II, who was on the throne in or about 760 B.C. (2 Kings 14:23-27). Damascus, possibly owing to Assyrian pressure, was unable to maintain her conquests to the east of Jordan, and Jeroboam succeeded in recovering the captured territory, including the two cities of Lo-debar and Karnaim. The Hebrew historian claims him as a great deliverer who re-established the frontiers ascribed to Solomon, and it is clear that the territory over which he ruled far exceeded that of his immediate predecessors. His reign certainly marks the high-water mark of Israelite prosperity, and in the large cities wealth and luxury reached a point which they had never before attained. Commerce and a regular financial system tended to the growth of a moneyed class, and the great cities were adorned with the palatial buildings of the merchant princes of Israel. They had separate residences for summer and winter, their walls were paneled with ebony and ivory, they used the costliest fabrics for their couches, enjoyed the finest of perfumed unguents, ate the most extravagant of foods and drank rich wine without sparing, while in music, if not in other arts, they claimed to be second to none.

(For a clear picture of religious, moral and social conditions in Israel at this time see the books of Amos and Hosea; for conditions in Judah, Isaiah and Micah.)

But a clearer eye could see that all this magnificence, wealth and luxury was but superficial, and that underneath the brilliant surface lay a rotting mass of hopeless misery and corruption. During the century which preceded the appearance of the prophet Amos at Bethel a fatal change had passed over the social and economic order of Israel, both in the north and (so far as the agricultural districts and the commercial cities were concerned) in the south. In the ninth century Palestine had been a land of small peasant farmers. Many of the holdings were very small; a type is presented to us by Naboth, whose farm would serve Ahab as a garden (1 Kings 21). The men bred by such a system have their faults; they are often slow, unimaginative, conservative; but all experience goes to show that they are vigorous and sturdy, and will resist to the death any form of oppression, whether from without or from within. Such were the men of Marathon, the men who laid the foundations of Roman greatness, and the men who at Karkar checked the advance of the Assyrian Empire. But in the eighth century all was changed. The peasant proprietor had almost disappeared, and his place had been taken by the capitalist who either let the land to a tenant farmer—at an oppressive rental—or worked it by slave labor. Lurid pictures of the prevailing conditions are drawn for us by the eighth century prophets, especially by Amos and Micah, while neither Hosea nor Isaiah is blind to the facts and their attendant dangers. Such conditions, as history, ethics and religion combine to teach, are wholly disastrous. The oppressed classes may not be finally crushed; they may retain something of the true human spirit, and this in the end will lead to such an internal explosion as wrecked France in the eighteenth century and has had such fearful effects in Russia in our own day. On the other hand the spiritual reduction of the people generally may be complete, and this can produce nothing but a national emasculation which leaves the country an easy prey to the first serious invader. It was so that Israel fell in the end, and it was so that the old Roman world, with its massed slave population, yielded to the hardier barbarians from the north.

The Overthrow of Israel. The death of Jeroboam II revealed the true position of northern Israel (2 Kings 15). His son and successor was assassinated after a short reign, but the murderer's career was cut short a month later by Menahem. Assyria was once more stirring, and in 738 B.C. Menahem, perhaps to secure his newly won throne, perhaps in despair of effective resistance, paid tribute to Tiglath-pileser III. His son, Pekahiah, was overthrown by a party acting in the interests of national independence, headed by Pekah, and he, in alliance with Rezon, king of Damascus, attempted to revive the old league which had successfully resisted Shalmaneser III a century earlier. But times had changed, and when the allies tried to force Ahaz of Judah into their confederacy, or, failing that, to substitute an Aramæan prince for him, they were not strong enough to coerce their southern neighbor, and he appealed for help to Assyria (cf. Isa. 7[1-9]). This step was probably unnecessary; Tiglath-pileser was not the man to overlook such a challenge as that of the allies, and in 732 B.C. Damascus was captured and Pekah replaced by Hoshea, who was permitted to hold his crown as a vassal of the Assyrian court (2 Kings 16).

Judah also was now subservient to Tiglath-pileser. We have the record of a new altar, whose pattern was sent by Ahaz from Damascus, where he had gone to render homage to his overlord (2 Kings 16[10-16]). Though no foreign worship is mentioned, we may suspect that, in accordance with Assyrian policy, some form of state cult accompanied the new piece of machinery, and that, in one way or another, Ahaz was compelled to recognize the official religion of Nineveh. The charge of human sacrifice is brought against him by biblical writers, and this also may be due to Assyrian influence, though the parallel instance in the story of Moab suggests that a more probable occasion was the attack on Judah made by Pekah and Rezon. But whatever be the reason, there is no ground on which the fact may be doubted, and it is clear that during the lifetime of Tighlath-pileser the whole of Palestine was practically an Assyrian province.

That great empire, however, was held together by the personality of its monarchs, and the accession of Shalmaneser V in 727 B.C. was the signal for widespread revolt. Egypt, though in great political confusion, still felt the possible danger of Assyria, and Hoshea fell under the influence of a certain So, who has not been certainly identified; probably he was either Shabaka, not yet at the height of his power, or some other local dynast of the Delta The inevitable result was a new Assyrian invasion. The dates are somewhat confusing, and there seem to have been errors in the transmission of the biblical figures. The best explanation of the records, taking into account both the Hebrew and the Assyrian chronologies, is probably one which allows Hoshea to be captured and destroyed before the siege of Samaria began. That undertaking lasted three years, and was not complete when Shalmaneser died in 722 B.C., the city actually falling to Sargon in 721. We have no details from any source of the dispositions made by Sargon in the Northern Kingdom, but we may conjecture that at least a large part of northern Israel was committed to the king of Judah. The uncertainty of our dating makes it impossible to decide without reservation whether or not Ahaz had been succeeded by Hezekiah, though in the opinion of the present writer it is more likely that the former king died in 725 (see 2 Kings 17).

From Hezekiah to Josiah. As far as we know Palestine remained duly submissive, and therefore in comparative peace, throughout the reign of Sargon. But the Assyrian invasion of Philistia in 711 (cf. Isa. 20¹) alarmed Egypt, now gradually emerging from a long confusion under Shabaka. The death of Sargon in 705 was the signal for almost universal revolt against Assyria, and Sennacherib, the new king, had to fight for nearly every province in the empire. In the west Padi, king of Ekron, was the only ruler who remained faithful to Assyria, and he was dethroned by his own subjects and imprisoned in Jerusalem. Hezekiah carried through a religious reform, endeavoring to sweep away all cults which seemed at all to conflict with the sole worship of the national God, Jehovah. While there is no reason to doubt his sincerity or his devotion to the cause of his God, it is not improbable that his action had a political aspect, and was interpreted by his own age, at home and abroad, as a gesture of defiance to Assyria.

Sennacherib found time to embark on a western campaign first in 701 B.C. The whole of Palestine was terribly ravaged, and in the territories of Judah alone the Assyrian king claims to have destroyed forty-six fortified cities and innumerable villages, while he claimed 200,150 as captives. But he failed to take Jerusalem and the biblical record ascribes the safety of the city itself to a disaster which overtook his army. It may well be that during his operations against the Egyptians, whom he utterly defeated at Eltekeh, his forces were attacked by bubonic plague. But though he failed to capture Jerusalem, Sennacherib inflicted an enormous fine on Hezekiah, and imposed a heavy tribute, besides reducing the dominions of Judah to very small limits (2 Kings 18, 19; also intro. to Isaiah in the present volume).

Sennacherib's invasion of 701 was the last appearance of a hostile Assyrian army in Judah. Manasseh, who followed Hezekiah, is strongly condemned for cruelty and apostasy, and this may well be due to his faithfulness to his Assyrian suzerain (2 Kings 21). The Chronicler speaks of his being carried captive to Babylon (2 Chr. 33¹¹); but there is no mention of this in Kings, and the Assyrian records, very full for this period, contain no reference to an attack on Judah. Probably there underlies this story a reminiscence of a visit Manasseh paid to Phœnicia, where, in company with all the kings of the west, he did homage to Esarhaddon. Till the decay of the Assyrian Empire between the years 639 and 612 B.C. Judah enjoyed comparative peace from foreign invasion.

Manasseh was succeeded in 641 by his son Amon, who was assassinated after a reign of two years. The boy Josiah, who followed his father, was still too young to take any active part in politics, and in 626 an event occurred which helped to change the face of the east. Wild hordes from the north broke through the political barriers established by the Assyrians, and made their way into the fertile crescent. The western stream of these people, known to Greek historians as Scythians or Cimmerians, followed the coast, and marauding bands devastated Judah. Reflections of the sufferings of the land are to be seen in the prophecies of Zephaniah and in various oracles of Jeremiah. The invaders were not of a type to establish a firm empire, but they struck a blow at Assyria from which she never recovered, and it must have been widely realized that her power over the west was at an end.

It was, perhaps, under the influence of this feeling that Josiah in 621 undertook a religious reform. As we have seen in speaking of Hezekiah, it is impossible to separate religion and politics in the ancient world, and there is no reason to doubt Josiah's sincerity. The repair of the Temple, which had suffered from neglect during the king's long minority, brought to light a book of the Law, commonly identified with the whole or a part of Deuteronomy (the identification has been questioned in recent years; some scholars, including Oestereicher and Welch, placing the book earlier, others, such as Kennett and Hölscher, dating it later; see the commentary on Deuteronomy in the present volume, and cf. the notes on 2 Kings 22, 23). Under the influence of this discovery, the worship of Jerusalem itself was first purified, and a mass of strange and debasing cults was swept away. An attack was then made on the local sanctuaries throughout Judah and as far north as Bethel. These were probably the seats of ancient Canaanite cults which had been adapted by Israel to the worship of Jehovah, though in their ritual they probably retained much of the traditional ceremonial.

But now all worship of Jehovah was to be concentrated in Jerusalem, and sacrifice was to be valid only when offered at the great altar on Mount Zion.

While it is impossible to exaggerate the religious effects of this step, its immediate political importance was comparatively slight. Assyria was dying, and could not avenge any insult which might be read into Josiah's action. Babylon had finally achieved her independence of Nineveh under a new Chaldean dynasty, and in alliance with the Medes and Scythians was beginning her final assault on Assyria. Nineveh fell in 612 B.C., and one of the most vivid pieces of descriptive poetry in all literature is the prophet Nahum's exultant ode over the sack of the city. Strangely enough, the only help she received came from Egypt, where the twenty-sixth dynasty had succeeded in uniting the country. Necho, the second king of this line, may have felt that the great danger would now come from Babylon, not from Nineveh, and that Assyria might be useful, if her existence could be preserved, as a buffer state. He made repeated expeditions eastward, which did not cease even with the fall of Nineveh. Finding reason to believe (possibly as a result of the religious changes made thirteen years earlier) that Judah was hostile, he summoned Josiah to Megiddo on one of his marches, and there put him to death. (The Chronicler records a battle, but this is hardly consistent with the narrative in Kings, and may be due to a tradition of a skirmish in which Josiah's attendants were involved.) He could not stay to settle the affairs of Judah, and popular choice elevated Josiah's second son, Jehoahaz, to the throne. Three months later, probably on his return to Egypt, Necho marched on Jerusalem, deposed Jehoahaz, who may be suspected of having maintained his father's policy, and set his elder brother, Jehoiakim, on the throne (2 Kings 23[31-35]).

Fall of Judah. For three years Egyptian influence was dominant in Judah, and it is possible that the condition of the country is reflected in the prophecies of Habakkuk (see the commentary on that book). But in 605 B.C. Necho was finally defeated at Carchemish, on the Euphrates; the victorious general, Nebuchadrezzar, succeeded to the throne a few months later, and the ultimate conquest of Palestine by the Chaldeans became certain. Nevertheless, for eight years Jehoiakim held his position, and proved himself to be one of the most oppressive kings who ever sat on the throne of David. His father had been essentially a sovereign of that democratic type which appealed so strongly to Israel, and had concerned himself first and foremost with sound administration and impartial justice. Jehoiakim's aim was to be another Solomon, and he adorned Jerusalem with magnificent buildings, erected at the cost of his people and by forced labor. But he was a strong character, and men crossed his will at their peril. He is the only king of whom it is recorded that he put to death an authorized prophet of Jehovah; even men suspected of high treason like Amos and, later, Jeremiah, were held to be sacrosanct if they were possessed by the Divine Spirit. It is a vivid picture of Jehoiakim that is drawn for us by the contemporary prophets (especially Jeremiah).

We have no details of the policy he followed. It seems not unlikely that Nebuchadrezzar left the west alone for a time, and Judah may have continued to be under Egyptian influence. But, as Jeremiah had foreseen, the battle of Carchemish had changed the course of history; it was the last time that an Egyptian king ever made a bid for world supremacy. Sooner or later Babylon would be mistress of the west, and the blow fell on Judah in 597. Before the actual capture of Jerusalem, Jehoiakim died, to be succeeded by his young son Jehoiachin, whose short reign ended three months later with his unconditional surrender to the besieging Chaldeans. He was carried to Babylon, and remained in captivity till the death of Nebuchadrezzar. With him went the flower of the Jewish nobility, and many others of the type that formed the best element in the country. (See 2 Kings 24.) We may conjecture that the exiles included not only Ezekiel but also the unnamed author of Psa. 42, 43.

For once Nebuchadrezzar had made a political blunder. The new nobility, the men who necessarily took the place of the deportees, were shallow, unsound, haughty, and capricious; men in whom obstinacy took the place of firmness and thoughtless jingoism the place of true patriotism. Another error was the choice of a successor to Jehoiachin, on whose throne Nebuchadrezzar placed a third son of Josiah, Zedekiah. Even from the Babylonian point of view it was necessary that a state so dangerously exposed to Egyptian influence should be controlled by a strong ruler, who could exhibit firmness as well as loyalty. Zedekiah was not a positively bad man, and in happier circumstances might have enjoyed a long and prosperous reign. But if he was no Jehoiakim he was equally no Josiah, and his character and temperament rendered him quite incapable of meeting the conditions with which he was faced. Early in his reign his loyalty seems to have been tested by a conspiracy in which Phœnicia and other western states shared. As far as we know matters never came to an open revolt, perhaps because Zedekiah held aloof. But it seems to have been necessary for him to send a special embassy to Babylon, and it has been conjectured that its purpose was to protest and prove his fidelity. At length in 588 B.C. Egyptian intrigues prevailed, if not with Zedekiah, at least with the turbulent nobility into whose hands he had fallen, and Judah revolted. In January, 587, a Chaldean army appeared under the walls of Jerusalem; the garrison was weakened by desertion and by famine, and, at last, in July, 586, the walls were pierced and the city taken. For the moment Zedekiah escaped, but, deserted by his guards, he was captured and taken to northern Syria, where Nebuchadrezzar had made his headquarters. A small detachment of the Chaldean army had been all that was necessary for the reduction of Jerusalem. Zedekiah's sons were killed before his eyes, he was blinded, and taken away into captivity. If Nebuchadrezzar's action seems cruel when judged by modern standards, it must be remembered that the victim had been guilty of the grossest ingratitude, and that the position he had tried to betray was one of the important frontier posts which kept Egypt from encroaching on the Babylonian Empire. (See 2 Kings 25; cf. Jer. 37–42.)

Jerusalem was laid in ruins, and a second deportation took place, leaving only the peasantry in the land. An attempt was made to establish some form of government under Gedaliah, a member of one of the few noble houses to be left in Judah in 597. Honorable, fearless, and chivalrous, he seemed the right man to restore the fallen fortunes of the land. But his very good qualities proved his ruin. The jealousy of Ammon sent Ishmael, a member of the house of David, to assassinate the unsuspecting governor, and the crime was carried out with indiscriminating cruelty. Ishmael himself fled, and the leadership devolved on a certain Johanan, who could think of no other course than to escape to Egypt, in fear of a fresh Chaldean invasion. With him went the last semblance of a real Hebrew state. (For a fuller discussion of Hebrew history in the eighth and seventh centuries B.C., see the present writer's *Decline and Fall of the Hebrew Kingdoms.*)

The Restoration. The old tradition, brought first into Palestine by the invading Hebrews a thousand years earlier, still lived on (and, like all living things, grew) in Babylon. The Jews seem to have formed a separate set of communities, and to have kept alive their national life and religion. Some of the noblest of the utterances of Israelite prophets and poets come to us from Mesopotamia, and the people still looked to their old home in Jerusalem, and still longed for an opportunity of reconstructing their national life in the old land. Their attitude toward their conquerors underwent a change. Jeremiah and Ezekiel are, if anything, pro-Babylonian, but the great mass of anonymous prophecy (e.g., Isa. 40–55), which comes from the reign of Nabuna'id, is bitterly hostile to the government, and looks forward with exultation to the approaching destruction of the city. Possibly the religious policy of the last king of Babylon had involved persecution of the Jews.

Once more the political face of the east underwent a change. Babylon fell, and Persia took her place. One of the first acts of Cyrus was to permit the Jews to return to their own land, and an expedition was made by a small group of exiles under Sheshbazzar in 538 B.C. (Ezra 1, 2). But the glowing hopes of the exiles were far from being realized. Other tribes had pressed into the land, and while the restored Jews were able to occupy Jerusalem, there was little of the old territory which they could call their own. After the confusion following the death of Cambyses in 522 B.C. and the assumption of power by Darius in 520, a scion of the house of David, Zerubbabel by name, was appointed governor of Palestine. Under his rule the Temple was rebuilt, and it is possible that he tried to win by force an independent position for himself and his people. Though we have no direct information on the subject, it is clear that the attempt, if it ever was made, proved a complete failure, and Judæa remained a small district under the satrap of the country "beyond the River," though with a subordinate governor of its own (cf. Haggai, Zech. 1–8 Ezra 3–6).

Except for such information as we can glean from prophetic writings of the period (among which "Malachi" is the best known) we are completely in the dark as to the history of Judæa for many years after the rebuilding of the Temple. It is not till Nehemiah is appointed governor that fresh light falls upon Palestine. The date of his governorship is uncertain. It is often placed in 445–4 B.C., but the king who appointed him is simply called Artaxerxes, and may equally well have been the first or the second of that name. If the second be right, then the coming of Nehemiah to Jerusalem will have taken place in 398, not in 445–4. The Aramaic papyri, recently discovered near Assouan, the relics of a Jewish military colony established there before the days of Cambyses, contain references which favor a later rather than an earlier period. But, whatever be his exact date, Nehemiah and his ecclesiastical colleague, Ezra, mark the real beginning of the new life of Judæa (cf. Ezra 7–10; Nehemiah). It is sometimes said that Judah went into exile a nation and returned a church, but this was not the immediate effect of the restoration, and becomes true in practice only with the establishment of the full Law by Ezra as the code governing Jewish life. Henceforward, to the genuine Israelite, political freedom and power were not an end in themselves; they were a means to the enjoyment of their peculiar faith and worship. If that could be secured there was no cause for unrest among the people. (See further the intro. to commentary on Ezra-Nehemiah in the present volume, p. 454.)

The Maccabean Struggles. The generations that followed Ezra and Nehemiah have left little or nothing behind them. From Josephus we hear of trouble with Persia in the days of Artaxerxes III, and it is possible that the Samaritan schism took place about 333. The conquests of Alexander made little change in the status of Judæa, but with the division of his empire the conditions which preceded the Babylonian conquest were repeated, and Palestine became once more a buffer state between an Asiatic power on the one hand and Egypt on the other. Egypt, under the Ptolemies, retained possession of the country (though at times insecurely) throughout the third century, but in 198 Jerusalem passed definitely into the hands of the Seleucid kings of Syria. Now began a desperate struggle between the two influences of the new Hellenism and the old Hebraism. Gradually the former sapped the strength of the people, and the story of the high priests of the first half of the second century is painful reading. To this period, perhaps, we owe some of the Psalms which draw so strong a contrast between the suffering righteous and the successful wicked. Judaism, as a faith, was in danger of being strangled by the culture of Greece, as it was mediated by the Syrian court and people.

There seems every reason to believe that the steady infiltration of foreign ideas would, in the long run, have undermined the resistance of the true Israelite spirit but for the precipitate action of Antiochus IV, known to his contemporaries by the name of Epiphanes. The method of "peaceful penetration" was too slow for this man, who was an enthusiast and a fanatic, determined to impose the culture of Greece on all his dominions in the spirit of the Oriental tyrant. In the Jews alone he found a people who, from his point of view, were too stubborn and narrow-minded to accept his principles. Rightly seeing that their resistance had a religious basis, he determined to force all Jewry into compliance. He entered Jerusalem, took possession of the Temple, and offered heathen sacrifices on the altar of Jehovah. Further, those practices which were characteristic of Judaism—circumcision and Sabbath observance—were made capital offenses, and it was decreed that the mere possession of a copy of the Law should be punished with death. (The struggles are described in First Maccabees; the book of Daniel reflects the Maccabean struggles. Cf. p. 192b.)

Such measures were bound to challenge resistance from the more conservative and more deeply religious elements in the people. Commissioners were sent through the whole country to enforce the policy of the Syrian king, and the first outbreak took place at the village of Modin. Here the commissioner was killed in the open city by one of its elders, Mattathias by name, and he and his sons, together with numbers of sympathizers from other parts of the country, took refuge in the hills. Under the leadership of Judas, one of Mattathias' sons, they carried on a guerilla warfare for a time, and finally met and defeated in pitched battles the forces that were sent against them. Jerusalem was recaptured (though the citadel was held for many years longer by a Syrian garrison), and the Temple was purified. The defiled altar was removed and a new one built, whereon the normal sacrifices were offered till the final destruction of the Temple by the troops of Titus in 70 A.D. Though Judæa was nominally still a province of Syria, practical independence was maintained till Pompey, in 63 B.C., invaded the country, and brought it under Roman domination.

The Jews Under Roman Control. For over a century Judæa remained virtually in Roman hands, but no portion of the empire gave the government more trouble. Originally included in the province of Syria, it was disturbed by such unrest that an Idumæan, Antipater by name, whose cleverness had enabled him to secure a large measure of power in the country, was appointed procurator, and his son, Herod, king. Though the rule of the latter was hated by the Jews, he succeeded in maintaining his position till his death in 4 B.C. His son Archelaus proved unfit for the task laid upon him, and was deposed in 6 A.D., Judæa being henceforward governed by Roman officials. No district needed more careful and sympathetic handling, and by some terrible irony none had such cruel, unscrupulous, and incompetent governors. Revolts were frequent, and the end came in 70 A.D., when the armies of Titus captured the city and destroyed the Temple. The cessation of sacrifice practically ended the history of Israel as a people.

Religion and History. It is a long way from

Abraham to the destruction of the Temple, yet through the whole two thousand years there runs a single thread—the religion of Israel. It was that, far more than even a sense of kinship, which gave strength to Israel's blood and continuity to her history. All historic religions have grown with the passage of time till their vitality has become exhausted and they have started on the path that leads to decay and death. But no other of the faiths of the ancient world can be traced with such accuracy as the religion of Israel. We can see how, at each stage in the political history of the nation, it manifested appropriate peculiarities, and how, whether because of them or in spite of them, it moved steadily forward. There is little enough in common between the creed and religious practice of the wandering Aramæan and those of the Pharisee or of the Zealot, but the movement from the one to the other is continuous and unbroken. Each stage, each new feature, springs out of a historic situation and must be seen against a historic background. Unless we can form some picture of the story of the Hebrew people as shown to us in the O.T., it is impossible for us to appreciate the progress of that divine revelation which, out of the darkness, shone with ever-increasing brightness, till it reached its perfect day in Jesus.

Literature: Kent, *Biblical Geography and History;* Kent, *The History of the Hebrew People,* 2 vols.; *The History of the Jewish People;* Riggs, *The History of the Jewish People;* Ottley, *A Short History of the Hebrew People;* Foakes-Jackson, *The Biblical History of the Hebrews;* H. P. Smith, *O.T. History.*

BIBLE MANNERS AND CUSTOMS

By Professor LESLIE E. FULLER

The Immovable East. For decades following the birth of modern interest in Bible lands emphasis was placed on exploration and geographical survey, for the purpose of identifying biblical sites and assisting the modern traveler in his journeys, and on excavation, for the purpose of determining from archæological remains the character of ancient Hebrew life and civilization. Little attention was given to dwellers in Bible lands—their mode of living, social and religious customs, legends and folklore, methods and processes of thinking.

In more recent years the value of a knowledge of present-day life and customs in the East as an aid to Bible interpretation has come to be appreciated. As a result modern travelers, excavators and explorers, trained residents and other observers, with insight and discrimination, all co-operate to make available for study the rich treasures of present-day Oriental life; and the investigation and evaluation of manners and customs in Bible lands is now one of the most fascinating studies of the Bible interpreter.

The reason for this widespread interest is to be found in the recognition of the primitive character of the Oriental's ways of thinking, expressing, and living. He has not changed to any perceptible degree since biblical times. Bible lands are a part of the immovable East. Economic conditions are such that the Oriental has escaped many of the evils of congestion so common in the West; he is content to remain in the open stretches of his deserts, or prefers the tranquil existence of his small villages. The inhabitant of the Near East has always expressed himself in realistic fashion, remaining close to life and its everyday occurrences: his language is realistic and devoid of abstract and philosophical terms. How we have been attracted by his touches of local color and his realistic pictures of human experience! Note, for instance, the contrast between Jesus and Paul. Paul is more Western than Eastern in his approach; his writings contain little local color; on the other hand, the parables of Jesus, couched in few words, breathe the outdoor life of Palestine. The old Semitic idiom with all its vividness and realism is apparent throughout the Gospels, though there this characteristic has come down to us in Greek form. This nearness of the gospel stories to the common and everyday life of Palestine constitutes one of the reasons why these narratives have continued to touch the hearts of men throughout the centuries. (See art., *Parables of Jesus*, p. 916b.)

The manners and customs of Bible lands may be studied under two heads: (1) the life of the nomads or desert dwellers, and (2) the life of the peasants or village and city dwellers. The first study would cover a wide range of travel and observation, noting the physical features of desert lands, tribal organization, characteristic social customs, food, methods of warfare, mental traits, and religious concepts. Under the second head attention should be given to the physical and economic features of Palestine, types of semi-nomadic and village life, and the customs of the peasantry. Throughout the study emphasis should be placed on daily life, types of dwelling, domestic and family life, community administration, education, legends and folk tales, religious beliefs, religious festivals and pilgrimages. The space allotted to this article is far too limited to permit covering this entire field or showing in any complete way the value of all these studies for biblical interpretation. Hence, the purpose of the article is simply to give a short summary of some of the more fundamental and basic features of life, especially desert life, in Bible lands.

Physical and Economic Features. The physical and economic features of Palestine have exerted a powerful influence upon the thought and life of its peoples. Always a buffer state, or a bridge head between warring nations on either side, it was and still remains the battleground of the Near East. The constant threat of war, pillage, and invasion was a vital part of the background of the Hebrew prophets with their messages of fire and earnestness. The fact that it was a land of little fertility, with a scanty supply of water, has left its impress on the life of the people and on the pages of the Bible. The Bible is an Oriental book, bearing all the earmarks of being written on the edge of the desert, containing graphic pictures of famine, thirst, the blasting of vegetation by the east wind and the deadliness of sandy desert wastes (cf. the reference in the last book of the Bible to the future state as a condition in which there will be no suffering from thirst). Again, Palestine always has been a land with a very small surplus of food, too small either to invite trade or to feed a large population; indeed its inhabitants were constantly threatened with starvation. Most of the peasantry lived from hand to mouth and in times of excessive famine and drought they moved away or died for lack of food. The presence of the poor as one of the necessary constituents of society was considered inevitable (Mt. 26^{11}).

Organization. The social and political organization always has been and still is essentially democratic. Among the desert folks, social organization assumes the form of a patriarchal clan, in which descent is reckoned through the father. There is good evidence, however, that originally the form may have been matriarchal, with kinship reckoned through the mother (cf. Gen. 2^{24}). The democracy of desert folks is noteworthy. A chieftain rules not by the right of inheritance, but by personal capacity and courage as the first among equals. All initiated men and boys constitute the governing body of the clan. The change from the nomadic type of life to the semi-nomadic or peasant type caused some changes, but much of the desert democracy was carried over. The village community of Palestine is nothing more than a patriarchal clan within the more compact organization of village life. The ruling body of the village is made up of the "elders." In a small village every male beyond a certain age has a voice in the government of the community; but as the village grows larger the governing power passes into the hands of a small group, such as the wealthy land owners, the military leaders or the priests. In the days of Jesus, when a much more complex social and political life had developed, much of the governing power resided in the synagogue, an institution that retained much of the old Semitic democracy.

Sacrifice. Sacrifice is one of the most universal practices in Bible lands (cf. Gen. 4$^{1-8}$). In the desert there is no private slaughter of an animal; such an act always assumes a sacrificial significance, and, therefore, is carried on according to a certain ritual. Through this primitive ritual of consecration, the sacrifice is turned over to the deity and thus is made holy. The blood of the animal is usually poured on the threshold; the flesh of the sacrificial animal is eaten by the worshipers presenting the offering as a communal meal, based on the idea of appropriating, through the eating of the flesh, the life and character of the sacrificial animal; and since all the members of the tribe, including the animals, were held to be in kinship with the tribal deity, such appropriation would imply sharing the life and character of the deity itself.

Taboo. Closely related to sacrifice is the *idea of holiness* or taboo. The district about a shrine, an oasis in the midst of the desert, a tree, a bush, or even an animal may be considered holy, that is, it may be thought to possess certain unusual qualities, which are traced to divine manipulation or possession (cf. Ex. 3^{5}). An animal that strays within a holy area becomes the property of the shrine. Trees growing within a sacred area must not be cut down; if unwittingly such tree is cut down, and later it is discovered that it belongs to holy ground, all tools used and clothes worn by the workmen must be left within the district, so that they are forever withdrawn from profane use. When interpreted in the light of present-day practices, further illustrated by the comparative study of religions, some of the practices recorded in the O.T. are more easily understood. For instance, taking into consideration the blood kinship of clan and deity, human sacrifice assumes a new meaning; for it meant the use of the clan blood as the most valuable offering (Mic. 6^{7}). The prohibition of swine's flesh is best explained on the assumption that a pig was the sacred or taboo animal of a neighboring people, so that the use of its flesh or blood would involve participation in the life and character of the god of that people.

Covenants. Another widespread practice or custom is seen in the making of covenants, such as the blood covenant, the bread covenant, and the salt covenant. The oldest of these is the blood covenant, which, like animal sacrifice, is based on the idea of blood kinship of god and clan, and of individual members of the clan. Hence any contract or covenant between members of the tribe, or individuals to be taken into the tribe, is ratified through the mingling of the blood of the individuals concerned or of the individual and of an animal belonging to and thus representing the tribe. The place of ratification is the threshold of the tent or house, which is regarded as an altar; later the ratification takes place in or near a shrine.

The covenant of bread or salt ratified through eating together carries with it some of the same ideas, for bread and salt are "live" substances like blood. The moment a person shares in a meal covenant of bread or salt with another person the two become kinsmen, for a time at least, and are in duty bound to protect one another; even enemies, when they have partaken of bread or salt together must protect one another. When interpreted from the standpoint of these practices many O.T. passages assume a much deeper meaning. When, for instance, the prophet promises the establishment of a new covenant (Jer. 31^{31-34}) it means that God will enter again into the closest relationship of kinship with his people. The covenant relations, once established, opened the way to the disclosure of the most intimate and personal thoughts and emotions. The moment Jesus established the covenant relation with the woman at the well of Samaria, intimate problems of personal concern could be and were discussed.

Blood Revenge. Blood revenge has retained to the present much of its primitive significance. The custom is clearly an outgrowth of the idea of the blood kinship of the tribe. Any injury inflicted on a member of the tribe affects the entire tribe; in a real sense it is a tribal injury, and all members of the tribe are under obligation to avenge the injury. In actual practice, however, only the nearest of kin, on the male side, are expected to become the avengers. If the immediate male relatives are not living, those next in line to the fifth generation are under direct obligation. The law of blood revenge demands reparation, according to the *lex talionis*—a boy for a boy, a man for a man, the son of a chieftain for the son of a chieftain, an eye for an eye, and a tooth for a tooth (cf. Ex. 21^{23-25}). In case of murder done wittingly or unwittingly the slayer may flee to the nearest shrine, or altar, thus seeking the protection of the deity. (Sometimes, to escape blood revenge, the slayer flees to another tribe, thus relinquishing his tribal allegiance and becoming a proselyte to the new tribe.) The slayer has the right of asylum for a period of three days, the purpose being to give him a chance to prove his innocence (cf. Josh. 20). In some cases the slayer may escape the death penalty by the payment of a stipulated sum known as blood money. Frequently, in attempting to avenge a murder too much blood is spilled; then an effort is made to square accounts again, and thus a feud is started which sometimes lasts long after the original cause is forgotten. Tribal feuds are more frequently settled by the payment of blood money than are personal feuds.

The custom of blood revenge throws much light on the incident of the murder of Abel by Cain, and Cain's subsequent banishment (Gen. 4^{9-15}). Cain becomes a wanderer on the face of the earth with no tribal protector—the most terrible situation in the desert. Finally, when he cries to Jehovah for protection or the rights of kinsmanship, Jehovah promises to become his protector. The partial breakdown of the desert custom and its rigid application are seen in the stories of David's relations with Abner and Joab. Abner kills a brother of Joab; according to custom Joab was the first in line to avenge his death; later, when Abner went to Hebron he was under the protection of David and David was bound, according to the law of hospitality, to protect him. In spite of these implied rights of the visitor Joab sought an opportunity to meet Abner, and when he met him killed him (2 Sam. 3^{30}). According to the desert law David, in turn, was bound to kill Joab, which he did not do. David did not have the courage to slay the military leader who was so essential to his success; but when he was about to die he charged Solomon to kill Joab. One of the first acts of Solomon was to kill Joab and thus clear the house of David from guilt (2 Sam. 2, 3; 1 Kings $2^{28f.}$).

Hospitality. The law of hospitality plays an important rôle in Bible lands. The law is an outgrowth of the economic conditions of the desert. No one travels in a desert country for pleasure. A man may endure desert travel for one of two reasons: either as a fugitive or an outcast from his tribe, or in the performance of a religious vow, or a pilgrimage to some distant shrine. Hence the entertainment of strangers or travelers becomes a sacred duty, for no one knows what the errand of the traveler may be and, thus, how soon the extreme rigors of the desert might force a pious pilgrim to break his vow. And even if the stranger should prove a fugitive, he might be innocent of the crime charged. Of course, the law of hospitality could be abused, for the moment a person touched a tent rope, the occupants of the tent were duty bound to furnish food and protection, even though the traveler might turn out to be an enemy. There are numerous instances on record in which food was gladly and freely given with much personal discomfort to the host. There are also records of instances in which an enemy asked for entertainment, was given food and protection for the night, and on the following day was given the fastest animal in the encampment in order to make good his escape.

The usual limit for entertainment is three days. In some places, especially along caravan routes, the matter of entertainment becomes an unbearable burden; and yet the law of hospitality is scrupulously observed. The case of C. M. Doughty is a good illustration of the extent to which travelers may depend upon this desert law. For two years he traveled through the desert regions of northern Arabia, depending wholly upon the rights and privileges assured him by the law of hospitality. Only once or twice was he in real danger of his life.

In the transition from the nomadic to the peasant mode of living the law of hospitality was sometimes disregarded, which is quite in line with the fact frequently observed that the change from one stage of civilization to another tends to weaken the social and religious sanctions of the former. Jael's killing of Sisera (Judg. 5[26]) is wholly unjustified by the standards of the desert. The same breakdown in the law is seen in Judg. 19 and 2 Sam. 3[27f.] There are many fine examples of dependence on the law of hospitality in the N.T. Jesus' commission to his disciples to go without scrip, bread, or money is typical of the East. Again, when Jesus commands the disciples to go into the village and prepare for the Last Supper, they are commanded to follow a man bearing a pitcher of water and to demand of the servant's master the use of the guest room and the rights of hospitality (cf. for additional examples of the influence of the law of hospitality Mk. 6[8] 14[13f.] Lk. 11[5f.] 19[7f.]).

Marriage Customs. The marriage customs of the East constitute another basis of suggestive comparisons with biblical material. Marriage is a commercial contract. The betrothal, usually arranged between the families concerned, is as binding as marriage itself. A betrothed couple are designated as husband and wife, and are so treated before the law (Deut. 21[10f.]). Most of the marriages occur in the spring, at the close of the barley harvest, or in the fall, at the close of the grape harvest. The village usually sets aside a week for marriage festivities, the period being known as King's Week. The week is devoted to games, athletic contests, and feasting. The bridal couples are enthroned on the threshing floor and crowned king and queen for a day; they receive a name of some king or queen well known in history, such as Solomon and Sheba. The marriage ceremony proper comes at the close of the King's Week. One of the most significant parts of the final ceremony is the sword dance—accompanied by fencing—which in some parts of Palestine is danced by the bridegroom and in some parts by the bride. The primary motive of the sword dance is to exhibit the physical prowess or endurance of the bridegroom or the bride. There are several examples of the sword songs in the Song of Solomon (4[1f.] 5[10f.] 7[10f.]).

Burial Customs. These throw a flood of new light on many sections of the Bible. Death is considered as a break in the usual run of events, a very inauspicious happening, which must be accompanied by expressions of deep concern. The accompaniments are excessive weeping, wailing, and physical tortures, such as tearing of the hair, cutting of the flesh and beating of the breast (Jer. 16[5f.] Ezek. 24[15f.] cf. Deut. 14[1]). The origin of these acts of physical torture can be traced back to a very early period, where they were used with magical significance. The women do most of the wailing, the men rend their clothes and weep. Tear bottles were used in Bible times (Psa. 56[8]). The spirit is supposed to hover over the grave for three days after burial. In the story of the raising of Lazarus it is stated that he was raised on the fourth day, which added to the wonder.

Religion. The religious practices and conceptions of the peoples of Bible lands have received much attention, and their value for biblical interpretation cannot be overemphasized. For present purposes it may be sufficient to mention some of the results of researches in the field of the primitive conceptions of God. The present desert dwellers are nominally Mohammedan, but many of the conceptions of deity, easily discoverable in Mohammedan disguise, are to-day practically what they were in the days of the patriarchs. These conceptions are not the result of reflection or speculation, but the direct outgrowth of daily life and experiences. The deity is thought to manifest himself in wells and fountains, trees, rocks, caves and mountains. God is anthropomorphically conceived; he moves frequently on a level with human beings. Again he is conceived as the prime mover in well-known cosmic events: If it rains, God causes it; if there is a drought, he is responsible for it. If a city is destroyed, the deity is the cause of its destruction. Good and evil, prosperity and misfortune, all come from God. Finally, God is conceived as acting not always in a moral and consistent manner; he is a God of moods and subject to sudden changes of mind. Some of these primitive conceptions appear in the earlier records of the O.T. The recognition of these primitive elements only sets into clearer light the loftier conceptions set forth by the prophets which have given to the religious message of the O.T. its permanent value and significance. (See art., *Religion of Israel*, p. 165; art., *O.T. Conception of God*, p. 158.)

Literature: Trumbull, *Studies in Oriental Social Life;* Mackie, *Bible Manners and Customs;* Tristram, *Eastern Customs in Bible Lands;* Baldensperger, *The Immovable East;* Rihbany, *The Syrian Christ;* Mrs. Goodrich Freer, *Arab in Tent and Town;* Doughty, *Travels in Arabian Deserts.*

TIME, MONEY, WEIGHTS AND MEASUREMENTS

By Professor CHARLES F. SITTERLY

Two facts must be kept in mind in studying the customs and usages of the Hebrews in respect of time, money, weights, and measurements: (1) The national life of the Hebrews was relatively late in its development, following by hundreds of years that of Egypt and Babylonia. (2) Their location between and dependence alternately upon those two great ancient civilizations made them the direct heirs of systems already perfected and widely practiced. It is not strange, therefore, that in these respects, as in its literary form, the O.T. reflects oriental practices and customs. The N.T., on the other hand, reveals the influence of Greek and Roman standards; in other words, it reflects the life and customs of occidental peoples.

Time. The word "hour" does not occur in the O.T., except in the Aramaic section of Daniel, but the division of the night into three *watches*, the beginning, middle, and last (also called the morning watch), and of the day into morning, noonday, and evening, as well as the marks on the sundial of Ahaz (Isa. 38[8]), shows a tendency to subdivide the period of daylight and darkness.

The term "day," used to designate the period of twenty-four hours from sunset to sunset, after the Egyptian style, or the twelve hours of daylight, longer or shorter according to the season, after the Babylonian style, is found in all levels of Hebrew literature, while its indefinite or poetic use as of a set time or period, and its apocalyptic use as "the day of the Lord" are very frequent.

The interval "between the two evenings" (Ex. 12[6] 30[8] Num. 9[3] R.V., mg.) refers to the time between sunset and darkness, also called "the cool of the day" (Gen. 3[8]) in contrast with "the heat of the day" or high noon (Gen. 18[1]).

The word "week" is not much used either in the O.T. or N.T., though the idea is common enough and the marking of the Sabbath or seventh day as peculiarly sacred was observed long before the Mosaic law—the Fourth Commandment enjoining its due remembrance—was formulated. The secular days of the week throughout the Bible are indicated by ordinals, though the sixth day came to be called in later Judaism, because of its relation to the Sabbath, the day of preparation (Lk. 23[54]).

Observance of the moon's phases marked the *month* from early times, and both numerals and names are used to designate them. Traces of Canaanite survivals are found in the descriptive names "Abib," month of earing; "Ziv," month of flowering; "Ethnanim," month of perennial streams; and "Bul," possibly the month of early rains. Following the Exile, and partly due to it, a new list of proper names was adopted, and priestly influence seized the opportunity to accept the Eastern method of beginning the year with the spring to emphasize the ritual priority of Passover, making the first month of the former or civil year the seventh of the new or sacred year as follows:

1. *Nisan.* Mid-March to mid-April; coincident with Abib, 7th month of the civil year.
2. *Iyyar.* April to May; coincident with Ziv, 8th month.
3. *Sivan.* May to June; found only in Esth. 8[9].
4. *Tammuz.* June to July; so called in later times.
5. *Ab.* July to August; so called in later times.
6. *Elul.* August to September; found only in Neh. 6[15].
7. *Tishri.* September to October; so called in later times;=Ethnanim, 1st month of the civil year.
8. *Marchesvan.* October to November; so called in later times;=Bul, 2d month.
9. *Chislev.* November to December; found only in Neh. 1[1] and Zech. 7[1].
10. *Tebeth.* December to January; found only in Esth. 2[16].
11. *Shebat.* January to February; found only in Zech. 1[7].
12. *Adar.* February to March. The intercalary month was Second Adar.

It seems probable that the *year* of patriarchal times was lunar, but as it was found that the seasons receded and the intercalary month had to be added about every third year (or 7 in 19) the solar system was adopted. The naming of the months indicates this; first the giving of names descriptive of the seasons, and second the assignment to certain months of the harvest feasts according to priestly ritual. Thus again Babylonian influence, which began the year with the vernal equinox, confirmed the change of priority from the Feast of Trumpets or New Year's in the autumn to that of Passover in the spring.

The elaborate system of *sabbatical years* every seventh year, culminating in the *year of Jubilee* every fiftieth year, though logical and finally legal, exerted no widespread influence on common culture either in O.T. or N.T. times.

Money. Lying directly on the travel route between the Nile and the Euphrates valleys, Palestine adopted the trade systems of the enlightened nations occupying these regions from early biblical times. The method of mere barter even among nomad chieftains was passing at least by the time of Abraham. His transactions with Abimelech, in Genesis 20 and 21, mingle barter with the exchange of currency, and by the time he buys the Cave of Machpelah "current money of the merchant" to the extent of four hundred silver shekels is weighed out to Ephron (Gen. 23[16]). Rings or bracelets, after the Egyptian manner, and wedges or ingots or "pieces of money," after the Babylonian, both in gold and silver, antedated true coins of the mint, but they appear to have been variously stamped, as with lambs, lions, and so forth, and cut into convenient forms and weights, so that by the use of balances satisfactory exchange could be effected (Gen. 24[22] 42[35] Josh. 7[21] 24[32] 1 Sam. 9[8] Job 42[11]).

According to Herodotus coinage was invented in Lydia as early as the seventh century B.C. From there it was introduced into the East by Cyrus and further developed by Darius, whose gold darics corresponded to the drachmas of the Greeks. A silver daric, thought to have come from the same mint, may be referred to in Neh. 5[15]. Meanwhile the Phœnician cities Aradus, Sidon, and Tyre had been allowed to coin silver and bronze, though not gold, and these coins were circulated in Jerusalem as early as the Restoration under Nehemiah (Neh. 13[15, 16]).

A new Greek standard of coinage called the Attic was introduced into Syria by Alexander and had a wide but brief vogue. The Ptolemies followed for a century and controlled the coinage of Palestine as far as Ptolemais. Their system was nearer to that of the earlier Phœnicians. Again the Seleucids reverted to the Attic usage and made a great effort, with varying success, to Hellenize the Jews in all things. At last came the Maccabean revolt, which involved from the first the question of tribute, until finally Simon succeeded for a brief period in gaining the right to coin both in silver and bronze. Of his silver half-shekel there seem to be true examples for four years and at least one whole shekel of the fifth year. Some experts declare that these so-called coins of Simon really belong to another Simon of the time of the rebellion of 66–70 A.D., but this view is less probable.

The privilege of coinage at least in bronze or copper was tenaciously held by the Jews through the many changes of government, down to the end of the Herodian house under Agrippa II. Again, when Bar Kochba led the Jews in their final revolt against Rome, he made an attempt to mark their independence by restamping the imperial silver and bronze coins with Hebrew symbols and inscriptions.

The Hebrews have always been keen in money transactions and from the days of Jacob have prospered in trade. Solomon acquired as well as dispersed vast wealth, and talents of gold became common, while silver was spoken of as plentiful as stones in Jerusalem (1 Kings 10[27]). The heavy *gold talent* stood at the head of the biblical coins. Solomon's revenue is given as six hundred and sixty-six such talents (1 Kings 10[14]). A gold talent was equivalent to at least thirty thousand dollars. Next came the *gold mina*, worth about five hundred dollars, then the *gold shekel*, about ten dollars.

The heavy *silver talent* was worth about two thousand dollars, the *silver mina*, about thirty-three dollars, and the *silver shekel*, sixty-six or sixty-seven cents. Besides the "heavy" there was a "light"-weight standard of half value, and there was also a "royal," i.e., slightly higher, scale employed in payments to the king's treasury, but in the O.T. the common and heavy norm is usually meant. Then there were a Babylonian or Persian talent, mina, and shekel, both heavy and light, on a scale of three to two as against the Jewish or Phœnician coinage which the Bible commonly employs. The shekel, either of silver or gold, was the unit of value, the mina being referred to only rarely and after the Exile, and the talent almost as rarely either before or after.

This common, so-called Phœnician, silver shekel became the "shekel of the Sanctuary" so often referred to in later priestly legislation (Lev. 27[3, 25]). In N.T. times the Roman system prevailed in civil affairs, while the Jewish or Phœnician still persisted in sacred affairs. The talent of Mt. 18[24] stood at twelve hundred dollars. The *pound*, equivalent to one sixtieth part of a talent, was worth about twenty dollars (Lk. 19[13f.]). The new Roman gold aureus, equal to five dollars, ruled the Imperial system, and the denarius, about twenty cents, in silver, was its unit. It may be considered as the laborer's daily wage (Mt. 20[2]) and was probably the coin with Cæsar's superscription which was handed to Jesus (Mt.

22[19, 20]). The "tribute money" of Mt. 17[24] was of course the half-shekel of the Temple.

Of the copper coins there were the *farthing*, or *assarion* (Mt. 10[29]), equal to about one and one eighth cents, the *uttermost farthing*, or *kodrantes* (Mt. 5[26]), about three tenths of a cent, and the *mite*, or *lepton* (Mk. 12[42]), one half the latter, which was the smallest coin of all.

Weights. As money weights and those of merchandise were at first identical, caution must be used in exegesis. The merchandise weights were of stone or bronze and carried in a bag (Deut. 25[13] A.V. mg.; Mic. 6[11]). The shekel was the unit, and as in the case of money there were the heavy, which was double the light weight, and the earlier or Babylonian and later or Phœnician scale. Later still Græco-Roman influence was felt. The chief weights, based on inscribed stones which have been found, are as follows:

1 shekel (light) = 126 gr. Troy or 0.36 oz. avoirdupois.

1 shekel (heavy) = 252 gr. Troy or 0.72 avoirdupois.

1 mina (light) = 7580 gr. Troy or 1 1-12 lbs. avoirdupois.

1 mina (heavy) = 15160 gr. Troy or 2 1-6 avoirdupois.

1 talent (light) = 454800 gr. Troy or 65 avoirdupois.

1 talent (heavy) = 909600 gr. Troy or 130 avoirdupois.

The Gerah or $\frac{1}{20}$ of a shekel and the Bekah or ½ shekel, as well as a ⅓ and ¼ shekel, are referred to. The only weight pounds referred to in the N.T. are of the Roman system (Jn. 12[3] and 19[39]).

Measurements. 1. Of *Length* and *Area.* Like the Egyptians, the Hebrews took the forearm for their first standard. The *fingers* (Jer. 52[21]) up to four made a *handbreadth* or *palm* (1 Kings 7[26]), three handbreadths a *span* (Ex. 28[16]), two spans a *cubit* (Deut. 3[11]), the entire forearm or "cubit of a man" being the ordinary working cubit. The so-called royal cubit of seven handbreadths was employed in both Solomon's and Ezekiel's Temple measurements (2 Chr. 3[3], Ezek. 40[5]). Possibly the shorter cubit was commercial and the longer for building purposes. There was also the *reed* or rod, which equaled six large cubits (Ezek. 40[3, 5] 42[16]).

As the Babylonian displaced or modified the early system it is impossible to determine exactly the above table in our terms, but we accept the following scale of equivalents:

The finger equal to about ¾ inches.

The handbreadth to about 3 inches.

The span to about 9 inches.

The common cubit equal to about 18 inches.

The longer cubit equal to about 20½ inches.

The reed equal to about 10 feet.

The *yoke* (1 Sam. 14[14]) doubtless meant to cover as much land as a team of oxen could plow in a day.

In the N.T. the *mile* (Mt. 5[41]) was equal to about 4,854 feet; the *sabbath day's journey* (Acts 1[12]) equal to 2,000 cubits or about 3,600 feet; the *furlong* (Lk. 24[13]) about 606 feet; and the *fathom* (Acts 27[28]) about 6 feet.

2. Of *Liquid Measure.* Although the more truly scientific Babylonian sexagesimal system has largely displaced the Egyptian or decimal, yet the two are mingled in O.T. usage, and in measurements of capacity are less accurately employed.

The *log* (Lev. 14[10]) contained about 1 pint.

The *kab* (2 Kings 6[25]) contained about 2 quarts.

The *hin* (Ex. 29[40]) contained about 6 quarts.

The *bath* (1 Kings 7[26]) contained about 9 gallons.

The *cor* (Ezek. 45[14]) contained about 90 gallons.

In the N.T. *bath* is referred to in Lk. 16[6] (R.V., mg.), and *firkin* (Jn. 2[6]) has approximately the same capacity.

3. Of *Dry Measure.* The unit, as in liquid measure, is the log, and the kab is also used in both tables.

The *log* (Lev. 14[10]) contained about 1 pint.

The *kab* (2 Kings 6[25]) contained about 2 quarts.

The *omer* (Ex. 16[36]) contained about $7\frac{1}{5}$ pints.

The *seah* (Gen. 18[6], tr. *measure*) about 1½ pecks.

The *ephah* (Ex. 16[36]) contained about 1 bushel, 4 quarts.

The *letek* (Hos. 3[2], mg.) contained about 5½ bushels.

The *homer* (Isa. 5[10], R.V.) contained about 11 bushels.

In the N.T. *bushel* (Mt. 5[15]) represents the O.T. seah of about 1½ pecks, and *measure* (Rev. 6[6]) about 2 pints.

Literature: Articles on "Weights and Measures" in the following Bible Dictionaries: *Hastings'* (five volume and one volume); *Temple; Standard; International Standard.*

ENGLISH TRANSLATIONS OF THE BIBLE

By Professor LAURA H. WILD

Determining Factors. The history of the English Bible is more than the history of the text; it is, indeed, a romance. One may recite translations, dates, and revisions, and get no adequate idea of its importance. It is the history of the repeated emergence of a foreign literature to supreme influence in the English tongue, for behind all versions lies the original, with its inherent beauty and vitality. However men have erred in doctrines imputed to it, in ecclesiastical structures built upon it, in the kind of book they have taken it to be, they have not erred in calling it holy, in attributing to it rare, surviving qualities, an influence more than human.

The Latin Bible came first to England. Afterward a translation of this translation made biblical truth clear, and a shift occurred in the attitude of the whole Western world toward authority, the Bible playing a most important part. From a subordinate place it rose to highest prominence. Man was to be guided not by church dictum but by Scripture; therefore the common man must have it in common language. Thus it filled a unique place for generations, but fear finally overlaid reverence and distorted its truth, blind authority becoming a shackle. It took another era to discard mechanical interpretations, and again release its living power. It weathered this third intellectual change when the scientific method of attaining knowledge altered the whole platform of regard. Reason then mounted the throne and it looked for a time as if the authority of the Bible was gone with church authority. But although dethroned from its high place of arbitrary control it is still acknowledged as a guide to man's reason when taken in the light of modern historical interpretation. Conscience is once more thrown back on the Bible, seeing there the progress of great transforming ideas of God and brotherhood.

Another salient fact is apparent in the history of the English Bible. Its vitality is inseparable from the vitality of its translators, the highest personal qualities helping to produce it. Somehow its quickening power brought forth courage undaunted, zeal unflagging, and an apprehension of meaning which resulted in the clearest, simplest, most pungent and pithy expressions known in English literature. Never could this have been attained without the strain of the difficult. Persecution of heretics has been the test in each era. Opposition has repeatedly arisen against the effort to tear away the artificial and introduce the heart of man to the heart of the book. Wyclif was persecuted because Latin was exchanged for English. Tyndale was martyred because of his translation from Hebrew and Greek. The Authorized Version was considered too sacred to alter when scholars gave us the Revised Version. Modern scholars are criticized for seeking to bring the meaning of an ancient book close home to everyday people in words they speak themselves.

During this period have occurred the Renaissance, the Reformation, the discovery of printing, and the reign of science, and the Bible has figured largely in them all. It has had more influence in molding the English language and literature than it has had upon any other tongue or literature. By Elizabeth's time, says J. R. Green, England had become "the people of a book, and that book was the Bible. . . . The English Version remains the noblest example of the English tongue . . . the standard of our language."

Wyclif and His Lollard Bible. The significance of Wyclif's Bible appears when we transfer ourselves to fourteenth-century England. There was wealth and display at court and among lords and prelates, but ignorant peasants faced wretched living conditions and deadening isolation, spelling laziness and vice. In Oxford "the dirt was sublime," with piggeries in the streets, the stream running through the town thick with rubbish and offal, its waters used for making bread and ale, while dead animals lay unburied. No wonder the Black Death scourged England. Among students drinking and riots prevailed and sexual vice was the dominant sin of both laity and clergy. Priests were often as ignorant as their parishioners. The rich were known to bribe the courts annually to stop embarrassing inquiries. Gross amusements corrupted court life. The land was rent by political quarrels with France and Rome.

Wyclif the Man. In such a setting we find Wyclif, "the flower of Oxford scholarship." Of blameless character, his greatness lies in his ability to understand his time and to inspire others to carry out his ideas. Although primarily a scholar he sympathized with the peasantry, for as parish priest he knew their needs and the corruption of the priesthood as well. Deft in unraveling England's knotty problems of state, he became indignant at Rome's intrigues to shackle her liberty, to bleed her for money, and to smother free speech. Sham he hated and dared lay bare, in his undaunted loyalty to truth seizing upon errors most needing exposure. In the violent language customary for his age, the Pope was to him "a more horrible idol than a painted log"; the bishops he called "dumb hounds"; and ignorant vicars were "full damnable before God." A keen intellect, intense feeling for the right, and fearless courage made him a formidable foe. He has been called "the Morning Star of the Reformation."

At first much attracted by the Franciscans who came to England originally with their founder's simple life and spiritual principles, he afterward became disgusted with their selfish, materialistic policy. A common saying was "This is a friar and therefore a liar." But he had been influenced sufficiently by them to adopt a simple dress of russet brown with bare feet. His "Lollards," or itinerant preachers, traveled thus over England with only a staff, somewhat as Franciscans had wandered over Italy spreading the gospel of their leader.

The Story of His Work. John Wyclif was born about 1320 in the north of England, whence Chaucer made the Devil appear. For years an Oxford scholar and teacher, he began his main work at about the age of fifty in the village rectory of Lutterworth in Leicestershire, where his sympathy for the people crystallized. At the University his ideas had been regarded as decidedly new and not altogether welcome, yet he could have stayed there had he been willing to compromise. In loyalty to his country he threw away the protection of highest government officials, striking straight at the heart of the impotence of England. To lead a godly life was what the clergy, the court, the scholar and the peasant alike needed for salvation. "Back to Christ" was his slogan as well as ours.

But how could a man get there except through the Bible? And how could he get at the Bible when by Pope, priest and friar it was closed to him? Setting himself to write and talk against papal authority and in favor of the authority of the Bible, against superstition and for the enlightenment of the masses, Wyclif became a dangerous man, for he said that worship depended on neither priest nor ceremony; that "each man that shall be damned shall be damned by his own guilt and each man that is saved shall be saved by his own merit." He frowned upon the "Pardoner" with his indulgences, the wealth and selfishness of monasteries, the whole materialism of his age. Since society, politics, and religion were all closely interwoven he could not say such things without becoming a revolutionist. Persecution was in the air. He himself escaped such tortures as awaited his illustrious followers, John Hus of Bohemia and William Tyndale his countryman, although in his last days he was summoned to Rome, being, however, unable to go, and he frequently referred to the possibility of death for his views. He was buried at Lutterworth, but later his bones were dug up, burned and thrown into the river "to the damnation and destruction of his memory."

It was in his very latest years (1380–84) that he accomplished his most famous work, a vernacular Bible, inspiring devout preachers to carry it to the people. But the Wycliffite Bible was not his translation alone. His disciple, Nicolas de Hereford, chancellor of Hereford Cathedral, was responsible for the larger part of the O.T. and John Purvey for most of the N.T., Wyclif doubtless laying the foundation for the N.T. in translations and paraphrases in his commentaries and sermons. The whole work was finished and thoroughly revised by Purvey. The Black Friars Synod of 1382 condemned Nicolas as well as Wyclif for heresy, and later the Pope sentenced him to life imprisonment at Rome. He was released, returning to England only to hide because of orders for rearrest. Captured and "grievously tormented" he recanted under the torture.

Wyclif's closest friendship was with Purvey, "a noted doctor," an Oxford student when Wyclif's fame there was at its zenith. Accompanying him to Lutterworth, he "drank deep of Wyclif's most secret teaching." He was a careful scholar, and his principles for translation hold to-day. His task was no easy one, but finally a simple, vivid, readable text was produced. Some of the words and phrases, absorbed in later translations, have entered into the body of our language.

The Result of His Work. Thus the Bible, which had been a sealed book to ordinary people, became common possession. To some this was shocking. They said, "The jewel of the clergy has become the toy of the laity." Moreover, Latin, so long associated with the Holy Word that it was considered by many a holy language, was displaced by a tongue as harsh as "the grunting of pigs or the roaring of lions." The Wycliffite Bible appeared in manuscript, printing being unknown until a century later. Of the copies painstakingly made one hundred and seventy are known to-day, one hundred and forty of them being Purvey's final version. Some were made on vellum, richly illuminated; the majority were cheaper, smaller, more perishable copies for the common people. In 1731 the N.T. was printed, and in 1850 the whole Wycliffite Bible—a fitting tribute to the great translator and his friends.

The forty years following Purvey's translation were busy ones for scribes. By 1395 Parliament, alarmed at its popularity, attempted to obliterate it. In 1396 a squire had to swear neither to read nor to own it. By 1401 English Bibles were ordered burned. By 1407 to possess a copy without a license was the first step to persecution. In 1415 we read, "It is forbidden under pain of cursing that no man should have or draw any text of holy scripture into English without license of the bishop." But Wyclif's "Poor Preachers" had aroused an appetite not easily suppressed and had lighted a fire that sent some to the stake.

Wyclif died of a paralytic stroke before the storm of persecution broke in its fury. Purvey was arrested and finally recanted, "grievously tormented and punished" in a "foul, unhonest prison." But the Bible had come into the possession of the English-speaking people to be theirs in a peculiarly intimate way. For while the Wycliffite Bible was a translation from an imperfect Latin translation with no Greek and Hebrew at hand, it was made by men vigorous, graphic and colloquial in expression, in the formative period of English speech when the sonorous qualities of the Latin had not been forgotten. It was the one book read, quoted and talked about.

Tyndale's Translation. A century and a half later Tyndale enters the lists. The stage is set for a hero and a tragedy. The situation was quite different from that which confronted Wyclif. The New Learning was quickening all Europe, classical studies were becoming popular, the new humanities were broadening men's interests, the Reformation was clarifying morals and motives. England was still rugged and rural, but this sudden stimulus caused brainy men to emerge from the yeoman's plow and the butcher's business to take the highest posts in the land. It was an age of ready wit and racy speech, subtle argument and intrigue, caustic and bitter retort, harsh and cruel punishment. The church had reasserted itself since the Lollard disturbances, the Wycliffite Bible was almost forgotten, conditions were corrupt, and the clergy ignorant as before. Yet national consciousness was arising; hence foreign influences were opposed. The Roman Catholic Church had its iron grip on Cardinal Wolsey and Sir Thomas More, flattering King Henry as "Defender of the Faith." An old law forbade private persons to translate the Bible; to study it in the original was frowned upon. Wolsey, alarmed at the spread of German ideas, required all Lutheran works to be surrendered.

Tyndale the Man. Tyndale came between the old era and the new. At first he became a heretic because he embraced the new scholarship, desiring to share its best with even the plowboy. Fleeing to Europe to pursue his project, in constant danger of being hunted down, his work interrupted repeatedly and bonfires made of his books, he lived to see the tables turned, his English Bible recommended and freely read, his persecutors themselves prisoners of the Tower, while England's king reigned supreme without papal dictation. But his life was a battle. His integrity and consecration were no match for the wiles of Henry's court. Yet we might not have had our Bible in its consummate English but for such a struggle, for Tyndale the scholar reflected Tyndale the man.

None surpassed Tyndale in argument. His humor was keen, his sarcasm cutting, but his sincerity was absolute and his affections real. He was plain, grave, quiet in appearance, spare in form, poor in purse, but rich in intellectual and moral power. He had an insatiable appetite for languages and an enviable fund of historical knowledge, even his enemy, More, calling him "full prettily learned," a learning guided by common sense. He handled words with unusual facility, having a long memory and a large vocabulary, with a sense of fitness and a mental precision. He Saxonized his English, modifying prevalent Latin forms and French elegancies. A good Greek scholar, and for his day efficient in Hebrew, he endeavored to understand the genius of those languages and to a remarkable degree caught the Hebrew idiom and rhythm. A simple, dignified, melodious style resulted. His scholar's instinct opposed fanciful allegorical interpretations of Scripture. He believed, like Wyclif, that to read the Bible in one's native tongue was the remedy for England's ills. Never did he indulge in the delights of scholarship for their own sake, but always with the purpose of helping England.

The Story of His Work. William Tyndale was born about 1484 in Gloucestershire, an agricultural community. Attending Oxford when very young, he gained a reputation as studious, upright, and much in earnest. The Bible became his standard of conduct, freeing him from subservience to other authority. Colet's lectures on Paul were then thrilling Oxford, brushing away centuries of scholastic rubbish. At Cambridge, he heard the learned Erasmus on the Greek Testament. Thence returning to his native county as chaplain or tutor to a manor-house, he came close to the common people. Reasoning with the ignorant clergy by straight appeals to Scripture, as Erasmus had taught, he was led to make his famous declaration to a learned man: "If God spare my life, ere many years I will cause a boy that driveth the plough-share know more of the Scripture than thou doest." Erasmus, with exceptional broadmindedness, had approved of vernacular translations, saying that he "would wish even all women to read the Gospel and the Epistles of Paul." Colet had translated the Lord's Prayer into English. The printing press had arrived. But tools for translation were rare and expensive; grammars and lexicons were scarce; and there was no Greek text except that of Erasmus. (See art., *Transmission of N.T.*, pp. 860–1.)

From Gloucestershire Tyndale went to London, hoping to interest the scholarly Bishop Tunstall in publishing his N.T. translation, already begun. But Tunstall refused, and Tyndale determined to push his enterprise on foreign shores with the help of the wealthy Monmouth. Merchants were often more progressive than the clergy. Traveling freely, they felt the vital currents sweeping the world along, and many of them heroically supported progressive leaders. Such a friend did Tyndale find in Monmouth, afterward put in the Tower for his loyalty, and such was Philip the Magnanimous of Marburg.

In 1524, Tyndale sailed for Hamburg never to return. Probably visiting Luther at Wittenberg, he soon settled in Cologne, a place famous for printers and with facilities for shipping books to London. Here he got three thousand copies in press when suddenly the work was stopped, Tyndale disappearing with what sheets he could save. At Worms, a city sanctioning the Reformation, he succeeded in printing six thousand copies, which were smuggled into England and Scotland and distributed secretly. Henry and Wolsey, however, were warned. Tunstall insisted on some drastic measure and the king ordered the books burned. The spectacle was staged at Paul's Cross, London. The cardinal was there in all his pomp, surrounded by his prelates. After Tunstall had denounced these "naughtily translated" books as containing "pestiferous and pernicious poison," noted heretics were required to cast them into the flames. Such publicity caused increased sales, merchants investing in the books for profit. Unauthorized editions were issued and the government spent large sums in vain to destroy them. An old Chronicler wrote that the Bishop thought "he had God by the toe, when indeed he had, as after he thought, the Devil by the fist." At any rate, Providence favored the Bibles until rigorous searching sent scores of people to prison.

In 1527 Tyndale went to Marburg, and under the protection of the Landgrave, who had founded the first university of the Reformation, enjoyed a period of undisturbed study. Here he engaged in translating the Hebrew O.T., and completed the Pentateuch with pertinent and pungent marginal remarks. When the Treaty of Cambray was signed between England and Germany, More and Tunstall were watchdogs, seeing to it that heretical books printed in one country were forbidden in the other. In January, 1530, the Pentateuch appeared. In May it was burned in London. In 1531 several of Tyndale's best friends were persecuted or burned. Tyndale completed the historical books as far as Chronicles, adding Jonah, but his O.T. remained unfinished.

When Wolsey fell, Thomas Cromwell directed agents to *persuade* Tyndale to return to England under guise of protection, then orders came to *apprehend* him. Tyndale got out of the way, but his disciple, Fryth, was taken. Now the Inquisition was in energetic action, yet Tyndale lived two years in Antwerp reprinting the O.T. and revising the N.T. This second edition has been called his noblest monument. Every word was carefully reconsidered and where possible improved. Annoyed that one George Joye had officiously undertaken revision, Tyndale in self-defense made a third revision but was arrested before its publication. Therefore it was printed imperfectly.

In England Henry had abolished papal authority. Persecution now relaxing, people dared read the Bible in their own tongue. Prominent persecutors were in the Tower, and it looked as if Tyndale might end his life in scholarly quiet. But the enemies of Protestantism in England could wreak vengeance on a countryman outside. Tyndale was finding a home in Antwerp's residence for English merchants when an agent lured him out to dinner, where officers were ready to carry him to the Vilvorde prison. There during sixteen months he was allowed some freedom. A letter begs for "a candle in the evening, for it is weary work to sit alone in the dark," and another for his Hebrew books. The trial dragged on, Cromwell's efforts at interference failed, and the judges were in a dilemma because pardon meant offending the church and death meant offending Henry. But the death verdict prevailed. Tyndale was martyred October 6, 1536, more mercifully treated than some, being strangled before burning. Just before his death he cried, "Lord, open the king of England's eyes." Eight years before he said, "If they shall burn me, they shall do none other thing than I look for."

The Result of His Work. Tyndale has been called "the true hero of the English Reformation." His life was a testimony to the power of the Bible. He had access to the best means of study of his day, doubtless having before him the Vulgate and other Latin translations, Luther's German Bible, and Hebrew and Greek texts. Probably he did not see any of the manuscripts which were the basis of the texts, but now we know that the Hebrew texts were fairly good, that the Greek were not the earliest and contained many errors, and that the Latin versions were quite corrupt.

Such was the work of Tyndale, not again to be approached, so far as the Bible is concerned, in scholarly daring and influential achievement. It was the molding of a living medium to express a vital force. From Tyndale's efforts came a book which was to permeate the life of English-speaking people not only with religious truth but with beautiful, majestic and forceful diction. "After nearly four centuries and all the action and reaction of time," says J. H. Gardiner, "it is still true that the type of prose style which no good writer can forget, and about which all varieties of prose style center, is the style of the first man who ever made printed English speak to the whole nation."

Between 1535 and 1611. The right to a vernacular Bible was indubitably established in the next seventy-five years, five English versions appearing. Mainly revisions, all were based on Tyndale's translation except the Douai version. None of the scholars undertaking the task equaled Tyndale in intellect or linguistic talent, but Miles Coverdale with his literary gifts permanently influenced our Bible.

Coverdale. Born in 1488, Coverdale studied at Cambridge. He became known for his persuasive preaching and modern sympathies. In 1534 Convocation asked for royal approval of a translation. The astute Cromwell, realizing that Henry would soon welcome such a popular appeal as an authorized English version would make, had started his friend Coverdale, now abroad, on such an edition. This appeared in England before Tyndale's death. A lover of books, versed in Latin and German, but not in Hebrew or Greek, Coverdale was an editor rather than a translator, depending upon Tyndale's version and Latin and German texts. He sensed the need of his time, for this was the first complete English Bible. It left unchanged words cherished by ecclesiastics, omitted controversial notes, placed the apocryphal books apart, and contained wood cuts. This Coverdale Bible became immediately popular, two editions appearing in 1537. In 1538 the N.T. was revised and reprinted with the Latin in a parallel column. Without Tyndale's convictions, Coverdale had more delicate feeling for melody and felicitous phrasing, many of his changes being preserved in the King James Version and his translation of the Psalms in the Psalter of the Prayer Book.

Matthew's Bible. Matthew's Bible appeared next, dedicated to King Henry and Queen Jane. "I like it better than any other translation made," wrote Cranmer, asking Cromwell to secure the king's license "that the same may be sold and read of every person." This version was actually Tyndale's work intrusted in prison to John Rogers, plus Coverdale's translation of the parts lacking. It got its name from publisher or patron, as Tyndale's signature would be unacceptable, and received royal sanction within a year of Tyndale's martyrdom and within ten years of the spectacular burning of his Testaments.

The Great Bible. Uneasy at the popularity of this Bible, with its obvious dependence upon Tyndale, Cromwell conceived of a *de luxe* edition of Coverdale's (mostly a revision of Tyndale's as we know), sending him to France where such a book could be printed. Confiscated, and some of it sold as waste paper, its sheets were recovered and sent secretly to England. It had a notable frontispiece, a Holbein engraving of King Henry handing the Bible to his subordinates. Because of its size and elegance it was called the Great Bible, and two years saw at least seven imprintings. Cranmer's elaborate preface to the second edition occasioned the name Cranmer's Bible. The fourth edition bore the sanction of Bishop Tunstall, Tyndale's persistent persecutor. A copy was ordered placed in each church, that "parishioners may most commodiously resort to the same and rede yt," but excited public discussion called forth an edict forbidding "any open reasoning in your taverns or alehouses." This was the officially authorized version, not the King James.

The Geneva Bible. After twenty years came the Geneva Bible. Mary's persecutions made Calvin's home the refuge of exiled reformers. A group, including Coverdale for a short while, produced a truly Calvinistic English Bible, the expense being borne by the Geneva congregation. This was more scholarly than the Great Bible, though based upon its O.T. and Tyndale's N.T. edited by Whittingham, Calvin's brother-in-law. This book, presented to Elizabeth at her coronation, went through sixty editions in her reign, one hundred and forty by 1644. Smaller than usual in size, using Roman rather than black-faced type, with text broken into chapters and verses after Stephen's Greek Testament, containing an introduction by Calvin, notes Calvinistic in tone, graphic pictures and the innovation of maps, this became the household book of England and Scotland.

The Bishop's Bible. The Bishop's Bible appeared in 1568. Archbishop Parker thought too many unsanctioned versions existed and directed a committee of scholars, including nine bishops, in a new revision. Through lack of consultation the style was uneven and it had no especial merit, although the N.T. possessed commendable points. Its use of verse divisions confirmed an unfortunate custom. Prescribed for churches, it soon superseded the Great Bible, holding sway forty years.

The Douai Bible. Alarmed at the inroads of the vernacular Bible, the Roman Church in self-defense authorized a translation by Catholics. The Douai version appeared in 1609 in such awkward English and literal Latinisms that it has never been read with any satisfaction by clergy or people. It was begun and finished at Douai, Flanders, where English priests were educated. The N.T., issued in 1582 at Rheims, was called the Rhemish N.T. Roman Catholics for some years have acknowledged their need of a better translation, which is now in the making.

The King James and the Revised Versions Compared. The King James is usually known as the Authorized Version (A.V.). It is the basis of both the English Revised (R.V.) and the American Standard Versions (A.S.V.).

Occasion for King James Version. In 1604, the year after his coronation, James I called a conference to examine into "things pretended to be amiss in the church." Because of "the most corrupted translation" in the Prayer Book, James, himself an earnest Bible student, became interested in a proposal for retranslation. Confusion in the use of versions had arisen and additional sources and better knowledge of Greek and Hebrew were now available. Accordingly fifty-four noted scholars, representing all phases of belief, were appointed to make the best version possible. Working in sections, using the Bishop's Bible as a foundation, and consulting all possible texts, they collaborated harmoniously and skillfully. In 1611 the masterpiece appeared, called "the noblest and most beautiful book in the world." Everywhere one meets comments like these: "A monumental work," "A book which, if everything else in our language should perish, would alone suffice to show the whole extent of its beauty and power." By the middle of the century it had displaced the Bishop's Bible in churches and the Geneva Bible in homes, and for two hundred and fifty years held undisputed sway in English-speaking countries. Even to-day it is *the* best seller, notwithstanding more recent versions and the popularity of other reading.

Secret of its Excellence. What is the secret? A few of Wyclif's phrases are here, Tyndale is largely responsible for it, Coverdale put his delicate touch on it, the sturdy tone of the Geneva text and the Latinisms of the Rhemish Testament modified certain sentences. Behind it were the world's profoundest religious truths, uttered by the Hebrews, in concrete, vivid, figurative expression. All was cast into a crucible heated hot with religious fervor, with the zest of a new intellectual awakening, a new freedom of the individual, a new national loyalty. Out of it came this book, so simple, direct, and suggestive in language, so beautiful and resonant in rhythm, so majestic and inspiring in tone that as literature many claim that it surpasses the original. No one influence has been so great in the life of English-speaking people, religiously, morally, socially, politically, as has this version. It still holds its own in many homes and pulpits. Why was there any attempt to displace it?

Reasons for the Revised Version. By the middle of the nineteenth century a great intellectual change was taking place. Science and historical research had brought to light a new world of learning, all study falling under the spell of the scientific method. Evolution was quickening imagination, fascinating finds in archæology were luring men to reconstruct the background of ancient literatures, and the centuries of development necessary to produce our Bible were clearly appearing in outline. Biblical studies were leaping ahead in scholarly skill and in available materials, old conceptions of a static world and an infallible book were giving way. In other words "biblical criticism" had come, and scholars felt it time for a new translation. The Revision Committee, gathered together in 1870, was guided by four considerations: the possession of several early uncial or capital-letter Greek manuscripts from the fourth and fifth centuries as opposed to the miniscules and cursives of the tenth to the sixteenth centuries known in 1611; the refinement of Hebrew and Greek scholarship and discoveries like that of the principles of Hebrew poetry; the light thrown upon obscure passages by historical studies; and changes in the English language itself. (See art., *Transmission of the N.T.*, p. 861.)

About seventy-five Greek and Hebrew scholars from England and America assumed the task. In 1881 the N.T. was published, in

1885 the O.T., and in 1901 an American edition embodying readings deemed preferable by the American members of the committee. Schools and colleges seized upon it as a textbook. Ministers of the advanced type used it in the pulpit, commentaries and lesson-helps incorporated it. Protest came from the theologically conservative, who regarded the King James Version as sacred, and from people of literary taste for displacing a beautiful classic by a rough revision. Both protests still hold, the former decreasingly, the latter increasingly.

Merits of the Revision. What are its merits? Scarcely any manuscript finds have been so thrilling as those of Tischendorf in 1840–44. He discovered or made available three of the four earliest manuscripts (see pp. 861–3). The fourth, sent to James by the patriarch of Constantinople when he heard of the king's interest in the Bible, did not reach England in time for use in the 1611 version. With so many sources available, the art of collation was developed and the discriminating sense of historian and linguist brought to bear on the probable original. Mistakes which had crept into the manuscripts were recognized and new shades of meaning in old words revealed. Many passages, aside from the Psalter, were printed in poetical form, the text was presented in paragraphs rather than verses, and extraneous material was omitted. The resulting version is accurate rather than beautiful, yet not truly accurate, for much improvement has since been made in pushing these principles of study further. It is a translation *per se*, not a book of literary excellence.

The Latest Vernacular Versions. Recently there has been a renewed outburst of scholarly industry in translating the Bible, especially the N.T.—fresh translations, not more revisions. Their popularity seems to indicate a new era for the vernacular Bible.

Reasons for New Translations. The reasons lie again in the age, an age of freedom, of demand for the real and for scientific scholarship. Fifty years have shown such enormous progress in biblical studies that advanced students discard much of the old. The whole foundation of judgment has shifted as the former basis of "a closed canon" and "an infallible rule" has crumbled. This critical age has handled roughly some sacred traditions. Passion for truth has outrun loyalties of sentiment. The air is electric with new interests. It is no longer a world of one book, and books that appeal are modern. The Bible seems as archaic as an ancestor's portrait in ruff and wig, for the English of 1611 is not the English of to-day and the version of 1885 is not colloquial. Biblical phrases rich in content to our fathers have become meaningless to this generation. Expositional sermons are displaced by current events and public Scripture reading has become trite. The fruit of familiarity minus understanding is boredom, the fruit of no reading at all is disregard; moreover, the shift is not yet popularly made from a Bible every word considered sacred, to a Bible held as a guiding star because showing the development of religious thought. Thus active personal regard for it is ceasing in many homes and schools, and so extensive is the ignorance that a nation-wide movement for religious education has been inaugurated. Also the popular mind is suddenly being stretched in two directions, to compass an international world where nations remote in miles have become political and commercial neighbors, and to compass in understanding ancient historic cultures. The latter has lagged while the former has progressed, and biblical students whose specialty is old civilizations have been searching for means to break the spell of indifference to the Bible. Awakened to the importance of its message in helping to solve the problems of our day, even as were Wyclif and Tyndale for theirs, they want the people once more to become familiar with its literature.

Such scholars as Weymouth, Moffatt, and Goodspeed have undertaken the hard task of once more bridging a chasm between the Bible and the people. The N.T. has received most attention. Only Moffatt's and *The O.T.: An American Translation*, contain the O.T. However, commentators have been publishing translations of O.T. sections which no student should miss. (Cf. G. A. Smith's *Jeremiah;* also Deut. 32, 33, in this Commentary.) A list compiled in 1925 (see J. V. Madison, *Journal of Bib. Lit.*, vol. xliv, 1925, iii, iv) enumerates one hundred and sixty-one N.T. translations since Tyndale; twenty-nine since 1900, when *The Twentieth Century N.T.* appeared, the majority American. These vary in excellence as well as in faults. Not all will live, but great praise is due some.

Estimation of the New Translations. In estimating these one must consider the difference between an accurate translation and a book of literature. Making a translation is a science, making literature is an art to be bound as little by too much learning as by too much convention. It is the height of skill to translate well and also write well. Tyndale was such a consummate genius and the Authorized Version is the fruit of the rarely gifted Elizabethan period. Criticisms of recent versions, highly commendatory as well as adverse, fall into these two categories. The N.T. was undoubtedly intended for common folk, yet that this need not preclude a book of literature springing from the pen of a common man, John Bunyan is witness. The gains of new translations are clear, plain language, striking home to the modern mind, and, in the form of the book, printed like other books. Yet Latin derivatives increase and vivid figures diminish, although Latin words are the language of abstractions which the Hebrews did not possess. They reveled instead in picturesque symbols. Excellent as these translations are as commentaries, exactness sometimes fails; and notwithstanding attempts to present poetry as such the original cadences often seem lost. Neither must we forget that literary masterpieces are found in the O.T., our finest writers and orators having whetted their style on the eloquence, poetry, and subtle satire of the prophets. However, criticism is easier than construction, and these scholars might well quote Tyndale: "If any man find faults either with the translation or aught beside (which is easier for many to do than so well to have translated it themselves of their own pregnant wits), to the same it shall be lawful to translate it themselves."

Ours is not an era of creative English but, rather, of learning to master the tools of research. Like that of Wyclif, it is an age awakening to a new world. Like that of Tyndale, it is a period of reforming philosophies and rediscovering values. It took great individuals to blaze the trail then. Groups followed in harmonious collaboration, the work of individuals being absorbed into a national classic. The cycle seems to be returning. Individuals are leading in something unique. Perhaps in due time their work, cast into a newly heated crucible, may produce once more a version of plain, pithy, suggestive words, with poetic symbolism and musical phrases, and another genius may appear to match the Hebrew idiom to the English and create a classic. Perhaps the flaming spirit of God's word will again break through the hard crust of convention in translation, and give us the radiant vision Erasmus had when he said that the N.T. pages "will give you Christ himself . . . in an intimacy so close that he would be less visible to you if he stood before your eyes."

Literature: Trevelyan, *England in the Age of Wyclif;* Poole, *Wyclif and Movements for Reform;* Demars, *William Tyndale;* Cooper, *The Life and Work of William Tyndale;* Gardiner, *The Bible as English Literature;* Goodspeed, *The Making of the English N.T.;* Hoare, *The Evolution of the English Bible;* Kenyon, *Our Bible and the Ancient Manuscripts;* Price, *The Ancestry of our English Bible;* Westcott, *History of the English Bible.*

II. ARTICLES
THE OLD TESTAMENT

THE FORMATION OF THE OLD TESTAMENT
THE TRANSMISSION OF THE OLD TESTAMENT
THE CHRONOLOGY OF THE OLD TESTAMENT
THE OLD TESTAMENT IN THE LIGHT OF ARCHÆOLOGY
THE OLD TESTAMENT AND SCIENCE
THE OLD TESTAMENT AND CRITICISM
THE PENTATEUCH—ITS ORIGIN AND DEVELOPMENT
THE LEGAL AND HISTORICAL LITERATURE OF THE OLD TESTAMENT
THE PROPHETIC LITERATURE OF THE OLD TESTAMENT
THE POETIC AND WISDOM LITERATURE OF THE OLD TESTAMENT
THE OLD TESTAMENT CONCEPTION OF GOD
THE RELIGION OF ISRAEL
ISRAEL'S MESSIANIC HOPE
THE LITERATURE OF THE INTERTESTAMENTAL PERIOD
THE RELIGIOUS DEVELOPMENT OF THE INTERTESTAMENTAL PERIOD

THE FORMATION OF THE OLD TESTAMENT

By GODFREY ROLLES DRIVER

MAGDALEN COLLEGE, OXFORD

General Contents. It is customary to speak of both the O.T. and the N.T. as "canonical." The application of the term "canon" to the Scriptures is not found before the fourth century A.D., and it is of strictly Christian origin. Nevertheless, the word may be and is conveniently used also with reference to those Hebrew Scriptures which Christians call the "Old Testament" (cf. 2 Cor. 3[14], where *vetus testamentum* is used by Jerome). The Hebrew Bible is divided into three parts; the "Law" (Hebrew *Tôrāh*), the "Prophets" *Nĕbhî'îm*), and the "Writings" (*Kethubhîm*), for the last of which Christian writers have substituted the Greek title *Hagiographa*, "Sacred Writings." Each group, with unimportant exceptions, consisted of the same books throughout its history, but the order within each varied considerably from time to time; it remained almost invariable only in the "Law," whose five books were always arranged as they still are in modern Bibles, unless it is conceded that the manuscripts of the list drawn up by the Christian bishop Melito (*cir.* 170 A.D.) point to an arrangement in which Numbers preceded Leviticus. The reason for the variations is obvious: each book was till comparatively recent times written on a separate roll, so that the question of the order in which the books should stand did not arise; but the obvious historical sequence of the books of the Pentateuch insured a chronological order from the first time on which each separate group, or the whole of the O.T., was copied on the same scroll, probably in or soon after the first century A.D. Similarly, there is never any variation in the arrangement of the historical books of Joshua, Judges, Samuel, and Kings.

Early Traditions. The formation of the Hebrew canon is an obscure subject, for no historical account of it exists, and the allusions found in the Apocrypha (2 Macc. 2[13-15] and 2 Esdras 14[19-48]) are purely legendary. Hardly more reliable are the stories which connect the men of the Great Synagogue with the work of forming the O.T. canon (Elias Levita), since this appears to be nothing but a fictitious assembly based on that at which Ezra promulgated the Law (Neh. 8–10), for which there is no evidence earlier than the Mishnah, namely, about the end of the second century A.D. All that can be said in support of the tradition is that much of the work must have been carried out by successive generations of scribes at Jerusalem. There is, indeed, no external notice touching the formation of the canon till several centuries after its close. Yet there probably underlies the story of Ezra's association with the work as outlined in the 2 Esdras passage already referred to, this much truth, that he was connected with the preservation and promulgation of the Law. Fond imagination has transformed this into an official establishment of the text of the Hebrew Scriptures as an authoritative canon of Scripture.

Principle Underlying Canonization. It may now be asked what is meant by the formation of the canon. It has, for example, been suggested that the canon contains merely those remnants of ancient literature which, having survived the accidents of time, came to be regarded by later ages as a collection of sacred writings; this is made improbable by the lateness of some of the books—e.g., Daniel (*cir.* 165 B.C.)—which have found a place in the canon. Nor is it merely an anthology of Hebrew literature; for such a conception, while accounting for the omission of certain known works—e.g., the "Book of the Wars of Jehovah" (Num. 21[14]) and the "Book of Jashar" (Josh. 10[13] 2 Sam. 1[18]; cf. also 1 Kings 8[53], LXX)—from the final collection, overlooks the religious purpose which appears clearly to have been the principle governing the selection. From a number of early sources comes the suggestion that the reason for setting the books apart is to be found in the fact that those responsible for the decision believed that they could hear the divine voice in the messages contained in the books. This recognition presupposes a people not only so far developed as to be conscious that the revelation of the divine will through human literature was possible, but also ready to accept such a revelation as authoritative (Ryle).

Composition and Compilation. Before the selection implied in the existence of a canon could be made two processes were necessary: in the first place, the composition of the original documents and, secondly, as numerous passages show, the compilation of the various books of the O.T. out of material selected from these documents. Oral tradition preceded written books. Thus there appear to be references to national songs so preserved (e.g., Num. 21[27]) before they were written down in such books as those whose titles have already been cited. These collections must have been in circulation for a long while before they were committed to writing, perhaps as early as the ninth century B.C. The motive assigned as the reason for which they were to be written down is definitely religious (Deut. 31[19]), and this same purpose, it may be inferred, underlay every step taken by the Hebrews to insure the preservation of their ancient Scriptures. Again, the compilers of the books of Kings continually refer to the extra-canonical sources from which they drew their material, such as the "Book of the Acts of Solomon" (1 Kings 11[41]), the "Book of the Chronicles of the Kings of Israel," and the "Book of the Chronicles of the Kings of Judah." The Chronicler also makes mention of the "History of Nathan" (1 Chr. 29[29] and 2 Chr. 9[29]) and the "Book of Jehu" (20[34]), in addition to allusions to canonical books which are preserved in the Bible; he quotes too the "Commentary of the Prophet Iddo" (2 Chr. 13[22]) and the "Commentary of the Book of Kings" (24[27]). Other compilers, like those who put together the Pentateuch in its present form, hardly ever or never cite their authorities; none the less, modern criticism has made it abundantly clear that most of the books of the O.T. owe their actual form to compilers of varying skill. Both the composition and the compilation, therefore, of a work preceded its admission to the canon.

Preliminary Stages in Canonization. In the period before the reforms of Josiah (*cir.* 640–608 B.C.) there was one thing which was invested with a semi-canonical sanctity: this was the Decalogue, which was preserved on the two Tables of Stone in the ark within the Holy of Holies (1 Kings 8[9]; cf. 2 Kings 11[12] 2 Chr. 23[11]). These laws composed, indeed, the charter of the constitution, but they are not to be confused with a canon of Scripture.

The first case in which a book appears to exert canonical authority is afforded by the discovery of the "Book of the Law" in the Temple in 621 B.C. in the reign of Josiah (2 Kings 22[3-20]; cf. 2 Chr. 34[8-28]). This is acknowledged to contain the words of Jehovah, and its authority is unhesitatingly accepted. Yet it is clear that it did not contain the whole of the Law, nor does the fact that it was called the "Book of the Covenant" (2 Kings 23[2, 21]; cf. 2 Chr. 34[30]) make it necessary to identify it with the Sinaitic legislation (Ex. 20–23; cf. 24[7]); for a number of reasons combine to show that it designates rather a part, possibly the bulk, of Deuteronomy or else a collection of Deuteronomic laws. The book of Deuteronomy is primarily not legal, but hortatory; in the effect which its discovery had on the minds of the king and of the nation may be recognized a forecast of the authority and the sanctity which books acknowledged to be canonical were afterward to receive.

Canonization of the Law. The fact that the first works to become authoritative were laws prepares us to find that the first part of the O.T. to receive canonical recognition was the Law (namely, the first five books, commonly called the "Pentateuch"). This is confirmed by the testimony of Jeremiah, who makes evident allusion to a written law (Jer. 8[8]); yet he does not introduce his quotations with any set phrase indicating that he is citing a sacred book, as the compiler of the books of Kings does (e.g., 1 Kings 2[3] 2 Kings 14[6]). But the Deuteronomic collection is still the only canonical book; for both these authors refer to it alone and both closely imitate its style. It must, however, be borne in mind that it did not occupy the position held by the canonical scriptures at a later period; for, in the first place, the prophets were still living and exercised a greater influence than any written law could do; and, secondly, the Deuteronomic Law alone was insufficient to constitute a national Scripture. Its history as well as its laws rested on the great works of the "Jehovist" and of the "Elohist," which appear to have been combined into one composite narrative before the beginning of the seventh century B.C. (See discussion in art., *Pentateuch*, p. 138.) The miseries of the Exile and the hopelessness of the future prospect must have driven the pious few to look back to the past glories of their race; and the veneration felt for the ancient records may well have given rise to a demand to bring them into connection with this Book of the Law. It is, therefore, a very plausible conjecture that, when the prologue and epilogue had been added to provide it with an historical setting, the scribe who edited the Jehovist-Elohist version of the book of Joshua in the spirit of the Deuteronomist attached that work to it, while about the same time a redaction of the whole narratives of the Jehovist and the Elohist was prefixed to it. Thus the so-called Hexateuch was formed in the early period of the Exile; but it is improbable that Joshua was separated from the Law prior to the close of the age of Nehemiah (a somewhat different view is expressed in the art., *Pentateuch*, pp. 142–4).

During the same period, other groups of laws were probably being gathered together; for, while Jeremiah does not, Ezekiel does show acquaintance with the Law of Holiness. But it is not probable that the Priestly Code as a whole was finally put together till after the return from the Captivity, since Zechariah nowhere appeals to it and Haggai speaks of the priests as if they still gave their decisions on their own authority. While, therefore, various groups of priestly laws were being brought together during the Exile, not, indeed, for public use but for the convenience of the priests, their codification in the Priestly Code must be put after 536 B.C.

Nearly a century later it was to the Deuteronomic law that Ezra appealed in support of his action against mixed marriages (Ezra 10[3]; cf. Neh. 13[1-3]); and other points emphasize the influence of Deuteronomy on Ezra and Nehemiah. The priestly law can hardly have been hitherto handed down otherwise than by word of mouth and in parts, for it is stated that both priests and people were ignorant how to celebrate the Feast of Tabernacles until they had been instructed by Ezra (Neh. 8[13-18]). The Priestly Code cannot, in fact, have been fully known at least to many of the priests and most of the people, before 444 B.C. That Ezra then publicly revealed it is the true inference from the accounts of what then happened and from the biblical descriptions of him (Ezra 7[6, 11, 14]). But these descriptions give no support to the theory which was based on them, that Ezra was inspired to dictate all the twenty-four books of the Hebrew canon which had been destroyed at the fall of Jerusalem (2 Esdras 14[38-48]). Beyond this it is impossible to go, for we have not sufficient facts on which to base any endeavor to ascribe this work of compilation to any single man. The process is more likely to have been gradual than otherwise; one school or generation of scribes, in all likelihood, compiled the Priestly Code and another combined it with the rest of what now comprises the Pentateuch, while on the trustworthy authority of the almost contemporary Chronicler it was Ezra who promulgated the "Book of the Law" in Jerusalem (Neh. 8–10); but there is no evidence to show whether the Law then revealed was only the Priestly Code (Wildeboer) or the whole Pentateuch (Ryle). In any case, it was the age of Ezra or the immediately following age which saw the full recognition of the first part of the Hebrew canon, namely, of the "Law."

Yet the Priestly Code of Ezra was not so extensive then as it afterwards became; for various practices, which are now found in it but which appear not to have been made in Nehemiah's time, must have been added at a subsequent period. Inversely, certain recent regulations, though "written in the law"—namely, the traditional law of the priests—never found a place in the canonical "Law." These facts are inconclusive; but from external evidence it may be inferred that a considerable time must have elapsed before the letter of the text was regarded as sacrosanct, since the Pentateuch translation of the LXX, made probably in the third century B.C., exhibits considerable divergencies from the Hebrew text in at least one long section (Ex. 35–40).

Finally, there are several facts that go to prove that the "Law" alone was the first Canonical Scripture: (1) It is named separately as a group distinct from the "Prophets" and other "Writings" in the first mention of the threefold canon (Prologue of Ecclus.); (2) it is treated with exceptional reverence by the post-exilic writers of the O.T. (e.g., Mal. 4[4]) as well as by the later Jews (e.g., Ecclus. 24[23-29] 1 Macc. 1[57]); (3) it is the part of the O.T. which was first and best translated into Greek; (4) in the beginning it alone was read systematically in the services of the synagogue; it was some time before lessons were taken also from the "Prophets"; (5) it was long used as a general title for the whole of the Hebrew Scriptures; (6) finally, it alone was recognized as canonical by the Samaritans; none of those scriptures which became canonical after the Schism (*cir.* 423 B.C.) was so accepted by them. This event, therefore, fixes the *terminus ad quem* for the closing of the first part of the Hebrew canon.

Canonization of the Prophets. The law without prophecy, it has been said, was a body without a soul (Dillmann). The next stage, therefore, when the voice of prophecy was finally silent, was the formation of the prophetic canon. This group was divided by the Jews into two parts; of these the first, called the "Former Prophets," comprised the historical books from Joshua to Kings (except Ruth), and the second, called the "Latter Prophets," consisted of the three great Prophets, Isaiah, Jeremiah and Ezekiel, and the twelve Minor Prophets.

Joshua, which had probably been compiled during the early part of the Exile, was at first combined with the Pentateuch; but by the end of Nehemiah's age it seems to have been separated from it, either because its narrative contained neither distinctive religious nor legal teaching or because the "Law" seemed to reach a more fitting close with the death of Moses. To the same period too must be assigned the compilation of Judges; of this the middle portion shows signs of having been edited by a compiler of the Deuteronomic school, while the first and last sections of the book, which exhibit no Deuteronomic traces, were probably added to the main part (Judg. 2[6]–16[31]) as a beginning and an end by a later hand. The whole book, therefore, must have been put together after the Deuteronomic age, namely, at some time during the Exile or later. To this general period also belongs the compilation of the books of Samuel, which show sporadic traces of Deuteronomic redaction. The books of Kings are the most markedly Deuteronomic of all the historical books and their compiler seems to have been, though not Jeremiah himself, yet a man like-minded with him and almost certainly a contemporary who lived and wrote under the same influences. They probably belong, then, to the last decade of the seventh century B.C., in which case a few additions must have afterward been made to them, since they carry the narrative down to 562 B.C. The reason why all these works were classed with the "Prophets" is clear: as Deuteronomy represented the law infused with the spirit of prophecy, so the historical books contained the record of Jehovah's dealings with his chosen people seen through the prophets' eyes, and were intended to teach the people great prophetic truth.

Hitherto, however, the sayings of the prophets were only transmitted orally (cf. Jer. 26[17, 18]) or preserved in written form by their disciples (cf. Isa. 8[16] 30[8]). Now, when a great age had come to an end and the gift of prophecy became ever rarer, the reverence for their teaching increased; while the records of them were through the ravages of time in danger of being altogether lost. Tradition claims that it was Nehemiah who gathered together the books concerning the kings and the prophets (2 Macc. 2[13]). Yet this does not mean that he drew up the Prophetic canon; it merely connects the preservation of some of the national records with him personally or with his generation. This is clear from the fact that, while there are clear allusions to the "Law" in the books of Ezra and Nehemiah, references in them to the great events of later history are vague and general; nor is there in them any mention of any of its great characters.

The ministry of Isaiah lasted roughly from 740–700 B.C.; but the compilation of the book which bears his name cannot be put till long afterward in view of the lateness of the prophecies (*cir.* 450 B.C.) which now form the last eleven chapters of it. These could not have been ascribed to Isaiah or appended to his collected prophecies till sufficient time had elapsed for their authorship to have been completely forgotten—probably a full century rather than anything less; and this brings its compilation down to a date not earlier than 350 B.C. Jeremiah cannot have been put into its present form till after the compilation of Kings, from which certain passages have been incorporated into it; further, the great divergencies from the Hebrew text which the version of the LXX exhibits points to the currency of different texts, possibly of different collections, till after the composition of the Greek translation. The middle of the fourth century B.C., therefore, should be late enough for the three great Prophets. The Minor Prophets necessitate a somewhat later date. Malachi was composed about the middle of the fifth century B.C.; the extensive prophecies consisting of six chapters, attached to the end of Zechariah (*cir.* 330–300 B.C.), could not have been added while anyone who knew the author personally was still living; it may be, therefore, that, as in the case of the addition to the original Isaiah, a century must be allowed before the compilation of this book could have been completed. This brings the editing of the whole book of the Minor Prophets down to the middle of the third century B.C. It may be added that they seem to have been treated as a single work before they were incorporated in the canon; for they show traces of one and the same editorial hand in the various headings prefixed to several of the books and to distinct prophecies.

Although, however, the collection of the "Prophets" appears to have begun in the age of Nehemiah, the divergent texts exhibited by the LXX in Samuel and Jeremiah, to which attention has already been drawn, shows that none of them can have become strictly canonical for at least another century. In fact, the Greek translation must have been completed before their canonicity was recognized, at least in Egypt, although this may have happened somewhat earlier in Palestine. The *terminus a quo*, therefore, for recognition of the "Prophets" as canonical will be certainly after 300 B.C. and probably not long, if at all, before 250 B.C. The *terminus ad quem* can be easily fixed from external evidence: for (1) Jesus the son of Sirach (*cir.* 180 B.C.) clearly recognizes them, in the order in which they are now found in the Hebrew Bible, namely, Joshua (Ecclus. 46[1-6]), Judges (46[11, 12]), Samuel (46[13]–47[11]), Kings (47[12]–49[3]), Isaiah (48[20-25]), Jeremiah (49[6, 7]), Ezekiel (49[8, 9]) and the Twelve Prophets (49[10])—a citation which proves that the Minor Prophets were already known collectively as the "Twelve Prophets"; (2) the author of Daniel (*cir.* 165 B.C.), refers to a group of books which includes the words of Jeremiah (Dan. 9[2]), and which appears to designate the prophetical Scriptures; (3) the grandson of Jesus the son of Sirach (*cir.* 132 B.C.), three times mentions the "Prophets" as forming the second part of the threefold canon (Prologue of Ecclus.). Thus the Prophetic canon is found to have been fully recognized between 180 and 130

B.C. Its compilation, then, may safely be put in the last half of the third century B.C. (Ryle) or in the first half of the second century B.C. (Wildeboer). Thus the "Prophets" acquired canonical authority just in time to strengthen the national feeling and so to form a bulwark against the Hellenization efforts of Antiochus Epiphanes (175–164 B.C.) and the renegade Jews who seconded his efforts.

There is, finally, little, if any, evidence in support of the view that the Prophetic canon was not closed till the latter part of the first century B.C., because of the doubts then current about Ezekiel's place in the canon (Fürst); if that had been the case, it is strange that Daniel was not classed with the "Prophets" (Wildeboer). With their recognition came also without doubt the reading of extracts from them as lessons in the service of the synagogues; but there is no evidence that this custom actually arose during the persecution of Antiochus Epiphanes (Elias Levita). In the N.T. mention is made several times of reading from the "Prophets" as well as from the "Law" (e.g., Acts 13[15, 27]); but it looks as if there were no systematic arrangement of the lessons from the "Prophets" as there was of those from the "Law," since the reader seems to have himself selected any suitable passage (cf. Lk. 4[16, 17]). That the reading of lessons from them preceded and so was the reason for their canonization (Ryle) cannot be proved; for it is not known when these lessons were first introduced, while the first mention of them occurs in the N.T. What might have delayed their recognition was perhaps the opposition of the Sadducees, who were loth to add anything to the canon of the Law (Budde).

Canonization of the Writings. The third group in the Hebrew canon is that called the "Writings" which is separated from the preceding "Prophets" not so much by a difference in its contents (Oehler) as by a chronological distinction (Wildeboer). It comprises (1) the poetical books: Psalms, Proverbs, Job; (2) the five "Rolls" (Hebrew, *Mĕghillôth*)—a late and artificial designation given to them because they alone of this group were employed in the worship of the synagogue (Wildeboer): Song of Songs (or Canticles), Ruth, Lamentations, Ecclesiastes, Esther; (3) the remaining books: Daniel, Ezra and Nehemiah (which form one book in the Hebrew Bible) and Chronicles. Of these, Ruth and Lamentations are reckoned with the "Prophets" in the Greek (as in the English) Bible, whence some have thought that they were originally so placed also in the Hebrew Bible and that they were transferred to their present position among the "Writings" by the mediæval Jewish doctors. The Hebrew evidence, however, is uniformly against this view.

A tradition, enshrined in what is without doubt a spurious epistle, claimed that Judas Maccabæus gathered together the writings which had been scattered by reason of the Jewish war of independence (2 Macc. 2[14]); from this it may safely be inferred that the losses incurred in the religious revival inaugurated by the war led to a demand that steps should be taken to preserve the relics of the national literature and to gather it together into an authoritative edition. Apart from those works which have been so collected, much of what was afterward incorporated in the "Writings" must have been already held in high esteem at the time when the "Prophets" became canonical. But, apart from what was thus recognized, there must have been many works which, through not having been declared canonical, had been less carefully preserved. These must have been fairly numerous; for the author of Ecclesiastes, who lived probably toward the end of the third century B.C., already laments the many books that are made (Eccl. 12[12]). It would be natural to find many of the books in this group among the "Prophets." Some—e.g., Chronicles, Ezra and Nehemiah, Ruth or Esther—failed to be so classified because the lateness of their composition had prevented as yet their canonical recognition; others—e.g., the Psalter or Daniel—because they had not yet been compiled or even written; others again—e.g., Lamentations, Song of Songs, or Ecclesiastes—because of their subject matter. Yet all were works of a religious character, of which the date could be supposed to go back to the end of the prophetic period, namely, the time of Ezra, some as resting on earlier names, others as supposedly contemporary with the history which they record; but without doubt questions of taste as well as of doctrine must have been taken into account.

The importance of the Psalter for devotional and liturgical purposes makes it a plausible conjecture that it was the first work to be admitted to the canon of the "Writings"; and its position at the head of this group is an indication of this priority. The fact that several of the Psalms in it appear to belong certainly to the Maccabæan age proves that the final redaction cannot have been made before the Maccabæan revolt; yet it cannot have been recognized much later, since it is soon freely quoted (e.g., 1 Chr. 16[7-36]) and cited as scriptural (e.g., 1 Macc. 7[16, 17]).

The date of the admission of the rest of the "Writings" is largely conjectural, owing to the lack of direct evidence. Job, which dates from the exilic or, even more probably, the post-exilic period, naturally obtained a place there through its fresh contribution to religious thought, while the fact that the Jews regarded it as an historical work increased their veneration for it. That it was not for this reason included in the "Prophets" may be due to the individual, rather than national, nature of its theme. The date of Ruth is uncertain; but it too, as a book dealing with the history of an individual family and not with that of the nation, obtained a place among the "Writings" rather than among the "Prophets," where it is found in the Greek Bible. The tradition that Jeremiah was the author of Lamentations caused this book to be attached to the book bearing his name, namely, among the "Prophets," in the Greek Bible; but its subject is in the highest degree unsuited to form the conclusion of a prophetical work, especially of one which closes with an historical narrative; further, if that had been its original position, the tradition that it was the work of Jeremiah would have been against removing it from the "Prophets" to the "Writings." Its poetical form, on the contrary, made it a suitable work for inclusion in the same group as the Psalter. Proverbs contains materials of diverse periods, some of considerable antiquity, others of a much later age; it appears to have reached its present form about the middle of the second century B.C. The variety and edifying nature of its contents, as well as its association with Solomon, may well have combined to win it a place in the canon soon after its final redaction. Lastly, Ezra and Nehemiah originally, it is generally held, was the concluding part of Chronicles. Its separation from that book is best explained by the following theory: Kings came to an end with the middle of the Exile, when the Babylonian monarch lifted up the head of the captive Jewish king about 560 B.C. (2 Kings 25[27f.]); to complete the story of the restoration of the Jews that portion of the Chronicler's work which began with the story of the Persian king's kindness to the Jewish exiles in 536 B.C. (Ezra 1[1f.]) was afterward selected for inclusion in the Scriptures. It could not be attached to Kings, since the Prophetic canon was closed; it was, therefore, inserted as a separate work in the "Writings." But, when once a part of the Chronicler's work had found acceptance, the claims of the rest of it could hardly have been resisted, especially as it provided much genealogical material not found elsewhere; consequently, it was admitted to the last place in the Hebrew canon. Thus Christ, in quoting from the first and last books of the Hebrew Scriptures (Mt. 23[35] Lk. 11[51]), refers not to the limits of time but to the limits of the canon. The date of the inclusion of Daniel can be closely defined. Jesus the son of Sirach makes no mention of Daniel in his famous list of Jewish heroes; but in a similar list, composed about a century later, there is an allusion to Daniel and the three children in the den of lions (1 Macc. 2[59, 60]; cf. 1[54]). From the middle of the second century onward it seems to have been well known.

Lastly, there are certain books whose claims to canonicity were much disputed. The Song of Songs was early accepted with the other poetical books among the "Writings"; but no allusions to it are found in literature until it appears in a Christian list of the last half of second century A.D. Ecclesiastes too, which belongs to the third century B.C., was accepted, possibly owing to its connection with Solomon, before any objections to it were seriously felt. According to a Jewish story, it was quoted as scripture in the reign of Alexander Jannæus (105–79 B.C.). The greatest doubt was felt about Esther. In some quarters it was the most popular book in the "Writings" owing to its intense nationalism, especially in the early period when the memory of the persecutions of Antiochus Epiphanes had not been entirely forgotten; in others it met in the course of time with such strong disapproval, possibly because of its insistence on a feast not prescribed in the "Law" or because of the absence of all mention of the Divine Name in it, that some Jews in the first century A.D. omitted it entirely from the list of sacred books. Mention is made of the day of Mordecai in a work of the first half of the first century B.C. (2 Macc. 15[36]); but this does not prove that this book had then been admitted into the canon. Josephus is the first author who appears to recognize it as canonical; yet it was omitted by Melito (*cir.* 170 A.D.) from his list, presumably on the authority of his Jewish informant.

The external evidence for the third group of the canon as a whole is vague. The grandson of Jesus the son of Sirach (*cir.* 132 B.C.) refers to the "Law," the "Prophets" and the "other books of the fathers" (Prologue to Ecclus.); but the phrase is too indefinite to imply that a special collection known as the "Writings" had as yet been gathered together. Nor does it tell us how many of these books had already been translated into Greek; but there is some evidence to show that the Greek version of Esther was known by 178 B.C. and that of Chronicles by 150 B.C. It has, in fact, been argued with some reason that the versions of some of these books—e.g., of Daniel and Esther—in the LXX are so unequally and so badly executed that the Alexandrian Greeks can hardly have recognized their canonicity.

The Jewish philosopher, Philo, who died about 50 A.D., refers to the threefold grouping of the canon in speaking of laws and oracles uttered by the prophets and hymns and other works of a pious nature; but, although he introduces frequent quotations from the "Law" and the "Prophets," he makes no use of Ezekiel, Daniel, Ecclesiastes, the Song of Songs, Esther, Ruth, Lamentations, or possibly of Chronicles. Citations are found in the N.T. from all the books of the O.T. except Obadiah, Nahum, Ezra and Nehemiah, Esther, the Song of Songs and Ecclesiastes. But the fact that there are prophets to whom neither Philo nor the writers of the N.T. refer is nothing more than an *argumentum e silentio* and singularly weak, for it is certain that the Prophetic canon was well established long before their time. Jesus, indeed, seems to imply at least the beginnings of the third group in his reference to the Law of Moses, the Prophets and the Psalms (Lk. 24^{44}); but it can by no means be decided from this whether the "Writings" as a whole were or were not at that time a distinct and recognized group of the canon. He also alludes clearly to Daniel (Mt. 24^{15}); and Ezra and Nehemiah are covered by his reference, already mentioned, to Chronicles. The omission of any quotations in the N.T. from Esther, the Song of Songs, and Ecclesiastes may be due, not to their absence from the canon, but to the fact that they supplied no suitable matter for such a purpose.

The frequent references to the "Scriptures" or the "Holy Scriptures" and similar phrases in the N.T. convey the impression that the writers are thinking not of isolated works but of a sacred national collection; yet it can be argued on cogent grounds that the N.T. does not necessarily imply a fixed canon. That this collection was the twenty-four books of the canonical Scriptures admits of little doubt. An unknown writer of the last decade of the first century A.D. speaks, according to the best manuscripts, of "the ninety-four books" (2 Esdras 14^{45-47}); by these he appears to mean the twenty-four published books of the canon and seventy others which are separated from them, as not yet to be published. Lastly, the Jewish historian Josephus, who was born in 37 or 38 A.D., speaks of the twenty-two books of the Scriptures: the five books of Moses containing the Law and the earliest traditions from the creation of the world till the death of the law-giver; thirteen books of the prophets who followed him till the death of Ahasuerus; and four documents comprising hymns and practical precepts. Thus, while recognizing the same canon, he does not follow the threefold division of it found in Hebrew tradition. The five books of Moses are the Pentateuch; the thirteen Prophets are probably Joshua, Judges and Ruth, Samuel, Kings, Chronicles, Ezra and Nehemiah, Esther, Job, Daniel, Isaiah, Jeremiah and Lamentations, Ezekiel, the Twelve Prophets; the four volumes of hymns and precepts are probably Psalms, Song of Songs, Proverbs, and Ecclesiastes. It seems preferable thus to count Ruth and Lamentations with Judges and Jeremiah respectively than to place them in the last group and omit altogether the Song of Songs and Ecclesiastes, on the grounds that they had not yet become canonical (Grätz); for such a theory is unsupported by subsequent lists.

It may be concluded, therefore, that the canon of the "Writings" had been determined by the time of Josephus. No attempt, however, to read them in the synagogue was made till a much later age, although they might have been used there for purposes of exposition. That twenty-four was regarded as the canonical number is shown by the use of the term the "Four and Twenty Books" (beside "the Law, the Prophets, and the Writings," the "Holy Writings," or even the "Writings" alone) by the later Jews as the usual designation of the O.T. Moreover, between the beginning of the first century B.C. and the end of the first century A.D. external wars and internal dissensions, both political and religious, make it unlikely that anything new was added to the canon, even though no formal act of ratification ever took place. It is, therefore, in the highest degree unlikely that any of the apocryphal books were ever included in the Hebrew Scriptures, so that the addition of the Epistle of Jeremiah and presumably of the Book of Baruch to it in Origen's canon can hardly be accepted as authoritative; even more improbable is the modern suggestion that Ecclesiasticus once found a place within the canon (Cheyne). Although, indeed, attempts may have been made to introduce 1 Maccabees and Ecclesiasticus into it, there seems to have been no real approach to success in either case; both were modern and both lacked the stamp of originality.

Final Ratification of the Canon. There remains, finally, the question whether the canon was ever formally ratified by the Jewish authorities. In answer to this it may at once be said that there is no scrap of evidence in support of the conjecture that its limits were finally fixed at an assembly in 66 A.D. (Grätz), and that nothing more substantial than a vague tradition underlies the theory that it was settled by the Pharisees soon after 70 A.D. (Wellhausen). Now, the polemic of the author of the Wisdom of Solomon, of which the date is still a matter of dispute, against the teaching of Ecclesiastes (Wisdom 2[1-22]) contains the first hint that doubts were felt about certain books on the grounds of their contents. The *Mishnáh*, which had been current orally for some time before it was committed to writing at the end of the second century A.D., bears later witness to feelings of uncertainty about several books—notably Ezekiel, Jonah, Proverbs, Song of Songs and Esther; but the reasons concern neither the date nor the authorship of any given work, but rest for the most part on points of trivial importance in the interpretation of the text. There is some evidence that many of these points were discussed and settled in the schools at Jamnia (Hebrew *Yabhneh*), a Jewish seat of learning near Jaffa. Here, it is recorded, there was held a council in 90 or 91 A.D., followed possibly by another in 118 A.D., at which a number of problems, principally of a practical nature, were discussed and settled. One or the other of these meetings, therefore, has been held to be the official occasion on which the Jewish authorities finally fixed the limits of the canon. The fact, however, is that the evidence for connecting the actual settling of the canon with either of these meetings is very slight. All that is definitely known, apparently, is that one Ben 'Azzai seems to state that the canonicity of the Song of Songs and of Ecclesiastes was decided by a Sanhedrin at Jamnia on the day on which Rabbān Gamaliel (a son of that doctor of the law named Gamaliel, at whose feet Paul was brought up) was deposed from the presidency. But, since problems of great practical importance are known to have been settled on the same day, it is difficult to see how there could then have been time for the discussion of vexed questions connected with the canon; further, although some of these difficulties were resolved at one or other of these meetings at Jamnia, others, especially those concerning Esther, Song of Songs, and Ecclesiastes, lingered on into the third century A.D. There is, therefore, reason seriously to doubt the view that the canon was finally settled at Jamnia.

The most that can be safely affirmed is that all the books eventually included in the canon had probably met with some sort of recognition, even if they had not already come to be regarded as canonical, by the end of the second century B.C.; consequently, the doubts about these works concern the revision of a canon already fixed rather than the admission to it of books about which there had been hitherto little more than a fairly general agreement. There are, indeed, no sure indications of the close of the canon at any time during the last century B.C. or the first century A.D. No portion of the O.T., therefore, it may be concluded, was ever formally canonized by any judicial or ecclesiastical authority; but the various books gradually made their way to universal acceptance in the synagogue, just as those of the N.T. came to be accepted in the church. In the disputes on the part of individuals or schools the process of canonization may be seen in operation. The formation of the canon was a work of unconscious selection, spread over a period of two or three centuries, not a deliberate act of judicial or ecclesiastical authority carried out on any single day. The intrinsic worth of the books so selected under divine guidance alone caused them to be recognized as authoritative Scriptures and needed no human agency to insure their veneration.

Literature: Briggs, *General Introduction to the Study of Holy Scripture;* Buhl, *Canon and Text of the O.T.;* Budde, *Encyclopedia Biblica*, article, "Canon of the O.T."; Green, *General Introduction to the O.T.—The Canon;* Ryle, *The Canon of the O.T.;* Woods, *Hastings' Dictionary of the Bible*, article, "Canon"; Wildeboer, *Die Entstehung des alttestamentlichen Kanons.*

THE TRANSMISSION OF THE OLD TESTAMENT

By Professor IRA M. PRICE

I. The Languages

Hebrew and Aramaic. The O.T. is written for the most part in a language which we call "Hebrew," though the term is not used in the book itself. The ancient Hebrews are said to have spoken "the Jewish language" (2 Kings 18[26, 28]). Isaiah designates it as "the language of Canaan" (Isa. 19[18]). In addition to the parts written in Hebrew, the O.T. contains smaller portions and fragments in another tongue, now named "Aramaic," formerly, "Chaldee." This for some centuries had been the language of northern Syria, western Mesopotamia, and southeastern Asia Minor, and was familiar to the educated and "traveled" officials in Isaiah's day, as seen from the narrative of the conference cited above. The portions of the O.T. written in Aramaic are Jer. 10[11] Dan. 2[4]–7[28] Ezra 4[8]–6[18] 7[12-26]; Aramaic words occur now and then throughout the O.T. (e.g., Gen. 31[47]), and are sometimes explained by an accompanying Hebrew word.

Besides Hebrew and Aramaic the O.T. contains isolated words in other languages, such as Egyptian: *abrech*, probably, "bow the knee," and *Zaphenath-paneah*, "Revealer of secrets" (Gen. 41[43, 45]); Amorite and Sidonian: *Senir* and *Sirion*, respectively (Deut. 3[9]); Daniel gives the Greek names of several instruments of music, and Esther contains some Persian terms. Officers of other nationalities than Hebrew usually carry their native titles when mentioned in the O.T. Several Babylonian and Sumerian words have also been recognized in recent years.

Semitic Languages. Hebrew and Aramaic belong to the Semitic family of languages, which is broken up into the north, middle, and south divisions. In the north division we find Assyrian (and Babylonian), Aramaic and Syriac; in the middle zone, Hebrew and Phœnician; in the south, Arabic, Ethiopic, and Amharic. Closely related to the Hebrew are the kindred tongues of the Moabites, Ammonites and Edomites, as also those of the Phœnicians, Canaanites and Amorites.

Peculiarities of Hebrew. Since Hebrew is a Semitic language it possesses the characteristics of that group of languages. All these languages resemble each other in the possession of a triliteral stem of verbal roots, the general structure of the verb system, likeness in methods of noun formation, the use of few particles, the lack of compounds, and the general use of prefixes and suffixes, instead of independent pronouns as in the Indo-European languages.

Hebrew also has another rather interesting peculiarity, namely, the absence of tenses in the strict sense of that term. The Hebrews looked upon acts simply as finished or unfinished, complete or incomplete, without any regard to time. The speaker or writer in imagination transported himself into the past, present, or future whence he viewed the actions taking place as complete or incomplete; and it is not always easy for the modern interpreter to put himself in the place of the ancient writer.

The Writing of Hebrew. The primitive form of Hebrew writing is known only from a few inscriptions of varying length belonging chiefly to the period of the dual monarchies. Mesha, king of Moab, set up about 850 B.C. the so-called "Moabite Stone," to celebrate his relief from the oppression of Omri and Ahab. This well-known monument found in 1868 on Moabite soil is written in a script practically identical with that of the original O.T. "The Hebrew-Inscribed Tablet of Gezer" carries seven lines of inscription of a slightly later form than that of the Mesha stone.

The Siloam inscription found in the mouth of the aqueduct leading into the pool of Siloam dates probably from the time of Hezekiah and preserves for us a still later form of the script. Some seals and a large number of potsherds found at Samaria by the Harvard excavations preserve proper names and other words in the primitive script of the same period. Phœnician inscriptions, few in number, also help to establish the character of the Hebrew alphabet current in the centuries of the monarchies.

Some time after the adoption of the Pentateuch by the Samaritan community, in the fourth or third century, B.C., appears gradually the change of the old Hebrew script into the square characters found in the MSS. and printed editions of the Hebrew Bible. The oldest inscription in square characters dates from 176 B.C., and was found in a cave near Heshbon.

The Hebrew language used by the O.T. writers had only twenty-two letters—all consonants; some of these can scarcely be represented by our English letters, or spoken by our vocal organs. In this respect again Hebrew is similar to Phœnician, to Moabite as it appears on the Mesha stone, and to ancient Arabic and Syriac. The pronunciation of such vowelless Hebrew words presented grave difficulties to the reader, since there are many words whose intended meaning could be radically changed by altering the vowels between consonants, without disturbing the latter in the least. Even in English we can appreciate the hazard in pronunciation involved in this system of writing; e.g., b(a)d, b(e)d, b(i)d, b(u)d, l(a)g, l(e)g, l(o)g, l(u)g. In the course of the ages the pronunciation of Hebrew began to slip away from the Jews; hence they took steps to hold it. Somewhere about the sixth or seventh century A.D., no one knows exactly when, the learned rabbis—the Massoretes—invented an ingenious and elaborate vowel system to preserve the traditional pronunciation of the Hebrew of the O.T. These vowel points were written not between but under, in, and over the hitherto vowelless consonants.

We now depend for our pronunciation of Hebrew on the Massoretic system of vowels, the transliterated Hebrew words in the Greek versions, and the names and words found in the cuneiform texts of Assyria and Babylonia. The Massoretic pointing naturally reflects the interpretation put upon the text by the inventors of the vowel system, which in some instances cannot be accepted as correct.

Changes in the Old Testament Languages. The Hebrew language occupied a place all its own in the history of Israel. While developed contiguous to other peoples and languages, it maintained a purity quite marvelous. Outside races, however, gradually edged their way into Israel's life, language, customs, and religion. The classical period of Hebrew writing, from the eighth to the fifth century B.C., gave way before the impact of the Aramaic sweep to the south. The later books of the O.T. are dotted with Aramaisms in vocabulary and syntax, revealing the weakness of the old defenses against the encroachments of foreign influences. These intrusions leave their precipitates in the Aramaic sections of Ezra and Daniel noted above, as well as in the general style of the post-exilic literature. The difference between the style of Kings and Chronicles is exactly the difference between the best type of literature of the classical period and the loose, less explicit style of the post-exilic era. When we think of the thousand years over which the languages of the O.T. stretched, we marvel at the comparatively few changes which appeared in that long period of time.

II. The Text

Early Oral Transmission. The Hebrew O.T. contains many primitive stories, fragments of poetry, everyday proverbs, and naïve expressions, which were carried down through generations by word of mouth. It is not improbable that the substance of the earlier books was transmitted for some time in the same manner. True, documents have been found in Babylonia and Egypt dating from long centuries before Abraham migrated from Ur of the Chaldees; but no mention is made of any writing by the patriarchs or anyone else in the book of Genesis. Moses doubtless learned in Egypt how to write, and several definite statements are made in the Pentateuch regarding that ability; and writing is presupposed in the last four books of the Pentateuch.

On the other hand, when we look for samples of the oldest Hebrew or Canaanitish writing we do not get far beyond about 1,000 B.C. In the fourteenth and fifteenth centuries B.C., the written language of Syria-Canaan was the cuneiform of Babylonia, as may be seen in the Tel-el-Amarna tablets, most of which represent letters from Syria and Palestine addressed to the kings of Egypt. Is it not reasonable to suppose that Babylonian was used probably because Canaan had no written language of its own at that date? If so, it may well be that Israel's earliest historical narratives, stories, legends, traditions, and scraps of poetry were transmitted orally down to about the year 1,000 B.C. Soon after that date, some of these materials, especially the poetry, groups of laws, and dramatic or tragic events, may have been put into writing; and these small beginnings mark the first steps in the composition of the O.T.

Earliest Writings Quoted. The writers of the books of the O.T. availed themselves of whatever sources were to be found. They used written documents at hand, oral transmissions found among their friends, personal experiences, anything their judgment approved. The first source book mentioned by an O.T. writer is "the book of the Wars of Jehovah," out of which the writer copied a snatch of poetry (Num. 21[14]); another early book quoted is "the book of Jashar," which the writer gives as his source for the poem describing the sun standing still (Josh. 10[13]); it is also given as the source of David's lament over Saul and Jonathan (2 Sam. 1[18]).

In addition to these incidental books called

by name, the writers of the earlier books of the O.T. employed some anonymous documents, two of them now named by scholars the "Judæan" (J), assigned to the early period of the dual monarchy, and the Ephraimitic (E), placed in the early eighth century (for the meaning of these symbols see art., *Pentateuch*, p. 137a). These documents may be traced by their style, vocabulary, theme and purpose through the Pentateuch and Joshua and, according to some, also through Samuel and Kings. Next came the prophets of the Assyrian period, Amos, Hosea, Isaiah, and Micah, followed by the seventh-century prophets and Deuteronomy.

Writers of the Old Testament. Who wrote the books of the O.T.? There is an occasional reference to writing, to secretaries, and to scribes. The Song of Deborah speaks of "the staff of the scribe" (Judg. 5[14], mg.). During the dual monarchy court officials, prophets, and kings are said to have recorded the events, decrees, and wisdom of their day. Samuel (1 Sam. 10[25]), David (2 Sam. 11[14]), Nathan the prophet, Gad the seer (1 Chr. 29[29]), and many others are said to have made records in writing. Immediately before, during, and after the Exile there were many who were able not only to record events, but also to compile history, arrange prophecies, and to select songs and psalms for the use of their own day and of succeeding generations.

The Hazards of Destruction. Every document written on papyrus or skin was always in danger of being lost or destroyed. To preserve it and to increase its usefulness it was laboriously copied by hand, time and time again. For convenience in handling the sheets were made into rolls. The ravages of war always endangered such perishable materials. There were a few events which threatened the very life of the precious Hebrew rolls. The first was the destruction of Jerusalem and its temple by Nebuchadrezzar in 586 B.C., although Ezekiel may have taken with him to Babylon, in 597 B.C., some parts of the O.T. When Antiochus Epiphanes (167 B.C.) issued a decree that all copies of the law should be destroyed (1 Macc. 1[56, 57]), his order did not include Babylonia, where Ezekiel and Ezra had been active during earlier centuries as teachers of their people, and where copies of O.T. books must have been extant, but many Palestinian copies undoubtedly disappeared forever during this crisis. (In Egypt also there must have been copies which served as the basis of the LXX translation.) The destruction of Jerusalem by Titus, in 70 A.D., also endangered the life of the O.T., which by that time was practically as extensive as it is now—for the Babylonian Talmud says that Titus destroyed copies of the law. In these perils probably many copies of the O.T. as well as the sources from which some of the books were compiled perished. Of books or rolls mentioned or quoted in various parts of the O.T. twenty-four have not survived.

The Hazards of Corruption. The plain unpointed text (see below, section on "Oldest MSS.") of the earliest copies of the O.T. were written in the script of the Moabite Stone. On this stone and in the Siloam inscription the words are separated by a small dot. The same dot is found between words in the Samaritan Pentateuch. When the square characters (the characters found in the printed Hebrew Bibles) were adopted this dot seems to have fallen out. This has resulted in some cases in the contraction of two adjacent words into one; in others, in the division of consonants intended to form one word, so that they appear as two.

The multiplication of copies of books by the pen of man created the possibility of errors. (If this is not self-evident, try to make an exact copy of ten pages of any written or printed document, and see how many simple and aggravating errors you will make.) To add to the hazards of error we must remember that the MSS. had neither verse, chapter, nor clearly marked paragraph divisions. Even the psalms were not separated, as we learn from the disagreement in the numberings in the Hebrew Bible as compared with the LXX. Thus, the copyist had both a difficult and a precarious task before him.

Origin of Variations in the Text. Copyists appear to have made two kinds of errors—intentional and unintentional. Intentional changes may be attributed to a desire (1) to correct some manifest error in statement, or a slip of a preceding copyist; (2) to use a euphemistic word or phrase in place of a coarse or indelicate one found in the text, this latter being usually consigned to the margin; and (3) to bring a statement into harmony with the theological ideas of the copyist or his age.

But the largest number of variations may be classed as unintentional. Scholars have practically agreed on a reasonable classification of these and of the sources from which they have come as follows:

(1) Failure to see the true sense of a passage has led to incorrect division of groups of consonants; as in Psa. 73[4], "For there are no pangs (mg.) in their death; but their strength is firm." By dividing the word translated "in their death," we may translate, "For they have no pangs; sound and firm is their strength"—a sense that suits both context and parallelism.

(2) Errors chargeable to the eye: (a) Repetitions: in Lev. 20[10], omit the five words repeated; 1 Chr. 9[35-44] has been repeated from 1 Chr. 8[29-38]. (b) Omissions: Prov. 10[10b], "He that rebuketh boldly is a peacemaker" (LXX). (c) Transposition of letters or words: 2 Chr. 3[4] says the porch of the temple was one hundred twenty cubits high; the LXX reads twenty cubits, and the Hebrew by a simple transposition of two letters and two words may be made to read twenty cubits, which is doubtless correct. Many cases are found where the copyist took one letter for another; for instance, "Nebuchadrezzar," the only correct reading, often appears as "Nebuchadnezzar," due to the mistaking of a Hebrew *n* (נ) for an *r* (ר). The same kind of error is seen in "Hadarezer," read for "Hadadezer," mistaking the Hebrew *d* (ד) for an *r* (ר).

(3) Errors chargeable to the ear: When a person read aloud to a copyist, the latter might easily write one Hebrew word for another of almost or exactly the same sound. A good example appears in Psa. 100[3], where "and not we ourselves" (A.V.), should be read "and we are his" (R.V.).

(4) Errors of memory: A copyist might carry in his mind the thought rather than the exact words of what he was copying. He might in this case use a synonym or nearly such in place of the word found in the original. Jer. 27[1] contains "Jehoiakim," where the context (v. 3) requires "Zedekiah" (cf. mg.).

(5) Errors chargeable to carelessness or ignorance: This is a numerous class. In 1 Sam. 13[1] we find: "Saul was ——years old when he began to reign"; some copyist neglected to write the number; 1 Sam. 12[11] reads "Bedan" where the Versions and the original in Judg. 4 has "Barak."

These classes of errors were copied from MS. to MS., together with new ones made by each succeeding scribe, until the whole text was finally put into printed copies in the fifteenth century. As a check on the continuous multiplication of errors the scribes counted the verses (even though they were not yet formally numbered), and even the letters in the different books, making note of the middle verse, the middle word, and the middle letter of each book. These numbers are found at the end of each book of our Hebrew Bible to-day. The middle verse of the Pentateuch is Lev. 8[7]; of Joshua it is 13[26]. The middle verse of the Hebrew O.T. is Jer. 6[7]. When a scribe had finished his work his count must tally with the established numbers; if it failed in this, he was required either to correct his copy or to discard it. But even with such care errors crept in.

III. Hebrew Manuscripts and Printed Editions of the Old Testament

Oldest Manuscripts. Hebrew MSS. of the O.T. are comparatively modern. The oldest one dated is of the Prophets, now in Petrograd (=Leningrad), which bears a date equivalent to 916 A.D.; it consists of two hundred and twenty-five folios, each of two columns of twenty-one lines, and contains Isaiah, Jeremiah, Ezekiel and The Twelve. Ginsburg located in the British Museum a MS. of the Pentateuch (Orient. No. 4445), which he is inclined to date "at least half a century earlier." This has one hundred and eighty-six folios, fifty-five of which were added in 1540 A.D. Every page carries three columns of twenty-one lines each, the *Massorah magna* occupying the space above and below the columns, and the *Massorah parva* the space on the side margins (see paragraph below on "Massorah").

The oldest MS. of the entire O.T. is one of the famous Firkowitzsch collection, dated 1010 A.D., though the correctness of this date is doubted by some investigators. There are very few MSS. of the whole O.T.; though fragmentary MSS. are numerous—about 1700.

Resemblance of All Manuscripts. Why do all existing Hebrew MSS. so closely resemble each other? Scholars have concluded that long before the invention of the Massoretic system of vowels, Hebrew MSS. were reduced to one type; every subsequent copy being made to conform to that model. Divergent MSS. soon disappeared from usage or were deliberately destroyed. This standard text is called the text of the *Sopherim*, i.e., of the scribes. The fixing of the official text followed soon after the final decision regarding the contents of the O.T. canon (cf art., *The Formation of the O.T.* pp. 97–8), i.e., in the second century A.D. At about the same time even the text came to be regarded as sacred; hence greater care was exercised in the copying of it; which accounts for the presence of so few variants. Another protecting factor was the introduction of the vowel points, which by fixing permanently the pronunciation helped to stabilize the text itself.

The Massorah. The Massorah ("Tradition") consists of the notes written on the margins of codices by the Tiberian scribes (Tiberias became a center of Jewish learning after the fall of Jerusalem) during the centuries between the reduction of the texts to a single type and the date of the oldest known MSS. These notes take into account peculiar and abnormal words, letters, spelling, pronunciation, vocalization, with such mechanical notations as the number of letters, words, sentences in each document. They also noted supposed errors in reading, and on the margin put what they conceived to be the correct form. In short, the margin of all codices became a kind of running commentary on all items in the text that required special attention.

Printed Editions of the Hebrew Bible. The first complete edition of the Hebrew O.T. based on the Tiberian system of vowel points (the scholars in the Babylonian centers of Judaism used a different system) appeared at Soncino in 1488 A.D. It next appeared at Naples in 1491–93. The third edition—the Brescia Bible—was issued in 1494, the text later used by Luther. A fourth edition came out at Pesaro in 1511–17. These four editions appeared under Jewish authorship, and were based on a direct collation of MSS. which gave them a text-critical value. The chief rabbinic Bible issued in those early years of printing was edited by Jacob ben Chayyim, and published by Daniel Bomberg at Venice 1524–25 in four folio volumes. It represented the standard text of the Tiberian school and has become the "Textus Receptus" of the Hebrew Bible for modern times.

The first edition of the Hebrew Bible to be printed under Christian influence and authority is found in the so-called Complutensian Polyglot; which carries in parallel columns the Hebrew text, the LXX, the Vulgate, and the Aramaic paraphrase (or Targum of Onkelos) of the Pentateuch. It was edited by Cardinal Ximenes and printed at the University founded by him at Alcala (Latin, *Complutum*), Spain, 1514–17 A.D. The critical value of this first polyglot is slight. Since then many new editions have been printed, some of them based on patient study and investigation; until the printed Bibles now in circulation furnish the best available reproduction of the Massoretic text. The Hebrew Bible to-day is divided into chapters and verses. The former are based on the Vulgate, in which they were introduced in the thirteenth century; the work is credited to several notable scholars, but none of the traditions can be verified. The first Hebrew text, published by itself, to insert chapter numbers appeared in 1573–74; though they are found in the Complutensian Polyglot published half a century earlier.

Collections of Variants. The immediate result of the printing of so many editions of the Hebrew Bible, based on the readings of many MSS., was uncertainty and confusion as to the true readings of the original text. The solution of this problem was found in collecting and comparing these variants, and culling from them what in the light of all the evidence might be accepted as the most probable reading. Passing over earlier efforts of this kind, mention should be made of the first great collector and publisher of these variants, namely, Kennicott, an Englishman, who collected and published, in 1776–80, in two folio volumes the variant readings of 694 MSS. and of a great number of editions. A little later De Rossi, professor at Parma, Italy, collected the variants of 732 MSS. and 310 editions, of which Kennicott had seen only 80. In 1784–88 he published four volumes in quarto, and in 1798 a supplemental volume. These two scholars together compared 1,346 different Hebrew MSS. and 342 reported editions, or a total of 1,688 different texts. The real and conclusive outcome of this tremendous task was the establishment of the fact that the basal Hebrew text of all the examined MSS. was practically one and the same, namely, the official text fixed during the second or third century A.D.

IV. The Versions

The Samaritan Pentateuch. This text of the Pentateuch is not a translation of the original Hebrew, and hence cannot be called a version. It is, rather, an independent Hebrew text, written in the Hebrew characters extant before the adoption of the square letters. Its chief value is found in its independent transmissions of the Hebrew text from the time of the Samaritan schism, about 400 B.C. Its variations from the Massoretic text have been carefully collated and amount in all to about 6,000 items, only about 1,000 of which, however, have any significance in textual work. Some of these variants, however, are so important that no commentator on the pentateuchal books can afford to disregard them, and no textual critic would venture to omit them. The oldest MS. of the Samaritan Pentateuch is not thought to be older than the tenth century A.D., though the claims of the Samaritans at Nablous, the only extant colony of Samaritans, reach back to the conquest of Canaan.

The Greek Bible: The Septuagint (LXX). The founding and growth of Alexandria, subsequently to the conquest of the Near East by Alexander the Great, the settlement there of a large Jewish colony and the smothering effect on the Jews of the Greek language, religion and culture, created a demand for a translation of the Jewish sacred writings into Greek. The Jews, with the co-operation of Ptolemy Philadelphus (285–247 B.C.), undertook the task of at least beginning a translation of the Hebrew Bible. The books were translated at different times by men unequally prepared for the task, the whole process extending over a period of approximately two hundred years, from about 250 to about 50 B.C.

The translation of the Law was in the nature of an official translation, and was made with considerable care. In the other portions the translators took some liberties with the text itself and with the arrangement of the material; e.g., after Jer. 25[13] they inserted chs. 46–51 rearranged in an order to suit their own opinions; the Hebrew order is resumed beginning with 25[15]. Most of the liberties taken with the Hebrew text may be explained by the purpose which the translators had in view. The plan was so to present the Hebrew Bible in Greek dress as to make it acceptable to the Greek-speaking Jews of that day. For this end fidelity to sense was emphasized rather than a stiff literal rendering of the original; hence the translators felt free to make slight changes or additions to round out the sentences or to reproduce figurative expressions by more easily understood words.

Moreover, due perhaps to pressure exerted by the more liberally minded Jews of Alexandria, the translators added to the collection a number of books not recognized as sacred by the Palestinian Jews (see art., *Intertestamental Literature*, p. 187, and art., *Formation of the O.T.*, pp. 97–8).

Although the oldest Hebrew MS. dates from the tenth century, there are numerous earlier Greek MSS. of the LXX. The earliest and most important of these are: (1) The oldest and most complete (covering the whole Bible), is the Codex Vaticanus ("B" in catalogues), in the Vatican library in Rome—of the fourth century; (2) the next in value is Codex Alexandrinus ("A" in catalogues) in the British Museum—of the first half of the fifth century; (3) Codex Sinaiticus ("א"), as old as "B" but fragmentary, in Petrograd or Leningrad; (4) Codex Ephræmi ("C") of the fifth century, a palimpsest, in Bibliothèque Nationale in Paris. (See art., *Transmission of the N.T.*, p. 862.)

The first printed copy of the LXX appeared in the Complutensian Polyglot. Swete's three volume edition (1887–94) of the LXX has been standard since its appearance, though the new Cambridge edition by Brooke and McLean records a much larger amount of material for critical study.

Rival Greek Bibles. The adoption of the LXX by the Christians of the first century prejudiced its value for the Jews of that age. Several rivals appeared, each claiming to be the most accurate rendering of the Hebrew. (1) The first response to a call for a new translation was made by *Aquila*, a proselyte to Judaism in Pontus, Asia Minor, about the middle of the second century. His translation is known to have been in use in 177 A.D. To satisfy the demand for an absolutely accurate translation he made his renderings slavishly literal, trying to translate every word and particle, regardless of sense, the requirements of the Greek language, or the expression of clear thought. Nevertheless, the translation of Aquila became the official Jewish Greek version of the O.T.

(2) The Christians of the second century resented such a rival translation; and a new translator, an Ebionite Christian of Pontus, or of Ephesus, bearing the name *Theodotion*, came to the front. His translation appeared about 180–192 A.D. in the reign of Commodus. Though based on the Hebrew text, it is in reality a revision of the LXX, showing many improvements over the original LXX, and expressing itself in much more correct and idiomatic Greek. The work was so well done that its Daniel has displaced the original LXX translation of that book in the extant Greek version; Theodotion also filled up the gaps in the LXX text of Job.

(3) The third great Greek translator was *Symmachus*, an Ebionite. His activity falls in the reign of Severus (193–211 A.D.). His version displays remarkable fidelity to the original Hebrew, uses clear and idiomatic Greek, and reveals keen appreciation of literary form. The excellence of the translation aroused the admiration of Jerome, who said of the three rivals: "Aquila translates word for word, Symmachus follows the sense, and Theodotion differs slightly from the LXX."

Origen and His Hexapla. The greatest biblical scholar of the early Christian centuries was Origen, born at Alexandria in 186 A.D., who laid the foundation of historical biblical study. When he entered upon his task he found the O.T. in Hebrew, the LXX, and the three versions mentioned in the preceding paragraph. As a result of somewhat close study he came to the conclusion that "every MS. differs from every other MS." He then conceived the idea of making a comparative study of the different versions and MSS., in order to find the one best MS. or version. To accomplish this, for himself and other biblical scholars, he planned a monumental work, called "The Hexapla" (i.e., the "sixfold" book), upon which he spent twenty-eight years of his life. In this he arranged in six parallel columns (1) the Hebrew text of the O.T., (2) the same Hebrew text in Greek letters, (3) the Greek translation of Aquila, (4) the Greek translation of Symmachus, (5) the LXX, with his own revision, (6) the Greek translation of Theodotion.

The purpose of the *Hexapla* was to make available a Greek text that would properly represent the original Hebrew. Origen's *Hexapla* has survived only in fragments here and there in works of ancient writers, or on the margins of MSS. The original MS. was seen in the library of Cæsarea at the beginning of the seventh century, where at an earlier time Jerome consulted it. Bishop Paul of Tella translated the fifth column, Origen's revision of the LXX, into Syriac, 617–618 A.D.

Origen's work, in turn, inspired three great scholars of the third century: (1) Eusebius of Cæsarea (260–340), (2) Lucian of Samosata (martyred 311), and (3) Hesychius in Egypt. These three furnished Greek revisions for all the east coast of the Mediterranean Sea, Eusebius for Palestine, Lucian for Asia Minor, and Hesychius for Egypt. These three revisions, however, never superseded the LXX; they give us, however, valuable critical material for approaching the original text of that version, and for determining the true reading of some difficult passages in the Hebrew O.T.

Latin Bibles: the Vulgate. While Greek was the prevailing language of the Christian Church down into the third century, the dominance of Rome gradually crowded it out of official use. Latin became so prevalent, especially in North Africa, that demands arose for the translation of the Bible into Latin. The earliest Latin translations are commonly called "Old Latin," the O.T. being a translation of the LXX, not of the original Hebrew. In course of time revisions were made on the basis of the best Greek texts available. At the request of Pope Damasus, Jerome, the most distinguished biblical scholar of that day, undertook one of these revisions—that of the Old Latin Psalter. His experience soon convinced him that he could accomplish better results by translating directly from Hebrew into Latin than by attempting a revision. A careful study of Hebrew under competent Jewish teachers, and a first-hand acquaintance with the topography of Palestine, gave him a background for the task. From about 390 to 404 he worked assiduously at Bethlehem and translated the entire O.T. from Hebrew into Latin. He also put into Latin the apocryphal sections of Daniel and Esther, and the apocryphal books of Tobit and Judith.

Jerome's translations were bitterly assailed on account of his elimination of well-worn words and phrases that appeared in the Old Latin; and he was so deeply affected by these criticisms that he died a broken-hearted man. During the next three centuries, however, the translation gradually gained recognition on the part of the church Fathers until it became the leader among the Latin versions of the O.T., a position which it has maintained to the present time. (See further on Latin Bibles, the Syriac Bible, and other Versions, art., *Transmission of the N.T.*, pp. 864–5.)

V. Textual Criticism

The Problem. In the preceding discussion attention has been called, among other things, to the fact that following the establishment of the O.T. canon and the fixing of the official text considerable care was exercised in the transmission of this text. But there is no evidence of similar care during the period between the writing of the autographs and the final determination of the text and its pronunciation; on the contrary, there is much internal evidence to show that much liberty was taken with the text. True, Philo asserts that the Jews never altered a word written by Moses, and Josephus maintains that nothing was added to the text of Scripture or taken therefrom, but it has long been recognized that these, like other Jewish traditions, cannot be accepted at face value. There is, of course, little to support the charge that the Jews corrupted the text willfully, from dishonest and polemical motives; but when we consider the abundance of possible sources of alterations or errors it is readily seen that changes may have been introduced unintentionally or from motives not dishonest (see above on "Origin of Variations").

The belief that even the earliest Hebrew MSS. present a text which cannot be considered an exact reproduction of the autographs is based upon considerations like these: (1) The O.T. contains passages in which the Hebrew text as it stands cannot be translated without violence to the laws of grammar, or which are irreconcilable with the context or with older passages (e.g., 1 Sam. 13[1]; cf. A.V. with R.V.). (2) Parallel passages found in more than one book differ in such a manner as to make it clear that the variations are due largely to textual corruption in the course of transmission (cf. 2 Sam. 22 with Psa. 18). (3) The ancient versions, some of which were made before the fixing of the official text, contain various readings which often bear a strong stamp of probability and remove, or lessen, the difficulties of the Hebrew text (see in R.V. footnote to Psa. 22[16c]).

Most of these changes from the original are due to accident; others, however, are in the nature of intentional alterations (see above). There seems to have been a time when the letter of the sacred books was thought of less importance than the spirit, when the words were not regarded as so sacred that to alter them would be sacrilege. If an expression seemed likely to cause misconception, or sounded irreverent, there was no hesitation about altering it; and even when the text as a whole was regarded as sacred, the early scribes believed that its sacredness would be preserved better by removing the offending expressions than by superstitious regard for the mere letter.

Considering all these facts it is vain to deny the existence of errors even in the oldest MSS. now in existence. To discover and, insofar as possible, to remove these errors is the task of the textual critic; for textual criticism may be defined as the effort to remove from a literary production all textual errors and blemishes and to restore the *ipsissima verba* of the author. In the case of the O.T. the problem is complicated by the fact that the available MSS. represent not the text of the autographs but a text fixed several centuries after the books were written. This means that the ordinary methods of textual criticism, the comparison of MSS., would take us not to the autographs themselves but to a text upon which the noncritical judgment of the scribes settled some time after the opening of the Christian era. Surely, the textual critic cannot be called too ambitious if he sets as his goal the restoration of the earliest reading attainable, which is the text of the autographs. The material on hand may not be sufficient to enable the critic to retrace the exact steps of transmission, and thus to remove the errors in the order in which they crept in; moreover, the restoration of the autograph text may never be more than approximate, the degree of approximation being determined by the amount of available evidence; nevertheless, to stop at a certain amount of correction when the material is not exhausted is to be unfaithful to an opportunity.

Method of Textual Criticism. How, then, may the original text of O.T. books, or at least an approximation to such text, be secured. For reasons already stated it cannot be done simply by a comparison of MSS., as in the case of the N.T. or of the classical writings. May we depend upon conjecture? Now, undoubtedly, conjectural emendation has its place; but it ought to be the last resort of the critic, to be employed only in cases of necessity. How easy it would be for the critic to impress upon his emendations the stamp of his own prejudices, to say what he thinks the author ought to have written rather than what he actually wrote! Surely, conjecture is a dangerous tool, an edged tool, with which, the proverb says, children and fools must not play. Many dark passages have, indeed, been illuminated by conjecture, but one cannot and must not depend upon it entirely or exclusively.

While Hebrew MSS. are of little value in attempting to restore the original text, and while conjectural emendation cannot always be relied upon, the critic has access to a valuable apparatus in certain recensions of the O.T. books which contain texts nearer in point of time to the autographs than the official text fixed in the second century A.D. These are the recensions preserved in the ancient translations, some of which were made earlier than the fixing of the official text, while others, though produced later, evidently had access to MSS. not affected by the official text. The four translations of greatest value for purposes of textual criticism have received attention in the section on "Versions" in this article cf. also art., *Transmission of the N.T.* (pp. 864–5). They are the Greek translation called the Septuagint (LXX), the Aramaic translation or translations known as the Targum or Targums, the Syriac translation commonly called the Peshitta, and the Latin translation of Jerome, the Vulgate. Other Greek translations made from the original Hebrew, those of Aquila, Theodotion and Symmachus, insofar as they are preserved, make valuable contributions. Some help is given by some ancient translations based chiefly on the LXX, but in the consultation of these the critic must always bear in mind that they are not derived directly from the Hebrew. Their chief value lies in the fact that they enable us to determine with greater accuracy the text of the LXX.

The use of the ancient versions for purposes of textual criticism is not without its difficulties: (1) Sometimes the text has not been transmitted in its original purity; the translations have suffered in transmission as much as has the original Hebrew text; (2) different parts of an ancient translation were translated by different men; some appear to be accurate and literal reproductions, while others give evidence of much freedom and even carelessness; at times it is not easy to determine the Hebrew text underlying the translation. Consequently, before using the translation for purposes of textual criticism the critic must reasonably assure himself that he possesses the translation in its original purity. Having done this, he must eliminate such variants as have the appearance of originating with the translators (some variants may be traced to difference in idiom; others to a desire to make rough places smooth; still others to certain theological tendencies of the age in which the translation was made). The remaining variations will be due to difference of text in the MS. or MSS. used by the translator or translators. These the critic must compare carefully with the text in the existing Hebrew MSS., in order to determine on which side the superiority lies. For many years scholars have labored on this difficult and somewhat tedious task and as a result of these patient and painstaking labors we are to-day in possession of a text of the Hebrew Bible that is far superior to the text embodied in the Hebrew MSS. or in the printed editions of the Hebrew Bible.

The Essential Trustworthiness of the Transmitted Text. The foregoing discussion reveals the fact that it is not possible to trace with absolute accuracy the successive stages in the transmission of the O.T. Evidently the earlier copyists were not as painstaking as were those of the period following the fixing of the official text. As a result not only have accidental changes crept into the text, but even intentional alterations were made. But while the presence of errors and intentional changes must be recognized, the biblical student should not feel unduly disturbed by the uncertainties and obscurities presented in the available MSS. (1) Numerous as are the deviations from the original, they are not more so than might be expected in a book that was handed down by copyists for so many centuries. (2) The changes from the text of the autographs do not affect the fundamental thought or teaching of the O.T. books; the reader may rest content that by studying the text reproduced in the English translations he gets close to the heart of the biblical message. (3) The task of the textual critic is not an easy one. But as a result of the patient labors of experts we have to-day a much more accurate Hebrew text than was available for any preceding generation. And we may turn to the study of this text in the full assurance that if we use the right method in the right spirit we may come to understand and appreciate the words written by holy men of God, as they were moved by the Holy Spirit.

Literature: Buhl, *Canon and Text of the O.T.;* Geden, *Outlines of an Introduction to the Hebrew Bible;* Green, *General Introduction to the O.T.—the Text;* Kenyon, *Our Bible and the Ancient Manuscripts;* Price, *The Ancestry of our English Bible;* Weir, *A Short History of the Hebrew Text of the O.T.*

THE CHRONOLOGY OF THE OLD TESTAMENT

By Professor ELMER A. LESLIE

The limits of space for this discussion demand that we restrict ourselves to results rather than to processes, for few subjects bristle with more difficulties than does this. For a compact and discriminating statement of the processes by which these results are obtained consult *The Cambridge Ancient History*, vol. i, ch. 4.

The Assyrian inscriptions furnish the following fixed dates:

854 B.C. The Battle at Qarqar or Karkar (Ahab participating).

842 B.C. Jehu's tribute to Shalmaneser III.

738 B.C. Menahem of Israel tributary to Assyria.

734 B.C. The Syro-Ephraimitic War.

722 B.C. The Fall of Samaria.

701 B.C. The Invasion of Judah by Sennacherib.

These form fixed points from which the chronologically less reliable biblical data may be approached.

This article presents: (1) The significant events in Hebrew history in chronological order, following a fair degree of consensus of scholarly opinion. (2) A synchronizing of Hebrew history with that of contemporary related peoples. (3) The various portions of the O.T. literature dated approximately and connected chronologically with the era from which they come.

Semitic Origins. The cradle and spreading center of the various Semitic peoples was the vast Arabian Desert in Western Asia, which is regarded by some scholars also as the original Semitic home. From this as a center in periodic migrations, layer after layer of Semites have deposited themselves in Egypt, Mesopotamia, Syria, and Palestine.

(1) In prehistoric times, in an epoch that lies beyond the remotest horizon of history, Semites entered the Nile Valley and mingled with the population already there, impressing their language upon the region.

(2) The first migration of historic times is the Akkadian, which began in the 5th or 4th millennium B.C. (Kraeling). These Semites migrated into the Tigris-Euphrates Valley and drove out and assimilated the Sumerians, taking over their cuneiform script. They became the peaceful Babylonians, and later the military Assyrians who sprang from them (becoming independent before 1400 B.C.).

(3) Probably in the third millennium B.C. the Hittites (non-Semites, *Khatti*, *Kheta*, *Heth*—earliest written record from annals of Babylonian king Samsu-ditana, whose reign ended 1924 B.C., according to Barton) established kingdoms at Mitanni, Boghaz Keni, Carchemish, Hamath, and elsewhere. For a time they ruled Babylon.

(4) About 3000–2500 B.C. came the Amorites (possibly so called from the Babylonian city, Amurru). Driving out the non-Semitic cave-dwellers of Palestine and strengthened by later forces, they set up the first dynasty of Babylon (2210–1924 B.C.), thus ending the period of Babylonian city kingdoms (Ur, Erech, Lagash, Nippur, Agade). Hammurabi, the greatest king of this dynasty (2130–2088 B.C., so Ungnad) gave to Babylonia the famous Hammurabi code of laws with which later Hebrew law has points of contact. If the Amraphel of Gen. 14⁹ is to be identified with Hammurabi, Abraham would be a contemporary of Hammurabi. But this identification is precarious.

(5) Between 1800 and 1750 B.C. the non-Semitic Kassites from the region east of the Tigris invaded Babylonia and founded the third Babylonian dynasty.

(6) Contemporary with them came the Canaanite migration. They settled chiefly along the Mediterranean and in the region east of the Jordan.

(7) In the early 17th century B.C. came the Aramæan migration into Mesopotamia. Out of this was to come later the vigorous Aram. Probably the biblical narrative of Terah's journey from Ur-Kasdim (Gen. 11) reflects this migration. Cf. Amos 9⁷, Kir = Uru (Sumerian); thus Amos 9⁷ supports Gen. 11³¹ (Kraeling).

(8) In 1680 B.C., the Hyksos, "the shepherd kings," probably Semites, secured control of Egypt.

(9) The middle of the 17th century B.C., when Egypt was occupied by the Hyksos, is the most suitable time for the Aramæan migration of the Hebrews, under Abraham, which brought to Palestine ancestors of the Israelites, Ammonites, and Moabites.

(10) These settlers were re-enforced by an-

other Aramæan branch later in the seventeenth century B.C. This is reflected in the Jacob narratives. This included the Edomites.

(11) While the Hyksos were still on the throne of Egypt (so Breasted) in the late years of their rule, the Rachel tribes migrated to Goshen, as is reflected in the Joseph stories.

(12) The Aramæan migrations reflected in the narratives of Terah, Abraham, and Jacob are forerunners (C. Noyes) of the Habiru, Semites who invaded Palestine in the 14th century when Egypt's control had weakened. (Cf. Tel-el-Amarna tablets; see p. 251b).

Israel in Egypt. Israelite tribes were in Goshen, on the eastern border of Egypt, probably during the brilliant 18th and 19th dynasties. The important kings and achievements of this period follow:

Ahmose I, 1580–1557 B.C., expelled the Hyksos.

Thutmose III, 1501–1447 B.C., conquered and compactly organized Palestine, Phœnicia and Syria into an empire. Jacob-el and Joseph-el appear in his geographical lists as Palestinian place names.

Amenhotep III, 1411–1375 B.C. Under him the power of Egypt was at its height.

Amenhotep IV (Ikhnaton) 1375–1358 B.C. Under Ikhnaton and his predecessor the Tel-el-Amarna correspondence took place. He was a brilliant idealist who attempted a monotheistic (pantheistic) reform. Breasted calls him the first individual and the first idealist of the world.

Rameses II, 1292–1225 B.C. The Pharaoh of the oppression. He built Ramses and Pithom (Ex. 1^{11}). In 1272 B.C., he made a formal treaty with the Hittites. Cf. *Cambridge Ancient History*, vol. ii, pp. 149f.

Merneptah, 1225–1215 B.C. The Pharaoh of the Exodus. In 1223 B.C. he quelled the revolt of Asia against him and engraved upon a granite stela a hymn of victory in which occurs the name "Israel" as the name of a people. Until recently it was the only known place outside the O.T. where the name Israel occurred. It has been shown by Scheil, however, that the name occurs as a personal name, "Israel, son of Rishzuni," on a Babylonian seal cylinder from before 2600 B.C. (Cf. Barton, *Archæology and the Bible*, p. 326). The name in the Merneptah inscription is, however, the first extra-biblical appearance of "Israel" as the name of a people. It proves that only a part of Israel sojourned in Egypt. The Exodus under Moses occurred about 1220 B.C.

Table of Dates. The following tables connect the O.T. literature with important contemporary events. The dates are all B.C. A comparison, however, with dates suggested in the commentaries in the present volume on the historical books and on the prophets will show that on some of these dates there is still a difference of scholarly opinion.

First Period: 1200–1013 B.C.

ISRAEL (BEFORE THE DIVISION), THROUGH THE REIGN OF SAUL

1200–1028 Period of Invasion and Conquest.
1150 Battle of Barak against Canaanites under Sisera.
1155–1080 Eli.
1100 Gideon and Abimelech.
1100–1020 Samuel.
1080–1028 Philistine domination.
1065–1013 Saul.
1028–1013 Saul's reign.

OTHER NATIONS

1194 Settlement of the Philistines in Palestine.
1100 Report of Wen-amon (Barton, *op. cit.*, pp. 410f).

FRAGMENTS OF O.T. LITERATURE BEFORE 1000 B.C.

Song of Lamech, Gen. 4^{23-24}.
Song of Miriam, Ex. 15^{21}.
The Ritual of the Ark, Num. 10^{35f}.
The Oath Concerning Amalek, Ex. 17^{16}.
The Song of Satire on the Amorites, Num. 21^{27-30}.
The Song of the Well, Num. 21^{17f}.
A Fragmentary Station List from the Book of the Wars of Jehovah, Num. 21^{14f}.
A Fragment from the Book of Jashar, Josh. 10^{12f}.
The Song of Deborah, Judg. 5.
A Proverb "of the ancients" quoted by David, 1 Sam. 24^{13}.
Two Riddles and a Triumph Song of Samson, Judg. $14^{14, 18}$ 15^{16}.
The Fable of Jotham, Judg. 9^{7-15}.
The Curse and Blessing of Noah, Gen. 9^{25-27}.
The Blessing (a summary of tribal history) of Jacob, Gen. 49.
The Oracles of Balaam, the Seer, Num. 23, 24.

Second Period: 1013–933 B.C.

ISRAEL (BEFORE THE DIVISION), THROUGH THE REIGN OF SOLOMON

1050–973 David.
1013–973 David's reign.
973–933 Solomon's reign.

OTHER NATIONS

1000 The Aramæan occupation of Syria.
969–936 Hiram of Tyre.
950 Rezin founded the Aramæan kingdom of Damascus. His successors Hezion, Tabrimmon.

FRAGMENTS OF O.T. LITERATURE FROM THE TIMES OF DAVID AND SOLOMON

A song celebrating the prowess of David, 1 Sam. 18[7] 21[11] 29[5].
The Benjamite Battle Cry, 2 Sam. 20[1].
David's Lament over Saul and Jonathan, 2 Sam. 1[19-27].
David's Lament over Abner, 2 Sam. 3[33f].
The Parable of Nathan, 2 Sam. 12[1-4].
The Blessing (a summary of tribal history) of Moses, Deut. 33.
The Book of the Wars of Jehovah.
The Book of Jashar (of the Valiant?).
The early strand of narrative in Samuel (1 Sam. 9, etc.).
The Court History of David, 2 Sam. 9–1 Kings 2.
The Book of the Acts of Solomon.
The kernel of the Temple narratives.
The Code of the Covenant, Ex. 20[23]–23[19].
The so-called "J" Decalogue, Ex. 34.

Third Period: 933–843 B.C.

ISRAEL (THE NORTHERN KINGDOM) FROM JEROBOAM I TO THE REVOLUTION OF JEHU

933–912 Jeroboam I.
912–911 Nadab.
911–888 Baasha.
888–887 Elah.
887 Zimri.
887–876 Omri.
880 Omri conquered Moab.
876–854 Ahab. Prophetic activity of Elijah.
858, 857, 854 Three wars with the Aramæans.
854 Ahab allied with Benhadad II of Damascus against Shalmaneser in the battle of Qarqar (Karkar).
854–853 Ahaziah.
853–842 Joram. Wars against Benhadad II of Syria.
850 Mesha throws off the Israelite yoke (Inscription of Mesha).
850 Prophetic activity of Elisha.

JUDAH (THE SOUTHERN KINGDOM) FROM REHOBOAM'S ACCESSION TO 843 B.C.

933–917 Rehoboam.
917–915 Abijam.
915–875 Asa.
875–851 Jehoshaphat.
851–844 Joram.
844–843 Ahaziah.

OTHER NATIONS

954–924 Sheshonk I (Shishak) of Egypt, campaign against Israel and Judah.
900 Benhadad I of Damascus conducts war against Israel.
884–860 Ashurnazirpal of Assyria approaches Hebrew territory.
859–825 Shalmaneser III of Assyria.
849 and 846 Campaign against Damascus and allies.
845 Hazael of Damascus wars against Israel.

O.T. LITERATURE OF THE NINTH CENTURY B.C.

The kernel of the Elijah narratives, 1 Kings 17–19, 21, 2 Kings 1, 2.
The kernel of the Elisha narratives, 2 Kings 2–8 13[14-21].
The revolution of Jehu, 2 Kings 9, 10.
Chronicles of the Kings of Israel, similar to the Book of the Acts of Solomon.
Chronicles of the Kings of Judah, similar to the Book of the Acts of Solomon.
The J Document, about 850 B.C.

Fourth Period: 843–722 B.C.

ISRAEL (THE NORTHERN KINGDOM) FROM JEHU TO THE FALL OF SAMARIA UNDER SARGON IN 722

843–816 Jehu.
842 Jehu pays tribute to Shalmaneser III of Assyria.
816–800 Jehoahaz.
800–785 Joash.
785–745 Jeroboam II.
760 Prophetic ministry of Amos.
750–735 Prophetic ministry of Hosea.
744 Zechariah.
744 Shallum.
743–737 Menahem.
738 Menahem pays tribute to Tiglathpileser III (Pul).
737–736 Pekahiah.
736–734 Pekah.
734 Syro-Ephraimitic war. Rezin (Damascus) and Pekah (Israel) against Ahaz (Judah).
733–732 Tiglathpileser places Hoshea on the throne of Israel.
733–722 Hoshea.
722 Sargon captures Samaria. Fall of Israel.

JUDAH (THE SOUTHERN KINGDOM) FROM QUEEN ATHALIAH TO THE DEATH OF AHAZ

843–837 Athaliah.
837–798 Joash.
798–780 Amaziah.
780–740 Azariah (Uzziah).
740–735 Jotham.
740–701 Prophetic activity of Isaiah.
735–720 Ahaz.
725–690? Prophetic activity of Micah.

Assyria

842 Shalmaneser III makes his fourth campaign against Damascus.
810–782 Adadnirari III conquers the west including Israel ("the land of Omri"), Phœnicia, Edom, Damascus, but not Judah.
745–727 Tiglathpileser III of Assyria.
738 His western campaign.
733–732 Tiglathpileser III makes campaign against the west.
732 Fall of Damascus.
727–722 Shalmaneser V.
722–705 Sargon of Assyria.
722 Sargon carries 27,290 Israelites captive.

O.T. Literature of the Eighth Century B.C.

Continuation of Chronicles of the Kings of Israel.
Continuation of Chronicles of the Kings of Judah.
The E Document, about 750 B.C.
The Writings of Amos.
The Writings of Hosea.
The Writings of Isaiah 1–39 (excluding 24–27, 13^{1}–14^{23} 21, 34, 35).
The Writings of Micah, 725–690 B.C.

Fifth Period: 722–538 B.C.

Judah from the Fall of Israel (the Northern Kingdom); the Jewish Exiles (after 597) to the Return

720–692 Hezekiah.
711 Judah "punished" by Sargon.
701 Sennacherib besieges Hezekiah, who becomes his tributary.
692–638 Manasseh, a vassal of Esarhaddon.
638 Amon.
638–608 Josiah.
627 Prophetic activity of Zephaniah.
626–585 Prophetic activity of Jeremiah.
621 The discovery of Deuteronomy and the Deuteronomic reform.
615 Prophetic activity of Nahum.
612 The fall of Nineveh.
608 Battle of Megiddo, death of Josiah.
608–597 Jehoiakim.
605 Battle of Carchemish.
600 Prophetic activity of Habakkuk.
597 Jehoiachin. The first captivity.
597–586 Zedekiah.
592–570 Prophetic activity of Ezekiel (in Babylonia).
586 The destruction of Jerusalem. The second captivity.
561 Release of Jehoiachim by Evil-Merodach.
540 Prophetic activity of Deutero-Isaiah (Isa. 40–55).
538 Cyrus gives exiles permission to return.

Assyria and Babylonia

722–710 Merodach-Baladan of Babylon struggles for the mastery of Assyria.
711 Sargon's expedition against Azuri of Ashdod.
705–681 Sennacherib of Assyria.
703 Sennacherib's expedition against Merodach-Baladan of Babylon.
701 His campaign against the west. Shuts up Hezekiah "like a caged bird" in Jerusalem. Carries away 200,150 people and much booty.
681–668 Esarhaddon of Assyria.
668–626 Ashurbanipal of Assyria.
625–604 Nabopolassar of Babylon founds the Chaldæan kingdom.
612 Fall of Assyria to Nabopolassar, Medes and Scythians.
605 Nebuchadrezzar of Babylon defeats Necho at Carchemish.
562–560 Amel-Marduk (Evil-Merodach).
560–556 Neriglissar.
556–538 Nabonidus.
553–529 Cyrus of Persia masters Media, Lydia and Asia Minor and at length, 539, Babylon.

Egypt

712–700 Sabaka.
700–689 Shabataka.
689–664 Taharka.
664–661 Tanutamon.
663 Destruction of Thebes by Ashurbanipal.
663–609 Psammetichus I.
609–593 Necho.
605 Necho defeated at Carchemish.
593–588 Psammetichus II places a Jewish garrison at Elephantine.
588–566 Apries (Hophra).

O.T. Literature from the Seventh Century to the Persian Period

Combination of J and E Documents.
Deuteronomy written 650. Introduced 621.
Zephaniah, 627.
Jeremiah, 626–585.
Nahum, 615.
Habakkuk, 600.
Portions of Lamentations, 586–570.
Ezekiel, 592–570.
Code of Holiness (Lev. 17–26), 560.
Combination of J, E, D, 560.
The Deuteronomic editing (late 7th century) and the exilic re-editing (c. 550) of the Books of Kings.
Deuteronomic narratives of Joshua, Judges, and Samuel.
The Song of Moses (Deut. 32).
Isaiah 13^{1}–14^{23} 21.
Deutero-Isaiah (40–55).

Sixth Period: 538–323 B.C.

FROM THE RETURN TO THE DEATH OF ALEXANDER THE GREAT

JUDAH RESTORED

538 Return of a band of exiles under Sheshbazzar.
537 Altar for burnt-offerings rebuilt.
536 Foundation of temple laid.
520–518 Prophetic activity of Haggai and Zechariah.
520–516 The rebuilding of the temple under Zerubbabel and Joshua.
460 Prophetic activity of Malachi.
444–432 Nehemiah's first and second visits to Jerusalem. The rebuilding of the wall. Eliashib high priest.
411 Jehohanan high priest at Jerusalem.
407 Bagoas, governor of Judah (Elephantine papyri).
397? Activity of Ezra. Introduction of Priestly Code.
351 Jaddua high priest.
350 Jerusalem taken by Artaxerxes III.
335 Samaritan schism. Samaritan temple built on Mount Gerizim.
331 Syria and Palestine mastered by Alexander the Great.
323 Death of Alexander and partition of his empire.

PERSIA 538–331 B.C.

538 Cyrus in control of Babylon.
529–522 Cambyses.
525 His Egyptian expedition.
522–521 Gaumata.
521–485 Darius I.
485–464 Xerxes I.
464–424 Artaxerxes I.
408–358 Artaxerxes II (Mnemon).
358–337 Artaxerxes III (Ochus).
337–331 Darius III.

EGYPT TO 331 B.C.

525 Cambyses masters Egypt. Does not harm Jewish temple in Elephantine.
411 Destruction of Jewish temple in Elephantine.

O.T. LITERATURE FROM 538 B.C. TO THE GREEK PERIOD 331 B.C.

Isa. 63^7–64^{12}, 538–520.
Haggai and Zechariah 1–8, 520–518.
Majority of the Psalms collected, many preexilic in origin.
Malachi, 460.
Obadiah, 460.
Trito-Isaiah 56–66 (excluding 63^7–64^{12}), 460–450.
Isaiah 34 and 35, 450.
Job, 450–400.
Priestly code and priestly redaction of Pentateuch, 500–400.
Memoirs of Nehemiah, 444–432, and Ezra? after 397.
Ruth, 400.
Joel, 400.
The "little Apocalypse," Isa. 24–27, 340–332.

Seventh Period: 323–150 B.C.

FROM THE DEATH OF ALEXANDER TO THE END OF THE O.T. PERIOD

JEWISH COMMUNITY

323–198 Palestine under the (Egyptian) Ptolemies.
321 Ptolemy takes Jerusalem.
198–164 Palestine under the (Syrian) Seleucids. Onias III high priest contemporary with Seleucus IV.
175 Jason is high priest, contemporary with Antiochus IV.
171 Menelaus secures highpriesthood.
168 Antiochus attempts to suppress the Jewish religion.
168–163 The Maccabæan era.
168–160 Judas Maccabæus.
165 The rededication of the altar.
161 Alcimos is high priest, leader of Hellenistic faction.
160–142 Jonathan ruler, and from 153 high priest.
142 Jews under Simon (142–135) gain political independence.

SYRIA

323 Seleucus I Nikator of Babylon.
316 Seleucus driven out by Antigonus.
312 Seleucus founds Seleucid (Syrian) dynasty.
312–280 Seleucus I (Nikator).
279–261 Antiochus I (Soter).
261–246 Antiochus II (Theos).
246–226 Seleucus II (Callinicus).
226–223 Seleucus III (Ceraunos).
223–187 Antiochus III the Great.
186–176 Seleucus IV (Philopator).
175–164 Antiochus IV (Epiphanes).

EGYPT

323–285 Ptolemy I (Soter)
285–247 Ptolemy II (Philadelphus).
247–222 Ptolemy III (Energetes).
222–205 Ptolemy IV (Philopator).
205–182 Ptolemy V (Epiphanes).
182–164 Ptolemy VI (Philometor).
170–164 Ptolemy VII (Euergetes) jointly.
164–146 Ptolemy VII (Euergetes) alone.

O.T. LITERATURE FROM THE DEATH of ALEXANDER TO THE END OF THE O.T. PERIOD

Jonah, 300.
Song of Songs, 300.
Zechariah 9–14, 300–250.
Proverbs compiled 300–250, many very old.
Chronicles, Ezra and Nehemiah, 300–250.
Beginnings of Greek translation of O.T. (LXX), 250.
Ecclesiastes, 250–200.
Daniel, 167.
Esther, 150.
Psalms (final edition), shortly after 150.

Literature: Cook, *The Cambridge Ancient History*, vols. i-iv, esp. vol. i; Breasted, *History of Egypt;* G. A. Smith, *Jerusalem from Earliest Times to A.D. 70;* Barton, *Archæology and the Bible*, 5th edition; Creelman, *An Introduction to the O.T. Chronologically Arranged;* Bewer, *The Literature of the O.T.*; Article, "Chronology of the O.T.", in Hastings' *Dictionary of the Bible;* Chronological Table at close of T. H. Robinson, *Decline and Fall of the Hebrew Kingdoms.*

THE OLD TESTAMENT IN THE LIGHT OF ARCHÆOLOGY

By Professor CHRISTOPHER R. NORTH

Definition of Term. The term "archæology" has a wide range of meaning, and it is necessary to define the sense in which we use it. In its widest application it denotes the study or science (Greek *logos*) of ancient things (Greek *archaia*), and is practically equivalent to the history of the remote past. Thus the study of the O.T. itself may be called archæology. A somewhat narrower definition is necessary for our present purpose, since we are concerned with the O.T. in the light of archæology. To most people archæology suggests the spade, and means nothing more nor less than excavation. Roughly, this is correct, though it should be remembered that in Egypt especially many monuments are above ground, and that when Edward Robinson in 1838 and 1852 traveled in Palestine identifying biblical sites he was an archæologist, even though he used no spade. The following may serve for a working definition of the subject: The O.T. in the light of what exploration has revealed of ancient Palestine and the adjacent countries (Egypt, Syria, Phœnicia, the Euphrates-Tigris Valley, etc.).

The importance of the study is obvious, since it supplies us, so far as its materials go, with facts contemporary with the O.T. period. A large number of inscriptions are exactly dated. It is true that the majority are more or less mutilated; but what we are able to read of them is contemporary, as a rule, with the events recorded in them, and presents no difficult textual problems of the kind with which we are familiar in the study of the O.T. text.

History of Archæological Research. The materials are already vast, though, as might be expected, they are more full for some localities and periods than for others. It is only just over a hundred years (1822) since the first ancient Egyptian text, that of the Rosetta Stone, was deciphered, whilst Babylonia did not begin to yield up its secrets until the middle of the century. Both languages, as well as the pre-Babylonian Sumerian, can now be read with tolerable ease, and the histories of the Nile and Euphrates-Tigris Valleys traced with some confidence and fulness as far back as the fourth millennium B.C. Perhaps the most surprising discoveries are those which have more recently come to light on the Mediterranean (Cretan and Ægean) and Hittite civilizations, of which scarcely the memory had been preserved. The languages of these last still await decipherment, though substantial progress has been made with cuneiform, as distinct from hieroglyphic, Hittite; but a great variety of inscriptions is available in Egyptian, Sumerian, Assyro-Babylonian, Phœnician, and Moabite (both of which differ only dialectically from Hebrew), and in various dialects of Aramaic. These have thrown a flood of light upon the language, history, and religion of the O.T. Up to the present, excavation in Palestine has yielded little in the way of inscriptions, but materials of a scarcely less valuable kind have been forthcoming. Excavations have been undertaken on the sites of Gezer, Taanach, Megiddo, Jericho, Samaria, Beth Shean, on several sites on the edge of the Philistine plain, and on Ophel, the ancient Zion or City of David. Much has been learned of the culture, such as it was, of ancient Israel, and a tolerably complete picture may be drawn of the everyday life of O.T. times.

Necessary Cautions. It is necessary at this point to enter a caution. The Assyriologist, e.g., is interested in Assyria for its own sake, for what it adds to the sum of knowledge. Naturally, however, the interest of a Babylonian story of the Deluge is enhanced by reason of its relation to the O.T. story, especially for the student whose first concern is with the Bible. But there is some danger that we may have no interest in archæology except as it confirms, or, it may be, negates what we are told in the Bible. And it is necessary to say that if our interest is one-sidedly utilitarian, if we are only concerned to affirm or deny the truth of the O.T., we shall not obtain the best results from our study. Obviously, a great deal of the archæological material has no direct bearing upon particular O.T. texts. But it would be foolish on that account to neglect it. What archæology gives us is, broadly, a contemporary background of ancient civilization, into which we may set the O.T. as part of a larger whole. That is not to deny the uniqueness of the part; it is to say that the whole, quite apart from particular details in it, is a very valuable commentary on the part. The O.T. is endowed with new life and freshness as we study it in its context, that of the stirring and multitudinous life of the ancient East.

We have entered this caution, partly in the interests of that larger appreciation of the O.T. which a study of archæology should give, and partly because, if our first concern is either to prove, or disprove, the O.T., we are in danger of putting theories before facts. We must avoid making an unconditional ally of archæology. This is done by two classes of writers. On the one hand, we hear of "monumental facts and higher critical fancies," and those who set out with that thesis may easily make believe that archæology confirms the O.T. when, indeed, it does nothing of the kind. On the other hand, those who have a theory to prove may easily be misled by verbal similarities between the O.T. and extra-biblical writings into supposing that the Hebrews had no original ideas, that they were slavish borrowers who tricked themselves out in the thought-forms of older and more advanced civilizations. So they may regard Hebrew religion as a branch of Babylonian religion, and reduce the O.T. to a complicated system of astral mythology.

Archæology and Criticism. Before we proceed to examine detailed correspondences between archæology and the O.T. it may be well to say something more regarding the first of the errors above, since it is that to which readers of the Bible are most prone. The untenability of the "pan-Babylonian" theory, representing the second error, will appear as we illustrate the parallels between the Babylonian material and the religious ideas of the O.T. It is well known that criticism has referred the oldest considerable portion of the O.T., the J document of the Pentateuch (see art., *Pentateuch—Its Origin and Development*, p. 142), to the ninth century or thereabouts B.C. This conclusion was arrived at, not upon archæological grounds, but simply from a study of the O.T. itself. But the critical theory for long received, as it were, negative confirmation from archæology in that the earliest known writing in the old West Semitic alphabet was the Moabite Stone, *cir.* 850 B.C. Some bronze fragments of bowls discovered in Cyprus, and inscribed with Phœnician characters, were assigned by Lidzbarski to the second millennium B.C., but there were no means of dating them exactly. The upholders of the Mosaic authorship of the Pentateuch accordingly fell back upon the theory that Moses wrote in cuneiform, the arrow-shaped writing of Babylonia. Cuneiform, of course, is a script, not a language. Hebrew might be written, more or less accurately, in cuneiform, and so, for that matter, might English. There are two theories: (1) that Moses wrote in cuneiform, in Babylonian, and that what he wrote was later, when the West Semitic alphabet was invented, translated into Hebrew; (2) that he wrote in cuneiform, but in Hebrew, and that this was later transcribed into the Hebrew characters. In support of this second theory it is urged that there are Canaanite, that is, substantially Hebrew words, in the Tel-el-Amarna letters, *cir.* 1400 B.C.

An inscription in the Phœnician script has recently been found at Byblos, dating from the thirteenth century B.C. That Moses might have written in the Hebrew language and script can therefore no longer be doubted. To say that the Phœnician script was in use in the age of Moses does not, however, prove that Moses used it; still less does it prove that he wrote the Pentateuch. The documentary theory of the Pentateuch was formulated before the Moabite Stone was found, and it depends on considerations, partly linguistic, which archæology cannot very well overthrow, partly historical, which archæology has done much to confirm. If archæology can prove that the Aaronite priesthood goes back to Moses, or that the principle of sacrifice at a single sanctuary is earlier than the seventh century B.C., to mention only two matters of importance, it may overthrow the critical position, but so far it has done nothing of the kind.

But while archæology has not overthrown the critical position it is in some details tending to modify it. Sellin in Germany, and Welch in Britain, though avowedly critical in their methods, represent a movement to date the documents earlier than the Wellhausen school had done. The reason would seem to be that they are influenced, consciously or unconsciously, by archæology. The importance of Babylonia and Egypt for O.T. study has of late years become increasingly obvious. Here were advanced civilizations going back to the fourth and fifth millenniums B.C., civilizations, moreover, which early and profoundly influenced life and thought in the land subsequently occupied by the Hebrews. What necessity, then, to postulate a late date for the development of O.T. religion, as though the Hebrews had to live entirely to themselves, and to find their way unaided? Why may not much of it be early, Mosaic? The reaction is at present, perhaps, rather too strong; archæology cannot dictate to criticism. It may be, however, that the criticism of the later nineteenth century will be modified along the lines of recognizing (1) that Hebrew origins go further back than had been supposed; and (2) that the documents of which the Pentateuch is composed were not entirely *ad hoc* writings, but included a considerable amount of material that is older than the dates at which they were finally reduced to writing; e.g., there are close parallels between the Book of the Covenant (Ex. 20^{22}–23^{33}) and the Laws of Khammurabi (c. 2100 B.C.).

The parallels between the archæological materials and the O.T. may be summarized under two heads: (1) Historical; (2) Moral and Religious.

1. Historical Material

The Patriarchal Age. The first Hebrew king to be named on an Assyrian monument is Ahab, by Shalmaneser III (853 B.C.), while the Moabite Stone makes mention of Omri, who was, however, dead when the inscription was cut. For the period prior to the Omri dynasty archæology and the O.T. appear to be engaged in a most tantalizing game of hide-and-seek. We read on a Babylonian tablet from Dilbat, near Borsippa, of one *Abarama,* probably some Babylonian Abram, who hired an ox (1965 B.C.). Another (his name is spelled *Abamrama*) in 1963 B.C. tenanted a farm and duly paid his rent (Barton, *Archæology and the Bible*, pp. 316f.). It is probable, then, that Abram was a common name in Babylonia about the time when the biblical Abraham is said to have lived. It is likely that the Amraphel of Gen. 14^{1} is the famous Khammurabi, but that neither proves nor disproves that Gen. 14 is history.

The name *Jakub-ilu*, or *Jacob-el,* is found in Babylonia during the Khammurabi period, and once the shortened form *Jakub.* The names *Ya'kb'ra* and *Yashap'ra,* the former certainly, the later probably, the Egyptian equivalents of *Jacob-el* and *Joseph-el* respectively, appear in the list of Canaanite cities captured by Thothmes III in the fifteenth century B.C. (Barton, *op. cit.*, pp. 325f.).

About fifteen years ago a Babylonian cylinder seal was found bearing the name *Israel* son of Rishzuni. It may with some confidence be assigned to the time of the dynasty of Sargon of Agade, which flourished between 2800 and 2600 B.C. It is to be noted that it is a personal and not a tribal name (Barton, *op. cit.*, p. 326).

It would be precarious to identify the persons bearing these names with the patriarchs of Genesis; still less do they guarantee the historicity of the patriarchal stories. It may be, however, that similar discoveries await the archæologist, and that ultimately sufficient evidence may be forthcoming to show that Hebrew origins lie further back in the past than many in recent years have thought.

From the Exodus to the Division of the Kingdom. With regard to the Exodus the most natural conclusion from the book of Exodus is that it took place in the reign of Merenptah *cir.* 1220 B.C. (Ex. 1^{11} 2^{23}, notes). Any extra-biblical reference to a relation between Merenptah and Israel is, therefore, to be eagerly welcomed. Sir Flinders Petrie in 1896 discovered such a reference in Merenptah's funeral temple at Thebes. Unfortunately, it creates as many difficulties as it solves. Merenptah includes Israel in a list of peoples whom he had subdued. His exact words are, "Ysiraal is desolated; its seed is not." The context makes it clear that Israel was a people already located in south Palestine. Needless to say, the O.T. knows nothing of such an encounter, since the Red Sea incident can hardly have such a reference. The question is raised whether on the basis of archæology the Exodus must not be dated earlier than the reign of Merenptah. The O.T., if its chronology is anything to go by, does preserve another tradition of the date of the Exodus. In 1 Kings 6^{1} we read that Solomon began to build the Temple in the fourth year of his reign, and in the four hundred and eightieth year after the Exodus. The date of Solomon's reign is about 977 B.C., which would give us about 1450 for the Exodus. This is two centuries earlier than Merenptah, but it is fifty years before the Tel-el-Amarna tablets. In the Amarna period Palestine was a province of the Egyptian empire, and the tablets consist largely of letters from petty kings and governors in Palestine to their Egyptian overlords. (The fact that the letters are written in Babylonian is eloquent testimony to the cultural influence of Babylonia over the "Westland." It may also be mentioned in passing that Jerusalem is already in the Amarna letters called Urusalim.) Now, the letters of Abdi-Khiba of Jerusalem contain references to the incursions into the country of a people called *Khabiru.* Are these Khabiru Hebrews, or in any way connected with them? It may be confidently affirmed that in cuneiform writing the equation is quite possible, that, indeed, the word *'Ibhri* (Hebrew) could only have been written with the consonants of the word *Khabiru.* There are other notices of these *Khabiru.* They appear as mercenaries in southern Babylonia in the third millennium B.C. In the first half of the second millennium they again appear as mercenaries, this time in the service of the Hittites. And it is likely enough that they are the *Aperu* whom we meet with in Egypt in the period 1300–1100 B.C. It is not necessary to equate the *Khabiru* absolutely with the Israelite-Hebrews of O.T. story. Gen. 10^{21-25} $11^{16f.}$ show that the name "Hebrew" had a wide connotation, wider than "Israelite," while in 1 Sam. 14^{21} Hebrews and Israelites appear to be distinct.

It is difficult to fit the Amarna letters into the simple story of the O.T. Any construction we may put upon the evidence can only be tentative. It is hard to believe that there is not some connection between *Khabiru* and Hebrews. On the other hand, the O.T. tradition of an Exodus in the reign of Merenptah is too strong to be set aside entirely. Is it possible that only some of the tribes went down to Egypt, perhaps the Joseph tribes, which are specially associated with Egypt? That these came out of Egypt in the time of Merenptah, and that they were joined, perhaps at Kadesh Barnea, by related tribes who had been in Canaan all along, or who had entered two centuries before with the *Khabiru*, or, possibly, as a part of the *Khabiru* movement? Some O.T. passages, e.g., Gen. 33^{18}–34^{31} 48^{22}, seem to be reminiscent of wars of conquest before the days of the Egyptian sojourn. Still other tribes—there is reason to believe Asher—only joined the Hebrew confederation after the actual settlement in Canaan. (For a discussion of this question see F. C. Eiselen, *The Prophetic Books of the O.T.*, pp. 29–35.) Finally the tradition of the Egyptian sojourn and the Exodus became the common possession of all the tribes.

Excavations at Beisan (Beth Shean), begun in 1922 and still in progress on behalf of the University of Pennsylvania, have brought to light a stele of Rameses II (1292–1225 B.C.), in which, report states, the Pharaoh claims to have built the city of Rameses with Semitic labor (cf. Ex. 1^{11}). Beth Shean was still occupied by the Egyptians in the reign of Rameses III (1198–1167 B.C.), well after the traditional date of the Exodus. From the Egyptians it passed into the control of the Philistines, a fact that enables us to understand the stranglehold which these peoples of the sea had in the days of the Judges and Saul upon the country that was later called after them. (See Macalister, *A Century of Excavation in Palestine*, pp. 73f., 158, 171f.)

Macalister's own work on Ophel (see map 3, end of Commentary) for the Palestine Exploration Fund has finally proved that the eastern and not the western hill of Jerusalem was the Zion, or David's City, of the Bible (cf. 2 Sam. 5^{7}). Portions of the Jebusite wall have been uncovered, and the identification of the enigmatical Millo (2 Sam. 5^{9}) proposed with some confidence. The word, which denotes a "filling," is an apt description of some masonry which seems to have been intended to close up a breach in the north wall of the Jebusite city (cf. 1 Kings 9^{24} 11^{27}). (See Macalister, *op. cit.*, pp. 104f.)

Divided Monarchy. For the time of the divided monarchy correspondences between the O.T. and the monuments are frequent, and go to prove the substantial reliability of the Bible narrative. Pharaoh Sheshonk I (954–924 B.C.), the Shishak of 1 Kings 14^{25-28}, left a long list of conquered Palestinian cities. These include places in the Northern Kingdom as well as in Judah. The Bible gives no hint of an invasion of Israel. The monarchs of ancient time were nothing if not bombastic, and frequently credited themselves with victories more sweeping than they actually achieved; but it is likely enough that Israelite cities sent presents to Sheshonk, if only to keep him out of their territories.

Shalmaneser's mention of Ahab as fighting with the Arameans of Damascus and others against him at the battle of Karkar (853 B.C.) has already been referred to. The Bible is silent about this. It does, however, help us to understand Ahab's sudden change of policy toward Damascus (1 Kings 20^{34-43}). Safety from the Assyrian menace had to be purchased by the putting aside of old animosities. Similarly, we may assume, the marriage of Ahab and Jezebel, which had such disastrous religious consequences, was in the first instance a political measure directed against Damascus.

The so-called black obelisk of Shalmaneser III tells of tribute received from Jehu in 842 B.C. Again the O.T. is silent. Jehu founded a new dynasty. Moreover, he had waded to the throne through torrents of blood. And however his own generation may have accepted him, we know that the prophet Hosea, a century later, thought his revolution a very inglorious affair that merited retribution (Hos. 1^{4}). Jehu himself apparently did not feel too secure, and purchased protection from Shalmaneser by paying him tribute. It is worthy of note that Shalmaneser calls Jehu "the son of Omri." Jehu was not a descendant of Omri; indeed, it was he who brought to an end the dynasty of Omri. But that he should be called the son of Omri, and Israel generally on Assyrian monuments "the land of the house of Omri," is evidence that Omri was a more remarkable man than the very summary account of his reign (1 Kings 16^{23-28}) would lead us to suppose. The Moabite inscription of Mesha (cf. 2 Kings 3^{4}) with its statement that "Omri oppressed Moab many days" points in the same direction. Several of its phrases echo the religious ideas of the O.T., and the whole suggests that at this time Israel and Moab were on much the same plane of cultural and religious development.

Valuable light is thrown upon the last days of the kingdom of Israel by the inscriptions of Tiglath-Pileser III (745–727 B.C.) and Sargon (722–705 B.C.). In particular the Assyrian annals enable us to correct the unsatisfactory Bible chronology of the period. (See art., *Chronology of the O.T.*, p. 108.) The submission of Ahaz of Judah to Assyria is confirmed by Tiglath-Pileser's statement that he received tribute from him (cf. 2 Kings 16[8]). Menahem's tribute (2 Kings 15[19f.]) is also recorded, likewise the discomfiture of Pekah (2 Kings 15[29f.]). We also learn, what is not obvious from the Bible narrative, that Hoshea, the last king of Israel, was a creature of Assyria. We should imagine from 2 Kings 17[3-6] that Samaria was reduced by Shalmaneser IV (727–722 B.C.). The Assyrian account makes it clear that while the siege was begun by Shalmaneser, the city only fell after the accession of Sargon. It is not likely that the new monarch, who was a usurper, and would have much to do to consolidate his position on the throne, was present in person. Sargon tells us that he carried away twenty-seven thousand two hundred and ninety people from Samaria, and that he peopled the land with settlers from other parts of his empire. The majority of the inhabitants were suffered to stay where they were, for Sargon distinctly states that he permitted the rest to keep their possessions, that he appointed a governor over them, and imposed upon them the tribute of the former king. There is, therefore, no need to make a mystery of the "lost ten tribes." Those who were deported lost their identity in the land of their exile. Those who remained intermarried with the settlers brought in by Sargon, and became the ancestors of the Galilæans and Samaritans of N.T. times.

The most circumstantial parallel between an Assyrian record and a historical passage of the O.T. is the beautifully preserved cylinder of Sennacherib (705–681 B.C.) describing his campaign of 701 B.C. For the critical problems arising out of the biblical account (2 Kings 18[13]–19[37] Isa. 36, 37), which appears, at least in Kings, to be drawn from three sources, the reader is referred to the commentary on the Kings passage. Sennacherib tells how he shut up Hezekiah "like a caged bird, in Jerusalem, his royal city," how he imposed upon him a tribute of thirty talents of gold, eight hundred of silver, and accessories. (2 Kings 18[14] gives the figures as thirty talents of gold and three hundred of silver.) Sennacherib naturally does not mention the appalling disaster that befell his army, but it is significant that he does not claim to have entered Jerusalem. Some scholars, among them Rogers (*Cuneiform Parallels to the O.T.*, pp. 337f.), believe that Sennacherib made two campaigns in the west, one in 701 B.C. and the other some fifteen years later; that two of the sources in 2 Kings (18[13-16] 18[17]–19[8]) refer to the earlier, while the third (19[9-35]) with its story of the Assyrian disaster and its reference to Tirhakah (v. 9), who did not become king of Egypt until 693 at the earliest, refers to the later campaign. Although this solution of the problem is very attractive, it cannot be said to be conclusively proved. The only notice we have of a campaign of Sennacherib in the west after 701 is a fragment describing an expedition against *Arabia* some time between 688 and 682 B.C.; and it is by no means certain that Isaiah and Hezekiah, who figure so prominently in the Bible story, were alive at that time. However that may be, the disaster that befell Sennacherib's host was almost certainly bubonic plague. Herodotus has a story (Book II, 141) to the effect that the quivers and bowstrings of the Assyrians were devoured by field mice. This may point to the spread of disease by rats, and we know from 2 Sam. 24[16f.] that the angel of Jehovah, who figures in 2 Kings 19[35], was regarded as the agent of pestilence. Before passing from the reign of Hezekiah we may mention the famous Siloam inscription, which describes the construction of the long tunnel between the Virgin's Spring and the Pool of Siloam (see map 3). Although it consists of six lines only it is the longest ancient Hebrew inscription yet found, and throws valuable light upon the defensive measures undertaken by Hezekiah for the safety of his capital (cf. 2 Kings 20[20]).

The recent discovery of a Babylonian chronicle throws valuable light upon the closing days of the kingdom of Judah. It appears that Nineveh fell in 612 B.C., not 606 as hitherto supposed, and that when Pharaoh Necho led his armies into Syria he was in alliance with the remnant of the Assyrians, and not hostile to them. (Contrast 2 Kings 23[29] and cf. Gadd, *The Fall of Nineveh.*)

The Exile and the Restoration. The inscriptions of Nebuchadrezzar are mostly concerned with his building operations, and make no mention of the fall of Jerusalem. Neither is there any exact parallel to the Edict of Cyrus (2 Chr. 36[22f.] Ezra 1[1-4]), though an inscription of his has been found proclaiming a general amnesty, and affording facilities to gods and peoples to return to their own dwellings.

A welcome addition to knowledge of the little documented post-exilic period is afforded by a collection of well-preserved Aramaic papyri from Elephantine, in Upper Egypt, written in the fifth century B.C. They are the literary remains of a Jewish colony of the Persian period, and include conveyances, contracts for loans, marriage settlements, and the like, drawn up with all the thoroughness of a modern lawyer. The most important of them is a copy of a letter sent in 407 B.C. to Bagoas, the Persian governor of Judah. These Egyptian Jews had a temple, with all appurtenances for sacrifice. They worshiped Jehovah under the name of Yahu, and with him they associated four other divine beings, one of them certainly a goddess. Three years before they wrote to Bagoas their temple had been destroyed and burned by their Egyptian neighbors. When this disaster came upon them they had written to Johanan, the high priest in Jerusalem (see Ezra 10[6] Neh. 12[22f.]), but he had not vouchsafed any reply. They now ask the governor to give permission for the temple to be rebuilt and its sacrifices reinstated, and add that they have sent a similar request to Delaiah and Shelemiah, the sons of Sanballat (Nehemiah's old enemy, Neh. 2[10], etc.). There is also a note, apparently in the messenger's handwriting, purporting to give the verbal permission of Bagoas and Delaiah to rebuild the temple and to offer meal offerings and incense as formerly. Note that nothing is said of burnt offerings, though these had been included in the petition. The omission is significant, and probably intentional.

All this is surprising. The reason why no reply had been forthcoming from the high priest is obvious: these Egyptian Jews were schismatics, with their temple outside Jerusalem. Equally obviously, they were not conscious of being schismatics, or they would not have risked being snubbed by appealing to such a dignitary as the high priest. But how came they to have a temple at all? The answer must be that they knew nothing of the Deuteronomic law of one legitimate sanctuary. Neither did they keep the Passover and the feast of unleavened bread until, in 419 B.C., they were ordered to do so by one "brother Hananiah." Who this Hananiah was is uncertain, but he appears to have come to Egypt on a mission similar to that of Ezra and Nehemiah to Jerusalem, for the purpose of enforcing a stricter obedience to the law. In another papyrus complaint is made that since the advent of Hananiah in Egypt things have gone ill with the Jews. And when the orthodox party in Jerusalem failed them they appealed to the civil authority and the Samaritan faction. These papyri contain startling matter, but of their importance there can be no question.

The above summary will sufficiently illustrate the value of archæology for the O.T. historian. It is clear that archæology and criticism must each pursue their own course, without prejudice from the other. Sometimes archæology confirms the O.T., sometimes it supplements it, occasionally it corrects it. Nevertheless, it must be apparent to every unbiased student that the monuments when read intelligently neither set aside nor discredit the O.T. documents. They offer their services, not as a substitute, but as a supplement, by the aid of which we may study from without the history of the Hebrew people.

2. Moral and Religious Material

Art and Culture. Before we pass to parallels strictly religious a few words may be said about the light thrown by archæology upon the cultural life of the Hebrews, since art and culture stand in a middle relation between the material and spiritual elements in the life of a people. In this connection we are reminded of the principle that God chose the foolish things, and the weak things, and the base things, and the things that are despised, and the things that are not (1 Cor. 1[27f.]). It may be said quite summarily that except in the realm of literature the artistic achievements of the Hebrews were poor indeed. Living in the very center of cultural influences from Egypt, the Mediterranean, and Babylonia, they nevertheless developed no new artistic forms, and what they copied they mostly spoiled. This is sufficiently shown in their pottery, which consists of feeble copies of foreign models.

As far as Palestinian excavation illustrates the religious life of the Hebrews it is mostly on its darker side. The standing pillars of Gezer enable us to picture the orgiastic rites at the "high places." The jars containing infants' bones are gruesome testimony to the revolting practice of child sacrifice (cf. Mic. 6[7]). The nude and coarse Astarte figures that are found in all strata of the pre-exilic period give added emphasis to the fierce denunciations of the prophets (cf. Isa. 2[8] Jer. 2[28] 44[17f.] Hos. 4[17], etc.). The name *Egeliah* ("bull-calf of Yah") on a potsherd from Samaria shows how far reaching was "the sin of Jeroboam the son of Nebat, who made Israel to sin." The religion of Elephantine is a survival of these crudities. It is evident that the prophets were voices crying in the wilderness, and that few understood or gave them heed. When we consider their surroundings we can only marvel at their greatness, the memorial of which endures for all time in the pages of the O.T.

Types of Literature. The literature of the O.T. is various, and parallels have been quoted for almost every department of it. More than one Babylonian parallel has been cited to the book of Job. There are Babylonian and Egyptian psalms, and the forms of these, and sometimes the ideas and phraseology, are similar to those of the O.T. Both Babylonia and Egypt had also Wisdom literatures, from which correspondences have been cited to Proverbs and Ecclesiastes. Poetry similar to the Song of Songs also existed outside of Israel.

It is obvious that sensuous love poetry like that of the Song may be produced quite independently all over the world. The theme of the suffering righteous man too is sufficiently familiar to recur independently. It is convenient to speak of Babylonian Job texts, though the name "Job" does not occur in them. The book of Job is one of the greatest—some say even the greatest—single piece of literature that any age or country has produced; and it may be said without fear of contradiction that its religious conceptions are incomparably higher than those of any alleged Babylonian parallel. (See art., *The Bible as Literature*, p. 19; cf. p. 483.)

Creation and Flood Stories. The purpose of the present article may be met by a comparison of the Hebrew accounts of the creation and the Flood with those current in Babylonia. There are obvious resemblances:

1. *Between the Hebrew and Babylonian Creation Epics.* The first thing that strikes us is the arrangement by sevens: the Babylonian has seven tablets, or cantos, with which compare the Hebrew seven days. Though there are differences the order is, in general, the same; e.g., the heavenly bodies are created in the fourth epoch, man in the sixth. Both conceive of an original watery chaos or abyss, denoted by what is essentially the same word—Hebrew *tehôm*, Babylonian *tiâmat*. The Hebrew *tehôm* was originally a personal name, for it is used without the article: "Darkness was upon the face of *tehôm*." The Babylonian *tiâmat* is a she-monster against whom the god Marduk engaged in mortal combat. Both accounts conceive of a super-celestial ocean upheld by a firmament. The Hebrew word denotes something beaten out, usually of metal. The Babylonian speaks of a "covering," and describes how the victorious Marduk formed it by splitting Tiâmat like a flat fish into two halves, making one of them a covering for the heavens. The conception of a world-encompassing ocean is found elsewhere in the O.T., notably in the Flood story, which speaks of the fountains of the great deep (*tehôm*) being broken up and the windows of heaven being opened (Gen. 7^{11}).

2. *Between the Hebrew and Babylonian Accounts of the Flood.* The resemblances between the Hebrew and Babylonian accounts of the Flood are even more close. In the genealogy of the Priestly Code in Gen. 5 the number of antediluvians is ten. As the Jehovistic genealogy of ch. 4 now stands the antediluvians of the line of Cain number eight, but it can be shown with reasonable probability that in the original tradition the number was ten, as in P. The Babylonians, like the Hebrews, divided history into an antediluvian and a postdiluvian period. According to their story the number of antediluvians was ten, with an average longevity of forty-three thousand and two hundred years. As in the Bible story, the tenth patriarch, Ut-napishtim, escaped from the Flood. He, like Noah, is warned of the approaching catastrophe by the god Ea, whose favorite he is. Instructed by Ea, he builds a ship, making it watertight with bitumen (cf. Gen. 6^{14}), and embarks in it his possessions, his family and kindred, craftsmen, animals domestic and wild. He shuts the door of the ship. (In the Bible it is Jehovah who shuts the door—Gen. 7^{16}—but the similarity of the phrase, occurring as it does at the same point in the story, is remarkable.) As in the Bible the ark rests on the mountains of Ararat, so Ut-napishtim's ship is held fast by the mountain of Nisir. In addition to a dove and raven Ut-napishtim sends out a swallow. When he comes out of the ship he sacrifices on the top of the mountain. As Jehovah smelled the sweet savor of Noah's sacrifice, so does the Babylonian story tell with reiterated emphasis how the gods smelled the savor, the sweet savor, and gathered like flies over the sacrificer. Finally, as in the Bible, a promise is given that never more shall a flood destroy mankind.

Evidently, there is dependence somewhere. How may it best be accounted for? The hypothesis of direct borrowing either way is improbable, especially for Gen. 1, which comes from an exilic writer who would only have been revolted by the Babylonian epic if he had first met it in all its mythological crudity in the land to which he had been deported.

Nor is it likely that the two recensions go back to a proto-Semitic source: it is difficult to think that stories in which water is such a prominent element could have grown up in the arid steppes of Arabia. The stories, it is most likely, are native to the Euphrates-Tigris valley; they were Sumerian in origin, were taken over by the Semitic Babylonians, and became naturalized in Palestine when Babylonian culture spread to the Mediterranean before the Hebrew conquest. In the same way we may account for the similarities between the Book of the Covenant and the laws of Khammurabi. (For the details see W. W. Davies, *The Codes of Khammurabi and Moses.*) When the Hebrews entered Palestine they inherited from the Canaanites much that the Canaanites had in their turn learned from the ancient civilization on the Euphrates. Some will prefer to believe that a nucleus of Babylonian story and legal procedure was carried to Palestine by Abraham, but in the present state of our knowledge of the patriarchal period this cannot be asserted with confidence, although the probability of it may be conceded.

Unique Elements in the Old Testament. However we may explain the relationship, what the Hebrews learned from their neighbors they used in their own way, and in the realms of literature and religion they touched nothing they did not adorn. It is when we note, side by side with the resemblances, the differences between the Hebrew and Babylonian stories, that we see the uniqueness of the O.T. Underlying the Babylonian stories is an exceedingly gross polytheism: the gods emerge out of the chaos. It is improbable that Gen. 1 teaches the doctrine of creation out of nothing; but God is one, supreme, and he forms the creatures with his word. The Babylonian gods decide to have a flood for want of something better to do: "their hearts prompted them," so the story goes. The creation epic does not scruple to describe how they celebrated their exaltation of Marduk by getting drunk. When the Flood is in progress they are desperately frightened, and sit cowering like dogs in heaven. When it is over they fall to unseemly wrangling about the responsibility for it. The Hebrews needed to be inspired by the Spirit of God when they set out to transform such unpromising material.

Nothing has been said of extra-biblical parallels to the *prophets*, for the sufficient reason that there is nothing that demands comment. A few parallels are adduced, but they only touch the circumference, and do not penetrate to the real inwardness of prophecy. It is extremely unlikely that any parallels that go to the heart of the matter will ever be found; had there been any to find, some tidings of them would have been heard by now. The prophets believed that they stood in the counsels of the Most High, that the very words they uttered were given them by God. The silence of archæology in face of this claim is eloquent. The prophets are the miracle of the O.T. Archæology cannot explain them; it has nothing to do but pay them homage.

In conclusion: The monuments have not spoken their last word; but if we are justified in drawing inference from that which is known, it is safe to assert that though the monuments may swell into infinity they will offer nothing to equal, much less to supersede, in substance and spirit the O.T. We may receive gratefully every ray of light, but the time has not yet come, nor ever will come, when we may lay aside the O.T. and substitute the hymns and prayers of Babylon or Egypt to give to us the bread of life Jesus found in the pages of the sacred book of his people. Let us welcome the light and knowledge God has bestowed upon us; let us rejoice in them with perfect assurance that they are for good and not for evil; let us learn to use them wisely and honestly, and let us still be ever alert listening for other words, uttered ages ago, but not yet audible to modern ears. "It is for us to catch these messages, and to understand them, that we may fit them into the great fabrics of apprehended truth to the enrichment of ourselves, and to the glory of our common Lord."

Literature: Barton, *Archæology and the Bible;* Rogers, *Cuneiform Parallels to the Old Testament;* Driver, *Modern Research as Illustrating the Bible*; Handcock, *The Latest Light on Bible Lands;* Wardle, *Israel and Babylon;* Macalister, *A Century of Excavation in Palestine.*

THE OLD TESTAMENT AND SCIENCE

By Professor W. G. JORDAN

Preliminary Remarks. It is important to define clearly the scope and limitation of the subject. It is not science and religion: between these two spheres of life, it may, in a sense, be said that there is no direct conflict. Devout men holding different views and standing at different stages of culture have had similar experiences of repentance, faith in God and loyalty to Jesus Christ. One of the keenest controversialists of the last century has expressed this fact in his own forceful fashion. Speaking of the great passage Mic. 6[6-8], Huxley says, "In the eighth century B.C., in the heart of a world of idolatrous polytheists, the Hebrew prophets put forth a conception of religion which appears to me to be as wonderful an inspiration of genius as the art of Phidias or the science of Aristotle." "But what extent of knowledge, what acuteness of scientific criticism, can touch this, if anyone possessed of knowledge or acuteness could be absurd enough to make the attempt? Will the progress of research prove that justice is worthless and mercy hateful; will it ever soften the bitter contrast between our actions and our aspirations, or show us the bounds of the universe and bid us say, Go to, now we comprehend the infinite?" Without reducing religion to mere feeling we may maintain that on definite actions the real conflict is not here.

Neither is it the conflict between science and theology with which we have to deal. That is a large subject to which much thought has been given and on which much has been written, and the positions of opposing parties have been constantly changing with the increase of knowledge and the varied outlook on the natural and spiritual worlds. These two disciplines have each their own sphere and purpose—one seeking to find the laws that rule in the world in which we live, the other to find God and vindicate the ultimate spiritual nature of life. Their relationship is not likely to be finally settled, at any one period, so that discussion will end; and that is well, because the intellectual movement is an essential part of a living religion. It is impossible for us to stand still or to go back to the simplicity of earlier days, but "it is important for us to note that in the early Hebrew religious system, as in the other religions of the Ancient East, there is no trace of a suggestion that natural knowledge, or any conception of the nature of the world, was regarded as an impediment or handicap to religion. Thus the fields of religion and science have not yet been differentiated. It would, therefore, be idle to seek here evidence of any opposition between the two" (C. Singer, in *Science, Religion and Reality*, p. 90; edited by Needham, published by the Macmillan Company).

But, as the same writer points out, opposition was bound to arise. With regard to the cosmologies through which the ancient religions sought to give a rational view of the world, we have to admit that "historically we now know that on another mental level such cosmologies form an obstacle when they once were an aid." We are now concerned, in a limited form, with this historical question as it affects the interpretation of the Bible and especially that of the O.T. The same scholar maintains with regard to Greek culture that considering the enormous mental energy that it displays and the vastness of its interests, "the comparative backwardness of the religious development of that culture is a very striking feature. Greek religion—using that word in the restricted sense—never reached the rational standard of the Hebrew religion" (*op. cit.*, p. 91). We must try to show that the growing monotheism in Israel was the cause of the unity of view, and also how it is that the science of a particular period is not inseparably bound up with religious faith. The lack of unity, due to polytheism, is even more marked in the earlier nations; of Egypt it is said: "In the sphere of cosmology no reasoned system was developed: besides *Ptah*, the potter Hnum of Elephantine, as well as other gods, claimed to have been creator. Nowhere can any uniform dogma be found" (*Encyclopædia Biblica*, vol. ii, p. 1217, published by the Macmillan Company).

The Problems Not Absolutely New. For many centuries there was no progress in what we call "natural science," and the critical discussions, stimulated by the Greek spirit, gave place to dogmatic theology and practical ecclesiastical organization. But there were anticipations of the questions which had to be faced more fully in the later periods. We are told that Aristarchus of Samos (about 250 B.C.) was denounced by the Stoic Cleanthes for attempting to show that the earth moves round the sun just as Galileo was condemned by the theologians of the seventeenth century. For the influence of Pythagoras (582–500 B.C.) and others, and "the reversion of Aristotle to the geocentric point of view," see Simpson, *Landmarks in the Struggle Between Science and Religion*, p. 23. Philo (born 20 B.C.) had to exercise his ingenuity upon the text of Scripture to make the story of creation square with his philosophy; and with the early Fathers the allegorizing method, used by the Stoics in their interpretation of Homer, was the favorite method of evading difficulties that sprang from the literal interpretation of Scripture.

The Modern Movement. The story of the growth of physical science and the conflict between men of science and theologians is a long one. We have to admit that the official theologians have in many cases fought a losing battle. It is well that supposed new facts should be carefully scrutinized and that new ideas should be shown to rest upon adequate reasons. But it is unfortunate that loyalty to the Bible has so often been invoked to oppose discoveries which have finally been proved by unanswerable arguments and convincing experiments. In our own generation we have watched the discussions connected with biological science and seen the belief in "evolution" steadily gaining ground among all classes of thinkers and working its way into the study of history, literature, and philosophy. Whatever may be the final form that it will take, it has been, especially since Darwin, the leading principle in scientific thought. Some zealous Christians regard the whole scientific outlook as skeptical, if not atheistic, and "a proportion of scientific men, incensed by the mere discrepancy of the biblical and scientific record, have abandoned more or less completely their relation to religion" (Singer, *op. cit.*, p. 148). The historian tells us that the conflict over the new astronomical views, three hundred years ago, which removed the earth from the center of our system and set the sun in its place, was even more bitter. Pains and penalties were then more easily inflicted. But most of us still feel that "the heavens declare the glory of God, and the firmament showeth his handiwork." It is clear, then, that it is necessary to seek a definite statement of what is involved in the supposed "discrepancy between the biblical and scientific record."

The Elements in the Modern Situation. The history of criticism and apologetics shows us that, with rare exceptions, the representatives of the churches have been intensely conservative. They have clung as long as possible to traditional views regarding the dates of ancient documents and have presented a stubborn resistance to a superficial "rationalism" with its sweeping assertions regarding miracles and the supernatural. There is a certain satisfaction in this because, first, it showed a determination not to be ruled by mere negation, not to lose hold of the realities of inspiration and revelation, but to wait until they were transformed by the new light into richer and nobler forms. And, second, this very tenacity in the defense of orthodoxy drove scholars back to a more careful study of the nature of Hebrew literature. Modern scholarship, in its general movement, has been controlled by facts, discovered in different departments and pointing to the same conclusion.

(1) *Physical Science.* Here we have been brought from the small limited world of the ancients to the vast universe revealed by modern astronomy. The world of the Hebrews was a small affair of three stories, the heavens above, the solid earth, and the regions under the earth. The Babylonians had a larger view of the world and a longer historical perspective. To-day the round earth rolling through space and the immensity of the starry sky are conceptions familiar to us all. With this goes the thought of the great age of the earth and the long history of lower and higher forms of life on it. Without considering hypotheses concerning the origin of worlds and of life it is evident that our view of the universe, built up through centuries of observation and experiment, is vastly different from that of the Hebrews.

(2) *The History of Mankind.* Though the word "history" does not receive its full application in reference to those periods when there were no written documents, yet it is clear that even then there was movement, progress in the conquest of nature and the acquiring of instruments to meet common needs. In those days, when men were laying the foundation of all that was to follow, they had a keen sense of the invisible and in their own way were seeking God, "if haply they might feel after him and find him" (Acts 17^{27}).

(3) *Archæology*, in the stricter sense, has proved the existence of great civilizations, in full swing, thousands of years before the Hebrews came upon the stage. A hundred and fifty years ago all that was known of the nearer East was found in the O.T. and a few fragments of Greek literature; now our museums and libraries have rich stores of monuments and documents which reveal to us the great empires of Egypt and Babylon, in all

their splendor, with their roots reaching into the remote past. (See art., *O.T. and Archaeology*, p. 114.)

(4) *Biblical Criticism.* The facts acquired from outside have shed light upon the origin and history of the Hebrew people, but the most powerful influence in changing the views of theologians has been the patient study of the sacred text in the endeavor to gain its permanent message by relating it to the life out of which it sprang. In dealing with any great subject that is involved in the study of the O.T. the real problem is to place the whole book in its true position in the history of the world. We can see clearly that the Hebrew people were not "scientific" in our sense of the word; they were not curious and speculative in the same sense as the Greeks; their sense of the nearness and direct action of God upon life did not lead them to the investigation of "the laws of nature." Hence, while they prized the story of the past, and found God in it all, the conception of its slow processes and gradual development was foreign to their type of mind. That we have been compelled to lay aside many of their traditions is not on account of abstract reasonings, but because the study of the documents has made possible a more living view of the growth of this literature and of the divine guidance running through the whole history. (See arts., *O.T. and Criticism*, p. 129; *N.T. and Criticism*, p. 885.)

The Documentary Theory. The most radical change in regard to the nature and origin of any of the parts of the O.T. is the investigation carried on for over a hundred and fifty years into the structure of the Pentateuch. (Something similar, on a smaller scale, may be seen in the analysis of the book that bears the name of the prophet Isaiah.) The taking over of the O.T. from the Jews by the Christian Church along with a solid body of literary traditions involved the acceptance of certain views as to the origin of the earth and the form of the solar system, which were regarded as inseparable from its theology. After remaining almost stationary a long time these two systems of tradition dominating science and theology broke down under the influence of the new knowledge. The philosophy of Aristotle and the cosmology of the O.T. ruled side by side for about two thousand years. They were both assailed by the new spirit of adventure and discovery, of observation and experiment. After the fresh living movement of the Reformation, the Book was placed by Protestants in the position of the Pope and its infallibility claimed in a rigid mechanical fashion. It is worth repeating that orthodoxy could and did stand against attacks in the name of "reason," and that a freer, larger view could maintain its place in the church only through the patient minute study of the sacred text. In the abstract we have to concede the possibility that God could inspire a man who never crossed the Jordan to write the first five books of the Bible. But when the contents and nature of the books were carefully examined by scientific methods the conviction was gradually formed, and in many ways confirmed, that this had not been the case. The evidences of compilation and the use of various names for the God of Israel had long been noted, but when, with other varieties of thought and expression, they were brought to bear upon the analysis of the documents, it was seen that the different parts of the Pentateuch could be related to the various periods of the life of Israel, as it was lived not in the wilderness but in Palestine. We are closely concerned with this fact, as we shall see, because it bears strongly upon the central point of our subject, the cosmogony in Genesis. True, science touches the biblical story at other points, but limitation of space makes an exhaustive discussion impossible. Moreover, the consideration of a particular subject transfers the entire subject to the realm of the concrete; besides, the underlying principles remain everywhere the same.

Old Testament Reference to the Universe. Before discussing the particular problems connected with the first chapter of Genesis we need to remember that similar views as to the structure of the world are implied in allusions scattered throughout the Bible. The exact nature and form of the earth beneath and the heavens above are not *discussed;* they come out incidentally in prose and poetry as the physical features of the world in which the writers live. The general outlines are there, but when we try to make a complete picture and ask questions as to what is the condition of things under the earth and how precisely "the firmament" encircles it above and around, there is no clear information. The three features are always there—the waters around and below the earth, the green earth itself with its varied forms of life, the firmament and the heavens above:

(1) "The earth is the Lord's and the fullness thereof; the world, and they that dwell therein. For he hath founded it upon the seas, and established it upon the floods" (Psa. $24^{1, 2}$). "On the same day were all the fountains of the great deep broken up" (Gen. 7^{11}). "When I shall bring up the deep upon thee, and the

great waters shall cover thee" (Ezek. 26[19]). The word "deep" is the same as in Gen. 1[1]. There is a suggestion that the waters under the firmament are connected, but it is in a late book where we meet the thought of a system. "All the rivers run into the sea, yet the sea is not full; unto the place whither the rivers go, thither they go again" (Eccl. 17).

(2) References to "the earth" are plentiful, often with joy in the God-given showers and sunshine that make it fruitful: "Of old hast thou laid the foundations of the earth; and the heavens are the work of thy hands" (Psa. 102[25]). "He causeth the grass to grow for the cattle, and herb for the service of man; that he may bring forth food out of the earth" (Psa. 104[14]). "The earth is full of the loving kindness of the Lord. By the word of the Lord were the heavens made; and all the host of them by the breath of his mouth. He gathereth the waters of the sea together as an heap: he layeth up the deeps in storehouses" (Psa. 33[5, 6]).

(3) It is difficult for us, when we have passed beyond childhood, to realize that men once thought of the heavens as a solid vault above which God held his royal court. The firmament appears to be a solid structure forming a division between the waters and into it the stars are set. "It is he that sitteth upon the circle of the earth, and the inhabitants thereof are as grasshoppers; that stretcheth out the heavens as a curtain, and spreadeth them out as a tent to dwell in" (Isa. 40[22]). "Canst thou with him spread out the sky, which is strong as a molten mirror?" or, as it has been rendered, "So strong—so like a molten mirror smooth?" (Job 37[18]; cf. Ezek. 1[26].) These incidental references in prose and poetry show the simple view of the size and structure of the world that prevailed; it is a popular presentation of nature as it appeared to men who had not attained to systematic observation and had no instruments to assist their eyes and ears. In the later periods there might be some speculation as to the heaven or heavens, the highest heavens or the shadowy underworld, but, as a rule, men did not venture over the ragged edges and outward fringes of the visible world. The world, as thus viewed, can kindle varied emotions: the glory of the sun (Psa. 19), the splendor of the starry sky (Psa. 8), the awe-inspiring storm, the peals of thunder as "the voice of the Lord" (Psa. 29), "the showers that water the earth," symbol of kindly rule (Psa. 72[6]), the darkness and mystery of night, the bright day that invites to labor—all this and more summed up in words of adoration and gratitude: "O Lord, how manifold are thy works. In wisdom hast thou made them all: The earth is full of thy riches" (Psa. 104[24]). The Hebrews were neither speculators nor mystics, but had a wholesome joy in the order and beauty of the world.

It is round the system of cosmogony and chronology that the discussions turn in the time of the early Christian fathers, and still more when science reached its modern stage of careful observation and exact measurements. The case is well summed up by a recent writer from the standpoint of science in two brief statements; after quoting them, it will be our business to show that biblical criticism has made it possible for us to justify them. For, while the movement of science forced a reconsideration of the whole subject, the intensive study of the Hebrew literature has shown the advance in Israel from early tradition to scholastic learning. "Finally, the cosmogony of Scripture is in great part the common-sense outlook in the pre-scientific age in the modern acceptance of the term 'science'; it is the cosmogony of the childhood of the race. Yet it also corresponds to the science of the age, for the creation narratives embody definite attempts at explanation of how all things came into being. At the same time they show the transforming Spirit of God at work upon myth and naïve observation, even as it works upon the heart of man." "The fact remains that the spiritual leaders of a people whose religious sensitivities were the most exquisite that the world has ever known took the inherited cosmogony of the racial group, and under the illumination of the inspiring and enlightening Spirit of God, made of it a vehicle for the proclamation of eternal truths that are at once independent of the categories of any age and yet must be represented through those of each particular age in order to be made real to the age" (J. Y. Simpson, *Landmarks in the Struggle Between Science and Religion*, Doran, pp. 56, 57).

The Chronology. The O.T. contains data from which a chronology has been compiled extending from the creation of the world to the destruction of Jerusalem by the Chaldeans in 586 B.C. Three different available texts of the Pentateuch give different numbers for the period from the Creation to the Flood: the Hebrew, 1,656 years; Samaritan, 1,307 years; Greek, 2,242 years. The question as to which of these numbers may be original cannot be settled and is of little interest now that we know that they are not to be accepted as historical. An examination of the different periods shows that there is a mingling of traditions with attempts at systematic arrangement. Dates before the founding of the kingdom of David (about 1000 B.C.) are uncertain; the chronology of the later period can, in a measure, be corrected from Assyrian records, and after the Exile a nearer approach to accuracy is possible. (For a more detailed discussion see art., *Chronology of the O.T.*, p. 108.) In modern times Bishop Usher (1580–1656), using the data offered by the Hebrew text, proposed a scheme of biblical chronology that was generally accepted, and until recently was printed in the margin of the English Bibles. It placed the date of the creation of the world at 4004 B.C. To reject this date it is not necessary now to turn to physical science, as it has been proved that four thousand years before Christ great civilizations existed, already having behind them a long history. The theory of documents throws light on this branch of the subject in that it shows that the section in which this elaborate chronology appears is the latest of those which form the Pentateuch. In Gen. 5[1-5] the chronology starts with the nine hundred and thirty years of Adam's lifetime. Adam (the Hebrew word for "man") is here used for the first time as the name of an individual. So the ideas of a world about six thousand years old and Adam as the name of the first man stand or fall together. This we now see, when we examine the nature of the latest document; "the Priestly Code" is not primitive tradition but late Jewish learning, which served a noble purpose in its time but belongs to the sphere of religion rather than to that of science. Comparing this with earlier documents, it is clear that chronology, like all other forms of thought, had a development. The early stories refer to things that happened "once upon a time"; striking events such as an earthquake (Amos 1[1] Zech. 14[5]) were used to mark a point of time; later the accession on the death of a king could be used to fix a date (Isa. 6[1]). An elaborate chronology was the achievement of a later time; this particular one has now fallen to pieces, but the thought that prompted it, namely, the desire to place the life of this small nation in the larger framework of the world's life implies a wonderful faith in the one God and in the unity of the world.

The Cosmogony. When we survey the long history of interpretation and the controversies of ancient and modern times, we can easily understand that the great passage Gen. 1[1]–2[4a] has been the real battle-ground. This is explained by the fact that it is in its own way an orderly scientific statement. Even before the difference in age, substance, and style of the two chapters was clearly demonstrated, the beautiful story beginning Gen. 2[4b] was felt to be in a different atmosphere. Huxley, the most persistent critic of traditions, did once refer to the building up of a man's rib into a woman as "this monstrous legend," but surely that was a slip, for as a "legend," a symbol of the fact that man and woman were made for each other, the story, though childlike, is beautiful. This wonderful short story of man's entrance into the world, the first shock of temptation, the failure and shame, the sympathetic thought of the pains of motherhood, and the depressing influence of hard, grinding toil which has made labor seem to be a curse—there is something here when it is not turned into rigid dogma that tends to disarm criticism. "Dust thou art, and unto dust shalt thou return" (Gen. 3[19]; cf. Job 1[21]) is a mournful refrain that comes to us even in brighter circumstances.

The Real Meaning of the Cosmogony. This noble statement which stands at the beginning of our Bible, according to the view that is now held, would not maintain its present position if the order were historical; with such an arrangement one would place first the simpler story that follows it (2[4b-23]). But for a version intended for use by the great mass of people no sensible person would venture now to disturb what has come to be a noble preamble to the whole book. The time for subtle apologetics and artificial harmonizing has passed and we can do justice to both these chapters in the light of the knowledge that we have gained. We do not attempt to reconcile them with each other or with the science of our own day. In the one we have the dry land as yet unvisited by rain, man made out of the dust of the earth, the animals presented to him, and finally woman formed to give the companionship which they cannot completely supply; the other has behind it the great watery chaos, suggestive of Babylonian floods. To this wonderful chapter we must devote a few words, stating its present situation in the realm of biblical study, and acknowledging that modern science compelled a reconsideration of the whole question. It is needless to give in detail the many attempts to harmonize the account in Genesis with the views held by men of science, at various periods, as to the origin of the world and the appearance of living creatures. (See Eiselen, *The Christian View of the O.T.*, ch. 2.) Those scholars who accept the documentary theory regard that as a closed chapter. They surrender the science but see more clearly the high place of the chapter in the history of science and religion.

Some have regarded Gen. 1 as poetry in form, but that is not generally accepted. "The Poem of Creation" is an attractive title which has been used to remove the subject from the sphere of scientific discussion. The orderly movement with the repetition of stately phrases does suggest a certain poetic effect. The modern scholar takes the statement literally so far as it can be clearly interpreted. The earth was in a chaotic condition when God formed it into an ordered world by the separation of the waters into two divisions above and below the firmament, and by the separation of those below the heavens from the land. The land and water were then supplied with inhabitants in a certain definite order. The agency that brought this about was the word of God. "For he spake, and it was done; He commanded, and it stood fast" (Psa. 33[9]). The brooding spirit is mentioned at the beginning but plays no part in the later movement. The word "create" (*bārā*) does not appear to be used in the canonical literature with the sense of "making out of nothing." (2 Macc. 7[23] is claimed as making the first use of it in that sense.) The creation took place in a certain definite order, and definite orders or species were fixed (each "after its kind"). The process lasted six days and was brought to an end by "the rest of God" on the seventh day. Here a reason is given for the sanctity of the Sabbath. This was a very noble and reasonable view to be held by a small nation two thousand five hundred years ago. Even after the solid framework breaks to pieces there are permanent truths of religion that have played a tremendous part in the history of the world.

The thing that has become clearer the more the matter has been investigated is that this cosmogony, simple as it seems, has had a long and eventful history within and outside of Israel. The connection with the ancient Babylonian cosmogonies is now generally conceded (cf. on Gen. 1). The background is that of the vast Babylonian plains, the region of great floods. The principle of division producing the heavens and the dry lands is present in both. But we are a long way from the grotesque mythologies and crude polytheism of early Babylonia, not to speak of the still earlier Sumerian prototypes. Just when or how these ideas came into the life of Israel is an unsettled question. Further, it is probable that the growth of the statement into the form that we now have, involves a slow historical process. The order of creation with its eight works may have existed before it was brought into the six-day scheme. We know that the late period in which the process was completed was a time when the sanctity of the Sabbath was coming to a supreme place. The idea of long struggles after a rational view of the world coming here to clear expression, adds to the final result both dignity and strength.

The most striking feature of this cosmogony, considering the period when it arose, is its clear monotheism. That the monotheism had its own history is a fact which cannot be dwelt upon here. At the time the narrative was written the Babylonians still worshiped the stars, but a Hebrew prophet could cry, "Lift up your eyes on high, and see who hath created (*bārā*) these," etc. (Isa. 40[26]). The stars played little part in the life of the Hebrews; in the story of creation there is a slight allusion to them—"the stars also." Here there is neither astronomy nor astrology; the heavenly bodies do not dominate the life of man, which is in the hand of God; they simply "rule" day and night by giving light for man to labor, fixing his period of rest and settling the times of the seasons for the church festivals. It is a small world, a limited conception, but it enshrines a great principle which, when the world is enlarged, is liberated for fuller service.

Conclusion. The conclusion, then, to which we have come is that in this cosmogony there is science, the science of the times in which it was written, and that science here as elsewhere must grow old, become, as we say, "out of date." This, indeed, is a process which takes place much more rapidly now than it did in ancient times. To claim present authority for dead science because it is in the Bible is foolish and harmful. What we are seeking is a clear view of the case as it has emerged from disputes in which sometimes there has been more heat than light. And while not aiming at elaborate apologetic, there are two remarks that need to be made in regard to the service rendered to science and religion by this cosmogony. Tyndall, in his famous Belfast presidential address, quotes Lange on the impossibility of continuing scientific investigation with the belief in a number of gods thus: "But when the great thought of one God acting as a unit upon the universe has been seized, the connection of things in accordance with the law of cause and effect is not only thinkable but is a necessary consequence of the assumption." This is no doubt correct from the point of view of the man of science, but the historian recognizes that this monotheism is not a mere assumption but an achievement of humanity, toward which the Hebrew race has played an important part and which finds, in the chapter that has provoked so much discussion, its highest and most formal pre-Christian expression. We may concede that the authoritative position gained by the Hebrew cosmogony checked speculation and retarded the progress of the modern scientific movement, but for centuries it preserved the ideas of the oneness of God and the unity of the world in a form suited to the capacity and knowledge of the Christian world. Science can make little progress in the primitive communities where polytheism and magic hold sway.

The three strong aggressive religions of the world—Judaism, Christianity, and Mohammedanism—rest upon this monotheistic belief, though it may not have reached in any of them its full and final perfection in its application to theology, science, and art. The long story has often been told of the struggle in various ages between these different aspects of human thought. For the world at large it is not yet a closed chapter, but students of science and of Scripture are coming more and more to an understanding that recognizes in this ancient cosmogony permanent elements and admits that the framework shattered by advancing knowledge did in its own time and way render service to the higher intellectual life. We cannot accept, as the final verdict, the words of one so high in the ranks of science as Tyndall when he said of Gen. 1: "It is a poem, not a scientific treatise. In the former aspect it is forever beautiful; in the latter aspect it has been and will continue to be purely obstructive and hurtful." When we no longer demand for it literal acceptance or spend our time in seeking to harmonize things that are worlds apart, we are all the better prepared to do justice to the place that it has held and the influence it has exerted in the past. The Bible has in it many poetic expressions regarding the world which should not be hardened into rigid science, but a survey of the whole subject warns us against attempting to dissipate its real science into poetry, as the simple science has its own tale to tell of the progress of humanity in its search for God. Of this great chapter we may still say: "It shall be to the Lord for a name, for an everlasting sign that shall not be cut off" (Isa. 55[13]).

The whole matter may be summed up in these words: Permanent harmony between science and the Bible will be secured when each is assigned to its legitimate sphere. Science has a right to ask that, when men are seeking purely scientific information, they should turn to recent textbooks in biology, geology, astronomy or other sciences; but in the sphere to which Jesus and the N.T. writers assigned the O.T., science cannot deny or seriously question its inspiration or permanent value. Unprejudiced science has never done this. It is perfectly ready to recognize the inestimable religious and moral value of even those biblical narratives which refer to scientific facts, not because of their scientific teaching, but because of the presence of eternal truth in the form of primitive science. If anyone wishes to know what connection this world has with God, if he seeks to trace back all that now is to the very fountain head of life, if he desires to discover some unifying principle, some illuminating purpose in the history of the world, he may still turn even to the early chapters of Genesis as a safe guide.

Literature: Temple, *The Relation Between Religion and Science;* Huxley, *Science and Hebrew Tradition;* Tyndall, *Fragments of Science*, vol. ii; Draper, *The Conflict Between Religion and Science;* White, *A History of the Warfare of Science with Theology;* W. S. Jordan, *Ancient Hebrew Stories and Their Modern Interpretation;* J. Y. Simpson, *Landmarks in the Struggle Between Science and Religion;* Needham, editor, *Science, Religion and Reality;* Commentaries on *Genesis* by Driver and Skinner.

THE OLD TESTAMENT AND CRITICISM

By Professor CHRISTOPHER R. NORTH

Meaning of Term. Criticism, by those who are opposed to it, is so often assumed to mean adverse criticism, "censure," that it is perhaps necessary to remind ourselves that in itself the word bears no such sinister meaning. It is derived from the Greek word *krinō*, "to judge," of which the Latin equivalent is to be seen in the second part of the word "discern." Criticism is discernment of the qualities of an object. Wesley reminded his preachers that the judge is always supposed to be on the prisoner's side. In the same spirit criticism seeks to approach its subject matter without preconceived ideas of any kind, and to arrive at conclusions strictly in accord with the evidence. As applied to any ancient writing the task of criticism is to discover how the document originated; if the document purports to be historical, whether in fact it is so; finally, whether the moral and religious ideas it contains are worthy expressions of divine truth.

Legitimacy of Criticism. The legitimacy of criticism as applied to the O.T. has been questioned on two grounds: (1) that as applied to a sacred and inspired writing it is at once unnecessary and even impious; (2) that our Lord gave his sanction to certain beliefs about the authorship and historicity of some of the O.T. books, and that these beliefs must therefore be accepted as final.

With regard to the first of these objections it may be urged that although the inspiration of the Scriptures has always been an article of faith in the Christian Church, no attempt has been made to define the *manner* of their inspiration in such a way as shall be binding upon all Christians. The second objection is perhaps more serious. It is urged that our Lord spoke of the Law of Moses (Mk. 1[44] Lk. 24[44]) and the book of Psalms (Mk. 12[36]) in such a way as to invalidate forever any discussion as to the authorship of these books; and that he referred to Jonah in such a way as to guarantee the truth of the story concerning him (Mt. 12[40]).

Now, if our Lord was possessed of absolute omniscience, this objection would perhaps have to be accepted as final. But have we any warrant for claiming such omniscience for him? All the indications are that his was a true humanity, which would seem to rule out omniscience. He is reported to have asked questions, from which the natural inference is that he needed information. On one point he definitely disclaimed knowledge (Mk. 13[32]). The phrase "he emptied himself" (Phil. 2[7]) seems to mean that when he came to earth Jesus laid aside certain prerogatives of divinity, and accepted for himself the limitations that are incident to the state of being a man. We read that he advanced in wisdom (Lk. 2[52]), that it behooved him in all things to be made like unto his brethren (Heb. 2[17]), from which it would seem to follow that his intellectual attainments were such as might be acquired by study, and that his knowledge of secular and scientific subjects was such as was open to men in the first century.

We must take it, then, that reverent criticism of the Scriptures is a legitimate proceeding. We may further be sure that in a universe of which God is the author and guardian of truth no criticism can do any ultimate harm to the Scriptures. If criticism is undertaken with unworthy motives, it must come to naught. And even if its motives are pure, if its conclusions are unsound those conclusions will be shown to be false. If traditional beliefs have been wrong, ultimately they must be replaced by better. In any case there is no need for men of faith to tremble for the ark of God.

Types of Criticism. It is convenient to consider criticism under four heads: (1) Textual or "Lower" Criticism; (2) Documentary or "Higher" Criticism; (3) Historical Criticism; (4) Moral Criticism.

1. Textual or "Lower" Criticism. The purpose of textual or, to use the technical term, "lower" criticism, is to recover, as far as possible, the actual words of any writing as it left the hands of its author. The oldest extant Hebrew MS. of the O.T. of certain date is not older than the tenth century A.D., well over a thousand years after the autograph copies from which it is descended. What were the fortunes of the text during that long period, and how far does the text of Hebrew Bibles to-day represent the actual words of the O.T. writers? For the answers to these questions the reader is referred to the article, *The Transmission of the O.T.*, pp. 99f. It is, however, not out of place to point out here that if God had been pleased to communicate to men Scriptures verbally inspired, he would surely have provided that their text should be transmitted without error. It is small comfort that the Scriptures should once have been inspired in the very letter if, owing to the accidents of transmission, that letter is sometimes uncertain. And all the indications are that the text has in places suffered beyond sure hope of recovery. The logical inference is that verbal infallibility is not a necessary condition of divine revelation, from which we are led to look beyond the letter to the spirit that giveth life (2 Cor. 3[6]). A further reason why mention should be made of "lower" criticism is that only so can we understand the true meaning of the, as it has proved, unfortunate term "higher criticism."

2. Documentary or "Higher" Criticism. If the term "criticism" has given rise to misunderstanding, the misunderstanding has only been deepened by the use with it of the adjective "higher." It should, however, be noted that the words "lower" and "higher" in this connection are technical terms, and that they were in use long before anyone thought of applying critical methods to the study of the Bible. "Higher" criticism was never intended to mean a method applied by men who think themselves superior to their fellows in critical acumen. It was so called simply to distinguish it from "lower" or textual criticism, the purpose of which has already been indicated. The function of "higher" criticism is to determine, if it be possible, the authorship, date, and place of origin of any writing. In a modern printed book these particulars are usually given on the title page. In the case of a book written in antiquity they must be inferred from whatever internal and external evidence is available. Such criticism is called "higher" because it deals with problems nearer to the source of the writing than textual criticism does. Obviously, a book must be in existence before its variations of text can become an object of study: it is the task of the higher or documentary criticism to find out how it came into existence. The problem thus dealt with is usually more difficult of access than a textual problem. Again, therefore, the term "higher" criticism is in some measure justified. Strictly speaking, any man is a higher critic who seriously gives himself to the study of the authorship of the books of the O.T., no matter how conservative his conclusions may be. It is further to be noted that the "higher" criticism as such does not concern itself with the historical accuracy of the documents with which it deals.

It is quite possible for a higher critic to conclude that Moses wrote the Pentateuch. Generally speaking, however, the trend of critical opinion has been away from the traditional positions as taken over by the church from Jewish rabbinical scholars. For the methods of criticism, and its results as applied to the several O.T. writings, the reader is referred to the "Introductions" to the books concerned, and in particular to the article, *The Pentateuch—Its Origin and Development*, pp. 134f.

If we consider the O.T. as a whole, the outstanding conclusion of literary criticism lies in its affirmation that the prophets are earlier than the Law. There are, of course, portions of the Pentateuch that are earlier than the earliest writing prophets; there are perhaps portions of the prophetical books that are later than anything in the Law. But, broadly speaking, the statement holds good that, whereas the order of acceptance of the books by the Jews was Law—Prophets—Writings (see art., *The Formation of the O.T.*, pp. 91f.), the actual order of writing was Prophets—Law—Writings. This means that the creative impulse in O.T. religious development came from the prophets. The Talmud stands committed to the statement that the "Men of the Great Synagogue," whoever they may have been, wrote Ezekiel and the books of the Minor Prophets. But if there is one book of the O.T. which more than any other bears the stamp of its author, it is the book of Ezekiel. However negative criticism may sometimes have appeared, it certainly has brought the prophets out of the obscurity in which for so long they were hidden. That is as it should be. What we have in the Law is the application to the daily life and needs of the ordinary Israelite of the ethical monotheism proclaimed by the prophets of the eighth to the sixth centuries B.C. It is true that there was some descent from the heights on which the prophets themselves moved. The master truths of prophecy, born in the experience of a succession of the greatest souls of all time, were, consciously or unconsciously, adapted to average Israelite capacities. But although sacrifice, so strongly denounced by the prophets (Amos 5[21-25] Isa. 1[11-15], etc.), riveted itself more firmly on Jewish practice, it is significant that in post-exilic times we hear no more of those constant lapses into idolatry that are so characteristic of the whole period prior to the Exile.

A little thought will make it apparent that no literary criticism can lessen the religious value of the O.T. The O.T. is what it is, and ultimately it must be judged by its intrinsic religious worth. Nor can literary criticism diminish the contents of the O.T.; it can only rearrange them in a somewhat different order. No critic proposes to abridge the O.T., nor in any way to interfere with the canon. So long as the materials for any study are not in their proper time sequence it is not possible to see in them anything other than a more or less imperfectly related series of fragments. Once that order has been properly determined, it is possible to see the living unity of the whole. What criticism has done is, by endeavoring to redistribute the O.T. sources in the order in which they were written, to make possible a more coherent and convincing conception of the organic growth of O.T. religion. By this means a new suggestiveness is given to the profound Pauline phrase, "when the fullness of the time came" (Gal. 4[4]). To this fullness more minds have contributed than was once supposed. For example, the book of Isaiah contains the work of many others besides the eighth-century Isaiah of Jerusalem. Some of the most inspired utterances in the O.T. are anonymous (e.g., Isa. 40–66). God gave not the Spirit by measure (Jn. 3[34]), and those who received it were careless of their own fame. What criticism reveals is not a revelation that is external and unrelated to human experience, communicated through a few; but a revelation of God in the history, thought, and experience of a people, a revelation that many witnesses have contributed to record.

3. **Historical Criticism.** It has already been said that the higher criticism as such is not concerned with the historicity of the documents with which it deals. It is, however, obvious that one of its results must be to raise the problem of historicity. Thus, if it is a conclusion of literary criticism that a certain document was written five centuries after the events it describes, we are bound to ask whether its account of those events is a true one. In the absence of any indications to the contrary we may decide that it is. But when we have two accounts of the same incident, as of the institution of the monarchy (1 Sam. 8, 10[17-24]; contrast 1 Sam. 9[1]–10[16], and see commentary), or of David's introduction to Saul (1 Sam. 16[14-23]; contrast 17[55-58]), the question must then be asked, which of the two accounts, if either, is the true one? And it will sometimes appear that we cannot claim literal accuracy for both without resorting to the most desperate harmonizing expedients. It is just here that criticism has raised serious misgivings in many devout minds. It is not "higher" criticism in its narrower meaning that is feared, but its implications for history. If some parts of the O.T. are not historical, how are we to know what is true and what is not? Can we even be sure that any of it is? Are we not shut up to the alternatives all or nothing?

To this the answer must be in general terms that most either-or propositions are of the nature of false disjunctives, and untrue to life. Even the wildest critic would decline to say that the O.T. contains no history at all; while every critic who values his reputation as a historian knows that it contains a good deal. We cannot therefore accept the negative horn of the dilemma. To accept the positive, and assert categorically that the O.T. contains no historical inaccuracy, is to be in a position equally untenable. Thus, according to some portions of the Pentateuch, sacrifice was to be permitted only at one central sanctuary, and the only persons who were competent to officiate were priests descended from Aaron. That being so, laymen like Gideon (Judg. 6[24]), Manoah (Judg. 13[19]), Samuel (1 Sam. 9[13]), David (2 Sam. 6[13]), were not competent to sacrifice at all, much less to build altars. Nor were the sons of David, a Judahite, qualified to be priests (2 Sam. 8[18], where the R.V. text is the only possible translation of the Hebrew). Moreover, if there was only one legitimate altar, that in Jerusalem, it is incomprehensible that so zealous a champion of Jehovah as Elijah should complain that the altars of Jehovah had been thrown down (1 Kings 19[10]), and that he should repair the desecrated altar on Carmel (1 Kings 18[30]). It is no remedy to say that these are declensions from the right statute: David and Elijah were devout worshipers of Jehovah, and evidently knew no better than to do as they did. The difficulties vanish when we recognize that the Pentateuch contains also an earlier law of the sanctuary than that which permits one altar only (Ex. 20[24f.]), and that while quite early after the settlement in Canaan Levites began to acquire priestly functions (cf. Judg. 17[13]), it was only gradually that the family of Aaron came to have a priestly monopoly. (Cf. Deut. 18[1-8], seventh century, where all Levites are priests; Ezek. 44[10-16], sixth century, where the non-Zadokite Levites are excluded; and the Priestly Code, fifth century, where the family of Aaron alone among the Levites are qualified to sacrifice.) It has been noted above that, speaking generally, the prophets are earlier than the Law. It is only as we apply this principle to the history of Israel that the historical books, Judges, Samuel, and Kings, become really intelligible. If the Law was complete before the Conquest, the history of the following centuries is full of insoluble enigmas. If in its present completed form it is post-exilic, the main features of the history and religious development become convincingly clear.

Although this is not the place to deal at length with the miraculous element in the O.T., it may be noted that many of the difficulties felt by the modern mind are removed by the method of comparative treatment of sources. Thus the stories of the plagues (Ex. 7:14–12:36) and of the crossing of the Red Sea (Ex. 14) are composite, and consist of elements from the three main Pentateuchal sources, J, E, and P (see art., *The Pentateuch*, p. 137b). Analysis shows that the miraculous element in the stories is least developed in J, the earliest, and is most prominent in P, the latest of the documents. The inference is clear: the plagues have a basis in fact, being all more or less related to physical conditions in the land of Egypt; they became magnified into the portents of P by frequent and triumphant repetition.

Rightly understood, there is no part of the O.T. that is without historical value when put into its proper time setting. A narrative may or may not be historically trustworthy as an account of what happened centuries before it was written; it is always of value as reflecting the thought of the time when it was written. And in a very proper sense the thought of a people is as real a part of its history as its commercial and political fortunes. To take an extreme example: the book of Leviticus contains a maximum of legislation and a minimum of action. But if we want to picture the everyday sacrificial ritual of the second temple, we need nothing more detailed and circumstantial than the first seven chapters of Leviticus. If we wish to know the procedure that was followed from the Persian period down to the time of our Lord, when a new high priest was consecrated, we need only turn to the account of the consecration of Aaron in Lev. 8.

The O.T., then, contains the materials from which, with the supplementary aid of archæology, a trustworthy history of Israel may be written. We may even go so far as to say that the O.T. writers came nearer to being historians in the modern sense than any ancient writers prior to the time of Herodotus. Their historical writing, however, was not exactly history in our sense of the word. What they give us is a philosophy of history rather than a scientific and unimpassioned description of the past. They were before all things preachers of righteousness; their main purpose was to influence the life and thought of their contemporaries. It is not that they were entirely uninterested in the past for its own sake; the early writers in particular tell of the past with a naïveté that is entirely free from theological bias. But the editors who gave their final form to the historical books were continually reading out of the past lessons for their own present, and inevitably their conception of the past was colored by the needs of that present. It is only what we should expect. The demand for history uncolored by the prejudices and ideals of the author is something essentially modern, and we have no right to expect it of the O.T. What we have there is in its own way warmer and more moving than history after the modern fashion; and if we want scientific history, we can with patience obtain it from the materials which the O.T. itself supplies.

4. Moral Criticism. It has already been said that the O.T., like any other literature, must stand or fall by its own intrinsic quality. This principle has led many quite confidently to announce its approaching dethronement from the high position it has so long occupied in the literature of the world. Rationalistic writers have openly made jest of some of the stories it contains. Many Christian people have been puzzled by what appears to be its imperfect morality, and have sought refuge in a deeper devotion to the N.T. and a tacit neglect of the O.T.

Now, if we are going blindly to insist on the dogma of an equal inspiration of every verse in the Bible, we must inevitably defeat the purpose we have in view. Instead of persuading people to love the Bible more we shall only succeed in making them skeptical of its claims to reverence. Frankly, the O.T. does contain stories that are unedifying, some of them even told without apparent moral censure. We think of Noah's drunkenness (Gen. 9:20-27); of Lot's incest (Gen. 19:30-38); of Jacob's theft of the blessing (Gen. 27); of the command to Saul to slaughter all the Amalekites, and the censure passed upon him for not fulfilling it to the letter (1 Sam. 15); of the, from the standpoint of to-day, barbarous conception of corporate responsibility that demanded the hanging of the seven sons of Saul (2 Sam. 21). The conclusion seems unavoidable that much of the morality of the O.T. is imperfect as judged by Christian standards. This was quite frankly recognized by our Lord himself (Mt. 5:21-47). It also seems to have been recognized in one form or another by all the leading N.T. writers; by Paul (Rom. 8:3); by John (Jn. 1:17); and by the writer of the Epistle to the Hebrews

(10^{1-4}). At the same time it is undeniable that our Lord nourished his own soul from the O.T., and that "the Scriptures" was the common designation of the O.T. in N.T. times (Lk. 4^{21} Jn. 5^{39} Acts 17^{2}, etc.). There must, therefore, have been that in the O.T. which satisfied the conscience and ministered to the spiritual life of Jesus and his apostles. In other words, the O.T. contains, besides much that is imperfect, much also that reaches heights that are nothing short of sublime. No pre-Christian literature ever produced a passage like that describing the martyrdom of the Suffering Servant in Isa. 53. (See art., *The Divine Element in the Bible*, p. 28.)

To say this means that the O.T. itself is quite capable of passing judgment on its own imperfect morality, does, indeed, tacitly pass such judgment insofar as it shows how that which was unworthy gradually gave place to what is above sane moral criticism. In some passages we can actually see the judgment of a more enlightened conscience being passed on earlier and crude conceptions. For example, there is little doubt that the three "sister-wife" stories in Genesis (12^{10-20} 20, 26^{1-11}) are variants of the same story. In two of them the sister-wife fiction is simply a lie; in the third, which comes from the comparatively late E document, the writer is at pains to explain that Sarah really was Abraham's half-sister (Gen. 20^{12}). That may be only a fiction, but it shows the way in which men's minds were moving. Of King Amaziah we read that he deliberately mitigated the severity of the old custom of putting to death innocent children with a guilty father (2 Kings $14^{5f.}$; contrast 2 Sam. 21 above). A comparison of the two accounts of David's numbering of the people (2 Sam. 24^{1} 1 Chr. 21^{1}) shows quite clearly how men's ideas of the moral character of God could change. Actions that they had no difficulty in ascribing to God in the tenth century they could not bring themselves to ascribe to him in the third.

Once more, the solution of the problem is to be found in the analysis and dating of the sources of which the O.T. is composed. By that means we are able to see how God progressively revealed himself to men as they were able to receive him. As one lesson was learned another was taught. It could not be otherwise. Moreover, a careful analysis reveals the fact that the transient elements in the O.T., such as the "ban" (see e.g., Josh. 7), polygamy, and the law of blood revenge, are roughly those that are pre-Mosaic, while those that are permanent and that were received into and perfected by the gospel of Christ, are those that sprang from the new impulse that Moses gave to religion for his countrymen and for the world. It is true that the transient elements did not at once die out. For long they persisted side by side with higher conceptions; but their disappearance was only a matter of time.

It may confidently be predicted that the canon of the O.T. will never be abridged. Men will naturally turn more frequently to some portions of it than to others. They always have done so. It may be that an occasional abridged volume for devotional purposes will do no harm if it gives us wider margins and larger print. *But the canon will never be revised.* If we are rightly to value our Christian heritage, we need to be at once humbled and encouraged by the view backward over the whole of the long road by which God has led us to it. And no one possessed of imagination and sympathy with the race in its upward striving toward God will wish to see a single verse of the marvelous record perish from the affection of his fellows. We conclude, then, that so far from the O.T. being discredited by criticism, its title to reverence has been abundantly vindicated. It stands for all time as a memorial of the goodness and severity of God (Rom. 11^{22}) that prepared the way for the coming of Him in whom all its promises are fulfilled.

Literature: Peake, *The Bible: Its Origin, Its Significance, Its Abiding Worth;* G. A. Smith, *Modern Criticism and the Preaching of the O.T.;* W. R. Smith, *The O.T. in the Jewish Church;* Driver, *Introduction to the Literature of the O.T.;* Simpson, *Pentateuchal Criticism;* McFadyen, *The Approach to the O.T.*

THE PENTATEUCH—ITS ORIGIN AND DEVELOPMENT

By President FREDERICK CARL EISELEN

Meaning of the Term Pentateuch. According to the arrangement in the Hebrew Bible the O.T. consists of three parts, called Law, Prophets, Writings, or, in Hebrew, *Tôrâh, Nebhîîm, Kethûbhîm.* The first division, the Torah, so called because it embodies practically the entire legal system of the Hebrews, is sometimes called "The Five Books of Moses"; the early rabbis speak of it as "The Five-fifths of the Law," an indication that the fivefold division was introduced at a very early date; and the early church Fathers, beginning with Tertullian, employ the term, still in common use, "the Pentateuch." The full form of the name in Greek would be *pentateuchos biblos*, translated "fiveroll book"; but in common usage the noun is omitted and *pentateuchos* comes to have the meaning of the complete expression freely rendered "the fivefold book." Strictly speaking *teuchos* denotes not the book or roll itself, but, rather, the box or chest in which it was kept; but Symmachus, an early translator of the O.T. (see art., *Transmission of O.T.*, p. 104b), uses it as the equivalent of the Hebrew word *megillâh*, or "roll."

The five books in the Pentateuch are: Genesis, Exodus, Leviticus, Numbers, Deuteronomy. Even the English reader can see that Genesis forms a book by itself, and so does Deuteronomy. The general contents and characteristics of Leviticus separate it from the books on either side; while the opening words of Exodus (1^{1-7}) and the closing words of Numbers (36^{13}) clearly show that these two books also are considered complete in themselves.

General Contents. All the material in the five books, varied as it is, may be arranged under two heads: (1) *History:* The historical portions of the Pentateuch cover the period beginning with the creation of the world and ending with the encampment of the Israelite tribes in the plains of Moab. This period may be divided as follows: (a) the beginning of all things (Gen. 1^1–11^9); (b) the Hebrew patriarchs (Gen. 11^{10}–50^{26}); (c) the Exodus from Egypt and the organization of Israel into a more or less compact national unit, with a national consciousness (the historical sections of Exodus, Numbers, Deuteronomy). No attempt is made by the authors to furnish a complete history; many events of considerable importance from the point of view of the historian are treated briefly or are passed over lightly; nevertheless, the stream of history is never wholly interrupted, and though at times it almost disappears, it always reappears and flows on to the end. (2) *Law:* The early readers focused their attention upon the legal elements in the Pentateuch; consequently, the books came to be known as Law or Torah (see above). Leviticus consists entirely of legal material; Exodus and Numbers are a mixture of law and history; Deuteronomy consists mainly of addresses embodying law; and even Genesis, which is chiefly narrative, mentions the laws of marriage and of the Sabbath as given in primeval times, gives regulations concerning food in the days of Noah, and relates the institution of circumcision in the time of Abraham.

The Hexateuch. It is customary among scholars at the present time to group together not only the first five books and call the collection the Pentateuch, but to add Joshua and designate the whole as the Hexateuch, i.e., the sixfold book. Joshua is added because "its contents, and, still more, its literary structure, show that it is intimately connected with the Pentateuch and describes the final stage in the history of the *origines* of the Hebrew nation" (see for details the commentary on Joshua). The divine promise that the descendants of Abraham should occupy Canaan, repeatedly made in Genesis and never lost sight of in the succeeding books, attains its realization only in Joshua. The following considerations probably account for the separation of the material in Joshua from the Torah: (1) Moses could not be connected with this material as its author; (2) the contents made it impossible to set it apart with the books of the Pentateuch as Torah, i.e., as an authoritative rule of life. (Much of what is said in the succeeding paragraphs concerning the Pentateuch would be valid in a discussion of the Hexateuch.)

Mosaic Authorship: the Arguments. In the latest portions of the O.T. it seems to be assumed that the Law, or Torah, is the work of Moses (Ezra 3^2 7^6 2 Chr. 34^{14}); but it is by no means clear that in these passages "Torah" is used of the entire Pentateuch; it may refer simply to the legal system embodied in the Pentateuch, or, possibly, to only a part of this system. But whatever the significance of these and similar O.T. passages may be, Philo of Alexandria, and Josephus, the former writing near the opening of the Christian era, the latter during the closing decades of the first century A.D., proceed on the assumption that Moses wrote the entire Pentateuch, and the same may be true of some N.T. writers (Mt. 8[4] Mk. 7[10] Lk. 20[37], etc.). The Babylonian Talmud (*Baba bathra*, 14[b]), embodying early official Jewish tradition, makes the definite claim: "Moses wrote his own book, the section about Balaam and Job." Only the closing verses of Deuteronomy are ascribed to Joshua, on the reasonable assumption that Moses could not have written during his lifetime the statement, "And he died there" (Deut. 34[5]). However, a commentary on this verse in the Gemara assigns even these verses to Moses, stating that he wrote them "with weeping."

The view that Moses wrote the entire Pentateuch, with the possible exception of the closing verses, maintained itself without serious opposition until the time of the Reformation; the objectors were few and exerted little influence. Conditions changed during the period of the Renaissance and the Reformation; and since then, as will be pointed out more in detail below, scholars in increasing numbers have become convinced that Moses could not be the author of the Pentateuch in anywhere near its present form (see succeeding sections of this article). On the other hand, arguments in favor of the Mosaic authorship have been put forward with much skill by those who still defend the traditional view. Limitation of space will not permit a detailed presentation of these arguments. (For a full discussion see Eiselen, *The Books of the Pentateuch*, chs. 4–7.) Here it may be sufficient to state the several lines of argument and to give a brief evaluation of them.

The arguments may be arranged in four groups: (1) Indirect evidence, which includes such considerations as lack of unanimity among those who deny the Mosaic authorship; the manner of literary composition practiced among the ancients; and the unity of theme and plan. (2) External evidence is found in N.T. statements, especially in the words of Jesus, in the traditions current among Jews and Christians, and in the testimony of O.T. books other than the Pentateuch. (3) Direct internal evidence consists of statements in the books of the Pentateuch themselves that Moses *wrote* something. (4) Greatest reliance is placed on what may be called indirect internal evidence, i.e., evidence found in the contents of the books apart from definite statements which point to Moses as the author. This argument is cumulative, and may be presented under various heads: (a) Evidence pointing to the origin of the Pentateuch in the desert; (b) the influence of Egypt reflected in the Pentateuch; (c) the lack of personal acquaintance with Palestine on the part of the author; (d) the apparent influence of Israel's nomad life on Pentateuchal legislation; (e) linguistic characteristics pointing to an early date.

What is the weight and value of these arguments? Of course, if it were possible to limit consideration to the facts and phenomena emphasized by the defenders of Mosaic authorship, and if the conclusions reached by them could be accepted without question, the arguments might appear quite formidable, if not overwhelming. However, without going into details, it may be well to keep in mind some rather important considerations (the facts presented in the succeeding sections are of great significance and should be studied in this connection; but for the present attention is being confined to a few general considerations and conclusions): (1) One cannot escape the conviction that the method followed by the defenders of the traditional view is neither fair nor scientific. Only the facts that can be interpreted in favor of Mosaic authorship are taken into account; contradictory facts are passed over lightly or are entirely ignored. (2) The only argument that has anything to do directly with the writing of the Pentateuch is the linguistic argument; but this has proved so unsatisfactory that it is now rarely used by those who know Hebrew, for the simple reason that further study has disproved the high antiquity of the alleged archaic words and forms. (3) The student of the Hebrew legal system as a whole, not of a few well-chosen examples apart from the larger context, finds it exceedingly difficult to believe that the desert wanderings furnished an opportunity for framing the intricate criminal, civil, moral, and ceremonial codes embodied in the Pentateuch.

Indeed, all that the facts presented may prove is that the Pentateuch *may* contain some elements originating in Mosaic times; they cannot prove that these elements were preserved in written form. Nor is it possible to point out definitely any of these Mosaic elements, for they may have undergone in the course of transmission either accidental or intentional alterations. The only conclusion warranted by the facts may be briefly expressed in these words: Whatever may be the time of the final composition or compilation of the Pentateuch, it contains elements, both historical and legal, which may have originated in the days of Moses. These elements were later modified in the spirit of the first great leader; and the result of this development, continuing throughout several centuries, is embodied in the present Pentateuch. If there were no evidence to the contrary, it might be legitimate to take a further step and ascribe the entire work to Moses. But if such a step is taken, it is in the nature of an inference and nothing more. On the other hand, fairness requires that in case there are facts that seem to militate against acceptance of Mosaic authorship, these too must be carefully examined before the final verdict is given. This examination is undertaken in the succeeding paragraphs.

Progress of Pentateuchal Criticism. As stated in the preceding section, few questions based on careful examination of facts were raised regarding the Mosaic authorship of the Pentateuch prior to the Reformation. In the tenth or eleventh century a Spanish Jew, Rabbi Isaac ben Jasos, pointed out that Gen. 36[31] must be later than the founding of the Hebrew monarchy, and in the twelfth century Ibn Ezra called attention to certain passages which he found difficult to harmonize with belief in Mosaic authorship. The Renaissance and Reformation caused a marked change. The Renaissance aroused men's interest in literature and science; the Reformation aroused their interest in religion as a personal experience. In the Renaissance men began to think for themselves in matters of science and literature; in the Reformation they began to think for themselves in matters of religion. It was inevitable that the awakening of thought and the substitution of reason for authority in science, secular literature and secular history should ultimately affect sacred literature and sacred history as well. At any rate, some of the leaders in the Reformation movement, like Luther and Karlstadt, did not hesitate to express independent judgments with reference to the Mosaic authorship of the Pentateuch. Similarly, Andreas Masius, a learned Roman Catholic, maintained that the Pentateuch received its final form from Ezra or some other man of God.

The general church, Protestant and Roman, did not adopt the liberal attitude of these leaders, but continued to regard belief in the Mosaic authorship of the Pentateuch an essential article of faith. Nevertheless, the facts to which earlier writers had called attention continued to assert themselves, and new facts came to be discovered; hence it is not strange that scholars within and without the church continued to insist that the belief in Mosaic authorship was not well founded (e.g., Spinoza, Hobbes, Peyrerius, Simon, Clericus, etc.), and to propose various theories in explanation of the facts. The value of these and similar discussions lies not in the conclusions reached, but in their insistence on the facts which demanded consideration and explanation.

Jean Astruc, physician of Louis XIV and professor of medicine in Paris, gave new direction to the whole investigation. He did not deny the Mosaic authorship, but following out suggestions made by earlier writers, he maintained that Moses used several literary sources, which he incorporated, practically without alteration, into the Pentateuch. On the basis of his discovery that in some sections of Genesis the divine name *Elohim* (God) was used, and in others *Yahweh* (Jehovah), he analyzed the book into two principal sources—the Elohistic and the Jehovistic—admitting at the same time the presence of smaller sections from nine or ten minor sources. Having compiled Genesis in this manner, Moses, he said, then wrote the remaining four books of the Pentateuch. (The *Conjectures*, in which this theory was set forth, was published in 1753.)

Theories of the Composition of the Pentateuch. The investigations begun by Astruc were continued by scholars during the latter part of the eighteenth and the first half of the nineteenth century. Among them were J. G. Eichhorn, W. M. L. De Wette, F. Bleek, H. Ewald, F. Tuch, K. D. Ilgen, H. Hupfeld, K. H. Graf, each of whom made one or more definite contributions to the advance in knowledge. In the course of these and later investigations, various theories were proposed to account for the complicated facts discovered by the investigators as follows: (1) *The Fragment Theory*, which looked upon the Pentateuch as "an agglomeration of longer and shorter fragments, between which no threads of continuous connection could be traced." The arguments in support of this theory were drawn chiefly from the middle books of the Pentateuch in which, because of the presence of extensive legal sections, the transitions are frequently quite abrupt. (2) *The Supplement Theory*, based upon a better appreciation of a common plan and purpose running through the entire Pentateuch. According to this theory, the Elohistic portion of the Pentateuch was the oldest; subsequently this was revised by the Jehovist, who annotated the older work and added to it a considerable number of new and independent sections. Deuteronomy was thought to be the latest addition. (3) *The Document Theory*, which is a modification of the Supplement theory made necessary by advance along two lines: (a) The discovery in 1853 by Hupfeld of a second Elohim source; (b) a better understanding of the interrelation of the different literary layers in the Pentateuch. The theory owes its name to the fact that by those who accept it the Pentateuch in its present form is thought to be the result of the compilation of material coming from at least four documents, each of which is thought to have had originally an independent existence. (In a sense the Fragment Theory as well as the Supplement Theory might be called Document theories, because both of them recognize the presence of material coming from different sources; but in each of the three cases the term used is descriptive of the most significant characteristic.) Though in the course of time various symbols have been used to designate the four documents, and though even now complete uniformity is lacking, at present the four documents are generally known as J, E, D, P. The first, called J, i.e., the Jehovistic document, uses in the sections narrating events prior to the call of Moses the divine name *Jehovah;* E, the Elohistic document, uses in the corresponding sections the divine name *Elohim;* D, the Deuteronomic Code, furnishes the heart of the present book of Deuteronomy; P, the Priestly Code, is a document combining both history and law, which owes its name to the fact that it is written from a distinctively priestly point of view. These four documents in turn are thought to embody material taken from still earlier sources which had an independent existence in written or oral form.

The Graf-Wellhausen Theory. The Document Theory is the prevailing theory at the present time, but not in the form in which it was first presented. After undergoing various transformations it emerged in a form now commonly known as the *Graf-Wellhausen Theory*, or the *Development Theory*, and it is in this form that it is most widely accepted at the present time. The theory derives its name from the fact that two of its most convincing exponents were K. H. Graf—a pupil of Edward Reuss, one of the first scholars pointing the way to the new view—and Julius Wellhausen, one of the foremost O.T. scholars of the past generation. The special contribution of the theory to Pentateuchal research was the determination of the chronological order and of the dates of the several documents. The four documents are thought to have originated in the order J,E,D,P, and their dates, not considering later additions, were fixed as follows: for J, about 850 B.C.; E, about 750 B.C.; D, about 650 B.C.; P, about 500–350 B.C. Other scholars assisting in the development of this theory are: W. Vatke, J. F. L. George, A. Kayser, A. Kuenen, etc. Modern scholars, with few exceptions, accept in all essentials the conclusions of the Graf-Wellhausen school regarding the order and dates of the Pentateuchal documents. A few still date E earlier than J, and a smaller number date P earlier than D; and there are some who, while accepting the theory in substance, assign the documents to dates earlier than those given above.

In more recent years scholars who accept the general position of the Graf-Wellhausen theory have given special attention to the determination of the age of the material embodied in the several documents. The earlier adherents of the theory were inclined to assign not only the completed documents, but also practically all the material embodied in them to relatively late dates. Later investigations have clearly shown that this tendency was unwarranted, and that much of the material, both historical and legal, originated very early and was handed down, orally or in written form, until finally it was given a place in the longer documents. H. Gunkel, A. Merx, H. Winckler, A. Jeremias, R. Kittel, and others have been very active in the pursuit of this particular line of study.

Criticism of These Theories. It must not be thought that during all these centuries no efforts were made to uphold and defend the Mosaic authorship. During the earlier post-Reformation period several defenders of the traditional views came to the front, among them Huet, a Jesuit; Heidegger, a Calvinist; and Carpzov, a Lutheran; others, while admitting the possibility of later additions and revisions, insisted that the Mosaic authorship of the Pentateuch in substantially its present form might be maintained. Among these writers the more prominent were Du Pin, Witsius, Spanheim, Prideaut, Vitringa, Calmet. During the nineteenth century Hengstenberg, Haevernick, Keil, Green, and a few others, all of them splendidly equipped from the point of view of scholarship, did their best to uphold or re-establish the traditional views. The twentieth century has not produced a single defender of the Mosaic authorship who can compare with these men in intellectual power, in a grasp of the problems involved, or in ability to marshal his arguments.

Some scholars, admitting a degree of truth in the newer views, but unwilling to accept them in their entirety, have proposed theories of their own, which, they believe, explain the facts without departing so far from traditional views. Here belong men like A. Klostermann, Jas. Orr, B. D. Eerdmans, J. Dahse, A. Troelstra, H. M. Wiener, and others. Most of these more recent views do not represent a return to the old traditional position, but are a combination of the Supplement Theory and a modified Document Theory. Unfortunately, as has been pointed out so forcefully by Professor Skinner (*The Divine Names in Genesis, passim*), the textual-critical foundations on which these views are largely based are rather insecure. In other words, though many minute questions of Pentateuchal criticism are still obscure, and though some of the views now held may have to undergo modifications, the Document Theory, as presented in its main outlines by the Graf-Wellhausen school, appears to have the better of the argument at the present time.

The Pentateuch a Compilation. The modern critical view of the origin and development of the Pentateuch includes the following items: (1) The Pentateuch is a relatively late compilation of material taken from written sources, all of which reached their final form subsequently to the time of Moses. (2) The compiler depended chiefly upon four documents: J, traces of which are found throughout the entire Pentateuch; E, closely interwoven with J and, like it, found throughout the Pentateuch; D, found chiefly in the book of Deuteronomy, though traces of it are found also elsewhere; P, which served as the groundwork for the entire compilation. (3) D is identical with the Book of the Law that served as the basis of Josiah's reform in 621 B.C.; it was in existence separately at that time; hence the Pentateuch in its final form cannot be older than that date, though some of the material embodied in it may be much older. (4) J and E are both older than D, and, according to most investigators, D is older than P. (5) The several documents show such striking differences that, on the whole, it is quite easy to separate them.

Any adequate discussion of the modern view must therefore include at least four points: (1) The Pentateuch is a compilation of material from different documents written at different times. (2) The Pentateuch contains some material that originated subsequently to the time of Moses. (3) The Book of the Law found in the days of Josiah was not the Pentateuch in its final form but the Deuteronomic Code. (4) The Pentateuch in its present form is the result of gradual growth during several centuries following the age of Moses.

In support of the claim that the Pentateuch is a compilation of material taken from different sources, attention is called to the following facts:

(1) The peculiar use of the divine names *Jehovah* (*Yahweh*) and *Elohim* in narratives of events prior to the call and commission of Moses. There are large sections of Genesis and of the opening chapters of Exodus which systematically use the name *Jehovah,* while others with equal consistency use *Elohim.* (See the table in Eiselen, *The Books of the Pentateuch,* p. 125.) Is there any significance in the fact that in Gen. 1[1]–2[4a], the account of creation, Elohim is used thirty-five times and Jehovah not at all, while in 2[4b-25], also dealing with creation, the combination Jehovah-Elohim is used exclusively? Does it mean anything that in Gen. 12–16 Jehovah is used twenty-seven times and Elohim not at all? Or, why is it that in Gen. 33–50 Jehovah occurs but once, while El or Elohim is found fifty-seven times? Is it strange that even with only facts like these before them scholars should reach the conclusion that the peculiarity in this use of the divine names points to the use of at least two distinct documents in the composition of Genesis? (This was the Document Theory as presented by Astruc; later investigation led to the discovery of a third document in Genesis, and finally to the recognition of the composite character of the entire Pentateuch.) Of course various attempts have been made to explain the usage described without assuming the use of different documents (see Eiselen, *The Books of the Pentateuch,* ch. 8), but the present writer is quite convinced that the facts in the case receive a natural and satisfactory explanation only on the assumption that the author had access to at least two different sources, one believing that the name *Jehovah* was known from the beginning, the other, that it was first revealed to Moses (Ex. 3[13-16] 6[2, 3]).

(2) The presence of repetitions and discrepancies both in the narrative and the legal portions of the Pentateuch. Would such duplications appear in a work coming in its entirety from one and the same author? We find them in both the narrative and the legal portions, as follows:

(a) In the *narrative* portions: Repetitions and discrepancies, which are found in large numbers, are of three kinds: (i) In some instances the duplicate narratives appear side by side, as in the case of the story of creation (cf. Gen. 1[1]–2[4a] with 2[4b-25]). While attempts have been made to deny the presence of parallel accounts, as a matter of fact these two chapters cannot be satisfactorily explained except on the assumption that we are face to face with two distinct accounts, which must be traced to two different authors. (ii) In other cases it may seem to the casual reader that he is dealing with a single continuous story; and yet closer study reveals the presence of repetitions and even discrepancies which show that the narrative in its present form is the result of compilation. Thus a careful reading of the narrative of the Flood (Gen. 6–9) reveals two accounts of man's corruption and God's consequent displeasure; also repetitions in the statements concerning the entering into the ark, the rising of the water, the perishing of all living creatures and the drying of the earth; some passages speak of one pair of every kind of animals being taken into the ark, while others distinguish between clean and unclean animals and state that of the former seven pairs of each were preserved; according to some verses the Flood continued for forty days, according to others, one hundred and fifty. (iii) There are, in addition to these cases pointing in the direction of compilation, some parallel accounts of the same events, not placed side by side, but found in different parts of the Pentateuch. Under this head may be mentioned duplicate accounts of the origin of names like Beersheba (Gen. 21^{31} and $26^{32, 33}$), Bethel (Gen. $28^{18, 19}$ and 35^{15}), Israel (Gen. 32^{28} and 35^{10}); there are two accounts of the promise of a son to Abraham (Gen. 17^{16-19} and 18^{9-15}); the father-in-law of Moses bears two different names (Ex. 2^{18} and 3^{1}); there are two accounts of the sending of manna and quails (Ex. 16 Num. 11), etc.

(b) In the *legal* portions. Repetitions and discrepancies here are equally numerous, but again only a few typical illustrations may be given: (i) Attention may be called to differences in the legislation concerning the place of sacrifice. According to the Book of the Covenant, Jehovah may be worshiped in different places —in every place where he may record his name, and the altar must be built of earth or unhewn stone (Ex. $20^{24, 25}$); the Deuteronomic Code prohibits repeatedly and emphatically the worship of Jehovah at local sanctuaries, and insists with the same emphasis that his worship should be centered in one place (Deut. 12^{2-7}; cf. 14^{23} $16^{2, 6, 7}$, etc.); the Priestly Code specifies that the same altar which, according to Ex. $20^{24, 25}$, is to be made of earth or unhewn stone, is to be built of acacia wood (Ex. 27^{1}). (ii) Similar differences may be seen in the laws with reference to the priesthood. The Book of the Covenant knows no priestly race; it agrees with the earlier historical records, which assume that the priests may be taken from any tribe, and that the heads of families may offer sacrifice (e.g., Judg. 13^{19} 1 Sam. 7^{17} 20^{29} 1 Kings $18^{30f.}$, etc.); Deuteronomy recognizes a priestly tribe—the Levites ($17^{9, 18}$ 18^{1} 21^{5}), implying everywhere that the priesthood was limited to the tribe of Levi and, also, that all the members of the tribe of Levi were priests; the Priestly Code expresses a still different view, namely, that the priesthood is limited to a particular family within the tribe of Levi, the sons of Aaron; while it assigns to other members of the tribe the lower offices and tasks connected with the sanctuary (Ex. 28^{1} Num. 3^{5-10} 18^{1-7}).

(3) Differences in theological conception, style, and vocabulary constitute another argument in favor of the composite character of the Pentateuch. These differences are discussed in greater detail in the succeeding paragraphs; hence it may be sufficient here simply to call attention to some striking differences in the two stories of creation (Gen. 1^{1}–2^{4a} and 2^{4b-25}). Note, for instance, the primitive God concept reflected in the second, which is the earlier, of these stories: "Jehovah-Elohim" is said to "form" or "fashion" man and the animals, and to "breathe" into man's nostrils the breath of life; he "takes" a rib from the man's body, "closes up" the opening, and "builds" the rib into a woman; he "plants" the garden, "takes" man and "sets him down" in it, etc. It requires no extraordinary powers of observation to see that the conception of Deity in the first, or later narrative in ch. 1 moves on a much higher, more spiritual, and more ethical plane. Moreover, even the English reader of these stories can appreciate certain striking differences in style, and at least the student of Hebrew is impressed by certain easily traced differences in vocabulary. Then when we remember that the same differences characterize the rest of the Pentateuch it becomes practically impossible to escape the conviction that, whoever may have been responsible for putting the Pentateuch in its present form, he must have drawn material from different literary sources composed by different authors.

Characteristics of the Four Principal Pentateuchal Documents. For the sake of clearness a brief statement may here be made regarding the peculiarities of language, style, and thought which differentiate the principal sources used by the compiler.

(1) *Peculiarities of language.* A full appreciation of the facts here enumerated requires a knowledge of Hebrew; but even the English reader can recognize some of the linguistic peculiarities. The following words are characteristic of J: "Jehovah" is the name of the God of Israel in the narratives of pre-Mosaic times; "Sinai," not Horeb, is the name of the mountain on which the Law was given; "Israel," not Jacob, is the name of the third patriarch, following the birth of Benjamin; "Canaanites" is the name used to designate the inhabitants of Palestine; "Aram Naharaim" is the regular name for Mesopotamia; "Egypt" is used as

the equivalent of Egyptian. Characteristic phrases are: "To find favor (or grace) in the sight of . . . "; "to call on the name of . . ."; "to run to meet . . . "; "took him a wife"; "to preserve seed alive"; "to dwell in the midst of. . . ." The longer form of the pronoun of the first person, *anôkhî*, is used, not *anî;* the Hebrew particle *na* is frequently used with the imperative for the sake of emphasis.

As characteristic of E may be noted: "Elohim," not Jehovah, is the divine name in the E sections of Genesis; "Amorites," not Canaanites, is the name of the pre-Israelitish inhabitants of Palestine; "Horeb," not Sinai, is the name of the mountain of God; "Jacob" is used in preference to Israel as the name of the third patriarch, from Gen. 32[32] on; "Jethro" is the name of the father-in-law of Moses. Among characteristic expressions are: "the man Moses"; "to bring up" (from the land of Egypt) instead of "to bring out," as in J.

D also has its characteristic words or phrases (for since J and E were in existence when D was written, we might expect to find indications that the author was influenced by the language of both these earlier documents): As in E, "Horeb," not Sinai, is the name of the mountain on which the Law was given. Some of the striking phrases are: "that your days may be long"; "a mighty hand and a stretched out arm"; "the stranger, the fatherless and the widow"; "and remember that thou wast a bondman in Egypt"; "to do what is right (or evil) in the eyes of Jehovah"; "with all the heart and with all the soul"; "to observe to do."

The linguistic peculiarities of P are exceedingly numerous. Driver (*Introduction to the Literature of the O.T.*, 1910 edition, pp. 131f.) enumerates fifty expressions characteristic of the narrative sections of P, many of which appear rarely or never elsewhere, some of them only in Ezekiel: "Elohim," not Jehovah, is used in Genesis; "Paddan Aram" is the regular name for Mesopotamia; "Sinai," as in J, not Horeb, is the mountain of God; *anî*, the shorter form of the pronoun of the first person, is used one hundred and thirty times, the longer form *anôkhî* only once; *ammim*, literally "peoples," is used in the sense of "kinsfolk," especially in the two expressions, "That soul shall be cut off from his kinsfolk," and "to be gathered unto one's kinsfolk." Other characteristic phrases are: "to be fruitful and multiply"; "this selfsame day" (literally, "the bone of this day"); "after their families"; "soul" (Hebrew, *nephesh*) in the sense of "person"; "throughout their generations"; "congregation of the Israelites"; "according to the mouth (i.e., command) of. . . ."

(2) *Peculiarities of style.* Even the reader of the English Bible can "feel" certain differences in the style of different sections of the Pentateuch. As in other matters, the differences between J and E are not as great as those between JE on the one hand and D and P on the other; which is due to the fact that J and E come from approximately the same age—the creative age of prophetic narration, both of them representing the same general point of view. It may be noted, however, that J dwells less than E upon concrete particulars, while it excels in the power of delineating life and character. Its author is, indeed, the best narrator in the Bible. E is perhaps a little more terse in style, but its narratives are on the whole so well told that it is not easy to see wherein they fall short of J, except that at times they lack the spontaneous charm and strength of the other. The style of P is much less spontaneous; it is "stereotyped, measured, and prosaic"; the descriptions are "precise and methodical"; there is a tendency to describe an act or event in full each time it is mentioned; P shows a preference for "standing formulæ and expressions." In general, it seems that the author's practical acquaintance with the Law created certain habits of thought and forms of expression which he carried over into his treatment of purely historical subjects. In a comparison of style D might almost be left out of consideration because, while J and E are chiefly historical, D represents legal literature; this difference in subject matter would inevitably produce differences in style, even though the author were the same. However, it is possible to institute comparisons between D and the legal sections of P: The style of the latter is cold, legal, formal, and precise; that of the former rhetorical and hortatory, closely resembling that of the great prophets. The differences in style and vocabulary—much more numerous than this brief list would seem to indicate—cannot be explained, as has been attempted, on the basis of difference in theme or subject matter, because in many instances the differences appear in sections dealing with one and the same theme.

(3) *Peculiarities of theological thought.* J reflects a very primitive and pronounced anthropomorphic conception of the Deity. Jehovah is represented not only as forming human resolutions and as swayed by human emotions, which is common in other and later books, as well, but also as performing his acts in a human way (cf. illustrations from the story of creation, above, under section (3) of "The Pentateuch a Compilation"). J shows less tendency than is seen in other parts of the Pentateuch to explain significant events by appeal to

the extraordinary, supernatural, miraculous; there is more general recognition of the play of natural forces. This appears, e.g., in the stories of the plagues of Egypt (Ex. $8^{1-4, 20-32}$ 9^{1-7}, etc.; compare these with 8^{5-7} 9^{8-12}, etc), and of the crossing of the Red Sea (Ex. 14^{21}). E reflects different and more advanced theological ideas. True, these narratives still recognize the legitimacy of the local sanctuaries and their equipment, but they give no support to unspiritual practices of worship, and the putting away of "strange gods" meets the author's full approval. The God of these parts does not appear in bodily form but in dreams (Gen. 20^{3} 31^{24} Num. $22^{9, 20}$), and he carries out his plans through the ministry of angels (Gen. 21^{17} 22^{11} 28^{12}). Closely connected with this conception is the representation of Abraham as a prophet (Gen. 20^{7}), while Moses, though not called a prophet, is intrusted with a prophetic mission (Ex. 3). Though the standpoint of both J and E is prophetic, there is in E less evidence of conscious ethical and theological reflection. D also has its own characteristic theological conceptions. It will have nothing to do with the local sanctuaries, because they have corrupted Jehovah worship and have led to such differences in the conception of Jehovah that in reality Israel was worshiping at its various sanctuaries not one Jehovah but a number of different Jehovahs; hence the insistence in Deut. 6^{4}, "Jehovah our God is one Jehovah" (cf. 6^{5} 10^{12} $11^{1, 13, 22}$ for a statement of the fundamental law of Deuteronomy). While J and E consider the "pillar" perfectly legitimate, D prohibits it (Deut. $16^{21, 22}$); unlike J and E, D insists again and again that there is only one legitimate place of worship (Deut. $12^{5, 11, 14, 18, 21, 26}$, etc.); unlike P (see next paragraph) D recognizes all the Levites as priests (Deut. $17^{9, 18}$ 18^{1} 21^{5}).

The theological conceptions of P present striking contrasts to those of the other sources. The representation of God is much less anthropomorphic, and there are no angels or dreams as means of divine communication. The author's outlook is narrow; the promises made to the patriarchs are restricted to Israel, and the writer's ideal is the Israelitish theocracy. In the legal sections of P religion is defined largely in terms of ritual and form, which is at variance with the spirit of J and E; there is an elaborate ritual for the offering of sacrifice, and great prominence is given to sin and trespass offerings, not mentioned elsewhere in the Pentateuch. A sharp distinction is made between the priests and the Levites (see above); only here is introduced the high priest with all his functions and privileges.

Post-Mosaic Elements in the Pentateuch. Astruc, who saw evidences of compilation only in Genesis, could hold that Moses was the compiler of Genesis and then wrote the rest of the Pentateuch (see above, under "Progress of Pentateuchal Criticism"). Later investigation, as has been pointed out in the preceding paragraphs, has convinced scholars that the entire Pentateuch is a compilation. If this conclusion is warranted—and the present writer believes that it is—belief in the Mosaic authorship becomes practically impossible. Some time must have elapsed between the last event recorded—the death of Moses—and the production of the compilation in its present form. There are, however, some additional specific considerations that strengthen the conviction that Moses was not the author, such as the presence of references and passages which by their very contents imply that they were written subsequently to the time of Moses (for details see Eiselen, *The Books of the Pentateuch*, ch. 11). There are, for instance, certain literary considerations, e.g., the use of the third person in referring to Moses (Ex. $6^{26, 27}$ Num. 33^{2}), or the account of Moses' death (Deut. 34^{1-8}). Some of the geographical terms point in the same direction. The territory east of the Jordan is called "beyond Jordan" (Num. 32 Deut. 1^{5} $4^{41, 46, 47, 49}$), implying that the author lived west of the Jordan, which would not be true of Moses. Residence in Palestine is suggested also by the use of the geographical term *neghebh*, i.e., the southern portion of Judah, with the general meaning "south," and of the term "sea," i.e., the Mediterranean Sea, with the general meaning "west." The name "Hebron" (Gen. 13^{18} 23^{2} 37^{14} Num. 13^{22}) was of post-Mosaic origin (Josh. 14^{15} 15^{13}); the same is true of the name "Dan" (cf. Gen. 14^{14} Deut. 34^{1} with Judg. 18^{29}). In the same direction point passages like Deut. 3^{14} (cf. Judg. $10^{3, 4}$) and Gen. 40^{15}.

A number of historical statements or allusions also imply a post-Mosaic date. Thus Gen. 36^{31} presupposes the establishment of the monarchy in Israel, generations after the time of Moses; the expression "the Canaanite was then in the land" (Gen. 12^{6} 13^{7}) has no meaning unless it was written at a time when the Canaanites had disappeared at least as an independent people. Deut. 2^{12} refers to the conquest as an accomplished fact; Ex. $15^{13, 17}$ presupposes the establishment of Jehovah's sanctuary on Mount Zion, which was not the case until the days of David. If Moses wrote the entire Pentateuch, is it not strange that he was in doubt regarding the name of his own father-in-law (cf. Ex. 2^{18} Num.

10[29] with Ex. 3[1] 18[1]). Moreover, the characterization of Moses in certain passages reads as if it came from someone other than Moses (e.g., Ex. 11[3] Num. 12[3] Deut. 34[10]). The legal sections of the Pentateuch contain some enactments which presuppose a background other than that of the desert (e.g., Ex. 23[19] Deut. 19[14]), and there are some archæological notes which seem to have originated at a relatively late date (e.g., Ex. 30[13, 34] 38[24-26] Deut. 3[11]).

Frequently the assertion is made that there is no good reason for denying the passages mentioned and others of a similar nature to Moses, that practically all of them can be interpreted as coming from him, and that the few exceptions may be regarded as later interpolations, without assuming that the whole work is a relatively late compilation. But while it is true that Moses might perhaps have written some of the passages enumerated, others cannot possibly come from him; and in every case the only natural interpretation is that which ascribes the passage to another author. Again, while some of the passages might perhaps be thrown out as interpolations, others are so closely bound up with their context that they would carry with them large sections of the Pentateuch, and the resulting breaking up of continuity in narration would increase rather than diminish the difficulties. On the other hand, the difficulties disappear if it is admitted that the narratives or the legal sections in which the alleged post-Mosaic elements are found were written in the periods to which modern scholarship assigns them.

Chronological Order of the Pentateuchal Documents. Is it possible to arrange in chronological order the documents from which the material used in the compilation of the Pentateuch was taken? Scholars have sought to find an answer to this inquiry by studying the documents along the following lines: (1) the historical situation reflected in the documents; (2) the theological standpoint expressed or implied; (3) the relation of the Pentateuchal documents to other O.T. writings; (4) peculiarities of vocabulary and style; (5) the relation of the documents to each other.

The conclusions reached may be summarized as follows: (1) J and E reflect the historical situation of the period of the Judges and of the early monarchy; D that of the later monarchy, especially conditions reflected in the account of Josiah's reforms in 621 B.C. and in the utterances of Jeremiah; P that of the later exilic and the post-exilic period, especially the age of Ezra and Nehemiah. (2) In the case of each of the four documents the theological standpoint agrees with what is known of Hebrew theological thinking during the period to which it is assigned on the basis of the historical situation reflected in it. (3) J and E have points of contact with O.T. writings known to have originated before 650 B.C. (e.g., the prophetic books of the eighth century); D with the literature that originated between 650 B.C. and the Exile (e.g., Kings, Jeremiah); P with that of the post-exilic period (Malachi, Ezra, Nehemiah, Chronicles). D seems to have been unknown prior to the seventh century, P before the Exile. (4) The style and vocabulary of each document are what they might be expected to be if the documents were actually written during the periods to which the historical background assigns them. (5) In their legal as in their historical sections JE, D, and P represent three successive stages of development—P implies the prior existence of D, D the prior existence of J and E. (6) The available evidence points to the following approximate dates for the documents: J belongs to the early centuries of the monarchy, perhaps about 850 B.C.; E originated not long before the appearance of the eighth-century prophets, about 750 B.C.; D presupposes the activity of the eighth-century prophets and may have been written during the reactionary reign of Manasseh, about 650 B.C.; P originated among the descendants of the exiles in Babylonia, about 500 to 450 B.C., and was completed in Palestine in the days of Ezra-Nehemiah, before 400 B.C. This statement regarding the dates of the documents does not exclude the possibility of some material having been added subsequently.

Growth of the Pentateuch. The successive stages in the development of the Pentateuch may be outlined as follows:

(1) The earliest literary period in Israel, as among other peoples, was preceded by an age of song and story. The songs, which centered around significant happenings in the life of the family, clan or tribe, or portrayed the heroic exploits of individuals, were highly prized, and were recited or sung both by the common people and by professional singers. Alongside of these songs grew up stories and legends glorifying important persons and events. Some of this material undoubtedly goes back to pre-Mosaic times.

(2) In time collections of these songs were made (cf. Num. 21[14] and Josh. 10[13]; also art., *The Poetic and Wisdom Literature*, p. 154). Similarly individual stories came to be combined in cycles, each cycle centering around an outstanding personality (cf. the patriarchal narratives).

(3) Following the occupation of Palestine, the Hebrews assimilated in large part the na-

tive population and rededicated to Jehovah many of its local shrines. With the sanctuaries some of the traditions which had grown up around these sacred places were taken over by the conquerors.

(4) Gradually the new religion introduced by Moses permeated the pre-Mosaic material and led to various modifications that brought this material into harmony with the new and higher religious and ethical conceptions.

(5) The entrance into Palestine meant the transition from a nomadic to a more settled mode of living. This forward step necessitated the adaptation of old laws and the formulation of new laws to meet the new needs. At some of the sanctuaries collections of such laws may have been made (e.g., the Book of the Covenant, Ex. 20[22]–23[19]). In the same places efforts may have been made to preserve in connected and more permanent form the early songs and stories.

(6) During the period of the United Monarchy traces of connected prose writing first appear. After the division of the kingdom this new literary interest continued to flourish. Finally it resulted, in the prophetic circles, in the collection of ancient songs and stories, their revision under the influence of the prophetic ideas and ideals, and their compilation into extensive "histories," tracing human history back to the beginning of man's life upon earth. Several of these "histories" may have been produced, but only two of them, J and E, the former written in Judah, the latter in Israel, seriously affected the growth of the Pentateuch.

(7) Probably during the reactionary reign of Manasseh, when the lessons taught in J and E needed to be impressed upon the people, the two documents were combined into a single continuous narrative. J was made the basis of the combination, because (a) J was a document of Judah, where the combination was made; and (b) the Northern Kingdom had disappeared in 722 B.C.; consequently E, as the product of a foreign and no longer existent people, had to be content with a secondary position.

(8) At approximately the same time D assumed literary form. In a sense, D is a compromise between priestly and prophetic ideals. The author (or authors), who possessed all the moral fervor of the eighth-century prophets, sought to make the prophetic teaching more effective by making it more concrete. Hence he retained, as far as possible, existing forms, usages, and traditions and poured into them a deeper and more spiritual significance.

(9) After the acceptance of D as the law of the land, during the reign of Josiah, the desirability of combining the new law code with the earlier documents, JE, which had come to occupy an important position, was recognized. This feeling was strengthened by the dissolution of the national life, when the few remains of national and sacred literature came to be highly prized. Consequently, some time during the sixth century B.C., D was united with JE, the compiler, or compilers, introducing into the older work such modifications as were necessary to maintain or establish logical connection.

(10) The publication of the "prophetic" D caused the priests to feel that their own interests were in danger and that the phase of religion represented by them might suffer; hence, shortly before the Exile in 586 B.C., they collected the laws dealing with priestly interests and ideals into a short code, which by modern scholars is called the "Law of Holiness" (Lev. 17–26; see commentary on Leviticus).

(11) During the Exile, especially through the efforts of Ezekiel, Deutero-Isaiah and their colaborers, religion became spiritualized. But while this spiritualizing process was going on the question seems to have arisen in the minds of some: The higher stage of religion having been reached, how may the lapses of the past be avoided? The answer was: By insisting upon obedience to definite rules and regulations. With the promulgation of D the reign of written law had its beginning; the Law of Holiness and the laws of Ezekiel (chs. 40–48) mark further steps in the development of legalism; but the culmination of the legalistic tendency may be seen in P, which originated among the exiles in Babylon.

(12) The new law, backed by the authority of Moses, soon came to be accepted as final authority. The seat of authority was transferred from the present experience of communion with God to laws which were thought to have originated at a time when God was believed to have been especially close to his people. This new interest in the law impelled a priest or priests who were under the influence of the new point of view to rewrite the early history of Israel, tracing it back to creation, perhaps for the sole purpose of furnishing a proper historical setting for the laws of P.

(13) The necessity of amalgamating the two parallel histories of the Mosaic and pre-Mosaic ages, JED and P, must have been felt soon after the compilation of P. As long as the two existed as separate works side by side, they would seem to compete for recognition as the authoritative word of Moses or of Jehovah. Serious conflict could be avoided only by uniting the two into one continuous work. The

task may have been undertaken by Ezra, or, if not by him, by some contemporary who was in hearty sympathy with the ideals of P.

(14) Thus, aside from minor alterations made at a still later time, the Pentateuch reached its completed form before 400 B.C. The finished work was called *Torah* or *Law.* Subsequently it was divided at natural dividing points into five parts or books, so that the whole came to be known as the *Five-fifths of the Law;* from this designation came the name *Pentateuch,* meaning *Five-Roll Treatise,* which was coined by Greek writers, from whom it passed into Latin and other western languages.

Permanent Value of the Pentateuch. In the introduction to the commentary on Genesis attention is called to the permanent value of that book from the standpoint both of history and of religion, and in the proper places brief statements on the same subject are made in connection with the other books of the Pentateuch. Consequently, it is not necessary in this connection to do more than to sum up in a few words the entire situation with reference to the permanent value of the Pentateuch. Elsewhere the present writer has written concerning Gen. 1–11: "The purpose of the narratives being primarily religious, it is only natural that the lessons reflected in them should be religious lessons. The one supreme truth taught throughout the entire section is 'In the beginning God'; but each separate narrative teaches its now characteristic lessons." (For a concise statement of the more important truths expressed or implied, see Driver, *The Book of Genesis,* p. 70.) The patriarchal narratives which follow are of the highest value both historically and religiously; and a similar statement may be made with reference to the other narrative sections of the Pentateuch. All the important incidents in the early history of Israel as recorded in the Pentateuch remain unaffected by modern conclusions regarding the origin of these books; nor is their religious value affected. These narratives still reveal the hand of God in the events culminating in the organization of Hebrew national life, and they still furnish striking illustrations of the reality of a Divine Providence.

The inherent value of the laws embodied in the narrative portions remains the same whether they come from Moses or were, as modern scholars believe, the product of the divinely guided experience of the nation from Moses to Ezra. The modern view does not alter the fact that the Hebrews were the first to learn and to teach that the supreme goal of life is righteousness and to give expression to pure and lofty ethics in objective law. The principles of Hebrew legislation, whether they were established by Moses or by some other man or men of God, remain to this day the "bone and marrow" of the world's greatest legal systems. Whenever the Decalogue assumed literary form, "the marvelous perfection of this summary of moral law, its intrinsic excellency, the universal applicability of its several precepts, and their abiding and unchanging nature, place these commandments in advance of anything to be found elsewhere in the annals of human legislation" (Terry, *Moses and the Prophets,* p. 28). Thus it is with the entire legal system. Modern scholarship does not tend to deny or doubt that the laws of Israel are permeated by a Divine Spirit, for the important question is not, When, where and by whom were these laws written? but, Do the character and spirit of the laws bear witness to the presence of God?

Literature: Keil, *Introduction to the Canonical Scriptures of the O.T.;* Raven, *O.T. Introduction* (these two represent the traditional point of view); Driver, *Introduction to the Literature of the O.T.;* McFadyen, *An Introduction to the O.T.;* Bewer, *Literature of the O.T.;* Green, *The Higher Criticism of the Pentateuch* (traditional); Wiener, *The Origin of the Pentateuch* (traditional); Brightman, *The Sources of the Hexateuch;* Simpson, *Pentateuchal Criticism;* Eiselen, *The Books of the Pentateuch.*

THE LEGAL AND HISTORICAL LITERATURE OF THE OLD TESTAMENT

By Professor W. G. JORDAN

Literature and Life. Literature suggests life; it is often defined as an expression and criticism of life. Law, on the other hand, is apt to be regarded as something cold and hard. But both law and "literature" existed before "letters"; and in diverse literary forms the records of ancient customs and traditions have been preserved. It will be our purpose in this brief sketch to show that in different forms and degrees they are revelations of a growing experience through which the spirit of God has given a unique and permanent gift to the world's religious life.

The literature with which this article is concerned arose in Palestine during the period between 1200 B.C. and 150 B.C.; but it had its roots in a more distant past and its successors in later Jewish literature. It passed through various stages as oral transmission, general literature, sacred literature and finally canonical literature. (See art., *Formation of O.T.*, p. 91.) While the dates of the different parts of this literature can be fixed only approximately, a fairly reliable outline has been reached which shows a living movement not accounted for by the genius of any group of men or the toils of any one generation but suggests "a discipline" (Deut. 8^{1-5}) which links all these into an organic whole and gives an impression of spiritual unity. This outline has been made possible by the study of separate yet related lines of history, political, literary and linguistic, ecclesiastical and religious. It can claim to have solved some large problems and revealed many smaller ones not easy to solve. Both in the region of law and history it has shown that there are strata in the documents which reveal separate stages in a life that was never at rest and never as simple as a superficial view would suggest.

Modern investigations have given a large background to the Nearer East. Archæology and comparative religion have made clear two things: (1) the great age of "civilization," thus making Hebrews and Greeks comparatively modern people, and (2) the fact that though a religion may in a real sense be traced to a great man as its founder, e.g., Moses, it was not written upon an empty page but was cast into the soil as a living seed which had to struggle for its life in the midst of a luxuriant crop of what came later to be regarded as "weeds." In Palestine to-day types of religious belief and practice may be found against which the men of prophetic spirit, in Israel, had to fight through those thousand years of conflict and progress. In the beginning criticism tended to be negative in its view of the primitive period; further investigation, however, has clearly shown that the origin of the national unity of the Hebrews and the foundation of their religion were linked together in the great crisis in connection with which they came into the land which was to be the scene of their historical and religious life. The sublime figure of the great leader, Moses, who himself never crossed the Jordan, is magnified rather than dwarfed by the mists that surround "the Exodus."

The Law-Literature

A religious movement in early days was bound to center round a great personality who, in a simple form, united in himself some of the qualities of priest, prophet and statesman. Many modern scholars maintain that the "Ten Words" of Ex. 20^{1-17} can, when freed from later expansions, be traced back to Moses. That question, as also the relation of this small group of laws to Deut. 5^{6-21}, is too complicated for discussion here. We must, however, conceive of Moses as one who, by uniting a number of tribes in the worship of Jehovah, lifted religion above the low nature worship, and thus started a movement which could reveal all that was implied in it only through the struggles which at times threatened to destroy it, and through the God-given teachers who in defending the teaching of Moses raised it to a higher level. (Ex. 34 probably contains an older and ritualistic decalogue.)

Babylonian and Hebrew Law. Questions have been raised about the background of the Hebrew law-literature, especially since the discovery (in 1901) of the Code of Hammurabi, who was king of Babylon about 2,000 B.C. The Empire of Babylonia was then in a flourishing condition and the Hammurabi code reflects the life of a highly organized community whose social conditions and commercial interests had to be carefully defined and regulated. The contrast between the circumstances and needs of this vast Babylonian organization and the small settlements of Hebrew tribes is very great. The superiority of Babylonian civilization is reflected in the existence of law and judicial procedure far in advance of anything that Israel could have required; nevertheless, the similarities between the two systems are striking, one conspicuous example being the retention of the primitive "law of like" (Mt. 5[38]). Some have traced these similarities to direct literary dependence; however, in most instances it is not a question of "borrowing"; the two peoples belonged to the same racial stock, known as the Semites; their roots went back to a common life in the distant past. From the common Semitic culture developed both the Babylonian and the Hebrew civilization, the Semitics of Babylonia reaching an advanced degree of civilization long before the younger branch that we call Hebrews had passed the semi-nomadic stage. (See further art., *O.T. and Archaeology*, p. 114.) The connection of the Babylonian code is closest with the collection of laws called "The Book of the Covenant" (Ex. 20–23).

The Book of the Covenant. In very early times short lists of rules were arranged in fives and tens to help retention by memory. Later longer codes grew out of these and were absorbed into still larger collections. The Book of the Covenant (Ex. 20[22]–23[33]) is the earliest of these. This collection of laws has been subjected to a searching analysis, which has revealed the fact that while it consists of various elements, it is, on the whole, the code of a pastoral people. There seems to be a distinction between "words"—direct and absolute divine commands—and "judgments"—judicial decisions or common law. The aim throughout is the rule of Jehovah's people by laws that are just to all classes, slaves as well as free men.

The Deuteronomic Code. Deuteronomy comes into the life of the people two or three centuries later, after the Northern Kingdom had been broken. The book in its present form consists of three elements—historical reviews, exhortations, and laws. It is with the latter that we are now concerned. Those laws are called specially "Deuteronomic" that are linked to the demand for centralizing the worship of Jehovah in Jerusalem. The effort to centralize Jehovah worship grew out of the conviction that while there had been many Baals, Jehovah is *One,* and that the purity of worship could be maintained only if it were confined to a single sanctuary. The general impression made upon the careful student is that so far as the substance is concerned this code is largely in the nature of a repetition and expansion of the earlier code, "The Book of the Covenant." However, the influence of the prophets is clearly seen, and the element of persuasion is prominent. In all probability the Deuteronomic Code in its original form was the law book which formed the basis of King Josiah's reforms (2 Kings 22, 23; 2 Chr. 34, 35. See further commentary on Deuteronomy, and art., *Pentateuch*, p. 143).

The Priestly Code. In the two codes considered thus far the observances of festivals and the rules of ritual appear alongside of social legislation, and the humanitarian emphasis is quite marked. In the Priests' Code, found mainly in the middle books of the Pentateuch, the ritual of worship and sacrifice is the chief feature. But even here there are traces that the prophets have not preached in vain, that the ideas of sin and purity are seeking symbolic expression and a deeper religious significance. One must resolutely put aside the thought of this great body of ritual legislation, upon which later Judaism on its priestly side came to rest, as a late invention. Many of the ritual provisions are survivals from prehistoric times, and the development of the code represents a long and slow process. In the code in its final form were included not only individual laws which had come down from earlier days but also smaller collections formed in earlier centuries. The so-called Holiness Code in Lev. 17–26 is an example of such an early collection of laws. The Holiness Code has striking points of contact with Ezek. 40–48, and may come from the priestly circles in exile.

A definite claim for Mosaic authorship of the whole Pentateuch is not found until a relatively late period (cf. 2 Kings 14[6] with 2 Chr. 25[4]); yet the rise of such claim is easily understood when we observe the living thread which connects the earliest laws with the latest, and at the same time keep in mind the tendency to mass the results of a long movement round the names of a single great leader, preferably one appearing in the early stages of the movement. In this connection the history of the word *Torah*, commonly translated "Law," is of real interest. In the beginning it had the general meaning "teaching," then it came to be used of definite precepts resulting from such teaching, later it was applied to a body of such precepts, and then finally it assumed the technical meaning "the five books of Moses." This is the meaning it has had for orthodox Jews during many centuries. No other section of their Scriptures was placed by them on the same level. Whatever part foreign influence may have played at different points, this "law-literature" is a genuine production and reflection of Hebrew life and religion. It played its part in building up the solid Judaism which saved the O.T. for the world and enabled the race and religion to survive the loss of the temple and the land. (For the glorification of this law-literature cf. Psa. 1, 19 and especially 119.)

Historical Literature

For a proper appreciation of the historical literature more than critical ability is required; it calls for an attitude of sympathy and for imagination. There is a certain clearness and precision in law and ritual. "Thou shalt observe this festival at a certain time and in a definite manner." "This thing thou shalt not do." Such commands and prohibitions are intelligible; though, at times, their origin and meaning may call for careful research. In the interpretation of historical literature the difference between the Oriental and the Western mind must be considered; moreover, in the days when the biblical records were written our modern division of science and art, fact and fiction, philosophy and theology had not come to any clearness. The Hebrew view of such things was simpler than our own or that of the Greeks. (See further arts., *O.T. and Science*, p. 125, and *Formation of O.T.*, p. 91.)

Literature Dealing with the Prehistoric Period. Our present concern being with *historical* literature we cannot deal at length with what must be regarded as the prehistoric period; i.e., as commonly understood, the period prior to Moses. The "historical" narratives in the O.T. begin with the story of creation and the origin of the various elements constituting what may be called early civilization. In these narratives (Gen. 1^1–11^9) numerous evidences of Babylonian influence have been discovered; but it is well to remember that the real significance of the early chapters of Genesis is found not in these common elements, but in that which represents the differences—the general spirit and atmosphere. Whatever the Hebrews may have drawn from the past they transformed under the influence of the Divine Spirit and used it for their own purpose, which had a constant relation to their God Jehovah; for they regarded their God as the God of history, first of their own nation, and then of the whole world. That this simple non-scientific people should feel the need of placing themselves in the large framework of the world's history, is the *wonderful* thing in these early narratives. The explanation of the origin of language (Gen. 11^9) may be unscientific, but the protest against the arrogance of overgrown power that forgets God is a permanent contribution. Thus in many other instances the real significance of a story is to be found not so much in a statement of fact as in the teaching of a great truth.

The same remark may be made in connection with the patriarchal stories. Though compiled from different documents belonging to different periods there is a similarity of purpose discoverable throughout these sketches. The material was not at hand for complete biographies or consecutive chronicles, but the precious fragments pieced together have gained a unity and spiritual influence of their own. Abraham, in the view of all the writers, is the type of the man of faith to whom the will of his God is supreme. Jacob suggests the clever contriver of his own destiny who must face the ghosts of the past and finds God in them. Nowhere is the idea of Providence that overrules evil for good more dramatically set forth than in the story of Joseph.

The Historical Period. When we pass into the actual historical period we have to admit that in many cases the records are scanty and that history and story stand side by side. The compilers of the books of Kings refer to certain chronicles (events of the days) from which they drew information, but no trace of these chronicles can be found. All such archives have perished except the lists of kings and certain facts concerning the history of the temple that have been preserved in the canonical books of the O.T. More elaborate chronicles are found in the ancient inscriptions from Babylon and Egypt. We may regret the small supply of interesting facts, but we must remember that a book destined to come down through the centuries would have been overburdened by a large freight of that kind and that we have ample compensation in what have been termed "family stories," as these give vivid pictures of real life.

The general outline is clear even if there is much darkness in places where we would desire a clear strong light. For instance, the seventh century is one of the most important in the history of religion, and yet little exact information is given. But let us glance rapidly at what we have. The older portions of the books of Joshua and Judges show the various tribes not yet united, fighting fiercely against the Canaanites for their existence in their new home. The suggestion of prolonged struggles with the Philistines is there also. In Samuel we meet the final conflict between Hebrews and Philistines for the supremacy of Palestine. Saul's career, with its tragic close, is the prelude to this great conflict; David comes upon the scene, settles that problem and builds a kingdom; his choice of a capital gives Jerusalem a place in history that it has never lost. In the early chapters of Kings, Solomon's extravagant, luxurious court, which sowed the seeds of disruption, is brought vividly before us. The experience of the Northern Kingdom with its alternate scenes of brilliant success and sordid failure is enrolled in a few wonderful pages of history, always interesting, often tragic. Assyria now comes upon the scene and from that time on we name the periods of Israel's history from the great world conquests that overshadowed her life: Assyrian, Babylonian, Persian, Greek, Syrian, Roman. These names call up a succession of tragedies through which the nation shrinks but the religion grows. When Judah is left alone we can trace her history through and after the exile and note the various steps in the building of the Jewish church and the preparation for Christianity. A real history is this, quivering all through with restless life. (See art., *History of Hebrew People*, p. 60.)

Specimen Narrative. A wonderful picture of real life is given in 2 Sam. 21[1-14]; though found at the end of David's life story, in reality it probably belongs to the beginning, showing that it comes from a source that had escaped the compiler of the book. No one questions its substantial historical accuracy; and from the religious point of view it is of the greatest significance. It interprets the famine as God's punishment *for the broken treaty:* "there is blood upon the house of Saul"; this is a very primitive view (cf. the advance on this in Deut. 24 Ezek. 18 Lk. 13[3]). The picture of the mother watching over the bodies of her sons so that they might have the burial without which there is no rest; the gratitude of the men of Jabesh-gilead; every touch, in a story that to us is strange and sad, brings out some feature of ancient thought; men seeking to interpret nature, trying to find justice and atonement, in other words, desiring to find God in their life. Such a picture is a treasure for those who are interested in the life of humanity and the progress of revelation.

Students of the O.T. regard the story of Absalom's rebellion (2 Sam. 13–18), an episode in the history of David's court, as "the richest jewel in the antique historical writing in Israel" (Gunkel). It should be read as one piece; the evil counsellor, ever at hand to encourage the adventure in wickedness; the unnatural outrage delicately told; the brother justly indignant waiting for his revenge; the sorrow of the father and the exile of the favorite son. This is at first a family affair, but when Absalom returns, plunges into politics and plays the demagogue, it becomes a thing of national importance. Then the scene becomes crowded with actors, and each leading man must make his choice and assume his position in relation to the king. The account of the deciding battle, the grim determination of Joab, whose patience is at last worn out, and the pathetic cry of the father—"Would God I had died for thee, O Absalom, my son, my son"—is an impressive climax which will never lose its power to move the hearts of men.

When we turn to consider stories which have been the subjects of keen controversy as to whether they can be placed on the same plane of historical accuracy or are, rather, symbolic pictures, we meet the claim, in some cases at least justified, that the freer interpretation gives a larger meaning. Why should we trouble as to who slew Goliath (1 Sam. 17[50] 2 Sam. 21[19] 1 Chr. 20[5]) when the simple story is such a splendid illustration of the fact that it was David, the youth from Bethlehem, who was destined to settle the Philistine problem? "Coming events cast their shadow before them" was an ancient belief even if not explicitly stated. The same question on a greater scale comes up in connection with the Elijah stories, especially the magnificent scene on Carmel. True, when we examine the records we find that the Elijah stories are set among political annals of Ahab's reign with which they have little or no relation. In the former Elijah stands out alone, a great figure representing courageously the religion of Jehovah; it is in his experience that the conflict with the Phoenician Baal finds supreme expression. Surely, it is impossible to find in all literature a finer picture of the decisive conflict between two types of religion (1 Kings 18). Alongside of this must be placed the scene in which the bold prophet denounces the base cruelty, the ruthless avarice of a despotic king (1 Kings 21). There may be differences of interpretation as to details but there is general agreement that these narratives represent historical and religious literature of the highest order.

Christian scholars did not abandon the literal and photographic interpretation of the wonderful stories in Daniel until they came, by historical research, to see that it was a nation (and not a few individuals) that was cast into the fiery furnace and the den of lions. Worthy record is this of the first great attempt to destroy by persecution a nation's religion and literature, and of the sublime faith with which the loyal worshipers of Jehovah met the crisis.

Primary Purpose. In conclusion attention may be called once more to the fact that the purpose of the historical literature of the O.T. is essentially and predominatingly religious. This is clearly recognized by the Jews, for they do not call any of the so-called historical books by that name. The five books of the Pentateuch they designate as Law, because in these books practically all Hebrew legislation is embodied. Joshua, Judges, Samuel, Kings they include in the list of prophetic books, because they recognize the essentially prophetic purpose of the authors. The other "historical" books belong to the third division of the Jewish Canon, called the Writings. Concerning the books of Kings, which are the principal historical records of the O.T., it has been truly said: "Kings, by virtue of its contents belongs as much to the prophetical books as to the historical. It is not a continuous chronicle; it is a book of prophetic teaching in which, sometimes history, sometimes story, is employed as the vehicle of teaching. It enforces the principle that God is the controlling power and sin the disturbing force in the entire history of men and nations." In a similar manner the religious purpose dominates the other O.T. historical books. The writers embodied only such historical material as was thought to illustrate the self-revelation of God in the history of individuals and of nations, or to bear in some marked way upon the coming of the kingdom of God. A modern secular historian is disappointed at many omissions which would be unpardonable in a strictly historical production. But it is readily seen that the religious purpose of a narrative or group of narratives may be served, and the didactic value may remain, even though there should be discovered omissions or inaccuracies with reference to details.

Literature: Gardiner, *The Bible as Literature;* Strachan, *Hebrew Ideals;* Peters, *Early Hebrew Story;* Gordon, *The Early Traditions of Genesis;* Jordan, *Ancient Hebrew Stories and their Modern Interpretation; History and Revelation, or The Individuality of Israel;* McFayden, *The Messages of the Prophetic and Priestly Historians.*

THE PROPHETIC LITERATURE OF THE OLD TESTAMENT

By Professor A. R. GORDON

The prophetic literature is in a peculiar sense the creative part of the O.T. Through the personalities of the prophets the light of revelation broadened "unto the perfect day." And in their application of the great principles of faith and morals the prophets are abiding sources of inspiration for all who seek after righteousness.

Seer and Prophet. Our English word "prophet" is derived from the Greek *prophetes*, "spokesman" (for a god). To this correspond two sets of terms in Hebrew: *ro'eh*, "seer," with its cognates *hozeh*, "gazer," *sopheh*, "spyer," and *shomer*, "watchman"; and the more specific *nabi*, "prophet," literally "spokesman," with its cognates *mal 'ach*, "messenger," and *melis*, "interpreter" (of Jehovah). In the interesting note, 1 Sam. 9^{9}, the "seer" is referred to as the spiritual forerunner of the "prophet." Originally, however, the two formed separate orders, the seers being related to the augurs or diviners of other nations, and the prophets to the ecstatics. Neither at first enjoyed a high reputation in Israel, the insight of the seers lending itself all too frequently to charlatanry and greed (cf. Amos 7^{12}), and the enthusiasm of the prophets tending to evaporate in sheer fanaticism. Both orders were ennobled by their common devotion to Jehovah. Increasingly, under his influence, the insight of the seers became insight into his character and purpose, and the enthusiasm of the prophets enthusiasm for his name and honor. In the greater prophets the qualities of both were blended. The prophet may be defined, indeed, as a man who with his inward eyes open to the eternal realities "sees the vision of the Almighty" (Num. 24^{4}), and inspired by his vision speaks in burning words of that which he has seen. To adapt Emerson's phrase, he is a seer who becomes a sayer.

Prophetic Inspiration. The prophets all felt that they were inspired by the living God. It was he who opened their eyes to see. As Amos expressed it, "Surely the Lord God will do nothing, but he revealeth his secret to his servants the prophets" (3^{7}). It was he also who inspired them to speak. His spirit "came mightily" upon them—literally "rushed" or "leaped" upon them—and compelled them to prophesy (1 Sam. 10^{10}). He took one from following the flock, and said to him, "Go, prophesy unto my people Israel" (Amos 7^{15}). He laid his hand upon another, and instructed him how to speak and act (Isa. 8^{11}). He put his words in the mouth of another (Jer. 1^{9}; cf. 20^{9}). He actually gave another his word to eat (Ezek. 3^{3}). Thus the prophetic message was an "oracle of Jehovah," a "burden of Jehovah," a "thus saith Jehovah." And the people accepted it as such. Even while they rebelled against the message, they recognized that God had been speaking to them through his servants the prophets (Jer. 7^{25} Ezek. 2^{5} etc.). No doubt, an ecstatic element clings to the noblest of the prophets; but this in no way detracts from the reality of their inspiration. In all genius there is something of the ecstatic. The inspired poet or painter is transported above the common plane, and in his "fine frenzy" sees those visions of beauty which he molds into works of art that are "a joy forever." In his moments of spiritual exaltation the prophet also is raised to the heights, sees his vision of the Almighty, and in his own style and measure speaks to us "the words of eternal life."

True and False Prophecy. An appreciation of the issues involved in the conflict between true and false prophets will help us more clearly to understand the nature of prophetic inspiration. This conflict emerges as early as the reign of Ahab, when the prophet Micaiah does not hesitate to describe the four hundred "prophets of Jehovah" who encouraged the king to go up against Ramoth-gilead, for "the Lord would deliver it into his hand," as inspired by "a lying spirit" which the Lord had put into their mouth (1 Kings 22^{23}). The later prophets have much to say of these false prophets, Micah denouncing them as "prophets that make my people to err" (3^{5}), Jeremiah as those "that prophesy lies in my name" (23^{25}), and Ezekiel as those that by their "lying divinations" hunt lives "for pieces of bread" ($13^{18f.}$). On the surface there is little to distinguish the true prophets from the false. Both introduced their prophecies by "Thus saith Jehovah." Both conscientiously believed they were speaking in his name and by his authority. There was a marked difference, however, alike in the tone and in the content of their prophecies. In the glib assurances of the four hundred prophets of Ahab's time, for example, Jehoshaphat detected too obvious a readiness to say what would please the king (1 Kings 22[7]). The same weakness characterized the false prophets throughout. As Micah says, they spoke of peace when they "bit with their teeth," and proclaimed war against such as "put not into their mouths" (3[5]). In fact, they were professional prophets, who made their prophecies suit their payment.

On the other hand, the true prophet was "full of power by the spirit of the Lord, and of judgment, and of might, to declare unto Jacob his transgression, and to Israel his sin" (Mic. 3[8]). In his classical analysis, Jeremiah (23[1f.]) carries the difference back to its ultimate source in the heart. The false prophets, he says, had no personal knowledge of God. In his fine image, they had never stood in the council of Jehovah (v. 22)—had never entered into immediate touch with him, or felt his spirit moving in their hearts. Thus they harped continually on the same old string, merely repeating what former prophets had said, or "stealing my words every one from his neighbor" (v. 30), instead of waiting upon Jehovah himself, and from his never-failing treasury bringing forth "things new and old." Hence, also, they had no real message for their generation, but glossed over truth and judgment by honeyed words of peace (v. 17). In other words, the false prophet was a materialist, who "divined for money" or selfish advancement, a traditionalist, who clung to the past and refused to advance in the knowledge of God's mind and will, an easy moralist, who preached the gospel of "peace, peace, when there was no peace," and himself followed the doctrine he preached; the true prophet was an idealist, who drank of the living wells of religion, a progressive, who continually advanced in knowledge and grace, an earnest moralist, whose words were no vain repetition of an empty "dream," but a fire that pierced to the conscience of his hearers, or a hammer that broke the stoniest heart in pieces (v. 29).

The Prophetic Call. The greater prophets were launched upon their ministry by a definite call. As a rule, this took the shape of a vision, which was either the precipitate of thoughts and feelings that surged within the mind of the prophet, or the lighting up by a sudden flash of illumination the experiences through which he passed. Occasionally the vision was determined by external stimuli, like the sight of a man with a plumbline testing a wall (Amos 7[7]), or someone carrying a basket of late autumn fruit (8[1]), a twig of almond blossom in the spring (Jer. 1[11]), or a boiling cauldron at a cottage door (1[13]). In describing their visions the prophets throw them into dramatic molds. Jehovah opens their eyes, and they see. He asks them what they see, and then he explains the meaning of it. Of course this is but the objectifying of a real psychological experience. Illumined by the light of the Eternal, the prophet sees into the heart of things, grasps the inner meaning of the facts of nature and life.

The vision is thus intimately related to the personality of the prophet, and gives the keynote to his future ministry. The austere herdsman Amos saw visions of impending judgment, and thus became the prophet of justice. The more sensitive Hosea felt the touch of God's love in the tragedy of his home, and became the prophet of love. The kingly Isaiah saw the Holy One on his throne high and lifted up, and became the prophet of holiness. Jeremiah read the lesson of his life as he walked in the fields round Anathoth, and became the prophet of personal religion. Ezekiel saw the vision of the glory of Jehovah, and became the prophet of regeneration. The nameless singer of the Exile heard heavenly voices of comfort, and became the prophet of comfort. Zechariah saw visions of the New Jerusalem, and became the prophet of hope.

Spheres of Prophetic Activity. It will already be evident that the prophets were interpreters of the mind and purpose of God, in the fullest sense of the term. They had seen the vision of the Almighty, and their task was to make the vision real to their fellows. To begin with, they were progressive revealers of the character of God. Through them God unveiled himself "by divers portions and in divers manners," until in the fullness of time he appeared to men in the person of a Son. But the prophets were as directly concerned with the conduct which God required of his people. Thus they became the great moral teachers of Israel. The people as a whole believed that God was satisfied with the ritual obligations of Sabbath-keeping, sacrifice, and prayer; the prophets insisted that he cared above all things for justice, mercy, and loving-kindness.

A great part of their teaching was devoted to social questions. In the most emphatic terms they denounced the social sins of graft, monopoly, greed, oppression and exploitation of the poor, bribery, luxury, sensuality, and drunkenness; with the same boldness they called for honesty, truth, good will and humanity in all men's dealings with one another. Nor did they hesitate, if need arose, to lay hold on the affairs of state, and try by wise counsel and direction to guide the destinies of the people along the right paths. In doing so, however, they acted not as political partisans, but as divinely commissioned representatives of the kingdom of righteousness, love and peace, which God was establishing on earth, and for which they were appointed to prepare the way.

The Prophets' Outlook on the Future. Though prediction is not of the essence of prophecy, the prophets were as vitally interested in the future as they were in the present. Being in such intimate touch with the mind and purpose of God, they were able to forecast the broad lines of his activity for Israel and the world in general. Their predictions bore mainly on the immediate future. While in details they might be vague, and occasionally mistaken, they did correctly anticipate the issues of history, and prepared their people for what was to be. They had also their gaze directed to the farther horizon. The earlier prophets, Samuel, Nathan, and Elijah, no doubt expected that the kingdom of God would be built upon the basis of the kingdom of Israel as it then was. A later generation foresaw nothing but doom for Israel. But out of the wreckage of the empirical kingdom the boldest of the prophets beheld the emergence of an ideal kingdom, which should embrace all the nations of the earth, a kingdom ruled by a Messianic King, Prince, or Shepherd, he and his ministers governing in the spirit of justice and love, binding the peoples together in the bonds of brotherhood, and thus inaugurating a new age of harmony and peace. (See art., *Israel's Messianic Hope*, p. 177.)

Forms of Prophetic Speech. The original prophetic preaching would seem to have been a kind of elevated chant. As late as Elijah and Elisha this preaching was purely oral. With Amos we reach the stage of written prophecy. An interesting illustration of the literary method of one of the prophets is given in Jer. 36, where we read how Jeremiah dictated to his secretary Baruch "all the words of the Lord, which he had spoken unto him," issuing a second edition, with "many like words added unto them," when the first book was destroyed in the fire by King Jehoiakim. The written prophecy would thus be a substantial reproduction of the spoken word, occasionally revised and brought up to date in the light of subsequent events. The prophecies of Amos and his great successors are in the form of elevated poetry. The language is "simple, sensuous, and passionate," the context being studded with brilliant gems of imagery. The movement is rhythmical, with meter, parallelism, and strophic arrangement as in the poetic books proper. (See art., *Poetic and Wisdom Literature*, p. 154.)

In Amos, Hosea, and Isaiah only a few narrative sections are in prose. With Jeremiah, however, prose begins to play a larger part; and broad tracts of Ezekiel are as prosaic as Leviticus. The authors of the glowing prophecies in Isa. 40–55 and 56–66 revert to poetry, though here the style is literary, not the deposit of the spoken word. In the later prophets, Haggai, Zechariah, and Malachi, the speech of prophecy passes into the dialectics of the rabbi or teacher. The same tendency appears in the apocalyptic prophets (see below). While the earlier Apocalyptists write in highly colored poetry, the characteristic product of Apocalypse in the O.T.—the book of Daniel—is almost entirely in prose. And the more developed Apocalypses of the intertestamental period are cast in the same mold.

Primitive Prophecy. The first clear instance of prophetic inspiration in the O.T. is seen in Deborah, who roused the people of Jehovah to the battle for independence against Sisera (Judg. $4^{4f.}$); but the typical prophets of this early period appear in the bands of religious enthusiasts who enter the scene during the stress of the Philistine peril (1 Sam. $10^{5f.}$), and in later crises sweep through the land on Jehovah's errands, clothed in the hairy mantle and leathern girdle of their order (2 Kings 1^{8}), often with the "sign of Jehovah"—the letter *tau*, resembling the Saint Andrew's cross—tattooed upon their forehead, breast, or hands (1 Kings 20^{41}, etc.), their whole appearance and behavior conveying to more sober minds the impression of madness (2 Kings 9^{11}). In outward guise these "sons of the prophets" are hardly distinguishable from the prophets of Baal or of other gods. What gave the promise of higher things was their enthusiasm for Jehovah and his people.

The greater personalities who soon emerged above the common crowd shared their enthusiasm. Only they moralized it. Samuel was supremely concerned for the deliverance of his people; but he saw that the king who should deliver them must be "a man after Jehovah's heart," counting that "to obey is better than sacrifice, and to hearken than the fat of rams" (1 Sam. 15^{22}). Nathan was equally concerned for the honor of Jehovah and his people, and boldly denounced David for the evil he had done in the sight of Jehovah by robbing the poor man of his wife (2 Sam. $12^{7f.}$). His successors were zealous defenders of the liberties of the people. It is significant that at the disruption of the kingdom under Rehoboam the prophetic party supported Jeroboam as the champion of popular rights, Ahijah the Shilonite as Jehovah's representative giving him the Northern tribes as his lawful possession (1

Kings 11$^{29f.}$), and the prophet of Judah, Shemaiah, assuring Rehoboam that "this thing was of Jehovah" (12$^{22f.}$). Elijah raised the twofold struggle to a definite issue, contending on Carmel for the sole supremacy of Jehovah (1 Kings 18$^{21f.}$), and at Naboth's vineyard for the privilege even of the humblest citizen to enjoy his own inheritance against the encroachments of the king (21$^{17f.}$). Elisha carried the former cause to victory through fire and sword; and at the same time by his acts of love and mercy he showed the people that Jehovah is best honored by a life of human sympathy and kindness (2 Kings 4$^{1f.}$).

Prophets of the Assyrian Age. The most creative period in the history of prophecy is that which opens with Amos of Tekoa toward the close of the reign of Jeroboam II of Israel (about 750 B.C.). In the course of a generation he and his successors, Hosea, Isaiah, and Micah, brought the principles of ethical monotheism into clear expression. Taking their point of departure from Samuel's antithesis of sacrifice and obedience, they sharpened the antithesis, and likewise gave practical content to the abstract notion of obedience. First, Amos insisted that what Jehovah required of his people was not sacrifice but justice (5$^{21-24}$); then his contemporary Hosea insisted that what he required was not sacrifice but love (6^{6}); Isaiah insisted that what he required was not sacrifice but holiness, which for him was a blend of justice and love (1$^{10-17}$); while Micah in his classical definition of religion pure and undefiled, summing up the teaching of all three, insisted that what he demanded was not sacrifice, however extreme, but "to do justly, and to love mercy, and to walk humbly with thy God" (6$^{6-8}$).

Prophets of the Decline and Fall of Judah. After a period of quiescence under the reactionary King Manasseh, prophecy came to life again through the menace of the Scythian invasion about 627 B.C. The first of the new galaxy of prophets was Zephaniah, the prophet of the Day of Jehovah. But the brightest star in the cluster was Jeremiah, the prophet of personal religion, who was led through the failure of the Deuteronomic Reformation to his epoch-making conception of the New Covenant, not of the letter, but of the spirit (31$^{31-34}$). Contemporaries of Jeremiah were Nahum, the prophet of the fall of Nineveh, and Habakkuk, the prophet of faith. But his true spiritual successor was Ezekiel, who carried his principle of individual responsibility to its full logical conclusion (18$^{1f.}$).

Prophets of Restoration. Ezekiel forms the link of connection between the earlier prophets of doom and the later prophets of restoration. Up to the day of the destruction of Jerusalem he prophesied of "lamentations, and mourning, and woe" (2^{10}); then he became the prophet of regeneration, the herald of the coming deliverance, and the father of Judaism. The true prophet of restoration, however, is Deutero-Isaiah (Isa. 40–55), with his good news of salvation, and his interpretation of the sufferings of Israel as the ransom for the sins of the world (cf. p. 168b). A generation afterward, Haggai and Zechariah encouraged the despondent people to press on with the building of the Temple; while about the middle of the fifth century B.C., Malachi and Trito-Isaiah (Isa. 56–66) sought to relieve the depression of their time by renewed insistence on devotion of heart and life as the one condition of salvation, the latter heightening the force of his appeal by his pictures of the new heavens and the new earth. The author of the matchless little book of Jonah, some two centuries later, aimed at quickening the sense of missionary obligation among his people by the story of God's love and mercy toward sinful but repentant Nineveh.

Transition Toward Apocalypse. The later prophets had their eyes increasingly turned toward the future. This tendency finds its characteristic expression in Apocalypse, that peculiar literary form in which spiritual truths are impressed, not by direct appeal to heart and conscience, but by a series of visions in which the destinies of Israel and the other nations are unfolded, these visions converging on a final Judgment scene, when the Ruler of the nations separates the sheep from the goats, and gives his people dominion over all their enemies, within and without. An approach to Apocalypse is found in Ezekiel's prophecy of Gog (chs. 38, 39); but the type assumes its first definite shape in the ardent utterance of Obadiah, contemporary with Malachi and Trito-Isaiah. Apocalypse takes on vividness of coloring in Joel, Zechariah 9–14, and Isaiah 24–27, all of them products of the late Persian and Greek eras. Finally, it comes to maturity in the book of Daniel, written to face the emergency under Antiochus Epiphanes (168–165 B.C.), which forms the model for the elaborate works of the Apocalyptic school during the next two centuries. (See art., *Intertestamental Religion*, p. 200.)

Literature: Eiselen, *Prophecy and the Prophets;* Gordon, *The Prophets of the O.T.;* Knudson, *The Beacon Lights of Prophecy;* T. H. Robinson, *Prophecy and the Prophets in Ancient Israel;* J. M. P. Smith, *The Prophets and their Times;* W. R. Smith, *The Prophets of Israel;* N. Micklem, *Prophecy and Eschatology.*

THE POETIC AND WISDOM LITERATURE OF THE OLD TESTAMENT

BY PROFESSOR A. R. GORDON

It is now recognized that a large part of the O.T. is poetic in spirit and structure. This applies not merely to the poetic literature proper, but also to the bulk of the prophetic books. The Revised Version has rendered a great service in printing the former in parallel lines. Unfortunately, it has not extended the same principle to the prophetic literature. Thus the poetic quality of these books continues to be obscured for the English reader. One of the chief merits of the more modern translations is to reveal the poetic form wherever it appears in the original. Our enjoyment of the literature is much enhanced thereby. (See art., *The Bible as Literature*, p. 19.)

General Characteristics. "All good poetry," says Wordsworth, "is the spontaneous overflow of powerful feelings." This is peculiarly true of O.T. poetry. The Israelites belonged to a race endowed with vehement passion; and their poetry is surcharged with this spirit. Hence the force of its appeal. "Deep calleth unto deep" as heart speaks unto heart.

If poetry be the overflow of feeling, the best poetic speech is that which gives the most adequate expression to feeling. For this purpose the O.T. poets had an almost ideal instrument in Hebrew. No language could more perfectly fulfill Milton's requirement that poetic speech must be "simple, sensuous, and passionate." With a childlike simplicity of form it combines a singular intensity of feeling and a pictorial power that lends itself to the boldest play of imagination. Figure crowds upon figure; mixed metaphors are common, and hyperboles a matter of course. The Hebrew poets can quite naturally picture the floods clapping their hands, the hills singing for joy, the stars from their courses fighting against Sisera, and the sun and moon standing still "until the nation had avenged itself of their enemies."

Poetic speech is also musical. The origins of poetry are found in song; and the language of poetry retains the music of song. The O.T. poets are as sensitive to musical charm as those of other nations, and show often surprising power in the wedding of sounds to tones of feeling, as in the reproduction of the gallop of war-steeds at the battle of Megiddo (Judg. 5[22]), or the brilliant picture of the flashing of chariots in the assault on Nineveh (Nah. 2[3f.]). Many of the psalms also, and the finer passages of Job and the Song of Songs, are real studies in harmony. Rime is rarely found, except in the older folk-poetry; but assonance and alliteration are frequent, and elaborate acrostics are found in Psa. 9, 10, 25, 34, 37, 111, 112, 119, and 145, Prov. 31[10-31] Lam. 1–4, and the reflective poem in Nah. 1.

A more specific quality of poetic speech is rhythm. Being the language of the heart, it moves with a beat resembling that of the heart. This movement is not peculiar to poetry, for in its more elevated moods prose also may be rhythmical. The distinction is, that in prose the rhythm is "unbound," or free; in poetry it is "bound," or metrical. A poem is a work of literary art, composed of a number of parallel lines, marked by a measured movement of pulse within the lines, and as a rule also by a measured movement of thought between the lines.

The presence of a metrical movement within the lines was long denied in the case of Hebrew poetry. Recent research has tended more and more strongly to establish it. As the result of an extended series of investigations it may now be asserted that Hebrew meter, like English and Germanic, is governed by the number of strong accents, the intervals being filled by a somewhat free choice of weaker elements, the number of which is limited only by the demands of musical time. The most frequent measure in Hebrew poetry consists of three such accents to the line. There is, however, much less rigidity than in modern verse. Thus in the more majestic psalms and odes a broader rhythmical effect is gained by the breaking in of a measure consisting of four accents to the line. This again may resolve itself into musical phrases of two pulses each, a variety which adds much to the life and energy of the poetry. But the most interesting measure in Hebrew is the elegiac—associated mainly with lamentations, though also with songs of joy and mirth—a combination of the three-pulse and two-pulse measures, which well reflects the choking of the voice under the influence of any strong emotion, whether of sorrow or of joy.

The movement of thought between the lines was first clearly recognized by Bishop Lowth, who in his famous lectures *On the Sacred Poetry of the Hebrews* (1753) developed the principle of parallelism, defining it as "a peculiar conformation of sentences, whereby the poets repeat one and the same idea in different words, or combine different ideas within the same form of words, like things being related to like, or opposites set in contrast to opposites." Lowth distinguished three types of parallelism:

1. *Synonymous*, where the original thought is repeated "in different but equivalent terms," as in the opening bars of the songs of Lamech and Deborah (Gen. 4^{23} Judg. $5^{2f.}$), or in Psa. 1^{1}, where we have an instance of what Lowth describes as a "triplet parallelism."

2. *Antithetic*, where "a theme is illustrated by contrast with its opposite," as in Gen. 4^{24} Judg. 5^{19} Psa. 1^{6}, and normally in the "Proverbs of Solomon" (Prov. $10^{1f.}$).

3. *Synthetic*, where the idea is expanded in certain directions, as in Ex. 15^{1} Judg. 5^{16} Psa. 2^{6}, and generally in the "Hezekiah" collection of proverbs (Prov. $25^{1f.}$).

Of this third type of parallelism there is a variety, described as *Spiral*, *Progressive*, or *Climactic*, where the changes are rung on some key word, as in Judg. 5^{30} Psa. 1^{3}, and especially in the "songs of Ascent," e.g., Psa. 121, with its play on the words "help," "keep," and "slumber."

The normal unit in Hebrew verse is the distich, or couplet, of two parallel lines, though the monostich, or single line, occurs sporadically, as in Psa. 18^{1} 87^{1}. Examples of the tristich, or combination of three parallel lines, are found in Psa. 1^{1} 5^{11} $45^{1f.}$ Prov. 25^{13}; the tetrastich, or four parallel lines, in Psa. 1^{3} 55^{21} Prov. $27^{15f.}$; the pentastich, or five parallel lines, in Psa. $6^{6, 7}$ Prov. 24^{23-25}; the hexastich, or six parallel lines, in Psa. 99^{1-3} Prov. 30^{21-23}; and still larger combinations in the latter context, and elsewhere.

The occurrence of selahs and refrains (the latter, e.g., in Psa. 42, 43, 46, 49 Isa. 9^{8-21} Amos 4^{6-11}) is evidence that the parallel units coalesce to form more extended groups. Attempts have recently been made to force practically the whole of Hebrew poetry into four-lined stanzas, each composed of two parallel units. Such a scheme may easily enough be applied to many of the psalms, the idyls in Songs, and even the speeches in Job; but it cannot be imposed on the folk-songs and the prophetic literature in the main without doing grave violence to the text. The selahs and refrains show that in the psalms also the stanzas are by no means of the uniform length of two parallel units. Again, therefore, we must allow for more freedom than rigid theory is willing to concede.

Folk-Poetry. Poetry begins in folk-song. Much of the earliest folk-song is of battle. This is as true of Israel as of other nations. The first recorded poem in the Bible is the battle-song of Lamech (Gen. $4^{23f.}$). And long after Israel had risen to a higher stage of civilization, the joy of battle continued to fire the hearts of the people, and inspired their most stirring strains. The tribes were roused to battle by the wild notes of the war-chant (Judg. 5^{12} 2 Sam. 20^{1}); and the returning warriors were welcomed with repetitions of joyous couplets, sung by the women in responsive chorus, to the accompaniment of music and dancing (Ex. 15^{21} Judg. 11^{34} 1 Sam. 18^{7}). Out of these emerged in due course songs like those of Moses (Ex. 15^{1-18}), Joshua (Josh. $10^{12f.}$), and Deborah (Judg. 5^{1-31}), which for daring imagination, combined with swift, dramatic movement, force and fire, are worthy to be placed alongside the most splendid battle-songs in any language.

Songs of victory pass occasionally into satire, as in the taunt-song over stricken Moab (Num. 21^{27-30}), and the coarse lampoons of Samson and the Philistines at each other's downfall (Judg. 15^{16} 16^{24}). A nobler development appears in songs of national hope and aspiration, like the Blessings of Noah (Gen. 9^{25-27}), Isaac (Gen. 27^{27-29}), Jacob (Gen. 49^{1-27}), and Moses (Deut. 33^{1-29}), but especially the four Blessings of Balaam, the son of Beor (Num. $23^{7-10, 18-24}$ $24^{3-9, 15-19}$), with their glowing pictures of future prosperity for Israel.

Songs of labor also fill a large place in the folk-poetry of Israel. The culture of the vine is peculiarly associated with song. It is probable that the fragment, "Destroy it not, for a blessing is in it" (Isa. 65^{8}), is a snatch from some old vintage song. The "joy of the fruitful field" is coupled with that of the vine-dressers (Isa. 16^{10}), and the "joy in harvest" compared with that of men "when they divide the spoil" (Isa. 9^{3}). The song of Deborah alludes to shepherd-songs, accompanied by "pipings for the flocks," around the troughs (Judg. $5^{11, 16}$). The opening of a well in the desert inspires the charming well-song (Num. $21^{17f.}$). Other songs of nature are suggested by such headings in the Psalter (see mgs.) as "The hind of the morning" (Psa. 22^{1}); "The dove of the distant terebinths" (Psa. 56^{1}); and "The lilies" (Psa. 45^{1} 60^{1}, etc.).

The only suggestion of a wedding song in the earlier literature is found in Gen. 24^{60}, where Rebekah is sent to her new home with the naïve wish that she may become the mother of thousands of ten thousands. There is abundant allusion, however, to songs of social life, e.g., the "sounds of mirth and song" that sped the parting guest on his way (Gen. 31[27]), the jests and riddles of the bridal week (Judg. 14[10-20]), the singing of men and maidens at the gate (Job 21[11f.] Lam. 5[14f.]), the senseless reveling at the tables of the rich (Isa. 24[9] Jer. 7[34] Amos 6[5]), which often degenerated into brutal scorn of the poor and unfortunate (Job 30[9] Psa. 69[12]). Reference to dirges for the dead is also common (Gen. 50[10] Judg. 11[40] 1 Kings 13[30] 2 Chr. 35[25] Jer. 9[17-22] Amos 5[16], etc.), while two classical laments of David have been preserved to us, that most tender expression of manly sorrow for Saul and Jonathan (2 Sam. 1[19-27]), and the equally sincere, if less poignant, utterance of grief over Abner (2 Sam. 3[33, 34]).

Even the most secular of the folk-songs of Israel are touched with religious emotion. The songs of Moses and Deborah might, indeed, with equal propriety be described as hymns of praise to Jehovah, who is regarded as the real Lord and Leader of Israel's hosts, the inspirer of heroic deeds, and the giver of victory (Ex. 15[1f.] Judg. 5[1f.]). The ark, which was the visible symbol of his presence among the people, was accompanied to and from the battlefield by sacred strains (Num. 10[35f.]). The simple greetings of daily life and work had likewise their religious note (Ruth 2[4] Psa. 129[8]). Naturally, the worship of the sanctuaries was attended by songs of a more distinctively religious character (Amos 5[23]), while the service of God in the Temple was inaugurated by Solomon's hymn of dedication (1 Kings 8[12f.]), a worthy forecast of the nobler songs that were afterward to exalt "the place of his habitation."

Proverbial Lore. The simplest mental life is no mere bundle of feelings; it consists equally of observation and judgment. And as men give voice to their feelings in song, they embody their judgments in those terse, sententious sayings we call proverbs. The Edomites, near kinsmen of Israel, have been justly celebrated for the wealth and brilliance of their proverbs, and the Israelites themselves shared to the full in the racial inheritance. The historical literature of the O.T. enshrines not a few pointed aphorisms, while in the book of Proverbs we find the noblest treasury of proverbial wisdom that any nation has to show.

The generic name for proverb in Hebrew (*mâshâl*) implies likeness or comparison. Good examples are found in the earliest proverb quoted in the Bible, "Like Nimrod a mighty hunter before the Lord" (Gen. 10[9]), and in the popular saying, "As is the mother, so is her daughter" (Ezek. 16[44]). Other primitive proverbs are apt illustrations of general principles, like the "proverb of the ancients" cited in 1 Sam. 24[13], "Out of the wicked cometh forth wickedness," or the barbed arrow shot by Ahab, "Let not him that girdeth on his armor boast himself as he that putteth it off" (1 Kings 20[11]). A proverb deriving its point from the sense of contrast to ordinary expectation is found in the taunt leveled against Saul—"Is Saul also among the prophets?" (1 Sam. 10[12]). This type of proverb leads to the fully developed antithetical couplet, illustrated in

"The fathers have eaten sour grapes,
And the children's teeth are set on edge"
(Jer. 31[29] Ezek. 18[2]).

As implying likeness or comparison, the proverb is linked, on the one hand, to the riddle, and, on the other, to the parable. The riddle may be described, in fact, as a veiled proverb, and the parable as an expanded proverb. A good example of the former is found in Samson's riddle (Judg. 14[14]), and of the latter in Jotham's parable (Judg. 9[7-20]).

The main development in proverbial lore is associated with the name of Solomon. In 1 Kings 4[32] he is credited with no fewer than three thousand proverbs, while aphorisms of a certain literary stamp are technically known as "proverbs of Solomon." Here the original one-lined shaft passes definitely into the couplet form, with parallelism in all its types, which is so characteristic of the book of Proverbs.

In later times the cultivation of the art was carried on in the schools of the wise, who more and more replaced the prophets as moral guides and teachers of the people. To these Wise Men we owe the main part of the book of Proverbs. They played also the part of popular preachers, rendering their appeal more effective, as Jesus did, by an abundant use of illustrative parables. (See intro. to Proverbs.)

Collections of National Song. The songs of which we have spoken were inspired by no literary ambition. The old "makers" simply poured forth the feelings of the moment, and for the most part their poetic effusions passed away with the occasion that gave them birth. Only a few select gems found a lodgment in the hearts of the people, or were handed down by *môshelîm*, professional balladists or reciters (Num. 21[27]), who sought to keep alive the memory of the brave deeds of old. Not till the establishment of the kingdom under Solomon does any attempt seem to have been made to preserve this inheritance in written shape. About this time, however, we meet with two separate anthologies of folk-poetry:

1. *The Book of the Wars of Jehovah*, a collection of battle-songs from Israel's wars of conquest and independence, which is referred to as the source of the curious fragment of place-names in Num. 21[14f.], but to which also may plausibly be assigned the song of Deborah (Judg. 5) and the songs of the ark (Num. 10[35f.]).

2. *The Book of Jashar*, or *the Upright*, that is, probably, *The Book of Israel's Good Men*, a collection more varied in its range, being (unless the "Upright" be Jehovah) cited as the source of Joshua's battle-song (Josh. 10[12f]), David's lament over Saul and Jonathan (2 Sam. 1[19f.]), and Solomon's hymn of dedication (1 Kings 8[12f.]), according to the LXX rendering.

The Poetic Books. The earliest of the poetic books proper may be Lamentations, a collection of five elegies on the downfall of Jerusalem, belonging to various dates within a century or two after the tragedy, and reflecting the sorrow of city and people under the chastening hand of Jehovah.

The real heart of the poetic literature, however, is found in the Psalter, "the Hymn Book of the Second Temple." As at present arranged, it is composed of five books, after the analogy of the Pentateuch; but it is clearly a complex of earlier collections, such as "the psalms of David," "the prayers of David," "the psalms of Asaph," "the psalms of the sons of Korah," and "the songs of Ascent," dating from various periods after the Restoration, and reflecting the varying moods of the devout soul in its approach to God. (See intro. to Psalms, pp. 509f.)

The loftiest heights in O.T. poetry are reached in the book of Job, a spiritual drama on the problem of suffering, set in a prose framework, no doubt based on popular tradition, both elements belonging to the fifth century B.C., and reflecting the triumph of faith in its struggle with the sorrows of the time.

A book of very different quality is the Song of Songs, which is now generally regarded as a choice anthology of Hebrew love songs, dating from the earlier half of the third century B.C., and reflecting the happiness of youthful love in the villages of Palestine.

The Wisdom Literature. As we have seen, the characteristic expression of wisdom among the Hebrews takes the form of proverbial sayings. The most complete collection of these is found in the book of Proverbs, a post-exilic compilation of "proverbs of Solomon" and "sayings of the wise," to which are added as appendices "the words of Agur," "the words of King Lemuel," and the praise of the good wife. The book is thus a compendium of Hebrew wisdom at its purest and best. While never rising to the heights, it keeps true to the "paths of righteousness," and remains an invaluable guide for the man who wishes to live an honest and fruitful life.

The introductory chapters of Proverbs are more hortatory in style. The general tone of these chapters is still essentially practical; but in ch. 8, doubtless as the result of Greek influence, the majestic figure of Wisdom becomes the subject of a speculative effort which makes her the foster child, associate, and representative of God. A grave protest against such incipient gnosticism is raised in "the words of Agur" (Prov. 30), where the possibility of any kind of speculative knowledge of God or his manifestation on earth is dismissed. Brilliant poetic expression is given to the same agnostic tendency in the Ode on Wisdom incorporated in Job 28, where Wisdom is known only to God, who discovered her when he established the laws of the universe, and who has no intention of revealing the secret to man. But the classical instance of negative philosophizing in the O.T. appears in the book of Ecclesiastes, with its haunting refrain, "Vanity of vanities, all is vanity," a book which is redeemed from absolute pessimism only by its Hebrew inheritance of faith and sanctified common sense.

For a fuller treatment of the poetic and Wisdom books see the introduction to the individual books in the commentaries.

Literature: W. T. Davison, *The Praises of Israel* and *The Wisdom Literature of the O.T.*; Eiselen, *The Psalms and Other Sacred Writings;* Gordon, *The Poets of the O.T.*; Gray, *The Forms of Hebrew Poetry;* G. A. Smith, *The Early Poetry of Israel.*

THE OLD TESTAMENT CONCEPTION OF GOD

By Dean A. C. Knudson

It might with some plausibility be maintained that in the O.T. we have to do not with one but with many conceptions of God. The people of Israel were not at any time so completely unified that they all shared the same world-view, and even if they had been, their thought varied from age to age so that in such a national literature as that of the O.T. we would still have no uniform body of teaching. What we actually have in it are developing and divergent opinions. But while this is true, each generation or age had its own dominant ideas, and these gave to the current thought of God a certain unity. Then, too, the view of God in one age of the nation's history stood organically related to the views of earlier and later ages so that what we find in the O.T. is not a number of independent conceptions of God but, rather, one conception unfolding through the centuries.

General Characteristics. The O.T. conception of God had four general characteristics. First, it was *practical*. It grew out of and was sustained by life. The theoretical reason had very little to do with it. No doubt the belief in God answered various questions that the early Hebrews raised with reference to the world and the course of events in it. But it did not owe its origin to these questions nor was it to any appreciable extent supported by speculative considerations. There are in the O.T. no arguments that seek to prove the existence of God or the possibility of our knowing him. His being and self-revelation were taken for granted. The heavens might declare his glory (Psa. 19[1]), but this was because people already believed in his existence. There was in ancient Israel no theoretical atheism or agnosticism. The fool might live as though there were no God (Psa. 14[1]) and devout men might be deeply impressed with the limitations of their knowledge of him (Job 11[7] 26[14] Isa. 55[8, 9] Prov. 30[1-4]), but that he actually existed and that he could to some degree be known was not disputed. Life itself, history, prophecy, the consensus attested his being, and the needs alike of the nation and the individual confirmed it.

In the second place, the O.T. *conceived of God as personal*. It represented a standpoint sharply distinguished from polydemonism, on the one hand, and pantheism on the other. No doubt the belief in vague impersonal spirits was to be found in ancient Israel; it persisted as a relic from an earlier period or was taken over from the Canaanites. But it had no recognized place in the national faith as expressed in the O.T. Indeed, it was distinctly rejected as foreign to the worship of Jehovah. Nor was there any tendency to identify Jehovah with the impersonal forces of nature. Throughout the whole of O.T. history he remained distinct from them—their personal master. One reason for this theistic or personalistic cast of Hebrew thought was the fact that Jehovah from the very beginning was regarded as primarily a God of history rather than of nature. It was as a directing agent in the affairs of men rather than as the cause of the orderly processes of nature that he revealed himself to Israel; and hence a clearly defined personal character was uniformly attributed to him.

This appears in the personal name which he bore. Whatever may have been the origin and derivation of the name "Jehovah" (see Gen. 4[26] Ex. 3[13-15] 6[2, 3]), it differentiated the God of Israel from all other gods, and even after the belief in the existence of other gods had ceased in Israel it still continued to give to him a uniquely individual and personal character. This is evident from the anthropomorphic methods of expression which we find throughout the O.T. These anthropomorphisms are somewhat more refined in the later books, more psychological and less physical in nature. But this, if anything, only makes them all the more personal in their implications. God everywhere in his relation to Israel is represented as a living, feeling, acting Being. That he is also free is likewise everywhere assumed. Creation was his free act, and the course of human history is freely determined by him. He is not bound by the laws of nature but through miracle can work out his own purposes. Nothing is more characteristic of Jehovah than what we call personality.

Another general characteristic of the O.T. conception of God is found in its inherent *tendency toward monotheism*. This tendency appears from the very outset in the exclusiveness of Jehovah. "Thou shalt have no other gods before me" was the foundation stone of the Mosaic religion and of the Israelitic religion as a whole. This commandment, it is true, did not at first exclude the belief in the existence of other gods, but it did by a practical logic of its own point in that direction, and it successfully resisted every attempt to introduce a female deity by the side of Jehovah and also every movement to break him up into a number of local Jehovahs. The Canaanitic and other Semitic religions had female deities, and they were not unknown to the Israelites, but Jehovah himself remained lone and solitary. He had no female counterpart, and all the immoral religious practices associated with the sexual principle he indignantly repudiated. His oneness thus saved his moral purity; and it also preserved his greatness. Had he followed the example of Baal (cf. Hos. 2[13, 17]) and permitted himself to be divided up into a number of local Jehovahs, he would have lost that magnitude of being which belonged to him as God of the entire nation and as the sole Being worthy of worship. Poly-Jehovism was as foreign to the true genius of Israelitic religion as was Baalism itself (Deut. 6[4]). The Hebrew heart insisted on absolute loyalty, and such loyalty could be directed only to *one* Being. Monotheism was thus implicit in Israel's religion from the very beginning.

A fourth characteristic of the Hebrew idea of God was its *ethical quality*. There has been some question as to whether the Mosaic Jehovah was a moral Deity. And it is no doubt true that Moses did not make moral obedience the essence of religion in the same explicit way as the eighth-century prophets. But that he insisted on loyalty to Jehovah as the basal virtue, and that this loyalty in view of its ideal and sacrificial character was essentially ethical, can hardly be questioned. There is nothing in the work of Moses more distinctive and more significant than the passionate and sustained devotion to Jehovah that he evoked among the Israelitic tribes. It was this that formed the basis of their national unity, it was this that differentiated them not only formally but qualitatively from other peoples, and it was this that made of Jehovah—instead, for instance, of Chemosh—the God of righteousness and the Creator of the world. We are then justified in saying that the Mosaic Jehovah, who by a marvelous act of deliverance won the undying loyalty of his people, was in principle a moral Deity, and that it was no accident that the later prophets laid such a unique stress upon his absolute rectitude. In so doing they simply put out at interest the pound they inherited from Moses.

The O.T. conception of God was, then, *practical*, *personalistic*, *monotheistic*, and *ethical*. These were its fundamental characteristics. But it was only gradually that they came to full expression, and no exposition of the O.T. teaching concerning God would be adequate that did not take account of the different stages through which it developed. The most important contributions to O.T. theology were made by the literary prophets. These men belong to the middle period of Hebrew history. So in outlining the history of Hebrew thought it is customary to distinguish three periods: the preprophetic (1200–750 B.C.), the prophetic (750–450 B.C.), and the post-exilic or legalistic (450–150 B.C.). With the idea of God in each of these periods we will deal briefly.

The Preprophetic Period. Before the time of Moses the Hebrews were probably polytheists (Josh. 24[2, 14f.] Ezek. 20[7f.]), though this did not necessarily exclude the belief in one supreme Deity on the part of some of the more enlightened members of the race. It was Moses who transformed the religion of Israel into a monolatry, i.e. the worship of one God, and with him the history of the religion of Israel in the proper sense of that term begins.

1. *Jehovah and Baal.* The period from Moses to Amos was characterized by a fusion of Jehovah with Baal. The name "Baal," which means lord or master, was applied to Jehovah (Hos. 2[16]), and by many he was conceived of in much the same way as Baal was by the Canaanites. The same rites and customs were adopted in his worship. Evil practices, such as prostitution and the use of images, crept into his sanctuaries. He became the God of the land, the giver of its grain, its new wine and its oil, losing much of his earlier ethical sternness as a desert Deity. With the Israelitic settlement in Canaan he nominally triumphed over Baal, but actually he later to a large degree succumbed to him.

2. *Divergent Conceptions.* This, however, was true only of the popular religion. The purer Mosaic faith continued to have its representatives, especially in prophetic circles. It was linked up with the higher national interests and with civic justice. But it was not carried out to its logical consequences, nor was it differentiated as sharply as it might have been from the popular beliefs and practices. Between the Baalish and the genuinely Jehovistic tendency in preprophetic Israel there was a distinct difference of spirit, and this gave rise to a certain tension in the religious life of the nation. But the difference or the tension was felt rather than clearly formulated. The result was that no thoroughly consistent view of God was developed. Cruder and more

adequate views lived side by side. In estimating these a distinction needs to be made between theoretical beliefs and practical postulates. The latter as expressed in prayer and the living faith of the people outran the former. Men did not in those days devote much attention to what we would call theological questions. They did not set themselves the task of bringing out the intellectual implications of faith. Everything was spontaneous or traditional, and hence we should not expect to find a homogeneous body of beliefs in the documents that have come down to us from them.

3. *Divine Unity.* In discussing the nature of God it is customary to distinguish between his metaphysical and his ethical attributes, and this distinction will in a general way be observed in the present article. The metaphysical attributes of the preprophetic Jehovah may be reduced to three: personality, unity, power. With the first two we have already dealt briefly. They were characteristic of Jehovah as conceived in the entire O.T. There was, however, one important contribution made to the development of the idea of the divine unity in the preprophetic period, of which note should be taken. This came from Elijah. He seems to have identified Jehovah with deity in such an exclusive sense as to imply the nonexistence of Baal (1 Kings 18[27]) and of other gods in general. At least it is evident that he meant to deny that Baal or any of the other gods, whether they existed or not, was for Israel God in the proper sense of the term. For his own people he regarded Jehovah alone as truly divine. While not thoroughly monotheistic, this was a significant step in that direction.

4. *Divine Power.* So far as the power of Jehovah, the most fundamental of his metaphysical attributes, is concerned, there are several divergent representations in the preprophetic literature. In not a few instances he seems to be represented as a localized deity or at least as a deity with a limited sphere of influence. He had a home. At first it was Sinai or Horeb (Judg. 5[4f.] 1 Kings 19[8]). Later it was the land of Canaan (1 Sam. 26[19]), and especially the sanctuaries in the land (Gen. 22[14] 28[16f.]). He was spoken of as "a man of war" (Ex. 15[3]), and so closely was he associated with the armies and wars of Israel (Ex. 17[15f.] Num. 21[14] Judg. 5[23] 1 Sam. 17[26, 36]) that it has been held that his power was limited to the battlefield and had nothing to do with the everyday affairs of men. Again he was so intimately identified with the Israelitic people that he seemed inseparable from them and limited in his power by them. Outside of Israel he received no recognition and apparently exercised no authority (Ruth 1[16]).

But while there are many passages that seem to represent Jehovah as thus limited geographically, racially, and otherwise, there are other passages that leave with us a distinctly different view. Some of these for instance speak of him in a way which implies that he had his abode in heaven rather than at any particular place on earth (Gen. 11[5, 7] 18[21] 22[11, 15-17]). And while heaven itself was no doubt thought of as a place, it was not apparently regarded as attached to any particular region but as offering direct access to every part of the earth. It suggested, therefore, a kind of omnipresence. From other passages it is also clear that Jehovah was not confined to Canaan. In the early patriarchal narratives we find him manifesting himself to his servants wherever they might be, in Egypt or the distant East (Gen. 12[1] 24[12f.] 26[12f.] 46[4]). Nor was his power circumscribed by that of the nation. He was superior to his people, both punishing and helping them. He could save by few as well as by many (1 Sam. 14[6]). There was nothing too hard for him (Gen. 18[14]). He was equal to all the needs of those who sought his aid.

5. *Divine Creation and World-purpose.* In the literature before Amos there are very few references to Jehovah's relation to the world of nature and to human history as a whole. Some have, consequently, concluded that the ideas of creation and of a divine world-purpose were entirely foreign to the preprophetic period. But this is hasty and unwarranted. The analogy of other peoples would suggest that Israel must have had its creation stories at an early date. The narrative in Gen. 1 (notes) probably represents the finished form of a story that had been current in Israel for centuries. An earlier form of the story seems originally to have stood at the beginning of the J document (Gen. 2[4b]), which dates from the ninth century B.C. A few poetic fragments from an earlier date (Judg. 5[20] Josh. 10[12, 13] 1 Kings 8[12, 13]) also suggest the idea of Jehovah's creatorship. The idea of his universal rule and world-purpose is not so distinctly alluded to, but it seems to have been implied in the popular belief in a day of Jehovah (Amos 5[18-20]) and was assumed by the eighth-century prophets as known to the people of their time. There is, then, good ground for holding that the preprophetic Jehovah was both super-national and supra-mundane. Both creative activity and a power that transcended Israel were ascribed to him.

6. *Spirituality.* In the metaphysical sense of the terms he was also a "spiritual" and a "holy" Being. But these attributes did not

in this early period differentiate him from other gods. They too were spirits, beings of an ethereal nature, endowed with a more than fleshly power; and they too had a mysterious, indefinable, fear-inspiring quality called holiness. In these respects there was no difference between them and Jehovah, except that these characteristics were ascribed to him in an accentuated form. So far as their practical effects were concerned, there is only one point that needs to be noted. The "spirituality" of the other gods did not exclude the use of images in their worship, but the case seems to have been different with Jehovah. There is a well-established tradition that Moses prohibited image-worship. This prohibition was to a large extent disregarded in later times, but there is no adequate reason for rejecting the tradition as unhistorical. What the exact basis of the Mosaic prohibition was we do not know, but it would seem that it must have grown out of the ascription to Jehovah of a higher degree of "spirituality" than that attributed to the heathen gods. In other regards the worship of Jehovah did not apparently differ much in early times from that practised at the Canaanitic shrines.

7. *Ethical Character.* We have already pointed out that there was a profoundly ethical bent to the conception of Jehovah from the beginning. But this was imperfectly developed during the centuries that intervened between Moses and Amos. Capricious anger (1 Sam. 6[19] 2 Sam. 6[6f.]), jealousy (Gen. 3[22] 11[6f.]), favoritism (Gen. 12[10-20] 20[1-16]), incitement to evil (Judg. 9[23] 1 Sam. 26[19] 2 Sam. 24[1]), and other ethical shortcomings were not infrequently attributed to him. Over against such facts as these, however, must be put others in which his moral character comes to clear and striking expression. Note especially Nathan's arraignment of David for his sin against Uriah the Hittite (2 Sam. 12) and Elijah's denunciation of Ahab (1 Kings 21). Then, too, the regular administration of justice was regarded as under divine protection. This is illustrated by the Book of the Covenant (Ex. 20[22]–23[19]), which deals to a large extent with questions of right and of humane regard for those in need.

The Prophetic Period. With Amos and Hosea we enter upon a new stage in the development of the idea of God. The preceding period had prepared the Israelites for a purging process. Their amalgamation with the Canaanites had contaminated the Mosaic religion but had not destroyed it. The introduction of Baalish rites and beliefs had produced revulsion as well as attraction. The difference between Jehovah and Baal was too great to be concealed or overlooked, and with the lapse of time it deepened into a sharp antithesis. This antithesis must have been felt to some extent by devout minds ever since the settlement in Canaan, but it did not receive a radical expression until the time of the eighth-century prophets. Through these men the Israelitic religion sought to cast off the foreign elements imported into it and to restore Jehovah to his original and unique pre-eminence. The new era thus inaugurated is one of the most important in the religious history of mankind. No movement quite comparable to it is anywhere else to be found. It raised the thought of God to a new level and gave to it an expression so striking that it has been to a large extent normative for all subsequent ages.

The eighth-century prophets and their successors in the next two centuries did not discourse on the nature of God nor on his metaphysical and ethical attributes; they were not teachers of theology. But they nevertheless did have fairly definite and consistent views on these subjects and they did much to elevate and clarify thought with reference to them.

1. *Monotheism.* The unity of Jehovah they developed into an explicit monotheism. They applied Elijah's negative attitude toward Baal to the foreign deities in general. These deities were perhaps not denied existence altogether. Some sort of being they apparently had apart from their idols. The prophets were probably none of them strict metaphysical monotheists or monists. But they were religious monotheists. For them there was but one God; other deities were "no gods." An explicit statement to this effect we do not find in the eighth-century prophets, but the idea is everywhere assumed (Hos. 8[6] Isa. 2[8]). And a century later, in Jeremiah (2[11] 16[20]) and in Deuteronomy (4[39] 6[4]), it is plainly affirmed. Not until the following century, however, did it become an outstanding feature of prophetic teaching. It was Deutero-Isaiah who first developed it, repeatedly affirmed it (Isa. 43[10, 11] 45[5, 21]), and supported it by arguments. One argument was drawn from the power of prediction which Jehovah alone possessed (Isa. 41[21-29]), another from his work as Creator (Isa. 40[12] 42[5] 44[24] 45[12, 18]), and a third from the absurdity of all idolatry (Isa. 40[18-20] 41[6f.] 44[9-20]). The heathen gods, according to Deutero-Isaiah, were inseparably bound up with their idols; they had no creative power and no power to predict the future; they were, therefore, no gods. Jehovah, on the other hand, and he alone, had no connection with man-made images; he alone knew the future; he alone was Creator of the world; hence he alone was God. In Deutero-Isaiah we thus have an absolute and explicit religious monotheism.

2. *Universal and Creative Power.* The power of Jehovah, as we have seen, was even in pre-prophetic times connected with the idea of his creatorship and universal rule. But the connection was loose and undeveloped. It was the writing prophets who first made the universal and creative power of Jehovah a matter of religious significance. Amos saw in his universal sway a ground for rebuking the pride of the Israelites (9⁷) and also a ground for asserting the certainty of their impending doom (9²⁻⁴). Isaiah found in it a basis for the belief that the evils suffered at the hands of Assyria were a divine punishment for the sins of Israel (10⁵). Indeed, in a generalized form this message was the burden of pre-exilic prophecy. The prophets also, and particularly Deutero-Isaiah, saw in the unlimited power of Jehovah a guarantee of the ultimate redemption of Israel. He had a purpose in the world, a purpose bound up with the fate of Israel, and the fulfillment of this purpose was made certain by the range of his power.

It was in this connection also that the creatorship of Jehovah was brought into prominence and made a fundamental article of belief. The pre-exilic prophets say little about it. Their message was primarily one of reproof and doom. But with the Exile the situation changed. Now the message needed was one of comfort and hope. Deutero-Isaiah, consequently, seized upon the idea of Jehovah's creatorship as one that furnished the firmest ground of assurance, and made it such a prominent element in his teaching that some have ascribed its origin to him. This, as we have seen, is a mistake. The idea was old. It was not the novelty of the idea that led Deutero-Isaiah to revert so frequently to it, but the novelty of the situation that confronted him. The idea had a religious value for his time that it had not had for earlier times, and this it was that led him to dwell with such fondness upon it. Later writers followed his example, and after his day it was an important article in the Israelitic creed (Gen. 1, Psa. $8^{3f.}$ 19^{1} 33^{9} $104^{2, 5}$ 148^{5} Prov. 8^{22-31} Job 26^{14}).

3. *Spirituality and Holiness.* Spirituality and holiness continued to be ascribed to Jehovah in the prophetic period, but they were given a more refined interpretation, and the tendency was to conceive of them in an ethical as well as a metaphysical sense. In Isa. 31^{3} we have the nearest O.T. approach to the N.T. declaration that God is a Spirit. Isaiah here in two parallel lines opposes God to man and spirit to flesh, thus practically identifying man with flesh and God with spirit. This sharp distinction between flesh and spirit gave a unique and more exalted character to the conception of the divine nature, and this in turn had an important influence upon the conception and practice of worship. Worship heretofore had to a large extent taken the form of rites and ceremonies; it had been closely bound up with the land of Canaan and the sacred places in it; it had also, in spite of the Mosaic prohibition, not been free from the use of images. In each of these respects the prophetic teaching marked a significant advance. Some scholars hold that the pre-exilic prophets repudiated all sacrifices and other external rites as unworthy elements in the worship of such an exalted and spiritual being as Jehovah (Amos 5^{21-24} Hos. 6^{6} Isa. 1^{10-17} Mic. 6^{6-8} Jer. $7^{21, 22}$). But this conclusion is not warranted by the text. Isaiah, for instance, in his condemnation of the current cultus, associated prayer with sacrifice (1^{15}), but it is evident that he did not mean to condemn prayer as such. What he condemned was a merely formal prayer (29^{13}), and so it was also with his condemnation of sacrifices and other religious rites. These rites as merely formal exercises were denounced as worthless, but when accompanied by the proper spirit they were not repudiated.

The first prophet clearly to recognize that the worship of Jehovah could be completely detached from the land of Canaan was Jeremiah (29^{1-13}). But in principle this independence was implied in the prophetic conception of religion. The Israelitic antipathy to image-worship antedated, as we have seen, the writing prophets. But it was transformed by them, especially by Hosea ($8^{4, 6}$ 13^{2}), into a crusading spirit, and in the Deuteronomic reformation was carried to a triumphant conclusion. A century later it was reaffirmed by Deutero-Isaiah in terms of biting satire (44^{9-20}) as over against the Babylonian religion, and from that time on remained a characteristic feature of the Jewish faith.

The holiness of Jehovah was impressively proclaimed by Isaiah ($6^{3f.}$), and his message at this point was echoed by Deutero-Isaiah ($41^{14, 16, 20}$ $43^{3, 14}$, etc.). Ezekiel also laid stress on the divine holiness ($36^{21f.}$). The term with them lost its earlier suggestion of the incalculable and irrational and denoted the unapproachable greatness of God. It also tended to become identified with some one distinctive attribute such as the power, purity, or righteousness of God.

We thus see that the writing prophets represented a distinct advance beyond the earlier period in their conception of the metaphysical attributes of deity. But it was especially in the ethical realm that their thought of God transcended that of their predecessors. It has just been noted that there was a tendency on their part to identify the holiness of God with his righteousness.

4. *Righteousness.* This suggests one of the most characteristic elements of their teaching, namely, that they ascribed to righteousness an absolute character. They saw in it the unique and most essential element in deity.

This insight they expressed in various ways that brought them into conflict with the traditional religion. For one thing, they insisted that sacrifices and other religious rites were no divine requirement; they lay outside the law of God. God for them was no ecclesiastical disciplinarian. Again, as the positive counterpart of this they maintained that the essence of true religion is to be found in righteousness. God's only requirement is an obedient will (Amos 5[24] Hos. 6[6] Isa. 1[16f.] Micah 6[8]). What he abhors is impurity, injustice, and inhumanity. The rich, insofar as they are guilty of these sins, are the special objects of his wrath. Then, too, they represented the impending day of Jehovah as one in which an even-handed justice was to be meted out to all nations. No special favor was to be shown to the Hebrews. Rather were they to be called to all the stricter account because of the privileged position which they in the past had enjoyed (Amos 3[2]). The day of Jehovah was thus to be one in which the eternal ethical ideal was to emerge in the order of time and God was to manifest himself as the absolute and righteous ruler of the world.

The righteousness which Jehovah, according to the prophets, demanded of his worshipers was as deep and broad as the ethical nature itself. It was subjective (Jer. 4[3f.] Ezek. 36[26]) as well as objective (Isa. 1[17]), personal as well as social. It involved mercy as well as justice. God for the prophets was "a just God *and* a Saviour" (Isa. 45[21]). Some of them stressed one attribute and some another. To Amos Jehovah was pre-eminently the God of moral law, to Hosea the God of love, to Isaiah the sovereign Lord of mankind, to Jeremiah the Searcher of hearts who enters into personal relations with men, to Ezekiel the jealous Guardian of an inflexible justice, to Deutero-Isaiah the Redeemer of Israel and of the world. But all of them saw in him the complete embodiment of their ethical ideal; no imperfection attached to him. Their view of the world, at least in intent, was an absolute ethical monotheism.

The Legalistic Period. The period following the decline of prophecy was more complex than might be suggested by its designation as "legalistic." The Law was the most prominent characteristic of the religious life of the period, but it did not exclude other important currents of thought. The prophetic teaching did not become extinct. It was presupposed by the Law, and expressed itself in the form of messianism (Joel, Isa. 24–27, Daniel) and of individual piety (Psalms). There was also a strong "humanistic" movement which we find reflected in the Wisdom Literature (Proverbs, Job, Ecclesiastes). These three different types of religious life and thought differed not a little from each other, but in their conception of God they were virtually at one. They all at this point accepted the teaching of the prophets; but they did not merely passively reflect it. They modified and developed it in various ways.

1. *Absoluteness.* To a certain extent the post-exilic period was reactionary. It was marked by a revival of ceremonialism and national exclusiveness that ran counter to the prophetic spirit. But while these reactionary tendencies affected seriously the practical religious life, they had little, if any, effect on the current theology. In theory post-exilic Judaism was rigorously monotheistic. No matter how much of a martinet Jehovah may seem to have been in his relation to the Jews, he was nevertheless regarded as "God of Heaven" and "Most High God" (Ezra 6[10] Neh. 2[4] Dan. 3[26] Psa. 78[56]). Instead of limiting the absoluteness ascribed to him by the classical prophets the post-exilic writers accentuated it. They dwelt at length upon his work as Creator and represented him as superior both in knowledge and power to the limitations of time and space (Psa. 8, 104, 139[4-12]).

2. *Transcendence.* The transcendence thus attributed to God no doubt obscured to some extent his immanence. The tendency was to detach him from nature and to think of him as above the world and apart from it, as One who in a miraculous way occasionally intervened in it. In other words, the tendency was toward a dualistic view of the world. This also had the practical effect of emphasizing the divine sovereignty rather than the divine Fatherliness. But while the post-exilic stress on the divine transcendence in these respects represented a decline in religious insight, it prepared the way for a significant advance. Jehovah heretofore had been a God of this world, a God of the living, not of the dead. This was true of the prophetic as well as the Mosaic and the popular conception of him. His power extended to heaven and to the underworld (Amos 9[2]), but for actual human life this had little or no significance. His real value to men was confined to the world as we see it. This world might be miraculously changed by

a divine intervention, but it was still thought of as a world in which decay and death had their place. Not until the post-exilic period did the conception arise of a new heaven and a new earth from which death and sorrow would be forever banished (Isa. 25[8]). And this was made possible only by the higher degree of transcendence now ascribed to Jehovah. He was now thought of as so superior to the order of nature that he was in no way bound by it but was able to destroy it (Isa. 51[6]) and to create a new world-order in which the ideal values of the spirit would be eternally conserved. It was at this point that post-exilic Judaism made its most important contribution to the development of the idea of God. The transcendent character now attributed to him made possible the belief in the resurrection and the life to come (Isa. 26[19] Dan. 12[2]) and so transformed Israelitic religion from a this-world religion into a religion that knows no spatial or temporal limits.

Comparison with Greek Thought. In order to appreciate the uniqueness and greatness of the O.T. conception of God it is important to compare it with Greek thought on this subject.

1. *Conception of Spirit.* In one respect Plato and his followers had a higher or more refined conception of spirit and of the divine nature than did the Hebrews. The latter thought of spirit as an ethereal substance, an attenuated form of matter, and so ascribed to God a semi-material nature. Plato, on the other hand, introduced the idea of an "immaterial" form of existence and applied it to God. This manifestly represented a higher and more "spiritual" conception of the divine nature from the philosophical point of view; it was later incorporated into Christian theology under the influence, especially, of Origen and Augustine.

2. *Transcendence and Dualism.* In another respect there was a rapprochement between Greek and Hebrew thought. Both inclined toward an exaggerated conception of the divine transcendence and a resulting dualism. This was more pronounced with the Greeks than the Hebrews, but toward the close of the O.T. period, as we have seen, it became a prominent characteristic of Hebrew thought. There was, however, this difference—that the Hebrews looked upon the world as created by God, while to the Greek idealists matter remained more or less independent of the Deity, a resisting element. Greek dualism was thus more deep-seated than that of the O.T.

3. *Personality.* The main difference between Greek and Hebrew theology is to be found in their view of the divine personality. On this point Hebrew thought, as we have seen, was explicit. It conceived of God as a thinking, feeling, and willing Being. This conception was, of course, not altogether lacking with the Greek thinkers. But it was obscured in various ways. Plato, for instance, found true reality in the universal: for him, the more individual or particular anything was, the less real it was, and this prevented a proper recognition of that unique individuality which is a constituent element in personality. Aristotle rejected this phase of Plato's teaching, but represented God as so devoid of feeling and of will that while the world loved him he did not love the world. Such a God was manifestly not a person in the proper sense of the term. But while defective from the practical and popular standpoint, the Greek view of God carried with it an ethical and spiritual idealism that brought it into close kinship with Hebrew thought. This is a most significant fact. That Greek philosophy led to a world-view similar in its fundamental outline to that of Hebrew prophecy is striking evidence that the intellect as well as the heart demands for its satisfaction an intelligent Being as the ultimate cause of the world.

Relation to New Testament. The God of Abraham, of Isaac, and of Jacob was also the God of Jesus (Mk. 12[26]). It is impossible to understand Jesus' conception of God apart from that of the O.T. Yet there is a difference between them. The O.T. conception in spite of all its greatness did not arrive at completeness and unity. It represented a developing process, a development from nationalism toward individualism, from particularism toward universalism, from naturalism toward an ethical spiritualism; but the goal of a universal, individual, and ethical faith was not attained. The God of the O.T. remained bound more or less to Jewish nationalism and particularism. He also failed to rise to the level of self-sacrificing love so as to evoke from men the instinctive cry of "Abba, Father." Here it was that Jesus transcended the O.T. He conceived of God as Father and as Father of all men in a way that rendered obsolete all earlier nationalistic, particularistic, legalistic, and royalistic conceptions of him. It was in this sense that he fulfilled the law and the prophets. He lifted their conception of God to the plane of an absolute ethical perfection.

Literature: Addis, *Hebrew Religion;* Badè, *The O.T. in the Light of To-day;* Barton, *The Religion of Israel;* Budde, *Religion of Israel to the Exile;* Davidson, *The Theology of the O.T.;* Knudson, *The Religious Teaching of the O.T.;* Marti, *Religion of the O.T.;* Orchard, *The Evolution of O.T. Religion;* Ottley, *The Religion of Israel;* Peters, *The Religion of the Hebrews;* H. Wheeler Robinson, *The Religious Ideas of the O.T.;* H. P. Smith, *The Religion of Israel.*

THE RELIGION OF ISRAEL

By Principal H. Wheeler Robinson

A group of Arab chieftains were scanning the night sky with Colonel Lawrence's glasses, surprised at the revelation of stars before unseen. The talk was of telescopes of ever greater power, revealing more and more stars. "When we see them all," one said, "there will be no night in heaven." But another asked, "Why are the Westerners always wanting all? Behind our few stars we can see God, who is not behind your millions." (Lawrence, *Revolt in the Desert*, pp. 138, 139.)

The Arab's words explain why a Semitic book, notwithstanding its limitations of "scientific" knowledge, still forms part of our greatest religious inheritance; behind its few stars it shows us God. The path by which that supreme knowledge was reached might be not less fitly described by some further words from the same book, in which the author pleaded with his Arab allies for a desperate venture: "There could be no honor in a sure success, but much might be wrested from a sure defeat" (p. 232). There speaks the veritable spirit of the great prophets who were the makers of the religion of Israel. Their persistent purpose became a crucifixion; it is always a cross that shows most of God. The moral struggle by which they reached God became itself a revelation of his nature.

When we look at the religion of Israel as a whole, we are justified in saying that the prophetic consciousness was to the nation as is the soul to the human body. We cannot, of course, make a clear-cut division of personality into these two elements. (Hebrew psychology never made the attempt, though the Greek psychology did. See the essay on "Hebrew Psychology" in *The People and the Book.*) But there is unmistakably something in human life which cannot be explained by external or physical categories, something we agree to call "soul," to denote the unifying center or nucleus, assimilating the external and the physical to itself, and transforming them into new products. This is what we see in the religion of Israel. It has its history, the history of a development extending over a thousand years, through which the activity of many factors can be traced—racial, geographical, political, economic, and social. We study the literature of the O.T. to-day in exactly the same critical fashion as we study any other body of literature.

But when we have gone behind the literature to the history it reveals, and have traced in that history the growth of a religion which has claimed and found a unique place in the world, the study of the religion brings us face to face with a comparatively small group of men who are, humanly speaking, its makers. These are the prophets of the great formative period from the eighth to the sixth centuries. The secret of their power and influence lies in their inner conviction that God is speaking to them and through them. This is the prophetic consciousness, and it is the soul of Israel's religion. All that went before—Semitic animism and Canaanite Baalism and Babylonian mythology—is so much "material" from which the soul assimilates all that is not alien to its controlling purpose. All that came after—the ritual of the Temple, the worship and piety of the Psalter, the ethics of the Wisdom Literature, the hopes of apocalyptic—can be truthfully described as the product of the prophetic consciousness, not in its substance, but in its dominating spirit and character. This is the point of view from which the present article is written, for it gives the Pisgah-view of Israel's religion.

I. The Early Religion of Israel

1. Semitic Animism. The Hebrews emerge into the light of history from the nomadic life of the desert. In Doughty's *Arabia Deserta* we get a vivid impression of what that life was through what it still is, for the Moslem creed has left the deep convictions of the desert largely unchanged. Animism—the belief in souls and spiritual beings—is a living faith among the Bedouins of to-day, who still believe in demons to whom the diseases of mind or body are traced. The belief in psychical influences is illustrated by the power ascribed to "the evil eye." The worship of ancestors still finds expression in a sacrifice to the dead. There are blood-rites which take us back to what is probably the most primitive element in Semitic sacrifice—the disposal of the blood of a slain animal, to escape from its weird powers and taboos. The rising of the new moon (with which the Hebrew Passover seems to be linked) is still something of a festival to these Bedouins. We may, even now, find examples of the fetishism which underlies stone-worship, together with the equally ancient tree-worship.

Survivals of all these practices are recorded also in the O.T., though their grosser elements have naturally been eliminated or transformed by the prophetic religion. Comparatively little trace remains of the belief in demons (Isa. 13[21] 34[14] Lev. 16[8] 17[7]; cf. 1 Kings 22[21]), for this was inconsistent with a developed belief in Jehovah. Ancestor-worship is reflected in a number of the customs and beliefs concerning the dead (Lev. 19[31] Deut. 14[1] 18[10, 11] 26[14] 1 Sam. 28[13] Isa. 8[19] Jer. 16[6]) and seems to be the original explanation of the teraphim (Gen. 31[34] Judg. 17[5] 1 Sam. 19[13] Hos. 3[4]). The blood-rites of the O.T. are too numerous even to be summarized here (e.g., Ex. 24[6-8] 1 Sam. 14[32f.] Ezek. 24[8]), but blood-revenge left its notable mark on early Hebrew law, as blood-communion with the Deity did on Hebrew sacrificial ritual. Another blood-rite is that of circumcision, which originally belonged to puberty (preceding marriage), and was transferred to infancy (Ex. 4[24-26]). In ancient Israel the festival of the new moon was as important as that of the Sabbath became to Judasim (2 Kings 4[23] Hos. 2[11] Isa. 1[13]). The idea of sacred stones and trees is continued in the *Mazzeba*, or stone pillar, and the *Ashera*, or wooden post (standing as substitute for the sacred tree), which were constant features of the worship at the "high places" of Canaan, so that these invading nomads would find nothing strange in their use. It is possible also that something akin to totemism is represented in the list of "unclean" animals, and in some of the tribal and personal names (see art., *Bible Customs*, p. 74b).

2. Primitive Ideas of Jehovah. But we must not forget that some, at least, of the Hebrews who settled in Canaan brought with them a higher faith, in which was already to be found the germ of the prophetic religion (for fuller details, see art., *The O.T. Conception of God*, p. 158). The escape of Israel from that Egyptian control which had temporarily modified their nomadic life was bound up with the faith of a great leader, really the first of the prophets. Moses did for the name of Jehovah what Mohammed did for Allah—he gave it a new content, as that of Israel's deliverer from bondage. The name was old, but the meaning was new. The God whose power and grace Moses proclaimed was a local God, whose seat was Sinai; a storm-God, whose favorite "theophany," or manifestation, was in the phenomena of the thunder, conceived as his "voice"; a war-God, whose battle-song was chanted when the ark moved; an oracular God, who gave decisions in disputes about tribal custom. By transmitting the divinely given decisions to his people Moses became a lawgiver in very much the same sense in which the sheikh of the desert still settles the disputes of his group of nomads.

But when all this has been said, we are still left asking what there was to separate Jehovah, thus conceived, from the gods of other peoples surrounding Israel, and of the same Semitic stock—e.g., from Chemosh, the god of Moab (see on Moabite Stone, p. 117b). Two things at least we may say, and they take us far: (1) The power and purpose of Jehovah had been revealed in a great act of deliverance, an act which became a constant source of inspiration to the memory of the subsequent generations (Amos 2[10] Hos. 11[1]). He is a saviour-God from the beginning, who makes history the channel of divine revelation. History is the sacrament of the religion of Israel, a sacrament which grew in meaning and power with the progress of the history. God is known for what he is by what he does, and what he does is the history of his people. (2) The second distinctive feature of this primitive faith in Jehovah is that the relation between him and Israel is ethically conceived from the outset. He is not a merely tribal God, so tied to Israel that his co-operation might be taken for granted. The words of Jesus, "Ye have not chosen me, but I have chosen you," might be applied to the Jehovah of Moses. He acts of his own initiative, and in that freedom of divine grace there is the necessary basis of a moral relation. Here is the germ of the later prophetic teaching (cf. Amos 3[2]), which carried this moral conception to its true issue by liberating it from nationalistic limitations.

3. The Influence of Canaan. This austere faith of the nomad Israelites was as much higher than the religion of the land they invaded as nomadic culture was lower than that of Canaan. For many centuries Canaan had been under the civilizing influence of the great empires, Babylonia and Egypt, east and west of it; it is, e.g., in the Babylonian language that the petty kings of Palestine correspond both with Egypt and with one another (see on Tel-el-Amarna Tablets, p. 116). The excavation of some of the walled towns of these Canaanites has told us much about their life, their religion, their burial practices, and their pottery. They had advanced far beyond the polydemonism of nomadic religion. The "phallic" emblems found at their high places show that the worship was of the reproductive forces of nature. Their goddess Astarte (Ishtar) stood for sexual love and reproduction. Baal, or "lord," was not a proper name, but a common designation of the local deity, the giver of fertility. Agriculture was bound up with religion, and the existence of temple-prostitutes shows the depth to which such nature-worship could fall. We get a glimpse of a Canaanite festival in Judg. 9[27]; the three great festivals of Israel, namely, Unleavened Bread (as distinct from the Passover subsequently combined with it), the Feast of Weeks, and the Feast of Ingathering, were all agricultural festivals, doubtless borrowed from the Canaanites, like so much else.

It was inevitable that the new environment should profoundly affect the religion of Israel. At first, Jehovah was conceived as the God of Sinai, who comes thence on occasion to help his people (so in the Song of Deborah, Judg. 5). But when he became "naturalized" in Canaan (cf. 1 Sam. 26[19] Hos. 9[3, 4]) in the sense of being the God of the land, there arose the grave peril that he should be "naturalized" in another sense, and made to conform with the naturalistic Baals of Canaan. This was the issue that Amos and Hosea had to face—not that of Elijah's earlier challenge to choose between Jehovah and the Tyrian Baal, but to choose between a higher and lower idea of Jehovah.

4. "Prophecy" Before the Prophets. Primitive prophecy, in the sense of ecstatic and dervish-like products of abnormal psychology, may have sprung from the Canaanite religion, for an Egyptian document of 1100 B.C. (Wenamon) tells us that a frenzy came upon a Canaanite youth during a sacrifice, in which he uttered a prophetic message. This incident connects with the frenzy of the prophets of Baal on Carmel (1 Kings 18[28]), and the less violent, but none the less abnormal, behavior of those prophets of Jehovah whom Saul encountered (1 Sam. 10[5f.]). He was drawn to share it by psychical sympathy; so at a later period the Spirit of God constrained him to "prophesy," throwing off his clothes and lying naked a day and a night. It is significant that we should first hear of such Hebrew prophesying at the time of the Philistine occupation, as again, in the time of Elijah and Elisha, it seems connected with an outbreak of nationalistic zeal against the Tyrian Baal, introduced by Jezebel (2 Kings 9); the prophets, lower or higher, were always prophets of Israel, even when patriotism seemed to go with pessimism.

But our literature also reveals a succession of prophets prior to the eighth century who evidently stand, as Moses did, head and shoulders above these ecstatic bands. We can say little of Deborah, and Balaam was not an Israelite prophet, but there are Samuel (called not a prophet but a seer, 1 Sam. 9[9]), Gad (1 Sam. 22[5] 2 Sam. 24[13]), Nathan (2 Sam. 12 1 Kings 1[8f.]), Ahijah (1 Kings 11[29]), Micaiah (1 Kings 22[8f.]), besides the outstanding figures of Elijah and Elisha. Thus we must not think of eighth century prophecy, in either its lower and psychical or its higher and moral aspects, as something wholly without precedent (cf. the religious and moral ideals of the early stories of Genesis, etc., which assumed literary form prior to the eighth century).

II. Prophecy

1. The Prophetic Consciousness. The psychology of the Hebrews was very different from that of to-day. It sprang from three main ideas, namely, those of (1) a principle of life and consciousness identified with the breath (*nephesh*); (2) psychical functions ascribed to the physical organs, e.g., the heart, kidneys, bowels (not the brain); (3) an invasive, wind-like spirit (*ruach*), accounting for anything abnormal in human character or conduct. The earlier forms of Hebrew prophecy sprang from an abnormal psychical and physical state (e.g., trance, ecstasy, dream), and some of these earlier phenomena remain in the later developments (Isa. 6, 8[11] Jer. 20[9] 4[27] Ezek. 3[14, 15] Amos 7–9). But, in the case of the greater prophets, such features are altogether subordinate to moral and spiritual experience of the highest type; the abnormal, in their case, has been transferred from the center to the circumference of their consciousness.

The prophets believed in the "objective" reality of what they saw and heard, just as did Augustine and Bunyan, and their abnormal states were probably essential to a prophetic "call," and were generally regarded as guaranteeing prophetic inspiration (cf. George Fox and the early Quakers); but the cardinal fact for us is that they were led to interpret their own moral and spiritual experience as a message of God to Israel. That which their own conscience condemned they taught that their God condemned; in this "value-judgment" lies the ultimate secret of divine inspiration. The movements of the world-powers (Assyria and Egypt, Babylon and Persia) around the politically unimportant Israel became morally explicable as controlled by Divine Providence and expressive of divine judgment. These prophets were primarily speakers, not writers; they were led to write, as a testimony against the refusal to hear (Isa. 8[1, 16] 30[8] mg., Jer. 36). It is around these testimonies, recorded by the prophets or their disciples, and much expanded by later editors and readers, that the O.T. has gathered. Thus the truth of its inspiration depends on the philosophical issue of the kinship of human spirit with divine, for this, in the last resort, is what "revelation" will mean. Is that which is true of the human spirit also true of the divine, in which it lives and moves and has its being?

2. The Protagonists of Prophecy. The truth which issued from this prophetic consciousness was cumulative, as the opening verses of the Epistle to the Hebrews declare; as W. Robertson Smith has said, one truth was enough to make a Hebrew prophet (*The Prophets of Israel*, p. 182). Thus we see Amos and Micah animated by the strongest democratic sympathies, and convinced that luxury and greed, injustice and hard dealing with the poor are hateful in God's sight; for these things the enthusiastic religion of the high places will never atone. They are the prophets of a righteous judgment, but Hosea is something more. He penetrates to the need for a changed spirit that shall issue in a changed national life; he believes in a God of covenanted love, as well as of righteous judgment.

The most majestic conception of God in the eighth century is that of Isaiah, the prophet of the "holy," i.e., of the transcendent God, revealed so impressively in the narrative of the prophet's call (Isa. 6). God desires from his people the holiness of moral innocence, justice, and humanity ($1^{16,\ 17}$ 5^{16}), not that of mere ceremonial ($1^{11f.}$ 29^{13}). The emphasis falls on the necessity for faith (7^{9} 8^{17} 28^{16} 30^{15}) in spiritual, as against material forces (2^{22} 31^{3}). The symbolic names which he gave to his children (7^{3} $8^{1f.}$) show his recognition of the divine commission given to Assyria, and his conviction that a "righteous remnant" (cf. 6^{13}) would be left to Judah, after the divine judgment (cf. $2^{5\text{-}22}$), namely, the laying waste of the fruitless vineyard ($5^{1\text{-}7}$); and that this remnant ($1^{25,\ 26}$; cf. $8^{16f.}$) would be established in Jerusalem ($28^{16\text{-}18}$ 31^{5}), the dwelling place of Jehovah (8^{18}). Isaiah lifted the idea of God to a new level by the definition of "holiness" in ethical terms.

In strong contrast with Isaiah stands Jeremiah, the prophet of spiritual individualism, whose autobiographical poems (the best translation is that by Skinner, in *Prophecy and Religion*) describe his call ($1^{4\text{-}10}$), his mission ($1^{11\text{-}19}$), his anxious sympathies (4^{19} $8^{18f.}$ 13^{17} 23^{9}), his sense of Jehovah's power ($4^{23\text{-}26}$), his lonely sorrows ($15^{10\text{-}21}$), the divine compulsion which kept him to his task in spite of its difficulty ($20^{7\text{-}18}$). The special contribution to religion made by Jeremiah is along this line of a direct personal fellowship with God developed through outer misfortunes and inner sorrows. His ideal is of an inward relation to God, as contrasted with dependence on the Temple and its worship (7^{4}) and conformity to an external law written on stone; i.e., he anticipated a time when all would share in the prophetic consciousness. This may be seen in his culminating prophecy of the "New Covenant" ($31^{31\text{-}34}$).

We find again another type of prophet in Ezekiel, the sacramentalist. His cardinal ideas are four: (1) the self-revelation of the holy and glorious God in history, and especially in the history of Israel; this explains both the doom of Jerusalem and its subsequent restoration; (2) the individual moral responsibility of men before God, as in ch. 18; (3) the supernatural work of the Spirit of God, in changing human hearts ($36^{24\text{-}29}$) and in restoring the nation to vitality, as in ch. 37; (4) the sacramental realization of the holy presence of God in the restored Temple and city, as in chs. 40–48; the keynote is, "Jehovah is there," 48^{35}. The influence of Ezekiel on post-exilic Judaism was destined to be very great.

In his fellow-exile, Deutero-Isaiah (Isa. 40–55), the sacramental emphasis is replaced by the evangelical. The aim is the "comfort" of Israel ($40^{1f.}$) through the promise of a speedy deliverance from exile by the hands of Cyrus, the "anointed," i.e., the Messiah of Jehovah, who will overthrow Babylon and restore Israel to its homeland. This confidence is based on the power of Jehovah over nature ($40^{12f.}$) and history ($41^{2f.}$), and his knowledge of the future ($41^{12\text{-}29}$; contrast the folly of idolatry, $44^{9f.}$). There also emerges a new and most impressive conception of the mission of Israel as "The Servant of Jehovah"—a clearly drawn and fully individualized figure, prophetic in function, patient and gentle in spirit, conscious of being a weapon in the divine hand, sustained by companionship with Jehovah, given the task of bringing the world to his feet, facing suffering in that mission, at last victorious through this very suffering endured for others (Isa. $42^{1\text{-}4}$ $49^{1\text{-}6}$ $50^{4\text{-}9}$ 52^{13}–53^{12}). This conception has more profoundly affected Christian than Jewish thought; for it had great influence on the consciousness of Jesus and on the N.T. (Cf. H. Wheeler Robinson, *The Cross of the Servant*, and in this Commentary the note on the Suffering Servant, p. 664.)

3. The Response to Prophecy. How far did the religion of the nation Israel as a whole reflect the great conceptions of its pioneers? Very little, to judge from our literary evidence, so far as the contemporaries of the prophets were concerned. We see that Isaiah formed a circle of disciples (8^{16}), so creating the "righteous remnant" and inaugurating the idea of the church, as a spiritual and not simply as a national body (Buchanan Gray, *Isaiah*, p. 155). An attempt at national reformation on prophetic lines was made, first by Hezekiah (2 Kings 18[3f.]), and in much more drastic and influential a fashion by Josiah (2 Kings 22 and 23). This is the reformation usually associated with our book of Deuteronomy, part of which seems to have been the mysterious "book of the Law" found in the Temple. It was probably drawn up by disciples of the prophets, who found their aspirations checked during the "heathenism" of Manasseh's reign; the book of Deuteronomy largely reflects the teaching of the eighth-century prophets, especially of Hosea. (See the Commentary on *Deuteronomy* in the New Century Bible, pp. 33, 34.) The ideals of the prophets are not left in the air; they are to be realized by centralizing all worship at the one sanctuary of Jerusalem, where presumably it can be kept free from corruption and abuse; the humanitarian desires of the prophets are now applied in the restatement of ancient laws and customs.

The reformation carried out by Josiah might have been no more than an episode in the history of Israel's religion; but the stern teaching of the capture of Jerusalem and the deportation of many of its chief inhabitants within the next generation gave a re-enforcement and a sanction to the words of the prophets which no king could command. It was inevitable that in thus becoming sacrosanct they should crystallize, losing the fluidity of origin; it was inevitable also that the reformation worked by the Exile in the popular religion of Israel should be something very different from anything these prophets had sought. That is true, however, of all history and all reformers, as it is true of life; the price of realization is always a loss of ideality.

III. The Transformed Religion of Israel

The religious community which gathered in and around Jerusalem after the Exile was very different from the political state of which the decline and fall had been watched by the mournful eyes of the prophet Jeremiah. It was geographically and numerically small, politically dependent on Persia, economically impoverished. Its first struggles to exist, which are reflected in the pages of Haggai and Zechariah (chs. 1–8), were accompanied by political hopes doomed to disappointment, and the resultant disillusionment is seen in the book of Malachi, some seventy years later. But the wise and patriotic administration of Nehemiah, and the religious leadership of Ezra (see Neh. 8), marked the beginning of a new period, for which the discipline of the Exile and the new reverence for the teaching of the prophets had cleared the way. Henceforward we can speak of "Judaism" as a compact and definite body of belief, the strength of which was to be manifested in the second century B.C., when it had to meet the shock of Hellenistic propaganda and persecution. The characteristics of this religion of early Judaism can be seen in four bodies of literature now incorporated or partly incorporated in the O.T., namely, the Law, the Psalms, the Wisdom Books, and those beginnings of apocalyptic which were to have so rich and influential a development beyond the canon of the O.T. (see art., *Intertestamental Literature*, p. 188).

1. The Ritual of the Temple. At the center of the post-exilic religious community was the worship offered to Jehovah in the Temple. Many of its details went back to the pre-exilic and indeed to the pre-prophetic days, for a priesthood is naturally conservative, and the old laws and customs of ancient sanctuaries had been collected and were carefully treasured. To understand them we have to go back to the codes of law of earlier date now enshrined in the "Torah" or Pentateuch—the Book of the Covenant (Ex. 20[22]–23[19]) of perhaps the tenth century, the book of Deuteronomy of the seventh, the Law of Holiness (Lev. 17–26) of the sixth, and the "Priestly Code," which seems to have formed Ezra's Book of the Law, in the fifth. These codes contain much that we should call secular, as well as the ordinances of worship; but we must remember that the distinction is ours, not theirs; Jehovah is the ultimate lawgiver whatever be the law, just as the god Shamash is regarded as the inspirer of the Code of Hammurabi, and the community in all its life and activities is conceived as a "theocracy."

In the light of these earlier codes we can see the general trend of development and mark the new emphasis. Thus the new ceremony of the Day of Atonement (Lev. 16) takes its place by the side of the ancient festivals of the Passover (and Unleavened Bread), the Feast of Weeks and the Feast of Booths, and, indeed, becomes the most important of all the holy seasons. A new solemnity, a deeper sense of sin—indeed, a new conception of sin on prophetic lines—are characteristic of the Day of Atonement. We also find new types of sacrifice emerging after the Exile. Prior to it the typical sacrifices were the peace-offering, a communion-feast of the worshipers, at which only the blood and certain portions of the fat were reserved for the Deity, and the burnt-offering, a rarer form of animal sacrifice, in which the victim was wholly offered to God. But in these later days we hear of the sin-offering and the trespass-offering. The sin-offering was specially "holy," and was burned away from the altar, when offered for the high priest or the community; otherwise, it was, because of this special holiness, consumed by the priests (Lev. 6[26f.]). This should prevent us from thinking of the victim as penally substituted for the sinner; it is, rather, a gift to restore a broken relation. The peculiarity of the trespass-offering was that it accompanied the restitution of misappropriated property, *plus* a fifth of its value (Lev. 6[1f.]). But in both cases there is no attempt to deal with deliberate sin (Num. 15[30]).

There has been a similar transformation of the priesthood. In earlier times anyone might sacrifice—no priest is mentioned in the Book of the Covenant, and David's sons were priests (2 Sam. 8[18]). The professional "Levite" hired by Micah (Judg. 17) belonged to Judah. By the time of Deuteronomy (18[1]) the priests are identified with the Levites, the priesthood not yet being confined to Aaron's sons, as in the later Priestly Code (Lev. 1[5]). In the poem known as the "Blessing of Moses," probably belonging to the eighth century, the tribe of Levi is represented as a priestly community (Deut. 33[8-11]). Ezekiel confined the priesthood to descendants of Zadok (44[13-15]). But in the time of the Chronicler (*cir.* 300 B.C.) to be a priest is to be descended from Aaron (1 Chr. 6[49-53]). In this transformation of both sacrifices and priesthood we can see at once the new emphasis on the holiness of God and therefore on the holiness of those who approach him, but we can see also that the spirit of the old taboos still remains to limit the moralization of religion which the prophets so strongly urged. They would have found something to approve and something to condemn in the religion which developed as a result of their teaching. We must, however, not set the priest in too sharp an antithesis to the prophet, as is often done. If there were worldly priests of the type of Caiaphas, there were also pious priests of the type of Zechariah, the father of John the Baptist. Let anyone who would realize the inspiration of the Temple ritual within a responsive heart read from the Apocrypha the fiftieth chapter of Ecclesiasticus.

2. The Piety of the Psalter. But we need not turn from the O.T. to the Apocrypha to realize what the ritual of the Temple meant for religion. The book of Psalms is in form primarily a collection of liturgies, though it contains elements not intended for liturgical purposes. Its piety largely clusters round the ritual of the Temple, as many a familiar phrase bears witness (24[7] 26[6] 27[4] 42[2-4] 43[3] 84[7] 134[3]). Without the Temple, we should have had no book of Psalms, to the incalculable loss of man's devotional approach to God. It is in this book that we see the finest product of the prophetic spirit, working itself out in the praises and prayers of the devout. This is what the religion of Israel actually means in its noblest application to life. If in the Psalms we have lost the freshness and originality of the prophetic pioneers, we have gained by the translation of ideas once novel into the familiar language of piety. Of course there is much in the book of Psalms which goes back behind the prophets. But it is *their* spirit that animates the book, whether the psalmists look on nature, the handiwork of God, or on man, exalted by him to so high a place, and (in the case of the chosen Israel) dignified with so noble a history of Divine Providence.

The book of Psalms is indeed a compendium of both the religion and the theology of early Judaism, and we recognize in it again and again the great ideas of the prophets. (1) The idea of God is fully and confidently monotheistic, (e.g., Psa. 115)—the position reached for the first time by Deutero-Isaiah. To this one and only God belong both mystery and majesty, both "righteousness" and "loving-kindness." His majesty is expressed by the language of the old theophanies, though the emphasis now falls on the ethical attributes (Psa. 97), without elimination of what Otto has called the "numinous," or awe-inspiring elements (6[2] 44[17f.] 85[5] 90[8]). The quality of loving-kindness, originally brought out by Hosea, is finely hymned in Psa. 36[6-10], where the companion quality of "righteousness" also appears—that "rightness" which is justice in weights and measures or in loyalty to a covenant promise. But always the mystery in God's personality remains, that distinctive something which cannot be reduced to our terms of right and wrong. The psalmists, as well as Deutero-Isaiah, repeatedly say that his thoughts are not as our thoughts. (2) This majestic God is the God of nature, though of a nature much more simply and crudely conceived than we usually think. The nature Psalms (8 19[1-7] 29 65 104 148) together exalt both man and God; for if they show the wisdom and power of the Creator, they also show something of the dignity and meaning of human life, to which so wonderful a setting and so high a place have been given. The cosmology is still that of Babylonian myth—a flat earth, supported by mountain pillars, which also hold up the heavens; all around the earth the primæval ocean and its monsters; underneath it the gloomy abode of Sheol, from which there is no return; above the solid heaven is the palace of Jehovah, and the heavenly court of angels. But there is a noble conception of God as Creator which lifts these crude ideas to a level never reached by Babylon,—a conception which is due to the prophets of Israel. (3) This uniqueness is seen also in the intimate interrelation of God and human history. Religion grows out of experience, and the psalms which interpret the history of Israel (78 105 106 114 136) are characteristic of the religion. (4) It is further seen in the interrelation of God with human society. It is God's concern to find or create a community of worshipers, to oppose and overthrow the ungodly, within or without Israel. This partly explains the passionate imprecations against Jehovah's enemies (58 59 69 83 109 137), as it does explain the peculiar consciousness of a community within the community, a righteous remnant to whom God's honor is committed. Here we notice again how directly the work of the prophets is continued in these disciples of theirs, the psalmists. (5) Finally, we come to the personal religion of the Psalter, of which Jeremiah was the pioneer and chief inspirer. It is not "individualism" in our modern sense, as something consciously antithetical to "socialism"; it is, rather, an individual-social consciousness which merges itself easily into "corporate personality" and identifies itself with the community, so that we often find it difficult to know whether an individual or a group is speaking to us in the Psalms.

The notes of this personal religion, whether it be individual or social, are a strong trust in Jehovah (16 23 91), thankful joy in God (107) and constant dependence on him (103) who is omnipresent (139). The standards of conduct inspired by this trust are prophetic (15 24); the chief if not the only sacrifice is that of obedience (40) and uprightness of conduct (50). Sometimes the consciousness of "righteousness" is too prominent to satisfy a Christian conscience ($18^{22\text{-}24}$ $26^{1\text{-}6,\ 11}$; cf. 143^{2}); but the penitential psalms (6 32 38 51 102 130 143) show how well the prophetic lessons have been learned. There is also too much insistence on outward prosperity as the sign and proof of divine approval, and on adversity as always penalty; but this is bound up with the limitations of outlook in regard to life after death (see below, p. 173). Notwithstanding these limitations, the sense of fellowship with God seems to defy all barriers, as in the remarkable close to the seventy-third psalm, which is, by common consent, the "high-water mark" of the religion of the Psalter.

3. The Ethics of "Wisdom." Alongside of the piety of the Psalter there is another result of the prophetic transformation of religion, to be seen in the "Wisdom" literature, namely, the canonical books of Proverbs, Job, and Ecclesiastes, and the apocryphal books of Ecclesiasticus and the Wisdom of Solomon. It must be remembered that this literature largely belongs to the same post-exilic community which we have just seen in the Psalms, and gives us another side of postexilic life. The ascription of the "Proverbs" and "Ecclesiastes" (as later of the Greek book of "Wisdom") to Solomon is simply one of those literary traditions which are seen also in the general ascription of Psalms to David or of laws to Moses: Solomon became the prototype of "wisdom," by which was meant practical sagacity (1 Kings $3^{16f.}$) rather than purely intellectual knowledge. Under the influence of the prophets the idea was extended to include moral and religious wisdom; the "wise men" (Isa. 29^{14} Jer. 9^{23} 18^{18}) became the mediators of prophetic teaching, without claiming the direct inspiration of the prophet; they appealed to reason and experience on a universal or "humanistic" basis. (See art., *Poetic and Wisdom Literature of O.T.*, p. 157b)

The wisdom literature of Israel gives us the nearest approach of the ancient Jewish mind to philosophy. It is predominantly religious, because there could be no Hebrew "philosophy" of life apart from religion (even Spinoza illustrates this). It is chiefly practical and ethical (or prudential), passing into speculation only in regard to certain religious problems, such as the divine method of creation, the revelation of God in nature and history, and, especially, the principle of moral retribution in relation to the problem of suffering. Its ethics moves between the utilitarian and the intuitional standpoints, and great emphasis is laid on the value of moral education. The moral ideas inculcated are chiefly those of justice, helpfulness, forgiveness, humility, self-restraint, industry, while violence, sensuality and greed, slander and gossip are condemned (for the noblest account of Hebrew ethics see Job 31, rising far above the Decalogue in moral quality). The familiar contrast of "Wisdom" and "Folly" in the opening chapters of Proverbs illustrates this practical appeal for an individual choice, because virtue will bring prosperity and vice adversity. The fear of Jehovah is the beginning of wisdom (Prov. 9^{10}); it is folly to be irreligious. There is real kinship between the partial wisdom of man and the complete wisdom of God. The Divine Wisdom is personified as God's agent in creation (Prov. 8; Wisdom 7^{22}–8^{8}), the shaper of the cosmos, natural and social.

But across this mechanical application of the prophetic doctrine of retribution, as in most of the psalms, there comes also from the wisdom literature a powerful challenge of this conventionality, a challenge truer to the spirit of the prophets than any slavish acceptance of the doctrine of retribution (how often the true heir of a great leader is the man who opposes the consequences of his leadership!). The prophets taught that God administered the government of the world on lines of the strictest retributive justice, and they applied this to nations. But when some of their own number (Jeremiah and Ezekiel) applied this truth to individuals, they set the "wise men" thinking about life along lines that at last issued in the books of Job and Ecclesiastes. Neither of these books believes in a life beyond death; the justice of God must be vindicated here and now, if at all. Ecclesiastes gives up the attempt in pessimism and agnosticism (not atheism—the modern and Western attitude), but tells us to make the prudent best of things, though all is vanity. Job gives us the splendid thought (see Job 1^{1}–2^{10}) of a divine mystery in the suffering of the innocent which conceals a sufficient divine purpose—if we could know it—witness-bearing to the reality of disinterested religion ("Doth Job fear God for naught?").

4. The Hopes of Apocalyptic. The fourth and last great result of the prophetic transformation of religion for both faith and literature is that known as "apocalyptic," by which is meant the "uncovering" of the future. So far as literary form goes, this is the most direct continuation of prophecy, and it is not always easy to say where prophecy ends and apocalyptic begins. (See art., *Intertestamental Literature*, pp. 189–91; *Backgrounds*, p. 843.) The central doctrine of an imminent judgment was common to both. From the time of Amos, if not earlier, the belief in the "Day of Jehovah" as a day of judgment, and in its near approach, formed a common feature of prophecy. Indeed, it has been said, and probably with truth, that the origin of apocalyptic is partly due to the re-editing of unfulfilled prophecy (Charles, *Eschatology*, 2nd edition, pp. 108, 134–190). Thus, whilst Jeremiah reapplied his own "Scythian" prophecies (4^{5}–6^{19}) to the Babylonians, and found their fulfillment in the destruction of Jerusalem in 586 B.C., Ezekiel makes a new application of them (38^{14-17}) to the "eschatological" enemy whom he calls "Gog," lured to attack Israel by its apparent defenselessness, so that Jehovah may demonstrate and vindicate his honor against this enemy.

The most important piece of apocalyptic in the O.T. prior to the book of Daniel (165 B.C.) is Isa. 24–27, which illustrates the character of this kind of literature in its transitional stage. Here we find the declaration of the coming judgment (24^{1-20}) which will overthrow the city of chaos, and be manifested in a series of inevitable disasters. Next follows the imprisonment, with a view to punishment, of the patron-angels and the earthly kings of the nations ($24^{21, 22}$), and Jehovah begins his reign in Zion in visible glory (24^{23}; there is no Messiah). He proceeds to celebrate his coronation-festival, and to remove the sorrow of all the peoples of the earth by the abolition of death (25^{6-8}). During the time of wrath against Jehovah's enemies on earth and in heaven, his people withdraw into safety (26^{20}-27^{1}). Finally, the trumpet sounds to recall the Jews of the Dispersion to Jerusalem ($27^{12, 13}$). Here we see the outline of apocalyptic about 300 B.C. (the interspersed songs have been left unnoticed).

In the later book of Daniel both the angelology and the symbolism are elaborated, though not so far as in the contemporary apocryphal apocalyptic, the so-called Dream-Visions of Enoch (83–90). The use of traditional names —Daniel, Enoch, Moses, Baruch, Ezra—for the recipients of the revelation is characteristic and significant; the writers of apocalyptic, though doubtless conscious of inspiration, must shelter themselves under the venerable names of the past. Just as a Jewish commentator (Rashi) imagines that a vision of Israel's future history was granted to Moses on Pisgah, so that he saw its striking scenes unrolled before his eyes, even so the apocalyptists in more elaborate literary form, and with use of much conventional material, imagine a vision of the great successive epochs of the world's history; but the culminating point is always the absolute and complete kingly rule of God. This is conceived as due to supernatural intervention, not to any slow evolution of good within the world, so that the "kingdom of God" for the apocalyptists is something very different from modern ideas of the world's future. It is customary to call this kingdom "Messianic," because it is sometimes linked with the idea of a "Messiah," i.e., an "anointed" representative of Jehovah (see art., *Israel's Messianic Hope*, p. 181); but the Messiah is not necessary to the idea of the Kingdom. The main conceptions of it are that Israel is in the right against the world, that Israel itself needs sifting in order to yield a righteous remnant, and that the Kingdom will be characterized by moral and physical perfection, or at least by great advance on present conditions of earthly life. In the later developments of apocalyptic the realms of heaven and Sheol come into the reckoning and the emphasis is shifted to them. The whole lurid panorama is thrown into the future, perhaps at long intervals of time, though the beginnings are conceived as close at hand. Consequently, the doctrine of resurrection and the ethical differentiation of the eschatology become of the greatest importance.

IV. The Life After Death

At first sight, it is strange that the O.T. should have so little to say about the life after death, when we remember how prominent this becomes in Jewish and Christian apocalyptic. Yet fuller inquiry will teach us that the gradual and late development of the idea was the very condition of its eventual vigor and value. There was time for many factors to co-operate, for men to become conscious of real needs—the first step toward seeking real satisfactions of them—and for the momentum of ethical monotheism to be brought to bear on the problems of human destiny, individual as well as national. It cannot be too clearly realized, especially at the present time, that a doctrine of life after death which means simply survival—a mere extension of this life—is of little value. The real significance of the Christian doctrine of immortality—which goes back to the Jewish in its origin—is in its *content*, not in its form. It is born of religion (as, indeed, was the Greek doctrine of immortality), and the values of religion flow into it. Its concern is with quality rather than quantity, and this characteristic is originally due to the religion of Israel. There was no moral or religious quality in the original Hebrew belief in "Sheol"—that vast, underground cavern in which the "shades"—not the souls or spirits—of the dead were gathered, just as they were in the Babylonian *Aralu* or the Greek *Hades*. To pass from the warm realities of life upon the earth to the cold semblance of that ghostly existence in Sheol could attract only a man utterly weary of living at all (Job 3^13-19^). To go down to the shades is literally to be humbled to the dust, a fitting fall for some tyrant conqueror of earth, whose corpse is left unburied upon it (Isa. 14^9-20^). In Sheol, the nations are grouped apart, as in a sort of allocated cemetery, but their mighty men are reduced to a common helplessness; there is no moral or religious differentiation in this shadow-existence (Ezek. 32^17-32^). A man will shrink from the gloom and deep darkness of Sheol as from the last enemy of all—for this is just what death means (Job 10^20-22^). There is no return from Sheol for him who has once entered it (Job 7^9^)—though Job wishes it were but a waiting room for him, until God had forgotten to be angry, and called once more for his unjustly treated servant (14^13f.^). Even if the "soul" lingers temporarily about the mouldering corpse (14^22^), it is the "shade" or ghost that goes to Sheol, the pale replica of the whole man, and not only the spiritual part of him. Where psalmists speak of being brought up from Sheol (e.g., Psa. 30^3^), they mean that they have narrowly escaped dying. The fact is that the body is essential to the Hebrew idea of personality, and there could be no conception of life after death until there was a doctrine of "resurrection," i.e., of the restoration of the body, the real "self" (*nephesh;* even a corpse can bear this name).

There are two passages, and only two, in the O.T. which speak clearly of a resurrection of the body, and therefore of life in the real sense after death. The earlier of these is found in the apocalypse already noticed (Isa. 24–27) of about 300 B.C. In 26^19^ it is declared that (righteous) dead who have given up their lives for their religion will be brought to life upon the earth again, their corpses arising from the dust. The later reference is also to be found in an apocalypse, that of "Daniel," about 165 B.C.; here there is a resurrection not only of the specially good, but also of the specially bad, to receive those deserts which they have somehow missed in the unprecedented upheaval of persecution (Dan. 12^2^). The moral and religious motive is plain, in this earliest emergence of faith in the resurrection. The motive becomes most apparent in other passages which, though they do not speak of life after death, do assert an intimacy of fellowship with God or faith in him, of which the *implicit* logic would be that death could not separate man from him. The most notable of these passages is Psa. 73^23-25^, that noblest assertion of dependence on God and confidence in him. Yet even here the inference is not drawn—the inference that because God is the rock of the believer's heart and his portion forever there must be life after death to confirm and realize this truth. Indeed, some of the passages in which this faith has been plausibly found require a more historical explanation. The famous passage in Job (19^25f.^)—"I know that my Redeemer liveth"—seems, when properly translated, to signify a temporary and bodyless return to "life," in order to see the delayed vindication of justice. In this and other passages (e.g., Psa. 16^10f.^ 17^15^ 49^14^), the Christian is naturally inclined to read a fuller meaning into Oriental imagery than is strictly justifiable; the figure of "waking" in the morning is a common one for deliverance (e.g., Psa. 30^5^), without regard to any life beyond death.

But though these expressions of confidence in God add nothing to the form of faith in immortality, they are very significant for its content, and, indeed, constitute the substance of that faith. It was the answer, as we may see from the book of Job, to the sorest need of the Hebrew mind and heart—the apparent injustice of life which seemed to deny, not God's existence, but his justice. No problem is more prominent in the religion of Israel than this, and none has created a more abundant literature. It was vital to the kind of faith in God which Israel possessed; it was a practical issue which must somehow be met, when the religious emphasis shifted from the national to the more individualized fortunes of men. The book of Job would be unintelligible if its background had been an assured faith in immortality; but instead, the book shows us a poet-thinker wrestling for a solution of the problem without that one solution which seems to us most obvious—that life beyond death will readjust all injustices of this life. There are other answers in the O.T., or approaches to answers, such as the exhortation of the psalmists to wait and see what will happen (here on earth, and before death) to the suffering innocent and to the prosperous guilty, or the gloomy skepticism of the book of Ecclesiastes; the highest point is reached in the great conception of Isa. 53, that the innocent may suffer vicariously and sacrificially for the guilty. The problem was such a pressing one just because it was so central to the teaching of the prophets. Their whole message stood or fell with the retributive justice of God. It is broadly true that this is vindicated within this life, and in the long run in the case of nations, because they do have a run long enough to work it out; it is not so true of individual lives which may, at least outwardly, miss their retributive award of good or evil. Thus the very criticism of prophetic truth in its individualized application was destined to issue in the great step forward into faith in a life beyond death as the necessary arena for the vindication of God's character and purpose.

V. The Conception of Salvation

Meanwhile men had their earth here, however unknown or uncertain heaven or hell might be. What did the religion of Israel make of this life, lacking the reference of its problems to another? What, in fact, could faith in Jehovah do for Israelites, seeing it gave them no outlook beyond death? The answer to these questions is the conception of salvation, always central for a religion, always conditioned by the idea of what men are saved *from* as well as *to*. The religion of Israel is characterized by a strong realism, a strong emphasis on the worth and value of this present life, taken in itself. To be deprived of it is the greatest evil, and moral exhortation can offer no more impressive choice than that between life and good on the one hand, and death and evil on the other (Deut. 30[15f.]). Of Wisdom, it is said that "length of days is in her right hand, in her left hand are riches and honor" (Prov. 3[16]). If we add to these "goods" of life the children who continue a man's life even after his death (by that "corporate personality" which makes the whole family a unit), we know the best that could come to the Hebrew, the most convincing signs and evidences of the moral approval of God, when the prophets had succeeded in moralizing the idea of God. In fact, Israel's life is positive and intense in its consciousness of value just because death is the absolute negation of it, and not the doorway to a life that can outrival it. The Israelite, therefore, appeals to Jehovah to save him from a premature death, or from the suffering of sickness, disgrace or poverty.

But the thought of these evils is crossed by another, as the religion deepens in moral quality. From the most primitive forms of religion in Israel, as elsewhere, there had been non-moral "taboos"—things which must not be done because of the fatal consequences they might bring, and some of these survived into the most developed faith (e.g., Deut. 22[9], or the last clause of Ezek. 18[6]). But the general trend of the prophetic teaching was, as we have seen, to emphasize the moral aspects of "sin" as well as of "God"—neither of these religious terms being originally moral at all. Sin—which then becomes the religious aspect of moral evil—is presented in the O.T. chiefly under four aspects, so far as the terminology is concerned. It is deviation from the right way; the word most often rendered "sin" denotes "missing the way" (Prov. 19[2]; cf. Judg. 20[16]), while the word rendered "iniquity" (1 Sam. 3[13]) also means a "going astray," the same metaphor also appearing in the very familiar "turn aside" (Judg. 2[17]). Again, sin may be described juristically as guilt before a judge, the antithetical term being "righteousness," the status of a person acquitted before the tribunal, not to be confused with moral rightness, though often including it (cf. Ex. 9[27]); this was a favorite figure with the prophets. The most significant and characteristic term of all is that rendered "rebel," used of subjects revolting against their ruler (2 Kings 8[20] Isa. 1[2, 3]). A fourth class of terms denotes sin by its intrinsic character as something evil or as bringing evil to its doer (1 Sam. 12[17] Prov. 22[8]) and therefore "senselessness" (Deut. 22[21]). This usage comes nearest to our "vice."

The common feature of all these is, of course, opposition to the will of God; moral good is conceived not in the Greek terms of an ideal but in Hebrew terms, as a law.

Over against this conception of human sin we must put that of divine grace. We have already encountered the great word rendered "loving-kindness," and meaning the "duteous love" which man may show to man, or man to God, or God to man. In the pre-prophetic times, this "grace" of God is as unmoralized as the idea of sin; grace is the arbitrary favor of Jehovah, on which Israel is apt to presume (Amos 3[2]). The relation of Jehovah to Israel throughout the whole period of Israel's religion is conceived in terms of a "covenant" (the word used denotes a "bond" of some sort). The covenant relation is not a bargain, but the obligation of a growing friendship. There was the covenant at Sinai (Ex. 24[3-8]), a blood-communion between God and man. There was the covenant of Deuteronomy (29[1]; cf. 26[17, 18]), which was a mutual engagement, inspired by the teaching of the eighth-century prophets. There was the covenant with Abraham (Gen. 17[7, 8]), as conceived in the late Priestly Code, which was a divine promise, fulfilled in many institutions. Thus we may say that the idea of a covenant is the constant background to the idea of salvation or redemption. We can never hope to understand it by taking a particular sin or a particular sacrifice out of their context, and trying to understand them apart from their background. If the offering of a sacrifice does avail to secure forgiveness of sin, and the proof of this in recovered health or prosperity, it is always because of the renewal of the covenant of "duteous love"—though low minds might construe it as a mere bargain.

The fact that the predominant significance of Hebrew sacrifices is that of a gift brought to a superior must not mislead us; this is customary in the East. In fact, the whole practice of sacrifice in the religion of Israel is less important as "atonement" than we are apt to think, and belongs, rather, to a general conformity with religious ritual as God's requirement. The atonement that was made by sacrifice (in its whole setting) was a renewal of the broken covenant, not the suffering of a penalty; in fact, we do well to keep quite apart the ideas of a forensic "righteousness" and the acceptance of an offering, though they may be used to refer to the same event (cf. Rom. 3[25]). We must not say that the prophets condemned sacrifice as such; what they condemned was the substitution of this external expression of worship for the more difficult realization of the will of Jehovah in moral conduct. This is finely seen in the well-known prophecy of the New Covenant (Jer. 31[31f.]), which we may regard as the democratization of the prophetic consciousness. What Jeremiah seeks in fact is the creation of a nation of Jeremiahs—i.e., of Israelites indeed. The old, external, national covenant has failed; the new must be constituted in an inner relation with the individual Israelite, so that external teachers will no longer be needed to impart the "knowledge" of God (which is volitional as well as intellectual). All this becomes a possibility only by an act of divine grace—a forgiveness of past sin, preparatory to this new creation, which is a free exercise of that duteous love of God toward man out of which his covenants, old and new, always proceed.

VI. The Unity of the Testaments

There could be no more suggestive point of contact between the O.T. and the N.T. than that which has just been named. The greatest prophecy of the most spiritual of the prophets is linked with words spoken in the upper room; it was both echoed and fulfilled in the "New Covenant" initiated by Jesus Christ. The Bible is a unity, and it is not critical study which disintegrates it, but such literalistic use of the Bible as treats it like a "jig-saw" puzzle. There are great and permanent ideas which run through the whole Bible and slowly emerge into a disclosure of their full meaning in the pages of the N.T. Some of these, such as the ideas of life after death, cannot be consecutively traced without reference to the Apocrypha and Pseudepigrapha (see the articles on the Intertestamental Period, pp. 187–213), with which every student of the Bible should have some acquaintance. But the dominant ideas of the N.T. may be seen already in the O.T. and unless we understand the religion of the old Israel we shall never know that of the N.T., which stands in such direct continuity with it.

We may think, for example, of the idea of God (always avoiding that frequent confusion between the development of the idea of God and the idea of a developing God, which is a contradiction in terms); that great conception of holy Fatherhood which distinguishes the teaching of Jesus, and is born of his filial consciousness, completes and rounds off the moral conception of Jehovah which the prophets achieved. Again, when we think of the cross of Christ as the nucleus of divine activity within this world's history, we have to remember that the achievement of Jesus was to bring together in word and deed those two conceptions which had never been united in Judaism, those of the Messiah and the Suffering Servant of Isa. 53. The newly made unity was his; but the materials he used, the elements of the conception, were drawn from the O.T., and they made the significance of his cross, which we see foreshadowed, not in every reference to wood within the O.T., but in the suffering for God *and with God* of a Job, a Jeremiah and a Hosea. The doctrine of the Holy Spirit is the very heart of Paul's teaching about Christian experience, and occupies a cardinal place in the fourth Gospel; that doctrine goes back to the wind (*ruach* = "spirit") that blew across Semitic deserts, the phenomenal energy that animated Hebrew leaders from time to time, the prophetic conviction that a "supernatural" influence must be brought to bear on the character and conduct of Israel to enable it to accomplish its destiny. The modern conception of human personality, which holds so central a place in the higher thought and philosophy of to-day, goes back to the N.T. teaching about man, and the dignity given to him by Jesus as a child of the heavenly Father, however degraded; but that conception itself points further back to such a passage as the eighth psalm, whilst the Christian doctrine of resurrection, as we have seen, is the direct product of Hebrew psychology. When we think of the Pauline conception of the church as the body of Christ, or the conditions of that mystical relation in which his life and that of the Christian are conceived as one, or the "representative" position which Jesus Christ holds as the head of a new race over against Adam, we are working with a conception of "corporate personality" which dominates much of the O.T., not only in the cruder forms which led, e.g., to the destruction of Achan's family, because Achan had broken a taboo, but also in the noble and spiritual transitions from the individual to the group and the group to the individual which characterize the "Songs of the Servant" in Deutero-Isaiah, and so many of the psalms and prophecies of the O.T.

It would be easy to show that the religion of Israel has left its imprint on practically every page of the N.T., and no writer or teacher or student of the N.T. can afford to neglect the O.T. The O.T. shows us the human in the divine; the N.T. shows us the divine in the human. Whether we study the prophetic consciousness in the O.T. or that supreme union of the human and the divine in the N.T., which we call the Incarnation, the crucial point is the same—the validity of a human experience to prove that the divine is really present and active, and that, in the greater or less degree, God is manifest in the flesh. Thus the prophetic consciousness which we found to be central historically is seen to be central also for philosophy and theology; in studying it we must meet the same challenge of auto-suggestion and self-illusion that religious experience to-day encounters, and the religion of Israel is thus brought into closest relation with the supreme issues of our own experience.

Literature: A useful list of books in English will be found in *A Scripture Bibliography* drawn up by the (British) Society for O.T. Study. The following may be named either for their importance or as suited to the needs of the readers of this Commentary: W. R. Smith, *The Prophets of Israel* (ed. Cheyne); Cornill, *The Prophets of Israel;* Budde, *Religion of Israel to the Exile;* Kautzsch, article, "Religion of Israel," in Hastings' *Dictionary of the Bible*, vol. v., pp. 612f.; Marti, *The Religion of the O.T.;* Hamilton, *The People of God;* Welch, *The Religion of Israel under the Kingdom;* H. W. Robinson, *The Religious Ideas of the O.T.;* H. P. Smith, *The Religion of Israel;* Gordon, *The Prophets of the O.T.;* J. M. P. Smith, *The Religion of the Psalms;* Skinner, *Prophecy and Religion;* T. H. Robinson, *Prophecy and the Prophets in Ancient Israel;* G. A. Smith, *Jeremiah;* Gray, *Sacrifice in the O.T.;* Peake (ed.), *The People and the Book;* Kittel, *The Religion of the People of Israel;* D. C. Simpson (ed.), *The Psalmists;* Welch, *The Psalter in Life, Worship and History;* H. W. Robinson, *The Cross of the Servant.*

ISRAEL'S MESSIANIC HOPE

By Professor J. E. McFadyen

The most scientific study of Israel's Messianic hope would be an historical study. It would compare and contrast this hope as it was cherished in Israel with cognate hopes in other parts of the Oriental world, notably in Babylon and Egypt. It would trace that hope to its earliest beginnings, it would show how it was affected and colored by the contemporary historical situation, and how it was gradually transformed by the deepening spiritual experience of the people or at least of their noblest representatives. It would show how the victory, prosperity, fertility, which earlier ages had counted as the things most devoutly to be wished for in the happy day to which they looked forward gradually gave place, under the impact of prophetic teaching, to ideals which placed the supreme emphasis upon moral and spiritual values—how the warrior was merged in the martyr, how the victory achieved by the sword came to be felt as nothing in comparison with the victory achieved by the patient endurance of wrong, how deliverance from the enemy would have been but a poor salvation if unaccompanied by deliverance from sin, how the deliverer, once seen as a King prancing upon his war-horse, appeared to the purged eyes of a later time as one meek and lowly of heart, riding upon an ass, and how later still the old earthly materialistic hopes of conquest, victory, and dominion revived, sometimes obliterating, and sometimes blended with, the nobler ideals that had been achieved in the process of the ages. This would be a fruitful and illuminating study; but, while not ignoring the historical affiliations of the hope, we shall concentrate rather on its religious aspect, partly because that is the aspect of the Bible which this volume keeps more particularly in view, and partly because, while the broad outlines of the development are clear enough, an historical study frequently raises questions of the date and authenticity of particular passages to which it is not possible to give any definite answer and concerning which the opinions of competent scholars often diverge very widely.

Our study of the question, then, will be determined by these considerations. We shall consider first, the contents of the Messianic hope, and then the various types of personality who were to incarnate that hope or to inaugurate the Messianic age.

I. The Messianic Hope

Triumph Over Evil. We may begin with the time-honored verse in Gen. 3[15] which forms part of the divine curse upon the serpent for tempting Eve to her fateful disobedience. "I will put enmity between thee and the woman and between thy seed and her seed: it shall bruise thy head, and thou shalt bruise his heel." This verse has long been known as the "protevangelium," the first expression of the gospel, and it has been interpreted as a promise of man's ultimate victory over sin. The *it*, which is to bruise the serpent's head is the seed of the woman just alluded to, i.e., her descendants—humanity. Not without reason has it been questioned, however, whether, even in the broad sense, this is a Messianic text at all. For, taking the story literally, the struggle is between the race of men and the brood of serpents; for the serpent is a literal serpent, doomed henceforth to crawl on its belly (cf. 3[14]). And—again not without reason—it has been pointed out that the verse does not speak explicitly of the ultimate victory of man but, rather, of an eternal enmity and struggle between him and the serpent. But in answer to these objections it may be fairly urged that the serpent of the story is more than a literal serpent; it is the embodiment of an evil principle, a fit emblem of the glittering baleful fascination of sin which deflects men from obedience to the reasonable voice of conscience and of God. And, again, it is perhaps not straining the sense of the verse too sorely to say with Dillmann that a struggle ordained of God cannot be without prospect of success. Man was destined for dominion (cf. 2[19] 1[28]), and though "now we see not yet all things subjected to him" (Heb. 2[8]), we can believe it to be the divine will that that dominion will one day be achieved, and indeed we see it achieved when "we behold Jesus" (Heb. 2[9]). So while the significant words of Genesis are in no sense a direct prophecy of Jesus, and not even an explicit promise of man's ultimate victory over sin, it may be fairly enough contended, in the larger light of revelation, that they are an implicit promise of that victory; and with wonderful appropriateness they are set at the beginning of our sacred Book, whose theme from beginning to end is salvation.

The Messianic People. Now this salvation,

which is the will of God for men, is historically mediated; it comes to humanity through Israel, which holds, so to say, the religious secret of the world. Israel is very conscious, and very early conscious, of her unique place in the purpose of God for humanity. This consciousness expresses itself with varying degrees of spiritual insight; sometimes, indeed, it expresses itself in terms almost wholly materialistic. The promise to Abraham, e.g., in Gen. 12[2f.] is that his descendants are to become a great nation and so conspicuously prosperous that other nations could wish for themselves nothing better than a prosperity like theirs. That—and not that Israel is to bring blessing to the world—is the real meaning of the clause rendered, "In thee shall all the families of the earth be blessed." But that rather materialistic hope takes on a much more spiritual complexion in Ex. 19[5f.] which promises that, if Israel obeys Jehovah's voice and keeps his covenant, they shall be "a kingdom of priests and an holy nation," and in this sense Jehovah's "peculiar treasure from among all peoples." Whether we interpret this as a promise that the Hebrew people are destined to be the priests of humanity, or simply that each of them, priestlike, will have direct access to God, this is one of the most fundamental passages of the O.T. We may say that we have here the dawn of the great conception of the kingdom of God. The passage occurs in connection with the exodus of Israel from Egypt, the act which sealed Jehovah's redeeming love for Israel, and to which later generations perpetually recur, as attesting the kindness, the power, the essential nature of God. The covenant then established had its moral and religious conditions; the people are to be a *holy* people, they are to be "a peculiar treasure" *if they obey*, and it is significant that the next chapter contains the Decalogue (20[1-17]) which shows the nature of the law they are expected to obey. It follows by implication that disobedience would be drastically punished (cf. Amos 3[2]), but the redemptive end would be kept ever in view. This idea of punishment which was essentially disciplinary with its issue in redemption is beautifully worked out by Hosea in ch. 2, where Jehovah is represented as luring his foolish and idolatrous spouse Israel into the wilderness (2[14]) where, after a discipline of many days, the wedding-bond is renewed forever, and Israel receives the promise that wild beasts and war and all that had harmed shall harm her no more (2[18]).

Messianic Promises: 1. *Return from Exile.* The promise ran, "The Lord will keep thee from *all* evil" (Psa. 121[7]). Contrary to this promise Israel suffered severe affliction, and grimmer and more fatal to her high destiny than the evils mentioned in the preceding paragraph was the experience of exile. This seemed not only to blight Israel's hopes but to destroy them, unless that experience could be reversed. But the love of their God reversed it. He who had long ago saved them from Egypt must save them from Babylon. So at a time when Hebrew hearts were sore and men wept as they remembered Zion (Psa. 137[1]), in days when they were saying that they were being forgotten and ignored by their God (Isa. 40[27]), a great prophet came forward (Isa. 40–55) with the inspired assurance that the sorrow would soon be lifted, Jehovah was coming to lead his people back across the transformed wilderness to their own dear land; "for ye shall go out with joy, and be led forth with peace" (Isa. 55[12]); and through the agency of the foreign Cyrus, Jehovah's own Anointed (i.e., Messiah), that promise was to be fulfilled in the near future (cf. Isa. 45[1-5]).

2. *Transformation of Wild Beasts.* From *all* evil—from exile, from wild beasts, from war, from idolatry. The last three points, lightly touched by Hosea, are taken up and developed by subsequent prophets. The first of the three receives immortal expression in the beautiful verses of Isa. 11[6-8], where the wild animals that had ravaged the land are to have their nature so transformed that they will peaceably consort with the tame animals—"the cow and the bear shall be friends"—and so gentle will they be that a little child can lead them.

3. *Destruction of War.* But worse than the ravages of beasts are the ravages of war, and this too must vanish in the good time that is coming. How fearfully the burden of war must have weighed upon the ancient Hebrew heart, and how alien it was felt to be to the purpose of God for men is evidenced by the fact that the great oracle announcing its abolition "in the after-time" occurs twice in the prophetic books (Isa. 2[2-4] and Mic. 4[1-4]). In the early days Israel had glorified war and had looked up to the God she worshiped as "a man of war" (Ex. 15[3]): now she knows better. The prophets were living in a world that was torn with strife, drenched with blood, and peopled by quarrelsome nations armed with swords and spears (Isa. 2[4]), and they felt that this must end and would end in the Messianic age. But it is too often forgotten that the heartening words, "Nation shall not lift up sword against nation, neither shall they learn war any more," are not merely a prophet's or a poet's dream. The prophets were realists as well as idealists, and in the most practical way they showed how this dream would become reality. It is not merely an aspiration, but the inevitable result

of the program sketched by the prophet in sublimely simple words. He represents the nations who have some quarrel on foot as suddenly inspired by the great thought of carrying their quarrels to Zion for arbitration; for they say, "Out of Zion shall go forth instruction [*or* guidance], and the word of the Lord from Jerusalem." With men like Isaiah and Jeremiah, whose souls were set on justice, to pronounce the word of the Lord, they could confidently anticipate an impartial decision. And through such men Jehovah would "judge between the nations and arbitrate concerning the peoples," and so wise and fair would the decision be that the nations would gladly accept it and go away content, resolved never again to wield the sword and spear for which they have now no more use, but to transform them into peaceful plowshares and pruninghooks. The abolition of war and the reign of eternal peace are to be secured by arbitration, and those things will come to pass when the natures of men are no longer swayed by passion but by reason and religion, when they abandon the bloody way of the sword and learn the way to Zion.

4. *Disappearance of Idolatry.* Further, in the coming age idolatry would be as intolerable as war, and, like war, it must disappear, the more so as the Messianic hope rested on Jehovah's covenant with Israel, and that covenant is rightly interpreted in the second commandment as excluding idolatrous worship of every kind. In keeping with this ideal, Mic. 5[12-14] describes the coming age as one in which not only every practice that savored of magic or superstition, but also all the heathen paraphernalia, such as stone pillars and asherim or wooden poles, that had for so long been associated with the worship of Jehovah, would disappear. This, however, was only a negative ideal, the positive counterpart of which was worship in the spirit. Of this we shall later have more to say; suffice it here to quote significant words of Jeremiah (3[16]) which look forward to the day when men would speak no more of the ark of the covenant of Jehovah; it would never enter their minds, they would never think of it nor miss it, nor would they ever again make another. When we remember the stupendous place that the ark had filled in the early history and how its presence on a battlefield was believed to guarantee the presence of Jehovah himself (cf. 1 Sam. 4[3]), these words of Jeremiah, which soar above the need for a material expression of religion into the region of pure spirit and which can gladly dispense with its most ancient and venerable symbols, are nothing less than wonderful.

5. *Forgiveness of Sin.* Most fatal of all to the communion with God at which the covenant aimed was sin, and an indispensable feature of the Messianic age would be the forgiveness of sins. "I, even I, am he that blotteth out thy transgressions, and I will not remember thy sins" (Isa. 43[25]). This promise, of course, like everything else in the O.T., has historical relations; it was given to the exiles in Babylon, and the experience of exile, which was interpreted as due to the wrath of God (cf. Isa. 40[2]), had greatly deepened the sense of sin. But by the deliverance from exile the divine forgiveness would be sealed, the love of God would have free course, and the people who were worthy to "inherit the land forever" would be a people who were "all righteous" (cf. Isa. 60[21]), saved not only from war and idolatry but from sin, and rejoicing in their forgiveness.

6. *Conquest of Death.* But "the last enemy is death" (1 Cor. 15[26]), and this too must be finally destroyed. The O.T., which confines its vision almost uniformly to this life and can do this the more contentedly as it is so radiantly sure of God and his presence in the world that now is, has very little to say of a life beyond the grave (see further art., *Religion of Israel*, p. 173; cf. art., *Backgrounds*, pp. 845–6); but we can rejoice that one of the later prophets has expressed his confident hope in the daring and splendid words, "He hath swallowed up death forever" (Isa. 25[8]), words so adequate that the great apostle can find no better with which to conclude his magnificent argument for immortality (1 Cor. 15[54]).

7. *Exaltation of Jerusalem.* It is not to be wondered at that the Hebrews, who were nothing if not patriotic, should have assigned a special place to Jerusalem in the glorious days to which they looked forward. We have already seen (cf. Isa. 2[2f.] Mic. 4[2]) that it is to Jerusalem the nations are pictured as journeying to have their disputes settled by arbitration, for "it is from Zion that direction goes forth" such as is to be found nowhere else in the world. But it is good to remember that sometimes even this very pardonable limitation is transcended. There is nothing finer in the O.T. than the vision in Isa. 19[23-25] of Egypt and Assyria, ancient and recent enemies of Israel, united with Israel in the latter days in a triple alliance, and united simply as joint worshipers of Jehovah. Nothing is here said of Jerusalem as the necessary center of that worship; there is nothing here like the narrower hope of a later day expressed in Zech. 14[16] that the nations who are to worship Jehovah must not only come to Jerusalem, but that there they must celebrate the distinctively Jewish feast of tabernacles. But while it may be frankly conceded that the hope seldom takes so pronouncedly Jewish a form as this, it has to

be admitted that Jerusalem—doubtless for reasons that are historically quite intelligible—is usually in the center of the picture, and that therefore the universalism is hardly ever complete. In the fine passage from which we have already quoted the prophecy of the abolition of death (Isa. 25[6-8]), it is upon Zion's hill that the rich feast is to be spread, of which all nations are represented as partaking; it is there that the veil of mourning is to be rent in twain and the tears wiped from every eye. Similarly in Jer. 3[17] Jerusalem is "the throne of the Lord; and all the nations shall be gathered unto it, to the name of the Lord, to Jerusalem." This emphasis upon Jerusalem may seem in strange contrast to the preceding verse which, by denying the importance of the ark, had seemed to carry us into an atmosphere of the spirit, to which material symbols and a special locality were irrelevant, and for this reason the verse has been denied to Jeremiah. However that may be, it embodies a characteristic Jewish limitation in the thought that it is only through the gates of Zion that men enter the city of God.

8. *The New Heart.* Having considered some of the blessings to be enjoyed by those who are privileged to share in the Messianic age—and these, as we have seen, include, according to some of the prophets, men of all peoples (cf. Isa. 45[22], "Look unto me and be ye saved, *all* the ends of the earth")—let us now consider the character of the participants. They are to be, first of all, men of a new heart. This is a point emphasized more than once by Ezekiel (cf. 11[19] 36[26]). When exiled Israel has been brought back and settled in her own land and has given evidence of her sincerity by putting away all the abominable habits and idolatrous practices that had separated her from her God, then Jehovah will interpose with the inward regeneration which he alone can secure. "I will give them another—so LXX, with a very slight change from the Hebrew *one*—heart, and I will put a new spirit within them." The words that follow define the meaning of this promise, explaining that for the stony heart, hard and impervious to the appeal of Jehovah's redeeming love, will be substituted a heart of flesh, i.e., soft, impressionable, responsive, yielding, obedient. This is a great prophecy, recognizing as it does the need of transformation, yet it is more limited in its outlook than one might suspect, for the succeeding words have a distinctly legal tinge. The people will evidence their transformation of heart by "walking in my statutes and keeping mine ordinances" (11[20]). Here the influence of Deuteronomy, which had been published about thirty years before, is very plainly felt. Obedience is to be not to the law of the spirit but to the written law; and so the promise which seemed to breathe the pure spirit of prophecy turns out to be conceived in the temper of legalism after all. All the same it is a great word, and if we ignore its legalistic limitations, it can be adopted as a motto—there is none better—for the character of the Messianic kingdom. On another occasion (18[31]) when Ezekiel is seeking to stimulate the sluggish consciences of his people, he urges that it is *their* duty to "make a new heart and a new spirit for themselves"; but in 11[19] 36[26] he regards the new heart and the new spirit as God's own gift to them. It is the everlasting antinomy of religion: "Work out your own salvation, for it is God that worketh in you" (Phil. 2[12f.]).

9. *The New Covenant.* But a greater than Ezekiel uttered a prophecy peculiarly precious to our Lord (Lk. 22[20] 1 Cor. 11[25]) and to the writer of the Epistle to the Hebrews (8[8-12]), which carries us into the region of pure spirit unsullied by any suspicion of legalism. Jeremiah (31[31-34]) foresees the coming day when Jehovah—it is always he who, of his grace, takes the initiative—will make a new covenant with Israel and Judah. This he expressly contrasts with the old covenant made at the Exodus, and by implication, with the Deuteronomic covenant made a few years before (cf. 2 Kings 23[3]). Those covenants involved obedience to an external law, but the law of the new covenant was to be written on the heart. Obedience would no longer be deliberate conformity to an imposed law, but the spontaneous expression of an inward communion with God resting upon the knowledge of his will, knowledge which would not have to be communicated by one to another, but would be the common and inalienable possession of all. Though this covenant is represented as being made with Israel and Judah, its nature is such that it is destined to be universal. The law written upon the heart—the human heart and not Israel's alone; the direct and unmediated knowledge of God—these things point beyond Israel to the whole human race. Glorious as is this word of Jeremiah, even within its somewhat nationalistic context, he spoke even better than he knew.

10. *The Outpouring of the Spirit.* There is one other prophecy, held by Peter to have been fulfilled at Pentecost (Acts 2[17f.]), which in spirituality and generosity of outlook would seem to rival this word of Jeremiah, and in a sense to be even more daringly explicit. It occurs in the picture of the latter days drawn by Joel (2[28f.]); "I will pour out my Spirit upon all flesh; and your sons and your daughters

shall prophesy, your old men shall dream dreams, your young men shall see visions; and also upon the servants and upon the handmaidens in those days will I pour out my spirit." Here Jeremiah's "all, from the least to the greatest" is defined in detail, and we seem to be confronted with the wonderful vision of a world whose every inhabitant is, so to speak, an inspired prophet—every man and woman, even those of humblest social status, in possession of the Spirit. But, despite the "all flesh," Joel's vision is not quite so generous as that. The blessing is for Judah; the fate reserved for "the nations" is judgment in the valley of Jehoshaphat (cf. 3[2]). Joel does not say, "Not only you, but also the heathen"; what he says is, "Not only you, but also your servants and handmaidens." So this fair vision is marred by a certain narrow nationalism after all; nevertheless, in the light of the Christian revelation, we may legitimately expand the words to a sense beyond that intended by Joel and regard the promise, "I will pour out my Spirit upon all flesh," as descriptive of one of the features, indeed, the profoundest and most essential, of the happy time to which the O.T. looks continually forward.

What a glorious hope it was! Limited, if you like, at points, by features peculiar to the nation in which it was born—for was not Jerusalem to be the metropolis of the better world to be? But what a noble world! One from which war, sin, and death would be banished forever, and one whose every inhabitant would be possessed of the Divine Spirit and have the law written on his heart.

The Messianic Figure

Even in the O.T., to say nothing of the N.T., this hope is frequently connected with a person. The character of the figure at the head of the redeemed theocracy may change with the historical situation, but there is usually such a figure. Usually, but not always; there is no "Messiah," e.g., in Amos, or Zephaniah, or Nahum, or Habakkuk.

The Messianic King. In most cases that figure is a king. Not, indeed, that the word *mashîach* ("anointed") has any specific or exclusive connection with royalty. Other leaders of the people were, or might be, also anointed. In Ex. 29[7] the high priest is anointed, and in 28[41] the other priests as well. In 1 Kings 19[16] Elijah receives a divine commission to anoint not only Jehu to the kingly, but also Elisha, his successor, to the prophetic office. The word could be applied even to a foreign ruler, as by the great-hearted prophet of the Exile to Cyrus (Isa. 45[1]), whom he regarded as consecrated by Jehovah to the task of delivering his people from exile. But the term is pre-eminently applied to the king. No official was comparable to him. He was the head of judicial and religious as well as of civil and military affairs. He was in a peculiar sense Jehovah's "son" (cf. Psa. 2[7]), a term otherwise applied only to the people (cf. Ex. 4[22]). It has, of course, to be remembered that Jehovah is the real king of Israel; so strongly is this felt that the later source in Samuel regards the demand for a king as an implicit rejection of the kingship of Jehovah (cf. 1 Sam. 8[7]). He is the glorious King (Psa. 24[7, 10]) and essentially the earthly king is but his viceroy. But, as his viceroy, he is all-important, and, in some form or other, monarchy is felt to be the most essential element in Messiahship. Again and again this comes out in the N.T. In all the versions of the superscription on the cross (Mt. 27[37] Mk. 15[26] Lk. 23[38] Jn. 19[19]) Jesus is described as the King of the Jews, he claimed to be Lord of a kingdom though not of this world (Jn. 18[36]), and after the resurrection the disciples ask him, "Lord, dost thou at this time restore *the kingdom* to Israel?" (Acts 1[6].)

The Ideal Prophet. Before proceeding to a discussion of the references to the king, let us look at the promise in Deut. 18[15] put into the mouth of Moses, "The Lord thy God will raise up unto thee [i.e., Israel] a prophet from the midst of thee, of thy brethren, like unto me" (cf. v. 18)—a promise which Peter (Acts 3[22]) and Stephen (Acts 7[37]) claim to have been fulfilled in Jesus; and it is doubtless with this text in view that the Samaritan woman says, "I know that Messiah cometh; when he is come, he will declare unto us all things." The Samaritans apparently conceived Messiah as a prophet. It is abundantly clear, however, from the context of the promise in Deuteronomy that it involves no reference whatever to a coming Messiah. There the speaker is denouncing the unworthy and superstitious ways of ascertaining the will of God practiced by Israel's heathen neighbors by means of sorcery, necromancy, etc.; and in contrast with these religious charlatans he assures Israel that she will always have prophets, men like Amos, Hosea, Isaiah, Jeremiah, to interpret the divine will. It would be no comfort to Israel, when entangled in any historical perplexity, to be assured that hundreds of years afterward a prophet would appear. Strictly speaking, the text is not a Messianic text at all. Yet it is not without some Messianic significance. While not predicted of Christ, it was certainly fulfilled in him, for in opposition to all the unworthy or inadequate expositions of the will of God, he is the perfect revelation of that will.

Messiah, when he comes, must be just such an one. The text is, in a sense, an anticipation of the character of the coming ruler as set forth in Isa. 11^{1-6}, and Peter and Stephen are true to its inner meaning when they claim it for Jesus.

Permanency of the Davidic Dynasty. To return to the king. A passage of much significance for the Messianic hope is Nathan's reply to David when he had proposed to build a worthy house for God (2 Sam. 7^{8-16}). David was not unnaturally regarded by later generations as the real founder of the monarchy, and the coming king of the ideal age is therefore usually identified with one of his descendants (cf. Isa. 9^{7}). The passage before us anticipates an unbroken succession within the Davidic dynasty (v. 12). It regards the king as the possible subject of the divine chastisement (v. 14), and it were therefore idle to look in it for any promise of an ultimate ideal king. All that is here promised is that the throne of David shall be everlasting, that Jehovah will always be a father to the reigning king (cf. Psa. 2^{7}), and that his mercy will never depart from him (vv. 13–16).

Character of the Messianic King. But with Isa. $9^{6f.}$ we approach the definite delineation of a character. Associated with the deliverance of Israel from the Assyrian yoke is the birth (or the *gift*, as the prophet calls it) of a child, destined to be none other than the Messianic King, for the insignia of government rest upon him. Wisdom and power are the two qualities singled out for special emphasis as fitting him to secure the peace, i.e., the welfare of his people. He is gifted with miraculous wisdom and divine strength, he is Wonderful Counselor and Warrior Divine (or Hero of Superhuman Might, as we might translate). Despite the traditional English translation ("Mighty God") the words do not imply that he is very God: this is not a prophecy of the incarnation. Deity is in him, but he is not Deity. Unfortunately, some ambiguity attaches to the meaning of the words rendered "Everlasting Father"; but here again there is quite certainly no prophecy of the incarnation. The words probably simply mean "Father," i.e., protector or benefactor (cf. Job 29^{16}) "forever"—"the benevolent guardian of his people so long as he and they endure" (G. B. Gray). In virtue of his wisdom and his power he becomes a veritable Prince of Peace: and the perpetuity of his kingdom for all time is guaranteed by the simple fact that his throne is supported upon those ethical qualities of justice and righteousness which alone are eternal. The verse preceding this fine description (v. 5) had, like 2^{2-4}, declared the abolition of war to be one of the features of the Messianic age: and the coming king, though depicted first as a warrior in order to secure the destruction of all that is opposed to his righteous will, uses his strength, as his wisdom, for the welfare of his people. His empire will be eternal, because it is built upon the indestructible foundation of righteousness. It is not unnatural to see in these great words an adumbration of the empire established by Christ, though it is not, of course, a prophecy of him. (See further the notes on Isa. $9^{6,7}$.)

The figure portrayed in Isa. 11^{1-5} is an advance upon the last, as it departs entirely from the wárrior ideal and lays much more elaborate emphasis upon his moral and religious quality. Still of the Davidic line (v. 1), he is, as Schultz (*O.T. Theology*, vol. ii, p. 405) well says, "perfect alike as Sage, King, and Saint." The Spirit is to *rest* upon him, i.e., as his permanent endowment, and the quality of this spirit will manifest itself in the three different spheres of intellect, of practical life, and of religion. It will equip him with general wisdom and insight into the meaning and conditions of his office, with a penetration which will enable him to discover the ways and means to secure the ideal ends of his Kingship, and a strength to carry them out, and finally with a real appreciation of and reverent regard for the will of Jehovah whose servant he is. It is characteristic of the passionate regard of the Hebrew prophets for the defense of the rights of the exploited and defenseless members of society that the one feature of Messiah's reign singled out for special comment is his interest in the poor and the needy. Like a skillful and inflexibly honest judge, he will examine the cases that come before him with the sole desire to reach the truth, undeflected by specious appearances or plausible statements, and when he brings to book the wicked oppressors of the down-trodden, he will use his power to make an end of them (cf. Psa. 72^{4}).

The passage from Mic. 5^{2} which is quoted in Mt. 2^{6} adds little that is substantial to the figure already drawn, and that little has been frequently misunderstood. Out of Bethlehem Ephrathah one is to come forth "that is to be ruler in Israel; whose goings forth are from of old, from everlasting." The last phrase almost inevitably suggests the pre-existence of the ruler whose historical appearance is here predicted, and nothing was more natural than to apply the prophecy to Christ, which was done the more readily on the strength of the pointed allusion to Bethlehem. But with the marginal translation of the last phrase, "from ancient days," the pre-existence disappears. The truth is that the words rendered "from everlasting" reappear in 7^{14}, where they denote a time no further back than the days when Israel occupied territory on the east of the Jordan, while in 7^{20} the other phrase, "from of old," signifies the days of the patriarchs. So far, therefore, from these phrases suggesting the pre-existence of the coming ruler, they mean nothing more than that he comes of an ancient family. The point of his origin in Bethlehem has also been usually missed; it is not that Bethlehem was David's home, but, rather, that not from the splendid capital Jerusalem but from the simple village or country town, "smallest among the clans of Judah," was the Saviour King to come. It is another aspect of the familiar biblical truth proclaimed by Paul that God chooses the weak and despised things to confound the mighty (1 Cor. $1^{27f.}$).

With this passage may be taken the prophecy from Isa. 7^{14} quoted in Mt. 1^{23}, "A virgin shall conceive, and bear a son, and shall call his name Immanuel." This has for ages been taken as prophetic of the virgin birth of Jesus, and some recent scholars are prepared to defend the view that a miraculous birth is here intended. But a glance at the margin, which for the crucial word "virgin" reads "maiden" (the word practically means "marriageable woman") shows that the verse will not bear the heavy weight which traditional interpretation has put upon it. It is to the Greek version we owe the word "virgin," for which Aquila, a later translator, was quite justified in substituting the Greek word for "young woman." It is not even quite certain that the prophet has any particular young woman in view; but it is quite certain that the birth of the promised child is expected not only within that generation but soon. The sign is explicitly said to be given "to you," i.e., to Ahaz (and his court), whom Isaiah is addressing, but a birth to take place seven hundred and thirty-five years afterward would have been no sign to them. The prophecy is, therefore, not a prediction of Christ, nor does the name of the child imply that he is God incarnate. "Immanuel" means "God is with us," and the giving of the name is a confession of his mother's faith that God is manifesting himself in the history of her people.

More than a century later Jeremiah again takes up the Messianic promise ($23^{5f.}$). In the coming days Jehovah will raise up a righteous "branch" or "shoot"—note the word, for it is applied less than a century after by Zechariah (3^{8} 6^{12}) to Zerubbabel—who will belong to the Davidic line, and who, as King, will execute justice and righteousness and so bring security to the land and people. We welcome again the old emphasis upon ethical interests and on the King's passion for justice, but the new thing in this oracle is the king's name, "Jehovah [is] our righteousness." The Hebrew for this is almost certainly suggested by the name of the reigning king, Zedekiah (="Jehovah is my righteousness"): the coming king and the people he governs will be indeed all that one called Zedekiah ought to be. They will all recognize Jehovah as the source and the giver of their salvation. This ideal is thus more distinctively religious than those which had preceded it. For reasons which are historically intelligible in the Exile, Ezekiel almost uniformly and no doubt deliberately avoids the word "king," substituting for it "prince"; but the royal figure, whatever we may call him, is charged with the old task of "removing violence and executing justice and righteousness" (45^{9}).

The Servant of Jehovah. But the fairest figure in the O.T., and the one which more than any other molded the consciousness of Jesus so far as that was molded by the literature of his people, is the suffering Servant of the great anonymous exilic prophecy preserved in Isaiah 40–55, and more particularly in the so-called Servant Songs (42^{1-4} 49^{1-6} 50^{4-9} 52^{13}–53^{12}). Though there is general agreement that the prophecy as a whole falls about 540 B.C., just before the close of the Exile, unhappily the fiercest controversies have been and are still being waged round the original meaning of the Servant Songs. Into these we do not propose to enter; suffice it here to say that one group of scholars regards the Servant as an individual, another as the community of Israel. Undoubtedly, in the prophecy outside the songs the Servant is Israel, not an individual (cf. 41^{8}), but whether the Servant of the songs is an individual or not does not really matter for our purpose; for nothing is more certain than that the ideal they embody and the character they portray were never completely realized by the community of Israel nor in any historical individual except Jesus Christ. (See the discussion on these various passages in the present volume, especially the note on p. 664.)

What was that ideal? It was the ideal of one who knew himself to be the servant of God and of humanity, commissioned to convey to the world the truth about God, one who dealt gently with the weak and discouraged and who discharged his high mission in self-effacing and unobtrusive ways (42^{1-4}), one who maintained unflinchingly his faith in God even when he seemed to have labored in vain (49^{1-6}), one who suffered violence and scorn unspeakable from those whom he came to help, but who never lost faith in the ultimate triumph of the cause he represented (50^{4-9}); it was the ideal of a man of sorrows, despised and rejected, unmurmuringly surrendering himself to a violent and dishonored death, but by this very suffering and death winning the guilty for God, and so lifted beyond death to a place of the highest honor as the acknowledged Saviour of the world (52^{13}–53^{12}). It was surely a true instinct that led the N.T. church to see in these marvelous songs an adumbration of the sufferings, the work, and the triumph of her Lord and ours (cf. Mt. 12^{18-21} Acts 8^{32-35}, etc.). In this martyr whose death brought healing and salvation to those who had so cruelly wronged him, we have traveled immeasurably far from the old ideal of the Warrior King. Strictly speaking, such a figure is not in the Messianic succession at all: but in its religious inwardness and in its apprehension of spiritual reality, it is beyond comparison the greatest figure of them all. Small wonder that it appealed so powerfully to Jesus, or that the early church identified him with the figure there so graphically portrayed.

King and Priest. With the return from exile political hope revived. This hope is reflected in the cluster of oracles which in the pages of Haggai and Zechariah gather round Zerubbabel, and it was the more passionately cherished as Zerubbabel was in the direct Davidic line. From the closing verses of Haggai (2^{21-23}) it is clear that that prophet reposed the most extravagant hopes in him, and the epithets with which he honors him attest his unique importance for the coming days. He is to be precious to Jehovah as the signet-ring upon his finger, and the instrument whereby his purpose is to be sealed; he is the elect one—"I have chosen thee"—the very title applied in Isa. 42^{1} to the Servant. It is as if in him Haggai saw that prophecy fulfilled, just as Zechariah (3^{8} 6^{12}) undoubtedly saw in him the "branch" or "shoot" predicted by Jeremiah (23^{5}). But it is of much significance that alike in Haggai and Zechariah, Zerubbabel the civil ruler is associated with Joshua the high priest (cf. Hag. 1^{1} 2^{2}, etc.), and even more emphatically by Zechariah than by Haggai. An oracle which was subsequently altered because the hopes it expressed had been disappointed (Zech. 6^{11-13}, see notes there) had represented Zerubbabel as the "branch," crowned as Messianic King, with Joshua the high priest seated at his right hand. Considering the importance of the Temple for that period (see pp. 815–17) the presence of the high priest as almost co-ordinate in importance with the king is very natural, but it is none the less ominous; it is an indication that the old prophetic interest, whose glory it was to emphasize ethical ideals, is now being deflected in the direction of ritual—a tendency which received conspicuous development in the century that followed. The thing that makes Haggai and Zechariah, however, unique among the prophets, apart from the place they assign to the priest, is that they do not look forward to the Messiah, they find him in the prince who, they thought, by the building of the Temple, inaugurated the Messianic age.

A truly chivalrous figure emerges in the same prophetic book, though drawn by a later hand—the King who is seen approaching Jerusalem, "just and having salvation, lowly and riding upon an ass, even upon a colt the foal of an ass" (Zech. 9^{9}). In the following verse he is represented as annihilating the instruments of war, chariots, horses, bow: he rules not by force, but by reason, by the word, and the word is such that, when he declares it, there is peace among the nations. And nothing is more natural than that a King of such a character and with such a policy should exercise universal sway, "from sea to sea, and from the River [Euphrates] to the ends of the earth" (cf. Psa. 72^{8}). Nothing is here said about his relation to the Davidic dynasty, perhaps the fall of Zerubbabel had dealt a deadly blow to that faith: but all the more does this figure make a more universal and persuasive appeal. The same hatred of war animates this oracle as inspired some of the earlier oracles with which we have dealt (cf. Isa. 2^{4} 9^{5}), the same delight in the "word" as the only means by which the world's peace may be permanently secured (cf. Isa. 2^{3}), and the same faith that the truly glorious figure is not the Warrior King but the Prince of Peace (cf. Isa. 9^{6}). This would be true, if with one of the margins we read "just and having victory," i.e., just and victorious: if this means victorious in fight, at any rate he uses his power to abolish violence and to establish the reign of reason, justice, and peace. It would be still more true, if with the other margin we read "just and saved," i.e., saved and justified, i.e., vindicated, in the sense in which Deutero-Isaiah applies these words to the suffering Servant. But it would be truest of all, if with Sellin, following the LXX, we read "just and the savior of the meek (or poor), riding upon an ass, etc." This would present the Messianic King in the old grand prophetic light as champion of the defenseless (cf. Psa. 72^{4}). In any case the point of the passage is that the King approaches not upon a war-horse, but upon an ass which was the symbol of peace. A King content to ride into Jerusalem on a beast which so little suggested military glory could inaugurate only a reign of spiritual dominion, very different from the nationalistic ideals of popular hope; and Jesus, in thus riding into Jerusalem, was doubtless not only claiming this ideal as his own, but claiming to be himself the King to whom the prophecy pointed.

The Son of Man. In one of the latest books of the O.T., if not the latest, appears a figure girt about with mystery, the figure known as "one like unto a son of man" (Dan. 7[13]). The chapter in which this phrase occurs presents a curiously impressive and sadly realistic view of history by means of imagery drawn from the animal world. Four fierce beasts are seen emerging from the sea—a lion, a bear, a leopard, and a beast more fiercely terrible still. Later, before the heavenly Judge, appears one like a son of man. As it is practically certain that the beasts represented four empires (see ch. 2, 11[1-3], notes) which the writer regards as resting upon brute force and therefore appropriately symbolized by wild beasts, it is very tempting to regard the one like unto a son of man as placed in deliberate contrast to them in order to symbolize the humane and therefore truly human empire by which they shall be followed and which is destined to be everlasting. Other verses of the chapter (e.g., 18, 22, 27) seem to bear out this interpretation, as the dominion which in v. 14 is promised to the one like a son of man is in these verses promised to "the saints of the Most High"—a phrase which, in its historical context, would be practically synonymous with the faithful Jews. In that case the passage would hardly be Messianic, in the narrower sense, at all. But the significance of the phrase is probably deeper than that. The figure, sprung upon us so suddenly and appearing only to disappear, may have been more familiar to the writer's contemporaries than to us. It is to be noted that he comes "with the clouds of heaven" (v. 13), and this may conceivably point back to a belief in one—no longer called a king, nor is anything said of his relation to the Davidic dynasty—who belongs to the transcendental heavenly world and who, as such, is fitted, as no king dreamt of by earlier prophets was fitted, to inaugurate the everlasting reign of the saints. The older ideals, tinged for the most part with nationalism, would by this ideal be thus definitely transcended, and we should have here a real foreglimpse of Jesus, who, though son of Israel, was also Son of man and Son of God in a sense which could not be predicated of any other son of Israel (cf. art., *Backgrounds*, pp. 845–6).

Fulfillment in Jesus. When we speak of Jesus as the Christ, we mean that Jesus is the Messiah, who fulfilled the hopes and the yearnings expressed in "divers portions and in divers manners" (Heb. 1[1]) by the inspired men of the olden time. He fulfilled them, indeed, in a far deeper sense than most of them dreamt of. For some aspects of this hope, notably as it appears in prophets like Haggai and Zechariah, were political, and there is something to be said for the view that some of the formulations of that hope, nationalistic and political as they were, made it difficult, especially for the less spiritually minded of the people, to recognize the incomparable worth of Jesus when he came and to see in him the culmination and the crown of the whole movement of the Spirit of God within Israel which is represented by the long story of the O.T. But it would surely be doing pathetic injustice to that great literature not to recognize the spiritual passion which animates so much of it and the profound insight which saw so clearly what must be the essential features of any coming age worth looking forward to and the essential character of the one who would be worthy to preside over it. The nature of the hope and of the ruler who is to inaugurate it may change with the changing years. At one point in the development—during the Exile, when the monarchy is no more—the hope is no longer centered upon a coming king, but upon a Servant who triumphs through his suffering and vicarious sacrifice: at another point—just after the Exile, when an attempt is made to reconstitute the national life—that hope becomes associated with the Temple, and at the right hand of Zerubbabel sits Joshua the high priest, sharing, though it be in subordinate degree, the dignity of the Messianic King. But, taken as a whole and at their best, how noble is the future that the finer spirits of Israel conceived as laid up in the purpose of God, and how attractive, as they portray him, is the figure of him who is to usher in or to preside over this better day. Conceived by Jewish hearts and drawn by Jewish hands, yet how human and how universal they are. War, idolatry, sin, death—every evil and hurtful thing abolished; glad free worship offered unitedly to the great God of all by men who had been erstwhile bitter enemies—such was their hope for the future, and the personality, when there was one, with whom they associated that hope, was one who used his power to secure justice and peace, and whose ambition was so remote from military glory that he could ride into his capital city on the foal of an ass. Jesus fulfilled this and every other worthy hope of the O.T. (Cf. note on the identification of the Suffering Servant, p. 664.)

But while he fulfilled particular prophecies such as the one last quoted, it is far more true to say that he fulfilled all prophecy. There is a sense in which all prophecy is Messianic prophecy, inasmuch as it is, in virtue of its moral and religious demands, a presentation of the character to which God would have his people conform and which in the fullness of the time was to be perfectly exhibited in his elect Servant. It is a fact of curious and profound significance that, unlike the evangelists and the apostles, Jesus rarely appeals to specific texts. He claims to fulfill the Law and the prophets (Mt. 5[17]), and to the disciples on the way to Emmaus, "beginning from Moses and from all the prophets he interpreted to them in all the scriptures the things concerning himself" (Lk. 24[27]); yet, though the contents of this exposition are broadly indicated in Lk. 24[46, 47], there is no detail and no such appeal to particular texts as have for ages formed the staple of the Messianic argument in the Christian Church. What he fulfilled was not so much the parts as the whole, for the essence of the whole was love (cf. Mt. 22[40]). He is the consummation and the satisfaction of all the noblest aspirations cherished by holy men of old. Not only does he say "Yea" to them all, but he is himself "the Everlasting Yea" (2 Cor. 1[20]). Wherefore it becomes the church, looking with adoring reverence upon this incarnate Affirmation of the gracious purpose of God for the world, to respond with its "Amen" to the glory of God (2 Cor. 1[20]).

Literature: Riehm, *Messianic Prophecy;* Briggs, *Messianic Prophecy;* Delitzsch, *Messianic Prophecies;* F. H. Woods, *The Hope of Israel;* G. S. Goodspeed, *Israel's Messianic Hope;* Adeney, *The Hebrew Utopia;* Ottley, *Aspects of the O.T.* (Lecture vi); A. B. Davidson, *O.T. Prophecy* (chs. xviii-xxiv); Edghill, *An Enquiry into the Evidential Value of Prophecy;* W. J. Moulton, *The Witness of Israel.*

THE LITERATURE OF THE INTER-TESTAMENTAL PERIOD

By Professor LESLIE E. FULLER

Importance of the Literature. It is almost a fixed tradition in some branches of the Christian Church that the span of centuries between the O.T. and the N.T. is a "period of silence." The claim is that from the time when the last O.T. book was written to the period of the writing of the first N.T. book the voice of inspired prophecy was silent, there were no other worthy mouthpieces of God, and as a result of this lack not a single page of literary material worthy of consideration was handed down.

To the literature that survived the term "apocryphal" was applied, carrying in the minds of many people the idea of something false or untrue. Although for a long time this literature has proved a fruitful field of study for scholars, many students of the Bible have remained completely ignorant concerning this intertestamental age, with its historical, literary, and religious problems.

There are, however, certain factors at work in the modern study of the Bible that are tending to alter this condition. The first of these is in the field of Introduction. Until recently it was assumed that the last book of the O.T., Malachi, was the last book to be written (about 450 B.C.). The period of silence was then thought to extend from about 450 B.C. to about 50 A.D., the time of the first written records of the N.T.—a period of about five centuries. Now, we know that several books of the O.T., such as Job, Ruth, Jonah, and a number of the psalms, were written in the fourth century B.C. or even later. At least Ecclesiastes and Esther are dated as late as the second century B.C. Thus the interim between the Testaments has been shortened from five to about two centuries.

A better appreciation of the history of religion, especially the religion of Israel, is another factor responsible for the rehabilitation of this period. The complete story of the religion of Israel cannot be told with the O.T. as its only source. Much essential information is secured from the study of the languages and literatures, as well as the religious, social, and political organizations, of contemporary peoples, a study made possible chiefly through exploration and excavation in Bible lands. The history and significance of the religion of Israel could not be fully understood or appreciated if we were deprived of the light from Arabia, Babylonia, Assyria, Egypt, and Canaan.

But the greatest single factor revealing the importance of the intertestamental period for the student of the O.T. as well as the N.T. is a fuller understanding of the entire Hellenistic world during the centuries concerned. The N.T. cannot be studied apart from Palestinian and Alexandrian Judaism, during the centuries immediately preceding the opening of the Christian era; equally important is a knowledge of general Hellenistic civilization with its religious and philosophical systems. If we are ever to have an adequate picture of the marvelous personality of Jesus, we must study it upon the background of Palestinian Judaism; if we are to understand the expansion of early Christianity we must take into consideration the preparation of the field by Judaism and Hellenism as reflected in the literature of the late pre-Christian centuries.

The purpose of this article is to make a survey of the Jewish literature of Palestine and the Dispersion in the intertestamental period extending from about 200 B.C. to 100 A.D. (The term "intertestamental" is hardly adequate, as some of the latest sections of the O.T. were written as late as 150 B.C. and some of the earliest books of the N.T. were written about 50 A.D.; which means that there is an overlapping at each end of the period.) It should be noted also that the survey will cover only the Jewish literature which shows more or less intimate relationship with the Palestinian or Alexandrian canon of the O.T.; Jewish writings not thus related are omitted. Thus the Palestinian portions of the Talmud and the works of Philo and his contemporaries do not come within the scope of this article.

Explanation of Terms. There are various terms applied to this literature which need explanation. The first of these is the term "Apocrypha." This term is derived from a Greek word meaning "something hidden." Originally it was used in a laudatory sense of literature hidden from the eyes of the uninitiated, and intended only for the wise. Later the term came to be used in a derogatory sense and was applied to literature of secondary value, and still later, in the days of Origen and Jerome, it was applied to literature considered false and heretical. There are those to-day who accept the last mentioned meaning; but, generally speaking, the modern use of the term does not involve such unfavorable judgment; it is used simply as a convenient designation of the non-canonical literature closely related to the O.T. and the N.T. In its broadest sense it includes the O.T. Apocrypha, the N.T. Apocrypha, and various other Jewish writings of a pseudepigraphal and apocalyptic character (see explanation of terms below). In a narrower sense the term is restricted to the O.T. Apocrypha or the N.T. Apocrypha.

The term "Pseudepigrapha" (meaning "writings under assumed names") is used with a narrower meaning than Apocrypha. Generally it is applied to all Jewish literature of the intertestamental period outside of the O.T. Apocrypha proper; but, as the term suggests, it is really intended to cover all the Jewish writings written under assumed names, such as Enoch, the Twelve Sons of Jacob, Moses, Ezra, etc. And there are some books of a pseudepigraphal nature in the Apocrypha proper, such as 1 Baruch, Epistle of Jeremy, and 2 Esdras.

The word "Apocalypse" calls for more extended explanation. Etymologically it means "revelation" or "disclosure."

Origin of Apocalyptic Literature. Apocalyptic literature (a subdivision of the pseudepigrapha—for the apocalyptic books are written under assumed names) represents a distinct literary movement in Judaism, continuing from the second century B.C. to the thirteenth and fourteenth centuries A.D. Its origin is still a matter of some discussion. One of the oldest theories traces the origin to Persian sources. Although this view was once very popular, it has few adherents at the present time. Some have advanced claims that the movement started among the Essenes, a communistic sect living in southern Palestine, but apocalyptic literature is far too loyal to the Temple and its attendant rites to have emanated from a heretical source. Others have defended the theory that the literature originated in the Dispersion, and represents a Jewish apologetic to the Hellenistic world and its culture. But, while some of the apocalyptic writings undoubtedly were produced by the Jews of the Dispersion, a majority of the writings originated in Palestine. Therefore, though the play of foreign influences on the Jewish mind must be recognized, in this case it is far more plausible to assume that apocalyptic literature was largely indigenous to Palestinian soil and represents a normal Jewish development.

The location of Palestine with its constant threat of invasion and war gradually prepared the soil for a persecution complex, which always forms the background of apocalyptic thinking. Unmistakable evidences of this appear as early as the days of Ezekiel; additional illustrations are seen in Zech. 9–14, Joel, Isa. 24–27 and 56–66. With this psychological condition already created, the Hellenizing policy of Antiochus Epiphanes and the oppression of the Romans were the one thing needed to crystallize the reaction to persecution into a philosophy and a literature of control. Again, the authors of apocalypses were members of the Pharisaic party, a party of laymen acting as champions of the common beliefs and hopes of the laity. This accounts for the fact that the apocalypses are in reality specimens of lay literature sponsoring popular beliefs in angels, demons, world judgments, Messiahs, catastrophic world endings, near approach of a Golden Age, bodily resurrection, the terrible punishment of the wicked and the sensuous and materialistic enjoyment of the righteous. The popularity and influence of this literature were greatest among the common people of Palestine, and especially in Galilee, the center of so many uprisings of the peasantry. In all probability the apocalyptic writings had their origin in lay circles outside of Jerusalem, and, as most scholars suppose, in Galilee.

The problem of all apocalyptic writing is the reconciliation of the current disasters with the power and the justice of God. In the case of Jewish apocalyptic thinking it must be remembered that many of the ancient worthies had promised the speedy coming of the Golden Age; but century after century passed with one disappointment after another. Foreign oppression continued unchanged and the question presented itself: How can this continued persecution be explained in view of the fact that Israel is the chosen race of God and God must still love his folk? Apocalypticism meets the issue squarely and, we maintain, honestly, especially in consideration of the day and age in which it was written. It attempts to create hope and encouragement for the dark days of persecution by picturing the wonders of God's power in the past and the approach of even greater and more wonderful manifestations in the near future. O.T. stories are rewritten and enlarged to show the special providence of God in protecting and guiding the destinies of Israel; and there are vivid and graphic pictures of the glories of the future wherein God arises to deliver his people from the domination of the Gentile and to mete out a much-deserved punishment to the wicked.

The method of the apocalyptic writers by which they sought to create hope and faith in God and loyalty to Jewish institutions forms one of the most interesting phenomena in religious literature. The writers place their revelations in the mouths of some famous personage of the past, such as Enoch, Moses, and Ezra; they always refer to their enemies, foreign nations, and kings in veiled and esoteric terms (the latter characteristic must not be taken as evidence of cowardice, for the prophets of the O.T. frequently followed the same method). Foreign nations are referred to as wild and ravenous beasts, domesticated beasts refer to Israel or a group or a leader in Israel; horns refer to kings and other rulers; stars refer to angels or superhuman beings. Apocalyptic literature was not misunderstood in its own day; e.g., the "abomination of desolation" in Daniel, which meant the desecration of the Temple by Antiochus Epiphanes in 168 B.C., was understood without difficulty by all the faithful in Israel living at the time the book was written. (Of course, later it was interpreted as referring to Rome and subsequently it received a different interpretation in every troubled age of the church.)

Major Differences Between Apocalypticism and Prophecy. A study of the points of contrast between apocalypticism and O.T. prophecy is necessary for a clearer understanding of the purpose and characteristics of apocalyptic literature. There are, of course, points of similarity. For instance, both claim to be true revelations of God, and both possess an eschatology, though in varying degrees. The differences, however, are far more significant.

(1) The prophetic message is sent forth under the name of its own author; apocalyptic literature assumes as its author the name of some great personality of the past. When prophecy is anonymous, as happens in a few instances, it makes no effort to go back to the distant past for its authority. To the writers of apocalyptic literature the O.T. canon was closed, the day of revelation was past, the present age of persecution was wicked and hopeless. Therefore the authors of apocalyptic writings preferred to remain unknown and, for the purpose of enhancing their authority, to place their writings under the name of some person within the period of revelation; such as Enoch, the Twelve Sons of Jacob, Moses, Baruch, Ezra, and many others. A typical apocalypse purports to start with the age of its assumed author and traces the history of mankind down to the Maccabean or Roman period (the time of its actual writing), and then to the Golden Age to come.

(2) Apocalyptic literature is largely a reinterpretation of prophecy. One prophet after another predicted the coming of the rule of God, but their predictions failed to materialize. The apocalyptic literature seeks to explain the failure and to reiterate the older promises in a manner adapted to the new conditions. The most remarkable reinterpretation of prophecy in apocalyptic literature is that of the seventy years of Jeremiah. Jeremiah said Israel would go into captivity for seventy years, to be followed by the restoration of Israel to Palestine and the coming of the kingdom of God. Originally the number seventy was a general term, representing most probably a lifetime, threescore years and ten. When at the close of the Exile and during subsequent centuries the Golden Age did not appear, the apocalyptic book of Daniel, written during the Maccabean crisis, reinterpreted the seventy years of Jeremiah as seventy weeks of years, or 490 years. In the thought of the author sixty-nine and a half weeks had already passed, leaving only one half of a week or three and one half years. When the three and one half years are completed, the Temple, which Antiochus Epiphanes desecrated in 168 B.C., will be cleansed, the daily sacrifice will be renewed, the resurrection will take place, and the Golden Age will be ushered in by the power of God. In Enoch the seventy years are interpreted as the rule of seventy patron angels, and the current age is placed in the rule of the seventieth angel, implying that the Messianic age is near at hand. In 4 Ezra (2 Esdras; see below) the seventy years or weeks of years of Daniel are reinterpreted so as to include the rule of Rome.

(3) The extensive use of symbolism, imagery, and vision is a striking characteristic of the apocalyptic writings. Few of these features appear in the prophetic books of the O.T., and to any considerable extent only in the writings of the post-exilic prophets, when prophecy had begun to decline. The origin of the use of this symbolism, so common to all the apocalyptic books, is still a matter of conjecture. It is possible that one of the motives for its introduction was a desire to create an atmosphere of antiquity, in keeping with the assumed name of the ancient author.

(4) The expectation of a catastrophic end of the present world is another peculiarity of apocalyptic literature. The idea of a spiritual transformation of the world is not foreign to the O.T.; but nearly all of the apocalyptic writers considered the present earth too wicked to contain the kingdom of God for more than

a limited period of time. According to some passages the present earth and the present heavens are to be renewed by God (Enoch 37–71), but other passages announce that the entire world will be consumed by fire; following this catastrophe there will be seven days of silence, and then a new earth will be created (4 Ezra).

(5) Prophecy is always conditional in its prediction of future events; apocalyptic literature predicts the end of the age at a certain time, as a part of a predetermined and unchangeable plan of God. The prophets believe that sin will be punished, but if the nation will repent, captivity or other calamities may be averted. In apocalyptic writing the entire history of the world has been predetermined from the beginning; the current evil age is a forerunner of the coming rule of God, but it must run its course. The book of Daniel says that the new age will come in three and one half years, the Assumption of Moses says seventeen hundred and fifty years after the death of Moses. This new age cannot be hastened or retarded, it will come irrespective of human conduct.

(6) The doctrine of the future life of the individual is a unique contribution of apocalypticism. The prophets believed in a semiconscious, nerveless existence after death, in an underground abode, beyond the bounds of communion with the nation and communion with God. This place, called Sheol, was without moral distinction; all the dead went there and remained there forever. One of the greatest contributions to religious development made by the apocalyptic writers was belief in a future life of the individual and in moral distinctions after death (the two O.T. passages, Isa. 26[19] and Dan. 12[2], in which the resurrection of individuals is taught belong to the apocalyptic literature); the earliest expectations were rather crude; the pious were promised a bodily resurrection, to dwell in an earthly kingdom, for the purpose of witnessing the punishment of the apostate and enjoying the external prosperity of the new age. In later books appears the more spiritual conception of an eternal existence of the righteous in heaven, i.e., the dwelling place of God.

Minor Differences Between Apocalypticism and Prophecy. Besides the major differences considered above, there are a few minor differences which should be mentioned.

(1) The concept of a new heaven and a new earth, found only once in the O.T. (Isa. 65f.), becomes a permanent expectation of apocalypticism. The finest descriptions of the new heaven and new earth are found in Enoch 37-71 and 4 Ezra.

(2) The scope of eschatology in apocalyptic literature is much larger than in prophecy. The eschatology of the prophets was an eschatology of the nation. In the apocalyptic writings the eschatology of the individual comes to the front, although at first associated with an eternal kingdom on earth. Finally, when the earthly kingdom came to be regarded as temporary, the eschatology of the individual came to stand alone, apart from any period of national triumph on earth.

(3) Points of practical interest are quite different in the two types of literature. For example, the prophets were primarily interested in their own day and its immediate problems. They were preachers of a moral righteousness and champions of the social and religious integrity of the nation of Israel. They had the beginnings of a philosophy of history, but gave little attention to the future. If they manifested any interest in the future, it was only the immediate future. On the other hand, the apocalyptic writers gave little thought to their own age. They trusted in an all-powerful God and a God in close contact with his world; but as for their own age manifestations of God's power are withheld; demons and evil men are working the ruin of the world. The points of emphasis in apocalyptic writing are God's activities in the past and his expected activity in the future. Thus the prophets had a social gospel, which is practically wanting in apocalypticism.

Classification. The historical occasions for literary activity in the intertestamental period are varied. Perhaps the most significant occasion furnishing incentives for literary endeavor was the Dispersion of the Jews to every large center within the Mediterranean basin. The literature of the Dispersion was motivated by three objectives: (1) to control and retain racial identity; (2) to demonstrate the antiquity and priority of the Jewish Law; and (3) to construct a synthesis of Jewish and Greek thought that would be attractive to both Jew and Gentile. The occasions for literary activity in Palestine were the Maccabean Rebellion, the glories and triumphs of the Maccabean rulers, the party strife of the Pharisees and the Sadducees, the oppression of the Romans, and the Fall of Jerusalem. These occasions were periods of war, civil discord, persecution, foreign domination, and destruction of nationality. As a result, much of the literature carries a note of cynicism and pessimism.

The Jewish literature of the intertestamental period falls naturally into two large groups, the Apocrypha proper and the Pseudepigrapha. The books listed as O.T. Apocrypha proper are as follows: 1 and 2 Esdras, Tobit, Judith, Additions to Esther, Wisdom of Solomon, Ecclesiasticus, 1 Baruch, Epistle of Jeremy, Prayer of Azariah and Song of the Three Children, Susanna, Bel and the Dragon, Prayer of Manasses, 1 and 2 Maccabees. Generally speaking, these books represent the excess of the Alexandrian canon of the O.T. over the Palestinian or Hebrew canon. The Alexandrian canon is in Greek and is known from the early Greek translation called the Septuagint (LXX). Some manuscripts of the Septuagint contain also the Books of 3 and 4 Maccabees. At the Council of Trent, in 1546, the Roman Church declared all the books of the Apocrypha proper canonical, with the exception of 1 and 2 Esdras and the Prayer of Manasses.

The books of the Pseudepigrapha are listed as follows: 3 and 4 Maccabees, Enoch, Testaments of the Twelve Patriarchs, Jubilees, Letter of Aristeas, Sibylline Oracles, Psalms of Solomon, Zadokite Fragments, Assumption of Moses, 2 Enoch, 2 Baruch, 3 Baruch, Martyrdom of Isaiah, and the Books of Adam and Eve. 4 Ezra, which is the same as 2 Esdras 3–14, is frequently classed among the Pseudepigrapha.

The intertestamental books may also be classified according to the places of their origin and composition. Popular tradition, beginning as early as the third century A.D., assumed that all the books of the Apocrypha proper were originally written in Greek. The tradition reasoned that since the manuscripts were found in the Greek they must have been written in that language, and therefore they must have originated among the Jews of the Dispersion. Recent studies have definitely established the fact that many of them were composed in Hebrew or Aramaic. The same is true of many of the books of the Pseudepigrapha. Although the only extant manuscripts are in the Greek, it can be demonstrated that the Greek is a translation from a Hebrew or Aramaic original. Consequently, it is quite clear that while a part of the intertestamental literature comes from the Dispersion, especially Alexandria, a considerable portion originated in Palestine. The Palestinian group includes the books that bear proof of origin in Palestine and evidence of having been written originally in Hebrew or Aramaic; the Alexandrian group includes all books written by the Jews of the Dispersion, and bearing evidence of original composition in Greek.

1. Palestinian Group.

(1) *General:* Ecclesiasticus, Judith, Jubilees, 1 Maccabees, Epistle of Jeremy, Susanna, Bel and the Dragon, Psalms of Solomon, Zadokite Fragments, 1 Baruch, Martyrdom of Isaiah.

(2) *Apocalyptic:* Enoch, Testaments of the Twelve Patriarchs, Assumption of Moses, 2 Baruch, 4 Ezra (same as 2 Esdras 3–14).

2. Alexandrian Group.

(1) *General:* Tobit, 2 and 3 Maccabees, 1 Esdras, Prayer of Manasses, Prayer of Azariah and Song of the Three Children, Additions to Esther, Wisdom of Solomon, 4 Maccabees, Letter of Aristeas, Books of Adam and Eve, Sibylline Oracles 3–5.

(2) *Apocalyptic:* 2 Enoch, 3 Baruch.

The literature of the O.T. Apocrypha and the Pseudepigrapha is also arranged according to century and date of origin. (Many of the books being composite, they are divided into sections, each section being given with its date. Most of the dates are in round numbers and can be regarded only as approximate).

1. SECOND CENTURY B.C. (200–100 B.C.)

(1) *General:* Tobit (200); Ecclesiasticus (180); Judith (150); Jubilees (110); Sibylline Oracles 3 (125–100).

(2) *Apocalyptic:* Enoch 1–36, 83–90, 106–7 (200–160); Enoch 72–82 (125–100); Testaments of the Twelve Patriarchs (125–100).

2. FIRST CENTURY B.C. (100–1 B.C.)

(1) *General:* 1, 2, 3 Maccabees (100); 1 Esdras (100); Prayer of Manasses (100); Epistle of Jeremy (100); Prayer of Azariah and Song of the Three Children (100); Susanna (100); Bel and the Dragon (100); Additions to Esther (100); Letter of Aristeas (100); Wisdom of Solomon (50); 4 Maccabees (50); Psalms of Solomon (50); Zadokite Fragments (50).

(2) *Apocalyptic:* Enoch 37–71 (105–91), 108 (100–75).

3. FIRST CENTURY A.D. (1–100 A.D.)

(1) *General:* 1 Baruch (100); Martyrdom of Isaiah (100); The Books of Adam and Eve (100); Sibylline Oracles 4, 5 (80–130).

(2) *Apocalyptic:* Assumption of Moses (1–30); 2 Enoch (50); 2 Baruch (50–90); 3 Baruch (100); 4 Ezra (60–120).

The literature of the intertestamental period may be further classified under certain descriptive titles indicating the general types or kinds of literature.

1. *History:* 1 Maccabees, 2 Maccabees, 3 Maccabees, Zadokite Fragments.

Not all these books are history in any strict sense of the word. Indeed, 1 Maccabees is the only book of the group that measures up to modern historical standards; 2 and 3 Maccabees are only semi-historical; and the Zadokite Fragments are classed here only because they furnish the history and covenant of the Zadokite Sect.

2. *Recensions of and Additions to O.T. Stories:* Jubilees, Prayer of Manasses, Epistle of Jeremy, Prayer of Azariah and Song of the Three Children, Susanna, Bel and the Dragon, Additions to Esther, 1 Esdras, 1 Baruch.

Most of this material represents enlargements of O.T. narratives, sometimes the additions are appended to the canonical books, at other times they are inserted in the midst of the narratives, as is done, e.g., in Daniel and Esther. The book of Jubilees contains an apocalyptic reinterpretation of the book of Genesis from the standpoint of the later concepts of the Law.

3. *Stories* and *Homilies:* Tobit, Judith, Letter of Aristeas, 4 Maccabees, Books of Adam and Eve, Martyrdom of Isaiah.

The books in this group are largely works of fiction. Their purpose is to glorify Jewish customs and institutions.

4. *Wisdom Literature:* Ecclesiasticus, Wisdom of Solomon, Psalms of Solomon, Sibylline Oracles.

This literature is modeled on the Wisdom literature of the O.T., such as Proverbs and some of the Psalms. The Sibylline Oracles contain some apocalyptic material. They are cast in the form of short verses and epigrammatic statements. (The Proverbs and Parables of Achikar are omitted from this list, as they antedate the period of the intertestamental literature).

5. *Apocalyptic Literature:* Enoch, Testaments of the Twelve Patriarchs, Assumption of Moses, 2 Enoch, 2 Baruch, 3 Baruch, 4 Ezra (same as 2 Esdras 3–14).

Brief Survey of the Separate Books. This general survey of the intertestamental literature is here followed by a brief discussion of the separate books. (For the teaching of this literature see art., *The Religious Development of the Intertestamental Period*, pp. 200f.; and for details of interpretation the commentaries on the individual books in Charles, *Apocrypha and Pseudepigrapha of the O.T.*) Only a few of the more important features of the different books can be noted, such as title, date and place of origin; there is also a brief statement of the contents and their value. (These notations follow the order of books suggested in the classification according to the types of literature represented by the books.)

I. History

First Maccabees. A valuable historical work concerning the Maccabean Rebellion, produced in Palestine about 100 B.C. The name "Maccabee" was first applied to Judas ($2^{4f.}$), and later to the entire family. The author was a man with Sadducean tendencies, tolerant, but loyal to his nation and the institution of the priesthood. The name of the Deity does not occur in the book.

The book opens with a short introduction starting with the conquests of Alexander the Great, and then treats in some detail the history of the Maccabean uprising, 175–135 B.C. The greater part of the book centers in the exploits of Judas, apparently the most remarkable figure of the rebellion. The book concludes with a short history of Jonathan and Simon to the year 135 B.C.

It is the most valuable because the most trustworthy record of the Maccabean Rebellion.

Second Maccabees. This book is not a sequel to 1 Maccabees, but simply a second book on the Maccabean Rebellion. It was written by a Pharisee, or a man with decided Pharisaic tendencies. It was written in Greek about 100 B.C.

The book purports to be an epitome of a larger work of five volumes (not extant) by one Jason of Cyrene. It treats of a much shorter period of history than 1 Maccabees, the period of 175–161 B.C., states the causes of the revolt and outlines the campaigns of Judas. Great detail is given as to the extent and drastic policies of Antiochus Epiphanes in his persecutions of the Jews.

The value of this book is more in the field of religious belief than history. It attained to great popularity in later centuries in the literature of the martyrs. The Roman Church uses certain portions of it to support the dogma of prayers for the dead ($12^{43f.}$) and intercession of the saints ($15^{11f.}$).

Third Maccabees. A product of Alexandrian Judaism very similar to the Letter of Aristeas. It was written in Greek about 100 B.C. The title is a misnomer, unless it be taken as synonymous with "persecution" or "persecuted folk."

The book is only semi-historical; many of its details are purely imaginary and fanciful. The story centers in an attempt of Philopater (Ptolemy IV) to enter the Temple at Jerusalem; he is frustrated by a timely divine intervention, returns to Egypt and begins a wholesale persecution of the Jews. Great multitudes are forcibly driven from their homes in all parts of Egypt and assembled in the Hippodrome in Alexandria. The king commands that the assembled multitude of Jews be trodden under foot by drunken elephants. Three times the day set for their destruction dawns, and each time some divine act of intervention occurs. The first time God causes the king to oversleep, the second time the king is thrown into a spell of confusion and forgetfulness, and the third time God sends a vision of angelic forms. The Jews are released and banqueted, and the king repents and becomes a patron of the Jews. Just as in the Book of Esther, the delivered groups are allowed to work their vengeance on the apostates until three hundred are killed.

The story possesses some real merit from a literary point of view, although at times its style is bombastic. Its prayers are among some of the finest in intertestamental literature. The story is a fine example of the type of literature current among the Jews of the Dispersion.

Zadokite Fragments. Written in Palestine in the middle of the first century B.C. The name "Zadokite" comes from the name of the sect whose covenant is found in the book. The text is fragmentary and incomplete. It was discovered in the ruins of a synagogue in Cairo in 1896.

The Fragments give a semi-historical narration of the founding of a new sect in Judaism, a group of dissenters who journeyed to Damascus and there drew up their covenant in 196 B.C. The Fragments contain chiefly a series of laws, which constitute the main part of the covenant. The new party consisted of a company of priests, hence the name "Zadokites." They dissented from the priestly circles at Jerusalem; they accepted the Law as final authority, but went a step further and ascribed canonical authority to the Prophets. The Fragments contain many laws which bear marked resemblances to the oldest sections of the Talmud, as the laws on the Sabbath, calendar, religious festivals, divorce, and many other social and religious matters. One of the most interesting features of the Fragments is found in their eschatology. Their authors expected a Messiah from Aaron (i.e., the family of Levi), to be preceded by a "Star" or a "Lawgiver" and "Teacher of Righteousness." This differs from the O.T. tradition of a Messiah from the tribe of Judah.

The value of the Fragments lies in the fact that they furnish information concerning a hitherto unknown sect in Judaism. Also they help to piece out our knowledge of the development of legalism in pre-Christian Judaism.

II. Recensions of and Additions to Old Testament Stories

Jubilees. A Palestinian product from near the end of the second century B.C. It is a rewriting of the book of Genesis from the standpoint of late Jewish legalism, and for that reason at times has borne the title "Little Genesis." It carries over much of the text of Genesis intact; however, at times it discards whole sections; more often it introduces whole new sections, to suit its later theology. Its present title is taken from the chronological scheme into which the framework of the book is fixed: all the events of the book from creation onward are dated according to a series of jubilees.

The book opens with a much enlarged story of the creation of the world. The acts of creation, based on the six days in Genesis, are expanded to twenty-two distinct creative acts. Stories of angels and the introduction of a counter kingdom of evil, fallen angels and demons, constitute a vital part of the rewriting. All incidents derogatory to the Patriarchs are left out, and they are purged of all deceit and falsehood. The great age of Methuselah is largely accounted for by the fact that he spent the first seven years of his infancy in heaven with the angels. The rite of circumcision is made pre-existent, for the angels are circumcised. Many other late priestly institutions are traced back to ancient times; for instance, the daily incense offering is traced to Adam, the Feast of the Weeks to Noah, the law of the tithe to Abraham, and the Day of Atonement to Joseph. The book is highly particularistic: it opposes all intercourse with the Gentiles, and believes in the future total annihilation of the Gentiles.

The value of the book lies chiefly in the fact that it demonstrates and illustrates the tendency in later Judaism to trace late beliefs and institutions back to the earliest times, for the purpose of giving to these institutions greater antiquity and thus greater authority in the face of Hellenistic opposition. The book is also very valuable for the purpose of textual comparisons with the text of Genesis. Its conception of the Law, angels, and demons is of interest from the standpoint of history of religion.

Prayer of Manasses. A product of Hellenistic Judaism about 100 B.C. It was intended as a prayer of penitence uttered by Manasseh in connection with his Babylonian captivity recorded in 2 Chr. 33. It is a prayer consisting, according to the generally accepted arrangement, of fifteen verses, opening with a note of adoration, vv. 1–7, followed by confession of sin, vv. 8–10, and an appeal for forgiveness and a short doxology, vv. 11–15.

It is one of the finest prayers in the apocryphal literature; its diction is chaste, its spirit reverent and devout. It received some well deserved recognition in the English versions of the Reformation period.

Epistle of Jeremy. A Palestinian work of the beginning of the first century, not far from 100 B.C. It purports to be a letter from the prophet Jeremiah to the Babylonian exiles. In reality, it is a short prosaic composition of seventy-three verses, possessing very little originality or depth of feeling. It is full of repetitions and lacks the fire of the prophetic movement of which it claims to be a part. Its principal message is a condemnation of idolatry.

Prayer of Azariah and Song of the Three Children. A Greek product of about 100 B.C. In the LXX it is an integral part of the book of Daniel, inserted after Dan. 3^{23}. As a part of the book it did not bear a separate title for a long time. It is frequently referred to as the "First Addition to Daniel."

Vv. 3–22 contain the prayer of Azariah, one of the Three Children cast into the fiery furnace, a prayer of praise and adoration, and a request for deliverance in accordance with God's promises. Vv. 23–27 form a prose section narrating the increase in the heat of the furnace, and the appearance of an angel of the Lord, who protects the Three Children. Vv. 28–68 are in the nature of a song of praise calling upon all creation to praise God. A refrain urging such praise is used throughout the composition.

The "Addition" has little real value. It lacks the power and impressiveness of diction found in the Prayer of Manasses. Perhaps its chief interest lies in the fact that it illustrates the ease with which a second-rate piece of literature could become a part of the O.T. canon of the Jews of the Dispersion.

Susanna. A Palestinian product of about 100 B.C., frequently found in Greek versions at the end of Daniel. Hence it became known as the "Second Addition to Daniel."

It is a story or a parable intended to illustrate the necessity of more thorough cross-examination of witnesses, and at the same time to exalt the great wisdom and foresight of Daniel. It narrates a story of two elders who lusted after the same woman; being repulsed in their advances they resolved to accuse the woman of unchastity. A trial is held and the two elders present their charge of adultery. On the basis of their testimony, Susanna is found guilty, and is about to be put to death, when Daniel intervenes. He proves their charges false; whereupon the elders are condemned to the same fate which they had proposed for the woman: they are thrown into a ravine, and fire from heaven consumes them.

The value of this "Addition" also is very slight. Again we may wonder at the ease with which a story of little moral value became a part of the Alexandrian Canon of the O.T.

Bel and the Dragon. The third of the "Additions" to Daniel, produced in Palestine about 100 B.C., and usually found at the end of Daniel.

The story is told to illustrate the wisdom and cleverness of Daniel. The first story of Bel, a heathen god whom Daniel refused to worship, is the story of a heathen idol that was credited with devouring great quantities of food. Daniel cleverly used some ashes to detect the footprints of the men who carried away the food. The king then orders the priests of the idol slain and the idol itself destroyed. The story of the great "Dragon" (better "serpent") also adds to the fame of Daniel. Daniel kills the serpent, and an enraged populace has him thrown to the lions. He suffers no harm, being supplied with food through the prophet Habakkuk, who is transported miraculously from Palestinian harvest fields to Babylon, and then returned safely. Finally Daniel is rescued from the lions' den, and his accusers are thrown to the lions. (The story of Habakkuk appears to be an interpolation.)

Very little value can be attached to these stories. The book of Daniel with its many symbolical and miraculous elements must have been very popular among the Jews of the Dispersion to give rise to so many expansions, at least some of which drifted into the Greek versions of the book.

Additions to Esther. Composed in Greek about 100 B.C. The Additions consist of six passages of one hundred and seven verses, which bear the marks of diversity of authorship. The purpose of the additions is to furnish details with reference to certain parts of the canonical book of Esther, to supply the name of God absent from the canonical book, and to soften down a little of the hatred for the foreigner reflected in the O.T. book. There is little literary merit or value of any kind in the Additions, but they are of interest to the student of textual problems as illustrating the methods and processes of interpolation.

First Esdras. An Alexandrian work from about 100 B.C.; sometimes called the Greek Ezra to distinguish it from the book of Ezra in the Hebrew canon. It is a free Greek translation or paraphrase of the more important sections of the O.T. books of Ezra and Nehemiah. The book opens with some of the incidents of Josiah's Passover narrated in 2 Chr. 35, continues through Ezra and extends to Neh. 8. The one striking difference between this book and the canonical texts is the story of the Three Body Guards and the Decree of Darius. The Three Body Guards carry on an oratorical contest to determine which is the strongest: wine, the king, or women. The third Body Guard, who speaks in praise of women (with an appended story glorifying truth), wins the contest. Darius decrees the restoration of Jerusalem. The minor differences between this book and the canonical books are largely in matters of arrangement and offer a fascinating field to students of textual problems.

First Baruch. A small pseudepigraphical work, written in Palestine about 100 A.D. It is found in all the editions of the LXX, where it bears the name of Baruch (it is here called 1 Baruch to distinguish it from the other books credited to Baruch), the amanuensis of the prophet Jeremiah (Jer. 36^4). The Fall of Jerusalem certainly constitutes part of its background.

1 Baruch is a composite book illustrating various types of literature. Chs. 1^1–3^8 are in prose, dealing with conditions of the exiles in Babylon and containing a series of confessions of sin and statements of the causes of these sins. In the remainder of the book we find poetic material, some of it jubilant and some of it in the form of lamentations. Some of the contents resemble the Wisdom literature of the O.T. The book finally closes with a promise of the return of the dispersed Israelites and of the glorious future for Israel.

III. Stories and Homilies

Tobit. A product of Alexandrian Judaism, written as early as 200 or even 250 B.C. Not long ago it was thought to be Persian in origin, but now its Egyptian origin is definitely proved. The story centers around the journey of Tobias, son of Tobita, a God-fearing man, to a distant land, the consummation of a happy marriage, and his safe return home. Raphael, one of the archangels, accompanies Tobias on part of his journeys and protects him in times of peril. The story undoubtedly draws some of its material from current folk lore. Indeed, there are three folk stories now known all of which seem to have some relationship to Tobit; the story of Achikar, the story of the Egyptian god, Khons of Thebes, and the story of the Grateful Dead. Tobit contains several quotations from the proverbs and fables of Achikar, a reputed wise man once a prime minister of Sennacherib, king of Assyria. The story of Khons, god of Thebes, is an Egyptian story (some of Achikar's wonderful deeds centered in Egypt) of a certain princess living in a distant country, who was possessed with a demon, but was healed through the instrumentality of Khons. The story of the Grateful Dead was really a cycle of stories well known throughout the Hellenistic world. In brief, it was the story of a traveler who, finding the dead body of a debtor, with a fine exhibition of self-sacrifice gave it a decent burial. The spirit of the dead man followed his benefactor in human form, delivered him from many perils and rewarded him in various other ways.

The purpose of the book was to offset some of the dangerous superstitions of Egyptian paganism as it affected the Jews of the Dispersion. Hence, by using some of the popular stories afloat it tried to show the sovereignty of Jehovah over all other gods. It also endeavored to teach loyalty to parents, respect for the dead, prayer, almsgivings, and fasting. Its conception of angels and demons marks a transition between the O.T. conception and that of later Jewish literature. The story reveals the tremendous grip which popular stories and superstitions may have on the popular mind.

Judith. Written by a Palestinian Jew about the middle of the second century B.C. The title "Judith" is taken from a Hebrew word meaning "Jewess." The purpose of the book is not historical but didactic. The author belonged to an orthodox party like the "Chasidim," who were the forerunners of the Pharisees.

The book falls naturally into two sections: an introduction, chs. 1–7, and the story of Judith, chs. 8–16. The introduction, though somewhat overloaded with details of military plans, possesses real literary merit. Nebuchadrezzar had declared war against Media, and had asked aid from his western dependencies, including Palestine. The latter did not respond, so he determined to punish them, and accordingly set out with an army of 120,000 footsoldiers and 12,000 mounted archers, all under the command of Holofernes. After conquering all the lands to the north of Palestine, Holofernes laid siege to Bethulah in north Palestine with an army of 170,000 footsoldiers and 12,000 mounted men. After the city had been reduced to a point of starvation, with its water supply exhausted, Judith appeared on the scene as heroine and deliverer.

Much emphasis is placed on Judith's piety, regular habits of prayer and fasting, her beauty and her daring. Alone with her maid and a bag of clean food she makes her way into the camp of the enemy and into the presence of Holofernes. She finally accepts his invitation to a feast, but does not eat except from her own supply of clean food. At the close of the banquet, being left alone with Holofernes, who is now intoxicated and helpless, she, with a prayer to God on her lips, cuts off his head with two strokes. The head is carried to the village, where Judith is proclaimed victor and deliverer. The siege is lifted and Israel is saved from disaster. The book concludes with a hymn in eulogy of Judith, and with Judith dedicating her share of plunder to God. She dies at the age of one hundred and five years, and the land of Israel enjoys peace for a long time.

The purpose of the book is to create faith in and loyalty to the Jewish religious institutions. Its chief value is not historical but theological and religious. It furnishes an excellent cross-section of some of the beliefs of orthodox Judaism during this second century B.C. Judith is pictured as a strict observer of the Law, a fine type of Pharisaic righteousness. She keeps the later Jewish festivals enjoined in the Pentateuch, as the festival of the Sabbath, the New Moon and the Eves of the Sabbath (8^{6}); she also fasts, prays continually and abstains from unclean food.

Letter of Aristeas. A product of Alexandrian Judaism from about 100 B.C. Aristeas poses as a court official in the court of the Ptolemies in Egypt, narrates a series of incidents leading up to and including the translation of the Law (=the Pentateuch) into the Greek, i.e., the so-called LXX. The purpose of the letter is to glorify the Law and the priesthood, and to give general approval of the translation of the Law into Greek. Incidentally, it endeavors to answer the many objections to the translation. It is a typical product of the Dispersion, having as its ultimate aim the presentation of Jewish institutions in the most favorable light and at the same time to steady the wavering faith of many of the widely scattered Jews. The letter does not possess great literary merit, but gives a vivid picture of the life of the Jews of the Dispersion and of their interests.

Fourth Maccabees. A typical Alexandrian production from the middle of the first century B.C. It is a homily on the supremacy of "inspired reason" over passion. The book, adopting the terminology of the Platonic and Stoic systems, seeks to show that obedience to the Law is one way of attaining ultimate ideals. The author claims that the passions of men came from God; hence they cannot be eradicated, but can be controlled. Reason, exercising such control, becomes an opponent of the passions. Most of the illustrations are from the stories of biblical heroes, and more particularly from the story of Eleazar, and the Seven Sons in 2 Macc. 7. The writer shows how these seven sons bore up under the terrible tortures of Antiochus Epiphanes and uses their fortitude and steadfastness as an illustration of the conquest of reason over the passions. Its chief interest lies in its efforts to adapt Jewish ideas to Greek thought. It is a fine example of control literature.

Books of Adam and Eve. A Hellenistic-Jewish work from the end of the first century A.D. The work exists in two versions, one in Latin, the other in a Slavonic dialect. It has suffered much at the hands of Christian redactors.

The stories narrated represent a type of popular legends such as grew up around many of the biblical characters, and are embellished with many details. We may take as an illustration of the interest in details the story of Adam's death: The death of Adam is foretold to Eve in a dream; the death-bed scene is a memorable one as he is surrounded by his sixty-three children; Adam traces the cause of his death back to his fall; some efforts are made to avert his death, but all are of no avail; Adam is buried by the archangels, and Michael carries his spirit to Paradise. At the close of the books Michael warns against mourning on the Sabbath Day. It is of interest to note the great popularity enjoyed by these and other Jewish legends, and to see the way in which they were worked over and adapted by the early Christians.

Martyrdom of Isaiah. A Palestinian work from about 100 A.D., part of a larger work known as the Ascension of Isaiah. The latter consists of three sections; two are of Christian origin and are known as the Vision of Isaiah and the Testament of Hezekiah; the third, which is of Jewish origin, is known as the Martyrdom of Isaiah. The story is fragmentary. It is a legendary account of Isaiah's death by being sawn asunder in a tree trunk (cf. Heb. 11^{37}). The legend enjoyed great popularity and may underlie the N.T. statement.

IV. Wisdom Literature

Ecclesiasticus. Written in Palestine previous to the Maccabean Rebellion, about 180 B.C. The title comes from the Vulgate, where, according to some, the word has the meaning "Church Book." Sometimes the book is called "Sirach," or by the Hebrew name of the author, "(Jesus) Ben Sira." The author appears to have lived in Jerusalem, where he was head teacher of a school; apparently, he was a man of wealth and a traveler. The book was translated into the Greek by the grandson of the author in 132 B.C.

In contents the book is somewhat similar to the book of Proverbs in the O.T. It contains numerous proverbs, maxims, and practical observations on human conduct, such as the observance of the Law, the need of wisdom in social and religious affairs, the punishment of the wicked, the reward of the righteous, the care of the poor and the needy, right conduct toward women, friendships, the training of children, need of self-control, chastity, and respect for parents and the aged; also warnings against falsehood, pride, intercourse with wicked men, and the misuse of power and wealth. Wisdom is defined as that faculty of common sense that enables one to distinguish between what is to one's advantage and what is harmful; it is personified and is represented as eternal and pre-existent; it is also identified with the Law, which is also declared to be pre-existent. Throughout the book there is the constant assumption of a strict monotheism, and a firm belief in Israel as the chosen nation of God.

Ecclesiasticus is one of the most suggestive books of the intertestamental literature; and probably was omitted from the O.T. canon only because it was written too late for its admission.

Wisdom of Solomon. Produced in Alexandria, about 50 B.C. The name "Solomon" in the title is purely a literary device as in the canonical book of Ecclesiastes. The book may have been written to combat the cynicism in the philosophy of Ecclesiastes. It can be divided into three parts: chs. 1^{1}–6^{8}, dealing with the destinies of the righteous and the wicked; chs. 6^{9}–10, setting forth the author's concept of wisdom; and chs. 11–19, which give an historical survey of Israel's history, express the author's theory of punishment, and condemn idolatry and its attendant evils. The general teaching of the book is a synthesis of Jewish and Greek ideas; the more important subjects covered are God, immortality, universalism, and the pre-existence of the soul. God is regarded as transcendent and removed from the world; he works through an intermediary, namely, Wisdom, which is personified and represented as co-architect with God. God loves all men ($11^{23f.}$). Immortality is immediate, that is, there is no intermediate state, no resurrection, nor elaborate final judgment. The pre-existence of the soul may be carried over from Greek thought ($8^{19f.}$). The religious ideas expressed or implied in the book are among the noblest produced in Hellenistic-Jewish centers during this period, and they find many an echo in the N.T.

Psalms of Solomon. Written in Palestine, about 50 B.C.; the writers were Pharisees; hence, by some writers the Psalms have been called the Psalms of the Pharisees. The use of the term "Solomon" in the title is in line with the general tendency of the age to produce pseudepigraphal literature (see above, under section on "Explanation of Terms"). The Psalms number eighteen and are modeled on the Psalms of the O.T.; many of them are very bitter in their condemnation of the sinners, i.e., the Sadducees, and the Gentiles. Psalm 17 looks forward to the near approach of an ideal temporary kingdom, with a Messiah from Judah; the hostile Gentiles will be destroyed, others will be converted, to serve in the kingdom. The Psalms throw much light on the sectarian strife which troubled Judaism during the first century B.C.

Sibylline Oracles. Books 3–5 of the Sibylline Oracles are largely Jewish in origin; they were written in the Dispersion and date from 125 B.C. to 130 A.D. The Jewish oracles are a part of a great mass of oracular utterances coming from different centuries and various religions. They are to be traced to a widespread practice in the Hellenistic world to seek divine guidance by means of inspired messages received from some Sibyl, generally a woman associated with a shrine; the oracles are given usually in verse form. Many of these Sibyls exerted great influence and enjoyed popularity extending over long periods of time. Religious cults were quick to recognize the power of these popular oracles for propagating belief; the Jews and later even the Christians did not hesitate to use them for their own propaganda. The Jewish Sibylline oracles are easily distinguished from non-Jewish by their subject matter, such as references to God, the Law, Israel, Beliar, the coming of the Messiah, and the typically Jewish condemnations of the evils of idolatry. The value of the oracles is slight, except as they reveal ancient methods of religious propaganda.

V. Apocalyptic Literature

Enoch. A series of apocalyptic writings, Palestinian in origin, coming from about 200–75 B.C. It would be quite proper to speak of the *books* of Enoch, for there is unmistakable evidence of at least five divisions, coming from different periods.

Chs. 1–36 comprise the oldest part of the book, built around a still older fragment (chs. 6–11) of an "Apocalypse of Noah."

Most of this section was written before the Maccabean Rebellion, between 200 and 170 B.C. This portion deals with the fall of the angels and their lust after the women of earth, with the consequent introduction of all sinful practices and demonic influences. The lot of the wicked and of the righteous, the names of the archangels and their functions, the journeys of Enoch through earth, Sheol, and the heavens are other subjects receiving attention.

Chs. 83–90 were written in the same period as Daniel, about 175–160 B.C. This section relates a series of dream visions covering time from the beginning of man's history to the coming of the final judgment and the eternal earthly kingdom. Past disasters are treated as a series of world judgments culminating in the last world judgment or the final Judgment, which is still in the future.

Chs. 72–82 constitute a semi-apocalyptic work, written in the last part of the second century, about 125 B.C. It consists of minute descriptions of the heavens, the movements of the sun, moon, and stars, the divisions of the year and the succession of the seasons.

Chs. 37–71, better known as the "Parables of Enoch," are among the best examples of apocalyptic literature. They were written in the first part of the first century, about 100–75 B.C. There are three parables, dealing with the coming of the divine, pre-existent Messiah, the Son of Man, and the Kingdom of God, which is to be eternal, in a new heaven and a new earth.

Chs. 91–108 may be considered together, though they come from different sources. Chs. 91–104 are largely a unit, coming from the first part of the first century, about 100–75 B.C. Chs. 106, 107 are fragments of the Noah Apocalypse (see on chs. 1–36) and belong in the second century B.C.; chs. 105, 108 come from the same age as 91–104. All the sections deal with the coming of a temporary kingdom and the resurrection of the spirits of the righteous.

The apocalyptic sections of Enoch unquestionably furnish the richest background material for the study of the N.T. (Cf. art., *Backgrounds*, p. 846.)

Testaments of the Twelve Patriarchs. The Testaments are apocalyptic writings ascribed to the twelve sons of Jacob; they were produced in Palestine in the last quarter of the second century B.C., during the early, more prosperous days of the reign of John Hyrcanus. The author was a close adherent of the Chasidim, the forerunners of the Pharisees. The book has suffered much at the hands of redactors, both Jewish and Christian. The Jewish redactions consist chiefly of a few first century B.C. additions, returning from the teaching in the earlier portions of a Messiah from Levi to the more ancient belief in a Messiah from Judah; the Christian additions are easily distinguished and comprise about one twelfth of the entire book.

In literary form the Testaments leave much to be desired; some of the finest ethical teaching is expressed in the most unpromising literary form. Each Testament follows a regular literary standard and presents its material in a threefold division: The first division gives a historical survey of the life of the Patriarch, the second summarizes the lessons and warnings to be drawn from the virtues or sins of the Patriarch, and the third contains the apocalyptic material dealing primarily with the immediate future of the writer's own age.

The Testaments reach the high-water mark in Jewish ethics; they contain a body of ethical principles that bear close resemblance to certain utterances in the Sermon on the Mount. The command of Jesus to love God and one's neighbor is stated three times in the Testaments (Issachar 5^{2} 7^{6} Dan 5^{3}), but with this difference: that one's neighbor is conceived of as a fellow Israelite. The doctrine of forgiveness also resembles the conception in the Gospels: divine forgiveness is conditioned on willingness to forgive one's fellow; and even though the offender will not repent when repeatedly forgiven, the spirit of hatred and resentment must be banished from the heart (Gad 6^{3-7}; cf. Mt. $18^{15f.}$). The Testaments are among the choicest products of the apocalyptic movement.

Assumption of Moses. A Palestinian writing, from the first part of the first century A.D.; that is, it was written during the lifetime of Jesus. The author evidently was a Pharisee with pacifistic tendencies. Originally the book consisted of two parts, the Testament of Moses and the Assumption of Moses. The present text depends largely on the Testament; only fragments of the Assumption have been preserved. The book is the protest of a Pharisee against the growing tendency of his party to blend political ideals with the Messianic hope; hence, while believing in the coming of the Kingdom, he has no room for a Messiah. The advent of the Kingdom is to be preceded by a period of repentance and a series of woes and supernatural signs. There is also a fragmentary account of the last days of Moses, his death, burial, and his assumption to heaven. It is significant that this little book, written during the lifetime of Jesus, agrees with him in the protest against the fusion of political and religious ideals. Some of the material in the book reappears in the brief Epistle of Jude (see notes there).

Second Enoch. An apocalyptic writing, from Jewish-Hellenistic circles, written in Greek in the middle of the first century A.D.; sometimes called the "Slavonic Enoch," because most of the extant sources are in Slavonic; also known as the "Secrets of Enoch." When the book was first discovered it was thought to be a variant of the better-known book of Enoch, but further study has established it as a separate work.

The incidents or stories in the book are concerned with the journeys of Enoch through the several heavens into the presence of God. A full description is given of each heaven and its contents. Arrived in the presence of God, Enoch is shown all the secrets of the world, including the heavens. These revelations he embodies in three hundred and sixty-six books. The closing chapters of the book deal with further revelations of the secrets of creation and other events; there is also a short history of Adam and his descendants. Finally Enoch returns to earth and instructs his children both in the past and the future.

The significance of the book lies in its teaching with reference to the final Judgment, angels, the pre-existence of the soul, plurality of the heavens and the temporary Messianic age of one thousand years. This is the only reference in Jewish literature to a temporary kingdom of one thousand years, that is, a millennium (cf. Rev. 20[1-8], notes).

Second Baruch. A composite book of apocalyptic type, largely of Palestinian origin; some of its material was written just before the Fall of Jerusalem in 70 A.D., and some later. In order to distinguish it from the apocryphal book of Baruch it is sometimes called the "Syriac Apocalypse of Baruch," due to the fact that the finest MS. of the book is written in Syriac.

There are two types of narratives in the book; one set is optimistic and patriotic in tone, the other is pessimistic. Chs. 27–30, 36–40 and 53–74 are the optimistic sections, written before the Fall of Jerusalem; chs. 1–26, 31–35, 41–52, and 75–87 are largely pessimistic, probably because they were written after Jerusalem was destroyed. With a few minor exceptions the entire book is the product of Palestinian Judaism. In the optimistic portions the hope of an age of triumph prevails, with a Messiah playing an active part; in the pessimistic sections the figure of the Messiah disappears, and the idea of a kingdom of triumph is abandoned.

It is one of the most interesting of the late Jewish apocalyptic writings contemporary with the N.T., especially in its ideas of sin, which resemble those of Paul, and its idea of the future as an age of incorruptibility following an age of corruption.

Third Baruch. An apocalyptic writing, of Greek origin, from about 100 A.D. It has suffered much at the hands of Christian redactors; frequently it is referred to as the Greek Apocalypse of Baruch. The book consists largely of a descriptive narrative of the contents of five of the seven heavens, with a description of the movements of some of the heavenly bodies and their attendant angels. It is of special interest because of its doctrine of the intercession of angels, and the further elaboration of the doctrine of the plurality of heavens. Its doctrine of sin is somewhat like that in 2 Baruch. The devil causes the fall of Adam, but no mention is made of inherited guilt.

Fourth Ezra (Esdras). A composite apocalyptic work, originating about 60–120 A.D. in Palestine. It is the same as 2 Esdras 3–14. The heart of the book is found in chs. 3–10, known as the Salathiel apocalypse. In this part apocalyptic literature reaches the highest point of rationalization on the meaning of sin and suffering and its reconciliation with the justice of God; a closely related question concerns the problem raised by the persecution of Israel, the chosen race. Chs. 11 and 12 contain the famous "Eagle vision"; in ch. 13 is the "Man from the Sea vision"; and in ch. 14 the "Ezra legend."

This book and 2 Baruch represent two of the most suggestive among the apocalyptic writings. In other apocalyptic literature obedience to the Law as the final hope of salvation is never abandoned; in 4 Ezra final salvation through the Law is questioned. The latter is the most deterministic of all the apocalyptic writings; the whole history of the world is pre-determined from the beginning. It is the only apocalyptic writing outside of 2 Enoch that places a limitation on the temporary Kingdom; but while the latter mentions one thousand years, in 4 Ezra the period of the renewed Kingdom is limited to four hundred years.

Literature: G. A. Smith, Jerusalem, vol. ii; Fairweather, *The Background of the Gospels;* Charles (editor), *The Apocrypha and Pseudepigrapha of the O.T. in English;* Oesterley, *The Books of the Apocrypha: Their Origin, Teaching and Contents.*

Also literature cited under article, *Religious Development of Intertestamental Period*, p. 213, and part IV of article, *Backgrounds*, p. 852.

RELIGIOUS DEVELOPMENT OF THE INTERTESTAMENTAL PERIOD

BY PROFESSOR LESLIE E. FULLER

Four distinct stages may be recognized in the religious development reflected in the O.T. (1) The nomadic stage, which was an age of origins and small beginnings; (2) the agricultural stage, which experienced a syncretism of the nomadic religion with elements contributed by the earlier inhabitants of Palestine, who had already attained to an agricultural mode of life; (3) the prophetic stage, which, pressed forward by the moral and religious problems created by the strange mixture of Canaanitish and Hebrew religion and the increasingly complex general culture, raised the religion to a very high level of spiritual and ethical appreciation and emphasis; and (4) the legalistic stage, which sought to preserve and protect the gains of the past by emphasizing implicit obedience to formal law and the painstaking observance and use of religious forms and institutions. The study of this development has commanded for a long time the best thought and effort of O.T. scholarship, which has been greatly aided not only by recent advances of knowledge in the fields of O.T. language, literature, and history, but also by the conscientious labors of archæologists and other students of contemporary history, religion, and civilization in general. As a result of this prolonged investigation and research O.T. religion, at least in its general outline and development, can now be presented in a perfectly clear and easily intelligible manner.

Scope of This Article. This article presents the stage of religious development immediately following that of the O.T. period, namely, the religious development of the intertestamental period. The ground work necessary for this study has been completed. Ancient literary remains have been recovered, carefully edited, and translated; commentaries, representative of the best scholarship, have been produced, and furnish a rich mine from which materials may be gathered; experience gained in the study of O.T. religion has aided in the solution of similar problems discovered in the intertestamental field. The several types of literature furnishing the source materials have been discussed in another connection (see art., *Intertestamental Literature*, pp. 190–2); where attention is also called to the various crises responsible for the literary activity, such as the Maccabean Rebellion, the domination of Palestine by Rome in the first century B.C., and the fall of Jerusalem in 70 A.D.; the influence of sectarian strife between Pharisee and Sadducee; the unifying forces running through large sections of the literature, such as loyalty to the Law, and the modifying influences exerted on the degree of loyalty to the Law by the appearance of another loyalty, namely, loyalty to the Messianic expectations. Excessive loyalty to the Law tended to crowd out emphasis on characteristic features of the Messianic hope, while intense loyalty to the Messianic hope tended to render the influence of the Law less absolute. The influence exerted on the authors by local and cultural environment has also been considered. Books written in Palestine follow closely the O.T. traditions, while the literature of the Dispersion reveals an attitude of receptiveness toward Greek thought.

The importance of the study of the religious development of the intertestamental period is determined by its relation to O.T. and N.T. religion. Apart from the Bible much of this literature would possess little or no interest. The intertestamental religious development must not be considered an orderly process of development. The literature as a whole presents many inconsistent ideas and even in a single book, which may be regarded as the product of one man's thinking, such inconsistencies are found. As compared with the O.T., there are points of advance, but also points of retrogression; and some of the earliest ideas are found even in the latest books written. Limitation of space makes an exhaustive discussion of the entire subject impossible; hence the present article will confine itself to the following ideas: God, man, angels, demons, preliminary and final judgments, kingdom of God, Messiah, resurrection, and life after death.

THE IDEA OF GOD

The idea of God in the O.T. is built upon an earlier Semitic conception of a God confined to one tribe and one locality. Other elements carried over from pre-Mosaic and early Semitic days include: (1) a vivid sense of the reality of the spirit world; (2) a belief in the far-reaching effects of divine power; and (3) a more or less deterministic or fatalistic view of the relation of Deity to the general world-order. The distinctive contribution of Israel to the God concept, made chiefly through the prophets, is (1) the insistence that there is only one God—monotheism; (2) the description of this one God as a God the very heart of whose being is holiness; and (3) the conviction that this God will establish his rule of holiness and righteousness upon earth—the kingdom of God (see pp. 158–64).

The intertestamental period causes little change in the essential character of the idea of God; but some of the more basic and inherent elements in the God concept are elaborated in some details, and descriptions are expanded as well as multiplied. One of the more striking features of the intertestamental literature is the great number of titles or names ascribed to God. The names applied to God in the O.T. are comparatively few in number, though in the later post-exilic writings a tendency to increase the number may be noted. The intertestamental writings furnish nearly one hundred divine titles and names. The succeeding paragraphs give a summary of the facts presented in the three groups of writings to be examined: (1) the non-apocalyptic books of Palestinian origin; (2) the apocalyptic books originating in Palestine; and (3) the literature of the Dispersion.

The Idea of God in Palestinian Non-Apocalyptic Writings. In this group of books Ecclesiasticus furnishes the best example of the enlargement and development of typical O.T. concepts. The author is a patriotic and loyal Jew and continues the best traditions of his race. He stresses the oneness of God, his eternal existence, his unlimited knowledge and wisdom, and his great power manifesting itself in the control of the world and the affairs of men. God is interested in all men, but he holds Israel as the chief object of his love and concern. The Book of Judith enjoins strict obedience to the Law as the main approach to God. Israel is God's own folk, and no matter how desperate their need, God always arises to the defense of his people. He uses the weak things of the earth to confuse the mighty. In Jubilees the Israelites are represented to be God's children. Only in a few places he is pictured as God of all men (1^{28} $22^{10f.}$ 30^{19}). The name of the Deity does not appear in 1 Maccabees, though there are several references to the protecting power of heaven. Most of the literature in this group is highly particularistic, though the universalistic note is not entirely absent.

The Idea of God in Palestinian Apocalyptic Literature. The apocalyptic literature presents the most noteworthy developments in the conception of God. Frequently the rich imagery and symbolism have obscured the real meaning and purpose of apocalyptic literature; and much of this formal and external element seems fantastic and unreal; but when we hold in mind that this literature was the product of the lay minds of Judaism, and that it represents a cross-section of popular belief, we may be able to appreciate the fact that even these fantastic expressions represent legitimate attempts to rationalize the world and God's relation to it. The vision or picture element served to make real and impressive the power of God.

The numerous pictures of God's heavenly court, with its angels, archangels and the entire heavenly host, tend to display his glory and power. Many have looked upon this idea of a heavenly court as an intrusion from Persia; it is much more probable, however, that we are dealing here with a natural Jewish development, an attempt to display the glory, majesty, and power of God by picturing the extent and splendor of his court, and placing at his disposal multitudes of messengers and other helpers to assist him in governing the universe. Most people tend to describe superhuman realms in terms of their own social order. The typical political organization of the intertestamental period was the monarchy, the power of which was centered in the person of the ruler, whose power was gauged by the size and magnificence of his court and the number of his court attendants. Nearest to him stood his prime ministers, followed in order by officers of lower ranks to the most lowly attendant. In apocalyptic literature we have God represented as a King of great glory and majesty; archangels play the rôle of prime ministers, to whom only matters of supreme importance are intrusted. In addition to the archangels the heavenly court includes numerous angels of a lesser rank, down to the unnumbered myriads of heavenly attendants and ministers.

God's unlimited wisdom and knowledge are repeatedly emphasized. His knowledge is unlimited; he alone knows the end of the age; he knows all the secret and hidden things of men. His knowledge is so great that he knows the number of all the raindrops in the world. Much of this detail is an enlargement of O.T. ideas, especially as expressed in Isa. 40–55, where God is conceived as measuring or spanning every detail of the heavens. God's intimate knowledge of the world is always emphasized in apocalyptic literature for the purpose of showing that his concern for the most insignificant problems of mankind is of truly practical value and significance.

Perhaps the most suggestive contribution of apocalyptic literature consists in its reconciliation of present persecution and disaster with a belief in the power and righteousness of God. Apocalyptic writers considered their own age as hopeless; an age in which the power of God is temporarily withheld; during which many forces are arrayed against God and his people; demons and Satans are abroad and there is little to restrain them; the pride and arrogance of the wicked and apostates are unchecked; the domination and power of the Gentiles are in the ascendancy. How can such condition exist if God is a God of righteousness and power? The problem was very real; and in order to give encouragement and inspire hope the apocalyptic writers constantly emphasized the activities of God in the past, and promised that he would do even greater things in the immediate future. The wonders of creation, the guidance and protection of his chosen people, acts of special divine intervention and great miracles are stressed as manifestations of God. Moreover, when the people sinned he revealed the same power by sending some great disaster as punishment for sin. The current age of sin will come to an end in a terrible world judgment; and as soon as it has accomplished its purpose God's rule or kingdom will come and even greater wonders will be performed. Thus the sinner will be punished, and the saint who maintains his faith in the hour of persecution and suffering will find his reward.

Some students of Judaism have characterized the above view as a species of dualism; some have even called it deism. Both designations fall short of the truth, for nothing was so foreign to the Jewish mind of these centuries as the idea of a God who at any time is incapable of carrying out his purpose. There might, indeed, be periods when he would not interfere in the affairs of men, but even then they believed that he was active in the universe, maintaining the natural course of events. And even though Satan was considered the Prince of this world, and the demons were thought to be working the ruin of men, they were subordinate to God, and with the coming of the final Judgment they would be punished and banished from the world.

The tendencies toward universalism, on the one hand, and particularism on the other, found in the O.T. reappear in the apocalyptic writings. Most of the latter are decidedly particularistic. In Daniel all the hostile nations are destroyed. The same is true in Enoch 91f.; 1–36; and 83–90. In Enoch 94^{10} God is pictured as rejoicing over the destruction of the wicked. Only in the Testaments of the Twelve Patriarchs are there pronounced evidences of universalism: all the Gentiles are to be saved; Israel with its Law is to be the medium of their salvation. To illustrate God's concern for some individuals among the Gentiles, it is stated that in the final Judgment Israel is to be judged by the best of the Gentiles.

The Idea of God in the Literature of the Dispersion. The idea of God in the literature of the Dispersion offers some striking contrasts to the orthodox position of Palestinian Judaism. There are far greater tendencies toward universalism; miracles and acts of divine intervention are numerous (cf. 2 and 3 Maccabees). Moreover, definite attempts are made in the direction of a synthesis of Greek and Jewish ideas, a synthesis wherein the basic principles of Jewish thought are retained and harmonized with Greek ideas and in some instances proven to antedate Greek thought. Both Philo and the Wisdom of Solomon retain belief in a personal God, although at times they approach pantheism. The motive of these writers in making a combination of Jewish and Greek thought was to combat the materialistic tendencies in Hellenistic life and culture and to furnish to their countrymen in the Dispersion a religious basis for everyday living. In the Wisdom of Solomon God is a creative force creating the world out of formless matter (11^{17}); he does not work alone, for Wisdom, a personified force, labors with him. 2 Enoch 24^{2} speaks of the earth being created out of nothing. The influence of Greek thought is seen in the Wisdom of Solomon 13^{3}, where God is called the author of beauty. The same book gives some fine examples of God's mercy and graciousness (4^{15} 12^{13}).

The Idea of Man

The O.T. is not very explicit in its conceptions of the nature of man, its point of focus being, not man and God, but first God and his requirements and then man. In other words, the O.T. is theocentric rather than anthropocentric. According to the earliest records man consists of two elements, body and soul (Hebrew *nephesh*); soul and spirit (Hebrew *ruach*) are not differentiated. In later records, a third element is added, so that man is thought of as having body, soul, and spirit. All the component parts of man's being in either the twofold or the threefold conception are needed to make a complete personality. Under the sway of the threefold concept, when a man died his body remained in the grave, his soul as a bearer of at least a portion of the personality went to Sheol, and his spirit went back to God. (While this may be regarded as the most systematically developed concept it is by no means consistently held even in the later writings.)

The Idea of Man in the Palestinian Literature. Comparatively few changes are made in the O.T. concept of man in the Palestinian literature of the intertestamental period. There seems to be a return to the older twofold concept, for in apocalyptic literature, especially, the spirit is mentioned more often than the soul as dwelling in Sheol. Thus the soul and the spirit are represented as bearers of the personality to Sheol. The significance of the change is readily seen in connection with the question as to the possibility of a return of the spirit part of man to the body, which is implied in the early ideas of the resurrection of the body. Man's personality, even though subject to the experiences of death and Sheol, lives on forever. This applies to the righteous and the wicked; there is no idea of total annihilation.

The Book of Ecclesiasticus (17[1f.]) explains or enlarges the thought in Gen. 1[26], which refers to man made in the image of God. (It seems rather odd that this term "image" is restricted to so few passages in Genesis.) God has endowed man with a mind and a heart and many other priceless gifts; but the supreme evidence of man's likeness to God is seen in his power to control nature.

The Idea of Man in the Literature of the Dispersion. Greater deviations from the O.T. idea of man are found in the literature of the Dispersion. Insistence on the pre-existence of the soul is the first and most radical departure from the Palestinian view (Wisdom 8[19, 20]). Man is made up of the body and this pre-existent soul, a kind of dualism foreign to the O.T. and the Palestinian intertestamental literature. The soul is immortal and is loaned temporarily to the body, which in some passages is thought of as a hindrance (15[8] 2[23] 3[1]). Philo turns the Genesis story into an allegory, with these same dualistic tendencies interwoven. The most natural result of this Greek-Platonic idea of the pre-existence of the soul is that the Jews of the Dispersion abandoned the Palestinian concept of the resurrection. According to the Wisdom of Solomon, the soul enters directly into eternal life at the time of death; thus the need for an intermediate state for the soul disappears. 2 Enoch 23[5] contains another reference to the pre-existence of the soul; 4 Maccabees 18[23] refers to the immortality of the soul, and further implies the pre-existence of good and bad souls. Josephus asserts that the Essenes believed in the pre-existence of the soul; whether they did or not, the idea was adopted by the later rabbinic writers.

In 2 Enoch the souls of men are created before the creation of the world, and at the same time future abodes for each soul, good or bad, are prepared (23[5], 49[2]). Wisdom is the creator of men out of seven substances (30[8]); flesh from the earth, blood from the dew, eyes from the sun, bones from stone, intelligence from angels and clouds, veins from grass, and souls from God and wind. The Hebrew designation of man, *adam*, is derived from the names of the four angels or stars guarding the four corners of the earth (30[13]). Man possesses free will, but the limitations of the body force the majority of men to choose evil instead of good. Death is the fruit of sin.

The fall of man is referred to again and again and certain theological implications are stressed, but it does not yet assume the position of a fully developed dogma. The story in Genesis is very simple: Adam and Eve disobey, and then they are expelled from the Garden of Eden; certain penalties followed; e.g., labor for food, pains of childbirth, thorns in the field and enmity between the seed of the woman and that of the serpent. (It is of interest to note that some of the penalties fall on nature.) There is no mention of any demonic incitement, no identification of the devil with the serpent; nor is there any hint of an hereditary tendency to evil being handed down to the race.

The Book of Jubilees carries over the Genesis story almost intact, with one exception, namely, Jubilees states that as a part of the punishment the animals were deprived of speech; which implies that prior to the Fall the animals talked like men. The first identification of the devil with the serpent appears in Wisdom of Solomon 2[24]; in other places the fall of man is traced to the evil communicated to men by the fallen angels (Enoch 69[11] 2 Enoch 31[3]). Man was righteous and immortal before he listened to the evil counsel of the fallen angels. A great number of penalties due to the Fall are specified in 2 Baruch 56[6f.], such as death, trouble, pain, sorrow, disease, sexual passions, birth of children, humiliation of mankind, and the extinction of goodness; the hereditary tendency to sin starts with the transgression of Adam and affects all mankind. The clearest statements in regard to this fact are found in 2 Baruch and 4 Ezra.

There are a number of references to the origin of sin. Ben Sira in Ecclesiasticus denies that it originated with God (15[11f.]), but implies in another verse (14) that God implanted in Adam an "inclination" (*yetzer*). This might mean that God created evil, as later rabbinic writers claim that the evil "inclination" was the older of the two inclinations in man. As a matter of fact, Ben Sira's ideas of the origin of sin are by no means consistent; in one place its origin is traced to Eve's transgression (25[24]) and in another place it is traceable to each man's own choice (21[27f.]). Enoch 1–36 and Jubilees trace the origin of sin back to the Flood, when the fallen angels lusted after the daughters of men. Later sections of Enoch imply a rebellion in the heavens before the creation of the world. Several first century B.C. writings trace the beginnings of sin to the transgression of Adam and Eve in the Garden of Eden (Wisdom 2[24] Enoch 69[6f.] 2 Enoch 31[3]). In 2 Baruch the origin of sin is traced to Adam's transgression, and it is stated that certain penalties are handed down to his descendants. 3 Baruch pictures Sammael, another name for Satan, as planting a vine—interpreted as the forbidden tree—in the Garden of Eden and deceiving Adam (4[8]). 4 Ezra places the origin of sin in the heart of Adam; the moment Adam yielded to temptation there was planted in his heart an evil heart (*cor malignum*); as a result there was introduced into the race an hereditary tendency to sin. All the evils of the world are traceable to this original sin of Adam (3[21f.] 4[30]).

Teaching Concerning Angels

Angels, conceived as intermediary beings, play a relatively small part in the O.T. In the pre-exilic sections the "angel of Jehovah" is not a being distinct from Jehovah, but closely associated, if not identical with him; indeed, most of the appearances of the "angel of Jehovah" are theophanies. In the post-exilic portions, with Ezekiel and Zechariah marking the transition, angels become distinct from Jehovah and act as mediums of revelation and interpreters. The earlier prophets received their revelations direct from God and had no need for these interpreters; during the later period the sense of direct and immediate contact with God became obscured and greater stress was laid on the activity of mediators. In general, angels in the O.T., even after they become distinct from Jehovah, are non-personal and rather undefined beings possessing no moral character. The references to angels are confined to small sections of the post-exilic literature; the most developed conception of angels appears in the apocalyptic book of Daniel, where ranks among angels are recognized; the patron angels of Israel and other nations are mentioned, and a personal name, Michael, is given to the "prince" of Israel.

The general absence of a developed angelology in much of the O.T. is traceable to a rigid application of monotheism, which excluded the idea and function of intermediate divine or semi-divine agencies. Some of the intertestamental literature follows the general O.T. practice of making few or no references to angels. There are, for instance, no references to angels in Ecclesiasticus, 1 Maccabees, Wisdom of Solomon, and in other parts of the Apocrypha proper. The greater number of references to angels are in apocalyptic literature.

The appearance of a well-defined angelology in this period is due in part to the tendency of removing God more and more from direct contact with men, of stressing the divine transcendence and, in part, to a desire on the part of men to make real and vivid the power of God by picturing the resplendent glory of God's attendant retinue. Possibly also the matter of God's power as related to the manifold greater and lesser processes of natural phenomena hastened the differentiation of function and the personalization of forces. The primary function of angels was to display the glory of God; the more numerous and powerful the heavenly courtiers, and the larger the armies and legions of angels, the more convincing the evidence of the power of God. Many of the more powerful angels attain to personality and specialized functions, but myriads of them remain undefined and non-personal.

The Book of Jubilees traces the origin of angels to the first day of creation. 2 Enoch traces it to the second day, while other books assume a pre-existent state for angels. Later rabbinic tradition, in harmony with 2 Enoch, traces their origin to the second day of creation. In one place they are said to be made out of fire (2 Enoch 29[1f.]). All the angels, except the two highest orders, are inferior to men.

Angels are designated by a great variety of names and are arranged in a number of significant groups. The most general names are Sons of Heaven, Sons of God, Holy Ones, Watchers, Angels of the Presence, and Angels of Sanctification; in some of the dream visions they are called stars. The smallest group, four in number, is the order of the Angels of the Presence; it consists of four archangels, namely, Michael, Raphael, Gabriel, and Phanuel. (In one list Uriel is found in place of Phanuel.) Another group consists of seven archangels, namely, Uriel, Raguel, Michael, Saraquel, Gabriel, Raphael, and Remiel.

Mention is made also of a group of twelve and a group of seventy; this latter group is an order of patron angels of the nations, based on the seventy years of Jeremiah and the later reference in Daniel. Organized under the leadership of these higher orders of angels are the great hosts and armies of angels, which form an unnumbered multitude.

The various personal functions of the archangels are worthy of note. Michael occupies the highest position. As the special patron angel of Israel (cf. Dan. 10^{13}), he rules over the best of men and Chaos, and is the giver of mercy and loving-kindness. Gabriel sits at the left-hand of God, presides over Paradise, the serpents, and the cherubim. Uriel is the keeper of the heavens and the starry hosts and presides over Tartarus. Raphael is the angel of healing. Remiel, probably the same as Jeremiel, presides over the souls of men or, more specifically, the treasuries of the dead, those awaiting the resurrection and the final Judgment. Saraquel (Sariel) is placed over those who sin in the spirit. Phanuel is in charge of the repentance of men.

The character and functions of angels are described in great detail. Angels are regarded as beneficent creatures, closely related to men, and bearing many of the physical and mental characteristics of men; they possess high moral character, but carry certain limitations in knowledge. Their primary functions are to display the glory and power of God and at all times to praise and magnify his majesty. Other general duties are to act as messengers and interpreters of the will of God to men. In the distant past they acted as media of revelation, mediating the Law, considered as pre-existent, to men (cf. Gal. 3^{19}). They convey the prayers of men to God, and in some instances they keep records of the good and bad deeds of men; they intercede at the throne of God for men (cf. especially 3 Baruch). All nations have special patron angels, Israel being especially favored in having the highest archangel, Michael, as its patron angel. All righteous Israelites have individual guardian angels; an idea which first appears in the Book of Jubilees (35^{17} cf. Mt. 18^{10}). All cosmic forces and events are under the control of a lower type of angels, angels of natural phenomena, like wind, rain, fire, snow, frost, etc. These angels of natural phenomena do not keep the Sabbath, as the processes of nature must be carried on at all times (Jubilees $2^{2f.}$; cf. Rev. $7^{1f.}$ 14^{18} 16^{5}).

Teaching Concerning Demons

In early Semitic religion God was conceived as the prime mover in all unusual events, everything that could not be explained as due to the activity of man, whether it was morally good or bad, was traced to direct divine interference. As time went on and the God concept became increasingly spiritualized and ethicized, it came to be felt that occurrences of a questionable or immoral nature could not be credited to Jehovah; hence a tendency arose to impose responsibility for such things upon other agencies. This tendency, of course, developed slowly, and the earliest references to "evil spirits" associate such spirits rather closely with Jehovah himself (1 Sam. 19^{9} 1 Kings 22^{19-23}).

Strictly speaking the O.T. is without a demonology, i.e., a systematized doctrine of evil spirits. There are only three sets of references to Satan as a separate and distinct personality in the entire O.T. In Zechariah (3^{1}), 520 B.C., he appears as subordinate to God and easily disposed of, with no independent control over evil. In the prose sections of Job ($1^{6f.}$), 450 B.C., he is introduced as a member of the court of Jehovah, who is commissioned by Jehovah to test Job within certain limits fixed by Jehovah; the Satan has no power not committed to him by Jehovah. Only in First Chronicles (21^{1}; *cir.* 300 B.C.), does Satan use the power of temptation apart from Jehovah, and only here is he opposed to the will and purpose of Jehovah (but cf. 2 Sam. 24^{1}).

The demonology of the intertestamental period is closely associated with the question of the fall of some of the angels from heaven. The stories of this event are not in agreement as to the time, place, or manner of the fall. Enoch $6^{1f.}$, which gives an enlargement of the story in Gen. $6^{1f.}$, places the incident just prior to the Flood, when a band of two hundred angels under the leadership of Semjaza came to earth, lusted after the daughters of men, and raised up from their union with the earth women several races of giants. The fallen angels instructed men in all sorts of evils; and when the giants died their disembodied spirits became the evil spirits or demons. In Jubilees 4 and 5 the angels are sent to earth to instruct men in the ways of righteousness, but while on earth they lusted after the daughters of men. The same results followed. According to a variant of the story in Enoch 69 and 2 Enoch 18 a few leaders of the angelic court started a rebellion in heaven before the creation of man; then, when man was created they acted as the agents of his temptation and downfall. In every case the fallen angels are represented as imprisoned, subject to some preliminary judgments and awaiting the final Judgment.

The greater part of the intertestamental literature presents, or at least assumes, the existence of a kingdom of evil spirits opposed to the kingdom headed by God. This counter kingdom is composed principally of evil spirits or demons, the disembodied spirits of the giants, who were the offspring of the fallen angels and human women. The ruling demons are designated as Satans, who, according to references in the later literature, were in existence as evil agencies even before the fall of the angels. The entire kingdom of demons is ruled by a chief demon, to whom at different times different names are given. The most important of these names or titles are Satan, Devil, Prince, Asmodeus, Mastema, and Beliar. The special domain of this counter kingdom of evil spirits is the earth and the air above the earth (cf. Eph. 2[2]). The power of the demons over the earth and its inhabitants is almost complete, at least for a limited period.

The most significant contribution toward a better understanding of intertestamental demonology is made by the Testaments of the Twelve Patriarchs. There the evil things in human experience, such as envy, lust, anger, hatred, lying, adultery, and fornication, are all conceived as personal evil spirits, frequently called spirits of deceit. The various sins of men are traceable to incitement by these ever-present evil spirits. The righteous man is given a power to tread on these demons; and as long as he obeys the Law and remains watchful he is enabled to ward off all their incitements. Beliar is the chief demon, in command of this kingdom of evil spirits. One of the principal functions of the Messiah will be to subdue Beliar and deliver the righteous from the possible temptations of the evil spirits.

The general functions of the demons are much the same throughout the entire intertestamental period. Their normal functions are to tempt, to accuse the fallen, and to torment the condemned. The first of the functions is stressed almost exclusively in the Testaments of the Twelve Patriarchs. They possess the power to reside in men, and more than one demon may possess a single individual (cf. Matt. 12[43-45]). Seduction is a special function of the demons, operative especially in the case of women. They report all evil of men, a function closely akin to one of the functions of the angels. Many of the bodily ills of men are traceable to the work of demons.

The final destiny of the demons is determined at the final Judgment. Until that time the earth is their sporting place, but in the final Judgment they will be punished and banished from the earth. Their rule of the earth and the air is an accompaniment of the evil age, but at the consummation of that age their rule comes to an end. Their punishment and torture will continue forever.

Preliminary and Final Judgments

The O.T. idea of the "Day of Jehovah" forms the basis for much of the later thought of a final Judgment or judgments. The origin of the Day of Jehovah is to be found in the old Semitic conception of a tribal god fighting for his people. During the preprophetic period this tribal view obtained and the people believed that on the Day of Jehovah their God would arise to destroy his enemies or the enemies of Israel and permanently exalt his own people. In other words, the Day of Jehovah was expected to bring a vindication of Israel irrespective of moral character or conduct. In the hands of the prophets this conception underwent a radical change; they lifted the idea into the moral realm, and insisted that while the day would bring the destruction of Jehovah's enemies and the exaltation of his friends, he must determine his friends as well as his enemies on the basis of moral, not racial considerations. Consequently, Israel, not meeting the ethical standards of Jehovah, must suffer punishment; the Day of Jehovah means its destruction, not its exaltation.

The Day of Jehovah is described as a day of terror and great dread, a day of punishment and judgment. Primarily, the day comes in order to punish a sinful people, but its results are to be felt by the entire world-order; there are to be great disturbances in the cosmic order; even the fish of the sea come under its drastic and far-reaching punishments. The time of its coming and its duration are by no means clear. Frequently the prophets saw in a threatened foreign invasion the harbinger of Jehovah's coming day. In some cases the Day of Jehovah is conceived as a great exhibition or demonstration of the divine power to the world at large. Finally, the day is expected to usher in a new world order, the rule of God which will last forever.

Many details of the O.T. conception of the Day of Jehovah are carried over intact into the intertestamental literature; there are, however, some rather marked changes, only the most significant of which can be noted here. According to Daniel, an apocalyptic book of the second century, which has found a place in the O.T. canon, there will be a preliminary judgment for which the sword will be given into the hands of the "saints of the Most High." This preliminary judgment will be followed by the final Judgment, which in turn will be succeeded by the eternal kingdom or rule of God on earth. Enoch 83–90 in sketching the entire history of the world interprets the great disasters of the past (for instance, the Flood and the Babylonian Exile) as a series of world judgments; the writer's own age is about to close with the final Judgment, which will mark the conclusion of the cycle of world judgments. The Book of Jubilees introduces as the first step a series of Messianic woes or signs (ch. 23), which will be in the nature of preliminary judgments; then the kingdom of God, a kingdom of temporary duration, will be established; this will be followed by the final Judgment, and the eternal heavenly kingdom. In every book originating in this century, except in the Testaments of the Twelve Patriarchs, God is the sole agent of judgment; the Messiah has no share in it. The objects of the final Judgment are the hostile Gentiles, the fallen angels, the demons, and the apostate Jews.

There are two divergent views in the first century B.C.: (1) Enoch 37–71 looks upon the earth as too wicked to become the *locus* of the kingdom of God; hence the author promises a complete renewal of heaven and earth. The final Judgment is to be a great exhibition of God's power and will usher in this new world order. God himself will be the supreme judge, but he will place most of the actual work involved in the judgment in the hands of the divine Messiah. The fallen angels, the kings and the mighty ones, and the wicked Israelites are the particular objects of God's wrath. The new heaven and the new earth will endure forever. (2) The Psalms of Solomon present the second view, which looks for a temporary kingdom similar to that described in Jubilees. All hostile Gentile nations are destroyed; the remaining Gentiles are converted and made to perform the menial tasks of the kingdom. The agents of these preliminary judgments are God and the Messiah. The final Judgment comes at the close of the temporary kingdom, and precedes the ushering in of the heavenly kingdom. No time limit is fixed for the duration of the earthly kingdom. Possibly it was to last only during the lifetime of the Messiah.

The literature of the first century A.D. fixes a definite time limit for the temporary kingdom. 2 Enoch limits it to a millennium, i.e., a thousand years, and 4 Ezra limits it to four hundred years. In each one of these two cases the final Judgment comes at the close of the temporary kingdom and preceding the eternal age to come. In some of the sections in 2 Baruch, written after the Fall of Jerusalem in 70 A.D., where the temporary kingdom is abandoned altogether, the final Judgment comes at the end of the age of corruptibility and ushers in an eternal age of incorruptibility. Only in rare instances in the literature of this century does the Messiah function as an agent in the final Judgment.

The most significant contribution of the first century A.D. to the idea of final Judgment is the introduction of a series of Messianic woes or signs. The sufferings and persecution endured by the Jews during this century may account for their presence. The Assumption of Moses presents a series of signs or travail pains of the new age, such as earthquakes, the turning of the moon into blood, the darkening of the sun, the retirement of the seas into the abyss, and disturbances of the orderly course of the stars (10³ᶠ·). 2 Baruch divides these travail pains, indicating the coming of a new age, into twelve groups. The principal ones are wars, assassination of kings, death, famine, earthquakes, fall of fire, rape, unchastity. The climax is reached in the twelfth woe, wherein all the preceding woes are mingled together (27, 70³ᶠ·). Another vivid description is found in 4 Ezra 5. The signs preceding the new age will be: lack of truth and faith, great increase in iniquity, the sun and the moon will be moved out of their natural order, general disturbances in all the orderly processes of nature, great wars, women will bear monsters, children will be born prematurely, and wisdom will hide itself (cf. Matt. 24).

The Kingdom of God

"Kingdom of God" is a term applied to the ideal future which the O.T. prophets expected soon to become a reality. During that age the will and purpose of God would be supreme; it would be, in a true sense, a theocracy; and conditions in the kingdom would be an expression of the character of God himself. Its seat is to be upon the earth, with Palestine as its center and Jerusalem its capital. The kingdom will continue forever, but this does not necessarily imply that individual members will enjoy eternal life; successive generations will guarantee the continued existence of the kingdom—a national immortality. The Messiah appears in only a few instances, and bears no organic connection with the kingdom. The glories of this kingdom consist in large part of external prosperity: e.g., the dispersed Israelites return to Palestine; the Temple is to be rebuilt; the Temple area is to be the center of a new fruitfulness; the whole land is to be well watered and the waste places restored to fertility like that which blessed the garden of Eden; animals of all kinds are to forget their fierce and savage habits and become the friends of men. Men are to enjoy the right of personal property and all kinds of material blessings will be theirs.

It would be a mistake, however, to think of the blessings as only material and external. There are also rich spiritual gifts anticipated. To begin with, admission to the kingdom depends upon proper spiritual qualifications—intimate personal relationship with God; sin has no place in the kingdom and consequently will be destroyed; it will be a kingdom of joy because the Fatherhood of God and the brotherhood of the citizens will be realized; there will be peace not only between God and man, but also between man and man, and between man and the animal world. And all these blessings will become possible because God himself will dwell in the midst of his people.

The second century B.C. literature retains many of these O.T. conceptions. The materialistic aspect of the blessings is highly elaborated. The members of the kingdom are to live for a thousand years and beget a thousand children; the restored fertility of the soil will be such that the yield of all fruits and grains will be ten thousand fold; every vine will have a thousand branches, every branch a thousand clusters, and every cluster a thousand grapes. Israel is at the center of the kingdom, with only very few Gentiles being admitted; even in the Testaments of the Twelve Patriarchs, where the salvation of the Gentile is clearly asserted, he is subordinate to Israel. Throughout the century the kingdom is expected to be eternal. The Messiah is absent, except as he may be seen in the person of a contemporary ruler, for instance, John Hyrcanus.

Two new features are introduced in this century: (1) In Enoch 90[28f.] the old Temple is folded up and carried away with its pillars and its ornaments; then God brings a new and much larger Temple, with new pillars and ornaments, and sets it up on the old Temple site. (2) The second feature of great interest is furnished by the Book of Jubilees (ch. 23). The advent of the kingdom is preceded by a series of woes, or signs; then the kingdom comes in gradually, by a slow and general repentance of the Israelites. For the first time in Jewish literature the kingdom is represented as temporary, with the final Judgment coming at its close. This marks the first breakdown in the idea found throughout the O.T. and the earliest intertestamental literature of an eternal earthly kingdom of God. Undoubtedly, the change is due to the growing belief that the earth is no longer a fit place for an eternal kingdom. This temporary kingdom will experience a reign of peace and joy, for Satan is to be banished; there will be no old men, all will appear young and live for a thousand years. There are no indications as to the length of duration of this temporary kingdom. Following the final Judgment an eternal age will begin, but details of description are wanting.

The literature of the first century B.C. presents some additional changes in the conception of the kingdom. In Enoch 37–71 the kingdom is eternal, but its establishment is preceded by a complete transformation of heaven and earth. The members of the kingdom are the righteous Israelites, who are resurrected and given transformed bodies; they will live forever, growing and developing all the time. In Enoch 91f. the earthly kingdom is retained, but it is considered temporary; it is designated as the eighth week in the world's history, wherein the wicked are delivered over to the righteous; an idea which may be based on the announcement in Daniel regarding a preliminary judgment by the saints of the Most High. The Psalms of Solomon (ch. 17) furnish another example of a temporary kingdom conceived from a decidedly particularistic point of view. The hostile Gentiles are to be destroyed, those who repent are to be saved to perform the menial tasks of the kingdom. In the latter passage the Messiah first appears in connection with a temporary kingdom. Neither passage fixes the exact duration of the earthly kingdom. The final Judgment comes at the close of the temporary kingdom, and will be followed by an eternal age that will bring rewards to the righteous and punishments to the wicked.

More significant changes in the concepts of the kingdom are introduced in the literature of the first century A.D. The writer of the Assumption of Moses, a contemporary of Jesus, announces that the kingdom will be established without fail 1750 years after the death of Moses; its advent is to be preceded by a period of repentance and a series of woes or signs. The earthly kingdom, which is to be temporary, no longer claims supreme attention; the point of emphasis is shifting to the eternal, heavenly age of blessedness. There is no mention of a Messiah, God being the sole agent of punishment and judgment. 2 Enoch, in accordance with the idea of God creating the earth in six days and resting on the seventh day, arranges the entire history of the world in six periods of a thousand years each, giving a total of six thousand years; the seventh period of a thousand years will be a period of rest, which is the kingdom of God. In other words, we have here a temporary kingdom of one thousand years ($33^{1f.}$). At the close of the temporary kingdom there is to be an eighth period, with no limit in time, an eternal age. This is the only reference in the Jewish literature of the intertestamental period to a temporary earthly kingdom of one thousand years' duration. The origin of the conception may be traced to the idea that a day in the sight of the Lord is as a thousand years (2 Pet. 3^{8}; cf. Psa. 90^{4}.)

The books of 2 Baruch and 4 Ezra furnish other interesting ideas concerning the kingdom. 2 Baruch considers his own age as an age of corruption, to be followed by an eternal age of incorruption, the interval between the two being bridged by an earthly kingdom of temporary duration; which, however, is reckoned a part of the age of corruption. It is a period of triumph over the enemies of Israel; in a few instances the Messiah plays an active part in the punishments inflicted upon the latter. In one part of the book the earthly kingdom is abandoned altogether; the resurrection of the righteous is directly to the glories of the eternal age. The original portions of 4 Ezra (chs. 3–10) seem to abandon the age-long hope of Israel for a kingdom of God on this earth. The present age of corruption will be brought to an end by means of a great cataclysm, which is a part of God's predetermined plan for the world; the time of its coming is known to no one but God himself. It is useless for man or angel to make any effort to understand the end of the age. The editorial additions to these chapters present a different view: The end of the present age is announced by a period of woes or signs; then the Messiah will come; his advent will usher in a temporary kingdom *of four hundred years;* at the close of this kingdom all men, including the Messiah, will die and the earth revert to a period of silence for seven days; then the eternal and incorruptible age will appear. (The limitation of the temporary kingdom to four hundred years is intended to offset the four hundred years of the Egyptian bondage.)

Work and Character of the Messiah

In the O.T. the term "Messiah" is most commonly used of a contemporary or future king of Israel; once it is applied to a Persian ruler, namely, Cyrus. Whenever the term refers, as it often does, to an ideal king in the future, the latter is thought of as coming from the tribe of Judah and the dynasty of David; indeed, he is to be a second David; he will rule over the earthly kingdom of God; (but there are a number of passages describing the kingdom which make no mention of a Messianic ruler). As a representative of God he is endowed with superhuman powers (cf., especially, Isa. $9^{6,\ 7}$ $11^{1\text{-}5}$). For a fuller discussion of the entire subject, see the article, *Israel's Messianic Hope*, pp. 181–6.

The Messiah is rarely mentioned in the literature of the second century B.C. In Enoch 90 there is one reference to a Messiah, who is described as a human being coming from the nation Israel; he appears as a white bull, which is subsequently changed into a lamb with black horns ($90^{37f.}$); he does not come until after the final Judgment and is a purely passive figure. The only other references to a Messiah during the second century are in Jubilees and the Testaments of the Twelve Patriarchs. Jubilees $31^{18f.}$ refers to a Messiah from Judah; a contemporary ruler, John Hyrcanus, is to prepare the kingdom for this coming ruler; to the Messiah no special function is assigned.

The most important second century reference to a Messiah is found in the Testaments of the Twelve Patriarchs. The author evidently is a loyal supporter of the Maccabean dynasty, which traced its origin not to the tribe of Judah but to the tribe of Levi. The Testaments of the Twelve Patriarchs being written during the reign of John Hyrcanus, when the glory of the Maccabees was at its height, it is not strange that the author should connect the Messianic hope with John Hyrcanus and his predecessor, Simon. The Testaments, therefore, set aside the age-long hope of a Messiah springing from Judah and instead promise a Messiah of the tribe of Levi. The Testament of Levi (ch. 18) is a Messianic hymn in eulogy of John Hyrcanus (it is similar in part to Psa. 110, which is considered by many to be a hymn in praise of Simon Maccabeus), who is expected to be the founder of a Messianic dynasty from the priestly tribe of Levi. He is called Priest, Prophet, and King; he is to make war against the enemies of Israel, to oppose the power of Beliar and the demons, and to arise in the defense of the righteous; he is to act as a mediator to the Gentiles; he possesses meekness, righteousness and even freedom from sin; in the near future he is to open the gates of Paradise to the righteous, and to give them to eat of the Tree of Life. In the first century additions to the Testaments of the Twelve Patriarchs, after the Maccabean leaders had broken with the Pharisees the hope of a Messiah springing from the tribe of Judah is revived. (Testament of Judah $24^{5f.}$).

The literature of the first century B.C. presents two of the most remarkable pictures of the Messiah. Enoch 37–71 presents the first description of a divine Messiah in the history of the Messianic hope. The Messiah is pre-existent, being in existence before the foundation of the world, and bears altogether divine and supernatural characteristics. He has four titles, Messiah, the Elect One, the Righteous One, and the Son of Man; all of which reappear in the N.T. His duties cover a wide range of activities: he is to play a prominent rôle in the final judgment, judging the kings and the mighty ones, the fallen angels and the wicked; he is to be the special defender and champion of the righteous; he possesses great power and great wisdom, which enable him to discern all the hidden and secret things of the world.

According to the Psalms of Solomon (17, 18) the Messiah is a human king from the tribe of Judah; in addition to Messiah he is called Son of David. His advent is to be preceded by great disasters, and it is known only to God himself; he is to be raised up by God and is to be known as his official representative. His mission is two-fold: (1) to destroy the hostile Gentiles and the sinners, i.e., the Romans and the Sadducees respectively; (2) to restore the dispersed tribes of Israel to Palestine. He is not a political and a warlike Messiah, for he relies on spiritual forces; holiness and freedom from sin are constantly stressed; he possesses great wisdom and a true sense of justice; his acts of judgment are always tempered with mercy. His subjects are called the sons of God.

The Messiah concepts of the first century A.D. reveal few changes. There is no Messiah in the Assumption of Moses, whose author is protesting against the political ambitions of the Pharisaic party; God alone avenges, judges, and rules his kingdom. A Messiah figure appears several times in the early sections of 2 Baruch. In one place he is revealed from heaven, following a series of Messianic woes or signs, and then returns to heaven. This implies that he was a divine or semi-divine being; no special function is assigned to him (29^{3} 30^{1}). In two other places he appears playing an active rôle in the punishment of the wicked ($39^{7f.}$ $72^{4f.}$); he personally convicts one of the Gentile leaders and puts him to death. In another place he gathers all the nations together in one great assize and kills all the hostile peoples that have oppressed Israel; the rest he spares. The Messiah is not mentioned in the late or pessimistic sections of 2 Baruch, nor in 2 Enoch.

The earliest sections of 4 Ezra contain no references to a Messiah; such references are found only in late passages and in editorial additions. As in 2 Baruch, the Messiah is revealed from heaven, but here he is accompanied by some immortal companions, most probably Enoch and Elijah. This heavenly or divine Messiah rules for the period of the temporary kingdom, a period of four hundred years; at its close he dies along with the rest of mankind ($7^{28f.}$). In 12^{32} is mentioned a Messiah who is pre-existent and of divine origin. (The latter part of the verse, which states that he will spring from the house of David, and thus implies an earthly Messiah, is probably a later addition.) The Man from the Sea Vision, the thirteenth chapter, presents a Messiah who is a divine being and uses certain supernatural means of destruction. His chief functions are to annihilate the hostile Gentiles, restore the lost tribes of Israel, and inaugurate a reign of peace. One other reference to a divine Messiah is found in 14^{9}, according to which Ezra takes up his final abode with the Son, the Messiah. Enoch is granted a similar privilege of transfer to one of the highest heavens (Enoch $70^{1f.}$).

The Future Life

The Idea of Resurrection. The idea of resurrection cannot be treated apart from the question of life after death (see succeeding section). The prevailing view on life after death in the O.T. is that man after death enters Sheol, an underground compartment, far beyond the affairs of men and the control of God. There are no moral distinctions in Sheol, and man once there has no hope of escape. Beginning with the eighth-century prophets two developments in the general religious thinking of the Hebrews began to exert an influence on the thought concerning life after death: (1) The growth of monotheism was bound to influence the thought concerning the extent of the divine power. Could Sheol be outside of God's sphere? (2) The greater emphasis on individualism, beginning with Jeremiah and Ezekiel, brought to light troublesome inequalities of life; righteous men did not receive adequate reward in this life, and many wicked men did not receive their full share of punishment. Was there any time or place for the straightening out of these inequalities? If the God of the whole earth is a righteous God, must he not provide a way out of this difficulty?

There are few references to resurrection in the O.T. There are, however, some indications that, inspired by the problems referred to in the preceding paragraphs, some of the saints of Israel revolted against a life after death in which Sheol was the last word. They cried for escape from Sheol, so that their fellowship with Jehovah and the saints might continue without interruption (see especially Psa. 16, 17, 49, 73). In these passages the hope is not that the dead might be brought out of Sheol; but rather that the pious at the time of death might be taken to the dwelling place of God, without first entering Sheol. There are only two references to a resurrection of individuals: Isa. 26^{19}—an apocalyptic section—speaks of the resurrection of pious Israelites, and Dan. 12^{2}, another apocalyptic passage, speaks of the resurrection of the Jewish martyrs and apostates, who will be raised so that they may receive adequate rewards and punishments. (Cf. p. 173.)

There are few references to resurrection in the entire body of intertestamental literature. Indeed, the references are so few that some students of the subject have raised the question as to whether the idea of a resurrection is an essentially Jewish product, or may not have been taken over from outsiders like the Persians. The earliest conceptions of individual resurrection expressed in the intertestamental literature are of a bodily resurrection. This idea of a bodily resurrection bears all the evidence of being indigenous to the Jewish mind. The chief motive for an escape from Sheol is a desire to return to earth and enjoy an uninterrupted communion with God and to take part in some of the physical joys and pleasures of the kingdom; also to witness the physical torments of the apostate Jews enduring punishment in the valley of Hinnom. To enter into all these experiences the body was necessary.

Practically all the references to resurrection in the literature of the second century B.C. speak of a resurrection of the body. Enoch 1–36 promises a bodily resurrection to all the righteous and some of the wicked in Israel. The righteous who are raised from the dead will share in the prosperity and glories of the kingdom of God, and at the same time they will have the satisfaction of witnessing the torments of the apostate Israelites in the valley of Hinnom or Gehenna. In Dan. 12^{2} there is a bodily resurrection of some of the righteous and some of the wicked Israelites. The pre-eminently righteous are raised to receive some delayed rewards, and the preeminently wicked are raised to receive some of their long deserved punishments. According to Enoch 83–90 all the righteous Israelites will be raised; the wicked remain in Sheol. The late second-century books introduce some changes. Jubilees has a resurrection of the righteous spirits only. The Testaments of the Twelve Patriarchs, a book with universalistic tendencies, announces that Israel and all mankind will be raised. The patriarchs Abraham, Isaac, Jacob, and the twelve sons of Jacob are to be raised first, then the rest of mankind (Testament of Benjamin $10^{6f.}$).

A variety of conception appears in the literature of the first century B.C. The first, carried over from the second century, looks for a bodily resurrection of the righteous Israelite only, a resurrection to eternal life in the kingdom of God (2 Maccabees). Another view finds expression in Enoch 91f., and the Psalms of Solomon, which promise a resurrection of the spirits of the righteous Israelites only. The Parables of Enoch 37–71 anticipate that all the righteous Israelites are to be raised and given transformed bodies, clothed in which they will enjoy eternal life in the new heaven and on the new earth. The wicked are raised to the final Judgment, which consigns them to eternal torture.

Similar diversity of opinion is found in the literature of the first century A.D.; sometimes one and the same book expresses more than one idea or gives other evidence of much uncertainty. The Assumption of Moses looks for a resurrection of the spirits of the righteous only, after the final Judgment. The righteous are then exalted to the heavens, whence they can look down and see the tortures of the wicked in Gehenna. 2 Enoch has no resurrection in a strict sense of the word, since the writer believes in the pre-existence of the soul. The righteous are gathered after the final Judgment and placed in the third heaven. According to 2 Baruch 30 only the righteous are raised; but according to 50f. both the righteous and the wicked are raised in a bodily resurrection, so that the resurrected people will recognize one another. After the final Judgment the righteous will be transformed and will become increasingly beautiful, while the wicked will become more and more ugly. In the earliest sections of 4 Ezra, the writer sets forth the view that the body is corruptible, and that the material of which the body consists is annihilated at death. An obscure passage ($8^{38f.}$) seems to imply a resurrection of the righteous only at the time of death. The later redactions of 4 Ezra introduce the idea of a first and second resurrection. In the first resurrection, at the beginning of the temporary kingdom of four hundred years, the Messiah and his companions, Enoch and Elijah, will appear ($7^{28f.}$). Seven days after the close of the temporary kingdom there is to be a general bodily resurrection of all mankind, Israelite and Gentile, good and bad.

Life After Death. The O.T. idea of life after death is similar to that which is found among the Babylonians and other ancient peoples.

The final abode of departed men is Sheol, a dark and dismal subterranean cavern, a land of shades and a land of no return; social distinctions obtain, but there are no moral distinctions; nor is Sheol a place of reward or punishment, for rewards and punishments are meted out to men before they die. Men in Sheol are cut off from the world of the living and are beyond the control of God.

Much of this early view is carried over into the intertestamental literature. For instance, to the writer of Ecclesiasticus the only hope of man beyond this life was to leave behind him a good family name and a line of stalwart sons to perpetuate the family traditions. Sheol is the final abode of all men, a land of no reproaches, a land of no delight, and wholly apart from happenings on earth and from God. Some of the later additions to the book introduce into the idea of Sheol an element of punishment and moral distinction. Essentially the same view appears in Tobit, the Psalms of Solomon, 2 Baruch, etc.

The first evidence of the moralization of Sheol appears in Enoch 22, with its threefold division of Sheol. Two factors contributed to the creation of moral distinctions in Sheol: (1) the making of some provision for meting out reward and punishment after death; (2) the desire on the part of pious Israelites to be permitted after death to return to earth and share in a renewed communion with God and the fellowship of the restored nation. Two of the three divisions mentioned in Enoch 22 serve as intermediate abodes, one for the righteous Israelites, and one for those wicked Israelites who did not receive adequate punishment on earth. The third division serves as the final dwelling place of all the other wicked persons. The two groups in the intermediate abodes will remain there until they participate in the bodily resurrection that will bring them back to earth, in order that they may receive their rewards until then denied, or their deserved punishments. In some of the books Sheol becomes an intermediate state for all the Israelites; then after the resurrection and the final Judgment the wicked are returned to Sheol for eternal torment of fire, while the righteous are assigned to heaven. In still other writings Sheol becomes only a place of fire and torment, and the final abode for the wicked.

The concept of Gehenna is closely connected with the moralization of Sheol. The term "Gehenna" originally referred to the valley of Hinnom, located south of the walls of Jerusalem. In ancient times refuse was burned there, and later Moloch worship was practiced in that locality. Because of the uncleanness of the place and its heathen association it is used in the intertestamental literature as a place of uncleanness, horror and punishment. In Enoch it is the scene of the bodily and spiritual punishment of the apostate Jews, in the presence of the righteous. Later it becomes a place of spiritual punishment alone. When Sheol becomes a place of fire, Gehenna is no longer associated with a location on the surface of the earth, but becomes practically synonymous with Sheol or comes to denote the place of hottest fire in Sheol.

Not all punishment is confined to Sheol and Gehenna. There is mention of a place of punishment in the third heaven: the northern part is a terrible place of torture; the southern part, separated from the northern part by a gulf, is Paradise (see next paragraph). The fallen angels are confined and punished in one of the other heavens; Tartarus is an intermediate place of punishment for the faithless angels; while the Abyss of fire is their final place of punishment.

The introduction of the idea of reward and punishment following the resurrection and the transformation of Sheol into the final abode of the wicked necessitated the finding of a final dwelling place for the righteous. This place is called Paradise in the intertestamental literature. The term as applied to the Garden of Eden is not found in the O.T.; it first appears with this meaning in the LXX translation of the O.T. Paradise in this sense is used also in the intertestamental literature. Enoch visits Paradise (=Garden of Eden) in his travels in the east (32^{3}); in other places Paradise is located in the north and in the northwest. These earthly locations of Paradise were soon abandoned. In some passages it is located in the third heaven (2 Enoch 8^{1}; cf. 2 Cor. $12^{2f.}$); there is also some evidence that for a time it was associated with Sheol (Enoch 22, 4 Ezra 7^{48-56}; cf. 1 Pet. $31^{18f.}$). The place is pictured as a garden, which contains the Tree of Life. One of the chief functions of the Messiah will be to open Paradise to the righteous, and to give to them the privilege of eating from the Tree of Life. In some passages Paradise is mentioned as an intermediate place for the righteous, but in later literature it appears uniformly as the final abode of the righteous, where they enjoy an eternal life of joy, peace, and freedom from all the sorrows of earth.

The Jewish literature of the Dispersion presents some interesting points of contrast as compared with the Palestinian views of life after death. The Jews of the Dispersion, under the influence of the Greek idea of the immortality of the soul, practically omitted the time quality from their eschatology.

They saw little need for a final Judgment, for they thought of judgment as immediate and self-executing. The soul was pre-existent, living only for a short time in the body; the body was evil and proved a hindrance to the soul; death meant the immediate release of the soul from the evil body to eternal life; there was no need of an intermediate state or a resurrection. There seems to be a slight trace of this in Jubilees 23[31], where the bodies of men rest and their spirits rise. In 2 Baruch there is an immediate transference of the resurrected righteous spirits to the new age, without any thought of a kingdom of God on earth; a fine example of the eschatology of the individual totally divorced from the eschatology of the nation. (See further, art., *Backgrounds*, pp. 843–7.)

Literature: Porter, *Messages of the Apocalyptical Writers;* Charles, *A Critical History of the Doctrine of a Future Life in Israel, Judaism and Christianity;* Charles, *Religious Development between the Old and the New Testaments;* Walker, *Teaching of Jesus and the Jewish Teaching of His Age;* Leckie, *World to Come and Final Destiny.*

For notes and comments on the different books, consult *The Apocrypha and Pseudepigrapha of the O.T. in English,* edited by Charles.

III. COMMENTARY ON THE BOOKS OF THE OLD TESTAMENT

GENESIS

By Professor THEODORE H. ROBINSON

Introduction

Purpose and General Outline. Christ first, Christ last, Christ all in all—that is the Christian attitude. Yet Jesus did not come into the world as an isolated and wholly independent phenomenon. There is much in his outlook and teaching which has to be understood in the light of his direct antecedents. It was not for nothing that he was a Jew, and his followers have rightly accepted the Jewish Scriptures as an integral portion of their own Bible. While men may love to see in him the fulfillment of all truth, wherever found and however uttered, he is in a special sense the climax of Hebrew religion. Behind him lies a long history, the spiritual experience of his people, and we cannot be too thankful that this experience has found an enduring literary expression in our Bible. Without the O.T. Jesus would be unintelligible, for there we have an "introduction" which explains much that he never explained, because he could take it for granted. (See art., *The Bible—a Library of Religion*, p. 15; cf. p. 175.)

It is, then, only as the record of spiritual experience that we can rightly study the O.T. It is not the soul-history of an individual, though it contains many such histories, and the world could ill have dispensed with the record of the inner life of a Hosea, a Jeremiah, or a Job. But these are items or stages in the larger whole, which is the story of a great people, and of the way in which their unique religion prepared the way for one yet greater. In a real sense Jesus was the inheritor of the life of all who had gone before him, and we can trace in the religion of Israel the long slow growth of discovery and of revelation (two sides of the same process) which finally made him possible. Other races began as high as Israel did, or higher, but by the time Jesus came she occupied a religious position above any other that the world had yet known.

Just as the O.T. as a whole is the "introduction" to Jesus, so the book of Genesis is the "introduction" to the O.T. The story of Israel's nationality begins with the Exodus; the story of her religion with Sinai. Her first national act was the flight from Egypt, and it was at the sacred mountain that for the first time she came into contact as a nation with that God who was to be the fountain of her spiritual life (see Ex. 3:13-22, notes). What is contained in the first book of the Bible is the story of the pre-Israelite world as conceived by the Hebrews.

The book falls into four divisions. The first tells the story of the world as a whole, tracing the record from the first appearance of man to the point at which a line of demarcation appears between the direct ancestors of Israel and those of other nations (chs. 1–11). Next we have an account of the oldest of the Patriarchs, Abraham, who is recognized as the ancestor not only of Israel but of other tribes and nations as well. This carries us from 12:1 to 25:18. The third section (25:19–36:43) tells the story of Jacob, and the last section (chs. 37–50) relates the history of Joseph, through whom the ancestors of Israel found their way to Goshen, and came into close contact with the Egyptian power.

Source Materials. Recognizing the broad aims which the writer—or, perhaps we should say, the compiler—of this book had before him, we must next ask ourselves whence he derived the information from which he constructed it. As soon as we look at the narratives we see that they come from many sources. There are traditions which have clearly come down from ages far older than Israel, snatches of song relating to peoples of whom all other traces have been lost, race memories enshrined in language which could not die. There are stories which are the common heritage of many peoples, finding parallels in the lore of other portions of the world, particularly of the ancient East, and it is significant to compare these with their foreign forms, and see how the spiritual genius of Israel modified, purified, and ennobled them. There are tales told age after age round the shepherds' watch-fires, sacred stories of the famous centers of worship, in which every visitor must have been instructed by the attendant priesthood, biographies of personified clans, through whose thin veil we can dimly trace the record of tribal history, genealogies such as are found elsewhere preserved in the tenacious memories of unlettered peoples, local traditions which explain how this or that spot came by its name and its importance. Every possible source of information has been ransacked, and the materials thus collected have been woven into a single whole, dominated by a single purpose, controlled by a single thought—the divine preparation for Israel.

A scientific study of these narratives shows that they fall into several well-marked groups. Two of these are similar to one another, and but for the fact that their narratives are sometimes interwoven with one another we might have remained oblivious to the distinction. (For a discussion of this interweaving and of the methods of analysis, the reader is referred to the article on *The Pentateuch*, pp. 134, and also to the chapter on "The Methods of Higher Criticism" in *The People and the Book.*) There are, however, some significant differences between stories derived from these two groups. One of them seems to show greater interest in southern Israel than in the north, and prefers to use the personal divine name "Jehovah"—hence it is commonly known as J. The other seems to have been current in the north—"Ephraim"—and, in Genesis, prefers the more general word for God—in Hebrew *Elohim.* This, therefore, is generally cited by the symbol E. It is often held that each group once formed an independent book; and if this opinion be correct, it is clear that the writers were drawing on material far older than their own day, sometimes older than Israel itself.

A third group stands widely apart from these two, and bears all the marks of coming from a different age. J and E, in the form in which they were embodied in Genesis, were practically contemporaries, reflecting the same general cycle of ideas and the same level of cultural and religious development. But this third class of passages differs widely from both. In Genesis it, like E, prefers to use the divine name *Elohim* instead of *Yahweh* (a word which appears in our versions as Jehovah or the LORD). But there is little else in which this type of passages resembles either of the others. The whole tone is loftier, and reflects the thought and feeling of a much more advanced age. The conception of God is less material and more spiritual, and while there is comparatively little narrative to be included under this head, what there is bears the impress of a very striking style. Genealogy is a favorite theme here, and, indeed, it might almost be said that in Genesis this group consists of genealogy, with an occasional narrative inserted. It is worth noting too that there is a fondness for exact figures, and that where events, as distinct from mere names, are recorded, they always have in them a legal element, and point to the establishment of some principle well recognized in the later Law. Passages of this class are commonly indicated by the letter P ("Priestly"), and are usually supposed to have been taken from a long comprehensive work, which included not only an outline history of Israel down to the end of the wanderings, but also the great mass of the Law as it appears in Exodus, Leviticus, and Numbers. (There are, of course, other passages of various length which cannot be traced to these three clearly defined sources; some of them probably were derived from otherwise unknown sources, while others undoubtedly originated with the compiler.)

Use of the Material. We have next to notice the way in which these passages have been put together to produce the final form in which we have the book to-day. It is clear that the sections which are grouped under the letter P have been used as a kind of framework into which narratives belonging to the other two groups or derived from other sources have been fitted. For the most part, as has already been noted, this framework consists of genealogies with the bare mention of one or two outstanding events in the lives of the more important persons named. There are, however, some half a dozen more extended narratives with the characteristics of P, each of which is clearly introduced with a special purpose, to which the same treatment is given as to narratives derived from other groups. Each is inserted in its place in the life of the person to whom it refers. Usually the narratives are simply placed side by side, but where similar accounts are derived from different groups, they are woven together, sentences or paragraphs from the one being inserted alternately with those drawn from the other. It is usually a simple matter to disentangle them, for it is really through discrepancies in the passage that attention is called to its composite structure. The method of literary composition or compilation used is familiar to every student of ancient literature, especially of ancient Oriental literature. There are many other examples in the various types of O.T. literature. (See art., *Pentateuch*, p. 134, and introductions to other historical books of the O.T. in this Commentary.)

Permanent Value and Significance. Each of the two main sections of Genesis—that which contains the ancient general history (chs. 1–11), and that which contains the stories of the Hebrew patriarchs (chs. 12–50)—has its own value and significance.

(1) *The Ancient General History.* Much controversy has raged around the first eleven chapters of Genesis (see art., *O.T. and Science*, p. 126). Formerly they were accepted as an accurate account of creation and the early history of mankind. At the present time less emphasis is placed on historical accuracy and

more on religious value. The position of modern scholars may be summarized as follows: If anyone is in search of accurate information regarding the age of the earth, or its relation to the sun, moon, or stars, or regarding the exact time or order in which plants and animals have appeared upon it, he should go to recent textbooks in astronomy, geology, paleontology and other sciences. It is not the purpose of the biblical writers to impart such instruction, or to enlarge the bounds of scientific knowledge. So far as the scientific or historical information furnished in these chapters is concerned, it is of little more value than the similar stories of other nations. And yet the student of these chapters can see a striking contrast between them and extra-biblical stories describing the same unknown ages handed down from pre-scientific centuries. Here comes to view the uniqueness of the Bible. The other traditions are of interest only as relics of a bygone past. Not so the biblical statements: they are and ever will be of inestimable value, not because of their scientific teaching, but because of the presence of sublime religious truth in the crude forms of primitive science. If anyone wishes to know what connection the world has with God, if he desires to discover some unifying principle, some illuminating purpose in the history of the earth, he may turn to these chapters as a safe and reliable guide.

(2) *The Patriarchal Narratives.* The experience of centuries furnishes abundant evidence that the patriarchal narratives are of inestimable value as means of impressing lessons of the reality and providence of God and of encouraging faith and confidence in him. Moreover, not one iota of their value for purposes of instruction in righteousness have these records lost because doubt has been cast on their absolute historical accuracy. "If," says Professor McFadyen, "it should be made highly probable that the stories were not strictly historical, what should we then have to say? . . . The religious truth to which they give vivid and immortal expression would remain the same. The story of Abraham would still illustrate the trials and rewards of faith. The story of Jacob would still illustrate the power of sin to haunt and determine a man's career, and the power of God to humble, discipline and purify a self-confident nature. The story of Joseph would still illustrate how fidelity amid temptation, wrong and sorrow is crowned at last with glory and honor" (*O.T. Criticism and the Christian Church,* p. 335, Charles Scribner's Sons, publishers.) This does not mean that these narratives are without historical worth; on the contrary, they are historical documents of immense value. Nevertheless, it may not be amiss to remind ourselves that the N.T. points the Christian reader to the O.T. not for instruction in ancient history but for teaching, for reproof, for correction, for instruction which is in righteousness; and these records, whatever may be their historical shortcomings, are most assuredly profitable for all these purposes (2 Tim. 3^{14-17}).

Literature: Bennett, *Genesis* (New Century Bible); Driver, *Genesis* (Westminster Commentaries); Ryle, *Genesis* (Cambridge Bible); Skinner, *Genesis* (International Critical Commentary); Frazer, *Folklore in the O.T.;* Gunkel, *The Legends of Genesis;* Gordon, *The Early Traditions of Genesis;* Ryle, *The Early Narratives of Genesis;* Kent, *Narratives of the Beginnings of Hebrew History* (Students' Old Testament); Orr, *The Problems of the O.T.;* T. H. Robinson, *Genesis in Colloquial Speech.*

I. Chapters 1^1 to 11^{26}: Early Days

The first main division of the book of Genesis falls into five sections, each marked by a "genealogy." Twice the genealogy is accompanied by a longer narrative of events, one of which stands by itself, while the other has been incorporated with another account of the same event. The sections are: 1. The Beginning of Things (chs. 1–4). 2. Antediluvian Man (5^1–6^4). 3. The Flood (6^5–9^{29}). 4. Recovery of Man and Repopulation of the Earth (10^1–11^9). 5. The Ancestry of Abraham (11^{10-26}).

Chapters 1 to 4: The Beginning of Things

This section describes the creation of the world and the outstanding features of the life of the first human generation. It contains five narratives: (1) an account of creation, (2) a second account of creation, (3) man's temptation and fall, (4) Cain and Abel, (5) Lamech and his song.

CHAPTER I

The First Account of Creation. (From P; 1^1–2^{4a}.) It is impossible to read this narrative without being struck by its dignity and lofty tone. The whole is arranged under a series of days, and to each day are assigned portions of the universe. The events are fitted into a framework which consists of certain formulæ, repeated at the beginning and end of each separate act; throughout a definite and progressive order is observed. The theology is advanced; God needs no physical means or material agency; his word suffices. The whole narrative is an expression of the supreme truth that God is the author of the universe, expressed in a form suited to a people of high intelligence, developed culture, and lofty religious thinking.

The common mythology of the nearer East —which includes the land of Palestine—told of creation as the result of a divine victory over "Tiamat," a chaos-monster who led the powers of darkness. Some such tale was current in ancient Israel, with Jehovah as the victorious hero-God (cf. Job 9:13 26:12, 13 Psa. 74:12-17 89:8-12, etc.). But even if the writer of this chapter had such a story in mind, we can see how the grosser elements have been purged away, and have left us with the noblest and most spiritual record of creation that any religion has offered the world.

Strictly speaking, there are only three acts of "creation." The term is used to describe the introduction of an element which cannot be explained by what has gone before. The intermediate acts are in a sense "evolutionary," i.e., the readjustment of material already present to form new combinations, and the word used to describe them is not "create," but simply "make."

1, 2. The "Creation" of "The Heavens and the Earth." There is no order, no shape, no distinction between solid and liquid, nothing but a confused indiscriminate mixture, and, hovering above it as a bird over its nest, the Breath of God, already, it seems, personified. (See discussion of the Spirit on p. 176.)

3–5. Light. In formulæ which persist through the chapter, the "making" of light is described. It is, to the Hebrew mind, independent of luminaries, which are rather concentrated masses of the pervading substance; it stands in eternal contrast and opposition to the darkness.

6–8. The Firmament. The process continues with the making of a *firmament*—a plate of hard material, probably pictured as dome-shaped. This gives a needed point of departure, a fixed spot in the midst of the chaos from which a start can be made. This done, the organization of the universe can follow, and it occupies the second *day*. (For the ancient view of the world, see p. 126.)

9–13. The Earth and Vegetation. The *third day* is given to the "making" of the earth as man knows it. The account starts from the "firmament," which is surrounded on all sides by the half-liquid, half-solid matter of the chaos. At the divine command this recedes from below the firmament, and an empty space (air and other gaseous substances are not recognized as material) is left under the dome. The pressure is so great that it separates the solid from the liquid elements, and the latter are collected to form the sea, while the former become the dry land. From the ground thus formed sprang the natural vegetable products of the soil, which, though not endowed with life as the Hebrews understood that term, yet grow and yield their fruits, and God sees that all is good.

14–19. Heavenly Luminaries. The sky above the completed earth is still empty, and the *fourth day* is occupied in the making of bright radiant objects. They are not merely celestial ornaments; their purpose is to indicate time. They mark day from night, but that is not all; they tell men when the seasons change, and when the festal occasions are due. These sacred times are older than man, and exist independently of him; when he is formed he must see that they are duly observed. The presence of these heavenly bodies will leave him without excuse, for they are good; they are all that man needs for this religious duty, and all that God intends.

20–23. Birds and Fish. This is as far as the products of matter can be carried, and in the account of the *fifth day* we meet once more with the word "create." A new element has to be introduced—that of life. As we have already seen, vegetable life does not properly come under that head for the ancient East. In animal life we have a factor for which there is no existing basis in matter or in its products; God must step in and fashion something entirely new. So the waters swarm with life, manifested first in the creatures of the seas and oceans, then in the winged things that fly in the empty space between the earth and the heavens. And this time it is not enough that God should merely pronounce them good. He has a special relation to these beings in whom there is implanted a second grade of his creative power; he blesses them and bids them multiply. This is significant for the writer's point of view. The reproduction of plants, their seed and fruit-production is automatic; that of the animal kingdom is due to conscious will, and needs both divine authority and divine command.

24–31. Land Animals and Man. To the *sixth day* are assigned the two final acts. The first of these is the production of the terrestrial animals, who are drawn from the earth as the fish have been drawn from the sea. Linked in a certain way with them, through the elements which compose his physical frame, comes man. God is represented as consulting (*us—our*) as to the formation of humanity, in language which suggests (though other explanations have been given) that we have here a relic of the old polytheistic phraseology which has escaped the careful expurgation of the writer. A further hint of a lower theological position has been seen by some in the repeated phrase *in our image, in his image, in the image of God,* which is thought to point to a time when men believed that God had a material frame like that which man possesses. Yet it is more probable that the expression *in the image of God* has no physical implications, but is meant to suggest that man differs from all the rest of the creation in the possession of self-conscious personality, in which he alone of all creatures resembles God. (See art., *O.T. Conception of God,* p. 158.)

In v. 27 for the third time we meet the word *create.* Again a new element has been introduced into the world, and previous acts of creation will not account for it. Man shares in the physical nature of the universe, and in the life found in fish and bird and beast. But these two factors alone will not account for him; he is created in the image of God, and, unlike any other being, has something possessed by the Creator and not merely by creation.

Man is thus the crown and supreme glory of the whole universe—just because he is greater than the universe. Physically feebler than many of the animals, he is yet their lord. We have a picture of a natural kingdom, with no internal warfare, but with a monarch. All live at peace with one another, since the vegetable world supplies all needed food. Over all, as God's vicegerent, stands the one being who really resembles his Maker—man.

CHAPTER II

1–4a. The Sabbath. The story of creation finds its climax in an item of ritual which was fundamental to the pious Jew. God's *work* has occupied him six "days," and he takes the *seventh,* the day of "cessation," for himself. There is thus a "tabu" on it; it is "holy," set apart from the affairs of ordinary life. Such a *seventh-day* festival seems to have been customary in Mesopotamia, and parallels observed in the O.T. and elsewhere have suggested that originally the "Sabbath" of the western Semites occurred not once a week but at the full moon only. The transference of the name to a weekly festival will then have taken place under Babylonian influence, possibly during the Exile. It may be well to insist once more that no one has ever supposed the narrative to be the free invention of the exilic or post-exilic period. It undoubtedly contains and is based on far older material, but this does not exclude the possibility that it was only at a comparatively late period that the form we have in our Bibles was attained.

A Second Account of Creation. (From J; 4b-25.) The J account of creation presents striking differences from P. There is no true cosmogony; except for the absence of rain (which is not mentioned in any J passage till the Flood), the world as we know it is assumed. The order of events is different; man is the first object created, woman the last, and her formation is due to man's spiritual need for companionship, not to the necessity for reproduction. There is some strange geography; the rivers Pishon (the Oxus?), Nile, Tigris, and Euphrates have a common source. The conception of Jehovah is extremely primitive. The story, with all its naïve beauty, is intended for an audience intellectually and spiritually immature.

4b–17. Man in the Garden of Eden. Jehovah, finding the clay moistened by the heavy mist, models a man. This might be done by any skilled potter, but Jehovah does more; he breathes into the figure, and so the man comes to life, not merely a toy, but a living soul. There is as yet no suitable home for him, but the need is met by the planting of a garden, whose trees are made to grow out of the ground. The garden is situated in Eden, to the east, and its produce includes trees good for food, ornamental plants, and two others with special qualities, the tree of knowledge and the tree of life.

In the garden the man is placed, with a double duty to perform. First, he has to be the servant of the ground, rendering to it those offices which it will naturally reward with its fruits; and, in the second place, he has to protect it against unnamed enemies. Finally the man may enjoy the fruits of his work; the fruit of the tree of the knowledge of good and evil alone is reserved. If man knew what was good for him—not necessarily morally good—he would be on a level with Jehovah. So the penalty for disobedience is instant death; the man will not be allowed to live out his natural term.

18–20. Creation of Animals. Jehovah is deeply concerned with the interests of his man, and observes his loneliness. But he does not know how the need is to be met, and, as a first experiment, constructs other beings in the same way as he had made the man—though it is not said that he breathed into them. In order to find out whether the experiment is successful, he brings the animals to the man. As each beast comes before him, he utters an exclamation, from which Jehovah judges whether the particular animal is suitable or not. Surely, among so many forms one at least will be satisfactory? As each beast appears, the man utters a sound, which becomes its name—a name is usually the first exclamation of the parent on seeing the newly born child; that is why so many Hebrew names are prayers—but though there is a large variety of exclamations, and, therefore, of names, the man says nothing to any of them which indicates that he has found what he needed.

21–25. Formation of Woman. The experiment has, therefore, failed, and Jehovah has recourse to a totally new method. He sends the man into a deep anæsthetic sleep, such as that which a divine power may always use when it seeks to work on man, and—though the man seems to know what is happening—without hurting him takes a rib from his side. This he "builds" up into a fresh shape, though he is first careful to close up the hole left in the man—he will not have his creature damaged. Then he brings the new object back to the man, and is greeted with an exclamation which shows that this time the experiment has been entirely successful. Classical English has no phrase which comes near to being an equivalent to the Hebrew idiom here used. "This is the stroke" would be a literal rendering, and we may compare slang expressions such as "to hit the nail on the head," "this is absolutely *it*," to convey to our minds something of the feeling which lies behind the Hebrew words. Thus the words put into Adam's mouth by Milton: ". . . so absolute she seems, and in herself complete" (*Paradise Lost*, bk. viii, 547–8). Then follows the man's reason: the new being is of his very substance. So the exclamation for her shall be *Wo-man*, for "from-man" was she taken. The narrator adds a note to the effect that this explains why men leave their parents but not their wives, why they make new homes for themselves with their wives. Finally it is noted that, in the absence of knowledge, there is no such thing as sex-consciousness in them (cf. 2¹⁻⁷, notes).

This is not history, nor is it science—it was never intended to be either. Some would call it folklore, and would point to many parallels in the early stories of other races. It—to repeat a principle which ought never to be forgotten—must be remembered that each age, each grade of development, has its own special method of instruction, and that to a comparatively unsophisticated people such a story as this is the best, perhaps the only, means of conveying Truth. It is of primary importance that even such people as those to whom this narrative was first addressed should realize the great fact that man owes to his God his own origin and also every benefit he possesses. It is instructive to compare this with similar stories elsewhere, and to appreciate the religious gulf which thus early separates Israel from other nations. If any insist on calling this folklore, let him do so in all reverence, remembering that it is consecrated folklore. (See further pp. 20, 226, 368b, and cf. Frazer, *Folklore in O.T.*)

CHAPTER III

Man's Temptation and Fall. This is really the story of the way in which man lost his chance of immortality. A story with the same general purpose was current in Babylonia, though, as usual in such cases, the details are widely different from what we find here. The Mesopotamian tradition sent a man, in despair at the common lot of death, to seek for the fruit of immortality, and explained how he was cheated by one of the gods into eating the fruit of death.

1–7. Temptation by the Serpent. The crafty enemy is the snake. He is the cleverest of all the beasts that Jehovah made; he stands erect and speaks with a human voice. Clearly he is not such a snake as men knew in later days. Still less is he the devil (a conception arising in Israel centuries after this story reached its present form; see p. 205), though he tempts man to do evil.

The conversation between the snake and the woman suggests with extraordinary psychological fidelity the main features of normal temptation. There is first the doubt cast on God. The attitude of Jehovah is misrepresented, and the snake asks, "Has God set you in the midst of this lovely garden, and yet denied you all its advantages?" His question implies that none of the fruit is permitted to the pair who have to work so hard to produce and preserve it. This misrepresentation is corrected, and the next step is to say: "God has forbidden you this one tree because he is jealous. He is afraid that you may be as good and as great as he is." The tempter next suggests the possibility of impunity. The terms of the divine command have implied that the tree is deadly poison; this, says the snake, is not true. On the contrary, it is a most valuable tree, and its virtues are more than medicinal. "To eat of it will raise you at once to the divine level, for all that you now lack is knowledge"—so he recommends the article which he wishes man to take. It may be remarked that there is nothing in the story as it stands which indicates that he is telling a lie, and we are free to suppose, if we wish, that he really stated the facts as they were known to him. Finally the desirability of the sin itself is emphasized, not only in the words of the snake but in the mind of the woman herself. Here, once again, we have an epitome of all temptation, and the woman falls. She takes some of the fruit, eats it, and gives it to her husband.

All that the snake has said comes true. They do not die, and they attain to knowledge. But, though clever, the snake is not as clever as Jehovah; though he knows a great deal, he does not know everything. He does not understand—at least he has not told the woman—what the first effect of the knowledge will be—a sex-consciousness which brings shame into the minds of the man and of the woman. It is to be noted that this is a peculiarly Semitic feeling. There are many races who have no objection to nakedness, because it does not awaken improper feelings in them, and evangelists as wise as Chalmers of New Guinea have not felt it necessary to insist on clothes as a necessary preliminary to a moral Christian life. But among Semitic peoples the attitude here represented is almost universal, and nudity is a terrible thing. Even the aprons of fig-leaves (which, perhaps, gave rise to the eastern tradition that the tree of knowledge was a fig-tree) do not give an adequate sense of protection in the presence of Jehovah.

8–21. Punishment for Disobedience. Jehovah delights to walk in the garden when the morning or evening breeze is blowing cool, and to enjoy the company and the conversation of his living toys. But now he cannot find them, and calls till they answer him. And though he is not omniscient, he is far wiser than the man or the snake, and he knows that this new shyness can have only one cause. The man's defense is not an attempt to blame the woman. He says, in effect, "You gave me the woman, so I supposed that anything she brought me had your sanction." If he blames anyone, it is Jehovah himself. But this explanation is not accepted; the woman is as free an agent as the man, and when Jehovah turns to her, she throws the final charge on the snake.

Judgment is then delivered. The snake is not even invited to make a defense, for his guilt is too obvious. He loses his erect posture, and is forbidden the vegetable food which he has hitherto shared with man and all other animals, and is condemned to eat earth. There is to be endless hostility between snakes and men, the one crushing the head of the other whenever opportunity arises, and the snake striking at the heel of man. Ancient zoology is often strange to us, and there is other evidence to show that the old Hebrew believed that earth was the normal food of snakes. It is certainly true that most snakebites are inflicted on the foot. Our narrative explains this as part of the "curse" or doom laid on the creature for having misled the woman.

The details of the woman's punishment are not certain, but it is clear that we have here also the explanation of familiar facts, which include the social inferiority of women as it appears in the East. There are references to the sex life, and, in particular, to the pains of childbirth, to which Hebrew women seem to have been more subject than others in the ancient world.

Jehovah then deals with the man. He too has to suffer, and the ground is placed under a curse which will react on him. He has always had to work, but his labors have hitherto been productive and comparatively painless. In future they will be exhausting and futile. It is not work that is the punishment, but the grim struggle against a hostile nature, which, unless he utterly spends himself, will give him only weeds instead of the plants he needs for food. At the close of the sentence the narrator appends two notes, one explaining the name the man gave to his wife and the other describing Jehovah's method of clothing the man and his wife. They are allowed to wear skins, though there is no hint as to the way in which these are procured. Probably neither the narrator nor his first hearers speculated as to whether any animals were killed, and, if not, whence the skins were derived.

22–24. Expulsion from the Garden. The snake's promises have thus been fulfilled, though with disastrous further consequences. The man has attained to knowledge, and he has not been immediately put to death. Yet death will one day be his portion, and he is condemned to a life of struggle. He has gained knowledge, but he has lost the friendship and confidence of his God. It would even seem that he has aroused Jehovah's fears, and there seems to be a real apprehension lest he should make use of his new powers still further. For in the garden there stands, not only the tree of knowledge, but also the tree of life; and if he once tastes of this he will be immortal, and the one divine prerogative that remains will be taken from Jehovah. So, in addition to the penalty already imposed, the guilty pair are driven out of the garden, and now he has to till the soil outside. Lest he should return Jehovah places a guard over the way. We often find in the ancient East figures of strange beings, half human and half animal, placed at the doors of palaces and of temples. It is clear that they represent guardian spirits, and, to judge from the description given by Ezekiel, and from other hints, they were known by the name of Cherub. Creatures of this kind are now stationed to the east of the garden, and (apparently in addition) a whirling sword of living flame keeps the way to the tree of life. Man has lost his last chance of immortality.

On the whole narrative one further remark may be made. We note a presentation of God and of his character, an ideal of religion, which are typical of a certain stage in the development of Israel, and, perhaps, of other nations as well. We see that Jehovah insists on his own superiority as compared with the man whom he has created. His only command is that the man shall not eat the fruit of the tree of knowledge, for to acquire what that food will give him will help to raise him to the level of God. When that command is broken a further danger is imminent, that the man will attain to immortality, and then there will be no difference at all in powers and in status between the Creator and the creature. This must be prevented at all costs, and the final act in the passage secures the permanent inferiority of man. Religion must consist in the reverent submission of the inferior to the superior, and in the recognition and maintenance of the supremacy of God over man. Friendship and affectionate association are certainly not excluded, but their basis must be the condescension of God and the humility of man. We shall meet with the same conception elsewhere in this book, and, indeed, it forms an outstanding feature of the religious thought of Israel throughout the history of the nation.

CHAPTER IV

1–16. Cain and Abel. The human race has now started on its career, and the more important conditions of life known in the early days of Israel have been explained. There are, however, further details which are to be traced back to the primitive world. There is, for instance, the distinction in the social order between the shepherd (usually a nomad) and the farmer, who must have a settled home. Further, there is need for an account of how crime, the wrong of man to man, first entered human life, and, it may be, it is felt that certain peculiarities of the life of two ancient tribes demand explanation. All these needs are met by the account of Cain, Abel, and Lamech, the first people to be mentioned after the initial pair. In all probability we are not intended to think of them as individuals primarily, though there are individual features in the story; they are types, and we may detect an element of tribal history. There is always antagonism between the nomad and the farmer, and the Kenites (cf. this name with Cain) formed a tribe in the early days of Israel (see 15[18, 19], and cf. Num. 24[21, 22]).

Cain's name is connected with the word "gotten" (v. 1); though this is an assonance rather than a derivation. Next comes Abel, the shepherd, apparently younger than the farmer—not the order usually accepted by modern students of social history. The contrast between the two comes out when each brings an offering to Jehovah, who prefers the produce of the shepherd to that of the farmer. Cain is jealous, and, since the story seems to be set in a world already well populated, lures Abel into the open country and kills him. Abel's blood lies uncovered on the ground, and blood, as the chief seat of life in the body, is, to the Hebrew mind, almost personal. It cries aloud to Jehovah, that the demand of the blood-feud may be satisfied (see art., *Bible Manners and Customs*, p. 75), for Jehovah, the God of these two, is the guardian of their blood. Cain's denial of his crime is futile, for Jehovah has the evidence of the blood before him, and passes on to give sentence. It is worth noting that Jehovah does not impose an arbitrary penalty on Cain; he merely states the inevitable effect of his crime. The ground has been compelled to receive a draught of that which it loathes; therefore its anger is roused against the person who has forced this upon it, and it will no more cooperate with him in the work of agriculture. Cain can no longer remain on the "ground," and he must be a wanderer, without home and without kin.

The world, as we have noted, is thought of as already well filled with men and women, and an unprotected and isolated stranger with neither kindred nor God to avenge him has small chance of escaping disaster. Jehovah himself has no animus against Cain, and, in order to protect him while he is far away, he sets a mark on him. Here we pass at once into tribal history. Cain is no longer an individual, but a clan, whose members are distinguished by some special mark which they bear. Anyone who sees that mark knows that the man who carries it belongs to a fierce and terrible people. Normally, if a member of a tribe is killed, the survivors exact a life for a life, but for each man killed this tribe will demand seven lives from the tribe of the offender (v. 15). The story of this fierceness has been combined with the old story of the murder of Abel and its consequences, and the latter now explains the habits of this clan. So, though the Cainites no longer dwell in the land which Jehovah is thought to hold as his own, his power can still reach and avenge.

17–26. Lamech and His Song. V. 17 begins a short genealogy, which differs markedly from those so frequent in the group which we call

P. Its purpose seems to be to connect Cain with Lamech, and there is a note of the building of a city called Enoch, so named after a son of Cain. There seems to have been some error in the transmission of the text, and probably Enoch himself was the founder of the city in question. The genealogy is carried to a generation beyond Lamech, and gives the origin of the tent-dweller, the musician, and the smith—all, curiously enough, features of life found among the nomads. This serves to introduce the very ancient song of Lamech, clearly a tribal saying. The men of the tribe are represented as telling their wives how savagely they avenge injuries. For an actual wound they are ready to take the life of a man, and even for a blow they will kill a boy. They compare themselves with the tribe of Cain, and claim that they are ten times as bloodthirsty as that bloodthirsty tribe, demanding, not seven lives for one, but seventy (cf. Mt. 18^{21-22}, notes).

The chapter and the section close with a note of the birth of Seth and of his son (vv. 25, 26). The latter is named Enosh—another word for "man"—and the remark is made that it was during his lifetime that the worship of Jehovah was first introduced.

Chapters 5^1 to 6^4: Antediluvian Man

This section forms a link between the story of creation and the next important point, the Flood. It illustrates the desire of the historian to narrow the range of interest till it centers on the immediate ancestors of Israel. Following Adam, Noah is the outstanding character, and this passage explains his antecedents and the reasons for the Flood. It falls into two parts: (a) a genealogy, bridging the period from Adam to Noah (ch. 5); (b) the sons of God and the daughters of men (6^{1-4}).

CHAPTER V

The Genealogy. This (from P) traces man through Seth, the third son of Adam. The word, *Adam*, here for the first time used as a proper name, means in Hebrew "a human being," or rather "humanity" as a species. In 1^{26} 2^5 and 5^1 it is clearly used in this general sense—elsewhere in these chapters it is used with the article, which should probably be inserted also in 3^{17}.

It is interesting to compare this passage with the Cainite genealogy (J) in 4^{17f}. Here we have nine generations, there six. Omitting the first three names in ch. 5 we find that of the remainder two, Enoch and Lamech, are identical with names in ch. 4, while there are close similarities in the rest. It is difficult to escape the suggestion that we have two recensions of one and the same genealogy, diverging at an early period, and current in different circles, yet both springing from the same source.

The names in themselves convey very little. They have been compared to the traditional lists of Babylonian antediluvian kings, but while the names have much in common, reigns of enormous length are assigned to the Mesopotamian monarchs; and if the material goes back to a common source, the Hebrew writers have introduced significant changes. *Methuselah* is remembered as the man who lived longest on earth, and the figures suggest that in the end he perished in the Flood. *Enoch* alone stands out as a real personality, and of him we have the simple statement that he walked with God, and he was not, for God took him. His is by far the shortest life in the list, and the explanation of this fact is that he made himself the familiar companion of God, and that God conferred on him the gift of immortality, taking him to dwell with himself. It is natural enough that legends should have grown about his name, and he became in later Judaism the center of a large eschatological literature (see art., *Intertestamental Literature*, pp. 197–8.)

CHAPTER VI

1–4. The Sons of God and the Daughters of Men. In this passage we are introduced to a strange old story which has largely escaped the modifications which a later theology might have made. Many explanations have been given; the *sons of God* are sometimes interpreted as angels, who for the sin described were driven from their heavenly abode (see art., *Intertestamental Religion*, p. 204). Evidently we have here a narrative which originated in days so early that men still believed in the existence of a multitude of deities. Alongside of—almost compared with—the "gods" of vv. 2 and 4 we have *Jehovah* in v. 3, and we are led to suspect that he is still only one of a number of beings of the same order and species as himself, though he may be superior to the rest. The full significance of the name came much later (see Ex. $3^{13, 14}$, notes).

These other divine beings regard the daughters of men as suitable mates for themselves, and from their marriages spring the famous heroes and giants of whom ancient legend told. Jehovah, on the other hand, looks on them as his creatures, and sees to it that his Spirit, that power which at the first gave man life, shall not dwell for unlimited periods in man. To ancient Hebrew thought man was an animated body, and when the spirit was withdrawn, he ceased to live. That spirit had been bestowed by Jehovah; it was, as we have already noted, a power almost personal, and it could be recalled by him who had given it. A limit of a hundred and twenty years is fixed, that man may not live long enough to encroach on the prerogatives of his Maker.

CHAPTERS 6^5 TO 9^29: THE FLOOD

The story of a universal Flood which destroyed nearly every living thing is found in the folklore of many peoples. These traditions differ in details very widely, though occasionally we find resemblances which suggest a common origin. Whether all go back to a single catastrophe, or whether similar events took place in different parts of the world, is a question which must be left to the individual student for decision. The two traditions—taken from J and P—preserved here are not dissimilar, but are yet different enough to make it advisable to look at them separately. (This may be done more conveniently by disregarding the chapter divisions; the succeeding paragraphs, therefore, are based on chs. 6–9.)

5–22. See below under chs. 7–9.

CHAPTERS VII, VIII, IX

The Flood. Throughout the J story we note the naïve outlook of the narrator, and his very elementary theology. Jehovah is described in anthropomorphic terms: He shuts Noah into the ark and uses the natural rain, though in an unnatural quantity, to produce the catastrophe; he suspects he has made a mistake in creating man, and is so affected by the smell of sacrifice that he realizes that he has come near to making a greater mistake in destroying man. Yet there are signs of a high moral standard; it is because of man's wickedness that he punishes him, and it is Noah's high character which appeals to him, and induces him to warn and save him. It will be noted that he leaves Noah to find out by his own experiment when the earth is dry enough for him to come out of the ark. As subsidiary features we observe that the Flood lasts for less than seventy days, and that, as in the Abel story of ch. 4, the use of animal food is assumed.

In the P narrative we find ourselves in a different atmosphere, though the facts are the same: We have the same ethical basis for the action of God, and the same recognition of Noah's goodness—like Enoch, he "walked with God"; we have the exact details of the ark and the dates of the stages in the Flood itself. The catastrophe is not produced simply by rain, but by a temporary collapse of the structure of the cosmos, through which water streams in above and below from the chaos outside (cf. p. 120). The conditions are maintained for a hundred and fifty days, and the whole duration of the Flood is at least a year. (For the distribution of the material among the two sources see Brightman, *Sources of the Hexateuch*, pp. 36–38; 215–218.)

The Survivors. Following the Flood the story of humanity begins anew. Just as the first human pair were ordered to increase and fill the earth, so the survivors of the Flood are instructed to repopulate it. The authority originally conferred over all the lower orders of being is confirmed, and one new element is introduced into life—the flesh of animals may in future be used as food. To this permission, however, a restriction is added. The sanctity of blood must be maintained, and in no circumstances whatever must it be eaten. The same principle will apply to man as to the beasts; whoever sheds the blood of another must submit to the law of blood-revenge, for the blood is a living, almost a personal entity, and will not be satisfied till it has been appeased by the blood of the slayer himself. And God proclaims himself its Vindicator against the aggression both of man and of beast.

The Rainbow. Lest man should have to live in constant dread of a repetition of the disaster which has thus ended the first age of his history, God grants a promise and a covenant: he will never again bring such a Flood over the earth. And as a sign, to reassure men when they are fearful in time of rain, he calls attention to the bow in the cloud. It is not suggested that there had been no rainbow before the Flood, but it is to have a new function in the life of the world, and men are to remember that He who set it there will keep his word (9^8-17).

Once again we have a story common in its broader outlines to many peoples. The forms in which it has come down to us clearly did not originate in Palestine, but in some country of wide level plains such as Mesopotamia, and the story which shows the closest resemblances is that which we know from Babylonian sources. But, again, the differences are more significant than the resemblances, for the old story is made to play a new part in the history alike of religion and of human development. It marks a fresh stage in that human order whose basis, to the mind of the writer, is the relation of man to God, and dwells not merely on the power of God, but also on his fidelity. Some would call this too folklore; if so, once more, it is consecrated folklore (cf. Frazer, *Folklore in O.T.*).

Noah's Drunkenness. This story (9^{18-28}) presents us with a new picture of Noah, the first cultivator of the vine and the first man to suffer from drunkenness. It also includes a very ancient curse on Canaan and a blessing on Japheth. These last two must be very ancient indeed, and belong to the early days of the Semitic race. The story of Noah is difficult to reconcile with the presentation given in the Flood narrative, and probably comes from a different cycle, though as it stands it belongs to the same general group of passages.

It seems that two different themes have been combined. In the first place we have the sin of Ham, and in the second the curse of Canaan. Though the latter is introduced as the son of Ham, yet the curse has every appearance of having been independent in origin of the preceding narrative, and of having sprung from the days when Israel was still struggling with the older inhabitants of the land. It is interesting to notice that Ham and Canaan were connected by ancient Israel, for the Canaanitish peoples were of true Semitic stock, and spoke Hebrew, a language akin to the Aramaic of the ancestors of Israel, while the other Hamitic peoples are all African. The connection of the two races may be due to the fact that Palestine was an Egyptian province at the time when Israel entered the land.

Noah's drunkenness, the mockery of Ham, and the modest piety of Shem and Japheth bring out strongly the Hebrew sense of shame. None but a drunken man would allow himself to be exposed, and the worst insult that one man could put on another was that which Ham offered his father (3^{7}, notes). The incident is, no doubt, due to very ancient tradition, and is used to introduce the curse on Canaan. With the latter are combined blessings on Shem and Japheth. The text seems to have been incorrectly transmitted in the former, and it has been suggested that it ran, "Bless, O Jehovah, the tents of Shem, and let Canaan be servant to him." The latter is a play on the name of Japheth.

Chapters 10^{1} to 11^{9}: Recovery of Man and Repopulation of the Earth

This section bridges the space between the two critical personalities, Noah and Abraham. It falls into two parts: (a) a genealogy which occupies ch. 10; (b) an account of the way in which differences in language arose (11^{1-9}).

CHAPTER X

The Descendants of Noah; Three Groups. The genealogy in ch. 10 is clearly composite, one element connecting itself with the type of genealogy we find in ch. 5 (P), the other, with its occasional personal notes, belonging to J. (See Brightman, *op. cit.*) Both seem to proceed on the same general principle—that of describing racial and geographical affinities as though they were family relationships. This was a familiar method in the ancient East, and even the Greeks used it in describing the main divisions of their people.

The arrangement in P is comparatively simple. There are three main groups of peoples, northern, southern, and eastern. The first are derived from Japheth, the second from Ham, and the third from Shem. Most of the names in the first group are familiar to us from other sources, and all except the Medes belong to Asia Minor or the Mediterranean coast lands. The geographical knowledge of the day evidently did not extend as far as continental European Greece, though the islands (v. 5) may include the Greek settlements in the Ægean. Most of the peoples in the second group also are referred to elsewhere in ancient records. They are not all African, for Seba was a district in southern Arabia and, as we have seen, Canaan is reckoned with Egypt. The third table includes the chief races of Mesopotamia, though it is curious to find that there is no mention of the Babylonians. Possibly the list was compiled at a time when Babylon was subject to Assyria and was not thought worthy of separate mention.

The other table of nations (in J) begins with the mention of Cush, who is not the descendant of Ham already mentioned, but the eponymous ancestor of an entirely different group, that of Mesopotamia. Notable among these names is that of Nimrod, who is not a people but an individual, regarded as the first man who attempted to form a great empire. No name resembling this has yet been found among early Mesopotamian monarchs, but the picture of the great king who was also a mighty hunter is one with which we are very familiar in Assyrian sculpture and records. The distribution of the "sons" of Egypt reflects the political situation of the second half of the second millennium B.C., with nominal Egyptian control over Palestine and Phœnicia, and with Hittites and Philistines in the country, though neither is dominant. The name "Shem" is here used simply to cover the descendants of Eber, the eponymous ancestor of the Hebrews (a much wider term than Israelite), and it is curious to note that most of the tribes under this head which can be identified at all seem to come from southern Arabia—in the other genealogy assigned to Ham.

CHAPTER XI

1–9. The Origin of Different Languages. It is always unintelligible to primitive peoples that there are differences in speech between the various tribes and nations, and many early peoples have stories which are intended to explain this fact. Israelite tradition connected the differences with the building of Babylon or of one of the great temple-towers or *ziggurats*, characteristic of Babylonian temples. The name "Babel" (of which "Babylon" is a later Greek form) means literally "gate of god," but is connected in this narrative with a Hebrew word *bālal* = "mix," "confuse." We may keep the assonance—though not the exact idea—by using the word "babble."

Mesopotamian theology held that the true home of the gods was in a mountain, far north of Babylonia, and to make a suitable home it was necessary to imitate this mountain home as far as possible. Hence the temples always had great towers, with successive stories of decreasing height. They were built, as the narrative correctly states, mainly of unburned bricks, though faced with harder material, for there is no building stone in southern Babylonia, and where mortar of any kind is needed bitumen is used. In the narrative we notice the naïve and elementary theology which we have observed elsewhere. The building of the tower is interpreted as an attempt to invade the sky, the home of Jehovah, though the reason is ostensibly that there may be a central rallying point for all mankind. Jehovah is alarmed at this invasion of his privileges; hence his action is a defense of his prerogatives.

We thus reach the end of the first epoch in the history of man, as conceived by the pious Israelite. The human race has been brought into being, in a world especially prepared, and the interest has gradually narrowed till it rests on a single family. One great critical event, the Flood, stands half-way down the story, and a minor occurrence, the building of Babel and the scattering of the nations, has been mentioned. All that has happened is the work of a single power; Jehovah has been preparing the way for his people. He made the world, he created man, he eliminated the hopelessly sinful, he scattered men throughout the world. In everything that has taken place his will has been manifest. Nothing has been without a reason. After long preparation the stage is now ready for his particular action upon those who are to be the ancestors of the Chosen People.

II. CHAPTERS 11^{10} TO 25^{18}: ABRAHAM

10–26. Abraham's Ancestry Traced to Noah. This is a simple genealogy, in P's usual formulæ, bridging the period from Noah to Abraham.

27–32. The Genealogy of Terah. As it is to Abraham that later Israel looked as the real founder of the nation, this division of the book of Genesis properly gives his genealogy, taken from P, which explains how Abraham came to western Asia. His father, Terah, is represented as moving from southern Babylonia —from Ur of the Chaldees—at an advanced age, after one of his sons had died. Since it is expected that the son will survive the father, special note is taken of the fact that Haran dies *in the presence* (or *sight*) *of his father*, i.e., while his father was yet living (v. 28); Terah takes with him his remaining two sons, Nahor and Abram, and his grandson, Lot, son of the dead Haran. The names of the wives of Abram and Nahor are given, and it is observed that Sarai had borne Abram no son. The migration reaches Haran, an important center roughly midway between Mesopotamia and Palestine, and there the aged Terah dies.

CHAPTER XII

1–9. The Promise Made to Abram and His Journey to Palestine. The thread of 11$^{27-32}$ is continued in vv. 4b (from *and Abram was . . .*) and 5, inserted by the compiler in the main narrative, which clearly comes from the southern group of traditions. Except in v. 5 (which implies a fairly long residence in Haran) there is no mention of Abram's original home, and the southern tradition leaves us free to assume that his call came to him either in Ur or in Haran. But that is a minor detail and does not affect the main facts. Wherever he was at the time, Abram heard the voice of Jehovah, and received his promise of blessing. He will be so prosperous that when in after ages men wish to invoke the highest good for themselves or for one another they will say, "May you be blest as Abram was" (this is probably the meaning of v. 3b; cf. 26^{4} mg.).

With this promise, Abram moves westward till he reaches Palestine, and then turns southward through the country. Several places are mentioned where later tradition recorded his presence. One of these is in the *Shechem* district, and there Abram receives a theophany at the Terebinth of Divination, a sacred tree whose name was probably explained by the story. Here he builds an altar, and a second at some spot not closely specified between Bethel and Ai. We have thus two ancient sanctuaries whose foundation is carried back to Abram. Thence he continues his journey southward till he reaches the Negeb, the dry pasture-land to the south of Judah.

10–20. Abram in Egypt. Temporary migration to Egypt in time of famine was not infrequent in Palestine and northern Arabia, for Egypt was one of the most fruitful countries in the ancient world. It is, therefore, by no means unnatural to find Abram following the usual custom. We may be sure that the Israelite tradition loved to dwell on the physical beauty of its great ancestress, with the implication that she was unapproached by any of the Egyptian women. Abram himself does not appear in a favorable light, especially when contrasted with the mild and generous Egyptian king. Nothing is said as to the means whereby Pharaoh discovered the cause of the plagues, and it is significant that when the deceit is detected no harm befalls the deceiver. Judged by modern moral standards, Abram's conduct is indefensible, and the story helps us to realize how much men have learned in the succeeding centuries. To early Israel it was probably a source of glee that their forefather could so successfully hoodwink the mighty king of Egypt, and in the end make capital out of his very difficulties and dangers.

CHAPTER XIII

Abram Separates From Lot; Abram's Magnanimity. The narrative introduces us to the beauty and richness of the southern end of the Jordan Valley. It is possible that the writer means us to think that there is as yet no Dead Sea; it certainly is implied that the catastrophe which turned the district to the south of it into a barren desert has not yet taken place. Lot, given the choice by Abram, who is ready to surrender his rights rather than engage in strife, selects this as his home, though it brings him into contact with the city dwellers. To the wandering shepherd, the city often appears a nest of iniquity; and this is one of the many passages in J which glorify the moral value of pastoral life as compared with that of the settled community. There is a lofty hill near the site of the ancient Bethel from which a wide view can be obtained, and Abram is depicted as standing on its summit and seeing the country stretch away to the far horizon on every side. This, says Jehovah to him, is to be his possession, and, in the persons of his descendants—so numerous as to outnumber the grains of sand on the seashore—he is to be its owner. (See art., *Land of Palestine*, pp. 56–7.)

The passage sets before us Israel's ideal man, peaceful, generous, humble, receiving the ideal blessing, namely, the expansion of his own personality into a great nation and the ownership of wide, fruitful lands.

CHAPTER XIV

Abram and the Mesopotamian Rulers. Perhaps no narrative in the whole story of the Patriarchs has aroused more discussion than this. It comes from a source which is independent of the main groups of tradition represented elsewhere in the book, and links the life of Abram with the great world even more closely than the references to Egypt. The latter give us no direct indication as to the Pharaohs with whom Abram and his immediate descendants came into contact. In addition to the Mesopotamian kings, we hear of *Melchizedek*, king of Salem (vv. 18–20; cf. Heb. 5[6-10], notes), but Abram's meeting with him is not necessarily a part of the original narrative; it is introduced most abruptly, and v. 21 follows naturally and immediately on v. 17.

The historical *possibility* of such an expedition has never been questioned, though certain details have been doubted; for instance (a) the exact line of march followed by the Mesopotamian kings, which took them through lands where the water supply is quite inadequate for any considerable armed force; (b) the names of the five *Canaanite* kings, which look like the inventions of a hostile narrator, since they all suggest wickedness and hatred; (c) the number of Abram's servants, which is identical with that which can be obtained by adding up the numerical values of the letters composing the name "Eliezer" (see 15[2, 3]). The Melchizedek incident, also, has aroused some suspicion; but, as we have seen, it may have been a later insertion in the story.

The discoveries of the last half century have thrown a flood of light on early Mesopotamia, and it has been claimed in some quarters that the historical accuracy of this narrative has been fully substantiated by archæological evidence. However, it may be stated clearly and emphatically, that not one of the points mentioned above has received the slightest support from any archæological material that has come to light. Moreover, with reference to the events in which the Mesopotamian kings participated, archæology goes no further than to reveal certain names which may be identical with at least some of the names given to the four kings. Thus Khammurabi of Babylon is possibly—even probably, though Assyriologists have not always agreed on this point —the original of *Amraphel*. A king of Larsa, a generation before Khammurabi, was called

Warad-Sin, which name, owing to the peculiar script used in ancient Mesopotamia (cuneiform ideographic and syllabic writing) may have been equivalent to Eri-aku (=*Arioch*). *Tidal* has been identified with a certain Tu-ud-khu-la, whose name appears as that of a contemporary (roughly) of Khammurabi, though he is nowhere described as a king. *Goiim* may be a corrupt form of "Gutim," a geographical name of the period, or (with the meaning "nations") it may refer to hordes from the north, possibly the ancestors of the Medes. Finally *Chedorlaomer* is probably a Hebrew way of writing the name "Kudur-lagamar," a perfectly good Elamite name, though it has not yet been identified for certain on any inscription. But the father of Warad-Sin was an Elamite king Kudurmabuk, which name contains the name of the same deity and is formed on the same general principle.

The style of the narrative is archaistic (rather than archaic) and suggests an imitation of ancient records. Obviously, the fact that the names of the persons mentioned are genuine does not certify the historicity of the events in which they are said to have played a part. In all probability, a comparatively late writer, finding an ancient tradition of a Mesopotamian raid into Palestine which took place not long before 2000 B.C., fitted it into the story of Abram, in order to show the valor and military prowess of his hero. We see Abram, not merely as the peaceful shepherd, but the man of action, faithful to the duties imposed by ties of kinship, bold, swift to move, generous and unselfish.

The interlude of *Melchizedek* is most significant, as it traces back the sanctity of Jerusalem (clearly the place indicated as *Salem*) to a very early period, and implies that even the earliest ancestor of Israel recognized this as the proper place at which tithes should be paid. In its present form, then, the story dates from a comparatively late period, when attempts were being made to insist on Jerusalem as the one legitimate sanctuary for all Israel, though we may safely assume that the narrative is based on ancient, possibly very ancient, tradition. It is noticeable that the divine name used is "El Elyon"—*the Most High God;* evidently, those responsible for the present form of the story are aware of the view that it was not till Israel reached Sinai that the name "Jehovah" was revealed (see Ex. 3^{13-22}, notes).

CHAPTER XV

The Covenant With Abram. It would appear that we have here an interweaving of two narratives, one of which is very incomplete. (This is suggested by the repetition of the same idea in vv. 2, 3, and by the fact that while v. 5 gives us a night scene, vv. 7–21 describe events which took place in the daytime, and ended only as darkness was falling.) According to one—the more fragmentary—Abram complains that in spite of the promises which have been made to him, he has no son to carry on his life and personality, and his successor must be a slave, one born to slavery in his own household. (So much seems to be clear, though the meaning of v. 2b is uncertain and its text doubtful.) The answer is that his descendants shall be as numerous as the stars (v. 5); in vv. 13–16 a brief account of their history up to the time of their actual occupation of the land is given.

The other narrative records a covenant made between Jehovah and Abram. Once more we meet with the naïve presentation and the anthropomorphic theology characteristic of other stories of this type (cf. 2^{4b-25}, notes). The covenant is ratified by means of a ceremony which is familiar to us also from other quarters: Certain victims are slain, and their bodies are cut into two parts across the middle; the parts are then placed on the ground, with a space between them; naturally vultures and kites come down on the carcasses, but Abram drives them away, till, toward evening, as the sun is about to set, he falls into that peculiar state into which God throws men when he wishes to act directly upon them (cf. 2^{21} Job 6^{13}). Though the sun is not yet below the horizon, the world grows suddenly and mysteriously dark to his senses, and in the midst of the gloom he sees Jehovah, in the form of fire, passing between the pieces of the victim. Doubtless previously he himself had walked between them, for the essence of this form of covenant ritual lay in the fact that both parties walked between the pieces of the victim. Thus they both entered into it, became part of it, formed one continuous living entity with it, and therefore with one another. In the life taken from the slain creatures they found a unifying force which bound them to one another; and so, for the purposes of the covenant, they were no longer two separate entities, but one (cf. Heb. 6^{13-20}, notes). The terms to be observed by Abram are not stated, but the divine promise is clearly set forth; Abram, in the persons of his descendants, is to possess the whole of the land of Palestine.

CHAPTER XVI

Hagar and the Birth of Ishmael. This narrative is intended to illustrate the relationship between Israel and certain Bedouin tribes who went under the general name of Ishmael. The Arabs to this day believe themselves to be the descendants of Abram and Hagar. The characters are clearly brought out: *Abram,* kindly, patient and just, longing for a son, yet not suggesting means whereby he might obtain one; *Sarai,* the typical Oriental woman, unable to endure the disgrace of childlessness, and willing to bear a son by proxy, yet bitterly jealous and unreasonable when the desired event happens; *Hagar,* the slave, unable to behave modestly when she feels that she has risen above her mistress, and without strength of character to bear patiently her mistress' harshness; finally, *Ishmael,* the "wild ass of a man," the free, uncontrolled, swift, and unaccountable son of the desert, such as the Bedouin often are to this day.

There are other points of importance. For the first time we meet with a type of theophany through *the angel of Jehovah.* This seems in the first instance to have been simply another way of describing Jehovah himself, but there is beginning to arise a feeling that it is beneath his dignity to appear in all his fullness; consequently, the "angel" may be regarded as a subordinate manifestation, though not yet a distinct personality (cf. Ex. 13[21, 22] 14[19, 20] 33[14], notes). We observe too that it is from the events recorded here that a certain well gets its name. As the text stands the whole name is not explained, but it is possible that the latter part of v. 13 should read *I have seen a God and have survived after seeing him.* If so, the word "survived" would give a clue to the element "Lahai." This, however, is pure conjecture, and it may well be that this part of the name of the well had no explanation at all in the original narrative.

CHAPTERS 17[1] TO 18[15]: GOD'S COVENANT WITH ABRAHAM, AND THE PROMISE OF ISAAC

This section includes two narratives, both promising Abraham—17[5] records the change of the name from Abram to Abraham—a son. Both give an explanation of the name "Isaac," interpreting it as "laughter." This is more obvious in the former of the two, where Abraham is expressly told that the name is to be Isaac (17[19]); but it is equally clear from the other account that a reason for the name is being offered (18[12]).

CHAPTER XVII

Rite of Circumcision; Abraham to Have a Son. It will have been noticed that up to the present we have had only two extended narratives in the P group. One of these is the story of the creation and the other the story of the Flood. Each of them ends with the establishment of some feature of the ceremonial or religious life, creation culminating in the Sabbath, and the Flood in the permission to eat animal flesh, a permission which is connected with the prohibition of blood, and with the law of blood-revenge. This second narrative is concerned also with a "covenant," made by God with Noah, thus narrowing down, if we may use such a phrase to represent the view of the writer, the area of God's special interest to the sons of Noah. We notice the same general features here. We have a "covenant" made with Abraham (cf. the "covenant" in ch. 15), who is promised, not only that his posterity shall be very great, but also (when he suspects that the reference is to Ishmael) that a son will yet be born to Sarah, in spite of her apparently prohibitive age. The mention of Ishmael occasions the promise that he too will become a great nation, though, while the sons of the unborn child are to include kings, Ishmael's posterity will attain the rank only of princes. The superiority of Israel over Edom is thus doubly indicated by the higher title of its rulers and by its descent from the free wife, not from the slave (cf. Gal. 4[21-31], notes).

Just as the covenant with Noah is confirmed by the rainbow, the covenant with Abram is attested by three new names. The first is that of God himself, who reveals his name as "El Shaddai" (*God Almighty*). The precise meaning of this term has not been ascertained, and it was not understood even by the Greek translators of the Pentateuch in the third century B.C. But it is clear that it involved the communication to Abram of some special character in God; for a name to the ancient Hebrew was never merely a name; it was an essential element in the personality of him who bore it, and the communication of a particular name by God indicated that in a special way he was to be known to the man or men to whom the communication was made (cf. Acts 2[38], notes). Further, the name of Abram is to be *Abraham*—again a change whose significance is not clear. At the same time the woman, through whom El Shaddai will fulfill his part in the covenant, is called *Sarah,* instead of Sarai. Once more we have to confess that the difference between the two names is not clear. Either might mean "princess" in Hebrew, but, as the family is represented as coming from Mesopotamia, it is more likely that the Babylonian significance—"queen"—is intended.

All this is God's side of the covenant. On the human side a new rite—new at least to Abraham—is established, that of *circumcision.* This was practiced by the Egyptians (and many other African peoples), and, in historic times, by all the nations round Israel except the Philistines. But it was not a Mesopotamian custom, and its institution here marks a clear and definite break with the past. Abraham, here as in all else the faithful worshiper, loses not a single day in fulfilling his part in the covenant; and we are allowed to suspect that it is as a result of this that Isaac, the first person to be born under the covenant, comes into being.

Thus is inaugurated a new stage in the history which the priestly writer has set himself to trace. The first is indicated by the creation, the second begins when humanity, purged of its wicked elements, makes a fresh start with Noah; here we have the further revelation signalized by circumcision and the new name, El Shaddai. The fourth is yet to come, and in Ex. 6^{3} for El Shaddai is substituted the "final" name for Israel's God, Yahweh, and in the covenant made through Moses, the true founder of the nation, the writer finds the completion of revelation as he understands it, and the goal toward which his history leads (cf. Ex. 3^{13-22}, notes).

CHAPTER XVIII

1–15. The Promise of a Son again Repeated to Abraham. This second narrative of the promise of Isaac exhibits all the characteristics which we have learned to associate with J. Abraham is still under the terebinth at Mamre (cf. 13^{18}), near Hebron. Revelation comes to him through a theophany; though it is noticeable that Jehovah does not come alone, and we may have here a relic of ancient polytheistic views which has been overlooked by the writer of the narrative. (Other explanations of the three persons have, of course, been given by both Jewish and Christian theologians.) We see Jehovah appearing as an ordinary traveler, and accepting the rich hospitality of a generous sheikh. No serious conversation is attempted till the visitors are served, and the courtesy of Abraham is carried to such lengths that he ministers to his guests in person, instead of committing the task to one of his numerous slaves. We have too the picture of Sarah, like a true Oriental woman, concealing herself from the visitors for whom she has cooked food, yet listening to what is being said, and ashamed of the laughter which has been forced from her by the suggestion that these two old people are to have a son born to them. But we have also a very important note—perhaps the climax of the whole passage—in v. 14; *nothing is too hard for Jehovah.* As sole Lord of creation he could do as he pleased; it was he who had made natural laws, and therefore he could "suspend" them.

Chapters 18^{16} to 19^{38}: The Destruction of Sodom and the Escape of Lot

Narratives which deal with Lot form no part of the more or less continuous story of the ancestors of Israel proper, and are digressions which explain the relation of Ammon and Moab to Israel. The narrative falls into four sections: (a) 18^{16-33}, the conversation between Jehovah and Abraham; (b) 19^{1-14}, Lot's entertainment of the divine messengers; (c) 19^{15-29}, the escape of Lot; (d) 19^{30-38}, the ancestry of Moab and Ammon.

16–33. Jehovah and Abraham. The aim of this section is to magnify the hero-ancestor of Israel. To the ancient mind God is always terrible; it is Jesus who alone has fully delivered the religious spirit from the dread of the "numinous." How great, then, must he be who not only dares to meet Jehovah face to face and to argue with him, but also succeeds in obtaining his request! We are already far on the way which led to the prophetic designation of Abraham as the "friend," the "lover" of Jehovah (2 Chr. 20^{7} Isa. 41^{8}). Further, we should note that Abraham's whole appeal is based on the assumption of the supremely moral character of Jehovah (v. 25). Here again we have a link with the teaching of the great prophets, and find an illustration of one of the fundamental distinctions between the faith of Israel and that of all other peoples of the ancient world.

CHAPTER XIX

1–14. The Sin of the Men of Sodom. There is hardly any passage in which the fundamental contrast between the good man and the wicked is more strongly brought out than it is here. On the one hand we have the Sodomites, first of all, presented as failing in the elementary duties of hospitality, and leaving them to a comparative stranger to perform (vv. 1, 2). Then we have them shown as given to that loathesome vice which owes its name to their behavior, and prepared to go to any length to gratify their lust (v. 5). Over against them stands Lot, fulfilling the duties of a host, and pressing on the strangers the courtesy which at first they are politely reluctant to accept (vv. 2, 3). Finally he feels so strongly the claims of his position as a host that he is prepared to make a sacrifice almost incredible in a Hebrew hero, and offer his own daughters to save his guests from indignity (v. 8). Once more we notice the stress laid in the patriarchal stories on the virtue of hospitality as one of the first and most exacting of all human duties. This is further illustrated by the fact that Lot's behavior meets with immediate reward; he is warned of the impending fate of Sodom, and given an opportunity of saving not only himself, but also any who are connected with him. Yet even his sons-in-law are men of Sodom, and he alone is righteous (v. 14).

15–29. Sodom and Gomorrah Destroyed; Escape of Lot. Since Lot's descendants were later located to the east of the Dead Sea, not to the south, it is sometimes supposed that the original story did not mention Zoar, and that vv. 17–22 are a later addition intended to explain how this little town continued to exist in the region of the catastrophe. Whatever one may think regarding details, it is clear that some tremendous event must have occurred in the Dead Sea region which later generations never forgot. V. 25 suggests a double tradition, for the word *overthrow* suggests an earthquake. Some have thought of an explosion of bitumen wells, others of a volcanic eruption. But whatever the physical cause, the moral and religious lesson remains unaffected. The sin of the cities meets with divine vengeance, while Lot's righteousness secures his safety in the midst of a disaster so great that in faraway Hebron Abraham can see the signs of it.

30–38. The Origin of the Moabites and Ammonites. These verses have been interpreted as a bitter sneer at Moab and Ammon. But it is possible that we have here a relic of a tradition which made the disaster universal, as was the Flood. In that case Lot's daughters must be regarded as heroines who adopted desperate measures to repopulate the earth.

CHAPTER XX

Abraham and Abimelech. This story (E) has parallels in chs. 12 and 26; each of the three narratives having its own characteristics. Even though Abimelech has done no intentional wrong, he and his realm are made to suffer. But God intervenes to prevent the worst happening, and warns the king of Gerar (between Beersheba and Kadesh) of the wrong he has nearly committed. God is interested in preventing sin, especially when it might defile or endanger the race which he has chosen as his own.

Abraham appears in a somewhat better light than in ch. 12. His lie about Sarah is not so direct a lie; it is true that they agree to conceal the fact that she is his wife, but at the same time the actual statement that they make is not false—she is, in a sense, his *sister* (v. 12). Further, Abraham, in spite of his cowardice, is represented as being a religious hero. He is great in the sight of God, and his prayer will avail for the healing of Abimelech.

Abimelech himself is favorably presented. Though he has sinned—or nearly sinned—in act, his conscience is clear, and he is prepared to make what restitution is possible, compensating both Sarah and Abraham. There is a touch of sarcasm in the way in which he insists on the brother-sister relation of Abraham and Sarah in making his expiatory gift. Unlike Pharaoh, he is magnanimous enough not to send Abraham away, but invites him to make his home where he will in his land.

CHAPTER XXI

1–21. The Birth of Isaac and the Expulsion of Ishmael. In the opening verses, describing the birth of Isaac, we have all three groups of narrative represented. E supplies only v. 6a. Since this single sentence taken from E is obviously a fragment of the tradition, it will be enough to note that it simply records a reason for Isaac's name—Sarah finds such joy in the event that she says "God has made laughter for me," i.e., "God has made me laugh."

P's stately, though summary narrative resumes the story of ch. 17; it records the fulfillment of God's promise, the naming of the child in accordance with the command given in 17^{19}, and his circumcision in accordance with the command recorded in 17^{12}.

J's narrative gives yet another explanation of the name of Isaac, and since this type of passage has already explained the word in 18^{12}, we may have here a later addition to the original J. Sarah gives her son his name because everybody will laugh at her for becoming a mother at such an age (cf. note above on v. 6a, which gives E's explanation of the name).

The continuation of the story in vv. 8–21 comes entirely from E, and is to some extent parallel with J's narrative in ch. 16. There is, of course, no discrepancy between the two stories, for J deals with the period before the birth of Ishmael. In both stories Sarah is represented as the rather small-minded, jealous woman. At the weaning-festival she sees Ishmael playing with her son (so probably the original text of v. 9) and is filled with anger at the thought that there is someone who may claim a share in the inheritance. In contrast to ch. 16, this passage represents Abraham as unwilling to accede to his wife's demand until he is directly ordered to do so by God himself.

The suffering and despair of the child and his mother are finely depicted. He is still small; the language of the passage implies that Hagar carried him until she was compelled to lay him under a bush. Especially touching is the mother's dread of seeing her child die. But her tenderness is matched only by that of God himself. He hears the cry and rescues the little one, showing Hagar where water may be found. It may well be that originally this story explained the name *Ishmael* = "God hears"; these words are at all events the key to the whole narrative. It is just because God hears the cry of the sufferer at the last extremity that Ishmael grew up to be the founder of the archer tribe that in after years bore his name (v. 20).

22–34. Abraham and Abimelech. This narrative is clearly composite, giving two reasons for the name *Beersheba*, the one being that current in the north—"the well of the oath"; the other that peculiar to J—"the well of the seven."

E's story connects with ch. 20. We are to suppose that, according to that group of narratives, the birth of Isaac and the expulsion of Hagar and Ishmael took place in Gerar. Curiously enough Gerar seems to be placed in v. 32 in Philistia. This is in any case an anachronism, for there were no Philistines in Canaan for centuries after the time of Abraham. The kindness and forbearance which Abimelech has shown to Abraham are not wholly disinterested, for the latter is very prosperous, and Abimelech and his chief captain Phicol (a name referable to none of the known languages of Canaan) seek to make a formal treaty with him. This is done by the exchange of gifts and by the oath of a covenant.

J assigns a different motive for the agreement. There has been a dispute over the ownership of certain wells. To settle the matter Abraham, who has failed to get satisfaction in answer to his complaints, sends seven sheep to Abimelech. By accepting them the latter acknowledges the giver's right to the wells in question, and they thus receive the name by which they are ever after known.

CHAPTER XXII

1–19. The Sacrifice of Isaac. This very familiar narrative is to be attributed in the main to E, though there is some ground for regarding vv. 15–19 as an appendix by a later editor. The story is told with matchless art, and with a masterly reticence which enables us to understand and interpret the feelings of the actors in spite of the fact that these are never mentioned. There are several points which need to be considered.

The first of these is the original significance of the story in its primitive form. No place named *Moriah* is known to us (2 Chr. 3[1] is probably based on a late and erroneous interpretation), but some scholars, finding a clue in v. 14, identify the spot with a certain Jeriel mentioned in 1 Chr. 7[2]. It is supposed that there was here an ancient sanctuary at which the first-born sons were commonly offered, and that this passage (in its original form) offered an explanation of the practice. Later Hebrew feeling modified the earliest tradition by the introduction of the surrogate. Others have thought this to be an explanation of the practice of substituting animals for the human victims, human sacrifice being common among Semitic peoples and others (cf. 2 Kings 3[27]). In favor of this view it may be pointed out that Abraham is certainly represented as believing that God might legitimately make such a demand of him, though fuller light must show that such an impulse must come from another source.

In the second place we have to note the use made of the old story by the writer. It is a test of Abraham's faith, and as such has been universally recognized. He can trust God, however strange his command may seem to be; the appendix recognizes that such confidence will meet with its reward in the reaffirmation of the divine promise (cf. Rom. 4, notes).

But there is yet a further significance to the narrative. As with the story in ch. 20, we have the picture of the divine plan surviving apparent difficulties. God's purpose is again on the verge of being finally frustrated, this time by the death of the person through whom its fulfillment is to be secured, but he finds again a way of escape, and triumphs over the obstacle. It is as though he were offering to man a supreme gift which is always imperiled but never destroyed—and he himself would not have it otherwise.

20–24. An Aramæan Genealogy. This is, apparently, from J, and is an account of the relation between Israel and the Aramæan tribes to the northeast of Palestine. It is necessary from the narrator's point of view, in order to explain events which are to be recorded later in the story of Jacob.

CHAPTER XXIII

The Death of Sarah and the Purchase of the Cave of Machpelah. It seems that this whole narrative comes from priestly sources; it was introduced to give an account of the way in which the first plot of ground passed into the possession of Israel. There is a stately courtesy about the narrative, which reflects the later view of the patriarchal life. Abraham has but his tent, and seeks a permanent resting place for his dead. In lordly fashion *Ephron*, who is not approached directly—another Oriental trait—offers not only the cave but also the whole field in which it is, for nothing. At the same time he mentions a very high price, which he regards as a trifle, and Abraham pays without a trace of that haggling which is the universal accompaniment of business in the East. So Abraham's first foothold in the home of his posterity is won through his bereavement.

CHAPTER XXIV

The Marriage of Isaac. The story as it has come down to us is essentially in a form current in the south, therefore J. But there are various slight divergences in the narrative which make us suspect we have here represented a double tradition, and that elements of both have been interwoven to produce the present narrative, though any detailed analysis must be uncertain. The narrative is a perfect specimen of the story-teller's art. We have the old *father*, at the point of death (he is clearly dead by the time the caravan returns), anxious above all things for the purity of the blood of his descendants, and refusing to allow it to be contaminated by intermarriage with the settled inhabitants of the land. There is the faithful and pious *slave*, concerned only to do the will of his master, and recognizing the divine aid which is granted to him.

On the other hand, there are the *Aramæans*, an interesting family: of the parents little is said; but they recognize that since Jehovah has so clearly shown his will, the matter is out of their hands. Yet they press on the slave an extensive hospitality, which he refuses only on the ground that it might be a betrayal of that divine grace which has so consistently been shown to him. At the same time (and this is one of the discrepancies in the narrative) *Rebekah* is left to make a perfectly free choice. Her decision is in full accord with her general character, and she is pictured as an ideal figure of Oriental girlhood, modest, kindly, generous, and pious. Her brother *Laban* is already displaying features which manifest themselves even more strongly in later life (see chs. 29–31). What convinces him is neither the demand of kinship nor the will of God, but the sight of the costly jewels on his sister's arm. Finally we have the presentation—lightly drawn as are all the personal references to *Isaac*—of the young bridegroom, whose mother's death, years before, has left a gap in his life which is only filled when another woman comes to enter into a yet closer and dearer relationship. It only remains to add that in v. 60 the narrator has included a bridal blessing which may go back to a very ancient time.

CHAPTER XXV

1–6. The Children of Keturah. This is apparently from J, and is intended to state the connection between Israel and certain tribes of the eastern and southern wilderness which Israel regarded as somewhat distantly related. The best known of these is Midian, for the Asshurites mentioned here are clearly not to be identified with the Assyrians, in spite of the similarity in name. By describing these tribes as descended from a secondary wife, the Israelite historian suggested that while the kinship was admitted, these others stood on a lower level. The same point is brought out by the statement that Abraham dismissed the sons of the concubines (probably including Ishmael) with gifts, that they might not in any way interfere with Isaac, the legitimate son of the promise.

7–11. Death and Burial of Abraham. This is clearly from P. We notice that there is apparently no hint of the expulsion of Ishmael or of the birth of other sons. Isaac and his half-brother seem to be living together, at least till the death of their father, and to unite in paying him the last rites due to the dead.

12–18. The Genealogy of Ishmael. This genealogy rounds off the story of Abraham, by tracing, as far as is necessary from the point of view of the writer, the other branch of Abraham's family. This done, the narrative can now concentrate on Isaac and his children.

19–34. See below.

III. Chapters 25^{19} to 36^{43}: Jacob

This section of the book of Genesis falls into three parts, illustrating (a) the relations between Jacob and his brother Esau (25^{19}–27^{46}); (b) the relations between Jacob and Laban (28^{1}–32^{3}); and (c) the narratives of Jacob's residence in Canaan, leading up to the fourth section of the book, the story of Joseph. There are a few obtrusive incidents and passages, of which the most noticeable is ch. 26, which deals with the fortunes of Isaac, and strongly recalls incidents recorded of the life of Abraham. The three main types of narrative—southern, northern, and priestly—still appear, though there is very little priestly narrative, those parts of the section being mainly confined to lists of names.

CHAPTERS 25[19] TO 27[46]: JACOB AND ESAU

There are two main incidents, the exchange of the birthright and the theft of the blessing, designed to explain two facts, the hostility of the semi-nomad or even semi-Bedouin people of Edom to Israel, and the fact that the former was, throughout a great part of the monarchic period, subject to the latter. There is a suggestion, borne out by occasional references, that originally Edom was the stronger of the two. In exilic and post-exilic times Israel developed a bitter and vindictive hatred of Edom, which goes back to the part played by the southern people in the sack of Jerusalem, 586 B.C. (See the commentary on Obadiah.) Our present narratives took form some centuries before this event, and show no signs of its effect on the mind of Israel.

19–28. The Birth of Isaac's Sons. The two boys are more than mere individuals; they are types of humanity, and the rivalry between the two is foreshadowed even before they are born, in the oracle granted to their anxious mother. The narrative explains their names: *Jacob* is connected with a noun meaning "heel," from which is derived a verb meaning "trip up," "overreach." *Esau* is often known by two other names, and, curiously enough, it is these that are alluded to here, *Edom*, meaning "red," and *Seir*, meaning "hairy." There is also an indication of the sociological contrast between them: Esau is the typical Bedouin chief, a hunter who has no property beyond his weapons, and lives on wild game, besides (presumably) what he can gain by plundering his neighbors. Jacob, on the other hand, is "civilized"—that is why his mother likes him more than his brother—the typical nomad shepherd, who has a tent and flocks of his own, and so he stands for the higher, more developed social order (v. 27). In a sense the rivalry between the brothers is the conflict between the two levels of culture.

29–34. Jacob Gains the Coveted Birthright. We have here an explanation of the fact that, though Edom came to its national heritage earlier than Israel, it nevertheless had to take second place. The narrative furnishes at the same time an extraordinarily valuable character sketch of the two chief actors. On the one hand, the hunter, failing in his quest, finds the man of higher culture stewing a lentil porridge, and, knowing nothing of civilized cookery, he simply cries out for some of the "red stuff" to stay his hunger. On the other hand stands the more sophisticated man—clever or cunning according to the point of view from which he is regarded—who sees his chance of attaining supremacy and takes it. We need not doubt that to the early tellers and hearers of this story Jacob's craftiness and address were a matter for pride. This was the way in which the "smart" Israelite might be expected to get the better of the "dull" Edomite.

CHAPTER XXVI

Isaac Among the Philistines. This narrative may have stood originally before 25[21]. Of the three patriarchs, Isaac is by far the least clearly drawn. In this, the only narrative in which he appears as the chief actor, we have little more than a reflection of events which occurred in the life of his father. There are slight differences, indicating a more developed attitude toward life and religion. Gerar is now definitely a Philistine city. Rebekah is not actually taken into the royal harem; the deceit is discovered (and by purely human means, not by divine revelation) in time to prevent matters going thus far (cf. ch. 20).

Vv. 17–22 give an account of strife over water, recalling 21[25]. Vv. 23–33 give a description of the naming of Beersheba, which is parallel to the E element in 21[22-33], though some of the details are different. We may conjecture that the same story was told about both Abraham and Isaac, but that it was applied by E to Abraham and by J to Isaac.

V. 34 is P's notice of the marriages of Esau, and prepares the way for its account of the departure of Jacob in 27[46].

CHAPTER XXVII

Jacob Steals Esau's Blessing. Except for the last verse (P), this narrative is a closely woven composition taken from J and E. The separation of the two is not easy. (For a possible division of the chapter between the two sources, see T. H. Robinson, *Genesis in Colloquial Speech*, pp. 31f. and 61f.)

Exactitude in the critical analysis of this chapter matters the less since the essence of both narratives is the same. In both we have the foolish and deceitful mother, the cunning and treacherous son, the blind old father, and the vigorous but simple-minded victim. The full extent of the harm done, however, is only revealed in E, when, in answer to the pressure of his unfortunate son, Isaac at length speaks. But, being in that prophetic mood which, to the Hebrew mind, so often immediately precedes death, he is unable wholly to control his language, and the words he actually utters are a ghastly parody of the blessing he has pronounced on Jacob. The keen edge of the oracle lies in the double meaning of a preposition, unfortunately misunderstood by many translators, ancient and modern. It may be partitive in sense, and is so used in the blessing of Jacob—*some of the dew of the heavens, and some of the fat of the land* (v. 28). But it may also be privative, and bears this sinister meaning in the words spoken to Esau—*far from the fat of the land . . . and far from the dew of the heavens* (v. 39). So it comes to pass that with almost identical words Jacob is blessed and Esau cursed. Small wonder that both Rebekah and Jacob knew there was reason to fear the rage of Esau. But, as Rebekah sees (this point is from J alone), her elder son is incapable of sustained purpose, even in his wrath (v. 45), and she is confident that the lapse of time will wipe out from his mind the memory of the wrong he has suffered at his brother's hands.

Jacob's action (and Rebekah's) is morally indefensible. The words of the dying father especially, when his spirit is fortified by his favorite meal, will have a validity of their own, a real value and force as active and efficient agents whose strength will not be exhausted by the passage of time. To some extent the words are independent of the speaker; he can control them partially in the act of utterance, but when once they have passed his lips they are entirely independent of his will; he can neither retract them nor modify their application. He did not mean to bless Jacob; but when once the fateful syllables have been pronounced he is helpless.

All the actors in the story know this, and the two conspirators are prepared to go to any lengths to secure for Jacob the desired victory. Yet the story is told without a hint of disapproval, and, as in the birthright story, there may be even a suppressed delight in the cunning of the ancestor of the nation, who thus cleverly built up for all time the prosperity of his descendants and their superiority to their southern neighbors. Not the least valuable element in Scripture is the way in which it shows the growth of the moral and religious sense, preserving for us the obsolete, the inadequate, the false, that we may contrast with these things the growth of the permanent, the perfect, the true (cf. Mt. 5$^{17-48}$, and art., *The Divine Element in the Bible*, p. 26).

CHAPTERS 28^{1} TO 32^{3}: JACOB AND LABAN

The scene is now transferred to northern Mesopotamia, a district called by J Haran, by E the land of the sons of the East, and by P Paddan Aram. Just as the last division of the Jacob stories has thrown back into the past the relations between Israel and Edom, this section explains the connection between Israel and Syria. Again emphasis is laid on the superiority and cleverness of the former, though it may be well to note that these qualities are illustrated not by deliberate deceit of the rival, but by Jacob's success in meeting and overcoming the attempts of Laban to get the better of his younger relative.

CHAPTER XXVIII

1–9. Occasion of Jacob's Journey to Paddan Aram. These verses (from the source P) contain the account, from the priestly point of view, of the reasons which sent Jacob to Paddan Aram. Just as the holy race must not be contaminated at its source by admixture of Canaanite blood through Isaac's marriage (ch. 24), so Jacob in turn must avoid repeating the offense of his brother (26^{34}–27^{46}), and must seek a wife from among the kinsfolk of his mother. It is noticeable that P ignores the hostility between Jacob and Esau, that he does not suggest that Jacob had anything to fear by remaining in Palestine, and that the only mention of a blessing given to Jacob is the natural dismissal of the son by a father. The immediate effect on Esau is noted: he does not feel anger against Jacob, but tries to put right what is wrong in the eyes of his parents, and takes a wife from the subordinate kinsmen of his family, i.e., from the tribe of Ishmael. There may have been a tradition of an Ishmaelite element in the Edomite blood.

10–22. Jacob's Vision at Bethel. The remainder of the chapter is a combination of elements drawn from both J and E. While differing characteristically in details (cf. vv. 10, 13–16, 19, with the rest of the section), the two narratives tell substantially the same story, and describe the first great critical experience in the religious life of Jacob. He comes into direct touch with his God, for the first time, and unexpectedly. As special revelations have been made to his grandfather (15$^{1-17}$, notes) and to his father (26$^{1-5}$, notes), so he himself learns from the mouth of Jehovah that he is in the direct line of promise. At the very moment in which he leaves the land promised to his posterity, he is assured of his return under divine protection, and of the fulfillment of the will of God through him.

Both forms of the story probably represent a sacred narrative told at Bethel, explaining the presence of a particularly holy sanctuary there, and giving the reason for one of its cultic objects, the sacred pillar. It is noticeable that E records the establishment of this emblem and the adoration paid at it without the least sense of wrong, though later Israel held these pillars to be idolatrous, and condemned worship there (2 Kings 23[14]). To those who paid their vows on this spot in later days it was enough that God had shown himself there. True, he could be everywhere, but there were special places in which he dwelt, and these could be made known only through his willing appearance to his worshipers. Jacob's dream convinces him that this is one of the homes of God—probably in the earliest forms of the story the home of an "El," or spirit—for in early days men often believed that unseen beings dwelt in such objects—and it therefore becomes holy for all the generations that follow him. It would seem too that E, at any rate, traces back to the very beginning of the sanctuary the custom of offering tithes there (cf., e.g., Amos 4[4]).

CHAPTER XXIX

1–30. **Jacob's Two Marriages.** Scholars recognize here a double thread, but the disentanglement of the two elements is difficult and the result hardly certain. The analysis is not a matter of great importance, as there are no serious differences of presentation between the two narratives.

A passage like this enables us to see the ideal man as conceived by Israel in the days of the early monarchy. Evidently the moral standard was not as high as that of prophetic and post-prophetic Israel; nevertheless, in his dealings with Laban, Jacob appears in a less unfavorable light than in his triumphs over Esau. And we can readily imagine how early Israel loved to dwell on the skill with which their ancestor met the crafty Aramæan and defeated him with his own weapons.

There is, of course, more than this in the story. The abnormal physical strength of Jacob, aroused by the appearance of his cousin, is emphasized by his ability to do a piece of work which usually demanded the united efforts of all the shepherds of the district (vv. 9–11). We are inclined to take his part when we see how his love for Rachel allows Laban to drive a hard bargain with him. We sympathize too, when, at the end of the seven years of service, the wrong woman is palmed off on him, with the excuse that custom (attested by the practice of other peoples) demands that the elder shall be married before the younger. A new agreement is made and he receives Rachel as soon as the wedding of Leah is over, and faithfully spends the next seven years paying the service which is the purchase price for what he has already received. We are constrained to admire the fidelity which kept him to the terms of his bargain.

31–35. See under 30[1-24].

CHAPTER XXX

1–24. **Jacob's Children.** Here must be considered also 29[31-35], which narrates the birth of four sons of Leah. J and E must have had very similar records here, for the narrative draws on both types of story.

This narrative introduces us to the traditional tribes of Israel. They undergo slight modifications later, but even here we have the main outline of the national groups. How are we to interpret this story? Undoubtedly ancient tradition told of incidents in the personal life of Jacob; but at the same time there is much to be said for the view that the chapter presents tribal history in the form of personal biography. Like the ancient Greeks, the Israelites felt themselves to be of common stock, though of different tribes, and they explained this fact by saying that they were all descended from a common father, though by different mothers. The description of *Bilhah* and *Zilpah* as slaves suggests that the tribes originating with them were subordinate to the Rachel and the Leah tribes respectively. We have thus a people produced by the amalgamation of two main groups of tribes, which had, presumably, achieved some kind of unity within themselves at an earlier period. These included: (a) Reuben, Simeon, Levi, Judah, Issachar, and Zebulun, with the subject clans of Gad and Asher; (b) Joseph (and, later, Benjamin), with the subject clans of Dan and Naphtali. A further point of speculative interest is raised by the two mother-names. The fact that *Leah* probably means "wild cow," and *Rachel* certainly means "sheep," has led to the suggestion that the two names indicate a totemistic stage in the development of Israelite life. The theory, while attractive, is weakened by the complete absence of a similar explanation for the names Bilhah and Zilpah.

25–43. **Jacob Acquires the Flocks of Laban.** Once more a composite narrative. In some parts, however, J and E are so closely interwoven that the two strands cannot be separated. Again, both narratives tell the same story, though with different details.

At last the long years of service are over. Women and children are negotiable property rather than independent human beings, and through all this time, though Jacob has had the use of them, they have belonged to Laban. Now the full price is paid, and they pass legally into the possession of the younger man. He has been so good a servant that his father-in-law is reluctant to let him go, and is prepared to pay him high wages to keep him. But the situation is not what it was fourteen or seven years earlier. Romance is over; the way is cleared for business. It is no longer Jacob but Laban who is the suppliant, and who has to accept the terms offered to him.

While both original forms of the story make Jacob offer conditions which seem unusually favorable to Laban, the two differ in details. In E Jacob simply separates the colored animals, far less numerous than the plain white sheep or the plain black goats, and forms herds of his own. His property will then grow simply by natural increase, though it seems that Jacob took measures to maintain the variegated coloring. In J, on the other hand, the conditions appear still harder for the herdsman. Laban himself goes through the herds, removes all the abnormally colored animals, and sends them three days' journey away from the main flocks, putting them in charge of his own sons. There can, then, be no risk of interbreeding between the two sets. Jacob remains with the flocks of plain animals, which it is still his duty to tend, and his pay is to consist in any abnormally colored specimens that may be born from them. Clearly, there is no reason why Laban should suspect that the bargain will deprive him of many of the young lambs.

But Jacob is a skilled and crafty breeder, and he has means whereby he can produce the abnormal forms when he pleases. It is said that his methods were often practiced in the ancient East, and they may well have been familiar to the shepherd audiences to whom these stories were told in ancient times. Thus he can increase his flock almost at will, and is careful to apply his methods only to the stronger animals. In the end the flock of Laban, in spite of his precautions, is the smaller and the weaker; Jacob has, by perfectly fair means (at least to the ancient mind —he had kept to the letter of his bond), justified his name and "overreached" his would-be clever rival.

CHAPTER XXXI

The Parting of Jacob and Laban. (Continued in 32:1-3.) All three of the groups of tradition found in Genesis are represented in the passage, though P is confined to v. 18, and even there the first few words belong to the narrative of the preceding verse. Analysis as between E and J is not very easy. The entire narrative falls into five sections, the fifth being 32:1-3.

1–16. Jacob Consults His Wives. Each source gives a divine and a human impulse to Jacob's departure. The latter in J is the complaint of Laban's sons, who see the whole of their patrimony being absorbed by their crafty cousin; in E it is the displeasure of Laban himself, who realizes that his trickery has turned against his own interests. His behavior has alienated the affection and confidence of his own daughters, who feel that he has treated them like foreign slaves, not like members of his own family, and they are prepared to cast in their lot with their husband. Jacob is further impelled to flee by the direct command of the Deity who has appeared to him twenty years before, and still watches over him for good. Having enriched himself in Aramæan territory, he must now return to the land promised to his posterity.

17–25. Jacob's Flight and Laban's Pursuit. Jacob "steals Laban's heart," i.e., cheats him, by taking advantage of his absence—incidentally, we notice how wealthy Laban still is, since his flocks graze over so wide an area. Rachel has something of the quality of her father and of her husband, and takes the family god, the *Teraphim*, with her. This seems to have been an image in human form, possibly representing the family "genius," and may be a relic of primitive ancestor worship. It is noticeable that the writer (the Teraphim incident is peculiar to E) has no word of blame for Rachel, either because of her dishonesty or, still more surprising, because she is apparently addicted to idolatry. Even in David's house Teraphim were found at a much later time (1 Sam. 19:13, 16). Moving slowly with his flocks, Jacob crosses the Euphrates and marches toward Canaan. Laban is three days' journey away, but the news is carried; and so much swifter is he that in seven days he overtakes the caravan in Mount Gilead, i.e., in territory which afterward belonged to Israel on the east of Jordan. The sequel leads us to suspect that Jacob is still only on the border of this land. We note that the divine protection is still with Jacob, and shows itself in a dream which forbids Laban to interfere with his nephew.

26–43. The Argument. The prohibition against "saying anything good or bad" (v. 24) to Jacob is not taken too literally by Laban, though he is clearly at a disadvantage when arguing with Jacob. Indeed, of the three charges he brings against Jacob—stealing his daughters (v. 26), leaving without notice (v. 27) and stealing his god (v. 30)—the last is the only one which would provide Laban with a real excuse for action, and Rachel's "cleverness" puts her father in the wrong here. Then it is Jacob's turn, and while his language is probably a little exaggerated (e.g., v. 41b), there is no doubt that he has a grievance. His is the complaint of the faithful and honest servant who is accused of stealing, and his concern is to show that he has been honest. Indeed, he has been more than honest, for he has not even claimed his due. The ancient rule, reflected in the life of later Israel, was that a shepherd was responsible for any animal which was lost, but if it were taken by a beast of prey, then he was free from blame and his employer had to bear the loss. Only he must produce a portion of the carcass as evidence (Ex. 22[13]; cf. Amos 3[12]). Jacob has not even availed himself of his right to this protection; he has been the model of a faithful, indeed, of a generous servant.

44–55. The Covenant at Gilead. Neither Jacob nor Laban is alone; each is the leader of a clan, and it is clear that we are reading the story of the way in which a boundary between two tribes came to be established. It seems that there are two traditions, one explaining *Mizpah*, the other *Gilead.* The first is based on the word meaning "watch"; instead of being a simple watchtower, this Mizpah (and there were many of them) has become the residence of a spirit, or perhaps even the Spirit itself, which will "watch" over the two parties and see that they keep their bargain, even when they cannot keep one another under observation. The other tradition traces the name Gilead back to a heap of stones—again, probably, though less certainly, the home of a spirit—which marks the frontier between the Hebrew and the Aramæan peoples. The name is given both in Aramaic and in Hebrew. The treaty is solemnized by a common meal in which both tribes share; afterward Laban takes his departure for his own land.

CHAPTER XXXII

1–3. Meeting with the Angelic Hosts. The origin of the name *Mahanaim,* which means "two hosts." The verses serve as a transition to the next section of the Jacob stories.

Chapters 32[4] to 36[43]: Jacob's Return to Canaan

This section falls into two divisions; the first, ending with 33[20], describes further incidents on the journey; the second records events which took place after his arrival.

4–22. Jacob's Preparations for Meeting Esau. The analysis is simple; vv. 4–14a belong to J, with perhaps a later addition in the prayer of Jacob (vv. 10–13), the rest to E. The main outline was probably common to both.

Twenty years have passed since Jacob fled from his brother's just anger. But Jacob has not forgotten the facts, and he fears that Esau also will remember. In J he tries to secure comparative safety by dividing his property; in E he prepares a present which is intended to illustrate at once his own prosperity and his desire to atone for the old wrong. This is sent forward, and, apparently, Jacob remains on the northern bank of the Jabbok.

23–33. Penuel. J and E seem here to be intimately interwoven, and analysis is rather difficult. But the main outline of the narrative is quite clear.

The passage explains several names. There is first the new name of Jacob himself, who is hereafter to be known as *Israel* (v. 28). Secondly, we have the origin of the name of the place (v. 30). Possibly also the name of the river itself, *Jabbok* (the modern Wadi Zerka), is to be connected with the unusual Hebrew word employed for wrestling. There is also the explanation of a "tabu" on the eating of a certain joint.

The earliest tradition probably represented Jacob as met at the river brink by the spirit of the stream, who seeks to prevent him from crossing. Such beings can move only at night, lest they be seen by men, and Jacob first discovers the identity of his antagonist near the dawn, when his demand to be let go becomes insistent. Jacob then uses his opportunity to secure a blessing, and, in one version of the story certainly, probably in both, his name is changed to Israel.

This ancient tradition has been used by the sacred writer to describe the second great spiritual crisis in the life of Jacob. The first was on his outward journey, when, alone, without friends or property, he found himself all unaware at the very house of God (28[10-22]). Now he has wealth, family, friends, but, nevertheless, he is menaced with danger from his brother. A still more terrible peril unexpectedly confronts him, and, though he does not come through unscathed, he yet wins something which will secure him against the thing he most fears, and assure him the final success which he seeks. Whether he recognizes in his opponent the God of Bethel or not, he can go on his way to meet his brother in the assurance that he is under divine protection, with the divine blessing and with the new God-given name. The kind of power that met him twenty years before, as he left the land, meets him again on its threshold as he returns to it.

CHAPTER XXXIII

Jacob Re-enters Canaan. The main portion of the narrative seems to be J, with phrases and sentences from E. The mention of Paddan Aram in v. 18 is probably due to a note extracted from P.

It is clear that Jacob is not wholly reassured by his precautions. But Esau is not the same man that he was twenty years before. There seems to be no trace of malice in him, and he is presented as a noble chief of Bedouin, with a generous heart and a strong sense of family duty. His affectionate greeting of Jacob and his refusal to accept the present offered till he is pressed, together with his own statement that he too is a man of substance, offer a very different picture from that which might have been expected.

Yet Jacob does not wholly trust his brother. He insists on his accepting one of the two divisions of his property. This is not the "present" of 32^{14-22}, for that does not appear in J's narrative; it is, rather, one of the two companies into which Jacob had divided all his wealth ($32^{7,\ 8}$). This will prevent Esau from carrying out any hostile design he may cherish. To this gift Jacob adds the most obsequious form of greeting, that offered by the subject to the sovereign, and he is followed in this by his wives and children. In the arrangement Jacob shows his fear. He goes first himself, but brings the others in the inverse order of their value to him, those whom he loves least coming first. Finally, he refuses the escort Esau offers him, and promises to follow leisurely to the south. But as soon as Esau and his men are gone, Jacob settles down for a time at Succoth, on the east of Jordan, and makes that for a time his home. It is noticeable that J does not make Jacob cross the Jordan at all, whilst E places him in the district of Shechem at once, and there he actually buys a field (v. 19). Finally he performs the ritual which leads to the establishment of a sanctuary there.

CHAPTER XXXIV

The Outrage on Dinah and the Sack of Shechem. A double thread (indicated in the following analysis as I and II) can clearly be traced through this chapter, though in places disentanglement is uncertain. The chief points of difference between the two: (a) in II the conditions on which Dinah may be married to Shechem are not stated, while in I circumcision is demanded, and, indeed, furnished an opportunity for the massacre; (b) in I Dinah is allowed to return to her father's house after the seduction, while in II she is kept in the city till taken thence by her brothers; (c) in I Jacob's sons generally slaughter the Shechemites, in II the deed is done by Simeon and Levi alone. The provenance of the two narratives is a little difficult to determine. It is possible that we have here two independent narratives, neither belonging to the main line of one of the great traditions, but emanating from the same general circles as J and E.

On the whole we may best interpret the chapter—whose salient features are the same in both recensions—as a piece of tribal history. We are still somewhat uncertain as to the exact details of the conquest of Canaan in later times by Israel, and it is possible that we have here an early tribal victory thrown back by tradition into the patriarchal period. Both Simeon and Levi disappeared early from among the territorial tribes of Israel, and their submergence may be due to acts of ruthless cruelty such as this. Apart from the fact that the ancestors of Israel are normally represented as peaceful shepherds, the narrative brings out once more some of the characteristics attributed to them all, but particularly to Jacob. We have especially the very high value set on female chastity, and the craft (particularly evident in the element classed as I) shown in overcoming those who have wronged or who would wrong Israel and his family. There may have been also in early days a glow of satisfaction felt when the tale of the conquest of a great Canaanite city was told, but to us the story is mean and repulsive; even the rebuke of the old father is based not on the moral aspects of the case, but on the danger to which it exposes him and his.

CHAPTER XXXV

1–15. Jacob's Return to Bethel. It is not impossible that the compiler of this story means us to suppose that the command to leave Shechem and go up into the hills to Bethel was in part due to the tragedy of Shechem. This, however, does not seem to have been in the thought of the original narrators of the story, to whom the completion of the cultic apparatus at Bethel is the important matter. We observe again that in E Jacob is more than the father of a wandering family; he is the head of a clan, and in that capacity orders all the *strange gods* to be removed (v. 2), thus anticipating the first of the Ten Commandments (Ex. 20^3). The strange gods may be taken to be the family deities and other gods whom the individual tribes worshiped before their amalgamation into Israel, and it is possible that we have once more a Mosaic regulation thrown back into the patriarchal age. Be that as it may, it is clear that to the mind of E the God of Bethel will tolerate no rival near his shrine.

P gives another of the series of divine blessings which began with the creation of man. There is an obvious reference to 1[28] in v. 11, and it is possible that we have here accounts of two incidents which the priestly writer originally intended to be kept separate, one contained in vv. 9, 10, the other in vv. 11–13. The first of these, indicating Jacob's change of name, takes in P the place of the Penuel incident in JE (cf. 32[29]).

E adds a note of the death and burial of *Deborah*, Rachel's foster-mother (v. 8), probably for the purpose of explaining the sanctity of the terebinth (*oak*) mentioned. It is doubtful that there is any connection with the "palmtree of Deborah" mentioned in Judg. 4[5].

16–20. The Birth of Benjamin and the Death of Rachel. The tragedy of this record (which is E throughout) appears not only in the facts themselves but in the names given to the child. The name is the parent's first exclamation on seeing the child (cf. note on 2[19]), and since the name given by the mother is inauspicious, the father changes it. The fact that Benjamin is born in Palestine may mean that this tribe had no traditions carrying it back to the nomad stage.

21, 22a. Reuben's Crime. A part of J. Another reference is made in the blessing of Jacob (49[4]), and, as in the account of the ancestry of Moab and Ammon, there may be some ancient slur cast on the character of the tribe of Reuben. The sentence is broken off suddenly; it may once have stood at the head of the short poem on Reuben now preserved in ch. 49.

22b–26. A List of the Sons of Jacob. A priestly summary of the ancestors of the twelve tribes.

27–29. The Death of Isaac. Also from P. The patriarchal home is still at Mamre, where the family tomb is situated (cf. 23[17]). P ignores any disagreements or differences between Jacob and Esau, and represents them as burying their father together. Similarly, he has taken no notice of the separation of Isaac and Ishmael (cf. 25[9]).

CHAPTER XXXVI

An Edomite Genealogy. The general style of the passage suggests P, but there are several features which make it unlikely that it comes from the main thread of that document. In particular the names of Esau's wives do not wholly agree with those given in 26[34, 35] 28[9]. There are also doublets within the passage (especially in vv. 9–14, 15–19) which suggest a combination of different sources.

The chapter is a summary history of Edom down to the time of the establishment of the Hebrew monarchy. It falls into no less than eight sections.

1–5. These verses are intended to indicate that there were at least four racial elements in the later people of Edom, one closely related to the Aramæan ancestry of Israel, one Canaanite, a third derived from the aboriginal inhabitants of the southern hills (Horites), and a fourth from a Bedouin tribe connected, but more remotely than Esau himself, with Israel. **6–8.** The migration which resulted in the settlement of Edom in the south. The writer ignores the rivalry between Israel and Esau, and assumes that the migration was due to economic causes like those which led to the separation of Abraham and Lot. It will be noted that in v. 8 "Edom" is used as an alternative name for the tribal ancestor, Esau. **9–14.** Edom is here used for the whole nation, and the interrelation of the Edomite tribes is traced through the *sons* of Esau. **15–19.** Largely a repetition of the preceding, except that the *sons* of Esau are no longer personified tribes, but rather individual chiefs of the tribes that bore their names. **20–28.** A list of Horite clans, evidently unified with Edom in later times. **29, 30.** A list of Horite chieftains bearing to some extent the same relation to vv. 20–28 as vv. 15–19 do to vv. 9–14. **31–39.** A list of Edomite kings. It is clear that though Israel claimed superiority over Edom, it was recognized that the latter had been the first to attain to an organized constitution. The same belief is expressed in the stories of the birth and of the birthright (25[24-34]), and in that of the stolen blessing (ch. 27). **40–43.** Another list of chieftains of Edomite clans, whose names seem to be taken almost indiscriminately from the preceding; Oholibamah, for instance, is now a chief, not a wife of Esau.

In general it may be pointed out that many of the names are common to Palestine and the surrounding districts. The name "Hadad," for instance, appears more than once, and is that of an Aramæan deity; other names also may be divine names. But, apart from the single mention of an Edomite victory over Midian in v. 35, the chapter throws comparatively little light on the early history of Edom.

IV. Chapters 37[1] to 50[26]: Joseph

The last division of the book of Genesis contains an account of Joseph, explaining how Israel came to be in Egypt. It contains twelve sections, of which two (chs. 38 and 49), which do not deal primarily with Joseph, must be regarded as digressions. All three of the main sources are represented, P, as usual, being little more than a summary framework. J and E are sometimes closely interwoven, but the analysis is usually fairly easy. The stories are rather different in type from many in the earlier divisions of the book; there is little that explains names or customs, and, apart from chs. 38 and 49, practically no tribal history. There seems to be a fairly accurate acquaintance with matters Egyptian, particularly in the E sections, though it is the Egypt of the tenth and ninth centuries, not that of the patriarchal age, with which the writers are familiar.

A judgment as to the historical value of the division must depend to some extent on the view held of the Exodus. We cannot question the historicity of that event; for without it it is impossible to explain the dominating influence of the tradition on the thought of later Israel. The people—or at least some of them—must have found their way into Egyptian territory, and the migration which led them there is involved in the story of Joseph. Joseph may safely be accepted as an actual person, under whose leadership or influence the tribes settled in the Goshen area.

It seems fairly clear that this immigration must have taken place during what we know as the Hyksos period, when Egypt was dominated by shepherd kings who came from the northeast. There are those who hold that the story of the Exodus is the Hebrew account of the expulsion of the Hyksos (about 1600 to 1550 B.C.). Those who favor this view (which, however, is far from being certain) are inclined to see in the story of Joseph an account of the entry of the Hyksos into Egypt. It is more probable, however, that the Hyksos were in the country at the time and that the Pharaoh who exalted Joseph was one of the earlier Hyksos kings. The required date (about 1750 B.C.) would not be seriously out of harmony with the synchronism which places Abraham in the age of Khammurabi. (See art., *History of Hebrew People*, pp. 60–1; cf. intro. to Exodus, section on "Contemporary History," p. 250.)

CHAPTER XXXVII

Joseph and His Brethren. Apart from vv. 1, 2, which seem to form P's introduction to the whole division, this chapter is a combination of J and E. The sources are easy to separate. Each story forms an almost continuous narrative, and though the main fact is the same, the details are different and, sometimes, inconsistent. In J the jealousy of the brothers is due to the father's favoritism, in E to Joseph's own dreams, and to the conceit which is supposed to have produced them. In J it is Judah who saves Joseph, by proposing to sell him to an Ishmaelite caravan which all the brothers see as they eat; in E it is Reuben who saves him by persuading them to put him into a dry pit, and he is terribly distressed when he finds the boy gone. In E it is Midianites, not Ishmaelites, who have drawn the lad out of the pit, and they have not been seen by any of the brothers. Finally, according to J, the brothers prove Joseph's fate by bringing the blood-stained coat; in E they simply tell their father that he has been devoured.

In the combined story which we now have before us, the interest centers on Joseph's weaknesses. He is his father's favorite, wears a long-sleeved coat, showing that he is to be a "gentleman" and do no work (cf. the garment worn by the princess Tamar, 2 Sam. 13[18]). He is also a conceited tale-bearer, and the result is what might be expected. The brothers—especially the sons of the slave wives—are not good men, and they will certainly take every possible chance of vengeance. It is only the compassion of an elder brother that saves the boy from immediate death, and even then his lot is not much better. While the sequel shows Joseph to be a fine character in many ways, these early failings are there, and meet with their inevitable reward.

CHAPTER XXXVIII

Judah and Tamar. This unpleasant story appears to come from southern Israel, and is, therefore, to be connected with J. But it is clearly not in the direct line of even the southern tradition, and may be regarded as an isolated narrative introduced in order to explain certain facts.

We note, then, first of all, that Judah is no longer in the same social group as his brothers, and, it would seem, is permanently settled in the land. This accounts for the practically complete separation of Judah from the rest of Israel throughout the early period of the conquest, a separation which was ended only in the time of David (2 Sam. 2[1-11]). We also observe that this story implies a large admixture of Canaanite blood in Judah; the clans which survived have a Canaanite ancestress. The sin of Er is not mentioned, but the details given of Onan suggest that possibly the original story ascribed to the elder brother a similar offense. In that case we may have here a relic of a belief in a demon who haunted the marriage chamber, such as forms the motif of the Book of Tobit. Naturally the Israelite writers have substituted Jehovah, to whom they ascribed all superhuman action. The narrative certainly shows that the law of levirate marriage (cf. Deut. 25[5f.]) is based on primitive custom; and it presents Tamar as a clever and praiseworthy woman, who succeeds, at risk to herself, in fulfilling her responsibilities to her dead husband.

CHAPTERS XXXIX, XL

Joseph as a Slave in Egypt. The two narratives of ch. 37 are continued here; in the main ch. 39 belongs to J and ch. 40 to E, though in each there may be words and phrases taken from the other source. The last verse of ch. 37, in fact, belongs rather to this section, for it forms the beginning of E's account of Joseph's adventures in Egypt, and it seems probable that the words in 39[1], "Potiphar, Pharaoh's eunuch, the chief of the executioners," have been introduced from 37[36] and are no part of the original narrative here.

In fact, in J's story Joseph's master is not a eunuch, nor is he necessarily a royal official. He is simply an Egyptian gentleman, who buys the Canaanite slave. The story has numerous parallels elsewhere, but is of particular significance in Joseph's career. It shows that the divine favor which has given him his high position in his master's house is due to his character, and, though tried so terribly, he proves worthy of the trust placed in him by God and man. Even when punishment falls upon him for the very crime he has refused to commit, his spirit is unbroken and his character again wins him favor and responsibility. Everyone who meets him reacts favorably to him; his master, his mistress—though her favor is disastrous—the jailer, all find him reliable and successful in all that he undertakes, and when distinguished prisoners join him he soon wins their confidence too. The earlier weaknesses in his character are being purged away by what he endures.

In E the person who buys Joseph from the Midianites is a eunuch, Potiphar, the chief executioner. As in the other narrative, Joseph finds favor in his master's sight and is made his personal servant (39[4a]). In this form of the story there is no general state prison; the officials under suspicion (probably of having tried to poison the king) are shut up in the house of the chief executioner, Joseph's master. They are great men, and may be restored to favor; moreover, there may be a risk in allowing them to be waited on by an inferior person, who may be bribed to help them escape; so the chief executioner places them under the care of his own confidential attendant (40[4]). The telling and interpreting of the dreams follow; the importance of the dream is a characteristic feature of E. The power of interpretation is a special divine gift, and is a further mark of the favor God has bestowed on this wonderful youth. The final evidence is offered when the fate foretold to each actually befalls him.

CHAPTER XLI

Joseph's Elevation. The main source for the story as we have it now is E; but numerous excerpts from J are also found. The notice of Joseph's age in v. 46 is probably derived from P. It may be doubted whether the dreams were mentioned at all in J, and possibly Joseph appeared in that narrative merely as one who could foretell the future. Egyptian literature contains several examples of "prophecies" uttered before kings; however, those which have survived are usually more like Jewish apocalypse than Hebrew prophecy. (See art., *Intertestamental Literature*, pp. 189, 190.)

The chapter falls into three parts: (a) Pharaoh's perplexity (vv. 1–13); (b) Joseph's solution (vv. 14–36); (c) Joseph's appointment (vv. 37–57). The first and last serve to emphasize the importance of the second. Joseph succeeded where Pharaoh and his wise men failed; and so greatly were all affected both by his understanding of the dream and by the wisdom of the measures he suggested that everyone felt that he was the proper person to carry out his own ideas. The sudden elevation and the autocratic power of the king, together with the authority conferred on the favorite, are characteristic features of Oriental stories. Here, however, the stress is laid throughout on the genuinely religious significance of the events described. It is because God is with Joseph, and because in all his conduct in Egypt he has shown himself worthy of the divine support that honor and power are bestowed on him. Even the heathen Egyptian recognizes that the secret of Joseph's power lies here, and we have to read the story as testimony to the superiority of Israel's faith over even the great religion of Egypt. (For a parallel, see Dan. 3[28-30] 6[25-27].)

CHAPTER XLII

The First Meeting Between Joseph and His Brothers. This chapter is almost entirely E, though it is clear that there are occasional phrases drawn from J, e.g., vv. 2, 5, 7, 9b–11a, 27, 28, 38. There are references in ch. 43 which show that in outline J had a similar story, though there were differences in point of detail.

Joseph has achieved a great triumph in being raised to the position he holds in Egypt, but that triumph is not complete till he has exercised that lordship over his brothers which his boyish dreams have promised him. The opportunity comes when they are driven to buy corn in Egypt, which from very ancient times was a storehouse of food for the civilized world. Now at last Joseph can take his revenge, and the first element in it is his refusal to believe in the good faith of his brothers. They recognize that the treatment they receive is a just punishment for that which they gave to Joseph years ago, but they cannot, in the nature of the case, fathom Joseph's further motives. He is actuated by love of Benjamin even more than by the desire for vengeance, and longs, first to assure himself of the safety of the boy, and, secondly, to see him once more. These ends he secures (after giving them all a serious alarm) by keeping Simeon while the rest are sent home. He seems to have chosen Simeon because he was the second in age; and he had not forgotten how the eldest, Reuben, had befriended him. Finally, terror is instilled into the brothers by the discovery that their money has been returned to them. This is placed by J at the first halt on the journey (v. 27); by E on their reaching their home (v. 35)—striking evidence of two narratives—and must have seemed to them either a piece of magic or an attempt to prove them thieves. Their difficulties are, throughout, increased by the fact that they have to speak through an interpreter—the only place in the patriarchal stories in which differences of language are recognized (v. 23).

The full result of this terror is only evident when the brothers reach their father. The sequel to E's story has not been preserved, except in fragments, but it is clear that an immediate return with Benjamin is contemplated in order to release Simeon, and that Jacob's natural objection is overcome only when Reuben gives his own children as hostages (v. 37). Once more, as in ch. 37, a prominent part is played by Reuben, and this suggests that these stories took shape among the shepherd community to the east of Jordan at a comparatively early date, when the tribe of Reuben (which disappeared soon after the conquest of Canaan) still held a leading position in Israel.

CHAPTER XLIII

The Second Meeting Between Joseph and His Brothers. The passage is almost entirely J; to E belongs only the note in v. 23, which tells of the release of Simeon.

As in E, so in J, the brothers have been harshly treated by the Egyptian Grand Vizier. But he does not seem to have detained any of them; rather he has dismissed them all, with the order that they shall not return at all unless they bring Benjamin with them. The question, therefore, does not arise till the stocks of food brought from Egypt are exhausted, and it is only when they are bidden to return for more that Judah tells his father of the conditions laid down by Joseph. From the dialogue which follows it appears that the brothers had not volunteered information about their family, but had given it under cross-examination (v. 7). It is Judah, not Reuben, who overcomes the reluctance of his father (in J called usually Israel rather than Jacob; cf. v. 6 with 42^{1}).

Joseph keeps his word—to all appearance. The strangers have satisfied the test imposed upon them, and they are liberally received. Their fears that this may be a trap are lulled by Joseph's steward (vv. 18–25), and though Joseph, as an Egyptian, cannot eat at the same table as they do, lavish hospitality is shown to them, especially to Benjamin (v. 34), while further evidence of Joseph's extraordinary powers is shown in his correct arrangement of his visitors according to age (v. 33).

CHAPTER XLIV

Joseph's Cup Found in Benjamin's Sack; Judah's Intercession. (Still from J.) The brothers' difficulties, however, are not yet over; indeed, they have not yet reached their height. Joseph is a magician, and one of his instruments, a magic cup, is secreted in Benjamin's sack (v. 2). Discovery and accusation naturally follow, and Judah, Benjamin's protector, makes a noble speech pleading for the lad. Joseph is satisfied at last. Just as his own sufferings have purified and ennobled his own character, so he finds at last that his brothers are not bad men at heart. They still care for their old father, and are still ready to make sacrifices for their youngest brother. He has achieved all that he had hoped by his tests; the brothers have learned their lesson, and the way is open for the dènouement.

CHAPTER XLV

1–24. Joseph Reveals Himself to His Brothers. The account chiefly used here is that of E, but J also has made some contributions. Vv. 1–15 form the climax of the whole Joseph story, for they narrate the reunion of the family, at length freed from the petty jealousies and the selfish passions which had manifested themselves in younger days. Great wrongs have been done and great sufferings have been endured. But all this is now past; peace, safety, and prosperity have been fully attained. What we see more than anything else is the working out of a divine plan. Human nature, even human sin, cannot interfere with the gracious and kindly purpose of a friendly God, who cares, not for his chosen people alone, but for others also. Egypt has been saved from starvation as well as the family of Joseph, and the king of the country gladly recognizes the obligations which he and his people owe to Joseph (vv. 16–24). For his sake these shepherds are welcomed, in spite of the normal Egyptian antipathy to the Asiatic nomad, and a suitable home is found for them. Thus we come to understand the full value of the man with whom God lives, and whom he favors. As the chief instrument in effecting the divine purpose, Joseph has not merely attained to wealth, influence and authority himself, he has also saved Egypt and established his own family in a place of safety.

25–28. See under chs. 46, 47.

CHAPTERS XLVI, XLVII

Jacob's Migration to Egypt. This narrative extends from 45^{25} to 47^{12}. The former of the two sections taken from P (46^{6-27}) is a normal priestly list of the persons—all, presumably, heads of clans—who came into Egypt with Jacob, and thus gives an account of the extent of the "nation" at this stage. 47^{5-11} is almost, so to speak, the formal charter of occupation granted by Pharaoh to Jacob and to his descendants; but we notice that, while the king makes the grant of land, Jacob takes the position of the superior, and bestows his blessing on Pharaoh.

The combined narrative JE gives a detailed account of the journey, the meeting of the old father with his long-lost son, and the reception accorded to the newcomers by Pharaoh. With its freshness and its psychological insight, the passage offers a solution of two problems. One of these is peculiar to J, the other to E. In J Pharaoh has known, as far as we are told, nothing of the coming of Joseph's family, and the latter thinks it best to see them safely established in Goshen before presenting them to the king (46^{31}). Then, in 47^{1-5}, when it is too late for Pharaoh to interfere, Joseph brings him the news. It is graciously received, though Pharaoh, bearing his subjects' prejudices in mind, assigns to the newcomers a district on the northeastern frontier, removed from the center of Egyptian life. At the same time he offers to give royal appointments to any of Joseph's brothers who seem fit for them. This difficulty, that of their reception by Pharaoh, is safely met.

The other problem is peculiar to E, and is not so much stated as assumed. Canaan is the promised land; is Jacob justified in leaving it? Still more, is he justified in leaving it for Egypt? The answer comes to him when he reaches the home of his father at Beersheba (46^{2-4}). There, at the ancestral sanctuary, he receives a divine revelation which assures him that the God of his father will not desert him; consequently, he may go into Egypt with safety to himself and to his descendants. Thus early we find traces of a conception of a God who is not limited to a single locality or to a few, but who can make his presence felt at any spot on earth's surface. These stories took shape far back in the past, centuries before the time of the great prophets; and yet we can detect the germs of a doctrine which led Israel, in the end, to the conviction that there was but One, the Living and True God.

Joseph Secures the Land of Egypt for the King. (47^{13-26}.) This section comes from J. It is an explanation of the Egyptian system of land tenure, which is entirely different from that of Israel. In Palestine men held their land freehold, except insofar as the later law recognized that they were tenants of Jehovah (Lev. 25^{23}). In Egypt, on the other hand, all land was the property of the sovereign, at least from the eighteenth dynasty onward. We may not approve of Joseph's action, as judged by modern social standards, but it is clear that Israel took a pride in him as the founder of one of the peculiar institutions of Egypt.

For vv. 27–31, see under ch. 48.

CHAPTER XLVIII

Jacob's Last Days. All three accounts, J, E and P, contain the blessing of the sons of Jacob. That of P is almost in the form of a will, in which the patriarch devises his property to his children, and makes special provision for Ephraim and Manasseh as separate tribes.

This is less explicitly stated in J and E. In the former narrative, Jacob makes Joseph swear to bury him in the ancestral grave at Machpelah (47^{29-31}). There seems to be some special symbolism in Jacob's bowing over the head of his bed (it may be remarked in passing that the quotation in Heb. 11^{21}, "worshiped, leaning on his staff," not "his bed," involves a different vocalization of the same Hebrew consonants that we have in the traditional text here—*matteh* for *mitteh*). In both these narratives of the blessing of the sons of Joseph, Jacob deliberately puts Ephraim before Manasseh. In the period of the Judges it seems that the latter was the stronger branch, but throughout the monarchy the relative positions were reversed, and Ephraim was the more prominent. This fact is explained in this passage as due to the fateful words of the dying Jacob. V. 22 seems to be an isolated utterance, representing a tradition which ignored the residence of Israel in Egypt, and suggesting a story of conquest which has otherwise disappeared, unless there be reminiscences of it in ch. 34.

CHAPTER XLIX

1–28a. The Blessing of Jacob. This is a very ancient poem in which are gathered together short characterizations of the various tribes. It is interesting to compare it with the blessing of Moses in Deut. 33. It seems to be the earlier of the two, and we notice that Joseph is still undivided, that Simeon and Reuben still appear as important tribes, and that Levi is a secular, not a priestly clan. The poem has been very carefully studied, and there is reason to suppose that it has a fairly long literary history.

(a) *Reuben* (vv. 3, 4), though the first-born, with natural rights of superiority, has sacrificed these things. The reference to 35[22] is obvious.

(b) *Simeon* and *Levi* (vv. 5–7) are linked together as cruel and passionate men, to whom such a crime as that described in ch. 34 would be only natural. They are deficient in ordinary humanity, and love only to give pain; when they are in a bad temper they are dangerous murderers, and even when they are in a gracious mood the best that can be expected of them is that they should mutilate cattle.

(c) *Judah* (vv. 8–12) dwells in a land rich in vines and pasturage, and is powerful in war. The disappearance of the three senior tribes leaves the fourth dominant and royal, and there may even be some primitive Messianic reference in the mysterious phrase *till Shiloh come.* (For a detailed discussion see modern commentaries on the book of Genesis.)

(d) *Zebulun* (v. 13) is not described; his geographical position, near Phœnicia, alone is given.

(e) *Issachar* (vv. 14, 15) is a tribe with a slight sense of the value of freedom, who, in order to secure material ease and comfort, is prepared to surrender the rights of liberty.

(f) *Dan* (vv. 16, 17) appears to be still in his original home in the southwest, lying across the great caravan road, where he can fall suddenly on travelers from an ambush.

(V. 18 forms no essential part of the poem, unless it be intended to mark a rest in the middle of it. As Simeon and Levi are grouped together, there are only eleven of these irregular stanzas, six before and five after this division.)

(g) *Gad* (v. 19), on the east of Jordan, is exposed especially to raids from the desert, but the Bedouin who make the attempt are in danger of suffering vigorous reprisals.

(h) *Asher* (v. 20) is noted for the richness and delicacy of his living.

(i) *Naphtali* (v. 21) is noble, free, adventurous, swift, and is noted for the beauty of his youth.

(j) *Joseph* (vv. 22–26) receives the most striking blessing of all, with the possible exception of Judah. Certain parallels are to be found in Deut. 33[13, 16]. He is exposed to danger, but will triumph over it all, and on him are showered the concentrated blessings of heaven and earth, farm and home, past and present. It is clear that at the time when the poem reached its present form Judah and Joseph divide between them the supremacy of the nation.

(k) *Benjamin* (v. 27) is described as a ravenous wolf greedily devouring his prey.

28b–33. See under ch. 50.

CHAPTER L

1–21. Death and Burial of Jacob. (Including 49[28b-33].) The patriarch's bones must not be allowed to rest on foreign soil. In P Jacob arranges to be buried in the ancestral cave at Machpelah (49[30]), and his wishes are carried out. But in J (what remains of E makes no mention of the burial of Jacob) the instruction is less definite (v. 5), and, as a matter of fact, after the due embalming the interment takes place on the east of Jordan, the last rites being performed in the presence of a great company of Egyptians, officials and others, who make an expedition for the purpose. Thus the name *Abel Mizraim* ("mourning of Egypt") is explained (v. 11).

Even the years they have spent in Egypt and the kindness they have received have not wholly obliterated from the minds of Joseph's brothers the wrong that they did him in his boyhood, and a narrative due to E records their anxiety. But once more the nobility and piety of Joseph's character are manifested. He realizes the fact that all history is the working out of a divine plan (v. 20), and that it is not for him to entertain thoughts of vengeance against the brothers whose misdeeds, under divine guidance, have led to such magnificent results. On the contrary, his kindness and his help will remain in no wise abated through the death of his father; his forgiveness is complete.

22–26. The Death of Joseph. Except possibly for v. 22, the whole of this passage is from E.

To the ancient Hebrew mind, no man could be called happy till he was dead, and till the seal had been set on his prosperity by long life and a peaceful end. So the story of the magnanimous hero is imperfect till the last record has been made and he lays down the tasks of life in a good old age, seeing his posterity well established, with the assurance, so far as any man can have it, of a continuance of his name and blood on earth. Yet he knows that this is not the final resting-place for his people. Like his immediate ancestors he looks on Canaan alone as the true home for Israel, and he anticipates the time, still centuries distant, when Israel shall take possession of its inheritance. So the book closes with the intimation that its story is one of preparation, and that completion is possible only in God's good time—it is but a book of Genesis.

EXODUS

By Professor J. F. McLAUGHLIN

Introduction

Period Covered. The book of Genesis brings the history of the ancestors of the Hebrew people down to the settlement of the family of Jacob in Egypt and the death of Joseph. Exodus continues the history to the departure of Israel from Egypt and the encampment at Sinai under the leadership of Moses. It covers, therefore, very briefly the period of sojourn in Egypt, gives an account of the oppression under which the people of Israel suffered toward the end of this period, then tells at much greater length the story of the birth and early life of Moses, his long residence in Arabia, his call to be the deliverer of his people, his return to Egypt and interviews with the Egyptian king, and his leading of the people out into the freedom and adventure of the wilderness. In the second half of the book is given an account of the encampment at Mount Sinai, the revelation of God in the mountain, the preparation of the first codes of law and the organization of a system of government, and the establishment of the religion and worship of Jehovah on a firm basis by a covenant bond, an organized priesthood, and a tent sanctuary or tabernacle.

Contents. The contents of the book may be conveniently arranged and remembered as follows:

I. *To Sinai.* 1. Oppression of Israel, birth, early life, and flight of Moses to Arabia, chs. 1, 2.

2. The call of Moses, his interviews with Pharaoh, the ten plagues, and the departure from Egypt, chs. 3–13.

3. The crossing of the Red Sea and the wilderness journey as far as Mount Sinai, 14^{1}–19^{1}.

II. *At Sinai.* 1. Events at Sinai and the giving of the law, 19^{2}–24^{18} and chs. 32–34.

2. The priesthood and the sanctuary, chs. 25–31 and 35–40.

The following passages should be noted as having peculiar interest and value:

The vision and call of Moses at Horeb, 3^{1}–4^{17}.

The plagues of Egypt, chs. 7–11.

The institution and law of the Passover, 12^{1}–13^{16}.

The song of Moses, 15^{1-21}.

The decalogue and book of the covenant, chs. 20–23; cf. 24^{7}.

The worship of the golden calf, ch. 32.

Name. The name of the book, Exodus, is the Latinized form of the Greek word *exodos*, which means "outgoing" or "departure." The word is so used in the Greek translation of the LXX, 19^{1}, and in the title of the book in that version. The form of the word in our English version is the same as that in the Latin Vulgate. The Hebrew title is simply the first three words of the first chapter, "And these are the names."

Structure. The literary structure of this book is similar to that of Genesis, Numbers, and Joshua, and can be seen to have, in certain features, a close relationship to Leviticus and to Deuteronomy. Two histories have been intricately woven together, the older of the two compiled, it is believed, by prophets of the age of Isaiah from still older written documents of their time, and the other, somewhat later, by devout men of the priestly order. The editors, or compilers, who carefully put these histories together in their earlier and later form, appear sometimes to have added brief notes or comments of their own, intended to convey an exhortation or to impress the moral and religious lesson of the passage. Extremely interesting attempts have been made by modern scholars to analyze the contents of Exodus, as of the other books above mentioned, so as to indicate the source or sources from which each portion of the book is taken. These will be shown at length in any good recent commentary, as, e.g., in the Cambridge Bible, the Century Bible, and the Westminster series. Reference will be made here, in our commentary, to such analysis where it seems necessary to make clear the meaning of a passage. (See art., *Pentateuch*, pp. 136–9.)

Authorship. In the N.T. and in early Jewish and Christian literature the books of the Pentateuch are commonly referred to as the book, or books, of Moses. Quotations in the Gospels from these books, especially from the laws contained in them, are usually introduced by the words "Moses said," or "Moses commanded." No doubt it was then the common belief that Moses was the author of the laws, but the naming of the books after him may simply mean that he is the chief person in them, just as the books of Joshua and Samuel are named after the great men whose words and deeds they record. It is not a proof of authorship. A Jewish tradition preserved in the Talmud states that "Moses wrote his own book," but evidence of the truth of this statement is lacking. The Pentateuch is written about Moses, not by Moses. (The article on the *Pentateuch*, p. 134, deals more in detail with the authorship of this and the other books of the Pentateuch.)

Nevertheless it is historically probable—and there is some evidence—that Moses did leave behind written memorials, including laws, and statistical and other records, and sayings or speeches which may have been written down and preserved with care by those who were associated with him. See, e.g., Ex. 17^{14} 24^{7} Num. 33^{2} Deut. $31^{9, 24\text{-}26}$, and compare 1 Sam. 10^{25}. This being admitted, we can readily understand that much, perhaps all, of such first-rate historical material, along with oral traditions handed down from the times of Moses, genealogical and family records, and priestly records, would be preserved in the early histories which have been woven into the structure of the Pentateuch.

Historical Value. We may confidently say, therefore, of the book of Exodus, as an important part of this composite work, that it has high historical value. Put into its present form by prophetic and priestly writers of a much later time, it contains much that was handed down to them from the past. Their interest was, no doubt, chiefly to promote true religion and the observance of the ancient sacred Law, but they desired for this very purpose to preserve the memory of the great deliverance which God had wrought for them from the bondage of Egypt, and of the great and heroic figure of the man whom God had raised up to be their leader and their lawgiver.

Religious Value. The book has also a very high religious value. It seeks to show, in every part, the divine interest in human affairs, God's watchful care over an oppressed and enslaved people and his rebuke of their oppressor, his guiding and sustaining hand, his judgments tempered by mercy. It identifies the laws of Jehovah, Israel's God, with the fundamental principles of justice, and sets forth high ideals of individual moral conduct and of public service. It reveals a God mighty to bring salvation to his people, their true King and Lord, not enthroned on high above them but dwelling with them, sharing their life, fighting their battles, and through his chosen and inspired servant administering their laws.

The great influence which this book has had upon the religious thought and life of Jew and Christian alike is manifest both in the many references to it in the O.T. and the N.T., and in the frequent use of its narratives and laws in the literature of Christian nations. For a very few examples see the historical Psalms 78, 105, 106, 114, and such passages as Psa. $68^{7, 8}$ $77^{13\text{-}20}$ and $103^{6, 7}$; also Isa. $43^{16\text{-}19}$ 51^{10} Jn. 6^{31} Acts $7^{20\text{-}44}$ 13^{17} 1 Cor. $10^{1\text{-}5}$ Heb. $11^{23\text{-}29}$. See also Milton's *Paradise Lost*, bk. xii, 155–244; Keble, *The Burning Bush*, *Song of the Manna-Gatherers*, and *Moses on Sinai;* Trench, *Moses and Jethro*; George Herbert, *Aaron;* Cowley, *The Destroying Angel;* Cecil Frances Alexander, *The Red Sea*, and *The Camp at Elim;* Moore, *The Song of Miriam;* Scott, *The March of Israel;* Bonar, *Marah and Elim;* Clough, *Moses Hidden in the Cloud;* Plumptre, *With Open Face Beholding*. (See *The Poet's Bible*, edited by W. Garrett Horder).

Contemporary History. It is said in Ex. 1^{11} that when Pharaoh subjected the people of Israel to forced labor they built for him "store cities, Pithom and Raamses." Now, the story of the oppression in Exodus makes it clear that the Israelites labored in the vicinity of their own homes, and it might therefore be expected that the site of these store cities would be found in or near the land of Goshen in which they were settled. This land, which was almost certainly in the northeastern part of Egypt bordering upon Arabia, is called in Gen. 47^{11} "the land of Rameses," and, according to Ex. 12^{37}, it was from Rameses that the Israelites set out upon their journey to the Arabian wilderness. The names "Raamses" and "Rameses" are clearly identical. The spelling in English corresponds to a slight difference in the vowels of the Hebrew word. In 1883 a well-known French explorer, M. Naville, excavated a mound of ancient ruins about sixty miles northeast of Cairo, where there is still a statue of Rameses II, a great king of the nineteenth Egyptian dynasty, seated between statues of the two solar deities Ra and Tum. Here he found inscriptions which seemed to show unmistakably that the ancient name of the place was Pi-Tum, or "house of Tum," a name which is without doubt the same as the Pithom of Exodus. The ruins show it to have been a city about two hundred and twenty yards square, inclosed by immense brick walls, and containing many chambers built of brick which were probably used for the storing of grain. The inscriptions show that the city was built, or rebuilt, by Rameses 11 (*cir.* 1300–1234 B.C.), and would, therefore, point to him as the Pharaoh who oppressed Israel. The site of the other store city, called after the king's own name, has not been identified with any certainty, but it was probably in the same region, and may have been the place of the king's residence, where he could easily be approached by the representatives of Israel. Professor Flinders Petrie claims to have discovered the site of Raamses at a place about eight miles west of Pithom, where there is a temple of Rameses II and part of the tomb of an official who was over storehouses of Syrian produce. The identification both of Pithom and Raamses has been disputed in favor of other localities in the northeastern parts of Egypt by recent writers. (See Gardiner in *Journal of Egyptian Archæology*, vols. v. and vi, and Peet, *Egypt and the O.T.*) The Pharaoh of the Exodus must, therefore, have been one of the immediate successors of Rameses II, probably Merenptah, who reigned from about 1234 to 1214 B.C. (See Ex. 2[23] 4[19]; Breasted puts the date of his accession about nine years later.) In his reign the power of Egypt, which had for three centuries extended over the nearer parts of Asia, began to decline, and it became possible for the Hebrews to escape from Egypt into parts of Asia free from Egyptian domination. An inscription dating from the king's fifth year mentions a victory over Libyan invaders from the west, peace with the Hittites of Syria, the suppression of revolt in Canaan, and the annihilation of Israel (*Ysiraal*). The last statement may simply be the record which the king chose to make of his dealing with the enslaved people who had escaped from his kingdom. (See art., *The O.T. in the Light of Archæology*, pp. 116–7.)

There is, however, another possible view of the date of the Exodus, supported by the statement made in 1 Kings 6[1], that Solomon began to build the Temple in Jerusalem in the four hundred and eightieth year after the coming out of Egypt. The date of the beginning of Solomon's reign has been fixed approximately at 970 B.C. The Temple was begun in his fourth year, i.e., in 966 B.C. Adding to that 480 we get the year 1446 as the date of the Exodus. At that time the reigning king in Egypt was Amenhotep (Amenophis) II, who succeeded the great Thothmes III (1503–1449 B.C.), who had raised Egypt to its highest point of imperial power and had carried Egyptian arms as far as the Euphrates. The predecessor of Thothmes III was the great queen Hatshepsut, daughter of Thothmes I, who has been supposed by many writers to have been the princess who rescued the child Moses and adopted him. Interest in her has been revived by the claim recently made by a German scholar that he had deciphered and translated certain strange non-Egyptian inscriptions occurring in the peninsula of Sinai on rock tablets and statues. In one of these he finds what he thinks to be letters indicating the name of Moses, who writes that the queen Hatshepsut had been friendly to him, had drawn him out of the Nile, and had made him ruler of a temple in Sinai. The claim of this scholar to have read and translated these curious inscriptions accurately is based largely on guesswork and still awaits verification. We cannot, with our present knowledge of them, assert either that they were written by Moses or that they make any reference to him. There is this further difficulty to be met, that if Moses lived in the fifteenth century B.C., and if the departure from Egypt and the settlement in Palestine took place toward the end of that century, then for four hundred years and more, down to the reign of Solomon, Hebrew history makes no reference to Egypt and gives no slightest hint of the numerous warlike campaigns in Palestine and Syria carried on during those centuries by the great kings of the eighteenth, nineteenth, and twentieth dynasties. The claims, however, of the earlier date, supported by 1 Kings 6[1], cannot be lightly set aside. This date is supported also by certain of the Tel-el-Amarna tablets, which contain correspondence of Egyptian governors of Canaanite towns, including Jerusalem, dating from about the year 1400 B.C., imploring help against invading hordes called Khabiri, which some modern scholars would identify with the Hebrew invaders under Joshua. (See art., *History of Hebrew and Jewish People*, p. 63.)

In the present state of our knowledge we cannot decide with any degree of certainty between the earlier, fifteenth-century date, and the later, thirteenth-century date. Both present difficulties, and neither can be shown to be in perfect agreement with the biblical narrative. We shall look hopefully for further light upon this problem which may come to us from new discoveries, such as are being constantly made by the indefatigable zeal of archæologists and explorers in the seemingly exhaustless mines of Egyptian antiquity.

Literature: Commentaries on *Exodus* by Driver (Cambridge Bible); Bennett (Century Bible); McNeile (Westminster Commentary); Chadwick (The Expositor's Bible). On the critical and historical questions: Breasted, *History of Egypt;* Kent, *Israel's Laws and Legal Precedents;* Wade, *O.T. History;* Foakes-Jackson, *Biblical History of the Hebrews;* Bacon, *Triple Tradition of the Exodus;* Shaw, *The Tabernacle: Its History and Structure;* Palmer, *The Desert of the Exodus;* Petrie, *Researches in Sinai* (chapters by C. T. Currelly). See also literature cited above under section on "Religious Value," p. 250.

CHAPTER I

1–7. Introductory Statement. The writer prefaces the history with a general statement regarding the settlement of Israel in Egypt and the sojourn there. The latter part of v. 1 should be rendered, "who came each man and his household with Jacob." Compare the list of names of Jacob's sons and grandsons in Gen. 46[8-27], where the total of seventy is made up by including Jacob himself and Joseph with his two sons. The LXX counts seventy-five, perhaps including the grandsons and great-grandsons of Joseph named in Num. 26[28-37]. Cf. Deut. 10[22] and Acts 7[14]. The passage in Acts is evidently based upon the LXX.

The story of Joseph's death and burial in Egypt has been told in Gen. 50[22-26]. There it is also related that he predicted the return at some future time from Egypt to Palestine, and that he made the Israelite people promise on oath that they would then bring his body to be buried in the land of his fathers. The period of the sojourn of Israel in Egypt, during which they *multiplied and waxed exceeding mighty,* is given as four hundred and thirty years, 12[40, 41] (cf. Gal. 3[17]), and as four hundred years, Gen. 15[13] (cf. Acts 7[6]). *The land* which *was filled with them* was that part of Egypt called in Gen. 45[10] and other passages "the land of Goshen," and in Gen. 47[11] "the land of Rameses." It seems to have been in the eastern part of the Delta.

8–22. The Oppression. *A new king* (v. 8), in all probability, implies a new dynasty. If, as is commonly believed, the king who made Joseph his prime minister was one of the Hyksos, or Shepherd Kings, invaders from Asia who held sway in Egypt, with their capital at Zoan (or Tanis) in the northeastern part of the Delta, the new king may have belonged to the eighteenth native Egyptian dynasty, by whom the Hyksos invaders were expelled from Egypt about 1580 B.C., or to the nineteenth dynasty founded about 1328 B.C. If the Exodus took place in the reign of Merenptah (1234–1214 B.C.), the king here mentioned must have been his predecessor, Rameses II. The favor shown the Hebrew settlers by the Hyksos kings, who were themselves, like the Hebrews, of an Asiatic race, was not continued by the native Egyptian kings who followed them. They may have feared another Asiatic invasion, and that the Hebrews, whose territory was on the frontier, would take sides with their enemies. Accordingly the Egyptians imposed upon them forced labor on the king's buildings and other public works. Doubtful of the loyalty of the Hebrews, they nevertheless did not want to lose them from the country, and so reduced them to a condition of slavery. Many of the great public works of Egypt, as of other ancient countries under despotic rule, were built in this way by the forced labor of slaves, or even of the common people of the country themselves.

The name *Pharaoh* is a compound of two Egyptian words which mean "Great House," and is used here as a title of the king, and not as his personal name. It is remarkable that the personal name is not given here as in the references to Egyptian kings in later centuries (1 Kings 14[25] 2 Kings 17[4] 19[9] 23[29] 2 Chr. 14[9]). This may be due to the fact that the history in its present form was not written until three hundred or more years later, when the personal names were not known.

The *store cities* (v. 11) were built for the storing of provisions against a period of famine, or of supplies for the army in time of war, or possibly also as convenient centers for trade (cf. 1 Kings 9[19] 2 Chr. 17[12]). *Pithom* is mentioned by the Greek historian Herodotus (fifth century B.C.) as on the canal made by Necho (610–594 B.C.) to connect the Nile with the Red Sea, a canal which had been begun by Rameses II, and was finally completed by the Persian ruler Darius. The site of *Raamses* (or Rameses) has not been certainly identified but it must have been in the same region, in the eastern Delta, where we know Rameses II to have carried on many building enterprises. (See also intro., section on "Contemporary History," p. 250.)

They were grieved (v. 12). The Hebrew word means both dread and dislike. They became alarmed and dreaded the growth of their Israelite neighbors. The same word is rendered "was distressed" in Num. 22[3], and "abhor" in Isa. 7[16]. The word rendered *rigor* (vv. 13, 14) is comparatively rare. It contains the idea of crushing force. The *mortar* was the black mud of the Nile or its canals, which was mixed with fragments of pottery. For the making of brick this mud was sometimes mixed with sand, and, to give it greater coherence, with chopped straw and chaff. In a semi-liquid state it was poured into molds and afterward dried in the sun. Such bricks were used both in Babylonia and Egypt for all kinds of buildings. The *service in the field* would include irrigation work of all kinds, the construction of dams and canals and the laborious lifting of water from the river or pools to the higher levels.

The Hebrew midwives refused to obey the king's inhuman command, and, it is said, as a reward for their piety God *made them houses,* (v. 21), i.e., families who perpetuated their names in times long after. It is thus that their names are remembered and recorded here. Since only two of these women are mentioned it is evident that the Hebrew community cannot have been very large.

CHAPTER II

Verses 1–22: Birth and Early Life of Moses; his Flight to Midian

1–4. Birth of Moses. The father of Moses was *a man of the house of Levi,* i.e., of the clan, or family group, which claimed Levi, third son of Jacob, as its ancestor. His mother was *a daughter of Levi,* or perhaps more correctly, as in the LXX, "one of the daughters of Levi." Like her husband, she was a member of the Levite clan, not literally a daughter of Jacob's son. Compare the name *daughters of Israel* given to the Hebrew women in Judg. 11[40]; *daughters of Canaan,* Gen. 28[8]; and *daughters of Judah,* Psa. 48[11]. But see also 6[14-20] Num. 26[57-59] (cf. 1 Chr. 23[6-13]), in which Amram, Moses' father, is said to be a grandson of Levi, and Jochebed, his wife, to be his father's sister, and so a daughter of Levi. If, however, there really was this close relationship between the patriarch Levi, who went down into Egypt with his father Jacob, and Moses, it is difficult to account for the four hundred years, or four hundred and thirty years (Gen. 15[13] Ex. 12[40, 41]) of the Egyptian sojourn.

The narrative here is concerned chiefly with Moses and he alone is mentioned (v. 2), but we learn further on that he had an older sister, Miriam (v. 4, 15[20] Num. 26[59]), and an older brother Aaron (7[7]). For the goodly appearance of the child Moses see also Acts 7[20] and Heb. 11[23].

The *ark of bulrushes* was made of the long stems of the Nile rush or papyrus, woven or bound tightly together and plastered with bitumen (rendered here *slime*) and pitch to make it water-tight. The pith of the stems of the same plant was cut into strips which, laid side by side and crossed at right angles with a second layer of the same, then glued together in sheets of convenient size, made a sort of paper used in Egypt and other neighboring countries as writing material. It had many other uses, such as for mats, sails, cloth, and baskets. The ark was, no doubt, shaped like a small boat. Such light boats are mentioned in Job 9[26] and Isa. 18[2]. A story has been found of an ancient Babylonian king, Sargon I, who was born in secret, committed to the river by his mother in a basket of rushes, and found and reared by one who used the river water to irrigate his fields.

5–10. Adoption by Pharaoh's Daughter. *The daughter of Pharaoh* is called by Josephus *Thermouthis,* and by Eusebius *Merris.* An inscription of the reign of Rameses II says that he had sixty sons and fifty-nine daughters. Among the names of his daughters there is one *Meri,* who may be the princess of our story. Knowing of the king's cruel edict, and her womanly compassion being aroused by the pitiful cry of the child, she adopted him, and by the ready wit of Miriam he was given to his own mother to nurse. As Moses grew from childhood to manhood he had, therefore, the double advantage of a knowledge of his own home and his own people, and of such education as the court and palace of an Egyptian king could afford. The story assumes that the king had a residence in or near the place where Moses was born and, therefore, in the Eastern Delta, and this seems to be confirmed by the discovery of many evidences of the presence of nineteenth-dynasty kings in that region.

The name *Moses* is pronounced in Hebrew *Mōsheh* and is the participle of a verb which means "draw." See Psa. 18[16], where there may be a reference to the deliverance of Moses. The word, however, is rare in Hebrew, and it has been supposed that it may have been originally an Egyptian word, which suggested the meaning "draw" only by its similarity in sound to the Hebrew word. If this be true, its original meaning may have been "son," or "child" (Egyptian *mes,* or *mesu;* see p. 62a). Driver (*Commentary,* p. 11) suggests *mosi,* "born."

11–15. Flight to Midian. The story told in vv. 11–15 throws light on the character of Moses in his earlier years. Though adopted by a princess and educated in the palace, he is not forgetful of his own people and of their *burdens.* In his interference on behalf of one who was being abused by an Egyptian he shows a rash and hasty temper, in marked contrast to the patience, forbearance, and self-control of later years. Two incidents, however, of those years of leadership in Israel show the same hot temper blazing forth under great provocation (see 32[19-22] Num. 20[1-13]).

Josephus, the Jewish historian of the time of Christ, tells another story to the effect that Moses attained a high command in the Egyptian army and led a successful expedition against the Ethiopians, in which he won the daughter of the Ethiopian king as his wife, and that, as a consequence, Pharaoh was jealous of his success and sought to kill him (*Antiquities*, bk. ii, chs. 10, 11; cf. Num. 12[1]).

The land of Midian (Vulgate, *Madian*) lay to the eastward of Egypt, across the Asiatic boundary. Its exact location is now unknown. If the traditional placing of Mount Sinai (=Horeb) in the southern part of the Sinaitic peninsula be correct, then we would look for the land of Midian in the same region, probably on the western side of the Gulf of Akaba, the northeastern arm of the Red Sea. Ptolemy, a celebrated Egyptian writer on astronomy and geography of the second century A.D., and Arabian writers mention a place called Modiana, or Madyan, east of the gulf of Akaba. In the O.T. Midian appears in the neighborhood of Moab and Edom (Gen. 36[35] Num. 22[4] 25[16-18]), and along with Amalekites and "children of the east," invading Israel from the east (Judg. 6–8). The Midianites are represented as, like the Hebrews, descended from Abraham (Gen. 25[2]), and so closely related to them. They were sent away by Abraham "eastward, unto the east country" (Gen. 25[6]). They are represented as caravan traders (Gen. 37[28] Isa. 60[6]), as shepherds (here), and as enemies of Israel (Num. 25[16-18] 31[1-12] Judg. 6–8). As a nomadic Arabian people they may have had several branches, and may have had more than one home in the northwestern Arabian wilderness.

16–22. With the Priest of Midian. *The priest of Midian* was, no doubt, the chief priest of the tribe and a person of importance. He may have been the guardian of the local shrine or sanctuary. In ch. 18 he appears to be a worshiper of Jehovah. His daughters cared for the flocks of sheep, according to a custom which still exists in the peninsula of Sinai. The name given to the priest in v. 18, *Reuel* (LXX Raguel), appears again in Num. 10[29]. In ch. 3 and elsewhere he is called Jethro. (Cf. Judg. 1[16] 4[11].) He may have actually had two names, or the difference in names may be due to difference in tradition. He appreciates the kindness of the stranger to his daughters and offers him the ready hospitality of the highborn Arab. The daughters called Moses *an Egyptian* because his clothes, and possibly his language, were Egyptian. The name *Zipporah*, which is feminine in form, means "bird," and *Gershom* (LXX Gersam) "a sojourner there."

Chapters 2[23] to 4[17]: Vision and Call of Moses

The cry of the people suffering a cruel bondage in Egypt reached the ear of God, and he raised up for them a deliverer. Moses, whose birth, education, and experience in the Arabian wilderness qualified him in an exceptional way for the task, was the man chosen. In a vision in the sacred mountain of Horeb God appeared to him, and revealed a new name by which he was henceforth to be known in Israel. In response to Moses' reluctant pleas and excuses he gives assurances and signs of his unfailing presence and help.

23–25. Israel's Cry of Distress. *The king of Egypt*, if we accept the later date of the Exodus, was Rameses II, who began the oppression and enslavement of Israel. He died about 1234 B.C. The writer of this history is assured of God's interest in the affairs of men, and that their sufferings do not go unnoticed by him. *God heard*, he *remembered his covenant*, he *saw*, and he *took knowledge*. For the covenant with Abraham see Gen. 15 and 17.

CHAPTER III

The story of Moses' vision at Horeb, in chs. 3 and 4, is drawn almost entirely from the Prophetic History Book, the oldest of the sources of the Pentateuch. It contains a remarkable and exceedingly valuable interpretation of Moses' religious experience and of the significance of the divine Name revealed to him.

1–3. The Burning Bush. *The back of the wilderness*, where the vision occurred, was, according to the usage of the language, the western part. If we accept the ordinary and traditional view that Horeb was in the southern part of the peninsula of Sinai, then the region referred to will be the country west of the Gulf of Akaba, in which there are several mountains from 6,500 to 8,500 feet in height. The farthest east of these, called by the Arabs *Jebel Musa*, or "the mount of Moses," is the one commonly identified with Mount Horeb.

It must be remembered, however, that there are strong reasons for believing that Mount Horeb was much farther north. For example, the place called Meribah, where Moses smote the rock and obtained a supply of water (17[1-7]), is placed in the corresponding story in Num. 20[1-13] at or near Kadesh (see map), and yet the rock is described as "the rock in Horeb" (17[6]; cf. Num. 27[14] Deut. 32[51]). If Horeb and Sinai are identified, or if they belong to the same range or group of mountains, there is additional reason for believing it to be near Kadesh. In Num. 10[12] the first stopping place in the march of the Israelites from Sinai is the wilderness of Paran, and from this wilderness of Paran Moses sent the spies (Num. 13[3]) northward into Canaan, who returned to him to Kadesh (Num. 13[26]). In Num. 20[16] Kadesh is said to be on the border of Edom.

In Deut. 33[2] Sinai seems to be identified with Seir, the name given to the mountains of Edom (cf. Judg. 5[4, 5] Hab. 3[3]). As against this view and in favor of the traditional site in the peninsula must be mentioned the fact that in the list of the journeys of the Israelites in Num. 33, there are twenty stations between Sinai and Kadesh, and that, in Deut. 1[2], it is said that "It is eleven days' journey from Horeb by the way of mount Seir to Kadesh," and that it is through a "great and terrible wilderness." (See McNeile, *Exodus*, pp. cii-cvi, who endeavors to prove that Horeb and Sinai are not identical, the former being east of the gulf of Akabah, and the latter near Kadesh on the western border of Edom. The exact position of the sacred mountain of Moses' vision is still an open question. An extremely interesting and full discussion of the subject will be found in Driver, *Exodus*, pp. 177–191.)

Here, as in a number of other passages, *the angel of the Lord* represents the Lord himself (v. 2; cf. vv. 4, 6). In Isa. 63[9] it is "the angel of his presence" (cf. 23[20-23] 32[34] 33[14] Mal. 3[1]). The mountain is called the *mountain of God,* perhaps because it was already held by the Midianites to be a sacred place, an ancient sanctuary. It may have been, therefore, that Moses, the shepherd, approached the place in a spirit of reverence and worship, and so was prepared in mind and heart for the vision which came to him there. There he saw a *great sight,* a bush which *burned with fire, and the bush was not consumed.* It is, perhaps, useless to try to explain just what Moses saw, or to find any phenomenon of nature which might have assumed this strange and startling appearance. No doubt nature does, at times, clothe herself in flaming colors. Whittier, with this experience of Moses in mind, has written of one who saw God in the "miracle of autumn," when

> "All the woods with many-colored flame
> Of splendor, making summer's greenness tame,
> Burned, unconsumed; a voice without a sound
> Spake to him from each kindled bush around,
> And made the strange new landscape holy ground."

Every one will be familiar too with Elizabeth Barrett Browning's lines:

> "Earth's crammed with heaven,
> And every common bush afire with God;
> But only he who sees takes off his shoes."

4–12. Call and Commission. There is no vision and no glory to him who does not see. Whatever the explanation, the fact remains of a profound experience of the Spirit, a real coming face to face with God (Deut. 34[10]). It is certain that Moses, during his banishment, had pondered much upon the affliction of his brethren in Egypt; and that the question how or by what means they might be delivered had often occurred to him. Now the call of duty comes home to him. It is the voice of God. He is the man divinely chosen for the task. The God of Horeb is the God of his fathers; it is therefore no strange voice that speaks. There is a new and significant name, but the same God.

The removing of the sandals and the hiding of the face by Moses are tokens of reverence. The Samaritans to this day remove their shoes at their sanctuary on Mount Gerizim, and the Mohammedans at the door of the mosque.

I am come down to deliver (v. 8). That is God's word of assurance and of promise. Moses is the chosen instrument of his will and purpose, but God himself is the deliverer. See the spirited poetic description of God's work on behalf of Israel in Psa. 105[26-45].

The description of the land of Canaan, the home of their fathers, in v. 8 (cf. v. 17), is repeated from Gen. 15[18-21], and appears again in 13[5] 33[2, 3] Lev. 20[24] Num. 13[27-29] 14[7] Deut. 26[9-15] Jer. 11[5] 32[22] Ezek. 20[6] (cf. Deut. 8[7-9]). The terms *Canaanite,* and sometimes *Amorite,* are used in a general way for the native inhabitants of Canaan. Where there is a distinction the Canaanites appear to be regarded as inhabitants of the coast lands and the Jordan Valley, and the Amorites of the higher lands both east and west of Jordan. The *Hittite* was representative of a great nation whose proper home was much farther north, in Syria and Asia Minor, but of which some settlements existed in Palestine from the days of Abraham (Gen. 23[5], "the children of Heth"; cf. Num. 13[29]). The *Perizzite,* a people of central Palestine, are supposed by some to have been simple peasantry, country-folk, living in unwalled villages (cf. Deut. 3[5] 1 Sam. 6[18]). The *Hivite* and the *Jebusite* were comparatively unimportant peoples of central Palestine, the latter of whom maintained themselves in Jerusalem until the reign of David.

Moses said unto God, Who am I? (V. 11.) His humility and his shrinking from so great a task, together with distrust of his own powers, are not altogether to his discredit. Compare Jeremiah's self-distrust in the presence of God's call (Jer. 1[6]), and the modest protest of Gideon (Judg. 6[15]). The answer of God to Moses, as to Gideon and to Jeremiah, is

Certainly I will be with thee. The God who dwells in the flaming bush upon the mountainside is also the God of human life. He will be with the man he has chosen, and he will dwell in the midst of the community of his people. The *token* suggested to Moses is to be a proof that he is really sent by God. We can imagine that it would make a strong appeal to his mind. If he can succeed in bringing the people of Israel out of Egypt, he will lead them to this very mountain, to this place now doubly sacred to him, and here he and they will worship God together. That will, indeed, be a proof of the reality and truth of the vision.

13–22. Jehovah, the God of Israel. Four apparently serious difficulties present themselves to the mind of Moses. The *first* (vv. 11, 12) is his fear that he is not the right person to undertake the task, that he has not the ability to perform it. This fear is removed by the promise of God's ever-present help. The *second* difficulty (vv. 13–22) is his fear that the people will not believe that it was really the God of their fathers who had spoken to him. Those were days of the worship of many gods. The Israelites were surrounded on every side by Egyptian temples and altars. No doubt the wilderness to which Moses had fled had its gods also—so they would naturally think. Much depended upon the name, the personal name, of the deity with whom he had held communion. *What is his name?* they will be sure to ask. *What shall I say?*

The answer to Moses' question (v. 14) contains either a new name, or a new interpretation of an old name of God already known to Moses. The latter seems to be the more likely explanation of it. The words *I am that I am* are evidently intended as an interpretation of the name "Jehovah," which was pronounced in Hebrew *Yahweh.* According to the popular etymology of this passage the Hebrew word was understood to be the third person singular masculine of the imperfect tense of the verb "to be" in its older form (found in a few instances in the Hebrew text and common in Aramaic), meaning "He is," or "He will be"; or, if regarded as derived from the causative stem of the verb, "He causes to be." The divine voice says "*I am,*" Moses interprets "*He is.*" There is some reason to believe that the name was known before this revelation of its meaning to Moses. If Professor Hubert Grimme's recent attempts to translate certain obscure inscriptions found in the peninsula of Sinai can be relied upon (see intro., p. 251) there was a temple there to Yahu (=*Yahweh*) in the fifteenth century B.C. The name may have been used by the Midianites with whom Moses was living. In passages of Genesis drawn from one of the early prophetic historians of Israel it is represented as freely used by the patriarchs. It is true that, in another account of this vision (6^{2-9}), the statement is made that by the name "Jehovah" (=*Yahweh*) God was not known to Abraham, Isaac, and Jacob, and was made known first to Moses, but this is quite evidently drawn from another source, and may be an inference from the story in ch. 3.

There is no doubt that the name, whatever its original meaning and use may have been, came to designate for Moses and for Israel the living, self-existent God, the One who is and will be, and who has within himself the exhaustless resources of being. He is not defined by one event, or by one circumstance, or by the experience of one age or nation, but is ceaselessly renewing the revelation of himself in the world of nature and in human history. His being is expressed in action. He will be with his people, guide, counselor, warrior, lawgiver, and mighty deliverer. See Psa. 68^4 89^8 (where the name is contracted to *Jah,* more correctly, *Yah,* or the word may represent an earlier form of the divine name) Jn. 8^{58} Heb. 13^8 Rev. 1^4 4^8.

It should be explained here that, in the Authorized Version and in the English Revised Version the name is most commonly translated "Lord." The American Revised Version prefers to use the form "Jehovah." This form has resulted from a curious mistake made by a mediæval Christian scholar, who, in endeavoring to read and translate the Hebrew text, combined the consonants of the divine name with the vowels of another word (*Adonai* = Lord) which was commonly substituted for it by Jewish readers.

The request which is to be made of Pharaoh (v. 18) is, no doubt, intended to be preliminary to further demands. The Egyptian king will realize that if the enslaved people are allowed to escape into the freedom of the wilderness they will not return. He will, of course, be unwilling, and his refusal will be *by a mighty hand* (v. 19), i.e., accompanied by the exercise of compelling force. But it will be better to adopt here the reading of the LXX, "except by a mighty hand," i.e., by the compelling power of the hand of God (so also v. 20, 6^1 13^9 32^{11}, and frequently in Deuteronomy and elsewhere).

The request is that they may be permitted to go a certain distance into the eastern wilderness to offer sacrifice and to hold a feast (5^1) unto their God. This may have been intended as the revival of an ancient spring festival, neglected during the sojourn in

Egypt, in which the first fruits of the harvest and the firstlings of flock and herd were offered in sacrifice, a festival afterward associated with the Passover and made to commemorate the deliverance from Egypt (see 13^11-16 Lev. 23^9-14 Deut. 16^1-8).

The people are to be instructed, when permission is given them to go, to ask presents of their Egyptian neighbors, and so to *spoil the Egyptians* (v. 22). The asking and giving of presents was a frequent incident marking the interchange of courtesies as well as of diplomatic missions in those days (cf. Job 6^22). The apocryphal book of Wisdom (10^17) interprets this, perhaps quite rightly, by saying that thus wisdom "rendered to the righteous a reward of their labors."

CHAPTER IV

1–9. Confirmatory Signs and Promises. Moses' *third* difficulty (cf. 3^13-22) lies in his fear that the people will not believe him nor listen to him when he comes to them with his message from God. His fear is met by signs which will be convincing, namely, the rod changed to a serpent, the leprous hand infected and then healed, and the water become blood. In ch. 7 we are told that when Moses exhibited these signs in the presence of Pharaoh the magicians of Egypt did likewise with their enchantments, and Pharaoh was unconvinced.

The insertion of parentheses in vv. 4 and 7 appears to be quite unnecessary, and is not required by the sense. There does seem, however, to be an omission at the beginning of v. 5, which should, perhaps, be directly connected with vv. 8, 9, and be preceded by some such words as "And the Lord said unto him, Do this," etc.

10–17. Moses' Reluctance Overcome. The *fourth* objection of Moses (v. 10; cf. 3^13-22) is that he is not *eloquent*, in Hebrew "not a man of words." The answer which he receives is that the God who made man's mouth will be with him and will teach him what to say. This assurance was abundantly fulfilled in the experience of Moses, who "was mighty in his words and works" (Acts 7^22). If the speeches attributed to him in Deuteronomy were his own words, and not an exposition of his teaching by later writers, we would indeed have to believe him to have been a speaker of notable eloquence and power.

Moses finally yields, but with apparent unwillingness, to the call of God (v. 13), and is now promised that Aaron, his brother, who *can speak well* (v. 14), will be associated with him. It may be noted in passing that the description of Aaron as *the Levite* makes it quite clear that this story was not written by Moses himself, but by others about him long afterward, when it was necessary to explain who Aaron was in this place where his name is first mentioned (cf. 6^20 7^1, 2). Aaron, Moses is told, is coming to meet him (see vv. 27, 28). He is to be Moses' *spokesman unto the people*, but the supreme authority is to rest with Moses, who is to be *to him as God.*

CHAPTERS 4^18 TO 5^23: MOSES RETURNS TO EGYPT; PETITIONS PHARAOH IN VAIN

18–31. The Return of Moses to Egypt. According to the patriarchal custom which prevailed in Arabia, Jethro was head of the family group or clan into which Moses had entered by marriage. Moses now asks and receives his permission to return to Egypt. The abrupt introduction of another command of God in v. 19 is one more indication of the fact that the narrative is compiled from different older sources. There is close connection here with 2^23a. Note the difference, however, between the reference to Moses' son in v. 25 (cf. 2^22), and the plural "sons" in v. 20 (cf. 18^1-5), still another indication of the composite character of the narrative.

Moses is bidden to present himself on his return to Pharaoh and to demand the release of his people, but is warned of the hardness of Pharaoh's heart (cf. 7^13, 22, etc.). That which we might regard as the natural and inevitable result of Pharaoh's cruelty and perverseness is here said to be the act of God (cf. Rom. 9^17, 18, notes).

Israel is my son, my firstborn (v. 22). God is thus declared to be the father of his people, and the close relationship which this represents is often assumed both in the O.T. and N.T. See Isa. 63^16 Jer. 31^9, 20 Hos. 11^1. The threat in v. 23 anticipates the tenth and last of the plagues (11^4-6).

The curious story told in v. 24 can only be understood as coming from a great antiquity and as representing an early and very primitive way of thinking. Moses is taken seriously ill at the lodging-place. His illness is attributed to the anger of God against him because he has neglected the sacred duty of circumcision in the case of his son. It is not to be inferred that it was neglected in his own case (Driver, *Exodus*, p. 33), which not only would be most unlikely, but is excluded by the statement of Josh. 5^4, 5. It was a custom, however, which was probably not practiced by the Midianites among whom he had been living, and seems to have been now reluctantly performed by his wife as, to her mind and to his, the only means of turning aside the anger of God and saving his life. So, when God *let him alone,* i.e., ceased to afflict him with sickness, she declared him to be *a bridegroom of blood,* saved to her by the blood of her son. According to the story in Genesis (17^{10-14}), the custom was introduced in the time of Abraham, and became a sign of the covenant bond between Jehovah and his people. It is known to have been practiced also by the neighboring and closely related peoples of Edom, Moab, and Ammon, by some Arabian tribes, and by Egyptians at least as early as the age of Moses. It can readily be understood that Moses, returning to Egypt to face the elders of his own people as their divinely appointed leader, might have been seriously disturbed in his mind by the neglect to circumcise his son and by the effect which this might have upon their minds and so upon the success of his mission. It is quite possible, also, that the apparent disagreement between Moses and his wife, which is suggested by this incident, led to her being sent back to her father, while Moses went on with his brother to Egypt (see 18^{2}).

Aaron, Moses' brother (v. 27), henceforth occupies a large place in the history of the Exodus; and, in the organization of the nation which takes place at Sinai, becomes the religious head, the chief priest, of Israel, as Moses becomes its lawgiver and judge, the authority of Moses being, however, always recognized as supreme (see 28^{1-3}).

CHAPTER V

1–9. Moses' Petition and Pharaoh's Refusal. The word rendered *feast* (v. 1) means both a pilgrimage and a sacred festival. It is identical with the word still used by Arabs and Egyptians to describe the pilgrimage to Mecca. The request of Moses and Aaron is that the people be permitted to make pilgrimage to some shrine or sanctuary in the wilderness. Perhaps Horeb was the place which they had in mind, although it was distant much more than three days' journey. Pharaoh does not recognize *the Lord* (in Hebrew *Jehovah*) as having anything to do with him. His question is contemptuous: *Who is Jehovah, that I should hearken to his voice?* The events which followed humbled that false pride (see $8^{8,\ 28}$ 9^{28} $10^{16,\ 17}$).

The visit of Moses and Aaron to the elders of Israel had become known (4^{29-31}), and the people, in the natural excitement at the hope of deliverance thus awakened in their hearts, had relaxed their diligence in labor upon Pharaoh's works. The king lays the blame upon Moses and Aaron. He determines to increase the burden of toil and commands, *Let heavier work be laid upon the men that they may labor therein* (v. 9). Straw had formerly been supplied to the men who made bricks of the Nile clay, but it will be supplied no longer; yet the full *tale of the bricks* will be required as before. The straw was useful in binding the clay more firmly together and so making a better and more durable brick, but brick seems often to have been made without it. The hardship of the new orders was increased by the demand that the full number of bricks should be made each day, so that it was not possible to concentrate upon the gathering of stubble one day with the hope of doubling the number the next (v. 13)—a good example of unreasoning, inhuman tyranny and cruelty.

10–19. Increased Burdens. The *taskmasters* of Pharaoh had appointed *officers* of the Hebrews themselves, whom they had set over the labor gangs, and whom they held responsible for the full quantity of work assigned. It was they, therefore, who were beaten, and who brought their complaint to Pharaoh. In v. 16 we should read in the last clause, with the LXX, "and thou shalt be guilty of sin [or a wrong] against thy people."

20–23. Discouragement and Complaints. (See 6^{1}.) Returning from their unsatisfactory interview with Pharaoh, and seeing themselves to be indeed *in evil case,* the officers, in their turn, bitterly accuse Moses and Aaron of being the cause of all their trouble. The net result of this first move toward deliverance was to sink the people into a deeper bondage and a blacker despair. They say to Moses. "You have brought us into exceedingly bad odor with Pharaoh and his officers, giving them an opportunity and an excuse to destroy us" (v. 20).

It was the habit of Moses, in the simplicity and purity of his faith, to turn to his God, whose promise at Horeb (3^{12}) he never forgot. See also $6^{12,\ 30}$ 17^{4} 32^{11-13} Deut. 9^{26-29}, etc. The answer to his prayer here lies in the power of God, in the *strong hand* by which the Lord will compel Pharaoh to let Israel go. In the calamities which came thick and fast upon Egypt in that tragic year he was to see the exercise of the compelling power of that strong hand (cf. 3^{19} notes, 13^{3}).

CHAPTERS 6^{1} TO 7^{7}: A SECOND ACCOUNT OF MOSES' VISION AND CALL

We have here (omitting 6^{14-27}) a second and shorter account of the experiences in Arabia and Egypt which led Moses to take up the great task of Israel's deliverance. This may fairly be regarded as taken by the compilers of the history from a different source, most probably from the Priestly History Book from which we have also 6[14-27] 7[8-11] 12[1-28], and many other passages of a similar character. The portions of the book of Genesis which appear to be taken from this same source do not use the name "Jehovah," so this writer is quite consistent in his statement that the name was now revealed for the first time to Moses. In 3[14] (see notes) there seems to be rather a new significance attached to an old and already known name.

CHAPTER VI

1–8. Call and Commission. In the Hebrew *El Shaddai* = "God Almighty," we have another of the very old Semitic names of God. *El* occurs frequently in the O.T., both alone and in compounds such as Beth*el*, "house of God," *Eli*jah, "my God is Jehovah," etc., and in the titles "Most High God" (Gen. 14[18]), "Everlasting God" (Gen. 21[33]), "Jealous God" (Ex. 20[5]), etc. The combination El Shaddai, or Shaddai alone, is found in many passages, as, e.g., Gen. 17[1] 28[3] Num. 24[4, 16], etc. The original or root meaning of the words is unknown. (Cf., however, the larger commentaries.)

The *covenant* (v. 4) with Abraham is made the starting point of all Israel's religious history. As developed in the teachings of priest and prophet it has become one of the most fruitful of all religious ideas. The Hebrew word means a "bond," and is used to signify an agreement freely entered into between men, and here between man and God, and confirmed by solemn oaths and engagements. Freely undertaken by both parties it becomes the most binding of all obligations, the fulfillment of its terms being a proof of honor and of fidelity. In the sphere of religion it represents man and God as thus bound together by mutual ties of faithfulness and high responsibility and honor, there resting upon the man who enters into it the same moral obligation to keep his oath and promise as upon the God he serves. In this passage the covenant with the patriarchs is recalled, with the assurance that it stands firm in the faithfulness of God and will surely be fulfilled. See, e.g., Gen. 15[13-21] 17[1-9]. Its fulfillment involves deliverance of Israel from Egypt and restoration to the land of their fathers, a task to which Jehovah will now set his hand. Jehovah will *redeem* his people from their bondage. The covenant made with their fathers he will renew with them as a nation, they to be his people and he to be their God (vv. 6–9). It is thus that Jehovah first of all earns and receives his title of *Redeemer* (cf. 15[13] Psa. 74[2] 77[15] 78[35] 106[10] Isa. 41[14] 43[14] 54[5]). The lifting up of the hand (v. 8; cf. A.S.V. "sware," and mg.) signifies the oath by which he had bound himself in covenant bond.

9–13, 28–30. The People's Unbelief and Moses' Hesitation to Approach Pharaoh. The expression *uncircumcised lips* is apparently Moses' way of saying that he has not the gift of eloquent speech (as in 4[10]). Evidently, circumcision meant consecration of the body and its life to God, and such consecration would be regarded, ideally at least, as fitting the man for God's service. Moses feels his unfitness in this regard. (See notes on ch. 3.)

14–27. The Tribe and Family of Moses. These verses evidently contain part of a genealogical record of the sons of Jacob. The writer's purpose is, however, to show the descent and kindred of Moses and Aaron, and so he limits himself, from v. 16 onward, to the tribe of Levi. Cf. 1[2] Gen. 35[23-26] 46[8-27] Num. 26[5-62]. The term *fathers' houses* means "family groups," or "clans." The Syriac version adds, in v. 20, "and Miriam."

28–30. See under vv. 9–13.

CHAPTER VII

1–7. Commission of Moses and Aaron. The answer of God to Moses' confession of unfitness is, as in 4[14-16], the choice of Aaron to be his spokesman. The Hebrew word here rendered *prophet* (v. 1) means "spokesman." Just as the prophet speaks the words which he receives from God, so will Aaron speak for Moses.

God will harden Pharaoh's heart, thus not only punishimg him by increasing hardness of heart for his crime against Israel, but providing an opportunity to show his signs and wonders in Egypt and thus to convince the Egyptians that he is indeed the sovereign Lord. Such a conception would have been impossible if at this early time Jehovah had been thought of as a God of righteousness and holiness. (See notes on chs. 4, 5.)

Chapters 7[8] to 11[10]: The Signs and Plagues

The plagues which visited the Egyptians during the greater part of a year after the refusal of Pharaoh to let Israel go are ascribed by the narrative to the direct working of the mighty hand of God on behalf of his oppressed people. At the same time it is made quite clear that they were natural phenomena, familiar to the people of Egypt, but extraordinary in intensity and violence and in their destructive effects. The writers (for we have here as in the earlier chapters material drawn from two or more sources) see the divine energy expressing itself in these events and using them both to achieve the deliverance of Israel and to make God's power known in Egypt and throughout the world ($7^{4, 5}$ 8^{10} $14^{4, 18}$ Psa. $77^{14, 15}$). They have the merit of seeing God not only in the extraordinary and supernatural but also in the natural, bending nature to his will, making the forces of nature obey him, and using them both for the good of his people and the discomfiture of their enemies.

Ten plagues are mentioned here, but in the two great historical poems, Psa. 78 and 105, only eight. It is possible that in two instances the story has been duplicated. The *lice* (or, rather, *mosquitoes* or *sand flies*) of 8^{16-19} may be the same as the *swarms of flies* of 8^{20-32} (cf. Psa. 78^{45} 105^{31}), and the *murrain* (or pestilence) of 9^{1-7} and *boils* of 9^{8-12} may also be identical (cf. Psa. 78^{50}).

8–13. The Sign of Aaron's Rod. The *rod* when first mentioned was in the hand of Moses (4^{1-4}). It was used by him to convince the elders of Israel of his divine commission. Now, in the interviews with Pharaoh it is borne by Aaron. There is no parallel in magical arts to this turning of a rod into a serpent. But snake-charmers in the East do, even in the present day, by a sort of hypnotism, render snakes rigid so that they can be held in the hand as rods. This may have been what Pharaoh's wise men did.

14–25. The First Plague: Water Turned to Blood. Apparently, Pharaoh was accustomed at certain times to go to the river, perhaps for some religious ceremony. There Moses and Aaron met him (v. 20). The rod was lifted up and the waters of the river were turned to blood. We are told by those familiar with Egypt that each year, when the Nile begins to rise in flood, toward the end of June, the water becomes discolored, partly from decaying vegetable matter and partly from a reddish marl brought down from the mountains of Abyssinia. It is first green, then red, and at this stage the river is called by the natives the Red Nile. But the Red Nile water is not unwholesome, and does not cause the fish in the river to die. It is evident, therefore, that there was something quite unusual and extraordinary in this seven days' plague. For another instance of water appearing like blood see 2 Kings $3^{22, 23}$; cf. Psa. 78^{44} 105^{29}. The magicians of Egypt produced the same change in some small body of water, or perhaps in vessels filled with water from the wells (v. 24).

In v. 17 the abrupt change from the words spoken by the Lord in the first part of the verse to the words of Moses in the second part is most likely to be accounted for by the method of the author or compiler, who pieces together his narrative from the different sources. Thus v. 17a is from one source and v. 17b from another.

CHAPTER VIII

1–15. The Second Plague: Frogs. If it may be supposed that the discoloration and corruption of the river water was due to the presence of great quantities of decaying vegetable matter swept down from its southern sources by the Nile flood, this condition would be favorable to the multiplication of frogs. And so *the frogs came up and covered the land of Egypt.* They entered the houses, and the earthenware stoves or *ovens*, and the shallow wooden *kneading troughs.* The magicians, also, by some clever trick, were able to produce frogs where there had been none. But Pharaoh was sufficiently impressed to send for Moses and Aaron and to beg them to *intreat the Lord that he take away the frogs.* This is a decided change from the contemptuous pride with which he greeted them at their first interview ($5^{1, 2}$).

The words of Moses in v. 9 are usually understood as a polite way of saying to the king, "Let the honor be yours of appointing the time." The Hebrew text, however, suggests the idea of a boast on the part of Pharaoh, and the meaning intended may rather be, "Have your boast that you have gotten the better of me in this matter: against what time?—" etc. Moses reads truly the falsehood in Pharaoh's promise (v. 8), but nevertheless yields to his request. He is willing that this time the king may boast to his princes and people that he has outwitted the insistent and troublesome Hebrew. At the same time he would give him unmistakable evidence *that there is none like unto the Lord* (v. 10). In v. 12b we should render (as in mg.) "as he had appointed (or promised) unto Pharaoh."

16–19. The Third Plague: Lice. The Hebrew word here rendered *lice* more probably denotes "gnats" or "mosquitoes" (Isa. 51^{6} mg.), which are abundant in Egypt. The ancient versions interpret both ways, some as lice and some as gnats. The fact that they attacked both man and beast is in favor of the latter meaning. While the Nile is in flood, especially in the autumn, they rise in swarms from the flooded rice-fields and "the air is sometimes darkened with them. Their sting occasions swelling and irritation." (See Driver, *Exodus*, p. 65. He adds, "The gnats in Egypt often look like clouds of dust.") Here the magicians of Egypt scored their first failure (vv. 18, 19), and *said unto Pharaoh, This is the finger of God.*

20–32. The Fourth Plague: Swarms of Flies. This plague, as previously suggested, may be identical with the preceding, the story of it having been drawn from two different sources. In that case the *swarms of flies* will have been the stinging gnats or mosquitoes. From these the Hebrews in their settlements in *the land of Goshen* are to be free. Pharaoh yields this time so far as to permit the Hebrews to keep their feast and offer their sacrifice within the land which they occupied in Egypt. The answer of Moses is to this effect: "The Egyptians are our near neighbors. Our customs of sacrifice would be exceedingly offensive to them." The reason for this statement lies in the fact that certain animals which the Hebrews were accustomed to offer in sacrifice were held sacred by the Egyptians, such as the cow, which was sacred to Isis, the bull to Apis, the sheep at Thebes, etc. Pharaoh goes still further and permits them to go into the wilderness, but not far away; but, when the plague is removed, he hardens his heart again and withdraws his permission. As Moses plainly said, he *dealt deceitfully* (v. 29).

CHAPTER IX

1–12. The Fifth and Sixth Plagues: Murrain and Boils. The *very grievous murrain* (in Hebrew, literally "a very heavy plague, or pestilence") and the *boils* represent diseases of men and cattle, the nature of which is quite unknown to us. The second is described as *a boil breaking forth with blains*, or pustules, i.e., distributing itself in painful blisters or ulcers. The LXX rendering suggests smallpox. The *furnace* (v. 8) "was a kiln for baking pottery or burning lime."

13–35. The Seventh Plague: Hail. In v. 14 the phrase *upon thine heart* means simply "upon thyself." The Hebrew word for heart has frequently this meaning (cf. Gen. 8[21]). The words *I had put forth my hand* (v. 15) are hypothetical. The Lord would have done this and Pharaoh would have been cut off, but God had kept him alive for this very purpose —to show him his power, and that *his name might be declared throughout all the earth* (v. 16; cf. Rom. 9[17]). God is not thus regarded as unjust, as dooming a man to destruction or using him in an arbitrary way, but, rather, as overruling even human perversity, which brings punishment upon itself, for the accomplishment of his beneficent purposes.

Hail storms are rare in Egypt, and when they do occur it is usually in January. That is the month here indicated by the statement that *the barley was in the ear, and the flax was bolled* (or in bud), and *the wheat and the spelt . . . were not grown up* (vv. 31, 32). It is evident that not all the cattle of Egypt had died (v. 6), or that fresh herds had been found, for Moses warns Pharaoh to provide for their safety.

There was *fire mingled with the hail* (v. 24), literally "fire taking itself in the midst of the hail." The reference is, no doubt, to incessantly recurring flashes of lightning (see mg.). Pharaoh was evidently alarmed by the awful spectacle of the storm and the destruction which it caused, but he was in no sense penitent. His confession of sin in v. 27 does not ring true.

Barley was very commonly grown in ancient Egypt, and from it was made a coarse kind of bread. The barley harvest began early in March. The *flax* in Egypt flowers in February. *Spelt* is a kind of grain much like wheat. It is known to have been used in Egypt. Jerome renders the Hebrew word here by the Latin for *vetch*, and that may be correct.

Moses' expectation that Pharaoh and his servants would not yet *fear the Lord God*, and so cease their stubborn opposition to his will, was fulfilled in the end by another refusal (vv. 30, 35).

CHAPTER X

1–20. The Eighth Plague: Swarms of Locusts. We have here again (vv. 1, 2) the declaration that God is making an example of Pharaoh, in particular that the people of Israel may know and may tell their children that he is indeed their Lord, the one God whom alone they are to worship and serve. The pronoun *thou* (v. 2) is used not of Moses only but of all Israel (cf. Deut. 4[9]). The words *what things I have wrought* (v. 2) should be rendered (as in mg.) "how I have mocked the Egyptians," but this sounds harsh to our ears. It is difficult for us, from the Christian point of view, to think of God as mocking, or, literally, making a toy or plaything of a people, diverting himself by their sufferings. The O.T. writers, who in this way endeavor to interpret for us the mind of God, had still much to learn.

For a description of the locust swarms which are common in the East, and occasionally visit Egypt, see Driver, *Joel* (pp. 37–39, 48–53, 87–91). Travelers tell of seeing the locusts brought up by a southwest wind from the Libyan desert, and in another instance from the east, and driven back into the desert when the wind changed. For the devastation wrought by them see Joel 1[4-20] 2[2-10] (notes). Pharaoh gives only a partial consent. The men may go, but not the women and children. His words in v. 10 are ironical. Moffatt renders, "Well, said the Pharaoh, may the Eternal be with you if ever I let you and your little ones go. Let you go? Plainly you are out for some mischief. No, no!" This time, in the sequel (vv. 16, 17), Pharaoh seems to be really humbled, but when the plague was gone he refused again to let Israel go.

21–29. The Ninth Plague: Thick Darkness. The *darkness which may be felt* was, in all probability, produced by a sand-storm, such as occurs frequently in the months of March and April. During a period of fifty days a scorching hot wind from the desert is liable to blow in over the cultivated lands of Egypt, for two or three days at a time, bearing such quantities of fine sand and dust that the air is darkened. The darkness has been compared to that caused by a London fog. The wind is said to travel sometimes in a narrow zone leaving the air clear on either side of the storm. There is a remarkable description of the terrors of this night of darkness in Wisdom 17. Another account of the final interview of Moses with Pharaoh (vv. 28, 29) occurs in 11[4-8]. This latter passage, however, may have originally followed the closing verses of ch. 10 in the narrative from which it was taken.

CHAPTER XI

The Tenth and Last Plague: Death of the First-born. Ch. 11 contains the announcement of the plague; the execution of the threat is recorded in 12[29-36]. This time, it is said, Pharaoh will not only give consent but will be so eager to get rid of the Israelite people that he will *thrust* them out. But before they go they will ask and receive presents of their Egyptian neighbors (cf. 3[21, 22] notes, 12[35, 36]). The fact that this was possible, and that *the Lord gave the people favor in the sight of the Egyptians,* shows that the relations between the two peoples were not unfriendly. The fault must have lain with the king and his counselors, yet the people suffered for the crimes of their rulers.

The last and most dreadful plague was that which carried off the first-born of Egypt (cf. 4[23]). The story contains a reminiscence of some terrible plague which afflicted Egypt, and which was regarded by the Israelites as a just punishment for the slaughter of their infant sons by Pharaoh and for his holding them in a cruel bondage.

The *mill* (v. 5) consisted of two round stones, probably held together by a sort of spindle, the upper one of which was rotated upon the lower. The corn which was to be ground was poured in through a hole in the upper stone, and the work was usually done by the women.

Chapters 12[1-28]+12[43] to 13[16]: The Passover and Passover Laws

It is evident to the reader that the laws contained in these chapters cannot have been framed and given to the people by Moses at the time of their hasty departure from Egypt. They are, rather, intended to provide for the celebration of this event in subsequent years. The instructions given in 12[21-28] are in part appropriate to the occasion, but not the elaborate regulations of 12[1-20] and 12[43-49]. Moreover, we have in ch. 13 the law governing the feast of unleavened bread and the sacrifice of the first-born. The presence of these laws illustrates the method of the author, or compiler, of this history. Not only does he bring together the various narratives which were in existence in his time, but he adds also individual laws or groups of laws in connection with the events which produced them, or which they were intended to commemorate, even though the formulation or codification of these laws as he gives them did not take place until long afterward. For other Passover and related laws in the Pentateuch see 23[15] 34[18] Deut. 16[1-8] Lev. 23[5-14] Num. 9[2, 3] 28[16-25].

CHAPTER XII

1–20. Institution of the Feasts of Passover and of Unleavened Bread. *This month* (v. 2) was the month *Abib* (13[4]), i.e., the month of the green ear. The Hebrew month was regulated by the phases of the moon, and Abib, which was in later times called by the Babylonian name Nisan (Neh. 2[1] Esth. 3[7]), came in the latter part of March and first part of April, the middle of this month corresponding closely to our Easter. (See art., *Time, Money,* etc., p. 77b.) The Hebrews had two methods of reckoning the year. According to one, which is still in use by the Jews, the year began in the autumn; according to the other, which is here used, in the spring. This latter method prevailed after the Babylonian Exile. In this month Abib, in Palestine, the barley was beginning to ripen, and the barley harvest began. (See further notes under vv. 21–36.)

21–36. The First Passover Celebrated. The first Passover celebrated by Moses and the Israelite people is described here (cf. vv. 43–51). A lamb or kid is taken from the flock and killed and its blood is smeared with a bunch of hyssop on the lintel and side posts of the door. When the Lord passes through the land to smite the Egyptians with a deadly plague he will see and pass over the houses of the Israelites which are so marked, *and will not suffer the destroyer to come in* (v. 23). It is significant that the word *Passover* is used here (v. 21) as though it were an institution already known. It is, indeed, quite possible that it was an ancient spring festival, associated with the offering of the firstlings of the flock and the firstfruits of the harvest. The smearing of the blood of the animal thus offered upon the lintel and door posts may have been regarded as a means of securing divine protection from plague or any kind of injury. This may have been the feast, long neglected by the Israelites in Egypt, which they now asked Pharaoh to permit them to celebrate in their own way in a wilderness pilgrimage to some sacred spot. Forever afterward, therefore, it was associated in their minds with the deliverance from Egypt. For a full discussion of the whole subject see McNeile, *Exodus*, pp. 62–68.

The Hebrew word translated "Passover" comes from the same root as the verb rendered "pass over" (vv. 13 and 23). In the ritual of the later age, as prescribed here in vv. 1–20, it is joined with the eating of unleavened bread (Hebrew *mazzoth*), and this custom may also have marked the older festival.

The *fathers' houses* (v. 3) were the family groups or clans. In later usage ten persons was the minimum number to join in the celebration. The animal chosen must be perfect, as in the regulations for animal sacrifice in Lev. 22^{17-25} (cf. Mal. $1^{8, 13}$). The prohibition of leaven may have been due to the fact that it was associated in the minds of the people with corruption or decay (cf. Lev. $2^{4, 5}$ 6^{14-18} $7^{11, 12}$ Num. 6^{13-21}, etc.). As made by modern Jews for the Passover the unleavened cakes are round, about twelve inches in diameter, and a quarter of an inch thick. In Deut. 16^{3} they are called "bread of affliction," and below, in v. 39, the explanation is offered, not that the law required their use, but that *they were thrust out of Egypt, and could not tarry, neither had they prepared for themselves any victual*, and, therefore, they baked unleavened cakes of the dough which they brought with them.

37–42. The Departure. The exact sites of *Rameses* (=Raamses, 1^{11}) and of *Succoth* are unknown, but the former has been located with some degree of certainty in the Wādy Tumilat, a strip of cultivated land extending from the Delta to Lake Timsah, northeast of Cairo, through which in ancient times a branch of the Nile flowed into a northern extension of the gulf of Suez. Succoth was probably about ten miles farther east, close to or perhaps identical with Pithom (1^{11}; see intro., section on "Contemporary History," p. 250.) The number of *six hundred thousand* men, besides children, presents a real difficulty (cf. 38^{26} Num. $1^{46, 47}$ 4^{48} $26^{51, 62}$). Counting women and children there would be at least from one to two millions. Added to these we are told was a *mixed multitude, and flocks, and herds, even very much cattle.* In four generations (Gen. 15^{16}), or even in four hundred or four hundred and thirty years (Gen. 15^{13} Ex. 12^{40}), seventy persons (1^{5}) could not have increased to so many. Besides, the movement of such an immense host would have been very slow, and it would have been impossible, unless miraculously supplied, to find food in the wilderness for them all. It may, however, have happened that this account, written some hundreds of years later, was based upon an older reckoning by families, in which the Hebrew word here translated "thousand" was used in the sense of "family," or "clan" (as, e.g. in Judg. 6^{15} 1 Sam. 10^{19} 23^{23}). The original reckoning, then, would have been six hundred families, which is a quite possible number. (See Flinders Petrie, *Researches in Sinai*, pp. 207–217.) This explanation is attractive but does not quite explain the fact that men only are counted, while the family or clan would have included all its members. The mixed company must have included Egyptians, and other co-laborers, who may have intermarried with them and now sought with them this way to freedom.

For the period of sojourn in Egypt see introduction, under "Contemporary History." The night of watching (v. 42 mg.) and the day of moving were indeed memorable in the history of Israel, *to be much observed* in annual festival even down to the present day.

43–51. The Passover Forbidden to Aliens. (Cf. notes under vv. 21–36.)

The application of the words of v. 46b (cf. Psa. 34^{20}) to Christ (Jn. 19^{36}) reminds us that in the symbolism of the N.T. our Lord has become the paschal (passover) Lamb slain for the world's redemption.

CHAPTER XIII

1–16. Consecration of the First-born: Feast of Unleavened Bread. (Cf. notes under 12^{21-36}.) For the dedication of the first-born to the Lord (v. 1) see more fully Num. $3^{11-13, 40-45}$ 18^{15-18}. The injunctions of vv. 9, 16, were taken literally by Jews of the later ages, and strips of parchment with passages from the Pentateuch written upon them (such as vv. 9, 16, Deut. 6^{8} and 11^{13}), inclosed in little leather cases, were worn upon the forehead and upon the arm, a custom which is still continued by devout Jews at morning prayer.

17–22. Early Wanderings of the Fugitives. *The way of the land of the Philistines* was, of course, the shorter way, following the sea shore, to Palestine. It is quite certain, from mention of them in Genesis (21^{32-34} 26^{1-18}), that Philistines were already settled in the southwest of Palestine. They had come originally from Crete (probably same as Caphtor, Amos 9^{7} Jer. 47^{4}), and were followed by others in the reign of Rameses III, after the Exodus. This road was, no doubt, strongly guarded by frontier garrisons of Egyptian troops past whom the Israelites would have had to fight their way. They were not yet ready for war.

The Red Sea is in Hebrew "Sea of Reeds"; the body of water here referred to was most likely a fresh-water lake to the north of the Gulf of Suez, perhaps Lake Timsah, surrounded by reedy marshes, and connected in ancient times with the gulf by a shallow channel. The exact route taken is, however, a matter of conjecture. For v. 19 cf. Gen. 50^{25} Josh. 24^{32}.

The *pillar of cloud* which guided them represented to them the presence of God. By night it was a *pillar of fire*. Cf. 34^{5}, "The Lord descended in the cloud." An ancient custom, still in use by Arabian caravans, of carrying braziers with burning wood at the head of a marching company has been cited as a possible explanation of the phenomenon. If so, it was no doubt given a religious significance, and was regarded as an altar fire symbolizing the divine presence. See Sir Walter Scott's hymn, "The March of Israel."

CHAPTERS 14^{1} TO 15^{21}: CROSSING THE RED SEA; THE SONG OF DELIVERANCE

By whatever means the people succeeded in crossing "the Red Sea" (13^{18}, notes) and escaping the pursuing Egyptians, the remarkable song in which they celebrated the deliverance bespeaks their confidence that they were under divine protection.

CHAPTER XIV

1–9. Pursuit by the Egyptians. The places named in v. 2 are unknown to us, and the place where the Israelites approached the sea is likewise unknown. It should be remembered that the term "sea" is applied in the Bible to a lake or river as well as to the larger body of salt water (cf. Num. 34^{11} Isa. 18^{2} 19^{5} Nah. 3^{8}, etc.). It is possible, therefore, that one of the lakes in the Isthmus of Suez may be intended, preferably Lake Timsah, or the Bitter Lakes (see map), which may, at that time, have been connected with each other and with the gulf to the south. It is inconceivable that Moses should have led the people to an impassable sea, trusting in a miracle for deliverance. Much more likely is it that, having turned back from the more direct and more frequently traveled road to Palestine, he followed another road by way of these lakes to a place where he expected to be able to cross, perhaps by a shallow ford. The name "Migdol," which probably means "tower," may designate a frontier post of the Egyptian army guarding this "way of the wilderness" (13^{18}). This way, apparently, offered a more favorable opportunity than the other of escape from pursuit and recapture by the Egyptian army. The Egyptian war *chariot* carried two men, one driving and the other, the captain, fighting with bow or spear, and shield.

10–20. The People's Murmurings and Jehovah's Promise to Moses. Moses had here another experience (cf. $5^{20, 21}$) of the ungrateful murmuring of the people against him whenever they were confronted by danger or suffering from the hardships of the way (cf. 16^{3} 17^{3} Num. 11^{4-6} 14^{3}, etc.). Over against this craven fear stands in bright relief the courage and faith of their great leader. *Fear ye not*, he said, *stand still and see the salvation of the Lord* (v. 13). The command is issued, not to turn back or to yield, but to *go forward* (v. 15). There is a time for prayer and a time for action. The time for action has come.

During the night *the angel of God*, no doubt representing the Lord himself in *the pillar of cloud*, removed and went behind the Israelite host. The joining of two older narratives is evident here (v. 19), in one of which the divine protector is the angel of God, and in the other the Lord in a pillar of cloud ($13^{21, 22}$). V. 20 is explained, in part at least, by Josh. 24^{7}, "He put darkness between you and the Egyptians." It is suggested by the Hebrew text that the cloud presented a dark side to the Egyptians, but lighted up the night on the side of Israel.

21–31. Crossing of the Red Sea. Throughout the night *a strong east wind* (which may have been from the southeast) drove back the waters. If the passage was made at the southeastern end of the Bitter Lakes, this can easily be understood. In the Gulf of Suez an east wind would have the opposite effect (see map). There may have confronted them an arm, or channel, of the lakes, fordable at low water. Such was the force of the wind that the bed of the channel at the ford was laid bare, while the deeper waters on either side were as walls to the people as they crossed over, preventing a flank attack upon them from either side.

The Egyptian army followed when there was light enough to see. The *morning watch*, with the Hebrews, was from two to six o'clock. Then *the Lord looked forth*, perhaps in flashes of lightning from the cloud. The discomfiture of the Egyptians was his doing. He *bound* (v. 25, mg. as in LXX, not "took off") *their chariot wheels*, which sank and stuck fast in the muddy bottom. There may have been a change of wind which brought the waters back in flood (15^{10}). According to Psa. 77^{17-19} there were torrents of rain with thunder and lightnings. *And the Lord shook off* (v. 27, mg., for "overthrew") *the Egyptians in the midst of the sea* (cf. 15^{1} Psa. 136^{13-15}). See also Deut. 11^{4} Psa. 78^{53} Heb. 11^{29}.

This signal deliverance from their dreaded foe convinced the people of Israel that Jehovah was indeed the God of their fathers and mightier than the gods of Egypt (15^{2} Psa. 106^{7-12}), and confirmed them in the recognition of Moses as their appointed leader and the true servant of God. It became to them the assurance and promise of deliverance in every trouble which came upon them in after years (cf. Isa. $43^{1, 2, 16-19}$ 51^{9-11}).

CHAPTER XV

1–21. The Song of Deliverance. The song is undoubtedly one of the finest passages of Hebrew literature. It is poetry of a high order. It breathes the very spirit of the time, the exultant joy of the multitude escaped from a hated bondage, the sea between them and their enemies. It declares their new-found faith and confidence in Jehovah, their God and their fathers' God, whose power is manifest in the overthrow of the Egyptian host which they had thought invincible.

The original song seems to have ended with v. 11. What follows is in a more reflective and reminiscent tone, and presupposes the passing through Edom and Moab and the conquest of and settlement in Canaan. This latter section we may believe to have been added by a poet of a later age. The first part can hardly have been other than a contemporary production, expressing the triumphant joy of victory. The style and language may fairly be regarded as marking an early date. (For a different view see McNeile, *Exodus*, pp. 88, 89.)

In v. 1 no doubt by *the horse and his rider* is meant the horse and the charioteer. These first lines formed the refrain, perhaps appended to each stanza of the poem (v. 21). In v. 2 (Hebrew) we have the shorter form for "Jehovah," namely *Jah*, better, *Yah*, an evidence in support of the view that the true pronunciation of the longer name in Hebrew was Yahweh (3^{13-22}, notes). The word *salvation* means here "deliverance," and has reference to the deliverance from the Egyptians. For the conception of the Lord as *a man of war* see Josh. 5^{13-15} and Psa. 24^{8}. The language of v. 8 is of course, the figurative language of poetry, with which the Oriental mind is well acquainted.

In v. 13 the Lord is declared to have led the people to his *holy habitation*, i.e., to Canaan, or possibly to Zion, if this part of the song was written in or after the time of David and Solomon (cf. 2 Sam. 15^{25}). The fear which took hold of the peoples mentioned (vv. 14–16) must have been the result of the conquest of eastern Palestine by Israel and the subsequent victories in western Palestine. The references in v. 17 seem clearly to be to Mount Zion and the Temple. *Miriam* may have been regarded as a *prophetess* because of her gift of song. She may herself have been the author of the original of this song. Her *timbrel*, or tabret, was a metal or wooden ring over which a skin was tightly drawn, which was held in one hand and beaten by the other.

CHAPTERS 15^{22} TO 18^{27}: THE JOURNEY TO SINAI

If the traditional site of Sinai be accepted, the direction after the crossing of the sea will have been southeastward, parallel to the eastern shore of the Gulf of Suez for some seventy or eighty miles, then eastward into the heart of the peninsula. If, on the other hand, with some recent authorities, we locate Sinai near the head of the gulf of Akaba, or farther north on the border of Edom, the direction will have been generally eastward.

22–27. From the Red Sea to Elim. The *wilderness of Shur* is apparently the same as "the wilderness of Etham" (Num. 33^{8}). Where mentioned in Gen. 16^{7} 20^{1} 25^{18} 1 Sam. 15^{7} 27^{8} it is described as south of Palestine and "in front of" or "before," i.e., east of Egypt. *Marah* cannot now be identified, but two places on the road to Sinai have been suggested, one about ten miles southeast of Suez and the other about fifty miles, where there are springs of bitter or brackish water. The Hebrew word *Marah* means bitter (Ruth 1^{20}). It is possible that Moses while living in the wilderness may have learned of a tree whose fruit, leaves, or bark had power to sweeten such water, and de Lesseps is quoted as saying that a species of barberry is so used, but this is not certainly known. What the statute and ordinance mentioned in v. 25 was is not stated, but it is evidently intended by the writer to show that Moses began here the proper organization and regulation of the life of the people, which he completed at Sinai.

The name *Elim* (v. 27) means "terebinths." The place has been identified, though not certainly, with a charming oasis about half way to Sinai, but it may have been much farther north. Others identify it with Eloth, at the head of the eastern gulf.

CHAPTER XVI

Sending of Quails and Manna. *The wilderness of Sin* (v. 1, 17¹), like the other places mentioned, cannot be certainly placed. It bears a name which indicates proximity to Sinai, the two names being probably from the same root word (the name of the Babylonian moon-god Sin).

The providing of food for so large a company in that comparatively barren wilderness must have been a serious problem. The people begin to feel the pangs of hunger and as usual put the blame upon their leaders (vv. 2, 3). The promise of *bread from heaven* is directly related here to the observance of the Sabbath day. The bountiful gift of food is to be made a test and a means of discipline, that the people may learn obedience to the law of God (v. 4). The promise, *At even then ye shall know . . . and in the morning then ye shall see,* is explained by vv. 12–14. The *quails* came in the evening, and the *manna* with the dew in the morning, both as evidence of God's care and manifestation of his glory. The words *looked toward the wilderness* (v. 10) are hard to understand, for the wilderness was about them on every side. It may be understood, however, that the pillar of cloud remained outside the camp, so that looking toward it means looking out from the camp circle or inclosure. Just what the people saw we do not know, but it may have been the gleam of fire through the cloud.

Quails, or partridges, are said to be common in the Sinaitic peninsula. In spring they move northward in great numbers, flying low, and when they drop exhausted to the ground can be easily caught. They now provided meat for the hungry wanderers. In the morning they found the *manna.* They had never seen it before and they said, *What is it?* The question in Hebrew is *man-hu* (the form *man* = "what," is Aramaic rather than Hebrew), which may also be rendered, "It is *man.*" If the latter rendering be accepted, the Hebrews would have used an Egyptian word *man,* meaning "sap" or "gum" from trees. Our word *manna* is taken from the Greek rendering of Num. 11⁶, etc. The description of it in v. 14 is supplemented in v. 31 and Num. 11⁷⁻⁹. Just what it was we do not know. No entirely satisfactory account of it as a natural product of that region has been given. The sweet juice of the Tarfa tree (a species of tamarisk) has been suggested. Exuding from the trunk and branches by night in summer, it forms "small round white grains, which partly adhere to the twigs of the trees, and partly drop to the ground. In the early morning it is of the consistency of wax, but the sun's rays soon melt it" (Driver, *Exodus,* pp. 153, 154). The Arabs gather and use it, calling it manna, but the quantity found is very small, and could not ordinarily provide food for many people. The writers of this history can only account for it as the gift of God, who thus provides for the wants of his people (see Psa. 78²³⁻²⁵ 105⁴⁰).

The *omer* (v. 16), a measure of quantity, is described as *the tenth part of an ephah* (v. 36), i.e., about six and one half pints (see art., *Time, Money,* etc., p. 79).

It is evident from ch. 16 that the Sabbath, or seventh day of the week, was already regarded as a holy day to be strictly observed (cf. Gen. 2², ³ Ex. 20⁸⁻¹¹ 31¹²⁻¹⁷ 34²¹, etc.).

Aaron's pot of manna was to be laid up *before the Testimony* (vv. 33, 34), i.e., in the sanctuary, which was not yet built, before the ark, or sacred box, which was to hold the tables of stone upon which the Ten Commandments were written. These Commandments (20¹⁻¹⁷) are frequently called the Testimony (25¹⁶, ²¹ 27²¹ 31¹⁸ 32¹⁵, etc.), or Witness, bearing witness as they did both to the divine law given through Moses and the covenant engagement which was based upon it (24⁷, ⁸).

CHAPTER XVII

1–7. Water From the Rock at Rephidim. The location of *Rephidim* is unknown. The joining of two narratives is illustrated very clearly in vv. 1–3, where the central facts—no water and the complaint of the people—are twice told. The name *Massah,* in Hebrew, means "tempting" or "proving"; *Meribah* means "striving," or "strife" (v. 7 mg.). A similar story is told in Num. 20¹⁻¹³, which is, quite possibly, a duplicate of this. If so it is probable that the event is out of its proper place here and belongs rather to the sojourn at Kadesh. This, again, seems to point to Horeb as being near Kadesh (v. 6; cf. Num. 27¹⁴). It is, of course, not impossible that two different places, for a similar reason, received the name Meribah. A legend in the Targum of Onkelos (cf. p. 106a) relates that the waters of the well of Beer (Num. 21¹⁶⁻¹⁸) followed the Israelites in their subsequent journeys, and this is used in 1 Cor. 10⁴ with a reference to the smiting of the rock. The story here and in Num. 20 may refer to the finding and opening up of a new well.

8–16. War With Amalek. *Amalek,* an Arabian tribe, is mentioned in other passages as inhabiting the country south of Palestine and near Kadesh (Num. 13[29] 14[25, 43, 45] 1 Sam. 15[6, 7]; cf. Gen. 14[7]). Hence the Amalekites seem to be out of place here, so far south, in the Sinaitic peninsula; and this may be further evidence that Horeb, which Moses was now approaching, was in the region of Kadesh. *Joshua* appears here for the first time and is leader of the armed forces of Israel (vv. 8, 9). In 33[11] he is said to have been Moses' minister, and a young man. Forty years later he succeeded Moses as ruler of Israel. It may be that this narrative, like the preceding, properly belongs to a much later period of the wilderness wandering. *Hur* is mentioned again in 24[14] as a man of rank and standing in Israel. Josephus says that he was Miriam's husband. Moses is represented here as an aged man, not participating in the battle, but with his two friends remaining upon a hill overlooking the field, in an attitude of prayer. The crime of Amalek against Israel is more fully described in Deut. 25[17-19]. They had hung upon the flank and rear of Israel's march, cutting off stragglers and those who were feeble, faint, and weary (cf. Num. 24[20] 1 Sam. 15[2, 3]).

The art of writing (v. 14) was well known in Egypt in Moses' time, and had been practiced there for many centuries. There is no doubt, therefore, that Moses and others of the Israelites may have learned to write. The oldest Hebrew writings actually known to us, however, belong to the tenth and ninth centuries B.C. The *altar* (v. 15) was, no doubt, built of stones of that place, for the offering to God of a sacrifice of thanksgiving. The name given it means "Jehovah is my banner" (R.V. mg.). The form of the oath in v. 16 is remarkable and, probably, very ancient. It is, literally, "A hand upon the throne of Jah," and should be translated, "I swear by the throne of Jehovah." The speaker is Moses (see R.V. mg.). The lifting up of the hand in making an oath was a common custom (6[8] Gen. 14[22] Num. 14[30] Psa. 106[26]).

CHAPTER XVIII

1–12. Visit of Jethro. The visit of Jethro to Moses took place *where he was encamped at the Mount of God*, i.e., at Horeb. According to 17[6] Moses was already at Horeb, but in 19[1] the Israelites are said to have come to Sinai, which, whether rightly or not, has been commonly identified with Horeb. The order of events is not clear, but the explanation lies in the effort of the authors to combine older narratives. Moses' wife *Zipporah* evidently had been sent back to Midian, perhaps after the disagreement at the inn (4[24-26]). She now comes to Moses with her father and two sons. For the name *Gershom* see on 2[22]. *Eliezer* means "My God is a help." Jethro acts as mediator in reuniting the divided family, and receives a cordial and affectionate welcome. Jethro recognizes the greatness of Jehovah and the great things he has done for Israel. He was, most probably, already a worshiper of Jehovah (cf. v. 12).

Some words have been lost from the latter part of v. 11, and the meaning is not clear. It may be that v. 10b, which is omitted in the LXX, should properly come at the end of v. 11, which would then read, "For in their proud dealing against them he delivered the people from under the hand of the Egyptians."

13–27. Appointment of Judges. The scene described in vv. 13ff. is of extraordinary interest as showing us quite clearly in what way some of the laws of Israel were made. The decisions of Moses, and no doubt of other judges after him, were remembered, and, in important cases, written down. Moses' judgments were received as *the statutes of God and his laws*. *The people come unto me*, he said, *to inquire of God*. He believed that he was as truly inspired and instructed of God while sitting in the seat of judgment with the people thronging about him as when alone in meditation and prayer in the mountain (19[3, 20]). Of the two classes of laws, the *words* (20[1]), or divine commandments, were the product of those days of retirement and communion with God in the mountain (31[18]), and the *judgments* (21[1]), mostly in hypothetical form, were such decisions of Moses and other great judges of subsequent times as are here referred to.

Jethro counsels Moses that the task which he has undertaken is too great for one man. Under so heavy a burden he will wear out his strength. He advises the appointment of others to share the burden with him, and gives a memorable definition of the sort of men who should be chosen, *able men, such as fear God, men of truth, hating unjust gain* (v. 21). Happy indeed the people ruled by such men! The people are to be divided into thousands, probably family groups rather than exact numbers (12[37-42], notes), and these subdivided into lesser groups, each of which will have its own magistrate or ruler, and will be responsible for good order within its own ranks. The ideal here presented is a worthy one, even though it may never have been fully realized. Moses was to retain the supreme authority, and to his court was to come *every great matter* (v. 22).

Chapters 19[1] to 20[21]: The Theophany on Mount Sinai; the Decalogue

The arrival at Sinai was followed by God's self-revelation to Moses, in the course of which Moses is said to have received "the Ten Commandments." For the relation between the Decalogue and other ancient codes, see art., *Legal and Historical Literature*, p. 145, and cf. notes on Deut. 6[6-21].

CHAPTER XIX

1. Arrival at Sinai. *In the third month* Israel came into the wilderness of Sinai. Assuming that the traditional location of Mount Sinai is correct, there is still some doubt as to which of two mountains was the one before which Israel camped. The choice seems to lie between Serbal and Musa, the latter in the center of the wedge-shaped mass of mountains in the heart of the peninsula. At the foot of this latter mountain is situated the convent of Saint Catharine, built originally in the sixth century A.D., and occupied by monks of the Greek Church. This site is the one which is most favored in Jewish and Christian tradition, and the surroundings of it would have been most suitable for a large encampment.

2–6. Moses and Jehovah in the Mount. Moses is said to have gone up into the mountain several times, sometimes alone and sometimes in company with others (vv. 3, 20, 24[9, 13-18] 34[4]). There may have been some sacred shrine which he visited there, perhaps the very place where he had the vision of the burning bush, and had been assured by God that he would return with the people of Israel to this mountain (3[12]). In any case his purpose was primarily communion with God.

In language of profound significance and great beauty Jehovah declares (vv. 3–6) he had chosen Israel both that they might be in a peculiar sense his people, a *peculiar treasure*, and that they might render a high service to humanity as *a kingdom of priests*, ministering in holy things. The fundamental conception here is that God chooses and calls an individual nation, as he chooses and calls an individual man, not only to special privilege but also to special service (cf. Isa. 42[1-4] 49[1-6], and notes on Rom. 9–11.) All are his, but there are special gifts and ministries. God reveals himself and accomplishes his purposes of good through and by means of human agencies. The mention of the *covenant* (v. 5) anticipates the account of the national covenant in 24[3-8]. As a kingdom of priests they will have the right both of knowledge of and direct approach to God on their own behalf and on behalf of others (for an interpretation of the function of the priesthood see Mal. 2[4-7], notes). And as *an holy nation* they will be set apart in a very special way for the service of God.

7–25. Jehovah's Appearance to the People. In v. 8 the people, anticipating further revelation to them of God's will through Moses, promise obedience (cf. 24[3-7]). The command to *sanctify them* (v. 10) must have involved some ritual of purification, perhaps washing their bodies as well as their garments (cf. Gen. 35[2, 3]). The *bounds* set for the people were, no doubt, marks of some sort about the base of the mountain, over which they must not pass, for the whole mountain is now regarded as a sacred place, not to be entered upon but with the utmost reverence and only by those whose duty it is to draw near to God on their behalf. A new conception of the way of approach to God arose in the teaching of the later prophets and in the N.T. (cf. Isa. 55[1-3, 6, 7] Heb. 12[18-24]). The *trumpet* of the earlier times was a ram's horn; later it was made of metal. When the hour for the solemn religious service comes the trumpet will sound the warning, the people will come up to the mountain but will not pass the barrier into the forbidden area.

The divine appearance on the mountain was in cloud and storm. From ancient times the thunder was spoken of by the Hebrews as the voice of Jehovah, and the lightning as his messenger, or as his flaming dart (v. 19, Psa. 81[7]; cf. Psa. 29). For other descriptions of this revelation of God in storm cloud, lightning and thunder, see Deut. 4[10-12] 33[2] Judg. 5[4, 5] Neh. 9[13].

CHAPTER XX

1–17. The Decalogue. The Decalogue (or Ten Commandments) appears again, with slight differences, in Deut. 5[6-21] (notes). It has been commonly regarded as the gift of God, through Moses, to the Israelite people. The doubt regarding Mosaic authorship, which is entertained by some, rests chiefly upon the second commandment (vv. 4–6). It is difficult to explain why, if Moses forbade the making of images, he himself should have made a serpent image, which afterward became an object of worship (Num. 21[9] 2 Kings 18[4]), and why images seem to have been generally in use as sacred objects down to the time of the Exile six hundred years later (Judg. 8[24-27] 17[1-5] 1 Sam. 19[13-16] 1 Kings 12[28-30] Hos. 3[4], etc.). It is possible that this commandment and others have undergone some change under the influence of the teaching of the prophets who denounced image worship, but the substance of these laws, dealing with simple and fundamental religious duties and human relationships, may very well have been the work of Moses. The belief that they were spoken by God rightly put emphasis upon their authoritative character and universal application.

The *first commandment* (v. 3) does not deny the existence of other gods, but declares that for Israel there is only one, that is Jehovah (cf. Deut. 5[7] 6[4] 2 Kings 17[35, 36] Jer. 25[6]). The full monotheistic conception of God came later (Isa. 43[10-13] Jer. 10[1-16]).

The *second commandment* (vv. 4–6) prohibits the making of images, evidently as objects of reverence or worship, for Jehovah is *a jealous* God and will have no rival in the affections of his people (cf. 34[12-17] Lev. 26[1] Deut. 4[15-24]). It is not easy for us to recognize the truth which lies in the words, *visiting the iniquities of the fathers upon the children*, but the actual facts of human life, consonant with the laws of nature, show that children do suffer for the sins of their parents. And these laws of nature are the laws of God. The complementary truth of individual responsibility is presented in Jer. 31[29, 30] Ezek. 18.

The *third commandment* (v. 7) does not forbid the taking of an oath, but false swearing, and the light, irreverent, or insincere use of the name of God. Ordinary profane language is forbidden, even that which veils the name of God under apparently meaningless imitations of it (Lev. 19[12]; cf. Mt. 5[33-37]).

The *fourth commandment* (vv. 8–11) enjoins the observance of the Sabbath as an holy day and a day of rest. There is a reference in v. 11 to the story of creation (Gen. 1[1]–2[3]) where the work of God is presented, under the figure of the days of the week, as proceeding by orderly stages to completion and rest. The reason for the observance of the Sabbath, in the parallel passage in Deut. 5[12-15], is simply that working people may rest (cf. 31[12-17] Lev. 19[30] Isa. 58[13, 14] Jer. 17[19-27]). The word *Sabbath* is taken directly from the Hebrew and means "rest" or "ceasing from labor." (For a discussion of the origin of the Sabbath see McNeile, *Exodus*, pp. 121–123, and Driver's art., "Sabbath," in Hastings' *Dictionary of the Bible*.)

The *fifth commandment* (v. 12) is called by Paul "the first commandment with promise" (Eph. 6[2, 3]). See also Lev. 19[3] Deut. 5[16] Mt. 15[3-6] Ecclus. 3[1-16].

The *sixth to the ninth commandments* (vv. 13–16) are directed against the crimes of murder, adultery, theft, and falsehood in witness-bearing.

The *tenth commandment* (v. 17) forbids both the entertainment of covetous desire and the acts of cheating, violence, and oppression which spring from it (cf. Mic. 2[1, 2]). The story of Ahab's covetous desire for the vineyard of Naboth and the crime to which it led furnishes an example (1 Kings 21[1-16]). Compare our Lord's teaching in Lk. 12[15-21].

18–21. Terror of the People. The story of the theophany upon Mount Sinai, begun in ch. 19, is completed here, with special mention of the fear with which the people looked upon the sublime spectacle of the cloud-encompassed mountain and the thunderings and the lightnings of the storm. They appealed to Moses to be their mediator and to bring to them the words of God.

22–26. For notes on this section, see below. "The Book of the Covenant," under (1) *Religious Worship, etc.*

CHAPTERS XXI, XXII, XXIII

THE BOOK OF THE COVENANT (see also 20[22-26])

The collection of laws which we have in 20[22]–23[33] is, along with the Decalogue and some other fragments of legislation (such as 34[17-26]), the oldest Hebrew code which we possess. Next in order of time, and most closely related to it, is the code in Deut. 12–26 (see notes), and, latest of all, the laws contained in the books of Leviticus and Numbers. A careful comparison of these codes, in their general features and in detail, will provide convincing evidence that they have not all come from one hand, nor are they the product of one age. Even in the collection before us are found some laws suitable only to an agricultural people in a settled and cultivated land, and having no value for the people under Moses in the tent life of the wilderness (cf. 22[5-8] 23[10-16]). The strong probability is that to the laws left by Moses were added from time to time laws made by other judges, or decisions of the courts in famous cases, all of which are grouped together here in a code which fairly represents the ordered life of the people in the period of the judges and early monarchy (see art., *Legal and Historical Literature*, p. 145).

The laws cover (1) the ordering of worship and other religious observances (20[23-26] 22[20, 28-31] 23[10-19]); (2) the rights of slaves and strangers, kindness to the widow, the orphan, and the poor, and even to an enemy, and the impartial administration of justice (21[2-11] 22[21-27] 23[1-9]); and (3) penalties for crimes against life and property, and other offenses (21[12-36] 22[1-19]).

(1) *Religious Worship, etc.* (A topical treatment of the several sections of the Book of the Covenant, involving a disregard of the chapter divisions, is followed in this exposition.)

It will be observed that this code begins with certain regulations regarding *the place of worship* (20[23-26]), and that the code in Deuteronomy begins with the same subject (Deut. 12), as also an ancient priestly code found in Lev. 17–26 (see notes; cf. 17[1-9]). It is here forbidden to make images of or to worship other gods. It is ordered that wherever there is a signal manifestation of the divine presence and power, as in deliverance from famine or plague, victory over enemies, or even an abundant harvest (20[24]), there the people shall build an altar to their God and offer to him their sacrifices. The altar must be of earth or of unhewn stone. In this latter requirement and the reason given for it (20[25]) one may see the primitive character of the law (cf. Deut. 27[5-7] Josh. 8[31]). It is not easy to understand, however, how the altar for the tabernacle (27[1-8]), or the altar for Ezekiel's plan of the new Temple (Ezek. 43[13-17]), could have been made without tools; Ezekiel's altar also was to have steps. In this oldest law of the altar nothing is said of the priest. There was as yet no priestly order; every Israelite might approach the altar, or build an altar for himself, and offer his sacrifice to God. Compare the law in Deut. 12[8-14], where it is commanded that there shall be only one central sanctuary and altar for all Israel. The custom recognized here, however, prevailed throughout all the earlier period of the history down to the reign of Josiah (639–608 B.C.), and altars were multiplied in every part of the country.

The law forbade under the most severe penalties the worship of any other god. Anyone guilty of such an offense was put under the ban, and so given over to destruction (22[20]). He could no longer have any part or lot with the people (cf. Num. 25[2-8]). It is forbidden to *revile God* (not *the judges*, as in mg. of 22[28]), and to *curse a ruler* (cf. Lev. 25[15] Acts 23[5]).

The first-fruits of the threshing-floor and of the wine-press, and the first-born of man and beast are to be given to God (22[29, 30]). But the first-born sons were to be redeemed (cf. 13[2, 13, 15] Num. 3[44-51] 18[15, 16]). A sabbatic year is enjoined (23[10, 11]), when they enter upon the cultivated lands of Palestine, and in that year the produce of the land is to be for the poor (cf. Lev. 25[1-7]). A comparison of Lev. 26[34, 35] with 2 Chr. 36[21] would seem to indicate that before the Exile this law was not observed.

There are to be three sacred festivals in each year (23[14-17]). The first is called by what was probably its original name, *the feast of unleavened bread*, later known as the Passover. It is to be celebrated in the month Abib (cf. 13[4], and notes on 12[1-36]). The second is *the feast of harvest*, or *feast of weeks* (34[22]), seven weeks and a day later (hence known to us by the Greek word *Pentecost*, which means "fifty"). The third is *the feast of ingathering* (23[16]), or feast of tabernacles (Deut. 16[13]), in the seventh month (Sept.-Oct.), *at the end of the year*. The year is here the old economic year (see note on 12[2]). The festival in this month celebrated the final ingathering of the produce of the year, corn and wine and oil, and also commemorated the period of dwelling in tents in the wilderness. For a fuller account of these feasts see Lev. 23[4-21, 33-44] Deut. 16[1-17], and notes there.

According to 23[18] *leavened bread* was not to be offered upon the altar. The prohibition applies generally, but has special relation to what was known as the meal offering (Lev. 2[11] 6[17]). There may have been in the fermentation produced by the leaven the suggestion of taint or decay, and so of unfitness for use as an offering to the Lord. *The fat of the feast* (23[18]), i.e., the fat portions which are to be burned on the altar (Lev. 3[3-5]), is not to be left over till morning, but all burned up on the same day. If left over, it might become stale or tainted. The best of the first ripe fruits is to be brought as an offering to the sanctuary (cf. 22[29]). The last injunction in 23[19] may perhaps have reference to some ancient superstition.

(2) *Slaves, strangers, widows, and the poor.* The law does not sanction slavery but attempts to regulate it. The Hebrew slave (21[2-11]) may be held for six years only. Compare the further humane provisions of the parallel law in Deut. 15[12-18], and the fact that the right of freedom which is denied to the woman slave in Exodus (21[7]) is granted in Deuteronomy (15[17]). In the later Levitical legislation it is forbidden to hold a Hebrew as a slave; he may serve only as a hired servant (Lev. 25[39, 40]). The word *God* in this passage (21[6]) cannot properly mean *judges* (as in R.V. mg.). The meaning must be that the slave is taken to the local sanctuary, or to the sanctuary in his master's house, if there be one (see Judg. 17[5]), and there, as in the presence of God, marked slave for life.

Justice to the stranger, the widow, and the orphan (22[21-27]), is commanded, and kindness to and consideration for the poor. The words *not as a creditor* (22[25]) are significant. Not as a creditor but as a friend, a neighbor, a brother.

The law makes strict provision for the administration of justice (23[1-9]). It is forbidden to take up and carry about a false report, to follow the crowd in doing evil, and to bear witness in a cause favored by the crowd which is clearly unjust. Even an enemy must be dealt with fairly ($23^{4, 5}$). He who has the responsibility of bearing witness or exercising judgment must not take a bribe.

(3) *Crimes against life and property.* A distinction is made in the code between willful murder and accidental killing. Of the latter it is said, in the language of that day, *but God deliver him into his hand,* literally, "make to fall to his hand." In such a case there will be appointed a place of refuge to which the killer may flee, and where he will be assured of a fair trial. In the wilderness, and in the early years in Palestine, while there was no assured and strong government, the relatives of the slain man took upon themselves the execution of vengeance upon the slayer, and that often without inquiry or trial. For the appointment of cities of refuge see Num. 35^{9-34} and Deut. 19^{1-13}. In some instances the sanctuary or altar was regarded as an asylum; but for the willful murderer that was not to avail (21^{14}).

21^{23-25} contains what has been called the *lex talionis*, or law of retailiation. Since the law is general, and refers to injuries which might be inflicted in a variety of ways, it is clear that it is not here in its proper place. The first part of 21^{23} may have originally been followed by words defining the penalty in that case. The more general law may originally have followed $21^{18, 19}$. Compare Deut. 19^{16-21} and Lev. $24^{19, 20}$.

The principle of ransom, or redemption price, is recognized in 21^{30-32}. But in the case of a slave, who is regarded as his master's property, the price of the slave must be paid, *thirty shekels of silver*, a shekel being worth about sixty-six cents.

Crimes of theft, or burglary, are severely dealt with, and the penalties are heavy. For damage willfully or carelessly done restitution must be made ($22^{5, 6}$). Where there is suspicion of theft, or wrongful possession of the property of another, but no clear evidence, the parties are brought to the sanctuary, and in the presence of God, and of the appointed judge or judges, an *oath of the Lord* is taken (22^{11}). The final decision, no doubt, rested with the judge, but was held to be, as in Moses' court ($18^{15, 16}$), the decision of God (22^{7-13}).

For the amount of the *dowry* ($22^{16, 17}$), see Deut. $22^{28, 29}$. The daughter is regarded as her father's property.

The law on the whole maintains a high standard of justice. It endeavors to preserve the purity and simplicity of the primitive religion and of religious practices. It enjoins kindliness and consideration for the rights and well-being of others in all the relationships of life. Especially does it require just and considerate treatment of the stranger, for, it is said, *Ye know the heart of a stranger, seeing ye were strangers in the land of Egypt* (23^{9}). Even the *lex talionis* marked a distinct advance upon the current code of the wilderness, in which trifling offenses or injuries often led to prolonged feuds and much loss of life. It strictly limited the penalty which might be exacted to an equivalent for the injury. Above all, the supreme value of the law lay in its identification of justice and righteousness, both in the individual and in the common life, with the will of a righteous God.

There follows (23^{20-33}) an earnest and impressive exhortation to obedience, accompanied by promises of divine leading and blessing, and of victorious entry into and possession of the land of their fathers. The angel of God, in whom God himself is present (32^{34} 33^{14} Isa. 63^{9}), will go before them, a stern but faithful monitor and guide. They must not forsake Jehovah for the false gods of the Canaanites, but must break down their altars. The *pillars* (23^{24}), which they are ordered to destroy, were large stones set up beside or near the altar, sometimes several in a row, and perhaps regarded as in some sort the dwelling place of the deity. They were used in the earlier time at the altars of Jehovah (24^{4}), but were forbidden by the later law codes because of their heathen associations (Deut. 16^{22} Mic. 5^{13}). The promise that the Lord will drive their enemies out of the land promised them *not in one year*, but *by little and little* ($23^{29, 30}$), is in harmony with the account of the conquest given in Judg. 1–3 (but cf. intro. to Joshua, p. 346.)

CHAPTER XXIV

The National Covenant. There is a break here in the continuity of the story, for, according to 20^{21}, Moses was in the mountain holding communion with God, while here (v. 1) he is bidden with others to *come up unto* the Lord. Then, in vv. 3–8, he is represented as telling the people the laws contained in the preceding chapters and securing their promise of obedience. The sequel to vv. 1, 2 follows in vv. 9–11. This is but another evidence of the composite character of the book.

Of the company which is called up into the mountain, *Nadab* and *Abihu* are the sons of Aaron, and the *elders* represent the people. The vision which they saw (vv. 9–11) was perhaps the glory of a sapphire-blue sky, swept clear of the clouds which had enveloped the mountain during the storm. In this they saw, with renewed spiritual understanding, the majesty and glory of the God of Israel (cf. Gen. 32[30, 31] Ex. 33[20-23] Psa. 19[1]). In spite of the injunction of 19[21-24], forbidding the people to come up into the mountain, these nobles of Israel who came up with Moses saw the vision and were not harmed (v. 11).

On the basis of the laws which he now presents to the people, Moses brings them into covenant bond with Jehovah. They promise to obey the laws as the very words of God (vv. 3, 7), and they receive in return the assured promises of God (23[20-33]). For this reason the code of chs. 20–23 is called here *the book of the covenant* (24[7]). The laws are described as *the words*, i.e., specific divine commandments (as the Decalogue and most of ch. 23), and *the judgments* (v. 3) or decisions of the court (usually in hypothetical form, like most of chs. 21, 22). This code is said to have been written by Moses, and was handed down to subsequent ages under his name and authority. Thus his name came to be inseparably associated with Israel's laws, and the later codes of Deuteronomy and Leviticus were also ascribed to him. The covenant was ratified by sacrifice and by the sprinkling of blood upon the altar and upon the people, thus signifying their union in this bond with their God (v. 8; cf. Psa. 50[5]).

The *tables of stone* (v. 12) are frequently mentioned in the following chapters and in the book of Deuteronomy. They are generally believed to have had inscribed upon them the Ten Commandments, but that is not certain. See also 31[18] 32[15, 16]. Joshua is described here as Moses' *minister* (cf. 33[11] Num. 11[28] Josh. 1[1]). On this occasion (v. 13), apparently, he accompanies Moses into the mountain and the elders are left, with Aaron and Hur, in charge of the camp.

Chapters 25 to 27: The Sanctuary and its Furnishing

There is to be a tent-dwelling for Jehovah in the camp of Israel. The Lord's commandment to Israel is, *Let them make me a sanctuary, that I may dwell among them* (25[8]). This sanctuary is to be both Jehovah's dwelling and a place of meeting, where he will meet with those who come to seek him, in thanksgiving, in prayer, or in penitence. Moreover, it is to contain the tables of stone upon which are written the Commandments, a perpetual testimony to the covenant bond between Jehovah and Israel, and to Jehovah's claim upon Israel's obedience under the terms of that bond. Hence it is called the *tabernacle*, or dwelling, the *tent of meeting* (27[21] 33[7]), and the tent, or tabernacle, of the testimony (38[21] Num. 17[7]). The oldest account of it is to be found in 33[7-11]. There it is described as pitched *without the camp, afar off from the camp*, and was under the constant care of Joshua (cf. references to it in Num. 11, 12 and Deut. 31). The account given of it here is later and from a priestly source, and there is reason to believe that it is to some extent idealized. Moses is represented as receiving the pattern of the tent-sanctuary and of its furnishings, with instructions regarding the making of it and them, in the mount from God (25[9, 40]). Compare the description of Solomon's Temple in 1 Kings 6, 7, and 2 Chr. 3, 4; see notes there.

CHAPTER XXV

1–9. Offerings for the Sanctuary. There was first the collecting of material for the sanctuary, and the people were invited to make an offering. There were gold, and silver, and brass for the vessels, for the gilding of the ark and its covering, for the candlestick, for chains, and rings, and hooks, and many other uses. There were blue, and purple, and scarlet stuff, and fine linen (not *cotton*, v. 4 mg.) for the curtains, fabric of goats' hair for a first covering over the curtains, and skins for a second and third covering. What the *sealskins* were we do not know, but the word used may be Egyptian and mean simply "leather." Acacia wood was required for the framework, and precious stones for adornment of the priests' garments.

10–22. The Ark. The chief and most sacred part of the furnishing of the sanctuary was the ark. A simple box, or chest, it represented the actual dwelling place of Jehovah, in the innermost and most holy part of the tent-sanctuary. Since a cubit measure is about eighteen inches in length it will be easy to reckon its dimensions. There was to be a *crown*, probably a molding, round about the cover, and rings upon the feet which supported it, through which *staves*, or rather poles, would be thrust with which to carry it. The *testimony*, i.e., the tables of stone containing the Commandments, was to be put into it. The covering of the ark, a slab of pure gold, is here called the *mercy-seat*. The Hebrew word means "place of propitiation." This covering became to ancient Israel most sacred. Over it, though invisible, was the very presence and dwelling of God, called by the Jews in later times the *Shekinah* (i.e., "the Dwelling"). The making of the *cherubim*, angelic winged figures (vv. 18–20), shows clearly that the second commandment (20[4-6]) was not understood as prohibiting all images, but only those which were made objects of worship.

23–30. The Table of Shewbread. The *table* was to be of the same length and height as the ark, and was to bear the dishes upon which the loaves of bread were to be brought in, and cups, or flagons, for the wine. The *shew-bread*, or Presence-bread, was bread placed, so to speak, in the presence of Jehovah (cf. Num. 4[7] 1 Sam. 21[6]) and for his use. It may have come to represent the hospitality of Jehovah, in whose tent the table was always spread and the fire always burning.

31–40. The Candlestick. More correctly, "the lampstand"; it had six branches bending outward and upward from a central stem. Upon this central stem and on the six branches seven lamps were to be placed, to be cared for and kept burning by the priests (27[20, 21]). The branches were each tipped with a *cup*, consisting of *knop*, or knob, and *flower*, i.e., calyx and corolla, like an almond blossom. Vv. 34, 35 are not very clear, but may mean that the three pairs of branches left the central stem at three successive levels, and that there were four of these cup-shaped blossoms in the central stem, two above and two below the branches, and one under each point of junction of the branches with the central stem. The *talent of pure gold*, of which the candlestick was to be made, is estimated as about ninety-six pounds avoirdupois, worth upwards of twenty-five thousand dollars.

CHAPTER XXVI

The Tabernacle. The sanctuary is to be thirty cubits long and ten cubits wide (forty-five by fifteen feet), and ten cubits (fifteen feet) high. There were to be two rooms, the outer or holy place, thirty by fifteen feet, and the inner shrine, separated from it by curtains, fifteen by fifteen feet and fifteen feet in height, a perfect cube. Compare the dimensions of Solomon's Temple (1 Kings 6[1, 2]), which were twice those of the tabernacle.

The solid structure was to be made of upright wooden frames fitting into bases or pedestals of silver, and connected at the top, middle and bottom by cross rails or bars (vv. 15–27; for fuller detailed description see Driver, *Exodus*, pp. 285–289, and Kennedy's art., "Tabernacle," with illustration, in Hastings' *Dictionary of the Bible*). The word *boards* is to be understood as used of such frames, each consisting of two upright pieces (here called tenons) joined at the top, middle, and bottom, by short crosspieces. Twenty such frames, with their cross-bars, would form the solid structure on the south side and twenty on the north, and six at the western end, with double frames at the corners (vv. 23, 24).

CHAPTER XXVII

1–8. The Altar. The altar of burnt-offering had to be of light construction so that it might be carried from place to place. It is described as a hollow frame of acacia wood, overlaid with brass (or, rather, bronze), and at each corner a brazen horn. A ledge surrounded it, half-way up, upon which the officiating priest might stand, and this was supported by a network of brass. This is, of course, very different from the altar prescribed in 20[24-26], which might have been quickly built anywhere, and just how it was to be used for a burnt-offering we do not know.

9–19. The Court. Round about the tabernacle was to be a great court one hundred cubits in length from east to west and fifty cubits wide, completely surrounded and shut in by curtains of fine linen. The altar of burnt-offering was centrally placed in the eastern part. The tabernacle itself was in the western part, its door facing to the east.

20, 21. An Unfailing Light. A short paragraph prescribes the care of the lamp (cf. 25[31]) by the priests in the Holy Place, and provides for a supply of *pure olive oil beaten for the light.*

Chapters 28 and 29: Priesthood and Sacrifice

Aaron and his four sons are designated as priests. The names of the sons are given in 1 Chr. 24[1, 2]. The need of a priesthood in such a community was very great. The people were ignorant and needed instruction. It was important that the exercises of worship should be conducted with dignity and kept free from the taint of idolatry and from cruel and immoral practices. A well-trained and high-minded priesthood could render this service. The priests cared for the altar, instructed the people in religious and moral duties, conducted the regular services of worship, and often acted as judges, alone or in association with the appointed judges of the civil courts. See, for an account of the service rendered by a true priestly class, Mal. 2[4-7], notes.

CHAPTER XXVIII

Description of the Garments of the Priests. The priest must be clothed in garments befitting his high office. Wise-hearted workmen are needed to make such garments (vv. 2, 3; cf. 31[1-11]), *for glory and for beauty.* The *breastplate* (v. 15) was more probably a pocket or pouch of some sort in which were to be put the two precious stones (v. 30) which were used for casting the sacred lot. The *ephod* was probably some sort of tightly fitting garment, a kind of waistcoat, or, perhaps, apron, supported by two shoulder pieces, like suspenders, and to it the pouch, or pocket above mentioned, was probably attached (cf. 1 Sam. 14$^{18, 19}$, R.V. mg.). The word *ouches* (vv. 11, 13) might be rendered "filagree settings," or "rosettes." The LXX has "little shields." The *breastplate* (or, rather, *pouch*) of judgment (v. 15) was so called because of its use when the priest consulted the oracle of God, by means of the sacred lot, on matters which were brought before him for decision (vv. 29, 30; cf. 1 Sam. 14^{41} R.V. mg., 28^{6}). This custom of trying to obtain guidance from God by casting a lot belongs to the earliest times and to a very primitive kind of thinking. In later times more spiritual conceptions of religion were introduced by the teaching of the prophets and it fell into disuse. The term *ephod* seems to be used in a different sense, perhaps of a plated image, in Judg. 8^{27} 17^{5} 18$^{14-20}$. A very similar Hebrew word, from the same root, is used of the gold casing or plating of an image in Isa. 30^{22}. What *the Urim and the Thummim* (v. 30) were is not certainly known. The words are plurals in the Hebrew language and may be used as abstract or intensive nouns, meaning "light" and "perfection," or "beauty." They may have been names given to small carved objects, or precious stones used in casting the lot, one of which would give a favorable, or affirmative, and the other an unfavorable, or negative answer to the question asked (cf. 1 Sam. 23$^{2-4, 6-12}$).

The engraving upon the gold plate to be worn upon the front of the high priest's miter (vv. 36, 37) was a continual reminder of the holiness of the priest's office. He was set apart and solemnly ordained and consecrated (v. 41) to the service of God on behalf of and as the representative of the people. In that capacity he, so to speak, took upon himself the sin of the people (v. 29), in any error or neglect of their religious duties, making sacrifice and confession on their behalf, and seeking for them forgiveness from God.

CHAPTER XXIX

The Consecration of the Priests. An elaborate ceremonial is prescribed for the consecration of Aaron and his sons and their successors in the priesthood. It consists of washing, clothing, and anointing the priest, the offering of a bullock and two rams in sacrifice at the altar, and the waving to and fro before the altar of certain portions of the second sacrificed ram with bread, all of which are then burned upon the altar, and, finally, the setting apart, after lifting up and waving before the altar, of portions of the meat as the priests' due, to be eaten by them at a sacrificial meal at the door of the tent sanctuary. Compare Lev. 8, where the ritual of consecration here commanded is described as performed in detail. For the washing (v. 4) a laver of brass was to be provided in the court of the sanctuary (30$^{17-21}$). A specially prepared fragrant oil was to be provided for the anointing (30$^{22-33}$; cf. Psa. 133^{2}), a symbol of unity and of joy as well as of consecration. The word *consecrate* (v. 9) means literally "to fill the hand," and probably refers to placing in the hand of the priest something which is a symbol of his office, as in our day when the bishop or presiding minister places a Bible in the hands of the newly ordained candidate, saying, "Take thou authority to preach the word of God," etc. (cf. 32^{29} Judg. 17$^{5, 12}$ 1 Kings 13^{33}). The sacrifice of the bullock is described as a sin-offering (v. 14; cf. Lev. 4), and was intended as a propitiatory gift to God bearing the earnest prayer of the offerers for the forgiving and cleansing grace of God, that the place (Ezek. 43$^{18-27}$ 45$^{18-20}$) or person (as here) consecrated may be regarded as free from sin and pure in his sight. The first ram was offered as a whole burnt-offering, and was intended as a gift to God, signifying the recognition of his sovereignty and the giving to him of the life in wholehearted loyalty and obedience (cf. Lev. 8$^{18-21}$, Psa. 51$^{16, 17}$). The second ram was the *ram of consecration* (v. 22). Its blood, which in the ritual represented life, was touched to ear, hand, and foot (v. 20), that the whole body in all its members might be consecrated. Here Moses performs an essential part of the ceremony (v. 24) which in some way seems to have symbolized the installation of the priest in his office.

A provision is added (vv. 38–42) for the daily ritual of worship by sacrifice at the sanctuary, morning and evening, through future generations. The chapter concludes with gracious assurances and promises. The sanctuary and the priestly ministry will be honored and blessed by God, and there he will meet and dwell with his people (vv. 43–46). These verses form a fitting conclusion to the body of instructions in chs. 25–29, and show the depth of religious feeling and the real and sincere faith which found expression in its elaborate detail.

CHAPTERS 30 AND 31: ADDED INSTRUCTIONS REGARDING SANCTUARY AND SABBATH

Further, and perhaps later, instructions are here given regarding the furnishing and maintenance of the sanctuary. The instructions reflect the usages of a later age.

CHAPTER XXX

1–10. The Altar of Incense. Nothing is said, in the previous chapters, of an altar of incense, and in Lev. 16, in the ritual of the day of atonement, it is not mentioned, but censers are to be used for the burning of incense (cf. Num. 16). There seems to have been no second altar in Solomon's Temple (1 Kings 6, 7), nor in Ezekiel's plan of the ideal Temple of the future (Ezek. 41f.). In the post-exilic Temple there was an altar of incense, called in 1 Macc. 1[21] "the golden altar" (cf. Heb. 9[4]). The *strange incense*, which is here forbidden (v. 9), was that which was not made according to the prescription (vv. 34–38). The true incense, compounded of fragrant oils, resins, and gums, with salt, when burned made a fragrant smoke, appropriate and beautiful symbol of the prayers of the people (cf. Rev. 5[8], notes).

11–16. The Atonement Money. A tax is to be imposed upon the people to provide for the upkeep of the sanctuary and its services, the people to be required to give *every man a ransom for his soul unto the Lord.* The silver *shekel* is believed to have weighed a little more than an English half-crown (see p. 79[a]). Compare the Temple tax of later times (Mt. 17[24-27], notes). In this simple way the law recognized the duty of every man to discharge his debt to his God and to support the services of worship.

17–21. The Brazen Laver. The laver was made from the polished metal mirrors, given as their contribution by "the serving women who served at the door of the tent of meeting" (38[8]). Compare the ten lavers of Solomon's Temple (1 Kings 7[38, 39]). It was an admirable provision to secure cleanliness at all times on the part of those who ministered in the sanctuary.

22–33. The Anointing Oil. The holy anointing oil was to be prepared by mixing olive oil with liquid myrrh (probably a sort of fragrant syrup now called "balsam of Mecca"), cinnamon, sweet cane (Jer. 6[20]), and cassia (inner bark of a species of cinnamon tree; cf. Psa. 45[8]). The *hin* measure (cf. 29[40]) was equal to about one and one third gallons (see p. 79[b]).

34–38. The Incense. See notes on vv. 1–10.

CHAPTER XXXI

1–11. Bezalel and Oholiab. Two skilled workmen are named who are to do the work, or to superintend the work, of construction. They are declared to be *filled with the spirit of God, in wisdom, and in understanding, and in all manner of workmanship.* It is freely recognized that God chooses and inspires the workman, qualifying him for his high and honorable task, as surely as he chooses the priest, the prophet, or the king. The gifts and operations of his Spirit are very widely bestowed. The Spirit of God, in the O.T., is regarded as the divine energy working in nature and in human life, creating, reviving, instructing, and giving special and extraordinary power to men called to special and important tasks (cf. Gen. 1[2] 41[38] Num. 11[17, 25-29] Deut. 34[9] Judg. 3[10] 1 Sam. 10[10] 11[6]; notes on 1 Cor. 12[4-31]; also art., *Religion of Israel*, p. 176[a].)

12–17. Sabbath Observance. For the instructions regarding observance of the sabbath day see notes on 20[8-11] Deut. 5[12-15]; cf. Jer. 17[19-27] Isa. 58[13, 14].

18. The Two Tables. *The tables of the testimony*, containing the ten commandments, have been already referred to in 24[12] and 25[16] (cf. 32[15, 16] 34[29] Deut. 9[10]). As to the statement, *written with the finger of God*, may we not understand it to mean that God was the source and author of these laws, but that he used human agency, both the voice and the hand of Moses, in delivering them to the people?

Chapters 32 to 34: The Worship of the Golden Calf and Events Following

CHAPTER XXXII

The Making of the Calf; the Punishment. According to the exceedingly interesting story here told, Moses was so long away from the people, communing with God in the mountain (24[18]), that they grew weary of waiting. Many of them, it appears, in spite of the evidence given them in Egypt, at the Red Sea, on the journey, and at Sinai, were not convinced of the reality of Jehovah, in whose name Moses had come to them. They remembered the images of the gods in Egypt, and had, probably, often been present at the elaborate and highly sensuous ceremonial of their worship, but they had no image by which to make Jehovah real and visible, and the ritual of his worship was slow in taking shape. No doubt, too, they longed for the joyous excitement of the feast which accompanied the sacrifice, and the riot of singing and dancing that usually followed (cf. Judg. 21[19-21]). Therefore they persuaded Aaron to make them an image, apparently an image of Jehovah in the form of a young bull, like the images Jeroboam set up long afterward at Bethel and at Dan (1 Kings 12[28-33]).

Aaron yielded to their request, and made the image of wood overlaid with gold, and then proclaimed a feast. This was in full celebration when Moses came down from the mountain bearing the tablets of stone inscribed with the commandments of God. The anger of Moses, the breaking of the tablets, and his intercession for the people are vividly pictured. The riotous outbreak developed quickly into open revolt against Moses and against Jehovah whom he professed to represent. The Levites, members of his own tribe, rallied about him. A sharp conflict ensued in which many were slain, greatly to Moses' distress, who again sought the Lord in agonizing prayer. He confesses the people's sin, pleads for their forgiveness, and, if God is not willing to forgive, that he may perish with them. The character of Moses shines out very brightly throughout. Intensely in earnest, utterly unselfish, loyal to his God, striving to save the people committed to his care from the gross idolatry of their Canaanite and Arabian neighbors, into which they were now in danger of falling, with all its moral uncleanness and degradation, he is the ideal statesman as well as prophet, a true man of God.

In his prayer (vv. 11–13) Moses seems even more zealous for the honor of God than for the deliverance of the people. On the other hand, in vv. 31, 32 the emphasis appears to be on the deliverance of the people (cf. Num. 14[13-19]). For the sworn promise to the patriarchs (v. 13) see Gen. 22[16-18]. The broken tables (v. 19) were later replaced (34[1-4, 28, 29]). Aaron's apology (vv. 22–24) is evidently a quite insincere attempt to evade responsibility. A frank and manly confession of guilt would have been much more to his credit.

The meaning of v. 25 is obscure, but the following verses make it clear that there were already two parties in the camp, those who were for Moses and those who were against him. The latter seem to have been ready to reject the worship of Jehovah as well as the authority of Moses. Aaron had *let them loose* in their revelry, but it is quite wrong to say that he was their leader. If that had been the case, the hand of Moses and the armed Levites, men of his own tribe, would have been against him. Guilty as he was in the first instance, he was now on Moses' side, and his action had been intended to bring the intoxicated revelers into derision with those who had risen up against them. The situation was so serious that Moses felt compelled to rally the Levites to his defense, together with all who stood for Jehovah and his laws. Following the LXX we should read in v. 29, "Ye have consecrated yourselves (literally, filled your hands) this day unto Jehovah, every man against his son and against his brother, so that he may bestow a blessing upon you" (see 29[9], notes). It is too much to read into the figurative language used here of warfare a consecration to the priesthood (so Moffatt's translation), though that may have been anticipated in the promised blessing (cf. Deut. 33[9-11]). An entirely different reason is given for the consecration of the Levites in Num. 8[5-22]. Just how Moses hoped to *make atonement* for the people's sin is not clear (v. 30); it may have been by the offer of his own life in their stead. The Hebrew word thus rendered means, literally, to cover, and so to put out of sight, the sin.

The conception of a book of life (v. 32) is apparently taken from the custom of keeping a register of the citizens of a community (cf. Psa. 69[28] Isa. 4[3] Jer. 22[30] Ezek. 13[9]; notes on Rev. 3[5] 13[8], etc.). Moses' prayer is, therefore, simply that he may die for or with the people he has led (cf. Num. 11[15]).

CHAPTER XXXIII

Jehovah's Anger Turned by Moses' Prayer. In ch. 33 there is an account of further communion of Moses with God, interrupted by vv. 7–11, which describe the placing and using of the sacred tent. V. 2, it will be seen, breaks the connection of vv. 1 and 3, and anticipates the promise of v. 14, for the *angel* everywhere represents the divine presence (see 23[20, 21] 32[34]). Here Jehovah is represented as refusing to go farther with this stubborn people (vv. 3–5). The people, in token of penitence and grief, remove their ornaments. Then Moses intercedes for them again (vv. 12, 13), and receives in reply the gracious assurance that God will go with them. Without that assurance he would desire to go no farther but to remain at Sinai, where they already had the evidence of his presence and power. Better the Sinai wilderness with God, than the land flowing with milk and honey without him.

Moses makes another request. Wonderful as his experiences of the divine voice and presence had been, he was human enough to have his seasons of doubt and perplexity. He begs that he may see the glory of God, that he may have a convincing and satisfying vision of him (v. 18). But the full glory of the face of God is ever beyond the reach of human understanding. So Zophar declared in the drama of Job (11[7-9]; cf. Jn. 14[8]). Moses may not see God's face, but his goodness, his grace, his mercy, he may see and know, as men saw that glory in the incarnation of our Lord. He will be as one of whose passing by he has a glimpse, but whose face is not revealed. One can hardly imagine a more explicit declaration, in parable form, of the incompleteness and limitations of human knowledge, even of the knowledge of truly inspired men (cf. 1 Kings 19^{1-18} 1 Cor. 13^{8-10}).

The tent of vv. 7–11 is perhaps an earlier and simpler form of the sanctuary than that described in ch. 26. This is called the *tent of meeting,* because it represents the dwelling-place of God, the appointed place where a man may bring his gifts and his prayers to God (29^{42}). It was to be pitched *without the camp, afar off,* and cared for by Joshua, unlike the great tabernacle, which was to be "in the midst of the camps," and cared for by the Levites whose tents were to be pitched round about it (see Num. 1^{47-53} 2^{17}).

CHAPTER XXXIV

Renewal of the Two Tables; Sundry Laws. Again Moses is summoned to the mount of God (vv. 1–3) and is bidden to hew and bring with him *two tables of stone like unto the first* which he had broken (cf. Deut. 10^{1-5}). The revelation to him then of the character and attributes of God reaches one of the highest points in religious experience. The name "Jehovah" (see 3^{13-22}, notes) takes on a still richer and loftier meaning. In it divine compassion and grace, longsuffering, mercy, and truth are the accompaniments of justice. He is a God who forgives, and yet does not leave unpunished, in whom "mercy and truth are met together" (Psa. 85^{10}; cf. Num. 14^{18} 2 Chr. 30^{9} Neh. $9^{17, 31}$ Psa. 86^{15} 103^{8} 145^{8} Jer. 32^{18} Joel 2^{13} Jonah 4^{2} Nah. 1^{3}; also arts., *O.T. Conception of God*, p. 162, *Religion of Israel*, p. 174). The covenant bond, broken by the sin of the people, is renewed, with a repetition of the divine promises and a restatement of the law in very simple form. Again the people are warned against the seductive influences of Canaanite idolatry, in which lies their greatest danger. The Canaanite altars, with their stone pillars, and their wooden posts, *Asherim* (perhaps originally trees, or trunks of trees), are to be destroyed. The worship of such false gods is described as *a whoring*, for Jehovah has espoused his people, he is their true husband, and he *is a jealous God.*

There are close resemblances between the short code of laws contained here in vv. 10–28, and some of the laws of chs. 13 and 20–23, so close as to suggest a common original. What their history is and how to account for the differences and different setting we do not know. Compare, e.g., vv. 14, 17 with 20^{3-6} 23^{13}; vv. 18, 19 with $13^{1-7, 11-15}$; v. 21 with 20^{8} 23^{12}; vv. 22, 23 with $23^{16, 17}$; vv. 25, 26 with $23^{18, 19}$. It is possible that this short code, with the Ten Commandments, may be, or approximate very closely to, the original of the Book of the Covenant (24^{7}), of which chs. 20–23 are a later expansion. Throughout this entire history we must recognize the fact that it is compiled from older documents, legal and historical, and that the extracts used are often fitted very loosely together (see art., *Legal and Historical Literature*, p. 145; art., *Pentateuch*, pp. 136–7.)

The shining of Moses' face was a reflection of the Divine Presence. Cf. the interpretation put upon this story by Paul in 2 Cor. 3^{7-18} and 4^{3-6}. So did men see with a brighter radiance "the glory of God in the face of Jesus Christ."

CHAPTERS XXXV–XL

The Building of the Sanctuary

These chapters repeat almost word for word chs. 25–31, and tell in detail how the instructions there given to Moses were carried out. There are some unimportant differences in the order of contents and concluding statements which tell of the dedication of the sanctuary and its occupation by the divine glory. Compare the description of Solomon's Temple in 1 Kings 6–8, 2 Chr. 3–6, notes, and of the ideal Temple in Ezek. 40–48, notes.

This section of the book begins with a repetition of the law of Sabbath observance (35^{1-3}). 35^{3} has a parallel in 16^{23}.

A very fine picture is presented in 35^{20-29} and 36^{2-7} of the liberality of the people, who not only brought more than was required for *the service of the work*, but offered of their labor freely as well. *So the people were restrained from bringing.*

There is no parallel in the earlier chapters for 38^{21-31}. An account is given of the amount of gold and silver and brass used in the construction of the sanctuary, an almost incredible total for a people so situated, the value of which in modern reckoning would amount to upward of four hundred thousand dollars.

When the work was finished (40^{33}), the cloud, in which God is represented as accompanying Israel, *covered the tent of meeting, and the glory of the Lord filled the tabernacle* (40^{34}; cf. 16^{10}). In what form the glory appeared we do not know, but the words evidently convey the fact of some real and profound experience of the Divine Presence (cf. 1 Kings $8^{10, 11}$ 2 Chr. 5^{11-14}). Thus was fulfilled the promise of 29^{43-45}, and thus is the Lord represented as taking up his permanent abode with his people.

LEVITICUS

By Professor CHRISTOPHER R. NORTH

Introduction

Title and Contents. The title "Leviticus" is derived from the Greek version of the O.T. (LXX), and means "that which relates to the Levites." Since, however, the Levites are mentioned only in 25:32, 33, it is necessary to give to the term a somewhat different emphasis from that which strictly attaches to it. All priests were Levites, but not all Levites were priests; and even a hurried reading of the book is sufficient to show that the laws contained in it have a much closer relation to the duties of the priests than to those of the Levites. The term "Leviticus" is, therefore, to be understood in a sense similar to that in the phrase "the Levitical priesthood" of Heb. 7:11.

The contents of the book fall into five well-defined sections: (1) Chs. 1–7, The Laws of Sacrifice; (2) Chs. 8–10, The Consecration of the Priests; (3) Chs. 11–15, The Laws relating to Uncleanness, with which may be taken ch. 16, The Ritual of the Day of Atonement; (4) Chs. 17–26, The Law of Holiness; (5) Ch. 27, An Appendix on the Commutation of Vows and Tithes.

Sources and Date. The critical problems presented by the book are comparatively simple. The contents belong as a whole to that great body of material in the Hexateuch known as the Priestly Code (P), for the date and character of which see the article *The Pentateuch—Its Origin and Development* (pp. 138f.). An exception may be made for the Law of Holiness (ch. 17–26), which embodies the priestly ideal in the earlier stages of its development. The distinctive features of the Law of Holiness are indicated in the introduction to chs. 17–26.

It will appear from the foregoing that the book is really a post-exilic compilation. This does not mean, however, that it contains nothing but post-exilic materials. Every present has strong links with the past, and no system, whether of social ethics, or of civil government, or of religion, can expect to obtain a firm hold on the allegiance of men if it breaks entirely with the past. In the book of Leviticus we see the Jewish sacrificial system in what is very nearly its latest stage of development. But embedded in the laws are many customs and precepts of Mosaic or even pre-Mosaic antiquity. It is, of course, not always possible to disengage these from their context, but in the following notes an attempt has been made to indicate the most obvious of them.

Historical Value of the Book. The book contains a maximum of precept and a minimum of action. And since the passages containing the latter were written many centuries after the events described, it is impossible to insist on their literal historicity. It would, however, be a serious mistake to think of the book as destitute of historical value. Every piece of literature is historically valuable insofar as it reflects the ideas and practices of the age when it was written. Leviticus is of inestimable value to the historian because it mirrors so faithfully the ecclesiastical system of Judaism in the otherwise little documented post-exilic period. (See further intro. to Ezra-Nehemiah, p. 454.) The "tent of meeting" and its sacrifices are an ideal projection into the past of the daily Temple ritual that lasted until after the time of Jesus. The study of Leviticus is, therefore, a valuable aid to the understanding of a not unimportant element in the background of the life of our Lord.

Religious Value of the Book. If it be true that Psalms is the most frequently read, it is perhaps equally true that Leviticus is the least read book in the O.T. Even for the Jews most of its laws have been a dead letter since the destruction of the Temple, and it is doubtful whether they would reinstitute the sacrificial system even if they had the opportunity. The Christian thinks of Leviticus as containing a larger proportion of those things which are done away in Christ than any other book in the O.T. And yet, paradoxical as it may seem, neither Leviticus nor the Psalms can be properly understood apart from the other. At least the student of the Jewish background of Christianity must know both, for the reason that they were held in equal veneration by Jewish piety in the time of our Lord. The Psalter was the prayerbook of the Temple; Leviticus provided the rubrics. This will be appreciated if vv. 16f. of Psa. 51 are compared with the later addition in v. 19: it is evident that a psalm which in its original form had no place at all for sacrifice has been adapted to the sacrificial ideal. The opinion is growing that the origin of a large number of psalms is to be sought in the Temple worship. It was Zacharias, a priest, who composed the *Benedictus* (Lk. 1⁶⁷⁻⁷⁹), and Simeon, a devout frequenter of the Temple, who uttered the *Nunc Dimittis* (Lk. 2²⁵⁻³²). These considerations should at least commend Leviticus to the sympathy of Christian readers.

Literature: Commentaries in English by Kennedy, *Leviticus* (Century Bible); Chapman and Streane, *Leviticus* (Cambridge Bible); Driver and White, *Leviticus* (Sacred Books of the O.T.); Lofthouse, *Leviticus* (Peake's Commentary); in German by Baentsch and Bertholet. Other literature: Gray, *Sacrifice in the O.T.;* W. Robertson Smith, *The Religion of the Semites* (2nd edit.); articles on "Sacrifice," and on "Cleanness and Uncleanness" in Hastings' *Dictionary of the Bible* and in the *Encyclopaedia Biblica.*

Chapters 1 to 7: The Laws of Sacrifice

There are two main divisions to this section: (1) 1^{1}–6^{7}—regulations for the proper observance of the five orders of sacrifices, namely, Burnt-offering (ch. 1), Meal-Offering (ch. 2), Peace-offering (ch. 3), Sin-offering (4^{1}–5^{13}), Guilt-offering (5^{14}–6^{7}). These regulations are mainly addressed to the people (1^{2} 4^{2}). (2) 6^{8}–7^{38}—details of procedure mainly for the guidance of the priests ($6^{9, 25}$).

CHAPTER I

The Burnt-Offering

1, 2. Introduction to the Whole Section. The laws are said to have been delivered to Moses *out of the tent of meeting.* This was properly the covering of the tabernacle (Ex. 35^{11}), but in the Priestly Code the tent of meeting and the tabernacle are usually synonymous. For description of the tabernacle and its coverings see on Ex. 26. It was not a place for congregational worship (the A.V. *tabernacle of the congregation* is incorrect), but a place where Jehovah met with Moses, and through him revealed the Law.

The general term *oblation*, covering all kinds of sacrifice, is *korban* (cf. Mk. 7^{11}, notes). It means literally "something brought near," in the Bible always of a gift to God. Note that only domestic animals are admissible as sacrifices. Certain other animals might be eaten (Deut. 12^{22}), but their use as food had no religious significance.

3–17. Procedure for the Burnt-Offering. For additional details see 6^{8-13}. The word translated *burnt-offering* (*'ôlâh*) means literally "that which ascends," either to the altar, or from the altar in sacrificial smoke. The special feature of the burnt-offering was that no part of the victim was consumed by the worshiper. Burnt-offerings might be either (1) public, or (2) offered by private individuals. For the occasions when burnt-offerings were made on behalf of the community see Ex. 29^{38-42} Num. 28, 29. These included the daily burnt-offerings, together with additional offerings on the Sabbath, at new moon, and at various annual feasts. An individual might offer a burnt-sacrifice at any time, whether in fulfillment of a vow, or as a spontaneous recognition of God's goodness to him (22^{18} Num. 15^{3}). The present passage seems primarily to have in mind the offerings of individuals. The victim might be taken from cattle (vv. 3–9), or from the flock (vv. 10–13), according to the means or discretion of the offerer. A further inexpensive option was provided for the very poor, who might bring one or more turtle-doves or young pigeons (vv. 14–17; cf. 12^{8} Lk. 2^{24}). This concession seems to be an afterthought, since birds are not mentioned in v. 2.

The ritual for sheep and goats is the same as for cattle. Sheep or goats are equally eligible, a poor man's goat being as acceptable as a richer man's sheep. Any animal offered must be a male without blemish. For list of disqualifying blemishes see 22^{19-24}. The donor was to *lay* (literally "lean" or "press," and compare the vivid picture presented by the word in Amos 5^{19}) *his hand* upon the animal, probably in token of dedication. The idea that it dies in his stead cannot be sustained. Even though the offering is said to make "expiation" (so render for *atonement* in v. 4; cf. Gray, *Sacrifice in the O.T.*, p. 74), the O.T. contains no theory of how this is effected. The conception of sacrifice uppermost in the O.T. is that it was a gift to God, who accepted the gift as expiation (so Gray, *op. cit.*, frequently). The animal is slain and dismembered by the offerer. This is done *before Jehovah*, or as v. 11 explains, close by the altar, on its north side. The blood, which everywhere in the O.T. is thought to be of peculiar sanctity, is received into a vessel by the priest, who "dashes" (the word is different from the "sprinkle" of 4^{6}) it against the four sides of the altar. The various parts of the animal are arranged on the altar, special mention being made of the intestinal *fat*, which was considered a great delicacy, to be offered always to God, and never to be eaten by man. A relic of the old idea of sacrifice as the food of the gods is preserved in v. 9b; cf. the Babylonian story of the Deluge, where the gods smell the sweet savor, and hover over the sacrificer. We gather from 7⁸ that the skin of the offering was the perquisite of the officiating priest. That the ritual preserves ancient custom may be judged from v. 7, where fire is to be kindled on the altar as occasion required. Contrast the (apparently) later regulation of 6^{13}, which requires that the altar fire shall never go out.

The ritual for birds (vv. 14–17) necessarily differs somewhat from the preceding. These are too small to be dismembered. The head is to be pinched, without being severed from the body (cf. 5^{8}).

CHAPTER II

The Meal-Offering

(For additional details see 6^{14-23} Num. 15^{1-16}.)

1–3. Materials and General Procedure. The word translated *meal-offering* (Hebrew *minchâh*) means literally a "gift." Unlike *korban* (cf. 1^{1}) it may be used of a present from one man to another (Gen. 32^{13}); or of tribute from a conquered foe (2 Sam. 8^{6}). In early times as a gift to God it was applied to both vegetable and animal offerings (Gen. $4^{3,\ 4}$). In the Priestly Code it is used only of cereal offerings, usually the accompaniment of a flesh offering (7^{11-21} Num. 15)—to eat flesh alone would be barbarous—but here, it would seem, independently.

The materials for the offering consisted of finely milled flour, olive oil, and frankincense. For the quantities prescribed when accompanying the several flesh offerings see Num. 15. The regulation *flour* is described as luxurious food (Ezek. 16^{13}), used in kings' households (1 Kings 4^{22}), and set before honored guests (Gen. 18^{6}). *Oil* served the same purpose as butter with us. Salt was added as a condiment (v. 13). To eat a man's salt was to accept his hospitality, and as his guest to be under his protection. Hence the phrase "the salt of the covenant of thy God" (v. 13). *Frankincense* (the English word means "pure incense") was a fragrant resin, and non-edible. The priest was to take a handful of the flour and oil, together with all the frankincense, and burn it upon the altar. The portion so burned is called a "memorial offering" (so translate in vv. 2, 9, 16). The meaning of the term is obscure, but the intention probably is that the memorial offering would serve to bring the offerer to the favorable remembrance of the Deity. What was left over, i.e., the larger part of the ingredients, went to the priests. It was *most holy,* and as such might be eaten only by males of the priestly families, and by them always within the sanctuary precincts (6^{16-18}). Certain other priestly dues were merely "holy", and might be eaten by other members of the priests' households (10^{14}; cf. 10^{10-13}).

4–13. Further Details Concerning the Cooking of the Meal-Offering. *Leaven* and *honey,* being fermentative, may not be used in any offering destined for the altar. (In domestic cooking honey served for sugar—Ex. 16^{31}). *Salt,* on the other hand, is a preservative as well as condiment (cf. notes on v. 1). The flour and oil might be baked in the oven, or pastry fashion on a griddle (v. 5, cf. mg.), or boiled in a *saucepan* (the proper translation in v. 7.).

14–16. Meal-Offering of Firstfruits. There is here no time for milling the corn, which is therefore roasted, or presented in the form of crushed groats.

CHAPTER III

The Peace-Offering

(For additional details see $7^{11-21,\ 28-34}$ 22^{21-24}.)

The translation *thank-offerings* of the A.S.V. (v. 1, mg.) is unsatisfactory, since it applies to one only of three varieties of peace-offering, namely: thank-offerings, votive-offerings, and freewill-offerings (cf. $7^{11-13,\ 16}$ 22^{21}). The Hebrew term (*shelem*) has generally been understood to denote an offering that has the effect of establishing harmonious and peaceful relations with the Deity. The etymology of the word, however, is equally consistent with the translation "recompense-offering," i.e., payment for benefits received, or expected. Thank-offerings and votive-offerings appear to be of this nature, and Prov. 7^{14} strongly supports this interpretation.

In early times we read of peace-offerings on occasions of national rejoicing (e.g., 2 Sam. 6^{17}). But the only public peace-offerings prescribed in the later sacrificial system are at Pentecost (23^{19}), and in connection with the consecration of priests (9^{4}). With these exceptions the peace-offering was a private and family sacrifice. Flesh was not a daily article of diet among the Hebrews, but a treat reserved for special occasions. There is no doubt that in ancient times all killing of domestic animals for food was sacrificial, i.e., the occasion for a peace-offering. When at the end of the seventh century B.C. sacrifice was confined to Jerusalem, some relaxation of this rule was necessary (Deut. 12^{15}).

Materials and General Procedure. Peace-offerings might be made of cattle (vv. 1–5), or of sheep (vv. 6–11), or of goats (vv. 12–17). Females as well as males might be offered (contrast the burnt-offering, ch. 1).

Normally, the animal must be without blemish (vv. 1, 6), but an exception was allowed for freewill-offerings (22^{23}), which were in a sense offerings of supererogation. Much of the procedure was the same as for the burnt-offering, but since it was an offering of less sanctity than the burnt-offering, the victim was not slain by the altar (v. 2; cf. $1^{5, 11}$). The choicest internal fats, together with, in the case of sheep, the fat tail, were burned on the altar as a *sweet savor* to Jehovah (vv. 5, 9f., 16). By the expression *the caul upon the liver* (vv. 4, 10, 15) is usually understood the caudate lobe. When it is said in v. 17 that no fat is to be eaten, the reference is to the internal fats specified in the preceding; the prohibition does not apply to muscular fat. After the removal of the fats the breast and the right thigh went to the priests (7^{31-34}). The remainder of the flesh was consumed by the offerer and his friends.

Chapters 4^1 to 5^{13}: The Sin-Offering

(For additional details see 6^{24-30} Num. 15^{22-31}.)

CHAPTER IV

1, 2. Definition. The primary purpose of the sin-offering was to make expiation for sins committed in ignorance. It is to be remembered that primitive morality takes little account of motives, but only of actions and their results. When right conduct consists in not disobeying commandments, it is easy to err, especially when the commandments are numerous and predominantly ceremonial. A man must needs have all his wits about him to keep the Law entire. Hence the anxiety of the psalmist (Psa. 19^{12}) that he might be cleared from hidden faults, by which are meant not sins that he kept secret from others, but faults hidden from himself. When such "errors" were discovered expiation was provided by the sin-offering. For sin as we understand it, intentional and "presumptuous" sin (Psa. 19^{13}), there was no remission by sacrifice (Num. $15^{30, 31}$ Heb. 10^{26-31}).

In addition to serving the purpose indicated above, sin-offerings also figured in the high priestly consecration ceremonies (ch. 8), and were required from persons emerging from certain states of uncleanness, e.g., child-birth (12^6), and leprosy (14^{19}). The value of the animal offered, likewise the manipulation of the offering, depended upon the rank of the offender.

3–12. For the High Priest. If the high priest commits an unintentional transgression, the whole community will incur guilt, since he acts as their representative. To remove this, nothing less than a young bullock, obviously without blemish, will suffice. The high priest presses (see on 1^4) his hand on the head of the victim, and he himself as the offerer slays it. Before pouring out the blood at the base of the altar of burnt-offering he takes some of it into the sanctuary, *sprinkles it* (the translation here is correct) on the curtain separating the Holy Place from the Holy of Holies, and smears it upon the projections at the corners of the altar of incense. (For description of the incense altar, which was inside the sanctuary, see Ex. 30^{1-10}.) The internal fats of the bullock, specified as for peace-offerings (vv. 8f.; cf. $3^{3f.}$), are burned upon the altar of burnt-offering. The remainder of the carcass, including even the skin, is burned, not upon the altar, but in the place where the ashes from the altar are cast (vv. 11, 12). No part is available for human consumption, nor for priestly profit.

13–21. For the Whole Community. The victim and the procedure are the same. The elders, as the responsible heads of the community, lay hands on the victim. The offering makes expiation (v. 20; see on 1^4) and the people are forgiven.

22–26. For a Ruler, or Secular Chief. The offering is an unblemished he-goat. Any priest may officiate (v. 25; contrast v. 16). None of the blood is taken into the sanctuary, but the procedure differs from that for peace-offerings and burnt-offerings in that some of the blood is smeared on the projections of the altar of burnt-offering. The fats are burned as before. The remainder of the carcass is not burned; it is the due of the officiating priest (6^{26}), and belongs to the class of "most holy" things (see on 2^{1-3}).

27–35. For a Layman. The procedure is the same as for a ruler, but a she-goat or a she-lamb suffices for victim.

CHAPTER V

1–6. Examples of Sins that Require the Sin (or Guilt?) Offering. These verses appear to break the connection between 4^{35} and 5^7, which follow one another naturally, 5^{7-13} providing for the man who cannot afford the lamb required in 4^{32-35}. They also present two further difficulties: (1) the sin described in v. 1 can hardly be called a sin of ignorance; (2) according to the R.V. of v. 6a (cf. A.S.V.) they appear to relate not to sin-offerings but to guilt-offerings, dealt with in 5^{14}–6^7. With regard to the second of these difficulties, the first of the two translations of the R.V. mg., *for his guilt*, is barely possible, but it is not the natural and obvious translation. The most likely solution of the difficulty is that these verses come from a source other than that from which the rest of the chapters in which they are embedded are derived, a source that did not differentiate clearly between sin-offerings and guilt-offerings (note both terms in v. 6).

The first example (v. 1) is that of the man who remains silent when evidence has been called for under an *adjuration* or a curse (cf. Judg. 17² Prov. 29²⁴). Such evidence may be either at first hand (*whether he hath seen*), or at second hand (*or known*). The second example (vv. 2, 3) is that of the man who touches the carcass of an unclean animal (see ch. 11), or a person in a state of uncleanness (see ch. 12–15). The third (v. 4) is that of the man who takes a rash oath. The word translated *swear rashly* is used only twice outside this passage, in Prov. 12¹⁸, and of Moses in Psa. 106³³ (cf. Num. 20¹⁰).

7–13. Sin-Offerings of the Poor. In v. 7a R.V. has *guilt-offering* (cf. A.S.V.) as in v. 6a (see preceding paragraph). The explanation, however, is somewhat different from that suggested there. The LXX reads *he shall bring for his sin that he hath sinned*, from which it is probable that the Hebrew originally read "sin-offering," not guilt-offering. However this may be, that the paragraph refers to sin-offerings is clear from vv. 7b, 8f., 11f. The consideration of guilt-offerings proper is deferred until v. 14.

These verses provide that if a man from whom a sin-offering is due is too poor to provide the goat or lamb, he may bring two turtle-doves, or young pigeons, one for a sin-offering, and the other for a burnt-offering. After the blood had been drained from the first, its flesh was presumably eaten by the priest. The second was burned according to rule (cf. 1¹⁴⁻¹⁷). If a man could not even afford birds, he might bring fine flour (about 7 pints), without oil or frankincense. Of this a handful was burned on the altar; the rest went to the priest (cf. 2¹⁻³, notes).

Chapters 5¹⁴ to 6⁷: The Guilt-Offering

(For additional details see 7¹⁻⁷ Num. 5⁵⁻⁸.)

It has already been noted (see on 5¹⁻⁶) that sin and guilt offerings are sometimes not clearly differentiated. They are admittedly similar (cf. 7⁷), and in the present passage the situation contemplated in 5¹⁷ seems nowise different from that demanding a sin-offering. The word for guilt-offering (*asham*) is used in 1 Sam. 6³⁻⁵ of the golden tumors and mice sent by the Philistines with the returning ark, and in 2 Kings 12¹⁶, somewhat similarly, of money payments to the Temple treasury. These usages are akin to the provision in the present section, where the principle of the guilt-offering consists in the payment of dues withheld from God (5¹⁴⁻¹⁹), or man (6¹⁻⁷), together with a compensatory fine.

14–19. Guilt-Offering for Dues Withheld From God. If a man inadvertently neglects to render at the appointed time what is due from him to the sanctuary, he must, on discovering his error, make it good, adding a fifth by way of interest. In addition to this he must present a ram, the value of which, to be estimated by the priest, must be in shekels, i.e., it must be worth at least two shekels. Two shekels would be about $1.40, but their purchasing power today would be much greater. For the disposal of the ram see 7¹⁻⁷.

CHAPTER VI

1–7. Guilt-Offering for Dues Withheld from Man. The unneighborly acts specified may best be indicated by a paraphrase translation of vv. 2f.: "If a man sins and commits a breach of faith against Jehovah by acting dishonestly toward his neighbor; whether by neglecting to return at the due time that which his neighbor has deposited with him for safe custody, or as security; or by obtaining something from his neighbor by violence or extortion; or by finding something belonging to another, and then swearing it is not in his possession—." Nothing is said of the case being brought into court. (The translation of v. 5c is too definite, the Hebrew being simply "in the day of his guilt.") The requirement of the guilt-offering was for the man whose conscience prompted him to make voluntary restitution. He was to restore to the person he had wronged the property, plus one fifth of its value, and in addition he was to present a ram to the sanctuary. If the matter went into court, the consequences for the offender were more serious (see Ex. 22).

Chapters 6⁸ to 7³⁸:

Supplementary Regulations for the Guidance of Priests

Many of the details here given have been mentioned in the preceding expositions. Only those that are new need be specially mentioned in the following comments, and the reader is referred back to the foregoing chapters.

8–13. The Burnt-Offering. Cf. ch. 1. Unlike ch. 1, which has primarily in mind the offerings of individuals, these verses contemplate the public burnt-offerings presented daily. The conduct of the priest was, of course, the same for both classes. Private offerings were slain by the offerer (1[5]); public offerings were probably slain by priests and Levites (cf. 2 Chr. 29[34] 35[9f.]). For the garments worn by officiating priests see Ex. 28[40-43]. These had to be changed when the sacred precincts were left. For the contagion of holiness that necessitated this, see on vv. 27f.

14–18. The Meal-Offering. Cf. ch. 2. This passage also has in mind the public meal-offerings accompanying the daily and other burnt-offerings (Ex. 29[40, 41] Num. 28[5], etc.). The procedure is as in ch. 2.

19–23. Meal-Offering of the High Priest. This is described in v. 20 both as a consecration offering and as a daily offering (*perpetually*). The second of these is attested by Ecclus. 45[14] and Josephus. With regard to the first, the words *in the day when he is anointed* are probably a gloss in this context, though a consecration meal-offering was made in later times (cf. Ex. 29[2]).

24–30. The Sin-Offering. Cf. 4[1]–5[13]. This, like the burnt-offering, was slain close by the altar. The higher grades of sin-offering were not eaten (v. 30; cf. 4[1-21]). The flesh of the lower grades (4[22-35] 5[7-10]) was consumed by the priests, and was *most holy* (see on 2[1-3]). It must not be eaten outside the sanctuary area, for holiness was contagious, and if laymen were infected by it the consequences might be serious. God might break out, as he did upon Uzzah (2 Sam. 6[6f.]). Men thought of holiness as physical before they thought of it as moral. It had affinities with uncleanness in that both were "taboo," i.e., withdrawn from the sphere of common usage (see art., *Bible Manners and Customs*, p. 74a). Thus when the later Jews wished to say of the O.T. that it was canonical, they said it "defiled the hands," i.e., certain lustrations were necessary after handling it. The "holiness" of a brazen vessel could be purged away by scouring. But an earthen vessel must be broken after use, since the holiness of the sin-offering, getting into its more or less porous texture, could not be entirely gotten out.

CHAPTER VII

1–7. The Guilt-Offering. Cf. 5[14]–6[7]. This is *most holy* (see on 2[1-3] and 6[24-30]). The place of slaughter and the manipulation of the blood are as for the burnt-offering (cf. on 1[11], and read *dash* for *sprinkle*). The fats are burned as in the peace-offering. The flesh goes to the priest.

8–10. The Priests' Share of Burnt-Offerings and Meal-Offerings. For v. 9 cf. 2[4-7].

11–21. The Peace-Offering. Cf. vv. 28–34, and ch. 3. There are three varieties, namely, thank-offerings, votive-offerings, and freewill-offerings. The flesh would naturally be eaten with bread. The meal-offering to accompany thank-offerings is prescribed, and consists of three varieties of unleavened, together with leavened bread. It does not appear that any of the bread was destined for the altar (the leavened portion would be ineligible for that purpose, see 2[11]), but one cake of each of the four varieties went as a heave-offering to the officiating priest, to be eaten with his portion of the flesh. The Hebrew word translated *heave-offering* (*terûmâh*) contains no suggestion of throwing. It simply means what is "lifted up" from the whole as the priest's portion. The flesh of thank-offerings must be eaten on the day of offering (v. 15; cf. 22[29, 30]), but an extension of one day was allowed for votive-offerings and freewill-offerings (v. 16; cf. 19[6]). Care must be taken to keep the flesh from all contact with uncleanness. The penalty for neglect of this requirement is extreme—*that soul shall be cut off from his people* (cf. Gen. 17[14] Ex. 12[15], etc.). What this involves is not stated. The contexts in which the phrase occurs do not suggest judicial procedure and capital punishment. Nor are we to think of anything quite so formal as excommunication. Probably what is meant is that the offender was left to the judgment of God, with the expectation that he would come to an untimely end (cf. 17[10] 20[3]).

22–27. Prohibition of Fat and Blood. Cf. 3[17] 17[10-16]. By *fat* here is meant the internal fat specified in ch. 3 for burning on the altar. To eat the fat of non-sacrificial animals was not interdicted, provided they complied with the laws of cleanness (ch. 11). But the *blood* must first be drained off, since it is pre-eminently the seat of life (Gen. 9[4]), and as such belongs to God. The fat of domestic animals might be put to human uses, provided they had not been sacrificially slaughtered; but it might never be eaten.

28–34. The Priests' Share of Peace-Offerings. This consists of the breast and the right thigh (not *shoulder* as in R.V. mg.). The *heave thigh* (see on vv. 11–21 for the meaning of the term) goes to the priest who conducts the sacrifice. The breast was "waved" in the direction of the altar in token of dedication to God, and then back again in token that God had bestowed it upon the priests. It went to the common priestly store. (Cf. the greed of Eli's sons, 2 Sam. 2[12-17].)

35–38. Concluding Summary. These verses look back to the regulations of 6[8]–7[34]. At the beginning of v. 35 read *portion* with R.V. mg.

Chapters 8 to 10: The Consecration of Aaron and His Sons, and Their Assumption of Office

CHAPTER VIII

The Consecration

The chapter is practically a repetition of Ex. 29, and tells how the instructions there given to Moses were carried out. For the details the reader is referred to the notes on Ex. 29.

1–5. Preliminaries. Cf. Ex. 29^{1-3}.

6–13. The Washing, Clothing, and Anointing. Cf. Ex. 29^{4-9}. For the various items in the priestly vestments see on Ex. 28. The *Urim and Thummim* (mg. reading, *The Rights and the Perfections*) are not mentioned in Ex. 29, but they are included in the catalogue of Ex. 28. They were probably stones for casting sacred lots (see on 1 Sam. 14^{41}). Nothing is said in Ex. 29 of the anointing of the tabernacle and its furniture, but cf. Ex. 30^{26f.} For the *laver* (v. 11) see Ex. 30^{18}.

Note that Aaron alone is anointed, not his sons (cf. 10^{7}, where all the priests appear to be anointed). This anointing, and the garments he wears, constitute him a person of kingly rank. In post-exilic times, when the monarchy no longer existed, the high priest exercised civil as well as ecclesiastical authority.

14–17. The Sin-Offering. Cf. Ex. 29^{10-14}. Moses acts as priest, and Aaron, as the offerer, slays the bullock. For the procedure cf. 4^{3-12}, noting that here nothing is said of the blood being taken inside the sanctuary. This is an installation-offering, not a sin-offering for inadvertence.

18–21. The Burnt-Offering. Cf. Ex. 29^{15-18}, and for the ritual ch. 1.

22–32. The Installation-Offering. Cf. Ex. 29^{19-34}. The Hebrew word translated *consecration* in vv. 22, 28f., 31, is literally "fillings," and finds its explanation in v. 33b, where the Hebrew reads "he shall fill your hand seven days" (cf. R.V. mg.). To fill a person's hands was a technical term meaning to install him in office (cf. Judg. 17^{5}, mg., notes). Accordingly, Moses takes certain parts of the offering, and before burning them on the altar puts them upon the hands of Aaron and his sons, and *waves* them (v. 27; cf. on 7^{28-34}). It is this contact with the holy flesh, and its reception on the altar from their hands, which gives the priests their peculiar standing. To make the consecration more complete some of the blood of the ram is applied to the right ears, thumbs, and great toes of Aaron and his sons (vv. 23–27). The point is not so much that ears, hands, and feet are especially consecrated, as that the whole body is consecrated by the application of the blood to these extremities. Even the garments of the priests are sprinkled with a mixture of blood and oil (v. 30; cf. Ex. 29^{21}).

With these differences the installation-offering resembles an ordinary peace-offering. The fats are burned on the altar. With them goes the right thigh, which, though belonging in theory to Jehovah, was ordinarily waved back to the priests. But at present it is not their due, since they have not as yet officiated. Moses as the officiant receives the breast as his portion. (Note that in 7^{31f.} the individual priest receives the thigh, and the priests as a whole the breast. Here the intention seems the other way about, and the accounts must embody different traditions). The rest of the flesh is boiled and eaten by the priests (v. 31), as it would be ordinarily by those who offered a peace-offering.

33–36. The Foregoing Ceremonies to be Repeated Daily for Seven Days. During this time the priests are to keep within the sanctuary inclosure. For the reason for this see on 6^{24-30}.

CHAPTER IX

The Priests Assume Office

On the eighth day Aaron, now fully consecrated, conducts special inaugural sacrifices, assisted by his sons.

1–7. Preparations. These consist of materials for (1) a sin-offering and a burnt-offering on behalf of the priests (in v. 7 for *for the people* read *for thy house*, with LXX); (2) a sin-offering, burnt-offering, peace-offering, and meal-offering on behalf of the people. The victims for the burnt-offering are said to be *of the first year*. This has generally been understood to mean "less than a year old," but Gray is inclined to think it means "of a full year old" (*Sacrifice in the O.T.*, pp. 348–351; cf. A.S.V., v. 3).

8–14. Offerings for the Priests: (1) *The Sin-Offering* (vv. 8–11). The ritual is similar to that in 8^{14-17}. (2) *The Burnt-Offering* (vv. 12–14). Cf. 8^{18-21}, and for the ritual see on ch. 1.

15–21. Offerings for the People. (1) *The Sin-Offering* (v. 15). The phrase *as the first* refers to vv. 8–11. (2) *The Burnt-Offering* (v. 16). For *the ordinance* see on ch. 1. (3) *The Meal-Offering* (v. 17). See on ch. 2. The portion not burned was later consumed by the priests (10^{12}). The last clause of the verse is unintelligible and probably a gloss. (4) *The Peace-offering* (vv. 18–21). For the ritual see ch. 3 and 7^{28-34}, and for the consumption of the priests' portions, 10[14]. Nothing is said of any share for the people.

22–24. The Pronouncement of the Blessing and the Revelation of the Divine Glory. Aaron pronounces a blessing from the altar. The words of the benediction are not given, but were perhaps as in Num. 6[23-26]. He then comes down (the altar was three cubits high, Ex. 27[1]), and enters with Moses into the shrine. When they come forth they together bless the people, and the *glory of Jehovah* is visibly seen as fire descending upon the altar. For the association of the divine glory with fire see Ex. 24[17]. It was generally hidden from mortal sight by the pillar of cloud. Other examples of the spontaneous consumption of sacrifices by fire are related in Judg. 6[21] 1 Kings 18[38] 1 Chr. 21[26] 2 Chr. 7[1]. The *shout* of the people (v. 24b) is not a panic-stricken woe but a ringing cry of joy. The word is that translated "sing" in Isa. 42[11]. Exultation and reverence go together: "They gave a ringing cry, and fell on their faces."

CHAPTER X

This chapter is of the nature of an appendix to the two preceding, and is designed to show that the ministrations of the priests are to be conducted with scrupulous regard for the proprieties of worship.

1–7. The Sin of Nadab and Abihu. These were the eldest sons of Aaron (Ex. 6[23]). Together with their father, and Eleazar and Ithamar their brothers, they had just been consecrated (Ex. 28[1]). They now offered *strange fire*, and were immediately consumed by fire from Jehovah (cf. 9[24]). What is meant by offering strange fire is not certain. Perhaps they had not taken fire from the appointed place, i.e., the altar (16[12] Num. 16[46]); or perhaps the incense was not according to the proper receipt (Ex. 30[34f.]). Others suppose that by the word "fire" in v. 1b should be understood fire-offering, and that Nadab and Abihu had presumed to offer an unauthorized sacrifice. Their father and brothers were forbidden to mourn for them. For the expressions used cf. 13[45] 21[10] Ezek. 24[17]. The hair was unloosed by removing the turban; which explains the reading of the versions noted in the mg. What is intended is not that the surviving priests shall stifle their natural affection, and by remaining impassive show their disapprobation of the action of their dead kinsmen. But if they mourn, they will be temporarily unclean (Hos. 9[4] Deut. 26[14]), and so incompetent to minister (21[1-24], where, however, the strict rule applies only to the high priest). That the occasion calls for mourning is recognized, but it is the people who must mourn (v. 6b), and lest the surviving priests should contract uncleanness by touching the corpses (Num. 19[11]), these are to be removed by Aaron's cousins (v. 4), who are unconsecrated, and may therefore contract uncleanness without detriment to the community.

8–11. Alcohol Forbidden to the Priests While Officiating. Cf. Ezek. 44[21]. For vv. 10, 11, cf. Ezek. 22[26] 44[23]. *Common* was the opposite of *holy*, *unclean* of *clean*. For the difference between holiness and uncleanness see introduction to chs. 11–15. It is quite certain that priests were teachers of ritual before they had the monopoly of sacrifice, and the function is still part of their duty.

12–15. Laws Governing the Consumption of Priestly Dues. It is sufficient to refer to the notes on 2[1-3] 6[24-30] 7[28-34].

16–20. A Passage Relating to the Consumption of Sin-Offerings by the Priests. It will be remembered that when the blood of a sin-offering had been taken inside the shrine, as in 4[1-21], the flesh was not eaten by the priests, but burnt outside the sacred enclosure. When there was no special blood rite, as in 4[22-35], the flesh was eaten by the priests (6[24-26]). The sin-offering referred to in the present passage is that described in 9[15]. No blood had been taken into the sanctuary, and Moses was surprised that its flesh had not been eaten, but burned. He therefore remonstrates with Eleazar and Ithamar. Aaron explains that the reason for departure from the ordinary procedure is that the untoward happening to his eldest sons rendered such a course unpropitious; whereupon Moses expresses himself content. The story is a strange one. We may perhaps infer from it that priests sometimes hesitated to eat the flesh of sin-offerings, and that the story was designed to show that such eating was, in the absence of special circumstances, quite in order.

Chapters 11 to 15: Laws Relating to Uncleanness

It has been stated (on 6[24-30]) that holiness was in early times thought of as physical, and that it had affinities with uncleanness in that both were "taboo"; further (on 10[8-11]) that the opposite of the holy was the common, and of unclean the clean. The difference between holy and unclean would seem to be that the holy was what it was because it had been brought into contact with the holiness of God, the fount and origin of all holiness; while the unclean was what it was by reason of an inherent quality, usually of a demonic character. While the ideas contained in the following chapters are intensely interesting in themselves, it must be frankly recognized that they are not in harmony with Christian ideas. Nevertheless the attempt to understand them should give us an intelligent sympathy with the human race, whereof we all are members, in its upward struggle toward the light, and enable us to realize from what a bondage we have been delivered by Christ (Mk. 7^{1-23}). In their present form the laws are late. But the ideas underlying them go back to primitive Semitic religion, and are therefore far earlier than Moses. The best treatment of the whole subject will be found in Robertson Smith's *The Religion of the Semites*, and in the article by Peake on "Uncleanness" in Hastings' *Dictionary of the Bible*, vol. iv. (See also art., *Legal and Historical Literature*, pp. 145–7.)

CHAPTER XI

Clean and Unclean Animals. Cf. Deut. 14^{1-21}. The origin of the distinction between clean and unclean was not hygienic, but religious. This statement is not invalidated by the fact that those peoples would tend to survive whose ritual was in accordance with hygienic principles.

1–8. Mammals. Many considerations might lead to an animal being pronounced unclean in the first instance. Foremost among these would be association with foreign cult (cf. 1 Cor. 8). (The reason why we do not eat horseflesh is not that it is really more revolting than other flesh, but that the heathen Saxons regarded it as sacred to Odin, and it was therefore forbidden to them when they became Christians, to avoid any danger of compromise with the old ideas). This principle will account for several items in the chapter; e.g., swine (v. 7; cf. Isa. 65^{4} 66^{17}, and note that excavations at Gezer prove that swine were sacrificed by the pre-Semitic inhabitants of the place); the mouse (v. 29; cf. Isa. 66^{17}); the camel (Robertson Smith, *op. cit.*, p. 283); the hare (v. 6; *ibid.*, p. 382). The law that an animal to be eaten must be cloven-footed and chew the cud is an attempt to generalize from immemorial custom in particular instances. This is borne out by the fact that the rockbadger (v. 5, mg.) and hare are not really ruminants, though the movement of their jaws makes them appear so.

9–12. Fish. The law seems formulated to exclude eels, probably on account of their resemblance to serpents, which were credited with demonic powers (cf. Gen. $3^{1f.}$).

13–19. Birds. These fall into two main classes: (1) carrion birds and birds of prey, whose food consisted of blood (cf. 7^{26}); (2) birds inhabiting wastes, and therefore associated with demons (cf. Psa. 102^{6} Isa. 34^{11-15}).

20–23. Winged Insects. Here, perhaps, physical revulsion may be a deciding factor. Four species of locusts are allowed (cf. Mt. 3^{4}, although it is more likely that the "locusts" eaten by John the Baptist were the pods of the carob bean, the "husks" eaten by the prodigal son—Lk. 15^{16}, mg.).

24–47. Carnivora, Reptiles, etc.; Uncleanness by Contact With Carcasses; Conclusion. The section is miscellaneous, and difficult to systematize. Further prohibitions relate to carnivora (v. 27; see above on birds), and to creeping things, whether rodents, reptiles or vermin.

Contact with the carcass of an unclean animal produces uncleanness in a mild form (vv. 24, 27, 31). The same applies to a clean animal that dies of itself (v. 39). If the carcass is carried, the measure of uncleanness is greater, and necessitates washing (vv. 25, 28, 40). A clean animal may not be eaten unless killed for the purpose, though we should judge that the very mild penalty was not intended to act as an absolute deterrent. If a carcass comes into contact with any domestic utensil, the utensil must be washed, or, if of earthenware, broken (vv. 33, 35; cf. 6^{28}). If it falls into a fountain or cistern, uncleanness does not result except to the vessel in which it is removed. Presumably the solution of uncleanness is so diluted as to be negligible; or is it a prudential consideration? Moisture will render seed permeable to uncleanness; but if the seed be dry, it is immune (v. 38).

In these regulations we see the beginnings of that casuistry for which Judaism later became a byword (Mk. 7^{1-23}, notes).

CHAPTER XII

Uncleanness After Childbirth. After the birth of a boy the mother is unclean for forty days in all; for a girl the period is twice as long. Note the almost sacred number forty, and its multiple. A boy is to be circumcised on the eighth day. At the close of the total period of uncleanness the mother is required to present a burnt-offering and a sin-offering. Provision was made to bring the requirements of the law within the means of the poor. The mother of Jesus was glad to avail herself of this concession (cf. Lk. 2^{21-39}, the best biblical commentary on this chapter).

To us it seems strange that the sacred function of motherhood should require to be expiated by a sin-offering. Nor is there any obvious reason why the period of uncleanness should be twice as long for a girl as for a boy. Once more the original motives underlying the laws were not hygienic, but religious. Primitive peoples universally associate the processes of generation and birth with the mysterious and uncanny, and a woman in childbirth is commonly supposed to be surrounded by demonic influences. These influences are often thought to be more potent when a girl is born than when the child is a boy; hence the longer period of uncleanness. It is not necessary to suppose that the Jews in later times had any conscious remembrance of the original motives underlying the laws of this chapter, but they still observed the forms. And it helps us to appreciate the completeness with which our Lord identified himself with men (Heb. 2^{17}) when we reflect that he fulfilled in his own experience ideas so primitive as these (Lk. 2^{21-24}).

CHAPTER XIII

Leprosy: Its Diagnosis. (On the whole subject see the articles on "Leprosy" in Hastings' *Dictionary of the Bible* and the *Encyclopædia Biblica*, by Macalister and Creighton respectively.)

That the Hebrew word translated *leprosy* has a wide range of meaning is evident from the fact that a garment (13^{47-59}) or a house (14^{33-53}) may be "leprous." They are leprous not because they are worn, or inhabited, by leprous persons; they are leprous in themselves. Not only is the application of the word "leprosy" in this chapter very wide, but it has even been doubted whether true leprosy (*elephantiasis graecorum*) is contemplated at all. The symptoms described are nowhere those which are most obvious to the beholder in a case of true leprosy, and it is generally agreed that the disease described in vv. 29–37 is nothing more serious than ringworm. At the same time there is little doubt that true leprosy was known in Palestine in O.T. times, and if known it would hardly be excluded from the catalogue. It further seems clear from the at first sight rather puzzling enactment of vv. 12f. that the leprosy that makes a man unclean is of a more or less malignant character. These verses exempt from uncleanness the man who is suffering from what appears to be *psoriasis*, a non-contagious and curable skin disease. We shall probably be right if we think of "leprosy" in the Bible as covering a variety of skin diseases, including true leprosy. The reason why the characteristics of the latter are not more obvious to the reader is that the symptoms described are those of the disease in its earlier stages, before its more repulsive manifestations have had time to develop. It should be added that the identifications of most of the "leprosies" described are obscure, even to medical experts.

1–44. In Human Beings. The general principle is that the disease must be more than skin deep, and accompanied by discoloration of the hair. In doubtful cases two periods of quarantine may be necessary, of seven days each.

45, 46. Conduct of a Leper. He is to be habited as a mourner (cf. 10^6 21^{10} Ezek. 24^{17} Mic. 3^7); to dwell apart from his fellows (cf. 2 Kings 7^3 15^5 Lk. 17^{12}); and to advertise his whereabouts to all who pass by crying, *Unclean, unclean.* Like the pariah in India, he was untouchable. Contrast with the attitude of the Law that of Jesus, who, being besought to speak the word of healing, did not forbear to touch the suppliant (Mk. $1^{40f.}$).

47–59. "Leprosy" in Garments. The description points to some kind of mildew or to moth. For the now almost obsolete use of the word *fretting* (v. 51) cf. the Prayer Book version of Psa. 39^{11}, "like as it were a moth fretting a garment." The process of inspection, with its two periods of quarantine, is similar to that for human beings. Note the effort to avoid destroying the garment (especially v. 56). A suspected garment would usually be an old one, but clothes were precious (cf. Ex. $22^{20f.}$ and notes on Amos 2^{6-8}).

CHAPTER XIV

Leprosy: Its Purification. The whole ceremony consists of two well-defined parts, described in vv. 2–8a and 8b–20 (or 21–32) respectively. That the first rite is complete in itself seems clear from the closing words *and he shall be clean*, and it is probable that in early times it alone sufficed. The setting free of the bird is a survival of the extremely ancient idea of the transference of uncleanness to animals. This part of the ritual should be compared with the likewise ancient ceremony of the goat for Azazel on the Day of Atonement (16^{20-22}). Other details, the running water, and the cedar wood, scarlet, and hyssop (vv. 4–6) figure in the ceremony of the red heifer (Num. 19), which also embodies antique ritual. The second series of rites (8b–20 or 21–32) has all the appearance of being a later approximation to the normal types of sacrifice.

1–8a. Initial Rite. A candidate for purification must apply to the priest; and if the priest is satisfied that he is healed, he is to take two clean birds, together with cedar wood, scarlet cloth, and hyssop. Cedar and hyssop are contrasted in 1 Kings 4^33 as extremes of greatness and smallness. Hyssop was used for sprinkling (Ex. 12^22), and was symbolical of cleansing (Psa. 51^7). Both it and the cedar were aromatic. They were tied together by means of the scarlet cloth. One of the birds was to be killed and its blood drained into an earthen vessel containing water from a running stream. The priest sprinkled the candidate for purification with the blood and water, and after immersing the living bird set it free. The cleansed man then washed his clothes and his person, and shaved his hair. (Hair was frequently regarded as a source of pollution, perhaps with good reason! Cf. Robertson Smith, *Religion of the Semites*, 2nd edit., p. 333, note 5.)

8b–20. Additional Rites on the Eighth Day. These included the following offerings: (1) a guilt-offering (vv. 12–18), consisting of a he-lamb and oil (one *log* = a pint); (2) a sin-offering, a ewe-lamb (v. 19); (3) a burnt-offering and meal-offering, consisting of a he-lamb and three-tenths of an ephah of flour (about twenty pints) respectively (see p. 79). For the procedure for the several offerings see the relevant sections of chs. 1–7. Note, however, that the guilt-offering here differs in several respects from the normal described in 5^14–6^7. It is not, like an ordinary guilt-offering, a payment for a due withheld from God. The victim is a he-lamb, not the usual ram. Contrary to the usual practice, the whole is "waved" (v. 12; see notes on 7^28-34). Finally, the anointing of the patient's extremities with blood (v. 14) is a feature peculiar to this and the priestly consecration ceremonies (8^23f.).

21–32. Concession to Poverty. Birds are allowed for the sin-offering and burnt-offering, and one third only of the quantity of flour. The materials and procedure for the guilt-offering in no wise differ from the preceding. Evidently, it was the most important rite in the series.

33–53. "Leprosy" in Houses. The description points to some kind of fungoid growth. It was evidently not contagious in the modern sense, since, if the house were emptied before the official sentence of uncleanness was pronounced by the priest, the furniture was not affected. If the trouble were persistent, the house was condemned. The purification rite for a house restored to cleanness is similar to that in vv. 4–7.

54–57. Summary Conclusion. The verses look back to the regulations of chs. 13, 14.

CHAPTER XV

Issues. The affections described in vv. 2–15 and 25–30 are abnormal. The first of these may be gonorrhoea, but that is not certain. It is not known whether the Hebrews were acquainted with venereal disease, though a few passages like Prov. 5^11-22 7^23-26 may have such a reference. The sin-offering required is of the smallest (vv. 14, 15), as in vv. 25–30, where there is no suggestion of unchastity (cf. Mk. 5^25-33). Even if the first paragraph does refer to venereal disease, therefore, it would seem that the chapter does not intend to stigmatize any of the conditions described as due to "sin" in our sense of the word. The original idea underlying the laws is similar to that indicated in the notes on ch. 12, namely, that sexual functions are mysterious, and must therefore be surrounded by powerful taboos. If the chapter be read with this consideration in mind, its contents will be sufficiently clear.

There is every reason to believe that those who gave to the laws their present form were aware of their hygienic value. But it should be recognized that the motives underlying them were in the first instance religious, not hygienic. When we first grasp this principle we may be surprised to find that the hygienic value of the laws is so extraordinarily high. The conclusion forced upon us by the study of this and the foregoing chapters is that, on the whole, true religion is sound hygiene, and that in the days before man began to concern himself with hygiene for its own sake, God in his wisdom safeguarded health by teaching men right religion. "The fear of the Lord is the beginning of knowledge."

CHAPTER XVI

The Day of Atonement. Among the Jews of N.T. times this was simply called "the Day" (cf. Acts 27^9), and was the most important event in the calendar. It is therefore surprising to find that there is no reference to it in the historical books of the O.T. It is briefly mentioned in 23^27-32 25^9 Ex. 30^10 and Num. 29^7-10, but nowhere in the O.T. do we read of any actual occasion when it was observed. Since the date was the tenth of the seventh month (our September-October—see p. 77) we should expect some mention of it between Neh. 7^73b and 9^1, which gives an account of solemn ceremonies in the seventh month, perhaps of the year 397 B.C. But there is none. The conclusion seems inevitable, that the Day of Atonement was the latest development in the O.T. economy of sacrifice. This does not mean that it was wholly an innovation. There is not the least doubt that that part of the ceremonies which describes the transference of the sins of the community to the "goat for Azazel" is a survival of extremely ancient practice (cf. intro. to ch. 14). The elaborate rites of "the Day," therefore, embodying as they do the slow development of centuries, are the best that the old dispensation could afford to take away sins. If the blood of bullocks and he-goats could have sufficed, there would here have been ample sufficiency. Contrast the efficacy of the sacrifice offered by Christ (Heb. 9, notes).

1–10. Preparations. Aaron is not to enter the Holy of Holies whenever he will, but once a year only (vv. 2, 34; cf. Heb. 9[7]). For the *veil* see on Ex. 26[31f.], and for the *mercy seat*, Ex. 25[17f]. The clothes worn by the high priest are not the regal vestments of ch. 8 but the unpretentious linen garments described in Ex. 28[37-42]. For himself he is to take a young bullock for a sin-offering (cf. 4[1-21]), and a ram for a burnt-offering; for the people two he-goats for a sin-offering, and a ram for a burnt-offering. On the goats lots are to be cast, one *for Jehovah*, and the other *for Azazel*. The translation *dismissal* in the R.V. mg. here (cf. *removal* in A.S.V. mg.) is inadmissible, being based on a false etymology. What the word meant is unknown, but it should be retained as the proper name of a wilderness demon. There is no doubt that the earliest imagination pictured Azazel as real (cf. 17[7]). In the apocryphal book of Enoch (second century B.C.) imagination runs riot about him, and he is said to have been the leader of the fallen angels who contracted unions with the daughters of men (Gen. 6[1-4]), and to him all sin is ascribed. (See art., *Intertestamental Literature*, p. 197b.)

11–14. Slaughter of the Priests' Sin-Offering; The High Priest Enters the Veil. Before the blood can safely be brought within the veil, the mercy seat of the divine presence must be obscured by a cloud of incense. The blood of the bullock is then sprinkled on the mercy seat. This was the only occasion in the year when this was done. The blood of an ordinary sin-offering for the high priest was brought no further than to the curtain that separated the Holy Place from the Holy of Holies (4[6]).

15–17. Slaughter of the People's Sin-Offering. The application of the blood is as in vv. 11–14. Being in the center of a sinful community, the sanctuary contracts defilement, and must therefore be "unsinned."

18, 19. Cleansing of the Altar of Burnt Offering. This was done with the blood of both sin-offerings.

20–22. The Scape-Goat. The sins of the people are now transferred to the goat for Azazel, which is then led into the wilderness. Whether the priestly editors who gave final form to the ceremonies thought of the act as anything more than symbolical it is hard to say. We need not credit them with the riotous imagination of the Book of Enoch. But no doubt among the common people the old ideas persisted.

23–28. Completion of the Offerings. This is in accordance with the usual regulations for sin-offerings and guilt-offerings, special care being taken to insulate both the "holiness" of the high priest, and the "uncleanness" of those who have been charged with the more menial services of the day.

29–34. Concluding Notices. The date of the ceremony is to be the tenth of the seventh month of the *ecclesiastical* year (September-October). (Note that this was the *first* month of the *civil* year; see art., *Time, Money, etc.*, p. 77). The day is to be a fast day, and a day of complete cessation from work, alike for the Jewish born and for the resident alien. For the phrase *afflict your souls*, i.e., to fast, see Psa. 35[13] Isa. 58[3]. It will be remembered (see on ch. 4) that sins committed in ignorance were expiated by the regular sin-offerings. There might, however, be sins of ignorance committed during the year and still undiscovered by the offender. These were supposed to be covered by the ceremonies of the Day of Atonement.

CHAPTERS 17 TO 26: THE LAW OF HOLINESS

These chapters have for the past fifty years been generally recognized as coming from another, and earlier, source than the main body of the Priestly Code. They are known as the Law of Holiness, and denoted by the symbol H. They embody a collection of miscellaneous laws, beginning, as in the Book of the Covenant (Ex. 20[22]–23[33]) and the Code of Deuteronomy (Deut. 12–26, 28), with laws on sacrifice (ch. 17), and concluding with an exhortation (ch. 26). See further on the Law of Holiness the articles, *The Pentateuch*, p. 139, and *The Legal and Historical Literature*, p. 146, and cf. the introduction to Ezra-Nehemiah and to Ezekiel.

Many of the laws are very ancient, and not all of them are from the same source. Thus many of the precepts concerning prohibited degrees in ch. 18 are repeated in slightly different form in ch. 20. The laws appear to have been gathered together just prior to the Exile or during the early exilic period. (Ch. 26 appears to have the Exile in mind, but the period between 597 and 586 B.C. would offer a possible date for this chapter.)

The Deuteronomic law of the one sanctuary is also the law of H (at least in the present form of 17^{1-9}), and there are affinities with Ezekiel which point to borrowing one way or the other. Some suppose that H depends on Ezekiel, but the more general opinion is that Ezekiel was acquainted with H.

The original body of laws constituting H was worked over by a writer of the Priestly School; e.g., most of the introductions to chapters are from P. Although in many respects the viewpoints of H and P are the same, differences are still discernible, e.g.;

(1) In H the festivals still have a close relationship to agriculture (cf. ch. 23). In P this relationship is lost sight of, and the great days of the calendar are rather occasions fixed arbitrarily for religious observance.

(2) H makes no distinction, as do Ezekiel and P, between priests and Levites. (Levites are only mentioned in 25^{32-34}, which is universally regarded as later than the main body of H; cf. intro., section on "Title and Contents.")

(3) In H the high priest is still first among equals (21^{10}). In P he belongs to a separate order: Aaron is in a class by himself, and the other priests are his sons. (The expression "sons of Aaron" used of the priests in the introductions to chapters in H is from the later priestly redactor.)

The dominant note in H is that of the holiness of Jehovah. Israel is to be holy because Jehovah is holy (19^{2}). In ch. 19 we have ancient Israelitish ethics at its best, and the whole is a noble attempt to blend ceremonial with moral holiness. The concluding exhortation (ch. 26) is as fine as anything of its kind in the O.T.

CHAPTER XVII

Laws of Sacrifice. (Cf. Deut. 12)

1–9. Slaughter of Domestic Animals. Such slaughter is treated as sacrificial, and for this reason it must be performed at the central sanctuary. The passage refers primarily to peace-offerings; see therefore on ch. 3. In the earliest Law (Ex. 20^{24}, from the Book of the Covenant; see p. 146) sacrifice was permitted in any place where Jehovah revealed himself. This would regularize such sacrifices as those of Gideon (Judg. 6^{11-24}) and Manoah (Judg. 13). But the terms of the law were wide, and experience showed that they were open to serious abuses (Hos. $4^{13,\ 14}$). To those who were jealous for the purity of religion many sacrifices seemed nothing better than a propitiation of demons (v. 7, R.V. mg., *satyrs;* cf. Isa. 13^{21}), as, indeed, they half consciously may have been. Hence the law that all sacrifice must be at an officially recognized sanctuary. This was perhaps the original form of the law in this paragraph (the words *camp* and *tent of meeting* look like an expansion of P). Deuteronomy (seventh century) went further, and required that all sacrifice should be at the central sanctuary, i.e., Jerusalem (Deut. 12), and with this the present passage in its expanded form agrees (see notes on 2 Kings 22, 23).

From this point of view an irregular sacrifice is tantamount to murder (v. 4), a taking away of life (cf. v. 11) which belongs only to God. For the phrase *he shall be cut off* (vv. 4, 9) see on 7^{20}. The law is binding alike upon native Israelites and resident aliens (vv. 8–16), who, dwelling in Jehovah's land, would naturally, according to the ideas of those times, conform to the worship of Jehovah (cf. Ruth 1^{16}).

10–12. Prohibition of Blood. Cf. 3^{17} 7^{26}. The soul (so v. 11, mg.) of any creature was thought of as quasi-physical, and as identical with the blood (cf. v. 14, Gen. 9^{4}). Insofar as sacrifice made expiation, therefore, it was by virtue of the blood-soul that was in it.

13–16. Application of the Blood-Prohibition to Non-Sacrificial Animals. These might be eaten, provided they were "clean," but the blood prohibition applies also to them. Their blood must be poured out (cf. Deut. 12^{16}), and covered with dust (cf. Ezek. 24^{7}). The reason for the prohibition in v. 15 is that the blood has not been drained off. In the Book of the Covenant such flesh must be given to the dogs (Ex. 22^{31}). In Deut. 14^{21} it may be given to the resident alien, or sold to a foreigner. The present passage seems almost to invite the poorer Israelite to eat it, provided he is prepared to contract a slight measure of uncleanness (cf. 11^{40}). Evidently, the blood-taboo was beginning to lose something of its terror.

CHAPTER XVIII

Forbidden Degrees of Marriage (Cf. 20^{11-21})

What is forbidden in this chapter is not occasional incestuous relations, which are, of course, included in the general commandment against adultery and fornification, but marriage. The phrase "to uncover the nakedness of" means to marry.

1–5. Introduction. A warning not to conform to heathen practices, whether of Egypt or of the pre-Israelitish inhabitants of Canaan. Note the thrice repeated *I am Jehovah* (R.V. *the Lord*). The phrase is characteristic of the Law of Holiness, in which it occurs some fifty times.

6–19. Table of Prohibited Degrees. The

general principle governing the prohibitions is that of blood relationship. The degrees within which marriage is allowed are much the same as in Christendom to-day. It may, however, be noted that nothing appears to forbid the marriage of uncle and niece. Relationship in law is regarded as the same as actual blood relationship. This is because man and wife are "one flesh" (Gen. 2[24]). Any approach to a father's wife is therefore an atrocious insult to the father himself (vv. 7, 8; cf. Gen. 9[20-27]). In several particulars the laws show an advance upon early Hebrew practice. Thus v. 8 implicitly condemns the ancient Oriental custom whereby a king made good his succession by succeeding to his father's harem (cf. 2 Sam. 16[21, 22] 1 Kings 2[22]). Marriage with a half-sister, once legitimate (Gen. 20[12] 2 Sam. 13[13]), is forbidden by vv. 9, 11. The law of v. 16, if strictly enforced, would forbid "levirate" marriage (Deut. 25[5-10]). It does not, however, appear to have supplanted ancient custom (see Gen. 38, Ruth 1[11]; and cf. Mt. 22 [23-28]). It should be noted that v. 18 does not forbid marriage with a deceased wife's sister, but only with a second sister during the lifetime of the first. This is an advance on the custom that permitted such marriages as those of Jacob with both Leah and Rachel. Polygamy is recognized, but experience showed that it was productive of much domestic unhappiness (cf. 1 Sam. 1[6], where the word for "rival" is from the same root as that in v. 18 here), and it gradually died out. The antagonism would be all the more marked if the rival wives were sisters (cf. Gen. 30[15]).

19–23. Other Sexual Enormities. For these verses see marginal references. For the Molech worship condemned in v. 21 see on 20[1-5], where the subject is treated more fully. It is perhaps included here in accordance with the prophetic habit of branding heathenish practices as adultery, i.e., unfaithfulness to Jehovah, the divine Husband of the nation (cf. notes on Ezek. 23, 24, Hos. 1–3).

24–30. Concluding Exhortation. Note the past tenses in vv. 27, 28, 30 (in the Hebrew also in vv. 25, 26). The standpoint is unconsciously that of the period following the conquest, a minor confirmation of the critical theory of the origin of the Pentateuch.

CHAPTER XIX

This chapter contains a variety of precepts, and no arrangement by paragraphs is very satisfactory. Practically every commandment in the Decalogue is touched upon, and the whole is important as showing how the commandments were interpreted when the Law of Holiness was formulated. The conception of holiness is for the most part distinctly ethical, and shows unmistakable influence of the moral enthusiasm of the prophets.

1, 2. Israel to Be Holy Because Jehovah Is Holy. This motive should be compared with that of Deuteronomy, which requires Israel to *love* Jehovah because he first loved his people by delivering them from the bondage of Egypt (cf. especially Deut. 6).

3, 4. A Summary of the First, Second, Fourth, and Fifth Commandments. The order is reverse from that in Ex. 20. Idols are *things of nought* (mg.), "inanities," a contemptuous epithet first applied to them, so far as we know, by Isaiah (Isa. 2[8] in Hebrew). For *molten gods*, at one time distinguished from carved or graven images, cf. Ex. 34[17]. In later times the term "graven" included both molten (i.e., metal) and carved (i.e., wooden) images (Isa. 40[19, 20]).

5–8. Consumption of Peace-Offerings. Cf. 7[15-18] 22[30].

9–18. Exhortations to Humanity and Justice. For vv. 9, 10, cf. 23[22] Deut. 24[19-22]. The widespread custom of leaving the corners of a field unreaped goes back to remote antiquity. The original motive appears to have been to propitiate the corn spirits, who would otherwise forsake the field. For this a humanitarian motive has been substituted. The injunction not to show favoritism to the poor (v. 15) has only one parallel in the O.T., in Ex. 23[3], and there the reading is questionable. By v. 16b is meant giving false witness against a man on trial for his life, or, worse still, bringing a capital charge against him falsely. V. 17 shows a fine appreciation of the inwardness of the sixth commandment (cf. Mt. 5[21, 22] 1 John 3[15]); the man who sees his neighbor doing wrong, and fails to rebuke him, makes the wrong his own. The words "Thou shalt love thy neighbor, and hate thine enemy" (Mt. 5[43]) are a later casuistical interpretation of the fine precept in v. 18. The second half is not a quotation from the O.T., but is arrived at by placing undue emphasis on "neighbor" instead of on "love." Jesus showed the true spirit of the Law by widening the content of the word "neighbor" (Lk. 10[29-37]).

19–25. Hybrids Forbidden, Trees to Be "Circumcised." For the law against hybrids cf. Deut. 22[9]. There is evidence that cloth mixtures had associations with magic, which would explain the prohibition of v. 19b. Perhaps the command in v. 19a is a later argument from analogy (the Deuteronomic parallel is different); at any rate, mules were common in Palestine (2 Sam. 13[29] 1 Kings 10[25], etc.). V. 20 comes strangely here. The woman in the case is a slave concubine. If she were put to death, it would be her master's loss; for a similar motive cf. Ex. 21[20]. Vv. 23–25 require that for three years the fruit of newly planted trees is to be treated as "uncircumcised," i.e., unclean, and therefore not to be eaten. In the fourth year it is to be wholly given over as a sacred due. Thereafter it becomes the property of the owner. Here again the original motive for not eating the fruit of the early years was probably to propitiate the fertility spirits (cf. notes on v. 9).

26–37. Miscellaneous Precepts. Most of these have parallels elsewhere, and the marginal references should be consulted. The practices condemned in vv. 27, 28, are very ancient, and belong to the vague border line between religion and magic. Peoples of the lower culture almost universally think of the spirits of the dead as frequenting their former haunts. They are besides endowed with supernatural powers, and as spirits are capricious these powers may be used to hurt the living. The mutlilations, cuttings of the hair and beard, and tattoo marks referred to were attempts on the part of the living to make themselves unrecognizable by the dead. They are accordingly condemned as heathenish and magical. V. 29 is probably directed against sacred prostitution (2 Kings 23[7]; cf. on Hos. 4[14]). Excavations at Gezer show that the command in vv. 35, 36, was by no means unnecessary. Most weights found there are either below or over standard. It must have been common to keep two sets of weights, one for buying, and the other for selling.

CHAPTER XX

1–9. Molech Worship, Etc. Cf. 18[21]. The distinctive feature of the Molech cult was the passing of children, usually firstborn, through fire (18[21] 2 Kings 23[10] Jer. 32[35]; cf. Deut. 18[10] 2 Kings 16[3] 21[6] Mic. 6[7], etc.). The rite appears to have become frequent from the eighth century B.C. onward, when the precarious political situation of the Hebrews inclined them to pessimism. The center of the cult was the valley of Hinnom (Hebrew, *Ge-Hinnôm*), south of Jerusalem, which thereby obtained such an evil reputation that Gehenna, the place of torment, was called after it. The identification of *Molech* is not certain. The original pronunciation of the name was certainly *Melek*, the Hebrew word for "king." One passage (1 Kings 11[5-7]) seems to identify him with Milcom, the god of the Ammonites. But probably in the popular imagination Melek was none other than Jehovah himself (cf. Jer. 7[31] Mic. 6[7]). The penalty for Molech worship was death by stoning; i.e., the act of killing and responsibility for it were to be shared by the whole community. If the people refused to accept their responsibility, Jehovah himself would see that justice was done against the offender (vv. 5, 6; see on 7[20]). Cursing of parents is also a capital crime (v. 9), and those who carry out the sentence are to be beyond the operation of the law of blood revenge. That is the meaning of the phrase *his blood shall be upon him.*

10–21. Penalties for Sexual Enormities. Every verse in this paragraph finds a parallel in 18[6-23], where, however, the emphasis is slightly different. In ch. 18 certain marriage unions are forbidden; here penalties are assigned for what may be only occasional incestuous relations. Where the manner of death is not prescribed we may suppose it to be by stoning (cf. Jn. 8[5]).

22–26. Concluding Exhortation. Israel is to observe distinctions between clean and unclean because Jehovah, the uniquely holy, has separated her from other peoples. There was no intention on the part of those who formulated the laws of Leviticus to emphasize ritual to the exclusion of morality. They intended ritual purity to be the outward and visible sign of an inward moral holiness. Wherever this is done there is a risk of formality and externalism; but the perversions of the scribes and Pharisees were no part of the intention of the original authors.

27. Cf. 19[31]. The verse seems out of place, and should probably follow v. 6.

CHAPTERS 21 AND 22: REGULATIONS CONCERNING PRIESTS AND THEIR DUTIES

These two chapters are mainly concerned with the priests, and especially with the conditions under which they may minister. The second half of ch. 22 prescribes the conditions of soundness required of any animal proposed for sacrifice.

CHAPTER XXI

1–9. Regulations for Ordinary Priests. No priest may officiate while in a state of ceremonial impurity. And since to have contact with a corpse is to contract impurity (Num. 19[11], etc.), the occasions on which a priest may mourn must be reduced to a minimum. He may mourn for his immediate relatives, including an unmarried sister. But for a married sister he may not mourn (v. 4; this verse in R.V. and A.S.V. follows the accepted Massoretic text; read instead, "He shall not contract uncleanness for a sister married to a husband, to profane himself"); that must be done by her husband. Mourning customs having magical associations (v. 5; cf. $19^{27, 28}$) are naturally forbidden to a priest. He must not marry a harlot, nor a woman sexually dishonored, nor one who has been divorced. And if his daughter becomes a harlot, she is to be burned. In a word, a priest must do all in his power to preserve the holiness vested in him. For the original significance of the phrase *the bread of their God* (vv. 6, 8) see the explanation of 1^{9}.

10–15. Regulations for the High Priest. For the conception of the high priest's office indicated by v. 10 see introduction to chs. 17–26. Uncleanness by mourning is forbidden him altogether. For the outward signs of mourning in v. 10b cf. 10^{6} 13^{45} Ezek. 24^{17}, and for their original heathenish significance see on 19^{26-37}. The high priest must not only live within the sacred inclosure (cf. 10^{7}); he must never go outside it. To do so would be to bring the holiness of God into contact with all manner of defilement. He is not even allowed to marry a widow, but must confine his choice of wife to a virgin *of his own people*, i.e., probably, but not certainly, of one of the priestly families.

16–24. Bodily Defects That Disqualify a Priest. A priest who is physically disqualified may not conduct a sacrifice, but by virtue of his birth he is allowed an equal share with his brethren of all the sacred dues. For the distinction between the *holy* and the *most holy* see on 2^{1-3}. The sanity of the Levitical arrangements as a whole is remarkable. The Hebrews saw no virtue in extreme asceticism and mutilation, and not even the high priest was required to be celibate.

CHAPTER XXII

1–9. Conditions on Which Priests May Eat the Sacred Dues. The physical disabilities of the preceding paragraph are permanent, but do not disqualify from participation in the dues; the conditions named in the present paragraph are temporary only, but disqualify so long as they last. The reading *that they separate themselves* (v. 2) is perplexing, since there is no doubt that the priests were permitted to eat the flesh of sacrifices. It is true that in Zech. 7^{3} the word translated "separate" must be understood of fasting. But here the sense is fundamentally weakened, and what is intended must be that the priests are to exercise caution in eating the sacred dues. The priest who eats them while ceremonially unclean is to be *cut off* (see on 7^{20}). The uncleannesses specified have been fully treated in the notes on chs. 11, 13, and 15. In v. 4b the reading of the R.V. text should be followed, not of the mg.; any *thing* will of course include any *person*.

10–16. Members of a Priest's Family and the Sacred Dues. The *stranger* in vv. 10, 12f. is not the usual *gêr*, or resident alien (17^{8} and frequently in O.T.). The word is *zar*, and by it is to be understood a layman; see Num. 1^{51}, where that is quite evidently the meaning. Neither is the *sojourner* in v. 10 the more or less permanently resident *gêr*, but a temporary guest. A hired servant is not a member of the household; he receives wages, and provides for himself. A slave receives his sustenance from his master, though he would naturally eat only of the "holy," not of the "most holy" things (see on 2^{1-3}). By *such as are born in his house* are meant the children of a purchased slave. A priest's daughter married to a layman ceases to be a member of the household, but she may return if she is widowed, or divorced, and have no child. (A woman might be divorced at her husband's pleasure, and no suspicion of unchastity would attach to her; otherwise she would be treated as in 20^{10}.) A widow with children is still maintained by her husband's family, and the children of a *divorcée* are in the custody of the father. For v. 14 see the section on guilt-offerings (5^{14-16}), where, however, the law seems much more fully developed.

17–25. Sacrificial Victims Must be Sound. Only burnt-offerings and peace-offerings are mentioned. The ritual of sin-offerings and guilt-offerings was not fully developed until the Exile, i.e., after the Law of Holiness was written. For burnt-offerings, only males are allowed (v. 19; cf. 1^{3}); for peace-offerings male or female (3^{6}). With one exception, namely, for freewill-offerings, which were offerings of supererogation, victims must be without blemish. A list of blemishes is given in vv. 22f. Castration disqualifies even for freewill-offerings (v. 24 reading as R.V. mg.). This rule would, in a country where slaughter was generally sacrificial, tend to discourage the operation altogether (so R.V. text). The laws apply not only to animals bred by the Hebrews themselves, but also to those acquired from foreigners.

26–33. Supplementary Rules and Concluding Exhortation. For v. 27 cf. Ex. 22^{30}, where, however, the rule applies especially to firstborn animals. V. 28 may be compared with Deut. 22^{6}, and perhaps also with Ex. 23^{19b} and parallels. The thank-offering appears here to be thought of as a separate order of sacrifice. It is not mentioned in v. 21, but contrast $7^{11f.}$, where it is included in the category of peace-offerings. This is another indication that the laws of sacrifice were the result of a long process of growth.

CHAPTER XXIII

The Sacred Festivals

In this and the two following chapters the original nucleus of the Law of Holiness appears to have been much expanded by P; see intro. to chs. 17–26. The sources of the several sections are indicated by the appropriate symbols, H and P. In those that belong to H the old time relationship of the festivals to the land and to agriculture is still evident. In the priestly sections, written in Babylonia during the Exile, this has naturally become obscured.

1–3. The Sabbath. (P.) Cf. Ex. $20^{8\text{-}11}$. It would not be possible for the whole population to attend a *holy convocation* weekly at the Temple. The phrase refers to synagogue worship, which was a recognized institution before the close of the O.T. period (cf. Psa. 74^{8} R.V. text).

4–8. The Passover and Unleavened Cakes. (P.) Cf. Ex. 12; Deut. $16^{1\text{-}8}$. This is to be kept on the 14th of the first month of the ecclesiastical year, i.e., Nisan (March-April). For the phrase *between the two evenings* in the R.V. mg. of v. 5 cf. the English word "twilight" (twin-light), which is similar in origin and meaning. The Passover was probably a pre-Mosaic lambing festival. In the period following the Conquest it became associated with the agricultural festival of unleavened cakes, or firstfruits of the barley harvest, with which it nearly coincided in point of time; so v. 6 here.

9–14. Firstfruits. (Mainly H.) The ceremony here described has no parallel in the O.T., and is obviously very primitive. It directs that before anything of the harvest is consumed a sheaf of corn shall be presented at the (local) sanctuary. This was part of the ritual of the festival of unleavened cakes already mentioned in v. 6. The original motive for eating the first corn without leaven was probably that the harvesting operations allowed no time for elaborate cooking. In early times the beginning of harvest would vary in different parts of the country, but from v. 11b it would appear that it was customary to commence on the first day of a week. When later the date became fixed the Sabbath was that after the Passover. The meal-offering to accompany the burnt-offering was about seven quarts, and the drink-offering about three pints.

15–22. The Festival of "Weeks," or Pentecost. (Mainly H.) This marked the close of the wheat harvest, and fell fifty days after the festival of Firstfruits; hence the later name "Pentecost" (Greek fiftieth). Elaborate offerings are prescribed, for the manipulation of which see the appropriate sections in chs. 1–7. The meal-offering, intended for the priest (v. 20), and not for the altar, may now be baked with leaven, since the need for hurried preparation is past. V. 21 is from P. For v. 22 see on $19^{9\text{-}18}$.

23–25. The Festival of Trumpets. (P.) In early times the Hebrew year began in the autumn (see on Ex. 23^{16} 34^{22}), as the Jewish *civil* year still does (see art., *Time, Money*, etc., p. 77). The festival of Trumpets, which fell, according to the later reckoning, on the first of the seventh month of the *ecclesiastical* year, was reminiscent of the earlier calendar, and marked the beginning of the *civil* year. It was to be marked by complete cessation from secular work, together with synagogue attendance (see on vv. 1-3).

26–32. The Day of Atonement. (P.) See on ch. 16.

33–44. The Festival of "Booths." (Vv. 33–38, P; 39–43, H.) In Ex. 23^{16} 34^{22} this is called the festival of Ingathering. It was the final harvest home of fruit, vintage, and olives (v. 39, and cf. Deut. 16^{13}), and was happily observed at full moon in the seventh month, Tishri (September-October). It was originally, quite naturally, a time of rejoicing, as the verses assigned to H still testify, when the whole population lived for a week in the open, sheltered only by temporary *booths* of palm branches, etc. (The R.V. *feast of tabernacles* in v. 34 gives a wrong impression of these structures, the more so as the Hebrew word is the same as that rendered *booths* in vv. 42f.). Already in H the occasion was solemnized as a remembrance of the deliverance from Egypt. In the solemn legislation of P (vv. 33–36) the originally festive character of the week has been modified with a thoroughness that testifies to the impression made on the conscience of the Jews by the bitter experience of exile.

CHAPTER XXIV

1–4. The Sanctuary Lamp. (P.) Cf. Ex. 27^{20f}. For the seven-branched *candlestick*, or, better, "lampstand," see Ex. $25^{31\text{-}40}$. It was made of pure gold; hence the term *pure* lampstand. It was to be fed with the finest beaten olive oil, and tended by the high priest himself.

5–9. The Shewbread. (P.) For the *pure table*, overlaid with pure gold (cf. above), see Ex. $25^{23\text{-}30}$. The institution of the shewbread goes back to early times (cf. 1 Sam. $21^{1\text{-}6}$), and has its parallel, even to the number twelve of the loaves, in Babylonian ritual. Early imagination would think of the loaves as food for the gods (see 1[9]), but in the present passage they are a "memorial-offering" (see on 2[1-3]), and the number twelve is doubtless symbolical of the number of the tribes of Israel.

10–23. Blasphemy a Capital Crime: The "Lex Talionis." Of this paragraph vv. 15–22 exhibit the characteristics of H. Vv. 15, 16, ordain that blasphemy is to be treated as a capital crime. This law has been expanded by P in vv. 10–14, 23, who embodies it in a concrete precedent. A half-born Israelite, offspring of a forbidden marriage (Deut. 7[3]), has *blasphemed the Name.* He is taken outside the camp, as far as possible from the center of the divine holiness, and stoned (see on 20[1-9] for the significance of this). This is the only passage in the O.T. where *the Name* (i.e., of Jehovah) is synonymous with Jehovah himself. In post-biblical times the Jews had such an extreme reverence for the divine name that they ceased to utter it, and even its pronunciation was forgotten; cf. Mk. 14[61], where the high priest says to Jesus, "Art thou the Christ, the son of the *Blessed?*" One of the commonest substitutes was "the Name."

In vv. 17–22 is a statement of the "*Lex talionis,*" or Law of Retaliation, the principle of "an eye for an eye," etc. (cf. Ex. 21[23-25]). This rough-and-ready principle of justice is from the Christian standpoint rightly condemned (Mt. 5[38]). Jesus taught that men were to forgive until seventy times and seven (Mt. 18[22], notes), a measure of forgiveness exactly proportioned to Lamech's measure of vengeance (Gen. 4[24]). Rightly understood, then, even the *lex talionis* once acted as a check upon primitive savagery, and helped to conserve some kind of law and order in the "times of ignorance." On the whole, it helped to make life and property safe until the time when men could appreciate a higher law.

CHAPTER XXV

The Sabbath Year and the Year of Jubilee

1–7, 17–22. The Sabbath Year. (H.) Every seventh year the land is to lie fallow. Mention is made of a fallow year in Ex. 23[10f.], where the motive assigned is a humanitarian one. There is no reason to suppose that in early times this law was observed simultaneously throughout the whole land, though that appears to be the intention here, at least in vv. 20–22. The humanitarian motive is not primary here as it is in the Exodus passage. The reason is rather that *the land* may *keep a sabbath unto Jehovah,* an approximation to the idea underlying Gen. 2[2f.] (P), where the Sabbath is no longer an institution made for man, but is given a cosmic significance. It is difficult to resolve the apparent contradiction between vv. 5 and 6. Either v. 6 must be a later addition to mitigate the harshness of v. 5, or we are to take it to mean that while reaping was forbidden, the self-sown produce of the land might be gathered as occasion required. Any fear of scarcity is allayed in vv. 20–22, where promise is given of an enormous harvest in the sixth year.

The Year of Jubilee. (Vv. 8–16, 23–55). The groundwork of the section is from P, who has, however, taken up and welded into his own legislation portions of the Law of Holiness. These latter may be identified by their concern for the welfare of the poor (e.g., vv. 35–40a). That the Jubilee law embodies a high ideal needs no showing, but even the Jews are fain to admit that its provisions were never very thoroughly carried out.

8–16, 23. The Main Provisions. The English word "Jubilee" is derived from the Hebrew *jôbēl*, meaning "ram's horn" (i.e., "trumpet"). The year is so called because it was to be announced by trumpet blast on the Day of Atonement. The main provisions of the Jubilee are three, and are operative at the end of every fiftieth year: (1) An additional Sabbath year is to be kept, v. 11; (2) all slaves are to be liberated, v. 10; (3) all leases are to expire, vv. 10, 13. The reason for this last provision is that the freehold of the land belongs to Jehovah, and not to any man. No lease may therefore extend beyond the next Jubilee, and the purchase price of any holding must be calculated on this basis, since it is only so many years' crops that are sold, and not the land itself (vv. 15f.).

24–28. Reclamation of Land Sold on Lease. Land sold on lease may be reclaimed by the owner at any time, provided that either he or his kinsfolk have the means to compensate the lessee. Such a provision would make leasehold very insecure. But if it discouraged "big business," it made impossible the expropriation of the small holder and the accumulation of the land into a few large estates. It is assumed that nothing but need will induce a man to sell his possession, and then only so much of it as will bring him deliverance from financial straits.

29–34. Urban Property. The freehold of a house in a walled city may be transferred (vv. 29f.); but a house in an unwalled village is to be reckoned as part of the adjoining farm (v. 31). In the Levitical cities the right of repurchase is retained (v. 32), and the property returns to the freeholder at the next Jubilee

(v. 33, reading *if one of the Levites redeem not*, after the Vulgate; cf. mg.). The reason is not that the Levites are privileged, but that, having no individual landed estates, they must be allowed the right of repurchase on what property they have, namely, houses. This is not contradicted by v. 34, where by *suburbs* (mg. *pasture lands*) is meant commonlands, which no individual has the right to sell.

35–38. "Usury" Forbidden. (H.) By *usury* is meant "interest," no matter at how low a rate. Such situations as arise in modern business are not contemplated. The text is concerned with money lent to a fellow countryman in temporary need, not with loans for commercial purposes. Therefore no interest is to be charged (cf. Ex. 22[25] Deut. 23[19]). Deut. 23[20] permits the taking of interest from a foreigner, whereby Shylock may justify himself.

39–46. Only Foreigners to Be Enslaved. A comparison with the earlier legislation of Ex. 21[2-6] Deut. 15[12-18] is instructive. A man may still sell himself to a fellow Israelite. But instead of being put to the work of a slave he is to be treated as a hired servant. What he gains in status he loses by being kept until the next Jubilee, instead of being released in the seventh year, as in Exodus-Deuteronomy. Only Jehovah has full slave rights over Hebrews (v. 42). Therefore a Hebrew, if he requires slaves in the true sense, must obtain them of foreigners (vv. 44–46).

47–55. Repurchase of Hebrews Enslaved to Resident Aliens. If a Hebrew sells himself to a resident alien, his freedom may be repurchased at any time by any member of his family; or he may, if circumstances permit, repurchase it himself. The price of his freedom depends on the number of years to the next Jubilee, when he becomes free automatically.

CHAPTER XXVI

Hortatory Conclusion to the Law of Holiness

As an example of impassioned eloquence, rising sometimes to the level of poetry (v. 36) this chapter is unsurpassed by anything of its kind in the O.T. It should be compared with Ex. 23[20-33], the conclusion to the Book of the Covenant, and with Deut. 28, the conclusion to the Laws of Deuteronomy. The latter parallel is especially close, since both exhortations contrast the blessings of obedience with the curses of disobedience, and in both the curses are described at greater length than the blessings. Further, a study of the marginal references will reveal many similarities of thought and expression to Ezekiel. The concluding verses show that the possibility, if not the actuality of exile, was very real to the imagination of the writer. These facts make it probable that the chapter was written some time during the first half of the sixth century B.C.

1, 2. Idolatry Forbidden. For *idols* and *graven images* see on 19[4]. A *pillar* (mg. *obelisk*, Hebrew *massēbhâh*) was a standing stone. Every "high place" was furnished with one or more of these, and many have been uncovered by modern excavation.

3–13. Blessings of Obedience. These strike the modern reader as very materialistic. It must be remembered, however, that the conception of a blessed future life was foreign to the thought of the ancient Hebrews. Moreover, the religious unit was the nation, not the individual. With such limitations upon its exercise the goodness of God could hardly show itself in any other way than that described. The more spiritually minded would value material blessings not so much for their own sake, but as evidences of the divine pleasure. (See art., *Religion of Israel*, pp. 174–5.)

14–45. Curses of Disobedience. These, like the blessings, are materialistically conceived, and for the same reason. The horrors of siege and deportation are vividly pictured in vv. 27–39. The measure of punishment is to be seven times proportioned to the transgression (vv. 18, 21, 24, 28). This suggests that the chapter was written not later than the early years of the Exile. At the close of the Exile, when the lessons of that catastrophe had been learned, it was thought sufficient that Israel should have received double for all her sins (Isa. 40[2]). In vv. 40–45 the thought passes beyond the proximate calamities to a subsequent repentance, confession, and restoration. The order of the whole section is as it should be, and shows a fine appreciation of moral values.

26. Bread is the *staff*, i.e., support of life; cf. Psa. 105[16] Isa. 3[1] Ezek. 4[16]. The meaning is that ten families will have to subsist on the rations of one. **30.** *Sun-images*, better "sun-pillars," associated with the Phœnician sun-god Baal-Hammân; cf. 2 Chr. 14[5], Isa. 17[8] etc. **34.** Literally, "the land shall pay off her sabbaths." Evidently, the law of the Sabbath year was not kept, but accounts would be settled when the land perforce lay uncultivated because of the people's absence.

46. Final Subscription to the Law of Holiness. The words suggest that the Law of Holiness existed as a separate unit before being embodied in Leviticus. (See intro. to chs. 17–26.)

CHAPTER XXVII

The Commutation of Vows and Tithes

A Late Appendix. This chapter provides that votive-offerings and tithes may be commuted for a money payment. In post-exilic times the maintenance of the Temple was extremely costly, and the priests would be glad to receive "cash down" rather than promises which sometimes might not be due for payment until some time in the indefinite future. The businesslike character of the chapter betokens a late date, as does also the assumption of the Jubilee legislation (vv. 17-25).

1–8. Persons. In early times we read of the votive-offerings of Jephthah's daughter, who was actually sacrificed (Judg. 11[30-40]), and of Samuel, whose life was spent in the service of the sanctuary (1 Sam. 1[11-28]). To later reflection the former would be barbarous, the latter impossible, since no non-Levite could by any means enter the ranks of the priesthood. A money payment, therefore, offered a satisfactory settlement, and was determined according to the value of the labor of the person vowed. A shekel was the equivalent of about sixty-six cents, though its purchasing power would be several times greater.

9–13. Animals. A sacrificial animal once vowed becomes "holy," and therefore inalienable from the purpose for which it is assigned. An unclean animal must be sold and its price paid to the Temple treasury. If the offerer wishes to reclaim it, he must pay its value and one-fifth additional.

14, 15. Houses. The principle is the same as for unclean animals.

16–25. Land. The procedure here is complicated by the Jubilee year (ch. 25). The value of a field depends upon the amount of seed required for sowing it. A homer, approximately eleven bushels, would be sufficient for sowing about four acres. The price is calculated at a shekel per *sowing of a homer* per annum for fifty years. If the transaction falls between two Jubilees a reduction is made according to the number of years to the next Jubilee. This settles the matter if the man who makes the vow is only a leaseholder (vv. 22f.). A freeholder must pay an additional twenty per cent, otherwise the field will become ecclesiastical property at the next Jubilee (vv. 19f.).

26, 27. Firstlings. Firstlings of sacrificial animals are Jehovah's in any case (Ex. 13[2], etc.), and are therefore outside the scope of the commutation law. The rule for firstlings of unclean animals is as in vv. 11f.

28, 29. The "Ban." For the ancient Semitic institution of the ban, or *devoted thing*, see notes on Deut. 2[34] Josh. 7, 1 Sam. 15. The custom was extremely barbarous, and we read nothing of its being put into operation after the days of Samuel. The law in v. 28 here refers to objects privately banned. V. 29, if of anything more than antiquarian interest, must refer to those who have been condemned for capital crimes.

30–33. Tithes. For the law of tithes see Deut. 14[22-29] Num. 18[21-32]. A tithe on cattle is a large demand, and is mentioned only here and in 2 Chr. 31[6]. For *whatsoever passeth under the rod*, i.e., of the teller, cf. Psa. 23[4] Ezek. 20[37] Jer. 33[13]. If a man wishes to commute the tithe in kind for a money payment, he may do so as in other cases by adding one-fifth to the value. The addition would tend to discourage commutation.

NUMBERS

By Professor LINDSAY B. LONGACRE

Introduction

Name. The book of Numbers is but part of a larger whole, the Pentateuch (see pp. 134f.). The title, Numbers, is a translation of the Latin, *Numeri*, which was in turn a translation from the Greek, *Arithmoi*. These terms served as titles for the book in the Vulgate and the LXX respectively. The title is appropriate for the first few chapters, but inappropriate for the book as a whole. Far more suitable is the simple, "In the Wilderness" (1[1]), by which the book is popularly known to the Jews.

As a matter of fact, the book itself is almost a wilderness in the variety of its contents and the lack of any order in the arrangement of these contents. While this disturbs a Western reader, it must be remembered that the book is essentially an Eastern book in language, ideas, and atmosphere, and that the Eastern mind has moods and methods all its own.

Significance. To be properly appreciated the book must be read as it is and for what it is, namely, a miscellaneous collection of lists, laws, itineraries, and traditions, which later Israel had gathered up and preserved as part of its heritage of a past too distant to be distinct but too vital to be forgotten.

While some of these materials would be of interest for their own sake, a large part of them served mainly as a foundation on which to base the religious beliefs of a later time. It is this use that has preserved them. The book is not an ancient one, comparatively speaking, or one that comes from a time even approximating the date of the events it describes. As compared with many other O.T. writings it is a late book, and was designed to set forth and to confirm the religious ideas which the writers regarded as of paramount importance.

Date and Composition. The analysis of the book into its literary elements, and the assignment of those elements to their relative and approximate dates, is a process that has extended over many years; but it has been done so thoroughly and so convincingly that its literary character is clear beyond all reasonable doubt. The priestly writers living in the Exile and after prepared a document (P) which consisted almost exclusively of legal and ritualistic matter. For them, this document represented the last word in religious authority. They possessed other documents, however, older than their own (J and E), from which they made selections for insertion in P. It is because these selected materials were usually not rewritten but incorporated bodily that it is possible even at this late day to distinguish them from the P document in which they are now found. Although it is convenient to speak of P as though it were a single homogeneous work, it is really composite, representing the work of a school rather than of a single individual, and uniting within itself strata of different dates and backgrounds. In the following notes these will be indicated where it seems necessary. (For a more detailed discussion of the composition of the Pentateuch and its permanent significance see article on *The Pentateuch*, pp. 134f.).

Literature: Kennedy, *Numbers* (Century Bible); Gray, *Numbers* (International Critical Commentary); Kent, *Beginnings of Hebrew History* (Student's Old Testament); George Adam Smith, *Historical Geography of the Holy Land*; Hastings' *Dictionary of the Bible;* Cheyne and Black, *Encyclopedia Biblica.*

Chapters 1[1] to 10[10]: Before Mount Sinai

The book falls naturally into three parts: (1) 1[1]–10[10], Before Mount Sinai; (2) 10[11]–20[13], From Mount Sinai to Kadesh; (3) 20[14]–36[13], From Kadesh to the Plains of Moab. The first section, taken from P, gives in considerable detail an account of the arrangements immediately preceding the journeyings through the wilderness.

CHAPTER I

1–4. Census of the Men of War Ordered. V. 1 locates the events about to be narrated as in *the wilderness of Sinai*, and gives the time as, *the first day of the second month in the second year* after leaving Egypt. The definiteness of both statements gives an impression of great accuracy characteristic of the whole section. But the wilderness referred to was a large place, so that the expression leaves the exact location of the camp quite problematical. It may also be questioned whether a calendar was so carefully preserved that the writer in Babylon, five hundred years afterward, could give the exact day of these events; but cf. note on ch. 2. The census was designed to establish the fighting strength of the whole people; but the author does not tell of any special use that was made of this enumeration, and it can only be conjectured that it represents his thought of a glorious army appropriate to the importance of a triumphant nation.

5–19. Heads of the Tribes. There are many variations in the way the tribes are listed. The lists do not always contain the same names, nor do they give the same order of names. Levi, for instance, is sometimes included and sometimes omitted, so that the total number, twelve, is attained in very different ways. The differences are so striking that it almost seems that the number twelve represents an ideal into which the names of the tribes were fitted more or less arbitrarily. (A convenient tabular view of the various lists may be found in Hastings' *Dictionary of the Bible*, vol. iv., p. 811.)

20–46. The Census. Note the formula used for each tribe, repeated with mechanical regularity. The grand total of 603,550 is impressive.

47–54. The Levites. Although the census is completed, it is only now explained why the Levites were not counted. A Western writer would have placed this instruction before, rather than after, the census.

CHAPTER II

The Disposition of the General Encampment. The tribes are given their places with reference to the tabernacle, which holds the central place of honor and security. Four tribes are placed east of the tabernacle; four, south; four, west; and four, north; with the tribe of Levi next to the tabernacle itself (v. 17). The disposition of Levi, however, is not clear (cf. 10^{17-21}).

When it is remembered that the writers of these chapters were remote in both time and place from the events they record, and that the history of Palestine and its people during the intervening centuries makes the preparation and preservation of such detailed records so difficult as to be almost impossible, it will be recognized that the writers act, so to speak, "by faith, not by sight"; the pictures here painted of those ancient times are ideals, clear enough in the minds of the writers, but hardly to be interpreted as historical records in the modern sense of that term.

The numbers given in the census are an illustration of this principle. Modern vital statistics show that 600,000 men twenty years old or more imply a population of more than 2,000,000; whereas in the days of the monarchy the maximum population of the Northern and Southern Kingdoms did not exceed 1,000,000. A comparison of the numbers with each other gives the surprising result that there would have to be an average of fifty children to a family; and yet, on the basis of the number of first born, only one woman out of fourteen or fifteen would be a mother (cf. Gray, *Numbers*, pp. 10–15). How the numbers are to be accounted for cannot now be discovered. Presumably the writer had some basis for his statements, but what this basis was, and the principle according to which he built upon it, are subjects upon which there is no existing information. The fact that the Hebrew letters of *Bene Yisrael* (children of Israel) when used numerically give 603, may have something to do with it, yet this may be only a coincidence.

A similar difficulty attends the arrangement of the camp. The mountains and wadies of Sinai have no room for such an arrangement of such a multitude. All existing evidence goes to show that the country in which all these events are located is substantially the same now as it was then, and it is clear that whatever happened must have fitted the conditions of the country. But the testimony of those most familiar with the physical conditions in that part of the world makes it difficult to believe that such a multitude could have been accommodated. It is well, however, to remember that the real significance lies not in the numbers or the exact arrangement of the tribes, but in the idea which the author seeks to express in this concrete fashion—*the sanctifying presence of God in the midst of Israel.* Moreover, the Divine Presence must be guarded against sacrilegious approach; hence the "holy" priestly tribe of Levi is placed between the sanctuary and the other tribes; and the "most holy" portion, the sons of Aaron, are appointed to guard the entrance to the tent on the east.

CHAPTERS III, IV

The Levites, Their Number and Their Duties. For the priestly writers this subject was of great importance. They held that there existed from the days of Moses a distinction between priests and Levites, in which the priests, though coming from the tribe of Levi, belonged to special families within that tribe, and were definitely superior to the other Levites (3^{10}, *stranger*, includes the non-priestly Levites). These other Levites, however, were ritualistically superior to non-Levites, and not only were they especially assigned to the care of the tabernacle, but they were so placed, in the encampment and on the march, that they acted as a kind of protective guard of honor for the sacred shrine. The author returns to this subject in 8^{5-26} and 18^{1-7}. The passage includes more than one view of the status of the Levites: they are a gift to Aaron and his sons (3^{9}); they are substitutes for the first born who otherwise should have been offered to Jehovah. As the Levites, however, numbered only 22,000 (3^{39}), and the first-born males of Israel came to 22,273 (3^{43}), the extra 273 were redeemed by a money payment (3^{46-48}). The totals in $3^{22, 28, 34}$ amount to 22,300 instead of 22,000 as given in v. 39. It has been suggested that in v. 28 the word "six" was originally three. The spelling of these two words in Hebrew makes this mistake easy.

Chapters 5 and 6: Miscellaneous Laws

CHAPTER V

1–4. Keeping the Camp Ceremonially Clean. This was to be done by the simple method of expelling the three classes of people concerned (v. 2).

5–10. Restitution for Guilt. The instructions cover the case of a breach of trust, but it should be noted that a sin against a man is also *a trespass against the Lord.* **8.** The instruction here supplements Lev. 6^{1-7} (see notes).

11–31. The Case of a Wife Suspected of Infidelity. The essence of this procedure is the test called ordeal, in which a suspected person is compelled to subject himself to some peril which, if he is innocent, will not harm him, but which, if he is guilty, will cause him injury and perhaps death. While this is the only instance in the Bible, the custom is widespread, and familiar to all readers of history. As here described it moves in a world of magic which to-day seems far removed from true religion, but which always has been closely connected with the earlier stages of religious development. **17.** *Holy water*—an expression occurring here only and which, perhaps, should be *living water*, as in LXX. Back of the custom is the conviction that nothing can be hidden from the Deity.

CHAPTER VI

1–21. The Vow of the Nazirite. The vow is taken for a limited length of time decided upon by the man who takes the vow; but the period determined upon must be religiously kept. The case of Samson (Judg. 13^{7}) is the only clear one of a lifelong vow of this kind, though it is possible that Samuel also is to be regarded as a lifelong Nazirite. There are three requirements (vv. 1–8): (1) The idea of the sacred quality and function of the hair is not peculiar to the Hebrews. (2) Abstinence from any product of the vine is a symbolic assertion of loyalty to Jehovah the God of the desert as opposed to the baals of the cultivated land (cf. the Rechabites, Jer. 35). (3) The avoidance of defilement from a dead body connects with Lev. 21^{11}, where this requirement is specified for the high priest; and the supposition is near at hand that the Nazirites are to be regarded as a type of temporary lay priesthood. Vv. 9–12 make provision for an involuntary breach of the third requirement; and vv. 13–21 set forth the formal release from the conditions of the vow when the period is completed.

22–27. The Priestly Blessing. There could be no better illustration of the promiscuous character of this document P than the occurrence of this beautiful benediction in the midst of the mechanical details of the vows and offerings. The blessing itself, vv. 24–26, consists of three lines, of which the first contains three (Hebrew) words; the second, five; and the third, seven; while each line falls into two parts. V. 27 is an illuminating example of the way *the name* of God has a much wider significance than an English reader would give it. God is what his Spirit is; his name is his character. And his name is upon those who find in him their blessing, their joy, and their peace (cf. Mt. 28^{19} Acts $3^{6, 16}$ 19^{13}).

CHAPTER VII

Offerings Made by the Heads of the Tribes. (Ch. 7 has the distinction of being the longest chapter in the Bible.) On twelve successive days the heads of the tribes already named (see chs. 1, 2) bring their offerings for their respective tribes. The *wagons* seem out of place in view of ch. 4, which specifies the Levites as the carriers of the tabernacle and its furniture. The mechanical twelve-fold repetition of the formula describing the offerings is a literary characteristic of the P writers. V. 89 is a fragment having no connection with what precedes or follows. It tells how Jehovah used to speak with Moses and is an echo of Ex. 25^{22}.

CHAPTER VIII

1–4. The Golden Candlestick. The description of the candlestick is substantially a repetition of Ex. 25^{37}.

5–22. Purification and Presentation of the Levites. The manner and significance of the sanctification of the Levites are described in these verses (cf. chs. 3, 4). Proper offerings are specified, the children of Israel lay their hands upon the Levites, and then the Levites are presented before Jehovah at the tent of meeting as a wave offering (Lev. 8^{27}, notes). Just how the writer supposed these acts to be carried out is not stated. There is no hint that they are to be delegated or that they are symbolic; yet there is something almost grotesque in the thought of the whole congregation laying hands on the Levites, and of the Levites being waved in any literal sense. The writer was much more interested in the fact that the Levites were properly sanctified and that they were unmistakably set apart from the other Israelites than he was with any diagram of how the various steps were actually to be worked out. This indifference to exact facts and possibilities is of a piece with the freedom which in chs. 1 and 2 dealt in big numbers and vast territory. It is possible here as there because both the writer and his readers are removed from the conditions of a past so distant and irrecoverable.

23–26. Age of Levitical Service. This paragraph extends the period of service in both directions beyond that given in 4^{3}. Here it begins at the age of twenty-five years instead of thirty; and while active service ceases at the age of fifty, as in 4^{3}, voluntary service after that age is provided for.

CHAPTER IX

1–14. The Second Passover. A second Passover is provided for those who, by reason of uncleanness or of being on a journey, were unable to participate in the regular one. The fact that the provision grows out of an actual emergency is interesting in its reflection of the probable origin of many of these requirements, namely, that arrangements made to meet a special case developed into a formal law. Strangers may also keep the Passover. For an occasion when this provision was actually taken advantage of, see the account of Hezekiah's action in 2 Chr. 30.

15–23. The Cloud of Fire. The cloud over the tabernacle gives the sign for camping or marching. When it is taken up, the people continue their journey. When it abides, they encamp. Vv. 19–23 enlarge the statement of v. 18. On the cloud, cf. Ex. 40^{34-38}, notes.

CHAPTER X

1–10. The Silver Trumpets. Signals are arranged for, to be sounded on silver trumpets. These are not to be confused with the *shophar*, a ram's or cow's horn, also called "trumpet" in R.V. (e.g., Lev. 25^{9}). The calling of the congregation and the signal to march are obviously suitable to the desert situation; but vv. 9 and 10 imply the days of settlement in Canaan. The shape and approximate size of these trumpets are known from the triumphal Arch of Titus still standing in Rome, on which are portrayed some of the sacred spoils Titus brought back from Jerusalem.

This closes the first part of the book, the division at this point being justified by the fact that thus far the people are located at Sinai and have not started from there on their way to the promised land. All that has occurred up to this point is thought of by the writer as preliminary to the forward march. The book of Numbers may thus be regarded as a continuation of the book of Exodus, Leviticus constituting a kind of grand parenthesis dealing specifically and exclusively with matters of ritual. Ex. 19–24 had brought the people to Sinai, and the remainder of the book, chs. 25–40, had taken up in great detail the setting up of the tabernacle. With the final arrangements as laid down in Num. 1^{1}–10^{10} the people are ready to proceed. At least, this is the view of the writers of P, who nevertheless did not hesitate to interrupt the story for the insertion of various legal passages dealing with matters which, to a Western mind, are wholly irrelevant to the narrative.

CHAPTERS 10^{11} TO 20^{13}: FROM MOUNT SINAI TO KADESH

The P documents which make up the first part of the book are here continued, but this second part contains also passages from JE. This involves some duplication in the narratives as well as some differences in the points of view of the stories themselves. The most interesting aspect of the section is its brevity. It purports to cover nearly the whole period of the forty years spent in the wilderness, and in view of the place given in later thought to this forty-year period, it might be expected that there would be a fairly rich supply of traditions concerning what had happened during that time; but such traditions are lacking. Practically all are given in this short section, while the few that are preserved deal chiefly with sins or outbreaks of some kind which call for condemnation and punishment. In the literary analysis of the section there is general agreement on the parts belonging to P, as there is also general agreement on the fact that the parts not belonging to P represent at least two other sources, J and E. The sources J and E, however, have so many traits in common that, while there is no doubt that the two are present, it is extremely difficult in some cases to make a satisfactory separation between them.

11–28. Departure From Sinai. The people set forward in obedience to the rising of the cloud which had been resting on the tabernacle. Instead of being "in the midst of the camps" (2^{17}) the Levites are here arranged in two groups (vv. 17, 21), so that those who carried *the tabernacle* proper could have it set up and ready to receive *the sanctuary*, namely, the most sacred articles, 3^{31}; cf. 4^{15}, mg. *The wilderness of Paran*, the scene of the following events, is here named in anticipation of the completion of this stage of the journey. The term is as vague as *the wilderness of Sinai* mentioned here and in 1^{1}, and the location can be identified only in a very general way. It lay west of the continuation of the Jordan Valley, which extends south from the Dead Sea to the Gulf of Akabah, and perhaps some fifty to seventy-five miles south of Beersheba (see art., *Land of Palestine*, p. 56). It is in this wilderness that Kadesh is located—the most important stopping-place, after Sinai, of the whole forty years; see below on 13^{26}.

29–36. Leaving the Mountain of Jehovah. Moses urges his father-in-law to accompany them, as one who knew the country (on *Reuel* see Ex. 2^{18-22}, and cf. Ex. 3^{1} $18^{1, 2}$, notes). Judg. 1^{16} indicates that he consented, although the present fragment from J breaks off without giving an answer. **33.** The second *three days* is probably recopied by accident from the first. The idea that the ark got so far ahead of the people is contradicted by every other reference, to say nothing of the impossibility of such a plan. **35, 36.** A fragment of ark ritual. The ark represents Jehovah. Where the ark is, Jehovah is. So that an address to the ark is an address to Jehovah. This fragment gives the formulas used when the ark was taken out to battle, and when it was brought back (in triumph). It is quoted here as suitable for the desert wanderings. (Cf. Psa. $68^{1, 2}$.)

CHAPTER XI

1–3. Destruction of Murmurers at Taberah. The place is called "Burning" (Hebrew, *Tabherāh*). It is not always easy to decide, in the numerous cases of this kind which occur in the O.T., whether the name of the place originated in the event or whether the story of the event grew out of the name itself. It is a well-known fact that names of places may be very ancient, while successive settlers explain the origin of the name in different ways. Undoubtedly, however, such an event as described here would easily justify a significant name. (Cf. 17^{1-7} Gen. 20^{22-34} 26^{18-22}.)

4–35. Incidents on the Way. The place is called "Gluttons' Graves" (Hebrew, *Kibhroth-Hattaavah*). In this passage there are evidently combined parts of various stories. There are the accounts of the manna and of the quails already given in Ex. 16 (see notes there); a fragment of one of the complaints Moses made to Jehovah (vv. 11, 12, 14, 15); the bestowal of the spirit of prophecy on the seventy elders and on the two who remained in the camp; and finally the explanation of the name of the place where all these events occurred. The *manna* as described in this connection had much in common with a sugary sap that in June and July exudes from a kind of tamarisk growing in the Sinaitic peninsula. It is possible that this natural product may form the basis of the account which regards this food supply as provided miraculously. The word "manna" is popularly represented (Ex. 16^{15}, mg., notes) as the excited exclamation of the people the first time they saw it. The supply of *quails*, represented (vv. 31f.) as a miraculous event on a large scale, is still an annual occurrence when these birds of passage, able to fly only with the wind, cross parts of southern Palestine in their migrations, and are captured in large numbers by the natives (cf. the flight of the pigeons in Cooper, *The Pioneers*, ch. 22). In the limited space available here it is not possible to furnish a detailed discussion of these incidents; for further comments see notes on Ex. 16 and larger commentaries. Vv. 11, 12, 14, 15 have such a loose connection with their context that they are now generally regarded as belonging elsewhere. It has been suggested that they would fit very appropriately after Ex. 33^{3}. At any rate their spirit and content suit that context better than this.

The spirit of prophecy referred to seems to be the ecstatic kind illustrated in 1 Sam. 10^{5}. The line of prophets, and the corresponding conceptions of prophecy, ran through many grades from the earlier ecstatic type to the deeply spiritual type represented in Isaiah and Jeremiah. The primitive, ecstatic, mechanical conception of prophecy, however, is no farther removed from the later spiritual view than the conception of deity represented in vv. 1 and 33 is remote from the thought of God in, say, Psa. 139 or the teachings of Jesus. (See arts., *The Prophetic Literature*, p. 150, and *The O.T. Conception of God*, pp. 158.) The conceptions of deity and of prophecy both moved gradually from the mechanical and local toward the spiritual and universal. If the marginal reading of v. 28 (*from his youth*) is correct the statement would be more appropriate at a time near the close of the wilderness period than near the beginning, as here. For v. 34 cf. note on vv. 1–3.

CHAPTER XII

Moses vs. Aaron and Miriam. Another combination of different accounts. Are Aaron and Miriam jealous of Moses on account of his marriage (v. 1) or on account of his supreme place as revealer of God's will? (V. 2.) Were both Aaron and Miriam involved? If so, why was Miriam the only one to be punished? (V. 10.) A final answer to these questions cannot be given and, perhaps, is not necessary. More interesting and more important is the position ascribed to Moses. V. 3 is the basis for the familiar proverb, "As meek as Moses." As a matter of fact, everything that is said of Moses elsewhere represents him as anything but meek in the commonly accepted meaning of the term. It is rather suggestive that this single isolated statement should have been allowed to outweigh every other reference bearing on the subject. V. 4 indicates the E document in its location of the sacred tent outside the camp. Vv. 6–8 fall into poetical form and might be paraphrased as follows:

"Listen to me!
If there be a prophet of Jehovah among you,
In a vision do I make myself known to him,
In a dream do I speak to him.
Not so is my servant Moses:
In all my affairs he is fully trusted,
By word of mouth do I speak with him,
Straightforwardly and not in mystic enigmas;
Jehovah's very form doth he behold.
Why then do you not fear to speak
Against my servant, against Moses?"

This view of a prophet evidently implies a very different conception of prophecy from that of 11[25].

In spite of Aaron's claim in v. 2 to be equal with Moses, he does not have the courage to go straight to Jehovah with his complaint, but turns instinctively to Moses to act as intercessor. Why Aaron himself was not also stricken is not clear. According to vv. 1 and 5 he was as guilty as Miriam. The freedom of this conversation between Moses and Jehovah (vv. 13f.) confirms v. 8. The whole chapter is a striking illustration of the place of Moses in later thought. He was regarded as unique in his authority over his fellows. This authority the author regards as continuing down to his own day. *Hazeroth* is presumably the stopping place in *the wilderness of Paran*, into which the Hebrews had already come in 10[12].

Chapters 13 and 14: The Spies, Their Report, and Its Consequences

In a comparatively short time (according to P's chronology, less than two years) the Hebrews had made a triumphant escape from Egypt, had received from Jehovah elaborate instructions for their future conduct, had been promised a definite home in a fruitful land, and now with the beginning of ch. 13 are at the threshold of that land ready to enter and take possession. What stopped them? No wonder that the answer to this question perplexed later writers. It was hard to understand why the steady progress that had been made up to this point should suddenly be blocked so that the promised land was not entered till a generation—forty years—afterward. There must have been some reason; and the JE and P writers fixed upon the episode of the spies as the turning point. It is entirely reasonable that spies should be sent ahead in preparation for so momentous an advance, and equally reasonable to suppose that their report would have a decisive influence on the next step to be taken. There were different traditions of just how the crisis occurred, and these two chapters show clear evidence of being made up of different and sometimes diverging accounts. The spies start from the wilderness of Paran, 13[3, 26a]; or they start from Kadesh, v. 26b. They traverse the land to the extreme north, Hamath, v. 21; or only as far as Hebron, v. 22. The majority of the spies report a land of famine and starvation, v. 32; or they report a land of fertility, v. 27. Caleb dissents, v. 30; or Joshua and Caleb dissent, 14[6-10]. These facts along with others have led to many attempts to analyze the passage into its constituent literary elements. There is close agreement on the parts assigned to P; and if one would take the trouble to draw a line with a colored pencil around these parts, he would see clearly what a complete and consistent narrative they give. They are: 13[1-17] (to *Canaan*), [21, 25, 26] (to *Paran*), [32] (to *thereof*); 14[1] (to *voice*), [2, 5-7, 10, 26, 29, 34, 38]. The parts omitted would be found to contain duplicate statements and other phenomena indicating a composite character, but it is not easy to make a satisfactory separation. They are assigned to J and E and may have been abbreviated in the interest of the P version. Connecting statements have been made here and there by the compiler in order to make his narrative more continuous. In addition to these three accounts there is still another in Deut. 1[19-46] (see notes there).

According to P, what happened was as follows: From Paran Moses sends twelve spies, one for each tribe, Joshua and Caleb representing the tribes of Ephraim and Judah respectively. They travel through the land going as far north as Hamath (!) and in forty days they return. Ten of them bring back such an unfavorable account of the land that the people begin to complain to Moses and Aaron. Joshua and Caleb seek in vain to quiet them. The people are about to stone Moses and Aaron when the glory of Jehovah appears. Jehovah then announces to Moses and Aaron that the people shall be punished by being compelled to remain in the wilderness forty years, a year for each day of the spies' journey, until all the men twenty years old or more (except Caleb and Joshua) should die. The ten spies who brought the unfavorable report die on the spot. The two chief factors in the reports of both P and JE deal with the fertility (or sterility) of the land, and the size and strength of the inhabitants. On the former point there is contradiction. On the latter there is agreement; but the majority regard the inhabitants as too strong to be conquered, while the minority say it can be done with the aid of Jehovah. One who has made the journey from the barren desolation south of Beersheba up to Hebron can appreciate the enthusiasm of the favorable report; for even to-day in contrast to its surroundings Hebron is a jewel of verdure with its fields and trees, and above all its springs of water. (See art., *Land of Palestine*, p. 56.)

CHAPTER XIII

The Spies Sent Out; Their Report. *The Wilderness of Paran* (v. 3), according to the view of P, lies south of wilderness of Zin (v.21). *By the South* (vv. 17, 22), literally, into the Negeb, a word referring to the dry country extending from Hebron to Kadesh. **21.** *The wilderness of Zin*, in P's view, lies north of the wilderness of Paran. Kadesh lies here, and would be included in the territory the spies were sent to survey. In JE Kadesh has already been occupied and the spies start from there. *Rehob*, far in the north, at the foot of Mount Hermon. *Hamath*, an important city one hundred and fifty miles north of Rehob. The *entering in* probably refers to a mountain pass between Hermon and the Lebanon through which one entered from the south into the territory controlled by Hamath. **28.** *Children of Anak*, or Anakim, a people who lived in the vicinity of Hebron, always referred to as people unusually large. **26.** *Kadesh*—also called Kadesh-barnea. This has been identified with a place about fifty miles south of Beersheba which bears almost the same name to-day, *Ain Kadis*. Whether this identification be correct or not, Kadesh must have been not far from that general locality. The name indicates a sacred place, and as it bore this name before the Hebrews arrived it was evidently so regarded by the earlier inhabitants, just as Mecca was a sacred place before the time of Mohammed. It was the headquarters for the Hebrews during the thirty-eight years of the wilderness period, which is not to be thought of as a time of constant motion but (if one might be allowed the expression) of a kind of nomadic settlement, as Bedouins to-day confine themselves to a fairly well defined territory. It is the scene of a number of important events described in the following chapters and stands out as the most conspicuous and significant place of encampment during the desert period after the departure from Sinai. **29.** *Amalek:* the Amalekites were a tribe living on the edge of the desert. They were still dangerous as late as the days of David (1 Sam. 30^{1}). The *Hittites* had their chief seat in Asia Minor but many had settled in Palestine (see Gen. 23^{10} 26^{34}). The *Jebusites* lived in the neighborhood of Jerusalem (cf. 2 Sam. 5^{6}). *Amorite* and *Canaanite* are terms used in the sense suggested by the latter, that is, dwellers in Canaan; although at an earlier time the Amorites were farther north than the Canaanites.

CHAPTER XIV

The People's Rebellion; Jehovah's Threat; Moses' Intercession. The pathos and power of the scene described in vv. 11–25 are not diminished by the similar scenes in Ex. $32^{9\text{-}14, 30\text{-}35}$ $34^{6\text{-}9}$. One cannot read unmoved the description of a leader as great as Moses, who not only champions the cause of Deity in the face of a shortsighted, thankless, turbulent people, but who is at the same time so devoted to his people that he casts in his lot with them whatever happens. There can be no doubt of the splendor and heroism which these writers saw in this great leader. This Moses of their ideals was so great that he not only dared to take Jehovah to task but actually prevailed in the argument. Yet this same Moses is willing to throw himself away if that will preserve the life of his people or the honor of his God. (Cf. Abraham's intercession for Sodom, Gen. $18^{22\text{-}33}$, and Paul's willingness to be *anathema* for his brethren's sake, Rom. 9^{3}.)

CHAPTER XV

The accounts of events at Kadesh are interrupted by a small collection of laws supplementing items already noted.

1–16. The Amounts of Meal, Oil, and Wine That Should Be Used With Different Sacrifices. The amounts vary with the value of the animal offered. The requirement applies to the sojourner as well as to the Hebrews themselves. (See Lev. 23¹⁻⁸, notes.)

17–21. Reserving a Portion for Jehovah. A special case of an offering of first fruits. (See Lev. 23⁹⁻¹⁴, notes.)

22–31. Propitiation for Unintentional Wrongdoing. A much simpler and probably earlier treatment of the subject than Lev. 4 (notes). The law provides for unintentional breaches, but makes no provision for one who breaks it willfully, "with a high hand." Such a culprit is *cut off* from his people. It cannot be said definitely whether this means death or expulsion from the tribe; although in a country of nomads the latter might easily lead to the former. (See Lev. 7²⁰, ²¹, notes.)

32–36. The Sabbath-Breaker. Breach of the Sabbath punished with death. Cf. 9¹⁻¹⁴, note.

37–41. Fringes. *Tassels* (mg.) at each of the four corners of the outer garment attached with a blue cord are to serve as reminders of religious obligations (cf. art. "Fringes," in Hastings' *Dictionary of the Bible*, vol. ii).

CHAPTER XVI

The Authority of Moses and Aaron Challenged by Korah, Dathan and Abiram. (*On* also is named in v. 1 but is not mentioned again.) The analysis of the chapter is best begun by collecting the sections dealing with Dathan and Abiram. These are: v. 1b (from *Dathan*) to v. 2a (to *Moses*), vv. 12–25, vv. 25, 26, v. 27b (from *and Dathan*) to v. 32a (to *households*), and vv. 33, 34. These sections taken together make an almost complete story, continuous and consistent, yet entirely omitting Korah and his company. (The apparent exceptions, vv. 24b, 32b, are noted below.) These sections are generally assigned to JE. When they are set off by themselves it is seen that what remains, constituting the larger part of the chapter, deals with Korah and omits all reference to Dathan and Abiram. This separation of the two groups of passages is not an arbitrary separation based solely on an accident of names, but is confirmed by the way the two parties are always dealt with separately. When Moses is dealing with one no reference is made to the other. They come to different ends, Dathan and Abiram being swallowed up when the earth miraculously opens and engulfs them, while Korah and his company are burned up by fire from Jehovah.

The separation is further confirmed by the fact that Num. 27³ refers to Korah only, while Deut. 11⁶ refers to Dathan and Abiram only. The Korah sections are assigned to P. But these Korah sections are concerned with two different themes: (a) Korah with two hundred and fifty non-Levites denying the ritualistic superiority of the tribe of Levi; and (b) a struggle within the tribe of Levi itself in which the Levites challenge the exclusive priesthood of Aaron. These two themes are so different that they justify a further analysis of the chapter. The sections dealing with Korah and his two hundred and fifty non-Levites, *princes of the congregation, men of renown*, are: v. 1a (*Now Korah*), v. 2b (from *with certain*), to and including v. 7 (omitting from v. 6, *Korah and all his company;* and from v. 7, *Ye take too much upon you, ye sons of Levi;* on which see below), vv. 18–24 (to *tabernacle*), v. 27a (to *tabernacle*), and vv. 41–50. These sections, like the Dathan and Abiram sections, make a continuous, consistent, and complete story.

When these sections are set off by themselves, along with the JE sections, there remain two groups of passages: (1) the genealogy of Korah in v. 1, which connects him with Levi; vv. 8–11, 16, 17, and 36–40. These passages set forth the theme (b) mentioned above. (2) Phrases and clauses now seem to be designed to connect and harmonize the larger sections. They are: the two items in vv. 6 and 7 already noted; the combination of Korah, Dathan, and Abiram at the end of v. 24 and in the middle of v. 27; and the addition of Korah at the end of v. 32. These fragments are at such variance with their setting that they are best regarded as the work of a late editor who attempted (but failed) to make the chapter consistent. The group of passages which sets forth the (b) theme has so many characteristics of P that it is regarded as a secondary and later stratum of the basic P document which told about Korah and the two hundred and fifty.

There can be no doubt that the three narratives now combined in this chapter reflect actual situations. The criticisms made of Moses in the JE story are only too probable. Obviously, he had failed so far to bring the people into the promised land (v. 14); and it is easy to understand that there would be jealousy of Moses' authority on the part of men who were quite ready to charge him with self-importance (v. 13b); and even with taking advantage of his position to increase his private possessions (v. 15b). This last charge was made also against Samuel (1 Sam. 12³), and is one that is easily credible in the East, to-day as well as in ancient times. JE's charge is thus political and administrative, and it calls for no great effort of imagination to reconstruct the troubles of this kind that Moses must have met not once but many times. The second situation is equally credible. Why should the tribe of Levi be considered any holier than the other tribes? Tribal jealousy prompts the question. Korah organizes a representative committee of inquiry and challenges Moses as the representative of the favored tribe. The third situation is quite credible but not as a situation arising in the days of Moses. Down to the period of the Exile all Levites, as far as family relationships were concerned, were eligible to the priesthood. Not until after that was a distinction made within the tribe in favor of the descendants of Aaron—an innovation that could hardly have been established without jealousies and conflicts. The P document in its final form is quite late enough to reflect such disturbances. (Cf. art., "Priests and Levites," Hastings' *Dictionary of the Bible*, vol. iv.) Even the ghastly punishments meted out to the offenders are credible to those who hold the primitive view of Deity characteristic of the early pre-Christian teaching.

CHAPTER XVII

Jehovah's Choice of the Tribe of Levi Confirmed. This chapter reports the miraculous confirmation of the divine choice of the tribe of Levi (vv. 1–11); following appropriately on the preceding account of tribal jealousy. Vv. 12f. express a natural fear in view of the events just recounted.

CHAPTER XVIII

1–7. Duties of Levi. Closely parallel to 3[5-10] but with more detailed directions for the priesthood. *Bear the iniquity* (v. 1), or, better, *guilt*, means to take the responsibility of preserving the ritual requirement and to bear the consequences if that requirement be not met. The principle is part and parcel of the primitive conception of holiness, according to which holiness is a dynamic force almost physical and mechanical in its nature. Like electricity it can, and does, discharge itself or "strike" one who, unaware or unprepared, approaches a "holy" object. Ritual preparation serves as a kind of insulation rendering the persons involved immune from this otherwise fatal force. In this passage the *priests* are thus qualified to serve in the holiest (most powerful and fatal) part of the sacred tent and to handle the holiest (most dangerous) objects belonging there. The *Levites* are qualified to serve in matters that lie between the priesthood and the laity, especially in the handling and the protection of the sacred tent. As long as these instructions are obeyed, and unqualified persons avoid these dangerous contacts, there will *be wrath no more upon the children of Israel* (v. 5b). It hardly needs to be stated that this conception of holiness was destined to move on to one more deeply spiritual just as the conception of prophecy did (cf. note on 11[25]). *Stranger* (v. 7) is anyone not a priest, even though he be a Levite (cf. 3[10]).

8–20. Provision for the Support of the Priests. The priestly revenues ran a course closely parallel to the increasing importance held by the priesthood in Israel. Such instances as Judg. 17[10] and 1 Sam. 2[13f.] suggest that it was optional with the worshiper how much he should give the priest. From this point on there is a steady increase in the amounts up to and even beyond the generous allowance granted here. The present passage belongs to P and represents post-exilic regulations. *By reason of the anointing* (v. 8)—read as in mg. *Corn* (v. 12)—not, of course, Indian corn or maize, but grain, wheat. *Devoted* (v. 14)—set apart for the Deity. The custom, frequently mentioned in O.T., is ancient and not peculiar to the Hebrews. As observed in Israel it became a method of converting to the service of Jehovah persons or objects regarded as opposed to him. In practice this meant either seclusion or destruction of the devoted thing. Precious objects gained by conquest or offered in worship could be secluded, set apart, by being taken to the sacred tent (later, to the Temple), there to become "holy," i.e., the exclusive possession of Jehovah. Cities and populations, however, could hardly be thus set apart, so they were destroyed, rendered incapable of further opposition to Jehovah. The term is thus seen to apply to anything specially vowed to Jehovah, whether the vow is made officially by priests and leaders, or privately by individuals. (See notes on Lev. 27[21] Josh. 7—Achan; Judg. 11[29-40]—Jephthah's daughter; 1 Sam. 15—Samuel and Amalek; Mk. 7[11]—Corban.) Here the reference is obviously to things that could be used profitably by the priests. A money payment (v. 15) is arranged as a substitute for the first-born. *Covenant of salt* (v. 19)—an enduring covenant of fellowship, growing out of the ancient custom that united those who ate together; the sharing of food is the sharing of life (see art., *Bible Manners and Customs*, p. 74b).

21–24. The Dues of the Levites. The Levites shall receive tithes from the people as compensation for their special service and because they are to have no (territorial) inheritance of their own.

25–32. Tithes Paid by the Levites. The Levites are not exempt from the payment of tithes to the priests. Having no inheritance where they might raise crops of their own, they must give tithes of their tithes. The whole chapter belongs to P.

CHAPTER XIX

1–10. The Ritual of the Red Heifer. Although this chapter belongs to P, its subject is recognized as a most ancient one. Students of primitive religions are familiar with the almost universal feeling that one is defiled by contact with the dead. This defilement requires some method of purification. The present chapter sets forth a ritual so strange, so suggestive of a world of pure magic, that it has so far defied all attempts to account for its presence in the Hebrew legislation or to relate it satisfactorily to the religion of Jehovah.

1–6. *Heifer*—all other offerings of animals were of males. *The priest* has surprisingly little to do with the whole ceremony. *Without the camp* and away from the altar, where an offering to Jehovah would be made. *Toward the front of the tent* locates the place as east of, and at a distance from, the tent. Later discussions specified the size and amount of cedar, hyssop, and scarlet cloth. The ashes of these ingredients were as important as those of the heifer. (Cf. the notes on the ritual for cleansing from leprosy, Lev. 14, and for the day of atonement, Lev. 16.)

7–9. All persons concerned with the preparation of the ashes were rendered unclean and had to purify themselves after the operation.

11–22. Purification From Contact With the Dead. See the notes on similar legislation in Lev. 21[1-4, 10, 11]. The ashes put into living (*running*, v. 17) water made a mixture which, when sprinkled on the persons concerned, purified them from the defilement caused by contact with the dead.

CHAPTER XX

1–13. Water From the Rock. V. 1 contains three brief preliminary statements: (a) place; (b) time; (c) death and burial of Miriam. The statement of time omits the year which, according to P, would be the fortieth, while according to JE the Hebrews reached Kadesh soon after leaving Horeb-Sinai (13[3, 23], notes). In the desert one's first and greatest need is water, and it would be strange if the traditions of the wilderness, however few, should not include tales of thirst. At least three of these are preserved in Ex. 15[22-26] 17[1-7], and the present passage. This one in Numbers and the one in Ex. 17 are closely parallel, and it may be this close similarity that led later rabbis to the curious conclusion that the rock at Rephidim (Ex. 17) and the rock at Kadesh (Num. 20) were one and the same rock, and that in some miraculous way it had followed the Hebrews from Rephidim to Kadesh (cf. 1 Cor. 10[4]). *The rod* (v. 8) is apparently thought of as the special rod which Moses had used in Egypt in the time of the plagues. The account is vague as to the sin of Moses and Aaron which prevented them from entering the promised land. It may be that they associated themselves too intimately with Jehovah (*we*, in v. 10) and thus detracted from the divine glory. Or it may be that in some passage now lacking they had addressed directly to Jehovah their doubt that water could be thus supplied. This latter view would find confirmation in the reference to Moses and Aaron as rebels in v. 24 and in 27[14]. In this case the *rebels* in v. 10 would be Moses and Aaron, instead of the people, as the verse reads now. *Meribah* (v. 13)—another place name (cf. on 11[1-3]).

CHAPTERS 20[14] TO 36[13]: FROM KADESH TO THE PLAINS OF MOAB

The same kind of literary variety is found in this part of the book as in the two other parts. From 20[14] to 25[5], J and E predominate; from there to the end of the book the material is practically all from P. With 20[14] the departure from Kadesh has begun. The story then advances rapidly to the end of ch. 21, which finds the Hebrews encamped on the plains of Moab at a point opposite Jericho. This is as far as the book of Numbers takes them. Chs. 22–24 are occupied with the account of Balaam; and from there to the end of the book there are a miscellaneous succession of experiences in the land of Moab, a group of laws, an itinerary of the complete journey from Egypt to the Jordan, and instructions preparatory to the advance into Canaan. The time covered is less than a year, and that year is the fortieth after leaving Egypt. According to 33[38], Aaron died in the fifth month of the fortieth year. After his death the people mourned for him thirty days (20[29]), so that not more than six months remain for all that follows.

The geographical disposition of the journey is clear in its large outlines, but perplexing in many of its details. Having failed to effect an entrance into Canaan from the south, the people move eastward around the southern end of the Dead Sea and then northward into the territory of Moab, whence the land of Canaan can be approached from the east. The chief perplexities of the route arise in connection with the intermediate stations between Kadesh and Moab. The most explicit itinerary (E) takes the people south from

Kadesh as far as the Gulf of Akabah before they turn north toward Moab. This long circuit is made in order "to compass the land of Edom" (21⁴); and it is not surprising to find the people "much discouraged" (21⁴) with this roundabout journey. It is, indeed, difficult to see how it could all be compressed into the brief time of six months. P, however (33[37, 38]), indicates the view that there was no southward move from Kadesh, but that from Kadesh the people moved east and then northeast, advancing as directly as possible toward Moab. Instead of "compassing the land of Edom" they pass its northwest corner and then turn directly north into the land of Moab. This route would harmonize better with the brief time allowed for the events in this last stage of the wilderness period. The chief difficulty in accepting this version of the story is the uncertain character of ch. 33 (see notes).

The literary and geographical questions are further complicated by the passages in Deuteronomy which refer to this period (cf. Deut. 1, 2, notes). These variant accounts have never been satisfactorily harmonized and it seems most reasonable to accept here as, indeed, throughout the Pentateuch, the existence of the different sources, each one of which tells its own story in its own way.

14–21. Israel and Edom. (JE.) The Hebrews ask permission to cross the land of Edom, but are refused. It is a little curious that no further reference is made to the tabernacle and the cloud over it as supplying signals for the advance and the halt. The events that follow are, indeed, not favorable to all that would be involved in the elaborate arrangements connected with the tabernacle; but these ancient writers are not disconcerted by such difficulties, and one can only wonder why such an important object and such an elaborate ceremony simply drop out of sight without comment. Without any indication of divine direction Moses takes matters into his own hands, and on his own responsibility sends messengers to the king of Edom.

Thy brother Israel—a relationship frequently referred to and indicating that the people of Israel felt themselves closely related as a people to the Edomites, a relationship which made enmity all the more bitter (cf. Gen. 25[24-26] 36[8] Obad. vv. 10–12). *Kadesh* (v. 16)—the location here is an important clue to the probable site. As the Hebrews are still west of the Arabah, the territory of Edom evidently included territory on the west as well as on the east of this great gorge. Until one has been in a desert country it is hard to appreciate the value of water. Great as the temptation would be to go through fields and vineyards and take some of the grain and fruit, it would be much greater to take a drink of water at a well or spring. How Moses or any other leader could have prevented this, or could have estimated the quantity on which to pay, is hard to tell. Evidently the king of Edom would not take the risk. *The king's way* (v. 17) may have been that part of the ancient trade route which passed Petra and Kerak (Hastings' *Dictionary of the Bible*, vol. v, p. 370). Denied permission to cross Edomite territory the Hebrews turn south in order to go around it.

22–29. Arrival at Mount Hor and Death of Aaron. (P.) *Mount Hor* cannot now be identified. Like Kadesh it is on the border of Edom, so that it could not be near Petra (Sela) as shown on most maps. *Ye rebelled*—cf. on v. 10. *His garments*—his robes of office (cf. Lev. 8[7-9]). *Died there* (v. 28)—stated as mechanically as the exchange of priestly robes. The account is quite unconscious of the tragedy and pathos of the event it here describes. P is far more interested in the proper priestly succession than in Moses, Aaron, and Eleazar as mere human beings. The people weep thirty days for Aaron as they were to weep later for Moses (Deut. 34[8]).

CHAPTER XXI

1–3. Victories over Canaanites. (JE.) This fragment referring to battles with Canaanites and the destruction of Canaanite cities must refer to a time when the Hebrews, or at least some of them, were in Canaan, and is obviously out of its proper connection here; but it contains nothing to indicate what its original connection was. Judg. 1[17] may refer to the same situation, but this is not positive.

4–9. The Brazen Serpent. (E, except the words *from mount Hor*, which connect with P.) Another case where a complaint on the part of the people brings a plague on them, this time of poisonous serpents. *Much discouraged*—literally, *shortened;* as one might say, "gave out." They speak against God, Moses, and the manna (v. 5, mg., *vile bread*). *A serpent of brass*—the Hebrew word means copper or bronze. For Christian readers this brief incident has found its chief significance in the reference made to it in Jn. 3[14], which is in principle the same sort of use that the ancient writer made. In both cases the incident is pressed into the service of a later theology, and both tend to obscure the fact that it is but one illustration of a practice well known outside the Bible as well as within it, namely, making an image of a pest or affliction and presenting the image to the deity who, in turn, would banish the pest (cf. 1 Sam. 6[5]). A more modern attitude is represented in 2 Kings 18[4], and also in the words of the apocryphal Wisdom of Solomon (16[7]): "He that turned toward it was not saved because of that which was beheld, but because of thee, the Saviour of all."

10–20. From Oboth to Pisgah. (P and E.) The places cannot be identified, but the idea is apparently that the route was eastward across the Arabah directly toward Moab (cf. intro. to section 20[14]–36[13] above). According to the itinerary in vv. 12–20 the Hebrews have left the gulf of Akabah, and in their long journey northward have at last reached the border of Moab. No description is given of the long trail that intervened. The wady *Zered* has not been identified, but there is no doubt about the *Arnon.* This stream flows through a canyon nearly two thousand feet deep, narrowing sharply from approximately two miles in width at the top to forty or fifty yards at the bottom. This deep cleft forms a natural barrier to progress north or south and serves as a well-marked border line for the dwellers on each side of it. According to v. 13, the Moabites are at this time living south of the Arnon, with the Amorites on the north. Farther to the east, where the canyon broadens out and where a number of other streams join the Arnon, the Hebrews would not only be able to make a crossing, but would be eastward of the territory of both Moabites and Amorites.

In vv. 14f. a few lines of a poem are quoted showing that the Arnon had long been recognized as a Moabite border. The *valleys* (plural) in v. 14 are the ravines in which flow the streams referred to above which unite later with the Arnon proper. The lines quoted are taken from *the book of the wars of Jehovah*, a collection referred to here only and whose character can only be guessed from this title and the quotation. The "wars of Jehovah" are those fought in his cause and with his aid; warfare was a religious undertaking. *Beer* (v. 16)—a two-syllable word, *Be'er*, meaning, "a well" (cf. Be'er-Sheba). Vv. 17f.—another poetical fragment called "the Song of the Well." Its date and origin are as obscure as those of the previous fragment (vv. 14f.).

21–32. Defeat of Sihon King of the Amorites. (JE.) V. 22, cf. 20[17]. *Jabbok* (v. 24)—a stream about forty miles north of the Arnon. Both streams cut their way down through the high table-land to the low level of the Jordan and the Dead Sea respectively. They form well-marked boundaries for the territory which at this time was held by the Amorites. *Was strong* (v. 24)—better, with LXX, *was Jazer,* the place mentioned in v. 32. *All these cities* (v. 25)—implies a preceding list which is now lost. *Heshbon and all its towns* (v. 29)—i.e., the smaller towns that looked to Heshbon as their head. The Amorites had invaded the former territory of the Moabites and had driven the latter south of the Arnon. Vv. 27–30 contain another fragment from an ancient poem. It is ascribed to *they that speak in proverbs*, and is evidently introduced here as a reference to Sihon's conquest of Moab. While it is not impossible, it seems rather improbable that such an intensely patriotic document as JE should quote a triumph song of the Amorite enemies; and this, along with the utter obscurity of v. 30 in the original, has led to the opinion (1) that the song comes from the Hebrews; (2) that the first stanza, vv. 27b, 28, is ironical; and (3) that the second stanza, v. 29, voices a Hebrew triumph over Moab. V. 31 is evidently the close of a section; while v. 32 is a fragment from some other account of the conquest of the Amorites.

33–35. Occupation of Bashan. (D, practically identical with Deut. 3[1-4].) This account is regarded as having been taken from Deuteronomy rather than the passage in Deuteronomy from this one, because of the Deuteronomic expressions it contains which are not used by JE.

P's itinerary is continued in 22[1] from v. 11, and the Hebrews are now finally encamped on the plains of Moab opposite Jericho.

Chapters 22[1] to 24[25]: Balaam Blesses Israel (JE)

This is one of the most interesting sections of the book of Numbers. Like so many other episodes, it stands by itself and could be omitted without interfering with the account of the progress of the Hebrews toward the promised land. Indeed, it is not concerned with an itinerary. Its main theme is the security and triumph of the Hebrews through Jehovah's invincible protection. In this security any opposition to them, as, for instance, Moab's, is foredoomed to failure. The particular exponent of this glorious prospect is Balaam, one who is neither a Moabite nor a Hebrew, but a wise man from the East. He has been sent for by Balak, king of Moab, to curse the invading Hebrew host, but he can speak only what Jehovah gives him to speak, and that is a blessing and not a curse. The passage has a sweep and fervor that are unmistakable, and which give it a high place in the literature of Hebrew religious patriotism.

The literary analysis shows (1) a prose

narrative which supplies a setting for (2) a group of poetic oracles: 23^{7b-10}; $^{18b-24}$; 24^{3b-9}; $^{15b-17}$; $^{18, 19}$; ^{20b}; $^{21b, 22}$; $^{23b, 24}$. The prose narrative is not a unit. There are many indications of this, among which are: (1) the obvious duplicate in 22^{3}; (2) the alternation of the names "Jehovah" and "God"; and (3) the apparent contradiction between 22^{22-35} which represents Balaam as disobeying God in starting off with the two servants, and the two preceding verses, which tell of God's permission that Balaam should return with the princes of Moab. So that it is now generally recognized that the present narrative is a combination of a J and an E version of the Balaam story. There is also a general agreement that, roughly speaking, the J narrative is represented in 22^{22-35} and ch. 24; the JE narrative (but more E than J) in $22^{2-21, 36-41}$; and the E narrative in ch. 23. Many details, however, are uncertain, for which the critical commentaries should be consulted. Both J and E represent Balaam in a favorable light. Quite a different character is given him in P ($31^{8, 16}$ Josh. 13^{22}), and it is this latter representation that underlies 2 Pet. $2^{15, 16}$ Jude, v. 11, and Rev. 2^{14}. One's view of Balaam's character will thus depend on the documents on which the view is based. As soon as the independence of the documents is recognized the different representations of Balaam's character can be allowed to stand on their own merits. They do not have to be amalgamated or harmonized. Release from such a necessity, here and elsewhere, is one of the solid gains of the literary criticism of the Bible.

The date of the written narrative is, of course, the date of the documents in which they stand, but the traditions on which these are based may be far older than that—how much older, it is impossible to say; but not earlier than a time when Israel felt herself nationally secure and victorious. The poems may or may not be of the same date as the narratives. It seems probable, however, that they were already part of the tradition before the narratives were incorporated in the present documents.

The question as to Balaam's home and country is not easily answered. In the passage as it stands he is located at such widely different places as *Pethor by the River*, i.e., the Euphrates (22^{5}); *Aram*, which is the common term for the region about Damascus (23^{7}); and *the mountains of the East* (23^{7}), a general term for the mountainous country lying east of the Arabah. Larger commentaries must be consulted for detailed discussions. The view adopted here regards Balaam as one of the type of wise men referred to in 1 Kings 4^{30} Jer. 49^{7}, whose word would have magic power (cf. Josh. 13^{22}, "soothsayer"). He may have been a Midianite, as suggested by his connection with the kings of Midian (31^{8}; Josh. $13^{21f.}$), or more probably an Edomite, and for the following reasons: (1) On the practical grounds of mere distance the Euphrates and even Damascus (Aram) seem out of the question; (2) Gen. 36^{32} names a Bela, son of Beor, as a king of Edom, a name which, in Hebrew, is almost identical with Balaam; (3) the route along which Balaam proceeds—*Ar* (*city*) *of Moab*, at the Arnon (22^{36}); *Kiriath-huzoth* (22^{39}), a city west of Medeba (so Eusebius); *Bamoth-baal* (*high places*), near Dibon (22^{41}); *Pisgah* (23^{14}); and *Peor* (23^{28})—marks a line from south to north, i.e., from the direction of the Edomite country; and (4) *Aram* (23^{7}) may be an accidental change from Edom (in Hebrew the letters "d" and "r" could easily be confused, the difference in the names being, roughly speaking, the difference between a-d-m and a-r-m; cf. p. 100), a correction that is also called for by the necessary parallelism with *mountains of the east* in the next line. Most of the conditions are met by this view, and it may be added that no view meets them all.

Far more important, however, than the home and character of Balaam himself is the nature of this ancient story which tells about him. It is the kind, especially in the episode of the speaking ass, that is seized upon by those who regard the Bible as a mere relic of ancient superstition, just as at the other extreme it is regarded by others as a signal example of the miraculous power of God. It is neither. Such errors regarding biblical passages would not arise if the true literary character of these passages were recognized. The fact that this story is now in the Bible, and that it is told there in the interest of Hebrew history and of the Hebrew religion, should not obscure the deeper fact that it is an ancient story of exactly the type that would suit people who held the view of life, and the ideals of God and of man, held by the early Hebrews. No matter what later use may be made of it, its inherent and original nature and character can be overlooked only at the peril of a fatal misunderstanding of the true character of God and a blind misreading of the Bible. The interests of piety are not served by ignoring in the Bible distinctions which, outside the Bible, are not only obvious, but essential, and which are accepted as a matter of course; and there are few who would insist that stories of this kind, whether inside or outside the Bible, must be taken literally. Talking trees (Judg. 9^{8-15}) or talking animals (as in this case) have a perfectly proper and intelligible place in a certain type of literature, and not until the type is recognized can the true power of the tale make itself felt. For there *is* power here, and a passionate earnestness which must be permitted their own form of expression; and every obligation of reverence as well as reason is laid upon reader and student to recognize that form, and then to interpret it in obedience to its proper laws of structure and meaning. (See art., *Bible as Literature*, p. 19.)

CHAPTER XXII

1. See closing notes under ch. 21.

2–14. **The First Embassy to Balaam.** Vv. 2–4 are introduction: Moab is terror stricken before Israel. Balaam is sent for, but he declines to come. *Pethor which is by the river.* A month's journey by camel train. Too remote to suit the story, which calls for four journeys (cf. above). *Of his people*—read probably with Samaritan Pentateuch, *of Ammon* (final letter having dropped out in the Hebrew MS.). *Blessed . . . cursed* (v. 6). The power of a blessing or a curse was never doubted in ancient times, e.g., Gen. 27[12f.] Judg. 17[2]; such belief is still widespread. *Elders* (v. 7, J)—cf. *princes* in v. 8 (E). *The rewards*—from time immemorial everyone acting officially had his fee, whether priest, soothsayer, or what not. *As Jehovah shall speak* (v. 8)—the view of God underlying the whole story is that of an ancient primitive people. It would be highly misleading to import into such a narrative the view of God represented in such prophets as Isaiah, Jeremiah, or in the N.T. These accounts are not abstract theologies, but survivals from a time when men were "feeling after God" (Acts 17[27]), and were still thinking of him very much as they thought of each other. Such a passage as this must be allowed to be at home in its own world and must be recognized not so much as a revelation of how men should think of God now, but rather as a record of how men thought of God then. In keeping with this is the way Balaam is represented as a worshiper of Jehovah in spite of the fact that he was not a Hebrew and that different peoples had different gods with different names.

15–40. **Balaam; the Ass; the Angel of Jehovah.** A more honorable embassy wins Balaam's consent. According to vv. 22–34, the ass saves Balaam's life. Attention has already been called to the sharp contrast between this section and the verses which immediately precede it. In v. 20 Balaam is expressly directed by God to go with the men, a direction which he obeys, v. 21. The whole point of the present incident, however, is that Balaam has sinned in presuming to go in defiance of Jehovah. The difference is accounted for by the difference of the sources. If anything were needed to make the type of the story clear, it would be found in Balaam's utter lack of surprise at the idea of the ass speaking. And yet no one supposes that it was any more usual for asses to speak then than it is now. Note the effective way in which the story-teller leads up to the point where the ass asks, "Did I ever do this kind of thing before?" (v. 30), and then, instead of having the ass continue with an explanation, he lets Jehovah's angel step in and carry the action to its climax. V. 35, with its abrupt reappearance of the princes of Balak, is generally regarded as supplied by the editor in order to bring the story back to the point where it broke off at v. 21. Vv. 36–40 narrate Balaam's reception and his explanation of the only terms on which he consented to come. For v. 41 see under 23[1-10].

(For additional notes, see the introduction preceding ch. 22.)

CHAPTER XXIII

1–10. **The First Oracle.** The introduction to the first oracle is found in vv. 1–6, including also 22[41]. The sacrifices are not any that are ordered by the Hebrew ritual, but those which in various forms conventionally accompany any ceremony designed to inquire the will of Deity. *Seven*—different numbers are regarded as having mysterious importance. The sanctity of the number seven (the days of the week) is of high antiquity and not peculiar to the Hebrews. *To a bare height* (v. 3): the tablelands where these scenes are located descend rapidly on the west to the Dead Sea and the Jordan Valley, and have many bare heights any one of which would suit this situation.

7–10. This is the oracle itself. *Parable:* this translation is unfortunate in its suggestion of the N.T. parables, a literary form with which the Balaam oracles have no connection. The Hebrew term *māshāl,* here translated "parable," has as wide a variety of uses as the English word "song." In this case it is applied to an oracle in poetic form which praises the nation (Israel) especially blessed by Jehovah. *Aram*—rather, *Edom;* cf. note above on Balaam's home and country. 9. Better, *Does not reckon itself one of the nations.* 10. Read, with LXX, *Who has counted the myriads of Israel?* The two lines that close the oracle strike such a different note that some have regarded them as the comment of a later reader or editor. Whether originally part of the oracle or not, *the righteous* must be understood as the ideal Israelite. The oracle as a whole sees Israel as an established nation, secure, isolated, numerous, and (if the closing lines be included) one whose men lived to a good old age (Job 5[26]). This oracle and the three that follow quite ignore the situation set forth in the prose narrative and concern themselves wholly with Israel's days of national glory.

11–24. Interlude Followed by the Second Oracle. Balak is disappointed, but he will try again. It was a second call that had persuaded Balaam to come, perhaps a second oracle would be the curse that Balak had asked for. Balaam's word was too powerful to be lost through lack of persistence, so he is taken where he can see better. *Pisgah* is a locality where several bare heights (v. 3) are found. In the second oracle Jehovah's faithfulness is set forth as the basis of Israel's happy lot in the future. *King* (v. 21) must refer to Jehovah. The first message telegraphed between Washington and Baltimore was the last line of v. 23.

25–30. Beginning of Interlude Leading to the Third Oracle. Similar to the preceding one but more definitely in favor of Israel.

(For additional notes, see the introduction preceding ch. 22.)

CHAPTER XXIV

1–9. The Third Oracle. Following the completion of the interlude in vv. 1, 2, the oracle itself is found in vv. 3–9. *Whose eye was closed:* the impossibility of translating this line is sufficiently shown by the great variety of proposals that have been made as to just what it means. Other obscurities are found, especially in vv. 7f. In spite of these, however, one cannot fail to catch the note of pride and fervor in which the poet utters his patriotic exaltation. He even sees in Israel a test or touchstone which determines the welfare or ill-fare of other nations, depending on their attitude toward Israel.

10–19. Interlude Followed by the Fourth Oracle. Vv. 15, 16 repeat vv. 3, 4. *The star* is a king (a David or an Omri) who conquers Moab.

20–25. Three Independent Oracles. Patriotic enthusiasm has forgotten the situation in the days of Balak and has added three brief oracles on other nations. Each is such a brief fragment that no connection can be found for it, and the general obscurity is intensified by the uncertainties of the Hebrew text. V. 25 brings the story to a close, leaving the whole section not only complete in itself, but independent of its context.

(For additional notes, see the introduction preceding ch. 22.)

CHAPTER XXV

1–5. Idolatry. (JE.) The Hebrews are beguiled into idolatry by the Moabite women. They yield to the wiles of the women and are persuaded to share in the sacrifices and worship of the Moabite god, Chemosh. V. 3 states the case differently, mentioning idolatry only, and connecting it with the special baal of Peor. Two different punishments are threatened in vv. 4, 5, representing two different versions of the story.

6–18. The Zeal of Phinehas. (P.) An incident somewhat similar to the foregoing and yet definitely different. Here it is Midianite women and the Midianites that are concerned, and the Hebrews fall into flagrant immorality. The account opens abruptly. A plague is raging which has been sent as a punishment for this immorality. The people are penitent and are assembled before the sacred tent imploring Jehovah to stay the plague. At this point v. 6 takes up the story. *An everlasting priesthood* (v. 13): this connection of the priesthood with Phinehas does not appear again outside this reference, until the late book of Chronicles. This is another example of the way an institution existing in the writer's day is traced back to an ancient origin in a special incident. The introduction of Peor in vv. 16–18 seems to be intended to connect this story of the Midianites with the story of the Moabites in vv. 1–5, but they are clearly two different stories.

CHAPTER XXVI

A Census of the People. The priestly school of writers (this narrative comes from P) was much interested in genealogies and numberings of the people. Conditions toward the close of the Exile and after brought these subjects into a prominence they did not have before. The spirit of this passage differs widely from the feeling before the Exile that there was something wrong about taking a census (cf. 2 Sam. 24[1-17]). The present chapter is very similar to chs. 1 and 3. A second census is taken just before the advance into Canaan, as though to balance the one that had been taken at the beginning of the wilderness period thirty-eight years before. During that time, according to the view of the later writers, all the men of war had died except Caleb and Joshua, and, of course, except Moses himself. A new generation of warriors is now ready to proceed. The grand totals are surprisingly close to those of the first census (v. 51, cf. 1[46]), although some single tribes show considerable differences, particularly Simeon and Manasseh.

1–4. General Directions. Similar to 1[1-19],

but without the plan by which the numbering was actually to be done. The sense of the Hebrew is not clear in vv. 3 and 4. The words set in italics in R.V. do not appear in the original; and a full stop comes after "Moses" in v. 4. The rest of the verse then becomes a subject without a predicate. Evidently, something has dropped out which can be supplied only by conjecture. Better proposals have been offered than the one given in the present R.V., as, for instance, to supply the verb "were" at the close of v. 4. This would lead naturally to v. 5 as follows: "And the children of Israel which came out of the land of Egypt were"—etc.

5–51. The Census Proper. A double formula is followed, the first part giving the names of the families, and the second part giving the enumerations. Most of the clan names are found also in Gen. 46. Vv. 8–11 mark the first of two interruptions of the formula. V. 11 reflects the fact that in the days of the priestly writers there was an important group of *sons of Korah* (cf. Psa. 42–49, titles) which presumably were descendants of some of Korah's sons who had not perished when Korah and his company were destroyed in the fire of Jehovah (16^{35}). The second interruption is found in vv. 30–33. The case of *Zelophehad's daughters* comes in for special treatment in chs. 27 and 36.

52–56. The Distribution of the Land. The passage of the Jordan and the conquest of the land are taken for granted. The death of Moses before the Jordan was crossed is also overlooked; the distribution was carried out by Joshua, not by Moses. V. 54 gives a reasonable direction for adjusting the amounts of land to the numbers in the respective tribes. Vv. 55f. offer an entirely different method, incompatible with the first, unless one assumes either that the lot was miraculously controlled or that the lot referred to geographical location and not to the size of the several allotments.

57–62. A Census of the Levites. Cf. 3^{14-39}. The totals differ by one thousand. The gist of the section is in vv. 57 and 62. What intervenes is really irrelevant, and v. 58 is obviously a different version of v. 57. There is no doubt that the three families of v. 57 have a historic basis. For *Nadab and Abihu*, cf. 3^{4}.

63–65. Conclusion. The story concludes with the significant statement that there was not a man except Caleb and Joshua who had been counted in the first census at Sinai.

CHAPTER XXVII

1–11. Inheritance of Landed Property. The distribution of the land just arranged for left some questions unsettled. For instance, in view of the custom that inheritance goes to male heirs only, what shall be done if a man leave daughters, but no sons? This case is here taken up and carried on to a general law regarding the succession of land ownership (cf. 1 Kings 21^{3} Mic. $2^{1f.}$). Further questions arose even after this law was established, and these are considered in ch. 36 below. *In his own sin* (v. 3)—i.e., the general sin of the people in refusing to proceed at once into Canaan (14^{26-30}). In vv. 5f. the law is carried back to a divine origin, the special case being the occasion of further revelation.

12–23. Moses Makes Preparations for His Death. The preparations are two: (1) He is to go to the top of Mount Nebo (cf. the parallel passage Deut. 32^{48-52}) and see the land which he is not to enter. There are several mountains overlooking the north end of the Dead Sea from the east, any one of which would satisfy the conditions of the hitherto unidentified Nebo. On a clear day one can see the Palestinian ridge from Engedi, touching the west coast of the Dead Sea, to Hermon at the far north (cf. G. A. Smith, *Historical Geography of the Holy Land*, pp. 562f.). For v. 14 cf. on 20^{1-13}. (2) He is to select his successor. Moses is here, as ever, represented as a leader whose first and only thought is for his people, regardless of what happens to himself. Joshua is selected. Moses formally passes on his office of leadership, but he cannot pass on his own supremacy (cf. $12^{7f.}$). From this time forward, according to P, the political headship is subordinate to the high priest, and Joshua is subordinate to Eleazar, through whom, as priest, Jehovah will henceforth reveal his will. *Urim* (v. 21)—usually coupled with the *thummim* (cf. Exod. 28^{30} Lev. 8^{8}). Two small objects bearing these names were used in ascertaining the divine will in special situations. What they were made of, what they looked like, and how they were used, are among the secrets of the past, though there have been many conjectures. The clearest example of their use is in LXX of 1 Sam. 14^{41} (notes). Just when one expects an account of Moses' death, somewhat as Aaron's death is described (20^{28}), the story breaks off. The death of Moses is not reported until the last chapter of Deuteronomy.

CHAPTERS XXVIII, XXIX

Public Offerings. Chs. 28 and 29 (P) give a list of the daily and festival offerings for the congregation, a list which stands alone in its completeness, with the amounts to be offered on each occasion. Lev. 23 is approximately parallel, or this section may be regarded as a supplement to that chapter. A closer but still incomplete parallel may be found in Ezek. 45^{18}–46^{15}. This list belongs to a late stratum of P, perhaps 400–300 B.C. Eight occasions are listed with the offerings for each, as follows: **Ch. 28**—(1) the morning and evening sacrifice for every day, whatever other offerings may be brought by reason of the day being a special one, vv. 3–8; (2) extra offerings for Sabbaths, vv. 9f.; (3) for the new moons (the beginnings of the months), vv. 11–15; (4) for the feast of unleavened bread following the Passover, vv. 16–25; (5) for the feast of first fruits, better known as the feast of weeks, vv. 26–31. **Ch. 29**—(6) for New Year's day (civil year), the seventh month of the religious year, vv. 1–6; (7) for the day of atonement, vv. 7–11; and (8) for the feast of booths which extends through eight days, with the specification for each day, vv. 12–38. Vv. 39f. contain a closing direction that these offerings are to be in addition to those brought by individuals.

With the kind and number of animals specified for the sacrifices, the meal, oil, and wine are added according to the amounts already given in 15^{1-16}. There is a noticeable number of *sevens* in the list. The seventh month stands out among the months as the seventh day stands out among the days of the week. The two great feasts in the first and seventh months continue through seven days each. Sevens of lambs are also frequent. These feasts differ from the pre-exilic feasts in the larger number of sacrifices, especially of animals; in the fixed numbers and amounts, which in earlier times were left largely to the worshiper; and, perhaps most distinctively, in their solemn priestly character (burnt-offerings and sin-offerings which laymen did not share) as contrasted with the happy feasts of earlier times shared by priest and worshipers. One can appreciate the devotion of the post-exilic Jews who reverenced and observed this elaborate and costly ritual, but in the light of the humane and spiritual teachings of the N.T. the fact cannot and need not be hidden that to-day one is appalled at such a program of ruthless slaughter. Was it some of this travail of the dumb creation that prompted Paul to write Rom. 8^{22}?

CHAPTER XXX

1–16. Responsibilities for Vows. (P.) The general principle, which in the remainder of the chapter has special application to women, is stated in vv. 1, 2, namely, that when a man makes a vow he must keep it. V. 16 is a closing summary.

3–5. First Special Case: A young unmarried woman in her father's house. *Vow* and *bond* in this chapter stand for two ideas; the vow involves action and the bond abstinence. One *vows*, for instance, to make an offering of some kind; one *binds* himself to abstain from food or drink or from cutting his hair (as in the case of the Nazirite). The father is the responsible party when he hears the vow made. He can annul it then if he will. If he says nothing it stands; silence gives consent.

6–8, 10–15. Second Special Case: A married woman. The provision here is like the preceding, the only difference being that the husband of the married woman takes the place of the father of the young unmarried woman. *Afflict the soul* (v. 13)—commonly means to fast. The reference here is to all forms of abstinence. V. 15 adds the possibility that the husband may keep silence at first and then repudiate the vow later. In this case the husband must *bear the iniquity* of the broken vow.

9. Third Special Case: Widows and divorced women must take full responsibility. This verse is not well placed and breaks the otherwise close connection of v. 8 with v. 10. The sense and independence of the verse, however, are quite clear.

CHAPTER XXXI

Legislation Regarding the Spoils of War. (P.) The regulations here laid down purport to have arisen out of a special campaign against the Midianites. Even a superficial reading, however, shows the high probability that the account is more ideal than historical. This is seen in the numbers alone; they are round numbers and they are enormous under the circumstances. The Hebrew warriors number 12,000 men—1,000 for each tribe. This army, without the loss of a single man, kills every Midianite warrior as well as the five kings and Balaam. The women and children of the Midianites are taken captive, along with all the cattle, all the flocks, and all the goods. All the Midianite cities and encampments are burned. The spoil includes 675,000 sheep, 72,000 beeves, 61,000 asses, 32,000 virgin women, and gold ornaments to the amount of 16,750 shekels. The primary interest in the distributive legislation is seen in the space devoted to its repeated details (vv. 25–54), in contrast to the silence of the writer on any time or place of march or battle. Second only to the distribution is the matter of purification following contact with the dead (vv. 19–24; see notes on 19^{11-22} Lev. 21^{1-4}). Finally, if the account were literal history, the nation of Midian must have been wiped out, for not only are all women and children captured, but all males are killed (vv. 7-17). Yet they were very much alive at a later time (cf. Judg. 6-8).

A story of this kind is called a *midrash.* The root of the word means "to seek out," and it is applied to stories that seek out deeper meanings and present them for purposes of instruction and edification. Many passages in the O.T. are of this type. While they are not to be regarded as literal histories they are not for that reason misleading when once their method and purpose are recognized. Here, as always, the literary form of the passage is an essential guide to content and interpretation. (See art., *Bible as Literature,* p. 19.)

As a last act of Moses before his death the story seems rather horrible. *Vengeance on Midian*—see ch. 25. *Trumpets*—cf. on 10[9]. What *vessels of the sanctuary* are intended in this connection cannot be determined, but cf. on 10[11-28]. Just as a matter of arithmetic it is interesting to consider how the small number of Hebrews would handle the large number of captives and cattle, to say nothing of the limited space at their disposal on *the plains of Moab* (v. 12). For v. 19 cf. on 19[11-22]. The spoil is divided into two equal parts, one half going to *the men skilled in war*, the other half to *all the congregation* (v. 27). The men of war turn over one five-hundredth of their share to the priests, and the congregation one fiftieth of their share to the Levites. *To make atonement* (v. 50)—in pursuance of the instructions in Ex. 30[11-16], for having taken a census of the army. *Sixteen thousand seven hundred fifty shekels* (v. 52): the shekel was weight and not primarily a measure of money. This amount of gold would weigh about 600 pounds avoirdupois. (See art., *Time, Money,* p. 79.)

CHAPTER XXXII

Settlements East of the Jordan. (P.) The tribes Reuben and Gad prefer to settle east of the Jordan. A brief reference is also made to three families of the half tribe Manasseh (vv. 33, 39-42). The literary analysis of the chapter is not easy, and various analyses have been made. The material represents JE and P, but these strands have now been interwoven by a late priestly writer. The main outline, however, is clear and closely parallel to Deut. 3[12-17]. **1-15.** Reuben and Gad propose to locate east of Jordan. Moses misunderstands their plan and is very angry. The cities named in v. 3 all lie between the Arnon and the Jabbok. Vv. 8-13 repeat the story found in chs. 13f. **16-27.** Reuben and Gad explain their plan and Moses consents to it. **28-32.** The agreement is confirmed with Eleazar the priest. **33.** This would be more appropriately placed after v. 38. It breaks the connection in its present place. **34-38.** All the cities named here lie between the Arnon and the Jabbok. **39-42.** This is a fragment from a summary of the conquest (except the editorial v. 40), very similar in style and manner to Judg. 1.

CHAPTER XXXIII

1-49. A List of the Encampments During the Forty Years in the Wilderness. (P.) As far as the place and journeys are concerned the chapter raises more questions than it answers. It belongs to a late stratum of P, but reflects at least three sources: JE, P, and some source now unknown, for it includes names found in P, but not in JE; also names found in JE, but not in P, as well as names found in this chapter only and neither in JE or P. According to this list, the people start from Rameses and arrive at the plains of Moab. In between these terminal stations forty places of encampment are named. The number can hardly be accidental, yet it is not intended to indicate that the people stopped a year at each place; the list does not adjust itself to such an arrangement. The only notes of time are in v. 3, where the start is placed in the first year, and in v. 38, where Aaron's death is placed in the fortieth year. It would be a great satisfaction if one could take a map and trace these marches one after the other. But a map locating these places does not exist, and it cannot be made. Most of the places are but names, and there is now no way of finding out where they were. It is only natural that the chapter should have raised many discussions, for which the critical commentaries may be consulted. (Cf. also the arts., "Wanderings, Wilderness of" in *Encyclopædia Biblica,* and "Exodus and Journey to Canaan" in Hastings' *Dictionary of the Bible.*)

1. *Journeys*—better, *stages,* as in mg. **2.** *Moses wrote.* It would be natural for the late priestly writer to suppose that Moses wrote an itinerary, and certainly some of the documents from which P drew purported to come from Moses. But, as stated above, even if Moses had written such a list and the list had been preserved, it would be of little if any use, for the various localities mentioned have long disappeared. It seems more probable, however, that this clause is an editorial note, and that v. 1 should continue with the words in v. 2: *and these are their journeys,* etc. **3.** *An high hand*—in a high-handed fashion, boldly. **5-15.** These verses include the route from Egypt to Sinai. On account of the importance of the events at Sinai this may be regarded as the first section of the itinerary, in spite of the fact that the location of Sinai is still under discussion (cf. p. 268, and Ex. 19, note). **16–36.** *Sinai to Kadesh* may be taken as the next section on account of the importance of Kadesh. *Rithmah . . . Hashmonah.* These places and all those named between (vv. 18–29) are mentioned nowhere else, and their locations are quite unknown. **37–49.** Third and last section. The writer's interest is indicated in his interruption of his list at v. 38 in order to say a word about Aaron. The most surprising omission from the list is "the wilderness of Paran," which elsewhere is so prominent in P. So far this omission has not been satisfactorily accounted for.

The material in the book of Numbers is arranged to agree approximately with these verse-divisions, except that Numbers begins with Sinai, and has no material corresponding to vv. 3–15. See introductory note preceding ch. 1. Vv. 16–36 cover 10^{11}–20^{21}; vv. 37–49 cover 20^{22}–22^{1}.

Chapters 33^{50} to 36^{13}: Miscellaneous Laws (P)

Several regulations unrelated to each other, but which are all set forth in anticipation of the day when Israel should be settled in Canaan and these directions would be needed. While some of the material may rest on earlier sources, the present form comes from a late priestly writer.

50–56. Instructions Concerning the Conquest of Canaan. The Hebrews are to make a "clean sweep." The Canaanites, and especially their religion, must be put entirely out of the way. In view of the feeling represented in Deuteronomy and Kings, that the disasters which came upon the nation in the period of the monarchy were due to the insidious influences of Canaanite religion, it is quite natural that a still later writer should regard the extermination of everything Canaanite as the only safety. *Figured stones,* literally *figures;* but that stones were implied is indicated in Lev. 26^{1}. The stones would bear carvings or engravings of religious symbols. *Molten images, high places:* the books of Kings and of the prophets show that down to the time of the Exile Israel was continually yielding to the temptations of Canaanite worship. V. 54 is a parenthesis based on 26^{54}. The Exile was not unnaturally explained by later writers as the fulfillment of punishments of which the Hebrews had been warned before they entered Canaan.

CHAPTER XXXIV

1–15. The Boundaries. We learn here what the late writer thought the Hebrews should have conquered. The boundaries are indicated in the order, south, west, north and east. That they are to some extent ideal is indicated most obviously by the statement that the great sea marked the western border. As a matter of fact, it never did; the Hebrew territory always stopped some distance from the coast. That was Philistine territory. The southern border (vv 3–5) is indicated approximately as a line running from the lower end of the Dead Sea westward through Kadesh-barnea to the brook of Egypt (Wady el-Arish; see p. 54). The western boundary is given in v. 6; the northern boundary in vv. 7–9. This is quite vague on account of the impossibility of identifying the places mentioned. Even the *entering in of Hamath* (cf. 13^{21}) is not absolutely certain. This *Mount Hor* is mentioned here only and is not to be confused with the other mountain of the same name in 20^{22f}. The writer evidently regarded the boundary as running well north of the Sea of Galilee. The eastern boundary (vv. 10–12) runs south from the unidentified *Hazar-enan* (which must have been located some distance north of the Sea of Galilee), well to the east of the Jordan, until it met the southern boundary at some point southeast of the Dead Sea. *Sea of Chinnereth*—another name for the Sea of Galilee. These boundaries inclose the territory which was to be divided among the nine and one half tribes that remained after Reuben, Gad, and the half-tribe of Manasseh had been allotted their territory east of the Jordan.

16–29. The Distribution of the Land. The distribution of the land is to be managed by what might be called a distributing committee composed of the men here named.

CHAPTER XXXV

1–8. Levitical Cities. The Levites are to receive forty-eight cities. Of these, six are to be cities of refuge (see on vv. 9–34). The whole allotment is made by each of the other tribes giving up cities in proportion to the amount of its own size and holdings. After the explicit statements in ch. 18, that the Levites are to receive tithes instead of land, it is surprising to find this assignment of cities. The solution of the contradiction is found here, as elsewhere, in the different documents representing the respective views. An entirely different provision for the Levites is found in Ezek. 48^{8-14}. Both are ideal and were never put into effect. The very nature of the country makes such laying out of the territory impossible. It might be done on a western prairie, but not in Palestine. Furthermore, the arithmetic is impossible. The cities are imagined as squares and the 1,000 cubits extending in opposite directions from two opposite sides leave 2,000 cubits for the resulting sides only when the city itself is reduced to zero. Neither Ezekiel nor this writer is concerned primarily with maps and surveys, but both are intensely interested in the functions and the prerogatives of priests and Levites. In pursuance of this object Ezekiel idealizes the future and this writer idealizes the past, both portrayals being ideal settings for an ideal group in an ideal country.

9–34. Cities of Refuge. The provision of shelter cities, three on each side of the Jordan, leads into a careful statement regarding those who may use them. Their first use is to protect a man until his case can be fairly heard and judged. After that the man's safety and responsibility depend upon the judgment that is pronounced and upon the man's subsequent behavior. From time immemorial it was a custom having all the force of law that when one man killed another the dead man's next of kin should avenge the death by taking the life of the killer. The legislation in this passage provides for a mitigation of this custom by sheltering the killer in case the deed was accidental. (Cf. notes on Deut. 19^1-13^.) *The congregation* (v. 24)—regarded regularly by P as the sacred community, the holy people, whose voice is the voice of God, and whom he thinks of as living together in the "holy city." (Lev. 16^{33} Psa. 89^{5} and cf. Psa. 1^{5}.)

CHAPTER XXXVI

Supplementary Legislation Concerning Daughters. The legislation supplements that in 27^{1-11} (notes). The permission that daughters inherit property carried the possibility that by marriage the inherited property might pass to another tribe. V. 13 is a formal close for the book. The last verse of Leviticus is a similar close, indicating that what preceded belonged to the period at Sinai. This last verse of Numbers refers similarly to the plains of Moab, which would point back to 22^{1}. The similarity of the two closing verses has led to the conjecture that they both may have been added at the time the Pentateuch was divided into its present five parts.

DEUTERONOMY

BY PROFESSOR D. R. SCOTT

INTRODUCTION

Names. Deuteronomy, like other books in the Pentateuch, owes its name to the LXX. In 17^{18} the LXX translators rendered the Hebrew for "a copy of this law" by "this second lawgiving," and gave the name *Deuteronomion* to the whole book. The translation is mistaken, but it truly describes Deuteronomy, which contains the second codification of the Law of Israel, the first being that which is found in Ex. 20^{22}–23^{19}, with 34^{11-27} $13^{3-10,\ 11-13}$, in which the most important part is the code contained in Ex. 21–23, known as the Book of the Covenant. In the Hebrew text Deuteronomy has no title, but it was referred to by its opening words, "These are the words," or simply "The words." In the course of the book other names occur, "this law" (1^{5}), "this book of the law" (29^{21}), "the words of the covenant which," etc. (29^{1}), "this covenant" (5^{3}), "this commandment" (6^{1}), and the particular laws are spoken of as "the statutes and judgments"; but these names, in all probability, do not refer to the whole of Deuteronomy, only to certain parts. In our English version Deuteronomy is called the Fifth Book of Moses.

Contents. As the name rightly implies, Deuteronomy is, or, rather, contains, a code of law, but the most cursory reading shows at once that it is more than this, for it contains not only laws but historical narratives and exhortations, and the laws themselves are rounded off with hortatory motives. The book is presented as Moses' valedictory, consisting of three discourses addressed to Israel in the land of Moab, immediately previous to the crossing of the Jordan. As such it may be briefly summarized as follows:

It opens with an introduction giving the time and place of Moses' valedictory (1^{1-5}); then there follows the command to start from Horeb for the promised land, the appointment of the headsmen to assist Moses in the judicature (1^{6-18}); the command to attack the Amorites, the refusal of the people to make the attack and their subsequent repentance (1^{19-46}). Israel, then, is represented as spending thirty-eight years in aimless wandering in the neighborhood of Edom and then, at the divine command, passing peaceably through Edom (2^{1-8}). No attack was made on Moab or Ammon, but Sihon, king of the Amorites, and Og, king of Bashan, were defeated and their territory was apportioned to the tribes of Reuben and Gad and to the half-tribe of Manasseh, who were enjoined to help their brethren in the capture of the land to the west of the Jordan. Moses intimates that Jehovah will not allow him to cross the Jordan (2^{9}–3^{29}). This historical review is then closed and there follows an urgent appeal for obedience to Jehovah's laws with an insistence on Jehovah's spirituality and absoluteness. If this appeal finds no response, then Israel will be dispersed among the nations, be diminished and worship other gods; but, on Israel's repentance, Jehovah, true to his promises and to his ancient choice, love and wonderful providence, will forgive Israel (4^{1-40}). Here is interposed irrelevantly the appointment of three cities of refuge (4^{41-43}). Then 4^{44-49} contains a fresh heading which may have been the original introduction to Deuteronomy, the previous and longer introduction forming the First Discourse (1^{6}–4^{40}), having been added at a later date.

At ch. 5 begins the Second Discourse of Moses, which continues right on to chs. 26, 28. The first part, chs. 5–11, is hortatory, inculcating the fundamental principles upon which the particular laws are based; the second, chs. 12–26, 28 (in which is interpolated an historical section 9^{7b}–10^{9}) sets forth the particular enactments that are to regulate the daily life of Israel. Moses begins with "the ten words," the basis of the covenant of God at Horeb. Jehovah spake these words, wrote them on the two tables of stone, and "added no more." The people, dismayed by hearing the voice of God and by its accompaniments, the darkness and fire, request Moses to act as mediator between them and God. This request was granted (ch. 5); Moses then gives the charge declaring the God of Israel to be Jehovah alone (or one Jehovah), whom Israel must love, reverence, and obey, and teach the children so to do. This relation between Jehovah and Israel is based upon the deliverance out of Egypt (ch. 6). Israel must have nothing to do with heathenism in any shape or form, for Israel is Jehovah's peculiar possession. Obedience will bring the divine blessing, for Jehovah will continue to fight Israel's battles, and he will firmly establish him in the good land (ch. 7). Israel in the good land must be on his guard, for the wealth of the land will be a temptation to apostasy, and his prosperity may lead to self-righteousness (chs. 8–9^{7a}). Here (9^{7b}) follows an historical section, containing a detailed account of Israel's disobedience at Horeb—the making of the golden calf, the breaking of the two tables of stone, the hewing of new tables and the making of the ark. The section contains notes (10^{6-9}) on Israel's itinerary and the separation of Levi. Then follows 10^{12}–11^{32} with final exhortations which lead up to the detailed exposition of the Code.

At ch. 12 the Code proper, consisting of some seventy separate laws, begins. These laws cover the whole of Israel's life—religion, judicature, war, social and domestic life. No principle of classification can be found in the laws, but roughly the chapters may be divided thus: (1) Chs. 12^{1}–16^{17} contain religious laws which deal with the place of sacrifice, the extermination of every idolatrous person and influence, abstention from the flesh of unclean animals, the regulation of tithes and firstlings, the religious and generous consideration of the poor, and the sacred pilgrimages or feasts. (2) Laws dealing with the judicature, the duties of the king, the revenues and privileges of the Levites and with the position and authority of the prophets in contrast to diviners and augurs (16^{18}–18^{22}). (3) Laws dealing with murder, removing old boundary marks, witnesses, the conduct of war and exemptions, the communal responsibility for untraced murder, marriage with a woman captured in war, the rights of the first-born, rebellious sons and hanged malefactors (chs. 19–21). (4) Chs. 22–25 contain various laws dealing with social and domestic life—such as the laws of lost property, the sparing of the mother bird on the nest, the safeguarding of buildings, the wearing of clothes, the rights of a husband, adultery and seduction, the cleanliness of the camp, the treatment of runaway slaves, religious prostitution, the exaction of interest and pledges, remarriage, the payment of the wage-earner, the treatment of the poor, corporal punishment, Levirate marriage, weights and measures, etc. Ch. 26 contains liturgies for Israel's observance, and the whole Second Discourse ends with an impressive peroration (ch. 28) in which a blessing is pronounced upon obedience and, with much greater detail, a curse upon disobedience.

Chs. 29, 30 (the Third Discourse) are supplementary: in them Moses reminds Israel of God's goodness and warns them of the disaster that apostasy will bring, but—so gracious is Jehovah—even after apostasy repentance will insure restoration, and he concludes by placing before Israel the great choice of obedience that leads to life and disobedience leading to disaster and death. This ends the three discourses.

In a few concluding words Moses then heartens the people, encourages Joshua, who receives his commission, and orders the recital of the law every seven years (31^{1-13}). Then follows the introduction to the so-called Song of Moses and the song itself (31^{16}–32^{43}). Moses finally commends the law and, at the divine command, ascends Nebo to die (32^{44-52}). Ch. 33 is the poem called "the Blessing of Moses," with which should be compared Gen. 49 and in which are set forth the special characteristics and destiny of the tribes of Israel. The book ends with a narrative of the death of Moses (ch. 34).

Religion and Ethics. No synopsis can convey the peculiar distinction of Deuteronomy among the books of the Pentateuch. That distinction lies in its religion and ethics, in its conception of God and its moral ideal. Deuteronomy shares with the rest of the Pentateuch in the emphasis upon the ethical greatness of Israel's God, in the assertion that Jehovah's relation to Israel rests upon Jehovah's own choice, his act of redemption and his providences, and is not merely physical and political, but morally purposive; with the rest of the Pentateuch it emphasizes the spirituality of Jehovah and his greatness compared with heathen gods; and Israel's greatness depends on a true response to this conception.

But Deuteronomy goes beyond all this in its continued emphasis of the love of Jehovah. He is a God who has borne with Israel as a man bears with and chastens his son. He has clung to Israel and set his heart upon him. He is the giver of rain and all the wealth of the land and he fights Israel's battles, but, above and beyond all, he is the lover of Israel that has made his vow of loyalty and will not break it; he has himself chosen Israel to be his own peculiar possession. By his choice, by his great act of redemption, by his unfailing, marvelous providence Jehovah has bound himself to Israel. He has loved Israel and will never let him down nor forsake him.

This God demands from Israel the devotion of his whole heart. It is true that Jehovah is a great and terrible God and men should fear him; but this fear is no pagan dread, but reverence that hears and keeps the divine law. But fear or reverence is not the only demand; Israel has to love God with his heart, soul, and mind. Only once besides in the Pentateuch (Ex. 20^{6}) is man's love to God mentioned, but it runs through Deuteronomy narrative, exhortation and law, and sums up Israel's whole duty to his God Jehovah. It is the intense, whole-hearted love of God that demands a like whole-hearted devotion from man that is at the root of the separatism that is so marked a feature. Jehovah will not tolerate any sharing of his rightful due with other gods; there must be no traffic with heathen abominations, no converse with heathen worshipers; Israel must separate himself from all such by their ruthless extermination; the very platings of the idols were contamination to Israel and abomination to Jehovah. Jehovah has his own ancient ritual (though in Deuteronomy the emphasis is not on the ceremonial side of religion) and Israel must adhere strictly to it; Jehovah's feasts must be religiously and joyously observed, his dues paid and his vows kept, his symbols worn; his servants, priests, and prophets must be honored; but through all he himself as the one God of Israel must be reverenced, obeyed, and loved to the complete exclusion of every other religious and heathen attraction. God is Love, even in his discipline which is meant to prove and test Israel, and Israel must love him with all his heart, soul, mind, and strength.

This love of man for God is no mere emotion or passion; it functions in the love and service of a man for his fellows, and chiefly for those who have suffered and known something of life's hardness, for the widow, for the fatherless, for the stranger within the gates, for the slave, for the fugitive; it spreads itself out into the animal kingdom and takes in the mother bird with her young and the ox as he treads out the corn. This human love, that takes its rise in the heart of God, colors the whole social life of Israel; it aims at justice between man and man, "Justice, justice shalt thou pursue"; the place of justice must not be tainted by corruption and no man must be condemned without fair trial and sufficient evidence; and to justice are added kindliness and humane consideration; the daily wage-earner, the slave, the debtor are to be treated with fairness and generosity; the newly married has to receive military and other exemption; the rights of woman, as mother, wife, and maid are duly acknowledged. The distinction of the particular laws taken as a whole is not in their moral and humane advance upon other codes, though, it is true, there is, in most cases, such advance, but in the spirit of consideration, kindliness, and humanity that is reflected throughout the entire code.

This humaneness may seem to be contradicted by the severity of the penalties enjoined and by the ordination of "the Ban" (*herem*) against the Canaanites and the Israelite worshipers of and traffickers with other gods. But the sternness of the fight against heathenism has to be remembered and the great issue, Israel's very destiny as Jehovah's people, involved; to Israel there was no remedy against things that were an abomination and detestation to Jehovah short of ruthless extermination, and, as for other cases, like filial disobedience or adultery, it must not be forgotten that prisons were non-existent and the evil with its influence and defilement must be destroyed.

The utilitarianism of Deuteronomy's morality may be adversely criticized—the reward of virtue is length of days and prosperity in the land. This feature is referred to in the commentary proper; sufficient to say here that the ethics of Deuteronomy is not merely utilitarian, for the motives of conduct have their value as well as the results. In two respects the religion and ethics of Deuteronomy may be said to be deficient: they lack the missionary spirit and do not look beyond Israel, and there is no immortality. As a whole, the religion and ethics are absolute, there is none of our modern fondness for "extenuating circumstances." "Ye cannot serve God and mammon."

Deuteronomy and Josiah's Reformation. In 2 Kings 22, 23, there is an account of the discovery of a book in the Temple by the priest Hilkiah, which was read by the chancellor to the king. This book is called "the book of the covenant" (2 Kings 23[2]) and is held by modern scholars to be Deuteronomy (in part or whole), the precepts of which brought about the reformation of Josiah. This conclusion is reached partly by a process of elimination: this newly discovered book cannot be the Pentateuch, which would be too long to be read, as the new discovery was, twice in one day; the Book of the Covenant in Ex. 20–23 has no reference to some of the most important points in Josiah's reformation and lacks the severity of denunciation to create so quick and terrible an impression as Second Kings tells us its book of the covenant did—and partly by comparison of the precepts of Deuteronomy with the details of the reformation—"point for point the details (of the latter) are paralleled by injunctions in Deuteronomy, notably the abolition of idolatry, the concentration of worship at a single sanctuary, the abolition of witchcraft and star worship, and the celebration of the Passover"; some of these enactments, it is true, are found in other parts of the Pentateuch, but only in Deuteronomy are they collected into one code or book. Only in one important point is there a difference, the provincial Levites are not called up in the reformation to officiate at the central sanctuary, and it has been suggested that the priests already in residence objected to such increase in their numbers with a corresponding decrease in their incomes. The "book of the covenant" (2 Kings 23²) was found in 621 B.C.; this fixes its composition and thus the composition of Deuteronomy before that date; and, as Amos and Hosea (750–735) do not demand the actual abolition of the local sanctuaries and the centralization of worship—the latter regarded by Deuteronomy as something new —Deuteronomy was probably composed between 735–621; according to some scholars, in Hezekiah's reign, about 700 B.C., according to others, in Manasseh's, about 650 B.C.

Such, in briefest form, has been the generally accepted position: (1) Deuteronomy enacts the centralization of worship which is the predominant principle, and (2) on the basis of Deuteronomy's enactments the reforms of Josiah were carried out. But recently the whole question has been reopened. Adam C. Welch, in *The Code of Deuteronomy*, holds that purity of Jehovah worship, not centralization, is the prevailing aim, and that, on this view, the majority of the laws and religious regulations are more simply and naturally interpreted than on the commonly accepted critical view. "The place that Jehovah chooses to make his name dwell there" is not Jerusalem alone, but any and every sanctuary consecrated to Jehovah and his worship. Only in one place (Deut. 12^{5}) is the demand for the one altar definitely made; this paragraph ($12^{1\text{-}7}$), it is suggested not without reason, is a later insertion. May it be that this is one of the places where, as Jeremiah (8^{8}) says, "the pen of the scribes hath wrought falsely"?

On one point Welch is right: purity of worship (whether it leads to centralization or not) is the main aim of Deuteronomy. The most cursory reader might read the book without grasping the principle of centralization; he could not miss the passionate insistence that Jehovah must be given his own worship and at the place (or places) of his own choice. On Welch's view Deuteronomy would be even earlier than the period assigned by orthodox criticism.

At the other extreme there is the view that regards Deuteronomy not as the program of Josiah's reformation, but as its deposit. This view, associated with the name of Professor Kennett in England and Professor Perry in America, brings the date down to the time of the Exile or even later.

Origin. In studying the origin of Deuteronomy we will consider: (1) Relation to other O.T. codes; (2) Structure; and (3) Authorship.

(1) *Relation.* There are four legal codes in the O.T.: The Book of the Covenant, etc. (JE), the Deuteronomic (D), the Law of Holiness (H) and the Priestly Code (P). By a comparison of D with the laws of JE it is evident that Deuteronomy is dependent upon the latter, covering practically all the ground of Ex. 20^{22}–23^{33}; in certain cases D follows JE almost verbatim (cf. Ex. 23^{19} 34^{26} with Deut. $12^{5,\ 6}$); but the laws of Deuteronomy reveal a more advanced state of society; in its historical parts too Deuteronomy shows the same dependence on the narrative of JE as in the legislation. To the law of holiness (Lev. 17–26) Deuteronomy shows a certain parallelism, but the author shows no knowledge of P as a legislative system and what is true in this respect of the laws is true of the historical parts.

(2) *Structure.* The style, with its flowing rhetoric and oft recurring phrases, and the one religious spirit, tends to give the impression of unity, but a closer examination shows the book to be a compilation. Opinion is varied as to what was the original Deuteronomy. Certainly it included the code, chs. 12–26, 28 ($14^{4\text{-}20}$ is probably a later insertion), with or without its hortatory introduction, chs. 5–11. Chs. 1–4 are usually attributed to a different hand or hands from the body of Deuteronomy, as are also 9^{8}–10^{11} $14^{4\text{-}20}$ (P), chs. 27, 29–34. Some of these passages contain references to the Exile and, though the style is deuteronomic, cannot belong to the original Deuteronomy. There are also signs of editors' hands in archæological notes and itineraries. "The Song of Moses" and "The Blessing of Moses" are from unknown sources. The code itself shows dependence upon JE, but no doubt the laws peculiar to Deuteronomy have their sources in older collections; the rough grouping, the cross divisions and the fact that the form of the laws varies (e.g., in some the second person singular, in others the second person plural) all suggest compilation. (See art., *Legal Literature*, p. 145.)

(3) *Authorship.* Deuteronomy claims Moses as its author, but doubt is thrown at once upon this by the phrase "beyond Jordan," 1^{5} 3^{8} 4^{41}, i.e., the east side of Jordan, which shows that the author was living in western Palestine. Further, by the time the book was written, the Israelites had built houses (22^{8}) and had the boundaries of their properties fixed by "those of old time." To those who hold with the majority of biblical scholars that JE is not the work of Moses, the point requires no further proof. The author, in ascribing the work to Moses, follows a literary method of his day, and one that has been adopted by many of the greatest literary artists, a perfectly defensible

method, for if Moses was not the literary writer of Deuteronomy, he was its spiritual inspiration, and, in that sense, the real author not only of Deuteronomy but of all Israel's law and religion. (See for a more detailed discussion art., *Pentateuch*, pp. 138-9.)

Literature: Driver, *Deuteronomy* (International Critical Commentary); G. A. Smith, *Deuteronomy* (Cambridge Bible); H. W. Robinson, *Deuteronomy* (New Century Bible); Harper, *Deuteronomy* (Expositor's Bible); Welch, *The Code of Deuteronomy;* Johns, *Code of Hammurabi* (referred to in this commentary as *C. H.*); Eiselen, *The Books of the Pentateuch.*

CHAPTER I

1-5. Introduction. Moses undertakes to give instruction and to expound Jehovah's law to *all Israel* in the land of Moab. The writer of the introduction is on the west side of Jordan, Moses and his congregation are depicted on the east side. The verses give the time and place of Moses' discourses.

Wilderness, the usual term for the pasture land east of Moab and for the region of Israel's earlier wanderings; *Arabah*, the usual term for the deep depression running north and south of the Dead Sea; *Suph*, . . . *Di-zahab* are all uncertain; it is impossible to harmonize these places with the fact that Moses addressed Israel on the steppes of Moab. *Horeb*, in E and D = "Sinai" in P and J; vv. 1-5 are composite; v. 3 is in the style of P. For *Sihon* and *Og* (v. 4) see $2^{24f.}$ and $3^{1f.}$

CHAPTERS 1^6 TO 4^{40}: FIRST ADDRESS OF MOSES

1^6–3^{29} is historical material; 4^{1-40} is chiefly hortatory.

6-8. Jehovah's Command to Start From Horeb for the Land. *The Lord our God spake:* his word is the great initial driving power. Advance into the hill country of the Amorites (the usual name in D for the pre-Israelite population of Canaan) and the parts adjacent as far as the Euphrates (the ideal but never the actual limit of Israel's land). This command is given with the assurance that Jehovah is Israel's God and present with them (vv. 6f.), that he will be faithful, having bound himself with an oath and that he is generous to the obedient and greatly daring (v. 8).

When God calls men to great ventures he never fails to equip.

9-18. The Appointment of Judges. *At that time* (i.e., after the charge at Horeb) Moses, finding his burden too heavy, bade the Israelites to appoint headsmen or judges—*wise men, and understanding, and known* according to their tribes. This the people did and Moses set them in graded ranks (vv. 9-15). He demanded scrupulous impartiality, for judgment is really God's (v. 17). The harder cases are to be brought to himself (vv. 16-18).

Notice in the passage the generosity and wisdom of Moses (v. 11), the democratization of the administration of justice (v. 13); above all, the emphasis on the fact that such administration is a service rendered not simply to man but to God (v. 17).

Cf. Ex. 18^{13-26} Num. 11^{14-17}. Notice the absence in D of any reference to Jethro. (For the meaning of the symbols, J, E, P, D, H, used frequently in this commentary, see art. *Pentateuch*, p. 137.)

19-46. The Grapes of Eshkol. The Israelites broke camp at Horeb, passed through *the great and terrible wilderness* and arrived at Kadesh-Barnea. There they are commanded by Moses, on the authority of Jehovah, to take possession of the hill country of the Amorites (vv. 19-21). They demurred and suggested the sending of scouts (v. 22). Moses, accordingly, chose twelve scouts who explored the vale of Eshkol, and brought back a good report of the land and a sample of its fertility. None the less, the people refused to attack; they defied Jehovah, accusing him of taking them out of Egypt for the sinister purpose of destroying them at the hand of the Amorites (vv. 23-27). Apparently, the scouts had returned with alarming reports of the people (cf. Num. $13^{1f.}$, P). Moses attempted to rally the Israelites, assuring them of the help of Jehovah in the attack, and reminding them of God's loving care in the past. All to no purpose. They would not trust Jehovah, their faithful, never-failing Guide. Consequently, Jehovah was wroth and swore that only Caleb and Joshua of that generation would enter the land. The privilege would be their children's. As for the rest, they were sent again into the wilderness (vv. 28-40). At the outburst of Jehovah's wrath the people bitterly repented; they resolved to advance, but were divinely warned through Moses that the opportunity is gone. None the less, in presumption and self-will, they advanced, and were driven back by the Amorites, as bees chasing them. Broken in spirit the people wept before Jehovah, but Jehovah hearkened not (vv. 41-46).

The paragraph forms a very "human document." The Israelites tasted the blessings of the good land and were content, or, at least, had not the courage to do and dare what was necessary for complete possession and satisfaction. They ate the manna, as it were, and were dead as before; the clusters of Eshkol brought no new life and determination. Therein is a parable. Men are content with the grapes of Eshkol, with a few clusters, when the vine on which those clusters grow, might, at the cost of willing sacrifice, be theirs in full possession. A virtue or two with their corresponding happiness are enough. They will not dare the sacrifice that would make the very source of virtue and happiness their own. To refuse that sacrifice is not only to lose the vine of Eshkol, it is to be driven into the wilderness. The refusal of the best, when it is offered, may mean the experience of the worst. Christendom to-day, for instance, is called to possess the nations for Christ. Christendom may be content with the grapes of Eshkol; it may dread the sacrifice demanded. The refusal may mean the loss of the grapes of Eshkol, of already attained Christian virtue and blessing, and not only that, but wandering in the wilderness of strife and war.

Another moral lesson "writ large" in the paragraph is—it is dangerous to trust the report of a few men rather than the proved fidelity of God.

Cf. Num. 13[1f.] (P and JE) noting the differences between it and Deuteronomy which point to a double tradition in the Pentateuch.

CHAPTER II

Edom, Moab, Ammon. Defeat of Sihon, King of Heshbon. After the repulse of Kadesh the Israelites turned back and spent many days (thirty-eight years, v. 14) in circling round Mount Seir. Then Jehovah gave command to go northward and skirt the eastern border of Edom. Attack is forbidden on Edom, from whom Israel must purchase bread and water, for Israel can afford to be independent in view of God's providence these forty years (vv. 1–8). The same clemency is to be shown to Moab and Ammon and for the same reasons (vv. 9–25). Sihon, King of the Amorites, is to be attacked. Before doing so, Moses endeavored to come to terms (vv. 26–29). Sihon was defeated at Jahaz, the population was put to the ban, but the cattle and spoil of the cities were preserved (vv. 30–37). For "the ban" see 7[2].

For "the hardening" of Sihon's heart cf. Pharaoh (Ex. 7[13]). Jehovah's absoluteness does not, however, necessarily preclude free choice.

Vv. 10–12 and 20–23 are antiquarian notes. The *Anakim* (v. 10) were a legendary race of giants, also called *Rephaim, Emim* and *Zamzummim* (v. 20). *Rephaim* = Hebrew "ghosts" or "weak ones"; *Emim* (cf. Gen. 14[5]) perhaps = "the terrors," and *Zamzummim* perhaps = "whisperers." The giants had a ghostly and terrible reputation. *Heshbon* = modern Hesban.

CHAPTER III

1–17. Og, King of the Bashan. Bashan was a district of some extent north and northeast of Gilead, and was famed for its pastures and forests; it held sixty cities. *Og* was a formidable foe, the last of the Rephaim and the final barrier between Israel and the promised land. In his case no attempt was made at conciliation. He and his people were routed and his territory was given to the two and a half tribes (vv. 12f.). Og himself was slain; his immense body was put into a sarcophagus (*bedstead of iron*) and in Rabbah became a curiosity.

The story has points of interest. The ethics of Israel's attack would not be accepted by pacifists to-day. True, Og was a gross materialist and utter heathen. To-day we send missionaries to such; we do not exterminate them. But Og would not strike the Israelites (or even us) as a subject amenable to missionary zeal. And at this time Israel had not a gospel that could convert materialists like Og. Hence a procedure that might be right for Israel, and the only possible one, might not be right for us to-day.

However, Og stood a gigantic and ghostly terror, the impersonation of brute force blocking Israel's path. Israel, in Jehovah's strength, faced him and defeated him, with the result that Israel goes forward on his destined career, while this piece of gross materialism was laid in his iron coffin to be a ghostly curiosity. But this was not in Israel's history the end of Og. Time and again the victory over him was remembered, and Og actually took his place in the spiritual songs of Israel (Psa. 135[11] 136[20]). The great and ghostly terror became a great and spiritual inspiration. Before a man can enter the promised land there may be some gigantic evil to be met—there is always the elusive giant Self—but once defeated the evil may become an unfailing source of inspiration.

V. 9 is an archæological note; vv. 14–17, based on Num. 32[41], repeat vv. 12f.; *Havvoth* (v. 14), perhaps tent villages; cf. Judg. 10[4] 1 Chr. 2[22].

18–22. Instructions to the Two and a Half Tribes and Joshua. After the conquest of Og and partition of territory east of Jordan, Moses charged the two and a half tribes to send their warriors over Jordan to help their brethren, leaving their families and the cattle in the apportioned territory (vv. 18–20); at the same time he charged Joshua, bidding him be courageous, for Jehovah fighteth for Israel (vv. 21, 22).

Cf. Num. 32[16-32]. To the charge to Joshua *at that time* the Pentateuch has no parallel.

23–29. The Prayer of Moses and Its Re-

jection. At that time Moses entreated Jehovah to complete his kindness by allowing him to cross the Jordan and view the whole land (vv. 23–25). Angry with him on Israel's account, Jehovah refused and directed him to ascend the headland of Pisgah and from thence view the land (vv. 26f.). He was also to encourage Joshua (v. 28).

Notice the pathos in the prayer: it begins *O Lord God, thou hast begun* but not fulfilled. How true of life! the great game never played out, the great art never perfected, the task never complete. Failure is a mark of all experience, but a necessity for progress and life itself. "The lamp surcharged with oil chokes." "A man's reach should exceed his grasp." Always is it "the broken arc," never "the perfect round"; "the best is [always] yet to be."

Notice further Moses' heroism. In the greatness of Jehovah he places his confidence; refused, he bears no grudge; he is content with his vision and transfers his privilege to Joshua. So long as Israel's destiny is realized, that is to him everything. Cf. Danton's wish—"Let me be accursed so long as France is saved." V. 29 closes the retrospect.

CHAPTER IV

Vv. 1–40 give the second or hortatory part of Moses' first discourse.

1–8. Commands to Keep the Laws. Moses commands obedience to the statutes and judgments. This will insure life, entrance into and possession of the land. The laws are not to be tampered with in the interests of human weakness. The experience at *Baalpeor* (i.e., the place sacred to the local god of Peor) was a warning. Those who turned to heathenism are dead; those who resolutely clung to Jehovah are alive. If Israel will only be obedient, then his wisdom will be proved and his religion and morality will excite the admiration of surrounding nations.

This prophecy of Israel's future greatness has been literally fulfilled, signally among enlightened Greeks after the conquest of Asia Minor by Alexander the Great, and to-day it is the religion and morality of Israel that claim our interest. Israel's living God, nigh unto him (v. 7), hearing and answering prayer, with his law and its religious sanctions, are Israel's abiding distinction. After all, these two, religion and morality, are the strength of every civilization.

9–24. Against Idolatry. Israel must zealously keep in mind the spiritual worship of Jehovah and teach this worship to coming generations. Let the memory of *Horeb* abide. No form was then seen, only a voice was heard. The revelation was spiritual, demanding a spiritual response. Let Israel take heed not to corrupt this spirituality and themselves by any materialistic representation of Jehovah; let Israel keep clear of all heathenish practices —such as the worship of graven images and the host of heaven (vv. 9–19). Nature worship and materialism in every form must be avoided. Israel belongs to Jehovah, who brought him out of the iron furnace (v. 20), was angry with Moses on Israel's account (v. 21) and forbade his entrance into Canaan; so must Israel keep spiritual to insure the entrance denied to Moses; Israel must be strictly faithful to the covenant (v. 23), cleave solely and absolutely to Jehovah, for he is a jealous God (v. 24).

Jehovah is spirit. He speaks to the mind and conscience and demands a religion of the spirit. He has nothing to do with paganism or materialism. Worship of the Creator, not of the creature, is Jehovah's demand.

Statutes and judgments (v. 1): the distinction may be between positive institutions and legal decisions which became precedents, what we call "statute law" and "case law," or between religious ordinances and civil enactments; *covenant* (v. 13): generally any agreement guaranteeing friendly relations between nations and individuals, first used of Jehovah's relation to Israel in JE (Ex. 19^5 $24^{7f.}$); *which the Lord . . . all nations* (v. 19): an interesting statement; Jehovah is the God of Israel and the gods of the nations are appointed by him —an attempt to reconcile the truth of Jehovah as one god with the existence of other gods. On worship of *host of heaven* see 17^3, note.

25–40. Threat of Exile with Promise of Forgiveness on Repentance. *The Uniqueness of God.* The day will come when Israel will find spiritual religion stale and its first freshness faded; he will then turn to idolatry. That day will be Israel's downfall. Diminished, he will be driven into exile and to the worship of senseless gods. To Israel repentant Jehovah will be forgiving; he will not let Israel down; he will remember the old covenant (vv. 25–31). For assurance let Israel turn to the past. No god ever acted like Jehovah. He chose Israel, disciplined him to hear the divine voice and see the divine wonders. He led Israel out of Egypt, and out of love for their fathers has brought the children to the promised land. No god is like Jehovah with his personal love for Israel—and so in the day of apostasy and disaster (this is the implicit argument) he will be able to forgive and restore. But (with a return to the keynote in v. 1) keep the statutes and judgments (vv. 32–40).

41–43. Appointment of Three Cities of

Refuge on East of Jordan. In 19¹⁻¹³ six cities appear to be appointed for the first time; these verses (4⁴¹⁻⁴³) may be a later addition. Cf. Num. 35⁹⁻²⁴ (P) and Josh. 20¹ᶠ. In earlier times asylum was granted at any and every altar (Ex. 21¹²⁻¹⁴).

44–49. Superscription to the Deuteronomic Code. This seems superfluous in view of 1⁶–4⁴⁰. It may, therefore, be a later addition, or 1⁶–4⁴⁰ may be the later addition. Driver accepts *both* as original parts of Deuteronomy.

CHAPTERS 5 TO 26, 28: SECOND ADDRESS OF MOSES

The theme of this long second address of Moses is the exposition of the Law. It comprises two parts: (1) a hortatory section (chs. 5–11); and (2) the code of special laws (chs. 12–26, 28).

CHAPTER V

1–21. The Ten Words. Moses begins his delivery of the Deuteronomic Law by a reference to the covenant made at Horeb where all his hearers were present. The covenant consists, *according to Deuteronomy*, of the giving of the ten words which Israel, on his part, has to obey. The following are the main characteristics of the rendering in Deuteronomy of "the ten words"—(1) hortatory additions, (2) more definite and emphatic statement, (3) raising of the wife's status, (4) humanitarian motive for the observance of the Sabbath, (5) additional motives for honoring parents, (6) the addition of "ox," "ass," "manservant" and "woman servant" to the list of Ex. 20¹⁰. The relation of the two editions (Ex. 20¹ᶠ· and Deuteronomy's) to each other and to other words given at Horeb is difficult. It is by no means certain that Ex. 20¹ᶠ· is the earlier, for it contains Deuteronomic expressions and one sentence (vv. 5b 6) reflects P. Notice too that in Ex. 20 the giving of the ten words from Sinai-Horeb is not connected with a covenant, which is connected in Ex. 24³⁻⁸ with other words; again Exodus connects the ten words with other words (Ex. 20²²ᶠ· 21f.) while Deuteronomy says that only the ten words were spoken from Horeb. It is probable that "the ten words" of Deuteronomy and of Exodus are derived from a still more primitive and briefer code. To the present writer there seems no insuperable difficulty in the opinion that the morality of Israel with a code goes back to Moses himself. How this came to Moses is the secret of his spirit. In him there is the inexplicable element that marks all genius, not least, genius of the religious order. Even if we could construct Moses out of his past, there would still be a residuum outside the sphere of historical influences—a residuum, which, in the last resort, can only be attributed to the living God. Consult further Ex. 20f. in this commentary and article "Decalogue" in any Bible Dictionary. A few brief notes are here appended.

6. The Preface. The tenderness is characteristic of Deuteronomy. *I am the Lord thy God.* The basing of Israel's duty on a great redemption is characteristic of O.T. religion—grace comes before law.

7. First Commandment. No rival god, real or unreal, to Jehovah is permitted.

8. Second Commandment. Against images. Such materializing denies the spirituality of Jehovah and degrades worship.

11. Third Commandment. Prohibition against the use of Jehovah's name for any unworthy purpose (e.g., some superstitious practice). It is a demand for reverence; not only that, but for truth and reality. The man from whose lips the name of God falls carelessly and frequently will lose hold of truth and reality. Cf. the N.T. saying, "Not everyone that saith Lord, Lord."

12–15. Fourth Commandment. Cf. Exodus and notice the more humane spirit of Deuteronomy. The Sabbath is a divine institution made in the interests of man, that man may remember God not only on the Sabbath but always.

16. Fifth Commandment. As in Exodus, but two additions: (1) *as the Lord thy God commanded thee* and (2) *that it may be well with thee*, a Deuteronomic phrase impressing Deuteronomy's doctrine of providence.

17–20. Sixth, Seventh, Eighth and Ninth Commandments. As in Exodus; for the word, "false" (Ex. 20¹⁶) Deuteronomy (Hebrew) has a broader term—"groundless."

21. Tenth Commandment. This passes from the sphere of action to that of thought and feeling. Paul (Rom. 7⁷) selects this as exhibiting the spirit of the whole Law. Notice two differences from Ex. 20¹⁷: (1) the *wife* placed by herself; cf. Deut. 21¹⁰ᶠ· 22¹³ᶠ· 24¹ᶠ· for higher status of woman; (2) Deuteronomy adds *his field* (v. 21).

22–33. Request for a Mediator. After the giving of "the ten words" Jehovah *added no more* (contrast Ex.), but wrote them on the two tables of stone and handed them to Moses (v. 22). The overawed people then requested Moses to act as mediator (vv. 23–27). The request is willingly granted (vv. 28b–30). As for Moses, he is bidden to receive from Jehovah instruction for the people (v. 31). The paragraph closes with an exhortation in Deuteronomic phraseology to obey the new charge (vv. 32f.).

The request gives expression to the permanent need in national life of men specially gifted to interpret to their fellows the contemporaneous mind and will of God (*as the Lord your God hath commanded you* (v. 32), i.e., through Moses who is now about to give the new instruction to the people).

CHAPTER VI

1–3. The Benefits of Obedience. Moses states that he has now in Moab to fulfill the charge given in Horeb to expound the statutes and judgments. Obedience to these will result in reverence for Jehovah, length of days, and prosperity in the land which Jehovah has promised to give (cf. LXX).

4–9. The Fundamental Creed and the Fundamental Duty. This paragraph is the Jewish "Shema," so called from the first word in the Hebrew—*Hear*. With 11[13-21] and Num. 15[37-41] it is the first scripture taught to Jewish children and has for centuries been the confession of faith among Jews. Later law demanded its recital every day, morning and evening. *Jehovah our God is one Jehovah.* The four possible renderings given by R.V. and R.V. mg. can be resolved into two: (1) Jehovah our God is one and indivisible—there are not many Jehovahs with different characteristics and localities; and (2) Jehovah is Israel's only God. Taken together the two are almost, if not quite, a declaration of monotheism.

This God Israel is charged to love with all his mind and soul (a Deuteronomic expression) and with all his strength. The one God demands the whole man. This primary and complete duty (outside Deuteronomy and Deuteronomic passages only referred to once in the Pentateuch, Ex. 20[6]) is set forth with peculiar emphasis in Deuteronomy in all its prosaic details, in its pragmatic teaching of history; in all its exhortations there runs the one echoing refrain, the one haunting *motif*—love of God. These words then in vv. 4f. are to be engraven on Israel's memory, impressed on the imagination of his children; they are to be the subject of conversation at home and abroad, at the break and the close of the day; to be a sign upon the hand and for frontlets between the eyes, to be inscribed on the doorposts of the house and on the gates of the village; in a word, these sublime words are to become the daily inspiration and the daily practice of Israel (vv. 6–9).

Our Lord made these words (v. 5) "the first commandment of all." And the great religious and national ideal which they express is still the necessity and the guarantee of a nation's true prosperity. It can become an effective national ideal only through individual acceptance (notice the "thou" and "thy" in v. 2) and the individual can make this ideal only through the grace of God (see 1 Jn. 4[19]). On v. 8 consult article "Phylacteries" in Bible Dictionary.

10–19. The Testing Time. When Israel has entered into the enjoyment of a civilization to which he has not contributed (vv. 10f.), then let Israel beware of forgetting his Deliverer (vv. 12f.), of imagining that the new wealth is due to the gods of the land and of serving them; Jehovah is the real giver of it all and he is a jealous God (v. 15). Only by steadfast obedience will Israel prosper (vv. 16–19).

How necessary the warning still is for the individual and nation! Civilization believes so easily that it has created itself—its knowledge, art, literature, its politics and all its wealth—forgetting that it is God that hath made us and not we ourselves nor any other forces less than God. The remembrance that the creative power and redemptive grace are the sources of all would save nations and individuals from the danger and disaster of prosperity.

Vv. 16f. are probably an addition and scarcely relevant here.

20–25. The Origin and Meaning of Law. When future generations ask the meaning of Israel's law, the answer is, Jehovah redeemed us unto life, and to complete this redemption and to maintain the life, he gave law in obedience to which Israel will gain and keep the righteousness that is life.

The purpose of law, then, is to preserve the life created by redeeming grace. Law is founded upon grace. The Christian law of service rests upon grace. "We love because he first loved us." Further, the act of grace can be kept permanent and alive only by man's continued obedience to the principle of grace.

CHAPTER VII

1–11. No Compromise with Heathenism. Israel must have no private or public dealings with the heathen nations which Jehovah will deliver into his hand. These must be put to the ban (vv. 1–5), for Israel is a holy people, consecrated to Jehovah who chose Israel for his sacred possession, not because of Israel's greatness; indeed, Israel was least among the nations. All Jehovah's wonderful deeds and gracious dealing are due to his love and faithfulness alone (vv. 6–8); Jehovah is everlastingly loyal to the loving and obedient, and requites his enemies. Let Israel know this—feel the force of it—and be obedient (vv. 9–11).

Such enumeration of the nations as in v. 1 is common in JE and Deuteronomic writers—

the enumeration is rhetorical; for *pillars and Asherim* (v. 5) see 12^{3}, note.

12–26. The Rewards of Obedience. As a reward for obedience Jehovah will be steadfast in his loving-kindness. Every blessing will come to Israel, even health, while the diseases of Egypt will be reserved for other nations. Israel will devour his enemies and must have no pity (vv. 12–16). If Israel should think that the nations are too strong, let him remember that the great and terrible God is still with him. Jehovah will gradually and providentially drive out the nations and their kings (vv. 17–24.) In the hour of victory burn the heathen gods; let their gold and silver be an abomination and detestable, mere contact with which or even coveting would pollute Israel (vv. 25f.).

The idea of material prosperity as the reward for faithfulness is common to the O.T. And, no doubt, a righteous and God-fearing people means a healthy and prosperous people. On the other hand, immorality and irreligion are frequently among the factors of a prosperous population. With the individual the same law holds, but again with many exceptions. The best rewards of righteousness, however, are not in the market place, but in the soul. And to nations and individuals alike, it will be found, when life is viewed profoundly and broadly, that God never fails to pay his workmen in peace and joy.

Abomination (v. 25), that which is ritually and religiously unlawful and abhorrent; *detest* (v. 26): cf. noun, "detested thing," practically the same meaning as abomination; *devoted thing* = banned; cf. Josh. 7^{1} and article "Ban" in Bible Dictionary.

CHAPTER VIII

A Call to the Remembrance of God's Providence With Its Obligations. Israel is bidden to keep the whole of the Deuteronomic Law, nor should he forget any of the discipline of the wilderness which had as its purpose the humbling of Israel, i.e., the creating of the feeling of dependence. In particular, the manna had this purpose, teaching Israel his complete dependence upon God's providence, whether ordinary or extraordinary; the chastenings too were signs, not of God's hostility but of his fatherly providence (vv. 1–6); the latter statement is remarkable in Deuteronomy, which regards physical suffering as a punishment for sin.

This discipline, gracious and generous, with its consequent duties, needs to be specially remembered in view of the nature of the land which Jehovah is about to give to his people. Its fertility, its wealth of minerals, its easily acquired commodities and luxuries—the whole generosity of the gifts calls for exceptional care against pride, self-sufficiency and forgetfulness of the providential and redemptive past (vv. 7–16). The temptation will be great and subtle to believe and say, "My power and the might of my hand hath gotten me this wealth" —to forget God and follow after other gods. Should Israel forget God as the Giver of all, Israel will perish like the dispossessed peoples (vv. 17–20).

This reminder of Moses becomes more and more urgent with the advance of civilization. The very generosity of God in the growing wealth of civilization may have its end defeated by blindness of heart.

Brooks (v. 7) = wadys either with only a winter flow or a continual stream; *fountains* (v. 7) = perennial springs; *depths* (or *springs*, v. 7) = outbursts of water from underground; *oil-olives* (or *olive trees*, v. 8) = cultivated olives; *iron* (v. 9) = basalt or iron proper; *brass* (or *copper*, v. 9) = bronze mixed with tin, or pure bronze.

CHAPTER IX

1–7. Warning Against Self-righteousness. Israel is about to dispossess nations mightier than himself. Jehovah is with him and victory is sure and summary. Let not Israel be deluded into believing that Jehovah is giving this signal victory because of any exceptional righteousness of Israel. From the time Israel left Egypt, he has been stiff-necked and intractable; Jehovah is dispossessing the nations for their wickedness and in simple fidelity to his promises.

That the gracious dealings of God do not rest on man's merit is a truth emphasized by the N.T. Man can never be out of God's debt; all is due to God's grace alone.

8–29. Proof From the Past, and Especially From the Incident of the Golden Calf, of Israel's Obduracy, Which, Had Not Moses Interceded, Would Have Brought National Destruction. (Continued in 10$^{1-11}$.) This retrospect, in general style similar to chs. 1–3 and like it based on JE (Ex. 32, 34, etc.), is a composite, historical paragraph breaking in upon Moses' exhortation.

Israel is proved to be a stiff-necked people by his behavior at Horeb (v. 8), where, while Moses was on the mount receiving the tables of stone, he made a golden calf, thus arousing the wrath of Jehovah (vv. 9–14). Moses thereon broke the tables, fasted forty days and forty nights, in fear of Jehovah's wrath (vv. 15–19a). At Moses' intercession Jehovah pardoned both Aaron and the people, and Moses destroyed the golden calf (vv. 19b–21). Nor was Horeb the only place where the obdurate temper was shown (vv. 22–24). Moses intercedes for the people (vv. 25–29).

CHAPTER X

1–11. (See under 9^8-29.) Moses' intercession prevailed, for God gave commandment to hew out two other tables, and wrote again the ten words thereon, which Moses placed in the ark which he had been ordered to make (vv. 1–5). A fragment of an itinerary follows with mention of the death of Aaron (vv. 6f.). The separation of the tribe of Levi to the priesthood is mentioned (vv. 8f.). A renewed statement is given of Moses' intercession (probably going back to 9^26-29) on the mount with the command to lead the people forward (vv. 10f.). Consult articles "Ark" and "Levi" in Bible Dictionary.

12–22. Exhortation to Reverence and Love the Great and Righteous God. In conclusion, let Israel respond to Jehovah's demand—no complicated task—for what he demands is love, reverence, and practical obedience. He can demand these, for though Lord of all, he chose, of his own free love, the patriarchs and their seed for the purpose of revealing himself to them (vv. 12–15). Let Israel then circumcise his heart—become receptive—and cease from his obduracy. Hardness of heart and self-will are vain in face of the sovereignty and absolute righteousness of Jehovah, whose justice and love are shown impartially. Let Israel imitate Jehovah; love the sojourner as Jehovah loved Israel, when he was a sojourner in a strange land (vv. 16–19). Reverence, then, serve and cleave to Jehovah. Let him be the object of thy praise, for—to take a particular instance—out of seventy persons he has made thee a great nation (vv. 20–22).

CHAPTER XI

1–9. An Appeal to Experience. Let Israel, then, love and obey Jehovah. His greatness and his grace are not hearsay, nor are they based on any outward authority: they themselves experienced the discipline in the great and terrible acts of Jehovah—in the deliverance from Egypt, in the long tramp in the wilderness, in the tragedies of Dathan and Abiram. With that discipline, his own, let Israel guard the whole charge; on that depend his life and prosperity, as Israel knows for himself.

10–25. A Warning. Canaan is not like Egypt where hard industry could keep the land watered and fertile; Canaan is a land of hills and valleys, dependent for water upon the rain of heaven, a land which is under the continuous personal supervision of Jehovah and always dependent upon his consideration (vv. 10–12). Therefore in Canaan let Israel sedulously keep Jehovah's commandments and he will give the rain upon which depends the whole fertility of the country (vv. 13–15). The generosity of Jehovah, however, may be a possible source of temptation, leading Israel to believe that the fertility is due to the Baalim (the local gods) and to worship these, so arousing Jehovah's wrath and bringing disaster (vv. 16f.). Therefore let Israel remember Jehovah's commandments (vv. 18–21; cf. ch. 6). Obedience will lead to complete possession of Canaan (vv. 22–25).

Again an appeal to materialistic motives! Let it be remembered, however, that the appeal is to the nation as a whole, and that perhaps the most impressive way to present the worth of goodness to a nation is to emphasize its concrete and material results. After all, there is truth in the saying, that sound morality and pure religion are good economics. "Seek ye first his kingdom and his righteousness; and all these things shall be added unto you," said Jesus; the position of Deuteronomy is very similar: reverence and love Jehovah for what he is; put his laws into daily practice and it shall be well with thee.

Sowedst thy seed (v. 10). Only here are we told that the Hebrews practiced agriculture in Egypt. *Wateredst it with thy foot . . . herbs* (v. 10)—the meaning is uncertain; most likely it refers to the guiding with the foot of water through narrow channels, or it may refer to some machine worked by the foot, perhaps the *shaduf*, which carried water in a bucket from the river bed, or to water wheels—in any case to some method that might be used in Canaan for a small patch or garden of herbs, but would be impossible for general irrigation. *The former rain* and *the latter rain* (v. 14)—the former that breaks up the dry, sun-burned ground continues through winter till the latter rain, so important for the ripening of the crop, comes in April and May.

26–28. The Summing up of the Discourse. (Chs. 5–11; see introductory paragraph preceding ch. 5.) Obedience brings blessings; disobedience a curse (cf. 30^1, 15, 19).

29. An Outward Ceremony. This ceremony gives a certain sanction to the blessing and the curse (cf. 27^11-13). *Gerizim* lies to the south, i.e., on the right hand according to Semitic orientation, and regarded as the auspicious quarter; *Ebal* on the north, or left hand, the inauspicious quarter.

30. A Geographical Addition. (Cf. 1^2). *The way of the going down of the sun*, supposed to be the great road running north and south through western Palestine; *the Arabah* (cf. 1¹), not relevant here; *Gilgal*—stone circle; there was more than one place of this name, probably a Gilgal near Shechem is meant; *oaks of Moreh*—LXX has "the oak of the revealer" (cf. Gen. 12⁶).

31, 32. A transition to the actual code (chs. 12–16, 28).

Chapters 12 to 26, 28: The Special Code

These chapters form the second part of Moses' second and main discourse (chs. 5–26, 28; see introductory paragraph preceding ch. 5). They give the practical exposition promised in 1⁵, particularize the various statutes and judgments (seventy in all) by which Israel has to regulate his daily life and which form a legal code. But the code is not a mere code, for all through it the same motives and exhortations are urged that we have found in preceding chapters. In this feature the Deuteronomic Code distinguishes itself from the book of the covenant (Ex. 21–23). The arrangement of the laws is far from precise and consistent, but they fall roughly and with interruptions and overlappings into four main divisions of unequal length:

1. Laws of Sacred Institutions and Worship, 12¹–16¹⁷.
2. Laws of Office-bearers, Judges, King, Prophet, 16¹⁸–18²².
3. Laws Relating to Crime, War, Property, Evidence, 19¹–21⁹.
4. Laws Miscellaneous—Civil, Military and Domestic, 21¹⁰–25¹⁶. (25¹⁷⁻¹⁹, on Amalek.)

Hortatory Conclusion, ch. 26.

Peroration, ch. 28.

(Ch. 27 is an interruption and later addition.)

Chapters 12¹ to 16¹⁷: Laws of Sacred Institutions and Worship

CHAPTER XII

1. The Title. *Statutes and judgments*, as already stated (5¹), may be equivalent to statute law and case law, or *statutes* may refer to decrees dealing with religion and its institutions and *judgments* to civil and criminal laws. There is no reference to commandment or charge (Hebrew *mizwah*), perhaps because this is supposed to have been given in chs. 5–11.

2–7. Law of the One Altar. First Pronouncement. In Canaan the Israelites must destroy all the sacred places upon the hills and beneath spreading trees and not worship in these places and in heathen-wise (vv. 2–4). The places of sacrifice are to be cast down, the obelisks to be broken, the Asherim, or sacred poles, to be burned, the graven images hewn into pieces; every trace of all this idolatry is to be destroyed (v. 4 appears an addition disconnecting v. 3 from v. 5). But to the one place that Jehovah shall choose out of all the tribes shall the Israelites bring all their offerings and there shall they eat with all their household before Jehovah and rejoice in all their enterprises (vv. 5–7).

Pillars, or obelisks (v. 3), natural or artificial bowlders in which the Deity was supposed to reside; *Asherim* (v. 3), wooden masts representing the sacred tree, also the abode of the Deity; *heave offering* (v. 6)—what is lifted from the common mass, perhaps "personal contribution."

8–12. Second Pronouncement. The present irregular manner may be tolerated in Moab, for the Israelites have not come to the settled state which Jehovah intends to give (vv. 8f.). When they have come, they shall bring all their offerings to the sanctuary that Jehovah shall choose and they shall rejoice with all their house and the landless Levite (vv. 10–12).

13–19. Third Pronouncement. Practically the same as the two previous (vv. 15f. anticipate vv. 20–25 and disturb the connection).

20–28. A Relaxation in View of the New Law. When Jehovah has enlarged Israel's border in Canaan and when an Israelite living at an inconvenient distance from the One Altar desires to make a feast of flesh, he may kill of his stock, of the ritually clean or unclean, eat and rejoice, just as he would eat of game such as the gazelle or hart (vv. 20–22). But the blood must not be taken, it must be poured upon the ground for the Israelite's own sake, i.e., to prevent his ritual pollution (vv. 23–25). All holy sacrifice, however, must be at the One Altar (vv. 26f.). Keep this whole law (v. 28).

In early Israel all slaughter was sacrificial, but if there was only one place of legitimate sacrifice, an Israelite who desired to make a feast might be in a difficulty. So domestic animals were placed on the same level as wild animals taken in the hunt, which were not regarded as akin to man, and therefore need not be eaten sacramentally. So this relaxation (vv. 20f.) would prevent religion from becoming too burdensome and from interfering unnecessarily with social enjoyment. The blood was identified with the life, as such it belonged to the Deity, was inviolably sacrosanct; so, however keen an Israelite might be for the blood (see 1 Sam. 14³²), he must sternly restrain his desire.

29–31. Syncretism Forbidden. Neither curiosity nor self-interested desire must lead the Israelites in Canaan to traffic with Canaanitish gods and ritual. All such is intolerable to

Jehovah, for (to take an extreme instance) even children are sacrificed.

Syncretism in religion is always a wrong method, for truth is never attained by indiscriminate comprehension but by fidelity to fundamental and proved principles. The prevalent Semitic idea was that not only must the gods of an invaded land be propitiated but also that the local ritual or mishpat must be adopted (cf. 1 Sam. 26^{19} 2 Kings $17^{25f.}$). For child sacrifice (v. 31) see 18^{10}.

32. 13^{1} in Hebrew. See 13^{1-5}.

CHAPTER XIII

1–5. Miracle no Test of Prophetic Truth. (See also 12^{32}.) No prophet or dreamer whose word, even though it be attested by a marvel, implies defection from Jehovah is to be listened to (vv. 1–3a). By such a prophet Jehovah is actually testing the people's love. Cling to Jehovah (vv. 3b, 4). Such a prophet shall be put to death for his apostate speech against the Redeemer and for his attempted seduction of Israel. Exterminate, then, the evil. (Cf. Mt. 16^{3} Mk. $8^{11f.}$ Jn. 7^{17}.) *Thou shalt put away* (v. 5)—a formula peculiar to Deuteronomy, laying upon the community the duty of clearing itself from all complicity with the specified evil.

6–11. Against Heathenish Enticements from Kith and Kin. Should one of one's own kith and kin secretly entice to idolatry, such an one shall be ruthlessly stoned. The witness to the sin shall cast the first stone, then the community, for such an one is trying to seduce Israel from Jehovah the Redeemer. The sentence will act as a deterrent to all Israel. (Cf. "He that loveth father or mother," Mt. 10^{37}.)

12–18. A Short Way with the Corrupters of Society. A problem arises: certain base people are said to be corrupting a city. Let the matter be carefully sifted. If the charge is true, then the whole community is put to the ban in its completest form—an instance of Deuteronomy's policy of no compromise with evil. Leniency was too great a moral risk. *Base fellows*—sons of Belial—worthless, immoral men (cf. 1 Sam. 2^{12}, A.V.)

CHAPTER XIV

1, 2. Against Heathenish Mourning. Sons of Jehovah are the Israelites; let them not gash their bodies or set baldness between their eyes. Israel is holy, Jehovah's special possession. With v. 2 cf. 7^{6}; for these rites see Isa. 22^{12} Amos 8^{10} Jer. 16^{6}.

3–20. Clean and Unclean Foods. Cf. Lev. 11^{2-23} (P); 20^{25} (H); not in JE. There is no reference to this Law in the reforms of Josiah. V. 21a: cf. Ex. 22^{31} (E) and Lev. $17^{15f.}$ (H). V. 21b: cf. Ex. 23^{19b} (E) and Ex. 34^{26b} J).

22–29. Concerning Tithes. Tithes (specified) are to be taken and eaten in Jehovah's sanctuary. Such a practice will lead to reverence of the Giver of all (vv. 22f.). If an Israelite be too far from the sanctuary, he may turn the tithes into money, buy at the sanctuary and feast with his household and the Levite (vv. 24–27). Every third year, however, all the tithe is to be retained for the Levite and the poor (vv. 28f.); i.e., the tithe is to be "secularized" into a "poor rate." Not in JE; in Num. 18^{21-32} (P) the law is quite different. The differences are due to the fact that the laws come from different periods, reflecting different historical and social backgrounds. (For similar differences in laws dealing with other subjects, see art., *Pentateuch*, p. 139.)

CHAPTER XV

1–11. The Year of Release; Borrowing and Lending. Every seventh year all creditors shall religiously cancel their loans to fellow Israelites, but not to foreigners. But if Israel is faithful, there will be no poor: Israel will lend, not borrow (vv. 1–6). Nor must an Israelite take advantage of the approach of this year and refuse loans to the poor, who will always be with them (vv. 7–11).

The contradiction is understandable in view of Deuteronomy's two ideals: (1) of loyalty to Jehovah with its inevitable prosperity, and (2) of philanthropy to the poor. The law applies to charitable loans (and their whole remission is intended) and not to interest, for this class of loan yielded no interest. Not in the other O.T. codes.

Borrowing and lending is, no doubt, a precarious practice. The generous lender is often deceived and the generous borrower has, sometimes, no need of a specially proclaimed year of release. Polonius' advice is not a bad rule. "Neither a borrower nor a lender be; for loan oft loses both itself and friend, and borrowing dulls the edge of husbandry," but, on the other hand, to refuse to grant a loan might be, in certain circumstances, mean and cruel, and to refuse to accept one but a proud folly.

12–18. Emancipation of Slaves. A slave is to be set free in the seventh year of service. Nor must he (or she) be cast penniless upon the world, but be richly endowed, for the Israelites were slaves redeemed by Jehovah (vv. 12–15). At his pleasure and after the customary rite he may remain for life as an old retainer in his master's house (vv. 16f.). The owner shall not take the emancipation ill, for he has received six years' service, double the hire of a hireling (quite cheap labor), and himself has been in many ways blessed by Jehovah (v. 18).

The law does not institute slavery but regulates it as humanely as possible. Hebrews fell into servitude through crime or poverty, but their condition as slaves was good and their law reveals the possibility of happy relations between master and slave. *Through his ear* (v. 17), i.e., the organ of obedience; cf. Ex. 21^{2-6} (E); Lev. 25^{39-55} (H and P).

19–23. Of Firstlings. Unworked firstlings of oxen and unshorn of sheep are to be consecrated and eaten at a yearly feast by the owner and his house at the central sanctuary (vv. 19f.) A blemished firstling is not to be offered in sacrifice but eaten at home as ordinary food, provided none of the blood be taken (vv. 21–23). The parallels are Ex. 13^{11-16} $22^{28f.}$ 34^{19} (JE) and Ex. 13^{2} Num. 18^{15-18} (P); cf. Deut. 12^{20-25}. Deuteronomy does not treat the subject exhaustively, but aims at accommodating the existing law to the changed conditions of the one sanctuary: P makes the firstlings the perquisites of the priests—a position irreconcilable with that of Deuteronomy, according to which the offerer and his family enjoy them—an encroachment of the priesthood on the rights of the laity.

CHAPTER XVI

The Three Annual Festivals or Pilgrimages. (Vv. 1–17). The three feasts—the Passover with Mazzoth (unleavened loaves), Weeks, and Booths—were doubtless all originally connected with agriculture and were an acknowledgment of God's bountifulness in the fruits of the earth. "Passover" and "Mazzoth" celebrated the appearance of the young and ripening ears in the spring; "Weeks" or "Harvest" (Ex. 23^{16}) or "Firstfruits" (Num. 28^{26}) the completion of the wheat harvest, and "Booths" (D and P), or "Ingathering," that of the vintage. In time, however, they all attained an historical meaning, "Passover" commemorating the sparing of the first-born in Egypt; "Mazzoth," the unleavened cakes made by the Israelites at the time of their flight; and "Booths," the years spent by the Israelites in the wilderness (P). "Weeks" finds no historical connection in the O.T.; later Jews, however, connected it with the giving of the Law from Sinai.

Deuteronomy definitely connects "Mazzoth" with "Passover"; localizes all the feasts at the central sanctuary and emphasizes their social joyousness, especially that of "Weeks" and "Booths."

1–8. Passover with Mazzoth. To be held in the month Abib (March-April, the later Nisan), and kept by the sacrifice of a bullock or sheep (vv. 1f.). For seven days unleavened bread is to be eaten, the bread of affliction, commemorative of the trepidation that marked the Exodus from Egypt; no leaven shall be found in Israel's borders during these days nor any of the Passover-sacrifice after the first evening (vv. 3f.). The offering is to be boiled and eaten in the evening at the central sanctuary and in the morning the Israelites shall return home (vv. 5–7). For six days shall unleavened bread be eaten, and, in the seventh, a sacred convocation shall be held and no work done.

The passage is composite, for vv. 3f. break the connection of vv. 1f. with vv. 5–7; there is also a contradiction between *seven days* (vv. 3f.) and *six days* (v. 8); again v. 7 fixes the feast for one day, vv. 3f. and 8 for seven. Originally there may have been two distinct laws, one for Passover (one day) and another for Mazzoth (seven days) which are here combined—not too successfully. Cf. for "Passover," Ex. 12^{21-27} 23^{18b} 34^{25} (JE); Ex. 12^{1-13} Lev. 23^{5} Num. 9^{1-14} 28^{16} (P): for "Mazzoth," Ex. 13^{3-10} 23^{15} 34^{18} (JE); Lev. 23^{6} (H); Ex. 12^{14-20} Num. 28^{17-25} (P).

9–12. Weeks. This was a harvest festival celebrated seven weeks after the start of the harvest, with gifts, according as the offerer has been blessed by Jehovah, in company with his household, the poor and the Levite, at the central sanctuary. Cf. Ex. 23^{16} ("Harvest"), 34^{22} (JE) Lev. 23^{15-20} (H) Lev. 23^{21} Num. 28^{26-31} ("First-fruits"; P); Deuteronomy, unlike the other codes, mgkes no mention of firstfruits; v. 12 connects with manservant (slave) in v. 11; it is not relevant to the Law as a whole but is true to the spirit of Deuteronomy.

13–15. Booths. Another joyous harvest festival—the crowning one (cf. 1 Kings 8^{2-65})—celebrated for seven days after harvest and the vintage by the Israelite with his family dependents and the poor at the central sanctuary. Ex. 23^{16} ("Ingathering") (JE) Lev. 23^{39-43} (P).

16, 17. Summary. The limitation to "males" does not conflict with vv. 1–15; to males attendance was obligatory, to others voluntary.

Chapters 16^{18} to 18^{22}: Laws of Office-bearers, etc.

18–20. Appointment of Judges. Judges are to be appointed in the various towns; they are to exercise their office with scrupulous impartiality and purity of motive. Bribery (very common in the East) is to be sternly eschewed. Righteousness—that must be the one aim. The details of judicial institutions among the

Hebrews are unknown; the other codes in the Pentateuch simply presuppose the existence of judges and inculcate purity and impartiality (cf. Ex. $23^{1-3, 6-8}$ Lev. 19^{15}); *the officers* (v. 18) were probably subordinate officials, Deut. $20^{5, 8, 9}$ (cf. Johns, *Code of Hammurabi*, §5; hereafter referred to as *C. H*).

21, 22. No Asherah and No Massebah to Be Placed Beside Jehovah's Altar. Cf. 12^{3}, note. The Asherah is thought by some to have represented the female element and the Massebah (pillar) the male element in the Deity. Consult articles, "Asherah" and "Massebah" or "Pillar," in Bible Dictionaries.

CHAPTER XVII

1. Against Blemished Sacrifices. No bullock or sheep unless physically perfect is to be offered to Jehovah. Whatever may have been the original ideas behind this law (e.g., that sacrifice was the food of the Deity and should be of the best), there would be the natural temptation to offer the second best to Jehovah—the common abiding temptation to cheapen religion. Cf. Lev. 22^{17-25} (P); not in JE.

2–7. Punishment of Idolaters. If any idolater be actually discovered and the offense proved, the idolater, man or woman, shall be stoned (vv. 2–5), but the case must be conclusively proved on the word of two or three witnesses; in this way shall the evil be burned out; the witnesses shall cast the first stone (vv. 6, 7). The seductive worship of the host of heaven, a main feature in Babylonian religion, is alluded to frequently in O.T. (See 2 Kings $17^{6f.}$ $23^{4, 5}$ Zeph. 1^{5} Jer. 8^{2} 19^{13} Ezek. 8^{16}.)

8–13. The Law of Appeal. Where a case, criminal or civil, is too difficult for the local courts (see 16^{18-20}, with which this passage is naturally connected), it is to be taken before the Levitical priests and a judge at the central sanctuary, whose decisions must be literally carried out on the spot (vv. 8–11). The man who refuses to accept the decision of the priest or the judge shall be put to death and be an example to all challengers of authority (vv. 12f.). The decision, of course, through the priest or judge is regarded as that of Jehovah; hence the severe punishment for contempt of court. For the dual authority cf. 19^{17} and 2 Chr. $19^{8, 11}$.

14–20. The Law of the King. When Israel desires a king like other nations, he must be chosen of Jehovah and must be a native Israelite; he shall not amass cavalry nor encourage the people to trade with Egypt in horses (vv. 14–16); he shall not have many wives nor accumulate too much wealth (v. 17). Seated on his throne, he shall make a copy of this code before the Levitical priests and shall study it continually. This will teach him reverence and obedience, and save him from arrogance toward his subjects, who are his brethren (vv. 18–20). This law is peculiar to Deuteronomy; it has points of contact with 1 Sam. $7^{2, 17}$ 8, 10^{17-27a}, i.e., with the later of the two narratives in First Samuel dealing with the establishment of the monarchy (see introduction to Samuel, p. 381). It is doubtful whether Deuteronomy or the narration in First Samuel is the older. The reference to wives, wealth, and horses is to the conduct of Solomon and implies a memory of his reign. The statement that the king shall be no foreigner is strange, for at no time in Israel's history did this danger seriously emerge. The main purpose of the Law is theocratic, and it is meant to guard against foreign influence.

CHAPTER XVIII

1–8. Of Priestly Dues. The Levitical priests (the whole tribe), being landless, shall have Jehovah as their inheritance, receiving the fire-offerings and other specified sacred dues. Jehovah has chosen Levi to be his priests forever (vv. 1–5). If a Levite shall keenly desire to leave his village and officiate at the One Altar, he may do so and take equal rank and share with the Levite already in residence, besides retaining what he may have realized from his practice, or—another interpretation—any property he may have inherited (vv. 6–8). See on 10^{9}. The dues of the priest are different in P, Lev. $7^{31f.}$ Num. 18^{18}; the latter half of this law was not carried out in Josiah's reformation (2 Kings 23^{9}), perhaps because of the self-interested opposition of the priests already in residence.

9–22. Of the Prophet. In the promised land Israel must have nothing to do with any heathen superstitions such as child-sacrifice, divination, soothsaying, enchantments, sorceries, charms (by magic knots, spells, or incantations), ghosts, spiritualistic mediums, necromancy. These nine forms of superstition are to be strictly eschewed; they are abominations which have proved destructive to the heathen; let Israel have no traffic with them (vv. 9–14). Nor will this be necessary, for to Israel will be given a succession of prophets, raised up from among the people, representatives, like Moses, of Jehovah, just as the people had requested at Horeb. Let Israel hearken to these; from those that hearken not Jehovah will exact the fitting punishment (vv. 15–19). Any prophet who speaks in self-presumption, or in the name of other gods, will be put to death. And the test of a true prophet is that his word comes true (vv. 20–22).

This law of the prophet is peculiar to Deuteronomy, though throughout the O.T. the superstitions referred to are forbidden (1 Sam. 28[3]). The Law recognizes prophecy as a factor in the theocratic life of Israel; through prophecy are communicated the mind and will of God upon which Israel's life and destiny depend. Prophecy in Israel no doubt arose out of crude beginnings—out of the very superstitions which are here condemned—but the fact that it did rise and became *the* rational and spiritual power proves two things: (1) that there is a living God revealing his mind and will, and (2) that Israel, by God's choice and grace, was through its prophetic personalities in contact with that living God. The test of true prophecy in this passage is the fulfillment of the prophet's word (cf. 13[1-5]); no doubt, it is true that the higher Hebrew prophecy is interpretative, not predictive, has insight rather than foresight (of particular events), and is concerned chiefly with morality and religion—but the confirmation of prophetic interpretation, insight, and truth would be in events, and upon these the popular mind would rely. The true prophet in Israel was (and always will be everywhere) the interpreter of the contemporaneous mind of God. He is one who has stood in the counsel of God, who has God's passion for righteousness and truth and the courage to declare to Jacob (everywhere) his transgression and to Israel his sin. He supplies the word of truth and inspiration that is necessary to social, national, and world progress, and declares the way of life to individuals and nations.

CHAPTERS 19[1] TO 21[9]: LAWS RELATING TO CRIME, WAR, PROPERTY, EVIDENCE.

CHAPTER XIX

1–13. Of the Cities of Refuge. When Israel is settled in Canaan he shall set apart three cities, to be selected after a survey and division of the land into three parts, so that every manslayer may find refuge in one or other of the cities (vv. 1–3). And this is the method of dealing with the man-slayer who flees to a city for his life—if he has slain his neighbor by accident, say in hewing wood in the jungle, for such cases there shall be three cities of refuge (vv. 4–7). But if God extends Israel's border to its promised limits, then three more cities shall be added to prevent the shedding of innocent blood (vv. 8–10). But if a willful murderer shall arrive at a city of refuge, then the elders of his city shall send for him and deliver him up to the avenger and so the blood of the innocent shall not remain upon the land (vv. 11–13).

This law controls the vendetta—blood for blood—common among Easterners. The vendetta was not confined to individuals; it was the concern of the clan, and might be carried on to the third and fourth generation. The law, as it stands in Deuteronomy, controls the vendetta and, even in the case of actual murder, metes out through the elders a rough justice. Cf. 4[41-43] Ex. 21[12-14] Num. 35[9-34].

14. Of Landmarks. No encroachments on private property are allowed, the boundaries or "marches" of which go historically far back. This kind of law was known to the Greeks, where landowners were under the protection of Zeus Horios; Latin landholders, similarly, were protected by the god Terminus, in whose honor the annual festival of Terminalia was held. The right of private property and the passing of heritage are presupposed by Deuteronomy. But this right—in every age—is derived from society, and those who enjoy the right should not forget the duty to society which the possession and enjoyment of such right entail. Deuteronomy does not consider the state of matters where a right—even a time-honored one—is held to the exclusion of the public good. It rightly, as we believe, accepts the principle of private ownership, but of the abuse of this principle it says nothing, though we can assume that such abuse would find no favor, for land throughout Deuteronomy is God-given. Not in the other codes, but cf. Hos. 5[10] Prov. 22[28].

15–21. Of Witnesses. At least two witnesses are required for any conviction (v. 15). In case of perjury (literally, a witness of violence, i.e., one who prefers might to right) the perjurer and the man against whom he has borne false witness shall be brought before Jehovah in the persons of the priests and judges, and if the perjury be proved, the perjurer shall come under the *lex talionis*, and suffer the punishment which his evidence would have brought upon the man against whom he has borne false witness. Cf. 17[6] and Num. 35[30]: both passages refer to a capital charge; for the *lex talionis* cf. Ex. 21[24] (JE) Lev. 24[18-20] (H).

CHAPTER XX

1–9. Of Warfare and Exemptions from Service. When Israel goes to war with a foe stronger than himself, he shall not be afraid, for Jehovah, the Deliverer, is with him, and, through the priest he shall be exhorted and reminded that Jehovah will fight on his side and win his battles (vv. 1–4). The officers shall give exemption to the man who has (1) built a new house but not dedicated it, or (2) has planted a vineyard but not fulfilled the rites that bring it into common use, or (3) has betrothed a wife but not married her, and (4) to all who are faint-hearted, lest they may infect the others (vv. 5–8). Then captains shall be appointed (v. 9).

10–18. Of the Capture of Foreign Cities. When Israel in war approaches a city, he has to offer terms of peace; if these be accepted, the inhabitants shall be taken for task-service; if not, the siege must be begun, and when, through Jehovah, the city has been captured, every male shall be slain, but women, children, cattle and spoil shall be taken as booty (vv. 10–14). "The ban" (not in its severest form) is to be applied to a foreign city, but in its severest form to the heathen cities of Canaan, to save Israel from being infected with their abominations (vv. 15–18).

19, 20. Of Sparing the Fruit Trees. In a protracted siege Israel shall eat of the besieged fruit trees and not wantonly destroy them; other trees may be hewn down for siege works (read v. 19. *Is the tree . . . man?* i.e., human). These three laws do not regulate the entire conduct of war, a sacred business to the Hebrews. They tend to moderate certain cruelties of ancient warfare, and in the exemptions (vv. 5–8) they recognize human claims. The whole chapter reads like an interruption between chs. 19 and 21¹⁻⁹, perhaps it originally stood after 21⁹.

CHAPTER XXI

1–9. Expiation for an Untraced Murder. If a man is found murdered by an unknown in the open country, the elders and judges of the nearest village shall take an unworked heifer to a perennially running stream in some uncultivated spot, break its neck, wash their hands over it, and, in presence of the priests, shall declare their entire innocence of the deed. So will the land and the people be cleansed of defilement caused by the murder. Probably an old incorporated law, peculiar to Deuteronomy.

Chapters 21¹⁰ to 25¹⁶: Laws Miscellaneous

10–14. Of Marriage with a Captive in War. An Israelite may in war take captive a woman whom he desires for his wife, but he must not treat her as his wife till she has performed certain rites and mourned for a month for her parents (vv. 10–13). If he has no pleasure in her as a wife, he must let the woman go according to her will, but he must not sell her nor deal in a despotic way, for he has dishonored her (v. 14).

The *shaving* and the *paring* (v. 12) may be mourning rites or acts of purification, cleansing her from the impurities of her old environment, or they may express, symbolically, the fact that her forsaken condition is at an end now she has found a home and a husband. The case contemplated would be possible only in case of war with distant nations. Marriage with a Canaanite was forbidden. Peculiar to Deuteronomy.

15–17. Of Primogeniture. A man cannot transfer the double portion of his eldest son, born of a disliked wife, in favor of the favorite wife's son (cf. Gen. 27, 48).

18–21. Of a Rebellious Son. In the case of a rebellious son, a squanderer and a glutton, his parents shall bring him before the elders, and all the villagers shall stone him. So will the evil be exterminated and the punishment act as a deterrent. We see here how the old absolute parental authority (Ex. 21⁷) was limited, and how parental authority was guided and enforced by communal authority. Notice too that the mother has her say in the matter.

22, 23. Of an Exposed Corpse. The body of a criminal hung, after execution, upon a tree must be taken down before nightfall, for the hanged is cursed of God and defiles the land (cf. Gal. 3¹³; notice Paul's omission of "of God").

CHAPTER XXII

1–3. Of Lost Property. Cf. Ex. 23⁴ᶠ.

4. Of Assisting Fallen Beasts. Cf. Ex. 23⁵.

5. Against Interchange of Clothes. Not simply a law of conventional propriety but directed against those simulated changes of sex common in heathenism. Peculiar to Deuteronomy.

6, 7. Of Bird Protection. For regard for the animal kingdom cf. 22¹⁻⁴ 25⁴ Lk. 12⁶. As the same promise is attached to this law as to the fifth commandment, reverence for motherhood may be the motive of the law, which may, however, go back to the conception of "the right of use" in the bird to the extent of sharing its produce but not of entire possession of the user. Peculiar to Deuteronomy.

8. Of Roof Protection. Cf. Ex. 21³³ᶠ. ("pit"). The roof of an Eastern house was flat or domed, with a flat surrounding terrace, and was used for taking the air, conversation, or worship. The idea of solidarity is seen in the guilt falling upon the whole household. Peculiar to Deuteronomy. Cf. Johns, *C. H.*, §§229–233.

9–11. Of Mixtures. (1) Of Seed, (2) of Plowing Animals, and (3) of Wearing Material. The origin of these laws is obscure. The underlying conception may be that of distinction of species (cf. Gen. 1[11, 12, 24f.]): each species has its distinct and divinely given characteristics which are not to be interfered with (cf. Isa. 28[24-29]). *The fruit forfeited* (v. 9), i.e., consecrated to Jehovah, banned from common use, a proof that the prohibited mixture was a religious or ritual offense. The law on plowing (2) is peculiar to Deuteronomy as also are the words appended to (1); cf. Lev. 19[19] (H).

12. Of Twisted Threads or Knots. Cf. Num. 15[37-41] (P).

Laws on Chastity. Several of the important laws on this are stated in vv. 13–30.

13–21. Of a Husband's Charges Against His Bride. If a man marries and denies his bride's virginity, her parents shall produce publicly proofs of her previous chastity. The elders shall then corporally punish the husband for his wanton words, fine him one hundred shekels of silver (£13–£15 = $65–$75) paid to the father and deprive him forever of right of divorce (vv. 13–19). If the allegation be found true, then the woman shall be stoned before her father's door, for she has wrought senselessness in Israel, turning her father's house into a harlot's. Thus shall Israel exterminate the evil (v. 20f.); cf. Johns, *C. H.*, §§127, 142.

The absence of the physical evidence is not certain proof of unchastity and probably other evidence was allowed. The law may seem to us cruel and indelicate, but such proof was considered essential among ancient peoples in the case of all marriages and is still called for by certain tribes in Syria, Egypt, and Morocco. The case in Deuteronomy, it should be noticed, is where a man has married out of carnal desire, and who, after his passion is gratified, by a revulsion of feeling turns against his bride: by this law he is not allowed to do just as he would wish; he has to grant the woman justice, and, unless he has good grounds for his allegations, he will have to pay. The law shows an advance in social ethics, especially in the status of woman; and that such a law is not needed to-day is due, in part, to its enforcement in olden days. Peculiar to Deuteronomy.

22. Of Adultery. Both guilty parties put to death, probably by stoning. Cf. Lev. 20[10]; Johns, *C.H.*, §§129, 131, 133, 135.

23–27. Of Seduction. Of a betrothed virgin with consent (vv. 23f.), without consent (vv. 25–27). The former case is treated as adultery and both are stoned; in the latter case the man is stoned. Peculiar to Deuteronomy; cf. Johns, *C.H.*, §130.

28, 29. Of Intercourse with a Virgin not Betrothed. The man shall pay the bride-price, and marry her without right of divorce. Cf. Ex. 22[16f.]

30. Against Intercourse With a Father's Wife. Cf. Lev. 18[8] 15[8] Ezek. 22[10]; cf. Johns, *C.H.*, §157.

CHAPTER XXIII

1–8. Certain Classes to Be Excluded From Religious Communion With Israel. (1) Eunuchs, probably on the ground that their mutilation is an outrage upon the nature which God has created or because the eunuch carries on his body the sign of devotion to other gods (cf. Lev. 21[20]). In Isa. 56[3f.] the loyal eunuch is given a place in the future kingdom (cf. Acts 8[27-38]). (2) Bastards, i.e., children of an incestuous union to the tenth generation, i.e., forever. (3) Ammonites and Moabites, on the ground of their unfriendly treatment of Israel (contrast, however, 2[29]) (vv. 1–6). The Edomites and Egyptians, however, may in the third generation enter the congregation, for Edom is Israel's blood-brother and Egypt was his host. *The assembly* (vv. 1, 8) or congregation—the word not used elsewhere in this sense in Deuteronomy; the originality of vv. 4–6 is doubtful.

9–14. Of the Purity of the Camp. In camp, Israel shall avoid every evil (v. 9); in particular, if a man suffer pollution, he shall leave the camp, bathe, and then return; and a place shall be reserved outside the camp for natural necessities and all excrement shall be covered up (vv. 10–13). Israel's God, who walketh in the camp to give victory, must not gaze on indecent things (v. 14).

The ideas behind this law were religious; sexual uncleanness was a disqualification for the religious service of war (1 Sam. 21[5]) and, in the second case, there was the danger of exposed excrement being found by the enemy and used magically against one (Frazer, *Golden Bough*, vol. i, pp. 327f.). Deuteronomy adds an æsthetic reason in v. 14b. No sanitary reason is given, but the religious and æsthetic reasons led to sanitary results. Cf. Num. 5[1-4] (P), though the particular case of Deuteronomy is not mentioned.

15, 16. Of Runaway Slaves. If a runaway escape to Israel (notice *unto thee* (v. 15), suggesting that the slave is escaped from a foreign master), he shall not be returned to his owner, he shall dwell where he chooses, and unoppressed. Peculiar to Deuteronomy; cf. 15[12-18]; Johns, *C. H.*, §§15–20.

17, 18. Condemnation of Religious Prostitution. No Israelite, man or woman, shall be a hierodule. Nor shall Israel bring the wage of a harlot or hire of "a dog" to the house of Jehovah his God. The practice of religious prostitution (i.e., hierodulia) was common in Canaanite and Phoenician cults, as it is in modern India. For *dog* cf. Rev. 22^{15}.

19, 20. Of Interest. Interest is prohibited on loans (charitable) to fellow Israelites, but allowed on loans (probably commercial) to foreigners. The condemnation of interest is in harmony with Greek, Roman, and early Christian ideas on the subject. Peculiar to Deuteronomy; cf. 15^{1-11} Ex. 22^{25} Psa. 15^{5}.

21–23. Of Vows. To forbear to vow is no sin, but once made, a vow shall be paid without delay: this is God's demand. Cf. $12^{6, 11, 17, 26}$. See article "Vow" in Bible Dictionaries.

24, 25. On the Use of a Neighbor's Corn and Fruits. The law checks the spirit of meanness in the grower and greed in the passer-by. It justifies the action recorded in Mt. $12^{1f.}$ Lk. $6^{1f.}$ The rabbis regarded "plucking" as a kind of reaping, and "rubbing" as threshing, and so both were works unlawful on the Sabbath —an instance of legalism destroying the spirit of kindness. Peculiar to Deuteronomy.

CHAPTER XXIV

1–4. On Remarriage of a Divorcée. If a man, for some unseemly thing (probably immodesty), going through the proper process, divorce his wife, and if she marry a second husband and be divorced by him, or if this second husband should die (vv. 1–3), then, in such case, her former husband cannot remarry her; she is polluted. Such a remarriage is an abomination and brings sin upon the land (v. 4).

The Law does not institute divorce—indeed, there is no law of divorce *per se* in the O.T.—nor does it regulate the process exhaustively; it simply states a particular case, in which the legal requirements for divorce are all fulfilled, and then the divorcée marries again, is divorced a second time or loses her husband by death; in that case—the apodosis begins at v. 4—she and her former husband cannot remarry. The Law, then, prohibits the remarriage of a woman whom he has divorced and who meantime has been another's, thus preventing the easy passage of a woman between one man and another, and being, on the whole, in the interests of the woman. The second marriage of the divorcée is not sanctioned in v. 2 (it is tantamount to adultery as far as her first husband is concerned), though such marriage in early Israel was probably not unusual; cf. e.g., David and Michal (1 Sam. 18^{28} 25^{44} 2 Sam. $3^{14f.}$). Hosea's case is scarcely relevant here. Cf. 22^{13-21} Mt. $19^{8f.}$

5. Exemption from Public Service Granted to the Newly Married. No military service or other public office is to be imposed on a man during the first year of married life, for the sake of his wife and home. Peculiar to Deuteronomy; cf. 20^{7}; for *cheer his wife* read with Vulgate *be happy with his wife.*

6. The Mill or Upper Millstone Not to Be Taken in Pledge. This would be to pledge life itself by taking away an actual necessity. "The ancient Common Law of England provides that no man be distrained by the utensils or instruments of his trade or profession."

7. Against Man-Stealing. An Israelite convicted of stealing a brother and acting tyrannically toward him shall be put to death. Cf. Ex. 21^{16} (JE), which has "man" for *any of his brethren*; cf. Johns, *C. H.*, §14.

8, 9. Precautions in Leprosy. These as prescribed by the priestly Levites under divine authority shall be carefully observed by the people, remembering the case of Miriam (how she was secluded, Num. $12^{14f.}$). Leprosy was regarded as a stroke from Jehovah, and was under the supervision of the religious authorities. In v. 8b read with LXX, *all the Torah —the teaching or prescriptions—that the priests, the Levites, do teach you.* This Torah is not Lev. 13f. with its various cases, but some earlier priestly Torah expanded later in Lev. 13f. (P).

10–13. On Pledges. When an Israelite lends to his brother on the security of a pledge he is not to enter the house of a borrower who has the right to select his pledge. If the borrower be a poor man and pledges his mantle (used for sleeping in and for other purposes), it must be restored before nightfall (vv. 10–12). This will secure for the lender the gratitude of the borrower and be reckoned as a righteous act by Jehovah (v. 13). The same humane motive as in v. 6. Cf. Ex. $22^{25f.}$ (JE) for the second part; the first is peculiar to Deuteronomy; cf. Johns, *C. H.*, §241.

14, 15. On the Payment of the Wage-Earner. The wage-earner, Israelite or "guest," if he be poor, is to be paid at the close of each day: his very life depends upon his wage. Otherwise, he will cry to Jehovah (cf. 15^{10}—there was supposed to be a peculiar power in the voice) and the withholder will be guilty of sin. Cf. Lev. 19^{13} Jas. 5^{4}; Johns, *C. H.*, §§257, 261, 273f.

16. On Individual Responsibility. See 2 Kings 14^{6}, where Amaziah, putting to death his father's murderers, does not slay their children, the Deuteronomic editor of Kings quoting this law as authority for Amaziah's clemency. In ancient times the family was the unit and the guilt (as well as the disgrace) of the crime fell upon the whole family. Individual responsibility is proclaimed by Ezek. 18^{4} (cf. Jer. 31^{30}) and emphasized by Christianity. The law is not in conflict with 5^9, for there the children suffer through the self-acting operation of natural and divine law; this is no reason why men should deliberately increase the suffering of the innocent, rather the reverse. Peculiar to Deuteronomy.

17, 18. **Against Injustice to the Protected Stranger, Orphan and Widow.** Notice that the motive (v. 18) is the great act of redemption as in v. 22. Cf. Ex. $22^{21f.}$ 23^{6-9} (JE) Lev. 19^{33} (H).

19–22. **On Gleanings.** The gleanings of the cornfield, the olive-garden, and the vineyard are not to be gathered in a mean way, but are to be left for the stranger, orphan, and widow. Obedience to this law will bring prosperity (v. 19b) and the law is to be kept as an expression of Jehovah's will and in remembrance of the great redemption (v. 22; cf. v. 18). A spirit that grasps the last penny is contrary to the will of Jehovah and unworthy of his great redemptive act. Cf. Lev. $19^{9f.}$ (H), which adds "the corners" but omits "the olive-garden."

CHAPTER XXV

1–3. **On Corporal Punishment.** After a regular trial between two parties to a suit, if one is declared guilty and if he deserves beating, then the punishment shall be carried out in the presence of a judge; the number of strokes shall be in proportion to the gravity of the offense, but shall not exceed forty, for excessive punishment of this kind would be dishonor to a brother. The Law does not ordain corporal punishment; it accepts it as a fact and regulates it; later Jews reduced the number of strokes to thirty-nine, in case of a miscount. There are frequent references in the O.T. to corporal punishment: Ex. 21^{20} Prov. 10^{13} 17^{26} 19^{29} 26^{3} Isa. 50^{6} Jer. 20^{2}, etc.

4. **On Kindness to the Working Ox.** Cf. 22^{1-4}. Quoted 1 Cor. 9^{9} 1 Tim. 5^{18} to enforce the principle that the laborer is worthy of his hire. Peculiar to Deuteronomy.

5–10. **On Levirate Marriage.** In the case of two brothers living on the same estate and one dying without son, his widow is not to marry into another family; the surviving brother must marry her and the eldest son born to this marriage shall succeed to the name and estate of the deceased brother (v. 5f.). Should the surviving brother refuse, a public demonstration before the elders with the widow and recusant present shall be held, in which the widow is to strip the sandal from the recusant's foot and spit on him, so expressing publicly the fact that he has repudiated the obligation and that he and his family are the object of public contempt (vv. 7-10).

Levirate marriage ("Levir" is Latin for "brother-in-law") was an old institution in Israel (cf. Gen. 38^{8}). The institution was not confined to the Hebrew people, but in varying form is found among many peoples—Hindus, Arabs, etc. Its origin is uncertain; the practice of polyandry, ancestor worship (the marriage being part of the rites performed to the spirit of the deceased), and the principle of Baal-marriage (i.e., that the wife was the property of the deceased and passed with the rest of the estate to the next-of-kin) have all been suggested. The case of Ruth and Boaz was not a Levirate marriage. It is as Goel (kinsman), not as Levir, that Boaz takes Ruth, Naomi having no son to act the part of Levir. Lev. $18^{6f.}$ and 20^{21} (H) forbid marriage with a brother's wife; probably Leviticus gives the general rule, which is superseded by the special circumstances stated in Deuteronomy, in which the main features of the law are, that it is confined to the case of two brothers living on one estate, that there is no son, and that the Levir, by fulfilling the obligation, does not found a family and estate for himself but for his deceased brother. P (Num. 27^{1-11}) by allowing daughters to inherit, partly does away with the need for the Levirate law.

11, 12. **On Immodesty in Woman—a Typical Case.** It may be that the woman's hand became *tabu* through contact with the organs of generation, for this is the only case, apart from 19^{15-21}, where mutilation is prescribed as a punishment.

13–16. **On Strict Honesty in Trade.** Traders are not to have two weights and two measures. The trickery of diverse weights and measures (or two prices for different customers) is not righteous (straight) and is an abomination to Jehovah; v. 15 (interrupting the connection) gives length of days as the reward for honesty in business. Honesty, as a rule, helps peace of mind, no small factor of longevity; the words *upon the land*, etc., are not without meaning. Dishonesty with God-given gifts increases the offense. Cf. Lev. $19^{35f.}$ (H) Amos 8^{5} Mic. 6^{11} Ezek. 45^{10} Prov. 16^{11}.

17–19. **On Amalek.** Amalek's cruelty in smiting the stragglers in the wilderness is not to be forgotten. Exterminate him! Cf. Ex. 17^{14} 1 Sam. 14^{48} 15^{2f}. The treatment received from Amalek rankled in Israel.

CHAPTER XXVI

Hortatory Conclusion; Two Beautiful Rituals. These two rituals set forth Deuteronomy's ideal of worship, which should be national, carried out at one sanctuary by the different families with their dependents, full of joyous gratitude for the wonders of the past, and mindful of God and the poor.

1–11. Ritual of the First-fruits. Settled in Canaan, Israel shall take of the first-fruits in a basket to the central sanctuary and, coming to the priest, shall announce his presence before Jehovah in the land of promise; the priest shall then take the basket and set it before the altar (vv. 1–4). Then Israel shall say, *An Aramæan nomad was my father, who went down to Egypt*, etc.—all emphasizing the wonderful growth, sore bondage, mighty deliverance and guidance to the promised land (vv. 5–9); then, setting the first-fruits before Jehovah (in v. 3 the priest had already done this), Israel shall worship joyously with his household, Levites, and strangers (vv. 10, 11).

Notice that the name of God in various forms occurs nine times in the paragraph. All is of God, the wonderful history and the bountifulness of the land—Jehovah, not the Baalim, is the author, Jehovah alone. *A Syrian ready to perish* (v. 5)—an Aramæan nomad (mg.), a reference to Jacob and his Aramæan connections. In 18^{4} the first-fruits go to the priests, but this present passage does not make clear their disposal; perhaps only some of the first-fruits were put in a basket and the rest were eaten at the joyous feast of v. 11; if all were given to the priests, then the joyous feast may be one of the three great annual feasts.

12–15. The Ritual of the Tithes. When the tithe, every third year, has been collected and given to the poor, Israel shall confess that he has dedicated all that he ought and fulfilled all the laws pertaining to the tithe, namely, that he has not, as a mourner for the dead, eaten part of the tithe or given of it to a mourning feast or to the dead (perhaps as *viatica*) and thereby defiled the tithe (vv. 12–14); after this confession he shall appeal for the divine blessing on the God-given land (v. 15). The poor's portion is sacred.

16–19. Closing Exhortation. The obligations involved in the relation between Jehovah and his people are affirmed. Israel by accepting the obligations has made Jehovah say that he will be their God, and Jehovah has made Israel say that he will be Jehovah's people and possession, and this will bring to Israel power, praise, and honor and make him truly a consecrated people. *Avouched* (v. 17), literally, "made say"; Israel did not actually make Jehovah say that he would be their God; he himself chose Israel (7^{8}), but Israel confirmed the divine decision.

CHAPTER XXVII

An Interruption and Later Addition. This chapter, in the third person, interrupts the discourse of Moses; it connects neither with 26^{19} nor with 28^{1}. Ch. 28 forms the natural conclusion to the code (chs. 5–26) and connects well with 26^{19}. Further, the various parts of the chapter are themselves imperfectly connected, and, while there may be a Deuteronomic nucleus in vv. 9f., the chapter as a whole cannot be regarded as an original part of Deuteronomy.

1–8. Moses, with whom are associated the elders (the only time in Deuteronomy), ordered the people to set up stones immediately they have crossed the Jordan, to smear them with chalk and to inscribe on them the Deuteronomic code (vv. 1–3). This is to be done on Mount Ebal (v. 4); an altar too is to be built for whole-offerings and peace-offerings and for joyous worship before God (vv. 5–7); the code is to be written very distinctly. The difficulties in this paragraph are: (1) the repetition, vv. 2f. =vv. 4, 8; (2) the contradiction, v. 2 stating that the stones are to be set up immediately after the crossing of Jordan, and v. 4, that they are to be set up on Mount Ebal, which was more than a day's journey from the Jordan; (3), vv. 5–7 concerning the altar are an interruption, and *how is this law of the altar to be reconciled with the law of the One Altar?* The difficulties plainly mark the passage as composite.

9, 10. Cf. 26^{16-19}.

11–13. In 11^{29} the word "put" or "set" suggested some kind of ceremony in the "setting up" of the blessing and curse: this ceremony is evidently described in these verses and in vv. 14–26.

14–26. Vv. 11–13 appoint the pronouncement of blessings and curses, but in vv. 14–26 we have only curses which anticipate unduly $28^{15f.}$; again in vv. 11–13 Levi is placed on Mount Gerizim among the tribes that bless, but in vv. 14–26 Levi is chosen from all the tribes to pronounce the curses. Further, of the sins against which these curses are pronounced only seven are condemned in the Deuteronomic code; six are condemned in JE and nine in H. The whole chapter is full of literary and historic difficulties.

CHAPTER XXVIII

Peroration of Moses' Second Discourse. For the analysis of this discourse, see introductory paragraphs preceding ch. 5 and ch. 12.

1–14. The Blessings of Obedience. Israel will be exalted over all nations; prosperity will pursue him in the city and in the country; all manner of bountifulness will be his; his enemies will be destroyed and Israel, established as Jehovah's people, will win the respect of the world and be exalted to highest supremacy.

15–68. The Curses of Disobedience. Failure in every department of national life (vv. 16–19 corresponding to vv. 3–6), pestilential fevers, droughts, ruinous defeat in battle (vv. 20–26); loathsome diseases, madness and other afflictions, leading to Israel's oppression by foreign invaders, and ultimately to shameful exile and public shame (vv. 27–37); failure of crops, Israel becoming so impoverished as to become dependent on the foreigner in his land (vv. 38–44; v. 41 is out of place and repeats v. 32); the next two verses (45f.) form a conclusion to vv. 15–44, and all the calamities, enumerated in vv. 15–44 are due to Israel's disobedience (45f.); then vv. 47f. form an introduction to vv. 49–68. Israel has not served Jehovah with joy, therefore he will in want serve his enemies (47f.). Jehovah will bring against Israel a fierce, relentless foreign nation, which will desolate the country and besiege the inhabitants in their cities, till they are under the gruesome necessity of eating their own offspring (vv. 49–57): Jehovah will plague Israel with terrible afflictions and rejoice in his disaster; homeless and helpless, Israel will find life an anxious terror and a burden; any survivors will be carried off as galley-slaves to Egypt; there they will be exposed for sale, but none will buy (vv. 58–68).

This chapter, forming a fitting conclusion to the Deuteronomic code, is, for its sustained eloquence, one of the most striking in the O.T. No paraphrase or synopsis can do justice to its wealth of biting detail and burning invective: it is a furnace belching forth flames of moral indignation and threatenings of evil. Such a chapter shows that there was a living conscience in Israel. Right is right and wrong is wrong, and out of them come inevitably the joy and tragedy of life.

It is true that the consequences of good and evil are pictured as material, on the one hand prosperity, on the other, disease and death. But is not this just the ancient way of stating that the foundations of civilization are moral? If those foundations are sound, civilization will be a blessing, if rotten—immoral and irreligious—it will be a curse. Individuals may be wicked and prosper, but let their wickedness infect the community, as it certainly will, and the community is near the precipice. And yet the consequences are not simply material in this chapter; the heart, mind, and will, reacting to the consequences of evil, become demoralized, lose balance, insight, and foresight. Men become blind of heart, lose their way, and grope about in inconsequent futility.

Jehovah is conceived as a God of absolute integrity. He cannot change evil into good nor cancel their inevitable consequences. The moral law with all its consequences is enthroned in his very being. When the writer pictures Jehovah as rejoicing over the afflictions of evil Israel (v. 63), he seems to depart from that conception of love which he elsewhere emphasizes so strongly, or from the conception of Hosea, who argues from a broken-hearted husband to a broken-hearted God, or most of all from the Christian conception of God, with his deepest sorrow for sin, but we must not forget that the writer is being carried along on a flood of moral feeling. What he wants to drive home to Israel is that they are not to think, because they are Jehovah's pecple, he will not punish their iniquities (cf. Amos). He certainly will, and behind the punishment there will be profound emotion, as profound as Jehovah's joy over Israel's righteousness, for Jehovah is no bloodless God.

For *with the sword* (v. 22) read *with drought;* v. 24 refers to the sirocco and is an accurate description; for *tossed to and fro* (v. 25) read *thou shalt be a horror;* v. 32—there was a large deportation in 701; the chapter is not necessarily, in whole or in part, post-exilic; for *as the eagle flieth* (v. 49) read *as the vulture swoopeth;* for *who would not adventure* (v. 56) read *who had never ventured to set,* etc., i.e., because she had always been carried; *that are written in this book* (v. 58)—not compatible with the prevalent representation that the laws, etc., of Deuteronomy were *spoken* by Moses, nor with 31[9], that the law was only written down *after* this discourse; the verse betrays the fact that Deuteronomy was always a written book; *into Egypt* (v. 68)—a striking climax—back to the place from which Israel was delivered (cf. Hos. 8[13]).

Chapters 29 and 30: Moses' Third Discourse

This forms a kind of supplement to the Deuteronomic Code.

CHAPTER XXIX

1. An Editorial Addition. The verse was probably inserted as a subscription to chs. 12–28. In the Hebrew, it forms the last verse of ch. 28.

2–9. The Inspiration of the Past. Moses reviews before all Israel the wonderful goodness of Jehovah from the time of the deliverance from Egypt. The wonder of that goodness Israel had failed to perceive and understand, but now (since it has been plainly set forth by Moses) it should be the motive for Israel's wise and fruitful obedience.

10–21. The Covenant Binding on Present

and Future Generations. All Israel is gathered together for the completion of the covenant which will also be binding on future generations (vv. 10–15); those present know from experience the dangers and consequences of lapsing into idolatry (vv. 16f.); let no man or woman apostatize, thinking in self-deception to escape the general disaster (vv. 18–21).

Hewer of thy wood unto the drawer of thy water (v. 11)—a description used in a later age for menials of the sanctuary, here probably in a more general sense; *idols* (v. 17)—a contemptuous expression = "rolled blocks" or "doll-images"; *to destroy the moist with the dry* (v.19) —a proverbial expression, meaning to sweep away everybody and everything.

22–29. Certain Disaster of Apostasy. The dreaded disaster is now pictured as a certainty. The land is utterly desolate, strewn with sulphur, salt, and lava. Future generations and foreigners will ask the cause of this disaster to the whole land and people. It is because Israel has forsaken his God and has been disobedient to his commandments—his God in whose keeping are the secrets of the future, while Israel knows only the present. V. 29 with its first person plural reads like a closing liturgy.

CHAPTER XXX

1–10. The Promise of Restoration on Repentance. When Israel, an exile in a foreign land, repents, then Jehovah in compassion will restore Israel's fortune and will change his heart, giving to it a new spiritual perception, so that Israel may again love and obey God and live. The curses will fall upon Israel's enemies while Israel himself will enjoy every blessing, and Jehovah will rejoice in blessing Israel's obedience. Two abiding spiritual facts are declared in these verses: (1) that repentance is the condition of restoration, and to repentance God is unfailingly responsive, and (2) that for repentance divine help is necessary (v. 6; cf. Jer. $31^{31f.}$). *Return* (v. 8) does not necessarily refer to the Exile; it may be used (though only here in Deuteronomy) in a spiritual sense (cf. Isa. 10^{21} 19^{22} Jer. 3^{1-7}).

11–14. The Divine Will Present in the Conscience. The divine rule of life—what God wants from man—is not beyond man's power of apprehension nor outside the sphere of everyday life and practice. He who does his will will come to know his mind (see Jn. 7^{17}). Paul (Rom. $10^{6f.}$) makes a free reproduction of the words—to Paul the law was oppressive, but the living inspirational word of faith is in the heart and conscience. Vv. 11–14 do not connect with v. 10 and are probably an independent fragment.

15–20. Peroration to the Discourses. The choice of the two ways—of life and of death—is now. Therefore choose life and live. Vv. 15–20 are considered by some to have followed originally ch. 28.

Chapters 31 to 34: Moses Finishes His Work; His Song; His Blessing

These chapters are of the nature of an appendix containing a narrative of events connected with the close of Moses' life and incorporating two poems. The various parts of the narrative are not closely knit together nor are they homogeneous. JE is the main nucleus of the narrative with Deuteronomic additions and excerpts from P.

CHAPTER XXXI

1–8. Last Word of Encouragement to the People and to Joshua. Moses has run his race; he has seen but will never cross the Jordan, but Joshua and the people will. God will go before them, destroying every foe; he will not let them down nor desert them. Be strong therefore. Fear not. Cf. 31^{2} with 34^{7} (P).

9–13. The Writing and Recitation of the Law. Moses delivers the Law written by himself to the priests and elders and gives instruction for its reading to the assembled Israelites, once in every seven years at the Feast of Booths in the year of Release. *Thou* (v. 7); in v. 9 Moses is addressing the priests and elders.

14, 15. Joshua Commissioned by Jehovah. Moses and Joshua are commanded to present themselves at the tent of meeting (i.e., the tent of Revelation, P's expression), where Joshua is appointed as successor to Moses.

16–22. Prediction of Apostasy. After the death of Moses, so Jehovah predicts, Israel will go awhoring after strange gods (possibly to be taken in a literal sense in view of the practice of prostitution in Semitic cults). This apostasy will bring heavy disaster, and Moses is instructed to write the Song that will testify against such apostasy. *Imagination* (v. 21), frequently in O.T. of evil and rebellious imagination against God.

23. This verse goes back to v. 14; the subject is Jehovah.

24–30. Vv. 24–26 repeat 9f.; vv. 27–30 form a second introduction to the Song. Cf. v. 28b with v. 19; cf. v. 29 with vv. 20f.; v. 28, *these words*, i.e., the Song.

CHAPTER XXXII

The Song of Moses. This Song is a didactic

poem, and as such is unsurpassed for fire and force and sweeping rhetoric in the O.T. According to 31[20] its purpose is to testify beforehand against Israel, but the poem itself is in the main one of mercy and hope, and is full of God's faithfulness and grace to a sinful and repentant people. The poem makes no claim to be by Moses and depicts a situation and events long after his time; the people are settled in the land long enough to have become demoralized. The precise date is impossible to fix; in its thought and theology it has points of contact with the eighth-century prophets and it has been called "a compendium of prophetic theology." Driver, however, holds that the general thought of the poem and its predominant ideas have decidedly greater affinities with the prophets of the Chaldean period (Jeremiah, Ezekiel, Second Isaiah) than with the earlier prophets Amos, Hosea, Isaiah, and Micah. In that case the poem belongs to the eve of the Exile or is even later. It is uncertain, then, whether the poem is pre-exilic, exilic or post-exilic, but if it were either of the two latter, it is remarkable that the greatest of Israel's afflictions is not mentioned. Whatever may be its date, the poem has a certain appropriateness in the book of Deuteronomy, for it sets forth, in strong and sweeping verse, the lessons which Deuteronomy, in law and narrative, seeks to inculcate and which Moses is depicted as declaring plainly to Israel on the steppes of Moab.

The following is a new translation of the Song, embodying some textual changes suggested by the ancient versions or by modern scholars:

1–3. Exordium. The Universe as a fitting audience is called upon to listen to the poet's theme, the greatness of Jehovah.

Give ear, O ye heavens, and I will speak;
And let the earth hearken to the words of my mouth;
Let my message drop as rain,
May my word distil as dew,
As mist upon the tender blades,
And as showers upon herbs;
For the name of Jehovah will I proclaim.
Give ye greatness to our God!

4–6. The Central Theme: A Faithful God, a Faithless People.

The Rock,[1] perfect is his work,
Yea, all his ways are ordered,
A God of troth, no treachery in him!
They have fouled their truth, no sons of his,[2]
A generation twisted and crooked.
Is it Jehovah ye thus requite,
O senseless folk and unwise?
Is he not thy sire that got thee?
Is he not thy maker and thy founder?

7–14. Consider the Past, With Its Proof of God's Providence.

Remember the days of old,
Consider the years, age after age,
Ask thy father, let him shew thee,
Thine Elders let them tell thee.

(The Elders answer:)

When the Most High gave the nations their inheritance,
When he separated the sons of man,
He fixed the bounds of the peoples
According to the number of Israel's sons;
For the lot of Jehovah is his people,
Israel the range of his inheritance.
He found him in a desert land
And in a desolate and howling waste.
He circled round him, he scanned him,
He guarded him as the pupil of his eye;
Like a vulture that stirreth up its nest,
That hovereth over its young,
He spread his wings, he took him.
Jehovah alone was his leader
With no foreign god to help him.
He made him to ride upon the highest lands
And to eat[1] of the fruitage of the land,
Suckled him[2] with honey from the crag[3]
And with oil from the flinty rock.
Curd of kine and milk of sheep
With fat of lambs and rams,
Herds of Bashan and he-goats,
With the richest and finest of wheat,
And the blood of the grape thou drankest—a foaming draught.

15–18. Jehovah's Generosity Led Only to Thankless Satiety.

Jacob ate and was full;[4]
Jeshurun[5] waxed fat and he kicked;
Thou waxedst fat, grewest thick, wast gorged;
And he forsook the God that made him
And treated as a fool the Rock of his deliverance.
They made him jealous with strangers,
With abominations they vexed him,
They sacrificed to demons, a no-god;
To gods they had not known,
New gods that late appeared,
Before whom your fathers shuddered not;[6]

[1] Rock—the word is applied to Jehovah and to the other gods; it expresses the idea of unchangeableness.
[2] Text uncertain.

[1] Adopting the reading of the LXX.
[2] I.e., made him enjoy.
[3] I.e., out of most unlikely places.
[4] This line is in LXX.
[5] A poetical name for Israel derived from Hebrew word for "upright": here applied reproachfully.
[6] Or "to whom they never gave a look."

Of the Rock that got thee thou wast unmindful
And thou forgattest God that had travailed with thee.[1]

19–25. The Punishment Meted out by Jehovah on Israel's Defection.

But Jehovah saw and he spurned
Out of chagrin for his sons and daughters,
And he said: I will hide my face from them,
I shall see what their end will be.
For a generation of tricksters are they,
Sons in whom is no steadfastness.
They made me jealous with a no-god.
They vexed me with their vanities;
But I will make them jealous with a no-nation,
With a degraded people I will chagrin them.
For a fire is kindled in my nostril;
Yea, it hath flames to shoot beneath,
Yea, it devoureth the earth and its increase
And setteth aflame the foundations of the hills.
I will heap evils upon them,
My last arrow hurl against them;
Drained by famine,[2] devoured by fiery bolts of fever and bitter destruction.
And the teeth of beasts will I send against them
With the venom of things that crawl in the dust.
Without, shall the sword bereave,
And in the chambers, terror
Destroying, yea, both youth and maid,
The suckling and man of hoary head.

26–33. The Withholding of Jehovah's Vengeance and Dread of the Taunts of the Foe.

I would have said, "I will split them in pieces
And still their memory among men.
Save that I dreaded the taunt of the foe
And the blunder of their rivals.
Lest they should say, Our hand raised itself aloft,
'Twas not Jehovah did all this.
For a people lost in counsels are they[3]
And there is no discernment in them.
Had they been wise, they would understand this;
They would discern their latter end.
How could one have chased a thousand[4]
And two put to flight ten thousand,
Were it not that their Rock had sold them
And Jehovah left them to their fate?
For their Rock is not as our Rock,
With our foes as judges.

[1] Notice how both fatherhood and motherhood are applied to the Rock.
[2] Text uncertain.
[3] In v. 28 the poet resumes in his own person.
[4] With reference to some disastrous defeat of Israel.

For from the vine of Sodom is their vine[1]
And from the fields of Gomorrah;
Their grapes, grapes of poison,
Bitter clusters are theirs;
The poison of reptiles is their wine
And the cruel poison of cobras.[2]

34–36. Jehovah's Vengeance, Withheld From Israel, Is Reserved for Israel's Foes.

Is it not all stored with me,
Sealed in my treasuries?
Vengeance[3] is mine and requital
What time their foot shall slip:
Yea, near is the day of their destruction,
And their fate will rush upon them.
Yea, Jehovah shall judge his people
And relent for his servants' sake;
Yea, he seeth their hold is gone
And there is left nor fettered nor free.[4]

37–39. God Will Speak to Israel in His Need, Showing to Him the Folly of His Trust in Strange Gods.

And he will say: Where are their gods,
The Rock whereon they refuged,
That ate the fat of their sacrifice,
Drank the wine of their offering?
Let them arise and help you,
Let their shelter be over you.
See now I, yea, I am he
And there is no god beside me.
I slay, yea, I make alive;
I wound, yea, I heal,
And there is no deliverer out of my hand.

40–42. In Conclusion Jehovah Swears Vengeance on Israel's Foes.

For I lift mine hand to heaven
And say: As I live for ever
I will whet the lightning of my sword,
And on judgment my hand shall grip
To wreak vengeance on my foes
And requital on those that hate me!
Mine arrows I will make drunk with blood,
My sword's fodder shall be flesh,
The blood of slain and captive
And the scalps of the longhaired foe.

43. Conclusion.

Sing triumphantly, ye nations, his people;
Surely the blood of his servants will he requite,
And revenge will he repay to his rivals,
And sweep clean the land of his people.

44. Concluding Note. Tautologous with 31^{30}; the natural sequel to 31^{22}; so LXX. *Hoshea*, probably an error for "Joshua."

[1] I.e., their national stock is in nature like Sodom's.
[2] Do vv. 31–33 refer to Israel or his foes? Probably the latter.
[3] LXX for the day of vengeance.
[4] An alliterative phrase=everybody.

45–47. Moses' Final Exhortation. Obey the law; it is worthy of regard, for on obedience to it depends Israel's life.

48–52. Moses Bidden to Die. Moses is commanded to climb Mount Nebo and view Canaan and die there like Aaron on "Hor the mountain," because of their breaking faith with Jehovah at Kadesh. Only the sight of the land is to be his. Cf. Num. 27[12-14] (P), of which these verses are a duplicate with expansions.

CHAPTER XXXIII

The Blessing of Moses. This "Blessing" appears as an independent poem, the introductory verse connecting it but loosely with the rest of the book. The introduction (vv. 2–5) describes the advent of Jehovah, the giving of the Law and the establishment of the kingdom; the main part (vv. 6–25) consists of a series of eulogistic sayings (there are no curses, as in the similar poem in Gen. 49) concerning eleven of the tribes, Simeon being omitted; the conclusion (vv. 26–29) emphasizes the uniqueness of Jehovah and the blessedness of his chosen people. The "blessings" characterize each tribe by some salient feature in its history, situation, or character.

As in the case of the "Song of Moses" (ch. 32) internal evidence makes it impossible to consider Moses as the author; but it is not easy to determine its exact date. Perhaps the several utterances originated independently in different places and at different times. Later they were collected, probably in the Northern Kingdom. If so, the poem must be dated earlier than 722 or 721 B.C., the date of the dissolution of the Northern Kingdom. The favorable comments on the tribe of Levi have led some scholars to conclude that the author or collector was a member of that tribe.

The following is a new translation:

1. Editor's Introduction to the Blessing. Cf. similar introduction to the "Song" (31[30]).

2–5. Exordium. A Theophany in which the Law is Given.

Jehovah from Sinai came,
And beamed forth to them,
He shone from Mount Paran,
He came nigh to Meribath-Kadesh:[1]
At his right hand a burning fire for them.[2]
Yea, he hath love for his people;[3]
His consecrated are in his hand.[4]
And he sustains thy lot
And keeps his covenant with thee.[5]

[1] Wellhausen's conjecture of a very uncertain text.
[2] Dillman's conjecture.
[3] LXX.
[4] According to ancient versions.
[5] Bertholet's emendation, but the text is very uncertain.

A law did Moses command us,
A possession for the congregation of Jacob,
And he became king in Jeshurun[1]
When the heads of the people were gathered,
All together the tribes of Israel.

6. The Blessing of Reuben (cf. Gen. 49[3]).

Let Reuben live and not die;
But let his men be few.

7. Judah (cf. Gen. 49[8-12]).

Hear, Jehovah, the voice of Judah,
And unto his people do thou bring him.
His hands strove for him;
But a help from his enemies shalt thou be.

8–11. Levi (cf. Gen. 49[5-7]).

Thy Thummim and Urim[2] be to thy pious one
Whom thou didst prove at Massah,
With whom thou didst contend at the waters of Meribah;[3]
Who saith of his father and mother, I have not seen them;
And his brothers he hath not owned
Nor known his own sons.
For they keep thy saying,
And thy covenant they guard.
They show thy judgments to Israel,
They set incense in thy nostril
And whole offerings on thine altar.
Bless thou his strength, O Jehovah,
And the work of his hands do thou receive.
Smite in the loins those that rise up against him,
And those that hate him so they rise up no more.

12. Benjamin (cf. Gen. 49[27]).

The darling of Jehovah, he dwelleth in security by him;
Jehovah ever broodeth over him
And between his shoulders[4] he has dwelling.

13–17. Joseph (cf. Gen. 49[22-26]).

The blessing of Jehovah be on his land,
With the wealth of heaven above[5]
And waters of the deep that couch beneath,
With the wealth of the increase of the sun,
With the wealth of the yield of the moons,
And from the head of the mountains of yore
And from the wealth of the everlasting hills,
And from the wealth of the land and its fulness
And from the favor of the Dweller in the Bush,[6]
May all come on the head of Joseph,
Upon the crown of the prince among his brethren.

[1] An ideal poetic name for Israel; cf. 32[15].
[2] Cf. Ex. 28[30], note. Urim and Thummim were the two sacred lots used by the priest in making decisions.
[3] Inconsistent with other accounts of events at Massah.
[4] Alluding to the site of the Temple.
[5] Hebrew, "with the dew."
[6] Ex. 3[2].

The firstling of his ox[1]—its majesty!
With horns like those of the wild ox;
With them he thrusteth the peoples
Together to the ends of the earth.
These be the myriads of Ephraim,
These be the thousands of Manasseh.

18, 19. **Zebulun and Issachar** (cf. Gen. 49^13f.^).

Rejoice, O Zebulun, in thy strength;
And Issachar in thy tents.
Peoples to the mountain do they call;
There they offer sacrifices of righteousness,
For they suck the abundance of the seas[2]
And the buried stores of the sand.

20, 21. **Gad** (cf. Gen. 49^19^).

Blessed is the extender of Gad.
As a lion he dwelleth
And tears the arm, yea, the scalp;
And he sought out the choice part for himself,
For there was a commander's portion reserved:
And he came with the heads of the people,
He wrought the righteousness of Jehovah,
And his judgments along with Israel.

22. **Dan** (cf. Gen. 49^17^).

Dan is a lion's whelp,
He leapeth forth from the Bashan.

23. **Naphtali** (cf. Gen. 49^21^).

Naphtali, abounding in favor
And full of the blessing of Jehovah,
The sea and the south do thou possess.

24, 25. **Asher** (cf. Gen. 49^20^).

Blessed above sons be Asher.
May he be the favorite of his brethren,
And be dipping his foot in oil.
Iron and brass are thy bolts[3]
And as thy days so may be thy strength.[4]

26–29. **Epilogue.**

There is none like the God of Jeshurun,
Riding the heavens as thy help,
And in his pride through the skies.
The God of old is a dwelling place
And underneath are the everlasting arms.
And he drove out the enemy before thee,
And said, "Destroy!"
So Israel dwelt securely,
The fountain of Jacob alone,
Upon a land of corn and wine;
Yea, his heavens drop dew.
Oh happy art thou, O Israel; who is like thee?
A people delivered by Jehovah,
The shield of thy help,
The sword of thy pride.
So shall thine enemies feign and fawn before thee;
But thou on their heights shall trample them.

[1] Refers to Ephraim, Gen. 48^13-20^.
[2] Allusion to the wealth accruing to the two tribes from the sea.
[3] Perhaps a reference to Asher's geographical position which would require strong defense against invasion.
[4] "Thy strength"—the meaning of the Hebrew word is unknown.

CHAPTER XXXIV

The Death of Moses. Moses ascends from the steppes of Moab to Mount Nebo and is given a vision of the promised land—a magnificent panorama; he is told that he will not enter, and he dies alone in some undiscovered spot on the mountain of Moab. Jehovah buries him (vv. 1–6). His days were complete—one hundred and twenty years—but his strength and vision were unimpaired. For thirty days the Israelites bemoaned the loss; Joshua assumed the leadership (vv. 7–9). There is a final word on the greatness of Moses (vv. 10–12).

Moses, alone on the mountain, viewing the future glory of his people, not allowed to enter, dying in a strange land, the people mourning his loss, is all humanly pathetic and humanly true. But it is the implications in the passage that mark its distinction. Moses dies, his life's work is complete, yet "his eye was not dimmed nor his natural force abated." According to 31^2^, he was worn out, but (34^7^) he still possesses the spirit of immortal youth; his vision, his expectation, his power over Israel still live. How easy to have written, "his body was lost in some crevice of the rocks," to state the simple particular! How childlike to write, "He buried him!" Childlike yet universally true, for it is Jehovah that buries all his children. And a Christian might have written even more, for Jesus said, "It cannot be that a prophet perish out of Jerusalem." Jehovah buried Moses in Jerusalem, the home of the Eternal God.

The fact that Moses is no longer accepted as the author of Deuteronomy does not lessen its permanent value, for the significance of a book does not depend upon its authorship or literary history, but upon its inherent worth. Judged by this standard Deuteronomy ranks very high. (See intro., pp. 319f.; art., *Pentateuch*, pp. 139f.) The spirit of the entire book is preeminently prophetic. Service is ever placed above sacrifice. To love and to serve Jehovah and one's fellows with all the heart and soul is its supreme demand. No wonder Jesus and the N.T. writers used it so extensively. We may well agree with the judgment of McFadyen: "Deuteronomy is one of the epoch-making books of the world."

JOSHUA

By Professor LINDSAY B. LONGACRE

Introduction

Place in the Canon. In the Hebrew Bible the book of Joshua (named for its chief character, not its author) begins a new division. The *law* closed with Deuteronomy. After the Law comes the division called the *Prophets*. Of the two parts into which this division is itself divided, the Earlier and the Later Prophets, Joshua is the first book in the Earlier Prophets. This designation suggests that the book's interest is primarily religious. It is presented neither as a book of law nor as a book of history, but as a book of prophecy. This suggestion, however, needs two qualifications: (1) The term "prophecy" must here be taken in a sense that reaches far beyond the narrow field of prediction; it must include also exhortation and instruction. (2) The book uses historical traditions as the basis of its appeal, so that it may properly be used as a source of history.

In one respect, however, the division in the Jewish Bible is misleading. The book of Joshua does not simply stand *next to*, but *with*, the Pentateuch, and for two reasons: (1) The whole Pentateuch in all its constituent documents points forward to the possession of the promised land. Had it not been followed, completed, crowned by an account of that possession it would have, so to speak, died without issue, or, like Moses, would have hailed the land from afar but left it unattained. So that on the basis of historical continuity the story in the Pentateuch needed to be carried further. (2) One familiar with the Pentateuch does not have to get far beneath the surface of the book of Joshua to realize not only that it is composite, but that the literary elements of which it is composed are already familiar. Deuteronomy has left an unmistakable mark on Joshua. Here too are the familiar JE and P, establishing a literary connection between the Pentateuch and Joshua too close to be severed by the latter's assignment to a fresh division of biblical books. It is this close connection of the book of Joshua with the Pentateuch that has led scholars to substitute for the term "Pentateuch" the newer term "Hexateuch," so that this sixth volume of the Story of the Promised Land might be taken into its proper place in the family of its closest literary relatives. (See further the art., *The Pentateuch*, p. 134, and cf. p. 92b.)

Literary History. The literary form of the book is due chiefly to R^D (i.e., the Deuteronomic Redactor). Who is this R^D? The answer is not far to seek. It begins with the book of Deuteronomy, a book which reveals a very definite conception of the conditions under which the Hebrews should enter the land of Canaan; and this Deuteronomic point of view is unmistakably represented in Joshua. If one should read, for instance, Deuteronomy 1^{34-39} 3^{18-22} 11^{22-25} 31^{1-8}, and then turn to the first chapter of Joshua, he would realize the similarity between the two far better than any amount of second-hand description could tell him.

How does the book of Joshua get this Deuteronomic coloring? Probably because it was in large part written by someone who looked upon the past from the Deuteronomic point of view. This "someone," desiring to continue the ancient story beyond the death of Moses and on to the conquest of Canaan, collected his materials and set them down in the way a good Deuteronomist would. This compiler or redactor is designated, for convenience, R, and to indicate that his work was done in the spirit of Deuteronomy, a D is added; hence R^D.

The exact extent to which J and E, singly or in combination, are used in the book is a matter still under some discussion; but there is no doubt about their presence, and many passages show themselves clearly to belong to one or both of these early sources. P also is well represented, more especially in the second half of the book, and the characteristic style and point of view of this document are easily recognized. The main features of the literary analysis are indicated in the notes.

The Hero Joshua. The figure of Joshua is an elusive one. He moves through the book in a fashion that is not easy to follow. The book as a whole has idealized so much of its material that it is not surprising that the chief character should also be idealized. The name means "Jehovah is salvation;" in Greek it appears as "Jesus" (cf. Mt. 1^{21} Acts 7^{45}, mg). The connection of Joshua with the territory of Ephraim (19^{50} 24^{30}) suggests that back of the narrative there may lie a recollection of the conquest of that district by the tribe of Joseph in which Joshua may have been active. He is mentioned first in Ex. 17^{9} (E) as a mature warrior, although later (Ex. 33^{11}) he is represented as a young man (cf. Num. 11^{28}, mg). His special function in the book is to carry out the commands of Moses as these are set forth by D.

Historical and Religious Value. In estimating the historical value of Joshua two facts have to be kept in mind: (1) The book is primarily a book of prophetic teaching, and only secondarily a book of history. The author or compiler was much more interested in teaching religious truth by the use of historical material than in narrating facts of history. (2) The story of the conquest is told from two divergent points of view. According to the book as a whole, the invading Hebrews formed a single army under the leadership of Joshua, and the entire land of Canaan was conquered by this united army in the short space of seven years (see, e.g., 10^{40-43} $11^{16-20, 23}$ 21^{43-45}). Following the conquest the land was divided among the twelve tribes by Joshua and Eleazar. Then there are other passages which clearly show that, though in the beginning the armies of Israel may have been united, they soon separated into several groups, each group fighting its own battles. According to the same passages the conquest was less rapid and less complete (see, e.g., 13^{13} $15^{14, 63}$ 16^{10} 17^{12-18} $23^{4, 5, 12, 13}$; cf. also the brief summary in Judg. 1).

On account of the primarily didactic purpose of the book, the divergence in the points of view of different sources embodied in the book, and the absence of definite extra-biblical information concerning this early period, it is exceedingly difficult to trace with any degree of assurance the successive stages in Israel's conquest of Canaan; indeed, it may never become possible to determine exactly the steps by which the Hebrews made themselves masters of the land. Nevertheless, there is insufficient reason for doubting that the biblical narratives rest upon a substantial historical basis; on the contrary, there is every reason for believing that the Joshua narratives, especially those going back to the J and E documents, when properly interpreted, possess great historical value.

Since the interest of the compiler was primarily religio-didactic, it is only natural that the book in all its parts should be permeated by an intensely religious atmosphere. Not to mention specific truths suggested in individual narratives, the book as a whole reflects a sublime faith in Jehovah the God of Israel, in his purpose for the nation, and in the ultimate triumph of this purpose. There is also the irrepressible conviction that the tribes fighting the battles of Jehovah were sustained by the unlimited powers of heaven. Inspired by this faith and conviction, the hero, Joshua, is made to emphasize, in his farewell address, the importance of uncompromising loyalty to Jehovah as a condition of national permanence and prosperity.

However, these lofty conceptions did not completely blot out the survivals of cruder and more primitive ways of religious thinking. Such ideas as blood-revenge, the ban (i.e., consecration to Jehovah by destruction), sacred trees and stones, the use of various forms of primitive magic, all reflect a very early stage of theological thinking, before the purer Jehovah religion had succeeded in driving out or transforming the elements which came to the Hebrews as a part of their common Semitic inheritance. Thus the book of Joshua throws much light on the earlier stages in the development of the religion of Jehovah. (See further the art., *The Religion of Israel*, pp. 165-7.)

Literature: H. Wheeler Robinson, *Deuteronomy and Joshua* (New Century Bible); G. A. Smith, *Historical Geography of the Holy Land;* Kent, *Beginnings of Hebrew History* (Students' Old Testament); Eiselen, *The Prophetic Books of the Old Testament;* Driver, *Introduction to the Literature of the Old Testament;* articles on "Joshua" in modern Dictionaries of the Bible.

Chapters 1 to 12: The Invasion and Conquest of Canaan

The book of Joshua falls into two parts; the first of these includes chs. 1–12. In contrast to the books of the Pentateuch, no further laws are given. Everything is ready for the advance. The striking aspect of the story is its directness, its completeness, and its speed. The Hebrews are encamped at Abel-Shittim, the point to which they had been brought at the close of the book of Numbers. Moses is dead and Joshua has succeeded to the leadership. After the start is made the campaign proceeds rapidly. Jericho is captured and an entrance is effected into the hill-country. Next comes a southern campaign. This is followed by one in the north; and the task is done.

CHAPTER I

Preparation for the Crossing of the Jordan. Joshua is exhorted to advance; rations are prepared; the two and one-half tribes east of the Jordan reassert their loyalty. The chapter is characteristically Deuteronomic. *All this people* (v. 2)—not only the fighting men. The whole nation is thought of as invading the land and taking forcible and complete possession. Joshua, an ideal hero according to Deuteronomic conceptions, is promised complete success. The idea that God would take or need an oath (v. 6) has its place in early conceptions of Deity, but one could hardly imagine such an idea held by Jesus, who taught that even men (let alone, God) should be too trustworthy to need an oath (Mt. 5[33-37].) The ideal of a good man set forth in v. 8 has its most familiar memorial in Psa. 1. *Beyond Jordan* (v. 14)—evidently written west of Jordan, hence not by Moses, for the territory of these tribes was east of the Jordan. *He shall be put to death* (v. 18): in his zeal for Moses, R^D lets the two and one-half tribes speak as though they were the special defenders of Moses.

CHAPTER II

The Spies and Rahab. *Sent spies*—as Moses had done before the first futile attempt to invade the land. *Jericho*: there have been at least three cities of this name in the same general location: the Jericho of to-day, the Jericho of N.T. and Roman times, and the Jericho of the O.T. They are quite distinct and lie a few miles from each other. The first two are now unimpressive villages. The third is a mound of ruins. Excavations carried on here in 1907-09 disclosed at the lowest level remains of a prehistoric settlement, above which were remains of a Canaanite city, which may well have been the one existing at the time of the Hebrew invasion. This city was a small affair with walls 12 to 14 feet thick, walls and houses being built mostly of sun-dried brick. It showed evidences of destruction by fire (6[24]). The desolate Judæan mountains rise rapidly about a mile west of the place; and as far as the present chapter is concerned the narrative is wholly credible. (See G. A. Smith, *Historical Geography of the Holy Land.*) *Rahab.* (Cf. art. in Hastings' *Dictionary of the Bible.*) Mt. 1[5] makes her an ancestress of Jesus; and she is highly praised in Heb. 11[31] and Jas. 2[25]. Her treachery to her own people, however, should not be overlooked.

The king of Jericho (v. 2)—an interesting side-light on the political conditions the Hebrews had to meet. The Canaanite cities had their own kings, as confirmed by the Tel-el-Amarna correspondence (about 1400 B.C.). If these kings had been united in a confederation, it would have been a much more difficult task for the Hebrews to make their way into the country. As it was, they faced comparatively small units of inhabitants, each Canaanite city acting for itself. *There came men of Israel:* taking the story as it stands, it must be supposed that both king and people of Jericho would be very much disturbed as to what might happen at the hands of the horde of invaders camping only a few miles away across the river (v. 9). *Pursued after them to Jordan* (v. 7)—supposing, of course, that the spies had hurried back to their own people. In vv. 10f. R^D represents Rahab speaking like a good Deuteronomist (cf. Deut. 2[25] 4[39] 11[25]). She urged the men to flee *to the mountain* (v. 16), which was nearer than the Jordan and in the opposite direction, with many caves where it would be easy to hide. *Which thou didst let us down by* (v. 18)—refers to the window, not *the line of scarlet thread*, nor the *cord* (v. 15). The scarlet thread may have been something worn by one of the spies and he hastily takes it off, to use as a convenient and not too conspicuous signal (cf. Gen. 38[18]).

CHAPTER III

Crossing the Jordan. Two chapters are devoted to a description of events connected with the crossing of the Jordan. *All the children of Israel* would be approximately two million people (cf. note on Num. 1, 2). *Sanctify yourselves* (v. 5): the advance is an act of God and as such must be prepared for. The people must be ceremonially clean before they are fit to share in the divine act. The sanctifying would consist in the washing of garments and bodies as well as abstaining from any act or object regarded as unclean (cf. 7[13] and Ex. 19[10]). The most vivid commentary one could have on the principle involved is to see a Mohammedan to-day making his ceremonial ablutions before going into the mosque to pray.

The accounts in vv. 8f. are not quite clear; one represents the priests as standing on the east bank of the river until all the people have passed over, the other places the priests in the bed of the stream which had become dry. Evidently, materials from two different sources are used by the compiler. The close of v. 8 looks like a note intended to harmonize the two conceptions. It is easy to read the story without realizing all that is involved in dealing with such a great number of people. The selection of twelve men, first mentioned in v. 12, is ordered a second time in 4[2], where the purpose of the selection is explained. In its present position the direction has no connection with the story. *At Adam* (v. 16) the Jordan is a very crooked river, and it happens on rare occasions that the bank becomes so undermined that a huge mass of earth and rock falls into the stream, forming a temporary dam and entirely blocking the flow of water for a time. Such a case is reported to have happened in the year 1257 A.D. (See Kent, *Beginnings of Hebrew History*, p. 259, note; and Hastings' *Dictionary of the Bible*, vol. ii, p. 765.) An occurrence of this kind might easily form a basis for the present narrative; although this, from the point of view of the compiler, would only transfer the miraculous element, which is central in the narrative, to a point farther upstream. There are many places where the Jordan can be forded in the dry season, but this crossing did not occur at such a time (cf. v. 15 and 4[18]).

CHAPTER IV

The Twelve Memorial Stones. *Take twelve stones:* there is nothing in Palestine quite so plentiful as stones; they are everywhere, and they supply the natural and universal material for boundaries, monuments, and memorials. *Twelve men* (vv. 2, 4)—cf. on Num. 1[6-15]. Vv. 6–9 are another indication of the ideal character of the story. The writer evidently regards the pile of stones as conspicuous throughout many generations and the Hebrews as being where such a question might frequently be asked. This view, however, overlooks the ease with which such a pile of stones would lose its identity among the stones of the land and its innumerable stone piles, as well as the fact that the biblical narratives of later times represent the Hebrews as living in the high lands of Judah rather than near Jericho, so that at best there would be comparatively few children to ask this question.

Set up stones in the Jordan (v. 9)—apparently another tradition about twelve memorial stones. Obviously, they could not be set up in the bed of the river and also taken to the camp (v. 8). *The people hasted* (v. 10). This is the only hint that the writer had considered at all the magnitude of the operation involved in moving two million people with their camp equipment. Haste would be imperative. *Forty thousand* (v. 13)—but cf. Num. 26[7,18, 34]. *The first month* (v. 19)—Nisan, i.e., April, so that the time of year would not be the dry season, when it might be practicable to ford the river (cf. note on 3[16]). *Gilgal*—a name of several localities in Palestine. The word is used generally for a circle of stones having religious significance, a cromlech. The natural sense of the passage is that the place here referred to had this name before the Hebrews took it, which means that it was a place sacred to the Canaanites. But 5[9] explains the origin of the name differently. It may be that the writer regarded Gilgal as the place where the Hebrews lodged that night (vv. 3, 8), yet two different places seem to be intended by these terms.

CHAPTER V

1. Belongs rather to the preceding chapter, bringing to a close the compiler's comment on the crossing of the Jordan.

2–12. Circumcision and the Passover. The practices of circumcision and the keeping of the Passover are intended to consecrate the new stage of the march. *Circumcise:* on the subject of circumcision consult Hastings' *Dictionary of the Bible*, *Encyclopædia Biblica*, and the *Jewish Encyclopædia*. *Knives of flint*, instead of metal, used probably because they were felt to be more in keeping with ancient custom. In vv. 4–7, R^D offers an elaborate statement that the men had not been circumcised, without indicating why this had not been done. V. 9 looks as if circumcision had not been instituted in Egypt (cf. Ex. 4[25]) and that this *reproach* is only now *rolled away*. The words *again* and *the second time* in v. 2 may have been added by R^D in order to connect the two points of view. A quite different representation of the introduction of circumcision among the Hebrews appears in Gen. 17, which carries the rite back to an origin that has no relation to Egypt. *Gilgal*—derived from the Hebrew verb, *galal*, "to roll," but this form does not mean *rolling* (v. 9, mg.; cf. note on 4[19]). The precise details mentioned in vv. 10–12 are all characteristic of the priestly writer who felt sure that no "uncircumcised" would eat the Passover, and also that the manna would hold out until native food was available.

13–15. Vision of Joshua. *Joshua was by Jericho:* in view of the preceding chapters, according to which Joshua with the people have been by Jericho for two or three weeks, this statement is for purposes of exact location both indefinite and unnecessary. It is, however, wholly appropriate and characteristic as introducing the story of the vision which dramatizes Jehovah's support of Joshua in the attack on Jericho. The location of Jericho made it the door to western Palestine through which the Hebrews would have to enter if they were to enter at all from this direction, and its conquest was imperative. One never knew when he was in the presence of divine messengers and forces (e.g., Num. 22[31] 2 Kings 6[17]). *Put off thy shoe*—as Moses was bidden to do (Ex. 3[5]), and as the Mohammedan does to-day before entering a mosque.

CHAPTER VI

The Capture of Jericho. *The Lord said:* if this is a continuation of 5^{13-15} the writer has lost sight of the *captain* with his drawn sword. But more probably the original continuation of 5^{13-15} has been omitted in favor of the story which here begins afresh. Vv. 6–11 describe the march which is made in obedience to the instructions in vv. 2–5. The order (v. 9) seems to be: (1) armed men; (2) priests bearing trumpets; (3) the ark; and (4) a rear guard. The word *priests* that is printed in italics does not appear in the Hebrew text, either here or in v. 13. The statement in both verses is simply that *the rear guard went after the ark blowing with the trumpets as they went;* although nothing has been said about supplying the rear guard with trumpets. The repetition of *compassing the city seven times* (v. 15) is an obvious duplicate due to separate sources. Vv. 17–19 hardly belong here; v. 16 should be followed immediately by v. 20. These directions belong earlier in the story. At this point there is no time for further instructions and there would be too much noise to have heard them had they been given after the order to shout. *Devoted*—see Num. 18^{14}, note. The presence of *the devoted thing* in the camp would cause the whole camp to be *devoted* (cf. mg. of v. 18 for *accursed*).

The fall of Jericho is a subject which has long had its place in the familiar picture gallery of O.T. scenes. Yet somehow the story does not read convincingly to men whose thoughts move naturally in the world as it is known to-day. But why should it? It was written by and for men who regarded the world, not as a unity but as a diversity in which the familiar course of events could be interrupted or reversed without in the least disturbing adjacent objects or interfering with (unknown) laws of nature. The real root of the modern reader's perplexity over the passage is his failure to distinguish between the overthrow of Jericho as a fact of history and the writer's explanation of its cause and method—the distinction between the "what" and the "how"; for the two are distinct and separable. The former is easily disposed of: the conquest of Jericho by the Hebrews is reliable history. It is the latter question which calls for comment.

The writer does not claim to have witnessed the event. He was dependent on the traditions which had come down to him from an earlier time. The difference between his own point of view and that of a modern reader is seen, for instance, in his apparent unconcern that his narrative represents Rahab's house as being on the town wall (2^{15}), that the walls fell down flat (6^{20}), and yet that Rahab's house is still intact (6^{22}). There was no doubt, however, that Jericho had been overthrown. As a matter of fact, the Hebrews were not the only ones who had taken this city at one time or another. Further, the sacred ark was regarded as having magic power, even if it was not always victorious (cf. on 1 Sam. 4–6). Also, belief in the power of a united shout was easy to one who believed in the objective power of a blessing or a curse (cf. on Num. 22^{6}). So that materials were at hand for just such an account as is given here, provided one lived in a world where these views were valid. And that is where the writer lived. And the modern reader, if he would appreciate these narratives, must be willing and able, in imagination, to place himself in that ancient world so different from his own. (See art., *How to Study the Bible,* pp. 5–7.)

These narratives are imaginative, but they cannot fairly be called fictitious. They are products of a pious imagination whose underlying motive is faith, not fancy. Once the capture of Jericho is established, along with its significance for the Hebrew people, it was as legitimate for the ancient writers to picture the scene in terms of their faith and of the world as they knew it as it is for the believer to-day to picture biblical history in terms of *his* faith and the world as *he* knows it (cf. the famous pictures of biblical scenes by the great painters). Thrilled with the vision of an ancient triumph, the biblical writer painted his picture, not in color with a brush on canvas, but in words with a pen on parchment; and he had a perfect right to do this, for he was preaching faith, not drawing diagrams. So that the obligation rests upon those to whom his words have come to understand his method and his purpose, and not to distort his meanings by forcing them into patterns they were never designed to fit. From time immemorial, sacred symbols, whether ark or crucifix, have fired men's hearts with courage, trumpets have sounded for assembly and attack, walls have gone down before invading armies, and all in the name of the God of Hosts; and this is what happened at Jericho. The destruction was probably not as complete as this passage indicates, for the city is apparently still standing in Josh. 18^{21} and 2 Sam. 10^{5}. On v. 26 cf. 1 Kings 16^{34}.

CHAPTER VII

1–5. Defeat at Ai. *Devoted*—see above on 6^{17}. *The anger of Jehovah:* it is only the familiarity of this phrase that obscures the primitive conception of Deity underlying it. *Ai*—up in the hill-country, well within the promised land. *To toil thither:* the ascent from Jericho in the Jordan Valley is by way of a steep gorge or wady whose ascent is extremely toilsome. *Thirty-six* out of three thousand does not seem such a terrible loss. The disaster lay in the fact of defeat, whether with or without casualties.

6–9. **Joshua Argues with Jehovah.** Cf. Deut. 9[26-29]. Joshua argues with Jehovah as Moses had done; a dialogue in which the writer dramatizes Joshua's humiliation and his discovery of the reason for the defeat. V. 9 shows clearly how closely united the welfare of Jehovah was supposed to be with the welfare of his people. In the thought of the early Hebrews the defeat of a nation was the defeat of its deity.

10–26. **Trespass of Achan and His Punishment.** To take *the devoted thing* was to rob God, a far worse sin than to rob a fellow man. (See notes on Lev. 27[28, 29] and cf. on Acts 5[1-11].) This brought upon the whole camp the ban under which the devoted thing had already been placed (cf. 6[18]). The deity's intervention (v. 13) must be properly prepared for (cf. on 3[5]). *Which the Lord taketh* (v. 14): the selection was probably thought of as having been made by some use of sacred lots, although just how this was done can only be conjectured. The ban is carried out against Achan and the place is named for the event. *A goodly Babylonish mantle* (v. 21) indicates in an interesting way the commerce of the day, as one might now have a gown from Paris. The inclusion of Achan's family with himself (v. 24) was inevitable. The separation of an individual from his family in matters of responsibility arose only at a comparatively late period. In this case all would have been contaminated by the devoted things. Death by *stoning* was a recognized form of execution. Stones big enough to be taken up in both hands were thrown down upon the victim until life was extinct (cf. Jn. 8[1-11] Acts 7[57-59] 14[19]). The confused text—stoning, burning, stoning—in this verse is due to the fact that the documents used are poorly combined. The name of the place *Achor* (v. 26) is attributed to this event by one of the popular etymologies so frequent in O.T.; cf. on 5[9].

CHAPTER VIII

1–29. **The Capture of Ai.** The camp having been purified in the drastic fashion just described, a second attack on Ai is made. The numbers in v. 3 seem too large (cf. v. 12). 4–7. A quite reasonable strategy. 8–13. *Among the people* (v. 9): the difference of one Hebrew letter would give the reading, "in the midst of the vale," as in v. 13. Vv. 10–12 are parallel to vv. 3–9. V. 13 reaches the same point reached in v. 9. 14–29. The strategy is successfully carried out. *At the time . . . Arabah* (omitted by LXX) gives no meaning. No previous plan of this kind (v. 18) has been mentioned. The idea is similar to that in the story of Moses (Ex. 17[11]). Joshua is apparently imagined to be on some high point where he could see and be seen, for he directs the outbreak of the men in ambush and also (v. 21) the return of the Hebrews who by apparent flight had drawn the people of Ai away from their city. The slaughter of the inhabitants (vv. 22–26) is carried out with the same thoroughness as in the case of Jericho. *A heap forever* (v. 28)—an echo of Deut. 13[16]. *Forever* must not be taken too literally; for, according to the author of Ezra 2[28], Ai was still a city in his day. The king is first killed and then his body hung on the tree (cf. Deut. 21[22f.]). *Heap of stones*—cf. 7[26] and 4[3], note.

30–35. **A Fragment About a Ceremony at Mount Ebal.** The location is at Shechem and presupposes settlement in the country. The passage does not relate to what immediately precedes or follows and interrupts the close connection between 8[29] and 9[1]. It apparently wishes to make clear that Deut. 27 was actually obeyed, but it plainly belongs elsewhere, having no place in the story until after the land has been conquered.

CHAPTER IX

1–15. **The Trick of the Gibeonites.** Vv. 1, 2 give a summary of the successful progress made up to this point, dramatically indicated by the fear of the Hebrews that is spreading through the country. *Perizzite, Hivite*—the names of two inconsiderable peoples of central Palestine; on the other names in this verse cf. Num. 13[29] and note there. Note the similarity between these verses and 5[1]. V. 3 begins the special story of the Gibeonites. *Gibeon* was five or six miles northwest of Jerusalem. In Solomon's day it was "a great high place" and the chief place for sacrifices before the Temple was built (1 Kings 3[4]). *Heard what Joshua had done* (v. 3). While this statement is appropriate to the course of the general narrative, it does not seem applicable to the story of the Gibeonites. The reason which they themselves give (v. 10) refers only to events previous to the crossing of the Jordan; and were it not for this editorial harmonization in v. 3b it would be most natural to suppose that the camp at Gilgal (v. 6) was the one pitched immediately after the river had been crossed (ch. 4). This would agree with the implied smartness of the Gibeonites, who would then be represented as realizing their danger, and as taking immediate and timely steps to save themselves.

The success of the strategy described in vv. 4, 5 (in v. 4 follow the reading of the versions; see mg.) is attributed to two causes, either of which would have been sufficient; the twofold explanation probably indicates different versions of the story. These causes are: (1) that the Hebrews were deceived; and (2) they failed to *ask counsel of Jehovah.* The existence of the two versions also explains the change from Gibeonites to Hivites (vv. 3, 7; cf. 11^{19}), and the alternation between Joshua and the men of Israel as leaders in the negotiations for the Hebrews. *The princes of the congregation* (v. 15b) connects this clause with the version of the story given in vv. 17–21. This v. 15 is a good illustration of the textual conditions which raise questions of literary analysis. Here are three well-defined statements: (1) Joshua made peace with them; (2) he made a covenant with them to let them live; and (3) the princes sware unto them. These appear to be too many statements for a single operation; and when they are crowded together like this their presence is most reasonably explained on the basis of the composite character of the present text.

16–27. The Resulting Status of the Gibeonites. V. 16 connects with the covenant in v. 15 and is continued in v. 22. Vv. 17–21 give a parallel account. *House of my God* (v. 23) connects with *place which he should choose* (a Deuteronomic phrase) in v. 27, both referring to the Temple. There was, of course, no Temple in the days of Joshua, but when these documents were written it had long been the center of the nation's religion. This verse is continued in v. 26. V. 22 does not call for any answer. The phrase, *hewers of wood and drawers of water* (v. 27), has become a current term for any persons who are condemned to menial service.

CHAPTER X

1–15. Gibeon Attacked by Five Kings in Southern Canaan, Rescued by Joshua. The covenant made with the Gibeonites obligates the Hebrews to come to their defense when threatened by the five kings. Under Joshua's leadership, and with the aid of a thunderstorm sent by Jehovah, the five kings are utterly defeated. The territory indicated would be included approximately between lines drawn from Jerusalem west to the coast, from Jerusalem south to Hebron, and then from Hebron west to the coast. Throughout all this campaign the headquarters of the Hebrews remains at Gilgal, where they first encamped after crossing the Jordan (4^{19}). It could not have been an entirely satisfactory location because, lying in the low Jordan Valley, every move into Canaan would have to start with the steep ascent up to the high-lying hill-country which was the object of the invasion and of the conquest. *Ascent of Beth-horon* (v. 10). There were two Beth-horons, the upper and the lower, near together and only a few miles northwest of Gibeon. In the pursuit from Gibeon the upper Beth-horon would be reached first, a descent leading down from there to lower Beth-horon, a little distance beyond. *Azekah and Makkedah* must have been in the same general neighborhood, though the exact sites cannot now be located. *The Lord discomfited them.* These were the wars of Jehovah (cf. Num. 21^{14}) and Jehovah was the final factor in all victories. V. 11 pictures Jehovah's direct co-operation in the sending of a terrific hailstorm (cf. Judg. 5^{20}).

Vv. 12–14 contain the famous reference to *the sun standing still,* which, like so many other familiar passages, would never have been misunderstood if its literary form had been recognized. There is here a four-line fragment of a poem. Taken by itself, it is plainly a poetic expression of the idea that the day was long enough for a complete victory. It is quoted from the *Book of Jashar;* Jashar meaning "upright," and referring to the nation as a whole or to the nation's heroes, or to Jehovah himself (cf. 2 Sam. 1^{18}). But the writer of the book of Joshua, in his zeal for Jehovah and for Joshua, has taken the poetry as though it were mechanical description and has made a nature miracle out of a poetic expression (vv. 12a, 13b). Later readers, ignoring the distinction between prose and poetry, and themselves as interested in signs and wonders as the author of Joshua, have been equally prosaic and mistaken in their reading of the poem. (See art., *Bible as Literature,* p. 19.) V. 15 is more suitable at v. 43, where it also appears. At this place it is premature; the fighting is not over.

16–27. The Fate of the Kings. The reference to the *cave* is true to the country; caves there are still numerous, and still used for various purposes. *To put one's foot upon the neck of his foe* (v. 24) was no mere gesture of triumph, but was supposed actually to complete the victory. In v. 25 R^D adds his familiar exhortation. The kings are treated as the king of Ai had been (8^{29}).

28–43. Review and Summary. R^D reviews and summarizes the campaign of which details have already been given. He views it as a complete subjugation of southern Palestine. *Kadesh-barnea* (v. 41) marks an extreme southern outpost fifty miles south of Beersheba. From here the Hebrews have conquered the country extending as far north as Gibeon and Ai, and from the Jordan Valley westward to the sea. It was a "whirlwind campaign," a "clean sweep"; but see below on 13[3], and also introduction, section on "Historical and Religious Value," p. 346.

CHAPTER XI

1–15. Conquest of Northern Canaan. Just as the possession of southern Canaan had been won by a single victorious engagement (ch. 10), so the possession of northern Canaan is now won by another complete victory over a northern group of Canaanite kings (vv. 1–9). The places and peoples named in vv. 2, 3, are intended to indicate all Palestine lying north of a line through the plain of Esdraelon and the southern end of the Sea of Galilee (*Chinneroth*). The name of *Jabin* (v. 1) and the location of the battle (vv. 4–9) are points of contact with the similar engagement doubly described in Judg. 4 and 5. *Waters of Merom* (v. 7)—identified by many with Lake Huleh, but a location more appropriate to the narrative would be nearer to the modern Meron, southwest of Hazor. The Hebrews never maintained control of the more open and level parts of the country and so had little use for either chariots or horses (v. 6). This fact may have had its influence on the burning of the chariots and the brutal mutilation of the captured horses (cf. 2 Sam. 8[4]). *Great Zidon* (v. 8): the familiar city on the coast north of Tyre is meant, but this seems too far away. The *Misrephoth-maim* may be the modern Musherfe, which lies on the coast almost directly west of Hazor. If the *Mizpeh* of this verse is the same as the *Mizpah* of v. 3, then the flight took place in two directions, some of the fugitives going northwest toward the Sea and others northeast back toward Hazor. Vv. 10–15 (R^D) complete the story, specifying that the king of Hazor was slain, that the Canaanites were exterminated, and particularly and characteristically that Jehovah's commands to Moses were fulfilled to the letter.

16–20. Summary of the Conquest of Canaan. A summary of the two campaigns which, according to this narrative, gave the Hebrews complete possession of Canaan. *Seir* and *Lebanon* (v. 17) represent the extreme south and the extreme north similar to the more familiar "from Dan to Beersheba," although these are named in the reverse order and do not embrace quite so much territory. *A long time* (v. 18)—cf. on 14[10]. To the early Hebrew it would appear no more strange that Jehovah should operate on men's *hearts* (v. 20) than that he should fight with hailstones (10[11]). The word "heart," however, must be understood in the biblical sense, namely, of men's thoughts and ideas, not of their feelings and emotions. The expression, "a hard heart," is equivalent to the modern expressions "headstrong," "self-willed."

21–23. The Anakim. These verses contain a final note concerning the giants who, according to tradition, lived near Hebron and in the Philistine country, as did the later Goliath of Gath (1 Sam. 17[4]).

CHAPTER XII

The Kings That Were Conquered by Moses East of Jordan (1–6) and by Joshua West of Jordan (7–24). Chs. 10, 11, telling of the conquest of the south and north respectively, had each closed with a summary of successes. Now that the conquest of the land is completed, there is given a summary of the whole enterprise. On vv. 1–6 cf. Deut. 2, 3. Vv. 7–24, which sum up the exploits of Joshua, repeat the names already mentioned in the preceding chapters with fifteen names in addition.

The following facts should be noted of the book so far: (1) The northern and southern campaigns left unmentioned a considerable extent of territory in central Canaan. This was eventually occupied by the Hebrews. Some of the names in this chapter, Bethel for instance (v. 16; cf. 8[17]), may be echoes of the invasion of this part of the country; as may also the isolated fragment, 8[30-35]. (2) The conquest as represented in this part of the book was accomplished with conspicuous thoroughness ("there was none left that breathed," 11[11]). (3) It was carried through quickly. The undertaking really reduced itself to two decisive battles, one against the kings of the south and the other against the kings of the north. The Hebrews acted unitedly under Joshua's leadership. This representation of the conquest is emphasized because it differs so widely from another one that appears later in the book (see on 13[13]), in comparison with which the one given here shows itself clearly as an idealization of the story in terms of an ideal fulfillment of the Deuteronomic command that the Canaanites should be exterminated (see intro., p. 346).

CHAPTERS 13 TO 24: THE DISTRIBUTION OF THE LAND AND JOSHUA'S FORMAL FAREWELL

The first part of the book consists mainly of narratives compiled from JE with frequent expansions by R^D and a few additions from P. The subject is primarily the conquest of the land. The second part consists mainly of geographical lists from P with only occasional brief extracts from JE and comparatively little of R^D. The subject is primarily the distribution of the land among the tribes. Additional matter includes the assignment of cities to the Levites, release of the tribes settled east of Jordan (cf. Num. 32) who had helped in the conquest, and two versions of a farewell address by Joshua. The first part of the book closes with Joshua's triumph, the second with his death.

CHAPTER XIII

1–7. Jehovah Orders Division of Canaan Among the Tribes. *Remaineth* (v. 1) may have referred originally to parts of the country lying within the territory traditionally occupied by the Hebrews (see below on v. 13), but R^D immediately applies the statement to border districts never occupied, and, indeed, never claimed (except ideally), by the Hebrews. The five Philistine cities named in v. 3 are frequently referred to (e.g., Judg. 3³ 1 Sam. 6⁴). Something has dropped out between v. 8 and the preceding verses; v. 7 is speaking of the Manasseh west of the Jordan, while v. 8 is speaking of the eastern part of the tribe. Furthermore, *him*, v. 8, has no proper antecedent in the present text.

8–33. Inheritances East of the Jordan. For the various sites and cities mentioned in these verses the critical commentaries and Bible dictionaries should be consulted; no attempt is made here to discuss them all.

V. 13 is the first of a series of fragments which represent a view of the invasion so different from the ideal view set forth in the book as a whole that it deserves more than casual mention, not only as an interesting item of literary significance, but more especially because of its bearing on the historical course of events (see also intro., p. 346). The other fragments are 15¹⁴⁻¹⁹, ⁶³ 16¹⁰ 17¹¹⁻¹⁸ 19⁴⁷. With these should be compared Judg. 1, where they are substantially repeated in combination with additional material. These passages are from J and represent the oldest and most reliable view of the history. According to their testimony, the settlement in Canaan was made gradually and partially, not by a single victorious movement; and it was carried out by single tribes or small groups of tribes acting independently, rather than by a united campaign undertaken by the whole nation. Treaty as well as warfare played its part in the story. The outcome was that the Hebrews established themselves in the hill-country, but they were unable to occupy the broader and more level districts and many of the cities. There are many reasons for regarding this as the actual course of the history, not the least being its correspondence with the conditions indicated in the books of Judges, Samuel, and Kings. It offers such a contrast to the idealization of the past which is characteristic of the present book of Joshua that the two must be regarded as mutually exclusive. Of the two the earlier testimony must be recognized as the more historical.

With v. 14 cf. ch. 21. *Medeba* (v. 16)—interesting to-day chiefly on account of the mosaic map, dating from the sixth century A.D., in the floor of the Greek church there (cf. Cobern, *New Archæological Discoveries*, pp. 367f.). *Plain* (v. 17)—better, with mg., *tableland;* for while the district referred to is one of broad fields, it lies high above the level, not only of the Jordan Valley, but also of the Judæan ranges to the west. *Balaam* (v. 22)—cf. on Num. 21–24. With v. 23 cf. ch. 22.

CHAPTER XIV

Assignment of Hebron to Caleb. *Eleazar and Joshua* were the successors respectively of Aaron (Num. 20²²⁻²⁹) and Moses (Num. 27¹⁵⁻²³); but whereas Moses took precedence over Aaron, Eleazar takes precedence over Joshua. Vv. 6–15 give an explanation of the fact that *Caleb* and his descendants possessed Hebron, one of the most important cities in the territory of Judah. Although named here with Judah, Caleb is usually represented as a descendant of Kenaz the Edomite (cf. Judg. 1¹³). There are grounds for supposing that his clan had penetrated the country from the south at an earlier period. *Forty-five years* (v. 10): this is the only statement in the book that bears on the length of time the conquest was supposed to cover. If the traditional forty years are taken as the correct number for the wilderness period, this verse would indicate that the conquest extended through five years. If the wilderness period was thirty-eight years (Deut. 2¹⁴), then the conquest would have covered seven years. *Anakim* (v. 12)—giants. Three are named in 15¹⁴; cf. on 11²¹⁻²³.

CHAPTER XV

1–20. Judah's Allotment. Roughly speaking, it included the territory west of a line drawn from the mouth of the Jordan at the Dead Sea to Kadesh-barnea, with the Mediterranean as the western boundary. *Gilgal* (v. 7)—not the place of the encampment near Jericho. "Gilgal" means "circle," and occurs frequently as a place name, indicating the site of a circle of stones having religious significance (see 4^{19}, notes). *Jerusalem* (v. 8)—another indication of the ideal character of the book, as Jerusalem did not come into the possession of the Hebrews until the time of David (2 Sam. 5^{6-9}).

Caleb receives his portion (vv. 13–19; cf. on 14^{6-15}) as though he belonged to the tribe of Judah, but he is *among the children of Judah*, i.e., he constitutes a different tribe. Vv. 14–19 are repeated in Judg. 1^{10-15}; and cf. above on 13^{13}. *Springs of water* (v. 19), rare enough in Judah, would make all the difference between desirable and undesirable fields. Hebron's value is due to its supply of water. V. 20 gives P's concluding formula.

21–63. List of the Cities of Judah. *Twenty-nine* (v. 32)—the total is incorrect; it should be thirty-six. A smaller error occurs in v. 36. For v. 36, cf. 13^{13}, notes.

CHAPTERS XVI, XVII

The Territory of the Children of Joseph. Joseph is not a single tribe but always is divided into the so-called half-tribes of Ephraim and Manasseh (16^{4}). Of these the more important and influential is Ephraim, who gives his name to the hill-country where he settles. Manasseh's chief share lay east of the Jordan. For 16^{10} cf. on 13^{13}.

For 17^{3-6} cf. on Num. 27^{1-11} 36^{1-12}. For 17^{11-13} cf. on 13^{13}. The towns here named are situated in or near the broad fertile plain of Esdraelon, which the Hebrews were never able to hold (cf. 17^{16}), a fact easily overlooked if the glowing idealism of the book of Joshua is not understood. 17^{14-18} (cf. on 13^{13}) furnishes further indication both of the partial failure of the conquest and also of the way the tribes act independently. *Thou shalt drive out*, etc. (17^{18}): the sense here should obviously agree with 17^{16}.

CHAPTER XVIII

The Tent at Shiloh; The Territory of the Children of Benjamin. In chs. 16 and 17, Judah and Joseph have had their lots assigned, but now there is a halt in the narrative. Seven tribes remain who have not been assigned to their inheritance. After long obscurity the sacred tent appears again and in a fragment from P is located at Shiloh in Ephraim's territory. *Slack* (v. 3) suggests again that the conquest was not as complete and triumphant as might otherwise appear. Joshua has to exhort the people to make a survey of the remaining territory with a view to final distribution. V. 7 is plainly from R^{D}, as is shown by its view of the Levites and its reference to the tribes east of Jordan. Beginning with the distribution to Benjamin at v. 11 the distribution to the seven tribes is set down in the same manner that had been followed in the case of Judah and Joseph.

CHAPTER XIX

The Distribution Completed. (Continued from ch. 18.) Vv. 15, 30, 38 contain numerical discrepancies which cannot now be explained. **47.** Cf. on 13^{13}. *Leshem* is probably the same as the *Laish* of Judg. 18^{29}. **49f.** Joshua, as national leader, and also as belonging to the tribe of Ephraim, is specially mentioned as receiving his portion within the bounds of his own tribe, although the commandment of Jehovah referring to it is not found elsewhere. **51.** Looking back from this verse to 18^{1}, it seems reasonable to suppose, as some do, that 18^{1} originally stood just before 14^{1}. This would make an appropriate beginning and unify the whole account of the distribution, locating it at Shiloh (cf. on 8^{30-35}) before the sacred tent, i.e., under divine auspices, with 19^{51} as the appropriate conclusion.

CHAPTER XX

Designation of the Six Cities of Refuge. Cf. on Num. 35^{9-34} and Deut. 19. The imperative custom of blood revenge required that if one person kill another the dead man's next of kin should kill the killer. The custom knew no exceptions and made no provision for accidents. These cities are provided for the protection, not of men who had committed a premeditated murder, but (1) to shelter the accused until his case could be heard and acted upon by proper judges; and (2) in case the death were accidental to provide for the accused a place where he could live in safety from the avenger. These six cities are located, three on each side of the Jordan, and each of the three in the northern, middle, and southern parts of the land respectively. They are included in the list of cities assigned to the Levites in the next chapter and were in all probability known already as places of religious importance. The text of the chapter differs considerably in Hebrew and LXX, the latter omitting *and unawares*, in v. 3, and all the vv. 4–6 except the phrase *until he stand before the congregation for judgment*, in v. 6. On blood revenge, see the article, *Bible Manners and Customs*, p. 75.

CHAPTER XXI

Cities Assigned to the Levites. Cf. Num. 35^{1-8}. Vv. 1–7 give the general statement of the number of cities involved, the tribes which should release them, and the Levitical families to whom they should be assigned. Vv. 8–40 give the cities by name; a kind of itemized list to accompany the general statement in vv. 4–7. *The children of Aaron the priest* (v. 4) constitute a special group within the family of Kohath, and their thirteen cities are priestly cities as distinct from the thirty-five remaining Levitical cities. The word translated *suburbs* means throughout the chapter lands close to a city where cattle could be pastured. Vv. 11f. reflect the compiler's embarrassment over the assignment to the children of Aaron of the cities that were already held by Caleb. Though *among the children of Judah* (15[13]), he is not treated as a Hebrew and would therefore be under no obligation to surrender any cities for the sake of a Hebrew religious requirement. In these verses the idea is that the children of Aaron received Hebron and the adjoining pastures while Caleb retained the fields and villages. Vv. 43–45 express the devout belief of the Deuteronomist that in ancient times in Israel everything turned out exactly as it should. Many people feel that way to-day about the past, instinctively idealizing and glorifying everything that happened then and correspondingly depreciating everything belonging to the present.

CHAPTER XXII

1–8. Return of the Transjordanic Tribes. A happy conclusion of an arrangement which when proposed threatened disaster (Num. 32). **8.** Better, omit with LXX, *spake unto them saying* and read *and they returned with much wealth. Your brethren* refers presumably to the men who had remained behind as a home guard after the departure of the quota of warriors promised to aid in the western campaign; cf. the provision in 1 Sam. 30[24].

9–34. An Altar Erected East of the Jordan. An example of the literary form called a *midrash* (cf. on Num. 31), a story designed to illustrate and to enforce a religious teaching. The teaching here to be illustrated is that the Hebrews should worship Jehovah at one sanctuary only, in this case Shiloh (cf. 18[1] and 19[51]). When the book of Joshua was written, Jerusalem was the sole shrine, and the principle of one central sanctuary is clearly laid down in the present *midrash.* Its late date is indicated by the principle which it embodies, a principle which had not been laid down in earlier days (cf. Ex. 20[24] and 1 Kings 19[10]), as well as by the suppression of the civil leader Joshua in the interest of the religious leader Phinehas, the son of Eleazar, the priest. The *midrash* may have as a historical foundation an actual altar somewhere along the Jordan in connection with which was told a story of threatened war between the tribes (cf. Judg. 19, 20). *To see to* (v. 10)—i.e., to look at, conspicuous. The establishment of an altar to Jehovah anywhere else than Shiloh (v. 16; later, Jerusalem) was regarded as nothing less than rebellion against Jehovah. V. 19 suggests that the land west of Jordan was the real Holy Land, the land east of Jordan was debatable. The English translation of v. 22 misses the impressive threefold name "El," "Elohim," "Jehovah," which appears also in Psa. 50[1], and which makes the following assurance a particularly solemn one. The characteristic of an altar is, of course, that it is a sacred place upon which offerings are made to a deity (v. 23). *A witness* (v. 28)—also in v. 34 where the words in italics in English do not appear in the Hebrew. This means that the Hebrew text does not give the name of the altar, but that the name is supplied here by the translators, perhaps under the influence of Gen. 31[47f].

CHAPTER XXIII

Joshua's Farewell Address: First Account. The Deuteronomic spirit, language, and point of view of this account will be quite evident to one who will compare Deut. 28, or even the little paragraph, Josh. 21[43-45]. The conquest has been completed; it was all Jehovah's doing, and now the remaining people of the land must be driven out; there must be no fellowship with them, under penalty of *all the evil things* (v. 15) that will come upon those who *transgress the covenant* by serving *other gods* (v. 16).

CHAPTER XXIV

Joshua's Farewell Address: Second Account. This is the address as E thought of it. The address leads into a renewal of the covenant on the part of Joshua and the people to be loyal to Jehovah. The details of the historical allusions can easily be traced by the use of a reference Bible. **1–14.** *Other gods* (vv. 2, 3): according to some modes of expression Abraham would be termed a heathen while he was in his home *beyond the River. Balak fought against Israel* (v. 9)—cf. Num. 22–24. *The men of Jericho fought against you* (v. 11)—this is not the impression one would get from ch. 6. *Amorite . . . Jebusite*—the familiar catalogue from RD. *The hornet* (v. 12)—may be meant figuratively (cf. Deut. 1[44]), or literally, in the way that Jehovah sent locusts and other pests; but the reference is not clear. The intention, however, is plainly to emphasize

Jehovah's agency as being the effective factor, and not Israel's *sword or bow*. The indication in v. 14 is that up to this point the Hebrews were not yet worshiping Jehovah only; but that earlier gods, from *beyond the River and from Egypt*, were still cherished (see v. 23). **15–18.** The people choose Jehovah because of his aid and guidance in the past. **19–24.** They confirm their choice by agreeing to be absolutely and exclusively loyal to him in the future. While Jehovah was merciful and forgiving, he was also jealous and, on some points, quite unforgiving (cf. Ex. $34^{6f.}$). Furthermore, the natural reading of the verse would make *jealous* explain *holy* (cf. on Num. 18^{1}). **25–28.** It would be interesting to discover the history lying back of the *covenant, statute, and ordinance* (v. 25), connected with Shechem, and what relation this covenant had, if any, to the one associated with Moses at Sinai. There has been much discussion concerning the book of the Law referred to in v. 26. If the verse came from R^D, it would be natural to think of the law book as the original Deuteronomy. Some have thought the reference to be the Book of the Covenant (Ex. 20^{22}–23^{19}; cf. Ex. 24^{7}). In any case the book referred to was evidently thought of as a book to which additions could still be made, and one that was separate from the book of Joshua. *The stone, the oak*—sacred stones and sacred trees are frequently mentioned in O.T., and are quite numerous in Palestine to-day, where they are still regarded in the primitive way indicated in v. 26. **29–33.** Cf. Judg. 2^{6-9}. The body of Joseph is probably thought of as embalmed according to the Egyptian custom (v. 32), which was not practiced by the Hebrews (cf. Gen. 50^{25} Ex. 13^{19}). Abraham had purchased a burial place at Hebron for his dead (Gen. 23), and so had Jacob (Gen. 33^{19}). With v. 33 cf. 21^{10-18}; there the children of Aaron receive no cities in the hill-country of Ephraim.

JUDGES

BY PROFESSOR W. O. E. OESTERLEY

INTRODUCTION

Title and Place in the Canon. The Hebrew title of the book is *Shôphĕṭîm*, the root meaning of which is "to govern" as well as "to judge," in the sense of discriminating and deciding between right and wrong. It signifies also "to vindicate," and thus "to deliver"; and it is in the sense of "deliverer" that the word is here used; see especially 2^{16-18}. Sometimes the Judge is spoken of as a "Saviour" because he saves his people from the hand of their enemies (see $3^{9, 15}$). The Hebrew canon consists of three divisions: the Law, the Prophets, and the Writings. The second division has two parts, the Former and the Latter Prophets. Our book belongs to the "Former Prophets," the subdivision consisting of Joshua, Judges, First and Second Samuel, First and Second Kings.

Contents. The Introduction (1^{1}–2^{5}) tells of how the Israelite tribes effected a settlement in Canaan; it shows that this was a long-drawn-out process, and that it was not brought about by any concerted movement, but that individual tribes acted independently. The book proper begins at 2^{6}, where the narrative is continued from Josh. 24^{27}; indeed, there is a slight overlapping at the start, for 2^{6-10} is more or less a repetition of Josh. 24^{28-31}. The main narrative runs to the end of ch. 12. There are, properly speaking, only six judges who come into account: Othniel (a somewhat shadowy person), Ehud, Shamgar (also little more than a name), Deborah, Gideon, and Jephthah. These deliverers are introduced in connection with six more or less serious crises: (1) The first of the Judges, Othniel, is said to have delivered Israel from a Mesopotamian king whose name is not given, but who is called Cushan-rishathaim, which means "the Cushite of double wickedness" (3^{7-11}). (2) Ehud, of the tribe of Benjamin, did his work in the south. Eglon, the king of Moab, had seized the city of Jericho, and imposed tribute on the adjacent territory. Ehud treacherously slew the king and, summoning the Ephraimites, succeeded in driving the Moabites across the Jordan (3^{12-30}). (3) Meanwhile the energy of the Israelites in the north was expended in attempts to conquer the land, but they were not altogether successful. In the course of time the natives prevailed against the newcomers, and the Israelites were threatened with complete subjugation. In this crisis Deborah, the prophetess, and Barak of Kadesh Naphtali assumed the leadership. The battle with the Canaanites was fought in the Plain of Esdraelon, and ended in a decisive victory for Israel. The power of the Canaanites was broken and Central Palestine was thrown open to the immigrants (4^{1}–5^{31}). (4) A new danger threatened from the east. Midianites began to cross the Jordan, and in a short time the Israelites, especially the tribes of Ephraim and Manasseh, were reduced to galling serfdom. From Manasseh arose the deliverer in the person of a brave, patriotic, God-fearing farmer by the name of Gideon. So great was the gratitude of the delivered tribes that they offered to make Gideon king, but he declined the honor. However, after his death, Abimelech, the son of Gideon and a Canaanite woman, secured the kingship, after slaying all the other sons of Gideon but one. The rule of Abimelech proved disastrous and soon came to an ignominious end (6^{1}–9^{57}). (5) The next crisis was caused by the Ammonites, another east-Jordan people. They took advantage of the unsettled conditions in Israel, and seized the Israelite territory east of the Jordan. In time they crossed the Jordan, and the Israelites, without a competent leader, were worsted. Finally they called to their aid Jephthah of the tribe of Gad, who defeated the Ammonites and dislodged them from all the Israelite territory (10^{6}–12^{7}). (6) The sixth and severest crisis was caused by the Philistines in the southwest. The book describes the exploits of Shamgar and, at much greater length, of Samson, but their deeds of personal daring were without permanent results. The struggles continued for several centuries, and ended in the complete triumph of Israel.

Five other judges are mentioned—Tola, Jair, Ibzan, Elon, and Abdon, concerning whom little information is given; hence they are commonly referred to as the Minor Judges. Samson, who is the twelfth, comes under quite a different category. He is not one of the Judges in the ordinary sense; and the cycle of the Samson stories (chs. 13–16) forms a distinct series of narratives radically different from the others. Another separate narrative is contained in chs.

17, 18, which describe the migration of the Danites from southern to northern Palestine, and tell how the sanctuary in Dan came to be founded. Finally, there is another story, and a very gruesome one, which gives an account of an outrage committed by the Benjamites of Gibeah, and of the almost complete annihilation of the guilty tribe by the rest of the tribes, means being found, however, of saving the tribe from total extinction.

Our book consists thus, strictly speaking, of five main parts, though they have been run into a more or less continuous narrative, namely, Introduction, 1^{1}–2^{5}; History of the Judges, 2^{6}–12^{15}; the Samson stories, chs. 13–16; the Danite migration, chs. 17, 18; and the Gibeah episode with its consequences, chs. 19–21.

This variety of content is of itself sufficient to show that the book does not form a unity, but is a compilation of material taken from different sources.

The Sources of the Book. It is within the nature of things that the exploits of tribal heroes should run from mouth to mouth, and that a more or less stereotyped form of the narratives should soon come into being. In each tribe such narratives would be preserved by being handed down orally; and thus there must have existed in the various Israelite tribes traditional material regarding their early history, which, in the first instance, floated about within the circumscribed area of the particular tribe. And, as the occurrences related must have been witnessed by many, different versions of the same event would naturally be current. How long it was before this oral material assumed a written form is, of course, impossible to say; but when it was written down more than one form would inevitably be preserved. After the stories of different occurrences had assumed written form, the next step would be that of gathering the written material together into a collection. Such a collection formed the original basis of our book.

Moreover, it is manifest from many indications in the book that more than one collection was laid under contribution in its compilation; indeed, it is generally recognized that at least two main collections are to be discerned. The older one, because it contains the well-established characteristics of the Jehovist document of the Hexateuch, is called J; and the later one, because of its Elohistic character, is called E (see art., *The Pentateuch*, p. 137). The former is a Judæan source; the latter a northern Israelite source. It must not, however, be supposed that these two sources, J and E, represent two individual writers; they stand, respectively, for Judæan and Israelite literary circles or "schools"; and each of the two sources was preserved within these "schools" for some considerable time quite independently, and no doubt received modifications and additions from time to time from different adherents of the two "schools" respectively. The redactor of Judges made use, then, of these two sources; however, he did not incorporate all that they offered; but what he did make use of from each he contrived to weld into a single narrative. Sometimes he succeeded in doing this well; at other times he was less skillful, and the twofold source becomes quite obvious. For example, in the Gideon story compare these two sets of passages: $6^{2-6, 11-24, 34}$ 8^{4-21}, on the one hand, and $6^{7-10, 25-32, 36-40}$ 7^{1}–8^{3} 8^{22-27}, on the other; and again in the Jephthah story: $10^{7, 17, 18}$ $11^{1-11, 29, 33b}$, 12^{1-16} represent one tradition; $11^{22-28, 30-33a, 34-40}$, represent the other. The same divergence is observable more or less throughout the book.

The next step in the literary history of Judges took place after the rise of the Deuteronomic school. Owing to the different religious point of view that resulted from the discovery of the book of the Law in the Temple in the reign of Josiah (621 B.C.), and the reforms this gave rise to, the religious history of the past came to be differently envisaged, and was interpreted accordingly. The written accounts of the history handed down from the past received the impress of this different envisagement. The marks of this in Judges are indubitable, so that we are justified in believing that it was subjected to a *Deuteronomic redaction.* Here, again, the work was not that of an individual; the book received from time to time additions from different members of the Deuteronomic school. A similar process took place finally with the rise of the Priestly schools. Again a somewhat different religious point of view developed, and again the nation's sacred records received the impress of this new school of thought. This too is observable in Judges. (Cf. art., *The Pentateuch*, p. 137.)

It is well to realize that, however alien to modern ideas of the sanctity of authorship the procedure just sketched may appear, it is one which was not only natural, but altogether justified. The guardians of the Hebrew Scriptures were also the religious leaders and teachers of the people. On them devolved the twofold task of preserving the ancient records intact, and of teaching the people in accordance with the development of their religious thought. They could not lay violent hands on the records and delete all which they did not accept; so they did the next best thing—they added here and there sentences and words more in accordance with their own higher views, and thus they sought to make a right impression, as they conceived it, on the reader.

Chronology. A brief consideration of the chronology of the age may assist toward a better understanding of the general course of events during the period of the Judges. (For a fuller discussion see Eiselen, *The Prophetic Books of the O.T.*, vol. i, pp. 44–50.) According to the chronological data furnished, the period of the Judges whose exploits are narrated in the book extended over 410 years. In 1 Kings 6[1] the statement is made that 480 years elapsed between the Exodus and the fourth year of Solomon's reign. Now, if we add to the 410 years suggested in Judges other events between the Exodus and the building of the Temple—some belonging to the generations earlier than the Judges, others to the years following the period covered in the book of Judges—the total would be at least 580 years, or about 100 years in excess of the total given in 1 Kings 6[1]. Even after a solution of this problem has been found other difficulties remain. The beginning of building operations on the Temple may be assigned to about 970 B.C. If to this date are added the 480 years of 1 Kings 6[1], the result is 1450 B.C. as the date of the Exodus. But, while there are some who favor such an early date for the Exodus, available evidence, though by no means absolutely conclusive, makes a date around 1200 B.C. much more probable, and this later date is accepted by the great majority of modern scholars. If, however, the Exodus is assigned to such a late date, the period of the Judges must be shortened to about 200 years.

A close examination of the records themselves increases the arguments in favor of such shortening. The chronological scheme totaling 410 years is a part of the framework of the book. It is the same framework that expresses the view that the Judges were saviours and rulers of all Israel, that they did their work for the *whole* nation, and that the land of *all* the Hebrew tribes had rest under them. On the other hand, the older narratives embodied in the framework, which are much nearer to the events, fail to support this view; they represent the Judges as local or tribal heroes, active within small districts in widely separated parts of the country; there is not the slightest indication that the power and authority of even the most prominent of these leaders extended beyond a limited area. In most cases, therefore, two or more Judges may have been contemporaries carrying on their activities simultaneously in different parts of the land. If this interpretation is correct, the period of the Judges may be greatly reduced; indeed, room can easily be found for all the persons and events of the age within the two centuries or less between the Exodus and the establishment of the monarchy.

Historical Value. Although the book of Judges presents us, in the main, with only local tribal history, its historical importance can hardly be overrated; and this in spite of the fact that it has been subjected to repeated revisions. It gives us a clear insight into the way in which the Hebrew tribes gradually acquired for themselves various districts in the land of Canaan and made for themselves a permanent home in face of strong opposition on the part of the original owners. The individual episodes recorded, it must be remembered, tell of times of crisis; we get little or no knowledge of the long intervening periods. When it is said, "the land had peace" for so and so many years, it may mean in some instances simply that the records of what happened during those periods were wanting. The original owners of the land did not acquiesce in subjugation for long periods without any attempts to oust the intruders. They were well equipped for defense and offense; and we may have to regard the episodes recorded only as illustrations of numberless similar ones, though the accounts that have been preserved may well represent the decisive and final struggles of a long series. Without any question, the most important of these was that recorded in the Song of Deborah, for this was something much more than a conflict between a single tribe and one particular foe; under Deborah and Barak occurs the first concerted movement of the Israelite tribes against a confederation of Canaanite rulers; and the vivid touches and minuteness of detail contained in the account impel the belief that it came from an eyewitness. The Song and other early literary fragments embodied in the book undoubtedly give an essentially true picture of conditions among the Hebrews—both the northern and the southern groups—during the generations immediately following their entrance into Canaan; the very simplicity and life-likeness of the narratives create confidence in their substantial accuracy.

Value for the History of Religion. The importance of our book from the religious point of view lies in the fact that it shows so clearly the retrograde tendency regarding both religious belief and practice which arose after the Mosaic period. This is to be accounted for (1) by the absence of any outstanding religious leaders to carry on the work of Moses; and (2) by contact with the religion of the Canaanites. The fundamental differences between the religious conceptions of nomadic tribes, such as the Hebrews were when they entered the Promised Land, and those of the agriculturists settled in Canaan, could not fail to produce a profound effect. Whatever counteracting influences there may have been among the Israelite tribes—and such undoubtedly existed—they were insufficient to stem, at any rate for a long time, the strong current of Baalism. That the religion of Jehovah did not become submerged during this period must have been due, on the one hand, to the presence of a small nucleus of true Jehovah worshipers which persisted on in spite of strongly adverse circumstances; and also because Jehovah-worship was adapted to Baalism. Spurious as the resultant religion was, it, at any rate, preserved the name of Jehovah among the people; and when, in due course, the spiritual descendants (i.e., the prophets) of the small body of worshipers who had preserved the Mosaic tradition preached what they had received, it was a known name which they proclaimed. So that even the spurious religion, insofar as it retained the name of Jehovah, was to the good. And it is this form of religion, Jehovah-worship adapted to Baalism, which is presented to our view in the book of Judges.

The ethical note in religion was very faint. The ideal man was the warrior; deeds of cruelty, if done to a national foe, were related with much glee. Jael is praised for treachery and murder, even though it involved the breaking of the law of hospitality, which was esteemed most sacred by all Semites. The story of Jephthah shows that human sacrifice was not unknown. In other words, the whole book pictures simple, primitive, and crude religious and ethical conditions during the period of the Judges, thus suggesting how much additional progress had to be made before Israel could become, as it did become, the teacher of religion and ethics to mankind.

Literature: Black, *The Book of Judges* (the Smaller Cambridge Bible for Schools); Budde, *Das Buch der Richter* (Kurzer Hand-Kommentar); Burney, *The Book of Judges;* Cooke, *The Book of Judges* (Cambridge Bible); Moore, *A Critical and Exegetical Commentary on Judges* (International Critical Commentary); Nowack, *Richter, Ruth, und die Bücher Samuelis* (Hand-Kommentar); Cooke, *The History and Song of Deborah;* Smythe Palmer, *The Samson-saga and its Place in Comparative Religion.*

Chapters 1[1] to 2[5]: Conquest of Canaan and Settlement of the Tribes

An introductory summary of the conquest, describing the events which happened after the death of Joshua. Victories are gained by Judah and Simeon. Caleb appears as the leader of the tribe of Judah, though he is not spoken of as one of the Judges. Then follows an enumeration of those districts which the Israelites were unable to conquer. The reason of this is revealed by the angel of Jehovah; it is because the people had not obeyed the voice of their God, but had made covenants with the people of the land, and had refrained from breaking down their altars. The people thereupon lift up their voices and weep—hence the name of the place, *Bôchîm* ("weepers," 2[5])—and sacrifice to Jehovah. The narrative then breaks off abruptly. Though not an original part of the book, this section has preserved a thoroughly reliable accurate account of the events during the early period of the conquest.

CHAPTER I

1–3. Introduction. The oracle is consulted as to which of the tribes is to begin the invasion of the land. Judah is designated, and invites Simeon to join him. *The Canaanites*—the J source uses this name of the inhabitants west of Jordan, the E source prefers "Amorites" as the name of the pre-Israelite inhabitants of the land. *My lot*—it is assumed that the land has been divided up into lots and assigned to the different tribes (see Josh. 17[14, 17]).

4–8. Defeat of Adoni-Bezek. V. 4 may be a gloss; v. 5 follows smoothly after v. 3. *Adonibezek*—better *Adoni-zedek,* king of Jerusalem (see Josh. 10[1, 3]); the mistake arose through the proximity of the place-name Bezek. In v. 7 it speaks of his having been brought to Jerusalem to die. It is probable that "king of Jerusalem" has fallen out after the name. *Cut off his thumbs*—the object of this was to incapacitate him from fighting. *Threescore and ten kings* (v. 7)—points to his having been a powerful and successful king. *Under my table*—not, of course, to be taken literally; the Hebrew word for "table" (*shulchan*) means a round piece of leather which was spread on the ground. *They brought him*—the reference must be to his own followers, not to the Israelites, for Jerusalem was not taken (see v. 21 and 19[11, 12] Josh. 15[63]). The assertion in v. 8 that Jerusalem was taken probably arose from a misunderstanding of "they brought him," which was thought to refer to the Israelites.

9–15. Caleb's Campaign. V. 9 is a later insertion. *The South*—called the Negeb, the arid district extending from south of Hebron to the border of the desert. *The lowland*—called the Shephelah=the valley in v. 19; it was the lower lying hill-country which extended from the center of the land westward to the maritime plain. With vv. 10f. cf. Josh. 15[13-19]. *Caleb* and *Othniel* in this context are not to be understood as individuals but as tribes; the name *Kenaz* = Kenizzite (see Num. 32[12]), i.e., non-Israelite. Othniel's marriage expresses a union between the two tribes. The narrative about Achsah's request being granted is the picturesque way of explaining how it originally came about that the fertile land with springs came into the possession of the Achsah clan instead of belonging to the older line of the Calebites.

16–21. Further Conquests of Judah and Simeon. *Kenite*—see 1 Sam. 30[29], for the friendly relationship between Judah and the Kenites. For *the children of the Kenite* we should probably read *Hobab the Kenite* (see 4[11]); a proper name is more natural in view of *Moses' father-in-law* (not *brother-in-law*) which follows (cf. Num. 10[29]). *The city of palm-trees*—(cf. 3[13]) i.e., Jericho (see Deut. 34[3] 2 Chr. 28[15]). *Utterly destroyed*—the word means "devoted" to entire destruction, *herem* ("ban") in Hebrew; Zephath receives the name of *Hormah* because it had been put to the ban. This etymology belongs, however, to later times. Hormah is similar in meaning to Hermon, "sacred," because it was a sanctuary.

Gaza, Ashkelon, Ekron, were Philistine cities in the low-lying land, which, as v. 19 says, Judah was unable to conquer. This verse comes from a later scribe who wished to make the section agree with Josh. 15[45-47]. *The three sons of Anak*—see v. 10 and Num. 13[22, 28]; they are spoken of as giants in Deut. 9[2]; they represent three clans which were driven out of Hebron by the Calebites. *Benjamin*—this, according to Josh. 15[63], should be Judah, which doubtless stood here originally; a later scribe changed it to Benjamin to bring it into agreement with Josh. 18[28].

22–29. Campaign of the House of Joseph. The tribe of Joseph conquered Bethel; but the Manassites and Ephraimites failed to drive out the Canaanites from several cities. These two tribes together formed the house of Joseph (see Josh. 17[17]); the passage, therefore, shows that when they fought side by side they were successful (vv. 22–26), but when independently, they were unable to overcome the enemy, and therefore settled down among them (vv. 27–29; cf. Josh. 17[11-13]).

30–36. The Northern Tribes. Zebulun, Asher, and Naphthali, being unable to assert themselves against the inhabitants of the district they attacked, settled down among the native population. Dan, however, is driven into the hill country. *Yet the hand of the house of Joseph*—this refers to later times. *Amorites*—the whole passage, especially v. 36, shows that this should be Edomites; the two names look very similar in Hebrew. *The ascent of Akrabbim* ("scorpions") was on the border of Edom (Josh. 15[1-3]), and *the rock*, or Sela, was an Edomite stronghold (2 Kings 14[7]).

CHAPTER II

1–5. The Words of the Angel of Jehovah. On the angel of Jehovah see note on 6[11-24]. These verses are obviously the work of a redactor, who wished to explain why it was that the chosen people of Jehovah, under whose guidance the promised land had been invaded, were unable to effect a complete conquest of the land. The central point of the speech lies in the rebuke to the people for not having broken down the altars of the Canaanites, and in the words *their gods shall be a snare unto you.* The section shows, what the prophetic books abundantly illustrate, that the religion of the Canaanites, i.e., Baalism, had fatally influenced the Israelites. And this is not to be wondered at, for Judg. 1 implies again and again that the Israelite tribes settled down among the native population; and as the Canaanites were far more cultured than the nomad Israelites, these latter were naturally impressed by what they saw in their new surroundings; and they adopted not only the customs and pursuits of the Canaanites but also what inevitably followed, religious rites, usages, and beliefs.

Chapters 2[6] to 16[31]: The History of Israel Under the Judges

6–23. Introduction Explanatory of the History that is to Follow. (3[1-6] is also included in this introduction.) Vv. 6–23 contain a philosophy of the period of the Judges. Vv. 6–10 constitute a link between the history related down to the end of the book of Joshua and that which is to follow in Judges. The rest of ch. 2 is the Deuteronomist's conception of the meaning of Israelite history during the period to be considered. Each "Judge" is regarded as having been specially raised up by God to deliver a repentant people from some enemy oppressor. The oppressor too has been raised up by God in order to punish the Israelites for apostasy. As soon as the people are sorry for their sin God is merciful to them and sends the deliverer. While it is impossible to deny that an element of artificiality enters in here, it must be recognized that the writer bears witness to a living truth, the full scope of which he could not, however, be expected to apprehend. Right living in the sight of God, whether national or individual, does bring prosperity; not necessarily material prosperity, but prosperity in the higher sense of spiritual contentment, just as the contrary entails, sooner or later, futility of effort and consequent degradation of life.

Unless this is remembered we shall be doing less than justice to one who, while not a historian in the modern sense, was imbued with the love of righteousness which was one of the glories of the prophets of Israel, whose follower the Deuteronomist was, and who therefore believed that the course of history was not unconnected with national morality and religion.

V. 6, cf. Josh. 24[28]; v. 7, cf. Josh. 24[31]. *All the great works*—i.e., the deliverance from Egypt, and the leading of the people through the wilderness, culminating in the conquest of Canaan. With vv. 8, 9, cf. Josh. 24[29, 30]. *The mountain of Gaash*—cf. 2 Sam. 23[30]. *Baal and the Ashtarôth*—see note on 10[6f]. *Have transgressed my covenant* (v. 20)—the two parts of the covenant are stated clearly in Deut. 26[16-19]; the people's part was to walk in the ways of Jehovah, and keep his statutes, etc. Jehovah's part was that they were to be "a peculiar people unto himself"; cf. Amos 3[2]: "You only have I known of all the families of the earth."

CHAPTER III

1–6. The Nations that were Left to Test Israel. (See also 2[6-23].) *The five lords of the Philistines;* the word for "lords" (*seren*) is used only in this connection, and is probably a purely Philistine title. *Hivites*—read *Hittites*. The suggestion is that in reality Israel did not succeed in driving out any of the nations already settled in the land.

7–11. Othniel as Judge. The narrative of Othniel introduces for the first time the stereotyped framework characteristic of the main part of the book. However, in distinction from the other occurrences, here the information furnished within the framework is practically nil. There is only the name of the deliverer Othniel and of the oppressor Cushan-rishathaim, and the statement of the conflict and Othniel's triumph. The lack of all specific details has raised questions in the minds of many scholars as to the historicity of the entire narrative, and one must admit that a good case can be presented in support of their view. In 1[13] Othniel is described as a Kenizzite, "the son of Kenaz," Caleb's younger brother and a leader in war; otherwise nothing is known concerning him. *Cushan-rishathaim* means, literally, "the Cushite of double wickedness"; evidently the word is to be regarded not as a proper name but a descriptive title expressing the contempt of the author. For *Asheroth*, v. 7, we should possibly read *Ashtaroth*, i.e., the female deities associated with the Baalim; or the Asheroth, i.e., wooden posts standing at the places of worship which must be regarded as symbols of these female deities. See also note on 10[6f].

12–30. Ehud as Judge. Apart from the working over by the Deuteronomist, two sources have been combined in this narrative. This can be seen by comparing vv. 19 and 20, which contain two accounts of Ehud's interview with Eglon; v. 26, moreover, gives two accounts of Ehud's escape. There are other indications of two sources having been combined, though they have been so intermingled that it is now impossible to disentangle them. Ehud's treachery was in accordance with the moral standard of his time.

The stereotyped Deuteronomic introduction is found in v. 12a. *A man lefthanded* (v. 15)—the Hebrew says "bound as to his right hand," i.e., lame in his right arm (see v. 16). But in 20[16] we read of 700 Benjamites who were lefthanded, so that in this case we must understand the term as meaning ambidexterous (so the LXX). In later Hebrew the expression has both this meaning and that of being lame in the right hand or arm. The translation *quarries* in v. 19 is uncertain, for the Hebrew word never has this meaning; elsewhere it always refers to a "graven image," or better a "hewn-out image." It is difficult to explain the expression here; no doubt it was plain enough in the original source. *His summer parlor* (v. 20)—the reference is to a chamber on the flat roof; cf. 1 Kings 17[19, 23] 2 Kings 1[2]s the lattice windows permitted the air to pase through, which cooled the atmosphere. *H-covered his feet* (v. 24)—a delicate way of ex; pressing that he was relieving nature (cf. 1 Sam. 24[3]).

31. Shamgar as Judge. That this verse is a later insertion is seen by the fact that it breaks the narrative; 4[1] is clearly the continuation of 3[30]. It was inserted to help to make up the number of the judges to twelve, and was probably suggested by 5[6] and 15[5-8].

CHAPTER IV

Deborah and Barak. A later prose parallel to the poem in ch. 5. Both undoubtedly record an historical event of great importance. Of special interest is the fact that two women, Deborah and Jael, appear as the heroines. It is the former who inspires Barak to attack Sisera, promising him victory. Sisera is defeated and takes refuge in the tent of Jael, the wife of Heber the Kenite; she kills him while asleep with a tent peg. It was a grievous breach against the law of hospitality; but the end was held to justify the means.

CHAPTER V

The Song of Deborah. As this magnificent poem is probably the oldest piece of poetry in the O.T., and contains some points of great importance for the study of the early phases of Israelite religion, it demands closer attention than any other portion of the book.

Vv. 4, 5 present a picture, which the poet constructs in his mind's eye, of the advent of Jehovah as leader of Israel's hosts. There is, of course, no reference here to the giving of the Law on Mount Sinai; indeed, in the Hebrew both rhythm and grammar make it probable that the words *even you Sinai* were not part of the original text. But their insertion is quite comprehensible, both because the imagery employed was reminiscent of the theophany on Mount Sinai, and also because Sinai was believed to have been the primeval dwelling-place of Jehovah. It lay in the south whence Jehovah would have come in passing through Edom to Canaan. The mention of Seir and Edom (they are identical, see Gen. 32[3]), in fact, implies the thought of Sinai being Jehovah's starting-point. Jehovah, therefore, was in the beginning not the God of Canaan, whose worship the Israelites found there when they settled down in the country, but he was the God who came with them when they invaded the land, and by whose help they were able to conquer it. They had learned to know him at Mount Sinai, his original place of abode (see Ex. 19[11, 18, 20] 34[2, 3] Deut. 33[2]), where he was sought on special occasions (Ex. 3[2f.] 1 Kings 19[8f.]). As by his help Canaan was conquered, he was later believed to have taken up his abode there, and Zion became his "holy hill."

The next point of religious interest would at first sight appear to be in v. 8. *They chose new gods, then was war in the gates*—but the text is corrupt, and we should render: *The sacrifices of God ceased, and the barley bread was exhausted;* i.e., as consequences of the state of the country described in the preceding verses, the people were unable to offer the usual sacrifices, and there was also the danger of famine.

20. *The stars in their courses fought*—the belief in the personality of the heavenly bodies was widespread in the ancient east (cf. Isa. 24[21] 40[26]). **23.** *Curse ye Meroz, said the angel of Jehovah*—the angel of Jehovah is the same as Jehovah himself; and the reference is to God as he was thought to reveal himself to men. The conception is very primitive: Jehovah curses those who did not come to his help when other mighty ones went forth to war. Jehovah is thus clearly conceived of as a battle-god in this early stage of belief; and the ideas regarding him were strongly anthropomorphic. It was an age when religion was largely utilitarian; Jehovah was called upon if it was thought that his help would be of use; presents, in the shape of sacrifices, were brought to him when anything was to be got out of him. He was worshiped if it was worth while; but if it paid to worship some other god, recourse was had to this other god. This was, briefly, the attitude of the bulk of the people toward God during the period of the Judges, and the Song of Deborah, insofar as it speaks of God, bears this out. **31.** This is the Deuteronomist's conclusion to the Song; it is composed in the spirit of the psalmists (see Psa. 19[4, 5] 68[2]).

Chapters 6 to 8: Gideon as Judge

The next enemy onslaught is that of the Midianites, a conglomeration of Bedouin tribes, living on the east of the Jordan. They are described as ravaging the settlements of the Manassites. These Bedouin wanderers over the steppe-land were in the habit of making sudden inroads into the cultivated land west of the Jordan on their swift camels, and, having looted whatever they could lay their hands on, made off as quickly as they came. On one of these expeditions the Midianite hordes attacked the Abiezrites, a Manassite clan. The head of this clan, Jerubbaal ("Let Baal contend") or Gideon ("hewer"), called together three hundred of his kinsmen, and went after the enemy; he came up with them soon after he had crossed the Jordan and was approaching the desert. He at once attacked them; the Midianites were defeated and their leader slain.

This narrative of Gideon's victory over the Midianites has been preserved in two forms; the earlier account is contained in 8[4-21], the later in 6[1]–8[3].

CHAPTER VI

1–10. Attack of the Midianites. The Deuteronomic editor prefaces the narrative with his interpretation of what is doubtless based on historic fact. With this hiding in dens and caves (v. 2) cf. 1 Sam. 13[6]. *When Israel had sown*—this reference to agricultural pursuits shows that settled life existed among some of the tribes, at any rate, by this time. The content of vv. 7–10 shows very clearly the thought of later times. Prophets were not yet known in Israel; and, above all, the words of v. 9 are a naïve contradiction of what is said in the previous verses.

11–24. Gideon's Call to Deliver His People. *The angel of the Lord*—it is to be noted that "the angel of the Lord" and the Lord himself are used interchangeably (see vv. 16, 21–23). The expression "the angel" or "messenger" of the Lord is used to express the divine presence. It may well be that "the angel of the Lord" was substituted for "the Lord" for reasons of reverential awe by some later scribe; but if so, he has not always been consistent; and the same applies to other books of the O.T.

The writers of the original records no doubt believed that the Almighty appeared at times in days gone by in bodily form. The more enlightened compilers of the biblical records who lived in later times conceived God as a Spirit and, consequently, could not believe in a bodily appearance of this kind. It is probable, therefore, that in redacting the biblical books their intention was to act on this principle: when an actual appearance of God was recorded they would interpret it in terms of a human being regarded as the representative or messenger of God (in Hebrew the same word is used for "messenger" and "angel"; cf. Malachi, interpreted in Mal. 1[1] mg. as "my messenger"); but where it was a question of divine communication coming direct to the recipient, Jehovah himself could be spoken of as imparting it, and this could take place without any appearance, as in the case of the prophets. Exceptions, as in the case of such outstanding personalities as Abraham and Moses, can be readily understood. If it be objected that this distinction is not always observed, the reply is that this ought not to cause surprise, for neither the exactitude, nor the logic, still less the consistency of thought, of moderns is to be expected in writers of a more or less remote antiquity. The point of vv. 20, 21 is that what was intended to be the offering of a meal on the part of a hospitable host became the offering or sacrifice of a worshiper.

25–32. The Destruction of the Altar of Baal. The marked differentiation here between Baal and Jehovah worship reveals the influence of the eighth-century prophets; for not until the time of Hosea is the application of the term "Baal" to Jehovah condemned (Hos. 2[17]). Prior to this the name "Baal," which means "lord," "master" or "husband," was applied to Jehovah without any thought of disloyalty.

33–40. The Narrative of the Midian Attack Resumed. *The valley of Jezreel*—not the great central plain which lies west of Jezreel, and is better known as the Plain of Esdraelon, but the broad valley east of Jezreel, which descends down to the Jordan. *The spirit of the Lord came upon*—literally, "clothed itself with him"; this curious expression describing the indwelling of the Spirit occurs elsewhere only in 1 Chr. 12[18] 2 Chr. 24[20]. For other ways of describing this see 3[10] 11[29], simply "was" upon; 13[25] "began to move," or "impel" him; and 14[6, 19] 15[14], "came mightily," literally, "rushed" upon him. Vv. 36f. well illustrate the naïve conception of God held at the time.

CHAPTER VII

1–8. Gideon's Army Reduced. The original number, 32,000, is first reduced to 10,000, and then to 300. The first reduction is apparently made in the light of Deut. 20[8], which would show that the redactor was acquainted with Deuteronomy (published 621 B.C.). The reason for the second reduction is given in vv. 5, 6, and has occasioned much questioning. There is, however, an easy solution of the difficulty if one recognizes, as is evidently the case, that a copyist or a later redactor was not quite clear regarding the matter, and made *as a dog lappeth* refer to the wrong people. The two types of drinkers are those who drink standing, *putting their hand to their mouth*, and those who bow down upon their knees; obviously, it is these latter who lap like a dog, since they are on all fours; but it is *the rest of the people* who do this, not the three hundred. So the three hundred are chosen because in standing to drink they can keep their eyes about them and guard themselves from sudden attack; whereas those on their knees are concentrating their attention on their enjoyment. The former are likely to be the better soldiers.

9–15. Gideon's Secret Visit to the Midianite Camp. Gideon, with his servant, steals into the Midianite camp, and overhears one of the Midianites telling his dream to his fellow. According to this dream a cake of barley bread fell into the Midianite camp, and turned a tent upside down. Gideon takes this as an omen of success, the cake of barley bread signifying the sword of Gideon, according to the Midianite.

16–25. Gideon's Victory. Even a cursory examination of this section necessitates the supposition that excerpts have been made from two accounts of the event. According to v. 16, Gideon puts into the hands of each of his three hundred men trumpets and empty pitchers with torches inside them (presumably lighted, since that was the object of holding them in the pitchers); according to v. 18 they are to blow the trumpets and shout; according to v. 20b, it is clearly indicated that they drew their swords. The carrying of pitchers and lighted torches would occupy two hands; the simultaneous blowing of trumpets and shouting would be an impossible feat. Further, one has only to read vv. 20–22 to see at once that two accounts have been, unskillfully, welded into one. A procedure such as this can occasion no surprise, for originally there must have been various accounts from those who had participated in the battle; more than one of these would ultimately have been reduced to written form; so that when the compiler of Judges wrote down his account of the episode it would have been a very natural thing for him to utilize all the material before him. *Oreb and Zeeb* (v. 25)—"raven and wolf"; in 8[5f.] the Midianite rulers are called Zebah and Zalmunna (cf. Psa. 83[11]); it is probable that two traditions are incorporated.

CHAPTER VIII

1–3. Jealousy of Ephraim. Cf. 12[1-6]. As the leading tribe Ephraim resents not having been invited to join in the attack on the Midianites (but see 7[24]); by a skillful piece of flattery Gideon assuages the anger of the Ephraimites; the mere gleaning of the Ephraimites is greater than the entire vintage of the Abiezrites, Gideon's tribe. The use of this species of proverb is interesting as showing that the construction of proverbs was in vogue among the Israelites in early times; many of the sayings in Proverbs owed their origin to spontaneous utterances of this kind. *Anger* (v. 3)—literally, "spirit"; for a similar use of the Hebrew *ruach* (spirit) see Prov. 16[32] 25[28].

4–21. The Pursuit East of Jordan. From vv. 18f. it is evident that this further pursuit was for the purpose of avenging the death of Gideon's two brothers. This section reflects yet another tradition of the Midianite encounter, for it differs from what has preceded: (1) One would expect the Ephraimites to have joined in this pursuit after what is said in vv. 1–3, but they are not mentioned; (2) Gideon has still only his three hundred men, whereas in 7[24] the whole countryside has been called together; (3) when it is said that Gideon and his men were faint with pursuing (v. 4) we have an incongruity with what has preceded, namely, a victory (7[25]).

5. *Succoth*—neither this place nor *Penuel* (v. 8) has been identified, but from Gen. 32[23, 30f.] 33[17] they were situated on the banks of the Jabbok. **7.** Read *I will thresh your flesh together with thorns*—cf. Amos. 1[3]; the threat is carried out (v. 16), where *threshed* should be read instead of *taught*. **10.** *Karkor*—another unidentified site. **11.** *Nobah and Jogbehah*—for the former, see Num. 32[42]; for the latter, Num. 32[35]. **13.** *From the ascent of Heres*—delete; it is a variant of "and discomfited all the host" (Burney); in Hebrew the two sentences look very similar. **14.** *Described*—read *wrote down;* perhaps this refers to Gideon; there is no reason, however, to doubt the possibility of the "young man" being able to write; the only surprising thing is that he should have been able to remember all the seventy-seven names. **21.** *Crescents*—hung on the necks of camels to avert the evil eye; according to Isa. 3[18] they were worn by women.

22–27. Gideon Refuses the Kingship, and Sets Up an Ephod. *I will not rule over you*—these words reflect the thought of later times owing especially to the teaching of Hosea (8[4] 13[11]); the succession of worthless rulers in the Northern Kingdom, during the period from the death of Jeroboam II (about 743 B.C.) to the fall of Samaria (722 B.C.), brought home the conviction that the existence of the monarchy was incompatible with the belief in the sovereignty of Jehovah. In 9[6, 16-19] it is assumed that Gideon was king, and it is also stated (9[22]) that Abimelech, his son, reigned after him for three years. **27.** *Ephod*—this sacred image, representing the Deity (cf. 1 Sam. 21[9]), must not be confused with the linen ephod, a priestly garment worn, e.g., by Samuel (1 Sam. 2[18]) and by David (2 Sam. 6[14]). The image-ephod was used for divination. *And all Israel went a-whoring*—for apostasy from Jehovah-worship described figuratively as adultery see Hosea *passim.*

28–35. Conclusion of the Narrative of Gideon's Judgeship. The hand of the Deuteronomist is clearly discernible in these verses. V. 33 especially comes strangely after what is told in v. 27. The worship of Baal-berith was, according to 9[4, 46], a purely local cult in Shechem; but it is spoken of here as though Baal-berith were the national god.

CHAPTER IX

The Reign of Abimelech. This narrative has been compiled from two sources, the sifting of which is no easy matter; and it is not to be wondered at that commentators differ in their opinions as to which parts belong to either source. Following Budde, it will be found that, apart from a few redactional elements, the two sources may be separated thus: Vv. 1–6, 26–33, 34–40, 46–49, 50–54; read in this order these verses form a coherent whole, and in all probability belong to J. Similarly, vv. 7–20, 23–25, 42–45, 56–57, belonging to E, follow in logical sequence.

1–6. Abimelech Becomes King. *Shechem*—the modern Nablûs, thirty miles north of Jerusalem. *His mother's brethren*—cf. 8[31]; she was what is called the *sâdika* wife of Gideon, i.e., female friend, who remained with her clan, and was visited from time to time by her "husband" (see Robertson Smith, *Kinship and Marriage*, p. 93). Abimelech thus belonged to his mother's clan in Shechem, not to that of his father in Ophrah, and could therefore speak of himself as bone and flesh of the Shechemites. With the wholesale slaughter referred to in v. 5, cf. 2 Kings 10[1-11] 11[1-3].

7–21. Jotham's Fable. A very interesting

example of the existence of the popular material out of which in later times the Wisdom literature grew. There are two difficulties which this fable presents: (1) If, as is widely held, it is intended to be a satire on the monarchy, it can hardly have been composed at this early stage. (2) There is no real parallel between the fable and the occurrence recorded; one has but to try to apply the fable to see this. Abimelech *acquires* the kingship; nobody offers it to him; in the fable the kingship is offered, but refused. The only point of parallelism is that the thorn destroys, and the implication is that this will be the case if Abimelech becomes king. It seems clear that the fable is an independent piece, and was inserted here on account of this last point. With v. 20 cf. vv. 56f.

22–49. The Revolt of the Shechemites. *Prince over Israel*—there was no consolidated Israel in the days of the Judges; the words reflect a later condition. *God sent*—with this primitive conception of God cf. 1 Sam. 16[14] 1 Kings 22[21-23] and see comments there.

28. The point of Gaal's words is that he contrasts the Shechemites with Abimelech; why should the Shechemites serve Abimelech, who is not really one of them, but the son of Jerubbaal, and belongs to a different clan? It is Abimelech and his officer Zebul who ought to be subservient to the Shechemites! Instead of *serve ye the men of Hamor*—read *they* [should] *serve the men*, i.e., the son of Jerubbaal and Zebul should serve the Shechemites. Gaal's words are intended to be a counterblast to what Abimelech said in v. 2. The abrupt mention of Zebul is noticeable; he must presumably have been the leader among those of Abimelech's "mother's brethren" referred to in v. 3. **29.** *And he said to Abimelech*—these words cannot have been spoken by Gaal; they have clearly got misplaced, and probably belong to v. 32: "And he [i.e., Zebul] said to Abimelech, now, therefore, increase thine army, and come out; rise up at night, thou and . . ." **31.** *Craftily*—read *in Arumah* (see v. 41); like several other places mentioned in Judges the site has not been identified with certainty, but possibly it is the modern Ormeh, not far from Nablûs. **37.** *The middle of the land*—literally, "the navel of . . ."; cf. Ezek. 38[12]; no doubt the expression is in reference to some height with a slight depression on the summit which would serve as an ambush (see end of v. 35). *The oak of Mĕônĕnim*—i.e., *the soothsayers' terebinth;* this was probably the ancient Canaanite name which in later days the Israelites called *Elôn Môreh*, "oracle terebinth" (Gen. 12[6] mg.); both names refer no doubt to the same tree, as in each case it is near Shechem.

45. *Sowed it with salt*—the action, which is not mentioned elsewhere, was symbolical, based on the idea, contained in such passages as Deut. 29[22, 23] Jer. 17[6] Job 39[6] Psa. 107[34], that the place would become like a "salt land and not inhabited." There was a similar custom among the Assyrians; Tiglath Pileser I strews salt over the conquered city of Hanusa, and Ashurbanipal over Susa after it had been laid waste (see Jeremias, *The O.T. in the Light of the Ancient East*, vol. ii, p. 42). **46.** *The tower of Shechem*—cf. the tower or *migdal* of Penuel (8[17]); the context shows that this was not in the city itself; it must, therefore, have been a strong place of refuge in the vicinity. *The hold*—from 1 Sam. 13[6], the only other mention of the word, this seems to have been below the ground; entrance to the tower from it is implied in v. 49. *El-berith*—cf. 8[33] 9[4]; LXX reads Baal-berith; the same temple is meant. **48.** *Mount Zalmon*—i.e., the *shady* mount.

50–57. The Death of Abimelech. *Thebez*—cf. 2 Sam. 11[21], possibly the modern Tubas, though the consonants, excepting the b, differ; it is twelve miles northeast of Nablûs. **54.** Cf. 1 Sam. 31[4].

CHAPTER X

1–5. Tola and Jair as Judges. *Tola the son of Puah*—according to Gen. 46[13] Num. 26[23] 1 Chr. 7[1], these two are brothers, the sons of Issachar, by which is meant that they were clans belonging to the tribe of Issachar. The site of *Shamir* is not known. *Jair*—likewise the name of a clan (cf. Num. 32[41] Deut. 3[14] 1 Kings 4[13]). *Havvoth-jair*—the name means "the tent-villages of Jair," and points to the transition from nomad life to more settled habitations. *Kamon*—the site of this place is not known, but it is possibly represented by Kamun "which is named by Polybius in connection with Pella."

6–16. An Explanatory Introduction to the Succeeding History. The Deuteronomist's conception of the history is again very evident in this section, but other hands have had a large share in it.

6. *Baalim*—cf. 2[13]; the reference is to the various local Baals of the Canaanite shrines. *The Ashtārôth*—the reference here is likewise to the Ashtarts, i.e., female deities, of the Canaanite shrines. The name Ashtart (=the Babylonian Ishtar) is written *Ashtoreth* in the Hebrew Bible, the vowels of the word *bosheth* ("shame") being substituted in order to indicate that the worship of this goddess was a shameful thing; cf. also Molech for Melech. *Bôsheth* is also substituted for Baal in Hos. 9[10] Jer. 3[24] 11[13] (cf. also the name "Ish-bosheth" = "Ish-baal," 2 Sam. 2[8] 1 Chr. 8[33], notes).

The goddess Ashtart (Astartê is the proper pronunciation) was, above all, a fertility goddess to whom the fruitfulness of the crops and fecundity of the flocks was believed to be due; hence the temple prostitutes, as with the Babylonian Ishtar.

11, 12. The names recorded here of the peoples who are said to have oppressed the Israelites give rise to considerable difficulties. As Moore points out, the editor "has accumulated the names of neighboring nations without any discoverable principle of selection or order. We read in it the names of some which nowhere else appear as oppressors, while we miss others, notably Moab and Midian, which we should certainly expect to find."

17, 18. See next paragraph.

CHAPTERS 10^{17} TO 12^{7}: JEPHTHAH AS JUDGE

Editorial Introduction to the Story of Jephthah. $10^{17, 18}$ is a summary of 11^{4-11}. *The children of Ammon . . . Gilead* is based on $11^{4, 5}$; *and the children of Israel . . . Mizpah* is based on 11^{11}; and v. 18 is based on $11^{6, 8}$.

CHAPTER XI

1–3. Introduction Proper to the Story of Jephthah. The name *Jephthah* occurs in Josh. 15^{43} $19^{14, 27}$, as that of a place; R.V. in those passages spells it "Iphtah," but in the original the two names are identical. *The son of an harlot*—not being the son of a lawful wife, nor even of a *sadîka* wife (see on 9^{1-6}), nor yet of a concubine, meant that he was fatherless; so that when it is said that "Gilead begat Jephthah" it simply means that Gilead was the land of his birth, and stands for his nameless father. Under such circumstances the legitimate sons of his father would have felt justified in driving him from their home. *The land of Tob*—an Aramæan district on the east of Jordan (see 2 Sam. $10^{6, 8}$ 1 Macc. 5^{13}). *They went out with him*—i.e., took to the road, became highway robbers.

4–11. Jephthah Invited to Lead the Gileadites Against the Ammonites. V. 4 is repeated in the first part of the next verse and should be deleted. Jephthah's exploits must have become notorious for him to have been invited to take the lead in this way; he is offered the leadership of his people if he will come and deliver them; he is naturally a little sceptical at first; but agreement is reached, and ratified before Jehovah. **11.** *Mizpah*—not to be confused with Mizpah in Benjamin (Josh. 18^{26}).

12–28. An Historical Discussion Regarding Israel's Right to Possess Gileadite Territory. It is immediately evident, in reading this section, that it breaks the course of the narrative; it must, therefore, be regarded as having been added from elsewhere. But it contains manifest marks of antiquity, and cannot therefore be a late insertion. From its general contents it is clear that the people with whom it is mainly concerned are the Moabites, while the context both before and after deals with the Ammonites. Burney gives good grounds for believing that we have here parts of two originally distinct narratives in which Jephthah appeared as the deliverer of his people from the Moabites and Ammonites respectively; and he constructs the basis of each narrative from these passages, substantially thus: to the narrative of the Moabite oppression belong 10^{17} $11^{12-28, 30, 31, 33-40}$; while from the Ammonite narrative the following are excerpts: 11^{1-11} (exc. parts of vv. 1, 2, 5), $^{29, 32, 33}$ (in part) 12^{1-6}. These two narratives were welded together, so that in separating the respective elements from each there are necessarily gaps which have to be conjecturally filled in; and this has been done skillfully and with great probability of correctness by Burney (*Book of Judges*, pp. 302f.). This seems to be the most probable solution of the difficulties raised by the presence and contents of this section.

12. *The children of Ammon*—on the basis of the solution of the difficulties here followed we must, of course, read *the children of Moab*, and so throughout this section. **13.** *Israel took away*—see Num. 21^{26}. *From Arnon even unto Jabbok*—a distance of about fifty miles. Cf. v. 17 with Num. 20^{14-21}, upon which it is evidently based. With v. 18 cf. Num. 21^{11-13}; with v. 19 cf. Num. 21^{21-23}; with v. 20 cf. Num. 21^{24-26}. **24.** *Chemosh*—the mention of this national god of Moab further bears out what is said in the introduction to this section. The god of the Ammonites was Milcom (see 1 Kings 11^{33} 2 Kings 23^{13} Jer. $49^{1, 3}$). For Chemosh see Num. 21^{29} 1 Kings $11^{7, 33}$ 2 Kings 23^{13} Jer. 48^{46}, and the Moabite stone. It is noticeable that Chemosh is here regarded as the god of the Moabites just in the same way as Jehovah was of the Israelites. The belief in God had not yet reached the development which is found among the eighth-century prophets. **25.** *Balak*—cf. Num. 22–24.

29–33. Jephthah's Vow, and His Victory Over the Ammonites. *Whatsoever cometh forth*—there is no justification for this rendering; the Hebrew *can* only mean "whosoever," which is further borne out by the words "to meet me"; this could be said only in reference to a person. The most likely person to welcome the returning victor would be a woman (see 1 Sam. $18^{6, 7}$ Psa. 68^{11}), and Jephthah must have expected this person to be his daughter; it is just herein that the essence and significance of his vow lay. The sacrifice of a child to Jehovah was not an unknown idea in Israel (see Gen. 22, Ex. 22[29, 30] Mic. 6[7] Ezek. 20[25, 26]); the more precious the gift offered the more likely would Jehovah be to grant what was required; this was the conception of the age; cf. the action of the king of Moab (2 Kings 3[26, 27]).

34–40. Jephthah's Vow Fulfilled. *With timbrels*—cf. Ex. 15[20]. *His only child*—note how this is emphasized; it enhanced the value of the sacrifice. **35.** *He rent his clothes*—cf. Gen. 37[29, 34] Josh. 7[6]; on the meaning and significance of this mourning rite see the writer's *Immortality and the Unseen World*, pp. 143–149. That Jephthah's daughter knows the reason of her father's sorrow without the necessity of any explanation is significant, for it shows that the terrible custom of such a sacrifice, rare as it was, no doubt, was perfectly understood. **37.** *And go down upon the mountains*—read *and wander about upon the* . . . , requiring only a very slight alteration in the Hebrew text. *And bewail my virginity*—to be deprived of motherhood was a grievous thing to a Hebrew woman; cf. Isa. 47[8, 9] 49[21], and see end of next verse, *she had not known a man.* **39, 40.** In all probability the sacrifice of Jephthah's daughter and the annual festival here spoken of were originally quite distinct; the former was a historical fact; the latter was the same festival as that spoken of in Ezek. 8[14] (the "weeping for Tammuz"), and was mythological in origin. The central act in the festival was the wailing for the death of the god, the personification of spring; this was explained as having originated through the lamenting of the women for Jephthah's daughter ("celebrate" in the R.V. should be read as in the mg. "lament"). It will be noticed that this is spoken of as *a custom in Israel*, not merely among the Gileadites, the significance of which speaks for itself.

CHAPTER XII

1–7. Jephthah Defeats the Ephraimites; His Death. With this section cf. 8[1-3]. *Passed northward*—but to reach Mizpah they would not go northward; R.V. mg. "Zaphon" (=Hebrew), a place in the Jordan Valley near Succoth (Josh. 13[27]), but this would involve going southward. It is impossible to say what stood in the text originally. **4.** *Because they said . . . Manasseh*—this reason for the conflict is quite different from what is said in the preceding verses according to which the Ephraimites attack Jephthah because he did not invite them to join him against the common enemy. The words evidently do not belong here; they are omitted by some LXX MSS. **6.** *Shibboleth*—it is interesting to note that there should at that time have been this difference in pronouncing the sibilant between two tribes closely connected racially, and living in adjoining territories. Even to this day the natives in and about Nablûs (Shechem) pronounce the word for "sun" *sems* instead of *shemsh. Shibboleth* means both a "stream," and an "ear of corn"; here, of course, the former is meant, as the scene described takes place on the fords of the Jordan. *Forty and two thousand*—that is too much; but numbers are often exaggerated in this book. **7.** *In* one of *the cities of Gilead*—the Hebrew reads *in the cities of Gilead;* there is some authority for emending the text so as to read *in his city, in Mizpah of Gilead.*

8–15. Three Minor Judges. See note on 3[31]. *Bethlehem*—this must refer to Bethlehem in Zebulon (Josh. 19[15]); not to the Bethlehem of Judah. This is the only place where the name "Ibzan" occurs. **15.** *The Pirathonite*—cf. 2 Sam. 23[30].

Chapters 13 to 16: The Samson Narratives

These narratives, which contain some of the most ancient material in the O.T., offer an extraordinarily interesting mixture of history, tradition, folk-tale, and glimpses of social life, together with religious and possibly even mythological elements. In all probability they were originally independent stories of a purely secular character, centering in the first instance around one or more village heroes; they were then gradually formed into a cycle, and finally they all became attached to one central figure. This material was then utilized for historical purposes, and some religious touches were added. A few examples of these different elements may be given. The most prominent feature is the folk-tale, which comes out in the exploits of the rollicking hero with his weakness for women; the rough humor and absence of moral sense stamps them as genuine village tales which are, certainly in some cases, based on fact. (See 14[1f.] 15[9f.]) Pictures of social life are seen, e.g., in 14[5] 15[12]; the historical element is clearly seen in that the whole cycle is brought into connection with the growing Philistine menace. Religious traits, at times rather incongruous, may be observed in 13[5f.] 14[4] 15[18, 19]. Mythological elements may be discerned, e.g., in the name of the hero (Samson="sun-man"), in the story of the foxes (15[3-5]), in Samson's seven locks of hair (=the sun's rays; 16[13f.]), and in the story of the water coming from the spring of Ramath-lehi (15[17f.]); the name of Delilah must also be mentioned in this connection, though space does not permit of this being more fully explained (see Jeremias, *The O.T. in the Light of the Ancient East*, vol. ii, pp. 169–173). It should be noted, however, that the use of mythological elements does not militate against the presence of a substantial historical nucleus.

CHAPTER XIII

1–25. Samson's Birth. V. 1, which is from the Deuteronomist, as the stereotyped words show, brings the whole cycle into connection with the growing Philistine aggression. The danger went on increasing, until it forced in Israel a centralization of government under the monarchy; it was not finally averted until the time of David. **2.** *Zorah*—the name is perhaps not without significance from the point of view of the mythological elements in these stories, for this place is in close proximity to Beth-shemesh ("the house of the sun"). **3.** For *the angel of the Lord* see note on 6^{11}. **5.** *A Nazirite*—cf. Num. $6^{1f.}$; one "consecrated" to Jehovah; the word is connected with a root meaning "to vow"; a Nazirite's vows bound him to abstain from all intoxicating drink, to let his hair grow, and to keep at a distance from a dead body. The vows could be taken either for a limited period, or, as in Samson's case, for life; *the child shall be a Nazirite unto God from the womb to the day of his death* (v. 7); the only vow Samson observes is that of letting his hair grow; he comes in contact with a carcase ($14^{8, 9}$), and drinks wine ($14^{10, 12, 17}$), for the word used for "feast" is *mishteh*, which means a "drinking-bout." *He shall begin to save*—apparently the remark of the redactor who knew that the deliverance from the Philistines was a long-drawn-out process. In vv. 16–19 the narrative does not run smoothly; the text is evidently a little out of order. **20.** *When the flame went up*—here the flame is from the sacrificial fire kindled by Manoah; in 6^{21} the angel strikes fire out of the rock. **21.** *But the angel . . . his wife*—these words break the connection; they would come more appropriately at the conclusion of the episode, after v. 23, where they probably stood originally. **22.** *We shall surely die, because we*—cf. $6^{22, 23}$. **23.** The wife's very practical argument is somewhat piled up, and reads rather artificially; probably an originally simpler phrase has been elaborated. **24.** *Samson*—the Hebrew *Shimshon* means a "little sun," or a "sun-man."

CHAPTER XIV

Samson Chooses a Wife. **1.** *Timnah* (cf. 13^{4} Josh. 15^{10} 19^{43} 2 Chr. 28^{18})—the modern Tibneh, a few miles southwest of Zorah. **2.** *Told his father*—see note on vv. 4–10; the arrangements for a marriage were made by the respective fathers of the man and of the woman; the mention of the mother here is quite unusual, but see below; with the exception of the marriage feast no mention is here made of the other customs usually observed, namely, the betrothal, the *mohar*, "dowry" (see Deut. $22^{28f.}$), the wedding processions, and the bridegroom's gift to the bride. But it is probable that in these early times the marriage feast, quasi-sacramental in character as it was, was the central rite, which placed the couple on a conjugal footing (see further under vv. 4–10). *Get her*—according to the ancient Hebrew view a wife was looked upon as bought property; this is implied by the paying of the *mohar*, cf. Ruth 4^{10}, where the word used is to "purchase"; this is not, however, the word here used. **3.** *Uncircumcised Philistines*—cf. 1 Sam. 14^{6} $17^{26, 36}$ 31^{4}.

4–10. The confusion manifest in the text here is due to insertions in later times when it was thought impossible that a hero in Israel should not have conformed to what (in those later times) had become the proper procedure in arranging a marriage. In order to rectify this the redactor inserted the references to Samson's father and mother (this applies also to vv. 2, 3), making it appear as though the marriage were arranged in the normal way. But the story as a whole shows that Samson did not contemplate a marriage in the proper sense; it was the case of a *sadîka* wife (see note on 9^{1}); this comes out clearly in the fact that Samson does not bring his "wife" to his house, but visits her in her home in Timnah, just as Gideon did in the case of his "wife" in Shechem (see 8^{29-31}).

8. *There was a swarm of bees*—taken in a literal sense this story is extremely improbable; but the point is that we have here the remnants of the mythological part of the narrative; "bearing in mind the phenomenal meaning so often attached to the lion as a solar symbol, we have no difficulty in understanding that the lion fostering the bees and producing honey is only another way of expressing the idea that the midsummer constellation with its warm, sunny weather favors the work of the bees. When the sun is in Leo, honey is plentiful" (A. Smythe Palmer, *The Samson Saga*, p. 99; see the whole of ch. ix). **11.** *Thirty companions*—these occupied the most important position at a marriage feast after the married couple and the friend of the bridegroom; in Cant. 3^{7} there are as many as sixty. From v. 16 it is seen that Samson's companions were Philistines. **12.** *A riddle*—cf.

Prov. 1^{6}, a "dark saying," the root meaning is "to turn aside"; the word, therefore, means something not straightforward, something indirect, and thus obscure. *Linen garments*—a rectangular piece of linen; in Isa. 3^{23} it is spoken of as worn by women. *Changes of raiment*—i.e., raiment worn on festal occasions. **15.** *Seventh* —read with the LXX *fourth. Entice thy husband*—this dishonorable proceeding is presumably justified by Samson's unfair act; as bridegroom his challenge could hardly be refused and yet the nature of the riddle made the answer impossible by fair means, since the companions, who did not know the facts, had nothing to go upon. *That he may declare unto us*—we should expect *unto thee,* it being taken for granted that she would repeat it to them. *Lest we burn*—somewhat drastic, but cf. 15^{6}. **17.** *The seven days*—i.e., the rest of them, since it was the fourth day (see above) on which the companions threatened her. **18.** *Before the sun went down*—these words are pointless here, a slight emendation of the Hebrew text enables us to read *before he went into the chamber* (see 15^{1}). It does not follow from this that the marriage was not yet consummated, as can be seen by 15^{1}. *If ye had not plowed* —a far from flattering insinuation against his "wife." It is very likely that v. 19, with the exception of *and his anger . . . house,* is a later insertion for the purpose of representing that Samson paid his wager. It is far more likely that in the original story Samson, finding that he had been deceived by his "wife," left her there and then; this would be the more justified as she was only a *sadīka* wife. Quite in accordance with the morals of the time Samson's "wife" is handed over to his "best man" (v. 20).

CHAPTER XV

1–8. Samson Avenges the Loss of His Wife. *In the time of the wheat harvest*—cf. v. 5. *Visited his wife with a kid*—this indicates the kind of relationship existing between Samson and his "wife"; note, too, that she is living with her father; but Samson's right to her is taken for granted. The father's action, however, is justified from his point of view because he thought, not unreasonably, that Samson had given up his "wife." **2.** *Therefore I gave her*—by this means the father had obtained a second payment for his daughter; his profit would be further increased by Samson taking the younger daughter. Revolting as these social conditions are to our ideas, it must be remembered that they were perfectly normal in those times (see Robertson Smith, *Kinship and Marriage, passim*). **3.** *Unto them*—perhaps we should read *unto him,* with the LXX, but it is not necessary; the verse simply describes what Samson was thinking; he is doubtless glad to have some excuse for venting his wrath. It might be thought that with his great strength Samson would have entered his "wife's" chamber in spite of the father's obstruction, instead of taking the vengeance described in vv. 4f.; but this would have eliminated the pretext for the fox-story. **4, 5.** To press the details in this account is quite unnecessary; it is simply an adaptation of a world-wide solar myth; for details see A. Smythe Palmer, *op. cit.,* pp. 101–111, and cf. Frazer, *Spirits of the Corn and of the Wild* (*The Golden Bough,* pt. v.), vol. i, pp. 296f.

9–20. Samson Slays a Thousand Philistines at Lehi. *Lehi*—"jaw-bone"; cf. 2 Sam. 23^{11f}. Burney draws attention to the similarity between the deeds of Samson, Shammah, and Shamgar (*op. cit.,* p. 75). The men of Judah, recognizing the superior strength of the Philistines, are at once prepared to deliver up Samson; being of a different tribe he had no claim upon their protection. Incidentally, this reflects once more what our book so often illustrates, namely, the entire lack of cohesion among the Israelite tribes. That it takes three thousand men to bind Samson is intended to be a witness to his prodigious strength. **13.** *They bound him*—a quite unnecessary precaution, as the sequel shows; but it enhances the graphic character of the narrative; the old Hebrews were past-masters in storytelling. **15.** *A new jawbone*—another graphic touch; a dry one would have been brittle. **18–20.** Being oppressed with thirst Samson cries out to Jehovah for help lest he should be overcome by his enemies; water is miraculously provided from the crag, and he revives; hence the name of the spot, *En-hakkore,* "the spring of the caller." There are a number of traits in this story which justify the contention of many scholars that we have here the adaptation of a solar myth; the subject is well dealt with by Burney, *op. cit.,* pp. 391f. *En-hakkore*—in 1 Sam. 26^{20} Jer. 17^{11}, "the caller" refers to the partridge which is common in the hill country of Palestine, and its call-note is often heard. The "Partridge spring" is probably the original meaning, which was adapted and given another meaning appropriate to the story. **20.** This is the Deuteronomist's addition; as it was here inserted too soon, it had to be repeated at the end of the Samson cycle (16^{31}).

CHAPTER XVI

1–3. Samson Carries Off the Gate of Gaza. *Gaza*—the southernmost of the Philistine cities, situated on the coast. **2.** *And it was told*—this has accidentally fallen out of the Hebrew text, but can be supplied from the LXX. As the words stand v. 2 is difficult to reconcile with what is said in the next verse, for if the Philistines were lying in wait in the gate all night, Samson would have other work to do before carrying off the gate. It is simplest to follow Moore and to regard the words *and they compassed him in . . . of the city* as a later interpolation added for the purpose of making Samson's escape more wonderful. The narrative runs smoothly if we read: *And it was told the Gazites, saying, Samson is come hither. And they were quiet all the night, saying . . .* **3.** *That is before Hebron*—i.e., to the east of Hebron. This was thirty-eight miles off! But in a wonder-story this is a trifle. Burney suggests a solar *motif*, which is extremely likely (see his commentary, p. 407).

4–22. Samson and Delilah. Samson's brilliant exploits are drawing to a close; he becomes entangled in the wiles of Delilah. After several attempts, she at last finds out that the source of his strength lies in his wonderful hair; by treacherously cutting this off while he sleeps she deprives him of his strength and delivers him to his enemies. They blind him and put him to shame. In none of the Samson stories does the solar myth *motif* come out more clearly than here. This cannot be illustrated in detail; but the following points indicate the lines along which the solar myth interpretation runs: After the brilliant exploits of his life's day, the first of which is to appear as a bridegroom (cf. Psa. 19[5]), Samson enters into the toils of Delilah (the name is connected with the Hebrew word for "night," *lāyĕlāh*); she weaves his seven locks of hair (=the sun's rays) with a web, i.e., night spreads her curtain over the sky (cf. Psa. 104[2]); by shaving off his locks she deprives him of his strength, i.e., the power of the sun's rays decreases as night overmasters them; ultimately he is blinded, i.e., night reigns supreme. In the *Midrash Tehillim*, on Psa. 19[7], it is said in reference to the sun: "He is like a hero who goes forth strong, and returns home powerless; thus the sun at his rising is a mighty hero, and at his setting a weakling" (quoted by Goldziher, *Mythology Among the Hebrews*, Eng. trans. by Martineau, p. 162).

4. *Sorek*—the site has been identified in the modern *Surik*, west of Zorah; the name means "choice grape" (see Isa. 5[2] Jer. 2[21]). **5.** *The lords of the Philistines*—five in number (see 3[3]). *Eleven hundred*—this from each of the five ("every one of us") would make an enormous sum for those days; but it is in keeping with the wonder tale. **6.** *Tell me*—the charming naïveté of the request shows that whatever foundation in fact may lie behind the story, it is artificially constructed. **7.** *As another man*—Hebrew, literally, "as one of mankind"; Samson's superhuman personality thus comes out quite incidentally. **9.** *So his strength*—i.e., the source of his strength. It is obvious that at the end of v. 13 something has fallen out of the text; it can, however, be supplied from the LXX: "And fastenest it with the pin, then will I become weak like any other man. And it came to pass that while he slept Delilah took the seven locks of his head, and wove them into the web"; then the Hebrew text continues, *and she fastened with the pin.* **17.** *There hath not come . . . womb*—an editorial addition (cf. 13[5, 7]). As soon as one attempts to take literally what is said in vv. 19, 20 one is launched into absurdities; a man would not sleep through the operation of having his head shaved, nor would this result in the loss of his strength. The editor brings in a religious note by adding, *but he wist not that the Lord was departed from him*, implying, no doubt, that this was because the Nazirite vow was broken by the shaving of Samson's hair; but Samson had no part in this. These words do not belong to the original text. **21.** *He did grind in the prison house*—"this representation may be due to the primitive conception that the sun, in performing his daily march around the sky, is performing a task of drudgery to which he is compelled by a law ('bound with fetters of brass') imposed upon him by a superior power" (Smythe Palmer, *op. cit.*, p. 161). **22.** *Howbeit*—this is added by way of explaining how Samson was able to accomplish his final feat of strength as narrated in vv. 29f.

23–31. The Death of Samson. *Dagon*—spoken of here as the national god of the Philistines; besides his temple in Gaza, he had one in Ashdod (1 Sam. 5[2f.]); widely separated places with names compounded with Dagon show that he was worshiped by the Philistines wherever they settled. That he was a fish-god is very unlikely; there is strong reason for believing that he was a corn deity; *dâgân* is the Hebrew word for "corn." A number of commentators transpose vv. 24, 25, which is certainly to be preferred, because *when the people saw him* (v. 24) must come after the call for him (v. 25). It is difficult to believe that v. 28, at any rate in its present form, with its strongly religious tone, can have formed part of the original narrative. **29, 30.** While it is, of course, possible that in this, as in the other Samson stories, a kernel of fact may have been utilized, occurrences such as those narrated in these verses show that imagination has played a large part in the construction of the stories. **31.** The redactor's conclusion.

Generally speaking, the biblical writers used

historical material primarily for the purpose of teaching religious lessons. This assertion can hardly be made of the Samson stories; for they were selected not so much for their religious value as for their popularity. Moreover, it is precarious to hold up Samson as an example of wholesome courage and virtue. Even when judged by the standards of his own age he reveals a lack of the moral qualities which make for true nobility.

It is, indeed, much safer to present him as a warning rather than as a type to be imitated. Although he was a worshiper of Jehovah and a hero who gripped the imagination of his age, he was governed largely by passion and selfishness; he had little regard for the rights and property of others; he was driven to some of his deeds by a spirit of vengeance, and finally died a victim of this very spirit. Samson represents one type of national hero during the primitive period of the Judges, but by no means the most exemplary; Deborah and Gideon, though not without weaknesses, illustrate a much nobler ideal, which found even fuller expression in the lives and messages of the later prophets. Thus the stories of Samson, as compared with later portrayals, show what remarkable progress was made in the appreciation of ethical ideals during the generations culminating in the eighth-century prophets (see Amos 5[24] Hos. 6[6] Isa. 1[16, 17] Mic. 6[8]).

Chapters 17[1] to 21[25]: Two Supplementary Narratives

First Narrative

Chapters 17, 18: The Danites and Their Sanctuary

The migration of the Danites and the founding of their sanctuary is the theme of chs. 17, 18. This section is by far the most important part of the book from the point of view of the history of religion and cult. It is seen how in these early times a sanctuary could be the private possession of an individual and that the prime requirement for it is an image of the god. We learn, too, that at this time any Israelite could be consecrated as priest, though it was preferable for a Levite to function as such. On the other hand, we learn that the priesthood claimed descent not from Aaron, but from Moses.

From the historical point of view also the section is important. It tells of the Danites having at one time been settled in the south of the land, which is borne out by Josh. 19[40f.], as well as by the Samson stories, before they migrated to the North, as here recounted.

The contents of these two chapters come from two sources; but the two forms of the narratives have been skillfully interwoven, and it is only here and there that repetitions, variations, etc., betray the existence of more than one source.

CHAPTER XVII

1–6. **Micah's Graven Image.** 2. *Micah*—this is one of the three names in the book which contain the abbreviated form of "Jehovah"; the others are Joash (6[11f.]) and Jotham (9[5f.]). It is evident that vv. 2–4 are not in order. They start in the middle of a conversation between Micah and his mother; the giving and receiving of the money is confused, and the sentences do not follow logically. Various reconstructions of the text have been proposed; that of Budde seems to read most smoothly, namely: "And he said unto his mother, 'The eleven hundred pieces of silver that were taken from thee, about which thou didst utter a curse, and didst also speak it in my ears, behold, the silver is with me, I took it; now, therefore, I restore it unto thee.' And he restored the money unto his mother. And his mother said, 'Blessed be my son of the Lord. I verily dedicate the silver unto the Lord from my hand for my son, to make a graven image and a molten image.' And his mother took two hundred pieces of silver, and gave them to the founder, who made thereof a graven image and a molten image; and it was in the house of Micah." One would have expected the narrative to have begun with the statement that the mother, finding that her money had been stolen, utters a curse against the thief; and the confused state of the present text supports the view that something to this effect has dropped out. At any rate, the narrative, implying that the son is terrified at the curse his parent has uttered, goes on to say that he returns the silver; the mother thereupon revokes the curse by pronouncing a blessing, and dedicates part of the silver to a pious use, the benefit of which is to accrue to her son. 3. *And a molten image*—probably a later addition; so, too, in the next verse. 4. *Two hundred*—this would have sufficed for the purpose; it is arbitrary to assume that the woman withheld the rest of the eleven hundred pieces out of avarice; had there been any intent to defraud the Lord, the point would have been brought out. Some commentators hold that the difference in the numbers is due to a difference of sources. 5. *An house of gods*—cf. 18[24]. *Ephod*—see note on 8[27]. *Teraphim*—see Gen. 31[19f.] 1 Sam. 19[13, 16]; from these passages it is clear that *teraphim* were images of gods in human form; they were a species of household gods, and in all probability were a remnant of ancestor worship. (See further, the present writer's *Immortality*, pp. 108f., 135f.) *Consecrated*—literally, "filled the hand" (cf. Ex. 28^{41} Lev. 8^{33}); it became the technical term for installing in the priest's office; originally it probably had a wider connotation and referred in general to investing someone with authority; that is the Assyrian use of the term, from which the Hebrew was derived. (See further, Nowack, *Hebræische Archæologie*, vol. ii, pp. 120f.) **6.** This may be the addition of a later scribe who wished to excuse the enormities (as they were to him) just mentioned; it is worthy of note that he thinks they were perpetrated because there was no king.

7–13. Micah Secures a Levite to Be His Priest. *Of the family of Judah, who was a Levite*—this seems to imply that the Levites were not a separate tribe, but members of a priestly caste who might belong to any tribe. On the other hand, many passages plainly state that the Levites formed a distinct tribe. It cannot be said that the problem has yet been satisfactorily solved. (See Burney's interesting note, *op. cit.*, pp. 436f.) **13.** *Now I know*—this gives us a very interesting insight into the naïve religious conceptions of the time; the point is that, since the Levites had formed a close entourage about Moses and had learned from him the proper way of conducting the worship of Jehovah, and that this tradition had been handed down among them, therefore there was a special advantage in having a Levite as priest, for by observing the correct ritual he would please Jehovah, and Micah would reap the benefit of this. A Levite would, moreover, be more skillful in consulting the oracle. Contrast with this artificial form of religion the prophetic ideals of the elements of true religion. Micah appears here as a worshiper of Jehovah; but in his worship of the ephod and the teraphim (v. 5) this would, at first sight, seem to be excluded; the truth is that just as in later days it was not thought incompatible to adapt the worship of Jehovah to Baalism, so Micah saw nothing incongruous in worshiping his household gods as well as Jehovah.

CHAPTER XVIII

1–6. The Danite Spies Come to Micah's House. *In those days . . . Israel*—a redactional addition (cf. 17^{6}). *Danites*—a small group in v. 11, but cf. Num. 1^{39}. **2.** Cf. with vv. 13, 14 for one illustration of many showing the twofold source. **3.** *They knew the voice*—i.e., they recognized the southern dialect; if the writer were thinking of the recognition of a personal friend whom the men had known before, he would have expressed it differently; the most obvious way of recognizing a friend is by seeing him. **6.** *Before the Lord is your way*—literally, *in front of*, i.e., *he sees right along it.*

7–10. The Spies Come to Laish. *Laish*—situated at the source of the Jordan. *After the manner of the Sidonians*—i.e., the Phœnicians, a peaceful people occupied with trade and commerce; and therefore easily overcome (see v. 10). *With any man*—read with the support of the versions, *Aram* ("Syria") for *Adam* ("man"); in Hebrew the two words were even more similar than in English transliteration; the emendation gives better sense. The verse means that the Sidonians were sufficiently distant from the city, on the one hand, while, on the other, there was no confederacy with Aram; so that there was no danger of interference in taking possession (see vv. 26, 27). The idea that what they are able to annex has God's approval is another illustration of the primitive moral sense characteristic of the times.

11–26. The Danites and Micah. When the whole body of the Danites arrive in the hill country of Ephraim the spies tell them of the shrine in Micah's house; they determine to steal the cult objects and to carry off the priest; the armed men hold the entrance to the city, while the five spies seize the former and lure the priest away with them. When the whole cavalcade has got some way from the city Micah and his fellow citizens pursue them and overtake them; but the thieves are too numerous; Micah suffers insult as well as injury, and returns home.

27–31. Laish Captured; the Setting Up of the Danite Sanctuary. The Danites take Laish and burn it to the ground; in place of it they build a new city which they call Dan, after their forefather. But the point of importance is the setting up of the sanctuary. An interesting detail about the priesthood is also added; this is traced to Jonathan, the grandson of Moses, and it is stated that it continued till the fall of the Northern Kingdom. **30.** This must be a later addition because the hitherto unnamed Levite is now paralleled by "Jonathan"; had the original narrator known anything about Jonathan being the name of this Levite, he would assuredly have mentioned it earlier in the narrative instead of adding it as a kind of after-thought at its conclusion. But the indication regarding the origin of the Danite priesthood is important, and no doubt historical. *Moses*—so the versions; but the Hebrew text has an "n" suspended over the text, making it "Manasseh," seeking thereby to obviate the distasteful fact that an idolatrous priest traced his descent from Moses. **31.** *Shiloh*—cf. 21^{19}.

SECOND SUPPLEMENTARY NARRATIVE

CHAPTERS 19 TO 21: THE OUTRAGE AT GIBEAH, AND ITS CONSEQUENCES

This extraordinary narrative runs as follows: A Levite from the hill country of Ephraim goes to fetch back from her father's house his concubine who has deceived him. At the father's request he remains with him for a few days. In the evening of the fifth day he departs homeward with his concubine. On the way they turn into Gibeah of Benjamin for the night; they have some difficulty in finding a lodging, but are ultimately received into the house of an old man (19^{1-21}). The house is surrounded by men with evil intent, and the Levite delivers up his concubine to their will. The next morning she lies dead on the threshold. The Levite takes the body to his home, where he cuts it up into twelve pieces and sends them throughout all the borders of Israel (19^{22-30}). The Israelites gather together, hear about the occurrence, and decide to punish the evildoers, for which purpose they assemble before the guilty city (20^{1-11}). The Benjamites are summoned to deliver up the culprits, but refuse to do so, whereupon war breaks out between the eleven tribes of Israel and the single tribe of Benjamin (20^{12-17}). During the first two days the Israelites are repeatedly defeated in spite of being encouraged to attack by Jehovah, whom they seek in Bethel. But on the third day they are able, by a piece of strategy, to take the city; the Benjamites are put to the sword, only six hundred escaping; these take refuge in the wilderness at the rock of Rimmon. The whole territory of Benjamin is ravaged, and everyone is slaughtered (20^{18-48}). The Israelites now mourn over the fact that one of their tribes has been thus exterminated. Six hundred had escaped, it is true; but as these were all men the tribe would die out, and all Israel had sworn not to give their daughters to the Benjamites (see 21^{1}). It is then discovered that none of the inhabitants of Jabesh-gilead had taken part in the war against the Benjamites; an army is, therefore, sent to punish the recalcitrant city; everyone is killed save four hundred virgins, and these are given to the Benjamites for wives (21^{1-15}). The two hundred other Benjamites, for whom wives had not been supplied, are bidden to hide in the vineyards during a vintage festival in Shiloh; when, according to custom, the maidens came out to dance, they are to rush out of their hiding places, seize a maid apiece, and carry her home to wife. This the Benjamites do, and then return to their inheritance (21^{16-25}).

Regarding this narrative it is to be noted, first, that the idea of united action on the part of eleven tribes is quite contrary to the conditions of the time as presented by Judges; the Song of Deborah, e.g., deplores the want of unity among the tribes ($5^{16f.}$), and that was at a time of far greater crisis than anything pointed to in this narrative. Again, the almost total annihilation of the tribe of Benjamin shortly before the hegemony of that tribe under Saul shows that what is here told cannot have taken place during the period of the Judges. Once more, the destruction of all the inhabitants of Jabesh-gilead at this period is not probable in view of the fact that soon after this time it appears as a flourishing city which is saved by Saul from the meditated attack of Nahash the Ammonite (1 Sam. 11^{1-11}).

On the other hand, that the narrative contains some historical kernel seems probable; for there are references in Hos. 9^{9} 10^{9} to Gibeah which seem to point to the event dealt with in these chapters. That the two sources J and E have been utilized and welded together may be regarded as certain; and in all probability some other source has also been laid under contribution. Furthermore, midrashic material appears also to have been added at some later period; and the redactional elements which occur are what we have been accustomed to look for.

CHAPTER XIX

1-10. The Levite's Visit to Bethlehem; the First Part of His Journey Home. For the first half of v. 1, cf. 17^{6} 18^{1} 21^{25}; it is the redactor's addition. **2.** *Played the harlot against him*—read with various commentators, following some LXX MSS. and the Vulgate, *was vexed with him;* this also suits the context better. **10.** *Jebus* (*the same is Jerusalem*)—there is no other evidence to show that this ever was the name of Jerusalem; it is called *Urusalim* in the Tel-el-Amarna letters (*cir.* 1400 B.C.); the city belonged to the Jebusites before David conquered it; and it may be that the redactor assumed that it was originally called Jebus after its owners.

11-21. The Levite in Gibeah. *Gibeah which belongeth* to *Benjamin*—for other places of the same name see Josh. 15^{57}, Gibeah in Judah, and Josh. 24^{33} mg., in the hill country of Ephraim. The name means "hill," and in each case the locality is, or was originally, a sanctuary. **18.** *And I am . . . Lord*—read following the LXX, *I am going to my house*, i.e., I am on my way home.

22-30. The Outrage on the Levite's Concubine. Cf. Gen. $19^{2f.}$ **23.** *Folly*—the word in Hebrew denotes moral delinquency (see Gen. 34^{7} Deut. 22^{21} 2 Sam. 13^{12}). In v. 30, the addition in some of the best LXX MSS.

should be read; then the whole verse would run: "And he commanded the men whom he had sent, saying, Say ye thus to every man in Israel, Was there ever such a thing since the day of the coming up out of Egypt of the children of Israel unto this day? Consider of it, take counsel, and speak. And it was so, that all that saw it said, there was no such deed done nor seen from the day that the children of Israel came up out of the land of Egypt unto this day." This evidently represents a more original form of the Hebrew text of this verse than the present form, which begins too abruptly.

CHAPTER XX

1–11. The Children of Israel Take Counsel in Mizpah. *The congregation*—this term is used only in post-exilic times; it is characteristic of the P document. LXX has "synagogue." *From Dan to Beersheba*—these were the northern and southern limits of the kingdom in the time of David and Solomon (see 1 Sam. 3^{20} 2 Sam. 3^{10} 17^{11} 1 Kings 4^{25}). *Mizpah*—the modern Nebi' Samwil, five miles northwest of Jerusalem; an ancient sanctuary (cf. 1 Macc. $3^{46f.}$). **5.** Cf. 19^{22-30}. **10.** *That they may do . . . Israel*—the reconstruction of the text suggested by Moore is preferable: "to do to Gibeah of Benjamin as all the wantonness which it has wrought in Israel deserves."

12–17. The Israelites Prepare for War. 15. *Twenty and six thousand men*—LXX reads twenty-five thousand, which is nearer the number given in vv. 44f. **17.** *Four hundred thousand men*—an impossible number; but it is not easy to determine the exact man power.

18–28. The Israelites are Defeated in Two Battles. The two sources have been very unskillfully combined in vv. 19, 20. **23.** *Went up and wept*—they went up either to Mizpah (v. 1), or to Bethel (vv. 18, 26). Altogether five acts are enumerated in v. 26: weeping, sitting before the Lord, fasting, burnt-offerings, and peace-offerings; such an accumulation of propitiatory acts would be sure to incline Jehovah to grant them victory. The verse gives a good insight into the religious ideas of the times. The words in brackets, in vv. 27, 28, are a later addition to explain why the ark, before which the oracle was given, stood in Bethel and not, as heretofore, in Shiloh.

29–48. The Israelites are Victorious in the Third Battle. 30f. Cf. for this stratagem, Josh. 8^{14f}. A good example of the two sources utilized is seen by comparing vv. 31–36a with vv. 36b–44. **38.** *A great cloud of smoke*—cf. Isa. 30^{27}. **40.** *The whole of the city . . . heaven*—cf. Deut. 13^{17}. **43.** The text here is very corrupt; according to Burney's skillful reconstruction (though he speaks of it as "extremely precarious") read *and they beat down Benjamin, and pursued him from Nohah as far as over against Geba towards the east.* Nohah (so LXX) was probably the name of a Benjamite city or village; it is mentioned in 1 Chr. 8^{2}. Drastic as this emendation is, Burney makes out a good case for it. **45.** *Gidom*—no such place is known; perhaps, following LXX, we should read *Geba.* As Moore points out, the word can also be translated *till they cut them off*, cf. 21^{6}.

CHAPTER XXI

The Destruction of Jabesh-Gilead; The Rape of the Shilonite Maidens. In this chapter the two sources are again clearly discernible, namely: vv. 1–14 and vv. 15–24; and some commentators would, not without good reason, discern signs of a third source, extracts from which have been inserted in each of the two main sources.

1–14. War Against Jabesh-Gilead. In order to provide wives for the Benjamites Jabesh-gilead is destroyed with the exception of four hundred virgins, who are handed over to the Benjamites. *Now the men*—this oath has not been mentioned; it must have stood, however, in the source from which this was taken (cf. vv. 7, 18). **2.** *To Bethel*—cf. $20^{18, 26}$. **4.** *And built there an altar*—but according to 20^{26-28}, there must already have been an altar there; this statement, therefore, can hardly belong to the original form of the story. **5.** *For they had made*—this also is not mentioned previously in the present text; but no doubt the account of taking this oath stood in the original source. At the end of v. 11 LXX adds: "but the virgins ye shall save alive. And they did so." This evidently stood in the Hebrew text originally. **12.** *To Shiloh which is in the land of Canaan*—cf. Josh. 21^{2} 22^{9}. **14.** *Sufficed not*—there were six hundred Benjamites who had escaped, but so far only four hundred wives had been provided.

15–25. The Remaining Two Hundred Wives Are Obtained. There is clearly a new beginning in v. 15; *had made a breach*—cf. 2 Sam. 6^{8} mg. **17.** *There must be an inheritance*—read following some LXX MSS., *How shall a remnant be saved?* **19.** *Behold there is*—these words must be understood as being addressed to the Benjamites. *Which is on*—these topographical details cannot have belonged to the original text; in very much later times it is likely enough that the site of Shiloh was not generally known; hence this insertion. **22.** *That we will say unto them*—read *that ye shall say unto them. Neither did ye give them unto them*—read *neither . . .*

to us. Else would ye . . . i.e., because they would have broken their oath (see v. 18). What the verse seems to mean is this: the Benjamites are bidden to say to the fathers of the stolen maidens, "Do not grudge us your daughters, because it is not as though we had captured them after a battle; on the other hand, you have not given them to us, so it is not as though you had broken your oath." This is clearly an extraordinary way of arguing, and it can scarcely be doubted that we have here an attempt to weld into one two accounts of what was said, and that the attempt has not succeeded. **25.** Cf. 17^6 18^1 19^1.

RUTH

By Professor WILLIAM C. GRAHAM

The book of Ruth is universally regarded as one of the most charming little idyls in all literature. The story has four distinct phases which are correctly indicated by its chapter divisions.

Textual Notes. The text is so clear and easy to follow that it is necessary to offer only a few brief notes. These will be found at the close of the discussion of each chapter.

The Interpretation. This follows ch. 4 on p. 378.

CHAPTER I

The Return of Naomi and Ruth to Bethlehem-Judah. This chapter tells of the return of Naomi to her native place, accompanied by Ruth the Moabitess, her daughter-in-law.

1–5. We have here the history of Elimelech's household prior to the action of the story. The time is the period of the Judges, since Obed, son of Ruth and Boaz, is said to have become the grandfather of David (4:17). Elimelech's household had been kindly received in Moab. The inference is that had it not been for the death of the two sons the household would have remained in Moab permanently.

6–15. Naomi, for all her years of residence as a foreigner in Moab, and for all the kindly treatment there accorded to her, still thinks of the wives of her own sons as foreigners. She sees no place for them in the life of her native country which she is about to resume. When urging them to part finally from her she assumes that because she has no more sons to marry them their matrimonial possibilities among the Hebrews are *nil*. There is no little irony in the situation, yet the author depicts Naomi sympathetically. She is quite unconscious of the narrowness of her attitude. Her fortitude in being ready to face alone her problematical future is touching.

16–18. Ruth's course is inspired by the altruistic motives of sacrificial love and service. Orpah, moved by utilitarian considerations, is ready to re-erect the barriers of national and religious feeling between her and her late husband's mother. Conversely, Ruth's course implies renunciation of her own people with all that that involves.

19–22. The unconsciously narrow and self-centered nature of Naomi is again sympathetically portrayed. Once back in the familiar scenes of her youth she gives way to a burst of self-pity which carries her close to rebellion against Jehovah. She fails altogether to regard the loving devotion of Ruth. All the latter's self-sacrifice has failed to break down the intangible barrier of national feeling.

Textual Note. 2. *Naomi* means "delightful." **20.** *Mara* means "bitterness."

CHAPTER II

The Meeting of Ruth With Boaz. Ruth's meeting with Boaz, described here, was apparently accidental, but the rest of the story turns on it.

1, 2. Further evidence of Ruth's altruism and of Naomi's real dependence on her. The latter was confronted by two alternatives: should she attempt to re-establish herself without Ruth's help, namely, penurious independence at the cost of grueling labor, or the humiliation of becoming an object of charity. Between her and either of these fates Ruth interposes the strength of her youth. She becomes a gleaner in the harvest fields. In doing so she braves not only the rigor of toil but also a certain amount of personal danger (cf. vv. 8, 9, 22).

3–17. Boaz's gracious attitude to the foreign gleaner who has chanced to seek permission to glean in his fields is here the theme. It is essential to the author's purpose that he should make a declaration of the motives which inspire his attitude. Thus Ruth is made to commit what is almost, if not quite, an indelicacy by inquiring of her benefactor, "Why have I found grace in thy sight, that thou shouldest take knowledge of me, seeing I am a stranger (=foreigner)?" Boaz's statement of his motives and his subsequent considerateness are tantamount to a declaration that Ruth is, for him, no longer a foreigner.

18–23. These verses further contrast the respective attitudes of Naomi and Boaz to Ruth. The elder woman is still unawakened to the deeper significance of the younger's relation to her. She blesses the man who has allowed Ruth to glean in so fruitful a field. She fails to bless the gleaner herself. She expresses gratitude to Jehovah when she learns the identity of Ruth's benefactor, tacitly assuming that her only hope lies entirely in her own kin. Yet her lack of appreciation is due not to any inherent harshness in her nature but entirely to her nationalistic prejudices.

Textual Notes. 1. *A mighty man of wealth.* The expression so translated means, "a man of great influence." Boaz was wealthy but his claim to mightiness lay in his magnanimity. 2. Cf. Deut. $24^{19f.}$ Lev. $19^{9f.}$ 23^{22}. 20. *One of our near kinsmen.* The word translated "kinsman" is *gô'el.* Its technical connotation is best suggested by the English words, "redeemer" or "avenger." His duties included the avenging of a kinsman's blood and the redemption of his person and property from seizure or forced sale (cf. Jer. 32^{8-12} Lev. $25^{25, 47-49}$).

CHAPTER III

Naomi's Stratagem. Naomi discloses to Ruth a stratagem which she has devised to stimulate Boaz to decision and action concerning his privileges and duties as *gô'el* ("redeemer") of her late husband's house.

1–5. The point here as before is again Naomi's attitude to Ruth. She thinks of herself as taking care of the latter, which, so far as the exercise of shrewd insight avails, she does. She cannot yet think of Ruth as taking care of her. Likewise it does not occur to her that her stratagem involves thrusting Ruth into a situation in which her honor may be imperiled. The latter is to take all the risk, which only enhances her more than filial submissiveness to the will of one who, all unconsciously, is using her as a pawn in the game of life.

6–15. Boaz is the hero of this incident. His morals do not crack under the strain to which they are subjected. The episode serves to make it perfectly clear that his regard for Ruth proceeds from worthy motives. Boaz is depicted as one who is meticulously upright in his observation of all the accepted social customs of his day.

16–18. These closing verses serve to intensify the previous delineation of Naomi as a shrewd, calculating, self-centered, though well-intentioned person, who, through the blindness induced by prejudice, utterly fails to recognize the sacramental love and sacrifice of one with whom she is daily thrown into the closest contact. Her anxiety about how matters have turned out with Ruth shows that she was aware of the risk which the latter, in obedience to her counsel, had incurred.

Textual Notes. 15. *And he went*—read *and she went.* 16. *Who art thou?* Naomi wishes to know not the identity of Ruth but what treatment she has received from Boaz (see mg.)

CHAPTER IV

The Marriage of Ruth and Boaz, and the Re-establishment of Naomi. The story comes to its climax in Ruth's marriage of her kinsman. On this marriage and what it implied the real message of the book depends.

1–12. That the marriage of Ruth and Boaz was a step taken under public approval, and only after every recognized custom of the day had been observed, and that by this marriage the assimilation of the foreign-born bride to her adopted people and country was consummated, is the theme of these verses. There can be little doubt that the author introduced the claims of the unknown kinsman in the preceding chapter, so that Boaz would be compelled to submit the whole matter to a council of the elders of the community. Thus it becomes clear that objection to the marriage of an Israelite to a foreigner, provided there are no barring circumstances, has no official warrant in the ancient social practice of Israel.

13–22. Similarly, the point here made is that such mixed marriages have often proved highly beneficial, not only to those closely concerned, but to the nation at large. So Naomi's neighbors, after the birth of Ruth's son, name him Obed, "Servant," typifying, perhaps, the values of his mother's life. Likewise they do not hesitate to declare to Naomi that her foreign-born daughter-in-law has been to her "better than seven sons."

But Ruth's crowning honor is that she becomes the ancestress of David, founder of the united kingdom of Israel. This is the real point of the story, to make which the tale is told.

Textual Notes. 3. *Selleth*—read *has sold* (cf. Lev. 25^{25}). 5. *Thou must buy it also of Ruth*—read *thou must also buy Ruth* (cf. v. 10). Naomi was the vendor of the land (cf. v. 3). The difference between the custom of the levirate marriage as reflected here and in Deut. 25^{5-10} should be observed. 7. Cf. Deut. 25^{9}.

The Method of Interpretation

The question of how the book of Ruth is to be interpreted is bound up with the author's motives in writing it. If it may be regarded as authentic historical literature, then there need have been no other motive than that of recording certain facts of historical value.

May the book, then, be so regarded? On this point the date of authorship is of importance. It must be borne in mind that the characters of the story are all otherwise historically unknown. Unless, therefore, the writer lived at a time approximately close to that of which he writes, the chances are that the tale is not primarily historical. This does not mean, however, that the author did not have access to or make use of valuable historical material.

By noting the descendants of Ruth as far only as the third generation, there is left with the reader the impression that the author may have lived close to the times of David. If this were the case, there would be less reason to doubt that the book is a genuine historical vignette.

There are, however, many considerations which point to the conclusion that the author was more probably a contemporary of Nehemiah than of David. These are: (1) This book, in the Hebrew Scriptures, has a place only in the third, latest, and least venerated group of sacred books known technically as "the Writings." (2) The diction and style show the influence of the Aramaic language, which is never found in genuinely early Hebrew literature. (3) The author in 4[7] feels the necessity of explaining, as a kind of obsolete social curiosity, a custom which was duly sanctioned by law in Deut. 25[5-10], itself only a late pre-exilic passage. (4) The idylic simplicity and pastoral beauty of the life reflected in the book of Ruth, when compared with the atmosphere of harsh and cruel necessity in which one moves as one reads the genuinely early stories in Judges, suggests later idealization.

But why should the author have chosen as the time of his story "the days when the judges judged"? Because he could not do otherwise, inasmuch as he wished to make Ruth an ancestress of David. In addition to this it may be said that any writer of fiction who chooses a historical *milieu* for his characters does so because he believes that in such *milieu* he will be able better to handle the problem of the story. The parallels between the period of the Judges and the days of Nehemiah are very great. This alone would account for the choice of the situation.

What, then, is the central problem of the book of Ruth? Surely, it is nothing else than the relation of the foreigner to Israel, a theme which runs through the whole book and to which the writer contrives to give commanding importance by many reminders that Ruth is a foreigner (cf. 1[22] 2[2, 6, 21] 4[5, 10]). There is, too, no doubt of his attitude on this question. His story shows that he wished to argue, first, that foreigners may be spiritually assimilated, and, second, that they may make contributions of essential value to society in general. If, then, we can find in history a time when this foreign question became acute, we shall be justified in interpreting the book as primarily didactic aimed at the propagation of the writer's views on that question.

The Historical Situation Which Stimulated the Author to Write the Book. It is definitely known that the problem of the relationships of Israelites with foreign-born or foreign-descended elements of the population did not become a public issue until the days of Ezra and Nehemiah. For an explanation of the circumstances which made that problem so acute at that time the reader is referred to the introduction to Jonah, section on "Historical Situation."

Here it will suffice to draw attention to the existence of three clearly defined groups in the population of Palestine in those days. These are: (1) The returning exiles and those descended from returned Babylonian Jews. (2) The foreign elements. (3) The native group who had never before come under the influence of the peculiar ideas and standards of their exilic compatriots.

The Interpretation. In the book of Ruth, surely by the deliberate intent of the author, the three leading characters, Naomi, Ruth, and Boaz, symbolize the three above-mentioned parties to the controversy which engaged public attention in the author's time. By attention to his delineation of these characters it is possible to see how he regarded each and what was his idea of the right policy for the time. Let us briefly review the characters of the story from this viewpoint.

1. *Naomi, the Returning Exile.* The widow of Elimelech manifests several characteristics which there is reason to believe were typical of the group she represents. She is given to self-pity and to brooding over the harshness with which life has treated her. She is inclined to be rebellious against the Divine Providence. She is essentially self-seeking and egotistical. This in turn makes her shrewd, calculating, cold, proud and inconsiderate even of those who serve her. Intellectually she is the strongest character in the story. Morally, she is the weakest. She will use, not only foreigners, but also her own kin to gain her ends. Apply this to the group which she represents and you have the author's rather shrewd appraisal of its limitations.

But the author is not hostile to the returned exiles. He is aware that great sorrow lies at the root of their shortcomings. He values, too, the loyalty to the homeland which even sorrow and long years of exile could not kill. He appreciates the courage which, alone and defenseless, would undertake the difficult journey home to a problematical future. Finally, he believes that the weaknesses he has exposed are not fundamental but accidental. Under happier circumstances, he hopes, they will be overcome.

2. *Ruth, the Foreigner.* It is manifest that the author sympathizes strongly with the foreigner. He is acutely conscious that the latter makes great sacrifices in leaving his own land. He cuts himself off from the social support offered by his kindred and must take his chance of integrating himself in the social fabric of his adopted country. In this difficult process of adjustment he, of necessity, passes through a period of humiliation which he may survive only by the exercise of moral strength of a high order. Such humiliations are usually imposed through the thoughtlessness and unconscious prejudices of essentially well-disposed people. The writer's evident belief is that a foreigner who can survive this period and prove himself a useful citizen, while, at the same time, coming to appreciate the spiritual heritage of those among whom he has come to live, is worthy of all acceptation.

3. *Boaz, the Native.* Boaz is a simple-hearted, unindoctrinated citizen. He is so occupied with his crops and herds as to have escaped altogether from the prejudices which are so strong in the exilic group. He is of a pragmatic turn of mind, little interested in racial and religious tags and labels. He is just such an ancestor as David might have had, jovial, hearty, manly, a "big man," mighty in toil, in the pleasures of life, or, if need were, in battle.

There are two influences at work in the life of Boaz, first, the clever mind of Naomi, who wishes to exploit the hold of kinship which she has upon him; second, the personality of Ruth the foreigner. Of these two the latter, in the author's judgment, is the stronger. Naomi's plans work out only because Ruth is her agent. Without her she would have planned in vain. This gives the key to the author's view of the social situation with which he deals. The success of the exilic party can be achieved only by the inclusion of the non-Jewish elements of the population in its plans. If the intellectually more able exilic group will follow the course taken by Naomi in the story, all three elements may relate themselves and harmony and prosperity ensue.

The ideal of the author for the future of his country was the re-establishment of a monarchy, brought about by a liberal policy which would unify all disparate elements of the population into one strong whole. This is the significance of the last words of the story (4^{17}), which tell how Obed, the son of Boaz and Ruth, became the grandfather of David. Let exile, native, and foreigner draw together in harmony and in three or four generations there may be another David and another united kingdom of Israel.

The Teaching Values of the Book. The social problem with which the author endeavored to deal is a live issue in our own day and will be to the end of time. One can hardly doubt that the universal acceptance of the principles laid down in this book in regard to the treatment of foreigners would result in increasing good will among men the world over.

But perhaps the greatest lesson of the book is that the way to happiness lies through intelligent co-operation with others. The individual virtues possessed by each character would not have sufficed in themselves to achieve the happy result. It is our human limitations, of which no one is free, which make us essential to each other. To give what we can in gracious co-operation with those who can give what we cannot—this is the path by which we may best serve, not only our own age, but posterity.

Literature: Eiselen, *The Psalms and Other Sacred Writings;* Thatcher, *Judges and Ruth* (Century Bible); Cook, *The Book of Ruth* (Cambridge Bible).

FIRST AND SECOND SAMUEL

BY PROFESSOR NATHANIEL MICKLEM

INTRODUCTION

Place in Canon and General Contents. In Hebrew MSS. and in the earliest printed editions of the Hebrew Bible the two books of Samuel are treated as one, but in the Greek Bible they constitute with First and Second Kings the four books "of kingdoms." The division of Samuel into two books, therefore, is only a matter of convenience, carried through rather arbitrarily. They deal with the beginnings of the Hebrew monarchy and cover the lifetimes of Samuel, Saul, and David.

Manner of Literary Composition. When we are told in 1 Sam. 27^{6} (cf. 1 Sam. 30^{25} and 2 Sam. 6^{8}) that "Ziklag pertaineth unto the kings of Judah *unto this day*," it is clearly implied that the writer lived several reigns at least after the time of David. But the question, When was Samuel written? is misleading unless we bear in mind the Hebrew method of writing history, so different from our own. If we judge by the O.T., we may conclude that the Hebrew historian worked by what may be called the "scissors-and-paste" method. His book would consist of a series of excerpts taken from earlier chroniclers and stitched together with a few connecting sentences or judgments giving the editor's point of view. The editor or final redactor of Samuel, therefore, may have lived long after the time of David, while some of the sources or chronicles from which he quotes may have been old books in his time and contemporary or nearly contemporary with the events they record. Thus questions of date, authorship, and reliability are very complicated and, except in broad outline, can be answered only very tentatively. Those who wish to follow the detailed arguments and analyses made by scholars can find them in the standard modern introductions to the literature of the O.T. Here only the surest and most generally accepted conclusions will be stated.

Source Materials. As to the *documents* which the editor of Samuel used it is impossible to arrive at certainty, but the various *types of tradition* which he has incorporated can be recognized even by the reader of the English translation.

1. Of one whole group of traditions *the prophet Samuel is the hero* (1 Sam. 1^{1-28} 2^{11}–4^{1a} 7^{2}–8^{22} 10^{17-27} 11^{12}–12^{25} 13^{7b-15a} 15^{1}–16^{13} 25^{1} 28^{3-25}). Whether or not these passages are taken from a single document, they represent a common and distinctive point of view: in the days of the Philistine oppression the national life and the national religion were at a low ebb, but before the lamp of God was quite extinguished (so some Jewish commentators mystically interpret 3^{3}), God raised up a political and religious leader in the person of Samuel. He became a *national* religious leader (4^{1}, etc.) and a *national* deliverer from the Philistine oppression (7^{13}); he judged *all Israel* (7^{15}). It was natural that his sons should succeed him in this work (8^{1}), but the people, not satisfied with the kingship of the Lord their God, exercised through Samuel, demanded a king (8^{5}); an earthly monarchy was for Israel a form of apostasy (8^{7}); none the less Samuel, at the divine command and with many warnings, selected Saul as king by means of the sacred lot (10^{21}). Samuel then makes a long farewell speech to the people ($12^{1f.}$). Saul's kingship is a failure from the first, for God immediately rejects him for disobedience (13^{13}). After a second act of disobedience on Saul's part (15^{19}) the breach between him and Samuel becomes final (15^{35}); Samuel anoints David in Saul's place (16^{13}). Samuel's death is the occasion of mourning on the part of all Israel, who gather at Ramah to bury him (25^{1}), but even after death Samuel dominates the situation ($28^{3f.}$).

There can be little doubt that in the main this picture of Samuel reflects a later rather than a contemporaneous point of view: Samuel did not judge "all Israel," for in reality "all Israel" was not united until the time of the monarchy, and in another and earlier tradition Samuel is represented as a relatively unknown local seer (9^{6}). Moreover, if, in fact, Samuel had destroyed the power of the Philistines, that task would not have remained for Saul and David. This does not mean that these stories are historically worthless, but only that the general picture they give idealizes the work and to some extent the character of Samuel. Further, some of the passages which give little historical information are, as we shall see, of great religious significance.

2. Another group of traditions deals with *the history and miraculous powers of the ark* (4^{1b}–7^{1}). Perhaps they were stories and legends

cherished by the Jerusalem priesthood who became the custodians of the ark. Whether these stories represent a written document by themselves or are taken from some document with a wider interest are questions we cannot answer.

3. Of a third group of traditions *Saul is the hero* (1 Sam. 9^{1}–10^{16} 11^{1-11} 13^{1-7a} $^{15b-18}$ 14^{1-52} 16^{14-23}). These tell how Saul went out to seek his father's asses and found a kingdom ($9^{1f.}$), how God's Spirit came upon him (10^{9}), how he first came to public notice by his deliverance of the people of Jabesh in Gilead ($11^{1f.}$), how he was successful in all his wars (14^{52}), and how at last he failed because the Lord sent an evil spirit upon him (16^{14}). These stories may naturally be thought to represent the Benjamite tradition. Whether they belong together in the sense of coming from a single document we cannot say. Their substantial historical accuracy there is no need to doubt.

4. A fourth group of traditions deals with *David's relationship to Saul* and David's exploits and sufferings before he became king (1 Sam. 17^{55}–19^{17} 20^{1b}–24^{22} 25^{2}–28^{2} 30^{1-31} 31^{1-13} 2 Sam. 1^{1-16}). These stories doubtless come from various sources; they are popular tales rather than history in the modern sense of that term; they all have David for their hero, and they are in many cases marked by a strong bias against the Benjamite monarchy of Saul; they are the traditions of Judah and of the south country where David was long outlawed; they are *bona fide* traditions and are based upon historical events, though doubtless the stories have been somewhat colored by the enthusiasms and prejudices of those who passed them down. These stories are not a literary unity.

5. There is a small group of stories which may be regarded as *romances* (1 Sam. 13^{19-23} 17^{1-54} 19^{18}–20^{1a}). These must be ascribed in large part to imagination, not history; they are intended as edifying stories, and possess much religious significance.

6. There is a series of narratives (2 Sam. 11^{1b}–12^{25} 13^{1}–20^{22}) dealing with *the family life and court history of David*, and in particular with Absalom's rebellion. These narratives are so vivid, so detailed, so well informed that it seems natural to refer them to someone who was actually in close touch with David and the court. These stories constitute a document of first-class historical importance; presumably they lay before the editor of Samuel in writing.

7. Most of the rest of Second Samuel is taken up with *narratives of David's reign* doubtless taken from various sources (2^{1}–7^{7} 8^{1}–11^{1a} 12^{26-31} 20^{23-26} 21^{1-22} 23^{8-23}). In general, these may be taken as reliable traditions; but for the most part we have before us traditions, not contemporary records.

8. Finally there is a group of *poetical or semi-poetical pieces* (1 Sam. 2^{1-10} 2 Sam. 1^{17-27} 7^{8-29} 22^{1-51} 23^{1-7}). One of these (2 Sam. 1^{17-27}) is quoted from the lost Book of Heroes (Jashar), another (2 Sam. 22^{1-51}) is found in a variant form in the book of Psalms (Psa. 18).

This analysis, it will be noted, is concerned with types of tradition rather than with documents. In the case of the Pentateuch the analysis of documents is relatively sure; in the case of Samuel it is quite uncertain. It constitutes a literary problem of great fascination to scholars, but of little direct importance to the ordinary Bible student. It is, however, of great importance to bear in mind the kind of sources, whether writen or oral, which the editor had before him. Through what stages and "editions" the books of Samuel may have passed before they reached their present state it is impossible to say. It seems fairly clear, however, that 2 Sam. 21–24 is an appendix added at some late stage to the book and giving items of information that should have come in earlier. The book reached its final form at approximately the same time as the books of Joshua and Judges, namely, about 400 B.C.

Purpose. What purpose did the editor put before himself in the compilation of Samuel? In the Hebrew Bible, Samuel, with Joshua, Judges, and Kings, belongs to the section called "the former prophets." Samuel was regarded, then, primarily as a prophetic book. It contains much historical material of first-class importance, but its purpose was not to give a scientific picture of a past age, nor to serve the purposes of archæology, but to edify the Hebrew Church; it is devotional literature or preaching, not scientific history such as we have learned to demand. The editor of Samuel fulfills Frederick Schlegel's definition of an historian as "a prophet who looks back into the past"; his interest lay in the moral order of the world, the righteous will and purposes of God. The editor was a preacher using the past as his text from which to give his contemporaries light upon the present, comfort, warning, and exhortation. From the documents and traditions available he chose such elements as served his purpose. These things are written, the editor of Samuel might say, that ye might believe that God has revealed his holy and righteous will in history, and that believing ye might have salvation and blessing in his favor.

The early Christian Church had no archæological interests. First and Second Samuel became Christian Scriptures because they were then, as they are still, useful for edification. No teacher finds difficulty in discoursing about the good Samaritan and the prodigal son because these are characters of fiction, not historical persons. The books of Samuel contain historical material of the greatest interest and importance, but the spiritual truth and value of the stories are very little affected by the minutiæ and uncertainties of historical criticism.

Permanent Significance. As has already been suggested, Samuel is of great importance as an historical document, not because it is history in the modern sense of that term, but because it contains some historical material of the highest order. Regarding the oldest sources used by the editor, the historian Eduard Meyer says: "It is something remarkable that an historical literature of this sort was possible in Israel at that time. It is far beyond anything that we know otherwise regarding the writing of history in the ancient Orient." The chief value of the later documents consists in their interpretation of the earlier history, which furnishes an interesting insight into the thought development of Israel's prophetic leaders. The rise of opposition to the monarchy revealed in the later portions is only what might be expected in view of the fact that as early as the time of Solomon the political developments incident to the maintenance of the monarchy threatened the very life of the religion of Jehovah.

Much may be learned from Samuel regarding *religious and moral conditions* during the period described: Enemies were tortured; the truth was held none too sacred; women and children were not exempt from the cruelties of war; polygamy was common among the higher classes. Evidence of progress, however, is not lacking. The rights of life and of property came to be more clearly defined and more carefully guarded. Even the poor had an opportunity of securing justice before a judge like David. Adultery was recognized as a crime. The law of blood revenge was gradually superseded by trial before an authorized tribunal. The centralization of government exerted a strong unifying influence on religious thought and practice. The offering of sacrifice was not yet restricted to the priesthood, nor was the priesthood restricted to the tribe of Levi, but the number of priests was increasing and their duties were becoming more clearly defined. The chief function of the priests was still the determining of the will of Jehovah. The care of the sanctuary, the offering of sacrifice, and other primary responsibilities were only gradually intrusted to them. Another person occupying a prominent place in the religious life was the seer, who was thought to possess the power of determining the divine will or, in general, of revealing secrets. Some persons might combine the two offices, but ordinarily the seers were concerned more with personal and temporal affairs, while the priests were interested in public and religious matters. Samuel was a seer, but a later writer thought him worthy of being called a prophet. In reality he marked the transition from the lower office of seer to the higher and more dignified office of prophet. As a prophet he was a worthy predecessor of Elijah, Amos, Isaiah, and other later prophets in Israel and Judah.

With all the advances in religious thought and practice, the age did not free itself entirely from religious shortcomings. Even the most enlightened had a relatively low conception of the character of Jehovah. David, for instance, considered departure from the land of Israel equivalent to exclusion from the presence and service of Jehovah (1 Sam. 26[19]). When Samuel slew Agag before Jehovah (1 Sam. 15[33]), and when king and people united in slaying innocent human beings to pacify Jehovah (2 Sam. 21), they gave conclusive evidence that they had not as yet fully comprehended his real character (cf. 2 Sam. 24). Succeeding generations had much to learn before the fullness of the perfection of Israel's God could be appreciated and proclaimed by the great prophets.

Condition of Text. The books of Samuel were written some two thousand years before the invention of printing; it is not surprising that in the course of those two thousand years mistakes and corruptions have crept into the text through the slips of copyists and other causes, nor that the Hebrew text, as it comes down to us, is sometimes unintelligible, often puzzling, and widely different from the Greek version (the LXX), which was made in the centuries immediately before Christ (see p. 103). Commentaries on the Hebrew text are largely taken up with attempts, that never can be more than tentative, to restore the text as it is supposed to have come from the author's pen. Almost all these discussions are concerned with points of literary but not religious interest. They are passed over in the following commentary except in cases where the English Version seems obscure or definitely misleading.

On dates, see art., *Chronology of O.T.*, p. 108. Variations indicate that as to some of these dates there is still difference of opinion.

Literature: H. P. Smith, *Samuel* (International Critical Commentary); Kirkpatrick, *Samuel* (Cambridge Bible); Kennedy, *Samuel* (Century Bible); Eiselen, *The Prophetic Books of the O.T.*, vol. i; Driver, *Introduction to the Literature of the O.T.*

FIRST SAMUEL

Chapters 1[1] to 4[1a]: The Birth and Prophetic Call of Samuel

CHAPTER I

1–18. Hannah's Prayer and Vow. The home of Samuel's parents, Ramathaim or Arimathea, cannot certainly be identified; it was perhaps due west of Shiloh. *Hannah* means "grace," *Peninnah*, "pearl" or "coral." In ancient Hebrew thought childlessness was the greatest disaster that could overtake a family; it involved annihilation for the family-soul in which all members of the family, past and present, participate. The duties of the priest at this early time are given in Deut. 33[8-10]; they were to divine the will of God by means of the *urim* and *thummim*—i.e., two lots used in divination—to teach the people the requirements of God and to offer the sacrifices. The covenant or Law, which they were to keep and teach, corresponds, in general at least, with the Book of the Covenant (Ex. 20[22]–23[19]). In v. 5 read with LXX *a single portion;* Jerome in the Vulgate says, "to Hannah he sadly gave a single portion, for Hannah was his love." *No razor* (v. 11)—a mark of special consecration to God (cf. the tonsure in Christendom). The word *Belial* (v. 16; cf. A.S.V., "a wicked woman") suggests negation, and connotes godlessness, emptiness, rottenness.

19–28. Answer to the Prayer and Performance of the Vow. The etymology of *Samuel* suggested in v. 20 is a popular etymology based on similarity in sound. Perhaps the writer means only that "Samuel" sounds in Hebrew like "asked of God." The reference to weaning suggests a period of at least three years, but more time seems implied. The sacrifice offered is an unusually valuable sacrifice. In v. 28 read *Samuel worshiped the Lord,* or *they worshiped the Lord there.*

As Mark, who tells of "great David's greater Son," begins with John the Baptist, so here David is introduced with the story of Samuel, who is represented as the son of his mother's vows (Prov. 31[2]). We see the simple piety of early days in Israel, the annual pilgrimage to Shiloh, where the ark was housed, the sacrifice there and the feast, the whole compared by Bennett to a Christmas and a Christmas dinner away from home. After dinner Hannah went into the sanctuary sadly to pray before the Real Presence represented by the ark. We note that the language of prayer has not changed, and that she leaves the sanctuary cheerful with the old priest's blessing. Much is implied of real understanding and affection between husband and wife; there is simple faith in the prayer-hearing God; and when at last the child has come and the time is ripe, his mother takes him to the sanctuary and dedicates him to God with thanksgiving and a special sacrifice.

Sacrifice is not a formality and empty rite; it is a gift; and in Hebrew thought everything that belongs to a man is, as it were, charged with his personality; therefore in the gift he gives something of himself; thus every gift is sacramental; nor is it a light thing to receive a gift, for the receiver in receiving accepts a personal obligation to the giver; he is bound by his acceptance. Sacrifice, therefore, is a solemn sacrament.

CHAPTER II

1–10. Hannah's Song of Thanksgiving. This, with its reference to the monarchy (v. 10), or possibly the Messiah, was hardly composed by Hannah on this occasion. Possibly it was inserted here because in later days it was used in the liturgy for the service corresponding to our "churching" of women. However, the psalm was used also as a song of victory and of thanksgiving on a variety of occasions. The wild ox symbolizes strength and victory; hence in v. 1 the metaphor of the horn. *Salvation*—deliverance from the shame of barrenness. Hannah's *Exultavit* (see v. 1) is the first draft of the Christian *Magnificat* (Lk. 1[46]); the *motif* of both songs is the same, and the one points to the other.

11–17. The Disgraceful Conduct of the Sons of Eli. In the latter part of v. 12 follow R.V. mg. Knowing God in Hebrew thought is always much more than knowing about God; it implies a personal relationship to God (cf. Jer. 22[16]). The custom described in vv. 13, 14 was an offense against courtesy. The priest's due should not be snatched in this way. The attitude reflected in vv. 15, 16 involved sacrilege, for the fat was a sacred part of the victim, belonging to God alone.

18–21. Samuel and Hannah. The story of Eli and his sons is interrupted by a few verses dealing with Samuel. *Ephod* refers to the priestly garment, probably a loin-cloth; the *robe* is presumably an outer garment, worn over the tunic.

22–26. Eli Reproves His Sons, but Without Effect. In an ordinary case of plaintiff and defendant, God, through his representative, the judge, can mediate between them; but when God is the plaintiff, his direct vengeance is to be expected (cf. Job 9[32f.]). *Would slay,* i.e., was to slay, as the event proved (v. 25).

27–36. A Prophecy Against Eli's House. In the light of the context *the house of thy father* must be the tribe of Levi, and the contrast seems to be between the Levitical house of Eli and the non-Levitical Samuel (that Samuel in the early stories was not a Levite is clear, for instance, from his mother's special vows for him); but the point of the later verses (30–36) is that the Levitical house of Zadok, the "faithful priest," shall supersede the house of Eli. Eli's sons, Hophni and Phinehas, died in battle (4^{11}). According to a doubtful tradition, the priests of Nob whom Saul slew (v. 33; 22^{11-19}) and Abiathar, whom Solomon banished (1 Kings 2^{27}), were descendants of Eli. These verses are certainly of late origin. In v. 18 the *ephod* is clearly a garment; in v. 28 this interpretation is doubtful. In the latter place, as in many other O.T. passages, it seems to be a solid object, probably a divine image, possibly in the form of a bull or a calf. (Cf. Judg. 8^{27} 18^{30}; see Budde, *Zeitschrift für Alttestamentliche Wissenschaft*, 1921, pp. 1f.) Instead of *wear*, therefore, read *carry*. The man not to be cut off (v. 33) is probably Abiathar (22^{20}). The reference in v. 36 presumably is to the plight of the country priests when all the worship was centered in Jerusalem (Deut. 18^{6-8}).

In the passage dealing with the rejection of Eli, which embodies material from different sources, the editor seeks to show three things: (1) that Eli, who was responsible before God for his sons, was rejected by God from the priesthood; (2) that at first Samuel took his place; and (3) that later the priesthood passed to the house of Zadok. The religious principle underlying the narrative is clear: There is no such thing as a "divine right" of priests, no "apostolic succession" that cannot be broken. God calls a man to a task, to its duties and its privileges; the sons may be expected to carry on their father's work; but if the duties are neglected, the privileges are withdrawn. "And say not within yourselves, We have Abraham to our father: for I say unto you, that God is able of these stones to raise up children unto Abraham" (Mt. 3^9).

CHAPTER III

The Prophetic Call of Samuel. (See also 4^{1a}.) The story is simply told. *Child* would better be rendered with v. 1 mg., *lad*. See comment on 4^4 for a discussion of the *ark*. On *sacrifice* and expiation (v. 14; cf. mg.) see closing paragraph on 2^{1-10} and on ch. 27. God will not accept Eli's gifts, and therefore will not accept or forgive Eli.

The daily opening of the doors was probably the occasion of a solemn service (v. 15). Samuel would be consulted on such questions as, whether a journey would be prosperous, and where lost objects would be found. All his oracles came true (vv. 19–21).

The subject of this chapter is the prophetic call of Samuel or the coming of a personal experience of God to him. When religion in Israel was at the lowest ebb (v. 1), God called forth a prophet. Samuel *heard* the voice of God, as did Saint Augustine in the garden (*Confessions*, viii, 12). Hitherto Samuel's religion had been traditional and at second hand; henceforward he knew God for himself (v. 7). As we have the story, the only message that comes to Samuel is a word of doom against the house of Eli, but a call to personal service on the part of Samuel is implied in v. 19 and in what follows. Eli, when he hears the message, consents to the law of God that it is holy and just and good. Possibly in v. 21 we should read that, not the Lord, but the *people* appeared again in Shiloh. Shiloh became the center of a religious revival, because it was known that God's word was to be heard there through Samuel. While these stories that make Samuel a national religious teacher may be late, they indicate the editor's conception of that prophetic office to which Christian ministers and teachers are also called, and of the experimental and personal religious experience which it implies.

CHAPTER IV

Defeat of Israel by the Philistines. The site of the battle with the Philistines, which led to the loss of the ark, is probably not far inland from Joppa.

For the *Philistines*, see on ch. 17. It is noteworthy that there is no mention of Samuel in this narrative. *The ark of the covenant of the Lord of hosts which dwelleth* (mg.) *amid the cherubim* is the fullest and longest title of the ark (v. 4); but it is not likely that this full title was used in these early days. Ark *of the covenant*—because as the visible representation of the God of Israel, inherited from the Mosaic era, it was a solemn reminder of the covenant between Israel and Israel's God. It was later supposed that the two "tables of the Law," the Decalogue, the basis of the covenant, were deposited within it. Lord *of hosts:* the hosts are primarily heavenly hosts of angels, stars, "sons of God," spiritual, demonic beings, but they may also include the armies of Israel. *Cherubim* are angelic beings, perhaps partly of human, partly of animal shape, attendant upon God; they were pictorially represented as guardians of the ark in Solomon's Temple, and it is doubtful whether they were associated with the ark and the religion of Israel before Solomon's time.

The ark was a box; such is the meaning of the Hebrew word *'aron*, translated *ark*. Later tradition supposed it to have contained various relics of the Mosaic period, the tables of the Law, Aaron's rod, manna, etc. The most probable suggestions as to original content are (a) that it contained nothing; (b) that it contained volcanic stones from the Sinai region. The God of Israel was the God of Sinai, and the region would be charged with his presence; therefore, in taking part of Sinai with them, Israel would be taking a potent talisman, would indeed be taking God himself; for, just as, in Hebrew thought, the whole family-soul is represented in each member of the family, to the whole of God, "God's presence and his very self and essence all divine," would be inevitably associated with the sacred stones from his own country. But it is no longer possible for us to know with certainty what, if anything, the ark contained. In later years, it may be, the ark came to be regarded as the throne of the invisible God (see further on ch. 6).

In v. 8 read *and with the pestilence* for *in the wilderness*. Only according to later theory was Eli a *judge* over all Israel (v. 18). Not only was the ark taken, but in all probability Shiloh itself was destroyed at this time (see Jer. 7[12]). This must have been a time of religious crisis for Israel. Much more after the capture of the ark must the elders have asked, *Wherefore hath the Lord smitten us to-day before the Philistines?* (v. 3). Were the gods of the Philistines stronger than the God of Israel? or had the God of Israel reason to be displeased with his people? Was repentance necessary? Many will have espoused the former view; it was a spiritual triumph that the latter prevailed. Eli, who *trembled for the ark of God*, betrayed an uneasy conscience (v. 13). National calamity, rather than success, is a time of spiritual growth. Yet this calamity was hardly on a national scale. No general is named; and if all Israel was concerned in the loss of the ark, not all Israel was engaged in the battle. This defeat may well have impressed upon all Israel the need for national unity and a king.

Chapters 5 and 6: The Mysterious Power of the Ark

CHAPTER V

The Ark No Blessing to the Philistines. The capture of the ark did not prove an unmixed blessing to the Philistines; even their gods suffered disaster. *Ashdod* was one of the five great cities of Philistia. *Dagon*, a fish or corn god, an old Akkadian sun-god. (See further comment on Judg. 16[23]). V. 5 offers an explanation of the habit in Ashdod of jumping over the temple threshold as a specially sacred or spirit-haunted place. The custom was widespread but forbidden to Israel as heathen (Zeph. 1[9]). In Solomon's Temple the threshold had a special guard (2 Kings 12[9]; cf. Esth. 6[2]). *Tumors*, better *plague boils*, i.e., bubonic plague (vv. 9, 11, 12). See further under ch. 6.

CHAPTER VI

The Ark Returned by the Philistines. Instead of *a guilt-offering* (v. 3), read *compensation*. *Mice* are a symbol of plague. The offering of golden *boils* to heal plague is a kind of homeopathic magic (see on 2 Kings 19[35]). A new cart and animals not broken in must be used for a sacred purpose (v. 7). To have the cows leave their calves and voluntarily take a certain road would be a kind of miracle. V. 15 seems to be a later addition. In later ages only priests might sacrifice. In v. 19 accept the marginal reading. Omit *fifty thousand men*. Kiriath-jearim (v. 21) was further up the Jerusalem road.

The burden of this passage is the mysterious and magical power of the ark, bringing destruction to the Philistines, and even to the Israelites, if it were not treated with due respect. There is nothing here of the God "whose property is always to have mercy." How differently do the heathen come to recognize the God of Israel according to some of the sublime prophetic utterances! That God has all power is a necessary idea in religion, but it is even more important to inquire how he exercises his power and to what ends. Religion develops as men moralize and spiritualize their conceptions of God's power. Christ might have summoned twelve legions of angels, but he sought a power over men's hearts which can only come by free consent. In the cross, more than in the creation, is shown God's omnipotence so far as religion is concerned.

Teaching of chs. 5 and 6. This section, by laying stress on the ark's magical powers, misses the religious significance of the ark for Israel. A probable clue to much of the religious history of the period may be found in the difference and opposition between the ark and the ephod. The ephod (see on 2[28]) was a divine image—an idol; the ark was a box, either empty or containing stones from the Sinai region (see on 4[4]), and thus constituted in a real sense a non-idolatrous symbol of the invisible God of Israel. Moreover, the ark was the symbol of the austere worship of the wilderness and of the religious foundations established by Moses. The ephod, on the other hand, was a Canaanite symbol taken over into Israel's religion, but never altogether freed from the degrading associations of Canaanite worship and the fertility-cults of Canaan.

After the ark had been captured by the Philistines, apart from these stories which are of somewhat doubtful historical worth, nothing is heard of it for some twenty years or more. It probably remained in Philistine hands at Gath (see 2 Sam. $6^{1f.}$); Saul seems to have made no effort to regain it; at least it is not mentioned in connection with Saul. His neglect of the ark may have been typical of his quarrel with Samuel. David's bringing up of the ark to Jerusalem is more than a sign of victory over the Philistines, more than a means of uniting north and south religiously; it is probably to be regarded as indicative of his general religious policy. David stands for the older and nobler religious traditions of Israel, the religious ideas of Moses. For this reason he builds no temple for the ark but houses it in a tent (see on 2 Sam. 7^{1-29}). We notice, moreover, that once David has taken the ark to Jerusalem, we hear no more of the ephod. He does not even take it with him in his flight from Absalom when he leaves the ark behind.

There is always a tendency in religion, as illustrated by these stories of the wonder-working of the ark, to externalize and materialize a spiritual miracle; thus feeding upon Christ by faith is easily externalized into the eating of bread, the moral glory of the saints into a halo round their heads, or justification by "faith" into justification by "orthodoxy."

CHAPTERS 7 AND 8: THE THEOCRATIC IDEAL

CHAPTER VII

1, 2. See on ch. 6.

3–17. Samuel Reappears as a Prophetic Leader. *Baalim* and *Ashtaroth*, male and female Canaanite deities, representing Canaanite religion generally, polytheistic, unethical, and often lascivious. The solemn libation of water (cf. 2 Sam. 23^{16}) is a part of the cleansing penitential ritual of the fast-day (cf. the rite of baptism). While the Israelites were engaged in religious rites the Philistines attacked them, but without success (v. 10), for they were supernaturally discomfited. If Samuel had really won so sweeping a victory over the Philistines, the work of Saul and David would have been needless. See further under ch. 8.

CHAPTER VIII

The Demand for a King Granted. In the earliest parts of the O.T. only twice (and even there not certainly) is God called "king" (Deut. 33^5 and Num. 23^{21}), but Gressmann thinks that from earliest times there was a close connection between the ark and the idea of the divine kingship (*Mose*, pp. 439f.; *contra*, Budde *Segen Moses*, pp. 13f.), and Mowinckel has given strong reasons for supposing that there was yearly in Jerusalem a festival of the "enthronement" of the God of Israel (see on 2 Sam. 6). The earthly king was always regarded as God's representative, but only in the Northern Kingdom, so far as we know, was there a repudiation of the earthly monarchy (for instance, Hosea). This section, therefore, presumably comes from a northern source. The description of the king's conduct seems the fruit of bitter experience.

Teaching of chs. 7 and 8. This section was written less to tell history than to set forth the author's theory of the destiny of Israel and of the significance of the kingship: Israel was intended to be a theocracy, a rule of God mediated, not through a king, but through a religious officer, prophet, priest and judge, such as Moses had been and such as, in the writer's view, Joshua and the Judges to Samuel must have been, till rebellious Israel asked for an earthly king. This ideal was realized after the Exile in the high-priestly rule; but this was legal rather than prophetic; it is at least partially realized in the constitution of the Roman Church. It is transcended in the N.T. idea that the Spirit is given to *all* believers; but the Christian Church is still a theocracy, not a democracy.

CHAPTERS 9 TO 11: SAUL'S ELECTION TO THE KINGSHIP

CHAPTER IX

Samuel Led to Select Saul. With 9^1 begins a new account of the establishment of the monarchy and the selection of Saul as the first king. *Saul* means "desired." The places named in vv. 4, 5 are unidentified. According to this narrative, Samuel was a local seer, not a national Judge and hero; evidently he is not known to Saul. The local sanctuary was usually on the hill above the town—a custom which dates from Canaanite times. Samuel is priest as well as seer. The monarchy in this story is regarded as of God's purpose and gift, while in ch. 8 it is traced to the people's rebellion. For *that which was upon it* (v. 24), read perhaps *the fat tail;* and for the last sentence perhaps *that thou mayest eat with the guests.* In v. 25 follow the marginal reading.

CHAPTER X

1–8. The Anointing of Saul. This is credited to Jehovah himself. Saul's choice by Jehovah is to be evidenced by several experiences predicted by Samuel. *To God* (v. 3) means "to worship at the sanctuary." The instruments mentioned in v. 5 correspond roughly to the guitar, tambourine, flute, and harp. *Prophesying* (vv. 5, 10–13) means "being in the prophetic frenzy." *Gibeah* (v. 5 mg.) means "hill." There seems from ancient time to have been some confusion between Gibeah, Geba, and Gibeon. It is probable that the Philistine prefect had his residence at Gibeon, and that Saul after his first successes against the Philistines made this residence into his palace. Thus, as Jerusalem later became "David's City," so Gibeon became Saul's Hill, or Gibeah. In 2 Sam. 21[6] Saul's Gibeah seems clearly to be Gibeon. Gibeon is here called "God's Hill," and it is likely (so Sellin) that the priests of Nob were the local priesthood here (see 22[11]).

9–16. The Return of Saul. Two interpretations of the surprise questions are possible: (1) Kish is an unlikely man to have a son among the prophets; (2) Saul is behaving in an abandoned way such as would not be expected of the son of Kish; these prophets are men of no family connection; no one knows who their parents were. The latter is much more probable.

17–27. The Kingship Viewed as Disloyalty to Jehovah. As in 8[4-22], the kingship is represented as due to the people's rebellion. Having demanded a king, who shall he be? The belief that God directs the sacred lot persisted into the Christian Church (Acts 1[26]). If in doubt, pray and then toss up, is the principle; it may be childish, but it is not irreligious where a man is entirely willing to do God's will if he can discover it. The phrase *God save the king!* was not a mere formality. According to primitive thought, to say "Hail!" to a man actually adds to his strength and dignity. Perhaps 8[11-18] gives the contents of the book alluded to in v. 25. See further under ch. 11.

CHAPTER XI

A Differing Account of Saul's Selection. With some additions this chapter continues 10[16] and gives another and probably more historical account of Saul's popular election as king. The *Ammonites* were nomad marauders; the *covenant* offered is presumably the right to a tithe of the crops. The *men of Jabesh* in Gilead were kinsmen of the Israelites. According to the ideas of the time, the Ammonites by putting out the right eyes would disgrace Israel; but even more—by taking away their honor, they would rob them of the strength of soul, their valor and prowess. The author here obviously knows nothing of the story that Saul was already elected king.

Every exceptional emotion or power, physical or spiritual, was traced by the early Israelites to Jehovah. The anger, boldness, and bravery of Saul could be explained only on this principle. The numbers in v. 8 may have been supplied subsequently. It is doubtful that the number of fighting men was so large at this time. Moreover, such an army could not be mobilized so quickly; and the mention of Israel and Judah presupposes the division of the kingdom. *Bezek*—almost opposite Jabesh on the west of the Jordan. Vv. 12, 13 are in the nature of an editorial addition, intended to connect the narrative in vv. 1–11 with the story in ch. 10, especially v. 27. V. 14 refers to the Gilgal near Jericho (Josh. 4[19]) which would lie on the return journey from Gilead. The term *renew the kingdom* (v. 14) is another editorial phrase to reconcile this chapter with the preceding: Saul had been privately anointed king by Samuel; he is now publicly elected.

Teaching of chs. 10 and 11. These chapters, which deal with Saul's election as king, describe the evoking of the hidden forces of his soul through God's Spirit making him a new man: God "turned him another heart" (10[9] mg.). Matthew Henry's comment is entirely along the lines of ancient Hebrew thought: "Whom God calls to service he will make fit for it. If he advance to another station, he will give another heart to those who sincerely desire to serve him with their power." But, as the sequel shows, ecstasy and spasmodic violent emotion are no substitutes for ethical insight and conviction. It is natural to compare and contrast this passage with the conversion of the N.T. Saul (Acts 9).

In this story we are first introduced to the *sons of the prophets* and the prophetic movement in Israel. These prophets, or "dervishes," as Moffatt translates or paraphrases the word, were bands of enthusiastic devotees, marked off from other men by their hairy mantle, their tattoo-marks or tonsure, who worked up the ecstatic frenzy by dancing, music, and other means. As organized bands we read of them now in connection with the Philistine peril and later in the time of the Syrian wars (1 Kings 22[6] 2 Kings 2[3], etc.). They would seem to have been the inspiration and backbone of the national resistance to the oppressor, carrying, as it were, "the fiery cross" from one end of the land to the other. For them religion and patriotism were inseparable.

Prophecy in its later and higher form came to be one of the distinctive elements in the religion of Israel, but the prophetic bands we meet here are part of a much wider movement which had its home in Thrace or Asia Minor. The "seer" appears to be of Semitic origin; not so the prophet; and the Dionysiac or orgiastic character of the prophetic frenzy would seem at first to have shocked the Israelites (see $10^{11f.}$). The movement was perhaps Aryan in origin and was possibly connected with the Aryan intoxicating sacred drink (*meth*, *soma*, *haoma*) associated with the moon-cult. It passed into Greece in the worship of Dionysius (Bacchus) and thus became the mother of the Greek tragedy (the word "tragedy" is from the Greek *tragos*, "a goat"; the goat-skins of the original dancing chorus from which the drama arose may be compared with the Hebrew prophet's hairy mantle). Through the Orphic cults it powerfully influenced the sublime mysticism of Plato; and through Plato, Plotinus, and Pseudo-Dionysius, the whole development of Christian mysticism. The movement passed to India, but there the ecstasy took the form of the absorption of contemplation, passive and ascetic; it seems to have passed to Iran, where Zarathustra (Zoroaster, possibly a contemporary of Saul but probably earlier), himself the closest parallel to the great Hebrew prophets, the enemy of the haoma-drink, seems to have regarded it with contempt.

In Israel it may well have been Samuel, as Kittel thinks, who laid hold upon this essentially un-Hebrew movement and turned it to the service of Israel's religion and Israel's God. In Israel some of the prophets became selfish and mercenary; they earned their bread by giving oracles and performing the functions of the seer in older days (Amos 7^{12} Mic. 3^{5}). Amos (7^{14}) and "Zechariah" ($13^{3f.}$) in particular dissociate themselves from the movement; yet the great Hebrew prophets are connected with these humble origins, even though they had outgrown or largely outgrown the primitive ecstatic elements in it. Finally, we may note that the prophetic movement came to Christianity, largely in its primitive form and from its early home, in the form of Montanism.

The prophetic frenzy was ascribed to the invasion of man's body by God's Spirit or breath. In the Bible we trace this primitive conception of God's Spirit through such passages as Isa. $11^{2f.}$ $61^{1f.}$, to Paul's doctrine of the Holy Spirit. There is always a tendency to see divine inspiration in states of high emotional tension (see notes on 19^{20}). Thus Joubert says of Madame de Staël that "she took the fevers of the soul for its endowments, intoxication for a power, and our aberrations for a progress."

CHAPTER XII

The True Religious Leader. The reference to the sons of Samuel (v. 2) is obscure; presumably the point is that they are men of mature years. For *Bedan*, v. 11, read *Barak*. V. 12 offers a rewriting and noticeable alteration of the story given in the preceding chapter. The wheat harvest (v. 17) took place in May-June.

This passage contains an address put into the mouth of Samuel protesting his innocence and laying down principles for the guidance of king and people in the light of God's dealings with Israel in the past. Whatever may be the historical value of the chapter, its religious significance is considerable, since it reveals the religious outlook and ideals of the age in which it originated. It depicts the true religious leader as one who instructs his people in "the good and the right way," who never ceases to pray for them (v. 23), who never uses his power and influence for his own personal advantage, never does violence to the rights of others or exercises favoritism (v. 3). As such Samuel is depicted. Again, the people can never prosper if they forget their past; and their nationhood is based upon the grace and goodness of God in days of old (vv. 6f.). God has shown special favor unto them; yet the past proves his moral order, and that his hand is heavy upon them when they forsake his ways and his law; but repentance has always been followed by deliverance (vv. 9f.). All past history pleads with them to walk in God's ways in gratitude and godly fear (v. 7). Not liberty primarily, not democracy, not empire must be the motive of the national life, but gratitude to God. The people's destiny depends neither upon wealth nor military preparedness, but on the pure religion of its members (v. 10). To forsake God and his ways is to turn to unprofitable emptiness (v. 21). God will punish sin, but his grace may be depended on forever, for it is his acknowledged purpose to make them a people unto himself, and he cannot allow his purpose to be thwarted in the end (v. 22). Such was "national self-consciousness" in Israel. Is it only with Israel that a prophet might *plead all the righteous acts of the Lord which he did to you and to your fathers?* (v. 7).

CHAPTERS 13 AND 14: THE VICTORY AT MICHMASH

CHAPTER XIII

A Composite Narrative. The narrative in ch. 13 contains material taken from different sources. Vv. 1–4 give the historical setting. The age of Saul is uncertain. The Hebrew text says that Saul was a year old at his accession; "thirty" in R.V. and "forty" in A.S.V. are alike mere conjectures. *Michmash* is the key to the mountains of Ephraim from the south. Instead of *Gibeah* read *Geba*, and in v. 3 *Gibeon* for *Geba* (see on 10^{1-8}).

Jonathan raises the standard of revolt by assassinating the prefect (not "garrison") of the Philistines. V. 4 is in the nature of an editorial addition to connect with vv. 7f. Gilgal does not fit this battle, and *all the people* were not with Saul (see vv. 6, 15, 20).

Vv. 7a-15a, led up to by the editor in 10[8] and 13[4], break the narrative. The section reflects relatively late ideas, and apparently is taken from a much later source. According to the earlier custom, Saul as king had a perfect right to offer sacrifice. Only according to later legislation was the offering of sacrifice restricted to the priests. The author of this story knows nothing of Ahijah (14[3]). V. 15b returns to the older narrative, which has no connection with Samuel. In v. 17 *spoilers* are "detachments," probably a technical term. Vv. 19–22 may again be a later addition, to enhance the extent of the victory. It is not probable that Israel was completely disarmed. V. 21 is so corrupt that no sense can be made of it without radical reconstruction of the text. See further under ch. 14.

CHAPTER XIV

Jonathan's Exploit. 14[1] returns to the main narrative. It introduces Jonathan's proposal to make an attack upon the Philistine garrison. In v. 2 read *Geba;* in v. 2 for *wearing* read *carrying* (see comment on 2[28]). The plan is carefully outlined by Jonathan; in due time the attack is made and proved successful (vv. 23, 30).

On discovering the flight of the enemy Saul inquired who was missing of his own camp (v. 17). He also sought to determine the further will of his God (v. 18). Apparently, the *ephod*—so read with LXX instead of *the ark*—needed manipulating and this took time, for Saul impatiently tells the priest to *take his hand away.* The instrument might fail to give any oracle at all (v. 37). The silence of the oracle implied the divine displeasure. Saul took steps to discover the cause of the divine wrath. In v. 41 read with LXX, *And Saul said, Lord, God of Israel, why hast thou not answered thy servant this day? If the guilt be in me or in my son Jonathan, Lord, God of Israel, give urim; but if thus thou say: It is in my people Israel, give thummim.* The urim and thummim were the sacred lots. Both Saul and Jonathan accept the decision by lot as final, and Jonathan professes himself ready to die. In harmony with the cruel custom of the age he would have been put to death, had it not been for the interference of the people. Possibly another victim, human or animal, was substituted.

Vv. 47–51 furnish a summary of Saul's activity. For *he vexed them* read *he was victorious* (cf. A.S.V. mg.). Presumably these stories of Saul's heroic exploits come from Benjamite traditions. There is no reference to Samuel, and in contrast with the following chapter, Saul's victory over the Amalekites is a subject only of congratulation. *Ishvi* (v. 49) is *Ishbaal.* In v. 51 the R.V. marginal reading is to be preferred. Saul failed in the task that David ultimately accomplished, but of Saul's heroic struggle for liberty there should be no doubt. We detect a strong bias against Saul in some of the (presumably) Judæan sources.

Teaching of chs. 13 and 14. This section is significant because it points to a religious problem of perennial interest. In the late fragment 13[7b-15a] Saul is represented as careless of the proprieties of religious observance, but in the rest of the narrative, which is doubtless more accurate historically, Saul seems to be depicted as scrupulous, even overscrupulous, in his ritual observances. It is true that in 14[19] he seems to lose patience with the priest who is busy with the oracle and bids his followers take advantage of the obvious panic in the Philistine camp. But even here he shows himself perfectly human, for when God delivers the enemy into your hands (or your neighbor is in want), there is no need to spend time seeking divine guidance. The curse pronounced in 14[24] against any who should eat during the day may be ascribed to a scruple against the appropriation of any of the booty before the first-fruits had been dedicated to God. Further, Saul's care for ritual matters is shown in his consternation when he finds that the hungry soldiers are eating food that has not been properly slain and prepared (14[33]). Jonathan, on the other hand, stands for a "common-sense" position (14[29]); victory is more important than ritual regulation and ceremonial niceties (cf. Mk. 2[25f.]). This may be taken as a higher point of view; but it is not clear whether the author's sympathies here are on this side. At any rate, once Saul has made eating *tabu,* God is angry when the *tabu* is broken (14[37]); even Jonathan does not protest against his fate, and the proposed night attack is dutifully abandoned (14[46]).

To divine God's will by means of chance remarks made by the enemy, 14[9f.], may not be a very spiritual proceeding, but it is here connected with the Hebrew conviction that the issues of all things are in the hands of God, and God is equally able "to save by many or by few."

CHAPTER XV

1–9. War Against Amalek. The divine command carries out the law of retaliation (see Ex.

17[8-16] Deut. 25[17f.]). *Utterly destroy* (v. 3) means consecrate utterly, make over to God by destroying. Saul does not hesitate to undertake the campaign, but he did not carry out the instruction to destroy utterly man and beast. The *Kenites*, or sons of Cain, were zealous worshipers of Israel's God, perhaps wearing a special "Jehovah mark" upon their foreheads; they were old allies of Israel. Amalek was not in fact annihilated (see 1 Sam. 30[1] 1 Chr. 4[43], etc.).

10–35. Saul Rejected for His Disobedience. Samuel, as the representative of Jehovah, could not keep silent in the presence of Saul's disobedience. *Carmel* was located south of Hebron. Saul set up a monument shaped like a hand (v. 12, mg.), or with a hand carved on it; a number of such monuments are known. To save the animals for sacrificial purposes would seem to deserve commendation. But the people may have been interested even more in the feast accompanying the sacrifice. The prophet recognizes no sin greater than disobedience to Jehovah. *For rebellion is the sin of witchcraft, and self-will is the guilt of teraphim* (v. 23). Whether teraphim were family gods, or waxen ancestral images, or idols, or oracular instruments, or healing talismans, or skulls, or sacred masks—all of which identifications have been suggested—we cannot say. They seem to have been of Syrian or Canaanite origin like the ephod. Instead of *delicately*, v. 32 (A.S.V., "cheerfully"), read perhaps *trembling;* for *the bitterness of death is past* perhaps *death is bitter*. The slaying *before the Lord* indicates that it was a solemn sacrificial slaying. With v. 35 cf. 19[24].

This narrative indicates the breach between Saul, the leader of the political party, and Samuel, the leader of the prophetic party. It is a curious mixture of primitive barbarism and sublime religion. The ferocious Samuel hewing Agag in pieces *before the Lord* is less attractive, if closer to history, than earlier pictures of him. On the other hand, the great saying in v. 22 contains the quintessence of the prophetic teaching: in religion it is the spirit, not the outward sacramental expression, which really matters. But the sublimity of this thought does not involve, as some have thought, that it must be a later addition under the influence of the great prophets, for a thousand years before this an Egyptian thinker had written, "Righteousness of the heart is better than the sacrifice of an ox brought by an unrighteous man."

It is in this chapter that we probably have the most authentic portrait of Samuel. The sin for which Saul is rejected is given as self-will or disobedience, perhaps aggravated by sacrilege; but the quarrel between Samuel and Saul had deeper roots than this one incident. Saul was ceasing to prove the mere tool of the prophetic-nationalist party; we may say perhaps that he exercised reasonable prudence in showing some moderation in his treatment of Amalek; to have slaughtered all his prisoners would have meant the impossibility of peace with the Amalekite tribes. But Samuel stands for the old-fashioned, fierce, inexorable ways of warfare in the desert in the time of Moses; there must be no accommodations for the sake of prudence and statecraft; disobedience to the absolute demands of the ban was to be repudiated as utterly as anything connected with Canaanite worship (the teraphim, which Samuel assumes to be illegitimate). See further on 2 Sam. 1.

CHAPTER XVI

1–13. David is Anointed by Samuel. These verses continue the narrative of the previous chapter. David is represented as a lad, the youngest in the home of Jesse, altogether unknown to fame, when the seer under the divine inspiration anoints him king in Saul's stead.

14–23. David is Introduced to Saul. In marked distinction from the preceding, David is here represented as a tried soldier, a musician and a story-teller. In ch. 17 he is again the shepherd lad, unknown and unhonored. These verses are the first of two different accounts of David's introduction to Saul; there is no reason to doubt their historical accuracy. Saul was troubled with some form of melancholia; his prowess, daring, and kingly power, gifts of *the spirit of the Lord*, left him, and an *evil spirit*, regarded as a "visitation" upon him for his sin, preyed upon him (see further on ch. 20). By the simple gift sent to Saul, Jesse at once bound himself to the king and the king to him.

The chapter raises difficult literary questions. There is no reason for doubting the historicity of the account in vv. 14–23, but neither this account nor the narrative in ch. 17 is consistent with the view that David has already been anointed as Saul's successor. But even though the historical value of vv. 1–13 may be open to question, the religious teaching in the whole chapter is perfectly plain. The author or editor believed that

". . . behind the dim unknown.
Standeth God within the shadow, keeping
watch above his own."

David's gradual superseding of Saul was no chance matter; when no one thought anything of David, God who knows men's hearts had chosen him and put his spirit upon him (v. 13), giving him a kingly soul. But there is here no doctrine of immutable predestination. David was chosen to receive the spirit because he was worthy (v. 7), and Saul who had been chosen was rejected because of his "rebellion." Phil. 2[13] gives the same idea in Christian form. Note, further, that though Saul's melancholia was regarded as sent by God, yet a remedy is also sent by God through music "that gentlier on the spirit lies than tired eyelids upon tired eyes."

CHAPTERS 17 TO 20: THE BEGINNING OF DAVID'S ADVENTURES

CHAPTER XVII

David Overcomes the Philistine Goliath. 17[1] opens the second account of David's introduction to Saul: David is a stripling, unknown to Saul and to fame (contrast 16[18-23]). It is interesting to note that there is an Egyptian tale of Sinuhe telling of his exploits in Palestine about 2000 B.C., closely parallel to the story of David and Goliath. In 2 Sam. 21[19] we are told that Goliath was slain by Elhanan (see also 1 Chr. 20[5]). The Philistines gathered in the mountainous country due west of Bethlehem. Goliath's armor was not unlike that of a Greek warrior. The Philistines probably came to Palestine from Crete, and they were not unconnected with the early migrations which issued in the Greeks of the historical period; they may be said to represent the early contact of Europe with the Hebrew race.

12. This appears to be a fresh introduction of David, without reference to ch. 16. **18.** *Pledge*, i.e., of their welfare. **29.** Presumably "it is not a matter of importance." **39.** *Proved* means "tried." **52.** For *Gai* read *Gath*, which was not far west. **54.** The reference to Jerusalem is late. (See 2 Sam. 5[6f.]). **55.** This is inconsistent with 16[14-23].

Heroic contests of the kind described here are common in many literatures, but the *nuance* given by the Hebrew writer is peculiar. David's concern throughout is for the honor of his God (v. 36); he ascribes his deliverances in the past and his confidence for the future, not to his prowess, but to the power of God (vv. 45f.). The omnipotence of God is accepted, speculatively by us, but practically by the Hebrews. Cf. Isaiah's doctrine of faith (Isa. 7[9] 28[16] 30[15-21]).

CHAPTER XVIII

1–5. The Friendship of David and Jonathan. This is one of the most beautiful incidents in all literature. In Hebrew thought the family makes a psychic unity; similarly, the friendship of David and Jonathan makes them psychically one. Henceforward in Jonathan's soul there is the conflict of loyalties between friendship and family (see on ch. 20). Jonathan's clothes and armor were part of his "soul"; these he gave to David. Similarly, Elisha takes up the mantle of Elijah (2 Kings 2[13]), and in the sixth book of the *Iliad*, Diomed and Glaucus publicly exchange armor.

6–30. Saul's Jealousy of David. It did not take long to arouse Saul's jealousy against David. The song, sung antiphonally by the women, could not have been composed early in David's career. The song was not necessarily a taunt at Saul; David's victories were Saul's victories while David served him. Nevertheless, it recognized David's superiority. Saul, moody and morbid, was easily carried to extremes. **10.** For *prophesied* read *behaved like a madman.* This story is repeated, presumably from another source, in 19[9f]. In 2 Sam. 21[8], apparently the same man named in v. 19 is described as Michal's husband. It seems that etiquette required that Saul should not take the initiative (v. 22). See further under ch. 19.

CHAPTER XIX

1–17. Saul in Jealousy Seeks to Kill David. David, it appears, would overhear the conversation. H. P. Smith thinks that in the original story this attempt on David's life was on the night after his wedding with Michal. For v. 13 see on 15[23]. *Pillow of goats* (v. 16)—Reimpell suggests a mosquito-net or wig. Michal pleads that her life would have been in danger had she prevented David (v. 17).

Teaching of chs. 18 and 19. The editor's interest in this section is in the inevitable way in which God's repudiation of Saul and blessing of David work out. Saul by virtue of God's Spirit had delivered Jabesh and vanquished the Philistines and had been regal in soul and power; but now he was rejected; his power was gone; he was a less successful warrior than David (18[7]); and Saul realized this (18[28]); Saul had no personal grudge against David, therefore he could be reconciled to him (18[17]); but he was bound to hate him in his struggle against the inevitable. David meanwhile has won the affection of Jonathan and of Michal; all the king's efforts to trap him are unsuccessful or redound to David's glory, for the Lord is with him. These narratives, therefore, are the stuff of a great tragedy such as the Greek tragedians loved to deal with. But the Hebrew writer is less fatalistic than the Greek, for Saul's rejection is his own fault; in God's world the fault, as in *King Lear*, brings its inevitable doom with it. Saul is not the wicked man;

he is the heroic figure who yet has missed his destiny and wrecked his life through self-will (see further on 1 Sam. 28, 2 Sam. 1).

18–24. David Compelled to Flee. To escape Saul's anger, David first took refuge with Samuel. These verses appear to be late, giving a second explanation of the famous proverb (v. 24) found also in 10^{12}. The supernatural protection of David here described is very different from the stories of his hard struggles against odds through long years of which we read in the succeeding chapters. *Naioth* is probably not the name of a village but some building, possibly the prophetic school in Ramah. The tradition which connects Samuel with the prophets, and the prophets with the founding of the Hebrew monarchy, is probably accurate. *Prophesied* means "fell into the prophetic frenzy" (v. 20). We can see from this and v. 24 how little of religious worth there was in this experience by itself, but all later mysticisms in all religions that lead to the ecstatic trance without issuing in any deeper understanding or ethical insight are of the same sort. These ecstatic feeling-states are often surrounded by a halo or seeming spiritual exaltation, but in reality they belong to the most primitive stages of religion, if to religion at all (see on ch. 11).

CHAPTER XX

The Covenant Established Between David and Jonathan. The first part of v. 1 is an editorial note connecting with the preceding. The subsequent story cannot be from the same source as 19^{11-17}, for in that case there could be no doubt of Saul's intentions in the minds of David and Jonathan. The festival of the new moon was always a solemn observance (v. 5). Since v. 10 implies that David and Jonathan cannot safely be seen together, v. 11 may be an interpolation. A somewhat clearer translation of v. 13, suggested by H. P. Smith, would be: *But if there be evil, God do so to Jonathan and more also if I bring the evil upon thee; but I will uncover thine ear. . . .*

Jonathan appears to be convinced that ultimately David will sit upon the throne of Israel. A better translation of vv. 14, 15 would be . . . *kindness of the Lord; and if I die, thou shall not cut off . . . for ever.* The rest of v. 15 and v. 16 is obscure; perhaps, *and when the Lord hath . . . of the earth, if the name of Jonathan should be cut off from the house of David, let the Lord require it at David's hand.* Saul appears to think (v. 30) that Jonathan has connived at David's escape upon a mere pretext. Vv. 40–42 appear to be a later addition; for the point of the shooting was that David was in hiding and Jonathan could not meet him personally. In v. 41 follow the margin.

Some of the tragic pathos of the idyllic friendship between David and Jonathan is lost upon us because in modern times the bonds of family have grown relatively loose. The modern point of view is put by Juliet:

> "'Tis but thy name that is my enemy;
> Thou art thyself, though not a Montague.
> What's Montague? it is nor hand, nor foot,
> Nor arm, nor face, nor any other part
> Belonging to a man. O, be some other name!"

This is modern because of its individualism; a name is a title only, not a reality. No Hebrew could speak like that. The name *is* the person; those who bear the same name share in the same soul. If two men whose families are at enmity have entered into a covenant with one another, they have by that covenant created an inward conflict for themselves that hardly admits of a solution (see on 18^{1-5}). We understand the situation better on the national scale. Jonathan's friendship with David was a sort of treason. Yet Jonathan is not blameworthy for this; though David is his brother, he must die fighting by his father's side, and bear the taunts of his father (v. 20) as one who had brought shame on the family soul; for the greatness of his family lay in the royal state and eminence in Israel, which his love for David has prejudiced (see on 22^{1}).

Some modern scholars have supposed that David was really guilty of treasonable intentions. But David's loyalty seems sufficiently attested by his unbroken friendship with Jonathan and by the dirge he wrote when Saul and Jonathan had fallen on Mount Gilboa (2 Sam. $1^{18f.}$). If, however, there had been a breach between Saul and the prophetic party represented by Samuel, and if the Philistine war was not prospering, and if Saul was largely incapacitated from the kingship by reason of his melancholia, it is not impossible that many would wish that another might take the reins from his failing grasp; that other would surely be Jonathan, the hero of Michmash. If this were so (but it is only a guess), David may well have favored the movement; but there is nothing to prove or make likely his disloyalty to Saul or Jonathan.

Saul did not die insane; his "madness" showed itself in fits of deep melancholia and in outbursts of ungovernable temper; it led him to suspect those about him and to break with his best friends. It was not inconsistent with a real devotion to the Lord's cause and with steadfastness and courage in the work he had undertaken. It is the kind of "madness" that is often found among religious people and has ruined and embittered many lives. This melancholia and jealousy are the marks of a man whose interest is still largely centered in himself; music might soothe him for a time, fits of repentance might follow fits of temper, but there was no real healing for him unless he could win real and complete freedom by being lost in a cause, by an enthusiasm for others which could burn up all smaller and pettier concerns. No Scriptures more surely than the story of Saul were written for our learning.

Chapters 21 to 27: Further Adventures of David

CHAPTER XXI

1–9. David in Flight; Assisted by Ahimelech. In his flight David appears at Nob, just north of Gibeon, without escort, food or arms; Ahimelech is anxious to know what such a visit may mean. This story seems to follow immediately after 19[11-17]. *Nob* may have been the Gibeonite sanctuary (see 2 Sam. 21[1-14]). The tradition that Ahimelech was descended from Eli may not be reliable. The soldier's task was to fight the wars of the Lord; therefore while on active service he was in a specially holy state, or, as we might say, was temporarily "in holy orders," which involved among other things abstinence from sexual indulgence. If David and his men, says the priest, have been loyal to these prescriptions there is no reason why they should not have the shew-bread. David satisfies the priest on this point; but his answer is obscure, and the text uncertain. The office that Doeg held at the court is uncertain.

10–15. David Feigns Madness at Gath. Pursued by Saul, David takes refuge with the king of Gath, in Philistia. That David ultimately became the vassal of the Philistines is sure; but this passage, which is a variant of 27[1f.], is out of place here. David would not go straight to Gath with Goliath's sword. That the passage is late seems indicated also by the strange reference to David as king in v. 11. It was written, suggests Gressmann, by someone who disliked the idea of David dwelling among the enemy and made a jest of it—as if there were not enough lunatics already among the Philistines! See further under ch. 24.

CHAPTER XXII

1–5. David's Regard for His Family. David had to look out not only for himself but also for his family. For *cave* read *stronghold*. Adullam was located some twelve miles southwest of Jerusalem. If David was in disgrace at court, his family at home would be in danger; a man and his family were one, each member of the family being, as it were, a manifestation or incorporation of the common family soul. This sense of family and racial solidarity lies behind Paul's teaching of the unity of the race in Adam and of the new race in Christ (see Dodd, *The Meaning of Paul for To-day*, ch. 8). David appears to have had Moabite blood in his veins (Ruth 4[21]; see also on 2 Sam. 8[2]).

6–23. Saul's Vengeance on the Priests at Nob. When Saul learned that the priests at Nob had helped David he swore vengeance upon them. For *in Ramah* read *on the height*. Saul is surrounded by Benjamites; he was presumably little more than the Benjamite chieftain, recognized as king by Israel as a whole only for purposes of war. He appeals to Benjamite prejudices and jealousies; upon Benjamite loyalty at least he might hope to depend. Saul's massacre of the priests at Nob would seem to be the ferocious act of a man out of his mind (v. 18). Possibly he suspected these priests of being involved in a conspiracy in favor of David (or Jonathan); see on ch. 20. The tradition that the priests of Nob were descended from Eli is open to suspicion; perhaps more probably they were the local priests of Gibeon, and if so, the Gibeonites later exacted a fearful vengeance. (See 2 Sam. 21.) For *Nob*, v. 19, read (very probably) *Gibeon* (see on 10[1-8]). *In safeguard* (v. 23)—cared for like a precious object intrusted to David's safekeeping. See further under ch. 24.

CHAPTER XXIII

Saul Pursues David. Saul gave David no rest; he pursued him from place to place. *Keilah*—a little town south of Adullam. Vv. 3, 4 were chosen by John Robinson for his text on the day of prayer and humiliation when the news came that permission was granted to settle in Virginia. The *ephod* (v. 9) is here the instrument of divination, not a garment as in 22[18]. See further under ch. 24.

CHAPTER XXIV

David Spares Saul's Life at En-Gedi. A narrative of an incident similar to one related in ch. 26: Saul falls into the power of David, who shows his magnanimity by sparing his life. The two chapters may represent two revisions of the same story; the one in ch. 26 may be closer to the original.

Teaching of chs. 21–24. This wonderfully graphic section consists of a number of disconnected stories of Saul's enmity against David and David's adventures. We read that "Jonathan strengthened David's hand in God" (23[16]), which means, "in the assurance that God was with him"; and the editor tells these stories to show how God was with David and what manner of man David was. By an excellent stratagem David overcame the hesitation of the priest at Nob and got not only food but an incomparable sword (21^{1-9}). Doom visits the innocent township of Nob, but David's obligations are satisfied by his care of Abiathar, the one survivor (22^{20-23}). Another fine exploit is his tricking of the Philistines. Once David escaped almost by a miracle ($23^{26f.}$). We are shown also David's religious scruples. Just as Saul's bodyguard declined to slay the sacred priests (22^{17}), so David will not put forth his hand against the Lord's anointed. In the thought of ancient and, to some extent, modern times, the divinity that hedged a king is not a mere sentiment of respect but a divine reality. To lay hands on the king was to lay hands on one in a special relationship to God, a holy person; therefore it was sacrilege. In these democratic days we are learning to look behind the uniform and consider the man; we have little respect for titles and offices; but the real sublimation of David's scruple would seem to be the realization that *every* person, as man, has a special relationship to God, and therefore must never, either in business or in war or in pleasure, be treated as a pawn in the game. A rather different idea is seen in $24^{18f.}$, where Saul recognizes that God delivered him into David's hand and that David, but for his generous magnanimity, might have slain him. Here David illustrates the Christian maxim, "Love your enemies."

CHAPTER XXV

The Folly of Nabal; David Marries Abigail. The relation of David to Nabal and the marriage of David to Abigail are here described at length. *Carmel* is the modern *Kurmul*, south of Ziph. In view of the fact that David was at the head of a band of freebooters the claim made in v. 7 is rather remarkable. David would also seem to have protected Nabal from other freebooters (v. 16). Some recognition was due to him. *A good day* (v. 8) is a feast day. Instead of *unto the enemies of David* (v. 22) read, with some of the ancient translations, *unto David. Nabal* means "fool." H. P. Smith suggests that the remark in v. 25 is as if she said his name was Brutus and he a brute. A present like the one referred to in v. 27 is in Hebrew called a "blessing," for it has a sacramental character (see on ch. 2). Perhaps in v. 37 a stroke is intended, and in the next verse a second. By his marriage to Abigail the outlaw David acquired social status and importance as a Calebite sheikh.

Nabal's name was Fool, and Folly was his nature. Nabal could be cheerful and expansive, it would seem, on occasion and when he was the center of the picture (v. 36), but with his wife and with his neighbors he was a churl and sullen as a mule; but not every Nabal has a wife like Abigail to save him from his folly. David was justly incensed at Nabal's discourtesy, and murder was in his heart; but he realized that this revenge would have been, to use Disraeli's phrase, "a just and unnecessary war," an offense to God; it is no part of a man's duty to stand upon his rights and avenge insults in this way; "Vengeance belongeth unto me," saith the Lord, "I will repay."

CHAPTER XXVI

David's Magnanimity. This narrative of David's magnanimity is generally supposed to be a different version of the same event as is described in ch. 24. If this is the case, we cannot be sure which account is nearer the facts; but there is something to be said in favor of the originality of the narrative in this chapter. For *flea* in v. 20 read *my life.* For the interpretation of the narrative, see under ch. 27.

CHAPTER XXVII

David Serves Achish, King of Gath. David, despairing of safety in Judah, enters the service of Achish, king of Gath. Perhaps Achish did not entirely trust David, and so sent him against the desert nomads rather than directly against Saul. *Geshurites* is almost certainly, and *Girzites* or *Gizrites* probably, a mistake; perhaps read *upon the cattlefolds of the Hagrites and the Amalekites* (v. 8). The Hagrites would be the descendants of Hagar. If David keeps his promise to his overlord, he is to be set over the king's bodyguard.

Teaching of chs. 26 and 27. In a literary sense, this section is not homogeneous, but the editor so uses his sources as to show the history, character, and religious ideas of David. We see how "primitive" in many regards was David's religious outlook and that of the writer who took him for his hero. David spares Saul's life on the ground that Saul, as the Lord's anointed, is a sacred and inviolable person (26^{9}). Again, personal vengeance is not for man; God will deal with the offender in his own way and his own good time (cf. 1 Cor. 5^{5}, where Satan is the Lord's minister). To venture into the king's camp was an exploit of much risk and only accomplished by God's help (26^{12}).

David, after taunting Abner (26^{15}), protests his innocence to the king, and asks why he is thus treated; he lays no blame on the king, but ascribes the king's conduct to instigation either from God or from ill-disposed persons. If God is responsible, then it must be in his own inscrutable and arbitrary purpose, for David has done nothing to deserve it. But if God is angry for some reason or other, it will not be difficult to placate him; let him "smell a sacrifice"; i.e., let him accept a gift as apology and compensation, and let the incident be closed (26[19] mg.). This is the most primitive form of expiation. The prophets later saw that even the sacrifice of man's most precious possession could not avail to wipe out sin, that God would be satisfied by no external act; he would be reconciled only to a man who did justly and loved mercy and walked humbly with him (Mic. 6[8]). In the N.T. we come to an altogether new and different conception of religion—that God is reconciled with man already, and that it is for man to be reconciled with God by accepting his forgiveness and his will (2 Cor. 5[18-20]).

If, on the other hand, it is men who have set Saul against David, David prays that the Lord's curse may be on them, for in banishing him from the Lord's own territory they have in effect told him to serve other gods, for only as a member of a community has one access to God; an individual cannot stand by himself; therefore, if a man went to live among a strange people, he would have to do homage to that people's gods (26[19]). It would seem to follow (though the conclusion is not drawn by the editor) that when a little later David became the vassal of Achish (27[2]), he must have worshiped the Philistine gods. It was the supreme achievement of the prophetic religion to discover that fellowship with God does not depend upon any place or temple or sacrament but is a matter of the heart, a personal relationship to God independent of place or circumstance (Jer. 29[1-14]). The astonishing principle that religion is a matter of locality was apparently accepted by the Lutherans at Augsburg in 1555 A.D., when it was expressed in the formula *cuius regio eius religio* ("A man's religion goes with his region"), and to this day the King of England is an Episcopalian in England and a Presbyterian in Scotland.

It is plain that in spite of David's valor and prowess and occasional triumphs his position as an outlaw was impossible; he had no option but to become the vassal of the national enemy, the Philistines. Later ages were uneasy about this and, as in 21[10f.], loved to show his cleverness and how he tricked and spoiled the Philistines, as if his vassalage were a triumph rather than a humiliation. Once David had submitted to the Philistines he was safe from Saul (27[4]). In 27[5] we see David's cunning; his request has the appearance of humility; in reality it is to further his designs. David is not regarded as deserving censure but praise for his lie to Achish when he told him that he had been engaged in forays against the men of Judah and their kindred. "God has given us tongues," said Heine, unkindly, of the French, "in order that we may say pleasant things to our fellow men." A man must have a "single eye" and no fear in his heart if he is to speak the truth. Once again David is too clever for Achish.

CHAPTER XXVIII

1, 2. David and Achish. David seems to promise Achish unlimited allegiance, but his heart's purposes are other.

3–25. The Story of the Witch of Endor. In fear of the Philistines Saul sought divine guidance. When he received no reply he turned for counsel to necromancy. Of the death of Samuel we have heard already in ch. 25. Saul had put away the *'oboth* and "adepts." The *'oboth* were spirits (in modern psychical language "controls," or objects used in necromancy). This form of divination was forbidden to Israel, presumably because it came from heathendom and could not be brought into relation with the God of Israel. Here again we see that Saul had been a scrupulous defender of Israel's religion. The *urim* and *thummim* would always give a *Yes* or *No* answer; therefore, if the *urim* are mentioned here (v. 6), the meaning must be that Saul could get no *favorable* answer. But since there is no mention of *urim* in v. 15, it is perhaps to be regarded as an addition here. *Saw Samuel* (v. 12), seems wrong. We should understand either that the name "Samuel" aroused the woman's suspicions, and then when she saw, or looked more closely at *Saul*, she recognized him, or that when she began to go into the trance, she knew that her interlocutor was the king himself. The word translated *god* or *gods* in v. 13 seems to mean no more than "a supernatural figure" or "spirit"; the departed are perhaps called "gods" because of their power over men. The essence of magic as opposed to true religion is that it exercises or claims to exercise a *compulsive* power over the other world.

Saul is not the villain of a melodrama but the central figure in a tragedy. His inspiration and sense of divine mission and divine good pleasure fail him just when once again he must fight for his life and the life of his people against the enemy. Saul is not afraid; he will do his duty; he will die with his face to the foe; his bitterness lies not in his outward lot but in the sense that God has rejected him; not a word will God speak to him of counsel or of comfort. In his desperation he turns to sources of illumination which in his happier and more glorious days he had condemned as illegitimate. The antique phraseology should not hide from us the fact that under these circumstances Saul did what so many in like case have done in recent years; *he turned to spiritism.* The "witch" of Endor was a "medium." A medium has the gift of reading or "tapping" what is in the mind, often the unconscious mind, of the person to whom she gives a sitting. She presumably goes into a trance and so describes the figure she sees that Saul recognizes that it is Samuel. She gives, as coming from Samuel, the answer to Saul which we should antecedently have expected anyone familiar with the situation to give, and Saul is prostrated in despair; only with difficulty is he persuaded to take food, and he goes into the battle a doomed man, knowing that he will be slain himself and, worse, his family will be blotted out also, and Israel will be defeated by the enemy.

We need not doubt that the phenomena of the spiritualist seance were familiar in Israel as they have been familiar in many parts of the world and many ages in Shamanism and other forms. A problem lies in the fact that Saul apparently did not doubt that he was actually in touch with Samuel, while he regarded the conjuring up of Samuel as an illegitimate practice. In these days it will be difficult to persuade men that if they can get into touch with the departed, it is wrong for them to do so. Into spiritistic claims it is impossible to enter here. Those who do not believe that converse with the departed is established will note that Samuel in the *seance* only says to Saul what his own conscience is presumed to have been telling him already; they will say, therefore, that the medium is only reading his unconscious thoughts. Those who believe in spiritism, on the other hand, will perhaps note that in this spirit-message there is much more of ethical and religious content than we have grown accustomed to expect.

CHAPTER XXIX

Achish Compelled to Dismiss David. David, mistrusted by the Philistine princes, is sent home by Achish. The word for *adversary* (v. 4), is "Satan" in the Hebrew. The Philistine leaders suggest that by treason to the Philistine cause David would have an admirable opportunity of being reconciled with Saul. Clearly, the writer of this narrative did not know the story that David had slain Goliath. After the words *that are come with thee* (v. 10) LXX adds, "and go to the place where I appointed you, and set no bitter (or pestilential) thought in thy heart, for in my sight thou art good." See further under ch. 30.

CHAPTER XXX

David Avenges an Amalekite Raid. When David reached home he found that the Amalekites had plundered Ziklag; he pursued and utterly defeated them. The captives were presumably to be sold in the Egyptian slave-market. David was perhaps to blame for leaving the town insufficiently guarded. The *Besor* (v. 9) flows into the sea south of Gaza. *Of the next day* (v. 17) must be a mistake, but the original text cannot be restored with certainty. V. 20 is unintelligible as it stands; perhaps the original stated that David's spoil consisted not only of the persons and flocks stolen from Ziklag but much other booty as well. David makes good and diplomatic use of his booty; he employs it for ingratiating himself with the sheikhs of Judah and of kindred tribes. Their acceptance of the gift (blessing) would bind them to David for the future. *Bethel* or Bethuel (v. 27) is in the neighborhood of Ziklag (Josh. 19^{4}). It is not the Bethel of Jacob (Gen. 28^{19}).

Twice in chs. 29, 30 we see David in a very awkward predicament, and on each occasion he issues from it triumphant. We cannot tell what his plans were had he been compelled to take the field against Saul; not only does he escape from that dilemma but he leaves the camp loaded with compliments from his overlord. On his return home he is nearly stoned by his followers for the disaster that has overtaken Ziklag; for a moment, we understand, he was overwhelmed, but *he strengthened himself in the Lord his God* (v. 6). This phrase, like the earlier phrase that Jonathan strengthened David's hand in God (23^{16}), is the kind of expression used by men who know what it is to stand alone or nearly alone against the world in the consciousness of right and of God's favor. No man has really found religion for himself who cannot, when his back is to the wall, *strengthen himself in the Lord his God.* The N.T. parallel is "The Lord stood by me" (2 Tim. 4^{17}). David's character and sense of fair play are shown in the regulation of vv. 24f. The writer clearly did not know the (presumably later) tradition that this ordinance came from Moses (Num. 31^{27}).

CHAPTER XXXI

The First Account of Saul's Death. (Cf. 2 Sam. 1^{5-16}.) This chapter continues the narrative from 28^{25}. Saul entered the conflict without hope. The LXX states that Saul was wounded in the stomach. The context requires something like this. Saul is wounded and is afraid of falling *alive* into the hands of the Philistines. V. 4 as it stands is unintelligible; the Philistines would not *abuse* him, i.e., mutilate and desecrate his body after death any the less because his armor-bearer had slain him. Omit, therefore, the words *and thrust me through* after *lest these uncircumcised come*, and understand by *abuse* such treatment as, for instance, Samson received at the hands of the Philistines (Judg. 16[25]). The news of the victory has to be brought to the Philistine gods in their temples. We may compare with this the way in which Hezekiah took the Assyrian letter into the Temple to "spread it out" before the Lord (2 Kings 19[14]). For *burnt them* (v. 12) read probably *raised the dirge*. Cremation was not an Israelite custom; and by *their bones* in the next verse we are hardly to understand *charred bones*. The tamarisk tree was undoubtedly a well-known sacred tree. See further under 2 Sam. 1.

SECOND SAMUEL

CHAPTER I

1–16. A Second Account of Saul's Death. The account is derived from a different source from that used for 1 Sam. 31. An Amalekite brings the news of Saul's death to David at Ziklag, claiming to have slain him. David and his men mourn the death of Saul, and the messenger and alleged slayer is put to death. It was usual for kings to go into battle in their *regalia*. It is not likely that, if the account of Saul's death in the previous chapter is authentic, an Amalekite would have chanced to find the dead Saul and make off with the crown and bracelet. If, therefore, the Amalekite did, in fact, bring these things to David, his own account of Saul's death is the more probable. The two narratives are in some parts irreconcilable. Gressmann accepts vv. 1–4, 8, 11, and 12 as an ancient and credible tradition; the other verses he regards as later and unhistorical.

17–27. David's Dirge Over the Death of Saul and Jonathan. This is one of the most beautiful elegies in all literature. There is no cogent reason why we should doubt David's authorship of it. The text of v. 18 is corrupt; and the meaning, especially of the first part of the verse, must remain uncertain. It is generally thought that the first part gives the first lines of the song. *The book of Jashar* is the book of the Upright, possibly Jehovah; or, if the reference is to men, the book of the Heroes. The reference is presumably a marginal note that has come into the text. Perhaps we should read . . . *and said* (*the sons of Judah should be taught it; it is to be found in the Book of Heroes*). The same book is mentioned in Josh. 10[13] as a collection of poetry.

The text of the dirge appears to be corrupt in several places and the meaning is not always clear. Following the announcement of the theme (v. 19) the author deprecates the spread of the news, for it will cause the enemies to rejoice; he pronounces a curse upon Mount Gilboa, where the heroes were slain; he glorifies the departed warriors and exhorts the daughters of Israel to lament and closes with an expression of his personal bereavement in the death of Jonathan. *Neither fields of offerings* (v. 21) is unintelligible. Perhaps *treacherous fields* or *fields of death*. The second part of the verse is obscure; the reference apparently is to the armor growing tarnished and rusty upon the battlefield. For *delicately* (v. 24) read *and with linen*. V. 25 should possibly be omitted; it is either corrupt or a mere variant of v. 19. V. 26 means, probably, man's love for woman, not *vice versa*.

Some of the traditions incorporated in Samuel show a strong bias against Saul and the brief Benjamite monarchy; but in this chapter and elsewhere we find for the most part a kindlier and doubtless juster judgment. The tragedy on Mount Gilboa is lightened by the action of the men of Jabesh (1 Sam. 31[11-13]), who remember Saul's early prowess and the hopes of his first days, and by David's noble tribute; Saul, he says, like Jonathan, was beloved and worthy of love; he was an heroic warrior, swifter than an eagle, stronger than a lion (vv. 22f.). Yet, says the editor, inasmuch as Saul failed in his task, God rejected him; his sin is said to have been "rebellion" (1 Sam. 15[23]) or self-will; he could not distinguish between God's will for him and what he thought God's will ought to have been. That this confusion should have arisen is not altogether strange in view of the environment in which Saul placed himself. Beyond doubt many lives of high promise and power have been rendered futile by just such self-will and unteachableness.

David's elegy shows him to have been a true poet. The claim made by many commentators that the poem is entirely without religious content is just only insofar as there is no reference to God or to religion. But when we reflect that in David's references to Saul there is not one word of bitterness or resentment at his own treatment, not a shadow of relief or satisfaction, we must conclude that the author must have been a man whose outlook was fundamentally religious in that he was delivered from personal pettiness and all that savored of mere personal ambition.

Chapters 2 to 6: David King of Judah

CHAPTER II

1–4. David Becomes King at Hebron. Gradually David had come to be recognized as the outstanding hero of Judah. It is not strange, therefore, that after the death of Saul he should be made king of his own tribe. Hebron was in the heart of the country that was well disposed toward David, difficult to reach from the coast, and, unlike Bethlehem which he might have chosen, out of reach of the fortress of Jerusalem. While it was a new thing for a tribe to have a "king," his tribesmen may have hoped that David would found a Judæan monarchy to take the place of the Benjamite rule of Saul. David remained a Philistine vassal for the present. As the friend of Achish he was the safest leader of Judah, and if the war with the Philistines was to be taken up anew, who could lead them as David could? On the other hand, would it be safe to arouse the enmity of a strong leader like David?

5–11. The Gileadites Make Ish-bosheth Their King. The message sent to the Gileadites would please the friends of Saul; but they were not ready to turn to David as their ruler. They made *Ish-bosheth* (v. 10) or Ishbaal (1 Chr. 8[33]), the only surviving son of Saul, king over North Israel. All the initiative is with Abner; Ishbaal—for that was his proper name—seems to have been only a boy. *Mahanaim*, the new capital, was located across the Jordan, and would be safe from David and the Philistines. While Ishbaal is called king of Israel, actually he seems to have reigned only over his Benjamite following. He also, we may suppose, would have to recognize Philistine suzerainty.

12–32. Abner's Opposition to David. (See also 3[1].) It was inevitable that the two kingdoms should soon come into conflict. Of the many battles fought one is related at length, the battle of Gibeon, because of its bearing on later history. It is commonly assumed that Abner was the aggressor, but since the battle was fought in Benjamite territory it is not impossible that David and his men were the offenders. The proposition of a tournament in which individual skill and valor might be tested is in line with Oriental custom.

Asahel's motive in pursuing Abner, and Abner alone (v. 19), was the desire for the glory that would accrue to him from slaying so notable a warrior. Abner's unwillingness to kill Asahel is presumably his realization that such an act, however justifiable, would involve a blood-feud with Asahel's family, which in its turn would make a general pacification more difficult. Abner apparently intended to wound, not to kill. But for Abner's appeal (v. 26), which was in effect an appeal for quarter, the pursuit, says Joab, would have gone on till next day. The continuation of the battle would have meant practically the wiping out of Israel or at least of Benjamin; from this the conscience of Judah might well recoil. If all the young men of Benjamin were destroyed, then the soul of Benjamin would be destroyed; Benjamin would be murdered. Individual life was cheap in ancient Israel, but the annihilation of a whole tribe or family was regarded much as we regard murder. The *Arabah* (v. 29) is the Jordan Valley. We can gauge the magnitude of the combat from the fact that the casualties were only some three hundred and eighty men.

CHAPTER III

1–11. The Weakening of the House of Saul. Events moved rapidly toward a reunion of Israel and Judah under David. Before taking up the events culminating in the reunion the editor inserts the names of six sons of David born to him by as many wives in Hebron. Abner, conscious of his power, trespassed on the prerogative of his king, and a quarrel ensues. The successor to the throne was naturally heir to his predecessor's harem. Abner's act was therefore treasonable.

12–19. Abner Proposes Submission to David. Thwarted in his desires, Abner opened negotiations with David for the submission of all Israel. David insists on the return of Michal; she is brought back and Abner continues his scheme. V. 12 is not quite clear. Perhaps, *all Israel is at my disposal to give it to whomsoever I will.* The restoration of Michal would give David standing as Saul's heir. "Usurpers," says Matthew Henry, "must expect to resign"; but Paltiel was innocent according to the ideas of the time. The idea of the permanence of the home was a spiritual achievement that came late.

20–39. Abner Completes Negotiations with David. When Joab, absent from Hebron at the time, returned he bitterly complained because David had not caused the death of Abner. When he could not move the king he himself slew Abner. We may perhaps suspect that, apart from the blood-feud, Joab was jealous of the great leader. If Abner came over to David's side, could David make so renowned a warrior less than commander-in-chief? David declares his innocence, and expresses his grief over the assassination of Abner in a dirge. There is no reason to doubt David's authorship of the dirge in vv. 33, 34. Was the noble and generous Abner, then, to die a rake's death, i.e., probably, an untimely death? Length of days Abner of all men might have expected! Was Abner to die the death of a common criminal? Read *as one putteth away criminals wast thou put away.* David, the fearless warrior, showed on many occasions that he had no great moral courage in dealing with members of his own family or court. (On Joab's blood-feud with Abner see p. 75.)

CHAPTER IV

The Murder of Ishbosheth. The death of Abner removed the main support of Ishbaal (see 2[8] mg.). Two of his officers murdered him and brought his head to David, expecting a reward. But David treated them as he had the confessed slayer of Saul. The note (v. 4) about *Mephibosheth,* or Meribbaal (for so we should read his name; cf. 1 Chr. 8[34] 9[40]), appears to be out of place. In vv. 6, 7 follow the LXX version as suggested in R.V. mg.

The chief figure in chs. 2, 3 and 4 is Abner. David fought hard, but he was not of those who belittle and detract their opponents; Abner was, he said, a prince among men, one who deserved to die in harness in the battle, or in peace and honor in a ripe old age (3[31f.]). There seems no doubt of David's innocence and detestation of Abner's murder. Abner was to have brought all Israel to David's side, and now the plan was spoiled. As David had treated the Amalekite (1[15]), so now he treats the murderers of Ishbaal (4[12]). David's generous and honorable feeling is connected with religion. He swears by *the Lord, who has redeemed him out of all adversity* (4[9]). God's cause is not to be served by shady or dishonorable devices.

CHAPTER V

1–5. David King Over All Israel. With Ishbaal slain, it was perfectly natural that the north should turn to David. He was anointed king over all Israel. "The Lord's anointed" may be king "by divine right," but he is a constitutional, not an absolute monarch, for his kingship is based upon a solemn covenant with his subjects; this covenant doubtless set forth the king's duties as well as his privileges. The anointing is a solemn religious act, but it is performed, not by the priests but by the heads of the tribes (v. 3).

Chapters 5[6] to 6[23]: Jerusalem the New Capital

6–16. David Captures the Fortress of Jerusalem and Makes It His Capital. The capture of Jerusalem was of the utmost importance to David. Not only was it a nearly impregnable fortress, but a national kingdom was almost impossible if the northern tribes were separated from Judah by an enemy fortress. Moreover, Jerusalem was central and had no traditions which would arouse tribal jealousies. The reference in v. 6 to *the blind and the lame* is not intelligible. Two alternatives to be considered are (a) that, with the R.V. and A.S.V. mg., we should understand v. 6 to mean that Jerusalem is so strong naturally that cripples could defend it, and assume that the text of v. 8 is hopelessly corrupt, having possibly once contained the information we get in 1 Chr. 11[6]; or (b) that we should assume that the reference is to some ancient pre-Israelite Jerusalem tradition or prophecy to the effect that Jerusalem could only be taken under certain hardly attainable conditions, such, for instance, as would imply that the conquering king was a divine hero ushering in the golden or Messianic age. The latter interpretation in some form is perhaps more probable. Possibly, however, the reference to the lame and blind covers merely a taunt at David, the point of which is now lost. The capture of Jerusalem by the Hebrews is an event of world-historical importance. Three religions look to Jerusalem as a holy city—Judaism, Christianity, and Islam; moreover, David's capture of the city nearly three thousand years ago has created some of the most perplexing political problems of to-day.

The following identifications may be suggested: *city of David* (v. 9) was on the low southeastern hill of the present Jerusalem; *watercourse* (v. 8)—perhaps the modern "Warren's shaft," a tunnel forty feet long bringing inside the walls the overflow of the Gihon spring (Duncan, *Z.A.T.W.*, 1924, pp. 222ff.); *Millo* (v. 9)—probably a fort on the southeast hill (see notes on 1 Kings 11[27] and *Z.A.T.W.*, *ibid.*). Not *Hiram* but Abibaal would seem to have been king of Tyre at this time (v. 11).

17–25. David Breaks with the Philistines. David's assumption of the united monarchy meant a breach with the Philistines. If Jerusalem was captured before the Philistine war, the *hold* must be Jerusalem; more probably the Philistine war came first, and perhaps Adullam is meant. *Rephaim* (v. 18) is the valley between Jerusalem and Bethlehem; *Baal-perazim* (v. 20) lay probably west of Jerusalem. David captured the Philistine idols as once the Philistines had captured the ark. For *Rephaim* (v. 22) read perhaps *Bekaim*, south of Gibeon. Tree-divination is common in antiquity, but here we get the magnificent conception that David is not to be precipitate, as Saul had been; he is to await God's time; when he hears the sound of marching in the tops of the balsam trees, he is to recognize the token that the Lord himself is marching to do battle for his people, then David is to bestir himself and follow. This method of determining the divine will is found among many primitive peoples.

CHAPTER VI

David Brings the Ark to Jerusalem; Michal's Scorn. David attempted to bring the ark to the captured stronghold, but an accident, interpreted as an expression of divine anger, interfered temporarily. A second attempt was successful. If Jerusalem was to be the political capital, it must be made the religious capital also. The ark (see on 1 Sam. 4) was the religious symbol of all the tribes and would tend, therefore, to draw their interest and devotion to Jerusalem. For *fir-wood* (v. 5) read *songs.* Harps, lutes, tambourines, triangles (?) and castanets correspond roughly to the instruments named. V. 6 is unintelligible in the Hebrew; the English translation seems illegitimate; for *put forth his hand* read perhaps *slipped against,* and for *stumbled* read *had been dunging* (Arnold, *Ephod and Ark,* pp. 45, 63). For *error* (v. 7) we may read *slip,* and suppose, if we will, that Uzzah broke his head upon the hard threshing floor. The king, according to the older ideas, was, of course, chief priest (cf. vv. 17f.). Thus he wore the priestly garment, the linen ephod (v. 14). For *play* (v. 21), read *dance.* Presumably David, in fact, separated from Michal.

David inaugurates his reign by defeating the Philistines and making Jerusalem his capital; the editor is far more interested in the religious than in the political side of the history; he gives little space to that great series of battles which broke the Philistine power forever (see Isa. 28[21]); he mentions the capture of Jerusalem, a notable exploit, very briefly, but describes in detail the bringing up of the ark. Here, again, we find primitive traditions of the arbitrary and wonder-working power of the ark to bless (v. 11) or to destroy (v. 7; see notes on 1 Sam. 6). Of great interest is the account of the sacred processional dance with which the ark is brought up to Jerusalem, a festival probably repeated on a smaller scale every year in Jerusalem at the great New Year feast of the Lord's Enthronement; no less than five different words are used to describe the motions; they may be translated, "dancing," "rotating," "jumping," "whirling," and "skipping"—the last in 1 Chr. 15[29] (Oesterley, *The Sacred Dance,* pp. 36, 54).

Ecclesiastical custom is always conservative; the priest's garment, the ephod, was doubtless the most primitive garment, a scanty loincloth. It is not clear whether the editor's sympathy is with Michal, "that much tried lady," as Bennett calls her; she here stands for the principle that religious custom must advance with the advance of civilization, and that a living church must not be tied to the customs and traditions that come from less enlightened ages. Or perhaps she stands for mere respectability in religion; that at least is David's defense; he protests against a religion of cold decorum; a man must be ready to be "a fool for Christ's sake" (1 Cor. 4[10]); but was David's "folly" of this kind? A processional dance of the kind described here is rich in emotional color, but poor in intellectual content, and we can gather little of the religious ideas associated with the bringing up of the ark. It is possible that it was for this occasion that Psa. 24[7-10] and 132 were indited (but see comments on these psalms.)

We know tantalizingly little about the religious traditions of Jerusalem prior to the capture of the city by David, but that they may have been of spiritual worth to the conquerors we may perhaps guess from such traditions as survive of the priest-king Melchizedek (Gen. 14[18f.] Psa. 110[4] Heb. 7). The author of the Epistle to the Hebrews lived too late to be a trustworthy medium of tradition; he shows, rather, the impression this mysterious figure, who ruled Jerusalem in the time of Abraham, made on the Hebrew people. The tradition in Gen. 14 points to a relatively noble and pure religion; Melchizedek is priest of "God Most High"; this is no animistic deity, no mere nature god or tribal god. Again, the ancient but corrupt Psa. 110 suggests the possibility of Messianic or quasi-Messianic ideas being derived from the old Jerusalem tradition (cf. note on 5[6-16]).

CHAPTER VII

1–18a. Why David Built No Temple. David, disturbed by the fact that the dwelling place of Jehovah was simply a tent, determines to build a temple; the prophet Nathan, whom he consults, at first approves, then opposes the plan. However, in recognition of David's desire a promise is made to him that his dynasty will endure forever. For *tribes* (v. 7) read *judges.* Sitting was not the usual posture for prayer, but the text in v. 18a may be right (cf. 1 Kings 18[42].)

This chapter, which is of composite origin, contains very ancient tradition. Solomon's Temple became the pride and joy of Israel and powerfully influenced the religious development. Later ages who idealized David had to explain why David did not build the Temple;

the answer given was that he made all the preparations for building it, but as a "man of blood" he was not allowed to undertake the actual building (1 Chr. 22[8f.]). Here (vv. 1–7) we get an entirely different tradition. David proposes to build a temple and consults the prophet Nathan; at first the prophet warmly approves, but when he has thought over the proposal and has slept on it, he comes back with a different message. The God of Israel, represented by his ark, had been housed in a portable tent throughout the days of Moses; these were the great days of Israel, when pre-eminently the hand of the Lord had been mighty to save. All the associations of the tent, therefore, were inspiring and uplifting; but a temple would be an innovation, a breach with tradition; all the associations of a temple were heathen. A temple, therefore, might be æsthetically splendid but spiritually disastrous. There are elsewhere traces of a protest against the idea of a temple. Solomon's Temple, even if erected solely to the glory of the God of Israel, had to be built by heathen workmen and on the model of heathen temples; it became, in fact, a snare to the Hebrews, so that later prophetic voices had to take up Nathan's burden (see Jer. 7 Ezek. 8, 9 Mk. 13[1f.]). Perhaps Nathan stood for conservatism and against progress, and perhaps a tent might have become a fetish no less than the Temple; but "consecrated bricks and mortar," more splendid services and ceremonies, do not necessarily tend to an increase of true religion. A tent is better than a temple as a symbol of the Christian Church, the pilgrim people of God, who have here no abiding city.

18b–29. David's Prayer and Thanksgiving. The rest of the chapter is really a psalm, though it is a matter of dispute how far it is actually metrical. No reporter was present at David's private devotions, and the psalm is to be treated as a religious composition possibly or probably dating, in the main, from David's time. In its context the chief point lies in its play upon the word *house.* David would build God a house; that is not to be; but God will build David a house, i.e., sons and posterity to follow him. In the N.T. also the house which God builds and for which God cares is in the souls of men; for it is men that are "the temple of the Holy Spirit" (1 Cor. 3[16]). We cannot say that the passage is personally Messianic; only the permanence of the Davidic dynasty is promised; but as the days darkened for Israel, this treasured promise tended to take on a more supernatural coloring, till men began to look for one who should be of "the root and the offspring of David, and the bright and morning star."

CHAPTERS 8 TO 10: THE GROWTH OF DAVID'S EMPIRE

CHAPTER VIII

An Account of David's Wars. David conquers in succession Philistia, Moab, Zobah, Damascus, and Edom. The narrative is supplemented by a list of David's officials. In v. 1b read *and he took the ark from Gath out of the hand of the Philistines* (cf. 1 Chr. 18[1]). The treatment of Moab would be regarded as a military precaution, not as an atrocity; it is to be hoped that many modern military precautions will before long be reckoned atrocities and discarded. The attack upon Moab seems strange in view of 1 Sam. 22[3f.] The end of v. 3 should probably read *when he* [David] *turned his hand against the Euphrates. Betah* and *Berothai,* (v. 8), are unknown, probably in the Antilebanon district. For *Joram* (v. 10), read *Badoram. Dedicate* (v. 11) probably means little more than "place in the royal treasury with a religious service of thanksgiving." The spoils of war were the spoils of the God of Israel; wealth thus dedicated might be used again for the Lord's battles and in cases of national emergency. For *Syria* (v. 12) read *Edom.* Similarly, in v. 13. In Hebrew the two words look very much the same. *Valley of Salt* is the depression south of Dead Sea. *Recorder* (v. 16), perhaps *private adviser. Scribe* (v. 17), presumably *keeper of the court records.* Hitherto the story of Israel had been conserved by ballad-singers, priests in their oral instruction and professional story-tellers; here first we come to exact historical records. There is no justification for the R.V. marginal translation *chief ministers* in v. 18. It was a much later theory that confined the priesthood to the supposed descendants of Aaron. *Cherethites* and *Pelethites,* i.e., Cretans and Philistines, formed David's bodyguard.

CHAPTER IX

David's Kindness to Mephibosheth. David shows kindness to the surviving son of Jonathan. *Lo-debar* was across Jordan, presumably near Mahanaim. See further under ch. 10.

CHAPTER X

David Overcomes Ammon and Syria. Insulted by the new king of Ammon, David makes war against him. Syria joins the Ammonites, but both nations suffer defeat. *Beth-rehob* (v. 6), probably in the Lebanon district. *Maacah,* at the foot of Hermon. *Tob* or *Istob* (v. 8), probably in the same region. The name of the Syrian ruler should be read *Hadadezer* (v. 16). The location of *Helam* is unknown, perhaps in the Yarmuk Valley. *Rabbah* (11¹) was located on the upper Jabbok.

Teaching of chs. 8–10. This section, which deals with the astonishing growth of David's kingdom, made possible by the contemporary impotence of the Hittite, Assyrian and Egyptian empires, seems to us almost barren of religious significance; not so to the editor, who saw in these victories the hand of God; the victories proved David as a man after God's own heart. It was usual for a new dynasty to destroy all the family of the preceding dynasty. It is true that a cripple was slight menace to David, and that the invitation extended to Meribbaal to eat at the king's table may have been due to David's determination to keep an eye on him (not without reason, as the sequel shows; 2 Sam. 19^25f.^); none the less, David spared not only Jonathan's sons but his grandson also, and, contrary to all custom, the house of Saul was allowed to grow and prosper in the land (see 1 Chr. 8^34f.^). David's generosity, therefore, and his loyalty to Jonathan need not be questioned.

Chapters 11 and 12: David Takes Bathsheba

CHAPTER XI

David's Sin Against Uriah. During the Ammonite campaign David committed the sin against Uriah and Bathsheba which darkened his entire subsequent career. Uriah, as his name shows, was a worshiper of Israel's God, though of Hittite extraction; presumably his family had been in Jerusalem before its conquest by David (cf. Ezek. 16³). David fails in his scheme to make it appear that Uriah was the father of the child. For v. 9 see above on 1 Sam. 21^1-9^. We notice that the ark is taken to battle as a palladium. See further under ch. 12.

CHAPTER XII

Nathan's Rebuke of David. Under Nathan's rebuke David repents, but the prophet makes it clear that he cannot escape punishment. Sin works in the body like a poison issuing in death. Death, therefore, is not so much the punishment of sin as its inevitable consequence. The poison is taken out of David's system and put into the child's! This conception of sin as a sort of physical affection of the soul is very crude, and the transference of the "sin" from David to his innocent baby seems to us, with our developed sense of individual responsibility and our weakened sense of the family as a psychic whole, to be immoral and shocking. But the underlying principle is clear: if suffering and sorrow did not inevitably follow upon sin, God's moral order of the world would be compromised. The Hebrew had no idea of what we call "the uniformity of nature" or the inexorable rule of natural law which largely dominates modern thinking, but he had a very vivid sense of history as the revelation of a moral order, which we often fail to observe (see art., *Religion of Israel*, pp. 167–9).

15b–25. David's Grief; His Faith in the Future. As announced by Nathan, the child of Bathsheba died. The Hebrew conception of life after death is difficult for us to grasp. The Hebrews shared the widespread belief that the departed lived a shadowy and unsubstantial existence after death in the underground realm called "Sheol," from which there was no escape. Such was the fate of the individual soul; but the most important fact about a man was not that he was an individual but that he belonged to a family, manifested and partook of the family-soul; after death he was, as it were, merged in the family, and if the family continued on earth, the whole family prospered. The Hebrews had no theoretical doctrine of a corporate or family-soul; some such term, however, is necessary to express their feeling that not the individual but the family is the real unity. David expresses the hope that he will be reunited with the child in Sheol. (See art., *Religion of Israel*, p. 173.)

26–31. Return to the War Against Ammon. In v. 26 either we should read *water-city* for *royal city*, and understand the city water supplies to be meant, or the *royal city* will be the royal quarter of the city. Once the water-supplies were captured, the city as a whole could not hold out long. The glory of the victory must be assigned to David (v. 28). This seems to us to smack of unreality, and rightly so; but to the ancient with his idea of national solidarity and of the nation's individualization in the king this seemed the only natural point of view; and even in our own day is it not true that those who do the work do not always get the praise? For *of their king* (v. 30) read *of Milcom*, their god. Also read *and in it was a precious jewel;* with this jewel (not the whole crown) David adorned his head. The captives were employed as state slaves.

Teaching of chs. 11 and 12. David's great sin, as has been frequently pointed out, would have been forgotten but for his repentance. That the king should be at liberty to take into his harem whom he would was doubtless an accepted maxim in the world of that day. The remarkable thing is not that David should have taken Bathsheba, but that he should have recognized and confessed that it was a sin. For such conduct was intolerable to Israel's God, and Israel's God alone; it was a crime against God (12^9). David, it will be noted, only contrived murder when his other efforts to avoid a court scandal had been thwarted by the steadfastness of Uriah. Bathsheba must have been a remarkable woman; she was David's favorite wife, who kept her ascendancy over him long after her youthful charms had vanished, and she was the mother of Solomon. Her part in this story is neither praiseworthy nor blameworthy; according to the ideas and etiquette of the time, she had no option. While there is no glossing over of David's sin, David's sincerity and insight are clearly displayed; he was humble enough to allow the prophet to speak and to accept, apparently without resentment, what he said. Moreover, his repentance was real and genuine.

Very remarkable too is his conduct with regard to the child; with prayer, fasting, and humiliation he beseeches God to spare the child; his earnestness and passion were so great that no one dared to bring him news of the child's death. But when he knows, he declines to have part in any of the mourning ceremonies which tradition and etiquette required. He shows himself impatient of formalities in religion and social life; everyone knew what he felt in his heart about the child. It is still customary to reserve tributes and kindly sayings and outward marks of affection till the object of them is dead. Christians at least should not be shocked at David's conduct. "Why," asks Ruskin, "should we wear black for the guests of God?" It would be better to pray for people when they are alive and to "anoint them beforehand for the burying" than to wait till they are gone, and only sad formalities remain.

Nathan undoubtedly risked his life in thus rebuking David. This is the true prophet who unasked, unwanted, and without regard to his personal danger rebukes sin, even in high places, in the name of the living God. But Nathan did more than denounce; he convinced. His parable came home to the king, so that the king could not but agree with the prophet's verdict. There have been many prophets in all ages to denounce vice, crime, and injustice, and to win the applause of those who are not guilty; but the true prophetic appeal is not *against* evil so much as *to* conscience. In this way the gentle John Woolman was perhaps more truly a prophet than most would-be reformers of men and morals.

Chapters 13 and 14: Problems of the Blood-feud

CHAPTER XIII

1–19. The Violation of Tamar. The violations of Tamar by Amnon was avenged by Absalom. As a result the latter was compelled to flee the country, but later, through the efforts of Joab, was recalled. For *sister* we should say *half-sister*. Court etiquette was strict; Tamar lived in Absalom's palace; how was Amnon to get her to his palace? If Amnon was sick, it would be proper for Tamar to go to his house. Amnon was to ask for certain cakes which, as was suggested, Tamar could make better than anyone else. *In his sight* (v. 8)—apparently from his bedroom Amnon could see into the outer room. "Folly" is the conduct of those who have no fear of God in their hearts. *Israel* (here represented by Tamar) is a civilized country; in those days there was no civilization apart from the fear of God. *Fools,* "wastrels." Tamar does not refuse to marry Amnon (v. 13). Marriage with a half sister was only later forbidden (Deut. $27^{22f.}$ Lev. 18^9 20^{17}). The garment was a long robe "with long sleeves" rather than multi-colored.

20–39. Absalom's Revenge. Absalom bode his time, but finally slew Amnon. After the murder he fled. LXX adds to v. 21, "but he grieved not the spirit of Amnon his son, for he loved him because he was his first-born." The sheep-shearing was a time of festival and rejoicing. The king of *Geshur* was Absalom's grandfather. Geshur lies southeast of Hermon. The close of v. 39 might be rendered freely, *he had recovered from the death of Amnon.* See further under ch. 14.

CHAPTER XIV

The Recall of Absalom by David. Joab devised a scheme which finally led to the recall of Absalom by David. "Wise" women (cf. 20^{16}) were probably those who were thought to have contact with spirits (witches), who interpreted dreams and signs and were credited with magic powers. The woman is put off with a vague promise. The *iniquity* (v. 9) would consist in the protection of a man guilty of murder; see below on blood-revenge. David has promised to protect the woman's son though he is a murderer; the woman now points the moral: Absalom, as heir-apparent, is the son of the people; David should protect him similarly, though he is a murderer; as long as he is banished, he is as good as dead to the nation.

The argument is not logically cogent; the woman has pleaded that her son, as her *only remaining* son, should be protected lest, in the event of his death, the family should die out. But Absalom is not the only possible heir of David, his last remaining son. In the East, as Hindu, Buddhist, and Jewish writings amply testify, an illustration, a parable, is convincing where a syllogism brings no conviction. This fundamental difference between Eastern and Western ways of thought should be borne in mind in the interpretation of N.T. parables also. The first part of v. 11 seems to mean that Amnon is dead, and it is useless to "cry over spilt milk." V. 14b is corrupt; possibly the wise woman indicates that God will not punish David for recalling Absalom. Vv. 15–17 may be a later addition; if not, they should probably be transposed to a position between vv. 7 and 8. V. 26 makes it clear that the hair was heavy, but the exact weight we cannot now determine. With v. 27 contrast 18^{18}.

Teaching of chs. 13 and 14. The theme of this section is the obligations of the blood-feud and difficult situations in connection with it. The family must avenge insults offered to its members upon the members of the guilty family. The blood-feud, which is intolerable in an organized and policed community, may well be necessary where crime would be unrestricted did not family or tribe take up the cause of the wronged. Absalom, according to the decencies and obligations of the time, was bound to avenge Tamar. But the blood-feud operates between families or tribes; an intolerable complication is involved when the offense takes place within the family, for there is a solemn obligation upon all members of the family to stand by one another. Here Amnon is the guilty party and Absalom's action was forced upon him by his father's inaction. David was angry, but did nothing. He might have insisted that Amnon should marry Tamar, or he might have cut off Amnon from the family. He did neither. When Absalom took vengeance into his own hands David was in a serious dilemma; he could neither blame Absalom nor could he countenance him, for this was murder within the family. David again showed his moral weakness by compromising.

The problem of the blood-feud introduced by the "wise woman" was somewhat different. It was right that blood should be avenged; but to slay the guilty member of a family is one thing, to blot out the whole family, leaving it without posterity, is another; what if the legitimate blood-feud involved the illegitimate annihilation of the family? David, apparently with some compunction, promises to defend the cause of the widow's family as a whole by refusing to allow the blood-feud in this case to be carried through. These problems in their ancient dress have long since ceased to interest us, but we also are often aware of the problem of a "conflict of loyalties," as, for instance, where a man can be loyal to his family as a whole only by not exposing one member of it, or to his state by being disloyal to the interests of a wider group, or to his denomination by being disloyal to the church of all believers. These chapters offer no solution of such problems, but they indicate the wretched consequences of David's weakness.

Amnon did violence to Tamar, and then turned her out "into the street"; public opinion to-day as in David's time would unanimously condemn Amnon, but see Jn. 8^{1-11}. We read that Amnon's love for Tamar immediately turned to hatred (13^{15}); perhaps for this reason David did not insist upon his marrying her. It is to be observed that when persons marry upon a basis of merely physical attraction without real mutual respect and without any regard to common ideals for life, those marriages tend to be miserable and to end in disaster. (See art., *Bible Customs*, p. 75.)

Chapters 15 to 18: Absalom's Rebellion and His Death

CHAPTER XV

1–12. The Ambition of Absalom Carries Him Away. First, he assumes the position of heir-apparent, and finally has himself anointed king at Hebron. Absalom, the Israelite Alcibiades, as Gunkel calls him, came forward as heir-apparent with all the pomp and magnificence to which the position would entitle him. It is likely that Bathsheba had used the time of Absalom's disgrace to get Solomon recognized as David's heir, and that Absalom's only hope of the succession lay in open rebellion. The king was the final court of appeal (v. 2). The first court was constituted by the elders of the township or by the local priest. It is likely that the country was better organized for war than for peace, and that the delays of the law were grievous for those who appealed to the king. In v. 7 some of the ancient versions read "four" for "forty," which is probably original. Absalom had already shown in the case of Amnon that he knew how to bide his time. Hebron was his family home. Just as there is felt to be a distinction, hard to define, between, for instance, Our Lady of Lourdes and Our Lady of Winchester and Notre Dame de Paris, so there was a distinction felt between "Our Lord of Hebron" and "Our Lord of Jerusalem" or "of Bethel." The Hebrew in v. 12 says *sent*, not *sent for;* we are not told where Ahitophel was sent. Presumably he was sent on some confidential journey to foment the rebellion. If, as is not impossible, Ahitophel was Bathsheba's grandfather, he may have felt himself bound to avenge Uriah if he could. *Giloh* was near Adullam.

13–18. David Taken by Surprise. David

was taken by surprise, but there was neither weakness nor indecision in his flight; he could not hold Jerusalem, for there was no time to summon the militia, and the bodyguard was insufficient for the purpose if he could not rely upon the loyalty of the populace. Numerous details connected with the flight are recorded in chs. 15 and 16. The presence of his wives and household would delay his retreat and was a risk, but David would not leave them to their fate. The ten women left were his own concubines (16$^{21f.}$). The king headed the procession from the palace and his supporters followed him; a halt was made at *Beth-merhak* (v. 17), perhaps the last house at the city gate. Here the procession reforms; the general body of supporters are in the van; then follows the bodyguard, and finally the king.

19–23. David generously advises Ittai to seek his fortune with the new king. Read, in v. 19, *an exile from thine own place.* Ittai (or Ateas), it appears, was a newcomer to Jerusalem; he had apparently taken service under David much as David in earlier years had taken service under Achish. The *little ones* are the noncombatants in his train.

24–29. The Ark Sent Back to Jerusalem. The ark was considered the symbol of the presence of Jehovah. Hence the priests brought it along. But David ordered it back to Jerusalem. Probably omit in v. 24, *and all the Levites with him,* and understand that after the passage of the Kidron the procession was met by Zadok and Abiathar with the ark. They put down the ark while the procession passed. Abiathar no longer carries "the ephod." V. 27 is not quite clear. David bids both Zadok and Abiathar each with his son to remain in Jerusalem. It would be advantageous to have some friends in the city. The expression *the fords of the wilderness* is obscure; the place appointed by David was west of the Jordan (cf. 17^{16}).

30–37. Mission of Hushai. When David learned of the disloyalty of Ahitophel he sends his friend Hushai back to counteract the influence of the traitor and advises him to cooperate with Zadok and Abiathar.

See further under ch. 16.

CHAPTER XVI

1–4. Ziba Brings an Accusation. David, it seems, had only just passed over the top of the Mount of Olives when Absalom reached Jerusalem. David accepted Ziba's story. Possibly Meribaal hoped that Absalom's rule would be a Judæan monarchy only, and that the rest of Israel would return to the house of Saul. It is by no means certain, however, that the story of Ziba can be accepted as true.

5–14. Shimei Curses David. One of the unpleasant incidents of the flight was the cursing of David by Shimei, a fellow tribesman of Saul of the tribe of Benjamin. If the incident recorded in 21$^{1-9}$ came early in David's reign the reference might be to events recorded there, or Shimei may be accusing David of complicity in the death of Ishbaal. The name of the place where the halt was made has been lost. Only a very brief halt would be possible till the Jordan was safely crossed.

15–23. Absalom's Final Breach with David. In v. 15 the narrative leaves David, in order to record what was happening in Jerusalem. Apparently, the populace sided with the usurper; and the counsel he receives is to push forward as speedily as possible. The act suggested in v. 21 would make the breach with David irremediable; it would be not only an insult to David but a definite claim upon the throne.

Teaching of chs. 15 and 16. One must admire the literary artistry of these and the following chapters dealing with Absalom's rebellion; their author is likely to be one who actually took part in the events of the time. The story lights up the character and religion of David as it was revealed in the hour of darkness. David was caught unawares by Absalom's rebellion, but, in spite of his love for his son, he never thinks of yielding to him. Retreat from the city is a military necessity, but he is careful to leave spies behind. Zadok and Abiathar remaining with the ark would not be suspected; Hushai, on the other hand, must play a double game. A man's friends are revealed by misfortune, and the story is therefore full of contrasts; Ittai, Abiathar, Zadok, and Hushai on the one side, Mephibosheth, Shimei, Ahitophel on the other. To Ittai David shows his thoughtful and singular generosity. Ittai is free to welcome Absalom if he will, and that at the moment when David's cause seemed desperate. The heathen Ittai's spontaneous and devoted loyalty warms David's heart when his own family is in arms against him. David's religion is shown in his refusal to take the ark with him. We have had many stories dealing with the miraculous power of the ark; had David shared in this superstition, he would have preferred the presence of the ark to the advantage of having Zadok and Abiathar in the city. If God was with him, he said, he would not need the symbol of God's presence; if God was not with him, the symbol would not help him. This is a far-reaching principle in religion. At Bahurim, says Gressmann, David found his Gethsemane.

As kinsman of Saul Shimei assumed the

blood-feud with David, but David had spared his life, and the meanness of his soul is obvious. But David's heart was too full of greater troubles to be concerned about peccadillos; in his calamity he recognizes the hand of God; he humbles himself; he does not refuse to drain to the dregs the cup of bitterness which God gives to him to drink; are not his sins and weaknesses being visited upon him? God has brought him to this, and God will deliver him if it is his will. In his calamity and sore need David does not curse his fate nor curse God nor feel bitterness even toward his enemies. There are many actors in the scene, and David must play his part; but the real meaning of it all is, as David sees it, that God is dealing with his soul, and he must deal not with men but with God in his trouble. This is religion, to see behind outward circumstances the hand of God, and amid the Babel of confusing voices to hear his voice and deal directly with him.

CHAPTER XVII

1–14. Ahitophel and Hushai. Hushai, the friend of David, counteracts the impression made by Ahitophel. David, it would seem, had left Jerusalem only about an hour before Absalom arrived; if Ahitophel could overtake him in his flight before he could get into position beyond Jordan, David's cause was lost. V. 3 appears to be corrupt; perhaps it should read, *I will bring back all the people to thee as a bride to her husband; the life of one man only thou seekest; with all the rest thou wilt be at peace.* Hushai's object is by any means to gain time for David; he suggests that an initial reverse, even if insignificant in itself, would ruin Absalom's cause, for it would be magnified by rumor.

15–29. David Crosses Jordan; Absalom Follows Him. Warned of his danger, David settled east of the Jordan, among the people who after the death of Saul had clung to Ishbaal. *En-Rogel* was situated where the Kidron and Ben-hinnom valleys meet. For *Israelite* (v. 25) we should probably read *Ishmaelite*. *Nahash* may be a mistake for "Jesse." Omit in v. 28 *parched pulse*. See further under ch. 18.

CHAPTER XVIII

1–18. David Defeats Absalom; Absalom's Death. The armies of David and Absalom finally met. David proposed to go with his men, but was persuaded to remain in a place of safety. He charged his officers to deal gently with Absalom. Absalom's army was defeated and Absalom was slain. For *forest of Ephraim* (v. 6), perhaps read simply *jungle*. *Ephraim* might be a mistake for "Mahanaim." Absalom's head was caught in a fork in the branches. The *servants* would be the bodyguard. V. 15 seems pointless if Absalom were already dead; and the Hebrew word does not mean "darts"; therefore it may possibly be right to read in v. 14 (after Klostermann): *grasped three branches with his hand and tore him down from the heart of the oak, and Absalom was still alive when he fell from the oak.* Once Absalom was dead, there was no need to continue the slaughter of brother Israelites. The origin of the custom referred to in v. 17 (cf. Josh. 7^{26} 8^{29}) may have been to prevent the slain man's ghost from rising to bring ill luck on those who had killed him, but we cannot be sure that in David's time the origin of the custom was remembered. The word translated "monument" (v. 18) means "hand" (see on 1 Sam. 15^{12}); this pillar was probably a sacred stone rather than a mere memorial. Absalom had perhaps arranged for services (like masses for his soul) to be solemnized there. The statement that Absalom had no son (cf. 14^{27}) may be a later addition.

19–33. David's Grief for Absalom. These verses describe David's grief on receiving the news of Absalom's death. *The Plain* (v. 23) is the Jordan Valley, which offered an easier road though less direct. Not *all is well* but *all hail* (v. 28); the word in Hebrew corresponds with the Arabic greeting, "salaam."

Teaching of chs. 17 and 18. Theme: in the providence of God Absalom's rebellion ends disastrously for him. The first part of the story deals with the duel between Hushai and Ahitophel. Ahitophel was a man remowned for his counsel (15^{31} 16^{23}). By this is meant more than that Ahitophel was a man of great sagacity; it implies also that he was a man of great force of character with the gift of persuading men to accept his counsel and the power to carry it through; in this force of accomplishing themselves the counsels of Ahitophel were like the oracles of God (16^{23}). But in God's providence (this is the meaning of 17^{14}) Absalom accepted Hushai's counsel and rejected Ahitophel's. When it finally came to the battle again God gave the victory to David; indeed, the country itself slew more than the sword (18^{8}). But the victory almost ends in disaster; so overwhelmed is David with the death of Absalom that the victorious army slinks back as if it were defeated (19^{3}). David had already gone far to lose the favor of the people, or Absalom's rebellion would not so nearly have succeeded. If he should now turn his victory into a cause of mourning and be more indignant with those who had ventured with him and saved him than with those who had rebelled, he would be a king with no loyal subjects, and the situation would be worse than ever before (19^{1f}). The situation is saved by Joab, who expostulates with the king and gains his point. David's affection for Absalom his son, in spite of all the past, is touching and reveals his noble character; and it may be that he blamed himself for what had happened. Had he been firmer with Amnon, how differently all might have gone! Absalom's estrangement from his father was the father's fault. David's attitude reveals weakness and indecision. What did he mean to do had Absalom been taken alive? He had put himself unreservedly in God's hands and God had given him the victory, and now he was repining. Moreover, his attitude was grossly unfair to his loyal men.

Chapters 19 and 20: The Settlement After Absalom's Rebellion

CHAPTER XIX

1–23. Joab's Counsel; Shimei's Confession. The chapter recounts various happenings connected with David's return. At first he seems inconsolable and loses all interest in government affairs. Joab rebukes him, and David, seeing the force of Joab's words, seeks to control himself and resumes his public duties. David remained beyond the Jordan waiting to be invited back. Absalom's death had thrown the country into confusion. Northern Israel was much more anxious for David's return than his own tribe. David evidently feels that he must exercise diplomacy with Judah and offer more than an amnesty, for he undertakes to put Amasa in Joab's place as commander-in-chief. Vv. 17 and 18 are obscure. Apparently, Ziba and his family rushed down to the Jordan and made themselves exceedingly busy helping the ferry to and fro.

24–43. David's Kindness to Mephibosheth and Barzillai. The incidents narrated in the closing paragraphs of the chapter throw light on the real character of David and on the far-reaching results of Absalom's revolt. Follow marginal reading in v. 25; for *to Jerusalem* read *from Jerusalem.* In v. 31 translate not *over Jordan* but *to the Jordan. Chimham* is presumably Barzillai's son. Among those who were present to escort the king there were twice as many from Judah as from the rest of Israel. V. 41 refers to *all the men of Israel who were there;* there was a quarrel about precedence and attendance on the king. Judah protests that they have not been bribed, neither are they recipients of any royal favoritism. Indeed, their enthusiasm for the cause of Absalom may have been due to David's failure to show them partiality. For *we have also more right in David than ye* read *we are the first-born before you* (v. 43). Judah, which indeed hardly appears in Israelite history till David's time, was regarded by the other tribes as a parvenu. For the moment Judah prevails. See further under ch. 20.

CHAPTER XX

1–3. Conflict Between Benjamin and Judah. The long-time conflict between north and south was accentuated by Absalom's rebellion and the events growing out of it. The revolt led by Sheba marks the last effort of Benjamin to regain the honor of the monarchy for itself, Saul having been a member of that tribe. So serious was the quarrel that only Judah attended the king to Jerusalem.

4–13. The Murder of Amasa. Joab shows the same cruelty in dealing with Amasa as he did in dealing with Abner (see 3^{27-30}). Joab's device is obscure. *Came to meet them* seems to mean *came up with them* (v. 8). It is probable (after Klostermann) that Joab in addition to his ordinary sword which he wore outside his military garment held also in his left hand another sword inside. The former fell to the ground and allayed any suspicion Amasa may have had. The soldier stood by the corpse and pointed the moral; to delay would mark a man as partisan against Joab, whose star was in the ascendancy again. Joab seems to have assumed the commandership which David had intrusted to Abishai, markedly passing over Joab.

14–22. Death of Sheba and End of the Revolt. The revolt was of short duration. With the death of Sheba peace was restored. The subject of the obscure v. 14 seems to be Sheba, who made his way up to Abel-beth-maacah, which is probably one of the northernmost Israelite towns in the upper Jordan Valley. The last part of the verse probably stated that his following was very small, perhaps that it consisted only of Benjamites. The wise woman's saw is obscure; does it end with the verse or with *faithful in Israel*? (V. 19). Its point seems to be that Abel had an old reputation for loyalty to Israelite traditions and institutions. Will Joab destroy a mother-city in Israel? A mother-city presumably because it was surrounded by smaller semi-dependent townships.

23–26. David's Officers. The officers of the administration are again given, with some variations from 8^{16-18}. We hear nothing of Joab's reinstatement; presumably David accepted the fact that Joab was the inevitable commander-in-chief. For *tribute* (*taskwork*, A.S.V., v. 24) read *corvee.* As regards these offices, see on 8^{16-18}. The names here are in part different from the earlier list. Doubtless, David changed his officers from time to time. *Ira*, who came of a Gileadite clan (cf. 23[38] 1 Chr. 25[3]), certainly did not belong to the Aaronic priesthood. He takes the place of David's sons in the other list.

Teaching of chs. 19 and 20. These chapters deal with the restoration of David to his former power. The death of Absalom did not end David's troubles. The pacification of the country was no easy matter. Judah had espoused Absalom's cause and feared reprisals. When they were assured on this head and David went out of his way to conciliate them, he thereby offended the northern tribes. His journey from the Jordan was hardly a triumphal procession, for the northern tribes refused to escort him, and one of them raised the signal for revolt in the words which, as Gressmann says, became "the Marseillaise" of Israel (20[1]). This revolution, however, was quickly and easily suppressed, and the bitterness between north and south seemed to be healed or at least allayed.

David's character again is revealed in the incidents of his return. With Judah he was diplomatic; with Shimei generous beyond the common manner of kings; there was to be a general amnesty to mark his return (19[22]). He seems to have suspected Meribbaal of treason, but gives him the benefit of the doubt. (Samuel uses "Mephibosheth"; in Chronicles the name is spelled "Meribbaal".) The figure drawn with the greatest sympathy is that of Barzillai, the aged country gentleman who has supported David in adversity, and now, coming down to escort David across the river, courteously declines the honors that David would heap upon him, asking only that his son may be taken to court (19[31f.]). Upon Joab, and only Joab, was David severe, and that unjustly. Joab had used great plainness with the king (19[1-8]), but David knew that he had spoken wisely and took his advice; yet he degrades Joab and offers his post to Amasa, Absalom's general. So it comes that Joab is in a way the hero of these chapters rather than David himself, and at the end we find Joab once again commander-in-chief, in virtue, it would seem, of the force of his character rather than the wish of David; and what a character! Fierce and relentless, slayer of Abner and Amasa and Absalom (murderer only of Amasa and even here "with extenuating circumstances," for Joab had been grievously wronged by the king); a soldier of many campaigns, and all of them successful; the hero of the capture of Jerusalem (1 Chr. 11[6]); forceful in counsel in the recall of Absalom and after Absalom's death; a man of courage and resource, of integrity and unswerving loyalty. He has been called "the Wallenstein of Israel." It was not for nothing that Jesus chose men like Peter and Simon the Zealot to be his disciples; they had much to learn, but they were the stuff of heroes.

Chapters 21 to 24: An Appendix

These four chapters are in the nature of an appendix, consisting in part of extracts from old records of the reign of David, in part of lists of David's heroes and their exploits, and in part of poems credited to David.

CHAPTER XXI

1–14. The Vengeance of the Gibeonites on Saul. The narrative of the prolonged famine and David's method of pacifying Jehovah throws much light upon the religious ideas of this early period. A massacre of the Gibeonites was in contravention of the covenant in Josh. 9; there is good reason to think that these Gibeonites were the priests of Nob (1 Sam. 22[18]; see on 1 Sam. 10[1-8]).

The narrative in vv. 1–14 is of unusual religious interest. S. A. Cook speaks of "the pacification of the Gibeonites" here, and rightly, but the point of the story is much more "the pacification of God"; for we have to do with human sacrifice to avert the anger of God as shown in a prolonged famine. A prolonged drought would be ascribed inevitably to divine displeasure. The oracle was consulted as to the cause of God's wrath, and the answer was, Saul's treacherous massacre of the Gibeonites. Inasmuch as more than six years at the very least must have passed since Saul's death, and presumably still longer since the crime, there is some ground for Gressmann's suggestion that David himself hinted to the priests that this might be the cause of the trouble in order that he might have a good and pious excuse for exterminating the house of his predecessor, a usual proceeding for a new dynasty in those days. This, however, is only a guess. The suggestion is at least as likely to have come from Abiathar, sole survivor of the priests of Nob. When "atonement," i.e., expiation or satisfaction, had been made by this human sacrifice on a large scale, God *was intreated for the land;* i.e., God put away his anger and sent rain (v. 14). That an expiatory sacrifice is intended is shown also by the phrase that Saul's sons were hanged up *unto the Lord* (vv. 6, 9).

This may appear barbaric religion. But is it fundamentally different from notions that have at times appeared in Christendom in connection with ideas of the atonement? For instance, "the blood that flowed from Calvary down and smoothed the Father's angry frown."

Yet we may find elements of truth and value in the sense of the seriousness of sin, in the realization that a family must pay the debts as well as receive the advantages of its forbears. In the N.T. we find an altogether different and new conception of religion, namely, that the task of religion is not the reconciling of God with man, but of man with God.

If a man's body was unburied, he could not rest in Sheol; to lack burial, therefore, was the most cruel fate. The heroism of Rizpah touched even that rough age as it has touched all ages since; her name is immortal as the type of a mother's love. The Greek parallel to the story of Rizpah is Sophocles' Antigone (see also Tennyson's poem *Rizpah*). Rizpah's fidelity was rewarded, for her sons were duly and decently buried at the royal command.

15–22. The Exploits of David and His Men During the Philistine Wars. The most interesting verse is 19, which credits the slaying of Goliath, not to David but to Elhanan. Is is likely that, if this feat had been performed by David, it would have been ascribed to this obscure person? On the other hand, David might easily be credited with what one of his heroes had done. (See notes on 1 Chr. 20.)

CHAPTER XXII

A Hymn of Thanksgiving. This poem is found in a somewhat later recension, in Psa. 18 (see the comments there). It purports to be a triumphal hymn sung doubtless to the accompaniment of sacrifice and festivity to celebrate David's victories. The hymn may have been adapted here and there for the liturgical purposes for which it was afterward used, but there is no good reason for doubting the substantial accuracy of the heading in v. 1.

CHAPTER XXIII

1–7. David's Last Words and Testament. There is no good reason for doubting that this psalm comes from the time of David, even if it was not indited by him on his deathbed. The text is in some confusion; presumably vv. 1–5 ran originally somewhat as follows (though much of the reconstruction is guesswork):

Thus saith David the son of Jesse,
Thus saith the man upraised on high,
The anointed of Jacob's God,
Lover of Israel's psalmody.

The Spirit of the Lord spake in me,
And his word was upon my tongue;
Jacob's God said to me,
Israel's Rock spake:

He that ruleth men righteously,
Who reigneth in God's fear,
He shineth like the morning light,
Like the sun on a cloudless morn,
Which maketh the green earth resplendent after rain.

But the godless are as wild thistles,
They are not grasped by the hand,
No man toucheth them,
Except with iron tools;
They are fuel for the fire.

Surely my house is not so with God;
He ordereth and sustaineth it;
For an everlasting covenant hath he made with me,
In him is all my salvation and my joy.

8–39. A List of David's Heroes. The paragraph is similar in nature to 21$^{15-22}$ and may be derived from the same document. It is a list of men who distinguished themselves in David's service and in consequence were made members of a separate group. For *the same was Adino the Eznite* (v. 8) read *he lifted up his spear*. The pouring out (v. 16) was in a sacramental libation. After *mighty deeds* (v. 20) read, probably, *he followed two young lions into their lair and slew them there; he went down also and slew the old lion. . . .*

In this chapter we have further fragments, first a psalm purporting to be David's last words, then a number of exploits performed by men who belonged to "the Three" or "the Thirty," probably popular honorific titles given to the notable sportsmen of the day. Two sections only have religious significance. The burden of David's psalm is not less moving for being simple; it says little more than that it is good to be good; but man can hardly say a profounder word than that.

It was for David a rare experience to be offered that which had been obtained at the risk of men's lives; for us the experience is common. The mining industry, deep-sea fishery, a thousand occupations and industries which minister to our daily comfort and convenience, are carried on at peril of men's lives. "The oppression of the slaves which I have seen in several journeys southward on this continent," says John Woolman, "and the report of their treatment in the West Indies, have deeply affected me, and a care to live in the spirit of peace and minister no just cause of offense to my fellow creatures having from time to time livingly revived in my mind, I have for some years past declined to gratify my palate with those sugars."

CHAPTER XXIV

The Census and the Ensuing Pestilence; David Purchases Araunah's Threshing-floor. Incited by Jehovah, David orders a census. Though it is divinely ordered, Jehovah is reported as angry (cf. 1 Chr. 21[1f.]). He sends a pestilence. The angel of Jehovah stops short of the destruction of Jerusalem. David is commanded to build an altar on the spot where the angel stood when the plague was stayed. This became the site of Solomon's Temple. *Araunah* seems to be a Hittite name, perhaps a title; for "Araunah" means "nobleman" in Hittite. This perhaps explains *Araunah the king* in v. 23 (mg.).

We have here a saga. The theology of the story is primitive and some elements in it at least are legendary, as, for instance, that David *saw* the avenging angel (v. 17). The story gave offense to later thought, so that we read in 1 Chr. 21[1] that Satan, not the Lord, moved David to the census. It is not clear to us why the census was a sin; probably because the growth and multiplication of a people is a sacred mystery into which one should not peer. The census may have been planned by David for the better organization of the militia or for purposes of taxation; in either case it might arouse much popular resentment. The conception that God being angry with his people should provoke the king to sin that he might be punished is primitive. Such stories have parallels from all over the world; it is not in such that the distinction and glory of Israel are seen. Indeed, such ideas we may regard even in David's time as *superstitions*, i.e., survivals from earlier thought not yet sloughed off.

FIRST AND SECOND KINGS

BY PROFESSOR D. C. SIMPSON

INTRODUCTION

Title and Place in the Canon. In the Hebrew, Greek, and Latin Bibles First and Second Kings follows First and Second Samuel. In the Greek and Latin Bibles, it is known as Third and Fourth Kingdoms (see intro. to First and Second Samuel, p. 381).

Contents. First Kings opens with a dazzling picture of the glories of King Solomon's reign and Second Kings closes with the restoration to honor of Jehoiachin, a prisoner of war in Babylon. Though this period is covered also by Second Chronicles, this latter work must be used as a supplement to, not as a substitute for, Kings. As a historical source, Kings is superior to Chronicles in many important respects (see intro. and notes to First and Second Chronicles). It is in the books of Kings that we can see the Northern Kingdom rise to power and influence, sink into moral corruption, and vanish from the stage of history; we watch the fierce conflict between wealthy Samaria and its weak little southern neighbor; we see the gallant resistance of Jerusalem to the fierce attacks of Sennacherib, and finally witness its fall before the onslaught of the king of Babylon. Again, it is in the books of Kings that we watch the historical struggles of real individuals for the higher and nobler ideal, alike in religion and in politics—Elijah against the prophets of the Tyrian Baal supported by the Tyrian princess Jezebel, Ahab against the Syrian forces, Jehoram and Jehoshaphat against the Moabites. It is from the books of Kings that we obtain a truer understanding of the evil practices of kings like Ahaz, and the earnest endeavor of Josiah to remedy a state of things which had become intolerable. Incidents such as these, together with many others, are put before us with such vividness and such dramatic power that they are indeed masterpieces of literary art. While they enthrall us as literature, they go far toward providing us with the knowledge of the historical and political background which is necessary for a true appreciation of the development of religion, ethics, and society during this formative period of the life-history of the chosen race.

But not even when they are supplemented from Chronicles do we find in the books of Kings a *complete* picture of those great movements, social, political and religious, which determined the lines upon which the national life progressed during this period. Hence, the student who wishes to reconstruct the true religious and social development of the period has to supplement the record found in these documents by the writings of the great prophets of the eighth century, together with those of Jeremiah and other famous prophetic leaders. Again, one who wishes to make a scientific reconstruction of the *history* of the period must read First and Second Kings in the light of, among others, such inscriptions as those found at Karnak, Nimrud, or Diban, if he would estimate the relation in which the Hebrews stood to neighboring nations. And yet, important as it is to supplement the records contained in these historical books both from the prophetical writings and from the inscriptions, it is equally important for the purpose both of the theologian and of the historian to examine carefully the literary structure and the successive redactions through which the books of Kings passed.

Authorship and Date. We owe the major portion of these books to the "compiler" (see below) who probably completed his work before the destruction of Jerusalem in 586 B.C., of which he betrays no knowledge. He probably lived in the reign of Jehoiachin, since it is here that the usual characteristics of his "framework" (see next paragraph) cease. His work was completed by a subsequent "editor" who belonged to the same school of thought but could tell of events as late as those of the reign of Evil-merodach (2 Kings 25[27-30]). A *few* additions were made to the text in the post-exilic period (see below under "Later Voices").

The Structure of First and Second Kings. The "compilatory" methods used by the Compiler of First and Second Kings are practically identical with those of many other historical writers of bygone days. They were used by the compilers of the Lives of Saint Francis of Assisi, by mediæval Chroniclers in Western Europe, by Justinian, using the Institutes of Gaius, by the Hindu Compiler of the great Law Book of Manu, by Arabic historians, by the Syrian Tatian in his Harmony of the Gospels, by the authors of the first and third Gospels, and, in the O.T., by the Compiler of the Pentateuch and Joshua, by the Compiler of Judges, by the Compiler of First and Second Samuel, and by the Compiler of First and Second Chronicles. Our Compiler, just as they did, utilized such records as were accessible at the time, choosing this account in accordance with his own earnest convictions, omitting that because he regarded it as irrelevant, and adding what he himself held to be essential. His record of Solomon's reign is in itself a small compilation, various sources being utilized, and the whole worked into a unity designed to drive home certain great religious truths. After the transition to the history of the Divided Kingdom (1 Kings 12) the story of each reign is (with a few exceptions) fitted into a definite and rigid "framework." First of all we have an opening formula (in which are given the date of the beginning of the reign, its length, the synchronism with the king of the other kingdom, and, in the case of Judah, the name of the king's mother); next comes the Compiler's "judgment" on the king in question (rarely containing historical items), and this precedes any extracts from his sources which the Compiler wished to insert; and finally appears the Compiler's "closing formula" (indicating where the curious reader may find further information, and recording the king's death, place of burial, and the successor's name).

The Sources. (1) Sources for the Reign of Solomon. The Compiler lived some three hundred years after Solomon's day, and set out to express his own religious philosophy of history. But it must not be thought that he was drawing on mere hearsay, still less on his own imagination, and that, therefore, his book is comparatively useless as a sober work of historical information. Sudden changes of style, coincident with differences in representation and varying emphasis in mental outlook and religious and moral presuppositions, are revealed in the various sections. They prove beyond question that the Compiler drew on *written* sources. Some of these sources were contemporary or nearly contemporary with Solomon; others were written some little time before the Compiler's day, although quite likely at some considerable distance from Solomon's reign. Thus the Compiler made use of (a) an intimate court history, (b) the official annals of the reign, (c) a biography of Solomon, (d) one document or more written in praise of Solomon's wisdom, and (e) a document concerned with his building operations. In the light of these various documents—even though they be of various dates and varying degrees of trustworthiness—the Compiler had every justification for seeing in Solomon, at least from *some* points of view, one of the greatest of Israel's heroes of old time.

(2) In the rest of his book the Compiler continued to quote from (a) the official Judæan Annals in connection with the reign of practically every Judæan king. For the history of the Northern, or Israelite, Kingdom he used similarly (b) the official annals of that kingdom. In addition he enriched his narrative by long extracts from works of which the chief were probably: (c) the "Acts of Elijah" (1 K. 17–19, 21; 2 K. 1^{2-17a}, see notes there); (d) the "Acts of Elisha" (2 K. 2, 3^{4}–8^{15} 13^{14-21}); (e) a history of the Syrian wars (1 K. 20, 22); (f) a history of Judah (e.g., 2 K. 11); (g) a history of the Temple (2 K. 12^{4-16} 16^{10-18} 23^{3-24}); and (h) a composite biography of Isaiah (2 K. 18^{17}–20^{19}).

On dates, see art., *Chronology* of *O.T.*, p. 108. Variations indicate that as to some of these dates there is still difference of opinion.

The Compiler's Date, Purpose and Message. His aim was not that of the merely scientific historian of a nation's internal and international political life: he lived long before the era of scientific history. His aim was primarily religious and didactic. He sought to chronicle such events of the past (beginning with the reign of Solomon) as had a message for the nation and the individual in his own day.

(1) The Compiler's aim in the history of Solomon's reign, as elsewhere in his book, was primarily didactic. He sought from the incidents in it to illustrate certain principles of religion, of religious policy and of conduct which were of importance for the nation and the individual in his own day. His three *chief* didactic themes, though interwoven and at times obscuring each other, stand out fairly clearly throughout his narrative.

His *first* theme is that true "Wisdom" (3^{4-9}) is from God, and that he who possesses it is endowed, potentially at least, with the requisite education and ability for dealing with the problems of any one of the various departments of human activity he pursues. Such activities include those of the law courts, of scholarship and general or specific culture, of the rich man with expensive tastes—a luxurious palace, a numerous household and an insatiable love of luxury—of the diplomatist anxious for the good name of his nation in the estimation of foreign powers, of the organizer of the naval and military forces of his nation, and even of the civilian population in regard to its personal duties and its financial obligations to the state, or of the promoter of commercial undertakings and the pioneer in the creation of new phases of a nation's material development.

The Compiler's *second* theme, to some extent

logically included in the first, and yet having a certain emphasis of its own, was the description of the buildings, especially the Temple, which, under the influence of the Divine Wisdom, assumed an increasingly larger place in the religious life of the nation for centuries after Solomon's day. It was to Solomon's Temple that the Compiler sought above all to attract his readers' attention and to cement their loyalty to it as the one legitimate place of sacrifice in their own day. We find expressed in First and Second Chronicles (especially in 1 Chr. 17, 22 and 2 Chr. 1–9, see notes there) a still more passionate devotion to the Temple, and that at a later stage of its evolution.

His *third* theme, necessitating considerable chronological displacement of the events of the reign, was distinctly less constructively optimistic than the others. It concerned a fundamental religious problem which is still discussed to-day. "Wisdom" inspires a man to high endeavor, so long as he consistently follows it. What, however, happens to a man who fails to follow Wisdom consistently? Insofar as he deserts her, what kind of reward may he expect? What kind of goal will he reach at his life's end? The Compiler, having no conception of a future life or of rewards and punishments beyond the grave (see discussion below), found, so far as Solomon was concerned, the answer to the riddle by creating a connection between, on the one hand, Solomon's love of foreign wives and their cults and, on the other hand, internal revolt and external military reverses. Consequently, he arranged his material to serve the purpose of showing (a) Solomon's predisposition at the very outset to make shipwreck of his life's ideals (1 Kings 3^{1}); (b) throughout the greater part of his reign his whole-hearted pursuit of the "wisdom" granted to him as a result of his vision (3^{4}–10^{29}); and (c) his later reaction from this pursuit of wisdom ($11^{1\text{-}13}$); resulting (d) in the punishment ultimately inflicted upon him through the instrumentality of his three "adversaries" ($11^{14\text{-}40}$).

(2) In conformity with his fundamental aim, the Compiler shows himself in the remainder of this history a whole-hearted follower of the prophetic and priestly supporters of Josiah's suppression of local sanctuaries and image-worship and of the consequent centralization of sacrificial worship at Jerusalem. Ever since Solomon's Temple had been built such centralized worship, it seemed to these reformers, had been possible: it was the only worship really acceptable to Him to whom it was offered and should therefore have been the only one practiced. Hence, in the Compiler's estimation, while Solomon's reign was an all-important step forward, the establishment by Jeroboam I of the Northern Monarchy, with its royal sanctuaries and bull-worship, was correspondingly retrograde and even fatal in its effects, in that henceforth all this cut off the Northern Kingdom from participation in that centralized worship and delivered it over almost entirely, and forever, to the hated bull-worship and other idolatrous practices connected in the Compiler's day with the worship at the local sanctuaries. A few only of the Judæan kings escaped a more or less complete condemnation when judged by this criterion; not one of the Northern kings was immune from it.

(3) The Compiler, moreover, sought to warn his readers that sin inevitably brings punishment, a warning still more emphatically and dogmatically stated in Chronicles. "Be sure your sins will find you out" is a motto of the book. He demonstrated that this was true not only when the sinner was otherwise a benefactor of religion like Solomon, but also when the nation was the sinner, e.g., the Northern Kingdom, and even the Judæan (see e.g., 2 Kings $17^{7\text{-}23}$ $23^{26,\ 27}$ 24^{3}). Since the conception of rewards and punishments beyond the grave had not yet arisen, all such correction of the sinner had to take place in this life. (See art., *The Religion of Israel*, p. 173.)

(4) The Compiler teaches, on the other hand, that rectitude on the nation's and on the individual's part, courageous faith, and, above all, prayer, have their reward and ultimately gain the victory—one of many lessons to be learned from the biographies of Elijah and Elisha, but more especially from that of Isaiah in connection with the great crisis of 701 B.C. (2 Kings 18, 19).

(5) The Compiler sought, too, to clarify, develop and deepen his readers' ideas of God, his attributes and providence in nature and in human history. These are the fundamental issues emphasized in the "Acts of Elijah and Elisha." It was probably with this end in view that he, unlike the Chronicler, included extracts from these "Acts" even though their heroes belonged to the Northern Kingdom. That kingdom in his estimation was otherwise spiritually dead and had been moribund from the outset, i.e., from the moment of its rejection of the Davidic dynasty, apostasy from the Temple, and establishment of the bull-worship as the state religion.

(6) In the political sphere the Compiler was a patriotic member of the Judæan kingdom. He saw, it is true, in his country's foes Jehovah's instruments of chastisement. He did not, however, adopt the passivist rôle; he gloried in the defense of Ahab (in spite of his hostility to that monarch's religious policy) against the Syrian invader (1 Kings 20). He was a loyal sub-

ject of the Davidic dynasty, denouncing only individual kings, especially Manasseh, who failed in their duty to Jehovah and to the state, but he never proposed the abolition of that dynasty. Hence his message to the reigning monarch of Judah was that he should live up to the highest ideals of Solomon, and to his fellow subjects that they should, as Paul long afterward counseled, "Fear God and honor the king."

(7) In the social sphere he appreciated the need for social reform, his sympathies being evidently with the Northerners in their protest against oppression (1 Kings 12), and with Elijah and Elisha.

Later Voices in First and Second Kings. (a) *Exilic additions.* After the Compiler had written his book, later members of his school of thought added 2 Kings 24^{8}–25^{30}, which tell of the nation's final downfall and experience in exile. It is, moreover, to these later editors that at least the concluding and finest part of Solomon's prayer must be attributed, with its universalistic outlook and its stress on intercessory prayer. (b) *Post-exilic additions.* It is necessary at this point, only to call attention to the insertions made in the otherwise very ancient record of the building of the Temple, 1 Kings 6$^{18, 20b, 21, 22b}$ 7$^{22, 42b, 48-50}$ 8$^{1, 2, 3a, 4b, 5}$, and to a certain number of small, but very significant emendations and additions scattered throughout the two books, e.g., 1 Kings 10$^{1b, 21-25, 27}$ 11^{5} 12$^{17, 32}$–13^{34} 18$^{29(?), 31}$ 20$^{35-43}$ 21^{23}; 2 Kings 23$^{7b, 12c, 14, 16-18(?), 19, 20}$.

Permanent Significance. The books of Kings, as already suggested, do not offer history in the modern sense of that term. The aim of the Compiler was not so much to write history as to show that the hand of Jehovah, the God of Israel, may be seen in the history of the chosen people. The selection or omission of material found in earlier sources was determined by this aim. Readers interested in affairs which in the opinion of the Compiler were of little or no religious significance are directed to sources in which such information may be found. The didactic tendency reveals itself especially in the framework, whose principal value consists in throwing light on the religious ideas and ideals of the Compiler.

Of very great historical value is the material which the Compiler took from the earlier sources, especially when he used it without serious modification. In many instances the brief and concise statements have every appearance of trustworthiness, and there are numerous indications of the fidelity with which the sources were preserved in their original form.

Perhaps the least satisfactory feature of the book is its chronology. No doubt the Compiler took some of the chronological data from earlier sources, but in the arrangement of this material and in the construction of the synchronisms he appears to have been under the influence of a more or less stereotyped and artificial scheme of generations. Fortunately the Assyrian chronology, which is fairly well established for the greater part of the period covered in Kings, makes it possible to place the biblical chronology on a more scientific basis. (See art., *Chronology of O.T.*, p. 108.) But in spite of some minor shortcomings the books of Kings are of the greatest interest and value to students of Israel's political and religious history. Indeed, they are far superior to any other historical records of the same age.

Literature: Skinner, *First and Second Kings* (Century Bible); Farrar, *The First and Second Books of Kings* (Expositor's Bible); G. A. Smith, *Jerusalem*, 2 vols; Kent, *The History of the Hebrew People*, vol. ii.; H. P. Smith, *O.T. History;* T. H. Robinson, *The Decline and Fall of the Hebrew Kingdoms* (Clarendon Bible); N. Micklem, *Prophecy and Eschatology;* and the works recommended in the present volume on the Writing Prophets of the period (e.g., Amos, Hosea, Micah, Isaiah, Habakkuk, Jeremiah, Ezekiel).

FIRST KINGS

Chapters 1 to 11: The Accession and Reign of Solomon (977–937 B.C.)

Chs. 1 and 2 serve as an introduction to Solomon's reign. They describe David's choice, made virtually on his death-bed, of Solomon as his successor and the steps taken to secure the latter's accession and subsequent security from the plottings of rivals. The whole of ch. 1 and much of ch. 2 are a transcript from an ancient source, written by a contemporary of the events narrated. The vivid description, the intimate knowledge of court life, and the keen partisanship, reflect the work of a supporter of Solomon, possibly one of the chief actors in the drama here recorded. For a note on the importance of Solomon's reign, see p. 422.

CHAPTER I

David's Last Days. (Continued in 2$^{1-12}$.) The author rises to superb heights of artistic skill in depicting the last moments of the aged king (vv. 1–4; David must now have been about seventy years old); the dangers of confusion in the leadership of the nation caused by the uncertainty as to David's rightful successor; the plots and counterplots within the court—Adonijah's hastily conceived plot and furtive banquet (vv. 5–10); the cunning subtlety, rather than statesmanship, of the aged Nathan, who had once been the bold exponent of the moral law of a God of justice and forgiveness (see notes to 2 Sam. 11^{2}–12^{31}) but now appears to be little more than a common wire-puller in a court torn by the claims of conflicting worldly interests (vv. 11–31); and the once beautiful, but now ageing, Bathsheba's equally guileful intervention on behalf of her beloved son (cf. note to 2 Sam. 12^{31}). The dramatic outcome of it all is seen in Solomon's immediate triumph (vv. 32–40; cf. 2^{10-12}), and in the crushing effects of the news of this on Adonijah's fellow banqueters and plotters (vv. 41–53).

CHAPTER II

The Accession of Solomon. (See also notes on ch. 1.) The hand of the same consummate artist is to be seen in the descriptions of the further march of events—the aged king's charge to Solomon (vv. 1–4); the tragic fall from royal favor experienced by David's oldest and well-tried ministers (vv. 5–7), involving, as it did, Joab's disgrace and death (vv. 28–35; for Joab cf. notes to 2 Sam. 19^{8b}–20^{26}); Abiathar's eclipse by Zadok and banishment to a despised village (vv. 26, 27); Shimei's thoughtless throwing away of his life through his over-zealous greed in pursuing his runaway slaves (vv. 36–46); and, not least, Adonijah's speedy punishment for his sinister attempt to secure, through Bathsheba, that which he dared not request directly from Solomon, whether the request was born of lust or of ambition to further his claims to the kingship (vv. 8, 9, 13–25).

The picture is not that of a number of stage villains pursuing each his own devious and disgraceful line of crime. All the *dramatis personæ* are necessary to the theme; and all act from motives which are never either wholly bad or wholly unselfish. All except Adonijah are men of courage and tact. Their self-confidence is born of a consciousness of the seeming justice of their respective causes and of their desire to secure the continuance of David's dynasty. That they differed in their conception of how best to attain this end was not their fault: that was directly due to the novelty of the monarchy as an institution. The uncertainty as to the succession resulted simply from the fact that the monarchy was a comparatively recent innovation. The first king, Saul, had been chosen as a military dictator, a last hope, to save his people from the Philistines. But his dynasty after Ishbosheth's (Ishbaal's) unhappy and ineffective reign, came to an abrupt end. The Northern tribes of their own free will chose David on his merits when he was already king of Judah. Was the next king to be called to the throne by popular vote, or was David to be allowed to found a dynasty? Both parties at this point in the reign of the dying David presupposed the latter alternative. But if it was to be adopted, was a strict system of primogeniture to be followed, or was the present sovereign to choose his successor?

On grounds of primogeniture Adonijah's claims were beyond dispute. We cannot tell how he would have dealt with the political and religious situation of his day had he become king. But it is evident that Solomon's selection by the dying monarch and the rôle which he subsequently played were fraught with vital consequences not only for the Hebrew people but also for the whole world. It was not Solomon's enthusiastic adherents at David's court, nor a mother's overweening ambition for her son's dynastic claims, nor Solomon's own greed of riches and power, but the Divine Providence, which was ultimately responsible for bringing Solomon to the throne and for the course which history followed during and as a result of his reign. Without Solomon's policy (in certain at least of its fundamental issues) the history of the pre-exilic Hebrew State could scarcely have developed on the lines which eventuated ultimately in the rise of the Judaism of post-exilic days. The latter, in turn, without the ideal of Temple worship which had its beginnings in Solomon's passion for building, could scarcely have endured long enough to become the earliest, and therefore the vitally important, environment of Christianity. Equally impossible without the discipline of the Temple rites would have been Judaism's continued survival after Herod's Temple had disappeared, to be one of the primary spiritual forces from which Mohammed drew his inspiration, and, by no means a negligible result, to be itself thirty centuries after Solomon's death still a living religion treated by its rivals with greater respect to-day than ever before, alike in the New World and in the Old.

Chapters 3 to 11: The Events of Solomon's Reign (cf. 2 Chr. 1–9)

CHAPTER III

1–3. Solomon's Marriage to the Egyptian Princess. The notice of Solomon's marriage to the Egyptian princess is placed at the beginning of Solomon's reign not as being the most important or the earliest of his adventures, but because, disapproving of it, the Compiler did not wish to include it among the adventures upon which Solomon embarked as a result of the gift of "Wisdom" (see intro., p. 413b).

4–28. Solomon's Choice of Wisdom: the Two Mothers. Solomon's sacrifice, vision, and the gift of wisdom to him at Gibeon (see Josh. 9[3-27] 2 Sam. 20[8] 21[1-9]), whence he returns to the sanctuary of Jerusalem, symbolizing the importance which was in future to be attached to the latter as compared with all other sanctuaries. His use of this divine gift of "Wisdom" is immediately illustrated (vv. 16–28) by his decision in the case of the two mothers.

CHAPTER IV

1–34. Description of Solomon's Home Policy. In vv. 1–19 (continued in vv. 27, 28, after which vv. 22, 23 should be placed) this policy is illustrated by a list of his officials, who are more numerous and have more clearly defined duties than David's (2 Sam. 8[17f.] 15[37] 16[16] 20[23f.] 1 Chr. 27[33]). This list belongs to the latter part of Solomon's reign, since his sons-in-law are mentioned. For *recorder* and *scribe* (v. 3) see notes to 2 Sam. 8[16, 17]. **7.** The twelvefold division of the country had as its object the maintenance of the royal household by the tribute in kind dispatched monthly by each officer in turn. **19.** *Gilead* is probably a corruption of "Gad" (otherwise unmentioned), which may have now occupied Sihon's territory, but *Og . . . Bashan* is probably a gloss (Bashan having been dealt with in v. 13). **20, 21, 24–26** are of later origin than their context (especially the phrase *on this side of the river*; cf. Ezra 4[17] etc.; Neh. 2[9]). They were inserted to enhance the width and extent of his kingdom and to exaggerate the value of his stables. **29–34.** The trend of Solomon's "Home Policy" is further emphasized by a description of his learning and especially his genius for creating "proverbs"—hence the ascription to him of collections of Proverbs (e.g., Prov. 10[1] 25[1] Eccles. 1[1] and the apocryphal Book of Wisdom), some of them (see v. 33b) being similar in form to the "Wisdom of Ahikar" which was the parent of Æsop's Fables.

CHAPTERS 5 TO 7: SOLOMON'S BUILDINGS—THE TEMPLE

This section is mostly from a special "Temple Source." It was written by a priest rather than by a courtier, since very much more interest is exhibited in the details of the Temple than in those of the secular buildings. The author of this source gives no hint that either Solomon or he himself regarded the Temple as designed to be the central and only sanctuary for the whole kingdom. That was an idea which only grew up shortly before Josiah's reformation, and of which the Compiler was an ardent exponent—hence the space given by him to the present extract from the "Temple Source." The description is mostly that of *Solomon's* Temple as distinct from (a) Ezekiel's proposals for its rebuilding after the Exile (Ezek. 40–48); (b) the Traveling Tabernacle of the Wilderness (Ex. 25–31, 35–40) which represents the attempt made in the Priestly Code to throw back the conception of one central sanctuary into the period of Moses; (c) the Temple as rebuilt by Zerubbabel 520–516 B.C., and (d) as again rebuilt and enlarged by Herod the Great.

CHAPTER V

1–12. The Preparations for Building. The congratulatory embassy evidently at the outset of Solomon's reign sent by Hiram (better "Hirom," Assyrian *Hirummu*, son of Abi-baal), king (969–936 B.C.) of Tyre, the paramount city of Phœnicia, which he improved architecturally, opened the way to definite negotiations for the supply of timber for building and to the completion of a treaty (see further 2 Chr. 2[3f.]).

13–18. Forced Labor. These verses, taken from an ancient source except perhaps vv. 16, 17, tell of the forced labor extorted by Solomon from his own Israelite (i.e., non-Judæan Hebrew) subjects, a fact afterward in part responsible for their determination to throw off the yoke of the Davidic dynasty. See note to 9[20-23]. **18.** *The Gebalites*: the inhabitants, skillful stone-masons, of the Phoenician city of Byblus (modern *Gebeil*, N. of Beyrut), where recent excavations have revealed important survivals of Egyptian and other cultures and religions.

CHAPTER VI

1. Date. The traditional date (cf. vv. 37, 38 and 7[1]) of the foundation laying seems to have been evolved in an artificial manner, 480 years being equal to 12 generations of 40 years each.

2–13. The Main Features of the Building. Its archetype cannot be determined, but the non-Israelite origin of its chief workman is consistent with the view of its being a copy of a foreign and therefore heathen sanctuary. Some compare its general outline with that of the temple of Amon-Re at Karnak, others with that of Syrian temples (but these are of later date). Lucian's description of the temple at Hierapolis bears a striking resemblance to it. The division into three sections is also found in temples in Sicily.

2. The Temple, situated east and west, was rectangular in shape, approximately (on the basis of a—royal—cubit being 20.7 inches) 104 feet long, 35 feet broad, and more than 52 feet high. It was "the house of habitation" of Jehovah himself conceived of as dwelling in the darkness of the inner shrine; it was not intended itself to hold the worshipers. The latter thronged the "Court" which lay to the west of the building. **3.** *House* has the wider, and Temple (or better "palace," i.e., of the Deity) the narrower connotation, the latter being here used for the larger (later known as "the Holy Place") of the two divisions of the interior of "the house." **5, 6, 8, 10.** The additional chambers or cells round the building were probably intended as depositories for the Temple appurtenances and treasures; the upper chambers were more roomy than the lower. The cross-beams of the floors were supported on the side of the Temple wall, not by being driven into the wall but by special supports attached to the wall for the purpose. **7, 9, 11–13.** These are probably a late editor's insertion.

14–35. Internal Arrangements of the Temple. Of the internal arrangements of the Temple described in these verses attention need be called here only to the following: **16.** The *oracle,* which was a cube with sides measuring 34½ feet, absolutely dark, later known as the "Holy of Holies." **19.** An additional *oracle,* the product probably of confusion on the Compiler's part, since there was only one oracle. **20b.** The *altar* of cedar wood, i.e., the table of shewbread, and, as LXX rightly states, *he made the altar of* instead of *covered the altar with* it. **21, 22.** The gilding of the house (cf. v. 30 end), probably the product of the post-exilic tendency to exaggerate the magnificence of Solomon's Temple. Huram-abi, though called an artist in gold in 2 Chr. 2[14], probably had no technical knowledge of the use of sheet-gold. **25–28.** The two *Cherubim* in the oracle. Here as in 2 Chr. 3[13] they stand on the floor of the oracle, whereas in Ex. 25[19] (P) they branch out of either end of the mercy-seat. On Cherubim in general see note to Gen. 3[24]. **31–35.** The *doors.* The phrase in v. 31b meant either that the door with its framework occupied a fifth of the space or that each was pentagonal (cf. 6[33] 7[5]), whereas the doors of Ezekiel's Temple were six cubits wide (cf. Ezek. 41[3]).

36–38. Final Details. The Temple *Court* (v. 36) in which stood the altar of burnt sacrifices (not mentioned in Kings: note to 2 Chr. 4[1]) was the *only* "court of the Temple" in pre-exilic days. The first proposal to construct *two* "courts of the Temple" came from Ezekiel (Ezek. 40f.); and the multiplication into those "of the Gentiles," "of the women," "of Israel" and "of the priests," to which reference is made in N.T. times, was one of the novelties of the Temple of Herod the Great. The Temple Court in our verse is defined as *inner* to differentiate it, not from any other Court *of the Temple,* but from the "Great Court" (7[12]) which surrounded not merely (a) the Temple in this *inner* court but also (b) the "middle court" which contained the royal palace and harem (7[8]) and (c) contained at its south end the buildings of 7[2-7]. These were never rebuilt in post-exilic days.

CHAPTER VII

1–12. Solomon's Buildings on Mount Zion. These were (a) his own palace buildings in their own court, which lay immediately south of the Temple Court, and (b) the rest of his buildings immediately south of this in the Great Court (cf. 6[36]). **1.** States the duration of the building operations; but whether the thirteen years should include the seven of building the Temple (6[1, 37]) or whether the sum total is twenty is uncertain. **2–5.** The *house of the forest of Lebanon* was so styled because of the numerous cedars from Lebanon used in its construction. It was the largest of the various buildings and situated farthest from the Temple. The upper story probably served as an armory (cf. 10[17] Isa. 22[8]) and the lower for popular gatherings, convened to discuss important affairs of state (Josephus, *Antiquities,* bk. viii, ch. 5: 2). **6, 7.** The *porch of pillars* was possibly intended to serve as the entrance or vestibule to the Hall of Justice. **8.** Cf. 6[36]. **12.** See note to 6[36].

13–51. The Furniture of the Temple and the Palace. The Temple was constructed by, or at least the work was done under the supervision of *Hiram = Huram-abi* (= "Huram my father"), as he is called in 2 Chr. 2[13] (his name in Kings having been assimilated to that of the well-known king of Tyre). The mention in v. 14 of his connections with Naphtali (but in 2 Chr. 2[14] with Dan) through his mother is due to a desire to make the chief workman of Jehovah's Temple as much an Israelite and believer in Jehovah as possible. Oholiab, mentioned in Ex. 31[6] as working on the Traveling Tabernacle of Moses' day, was also of Northern extraction, a Danite.

15–22. The Two Pillars. In the Temple Court, immediately in front of the entry to the Temple, were placed two tall pillars. It is difficult to obtain a clear idea of their appearance. But, by comparing the present account with 2 Chr. 3[15-17] and Jer. 52[17-23], we gather that each of the two pillars was surmounted by a sphere, or *chapiter*, rising out of *lily work* and covered by a network of metal, to which two rows of loosely festooned chains were attached at four points. They stood *beside* (see 2 Chr. 3^{15-17}), *not within* or *supporting*, the entrance. The fact that each had a particular name further suggests that they were not simply part of the architectural adornment, but originally bore some analogy to the pillars which, singly or in pairs, formed an important feature of Semitic sanctuaries. At Melkart's shrine at Tyre there were, according to Herodotus, two costly obelisks at which Melkart (and probably his wife-consort) was worshiped. Two pillars also stood before the temples in Paphos and in Hierapolis. Ashurbanipal on the occasion of his expedition to Egypt and Ethiopia recounts that part of his spoil included "two obelisks high with resplendent plating of fine workmanship . . . from the threshold of the gate of the Temple." Therefore these pillars at Jerusalem, built, like the Temple itself, by Phœnician workmen, were probably intended to be symbols of the Deity: they were an artistic refinement of the *Mazzebah*, or stone obelisk which, at many Israelite sanctuaries, still stood beside the altar in much later days. But it does not necessarily follow that Solomon and his subjects so interpreted the significance of these novel and foreign brass objects: for them the Ark in the "oracle" seems to have symbolized Jehovah. But it is possible that instead of *Jachin* (or Jakin, v. 21, i.e., "he [Jehovah] establisheth") the name "Jehovah" was carved on one pillar by Huram-abi and subsequently altered into this name; and *Boaz* (i.e., "in him is strength") may be a later substitution for "Tammuz," whose cult was very prevalent in the Semitic world (cf. Ezek. 8^{14}).

23–26. The Bronze Sea. This stood in the Temple Court to the southeast of the Temple building, between the latter and the altar of burnt-offering (cf. 2 Chr. 4^{2-6}). The present narrative offers no explanation of its purpose and use. The Chronicler does so, but his explanation is not very feasible. The priestly reconstruction of the Mosaic Tabernacle substituted an ordinary laver (Ex. $30^{18f.}$ $40^{7,30}$); Ezekiel had no need for it, as he introduced a Temple stream (Ezek. 47^{1-12}). The *primary* meaning originally attached to this vessel seems to have been symbolical. An *Apsu*, or deep, had a place in Babylonian temples and served for purificatory purposes. Moreover, Marduk, whose symbols are oxen, in Babylonian mythology represents the sun who, in spring, strives with the surging deep—the monster Tiamat—which he overcomes. These symbols may have been taken over by the Hebrews to represent the Israelite Deity (cf. the calf in Ex. $32^{1f.}$; and see 1 Kings $12^{28f.}$). For Jehovah as God of rain cf. Psa. 29^{10}, and as subduer of the primæval flood and chaos cf. Gen. $1^{2,6,9}$ Psa. 24^{2} 93^{3}.

27–39. The Ten Movable Lavers. If the large bronze bowl signified the sea (see note above), the smaller ones probably denoted the clouds, the sources of the heavenly or upper waters. In any case, the height of the lavers—about twelve feet—seems too great to allow of their proving of actual use in the practical affairs of the Temple. A laver of the kind which is here meant has been found in Cyprus; it differs from the Temple one chiefly in size.

40–47. A summary of "Hiram's" accomplishments.

48–51. A List of the Golden Implements of the Temple. For the existence of much of what is here mentioned (e.g., the golden altar) there is no pre-exilic evidence; the *bare* enumeration of golden articles is astounding after the careful mention of the bronze furniture, and may well be a post-exilic interpretation. The *golden altar* is the altar of incense which otherwise makes its first appearance only in the latest portion of the post-exilic priestly legislation (P). It was unknown in Ezekiel's Temple and therefore, in all probability, entirely foreign to that of Solomon. With reference to the *table* cf. 6^{20-22} with 7^{48-50}; the former mentions an altar, here appears a table; there it is of cedar, here it is of gold. *Shewbread:* literally "bread of the face, or presence," was so styled because it was placed before Jehovah (Ex. 25^{30} Lev. 24^{6} 1 Sam. 21^{6}). In 1 Sam. 21^{6} it is called "holy bread." In the post-exilic "Priestly Code" seven-armed *candlesticks* are mentioned (Ex. $25^{31f.}$ Lev. $24^{1f.}$). Such a candelabrum is depicted on the triumphal arch of Titus at Rome. The absence of any such ornament from the earliest list of Temple furniture (see ch. 6) makes the existence of this candelabrum as early as Solomon's time extremely doubtful. But some system of lighting, if only that of single bronze candlesticks, must have been in use from the first.

CHAPTER VIII

The Dedication of the Temple. (Cf. 2 Chr. 6^{1}–7^{10}.) Based undoubtedly on an ancient source, the account has been supplemented and revised by the Compiler and later editors. The insertions and revision in part betray themselves by their subject matter and in part are emphasized by their absence from LXX. But the substantial trustworthiness of the main facts is beyond question and it is enhanced when compared with the Chronicler's version.

1–11. The Removal of the Ark. Here is described the removal of the ark from Ophel, the southern end of the Eastern Hill, northwards to the oracle of the Temple, its last resting-place. The term *Zion* (v. 1), though often restricted to the site of the latter, is here used to denote the southern spur and is equated with the City of David. LXX retains of v. 2 only the words *in the month of Ethanim;* this verse creates a chronological difficulty since in 6[38] the *eighth* month, not the *seventh,* is specified. Either two distinct traditions have thus been preserved, or the dedication took place in the seventh month of the year following the completion of the Temple. Huram-abi's work may have caused this delay. **4.** Here are two traces of revision subsequent to the Compiler's work: the reference to *the tent of meeting* and the distinction drawn between priests and Levites are both, like *all of the congregation* of v. 5, characteristic of the Priestly School and of post-exilic usage (cf. note to 1 Chr. 13[1-5]). But the reference to *the priests* (not the priests and Levites as distinct from each other) in v. 6 doubtless belongs to the old narrative and illustrates the growing importance of this professional class; for a little earlier David, in bringing the ark from its earlier home, had not troubled about them (2 Sam. 6[13]). For the ark (v. 9) see notes to 1 Sam. 4[4] 5[1]–7[1].

12, 13. An early tradition (to be found in a still purer form in LXX) of Solomon's acts and words of dedication.

14–21. Preliminaries of the Dedication. This version was current in the Compiler's—the Deuteronomic—School. It is of considerable importance as reflecting the gradual liturgical growth of intercessory prayer not merely in his day but in that of subsequent editors of his work down to a late period in the Exile. In vv. 14–21 Solomon is made to address the people in terminology which at every turn, like that of the prayer which follows, recalls that of the hortatory sections of the book of Deuteronomy. The king, by virtue of his kingship, was head priest of his own sanctuary; thus Solomon was quite justified in assuming the rôle of a priest; the professional priests exercised their office only as the king's deputies (cf. 2[26] and 2 Kings 12[7] 16[10-16]).

23–53. Solomon's Dedicatory and Intercessory Prayer. This is one of the finest examples extant alike of an ideal dedicatory prayer and of intercessory supplication, and that too on behalf not merely of the petitioner's own nation and co-religionists, but of all the families of the earth, to the end that all may find and worship the true God. Solomon is made to pray first of all that the promise made to David may be honored (vv. 23–26); that prayers made in this Temple may be answered by Jehovah (vv. 27–30), whom he is made to recognize throughout the prayer as a God who' so far from being confined in and limited to this Temple (as in the original prayer in vv. 12, 13), is not merely supramundane but also transcendent; that the oath of ordeal (cf. Ex. 22[7-11] Num. 30) may be duly effective (vv. 31, 32); that confessions of sin in national defeat may be accepted (vv. 33, 34); that prayer in drought (vv. 35, 36) and in various calamities (vv. 37–40) may be rewarded; most important of all, and reflecting the universalistic missionary ideals of the Deutero-Isaiah and the Songs of the Suffering Servant, that even the *foreigner's* cry in this Temple to Jewry's God may be received by that transcendent Deity (vv. 41–43); that prayers in war, captivity and exile may also find a favorable hearing (vv. 44–53).

54–66. Benediction; The Final Festival. Faithfully transcribing his ancient source, the Compiler relates Solomon's blessing of the people in his priestly capacity (vv. 54–61; naturally omitted in Chronicles, where a story of the descent of heavenly fire is substituted). Vv. 62–64 enumerate the sacrifices of king and people; vv. 65, 66 the celebration of the Feast of Tabernacles. This is represented as kept in accordance with Deut. 16[13-15] and as attended by all Solomon's subjects from the extreme north to the extreme south of his dominion, the southern boundary being the Wady-el-Arish, or *brook of Egypt.*

CHAPTER IX

1–9. A Theophany. This answer to Solomon's prayer is a further insertion made by a Deuteronomic writer of later date than the Compiler. Vv. 6–9 in particular presuppose the destruction of Jerusalem and the Temple and are designed to answer the question: Why was this catastrophe a justifiable and necessary act of divine providence?

10–28. Solomon's Public Works and Political Policy. This series of notices relating to the public works and political policy of Solomon are but imperfectly connected. Josephus states that *Cabul* (v. 13) meant in Phœnicia "not pleasing." Altered to *Kabal* it would mean "as (i.e., equal to) nothing." *Galilee* here has a much smaller application than in N.T. times, chiefly referring to the territory of Naphtali. But, though small, this cession of Hebrew territory must have hurt national pride and so contributed to the growing disaffection of Solomon's northern subjects, which flared up at his death chiefly in reaction against his system of corvee (v. 15), imposed on them in the interests of his buildings and fortresses. *Megiddo* secured him against Phœnicia and commanded the highways of communication between Syria and the Nile. The acquisition of *Gezer* (v. 16), which had in the past resisted absorption by the Hebrews (cf. Judg. 1^{29}), even now fell not to Hebrew attack but to the military prowess of Egypt. It was a gift to Solomon calculated to impress him not only as to the friendship, but also, and more especially, as to the overwhelming military resources of his Egyptian father-in-law. Square towers, inserted at intervals along the wall, still survive, and are said to be probably the work of Solomon. (See *Palestine Exploration Fund Quarterly Statement*, Jan., 1905, pp. 30f.)

17–19. Solomon was a great builder. *Beth-horon* commanded the road from the sea-coast to Jerusalem; *Baalath*, probably the modern *Bel'ain*, was about two and one half miles north of Beth-horon. *Tamar*—the Roman Thamara, in the Judæan Steppe (see Ezek. 47^{19}), probably the modern (ruined) el-Kurnub, guarding against attack from the south. For the variant reading *Tadmor* see 2 Chr. 8^{4}. Chariots had not formerly been used by the Hebrews but by the Canaanites: they were useful for fighting in the less hilly districts (see Josh. 17^{16}).

20–23. Solomon had numerous bondslaves. These consisted of the five nations usually enumerated in Deuteronomic passages. The purpose of the passage (see also 2 Chr. 2^{17} 9^{20-22}) was to clear Solomon of the charge, made in the ancient sources included in this book, of enslaving his non-Judæan subjects, e.g., 5^{13-15} 11^{28}, the levy of Joseph 12^{4}.

24, 25. On v. 24, see note to 7^{8}. Solomon functioned as priest (see note to 8^{22}) at the three annual feasts inculcated in the "Code of the Covenant" (Ex. $23^{14, 16}$; cf. the little Code of the Covenant, Ex. $34^{22, 23}$). For the Chronicler's changes see note to 2 Chr. $6^{12, 13}$.

26–28. Solomon's navy and expeditions to Ophir are referred to again in $10^{11, 22}$. *Eloth* lay a little north of the modern *Kal'al el'Akaba*, at the north end of the Gulf of Akaba. The expedition must have taken place before the loss of Edom (see 11^{14-22}), unless Solomon succeeded in keeping the harbor and sea approaches (cf. 1 Kings 22^{48} 2 Kings 8^{20} 14^{22} 16^{6}).

CHAPTER X

1–13. Solomon Visited by the Queen of Sheba. Situated in southwestern Arabia with Mariaba as its capital, the fame of Sheba as a center of culture and political power is attested by Strabo, Pliny, and the Himyaritic inscriptions. It is often mentioned elsewhere in O.T. (e.g., Psa. $72^{10, 15}$ Isa. 60^{6} Jer. 6^{20}), with its caravans conveying Indian and Arabian produce to Tyre and elsewhere (Job 6^{19} Ezek. $27^{22f.}$ 38^{13}). It is not Solomon's juridical wisdom (as in $3^{16f.}$) but his general knowledge of life and its more abstract problems which is here held up for approbation. The hard questions were not concerned, as Jewish tradition suggests (cf. Mt. 12^{42}), with religious matters, but were perplexing questions like Samson's riddle (Judg. 14^{12}) and the riddle guessing in which Josephus asserts that Solomon and Hiram indulged (*Antiquities*, bk. viii, ch. 5: 3).

14–29. Solomon's Prosperity and Wealth. This section contains a number of disconnected notices relating to Solomon's prosperity and wealth, not dissimilar to 9^{10-28}. But though, like the latter, mostly based on the ancient Annals, parts of this section reflect traditions of the Compiler's own day, especially vv. 14, 15 (and even more so vv. 21–25, 27), and illustrate the tendency, increasing as time went on, to emphasize his wealth and personal gifts. The description of his golden age in vv. 23–25 rivals in its terms the Messianic forecasts of the future (Isa. 23^{18} $60^{2f.}$). It was probably Solomon who initiated the use of horses in war. They had previously been ridden only in times of peace as a mark of wealth (1^{5} 2 Sam. 15^{1}): most commonly the Hebrew of pre-Davidic days rode on asses or mules (Judg. 10^{4} 12^{14} 2 Sam. 13^{29} 18^{9}). For the later condemnation of horses see Hos. 1^{7} 14^{3} Amos 2^{15} Mic. 5^{10} Isa. 31^{1}; cf. also Deut. 17^{16}. The caravaneering of v. 29 was probably directed not to Egypt (Hebrew *Misraim*) but to *Musri* (cf. 2 Kings 7^{6}), a North Syrian land, situated, as Assyrian inscriptions attest, south of the Taurus, a direction in which Togarmah, also renowned for its horses, must be looked for (Ezek. 27^{14}). Instead of *in droves* (v. 28) read *and from Koa* (a district of Cilicia, north of the Taurus range), an emendation supported by many authorities.

CHAPTER XI

1–13. Solomon's Marriage of Foreign Princesses and Worship of Foreign Gods. For the place of this section in the Compiler's *third theme* see introduction, p. 414. The historical kernel of these verses is extremely important for the reconstruction of the history of Solomon's dominions and the causes of discontent at the close of his reign. Among the deities whom he worshiped (not instead of, but doubtless in addition to, Jehovah) was *Ashtoreth*, the chief female goddess as the consort of the male Baal. In Mesopotamia she revealed herself as Ishtar, goddess, among other things, of war; among the Canaanites and Phœnicians as Ashtart, the goddess of love and fecundity; she even penetrated at a very early time into

Egypt. Among some nations (e.g., the Sabæans) we find a masculine form of the word indicating a *male* deity. The worship of this deity, therefore, in one form or another was well-nigh universal. *Milcom* was the national god of the Ammonites. Solomon probably built his altars (vv. 7, 8) on soil brought from the native land of each several god, just as Naaman desired to worship Jehovah on Palestinian soil taken from Israel to Syria (see notes to 1 Sam. 26[19] 2 Kings 5[17]). *Chemosh* was the national god of Moab (cf. Num. 21[29] and the Moabite Stone).

14–22. Solomon's First Adversary. This first adversary is the Edomite Hadad (the name of a god among the Assyrians). The incident probably took place comparatively early in Solomon's reign and was seemingly relegated to the end by the Compiler to drive home his moralizing lesson. Two distinct stories seem to have been welded together in this narrative. According to the one, Hadad was an Edomite prince who in his childhood escaped David's massacre of the Edomites and was taken to Egypt: he was brought up by Pharaoh's wife, Tahpenes, and on the death of David returned as king of Edom. According to the other, Adad, a leader of Edomite troops, escaped from Joab, fled to Midian and from thence to Paran, and finally to Egypt, where he became the Pharaoh's brother-in-law. Hadad himself may have been a Midianite: vv. 17, 18a at least suggest that his connection was originally with Midian. Granted this, *Midian* may have given place to *Edom*, which in turn, when the close of the story was misplaced to the point which it now occupies (namely, v. 25b), was corrupted into *Aram* (=Syria).

23–25. Solomon's Second Adversary. This was Rezon of Damascus. The author of this story seems all unconscious of the terrible significance which this new power was destined to have for the Northern Kingdom: for two centuries Israel and Syria were deadly enemies until both succumbed before the onslaught of Assyria. V. 25a suggests that the revolt took place early ("*all* the days") in Solomon's reign. The close of the story and of this verse, which in the Hebrew has been misplaced (v. 25b belonging to v. 22), has been preserved by the LXX, which reads: "And Hadad returned to his own land. This is the evil which Hadad did, and he oppressed Israel and reigned in Edom."

26–43. Solomon's Third Adversary. This was not a foreigner but an Israelite tribesman, an Ephraimite. Whereas the other adversaries' efforts resulted in the loss to Solomon of some of the foreign vassal-states dating from David's time, this one stood forward as the champion of the rights of the enslaved Northerners (cf. 9[20-23]) and became their king at the death of Solomon. The Compiler's animosity toward this leader of revolt against the Davidic dynasty was due to the fact that his success made the religious unity of all the tribes in the worship of the Temple an impossible ideal. A somewhat different version of this rebellion appears in the LXX after 12[24]. It tells how Jeroboam, an Ephraimite, son of a harlot named Sareisa (or Sareira) and a servant of Solomon, was appointed overseer of the corvee of the tribe of Joseph. With a force of three hundred chariots he raised a revolt and, being compelled to flee to Shishak, king of Egypt, married Anoth, the sister of the Pharaoh's wife (this detail belongs to the story of Adad; see note on v. 19), who bore him a son Abijah (cf. v. 20). Upon Solomon's death Shishak unwillingly allowed him to return to his own country, where he collected the tribe of Ephraim and built a fort. The name of his mother *Zeruah* (i.e. "leprous woman") would appeal to the Compiler as being (like "harlot" in the duplicate narrative) a sign of the inherent badness of her son. But he lacked neither courage nor a sense of justice, as is shown by his action in vv. 27, 28. The support given him by the prophet in vv. 29, 30 is similar to that accorded to David and later to Jehu: it suggests that he was by no means the irreligious and self-seeking usurper whom the Compiler paints for us.

The Importance of Solomon's Reign. We are now in a position to estimate the importance of Solomon's reign, to which the Compiler has devoted so large a portion of his work. In what respects is it noteworthy? What were its results—good and bad—upon the character and subsequent history of the Hebrew people?

It should be clear that the whole effect of Solomon's reign was in the direction of revolutionizing Hebrew life; his influence is by no means to be judged only by the importance subsequently assumed by his Temple. It was he who hastened the inevitable transition of an originally nomadic people from a pastoral and agricultural stage of its evolution in the direction of its ultimate destiny as the nation noted for commercial instincts and trading acumen. Moreover, he gave to the Hebrews, for the first time in their existence, the status of a nation, and made them for the time being a closely united whole. Kingdoms and empires such as those of Egypt and Tyre had previously had little or no cognizance of the Hebrews as a *nation:* it was his aim to make them capable of negotiating on equal terms with such neighboring peoples, and of entering into treaty alliances with them. He, by his personal example, set forth, in the juridical sphere, an ideal of equity and insight into motives which allowed Hebrews of subsequent days to appreciate the teaching of Amos when he demanded "righteousness" in the law courts and in every other department of life, and of Jeremiah when he failed to find it anywhere in Jerusalem. Similarly, Solomon organized an efficient system of taxation and methods for its collection in a part of the world which to this day, except when under the direct authority of a Western power, suffers from the absence of such organization and from the peculations of minor officials thereby made possible. Lastly he gave an impetus to gnomic "wisdom," to the tendency, that is, to bring common sense to bear on life and conduct and to look below the surface to the heart of things. He did this so thoroughly that much literature, though written by others than Solomon, bears his name, e.g., the book of Proverbs (see Prov. 10[1] 25[1]), Ecclesiastes, and the apocryphal Book of Wisdom.

But neither a nation nor an individual can suddenly move forward in any of these directions without laying itself open to the dangers which always beset the path of progress. Thus Solomon, to insure the success of the beginnings of these changes in his people's life and outlook, was tempted to employ methods some of which are justifiable in no age whether for a nation or for an individual. In particular his efforts to raise the status of his kingdom in the estimation of its neighbors led him to establish an extravagant standard of luxury at his court. This in its turn led to excessive taxation of his subjects. His efforts to give dignity to his palace and public buildings tempted him to yield territory to Phœnicia and to enslave all his subjects other than the men of Judah, and this in turn led to the disruption of his kingdom at his death. Even during his lifetime, probably early in his reign, his concentration on these and other aspects of public policy, to the exclusion of any real interest in military preparedness, resulted in the loss of his father's foreign dominions.

Thus the results—good and bad—of Solomon's activities were remarkable and fully warrant the considerable amount of space allotted to them by the Compiler in his history. But the fact that the good effects were well-nigh counterbalanced by the bad in his lifetime and afterward, should warn us against an uncritical appreciation of his personal character. He desired "Wisdom" and was granted it in a measure far in excess of the amount and quality of it potentially present in other men of his generation. But he failed in his personal conduct and in some aspects of his official policy—more particularly in the social sphere—to rise far above the standards of other men of his day less brilliantly endowed. Solomon in all of his glory, said our Lord, was not arrayed like one of these lilies of the field, calling us away from the artificialities alike of luxurious and smart society and of ornate ritual and ceremonial to the simple beauties of nature and the worship of the heavenly Father "in spirit and in truth" (Jn. 4[24]).

1 Kings 12 to 2 Kings 17: The Divided Kingdom

The restlessness of Solomon's subjects became more manifest after his death. His son Rehoboam had a splendid opportunity to allay the dissatisfaction, but he refused to accept the better part. His policy led to a division of the kingdom—a division which was never healed.

Chapters 12[1] to 14[20]: The Revolt of the Northern Tribes

Solomon's reign of profligate luxury, diplomatic successes in the international sphere, and remarkable organization of the human and material resources of his realm was at an end. The Northerners, his oppression of whom had rendered this possible, were determined that his death should mark the end of that oppression. They chose for their first king Jeroboam the Ephraimite (937–915 B.C.).

CHAPTER XII

1–24. Rehoboam's Loss of His Northern Subjects. Rehoboam's failure to realize the gravity of the situation lost him his Northern subjects, and his attempt to continue the system of indentured labor cost him a general, and it drove the Northerners to the immediate choice of Jeroboam, whose efforts to alleviate their lot in Solomon's reign (11[26-40]) they remembered. In Judah, Rehoboam's determination to stamp out the rebellion by force of arms called forth a public and effective protest from the prophets, who were the religious leaders of Judah, which alone remained faithful to the Davidic dynasty. Thus prophetism, formerly the champion of resistance to foreign domination (see notes to 1 Sam. 9[1]–11[15]), ranged itself definitely on the side of the oppressed against the oppressor, and so laid at this time the foundations on which first Elijah, and later, on a very much higher plane, the prophets of a new type, Amos, Hosea, Micah, and Isaiah, were able to build their doctrines of a God whose own nature was essentially moral, and whose demands on his people and their rulers were also ethical rather than cultic, moral rather than blindly nationalistic. Whether the prophets in point of fact caused Rehoboam at once to acquiesce in the revolt is doubtful (see 14^{30}). In any case, the Northern tribes retained the monarchical form of government, though with many dynastic changes, which maintained its distinctness from Judah and its Davidic dynasty right up to its subjugation by Assyria (2 Kings 17^{6}). Later thought saw in this last event abundant evidence of the North's wickedness in rejecting the Davidic dynasty (cf. 2 Kings 17^{7-23}).

25–33. Jeroboam Builds Shrines for His People. The Compiler of Kings interpreted Jeroboam's most innocent acts and what was really an attempt to humor the old-fashioned and reactionary religious ideals of his Northern subjects as clear evidence of his determination to alienate his Northern subjects' affections from the Southern Kingdom and, in the Compiler's thought, the only legitimate sanctuary. To the Northerners, however, the Temple was only a reminder of their own indentured and unwilling labor, its symbolism the evidence of Solomon's foreign and therefore unpatriotic proclivities, while the idea of the central sanctuary did not arise till much nearer the reign of Josiah and the Compiler's own times. But a historical kernel underlies the statements contained in these verses. Jeroboam gave his subjects exactly what their conservative presuppositions demanded—sanctuaries of their own—two maintained at the royal expense—an ancient method of representing Jehovah as the God of physical force, a bull (cf. Ex. 32^{1-6}), a professional priesthood augmented from among the laity as need arose—its restriction to the tribe of Levi being as yet unknown—and a harvest festival at the time when crops were actually garnered in (i.e., roughly fourteen days later in the North than in the South). Because he was king he exercised his office as the national priest just as Solomon had done and as Uzziah long afterward did (see 2 Chr. 26^{16-19}) in the Temple.

CHAPTER XIII

Divine Punishment for the Alleged Apostasy: the Disobedient Prophet. Later generations asked: Could apostasy from Jehovah, such as the religious innovations of Jeroboam appeared to involve, have gone uncondemned and even unpunished? The present chapter contains their answer to this question. It seems to be an adaptation to Jeroboam I's reign of the incident related of the reign of Jeroboam II in Amos 7^{10-17}. It serves, too, to explain Josiah's strange omission to desecrate a certain tomb (2 Kings $23^{17, 18}$). It reflects, moreover, the post-exilic distrust of the "prophet" as distinct from *the man of God* at a time when the former were well-nigh extinct and were wholly despised. It contains the beginnings of that significant process which culminated in the personification of "the word" (cf. 1 Kings 20^{35}), which played so large a part in Johannine and later Christian terminology. It is not history but a didactic story. It carries with it a warning to every religious denomination to-day not to cast aspersions on the leaders of its rival schools of thought: it is a warning too to each individual to put first the voice of conscience as being the most sure means whereby the individual can apprehend God's will as to his place and purpose in the divine economy.

CHAPTER XIV

1–20. Additional Punishment for Jeroboam: His Death. The original story, which is still, however, replete with the thought of the parents' devotion for their child and their appeal to God through his human representative to save it, was gradually modified in course of transmission. The story was utilized to explain how the prophetism which had put Jeroboam on the throne expressed, even in his lifetime, its abhorrence of his religious program and predicted the ultimate overthrow of his dynasty. Thus did posterity, under the influence of changed ideals, pass an adverse judgment upon the policy of Israel's first king —that courageous soul who, even in Solomon's reign, had dared to withstand the tyrant's iron hand, and who appears, in point of fact, to have devoted himself throughout his reign to what at the time seemed to be the best interests of his subjects. Thus too in Christian times have good and courageous leaders of past generations been too hardly criticized and too hastily condemned by a subsequent generation which, because of its own changed ideals, has failed to see the past in its true proportions.

Chapters 14^{21} to 15^{24}: The History of the Judæan Kingdom

21–31. Rehoboam, the First King (937–920 B.C.). See 2 Chr. 10–12. The purpose of Shishak (960–950 B.C., first king of the Bubastide, the 22d Egyptian dynasty) in invading Judah is obscure. It may have been either (1) an attempt to reimpose the old Egyptian yoke upon Palestine and in particular upon the Hebrews, in which case the brevity of the Judæan historian's reference to the campaign is perfectly natural, since the invasion seems to have been for the moment quite successful;

or (2) an attempt to assist Jeroboam, as a protégé of Egypt (11[40]), by attacking the Davidic kingdom. The inclusion, however, of *Israelite*, in addition to Judæan towns, in the Pharaoh's own list of cities taken by him seems to militate against this latter hypothesis. The list is to be found on the southern wall of the great temple at Karnak.

CHAPTER XV

1–8. Abijam, the Second King (920–917 B.C.). See 2 Chr. 13.

9–24. Asa, the Third King (917–876 B.C.). See 2 Chr. 14–16. The Compiler found in Asa a man after his own heart—an iconoclastic reformer. Of his activities in this and other matters and of their religious significance for later generations we read still more in Second Chronicles. *Asherah* (v. 13), if used here to denote a goddess, means an image of Astarte (cf. note to 11[1-43] 16[32]). Against its use here in its ordinary sense of sacred tree or pole is the fact that prior to the Deuteronomic reformation (2 Kings 23) such trees or poles were more or less legitimate at the sanctuaries of Jehovah. Asa's diplomacy met the need of the moment (vv. 16–21), but had bad consequences: (1) His gift would be interpreted by Syria as an acknowledgment of Syria's overlordship of Judah; (2) an immediate loss of Northern territory ensued; and (3) the energetic Benhadad I, strong enough to defy the Assyrian king, Shalmaneser III, was encouraged to pursue his policy of interference in Palestinian politics to the future detriment of both kingdoms.

CHAPTERS 15[25] TO 22[40]: THE HISTORY OF THE NORTHERN KINGDOM (see 14[20])

The Compiler here interrupts the account of the history of Judah, and resumes from 14[20] the history of Israel, or the Northern Kingdom. He resumes the history of Judah at 22[41]. This alternation of the two histories continues to 2 Kings 17.

25–32. Nadab, the Second King (915–914 B.C.). Note (1) the recurrence of Israelite-Philistine hostilities, and (2) the description of the first dynastic change in the Northern Kingdom.

33, 34. Baasha, the Third King (914–900 B.C.). See also 16[1-7]. It would appear that just as Jeroboam owed his rise to the intervention of the prophets, and just as his dynasty was abruptly cut off through their activities, so Baasha owed his throne to them, but his policy was regarded by them as equally unsatisfactory and they determined as soon as possible to terminate his dynasty. The speech put into Jehu's mouth was, however, a free composition of the Compiler's, and 16[7] was a reflection of later days upon the fulfillment of the predictive element in prophecy.

CHAPTER XVI

1–7. See note on 15[33, 34].

8–14. Elah, the Fourth King (900–899 B.C.). With his death the dynasty of Baasha became extinct. The king would more profitably have been with the army, not at his capital; perhaps this was the cause of the army's discontent, which reached its climax in his assassination. Arza need not necessarily have been cognizant of the plot.

15–22. Zimri, the Fifth King (899 B.C.). Zimri's seven days' reign was ended by his suicide, but this by no means meant peace for the Northern Kingdom. Tibni held his own against Omri for four years (see vv. 15 and 23); it was not until Tibni and his brother Joram (so LXX in v. 22) were dead that Omri could feel secure on his throne.

23–28. Omri, the Sixth King (899–875). The Compiler rightly appreciated the importance of, and therefore recorded, Omri's founding of Samaria (on the west side of Mount Ephraim and at the head of the chief pass to the Mediterranean) and its use henceforth as the capital. Had he set out to write an ordinary instead of a religious history of his nation's past, he should have detailed the following important features of Omri's rōle in Israel's history: (1) The fame of Omri became widespread. From the reign of Shalmaneser III (854 B.C.) to that of Sargon (720 B.C.) the Northern Kingdom was alluded to on Assyrian inscriptions as "the land of Omri," or "the land of the house of Omri," and Jehu, although the founder of a new dynasty, was styled by the Assyrians, "son of Omri." (2) The only weakness of Omri's new dynasty, which endured for a half a century, was its blindness to the religious and conservative instincts of its subjects. (3) In addition to the partially successful wars against Syria referred to by the Compiler (20[1-34] 22[1-36]), Israelite overlordship of Moab was capably asserted, a fact recorded by Mesha, king of Moab, on the Moabite Stone. (4) The statesmanship of Omri and his dynasty is well illustrated by the treaty with Tyre (aimed at the hegemony of Syria) cemented by the marriage of his son Ahab with the Tyrian princess Jezebel, the alliance with Judah cemented by the marriage of Athaliah with Jehoram (see 2 Kings 8[18]), and the defensive alliance with Syria against Assyria (see 20[34]).

CHAPTERS 16[29] TO 22[40]: AHAB AND ELIJAH

29–34. Ahab, the Seventh King (875–853 B.C.). The policy of alliance with Tyre now began to bear its natural fruit. Doubtless it assisted Israel in maintaining something of its political independence of Syria. But it threatened Israel's religious independence and provoked a religious situation of which Omri had not dreamed and which was destined ultimately to lead to the extinction of his dynasty. Marriage alliance with the king of powerful Phœnicia could not be easily bought or lightly treated. Moreover, the Tyrian princess was a woman of character and determination, and, judged by the standards of her own nation, deeply religious. Jezebel was the daughter of *Ittobaal* (="Baal is with him"), king of Tyre (887–876 B.C.), who was therefore interested in Melkart, the chief male deity of Phœnicia, but had been (before he succeeded, according to Josephus, the usurper Phelles) a priest of Astarte. Ahab consequently established not only a temple of Melkart at Samaria but also one of Astarte (*Asherah* in v. 33, probably here used in this sense; see note to 15[13] and cf. note to 11[1-43]). These indications of royal favor for cults other than those of the purer forms of the worship of Jehovah naturally influenced popular feeling. The continuance of old superstitions, the recrudescence of Canaanitish Baalism, and, worst of all, the still more rapid fusion than heretofore of Canaanitish Baalism and popular forms of Jehovah religion, were all encouraged. For instance, the refounding of Jericho was marked by the old Canaanite custom (revealed by excavations at Gezer, Taanach, etc.) of immolating children at the foundation of a new city (v. 34). Unfortunately, the Compiler is silent as to what were the exact relative proportions of Canaanite Baalism, popular Jehovah religion, and new Tyrian elements which contributed to the composition of the religious party or parties now opposing themselves to the higher and purer forms of Jehovah worship. Whether or not the policy of the court and popular feeling favored Canaanite Baalism or a fused Jehovah-Baal religion or the Tyrian religion, they were moving definitely toward the position that, though, on the one hand, Jehovah was war God, the control of nature, on the other hand, including the bestowal of her gifts, and the increase of human, animal, and vegetable life, was vested in gods other than Jehovah. The ethical and moral claims of Jehovah were put on one side and forgotten.

CHAPTER XVII

Elijah Opposes Ahab's Innovations in Religion. In striking contrast to all this are Elijah's own religious position and message as revealed in the "Acts of Elijah" (i.e., chs. 17–19, 21), which undoubtedly contain a general substratum of historical facts though written to glorify the life-work of that hero and to incorporate the outstanding points of his teaching as this was understood by his disciples during the next two or three generations. Elijah proclaims that *Jehovah*, not Canaanite or Tyrian Baals, is the sole director of nature, the sole bestower and withholder of nature's gifts in Palestine (v. 1), a truth demonstrated by the story of Elijah's own experience in being fed by the ravens (vv. 2–7). Moreover, Jehovah is shown to be also the bestower of nature's gifts to *non-Israelite* dwellers in Palestine (vv. 8–16), and the sole and effective renewer of human life (vv. 17–24).

CHAPTER XVIII

The Trial of Creeds on Mount Carmel. Jehovah, for his part, proves himself a God able to nerve his prophet to defy the human king and call for a trial of creeds (vv. 1–19). This trial takes place on Mount Carmel (vv. 20–40). On an ancient altar of Jehovah (an apt symbol of Jehovah's ancient worship and former recognition as sole God in Palestine) descends the fire from heaven. It vindicated Elijah's mockery of the ineffective ritual, ceremonial, and gods of his opponents, and also his own faith in Jehovah as nature's God, alike as an earth deity and as a sky-god (the fire *from heaven*)—but it did *not* demonstrate either the *absolute* transcendence of Jehovah or his sole creatorship and direction of the *universe*. These latter issues were not in dispute, being beyond the ken both of his opponents and of Elijah himself. In vv. 41–45a Elijah is the herald of Jehovah in his capacity as the raingiver, the function of a sky deity. But he is still an *ecstatic* prophet, not without external affinities with the "sons of the prophets" of Saul's day (vv. 45b, 46). See note to 1 Sam. 9[1]–11[15].

CHAPTER XIX

1–21. Elijah's Flight: His Encouragement by Jehovah. Elijah is also a *true* prophet, and therefore hated by the arch-enemy of Jehovah (vv. 1, 2). In his flight he goes first to the ancient sanctuary of Beersheba (vv. 3–7), which was beloved of Northern tradition (see Gen. 21[31f.] 26[23]), and a favorite sanctuary of Northerners even in later times (see Amos 5[5] 8[14]). Finding no spiritual comfort here, he wanders into the adjacent "wilderness," where he receives *physical* succor from "an angel" from Jehovah. In search of Jehovah he visits Horeb (vv. 8–18), the scene of Jehovah's self-revelation to Moses and of his first covenant with the Hebrews.

In what did the revelation here made to Elijah consist? Many answers have been given to this question. No one by itself seems to exhaust the full potential significance of the passage as a whole. Jehovah's absence from the most potent forces of nature may have been meant as a warning to Elijah not to identify Jehovah too exclusively with these natural phenomena, as being only transient vehicles, not the essentials, of his self-revelation to Moses of old or to Elijah himself on Mount Carmel and at this moment. The *still small voice* (or, better, *the sound of a light whisper*) may have been intended to guide Elijah to higher and purer planes of prophetic intuition than those to which he had so far risen through his previous observation of the external phenomena of nature and its message. It may be, on the other hand, that the "whisper" was that of the desert waste. In this case its message was to communicate to Elijah that only after Israel's present social structure had crashed like the thunder and Canaanite civilization had passed away like the lightning, would Israel find Jehovah in a return to the silence and the simplicity of the desert. In this latter interpretation the "whisper" is itself the message. Elijah has received the call to be a revolutionary, an enemy of ordered society to an extent to which even he had not hitherto condemned it. No truth as to God himself, no comfort for Elijah's own soul, no constructive spiritual message was thus revealed to him: he was to become merely an exponent of "the eschatology of woe" and to preach that only *after it* and *through it*, if at all, was "a good time coming." If this interpretation is adopted, the narrative must be regarded as composite.

19–21. This seems to be a fragment of another tradition in which Elijah's revolutionary program was aimed only at the dynasty of Omri and not at civilization in general. It was to be worked out by political means (the Syrian wars and the new dynasty of Jehu) and by the commissioning of a successor, not by a catastrophic upheaval of society, nor by Elijah's own "whirlwind" methods. (See N. Micklem, *Prophecy and Eschatology*, pp. 83–104.)

CHAPTER XX

This chapter (see also 22[1f.]) interrupts the story of Elijah. Telling of certain aspects of Ahab's reign from an entirely different angle from that adopted in the preceding chapters, it is a valuable corrective of them. In chs. 17–19 Elijah was the hero, Jezebel the arch enemy and Ahab her weak tool, and the theme was Elijah's stand for the higher religion of Jehovah against those who, including Ahab and Jezebel, sought its eclipse or abolition. In ch. 20 (and again in ch. 22) Jezebel recedes entirely into the background, Ahab is the hero, courageous and capable.

1–12. **Ahab's Courageous Resistance to Benhadad.** Ahab, with much courage, resists Benhadad's demands for an increased tribute of money and a human freight of Israelites to serve as his soldiers and slaves. The cause of Syria's hostility to Israel at this moment is not clear. If, as we gather from v. 34, Omri's wars with Benhadad I had turned out disastrous for Israel, and if territory had therefore been ceded to Syria, the present campaign may have been intended to drive home on Ahab a full consciousness of those unfortunate facts. Possibly Benhadad's purpose was only to extort auxiliary troops from Ahab for his campaign against Assyria which culminated disastrously for Syria in the battle of Karkar (854 B.C.), though the triumph of Assyria was by no means decisive. The Assyrian account of the battle asserts that contingents were furnished by Ahab of Israel, Benhadad of Syria, the kings of Hamath, etc. It has, however, been supposed that at the time of this siege of Samaria, Benhadad had already been defeated at Karkar, and was now calling on Ahab for fresh assistance; Ahab, grasping the opportunity afforded him by Syria's weakness consequent on its defeat at Karkar, decided to refuse Benhadad's demand and to throw off the Syrian yoke—hence Benhadad's present campaign.

13–34. **Benhadad's Defeat; Ahab's Magnanimity.** It is because Ahab, though insolent in his attitude toward Elijah, implicitly obeys the message of a "prophet" that he succeeds in warding off the Syrian attack. In the estimation of the Syrians, Jehovah was so closely connected with Ahab's success that they, knowing him to be a God of mountain heights, decided to open the following year's campaign in the plains, over which, they thought, he had no control, and fixed on Aphek (see 1 Sam. 29[1]). On the other hand, in the thought of the writer, Ahab was so closely identified with the cause of Jehovah and Jehovah's people that "a man of God" revealed the Syrian plan to Ahab; as a result he was again successful. On Benhadad's abject surrender Ahab, in striking contrast to his treatment of Elijah, is represented as magnanimous in his sparing of the Syrian's life, contenting himself with the return to Israel of its lost trans-Jordanic territory, and the right to trading facilities in Damascus equal to those previously enjoyed in Samaria by Syria, terms which, though seemingly magnanimous, represent a victory of which Israel had every reason to be proud.

35–43. **Ahab Rebuked.** Note here, as in ch. 13, (a) the same blind obedience to a divine behest is demanded (v. 35), (b) disobedience is summarily punished by death (v. 36), (c) a lion is again the agent. In it an exilic redactor urges that the terms were scandalously mild, and appears to argue that this was the parting of the ways for Ahab: henceforth *the sons of the prophets* and Ahab took opposite paths (cf. however, ch. 22).

CHAPTER XXI

The Story of Elijah Resumed; Naboth's Vineyard. The Compiler, by making further extracts from "The Acts of Elijah," withdraws our attention momentarily from Ahab's military achievements and fixes it on the social and economic conditions of Israel. We have here the beginnings of the transition from small peasant ownership to that of large estates, from the privileges of the status of freemen achieved for the Israelites by Jeroboam I to the ills of a practical serfdom under large and wealthy landowners careless of the conditions of the newly made poor. All this came to a head in the prosperous reign of Jeroboam II (see Amos' denunciations of it) just as a similar economic crisis occurred in Judah in the prosperous years which preceded the Assyrian domination (see Micah's and Isaiah's descriptions).

The present narrative, however, shows very clearly that the economic revolution in the North was really a slow process, beginning in the prosperity which followed Ahab's alliance with Tyre and defeat of Syria. At the outset it was made possible, just as its climax was afterward assisted, by Assyrian pressure on Syria's other frontier. But more important even than the light thus thrown on the economic and social changes in Ahab's reign, is that thrown on the evolution of Elijah's gospel. The scene on Mount Carmel had demonstrated that Jehovah was *the* God in Israel; that on Horeb (if taken as a whole) that Jehovah speaks to the individual conscience if only in the whispers of the desert; the story of Naboth presupposes a God who is ethical and moral in his own attributes, demanding ethical and moral ideals and conduct in his worshipers, and yet extending his loving compassion even to Ahab when at last repentant (vv. 27–29). It thus reveals yet one more way in which Elijah did his part to keep alive and hand on to posterity that spark of the ethical and moral revealed to Moses centuries before on Mount Horeb, destined to shine more brightly and clearly in the writings of the eighth century prophets, and reflected in the Deuteronomic Law book of Josiah's reign (of the ideals of which the Compiler of Kings was an exponent) till at last when "Elijah redivivus" had come, in the person of John the Baptist, the Deity in all the fullness of his moral qualities, and not least that of Love, became himself incarnate.

CHAPTER XXII

1–40. Ahab and Judah; His Death at Ramoth-gilead. In ch. 22 the scene again changes. We are back in the general atmosphere of ch. 20, but important developments have come about during the three intervening years. Ahab's influence extends to Judah, whose king is now his subservient ally. So subservient indeed is he, that, though shocked at Ahab's thoughtless omission to consult the prophets and doubtful as to their credibility when they are consulted, he accompanies Ahab on this new and, for Ahab, fatal campaign. He even endangered his own life to carry out his share in Ahab's counter-plans to the Syrian plot to assassinate him. But the religious interest of the story is centered in Micaiah the son of Imlah. He gives hints of great value as to (a) the inspiration of false prophecy and true prophecy, both of which he attributes to the direct action of God; vv. 19–23 show how inadequate was the conception of the character of Jehovah during the pre-prophetic period, and how much we owe to the prophets of the eighth century for placing the ethical quality at the heart of the God concept; (b) the employment of symbolic actions by prophets of this period, a usage not indulged in by Micaiah himself but reappearing in Isaiah (Isa. 20) and especially in Ezekiel (e.g., Ezek. 4, 5, etc.; cf. also Jer. 28[10]); (c) the nature of God and of his heavenly court; his attendants are "spirits," a conception in its origins dating back to animistic times but in its results leading to the doctrine that God himself is Spirit (cf. Isa. 31[3] Jn. 4[23]).

CHAPTER 22[41-50]: THE HISTORY OF THE JUDÆAN KINGDOM (see 15[24])

41–50. Jehoshaphat, the Fourth King (876–851 B.C.). See 2 Chr. 17–20, in which are imbedded a considerable number of historical facts supplementary to this brief account of Jehoshaphat's suppression of vice, relations with Edom, and abortive mercantile expedition to Ophir. For vv. 47, 48 read *Now there was no king in Edom; and the deputy of king Jehoshaphat* (i.e., in Edom) *made a ship, etc.*

1 KINGS 22[51] TO 2 KINGS 8[15]: THE HISTORY OF THE NORTHERN KINGDOM (see 22[40])

51–53. See 2 Kings 1[1-18]. There is no good reason for the chapter break after 22[53] or the break between 1 Kings and 2 Kings at the same point.

SECOND KINGS

CHAPTER I

1–18. Ahaziah, the Eighth King (853–852 B.C.). See 1 Kings 22^{51-53}. In vv. 2–17a Elijah makes his reappearance. The picture in vv. 2–4 resembles that of Elijah in 1 Kings 17^{1}–19, 21. As there, so here, he appears suddenly; and as quickly he vanishes. He is here, as there, alike the prophet of doom to the royal house and the zealous proclaimer of Jehovah as the only true God in Israel, the only effective bestower of human life, and therefore the only one who may at will deprive a human being of his life. Vv. 5–18, however, seem to portray an Elijah of a very different type from the hero of vv. 2–4; moreover, the restraint in the use of miraculous power which is so marked a feature in the latter is conspicuously lacking here. The story—which has marked affinities with 1 Sam. $19^{18f.}$ and 1 Kings 13—was clearly intended to inculcate respect for the prophet and his office (see especially v. 13 and cf. $2^{23f.}$). It may have been inserted by the second redactor.

16. *Baalzebub* may mean either *baal* (i.e., *lord*) *of flies*, or *Zebub is Baal*. If such a place-name is rightly read on one of the Tel-el-Amarna tablets, the latter interpretation is correct and the reference is to the deity of a popular local shrine.

CHAPTER II

1–14. Elisha's Preparation for His Ministry. This chapter—unquestionably a unity—forms the introduction to the ministry of Elisha rather than the conclusion to the biography of Elijah. (1) The situation is quite different from that found in the Elijah narrative (1 Kings 17^{1}–19, 21). In the latter Elijah has no definite abode; he appears and disappears with lightninglike rapidity; here Elijah and Elisha live together at Gilgal. There Elijah is a "man of God" standing absolutely alone; here he is a teacher surrounded by numerous disciples. In 1 Kings 19^{19-21} Elisha is already invested with Elijah's mantle and is recognized as his successor; here even Elijah does not know who will carry on his work. (2) The situation is entirely in harmony with that found in the stories concerning Elisha and with the representation of life within the prophetic guilds as it is there described. (3)The contents of vv. 19–25 form a correct sequel to vv. 1–18—an impossibility if the latter belonged to the Elijah, rather than to the Elisha, biography. The story is rich in the ideas of early times and in the way of expressing those ideas then current—the prophetic mantle with its magic powers, the whirlwind as the symbol of Jehovah's presence, the translation of an outstanding saint to heaven. The purpose of this last feature (cf. Tobit $12^{20, 21}$ Lk. 24^{51} Acts 1^{9-11}) is to conduct him from this world to the heavenly one without his going by way of the grave or Sheol, the place of the departed. At the time at which this figure of speech arose death betokened the *end*, not, as with us, the consummation of communion with God. *Then* it was supposed that after death a man, instead of enjoying the beatific vision, ceased more or less entirely even to exist. (See art., *The Religion of Israel*, p. 173.) Unless Elisha beheld the actual translation of Elijah he could not hope to receive his spirit, for only to the preeminently spiritual was such a vision possible (cf. 6^{17} and 1 Cor. $2^{14f.}$).

15–25. The First Prophetic Acts of Elisha. The fifty members of the prophetic guilds, who were watching intently, did not see it, and consequently they doubted Elisha's word (vv. 16, 17) even though they had themselves seen Elisha's miraculous power exercised by means of the mantle of Elijah. Jehovah's power (vv. 19–22) is demonstrated over inanimate nature, and in vv. 23–25 his care for the well-being and dignity of his prophet is emphasized, though again the God concept reflected in the narrative reflects a rather crude stage in the religious and ethical development. For the reproach attached to baldness see Isa. 3^{17-24}. Here, however, the specific reference is to the tonsure of the strict prophets of Jehovah (cf. 1 Kings 20^{41}); they would be most unpopular in places such as Bethel and Samaria, which depended so much on the royal favor. The extracts from the "Acts of Elisha" are continued in 3^{4}–8^{15} 13^{14-21}.

CHAPTERS 3^{1} TO 8^{15}: THE REIGN OF JEHORAM

CHAPTER III

This Jehoram (called Joram in 8^{16}), son of Ahab and king of the northern tribes, must be distinguished from Jehoram, son of Jehoshaphat and king of Judah (see 8^{16-24}). The significance of this present section, however, is not so much in anything we are told about Jehoram, as in the fact that it records so many stories about Elisha.

1–3. Jehoram, the Ninth King (852–842 B.C.). If any real reformation was attempted, it must have been on a very small scale, for Jezebel was still alive and Jehu's sweeping reformation took place later ($10^{18f.}$). On 3^{2} see 1 Kings 16^{32}.

4–27. The Revolt of Mesha, King of Moab; His Defeat. Mesha had already erected the famous inscription (discovered at Diban in 1868; cf. p. 117b) to commemorate his expulsion of the Israelites from Moabite territory. He had now to withstand a fresh attempt to reimpose the Israelitish overlordship. Mesha, fearing an attack on the north, had thoroughly fortified the border cities (as stated in his inscription), and therefore Jehoram decided to march round the southern extremity of the Dead Sea and begin his campaign from the south. As the ruler of Edom (there was no *king* of Edom at that time, cf. 1 Kings 22[47f.] and 2 Kings 8[20]) was the vassal of Jehoshaphat, he would be compelled to allow the allied armies to pass through his territory. As for Judah, it was still under the suzerainty of the Northern Kingdom (cf. 1 Kings 22[4]), and Jehoshaphat was therefore compelled to furnish auxiliaries.

But important as is this story for the purposes of the historian, it is still more interesting to the student of Israel's religion. In connection, e.g., with prophetism it is noteworthy that Jehoram's relations with Elisha were considerably more strained than were those of Ahab with the true prophets of Jehovah (see 1 Kings 22). Elisha, moreover, seems to have retained the outward characteristics of the earlier ecstatic prophets to a greater extent than the more spiritually minded Elijah (cf. note on 1 Kings 18[45b, 46]). He was also intimately connected with the prophetic guilds, of which he was the head, but with whom Elijah had no dealings. Further, v. 27, the ideas of God presupposed by the Hebrew historian are important. In the days of Omri and Ahab Chemosh had "been angry with his servants" and had "afflicted Moab many years" (see Mesha's inscription). Mesha now attributes the temporary success of the Hebrews to the same cause and does his utmost to avert the wrath of his god by sacrificing his eldest son. The words *and there was great wrath against Israel* are important as showing the henotheistic (see p. 166) point of view of the author of this old story. He probably expressed himself in still clearer terms, which a later editor for theological reasons has modified. But even as it now stands, the sentence means that in the estimation of this Hebrew writer Chemosh turned his wrath from Moab, his own people, to Jehovah's people who had dared to enter the territory of the Moabite deity.

CHAPTER IV

Four Stories of Elisha's Power. Vv. 1–7 teach the same lesson as 1 Kings 17[8-16], and vv. 8–37 the same as 1 Kings 17[17-24]. Vv. 38–41 are, however, on a lower plane, somewhat crudely relating Elisha's power over the death in the pot. The miracle of the feeding of the multitude, vv. 42–44, on the other hand, is important, being a remarkable anticipation of that recorded in all four Gospels.

CHAPTER V

1–19. The Recovery of Naaman the Leper. This story is the masterpiece, both literary and religious, among these biographical sketches of Elisha. At this time the Northern Kingdom was the vassal of Syria, as the peremptory tone of the Syrian monarch's letter shows (vv. 5f.), and the Israelitish king interpreted the extraordinary message as a pretext to break an existing peace (cf. 1 Kings 20[7]). The only hostilities had been those of freebooters and marauding bands which harassed the borders of Israel; and it must have been during one of these raids that the Hebrew maid was captured. Vv. 17–19 are theologically of great importance, for not only do they show Naaman's religious point of view but also that of Elisha and of the Hebrews generally. Elisha does not dissent from the proposal made by the Syrian general, but at once acquiesces in it. We may infer therefore (1) that it was taken for granted that Jehovah was God of Israel, and of Israel only, and could only be worshiped on the *soil of Israel*—hence Naaman's request; (2) that other national gods, as real as Jehovah, existed, each of whom was the rightful god of his own nation and had certain territory upon which alone he could be worshiped; (3) that signal acts of deliverance at times brought home to individuals the wonderful powers possessed by some one god, who was therefore particularly extolled. Several other passages show, like this one, that, in the period prior to the reign of Josiah, the Hebrews' ideas of Jehovah were henotheistic, i.e., he was accepted as the God of Israel but not of other nations, e.g., Ex. 15[1-11] Judg. 11[23f.] Ruth 1[16] 2[12] 1 Sam. 26[19] 2 Kings 3[26f.] Amos 5[14] Hosea 9[3].

20–27. Avarice of Gehazi. These verses narrate the avarice of Gehazi, Elisha's servant, and his punishment. The ethical implications of the story should not be overlooked. Gehazi sought to obtain personal profit from a kindly deed done by another. He seems to have convinced himself that this was proper, but Elisha had a deeper insight into right conduct. Sophistry can never endure a close examination.

CHAPTER VI

1–23. The Lost Axe; the Syrians Smitten with Blindness. From the high level of the last story we drop back to the type which immediately preceded it. Elisha is again living in the community life of the prophetic guilds (vv 1–7). The story of Elisha's miraculous knowledge of Syrian military secrets in vv. 8–23 somewhat resembles 1 Kings 20[22-24], only here the religious significance of the story appears to be the primary object of the narrative—faith and hope unfalteringly growing the stronger the darker the situation becomes and communicating themselves to others previously possessed by coward fear: "Lord, open his eyes that he may see." In this critical moment Elisha indeed proved himself worthy of having seen Elijah's passing and of succeeding him. The vision of those horses and that chariot had remained vivid in his memory; hence he could pray that it might be revealed to whom he would. It is idle to endeavor to find a definite historical setting for these events. V. 23 shows that Israel is harassed by the inroads of small "bands" of marauders, not by the regular Syrian army. Neither king is mentioned by name, but the Israelite monarch is one with whom Elisha is on friendly terms (v. 21).

24–33. Famine in Samaria; Elisha is Threatened. Here and in 7[1-20] is recounted Elisha's triumphant emergence from another and more serious siege, this time not at Dothan but in Samaria. The background of famine is similar to that of 1 Kings 17. The mention of Benhadad does not fix a definite date for the siege. If there had been *only one* and not *three* kings of this name, the dating of the siege might be simpler. But the fact that history and tradition are inextricably woven together in these accounts makes it well-nigh impossible to say definitely in which reign the siege took place (see note on 5[5f.]). From the words *son of a murderer* (v. 32) it has been inferred (1) that the king must be Jehoahaz, the son of Jehu; but the prophet who had anointed Jehu for a special purpose would scarcely have branded him as a murderer for accomplishing his appointed task; and (2) that Joram (cf. 3[1] 8[16]) is the king referred to, for Elisha's taunt would well suit a son of Ahab, who had persecuted and slain the prophets. But the expression must be taken in its usual Oriental sense. The person actually addressed is the "murderer," not his father, for the Oriental defames his opponent's parent in order to make the defamation of that opponent's character the more complete (cf. 1 Sam. 20[30] Isa. 57[3]). Therefore no conclusion can be drawn from this phrase as to the monarch referred to.

CHAPTER VII

1–20. Elisha Predicts Plenty; the Syrians Flee. Elisha had doubtless advised the Israelites to offer a stout resistance to the Syrians when they appeared outside Samaria, and so he might be held morally responsible for the non-surrender of the city. But his promise (v. 2) that the *windows in heaven* should be opened, i.e., rain descend, shows that Elisha was chiefly blamed for the drought which had increased the horrors of the siege (cf. 8[1f.]). The Syrians could never have supposed (v. 6) that an alliance would be formed between the Hittites on the north and the Egyptians on the south of Palestine. Instead of *Egypt* (*Misraim*) should be read *Muṣri* (for this see note to 1 Kings 10[20]) as the ally of the Hittites. A king of Musri was defeated together with Syria and Israel at the battle of Karkar in 854 B.C. A combined attack by two such foes would be sufficient to cause panic among the Syrian forces.

CHAPTER VIII

1–6. Elisha Recovers the Shunammite's Land. This story is intended primarily to illustrate the fame of Elisha and his miracle-working powers. It has no connection with 6[24]–7[20]. Gehazi could not have been admitted to the king's presence (vv. 4, 5) if he was already a leper (5[27]). Hence it seems probable that 8[1-6] formerly stood between 4[8-37] (to which there is a reference in v. 1) and 4[38f.], which presuppose it.

7–15. Benhadad's Death at the Hands of Hazael. Elisha now seems to be well known in Damascus (cf. vv. 2f.). In the original account there was probably a statement that the journey was undertaken at the bidding of Jehovah. Doubtless, too, before the story was curtailed it contained some description of Hazael, who is referred to as a person already well known to the reader. It is remarkable that the command to anoint *both* Hazael *and* Jehu was given to *Elijah*, but that the former is anointed by Elisha and the latter by an unknown prophet.

CHAPTER 8[16-29]: THE HISTORY OF THE JUDÆAN KINGDOM (see 1 Kings 22[50])

16–24. Jehoram, the Fifth King (851–843 B.C.). Cf. 2 Chr. 21. After v. 21a the narrative must have told how Jehoram was surrounded in Zair by the Edomites, and v. 21b then narrated his defeat which is confirmed by v. 22. The people who fled to their tents were evidently the Judæans, and *the captains of the chariots* were Jehoram's own officers. A later writer by a scratch of his pen transformed Jehoram's crushing defeat into a victory. *Libnah* (v. 22) was a fortified and strategically important city (see 19[8]). Its inhabitants were for the most part non-Hebrews and were pro-

Philistine in sympathies. Possibly this revolt was connected with the incursion of Philistines and Arabians narrated in 2 Chr. 21^{16f}.

25–29. Ahaziah, the Sixth King (843–842 B.C.). Cf. 2 Chr. 22$^{1-9}$.

CHAPTERS 9^{1} TO 10^{36}: THE HISTORY OF THE NORTHERN KINGDOM (see 8^{15})

CHAPTER IX

Revolt and Reign of Jehu, the Tenth King (842–815 B.C.). The dynasty of Omri owed its extinction, and that of Jehu its rise, in the first place, to the army, which was probably discontented with the conduct of the war and ready to receive from the religious leaders the slightest hint that the latter would welcome a revolution. In the second place, Elisha, representing the prophets, intervened once more in political matters. He did so because he was exasperated by the low religious standard of Omri's house and was attracted by the apparent keenness of Jehu for conservative religious reform. In the third place, the Rechabites for once intervened in matters of state (see 10$^{15f.}$). These ascetics, by their abstention from wine and withdrawal from contact with civilization (see Jer. 35$^{6, 8, 14}$), represented a protest against the worship of the Baals. The latter were supposed to regulate the processes and gifts of nature, especially the vine and its potent derivative. "Do not drink the wine and you will not have to worship its giver," seems to have been their watchword.

CHAPTER X

Jehu the Oppressor; His Moral Failure. A kingdom, won by usurpation and itself profoundly debased, cannot be turned from its evil ways to good ones by persecution or the inquisitor's lash. Thus, though Jehu exercised the most utter frightfulness toward Jezebel, the arch enemy of Jehovah (9$^{30-37}$), toward the rest of the royal house (vv. 10–14) and toward the worshipers of Baal (vv. 18–28), such persecution failed to stamp out the rival religion. Civil war and the extermination, rather than the pardoning, of a defeated rival's supporters inevitably weaken a state. Jehu's methods, accordingly, played into the hands of Syria (vv. 32–36). After Jehu's cold-blooded murder of the Tyrian princess no help, diplomatic or military, could be expected from Tyre. Jehu was compelled to become the vassal of Shalmaneser III, king of Assyria, about 842 B.C., as the latter king states in one of his inscriptions. But Shalmaneser was no infallible protection against Syria. He twice failed to seize Damascus, and after 839 B.C. Hazael, having completely routed his formidable foe, found himself free to turn his attention to his weaker neighbor, Israel: to this vv. 32, 33 refer.

CHAPTERS 11^{1} TO 12^{21}: THE HISTORY OF THE JUDÆAN KINGDOM (see 8^{29})

CHAPTER XI

Athaliah, the Impious Usurper (842–836 B.C.). Cf. 2 Chr. 23$^{1-21}$. This is the first long narrative of events in the Southern Kingdom incorporated by the Compiler since the close of Solomon's reign. He rightly attached considerable religious importance to Athaliah's attempt to establish her own family, the Omri dynasty, now expelled from the North, upon the Southern throne, and to introduce foreign cults into Jerusalem such as Jezebel, her mother, had succeeded in introducing into the Northern Kingdom. But the Jerusalem priesthood, to its credit, took up Elijah's watchword; the palace guard remained true to the Davidic dynasty; and the populace approved of Athaliah's deposition and murder. The reference in v. 12 to *the testimony*, i.e., the book of the Law, reflects the practice of a period later than the reign of Josiah, before whose time no written lawbook was used in this connection. Ornaments, or more specifically bracelets (2 Sam. 1^{10}), were usually handed to the king; hence one or other of these words should be read here instead of "testimony."

CHAPTER XII

1–3. Joash (Jehoash), the Seventh King (836–796 B.C.). Cf. 2 Chr. 24.

4–16. The Temple Repairs. The narrative here is the more trustworthy because of its frank reference to the remissness alike of people and of priests. It sheds a remarkable light on the conditions which prevailed at this time. The king's power was evidently absolute; the Temple was still essentially the Palace Chapel, and the priests were royal nominees (cf. 16$^{10f.}$).

17–21. Joash Assassinated. Hazael's campaign in southern Palestine followed his attacks on the Northern Kingdom (10^{32} 13^{3}). The ignominy of Joash's method of meeting military invasion by financial payments probably proved too great an insult to the military party at court and led to his assassination.

CHAPTER XIII

THE HISTORY OF THE NORTHERN KINGDOM (see 10^{36})

1–9. Jehoahaz, the Eleventh King (815–798 B.C.). Israel was completely under the power of Syria throughout this reign. See 8^{12} and

Amos 1[3-5] for a graphic description of the devastation wrought by Israel's hereditary foe. *Saviour* (v. 5) does not necessarily refer to any particular person, but picturesquely utilizes language such as that of Judg. 3[9, 15]. The Assyrian kings, who by their attacks drew off the attention of Syria from Israel, and Jeroboam II (cf. 14[27]), who extended the territory of the Northern Kingdom, each performed the part of a "saviour."

10–25. Jehoash, the Twelfth King (798–782 B.C.). This Jehoash is to be distinguished from the Jehoash (Joash) of 12[1]. The tradition preserved in LXX (L), that Hazael had wrested from Jehoahaz Philistine territory extending from the Mediterranean Sea to Aphek is worthy of attention, for the writer evidently placed the campaign recorded in 12[18] in the reign of Jehoahaz. But the tide of Israel's fortune at last began to turn, though not so quickly as the prophets who now supported the king desired. This delay was attributed by Elisha to the king's lack of confidence in God and indecision of character. *Arrows* (v. 15) were frequently used in determining the future (cf. Ezek. 21[21]). The success of Jehoahaz, from the human point of view, was due to (1) the confusion in Syria consequent upon the accession of a new king, (2) Benhadad's own feeble rule, and (3) the energy displayed in extending his dominions westward by the Assyrian king, Ramman-Nirari III, who defeated Mari (identified with Benhadad), king of Damascus, between 806 and 803 B.C., and thus relieved Israel from the pressure of Syria.

CHAPTER XIV

VERSES 1–22: THE HISTORY OF THE JUDÆAN KINGDOM (see 12[21])

1–7. Amaziah, the Eighth King (796–789 B.C.). Cf. 2 Chr. 25. V. 6 marks a development toward the recognition of individual responsibility—a teaching which was not *fully* formulated till Ezekiel's day (Ezek. 18), though, in contradistinction to the barbarous and older practice (see Josh. 7[24] 9[26]) it was enforced in legislation as early as Josiah's Lawbook (Deut. 24[16]). The Compiler's purpose here is to emphasize this enactment. Effective Judæan suzerainty over Edom (v. 7) was certainly brief, since the Assyrian king of the period, Ramman-Nirari III, mentions it as a state tributary to Assyria.

8–22. It was apparently the populace, as opposed to the court, who, in the hour of defeat, failed to appreciate Amaziah's courage and patriotic intentions in attempting to free them from the suzerainty of the North, and on this account they assassinated him (v. 19).

VERSES 23–29: THE HISTORY OF THE NORTHERN KINGDOM (see 13[25])

23–29. Jeroboam II, the Thirteenth King (782–741 B.C.). During Jeroboam's long reign the Northern Kingdom experienced great material and political prosperity. That this prosperity resulted in a most disastrous lowering of the religious and moral tone of society and in economic conditions irksome to the poor is evident from the writings of the contemporary prophets Amos and Hosea. Both prophets throw a most vivid light upon the life, politics, and aspirations of the Northern Kingdom at this time. Jeroboam doubtless deserved praise for grasping the opportunity of enlarging his kingdom, but the conditions were extraordinarily favorable. The Assyrian kings Shalmaneser IV (787–772 B.C.) and Assurdan III (772–754 B.C.) threatened the very existence of Syria, Israel's hereditary foe. Syria, therefore, had no attention to spare for Jeroboam and his encroachments. Assur-Nirari, the next Assyrian king, failed to press home the attack on the Palestinian states, and Syria, for the time being, constituted merely a buffer-state between Assyria and Israel. Only an Amos could see that soon Assyria would swallow up Syria, and that Israel would be the next victim (Amos 6[14]).

CHAPTER XV

VERSES 1–7: THE HISTORY OF THE JUDÆAN KINGDOM (see 14[22])

1–7. Uzziah, the Ninth King (789–740 B.C.). Cf. 2 Chr. 26. Though the Compiler thought it necessary to reproduce only one verse (v. 5) of the Annals, this reign actually represented the high-water mark of national and political prosperity in the Southern Kingdom just as that of Jeroboam II did in the Northern one. See further details embedded in the post-exilic estimate of his achievements in 2 Chr. 26.

VERSES 8–31: THE HISTORY OF THE NORTHERN KINGDOM (see 14[29])

8–31. Zechariah, the Fourteenth King: His Four Usurping Successors. After the murder of Zechariah, the last of Jehu's dynasty, vv. 8–12, the Northern Kingdom entered upon the last phase of its chequered history, falling into the hands of a series of usurpers: *Shallum* (741 B.C.), vv. 13–16; *Menahem* (741–737 B.C.), vv. 17–22; his son *Pekahiah* (737–736 B.C.), vv. 23–26; *Pekah* (736–734 B.C.), vv. 27–31, whose successor was *Hoshea*, Israel's last king (see 17[1-6]). Their rivalries and misgovernment aggravated the moral corruption of the people and the divergent aims of the pro-Assyrian and pro-Egyptian parties in the state.

Hosea in his prophecies paints a vivid picture of these closing years before the final catastrophe, and a study of his book is vital for an appreciation of religious and social conditions during these reigns.

Considerable light is thrown on Israel's international politics by the Assyrian inscriptions. Tiglath-Pileser III states that in 738 B.C. he received tribute from a number of kings, among whom he mentions Rezon of Damascus and Menahem. Like his father, Pekahiah owed his throne to his Assyrian overlord, and remained true to him. Hence he became the victim of the anti-Assyrian patriots led by Pekah. The latter's triumph proved short-lived. He was a patriot with anti-Assyrian leanings and was, accordingly, committed to an anti-Assyrian confederacy with Syria and other Palestinian states. For the causes of the Syro-Ephraimite War, see note on 16^5-9. The revolution which brought his reign to a close would, therefore, have the approval of Tiglath-Pileser, who, in the record of his campaign of 734 B.C., describes how "Pa-ka-ha (Pekah) their king they slew; A-u-si (Hoshea) to reign over them I appointed." (See p. 118a.)

Chapters 15^32 to 16^20: The History of the Judæan Kingdom (see 15^7)

32–38. Jotham, the Tenth King (740–735 B.C.). Cf. 2 Chr. 27^1-9. His period of coregency in his father's reign (see 15^5b) is probably included in the total length ascribed here to his own reign. **35b.** Probably "the gate of Benjamin" (Jer. 20^2).

CHAPTER XVI

1–20. Ahaz, the Eleventh King (735–726 B.C.). Cf. 2 Chr. 28. The religious and political significance of the reign can best be appreciated only if full weight is given to Isaiah and his religious and political program. (For details see the introduction to the commentary on Isaiah in this volume, and the comments on the individual passages mentioned.) His "call" (with its emphasis on the holiness and sovereignty of Jehovah, and, in antithesis, the sinfulness of sin) practically coincided with Ahaz's succession to the throne (Isa. 6); he developed a definite policy in connection with the Syro-Ephraimitish struggle (see Isa. 7^1–9^7 and cf. Isa. 9^8–10^4 5^25-29 17, 18^1-4); he enunciated in this connection his doctrine of the "Remnant" (7^3 *Shear-jashub*, cf. R.V. mg., "a remnant shall return"), the conception of religious faith (7^9b), Immanuel (7^14-16), the esoteric teaching of chosen disciples (8^16). Moreover, much of his teaching in connection with morality and social reforms belongs to this reign (e.g., Isa. 1 in part, 2–4, 5 in part).

5–9. Pekah, king of Israel, and Rezin, or Rezon, king of Syria, formed a coalition against the impending onslaught of the Assyrians and invited the co-operation of the king of Judah. Ahaz, however, refused to join their confederacy. Therefore they endeavored to depose him and give the crown to a creature of their own, a Syrian, known as the "son of Tabeel" (Isa. 7^1, 2, 5, 6). Ahaz, in panic, appealed to Assyria for aid, thus attracting the latter's attention to Judah and at once making it Assyria's vassal. Tiglath-Pileser first advanced against Israel (15^29), and then after a two years' campaign conquered Damascus in 732 B.C.

10–16. The new altar was probably an Assyrian one upon which Tiglath-Pileser had sacrificed at Damascus; Ahaz may have regarded it as responsible for the Assyrian king's victories. **14.** As the text stands it means that the old altar was removed to allow the new one to be set in its place. The LXX, however, gives a better idea of what took place: in order to transfer the sacrificial holiness of the old altar to the new one, the blood of the victim was sprinkled first on the former and then on the latter.

CHAPTER XVII

The History of the Northern Kingdom (see 15^31)

1–6. Hoshea, the Nineteenth and Last Northern King (734–722 B.C.). The record of this reign has been much condensed, and it is difficult to reconstruct the actual course of events; the Assyrian inscriptions give no real assistance. It is possible here only to refer briefly to the most probable hypothesis: Hoshea had been raised to the throne of Israel as a vassal of Assyria by Tiglath-Pileser III (15^30); when, however, the latter was succeeded by Shalmaneser V, Hoshea seized the opportunity to rebel; but no sooner did his suzerain march against him than he hastened to placate him by presenting his customary tribute (17^3). Somewhat later, tempted by the king of Egypt, he again rebelled (v. 4a); this time he was taken prisoner (v. 4b), and Samaria was besieged (v. 5). The chief difficulties in this reconstruction are: (1) The reign of Shalmaneser V (727–722 B.C.) may seem too short to allow of *two* campaigns against Israel, especially since the Assyrian records state definitely that there was *no* foreign campaign in 726 B.C. (2) It looks as if Hoshea were taken prisoner, and presumably dethroned, three years before the fall of Samaria, though it is stated that Samaria fell in the "ninth" year of Hoshea. **4.** *So* is called *Shab'i* in Assyrian inscriptions and is usually identified with the Pharaoh Sabako or Shabako. Some Assyriologists, however, equate *Shab'i* either with the king of a small district east of the Delta, or with the commander-in-chief of the North Arabian kingdom of Muzri. **6.** Shalmaneser having died during the siege, it was Sargon, a usurper, who finally captured Samaria in 722 B.C. His inscription reads: "Samaria I besieged and conquered: 27,290 of its inhabitants I carried into captivity, fifty chariots I seized from them; the rest of them I allowed to retain their possessions (?); I set my officers over them; the tribute of the former king I laid upon them."

7–41. Causes and Results of Israel's Downfall. These verses contain reflections by the Compiler and by later editors of Kings on the causes and effects—chiefly of a religious nature—of the downfall of the Northern Kingdom. Special attention is given to the settlement of foreigners in Samaria and the resulting mixture in population and religion (vv. 24–41).

CHAPTERS 18[1] TO 25[30]: THE HISTORY OF THE JUDÆAN KINGDOM (see 16[20])

The Reign of Hezekiah, the Twelfth King (726–697 B.C.), is the subject of chs. 18–20. Cf. 2 Chr. 29–32. Chs. 18[13]–20[19] are practically identical with Isa. 36–39, though not without certain variations. On the whole, our text is preferable to that of Isaiah, which has a tendency (1) to suffer abbreviation, e.g., Isa. 36[2], (2) to suffer displacements in order, e.g., in Isa. 38[21f.], and (3) to include interpolations, e.g., Hezekiah's Song (Isa. 38[10-20]). Much of Isaiah's public activity belonged to this reign, and many of his prophecies (see Isa. 10[5]–11[9], 18, 19 in part, 20, 21, 28[7]–32) throw considerable light upon its political and religious problems.

CHAPTER XVIII

1–8. Hezekiah's Reforms and Good Reign. For the *serpent* (v. 4) cf. Num. 21[6f]. On Assyrian reliefs there are several representations of serpent worship and here (cf. "the stone of Zoheleth," i.e., of the serpent, in 1 Kings 1[9]) we have an illustration of its persistence among the Hebrews. It is difficult to define the extent and exact purpose of Hezekiah's reformation. It has been held, on the one hand, that it was confined to the Asherah and serpent of this verse, and that any destruction of high-places and altars which took place during Hezekiah's reign was not due to his initiative (see v. 22), but was the result of the ravages of war. The Chronicler, on the other hand, relates at great length a "thorough, godly reformation" carried out at the king's instigation. Josiah's Deuteronomic reformation does not preclude an earlier attempt at reformation; rather, it must have had its origin in part in some slight measure of reform such as that inaugurated by Hezekiah under the influence of the iconoclastic teaching of Isaiah (cf. Buchanan Gray, *Numbers*, p. 274). V. 8 is probably to be dated in the latter part of the reign.

9–12. Fall of Samaria. See on 17[1-6].

13–37. Sennacherib's Threat Against Hezekiah. When Sennacherib succeeded Sargon (705 B.C.) many tributaries of Assyria tried to regain their independence. Among them was Hezekiah, who, relying upon the help of Egypt and the support of certain Philistine cities, prepared to throw off the Assyrian yoke. In 701 B.C. a general revolt broke out in Palestine. Sennacherib acted promptly and effectively. He marched against Phœnicia, captured the chief cities and drove Elulai, king of Tyre, into exile in Cyprus. Therefore several princes hastened to make submission and to pay tribute, but the Philistine cities and Judah still defied the invader. A body of allied forces came to their help, but they suffered a decisive defeat at Altaku or Eltekeh (a village east of Ekron). Askelon, Ekron, Timnath, were captured in swift succession; Judah was invaded, one hundred and forty-six cities were taken, a number of persons deported, and Jerusalem itself was besieged. Hezekiah submitted and paid a heavy tribute. The Assyrian forces, however, which were advancing toward Pelusium, met with a sudden disaster, the nature of which can only be surmised, and Sennacherib returned home without having taken Jerusalem (see 19[35]).

Practically all scholars are agreed that chs. 18[17]–19[37] are excerpts from a biography or "Acts" of Isaiah. Nearly all moderns also hold that 18[17]–19[37] may be resolved in two narratives, i.e., 18[17]–19[8] (or v. 9a) and 19[9-37] (or 19[9b-35]; vv. 36 and 37 being variously assigned to one or the other of these), and that both those narratives are concerned with the operations conducted by Sennacherib after the battle of Eltekeh during his campaign of 701 B.C. which the Compiler has already summarized (from the Judæan Annals) in 18[13-15]. Neither in the extract from the first nor in that from the second narrative do we hear anything of the tribute recorded in 18[13-16] and also in Sennacherib's inscription (see p. 118).

CHAPTER XIX

1–36. Hezekiah's Prayer and His Deliverance. Sennacherib's own inscription would suggest that the *tidings* of v. 7 was connected not with the movements of Tirhakah (cf. note to v. 9) but with the revolt of Shuzub, a Chaldæan prince. The Assyrian king certainly returned to the North to begin his "fourth campaign" (701–700 B.C.) against Shuzub in the swamps of the land of *Bet-Jakin* (Prism Inscription, col. iii, 42f.). The mention (v. 9) of Tirhakah (Assyrian *Tarku*) is difficult. He did not come to the front until 690 B.C. at the earliest. The Ethiopian tyrant of Egypt in 701 B.C. was Shabako.

35. For *the angel of the Lord* see note to 2 Sam. 24[15f]. In Herodotus ii, 141, the Assyrian calamity is ascribed to field mice which gnawed the Assyrians' bow-strings (for mice as symbols of pestilence cf. 1 Sam. 6[4f.]); at Ptah a stone statue of an Egyptian king holding a mouse in his hand is said to have commemorated this event (see also intro. to Isaiah).

37. **Death of Sennacherib.** Sennacherib's death did not take place till 681 B.C., twenty years after the deliverance of Jerusalem. Sharezer's share in the murder is not mentioned elsewhere. The Babylonian Chronicle, col. iii, 34, 35, reads: "In the month Tebet, the twentieth day, his son slew Sennacherib, king of Assyria, in an insurrection." Esarhaddon reigned till 668 B.C.

CHAPTER XX

1–19. **Hezekiah's Illness; an Embassy from Babylon.** The date of both Hezekiah's illness and Merodach-baladan's embassy (vv. 12–19) presents a very baffling problem. Merodach-baladan, once king of Chaldæa, had made himself master of much of Babylonia, but he was expelled by Tiglath-Pileser in 729 B.C. He was able to defy Sargon from 721–710 B.C. and to retain his hold upon Babylon. But, once more expelled, he waited until Sennacherib's accession before making a third attempt to seize the throne. He was finally overthrown after he had been in possession of Babylon for a period of nine months in 702 B.C. It is generally thought that Merodach-baladan's embassy to Hezekiah took place *before* 710 B.C. at a time when, fearing Sargon's attack, he was endeavoring to make alliances with the neighboring states; more precisely, if Hezekiah's illness took place in 714 B.C., an embassy, under the pretext of polite inquiry as to his health, would arrive in Judah between the end of 714 B.C. and the spring of 712 B.C. Some, however, adopt Schrader's view that the embassy was sent between 704 and 702 B.C., and that it precipitated Sennacherib's invasion of Palestine. The real motive of the embassy, it is clear, was not to congratulate Hezekiah on his recovery, but to persuade him to join in a rebellion against Assyria. Hezekiah exhibited his reserves of gold to demonstrate the extent of the financial burden which he could undertake in the course of the proposed rebellion.

20, 21. **Pool of Siloam.** By means of the Siloam canal the water of the Virgin's Spring (=Gihon of 1 Kings 1[33]) was conducted to the Pool of Siloam. In time of siege the city was thus provided with a good water supply.

CHAPTER XXI

1–18. **Manasseh, the Thirteenth King** (697–641 B.C.). See 2 Chr. 33[1-20], and notes there. His reign was by no means destitute of positive importance in the political and religious development of the nation. Politically Judah must have been the vassal of Assyria, for the name of Manasseh is found in a list of tributary princes on two cuneiform inscriptions, one dating from the reign of Esarhaddon (681–668 B.C.), and the other from that of Ashurbanipal (668–626 B.C.). The impious religious innovations, and especially the worship of the host of heaven, which formed such a marked feature of this reign, were mainly due to the influence of Babylonian and Assyrian cults; the prophetic party, having protested in vain, suffered severe persecution (vv. 16, 24; cf. Jer. 2[30]) during which, tradition says, Isaiah himself suffered martyrdom. The tragic condition of the kingdom during this period has been admirably depicted by the prophet of whose work a fragment has survived in the book of Micah (6[1]–7[6]). There are, however, scholars who trace some positive good to the influence of these Babylonian cults, for they suppose that it was now Hebrew religious literature was enriched, e.g., in the earlier chapters of Genesis, by material which is essentially Babylonian in its origin. (See Budde, *Religion of Israel to the Exile*, pp. 161f.) It was during the stormy days of Manasseh's reign that the earliest portions of Deuteronomy were probably drawn up and the cleavage between the popular, national, and non-ethical conception of Jehovah, on the one hand, and the higher and more spiritual teaching of the ninth and eighth century prophets on the other, became for the first time clearly marked.

19–26. **Amon, the Fourteenth King** (641–639 B.C.). Cf. 2 Chr. 33. The conspiracy which ended the reign of Amon was the work of a *court* party, and was not necessarily caused by any dissatisfaction with the continuance of Manasseh's religious policy. His avengers were *the people of the land*, i.e., either the people generally in antithesis to the court, or the provincials as opposed to the inhabitants of Jerusalem.

CHAPTER XXII

1, 2. Josiah, the Fifteenth King (639–608 B.C.). See 2 Chr. 34, 35. The account of Josiah's reign extends from 22[1] to 23[30].

3–20. The Lawbook Discovered in the Temple. The Compiler relates at considerable length the repairing of the Temple in 621 B.C., the finding of the Lawbook, and the far-reaching character of the reformation thus inaugurated. The Lawbook has been long regarded, and, in spite of some recent expressions of dissent, is still generally regarded, as identical with part of Deuteronomy. It comprised, at any rate, practically all the legislative kernel of Deuteronomy, i.e., chs. 6–26; it represented an attempt to embody in legislation the lofty spiritual teaching of the prophets Amos, Hosea, Isaiah, and Micah, and was most probably drawn up by exponents of this purer religion of Jehovah during the bitter persecution of Manasseh's reign (see intro. to Deuteronomy).

CHAPTER XXIII

1–28. Josiah's Attempt to Enforce the Law. The immediate results of its enforcement, of which the centralization of sacrificial worship at Jerusalem and the abolition of images of Jehovah as well as of other deities were the most spectacular, are here stated. (See Simpson, *Pentateuchal Criticism*, ch. v, pp. 94–122, and McNeile, *Deuteronomy: Its Place in Revelation.*) Its ultimate results were still more vital to the development of Hebrew religion, forming as it did the basis from which exilic thought proceeded to press forward to new religious and spiritual achievements. The extension of the reformation to Samaria (vv. 16–20) would do much to commend the movement to the patriotic instincts of Josiah's subjects.

29, 30. Josiah's Death at the Battle of Megiddo. Josiah's ill-fated participation in the international struggles of his day, however, shook popular faith in the legitimacy of his reforms. It has been usually supposed that Necho II (Egyptian, *Neku*, 609–594 B.C., the son of Psammetichus I, and second king of the 26th dynasty) sought to wrest Syria from the Assyrians at a time when they were about to be overcome by the combined forces of Nabopolassar, king of the province of Chaldæa, and of Cyaxeres, the chieftain of the Medes. Necho had taken the road by the seacoast, and had not invaded Judæan territory. It has also been held that Josiah, as an Assyrian vassal, was compelled to march against him in defense of Assyria. 2 Chr. 35[20f.], however, lends color to the supposition that Josiah was anxious to secure the independence of his own realm, and on this account risked an encounter with the Egyptian army. But Gadd's recent decipherment of a certain Babylonian inscription fixing the date of the fall of Nineveh (the capital of Assyria) as early as 612 B.C. instead of 606 B.C. makes it clear that, since Assyria had already ceased to exist as an empire, Necho was not attacking Assyria nor was Josiah defending it. It may be that Josiah had already yielded obedience to the new (i.e., the Chaldæan) empire which succeeded the Assyrian and was defending *its* territories, while Necho was endeavoring either to come to the rescue of (translating "on behalf of" instead of "against") the practically defunct Assyrian empire or to seize as much as he could of its former territories before the Chaldæans had time to consolidate their new possessions (in which case Assyria is used loosely of the Mesopotamian oppressor as elsewhere). If we read the account before us independently of that contained in 2 Chr. 35[20-25], it might appear that Josiah, summoned by Necho, went to Megiddo accompanied only by "his servants" and without an army, to an *interview* with Necho, who, "when he had seen him," assassinated him. (See for Jewish attitude to Nineveh, intro. to Nahum.)

31–35. Jehoahaz, the Sixteenth King (608 B.C.). He was popular with the people because he stood for a strong independent national policy. On that very account he was deposed by the Pharaoh in favor of his elder brother, Eliakim, whose policy was pro-Egyptian. **33.** *Riblah*, of great strategic importance, was on the Orontes near the northern extremity of the Coelo-Syrian valley, about fifty miles south of Hamath. The Pharaoh, as v. 34b shows, was already retiring toward Egypt.

36, 37. Jehoiakim, the Seventeenth King (608–597 B.C.). See also 24[1-7] and cf. 2 Chr. 36[5-8]. Jeremiah fills in the picture and shows a despicable monarch, who was covetous (Jer. 22[17]), unjust and tyrannical (Jer. 22[13]), and a great builder (Jer. 22[14, 15a] Hab. 2[10, 11]).

CHAPTER XXIV

1–7. Jehoiakim Revolts Against Babylon. Jehoiakim remained faithful to his Egyptian master till Necho's defeat by Nebuchadrezzar at Carchemish in 605 B.C., then after three years' vassalage to Babylon, he revolted under Egyptian influence but apparently died before Nebuchadrezzar and his army arrived, but not before he had to resist freebooters encouraged by the Babylonians to attack him. His fate is uncertain. According to the Chronicler he was carried as a prisoner to Babylon (2 Chr. 36[6]). Jeremiah evidently regards his death as shameful, for in one place he says that he is to be buried with the burial of an ass outside Jerusalem (Jer. 22[19]), in another that his body is to be cast out unburied (Jer. 36[30]). Whatever his end may have been, it is clear that he did much by his home and foreign policy to hasten the ruin of Judah. Instead of *Syria* (*Aram*, v. 2) read *Edom:* the LXX of 2 Chr. 36[5] adds "Samaritans."

8–17. Jehoiachin, the Eighteenth King (597 B.C.). Cf. 2 Chr. 36[9, 10]. The king and country were involved in this disastrous war owing to the suicidal policy of Jehoiachin's father. Vv. 10–17 record the siege and capitulation followed by the exile in Babylon of the royal house and chief officials, lay and priestly: among the latter was Ezekiel (Ezek. 1[2] 8[1], etc.).

18–20. Zedekiah, the Nineteenth and Last King of Judah. (597–586 B.C.). See also 25[1-7] and cf. 2 Chr. 36[11-21], but especially Jer. 52[1-11] the text of which is better and fuller than Kings.

CHAPTER XXV

1–7. Zedekiah Overpowered by Nebuchadrezzar. Zedekiah appears to have begun his reign as a well-intentioned vassal of Babylon, welcomed by Jeremiah (Jer. 34[4f.], etc.) and almost to the end a believer, even if afraid to avow his belief, in Jeremiah (e.g., Jer. 37[17, 21] 38[10, 16]). But his court, an upstart one now that the old aristocracy had been taken into exile, along with the "false prophets" and the false promises of Egypt, drove him and Judah on to the supreme folly of revolt. The siege began in January, 587 B.C., lasting a year and a half all but a day. **3a.** Read as in Jer. 52[6]; cf. Jer. 39[2]. **4.** Restore the text from Jer. 39[4]. The breach to facilitate the flight was made at a spot on the southeast side of the city where the walls might be described as "two," i.e., double. Either an outer wall had been built to inclose the Pool of Siloam (which was unprotected by the inner wall), or the west wall of the Eastern Hill ran closely parallel to the east wall of the Western Hill at this point. The *Arabah* is the depression through which the Jordan flowed. **6.** *Riblah:* see 23[33]. **7.** Jer. 52[10] (cf. 39[6] and variants there) adds: "He slew also all the princes of Judah in Riblah." In addition to several other details in which Jer. 52 may preserve a superior text, it contains the probably true tradition that Nebuchadrezzar "put him to prison till the day of his death."

8–21. The Beginning of the Exile. Jer. 52[29] (supported by v. 27 below) contains the tradition that the destruction of Jerusalem took place in 587 B.C., the *eighteenth* (cf. v. 8) year of Nebuchadrezzar, a year earlier than the traditional date (586 B.C.). **11.** Somewhat hyperbolical. The exilic editor of Kings, unlike the Chronicler (2 Chr. 36[20]), did not believe that anything like *all* the people were either deported or made captive (see vv. 22–26). The "artificers" of Jer. 52[15] mg. is preferable to *the multitude* of our text. **13–17.** Jer. 52[17-23] contains a fuller list of the smaller Temple utensils which were carried away to Babylon. **18–21.** After this Jer. 52[28-30] contains a statement of the numbers of Judæans deported on different occasions by Nebuchadrezzar, but such an enumeration is absent not only here, but also in LXX of Jeremiah. Jeremiah, as a proved friend of the Babylonian conquerer, was among those allowed to remain in Palestine (Jer. 39[11-14]).

22–26. Rule of Gedaliah. A brief outline of the history of Judah under the governorship of Gedaliah; the assassination of Gedaliah and the flight of the people to Egypt; an abridgment of the full and detailed narrative contained in Jer. 39[11]–43[7].

27–30. Jehoiachin's Release. Jehoiachin is released and favorably treated in Babylon (see Jer. 52[31-34]) by *Amel-Marduk* (weakened into *Awel-Marduk*, whence *Evil-Merodach*), who succeeded Nebuchadrezzar in 562 B.C. and reigned till 560. He showed here the signal favor of granting to Jehoiachin precedence over other conquered monarchs similarly pardoned and gave him a fixed allowance from the royal exchequer (cf. 1 Kings 2[7]). Jer. 52[34] adds at the end "until the day of his death," but Kings ends on a note of triumph unmarred by this.

FIRST AND SECOND CHRONICLES

By Professor D. C. SIMPSON

Introduction

Title and Place in Canon. First and Second Chronicles, in the Hebrew Bible, are called "the events of days," i.e., daily happenings. In the Greek Bible, they are called "the things omitted concerning the kings of Judah." They are found in the latter, as in R.V., immediately after the books of Kings. In the Hebrew O.T., on the other hand, First and Second Chronicles appear at the very end of the third division of the canonical Scriptures. They owe their position there, in part, to the late date of their composition, and in part to the fact that they are probably the last books to be admitted to the canon. First and Second Chronicles, Ezra, and Nehemiah are a compilation by one and the same writer (see also intro. to Ezra-Nehemiah, p. 455), who will be referred to in the following pages as "the Chronicler."

Date. Since the Chronicler refers to a member of the Davidic dynasty of the sixth generation after Zerubbabel (1 Chr. 3^{19-24}), uses Persian terms (1 Chr. 29^{7}), seems himself to have lived later than the Persian period, and in Neh. $12^{10f., 22f.}$ refers to Jaddua, the high priest in the time of Alexander the Great, the compilation as a whole may well be adjudged as belonging to the Greek period, to a date between 300 and 250 B.C. The Compiler's literary style, theological presuppositions, religious interests and ethical outlook all point to this late date.

Contents and Structure. First and Second Chronicles consist of (a) a series of genealogies and other statistics (1 Chr. 1–9) extending from Adam to somewhere near the Compiler's own day; (b) the reign of David (1 Chr. 10–29); (c) that of Solomon (2 Chr. 1–9); (d) the reigns of the kings of Judah but not, as in Kings, of the Northern Kingdom (2 Chr. 10–36^{21}); (e) 2 Chr. $36^{22, 23}$ =Ezra 1^{1-3a}.

Sources. On the compilatory methods of Hebrew historians, see pp. 91, 381. Among the chief sources utilized by the Chronicler were: (1) Genesis-Joshua for much of 1 Chr. 1–9. (2) First and Second Samuel and First and Second Kings, from which he made numerous extracts which are indicated below and for comments on which the reader should refer to the notes on them in their earlier contexts in Samuel and Kings. The Chronicler utilized the "framework" of these as the framework of his own history of Judah. He also incorporated (3) a number of other narratives which have no counterpart in Samuel and Kings. These last may or may not be, probably are not, identical with the various works to which the Chronicler refers in 1 Chr. 9^{1} 29^{29}; 2 Chr. 9^{29} 12^{15} 13^{22} 16^{11} 20^{34} 24^{27} 25^{26} 26^{22} 27^{7} 28^{26} 32^{32} $33^{18f.}$ 35^{27} 36^{8}.

These passages are, it is true, mostly marked by the style, the phraseology, and, at times, also the mental and theological outlook which are characteristic of the remaining elements in Chronicles, elements which are obviously the Chronicler's own composition and reflect the Chronicler's own contribution to the volume. But from this it is not necessary to infer that their contents are nothing but the Chronicler's own inventions and that, therefore, they are historically untrustworthy. On the contrary, the Chronicler probably incorporated traditions of which many had hitherto been handed down only orally and had been well known to himself from earliest boyhood. To them he had always attached as much importance as to the other narratives which he took from written sources: just because they had become so much a part of himself he related them in his own characteristic style and phraseology. The historical worth of each story must be adjudged on its merits. Even where it is obvious that, in its present form as it appears in Chronicles, a given story has been *embroidered* by the Chronicler, historical facts, and those sometimes of the greatest value to the historian, will often be found embedded in such story.

On dates, see art., *Chronology of O.T.*, p. 108. Variations indicate that as to some of these dates there is still difference of opinion.

Purpose and Teaching. Some of the Chronicler's additions to the history of the past, as told in Samuel and Kings, are of considerable value to the historian for reconstructing the history of that past. But the Chronicler's object was not to collect information for a scientific reconstruction of past history. Like the Compiler of Samuel, and especially like the Compiler of Kings, his purpose was primarily religious. Just as, e.g., First and Second Kings had been compiled to meet the needs of religious men in the closing years of the pre-exilic period, so a new book of meditation on the religious experiences of the past was needed in the third century B.C. and was provided by the Chronicler. Without, for instance, in the least contradicting the religious teaching of First and Second Kings (see intro. to Kings), he put that teaching in a new perspective and added to it very considerably. Moreover, history had long since demonstrated the complete destruction of the old "Northern Kingdom." Men of the Chronicler's age and type were no longer interested in its fortunes: its fate was too obviously that of utter and final eclipse. Hence the Chronicler, unlike the author of Kings, omitted to recount its history reign by reign. It was on this account, not because of any antipathy to prophetism, in which he thoroughly believed (see below), that he omitted even to record the life-work and stormy episodes in the careers of the great Northern prophets, Micaiah ben-Imlah, Elijah, and Elisha. The Jerusalem Temple, on the other hand, had proved its own inherent sanctity and its importance for Judah by rising again in 520 B.C. to new life and activity after its downfall in 586 B.C. Its sacrifices, in the estimation of the Chronicler and his school of thought, constituted a great link between earth and heaven. Its Aaronic priesthood, and more especially its Levitical choir, Davidic Psalter and sacred music, seemed to the Chronicler to be the earthly counterparts to those of the heavenly Temple itself. This may not justify, but it explains, the disproportionate space given more especially to recording the preparations for and the building of the Temple, as well as the apportioning of the duties and privileges of its personnel, and the origin of its musical arrangements (see notes on 1 Chr. 21–29).

Moreover, between the compilation of First and Second Kings and the Chronicler's day, the developments of theological speculation, of religious practice, and of ethical and moral ideals had been very considerable. The Chronicler, therefore, set out to rewrite the history of the past in the light of such of these later developments as appeared to him and to his generation to be vital and necessary. By means of history thus rewritten he hoped to commend these doctrines and points of view to his contemporaries. One or two of his favorite themes have ceased to have even an indirect message for men of to-day, unless, by contrast, they remind us of the tremendous advance made (chiefly through the coming of the world's Redeemer) by religious thought during the years that lie between the Chronicler's day and ours. But others are of direct and permanent value: they will remain true to the end of time. To the first class belong, for instance, the veiled, but none the less bitter, condemnation of the Samaritan contemporaries of the Chronicler, with their schismatic Temple on Mount Gerizim (see notes to 2 Chr. 11[13-17] 13[3f.] 14[9-15] 20[35, 36] 25[6f.], etc.), the narrow-minded ecclesiasticism, and the stress on the externals of religion, which were often so disastrous in their effects. To the second class belongs the stress on monotheism (1 Chr. 29[10-19]), on the wrongfulness of idolatry (1 Chr. 14[12] 2 Chr. 14[3f.]), on the transcendental elements in the idea of Jehovah, who can still become immanent at least in the Temple (2 Chr. 7[1-3]), on his omniscience (2 Chr. 16[9]), on his omnipotence as the source of all (1 Chr. 29[10-19]) except of evil (1 Chr. 21[1f.]), on his providence over humanity in general (see note to 1 Chr. 1–9), and over his elect in particular, on his speaking to his people through Spirit-inspired human instruments (1 Chr. 17[1-15] 2 Chr. 15[1-7], etc.), on the solidarity of the human race (see note to 1 Chr. 1–9), and on faith and confidence in Jehovah (2 Chr. 14[9-15] 16[1-10]). Careful attention also should be paid to the Chronicler's teaching on the conditions which make war justifiable, successful or disastrous (2 Chr. 13[4-20] 14[9-15] 20[1-30]), on the relations between sin and punishment, goodness and reward (see notes to 1 Chr. 10[13f.] 2 Chr. 14[9-15] 24[15-24] 26[16-21]), on the fallacy of worldly wisdom (i.e., Hellenism, see on 2 Chr. 16[12-14]), and on the efficacy, duty, and comfort of prayer (1 Chr. 17[16-27] 29[10-19] 2 Chr. 6[1-42] 7[1-3]). These are all fundamental issues of permanent importance for the religious and moral life of every nation and every individual in every age. They lose nothing, on the contrary, they gain, by being discussed and taught in the Chronicler's way; i.e., not as abstract philosophical problems, but as practical issues worked out in the history of a nation's destiny and in the life-story of outstanding individuals of old time.

Permanent Value and Significance. In estimating the permanent value of Chronicles, its scope and purpose as outlined in the preceding paragraphs must be kept in mind. The general judgment of modern scholars is that in historical value it is inferior to that of the other canonical books, from which much of its material is drawn. If the Chronicler had access to extra-canonical reliable sources from which he drew material not found elsewhere in the O.T., the book becomes an important supplement to the other historical books. On the whole, the judgment of Professor Sayce with reference to the historical value of Chronicles is well founded: "The consistent exaggeration of numbers on the part of the Chronicler shows us that from a historical point of view his unsupported statements must be received with caution. But they do not justify the accusations of deliberate fraud and 'fiction' which have been brought against him. What they prove is that he did not possess that sense of historical exactitude which we now demand from the historian. He wrote in fact with a didactic and not with a historical purpose."

The religious teaching of Chronicles gives evidence of the limitations of the age in which it was written. There are, indeed, expressions of intense religious fervor, but, on the whole, the book defines religion in terms of ritual and ceremonial. Its attitude toward the moral problems of life is more or less superficial. The author believes in a mechanical correspondence between conduct and destiny. The reward of piety is prosperity; and in turn prosperity is an unfailing proof of piety. In the same way, the punishment of sin is adversity, and adversity is an infallible proof of sin. In its own day the book undoubtedly served an important didactic purpose—of encouragement and warning; but to the modern student of religion its chief value lies in the fact that it enables him to understand more clearly the ideas and ideals of the age from which it sprang.

Literature: W. Harvey-Jellie, *First and Second Chronicles* (Century Bible); E. L. Curtis, *Chronicles* (International Critical Commentary); on First Chronicles the works recommended in the present volume on First and Second Samuel; on First and Second Chronicles those recommended on First and Second Kings; *The Parallel History of the Jewish Monarchy*, Parts 1 and 2 (consisting of the text of First and Second Samuel, First and Second Kings in parallel columns with that of First and Second Chronicles) will be found useful for the comparative study of these books.

FIRST CHRONICLES

CHAPTERS I–IX

The Chronicler's General Introduction. Consisting of genealogical tables interspersed with geographical and historical items, these chapters serve as a rough-and-ready background to the whole book, an anticipation of the tables of dates, contents, and statistics to be found in modern works. It assisted the Chronicler to give a bird's-eye view of the times of which he wrote, but more especially it provided a skeleton history of events earlier than the period to which he wished to devote the greater part of his volume. Though somewhat dreary to the modern reader, these genealogies at times contain matter of considerable historical importance. They made too a peculiar appeal to the Chronicler and to many of his Jewish readers. The latter, especially if they were able to trace their lineage back to any of the families here enumerated, found the utmost satisfaction in perusing them. Genealogies too served as the touchstone of true Jewish lineage, making a definite cleavage between full Jewish, semi-Jewish and completely non-Jewish birth, at a time when such distinctions had become matters of vital importance in the estimation of all orthodox Jews. Moreover, with the help of these genealogies, culminating in the genealogy of Saul, the Chronicler was able to pass quite naturally in ch. 10 to his very full treatment of that monarch's successor, David.

Finally, by means of these seemingly lifeless lists the Chronicler sought to drive home important religious truths which had found little or no place in the works of earlier historians (e.g., First and Second Samuel, First and Second Kings); but which post-exilic Judaism, in spite of all its self-centered egotism, recognized and which (maybe for different reasons) still need emphasizing to-day: (1) The Divine Providence works out slowly but surely, choosing from among Adam's descendants this outstanding personality in one generation, that in another, to serve, as it were, as milestones on the long road of human endeavor; from the physical and spiritual descendants of these chosen vessels it finally builds up the church-community of the future. In the estimation of the Chronicler, for example, the members of his nation and church had Adam as their first physical father, Abraham as the first spiritual one, Moses as the giver of the eternal Law, David as the organizer of its Temple and of that Temple's personnel, music, and psalmody, Solomon as its builder, and so on up to the Chronicler's own day. (2) In spite of this highly selective theory of human destiny, and in spite of his ultra-ecclesiastical outlook, the Chronicler recognized the truth of the solidarity of the human race, the brotherhood of *all* Adam's descendants. For him they were all (except the outlaw Cain and his descendants) within the general orbit (as opposed to the special selection) of the Divine Providence. Consequently, he did not shrink from including in his work genealogies of all three sons of Noah (1^{5-27}), Abraham's descendants by his concubines (1^{29-33}), even the hated descendants of Esau the Edomite (1^{35-54}), and all the descendants of *all* the sons of Jacob, not merely of those three—Judah, Benjamin, Levi—who alone had, in his judgment, remained true to their election to membership in the Jewish Church.

All the genealogies are valuable, but since it is these three patriarchs in which he is *chiefly* interested, it is in theirs that we find most information over and beyond mere statistics. 2^{3}–4^{23} contains various genealogical lists and items of information concerning Judah, of which those concerning David's ancestry traced back to Ram (2^{10-17}) and his descendants right down to post-exilic days (3^{1-23}) are the most interesting. 7^{6-12}, like 8^{1-40}, purports to give the genealogy of Benjamin, but the former is perhaps that of Zebulun. 6^{1-81} sets forth the genealogy of the Levites. It is the fullest and most important of all. Especially noteworthy are its lists of the succession of high priests from Aaron to the Exile (6^{1-15}), the singers descended from Gershom, Kohath, and Merari (6^{16-30}), and from Heman, Asaph and Ethan (6^{31-47}). 6^{48-49} gives further information as to the services of Levites and Aaronites. 6^{54-60} provides a further list of high priests, this time to the period of David. David, we are taught, was the originator of the guilds of singers and of the musical services so characteristic of the Temple worship of post-exilic days. And it was with this thought paramount in his mind that the Chronicler, having given in 9^{1-34} a genealogy of the inhabitants of Jerusalem (i.e., of those who were his readers), proceeded to his account of David.

Chapters 10 to 29: The Reign and Life-Work of David

Chronicles and Samuel. Nearly all that is weakly human and much that is fresh and courageous in his character seems to have disappeared from the life story of David as here depicted. The reader will look in vain in these chapters for more than passing references to David's boyhood (see 17^{1}), his combat with Goliath (18^{2}) and his wild outlaw life (12^{1-23}), or his intimate domestic life. His career, moreover, at Saul's court is entirely omitted. In First and Second Samuel, David lives before us not only as the recipient of Messianic promises, but chiefly as the intrepid youngster, the slayer of Goliath, the patient harpist to the king, who is fast losing his reason and secretly seeking David's life, the outlaw chieftain who here refuses to take Saul's life, the composer of at least one *secular* lyric of outstanding merit, the faithful friend of Jonathan, the passionate lover of Bathsheba, the too indulgent father, at once the victor over the Philistines and Jebusites and the barbaric conqueror of trans-Jordanic lands—and yet a signal failure as the administrator of justice and as a unifying figure in his people's life in times of peace.

Many, on the other hand, of the other traditions of David preserved in First and Second Samuel were incorporated by the Chronicler sometimes *verbatim*, sometimes with modifications, in these chapters. The Chronicler also had recourse to other sources of information, these being often of no great antiquity and merely reflecting the traditions of his own day, sometimes possibly representing only his own subjective conception of what David *ought* to have been and *ought* to have done. But the total effect is striking. Not merely has David become an ideal figure who lacks most of the ordinary vices of his day, he has also become a passionate devotee of the ideal of the Temple which his son was destined to build. His life-work is all made to lead up to, and so to subserve, the interests of this climax of his career, namely, the preparation of the material for the erection of the Temple, the organizing of the personnel, especially the Levites, and, within this body, of those Levites whose lot it was to lead the musical and choral side of worship in the Temple. But the reader had best suspend judgment on the Chronicler's treatment of David till he has once again read both First and Second Samuel and these chapters with the notes which follow below. (See "The Chronicler's Delineation of David," p. 445.)

CHAPTER X

The Death of Saul. Vv. 1-12 almost = 1 Sam. 31^{1-13}, but vv. 13, 14 are the product of the Chronicler's own vivid conviction—expressed by him at times in a somewhat mechanical manner—that all things happen providentially. Since his theology contained no doctrine of existence after death or of rewards or punishments in heaven or hell, a man's fate in this life is, in his judgment, the final divine verdict on his character. Consequently, so cruel a fate for Israel's king appeared to him to stand in some relation to his conduct. He felt it to be necessarily connected with (a) that king's recent deviation from full trust in Jehovah and recourse to cults of the dead, and (b) the overruling Providence which had already designated David as the future king.

CHAPTER XI

1–9. David Reigns; He Captures Jerusalem. For vv. 1–3 cf. 2 Sam. 5^{1-3}. For *Hebron* see note to 2 Sam 2^{1}. For reference to Samuel see 1 Sam. 15^{28} $16^{1, 2}$. Vv. 4–9 are an abridgement of 2 Sam. 5^{6-10} (see notes there), with the addition of the notice of Joab's restoration of the city (as distinct from the citadel).

10–47. A List of Fifty-one of David's Heroes. Vv. 9–39=2 Sam. 23[8-9a, 11b-39] (with vv. 9b–11a inadvertently omitted), where a better text of the earlier part is preserved. For the description of the *Egyptian* (v. 23) cf. 1 Sam. 17[7] 2 Sam. 21[19].

CHAPTER XII

1–22. David's Followers During His Desert Wanderings. They appear as envisaged through the mists of seven hundred years by the Jewish Church of the Chronicler's day. David in 1 Sam. 22[1f.] was followed by a small faithful band of men who like himself were desperate outlaws; in Chronicles he has become the general of the flower of Israel's manhood. Men of the Chronicler's day would boast of their descent from this or that follower of the great David. Hence the interest which attached to the Chronicler's list and to the more or less graphic notes on their peculiarities and achievements.

23–40. David's Military Leaders. A similar interest would be aroused by the list (not based on Samuel) of military men who hailed David king at Hebron. Many of the names and notes in these lists are probably far more genuine and trustworthy than many similar items in the genealogical trees of well-known families of the last few centuries.

CHAPTER XIII

The Solemn Journey of the Ark From Kiriath-jearim. Less arbitrary than the autocratic David of pre-exilic days, and more ecclesiastical in his conception of the requirements of a religious procession, the David here idealized duly consults with the officers of his realm and summons the priests and Levites to take their appropriate part in the solemn progress (vv. 1–5). Thus, and thus only, could post-exilic Judaism conceive that David had acted—David, the ideal king, the benefactor of the priesthood, the originator of the various Levitical choirs. In David's day there was, in point of fact, no distinction between "priests" and "Levites." It was Ezekiel who proposed a distinction (between "sons of Zadok" and the *rest* of the tribe of Levi; see Ezek. 44[10-31]), and not till after the Exile was the Aaronic priesthood with the "Levites" as a subsidiary order established. **6–14.** Almost *verbatim*=2 Sam. 6[2-11] (see notes there), except that (v. 14) the piety of the Chronicler's day, recoiling from the idea of the ark resting in a private and secular dwelling, thought of it as placed "by" the house of Obed-edom, and as having "its own house," as the Hebrew should be translated.

CHAPTER XIV

1–7. David's Exaltation and Family. The Chronicler tells (vv. 1, 2) from an unknown source of the presents sent to David by Hiram king of Phœnicia (see note to 2 Sam. 5[11]), an incident chronicled as being illustrative of David's fame in the estimation of the leading nations of his day. **3–7.** Next he mentions David's sons born in Jerusalem (cf. 3[5-8] and see 2 Sam. 5[13–16]).

8–17. Defeat of the Philistines. Vv. 8–12 relate his victory at Baal-Perazim (=2 Sam. 5[17-21]; see note there to v. 20), which culminated, so post-exilic Judaism instinctively felt, not in David's soldiers treasuring the captured images of the Philistine gods (2 Sam. 5[21]) but in their immediately and appropriately burning them. **13–17.** David's further victory over the Philistines *in the valley* (based on 2 Sam. 5[22-25], where the valley is that of Rephraim; see notes there to vv. 20, 22) is stated to be the culminating reason for David's international fame.

CHAPTERS XV, XVI

Transfer of the Ark to Jerusalem. As compared with 2 Sam. 6[12-19] (see note there), these chapters contain a lengthy description of the journey of the ark (see note to 2 Sam. 6[3], and for its earlier history and significance see notes to 1 Sam. 4[4] 5[1–7][1]). Again it is the David idealized by post-exilic piety who makes both the general (15[1-15]) and the musical preparations (15[16-24]) for this most solemn journey. David appoints the Levites to serve before the ark (16[4-7] and see vv. 37–43) and appoints the "Asaph" division of Levites henceforth to be the chanters of the psalms of thanksgiving. The psalm used on this occasion (16[8-36]) was a combination of Psa. 105[1-15] 96, 106[1-48] (all probably psalms of post-exilic origin).

CHAPTER XVII

Nathan's Message to David Concerning a Temple; David's Prayer. As idealized in post-exilic days David's interest in the personnel of the Temple was extraordinarily great. Was he not the organizer of the priests but above all of the Levites, the inspirer of the Temple music, the author of its psalmody? Why, then, did Providence decree that not David but Solomon should be the founder of the Temple for which these Levites, this psalmody and music, were intended? The only possible answer to the riddle as it seemed to these worshipers in the post-exilic Temple was that contained in Nathan's message to

David (vv. 1–15) and David's prayer of thanksgiving (vv. 16–27). (See further notes to 2 Sam. 7[1-7]).

CHAPTER XVIII

Practically *verbatim*=2 Sam. 8[1-18].

CHAPTER XIX

For this and 20[1-3] see 2 Sam. 10[1-12] 11[1] 12[26, 30, 31].

CHAPTER XX

Wars Against Ammon and Philistia. For vv. 1–3 see under ch. 19. For vv. 4–8 see 2 Sam. 21[18-22]. In v. 5 the Chronicler states that "Elhanan . . . slew Lahmi the brother of Goliath the Gittite" instead of "Elhanan . . . the Bethlehemite (Hebrew, *Bethlamhi*) slew Goliath" (2 Sam. 21[19]). This is an interesting textual emendation by the Chronicler. Though he did not himself record it, he knew full well that it was David, not Elhanan, who slew Goliath. To reconcile the two traditions he turned the *lahmi* of *Bethlahmi* in Samuel into the name of a supposed brother of Goliath slain by Elhanan.

Chapters 21 to 29: Preparations for the Building and Administration of the Temple

Post-exilic piety, as already indicated (see on ch. 17 above), would have been well content that David rather than Solomon should have been the builder of the Temple, but Providence had decreed otherwise. Post-exilic historians, therefore, contented themselves with treasuring and preserving traditions which told of preparations made by David for the building of the Temple and his arrangement for its personnel.

CHAPTER XXI

The Census; the Plague; the Temple Site. The chief interest of the story of David's census and the plague (probably based on, though deviating in important respects from, 2 Sam. 24, where see notes) consisted for the Chronicler in the fact that it led to the revelation to David of the predestined site for the Temple. To us an important point of interest in this section consists in the Chronicler's attributing the temptation to *Satan*. Pre-exilic thought had, quite naturally and without an especial reflection or questioning, referred all facts and phenomena, and all kinds of human fortune, good and bad, to Jehovah himself as their immediate cause. But by the Chronicler's time, as a result of the prophetic emphasis on the righteousness and holiness of Jehovah, the cause of moral wrongdoing was attributed to Satan, once a member of the heavenly court, the divinely appointed tester of human motives (Job. 1[6-12] 2[1-7]; cf. Zech. 3[1f.]), but finally regarded as the head of the fallen angels, the enemy, by N.T. times, alike of God and man.

CHAPTERS XXII–XXVII

David as Ecclesiastical and Political Organizer. In 22[2-19] we have a selection of traditions also dear to post-exilic piety, reflecting, as they did, exactly what it conceived to be the justification for its own whole-hearted devotion to the Temple, for the regulations in force and for the services carried out by the clergy of its own day. Not only are David's general preparations for the Temple mentioned (vv. 2–5), but also his charge to Solomon (vv. 6–16), and to the princes (vv. 17–19). Ch. 23 contains his provisions for the Levites and their services, and 24[1-19] those for the priests. 24[20-31] contains a supplementary list of Levites: the courses for the singers are given in ch. 25, for the gate-keepers, treasurers, and other Levitical officials in ch. 26. David thus became famous as an organizer in the ecclesiastical sphere. Ch. 27 illustrates the traditions which grew up in praise of his organizing ability in the secular sphere of the army (vv. 1–15), tribal princes (vv. 16–24), royal treasury officials (vv. 25–31), and counselors (vv. 32–34).

CHAPTER XXVIII

David's Final Preparations for the Temple. The Chronicler and his contemporaries had no conception of the vital question of succession with its concomitant factions and animosities in the royal entourage vividly set forth in 1 Kings 1 (see notes). Instead they conceived of the attention of David and his court and subjects as being mainly concentrated on the various projects for the building of the Temple. It was this which was the ultimate purpose of David's communications to the people in a public assembly in connection with Solomon's succession (vv. 1–8). It was to this that David called Solomon's attention (vv. 9, 10). It was the *pattern*, the "architect's plans," as we should say, of the Temple and its various parts which Solomon received from David (vv. 11–21).

CHAPTER XXIX

1–25. The People Offer Willingly; David's Prayer and Thanksgiving. It only remained for David to make his last final appeal for free-will offerings for the financing of this same project, an appeal meeting with instantaneous success (vv. 1–9), and then (vv. 10–19) to utter his final prayer. The beauty, richness, and spirituality of this prayer bear ample testimony to the piety and religious insight of the Chronicler's co-religionists of the third century B.C., for whose edification the Chronicler included it in his book. It is the prayer of an undoubting monotheist, conscious of the need of a spirit of thankfulness and of a "perfect heart" as conditions of real personal relationship to the omnipotent and only God, the Creator, the Sustainer, and the ultimate goal of all the universe and yet still the God of Israel, the God of the patriarchs, and the God to whom the sacrificial worship is to be offered in this Temple to the end of time—"All things come of thee and of thine own have we given thee." Hence it was after the sacrificial banquet was finished that Solomon became king over a thoroughly satisfied and religiously privileged people with the full approval of his brothers (vv. 20–25).

26–30. David's Reign and Death. The Chronicler closes the reign of David with a chronological note (see 1 Kings 2^{11}) emphasizing the reputation as well as the age of the dying monarch (v. 28), and indicating the independent authorities from whose literary works still more information could be gleaned (vv. 29, 30).

The Chronicler's Delineation of David. Such is the Chronicler's delineation of David, his reign, his acts, and the goal of all his strivings. David has become a model of subordination of self to the highest religious destiny of his subjects, which only a few Christian princes, such as Constantine or Charlemagne, have excelled. The reader may, indeed, prefer the more strictly historical account of David in First and Second Samuel with its stories of David's boyhood at Bethlehem, the spontaneous courage and chivalry of his youth whether matched against a lion, fighting for his father's sheep, or against Goliath on behalf of the armies of Israel, his harpist career at Saul's court, his patient endurance of Saul's jealousy, his love for Jonathan, his outlaw life with its hair-breadth escapes from Saul's pursuit alternating with the twice repeated refusals to seize the opportunity of slaying Saul. The reader too may admire the skill displayed in David's elegy over Saul and Jonathan, his care for the burial of Saul's descendants, the stories of his adulterous love for Bathsheba, of his repentance when confronted by Nathan's "Thou art the man," his grief at his child's death, his failure to control his family, the tragedy of Absalom's rebellion. But let the reader be fair to the Chronicler in thus suppressing and even departing from some of these comparatively trustworthy stories. He may, indeed, have omitted some stories as unedifying. But since omissions were necessary in consequence of the comprehensive character and length of his history, the great bulk of what he omitted he probably chose thus to sacrifice as being that which he could best afford to omit, though much of what he suppressed probably made a real appeal to the Chronicler. He knew, for instance, accepted, and was a zealous believer in the story of David's victory over Goliath (see $18^{1, 2}$).

But, in order to appreciate the Chronicler's skill in accomplishing the task which he set himself, we have to keep in mind the fact that he was a stern exponent of contemporary orthodoxy at a time when many of his co-religionists were beginning to be attracted to Hellenism (cf. 2 Chr. 4^4). He was also a devotee of the Temple, which obviously could never have been built but for David's capture of Jebus. He was a keen exponent of the Temple worship at a time when that shrine was beginning to feel the effects of the (unintentional) rivalry of the synagogues springing up throughout the land. He was, perhaps most of all, a musician and (in spite of his own prosaic and somewhat overloaded style) a lover of poetry, an admirer of that Jewish hymn book, "The Psalter," which still to-day expresses the religious aspirations alike of Protestant and Catholic Christendom as well as of orthodox and modernist Jewry. He was a devoted admirer of the Levitical system rather than a student of the arts of war or learned in the shepherd's lore. As a keen musician he had year by year listened to the Temple music which, more even than the cultus itself, exalted him and put him into touch with the Unseen and the Infinite. Its appeal to his inmost being had stirred a desire within him to tell of its origins and its development. He had, in short, come to regard David not merely as ultimately responsible for, but also as the sole originator of, *all* the arrangements and liturgy of the Temple. *We* perceive that, in the form which they had assumed by his day, these were the result of a *long process* of development and that they were destined at times to obscure rather than to illuminate the essentials of true religion. But this the Chronicler did not realize. *He* loved all these things dearly—and to him who loves much, much shall be forgiven.

Moreover, in the Chronicler's day the worship of the Temple, external though it essentially was, had not yet become a caricature of true religion, and its priesthood was not yet the open enemy of positive goodness, which it is depicted as being in N.T. times. Had it already become this, it could not a hundred years or more after the Chronicler have called forth the Hasidæans' passion for martyrdom on its behalf when Antiochus profaned its altar in 168 B.C., any more than, just before the Chronicler's day, it could have roused the poetic muse which produced some of the finest of the psalms for use within its courts. Moreover, devotion to the Temple, even to Herod's Temple—in spite of its many abuses—must not be looked on as the mark of one who is merely interested in the external trappings of religion for their own sake and has no vision of the possibilities of immediate and mystical union with the Divine. Respect for the Temple was an element even in Christ's love of his fellow countrymen and their religious institutions. In childhood and in his public life he resorted thither (see Mk. 11^{15} 13^{1} and parallels in Mt. and Lk.; Lk. 2^{22-50}; Jn. 2^{13-22} 7^{14-44}, etc.). It was the scene of some of his most important sermons and discussions (Mk. 11^{15}–13^{1}). Because it was God's "house of prayer" he troubled to turn out the traders from its precincts (Mk. 11^{15-18}; cf. Jn. 2^{13-22}). Its impending overthrow was a matter of the deepest grief to him (Lk. 19^{41-43}). After his Ascension the first generation of his disciples constantly resorted thither to pray as well as to preach (Acts $3^{1f.}$). Not till the Hellenist Stephen became prominent were the Palestinian Christians charged with "blasphemy" against it (Acts 6^{13}). At the end of his third missionary journey Paul not only himself performed a religious obligation there, but at James' suggestion paid the fees to assist others to do so, even if in doing this he was only acting up to his principle of being "all things to all men" (Acts $21^{17f.}$). It would appear that the reader of Chronicles to-day, instead of criticizing the Chronicler for his one-sided view of history, ought rather to include the study of the origins and subsequent development of the Temple, its ministers and its part in Jewish life, among his own studies of the origins of Judaism as the parent of Christianity.

SECOND CHRONICLES

Chapters 1 to 9: The Reign of Solomon

For a parallel account, with differences, of Solomon's reign (977–937 B.C.) see 1 Kings 3^{1}–11^{43}.

CHAPTER I

1–13. Jehovah's Revelation to Solomon at Gibeon. See 1 Kings 3^{4-15}, from which vv. 6–13 are abridged. The Chronicler seeks in v. 3 to justify the sanctuary at Gibeon as legitimate on the ground that it was (in his estimation) the lineal descendant of the Traveling Tabernacle of the wilderness wanderings described in the Priestly Code (Ex. 25–31; 35–40) and a copy of the heavenly temple shown to Moses in the Mount. **9.** See the Messianic promise to David in 2 Sam. 7^{1-17}.

14–17. Solomon's Wealth. (Cf. 9^{25-28}). Practically = 1 Kings 10^{26-29}.

CHAPTER II

The Building and Dedication of the Temple. 2. Cf. vv. 17f.; 1 Kings $5^{15f.}$ **3–10.** Solomon's message to Hiram contains information (not recorded in 1 Kings 5^{1-6}) as to David's relations with Hiram (cf. 1 Chr. $14^{1, 2}$): a workman skilled alike in metals, cloth, and engraving is needed. Various kinds of wood are specified. The provision for the Phœnician workers is defined. **11–16.** Hiram's answer is based on 1 Kings 5^{7-9}. **17, 18.** Men of the Chronicler's age and school of thought, owing to the fact that the enslavement of *Hebrew* citizens had been forbidden long before their own day (Lev. 25; Neh. 5^{1-13}), could not conceive of the *corvee* as applied to *Hebrews* and therefore imagined that the impressed workers consisted entirely of aliens. That the idea of *alien* indentured labor did not offend them is not surprising in view of its being still allowed even in some possessions of European powers and in South America to the present day.

CHAPTER III

Building of the Temple Continued. 1, 2. Cf. 1 Kings 6^{1}. The identification of the site of Abraham's attempted sacrifice of Isaac with that of the threshing floor of Araunah (cf. 1 Chr. $21^{15f.}$) and of Solomon's Temple is here definitely affirmed. **3–7.** Dimensions of the porch and the holy place; cf. 1 Kings $6^{2, 3}$. **8, 9.** The most holy house. Cf. 1 Kings 6^{14-22}. *Six hundred talents* (probably=27,000 lbs.) would seem an exaggeration. **10–14.** Two cherubim. Cf. 1 Kings 6^{23-28}. The note as to the *veil*, not mentioned in Kings or in Ezekiel, is based upon the usage of the Chronicler's own day which was influenced by Ex. 26^{31}. **15–17.** Two pillars. Cf. 1 Kings 7^{15-22}. Their height is here double that ascribed to them in Kings.

CHAPTER IV

The Furniture of the Temple. 1. The altar is not mentioned in the Temple source of

1 Kings (but see 1 Kings 8[64]), either because it has there inadvertently dropped out of the text or because Solomon, in point of fact, sacrificed on the bare rock, the celebrated *es-Sakra*, now covered by the Mosque of Omar. The description here is probably based on the Chronicler's knowledge of the altar of his own day. **2–6.** Similarly, ignorant of their original use, the Chronicler here states the theories of his own day as to the brazen sea and the lavers; cf. 1 Kings 7[23-26]. **7, 8.** The candlesticks (cf. 1 Kings 7[49]), ten tables (possibly for the candlesticks, unless for shewbread), basins (cf. 1 Kings 7[40])—all probably described as the Chronicler saw them in the post-exilic Temple. **9.** Similarly, the Chronicler mentions not the *one* court of Solomon's Temple (see note to 1 Kings 6[36]), but the *two* of post-exilic days, **10–18.** The sea, etc. Cf. 1 Kings 7[39b-47]. *Zeredah* = Zarethan (1 Kings 7[46]). **19–22** (and 5[1]). The golden furnishings and the completion of the work (=1 Kings 7[48-51]; see notes there).

CHAPTER V

The Ark Installed in the Temple. The ark is brought to the Temple with due solemnity and escorted both by priests and by Levites (except in v. 5) in accordance with the post-exilic presuppositions based on the Priestly Code as to the constitution of the priesthood. **12.** A reference is made here to the presence and duties of the Levitical singers and musicians (entirely ignored in Kings), a topic in which the Chronicler was much interested. He made the descent of the cloud coincident with this musical outburst, as if attesting divine acceptance of the latter. Otherwise the amount of deviation from 1 Kings 8[1-11] is negligible.

CHAPTER VI

Solomon's Words and Prayer of Dedication. The whole, except vv. 13, 41, 42, simply repeats 1 Kings 8[12-50a]. To the Chronicler's generation the idea that Solomon should function as a *priest* was unthinkable—cf. the Chronicler's omission of Solomon's blessing of the people, though recorded in 1 Kings 8[54-61]. Consequently, it was supposed that he must have acted as the *preacher* on this occasion and have occupied an improvised temporary rostrum. **40–42.** These verses also reflect the piety of post-exilic days. The Deuteronomic era which produced 1 Kings 8[51-53] (which the Chronicler rejected in favor of these verses) had fixed its gaze, so far as the past was concerned, chiefly on the redemption from Egypt. The post-exilic period, with a richer theology and a wider experience of life gained both during the years of separation from the Temple and in the succeeding centuries of development of its services, evolved finer and fuller liturgical formulæ and terminology. **41.** The opening expressions are partly drawn from the post-exilic Psa. 132[8] and from the ancient address to the ark, Num. 10[35], etc., while the contents of v. 42 recall Psa. 132[10f]. Together they form a harmonious echo of a variety of O.T. passages requisitioned for liturgical expression.

CHAPTER VII

1–3. The Answer to Solomon's Prayer. Here is a remarkable and vigorous description of the divine acceptance of and answer to Solomon's prayer. Fire descends from heaven and consumes the sacrifices; the transcendent God, materialized as smoke, becomes immanent ("the glory of the Lord") in the "house" of the Lord. For this brief divine moment not even the priests, the consecrated human media of communion between the Divine and the human, have any special place in Israel's mystic union with its Divine Head. The people have an *immediate* vision of their God: they worship him in the most direct possible manner and themselves offer up thanksgivings. It is a descriptive narrative which finds no place in Kings, but is, on that account, not necessarily the less majestic and ancient. Like the similar description of the answer to David's prayer in 1 Chr. 21[26] (on the occasion when, after sacrificing on this same spot, according to the Chronicler he selected it for what it had now become), the imagery goes back to more primitive descriptions such as that of Elijah's moment of triumph on Mount Carmel. Probably the present passage in its turn served to supply in part the imagery for the description of an equally dramatic initial moment in the experience of the Christian Church—when at Pentecost the Spirit came down from heaven as cloven tongues of fire. It rested then, however, on and in no material building of human design, but on human beings who were God's spiritual creation. It denoted (though they did not at first realize this) the freeing of the early Christians from the deadening effects of the external sacrifices of the Temple and its ritual, in order to build up a *spiritual* Temple in each of them, a Temple destined to supersede as well as outlive Herod's reconstruction of Solomon's Temple on Mount Zion. No longer did "the children of" the *new* "Israel" need to "look on": they were themselves afire with the Divine Spirit: their task was to hand on to others the sacred fire of the good news of immediate access to God, and to hand it on burning more brightly, if possible, than when they received it.

4–7. The Dedicatory Sacrifices. The Chronicler utilized 1 Kings 8^62-64^, introducing, as was his wont, a reference to the choral and musical accompaniments of the sacrifice. Merely because he himself was interested in the Temple music, and referred to that of David and Solomon, in the terminology of his own day, it is wrong to assume either that he *invented* such references or that they cannot be historical. The assumption that religious music and psalmody among the Hebrews were exclusively of post-exilic origin is entirely false. (See *The Psalmists*, edited by D. C. Simpson, Essay I.) On the post-exilic distinction between Aaronic "priests" and the rest of the "Levites" see note to 1 Chr. 13.

8–10. The Feast of Dedication. Utilizing 1 Kings $8^{65, 66}$, the Chronicler interpreted the somewhat curious "seven days, even fourteen days" of Kings as referring to two separate festivals, first that of the Dedication of the Altar, and secondly that referred to in Kings, the Feast of Tabernacles. The latter he held to have been observed by Solomon, as it was observed in his own day, according to the provisions of the Priestly Code: he therefore naturally added a reference to the eighth day of *a solemn assembly* (Lev. 23^{36}).

11–22. Solomon's Vision. This appears to be a combination of 1 Kings 9^{1-9} with (in parts of v. 12, and vv. 13–15) matter from some other source.

CHAPTER VIII

Various Political and Administrative Notices. The divergences from 1 Kings 9^{10-26} are few, but, on that account, none the less interesting and instructive as reflecting the new light in which the matters in question were viewed by men of religious and political ideas in the Chronicler's day. Thus, vv. 1, 2, the incident described in Kings as a cession of cities by Solomon *to* Hiram was now regarded as a gift made by the latter to the former. Vv. 3–6 describe Solomon's fortifications and store cities. See 1 Kings 9^{17-19}. While the fall of Gezer was no longer of interest, the seemingly insignificant Tamar (in South Judah) of 1 Kings was interpreted as a mistake for *Tadmor*, i.e., Palmyra, northeast of Damascus, well known in later days, and of which in later times Zenobia, the powerful patron of the heretic Paul, Bishop of Samosata, was queen. It was a victory which, if achieved by Solomon, must have made his dominions far more extensive than is usually claimed for them.

CHAPTER IX

1–28. See 1 Kings 10.
29–31. See 1 Kings 11^{41-43}.

Chapters 10 to 26: The History of Judah from Rehoboam to the Exile

CHAPTERS X–XII

Rehoboam, the First King of Judah (937–920 B.C.). See 1 Kings 12^{1}–14^{20}. The Chronicler has assembled from other sources a wealth of additional information. Much of this latter is historically important, and still more of it is religiously instructive.

Rehoboam's fortifications (see 11^{5-12}), situated on the highway into Egypt and on the west Judæan hills, were very necessary, as is shown by the story of Shishak's (? earlier) invasion and devastation of the country. They were justifiable defensive measures as distinct from modern forms of aggressive militarism. In 11^{13-17} is related, in restrained terms, the glorious story of families who, like the Pilgrim Fathers of old, left their homes and kindred to migrate to a land where conscience told them they would find liberty to worship God in the highest and purest form known to them. To the Chronicler and his contemporaries, irritated by the Samaritan community and schismatic Samaritan Temple of their own day, this migration from Samaria to Judæa by pious men of ancient days must have appeared as glorious as do stories of early Christian martyrs and confessors to us in the twentieth century. 11^{18-23} shows that the Chronicler was not so narrow-mindedly immersed in ecclesiastical matters as not to be interested in the details of the royal household and its still extravagantly luxurious harem, far exceeding the resources of the small kingdom over which Rehoboam now ruled.

The section 12^{1-11} contains a much fuller account of Shishak's invasion than 1 Kings 14^{25-28}. In v. 12 the Chronicler stated for his contemporaries' benefit a truth which, if modern nations appreciated it, would transform the national and economic life of to-day: a nation's "goods" consist neither in its extent nor in its mere political influence, neither in its riches nor in its possession of financial magnates, but are to be measured by its ideals and by the realization of these in the daily life of its citizens.

CHAPTER XIII

Abijah, the Second King (920–917 B.C.). See 1 Kings 15^{1-8}, for part of which the Chronicler substitutes (a) a description of a war waged by Abijah against the backsliding Northern Kingdom (v. 3); (b) a statement of the religious and moral grounds which alone justified the declaration of war against a neighboring and kindred nation (vv. 4–12); and (c) the valuable comment (vv. 13–20) that victory comes from God alone, and comes not necessarily to the side with superior forces and technique (Israel) but to the one which has justice and right on its side (Judah).

CHAPTERS XIV–XVI

Asa, the Third King (917–876 B.C.). See 1 Kings 15[9-24], where Asa, unlike his two predecessors, is represented as a good and successful monarch. The present narrative contains ample justification of the verdict on Asa. 14[3-8] claims that Asa inaugurated a sweeping iconoclastic and anti-foreign religious revolution as well as a defensive military reorganization; 14[9-15] claims that as the outcome of his reliance on God he crushingly defeated both the Cushite invaders led by Zerah (either=Egyptians under Osorkon I or II, or the Arabian Cushites—see 1 Chr. 1[9], or people of Saba) and the Gerarites. The latter were thus taught that light-hearted interference in others' military struggles brings trouble to the intervener.

But, as interpreted by the Spirit-inspired Azariah, son of Oded (15[1-7]), this war taught Judah the still more important truths, often vindicated but often forgotten before and since, that (a) *The Lord is with you if* (when, while, or because) *you are with him*, and (b) *If ye seek him, he will be found of you* (cf. Isa. 55[6] Mt. 7[7f.], etc.), as well as (c) the message which inspires reformers of all ages: *Be strong . . . your work shall be rewarded.* Consequently in 15[8-19] Asa's reformation, only less sweeping than that of Hezekiah and Josiah, is carefully recorded.

Asa proved himself in the hour of trial, however, faithless to his own ideals and lacking in faith in God (16[1-10]). It was to Syria, not to Jehovah, that he turned for help against the Northern Kingdom. Hanani the seer, along with some of the people supporting him, was imprisoned for pointing out the truth which should have been, but was not, a source of comfort to Asa: *the eyes of the Lord run to and fro throughout the whole earth . . . in the behalf of them whose heart is perfect toward him.* As if in punishment for this, Asa became diseased, and died (16[12-14]). All the paraphernalia of burial rites suited to his royal estate were, however, enacted, including *a great burning* (not of his body but of funeral spices). In this connection the Chronicler incidentally expressed his views on a disputed question of his day. Men of meticulous faithfulness to the traditions of Judaism regarded resort in illness to physicians as an act of apostasy from the faith of their fathers, since the practice of medicine was then a profession newly introduced from non-Jewish, i.e., Hellenistic, sources. Hence the Chronicler's condemnation of Asa's resort to them. Others, like Asa, had no scruples in pinning their faith to the physician's skill. The *via media*, however, between these two extremes, which Christian thought would approve to-day, was reached soon after the Chronicler's day by Ben Sirach (see Ecclus. 38[1-14]). Unfortunately, our own age, with its materialistic outlook, tends to approximate to Asa's standpoint.

CHAPTERS XVII–XX

Jehoshaphat, the Fourth King (876–851 B.C.). To the information contained in 1 Kings 15[24b] 22[1-35a, 41-50], the Chronicler added narratives chosen by him to exemplify certain ideals of civic life which seemed to him of vital religious value. The first (see 17[7-9]) inculcates the provision of qualified teachers, not only ministerial ("priests and Levites") but also laymen (a real indication of a historical kernel underlying the story), to undertake the religious education of all citizens. In the second place (17[10-19]), the excellent effects of such education are exemplified (1) by the admiration shown by other nations for a state so instructed, especially, and in tangible form, by Philistines and Arabians (=desert tribes in Jehoshaphat's day, but in the Chronicler's day=the important Nabatæan state south and southeast of Judah), and (2) by the efficiency of the army. In the third place (see 19[1]–20[36]) the complete boycott of the schismatic Samaria and abstention from all relations with it are inculcated in the narrative of the message of the seer Jehu, the son of Hanani, and by the destruction of Jehoshaphat's fleet, as predicted by the prophet Eliezer, in punishment of his alliance with Samaria's king. This represents an attitude of sectarian aloofness and ecclesiastical bigotry. It was, unfortunately, far too deeply ingrained in the outlook of men of the Chronicler's day, and was condemned by our Lord's action in freely conversing with the woman of Samaria. It is still all too prevalent among Christian denominations in our own day. Next (19[4-11]) the lesson that national leaders with religious ideals should insist on the impartial administration of justice is taught by the narrative of the establishment of local courts and also a central court of appeal (Deut. 16[18-20] 17[18]). Lastly (see 20[1-30]), the necessity for facing national peril, and even actual invasion of national territory, not merely with well-drilled armies but in perfect confidence in the transcendent God (*God in heaven*), the invincible *ruler over all the kingdoms*, is exemplified in the Moab-Ammon attack (a seeming adaptation of 2 Kings 3[4-27]), the contents of Jehoshaphat's prayer, the Spirit-inspired utterance of the Asaphite Levite Jahaziel, and the triumph celebrated in the valley of Beracah (v. 26).

CHAPTER XXI

Jehoram, the Fifth King (851–843 B.C.). See 2 Kings 8[16-24]. The preceding reign provided the Chronicler with opportunities for emphasizing the beneficent results of the reign of a good king. The opportunity to drive home the unfortunate results of the political program of a decadent ruler is provided by the present reign: vv. 2–4, the weakening of the state owing to Jehoram's jealousy and murder of his own brothers as being possible rivals; v. 6, its degradation owing to his alliance (constituted by his marriage to Athaliah) with Israel and (through her mother Jezebel) with Tyre; vv. 8–11, the opportunity for revolt presented by Judah's lowered morale and seized on by Edom and Libnah. The religious significance and direful results of all this are emphasized in the "writing" (vv. 12–15) ascribed to Elijah. They are also emphasized by the pillaging expeditions of the Philistines and Arabians (vv. 16, 17), by the fatal tragedy of Jehoram's internal illness, by the absence of all forms of public mourning at his death, and by his burial elsewhere than in the dynastic mausoleum (vv. 18–20).

CHPATER XXII

1–9. Ahaziah, the Sixth King (843–842 B.C.). See 2 Kings 8[24-29]. The Chronicler emphasized the evil effects (a) of Jehoram's disastrous reign by hinting at a disputed succession in which the inhabitants of Jerusalem took sides (v. 1); and (b) of a bad mother's influence on the subsequent development of a child's character, and of that of bad counselors in an already corrupt court (vv. 2–4), resulting in Ahaziah's close alliance with Samaria (vv. 5, 6; see 21[6] above), and, as divinely predestined, in his death in Samaria (not at Megiddo as in 2 Kings 9[27f.]), where only his grandfather Jehoshaphat's merits sufficed to secure him decent burial (vv. 7–9).

10–12. The Reign of the Usurper Athaliah (842–836 B.C.) did not detain the Chronicler and he passed on to the career of Joash.

CHAPTERS XXIII, XXIV

Joash, the Seventh King (836–796 B.C.). See 2 Kings 11[1]–12[21]. In 23[1-21] we see the Chronicler freely modifying the story of 2 Kings 11[4-12]. Himself a devotee of the Temple, its etiquette, ceremonial, and ritual, and desirous of inculcating a love of the same in his readers, he transformed the foreign bodyguard of pre-exilic days (1 Kings 1[38, 44]; cf. 2 Sam. 8[18] and note there) into prominent Levites, allowing only priests and Levites within the Temple, as was the case in his own day. Not a small cabal, as in Kings, but *all* the Judeans of importance are here cognizant of a plot of which all religious men of the Chronicler's own day must needs have approved. Fidelity to the same presuppositions of his day explains the changes in 24[4-14] as compared with 2 Kings 12[4-12]. 24[15-24], however, contains valuable hints of the reaction which took place in the latter part of Joash's reign against the reforming policy of the now deceased Jehoiada—such reactions are inevitable after any reform. The more extreme the reformation is, the more sweeping will be the reaction. But, though needing to be resisted, such reactions should never disturb unduly the disciples of the cause of progress. They are ultimately brought to an abrupt ending, and reform in the long run always triumphs. Such, the Chronicler pointed out, was the fate of this particular reaction. Scarce had the blood of Zechariah, Jehoiada's son, the Spirit-inspired apostle and martyr of reform, dried on the pavement of the Temple court between the Temple and the altar (cf. Mt. 23[35] Lk. 11[51]) when the Syrian invaders (cf. 2 Kings 12[17f.]) swooped down upon Jerusalem. Though numerically weak they seized the reactionaries' leaders and plundered their possessions. They served, as it seemed to the Chronicler, the plan of Divine Providence in swiftly punishing the sinner in this life. Joash himself (24[25-27]) finally met with retribution—disease in his lifetime, assassination at the hands of his foreign or semi-foreign court-officials, and, after his death, deprivation of a place in the dynastic mausoleum. Truth and religion, as it seemed to the Chronicler, had, after all, triumphed—as, indeed, in the long run they must, though not necessarily as speedily or as mechanically as the Chronicler imagined.

CHAPTER XXV

Amaziah, the Eighth King (796–789 B.C.). See 2 Kings 14[1-22]. The Chronicler's important additions to the story of Kings are chiefly confined to its fuller description of the Edomite war (vv. 5–13). He sought once more to illustrate the truths which he had so much at heart: (a) the need for abstention from all relations with the Samaritans (vv. 6, 7); (b) the dire results of having even business relations with them (v. 13); (c) faith in God, and God only (vv. 8, 9), who, indeed, rewards such faith in him by granting victory to the man of faith (vv. 11, 12); (d) the danger of temptation assailing a man, thus rewarded for his faith, so that he falls subsequently into unbelief and sin, even into defiance of God's spokesman specially commissioned to warn him of his sin (vv. 14–16); and (e) the certainty of punishment in this life for those who yield to this temptation (vv. 17–24).

CHAPTER XXVI

Uzziah, the Ninth King (789–740 B.C.). See 2 Kings 15^1-7^, where Uzziah is called Azariah, but cf. vv. 13 and 30. This reign, in spite of the growing power of Assyria, was one of the utmost prosperity. This prosperity the Chronicler ascribed to Uzziah's obedience to the heavenly vision as revealed by Zechariah. **6–15.** Here is contained valuable information, not otherwise extant, as to Uzziah's military successes over the Philistines and certain Arabians, his vassalship over the Ammonites, and the material prosperity of his realm. **16–21.** The story of Uzziah's priestly act at the altar of incense is introduced by the Chronicler to explain the reason for his tragic physical suffering. But it is also valuable as showing that, even as late as the eighth century, B.C., the reigning monarch still claimed the privilege and duty of acting as head priest in the Temple (cf. notes to 6^{1-42}).

CHAPTER XXVII

Jotham, the Tenth King (740–735 B.C.). See 2 Kings 15^{32-38}. The notices in vv. 3–6, probably from ancient sources, of his building operations and success over the Ammonites, have been preserved for us only by the Chronicler.

CHAPTER XXVIII

Ahaz, the Eleventh King (735–726 B.C.). See 2 Kings 16^{1-20}. The Chronicler utilized both the narrative of Kings (which he considerably modified) and other available information in order to emphasize the doctrines for the propagation of which he had already contended in his record of previous reigns. Thus Ahaz's idolatry (vv. 2–4) is brought into immediate relation to its punishment not by a combined attack of the Syro-Ephraimites (as in Kings), but by the inroads first of Syria and then of the Northern Kingdom (vv. 5–7). **9–15.** He emphasized the value of the intervention of heaven-sent prophets; Oded this time carried conviction even to the (in the Chronicler's estimation, godless) Samaritans. **16–19.** The Chronicler emphasized too the divine purpose of chastisement in the inroads of the Edomites (cf. 2 Kings 16^{6}) and Philistines. **20–25.** To these divine warnings Ahaz reacted, not with repentance and contrition, but—so the Chronicler interprets Ahaz's motives—by committing the further sins of calling in the aid of Assyria, of adopting the religion and cults of Syria (not merely a Syrian altar, as in 2 Kings 16^{10-16}), and even of interdicting the worship of Jehovah and restoring the baser types of local sanctuary worship. Thus in Ahaz the Chronicler exemplifies how a man who has erred and has been divinely warned as to his conduct may refuse the divine discipline and persist in defying God: in 33^{1-20} he illustrates how another may heed the divine warning and so find spiritual refreshment and a return of material prosperity.

CHAPTERS XXIX–XXXII

Hezekiah, the Twelfth King (726–697 B.C.). See 2 Kings 18–20. In contrast to the apostasy of his predecessor, this king is envisaged by the Chronicler as a much more thoroughgoing reformer than in Second Kings, a reformer after the Chronicler's own heart.

Ch. 29. Hezekiah, for instance, reopened the Temple doors and called on priests and Levites alike (see note to 1 Chr. 13^{1-5}) to resume their faithful service.

Ch. 30. He kept the Passover, just as 2 Kings 23^{21-23} recounts that Josiah afterward did, but, unlike the latter, he invited to it all Israel and observed it for two weeks.

Ch. 31. The celebrations culminated (v. 1) in an iconoclastic orgy. Priests and Levites (see note to 1 Chr. 13^{1-5}), encouraged to perform their respective offices, now received their due support as they did in the Chronicler's own day (vv. 2–21). This may not be history, but, sympathetically read, it makes an appeal to the modern reader as being the daydream, the uncritical but none the less truly devout and mystical imagining, of one for whom the Temple was the gate of heaven, its clergy the earthly counterparts of God's own heavenly temple, and its festivals and sacraments the outward yet effective signs of a real spiritual grace.

Ch. 32. See on 2 Kings 18^{13}–19^{37}; cf. Isa. 36^{1}–37^{38}.

CHAPTER XXXIII

1–20. Manasseh, the Thirteenth King (697–641 B.C.). See 2 Kings 21^{1-18}. **11.** It is to the Chronicler alone that we are indebted for two exceedingly probable and enlightening items of information — Manasseh's rebellion against Assyria and his journey to Babylon to make obeisance to his conquerer. The historicity of these statements has been questioned on several grounds. But his name occurs in lists of tributary vassals both of Esarhaddon (681–668 B.C.) and of Ashurbanipal (668–626 B.C.). Moreover, in the latter's reign parts of Palestine are known to have been in revolt against that monarch and to have supported the rebellion of the viceroy of Babylon, the Assyrian king's brother. At *Babylon*, moreover, as the Chronicler here states, and not merely at Nineveh (as might have been expected since *it*, not Babylon, was the capital of Assyria), this monarch, according to inscriptional evidence, did indeed receive the obeisance of his vassals. Lastly, Manasseh, in having his life and kingdom spared to him (vv. 12, 13), received no greater boon than did Necho I of Egypt. Hence the probabilities are in favor of rather than against the tradition that Manasseh rebelled and made his submission at Babylon.

Interesting as they are to the archæologist and the critical historian, these historical questions occupied for the Chronicler a very subordinate, if any, place in his interests. For him, not the events themselves, but their religious significance, as that was interpreted in his own day, constituted the vital issue. Fortunate indeed was Manasseh if his adventure really involved for his own spiritual experience even a small part of what the Chronicler found in its results—resort to prayer, repentance, contrition, forgiveness, amendment, restitution. Fortunate too is every man who can see and realize these results as he reviews his own life-history, his own mental and emotional development, and his own spiritual and mystical experience and can express himself as Manasseh is made to do in *The Prayer of Manasses* preserved in the Apocrypha. (See art., *Intertestamental Literature*, p. 193b.)

21–25. Amon, the Fourteenth King (641–639 B.C.). See 2 Kings 21[19-26].

CHAPTERS XXXIV, XXXV

Josiah, the Fifteenth King (639–608 B.C.). See 2 Kings 22[1]–23[30]. The occasion, and even the *immediate cause*, of the vitally important reformation of his eighteenth year was doubtless the finding of the Lawbook (2 Kings 22[3f.]). But the *ultimate* causes must be looked for in the teaching of the great writing prophets, in their disciples' faithful preaching of those prophets' message, and in the predisposition of Josiah himself, probably from earliest boyhood, toward the realities of the spiritual life. This last was fully realized by the Chronicler; indeed he overemphasized it. In the narrative before us, *not in his mind simply*, but *even in official actions*, the young king, *when only twelve years old*, is made by the Chronicler ruthlessly to embark on the task of reformation—a task gigantic in itself and so momentous in its effects upon the later development of this nation's religion and, through it, on that of two thirds of the world to-day.

Once again the Chronicler lays himself open to the charge of being an uncritical historian; but as a psychologist he triumphs. Sudden conversion after adolescence does not more easily or more usually produce the balanced judgment and the inner self-dedication necessary alike for an individual's own spiritual development, and for his leadership in a nation's religious evolution, than does a childhood of piety and an adolescence of pure and holy thoughts fixed on God and unerringly devoted to ideals of service to humanity. The boy, thus self-dedicated to God and his fellow men, at twelve years of age is as likely to serve both, and do so as whole-heartedly as he whose ideals have remained undeveloped and undirected till the manifold calls and interests of manhood have well-nigh usurped the place which those higher ideals would otherwise have occupied. The story will have a real message for to-day and a blessing for posterity if, in addition to acting as a trumpet call to have done with mediæval superstitions and to spread a more spiritual and pure type of religion and morality, it drives home, *in the form in which the Chronicler gives it*, the desirability of our children being educated from their *earliest* days in *religious* knowledge, and that based on no reactionary presuppositions. It must be based on the results of the most modern biblical criticism and of the most recent ethical and moral conceptions of God, who himself will thus be revealed to the next generation more clearly and more fully than to any which will have gone before.

CHAPTER XXXVI

1–4. Jehoahaz, the Sixteenth King (608 B.C.). See 2 Kings 23[31-35].

5–8. Jehoiakim, the Seventeenth King (608–597 B.C.). See notes to 2 Kings 23[36]–24[7]. "Nebuchadrezzar" is a more correct form than *Nebuchadnezzar*.

9, 10. Jehoiachin, the Eighteenth King (597 B.C.). See notes to 2 Kings 24[8]–[17] 25[27] Jer. 52[31] and cf. 1 Chr. 3[16f.] for his descendants. Chronicles increases the length of his reign by ten days and puts his accession in his *eighth* year.

11–21. Zedekiah, the Nineteenth and Last King of Judah (597–586 B.C.). See notes to 2 Kings 24[18]–25[7].

22, 23. The Decree of Cyrus. Cf. Ezra 1[1-3a]. Just as Second Kings closes with a message of optimism and hope for the future, so the Chronicler's work as it now stands hints at a brighter future. The story of that future, as told by the Chronicler, now appears divorced from First and Second Chronicles in the books of Ezra and Nehemiah. The Compiler of Kings envisaged a restoration of the Davidic dynasty in Jehoiachin and his descendants: the Chronicler lived sufficiently late to see that, though David's dynasty no longer held the throne, David's *spiritual* creation, the Temple, was once more the spot where men might find David's God and offer up their adoration to Him to whom David had said, in words that have since become classic, "All things come from thee and of thine own do we give thee."

EZRA AND NEHEMIAH

BY PROFESSOR ROBERT W. ROGERS

INTRODUCTION

A Priestly History. There are many ways of apprehending or of accepting and explaining human ideas about God, and many ways also of teaching men about him. In the beautiful pages of the O.T. three of these ways stand out prominently, represented respectively by Priests, Prophets, and Wise Men. The reader who has not met already examples of these three has not yet read widely in this volume of popular presentation and interpretation of the O.T. If he has read Leviticus and Numbers, with considerable portions of Exodus, he has seen the priestly method of teaching about God and his relations with men. On the other side of the picture, he who reads Isaiah, Jeremiah, Ezekiel, and the Twelve Minor Prophets has the prophetic approach to the divine before his eyes, and then in Joshua, Judges, Samuel, and Kings he may read the prophetic view of history. In Proverbs, Ecclesiastes, and Job he will have before his delighted and interested eyes the thoughts of the Wise Men. Besides these greater and more comprehensive expressions of the three types of teachers, he will find many other examples of their work in other books. Thus in Genesis and Exodus he will find both priestly and prophetic teaching, and in the Psalms all three may often be followed, and in yet other books are here and there evidences of effort to bring men to God by any means. There still remain, however, for comment here, a most important collection of books which represent distinctly and insistently the priestly way of looking at the history of Israel.

During the Exile in Babylonia from 597 and 586 to 537 B.C., the priests who were earnestly seeking to save the Jews from dangerous contacts with the religion there in vogue were busily assembling, compiling, and preserving records and traditions of their people. They had the book of Deuteronomy, largely a prophetic book, and much of the material now in Joshua, Judges, Samuel, and Kings, together with many other bits of writing or of memorial tradition, and as they read it all over it was easy for them to see how much of it represented the prophetic viewpoint. Here were the prophets in complete possession of narrative history. "Why," said they among themselves, "why not a narrative history after the priestly way of thought?" See how Robertson Smith states their case: "Thus there seemed to be room for a new history, which should confine itself to matters still interesting to the theocracy of Zion, keeping Jerusalem and the Temple in the foreground, and developing the divine pragmatism of history, not so much with reference to the prophetic word as to the fixed legislation of the Pentateuch, so that the whole narrative might be made to teach that the glory of Israel lies in the observance of the divine law and ritual."

So did it come about that during the Exile and long afterward, as men brooded earnestly over these things, some man or men must finally begin the writing. The final product was Chronicles, Ezra, and Nehemiah. These were, I think, all one book, composed originally by the one set of hands, whether of one man or of several men. To understand Ezra and Nehemiah you ought first to read very carefully Chronicles, first by yourself and then with the aid of Professor Simpson's commentary on Chronicles in this volume. You should, however, do some work of your own. You will find (see p. 439a) in Simpson's commentary the evidence of the use which the Chronicler made of Samuel and Kings, and he will have set down for you (see p. 439b) lists of passages which show how and wherein the compiler of Chronicles has supplied materials of his own not found in the earlier books. But though you see and even read some of these, it will mean nothing of value to you unless you make some real effort to make the comparison for yourself. Long ago the lamented Professor Driver, whose pupil Professor Simpson was, told us how this should be done. He said: "The reader who desires properly to understand the method and point of view of the Chronicler should mark in his Revised Version—by underlining in the case of simple words or verses, and by drawing a line along the margin in the case of longer passages—these and the other passages peculiar to him. He will then soon discover that they have a character of their own, in language and expression, not less than in subject matter, which differentiates them materially from the parts transferred unaltered from Samuel or Kings." There precisely is the way to come to some understanding of the difference between a prophetic and a priestly view of Israel's history. He who would do that would have some knowledge that was really his own. And now do this in some measure, and read the books of Chronicles through and accompany the reading with Simpson's commentary. When you have done this you will be ready to begin your study of Ezra and Nehemiah.

You will then have learned that Chronicles-Ezra-Nehemiah, all forming one book, were probably written somewhere between 300 and 250 B.C., and that Ezra-Nehemiah were severed from the rest and received into the canon of Sacred Scripture, but that a dispute arose among the learned men of Judaism, and the books of Chronicles had a sore struggle to pass through before they were so admitted. This explains the reason why Chronicles is the last book in the Hebrew Bible, and is preceded by Ezra and Nehemiah, though the proper sequence of historical events would require the order to be Chronicles, then Ezra, and last of all Nehemiah. There are many haphazard strokes in the long process of the writing and compiling and canonizing of the sacred books. When we consider the long stretches of the years and remember the vagaries of men we shall have no excuse for surprise. The Bible is clearly not only a divine book, but also a human book. Let us not over-emphasize either of these two readily recognizable sides of its form and contents. God has spoken to men in these books, but he has spoken to them through men, and so though the books come into our hands trailing clouds of heavenly glory, they come also well sprinkled with earthly dust.

The Two Heroes. The two heroes of Ezra and Nehemiah are these two men. Let us see how we may place them historically, both in the order of time and in their several peculiarities, in their character and in their work. They represent two orders in the religion of Israel which are not found in the early days, for Ezra is a scribe and Nehemiah a statesman. The former corresponds in some respects to the priests of earlier days, but in other respects is very different from them, so different as justly to be placed in a separate category. The latter fulfills some of the functions of a king in the earlier days, for he was the governor of his people. Yet is he different, for though some of the kings were indeed under foreign domination, as, e.g., Hoshea under the Assyrian king Tiglath-pileser III and Zedekiah under the Chaldean king Nebuchadrezzar, still these had some authority of their own, while Nehemiah was governor only and entirely under Persian appointment. There was no longer an Israelite or Jewish state even nominally independent. The position of governor we find easy enough to understand, but perhaps a word about the office and work of the scribe may be useful to us in attempting to visualize Ezra in his proper person.

The Scribes. During the Exile there came slowly a great change in the religion of Israel. Slowly indeed, but surely the foundations were laid which transferred the people from the influence of the prophetic word spoken audibly into men's ears, into a nation bound to observe a rigid code of laws. The old freedom gave way before the new norm. Religion ceased gradually to be a communion with God, and became a walk, legally correct in all its details, according to a written standard. The simplicity of Deuteronomy, which, though it contains many laws, was yet prophetic in tone, was being supplanted, and in its place were coming the elaborate codes governing not merely the priest in his functions, but every act of everyday life. These fundamental laws we may now read in portions of Exodus and Numbers, and in still more elaborate and sustained form in Leviticus. But as men tried to observe these laws it soon became evident that difficulties of interpretation were continually springing up. Who should explain how the Law, in its letter, was to be interpreted when contradictions, or, at least, contra-indications seemed to appear between different passages? So to fill this new function there began slowly to arise a new order of men who sat during every hour that could be taken from their bread-earning laboriously poring over the sacred rolls of the books, comparing and contrasting laws, and carrying them forward to new uses by elaborate processes of deducing from them implied or supposedly implied new applications. These men were called *Sopherim*, or scribes, and soon formed themselves into a separate class. Ezra the scribe became the great exemplar of this new class. They who came after him did many things which he did not attempt, but he was their father in the Law, they were his sons, and in their eyes he became a splendid person. They became not merely editors and interpreters and expounders, but from them came pupils who were skilled in the copying of manuscripts, as we should say, calligraphists. The higher, abler, and more learned became jurists and gave themselves to the most elaborate expositions of Scripture. If we carry this story down into the Greek period, we shall there behold an elaborately organized separate order which had begun chiefly by recruits from priests and Levites but had drawn many devout laymen into their ranks. When Antiochus Epiphanes attempted to destroy the Jewish faith, martyrs were not wanting to cling to copies of the proscribed books, and their blood strengthened their ardor, and gave it a touch of heroism of which survivors might well be proud. After the Maccabee uprising they were accorded seats in the Sanhedrin as a separate class, and thereafter became more exclusive, opinionated, and determined in their zeal for the Law. They seem largely then to have become Pharisees, but there are hints enough to connect some of them with the Sadducees. In the N.T. period they had become avid of praise and of public and private honor. They were addressed as Rabbi, which meant, literally, "my Lord," but came to mean technically "my Master" or "my Teacher," and under that fine old title they wrapped themselves in honor and demanded it for themselves and commended its extension to their pupils. "Let the honor of thy disciple be dear unto thee as the honor of thy associate; and the honor of thy associate as the fear of thy master; and the fear of thy master as the fear of heaven" (*Sayings of the Fathers—Pirke Aboth*, iv, 17). They were sometimes addressed as Rabban, or Rabboni, which means "master and father," and placed themselves above the claims of family. If one's own father and one's own teacher were in any trouble or distress, the teacher must first have assistance.

As members of the Sanhedrin they had come into a quasi-judicial capacity, which they did not possess in their earliest development, but even above this they had duties more wide reaching and even greater in importance. The first of these duties here to be mentioned was teaching. It was their business to raise up disciples, whose bounden duty it was first to commit to memory all that the teachers imparted, and, second, never to depart from a master's word no matter what might happen or ensue. In N.T. times the pupils sat on the ground and the rabbis on a bench, much as do the Mohammedan teachers to this day. Even more important than this function was the duty of so studying the Law as to be able to interpret its every rule or precept or admonition and to apply these to every possible occasion in life. As social life developed this was often very difficult. Sometimes the Law simply could not be stretched or interpreted to meet every new occasion. Then they had recourse to some saying of a former rabbi which might be elevated into a tradition and so be added to the general body of instruction. Here, then, were the beginnings of the Mishna, which would creep on by repeated accessions into the fearsome, awesome masses of the Talmud. The principles laid down by the men of the Great Synagogue for the scribes were three: "Be deliberate in judgment; and raise up many disciples; and make a fence to the Torah." This "making a fence to the Torah" meant the devising and expanding of legal precepts to such a point that if a man were devout and attempted to follow them, he would be so bound up by rules and regulations and traditions that he would not be tempted to break the fundamental law in even the slightest degree. This accumulating mass of traditions and interpretations and legal determinations was grouped together under the word *Halachah*, which means primarily "a going," hence "a way," then figuratively "custom," "usage," "rule." As it grew in mass, it grew in favor and in reverence so that it came to be placed with even the original Scriptures as divine and then was projected into the remote past. The rabbis began to talk about Moses as having been taught by God not only the written Law but also the oral law. Some of them still held that the written Law was supreme, this as a theory, but in practice they assigned a greater authority to their oral laws, expansions, developments, and decisions (see Mt. $15^{2f.}$ and Mk. $7^{5f.}$). Edersheim (*Life and Times of Jesus the Messiah*, vol. i., p 97, footnote 5) quotes a rabbinic saying that, "An offense against the sayings of the scribes is worse than one against those of Scripture." "Scripture" here means the "Law," the five books of Moses; but if these were so treated, even with greater freedom did they handle the remaining sacred writings. They set forth the teaching of the other books in what is often translated "commentary," but really ought always to be known by its Hebrew name *Haggadah*. This word is clear enough in its meaning to those who have long studied the Scriptures and the traditions in Hebrew, but it is not easily defined for the general reader. For the present purpose it will be better to define it by means of a description rather than by the use of some definite English word. By *Haggadah* the scribes, in practice, meant a writing which gave a doctrinal and practical expansion and exposition of the sacred text, not excluding fabulous embellishments. *Haggadah* began early to be manifested among the scribes, how early we do not know, but there were actual written specimens of it available when the Chronicler made his book, for he refers specifically to the *Haggadah* ("commentary" in R.V.) of the prophet Iddo (2 Chr. 13^{22}) and to the *Haggadah* ("commentary") of the book of the kings (2 Chr. 24^{27}). These may have been only small beginnings, but the harvest was great and evil in later days.

But the reader may now be saying to himself, "What has all this to do with Ezra?" The answer is that it has much to do with any estimate of his work and worth. A man must be judged not only by his work but by the consequences of it. As Ezekiel is justly to be declared the father of ecclesiastical Judaism, so Ezra must bear whatever of honor or of reproof belongs to him as the father of the whole wearisome system of "scribeism"—if there be such a word. He did not will or wish it, but he fathered its beginnings and the result is with us still. Our Lord loved it not, nor need we feel any strong impulse to do so. It had its uses, and its value for its own day, and some returns has it made to us because of its devotion to the Scriptures, and its care of them in dark days, but it is probably just to say that the evils it has brought exceed the good. Let us now turn more definitely to survey the man Ezra.

Ezra the Man and His Work. We have no knowledge of Ezra beyond what may be gleaned from the books of Ezra and Nehemiah, and what may from these be gleaned has more difficulties than may properly be raised in this commentary, to say nothing of any close discussion of them. We can do no more or better than to draw out before our eyes such few facts as may be reasonably regarded as significant or important and therewith be content. There is, to begin at the beginning, a very fanciful, imaginative, and artificial genealogy given of him (Ezra 7[1-6]) which contains fifteen names of his supposed ancestors by which his line is carried back to Aaron. This is plainly an insufficient number to span one thousand years. By comparisons with the lists in Chronicles and in the apocryphal books of First and Second Esdras we can make up a list of thirty names, but one cannot but feel that the whole is artificial. Genealogies, whether ancient or modern, have a sad trick of following hopes rather than facts. When we come below to our little attempt to reconstruct the historical background of the books of Ezra and Nehemiah, we shall have a few words to say about Ezra's work, and there are other words in the commentary later to follow about his journey to Jerusalem and his work there. Let us here bring out an impression of the man rather than a biography in historical environment. It must be confessed at the outset that he is not a figure beloved among Christians in our age, nor is the book which bears his name a favorite book for devotional reading. His is, in general, a cold, austere figure, harsh in judgment and intensely severe and uncompromising in the execution of an imperious will. We must put forth a strong effort to excuse some of his deeds, and go back over his career with a fixed determination to judge him very generously, finding excuses for him in the spirit of his times. The book of Ezra is for the most part not inspiring reading, but there are two fine bits in it, and they are found written in 3[11-13] and 8[21, 22]. I advise the reader to turn to them and take comfort from them. He will not find anything elsewhere in the book to match them. This unfavorable view of Ezra goes far back in the history of Judaism. When Ben Sira calls the roll of heroes in a passage of the highest beauty (Ecclesiasticus 49[11-13]) at the beginning of the second century B.C., he mentions Zerubbabel, Jeshua, and Nehemiah, but gives no word to Ezra. In a later book (2 Macc. 1[18-36]) there is much glorifying of Nehemiah, but no mention of Ezra. But when a later tradition got a good chance it magnified Ezra beyond all rime or reason. He became then the actual founder of the Great Synagogue and the father of the scribes. In the apocryphal Fourth Book of Ezra he is presented as a man who restored the Law and rewrote all the sacred records which had been destroyed, and produced seventy apocryphal works! Then to others he was the man who closed the sacred canon, though it was, indeed, not closed until long after his death. What remains of his own personal writing will come up for mention in the commentary below.

Nehemiah the Man and His Work. Pleasant indeed is it to turn from Ezra even at his best to the far more attractive figure of Nehemiah. He was quite human enough to have positive faults, but there is yet so much that is noble, and he displays so much generosity, faithfulness to high ideals, a splendid patriotism, and quickness in action, that the modern man feels at once a sympathy with him quite impossible with Ezra. If one were to read passages from Ezra in public, he would speedily see that he had a listless following, but there are whole chapters of the book of Nehemiah which make the average congregation or assembly straighten up and listen eagerly. The mind of the common man knows what it likes and shows no small amount of wisdom in the choice. In one point only does Nehemiah display an unlovely side much like that of Ezra. He was intense in his attempt against those who had contracted marriages outside the Jewish pale. This zeal of his finds a characteristic expression in the words, "And one of the sons of Joiada, the son of Eliashib the high priest, was son-in-law to Sanballat the Horonite: therefore I chased him from me" (Neh. 13[28]). This proved in the sequel to have been a sad blunder, for it was a high contributing factor in the formation of the Samaritan religion destined long to be a thorn in the side of Judaism. It was a pitiful and cruel act to attempt to separate families many of them had founded years earlier. Here was a Hebrew who had married, quite innocently, a woman from a nearby village. She was a Canaanite, and had borne him three children. What rime or reason was there in Nehemiah's plan to say to this man, *You must put her away*—drive her out as was Hagar, with little Ishmael, driven out centuries earlier? Logic is good in its place, but forbearance is often better. To save Judaism it might be necessary to forbid any future mixed marriages, but to break up those already consummated was a horrible atrocity, and no amount of effort on our part to justify Nehemiah by an appeal to different customs in a different age should require us to justify these acts. The whole story besmirches his soul, disproves his possession of a sense of justice, and makes him, in this one particular, an intolerant monster. (This is great plainness of speech, let the reader bear it with whatever patience he may be able to command.)

But if this be a dark strain, the rest is nearly all good, clean, admirable, and the man otherwise a fine figure. He was a man of action, not only in the matters of social organization but equally in the physical affairs of his city. To him the city owed the reconstruction of its defensive external walls. He knew that a city in that age without walls might readily be the easy prey of some marauding tribe, or be conquered by an external enemy strong enough to snatch a bit of domain from the hand of the Persians, who now held it in what seemed to be a firm grip. He was too prudent to trust to future contingencies the exigencies of the present. He knew that hostile neighbors were near by and that none knew when signs of weakness among Jerusalem's leaders would encourage them to attack. He therefore made provision that even the men who worked on reconstruction should be armed with weapons and be ready to stand their ground and hold by force their own just possessions. There is a lesson here we do well to heed.

The Historical Background. It is idle to attempt to secure either knowledge or intellectual pleasure from the reading of the books of Ezra and Nehemiah without some attempt to reconstruct by the use of historical and archæological and critical methods the age in which the men lived. If to this knowledge we are able to call into service the priceless help of imagination, we shall then see them working in their own environment, and understand them far better. But to do this we must go back over a long and tumultuous stretch of history, the earlier part of which needs but little exposition, the latter part much.

1. *The Exile and the Restoration.* Let us remind ourselves that in 597 B.C. Nebuchadrezzar carried out of Jerusalem to be exiles in Babylonia eight thousand of its people. Among these was the aristocratic and very able figure of Ezekiel, who in 593 was called to be a prophet and was thenceforward quick to do his utmost to save his people from disintegration, and from absorption not merely into the economic but even into the religious situation in Babylonia. In 586 B.C. Nebuchadrezzar's army again besieged Jerusalem and carried thence to join the other band of exiles a larger company, who may have numbered forty-eight thousand, or perhaps even more. Here, then, in far distant Babylonia was a considerable Jewish colony, with representatives of every grade of society—artisans, farmers, city workers, and men of affairs, men of skill, men of knowledge, men of deep piety. The process of adjustment was neither easy nor quick, but in due time it was accomplished. Few races have ever inhabited this earth with more of a mixed endowment of industry, capacity, power of accommodation, patience, and skill in husbanding resources and of saving returns in money or other valuables. Some of them rose to power and to financial influence, and to their skill the great banking houses of Egibi and Murashu bear eloquent witness.

They were in Babylonia when one of the greatest events of ancient history came to pass. Beyond the borders of the great valley of the Tigris and Euphrates there was in process of formation a new empire. A man named Cyrus, born in an obscure province known as Anshan, or Anzan, in 559 B.C., became its king. and in 550 conquered Astyages, king of the Median empire, and annexed to himself this domain. Cyrus was now the chief ruler of Asia, and in it had only two rivals: far away beyond the River Halys in Asia Minor, was Crœsus, king of Lydia; and near at hand was Nabonidus, king of Babylon, a doctrinaire prince and far from any equality with this new and virile conqueror. In 546 B.C. the kingdom of Lydia fell into the hands of Cyrus, and in 538 Babylon was likewise taken. The Jews in Exile had seen or heard a shift in human history unparalleled before, the making of the greatest empire the world had seen up to that time, and all within little more than twenty years.

In 537 B.C. Cyrus issued a decree permitting all the Jewish exiles who wished to do so to return to their homeland. The news must have run like wildfire, and have imparted a shock comparable only to a bolt of lightning.

The devout and God-fearing who had heard or read the promises of the prophets may well have felt that dreams had become realities and prophecies fulfillments beyond compare. But permission to return was not compulsion to return, and the problem then set for the Jews was not easy. We must remember that the Jews in Babylonia were now divided into three clearly marked classes: (1) Some had been carried away in 597 B.C. They had now been fifty-nine or sixty years in Babylonia and all were now old; even those who were boys of ten or twelve years of age were about seventy years or above it. Some of them would be too old for the long, hard journey or unfit to face the struggle needed to gain a foothold in the old land of which they could have only shadowy memories. (2) Others carried away in 586 B.C. had been now forty-eight or forty-nine years in Babylonia. In that time they had founded homes, earned a livelihood, learned the language, and were in many respects Babylonians; and some of them had married Babylonian wives, adopted the civilization about them, and even had adopted the religious ideas and were following the worship of their neighbors. (3) There was still another and a very large class composed of those who were born of Jewish parents in Babylonia. They knew Palestine only by hearsay, and if they had met with success in business, would hardly be eager to go to a strange land, however much their fathers had loved it. When the decree was issued there would arise a serious question as to how many might seize the opportunity and who they might be. It seems a fairly safe conjecture that few of the first class would attempt the enterprise; and if they were willing, could hardly be regarded as valuable settlers—nay, they might even be a burden rather than an asset. Perhaps few of the third class would wish to go, and might need much pressure to induce them to undertake it. This, then, would leave the attempt chiefly to the second class. However that may be, the number that did actually return fell far short of expectation. How many they were we do not know, for the lists that have been preserved show wide divergence in the numbers, as the commentary to follow shows clearly enough. They who went were confronted with serious problems. The glories which the prophets had foreseen were elusive or undiscoverable. The lands which they or their fathers had owned had long since passed into other hands, and they must buy new property out of whatever means they had brought from Babylonia, or set themselves with the proverbial diligence and prudence of their race to make such livelihood as was possible. It must be a process of peaceful penetration much like that which their remote forefathers had carried out in many cases in the days of Joshua and his successors. The people whom Nebuchadrezzar had left behind in 586 had done nothing to rebuild the Temple or to restore the city walls. They had been a poor folk indeed; the energetic and enterprising were exiled, and they who remained were content to live humbly and put forth no great effort to emulate the greater deeds of their fathers. To those who now returned to join them the city must have presented a sorry sight. There lay the ruins of the Temple, still blackened here and there by the fire of long ago. The city walls were little more than ragged and jagged heaps of debris. Where were the hopes and dreams of the prophets? What could they now do? Their answer was that they must first provide housing for their families who would need shelter in a climate by no means bland, but, rather, often fierce and dangerous with wet and cold. They must lay the foundations of an ordered economic life, then something more and better might be secured. Whether they all knew it or not the gravest problem before them was the question, What could be or should be done about the Temple? There lay its ruins as Nebuchadrezzar had left them, and no man for fifty years had set hand and heart to the work of restoration.

2. *Rebuilding of the Temple.* It is fully established by the experience of the ages that no religion can exist and propagate without some visible place of assembly. There must be a meetinghouse, a church, a synagogue, or a temple. If they provided nothing of the sort, Judaism must die. They were confronted with the prospect of a real tragedy, not for them only but for all succeeding generations—nay, for us also. One might have supposed that whatever the motive or the reasoning, they would surely make an attempt at this imperative need. But they did not. There is justification enough for not undertaking any enterprise so great, but it is a sorry commentary on human weakness of will and lack of even ordinary foresight that they did so little. What they actually did was to set up the altar of burnt sacrifice. This was, indeed, something, some recognition of the just claims of the human heart for worship. But it was hopelessly insufficient. It was only a stop gap, and had really the effect of satisfying some scruples, and then they sank back into a dangerous content. So the years slipped by. They built homes, rude enough in the beginning, but soon made comfortable and then even embellished. Their religion was in grave danger. Sixteen years of religious inaction

followed, and in September, 520 B.C., and then on into the following January, a new prophet, Haggai by name, preached four little discourses urging action. His efforts were seconded by another prophet, Zechariah, and at once the work began. In four years the Temple was finished. It was not so large, so imposing, so richly adorned as had been Solomon's Temple, but it sufficed to save the faith. We have been following affairs in Palestine, let us now turn quickly to see what was going on in Babylonia during these fateful years.

3. *The Persian Rule.* Cyrus reigned from 558–528 B.C. and was succeeded by his son Cambyses, who lacked, indeed, many of the qualities of his father, but was nevertheless no mean king, and even added Egypt to his empire, which had now become the largest the world had known up to that day. But Cambyses lacked entirely the wisdom of Cyrus, and departed seriously from his generous treatment of conquered peoples. His life ended in a cloud, whether by his own hand, as has been reported, or not. His successor, Darius I, justly called Darius the Great (521–485 B.C.), was in administrative capacity greater, so far as we can see, than any king in any Oriental land before his day. It was he who organized what Cyrus had won, and Cambyses had left in disorder, and to him quite as much as to Cyrus is due the praise of men in his age for combining power and order with a considerable amount of peace. His successor was Xerxes I (485–465 B.C.), whose fame to us rests chiefly upon his fortunately unsuccessful attempt to conquer Greece, which failed by his defeat at Salamis in 480 and at Platæa in 479 B.C. This is here mentioned that we may connect in our minds the history of Greece with the O.T. history, for Greece is the foundation of our western culture, and the roots of N.T. doctrine are in the Hebrew thought and life.

The next king of Persia was Artaxerxes I, surnamed Macrocheir, Longimanus, "long hand," because his right hand was longer than his left (465–425 B.C.). He was a man well fitted, on the whole, for his great task. He held together by force widely separated provinces such as Bactria on the east and Egypt on the west, and so postponed for a time the downfall of the empire, which was certain to ensue in later days. During his reign, the Jews who had been carried away in 586 and had not accepted the permission to return home in 537, continued to live peaceably in his empire and especially in Babylonia. Many of them had become prosperous and there must have been men of considerable wealth among them. Some had reached posts of honor and of emolument in the empire, but with one distinguished exception their names have perished. This may well be due, in large measure at least, to the widespread habit of adopting other names either distinctively Persian or at least not clearly Jewish. To this the Jews in all ages have often been compelled by persecution or by artificial difficulties made and provided to stem their prosperity. Nor, as we know, has this device ceased to produce examples in many lands even in our own day.

Among the Jews in Babylonia were two men whose names have been preserved, Ezra and Nehemiah, and, yet more important, portions of memoirs of their own deeds and works remain in the composite book Ezra-Nehemiah which the Chronicler has rescued and copied. For this service only he deserves deep and abiding gratitude, and for it others of his all too obvious faults in recounting the past may well be forgiven.

4. *Return under Ezra.* To Ezra and to Nehemiah there had been coming from Palestine reports of the conditions there prevailing, to which story we have been making reference above. To an emotional man like Nehemiah the intelligence was distressing and he was anxious to give some help or inspiration to men who were obviously in a sad plight. Yet the opportunity came first to Ezra. In the seventh year of Artaxerxes (458 B.C.) he secured a royal decree of broad and generous compass which gave him permission to visit his people in Jerusalem. He gathered in Babylonia fifteen hundred compatriots who had resolved to cast in their lot with the restoration. They set out from Babylon and made a rendezvous at Ahava, a Babylonian district on a river of the same name. Neither the place nor the river has been identified, but they must have been near the capital city. A stay of three days made some organization possible, and permitted the making of provision for defense against possible attempts at robbery on the journey. Ezra might well have had a guard of soldiers, but he was ashamed to ask for them, "because we had spoken unto the king, saying, The hand of our God is upon all them that seek him, for good; but his power and his wrath is against all them that forsake him. So we fasted and besought our God for this: and he was entreated of us" (Ezra 8[22, 23]). In this there was a touch of fanaticism, for the taking of the ordinary and usual precautions would not in the least have dishonored God or made prayer to him for protection unnecessary. He who prays for his daily bread is not thereby

dispensed from taking every effort to earn it.

Ezra's company numbered fifteen hundred and ninety-six men, besides some priests, and he was bearing rich offerings to the Temple at Jerusalem not only from his own people but even from the king himself (Ezra 8:25-27). His caravan would have been a rich prize for some of the wandering tribes of the desert, but the long and very difficult journey was made successfully, and on the twelfth day of the seventh month (*Tishri*, October) the caravan entered the city. It must have awakened great enthusiasm, but many who rejoiced then quite probably were cheerless afterward when they had experienced the heavy hand of this new master. His first move was against mixed marriages, and many and cruel were the hardships then caused, of which in the case of Nehemiah there is some discussion above. This would very probably produce much irritation and would doubtless rouse local opposition to any other measure which he might propose. He had another and larger purpose and the long delay in beginning it is still a puzzle to our minds. The uproar over the marriage question may have been one factor in his waiting, but he who acted with so great severity in this may have been equally severe or autocratic in other matters. Whatever the cause, he was slow to act upon what would seem to have been his supreme desire. From Babylonia he had brought with him a roll of the law, a great body of religious practice and order which now forms a large part of the Pentateuch. The people in Palestine, insofar as they were maintaining the worship of Jehovah, were continuing the order found in the book of Deuteronomy. Ezra was bringing a far more elaborate liturgical law, which had been compied and arranged in Babylonia, which he undoubtedly hoped would have great value in intensifying religious zeal, in increasing devotion, enriching the forms of worship, and in the quickening of the spiritual life. But he delayed, hesitated, and perhaps was waiting a more auspicious occasion.

5. *Return under Nehemiah.* While Ezra was [illegible]sily engaged with reforms, whether wise and [illegible]essary or foolish and precipitate, help of [illegible]tinguished character and of the highest value was preparing in the east. In the winter of 445–444 B.C. the Persian court was in Susa, the ancient capital of Elam. There in a position of honor and influence was a Jew named Nehemiah, who is called cup-bearer to the king, but we know nothing of any office with such a title and can only draw the inference that he was in some way one of the king's ministers. From Jerusalem there returned a company of Jews, among whom was Hanani, own brother or near relative of Nehemiah. When questioned he gave a sorry report of the conditions in the Holy City. Nehemiah was overwhelmed and "sat down and wept, and mourned certain days; and I fasted and prayed before the God of heaven" (Neh. 1:4f.). He wished to return to Jerusalem to give help, and to inspire the people to make some effort. Four months passed before he saw a favorable opportunity of laying before the king the troubles of his people and the anxieties of his own heart. But when he finally laid the case before the king he found immediate acceptance of his plea. The king gave him four months leave of absence, with permission to go to Jerusalem, and undertake its reconstruction. He was strengthened by letters to the Persian governors west of the Euphrates, and to Asaph, keeper of the royal forest, to supply timber for the gates of the city wall and of the Temple. These letters to the governors would serve much as passports do now, and the gift of wood would be highly appreciated by a people who were poor enough to need it. Unlike Ezra, Nehemiah set out with an armed escort provided by the king, traveled unmolested, and reached Jerusalem in safety. For three days he studied the situation and then made a night inspection of the city walls. The story of this night ride, admirably and eloquently told, has captured the imagination and touched the heart of later ages.

Having arrived at a conclusion, he summoned the people, and in burning words laid before them the state of their city. Aroused by him, they took quick resolve to begin work upon the walls. All Jerusalem was roused to action, and far away from the city swept enthusiasm until men came to work from Jericho, Tekoa, Gibeon, Mizpah, Zanoah, and Keilah. It was a veritable outburst of a new national spirit. To the hard manual labor came many previously unaccustomed to it. Here were priests and Levites, goldsmiths and perfumers, even rulers of districts. A masterful man and a master of men had come and they were willing to accept his bidding and do his will. But the difficulties were many. Sanballat and Tobiah, old enemies of the Jewish people, assisted by one Geshem, or Goshem, of an Arabian tribe, sought to stop the work by getting word to the king that these were rebels against his authority, probably insinuating that they were rebuilding the city walls that they might use them against any troops he might send. When this failed they tried ridicule. Tobiah scoffed at the work they were doing, declaring it to be too weak to be of any value as a defense, saying,

"Even that which they build, if a jackal (mg.) go up, he shall break down their stone wall" (Neh. 4^{3}). Nevertheless, "the people had a mind to work" (Neh. 4^{6}). Ridicule having failed, Sanballat determined upon sterner measures. He raised a force of Arabians, Ammonites, and Ashdodites and planned a secret advance and a sudden attack. Nehemiah was prepared, and had even his workers armed. When Sanballat saw this situation he gave over the plan of assault and undertook a sort of siege. As Nehemiah was acting under royal decree, Sanballat had now made himself a rebel against Persia, which might end in a very uncomfortable situation.

The next move of Sanballat was a shrewd attempt to induce Nehemiah to enter upon a conference with him. Nehemiah refused. Then Sanballat tried a threat, declaring that there were rumors abroad that Nehemiah was seeking to make himself a king, and that he would do well to take steps to clear himself. Nehemiah decided to take the risk of a possible misunderstanding in Persia. These were difficulties enough to try even a strong man's soul. But there were dangers also among his own people. There were so-called prophets ready to act the traitor against the greatest leader whom these times had produced. The name of only one of these miscreants has been preserved, Shemaiah (Neh. 6^{10}), but there were surely some others, and perhaps even many of them.

In spite of all these forms of opposition, the policies of Nehemiah went steadily forward. The walls were reconstructed, the gates framed, and the city was again fit to be called a city according to the standards of that age. The time occupied in all this hard labor with the hands and struggle with enemies within and without cannot now be certainly learned. The mention of fifty and two days (Neh. 6^{15}) as the time consumed in the restoration of the wall is obscure because the year is not mentioned. Josephus gives two years and four months as the period of rebuilding, while Ewald has made an ingenious computation and offers the conjecture of five years, which seems none too much. The completion was celebrated with much acclaim, with two processions marching round the circuit in opposite directions, with Ezra at the head of one and Nehemiah of the other (Neh. 12^{43}).

The way was now fully prepared for Ezra's work of introducing the new code of laws which he had brought from Babylonia. With all pomp and dignified ceremonial the book was read in the ears of the people (Neh. 8–10). This was the book now commonly called the Priest Codex, with which were combined then and soon after other and earlier writings to form the Pentateuch—a book surpassed by none in all the history of literature when judged by the influence which it has exerted; for three great religions have their roots in it —Judaism, Christianity, and Mohammedanism. The people accepted it by popular acclaim and at once set about the introduction of its ceremonial provisions. This began a new era among the Jewish people; henceforth they were to be the people of a book, and not men attending upon the spoken word of the prophet. The prophet must decrease, while the scribe, the lawyer, the interpreter of a written Law, must increase. Ezra and Nehemiah had worked well together, each doing his own share in accordance with his own genius and qualifications, Nehemiah in political affairs and Ezra in morals and religion. Ezra's work would far outlast Nehemiah's, for the state would perish, but the book live on. (See art., *Pentateuch*, pp. 138–141.)

Nehemiah had proved well his right to be the governor of his people, to which office Artaxerxes had appointed him. He must now return to Persia to render account of his stewardship. There are unhappily some chronological difficulties which must be discussed in the commentary below. He left his province in a far better state than he had found it. But when his strong hand was removed, new difficulties and troubles, mostly internal, appeared. The Temple precincts were profaned (Neh. $13^{4f.}$); the Levits did not receive their lawful dues and had to seek a livelihood in the field (Neh. 13^{10}; cf. Mal. 3^{7-12}); the laws of Sabbath-keeping were violated; mixed marriages began again. It seemed as though the whole new structure of political and religious life so carefully set on foot was about to fall into pieces. The situation called loudly for the personal presence of Nehemiah, and in the year 433 B.C. he returned again to Jerusalem ready for vigorous measures of repression and of reorganization. He had no mock modesty; he knew his worth and fearlessly made mention of it. He concluded his labors with the bold words, "Remember me, O my God, for good" (Neh. 13^{31}). So ends our story of the background in history and of the work of Ezra and Nehemiah.

The Sources of the Books. It has been stated that we owe these books for their compilation and preparation to the Chronicler, from whose hand or hands came also the two books of Chronicles. It needs only that we here mention so far as known the materials which he used. His sources may be briefly enumerated here, and there will be some further hints and explanations.

(1) *The Memoirs of Ezra*, from which there were certain portions extracted verbatim, as, e.g., Ezra $7^{27f.}$ 8^{1-36} and 9^{1-15}, and these are of priceless value to us. Besides this he used the same source for material without making verbal extracts as in 7^{12-26}. Furthermore, he took still other portions and worked them over in his own way and in his own style.

(2) *The Memoirs of Nehemiah.* From these he has made verbatim extracts, as Neh. 1^1–7^5 and 13^{4-31}, and, as in the case of Ezra, utilized other portions, turning them over for his own special purposes.

(3) *Temple Records.* In the accounts of the building of the Temple there seems to be evidence of the use of some record or records which may have been preserved in the Temple precincts and made available. The passages which particularly suggest this are Ezra 4^{6-23} and 5^1–6^{15}. Furthermore, in the list of the heads of families, both priestly and levitical (Neh. 12^{1-26}), we may presumably conjecture that these also came from records preserved in the Temple.

(4) *Doubtful Sources.* There must have been much material derived from sources no longer in existence and not now to be differentiated or surmised by us.

Literature. In the case of Ezra and Nehemiah, as in that of every other book, the only sure method is to begin with repeated reading of the books in the R.V. He who will do this will have a reward to be secured in no other way. Reading and re-reading and reading again is the only way to gain familiarity. So, and so only, are supposed difficulties and obscurities removed, and then the real difficulties stand out clearly and we are ready to ask for help looking toward their solution. When this has been done and this commentary has done all that may justly be expected of it, the real student is ready for something larger and better. But he will now be confronted with a disappointment, for the literature available to those who read only English is not so extensive as in the case of the more popular books, such as Genesis, Isaiah, and the Psalms. The most helpful books are: Ryle, *Ezra and Nehemiah* (Cambridge Bible); T. Witton Davies, *Ezra, Nehemiah, and Esther* (Century Bible); Batten, *Ezra and Nehemiah* (International Critical Commentary); George Adam Smith, *The Book of the Twelve Prophets*, especially pp. 187–272 (Expositor's Bible); Foakes-Jackson, *The Biblical History of the Hebrews to the Christian Era;* Kent, *The Makers and Teachers of Judaism.*

EZRA

CHAPTER I

1–4. Cyrus Permits the Jews to Return Home. The book begins with an account of the issuance of a decree by Cyrus permitting the Jews to return to Palestine. The decree is unfortunately not given verbatim but in the words of the Chronicler giving in his own way the sense. In 2 Chr. $36^{22f.}$ the first three verses down to *let him go up* are repeated. They are original here, and were there quoted to give the book a cheerful conclusion. *In the first year* is 537 B.C., which was not really the first year of his reign as king, for he had been king in his own country from 559 or 558, but it was the first year of his reign as king of Babylon, which was taken in 538. For this reason the Jewish chronicler calls it the first year, i.e., the first year of Cyrus' rule over the Jews in Babylonia, who had before this been under the rule of Nabonidus, king of Babylon. *By the mouth of Jeremiah* means the seventy years as predicted by him in 29^{10} as follows: "For thus saith the Lord, After seventy years be accomplished for Babylon, I will visit you, and perform my good word toward you, in causing you to return to this place" (cf. 25^{11}). All sorts of antics have been performed by commentators to locate this seventy years, which is obviously a longer period than the Jews were in Babylon, for 597–537 is but fifty-nine or sixty years, and 586–537 is only forty-nine years. The true explanation is that "seventy" is only a general statement in a round number for a long period, and is not to be taken as a literally exact definition of the years of Exile. *The Lord stirred up . . . Cyrus.* Cf. Isa. 45^1, where Cyrus is denominated the Lord's anointed. *All the kingdoms*—a very great boast, but such were common among Oriental kings. The Chronicler goes on to declare that Cyrus acknowledged Jehovah as the God who inspired his deed (v. 2). But we see from the Babylonian and Persian inscriptions which we now possess that Cyrus was a polytheist and so remained. Whatever honor he showed the gods of other peoples was not done because of an acceptance of them but for political purposes. *Whosoever is left*—read *remaineth.* This sounds as though the decree bade peoples other than the Jews to help them. Though this might come about in some places where good relations existed it seems hardly likely to be commonly the case. The text as it stands is awkward in the Hebrew, and it seems most likely that the original meaning was that Jews who did not choose to return should help those who did go.

5–11. **The Return of the Jews Under Shesbazzar.** The Jews gave liberally to those who were going in the return, and Cyrus even ordered that the sacred vessels which Nebuchadrezzar had removed from the Temple (2 Kings 24[13] 25[14f.] 2 Chr. 36[7]) should be restored, and this was to be done by *Mithredath.* The name is in Persian *Mithradata,* which means "Mithras (the Persian sun god) has given," known to us in the Greek form *Mithridates,* or, more correctly, *Mithradates.* These vessels and other gifts were to be given to *Shesbazzar,* a name of uncertain derivation and meaning, which has long been a puzzle to commentators. He has often been identified with Zerubbabel, but this should not be done. He was quite probably the uncle of Zerubbabel, by whom he was succeeded in the office of governor. The numbers given in vv. 9–11 cannot be satisfactorily explained and must be regarded as exaggerated.

CHAPTER II

A Register or List of Those Who Returned. Some of the names are easy to interpret or understand, and some are of persons otherwise known or even famous. This simple commentary is not fitted either by space or its immediate purpose to discuss them one by one. Yet are they all interesting enough to deserve it. Here there must be a restriction to a few only. *Zerubbabel* (v. 2) means "Seed of Babylon," for there was he born, and the name is Babylonian, not Hebrew. *Jeshua* is a shortened form of "Jehoshuah," or "Joshua"; he was the high priest of the return, and the son of Zehozadak and the grandson of Seraiah, who was put to death by Nebuchadrezzar (2 Kings 25[18-21] Jer. 52[24-27]). *Nehemiah* is not the man who restored the walls of Jerusalem in 445–444 B.C. Upon these names there follows (vv. 2–35) a register of the men of Israel who returned. It certainly has been ill preserved, for it contains not only personal names, but even names of clans and cities, and in a considerable number of cases we are still uncertain as to which is which. After these (vv. 36–39) there is a list of the *priests,* and then (vv. 40–42) come the *Levites* and with them the *singers* and *porters,* or, rather, doorkeepers. The number of the Levites seems very small, only 431 when compared with 4,289 priests. Some had been compelled to resort to purely secular work in order to win a living, but the total here leaves us still surprised at its smallness. The next list (vv. 43–54) is of the *Nethinim,* which means "given," i.e., to the Temple. They were a low grade of slaves, some of them captives in war, and belonging to foreign nations, such as Meunim, i.e., Minæans, a people of Arabia. In vv. 55–58 we have *Solomon's servants,* a subordinate class of the Nethinim, and in vv. 59–63 priests who could not trace their descent, and were therefore not recognized as legitimate members of the tribes. The word *Tirshatha* (v. 63) is a Persian word corresponding to the Babylonian word *Pekhah,* or "governor." Lagarde thought that *Tirshatha* meant "him who is feared," but it is scarcely certain. *Urim and Thummim* were the sacred tools of the lot by which decisions were given. They have usually been explained as "Light" and "Perfection," but were, rather, Hebrew adaptations of the Babylonian *Urtu* and *Tamitu,* the tablets of Destiny; and the method of using them still remains uncertain (cf. comment on 1 Sam. 1[3]). In vv. 64–67 we have the summary of all who returned, and the total comes out at 42,360. But if they be added up as they have here been given, the total is only 29,818. The numbers given in Nehemiah foot up to 31,089, and in the apocryphal book of 1 Esdras the number comes out at 30,143; yet in these cases also the total is given as 42,360, which shows plainly that some editor has corrected them to make all three passages agree. The Bible has not been miraculously preserved from errors in numbers, or from their artificial editing and correcting. The difficulties about the numbers of persons who returned appear also in the enumeration of animals; so, e.g., the horses (v. 66) are numbered at 736, but in 1 Esdras as 7,036; and the asses are set down here and in Nehemiah as numbering 6,720, but in 1 Esdras the number of them is 5,525. Then the chapter specifies (vv. 68, 69) the contributions made for the restoration of the Temple. The amounts seem hopelessly exaggerated, for certainly most of those who returned were poor, many very poor. As a modern analogy one needs only to be reminded of the condition of the Jews now returning to Palestine, for whom large sums must periodically be raised among their rich brethren in America and in England who have no thought of returning.

CHAPTER III

1–6. **Restoring Religion: Rebuilding the Altar.** The first act in the restoration of the religious life was the rebuilding of the altar. The month was Tishri, the *seventh month* of the religious year and corresponding in part at least to our month of October. It was one of the most sacred months in the year, for in it there occurred on the first day the Feast of Trumpets (Num. 29[1]); on the tenth the Great Day of Atonement (Num. 29[7] Lev. 16[29]), and on the fifteenth the Feast of Tabernacles (Lev. 23[34-36, 39-44] Num. 29[12-38]). It would be difficult to find any month better fitted for the beginning of a work so important. There and then a great public assembly was held, and ceremoniously a beginning was made in rebuilding the altar, and the offerings prescribed for the Feast of Trumpets (Num. 29[1-6]) were made. *Upon its base* (v. 3)—read with the mg. *in its place.* The text of the next clause has not come down in good order, but the general sense seems to be that they were now assured of the divine protection, in the fear they had of their hostile neighbors. Then they kept the Feast of Tabernacles, the most joyous of all, for it celebrated the vintage and lasted seven days (Ex. 23[16] Lev. 23[34-42]). This was followed by the re-establishment of the daily offering, morning and evening, of a lamb of the first year (Ex. 29[38-42] Num. 28[6]). There followed in due order the observance of all the *set feasts* (v. 5), Sabbath, new moons, Passover, Weeks, Trumpets, Atonement and Tabernacles. But the Chronicler adds a note, *But* (or *although*) *the foundation of the Temple of the Lord was not yet laid.* By this he means to intimate that all this was provisional, unusual, extraordinary, for he could not think that all this could properly be done until the Temple was rebuilt.

7–13. Rebuilding of the Temple Begins. Before actual work on the Temple could begin they must first quarry new stone, which could be obtained on the spot, and arrange for the securing of wood from the Lebanon. This was a costly and difficult procedure. The great trees must be felled, and then dragged over the crest of the Lebanon, and slid down the slopes of the mountain range, then rafted to Joppa and dragged thence to Jerusalem. It was a big undertaking for people so poor. This next step was taken in the *second year* (536 B.C.), and the *second month* (Iyyar, corresponding in part to May) by the appointing of Levites to carry on the great task. The text of vv. 8–10 is too difficult to make anything of it save by extensive alteration, partly by subjective conjecture and partly by the use of the Greek Ezra (cf. p. 194b). The student must study this in critical commentaries. The ceremony connected with the laying of the foundation was elaborate and was accompanied by singing which was apparently done by two choirs antiphonally. The meaning seems to be that one choir sang, *O give thanks unto the Lord, for he is good,* and the other responded, *For his mercy endureth forever.* But among the people were old men who had seen the first Temple, and, as they now looked on, they wept, thinking how small seemed all these preparations in comparison with the grandeur of Solomon's Temple. (Cf. also Hag. 2[3-9] Zech. 4[10].)

CHAPTER IV

1–7. Hostility Toward the Undertaking. This is a chapter of struggle against great odds. The neighbors of the new community were quite ready to make trouble unless very tactfully handled, and perhaps in any case, or under any condition. The whole case is not difficult to understand. When Sargon took Samaria, capital of the Northern Kingdom, in 722 B.C., he carried off twenty-seven thousand two hundred and ninety of the inhabitants and settled them within the borders of his own kingdom. To occupy the space vacated by them he brought in colonists from a number of conquered peoples. During the reign of Esarhaddon, king of Assyria (681–668 B.C.), still others were brought in. The original Hebrew stock intermarried with these colonists and the mixed race thus produced came to be called Samaritans. These people now applied to the Jews, most of whom belonged to the tribes of Judah and Benjamin, to be permitted to unite in the work of rebuilding and so be received into the company of God's people Israel. They made the claim that it was their custom to sacrifice unto Jehovah (v. 2); there is, however, another reading, *yet we do not sacrifice* (R.V. mg.), but the first is preferable. This request was denied very haughtily, and one thinks, very unwisely. There would have been difficulties and dangers in their admission, but their rejection made bad blood and ill feeling, and unto our own day the evil effects continue, though now the Samaritans are but a pitiable remnant. *The people of the land* (v. 4) means all who were not of pure Israelite extraction. *Weakened the hands* might be rendered "disheartened" and *troubled them in building* should read *terrified them from building.* This attempt to stop the work went on during the rest of the reign of Cyrus. He was succeeded by Cambyses, who died or committed suicide in 522 B.C. In the same year came Darius to the throne. Now, we know from Haggai that the rebuilding was resumed in 520, the second year of Darius, and it would appear, therefore, that from 536 to 520 nothing was done. There is, therefore, a historical and chronological tangle in v. 5. The tangle is made much worse in vv. 6, 7, for here we have Xerxes, who began to reign in 485 B.C., and then Artaxerxes (464–424), and then in v. 8 we have another letter mentioned. No reasonable and solidly based solution to this problem has yet been found.

8–24. Letter to Artaxerxes, and the Reply. With v. 8 begins a long section of the book (4^8–6^{18}) which is an extract from an Aramaic document and is written in Aramaic, and not in Hebrew. It begins with a letter written to Artaxerxes with the purpose of preventing any further rebuilding of the city walls; following that letter's conclusion there comes the king's reply. Let us try to shed a little light here or there upon some portions of these letters. *Rehum* and *Shimshai* are both foreign names. They may be Persian, but that is quite doubtful. The list of nations or peoples for whom they acted are apparently all non-Hebrew. The king *Osnappar* (v. 10) is Ashurbanipal, king of Assyria, 668–625 B.C., to whom also is credited the bringing of colonists into Samaria. Now, Rehum and Shimshai as representatives of this long list of peoples appeal to Artaxerxes against the returned Jews in Jerusalem, and they attempt to prejudice the king against them by calling Jerusalem a rebellious and bad city. In v. 12 it is said that walls are finished and in v. 13 it is implied that they are still unfinished, and the petitioners pray that their completion be prevented. In v. 14 the petitioners represent themselves as being in the king's employ, which is the meaning of the expression *eat the salt of the palace.* (Cf. the English word "salary," *salarium*—"salt-money.") Then they ask the king to examine into the history, for there shall he learn that Jerusalem has been a rebellious city, and the inference that they desire to have drawn is that the king is in danger of losing all the province west of the Jordan. The king was deceived by these specious pleas and returned a reply (vv. 17–22) ordering the Jews stopped in their work; and this was done by force. After this there follows a long interval, a break in the narrative due to this Aramaic document. The document seems ill placed here, and makes us much difficulty in following the order of events (see the more detailed commentaries).

CHAPTER V

The Building of the Temple Resumed; A Letter to Darius. Now we come to the remarkable story of the resumption of work upon the Temple, after a suspension of sixteen years. The year of the resumption is given in 4^{24} as the second year of Darius, i.e., 520 B.C. and this chapter begins with some account of what led to this new effort. It was due to two prophets who fitted well into each other's work, Haggai and Zechariah. It would well repay the reader to turn to the messages of these prophets and read Haggai entirely and Zechariah 1–8, and take a look into the commentaries on these books in this volume. The last phrase in v. 1 should read as in the R.V. mg., *in the name of the God of Israel which was upon them.* Zerubbabel was now the governor and Jeshua was the high priest. Haggai and Zechariah had eventually won, and their ringing and urgent words had also won the people, so that the work began with leaders and people all in good heart. *Tattenai* (v. 3) was Persian governor over the whole district west of the river, and was therefore superior to Zerubbabel. We have found his name nowhere else. *Shetha-bozenai* was apparently a Persian name, the original form of which has been conjectured to be Shethar and boznai, a corruption of the title of the man's office (so Batten), but this is quite uncertain. Tattenai had perhaps been incited by the Samaritans, but, at any rate, he thought it his duty to ascertain definitely whether the Jews had authority for rebuilding the Temple. He sent therefore a letter to Darius asking that a search be made among the archives to learn whether any Persian decree had ever been issued giving royal permission. At the beginning of v. 4 both in A.V. and R.V. stand the words, *Then said we unto them.* The best solution yet offered is to read conjecturally, *Then spake they unto them.* The *Apharsachites* (v. 6) have not yet been identified. *The great king* (v. 11) was Solomon. In v. 16 what is said of Sheshbazzar is in contradiction of the statements in 3^8, where the work is ascribed to Zerubbabel.

CHAPTER VI

1–18. Darius Discovers and Confirms Cyrus' Decree. The king has a search made at Achmetha, i.e., Ecbatana, the summer residence of the Persian kings, and there was found a decree of Cyrus specifically ordering the rebuilding of the Temple in Jerusalem. The words of the decree as here set down are apparently not a literal copy but the substance of it in the words of the Chronicler. That which follows about supplying help to the Jews not only for the rebuilding but even for sacrifices afterward was very generous, and though not quite improbable is so much in the style of the Chronicler as to make one disposed to think it rather elaborated. The work went on rapidly thereafter and was carried to its conclusion (vv. 13–18). The success is ascribed primarily to God, but as helpers three Persian kings are mentioned, Cyrus, Darius, and Artaxerxes. The first two are correctly named here, but Artaxerxes is not, and the name is therefore probably an insertion by a later editor. The *third day of Adar* (v. 15) in the sixth year of Darius, 516 B.C., is the day of the finishing of the work (Adar is the twelfth month, approximately March). The foundation was laid in 537, and the work recommenced, as Haggai says, on the twenty-fourth day of the sixth month (Elul=September) of the second year of Darius, so that four and a half years of work had been given to it from that time to the completion. Then the dedication took place, but the sacrifices seem small when compared with those of Solomon (1 Kings $8^{5, 63}$) or of Hezekiah (2 Chr. 30^{24}) or of Josiah (2 Chr. 35^{7}). At the end of v. 18 the Aramaic language portion ends and with v. 19 Hebrew is resumed.

19–22. The Celebration of the Passover. This took place on the fourteenth day of the first month (Nisan). In only five places in the O.T. is a celebration of the Passover mentioned: (1) Under Moses (Num. 9^{5}); (2) under Joshua (Josh. 5^{10}); (3) under Hezekiah (2 Chr. 30); (4) under Josiah (2 Kings 23^{21}, 2 Chr. 35); and (5) this one under Zerubbabel. In every one of these cases there was some special or important rededication of the people to the worship of their God. Here two classes are mentioned as participating in the ceremony, namely, those who had returned from captivity and *all such as had separated themselves unto them from the filthiness of the nations of the land, to seek Jehovah, the God of Israel.* The filthiness of the land is idolatry, and the people here described are in large measure, if not wholly, Israelites left behind by Nebuchadrezzar who had drifted off into idolatrous practices but were now returning. The *king of Assyria* here meant is certainly the Persian king, who also ruled both Babylonia and Assyria since the days of Cyrus.

CHAPTER VII

1–10. The Return of Ezra the Scribe to Jerusalem. We come now to the second part of the book of Ezra, which is devoted to an account of the return under Ezra and to his work. It begins with a summary, setting down first Ezra's genealogy and then his return to Jerusalem. Between the preceding chapter and this a period of nearly sixty years is passed over silently. There had been an allusion to Xerxes (4^{7}) and into this reign is also fitted the episode narrated in the book of Esther, which, insofar as it contains any historical material, was deemed interesting and important, but it had no influence in the course of events, and the Chronicler could find nothing to tell. The phrase *Now after these things* is not uncommon (Gen. 15^{1} 22^{1} Lk. 10^{1}) but is otherwise insignificant. For the genealogy of Ezra see the introduction, p. 457a. The reign of Artaxerxes extends over the period 465–425 B.C., and the event now to be described occurred in 458. *A ready scribe* (v. 6). For the scribes and the significance of their work in later days see the introduction. Note that here the description of Ezra is given in the third person, and contrast the use of the first person beginning with v. 27. The enumeration of those who came up with Ezra is elaborate. Every possible order from priests to Nethinim is mentioned (on the last named see 2^{43-54} above), and this points to a very careful maintenance of communal life in Babylonia. Everything that could be done to hold the people to national and religious order seems to have been done. The *fifth month* (v. 9) was Ab, corresponding approximately to August. The rendezvous occurred apparently in the first month (Nisan) and the time occupied was in all about three months and a half, and the distance by the route which they had to take up the Euphrates and then down through Syria would be about nine hundred miles. The journey would be very hard in summer (April to August), and to avoid the blistering heat it would be necessary to bivouac during most of the day, traveling by night and in the early morning. (On the names of the Hebrew months here and following, see p. 77b.)

11–28. The Letter Given by Artaxerxes to Ezra. Here follows a copy of the letter of authority from Artaxerxes which Ezra carried. As to substance there is no reason to doubt it, but the Chronicler attempts only a synopsis, and his own views are discernible in it. V. 11 introduces it in Hebrew, and then with v. 12 Aramaic begins. The enumeration of gifts from the royal bounty, and the gifts of Jews who remained in Babylonia and of those met on the way made a considerable sum, but is not here added up. Ezra has complete authority for all expenditure and need have no fear about his responsibility (v. 18). He has even authority to draw for more on the royal treasure, but a limit was set of a hundred talents of silver (v. 22), which would be about one hundred and ninety thousand dollars, with an actual purchasing power of above three times that amount in the present day. It is not possible to estimate with any certainty the value of the goods which he was to have. Ezra is also commissioned to make judicial appointments and make provision for social order among his own people, so that he really exercises the authority of a governor, for even the power of death was given into his hands (v. 26). It has been said that this applies only to the religious reorganization, but it is not easy to see where the qualification appears. Ezra, according to the literal word, is made a sort of despot. And now, suddenly, in v. 27 the narrative switches back into Hebrew, and we read in two verses an outburst of joy and gratitude from Ezra, who prepares at once to exercise the authority committed to him. The deeds that follow show how willing he was to wield the scepter. Indeed, from his day until now there are few religious leaders who have not gladly exercised as much authority over secular affairs as they dared.

CHAPTER VIII

1–14. The Heads of Families Who Accompanied Ezra to Palestine. Some of the names are interesting, and they who have a care for genealogies might find it worth while to pursue their studies into the elaborate commentaries and dictionaries. It is not fitting to take up these minute problems here.

15–30. The Rendezvous at Ahava. The exact place is still unknown; nor has the name been found in any Babylonian document. It would seem to have been on one of the great irrigation and drainage canals not far from the capital. As the main company numbered fifteen hundred, and with all those who might be called camp followers there must have been eight thousand or more, a considerable space would be necessary for the camp. There they remained three days in tents, while Ezra made a numbering and a survey. He found that there were no Levites among them, and as one of his chief objects was the setting up of an elaborate liturgical form they were indispensable. He therefore sent messengers to a place called *Casiphia* (v. 17) whose site is quite unknown but must have been not far away, where was apparently a settlement of Levites and Nethinim, and thence drew to join them eighteen Levites of one family with twenty of another and two hundred and twenty Nethinim. Then a fast was proclaimed as a religious exercise (v. 21), and prayer offered for safety and guidance, as Ezra was unwilling to ask the king for a guard, which was really as needful in that journey then as it is now. In this matter Nehemiah displayed better judgment. When the religious ceremonies were over, Ezra set himself to have a reckoning made of the money and of the value of all the vessels for the sanctuary, and the total came out at nearly five millions of dollars, with a purchasing power perhaps thrice what it now has. It seems clear enough that the amounts have been greatly exaggerated.

31–36. The Journey and the Arrival at Jerusalem. As has already been said, the difficulties were enormous and the successful conclusion leaves to us only a desire to speak a word of praise for the management of the whole affair. Ezra proved himself equal to the task. Upon arrival offerings in large numbers and at much cost were made by those who had returned, and when these ceremonies were concluded Ezra was ready to begin his real work. It would be no easy matter, but he was eager for it.

CHAPTER IX

Enforcing the Principle of Nationalism. The first business that came before Ezra was the sorry story of the departure of the people from the principles which he regarded as essential to the national existence. The report was of intermarriages, evidently on a large scale, with the neighboring peoples, of whom there is a long list. Ezra was plunged into a fury, tearing his garments, plucking out both hair and beard, and then sat down in mourning posture until evening. Then, before the people, at the evening assembly he tore garment and mantle and began a confession in the name of the people. In v. 8 there is a curious and difficult phrase—*a nail in his holy place*—which is apparently a metaphor of some sort, if the text is correct. The Greek Ezra gives a simple text, reading, "a root and a name in the place of thy sanctuary." This may be correct. *Bondmen* and *bondage* (v. 9) are very strong words and ill suited to express the conditions under which the Jews were living in the Persian empire, but Ezra was not in a state of composure, and might say anything. *A wall in Judah and in Jerusalem* has reference to any means of defense, not the city walls which were in ruins until Nehemiah had them rebuilt. In v. 11 Ezra seems to be depending upon Deut. 7^{1-3} 23^{7} and these passages he links with the prophets in a dual authority. This is interesting, for we do not meet with such an identification earlier. We are here standing at the beginning of the new scribal era. In v. 12 Ezra is repeating in a general way the law in Deut. 7^{3}, but he makes it very strong, and that which had originally applied, in the full force of its severity, only to the Moabites and Ammonites, he now applies to all the neighboring peoples, though Edomites and Egyptians had been expressly excepted from the curse (Deut. 23^{7}). In vv. 13–15 Ezra declares that this deed of theirs is so evil that God might even have utterly consumed them. He has indeed punished them less than their evils deserved.

CHAPTER X

1–5. The People Confess and Make Promises. While Ezra was confessing and praying in public the people were gathering in a great assembly. The news would have spread widely and such a spectacle would create great excitement. And now the narrative shifts back into the third person. The Chronicler in the preceding passage has been quoting Ezra's memoirs, though in his own fashion. He now drops this method and, whether using the memoirs as a source or not, goes back into his own style. In a state of high excitement and under the leadership of a man named Shechaniah—a name with the almost ironical meaning here of "Jehovah has taken up his abode"—the people covenant to put away the foreign wives and their (little) children. And Ezra made them take oath to do this barbarous, cruel, atrocious deed. O religion, what crimes have been committed in thy name!

6–17. The Process of Putting Away Foreign Wives. The next step was to devise machinery and provide checks in the carrying out of this business. Ezra went aside to mourn and fast, not in sorrow for the poor women and the children that must suffer, but because these marriages had ever taken place. A little more mercy and pity would have made him seem more like a human being. But we need cast no stones. The spirit of intolerance survives the flight of time. All were now summoned to Jerusalem, and a time limit of three days set, after which the goods of those who did not appear would be forfeited (in Hebrew "devoted," i.e., "destroyed") and they would be excommunicated. The assembly was duly convened on the twentieth day of the ninth month (Chislev=approximately December) which was in the rainy season. There they sat in the broad place before the Temple, while the cold rain of the hills poured down upon them, for it is particularly called *a great rain.* There, in the wet, Ezra addressed them in minatory words, bidding them not only to separate themselves from the poor, miserable wives, but even from their neighbors. The LXX supplies in v. 12 an interesting reading, "Great is this thy demand for us to do," which suits well with the context. There were men of sense and feeling among them who mentioned the weather and measured the task as a great one. Perhaps some thought of postponement until better weather conditions might make it a little easier to drive out the women and the children. They even ask for the appointment of a commission. This was done and the commission sat during three months, hearing and adjudicating separate cases (v. 17). They began on the first day of the tenth month (Tebeth=approximately January) and sat through Tebeth, Shebat, and Adar, or three months, and made an end by the first day of the first month (Nisan=approximately April) which would certainly be a month more reasonably suited for the horrors of this family disruption. The climate of Jerusalem in April is usually pleasant. The wives could now take packs on their backs, and lead the children by the hand, and go out under God's blue sky with less peril.

18–44. A List of Those Who Had Taken Foreign Wives. There appear among them no less than seventeen priests, together with Levites, singers and doorkeepers. It is clear, therefore, that those who were religious leaders had a considerable share in breaking the laws. Ezra has shown no mercy. He has carried out the provisions of the matter as logic, not as mercy required. Some commentators provide unconscious humor in their desire to exculpate him. Let us leave him as he was and pass on to the next man, until we see Ezra again in another capacity.

NEHEMIAH

Introduction. For a discussion of the general questions connected with this book, see the introduction to Ezra-Nehemiah, pp. 454–463.

CHAPTER I

The Sadness of Nehemiah: His Prayer for the Prosperity of Jerusalem. We are now come to the work of Nehemiah. Ezra completed his work concerning the foreign wives on the first day of Nisan (April) of the eighth year of Artaxerxes (457 B.C.). We are now suddenly transported to Chislev (December), the ninth month of the twentieth year of Artaxerxes (445 B.C.). There is, however, a tangle in the dates, and it is best to admit it frankly. In Neh. 2[1] we read of events in the first month (Nisan), while here in this first chapter we read of the ninth month of that year. What took place in the ninth month surely did not precede what took place in the first month. Some compiler or copyist has blundered. The introductory words of this chapter were, apparently, placed here when Chronicles, Ezra, and Nehemiah ceased to be one, and became three books. They were then necessary to introduce Nehemiah as a separate book.

Nehemiah was now in Susa (for *Shushan*), the winter capital of the Persian kings, and was in the palace, or, rather, the royal castle.

There he received a visit from a man named Hanani, who was apparently a relative; the word describing him does not necessarily mean brother. With him came some other Jews from Jerusalem who brought a sorry report of the state of affairs at Jerusalem. Ezra's great marriage reform had borne no good fruit in an energetic policy of political and external progress. The walls and gates were still in ruin thirteen years later. What was needed was practical wisdom and efficiency rather than religious fanaticism. The news plunged Nehemiah into grief, which continued for days. He fasted and prayed and the prayer here ascribed to him (vv. 5–11) sounds much like a regular liturgical prayer which may have come from some sort of Temple prayer book. It is strongly charged with phrases from Deuteronomy. Everything in the prayer is so plain that it needs no exposition.

CHAPTER II

1–11. Nehemiah's Desire to Return to Jerusalem. Nehemiah was cupbearer to the king; we do not know what sort of office this was, but it is clear enough that it was a post of dignity and near to the king. The English version of v. 1b adds something to the Hebrew in describing Nehemiah's attitude. The Hebrew says only "I was not sad," but the king observed a change in his countenance, and Nehemiah, knowing that he must not be gloomy in the royal presence, was much perturbed, and confessed the reason for his demeanor. The king asked what he desired, and learned that Nehemiah wished to visit Jerusalem and see what he might be able to do for its rebuilding. Nehemiah asks boldly for permission to go, for letters of convoy, and for materials from the royal possessions to be used in restoration works. The memoir of Nehemiah which the Chronicler has been using must have been much abbreviated by him. We are whisked along swiftly over the long journey, which went probably from Susa to Babylon, and thence up the Euphrates, and across by way of Damascus and then down to Jerusalem. There Nehemiah waited three days, as Ezra had done before him in his time. He needed some rest, and he may well have made some ceremonial visits to men of promise in Jewry.

12–20. Nehemiah Surveys the Walls by Night. Following these preliminary labors, he was ready to make a personal survey of the situation. He decided to do it by night in order, as far as possible, to give no occasion for enemies to stir up trouble. He would probably ride on a mule or ass as much more surefooted than a horse, and so he made a circuit of the ruined walls. The various places mentioned—the valley gate, dragon well, and dung port—have been for ages matters of dispute among archæologists, and he who would know how uncertain and difficult they are still may consult the larger commentaries and read in George Adam Smith's learned, interesting, and monumental book on *Jerusalem*. But whatever way he took, or however he went, there can be no doubt of the interesting quality of the story. It is picturesque, and he who has not enough imagination to feel a stir as he reads of it deserves real pity. Then he got together the leaders of the people, and having told them of the impression which the moonlit sight had made upon him, he urged them to unite in a great effort to put the city in a state of proper defense by rebuilding its walls. The enemies whom he must now confront are named as three, *Sanballat*, *Tobiah*, and *Geshem the Arabian*. The first name is Assyrio-Babylonian; its form in that language would be Sin-uballit, which means, "Sin (the moon god) has given life"; he is mentioned in the Elephantine papyri as governor of Samaria. Tobiah was an Ammonite, but his name is Hebrew and means "Jehovah is my good." Geshem is called an Arabian, and his name is written "Gashmu" in 6[6], where the ending "u" is Nabatean. These opponents were an ill-assorted group of mixed nationalities, but perhaps likely to be all the more efficient in stirring up trouble if each had some of his own nationals as followers. Their present plan was to sneer and insinuate that Nehemiah and his followers were planning to rebel against the king of Persia by setting up here a city to be defended against him. Nehemiah, sure of his ground, repudiates them and declares his confidence in God's support.

CHAPTER III

An Independent Account of the Reconstruction. In ch. 3 we have an independent account of reconstruction work, which breaks the connection between 2[20] and 4[1], where the story resumes. It is clearly incomplete and must be an insertion from an independent source. The distribution of the work as here set down disagrees in certain particulars with that given in ch. 6, nor is our knowledge sufficient to enable us in every point to bring them into unity. *Eliashib*, now high priest, was the son of Joiakim and grandson of Jeshua (Ezra 3[2] Neh. 12[10]). He here co-operates with Nehemiah, but his association with Tobiah (13[4]) would seem to indicate that he was hardly in sympathy with Nehemiah in all points—perhaps not in Nehemiah's moves to bring about complete separation between the returned Jews and the peoples of the land. The localities here mentioned bristle with difficulties, and it is idle to attempt a solution for more than a few of them. The *sheep gate* lay on the north side of the Temple inclosure and may have been so named because through it sheep were brought to the sacrifice. The *tower of Meah* was northwest of this and corresponds to the *birah*, or castle, which Nehemiah mentions (2[8]), which appertains to the house of Jehovah (see also 7[2]). It was the residence of the Persian governor, and afterward of the Maccabean kings. It was rebuilt by Herod the Great and named Antonia. The *tower of Hananel* was further toward the northwest, not far from the present Damascus gate, which should probably be identified with Nehemiah's *fish gate* (v. 3). It was named from its proximity to the fish market to which resorted the fish dealers from the Sea of Galilee and from the Phœnician cities. The fish supplied were probably salted and sun dried. The *old gate* (v. 6) lay at the northwest corner of Solomon's wall and would therefore correspond approximately with the Jaffa gate. The *broad wall* (v. 8) corresponds to the present wall south of the Jaffa gate. The *tower of the furnaces* (v. 11) has been identified with the rock-cut foundations which have been found in the grounds of Bishop Gobat's school, and known to archæologists as Maudslay's scarp. The *valley gate* (v. 13) was at the southwest corner of Solomon's wall and the *dung gate* at the extreme southern side of the city. It has been excavated by Bliss, and was perhaps so named as the gate through which the refuse of the city was carried. The *fountain gate* (v. 15) lay near the pool of Siloam at the crossing of the Tyropean valley.

Next came the *pool of Siloam* (v. 15; see text and mg.) to which water was conveyed by a rock-cut from Gihon, called commonly the Virgin's Spring. The overflow from Siloam made a fertile spot in the mouth of the Tyropoeon which was called the *king's garden*. The *stairs of the city of David* are the rock-cut steps which may still be seen at the southern end of the eastern hill. *The tower that standeth out* (v. 25) was excavated by Warren, south of the Haram, on which stand now the sacred buildings of the Mohammedans. The *water gate* (v. 26) lay near this and gave access to the spring of Gihon. The *horse gate* (v. 28) was in Solomon's wall at the southeast corner of the Temple inclosure. The *gate of Hammiphkad* (or the "mustering"—v. 31) was the same as the old east gate of the Temple.

CHAPTER IV

1–6. The Samaritans Purpose to Stop the Work. The text beginning with v. 2 and onward is in grave doubt. Its difficulties are so numerous that we can only suppose that there are copyists' mistakes in it. The problems may be sought out in the larger commentaries. Here it need only be said that as the R.V. makes reasonable sense the ordinary reader will do well to be content with it. By the *army of Samaria* is probably meant not an army in the modern sense but, rather, groups or mobs of men more or less armed. The next phrase but one, *will they fortify themselves?* is unsatisfactory. Ryle most ingeniously proposes an emendation of the Hebrew which produces "will they commit themselves to their God?"—which seems almost too good to be true, though it does combine beautifully with the following clause, *will they sacrifice?* *Revive* should be translated *restore.* In vv. 4 and 5 we have a prayer interjected. All went well until the wall was raised to half its former height all the way round the city. It has been calculated from the foundations discovered by Sir Charles Warren that the original ancient wall had been two hundred feet high!

7–23. Nehemiah's Preparations to Meet the Opposition. In most printed editions of the Hebrew Bible the fourth chapter begins with v. 7 of ch. 4 in the English Bible. The story goes on now to describe a very dangerous critical situation. The success thus far attendant upon Nehemiah's reconstruction work had impressed the enemies strongly with the probability that the Jews would succeed in their enterprise unless other steps were taken. The three leaders already mentioned combined forces and secured also the aid of some allies from Ashdod, then probably the chief Philistine city on the coast. They decided now to resort to force and make a combined attack. Nehemiah had a sufficiently good intelligence service to learn of the danger and prepared to meet it. He prayed unto God, which was an admirable beginning, but only the beginning. He knew what were the realities, and prepared to do the duty of a man, and not imitate a rabbit to run away. Nehemiah had also to cope with cowardly Jews, who lived near the enemies and *ten times* (v. 12) warned his people of their danger and tried to get them to leave the works and return home. Nehemiah, in order to ward off any surprise attack, armed his people with swords, spears, and bows, and did his best to inspire them with courage and make them willing to fight, and so he got them to go on with the work, with half at work and half on the watch to repel an attack. Some even of the workers had a tool in one hand and a weapon in the other. So did this manly man keep men at work and on guard, and inspired by hope, and assured of God's help for those who help themselves. He is indeed a noble picture, a man to remember, a man to imitate in time of peace, or in time of war, to be ready in the former for the coming of the latter, if, when and as it may come.

CHAPTER V

1–13. Economic Difficulties. This passage would be reasonably clear in itself if we could be sure that it was here set in its proper context. There was a stringency in food supplies caused by something which is not here mentioned. The position of the passage implies that this was caused in some way by the work on the walls—perhaps by the withdrawal of agricultural laborers from their fields to work on the walls, or to take part in defense measures against the threats and acts of Sanballat and his followers. There are, however, difficulties in this solution, for in v. 14 Nehemiah is talking about affairs after he had been in Jerusalem twelve years, which was long after the walls had been completed. This, then, points to the economic disturbance as something long after the work on the walls, and due to some other cause, such, perhaps, as one of the famines to which Palestine had often been accustomed. It is a question we cannot answer, a problem we cannot solve. If we had all of Nehemiah's memoir complete instead only of the excerpts which the Chronicler has preserved, this might be made plain. *The people* who cried out in their want are the poorer classes, as distinguished from the aristocracy of riches or of rank such as the priesthood. Some had borrowed to buy food, others to pay the king's tribute, i.e., taxes. Nehemiah was very angry and provided for a conference to consider the matter, and learn who was responsible for usurious practices, and for selling people into slavery (v. 7). The laws of slavery had been changed several times, for those in Deuteronomy are quite different from those of Exodus, and again from those in Leviticus. He applied so far as he could a law of mercy and demanded restitution of lands and goods, and made priests swear that they would do this. He made a vigorous speech, and accompanied it with a symbolical gesture, pulling in his outer garment to his body and then shaking it out loose (v. 13). They would remember that. Ah, what a man he was! A man for that day indeed.

14–19. Nehemiah Enumerates Other Sacrifices and Work of His for His People. He is speaking of a period of twelve years, 445–444 to 433–432 B.C., during which he was governor. We do not know how much of his time he actually resided at Jerusalem. It is clear that at some time he had gone back to Susa (see 13[6f.]), and in 432 returned to Jerusalem. He did so much at Jerusalem that we must think of him as being there most of the twelve years, but it may not be so. We do not know, and conjectures do not carry us far. Here, again, we wish for the whole of Nehemiah's memoir. If only it had survived; if only it might yet be discovered—but there seems to be no probability. Alas, and alas! Nehemiah not only took nothing from the public purse but he spent lavishly upon entertainment of others, and as he concludes the survey he has the boldness to call upon God to reward him. There is no mock modesty in the prayer, and there is also nothing of a petty conceit or of self adulation in it. He knew he had done well. His conscience was clear. He had a just right to a decent degree of pride in his career, and was man enough to say so. Let the record stand.

CHAPTER VI

1–9. Another Attempt to Hinder Nehemiah. Here, now, owing to the bad arrangement of the different sections of this important book, we are carried back to the story of the rebuilding of the walls, which was interrupted by ch. 5. We are here again observing the efforts of Sanballat, and his motley crew, to prevent the conclusion of the work on the wall. They propose now to try chicanery, get Nehemiah into a conference and contrive some scheme to get him into their power. They invite him to *Ono*, which may be at Kefr Ana, north of Lydda (Ezra 2[33] 1 Chr. 8[12]). This would involve his absence for three or four days. He refused. This attempt was made four times, and then as a fifth attempt a letter was sent to insinuate that he had better prepare to defend himself against a charge that he was plotting a rebellion against the Persian king, and suggesting that he had better confer with Sanballat, who would endeavor to give him aid. Nehemiah responds, curtly denying the impeachment and goes on with the work, offering a word of prayer to God for help.

10–14. Nehemiah's Enemies Resort to Treachery. The narrative is so concise as not to be very clear to us at this long distance in time and space. So far as we can fathom it, it would seem that Nehemiah is warned that an attempt on his life is probable and he was advised to seek asylum in the inner sanctuary, accompanied by Shemaiah. Now, Shemaiah was *shut up*, that is ceremonially unclean (cf. Jer. 36[5]). No layman had a right to enter the inner sanctuary and Nehemiah was a layman. Moreover, to enter with a man ceremonially unclean would greatly increase the breach of law. But Nehemiah is too keen and quickwitted so to be entrapped.

15–19. Completion of the Walls. The walls are completed in fifty-two days in the month Elul=August-September. The time seems too short. See the remarks in the introduction concerning this matter, p. 462a.

CHAPTER VII

1–4. The Necessity of Continued Vigilance. The work was done, but there was now need to guard what had already been attained. The price of safety, then, as often since, was vigilance. Nehemiah ordered the gates kept closed until the sun was hot, though the usual practice was to open at sunrise. This precaution would prevent a surprise visit before the whole city was active. Even the late sleepers, then, as now, are a menace in the eyes of men of action. *The houses were not builded* (v. 4) does not mean that there were no houses within the walls but that there were unoccupied spaces; the city was not full of inhabitants.

5–73. List of Returned Exiles. Nehemiah found among the archives a register of those who had returned. This means probably those who returned under Zerubbabel, and this supposition is confirmed by its close resemblance to that in Ezra 2[1-70], with which there is also for comparison the Greek Esdras. There would be no profit for us in a minute examination of these names. Let us pass them by. We come now to the story of the great religious reform and to the interesting story of the introduction of the new Law. We have first the public reading of the Law.

CHAPTER VIII

The Great Religious Reform. The next three chapters contain a description of the great religious reform initiated by Ezra and Nehemiah.

1–12. The Calling of a Public Assembly. There is a great public assembly, brought about we know not how, for only parts of the original story have here been preserved. For even this much we should be very thankful. The assembly was held on the first day of the seventh month, which was the day appointed for the Feast of the Trumpets (Ezra 3[1] Lev. 23[23-25] Num. 29[1-6]). This month was Tishri, approximately October, and therefore a good season in most years, before the winter rains began. And now the name of *Ezra* appears for the first time in the book of Nehemiah. What had Ezra been doing all this while? This we do not know. We may speculate, which is harmless and sometimes amusing, but it carries us not very far. He may have gone back to Babylon. He may have remained at Jerusalem and gone on with his reforms, and we are left without information solely because the part of his memoir which contains information about his work has perished. Let us be thankful to the Chronicler for all that he has preserved and be as contented as we may without the rest. What we now have before us is the account of the promulgation of the Law. The assembly is present. Ezra has the roll as priests and scribes and lawyers had put it together in Babylonia. He is now, at long last, and after much preparation ready to read it. Ezra stood upon a *pulpit of wood* (v. 4), in Hebrew, a "tower"; it probably means some sort of a platform, for on the platform with him were a certain number of men. The number cannot now be definitely ascertained. The Hebrew makes the number six on the right hand and seven on the left, as does also the LXX, but 1 Esdras gives seven on the right hand and six on the left. Who were these men? Were they Levites? Where was the high priest, and why was he not present? It is idle to speculate. In v. 8 there seem to be confusions in the pronouns. The verse should probably read, *And he* (*Ezra*) *read in the book, and they* (*the Levites*) *gave the sense, and they* (*the people*) *understood the reading.* The word *distinctly* does not exactly correspond to anything in the Hebrew. The expression *gave the sense* is to be taken with this. The R.V. is paraphrasing rather than translating, but the result is good rather than bad. But we cannot successfully reconstruct the whole scene with any strong assurance. As good a guess as any is that Ezra first read a bit aloud, then offered some explanation, and the Levites followed with an exposition and interpretation, perhaps even translating some of the Hebrew words into Aramaic, which language must now have been in considerable use. The main point is that by some process the newly expanded and greatly enlarged Law, now represented as a whole and in a final form in the Pentateuch, was presented to the people for their acceptance. Then the people, much solemnized by the scene and the Law, wept, thinking how far short they came of all these requirements; but their leaders told them to go away rather and make merry and rejoice, and send gifts in token of the happiness with which they received the words of the Law of their God.

13–18. Celebration of the Feast of Tabernacles. In this new Law they found the regulations governing the Feast of Tabernacles. They seem to have known nothing of this before, but now prepare to celebrate it. The Law is found in Ex. 23^{16} Lev. 23^{29-43} Num. 29^{12-38} Deut. 16^{13-15}. Yet there are records elsewhere of its having been observed by Solomon (2 Chr. 7^{8} 8^{13}) and by Zerubbabel (Ezra 3^{4}) and it would therefore appear that the Chronicler had forgotten or overlooked these instances. In v. 18 there is some doubt as to whether we should understand *he read,* i.e., Ezra, or "one read," i.e., somebody else.

CHAPTER IX

1–5a. The Fast. The Fast and the Confession and the Solemn Covenant are described in chs. 9 and 10. The assembly of which we have been reading took place on the twenty-second of Tishri and after the lapse of only one day, on the twenty-fourth, there begins a great ceremony of national humiliation. And now the *seed of Israel,* they who had completely separated themselves from all their neighbors, put on the signs of mourning, not for their sins but as an expression of sorrow that they had not been keeping the Law which had now been made known to them.

5b–37. Prayer and Confession. Who offered it is not said. It needs no comment. The phrases are familiar, for they are taken from Scripture elsewhere, especially from the Psalter. It has the prophetic rather than the priestly tone and may have been inserted here from some earlier writing. The passage is liturgical and shows how rich is the biblical material in forms of prayer, and he who knows the *Book of Common Prayer* will there find how much the Bible has contributed to its rich and beautiful store of words of supplication.

38. The Hebrew begins ch. 10 at v. 38, and Luther has accepted this division for the German Bible.

CHAPTER X

1–29. Those Who Accepted the Covenant. Here is the covenant, and, as was later and very often an Oriental custom, the names of those who accept the covenant and agree to keep it are placed at the beginning, and not at the end as they would be in our usage. The first name is quite properly Nehemiah, the governor, whose title is here given as Tirshatha.

30–39. The Obligations of the Covenant. The first prohibition is the intermarriage with foreign women. This is the old bone of contention, which Ezra (9^{2}) had so strenuously and so severely tried to have carried out. The immense difficulty of even an approximate securing of compliance may be seen at a glance in Neh. 13^{23-28}. The next prohibition relates to the *Sabbath* (v. 31), which contains an extension over the phraseology of the Pentateuch. This was the beginning of a fearful series of extensions and refinements and casuistries prolonged through centuries until Another and a Greater should declare that the Sabbath was made for man, and not man for the Sabbath—yet are there many in Christianity still in the old bondage of law in this matter. With the Sabbath observance is linked also the seventh year (Lev. 25^{2-7}), but there is evidence enough that it was not carried through (Lev. $26^{34, 35, 43}$; 2 Chr. 36^{21}). There would appear to have been some efforts to do it in later times (1 Macc. $6^{49, 53}$ Josephus, *Antiquities,* bk. xi, ch. 8: 6). It is amusing to note that Tacitus ascribes this custom to national laziness (*History,* bk. v, ch. 4), but laziness has never been a Jewish vice. As to the exaction of debt on the seventh year it may be remarked that this does not mean extinction but only postponement until the next year. The law of poll tax (v. 32) follows and provides a charge of one third of a shekel, but, according to the written Law (Ex. 30^{11-16}), a half shekel was due. This shows that Ezra was quite willing to modify the Law to suit conditions. He was not a complete literalist. The next provision was the arrangement for the supply of *wood* for sacrifices (v. 34). The quantity necessary for the multitudinous sacrifices must have been great, and the maintenance of the supply very difficult, for the country was small, the soil poor and lacking in depth for tree growth. The last provision was for *first fruits and tithes* (vv. 35–39). The laws concerning tithe vary enormously in the O.T. and it is impossible here to discuss and disentangle them. They who really wish to know must have recourse to Bible dictionaries and to critical commentaries. It seems a pity that so many in the Christian Church still cling tenaciously to the idea of tithing as a perfectly clear, simple, straightforward, comprehensive divine law, though a few hours of study would show how little such adjectives would properly apply.

CHAPTER XI

Miscellaneous. We have come now to the very last section of the book which is comprised in chs. 11–13. It may well be called "Miscellaneous," and is conveniently taken in the order in which it stands. It has not much of interest for us, and seems to have been rather loosely put together. The first section of it (11^{1}–12^{26}) consists of lists of various kinds and of mixed importance.

1, 2. Increasing the Population of Jerusalem. We have already seen that Jerusalem was underpopulated, and that the city had unbuilt spaces within its walls. Here is an effort to remedy this situation. Lots were to be cast, so that people from the villages should be selected, one out of ten, to come and make homes in the city. In some cases this would involve a serious re-adjustment, for it might be difficult to find bread-earning labor. Some who came voluntarily were much honored for their patriotism and self-sacrifice.

3–24. Lists of Names of the Chief People in Jerusalem. There are first (vv. 3–9) the chief laymen; upon which there follow the priests (vv. 10–14); the Levites (vv. 15–18); the gate keepers (v. 19), with a few miscellaneous (vv. 20–24). We can see signs of the difficulty with which these lists have been preserved and handed on to us. Thus in the list of priests the total comes out at one thousand one hundred and ninety-two, but in the list in 1 Chr. 9[13] it is one thousand seven hundred and sixty. The king referred to in vv. 23, 24 is Artaxerxes, and this proves this list to belong to the time of Nehemiah.

CHAPTER XII

1–26. Another List. Names of those who returned with Jeshua and Zerubbabel, with sundry extracts from other lists. If we compare the lists here in vv. 1–7 and again in vv. 12–21 with 10[3-9], we shall find many discrepancies, the complete explanation of which is not easy. The only point of importance here to be noted is that the *Ezra* in vv. 1 and 13 is not Ezra the scribe; this Ezra appears in 10[3] with the name written Azariah.

27–43. A Narrative of the Dedication of the Walls. The natural place for this narrative would seem to be immediately following upon 6[15]. It is only another instance of the loose editing of the parts which compose the book. But however ill its placing here, it is of great value, for it is evidently based upon the authentic memoir of Nehemiah, as we may see from several verses (31, 38, 40), but the Chronicler has probably used it in his own way, making over its phrases into his own manner. We should like to have the original, but as fate has denied us that boon we do well to value what we have. The instruments used in the joyous celebration are still not any too well identified, but the *psaltery* was apparently a small, portable harp, played with the balls of the fingers, while the instrument here called *harp* corresponds more nearly to a zither and was picked with a piece of metal held between the fingers. There is not much that needs comment in this passage, save only here a word or two. The *house of Gilgal* (v. 29; *beth* is the Hebrew word for house) is probably the Gilgal of 2 Kings 2[1] 4[38] about fourteen miles north of Jerusalem, and so probably one of the most distant points occupied by these Jews. *Purified themselves* (v. 30) means by sacrifices and the sprinkling of blood. It would appear that even the gates and walls were sprinkled. The two processions which Nehemiah arranged set out from near the valley (that is the Jaffa) gate, the one proceeding northward and the other southward, and the two meeting in the open space east of the Temple.

44–47. Regulations Concerning Provisions for the Priests and Levites. In this section Zerubbabel and Nehemiah are mentioned by name and together. Here then in the third person we have something which did not come from the memoir of Nehemiah but was later written when these two men were heroes of the past.

CHAPTER XIII

1–3. The Separation of the Mixed Multitude. These verses are intended to serve as an introduction to the episode which follows. Let it be noted that the phrase is *they separated*, not "he separated." This indicates, of course, that Nehemiah did not do this, and that this does not come from his memoir.

4–9. Nehemiah's Second Visit to Jerusalem. In these verses we return to Nehemiah's memoir, in which we shall read what Nehemiah did, or sought to do, upon his second visit to Jerusalem. Nehemiah after twelve years of governorship in Jerusalem had gone back to the Persian king. From v. 6 it appears that in the year 433 B.C., he had gone back to Susa, where his stay must have been brief, for in 432 he was again in Jerusalem, drawn thither by his anxiety about the state of affairs. He had probably been only a few months absent. The expression *Now before this* (v. 4) refers to his second visit to Jerusalem which is mentioned, as we have just seen, in v. 6. This is a useful hint to us that the compiler often put down verbatim what he found in the memoir, without stopping to fit it in with what he had already written. How much before the second visit this difficulty occurred we do not know, nor do we know any way of finding this out. In vv. 4–9 we learn that Eliashib, the high priest, had taken one of the chambers of the Temple and fitted it up as lodgings for Tobiah. This was a shocking breach of order and propriety in the eyes of Nehemiah, and he took sharp action, casting Tobiah's goods and chattels out, and then had the place cleansed ceremoniously after such a desecration.

10–14. Nehemiah Befriends the Levites. Nehemiah discovers that the Levites were not receiving their lawful dues, and to support themselves were compelled to go out and work upon farms. He introduced a reform in methods and attempted to secure a proper payment of tithe. Let it here be noted that the tithe was then difficult to enforce or enjoin. And after this struggle Nehemiah again asks God to remember what he had sought to do. He had so spoken before (5[19]) and there is no impropriety or indelicacy in it.

15–22. The Difficulty of Sabbath Observance. Now, again, is Sabbath observance a difficult problem. Nehemiah definitely accuses his brethren of treading grapes in the wine press, and of bringing in sheaves of grain, and all sorts of burdens on the Sabbath day. Furthermore, the Tyrian fishermen were carrying on their traffic in fish, salted and dried. Nehemiah rebukes them and reminds them of former breaches of the Law (see Jer. 17[22, 23, 27]), and to prevent the traffic he ordered the city gates closed when twilight was coming on before the Sabbath and kept closed until the Sabbath was over. This only partially succeeded, for merchants then stayed outside the city walls to carry on trade, and he then had to threaten *to lay hands* on them and they knew that he would do it. Again he appeals to God to accept this from him and grant him a blessing.

23–29. Mixed Marriages Condemned. And now, yet again, comes up the vexed question of mixed marriages. There were children who spoke partly in a dialect of Ashdod and partly in the Jew's language, i.e., in Hebrew. Nehemiah could not endure it, and took savage means to end it. He strove with them and cursed them and beat them and pulled out their hair and made them swear to abandon the process. It's a sorry piece of business. It hurts Nehemiah's noble and splendid repute far more than those who suffered. O religion, religion, who shall restrain thine excesses!

30, 31. Summary. Nehemiah gives a scant summary of his reforms, omitting probably by simple inadvertence the reference to his attempts to secure a better Sabbath observance.

ESTHER

By Professor ROBERT H. PFEIFFER

Introduction

Contents. Ahasuerus, king of Persia, after divorcing his favorite wife Vashti, chose Esther, the cousin of Mordecai, as the queen. Haman, the chief minister, irritated by Mordecai's disdain, obtained from the king a decree ordering the extermination of the Jews. Esther, not without danger, brought about the downfall of Haman, whose place was taken by Mordecai, and the publication of a new edict which, without abrogating the former one, allowed the Jews to slaughter their foes. The festival of Purim was instituted to perpetuate the memory of that event.

Historicity. The chief argument for believing that the book is a record of actual events is the correct and detailed description of some Persian manners as we know them through Greek historians, and of the royal palace at Susa which has been excavated (M. Dieulafoy, *L'Acropole de la Suse*, 1890; cf. *Bibliotheca Sacra*, lxvi (1889), pp. 626–53). However, even disregarding the anachronisms, the extraordinary coincidences, and the improbable incidents that have been pointed out in the book, it is clear that the accurate reproduction of the local color and the comparative lack of discrepancies in the narrative do not necessarily prove that the incidents related are real. On the whole, the apparent exaggerations, the dramatic structure, the transparent purposes (the institution of Purim and the glorification of militant Judaism), and not a few incredible incidents, classify Esther as primarily a didactic work. The most elaborate and most recent attempt to prove the historicity of this book by conceding that the story would be unbelievable under Xerxes and by identifying Ahasuerus with Artaxerxes II (J. Hoschander, *The Book of Esther in the Light of History*) is far from convincing.

Date. The Book of Esther was written long after the time of Xerxes—in fact, when the Persian Empire was a dim memory of distant days (1[1]). Like the book of Daniel (which knows only four Persian kings) the Persian period (two centuries) is shortened so that, instead of being separated by a century, Nebuchadrezzar and Xerxes are practically contemporaries (2[5f.]; cf. Tobit 14[15]). The edict of Haman (3[8f.]) may be an echo of the measures of Antiochus Epiphanes in 168 B.C., and the victorious attack of the Jews upon their enemies (9[1f.]) may be an anticipation of the Maccabean rebellion (beginning in 167 B.C.). Forcible conversions to Judaism (8[17]) are historically unknown before the time of John Hyrcanus (135–105 B.C.), during whose rule the book was probably written.

Purpose. The author lived at the time when the Jewish nation, after saving its religion from the annihilation planned by Antiochus Epiphanes, had taken the offensive against the heathen, first for political independence, then for extended territory. Daniel (164 B.C.) was a call to arms in defense of the faith; Judith (about fifteen years later) was an appeal to fight for deliverance from foreign rule (attained in 141 B.C.); Esther (about 130 B.C.) was an invitation to a war of conquest and revenge. The story leads up to a wholesale massacre of non-Jews and the yearly celebration of that carnage. The festival of Purim (3[7] 9[19f.]), presumably of Babylonian or Persian origin, was at first not religious, but social and patriotic in character: the author wrote his book to keep alive the memory of the day in which the plan of Haman was reversed, to the glory of the Jews and to the ruin of their foes.

Religious and Moral Teaching. Esther is spiritually on a much lower plane than Daniel, and even than Judith. Ethical religion has no place in the book, its characters betray no religious aspirations or convictions. The Jews distinguish themselves from the heathen only because they have peculiar laws (3[8]), which, however, they readily disregard when it serves their purpose (2[9]), so that it becomes easy to conceal their Jewish extraction (2[10]). The moral teaching of the book can be summarized in the command: Love your kindred, hate your enemies. The individual Jew must disregard his own life when national existence is at stake (4[13-16]); the might of the Jews and the destruction of their enemies are the supreme moral ideals of the book. The lack of religious elements (which the LXX supplied in the apocryphal additions) and the moral conceptions totally at variance with those of Jesus may explain why the book was never quoted in the N.T.; among the Jews, however, it was very popular (two ancient Aramaic translations, or Targums, have come down to us), and chiefly because of this popularity it was admitted to the Hebrew canon of Scriptures.

The general spirit and attitude of the book are far removed from prophetic ideals or the teaching of Jesus. Its religion is a fierce, unethical nationalism. Its low moral and religious tone cannot be justified, but it can be explained. At a time when the extreme cruelties perpetrated by Antiochus were still fresh in the memories of the people, and when every pious Jew was convinced that his enemies were really the enemies of his God, the bitter fanaticism reflected in the book is quite intelligible. Moreover the popularity of the book shows that prophetic religion was far from dominating the Judaism of the second century B.C. It also explains in a measure why the lofty spiritual and ethical teaching of Jesus encountered such bitter opposition in representative Jewish circles.

Literature: Paton, *Esther* (International Critical Commentary); Eiselen, *The Psalms and Other Sacred Writings;* Streane, *Esther* (Cambridge Bible); Adeney, *Esther* (Expositor's Bible); Harper, *Esther* (Temple Bible); T. W. Davies, *Ezra, Nehemiah, Esther* (New Century Bible).

CHAPTER I

The Dismissal of Queen Vashti

1–8. A Festival Lasting Six Months. *Ahasuerus* (Xerxes I, 485–465 B.C.; not Artaxerxes II, 404–358 B.C., as in LXX and Josephus) ruled over a vast empire (cf. 10[1]), comprising 127 provinces (120 in Dan. 6[1]; 20 satrapies in Herodotus). To the acropolis of Susa, in Elam (Neh. 1[1] Dan. 8[2]), his spring residence (Xenophon, *Cyropaedia*, viii, 6.22), he invited the grandees and the army, presumably to celebrate his coronation. At the close of the period a seven days' feast was arranged for all who had gathered at Shushan for the occasion. White and blue (the national colors, 8[15]) draperies were fastened by means of white and purple linen cords to silver rings attached to marble pillars. Gold and silver couches stood on mosaic floors (alabaster, white marble, mother of pearl stone, and speckled marble). Wine was served in regal fashion, without restriction (LXX) or compulsion (Vulg.).

9–12. An Unruly Queen. Queen Vashti gave at the same time a feast to the women. Merry with wine, the king sent seven eunuchs to ask the queen to show her beauty to the drinking guests; with befitting modesty she refused. Women in Persia often sat at great banquets (Neh. 2[6] Dan. 5[2]); in Judæa usually not (Mk. 6[24]).

13–20. The Consultation and Verdict of the Wise Men. The court astrologers (*which knew the times*, cf. 1 Chr. 12[32]: experts in fixing the calendar) were jurists and formed a sort of supreme court (cf. Ezra 7[14]), although astrologers and judges were usually distinct persons. The queen, in the opinion of the wise men, was guilty in two respects: she openly defied her husband and she gave to all other wives an example of domestic insubordination. Her deed must be publicly reproved and she must be deposed: the publication of an irrevocable (8[8] Dan. 6[8, 12, 15]) decree to this effect will improve domestic discipline in the Persian empire.

21, 22. A Law for the Benefit of Husbands. Letters containing the decree outlined by the wise men were sent to the various provinces in the local language and script. Darius engraved an inscription on the rock of Behistun in Persian, Elamitic, and Assyrian (cf. the three languages of Switzerland). The last words of the chapter (*and should publish it . . .*) are uncertain: LXX omits them; Vulgate says *and it shall be published among all nations;* the Targums understand the clause to mean that in mixed marriages the wife must speak the language of the husband; some modern critics propose the reading, *and she shall speak whatsoever seems fit to him* (cf. A.S.V., v. 22).

CHAPTER II

Esther Chosen as the Queen

1–4. The Search for a New Queen. Noticing that the king, now in a calmer mood, regretted his summary rejection of Vashti, the chamberlains proposed a plan for the selection of another wife, which reminds us of 1 Kings 1[1-4]. The most attractive maidens of the realm should be brought to Susa: under the supervision of Hegai, the chief eunuch, they should prepare themselves by means of cosmetics for the royal inspection.

5–8. Esther. She was the cousin and foster daughter of Mordecai, a Benjamite descendant of Kish, the father of Saul (1 Sam. 9[1]), who had been deported with *Jeconiah* (Jehoiachin, 2 Kings 24[11f.]) in 597 B.C. and who, if the chronology of our author were not at fault, would now (482 B.C.) be at least one hundred and fifteen years old. Curiously Mordecai and Esther are named after Babylonian deities (Marduk, or Merodach, and Ishtar). *Hadassah* means "myrtle."

9–11. Esther in the Custody of Hegai. The chief eunuch liked her and gave to her beauty preparations and royal food, assigning to her seven maids and lodging her in the best part of the harem, where Mordecai came daily to see her. Esther did not, like Daniel (1[8]), observe the dietary laws of Judaism; she actually concealed her nationality. How Mordecai could have access to the harem, and how Esther's kinship with him, and therefore her race, could remain a secret are questions which are more disturbing to us than to the author, who likewise sees nothing wrong in this sacrifice of principles to worldly ends.

12–15. The Maidens Prepare for the Royal Inspection. After one whole year devoted to enhancing their beauty (six months with myrrh and six with balsam and other cosmetics) each one of the virgins was brought before the king and became then one of his concubines. Esther wisely let herself be guided by the judgment of Hegai, who besides being an expert in such matters must have known the taste of the king.

16–18. Esther Crowned Queen. In Dec.-Jan., 478 B.C., four years after the rejection of Vashti (the author knows nothing of the ill-fated expedition of Xerxes against the Greeks during the interval), Esther's turn came: she pleased the king instantly and was made queen. On the occasion of the feast of coronation a *release* (tax-relief? amnesty? holiday? discharge from military service? cf. Mt. 27^{15}) was granted to the provinces and *gifts* (of food?) were distributed lavishly.

19–23. A Conspiracy Disclosed by Mordecai. While he was sitting, as was his custom, at the entrance of the royal palace, Mordecai discovered a plot against the life of Xerxes (who was ultimately assassinated), whether through a Jewish servant of the conspirators (Josephus), or through his knowledge of seventy languages (Targum), or otherwise, the author does not say. Through Esther he communicated his discovery to the king. After an investigation the two guilty courtiers were hanged and Mordecai's service was recorded in the royal annals (cf. $6^{1f.}$ 10^2 Ezra 4^{15}). V. 19 is obscure; Gunkel reads: "when the [remaining] virgins [whose turn had not yet come] were brought into the second harem."

CHAPTER III

The Destruction of the Jews Planned by Haman

1–4. A Firm but Irritating Jew. Sometime between 478 B.C. (2^{16}) and 473 B.C. (3^7) Haman was made grand vizier. He was an *Agagite*, presumably a descendant of the Amalekite king defeated by Saul (1 Sam. $15^{8f.}$); the hostility between Agag and Saul is transmitted to their descendants Haman and Mordecai (see comment on 2^5 and 6^{12-14}). As Daniel's friends refused to prostrate themselves before the statue (Dan. $3^{12f.}$), so Mordecai remained conspicuously seated when Haman went by, either because he regarded the customary prostrations as acts of idolatry connected with emperor worship (Æschylus calls Darius "Persia's god born in Susa") or because he despised the descendant of Agag. His explanation to those who were curious to know the reason for his behavior was that he was a Jew. It was not long before Haman's attention was called to this matter.

5–11. An Enraged Minister. The pompous vizier, when he verified the report, was so furious that, regarding the execution of Mordecai as an inadequate revenge, he decided to destroy the whole Jewish nation within the Persian empire. According to a common conception (of Babylonian origin) there was an appropriate time fixed by fate for every undertaking (cf. Eccl. 3^{1-8}). To determine the proper day for the proposed pogrom, Haman had lots (*Pur*, an obscure word; cf. 9^{23-28}, notes) cast in his presence in March-April, 473 B.C. Every day was taken up in turn "and the lot fell on the 13th day of the (12th) month, which is the month Adar [February-March]." (These words were accidentally omitted in the Hebrew and are preserved in the LXX; cf. v. 13.) Haman then reported to the king that a certain race, which he does not name, had its own laws and did not observe the royal edicts; as an inducement for its destruction he promised to pay into the treasury a sum of about $18,000,000. The king, taking off his signet ring (the symbol of supreme jurisdiction, cf. $8^{2, 8, 10}$ Gen. 41^{42}) and placing it in the hands of *the Jews' enemy*, told him to keep the money (as a reward for ridding the state of an internal enemy) and proceed as he saw fit.

12–15. A Bloody Law. Eleven months before the fateful day (the author does not notice that the Jews had ample time to escape) the decree of Haman was drafted and dispatched posthaste to the satraps and governors (1^1); it was written in the local languages and scripts (1^{22}). On the 13th of Adar the Jews were to be killed and their goods plundered. The Jews of Susa were panic-stricken, whereas Xerxes and Haman drank to the success of the undertaking.

CHAPTER IV

Esther's Resolve to Save the Jews

1–3. A Nation in Mourning. Mordecai, who had unconsciously caused the impending calamity, and the Jews mourned according to the ancestral customs, which included tearing the upper garment (2 Sam. 3^{31}), wearing sackcloth (Isa. 15^3 22^{12}), putting ashes (or dust) on the head (2 Sam. 13[19]) or wallowing in them (Jer. 6[26]), fasting (2 Sam. 1[12]), and weeping (Jer. 22[18]). See also on 6[12-14].

4–11. An Appeal to the Queen and Her Answer. Esther sent to Mordecai a robe to replace his sackcloth, so that he could enter the palace (see v. 2), but he refused it and informed her through Hathach of the gravity of the situation, urging her intervention in behalf of the Jews. Esther replied that she could not intercede for her people before the king without risking her life. No one dared appear unsummoned in the presence of the ruler, or even enter the inner court, from which he could be seen (5[1f.]), under penalty of death, unless the sovereign held out to the intruder his golden scepter. The author does not reckon with the fact that one could have oneself announced to the king (Herodotus iii, 118; 140), either through ignorance of Persian etiquette or to enhance the heroism of Esther (see v. 16). Josephus (*Antiquities* xi, 6.3) solved the difficulty through an absurd guess.

12–14. A Warning. The reply of Mordecai was illogical, but, as often, a weak argument presented forcibly carried conviction. If the decree is executed, he argued, Esther will perish (but would not Haman make an exception for the queen, even if he knew her race?); if the Jews are saved without Esther's intervention, she will lose the opportunity of a lifetime (but why should she risk her life if there is such a possibility?). Humanly speaking (and the author does not count on divine help) it seems far more likely that the king would spare his beloved wife than that the Jews should be saved through their own efforts or through foreign intervention. Here and in the next verses religious faith, confidence in Jehovah in desperate straits, is deliberately suppressed to emphasize human ingenuity (cf. above on 2[9-11]). 1 Maccabees likewise attributes the military success of the rebellion to human shrewdness rather than to divine intervention.

15–17. A Heroic Decision. Esther's noble resolve to go to the king at the risk of her life is the moral high-water mark of the book, even though a cynic may remark that according to Mordecai's argument she had everything to gain and nothing to lose by doing it.

CHAPTER V

The Opposing Plans of Esther and of Haman

1–8. Taking a Chance. Tense with the consciousness that her life depended on a royal whim (4[11]) and wearing, with true feminine shrewdness, her royal apparel, Esther entered the forbidden inner court on the morning of the third day after her decision. Fortunately, the king, who spied her from the throne room, was in good humor and extended to her the golden scepter; approaching, she touched it reverently. On being asked what her wish was (it would have been a violation of etiquette to ask a favor from the king without being invited to do so: see Neh. 2[4]; cf. 1 Kings 1[16]), with the promise that it would be granted *even to the half of the kingdom* (v. 6, 7[2] Mk. 6[23]), Esther, postponing her real petition, simply invited the king and Haman to a banquet. After the meal, when according to Persian custom wine and fruit were served, the king again asked Esther to make her petition. Esther started out to implore the king to save the Jews when suddenly, her strength proving unequal to the ordeal, she procrastinated again and wound up with another invitation.

9–14. Gratifications and Vexations of Haman. Leaving the banquet in high spirits Haman met Mordecai (who had evidently removed his mourning garb when Esther promised her assistance), and at the sight of the unobsequious Jew he lost his good humor. At home he boasted of his wealth and progeny, and, not dreaming that it would be his undoing, of the invitation to the queen's table. But Mordecai was the fly in the ointment. No matter how much we have, one thing is always lacking: David and Ahab obtained it through murder (was it worth the price?); Haman met his doom in the attempt to get it. Haman's wife and friends advised that Mordecai be hanged on the morrow and swing in the wind while Haman would sit happily at the queen's banquet.

CHAPTER VI

Mordecai Honored by the King

1–3. An Unrewarded Service. Xerxes was sleepless that night and ordered the royal annals (2[23]) to be read before him, surprisingly without obtaining the desired result. Toward morning, when they came to the story of the conspiracy disclosed by Mordecai (2[21-23]), the king became interested and asked how the man who had saved his life had been rewarded; he was told that nothing had been done for Mordecai.

4–9. Haman's Irritating Blunder. Haman, who had come to the palace early to obtain permission to hang Mordecai, was summoned before the king to propose a plan for honoring a faithful subject. Imagining, in his conceit, that he himself was the person in question, Haman answered that this man should be mounted on a royal steed, crowned, and led through the streets by a high official making a proclamation before him (cf. Gen. 41:38-44).

10, 11. A Public Recognition of Mordecai's Loyalty. The shock to Haman in hearing that the man he was proposing to have hanged was to be honored with the dignities he expected for himself must have been as great as the shock to David when Nathan said, "Thou art the man" (2 Sam. 12:7); but, concealing his feelings, he carried through the ordeal unflinchingly.

12-14. Haman's Misgivings. After the unexpected demonstration of royal esteem Mordecai went back to his familiar haunt. But Haman went home *mourning and having his head covered* (cf. comment on 4:1-3 and 7:8 2 Sam. 15:30 Jer. 14:4). His wise men gave him no comfort. In the duel between the Jew Mordecai and the Agagite Haman (3:1) the doom of the latter was foreordained in the scriptural predictions of the fall of Amalek (Ex. 17:16 Num. 24:20 Deut. 25:17-19 1 Sam. 15:2f.). In the midst of these forebodings a chamberlain came to summon Haman to the banquet (cf. Lk. 14:17).

CHAPTER VII

The Downfall of Haman

1-6. Esther's Petition. While drinking wine after the meal (5:6) the king for the third time (5:3, 6) asked Esther for her wish. With impassioned words Esther begged for her life and for that of her people (without naming their nationality): they have been sold to be destroyed; had they been sold into slavery she would have said nothing. The end of v. 4 (*although*, etc.) is unintelligible in the Hebrew. Horrified, the king asked who had made the murderous plan; Esther, pointing her finger to Haman, forthwith accused him. Haman, who had not had the opportunity to vindicate himself, realized, in his panic, that he had unwittingly planned the death of the queen.

7-10. Haman's End. While the king had gone out in the park (1:5) to recover from the shock, Haman, wild with terror, fell at the feet of the queen, who was reclining on her couch (cf. Amos 6:4), for she alone could now save him. Xerxes, detecting him thus, misconstrued his intentions; Esther, adamant against all pity, took an unfair advantage of an absurd suspicion of the king and allowed Haman to be condemned for a crime he had not committed. Perhaps she surmised that Haman could have justified the decree against the Jews if given a chance, although later the king thought he had condemned Haman for his hostility against the Jews (8:7). The eunuchs covered Haman's head, in Greece and Rome a mark of capital punishment. Harbonah (1:10) mentioned the gallows erected in Haman's house for Mordecai (5:14), and the king, a man easily influenced and moody, took the hint. The author loved poetic justice: the dignities expected by Haman belong to Mordecai (6:6f.), and on the gibbet that he had erected for his enemy Haman was hanged himself: "Whoso diggeth a pit shall fall therein" (Prov. 26:27).

CHAPTER VIII

Mordecai's Elevation and the Rescue of the Jews

1, 2. Mordecai Made Prime Minister. As was done with people condemned to death (Herodotus iii, 129), Haman's property was confiscated and presented by the king to Esther, who intrusted it to Mordecai's administration. When the king heard that Mordecai was a cousin and foster father of the queen (2:7) he gave him the rank of the highest officials (1:14; cf. 1:10 7:9) and granted him the possession of the royal signet-ring (3:10). In power and wealth Mordecai was henceforth second only to the king.

3-8. The Appeal for the Jews. With unnecessary personal risk (4:11), for Mordecai was now the grand vizier, Esther made her petition in behalf of her nation; with disinterested and ardent patriotic zeal, now that her own safety was not in question, even before the golden scepter was stretched forth as a sign of immunity (4:11), she begged the king to revoke the edict that Haman had devised for his private vengeance (3:12f.). In spite of his favorable attitude the king was unable to revoke the edict (1:19), but he gave Esther and Mordecai full authority to make it harmless with another one (cf. 3:11).

9-14. A New Edict. Two months and ten days after the promulgation of Haman's edict (3:12) its counterpart was prepared and published with the usual procedure (3:12f.), only that to gain time especially swift and well-bred horses were furnished to the couriers. In the new law the prescriptions of 3:13 were reversed: the Jews were allowed to massacre and plunder their foes. Would any king of Persia ever have allowed the Jews to kill at will his faithful subjects?

15-17. Contrasting Reactions to the Edict. An ovation greeted Mordecai as he went forth from the palace with a royal garment (6:8, 11) of blue and white (1:6), crowned with a diadem (different from the royal crown, 1:11 2:17 6:8). In the provinces the Jews received the new edict with exuberant joy and proclaimed a holiday; the heathen were struck with terror: many, in their panic, actually became Jewish proselytes.

CHAPTER IX

The Revenge of the Jews and the Feast of Purim

1–5. The Day. On the 13th of Adar (February-March), when the two conflicting decrees (3^{13} 8^{11}) went into effect, the Jews assembled themselves for the fray while their disorganized enemies fell into a panic (8^{17}). The provincial authorities, now that Mordecai was at the helm, did not hesitate between the opposite instructions received from the king (3^{12} 8^{9}): siding with the Jews, they contributed to wipe out their foes, whether active or passive. It was not a battle but a massacre of Saint Bartholomew: the heathen did not attack, the Jews suffered no casualties. The murderous plan of Haman was simply reversed (for another instance of poetic justice see 7^{7-10}).

6–10. The Bloodshed in Susa. In the capital five hundred heathen were slain in addition to the ten sons of Haman, whose names are written in a vertical column in the Hebrew text "because they were hung (v. 13f.) perpendicularly one over the other" (Buxdorf). No property was plundered (in spite of 8^{11}), lest the heathen say, "I have made Abraham rich" (Gen. 14^{23}; so Grotius).

11–15. A Second Massacre. The king was so unconcerned with the slaughter of so many of his subjects that he offered to grant another wish of Esther. The cruel queen asked for a renewal of these atrocities on the following day and for an exhibition of the ill-fated sons of Haman upon the gallows (cf. on vv. 6–10). So it was done; three hundred more victims fell on the 14th in Susa, for no other reason than to justify the celebration of Purim on both days (cf. on v. 18f.).

16–19. The Feast of Purim. In the provinces the Jews slaughtered seventy-five thousand (LXX 15,000) heathen on the 13th of Adar and celebrated on the 14th; in Susa, where the butchery continued for two days, the celebration came on the 15th: thus the author explains why Purim was celebrated on the 14th in the villages and on the 15th in the cities (see, however, vv. 21f.). The reason for the divergence seems to be that the fast of the 13th, when the festival was introduced from the Eastern provinces into Jerusalem, had to be postponed to the 14th because the 13th was the celebration of the defeat of Nicanor in 161 B.C. (1 Macc. 7^{49}; cf. 2 Macc. 15^{36}).

20–22. Instructions for the Celebration of Purim. Mordecai ordered all the Jews to celebrate on both the 13th and the 14th, obliterating the difference between villages and cities in the date (vv. 16–19): Josephus asserts that in his time both days were observed, and the Mishna (200 A.D.) legalizes the two different dates of vv. 16–19.

23–28. The Significance of Purim. The name of the festival is derived from the word "Pur" (plural Purim), which is said to mean "lot" but cannot be identified in any known language. Haman had determined the day of the proposed pogrom by casting lots (3^{7}), but was ordered hanged together with his sons by the king (Esther's intervention is not mentioned here). The averted danger was to be celebrated yearly by the Jews and their proselytes, everywhere and in all future time. This summary does not agree in all details with the rest of the book.

29–32. A Second Letter of Instructions. Esther joined Mordecai in prescribing to the Jews of the one hundred and twenty-seven provinces (1^{1}) the observance of Purim, adding to the previous directions that one day (later the 13th was chosen) be devoted to fasting, in commemoration of the fasting of 4^{3} and of that of 4^{16f}.

CHAPTER X

The Epilogue

The author breaks off an account of the reign of Xerxes (a new tribute is mentioned) by referring the reader, after the pattern of the books of Kings, to the Persian royal annals (2^{23}). In his exaltation Mordecai did not forget, as often happens, his own nation: active in furthering the welfare of the Jews, he was free from envy on their part and was greatly beloved.

JOB

By Principal W. F. LOFTHOUSE

Introduction

Literary Classification. The book of Job occupies a unique position in the O.T. It stands outside all the recognized classifications of O.T. literature. It is neither Law (*Torah*) nor history; it has nothing in common with the Prophets, nor (for the most part) with the piety of the Psalms; it is often classed as part of the Wisdom Literature, but both in literary form and general outlook Job is different; still less has it anything in common with the apocalyptic books. A large part of the book may be called a dialogue; but the dialogue is rather a succession of elaborate speeches than the quick interchange of conversation, such as is often found in the narrative books. There is no direct attempt at edification; in fact, a great deal of the book would be, and actually was, found disturbing to Jewish orthodoxy; and although it is concerned with ideas that may be called theological, there is no formal theological system to be discerned. The author has, indeed, been classed among the "skeptics of the O.T.," and regarded as deliberately cutting himself off from all the traditions of his race. The first effect is bewildering to one who is familiar with the spirit of the rest of the O.T.

General Character. Certain things, however, are clear: the book is poetry (with varied but quite distinct rhythms, and all the parallelism which characterizes Hebrew poetry) set in a framework of prose; it is concerned all through with the relation of God's government of the world to suffering and evil; certain speeches, attributed to Elihu, could be removed without apparent detriment to the composition or symmetry of the rest of the book; the "speeches" of Jehovah at the end of the book, or something like them, are needed, and yet they seem curiously irrelevant to the questions which have hitherto been asked; and some few passages (notably ch. 28) fit very badly into their context.

Thus, four large questions immediately arise: (1) Is the book a compilation; and, if so, how did the compiler treat his material? (2) Were the materials used independent of each other, and what was their relation to the general current of Hebrew thought? (3) What is the date of the book in its present form, and of its materials, so far as they had a separate existence? (4) What was the purpose of the author or of the compiler and of the separate authors?

Every conceivable answer has been given to each of these questions, by professed scholars, and by "amateurs" like Froude in *Short Studies on Great Subjects* and (by implication) H. G. Wells in *The Undying Fire*. The details will be found in the longer commentaries. The following paragraphs, without explicit reference to existing theories, attempt to set forth the main considerations necessary to the reader of the book in forming his judgment.

The Problem of Evil. The subject of the book is commonly held to be the Problem of Evil; and at first sight the book contains five answers to the question, "Why is evil allowed?"—the answers (1) of the Satan (or adversary): to test a goodness that may be only skin-deep; (2) of the friends: to punish wickedness, recognized or unrecognized; (3) of Job himself: because God is really unjust; (4) of Elihu: to warn or to educate and train; and (5) of Jehovah: to bring home to man his ignorance. The arrangement by which these answers are contrasted with one another is as ingenious as it is effective; the first, being the most superficial, is naturally put into the introduction or prologue; the second and third are elaborated in three cycles of speeches, in each of which Job answers the separate Friends in turn; the fourth (for the literary independence of the Elihu section is not universally held) is placed in a set of discourses to which neither Job nor his friends, from their standpoints, could well make reply; and the fifth, like a mysterious storm suddenly gathering and then clearing the air, reduces all the speakers to an awed silence, and a brief Epilogue leaves us again, not inartistically, at the lower level of the Prologue.

Apparently no one of these five answers is meant to be decisive; the fifth, indeed, seems no answer at all, but only the denial of the possibility of an answer. The other four, undoubtedly, contain elements of truth; but each of them raises about as many new questions as it answers. The Satan is apparently right; Job utters curses which even to our ears sound shocking; the contentions of the Friends are in several places echoed, with a good deal more force, by Job himself; Job is condemned, yet divinely rewarded at the last; and what he is condemned for is not clear—certainly not for the sins of which the Friends had accused him, while nothing is said to suggest that Elihu's view of suffering is really wrong. Whatever the separate authors (supposing them to have existed) may have thought, can we imagine that the compiler had made up his mind?

The Main Question. The main interest of the book, however, is not so abstract; the Satan is not interested in general theology, or even in a theodicy; he wants to know, "How will a pious man stand the test of pain?" and, with all the writhing of the tortured thought in the chapters that follow, that question is never lost sight of. The Satan's own answer (which, it may well be, we are never intended to forget in the later chapters) is, "He will renounce God"; Job's answer, in the Prologue, is, "He will take what God sends," and then "He will pray to die," "He will deny God's justice," and "He will appeal from God to—whom?" The Friends, in tones that vary between courtesy and brutality, insist, "He will ask with confidence for forgiveness and release. It is to the wicked that suffering comes." The central part of the book shows Job twisting in the chains of this logic, and finally throwing them off: "I am not wicked, but you are unjust or God is! Let me die. Yet this cannot be God's last word; he will vindicate me at the last." Elihu takes even less account of the promethean struggles of Job than do the Friends; but he recalls our attention to the original question, and replies, "He will bear it with equanimity, knowing that there is a purpose in it all, to be understood in good time." And, with the practical issue in mind, Jehovah's addresses become less perplexing: "He will turn from his own sufferings to the vast magnificence of nature, and complaint will be silenced in awe."

Hebrew "Orthodoxy." The book, we said, is unique in Hebrew thought; yet it implies Hebrew thought on every page. Without the rest of the O.T. it would mean nothing. It is written, indeed, against a background of Hebrew "orthodoxy" and the perplexities that followed for the orthodox. Evil, as all that causes pain or suffering, must be distinguished in the O.T. from sin; but since God is regarded as the author of good and evil alike, it was natural to look upon all evil as the penal result of sin. This at once raised practical difficulties. If evil is punishment, it obviously falls upon the wrong persons. Why do the wicked flourish, and why are the righteous reduced to poverty? In Proverbs, indeed, the old-fashioned attitude is for the most part preserved: "Do good and you will be rewarded; do evil, and you will suffer for it." But what if the rule does not hold? This is the question that puzzled many of the psalmists; and the natural course was to fall back on one of two statements; either, "There is no need to fret; the wicked or their descendants will be punished in the end"; or, "The good suffer only for a time; the pious man will never starve" (cf. Psa. 37, 49, 73). Both these expedients seem at times to be pointing to something further: "The good can never really suffer; for goodness means the favor of God, whatever outward circumstances may be; and God's favor is the pearl of great price."

This conception, however, had not made its way generally into Hebrew thought, and the book of Job is very far from taking it for granted. As far as the central part of the book is concerned, the Friends and Job start on the same level; a modern psychologist might see in the Friends the expression of an element in Job's thought, projected outside him to gain fuller emphasis. It is as if the sick man says to himself: "This must be a punishment for my sin. Yet how have I sinned? It is a cruel thought. And God must be cruel too. But is he? Does he believe that I have sinned? Let him come into the open and charge me to my face. If he would, my innocence would be proclaimed. He terrifies me now; then, he would clear me. He will clear me. I could wait for that, even though he were to kill me while I was waiting."

Job's Reaction. Such are the quick transitions of Job's thought, as, on fire with resentment or longing or despair or anguish or rapture, he flings his guesses at truth against the ruthless reiteration of traditional beliefs, his friends', or his own; a reiteration which deepens in intensity and pitilessness as the dialogue proceeds. He hardly ever challenges them outright; in his agony he is made to double hither and thither like the hunted creature he feels himself to be, till he flies for refuge "from man's God to God's God." It is here that we are aware of the supreme art of the poem, for even if in the entire absence of action we do not call it dramatic, as we call an Elizabethan play dramatic, the author has taken the surest way to make us feel the triple contrast—the contrast between Job and his friends, between the more benignant and the more cruel forms that their orthodoxy (the orthodoxy of Psa. 37, be it noted) might take, and between the nervous shifting of Job's emotions and the steady advance to a conception of God of which they could understand and know nothing. If, on the other hand, the author wished to show the wrestling of an individual soul, stricken down by some immense woe, with the beliefs in which he had been brought up, but which, like some ancient idol, only brought terror when men craved for comfort, how could he have done it better?

Speeches of Elihu and Jehovah. When we pass to Elihu, we are on a lower level of experience. Elihu has not made up his mind; he has three theories, none of which appears to satisfy him. Elihu understands Job's agony as little as do the Friends. For a milder kind of suffering his suggestions might be, and are, well enough. And they take us further than most of the psalmists had traveled. But if we are intended to imagine him addressing Job as Job lies stretched on his dunghill, it is fit that no reply should be made to him. Job turns from the irrelevant youth with mute contempt. To turn from Elihu to the speeches of Jehovah is like turning from Wordsworth's Ecclesiastical Sonnets to the noblest of his Odes. Here we have Hebrew nature poetry at its best and most characteristic. It is entirely different from the romantic and imaginative nature poetry of the West. Neither Keats nor Shelley nor perhaps Byron could have written a line of it. Its real strength lies in its descriptive powers and its controlling sense of the unseen. For the Hebrew poet vision is much more than feeling. To another great poet (in Psa. 104) the world is a vast storehouse of wonders, whose usefulness for the human race is its chief glory.

Here, however, *not* as in Psa. 104, the poet takes the opposite line; his eye rests on all the elements in this varied world that man cannot use, nor even understand, and his thought trembles at the hidden operations that cause the changes he sees. The result is a series of rhetorical questions to which only one answer is possible, and which leave the mind half paralyzed, as if the repeated shocks of suffering were to be overcome by a yet deeper shock, of helplessness in the presence of the unknown and unknowable. Yet is this psychologically true? Would the restless moods of Job, embittered by the heartlessness of his friends, irritated by the well-meant commonplaces of Elihu, have been calmed by this majestic summons to humility? The description, indeed, of Job as darkening counsel by words of no understanding (if meant for Job) seems either beside the mark, or cruelly unjust. We may indeed be intended to conclude that there is no answer to the question, "Why does the good man suffer?" save *omnia exeunt in mysterium;* but what are we intended to say, now, to the book's central question, "What will the good man do under the test?" How does Jehovah in all this give his own answer to the Satan? Or are we intended to regard these addresses as an interlude, and, satisfied that Job has not really renounced him, find the real answer of Jehovah in his restoration of Job to more than his former prosperity?

Composition of the Book. At this point we must return to the subject of the composition of the book. Was it a compilation? We have now some data for a solution of this problem. The book can be called an intellectual unity, yet the joints between the different parts are clearly visible. Some of them become more visible when we consider the literary characteristics. The Prologue and Epilogue are in simple straightforward prose, with some of the qualities of the "folk-tale," but the narrator understands the value of repetition, and the scene in heaven is described with a very dignified reticence. Job himself is set before us as an august patriarchal hero, who might well have suggested the reference in Ezek. 14 or in Jas. 5^{11}. It is tempting to regard the Prologue and Epilogue as a single composition; but while the point of view is the same in both, and quite innocent of the deeper questions raised in the body of the book, the first verse of the Epilogue demands more than the narrative of the Prologue has actually given. When we pass to the Dialogues, and to poetry (of a very high order throughout), we notice at once a change in the use of the divine names; the name "Jehovah" is never used outside the prose sections (save in the "stage directions"); instead, the non-national names "El," "Eloah," "Shaddai," and "Elyon." These suggest, like everything else in the poem, a deliberate desire to keep the reader's thought away from any association with the chosen nation. When we approach the Elihu chapters, however, we find that he seems to have a special preference for the first of these names; there are other linguistic peculiarities which, taken together, are not negligible; and the prolixity of the style marks off these chapters. On the other hand, the Jehovah speeches show no noticeable differences in style or language from the dialogues.

Certain sections (namely, ch. 28 and parts of chs. 40, 41, 42) seem clearly out of harmony with their surroundings (see notes there), and other shorter passages, omitted in the LXX (see below), may have been inserted later; when allowance has been made for these, the possibilities of the composition of the book are almost endless. Were each of the four main divisions of the book independent—the Prologue and Epilogue (symbol PE in the following discussion), the Dialogue (symbol D), the Elihu speeches (symbol E), and Jehovah (symbol J), with a compiler to fit them all together later? Or did the author of one division (e.g., D) take the others and adapt them to his own work? Or was PE first in existence, and were the divisions added to it, at once, or gradually? The only point on which everyone seems agreed is that D is homogeneous, if some rearrangements are made toward its close (see notes prefixed to ch. 22). It is equally clear that D is not complete in itself. Something is needed, both by way of beginning and end. For this we have PE. (These are not the symbols J, E, P, D of the Pentateuch; cf. p. 137a.)

Many readers will think that if the author of D had written PE, he would have introduced into both parts of his work more cross-references. The frame seems to have been made with no thought of the picture. For this reason, PE has often been held to be an older tale of a half-legendary hero, which suggested D to some later thinker, as Holinshed or Saxo suggested Lear or Hamlet to Shakespeare. It is specially difficult (though of course not impossible) to think that a man who could write D would be satisfied with the rather "bourgeois" magnificence of the Epilogue. Yet is PE homogeneous? The story of Job's distress and his patience beneath it may well have been a popular tale; but the scenes in heaven, unreferred to in the Epilogue (see on $42^{7f.}$), do not belong to a folk-tale *motif*. They are nearer to Goethe than to Marlowe. Where certainty is unattainable, we can but guess that the author of D took (and perhaps rewrote) the beginning of the old story, added the episode of the Satan and Jehovah to lift it to the region in which his own thought was to move, and then, at the end, added (or left for another) the traditional conclusion.

What, then, of J? It must be remembered that the problem is simpler if we omit from J the dubious sections (40^{6}–41^{34}); but would not the author of D have been here more direct? Does Jehovah say what the argument of the book demands? On the other hand, we can well believe the descriptions of behemoth and leviathan to have been independent compositions. The conception of an address by Jehovah himself as the answer to the agonized cries of Job is masterly, and worthy of the author of D. Equally worthy is the elevated style and imagery of chs. 38, 39. But what is the answer which the author embodies in these chapters? The words out of the whirlwind make no reference to the Friends, nor (still more surprisingly) to Job's sufferings. And Jehovah's presence does not bring a moment's respite to Job's sufferings. Job is lying all the time in dust and ashes. Nor is there a single word of sympathy, still less of vindication (the last is left for the Epilogue). The effect on Job is best expressed by Rom. 3^{19}, "that every mouth may be stopped, and all the world may be brought under the judgment of God." But Jehovah vindicates his justice as little as he vindicates Job's innocence. Man must find peace, as Job (we are probably intended to believe) found it at the last, not in God's love to the individual sufferer (a thought quite foreign to the book) but in the contemplation of the broad sweep of his creative and providential wisdom.

But we must recognize, if this is true, that what is to us the real strength of the author's work lies in D. The picture of Job there is fiercely clear, and the reader is made to feel, almost with horror, that if, in the Prologue, God allows Job to be put on his trial, in D Job puts God on his trial. Perhaps, to the average pious Jew, this was enough to deserve the treatment Job receives in chs. 38, 39, with or without the addition of the Epilogue. But it is hardly possible for us to imagine that the author of D, *when* he wrote, e.g., 9^{17-35}, or 19^{1-27}, could have tolerated Job's submission (in ch. $40^{3f.}$) to such appeals as those of chs. 38, 39. The Jehovah of these chapters is neither the God with whom Job would take refuge nor the God whom Job attacks. He at least is never vindicated. Did the author think he would be? That is his secret. This leaves E to be considered. Most scholars have seen strong reasons for separating E from the author of D, though some have regarded it as the very center of the book. The thought is on a lower level. The style is distinctly inferior. The language has a number of dialectic peculiarities, and there are numerous cross-references to the rest of the book, though in word rather than in thought. But it certainly implies the existence of D. If then it did not come from the same pen as D, who wrote it? We can only suppose that someone later on, dissatisfied perhaps with the result of D, and perhaps of J, and unable to appreciate or understand the daring speculations of the author, added something intended to satisfy the more cautious readers, as a later editor seems to have "improved" Ecclesiastes.

But is this certain? Elihu (see on ch. 32) comes forward as an exponent of a kind of orthodoxy brought up to date. He thinks he has much to say; yet he practically says nothing, and with foolish pompousness. But he does clearly refer to Job's words, even if he (not unnaturally) misunderstands them. His main interest is that of the rest of the book—how should a good man behave under suffering? His denials of the need of a theophany, to the reader who knows that ch. 38 is coming, are full of "dramatic irony." May it be that the author, having brought the wisdom of antiquity to silence, wished to show that a revised or modernized traditionalism was still more futile, and so—gave us Elihu?

According to the view here outlined, the author of D, busied over his problem of the testing of the good man and its result, in his breaking away from tradition, used the existing story of Job, finding it the more convenient to his purpose because, lying outside Israel, it enabled him to neglect any special revelation from Israel's God; turning part of it into an introduction, and transforming it by a striking piece of imagination. He then left it on one side, and dramatized his own laboring thoughts; then, perhaps after an interval, he added E (if our conjecture will hold good) and J, and left the work to be rounded off with so much of the concluding parts of PE as were of use to it.

The general view, however, is that later on, when the book passed out of the control of the author of D and J, E was inserted. All this, we must confess, is at best speculation; though what is there to be done but speculate? Many have preferred to postulate a compiler, who took the independent PE, D, etc., and fitted them more or less clumsily together. Against this, however, "clumsy" is hardly a fair word. And the difficulty of seeing how J or E could have arisen apart from D remains. The present position of PE, too, is made far more intelligible by supposing that the author of D was responsible for it rather than a compiler. The most that can be said in this direction is that J may have been added later, as well as E. But if D was left without J, it must have been left without the concluding part, and therefore all, of PE. And we are back again where we started.

Date. PE (see note on 1^{17}) regards Job as living at an early period; and it may itself be early; many have regarded the view of the Satan (but see above and note on 1^{6}) as distinctly naïve; in D there are no indications of an early stage of thought. On the contrary, although Job is always represented as the patriarchal *seigneur*, his speeches are full of references to what may be called an advanced state of society; this is specially marked in, e.g., chs. 24 and 29. The extremes of wealth and poverty, the power of unscrupulous riches, the allusions to trade, and the development of political organization, all point to a period in Israelite thought very much later than that of Moses or even David. It is true that in the near East, in biblical times as today, what we call old and new live contentedly side by side; the Bedouin sheikh of to-day is really a contemporary of Abraham and Lot; and the Babylon of Hammurabi's time, and even long before, was more "modern" than Ahab's Samaria or Jehoiakim's Jerusalem. But (so far at least as our evidence goes) it was only after the Exile that the Jews were brought into contact with the very varied conditions of civilization with which the book presents us; and there is no sign that, before the Exile, the intellectual problem with which the author is dealing had risen before the Hebrew mind, or that the non-national point of view, already emphasized, would have been understood or entertained. Little is to be learned, indeed, from the considerations of style on which some lay weight; but the "Aramaisms" (idioms strange to classical Hebrew, but found in Aramaic, which after the Exile became more and more the language of everyday intercourse in Palestine as elsewhere in Western Asia) point, especially for E, where they are more frequent, to a post-exilic date.

Literary Relationships. On the other hand, the absence of any references to "apocalyptic" or to the deeper piety found in some of what are presumably the later psalms suggests a date not very long after the return. This, it is true, is not decisive; the author may have chosen to neglect them; but, if he had been writing when they were common property, he would have done so, with such a subject as his, rather at his peril. Other evidence may lie in the numerous similarities between Job and other parts of the O.T. The clearest example of these is in the "parody" of Psa. 8^{4}, in Job 7^{17} and perhaps 25^{6}. In most instances it is impossible to say which influenced the other; but the balance of probability seems to point to the priority of Job. If the author knew the earlier psalms, later writers had studied him. In any case, the book in its completed form must be placed before the end of the second century B.C., as is shown by its appearance in the LXX, and by its place both in that translation and in the Hebrew canon (see below).

Much discussion of late has centered round the relation of Job to a recently discovered Babylonian work, often known as the "Babylonian Job." This has survived in texts of the seventh century, though it is probably a far older work. In it the hero, a king, laments that he is in sore trouble, in spite of his meticulous piety. His sufferings remind us of Job's; and toward the truncated end of the poem they are apparently removed by the mercy of the gods. But there the resemblance ceases; for the Babylonian sufferer is outwardly very much more "pious" than Job, and is convinced that he must have transgressed unintentionally—a frequent *motif* in Babylonian "penitential" psalms (cf. Lev. 4^{2} 5^{14-19}, etc.); and he never suggests that heaven is unjust to him. Further, there is no dialogue; the Babylonian poems, which are usually quoted as instances of dialogue like the book of Job, and which date at least from the eighth century, are wholly different in thought and intention. That the Hebrews were influenced by Babylonian literature there is considerable evidence to prove (though it may easily be exaggerated); but to find motifs for Job one might as well go to Plato (possibly a contemporary) as to the poems here referred to.

On the other hand, Job is commonly connected with the Wisdom Literature of Judaism—Proverbs, some of the Psalms, Ecclesiastes, Sirach, and the Wisdom of Solomon. All of these books show a certain emancipation from the national standpoint which is prevalent in the Law, the Prophets, and the apocalyptic books; though all of them, except Job, some few psalms, and Ecclesiastes, echo the Hebrew's pride in the past and the future of his nation. But with Wisdom, in the three main senses in which we meet it in these books, Job has practically nothing to do. The word "Wisdom" may mean practical skill in the direction of life and its affairs; the half-personified agency by which God carried out his creation; or the humble yet confident piety which, starting from recognized beliefs, would "justify the ways of God to men." Our author's interest lies in quite other directions. Nor is he rightly called a skeptic, like the author of Ecclesiastes. Ecclesiastes illustrates the first kind of Wisdom; life can only be lived satisfactorily by taking things as they come or go; the author is content to "leave our Lord God out of the play." This is the last thing Job can do. He may question all the accepted views about God; but that God is there, and must "make it plain" at the last, he cannot doubt.

Place. The book itself contains many allusions to Edom; Edom was the home of the Friends; it is also suggested that the land of Uz may have been in or near to Edom; but this is quite uncertain. The wisdom of Edom appears as traditional in several passages of the Bible (cf. Jer. 49^{7} Obad. v. 8). Has the author of Job, then, any real connection with Edom, so bitterly hated by the Jews, yet so respected, it would seem, by her sages? This can hardly be maintained. Of the reputed wisdom of Edom we know nothing; and if the author brings three of his characters from Edom (Elihu has nothing to do with Edom, it may be noted), their point of view is entirely Jewish; and, whether it is Edomite or not, Job will have none of it. But is Job himself represented as living in Edom—as being an Edomite chief? This is equally doubtful. Life in Edom, in O.T. times, before the wonderful developments in Petra, was stern and hard; a long conflict with rock and desert. The Edomites (making all due allowance for the hatred of their traditional foes) were little better than brigands. The wealth and the wide agricultural and pastoral prosperity of Job's house and estates point rather to the Hauran, farther north, than to Edom. But the matter is of little importance. The author had quite enough skill to give his characters a non-Jewish environment; his thought is Jewish through and through.

Canonicity and Text. Reference has already been made to the place of the book in the Hebrew canon. When was the book accepted as canonical? It would not be surprising if a work so daring and even in places so irreverent had found difficulty in being accepted at all. This, however, is not the case. The book stands in the third part of the Hebrew canon, the Hagiographa, or the "Writings," following Psalms and Proverbs; in some Jewish lists and MSS. it precedes them, for the same reason that gained its general acceptance, namely, that it was believed to be a work of great antiquity, perhaps referring to the time of Moses. For this reason some Christian writers of antiquity placed it among the histories; its place in our Bibles is due to the position which was given it in the Vulgate, between the histories and the poetical books; and the esteem which led it to be almost universally regarded as historical saved it from the doubts that clustered around Ecclesiastes and Canticles.

From the fifth chapter on, the Greek translation (LXX) omits a number of clauses. In some books, such omissions furnish important evidence for the correction of the text; here they tell us little; occasionally, however, the LXX appears to have preserved the right order of verses where the Hebrew text has been disarranged; for the rest, the LXX shows that even when the book was first translated into Greek many words and phrases were felt to be very obscure, and textual variations were common.

Religious Value. No thoughtful reader can fail to be aware that he is here dealing with one of the great poems of the world. Even if we confine our attention to D, it is the longest sustained poetical composition in the Hebrew canon; and it never sinks below the high level on which it starts. Its terse phrases, its illuminating metaphors and similes, and its brilliant descriptions refuse to be dislodged from the memory. Note especially the dream, 4^{12-21}; the peace of the good man, 5^{18-27}; the disappointed caravan, 6^{15-20}; the hostility of God, 16^{11-14}; the misery of the outcasts, 24^{5-11}; the marvels of the heavens, 38^{31-35} (see notes in the commentary). Equally arresting is its penetrating ethical criticism; ch. 31 is the fullest exposition of Hebrew moral ideals that we possess. Even more surprising are its powers of psychological analysis; at first sight, Job's moods seem to follow one another with merely chaotic violence; closer study shows how each prepares for the next (note especially chs. 9, 10, and 19^{13-29}).

The very nature of the subject suggests that there will be but little positive religious teaching. And it may be said that the "orthodoxy" against which Job argues so unweariedly has long since lost all interest for us. As we have seen, Jehovah's speeches, where we might have looked for a revelation, appear to contain nothing but a sublime hymn to the power and mystery of nature. This seems to have been the feeling of the N.T. writers. Job is directly quoted only once (1 Cor. 3^{19}=Job. 5^{13}; and perhaps alluded to in Mt. 24^{28}=Job 39^{30}), and the reference in James (5^{11}) can no more than that in Ezekiel (14^{14}) be called a quotation from our book. But when the reader looks deeper, especially if he too has known suffering at all like Job's, he will find how much positive teaching and inspiration is to be found, especially in the speeches of Job himself. The question, "How will a good man act, and what should he think, when he is tested by suffering?" is one which most serious people face at some time or other. In the first place, suffering is felt, throughout the book, to be in direct relation to God—the impulse to hide ourselves in the dark when in pain, or the superstition, perhaps derived from Hebrew "orthodoxy," to think of God as angry with us receives here its death-blow. Secondly, Job's resolve never to deceive himself, to face the worst, and even "to tell God what he thinks of him," is not only a challenge to courage; it is the preparation for intellectual illumination. Thirdly, no one can read the book sympathetically without becoming infected by Job's faith, that even though both nature and experience "shriek against his creed," there is a reason and a purpose and an ultimate vindication of justice and goodness in things.

Unique in Hebrew literature, the book of Job finds a curious parallel in Æschylus' *Prometheus Vinctus;* a parallel and a contrast. Prometheus, chained to a rock in the Caucasus, has incurred the anger of Zeus, because he had brought to mortals the gift of fire—the means of civilized existence. He is visited there by nymphs, by the spirit of ocean, and by another sufferer from the tyranny of Zeus, and bidden by them, not in superior piety, but genuine sympathy, to submit. He refuses; he will wait till Zeus relents; or he speaks of a secret which will accomplish the doom of Zeus himself. Hermes comes to bid him reveal this secret. Again he refuses, and the earth opens, to plunge him into fresh tortures, and he disappears with the cry, "See the injustice of my fate." The same indignant accusation, the same wistful longing, the same assertion of the sufferer's righteousness, but a world of difference between the Greek and Hebrew outlook on God and the world. Prometheus finds sympathy from his friends, while Zeus is what Prometheus thinks him to be, relentless, savage, and himself under the stern empire of destiny. Job is condemned by men, but finds that God is not what he had been tortured into thinking, but the eternal source of wisdom and power and even of justice.

The Greek is pessimistic; the Hebrew is not. What he is can be seen by a comparison with Jeremiah. Jeremiah too comes perilously near to what respectability would hold blasphemous. But to both, what seemed neglect or injustice or positive tyranny became "a sting that bids not sit nor stand but go." If there was hidden from both the truth of the redemptive transformation of suffering, as it is learned in Isa. 53, we see in Job the wrestler who cries out to his terrible antagonist, "I will not let thee go except thou bless me." The dialogue (and, after all, the dialogue is the kernel of the book) ends, it is true, on a note of interrogation; but it is an interrogation that prepares the way for Rom. 8 and Jn. 17. Immortality, as the Christian understands it, is hidden from the eyes of the writer; but no one can rightly understand or value that crown of truth unless in some way he has been forced, step by step, as was Job, to look beyond the tragedy of this earthly existence to the eternal life which is rooted in communion with God. In the ordinary sense of the word, the book can no more be called an autobiography than it can be called history; but few will doubt that the author has dramatized questions and agonies of his own; and when we touch that brave spirit, we touch also the Captain of all those who, without us, shall not be made complete (Heb. 2^{10} mg.).

Literature: Davidson, *Job* (Cambridge Bible); Peake, *Job* (New Century Bible); Froude, *The Book of Job* (Short Studies on Great Subjects); Cheyne, *Job and Solomon;* McFadyen, *The Problem of Pain;* Jastrow, *The Book of Job*.

Chapters 1 and 2: The Prologue

The story of Job's testing, in five scenes: Job's piety and wealth; the Satan's first suggestion to Jehovah; its failure; the Satan's second suggestion; its failure. The whole is a skillful combination of terseness and subtlety, proving that real goodness is superior to anything that the Satan can effect.

CHAPTER I

1–5. Job's Piety and Wealth. *The land of Uz*—cf. Gen. 10[23] 22[21] 36[28]. There is no need to discuss its precise locality. Job is described as a great sheikh and a non-Israelite; *perfect*, a rounded or full-orbed character. *His day*—possibly, but not certainly, the birthday. *House*—cf. v. 19, might be used for "tent." *Offered*—was Job also a priest? The Levitical regulations would not apply outside Israel. *Renounce*—the word usually means "bless"; see v. 11, 2[5, 9]; *not* 3[1]. Perhaps here for "say farewell to"; or a euphemism inserted later in the text (cf. 2 Sam. 12[14]).

6–22. Job's First Test and His Faithfulness. *Jehovah*—the national name for God is used in the prose portions, not elsewhere. He is represented here as holding a sort of court of supernatural beings, *sons of god*, or *the gods* of whom the "adversary" (*Satan*) is one; the word occurs in Num. 22[22]; also as a proper name in 1 Chr. 21[1] and with the article in Zech. 3[1]. Note, in v. 8, the repetition from v. 1. *For nought* (v. 9), i.e., without due equivalent. Vv. 11, 12 show that the Satan is entirely dependent on Jehovah; and Jehovah, in accepting his suggestion, forbids him to go beyond it. Note in vv. 13–19 the literary force of the messengers' formula; blow on blow; though there is no climax till v. 18. *Sabæans* (v. 15)—traders from southwest Arabia (cf. Gen. 10[7, 28]). *Fire*—cf. 1 Kings 18[38] 2 Kings 1[12]. *Chaldeans* (v. 17)—an archaic use; later, identical with Babylonians. LXX has "horsemen." They rush the camels from three sides. *Blessed* (v. 21), as in 1[5], etc. (see note). Job here stresses God's power rather than his love. *Foolishness* (v. 22) = "savorlessness"; LXX uses a word which implies the opposite of "discretion."

CHAPTER II

1–10. Job's Second Test and His Faithfulness. *Holdeth fast* (v. 3)—cf. v. 9; Job's attitude throughout the dialogue. *Without cause*—cf. 1[9]. *Skin for skin* (v. 4)—apparently a quotation of some rough proverbial phrase; perhaps a reference to Bedouin blackmail. The loathsomeness of Job's disease is everywhere stressed as much as his actual suffering; the same is true of the sufferer in Isa. 53. It was perhaps elephantiasis, or possibly no definite disease was thought of. Blake, in his illustrations to Job, pictures his wife at his side continuously. *Foolish* (v. 10)—"heartless," or wanton; not the same word as in 1[22]. God can take away the good (1[10]) *and* give the evil.

11–13. The Coming of Job's Three Friends. The original story is now complete. The Friends have not been previously mentioned; but their mention here is needed as a linkage. *Eliphaz* (Gen. 36[4]) from Edom, the traditional home of wisdom. We have no clue as to the origin of the other names.

Chapters 3 to 31: The Dialogue Between Job and His Friends

We are now in a new atmosphere; the point of interest is changed. Job's attitude is the reverse of that of 1[21] 2[10]. Are we to understand that some time has elapsed? To the Friends, God is cosmic power, moral power, and justice, now manifested in ruthlessness, now modified by grace. To Job he is irresponsible power, caprice, neglect, cruelty, a kind of Nero; a tyrant in the court, before the judges, or himself the judge, a kind of Jeffreys. But Job does not forget (chs. 16, 19) the God of his earlier belief (ch. 31), a very different being. The Friends are traditionalists; they have no arguments or replies to Job. Why did they not see this? Their absence of reference to his sufferings, their accusations of impiety, and their often harsh and brutal language, surprising in themselves, are really a sort of "defense mechanism," which finally breaks down. Few discerning readers will doubt that this was Job's effect on the Friends. They could find no answer, and so condemned him (32[3], and, more vaguely, 42[7]).

CHAPTER III

Job's Passionate Cry for Death. Would I had died at birth (vv. 2–12); then, I should have had rest in Sheol (vv. 13–19). Why must the wretched continue to live? (Vv. 20–26.) With Job's cry, cf. Jer. 20[14-18]. A day that brought poor miserable man into the world should be forever of ill-omen. *Shadow of death*=thick shadow. The last clause of v. 5 is obscure. *Leviathan* (v. 8) is a sea-monster, like the Babylonian Tiamat. Hence, perhaps for *day* we should read (by small alteration) *sea*. Even if I had to be born (v. 11), why must I go on living? The father's *knees* (v. 12), when he acknowledged the new-born infant. Vv. 13–19 give a touching picture of Sheol, the abode of the dead; generally, as in Psalms and Isa. 38[18], dreaded (as the Greeks dreaded Hades). *Waste places* (v. 14)—better "pyramids." In Sheol there is no difference between infants and great lords. Job, once a lord, feels himself now no more than a serf. In v. 20, for the first time Job questions God. *Hedged* (v. 23)—one of the cross references to the Prologue (1^{10}). In despair Job cries out (v. 25), I have only to be afraid of something, and it is upon me.

Chapters 4 to 14: The First Cycle

Eliphaz opens (chs. 4, 5) in what is an attempt at reply to ch. 3; Job replies (chs. 6, 7, using singular, not plural) partly to Eliphaz, partly to God: *Leave me alone!* Bildad (ch. 8) is briefer and more pointed; Job (chs. 9, 10) replies rather to God than to Bildad; there is now a complete gulf between Job and God. Zophar (ch. 11) treats Job with contempt but ends much as Eliphaz and Bildad had done; Job (chs. 12–14) indignantly attacks both God and the Friends, and ends with a cry of despair.

Chapters 4 and 5: The Speech of Eliphaz

An elaborate and dignified statement of the traditional Hebrew view (how natural it would be in a psalm!) but with an unmistakably superior and patronizing tone.

CHAPTER IV

1–11. Security of the Righteous. Eliphaz begins with an apology for speaking at all (vv. 2–5); God is just (vv. 6–11); the vision, Shall man vindicate himself before God? (Vv. 12–21.) Affliction is not causeless, but a punishment. The theme is continued into ch. 5 (5^{1-7}); for all his might, God is a refuge to the needy (5^{8-16}); the humble will be preserved in inviolable peace; this is sure (5^{17-27}). In ch. 3, there is no reference to religion save perhaps in v. 23; Eliphaz is distressed at Job's apparent irreligion and implied attack on his own creed. Having strengthened others (vv. 3f.), surely you should stand firm. Yet you do fear God; then integrity should yield hope. The results of an attack on a den of lions are described in vv. 10, 11 (note the five different words for "lion"): they are rendered helpless; so are the wicked.

12–21. God's Righteousness, Man's Unrighteousness. Note the literary art of the description in vv. 12f. The weird nightmare horror reminds one of Gen. $32^{24f.}$; cf. Otto, *Idea of the Holy*. "Silence (v. 16) and then I could catch a sound." The R.V. of v. 17 is commonplace. Better, "be justified *by* God?" *Before* (v. 19)=either "more quickly than" or "like."

CHAPTER V

See notes under 4^{1-11}.

1–7. Suffering the Result of Sin. Since angels are inferior, there is no help from them; such folly as yours brings its own punishment (there is perhaps a suggestion of guardian angels here, the opposite of the "Satan"); as often, a statement calls up an associated picture (vv. 3f.). The doctrine of the "sour grapes" (Jer. 31^{29}) meets us constantly in Job. In v. 5, the reading is doubtful; perhaps omit *b*, and for *c* read *the thirsty drinketh the milk*. The sense, however, is clear. Trouble comes, not by chance, like weeds, but is inevitable—perhaps, because of sin. *Sparks* (v. 7)—this may be the meaning of the Hebrew phrase, literally, "sons of the flame."

8–27. The Benefits of Chastisement. One is safe with God, who is wonderful, especially in bringing down the mighty from their seats (cf. 1 Sam. $2^{4f.}$ Lk. 1^{51}). Some object for *saveth* is needed in v. 15. Vv. 7f. contain a beautiful passage; but how would it strike Job? For the use of numbers, six and seven, in v. 19, indicating an unlimited number, cf. Prov. 30^{18}. *Scourge*=(v. 21) "slander." The *stones* on the soil would naturally be as exasperating to the farmer as the wild beasts or vermin. *Miss* (v. 24); literally, "sin," i.e., miss the mark, get wrong in the "tale" or "count."

Chapters 6 and 7: Job's Reply to Eliphaz

Job's misery; the Friends' heartlessness; God's cruelty. **Ch. 6.** Job replies: God is doing his very worst; let him kill me! (Vv. 1–10.) You should have showed sympathy; instead, you have deceived me (vv. 11–20); you are unjust, willfully misunderstanding; be kind; I deserve it of you (vv. 21–30). **Ch. 7.** Surely, my misery can claim this (vv. 1–8). I am a ruined man, so I will let myself go (vv. 9–16); why does God torment me by making this cruel sport of me? (Vv. 17–21.)

CHAPTER VI

1–13. Job's Intolerable Wretchedness. How little the Friends understood Job's perturbation! In v. 4 is the first clear mention of God as the author of Job's calamities. The arrows are poisoned. You should know (v. 5) that there is always a reason for complaints. Instead of *fodder* I have only the most revolting food, *white of egg*, or, "slime of purslain," or perhaps "the ravings of a dream." V. 10c suggests that his righteousness would mean some gain for him after death; but this is a thought foreign to Job as yet.

14–23. Disappointment Over the Attitude of the Friends. Better (v. 14), "to him that is in despair." Note *brethren* (v. 15); not yet foes. A touching figure; cf. Jer. 15^{18} (applied to God; but Job has not yet reached this point). The caravan counts on reaching a stream; as so often in summer, the stream is dried up;

hence they must look despairingly elsewhere; in vain! They perish. *Tema*, in North Arabia; *Sheba*, South Arabia. Change v. 21 to read *so have ye been to me.* Why are they so disagreeable? He had asked nothing from them.

24–30. Appeal for Fair Treatment. "How do your attempted reproofs really reprove?" (V. 25.) Do not think of my words but of the despair behind them (v. 26). Ruthless creditors! (V. 27.) The chapter ends with pathetic self-defense—"I can tell if I am uttering 'calamities' " (the same word, probably, as in v. 2).

CHAPTER VII

1–10. Wearisomeness of Life. Man is like a soldier on hard service, or a sweated day-laborer—often treated worse than a slave. V. 6 expresses a double grief: he is going to die, yet he cannot die; at the heart of it is the absence of the old communion with God. With v. 9 cf. Hezekiah's prayer, Isa. 38^{18}. Sheol cannot be avoided; cf. 19^{27} (see comment there).

11–21. Challenge of God and Prayer for Death. There is no use in restraint. Perhaps this, like 6^{4}, is the real "renunciation" of God. Note the irony in v. 12; to the Hebrew, the sea is the element of disorder and chaos, symbolized by a mythical monster, Leviathan (3^{8}), Rahab (26^{12}), or (Babylonian) Tiamat (cf. also Rev. 21^{1}). Mental and physical sufferings are joined. Better be actually strangled (v. 15) than continue in the present condition —choking sometimes accompanies leprosy. For *bones* read probably *pains*. With vv. 17, 18, cf. Psa. 8^{4}. The word *visit* in Hebrew has two meanings—to approach an inferior either with grace and kindliness, or with condemnation and penalty. Cf. our word "inspect"; and 1 Cor. 4^{21}. Hence the bitterness of what must surely be a quotation here. Job's only wish now is to be let alone (contrast v. 6), even for a single moment. Have I sinned? (Vv. 20, 21.) Well, it cannot harm thee; forgive me now; it will soon be too late, and then *thou* wilt regret it.

CHAPTER VIII

The Speech of Bildad

Bildad Declares God's Justice. What rash folly! If you prayed for a return of prosperity, and deserved an answer, it would be given (vv. 1–7); the wisdom of antiquity would tell you that the wicked cannot prosper (vv. 8–19); but a good man cannot be lost (vv. 20–22). The tone of superiority is still evident; but there is nothing new in the argument. Bildad does not directly charge Job himself, but apparently his children, with having brought down the calamity; but his long account of the misery of the wicked suggests a more personal attitude.

In v. 4 is a cross-reference to the Prologue (1^{5}). No actual sin, however, was mentioned; 5^{25} and 14^{21} must not be pressed as suggesting that the sons were still alive. *Seek diligently* (v. 5) echoes 7^{21}. *Thou* is emphatic. The promise held out in vv. 6, 7 was fulfilled at the end of the story. Note the half ironical modesty in v. 9. The ancients are commonly but illogically supposed to be wiser than their children, who, as Bildad himself claims, inherit and can extend their experiences. *Rush* (v. 11) = "papyrus," a reed with a stem ten feet or more in height; once common in Egypt, and still found in the Jordan Valley, used as writing material; cf. the word "paper." *Withereth* (v. 12), merely by the withdrawal of water; so God has but to withhold his favor from the wicked (as he always will) and they perish (cf. Psa. $1^{4f.}$ 37^{2}). *Paths* (v. 13); better, *end.* In v. 14 substitute (giving a closer parallel) *their confidence rests on gossamer.* His estate is no better than a spider's web. V. 16 presents another simile; *before*, i.e., beneath the rays of the sun. V. 17 is difficult: *About the heap*, may possibly be *around the spring; he pierceth* (LXX, "he shall live in"), i.e., he forceth his roots right into the place of stones; or even "he taketh hold of the stones (in the wall)"; v. 17 is meant to strengthen vv. 16, 18f. The expression in vv. 18, 19 suggests a sudden crash; this is all the joy he has; and he is at once forgotten. Bildad's last words leave a sinister suggestion, which was doubtless intended.

Chapters 9 and 10: Job's Reply to Bildad

Ch. 9. God's might is immense (vv. 1–10); hence, it is impossible to answer him (vv. 11–16); but he is capricious; he cares nothing for moral distinctions (vv. 17–24); but oh, my misery; there is no comfort in God, who only uses his superhuman power to treat me as a criminal (vv. 25–35). **Ch. 10.** Yet I would appeal to him; he knows my innocence (vv. 1–7); and once he cared for me (vv. 8–12); now, how cruelly he is changed; whatever I do, he is my foe (vv. 13–17); if this miserable life is my fate, let me have one brief respite before the grave! (Vv. 18–22.) Job pays no attention to Bildad; he is still thinking of Eliphaz. He takes up $7^{17f.}$; his complaint at his woes is now sharpened into complaint against God, and a denial of his justice. If God is the author of suffering, and the function of suffering is punishment for sin, and Job has not sinned, what is the explanation of Job's experience? At the back of Job's mind is the figure of an adversary, now in battle, now in the law court, so powerful as to be beyond justice—once a friend, now a tormentor.

CHAPTER IX

1–21. Job's Helplessness in the Presence of God's Infinite Might. With v. 2 cf. 4^{17}, a slightly different expression. *Just*=counted as guiltless in the sight of God, with the recurrent figure of the court. The Hebrew word for "just" has two (not clearly distinguished) meanings; righteous, and (not always the same thing) pronounced innocent, or discharged with no further liability. In any legal contest with God man is at a decided disadvantage; moreover, God's might is destructive. The three particularly conspicuous constellations (if rightly identified), named in v. 9, are also mentioned together in Homer; but they are no more than probable translations of the Hebrew. *Chambers*, probably the southern sky and its constellations. In v. 10 Job quotes Eliphaz (5^{9}). God is pictured in v. 12 as a mythological hero; so v. 13; Rahab the primeval monster (=Tiamat); cf. 7^{12} Isa. 51^{9}; used for Egypt, Psa. 87^{4}. In the Babylonian Tablets of Creation some of the gods were the "helpers of Tiamat" in her strife with heaven (cf. notes on Gen. 1, 2; also art., *O.T. and Archæology*, p. 120). Even if I were in the right (v. 15), I should have to play the suppliant for pardon. *Call* (v. 16)="cite with a legal summons." V. 17 describes what he would do if he did answer the summons. Who will fix a time, as a judge, for my case to come on? (V. 19.) Though I be in the right, my own mouth would put me in the wrong (v. 20). But I *am* blameless (v. 21); beside that, I care not if I die; hence, I am not afraid of asserting God's complete indifference to justice.

22–35. God's Unfair Treatment of Job. God destroys the good with the bad: Job's innocence, therefore, is no protection. *Covereth* (v. 24), as a bribe might be said to do. "Who else?"—the most burning question of all. *Ships*—reed boats that skim over the surface of the water. Job's thought passes from the impossibility of getting justice to the horror of being treated as guilty, whatever he does. In v. 30 follow margin. The sentence is properly, *if I even washed, . . . that moment thou wouldst*. *Daysman*="umpire" (v. 33), to exert his authority over us both. V. 35 closes with the assertion, "I am not really the guilty person he pretends me to be."

CHAPTER X

1–17. God's Present Attitude Is Incomprehensible. Having reached this point of despair, Job will express himself freely, and cross-question God. "A human being might despise justice thus; but wilt thou?" *Work* (v. 3)—Job himself, or other men; v. 3c is superfluous. *Flesh* belongs to men but not to God (v. 4). In v. 7a read, preserving the parallel, *because thou knowest I cannot save myself*. For God as potter (v. 9) cf. Gen. 2^{7} Isa. 45^{9} Jer. 18. For God's care in the creation of man cf. Psa. $139^{13f.}$; the process of man's formation is summed up in vv. 10f.: the semen, the fœtus, the formation of the whole bodily frame, and the blessings of Providence that follow. *These things . . . this* (v. 13) refers to vv. 14f., God's cruel designs; vv. 14f. apply 9^{22} to Job himself; *looking upon* (v. 15), better, *sated with*. *Marvelous* (v. 16), not in providence now, but in tyranny.

18–22. A plea for a brief respite before death.

CHAPTER XI

The Speech of Zophar

Zophar, who has evidently listened intently to Job's previous appeal, now breaks in: Mere confident mockery (vv. 1–6), the idea that a futile human being can find out the designs of God (vv. 7–12); righteousness and piety bring light and peace; but as for the wicked—(vv. 13–20). Zophar repeats his companions' arguments (cf. vv. 18–20 with 8^{20-22}), but with an outspoken brutality as yet foreign to them.

1–6. Rebuke of Job's Challenge of the Divine Righteousness. Loquacity, boasting, mockery, self-righteousness, may all be urged against Job; but what of Job's excuse? Zophar repeats (v. 5), though with a different direction, Job's prayer of 10^{2}. V. 6c means "bringeth into forgetfulness, for thy benefit, a part of thy sin."

7–12. God's Wisdom, Man's Blindness. "Canst thou discover the vast range of God's being, or reach the bounds of the Almighty?" All the acts of God must be judged in the light of his infinite wisdom; the divine acts are not arbitrary or unfair; indeed, if Job would only realize it, his sufferings are less than he deserves. Over against the all-wise God is weak and foolish man. *Vain* (v. 12)—"empty," "futile." If the text of v. 11 is right, it contains another (softened) condemnation of Job (9^{22}). In v. 12 read margin: *A foolish man will get understanding, when a wild ass's colt* (type of indiscipline) *grows human*, i.e., tamed.

13–20. Exhortation to Repentance. *Thou* (v. 13), emphatic, wicked as thou art. With v. 17 cf. Job's words in $10^{21f.}$; LXX translates v. 17b, "thy prayer as the day-star." *Secure* (v. 18), literally, "thou shalt trust"; v. 18b means, after searching in vain for a possible foe, "thou shalt be at peace." V. 20 is an extension of Bildad's words in 8[22].

CHAPTERS 12 TO 14: JOB'S REPLY TO ZOPHAR

Ch. 12. What profundity! But as you see from my sufferings, there is no justice in God (vv. 1–6); all nature will tell you of the power and wisdom of its creator (vv. 7–13); but he is the great source of destruction in nature, and of deception and calamity in political life, causing nations to grow, only to fling them into confusion (vv. 14–25). **Ch. 13.** I have nothing to learn from you; you are defending God with mischievous arguments and lies but you cannot deceive with your maxims (vv. 1–12); but now, whatever happens, I will make the speech which declares my innocence (vv. 13–18); but oh, cease to terrify me thus; tell me why thou dost imprison me in helpless corruption (vv. 19–28). **Ch. 14.** Do not ask what poor feeble man cannot give (vv. 1–6); for man, unlike a felled or withered tree, can never live again (vv. 7–12); I would gladly die, if after that I might have a discharge from my term of service (vv. 13–15); but thou art relentless to my frailty; all nature decays, and man ceases to know anything but his pain (vv. 16–22).

This striking passage abounds in quick changes of mood—resentment against the Friends, irony, accusations against God, confidence, pathetic appeal, longing for some understanding with God, and despair.

CHAPTER XII

Job Admits God's Power, but Doubts His Justice. Another ironical outburst: Job's insight is not inferior to that of his friends. With v. 3 cf. 13[12]. The thought connection in vv. 4–12 is not easy to trace; v. 3 joins naturally to v. 13: Job takes up Zophar's thought, and extends it. God is all-powerful—for destruction! Yet it is unsafe simply to omit the intervening verses for this reason (but see below, vv. 7f.); in spite of the difficulties, the thought is suitable to Job; his consciousness of being despised (a kind of "inferiority complex" after his misfortune) the Friends, in their safety, can neglect. V. 6 brings a quick transition to the thought of divine injustice. For *speak* (v. 8) read probably *the creeping things of the earth. This* (v. 9), i.e., all this injustice and chaos (as in v. 6). Note in vv. 7, 8 the singular pronoun and verb (imperatives); it is found in Job's speeches (if correct) only here, 16[3], and 21[3]; see on 26[2-4]. Also note the use of "Jehovah" (v. 9), unique in dialogue. This, it is true, throws some further doubt on the authenticity of vv. 4–12. The argument in vv. 11–13 is: "I listen to you with discrimination; do you say that with aged men is wisdom? I reply, Wisdom is with God; and look how he uses it." Still, v. 13 follows best on v. 3. With v. 15b cf. 5[10]; "rain, yes; but only for a devastating flood." Vv. 17–21 suggest the vast political changes involved, for all the near East, in the fall of the Assyrian, Babylonian, and Persian Empires between 600 and 300 B.C. God does not only destroy; but destruction is Job's last word about him in these terrible verses; God is pleased to reduce men, in general, to the helplessness of intoxication!

CHAPTER XIII

1, 2. These verses should be taken with ch. 12: Job knows all the Friends know; but how differently he interprets it.

3–12. Worthlessness of the Friends' Defense of God. *Surely* (v. 3)="but of a truth"; the word is an emphatic adversative. *Reason*= "argue" as an opponent; the law court again. Convince, and even convict, and prove guilty. *Forgers* (v. 4)="plasterers" or smearers. *Reasoning* (v. 6)="attack," as in v. 3. *Pleadings*="accusing speeches." Job is accuser, not defendant. The Friends are regarded as giving, in the court, a verdict for God against Job and justice (cf. 9[33]) with partiality (v. 8a; cf. Lev. 19[15]). Are you prepared for the consequences? (V. 9.) Job implies that God, in spite of his contempt for justice, wishes for no help of this sort; cf. 12[2, 11] 42[7, 12].

13–28. New Challenge of God. *Wherefore* (v. 14) should be omitted (almost identical with the Hebrew letters for the last word of v. 13, cf. mg.). Then v. 14b means, "I am willing to endanger my life," and v. 14a must be a statement parallel to it, perhaps, "carry off, like a wild animal, my own flesh." The well-known A.V. translation of v. 15 is quite unsuitable to the context and is not in accord with the original Hebrew; instead of *for him*, or *it*, we should read *not*. Hence, "he is going to slay me; I will have patience no longer" is more suitable to the context. *Maintain*, same word as *reason* (v. 3). V. 16b means, either, the wicked would not be accepted, if they should approach God, or, would not desire to approach. Justice in God there must be, after all; v. 18b, "that I for my part (emphatic) shall be pronounced in the right." I fear no foe (v. 19), though, if I did, I should be content to perish in silence. In v. 20 confidence suddenly weakens; "God must not employ force; then I care not whether he replies or attacks." Yet there follow only questions and complaints; God acts as a condemning Judge (v. 26a), though Job does not profess to be wholly guiltless (v. 26b). V. 28

reiterates v. 25; the pride of v. 17 is now gone; and the way is prepared for ch. 14.

CHAPTER XIV

1–12. Frailty and Brevity of Human Life. It is absurd to think that weak, helpless man can stand up in court against God; for *me* (v. 3b) probably read *him*. V. 4 is rhythmically defective and may be a late marginal note or "gloss." V. 5 is probably the protasis to v. 6; i.e., "if it is true that his fate is fixed, allow him a respite," if life is short, surely some ease might be allowed. Man has not even the advantage of a tree! (Vv. 7f.) Vv. 10–12 express the same thought as 7^{7-10}; v. 11 is similar to and may be a quotation from Isa. 19^5. *Sea*—sometimes means, as here, inland lake; in Isaiah it is used of the Nile.

13–22. Hopelessness of Job's Condition. *Sheol*—the shadowy abode of the departed is man's destiny; if only one might be hidden there till God were kinder, so that he might then return to earth; but no! Job conceives of some idea of a life after death, only to reject it. Vv. 16, 17, better taken as a continuation of v. 15: "for now, in that case, thou wouldest guard my steps, and not watch them jealously; my transgression would be sealed up and done with." *And surely* (v. 18), the Hebrew is simply adversative. "As it is, as mountains, rocks, stones, and the solid earth perish, so does this poor human hope." *Changest* (v. 20), in death; *away*, to Sheol, where (vv. 21f.) there is no knowledge of events on earth (another allusion to Job's own family?) but there is pain (this may be a reference to decomposition in the grave); this is a darker view than was implied in $3^{17f.}$; Job's speeches regularly end in a deep sigh of misery.

Chapters 15 to 21: The Second Cycle

Eliphaz, having listened to Bildad and Zophar (and Job's replies to them), repeats their argument, in a more flowing and dignified but not less galling style, ending with an elaborate picture of defiant but helpless impiety. Job, specially moved by such words when coming from Eliphaz, breaks out into complaints against both men and God, and then appeals from God to a "witness" in heaven. But he has no hope; he is traduced; Sheol alone awaits him. Bildad's speech shows his irritation, but he has no argument save a further description of the fate of the wicked (of this he is never tired!). Job, in resentful tones, attributes his terrible isolation to God; and then for one moment thinks of a vindicator on earth, and turns on his persecutors. Zophar intervenes with a long homily which repeats Eliphaz and Bildad; and Job, now for the first time answering the implied argument, urges that the wicked live in happiness, and that even death is no real punishment to them. In this, the middle portion of the composition, as so often in Hebrew literature, the climax of feeling is reached.

CHAPTER XV

The Second Speech of Eliphaz

I can but answer you—so Eliphaz begins his speech—out of your own mouth (vv. 2–6); what presumption to criticize our traditional wisdom! (Vv. 7–12.) A puny and guilty being should fear to challenge the knowledge of past ages (vv. 13–19); an evil conscience never allows its owner to rest (vv. 20–25); defiance of God brings its own inevitable condemnation (vv. 26–35). Eliphaz's eloquence is still sonorous; but imaginative rhetoric cannot redeem platitudes, and he has no conception of an answer either to Job's sufferings or for his daring and tortured thoughts of God.

1–16. Rebuke of Job's Presumptuousness. The *east wind* (v. 2), from the desert, is the dangerous sirocco. *Belly* (cf. A.S.V.)—to the Hebrew, the seat of emotion rather than thought ("heart"). What a travesty of Job's agonized cries! In v. 4 Job is accused of diminishing or holding back the reverent musing which is the mark of true religion. Job's words are said (v. 5) to spring from an evil heart. What is old must be true (vv. 7, 8). Is Eliphaz thinking of 13^2? *Counsel* (v. 8), rather, *council*. Has Job attended there? *Consolations* (v. 11), uttered by me, but really coming from God. *Wink* (or "flash," v. 12), apparently (for the word nowhere else occurs) make hints or suggestions. With v. 14 cf 4^{17}; with v. 15 cf. 4^{18}. In v. 16 the reference is to man in general, though doubtless with Job in the speaker's mind.

17–35. Evil Conscience and Speedy Destruction of the Wicked. In v. 19 Eliphaz refers to the freedom of his tribe from contamination by new ideas from foreign political and cultural invasions. The powerful description in vv. 20f. may be taken to mean that the wicked is pursued by calamity all his life, which could hardly be asserted, save by a rhetorician; or that inward terrors plague him from the first. But is conscience always active? Cf. Shakespeare's delineation of Macbeth. In v. 22 LXX has "let him not believe." For *fatness* (v. 27), as a sign of crass stupidity, cf. Deut. 32^{15} Psa. 73^7. *Cities* (v. 28), under the curse of God, and therefore to be left in ruins, such as Sidon, or Jericho, rebuilt by Hiel (1 Kings 16^{34}). *In-*

habited, better, *should inhabit*. *Bend* (v. 29), like full ears of corn (cf. A.S.V.). *His mouth* (v. 30), i.e., God's, the metaphor being suddenly dropped; better, *his bud is whirled away by the wind*. The olive bears very little fruit in alternate years (v. 33).

Chapters 16 and 17: Job's Second Reply to Eliphaz

Ch. 16. Words are as easy as they are useless (vv. 2–5); they are indeed useless to me, the object of God's relentless fury (vv. 6–14); but helpless as I am, I can yet appeal to God to uphold my cause (vv. 15–22). **Ch. 17.** I am helpless and despised; where can I look for aid? Not to men (vv. 1–7); yet my calamities will strengthen the upright (vv. 8–10); I can hope for nothing now but death (vv. 11–16). Job now drops the image of the law court (save in 16[21] 17[3]), regarding himself as the victim of God's rage. There is a sudden and remarkable flash of confidence in 16[19]; but the speech ends with utter despair.

CHAPTER XVI

1–5. Reproach of the Heartlessness of His Friends. *Miserable* (v. 2), who (only) bring trouble. *Vain* (v. 3), literally, words of wind. In v. 3b Job turns, as very seldom, on an individual (see on 12[3-12]). *But* (v. 5) is not in the Hebrew, and should be omitted, for v. 5 continues v. 4, "I could have comforted you (as you have not comforted me!)"

6–17. Job's Sorrowful Condition: Forsaken by God and Men. Speech and silence are the same (v. 6). What is *my company?* (V. 7.) Is Job thinking of his former household? Substitute: *my evil has seized me*. *A witness* (v. 8), at any rate, to the traditionalists. *Torn* and *gnashed* (v. 9) suggest a wild beast; *persecuted*, literally, "hated." Vv. 9c–11 break the connection; it is difficult to understand the sudden reference (in literal terms to human adversaries); the verses suggest Psa. 22 and Isa. 51. V. 12 carries on the metaphor of v. 9; God is the leader of a band of archers (vv. 12a, 13; unless *archers* should be *arrows*), and then a warrior mutilating his foes (*reins*, archaic for "kidneys"), or besieging a city (not *giant*, v. 14, but *mighty man*). *Upon* (v. 15), i.e., next my skin. *Horn*, symbol of confident strength. In v. 17 Job repudiates lawlessness, like God's!

18–22. The Witness in Heaven. The *blood* (v. 18)=the life (cf. Lev. 17[11, 14]) of an innocent man is regarded as crying from the ground (cf. Gen. 4[10]) till his death is avenged by the "goël," or avenger of blood. The blood belongs even more to the tribe than to the individual. If it is covered, the cry is dulled. Job longs that his blood may cry out against his murderer—God. My appeal is not in vain (v. 19); I have a witness to my cause in heaven. Who is this? God himself? God, thinking of Job, as Job hopes later on, with a changed mind? *Even now* is against this. The witness could not well be other than God. But Job has not thought out the implication of his daring words. There is another flash in 19[27]. Only in a later age does it become an illumination. In vv. 20f., Job falls back into his old wish that he might be pronounced righteous, but with the significant difference that God is to umpire in Job's case against God, as also against his friends (neighbors), although he himself will not be living to rejoice in the verdict (v. 22).

CHAPTER XVII

1–9. Further Appeal to the Witness in Heaven. The connection of thought in the opening verses is not clear. Probably the meaning is, "Yes, I shall soon die; and even now men mock me bitterly; then let me find a surety in God." Or, v. 2 (translating *mockery* instead of *mockers*) may refer to God, giving the same antithesis as in 16[21]; the first half of v. 4 shows that Job has the Friends in his mind. *Strike hands* (v. 3), in giving the pledge. V. 5 carries on v. 4b, but the text is difficult and uncertain. Vv. 6, 7 revert to Job's persecution; vv. 8, 9 appear out of place; if the thought of the effect upon the good had occurred to Job here, it could hardly have been dropped immediately, and v. 7 connects with v. 11 rather than with v. 10 and its reference to the Friends.

10–16. Death the Only Hope of Deliverance. *Return*, i.e., to your argument; *all of you* is in the Hebrew, strangely, "all of them." How do the Friends change night into day? (V. 12.) By pretending that Job is not really in darkness? But when had they done this? In v. 13 the Hebrew points to "if I hope, (yet only) Sheol is my home"; the remaining clauses being categorical rather than conditional. Vv. 15, 16 are thus parallel to vv. 13, 14; but the Hebrew of v. 16 is hardly intelligible. Job ends on his usual note of despair.

CHAPTER XVIII

The Second Speech of Bildad

Your contempt for us is mere overweening conceit (vv. 2–4); the wicked will be put to confusion—ensnared by his own wickedness (vv. 5–12); calamity will seize both him and his descendants (vv. 13–21). After the customary brief outburst of resentment, Bildad enlarges on Eliphaz's theme, but stresses the fate of the wicked (brought on him by himself) as future, not present. This is not yet *peccatum poena peccati*, but *peccatum instrumentum poenae*.

1–4. Condemnation of Job's Rejection of Friendly Counsel. Bildad here retorts on Job with a *tu quoque:* it is you who need to think, instead of treating us as unintelligent brute beasts. *Unclean* (v. 3)—probably "stupid" or "silenced." In your own anger, not in God, is the cause of your anguish (v. 4). Is the order of things to be changed to gratify your private desires?

5–21. Calamity in this Life and Dishonor After Death the Lot of the Wicked. The law of the destruction of the wicked still holds good. V. 7b suggests that the trap (note the six synonyms) is successful because of the victim's folly rather than the hunter's skill (cf. 5[13]). *For his halting* (v. 12), better, *when he slumbers*, or *at his side.* The Hebrew cf. v. 13 (literally translated in R.V.) is obscure; is Bildad generalizing from a peculiarly brutal allusion to Job's own disease? *Brought* (v. 14), better *marched.* Note the impressive vagueness in v. 15a. *The street* (v. 17), better, the open country outside his lands (*earth*). *Where he sojourned* (v. 19), i.e., being only a stranger, with no rights of his own. Read in v. 20, *they that are of the West . . . and they of the East.* He is to leave *no* memory behind him.

CHAPTER XIX

Job's Second Reply to Bildad

Why do you still refuse to see that it is through God's injustice that I suffer? (Vv. 2–8.) He has brought me down to utter defeat, like a victorious foe (vv. 8–12); into utter loneliness and universal contempt; do not you be like God! (Vv. 13–22.) Would that my words might remain; yet I have a vindicator, and I shall somehow live to look on God; let my persecutors then beware! (Vv. 23–29.)

Job begins by manifesting a deeper and more indignant disappointment in the Friends, which leads him, in thinking on God's harshness, to concentrate on his own isolation. This leads, again, to a pathetic appeal to the Friends, which, as the thought of 16[18f.] suddenly returns, changes to the wish that, even if he dies, his defense of his cause might remain. But—by a surprising transition—better than that, he has a vindicator, and he will himself be satisfied. This is the magnificent though obscure climax of the whole dialogue; but Job ends immediately, as he began, with a bitter reference to the Friends.

1–6. Protest Against the Reproaches of the Friends. V. 4 reads literally, "If I really did err, is it with myself (emphatic) that my error is to remain as a lodger?" The verb properly means "to stay for a night only" (cf. Psa. 30[5]). Is this a parallel to 6[24] or 10[6]? Or is the second clause, like the first, a question? Job is hardly in a mood to admit even error (a milder word than *sin*). *Now* (v. 6), however, it surprises you. *Subvert*—the verb means to bend or pervert justice, treat a man dishonestly. These accusations against God appear in each of Job's speeches.

7–29. Job's Sufferings. In v. 7 read *I am crying out, "Violence!"* God is once more spoken of (vv. 10f.) as the ferocious invader (invading troops regularly destroyed the orchards; Deut. 20[19]). Vv. 13f. describe a yet deeper misery. If the author made use of, rather than invented, the Prologue, we can see how his imagination has been working on it. The proverbial expression in v. 20b should probably be *I plucked at my skin with my teeth;* as it stands, what can it mean? V. 22b is an echo of the Oriental phrase, "to eat the flesh," "to calumniate." *Book* (v. 23)—scroll or document of accusation. *Inscribed*—synonym of "graven" (v. 24b). Either, "in a book, or on lead tablets on a rock," or, "by graving on the rock filled in with molten lead." *The redeemer* ("goël," v. 25) is properly the next of kin, whose duty it is to avenge a murder, or buy up family property when it comes into the market (Ruth 4[1f.]), "I have more than a document; a champion who is alive [even when I am dead!]." V. 25b is very obscure; literally, "afterwards [at the last, as having the last word, or, simply, after my death], on the dust [on Job's grave, but contrast 16[19]] he will take his stand." V. 26a is too corrupt to be translated with any confidence; literally, "and after [i.e., afterward] my skin they have destroyed this"; *from my flesh*, i.e., "without [or, apart from] or out of [i.e., while I am still in it]." But, however we understand this, the important words are *I shall see God*, and this as "for myself" (v. 27 mg.), i.e., *on my side. And not another*, i.e., "and not as a stranger, or, as estranged."

Here Job extends and transforms the thought of 16[21]. The witness or "goël" is God, at last and firmly his friend, and Job is to behold him vindicating that very accusation of God which he has so constantly, daringly, and often despairingly, uttered. This is not an assertion of the (later) doctrine of immortality; we cannot be sure, from our actual Hebrew text, that Job expects by some miracle to come to life again, but he is certain, now, that the final authority in the world is moral ("appealing from man's God to God's God") and that death itself is subordinate to the real justice of God. If we substitute for "justice" God's communion with his children in Christ, we have the essence of the doctrine of eternal life as found in the N.T. V. 27c means, "I am consumed with passionate longing." But Job, even now (v. 28), cannot forget the Friends sitting before him; v. 28b is obscure; "seeing that I really am sincere and conceal nothing," or reading, as is possible, *him* for *me*, "since the cause of his suffering lies in himself and in his sin"; v. 29bc is also textually uncertain, but the general sense is clear. Job does not again reach the height of vv. 25f.; but this is quite in accordance with the Hebrew love of placing the most important assertion in the middle rather than the end of a composition. Psychologically, too, it may be verified. Tantalizing as is the state of the text, we can see how the long-drawn-out conflict between the two conceptions of God reaches its height in this second cycle; and the profoundest doubt is met by the most daring "guess at truth," as the old metaphor of the law court receives this startling extension of the "goel."

CHAPTER XX

The Second Speech of Zophar

Job's speech cannot go unanswered (vv. 2, 3); the prosperity of the wicked is short-lived (vv. 4–11); he cannot keep the wealth and pleasure that he has gained through dishonesty and violence (vv. 12–19); when he is about to satisfy his greed he suffers the terror of God's wrath; how great and conspicuous is his fall (vv. 20–29). Zophar is quite unable, like the rest, to understand Job; but he now stresses the dramatic suddenness of the fall of the wicked in language that might suit the calamity of Job himself (ch. 2) or the narrative of Lk. 12. In v. 3b read *with wind* [or, in argument] *void of understanding thou answerest me.* V. 10 stresses the greatest indignity. *His hands*, better, *his children*, or *their hands* (either is an easy alteration). *Hide* (v. 12), like a dainty morsel; a curious parallel in Ezek. 3^{3}. "His belly must be filled!" (V. 23.) One (i.e., God) will cast on him his fierce wrath (instead of the dainties he claimed); but the text is not certain. If he escapes one disaster, another ruins him (v. 24).

CHAPTER XXI

Job's Second Reply to Zophar

My complaint goes beyond my personal suffering (vv. 2–6); it concerns the prosperity of the wicked even when they openly defy God (vv. 7–15); their calamity is at best exceptional; let suffering come on *them*, not on their children (vv. 16–18); God is not mocked; happy or miserable, all die in the end (vv. 19–26); such arguments as you use about the wicked man bring no peace to me (vv. 27–34).

Here at last Job passes definitely beyond his own misery, and urges that God repudiates retributive suffering in his whole government of the world. He reproduces his opponents' arguments (hence the appearance of contradiction), only to overthrow them.

"Thou wilt mock on" (v. 3; addressed to Zophar himself); not a command if the text is right; but LXX has the plural. "Am *I* (emphatic) complaining about man?" (V. 4.) For the rhetorical effect of vv. 5f. cf. 4^{12-15}. V. 8 should follow vv. 9, 10. Job might be giving a picture of his own previous prosperity. *In a moment* (v. 13b), i.e., without his own long-drawn-out agony (cf. 3^{22}). In v. 16a Job perhaps quotes from the Friends; or the words might be a protesting interpolation of the Friends themselves after vv. 14, 15. V. 16b is repeated by Eliphaz in 22^{18}. *Sorrows* (v. 17), "snares" or "pangs, as of travail." In v. 19a, with a change in text read *let him* [God] *not lay upon.* Job here states his opponents' position; the opponents, however, have never actually asserted (what Ezek. 18, conscious of attacking a widespread belief, denies) that children suffer *instead of* parents. "Do you really think that I am trying to instruct God?" (v. 22) or (less conformably to the Hebrew, but logically more satisfactory) "Can anyone take God's place as a teacher?" Vv. 23–26 repeat 9^{22}. V. 30, as the text stands, may be a "dogmatic correction" of a later scribe; the change of one letter, however, would give "is spared *in* the day of calamity . . . is guarded *in* the day of wrath"; or, if not too farfetched, "your belief (v. 30) is founded on mere travelers' talk" (v. 29). *Keep watch* (v. 32); the subject is indefinite, or it may be the dead man's shade. "The very tomb [an imaginative *tour de force*] gives him pleasure (v. 33), such is the way of all flesh." Job's three speeches in the second cycle may be taken as containing three replies to his opponents: (1) his arguments have a higher authority (16^{19}); (2) he will personally be vindicated (19^{25}); (3) the opponents' position is untenable on the available evidence (ch. 21).

Chapters 22 to 31: The Third Cycle

Chs. 22, 23 are quite intelligible, but ch. 24 is difficult in the mouth of Job, if not impossible. Ch. 25 (Bildad) is unusually brief.

Ch. 26 might have been, and may still be taken to be, a continuation of ch. 25, rather than the reply of Job. 27^1-12 is a suitable reply to Bildad from Job, but 27^13-23 contains a flat contradiction of 27^1-12. In the text there is no speech at all from Zophar, and these verses might well be his reply to the preceding. Ch. 28 has no connection with the argument; it is more in the vein of chs. 38–41, or still more of Prov. 8, and is probably a quite independent poem (see on ch. 41). In chs. 29–31 Job winds up the whole discussion.

The course of the cycle will then be: Eliphaz charges Job with being like the wicked whom he has just described, repudiates Job's account of them, and in dignified and beautiful words appeals to Job to repent. Job, as if influenced by the appeal, laments that he cannot find God, and that the world's suffering is not conterminous with sin. Bildad now appeals, with real eloquence, but little logic, to the inscrutable might of God. To this Job only replies, "I know that I have not sinned; then how can you be right, or God just?" Zophar repeats his last argument, that the wicked has no pleasure in his ill-gotten gains. Job then draws an elaborate contrast between the probity and wide philanthropy of his old life and the bodily and mental suffering of the present, concluding with a magnificent statement of the ideals which he had actually carried out. Chs. 29 and 31 might well be taken as an elaborate commentary on 1^1, and ch. 30 on 2^6.

CHAPTER XXII

The Third Speech of Eliphaz

God has nothing to gain from man's goodness, or to fear from his sin (vv. 2–4); you have abused your position; hence your fall (vv. 5–11); do not be like the wicked; they do *not* prosper in the end (vv. 12–20); if you would make a friend of God, even now how completely he would receive and restore you! (Vv. 21–30.) A gracious and dignified appeal, if addressed to, e.g., Nabal (1 Sam. 25^2f.); but to Job!

1–5. Job's Sins the Cause of His Affliction. God cannot be punishing Job for his piety (*fear*, in good sense, cf. 4^6); therefore it must be for wickedness. Note in v. 5 the underlying assumption.

6–20. Enumeration of Job's Alleged Sins. V. 6 implies a disregard of the old Hebrew rule that a garment taken in pledge should be restored at nightfall (Ex. 22^26, 27; cf. Deut. 24^17). *For nought*, for a trifling debt, or for no debt at all. Though you neglected the poor, you acquiesced in the power of the (oppressive) rich (vv. 7–9). The treatment of widows and orphans is regarded as a kind of "acid test" of morality throughout the O.T. In v. 11 substitute *thy light is darkness, so that.* The thought of v. 12 is, "God, as we both admit, is as high as the stars; hence (v. 13), *you* will be asking, drawing the wrong conclusion . . ." Job had not said, however, that God could not see, but that he did not judge. Do not imitate the wicked (v. 15) whom you described (in ch. 21); for v. 18, cf. 21^16, note; you forget their real end (v. 19).

21–30. Exhortation to Repentance. *Acquaint thyself* (v. 21)—"grow used to," as an intimate friend. *The law* (v. 22), "instruction" (this is the true meaning of the Hebrew word); there is no reference here to the specific instruction or law given to Israel through Moses. *Lay* (v. 24), as worthless. *Delight* (v. 26), "take exquisite pleasure in." The Hebrew text of v. 29 is barely intelligible.

Chapters 23 and 24: Job's Third Reply to Eliphaz

Ch. 23. If I could but find God, all would be well (vv. 2–7); but he hides himself (vv. 8, 9); he must vindicate my innocence at the last (vv. 10–12); but, here and now, his plan is unintelligible (vv. 13–17). **Ch. 24.** Think of the high-handed oppression and abject poverty and furtive crime in the world (vv. 1–17); you may reply, "It is only for a time" (vv. 18–21); yet can it be denied that God preserves the wicked? (Vv. 22–25.)

CHAPTER XXIII

1–7. Job's Yearning for Access to God. Ch. 23 is entirely appropriate in the mouth of Job; neglecting Eliphaz he is holding, though insecurely, to the faith of 19^25 (cf. especially v. 7). How far removed is his world from the simple and elementary sequences of the Friends: "sin and be punished; repent and be forgiven!" The effect of the apparent contradictions of ch. 24 is increased by a very uncertain text, and the descriptions in vv. 3–7, though poignant, are, for Job, strangely detached. In v. 6 Job moves beyond 9^13; he now believes that the prayer of 13^20f. will be answered. *My judge* (v. 7)—is this God? If so, the thought of "God's God beyond man's God" is still implicit in Job's words.

8–17. Reassertion of Job's Innocence. Job is opposing the Friends' "world-order" to another, to which he is precariously advancing. This second order he cannot yet reach (v. 9), but he trusts it (vv. 10f.), though now the thought of it plunges his mind into confusion

(vv. 15f.). What Job is trying to say is that there must be an intelligible order in the universe, though as yet it is wholly unintelligible to him—another aspect of the conviction of 19[25].

CHAPTER XXIV

God's Indifference to Wickedness. Why does not God fix definite *times* for judgment for men (v. 1) (as for Job himself)? As it is, violence is unchecked. *Remove* (v. 2)—to steal their neighbors' lands; cf. Deut. 19[14] Isa. 5[8]. After v. 3 possibly v. 9 should be inserted. *Turn* (v. 4), literally or metaphorically; the one, as to-day, generally implies the other. The poor are "as homeless as wild creatures" (v. 5), or, "like wild creatures on the *open moor*" (the equivalent, to us, of both "desert" and "wilderness"—steppe). A description of some nomadic gypsy group, outcasts or wandering thieves. *Provender* (v. 6), mere fodder for cattle; "they pilfer the late-ripe fruit of the vines." *Wicked* should probably be *rich* (cf. Isa. 53[9] mg., for the reverse change). Vv. 10f. apparently refer to ill-used slaves, half-starved; vv. 12f., misery and wretchedness dwell in the city, which is also the hunting ground of the murderer, adulterer, thief. Possibly v. 14c should follow v. 15. *Shadow of death* (v. 17)=*profound darkness.*

Vv. 18–22 are intelligible here if put into the mouth of Job's Friends. V. 18c should read *no treader of grapes turns to their vineyard.* The Hebrew text of v. 20 is corrupt, but some such sense as expressed in the translation must be intended. Read v. 22b, *riseth up from sickness, but does not believe that he will live.* In v. 23 Job resumes his own argument, but v. 24 repeats vv. 18–22. The expedient by which the whole of v. 24 is secured as a part of Job's speech is not wholly satisfactory; possibly the confusion in the text suspected for ch. 25 begins earlier, and part of ch. 24 may even belong to ch. 25.

Chapters 25 and 26: Third Speech of Bildad

How impossible to justify oneself before the omnipotent! (25[1-6].) How vain, then, are your arguments! (26[2-4].) The whole framework of earth, sea, and sky is his creation, and how much must lie beyond! (26[5-14].) Bildad's exalted words, worthy to stand beside Psa. 104[1-9] or Job 36, are broken by 26[2-4], whose personal tone probably suggested Job as the author (cf. 12[2f.] 16[2-5]); but Job regularly uses the plural of the personal pronoun, while the Friends, to whom such language is by no means strange, use the singular (as here).

CHAPTER XXV

Man's Inferiority to God. *Armies* (v. 3) =*troops;* the hosts of heaven; hence, parallel with *light.* Vv. 4–6 are quoted from Eliphaz, 15[14-16].

CHAPTER XXVI

"The Outskirts of His Ways." "Do your words really aid him who feels himself helpless before God?" *Deceased* (v. 5), literally, "the shades"; perhaps, as LXX, the mighty dead of antiquity. *Inhabitants*=monsters of the deep. *Beneath* should probably be joined as an adverb to v. 5a. *Abaddon* (v. 6), Hebrew, by derivation, "place of destruction" (cf. Prov. 27[20]). *Stretcheth* (v. 7), like a vast tent-cloth, without any pole. Resting on the ocean is a partition ("the firmament"?) (v. 10); within it, the light of the heavenly bodies; without it, darkness. *Pillars* (v. 11) —mountains of the horizon; it would, however, be precarious to conclude (as is often done) that this literally represents the actual Hebrew views of geography. V. 12 contains another reference to Babylonian mythology (cf. 9[13]). *Outskirts* (v. 14), i.e., the earth and the world of earth and sky are at the edge and not the center of God's whole universe.

CHAPTER XXVII

Job's Third Reply to Bildad

In spite of God's treatment of me, I will hold to it that I am innocent (vv. 2–6); there is no real profit in wickedness, as all should know (vv. 7–12); the wicked may grow rich, but they have no joy either in their wealth or in their posterity, and destruction sweeps on them like a hurricane (vv. 13–23). The first six verses follow Job's argument in chs. 23, 24 quite naturally; at all events, Job knows he has nothing to confess which could justify his misery or put his Friends in the right (v. 5). Vv. 11 and 12 are clearly Job's, if only for the personal pronouns. But vv. 7–10 are unlike Job. Has he found a temporary refuge on the level of the Friends' thought? Or does he, rather, in sudden exasperation, think of those who would question his integrity as his enemies, rising up against him (v. 7), and threaten them with the very fate they had described? Certainly, it is not easy to see the reason for the personal touch in v. 7 if the verse belongs to Zophar; but if vv. 12–23 are Zophar's, he, having no fresh replies, and unconsciously echoing v. 8, repeats his general assertions in ch. 20.

1–6. Reaffirmation of Job's Innocence. In v. 2 note the irony of Job's oath. *Heart* (v. 6) =*thoughts* or *conscience.*

7–23. Mental Condition and Material Ruin of the Wicked. V. 10a is quoted from Eliphaz (22[26]). In vv. 11f. Job proposes another course of instruction; but could he really say anything fresh after chs. 19 and 23? So he breaks off: "you know it; why this futile refusal to confess it?" *Raiment* (v. 16)—a recognized investment or embodiment of wealth (cf. 2 Kings 5[22]). *Booth* (v. 18)—a mere temporary hut for a watchman in the gardens. *Gathered* (v. 19)—better, *but not again. East wind* (v. 21) =*sirocco,* as in 1[19] and 15[2]. Only at the end of the address is the action of God referred to (v. 22), though even here the word "God" is only implied in the Hebrew.

CHAPTER XXVIII

The Wisdom of God Unattainable by Man. This cannot be taken to be a part of the dialogue, as it has no connection with the preceding or following passages, nor with any part of the subject of the debate. If it were to be taken as an original part of the book, the speeches of Jehovah could hardly be thus anticipated. It belongs to a type of composition known as Wisdom Literature, "wisdom" in the Hebrew being used both in connection with God's providential creation and government of the world, and man's shrewd and provident (and therefore, pious) conduct in it. The subject is treated, from varying points of view, in Proverbs, Ecclesiastes, Ecclesiasticus, Wisdom of Solomon. (See art., *The Poetic and Wisdom Literature*, p. 157b.) Consider the skill and daring of the miner (vv. 1–4), and his magnificent achievement in the conquest of the treasures hidden in the earth (vv. 5–11); wisdom, hidden more deeply still, is more precious than all that mines can yield (vv. 12–22); God alone, the omniscient Creator, knows its secret and uses it (vv. 23–27); for man, the pursuit of wisdom is true piety (v. 28).

Surely (v. 1)—better *for;* this implies something to precede it, such as, "wisdom is harder to come by than gold or gems"; it can hardly refer to ch. 27. *Mine*—in spite of Deut. 8[9], mining was scarcely known in Palestine, but it was somewhat familiar to the Jews as carried on in Lebanon, Edom, Midian, Egypt. Sinai, at least in earlier times, had its copper and sapphire workings. Separation from the ore is regarded as part of the mining process. *An end* (v. 3)—apparently by letting in daylight or lamplight. *Shaft* (v. 4)—elsewhere, torrent or torrent-bed (wady). *Sojourn*—why this word? Perhaps we should read *lamp* or *light;* or perhaps (cf. mg.) *torrent* is the subject; and *hand* or *swing* (at end of rope, in descending) should be *are diminished* or *depart* (disappear). The poet seems not to have actually seen the operation. What a contrast in v. 5, cornfields and blasting! *Sapphire* (v. 6)=*lapis lazuli,* whose particles glint like gold. Bird and beast know not wisdom (vv. 7f.); man turns the hills upside down for it: a better order would be vv. 10a, 11a, 10b, 11b. *Channels, trickle;* read, with mg., *passages, weep. Price* (v. 13) —better, with LXX, *path. Ophir* (v. 16)—cf. 22[24]; *onyx*—Hebrew, *sheham;* mentioned in Gen. 2[11] Ex. 25[7] 28[20] Ezek. 28[13], etc.; the actual gem is uncertain. *Glass*—then, of course, a rarity; *rubies* should probably be *pearls. All living* (v. 21) refers to men; a better antithesis would be, with the addition of one letter, *all animals. Abaddon* (v. 22; cf. A.S.V. mg.), as in 26[6]. A better parallel would be secured to v. 26 if, with LXX, etc., v. 25 were made to read *when he was making and meting out* (cf. mg.). In later thought (Prov. 8, Philo and Jn. 1 where *logos* represents "wisdom" as it is used in vv. 12, 20, 28), wisdom is half-personified, as more than a model or tool—a companion; here, more simply, wisdom is definitely set forth in the primal acts of creation, in God's eyes and purpose (as in Gen. 1[3]). V. 28 is distinct from the rest of the chapter, and in prose; but not ineffective, as an application of the whole by a reference to the other kind of wisdom.

CHAPTERS 29 TO 31: JOB'S FINAL SURVEY OF THE CASE

Job does not now explicitly refer to Zophar's preceding speech (see introductory notes to ch. 27), nor, indeed, to any part of the previous dialogue. He has passed the stage of argument, or even of attack on God. He knows himself to be deserted by God. He no longer asks, Why? Yet indirectly this section is a powerful and final vindication of all that he has urged; his splendid record of far-flung beneficence, the appalling contrast of his present sufferings, and the unbroken probity of his old life. On the other hand, ch. 31 is not without difficulty; since, throughout, Job calls down on himself, if he should have been unfaithful, the very calamities from which he is now suffering, and to which, here, he makes no reference (see below).

CHAPTER XXIX

Job's Former Prosperity. I recall the general honor in which I was held (vv. 2–10), a protection to the poor, a terror to evildoers (vv. 11–17), and my confident expectation of continued prosperity (vv. 18–21); I was held in deep and universal reverence (vv. 22–25).

This is more than the portrait of a desert sheikh; a large and (as we might say) feudal land-owner, with the character of an idealized Abraham; yet the relations mentioned are social rather than political or tribal and all spring from the companionship and guidance of God.

Ripeness (v. 4)=*maturity;* many years of life were expected (cf. v. 18). *Secret*=intimate, friendship. *Gate* (v. 7), the open space where meetings were held, public questions decided, and justice administered. *Street*=*broad place.* Job is represented as equally at home in tent (v. 4) and city (v. 7). Vv. 12f. state the reason for this deep respect (cf. Psa. 72[12]). *He clothed* (v. 14); cf. Judg. 6[34]. *Diadem*= *turban.* For the metaphor, cf. Eph. 6[10f]. *Sand* (v. 18)—his days were to be as many as the grains of sand, or with a change in text, like a palm, or the phœnix (symbol of growth or renewed life). *Is renewed* (v. 20)=*shows freshness,* i.e., "is pliable." Vv. 21–25 really belong to the description of the assembly in vv. 7–11. Can one cast down the *light* of a face? (v. 24); perhaps, omitting "cast not down," join v. 25c to v. 24c ("the light of my countenance comforted the mourners").

CHAPTER XXX

Job's Present Humiliation and Wretchedness. Now the most miserable outcasts jeer at me (vv. 1–8); I suffer positive mob violence (vv. 9–15); my disease is horrible and relentless (vv. 16–18); God is the cause, tyrannical, unconscionably cruel (vv. 19–25); my old hopes are changed to utter dejection (vv. 26–31). Job here lays special stress (if the verses are rightly placed) on the contempt which he endures, as distinct from his bodily tortures. All this implies a considerable interval since his calamity, and a quite gratuitous popular *Schadenfreude*; it is more than an ill-natured glorying when "the mighty are put down from their seat." For the alliance of pain, loathsomeness and popular contempt, cf. again Isa. 53. V. 1 is an appropriate introduction to the chapter, but the text is very uncertain. *Ripe age* (v. 2)=*vigor.* Vv. 3f. imply much more than v. 1; famine-stricken, brutal pariahs (cf. 24[5f.]). *Bushes* (v. 4), where the shade gives the struggling desert plants a bare chance. *Broom*=the "juniper" of 1 Kings 19; the roots are said to be very bitter. The description would fit such a tribe as the Doms of Bengal.

Why are such loathsome creatures singled out for description? Are we intended to imagine an actual incident? Or have we an extended parallel to 24[5-8]? If the passage is not original, Job's second speech begins with v. 9, in strong contrast to 29[21-25]; and it becomes far more effective. Vv. 12–15 suggest an incident once more; but the circumstances of Job's downfall compel us to regard it as imaginative. *Stand up* (v. 20), as in a law court; cf. 13[3] 16[21]. The parallelism necessitates "lookest not." The Hebrew of v. 24 is obscure; possibly it contained a parallel to v. 25. Vv. 28f. refer to Job's disfigurement and repulsive appearance. Unless Job actually was the object of mob contempt and violence (vv. 12, 28), we seem to have here a phantasy suggested by 29[7f.] and his present misery; 30[1-8] may then be another phantasy. The parallels to Isaiah's "suffering servant" are noteworthy.

CHAPTER XXXI

Integrity of Job's Entire Life. Impiety, which I have shunned, would bring God's condemnation and punishment (vv. 1–8); this I should deserve, had I been guilty of unchastity or of harshness to my slaves (vv. 9–15), or of anything but the broadest charity to the poor (vv. 16–23); or of trust in wealth, of superstition, hatred, inhospitality or hypocrisy (vv. 24–34); I can justify my whole life fearlessly (vv. 35–40). Some rearrangement of the verses would make the order of thought more logical; e.g., 6, 5, 7, 8, 1–4, 9, 14, 23, 15–22, 38–40, 24–37. The suggestions for such rearrangement are tempting but call for much caution; yet we can hardly avoid placing vv. 38–40 in an earlier part of the chapter; vv. 35–37 are certainly the concluding words. An impressive and noble statement of O.T. (private) ethics at its best. It goes far beyond the Decalogue (being positive as well as negative) and embodies all the rules of conduct (in spirit as well as letter) found in the Torah and the prophets, and may well be compared and contrasted with Rom. 12[9-20] Col. 3[5-17]. But, in contrast with his previous speeches, Job's need has changed and softened. Then he cried, "God does not punish the wicked"; now, if not as the Friends, "God does punish them," yet "wickedness is a thing to be punished by God." This form of the traditional creed must be understood (though it is not explicitly stated as such, but note v. 23) as Job's conviction in the old days. Now, instead of denying the moral principles of God's government, he denies (implicitly) God's moral practice. "If only," he sighs, "my case could come up for hearing, how confident I should be of the verdict!" He no longer cries, as in 16[19] and 19[25], "My case must come on"; but the author leaves the conviction, after so full a statement of the circumstances, that it cannot be neglected, thus preparing the way for chs. 38f.

Covenant (v. 1), as often in Hebrew usage, practically equivalent to *rule;* like the mediæval ascetics, he will not look at what might prove a temptation. The thought of vv. 2, 3 is as contrary to, e.g., 9[22] 21[7, 17], as it is consistent with 20[5] (Zophar) and the Friends' position in general. But Job is expressing his older faith, as is clear if we compare vv. 4, 6 with 14[16]. *Vanity* (v. 5)=*insincerity.* V. 6 (cf. v. 35) implies that God would not judge at all rather than that he would judge wrongly. *Grind for* (v. 10), i.e., "become another's meanest slave"; a man's household is still part of himself. A crime such as is described in vv. 9–11 is odious even to man; how much more to God! Vv. 13f. present an exalted view of the duties of a slaveholder. For the varying position of the slave in Hebrew society, cf. Ex. 21[2f.], Saul's houseslave (1 Sam. 9[3f.]) and Jer. 34[9f.]; cf. also Philemon, where the bond is not a common humanity, but Christianity. *Grew up* (v. 18) —better, *he brought me up; was my guide,* i.e., God's care, for he taught me my duties to them; a very pregnant thought (cf. 1 Jn. 4[19]). V. 21b means, "because the judges would have given me a verdict." Vv. 26f. furnish a rare allusion in this book to false worship as distinct from false conduct; sun-worship was as old in Judah as the seventh century; *kiss*—such gestures were familiar in Babylonian worship. In v. 29 Job almost rises to Mt. 5[44]. No one has asked in vain even for meat, much less for bread (v. 31). All this makes 30[9f.] the more outrageous. *Like Adam* (v. 33)—better, *from* or *among men.* Vv. 35–37 contain the final appeal to be judged. *Signature,* Hebrew *tau* (mark or cross=X); the text, if right, shows that Job thinks of himself as putting in a written plea of innocence. The absence of symmetry suggests some insertion to balance what appears now in v. 35c., literally, "and the document [?] (which) my adversary wrote." *Adversary,* literally, "man who contends with me," i.e., God, who, far more than the Friends, is Job's terrible opponent. But, if so, he here regards God's refusal to listen to him as based on the absence of a definite complaint. If he had the document, so confident is he of his power to answer it, that he would make a public display of it (*upon my shoulder,* v. 36) and then, like royalty come into court, he would give the triumphant explanation.

After this, the Friends could say nothing more, and, as it would seem (unless we regard the Elihu speeches as a part of the original work; see intro.), the author passed on to Jehovah's response to Job's summons.

Chapters 32 to 37: Speech of Elihu

On the critical questions connected with this speech, see introduction, section on "Composition of the Book."

CHAPTER XXXII

After his introduction by the author (vv. 1–5), Elihu speaks: "Your helplessness must be my excuse for speaking (vv. 6–12); but while you have nothing to say, I, young as I am, am full of ideas which must find utterance" (vv. 13–22).

In a few prose sentences Elihu is introduced formally as a person of some position, but his tone, beginning apologetically, is almost ludicrously self-important. The author, however (whether different from the author of the rest of the book or not), says nothing to show whether he agrees with his summary of Elihu's feelings in vv. 2, 3.

Righteous (v. 1)=*in the right* as before. Elihu is represented in v. 2 as akin to Job (Gen. 22[21]). Short as this prose introduction is, there are repetitions in it which mark it off from the prose of chs. 1, 2. V. 8a is to be explained by 8b; it is not age but the breath of God which gives wisdom. *Man*—Hebrew, "man in his weakness." Are we to gather from v. 11 that others also were listening to the preceding dialogue? Job is not so clever that God alone can answer him (vv. 13f.); "he has not yet argued with me" (!). It may be noted that the word for "spirit" (v. 18) also means "wind." The metaphor in v. 19 is one of physical discomfort. *Refreshed* (v. 20)=*found relief. Respect* (v. 21)=*show partiality* (31[34] 34[19]).

Chapters 33 to 35: Defense of God's Justice Against Job's Presumptuousness

Ch. 33. Elihu begs Job to hear him, a young man with matured ideas, patiently (vv. 1–7). As against Job's self-defense he argues that God sends visions and suffering to preserve man's life (vv. 8–22); thus God is graciously pleased to restore man, as at last man himself recognizes (vv. 23–33). **Ch. 34.** I appeal to others against Job's impiety in his complaint (vv. 1–9); God recompenses strictly and cannot be charged with injustice to his creatures (vv. 10–19); he justly exercises complete power over mankind (vv. 20–28); and in whatever he does we must acquiesce (vv. 29–37). **Ch. 35.** Man cannot effect or draw up bargains with God (vv. 1–9); as a matter of fact, men neglect him when they should rather humble themselves before him (vv. 10–16). In each section Elihu begins by quoting Job, but there is little originality in his answers; he is made (though perhaps unconsciously) to echo the arguments of the dialogue with little variation.

CHAPTER XXXIII

Evidences of God's Desire to Help Man. With v. 4 cf. 32[8]. Here the thought is: "I am but man; you can argue with me; I cannot terrify you as God may do." V. 9 misrepresents Job's attitude. Elihu has as little sympathy (vv. 10f.) for Job as have the Friends. God does not refuse to answer (vv. 13, 14), as Job has complained. With v. 15 cf. Eliphaz' vision in 4[12f]. V. 15b should perhaps read *terrifies them with visions.* The text of vv. 17, 18 is difficult: *By the sword*—better, *through God's weapons,* or *into Sheol.* The description in vv. 19f. would recall Job's own pains. *Destroyers* (v. 22)—apparently, *destroying powers* (cf. 2 Sam. 24[16] 1 Cor. 10[1-13]). *If there be* (v. 23)—probably, *though there be;* another heavenly visitor, interpreting God's ways to man, out of a thousand detached for this purpose; this angel (v.24) then bids the angel of death release him, on payment of a ransom (his own confession of sin). With v. 26 cf. 22[27] (Eliphaz); the restored man then goes to the Temple (*before men,* v. 27), and there publicly recounts his experiences (cf. Psa. 27[6]). *Restoreth* should probably be *proclaimeth.*

CHAPTER XXXIV

The Exactness of God's Recompense. *Wise,* (v. 2)—either the Friends, or, more probably, others who are thought of as forming part of a larger group. With v. 7 cf. chs. 15, 16; but in v. 8 Elihu goes further than Eliphaz. V. 11b is, literally, "as is a man's path, so [God] makes it find him." God's recompense is exact. God can do no wrong (vv. 12f.) and he can never be called to account. Job had asserted the second, but had questioned the first; nor can the fact of God's power well be made, as Elihu argues, the ground of belief in his justice. With vv. 14, 15 cf. Psa. 104[29] Eccles. 12[7]. Injustice cannot continue in power (vv. 17f.); but can we condemn Him who combines justice with power, and who can say even to a king, ". . . who (v. 19) respecteth not . . . ?" V. 23—better, *to appoint a time for that* (cf. 9[32] 23[3f.]). V. 26 is, literally, "instead of the wicked, he striketh them in the place of beholders," i.e., in public; for *instead of* read *he smiteth.* Vv. 29–33 are a difficult and textually corrupt passage; the general sense appears to be (v. 29): "God does recompense, but (v. 31) you deny it, saying (v. 31b) you have suffered without sinning; what other plan (v. 33) do you propose? It is for you to say, and not for me." *Until the end* (v. 36)=*until he could argue no more. Rebellion* (v. 37)=*transgression;* a stronger word than that used for "sin." *Clappeth,* i.e., as a gesture of defiance toward God.

CHAPTER XXXV

Man's Complete Inability to Affect God. Do you think that you are vindicated (v. 3) by repeating that your goodness has done nothing for you? Elihu then sets out to show that goodness does "pay" (contrast the Prologue). *Companions* (v. 4)—here apparently the three Friends, who had not really answered Job. God is too high to be affected by your human acts (vv. 5–7; cf. Psa. 50[12]); these affect only men, who, when injured, may well appeal to God. But no one makes the right kind of appeal (vv. 10, 11). Men's cries are unheeded because they are vain (vv. 12, 13), i.e., misdirected and self-centered (cf. Jas. 4[3]); still less will you be answered (v. 14) when you openly disregard him; then, follow mg., or, read perhaps, *keep silence before him.* It is only because his wrath has not punished you (!) that you deny his real recompense of evil; i.e., you deny that goodness pays. *In vanity* (v. 16), i.e., "utters sheer folly."

CHAPTERS 36 AND 37: GOD'S PROVIDENTIAL DEALINGS WITH MEN

Ch. 36. Yet more, and not unimportant (vv. 1–4), God teaches all men by his appointment of their lot (vv. 5–11); he requites them justly, but uses their trouble to bring them to him, as he would have brought Job (vv. 12–17); let Job therefore be humble (vv. 18–21). God is above our criticism, as is shown by the beneficence and the terrors of creation (vv. 23–33). **Ch. 37.** Lightning, thunder, rain, snow and ice all serve the ends of his moral government (vv. 1–13); how can man teach the wielder of such enormous power, or even understand him? (Vv. 14–24.) In this last discourse, Elihu passes from God's government of human affairs to his conduct of the impressive processes of nature. In the first we can read his strict justice; the second forces us to confess that he is incomprehensible. We are reminded, now of the speeches of the Friends (especially chs. 11, 18), now of the address of Jehovah in the succeeding chapters. But nothing fresh is added (except perhaps in 36[15]), and neither the Friends nor Job have anything to say in reply.

CHAPTER XXXVI

1–15. Affliction Sent for Purposes of Warning. *Afar* (v. 3)—referring to the broad generalizations that follow. The modesty of tone in 32[6f.] is now quite forgotten. V. 7a would come better after v. 6a; then the humiliated and wronged would be more clearly contrasted with kings on their thrones. Even the good apparently may have done wrong (v. 8), and so may need correction through their sufferings (cf. v. 15; and, for the perversion of the good, Ezek. 18). *Unclean* (v. 14)—properly, temple servants devoted to a life of (ritual) unchastity (cf. Deut. 23[17]).

16–23. Exhortation to Patient Submission. V. 16, like vv. 17f., is very hard to translate; the general sense perhaps is as in R.V., though note mg., ("out of the mouth of confinement" —a curious metaphor) or, possibly, "He was actually enticing thee"; v. 17, either "you are filled full of the just punishment on the wicked," or "you wickedly criticise God, hence." The first phrase of v. 18 is uncertain; the parallel with v. 18b is best preserved if *wrath* is understood of God's anger, "let it not entice you to mockery, nor be misled by your ransom-price, i.e., your sufferings." V. 19, "will either wealth suffice without distress," i.e., "to deliver from distress?" V. 20 is obscure: Why should he desire the night, in order that calamity might come either on nations or on himself?

24–33. God's Unsearchable Greatness. V. 27 contains an interesting reference to evaporation, to which there is no reference in Jehovah's address where rain is mentioned. V. 29 is apparently influenced by Psa. 18[11f.]: his *pavilion=the storm cloud. Spreadeth* (v. 30), in the lightning-flashes. Why *covereth?*—perhaps, as in Psa. 18[15], *lays bare.* V. 31 breaks the connection, and should perhaps be removed as a gloss. He seizes, as it were (v. 32a), handfuls of lightning and hurls them at his mark. In v. 33b the reference to the sensitiveness of cattle to a gathering storm is out of place here; better, *kindling his anger in the storm.*

CHAPTER XXXVII

Vv. 1–13 continue the description of God's greatness in 36[24-33]. In stormy weather, men cannot work, nor wild beasts hunt (vv. 7, 8). For *chambers of the South* (v. 9) cf. 9[9]. But *of the South* is not in the Hebrew; *chamber= storehouse of storm* (cf. the cave of Æolus, Odyssey, bk. x); for *north* read *granaries. It* (v. 12), i.e., the lightning. In v. 13, either omit *or* or read *curse* for *land.*

Vv. 14–24 continue the exhortation in 36[16-23]. In v. 17 the reference is to the warmth of the clothes felt during the sirocco, the burning wind from the *south*, and the stillness of the earth beneath the blasts. The skies are regarded as hammered into a rigid "firmament" or inverted bowl (v. 18). *Darkness* (v. 19), i.e., of our minds. *Swallowed up* (v. 20), as (if the text is right) he would be, should he argue with God. *See not* (v. 21), because of thunder clouds. Babylonian mythology thought of the *north* as the radiant home of the gods (v. 22). Light is always with God. He is beyond us (v. 23), but he will not pervert justice. Hence (v. 24) he is feared. The conclusion of Elihu's speech is obscure; but it suggests (in spite of 36[4]) one who is "willing to wound, but yet afraid to strike."

Chapters 38[1] to 42[6]: Speeches of Jehovah and Job's Submission

Jehovah breaks in "from the whirlwind" and answers Job; Job confesses himself unable to reply. In chs. 38 and 39, after a brief challenge to Job, Jehovah recounts the wonders of earth and sea, light and darkness and storm, the creatures of the wild and the war-horse, in each instance asking Job if he understands or has planned or created it. This is followed by a pointed question to Job (40[2]), who replies with submission (40[3-5]). Jehovah then makes a further challenge and passes into long descriptions of "behemoth" and "leviathan" (ch. 41). Job then (42[1-6]) makes a further confession of his helplessness.

Jehovah's address, especially in chs. 38, 39, is impressive and majestic, but it raises two questions:

(1) How, in the mind of the author, is Job's position met? Job has called on God to state his charges against Job himself, on the ground of which Job has been made to suffer; to these Job was sure that he would be able to reply convincingly. But Jehovah makes no charges; instead he calls on Job to answer him and to consider the vastness of nature and his own insignificance; and then Job confesses that it is absurd for man to question God. This hardly "justifies the ways of God to man"; it does not explain why Job suffered. But if the author's main interest was in the problem of what a good man should do in deep suffering, it does seem to supply a definite answer; "he should remember the mighty sweep of God's power, the amazing variety of his creation, and so endure rather than question." In other words, the section appears to teach the answer that there is no real answer that will satisfy the mind; that the answer is one of faith, and that peace comes through recognizing this and holding on to God in the confidence that he knows how to manage the universe. Though this might not satisfy a Western philosopher, and though it comes short of the Buddhist teaching, "flee from the world of desire altogether," it is typical of much of Hebrew reli-

gious thought, which is anchored to the transcendence of God, and which comes to rest in contemplating his power rather than his attention to the desires of individual human beings (cf. p. 160). The passage, then, can take its place beside Psa. 104 (the adaptation of the whole world to the needs of the various creatures) and Mic. 6[8] (as typical of the prophets) —man's part is to live a life of morality (Job 31) and humility (42[1-6]).

(2) What is the purpose of the second address (chs. 40, 41)? The whole episode would end very effectively at 40[5]. But Jehovah is not content with Job's surrender. In 40[6-14] he appears to ask for something more; and in the rest of chs. 40 and 41 we are reminded of ch. 39; but the descriptions are much longer (ch. 41, indeed, is wearisome) and there are none of the questions which make chs. 38 and 39 so vivid. Ch. 41 ends without any further appeal to Job, and most of Job's short speech in 42[1-6] is a repetition of what he and Jehovah had previously said. We may conjecture that there was originally only one speech and one reply, and that there have been additions and displacements. We may join the substance of 40[6-14] to 40[2], and 42[1-6] (or parts of it) to Job's first reply in 40[3-5], regarding the "behemoth" and "leviathan" sections as no part of the original poem. Or, it may be even simpler to regard the whole of 40[6]–42[6] as an amplification of the one speech and one reply in 39[1]–40[5], whether by the original author or by someone else.

CHAPTER XXXVIII

Job's Ignorance of the Mysteries of Inanimate Nature. "Answer me," says Jehovah, "and expound the mysteries (vv. 1–3) of the creation of the stable earth (vv. 4–11), the light and the darkness (vv. 12–21), rain, snow and ice (vv. 22–30), the heavenly bodies, lightnings, and clouds" (vv. 31–38).

Vv. 1–38 stress Job's ignorance of inanimate nature on earth and in heaven. It is suggestive, but not necessary to connect the whirlwind (v. 1) with Elihu's description of the gathering storm (37[1-8]). *Who?* (V. 2.) Is this a direct reference to Job? But the words are hardly appropriate to chs. 29–31; better, to the substance of Job's earlier complaints, or, indeed, to chs. 32–37, the speeches of Elihu, if these are to be understood to be in their proper or original place. With v. 3 cf. Ezek. 2[1, 4f]. God as the architect of the world is a familiar figure in Hebrew poetry, but the phrases here are not necessarily intended to be taken literally. *Sons of God* (v. 7)—cf. 1[6]. There is no reference in v. 12 to the sun and moon; light and darkness are apparently thought of, as in Gen. 1[3-5], as existing independently. V. 13 uses an original metaphor: the dawn seizes the vast coverlet of the surface of the earth and shakes the wicked out of their concealment in it. How different from the Greek picturesque figure of the "rosy-fingered one"! The metaphor of the garment (the earth's surface) appears in a similar form in the Babylonian creation epic. The sea (v. 16) was always a solemn and terrifying mystery to the Hebrews (cf. Psa. 104[25] 107[23] Jonah 2 Rev. 21[1]). For *gates* (v. 17) suggesting impregnable power, cf. Mt. 16[18]. The irony of v. 21 echoes that of Job in 12[2]. As in Psa. 104, each section of creation has its purpose (v. 23), though (v. 26) this may transcend mere human needs. With v. 31 cf. 9[9] (note). Here in each case the names refer to constellations; *Mazzaroth* (v. 32; a plural) is quite uncertain. *Inward parts . . . mind* (v. 36)—the Hebrew words used here are otherwise unknown, but the R.V. translation is quite inappropriate to the context. *Pour* (v. 37)=*tilt;* like skin water-bottles, to empty them. Vv. 39–41: see under ch. 39.

CHAPTER XXXIX

Job's Similar Ignorance of Animate Nature. From inanimate nature Jehovah turns to the animal creation. With ch. 39 should be taken 38[39-41]. "Do you know the secrets of lions (38[39-41]; see comment below), of wild goats (39[1-4]), of the wild ass (vv. 5–8), of the wild ox (vv. 9–12), of the ostrich, stupid yet fearless (vv. 13–18), the high-mettled war-horse (vv. 19–25), the hawk or the eagle?" (Vv. 20–30.) Previously, the question has been, "Can you do what God does?" Now (in animated nature), "Can you control or teach the wild beasts?" Here the poem falls into stanzas of irregular length, each containing a vivid word-picture.

Hunt the prey (38[39]), as God their maker does (cf. Psa. 104[21]). For *raven* (38[41]) read *for him in the evening;* the mention of a bird is inappropriate, and the Hebrew words for "raven" and "evening" are almost indistinguishable. These wild creatures are beyond the care or notice of man but not of God, who makes pregnancy easy for them (39[1-4]). The Hebrew word for *wild ass* (v. 5) is quite distinct from that for "domestic ass," and vv. 5f. describe the contrast between the two. *Wild ox* (vv. 9f.); Hebrew, *re'em;* contrast *sor*, domestic ox; perhaps the aurochs. Even if he could be tamed, he could never be relied on (v. 12). The section beginning with v. 13 is not introduced by a question, like the rest, and seems out of place (between ox and horse); moreover, there is little suitability in the characteristics mentioned, stupidity and ferocity, while v. 13 is untranslatable. The mention of the *horse* in v. 18 connects this with the following section, and was perhaps the cause of the insertion of the short poem here. How that magnificent creature, the horse, throws man into the shade! (Vv. 19f.) *Quivering mane*, a guess, as is "thunder" (A.V.); though quite possibly right. *Valley* (v. 21), where chariots would naturally fight (cf. 1 Kings 20[28]). In v. 24b, follow the mg. Some species of *hawk* are said to be migratory (v. 26).

CHAPTER XL

See above, introductory paragraph (2) to section 38[1]–42[6], for a suggested rearrangement. *Jehovah:* Can you answer *me?* (Vv. 1, 2.) *Job:* I am silent! (Vv. 3–5.) *Jehovah:* Then answer! Can you imitate my magnificence, in my rule over the proudest of mankind? (Vv. 6–14.) The marvel of Behemoth (vv. 15–24).

1–14. Jehovah's Challenge to Job. Job has been quite ready to speak, but he has learned his lesson (v. 5). Now that he is lying helpless, the irony that follows (vv. 6f.) is futile. "If you criticize, seize my power, and proceed to govern; then I will acknowledge your independence." Note that Jehovah is here made to pass from his justice to his power; cf. Elihu, 36[22]. As a divine argument, the passage is only tolerable if we regard (as perhaps the author regarded) Job's criticism of God as, under any circumstances, glaring impiety.

15–24. Behemoth. The Hebrew word *behemoth* is plural, denoting, as the plural often does, size or strength. The beast here described is generally identified (from the terms of the description) with the hippopotamus, which, though now not found north of the second cataract, actually existed previously in lower Egypt and possibly in the Jordan Valley. The description of the monster's strength and habits is more leisurely than the descriptions in ch. 39, and exaggerated (vv. 17, 19). *Mountains* (v. 20)—at best, low hills near the river; *lotus* (v. 21)—a low scrub is meant, growing near the riverside; *brook* (v. 22), or "wady," which suggests, like v. 23, Palestine. No sudden rise in the water can disconcert him. *Snare* (v. 24), apparently the spike on which the bait was placed (cf. 1 Sam. 18[21]).

CHAPTER XLI

Leviathan. This word refers to various creatures in the O.T.; it seems to mean whale in Psa. 104[26]; and dragon in Psa. 74[14]. In Job 3[8] it is mythological or metaphorical, and a mythological explanation has been suggested for this passage (as also for ch. 40); but probably what is meant here is the crocodile, familiar on the Nile and also, apparently (to judge from proper names), at one time in Palestine. But the turgidity of the style (cf. ch. 40) shows that it could not have been a familiar object to the writer of the chapter. The main ideas are the creature's unapproachableness (vv. 1–11), the strength of his body (vv. 12–18), the terror he inspires, and his scorn of those who would conquer him (vv. 19–34).

The crocodile, like the hippopotamus, could be and was captured (vv. 1, 2); crocodiles are generally wary and suspicious (v. 3), and, since they can procure abundance of food, will seldom attack a man. Man might sport with a bird (v. 5); with "leviathan" only God can play (the rabbis imagined him doing so). *Barbed irons* (v. 7)=*harpoons*.

"If you should lay your hand . . . remember what a battle with him is like; you will not do it again!" (V. 8.) *The hope of* (v. 9), i.e., "to capture." Vv. 10b, 11 are obscure; perhaps intended as a boast in leviathan's mouth. In v. 12 the first person singular (as in v. 11) is strange. The reference in v. 13 is to scales and jaws. *Sneezings* (v. 18), i.e., spray breathed through his nostrils. In Egyptian hieroglyphics, the eye of the crocodile is the sign for dawn. *Ointment* (v. 31)—does this refer to odor? The crocodile possesses two sets of musk glands. V. 34a, probably should be read, with slight change, *every high thing feareth him.*

CHAPTER XLII

1–6. Job's Second Reply and Penitence. (But see on the whole passage, introduction to 38[1]–42[6] above.) V. 2 comes better after ch. 39 than chs. 40, 41. Vv. 3a and 4b are quoted from Jehovah's words in 38[2, 3] (cf. 40[7]). Job has been speaking about God's nature, which he now knows (v. 3bc) to be beyond his comprehension. V. 4a, like 4b, if correct, is apparently put into the mouth of Jehovah, but has no point here (cf. 38[3] 40[1]) where the words are in place. Job had prayed to see God (23[3]), but how different is the actual effect of the vision! (V. 5.) It convinces him (and this is given as his last word) that even in his agony he has sinned in questioning God.

CHAPTER 42[7-16]: THE EPILOGUE

The End of Job's Trials. This passage is on a distinctly lower level than the Prologue, in both style and thought. It points back to the dialogue, or to something like the dialogue; but the last clause of v. 7 (repeated in v. 8) does not fit either Jehovah's address to Job or Job's confession. Nor does it fit the Prologue, since the main interest of chs. 1, 2 in the Satan's question to Jehovah is not referred to. The whole conclusion—Job's last state better than the first!—is a very simple instance of what is known as poetic justice, accomplished by a *deus ex machina.* On the other hand, it may be said to satisfy, as far as it goes, the claims both of the Friends ("if a man is righteous, he will be delivered or rewarded at the last"), and of Job himself ("if God is just, he must vindicate me"). V. 8 describes a very large sacrifice; *folly*—the word which Job had used to his wife in 2[10]. *Accepted* (v. 9)—elsewhere, "accept the face" means "receive into favor." The Hebrew construction of v. 10 suggests a break or contrast between vv. 9 and 10. *Turned the captivity*—the phrase is usual of Israel's restoration from exile. With v. 11 cf. 19[13f]. *Piece of money*—the value could not have been large (cf. Gen. 33[19]). His possessions are doubled (v. 12); the number of children remains the same. The names of the daughters (v. 13), meaning respectively "dove" (?), "cassia," "horn of eye-paint," apparently are intended to suggest their beauty. *Inheritance* (v. 15)—cf. Num. 27; Job goes beyond the Hebrew custom. Job enjoyed length of life worthy of the patriarchal age (v. 16).

PSALMS I–LXXII

By Professor ELMER A. LESLIE

Introduction

(The present introduction covers the entire Psalter, and is by the author of the commentary on Psa. 1–72. For Psa. 73–150 see pp. 554–601).

Significance of the Psalms. In the book of Psalms we meet the religion of Israel at its greatest depth and its most passionate intensity. The psalmists fell heir to the profound insights and spiritual experiences of the prophets. These latter were Israel's intellectual and spiritual pioneers, blazing new paths to God and clearing new trails for human feet. The psalmists largely found ready at hand these insights. They took them up, lived their way into them experimentally, applied them to the life of individuals and of the community and linked them to the religious worship that centered in the Temple, all the while both deepening and intensifying them. The Psalter, representing as it does close to a thousand years of Israel's history, may be viewed as a transcript of the heart life of the Hebrew people. Coming from a vast variety of individuals who had learned both how to exult in unspeakable joy and to cry out unto God from the deeps of inexpressible anguish, it is a mirror of the life of the soul, not of Israel merely, but of humanity. It is the noblest book of devotion possessed by men, and comes down to us enhanced by the reverence of centuries to which it has contributed both strength and light.

The Terms "Psalms" and "Psalter." The Psalter is the first book of the *Kethubhim* ("writings"), the third section of the Hebrew Bible (see art., *The Formation of the O.T.*, pp. 95–7). It bears the title *Tehillim* ("praises"), yet only one of the psalms (145) is so designated. An earlier time called these poems *Tephilloth* ("prayers"; Psa. 72^{20}). The LXX uses the designation *Psalmoi*, the plural of a term meaning "a touching sharply," "a pulling or twanging with the fingers," which corresponds best with the term preferred in the titles, *mizmor*, or "melody." This term is used in the O.T. to designate only religious songs. It comes from a root meaning "to pluck" or "to pinch," which could thus be used of touching the strings with the fingers. In the Codex Alexandrinus the designation *Psalterion*, whence comes the term "psalter," is used. The word means primarily a stringed instrument, but by association of ideas it came to mean the songs sung to the accompaniment of the stringed instrument.

The Organization of the Psalter. The Hebrew Psalter is divided into five books, a division which is at least as early as the LXX. Each book closes with a doxology and the last Psalm (150) is itself a doxology to the entire Psalter. The divisions are as follows:

Book I. Psalms 1–41.
Book II. Psalms 42–72.
Book III. Psalms 73–89.
Book IV. Psalms 90–106.
Book V. Psalms 107–150.

Probably this fivefold division originated from viewing the Psalter as the counterpart of the Law, the response of the community to the summons of God in the Law (Kittel). "The Hebrews," says Epiphanius, "divided the Psalter into five books so that it would be another Pentateuch."

A careful study of these five divisions of the Psalter reveals the gradual amalgamation within these books of several originally separate collections. This view is supported by the following arguments: (1) Certain psalms in one collection are repeated in another with only slight changes (14 = 53; 40^{13-17} = 70; 57^{7-11} + 60^{5-12} = 108). (2) Psa. 72^{20} says "the prayers of David are ended"; yet we find many other psalms attributed to David in the succeeding books. Evidently, an early Davidic collection ended with Psa. 72. (3) Other individual collections are discernible: "of the Sons of Korah," 42–49, 84, 85, 87, 88; "of Asaph," 50, 73–83; *Maskîl* psalms, cultic songs, viewed as the product of special divinely endowed insight (Mowinckel), 52–55; *Miktām* psalms, of atonement or expiation, 56–60; the Psalms of Ascents, 120–134; the Hallelujah Psalms, 111–113, 115–117, 146–150; cf. also 105–107. (4) In 1–41 the name of Jehovah for Israel's God appears 272 times; Elohim only 15. In 42–84 Elohim appears 208 times; Jehovah, 48. A comparison of Psa. 53 with 14 reveals that the editor of 53 has changed "Jehovah" to "Elohim." These facts are explained as follows: Psa. 1–41 is an early collection; Psa. 42–84 is a later collection in which the editor, working at a time when the sacred name of Israel's God was no longer pronounced because it was considered too sacred for pronunciation, substituted as far as possible Elohim for Jehovah.

Steps in the Formation of the Psalter. The recognition of these originally separate collections helps us to discern the steps in the formation of the Psalter. (See Gray, *Critical Introduction to the O.T.*, p. 132, Charles Scribner's Sons, publishers):

1. The compilation of a Davidic collection with a doxology at the close, 3–41.
2. The compilation of a second Davidic collection with a doxology at the close, 51–72.
3. The compilation of a collection entitled, "of Asaph," probably a guild of Temple singers (Ezra 2[41]) 50, 73–83. J. P. Peters suggests that this collection originally belonged to the sanctuary at Bethel.
4. The compilation of a collection entitled "of the Sons of Korah," likewise probably a guild of Temple singers (2 Chr. 20[19]), 42–49. Peters suggests that this collection originally belonged to the sanctuary at Dan.
5. The redaction of an Elohistic Psalter, 42–83, out of psalms that were derived from the second, third, and fourth collections. The editor quite generally, but not consistently, substituted "Elohim" for "Jehovah."
6. The Elohistic Psalter was enlarged by the addition of 84–89.
7. The compilation of a collection entitled "Songs of the Ascents," 120–134.
8. The compilation of 90–150 around these "Songs of the Ascents" and other similar collections.

W. R. Smith maintains that these steps finally culminated in three separate collections 1–41, 42–89, 90–150; which subsequently were redivided so as to make the Psalter conform with the five-fold division of the Law.

Psalm Literature in the Old Testament Before the Exile. We approach the psalms aright only when we attempt to see them in the context of the whole psalm literature, both canonical and uncanonical, that came from the soul of ancient Israel. In Ex. 15[21], the song of Miriam, we have a fragment quite in the style of a psalm which probably comes from the time of Moses (*cir.* 1200 B.C.) In Judg. 5, the Song of Deborah, the earliest extant monument of Hebrew literature, dating from about 1150 B.C., we have a brilliant pæan of triumph, much in the style of a psalm, celebrating the victory of the Israelites under Deborah and Barak over the Canaanites under Sisera. 2 Sam. 23[1-7], which is quite similar to some of the psalms containing oracles, is possibly, as Sellin maintains, a product of early prophetic bands. The existence of this material outside the psalter, yet strikingly similar to it, suggests that psalmody in Israel has a long history that reaches back even behind the Davidic era.

The existence of psalms and references to psalmody in the pre-exilic prophets argues for the pre-exilic origin of many psalms. Gressmann calls these prophetic poems political psalms and believes they are largely fashioned upon the psalms of worship that were already in existence. Some of them are oracles concerning the future and were to be sung by the ideal community of the future. Such are Hos. 6[1-3] and 14[1f.] Isa. 2[1-4] (paralleled in Micah 4[1-3]), which may, however, come from the postexilic period, reminds us forcibly of Psa. 122, which is a summons to a pilgrimage to Jerusalem. Amos 6[5, 6] is interpreted by Gressmann as referring not to the ordinary banquet songs but to sacred songs accompanying the sacrificial worship, i.e., songs like the psalms (see Simpson, *The Psalmists*, pp. 8f.); he believes that psalms are as old as sacrificial worship. Isa. 30[29] seems to refer to psalms used in Temple worship at the feasts by the pilgrims to Jerusalem. A psalm closes the first great section of Isaiah's prophecy (ch. 12).

Amos 5[2, 3] is a national dirge or lamentation such as is frequently found in the Psalter, and such as must have been used in times of solemn national fast days (cf. Joel 1[8-14]). Jer. 14[7-9] offers a similar example; Jer. 16[19, 20] and Jer. 17[7, 8] are psalms, the latter serving as the pattern for the later psalm which forms the introduction to the Psalter. Hab. 3 is a psalm of a theophany very similar in parts to Psa. 18 and 97. Isa. 38[10-20], the psalm of Hezekiah, and that of Hannah, 1 Sam. 2[1-10], also have their counterparts in the Psalter.

Psalm Literature in Postexilic Judaism. Ezekiel's plan of the restored Temple had chambers for the singers (40[44]) and thus suggests a developed Temple choir even before the Exile. The exiles knew Temple songs (Psa. 137[3, 4]). In Deutero-Isaiah many psalms occur (Isa. 40[12-31] 42[10-12] 44[23] 49[13] 52[9] 54[1-10]). Gressmann maintains that no prophet so resembled a psalmist as did the author of Isa. 40–55. Trito-Isaiah (Isa. 56–66) also contains several psalms (Isa. 61[10, 11] 63[7]–64[12] 66[10-14]). Jonah 2[2-9] is a psalm inserted later into the original book of Jonah. Isa. 25[1]–26[10], originating in the early Greek period, is made up of hymns of thanksgiving. The Chronicler puts a psalm (a prayer) into the mouth of David (1 Chr. 29[10-19]) and prayers of lamentation and confession into the mouths of Ezra, Nehemiah, and the Levites (Ezra 9[5-15] Neh. 1[5-11] 9[6-39]).

Uncanonical Psalms. In still later, uncanonical, writings psalms are found. In

Ecclus. 39^{14b-35} (first quarter of second century B.C.) Jesus, son of Sirach, turns psalmist and in hymnic form sets forth his wisdom concerning creation. In 1 Maccabees (early first century B.C.) we have several lamentations (1 Macc. 1^{25-28} 2^{8-12}) and odes of praise (1 Macc. 3^{1-9} to Judas, and 14^{6-15} to Simon) quite in the style of the Psalter. In the Psalms of Solomon (middle of first century A.D.) we have psalms like those of the Psalter, which breathe the piety of the Pharisees. In the 42 Odes of Solomon (second century A.D.) we have Christian psalms resembling many in the Psalter which they attempt to imitate. Thus the psalms of the Psalter are but the most significant part of a psalm literature that dates from Mosaic times down to the second century after the opening of the Christian era.

Psalm Titles. One of the fascinating questions in the study of the Psalter is the interpretation of the superscriptions to the individual psalms. All but thirty-four of them bear titles, the exceptions being called by the Jews "orphans." These superscriptions, though not original with the psalm authors, go back to relatively ancient tradition. A comparison of the titles in the LXX with those in the Massoretic text shows that some of the terms were already unintelligible when this translation was made and that the superscriptions had not yet become fixed. Before any certainty can be achieved with regard to the significance of the titles we must understand the meaning of the technical terms used. And yet upon no question in the study of the Psalter is there more uncertainty than upon the meaning of many such terms. The recent researches of Sigmund Mowinckel (*Psalmen Studien*, I–VI, 1921–4) have opened the question afresh and are rich in suggestions concerning the use of the psalms in connection with the cult.

Suggestions Toward the Interpretation of Technical Terms in the Titles. The succeeding paragraphs present several of the most probable suggestions of Mowinckel. (1) Certain terms define the *general* or *special character* of the psalm. The term, *mizmōr* (3, etc.), ordinarily rendered "psalm," is a song accompanied by instrumental music. The term, *shîr*, "song," used alone only in 18 and 46, ordinarily designates profane as well as cultic songs, but in the Psalter, as might be expected, it is a designation of religious songs only. A whole group have the title, *Shîr hamma'alōth*, ordinarily translated Psalms of Ascents (120-134). The word "ascents" refers to the festal procession of the ark which took place annually on New Year's Day, celebrating the accession of Jehovah to his throne. *Miktām* (16, 56–60) is applied to songs suggesting the idea of atoning for or expiating sins; all such psalms are individual lamentations. *Maskîl* (32, 42 etc.) designates a song of worship accompanied by music, insofar as it is the product of special insight such as that of seer, prophet, priest, Temple poets and singers. *Shiggāyôn* (7), a term which probably came into the cult language of Israel through Canaan, is connected with the Assyrian lamentation psalm. It probably (cf. Hab. 3^{1}) has to do with the cultic acts which accompanied the singing of such songs. *Tᵉhillâ* (145) means "hymn"; *tᵉphillâ* (90, etc.) is the general word for "prayer," especially a prayer of petition.

(2) Other terms used in the title concern the *purpose* of the psalm: *Lᵉthōdhâ* (100) means "for (an expression of) thanks," which probably accompanied the offering. *Lᵉannōth* (88) means "for penitence," and was composed for use in the penitential phase of worship. *Lᵉhazkîr* (38, 70) means that the psalm was used "for bringing sins to remembrance," the psalmist's own sin (Lev. 5^{12}) or the unrighteous acts of the enemy from which he is suffering. *Lᵉ* or *'al yᵉdhûthûn* (39, 62, 77) means "for confession," i.e., a psalm of confessional and petitional content. The Chronicler misunderstood this title and attributed it to another Levitical guild of singers, along with those of Asaph, Heman, and Ethan. *Lᵉlammēdh* (60), "to teach," points to the revelation of Jehovah to a prophetically inspired worshiper (cf. the oracle of 60^{6-9}).

(3) A number of terms have to do with cultic acts or situations. *Lamᵉnaççeah*, found in fifty-five psalms, appears first in the title to Psa. 4. Ordinarily it is rendered "for the chief musician" or "for musical rendering" (Kittel). Mowinckel suggests that the root idea of the word is "to shine," and here means "to cause to shine," the object understood being "the face of Jehovah." Thus interpreted it would refer to such liturgical acts as would make Jehovah's countenance alight with mercy and gentleness so that he would hear and bless. If this interpretation is accepted, it might be paraphrased: "to put God into a gracious attitude."

'al yônath elîm (LXX) *rᵉhoqim* (56) does not refer to a melody to which the psalm is set. It means, rather, "concerning the dove for the far-away gods." The psalm is designated to be sung over the dove which symbolically carries away the guilt of the purified to the far-off gods. It is a sacrifice originally conceived as placating the evil spirits that were viewed as having caused the sickness or misfortune of the sufferer (cf. Lev. 1^{14} 5^{6-10} 16 and Zech. 5^{11}).

'al ayyeleth hashshahar (22), "concerning the hind of the dawn," refers to a cultic act, the sacrifice of a ewe, in connection with which the psalm was sung by the offerer or by the priests in his name. The sacrifice which was a sin-offering was brought at the first streak of dawn (cf. Job 1[5]).

'al shōshannîm (45, 69), *'al shûshan edhûth* (60), *'el shōshannîm* (80) are variants of the same title, which means "concerning the lilies of the ark" (Ex. 30[36] Num. 17[10]). It refers to the use of flowers in the sacrifice. According to the Mishna, those in festal procession (cf. Lev. 23[40]) carried branches of palm, myrtle, and willows up to the Temple, and after the procession about the altar the branches were placed around it to bless it. So probably these flowers were laid down on or before the ark while the psalm was being rendered.

'al mahalath (53, 88), "concerning illness." Psalms thus designated had to do with the purification ritual after sickness, which was viewed as caused by enemies of Jehovah; *'al* (LXX) *hanᵉhîlôth* (5) probably is a scribal error for the same phrase as the preceding. *'al 'alāmôth* (46). The same consonants appear in the subscript to 48. The term refers to a cultic liturgical act of which the playing of the harp and singing constituted a part (cf. 1 Chr. 15[20-22]); furthermore, it is a technical designation of a certain part of the festal ritual of the great autumn festival celebrating Jehovah's accession to the throne. Mowinckel, following the LXX, renders it "concerning the hidden things" and connects it with the unveiling of the future through the prophets of the cult, which was accompanied by playing on the harp (cf. 2 Kings 3[15f.]). *'al mûth labbēn* (9), "against the death of the son (of the king)," may possibly refer to the placating of the powers conceived as threatening the death of the royal prince. *'al hashshᵉmînîth* (6, 12), "concerning the eighth," designates a cultic act accompanied by the harp. It is the last and decisive act in the ritual of purification, following which perhaps came the prophetic oracle. *'al haggittôth* (LXX) (8, 81, 84), "over the winepresses." Thirtle connects the terms with the autumnal feast of booths. *'al tashᵉhēth* (57–59, 75), "destroy not." Mowinckel, citing Isa. 65[8], "Destroy it not, for a blessing is in it," connects it with a prayer liturgy of the congregation, "the vineyard of Jehovah," for protection and help.

(4) Finally, there are two designations that may be classed as musical references, one occurring in the titles, the other in the body of the psalms. (a) *bᵉ* and *'al nᵉghînôth* (6, 54, 55, 67). This indicates that the cultic action designated by *lamᵉnaççᵉah*, with which the phrase appears (see (3) above), was performed to the accompaniment of the harp. (b) A designation found in the body of the Psalms, not in the title, is *higgāyōn selāh* (9[16]). *Higgāyōn* is found alone in the text of Psa. 92[3] and *selāh* elsewhere alone. Probably the words are identical or parallel in meaning. The word *selāh*, which means "lift up," is simply the direction to the worshipers at that point in the rendition of the psalm to "lift up" the cultic cry, "He endureth forever and ever" (cf. Aquila and Targum). It is to be classed, so far as the content of the cultic cry is concerned, with "Amen" and "Hallelujah."

The Psalms in Jewish Usage. The psalms give us some further evidence of their use in worship. Psa. 30 was used at the festival of the Dedication of the Temple. Psa. 92 was a song for the Sabbath day. Psa. 100 was used in connection with the thankoffering. From the LXX we learn that Psa. 24 was attached to Sunday, 48 to Monday, 94 to Wednesday (also, according to Theodoret, 101), 93 to Friday. Later Old Latin and Armenian translations attach 81 to Thursday. The LXX designates 29 for use on the last day of the Festival of Booths. The Mishna (*Tamid* VII, 4) names Psa. 82 for Tuesday. The Talmud gives further directions concerning individual psalms and groups of psalms.

Our study of the titles and of the date concerning Jewish usage leads us to the conclusion that originally the psalms were connected with the sacrificial worship. This argues for the high antiquity of Hebrew psalmody. When worship in Israel changed its center from the Temple to the synagogue, the psalms became a spiritual liturgy.

The Question of Davidic Authorship. The titles offer data concerning the authorship of the psalms. Seventy-three are attributed to David, twelve to Asaph, nine to the sons of Korah, two to Solomon, one to Heman the Ezrahite, one to Ethan the Ezrahite, and one to Moses. To each of these names is prefixed the preposition "of" or "belonging to," which originally may have designated the collection from which the psalm was taken rather than authorship. But when the historical notes to the "of David" psalms were added, a process still going on about 200 B.C., the phrase was interpreted as denoting authorship.

Now we know that David was a musician (1 Sam. 16[14f.]), and that he wrote secular poetry (2 Sam. 1[19f.] 3[33f.]). He may therefore have written religious poetry. But the fact of Davidic authorship of any of the psalms cannot be maintained with absolute confidence. Gray has stated the matter accurately when he says, "There are psalms in the Psalter of which, if we may remove certain parts as later interpolations, a residuum remains of which it would be unjustifiable to assert that it was not written by David" (*Critical Introduction to the O.T.*, p. 139, Charles Scribner's Sons, publishers). The authors of some of the psalms attributed to David represent the peaks of O.T. spiritual insight, which appears inconsistent with the far more primitive views held by the David of the historical books. Moreover, the language of some of the "Davidic" psalms shows the strong influence of the encroaching Aramaic, an evidence of post-exilic date.

The Dating of the Psalms. The intimate association of the psalms with the Temple worship as revealed in the Psalter, in the titles and in the Talmudic references, suggests the most probable view of the date of the Psalter. It is the hymn and prayer book of the second Temple. Many of the hymns are pre-exilic in origin, but in every case in their present arrangement they have been collected and edited for the post-exilic period. In the absence of practically all external evidence—the chronological notes in the titles are later editorial additions—the date of a psalm must be determined almost entirely upon the basis of internal evidence. Four principles guide us in this: (1) the historical allusions; (2) the diction and literary style; (3) the relation to writings of known date; (4) the character of the religious ideas. A number of psalms can best be explained as dating from as late a time as the Maccabæan era. The Psalms of Solomon are not included, so the Psalter must have been closed by the time these psalms were composed. The reference to Psa. 79[2] in 1 Macc. 7[16, 17] (about 100 B.C.) views that psalm as Holy Scripture, which suggests that the Psalter was closed late in the second century B.C. This view, which maintains the presence of early, even pre-Davidic elements in the Psalter, and likewise the presence of very late, even Maccabæan elements, makes the Psalter a transcript of the entire religious history of Israel.

The Poetry of the Psalms. The Hebrews, with their burning religious passion, their spirited nationalism, their strong imagination, were poetically gifted to a high degree. Their poetry, of which the psalms offer excellent examples, is not primarily that of conscious art but, rather, that of simple, childlike utterance from the heart. It was Lowth (1753) who discovered the fundamental principle of Hebrew poetry, namely *parallelism*, the correspondence of one verse or line with another. Various types of parallelism are discernible (for details see art., *Poetic and Wisdom Literature*, p. 155). (1) Synonymous, Psa. 114; (2) antithetical, Psa. 30[5]; (3) synthetic or constructive, Psa. 19[7-10]; (4) introverted, Psa. 30[8-10]; (5) climactic, Psa. 121[1-4]. Ordinary meter and rime are absent, but Hebrew poetry has rhythm, of which G. B. Gray distinguishes two types—"balancing rhythm," where in the two lines there is an equality in the number of stresses, and "echoing rhythm," where there are in the first line a greater number of stressed syllables, and a smaller number in the second.

Comparison with Babylonian and Egyptian Psalms. Hebrew poetry shares with Babylonian the two principles of parallelism and rhythm, the former being the more marked of the two. A flood of light has been poured upon the development of Hebrew psalmody through the Babylonian psalms. (See Gressmann, *Altorientalische Texte zum Alten Testament*, 2nd edit., 1926.) Among the most important of these are two prayers to the goddess Ishtar, a hymn to Sin the Moon-god, and a hymn to Bel. (See Barton, *Archæology and the Bible*, 4th edit., pp. 458–461.) While these reveal many points of contact with Hebrew psalms, the latter are far loftier and profounder in the consciousness of sin.

There are likewise many points of contact with Egyptian hymns, the two most famous being from about 1400 B.C., a hymn to the Sun-god, and a hymn in Praise of Aton. (See Barton, *op. cit.*, pp. 462–466). While alive with deep feeling and religious insight, nevertheless the Egyptian poems lack the simple directness and deep passion of the Hebrew psalms. The relative antiquity of psalm literature among Israel's neighbors argues for an early development of psalmody in Israel.

The Classification of the Psalms. One question which meets the investigator of the psalms at every point has to do with the classification of the psalms. Several principles may be followed and all are illuminating. Barton (*Religion of Israel*, pp. 201f.), proceeding chiefly from various soul moods, divides them into ten groups: (1) Unregenerate hate; (2) hymns of war; (3) love for the law; (4) historical retrospects; (5) nature psalms; (6) Pharisaic spirit; (7) prayers for help; (8) reflective psalms; (9) expressions of trust; (10) progress in religious thinking.

McFadyen (*Psalms in Modern Speech*, pp. 246, 247), starting from a purely topical principle, suggestively divides them into the following groups: (1) Psalms of adoration; (2) psalms concerning Jehovah's universal reign; (3) psalms concerning the King; (4) psalms of reflection; (5) psalms of thanksgiving; (6) psalms in celebration of worship; (7) historical psalms; (8) imprecatory psalms; (9) penitential psalms; (10) psalms of petition; (11) alphabetic psalms.

The most illuminating principle of grouping, however, is that pursued by Staerk, *Die Schriften des Alten Testaments*, 2nd edit., by Kittel, *Die Psalmen*, and by Gunkel, *Die Psalmen.* They start from the use of the psalms in the worship of Israel. Staerk divides them as follows: The religious lyric, including hymns, cultic and individual; prayers of thanksgiving and of petition, both cultic and personal; and songs, spiritual and of the wisdom interest. The psalter furnishes but one illustration of the profane lyric (Psa. 45), and it has been adapted to religious use. Kittel groups them as follows: Public hymns of praise; individual hymns of praise; public prayers of thanksgiving; national prayers of petition; prayers for the king; individual prayers of petition; wisdom poems and spiritual songs. Gunkel distinguishes ten groups: (1) Hymns of praise; (2) hymns of Jehovah's accession to the throne; (3) national lamentations; (4) the king's psalms; (5) individual lamentations; (6) individual songs of thanksgiving; (7) smaller groups including blessings, curses, pilgrimage, victory and thanksgiving songs (all of these groups are lyrics); (8) prophetic poems; (9) wisdom poetry; (10) antiphonal poems and formal liturgies.

Religious Values for To-day in the Psalms. The prophets utter the mind of Israel concerning God. The psalmists utter the heart of Israel in experience with God. There is no body of devotional literature in the world comparable to the Psalms in expressing the reality, depth, and purity of religious experience. As Greece gave to the world sensitiveness to beauty and the stimulus to thought, as Rome contributed administration and law, so Israel's genius gave to humanity religion. And nowhere in the literature of Israel is this so apparent as in the Psalter. The two main directions in which it offers significant religious value for modern life are (1) in the idea of God it contains and (2) in the varieties of religious experience it portrays.

The Idea of God in the Psalter. Taking the psalms as a whole, they contain the conception of a majestic God. He is the Creator of the world. The heavens, the sun, moon and stars owe their being to him. Man too came to be through God's creative purpose. He is the summit of creation, made "but little lower than God." This whole area of creation is under the Creator's dominion. Nature reveals the very mind of God. The heavens declare his glory. The thunder is his voice. The recurring succession of the seasons, the passing of day into night, the mysterious productivity of the soil, the deepseated, instinctive processes of animal life—all utter the mind of God. He is all-powerful. He is all-knowing. He is everywhere present.

Moreover, this majestic God is the God of history. All human history moves toward a goal, the reign of God over all mankind, in all the earth. But this ultimate purpose of God is not viewed as achieved through the initiative and effort of men so much as through the direct effort and energy of God. To a unique degree this God of human history is the God of Israel's history. He created Israel and made himself known to her. He is the God of Moses and the Exodus, of Sinai and the wilderness, of the invasion and settlement of Canaan. And this God of Israel is the one sole God of the whole world, who uses Israel to reveal him to the far ends of the earth—a thought common also to the prophets.

Varieties of Religious Experience in the Psalter. The Psalter is the utterance of many individuals of different epochs and out of richly diversified situations. It is the deposit of the religious soul of Israel, conceived as a corporate unity. It is also the deposit of the religious experience of individual Israelites. Their names may not be known to us, but these heart utterances reveal a variety of mental and spiritual attitude that gives to the Psalter its universal quality. It becomes the mirror of the soul. There is no modern type of religious experience but what is mirrored forth, often in classic utterance, in the Psalms. Here is to be found upon every page the expression of *confident trust in God.* He is the psalmist's "light and salvation." With him one need not be afraid. The utterance of the *mood of gratitude* is a characteristic note. Here in utter sincerity is sounded the *soul's sense of guilt* and *sin* in all its ugliness and destructiveness. Fast upon this comes the *heart's cry for pardon, cleansing* and *restoration,* the hunger for *new inner creation* and *renovation.* Some few psalms introduce us to the *student of the law* who glories in this perfect revelation for the needs of life. Here too are *reflective psalms,* where some individual grapples with the problem of suffering, and at the climax of one of these there is given expression to a sense of *fellowship with God* so deep and rich as to illumine for modern men the nature of mystic union with God. Occasionally there blaze forth *passionate indignation* against men, and *impatience* with the seeming *aloofness* of God. These lower ground tones of the Psalter, however, but serve to lift into nobler clearness the more predominant moods of *aspiration* and *inextinguishable* hope, the *exulting life* of *forgiveness, restoration,* and *triumph.* At greater depths than can be said of any other book, the Psalms "find" us and give a vehicle of utterance for the diversified emotions and yearnings of humanity to-day.

Literature: Commentaries: Briggs (International Critical Commentary); Kirkpatrick (Cambridge Bible); Davison and Davies (New Century Bible); Cheyne, *The Book of Psalms.*

Other Studies: Eiselen, *The Psalms and Other Sacred Writings;* Simpson (editor), *The Psalmists;* Welch, *The Psalter;* J. M. P. Smith, *The Religion of the Psalms;* Peters, *The Psalms as Liturgies.*

Translations: McFadyen, *The Psalms in Modern Speech;* J. M. P. Smith, in *The Old Testament* (An American Translation).

PSALMS 1–72

Psalm 1. The Psalm of the Two Ways

This psalm reminds us of the opening sentence of *The Teaching of the Twelve Apostles:* "There are two ways, one of Life, and one of Death, and there is a great difference between the two ways." The characterization of the righteous man as an earnest student of the Law, and the interest in retribution contained in the psalm, mark it as dating from the Greek period. It stands under the influence of the legalistic and wisdom tendencies in Judaism. It has no title. Probably it was intended by the final editor of the Psalter to serve as an introduction to the whole book, and it serves that purpose admirably. The psalmist sharply contrasts the two ways of life, interpreting them both with his eyes upon the ultimate fate of righteous and sinful men.

1–3. The Righteous Way. The psalm begins with an exclamation, literally translated, "Oh, the happiness of the man!" The career of the righteous man is first considered negatively. He has nothing to do with evil men. He, accordingly, escapes their influence, which is graphically described as a mastery by degrees. He who associates with evil men may first merely *walk* with them, but soon he *stands* where sinners congregate, and at length he *sits* with them as one of their scoffing company. Vv. 2 and 3 characterize the righteous man in positive terms and strike a fundamental note in the psalms. He is a zealous student of the *law.* Making use of the pictures of Jer. 17[7, 8] and Ezek. 47[12] the author compares the righteous man to a tree planted on the bank of a stream with constant source of refreshment (cf. Rev. 22[1, 2]) and consequent regular and dependable fruitage. Whatever he undertakes he "brings to a successful issue."

4–6. The Unrighteous Way. For v. 4a read with LXX *Not so the wicked, not so.* The description of the career of the unrighteous man is implied in the negative characterization of v. 1, but here a graphic detail is added, taken from the familiar scenes of the threshing floor. As the grain is beaten out, the pursuing wind sweeps away the chaff from the wheat. Just as worthless and insubstantial as *chaff* are unrighteous men. Vv. 5 and 6 are eschatological and move in the prophetic ideas of the judgment that precedes the new age (cf. Mal. 3[17–4]2). In that judgment the wicked will go down to destruction. None such will be found among that sifted congregation of righteous men whose conduct Jehovah knows and values.

Psalm 2. Jehovah's Oracle to the King

This psalm is of great poetical and dramatic power. It contains an oracle of Jehovah to a Judæan king from the mouth of the king himself, uttered at the festival celebrating his accession to the throne (cf. Gunkel, *Die Psalmen,* p. 5). It is this which determines the distinctive character of the psalm. It is best understood as pre-exilic, coming from a time when the nation was surrounded by powerful foes and national feeling ran high. The linguistic arguments for a late date (Duhm considers it Maccabæan) are not conclusive. The psalmist is at home in the eschatology of the prophets (vv. 1–3, 12b), including the world dominion of the Messianic king, expressed in the O. T. as early as Gen. 49[10] (from the J. narrative; this poem, in its original form, may come from the tenth century B.C.). That which explains the oracle and gives the psalm its vibrant passion is the conviction that the king now ascending the throne is the Messianic ruler (cf. Isa. 11[1f.]; so also Kittel, *Die Psalmen,* p. 12).

1–3. The Agitation of the Nations. With vivid prophetic style (cf. Isa. 22[1]) the poet introduces the psalm with a query. Why this agitation? He answers his own question. The accession of a new king to the Judæan throne is the occasion of international excitement. Peoples hitherto submissive to Judah are plotting revolt. Their rulers are in secret conclave saying (literally), "Let us snap their bonds and fling off their fetters."

4–6. Jehovah Speaks to the Plotting Nations. In vivid contrast to the perturbed earthly rulers sitting in secret conference *sits* Jehovah, the sovereign God, exalted (cf. Isa. 6[1]) above them, derisively laughing (in vivid anthropomorphism) at their cunning intrigues. At length (v. 5) his laughter is broken by angry, terror-striking words to the plotting kings: "As for me," in contrast to the puny kings, "I have installed [Assyrian, *našaku*] my king." Their efforts against Jehovah's anointed will be unavailing.

7–9. The King Discloses His Oracle. The king speaks. He tells of a divine oracle he has received. For the ruler's access to the divine revelation see 1 Sam. 10[6] 1 Kings 3[5] and especially that of the Messianic ruler, Isa. 11[2]. The royal oracle contained a decree and a pledge. The decree is given through an ancient Oriental formula of adoption familiar in Babylonian law. (Gunkel, *Die Psalmen*, p. 7; also Driver in Simpson's *The Psalmists.*) The king upon his accession to the throne is accepted as Jehovah's son. From now on he will be dealt with by Jehovah as though he were his son. We recall at once also the oracle of Nathan to David (2 Sam. 7[14]). The baptismal oracle to Jesus (Mk. 1[11] and parallels) is reminiscent of this passage. The pledge follows (v. 8). Let the king but speak out his request and Jehovah pledges him participation in his world-wide sovereignty. As Jehovah's son he may assert Jehovah's dominion. This world domination is not conceived in the noble idealism of Isa. 19[19f.] or of Mic. 4[1-3], but in terms reminiscent of ruthless Assyrian dominion (v. 9).

10–12. The Poet Appeals to the Plotting Kings. Let them be submissive to Jehovah. *Kiss the son*—a sign of submission in the Orient (cf. Isa. 49[23]). Ashurbanipal records concerning his tributary kings: "Their tribute I received; they embraced my feet" (Barton, *Archæology and the Bible*, 3rd edit., p. 360). V. 12b implies that the day of Jehovah with its universal judgment is at hand. Safety lies only in submission to Jehovah and his king.

Psalm 3. Morning Confidence After Rest Amid Peril

1, 2. The Psalmist's Perilous Position. The psalmist is in the midst of grave peril, surrounded by enemies more numerous than he has ever known, deluged by discouraging, pessimistic comments over his situation from his friends (cf. Job 2[11-13]).

3, 4. Past Experience of Jehovah's Protection. *But thou* (v. 3) is in contrast with the "many" of vv. 1, 2. Jehovah has been to him in other days a shield of protection (cf. Gen. 15[1]), the supporter of his dignity, the restorer of his courage, and (v. 4) the answerer of his prayers. The tense of the verbs in v. 4 is frequentative: "As often as I call, he answers me" is what the verse suggests.

5, 6. Cheering Experience of Preceding Night. An experience just enjoyed (so Kittel) heightens his confidence. Amid the very perils and tenseness of the external situation described in vv. 1, 2 he had had a night of rest, undisturbed and refreshing. He awakened on the new day realizing that during the unconscious hours God had sustained him. He had learned the power of spiritual detachment through faith in God (cf. Harriet Beecher Stowe's hymn, "Still, still with Thee"). His confidence is enhanced. No multiplication of foes can daunt his courage (v. 6).

7, 8. A Brief Cry for Help. V. 7a is followed by an expression of conviction that the very countenances that have insulted him (cf. Job 16[10]), and the very teeth that have uttered cries of enmity (cf. on 58[6]) will be destroyed. (The tense used is what is commonly called the "prophetic" perfect or the perfect of "prophetic certainty.") Compare the note of triumph (v. 7) that closes the psalm with the note of lament that begins it. V. 8 is a later addition that attempts to adapt a purely individual experience to community use. The connection of the psalm with David as suggested in the title is not impossible, but v. 4b makes it improbable (see intro., section on "Titles of the Psalms," p. 511).

Psalm 4. A Summons to Self-Control and to Worship

The Jewish community has fallen upon hard days (vv. 1, 6). The harvests are diminished (v. 7b), and the leading classes (see v. 2) have turned against Jehovah, and are hurling insults at the loyal. Many are perplexed and profoundly agitated. The period of Malachi and Isaiah 56–66, about 450 B.C., is the most likely time in which to date this psalm.

1. The Psalmist Appeals to God. In a well remembered experience in the past he has been helped. He now craves similar deliverance for himself and all the faithful. He speaks as a leader in the inner circle of loyal Jews.

2, 3. Address to the Disloyal Who are Insulting the Psalmist. *Sons of men* (v. 2) does not refer to humanity as contrasted with Deity, but means the distinguished citizens, property holders in distinction from the poor people (cf. Psa. 49[2]). These distinguished men are slandering his reputation (v. 2a), but are themselves living superficial, empty lives. Read v. 3a, following emendation suggested by Graetz based on Psa. 31[21], *Know ye, that Jehovah hath made wonderful unto me his kindness.* In spite of the insults of distinguished fellow citizens he feels that his own life is a wonderful result of divine grace.

4, 5. The Psalmist Counsels the Loyal. Turning away from the indifferent with their empty lives to the inner circle of the loyal (cf. Mal. 3[13-18]), he summons them, in the very face of insult, to keep themselves in control. Translate v. 4 as follows, *Be agitated* [i.e., disturbed, provoked to wrath], *but do not sin. Speak with your own heart upon your couch and be silent.* They are counseled to keep their doubts and their insults to themselves. Instead of venting themselves in anger upon their insulters, he summons them to the practices of religion, particularly to those that centered in the sacrificial worship of the Temple (cf. Isa. 56[1-8] 60[6]). *Sacrifices of righteousness*—cf. Deut. 33[19] and Psa. 51[19]. The conception is not spiritualized here. Actual sacrifice is meant.

6–8. The Psalmist's Utter Trust in God. He quotes the pathetic craving of the despairing and the skeptical for better times. Read v. 6a as a wish: *Many are saying, Oh that we might see good*—i.e., good times, contentment, happiness. V. 6b is a prayer in the diction of the ancient benediction in Num. 6[24-26]. Swift upon the utterance of this prayer comes the confidence that God has heard. Some may complain and accuse but not the psalmist. In the very face of poor harvests and poverty he has experienced the richness of a joyful heart. In this confidence, this sense of security in God, the moment he lies down to rest he drops off into peaceful sleep.

Psalm 5. A Morning Prayer

This psalm is a lamentation of an individual suppliant. In origin it is closely associated with the Temple worship, as v. 3 clearly reveals; for it is a song sung in connection with the morning offering (cf. 2 Kings 3[20] Ezek. 46[13]). The psalmist, living amid arrogant, iniquitous fellow citizens, awaits a revelation of leadership from Jehovah, whose nearness the sacrifice guarantees. The atmosphere of strife between the righteous and wicked within the community is reflected in the prayer for the punishment of the wicked. The psalm probably dates from the middle of the fifth century B.C. and reflects the temper of Malachi and Isa. 56–66.

1–3. A Plea for Jehovah's Attention. The psalmist's plea is uttered in a morning prayer, accompanying his sacrifice; it is the prayer of a subject to his Sovereign (v. 2). *In the morning will I order* (v. 3). There is no object to the verb, but the term used is the customary word for the preparation of the offering (Gunkel).

4–7. Contrast Between the Arrogant Sinners and the Psalmist. The sinners are objects of Jehovah's hatred and destruction, but he is the recipient of the *loving-kindness* of God. He is conscious of an awesome sense of privilege in the worship of the Temple (v. 7; cf. 23[6b] 27[4b]). He is a devout believer in the efficacy of sacrificial worship. *Evil* (v. 4)—read with mg., *the evil man* (cf. 15[1]).

8, 9. The Prayer. The presence of enemies in the community adds concreteness, passion, and intensity to his prayer. He prays to be led in Jehovah's own way and to have that way made *straight*, or "level," or "smooth" before him. Evidently, the flattering, treacherous counsel of his insidious watchers, the "enemies" of v. 8a, has made Jehovah's will uncertain. Note the vigorous comparison in v. 9c. Enter into that treacherous, open mouth of the deceitful, arrogant man, and you will find yourself in a sepulcher! *Flatter*—literally, "make smooth" or "slippery."

10–12. Prayer for Punishment upon the Sinful and Blessing Upon the Righteous. The psalm here passes from the individual to the social note. The psalmist's own experience leads him to wider generalizations. V. 10 reveals the vindictive temper of the Judaism of this period (cf. Psa. 64). The contrast between a curse upon the sinful and a blessing upon the righteous is frequent in the Psalter (cf. 71[13, 14]). This psalm is an example of naïve self-consciousness of righteousness.

In v. 11 the psalmist prays that the loyal may live jubilant lives in the guardianship of God, their defender and protector. This note of joy is a characteristic contribution of the Psalter to religious experience.

Psalm 6. A Song of Lamentation

The psalmist is in physical distress (v. 2); he gets no rest but spends his nights in physical and mental pain (v. 6); death seems near (v. 5). But what intensifies the physical suffering which he evidently attributes to the disciplining hand of Jehovah (v. 1) is the anguish of spirit caused by the insults of his enemies (v. 7), the evildoers of the community (v. 8a). This anguish of spirit is the main theme of the psalm. The psalm probably comes from the late Persian period and reflects the inner struggles of the fifth century B.C. It has clearest contacts with 27[7-14] and 143.

1–3. The Psalmist's Passionate Prayer for the Abatement of His Punishment. He offers no protest and denies no guilt. He discerns the connection between his suffering and his sin, but he throws himself upon the mercy of God (vv. 1, 2a). In v. 2b read with slight change of text (following Buhl), *My bones have become old;* his suffering is ageing his physique, and disturbing his soul (v. 3a).

4, 5. Petition for Recovery. He appeals to the deepest quality in God, his loving-kindness (cf. 5[7]), as the basis for his petition. In v. 5a read, with LXX, *For no one in death remembereth thee.* His argument is "Save me so that thou wilt still have me to give thanks unto thee" (cf. the similar argument in 30^{9-12} and 88^{11}). *Sheol* is the abode of the dead where all have a dim, shadowy existence.

6, 7. The Nature of His Suffering. With Oriental exaggeration the psalmist says he has wept so much that his bed dissolves in his tears (v. 6). He has become enfeebled (v. 7), but the chief cause of his suffering is the insults received from his enemies, the ungodly Jews in the community. In v. 7 read, with the versions, *I have grown old*, and with Cheyne, *at the insult of my adversaries*.

8–10. The Petition Suddenly Turns Into a Song of Triumph. No longer does he quail before evil men. Now he has been heard by Jehovah. Jehovah is on his side and will humiliate his enemies.

Psalm 7. Refuge in God for the Persecuted

This is a psalm of lamentation of an individual. The psalmist is being bitterly and unjustly persecuted by enemies. He is being accused of infamous deeds and his life is being threatened. Kittel suggests that the psalmist is a high representative of the nation, whose personal affairs also concern the nation. This interpretation best accounts for the transition from the individual to the community at v. 7, and preserves the fundamental unity of the psalm. The psalm (v. 9b) shows familiarity with Jeremiah (11^{20} 17^{10} 20^{12}) and (vv. 7, 8) with the late prophetic eschatology; it probably dates from the early Greek period.

1, 2. Call to God for Help. The persecution is persistent and fierce.

3–5. A Solemn Protest. In passionate words the psalmist protests against the accusations brought by his enemy and declares his innocence. V. 4b is parallel in thought to v. 4a and should read *And if I have oppressed those who for no cause are hostile to me*, following suggestions from the ancient versions. Cf. Job $31^{5f.}$ for this whole section. *Him that was at peace* (v. 4)—read, with LXX, *My friends*. *My glory* (v. 5) = "My dignity," i.e., those in a covenant of peace with me.

6–9. Prayer for the World Judgment of Jehovah. His first petition is that against the outbursts of fury (plural) of his adversaries; but the psalmist is convinced that according to his own nature—i.e., by laws self-ordained—Jehovah will vindicate him. But swiftly the psalmist passes from the conception of Jehovah as his personal Judge to the vast eschatological conception of Jehovah as the Judge of the world, seated on high (so Buhl) above the nations (vv. 7, 8a; cf. Isa. 24^{23} Dan. 7^{10} Rev. 4^{10}.) In v. 7b, for *return thou* read, with Gunkel and others, *take thy seat*. In v. 8b he returns to the thought of personal vindication by the righteous Judge who knows and judges the hearts of all men (cf. Jer. 11^{20}).

10–13. His Calm Certainty of God. He is sure of God's protection (v. 10), and of his permanent attitude of indignation toward the sinner (v. 11). V. 12a refers to God who holds ready and in reserve his judgment. Read *surely* or *verily* (an asseverative particle) *he is whetting his sword*. This carries on the thought of v. 11.

14–16. The Scene Shifts from God to the Wicked Man. V. 14 presents a vigorous figure. The wicked man is portrayed in the birth throes, bringing forth an evil deed. The gradual growth of the evil deed from its conception in the mind to its expression in an act is suggested. Vv. 15, 16 depict the suicidal result of evil (cf. 28^{4} Jer. 18^{20} Prov. 26^{27} Obad. v. 15b). The evil man falls into his own trap. Harm planned for others harms the schemer himself. Here is enunciated a profound moral principle (cf. Esther 7^{10}).

17. The Vow. It is customary for a song of lamentation to close with a vow of gratitude and praise.

Psalm 8. "The Starry Heavens Above, the Moral Law Within"

This psalm is one of the most majestic in the Psalter. It is a hymn of adoration beginning in the realm of nature but moving in brilliant and surprising transition to man. It is manifestly later than the priestly account of creation (Gen. 1^{1}–2^{4a}), upon which it is dependent (vv. 6–8). It, accordingly, dates from some period subsequent to 500 B.C. It is probably a night song used in connection with the nocturnal festivals of Israel (Kittel). The author had a deep and sensitive appreciation of the beauty of an Oriental night (vv. 1, 3).

1, 2. An Exclamation of Reverent Awe. The majesty of God fills the psalmist's mind. V. 1, *excellent*—literally, "wide," "spacious," "majestic"—a poetic word; *upon the heavens* suggests vividly the appearance of the stars upon the dark background of the sky. The sincere praise of Jehovah by infant *babes* is stronger than the scheming hostility of God's enemies.

3–5. "The Starry Heavens and the Moral Law." The heavens are conceived as the work of the strong, skillful, sensitive fingers of the Creative Artist. The psalmist is exalted by the thought of the vastness, the mystery, the variety manifest in the heavens. We are reminded of Dante's frequent reference to the beautiful stars, the word "stars" ending each section of *The Divine Comedy*.

In swift transition the psalmist passes from nature to man, first to man viewed in his seeming insignificance in comparison with the vastness of the natural universe. Why should God remember man or follow him with his providence? *Son of man*=man. Then in surprising contrast he sees man in his dignity. V. 5a may be translated literally, "Thou didst make him lack little of God." Man is like a king. Instinctively we recall the great dictum of Immanuel Kant: "Two things there are which, the oftener and the more steadfastly we consider them, fill the mind with an ever new and ever rising admiration and reverence: the starry heavens above, the moral law within."

6–9. The Consequent Dominion Given to Man. The creatures of earth, air, and sea God has placed under human dominion. The psalmist makes implicit reference to the priestly narrative of creation (cf. Gen. 1[26, 27]). The psalm ends in deepened reverent wonder: v. 1 is repeated, but is now athrill with the total content of the psalm, hence enriched and deepened. Kittel considers vv. 1, 2 and 9 as sung by the choir; vv. 3–8 by a single voice.

Psalm 9. The Certainty of Judgment

Psa. 9 and 10 were originally one. They are so considered in several MSS. and in the LXX where 10=9[22-39]. Psa. 10 has no title and the two psalms reveal a common use of language (cf. 9[9b] and 10[1b], *in times of trouble*). Together they present the first example in the psalms of an acrostic, every other verse beginning with a different letter of the Hebrew alphabet, in successive order. Such poems are found likewise in Psa. 25, 34, 37, 111, 112, 119, 145 as well as in Lam. 1–4, Prov. 31[10-31] and Nah. 1. The model for this type of artistic poem is found in Babylonian literature (Jeremias). In the case before us the acrostic is incomplete, Psa. 9 carrying it through *k* (*d* is omitted), and Psa. 10 presenting only *l*, *q*, *r*, *s* and *t*. It is possible to discern also *n*, ', and *p*, and Gunkel, through slight reconstruction of the text, restores the original acrostic almost completely. It comes from the late Persian period, from a time when the different types of psalms had begun to fuse into one another. This fusing accounts for the variety of emotion and is at the same time our basis for maintaining the unity of the original psalm. It reveals the tense party strife of late Judaism.

1, 2. An Individual Utters His Thanksgiving. The psalm opens in the form of a hymn. The "marvelous works of Jehovah" (v. 1b) is a favorite hymn theme in the psalter.

3, 4. The Particular Reason for His Thanks. The psalmist's enemies have been humiliated and condemned by Jehovah, the righteous Judge.

5–16. An Eschatological Hymn. The idea of Jehovah as the Judge of the individual provides the transition to the eschatological conception of Jehovah as the future Judge of all the nations. The verbs are prophetic perfects, suggesting that the psalmist views the future judgment as a certainty. It is possible that this psalm was used in the ritual of the Feast of Tabernacles where, as Mowinckel thinks, the enthronement of Jehovah over all humanity was symbolically celebrated (cf. T. H. Robinson in Simpson's *The Psalmists*, p. 91). These verses portray Jehovah as Judge and King of the world, dealing out destruction to the nations (Isa. 17[12-14] 66[15, 16] and cf. Psa. 68) and providing safety for his loyal worshipers (vv. 9, 10). In v. 11 read with mg. *peoples*. V. 12a, literally, "as exactor of blood he remembereth them." Into the eschatological hymn is inserted the individual note of petition (vv. 13–15). Jehovah's mercy to the humble (v. 12b) recalls the psalmist's own need of safety from Jehovah's hand. Note the contrast between the gates of death (v. 13c), a Babylonian conception (the grave was guarded by 7 or 14 gates, according to Babylonian legend), and the gates of Jerusalem (v. 14b).

17–20. The Psalmist's Certainty of the Judgment of Jehovah Upon the Nations. The thought continues that of vv. 5–16. See also the notes on Psa. 2.

Psalm 10. The Certainty of Judgment (Continued)

1–11. A Lamentation Because of the Activities of the Godless. The psalmist gives vivid glimpses of the party strife in Judaism in the times of and preceding Nehemiah (see p. 461). Hostile, scheming, boasting, covetous, irreverent, prosperous (v. 5a, following Wellhausen), deceitful, treacherous men pounce upon the weak and overpower him. They maintain God does not see their deeds (v. 1).

12–16. A Passionate Plea—for the divine destruction of the wicked Jews and of the nations (with v. 16 cf. 9[17f.]).

17, 18. A Prophetic Note. The meek in heart have access to the protection of God.

Psalm 11. Refuge in God From Pursuing Enemies

The psalmist is a leader of the loyal. In discussion with his friends, who give him cowardly counsel, he utters his confidence in

God. It is a distinctly individual psalm and reflects the period of party strife which forms the similar background of Psa. 3 and 4. In situation it reminds us forcibly of Neh. 6[11]. In subject matter it has most in common with Psa. 64, 120, 140 and 142.

1, 2. Heroic Faith in the Face of Cowardly Counsel. His friends, knowing the ruthless pursuit of his enemies (v. 2) and the seeming impotence of righteous men in those degenerate times (v. 3) counsel him to "flutter to the hills like a bird" (v. 1c; cf. LXX). But he maintains that his refuge is not to be in cowardly flight but in Jehovah (cf. 27[1]).

3–7. The Reality of God's Rule in the Moral Order. The contrast between a society in which the very *foundations* are broken down, and an abiding, supreme spiritual order with Jehovah in control is powerfully portrayed. His all-seeing eyes are watching men, testing the righteous (v. 5), and punishing the wicked (v. 6). The psalmist's pictures of the punishment which Jehovah's judgment brings root in scenes of volcanic eruption (cf. 18[13] Isa. 30[27-33]). *The upright shall behold his face* (v. 7c). Probably this clause originally meant, as Gunkel suggests, "seeing the symbol of the God at the visit to the sanctuary." (We have examples of this in Babylonian and Egyptian literature; cf. also Ex. 23[15] (E), Ex. 34[23f.] (J), Deut. 16[16] (D), 1 Sam. 1[22] (Hannah), Isa. 1[12]). But this primitive expression comes to be filled with deep mystical content in the psalms (cf. 17[15] 27[4] 42[2]). The righteous have access to Jehovah's presence and the privilege of fellowship with him. The conception is not eschatological.

Psalm 12. A Liturgy of Lamentation

The psalm dates from the post-exilic period. It reflects dark times, a generation where evil has the upper hand in the Jewish community, when loudmouthed deceitful flatterers are making hard the lot of humble, godly men (vv. 3–6a). There is a quotation (v. 5b) from a late chapter in Isaiah (33[10]). Gunkel (cf. also Peters) interprets the psalm as a liturgy: vv. 1–4 are uttered by the congregation; v. 5 is spoken by the priest; vv. 6–8 are the response of the congregation.

1, 2. A Cry to Jehovah for Help Against the Deceitful. *Godly man* and *faithful* are parallel terms. Wellhausen reads the abstract nouns "love" and "faithfulness."

3, 4. The Longing for the Destruction of the Deceitful. Read v. 3 as an earnest wish: *May Jehovah cut off*, etc. In v. 4a, following the LXX, read *our tongue we will make mighty*.

5. The Oracle From Jehovah. In response to the uttered longing of the congregation the priest utters the divine oracle assuring the worshipers of Jehovah's help (cf. 20[7] 95[7]).

6–8. The Answer of the Congregation to Jehovah's Oracle. Upon such words (v. 6)—in contrast to the words of the flatterers—Israel can depend. This verse is quite in the style of 18[30] 19[7f.] 119[40]. In v. 7 the psalm rises into an expression of confidence which the priestly oracle has awakened. Now the faithful are not afraid among their godless contemporaries. It closes with a vivid picture of the proud self-consciousness of the latter, stalking about, unaware of Jehovah's promise to the faithful (v. 8). Read in v. 7, with LXX, *thou wilt keep us*, and with several MSS., *thou wilt preserve us*. Not the *words* of Jehovah, but his loyal ones are to be kept.

Psalm 13. Confident Amid Distress

The psalmist is in profound inner distress (v. 2), so weak in body as to feel death to be near (v. 3). But intensifying his physical pain is his mental anguish, occasioned by the exulting taunts of the irreligious and especially by the seeming futility of his faith. We are clearly in the time of strife between the loyal worshipers of Jehovah and the worldly-minded skeptics of the Greek or the late Persian period (cf. Psa. 64).

1, 2. The Psalmist's Lamentation. He feels himself to be forgotten by Jehovah. Four times he starts his lamentation with the reproachful phrase, *How long* (cf. the identical phrase in Babylonian psalms, "How long will the Lord who sleeps still sleep." Quoted in Simpson, *The Psalmists*, p. 132). Read v. 2a, with Gunkel and Kittel, *How long must I bear sorrow in my soul*.

3, 4. His Petition for Health and Justification Before His Troubles. Read v. 3a, with Ehrlich, *Consider my misery* for *Consider and answer me*. The lightened or brightened eyes indicate the light of health and happiness (cf. 1 Sam. 14[27]). The psalmist has no conception of immortality.

5, 6. His Trust and Praise. The psalm closes with an expression of confidence in God's "goodness," "kindness," "mercy," "love" (Hebrew *hesed*), that quality that is deepest in the prophetic conception of God. (The word is used frequently by Hosea.) The lamentation and the petition change to the mood of certainty of Jehovah's help which is expressed in a hymn of praise.

Psalm 14. Responsibility for Irreligion in the Community

This psalm dates from the Persian period

when degenerate priests were spiritual leaders in Israel. It mirrors the same situation that is reflected in Malachi. The psalmist, who is clearly a prophet in spirit, interprets the temper of his times as a practical atheism, and, as Gunkel's brilliant reconstruction has clearly shown, he attributes this lack of religion, as the prophets were accustomed to do, to the materialism of the priesthood. This psalm was originally identical with Psa. 53. A comparison of the two makes it possible to come closer to the original text, especially in vv. 5, 6, where we meet the greatest difficulties.

1–3. The Practical Atheism of the Psalmist's Day. The psalm begins in the manner of the Wisdom literature. The *fool* is the irreligious, churlish man, one who denies God and insults men, the opposite to "noble-minded" (cf. Isa. 32^{5}). These verses are a prophetic invective and remind us of Jer. 5^{1} and Isa. 59^{3-8}. V. 2 furnishes a vivid anthropomorphic touch (literally, "leaned over and looked down"). God is pictured as hunting for men of insight or understanding, but as unsuccessful in his search.

4–6. The Prophetic Psalmist's Threat to the Priests. The text of this passage is very corrupt. The prophetically-minded psalmist is laying the responsibility for such an irreligious age at the door of the religious teachers of the time, the priesthood. The best approach to his meaning is through Hos. 4^{6-12a} Jer. 23^{11} Ezek. 22^{26} Mal. 2^{1-9}. These priests eat the shewbread in the Temple (v. 4b), but cause the people to err. Nor do they call upon Jehovah. But He whom the priesthood does not fear will become a cause of fear. The profane priesthood (cf. Jer. 23^{11}) will be humiliated (Jer. 2^{26}), for God has rejected it (cf. Hos. 4^{6}). The verses should be rendered most probably as follows, (chiefly following Gunkel):

4. "Have they no insight, who do iniquity,
Who cause my people to stumble?
They eat the bread of Jehovah,
They do not call upon his name.
5. Will he (Jehovah) not become a terror,
For God will scatter his bones.
6. The profane he will put to shame,
For God hath rejected him."

7. A Prayer for the Intervention of Jehovah. The irreligiousness of the times is called a *captivity*, i.e., of the spirit.

PSALM 15. WHAT JEHOVAH REQUIRES OF HIS WORSHIPERS

This psalm is a Temple liturgy performed at the door of the Jerusalem Temple. The worshipers ask the question, "Who can worship in the Temple?" The priest answers, reciting the requirements of God for his worshipers, and as the people enter the Temple he pronounces the promise of stability. Kittel thinks the mingling of prophetic and priestly elements points to the time of Deuteronomy as its date, but probably the verbal similarity of v. 5a with Lev. 25^{37} (from the Code of Holiness) points to the early post-exilic period. Probably in earlier times the priests guarded the worship at the sanctuaries by such questions as, "Are you ceremonially clean?" (cf. 1 Sam. $21^{4f.}$); "Have you brought the prescribed offerings?" (cf. Ex. 23^{15} Deut. $26^{1f.}$). The activity of the prophets changed the character of the answers, but the questions must have been frequent in Israel, as certain references clearly show (cf. 24^{3-6} Mic. 6^{6-8} Hag. 2^{11} Zech. 7^{4-6} Isa. 31^{4-16}).

1. The Worshipers' Question. What does Jehovah require of those who would worship him in the Jerusalem Temple?

2–5. The Answer of the Priest. Peters suggestively sees here a "Temple decalogue" and maintains that we have nowhere else in the O.T. so full a statement of the obligations of holiness that made up the virtues of Jehovah's worshipers (*Psalms as Liturgies*, p. 123).

2. (1) "He is honest and righteous in life.
(2) He is truthful to the core.
3. (3) He refrains from gossipy slander. (Literally, 'He does not foot (it) with his tongue.')
(4) He does no harm to his friend.
(5) He does not insult his neighbor.
4. (6) He despises the man who has made himself odious (so LXX).
(7) He honors those who fear Jehovah.
(8) He keeps his oath though he suffer for it.
5. (9) He does not loan money at interest (cf. Ex. 22^{25} Deut. $23^{20, 21}$ Lev. 25^{35-37}).
(10) He cannot be bribed to stand against the innocent man."

V. 5c contains the Priestly Promise: He who expresses these virtues has gained stability. The psalm describes a class of men "who for centuries, and in every rank of life, have been an honor and strength to their church and country."

PSALM 16. A MEDITATION OF TRUST IN TIMES OF IDOLATRY

This psalm is more a meditation than a hymn (Welch). The psalmist lives at a period when a vigorous tendency toward the worship of other gods was felt in Judaism. The atmosphere of Isa. 57[3f.] and 65[3f.], from the Persian period shortly before Nehemiah, seems native to this psalm. He scorns these idolaters (v. 4), and trusts Jehovah utterly.

1, 2. A Prayer and a Confession of Faith. Jehovah is the psalmist's *summum bonum.*

3, 4. His Delight in the Loyal and His Scorn of the Worshipers of Other Gods. V. 3 is difficult. Read

"As for the holy ones who are in the land
They are the glorious ones in whom is all my delight" (cf. Driver, *Tenses*, p. 268).

The psalmist will have nothing to do with idolaters. These men he will not sacrifice, pouring out their blood as though in a drink offering to their god; he will not even soil his lips with their names.

5–8. His Utter Trust in Jehovah. Having nothing in common with the idolatrous majority, he is not lonely. He has his *portion* in Jehovah. As a guest he has from his host's hand his cup. The *lines* (v. 6) that fix the boundaries of his *lot* inclose good "land" (*heritage*); his "land," however, is not material; it is Jehovah. *Heart* (v. 7, A.S.V.)—literally, "reins," i.e., conscience (cf. Job 4[12f.]). V. 8 describes the practice of the presence of God (cf. 109[31] 121[5f.]).

9–11. The Psalmist's Exultant Joy in God. For *my glory* (v. 9) probably read, with Driver, literally, *my liver = my emotions.* Formerly v. 10 was understood as having reference to an after life (so Delitzsch). It is, however, to be interpreted in the same way as in 9[13] and 30[3] (see comments on the two passages; cf. also H. W. Robinson, *The Psalmists*, p. 57). God will not abandon him to death. *Thine holy one*, i.e., the psalmist himself will not be allowed to die. In v. 11 also the psalmist is thinking of this life. God alone can satisfy him with life that is life indeed. While there is no reference to immortality here, the emphasis on religious experience (cf. 73[25, 26]) takes us a long step in that direction.

Psalm 17. Rectitude and the Vision of God

This psalm reflects the same background as Psa. 16 and probably dates from the middle Persian period. It is a declaration of innocence. The psalmist is surrounded by insolent "men of the world" (v. 14), who are sleek and proud (v. 10), treacherous toward men of his spirit (vv. 9, 11), and who find their satisfaction in the earthly realm (v. 14). He, however, conscious of integrity (vv. 4, 5) and hoping for their destruction (v. 13), finds his satisfaction only in God (v. 15).

1–5. The Psalmist's Consciousness of Rectitude. He is conscious of the scrutiny of God upon his thoughts, words, and deeds; no wrong has been found in his life.

6–8. His Prayer for Protection. His past experience in prayer (v. 6) now leads him to pray. *Marvelous loving-kindness* (v. 7a)—render *make wonderful thy loving-kindness. Thy right hand*—i.e., the place of safety. *The apple of the eye*—literally, "The pupil of the eye," a synonym of preciousness.

9–12. His Enemies Described. These verses present a vivid contrast to vv. 1–5. Round about him are enemies—unfeeling, proud, and treacherous. For *their own fat* (v. 10a) read *their heart*, and translate *their heart they have closed*, i.e., to pity. In v. 11 the psalmist changes to first person plural. He speaks for all the righteous.

13, 14. His Vindictive Prayer. He summons Jehovah to *confront* his enemies with destruction. Vv. 13c, 14 vividly climax the description of the psalmist's materialistic enemies. The text is difficult and may be best translated as follows:

13c. By thy sword, free my life from the wicked.

14. By thy hand, O Jehovah, from the men,
From worldlings whose portion is (this) life.
Yea with thy treasure let their belly be filled.
Let (their) children be filled to excess.
Let them bequeath what they leave to their babes!

The words are spoken in bitter sarcasm. These insolent men are worldly in their interests. Let material blessings "satiate" them from generation to generation!

15. The Psalmist's Sole Satisfaction is God. In vigorous contrast to these men of the world who are sated with the material things of life, the psalmist has his satisfaction in the vision of God, i.e., in communion and fellowship with him. *When I awake*—Duhm interprets "from sleep," Cheyne and Kittel "from the sleep of death." This latter conception is late, the idea of resurrection being found clearly in only two passages in the O.T.—Isa. 26[19] (*cir.* 340 B.C.) and Dan. 12[2] (*cir.* 167 B.C.). The key to correct interpretation is furnished by the LXX. Read *When I gaze upon thy form* (cf. Gunkel). The passage refers, not to the vision of God after death, but to the vision of God in this life; i.e., mystic fellowship with God is the psalmist's thought. This preserves the vivid contrast with the satisfaction in this life of the wicked. *Thy form*—gazing upon the form of God (an anthropomorphism) means enjoying fellowship with God (Gunkel, Cheyne).

Psalm 18. The King's Hymn of Thanksgiving for Victory and Dominion

This psalm is found in another recension in 2 Sam. 22, where, however, the text is less perfectly preserved. Vv. 7–15 are very old, probably coming from the time of David or even from the same time as Judg. 5, the earliest extant piece of literature in the O.T. The rest of the psalm, while also pre-exilic, seems to have originated late in that period. The song was sung by the court singers to celebrate the victory and dominion of a Judæan king, possibly, as Kittel and Gunkel suggest, Josiah. We have examples of such royal psalms in Babylonia (Nebuchadrezzar), Assyria (Ashurbanipal), and Egypt (Ikhnaton).

1–3. A Hymn of Praise to Jehovah. Jehovah is described in vivid and familiar pictures in v. 2. He is *rock*, i.e., "crag," *fortress, deliverer, rock* (cf. Babylonian "god my mountain"), *shield, horn of salvation* (horn is a symbol of strength), *high tower*, i.e., "secure height."

4–6. The King's Need and his Cry to Jehovah. V. 4 may contain an implicit reference to Babylonian mythology. *Floods of ungodliness*—literally, "torrents of Belial," torrents of the land of no return, i.e., Sheol (Driver). Death is like a hunter, awaiting mankind with cords and snares.

7–15. The Revelation of Jehovah. Cf. 97[2f.] Judg. 5[4] Deut. 33[2] Isa. 30[27f.] Hab. 3[3f.] These verses, in imagery very ancient in Israel, describe the majestic and awesome appearance of Jehovah in earthquake, volcanic eruption, hail, thunder, and lightning. Gressmann, citing Ex. 19[18] (J), maintains that Mount Sinai, to which Moses led the Israelites, was volcanic, and amid the terrors of volcanic eruption the majestic appearance of God was experienced. This ancient experience gave Israel its traditional imagery for describing great theophanies. V. 11 may be translated:

"He made darkness his hiding place round about him.
His thicket a gathering of waters."

V. 14 has a parallel in Babylonian literature; of Marduk it is said:

"The lightning he set before him,
With a burning flame was his body filled."

16–19. The King's Deliverance. He tells how Jehovah rescued him from his peril.

20–24. The Reason for His Deliverance. It is due entirely to the righteousness of the king. The language of this section is Deuteronomic, especially v. 22.

25–30. A General Confession of Faith in Jehovah's Dealing With Men. From Jehovah's dealings with him individually the psalmist passes on to the broader conception of Jehovah's dealings with mankind. Here we have a picture of individualism in retribution in a distinctly sub-Christian atmosphere. In v. 29a read *For with thee I can crush a marauding band. Tried* (v. 30), literally, "smelted."

31–42. A Hymn of Praise to Jehovah. The second major part of the psalm begins here. His success, his skill as a warrior, comes from Jehovah. *Thy gentleness hath made me great* (v. 35): another possible translation is, *Thy condescension causeth me to increase.*

43–45. The King's Increased Prestige. His victory assures him widened dominion.

46–50. A Concluding Hymn of Praise. The king is here seen to be of the house of David, i.e., Judæan. V. 50 is of Messianic import.

Psalm 19. Revelation of God in Nature and in the Law

This psalm is composed of two originally independent poems. (1) *The Symphony of the Heavens* (vv. 1–6). (2) *A Hymn in Praise of the Law* (vv. 7–14).

(1) The first poem has for background Babylonian mythology, as the allusions in vv. 5c, 6 clearly show. The Babylonians and Assyrians personified the natural bodies and forces. Perhaps it was during the reign of Manasseh (7th cent. B.C.) through the worship of Shamash the sun god, then introduced (2 Kings 21[3f.]), that such ideas found entrance into the background ideas of Israel (Gressmann). But these ideas merely provide a kind of poetic vehicle for the loftier and profounder thought of Israel. This is one of the most majestic and beautiful of the nature hymns in the Psalter.

1, 2. The Language of the Heavens. Through Plato we know of the celestial harmony of the spheres, probably of Oriental origin. The heavens are uttering a marvelous melody. *The heavens declare*—better, *The heavens keep recounting* and *the firmament keeps revealing*—the participles suggest continuous action. They have as their theme *the glory of God*, i.e., the majestic nature of God. One day utters it to the next, pouring it out, bubbling it forth in eager, spontaneous utterance. One night declares (a poetic word) to the next, the wisdom at the heart of the majesty.

3, 4. The Celestial Harmony of the Spheres. No human ear hears this marvelous melody, yet it reaches the far corners of the earth. In v. 4 for *their line* read *their voice.*

5, 6. A Hymn to the Sun. Primitive man saw in the ball of the sun a god. On a tablet of Nabu-apalidin (860 B.C.) Shamash, the sun god, is said to have a tabernacle in the sea.

He too was a bridegroom, and his bride, Aia, dwelt in that tabernacle. Shamash goes forth out of the sea and pursues his course, overcoming demons as he fights his way (Gressmann, *The Psalmists*, pp. 16f.). An echo of this Babylonian conception provides the figures of speech for the loftier Hebrew thought. The sun is great, but behind the sun is Jehovah. The sun reveals his majesty.

(2) The union of vv. 1–6 and vv. 7–14 into one psalm is probably due to similarity of theme: the revelation of God in nature and in the Law. The key to an understanding of these verses is the attitude of Judaism toward revealed religion. G. F. Moore has stated this with clear insight. "The corner-stone of Judaism is the idea of revealed religion. God has not only made himself known to men, but has declared to them his will for man's whole life. This revelation the Jews possess in their Holy Scriptures and in its complement, the unwritten Law. . . . (Note—The oral Law was revealed at Sinai no less than the written Law.) . . . There is no duty toward God or man which is not either expressly or by plain implication contained in this twofold revelation" (*History of Religions*, pp. 68f. Charles Scribner's Sons).

The conception generally held by Christians concerning the Law is built upon the views of Paul in Rom. 7[14f.] and Gal. 3. These views, however, are not characteristic of normal Jewish feeling toward the Law. This psalm and Psa. 119, accordingly, provide a healthy supplement to what Schechter has suggestively called the "night of legalism," as life under law has ordinarily been interpreted. In these psalms, rightly understood, there is not monotonous repetition, but the joyous recall with infinite variation of the wonder and privilege Israel enjoys from Jehovah in the gift of the Law. The psalm dates from the days after the priestly Law had been accepted as the fundamental basis of Judaism some decades previous to the Greek period.

7–10. Praise of the Law. The Law is interpreted by six terms. Each illustrates some one aspect of this perfect revelation and each accomplishes some particular thing in the building of a godly life. Through paraphrase we shall make this clear:

(1) The Law conceived as the "teaching" or "instruction" of Jehovah is "complete," "entire" and "refreshes" the weary spirit (v. 7a).

(2) The Law viewed as giving *testimony* for Jehovah, a phrase characteristic of the priestly legislation, is "trustworthy," "dependable," and fills the "openminded" person with "wisdom" (v. 7b).

(3) The Law understood as the *prescriptions* of Jehovah for Israel is "equitable" and "just" and fills the "heart" with "joy" (v. 8a).

(4) The Law heeded as a set of *commandments*, a term characteristic of the Deuteronomic legislation, is *pure*, i.e., without moral defilement, and "illumines" with insight (v. 8b).

(5) The Law looked upon as an *object of reverence* has in it no power to "contaminate" or "render impure" and is "eternally valid" (v. 9a).

(6) The Law interpreted as a body of *ordinances*, i.e., judgments, decisions that later became precedents, is in "exact conformity" to justice, and conceived as a "unity" is *righteous* in its decrees (v. 9b). V. 10 refers to all the laws of Judaism—worth more than gold and sweet to the spiritual senses.

11–13. His Personal Application of the Law to His Life. He found through observing it "warning" from evil and "reward" for obedience. Conscientious as he is, he knows that he makes *errors;* moreover, inadvertently and unconsciously he may have become ceremonially unclean (cf. Lev. 5[2]); he, therefore, prays for acquittal from such *hidden* guilt (cf. a similar Babylonian prayer in Simpson, *The Psalmists*, p. 158). *Presumptuous sins* (v. 13) =conscious sins of rebellion or pride. (Root idea, to "boil up" or "seethe".) This kind of sin ("with a high hand," Num. 15[30]) alone is *great transgression.*

14. The Prayer of the Lover of the Law. As of old, the bringer of a sacrifice (Lev. 1[3] Isa. 56[7]) hoped that it might be acceptable, so in this period, when the prayer had taken the place of the sacrifice (Gunkel) it is words and thoughts that are conceived as a living offering, unblemished and acceptable to Jehovah.

Psalm 20. A Prayer For the King Before Battle

The king is about to enter into battle (v. 1). At a day of prayer preceding the fray he has offered his sacrifice (v. 3), as was customary (cf. 1 Sam. 7[9] 1 Kings 8[44f.] 2 Chr. 14[10]), and has prayed for victory (v. 4). The psalm is a prayer for victory. For a similar psalm see 144[1-11]. We cannot discern which king is meant. It is from the late years of the Judæan kingdom, therefore is pre-exilic and not Messianic.

1–5. The Prayer for the King. This is sung *to* the king by the priestly choir. Let Jehovah whose residence is in Zion (v. 2) accept the king's sacrifice and grant him victory (v. 4). If the king returns triumphant they will celebrate the victory, giving credit to Jehovah (v. 5).

6–8. An Oracle of Victory. The psalm changes to the third person. These verses are in the prophetic perfect and are an answer in the mood of prophetic certainty to the prayer in vv. 1–5. Moreover, vv. 6–8, as v. 6 shows, are sung by a single voice. The oracle is simply the assurance, spoken under prophetic insight, that Jehovah, not mere military force, is with the king (vv. 6, 7) and will make him victorious. The enemy will "fall" but Jehovah's people will "stand firm." In v. 9 the choir repeats its petition. Read with LXX, *Jehovah save the king. Answer us when we call.*

Psalm 21. A Song Extolling the King

This is a psalm for the king, to celebrate his birthday (Gen. 40[20]), or the anniversary of his accession to the throne (Hos. 7[5], Gunkel). He has been loyal to Jehovah (v. 8) and has been honored with material and spiritual blessings (vv. 3–7). He is also a mighty warrior. May he be victorious! Vv. 1–7 are sung concerning the king, by the Temple choir, and are a song of praise to Jehovah. Vv. 8–12 are sung *to* the king. The psalm comes from the period of the Judæan kingdom, probably shortly before the Exile.

1–7. Gratitude for Jehovah's Blessings upon the King. Jehovah has "confronted" the king with *blessings of goodness* (v. 3). He has received, perhaps in an oracle, the guarantee of long life (v. 5); and he enjoys full security in God (v. 7).

8–12. The Voicing of Hopes for His Victories. The verbs do not express certainties but wishes; e.g., v. 8, *May thy hand find out all thine enemies*, etc. For *in the time of thine anger* (v. 9) read *when thou appearest* (cf. mg). *They imagined a device* (v. 11)—literally, "they hatched up a scheme."

13. A Concluding Vow. If Jehovah reveals his strength in the king's wars Israel will sing his praises.

Perhaps (cf. Kittel) vv. 1–7 were sung by the Temple choir; vv. 8–12 by a single prophetic voice; and v. 13 by all the people. Psa. 20 and 21 represent the same type of psalms (concerning the king) but are independent of one another.

Psalm 22. From Forsaken by God to Triumph in God

The author of this psalm is a poignant sufferer. His physical pain is keen (vv. 14–16), but is intensified by the hostility of the godless in the community (vv. 16–18). Rightly understood the psalm is a unity, the vow (v. 22) following naturally the lamentation of vv. 1–21 and introducing the song of praise, vv. 23–26, that climaxes in a majestic hymn, vv. 27–31. The allusions of v. 29 especially point to the time of Isa. 56–66, the middle of the fifth century B.C., as its probable date. This is the "Passion Psalm," made sacred to Christians by the use of its opening line by Jesus on the cross.

1, 2. The Psalmist Feels Forsaken by God. (Cf. Mk. 15[34] Mt. 27[46].) V. 1a is the only word spoken on the cross that is reported in the earliest tradition. It was uttered by Jesus in Aramaic. No quotation could have more fittingly interpreted the depth of his mental suffering, and its use illumines Jesus' familiarity with the Psalter, as the whole lamentation, especially vv. 13–18, is descriptive of anguish such as he endured.

3–5. His Appeal to History. Using Isaiah's great word for "God" (*holy;* cf. Isa. 6[3]), he suggests that God has his being, his very "dwelling," in the praises from his children (cf. 116[15], literally, "Costly in the sight of the Lord is the death of his saints"). There is here an implicit argument for Jehovah's help. To keep the psalmist alive will mean another to praise Jehovah. The fathers were vindicated, not shamed, before their foes (vv. 4, 5).

6–11. He Contrasts His Own Shame With the Deliverance of the Fathers. Humiliated and despised, he suffers his enemies' gestures of contempt (v. 7) and sarcastic words (v. 8). Yet God has sustained him since birth (vv. 9–11). In v. 9b read *Thou art he that maketh me to depend upon my mother's breasts.*

12–18. His Treatment at Hostile Hands. His strong, vigorous enemies (v. 12; cf. Amos 4[1], where the prophet calls the sleek, selfish women of Samaria "cows of Bashan," the fertile pasture land of north Israel), with their cold, heartless staring, intensify his physical exhaustion until death seems near (vv. 14, 15). He feels like prey hunted down by dogs. With his hands and feet mutilated (so Duhm reads for *pierced* in v. 16c), with bones sticking out through the flesh (v. 17a), his hostile observers, in anticipation of his death, begin to divide up his belongings (v. 18). These verses gather up more than his own personal sufferings; the whole community is in his mind (vv. 12, 16).

19–21. His Cry for Deliverance. With vivid pictures of his peril he prays for deliverance. His foes are compared to pursuing dogs (cf. v. 16), lions, and wild oxen (v. 21). *My darling* (v. 20)—literally, "my only one," i.e., poetic for "my life" (see mg.).

22–26. His Vow and Song of Praise. When he was in the poignancy of his suffering he made vows (v. 25); which now, in the Temple, in the presence of the congregation and with profound gratitude, he pays in a sacrificial repast, for God has heard his cry (vv. 24, 26).

27–31. A Majestic Hymn. The psalmist's personal praise (vv. 22, 25) is lifted now into universal praise. This is similarly done in 69[34f]. He pictures the nations as Jehovah's subjects (v. 28), worshiping at his sanctuary (v. 29a; cf. Isa. 66[19-23]). Indeed, all humanity (v. 29) pay him homage, and one generation will bequeath to the next the heritage of his character (vv. 30, 31). Compare the praise of Ashur in the Assyrian account of creation (Simpson, *The Psalmists*, p. 155).

Psalm 23. Jehovah the Shepherd of the Godfearing Individual

The author of this priceless jewel of the Psalter has fallen heir to the great prophetic insights of Jer. 23[1-4] Ezek. 34 and Isa. 40[11], where Jehovah is represented as shepherd of Israel. Kings and officials were commonly so designated in Egypt, Babylonia, Israel, and Greece. But Israel with tenderest associations applied the term particularly to illumine the character of her God. The prophets, however, had not yet individualized the conception but applied it to Jehovah as leader of the nation. All the richness held in this national context the psalmist claims for himself. His clear dependence upon the prophets and the reference to the Temple (v. 6) show that the psalm cannot be Davidic. It is a product of the Persian period and came from a soul richly endowed with religious feeling.

1–3a. Jehovah as Shepherd Provider. The sheep whom Jehovah shepherds are conscious of no lack (v. 1). He provides the three things needed by sheep—pasturage, rest, and water. To find these together is not easy in Palestine. But the shepherd knows where to find the "fresh shoots of green grass" where he may let the sheep graze and *lie down* (v. 2a). He knows how to *lead* the flock along the current of the torrential mountain wadies, until he finds a clear, placid pool of *still water*, i.e., "waters of quietness," where the sheep may drink with comfort and safety (v. 2b), and find the refreshment that recreates and *restores* (v. 3a).

3b, 4. Jehovah as Shepherd Guide and Guardian. The shepherd leads his sheep in "right tracks" (v. 3b), in trails that lead somewhere, for the shepherd knows the paths over rocky highland and open valley, and his "reputation" (*name*) as a shepherd is at stake (v. 3b; cf. Jer. 14[7] Ezek. 20[9]). When the sun is sinking and the *deep* shadows (in v. 4a read mg.) fall upon the valleys and gorges bringing peril of attack from wild animals or robbers, the sheep are not afraid. There is their guardian with his "club" (*rod*) heavily nailed at the end, and with his *staff*, with which he beats down leaves (Koran 20[9]) for his sheep. With such protection the sheep are made comfortable (v. 4b). Through such Palestinian pictures of ordinary daily life the psalmist portrays what Jehovah is to him personally in life's valleys and highlands. The imagery applies both to his physical and spiritual life. The shepherd care of God is grounded in his very nature. *For his name's sake* (v. 3b) means that God's honor is at stake in caring for his own (cf. Ezek. 36[22f.]).

5, 6. Jehovah as Host. The figure changes. Jehovah, the psalmist's host, spreads before him a table of bounty. The psalmist is an honored guest and (what gives the picture peculiar zest) his *enemies*, the insulting, ungodly Jews, are looking on as Jehovah treats him with Oriental courtesy (v. 5a). As in the ancient Egyptian custom, a lump of scented ointment is placed upon the heads of banquet guests (see 133[2], and cf. Blackman in Simpson, *The Psalmists*, p. 196), so Jehovah anoints his head (v. 5b). A cup of wine brim full is handed him. One senses the lifting tone of wonder and gratitude which rises to its climax. What he now enjoys is but prophetic of what he will enjoy his life long. *Goodness* and *mercy*, personified as angelic spirits, will ever "pursue" him, and—here with tender, heartfelt exaggeration—he will practically spend his days in the Temple, where God is peculiarly near (cf. 27[4] 61[4]; also Anna in Lk. 2[37]). The Temple and its worship he views as the symbol of the favor of God.

Psalm 24. The Liturgy of Jehovah's Entrance into the Temple

This psalm is composed of three originally independent poems. Two of them, vv. 3–6 and 7–10, are concerned with entrance into the Temple. The two were brought together, prefaced by an ancient hymn, vv. 1, 2, and the whole constructed as a liturgy sung at the entrance of the ark into the Jerusalem Temple at the annual New Year's festival. Mowinckel connects it with the annual ritual of the enthronement of Jehovah (cf. Robinson's chapter, "Eschatology of the Psalmists," in Simpson, *The Psalmists*, p. 191). Vv. 1, 2 are very old and embody primitive cosmology; vv. 3–6 may be based upon Isa. 33[14-16] (cf. also Psa. 15, with which it has close contact); these verses may date (so Kittel) from the century preceding the Exile. Vv. 7–10 are also preexilic: Jehovah is a god of war; the Temple gates are already ancient (v. 7); we are therefore centuries beyond David and Solomon.

1, 2. A Hymn Celebrating God the Creator. Jehovah's world dominion, a favorite theme of Hebrew hymns, rests upon his creatorship. V. 2 contains a reference to the ancient cosmology which held that under the earth there was an enormous mass of water (cf. Gen. 7[11] 49[25d] Ex. 20[4]; see further, pp. 126–7). The Babylonians shared this view. But Jehovah has *established* the earth upon these chaotic floods, firm and enduring. The primitive cosmology here is subservient to the author's ethical theism.

3–6. A Liturgy of Entrance for Worshipers. This was rendered antiphonally. By the *holy place* is meant Jerusalem. The worshipers ask the question (v. 3), "Who can worship Jehovah in his Temple?" The answer is sung by the priestly choir (vv. 4–6). The requirements show the influence of the prophets (cf. the ancient answer in the Code of the Covenant, Ex. 23[1-4]). They are purity of action and motive, "lifting the soul," i.e., setting the desire not upon falsehood in action, but upon God. Such a worshiper will be welcomed by God and allowed to draw near to receive his revelation.

7–10. The Entrance of the Ark into the Temple. The festal procession has reached the doors of the Temple. It is the ark of the covenant, the ancient symbol of Jehovah's presence, that is entering, the *King of Glory*, i.e., the "Majestic King." The choir outside the Temple calls upon the *everlasting*, i.e., ancient, Temple doors to open. The expression involves a majestic personification. From within a single voice challenges, "Who is the Majestic King?" The choir without answers, glorifying Jehovah as a god of war. We feel the splendor of this deposit out of the heroic days of Israel. Again the choir without calls upon the doors to open (v. 9), and the single voice within again challenges. Once more the choir without answers, now calling him by the ancient name, "Jehovah Sabaoth," which means, "Jehovah of hosts," and emphasizes the warlike character of Israel's God. The connection of the word *glory* points with certainty to the ark, which symbolized Jehovah's presence, especially in battle (cf. 1 Sam. 4[21f.]). At the mention of his name, which the psalmist withholds until now (v. 10b), the gates open and the procession enters. This is one of the most majestic portions of the Psalter and retains an atmosphere of inexpressible grandeur.

Psalm 25. The Lift of the Soul to God

This psalm is an acrostic (cf. introductory notes to Psa. 9 and 10). With two slight emendations in v. 5c and v. 18a we have a perfect acrostic, every letter of the Hebrew alphabet being represented in twenty-one verses, the last, v. 22, being a liturgical addition. The psalm is late, revealing the influence of the great prophetic teachers and of the wisdom poetry (vv. 12–14 and 4b). The psalmist is in distress because of many enemies (vv. 2, 17, 19). But deeper than this is his sense of sin, which permeates the entire psalm. V. 7 recalls the sins of his youth; he is conscious that his iniquity is great (vv. 11b, 18b), and prays that "sinners" may be instructed in life's way (v. 8b). The alphabetic scheme somewhat binds him and makes it difficult to discern marked logical order in the arrangement of his thoughts.

1–7. An Utterance of Trust and Petition. The psalmist emphasizes as the basis of his petitions the ancient goodness of God revealed in history (vv. 6, 7).

8–15. The Character of God and His Gracious Dealings. He enumerates *justice, loving-kindness* and *truth*, i.e., loyalty—all prophetic characteristics—and considers the regard of Jehovah for his own honor as the ground of his request for forgiveness (cf. Ezek. 36[22f.]).

16–21. His Petitions. He prays in his weakness and isolation (v. 16) for Jehovah's gracious comradeship. In v. 17 read, with slight change of verb, *The straits of my heart enlarge.* Note in v. 21 the poetic and beautiful personification of two prophetic qualities, *integrity* and *uprightness*—literally, "straightness."

22. A Liturgical Addition. The ending adapts this individual psalm to the uses of congregational worship. Peters considers it a litany for the celebration of a fast. The keen sense of sin expressed would well serve such a purpose.

Psalm 26. A Declaration of Innocency

The psalmist's life, in common with that of others, is in peril (v. 9). Some sickness or epidemic is removing men right and left (v. 9). For many death is what they deserve, for their lives are full of infamy and corruption of justice (v. 10). But not so with him. In sincere though exalted consciousness of superiority to them in conduct and character (vv. 4f.), he pleads with God for escape from the fate in store for them (v. 9). The psalm is a lamentation of the individual and, according to our standards, has a strong Pharisaic note of self-conscious righteousness. The psalmist, however, is heir to the inward self-scrutinizing religious experience of Jeremiah. His words come from a time when psalm-singing was at its best in Jewish worship (vv. 6–8).

1–3. He Opens His Integrity to the Scrutiny of God. He does not fear but welcomes God's inspection even to the dominant affections of his heart. He is here using the familiar and characteristic thoughts of Jer. 17^{10} and 20^{12}.

4, 5. The Superiority of His Character. In what strikes us as bold self-righteousness he makes claim to superiority in character over those whose peril he shares. We are reminded of the Pharisee's prayer, "God, I thank thee that I am not as the rest of men" (Lk. 18^{11}). H. Wheeler Robinson reminds us, however, that historical exegesis would have to recognize the validity of his claim (*The Psalmists*, p. 54). But the righteousness here referred to is chiefly negative.

6–8. His Regular Participation in Temple Worship. The tenses of the verbs in v. 6 are frequentative imperfects, to be rendered not as futures but as what one is accustomed to do, i.e., "Again and again I wash my hands in innocency." He mentions in vv. 6, 7 three acts of the ritual which accompanies the sacrifice (cf. Deut. 21^{1-8} for a ritual used with the profession of innocency). Words and acts of ritual went together (cf. Gressmann, *The Psalmists*, pp. 11f.): (1) This symbolic washing of the hands (v. 6a) was probably the first act of the ritual. (2) The second act was walking around the altar (v. 6b; cf. 118^{27b}). Psa. 42^4 also just suggests such a picture—a throng of worshipers in joyous exalted emotion moving in rhythmic steps about the altar, the central point in the sanctuary. (3) The third is the song of praise (v. 7a), which probably accompanied the procession. The subject of the song is a characteristic theme of Hebrew hymns, the "wonderful acts" of Jehovah. This vivid glimpse which the psalmist gives of himself at worship is closed with a beautiful heart utterance of love for the Temple (v. 8; cf. 27^4 84).

9–11. His Plea for Jehovah's Special Concern. Because of his superiority in character and his scrupulous participation in worship (vv. 9, 10), because of his integrity mentioned yet once again (v. 11, cf. v. 1) he pleads for a special treatment. *They* deserve nothing better but *he* does.

12. He Will Praise Jehovah for Deliverance. In anticipation of Jehovah's answer he feels secure. In this same place, again will he join the congregation in their praise of Jehovah. The peril of the Judaism of our psalmist's day was that it should exhaust itself in outer rites while lacking a deep inwardness of piety that trusts less in self and more in God. This limitation is evident throughout the psalm.

Psalm 27. Fearless Trust in God

This psalm is composed of two originally independent poems. (1) *Jehovah the Highest Good* (vv. 1–6). (2) *The Disowned Psalmist Cries unto God* (vv. 7–14).

(1) The psalmist is one of the Dispersion, far away from Jerusalem, and his soul is filled with longing for the Temple worship (v. 4). It is his one prayer. Surrounded by enemies, faced by grave peril, which he compares to the attack of wild animals or the siege of an army (vv. 2, 3), he is not afraid. Trust in Jehovah has conquered his fear. Although he cannot worship in the Temple, he is sure of Jehovah's protection. It is one of the most precious of the songs of trust in the Psalter. It is both tender and majestic.

1–3. His Unconditional Confidence in God. Light, safety, place of refuge—all this is Jehovah to his life. His faith has cast out his dread.

4–6. His Greatest Desire—to live forever in the Temple (cf. 23^6). Three things the Temple gives him: (1) The first, to behold the *beauty*, i.e., pleasantness, loveliness, delightfulness—all conceived as moral qualities—of Jehovah. This reminds us of a line in an Egyptian prayer to Amon: "Grant unto me, that mine eyes may see thy beauty." The psalmist is not thinking of an image of God but of those sacred symbols in the Temple that make God real and bring him near. (2) The second, to *inquire*, i.e., to seek, consider, reflect. To behold beauty is at least in part physical. To inquire is mental, brooding over the meaning and message of the visible symbols. Note the union of adoration and the spirit of inquiry —not mutually antagonistic, but the one providing the right atmosphere for the other. (3) The third, the assurance that Jehovah will *keep* him—furnish a place of shelter in dark days. He employs three vivid pictures of Jehovah's shelter:

He will *hide* him in his thicket.
He will *conceal* him in the covering of his tent.
He will *lift* him upon an inaccessible rock.

He rises from this thought to a greater one. He is far away from the Temple but now, in this faith which the recall of the Temple has awakened, he is superior to his enemies, beyond the reach of their evil intent. In some future day again the privilege of sacrifice and song shall be his!

(2) The spirit of vv. 7–14 differs somewhat from vv. 1–6, but the two sections are alike in the reality of their trust in God. The psalmist is in a trying position. Forsaken by his parents (v. 10), falsely accused and cruelly treated by his enemies (vv. 11b, 12), and feeling himself under the displeasure of God, he cries out to him in a passionate lamentation. Briggs inclines to a Maccabæan date because of v. 10,

but there is no certain clue to the date of the psalm.

7–12. The Cry to God of a Heart in Misery. Gunkel emends v. 8, connecting it with v. 7b, the whole reading: "Have mercy upon me and answer me, my God, For my heart is distressed. Thy face, Jehovah, do I seek," connecting the last line with v. 9. Both Hebrews and Babylonians used the phrase "to seek the countenance of" with the meaning "to turn to" someone for aid (see 17^{15}, and cf. the letter in the Tel-el-Amarna tablets where a provincial governor is seeking the help of the Egyptian king: "My lord, my god, my sun, what more do I seek? Forever do I seek the beautiful face of my lord the king." Quoted from Simpson, *The Psalmists*, p. 133). V. 9 derives its pathetic intensity from the following verse. His parents have forsaken him. (Read v. 10a mg.) Let not Jehovah do the same! Vv. 10f. give the conception of Jehovah adopting him as a son (cf. 2^{7}, where the expression is used of a king). Here it is applied to an ordinary individual. His enemies have made life's *way* anything but *plain*—i.e., level.

13, 14. The Certainty of Jehovah's Answer. Read v. 13 (following J. M. P. Smith), *I believe that I shall see*, etc. In v. 14 he summons his own heart to assert the attitude of waiting for Jehovah.

Psalm 28. The Help of Trust in Peril

In imminent peril of death (v. 1d) from deceitful, treacherous persecutors (v. 3), the psalmist pours out a passionate lamentation unto Jehovah. His prayer is heard and the psalm suddenly changes, at v. 6, from petition into serene gratitude. Vv. 8, 9 adapt a purely individual psalm for use in the king's Temple at Jerusalem. The psalm is pre-exilic, coming from the late years of the Judæan kingdom.

1, 2. The Psalmist's Cry to God. His address to God as *my rock* may be compared to the similar Babylonian address "great mountain," or "God my mountain" (cf. 18^{2}, notes). If help does not come, death at the hands of his persecuting enemies is certain. V. 2b is a valuable source for the posture in prayers of lamentation. The suppliant either stands or prostrates himself before the Temple and stretches out his hands toward the *holy oracle*, i.e., the holy of holies (cf. 44^{20} 63^{4} 1 Tim. 2^{8}).

3–5. His Petition. He prays first for protection. *Draw me not away* (v. 3)—wicked men are threatening his life. He sees through their deceit and prays for escape from their plots. Mowinckel advances the novel theory that the *workers of iniquity* here and elsewhere in the psalms (especially 6, 26, 31, 35, 41–43, 51, 54, 63 and 120) are sorcerers, seeking by magic to accomplish their evil designs (cf. *The Psalmists*, p. 112). As for them, however (vv. 4, 5), let them have what they deserve (cf. 7^{16}, notes). He stands under the influence of an emerging individualism in retribution, which indicates a time close to Jeremiah (cf. Jer. $31^{29, 30}$).

6, 7. His Confession of Faith. The lament changes suddenly to eager praise. He is certain that his prayer has been heard and he has experienced the help of trust in God. A song replaces his cry of distress.

8, 9. A Petition for People and King. These verses are extraordinarily important. They are almost exactly like $61^{6, 7}$ 63^{11} 84^{9} (cf. also 1 Sam. 2^{10}), and all these passages are to be studied together. They are additions adapting an individual psalm to use in the Temple at Jerusalem, which is the place where the king worships. They are here a prayer for the king (v. 8b) and the people (v. 9a). They prove the pre-exilic origin of such psalms, and are not to be interpreted as Messianic.

Psalm 29. The Voice of Jehovah

Here is a nature psalm of marvelous descriptive and poetic power. The phrase *qôl Yahweh*, i.e., the "voice of Jehovah," seven times uttered, gives the impression of clap upon clap of thunder. Welch recalls Byron's, "From peak to peak the echoing crags among leaps the live thunder." The thunder is Jehovah's voice, not in anger but in awe-evoking, majestic power. The song is ancient, as its primitive color reveals. The idea of Jehovah as world King in this context is not late but a very early conception. The reference to Hermon as "Sirion" (v. 6b) according to the Phœnician usage, is evidence that it comes from the Northern Kingdom and so that it is earlier than 722 B.C.

The reference to far-away Kadesh (v. 8) recalls the experience of Moses at Sinai and the theophany in a storm (cf. Ex. 19^{19}). The terror of the storm causes the hinds to give birth prematurely. In v. 9b the text is imperfect. Gunkel emends to read, "It freights the chamois with lightning." The Temple, the majestic structure and all its magnificent appointments, responds to Jehovah's voice in the unanimity of a single word, spoken in awed recognition of his grandeur—*Glory!* In his mighty, seemingly destructive voice they hear a gracious accent and discover a steadfast purpose in which there is no caprice. (Cf. Coleridge, *Hymn Before Sunrise.*)

1, 2. The Adoration of the Heavenly Court.

The *sons of the mighty* are summoned to *ascribe* —literally, "give"—their tribute of praise to Jehovah. The phrase marks the superhuman character of those addressed. It may be paraphrased, "Ye heavenly powers" (Welch, *The Psalter*, p. 16). Compare the similar conception in Babylonian thought:

"When thy word rings out in heaven, let the Igigi throw themselves down on their faces;
"When thy word rings out on earth, let the Anunnaki kiss the ground."

The Igigi represent the stars, the gods of the upper world, and the Anunnaki, the gods of the lower world (G. R. Driver in Simpson, *The Psalmists*, p. 153). Note the ascending parallelism in v. 2a. *Beauty of holiness* (cf. A.S.V., "array")—garbed as priestly ministers the heavenly powers are to worship Jehovah.

3–9. The Seven Claps of Thunder. Peters calls the whole psalm, "The Song of Seven Thunders." Seven times occurs the staccato phrase, *qôl Yahweh,* the "voice of Jehovah." The assonance in Hebrew is indescribably effective, and descriptive in extraordinary degree of seven successive thunderclaps. There is here suggested likewise a primitive sense of awe which the mysterious thunder always awakens in men's hearts. No other physical phenomenon made so deep an impression upon the Hebrew heart as thunder. What the Babylonians attribute to Ramman and Adad, and the Hittites to Tesup, the Hebrews attribute to Jehovah. This shows the inevitable bent toward monotheism in Hebrew thought (cf. 18^{13} Isa. 30^{30} Jer. 25^{30} Amos 1^{2}, etc.). The psalmist pictures the effect of thunder upon (1) the sea and (2) the land; (3) in the animal world and (4) in the Temple. *The waters*—carries the atmosphere of the mythical primeval deeps (cf. $93^{3,\ 4}$, where the language is figuratively used). There is a primitive grandeur in this conception. The lightning splits the strong Lebanon cedars. The mountains Lebanon and Hermon tremble from earthquake. How vivid the anthropomorphism! This is their happy dance at the voice of Jehovah (cf. $114^{4,\ 6}$). According to the poet's conception the flashes of lightning are cloven into forks by the thunder.

10, 11. Jehovah King Over Israel. There is reference here again to the mythological conception of the subterranean deep over which Jehovah is master (cf. Gen. 1^{7}, etc.). The universalistic implications of the references to Jehovah's relations to nature are not followed out. In the last verse the psalmist focuses his attention upon Israel, Jehovah's people. All this majestic power, to which even all nature responds, is for Israel! It took the later thinkers to discover that it was for mankind.

Psalm 30. Thanksgiving for Recovery from Illness

The psalmist had been living in careless security, seemingly held in honor by Jehovah (vv. 6, 7). Then came the disillusioning experience of a serious illness in which he was at the doors of death (v. 3). In his dangerous condition he prayed for help (vv. 2, 8–10), and was restored to health (v. 1). In profound gratitude he celebrated a feast of thanksgiving (v. 11), the inner circle of the loyal participating with him (v. 4). He tells his experience in two parallel cycles (v. 1=11, 12; 2, 3=8–10; 4, 5=11, 12). The superscription which seems to connect the psalm with the feast celebrating the rededication of the Temple (Chislev 25, 165 B.C.; cf. 1 Macc. $4^{52f.}$) may have been intended originally as a subscription to Psa. 29, which better suits the occasion. Psa. 30 dates from before the Maccabæan era.

1–3. His Restoration From Severe Illness. His restoration to health has stopped the rejoicings of his enemies who hoped he would die.

4, 5. He Summons the Loyal to Celebrate His Deliverance. The psalmist was a leader of the loyal. His restoration was an occasion of public significance. He invites the loyal to his thanksgiving feast.

He interpreted his sickness as caused by the anger of God, which, in turn, his sin had aroused. His experience led him to make a general observation which he expressed in such perfect form that it has become a classic proverb:

"In the evening weeping may lodge,
But in the morning there is a shout of joy"

(so read v. 5b). Compare the votive stela of the 19th dynasty of Egypt:

"The Lord of Thebes passeth not a whole day wroth,
His wrath is finished in a moment and nought is left" (Blackman in Simpson, *The Psalmists*, p. 186).

6, 7. His Careless Sense of Security. These verses describe his life before his sickness. He had stood high in the regard of men and seemingly in the regard of God. Then had come the disillusioning crash. In v. 7 for *my honor* read, with LXX and Syriac, *my mountain.*

8–10. His Argument With God for Recovery. He bases his petition upon the worth to God of human praise and testimony. His argument (cf. 6^{5} 115^{17}) runs: "What do you gain by causing me to die? If I go down to the grave, there will be one less to utter your praises and tell others of loyalty to you." The psalmist is keenly conscious of the social worth of testimony, the grateful utterance to others of what God has done for us (v. 9).

11, 12. His Tears Turned Into Joy. His prayer is answered and he is restored. He mentions no word concerning a thank-offering, but the reference of v. 11 to the joyous dance about the altar clearly presupposes it (cf. also v. 4a, where he summons others to participate in singing). V. 12 implies the absence of such praise had Jehovah allowed him to join the silent company of the dead.

Psalm 31. A Cry From a Distressed Soul

The psalmist is entangled (v. 4) in grave difficulties (v. 9). He is in keen physical suffering that has dragged on for years (v. 10) and death seems near (v. 22). He evidently had become physically repulsive to those who knew him well (v. 11; cf. Job 30[9-31]), and a butt of his enemies' derision. And, what is worse than derision, by some he was ignored (v. 12). Abandoned to loneliness, he called upon God and found relief (v. 22). Kittel's attempt to see in this individual lamentation a prayer liturgy ignores the personal color of the psalm. It is late, certainly after Jeremiah (cf. Jer. 20[10] with v. 13); reminiscences of other psalms (e.g., 9[1] 18[2] 23[3] 38[4] 55[5]) suggest a late period in post-exilic Judaism. See also *his saints* (v. 23), i.e., his pious ones.

1–8. Petitions for Help and Assertions of Trust. He bases his appeal upon Jehovah's own honor. V. 5 is made sacred through its quotation by Jesus on the cross (cf. Lk. 23[46]); incidentally, a suggestion that this psalm was familiar to and loved by Jesus. His enemies were evidently idolaters (v. 6). *Large place* (v. 8) = "wide place," contrasted with *adversities* (v. 7) = "straits."

9–13. Lamentation From a Suffering Heart. In these verses are concentrated the circumstances that give rise to the passionate lament of a bursting heart. See introductory notes to the psalm.

14–18. Recovery for Him but Death for His Enemies! V. 15 is the source of Browning's familiar line in *Rabbi Ben Ezra*. What the wicked have desired for *him*, let happen to *them!* (V. 17.) Note (v. 18) the psalmist's sensitiveness to the *lips*, i.e., the "talk" of his enemies (cf. vv. 13, 20). His was a sensitive nature, akin to that of Jeremiah.

19–22. His Confession of Confidence. Between vv. 18 and 19, we are to infer, his prayer of vv. 1–8 has been answered. Note the vivid comparison in v. 21. In the onslaught of his difficulties he had felt like a besieged city.

23, 24. An Exhortation to the Loyal. This exhortation gains weight and concrete color through the experience of the psalmist. It is not a pious ejaculation but a stirring, personal testimony of the grace and judgment of God.

Psalm 32. Thanksgiving for Forgiveness

The psalmist was in keen physical pain. He was becoming more and more exhausted (v. 3), and the very sap of life seemed to be drying up (v. 4). He knew it was because he had sinned, but for a time he refrained from confessing it. At length, driven to the acknowledgment of his sin (v. 5), he was forgiven and his life preserved (v. 7). In the spirit of the sages of Israel he turns instructor (vv. 8, 9). His experience has qualified him to be a spiritual guide of others. This wisdom atmosphere in the psalm is a clue to its date, which is the late post-exilic period (cf. p. 157b).

1, 2. Beatitudes of Forgiveness. Translate (cf. Psa. 1) as exclamations, *Oh the happiness of him*, etc. In these opening verses rings the thrilling note of personal experience. The psalmist can say, "I know." He uses four words for moral offense: *transgression*, *sin*, *iniquity* and *guile*, i.e., treachery.

3, 4. His Guilt Unacknowledged. *When I kept silent*—i.e., he did not confess his sin, and consequently felt heavy upon him the punishing hand of God. His sickness he interpreted as the definite result of God's displeasure. This direct relationship between guilt and physical suffering was one of the most deeply rooted dogmas of Judaism. The converse doctrine was also held that whoever experienced misfortune was guilty of some known or hidden sin. Against this dogma great spirits like the author of Job hurled the weight of their genius. The psalmist suggestively portrays an implicit contrast. Before God he exhibited silence, but inwardly his conscience was crying out in distress.

5. The Way to Health and Peace. At length the hard pressure of God's hand (cf. v. 4) won out and brought him to courageous repentance. Jehovah forgave him and (it is implied) he was delivered from his illness (cf. Prov. 28[13]).

6, 7. The Practical Lesson of His Experience. The psalmist becomes exhorter and with a reminiscence of Isa. 55[6] he calls every one that is *godly* to prayer, evidently to the prayer of repentance. So will they escape the floods of misfortune into which the lack of the repentant spirit had brought him. In v. 7 he reverts to his own experience. *Songs*—literally, "ringing cries." Even when the spiritual experience of forgiveness (vv. 1, 2) is allowed to color these verses we sense a limitation in the psalmist's interest in forgiveness. It is too materialistic. He does not emphasize the painful memory of his sins, but rather lingers in the thought of escape from trouble (cf. v. 10). Nor does he call the sinners but the righteous to repentance (v. 6).

8, 9. The Psalmist Turns Sage. Note the change to the second person. In the manner of Proverbs he speaks to fiery youth and shows the influence of the wisdom temper in Judaism. The figures are not of stubbornness but of abounding energy that needs guidance.

10, 11. The Lot of the Godless and the Loyal. The limitation noted in vv. 6, 7 recurs here. The psalm ends in the mood of joy.

Psalm 33. Thanksgiving for National Deliverance

This is a song of national deliverance. Noting reminiscences of Isaiah (cf. v. 17 with Isa. 31[1f.]) and the atmosphere of marvelous deliverance (v. 10) that breathes through the psalm, Kittel inclines to connect it with Sennacherib's invasion in 701 B.C. (cf. Isa. 37[36f.]) and views it as coming from one who had heard Isaiah and had learned from him, but had not grasped his deepest thought. However, the clear influence of the priestly account of creation (cf. v. 6 with Gen. 1[6]), the reminiscences of Deutero-Isaiah (cf. v. 11 with Isa. 40[8] 46[10]), and other still later passages, make a post-exilic date practically certain. The psalm is tinged with views concerning divine speech and divine wisdom (v. 6) which consider them not merely as instruments but as agents in the process of creation (so Robinson in Simpson, *The Psalmists*, p. 30), a viewpoint fully developed in late Judaism, climaxing in Philo. The strong nationalism of the psalm, with Jewish self-consciousness running high (vv. 10, 12), points almost certainly to the Maccabæan period (Olshausen, Briggs), to some great victory that profoundly stirred the psalmist. The twenty-two verses seem built upon the existence of twenty-two letters in the alphabet, but do not form an acrostic.

1–3. Introduction to the Hymn. For the occasion celebrated no familiar song will suffice; so the Temple choir is called upon to sing a new song, probably this song written under the exalting influence of the very victory it celebrates.

4–9. The Word of Jehovah. This victory is no human achievement. Behind it was the creative *word* of Jehovah: (1) His word expresses his nature, which is "righteous," and "just" and "loyal." Literally, "the word of Jehovah is straight." (2) His word is creative. As at creation he said, "Let there be light" and "there was light," so now, what has happened is the awesome result of his word (vv. 8, 9). Only the strong instincts of monotheism could keep the word, thus conceived, unseparated from God's essence (cf. Jn. 1[14], notes). V. 7a offers a vivid comparison. For *as an heap* read, with LXX, *as in a skin*. This makes the parallelism with v. 7b complete.

10–12. Deliverance from Heathen Enemies. Wellhausen rightly translates *nations* as *heathen* and at once we feel ourselves in the Maccabæan struggles against the Hellenizing Syrians. Render the verbs as perfects. *Jehovah hath brought*, etc., *he hath made*, etc. (v. 10). In a single remarkable victory for the Jews, Jehovah has shown himself again the God of Israel, his covenant people (v. 12).

13–19. The Eye of Jehovah. The thought of deliverance by Jehovah leads the psalmist to speak in meditative vein about the all-seeing *eye* of God, first (vv. 13–15), penetrating into the plotting hearts of Israel's enemies, and second (vv. 16–18), seeing the dire need of his people and coming (*he*, not horses or armies) to their help. In their imminent peril of defeat and death he comes to those who trust in him (cf. Isa. 7[9] 28[16]). How much greater is the help of God than the help of horses and armies! He had learned of Isaiah (cf. 31[1f.]) the might of trust in God.

20–22. An Utterance of Confidence and Hope. The deliverance which has stirred the psalmist's soul leads him to an abiding attitude of trust in the *name* (v. 21)—i.e., the nature, of God. The psalm rises to the note of benediction. It begins with a ringing cry. It ends (see mg.) in up-reaching waiting before God (v. 22). These verses are specially fitted for utterance in a hymn.

Psalm 34. The Teaching Content of a Great Release

The psalmist had been in grave difficulties—in terrors (v. 4), straits (vv. 6, 17), and peril to life and limb (v. 20). He was not of the upper classes, but of the meek, "one of the poor, weak, and afflicted" in Israel (v. 2). He calls himself "this poor man" (v. 6). Yet—and the wonder of it is aglow in his heart—Jehovah had heard and delivered him! Released from his distress—what it was we do not know (Gunkel thinks illness)—he becomes evangelist, summoning his fellow Jews to experimental relationship with God (v. 8). His mood suddenly changes at v. 11 from evangelist to teacher and the psalm issues in a didactic poem quite in the style of Proverbs 1–9 and Ecclesiasticus. The psalm shows the influence of Isa. 56–66 (cf. v. 18 with Isa. 57[15]), and the didactic method of vv. 11f. points to the influence of the Wisdom literature. It probably comes from the times just preceding the beginnings of the Greek period, from the first half of the 4th century B.C. It is an alphabetic acrostic (cf. Psa. 9, etc.).

1–3. An Invitation to Praise. Out of a full heart overflowing with gratitude the psalmist invites others—the *meek*, i.e., the teachable and humble—to praise Jehovah with him. He knew the mutual enrichment and impetus that comes from common worship. *With me* and *together* are the strong words of v. 3.

4–7. His Experience of God. His experience he summarizes in a single verse; he sought and found God, and with it release from terror (v. 4). Then he expands it (vv. 5–7). Read v. 5 (following LXX and other ancient versions and MSS.) with Hitzig,

"Look unto me and be radiant
And your faces will not be ashamed."

He himself is an example of what God can do. "If filled with a sense of shame," he says, "look at me and remember God can do as much for you." This makes easy and natural the transition to v. 6 where he carries the note of personal experience further and rises to a classic generalization (v. 7). Note the military figure. The religious man is protected by the unseen power of Jehovah.

8–10. The Psalmist Turns Evangelist. His own experience leads him to summon others to the laboratory test of relationship with God. His reason is chiefly a material one (v. 10b). The promise of v. 10b gains in vigor of contrast when in v. 10a instead of *young lions* we translate the word, which is Aramaic, "deniers of God." While those who deny God suffer want, is his thought, the righteous are provided life's necessities.

11–22. The Psalmist Turns Sage. The psalm at this point moves into the didactic temper and deals with the problem of retribution. The experience of the psalmist has given him the right to teach others, which he proceeds to do. *The fear of Jehovah* is equivalent to "religion" (v. 11). He uses the question and answer method, characteristic of the wise men. V. 12 asks the question, vv. 13f. answer it. The way to *life* or to the *good* is (1) negative, "desist from evil words and deeds," for the Lord is against evil men (v. 16); (2) it is positive, "do good, devote yourself to peace"—the establishment of wholesome relations with all men and with God. Such men Jehovah "sees," "hears" (v. 15) and "delivers" (v. 17). V. 18 is a reminiscence from Isa. 57[15]. Vv. 19–22 expound the view of retribution characteristic of Judaism: the exact proportion of punishment to guilt and of reward to virtue. It was against this dogma which had a throttle-hold upon Judaism far down into the N.T. period that the author of Job, a little later, battled with the creative vigor of his pioneering mind.

Psalm 35. A Lamentation From One of the "Quiet in the Land"

The psalmist is a leader of the "quiet in the land" (v. 20b), the inner circle of peacemakers and patient followers of Jehovah. His cause (v. 27) is a matter of public concern. Surrounded by opponents (v. 1), pursued (v. 3), plotted against (v. 7) and even robbed (v. 10c), he utters his lamentation to Jehovah. When those now his enemies were his friends and ill, he had dealt with them as with his own people (vv. 13f.). But how differently they reciprocated! (V. 15.) He pleads for rescue from them and utters a vow of thanksgiving which upon deliverance he will pay in the Temple in the presence of the worshiping congregation (v. 18). The first cycle of his lamentation climaxes in this vow. At v. 19 begins a new cycle that parallels the first. Here the appeal is more directly for visible punishment upon his enemies (v. 26) and for visible evidences to the "quiet in the land" of his integrity. This second movement likewise closes with a vow (v. 28). The psalm shows reminiscences of other poems in the Psalter, having most contact with 55, 59, and 69. The psalm mirrors the background of Isa. 56–66 (460–445 B.C.).

1–8. A Passionate Prayer for Deliverance From His Enemies and for Judgment Upon Them. *My soul*, as so often in the psalms, means "my life." Note, in vv. 5, 6, the two pictures showing the psalmist's enemies in precipitate defeat—*chaff before the wind*, and as "pushed from behind" in *dark* and *slippery* places; in both cases behind them and hurrying them to destruction is the angel of God. Omit *in a pit* (v. 7).

9, 10. His Contemplated Joy at Release. *Soul* (v. 9) and *all my bones* (v. 10), i.e., the psalmist's whole being, will rejoice.

11–17. His Treatment by His Enemies Contrasted with the Treatment He has Given His Enemies. Those now his enemies deal with him as with a clandestine malefactor (v. 16; cf. Job 30[25]). In this section we are in closest contact with the similar portrayal in Job, for those who now are his enemies were once his friends (vv. 13, 14). Their attitude now reminds him of lions roaring as they leap upon their prey. In v. 16a read, with LXX, *They tried me, they held me in derision. My darling* (v. 17)—cf. 22[20], notes.

18. His Vow of Public Thanksgiving. If released, he will offer a thank-offering before the congregation in the Temple.

19–21. He Reverts to His Enemies' Treat-

ment of Him. *Wink with the eye*—in sly deceit. *Quiet in the land*—i.e., the peacemaking religiously-minded circle from which in large part came the Psalms (cf. Lk. 1^5–2^39).

22–26. His Final Appeal to God. Note vigorous contrast between *Thou hast seen* (v. 22) and *our eye has seen* (v. 21).

27, 28. A Prayer for Joyous Vindication before his followers and a restatement of his vow.

PSALM 36. THE TRIUMPHANT MIGHT OF THE GOODNESS OF GOD

The psalmist, in peril at the hands of evil men (v. 11), portrays the sinful heart of man as an evil spirit uttering to his innermost being an oracle (v. 1a). The content of the oracle is left a mystery, but the depravity it gradually accomplishes is brilliantly described (vv. 1b–4).

At v. 5 the psalm swings with dramatic abruptness from "the rise and progress of sin" (McFadyen) to the contemplation of the goodness, the kindness and the mercy of God alike in nature (vv. 5, 6) and in human life (vv. 7, 8). The meditation rises into prayer (vv. 10, 11) for the triumph of Jehovah's loving-kindness over the arrogance of the evil men (cf. vv. 1–7). The psalmist leaves us solemn and awe-struck in the presence of his vision—the forces of evil decisively and finally defeated (v. 12).

The psalm, in spite of the sharp break of thought at v. 5, is a unity. The first four verses are but a foil brilliantly used to form a background of moving darkness against which to picture the goodness of God. With splendid restraint vv. 11, 12 bring us back into the theme of vv. 1–4. V. 12 bears to vv. 1–4 and vv. 5–8 the relation of conclusion to minor and major premises. The psalm comes from post-exilic times; it was written in a period of party stress within Judaism.

1–4. The Progress of Evil in the Sinful Man's Heart. The progressive mastery of the "evil spirit" at work within the human heart is expounded: (1) The oracle it utters within his heart encourages him to believe his sin will not be found out. In v. 2a read with mg. *It* (i.e., sin) *flattereth him in his eyes.* (2) His words become deceitful and his actions careless (v. 3). (3) With deliberation he sets himself at sinful matters without revulsion (v. 4).

5–9. The Goodness of God. Here in five verses is one of the most beautiful hymns in the Psalter. Vv. 5, 6 deal with the goodness of God in the natural universe. Through figures of vastness—the wide expanse of the heavens and the immeasurable height of the skies, the rugged steadfastness of the *mountains of God*, and the unsoundable profundity of the mythical *deep* (in Babylonian doctrine "the deep sea" was considered the seat of wisdom)—the character qualities of God, his loving-kindness, his loyalty, his righteousness and his justice are suggested.

Vv. 7–9 deal with the goodness of God in the human world, but every blessing dealt with is spiritual and the atmosphere of personal experience is felt. Here is deep spiritual religion. This great God, so he feels, is for us—for us poor human beings—even *the children of men.* Note the beautiful metaphor of protection in v. 7b. The psalmist is a loyal worshiper in the Temple (v. 8) and prizes the sacrificial meal, i.e., *fatness* and *drink* as sacraments, symbols of a divine bliss which these help him to express. Where God is—for him primarily in the Temple —are *life* and *light* (cf. Num. 6^25, 26). What life and light he enjoys have their source in the heart of God—great and deep thoughts in Israel's religion at its best.

10–12. Jehovah's Triumph Over Evil. The psalmist prays that this goodness, this *loving-kindness*, may guard him against his arrogant enemies. *There* (v. 12)—i.e., in a vision that fills him and us with the mood of awe—he pictures the evil forces, which in vv. 1–4 were mustering into aggression, as utterly, finally and irretrievably defeated by the might of the character of God.

PSALM 37. GOD'S CARE OF THE LOYAL

This is an acrostic poem. It is one of the wisdom psalms, having closest contact with Psa. 49 and 73. It is full of exhortations and warnings, proverbs and promises. The speaker is an old man (v. 25) and in his observations one feels the weight of his mature experience (vv. 35f.). The subject of the psalm is the doctrine of retribution (cf. Jer. 12^1f. Mal. 2^17), a characteristic theme in the late Wisdom literature (cf. Prov. 24^19 Job 21^7f. Eccl. 8^14). The author does not expect Jehovah to intervene, to strike down the wicked man. Contrast the psalms of lamentation. He believes that wickedness has no stability. It falls of itself. Moreover, the retribution of God is not conceived as taking place at the judgment. It, rather, is expressed from the standpoint of the righteous peasant who compares the permanency of his hold upon the ancestral soil (v. 11; cf. 25^13) with the rapid, traceless vanishing of the wicked.

The author is dependent upon Job and has reminiscences of many psalms and proverbs, but his ideas do not improve upon the thoughts uttered by the three friends of Job. Kittel draws attention to the two limitations in his solution of his problem: He lacks the idea of an inner judgment not mirrored in outer circumstances, and also that of equalization of lot in after life. The poem is very late, possibly Maccabæan. Those who put it early (e.g., Davison, time of Hezekiah) ignore the connection with other late literature. Tertullian called this psalm "a mirror of Providence," and Luther called it "a garment for the godly with the inscription 'Here is the patience of the saints.' "

1–11. Admonitions for Periods of Stress and Strain. It is foolish to complain at the seeming prosperity of the wicked. The psalmist counsels the afflicted to wait and see what will happen. The prosperity of the wicked will not last, nor will his memory endure. V. 11 furnishes the source of Mt. 5[5]. A quiet, unobtrusive religious optimism is expounded in this first section.

12–20. The Destiny of the Sinful. Evil is suicidal; it is self-destroying. Righteousness makes for permanency; but sinners are as transient as dry grass to which a match has been struck.

21–31. Jehovah's Considerate Care of the Faithful. The note of personal experience, in v. 25, is a welcome release from the typical and somewhat monotonous wisdom style of address. From youth to age his eye sweeps the horizon of the years. He has never seen righteous men abandoned nor their descendants beggars. In a land where beggars are numerous this takes on new color. V. 31 reveals the interest of the loyal in the Law. Religion is life under the Law.

32–40. Observation of the Retributive Principle. The prosperity of the sinful is but transient. The righteous man may suffer for the present but he will end his life in peace.

Psalm 38. The Prayer of a Penitent Sufferer

This is a lamentation of an individual. The psalmist is very ill (v. 3), with a painful (vv. 2, 7) and loathsome (vv. 5a, 11) skin disease (vv. 3a, 7b). This illness he attributes to the discipline of Jehovah, which he has brought down upon himself by his sin (v. 4) and folly (v. 5b). His kinsmen consequently have abandoned him (v. 11) and have become his enemies (v. 12). Yet he does not retaliate in kind (vv. 13b, 14b) but turns a deaf ear to his critics and enemies (vv. 13a, 14a). In his loneliness he looks to God for relief (v. 15). He confesses his sin (v. 18) and, confident of an answer (v. 15b), closes with a petition for speedy help (v. 22). This psalm has many reminiscences of Job (see especially 19[13-19]) and of Jer. 4[19] 20[10]. These facts, combined with the use of an Aramaic word in v. 3, point to a late date, probably shortly after 400 B.C. To consider it as "the complaint of the afflicted community" is to miss the intense individualism of the psalm. In the prayer book of the Church of England this is one of seven penitential psalms (the others being 6, 32, 51, 102, 130 and 143).

1–10. His Lamentation Over His Suffering. The psalmist attributes his intense pain to the arrows of God (cf. Job 6[4] and Homer's *Odyssey* 7[64] 15[402] 17[251, 494]). His condition reveals the way in which God shows indignation against sin. Vv. 5–10 describe his suffering more concretely. It reminds us of that of Job and the description points clearly to a burning skin disease which seemed to have its roots deep down within his body. His pain wrings from him groans (vv. 8, 9) and robs life of its joy (v. 10b).

11, 12. The Effect of His Condition on His Friends. His situation dissolves ties of friendship. Read, with Briggs, *my lovers and my friends are at a distance from me* (v. 11a). *They* (v. 12) refers to his lovers, friends and kinsmen. These have now turned against him.

13–20. How He Reacts to Their Treatment. He has no bitter words of condemnation against his enemies. He has nothing vindictive in his heart (vv. 13, 14). His refuge is in God (v. 15), and although he feels himself growing weaker under the strain (v. 17), God will not allow him to be humiliated before those who have treated him disloyally (v. 16). V. 18 connects with v. 15 in thought. His basis for hope in God is his confession of sin and his penitence before God, although he realizes that his attitude of doing what seemed good to him (v. 20b) made his enemies all the more aggressive (vv. 19, 20a).

21, 22. His Petition for Help. He is certain of being heard. Points of contact with this psalm are found in Babylonian psalms of penitence (for vv. 5, 6 see G. R. Driver in Simpson, *The Psalmists*, pp. 129, 135).

Psalm 39. The Transiency and Futility of Human Life

The psalmist, wasting away under a severe illness (vv. 10, 11), due as he thinks to his sin (v. 8), is sorely tempted to impatient utterance in the presence of wicked men. But in spite of the hot fires of his soul's emotion (v. 3) he kept himself in control (v. 2) until his thoughts took definite shape. Then out of this experience comes the burden of the psalm, teaching uttered in meditative prayer—the transiency and futility of human life (vv. 4–6). He prays God for release (vv. 7–11) and recovery (vv. 12, 13). The psalm dates most likely from shortly after the writing of the book of Job, probably in the early fourth century B.C. It came from a creative psalmist of inner richness of spirit.

1–3. The Psalmist Keeping Himself in Control. Severely tried by his suffering and gloating enemies, he kept his mouth closed, refusing to utter words against the divine order. Contrast with Mal. 3[14, 15] and Job. He is not tempted to speak wrongly against his enemies, but against God.

4–6. The Psalmist's Melancholy Resignation. These verses show this psalm to be transitional to the spirit discernible in Ecclesiastes (Balla). He stresses the two major thoughts of the psalm, the transiency of life (vv. 4, 5ab) and the futility of it (vv. 5c, 6). In v. 6 for *in a vain show,* read, with mg., *as a shadow.*

7–11. A Prayer for Release from Discipline. Here the personal note recurs. In confession of sin (v. 8) and in utter dependence upon God (v. 7) in his weakness, he prays for release from the harsh chastening he is experiencing.

12, 13. A Prayer for a Bit of Brightness Before Death. Man is a guest in the household of God, but is destined soon to depart. If he is to have any joy it must come to him during his brief sojourn. In v. 13 read, with mg., *look away from me that I may brighten up.* He seems to feel the persistent and sternly disciplinary eyes of God upon him. "Let God take his eyes off" is his prayer (v. 13), so that he may enjoy a brief respite before his death (cf. Job 7[19] 10[20f.] 14[6]).

PSALM 40. THE THANK-OFFERING JEHOVAH DESIRES

The psalmist, in imminent peril of death (v. 1), has been brought back to health. In gratitude he composes a new song of praise (v. 3), which he proceeds to sing (vv. 4–11). The main theme of the hymn (vv. 6–10) is that while Jehovah requires no sacrificial offering from him, he feels obligated to be a herald of God's goodness to the congregation. The hymn closes with a personal petition. Vv. 1–11 have fallen heir to the richest teaching of the prophets. They come from a period when the Law was at the center but when it was freely interpreted—after Ezra, in the fourth century B.C.

At v. 12 a new poem begins which originally had no connection with vv. 1–11. "The Magnificat is precipitated into the plaintive *De profundis.*" Vv. 13–17 appear again in the Psalter as Psa. 70. They form a lamentation of an individual. Persecuted by enemies (vv. 14, 15) he seeks help for himself from Jehovah (vv. 13, 17) and comfort for the loyal (v. 16). V. 12 is a later addition binding the two psalms into a liturgical composition. This second poem probably dates from before Nehemiah in the first half of the fifth century B.C.

1–3. The Psalmist Relates His Experience. From some situation where death seemed certain, he had been rescued after patient waiting. The underworld, i.e., the *pit,* is here conceived as a deep cistern (cf. 28[1] 30[3, 9] 69[2, 14]). From *miry,* slimy underfooting, so he pictures it, he has been set firmly upon a *rock.* The gratitude of deliverance finds utterance in a *new* song.

4–12. His Hymn of Praise. The hymn begins by praising God indirectly, through a beatitude for his loyal ones; then proceeds in a characteristic hymn theme to praise God for his *wonderful works,* also adding an element not so common—for his *thoughts.* Read, with mg., for v. 5c *There is none to be compared unto thee.* Note that he speaks not of thought but of separate single thoughts.

God requires not sacrifice and offering but heart gratitude (vv. 6–8). The psalmist uses four technical terms of the sacrificial system, *sacrifice,* meal *offering,* in which the worshipers participated, and whole *burnt-offering* and *sin-offering.* But he lines himself up with the great prophetic words of 1 Sam. 15[22] Amos 5[21f.] Hos. 6[6] Isa. 1[11f.] Mic. 6[6-8] Jer. 7[22f.] and similarly minded psalms (e.g., 50[8-13] 51[16f.] 69[31]; cf. Heb. 10[5-7]) in insisting that Jehovah does not require such sacrifice. This is the more significant when we note that he was living under the priestly law, i.e., *the roll of the book* (v. 7), where the sacrificial system was accepted as of central importance. We see that among many spiritually minded circles of the laity the spirit of the prophets still lived. They were able to read the Torah, the Law, with prophetic eyes (vv. 9, 10).

With this psalmist, what in earlier days would have merely accompanied a thank-offering takes the place of it. A hymn sung in connection with the thanksgiving offering becomes simply a spiritual song of thanksgiving, but, as was the case with that accompanying the sacrificial rite, he sings it in the great congregation of the Temple. He does not keep his praise to himself.

Lo, I am come (v. 7)—probably into the Temple. Read, with mg., for v. 7b, *it is prescribed to me.* He comes as did men of old to do the will of God, but this will is not legalistically conceived as the fulfillment of external prescriptions. The Torah he obeys is that expounded in Jer. 31[31f.], the inner prescriptions of the heart. With this section compare the Instruction of Merikere (Egyptian), "more acceptable (to the sun god) is one righteous of heart than the ox of one that worketh iniquity" (Blackman, in Simpson, *The Psalmists*, p. 190). The hymn (vv. 4–11) closes with a personal petition. V. 12 is a harmonistic verse joining the originally separate psalm of lamentation (vv. 13–17) to the foregoing psalm of thanksgiving. Vv. 1–11 deal with his iniquities; the lamentation deals with his enemies.

13–17. A Petition for Personal Deliverance and for Judgment Upon His Enemies. (Cf. Psa. 70.) The circle of the loyal (v. 16), seeing the destruction of the enemy, will praise Jehovah. With great pathos the psalmist reiterates his petition, and the psalm closes with the soul awaiting his urgently needed help.

Psalm 41. A Hymn of Thanksgiving for Deliverance From Illness

Beginning in a manner that shows the influence of the Wisdom teachers of Israel, the psalmist gratefully acknowledges Jehovah as the source of his deliverance from illness. Indulging in reminiscence, he recalls his treatment when ill, at the hands of his enemies and of his intimate friend (vv. 5–9), as well as his former prayer (vv. 4, 10) for relief and restoration to health. His prayer was answered and he recovered. The psalm is post-exilic, showing dependence upon Jeremiah and Job.

1–3. Jehovah the Source of His Recovery. After his recovery the psalmist seems to have meditated upon the question, "Who has a right to expect from Jehovah recovery from illness?" He is not satisfied with saying "he that confesses his sin" (v. 4b). He goes a step further. In addition to this it is "he that showeth consideration to the weak" (v. 1). In words characteristic of the sages in Israel he puts this thought into a beatitude at the very beginning of his psalm. It is Jehovah that kept him alive, when he was languishing upon his bed. The text of v. 3b is uncertain. Gunkel reads, "All his suffering thou turnest into strength."

4–10. His Lamentation Uttered in His Illness. Two things pained him most. First (v. 4b) his consciousness of sin, which he frankly confesses, without revealing its nature; second (v. 5), and this weighs yet more heavily upon him, the treachery and evil hopes of his enemies, who want him to die. They visit him with seeming interest, but are merely seeking information as to his physical condition, and even during the visit they are thinking what they can tell their comrades, secretly confiding to them and exulting over it, that he cannot recover (vv. 7, 8). The climax of this suffering comes when his *own familiar friend*, literally, "the man of my covenant," he who had eaten bread with him at his table, turned traitor (v. 9; cf. Jer. 12[6] Job 19[13-19]). The passionate desire for requital is beneath the temper of the psalm as a whole.

11, 12. His Prayer Has Been Heard. His recovery and the failure of his enemies' hopes are proof of Jehovah's forgiveness. *Forever* he will have the privilege of worship *before thy face*—i.e., in the Temple.

13. The Doxology. Each book of the psalms closes with a doxology (see intro., section on "The Organization of the Psalter," p. 509b).

Psalm 42. Longing for Pilgrimage to the Sanctuary

Psa. 42 and 43 were originally a single poem. Psa. 43 has no superscription, and the refrain found in 42[5, 11] 43[5] conclusively proves the essential oneness of the two psalms in thought and artistic construction. The psalmist is deeply depressed (cf. the refrain) and for some reason unable to make the pilgrimage to the sanctuary. This psalm was possibly a liturgy for the Feast of Ingathering (Ex. 23[16]), a feast of great merriment and one celebrated by a pilgrimage to a shrine. Peters believes that it was a festival hymn of the Dan temple. He thinks that with the ravaging of northern Israel by Tiglath-pileser IV in 734 B.C., some of the priests with their liturgies migrated to Shechem or Bethel, and in 722 B.C. from there to Jerusalem. Thus psalms originally used at local Jehovah sanctuaries got into the Temple Psalter. The date is probably toward the middle of the eighth century B.C.

1–5. Longing for the Sanctuary. The psalmist interprets his longing to worship God at the sanctuary under the picturesque simile of the thirst of the stag in summer (vv. 1–3). He seizes upon physical thirst and that of an animal that cannot hide it as the best figure through which to portray his passion for God. In such a pilgrimage he would find buttress and defense against his taunting enemies who have plagued him to tears. He recalls earlier pilgrimages when he used to lead the pilgrims in festal procession to the Temple (at Dan?), a boisterous, happy throng (v. 4). V. 5 contains the refrain. This is the finest, the most poetic, and the most spiritually rich refrain in the Psalter. It recurs in v. 11 and 43[5]. His higher self encourages his despondent self by hope of a future pilgrimage. Peters thinks v. 5 is the cry of confidence from the hard pressed people that Jehovah will yet help them.

6–11. Joyful Memories Contrasted with the Painful Present. The pilgrimage, in the psalmist's memory, has reached the sources of the Jordan at the foot of great Hermon. *Mizar* ("little") is the little hill by the spring of the Jordan, on which stood the Temple. "V. 7 is a vivid description of the impression made on the mind by the rushing torrents, with their roaring sound . . . especially impressive is the great fountain at Tel Kadi, the ancient Dan, where with a mighty roaring, as of a distant cataract, a river springs full-born from the ground . . . the water rushing out through its subterranean channels, the deep below crying out to the deep above, pouring forth in waves and billows in which the pilgrims bathe." (Peters, *The Psalms as Liturgies*, pp. 63, 277. The Macmillan Company, publishers.) Omit in the translation of v. 8 the first word, *yet*, which is not found in Hebrew. On the pilgrimage God's mercy cheers him by day and the pilgrim songs and prayers at night.

But from such happy memories he awakens with a jolt (vv. 9, 10), to utter a lamentation over the enemies' taunts that he and his fellow countrymen have no god who can protect them. *Where is thy god?*—here as in v. 3b a sneering challenge from boasting foes who see in their victory the downfall of the defeated enemies' gods. For the refrain in v. 11 see comment on v. 5.

Psalm 43. The Goal of the Pilgrimage

Vv. 1, 2 are an appeal for the decision, i.e., the judgment of God against the deceitful heathen enemies. In vv. 3, 4 the psalmist appeals for the personified spiritual forces of light and truth to lead him even as he had led others (see 42⁴) to the sanctuary and the booths. (Even if the sanctuary were originally Dan—see on Psa. 42—the words were later interpreted as referring to Jerusalem.) There he will make his offering. The final refrain carries the atmosphere of triumphant expectancy.

Psalm 44. A National Song of Lamentation

There is a great crisis on in Judaism (v. 9) and Israel seems abandoned by God. Interpreting hopefully God's past leadership of the nation (vv. 1–3), the psalmist appeals for his immediate help in the present crisis. The most likely background of the psalm is the Maccabæan era. Kittel calls it the "Song of Lamentation of the Maccabees," and thinks the occasion of it was the slaughter of the Jews referred to in 1 Macc. 2[29-38].

1–3. God's Hand In Israel's Past. The psalter is alive with the sense of history and sees Jehovah's hand in every step of Israel's career. V. 1 pictures one generation telling to the oncoming generation of God's dealings with Israel in the past. What Israel achieved at the conquest (vv. 2, 3) was not due to her prowess but to God.

4–8. Confidence in God's Help in the Present Crisis. In his historical recall the psalmist takes hope. Not by military equipment (v. 6), or by the people's own strength. but from God will come victory. This is an attitude characteristic of the book of Daniel (*cir.* 167 B.C.).

9–16. Seemingly God Has Forsaken Israel. The lamentation begins here. Israel's armies are defeated (vv. 9, 10). Successive exiles have scattered her forces. In bitter sarcasm Jehovah is accused of selling Israel (to the Hellenizing Syrians) cheap (v. 12). She has no standing among the nations (vv. 13–16). This, since the time of Ezekiel (cf. ch. 36), was a sensitive point with the Jews.

17–22. Yet Israel Has Been Loyal to God. The psalmist is evidently in a desolate wilderness and a dark valley (v. 19). Israel's loyalty does not deserve such treatment (v. 21). V. 22 may be a reference to the severity of persecution by Antiochus Epiphanes, who ruthlessly attempted to Hellenize Judaism (see p. 755).

23–26. A Passionate Appeal for God's Help. V. 25 implies the situation mirrored in 1 Macc. 2[29-38]. The basis of the appeal now is not Israel's self-respect among the nations but, rather, the nature of God.

Psalm 45. A Song Celebrating a King's Marriage

We have here a wedding song for a king. Sellin considers it a song celebrating the marriage of Jeroboam II with a foreign princess. Other suggestions offered are the marriage of Solomon with the daughter of Pharaoh, Ahab with Jezebel or Joram with Athaliah. The psalm is not Messianic but belongs to a group of psalms concerning the king. As to date we can be certain only that it is pre-exilic.

1. Prelude. The poet proposes to sing a song concerning the king. *My heart overfloweth*—the poet sings "the things of my making," i.e., his own poetic composition. In old English "maker" = poet.

2–9. Praise of the Groom. He begins with the king's "beauty" (v. 2) and *grace*—a mingling of favor, kindness, and elegance. Then (vv. 3–5) he praises him as warrior. Calling him to array himself for battle, he exclaims, *Thy glory and thy majesty*. In v. 4a read, with McFadyen, *Good fortune attend thee as forth thou dost ride*. He goes forth riding majestically upon his horse, fighting in behalf of (so read with mg.) loyalty, gentleness and righteousness. *Terrible things* refers to deeds arousing dread. V. 5 means "pierced to the heart are the king's enemies."

Translate v. 6 with G. R. Driver (Simpson, *The Psalmists*, p. 124), *Thy throne is God forever and ever*, i.e., *thy throne is like God's throne.* The king is addressed in hyperbole as God. We find a similar usage in the Babylonian "Epic of Creation" concerning Marduk. Kittel renders *Thy throne, thou divine one, stands always and ever.* The emendation of the text to read, "Thy throne will stand forever and ever" (Wellhausen) is not necessary. V. 7 asserts the king's right to rule. V. 8 describes the royal wedding garments and the instrumental music; and v. 8 refers to the foreign princesses, the attendants of the bride. At the king's right stands a foreign queen.

10–12. The Singer Counsels the Bride. She is to forget her own country and reverence her new husband, the king. Read v. 12, *And the Tyrians shall come with a gift.*

13–15. The Royal Bride Described. She is a foreign princess. We get a glimpse into the palace where she waits, dressed in golden bridal array. Soon, accompanied by the joyous young women of the bridal party, she will be led to her new home, an important part of the marriage ceremony in the East.

16, 17. Anticipation of the King's Fame. He is to have the forward look, his eye upon his posterity, building a name to endure through the generations.

Psalm 46. God Our Refuge and Strength

Various views are held concerning the interpretation of this great psalm. Briggs thinks it expresses the confidence of King Josiah amid the international commotion occasioned by the Scythian invasion. Wellhausen connects it with the revolution in the near East caused by the mastery of Alexander the Great. Cheyne and most expositors connect it with the invasion of Sennacherib in 701 B.C. Peters views it as originating in the northern sanctuary at Dan, the topography of which region it depicts. But the profoundest and most consistent interpretation is that of Gunkel, who views it as an eschatological hymn of Zion like Psa. 47 and 76. Our interpretation owes much to his masterly exegesis. This psalm stands under the profound influence of prophetic teaching concerning the end of the days. It reveals the depth of religious feeling and the power of inspiration that eschatological ideas contained for ancient Israel. It comes from a period after the greater prophets had done their work, probably shortly after the time of Deutero-Isaiah. This psalm gave rise to Luther's majestic hymn, "A Mighty Fortress Is Our God." It has been called "the sublime song of faith." The author moved not only in eschatological conceptions but also in the ideas of Gen. 15:6 Isa. 7:9 30:15 and Hab. 2:4. Possibly some historical incident gave occasion for it, but the whole burden of the psalm has to do with the awesome future—the time of the end.

1–3. The Expectation of Jehovah's Intervention. The pictures of the convulsions of nature are the conceptions largely inherited by the prophets and sketched by them to picture the terrible, final catastrophe which will precede the new era. The pictures are of volcano (read in v. 2a *though the earth melt*), earthquake (vv. 2b, 3b), and flood (v, 3a). It was expected, according to old Hebrew thought, that as at the time previous to creation there had been a chaotic mass of primeval waters which with roaring destructiveness were in control until Jehovah mastered them (cf. 89:10 104:6-9 Job 38:11), so in the last days a new destructive flood would lift itself against Jehovah's creation (cf. Jer. 47:2) as an overflowing scourge.

But in such a time Israel need not fear. God is our shelter and strength. The destructive waters cannot shake *Him* nor those whom he protects. Probably the refrain (vv. 7, 11) sung by the congregation has dropped out and should also appear after v. 3. *Jehovah of hosts* —this name re-echoes the early thought of Jehovah as God of war.

4–7. Jehovah's Victory and the New Era. V. 6 portrays the armies of the nations, i.e., heathendom, arrayed against Zion in final attack, raging in enmity and threatening (cf. Isa. 17:12-14 Ezek. 38:14–39:20). But the city need not fear, for in Jerusalem (Isa. 37:35) is Jehovah, and even at the darkest hour, "at the turning of the morning," Jehovah will reveal his mighty presence as of old (cf. Ex. 19:18), the uproar will cease and the earth as in terror shall quake. Amid all the chaos and raging the one center of calm is Jerusalem, for Jehovah is there.

In graphic contrast to the seething, destructive waters of chaos the psalmist pictures other waters not destructive but productive, not terror-inspiring but peace-bringing—the waters of the ever increasing stream of Ezekiel's vision (ch. 47), flowing out from under the threshold of the Temple, bringing life and health wherever they flow. With awesome poetic power the psalmist awakens in this section the *mysterium tremendum* which Rudolf Otto calls the deepest element in religion.

8–11. The Result of Jehovah's Intervention. The battle of Jehovah with the raging nations is over. He has compelled and conquered the opposing powers of the world (cf. Isa. 59:15b-20

63[1-6]). V. 8 summons Jehovah's people, protected in the final catastrophe by his power, to view the field of his victory. He is master of the earth. No combination of forces can ever conquer him. The implements of war are scrapped (cf. Isa. 2[1-4]). God now ascends the throne of the universe and utters his summons to humanity: *Be still* (v. 10)—i.e., desist, refrain from all lack of confidence in me, from all enmity against me, recognize who I am! Jehovah! king over the nations, king over all the earth! The last refrain, in v. 11, is imbued with the atmosphere of triumph.

Psalm 47. The Enthronement of Jehovah

This is a psalm, similar to Psa. 93, 95–100, celebrating the enthronement of Jehovah as king of the whole earth. It is an eschatological hymn with a liturgical character. In Babylonia on each New Year's Day there was a ritual in which the Babylonian king "took the hands of Bel." Likewise, on this day was recited the Babylonian epic of Creation, which interests us because in one of these "accession" psalms Jehovah's creation of the world is celebrated (see 95[5]). Mowinckel has recently maintained (*Psalmenstudien* II, especially p. 31) that the accession of the Hebrew king was celebrated as an annual festival in the autumn, coinciding with the Feast of Booths. This gave the model for the psalms of Jehovah's accession which were used liturgically. The festival was celebrated on New Year's Day by a procession with the ark from some spot in Jerusalem to the Temple. While in part historical (cf. 2 Sam. 6[12f.]) such a celebration is likewise eschatological in that it looks forward to the day when Israel s faith will be vindicated and Jehovah will be supreme. References in v. 5 (cf. Lev. 23[24] Num. 29[1]) point to a date in the late fifth or early fourth century B.C., later than Isa. 56–66 and close to the compilation of the priestly code.

1–4. The Summons to Rejoicing Over the Enthronement of Jehovah. The jubilation accompanying the enthronement of an earthly monarch creates the conceptions for this (cf. 1 Kings 1[34, 39], Solomon; 2 Kings 11[12], Jehoash). Jehovah is more than king over Israel, yet to Israel he has a unique relation (vv. 2b, 3, 4).

5–7. Jehovah's Accession to the Throne. Amid the popular acclaim of all, He ascends his throne to reign over *all the earth,* i.e., over humanity.

8, 9. The Unity of Humanity in God. All the nations are here viewed as, spiritually, the people of the God of Abraham. Here is a universalism lifted high above the prevailing nationalism. This psalmist had fed upon the ideals of the Second and Third Isaiahs (cf. Isa. 49[1-8] 66[18]).

Psalm 48. A Processional Hymn

This is a hymn sung by the congregation in the Temple (v. 9) at the beginning of the festal procession, probably at the Feast of the Passover. Those who participate have evidently come from a distance (v. 13), possibly the only time some of them will ever celebrate a festival at Jerusalem. The psalm is strongly colored with eschatological conceptions. It dates most likely from the late Persian period.

1–3. A Zion Hymn in Praise of Jerusalem. It is not the actual Jerusalem of which the psalmist sings, but the Jerusalem of prophetic hope (cf. Isa. 2[1-4]), when it will be the center of the Messianic kingdom, which will include the whole earth. *The sides of the north* is probably in origin a mythical conception. *The north* is the abode of the gods. This ancient popular idea has been taken over and applied to Jerusalem.

4–7. The Final Attack of the Nations Upon Jerusalem and Her Supernatural Deliverance. This conception is familiar in eschatological ideas (cf. Ezek. 38, 39, Joel 3[12f.]). Not by human warfare but by Jehovah's supernatural interference was Jerusalem saved. We do not have here the portrayal of an historical event, for Jerusalem's population had no share in it.

8. The Pilgrim's Wonder at Jerusalem. We sense here the awe of the pilgrim who at last finds himself in the beloved city of which he had been told so much. Now he has seen with his own eyes the eternal city.

9–11. The Festal Celebration. It included worship in the Temple, the singing of Jehovah's praise, and the free jollification of the city.

12–14. The Festal Procession. Perhaps the procession went around the city walls. At any rate, it went from place to place, recalling scenes having to do with David and Solomon, Josiah, Isaiah and Jeremiah. The pilgrims must note these things well. In their far-away homes they must tell to the children what they have seen. What God has been and done in the past gives confident expectation for his continued help.

Psalm 49. An Intimation of Immortality

This is not a hymn but a meditation (Welch, *The Psalter*, p. 78; cf. Psa. 16 and 90). The psalmist is perplexed by the problem of the prosperity of the wicked (vv. 5, 6). Regardless of their wealth they all go down to Sheol (v. 14) and never again see the light (v. 19b). But as for him, Jehovah will ransom him from Sheol's power and receive him to himself. We have here a fairly clear intimation of immortality. The psalm comes from one of the sages of Israel and has closest contact with Psa. 37 and 73. It is very late—probably from the Greek period. The text is very imperfect and at points needs reconstruction.

1–4. His Appeal for Attention. The psalmist would reach not only Israel, and not only the well-to-do, but humanity of all classes (vv. 1, 2). He has a message of wisdom for mankind and evidently believes in the stimulus of music to thought (v. 4). For v. 4b read *I will open my perplexing question upon the lyre.*

5, 6. The Problem Stated: Why Worry Over the Prosperity of the Wicked? Following Origen, v. 5 should be rendered, *Why should I fear in the days of trouble when the iniquity of those persecuting me surrounds me? They that trust* (v. 6), i.e., those persecuting me.

7–14. All Mankind Has the Same Fate. Read v. 7, *Yet* (this word implies a conclusion reached after a long process of thought) *man surely cannot ransom himself; nor give to God his price.* Man cannot buy perpetual life. Omit v. 8 as a later gloss and read v. 9a, *that he should live always and ever.*

Vv. 10–12 state that the wise and the stupid come to the same end—Death. In v. 11 read, with mg., *Their graves are their houses forever,* and v. 12a, *But man in honor without discernment is,* etc. A man who lacks insight, though he may have material splendor, perishes like a beast. Read v. 13a with mg., *This is the way of them that are foolish;* read v. 13b following J. M. P. Smith (*The Religion of the Psalms,* p. 119), *And the path of those who delight in their own speech.* In connection with v. 14 Cheyne (*The Psalms,* p. 138) quotes an Arabic poem: "And to-day they wander, a trembling herd, their herdsman Death." Read v. 14cd, following Buhl,

"They go down with the upright to the grave
And their form is for wasting.
Sheol is their dwelling."

15–20. The Abandonment of the Unrighteous Rich in Sheol but the Immortality of the Righteous. This is one of the very few places in the O.T. where is to be found a suggestion of a noble destiny beyond the grave for the individual (see p. 173). The psalmist speaks only of what he believes his own fate will be, in dramatic contrast to those whom he has been criticizing. He merely mentions his hope in v. 15, and it does not affect the rest of the psalm except by the sharpness and vigor which it puts into the contrast. Yet the climax of the psalm is here. He will not go down to Sheol but will be received by God (cf. 73[24]). Jehovah will not allow him to come into Sheol's power. Gunkel considers this verse a late addition, but Duhm rightly sees in it a passage similar to Isa. 26[19] and Dan. 12[2].

Read v. 18b, following Duhm and Gunkel, *And praised it when it did well for itself.*

Psalm 50. The Sacrifice God Requires

The psalmist is a student of the prophets and in his psalm we find a type of thought and a manner of utterance that is characteristic of Israelite prophecy at its best. What he says concerning sacrifice connects him at once with the utterances in 1 Sam. 15[22f.] Amos 5[21f.] Hos. 6[6] Isa. 1[11f.] Mic. 6[6f.] Jer. 7[22f.] Yet while a student of the prophets he is likewise loyal to the Law, which he reads and obeys in the prophetic spirit. The psalm dates from the post-exilic period, probably the fifth century B.C., when the Deuteronomic Law was still supreme, and before the priestly code had been accepted as the basis of Jewish life and conduct. (See notes on 40[4-12].)

1–6. The Appearance of God. God in a revelation that affects the whole earth (vv. 1, 4) comes to scattered Israel to gather them together (v. 5) and judge his people. As the ancient poems (cf. Judg. 5[4f.]) represented him as coming from Sinai, this psalm pictures him as coming from Jerusalem, but the old natural accompaniments of the theophany are present (cf. Ex. 19[18, 19]).

7–15. God's Oracle Concerning Sacrifice. The oracle addressed to collective Israel opens in prophetic style. As to sacrifices, Israel is scrupulously faithful, but Jehovah does not desire sacrifice, for all the animals used in sacrifice already belong to him (vv. 8–13). What God wants is not the sacrifice of animals but of the heart in gratitude, in the payment of vows, and in prayer (vv. 14, 15a). Gunkel says that v. 15 summarizes in brief, powerful manner the life of the pious: need, call unto God, deliverance, and praise. The psalmist's emphasis on heart gratitude and prayer goes even beyond the prophetic teaching cited in the introduction.

16–23. Superficial Legalism. The wicked are severely (v. 22) condemned for their superficial confidence in the Law, which they disobey. Evidently he has in mind the Ten Words (cf. Ex. 20[1-20], especially [14-16]), as the summons in v. 7 also suggests (cf. Deut. 5[1] 6[4]). The psalm links together in the closing verse prophetic piety and piety under the Law.

Psalm 51. Cry of a Soul for Cleansing and Pardon

This penitence psalm is one of the deepest in the Psalter. The psalmist is heir to the prophets who interpreted religion chiefly as an inner heart experience. In origin it goes back to the early ritual of worship. A man sick (v. 8b), and accordingly feeling himself under the censure of Jehovah, goes to the priest at the sanctuary to be cleansed and pardoned. Using the ritual form, the words being accompanied by ritual acts, he would say, "Purge me with hyssop and I shall be clean" (v. 7a). He is profoundly depressed (v. 8a), for his life is in peril (v. 14a). His sense of sin in keenness and depth is unsurpassed in the Psalter. The poet lived after Isaiah (cf. Isa. 1^{16-18}), but before Haggai and Zechariah. His indebtedness to Jeremiah and Ezekiel marks the psalm as exilic or early post-exilic. Vv. 18, 19 are an editorial adaptation dating from the Judaism of the fifth century previous to Nehemiah.

1, 2. A Cry for Forgiveness. From the depths of his soul the psalmist cries for pardon. Three terms are used for sin and three for forgiveness. He prays that his *transgressions* may be blotted out, that his *iniquities* may be milled or treaded out (the method of washing) and that from his *sin* (root = to miss the mark) he may be pronounced clean. *Cleanse* (v. 2b)—originally a ritualistic, ceremonial term, which here has achieved moral significance.

3–6. The Psalmist's Confession. This confession, which expresses deep penitence, is the basis of his petition. His sense of sin stands ever at the center of his consciousness (v. 3b). This broad, central confession is deepened by the addition of two thoughts: (1) His sense of sin is so keen and deep that he views it as more than transgression against men. Gunkel (who in v. 14 instead of *Deliver me from bloodguiltiness* reads *Deliver me from silence*, i.e., of the underworld = death) maintains that the sin of which he is conscious is not sin against men but, rather, that of inadvertence and, therefore, against God (for the procedure in "unwitting" sin see Lev. 4, notes). But this interpretation does not sound the depths of the psalmist's consciousness of sin (cf. v. 3). To view all sin as, in the last analysis, sin against God is an evidence of moral inwardness and spiritual depth. His confession of this opens the way to pardon, justifying God in exerting his sovereign prerogative in pronouncing him, i.e., judging him, forgiven regardless of those who think he deserves differently (cf. v. 14). The connection between v. 4ab and v. 4cd is best brought out by supplying the thought that is hidden in the pregnant utterance of the psalmist: This confession of ultimate guilt before God I make so that God may be warranted (justified) in uttering the words (so LXX for "when thou speakest") of pardon—originally referring to the priestly pronouncement of cleansing and forgiveness following the worshiper's confession. It is a misunderstanding to interpret the meaning of the text to be that human sin was designed to bring into clear prominence the grace of God (cf. Rom. $3^{4, 5}$).

(2) The second thought, supplementing the broad confession of v. 3, is that the psalmist as an individual is also implicated in the sin of the race (v. 5). Not "original sin" is maintained here, but a universal tendency toward sin (cf. Isa. 6^{5}). But in the psalmist's mind this does not excuse but deepens his guilt, for in v. 6 he utters another pregnant sentence like v. 4bc, which means, "I would not speak such words unless I felt it essential that my confession be without reservation, that it open to the scrutiny of God the innermost moral recesses of my nature." *Inward parts*, and *hidden parts*—literally, "covered," "concealed," "hidden" and "shut-up," "corked up." There is an utter sincerity and transparency in his confession, in which attitude of soul God instructs him. Gunkel's interpretation of an esoteric secret wisdom is not adequately based.

7–12. His Petition for Cleansing and Renewal. Vv. 7–9 are a prayer for cleansing. The references to hyssop and washing probably go back to ritual acts which were accompanied by pronouncements of the priests. Peters thinks we have the very words from the familiar language of the ritual. It concluded in cries of joy and praise (v. 8a). *Hyssop* is a shrublike herb with strong aromatic leaves to which ancient peoples ascribed purifying power. It was used to sprinkle the worshiper (cf. Lev. $14^{4f.}$ Num. $19^{6, 18}$). *Bones which thou hast broken* (v. 8)—not to be taken literally but symbolically of his total crushed and despondent condition (cf. 35^{10} Isa. 38^{13}).

Vv. 10–12 are a prayer for renewal. Using the term that recalls the marvel of God's creative act which called the world into being, he prays for a "new creation," a cleansed heart (heart = "the practical reason," Kittel), and the renewal of his former unwavering and confident disposition. Pardon is not enough. Something creative reaching the moral and spiritual aspects of life is essential. The author is the heir of the deep ideas of Jer. 24^{7} 31^{33} and especially Ezek. 36^{25}. A nobler conception of the Spirit of God as an abiding power for good in the individual life (v. 11) is not found elsewhere in the O.T. He seeks the renewal of his former joy of fellowship with God and an obliging and willing spirit (v. 12).

13–17. His Vow. If Jehovah will pardon and restore him, he will act as an evangelist for him. The speaker was in peril of violence from men who felt he deserved differently at the hand of God. He prays for deliverance from an act that would make its perpetrator guilty of murder. Released from his crushed condition, he will proclaim abroad what Jehovah has done for him (v. 14). Like the poet of Psa. 50 (especially 8-15), this psalmist (vv. 16, 17) represents the prophetic attitude toward sacrifice. Welch points out that the sacrificial system had to do with atonement for sins of inadvertence only and hence did not go deep enough to reach the psalmist's sense of sin, for he had sinned with knowledge and out of weakness of will. This was the fundamental limitation of the liturgies of Israel—their shallowness in dealing with the ultimate question of sin (cf. *The Psalter*, pp. 109f.). The sacrifices God requires are not burnt-offerings but humility of spirit (cf. Cheyne's references to the Jewish service for the Day of Atonement).

18, 19. **An Editorial Adaptation.** A later writer corrects the liberal prophetic teaching of the preceding verses by adapting the psalm for use in the second Temple, an institution which attached great significance to sacrificial worship. This addition comes from the time previous to the rebuilding of the wall by Nehemiah (v. 18). It is in fundamental clash with vv. 16, 17, but in harmony with Psa. 66 13-15. "The use of such a psalm as the fifty-first alongside of the ritual it transcends and supersedes may remind us that the Temple worship, like all ritual, was really a framework of different spiritual values experienced by the differing worshipers" (H. W. Robinson in Simpson, *The Psalmists*, p. 62).

Psalm 52. The Fall of a Rich Boaster

This is a psalm of lamentation in the form of an address to him who is the occasion of the lament. The person addressed is one of the leaders of the proud materialists in the community. His perverse, boastful talk is what arouses the righteous indignation of the psalmist (vv. 2–4), who looks confidently forward to his destruction (v. 5).

1–4. **His Boastful Evil Talk.** Addressing the boaster in fine irony as a *mighty man*, the psalmist asks him why he behaves so proudly toward the loyal all the days (v. 1b; so Wellhausen following the Syriac). His sharp tongue is compared to a treacherous razor.

5–7. **His Judgment at God's Hands, the Righteous Looking On.** His seeming security is only apparent (v. 4). The verbs of v. 5 express petition, "May God destroy thee," etc. The terms are picturesque and suggestive. May God demolish thee, shatter thee, tear thee away without a tent, uproot thee (cf. Isaiah's vigorous reprimand to Shebna, 22 16-19, which is very similar). The judgment of God is strengthened by the righteous looking on, who point to him and laugh tauntingly at him, recalling his irreverence and materialism. In v. 7a read with mg. *stronghold* for *strength*, and with Syriac and Targum read *in his wealth* for *in his wickedness* (v. 7c).

8, 9. **The Contrasted Attitude of the Psalmist.** In the court of the Temple flourished olive trees which were viewed as being under the special protection of God. Conscious of fresh, inner vitality, the psalmist compares himself to such trees. So certain is he of the future judgment upon this boastful leader that he views it as already accomplished and vows the singing of a song of thanksgiving among the loyal forever.

Psalm 53. Man's Folly and Wickedness

Psa. 53 is practically identical with Psa. 14. See notes and comments there.

Psalm 54. A Prayer Against Insolent Foes

This is a lamentation of an individual. The psalmist is in peril at the hands of insolent, godless men who are seeking his life (v. 3; cf. Psa. 64). But he trusts in God (v. 4) and hopes for their destruction at God's hands (vv. 6, 7). In certain anticipation of this (v. 7) he vows a freewill offering of thanksgiving (v. 6). The situation is similar to that of Psa. 64 and comes from the period of party strife in late Judaism.

1–3. **The Psalmist's Petition for Help.** He speaks of the *name* of God as having marvelous power (cf. Acts 3 6, 16 4 7, 12). He needs the divine help because he is hunted down by violent men (v. 3). Psa. 86 14 practically parallels v. 3. From there restore (so also several MSS. and Targum) *insolent men* in place of *strangers*, or foreigners. The insolent are not Gentiles but godless Jews. *Violent men*, literally, "terror-striking" men.

4, 5. **His Confidence in God.** In vivid contrast to the godless his confidence is in God. He has others who are helping him but "among those who are supporting his life is the Lord." V. 5a is a wish. Translate *May the evil fall back upon those insidiously watching me. Truth* = loyalty. God's loyalty to the psalmist means extermination for his enemies.

6, 7. **His Vow in Anticipation of Deliverance.** The psalm issues in a vow. He will offer a *freewill-offering* (cf. Lev. 7 11f. 22 17f.)—not a regular, specified sacrifice but a thank-offering brought voluntarily.

Psalm 55. Treachery and the Shattering of Friendship

This psalm combines two originally different poems, both being lamentations because of disloyalty. Because of this similarity of theme they were later brought together into a single psalm. The text is at many points imperfect, but the two poems can still be separated. The first is composed of vv. 1–18a, 22. This is a lamentation of an individual. Persecuted by enemies (v. 3) and in peril of death (vv. 4, 5) he longs for escape into the wilderness (vv. 6–9a). The evil remnant in the city is described (vv. 9–11). The deep pathos of the lamentation, however, appears in vv. 13, 14, where we learn that the leader of his enemies was once his familiar friend, with whom he had gone in festal procession into the Temple (cf. on 42[4]). He passionately prays for the destruction of his enemies, and utters his intention to petition persistently for help (vv. 16, 17). He concludes (v. 22) with a moving exhortation to his own soul. This psalm has closest contact with Psa. 42 and 120. Since Theodore of Mopsuestia, scholars have inclined to a Maccabæan date for the poem, but Kittel maintains it might fully as well come from the time of Jeremiah. This part of the psalm is most likely post-exilic.

The second is composed of vv. 18b–21, 23, being evidently a fragment of a lamentation from a psalmist of the dispersion who while in northern Arabia, probably as a trader (?), had entered into a covenant with certain Arabian tribes (v. 19; see below), under whose protection he was sojourning. This covenant of peace (v. 20) they had ruthlessly broken and had, in fact, become his enemies. Although through smooth speech they still simulated friendship (v. 21), God, in whom the psalmist trusts, will destroy them.

1–5. The Psalmist's Lamentation Unto God. He is being so oppressed and so cruelly dealt with that he is overwhelmed with terror.

6–9a. A Lyric of Escape. Here is a tender bit of poetry quite different from the lament, having in it a beautiful imaginative touch. The persecution he is enduring is compared to a tempest—a storm of destructive speech. V. 9a belongs to the preceding, rather than the following verses. Read, following Gunkel's reconstruction:

"From the destructive storm of their throat,
From the torrent of their lips."

9b–11. The Wickedness Rampant in the City. A vivid portrayal of the wickedness of the city in which the various types of evil are personified. What city? Gunkel raises the question of a possible reference to a pagan city. Ewald and most moderns think of Jerusalem, which seems (cf. v. 14) most likely.

12–15. The Treachery of an Intimate Friend. The psalmist's plight is made the more pathetic in that the leader of his enemies is a former friend with whom he had been on most intimate terms, with whom he had shared the most sacred hours of festal celebration with thronging worshipers in the Temple (v. 14; cf. 41[9], notes). This fact puts passion and intensity into his prayer for sudden destruction of his enemies.

16–18a, 22. A Concluding Utterance of Dependence Upon God. With v. 17 cf. Dan. 6[10] for the prayer three times a day. Read v. 18a, with the LXX and following Wellhausen, *he shall redeem.* Speaking to his own soul the psalmist says, *Cast upon Jehovah thy lot* (v. 22), i.e., the care or anxiety of which he has been speaking.

18b–21. The Treachery of the Sons of the Desert. This difficult section does not refer to vv. 12–14. Clearly the text is corrupt and demands reconstruction. Read v. 18b, following mainly Gunkel's reconstruction of the text:

"For there are attacking me archers,
They have become opposed to me."

Ehrlich's brilliant conjecture is the key to the correct understanding of v. 19, an exceedingly difficult verse. With a slight change in the consonantal text he perceives here the names of Arabian clans which we find mentioned in the Pentateuch—the familiar "Ishmael," and "Jalam," a son of Esau (cf. Gen. 36[5, 14, 18] and 1 Chr. 1[35]), i.e., an Edomite clan (cf. also on 120[5] for a reference to similar Arabian clans). Translate: "Ishmael and Jalam and the inhabitants (i.e., natives) of the East. He to whom there is no (such thing as) breach, i.e., of covenant" (cf. v. 20). The eponymous designation of these tribes is followed out by use of the singular, third person masculine pronouns in the following verses. These sons of the desert have turned traitor (v. 20). Outwardly friendly, they were actually treacherous.

23. Prayer for Destruction. This fragment ends with a passionate prayer for the destruction of the traitors and an assertion of the psalmist's trust in God.

Psalm 56. Unswerving Faith in God

This is a lamentation of an individual. The psalmist, who is of the Dispersion, has lived a wandering life (v. 8a), necessitated by his enemies (vv. 1, 2a, 6), who are figuratively portrayed as warriors (vv. 1b, 2b). But he trusts in God (v. 4), who is "for him" (v. 9b) and will put his enemies to rout (v. 9a). He vows thank-offerings in return for his deliverance from peril of death (vv. 12, 13). There is a beautiful refrain in v. 4 and vv. 10, 11. The psalm is probably from the early post-exilic period when the dispersion had set in. (The term "dispersion," or "diaspora," is used to describe the scattering of the Jews throughout the Near East, beginning with the Babylonian Exile of 597 and 586 B.C.; cf. pp. 847–9.)

1, 2. A Cry to God Because of Enemies. The psalmist's enemies are interpreted as warriors who *swallow* him—i.e., they are "crushing," "trampling upon" him.

3, 4. Trust in the Day of Fear. In the hour when tempted to be afraid he trusts in God against whom mere flesh cannot prevail.

5–7. Lament Over the Activities of His Enemies. He proceeds to a more detailed account of his enemies' dealings with him. Translate v. 5a, *All the day long they vex my affairs;* read v. 6a, *They spy out* (Gunkel), *they lie hidden.* In the psalmist's cry to God for their defeat we see that his enemies are not Jews but foreigners (*the peoples*). Read v. 7a, *For their iniquities weigh out to them*, i.e., retribution (Ewald).

8–11. His Confidence in God's Concern. Because of the strenuous enmity which he has experienced he has been a wanderer but has not been absent from the concern of God. His tears have been treasured up in God's *bottle*, the record of them set down in God's *book* (cf. Job 19²³ Mal. 3¹⁶) i.e., his commemoration book. The Babylonians also shared the idea that man's deeds are written down by the gods. In v. 9b is expressed the crisp, concentrated summary of his confidence: *God is for me.* His faith has in it the ring of certainty. Vv. 10, 11 repeat the refrain of v. 4.

12, 13. The Payment of His Vows. When he experienced his difficulties he vowed thank-offerings in case of relief. Help has come and the payment of his vow is now his duty. Jehovah has intervened. His loyal one has been delivered from premature death.

PSALM 57. MY HEART IS FIXED

This psalm is closely connected with the preceding and probably comes from the same period and author. The psalmist is of the Diaspora (v. 9) and has sensed the meaning of Jeremiah's counsel to the Judæans in far-away Babylonia (Jer. 29^{12-14}). He is passing through a storm of fiery, bitter enmity, expressed in sharp, biting speech that strikes to his very heart (v. 4). Yet he confidently trusts in God (vv. 2, 7), from whom he expects retribution upon his enemies. The psalm ends in a beautiful hymn of praise (vv. 7–11, which verses recur in 108^{1-5}). It is a song to be sung not in the Temple, but in the Diaspora among the nations.

1–6. A Cry for Mercy and the Psalmist's Trust in the Protection of God. He is enduring a "storm of ruin" (Cheyne). Until it passes he is under the protection of his God. His past experience leads him to present confidence in God, who accomplishes deliverance for him. V. 4 contains the psalmist's lamentation: His enemies are like *lions*, mad with rage, among whom he lies down to sleep in the atmosphere of constant peril of their sharp invective. From the harshness of human beings he rises to the hope of the ultimate universal sovereignty of God (v. 5; cf. 56^{4}). Furthermore, he rejoices in the certainty of God's judgment upon his enemies (v. 6). Characteristic of many of the psalms is the thought of the self-destruction of evil (cf. 7^{16} 9^{16}).

7–11. A Morning Hymn of Thanksgiving. The psalmist is asleep (cf. v. 4b), his lute and harp silent at his side. The slumber of night is upon nature. Then in gratitude the psalmist first awakens his own *glory*—the text should be changed so as to read "soul" (literally, "my liver," i.e., the seat of emotion)—then his silent lute and harp (v. 8a), and finally the slumbering dawn, to sing Jehovah's praise in a morning hymn of thanksgiving. Read, with mg., v. 8b, *I will awake the dawn.* This beautiful poetic conception has achieved a rich variety of expression in English poetry. Milton, "Cheerly rouse the slumbering morn"; Shakespeare, "the gentle lark . . . wakes the morning"; Tennyson, "cold winds woke the gray-eyed morn." The psalmist's determination to sing the praises of Jehovah springs not from the actual experience of the destruction of his enemies, for this is still in the future, nor simply from the conviction that his cry unto God has been heard, but rather, out of an abiding faith that has sustained him in the very experience of persecution. *My heart is fixed*—literally, firm, established, steadfast. Amid fears and subtle perils his heart remains steady through his confidence in God.

His hymn of praise is sung not among his fellow countrymen but away from the Temple among pagan peoples. This psalm has given courage and confidence to persecuted and scattered Judaism through the centuries. The recurring refrain in v. 11 brings the psalm to an exalted close.

PSALM 58. CORRUPTION OF JUSTICE IN THE EARTH

This is a lamentation of an individual. The psalmist is deeply concerned over the corruption of justice in the earth. His eye is upon the earthly rulers, who should be the dispensers of justice among men. But he addresses the heathen gods, whose instruments of evil these rulers are and under whose protection they stand (vv. 1, 2). He prays for the destruction of these malicious leaders (vv.

6–9) and asserts the vindication of the righteous and the triumph among the gods of the God who judges the earth. The psalm is later than Deutero-Isaiah; it probably comes from late Judaism. It has very close contact with Psa. 82.

1, 2. Address to the Gods. Read v. 1a with mg., *O ye gods,* instead of *in silence,* and construe *ye sons of men* as the object of *judge.* Instead of directly challenging the earthly rulers with the miscarriage of justice he addresses the gods, the guardian spirits of the rulers of the nations. Ultimately the corruption of justice among mankind is conceived as due to them, the real forces behind the present world disorder. Read v. 2b with Syriac (and Buhl), *But nay, all of you judge in the earth in iniquity* (see Eph. 6[12], notes).

3–5. The Malicious Behavior of the Wicked. The scene shifts. The psalmist now addresses the earthly puppets of these heathen gods. From birth their words, i.e., of judgment, have been like the poison of serpents so fierce that no charmer could soothe them (cf. 140[3] Jer. 8[17]).

6–9. A Vindictive Prayer for Their Destruction. Graphic and vigorous symbols are employed to depict the longed-for destruction: Lions robbed of viciousness by broken teeth (v. 6), vanishing streams (v. 7a), withering grass (v. 7b; accepting the emendation suggested by Cheyne, "Let them be as grass that quickly withers"), snails that melt and pass away, a premature birth (v. 8b), plants cut down like thorns, and borne away in the storm before they had produced fruit (v. 9a; accepting the reading suggested by Gunkel, "Before they bear fruit may they be cut off as thorns. In wind may he sweep them away as nettles").

10, 11. The Vindication of the Righteous. These verses illustrate the vindictive temper of late Judaism. Mankind shall see in this judgment upon heathen leaders a reward of righteousness and an evidence of the supremacy of Jehovah over other gods. *That judgeth*—in Hebrew the plural form of the participle; possibly a relic carried over from the plural conception of deity. Where used of Jehovah the plural has a certain literary force which can be felt but not rendered in translation (Gen. 1[26]).

Psalm 59. God is My High Tower

This is a psalm of lamentation. The psalmist is in the Diaspora and his enemies are Gentiles (v. 5), whose taunts and sharp speech create his problem (vv. 7, 12). The same vindictive spirit that moves the previous psalm is here found. He passionately beseeches God to destroy his enemies and thereby show the supremacy of Israel's God (v. 13). The sense of strain under which the psalmist lives is ominously suggested in the first refrain (v. 6, repeated in v. 14), and the relief of faith in hours of such strain is powerfully expressed in the second refrain (v. 9, repeated in v. 17). The psalmist probably writes from the post-exilic period, when the Diaspora had set in in full force.

1, 2. His Cry for Deliverance From Enemies. The psalmist is suffering persecution but he speaks with Oriental color. It is the speech of his enemies, not bodily peril at their hands, that disturbs him (cf. vv. 7, 12).

3–7. Their Activity Described and a Prayer for Their Destruction. His enemies are powerful and crafty (v. 3ab), and the psalmist is keenly conscious that he does not deserve such treatment; he has not sinned against them (vv. 3c, 4a). In the midst of his description he utters a passionate prayer for their punishment (vv. 4b, 5). He compares his enemies to hungry, prowling *dogs* moving around the *city* (v. 6). When they speak they *belch* forth sharp cutting words (v. 7). The city is probably not Jerusalem but a heathen city.

8–10. His Confidence in God. God will both protect him and accomplish the destruction of his enemies, which he desires. Read in v. 9, with LXX, some MSS., and v. 17, *Unto thee, O my strength, will I sing praises.* In v. 10 read *As for my God, his mercy comes to meet me.*

11–13. A Prayer for the Destruction of His Enemies. V. 11 seems to suggest that he wants their destruction to be gradual so that, as they are being destroyed, they may realize that Israel's God is supreme (cf. v. 13). It is again evident that it is the speech of his enemies that has disturbed him most. The prayer is passionate and vindictive.

14, 15. The Enemies Unaware of Their Certain Fate. With graphic poetic force he again pictures the enemy as before (v. 6), as ravenous, hungry dogs, wandering about the city seeking food. But now he does not fear.

16, 17. His Vow of a Morning Song of Thanksgiving. The psalm closes, as is frequently the case with such lamentations, with the pledge of a song of thanksgiving which he will sing at Jerusalem at the morning offering (v. 16), when release has come.

Psalm 60. Israel's Ultimate Triumph

This psalm is a liturgy of national lamentation. The lamentation is in two parts, vv. 1–4 and vv. 10–12. Between these two parts of the lament is inserted a priestly or prophetic oracle (vv. 6–9). The lamentation leads us into the atmosphere of depression caused by reversals in war. Israel has had to flee before the foe (v. 4b, mg.). God seems to have forsaken the armies of Israel (v. 10). Yet without his help the enemy cannot be defeated (v. 11). The oracle is reassuring in tone, emphasizing Jehovah's ultimate control of territory once Israel's, but now in enemies' hands (vv. 6, 7), and his final masterful domination of Israel's enemies, ending in a challenge to the Israelite forces (v. 9). This oracle probably dates originally from an earlier period than the rest of the psalms, probably from the early exilic period (see on v. 7). But this early oracle has become a part of a later liturgy which best fits the Maccabæan era. The psalm thus has closest connection with Psa. 44.

1–5. Public Lamentation and Petition. The reversals are compared, through characteristic classical eschatological symbols, with an earthquake (v. 2) and the forced drinking of the wine that causes reeling (v. 3b; cf. 11[6] 16[5] Jer. 25[15]). Israel has been experiencing hard days, which are viewed as evidences of the angry disapproval of God. V. 4 is an expression of grim sarcasm. The banner of Israel given by Jehovah does not lead them to victory, but, rather, into flight. Read, with mg., for v. 4b, *That they may flee from before the bow*, i.e., of the enemy. In v. 5 the lament rises into petition. Let Jehovah reveal his helping power to Israel his *beloved*.

6–9. The Divine Oracle From the Temple. This was uttered by a priest or prophet who was seized by the certainty of Jehovah's triumph and that of his people. Shechem and Succoth (cf. Gen. 33[17]) are in the hands of foreigners. Gilead, Manasseh and Ephraim are Israel's legitimate possession, but at the present other powers are in control (v. 7). According to Jer. 49[1], in exilic times Ammon was in control of Gilead, but the certain regaining of this region was a firm conviction of exilic and even late post-exilic prophecy (cf. Jer. 50[19] Mic. 7[14] Zech. 10[10]). These sections will be recovered, and Judah will be the center of rule of the regained and reunited kingdom (cf. Gen. 49[10]—very early—and from later times, Zech. 9[13]). Moreover, the ancient and the persistent enemies of Israel—Moab, Edom, and Philistia—will be under the domination of Israel (v. 8). The casting of the shoe (v. 8b) is an Oriental symbol of possession and dominion (cf. Ruth 4[7f.]); here it is also a symbol of contempt. In v. 8b read *Over Philistia will I shout* (cf. 108[9] and Syriac).

The oracle ends in a challenge to the forces of Israel. God's mastery for Israel of the mentioned region is a future certainty. Israel is summoned to initiative, beginning at the point of tensest enmity, to bring God's control into Bozrah, the Edomite capital. The bequest of God awaits the conquest by Israel. This connection of v. 9 with the preceding rather than the succeeding verses gives finish and meaning to the oracle.

10–12. Lamentation Changes to Confidence. In spite of the heartening oracle the psalmist, unable to shake off present depression, laments that God goeth not forth with Israel's armies. Unless divine help comes, human forces are unavailing. Then at length comes the psalmist's rebirth of confidence. The priestly oracle has done its work. The psalmist goes forward inspired by the potent presence of his God who will make Israel victorious.

Psalm 61. A Cry to God From Afar

This is an individual lamentation. The psalmist is one of the Diaspora (v. 2a). Far away from the Temple that he loves (v. 4), amid enemies that cause his spirit to flag (v. 2), he utters his lamentation (v. 1), and prays for help (v. 2), and vows songs of gratitude to God which he is certain will be performed daily in the Temple. Into this typical lamentation of an individual are inserted two verses (6, 7) that turn the lament into a petition for the king. The king meant is an actual reigning monarch, which marks the psalm as certainly pre-exilic.

1, 2. A Far-Away Cry for Help. Ready to faint, because of his enemies, the psalmist cries unto God. The burden of his cry is v. 2b, which read, following LXX and Syriac, *Lift me up upon a rock and set me down.* The rock is a place of security above the assaults of the enemy.

3, 4. His Confidence in God. In the past he has found refuge in God. He now craves the security and protection of God's presence in the Temple. Read v. 4, *I would dwell*, etc., *I would take refuge*, etc.

5, 8. His Certainty of Being Heard Expressed in a Vow. While still fainting, he is sure of God's response, for God grants the request of those who fear him (v. 5, reading *request* for *heritage*). He vows perpetual praise to him, which vow, not on one occasion merely but daily, will be fulfilled.

6, 7. Petition for the Reigning King. Probably to adapt it to use in the king's Temple, a later poet inserted between vv. 5 and 8, which clearly belong together, this petition for the prolonged life of the king and for his protection at the hands of God through his loving-kindness and truth, conceived here as angelic spirits.

Psalm 62. Confidence in God Alone

This is a song of trust that begins with a

lamentation and ends in an exhortation in the manner of the sages. The psalmist is conscious of weakness (v. 3), possibly illness, that is heightened by the ruthless and deceitful attacks of his enemies (v. 4). But with a quietude and resignation of soul that represents one of the noblest faith attitudes in the Psalter (vv. 1, 2, 5–7) he waits confidently for the help of God. At v. 8 the psalmist passes into the mood of the Wisdom literature in which he utters counsel based upon his own individual experience. The most probable date is the middle Persian period out of which came also the book of Job.

1, 2. The Psalmist's Soul in Quietude Before God. These verses form a strong refrain which recurs in slightly varied from in vv. 5, 6. They utter a profound expression of quiet, trustful resignation toward God, his "crag," his "salvation," his "secure high retreat," but with the tension of eager expectancy at its heart. Luther suggestively translates, *My soul is silence, waiting all hushed for God.*

3, 4. An Indignant Lamentation Directed to His Opponents. *A man* (v. 3)—most likely the psalmist himself. He feels weak and ready to fall like a swaying wall, like a "fence pushed in" from without. They are plotting to *thrust him from his excellency* (read *dignity*), openly friendly but inwardly his enemies. He uses a military figure to describe their actions.

5–7. His Silent Confidence in God. Repeating the refrain with which the psalm opens, and emphasizing out of his experience what God is to him, he turns sage and speaks to his nation.

8–12. The Psalmist Assumes the Rôle of Sage. This section shows how strongly the wisdom ideas penetrated into the circle of the psalmists (cf. on 37, 49[1f.]). Probably some of the psalms come from the circle of the sages. The author's confidence in God, based on his own experience, now strengthened by a special revelation (see below), leads him to counsel constant trust in God as opposed to trust in mere human beings, mere men, who when put on the scales with *vanity*—literally, "a breath," i.e., nothing substantial—are outweighed even by that! Trust in God is also opposed to trust in wealth, or in those methods by which it is often secured. This counsel he grounds in the narrative of a personal revelation from God (v. 11). In the manner of Eliphaz in Job 4[12f.], he reports an oracle that had come to him twice from God. Not through dependence upon men but through trust in God can men find help. He alone in the final analysis has power. Yet it is power in its more tender aspect of loving-kindness that moves the psalmist to his statement of a dogma of orthodox Judaism, the exact correspondence of lot to desert (v. 12). It was against this dogma that the author of Job contended with keen insight into its limitations.

Psalm 63. The Thirst of the Soul for God

This is a song of trust. The psalmist is one of the circle of deeply religious men in Israel, to whom the Temple and its worship were but symbols and helps to a deep, spiritual worship (v. 2). He is passionately eager for fellowship with God (v. 1), the need for it intensified by the peril of death in which he stands because of pursuing enemies (vv. 9, 10). The psalm is really a confession of deep spiritual trust. In depth of religious insight it compares well with 36[7-9] 73[25] and 94[16f]. The verse concerning the king (v. 11ab), which is a later addition, proves the pre-exilic origin of the psalm.

1–3. The Psalmist's Longing for Fellowship With God. Like 42[1], he uses the figure of physical thirst in a desert region to interpret his craving for God (cf. 143[6]). Coming with such craving to the sanctuary, through sacrifice, prayer, and meditation he *looked upon*, i.e., became conscious of God. To experience the kindness of God meant more to him than life itself.

4–8. The General Utterance of His Trust. His present soul-satisfying experience of God inspires him to sing perpetual songs of praise throughout his life. In the wakeful hours of the night God will be the theme of his meditation. In v. 7b for *will I rejoice*, read *I shall dwell;* v. 8a may be rendered, literally, *My soul hath clung close to thee.*

9–11. The Destruction of His Enemies. Here for the first time we see the fact that intensifies the psalmist's sense of need for God. He has enemies who are seeking his life. These will be destroyed by death (v. 9b); Sheol, the sword and dishonorable treatment of their dead bodies (exposed without burial to wild animals) will be their lot. In v. 11 read *May the king rejoice*, etc. This prayer for the king is a later addition (see on 61[6, 7]), intended to adapt the psalm to use in the king's Temple at Jerusalem (Gunkel).

Psalm 64. The Ultimate Defeat of Evil

The psalmist, overwhelmed by fear of the enemies that are evidently very numerous (v. 2b, mg.), laments unto God and prays for his protection. He describes graphically the activities (vv. 3, 4), and imaginatively the words, of their scheming councils. But the psalmist confidently awaits their destruction at the hand of God, with its consequent effect upon the world. The psalm is similar to 5 and 10. The enemies are forces within Judaism. We cannot overestimate the influence in Judaism's dark hours of such faith in the ultimate defeat of evil and the sure triumph of righteousness as breathes in this psalm. It comes from the late Judaism when party strife was tense.

1, 2. Lamentation and Petition. Dread of the enemies that are about him in a "throng" (so v. 2b, mg.), plotting against him in secret, portrays the situation of the psalmist.

3–6. The Activities of his Enemies Described. Here, as in many similar instances, the chief point at which the enmity is felt is in defaming, slandering speech, which is graphically compared to sharp swords and poisoned arrows (v. 3; cf. 57[5] Prov. 26[18f.]) shot unexpectedly from ambush. Vv. 5, 6 picture the enemies concocting their plots, and the psalmist imaginatively represents their speech. The text of v. 6 is corrupt. Read v. 5c, with Syriac and Vulgate, *Who shall see us?* and, with Gunkel, v. 6a, *And search out our secrets; the deception has succeeded*; literally, "the device (is) well thought out." V. 6b should be interpreted as the psalmist's meditative reaction to such plotting on the part of his enemies. Read, following suggestions from Jer. 17[9], where his reaction to his enemies is likewise the thought, *Yea the bosom* [i.e., of man] *is incurable and the heart is deceitful.*

7, 8. God's Victory Over the Enemies. Note the suggestive way in which the psalmist portrays their fate in terms of their activities. Their dealing returns upon them (cf. Obad. v. 15b). They had aimed arrows at him, God will shoot arrows at them. They had taken him unawares, God will treat them similarly. They had laid traps for his feet, God will cause them to stumble. Read v. 8a, *He* [God] *shall cause them to stumble against their own tongue* (cf. mg.). Their destruction shall be so terrible as to cause all who see it to "flee" in terror (cf. mg.).

9, 10. The Effect of the Defeat of the Evil Upon the World. In awe all men will recognize the retributive power of God. The righteous shall trust him all the more and shall triumph.

Psalm 65. A Psalm of National Thanksgiving

A psalm of rare poetic and imaginative power. The author may have found his inspiration in a thanksgiving festival, probably after the relief from dearth. This festival itself may have been held in fulfillment of a vow, probably made at some such occasion as that described in Joel 2[15f]. There is a distinct division discernible at v. 9; but Kittel rightly accepts the psalm as a unity, against Gunkel, who views it as originally two separate psalms. The psalmist's touches of universalism in vv. 2, 5, 8 and the implicit universalism of vv. 9–13 suggest a date after Deutero-Isaiah, probably in the early post-exilic period.

1–4. The Fulfillment of a Vow. The lines of the text need rearrangement, as Gunkel has seen. Read v. 1a, *To Thee praise is fitting, O God in Zion.* V. 2a, *O thou who hearest prayer*, connects in thought and meter with v. 1. For vv. 2b, 3, read *Unto thee all flesh brings matters of iniquity* (i.e., what has to do with humanity's sense of sin; cf. mg.). "Our transgressions have become too strong for us. Thou wilt propitiate them."

The thanksgiving festival for which the psalm was composed is itself the fulfillment of a vow (v. 1b), made in dark hours, perhaps of famine and failure of crops, a condition viewed as the result of sin (v. 3a). The forgiveness of God, suggested through the release from famine, is here not merely his gracious gift to Israel but evidently (see vv. 5b, 8) benefits all flesh, which, when compared with Gen. 6[12], means humanity as a whole. While only Israelites, the chosen people, can partake of the blessings of the Temple (cf. Psa. 15 and 24), all humanity may share in the grace of God. Kittel recalls in this connection the similar broad outlook toward the Gentiles in Mal. 1[11] (notes), that prayers, rites, etc., brought to the worship of other gods, if sincere, in the final analysis belong to Jehovah, the one true God, and are accepted by him.

5–8. Israel's God a God of Creative Power. These verses portray God in his grandeur, a God of marvelous acts that root in his righteous nature. This God, who has revealed himself as governor of Israel's history (v. 5a) and as lord of nature, master of mountain and sea, is also lord of humanity (v. 7b), his dominion reaching to *all the ends of the earth* and *the far-away isles* (so read v. 5d). Sunrise and sunset are the limits of his beneficent and happiness-creating control (v. 8). It is clear that this psalmist has grasped Deutero-Isaiah's conception of a universal God.

9–13. The Year Arrayed in Its Glory. Relief from the dearth of rain has come and with it evidence of the return of God's favor. The "heavenly stream," which is viewed as the source of rain, *the river of God*, has poured its waters upon the earth. God is the great Gardener (v. 10), "pressing down" (cf. mg.) *the ridges*, "smoothing out" the *furrows* with rain. The climax of the year is the period when the soil is producing. The psalmist pictures this as the year's beautiful "crown," placed upon it by God (v. 11a; cf. 103[4]). Wherever God, the great Gardener, walks across the garden of the earth there springs up fruitfulness.

The psalm ends with a beautiful poetic picture in which hills, pastures and valleys are personified:

"The hills gird themselves with rejoicing.
The pastures are clothed with green grass,
The valleys envelop themselves with corn.
Thus arrayed in festive garb they too utter their praise.
They shout for joy!
They sing!"

Kittel rightly exclaims in the presence of such marvelous imaginative pictures: "What a poet! What a Folksoul."

Psalm 66. The Payment of a Vow

This psalm has two distinct parts, vv. 1–12 being a national song of thanksgiving, and vv. 13–20 a narrative of the payment of the vow of an individual. Because of this many have found here two separate psalms. Rightly conceived, however, vv. 1–12 are really preliminary to the main part of the psalm, vv. 13–20. The psalmist conceives what God has done for Israel as a nation and through Israel for humanity as a whole as giving a background of strength and color to his own experience of the divine grace. The clear detail of how the psalmist pays his vow (vv. 13–16) is instructive in high degree. The psalm stands clearly under the influence of Deutero-Isaiah. Vv. 1, 4, 5, 8 and the mingling of two divergent types of psalm material also point to a post-exilic date. Such a psalm reveals how the sense of history buttressed the religion of the individual in Israel.

1–4. The Earth Is Summoned to Praise Jehovah. The awesome deeds of God (v. 3) in Israel's history lead the nations of the world to come cringing unto him. This suggests the world-wide significance of Israel's history. The whole earth (v. 1) is accordingly invited to praise him (cf. Isa. 2:1-4 Zech. 8:20f.). The universalism of Deutero-Isaiah is here apparent, although on a somewhat lower plane.

5–7. God's Hand in Israel's History. What God does concerns all mankind (v. 5b), so the nations are summoned to recall what God has done for Israel at the Exodus, where in unique degree his hand was revealed (v. 6). For v. 6c read, with mg., *There let us rejoice in him*—i.e., the revelation of God's hand in Israel's ancient past is a basis for present joy; here is suggested the solidarity of Israel throughout the centuries, and implicitly, the solidarity of humanity. V. 7 presents a graphic picture of Israel's God in perpetual watch of the nations. With his eyes upon them, they dare not attack Israel.

8–12. A Renewed Summons to the Nations. Because God has been so wonderful to Israel, even the nations are to praise him. The pronouns of the first person plural (vv. 9f.) all refer to Israel. Israel has been tested by grave peril (v. 9), by trial (v. 10), by defeat and by extreme danger (v. 12ab), but God has brought the nation into "a place of liberty" (v. 12c; so read instead of *wealthy*).

13–20. The Payment of the Vow of an Individual. Welch shows how individual vows made in sickness or in seasons of great joy were paid at the sanctuary, frequently at one of the great festivals. In the presence of all the people, the community participating in the rite, the worshiper paid his vow, explaining through ritual words the meaning of his sacrifice (vv. 13, 14, 16). It may be that, as was the case in Babylonia and Egypt, such liturgies for the use of private individuals were retained by the priesthood and were handed out for the use of worshipers (see Welch's instructive discussion in *The Psalter*, pp. 67–80). Such occasions give rise to public testimony in Temple worship. Here the worshiper is evidently a prominent man, probably the leader of the congregation. Read v. 17b, with Syriac, *And I exalted him with my tongue.* Read v. 18, with mg.,

"If I had regarded iniquity in my heart,
The Lord would not have heard."

He was conscious of no sin when the vow was made. The psalm ends with a passionate ascription of praise.

Psalm 67. A Harvest Song of Thanksgiving

This is a national psalm of thanksgiving for the harvest. It was probably rendered by the Levitical choir at the feast of booths or Pentecost. The psalmist is imbued with the thought of Israel's mission as a light unto the nations (cf. Isa. 42:6 45:22). It probably comes from a time after Deutero-Isaiah, in the early post-exilic period. Through the temporal blessings the psalmist views the eternal goodness of God to Israel and to the world.

1–3. A Prayer for Blessing Upon Israel for the Sake of the World. Part of the famous priestly blessing of the sons of Aaron is quoted with change to first person (v. 1; cf. Num. 6:24f.). The significant purpose of this petition is that through the blessing of Israel the nations shall be led to a knowledge of Jehovah. This leads to a summons to the nations, in the style of an hymnic introduction, to praise God

(v. 3), which summons forms a vigorous and effective refrain.

4, 5. The Nation's Hymn of Praise. The subject of their hymn is the uprightness of God's government of the world. The refrain recurs in v. 5.

6, 7. Thanksgiving for the Harvest. In v. 6 we learn the special theme of the psalm—gratitude for the harvest. But this is viewed as but a material symbol of the goodness of God. V. 7 is a prayer. May the nations far and near, through observing God's material blessings to Israel, be led to worship him. Gunkel here restores the refrain, which would give finish and symmetry to the psalm.

Psalm 68. Israel's Triumphal Ode

Here is an ode of great literary and poetic power, preserved in a text very imperfect in detail, yet as a whole reasonably clear. It is a mistake to see any single triumph as its background. Rather is it a review of God's victories across the centuries with a consequent hope of his ultimate and complete triumph. With remarkable restraint the psalmist keeps this psalm vibrant with the atmosphere of the early national triumphs, leaving it to make its own impression, and to awaken, as it may, hope for the future. The psalmist is steeped in the ancient traditions and heroic literature of his race (e.g., Judg. 5, Deut. 33); likewise is he familiar with Deuteronomy and the late prophetic teaching (especially Second and Third Isaiah), by which he is deeply influenced. Peters (*The Psalms as Liturgies*), ignoring this, and interpreting the psalm as hinting at ideas later developed by Deuteronomy and the prophets, places it in the time of Jeroboam II, the middle of the eighth century. But we are safer, in the light of the eschatological features of the psalm and the reference to Egypt (cf. v. 31; Egypt maintained its independence against Persia 408–343 B.C.), to date it from the fourth century B.C.

1, 2. An Adaptation of the Ancient Ark Ritual. The psalmist, in his prayer for the help of God against Israel's foes, makes use of the ancient ritual of the ark found in Num. 10[35]. The presence of the ark with Israel's forces meant the presence of God. So may he ever appear, bringing, wherever needed, destruction to the wicked, i.e., to the enemy.

3, 4. The Righteous Prepare for His Coming. The enemies that melt and perish before him form a foil for the righteous who, in a hymnic introduction, are invited to exult at his coming and prepare the way for him. There is reference here to Isa. 40[3] 57[14] 62[10]. *Yah* is the primitive form of God's personal name, which ordinarily has the form "Jehovah."

5, 6. The Pledge of Deliverance. This is the hymn introduced by vv. 3, 4. It celebrates Israel's deliverance from the bondage of Egypt. The *rebellious* were then the Amalekites and Edomites. The language is based upon Deuteronomy (cf. Deut. 10[18-22]), and the atmosphere of the triumph of the Exodus is here implicit for the Israel of the psalmist's day and for the future.

7, 8. The Wilderness Journey. The psalmist adapts to his use the verses of the song of Deborah that deal with the theophany in which Jehovah comes from his ancient habitation to defeat the Canaanites (Judg. 5[4, 5]). The experience of history becomes a basis for permanent hope.

9, 10. God's Marvelous Provision for His People. The sacrifice that celebrates in worship Jehovah's triumph and which includes the feasting of the people in a way dramatizes the appearance of God and his provision of manna and quails in the desert. Peters (*The Psalms as Liturgies*) reads v. 9,

"With a rain of freewill offerings
Thou besprinklest thy heritage."

11–14. The Songs of Victory. At the Exodus (Ex. 15[21]) and at the triumphs of David (1 Sam. 18[7]) the women proclaimed the triumph in songs. So here we have the first lines (so Peters) of several triumph songs, which are sung by the women (v. 11b). Their theme is the triumph of God. V. 12 is a song celebrating the triumph of Barak over Sisera; v. 12b refers to Sisera's mother awaiting her son's return, laden with spoil (cf. Judg. 5[30]); v. 13a is a taunt song against Reuben (Judg. 5[16]); v. 13bc is probably, as Ewald thinks, a fragment of an old song from "the Book of the Wars of Jehovah"; v. 14a is a fragment of a song of victory from the days of the conquest of Canaan; v. 14b refers to a region near Shechem (Judg. 9[48]).

15, 16. Praise of Zion. The psalmist is sensitive to beauty. Great as is the "mountain of summits," the mountain of Bashan (probably also a reference to an ancient song; so Ewald), God's mountain, Zion, puts the beauty of Bashan to shame. This is one of the songs of Zion, which the exiles found difficult to sing "in a strange land" (cf. 137[3]).

17, 18. The Entrance of Jehovah into Zion. Israel is now at rest in Palestine. The conquest is past. V. 17 is an adaptation of the ancient ritual used as the ark was brought back from battle (cf. Num. 10[36]). Now the forces of God are the thousands of his own people settled in Palestine. Jerusalem, the capital, and the place of Jehovah's abode, the new Sinai (read mg.), is supreme even after the

Babylonian Exile (v. 18), and is the receiver of the tribute of the nations (cf. 76[11]).

19–23. A Hymn Celebrating Jehovah in Salvation and Judgment. He is here celebrated as a burden-bearing and delivering God. He will deliver Israel from the fiery furnace (following a reading suggested by Lagarde) and from the depths of the sea—i.e., from fire and water—symbols of grave peril. But upon the enemies Israel may wreak its vengeance (v. 23).

24–27. The Festal Procession. These verses graphically portray the celebration of the triumph of the heavenly king in terms of that of a victorious monarch (v. 24). In the procession the Levitical singers are in the lead, followed by the maidens playing timbrels, and, bringing up the rear, the players of stringed instruments (v. 25). All are singing the praise song to God, the Lord, the fountain source of Israel. The procession celebrates no single triumph of Israel; the psalmist has in his imagination Israel's victories through the centuries. The little fighting clan of *Benjamin* (cf. Judg. 5[14], the fighting cry, "After thee, Benjamin"), which furnished the first king of Israel, is mentioned side by side with *Judah* of early promise and of later prowess (cf. Gen. 49[8f.]), along with the two heroic tribes, which in the song of Deborah are given place of honor, *Zebulun* and *Naphtali.* All march in the same triumphal procession. The psalmist thus looks across the centuries and pictures in his chambers of imagery a victorious procession.

28–31. The Ultimate Triumph of God. The imagination of the psalmist leaps from the contemplation of the past to the contemplation of the time of the end. The God who has thus been in Israel's history is now summoned to assert again his power. Read for vv. 28, 29a,

"Command, O God, thy strength,
That strength thou didst exercise for us
From thy Temple at Jerusalem."

He gazed into the final era when the kings of the nations shall worship Jehovah (cf. Isa. 49[7]). The enemies—the chief evidently being Egypt, *wild beast of the reeds*—portrayed here in apocalyptic fashion as animals (cf. Dan. 7[1-7], notes), will be destroyed (v. 30) and the once-enemy nations like Ethiopia will come to Jerusalem to worship (v. 31; cf. Isa. 19[19-25] Zech. 8[22].)

32–35. The Kingdoms are Summoned to Praise. In anticipation of the ultimate triumph of Israel's God the nations are summoned even now to praise him (v. 32), in a majestic hymn of praise (vv. 33f.), which is reminiscent of the ancient poem in Deut. 33. Here again is implied a sense of a world-wide mediating task for Israel.

Psalm 69. Unmerited Suffering for Loyalty to Convictions

The psalmist, a leader of the loyal, is near death's door (vv. 4b, 15c), which situation is made the more disturbing because it is to him direct evidence of God's disfavor (v. 26). Moreover, added to this is the overwhelming sense of disgrace in which he stands in the community (vv. 11, 12), and which shows itself in scornful and outspoken enmity (v. 4). But his zeal for God and the Temple remains constant and sincere. He prays for deliverance for himself and for judgment upon his enemies (vv. 14, 22f.). Upon the evident reversal of his fortunes he utters a song of thanksgiving (vv. 30–32) and a hymn of praise (vv. 33, 34). The most probable period out of which the psalm came is the fifth century B.C.

1–4. The Psalmist's Lamentation. The psalmist is in deep distress, struggling, as it were, in waters beyond his depth, discouraged beyond expression with unanswered prayers, and enduring insult at the hands of enemies, numerous and powerful.

5, 6. He Acknowledges His Sin. He is keenly conscious of the influence of his example upon the loyal, who evidently look up to him as a leader. If he is not restored, the loyal will fall away into dishonor.

7–12. The Lamentation Renewed and Detailed. His disgrace in the public eye is really due to his loyalty to God (v. 7), consumed as he has been with a passion for the Temple and its worship (v. 9a). He has identified himself with God's cause. His out-and-out loyalty has made the brunt of the community's enmity against God fall upon him (v. 9b). His loyalty to the rites of his religion has awakened scornful gossip (v. 12) and made him the sport of the community (v. 11).

13–20a. His Prayer. In keen distress of body (v. 17) and soul (vv. 19, 20a) he prays for deliverance from death—for the mouth of the grave seems wide open toward him—but also for deliverance from his enemies (vv. 14b, 18), and for vindication before them (v. 19).

20bc, 21. His Treatment. He had a right to expect pity but found in its stead only abuse and merciless treatment (cf. Mt. 27[34, 48]).

22–29. A Passionate Prayer for God's Retribution. These bitter words must be viewed in the illuminating light of v. 9b. *His* enemies were *God's* enemies, deserving of the divine destruction. Make their lives and their homes desolate! (Vv. 22–28.) For, not satisfied with the punishment from God which the psalmist is viewed as already suffering through his sickness, they add to this their persecution (v. 26). So let God add charge to charge against them (v. 27). Let their names be blotted out of the divine book (cf. Ex. 32^{32} Isa. 4^{3} Dan. 12^{1}), i.e., let them die (v. 28). But let the psalmist be saved and restored (v. 29). Cf. also the Babylonian tablets of fate, the tablets of good and the tablets of evil, kept by Nabu, the scribe of the gods. The conception here found is the Hebrew counterpart of the Babylonian idea (cf. 87^{6} 139^{16}).

30–32. His Song of Thanksgiving. Between the situations of vv. 29 and 30, his prayer has been answered. With a song in his heart, aware that the faith of the loyal has been steadied by his release (v. 32), he praises God. Not with sacrifice, but with song he worships, believing the latter more acceptable. This union of zeal for the Temple (v. 9) with the practical rejection of the sacrificial system is remarkable and links the psalm to the great prophetic utterances of the Psalter (cf. 40^{6} $50^{8f.}$ $51^{16f.}$).

33, 34. His Hymn of Praise. The song of thanksgiving issues in a hymn where all creation is summoned to praise the God who answers prayer.

35, 36. A Liturgical Adaptation. In the form that reminds us of Isa. 44^{26-28} and 65^{9} we have here, as Kittel rightly sees, a liturgical addition. These verses lack the intense individualistic passion of the rest of the psalm.

Psalm 70. A Prayer for Deliverance and Judgment

This psalm = 40^{13-17}, where see notes.

Psalm 71. Abandon Me Not in Old Age

The psalmist is an elderly man (v. 9). From his birth he has been undergirded by God (v. 6), and from childhood has been under his instruction (v. 17). Now, old and weak, he is surrounded by adversaries who desire to do away with him (vv. 11, 20). In the confidence induced by a lifetime of experience he waits for God's deliverance. He is conscious of the gift of inspired utterance (v. 15) and his desire to live (v. 20) is only that all day long he may teach the younger generation (v. 18) the nature of God (v. 24). We feel ourselves to be amid the party strife of the Persian period, probably in the fifth century B.C. The psalm is not a community psalm but is the lamentation of an individual, as the corrected text of v. 20 reveals.

1–8. Confidence in God With Petition for Deliverance. Vv. 1–3 = 31^{1-3a}, where see notes. In v. 3a read *rock of safety.* The words *whereunto I may continually resort* = "to save me" in 31^{2}. This psalm suggests the habit of communion. His enemies are both unrighteous and ruthless. The psalmist, now an old man (v. 18), looks back (vv. 5b, 6) to the day of birth. Translate:

> "By thee have I been supported (or braced) from birth.
> From the womb of my mother thou didst draw me forth."

From that moment until the present God has "braced" him. *Wonder*—better, *object of horror*—as he is to some (v. 7), God is his refuge. This section comes to its climax in a song that is a burst of gratitude (v. 8). Translate *All the day with thy beauty.*

9–13. Lamentation and Petition. Here he reveals his condition. In failing strength due to his age (v. 9), surrounded by plotters against him (v. 10), who, because of his condition, consider him abandoned by God (v. 11), he prays for God not to "fling him off" now (vv. 9, 12). He prays for reversal of fortune upon his enemies (v. 13). Let them be humiliated.

14–16. A Burst of Praise. Still in his dire distress he waits for the relief of God in the spirit of praise. He recalls the mighty deeds of God in his life.

17–21. A Song of Thanksgiving. The psalmist claims inspiration for the teaching which he has hitherto done, probably in similar songs (v. 17b). He has been taught of God since childhood (v. 17a). Now, *old and gray,* he prays for God's presence in strength to be with him until he has taught the next generation (so with Syriac, "the coming generation," v. 18). He is impressed with the righteousness of God (v. 19) which has followed him throughout his life. He is confident of restoration to health from the very gates of death (vv. 20, 21). Read *me* for *us,* with mg., in v. 20 (so Duhm, Cheyne, Gunkel, following the versions).

22–24. His Vow. When help comes he will sing God's praises and speak untiringly of his dealings. Then his enemies will be the humiliated party, and he will stand vindicated before them.

Psalm 72. A Prayer for the King's Righteous and Prosperous Reign

The psalmist, who is probably himself one of the poor in the nation (note the repeated references to the poor), prays that as a guiding principle God's justice may be granted the young (v. 1b) king. He wishes and confidently expects for him world-wide sovereignty (vv. 8f.), national prosperity (v. 16) and perpetual fame (v. 17). The psalm portrays an ideal monarch and an ideal rule. It dates from the time of the Israelitish kings, and is pre-exilic. Kittel inclines to associate it with Josiah.

1–4. Prayer and Wishes for a Reign of Righteousness and Peace. The psalmist prays that the young king, the rightful heir, probably just beginning his reign, may be imbued with God's spirit of justice. A similar prayer addressed to Ashur is found in Assyrian literature. The future tenses of the verbs throughout the psalm should be changed to jussives (so mg.), expressing the wishes of the psalmist. The poor of the people (vv. 2, 4) are of special concern to him. The productivity of hillside and mountains is the natural accompaniment of a righteous reign.

5–7. His Enduring Reign. As is the case with Assyrian and Egyptian monarchs, a long reign is hoped for, in which the outstanding mark will be peaceful, gentle productivity.

8–11. The Extent of his Dominion. The psalmist wishes for him world-wide dominion (cf. 2[8] 18[43f.]), extending from the Euphrates unto the extremities of the earth (v. 8). Desert tribes (v. 9), far-off kings from Spain, from islands in the Mediterranean, from South Arabia, from (probably) the coastlands of the Arabian sea (v. 10), commercial people of wealth and power will bring him tribute and pay him homage (v. 11).

12–14. The Reward of His Righteousness. Such sovereignty is granted him as a reward earned by his righteous rule, which recognizes the rights of the poor who otherwise would have no one to maintain their cause. In his sight even oppressed and powerless folk are of precious value. The verbs here are indicatives, not jussives.

15. The Reward From the Hearts of the Poor. Here is a sensitive and beautiful touch. These poor can do nothing of material significance for the king—this he does not need from them—yet may they continually pray for him! Probably the psalmist himself is of this class. V. 15a is a gloss which breaks the connection of vv. 14 and 15b. Similar attitudes of prayer for the king are found in Babylonian, Assyrian, and Egyptian literature.

16, 17. Resultant Rich Harvests and Enduring Fame. Read v. 16, following Gunkel:

"May there be plenty of corn in the earth,
On the top of the mountain may it wave,
Like Lebanon may its fruit flourish
And its sheaves as the herbage of the field."

May his reputation never fade!

18, 19. The Doxology. This closes the second book of the Psalter (cf. on 41[13]).

20. This verse is the subscription of a collection of "Prayers of David," which ended with Psa. 72.

PSALMS LXXIII–CL

BY PROFESSOR W. A. SHELTON

General Introduction. For the general introduction to the Psalter, see pp. 509f. The third book of Psalms (73–89) contains seventeen psalms: The first eleven are psalms of Asaph, while 84, 87, 88, and 95 are assigned to the Sons of Korah, 86 to David, 89 to Ethan, and 88 is assigned also to Heman. Asaph is said to have been one of the chief musicians of David, of whom there were three: Asaph, Heman and Ethan (cf. 1 Chr. 15[16, 17] 16[5], etc.). It is not to be thought that all of the psalms assigned to Asaph were written by him. Indeed, it is not necessary to hold that he wrote any of them. He was, rather, the one who organized and conducted choirs and orchestras and perhaps edited collections of hymns. He may have written some of them, set others to music, and merely readapted others. Some may have been dedicated to him and some composed by his guild. But his psalms are a type. They are distinguished by a prophetic note. God is a judge. He is presented as announcing a judgment in his own voice, as in Psa. 75 and others. The interpretation of the past for the purpose of teaching the proper conduct for the future is common in this collection. The oft-repeated figure of God as a Shepherd of his flock, and the use of Jacob and Joseph are characteristics of the Asaph psalms.

PSALM 73. THE SUFFERING OF THE RIGHTEOUS; THE PROSPERITY OF THE WICKED

The theme of this psalm is one that men can never escape (cf. Psa. 37, 49). It is the problem of Job. Why do the righteous suffer and the wicked remain prosperous? The psalm is divided into two parts: (1) The psalmist confesses his temptation and relates how nearly his faith has failed him (vv. 1–14). (2) He relates how he has come to see the error of his way and has come out victorious (vv. 15–28).

1. The Psalmist's Triumph. Surely, in spite of all that has been suffered, God is good, and only good, to Israel. *To such as are pure in heart*—a clean heart is the "open sesame" to the goodness of God.

2–9. The Psalmist's Danger. Here is the same situation in which Job found himself and, indeed, in which many saints have found themselves in every age. V. 2 states that the psalmist came near to apostasy; vv. 3–9 give the cause of his danger—the unbroken prosperity of the wicked. *There are no bands in their death*—the wicked seem to die well. They do not suffer as the saints suffer, even when facing the "last enemy." *Their strength is firm*—calmly they go to death. *Pride is as a chain about their neck*—pride adorns them as a necklace and violence clothes them as a garment (cf. Job 29[14]). *Their eyes stand out with fatness*—out of the grossness of their hearts comes their wickedness. *Against the heavens* (v. 9, mg.)—they would even speak against God. *Their tongue walketh through the earth*—they speak arrogantly.

10–12. The Evil Influence of the Prosperous Wicked. V. 10 probably means that the prosperous wicked gather many to their banners. The rich have many "hangers on." *How doth God know?*—this is said by those deluded by the wicked. *These are the wicked*—i.e., the men the psalmist has just been describing. Because they are always at ease, they prosper. Nothing interferes with their prosperity (cf. Job 21[7-13]).

13, 14. The Psalmist's Temptation. The psalmist says it is in vain that one lives a clean life; the other life pays better. I seek, he says, to meet the demands of righteousness, and for my pains I get only plagues and beatings, being chastened every morning.

15–17. Solution of the Psalmist's Problem. He is saying: "If I state the feelings of my heart with reference to these things, I shall be unfaithful to those whom I influence. I have no right to bring doubts to others. When I sought the solution to my problem, it was too painful to me. It was too hard to understand." *Until I went into the sanctuary of God.* There is the place to solve all problems. There went young Isaiah (Isa. 6[1]) when his king was dead or dying and his heart perplexed. Many have found the satisfying portion in times of deepest doubt in the house of the Lord. *Considered their latter end.* When in the midst of the services in God's house I thought with Him who sees the end from the beginning, I grasped the meaning of it all. Prosperity is but for a day and chastened character stands out brilliantly against the darkening skies of a day of reckoning. "Success," says Victor Hugo, "is a very hideous thing and its resemblance to merit deceives men."

18–20. The Ultimate Fate of the Wicked. When the veil is drawn aside the psalmist is astonished. *Slippery places.* A while ago it was the psalmist who thought he was in a slippery place. Now he sees clearly that it is the wicked even though he seem prosperous. Destruction, desolation, terrors—these are the heritage of those who prosper at the expense of right. Riches, palaces, plenty are no guarantee of happiness. These wicked are as one awaking from a dream; they find their prosperity nothing more than a mere phantasm. They only thought they were prosperous, whereas in reality they were poor and blind and wretched (cf. Job 20[4-11]).

21, 22. The Psalmist's Confession. *As a beast before thee.* The word translated "beast" is the Hebrew word *behemoth,* which is translated in Job 40[15] (mg.) as hippopotamus, the most stupid of all beasts. He is now down in the depths of humility.

23–26. The Saint's Permanent Fellowship with God. The psalmist contrasts his enjoyment of fellowship with God with his former outlook on life. *Thou hast holden my right hand*—the high God stoops to lead weak and foolish man. *Thou shalt guide me with thy counsel*—God will guide the one who puts his full trust in him. *Afterward receive me to glory* (v. 24b, cf. mg.). The question is: Does the psalmist have a conception of heaven as the N.T. writers had? Most modern scholars feel that "glory" here does not refer to the hereafter, but, rather, to that honor which stands in glad contrast over against the degradation which the writer felt when he was talking about the prosperity of the wicked. Just now he was as stupid as a behemoth, but since he has submitted himself to the leadership of God and realized his own inability, God will conduct him to high honor. However, the passage makes the impression, hard to get away from, that the eternal glory is meant.

V. 25 furnishes a grand climax. *Whom have I in heaven but thee? and there is none upon earth that I desire beside thee.* The psalmist begins with a wail of despair from the depths of spiritual depression; but out of it he comes, beginning with his going to the sanctuary of the Lord, and climbs to this stairway of spiritual attainment, where his confidence and faith overreach earth and sweep out into the heavens. God becomes his one great answer to all questions and the satisfaction of every desire. *Heart* and *flesh* shall fail, but God is sufficient for all of his needs.

27, 28. The Final Contrast Between the Wicked and the Righteous. The wicked whom I envied are marked for destruction, but the best thing for me is to *draw near unto God.*

Having achieved a spiritual triumph he has an inexhaustible theme for his songs of praise.

PSALM 74. GOD'S APPARENT INDIFFERENCE; A PRAYER FOR VINDICATION

God seems altogether to have abandoned his people. Their Temple is destroyed, their synagogues burned, no prophet is in the land and the people have been humbled. Both here and in Psa. 79 the idea is emphasized that if God's people are humbled his own honor is also involved; he is humiliated along with them. The psalmist prays fervently for the return of God to his stricken people. He reminds him of his mercy in the past and his responsibility in the present and describes the awful havoc wrought by the enemy.

It is very difficult to fix the exact date of this psalm or the occasion which gave rise to it. Some hold with Kirkpatrick (Cambridge Bible, p. 440) that it originated in the Babylonian Exile, perhaps between 586 and 566 B.C. If this be true, then it was most surely adapted to express the feelings of later ages. The whole atmosphere and expression, however, would best be suited to the time of Antiochus Epiphanes, probably between 168 and 165 B.C.; that is, in the time between the edict of Antiochus in 168, requiring the Jews to worship the Olympian Jove, and the success of the Maccabæan revolt in 165; during which period the Jews suffered the severest persecution of their whole experience (see pp. 192b, 755).

1–3. An Appeal to God. On *Maschil* (or *Maskîl*) see p. 511b. *Why hast thou cast us off forever?*—the people cease to hope for better times; God seems permanently turned from them. *Why doth thine anger smoke?*—the figure is a severe one. God's anger is fierce. The *smoke* is the outward sign of the fire of his wrath. Moreover, it is against his *sheep*—the true shepherd loves his sheep. The picture is of the meek, harmless ones. God's anger appears to be beyond all reason. *Thy congregation* (v. 2)—i.e., the assembly of thy people or the nation itself. *Purchased*—brought out of Egypt and formed into a nation to be God's own heritage. *Which thou hast redeemed*—cf. the song of Moses (Ex. 15[16], where the same word is used). The meaning is to set free by paying a ransom; it is often used for the deliverance of the children of Israel from Egyptian bondage (Ex. 6[6]), as well as with reference to the Babylonian Exile. *Thine inheritance*—the peculiar people of God. *Mount Zion*—remember the congregation and also the Holy Mount where the congregation meets. In v. 3 for *feet* read, with LXX, *hands;* some suggest a change which would give *eyes.* Lift up your eyes to behold the utter ruin. But "lift up your feet" to come to look upon the ruin would not be illogical. The prayer is for God to come to the place of his ancient dwelling and behold the utter ruin of it. *Perpetual*—the ruin seems to be permanent. The enemy hath wrought all evil in the *sanctuary.* The writer is horrified at the sacrilege committed.

4–9. The Desecration of the Holy Precincts. The adversaries of God have *roared.* The sacred area was filled with heathen foes instead of faithful worshipers. *Ensigns for signs*—literally, "their signs as signs." The heathen signs and symbols now take the place of those of Jehovah. They are like woodcutters felling entire forests. *Thicket of trees*—the carved work of the Temple was wrought out as a forest of palm trees and open flowers (1 Kings 6[29]); thus the ancient skilled workers constructed symbolic forests, and now these vandals are hewing them down.

In the building of the Temple there was heard not the sound of "hammer nor ax nor any tool of iron" (1 Kings 6[7]). Now the sound of *hatchet and hammers* was the sound of sacrilege. *They have set thy sanctuary on fire* (v. 7): this seems to indicate a complete destruction such as took place under Nebuchadrezzar (2 Kings 25[9]). V. 8 is a very important one, since *synagogues* did not originate until the Exile and probably did not come into Palestine until after the return. The first mention of them is here. The time when all of the synogogues were destroyed was after 168 B.C., by Antiochus Epiphanes. *Our signs*—the outward symbols of their religion. The Sabbath was no more kept, the sacrifices were not offered, there were no feasts as of old. Antiochus attempted to suppress all signs of the Jewish religion. No surer proof of religious decay can be found than the desecration of the symbols of religion, especially the Sabbath. *No more any prophet*—there was no prophet in the days of the Maccabees. Unhappy the people who have no holy man to lead them to God.

10, 11. Jehovah's Apparent Indifference. *How long?*—this expression appears often and always reflects the same state of mind; evidently, it was the conventional phrase by which the Jew poured forth his soul in times of extreme trial.

12–17. Past Manifestations of the Divine Mercy and Power. On second thought, the psalmist muses on the past goodness of God and takes courage in the wonderful acts of the great King in olden times. *Salvation*—literally, salvations or deliverances; many of them had been wrought for Israel by their King. Perhaps in his own good time he will visit his people again for good. *Thou didst divide the sea*

(v. 13; cf. mg.)—by the mighty power of Jehovah, the sea, i.e., the Red Sea, was divided at the time of the Exodus. *Dragons*—or "sea-monsters"; *leviathan*—the crocodile (Job 41[1], notes). Both terms may be used of mythical monsters which appear also in Babylonian literature and elsewhere in the O.T. If so, the author was hardly aware of the original usage; he uses the terms simply as symbols. God cuts in two the Red Sea and these other monsters, which represent Egypt and the Pharaoh and his army, who were left floating upon the waters of the sea. The Exodus is a favorite theme with the psalmists. *To be meat* (or *food*) *to the people inhabiting the wilderness* (v. 14b)—jackals and other animals. The bodies of the Egyptians washed up on the shores of the Red Sea were devoured by desert animals. God's wonderful strength is shown also in his ability to bring water out of the rock, i.e., a spring, to dry up the Jordan or other perennial streams. God is the Governor of all nature and sets a bound for it. He orders days, nights, and seasons according to his will (vv. 16, 17).

18–23. An Appeal to God to Remember His Saints. In the light of past experiences the psalmist is convinced that Jehovah will look out for the darlings of his heart, his *turtledove;* that he will remember his covenant with his people and not forget the arrogant cry of the adversary.

Psalm 75. The Presence and Power of Jehovah

A thanksgiving for a remarkable deliverance, probably in the recent past. The author is unknown. The time and occasion are uncertain. Some date it after the invasion of Sennacherib, king of Assyria (see 2 Kings 19), others, like Perowne, suggest the late Persian period. The psalm is lyrical, both in music and matter.

1. The Theme: Thanksgiving for a recent manifestation of the divine power. A suggested rendering for this verse is, "We give thanks unto thee, O God, we give thanks: and we call upon thy name: we recount thy wonderful acts." *Thy name is near.* If this reading is retained, it means "thou art near"; the name of God means the character of God in expression.

2–5. The Divine Warning Against the Foes. *I will judge*—God has not abdicated his throne; in his own good time he will take his place on the judgment seat and his judgment will be in righteousness. Though the earth dissolve and pass away, there is a moral order that stands sure and steadfast. *I said unto the arrogant:* Is the reference to Rabshakeh, the chief captain of Sennacherib? (Cf. 2 Kings 19[1, 2].) *Lift not up the horn*—deal not proudly. It is the meek that "shall inherit the earth."

6–8. Jehovah the Supreme Arbiter of Human Destiny. *Lifting up*—promotion. The north is the only direction not mentioned, it is thought by some because the Assyrian approached from the north. Help and exaltation cannot come from any direction; Jehovah alone can give it. Emptying the *cup* of judgment is a common figure. The wicked are forced to drain to the dregs the cup of their own iniquity (cf. Rev. 14[9-11], notes).

9, 10. A Vow of Praise. The psalmist declares his intention of ever singing the praises of Jehovah; v. 10 gives Jehovah's answer to this vow of praise. *I will cut off*—Jehovah promises to destroy the wicked and to exalt the righteous. The *wicked* is the proud and arrogant enemy; the *righteous* are the psalmist and Israel which he represents.

Psalm 76. A Psalm of Victory

The background of this psalm is furnished by a great historical event in which Jerusalem was delivered from some enemy, who was entirely overcome while most of his army was slaughtered. It sounds somewhat like the battle song of Deborah (Judg. 5). The occasion is probably identical with that reflected in Psa. 75.

1–3. Defeat of Israel's Enemies. *Judah . . . Israel*—both kingdoms find God sufficient in battle. The psalm was certainly written after the division. *Salem*—the word means "peace." Jerusalem means "city of peace." The psalmist possibly intends to use the word peace to describe not only Jerusalem, but the condition of the people after the victory, as well. *Zion*—may refer to the same place as Salem. While Zion came in after times to mean the Temple mount, it was first used of the western hill, on which the original city of David was located. The weapons of war are broken and worthless before Jehovah. The psalm may refer to the defeat of Sennacherib (2 Kings 19[35]).

4–6. Manifestation of the Divine Power. *The mountains of prey*—read, with mg., *more than.* Jehovah is more glorious than the high mountains, amid whose mysteries the daring hunter seeks his prey. *The stout-hearted are spoiled, they have slept their sleep* (v. 5)—defeat and death. Very poetical is the picture of death as an eternal sleep. The vivid description here is of the enemy (possibly the Assyrians) on the morning after the battle sleeping harmlessly and peacefully upon their broken arms, their hands impotent and unable to seize the weapons of war. Death has broken the strength of the mighty; the Hebrew patriot to-day walks among the slain, praising his God. *Chariot and horse*—how still they lie! But yesterday the horses were prancing and rearing, gnashing their teeth for the battle, ready in their fury to tread down the people of God; the chariots were rattling and thundering over the battlefield spreading dismay everywhere; but to-day they are silent and harmless.

7–9. The Irresistible Judgment of God. Who, in the face of this providence, can stand against God? He sweeps armies away with a breath. None is safe, save those who trust him. The seat of Jehovah is really in heaven, but his earthly dwelling place was in Jerusalem. He sits now as a mighty Judge and gives forth sentence upon those of earth who fight against his meek ones. *The earth feared, and was still* when God arose to judgment. What an awful time, when God marches forth to take his place upon the Judgment seat! The idea of the earth (v. 8b) entering into such experience is not confined to this passage. The evangelist tells that the earth expressed its sympathy when Jesus was crucified (cf. Mt. 27^{45-52}).

10–12. Praise of the Triumphant God. *Surely, the wrath of man shall praise thee.* How many times has this been demonstrated through the years! God is not the author of wrath, but when wrath is made manifest he is present, and the very works of Satan are sometimes turned into the glory of God. *Vow and pay* (v. 11)—let Israel now pay the vows she made to God in the time of peril. Many, when they face disaster, vow to give themselves or their time and property to God, but frequently they forget when the time of stress is over. Let everyone bring presents to him when no peril exists. Jehovah is the King of kings (v. 12).

Psalm 77. A Wail of Sorrow When Faith is Sorely Tried

Both date and author are unknown. Apparently it comes from a time of great distress —possibly when Jerusalem was so seriously threatened by the Assyrians in the days of Hezekiah. The likeness to the Psalm of Habakkuk is striking (cf. Hab. 3).

1–3. I Will Cry and God Will Answer. There is something of the wail of Job in these verses. The force of the tenses in Hebrew is not quite clear. Probably v. 1 is to be regarded as an expression of confidence in spite of past disappointments (vv. 2, 3). Many seek the Lord only in the days of trouble, and it is good that we can turn to him in our calamities; but sometimes it seems as if prayers were not heard. *My hand was stretched out*—in prayer; should probably read *my eye was poured out*—in tears. Unrelieved sorrow—even the night brought no restful sleep. V. 3, describing a past experience, should probably be translated: *When I would remember God, I was so disquieted that I could not; When I would complain* [or *muse in prayer*] *I was unable to do so.*

4–9. Musings on the Divine Mercies in the Past. God will not let the psalmist sleep but holds his eyes open. *Watching*—or watchers = eyelids; guards of the eyes. *Considered the days of old*—"Sorrow's crown of sorrow is remembering happier things" (Tennyson's *Locksley Hall*). He remembers when he sang even in the night. *Commune*—to commune with your own heart is to meditate, and here also to mutter, as if the psalmist were humming some old song from the days of better fortune. In his musing he diligently sought to fathom the ways of God. *Cast off forever?* Is this condition permanent? Is his mercy spent? How long? Has he forgotten to be gracious? (Cf. Hab. 3^2, "In wrath remember mercy.")

10–15. Jehovah's Power and Mercy Manifested in His Dealings with Israel. What troubles the psalmist most is that God has changed (in v. 10b read mg.). He is not what he once was. God's *right hand* was the hand with which he saved in the past (Ex. 15^6). Whatever may be the situation now, in the past God has shown himself able and willing to help (vv. 11–20). *The sons of Jacob and Joseph.* Jacob was the father of all the patriarchs. Joseph himself directly founded no tribe but was the father of Ephraim and Manasseh, two powerful units of Israel; the meaning here is all the tribes. The reference is not only to the experiences of the Exodus but to the entire past history.

16–19. God's Power Over Nature. A poem or a fragment of another psalm seems here blended with this one. This passage describes God revealing himself in the majesty of storm. Some see a reference to creation (cf. Psa. 29). The waters of the Mediterranean Sea have become troubled. Waves rise here and lash the shore. The storm clouds rise out of the Western sea. *Sound* (v. 17)—thunder; *arrows*—zig-zag lightning; *lightnings lightened the world*—sheet lightning. *Thy way was in the sea*—God governs the sea as well as the dry land.

20. Conclusion. *Thou leddest thy people*—expresses calm confidence in the final outcome of it all. As Jehovah led his people in the past so he will care now for those who put their trust in him.

Psalm 78. A Psalm of Teaching

A "wisdom" psalm. Its purpose is to instruct the present from the experiences of the past. It is impossible to fix a date with any degree of certainty. The Temple seems to be standing (cf. v. 69) and possibly the divided kingdom.

1–8. The Psalmist Recalls the Past as a Means of Teaching the Future. As we have received from our fathers the traditions of the past, so we must give them to our children and children's children (vv. 3, 4). This is a sacred duty, laid upon all parents according to the *testimony* (v. 5), the commandment, given to Israel long ago (cf. Ex. 10[2] 12[26, 27] Deut. 4[9], etc.). To obey these commandments is our only means of keeping faith with the fathers and preserving history for future religious education (v. 6). Thus successive generations may see how God dealt with his people. This knowledge will enable them to avoid the mistakes of the fathers and to maintain and intensify their own faith (vv. 7, 8).

9–31. Ephraim's Disobedience in Spite of the Divine Mercy. Ephraim did not trust God in battle. This was one of the disgraceful incidents in the traditions of the past. Ephraim represents Israel. The reference may be to a particular incident, or the words may be descriptive of the general cowardice or faithlessness of the people. *Zoan* (v. 12)—capital of the Hyksos, and near the land of Goshen, where they could see what God did for his people in the Exodus. The mighty works of God are described in detail in vv. 12–31. But the people sinned in spite of his marvelous works. *Lust* (v. 18) = appetite. *A table in the wilderness*—see on 23[5]; God was angry but still fed them with the *corn of heaven* (vv. 20–24), and plenteously provided his people in the desert with food (vv. 25–28). He cared for them in spite of their apostasy. The wrath of God comes at unexpected moments; the very food which they demanded was the source of their ruin (vv. 29–31).

32–39. Superficial Repentance. They continued in sin (vv. 32, 33); but finally, in the midst of disaster they remembered him (v. 34). *Rock . . . Redeemer* (v. 35)—familiar terms for "Jehovah." But they worshiped him with their lips only; their hearts were far from him (vv. 36, 37). *Covenant*—i.e., a contract with God. In spite of the people's baseness, God, being full of compassion, often turned away from his anger; he dealt with them not according to justice, but mercy. *Flesh* (v. 39) = the frailty of human nature (cf. Psa. 103[14]).

40–56. The More God Showed His Mercy the More They Rebelled and Forsook Him. Over and over the same story of apostasy is told and retold, but ever God's mercy holds. These verses give a complete survey of events connected with the Exodus and the desert wanderings. *The border of his sanctuary, to this mountain*—Mount Zion, on which the Temple was built, and the promised land of Canaan.

57–64. The Divine Leadings During the Period of the Judges. Once again God does everything good for them in giving them Canaan as a home, but they rebelled and apostatized again. In their settled state they forsook him and built high places (altars for the practice of pagan rites; 2 Kings 23[5f.]). Then God abandoned them to their enemies (vv. 60, 61). The ark, the symbol of his presence, was captured and he went out of the land with it (cf. 1 Sam. 4). *Shiloh*—where the ark had been located. *No marriage song* (v. 63)—no marriages were contracted because the young men had been taken away or killed. The priests were murdered and their widows made no lamentation. Can this be a reminiscence of the death of Hophni and Phineas and the death of the widow of Phineas on the news of her husband's death and the birth of Ichabod? (1 Sam. 4[12-22].)

65–72. Choice of Zion and of David. God seemed to them to be asleep (v. 65). In the time of Samuel vision was scarce. The figure of God awakening out of a sleep and suddenly realizing what was happening to his people, and then rushing out as a man stimulated by wine and smiting the army just leaving with the booty is a very vivid one. He rescued the tabernacle, but he selected for it a new location, namely, Zion in Judah, where he built his sanctuary. He also chose David his servant to be his king and the shepherd of his people (vv. 70, 71), and David, with the same skill which he had shown in feeding sheep and guiding them, guided Israel.

Psalm 79. Lament Over the Destruction of Jerusalem and Prayer for Help

This psalm because of its theme naturally follows Psa. 78. It is a brief but magnificent plea for God's help marked by deep pathos and earnestness. The hopes of the long years have been suddenly shattered and the psalmist saturates his prayer with the deep welling up of protest and pleading with God to make good his promise and not to remember too vividly the people's misdoings. The background is similar to that of Psa. 74 (see introductory paragraph there with reference to possible date).

1–4. Sufferings Endured by the Psalmist and His People. The land has been invaded; Jerusalem is in ruins; the Temple is desecrated. The conditions may be those of the days of Antiochus Epiphanes. *Heathen* = nations (mg.). *Inheritance* = Palestine or the Holy City. The happenings are recent. The dead are still unburied; blood has been shed like water. This happened many times, but in the most horrible manner about 168 B.C. (see intro. to Psa. 74).

5–8. Prayer for Help. *How long?*—an oft-repeated phrase (cf. 74^{10}, note). How long will God wait to relieve and avenge his people? *Forever*—seems out of place with "how long," but it is an idiomatic expression often used this way. *Pour out thy wrath*—the ethics of v. 6 may not be as high as N.T. ethics; but the prayer is quite in harmony with many O.T. expressions. It is inspired not by a spirit of personal vengeance but of outraged piety. The heathen nations had utterly despised them and violated all they held sacred; thus they had proved themselves not only Israel's enemies but also the foes of Jehovah. *Jacob* (v. 7)—for Judah is unusual. V. 8 contains the right kind of prayer; the psalmist confesses past sins but prays that God may not hold them against him. *Prevent*—old English for "go before," or precede.

9–12. Prayer for Deliverance, to Protect the Honor of Jehovah. *The glory of thy name.* If the people's sufferings will not move God, he should interfere to protect his own reputation. *Where is thy God?* The helplessness of his people justifies the suspicion that God has lost interest in them (v. 10; cf. 42^{3}). Let him now show himself in vengeance. *The sighing of the prisoner*—those appointed to die; they appear to be condemned to death. A vivid picture of the condition of the psalmist and his countrymen. Surely they need help. V. 12 is similar to v. 6. The people conceive of the reproach of Israel as reproach heaped upon God himself; hence their plea—*they have reproached thee.*

13. Vow of Thanksgiving. If God will do these things for the sheep of his pasture, i.e., Israel, they will pledge him the sacrifice of thanksgiving.

PSALM 80. PRAYER FOR DELIVERANCE FROM CALAMITY

This psalm is of the same strain as Psa. 79; it is a plea for God to return once more unto his people and restore them to the favor that was once theirs. It may have had its origin in the Exile as a prayer for complete national restoration.

1–3. Prayer to the Shepherd of Israel. The term *shepherd* is a tender and appealing one. *Joseph* = Israel; recalling the experiences of the desert wanderings. *Cherubim*—the figure on either end of the ark of the covenant, between which was the mercy seat over which God was wont to appear (see on Gen. 3^{24}). *Ephraim* and *Manasseh* were the sons of Joseph; *Benjamin* was his younger brother; Rachel was the mother of both; sometimes Rachel appears as the mother of northern Israel. *Us*—a national prayer. National repentance deserves national restoration. *Cause thy face to shine* = restore thy favor (cf. Num. 6^{25}).

4–7. How Long Will Israel Continue to be the Object of God's Displeasure? *How long wilt thou be angry?*—literally, "How long wilt thou be fuming?" *Against the prayer*—the divine anger is so intense that even prayer is futile. The bitter punishment has given occasion for the scorn of their enemies (vv. 5, 6). Vv. 3, 7, 19 are refrains, praying for restoration.

8–13. God's Former Care and the People's Present Plight. The metaphor of a *vine* describes the nation brought out of Egypt and established in Palestine. Jehovah carefully prepared the soil and caused it to take deep root. It was a mighty vine and became in its spreading boughs like goodly cedars (v. 10). This vine spread from the *sea* = the Mediterranean Sea, to the *River* = the Euphrates (cf. 72^{8}). But now God has broken down the hedges which protected it so that it is a prey to all that pass by (v. 12). The wild boar and other beasts of the woods devour it. This often happens in the vicinity of Mount Hermon (Tristram, *Natural History of the Bible*, p. 56; cf. Isa. 5^{1-7}).

14–19. Prayer for the Restoration of the Divine Favor. He who planted the vine should not go away to heaven and forget what he has done; he should at least look down from that high place and see what is happening to his vine and his vineyard. *Fire* (v. 16)—all this burning is due to God's anger; though Israel is Jehovah's son (v. 17). The restoration prayed for will furnish a new basis of praise and allegiance (vv. 18, 19).

PSALM 81. GOD'S DESIRE FOR ISRAEL SET AT NAUGHT

Some commentators hold that Psa. 81 consists of two originally independent psalms (vv. 1–5b and 5c–16). The first is interpreted as a festival summons, the second as a threat of punishment for disobedience. It is preferable, however, to accept the psalm as a unit, picturing God's goodness and Israel's waywardness. The date is uncertain; the Temple appears to be standing; some have dated it in the days of Josiah; others, however, place it after the Exile.

1–5b. Summons to Celebrate a Festival. Some think that v. 1 is addressed to the entire congregation; v. 2 to the Levites as the leaders of the Temple music; and v. 3 to the priests whose duty it was to blow the trumpets. V. 2

mentions the instruments with which the service was carried on: *Timbrel*—a tambourine or hand drum; *harp . . . psaltery*—both stringed instruments; *trumpet*—Hebrew, *shophar*, the horn as distinguished from the metal trumpet. *New moon*—according to the Talmud the reference is to the new moon of the month Tisri; if so, the second part of the verse refers to the Feast of Tabernacles, which began on the full moon of the same month. This festival had been divinely appointed.

5c–10. Jehovah and Israel. *I heard a language that I knew not.* A difficult expression. Probably a new beginning should be made with these words. If so, Jehovah would be the speaker; and the reference would be to his hearing the voice of the Egyptians lording it over Israel. He then delivered the slaves from servitude (vv. 6, 7). *Secret place of thunder*—render *I answered thee veiled in the thunder cloud*—referring to thunder on Sinai. *Waters of Meribah.* Meribah means strife; the experiences at Meribah may have been commemorated by the pouring out of water at the Feast of Tabernacles, to remind the people of that long strife between a long-suffering God and an obstinate people (Ex. 17^{7}). Vv. 8–10 emphasize the sole deity of Jehovah and urge the people to put their full trust in him who delivered them from Egypt. Why do they starve now? *Open thy mouth*—God was good to Israel; they owed him their very existence, and he was always ready to supply their needs; he did so in the past; he is willing to do it now; but he can fill their mouths only if they open them.

11, 12. Israel's Stubbornness. In spite of the divine mercy Israel would have nothing to do with Jehovah. *I let them go*—God punishes his people by letting them go on until they realize that without him they can but meet disaster.

13–16. The Eternal Mercy of God. If Israel would turn to him he would bless them abundantly; he would drive back their enemies and would make them come cringing to his people. The picture of God here is the same as in the parable of the prodigal son: he ever longs for the return of his prodigal children. *Finest of the wheat*—literally, "fat of wheat." The final consummation would be that God would give his people the best, and out of the hardest experiences he would bring them honey and rich bread. How wonderful are the mercies of God!

Psalm 82. God the Judge of All Human Judges

The date is uncertain. Unrighteousness was prevalent; but such a condition was not uncommon, and does not fix the date. The expression in v. 1, "he judgeth among the gods," has led some to believe that the psalm portrays a judgment scene in which Jehovah calls the gods of other nations before him to judgment; sternly he rebukes them for their partiality and misrule and exposes their futility. Others think the persons judged are rulers and magistrates in Israel, who in their representative positions stand for divine authority and rule. Still others think of the wicked rulers and governors of nations holding Israel in subjection. On the whole, the second interpretation appears to be the more probable. The theme is common in the prophets (cf. Amos 5^{10-15}).

1–4. The Arraignment of the Unjust Judges. *Congregation of God*—an assembly called by God himself for a judicial session. *Gods*—not divine beings, but judges who administer divinely given laws and possess divinely bestowed authority. The charge is that they practice injustice and partiality; they are exhorted instead to give special consideration to the poor and needy (cf. Isa. 11^{1-5}).

5–7. Their Sentence. The judges are morally blind and incompetent; hence judgment must fall. *Ye are gods*—Jehovah exalted them highly; but now they must die like common men; they shall fall like other princes who failed in their trust.

8. The Judge of All the Earth. The trial is over; God alone stands out as a righteous Judge. The psalmist appeals to him to take possession of all the nations as their Sovereign and Judge.

Psalm 83. A Plea for Judgment Upon the Enemies of Israel

It is very difficult to determine the probable time of this psalm, for no historical situation brings together at once all of the tribes and peoples mentioned here. Many scholars refer it to the time of Nehemiah, when every man's hand seemed against him in the rebuilding of the walls. Others think of the Maccabæan period.

The psalm falls naturally into two sections. (1) Vv. 1–8: the psalmist pleads with God not to sit by as an indifferent spectator and allow the enemy to close in from every side and utterly destroy the inheritance of Jehovah; (2) vv. 9–18: he prays God to humble the enemies as he has done in the past, that they may yield him homage, either voluntarily or by force.

1–4. Let God Speak and the Enemies Will Be Dispersed. It is God's silence and apparent indifference that allow the enemies to continue their attacks. The word *tumult* denotes an uproar, the noise of a great multitude.

Crafty counsel—there is a plot against Jehovah, for a plot against his people is a plot against him. *Thy hidden ones*—God's people whom he hides in the day of trouble. The plot is to blot out the very name and remembrance of Israel.

5–8. **Enumeration of the Confederates Against Israel.** The *Edomites* were the descendants of Esau, and inhabited the region southeast of the Dead Sea. *Ishmaelites*—Arab tribes of the desert. *Moab*—or Moabites, situated on the eastern side of the Dead Sea, north of Edom. *Hagarenes*—or "Hagrites," were from the Hauran, east of Gilead. *Gebal*—perhaps not the people used by Solomon from the old city of Byblos in Phœnicia, but, rather, a tribe of the Edomite mountains. *Ammon*—ancient and bitter enemy of Israel, east of the Jordan. *Amalek*—dwelt in the desert south of Beersheba, between the Arabah and the Mediterranean and extending into the Sinaitic Peninsula. From *Tyre* to *Philistia* includes the entire Mediterranean coast. *Assyria*—the Assyrians conquered northern Israel in 722 B.C. and after that colonized Israel with some of their own people, and it has been suggested that these—the forerunners of the Samaritans—may be meant. The *children of Lot*—i.e., Ammon and Moab. (For a fuller description of these names, see arts., *Land of Palestine*, pp. 53–8; *Hebrew History*, pp. 62–7).

9–18. **Prayer for the Destruction of Israel's Enemies.** The second part of the psalm is a prayer that the nations named may be dealt with as Jehovah has dealt with others in the past. *Midian*—whom Gideon subdued (Judg. 7, 8). *Sisera*—defeated by Deborah and Barak (Judg. 4, 5). *Dung* (v. 10)—the declaration is a contemptuous one. They became as fertilizer for the ground. *Oreb and Zeeb*—Midianite generals (Judg. 7^{25}); *Zebah and Zalmunna*—kings of Midian (Judg. $8^{5f.}$). *Who* (v. 12)—refers to present enemies. God's *habitations*—or "pastures," the lands which he has given his people. *Whirling dust* (v. 13)—anything whirled away by the wind may be meant. Thomson (*Land and the Book*, p. 563) thinks the head of the wild artichoke is meant. This breaks off and goes whirling across the desert, something like our own Western tumble weed. *Stubble*—this word and the one above mean that they shall be nothing but drifting chaff. Make them as a mountainside after a forest fire has swept up it. Let storms distress them. Let them be humiliated, that they may seek thee (vv. 14, 15). The prayer for punishment and destruction is in reality a prayer for the salvation of these people—that they may know Jehovah. Chastisement has for its primary object conversion.

Psalm 84. A Pilgrim Processional Expressing Love for the Temple

The 84th psalm should be studied in connection with Peters' great book, *The Psalms as Liturgies* (The Macmillan Company). With Psa. 84 begins the Korah collection. This psalm is a companion to Psa. 42, 43. It reveals the same devotion to the Temple service, and contains many like expressions; it may come from the same author. Peters thinks it was at first intended to be sung at the Dan altar and later adapted for the Jerusalem Psalter (*op. cit.*, p. 340). This psalm, probably written between the time of the fall of Samaria and the fall of Jerusalem (722–586 B.C.), is a pilgrim processional. The procession, according to Peters, begins on the western hill. This hill is higher than Mount Moriah, on which the Temple stood; so that the procession looking down from the western hill could see within the Temple area and behold the beauty of the buildings there.

The first stanza, vv. 1–4, ends with "Selah" (cf. p. 512). Peters thinks that the word was here used as a signal to stop the procession and "lift up" the censer. The second stanza, vv. 5–8, describes the route of the procession. The old Tyropæon valley was much deeper than it now is; and across it was a causeway. Across this the procession made its way down into the valley to the Pool of Siloam. This pool since Hezekiah's day has been supplied with water from the Virgin Spring, under the hill Gihon, through a tunnel called Silwan. The Pool of Siloam is a cistern and was once inside the walls of the ancient city. The spring furnishing water was outside the wall. This spring was tapped and its waters carried through this aqueduct, for five hundred eighty-three yards. The spring was then covered up from the enemy. Near the Pool of Siloam and about it were the graves of thousands; hence the name "the valley of Baca," or "Weeping." The eastern and western hills were connected by bridges, the remains of two of which have been discovered. From the Pool of Siloam the route would wind up the hill toward the Temple, over terraces or ramparts, until, after passing the king's house, the pilgrims found themselves at the gates of the Temple and finally inside. The first stanza, vv. 1–4, opens with a statement much like the refrains of the other stanzas, and this one has no other refrain. The third stanza, vv. 9–12, describes the blessedness of worshiping Jehovah in the sanctuary.

1–4. **The Psalmist's Delight in the Temple.** *How amiable are thy tabernacles*—the procession starts and looks down upon the beauty of the

the "Mother dear, Jerusalem" for all nations (v. 5). When Jehovah makes up his census he will write down the names of those who are born in her and those who have come in by the second birth (v. 6).

7. **Universal Rejoicing.** With rejoicing the children of Zion (v. 5) greet their mother. The verse may be rendered: "They that sing and they that dance shall say, 'All my springs are in thee' "—springs or fountains of salvation. All the good they enjoy comes from their mother, who in turn receives it from Jehovah.

Psalm 88. Prayer for Deliverance from Death

Called the saddest psalm in the Psalter. It may be a wail of Israel in Babylon; but in its present form it is a penitential psalm used liturgically. The Syriac Version prefaces this psalm by, "Concerning the people which was in Babylon."

1–8. **Cry for Mercy.** The psalmist pleads the intensity of his sufferings in the hope of arousing the divine pity. *Sheol* (v. 3)—the place of the departed; a gloomy place where the dead endure a sort of shadowy and uncertain existence. The psalmist is near death; by some he is already counted a dead man (v. 5). *Like the slain*—those slain in battle and buried in nameless graves. *Whom thou rememberest no more*—the dead are completely cut off from Jehovah. This is indeed a gloomy view of the future state. *Lowest pit . . . dark places . . . deeps*—all refer to Sheol and give some idea of the nature of the place. *All thy waves* (v. 7)—the torrents of affliction (cf. 42^7). In his affliction he was, like Job, forsaken by his friends.

9–12. **The Importunity of Prayer.** If God is thinking of helping him he must do it at once; his strength is failing; he will soon die, and with death he will pass from the control of Jehovah (see p. 173). *Wilt thou show wonders to the dead?* Vv. 10–12 express in various ways the thought that the person who enters Sheol is cut off from Jehovah; Jehovah cannot manifest his power in Sheol, nor can the dead sing his praises. If, therefore, Jehovah wants to help the psalmist he must do it before the latter dies. *Land of forgetfulness*—in Sheol one forgets and is forgotten.

13–18. **The Psalmist will Continue to Rely Upon God.** *In the morning* (v. 13)—the night passes and he still prays. Death has not actually overtaken him, and once again he spreads out his hands and lifts his voice to God. Perchance to-day he will be gracious. *Why?* (v. 14)—the eternal question. He prays and trusts where he cannot understand. *From my youth up*—must refer to an individual and not to the nation. He may have been afflicted with leprosy from his childhood. *Thy fierce wrath*—the fiery streams of thy wrath have gone over me. The figure is very intense. *Thy terrors*—a favorite word with Job. Like one caught by the tides, these terrors rise higher and higher each day to overwhelm him (v. 17). Read v. 18 *Lover and friend as well as acquaintance slip away and darkness takes their place.* The pathos of this psalm is remarkable. The whole reminds one constantly of Job. The psalmist comes to the end of his wail with no light on the difficulties which have confused him, but with one great outstanding victory. He has come to praise God though he seems utterly hostile to him. He has found that even if God is hostile, yet there is none other to pray to. God or nothing. And he decides to pray on though he cannot understand.

Psalm 89. Battle of Skepticism and Faith

The psalmist, dressing up his doubt with much praise, reminds God of his promises to David and his failure to carry them out. This certainly looks like a psalm of the Exile experience. The king seems to have been dethroned and a prisoner. The psalmist reminds God of his promises and his character and expresses astonishment, in view of these, that the king should be in such a state. If God is merciful and righteous, the present affliction cannot be the last word.

1–4. **Loving-kindness and Faithfulness of Jehovah.** *I will sing of the mercies of the Lord*—the mercy of the Lord is still the most amazing thing in heaven or earth. The *faithfulness* of Jehovah is the guarantee of his abiding mercy and of the carrying out of his promises. *For I have said* (v. 2)—I have come to this conclusion. Mercy and faithfulness are rooted in the depths and reach to the very heavens; these shall pass away but the attributes of God shall stand forever. In vv. 3, 4 Jehovah is the speaker. He sets forth his promise to David. *I have made a covenant*—a covenant established by Jehovah cannot be broken. *Chosen*—i.e., David. V. 4, giving the substance of the promise, is based on 2 Sam. 7^{1-29}, where God makes a covenant with David.

5–18. **A Hymn of Praise.** The power and faithfulness of Jehovah guarantee the fulfillment of his promises. *The heavens*—the whole celestial order. *Who in the skies?*—does he mean the sun, moon and other heavenly bodies, or does he mean the council of heaven itself? The psalmist must be excused for taking the "wings of the morning" and sweeping out into regions beyond mortal ken and singing of heavenly councils in the midst of which the incomparable God stands towering above them all. *God of hosts* (v. 8)—hosts of earth and of heaven. This heavenly host is often referred to in the O.T. (Gen. 32^{2} 2 Kings 6^{17}; cf. Lk. 2^{13}, etc.). *Rulest the pride of the sea* (v. 9). The sea, a symbol of unrest, was most terrible to the Hebrew. It was thought to be ruled by divine spirits, but Jehovah (*Jah*) was superior to them, as he proved at the Red Sea. *Broken Rahab in pieces* (v. 10)—refers to the utter annihilation of Egypt or, as some think, to the primeval monster which represented chaos and was overcome in the creation (cf. 87^{4} Gen. 1^{2} Job 26^{12}). *North and south* = all the world; *Tabor and Hermon* = east and west.

V. 14 offers a wonderful metaphor: God is sitting upon a *throne* whose foundations are *righteousness* and *judgment; mercy* and *truth* are his attendants. The throne of God is founded upon eternal and unshakable righteousness and justice; truth or faithfulness underlies that justice and assures it, while mercy (=loving-kindness) tempers justice (cf. on 85^{10}). Happy is the people who have such a God (v. 15). *In the light of thy countenance*—means in his favor and by his grace. *In thy name*—i.e., in the divine character as revealed in God's dealings with men. The basis of their *glory* (v. 17) is the power of God; they may safely lean on him. *Our horn shall be exalted*—the figure of a victorious wild animal with head up. *Our shield . . . our king*—the king was appointed by God and was the defender of Israel. *Holy One of Israel*—a term often used by the prophets, especially by Isaiah, who may have coined the phrase (see p. 162); the very holiness of God insures the redemption of his people.

19–37. The Divine Promise to David. The reference to the king in v. 18 naturally suggests the covenant with David (cf. vv. 3, 4), which the psalmist outlines in detail. *Thou spakest in vision*—perhaps the time mentioned in 2 Sam. 7^{1-29}. *To thy saints*—read, with mg., *saint;* the reference is to Nathan or David. *Laid help upon*—David, a mighty hero, was chosen and empowered to help his people. This is also the thought of vv. 20, 21: David was called for the purpose of helping Israel, and Jehovah promised to strengthen him. Moreover, Jehovah promised to give him victory in battle and thus exalt him (vv. 23, 24). His left hand shall be upon the Western Sea and his right upon the Euphrates, which shall be the boundaries of the land.

The relationship between Jehovah and David was to be intimate; *my father* (v. 26)—cf. 2^{7} 2 Sam. 7^{14}. *Firstborn*—David would cry "My Father!" In answer God would make him his son, with all the rights and prerogatives of the firstborn. *Mercy*—or "loving-kindness." The endurance of that kingdom shall be as the days of heaven, where the day never ends; i.e., *forever* (v. 29). *If his children forsake my law*—which they did—they shall be punished; but even then Jehovah will remember this promise, will have mercy and exhibit that same faithfulness (vv. 30–33). His throne shall be as enduring as the sun and the moon (vv. 35–37).

38–45. Contrast Between the Divine Promises and the Present Reality. The psalmist now comes to contrast the present plight of the nation and its king with these promises to David. This is the point to which he has been leading up all of the time. *Thou*—the psalmist boldly charges God with breaking his promise (v. 38). *Abhorred the covenant*—Jehovah has acted as if he had never made a promise; he ruthlessly took the crown from the head of the successor of David and cast it to the ground. His treatment of the king has brought disaster to the nation (vv. 40, 41). *Hedges* are broken down so that strangers pass through the land of Palestine and help themselves, leaving it in utter ruin, since there is nothing to shield it. The enemy has been favored (v. 42); Jehovah has not helped the king in battle as he promised in v. 23 (v. 43). *Days . . . shortened* (v. 45)—he has become prematurely old. The reference is probably to Jehoiachin, who was not more than eighteen when he was dethroned (2 Kings 25^{29}).

46–51. Prayer for a Removal of the Contrast. In vv. 46, 47 the psalmist pleads with God to withdraw his wrath, and to remember the transitoriness of human life (cf. Psa. 90). What man is so strong that he shall not see death? Time is short and the best of men must die (v. 48). What is the use of afflicting him? *Where are* (v. 49)—what has become of all past expressions of loving-kindness and mercy and of the oath to David, described in the preceding verses? *Reproach* (vv. 50, 51)—while the king and the nation are sufferers, the reproach also affects God. He too is dishonored in the dishonoring of his people. V. 51 may refer to the humiliation of Jehoiachin as he was led in dishonor through the streets of Babylon with a jeering throng dogging his footsteps (2 Kings $24^{15, 16}$).

52. Closing Doxology. This verse does not belong to the psalm proper; it is rather a doxology for the entire Book III.

Psalm 90. Jehovah the Unchanging the Refuge of Changing Man

Book IV of the Psalter consists of Psa. 90–106 (see intro., p. 509). Peters thinks this psalm was written during the so-called "Back to Moses" movement about 500 B.C.; others think of the death of Josiah, 609 or 608 B.C., as a suitable occasion. The sublimity and inspirational quality are entirely independent of its date. It inspired the great hymn, "O God Our Help in Ages Past."

1–6. God an Everlasting Refuge. *Lord*—Hebrew, *Adonai;* the title by which Jehovah is known as the ruler of the universe. *Dwelling place*—habitation, place of refuge; God is our home. *In all generations*—from generation to generation; i.e., at all times, forever. *Mountains*—thought to be the oldest of God's creation. *Brought forth* = begotten. *Thou hadst formed*—literally, "didst travail in birth with." The writer places himself back in the primordial time and conceives of God travailing in the struggle to bring forth creation. The Spirit of God was brooding over the abyss (cf. Deut. 32[18] Job 38[8, 28, 29]). Before all this took place, ere the "morning stars sang together and all the sons of God shouted for joy" (Job 38[7]), long ages before the beginning of creation, God was. He was and is (cf. Ex. 3[14]).

Not only the universe but man also is dependent entirely on God. *Thou turnest man to destruction*—or "dust" (v. 3; cf. mg.). Man in comparison with God is a thing of dust rapidly returning whence he came. *Return*—a call to a new generation to take the place of those so rapidly passing from the stage of action. *A thousand years* (v. 4)—another figure to impress upon the reader or hearer the eternal stretches of time in the mind of God as compared with man (cf. 2 Pet. 3[8]). A thousand year period when it is passing is but as the closing day, with all of its experiences fresh in mind. *A watch in the night.* In O.T. times the night was divided into three watches (Judg. 7[19] 1 Sam. 11[11]); the N.T. division into four (Mt. 14[25]) is of Roman origin. What passes more quickly than the hours in which we sleep! A thousand years to God are but as a watch through which one has slept. To God there is neither yesterday nor to-morrow; he lives in the eternal present. Time is purely a human element and only the finite "Shapes the shadow, Time." *Thou carriest them away as with a flood.* The entire sentence is but a single Hebrew word; it emphasizes the suddenness of destruction. *Sleep*—either, they are as those who are asleep; or "they fall asleep," in the sleep of death. In v. 6 man is compared to grass which, indeed, groweth up with the morning dews; but in the heat of the day it is scorched and in the evening withers and becomes worthless.

7–12. Misery of a Life Spent Under Divine Displeasure. It is bad enough that life is brief and uncertain; it is worse to live it under the cloud of God's wrath, caused by human sin. *We*—the nation Israel. *Troubled*—or dismayed, because of divine judgments. *Sins*—the light of God's countenance usually expresses his favor, but here it is like the searching rays of the noonday sun, from which there is nothing hidden; the people's sin stands revealed before him. *All our days are passed away*—our brief day has turned, without value, toward the evening. It has been a day of wrath and there is no sign of light at evening time. *A tale*—literally a sound, or sigh (cf. mg.). The years pass as quickly as a sigh, which is an expression of weariness or sorrow.

The life of man is at best but brief (v. 10). Three score and ten, or even four score years, is the most that men can hope for, and few realize such an old age; but if they do, they must confess at the end that it has meant nothing but weariness and disappointment. *Who knoweth the power of thine anger?* (V. 11.) Who can know how long it will last and how to fear him so as to protect himself against God's fierceness toward sin? Since man is ignorant, God must help him. *So teach us*—give us that discernment which we lack, so that we may know how to secure the divine favor and good will.

13–17. Prayer for Restoration of the Divine Favor. *Return* (v. 13)—a prayer that God may change his attitude and show that he has forgiven. *Let it repent thee*—the change in God's attitude is called repentance. Once it was interpreted literally (cf. Gen. 6[6]); but here the thought is not that God would find himself mistaken or regretful, but, rather, that he would find it in his heart to have mercy, overlook the worthlessness of his people and forgive their sins. *In the morning*—as though they were in a state of night through all of their troubles; they pray for the approach of the dawn. Let the joy of the morning be proportionate to the sorrow of the long night (v. 15). *Beauty* (v. 17)—or "pleasantness" = the gracious kindliness of Jehovah. Make the work of our hands worth while.

This is the funeral hymn of the ages and is well fitted for that service. It is in a minor key, but pathetically beautiful. There is a rhythm about it that reminds one of some mighty organ oratorio, sounding with solemn and measured tones. It needs, however, the radiant touch of the Christian hope.

Psalm 91. Jehovah the Sure Defense of Those Who Trust in Him

In the view of many scholars this is a national psalm, but there are also good reasons for considering it a personal one. The best of these is the impression it makes on the reader. The exquisite beauty of it and the deep trust and confidence reflected in it seem to be too profound to be the expression of national hope; they sound like the welling up of a deep emotional spring within the individual soul. The Targum thinks of this psalm as a dialogue between David and Solomon. David speaks: "I will say of Jehovah . . . for he will deliver thee Solomon my son." Solomon answers: "For thou Jehovah art my refuge, in a lofty dwelling hast thou placed the abode of thy Majesty." The Lord of the world answered and said thus: "There shall no evil befall thee." The date of the psalm is uncertain; probably it is post-exilic. The rabbis suggested that since Moses wrote Psa. 90, he also wrote its antithesis in Psa. 91.

1, 2. The Theme of the Psalm: Jehovah a Secure Defense. The Hebrew of the first line is very brief. The word "happy" may have dropped out at the beginning. If it is restored, the line would read, *Happy is the man who dwells in the secret place.* The general sense is clear. The one who takes refuge in the secret hiding place, or the safe retreat of God, is both happy and secure. *Almighty*—Hebrew, *Shaddai;* this is the name used for God in Gen. 17¹, where it occurs as *El Shaddai.* The term *Elyon*—the most high—is used for "God" in Gen. 14¹⁹⁻²¹. *Secret place* = covert, i.e., under the protection of God Almighty. There none but God can find him; the enemy cannot locate him. *Shadow of the Almighty.* God is sometimes presented under the idea of a "Rock in a weary land," which gives shade to the weary traveler and protection; or the words may refer to the protection of the mother bird, a figure used later (v. 4). The one who dwells in the secret covert of the Most High shall become his abiding guest. V. 2 is the expression of complete confidence and trust.

3–8. God's Providential Care. *Surely*—there can be no doubt about it. *Snare of the fowler*—the trap of the huntsman, who seeks human prey. *Noisome pestilence*—since pestilence is mentioned in v. 6, many accept the reading of some of the ancient translations, "from the destroying word," i.e., slander and gossip. *Pinions . . . wings*—there is tenderness and intimacy in that expression (cf. Mt. 23³⁷). The picture is of a mother bird which gathers her young under her wings in time of danger. One who abides under the shadow of the Almighty need not fear sudden surprises by *night* or open attacks by *day.* Day and night are both alike to Him in whom we dwell (v. 5). *Pestilence* and *destruction* (or "plague") are set forth as stalking demons seeking human prey; these too are impotent to harm as long as the divine protection is ours. *Thee* (v. 7c). The emphasis is upon this word. Whatever may happen to others he who trusts in God is safe. The psalmist may have had in mind here the deliverance on that last night in Egypt when the destroying angel passed through, but the Hebrews under the care of God were exempt from destruction (cf. Ex. 12¹³, ²⁷).

9–16. Renewed Assurance of Divine Protection. The translation of v. 9 is somewhat uncertain. Some read *For Jehovah is thine own refuge, the Lofty One thy place of safety* (cf. also mg.). The general thought, however, is clear; the psalmist describes again the safety of those who put their trust in Jehovah. The same theme is continued in v. 10. The psalmist once more reminds us of the basis of this confidence. *Plague.* Is it possible that trust in God will keep all physical plague away? Certainly it will keep away all spiritual evil. Jehovah will exercise a protecting care (vv. 11, 12). *He shall give his angels charge over thee*—cf. Ex. 23²⁰. *All thy ways*—the ways ordered by God for you, not those of your own choosing. The devil tempted Jesus by quoting this verse to him (Mt. 4⁶). *Lion and adder*—the adder was the cobra of Egypt which Cleopatra used to commit suicide.

In vv. 14–16 Jehovah speaks: *He hath set his love upon me.* Love begets love and responds to love. "We love him because he first loved us." God chooses any people to be his people who choose him to be their God. *I will set him on high*—out of the reach of his enemies and over them (cf. Esth. 6⁷⁻¹¹). *Call . . . answer* (v. 15)—he has stood the test. *I will be with him in trouble*—happy the man who has won such a place with God. "Can you trust God?" may give way to "Can God trust you?" *Deliver . . . honor*—not only saved, but saved to something and for something. *With long life*—this was the *summum bonum* of Israel's saints, to live long on the earth. *Satisfy*—I will make life worth living and allow him to live as long as he finds it worth while. *My salvation*—from every foe and every evil. This is the word that includes all that has gone before. Deliverance from the snare of the fowler, noisome pestilence, terror by night, arrow by day, pestilence of darkness and destruction of noonday, evil, plague, stones, lions, adders, trouble, and everything else. Thus salvation will be positive. Not only shall he be saved *from* all of these; but he will also be saved *to* a home in the Almighty, life in the midst of death, courage, the care of angels; he will be set on high, delivered, victorious, honored, satisfied.

PSALM 92. HYMN OF PRAISE FOR SOME GREAT NATIONAL DELIVERANCE

No author is suggested; it probably was written soon after the return from Exile. Its being set apart as a psalm for the Sabbath day is due to the fact that it glorifies the mighty works of Jehovah. The Sabbath was the day on which the works of creation were celebrated. The Targum gives this title, "A Psalm of praise and song which the first man uttered upon the day of the Sabbath."

1–3. The Joy of Praise and Thanksgiving. *Give thanks.* The most delightful occupation of man is to give thanks to God (v. 1). *Sing praises*—to make a joyful noise unto Jehovah. *Morning . . . night*—natural times for prayer and praise. See on 81[2] for the stringed instruments used in worship, the decachord, psaltery and the harp or lyre. *Solemn sound* =meditative.

4–8. The Sovereignty of Jehovah the Ground of Praise. *Through thy work*—thy working, or activity. *Works*—what the psalmist has in mind is the result of the divine workings, as he has observed them. God works his own way and brings forth the results in his own good time (v. 5). This the psalmist understands, but *the brutish man . . . the fool* (silly, v. 6) cannot see or understand the ways in which God works out his purpose. The wicked flourish for a time but soon are cut down (37[35, 36]). A brutish man is like a brute and sees and feels as a brute. To satisfy himself in the lowest forms of life is his deepest concern. The grandeur and profundity of God's works are beyond his conception.

9–15. Evidences of the Divine Supremacy. These evidences consist in the fact that the righteous flourish, the wicked perish. *My horn hast thou exalted*—the frequent figure (89[17]) of the tossing of the head by a wild animal as indicative of strength and vigor. *I am anointed with fresh oil*—as on some festive occasion, so that the face shines and there is an air of joy. V. 11 sounds rather harsh, but is in harmony with many other O.T. passages. There is a seeming gloating over the suffering of the enemies of Israel. *Flourish* (v. 12)—this is a familiar figure of strength and glory. The *palm* in the East furnishes food, drink, fuel, building material, and shade; the *cedar*, stately, fragrant, beautiful and desired by kings for building purposes. Both are evergreen and live to a great old age. In v. 13 the psalmist may have had in mind the trees growing in the Temple area as they do to this day. There was a "house of the forest of Lebanon"; and the front porch of the temple of Solomon was a forest of columns representing trees (1 Kings 6[3]); and on the walls of the Temple were carved trees (1 Kings 6[29]). *In old age* (v. 14) —the palm tree has been known to bear fruit at two hundred years of age. V. 15 is a final acclaim of confidence in Jehovah.

PSALM 93. THE MAJESTY OF JEHOVAH

Psa. 93–100, except 94 (and possibly 92 also), are sometimes called "Royal Psalms," because they all stress the sovereignty of Jehovah over Israel. This psalm has been called the "Prelude" to the entire group and should be studied in connection with the others. The LXX and the Talmud make this a Friday psalm, a psalm of the day before the Sabbath, or of the sixth day of creation, "when God peopled the world and began to reign over it." Reminiscent of this occasion and similar to it in significance was the restoration from exile, when God repeopled his own land, and again began to reign over it. It is a psalm of thanksgiving, which probably comes from the early period of the restoration.

1, 2. The Eternal Sovereign is Jehovah. *The Lord (Jehovah) reigneth*—has proclaimed himself King. During the Exile the very foundations of the moral order seemed tottering, but now God has once more assumed his royal place and the world has again become orderly. *Apparelled with majesty*—the picture of Jehovah returning and assuming the throne, resplendent with glory and inspiring in power, restoring confidence by his very presence, is a very vivid one (cf. Isa. 6[1]). *Of old*—Jehovah has always been king; he has only seemed to abdicate; his throne is eternal.

3, 4. The Powers of Earth Threaten Jehovah's Reign in Vain. Rivers at flood tide, oceans rising in the face of storms, thundering waters, and raging storms cannot shake the everlasting throne. Exile, persecution, and death may not destroy God's people. They can be destroyed only by themselves. In the midst of the storms and raging tumultuous waves rises the voice of God high above them all.

5. The Testimony of God is Sure. The divine testimony and the divine holiness answer all questions of doubt.

PSALM 94. PRAYER FOR VENGEANCE

Israel is greatly oppressed and prays that the righteous judgments of God be revealed upon all her enemies. The psalm seems to depend upon Psa. 73, and upon Job; but no definite period can be fixed for its origin.

1, 2. Vengeance Belongs to God and Not to Man. Appeal to God who has the power and right to punish. *Lift up thyself*—i.e., take the seat of judgment. He prays here for an assertion of the divine prerogative.

3–7. How Long Will Jehovah Keep Silent? V. 3 expresses the cry of the ages—*How long shall the wicked triumph?* V. 4 pictures the insolence of the arrogant petty rulers. *Prate* = boast; *arrogantly*—they indulged in loud talk. They crush Jehovah's people by arrogance and extortion (v. 5). *Thine heritage*—i.e., Israel. V. 6 is a kind of proverbial expression for inhumanity and treachery: They are cruel to those who have no defense, they violate all good custom, they are inhospitable, even slay the sojourners, who are under the protection of the sacred law of hospitality; they show contempt for God himself. *God of Jacob*—they think of him as one among many gods, in no sense superior to the others.

8–11. Jehovah a God of Unique Power. The psalmist turns to those among his own people who think with the heathen that God is impotent. *Brutish*—the men who have lost the finer sensibilities (v. 8; cf. on 92[6]). It is ridiculous to believe that the God who created the organs of sense does not possess them himself. He knows and will be able to judge wisely (v. 9). The psalmist looks even beyond Israel and sees that God is teaching all mankind. But if he teaches all men, is it not reasonable to suppose that he knows them, even their inmost thoughts? (Vv. 10, 11.)

12–15. Jehovah Ultimately Will Care for His Own. Happy are the victims of cruel oppression who wait upon God, for their time will surely come! It is an educational process. *Chastenest* (v. 12)—Israel is being divinely educated, and the teaching received will give Israel such an insight into God's ways that oppression will be endured calmly until the day of retribution. *Unto righteousness* (v. 15)—the administration of justice will be such that all good men will long for it and follow after it.

16–19. Israel Has No Helper but Jehovah. *Who will rise up*—no one but Jehovah. (Cf. Job 19[26-28].) The psalmist's experience confirms the hope of the aid of Jehovah (cf. Psa. 124). *My foot slippeth* (v. 18). He recalls that when he was about to stagger from the path of duty the loving kindness of God held him up; he gave himself up for lost but the divine love had hold of him all the time.

20–23. Deliverance of the Faithful; Destruction of the Tyrants. *Throne of wickedness*—temporarily wickedness may appear to triumph; but ultimately right and righteousness must prevail. *High tower . . . refuge*—place of protection and safety. *Their own iniquity*—God will cause their wickedness to return upon their own heads; while the innocent, whom they intended to destroy, will be delivered from their power.

Psalm 95. Humiliation of Babylon and Restoration of Israel

Israel is solemnly warned that in spite of the divine goodness, if they provoke God as their fathers did in the wilderness, they can expect no more exemption from punishment than their fathers received.

This group of Psalms, 95–100, were probably arranged to be sung at the services in the second Temple, dedicated in 516 B.C. The title of Psa. 96 as given by the LXX is, "When the House was being built after the captivity"; and of Psa. 97, "When his land was being settled." They are liturgical and lyrical reflections of Isaiah 40–66. All the psalms in the group may have originated soon after the return from exile.

1, 2. Call to Worship. *Rock*—a frequent designation of God in the O.T. *Presence*—in the Temple; i.e., come before Jehovah himself. *Thanksgiving*—ever due to God; ingratitude is the worst of offenses, especially against God to whom we owe so much.

3–5. The Greatness of God. God is not to be compared with the impotent gods of the heathen. *King*—the kingship of Jehovah is the main thought in this collection of "Royal Psalms." The tremendous places of the earth, unexplored by man, are all under his control. From ocean's mysterious depths to the mystical heights of the mountains is the sweep of divine control (v. 4). He is king over nations and nature. The *sea* and the *dry land* belong to their Creator. The sea seemed most mysterious and by many Jews was supposed to be outside the realm of Jehovah, but the psalmist reminds us that God made and governs all.

6, 7. Second Call to Worship. Based on the relation of Jehovah to Israel. The psalmist speaks from personal experience—the individual worshiper in group worship. *The sheep of his pasture*—no more expressive term could have been used (see on Jn. 10[1-18]).

8–11. Warning Against Obstinacy. It always leads to destruction. *Harden*—do not do as your father did at *Meribah*, and in the day of *Massah* in the wilderness (Ex. 17[1-7]). He remembers God's patience and kindness in the wilderness and also the apostasy of the people when they sorely tried him. God was tried and found true by the children of Israel. Meribah = "strife," Massah = "temptation" (cf. mg.). The children of Israel were not only wandering literally, but also in the ways they knew were not right; hence God was angry and for forty years he was displeased with the erring people. He would not let them *enter into rest*—

he could not allow them to enter the promised land; the people, by their own conduct, made it impossible for God to use them.

PSALM 96. PRAISE TO GOD THE RIGHTEOUS JUDGE

The LXX assigns this psalm to the time when the House was built after the captivity: and there is no reason to doubt that it originated soon after the return from exile.

1–3. Call to Universal Praise. *A new song* —the return from captivity called for a new song. The new Temple was to be a house of prayer for all peoples. The entire earth is called upon to join the glad voices of the returned exiles. This is an outburst of overflowing praise, free and spontaneous. *Salvation from day to day*—each new day demands fresh praise, for the divine expressions of love and mercy are daily renewed. *Nations*—all nations must know and love him. Tell to all the world the wonders of God's amazing love.

4–6. Jehovah's Worthiness to be Praised. It took a great God to deliver his children from captivity, and therefore his praises should be great. He is the incomparable God. The psalms in this collection continually refer to heathen gods as impotent and worthless, while Jehovah is very great. *Honor, majesty, strength,* and *beauty* are his characteristics. Honor and majesty, personified, wait upon him, while strength and beauty adorn his Temple.

7–9. The Whole Earth Exhorted to Acknowledge Jehovah. God is to be praised with our voices, with our substance, with lives of beauty and holiness. *Beauty of holiness* is ever the adornment of his saints; they need no other (cf. notes on 29[2]).

10–13. Jehovah the God of All Nations. Say among the heathen: God hath proclaimed himself King over all. Jehovah reigns not over Israel only but over all the world. He is so gracious and glorious that all nature is joyous in its expressions (v. 11). When the kingship of Jehovah is universally established, the whole universe will be permeated with a spirit of joy. Therefore (v. 13) let all nature rejoice in the day of his coronation: he comes to establish righteousness in the earth. This note of universalism characterizes many psalms, and was a developed feature of Israel's religion (see art., *Religion of Israel*, pp. 171b, 848).

PSALM 97. JEHOVAH REIGNETH

One of the most prominent thoughts in this psalm is judgment, the judgment by which the Lord accomplishes his righteous reign. The psalm is not an original composition; there is hardly a phrase that has not been borrowed, but the borrowing and arranging have been done with consummate skill. The psalmist himself is deeply moved, and, drawing upon psalmists and prophets, he has constructed a "costly mosaic with marvelous skill." The author or compiler is unknown; the psalm probably belongs to the early post-exilic period.

1–3. Jehovah's Dominion. Jehovah has proclaimed himself king. *Isles*=coastlands; a favorite word in Isa. 40–66; all the islands and coastlands of the Mediterranean. The whole near East would have cause to rejoice in the establishment of righteous government. Though *clouds* and *darkness*, as at Sinai, enshroud him, yet *righteousness* and *judgment*, or justice, are the foundation of his kingdom, and his people need not fear him.

4–6. Manifestations of Jehovah's Power. Probably a reference to Sinaitic experiences. Thunder, lightning, earthquake—these are but the manifestations of his power. How impotent are the hills, which seem to us so majestic, in the presence of God, and how readily they give way before him (v. 5; cf. Mic. 1[4]). *Heavens declare* (v. 6)—all the wondrous works of God are but the silent testimonies of his power and glory (Psa. 8[1] 19). All the people may see the story of his majesty and goodness in the heavens above and his glorious manifestations in the history of men.

7–12. Let Israel Trust in God Who is Supreme. Once again he turns to contrast idols of other nations with God (cf. 1 Sam. 5[1-5] 1 Kings 18[30-40] Isa. 42[17] 44[9-20]). History and experience have shown Jehovah supreme. *Zion*—Jerusalem hears of the ruin of Babylon and is glad. For v. 9 see 83[18]—God stands supreme above them all. Therefore let Israel trust in him and serve him. *Ye that love the Lord, hate evil*—live up to your profession. *Light is sown*—it is daybreak for the righteous; there will be universal diffusion of light (v. 11). Consequently, the righteous may well rejoice in the Lord. *His holy name*—literally, "the memorial of his holiness." His name brings to mind what God is and does (v. 12).

PSALM 98. A HYMN OF PRAISE

As in Psa. 96, man and nature are here urged to praise God for the merciful deliverance of his children from captivity. The writer was familiar with the latter part of Isaiah, and the psalm must have been written soon after the return of the Jews from Babylonia.

1–3. Praise Jehovah for His Mercy Toward Israel. *A new song*—the entire earth is called upon to join the glad voices of the returned exiles. *His right hand*—his own might was sufficient. Jehovah's kingdom is being established (v. 2). *Salvation*—his power to deliver; *righteousness*—his fidelity to the covenant with

Israel. The combination of the two terms is quite common in Isa. 40–55. All nations have seen that Jehovah is God. He has proclaimed and demonstrated his righteousness and truth to other nations by delivering Israel from exile.

4–6. Let the Whole Earth Worship God. Salute Jehovah as he assumes his seat upon his universal throne. Use the harp and all other kinds of music in praise of him. Use every means of giving him a great welcome at his coronation (see notes on Psa. 72).

7–9. Let all Nature Rejoice in Worship of the True God. Cf. 93[3] Isa. 55[12], where the trees are said to clap their hands and the hills shout for joy. When God assumes his throne of judgment all nature will rejoice. He is worthy of praise, for he will judge in uprightness (v. 9).

Psalm 99. The Holiness of God's Government

A call to worship Jehovah as the thrice holy God. The two subjects are the universality of Jehovah's rule and the righteous character of his government. Like the other psalms in the collection, this one comes from the early post-exilic period.

1–3. Joyous Utterance of the Wonderful Fact that Jehovah Reigns. Fear or respect for an earthly king is expected; how much more for the King of kings! *Upon the cherubim*—or "between"; on the mercy seat, the place of his earthly manifestation. *Zion*—the seat of his universal sovereignty on earth (v. 2). *Terrible name* (v. 3; cf. on 8[1] 31[3], etc.)—let all the earth praise the majestic name of God, who is holy; the ineffable name expresses the divine character. The Jews came to have such a profound reverence for the name of God that they adopted a number of equivalents for it. After using the name or its equivalent, such as "the Most High," or "the Blessed One," they would add —as they still do—"blessed be He!"

4, 5. The Righteous Character of Jehovah's Reign. *Loveth judgment*—his mighty power never exerts itself tyrannically. This great and terrible King, so strong, loves justice and establishes equity, so that the righteous need not fear him. Praise God and humbly, meekly worship him, for he is holy (v. 5). In ancient times the ark was God's *footstool;* here probably the Temple is meant.

6–9. The Holiness of Jehovah's Reign. The psalmist remembers that three holy men called upon God: *Moses, Aaron,* and *Samuel* all interceded for others and God answered them (Ex. 32[30-35] Num. 16[46-50] 1 Sam. 7[8, 9] 12[16-24]; cf. Jer. 15[1], "The Lord said, Though Moses and Samuel stood before me, yet my mind could not be toward this people"). Now he has relented, has heard their cry of intercession and has delivered the people from Babylon. V. 7 describes the manner in which God spoke to them—and they remembered. *Tookest vengeance* (v. 8)—God loved the sinner and hated his sin. The psalm closes (v. 9) with another call to worship the holy God.

Psalm 100. Exhortation to Thank and Praise Jehovah

A psalm intended from the beginning for public worship. In the second Temple it was used when the thank-offering was presented. It is the last in the collection of the "Royal Psalms" and, like the others, comes from early post-exilic times. It is the basis of "Old Hundred":

"All people that on earth do dwell
Sing to the Lord with cheerful voice."

In the Praise of Jehovah All Mankind is to Regain Its Lost Unity. One essential element of worship is "joy" (vv. 1, 2). Worship also includes the "recognition of God" (v. 3); *sheep of his pasture*—a figure dear to the heart of an Easterner. *Thanks* in worship is like Temple incense (v. 4). We enter into his gates thanking him for his mercy and praise him when we are in his courts. We enter God's temple not because of duty but because we love him; remembering all his goodness to us, we enter his presence with praise and pleasure. V. 5 further describes the character of God. God is more than just—his mercy is everlasting, and all generations will know the truth of him. The amazing thing to them and us is that, after all of our backslidings and meanness, God takes us back and loves us still. "Old Hundred" seems to burst forth from the psalmist's heart, after the contemplation of Psa. 95–99, while thinking upon Israel and all her backslidings and her restoration by a merciful God to a new home and a new Temple. As a Shepherd, God brought back his sheep to the home pasture.

Psalm 101. Profession of Uprightness

Called "David's Mirror for Rulers." It is used on the day of the coronation of English rulers. The origin of the psalm is uncertain. Some scholars accept the testimony of the title and interpret it as an expression of the high purpose which inspired David in his preparations for the transfer of the ark to the new capital. Others, however, assign it to a much later date, possibly as late as the Maccabæan period.

1–4. Preparation for the Coming of the Divine Guest. These verses may express David's longing for the ark to come to him, or the psalmist's longing for the individual presence of God. *I will walk within my house* *with a perfect heart.* The king would find difficulty in doing this; and if he is David, he most certainly did not live up to that vow. Royal palaces have often been places of intrigue and infidelity, but this ruler is cleaning house for the purpose of making Jehovah his guest. No ideal of baseness shall determine his path. *Turn aside*—he hates depraved things. They may tempt, but he will not entertain them.

5–8. Cleansing the Royal Household. The psalmist seems to be a ruler addressing himself to God; if so, he is very noble in his aspirations and ambitions. He first resolves to cleanse his own heart; but he goes further and determines to cleanse his court, as well, of evildoers, to put his house in order, so that Jehovah may be his guest. Moreover, he is always anxious to use only upright and honorable men in positions of trust.

Psalm 102. Complaint and Prayer of One Who is Afflicted

The psalm evidently reflects the late exilic period. Zion appears to be still in ruin, but the time of restoration is at hand (vv. 13, 14). The psalm appears to be dependent on Isa. 40–55 and several other psalms. The prayer is not only an individual petition; it is also a plea for the restoration of Israel and Zion.

1–11. Prayer for Speedy Deliverance. Vv. 1, 2 consist largely of phrases taken from other psalms. The suffering of the psalmist is intense. *Smoke*—a figure of transitoriness; *burned* —may refer to ravaging fever. In v. 5 the resemblance to Job is striking (19^{20}). He compares himself to lonely birds, like the *pelican* and *owl* (v. 6). The pelican inhabits desolate places and the owl is called by the Arabs "mother of ruins." They are found in practically every ruin of the near East. *I watch* or "keep vigil" (v. 7)—i.e., I lie awake nights. *Sparrow*—probably some nocturnal bird, like the owl, which sits upon the housetops while the tired and sleepless victim tosses upon his bed, hearing these weird birds of the night. Mourning and tears are as familiar to him as food and drink (v. 9). Apparently God has lifted him up for the sole purpose of casting him down (v. 10). His life is *like a shadow that declineth* (v. 11)—at evening time the sun casts a long shadow, but the longer the shadow the sooner it is gone. Withering *grass* is a common symbol for transitoriness (Isa. 40^{6-8}).

12–22. Jehovah a Sure Pledge of Restoration. Heretofore the psalmist has described things as they are; now he turns to lift his eyes toward the horizon of hope and to contemplate the eternity of God as the sure pledge of final redemption and restoration. *Time* (v. 13)—the time set in God's own purposes for the restoration has arrived. V. 14 contains a pathetic appeal. *Stones . . . dust*— the people love the very ruins of Jerusalem. To this day the Jews wail daily at one of the city's ancient walls, kissing the stones and often beating their heads against them. The restoration of Zion will be the prelude to the conversion of the whole world (v. 15). *Built up Zion*—the restoration of his people will result in the rebuilding of Zion. *Written* (v. 18)—the wonderful works of Jehovah shall be recorded for all generations, and the new nation growing out of the restored people shall praise Jehovah. Here first in the Psalms occurs the expression thereafter so familiar, *Praise Jehovah*—Hebrew, *Hallelujah.* That is what the generations will say who read the records of what Jehovah is about to do (v. 19). *Sighing* (v. 20)—God is in heaven, but he looks to see and listens to hear the moaning of the prisoner and the "children of death" (cf. mg.), i.e., those in danger of death. *Declare the name of the Lord* (v. 21)—the conversion of the world is to be a conversion to Judaism; at Jerusalem, all men are to praise Jehovah. *Gathered together* (v. 22)—Israel and other nations; the final result will be the spiritual development of the people of God consisting of Hebrews and non-Hebrews (cf. Isa. 2^{2-4} Mic. 4^{1-5}, notes).

23–28. The Unchangeableness of Jehovah Guarantees Deliverance From Present Distress. In v. 23 the psalmist returns to the present; its contrast with the future is striking. The future is glorious, the present evil; days are short, life fleeting and he may not live to see the good days to come. *Midst of my days* (v. 24)—prematurely; the contrast is between his own brief life and the eternal years of God. In vv. 25–27 God is compared with the age of the earth and the heavens. The most enduring things in the material universe pass away but God is from everlasting to everlasting; they grow old as a garment and are cast off, but God never wears out, he never goes out of style, and will abide forever (cf. Heb. 1^{10-12}, where these verses are quoted from the LXX and applied to Christ). The permanence of God guarantees the perpetuity of God's servants and their seed. They shall be reestablished in his land forever (v. 28). Cf. Browning's line in *Rabbi Ben Ezra:* "Earth changes, but thy soul and God stand sure."

Psalm 103. Hymn of Thanksgiving for God's Mercies

The hopes expressed in Psa. 102 have been realized; God has forgiven and restored his people; sorrow has been transformed into joy; now thanksgiving is in order. The psalmist exhorts all the world to join in giving thanks to the great and good Jehovah. As it stands the psalm has every appearance of a liturgical composition; it was probably used when the thank-offering was presented. Though ascribed to David, Aramaic characteristics of the language, dependence on Jeremiah, Isa. 40–66, and Job, as well as general matter and style, point to a post-exilic date.

1–5. Self-exhortation to Praise God. *My soul* = myself = my inner being. All the spiritual faculties and powers of self are summoned to praise God. *Holy name* = holy character, as shown in manifestations in history. *Forget not* (v. 2)—remember all that God has done for you. Count your blessings and praise God accordingly. The surcease from punishment is evidence of forgiveness (v. 3). *Diseases*—ailments, bodily, mental, and spiritual. God is the Great Physician, who can make men whole. He can snatch the sick man from the very jaws of death. *From destruction*—from the grave. God has redeemed the people from certain annihilation. *Crowneth*—a splendid metaphor. God's people are clothed with the garments of holiness and crowned with kindness and mercy (cf. Job 29[14]). Jehovah is the giver of every "good and perfect gift." *Thy mouth* (v. 5) = thy desire or appetite; possibly, "thy years" (cf. mg). The Targum interprets, "the days of old age." The translation "who adorns thee to the full with goodliness" brings out more clearly the usual meaning of the words. God is the fountain of immortal youth. *Like the eagle*—some think of the phoenix bird. The myth of the phoenix supposes that the bird burns up at five hundred years of age and then springs full grown but young and free from its own ashes. The eagle also was supposed to renew its youth by soaring far sunward and then plunging into the ocean. The plain meaning of the passage is that those who trust in Jehovah shall ever be strong and buoyant as the eagle (cf. Isa. 40[31]).

6–10. Jehovah Has Been Gracious to Israel in the Past. The general truth expressed in v. 6 has had a new and recent illustration in the deliverance from exile. *Moses*—God revealed his will to Moses in his Law and his doings to Israel in the Exodus (Ex. 33[13]), but also in subsequent events. *Compassion* (v. 8)—he has shown how great is his patience and sympathy. Over and over again he gave men still another chance. *Plenteous in mercy*—a very comforting expression. *He will not always chide*—he will not stay angry always. He must at times punish, but he will soon relent. *After our sins* (v. 10)—God does not deal with any of us according to our deserts, but, thank God, according to his plenteous mercy.

11–14. The Greatness of the Divine Mercy and Compassion. *High above the earth* (v. 11)—the description of the greatness of God's mercy bankrupts imagination. It is greater than the distance between earth and heaven. *Them that fear him*—true Israelites who maintain an attitude of reverence leading to obedience. Once more in v. 12 the psalmist tries to illustrate the mercy of God. *East . . . west*—the limits of the horizon, which meant much more to the man of the psalmist's day than to-day. How comforting is this thought to the penitent who has come to hate his sins with the deep loathing of an awakened sinner! V. 13 is one of the finest verses in the Bible. It deserves a place alongside of John 3[16]. The frailty of man is pleaded as a basis of God's pity (v. 14). *Our frame*—God remembers that he made man out of dust. He understands how much to put upon him, how much he can bear.

15–18. Man May Pull Away, But God's Mercy Endures Forever. In vv. 15, 16 is the familiar figure of grass to illustrate man's transitoriness. *Man* = mankind in general. Mankind moves like a swift river toward the sea of death. On the other hand (v. 17), God is eternal, and his mercy likewise never fails. Man may pass from the stage of action and another generation take his place—but the same God exercises the same mercy toward all the changing generations of men. *Children* are the inheritors of the grace vouchsafed to the fathers. All these promises belong to those who keep his covenant and remember his commandments to do them.

19–22. Universal Call to Praise. *Hath established his throne* (v. 19)—his throne is on high and his rule covers heaven and earth; he has proclaimed himself king over all, consequently all are urged to recognize his sovereignty and to praise him. *Angels*—heavenly beings are called upon to praise him; how much more man! (Cf. pp. 204–5.) *Fulfil his word*—the angels, full of might, are the messengers of God. *Hosts* (v. 21) = hosts of heaven; here, probably, the angelic hosts. *Ministers*—those who stand by his throne to do his pleasure (see on Zech. 4[14]). All the celestial hierarchy are called upon to swell the anthem of praise which the earthborn begin. *His works* (v. 22)—all creation is called upon to join the heavenly chorus. Then the psalmist returns to his starting point: *Bless the Lord, O my soul!*

Psalm 104. Jehovah's Care Over All His Works

Another hymn of thanksgiving, similar in its spirit to Psa. 103. While nothing is known about authorship and date, some are inclined to ascribe it to the author of the preceding psalm. Attention is sometimes called to the similarity between this psalm and the hymn of praise composed in the fourteenth century B.C. by Ikhnaton of Egypt to his god Aton (Breasted, *History of Egypt*, pp. 371–376).

1–4. Greatness of Jehovah Revealed in Creation. God has *clothed* himself with the wondrous garments of nature. These are the manifestations of his honor and majesty. *Light*—light was the first thing created. God creates the light and wraps it about him as a beautiful garment. Light reveals while it conceals. *Like a curtain*—the sky is stretched out like a blue curtain dotted with bright stars. *Waters*—the waters "that were above the firmament" (Gen. 1[7]). Here he lays the beams of his chambers, above the curtain of the sky. *The clouds his chariots*—God manifesting himself in a storm cloud is a familiar figure in the theophanic psalms (18, 29, Hab. 3). *Winds his messengers*—the great forces of nature are his agents. He makes use of them. The *flaming fire*—the lightning is his minister. On nature as God's "garment" see the conception of Goethe, in *Faust*, of nature as a weaver:

"'Tis thus at the roaring loom of time I ply,
And weave for God the garment thou seest him by."

5–9. The Formation of the Earth. The conditions of primeval chaos are here described, when the vast void was conceived as a liquid mass. If there were mountains, they had not yet appeared. We have here a remarkable description of God rebuking or driving back the waters. His thunder-voice frightens them and they hasten away. Mountains and valleys appear in the place he has prepared for them. He sets for them bounds that they should remain in their appointed places. The whole is a poetic parallel of Gen. 1[9, 10]. (See pp. 126–7.)

10–18. Beautifying and Fructifying the Earth. Jehovah created *springs* in the *valleys* among the hills, so that the *beasts* may drink from them. The trees grow about these springs and the birds live and sing in them. The valleys are watered by streams, but the mountains are watered from heaven, i.e., by rainfall—from his upper *chambers*. The earth is watered, refreshed, fertilized and fed by the rains, springs, and streams which God has provided, and thus is made fruitful. *Grass . . . cattle, herb . . . man*—God produces crops which may serve as food for man and beast. God gives the increase to the efforts of man in the production of food, but grass grows spontaneously for the cattle. Grain, i.e., wheat and barley, wine and oil were the chief products of Canaan (see art., *Palestine*, p. 59b). *The trees of the Lord* (v. 16)—the forests do well without the care of man; these are the gardens of God. The *stork* rarely builds in trees but on houses; but when no houses are available the fir tree is her favorite place. The high hills for the *goats*, the rocks for the *conies*—each animal seems to have provided for it a home suitable to its habits.

19–23. The Functions of Sun and Moon. A poetic elaboration of Gen. 1[17, 18]. *Moon for seasons*—the word "month" is from the word "moon"; the beginning of the month was the new moon; *the sun*—makes its daily round; God orders the journeys of both. When the sun goes down *darkness* comes and the *beasts of the forest* have their time. The *young lions* seek their food from God. When *the sun ariseth* the beasts that belong to the night steal away to their dens. *Man*, who belongs to the day, now goes forth to his labor, and God, who never sleeps, watches over them all.

24–30. Further Marvels of the Divine Creation. The psalmist cries out in wonder at the complexity of God's works and the wisdom exhibited in them all. Earth is full of the riches (mg., "creatures") of God. From this exclamation he turns to the wonders revealed in the *sea* (vv. 25, 26), stretching out before the psalmist's gaze, full of creeping things innumerable. The sea has always been full of the most alluring mysteries. It could feed, clothe, and fuel the whole world as well as form its great lines of travel and commerce; moreover, what unknown mines and mountain ranges, valleys, deep and broad plains, what fauna and flora must be there, beneath those mighty waters. *Ships*—stately and useful, with a sweep of freedom unknown on land. *Leviathan*—see on Job 41[1-34]. God is the great Householder; both land and sea animals seek their meat from him (vv. 27, 28); God gives life as well as food (v. 29). Day by day he gives them breath, and when he withdraws his sustaining influence they die and return to dust. When the present generation of animals die God's Spirit creates others to take their place (v. 30; cf. on Gen. 6[3]).

31–35. Concluding Prayer and Vows. Vv. 31, 32 contain a prayer for the continuance of these wonderful manifestations in nature. The psalmist vows that he will always praise God and think kindly of him even when he cannot understand (vv. 33, 34). V. 35 is a prayer for the elimination of all that mars the harmony of the universe. This psalm (cf. Psa. 103) begins and ends with *Bless the Lord, O my soul!* The psalmist then appends a single word in Hebrew, *Hallelujah;* which is translated, *Praise ye the Lord!* (But cf. introductory paragraph to Psa. 105.)

Psalm 105. Historical Psalm of Praise and Encouragement

The LXX places the word "Hallelujah" at the beginning of this psalm rather than at the end of Psa. 104. If this is correct—and it probably is—then Psa. 103, 104 begin and end with "Bless the Lord, O my soul," and Psa. 105, 106 begin and end with "Hallelujah." The two last mentioned psalms are closely related. Psa. 105 recapitulates the many ways in which Jehovah has proved his faithfulness to the covenant made with Abraham; Psa. 106, a penitential psalm, recites Israel's faithlessness and disobedience. Both psalms reflect conditions during the post-exilic period; they may be the work of one and the same author.

1–6. Summons to Proclaim Jehovah's Mighty Works for His People. *Give thanks . . . call upon his name* or "proclaim his name." God ever strove to teach Israel that her main business was to *make known* God to all the world (v. 1). *Sing . . . talk*—like a modern service, sing his praises and preach his gospel. *Holy name* = holy character (see on 99^{3} 103^{1}; cf. Acts 3^{6}). *Heart*—inward joy, inspired by the consciousness of his presence. *Strength* (v. 4) —Jehovah is the source of all our power. "The power of a life, like the power of a stream, is in proportion to the altitude of its source." *Face* = favor. *Remember* (v. 5)—cf. on Deut. 8^{11-20}. Israel had often forgotten. *Marvelous works*—at the time of the Exodus and later. *Judgments of his mouth*—on Pharaoh and others. *Abraham . . . Jacob*—Jacob was in reality the father of the race by whose name, Israel, they were called; but the Hebrews always traced their lineage back two steps further, to Abraham (cf. pp. 1155–6).

7–12. The Theme of the Psalm: Jehovah's Faithfulness. *The Lord our God*—"Jehovah" was the name applied to God as the God of Israel. Though he was the God of the whole earth, he bore a peculiar relationship to the Hebrews (Ex. $3^{13f.}$). *Covenant* (v. 8)—he remembers his covenant, for it is a word of a thousand generations; i.e., it is timeless, eternal. "Heaven and earth shall pass away, but my word shall never pass away." He made his covenant with Abraham (Gen. 13^{14} 17^{2} 22^{16}, etc.), with Isaac (Gen. 26^{3}) and with Jacob (28^{13}). It would not be enough to say he made it with Abraham, for Abraham had several sons, nor with Isaac, for he had two sons. It was through a chosen line of descendants. God made this covenant with them when they were a feeble folk. When they went from Shechem Jacob said of his family, "we are few" (Gen. 34^{30}).

13–24. Jehovah's Protecting Care of the Patriarchs. God watched over them among the nations. *Reproved kings for their sake*—as Pharaoh on account of Abraham and Sarah (Gen. 12^{17}; cf. also 20^{3}). *Anointed . . . prophets* (v. 15)—the patriarchs are thought of as kings and prophets. *A famine in the land*—that is one of the commonest occurrences in that land. Famine gave God a chance to show his faithfulness. *Staff of bread*—sustaining food. Even before the famine started, God sent a man on ahead to prepare to keep them alive. *Joseph,* however, whom he sent for this purpose, he allowed to go to prison (v. 17). As Job could not understand the ways of God, so Joseph must have been astounded that God should have seemingly forsaken him utterly; but (vv. 19, 20) he waited God's time till his release came and God's purpose in allowing him to go to prison was revealed. God sometimes allows his children to go very low, that he may lift them on high (cf. Eph. 4^{9-11}). He lifted Joseph from prison to be ruler of rulers (vv. 21, 22; cf. Gen. 50^{20}). *Israel* = *Jacob*—cf. 59^{13} 78^{5} Isa. 49^{6}. *Ham* = Egypt in Africa (v. 23). *Increased . . . stronger*—a slave people rose to such strength that it threatened the peace of the land.

25–36. Display of Jehovah's Power in Egypt. The enmity of Egypt furnished Jehovah special opportunity for the display of his power. *He turned their heart* (v. 25)—in the psalmist's conception, the hatred of Israel by Pharaoh was but another incident in the eternal purpose of God (cf. Ex. 4^{21} 10^{1}, etc). *Moses his servant*—as he had sent Joseph earlier in his program. *Aaron*—curiously Aaron nowhere occurs in the story of the Exodus until he is an old man, when he goes out to meet Moses, who was already eighty years old. He has been held in reserve until called upon the stage for his part at the appointed time. *His signs*—or, the words of his signs. The plagues were proclaimed as signs warning Pharaoh not to stand in the way of God's sovereign will (v. 27). *Darkness* (v. 28)—the ninth plague is placed first here, perhaps because the people of Egypt worshiped the sun and Jehovah showed his supremacy when he shut out the face of their god. Vv. 28–36 enumerate the plagues recorded in detail in Ex. 7–12.

37–45. From the Exodus Through the Desert to Canaan. *He brought them forth with silver and gold* (Ex. $12^{35, 36}$)—the ethics of this action has often been assailed and need not be defended. Probably the figure is of an army with the spoils of battle (which also cannot be defended according to Christian ethics), among whom none were faint or weary. The story of that last tragic night in Egypt and the dawn of the set day is thrillingly romantic and dramatic (cf. Ex. 12). *Egypt was glad* to get rid of them. Their presence had brought too much affliction and loss. Following the departure from Egypt Jehovah looked after the fugitives during the desert wanderings (vv. 39–43). *Rock* (v. 41)—at Rephidim. This must have been a very pleasant memory. Hot and thirsty in a land hopelessly desert, they receive refreshing water from the dry rock (Ex. $17^{1f.}$); he also gave them *bread* (Ex. 16). *Remembered* (v. 42)—he did not forget his holy promise then, nor will he forget now. *Joy . . . singing*—as at the Red Sea (Ex. 15). *The lands of the nations*—he gave them Canaan, civilized with the labors of a thousand years. No other peoples have ever inherited an old civilization complete (v. 44). The purpose of all of God's blessings upon his people is that they may do his will (v. 45). *Hallelujah*—cf. on 104^{35}.

Psalm 106. Israel's Ingratitude and Disobedience

Though Jehovah always showed himself gracious, the people disregarded his goodness and rebelled against him. This psalm is a confession of the baseness of the people's conduct, followed by a brief prayer for the people's restoration. It may be by the same author as Psa. 105 (see introductory paragraph there).

1–5. Call to Praise Jehovah for His Unfailing Goodness. Calling attention to the continuous mercy of God reveals the more clearly the baseness of the people's sins as described in vv. 6f. *Hallelujah*—or *Praise ye the Lord* (v. 1)—some of the early translations consider this a part of the title, not a part of the psalm proper. Israel was to keep the ordinances of God—the reward was prosperity and victory. Vv. 4, 5 contain a personal prayer by the psalmist, that he may participate in the full restoration of his people.

6. Theme of the Psalm: Confession of Sin. The nation's history is dark in deeds of disobedience and general apostasy. The psalmist means to confess not only the sins of his own generation, but also those of the fathers. There is a deep sense of national solidarity.

7–12. Experience at the Red Sea. In the face of God's wonderful manifestations in Egypt the people showed unbelief at the first provocation; but in spite of it God gave them deliverance (vv. 7–11). Their faith was renewed (v. 12); but only for a little while.

13–15. Murmuring for Food. They praised for a while and then they ceased to trust God to take care of them. *Lust*—they murmured for water and food, all of which God supplied (Ex. $15^{22f.}$ $16^{2f.}$ $17^{2f.}$); here the reference is to the lusting after flesh (Num. $11^{4f.}$). God gave them what they were lusting for and then they "turned to loathing."

16–18. Jealousy of Moses and Aaron. *Envied* (v. 15)—the rebellion against Aaron and Moses was also rebellion against God. Vv. 17, 18 describes the punishment of the rebels (Num. 16^{31-35} Deut. 11^{6}). But punishment did not heal the spiritual disease.

19–23. The Golden Calf. The incident is described in Ex. 32, Deut. 9^{8f}. They could not see God; they wanted an image that they could touch with their human hands. *Changed their glory*—i.e., Jehovah himself. They exchanged their glorious God for the image of a calf. *God their saviour*—had they remembered the many deliverances wrought by Jehovah they would not have turned so easily to a "calf." *He would destroy them*—over and over again they would have perished had it not been for Moses; Moses was their human saviour.

24–27. Cowardice on the Return of the Spies. After they had experienced so many blessings from Jehovah they might have believed that he would give them the promised land to possess. When they again showed lack of faith, Jehovah caused them to die in the wilderness and later scattered their descendants among nations.

28–31. Participation in Moabite Worship. By worshiping idols they brought destruction upon themselves (Num. 25). *Phineas* took God's part and fought against those who were sinning, and by this act of faith and fidelity, purchased unto himself an immortal name.

32, 33. The Sin at Meribah. Num. 20^{1-13} In this sin Moses became involved. *Spake unadvisedly*—the sin of Moses was impatience and want of faith (cf. Num. 20^{12} Deut. 1^{37} $4^{21f.}$).

34–46. Continued Disobedience After Entering Canaan. The whole history is a story of backsliding and coming back to God, only to backslide again; and, on the other side, repeated punishments for their wrong doing. *Distress*—when they were in distress because of their sins, they always came back to God for help, and as often as they came he pitied them and gave them another chance (v. 44); in spite of their rebellion, God remembered his covenant and showed mercy.

47. Closing Prayer. The climax and ending of the psalm. The confession has been made; God has been merciful again and again; let him show mercy once more by restoring the nation: "Gather us from among the nations, make us a people again."

48. The Doxology. This verse contains a doxology, taken from 1 Chr. 16^{36}, marking the close of Book IV. Cf. 89^{52} 105^{45}.

The division between Book IV and Book V

seems to be arbitrary; originally the two books formed a single collection (Psa. 90–150; see introduction, p. 509b).

PSALM 107. A CALL TO THANKSGIVING

In this psalm (which begins Book V) there is a call to thank Jehovah for deliverance, yea, for many deliverances throughout Israel's entire history. It was meant originally for the recently returned exiles from Babylon; by recalling the manifold mercies of God they might be encouraged to rely upon him when things looked dark in their own day. It comes, therefore, from the early post-exilic period.

1–3. A Call to Give Thanks. First Reason: the Return. *The redeemed of the Lord* (v. 2)—in post-exilic literature these words usually refer to those delivered from exile in Babylonia; more rarely to deliverance from bondage in Egypt. *Gathered*—the Jews have ever been a people of dispersion, and there may have gathered in Jerusalem after the Exile Jews from every point of the compass. Cf. the gathering at Pentecost (Acts 2[5]).

4–9. Deliverance of Travelers Lost in the Desert. Vv. 4–32 contain four pictures representing the goodness of God in rescuing people from extreme peril. The first is that of travelers lost in the desert. It is a vivid portrayal of a lost people—wandering in the desert between Egypt and Palestine, or between Palestine and Babylonia, more likely the former—recounting the mercy of God, how he led them through these troubles to a settled land and an inhabited city. This may be the experience of every soul lost from God. For such wonderful help men should ever praise Jehovah, especially those who had been the recipients of special grace (v. 8), such as are described in vv. 4–7. Here as in the similar passages, vv. 15, 21, 31, the exhortation is addressed to the persons whose rescue is described in the verses immediately preceding. God satisfies the hungry soul (v. 9). The reference is primarily to the satisfaction of the hungry desert travelers.

10–16. Second Reason for Thanksgiving: Jehovah Frees the Prisoner. Perhaps he has in mind the prisons of the Babylonian Exile. The exiles were, however, in no sense prisoners; they enjoyed almost as much freedom as had been theirs at home. The prison experiences are the results of disobedience to God (vv. 10–13); but when the prisoners cried unto him he saved them, as usual (v. 13); he released them from the prisons, even on the eve of execution (v. 14). Hence the exhortation to praise Jehovah for what he has done (cf. v. 8). *Gates of brass*—neither gates of brass nor bars of iron can keep Jehovah from releasing the prisoner.

17–22. Third Reason for Thanksgiving: Restoration from Sickness. A similar passage is found in Job 33[17-26]—men are *fools;* they sin, only to be afflicted because of their sins. *Abhorreth all manner of meat*—their afflictions spoil their digestion; they come to the verge of death, but "out of the depths they cry," and he saves them (vv. 18, 19). *Sendeth his word*—which possesses power to heal them; even though they are at the point of death (v. 20). For the refrain in v. 21 see on v. 8. To the praises of the lips are to be added *sacrifices of thanksgiving*—a thankful heart will inevitably be revealed with proper thank-offerings of our substance (cf. Mal. 3[8-10]).

23–32. Fourth Reason for Thanksgiving: Rescue of Sailors Caught in a Storm. *That do business*—sea merchants. See the eloquent description of the great merchant fleets of Tyre in Ezek. 27. *The works of the Lord*—the sea impresses one with the greatness and majesty of Him who makes and governs it. *The stormy wind*—God creates the storm, which at sea is especially terrible (vv. 25–27); but when the sailor calls upon God, he hears and brings calm, gladness, and a safe haven. For the refrain in v. 31 see on v. 8. V. 32 contains an additional call to praise him, in the *assembly* and in the *seat of the elders*—the legislature. Let church and state join in praising God.

33–43. God's Providential Government of the World. From specific instances the psalmist turns to more general manifestations of the divine mercy and power. Under the hand of God the very earth shifts. Fertile lands may be turned into desert because of the sins of their inhabitants; on the other hand, desert places may be made fruitful and glorious (vv. 33–38). Trouble may, indeed, come; but Jehovah will be present to help and deliver; which will bring joy to the upright and disappointment to the wicked (vv. 39–42). *Whoso is wise*—the wise man can learn useful lessons from observing the providential acts of God (v. 43; cf. Hos. 14[9]).

PSALM 108. A PRAYER FOR HELP AGAINST ISRAEL'S FOES

The material of this psalm is taken from 57[7-11] and 60[5-12]. It is later than the component parts; in other words, though ascribed to David in the title, it is undoubtedly post-exilic in origin.

1–5. Resolution of Joyous Thanksgiving, Followed by Prayer. His will and purposes are steadfastly *fixed* to sing the divine praises. Some ancient translations read *prepared.* *Awake, psaltery and harp*—they have been silent through days of exile. *I will awake right early*—better, *I will awake the dawn;* I will sing before the sunrise. I will celebrate the dawn of our deliverance. *Among the peoples* (v. 3)—in contrast to the thought of 137[4], "How shall we sing Jehovah's song in a foreign land?" Now he proposes to sing boldly the praises of Jehovah in the midst of the nations who had seen both Israel's downfall and deliverance. *Among the nations*—may indicate the composition of the psalm after the decree of Cyrus, but before the writer had returned. *Above* (read *unto*) *the heavens* (v. 4)—the greatness of God's mercy is incomparable. As God's mercy is high as the heavens, so praise to him should be just as high; and as God has given his people such wonderful evidence of his love and mercy, so his people should exalt him in their hearts and lives as well as with their mouths.

6–13. Prayer for Help and Expression of Assurance. *Beloved*—this term runs through the Bible; it is probably the forerunner of the technical term applied to a group or party in later Judaism—the "Hasidim." *In his holiness* (v. 7)—the holy aspects of God's character make it impossible for him to fail. God is the subject and the speaker. *Shechem . . . Succoth*—two cities connected with the history of Jacob, their father (Gen. 33[17, 18] Josh. 13[27]); the former represents the territory west of the Jordan; the latter, the territory east of the Jordan; similarly, *Gilead and Manasseh* represent the territory east of the Jordan and *Judah and Ephraim* that west of the river. *Moab*—proverbially proud, is compared to a basin for washing the feet. *Edom* is to be either a rubbish heap upon which cast off shoes are thrown, or a menial slave to whom the victorious warrior casts his dusty sandals. *Philistia*—over this most powerful of Israel's enemies God will shout in victorious triumph.

Beginning with v. 10 we are led to believe that the preceding has been only a hope. It now takes the form of a prayer for its accomplishment. *Fenced city . . . Edom*—the strong city of Edom was Petra, the ancient capital, carved out of solid rock and almost entirely inaccessible. God alone can lead to such a victory (vv. 11–13) and he will surely do it.

Psalm 109. Prayer for Vengeance

An "imprecatory" psalm. It opens with a prayer for help against merciless enemies; but when he thinks of the injustice which has been done to him as well as to others, he breaks out in bitter, uncontrolled denunciation. The psalm probably belongs to the post-exilic age.

1–5. Appeal for Help against Cruel Foes. *Hold not thy peace*—the psalmist prays that God will break his silence, in the midst of the noisy clamor of enemies. He does not mince words about his enemies. While God is silent, their mouths are open and pouring forth lies, they hate him, and this hatred is not only without cause but is returning evil for good.

6–20. Passionate Prayer of Retribution. The particular enemy condemned seems to be an officer; a class that have almost always been oppressive in the East. The psalmist prays that an accuser or adversary should always stand at the right hand of this cruel oppressor. *When he is judged*—let the case always go against him (v. 7). *His prayer turned into sin*—when a wicked man prays to God, without true penitence, he is asking God to take the part of the wicked and thus subvert the whole moral order. *His days be few*—long life was the *summum bonum* to the Jews; hence a short life was a curse of God. Let his misdeeds fall even upon his family. *Children vagabonds and beg*—this is an awful curse, but quite in keeping with ancient Oriental thought. *Desolate places*=ruined houses; perhaps, "driven out of their ruined homes."

Many read, v. 11, "Let a creditor ensnare all that he hath and foreigners plunder his labor." Let none show him mercy and none show pity to his fatherless children (v. 12). *Posterity be cut off*—this was a serious matter to the Hebrew, for, if that happens, in one generation his name will be completely forgotten. In vv. 14, 15 a curse is asked even because of the sins of the parents. In the case of the psalmist's enemy, may the ancient law (see Ex. 20[5]), according to which the sins of the fathers are to be visited on the children, be fully met.

The psalmist explains, in vv. 16–18, why he is asking such dire curses: the one cursed lacked mercy, persecuted the poor, and killed the broken in heart; he loved cursing, and therefore he is getting only what he fully deserved. He delighted not in blessing, and he is not to be blessed. *He clothed himself also with cursing as with his garment.* Therefore may cursing be his clothing and may it never get far away from him. *Reward*—there is ever an insistence that all this imprecation was deserved.

21–31. Prayer for Pity and Deliverance. The psalmist expects no help from his enemies; but God can and will have mercy on him. V. 22 is a confession; *poor, needy, wounded within*—heart wounds are the sorest of all. *Shadow* (v. 23)—see on 102[11]; his strength is completely gone (vv. 24–26); there is no one to whom he can turn but God (v. 27). However, if God will bless, let the enemy curse all he will (v. 28). Once again, in v. 29, he implores God to bring his enemies to such shame and confusion that he will be completely vindicated in the eyes of all about; then he will praise Jehovah (v. 30); for when the poor comes up for judgment the accusers may be there with lying lips, but Jehovah will stand at the right hand to bless and deliver them (v. 31).

Psalm 110. The Victorious King

The psalmist here asserts that Jehovah will exalt his lord to a place "at his right hand," from which he will exercise dominion over the conquered nations. The psalm is therefore regarded as Messianic. It is of special interest because of the use made of it by Jesus (Mk. 12[35f.] Mt. 22[41f.] Lk. 20[41f.]). In the title the psalm is ascribed to David, and there are those who believe that the words of Jesus make Davidic authorship certain. A closer study of Jesus' use, however, shows that the value of his argument is not affected by the question of authorship; which means that in this, as in all similar cases, the question must be determined on the basis of all the various kinds of evidence available; and on the basis of such evidence many modern commentators are inclined to date the psalm in the Maccabean age.

1–3. Jehovah's Decree Concerning the King. *My lord*—a title of respect and reverence. *At my right hand*—the place of honor, but more is implied, namely, that the king will share Jehovah's throne. *Thine enemies thy footstool*—it was an ancient custom for victorious kings to place their feet upon the necks of their conquered enemies—this indicates complete subjugation (cf. 108[9]). *Rod of strength* (v. 2)—read *scepter* (A.S.V. mg.); the scepter of power and authority is to be stretched out from Zion, the new capital. *Offer themselves willingly* (v. 3)—read *The people are freewill offerings in the day of the army muster.* Human agency is necessary to the accomplishment of divine tasks. *In the beauties of holiness*—read, with R.V. mg., *in holy attire;* probably connected with that which follows, *Out of the womb of the morning thou hast the dew of thy youth.* The first clause may refer to the holy mountains where the armies mustered; the morning was considered the mother of the dew. The general thought of the verses is that the new king will be strong, enjoying eternal youth, and will have the ready and enthusiastic co-operation of his subjects.

4. The Royal Ruler will Fill the Priestly Office. The ideal ruler will possess both priestly and kingly functions. This was true in the earliest days of Israel's history and again during the Maccabean period. *After the order of Melchizedek*—Melchizedek did not occupy the priestly office because of family relationship but, it is assumed, by divine appointment. Similarly, the Messianic priest-king might claim his priesthood on the basis of the immutable decree of God, who with solemn oath confirmed the appointment. He is to be such *forever*—this is no temporary assignment; continually he will exercise the prerogatives of a mediatorial priesthood. For the use made of this statement by the author of the Epistle to the Hebrews, see p. 1310. It should be noted that if the psalm comes from the Maccabean age, it reflects actual conditions in the Jewish community at the time: (1) Simon was the ecclesiastical as well as the civil head; (2) the Maccabees belonged to the priestly tribe of Levi.

5–7. The Priest-King's Victory. The scene is now upon the battlefield. *Thy right hand*—as chief support. *Strike through kings*—in the day of the judgment of the nations; nothing shall stand before him. In the great battle the king will not stop, but press on to glorious victory. This ruler is not a prince of peace, but a lord of war.

Psalm 111. The Power, Goodness and Righteousness of Jehovah

This is the first of the "Hallel" songs (Psa. 111–118; sometimes, however, the designation is given only to Psa. 113–118). They are so called (1) because of the frequent use of the term *Hallelujah* = *Praise ye Jehovah;* and (2) because they are the "Praise Songs" used at the three great festivals of Passover, Pentecost and Tabernacles. This and Psa. 112 are acrostics, each having twenty-two lines, the number of letters in the Hebrew alphabet, and the successive lines beginning with successive letters. The two psalms are closely connected also in language and contents; though in Psa. 112 some of the expressions applied to God in Psa. 111 are applied to godly men (see comments). Both undoubtedly belong to the post-exilic period, but the dates cannot be determined more exactly.

1. Promise of Praise. *Hallelujah*—no part of the main structure of the psalm; it is simply a liturgical call to praise. *I will give thanks unto the Lord with my whole heart*—not alone with lips but from the deeps of my innermost being will I praise him. *The council of the upright*—rather, in the intimate fellowship of the individual members of the group. *Congregation*—in the gatherings of those intimate friends in the house of God. The reference is to private prayer and public worship.

2–8. Grounds of Praise. There is every reason why the psalmist should praise God. *The works of the Lord are great*—he has wrought wonderfully for his people Israel and this is the ground of that great praise which is here proposed. *Sought out*—the works of God are manifest in their wondrous glory to all who have eyes to see. The saints of God seek to see his works and to delight in them. *Honor . . . majesty*—or "his work is honorable and glorious"; i.e., it expresses his great majesty. *To be remembered*—Jehovah has appointed ordinances and rituals that will remind all succeeding generations that *the Lord is gracious and full of compassion* (v. 4). *Meat*—literally, "prey" (v. 5, mg.). Possibly the expression means that Jehovah has snatched the prey from the mouth of their enemies and has given it to them for food. The word may be used simply for the purpose of securing the right letter for the acrostic. He is a covenant keeping God. *Heritage of the nations*—he made them inherit the land of Canaan, previously in possession of other nations. *Truth and judgment* (justice)—these are eternal attributes of God. V. 8 emphasizes the solidity with which the divine precepts and commandments are founded; they are resting upon truth and uprightness. These attributes of Jehovah are the sure proof that he will fulfill all of his promises and keep all of his covenants.

9, 10. Recapitulation of God's Mercies to His People. In contemplation of these wonderful works of God the psalmist breaks forth into animated exclamation: *Holy and reverend is his name. The fear of the Lord is the beginning of wisdom.* To fear Jehovah, i.e., to take an attitude of reverence toward him, is the beginning or the crown of all true wisdom (cf. Prov. 1^{7} 9^{10} Job 28). The praise of God will endure *forever* (v. 10). His wonderful works and mercies toward his people guarantee that men shall always praise him.

Psalm 112. The Prosperity and Blessedness of God-Fearing Men

The righteous character of the God-fearing man is a reflection of the character of God himself. On the contents, date, and relation to Psa. 111 see introductory paragraph to the latter psalm. There are no clearly marked divisions in the psalm. The characteristics of the God-fearing man are outlined; the rewards he receives from God are described; and the psalm closes with an announcement of the destruction of the wicked.

1–3. Blessed Is the God-Fearing Man. Such a man will want to do God's will; hence he studies his commandments ($1^{1, 2}$). *His seed*—his influence shall be so great that succeeding generations will be men of God and prosperous (contrast 109^{13}). An upright man creates a condition in the midst of which upright children develop. In accordance with general O.T. thought, honor and wealth are promised and come to the upright man (cf. Isa. $53^{10, 11}$).

4–6. Reward of the Righteous. V. 4 describes the righteous man; he is gracious and compassionate. *There ariseth light*—the light of prosperity. Fortunate the man who has the will power to turn his emotions into action. *Maintain his cause*—better "manage his affairs;" the God-fearing man will manage his own business so as to hurt no one. His prosperity is not temporary, but permanent.

7–10. Permanence of the Righteous, Destruction of the Wicked. *Afraid*—the righteous man has no premonitions of impending evil. *Fixed*—or steadfast, which gives him calm confidence. His trust is in Jehovah, and his purpose fixed (v. 8); consequently he is sure that ultimately his enemies will be defeated. *Dispersed*—almsgiving shall be remembered forever. The wicked behold the works of the righteous and are angry because of the thwarting of their own evil plans (v. 10); and they will die disappointed.

Psalm 113. Gratitude for Restoration from Exile

The first of the smaller group of "Hallel" psalms (113–118; see introductory note to Psa. 111). It is a call to praise Jehovah who, though exalted above the nations in heavenly glory, condescends to care for the weak and oppressed on earth. It is post-exilic in origin.

1–3. Call to Universal and Unceasing Praise. *Servants*—all true Israelites, ready to do Jehovah's will. *Name*—may mean either character, or manifestations of Jehovah, or Jehovah himself. The praise of Jehovah is to be universal (v. 3).

4–6. Ground of Praise: Jehovah's Majesty and Condescension. *High above all* (v. 4)—a picture of the majesty of Jehovah, enthroned in glory. *Who is like* (v. 5)—he is incomparable; there is no one like him. *Humbleth himself*—though enthroned in heaven Jehovah bows down to observe what is going on on the earth as well as in the heavens.

7–9. Jehovah's Condescension. Jehovah's interest in man and his doings has frequently shown itself. *The poor*—he concerns himself with earth's lowly, yea, with earth's lowliest; *dunghill*—a figure implying extreme degradation and misery. His concern is to lift up the needy. *With princes* (v. 8)—he takes those who trust him even from the dunghill and sets them with princes. *Barren woman*—he is kind even to the barren woman, so that she comes to know the joy of motherhood (cf. 1 Sam. 2^{1-10}).

PSALM 114. GOD'S DELIVERANCE OF ISRAEL FROM EGYPT

This psalm has been called a perfect poem, exquisite in form and marvelously artistic; its parallelism is faultless. It was used by Dante for his spirits on their way to Purgatory; at present it is widely used as a prayer for the dying. While it celebrates primarily the deliverance from Egypt, it was written after the return from Babylon as a celebration of Israel's second birth—the return from Babylon.

1, 2. The Exodus from Egypt. This marked Israel's birthday (Hos. 11[1]). *Out of Egypt*—a favorite theme; they had been strangers in the midst of strange people. *Judah . . . Israel*—the whole nation. *Sanctuary*—the Temple in Jerusalem. *Dominion*—external and temporal power. The thought is not that Judah was especially sacred or that Israel stood preeminently for dominion; it is simply an attempt to complete the parallelism and to state that the whole life of Israel came under God's control.

3, 4. Obstacles Overcome. Jehovah cleared the way of all obstacles. *Sea*—the Red Sea is personified and represented as seeing the people, with Jehovah marching at their head, and frightened, fleeing from his awful presence. "Awestruck nature recognized and obeyed its Master's will." A little later the Jordan was driven back. *The mountains* are likewise represented as frightened animals running here and there. Perhaps the disturbances at Sinai are intended (Ex. 19[16-18]; cf. Isa. 55[12]).

5, 6. Why Did Nature Act Like This? The psalmist here pictures himself as standing back with those early fathers, watching the mighty spectacle and addressing the personified objects of nature. "What was the matter with you, Sea? What ailed you, Jordan? Ye mountains and hills, what were you doing?"

7, 8. The Irresistible Power of Jehovah. The psalmist now turns to the present once more. No wonder nature does these marvelous things. There is a reason: God has revealed himself in its presence. He made a flinty rock a fountain of water (Ex. 17[6]). So shall he bring forth streams of blessing for his people.

PSALM 115. JEHOVAH AND IDOLS

The psalmist knows that the misfortunes of Israel have sometimes led their enemies to suggest that Jehovah was weak and incompetent, while their own gods were strong. This is not the case. Jehovah is far superior to the heathen gods who can do nothing for their worshipers. Let the people trust in him, and in his own good time he will bless them and deliver them. Apparently, the psalm reflects an experience of deep humiliation and a recent encounter with idols. It may look back to the Babylonian Exile. It is undoubtedly postexilic.

1-3. Appeal to Jehovah to Deliver His People and Thus Vindicate Himself. *Not unto us*—the prayer is for the vindication of Israel, for the sake of Jehovah's good name. *Where is now their God?* The gods of the heathen were such gods as could be handled and seen and catalogued; the Hebrew God could be seen only in his works; but the treatment of his people raised questions regarding his reality and power. The psalmist answers boldly: Our God is in the heavens—he is not within the house in the form of wood or stone or even gold. He is spirit. He has done whatever he pleased to do and here about us is the evidence of his master workmanship.

4-8. Contrast between Jehovah and Heathen Gods. How different! *Their idols*—human built and in human likeness, they do not even have the human intellect. They have every physical attribute of the human being but are utterly impotent to use any of them (vv. 5-7). *They that make them shall be like unto them*—as the gods, so the men. We are no better than the gods we make and we rise no higher than our conception of the Deity.

9-13. Exhortation to Trust Jehovah. *Trust*—not in perishable gods (described above) but in the eternal. *He is their help and their shield*—transition to the third person on account of the antiphonal character. Probably the first line was sung by the precentor and the answer by the congregation. *House of Aaron*—vv. 9, 10, 11, form parallel appeals; the main characters are Israel, Aaron, and those that fear Jehovah. Each in turn is urged to trust in Jehovah. Note the narrowing process: the address is first to the whole nation, Israel; then to the priestly order, the sons of Aaron; then to the inner circle of the true devotees who fear Jehovah. *Hath been mindful*—Jehovah will answer such a prayer and such trust; he will bless Israel, Aaron, and the fearers of the Lord; which means that he will bless all who trust him. *Small and great*—all, without distinction. Rank and reputation mean nothing to him; trust means everything.

14-18. Prayers for Divine Blessings and Promise to Praise Jehovah. May Jehovah increase the little congregation who had returned to Palestine. *Children*—while a large family was ever a matter of rejoicing to the Hebrew, it was even more so now when their numbers had been so sadly depleted in the Exile. The optimistic trust in Jehovah is justified by the greatness of his power (v. 15).

He made heaven and earth, in contrast to the heathen idols who are powerless; they cannot even feel or smell or see. Now is the time to praise Jehovah (vv. 17, 18). *The dead praise not the Lord*—a thought frequently expressed that the dead in Sheol can no longer praise God (cf. 6[5] 88[10-12] Eccl. 9[10], etc.).

Psalm 116. Thanksgiving for Deliverance from Imminent Danger of Death

The psalmist has apparently been in extreme personal peril, from which he has been delivered by the grace of Jehovah. The recovery of Hezekiah has been suggested (Isa. 38), but there are many indications of a later date, and the psalm may express the deep gratitude of any saint for deliverance from some grave danger. The language, with its strong Aramaic coloring, favors a late post-exilic date. In the same direction points the dependence on other psalms.

1, 2. Answered Prayer Demands Loving Gratitude. *I love*—one could never love an impersonal God, but since he concerns himself with our welfare, we can love him. We love him because he first loved us.

3, 4. Prayer in Peril. Death and Sheol, the most dreaded enemies of man, are visualized as huntsmen lying in wait with snares and pulling the cords close about the necks of their victims, or driving them into a narrow valley whence there is no escape. *Name* = the character of Jehovah (cf. on 113[1-3]).

5, 6. Revelation of God's Character. Jehovah not only hears, but he hears graciously, and mercifully. These are the amazing attributes of God. His sovereignty is a matter of course, and his justice all would expect, but grace and mercy for a sinful race are far more comforting (Ex. 34[6]). *Preserveth the simple* (v. 6)—how comforting that is! Earthly potentates are usually impatient with ignorance and weakness; not so God. The simple are the objects of his special care and sympathy. A proof that he preserveth the simple is that *I was brought low and he helped me.*

7–9. Self-Encouragement on the Basis of God's Mercy. *Return unto thy rest, O my soul*—cease taking anxious thought for the morrow, and rest in that blessed trust which walks with God in the night as well as in the light. Jehovah has delivered me from death, tears, and stumbling. Therefore since God has been so gracious to me, I, on my part, will walk before him, as his own, as long as I live.

10–14. Triumph of Faith and Thanksgiving. V. 10 begins a new section. Before, it was "I love," now, "I believe." The conception of this psalm is very high. Notice "love," "prayer," "grace," "mercy," "faith." *I believe*—better, *I believed;* I never lost faith in the heavenly Father; I did lose faith in men (2 Cor. 4[13]). *All men are a lie*—Hebrew, "liars." In his extremity they probably forsook him as men frequently do, but God was faithful. The psalmist senses his obligation to God and inquires what task God will set him that he may show his appreciation of his goodness to him (v. 12). *Cup of salvation* (v. 13) = cup of blessing. *Pay my vows*—I will acknowledge my obligation and proclaim my gratitude. The psalmist had been in peril and had made vows as to what he would do if he got well (cf. 50[14]).

15–19. Jehovah's Care for His Beloved. God cares for his people while they walk in the land of the living, he hears their prayers, he heals their infirmities, and when they come to die he is not unmindful of them. Many have felt in the hour when death enters the home that God has forgotten; but it is not so; even then he cares and his dying saints are precious in his sight. No wonder martyrs have gone to their death with these words on their lips. *Thy servant and the son of thine handmaid*—not only a servant but one born in the house, and so of "the household of God." *Thou hast loosed my bonds*—of infirmity, and so purchased me with kindness and placed me in the bonds of love and gratitude forever. *Sacrifice of thanksgiving*—more precious to God than all other sacrifices. Gratitude expressed in loving deeds is the greatest of all virtues. *In the presence of all his people*—stress is laid on public thanksgiving (cf. 22[25] 66[13]).

Psalm 117. Psalm of Praise

We get a glimpse here of the message of Deutero-Isaiah and of Jonah. The ultimate purpose of Jehovah in choosing Israel is that Israel may call all other nations to praise him. Its occasion may have been the celebration of some special deliverance, but more likely it is simply a clarion call to the universal praise of Jehovah. It is the shortest of the psalms.

All ye nations—this was a far reach for a Hebrew who was rather nationalistically inclined. *Mercy is great*—greater than their transgressions. *Truth*—mercy and truth are fundamental attributes of God.

Psalm 118. Song of Praise for Deliverance

The last of the "Hallel" psalms (see intro. to Psa. 111), in which the spirit of jubilant thanksgiving finds fullest expression. It seems to celebrate some great deliverance; the people came together and formed a procession which marched to the Temple singing the praises of their deliverer. Various dates have been suggested. Some scholars think that it may have been written at the time the second Temple was built. Baethgen makes the definite assertion that it was sung for the first time at the Feast of Tabernacles in the year 444 B.C. Cheyne thinks of the time of Judas Maccabæus. There is much to be said in favor of the time of the rebuilding of the walls under Nehemiah (v. 25 occurs in the prayer of Nehemiah, Neh. 1[11]).

1–4. **Call to Praise.** All Israel is urged to praise Jehovah because of his unfailing goodness. *His mercy endureth forever*—the same refrain runs through Psa. 136; it contains blessed promises, upon which men may always depend. *Israel*—the whole nation. *House of Aaron* = priests; let them take part in the great cry. Once again "the fearers of Jehovah" are named; perhaps "the saints."

5–9. **Israel Acknowledges Jehovah as Her Deliverer.** Out of the "straitness" of Israel among her enemies, Jehovah has loosened her bands and widened her boundaries, till now the people feel free and secure round about. "If God be for us who can be against us?" (Rom. 8[31].) *On my side* (v. 7)—there are those who help and those who hate, and since Jehovah takes the part of those who help, victory is certain. Trust in Jehovah is better than confidence in man (v. 8), or even confidence in kings or princes (v. 9).

10–14. **Victory Through Jehovah.** It was Jehovah's help that enabled them to withstand hostile attacks. *All nations compassed me about*—Israel was sore beset by encompassing enemies. But such circumstances were common throughout Israel's history. *Like bees . . . as the fire of thorns* (v. 12)—in great numbers and with destructive force. But no matter what they are, in the name of Jehovah triumph is assured. The onslaught against Israel was fierce but Jehovah helped and the enemy failed (v. 13). V. 14 reproduces some words from the Song of Moses after the crossing of the Red Sea, the great deliverance which was ever a theme of thanksgiving (cf. Ex. 15[2]).

15–18. **Grateful Rejoicing.** In grateful recognition of Jehovah's help the people rejoice. While the procession is passing the booths of the pilgrims they shout for joy. V. 16 contains the words of the shout they give. Israel has been sore beset and nigh unto death; but with full assurance she cries out: "I shall not die but live; he has chastened me sore but has not given me over to death."

19–24. **Entrance into the Temple Courts.** Vv. 19–21 represent the procession as reaching the gate and demanding entrance. The choir from within reminds the marchers without that it is the gate of the Lord, and that only the righteous may enter and praise Jehovah. *The stone which the builders rejected is become the head of the corner*—the metaphor may have an historical background. There is a tradition of a time when, in the building of King Solomon's Temple, a stone was found without seeming purpose and was thrown away; later it was discovered that the chief corner stone was lacking and the rejected stone fitted this most important place. Israel was rejected by her neighbors as a useless race, but they were found at last to possess the very elements upon which the structure of human society and salvation rested. So Jesus, despised and rejected of men, is found to be the chief corner stone of human salvation (Mk. 12[10, 11] Lk. 20[17] Acts 4[11] 1 Pet. 2[7]). *The Lord's doing* (v. 23)—this is the way the Lord does it, and we marvel at his miraculous power and amazing mercy. *This is the day* (v. 24)—this holiday which is being celebrated—God made it, preserved it; it is his, and we will celebrate it.

25–29. **Vows and Prayers, Blessings and Praises.** *Save now*—it is not enough to celebrate the victories of the past; the psalmist utters a prayer for carrying forward the work into the future. The procession enters the Temple and the priests cry this word of welcome and blessing (v. 26; cf. Mt. 21[9]). *Hath given us light* (v. 27)—the night of despair is over, and the morning of a new day dawns. The psalm ends as it begins.

Psalm 119. Meditations Upon the Law of Jehovah

The psalm was never intended to be sung or chanted, but was probably recited by the Levitical reciters of the choir. There is in the psalm a noteworthy passion for the Law. "O how I love thy law" and similar expressions indicate the ardor with which the psalmist went about obeying the law. It was to him no irksome task, no driving duty, but a passionate privilege that brought joy and comfort to him.

The author seems saturated with the teachings of Deuteronomy. The arrangement is interesting. It is, like Psa. 111, 112, and others, an alphabetic acrostic. There are twenty-two stanzas, each headed by a letter of the alphabet; each stanza contains eight verses and each of these begins with the letter which stands at the head of the paragraph. Every one of these lines refers to the Law. The vocabulary is varied. The fact of so many words used for "Law"—there are ten of these: Law, Word, Saying, Commandment, Statutes, Ordinances, Precepts, Testimony, Way, Path—is remarkable. This psalm made a great impression upon the early Fathers. It has been called the alphabet of love. The great teaching of the psalm is that love and law are never in conflict. This psalm is a splendid proclamation of the majesty of the Law. To the psalmist the law is but the will of God and his method of expressing himself in the world. It is more than stern justice; it is a helpful path by which the upright may see his way. It suggests the close relationship between God and man. Throughout this, the longest chapter of the whole Bible, there is kept before the mind of the reader the personality of God. He is in the world which he made and is greater than the laws which he has promulgated and moves with majesty amid those laws. They are, in fact, the revelation of him (cf. pp. 163–4).

Date and authorship are unknown. Some have suggested the period of the exile, about 560 B.C., others, the time of Nehemiah, about 440 B.C., still others, the early Greek period, about 250 B.C. Undoubtedly it is a late postexilic production, when the Law had come to assume a position of authority; it reflects the emotions of a pious soul who found the Law a real means of grace. The exact date cannot be determined.

In this commentary it may be sufficient to give the substance of each paragraph; for a more detailed study larger commentaries may be consulted. (On the place of the Law in postexilic times, see intro. to Ezra-Nehemiah, pp. 455–7, and cf. pp. 169–70.

1–8. Aleph. The psalmist makes a statement about the beauty of loyal obedience to the Law and utters a determined prayer that God's Law may become the fixed rule of his life.

9–16. Beth. Youth may be clean and prosperous by loving the Law of Jehovah. It is a safeguard as well as a joy.

17–24. Gimel. Nothing better can ever be done, in time of persecution, than to observe the Law of Jehovah. It will always prove a comfort and strength.

25–32. Daleth. The psalmist is in trouble and bowed to the dust. In his difficulty he prays for strength to keep him steadfast in the observance of the statutes, precepts, word, truth, testimonies, and commandments of Jehovah.

33–40. He. This whole paragraph is a prayer that the psalmist may observe to do the Law of Jehovah.

41–48. Waw. He still prays that Jehovah will keep him strong to bear witness even before kings.

49–56. Zayin. Jehovah's Law has been adequate in the time of affliction and trial and has brought hope and joy.

57–64. Heth. Once again he proclaims his devotion to the Law of Jehovah.

65–72. Teth. Affliction is a schoolmaster to teach us the way of right; it is one expression of Jehovah's interest and love.

73–80. Yodh. Affliction is all right if it does not last too long. The psalmist prays for surcease from his own sufferings, that the righteous may be comforted and the wicked brought to shame.

81–88. Kaph. Jehovah tries him almost beyond endurance, but he will be faithful as he has been through all affliction to the present moment.

89–96. Lamed. The impregnable rock of Scripture, the eternal Law of Jehovah, which cannot be shaken, remains forever the hope and encouragement of the saints of God.

97–104. Mem. This stanza pours out the passionate devotion of the singer to Jehovah and his Law. It is one of the few paragraphs containing no petition (cf. vv. 161–168).

105–112. Nun. The Law of God is the guide of his footsteps, and he vows to keep it forever, whatever risks it may involve.

113–120. Samech. The psalmist contrasts his own situation with that of those who disobey the Law. He finds safety and inspiration in his own loyalty and love.

121–128. Ayin. Because he has kept the Law, he pleads that fact as a reason why Jehovah should deliver and recognize him; the faithlessness of others only increases his own love for the Law.

129–136. Pe. The beauty of the Law of Jehovah and its benefits. His eyes are weary with weeping because others fail to see in it what he sees and do not keep the Law of the Lord.

137–144. Sadhe. Jehovah's Law is righteous and pure, and therefore it challenges the deepest devotion and the highest reverence.

145–152. Koph. The psalmist unceasingly prays that he may be kept faithful to the Law, in the midst of people who disregard it. He wants the Law to be the supreme rule of his life.

153–160. Resh. He prays for deliverance and works in a kind of refrain beginning with the word *Quicken*:

"Quicken me according to thy *word.*"
"Quicken me according to thine *ordinances.*"
"Quicken me according to thy *loving-kindness.*"

161–168. Shin. This stanza contains no petition (cf. vv. 97–104). The psalmist professes diligent observance of the Law and love for it.

169–176. Taw. A final outburst of determination to do the will of Jehovah and to delight in his law. A petition for Jehovah, in view of such fidelity, to seek his servant like a lost sheep.

Psalm 120. Cry for Help Against Quarrelsome Neighbors

Psa. 120–134 bear the title "Song of Ascents." This expression has received a variety of explanations. The most probable of these looks upon the psalms as a collection of "Pilgrim Psalms," used in connection with the pilgrimages to Jerusalem undertaken by pious Jews in Palestine and in the Diaspora. All of the pilgrim songs should be studied with the historical situation in mind: The pilgrims have come from afar, and they have had many hard experiences. They have traveled over robber-infested deserts, have been lost on the trackless wastes and buffeted by storms and hunger and thirst; many of them died on the way. The faithful Mohammedan to-day finds such difficulties on his way to Mecca and other shrines. All the psalms reflect conditions during the post-exilic period, chiefly in the days of Nehemiah.

If Psa. 120 is taken as reflecting the conditions in the post-exilic community, it may refer to the troublous days of Nehemiah, whose building enterprises were interfered with by the Samaritans. It may, however, be descriptive of experiences suffered by pilgrims from some distant land on their journey to Jerusalem. Liars misdirected them, robbers beset them; but when they cried to Jehovah, he delivered them.

1. Affirmation of Confidence in God. His experience has been that Jehovah answers prayer in the day of distress; hence he will trust him now.

2–4. Prayer for Deliverance from Unscrupulous Enemies and for Just Retribution. He prays that he may be personally innocent of those sins which he complains of in others, lying and slanderous words. What kind of punishment shall be meted out to the deceiver? (V. 3.) The retribution is described in terms suggested by the offense. *Sharp arrows* (v. 4)—the tongue, the deceitful tongue, has shot forth mighty arrows, piercing the vitals of those slandered by it (cf. Prov. 26^{18} Jer. $9^{3, 8}$). It, in return, shall be pierced with real arrows (Jas. 3^{2-10}). *Coals of juniper*—or "broom" (mg.). His slander has kindled fires of strife; the compensation will be similar.

5–7. Lament over the Pitiful Condition of the Psalmist. *Kedar*—desert tribe of Ishmaelites. The names are used in a typical sense, like "Turks and Tartars," of cruel, bloodthirsty enemies. *Peace*—I seek to promote peace, but I dwell in the midst of a people who ever counsel war. The pilgrim psalmist is recounting the difficulties he has experienced in the course of the pilgrimage, but God has kept him faithful, and he comes with unsullied hands to the house of God.

Psalm 121. Jehovah the Protector of His People

Israel has in all experiences the assurance that he who made heaven and earth will protect his own people. This, a pilgrim song may have been used by the pilgrims as the Temple mountain and the holy city came in view. The psalm is without clear divisions. The parallelism is climactic, succeeding lines being held together by the repetition of certain key words (see art., *Poetic and Wisdom Literature*, p. 154).

1, 2. Source of the Psalmist's Help. *Unto the mountains*—the Temple mountain and the mountains on which the city was built. May refer to the emotions aroused in the pilgrims by the first view of the holy city; or may express the determination to make a pilgrimage there. *My help*—the reference to the mountains might suggest that he is putting his trust in them. Not so! He depends entirely upon God. *Made heaven and earth*—he is powerful; therefore the psalmist need have no fear.

3, 4. The Power and Interest of Jehovah. The psalmist is perfectly safe. *He that keepeth Israel shall neither slumber nor sleep.* Not like Baal, of whom Elijah said on Mount Carmel, "Cry louder, perchance he sleepeth or is gone on a journey" (1 Kings 18^{27}). The ever-watchful eye of Jehovah watches over the destinies of his people.

5–8. Promise of Constant Care. A comforting thought. The divine care is described under various figures. *Shade upon thy right hand*—or south; the Jew faced the east. The sun is a constant peril to the traveler; but God may be "a rock in a weary land," under which the traveler may hide from the pitiless sun. *The moon by night*—the desert caravans move mostly by night. *Thy going out and thy coming in.* If it refers primarily to the pilgrimage, the meaning is "The Lord will be with the pilgrim when he starts on his pilgrimage and will bring him safely home again." It is, however, capable of a larger interpretation. The going out and the coming in may refer to all interests of human life. God preserves our going out across the threshold in the morning and our returning in the evening. He preserves the going out of youth from the home in the morning of life and its successful close. He preserves our coming into the world and will see to the crossing of the threshold into our Father's house eternal.

Psalm 122. A Pilgrim's Meditation

As the pilgrim beholds the Temple he remembers the history of the city and its significance. He, therefore, prays for the continued prosperity and peace of city and Temple. The psalm is used to the present day by Russian pilgrims to Jerusalem. The ordinary Hebrew text ascribes the psalm to David; but some of the ancient versions name no author. Most modern scholars infer from the contents, historical allusions and linguistic peculiarities that the psalm is late, coming probably from the days of Nehemiah, soon after the city was rebuilt and its population settled.

1, 2. Expression of Joy that the Journey Is Ended, the City Reached, With a Visit to the Temple Imminent. *Are standing*—the perfect of experience. Some said, "Let us go." We came, and we are here at last, after years of longing and waiting; our feet are actually pressing the pavement of the holy city. What a glorious sight! What overpowering memories!

3–5. Impressions Made by the Sight of the City and Memories Called up. The pilgrim begins to look about him. He observes the structure of the city. It is his first visit. The city is *compact*—he is from some place where space is more liberal. The walls of Jerusalem at the present day are two and a half miles in circumference with a population inside the walls of about thirty-five thousand. *Whither the tribes go up.* From the time of David on Jerusalem was visited both as the political and the religious capital of Judæa as a *testimony* (see A.S.V. mg.) of fidelity to Jehovah. *To give thanks.* Often the visitors made their pilgrimage in payment of a vow, made in some time of stress or danger. *Thrones of the house of David.* The rulers administered justice; this was another reason why the tribes visited the city.

6–9. Prayer for the Peace and Welfare of the City. The memory of the past glory leads the psalmist to pray for the future welfare. *Prosperity*—true prosperity can be enjoyed only in a time of peace. He prays also for those who remain at home and are not privileged to make the journey. *For the sake of the house of the Lord.* The psalmist is interested in the holy city (1) because of the bond which binds him to the city as a member of the Jewish community; but (2) even more because it is the religious center, the dwelling place of his God (v. 9).

Psalm 123. The Eye of Hope

A community prayer. In v. 1 the psalmist speaks as an individual, but in the succeeding verses, as he joins all the members of the community with himself in faith and prayer, he passes into the plural. The psalm is an expression of intense longing for the conscious presence of God in the time when men scoff and the soul is exceedingly sorrowful. There is no external evidence to indicate its date; it would fit into the age of Nehemiah.

1, 2. The Eye of Hope Turned Upward. In v. 1 the emphasis is on the word *thee.* There is something intensely personal about many of the expressions of the psalms, e. g., "Against thee, thee only have I sinned" (51[4]). This is the place to which every supplicant must come before he can hope for a satisfactory answer. *In the heavens*—the petitioner ever looks up. God is on high, at least in the sense of ethical conception. *Eyes of servants look unto their master*—watching to catch the first move of command, in order instantly to obey and if possible to anticipate the master's wishes. So the devout psalmist looks unto the hand of his great master, ready to receive or give, but ever ready to obey. *Until he have mercy*—we do not pray for justice but for the abounding and ever enduring mercy of God.

3, 4. Urgent Plea of the Scorned and Despised People. There is no hope unless Jehovah is gracious and ready to help. *We are exceedingly filled with contempt*—heaped upon us by others, or contempt for others. In either case the petitioner is a subject of God's mercy. In all probability the former is meant. *Scoffing . . . contempt*—of those that are at ease and proud. The soul of the writer is full; he can endure no more, and he is in danger of doing something that he ought not; therefore, he is begging for surcease from this condition.

Psalm 124. Thanksgiving for Rescue from Enemies

The pilgrims here sing of recent deliverances. As they remember the narrow escapes, and the many difficulties, and realize for themselves the dreams of a lifetime in the fact that they have actually arrived, at least have crossed the Jordan and are on their way up the steep ascents toward the sacred city, they ascribe all glory to God, who alone could have brought them safely thus far. This, however, may have been but an adaptation of an older psalm. Many think it was originally written to celebrate the deliverance from the Babylonian Exile; others connect it with the deliverance from enemies roundabout, such as Sanballat and Tobiah, at the rebuilding of the city walls under Nehemiah. Though in the Massoretic text the psalm is ascribed to David, contents and language favor a post-exilic date. Some of the early translations omit the reference to David. The central lesson of the psalm is that God is the only refuge in time of danger.

1–5. Unless Jehovah Had Taken the Part of the Singers Destruction Would Have Been

Certain. *If it had not been the Lord*—that is still the cry of the devout soul. God was on our side, therefore are we here to-day (cf. Neh. 4[20]). *When men rose up against us*—this was frequently the case in the days of Nehemiah. *Swallowed us up alive*—gobbled us up as some wild beast of prey. Then would friend and loved one look and wait for our return, but we should never have been heard from. In vv. 4, 5 the figure changes to *the waters*. If the reference is primarily to the experiences of the pilgrims, the thought is that they had been delivered from robbers; now they have reached the margin of the desert and must cross swollen and bridgeless streams. If the reference is to the experiences of the post-exilic community, the waters represent more general dangers. Some see in the figure a veiled allusion to the creation story. The *proud waters* would then be the primeval ocean of chaos threatening to sweep everything back into utter oblivion.

6–8. Thanksgiving for Past Help, Confidence for the Future. The figure changes again. The enemy has laid for them a *snare*. This would be an apt description of the experience of Nehemiah. But the snare is *broken* and the prey is *escaped* (cf. 91[3]). Jehovah himself, who made heaven and earth and has all power, is the only one to give adequate help.

Psalm 125. Security of God's People

We are to imagine bands of pilgrims crossing the river at Jericho and conducted up to Jerusalem by the Levites, and as they go up they sing of their adventures on the way. They have arrived on the Mount of Olives, or Mount Scopus, their eager eyes catch the first vision of the holy city, they utter a cry of admiration, and then fall to describing it and comparing it to the character of a faithful Israelite. Mountains ever played a great part in Israel's history—Sinai, Hor, Nebo, Olives, Ebal, Gerizim, Carmel, Gilboa, Tabor, Hermon, and Mount Zion, this last the most sacred of all. Mount Zion was the very center and symbol of Israel's religion and of her indissoluble solidarity. To it every devout Jew away from home looked when he prayed and to it each hoped some day to make a pilgrimage. What emotions must have stirred their hearts when first they came to look down upon the holy city from loftier heights, or when they gazed upon the mountains surrounding the hills upon which Jerusalem was situated. There is no definite indication of date. Kirkpatrick thinks of the time of Nehemiah, and suggests reading Neh. 6 in connection with this psalm. Undoubtedly the plot of Sanballat, Tobiah and Geshem would offer a most suitable occasion.

1, 2. Confidence of the True Israelites in Jehovah. They that trust in Jehovah are *as Mount Zion*—fixed, immovable, abiding forever (cf. Psa. 15). *As the mountains are round about*—all around Jerusalem are higher hills: east of the city is the Mount of Olives, southeast is the Hill of Offense (or Evil Counsel), on the north, Mount Scopus, and on the west the ground rises gradually to a higher plateau. *Round about his people*—like a mighty wall of mountains Jehovah shelters them. *Evermore*—these hills may pass away but Jehovah remains.

3–5. Protection for the Faithful, Destruction for Apostates. Confidence in Jehovah is not misplaced. *Scepter of wickedness.* Surely Jehovah will never again allow a foreigner to rule over the holy city. *The righteous put not forth their hand unto iniquity.* If foreign rule continued too long, the Jews might be tempted to amalgamate with other peoples, as Jews of the Northern Kingdom did in Samaria. *Do good*—show favor to the upright. But there can be only destruction for *such as turn aside* and sell out to the enemy, as some did in the time of Nehemiah and on many other occasions. *Peace be upon Israel*—a liturgical addition expressing a prayer.

Psalm 126. Thanksgiving for Past Help; Prayer for Completion of the Restoration

The psalmist remembers the joy which came to him and his countrymen when the return from exile or the change in fortunes was experienced. The present, however, is disappointing, and, in confidence, he prays that Jehovah may bring the restoration to a glorious completion. There is no definite indication of date. It would fit in the troublesome period soon after the return in 537 B.C. or in the time of Ezra and Nehemiah nearly a century later.

1–3. Jehovah Has Already Done Marvelous Things. *Captivity*—the phrase might be translated as in the text, or as in A.S.V. "brought back those that returned" (cf. mg.), or "turned the fortunes"; i.e., restored prosperity; in any case the reference would be to the changes following the Babylonian Exile. *Them that dream.* It seemed too good to be true; they wondered if they were really awake (Lk. 24[11]). When the reality dawned upon them, they were full of joyous laughter and singing. In the beginning of the captivity they refused to sing (cf. Psa. 137). Now they can once again blend their voices in joyous song. *Among the nations.* Even other nations remarked that their God had done great things for them, and, indeed, say the singers, the Lord *hath done* great things for us and that is the reason we are glad.

4. Prayer for the Completion of the Restoration. V. 4 implies a background of disappointed hopes such as did come after the return. But the remembrance of past help leads to the confident prayer that Jehovah will help again. *Streams in the south.* The streams of the Negeb were dry in the summer, but winter rains brought plenty of water and made the people rejoice. "Our summer," says the psalmist, "has been long and very droughty. Let our fortunes hereafter be as the winter rains, refreshing and life giving."

5, 6. Expression of Faith in the Final Outcome. *They that sow in tears shall reap in joy.* "So it is ever in God's kingdom. Precisely those undertakings which at first seemed hopeless and were begun under pressing troubles end in achieving the greatest good." It has been thought that these verses refer to the poverty of the people who returned from exile and undertook the task of rebuilding the land and starting the crop rotation again when there was but enough grain to keep their children from hunger; nevertheless, in order that they might live another year, they divided the grain, and while the children cried for bread they scattered it in the ground that it might die and live again in an abundant harvest which would bring joy continued through the coming year. So the father sowed, watering the ground with his tears, but at harvest time he will come again with rejoicing, bringing his sheaves with him. (Cf. Hag. 1[1-11] 2[15-19], notes.)

Psalm 127. Utter Dependence Upon Jehovah

This psalm has been called the Hebrew "Cotter's Saturday Night"—and not unfittingly. Man's labor without God's blessing is disappointing; he bestows his blessing only upon those who love him; a large family is a special blessing from God, for it will bring respect and influence to the father. The ascription to Solomon in the title (cf. Psa. 72) is not found in most recensions of the LXX. It is probably an inference from v. 1, which was interpreted as referring to the building of the Temple; as a matter of fact, it refers to the building of any home or the setting up of any family. The psalm resembles others in the collection of Pilgrim Psalms and may reflect the same post-exilic conditions (cf. Hag. 1[4] Neh. 4[9f.] 7[3, 4], etc.).

1, 2. Man's Dependence Upon God. There is no use to *build* unless you build unto God. Material building is all in vain unless great spiritual interests are housed therein. No use to *watch* a city unless Jehovah also keeps watch. There is no success without Jehovah. Nothing is fruitful in man's hands without God's sanction. The *house* is not the Temple, nor the *city* Jerusalem; house or home building and city watching represent samples of ordinary human undertakings. The most strenuous efforts are vain without God (v. 2). If you work with him, he gives all necessary things to you even "while you sleep." *Sleep*—better, with mg., *in sleep.* It has been suggested that the word *Shena*, "sleep," should be *Selah*, which would mark an interlude; then the verse would end: "For he giveth his beloved *what is necessary*." There is insufficient support for this suggestion. The verse is not to be interpreted as discouraging hard work—laziness is strongly condemned in the O.T., e.g., Prov. 6[9f.] 31[15, 27] (see p. 611); it means rather, that God's children should not spend all of their lives in the drudgery of accumulating material things, but take time for rest and social development. It is not enough to make a living, one must also live.

3–5. Children are God's Gift. The psalm is composite: this is the second half. Children are the joy and defense of their father—this is the theme. They are a *heritage* (v. 3b; expanded in Psa. 128). Children born in the father's young manhood (v. 4b) will be his protectors in his old age. *The gate* (v. 5c)—the place of council and judgment (cf. Isa. 29[21] Amos 5[10, 12, 15]). The father who has strong sons need not fear for his cause.

Psalm 128. The Fear of God the Best Basis of a Happy Family Life

This psalm is closely connected with the preceding. It presents the refreshing picture of a family contented and happy, prosperous and peaceful. One can almost see this happy farmer, returning at evening time from his fields of plenty to his home, where a happy loving family await him. Such homes form the bulwark of any nation. A happy family life has always been the glory and pride of the Hebrews. The psalmist knows that the fear of God is the best basis for it. The psalm may fall in the same period as Psa. 127. The scarcity of the population and the constant dangers from without presented grave problems. The psalmist offers a solution: Fear God, which will lead to a happy family life which, in turn, will mean prosperity for the state.

1–4. Domestic Happiness a Reward of Godliness. *Feareth . . . walketh*—happy is he who worships God and in whom this worship bears the fruit of right conduct. *The labor of thy hands.* Man must toil, but God will bless the labor of a righteous man; he shall be happy and prosperous, and the fruits of his toil shall not be taken from him by robbers. In addition to the necessities of life he will have what gives beauty, joy, and permanence. *Vine*—a symbol of gracefulness; *fruitful*—a large family of children; *olive plants*—a symbol of vigor and strength. Parenthood revealed the blessing of God; barrenness was considered a curse. *Innermost parts*—the women's quarters, farthest removed from the entrance. Surely the man who fears Jehovah shall thus be blessed.

5, 6. Prayers and Hope for the Welfare of the Community. These verses show that the psalm was used in public worship. May Jehovah continue to shower blessings upon the community, and may the people see and enjoy prosperity and peace forever. May there always be an abundance of pious men enjoying the blessings of a rich family life. *Peace be upon Jerusalem*—a separate liturgical benediction.

Psalm 129. Past Experience a Ground of Hope for the Future

This is a psalm of the community. Israel has suffered severe affliction throughout her entire history, but has not been utterly destroyed because Jehovah was on her side. The good fortunes of her present enemies will be brief, because Jehovah will put them to shame. There is no definite indication of date. It seems closely related to Psa. 124, only here the hope that the enemies will be subdued is expressed with greater confidence. It may have been written at about the same period, with reference to the dangers threatening the community in the days of Nehemiah.

1–3. Israel's Past Afflictions and Deliverances. Israel has always had a hard time even back in the early days when they were in Egyptian bondage. *Youth*—see Hos. 11^1. *Have not prevailed.* This has been the experience of God's people in all ages; God always protects and delivers those who trust in him. *The plowers plowed* (v. 3)—a picture of extreme cruelty; the nation is pictured as thrown upon her face, while the enemy plowed deep long furrows upon her back, like the marks of the lashes on the back of a slave.

4. Jehovah Has Broken the Chains of the Oppressor. Jehovah has cut the bond of captivity, has separated his people from the enemy, and has put the enemy to shame. *Righteous*—loyal to the covenant made with his people in the beginning.

5–8. Hope for the Future. On the basis of past experience the psalmist offers a prayer that Jehovah will continue the work of protection and deliverance. *Grass upon the housetop.* In the East many of the small houses are covered with earth and frequently a roller is run over this sod roof to keep it compact, just as a roller is used on playing-fields in this country. If this is neglected, a sparse grass springs up but soon dies. Grass cannot successfully grow on a housetop; as this grass soon passes away, so let the enemies of Israel be. *Reaper.* Just as the mower and reaper of such grass will be empty handed, so may Jehovah let those who plot against Israel waste their time. *They which go by*—ordinarily passers by would shout good wishes to the reapers, and the reapers would shout back; but there will be nothing of that sort with the oppressors of Israel; they will be silent, for there will be no harvest.

Psalm 130. Psalm of Penitence

We have in this psalm what seems to be the prayer of a representative Israelite, who offers a confession of sin and a petition for mercy not so much for himself as for the community. The most probable occasion is presented by the troubles through which the community passed in the days of Nehemiah (cf. Neh. 1^{4-11} and the confession of Nehemiah in ch. 9).

1–4. Cry of Penitence from Depths of Trouble. The psalmist is in danger of being overwhelmed by the sea of trouble and cries *out of the depths* to Jehovah, who is a God of pardon. Penitent, he prays to God (v. 2). *Shouldest mark iniquity* (v. 3). If God marked every sin carefully, who could stand? There would be hope for no one. The only hope is in the divine *forgiveness*. One reason for worshiping God is his willingness to forgive.

5–8. Assured of the Divine Forgiveness Psalmist and People Can Afford to Wait. *Wait*—the expectancy of the soul; sometimes God requires waiting as discipline; hope is in the divine promises; it is harder to wait than to work. *More than watchmen*—the soul waits for God's answer more eagerly than the watchman waits for the dawn. The repetition indicates earnestness. *O Israel, hope* (v. 7)—a strong exhortation to Israel to join the psalmist in hope, in faith in God, who is merciful and will give pardon graciously and "life abundant." God will surely take away the calamities that are the result of Israel's wickedness, and even wickedness itself.

Psalm 131. Childlike Trust in Jehovah

Subdued by suffering, the psalmist confesses humility; he will be satisfied with whatever lot Jehovah chooses for him. He has come to Jehovah after the sufferings and disappointments of his life, like a tired subdued child, at the end of the day, who lays his head upon the mother's breast and leaves life's problems with her; so the psalmist trusts in Jehovah.

Most commentators regard it as a community psalm. The psalmist represents the best elements in the community, and for himself and them renounces all worldly aggrandizement for Israel (cf. v. 3). The ascription to David is not found in all the ancient versions. The title may have been added because it was thought that the psalm illustrated the spirit of David's life (cf. 2 Sam. 7[21f.]). It comes probably from the same period as the psalms in whose midst it stands. The restoration had been pictured by the prophets in the most glowing colors; the reality fell short of the expectation. Many became discouraged but some high souls began to wonder if the hopes themselves might not have been misdirected. They were willing to trust God implicitly.

1, 2. A Haughty Heart Denied. Pride or arrogance has its seat in the heart and mind of man, it reveals itself in the countenance; it likes to move in the sphere of things beyond the arrogant man's ability. The verse breathes a spirit of humility. *Stilled . . . quieted*—before he resigned himself his whole being was troubled, full of passion and lofty ambition; but the victory has come. Says Perowne, "Two things are suggested here—the cost by which he gains this peace and the purity and unselfishness of the rest he gained."

3. Perfect Peace. In a spirit of contentment Israel may patiently wait for the development of God's purpose.

PSALM 132. PRAYER FOR JEHOVAH'S BLESSING UPON THE SANCTUARY FOR DAVID'S SAKE

Apparently written after the Exile, either in the days of Zerubbabel or of Nehemiah, probably the latter, for the purpose of encouraging the people by reciting how God had been merciful to David, their great hero. It is reminiscent of the bringing up of the ark from the house of Obed-Edom and placing it upon Mount Moriah. In those days it looked as if Jehovah had forgotten his people; and yet it was the beginning of the most glorious period in Israel's history. Though the present looks dark, Jehovah can remove the distress and once again bestow abundant blessing upon his sanctuary and the people. Cf. 42[6], "I remember thee from the land of Jordan and the Hermons, from the hill Mizar." The psalmist remembers the Lord from the time of David and his doings then. The interpretation of the psalm presents considerable difficulty. Indeed, it becomes possible only if the dramatic principle underlying the arrangements is recognized. Different sections must be assigned to different speakers.

1, 2. Prayer to Remember the Pains David Took to Establish the Sanctuary. David was willing to undergo all manner of hardship. *His affliction*—the pains he took in preparing for the building of the house of the Lord, beginning with his bringing up of the ark. *He sware.* Not necessarily that he actually made a vow to build the house of the Lord, for which there is no historical authority, but, rather, that he determined to build the house and made great preparation. It may well be doubted whether Solomon could ever have built the house, had David not prepared the way.

3–5. Contents of the Oath Sworn by David. David is serious about the matter. *Tabernacle of my house . . . bed.* I will not rest in luxurious ease while God has no earthly dwelling place. In 2 Sam. 7[1] David proposes to build a house for Jehovah, but is forbidden by Nathan. David is conscience-stricken when he remembers that he lives in a house of cedar but Jehovah within curtains. V. 4 is a proverbial expression (cf. Prov. 6[4]). *A place.* The ark was the symbol of the Divine Presence; hence the place intended for the ark was intended for Jehovah himself.

6, 7. The People's Hearty Cooperation. Israel entered enthusiastically upon the enterprise. *We heard of it,* i.e., the ark. *Ephrathah.* Elsewhere this is the name of Bethlehem or of the district in which Bethlehem is located (Gen. 35[16, 19] Ruth 4[11] Mic. 5[2]). Here it is synonymous with Ephraim, the territory in which Shiloh was located (cf. 1 Sam. 1[1f.]). They heard that the ark was in Shiloh; but when they sought it, it was no longer there, but *in the field of the wood,* i.e., Kiriath-Jearim (cf. mg.). The ark had a varied itinerary and the people are here represented as seeking it, making inquiries here and there, until it is found at Kiriath-Jearim (cf. 1 Sam. 7[1]). V. 7 is a mutual exhortation to worship in the sanctuary David has proposed to build. *Footstool.* Since Jehovah is enthroned upon the Cherubim the ark is his footstool.

8–10. Prayer that Jehovah May Recognize These Efforts and Take Possession of the Sanctuary. *Arise . . . thy resting place.* This is the formula used when the ark was brought up. The symbol of the Divine Presence was the ark, and this was now to come up to the threshing floor of Araunah on Mount Moriah as its permanent resting place. *The ark of thy strength*—the strength of Israel derived from the presence of the ark (cf. 1 Sam. 4) and so from the presence of Jehovah himself. *Priests*—a separate priestly order was introduced in Israel later than David and Solomon. *Saints* = favored ones, namely, the Israelites. The idea of righteousness being a garment is common (Job 29[14]). Happy the people who have priests of righteousness and who, therefore, may shout or joy. *David's sake* (v. 10)—the basis of the prayer from the beginning (cf. v. 1). *Turn not away the face*—which would mean to deny the petition. *Anointed*—refers to the king or to anyone else who has a mission from Jehovah. Here the reference is to the petitioners, who are conscious of a divine mission.

11, 12. **Recital of Jehovah's Oath to David.** This is the beginning of the divine answer contained in vv. 11–18. *The Lord hath sworn.* There is no record of an oath; we have here a poetical statement of the certainty of God's promise (cf. 2 Sam. 7); *in truth*—he made this promise to David, and he will surely fulfill it. *The fruit of thy body*—this is part of the content of the promise made to David. *If* his children will keep the law of Jehovah and observe to do his will, keeping his *covenant*, then the Davidic succession will be eternal. As long as they keep the law of Jehovah so long Jehovah will keep his promise, but whenever they break it the contract ends (cf. Heb. 8[9]).

13. **Jehovah Has Chosen Zion as His Earthly Dwelling Place.** This choice furnishes the basis for the oath in vv. 11, 12. *Zion . . . for his habitation.* The choice of Zion was made before the choice of David, and while the house of David may pass away because of disobedience, Zion may still have a chance if the successors of David, though not of the Davidic line, continue to be righteous.

14–18. **Direct Reply of Jehovah.** He will bless people and priests and restore the fortunes of the house of David. In Zion Jehovah will have a permanent resting place; his choice is made and he will abide by it (cf. v. 8). V. 15 promises that Jehovah will bless the people with material blessings. Prosperity will be upon the land when God shall come back to Zion. *Satisfy her poor*—Jehovah always gives special consideration to the poor and needy. V. 16 is similar to v. 9; there the prayer is that the priests may be clothed with righteousness; here the promise is that they will be clothed with *salvation;* i.e., they will become real channels of blessing for the worshipers, who then will have every reason to rejoice. *The horn of David to bud* (v. 17). His horn (symbol of power and vitality) has been cast down and is dead in the dust, but as in the valley of dry bones Jehovah made the dead to live, so the horn of David, entirely humbled, shall bud and be lifted on high. The promise that the sprout of David will come will be fulfilled (cf. Isa. 11[1] Jer. 23[5] Zech. 3[8], etc.). *A lamp for mine anointed*—a symbol of continuity: he will abide forever. Who? Either the promised sprout or the dynasty of David. Just as the priests of Jehovah are to be clothed with salvation and righteousness, so his enemies will be clothed with shame (v. 18). *Himself*—David as the personal representative of all his successors. *Crown*—or diadem, meaning not only the kingly crown, but also the glittering diadem of the priest. It may be that the expectation is, as in Psa. 110, that the ideal ruler will combine kingly and priestly functions.

Psalm 133. The Excellency of Brotherly Unity

This beautiful psalm of brotherly love is ascribed to David; but the title is not found in some MSS. and in the most important ancient translations. The psalm may express Nehemiah's ideal for the post-exilic Jerusalem community; it may be a call for the returned exiles to come and dwell together in this new community with true fraternity. The opening word, "Behold," may suggest that the psalmist actually had before his eyes an instance of the blessings of brotherly concord. May the psalm reflect the enthusiasm of those who volunteered to dwell in Jerusalem in the days of Nehemiah? (Neh. 11[2].)

1. **Brotherly Unity.** *Behold*—such a community is the joy and pride of all who see. *Good*—inherently valuable and useful; *pleasant* —æsthetically pleasing, pleasant to look upon. *Unity*—this thought is implied, but the word is not in the Hebrew text.

2, 3. **Blessings of Brotherly Love Illustrated.** V. 2 illustrates the "good" and v. 3 the "pleasant" of v. 1. *Precious oil*—oil is the symbol of joy; sometimes the term "oil of gladness" is used. The psalmist thinks of the sacred oil with which the high priest was anointed. *Aaron's beard.* Aaron stands as the personification of high priesthood and the representative of the whole nation; the copious anointing which poured down over his garments symbolized the solidarity of the group represented. *The dew of Hermon.* The heavy dews of Hermon are proverbial. Dew is nature's compensation for her failure to give rain and symbolizes refreshment and quickening. Palestine was desolate as the desert, until the brethren came together in brotherly fellowship; then, like the dews of Hermon, they brought freshness and life and the resurrection of ideals. *There*— in Jerusalem, Jehovah decreed the blessing which would mean life and prosperity forever.

Psalm 134. Greetings of the Night Watchers

A choir of pilgrims leaving the Temple for the night exhort priests and Levites to praise God. The latter respond with a benediction upon the worshipers. There is no definite indication of date or occasion. It may have been composed after the restoration of Temple worship under Nehemiah (12^{44-47}).

1, 2. Call to Praise Jehovah. The call is made by a group of worshipers. *Ye servants*—not worshipers in general, but, as the next clause indicates, those who actually "serve" in the sanctuary; *stand in*—the regular term for priestly or Levitical ministrations was "stand before" (Deut. 10^{8}). The Levitical singers were employed day and night in the Temple. As the people finish the evening worship they exhort priests and Levites to praise Jehovah as they minister in his name. For services at night cf. 1 Chr. 9^{33}. *Lift up your hands*—a gesture of prayer. *The sanctuary*, toward which the hands are extended, is the most holy place, the earthly dwelling place of Jehovah.

3. The Priestly Benediction in Response to the Call. *The Lord bless thee*—the priests call on Jehovah in the sanctuary to bless the people as they return to their homes. This is the last of the Pilgrim Psalms (120–134). It is in itself a sort of benediction, which forms an appropriate close to the entire collection.

Psalm 135.
Praise of Jehovah's Wonderful Works; Nothingness of Heathen Idols

The psalm is a collection of fragments from different parts of the O.T., skillfully put together to form an impressive hymn of praise. There is a careful survey of Jehovah's manifestations in nature and in history; these reveal his great power. The idols, on the other hand, are impotent; they can do nothing for themselves or their worshipers. Therefore let all Israel praise Jehovah. The psalm is, in a sense, an expansion of Psa. 134 (cf. also Neh. $9^{4f.}$). It is a post-exilic production, and evidently was intended for use in the services of the second Temple.

1–4. Call to Praise Jehovah. The call is addressed to *the servants of the Lord*—see on 134^{1}. *Stand in the house*—see on 134^{1}. Levites, priests, and the general worshipers are all urged to praise their God. He deserves such praise, because he *is good*—as shown in his choice of and care for Israel. Moreover, it is *pleasant*—it is delightful to sing the praises of Jehovah. *The Lord hath chosen*—based on Deut. 7^{6} or Ex. 19^{5}; God's choosing of Israel for his own is ample reason for praise.

5–7. Jehovah's Power Manifested in Nature. He who has eyes to see may know the kind of God Jehovah is. *Great . . . above all gods.* Whatever may be thought of the existence of the gods of other nations, Jehovah was greater and more powerful than all the others. He is sovereign in every sphere; his work in *heaven, earth* and in the *seas* calls for praise. He is master of them all. V. 7 is taken almost verbatim from Jer. 10^{13}.

8–12. Jehovah's Power Manifested in History—especially in the deliverance from Egypt, the guidance through the desert and the settlement in Canaan. Vv. 8, 9 describe manifestations of God's power in delivering his children from Egypt. Equally wonderful was his interference on their behalf during the desert wanderings, when he helped Israel to defeat her enemies; *Sihon* and *Og* were the most formidable (vv. 10, 11; cf. Num. $21^{21f.,33f.}$ Deut. $2^{30f.}$ $3^{1f.}$). He then helped them to conquer Palestine, the land of promise, and established them there (v. 12).

13, 14. Jehovah the Eternal God Will Have Mercy on His People. V. 13 is based on Ex. 3^{15} (cf. 102^{12}). *Thy name*—i.e., thy character (see on 75^{1}). This was the source of Moses' mission and the authority for his task; it is still the hope of Israel, for the name of Jehovah will endure *forever*. He will not forget the people who have cost him so much. His name is unchanged, his power unexhausted; therefore he cannot cast off his people; he must save them.

15–18. Jehovah Contrasted with Heathen Idols. These verses are taken with minor changes from 115^{4-8} (see notes there); v. 18 emphasizes the truth that we become molded in the likeness of our ideals; the object of our worship is the model by which we develop our characters.

19–21. New Summons to all Israel to Praise Jehovah. The threefold call of 115^{9-11} 118^{2-4} is here expanded to include the house of Levi. Let all the people praise Jehovah.

Psalm 136. Hymn of Praise

The psalm bears resemblance to Psa. 135, but here is added the refrain which forms the second part of each verse; the whole emphasis of the psalm is on this refrain. It is clearly a liturgical psalm; the first part of each verse may have been sung by the leader, with the response in the second part by the choir; or the first part by the Levites, the second part by the congregation (cf. Ezra 3^{11} 2 Chr. $7^{3,6}$).

1–3. Call to Thanksgiving. Praise and thanksgiving are due to God, for he is *good;* again and again he forgives his wayward children. *God of gods*—he is far superior to any other being thought of as divine; he is also above kings and magistrates.

4–9. Jehovah the Creator. He has supreme power; he is not dependent upon any other force or power. *Understanding*—the heavens declare his glory, wisdom, and intelligence. *Spread forth*—the ancients thought that the earth was spread out and rested on an abyss of waters referred to as "the deep." *Lights*—

sun, moon and stars declare his glory (vv. 7–9; cf. Gen. 1[16-18]).

10–15. Jehovah the Saviour of Israel. As frequently, the experiences of the Exodus are mentioned as outstanding examples of God's care for his chosen people and his mercy toward them.

16–22. The Conquest of the Promised Land. The incidents here mentioned are frequently enumerated as evidences of God's interest and power (cf. 135[10-14]).

23–26. Jehovah the Saviour of Israel and the Upholder of All. Vv. 23, 24 may refer to the Babylonian Exile, described as *low estate*, and to the people's deliverance from it. In v. 25 the psalmist passes from the specific care of Israel to the universal fatherhood of God, which makes him the supporter of all life. The psalm closes with another exhortation to give thanks, this time to the God of the universe.

Psalm 137. A Wail from the Exile

The psalm reflects the emotions of the exiles. Their hearts were sorrowful, so that they could not sing songs of Zion; but they were as loyal as ever—if not more so—to their God, to the holy city and to their old home. Their very loyalty to Jehovah makes them break forth in bitter denunciation of the nations responsible for their present plight, especially Edom and Babylon. The psalm is reminiscent of the opening days of the Exile; it may have been written soon after the capture of Jerusalem and the destruction of the Temple by Nebuchadrezzar, in 586 B.C. The reference to Jerusalem being destroyed impresses one as referring to something very recent. On the other hand, many modern writers hold that it was composed after the return in 537 B.C.

1–3. Sorrows of the Exile. The psalm reveals the triumph of spirit over matter, of a spiritual ideal over material possession. *By the rivers*—Euphrates and its canals, such as Chebar; possibly also the Tigris. Babylonia was a land of canals. Jerusalem was Jehovah's sanctuary and Palestine his home; in the thought of the exiles there could be no worship of him in any other land. *Willows*—there are still willow groves along the Euphrates amid the ruins of Babylon. *Songs . . . mirth.* The officers who had charge of them demanded that they sing their sacred songs as a matter of amusement. They had no heart for joyful music.

4–6. Loyalty to Jehovah and to the Sacred City. V. 4 emphasizes the impossibility of singing a song of Zion when they were away from Zion and Jehovah's land. *If I forget thee.* To sing Jehovah's songs to the Babylonians would be forgetting Jerusalem, and the psalmist prays that when he forgets Jerusalem he may forget how to play the harp at all. Rather than sing a sacred song for the captors, he would lose the gift of singing. Jerusalem to him was greater than anything in life (vv. 5, 6).

7–9. Prayer for Vengeance Upon the Enemies of the Chosen People. The Edomites had not only encouraged the destruction of Jerusalem but had actually helped the Babylonians in their cruel capture. The Edomites were cousins of the Hebrews, children of Esau; which made their crime the greater. Thinking of vengeance, the psalmist cries, Happy shall be the one who treats you as you have treated us; a consistent application of the law of retaliation. V. 9 amplifies v. 8. *Thy little ones.* Emphasis is on the word *thy*—even as you dashed our little ones against the stones. This is not Christian ethics; but it is what might be expected, in that period and in that situation, of persons who looked upon their own enemies as enemies of Jehovah, who by destroying them were threatening to destroy Jehovah religion. (See on Jer. 49[7-22] Amos 1[11] Obad. vv. 10–14.)

Psalm 138. Thanksgiving to Jehovah for the Fulfillment of His Promises

An expression of the gratitude and confidence of the restored community. While the title ascribes the psalm to David, it has all the marks of a post-exilic production. A number of the MSS. of the LXX add "of Haggai and Zachariah," which would point to a post-exilic date. This view finds support in the theological ideas expressed or implied. For instance, the idea of the universality of Jehovah's dominion is post-exilic; and there are echoes of certain doctrines of Isa. 40–66.

1–3. Jehovah Has Manifested His Loving Kindness and His Faithfulness in the Fulfillment of His Promises to Israel. The psalmist's faith in God is not shaken by the power of the heathen world. *I will give thee thanks with my whole heart*—with whole-hearted praise. *Before the gods.* The psalmist lifts his voice in the midst of powerful nations trusting in many gods; these do not baffle him in the least. The Jew always looked *toward the Temple* when he prayed. *Magnified thy word.* God, by keeping his promise and fulfilling his word, is now exceeding all previous revelations of himself. *Encourage me* (v. 3). God not only answers prayer but gives great courage of conviction. The psalmist was in dire distress and cried unto Jehovah, who gave him strength of soul.

4–6. The Whole World Will Praise Jehovah Because of His Faithfulness. The nations and their kings will unite in praising Jehovah when they hear of his favor toward the Hebrews. The way God has dealt with his people brings more glory to his name than the world which he has made. Jehovah is not too exalted to be interested in the *lowly*. The highest proof of greatness is consideration for the lowly.

7, 8. Jehovah will Continue to Deliver Israel. New difficulties will come, but God will be near. In time of trouble he will take care of his suffering children and protect them from their enemies. V. 8 expresses a sublime confidence in the promises of God. Jehovah will carry out his purpose.

Psalm 139. The Ever-Abiding Presence of God

One of the grandest psalms in the entire collection, if not, indeed, the best of them all. Its tone is high, and its conception of the personal and highly spiritual nature of God rises to glorious heights. It has been called "the crown of the Psalter." It might be called "The Psalm of the Unavoidable God"; its main theme is "God Cares." He cares personally and individually. It is the O.T.'s highest conception of the relationship of God to the individual soul. Though it is so stated in the title the psalm cannot come from David: (1) The language is very late; it is not pure Hebrew but has many Aramaisms; (2) the thought is late; it resembles in this, as in the language, the book of Job; (3) the conception of God also points to a late date. The psalm is undoubtedly postexilic.

1–6. God's Perfect Knowledge of the Psalmist. Jehovah knows all about me. He has searched me through and through and there is nothing about me unknown to him. God not only knows but he cares. *Thou*—emphatic. God considers the smallest experiences of my life. He knows the purposes of my mind even before they take thought form. *Thou searchest*—or "winnowest," "siftest," as wheat; *my path*—when I walk; *my lying down*—when I stop. He acquaints himself with *all my ways*. *Not a word in my tongue*—render, *For when a word is not yet on my tongue, lo, thou knowest it altogether*. Before a word is spoken, God understands what will be uttered. *Beset*—hemmed in as a city surrounded by an army; God has hemmed me in so I cannot escape him. Such knowledge is beyond human intellect (v. 6). *I cannot attain unto it*. The divine omniscience is inaccessible to human power. Humanity can stand in reverent wonder at its workings, but must ever be impotent to apply the canons of human reason to it.

7–12. God's Universal Presence. Jehovah is inescapable. *Thy presence*—literally, face. The face of God is ever before us. One cannot run away from God (cf. Jonah 1[3f.]). *If I ascend to the dwelling place of God*, as Enoch or Elijah; *Sheol*—if I descend into Sheol, which is the other extreme of the universe, I shall still face him. He is in heaven above and he goes down into Sheol. *The wings of the morning*. The dawn was described with the beautiful imagery of slowly spreading wings in the East, flying out over all the world and going down in the uttermost part of the Mediterranean. The wings of the dawn, the uttermost part of the sea, mean the whole sweep of the earth from east to west (vv. 9, 10). *Darkness shall overwhelm me* (v. 11). The religion of Jehovah was the only one whose God ruled the night as well as the day. Ikhnaton (Amenophis IV) of Egypt rose to a lofty height in his pantheistic conception, but his god was impotent during the night. But to Jehovah day and night are alike.

13–18. God Has Ordered the Psalmist's Entire Life. Many would transpose vv. 13 and 14, reading 14 first and making 13 the explanation of it. The thought in v. 13 is that God knows him because he created him; indeed, he knew him before the psalmist began to take form. *Possessed*—better, *formed* (cf. mg.). *Reins*—or, kidneys, the seat of passions and emotions. *Covered*—or, *knit me together*. Bones and sinews were knit together by the fingers of Jehovah. When the psalmist comes to consider his physiological composition, he bursts forth in praise to God for his workmanship. *My frame* (v. 15) = my skeleton, the frame work of my body. *Curiously wrought*—i.e., skillfully; the word means also embroidered with threads of many colors. Perhaps the psalmist thinks of the veins. *In the lowest parts of the earth*—here the womb. How could God do such skillful work in the hidden parts away from the light!

Mine unperfect substance (v. 16)—Jehovah's eyes were upon the undeveloped embryo, and he had a book in which were recorded all the members yet unformed. He had a plan by which the body was to be formed. Therefore *How precious*, etc. (v. 17)—God's thoughts for me are precious beyond expression and they are numberless. The word translated "precious" may mean also incomprehensible. If this translation is accepted the verse comes to suggest a contrast between God's thought of the psalmist and the latter's thought of God. *When I awake I am still with thee*—asleep or awake my thoughts are with God.

19–24. God Cannot Endure Wickedness; Neither will the Psalmist. This wonderful God must be intolerant of wicked men (many think this part of the psalm is a later addition). *I hate*. It is natural that one who loves God with the passion expressed in the foregoing would with the same intensity hate the sins which insult the God who is so good. These sins are connected, in the mind of the psalmist, with the sinners (v. 21); therefore he hates the sinners with the same fierce hatred. The psalmist closes with a prayer for himself that God may search his soul as he has searched and known his body and discover to him what is wrong and lead him in *the way everlasting* (vv. 23, 24) —the way leading to life and peace, the opposite of the way leading to ruin and an early death. (On the main thought of the psalm, see Francis Thompson, *The Hound of Heaven.*)

Psalm 140. Prayer for Protection Against Persecutors

Psalms 140–143 form a group generally thought to be late. These psalms seem inseparable; they are similar in theme, language, and form, and they are individual rather than national. The four psalms may be by the same author. The presence of the name David in the title may be due to the fact that at one time the psalms were a part of a Davidic collection. At any rate, dependence on other psalms, some of them late (e.g., 77), familiarity with Job and Proverbs, and other considerations, have convinced most scholars that the psalms came from the unsettled conditions of the post-exilic period.

1–3. Prayer for Deliverance from Unscrupulous Enemies. They are *evil* and *violent* (v. 1). The singulars are probably to be understood collectively; unless the psalmist wants to single out a particular individual, who is the leader in the plots. *Gather themselves together*—better, with mg., *stir up wars.* They are always trying to pick quarrels. *Sharpened their tongue* (v. 3)—they are deliberately planning to inflict a deadly wound by slander. Poison is on their lips.

4, 5. Repetition of Prayer for Deliverance. The psalmist prays again for deliverance from those who are determined to cause his downfall. *Snare . . . cords . . . net . . . gins* (v. 5). As the hunter traps his game, so they are trying to trap him. Four kinds of traps are named to show the variety and persistency of the attack.

6–8. Jehovah the Faithful Helper in Time of Need. The psalmist pleads the relationship he sustains to God, which entitles him to protection. *Covered my head* (v. 7)—God has protected him as a helmet does the head in battle; therefore he is confident in his prayer that the wicked enemies will be defeated and not exalted (cf. Eph. 6[10-17]).

9–11. May Deserved Retribution Overtake the Evil Doers. The petitioner asks that the mischief they are trying to do him may recoil upon their own heads (v. 9). *Burning coals . . . fire*—he asks that the fate of Sodom overtake the offenders. His imprecation grows heated and fierce (v. 10). Moreover, he has faith in God that calamity will pursue the wicked and drive them to destruction.

12, 13. Destiny of the Righteous and the Wicked. The *afflicted* righteous man will be protected, and the cause of the poor championed (v. 12). *Righteous . . . upright* (v. 13)—the destruction of the wicked is the guarantee of happiness and security for the upright.

Psalm 141. Prayer to be Saved from Sin and Sinners

See introductory paragraph to Psa. 140. The psalmist presents his prayer as an "evening sacrifice." The godless are now enjoying ease and prosperity; but he is confident that in the end right and righteousness will triumph. The destruction of the wicked will open the eyes of their followers and make them ready to heed the psalmist's teaching.

1, 2. A Plea for an Immediate Answer to Prayer. The psalmist has already offered his prayer; may the answer come speedily. May his prayer go up to Jehovah as the smoke of incense goes up, at an *evening sacrifice.* The evening sacrifice or oblation, i.e., meal offering (Ex. 29[38-42]), may be mentioned because the psalmist was in the habit of praying at that time.

3–5. Prayer for Strength to Resist Temptation. The psalmist prays that Jehovah will help him to say only the right thing. *Keep the door of my lips* is a prayer all need to offer. *Incline not my heart* (v. 4)—a prayer that he may not want to live the life of sensual ease, the wicked life. "Lead us not into temptation." *Reprove*—a prayer that he may welcome reproof and guidance from the righteous, and turn away from the evil deeds of the wicked. The marginal reading of v. 5d is preferable, "for still is my prayer against their wickedness."

6, 7. Effect of the Judgment Upon the Wicked. When the leaders of the wicked have been thrown from the cliff and thus executed, then the followers will welcome the advice of the psalmist. *Our bones*—better, *their;* the words may refer to the bones of the judges who were executed. It must be admitted, however, that the interpretation of vv. 6, 7 is exceedingly difficult.

8–10. A Prayer of Confidence in God. The psalmist has put himself under Jehovah's protection; and he makes this relationship the basis of his plea. V. 9 is a prayer to keep him from the sensual temptations with which the wicked are trying to entice him, and v. 10 a plea that the plots of the wicked may recoil upon themselves (cf. 7[15, 16] 9[16] 140[11]).

Psalm 142. Prayer for Personal Safety

The psalmist is hard pressed. In Jehovah is

the only basis of hope; he therefore turns to him for help, with the promise that he will express his gratitude and praise openly. For the ascription to David see introductory paragraph to Psa. 140. When the psalm had once come to be connected with David, it was easy to infer from the contents that it described the experience of David in the cave of Adullam (1 Sam. 22) or of En-gedi (1 Sam. 24).

1, 2. **Jehovah Alone Can Give Relief to the Psalmist in His Distress.** He prays *aloud* to Jehovah. His situation will not allow him to pray in silence; his emotions are too violent and his distress too intense. He will *pour out* (v. 2) his whole heart to God in complaint, even as one pours out a libation.

3, 4. **Comfort of the Assurance that God Knows Him.** He finds comfort in the thought that Jehovah knows all about him, even the perilous snares his enemies are laying for him; he pleads to Jehovah in his loneliness, for no man is near him or cares for his soul. Like one lost on a dark road, he looks fearfully around and finds himself still alone. *Right hand*—the place of a helper or champion. There was none to help.

5–7. **Prayer for a Speedy Answer.** In the midst of this lonely road, beset with snares, he cries unto Jehovah. He looked to the right hand and to the left, but there was none to help; then he looked up, for in Jehovah was his help; let him interfere (v. 6). *Out of prison* (v. 7)—may refer to a literal place of confinement, or may be understood figuratively of the depth of his distress. *That I may give thanks*—for the wonderful deliverance. Then the righteous will join in the psalm of thanksgiving at his release.

Psalm 143. A Penitential Psalm

The psalmist is afflicted, but he sees in his sufferings merited punishment for sin. He pleads not only for the removal of suffering but also for restoration of close fellowship with Jehovah, which will entitle him to the divine mercy and help. It probably comes from the same period as Psa. 140–142 (see introductory paragraph to Psa. 140) if not from the same author.

1, 2. **Appeal for Merciful Consideration.** Though feeling his unworthiness, the psalmist nevertheless pleads for a hearing with Jehovah (v. 1). He begins by pleading guilty (v. 2). He cannot stand trial, and his soul cries out "Unworthy" as he comes into the presence of Jehovah; he recognizes the necessity of mercy instead of justice (cf. Isa. 6^5).

3, 4. **Despair at His Position.** His case is bad. The persecutor has beaten him down to the very darkness of death. *My spirit is overwhelmed*—or *my spirit fainteth;* aware of his unworthiness he is paralyzed at the apparent hopelessness of his position.

5, 6. **Past Experiences Cause Him to Yearn for New Manifestations of God.** He remembers the past marvelous workings of God and prays for a fresh manifestation. *I spread forth my hands* (v. 6). The outward expression of the soul's passionate longing.

7–12. **Prayer for the Guidance and Deliverance of the Psalmist and the Destruction of His Enemies.** Unless the Lord looks down with immediate mercy, the psalmist feels himself ready to give up and sink into the pit of death (v. 7; the language here is borrowed from other psalms). In the darkness of despair he longs for the dawn of God's presence, bringing him guidance (v. 8). He takes refuge in Jehovah (v. 9), in the firm hope that he may hide him until the trouble is past; and that Jehovah will help him to conform his will to the divine will (v. 10). The assurance of the divine help brings about a quickening of the spirit: God will surely bring the soul out of trouble (v. 11). *I am thy servant* (v. 12)—therefore the psalmist has a right to expect the master's protection for himself and the master's punishment and destruction of all who seek to injure him (cf. Jn. 17^{6-11}).

Psalm 144. Praise for Help Received; Blessings Resulting from the Divine Protection

The psalm seems to be a compilation of material taken from different psalms (e.g., 8, 18, 23, 29, 104) and possibly from some poem which has not been preserved. Though the title refers to David, the character of the psalm as a compilation makes a late date highly probable.

1, 2. **Praise for Military Assistance.** The psalmist gives praise to God who teaches his hands the skill of warfare. *Fingers*—possibly for the use of the bow. Though vv. 1, 2 refer to help in the time of war, the more gentle qualities of Jehovah are also remembered. Jehovah is kind, strong; in him we may live and view the landscape of realities; he is deliverer, protector, who makes the psalmist a successful ruler (Psa. 18).

3, 4. **God's Goodness and Man's Insignificance.** Jehovah is so wonderful—who is insignificant man, that God thinks about him? (Cf. 8^4.) *Vanity*—Hebrew, "breath," a figure describing the brief span of man's earthly pilgrimage ($39^{5,\ 11}$).

5–8. **Prayer of the Manifestation of God's Power.** The descriptions of 18^9 104^{32} and other passages are changed to prayers. The enemy is wicked. *Right hand of falsehood*—they take oaths which they do not mean to keep. God has shown himself powerful in the past; let him do so again, and there is no chance for the enemies to endure.

9–11. **Promise of Eternal Gratitude; Renewal of Prayer.** The psalmist is confident that the deliverance asked for will be granted. *David* may denote the typical ruler of Israel (v. 10). V. 11 contains a prayer for deliverance from the wicked enemies.

12–15. **Prosperity of Israel Under the Protection of Jehovah.** An independent poem, probably taken from a source which is no longer known. Vv. 13, 14 describe conditions in a nation whose God is Jehovah (v. 15). In such a nation young men and women will be strong, vigorous, and beautiful (v. 12). There will be abundant material prosperity; the enemies will be driven away, sons and daughters will grace the home, and the barns be full of provision (v. 13). After a successful harvest the oxen are laden with fruits and grain, and there will be no hostile attacks by any enemy. All these blessings will come from Jehovah who "is the source and sum of all true happiness, temporal and eternal." Happy indeed is the people whose God is Jehovah!

Psalm 145. Praise of Jehovah for His Wonderful Goodness and Power

A collection of "Songs of Praise" (145–150) forms the close of the book of Psalms. Evidently all of them were composed for liturgical use; they are held together by similarity in thought and language and probably all come from the same period, namely, the days of Nehemiah. Psa. 145 is the only one in the entire book that is called "Praise," though the later Jews called the entire Psalter "Book of Praise." The marvelous beauty of Psa. 145 has inspired varied descriptions. It has been called "a noble doxology," "a bracelet, in which one beautiful bead is strung on after another, making a yet more beautiful whole." Its theme has been said to find expression in "Thine is the kingdom, the power and the glory, forever and ever." The speaker is Israel and the subject is the unspeakable majesty, goodness, greatness, providence, and love of God. There is a strong note of universalism running throughout. It is an alphabetic acrostic, each two line stanza beginning with a letter of the Hebrew alphabet in regular order.

1–3. **Chorus of Praise.** Israel announces the determination to praise Jehovah the eternal King (v. 1); *forever and ever*—Israel speaks with a consciousness of national immortality (v. 2). Jehovah is worthy of infinite praise; his greatness is beyond the goal of human search; man can never fully know it (v. 3).

4–11. **Character of Jehovah Calling Forth His Praise.** From one generation to another his praise shall go on; and yet it never will reach adequate expression, because the character and acts of Jehovah are beyond human comprehension. The glorious splendor of divine majesty shall be a continuous theme (v. 5). Men shall speak of his great strength, his mighty works and his weighty judgments (v. 6); they will also pour forth a perpetual stream of praise for his great goodness and righteousness (v. 7), his compassion and tender mercy (v. 8; cf. Ex. 34^{6}). The good Father, whose goodness and mercy is unto all men, manifests these same attributes in nature (v. 9). "All thy works shall praise thy name—in earth and sky and sea" (v. 10; cf. 19^{1-6}). God's people will talk of his glory and power (v. 11).

13–17. **Jehovah Desires to Make Known Himself, His Works, His Purpose.** The purpose of his manifestations is to reveal his mighty acts to the children of men (cf. v. 12). God's rule cannot be measured by time; it is yesterday, to-day, and forever (v. 13; cf. Dan. 4^{31}). One line of the acrostic seems lost here. Jehovah is the great comforter of the burdened heart and the helper of the fallen (v. 14). He is able to supply every need; he takes care of every creature; he is the great head of the house, the great provider for all the needs of his household, *in due season* (v. 15). Every living thing is satisfied from the bounty of Jehovah. When he opens his hand all of his household is satisfied (v. 16). God is holy (v. 17), eternally right and merciful.

18–21. **Jehovah Ready to Hear and Answer Prayer.** Jehovah will help any child that calls upon him sincerely, and he is ever near enough to hear (v. 18). When there is no response we have not called *in truth;* otherwise his righteousness, i.e., his loyalty, to the covenant relationship would surely bring an answer. Concerning vv. 19, 20, Kirkpatrick says: "Fear and love are the inseparable elements of true religion. Fear preserves love from degenerating into presumptuous familiarity; love prevents fear from being a servile and cringing dread" (Cambridge Bible, p. 817). V. 21 reiterates the resolution that the psalmist shall never cease to praise God, and he challenges all humanity to join in his praise.

Psalm 146. Jehovah the One True Helper

Israel is warned against trusting in men; Jehovah alone can supply her need, and he is willing to do so. Therefore, let all sing his praise. This is the first of the five "Hallelujah" psalms with which the book closes. Psa. 146 has several points of contact with Psa. 145 (see introductory paragraph there).

1, 2. Exhortation and Promise to Praise Jehovah. V. 1 contains a call to worship, in the spirit of Psa. 103. V. 2 expresses an absolute commitment of self to God (cf. 104[32]).

3, 4. Warning Against Putting Trust in Men. There is no need to trust in princes or any other man, for they return to the earth from whence they came, and their purposes with them. The grave levels every caste and irons out every difference of social standing; pauper and prince lie down together, inheritor of six feet of sod. God alone abides and retains his power.

5–10. From the Helplessness of Man to the Power of Jehovah. The psalmist contrasts the hopelessness of trust in man with the hope born of trust in God (v. 5); also the weakness of man with the might of the Creator who made heaven and earth (v. 6). This powerful God is also good (v. 7), as he has revealed again and again in the history of Israel and in his dealings with men in general (cf. 103[6] 107[9]). With this verse and v. 8 compare also Mt. 11[1-6]. *Strangers* (v. 9)—better, "sojourners"; i.e., resident aliens who have no right of citizenship; for these and all others who need his help he cares, but he destroys the wicked. His reign is not transitory as is that of earthly kings, but eternal (v. 10).

Psalm 147. Praise for Restoration, Providence and Prosperity

The psalm falls quite naturally into three parts (vv. 1–6, 7–11, 12–20), each one beginning with a call to praise. The three outstanding themes are (1) the goodness of God to Israel; (2) his beneficent care for all nature; (3) his moral government of the universe. Like the other psalms in the group it may come from the days of Nehemiah; "it is not an improbable conjecture that it was composed for the festival of the dedication of the walls of Jerusalem celebrated by Nehemiah (12[27-43])."

1–6. Praise of Jehovah as the Restorer of Israel, the Ruler of the World. V. 1 includes what may be regarded as the title, a call to praise and the statement that it is pleasing and satisfying to worship Jehovah. *Doth build up* (v. 2)—it is a continuous process; Jehovah is constantly rebuilding Jerusalem and gathering his people who have long been outcasts (cf. 51[18]). The loving-kindness of God exhibits itself in the restoration of his people and their healing (v. 3; cf. Isa. 61[1f.]). *Number . . . names* (v. 4). The God who knows the number and names of the stars will have no special difficulty in finding all his people. He is mighty, powerful, and there is no limit to his understanding (v. 5). He numbers the stars, but who can tell *his* wisdom? The power and love of God are manifested in his moral government of the world (v. 6).

7–11. Praise of Jehovah as the Beneficent Lord of Creation. The psalmist, contemplating the works of God, bursts into a new exhortation to praise him. Jehovah's marvelous works are shown in the mystery of rainfall and the growth of grass (v. 8). Further evidences of the divine beneficence are seen in the care of dumb animals and helpless birds (v. 9); the raven's cry goes not unheeded. Jehovah delights not in physical strength but in reverent trustfulness (v. 10). *Horse* refers to warfare; swiftness of foot was necessary to the warrior. Jehovah is not dependent on armies. In reality he is not on the side of the strongest military forces, as has been said, but with those who put their trust in him. He takes delight in spiritual rather than physical strength. *Hope in mercy.* Divine mercy is a source of permanent strength.

12–20. Praise of Jehovah as the Giver of Peace and Prosperity. Jerusalem is personified and called upon to praise Jehovah. Jehovah has established Jerusalem; it is his name that has made her glorious (v. 13); it is he, and he alone, who is the giver of peace and plenty (v. 14). *Commandment . . . word* (v. 15)—God's word is personified; it is sent forth as a swift runner (107[20]; cf. Isa. 55[10, 11]). *Snow* and *frost* are not altogether rare in Palestine and Jerusalem; but it is always a matter of wonder when a blanket of snow bedecks the earth with glory, and frost reveals much of nature's beauty (v. 16). *Ice*=hail; it is compared to morsels of bread scattered to the birds (v. 17). Just as he sends these things, so he also causes their disappearance (v. 18). The *word* of Jehovah, which is operative in nature, has taken in Israel a special form, the revelation of the divine law (v. 19). This is the unique privilege of Israel, for he has not revealed himself like that to any other nation.

Psalm 148. A Universal Hymn of Praise

Israel, rejoicing in her restoration, summons all nature, heavenly and earthly, to join in praise to the God who made them. Evidently, the psalmist thinks that the history of Israel has a significance for the whole world (see introductory paragraph to Psa. 145).

1–6. Call to the Heavens to Praise Their Creator. The call is universal. *Heavens . . . height*—perhaps the stars and moon. Let all the heavenly bodies praise Jehovah. *Angels . . . hosts*—the hosts are the troops of angels. Vv. 1, 2 call upon heavenly beings and heavenly bodies to join in the anthem of praise. *Sun, moon . . . stars of light*—are called upon to add their glad acclaim of praise (cf. Psa. 19). *Heavens of heavens* (v. 4)—not a plurality of heavens; the later Jews thought of either three or seven heavens—"the highest heavens" (cf. "Song of Songs," "King of Kings," etc.). *Waters . . . above the heavens*—cf. 104^{3} Gen. $1^{6, 7}$ and notes. The earth was supposed to be surrounded by water. God commanded, and they were created (v. 5). The conception is that of Gen. 1; God said the word, and heaven and earth were made. Thus, because God made them, he is entitled to their praise. *Established . . . made a decree* (v. 6). God has made the heavens and the earth, and they are given fixed laws which they cannot transgress; these laws are nothing more than the expressions of the divine will.

7–13. Call to the Earth to Praise Its Creator. The creatures of the earth should praise God. *Dragons, and all deeps*—the sea monsters of Gen. 1^{21}; these inhabitants of the sea with the sea itself. All that is in the sea is called upon to praise God; thus Israel, who feared the sea, is reminded that God governs the sea as well as the land. How beautiful is the thought (v. 8) that even the storms raging about us are but divine messengers. Lightning, hail, snow, vapor, and stormy wind are all doing God's will and are fulfilling his word. The summons in vv. 9–12 includes mountains, trees, beasts, creeping things, flying fowl, men, kings, princes, men and maidens old and young. All these, without distinction of caste or station, are called upon to praise God, catching the spirit of the general outburst of adoration. Let all of them praise him whose name is excellent and whose glory is above the heavens.

14. Israel Has Special Reason for Praising Jehovah. He has exalted *the horn of his people*—has restored their dignity and power. *A people near unto him*—the Hebrew people were his chosen ones and his saints.

Psalm 149. Song of Triumph

The first part of the psalm is a summons to praise Jehovah. The latter part is cruelly vindictive. It has been argued and possibly with some degree of reason, that it was written for the rededication of the Temple under the Maccabees in 165 B.C. or even after the capture of Acra in 142 B.C. In its vindictiveness it resembles the book of Esther, which comes from the same late period. It is doubtful, however, that the arguments for such a late date are conclusive. It is more probable that this psalm, like the others in the group, originated in the days of Nehemiah.

1–5. Israel Summoned to Praise Jehovah. The reason is twofold: (1) He is the "maker" of Israel; (2) he is her "restorer" to dignity and power. *New song*—new blessings demand new songs of praise. *Saints* = *Hasidim.* If the psalm is Maccabæan, the reference is probably to the Hasideans mentioned in the books of Maccabees (1 Macc. 2^{42}). But if it comes from the age of Nehemiah, the entire faithful community is addressed. *In him that made him*—Jehovah made them a nation and now restores that nation. The celebration is accompanied by a religious dance and instrumental music; *timbrel*—a hand drum (v. 3).

Taketh pleasure in his people—always, but especially in deliverance from national danger his favor is once more vouchsafed to them. *Will beautify*—or "adorn." The word "adorn" is often used of restoration, yet there is also another beautiful figure which often occurs, namely, the adornment of righteousness. The former is preferable here. *Salvation*—mg., "victory"; it denotes prosperity and general welfare as well as the restoration from exile (v. 4). Let Israel exult in the honor which God has put upon them. *Sing upon their beds*—in the East one lies down behind barred doors and with watchmen. When the Lord has wrought victory, the security is so great that the people may make a joyful noise upon their beds; there will be no danger of sudden attack and no need of silence and secrecy.

6–9. Triumph Over all the Nations and Their Destruction. The high praise of God is to be in their mouths, while a *two-edged sword* (or "devouring sword") is to be in their hands (cf. Neh. 4^{16-18}). While the mouth praises God, the hand is to wield a sword that will speak just as convincingly. *Vengeance . . . punishments.* The restored Israelites are to be the instruments in the hands of God to chastise the nations that will not hear or that have thought to destroy God's people. The Messianic nation here is bringing all other nations under subjection (v. 8); kings and nobles will be overcome; the victory is to be complete. *The judgment written* (v. 9)—judgment upon hostile nations is one of the favorite themes of the prophets. *This honor*—translate, "honor shall that be to all his saints." The complete defeat of the enemies brings honor to God's own people.

Psalm 150. An Expression of Highest Joy

This mighty burst of praise is a fit ending to the book which above all other books of the Bible expresses the whole range of human experience: Love, Life, Joy, Sorrow, Disappointment, Sin, Repentance, Comfort, Condemnation, Imprecation—every sort of human frailty and faith. But at last, when the whole question has been gone over and the conclusion of the whole matter is reached, there is the highest reason for praising God with the whole being and for shouting forth his praise with this trumpetlike song. The answer to all questions and all conditions of life and experience is: "Praise Jehovah; Hallelujah."

Praise God—Hebrew, *El*, the God of power; *sanctuary*=heaven, the abode of God; *firmament*—the foundation of his sanctuary, for God's dwelling is above the firmament. *Mighty acts . . . excellent greatness*—manifested in his dealings with men, in personal experience and in nature. *Trumpet . . . psaltery . . . harp*—praise him with all of the instruments which can be used (v. 3). Other instruments to be used in the ritual of worship are mentioned in vv. 4, 5. The picture is of a great holy day of spiritual exultation, when all of the choirs will join in songs of praise; first in heaven, or the sanctuary of God set upon the mighty firmament of the skies, where angels sing; then in the earthly temple, either with the voice of nature, which ever praises God, or with the instruments devised by the cunning hand of man, for this very purpose. Choir, orchestra and congregation are called into this mighty oratorio that wells up from earth and challenges the heavens until the psalmist, in a great finale, cries out, "Let everything that hath breath praise the Lord."

PROVERBS

By Professor EARLE B. CROSS

Objective and Method of Treatment. In preparing this interpretation of the book of Proverbs the author has tried to keep in mind the things which touch ground common to our modern life and the ancient Hebrew world. He has sought to discover what in Proverbs is of worth and interest to the present age. To do this he has not followed the usual commentary method, but has grouped together significant blocks of proverbs and has given them a connected topical treatment. A large part of Proverbs of little meaning for present day thought and life has been ignored in deliberately focusing on the old book the spotlight of what modern youth is thinking, in order to set forth in relief such part of its contents as has a vital message for to-day.

Literature: For those who desire to make a more detailed study of the book and who, therefore, wish to consult more comprehensive works on Proverbs, there are available the following helps: Toy, *Proverbs* (International Critical Commentary); Horton, *Proverbs* (Expositor's Bible); Elmslie, *Studies in Life from Jewish Proverbs;* Genung, *The Hebrew Literature of Wisdom;* Kent, *The Wise Men of Ancient Israel and Their Proverbs;* Kent and Burrows, *Proverbs and Didactic Poems* (Student's Old Testament).

I. Appreciation of Proverbs as Literature

Characteristics of Hebrew Poetry. The Hebrew poets seem to have been little concerned with a careful meter such as marks the classic Greek and Latin, or much of English poetry. The natural stress of the voice gives a rhythm which satisfied the Hebrew, and this suffers little in the process of translation. (See art., *Poetic and Wisdom Literature,* pp. 154; cf. also pp. 23, 341f.) Most of the lines in Proverbs are three stress lines, such as in 10[1, 2]:

"A wise son | maketh | a glad father:
But a foolish son | is the heaviness | of his mother.
Treasures of wickedness | profit | nothing;
But righteousness | delivereth | from death."

A second feature peculiar to Hebrew poetry is the rhyming of the thought. In the lines quoted above, the second of each couplet gives the obverse of thought in relation to the first. This balance of lines give a pleasing effect. Frequently, the second line of a couplet will repeat the thought of the first, but in a variance of words, as in 1[20]:

"Wisdom crieth aloud in the street;
She uttereth her voice in the broad places."

Less often, the second line extends the thought of the first by presenting a conclusion or sequence of idea, as in 1[10]:

"My son, if sinners entice thee,
Consent thou not."

The couplet is by no means the only grouping of lines in Hebrew poetry. Triads of lines are common, quatrains also, and groups of five, six, or seven lines. The more numerous the lines in a group, however, the more likelihood that subordinate divisions of the thought will appear (see p. 155). Couplets predominate in Proverbs 10[1]–22[16]. In the other parts of the book, a variety of groupings will be found.

Longer Poems in Proverbs. A sonnet—to borrow English terminology which does not exactly fit—a sonnet of interesting form occurs in Prov. 6[6-11].

"Go to the ant, thou sluggard;
Consider her ways and be wise:
Which having no chief,
Overseer, or ruler,
Provideth her meat in the summer,
And gathereth her food in the harvest.
How long wilt thou sleep, O sluggard?
When wilt thou arise out of thy sleep?
A little sleep!
A little slumber!
A little folding of the hands to sleep!
So shall thy Poverty come as a robber,
And thy Want as an armed man."

See the sluggard nod off into sleep! "A little sleep!" Bobs his head onto his breast. "A little slumber!" Again he nods. The next line suggests the snuggling of his body down into a more comfortable posture for a sound sleep, whereupon those two ruffians, Poverty and Want, burst upon the scene to strip the sluggard and leave him to rags and hunger. With a different prefatory setting this same refrain appears in 24:30-34. The teacher with imagination and dramatic instinct will know how to fix by pantomime the lesson of these lines upon the minds of children.

Another kindred poem is found in 23:29-35, in which the imagination sensitive to the dramatic may discover a dialogue. A drunkard complains at implied slurs of his friend, speaking in tones which would sound forth injured innocence were they not maudlin, and broken by an occasional hiccough:

"Who hath woes?
Who hath sorrow?
Who hath contentions?
Who hath complainings?
Who hath wounds without cause?
Who hath redness of eyes?" (23:29)

His sober friend responds, as the second person of the pronouns indicates in the answer to the questions, but to no avail (23:30-34). In alcoholic glee, the drunkard hails the drowning of his woes in the coma of his cups, as the variance in pronouns again indicates:

"They have stricken me, and I was not hurt!
They have beaten me, and I felt it not!
When shall I awake? I will seek it yet again."

The italicized words of our English versions in the first line of v. 35 are not in the Hebrew, but they do indicate that our translators recognized the drunkard as the speaker. A reader trained to express the proper inflection, tone color, and touch, can render the lines with adequate depiction of the ridiculous sot, unreasonable, enslaved by appetite, and glorying in the very insensibility which is his doom.

Imaginative Language and Figures of Speech. Imaginative language characterizes the Hebrew, as it does all other poesies. Simile, metaphor, allusion, metonymy challenge the best thought of the reader. As the writers seek to incite youth to the search of wisdom, they write:

"If thou seek her as silver,
And search for her as for hid treasures" (2:4).

If we may define wisdom for the moment as the expression in conduct of divine ideals for human life, we realize that in the simile cited the poet has chosen a figure embodying the chief rival of wisdom in human affairs—wealth. He would set his disciple to pursuing wisdom with all the zest with which the average youth was chasing the almighty shekel. He would have him, to use the amplified form in which a greater poet rendered the same figure, "go and sell all that he possessed, and buy the field in which wisdom lies hidden." The stupendous modern expeditions for the salvaging of sunken treasure ships may serve as illustrations commensurate with the superb modern apparatus for the acquiring of wisdom which is available for the willing disciple. Let the mind dwell on such figures in the Proverbs and the aptness, the stimulating suggestiveness of their art will quicken every alert mind.

Another couplet from Proverbs we cite, which appears in more ample form in Jesus' usage:

"When the whirlwind passeth, the wicked is no more:
But the righteous is an everlasting foundation" (10:25; cf. Mt. 7:25-27).

In this metaphor, profoundly true to life, wherein neither good nor bad can escape devastating storms, the superior worth of the righteous appears in his foundation upon which courage and faith may rebuild.

Imaginative expansion of the figures of speech in Proverbs is not only a fascinating process but also a profitable study. The point of illustration is not always obvious, however, for it is often obscured by faulty translation, or by the archaic nature of the allusion, when the text itself is not garbled. The more extensive commentaries will be of service in such cases. We venture to cite one instance, in which the pith of the lesson is obscured by the translation into English of the Hebrew word "taste" as "discretion." We hold to "taste" in precisely our usage of that word in the simile in 11:22:

"As a jewel of gold in a swine's snout,
So is a fair woman which is without taste."

Here is posed a bulk of bestiality dangling a ludicrous atom of beauty. In like manner does charm, physical or spiritual, dwindle to nothing against the coarse material reality of a lack of taste, be it in dress, manners, conversation, or religion. This taste may be in large measure a natural gift, but Proverbs is concerned throughout in depicting it as a matter of cultivation through self-discipline. (See below, section III.)

In some senses the ninth chapter of Proverbs is the climax of the book. The form of the poem is unique, fashioned upon the model of an arch. Stands Mistress Wisdom as the one pillar (vv. 1–6), Mistress Folly as the other (vv. 13–18). The arch contains couplets on the worth of discipline and a capstone on Wisdom:

"The fear of the Lord is the beginning of wisdom:
And the knowledge of the Holy One is understanding" (v. 10).

Without this arch and its capstone, the poet could not have set forth Mistress Wisdom over against Mistress Folly with confidence that the reader would detect the superior worth of the former. The style of the two pillars is worthy of note. Mistress Wisdom works with zeal and purpose. She builds a mansion, proportioned to seven pillars. She prepares a banquet, with invitations to which she sends forth her maidens. Mistress Folly, on the other hand, talks much—but does nothing. She sits idly at her door by the wayside. She has no disciples, and is unheeded by most that pass. The poet deftly indicates that Wisdom and Folly may not be easily distinguished at the first, when he places in the mouth of each the identical words of invitation:

"Whoso is simple let him turn in hither:
As for him that is void of understanding, she saith to him . . ." ($9^{4, 16}$)

What each says then follows. Wisdom, e.g., says that she has a simple feast of life and understanding. Folly has stolen waters, and promises of bread, which are made futile by death.

Proverbs is by no means the least of those works which have placed the O.T. upon a high pedestal in the hall of the world's great literature.

II. The Place of Proverbs in Hebrew History

Literary History. The book of Proverbs is a summary of the best contributions of Hebrew wise men from the earliest times to the days of the restoration following the return from exile in the fifth century. It is the last edition of a work which grew with the passing years. Many of the hundreds who doubtless contributed to its contents spoke words such as had pertinence to their own times only, so that they have been eliminated from the editions of succeeding generations. As we now have it, the book presents a nucleus of such ancient material as was consonant with the ideas of those writers who put forth this latest summary of wisdom on the eve of the closing of the canon of sacred writings, after which nothing more could find its way into the Scriptures. Kindred writings exist, which did not find recognition as Scripture, such as "Ecclesiasticus," or the "Wisdom of Jesus ben Sirach." (See art., *Intertestamental Literature,* p. 196b.)

Solomonic Authorship. Tradition attributes Proverbs to Solomon, as the editorial notation in 1^1 reveals. If Solomon was the author, we must date the book five centuries earlier than the date required by manifest facts. Solomon is referred to again in 10^1, and also in 25^1. The latter verse is, "These also are proverbs of Solomon, which the men of Hezekiah king of Judah copied out." Where had these proverbs been during the two centuries which separate the days of Solomon from Hezekiah? In any case, the last two chapters of the book are not to be ascribed to Solomon, for they are headed respectively, "The words of Agur the son of Jakeh, the oracle," and "The words of king Lemuel; the oracle which his mother taught him" (30^1 31^1). To the extent of these two chapters at least the book is composite. The ascription of the book to Solomon was probably due to the original impulse which that famous king gave to wisdom. The mass of such literature which grew up in later generations was attributed to him by proxy, even as the psalms are largely attributed to David and the writings of the Law to Moses.

This theory is strengthened when one considers how different the contents of the book are from what one would expect of Solomon's writings. A description in Kings states: "God gave Solomon wisdom and understanding exceeding much . . . And he spake three thousand proverbs; and his songs were a thousand and five. And he spake of trees, from the cedar that is in Lebanon even unto the hyssop that springeth out of the wall: he spake also of beasts, and of fowl, and of creeping things, and of fishes . . ." (1 Kings $4^{29f.}$).

The first twenty-nine chapters of the book contain but 850 verses in all, so that we can hardly claim to be in possession of more than a fragment of the 3,000 proverbs of Solomon, not to mention the 1,005 songs. After Kings has led us to expect a rather exclusive use of illustrations from animate nature, we are surprised to find in Proverbs but 38 verses of this type, 29 referring to animals, birds, or insects, with no reference to fish, and nine mentioning vegetable objects. Furthermore, the predominance of such nature proverbs among the 64 verses of the last two chapters of the book, where 13 are found, sets these chapters forth as more truly characteristic of the Solomon whom Kings describes than is the main portion of the book. Yet, as we have seen, these chapters are definitely assigned to writers other than Solomon. If Kings is right concerning the nature of Solomon's proverbs, then the book of Proverbs contains little from his hand. It is barely possible that the bulk of Solomon's work has been lost, and that only such material remains as is least like what Kings describes. This idea has but to be stated to be rejected.

The references to kings which are found in

Proverbs (16^{14} 19^{12} 20^{2} 25^{3}) have been cited by some as being so derogatory of the honor and majesty of monarchs that Solomon would hardly have written them. Let the student consider these references for himself, however, and he will be inclined to turn the argument about to support Solomon's authorship.

Characteristic Ideas of Proverbs: Their Bearing on the Date. The more cogent evidence for locating the book of Proverbs somewhere in the period following the Exile appears when one takes into account the attitude which is revealed in the book with regard to such outstanding ideas as the concept of God, the status of woman, and the social entity. In the stream of developing thought and social relations the position which Proverbs holds is such as to confirm the theory that it is to be dated in the later years of Hebrew history.

(1) *Conception of God.* Consider the evidence with regard to the idea of God in Proverbs. The fundamental conception of God for the writers of Proverbs is his creative power ($3^{19,\ 20}$). The surging primeval deeps were broken up and disposed as seas through the creative might of God; and the cool dew of evening slaking the thirst of vegetation is a gift of the same creative power. There is a similarity between the imagery in an outstanding passage of Proverbs (8^{22-31}) and the language of certain passages in the later chapters of the book of Isaiah ($40^{12,\ 21f.}$ 44^{24} $45^{11f.}$) and in the book of Job ($9^{5f.}$ $26^{7f.}$ $38^{4f.}$). Both of these latter sections of the Bible are products of the latest periods of Hebrew history. Can such a conception of God have been portrayed in the days of the early monarchy by Solomon?

David, the father of Solomon, thought of God as confined to Hebrew territory (1 Sam. 26^{19}). It was not till the time of the writing prophets that there began to appear an idea of God as God of all the earth. In Amos (see 9^{7}) the idea is hardly more than a query. (Amos 4^{13} $5^{8,\ 9}$ 9^{6} are generally regarded as marginal annotations from the hands of writers of a date following the Exile.) In any case, Amos did not come upon the scene until nearly two centuries after Solomon's time. Amos and his successors were responsible for the building of that splendid theology in which there came to flower at length the conception of God as sole Deity and Creator as well as Controller of earth. Proverbs appears to exist in a realm of thought where this conception of God has deep root. It is a book relatively late in Hebrew history. (See art., *O.T. Conception of God,* pp. 161–3.)

(2) *Status of Woman.* In the early days of the monarchy, polygamy prevailed. Certainly, all the kings of Israel and Judah had large harems, and the harem of Solomon himself has become proverbial. A fair inference from the privilege of the king might be drawn to the effect that the man of lesser rank might have the same right to a harem limited only by his ability to provide therefor. Elkanah, father of Samuel, had two wives (1 Sam. $1^{1,\ 2}$). Even more definite evidence comes from the legal enactments of successive periods. Deuteronomy in the seventh century recognizes the right of a man to have at least two wives (Deut. 21^{15}). Nowhere is there any law prohibiting polygamy. Yet in the later codes of the Priestly document of the Hexateuch, dating from the Exile, there is no repetition of such a clause as that which appears in Deuteronomy, countenancing polygamy. The probability is that any book produced before the Exile would reveal traces of plurality of wives, if there were any reference at all to marriage or the family.

The book of Proverbs, however, seems to assume monogamy as the type of marriage. Several passages refer to the family and woman's place in life (12^{4} 18^{22} 19^{14} 21^{9} 25^{24}). In each case the sentiment is more monogamous than polygamous. Again, in the somewhat stilted alphabetical acrostic in praise of the ideal woman (31^{10-31}), the wife appears as household manager. There is no reference to rival wives, or subordinate wives. The reasonable inference from the passage is that the dominance of one woman after this fashion in a household implies monogamy. Furthermore, in the discussion of sexual evil the implications, insofar as they bear upon the form of the family, seem to support the contention that monogamy was the type (see especially $5^{18,\ 19}$). There are no passages which require one to postulate a polygamous background. Such facts support the theory that Proverbs is a product of the period following the Exile.

(3) *The Social Entity.* Through the early years of Hebrew life the entity of social interest is the nation, or the family. In nomad life, the individual exists only as one of a group. Apart from his group he can hardly win food from the hand of nature, even if he can protect himself from the ravages of his fellow men. This nomadic influence persisted with the Hebrews into their settled life in Canaan. The story of Achan illustrates the close-knit life of members of a group in that the entire group paid the penalty of death with Achan for his violation of the ban against taking booty in the attack on Jericho (Josh. 7). The earlier prophets directed their sermons to the nation. Even Jeremiah and Ezekiel, to whom

credit is usually given for the discovery of the individual, preach largely to the nation as such.

It is, therefore, striking to find in the book of Proverbs no reference at all to the national entity. The words "Israel" and "Judah," or "nation," which are the commonplace of the O.T. with the exception of Job, are conspicuous by their absence. It is difficult in the face of this fact to regard either Job or Proverbs as the product of a writer of the days prior to the Exile, unless we premise some peculiar spirit in the wise men as such which led them to stress the individual rather than the group. The Dispersion was just such a cataclysm as would tend to emphasize the individual and obliterate the group in the welter of deportations and wide dissemination of the nation throughout the known world.

(4) *Linguistic Characteristics.* The linguistic evidence, which may be found in detail in more extended commentaries, reveals many late-word usages in the Hebrew of Proverbs. Aramaic words are of frequent occurrence with a few words of possible Arabic origin. One word occurs which may have been borrowed from the Greek, although the borrowing may have been in the opposite direction after all, by the Greek from some Semitic source kindred with the Hebrew. On general grounds of language and style, Proverbs obviously ranges with Job and Ecclesiastes, and the evidence which places these books in the period following the Exile, will necessarily weigh in favor of dating Proverbs there as well.

III. The Counsel of Proverbs

Outline of Book. The book of Proverbs naturally divides itself into six parts, two of which might be further subdivided into two parts each. These divisions are indicated in the book itself by captions at the several points of distinction. We outline the contents thus:

1. Prologue, whose chief theme is "The Praise of Wisdom" (chs. 1–9).
2. Disconnected aphorisms on various themes, chiefly emphasizing the superior worth of wisdom and moral conduct, and largely in the form of couplets. (10^{1}–22^{16}). Caption: "The proverbs of Solomon." 22^{17}–24^{22} may be considered part of this section, since there is no specific caption (cf., however, the exhortation, "hear *the words of the wise*," in 22^{17}); quatrains prevail here instead of couplets and there are some longer stanzas on particular themes, e.g., the drunkard (23^{29-35}).
3. A brief section of no especial distinction aside from the caption: "These also are sayings of the wise" (24^{23-34}).
4. A collection of aphorisms of a variety of forms and on various themes (25^{1}–29^{27}). Caption: "These also are proverbs of Solomon, which the men of Hezekiah, king of Judah, copied out."
5. Varied material, largely numerical riddles (30^{1-33}). Caption: "The words of Agur the son of Jakeh; the oracle."
6. Two poems on the king's duty (31^{1-9}) and the worthy woman (31^{10-31}). Caption: "The words of king Lemuel; the oracle which his mother taught him." The poem on the worthy woman might be distinguished as an anonymous poem from the words of king Lemuel and be considered a closing section for the entire book.

Principal Theme: The Worth of Wisdom. The dominant theme of the book of Proverbs is the superior worth of wisdom. In the usage of the book wisdom includes moral conduct as well as knowledge. The writers do not set forth the precise content of wisdom, but confine themselves to general exhortations to seek out and secure this priceless treasure. They personify both wisdom and folly as women. Wisdom first appears in person in the open square before the city gates, where were wont to assemble the elders of the people for counsel and for judgment ($1^{20f.}$). There is a dramatic quality in her appeal for a following. At first she proffers the untutored her spirit and the knowledge of her teaching (1^{23}). A pause ensues during which the imagination can readily picture the scoffer and the fool, to whom the appeal has been addressed (1^{22}), turning away in complacent scorn. Whereupon Wisdom continues, "Because I have called, and ye refused . . . I will mock when your fear cometh, when your fear cometh as a storm, and your calamity cometh as a whirlwind" (1^{24-27}). Another pause, storm-filled, follows these words, as the destruction of fools sweeps by. When the dust has settled, Wisdom speaks no longer to the scornful, for they have perished. The shifting of pronouns in reference to the scoffers from "you" and "your" to "they" and "their" supports this inference. The chapter then concludes with a masterly contrast between fools, quieted at last in death, and Wisdom's followers, dwelling "securely . . . without fear of evil."

Again, Wisdom appears in the open square to persuade men of the worth of her incomparable riches (ch. 8). Her origin is with God, and she is set against all evil of whatever hue. Wisdom is the basis of government, the producer of abundant wealth, the ancient creative power working with God in the framing of the habitable earth. " 'All they that hate me love death,' for I am the creative principle of life," she would say.

The third appearance of Wisdom in personification follows in the ninth chapter after a fashion which we have described above. This is possibly the supreme point of the entire book; certainly, it is the climax of the prologue.

Personification of Folly. The opposite of wisdom is also personified in the prologue in the figure of Mistress Folly, or in the words of the English versions, "The foolish woman" (9^{13}). The seventh chapter also is a personification of Folly in colors of an adulteress, secretly enticing the callow to their doom. This chapter is usually taken as a description of a lewd woman; but certain facts seem to warrant a broader interpretation. The proximity of the personifications of Wisdom (ch. 8; 9^{1-6}) and of Folly (9^{13-18}) about which there can be no two opinions, suggests that ch. 7 also may be taken as figurative. Furthermore, there is significant similarity between this chapter and the personification of Folly in the last verses of the ninth chapter. The one who is tempted is in each case "simple" and "void of understanding" (7^{7} 9^{16}). Not only is the woman in each passage described as "clamorous" (7^{11} 9^{13}), but the furtive manner of the seduction is alike, though tersely depicted in the one case and amplified in brilliant but horrid detail in the other. The concluding lines of each of the three chapters which contain these personifications (7, 8, 9) are practically identical. This, again, lends color to the idea that ch. 7 as well as the others contains a personification. The art by which the author chose the adulteress with all her wiles and seductive glamour for the figure of Folly, is apt and significant, for is not lewdness the epitome of folly? The moral sense of the poet prompted him to the choice, as it guided him also in painting the whole picture, not omitting the yawning pit and death at the end of the wanton fling.

Sexual Vice. This seventh chapter remains a graphic warning against sexual vice, even while it is regarded as an imaginative depiction of the worthlessness of folly. Beside this seventh chapter, the fifth also and the sixth, from the twentieth verse on, are built upon this theme—the deadliness of sexual sins. The point of view throughout is that of the man. It is women who are painted as the seducers, and a moral menace. This limited point of view is due to the fact that women were probably not in the educational scheme of those days at all; hence the address is always to the man's angle of vision. Nevertheless, now that we have grown to a broader educational program in which both sexes are equally prominent, the lesson of this ancient book is still pertinent. The terms for the feminine may be read in place of the masculine without greatly disturbing the picture, and without vitiating in the least the moral ideal which is set up. Evidently, the writers of Proverbs regarded sins of sex as the most deadly. At least, they gave greater space to denunciation of them than to warnings against any other type of sin.

Perils of the Moral Life. Ch. 6 epitomizes the writers' idea of perils to the moral life—sexual sins are denounced at length (6^{20-35}), going bond for a person (6^{1-5}), laziness (6^{6-11}), and general perversity (6^{12-15}). Tucked away in the midst is a numerical riddle answering the query, "What are the six or seven chief abominations of God?" The answer is, "Haughty eyes, a lying tongue, and hands that shed innocent blood; an heart that deviseth wicked imaginations, feet that be swift in running to mischief; a false witness that uttereth lies, and he that soweth discord among brethren" (6^{17-19}). The moral ideal and prudent counsel herein contained are as sound for this twentieth century as for the generation which read them first.

The Wise Man's Program of Religious Education. Proverbs begins with what might be called an ancient program of religious education (1^{2-6}). Its several clauses are worthy of study.

(1) *To know wisdom and understanding.* The word "wisdom" has been taken rightly to be the most comprehensive term for the intellectual interests of the Hebrews. Wisdom (*chokhmah*) is, however, superior to mere knowledge (*da'ath*), for it includes not only the significance of the latter term but also the expression of that knowledge in conduct, ethical and religious. Wisdom is the knowledge of how best to conduct oneself in God's world and action consistent with such knowledge. Coupled with wisdom in this first clause of the program is "instruction" (*musar*). A better translation would be "discipline." While it refers largely to the process by which teachers and advisers correct the seeker after wisdom, it involves also self-discipline. As a later clause indicates (1^{5}), discipline is indispensable throughout life.

(2) *To discern the words of understanding* is the second clause of the program. In the Hebrew there is a tautology which our translators have sought to avoid. We incline to believe that the authors deliberately wrote "to understand the words of understanding." The Hebrew root (*bi'yn*) indicates an active effort to see through things, to get at the root of

matters. One might well paraphrase the clause, therefore, "to understand the vocabulary of life's fundamentals."

(3) The program further proposes *to receive instruction in wise dealing, in righteousness and judgment and equity.* "Wise dealing," or, better, "wise conduct," is interpreted in the three terms which follow. The first of the three words, "righteousness" in the English, suggests the vertical plane, connoting the upreach after the divine which is an integral element of wisdom in Hebrew thought. "Uprightness" might preserve the color of the word best in a translation. The last word in the triad, "equity" in the English, means "straightforwardness," if one cares to observe the color of the original. The word suggests straight and narrow paths amid human affairs. The central word, rendered "judgment" in the English, is *mishpat* in Hebrew. Jeremiah used this word in a novel sense to convey almost the meaning which our modern word "religion" includes (Jer. 8[7], "ordinance" in R.V., "law" in A.S.V.). Again, in the superb Servant Songs the word flowers into the same meaning, "religion" (Isa. 42[1-3] 49[4], "judgment" in R.V., "justice" in A.S.V.). The new significance which was given to the word *mishpat* during the Exile must have been familiar to the authors of the prologue of Proverbs, and we incline to believe that in this program of the first chapter it should be translated "religion." "Wise conduct," then, is interpreted as "uprightness, religion, and righteousness." As the Hebrew often arranges his items, the middle word is of most significance, like the capstone of an arch; religion is therefore seen to be the predominant factor in moral conduct.

(4) *Young and old have a part in the program.* We can best set forth our interpretation of the lines dealing with youth by a fresh rendering,

"To give shrewdness to the untutored,
To the young man knowledge and thoughtfulness" (1[4]).

Maturity also is included in the scheme of the wise. Those who have had instruction can never cease to add to their store of learning, and even the "man of understanding" may still have ideals of accomplishment in striving to attain unto "sound counsels" (1[5]). The figure in the background of this last phrase in the Hebrew comes from life on the sea. "Sound counsels" is a secondary meaning, quite adequate, but not as vivid as "handling the ropes."

(5) Finally, the program looks to *the grasp of literary forms and their significance,* so that the difficult allusions and figures of speech in the presentation of truth may not be unappreciated. The word rendered "proverb" seems to cover the whole field of poesy, as a study of its usage in the Hebrew reveals.

"To understand poesy, and parables,
The words of the wise, and their figurative style" (1[6]).

Thus the whole program stands—the mastery of life's fundamentals through discipline; the attainment of moral conduct; the development of intelligence in youth and the perfection of wisdom in the mature; the appreciation of the noble forms which truth assumes. Here are the elements of philosophy, ethics, and æsthetics in this simple program, whereby it must be approved as culturally sound.

Religion in Proverbs. To the casual reader the book of Proverbs may seem to be less religious in tone than most of the other books in the O.T. Practical precepts, appeals to moral conduct, and aphorisms little related to religion are the gist of the work. These are the flower cluster. The great calyx which holds the many blossoms together is not much seen; but the major premise of the book is religious, witness what might be called the text of it all:

"The fear of the Lord is the beginning
(or, the chiefest part) of wisdom" (1[7]).

Even beneath such lines as 20[29]

"The glory of young men is their strength:
And the beauty of old men is the hoary head,"

lies this major premise, as a kindred aphorism suggests,

"The fear of the Lord prolongeth days:
But the years of the wicked shall be shortened" (10[27]).

Thus the religious sanction must be kept in mind throughout, for it is everywhere like unseen roots from which the individual proverbs spring up. The prologue itself also gives ample evidence of the religious sentiments of the authors and their regard for God as the source and purveyor of wisdom, and the guardian of moral conduct (2[6-8] 3[5-12, 21-26, 31-34] 6[16-19]).

IV. Proverbs Speaks to the Twentieth Century

The modern reader requires some classification of the material in Proverbs, particularly in the tenth and following chapters. (See the classification in Kent, *The Wise Men of Israel and Their Proverbs*). In the space at our disposal, disregarding irrelevant material, we shall hew to a single line, namely, the answers which Proverbs has to give to the problems of modern youth in their later adolescence. As we cannot afford space for discussion of problems of text, we shall consider only those passages which are fairly clear in meaning. (For a critical discussion of the book see Toy, *Proverbs*, in the International Critical Commentary.) The problems of modern youth may be summarized in four or five spheres—recreation, sex life and the home, economic activities, and cultural life.

Recreation. Modern youth asks in regard to recreation, "What is play? What is wasting time? Is amusement wrong and in what proportion? Is recreation contrary to religion? Is it improper to join in amusements with the opposite sex? How can one gain a right conscience on amusements? How can one find an interest in life?"

(1) *Play.* Proverbs has little to give directly in solution of these problems, for recreation had not come to the fore in those ancient days. Feasts and banquets on occasion, religious celebrations, impromptu matches of strength and skill such as are common to men who must keep fit for war—these appear in the records of the Hebrews. Children played their games of make-believe weddings, funerals, and the like; and no doubt games were invented by mature folk in their hours of relaxation. The nature of this recreation, however, was not such as to raise any very serious problems; nor was play of such prominence in the social order that it would be considered at length by those who were meditating upon moral and spiritual life.

(2) *Seriousness of Life.* The writers of Proverbs felt the seriousness of life, its burdens and its woes (14[13]). But theirs is by no means a pessimistic outlook. They maintain a sane balance. Though life may be hard, yet Proverbs is in favor of a genial, joyous attitude of mind (15[13, 15]). Play or recreation is a means for bringing joy and cheer into life, taking the mind out of its cloying rut and giving it new vigor. As such the book would seem to approve recreation. Yet all of life cannot be play. A man requires the bread and other staples of life besides honied sweets (25[16]). As to what proportion of life's program should be recreation, Proverbs would throw the burden of decision upon each individual. Wisdom is not a stereotyped body of knowledge or advice. Every man must work his own soil and grow his own crop; the wise man is one who has trained his mind to discern between good and evil, to seek after an ideal and an objective such as God in his perfection might set up for him. As a man must learn to control his appetites, so he must control his time and energies, must arrange his life's program in accord with the highest good, and so avoid the retching and painful surfeit of eating too much sweet (25[16]).

Riotous living is not recreation in the true sense of the word. It leads to all sorts of social strife. One must seek suitable recreation in some other mode (17[1]).

(3) *Helpful Recreation.* Recreation should not encroach upon life's serious business (21[17]). Proverbs opposes a stern front to laziness. Life develops through hard labor; the energetic man has the approval of the wise. Consistently, therefore, they would set limits upon recreation in life's program. There must be a definite objective in life for the wise man in contrast with a fool who simply enjoys life, who has his fling (15[21]). Would not the writers of Proverbs hold that recreation should serve life's objective? Health of body, soundness of mind, speedy co-ordinations of mind and body—these are indispensable. Such recreation as contributes to these ends furthers the attainment of life's objective.

(4) *Harmful Recreation.* Youth must be alert to avoid perils in such recreation as has proven the downfall of others. The book of human experience is wide open; the wise will read and heed. There is deadly play; as there is also healthful recreation (16[25]). Recreation should be in accord with wisdom. Perhaps no single verse is of more import on this matter than 10[23]:

"It is as sport to a fool to do wickedness:
And so is wisdom to a man of understanding."

The modern attempt to guide youth into constructive programs of recreation away from destructive and noxious mischief is in line with this. The ideals of fair play and sportsmanlike conduct which mark modern playing fields are one with the ancient spirit which the social order found to be good and upon which the Hebrews set their seal of approval.

Sex Life and the Home. In the sphere of sex life and the home, modern youth is asking such questions as these: Is sex appeal indecent? Why monogamy instead of polygamy? Is there harm in sexual intercourse outside of marriage? How can one control his passions? How does love differ from passion? Is woman the equal of man? What is a home? What is due honor to parents? Many of these questions which are of acute import to modern youth were not central in the world in which Proverbs was born. For one thing, marriage came much earlier then than it does now on the average. The requirements of modern life prolong the period of training, and youth cannot assume the responsibilities of matrimony for nearly a decade later than the Hebrew boy and girl did. This delay in the normal expression of sex life in marriage has given rise to grave problems of control of this master passion. Yet the basic principles of a well-ordered sex life are discoverable in Proverbs.

(1) *Sex Appeal.* Is sex appeal indecent? Not in its normal and proper satisfactions, Proverbs would say, as the hunger for bread is normal even though gluttony is to be abhorred ($23^{20, 21}$). The union of the sexes is a holy thing (18^{22}). The physical relationship of husband and wife is recognized as a fundamental good, quite as frankly as we are coming to regard it to-day ($5^{18, 19}$). The harlot and adulteress are denounced, and by implication the fools who are led astray by them are also scored ($5^{3\text{-}13}$ $6^{1\text{-}5, 20\text{-}35}$ $7^{4\text{-}27}$ 22^{14} $23^{27, 28}$ 29^{3} 30^{20}).

(2) *Standard of Marriage.* The standard of marriage in Proverbs is clearly monogamy. The writers do not argue the case, however, even though the earlier centuries of their people's history had been marked by the practice of polygamy. Their method seems to have been to state the conclusions to which by experience the social order had arrived, namely that monogamy was the ideal of marriage, and leave it to the individual to thresh out for himself the supporting arguments. Modern youth has a wealth of literature to peruse on this and kindred problems, in which he will find the wiser moderns supporting the conclusion of Proverbs.

(3) *Sexual Intercourse.* Is there harm in sexual intercourse outside of marriage? Proverbs is unequivocal in its affirmation of the perils in sexual promiscuity. Death is the penalty (see passages cited above). Possibly the writers have in mind the ancient penalty which their people had prescribed for adultery as a legal provision; more probably the perils of disease are intended (5^{11}), and the jealous vengeance of a wronged husband ($6^{29f.}$). Modern sociology agrees with the conclusions of Proverbs. Promiscuity in sexual relations exposes one to diseases of a most deadly nature, disrupts social bonds, and creates fatal antagonisms. Probably the writers of Proverbs had not come to appreciate the most deadly peril in promiscuity which modern writers find, in the breakdown of moral character and loss of the finer capacities of the emotional nature. Sexual life must be controlled and regulated not only before marriage but within wedlock. If Proverbs does not specifically teach this, yet self-discipline and control are keywords of the book.

Proverbs has no specific answer to the problem of sexual control, for early marriages prevented the rise of this question in large measure. (For modern discussion see Exner, *Rational Sex Life for Men;* Royden, *Sex and Common Sense;* Gray, *Men, Women, and God*).

(4) *Equality of Woman.* Is woman the equal of man? Proverbs is written from the male point of view, for its age was adjusted to male supremacy. The book expresses a higher regard for women, however, than any earlier period of Hebrew history had produced. Monogamy is assumed to be the normal order of marriage for one thing, and woman is highly exalted in her wifehood (18^{22} 19^{14}). These appreciative passages offset the repeated denunciations of garrulity in women which mark Proverbs ($21^{9, 19}$ 25^{24} 27^{15}). The worthy woman is praised in no measured terms (12^{4} $31^{10\text{-}31}$); but our English translations have rather perverted the significance of these passages by rendering a Hebrew word as "virtuous" which is best translated "good." Not only skill in management of a household colors the picture of the worthy woman, but social and moral, if not intellectual, abilities as well ($31^{25, 26}$). If Proverbs does not rise to the standard of our modern era in which woman is finding emancipation from the age-long conceit that man was her master, it should not be forgotten that in the interval between the writing of Proverbs and our own time the world has been profoundly affected by the teaching of the greatest Hebrew of all, Jesus.

(5) *Home.* In answer to the question, What is a home? the book of Proverbs supplies food for thought. Home is a kinship group centered about a father and a mother, inclusive of children and the aged of a former generation as well (17^{6}). The coherence of the group is mutual respect and honor (17^{6} 19^{26} 20^{20} 23^{22} 28^{24} $30^{11, 17}$). One of the prime objectives of a home is the development of worthy children. The home is a place of discipline and moral education ($13^{1, 24}$ 19^{18} $22^{6, 15}$ $29^{15, 17}$). Possibly Proverbs emphasizes the rod and chastisement more than many exponents of modern education would approve; nevertheless such rigorous discipline is better than the foolish renunciation by parents of all attempt to control the child on the principle of letting him "express his natural self." Discipline remains a cardinal principle of character education.

(6) *Children and Parents.* The supreme joy of parents is found in worthy children (10^{1} 15^{20} $17^{21, 25}$ $23^{24\text{-}26}$ 28^{7}). In their turn children are blessed in the worth of their parents (20^{7}). Home is a preparatory school for life, a culture center for wisdom, which we have defined in an earlier chapter.

Proverbs subscribes to the ancient law which demanded honor for father and mother. Paul interpreted the word "honor" by "obey"

(Eph. 6[1, 2]), and in this he was following Proverbs, which uses the word "hearken" in the sense of "obey," thereby strengthening the requirement of the more ancient Decalogue of Moses (13[1] 23[22]). The mother is included in the demand for respect and honor. The claims of parents upon children for honor and respect are still valid, ignored though they may be by such as Proverbs would call fools (19[26] 20[20] 28[24] 30[11-14, 17]). Changes in social custom and in the substance of human knowledge were not as stupendously rapid in those days as they are in our time, yet parents were doubtless "out of date" to their children then as they often are now. Proverbs maintains rightly that one important social bond is respect of youth for age.

Economic Activities. What is success? By what means can it be achieved? Is the making of a fortune a proper objective of life? Is not the policy of "number one first" indispensable? Is "honesty the best policy"? Do wealth and success inevitably attend a moral man? Is there a place for the "Golden Rule" in business? Such are the queries which modern youth is asking as to the sphere of economics.

(1) *Success.* What is success? Not riches alone (23[4, 5]), but wisdom (16[16]) and a good name (22[1]). After all, neither wealth nor poverty is the criterion of life, but one should aim to win the favor of God (22[2, 4]). God's favor is upon those who try to do right (11[20] 12[2] 16[7, 20] 21[3]). Success is difficult of definition, but Proverbs emphasizes diligence and hard work in so many passages that obviously the writers regard the lazy man as doomed to failure (10[4, 5, 26] 12[11, 24, 27] 13[4, 11] 14[4, 23] 16[16] 18[9] 19[15] 20[4, 13] 21[5, 25] 22[29] 24[30-34] 27[23-27] 28[19]). Generosity, good will, and unselfishness are also qualities which make for success (11[24-26] 13[7] 22[9]).

(2) *Fortune.* Is the making of a fortune a proper objective in life? In answering this question one has to consider what Proverbs has to say with regard to riches as compared with poverty; and in doing this we shall come across the answer to other questions in the list—"Is not the policy of number one first indispensable? Is honesty the best policy? Do wealth and success inevitably attend the moral man?" Riches bring power (22[7]); they add to the number of one's friends (14[20] 19[4, 7]); wealth gives a sense of security and self-confidence (10[15] 18[11]). Yet in a time of peril it is a man's integrity, after all, that saves him (11[4]). Riches may ransom a man, but a poor man has no cause to fear the threats of kidnappers (13[8]). A man may become hardened by wealth (18[23]). To get rich quickly is perilous (13[11]; LXX and Vulgate read "in haste" for "by vanity"); it is often accomplished at great risk to one's moral character (28[20]), and probably wealth thus won will soon be lost (28[22]). To get rich dishonestly is abominable to God (11[1] 16[11] 20[10, 23]). Poverty is no cause for shame (16[8] 17[5a] 19[1]), for it may be merely the result of injustices suffered (13[23]). Riches must be coupled with moral character and righteous conduct to be of value in the world (10[2, 16] 11[18, 28] 13[22, 25] 14[31] 15[6, 25, 27] [for *gifts* read *bribes*] 16[8] 19[1]).

(3) *The Golden Rule.* There remains the question, Is there a place for the Golden Rule in business? The answer rests upon the decision which one makes as to the ultimate objective of business. Proverbs sets up not simply wealth as the aim of economic life, but moral character must be inviolate as wealth is secured. In this we discover Proverbs to be one with Jesus, and the elements of his masterly summary of life's method in the Golden Rule are written in the work of the wise men three centuries before his day.

Cultural Life: (1) Personal Aspect. The problems of cultural life are in the main of two trends—the one personal and the other social. In the personal aspect appear such questions as: What is education and how can culture be secured? What is goodness? Why be good? Is goodness always blessed and prospered? What is the meaning of life? Is there a future life? What is religion? Is there a God? Of what value are religious exercises, prayer, etc.?

(1) *Appreciation of Values.* Culture involves appreciation of moral (12[3] 23[15-19] 29[18, 24]), æsthetic (11[22]), and spiritual (15[33a] 21[30]) values. The expression of this appreciation in conduct is assumed to follow in the manifestation of such virtues as those which we are about to enumerate. There is no evidence that the writers of Proverbs thought of such practical training as the modern educational program involves. Yet they deemed culture to be the result of rigorous discipline and self-correction (10[17] 12[1, 15] 15[5, 31, 32] 17[10] 22[6] 23[13, 14]), by observation (17[24] 19[25] 20[12]), and by endless effort (15[14, 21, 28] 16[16] 29[20]). Culture is not a commodity that may be bought (17[16]).

(2) *Goodness.* What is goodness? We may note here the virtues and admirable qualities of life which Proverbs exalts; they form a list which compares favorably with those of Paul in the N.T. We find humility (11[2] 15[33b] 16[5] 18[12] 22[4] 25[14] 27[2] 29[23]); various types of self-control (14[17, 29] 16[32] 17[27, 28] 18[13] 19[11] 20[1] 25[28]); veracity (10[10] 12[22] 13[5] 16[6] 19[22] 20[17]); kindness (11[17] 12[10] 16[6] 19[22] 21[21]); generosity 11[25] 21[26] 22[9] 28[25]); diligent activity (15[19])

22[13] 26[13-16]); good cheer (15[13] 17[22]); justice (21[15]); and fidelity (25[13]). All of these references will be found to be illuminating as to the moral ideals of Proverbs.

(3) *Why Be Good?* The questions, Why be good? and Is goodness always blessed and prospered? may be taken together. In a measure this problem has been considered under the caption of economic activities. The book declares that wickedness leads to disaster, whereas moral conduct has the favor of God (10[30] 11[3, 6, 8, 19, 20, 31] 12[13, 21] 13[6] 19[23] 22[5, 12] 28[18, 25, 26] 29[1]). The writers probably would allow that specific instances may seem to contradict this general assertion, but that, taking life as a whole and in the long run, the balance is greatly on the side of goodness. One essential difference between goodness and evil lies in the power of recuperation which the good man has in the common lot of humanity to suffer in storms and calamity (10[25] 24[15, 16]).

(4) *Meaning of Life.* What is the meaning of life? Proverbs traces life's significance primarily to God. Life is the reward of one who reverences God (19[23] 22[4]). The translations render "reverence" as "fear," but it is fear in the sense of awe which is intended. Reverence is a fountain of life (14[27]), and prolongs life (10[27]). Life has also a moral content (11[19] 12[28] 21[21]), and intelligence is an indispensable factor therein (10[17] 13[14], read mg.; 15[24], read, with LXX, *Ways of life are the thoughts of the wise, that he may turn away from Sheol and be saved*; 16[22]). The writers are usually concerned with this mundane sphere, and not with a hypothetical future life. As to the fact of an existence after what we call death, Proverbs says nothing clearly. The time had not yet come when such a doctrine should be shaped to serve as a corrective of the apparent injustices of this world. (See art., *Religion of Israel*, p. 173, and cf. p. 210.) The writers of Proverbs believed that this present life has its compensations (11[31]), and especially noted the superb stability and recuperative powers of a good man as against a bad (10[25] 24[16, 17]). Many passages in our English texts would seem to indicate a belief in a future life, but a careful study of the Hebrew text makes clear that the writers are thinking rather of this present life and its prolongation in this world by moral conduct (12[28] 13[14] 15[24] 22[4]; cf. also 10[25, 27], and see Toy's notes on these passages).

(5) *God.* As to whether there is a God, Proverbs never indicates a doubt. In a masterly passage we read that the rich may lose their need of God and the poor may think that God has forgotten them (30[7-9]), yet God still exists, supreme in wisdom (21[30]), and ruler over all (16[1, 2, 9] 20[24] 21[31]) as the disposal of lots indicates (16[33] 19[21]). Even kings are in his power (21[1]). God made mankind, and has his purpose for them (16[4] 20[12] 22[2]). He tests men (17[3] 21[2]), and defends and cherishes those that take his way (10[29] 12[2, 22] 14[26] 15[8, 9, 29] 16[5] 18[10] 22[12] 28[25] 29[25] 30[5, 6]). Nothing escapes his observation (15[3, 11] 20[27]—instead of *belly* read *soul* in the sense of "inner being.")

(6) *Religion.* Since the writers believe in God, they had a religion even though there may not be the equivalent of our modern word "religion" in the book (see discussion on p. 608b). The phrase which comes nearest to it is "the fear of the Lord." This reverence for God is a source of confidence and life (14[26, 27] cf. 15[33]). Trust in God is also involved in religion (16[20] 28[25b] 29[25b]). Practical righteousness, furthermore, is a prime element in religion, to which ritual is secondary in the minds of the writers of Proverbs (15[8] 21[3, 27]). Prayer also is a religious privilege, available for those whose conduct is righteous (10[8, 29] 28[9]).

Cultural Life: (2) Social Aspect. In connection with his group such questions arise in the mind of modern youth as: What is friendship or brotherhood? Does a man's group have a right to control him? Is charity a virtue? Is race antagonism natural and inevitable? War? Social cleavages?

(1) *Friendship.* Friendship, according to Proverbs, is a social bond far stronger than blood kinship (18[24]—a necessary textual correction in the first line, noted in Toy, gives the reading, "There are friends for mere companionship"—27[10c]). Friendship develops character (27[17]). Poverty is a severe test of friendship; it may alienate fair-weather friends (19[4, 7]). Wisdom counsels to beware of friends who are sponges (19[4, 6]). On the other hand, remember that friendship is not merely an anchor to windward. Work out your own salvation (27[10b]—Toy indicates that the lines in 27[10] are not properly parts of a single sentence, but disconnected lines dealing with the same theme; each is to be taken by itself). Friendship lies deeper in the being than professions in words; loud declarations of friendship may even cast doubt on the sincerity of the tie (27[14]).

Friendship appears to be an important theme in the estimation of our writers, if we may judge by the scope of their lines. They give counsel as to the preservation of friendship. Beware of gossip about your friends (16[28] 17[9]); some slander may injure them in your sight. Old tried friends deserve your loyalty (27[10a]). Avoid friendship with an irascible man

($22^{24, 25}$). True friends overlook occasions for quarrel (17^{9}; cf. 10^{12} 16^{28}). Let not friendship become so close that it becomes wearisome (25^{17}).

(2) *Brotherly Kindness.* The spirit of brotherly kindness pervades the book. Charity is exalted as one of the chief social virtues ($11^{25, 26}$ 14^{31} 21^{26} 22^{9} $28^{8, 27}$). Social cleavages are recognized as existent, particularly between the rich and the poor; but the writers' sympathies are with the oppressed and poor (16^{19} 17^{5} $22^{2, 16}$ 29^{13} 30^{10-14}). The spirit of Proverbs rises to superb heights in its ideal of love toward one's fellow men, even toward enemies (17^{13} 20^{22} $24^{17, 18, 29}$ $25^{21, 22}$). The verse last cited has become a commonplace wherever the Bible is known by reason of its vigorous imagery (see Mt. 5^{38-45} and Rom. 12^{19-21}, notes). The most poignant suffering that a vengeful man's hand might work upon his enemy could not as swiftly touch the citadel of his hostility and capture it as the satisfaction of the enemy's needs. Love and kindness toward an enemy are the most satisfactory kind of vengeance. Social frictions are deplored. Strife is termed the conduct of fools (20^{3}).

(3) *War and Peace.* While war and the more extended frictions of the social order, the strife of nation with nation, are not in the direct line of their vision, yet the writers of Proverbs have laid down the basic principles which point the way to peace and comity. War had not been outlawed (20^{18} 24^{6}). That a nation should have a conscience, however, and should study its march in the world to conform its steps to wisdom even as the individual is advised to do—this appears to have been the mind of the sages (14^{34}). It is not beyond possibility to say that they would have approved the extension of their advice for individuals to the broader sphere of national relationships.

(4) *Government.* The book recognizes the authority of social control as this is expressed in government. Monarchy was the typical order of those days. The right of the king to rule is unquestioned, but even the king is subordinate to God on high (21^{1} 29^{26}—"justice" is preferable to "judgment"). Revolutions are frowned upon as social upheavals ($24^{21, 22}$). Like Paul, they would say that constituted authorities are of God (Rom.13^{1}); revolution that is violent and destructive is often fatal even to the revolters. The way of amelioration of conditions lies in working within constituted channels of appeal for reform. A king must be righteous and a follower of wisdom (16^{12} 20^{28} 28^{15} $29^{4 \text{ mg. } 14}$). The virtues which should adorn the common man are the true crown of royalty.

(5) *Practice of Wisdom.* Our modern life is not ordered like that of the ancient world in which this book took form; but the basic principles of life by which the solution of moral problems may be achieved now, as then, are written upon the pages of this work. Wisdom is not a body of knowledge, nor a book of rules. It is an achievement through the discipline of an intellectual struggle. As one learns to play a game only by playing it, so with all helps of books and teachers, after all, a man learns wisdom by practicing it. "We learn to do by doing."

"Blessed is the man that heareth me,
Watching daily at my gates,
Waiting at the posts of my doors.
For whoso findeth me findeth life,
And shall obtain favor of the Lord.
But he that misseth me wrongeth his own soul:
All they that hate me love death" (8^{34-36}).

ECCLESIASTES

By Professor GEORGE L. ROBINSON

Introduction

Title. The name "Ecclesiastes," which comes to us from the Septuagint Version through the Latin Vulgate, means, literally, "a member of an assembly." It was doubtless intended to express in Greek the equivalent of the Hebrew name *Koheleth*, i.e., "master of an assembly" (cf. the similar phrase in Eccl. 12^{11}). In form the term *Koheleth* is a feminine participle, and is closely related to the noun "kahal," meaning "an open assembly," or an assembly which embraces what is "under the sun." Hence, as Kuhn has recently suggested, there may be embedded in the very title of the book the idea of a revelation which is only partial, the author knowing more than he is willing, or even able, to tell. The Targums hint of this deeper interpretation.

Author and Date. The author of *Koheleth* was a Hebrew philosopher, or Wisdom-sage, who lived probably quite late in Jewish history and endeavored to impersonate King Solomon. He writes as a theistic-agnostic, giving in his book a bit of his own biography. Both his language and his ideas point to the late Persian, or, more probably, to the Greek period, prior to the Maccabean uprising. He could not have been Solomon himself; for he tells us that he *was*, not *is*, king in Jerusalem (1^{12}), that the government is bad, that the king is despotic, the judges are corrupt (3^{16}), oppression reigns (4^{1-3}), bribery is rife (5^{8}); everything is crooked (1^{15}), and that society in general is in a deplorable state. Living in the midst of such conditions, *Koheleth* pours forth one long drawn out and bitter lament of pain and disappointment, because there was no escape from present misery either in this life or in that to come. The author's allusions to local conditions, however, are all so general and indefinite, that it is impossible to date his book with absolute certainty, but it is reasonable to conclude, from the hints we have, that it was not composed until long after the Exile, probably shortly before 200 B.C., as the author of the apocryphal book of Ecclesiasticus seems to have known Ecclesiastes (see Eccl. 8^{13} and Ecclus. 1^{13}, etc.; cf. pp. 196–7).

Purpose. *Koheleth's* obvious aim was to state rather than to solve the difficulties of life. Living amid confusing civil and social conditions, his one chief object seems to have been to discover the true value of life: Is life worth living? What profit, or net gain, can be expected? What is man's highest happiness? What is the *summum bonum*, the advantage, the surplus, the profit of all? *Cui bono?*

The author employs three synonyms to express the idea of profit, or net-gain: *yithron*, used six times (1^{3} 2^{11} 3^{9} $5^{9,\ 16}$ 10^{10}), *kishron*, used once (5^{11}), and *yother*, used twice ($6^{8,11}$). This particular concept is obviously the key-thought of his whole book; his estimate of life taking, as in Job $1^{9,\ 10}$, the form of a "profit-and-loss" account. Such an idea was wholly germane to any discussion of *Hokhma*, or "Wisdom"; for, to the Hebrew mind, "Wisdom" was a matter of economic concern, wisdom and profit being closely allied. Ecclesiastes is pre-eminently a book of wisdom (cf. $7^{11,\ 12}$ 8^{1} $9^{16,\ 18}$ 10^{10}).

Contents. Though the book is particularly difficult to analyze, yet one general idea, with something of an inherent dramatic element running through it, dominates the whole. As the late G. B. Gray observed, "It resembles Job more than Proverbs, and is fundamentally the work of a single writer devoted to a single theme." For, though different voices are constantly being heard in it, the book is no mere anthology or collection of separate and unrelated thoughts. Rather the author catalogues his varied moods of pessimism, hedonism, sophism, and faith; his method being that of an inductive philosopher who explores every possible field of knowledge before he draws his conclusion. In all, he makes some four separate quests for the *summum bonum*, or real profit, in life.

1. *The quest of wisdom*, practical wisdom; or as we might say, "sociology" (1^{12-18}). Like the good Arabian Khalif Haroun al-Raschid, he studies, first hand and in a practical way, the common miseries of men of all classes, and he discovers with tragic anguish of soul that crooked things cannot be made straight, and that in much wisdom is much grief (1^{15-18})—apart from God!

2. *The quest of pleasure* (2^{1-11}). *Koheleth* in pain and disappointment turns from wisdom, or sociology, to pleasure and enjoyment; very much as Goethe's Faust, who, having failed to solve life's riddles by study, plunges deep in delights, that he may thus "still the

burning thirst of passionate desire." Not, however, as a vulgar sensualist indulging himself in every excess, but as Solomon, building for his own enjoyment beautiful palaces, and surrounding himself with lavish luxuries, singers, servants, etc., all that royal wealth could buy. But, alas! pleasure and opulent ease bring him, as wisdom did, only pain and disappointment—apart from God!

3. *The quest of labor and riches* (2^{18}–6^{12}). *Koheleth* next devotes himself to labor and money-making. Surely honest toil, he thinks, ought to bring satisfaction; for was not labor ordained in the Garden of Eden before the fall? But in this quest also he is again woefully disappointed; and for manifold reasons: (a) the uncertainty of having a wise successor to inherit his fortune (2^{18-23}); (b) one's lot in life, which is wholly in the hands of an all-powerful and arbitrary God (3^{1-15}); (c) injustice in the law courts (3^{16-22}); (d) oppression, and no comforter (4^{1-3}); (e) competition (4^{4-6}); (f) the fact that money, after all, fails to satisfy (4^{7}–5^{12}); (g) that hoarded wealth is often lost through speculation and bad investments (5^{13-17}); (h) but especially the fact that a rich man is sometimes denied by Providence the power to enjoy his possessions (6^{1-12}). And so, in view of all these obstacles and discouragements, he at last gives up the quest of obtaining happiness through riches, declaring, as in the cases of wisdom and pleasure, that all is vanity and a striving after wind, endeavoring to win any real profit through the acquisition of money—apart from God!

4. *The quest of fame* (7^{1}–11^{8}). "A good name is better than precious ointment" (7^{1}). This quest *Koheleth* does not develop, or pursue, as we might expect; yet he does realize and comment on the emptiness of human praise (7^{5}), and discourses at great length on the relative values of wisdom and folly; e.g., wisdom censures, while folly flatters (7^{5-7}); wisdom is patient, i.e., is independent of public sentiment, folly feeds on what people think and say, and is therefore proud (7^{8-10}); wisdom is a defense (7^{11-14}); wisdom avoids extremes (7^{15-18}); wisdom is strength (7^{19-22}), and is exceedingly rare even in men, but entirely wanting in women (7^{23-29}); wisdom is patriotic (8^{1-9}); wisdom often goes unrewarded (8^{10}–9^{6}); wisdom works joyfully (9^{7-10}); wisdom, indeed, is often the victim of time and chance ($9^{11, 12}$), and is soon forgotten (9^{13-16}), loving peace, while folly loves war (9^{17}–10^{4}); yet wisdom is often triumphant (10^{5-7}); wisdom, accordingly, is "profitable to direct" (10^{8-11}), and speaks graciously, whereas folly talks foolishly (10^{12-15}); in short, wisdom is the attribute of kings (10^{16-20}), penetrates the future, encourages faith, and gives true perspective to life (11^{1-8}). Apart from God wisdom is impossible!

Koheleth's Philosophy of Life. Throughout the book *Koheleth* is obsessed with certain convictions which are forced upon him by his own experience and observation. One is that "all is vanity," i.e., human endeavor is absolutely without result. There is no net gain or surplus possible, anywhere. Another is that there is nothing better than to eat and drink and enjoy life as its blessings come and go, for this is man's divinely appointed portion; but the power to do even this is from God. A third is that there is no progress in the world, no evolution possible. All things move in a circle accomplishing nothing. There is nothing new under the sun; and nothing can be transmitted by one generation, or by one individual, to another. Still another postulate of his philosophy is that death ends all. Yet man's spirit is forever striving to transcend its earthly sphere. Accordingly, *Koheleth* yearns for the continuation of life, for immortality, that he may reap the rewards and conserve the gains of right living here. But, though he ardently longs for immortality, he does not actually discover it until near the very end of his struggle; when he finally exults in the revelation that, while the dust returns to earth as it was, *the spirit shall return unto God who gave it* (12^{7}); cf., however, v. 8, which makes it clear that v. 7 brings no real satisfaction to the author; the context suggests that the author has in mind, not individual immortality, but reabsorption—the body to the earth, the spirit to God—which means the disappearance of the individual. No wonder he considers this also "vanity". Kuhn, indeed, finds repeated hints of immortality throughout the book (cf. 3^{17} 6^{12} $8^{12f.}$ $12^{1-8, 14}$); but his interpretation is hardly justified by the language itself, by the immediate context and by the general thought of the book.

Unity. According to some scholars, few books have been edited and redacted, revised and supplemented, as often and as much as the book of Ecclesiastes. The grounds for thinking so are the apparent contradictions and anachronisms (some not as real as supposed) which are patent to every thoughtful reader. Yet it must be acknowledged that the modern idea of redacting and re-editing has, in the case of Ecclesiastes, been considerably overworked. While there are doubtless some interpolations and possible dislocations in the original Hebrew text of the book, it surely is not necessary to find so many different editors, as some allege, to account for them. As Barton wisely observes, "When a modern man realizes how many different conceptions and moods he himself can entertain, he finds fewer authors in a book like *Koheleth*." Many different theories have been advanced to account for the facts. Burrows has recently suggested that Ecclesiastes "may have originated, like some of the prophetic books, in a disciple's notes of his master's sayings." This, he thinks, would account for "the lack of orderly arrangement, the frequent recurrence of similar ideas, and the presence here and there of epigrammatic remarks having no direct connection with what precedes or what follows them." But whether this be so or not, the author was neither a cogent reasoner in the modern sense on the one hand, nor a conceited agnostic on the other; neither was he a cynic, nor a reformer, a Stoic, an Epicurean, a Buddhist, nor a scoffing unbeliever; but he was a frank and sincere interpreter of his own personal doubts, and he exhausted every possible experiment at his disposal to solve his difficulties. After all is said, the book of Ecclesiastes is a self-consistent exposition of common everyday skepticism, honestly presented and confessed, and just as sincerely and frankly answered and refuted in the light of an unswerving faith in God. *Koheleth* himself must have been a mature and experienced man.

Value. Primarily, the book of Ecclesiastes attempts a new theodicy, a new view of God's providence. To *Koheleth*, as to all other Hebrew sages of antiquity, "Wisdom" meant the recognition of God's world-plan for the individual and for society; and he answers the question, Is life worth living? by pointing to the Sovereign-God, urging young people to remember him while still in youth, and commending all men to fear him and keep his commandments. *Koheleth* was a child of his time; a voice crying in the night. But by crying he prepared the way for Christianity by showing the need of it. Had he known "Christ and the power of his resurrection," as Paul did, instead of crying, "Vanity of vanities, all is vanity," he would have shouted, "Value of values, all is of value in the light of Him who brought life and immortality to light!" The permanent value of Ecclesiastes, accordingly, consists in this: *Koheleth* faced one of the great questions of life, namely, Is life worth living? It is a question which still haunts the great majority of the human race, and one which cannot be answered except in terms of a reverent faith in an all-wise and all-loving God.

Literature: Plumptre, *Ecclesiastes* (Cambridge Bible); Cox, *Ecclesiastes* (Expositor's Bible); Streane, *Ecclesiastes, or The Preacher;* Martin, *Ecclesiastes* (New Century Bible); Barton, *Ecclesiastes* (International Critical Commentary); Tyler, *Koheleth;* Wright, *The Book of Koheleth Considered in Relation to Modern Criticism;* Cheyne, *Job and Solomon;* Genung, *Ecclesiastes and Omar Khayyam; Words of Koheleth; The Hebrew Literature of Wisdom in the Light of To-day;* Dillon, *Skeptics of the O.T.;* Scott, *Pessimism and Love;* McFadyen, *The Wisdom Books in Modern Speech;* McNeile, *Introduction to Ecclesiastes.*

CHAPTER I

1. The Title. *The Preacher*—debater, or orator; all possible English equivalents of the Hebrew name *Koheleth*, which is, of course, a suggestive term coined by the author for the occasion (see intro., section on "Title," and cf. 1[12] 7[27] 12[8-10]).

2–11. The Introduction. Announcing the Preacher's main inquiry or chief concern, namely, Is life worth living when there is no profit, or net gain, and there is no remembrance of one after death? *Vanity of vanities, all is vanity.* Thus *Koheleth* opens his so-called "symphony of pessimism," repeating these melancholy words like a knell, some forty times in all. What he means is that life is empty and without profit—apart from God! *There is no new thing under the sun* (v. 9). The phrase "under the sun" occurs some twenty-five times. Life is a weary monotony, an endless treadmill! New discoveries are but rediscoveries (v. 10; cf. 3[15]). Man's spirit transcends his sphere. *Koheleth's* soul longs for immortality (v. 11).

12–18. The Quest for Wisdom. *Koheleth* first seeks through wisdom for the *summum bonum*, or highest happiness. The author here impersonates Solomon, who, as a rich king, possessed the necessary resources to investigate and experiment, to travel far and to exhaust all possible sources of wisdom. By *wisdom* he means practical wisdom, especially God's plan for each individual life: "God's world-plan," or Providence. In ancient Israel there grew up a class of *Hokhma*, or "Wisdom" writers known as "the wise" (Jer. 18[18]), alongside the priests and prophets, who as philosophers cared almost nothing for the ritual of the former, and quite as little for the distinctively national ideals of the latter, but who interpreted life from the human point of view, and accordingly are sometimes spoken of as "the Humanists of Israel" (see art., *Poetic and Wisdom Literature*, p. 157). But *Koheleth* in his search for practical wisdom found that *crooked* things could not be made straight—apart from God, and that all his searchings were but *vanity and a striving after wind.* This last phrase, "a striving after wind," is a very strong expression, occurring seven times in the book (1^{14} $2^{11, 17, 26}$ $4^{4, 6}$ 6^{9}), and signifying, literally, "a feeding on wind," hence a disappointing desire. In v. 16 there is an obvious anachronism, inasmuch as David alone preceded Solomon as king in Jerusalem. *Koheleth* finds it difficult to impersonate King Solomon (cf. $2^{7, 9}$). In 2^{12} he gives it up altogether, dropping the mask of royalty which he had assumed at the beginning (1^{12}). His pathetic wail in v. 18 over his failure in not finding happiness in the investigation of "wisdom" reminds one of the Arabic proverb, "A wise man is never happy." Cf. Matthew Arnold's lines on Goethe:

"And he was happy, if to know
Causes of things, and far below
His feet to see the lurid flow
Of terror, and insane distress,
And headlong fate, be happiness."

CHAPTER II

1–11. Koheleth's Second Quest—through pleasure. Turning from wisdom to wine, the Sage plunges into all sorts of sensuous delights; not, however, as a vulgar sensualist. In v. 2 there is a touch of Buddhism, which teaches that if men would avoid disappointment and pain they must crucify their inordinate desires. Like Solomon, *Koheleth* built for himself beautiful palaces and secured concubines and servants very many, but his satisfaction was only superficial and temporary; for when he took an inventory of all his joys and pleasures derived from this source, all was emptiness, and there was no surplus or net gain in reserve. And so pleasure, like wisdom, failed utterly to satisfy—apart from God!

12–17. Wisdom and Pleasure. *Koheleth* pauses before making a third experiment to compare wisdom and pleasure; and he finds that while the one excels the other as far as light excelleth darkness, yet one event happeneth to them all, namely, *there is no remembrance forever* (v. 16). Both are equally a disappointment—apart from God! And so he concludes, "I hated life, because all was emptiness and a feeding upon wind." Life's compensations were altogether inadequate; the preacher's soul still yearned for something higher.

CHAPTERS 2^{18} TO 6^{12}: KOHELETH'S QUEST FOR HAPPINESS THROUGH WORK AND WEALTH

Since God ordained labor in the Garden of Eden before the fall, surely labor, *Koheleth* reasons, ought to yield happiness and satisfaction worth while. But alas, he finds that even labor and riches fail to secure genuine happiness, for various reasons:

18–26. The Uncertainty of Having a Wise and Worthy Successor. This is the first of eight obstacles to happiness. In view of this uncertainty the author recommends the sober enjoyment of life while it lasts. From the ancient Hebrew point of view, there was nothing foreign or Epicurean in such an attitude, but rather the general and accepted dictum of Hebrew monotheism (cf. Jer. 22^{15}). Material and physical enjoyments may be fleeting, but they are nevertheless real, and they are the gifts of God. *Koheleth* reiterates this teaching (cf. 3^{13} $5^{18f.}$ 8^{15} 9^{7}); for who can enjoy himself apart from God? (V. 25, mg., LXX reading.) V. 26 is regarded by some as wholly "discordant" with and as "totally opposed" to the other teachings of the book; but *Koheleth* ought surely to be allowed to discriminate between a moral life and one that is not!

CHAPTER III

1–15. Hopelessness of Struggle Against an Arbitrary God. A second obstacle in the way of obtaining happiness through labor and money-making is the fact that one's lot in life is wholly in the hands of an arbitrary God. This section, consisting of fourteen couplets, teaches that business success depends upon whether the times are propitious, and that only God can make them so. Everything is transient and temporary; what profit, therefore, in laboring for gain! God has even *set the world* in man's heart, *so that man cannot find out the work that God hath done from the beginning even to the end* (v. 11). The word *olam*, here translated "world," is used in later Hebrew in the senses of both "cosmos" and "eternity"; elsewhere in Ecclesiastes it is employed in the latter sense only, and so it seems preferable to render it as "eternity" here, as is done in the text of A.S.V. (cf. R.V. mg.). The author's aim was probably to set "eternity" over against "time" (the word "time" occurring some thirty times in the book). In v. 12 the thought of *doing good* is to be understood in the sense of enjoying life! And in v. 13 the idea of food and drink as "the gift of God" is anything but Epicurean! Being a reverent theist (v. 14), *Koheleth* found in God's unchanging purpose sufficient warrant to trust him.

16–22. Injustice in the Law Courts. The third obstacle to obtaining satisfaction and happiness through labor and riches was injustice in the law courts: *in the place of judg-*

ment, wickedness was there. This was true probably of both church and state. Some reject v. 17 as a later interpolation, on the ground that the original author never regards God as vindicating the godly; but it is better to allow that future retribution was one of the fundamental teachings of *Koheleth* (8[12, 13]; cf. 12[14]). God at least disciplines men to *prove them,* and to show *that they themselves are but as beasts;* both men and beasts alike being victims of chance (v. 19, mg.). Besides, *all go unto one place*; or, in the language of Lucretius, "Nature is the womb and tomb of all." There are other passages in Ecclesiastes, like these, which seem to intimate that *Koheleth* had lost completely all hope of immortality; but other O.T. saints did so too (Psa. 49[12, 20]). He does not explicitly deny that man's spirit may go upward; he only doubts it. In the end his skepticism on this point seems to vanish (12[7]); but the substitute proves equally disappointing, as before.

CHAPTER IV

1–3. Oppression. This is a fourth obstacle to thwart him in his quest. *And they had no comforter.* This so aroused *Koheleth's* feelings of compassion that, like the suffering patriarch (Job 3[11-16]), he *praised the dead which are already dead more than the living which are yet alive; yea, better than them both,* as Cicero and Sophocles also felt, is it never to have been (cf. 6[3] 7[1]).

4–6. Competition. A fifth obstacle is competition and envy—envy being but another form of oppression, for it can be as inhuman as tyranny. But inasmuch as the business man cannot altogether retire from the field, let him shun the rivalries and jealousies of the struggling business world; and, "having food and raiment, let him therewith be content."

7–16. Disappointment in Riches. The fact that riches do not satisfy is the sixth obstacle to *Koheleth's* struggle for satisfaction through wealth. The miser is never satisfied (4[8]; cf. 5[10]); in vv. 9–12, on the other hand, by means of a series of proverbial sayings, *Koheleth* shows the profitable advantages of business partnership. The school of Epicurus emphasized a similar type of friendship; but there are no distinct proofs of dependence of the one upon the other. This section closes with the familiar and oft-quoted maxim, *a threefold cord is not quickly broken.* This maxim, of course, should not be forced to refer either to the Trinity or to Paul's celebrated trilogy of faith, hope, and love (cf. 1 Cor. 13[13]). The continuation and conclusion of this section of the argument is found in 5[10-12], separated from these verses by a series of unrelated and miscellaneous utterances.

Verses 13–16 seem to point to some definite historical person, like Alexander Balas, or Ptolemy Epiphanes, who as youths rose up and usurped their thrones. Moffatt's translation of this section is most suggestive; its moral being that usurpation and anarchy avail nothing, inasmuch as even royal treasures are fleeting.

CHAPTER V

1–12. Miscellaneous Injunctions. In vv. 1–7 rash vowing and sham religion are condemned; because *God is in heaven,* and therefore transcendent, and it is impossible to bribe him. In attempting to bribe God by rash vow-making, the lips involve the whole body in sin; and an apology to the priest, or Temple-recorder, will be expected. Rather, he says, *fear thou God;* this being the second of a series of six references to "fear" in the book (cf. 3[14] 5[7] 7[18] 8[12, 13] 12[13]). To Hebrew wise men, "the fear of God" was the portico of "wisdom" (cf. Prov. 1[7]).

In vv. 8, 9, *Koheleth* encourages patriotism by exhorting his readers to trust in Providence, despite the fact that government officials, one rank above another, all accept bribes and are guilty of oppression; because, says he, *there is one higher than the high who regardeth, and there be higher than they* (referring to the king). In v. 9, he probably means that "it is in every way an advantage to a land to have a king devoted to the cultivation of the soil," as McFadyen translates it.

13–20. Unfortunate Investments. *Koheleth's* seventh obstacle to finding happiness through the acquisition of wealth is that large fortunes are often squandered through unfortunate investment and foolish speculation, causing bitter regrets. Better be less ambitious, and enjoy what you already have. To enjoy present good, indeed, is the gift of God (v. 19; cf. 3[13] 1 Tim. 6[17]). He who thus lives has less to guard, and he will not brood over the brevity of life (cf. Prov. 15[15]). "The miser is the Devil's dupe."

CHAPTER VI

Inability to Enjoy Riches. The eighth and last obstacle which seriously confronted *Koheleth* in his search for the *summum bonum,* through labor and wealth, is the fact that a rich man is sometimes denied by Providence the power to enjoy his riches. The strain and stress of obtaining them robs him of his ability to enjoy them (cf. 2[22, 23]). *If a man beget an hundred children,* and lives, cramped and unhappy, and dies without friends, *an untimely birth is better than he.* It is suggested that *Koheleth* here may refer to Artaxerxes II (Mnemon), king of Persia, 405–358 B.C., who is said to have had more than one hundred and fifteen sons, one of whom was Artaxerxes III (Ochus), who, after reigning twenty years, was assassinated and his body thrown to the cats. The burials of Jezebel and of Jehoiakim were likewise tragic (cf. 2 Kings 9[35] Jer. 22[19]). What *advantage* have such? asks *Koheleth;* and he answers, *Better is the sight of the eyes than the wandering of the desire* (v. 9); in other words, "A bird in the hand is worth two in the bush." Moreover, mortal *man* cannot cope with the fixed decrees of his Maker, but lives hemmed in by fixed and inexorable rules, and his fate is sealed in advance. Here *Koheleth* borders closely on sheer fatalism, but Isaiah and Paul also approximate this philosophy of determinism (cf. Isa. 45[9] Rom. 9[20]).

And so he concludes his long, vain search for happiness and profit along the line of labor and money-making by confessing, with pathos, that man's days of labor and toil are after all but a shadow, because there is no hereafter. So sorely disappointed is he that he seems again to abandon, temporarily at least, all hope of immortality.

Chapters 7[1] to 11[8]: Koheleth's Quest for Happiness Through Fame

While the principal thought of the section is as indicated in the heading, various other matters are touched upon; especially are there repeated glorifications of wisdom and descriptions of the folly of wickedness.

CHAPTER VII

Fame—Wisdom—Folly—Wickedness. He begins, *A good name is better than precious ointment;* punning on the Hebrew *shem,* "name," and *shemen,* "ointment." Plumptre, trying to reproduce in English the Hebrew paronomasia, translates, "A good name is better than good nard!" *Koheleth* adds, *And the day of death than the day of one's birth.* Herodotus tells of certain Thracians who were accustomed to meet and bewail a child's birth because of the woes and sorrows which it faced in life, while they buried their dead with joy and gladness, because they were at last set free from evils. This practice can be traced back also to primitive Buddhistic custom. *Koheleth* continues, *It is better to go to the house of mourning, than to go to the house of feasting.* Surely, one who speaks thus is no vulgar sensualist, no Epicurean. Jewish mournings lasted from seven to thirty days, affording ample opportunity for reflection on death. *Sorrow is better than laughter:* an aphorism which finds a reflection in the Greek proverb, "To suffer is to learn." *For as the crackling of thorns under a pot, so is the laughter of the fool.* Here again the author puns, this time on the Hebrew words *sirim,* "thorns," and *sir,* "pot"; the play upon words has been expressed in English thus, "as the crackling of nettles under a kettle!" In v. 10 a sentimental question, characteristic of old men, as to why *the former days were better than these* is discouraged. The ancient Greeks and Romans, like the Chinese, used to ask the same foolish question. In v. 22 *Koheleth* appeals to conscience (though the *word* "conscience" never actually occurs in the O.T.) when he affirms, *oftentimes also thine own heart knoweth.* In v. 28 he voices the ancient Oriental opinion of women (cf. 1 Cor. 7[27] 11[8, 9]); it was left for Jesus to give woman her true place. But even our author encourages honorable marriage as a source of happiness (9[9]).

CHAPTER VIII

Obedience to Rulers—Inequalities of Life. V. 2 is regarded by many as a hint of the date of the book: *keep the king's command, and that in regard of the oath of God.* It is supposed to point to the case of Ptolemy Soter (332–285 B.C.), who carried into Egypt large numbers of Jewish captives and bound them by solid oaths of fealty. V. 8 warns the readers that *there is no discharge in the war* against death. V. 10 describes how wicked men are often buried in great pomp; whereas good men are even excluded from the Holy City, and soon entirely forgotten. Vv. 12 and 13 are by some deleted from the original text of *Koheleth,* because they emphasize the fear of God; but it seems somewhat arbitrary to exscind all such passages (cf. 3[14] 5[7] 7[18] 12[13]).

CHAPTER IX

Mystery of God's Doings—Uncertainties of Life—Superiority of Wisdom. In ch. 9 the author reverts to the thought of death. He says, *All things come alike to all;* e.g., earthquakes, tempests, pestilences, and the like; just so death, which sweeps away all distinctions. *Neither have they any more a reward; for the memory of them is forgotten.* There is evidently an intended assonance here between the Hebrew word *seker,* "reward," of the first clause, and the Hebrew word *zeker,* "memory," of the second. Oblivion following death was to *Koheleth* the tragedy of life (cf. 1[11] 2[16]). Consciously or unconsciously he shared the pagan conception of "hope"; which, according to the myth associated with "Pandora's Box," was the last article to fly out, and of all the contents of that mystic chest it was the most disappointing of all—the acme of vanity! According to v. 6, even the three strongest and most vehement passions of man—love, hatred, and envy—are all destined to be hushed in the silence of the grave.

Still, says *Koheleth*, though death is the only fixed outlook man has, he should enjoy sensation and sunshine while they last. Therefore, *live joyfully with the wife whom thou lovest all the days of the life of thy vanity*, and, *whatsoever thy hand findeth to do, do it with thy might;* thus he lauds quiet home life, and encourages honest toil. His allusion to *Sheol*, "the grave," in v. 10, is his only reference to the place of the departed in the book. Continuing his induction, he finds that *the race is not to the swift*, alluding possibly to the contests of the Greeks; but the Greeks were not the only people of antiquity who possessed runners (cf. 2 Sam. 18[19-23]). And he also finds that *time and chance happeneth to them all;* "chance" being employed here in the sense of misfortune, or of "occurrence," as in 1 Kings 5[4]. Man can no more foresee his own fate than fishes caught in a net can anticipate their doom. In vv. 13–16 the author seems to have in mind some definite historical event such as the siege of Dor (1 Macc. 15), or, possibly, of Abel (2 Sam. 20[15-22]).

CHAPTER X

Wisdom—Charity—Industry. In v. 2, when the author affirms that *A wise man's heart is at his right hand, but a fool's heart at his left*, he does not intend to teach that there is a physiological difference in the bodies of fools and of wise men; he rather refers to their conduct. The Romans, however, seem to have accepted such a view, taking the language literally, for they called left-handed deeds "sinister" (cf. Mt. 25[31-46]). In v. 3 *Koheleth* tells us that the fool fancies everybody he meets is a fool too; while in v. 4 he advises any one who has offended his superior not to retaliate, or resign, but to defer to him, on the principle that "the least said is soonest mended." "Blessed are the meek!" His mention of *horses* in v. 7, according to Grieve, is an indication of late authorship; but Solomon is said to have had "forty thousand stalls of horses" (1 Kings 4[26]; cf. 2 Chr. 9[25]). Graetz imagines that *Koheleth's* reference to *servants upon horses* points to the reign of Herod the Great as the time of composition; but, as Barton observes, "almost any period of Oriental history must have afforded such examples."

In his continued praise of "Wisdom," our author declares that wisdom is profitable to direct both the woodsman to sharpen his blunt ax, and the snake charmer to avoid being bitten (v. 11); wisdom furnishes foresight. "Success depends upon foresight," says an ancient proverb. Fools, on the other hand, multiply words, their verbosity being the measure of their capacity. Ask a fool, for example, the way to the city, and his wordy, verbose, round-about directions will only confuse you. With true patriotism, *Koheleth* adds that a country is to be pitied when its king is a servant, or a usurper. Alexander Balas and Herod the Great are only two of many of ignoble birth. Feasting and wine-bibbing bring revelry; money squandered is the cause of both. *Curse not the king*, even a bad ruler; for "walls have ears" and "treason will out!"

CHAPTER XI

Generosity and its Reward. An enigmatical word of counsel, teaching benevolence: *Cast thy bread upon the waters.* Whether *Koheleth* had in mind the grain ships sent out from Alexandria to Rome and elsewhere in search of markets, or the custom in Egypt of sowing seeds upon the waters of irrigation, it is impossible to say, but he probably intended to teach benevolence. The added advice in v 2 confirms this interpretation: *Give a portion to seven, yea, even to eight;* i.e., Do not restrict your gifts to a selected few, for you don't know how soon you will need charity yourself. As the fixed and inexorable laws of nature encourage faith in the farmer, so they ought to encourage faith in the deeper things of God. In the chemical laboratory of the American University at Cairo a Moslem student woke up one day to the fact that, if like causes in nature always produce like effects, then Allah cannot be fickle and capricious after all, but trustworthy; his discovery in science completely revolutionized his theology.

In v. 7 *Koheleth* divests himself of his accustomed pessimism, and begins to recognize the supreme joy in just living. For he now sees that the days of darkness are sent in order to make men reflect. For vv. 9, 10, see under 12[1-8].

CHAPTER XII

1–8. Remembrance of God in Youth. (Including also 11[9, 10].) The book closes with a characteristic answer to *Koheleth's* oft-repeated inquiry, What profit is there in life? He proffers two noteworthy suggestions, namely, to *rejoice* (11[9]), and to *remember* (12[1]). In 11[9, 10], he advises to make the most of youth, through a joyful use of all that youth affords, but to do so conscious of a final reckoning; in 12[1-8] he advises to remember also the Creator in youth, before the storms of life overtake and all appetite for God vanishes because of the infirmities of old age. The latter section is highly allegorical and symbolic. To the Oriental such figures and symbols spoke with far more naturalness and force than they do to us.

Vv. 1, 2 describe a sirocco, or a hurricane. Vv. 3–7 describe the gradual breaking down of the physical body, and the inevitable effects of senility. *The house* probably refers to the physical body; *the keepers of the house* are the hands, which often shake and tremble in old age; *the grinders* are the teeth, which become fewer as the years pass; while *those that look out of the windows* are the eyes, which frequently grow dim toward the end of life. *The doors in the street* are the ears, which often lose their keenness in riper years; and *the daughters of music* are the failing vocal cords of those who sing. *The almond tree* may hint at the appearance of gray hair; and *the grasshopper* may symbolize any trifling weight which to old people seems heavy; while the *caperberry* probably suggests an artificial stimulant to failing appetite. In a similar manner *the silver cord* may refer to the spinal cord; *the golden bowl*, to the skull or cranium; *the pitcher*, to the heart; and *the wheel broken at the cistern*, to the prostate gland, or other abdominal parts, which so frequently give way during failing years. And then follows the climax of the whole book, which was a new revelation to *Koheleth;* not that *the dust returns to the earth* was new, but that *the spirit returns unto God who gave it.* At last *Koheleth* has discovered immortality in God. Like Job, he won the victory of faith (Job 19[25]). After a long life of struggle and doubt he has been given a new revelation, and it seizes hold upon him. Yet still he wails, *Vanity of vanities, all is vanity*, probably because all earthly gains and achievements, profits and emoluments (apart from God) are empty and disappointing. (But see intro., section on "Koheleth's Philosophy of Life," p. 615, for a more probable interpretation.)

9–14. Some Closing Exhortations. Vv. 9–14 are by many regarded as an editorial postscript to the book; while others, like W. P. Paterson, regard them as "very probably genuine." It is certainly strange that an author should speak of himself in the third person, and commend his own literary ability and wisdom, as is done in vv. 9–12. On the other hand, it has been suggested that vv. 13, 14 contain the only worthy conclusion to the whole argument. *Koheleth*, like Bacon, was an inductive philosopher. Having finished his inductions and investigations, he lifts up his voice, as it were, and announces: *This is the end of the matter; all hath been heard; fear God and keep his commandments; for this is the whole duty of man* (v. 13). These words are something more than an "orthodox conclusion," added by those who wished to secure for the book an entrance into the canon of Scripture; they constitute the principal teaching of the book—"the wisdom of God" *par excellence.* The word *duty*, which is printed in italics (because it has no Hebrew equivalent), can well be sacrificed for one that is far more characteristic of the entire book, namely, "profit," which, as we have seen, occurs in different synonyms some nine times. "Fear God and keep his commandments," says *Koheleth*, "for this is the whole profit of man!"

For God shall bring every work into judgment. This last sentence of the book contains the clearest statement concerning judgment in the O.T. According to *Koheleth*, life is an apprenticeship, one long, but not endless, discipline. To fear God, therefore, and keep his commandments is the very essence of the divine discipline, and the only way to wisdom and immortality. Let a young man remember his Creator in youth, and he will naturally continue to fear God and keep his commandments all through life, and when he dies his spirit will return unto God who gave it. On the other hand, as Thomas Fuller remarks, "Short preparation will not fit us for so long a journey."

THE SONG OF SONGS

By Professor ROBERT H. PFEIFFER

Introduction

General Character. The Song of Songs is a poem or a collection of poems depicting, with enchanting imagery, consummate literary skill, and a rare appreciation of nature's charms, the thrilling anticipation, the rapturous delights, and the exquisite torments of two lovers. Its theme is the love between a man and a woman, blooming in the meadows and vineyards of Palestine at the coming of spring, described with a fullness of detail and a naïve and spontaneous freedom of expression that are truly Oriental. This superb composition found a place in the sacred canon through an allegorical interpretation of the book on the part of Akiba and other rabbis living at the end of the first century A.D., although at that very time irreverent young people, not able to appreciate any hidden meaning, were singing it "as a kind of secular song" (*Tosephta Sanhedrin*, xii).

The Allegorical Interpretation. Only by detecting a deeper meaning under the plain sense of the book could it be classed as sacred scripture. The Jews at least as early as 90 A.D. saw in it an allegory of the love between Jehovah and Israel (cf. 4 Ezra 5[24, 26]), an interpretation fully developed in Targum and Midrash and adopted substantially by Augustine and Luther. In a Christian form (the love of Christ for the church) this view was presented by Hippolytus, Cyprian, and, in more recent times, Hengstenberg (cf. the chapter headings in the A.V.). More numerous are the Christian interpreters who see in Canticles (name derived from the Latin) not an allegory of the Old or of the New Covenant, but of the mystical relation of the individual soul with God or with Jesus Christ (Origen, Theodoret, Bernard, Madame Guyon). In our own day the religious interpretation has reappeared in an entirely new form: the book is said to be a pagan litany used in the worship of Osiris (N. du Jassy) or of Tammuz (Adonis) and Ishtar (Astarte) (W. Erbt, T. J. Meek); this view is criticized by N. Schmidt in the *Journal of the American Oriental Society*, vol. xlvi, pp. 154f.

The Literal Interpretation. Theodore of Mopsuestia (+429 A.D.) was the first writer to protest against the allegorical interpretation; and although he and others agreeing with him in later centuries were declared heretics, the literal interpretation has now become prevalent. Modern interpreters adopting the historical point of view regard the book either as a drama or as a collection of lyrics dealing with human love. Origen (about 300 A.D.) defined it as "a nuptial poem composed in dramatic form"; and since Jacobi (1771) the work has been fully dramatized in many conflicting ways by Stæudlin, Umbreit, Ewald, Boettcher, Delitzsch, Hitzig, Renan, Stickel, Oettli, Bruston, Driver, A. Harper, L. Cicognani, Adeney. A close examination of these attempts reveals the inherent weakness of the dramatic theory (for details see Eiselen, *The Psalms and Other Sacred Writings*, ch. 6).

The simplest and most natural interpretation, which is adopted here, is that Canticles is an anthology of love lyrics rather than a single poem, a collection of songs which Herder (who in 1778 first presented this view) aptly compared to a string of pearls (cf. pp. 19–20). Wetzstein (1873), after observing the wedding festivities among Syrian peasants, came to the conclusion that our book consisted of nuptial songs: for seven days after the wedding the bridegroom and the bride are enthroned as king and queen (cf. 3[11]); their charms are praised in extravagant terms; dances and sports are carried on before them, and the bride herself occasionally gives a short dance to display her queenly attire. This alluring interpretation was accepted by Stade, and fully developed by Budde, who was followed by Kautzsch, Siegfried, Cheyne, Jastrow, Bewer, and many others. It has been confirmed by the publication of Syrian and Arabic wedding songs, and by a comparison with ancient Egyptian and Assyrian love poems (a catalogue of the latter has recently been found; it is translated by Meek in the *Journal of Biblical Literature*, vol. xliii, pp. 245f., and by Barton, *Archæology and the Bible*, 4th edition).

It should be noted, however, that the book is not a haphazard collection, for there are throughout the song suggestions of a certain literary unity. Whatever the origin or original form of the individual songs may have been, they were probably worked over and put in their present form by one editor, whose aim was "to present a ritual to be used in the wedding ceremonies that would be both noble and chaste . . . While they do not adequately present the sanctity and beauty inherent in our modern ideal of marriage—for that ideal was unknown to the East—they do extol nobly and exquisitely the sanctity and beauty of true love between man and woman. Nowhere in literature has this divine passion been more beautifully described than in the words which the bride addresses to her husband as she enters his home, thereby making complete the marriage relation:

'Love is as strong as death;
Jealousy is as irresistible as Sheol;
Its flames are flames of fire,
A very flame of Jehovah.
Many waters cannot quench love,
Nor can floods drown it.' "

Date of Composition. If we admit that the book is a collection of folk songs recited at rural weddings, it is clear that they must have circulated orally long before they were published in written form or collected in an anthology. It is not unlikely that some of the material embodied in the book existed in pre-exilic times when Hebrew was still the vernacular. If in some form the songs were not older than the editor who published them, they would not have been in Hebrew. However, the presence of Aramaisms compels us, on linguistic grounds, to date the existing collection not earlier than 250 B.C., when Aramaic was the spoken language. Without attempting to distinguish the original songs and the editorial matter, as Jastrow does, we must admit that there are glosses (e.g., the word "bride," *my bride* in R.V., 4^9-12^ 5^1^) and marginal interpolations (according to Cornill: 2^9a^ 4^8^ 8^3, 4, 13, 14^).

Literature: Griffis, *The Lily Among Thorns;* Haupt, *The Book of Canticles;* Jastrow, *The Song of Songs;* Eiselen, *The Psalms and Other Sacred Writings;* Martin, *Proverbs, Ecclesiastes and Song of Solomon* (New Century Bible).

CHAPTER I

1. The Title. This *editorial superscription* characterizes the book as the most beautiful of the songs of Solomon, who was, according to 1 Kings 4^32^, the author of one thousand and five songs. On the real date of the book see the introduction.

Chapter 1^2-8^: Songs of the Bride Longing for her Bridegroom

2–4. Love's Yearning. The joys of love are associated, in Oriental fashion, with wine (4^10^ 7^9^) "which cheereth God and man" (Judg. 9^13^) and fragrant perfumes which "rejoice the heart" (Prov. 27^9^). The maiden pictures herself as the chosen one of a glorious monarch (the rustic husband), beloved by his (imaginary) women of the harem (cf. Psa. 45^14f.^). With slight emendations we should probably read *Kiss me with the kisses of thy mouth. . . . Bring me, O King, into thy chambers.*

5, 6. An Apology. Forestalling a criticism of the fair ladies of the harem (*daughters of Jerusalem*), the peasant girl explains that she is sunburnt because her brothers sent her to keep their vineyards at harvest time. She is dark like the tents woven by the Bedouin (*Kedar*, a son of Ishmael, Gen. 25^13^, is the poetical name of the Arabian nomads) out of goat's hair, but beautiful like the draperies of Solomon's palace. Brothers were, in the ancient East, the protectors of their sisters (Gen. 24 and 34; 2 Sam. 13) and had much authority over them. The heat in the vineyards was so intense that watchers made themselves booths (Isa. 1^8^; cf. Job 27^18^). Keeping their vineyard, she could not watch her own, i.e., safeguard her fresh complexion.

7, 8. The Rendezvous. The scenery shifts from the dream world of the royal harem in Jerusalem to the bride's familiar environment. The shepherdess asks her lover where he pastures his flock; he suggests that she follow the tracks of the sheep. She addresses him as *thou whom my soul loveth* (3^1-4^); he calls her the *fairest among women* (5^9^ 6^1^). *My soul* is a Semitic idiom meaning "I myself" (cf. Lk. 12^19^). In the heat of noontime (cf. Gen. 31^40^) the sheep rested in the shade of trees (Virgil, *Georgics* iii, 328–335). *One that is veiled:* the Versions render, by inverting the order of the first two Hebrew consonants, *one that wanders* (cf. mg.). Where she dreaded to be seen, wandering in search of him, is just where she will find him.

Chapters 1^9^ to 2^7^: Bride and Groom Praise Each Other

9–11. The Bridegroom Sings the Beauty of the Bride. He compares her to a noble mare; her jewelry is like the trappings of a royal steed. Such a comparison was not offensive to the ancients and was used by Theocritus, Anacreon, and Horace (Homer, *Iliad* xxii, 21–24, compared Achilles to a winning race horse). Amos (4^1^), however, is by no means complimentary when he addresses the ladies of Samaria as "ye kine of Bashan" (cf. Jer. 2^23f.^). The kings of Egypt ("Pharaoh" in Egyptian means "great house") were famous for their horses (Gen. 41^43^ Ex. 15^4, 21^, etc.); in Egypt and in Babylonia horses were unknown until 2,000 B.C.; although horses were known in Canaan at the time of the Exodus (cf. Judg. 5[22]) the Israelites did not use them before Solomon (1 Kings 4[26] 10[26]). The maiden had pendants in the form of coins hanging down from the head on the forehead and on the cheeks; on Hebrew jewelry see Isa. 3[16f].

12–14. The Reply of the Bride. She compares the charm of her beloved to the fragrance of sweet-smelling spices: steeds and chariots appeal to the man (vv. 9–11), perfumes to the woman. *Spikenard* is a perfume of great price (Mk. 14[3-5]) obtained from Palestinian herbs (4[13f.]); Horace calls it Assyrian nard, Tibullus calls it Syrian nard. *Myrrh* is an aromatic gum resin obtained by incision of a shrub growing in Arabia. The maiden carries the thought of her beloved in her heart just as she wore on her bosom a bag of myrrh. *Henna-flowers* are Palestinian (see Josephus, *Wars of the Jews*, iv, 8.3) and have clusters of yellowish blossoms; a toilet water is prepared from the leaves and roots. *En-Gedi* is a luxuriant oasis west of the Dead Sea.

15–17. A Duet of the Lovers. (Continued in 2[1-3].) The bride sings 1[16,17] 2[1, 3]; the bridegroom sings 1[15] 2[2]. *Thine eyes are as doves* seems to have been added from 4[1]. The words of vv. 16b, 17 can be understood literally of the couch of fresh grass out in the cedar forest, or imaginatively of the luxurious bed, fragrant like green grass from perfumes sprinkled on it (Prov. 7[17]), in the renowned "house of the forest of Lebanon" of King Solomon (1 Kings 7[2]). The meaning of the Hebrew word translated *rafters* is unknown. *Sharon* is the maritime plain between Cæsarea and Joppa (Isa. 33[9] 35[2] 65[10]). The *lily* was a wild red flower admired by Jesus (Mt. 6[28-30] Lk. 12[27f.]) for its gorgeous beauty.

CHAPTER II

1–3. With becoming modesty the bride compares herself to common wild blossoms, but the bridegroom turns her words into a compliment by contrasting the lily with the thistles; not to be outdone, she likens him to the apple tree, and longs for its cool shadow and its pleasant fruit, an allusion to the protection and joys of matrimony.

4–7. The Banquet; a Song of the Bride. The description of the feast in the house of wine over whose door hung the sign *Love* is an allegory of the delights of love. The playful adjuration in v. 7 (a sort of refrain appearing again in 3[5] 8[4]) by graceful wild animals may be compared with the humorous oaths of Socrates "by the dog" or "by the goose."

Chapters 2[8] to 3[5]: Reminiscences of the Bride

8–17. A Serenade in the Springtime. Once upon a time, when she was retiring for the night, her beloved sang before her house a song of spring and of love. To his invitation to follow him she modestly requested him to return in the morning. (1) **8, 9.** The arrival of the youth. His haste is pictured with poetical exaggeration (cf. 2 Sam. 2[18]). In v. 9 we should probably read *I looked out of the windows, I glanced through the lattice* (cf. Judg. 5[28]). (2) **10–15.** The song of the youth. This is the only instance in which direct speech is introduced in the book. This song is a delightful description of the coming of spring and reveals a delicate feeling for the charms of nature. *Winter* and *rain* are synonymous terms, for there are really only two seasons in Palestine: the dry (April-September) and the rainy season (October-March). The signs of spring are the singing of birds and the budding of plants. The *turtle* (turtle-dove) is a migratory bird (Jer. 8[7]) whose return is a sign of spring. The *vines* in blossom are not very fragrant; perhaps we should read (with 7[13]) "the mandrakes give forth their fragrance." The maiden, invisible behind the lattice, is compared to a dove in inaccessible places (Jer. 49[16] Obad. v. 3; cf. Jer. 48[28] Ezek. 7[16]); she is called *my dove* as in 5[2] 6[9] (cf. 1[15] 4[1] 5[12]). V. 15 introduces the one disturbing element in this idyllic picture of spring: the *foxes* that gnaw at the vines in bloom (cf. v. 13), a parallel to the ancient fable of the fox and the green grapes. (3) **16, 17.** The song of the maiden. In v. 16 (=6[3]) she speaks to herself; in v. 17 to her beloved. She tells him to come back swiftly at dawn. The meaningless *mountains of Bether* should probably be read, after the parallel verses (4[6] 8[14]), "mountains of spices."

CHAPTER III

1–5. A Dream of the Bride. Missing her beloved when she awoke at night, she searched for him in the city until she found him (cf. 5[2-8]). While going about in the dark narrow streets and in the wide city squares, she came across the watchmen (cf. Isa. 21[8, 11] 62[6] Ezek. 33[6] Psa. 127[1] 130[6]). Finding her beloved soon afterward, she brought him to her *mother's house:* maidens lived in special quarters with their mothers (Gen. 24[28]) or with other women (Gen. 24[67]); the various wives had separate dwellings (Gen. 31[33]). On v. 5 see 2[7].

Chapter 3[6-11]: The Palanquin of Solomon

This song describes, with elaborate imagery, the rustic wedding procession: the bridegroom,

King Solomon, accompanied by his friends, *three-score mighty men,* went to fetch the bride, who was brought with the bride's maids, the *daughters of Zion,* to the house of his parents (see Psa. 45^8-15 1 Macc. 9^37-41 Mt. 25^1-12).

6–8. The Procession Approaching in the Distance. As clouds of dust are perceived in the direction of the pasture lands along the Jordan someone asks: "What [not *who*] is this?" It is the sedan chair of Solomon (i.e., the young peasant bridegroom), fragrant with myrrh, incense, and all the powdered spices of the trader (cf. Psa. 45^8 Prov. 7^17). Sixty friends of the bridegroom, twice as many as Samson had (Judg. 14^11), armed with swords, protect the "king" against nightly perils (usually imaginary, but sometimes real: see 1 Macc. 9^37-41).

9–11. Description of the Palanquin and of the King. The *pillars* supporting the top are covered with silver, the framework of the seat is of gold, the cushion is of *purple* (crimson), the inside is inlaid (mg.) or plated with ebony (not *with love;* this error occasioned the addition of the gloss *from the daughters of Jerusalem*). The bridegroom was crowned like a king (Isa. 61^10; cf. intro.) by *his mother* (in Euripides, *Iphigenia in Aulis,* 905, the mother crowns her daughter as bride).

Chapters 4^1 to 5^1: The Lover Sings the Charms of the Maiden

CHAPTER IV

1–7. The Beautiful Features of the Bride. The description of the bride extends to minute details. The comparisons are highly imaginative and, to Western readers, farfetched. **1–3.** Eyes, hair, teeth, lips, and temples are compared with doves, goats, ewes, a scarlet thread (Josh. 2^18), and a crack on a pomegranate (or a grain of the same). **4, 5.** The neck and the breasts are compared to the tower of David (cf. Neh. 3^25-27?) and to the twins of a gazelle. The coins strung on a necklace around her neck (1^10f. 4^9) are like the shields hanging on the wall (cf. Ezek. 27^11 1 Macc. 4^57). **6.** Possibly an interpolation of 2^17 with some changes. **7.** The summary of vv. 1–5, recalling the beginning (v. 1a). Or should we read v. 7 before v. 6?

8. Invitation to a Maiden Living in the Hills. The scenic beauty of *Lebanon* (cf. 3^9, etc.) is celebrated in Isa. 60^13 Hos. 14^5 Zech. 11^1. *Amana* is the peak from which the river of the same name (Abanah in 2 Kings 5^12, now Barada) flows to Damascus. *Senir* is the Amoritic name of Hermon (Deut. 3^9). Amana and Senir occur with these meanings in the Assyrian records.

9–11. Insane With Love. With one of her eyes (6^5) and with the amulets hanging from her necklace (1^10f. 4^4) she has bewitched him, robbed him of his senses, driven him to distraction (the *heart* in the O.T. is the seat of the mind). On v. 10 see 1^2f.; on v. 11a cf. Prov. 5^3. **11.** This verse describes the sweetness of the kisses rather than of her words (contrast Psa. 119^103). Garments were perfumed with aromatic herbs (Gen. 27^27 Psa. 45^8).

12–16. The Enclosed Garden. (See also 5^1.) **12–15.** The bride belongs exclusively to her beloved; she is like a locked park, like a sealed spring. Springs were often closed with large stones (Gen. 29^2, 3 2 Sam. 17^18f.) and could conceivably be sealed (cf. Deut. 32^34 Dan. 6^17 Mt. 27^66 Rev. 20^3). The comparison of the wife with a fountain is more fully developed in Prov. 5^15-19. Garden and spring are parts of the same picture (Isa. 58^11): *a fountain of gardens* means a garden fountain. In connection with the garden the poet mentions valuable plants: pomegranates (4^3 6^7, 11 8^2), henna with spikenard (1^12, 14), saffron (crocus), calamus and cinnamon (ingredients of the sacred oil, Ex. 30^23), frankincense (Ex. 30^34f.), myrrh (1^13), aloes (Psa. 45^8 Prov. 7^17 John 19^39). **16.** The maiden uses the image of the garden to express delicately her wish to be with her beloved; he replies (5^1) with eager enthusiasm. The bride invites the winds to blow upon her garden (i.e., herself) and carry its fragrance to her beloved so that he may come to enjoy its fruits. He welcomes the suggestion, comes into his garden, gathers his spices, and eats his honey. *My spice*=my balsam (mg.): Josephus relates that this plant was introduced into Palestine by the Queen of Sheba (*Antiquities,* viii, 6:6); and he states that he has seen it thrive by Jericho (xiv, 4:4) and En-Gedi (ix, 1:2). *Eat, O friends,* etc., is incongruous in the mouth of the bridegroom; if the clause is not interpolated, it must be addressed by the wedding guests to the bridal couple.

CHAPTER V

1. See above under 4^12-16.

Chapters 5^2 to 6^3: The Lost Bridegroom

2–7. The Search: a Dream of the Maiden. (Cf. 3^1-5). The youth knocked at her door one night, but had vanished in the dark when she opened to him. Vainly she looked for him in the city: the watchmen treated her with contempt, for no respectable woman would be seen wandering alone at that hour. This recollection of the bride is best explained as a dream (so also 3^1-5): while this happened she was sleeping but her mind (*heart,* cf. on 4^9) was awake, dreaming, unless we should suppose that the maiden was a sleepwalker (Cicognani). When the young man knocked and asked the maiden to open she was sleeping after removing her tunic, which was worn directly on the person (the outer garment served as a bed covering for the poor, Ex. $22^{26f.}$) and after washing her feet before retiring (Gen. 19^{2} 2 Sam. 11^{8}), for she went barefoot during the daytime (shoes, 7^{1}, are part of the bridal apparel). The young man introduced his hand through a hole in the door (for the key or for looking out) apparently to pour in the liquid myrrh (cf. Lucretius, *The Nature of Things*, iv, 124f.), that stuck to her hands as she opened the door. The youth did not have the persistence of the man in Lk. 11^{8} and withdrew after she teasingly excused herself. *My soul . . . when he spake* seems to belong after v. 4.

8, 9. A Message. Meeting the daughters of Jerusalem (1^{5} 2^{7} 5^{16}, etc.) she requests them to tell her beloved that she is faint with love ($2^{5, 7}$); they ask for his description.

10–16. The Handsome Traits of the Bridegroom. As in the parallel description of the bride ($4^{1f.}$), the features are mentioned from the head downward. He is white and ruddy (Lam. 4^{7}), conspicuous among a myriad. His head is like fine gold (cf. Dan. 2^{32}); his locks are bushy (palm branches?), raven black; his eyes are like doves (1^{15} 4^{1}) by canals of water, perched on the rim (of a pool); his cheeks are like beds of balsam (5^{1}) raising perfumes (cf. LXX); his lips are like lilies (2^{1}); his hands are like jewels set with topaz (mg.; in Hebrew "Tarshish," a gem imported from that city in Spain); his body is like a slab of ivory; his legs are like marble columns; the whole of him is like Lebanon, choice (tall) like cedar trees; his mouth (palate, mg.) is like bonbons (or a sweet drink, Neh. 8^{10}).

CHAPTER VI

1–3. The Lover's Whereabouts. To the inquiry of the daughters of Jerusalem the maiden replies that her bridegroom is in his garden (5^{1}). This section seems to contradict the preceding ones in which the maiden was vainly searching for the youth, but strict logic should not be expected in imaginative poetry of this kind.

Chapters 6^{4} to 7^{9}: Songs Describing the Beauty of the Bride

4–12. The Charming Features of the Maiden. **4–7.** These verses are closely parallel and in part identical with 4^{1-7} ($6^{5b-7}=4^{1b, 2, 3b}$). The comeliness of the maiden is compared with the beauty of *Tirzah*, the capital of the Northern Kingdom from Baasha to Omri (1 Kings 15^{33}, etc.), and of *Jerusalem*, the capital of the Southern Kingdom. Tirzah is here chosen instead of Samaria on account of the meaning of the word ("pleasant") and on account of the bitter feelings of the Jews toward the Samaritans (Jn. 4^{9}; cf. Ecclesiasticus $50^{25f.}$). *Terrible* (vv. 4, 10)—on account of her bewitching eyes (v. 5, cf. 4^{9}). **8, 9.** She is more precious to the lover than a whole royal harem (cf. 1 Kings 11^{3}), just as his little vineyard is dearer to him than the opulent plantations of Solomon ($8^{11f.}$). The maiden is the only daughter in her family, but she has brothers (1^{6}). **10–12.** These verses do not seem to belong to their immediate context; Jastrow transposes vv. 11 and 10 (in this order) after 6^{3}; v. 12 is unintelligible in the Hebrew and probably corrupt. **13.** See under 7^{1-9}.

CHAPTER VII

1–9. The Dance of the Bride. (Begins with 6^{13}.) In 6^{13}–7^{5} the wedding guests sing the beauty of the dancing maiden, describing her features, not from the head downward, as elsewhere ($4^{1f.}$ $6^{4f.}$), but beginning with the feet, the most conspicuous part in a dancer, and moving upward. Naturally, the diction is far less restrained than in those other songs which confine themselves to the upper part of the body. The dance *of Mahanaim* (6^{13}, "the two camps" or better, with LXX and Vulgate, *of ham-mahanim*, the camp or war dance) is probably identical with the sword dance, still a part of the wedding festivities in Palestine (Wetzstein, cf. intro.). *Shulammite*—elsewhere in the O.T. *Shunammite* (1 Kings 1^{3}, etc. 2 Kings $4^{12, 25}$), a woman from Shunem (now Sōlem); the beauty of Abishag the Shunammite had evidently become proverbial and "Shulammite" is used here as a synonym of *fairest among women* (5^{9} 6^{1}). *Return*—turn around. *Why will ye . . .* What will ye see in the Shulammite as she engages in the military dance? The question in v. 13b should probably be changed to bring it in line with v. 13a. **1–5.** *Sandals* (v. 1)—cf. on 5^{3}. *Prince's daughter*—in Palestine the rural bride is still called daughter of a nobleman. *The joints of thy thighs*—better "the circling of thy thighs" (in dancing). *Jewels*—chain, necklace (Prov. 25^{12} is the only other passage in which the word is used). The allusions in v. 2 are of questionable taste; on v. 3 cf. 4^{5}. *Neck*—cf. 4^{4}; *eyes*—cf. 4^{1} 5^{12} (1^{15}). These *pools* are still in existence northwest of Heshbon. *Bath-Rabbim*—either a gate of Heshbon (meaning "the daughter of multitudes") or a village near by. *Tresses*—the

Hebrew word means "watering troughs" and is obscure in this context. **6–9.** The bridegroom compares the bride to a palm tree; his tone is more passionate than in the similar songs (4^{9}–5^{1}). *Love*—means probably "my beloved." *Palm*—the date-palm; Homer likewise compares Nausicaa to a palm tree (*Odyssey*, vi, 162f.); cf. Psa. 92^{12}. *Branches*—"panicles" (the Hebrew word occurs only here in the O.T. but is known in Assyrian). *Smell of thy breath*—literally, "of thy nose"; should probably read *the breath of thy nose. Wine*—cf. 1^{2} 4^{10}. *Of those that are asleep*—is meaningless; with a slight change of the text the ancient versions read "gliding through *my* lips and *my teeth.*"

Chapters 7^{10} to 8^{7}: Love Songs of the Bride

10–13. Love in the Springtime. See 2^{8-14}. V. 10 is an echo of 2^{16} 6^{3}; cf. Gen. 3^{16} 4^{7}. *Villages*—the same Hebrew word in 4^{13} means "henna" blossoms; with a slight change it could be read "vineyards" (cf. v. 12). Palestine had few walled cities and numerous villages (Deut. 3^{5}; Tacitus, *Histories*, v, 8). On v. 13 see 6^{11}. *Mandrakes*—cf. Gen. 30^{14}. *Precious fruits*—cf. $4^{13, 16}$.

CHAPTER VIII

1–4. "Oh that thou wert as my brother!" Then she could enjoy his company without fear of scandal, and even kiss him before people (as cousins could do, Gen. 29^{11}): the wish is pure and maidenly. *Mother's house*—cf. 3^{4}. *Who would instruct me*—neither this nor the rendering of the margin is satisfactory; LXX reads, with 3^{4}, *and into the chamber of her that conceived me.* The Greeks also knew the wine prepared from the *juice of pomegranate.*

5. Two fragments, without connection with the context: the first seems to be a variant of 3^{6}; the second is difficult (the maiden awakens the youth sleeping under the apple tree where he had been born).

6, 7. Love's Irresistible Power and Inestimable Value. Here the book reaches its climax; these verses deserve a place among the best amatory poetry of all times. The association of love and death, the picture of love as a flame, are well-nigh universal. *Seal*—worn, in Babylonian fashion, attached to a string around the neck (cf. Gen. $38^{18, 25}$) or as a ring on the finger (Jer. 22^{24}; cf. Gen. 41^{42} Esth. 3^{10} 8^{2}). *Jealousy*—cf. Prov. 6^{34}; some moderns translate "its passion." *The grave*—Hebrew *Sheol* (mg.), the pit wherein gather the shades of the departed: like a monster it opens wide its mouth (Isa. 5^{14}) and is never satiated (Prov. 27^{20} $30^{15f.}$). *Flame of the Lord*—is doubtful: it is the only occurrence of the divine name (here *Yah;* the versions omit it) in the book, and the expression is not common in Hebrew (in spite of "the fire of the Lord," Num. $11^{1, 2}$ 1 Kings 18^{38}). Possibly we should render "its flames are . . ." (a word accidentally omitted).

Chapter 8^{8-14}. Miscellaneous Songs

8–10. An Incident of the Bride's Childhood. Her brothers (cf. $1^{5f.}$) wondered what they should do if she were asked in marriage (1 Sam. 25^{39}) when too young, and teased her about her immaturity; now she can mock them. The brothers decided to fit their actions to her behavior: *if she be a wall*—repelling suitors—they will raise the wall still higher, adding their watchfulness to her chastity; *if she be a door*—welcoming the advances of lovers—they will nail a plank of wood on the entrance, barring all access to her. The first alternative proved true: she was adamant to all allurements like a wall, her very charms were defensive fortifications, and thus she found favor in the eyes of her future husband.

11, 12. My Vineyard. The lover, rejoicing in the possession of his little vineyard, does not envy the vast estates of Solomon. *Baal-hamon* is otherwise unknown. *Keepers*—guards, not laborers. *Every one* . . . the Hebrew cannot mean that every keeper had to pay one thousand shekels to the king, but that a man, if he bought the whole produce, would have to bring in payment thereof one thousand shekels. We can get a conception of the vastness of this imaginary estate when we consider that a vineyard with one thousand vines was worth one thousand shekels (Isa. 7^{23}). *My vineyard*—means, of course, "my bride" (cf. 1^{6} 2^{15}; see also $4^{12, 15}$). *Before me*—under my authority and supervision: "I need no keepers for it (for the idiom cf. Gen. 20^{15} 24^{51} 47^{6}): Solomon has to pay one fifth of the proceeds of his vineyard to his keepers, but I have no such expense." Expenses and cares increase in a far greater ratio than one's holdings.

13, 14. The Bride's Final Song. While she is in the gardens she is asked to sing; she responds with a verse from an earlier poem (2^{17}; cf. 4^{6}).

ISAIAH

By Professor ROBERT W. ROGERS

Introduction

Admonition. The book of Isaiah is one of the longest books of the O.T. as it is also one of the most important. Its influence is not so great as that of the Pentateuch, for the Pentateuch has exerted an influence upon the religions of mankind without parallel in any other book. It is the foundation of Judaism, and the roots of Christianity and of Mohammedanism also draw supplies from it or rest upon its solid foundations of the knowledge of God. The influence of the book of Isaiah upon Christianity is less than the influence of the incomparable book of Psalms, for in all periods of its history the Christian Church has sung its way out of tribulation in the hymns whose matchless beauty, grace, and emotion have welled up wherever men rejoiced or suffered, despaired or hoped. But when the Pentateuch and the Psalter are set aside there need be little doubt that Isaiah ranks next in power over Christian thought. The earliest struggle of Christians to win Jews to their faith drew largely upon the Messianic portions of this glorious book. Isaiah himself was not so great a prophet as Jeremiah, for there are no words in any of his sermons so profound in their meaning, so clear in anticipation of the Lord's own message as the prediction of the new covenant (Jer. 31[31-34]), but Jeremiah even at his highest pitch of eloquence was not so great a wizard of words as Isaiah again and again in the early chapters. And if we spring over the historical section and add to these chs. 40–55, then there surge in a mighty sea of eloquence words so magical, so musical, and withal so full of moving thought as are not easy to parallel elsewhere in Holy Writ.

Yet great and full of majesty, dignity, and worth as is this book of Isaiah, taken as a whole it is in its entirety but little known among us, and especially in America is this true. At the Advent season Isa. 9 and 11 are wont much to sound forth among us, and at other times ministers of religion are oft impelled to read in public chs. 40 and 53 and 60, largely perhaps because 53 suggests so wonderfully the sufferings of our Lord, while 40 and 60 are so eloquent that even the deaf must hear their music and the dumb must repeat it.

But if the ministry confines its exposition almost wholly to chs. 9, 11, 40, 53, and 60, there is no need that all God's people should learn so little of this portion of the sacred Scriptures. To learn more is easy enough with a bit of patience, a leavening of perseverance, and a gift of continuance. Come now, O thou reader of a goodly and of a godly spirit, essay this pleasant and most profitable task, lay down this Commentary for the nonce, seize the O.T. in the Revised Version, shut yourself up from the world, and read the book through as a whole. Did you give a sigh of doubt before and a deep sigh of relief after? It may be so. There were hard spots, none too easy to understand. So you say, and you are right. I should be telling you that shortly, but it is much better to have discovered it yourself. Knowledge self-acquired is a rich acquisition. And what was the nature of these difficulties? There were certain words difficult to understand in their connections. That is true enough. To meet these difficulties commentaries have been written. But there were also difficult allusions to events long gone by; yes, and for the full explanation of these, historical knowledge is needful, and histories and commentaries have been composed. But as you read you came upon places where there seemed to be an enigmatic break in the connection of thought, which you caught up and connected somewhat later. Even so; and to meet this men have invented and almost perfected systems of literary criticism by which they are able, however imperfectly, to show that portions of the book are widely separated in the time of their origin, and there are books which expound these processes and make the book more surely intelligible. Now, read the book through again, and yet again, and for the fourth time. You are increasing gently and surely in knowledge now. You are discovering the ways of the Lord of the Scriptures. It is the Lord who has been speaking, but he has not been speaking in fire or thunder or earthquake, but in and through the words of men. These men lived and worked in history. God spoke through them in human history, and other men collected their sermons or addresses or their writings and preserved them for us. God did not miraculously preserve them from ill arrangements of the prophetic words, nor prevent the corruption of word or phrase by careless copyists. Many of the difficulties thus introduced have been successfully sought out and garnered for our instruction, and libraries have been written by learned men to set forth all that has thus been won. We who now live are the heirs of all the ages in biblical learning, and for few books has so much been done as for this book of Isaiah. Come, then, and let us make a beginning; let us ask those who have gone before to select for us from the mighty aggregations of learning so much as we can duly assimilate, wisely use, and completely make our own. Let us be content no longer with chs. 9, 11, 40, 53, and 60.

The Purpose of the Author of the Commentary. The author aims no higher than merely to introduce the beginner to the accumulated stores of knowledge which the years have assembled and made available for us. Every generation stands on the shoulders of its predecessors. It sees farther afield because other generations have labored and the newcomer enters into their labors, possesses their results. Yet must each generation make, so far as it may, its own contribution. Science, art, and letters must make some advance, somewhere, somehow, or the minds of men must stagnate and progress cease. This progress is, however, achieved almost always at the hands of a few leaders. Others must be content to garner their results and pass them on down the long oncoming line. Real originality is far less common than the half-crazed optimists who prate in every market place would have us imagine. Yet even if it be absent in any large degree, every individual must cultivate in himself whatever spark of originality may be his, and with it seek to increase his own judgment, learn how to use, not as a slave but as a free man, the results attained and promulgated by the great leaders of thought. To do this he must be modest, be willing to be taught the ABC of the subject, whatever it may be. When these have been learned, the foundations are laid, and the building of an independent structure may begin. But this cannot even be begun, much less finished, without individual effort, the exercise of personal thought, the assembling of one's own materials, the testing of the results of others, the subjecting of them to thoughtful searching criticism. The swallowing whole of the work of others is not an intellectual enterprise. The swearing by the word of any master, however great he may be, is not learning. Yet are we everywhere surrounded by the loud-voiced repetition of catch phrases, borrowed anywhere, ill assorted, ill digested, but all the more cocksure and final. This little commentary on the book of Isaiah is not intended for technical scholars, who having already found their way are now walking serenely therein. It is writ only for beginners in the study of this prophet. It makes no pretense of breaking new ground. Its author could with much less labor and concern have written for scholars. He might then have set long lines of Hebrew words and phrases in array, and have made unrestricted use of such new light as the labors of recent years have brought to bear upon them. Selection of materials would have been easy, the ordering of them a light task, the need of seeking to make them interesting hardly worth consideration. On the contrary, in a study such as the present, the writer must avoid tediousness as a plague, must leave out much that he would fain discuss, must try to catch the thing which may be difficult to some mind, without making the matter a bore to those who have advanced beyond the need of such exposition.

The Apparatus. He who now begins his serious study of the book of Isaiah must begin his work with one absolutely indispensable piece of working apparatus, and for some time to come needs only one,—the Revised Version of the Bible. But its possession without daily use is valueless. Knowledge comes to him who works for it; to none other is it granted. Nothing worth possessing comes without some drudgery. This is fully as true of the knowledge of the book of Isaiah as of any other book, any other subject. The first, the very first call to be made is a call to read again and again and yet again the book of Isaiah. It ought to be read through at a sitting; then the first thirty-five chapters should be read separately, not once but repeatedly; then the historical episodes in chs. 36–39; then the splendid chs. 40–55 over and over again; and finally chs. 56–66 also repeatedly. This is foundation work, and without it no independence in study is possible. He who has the will to do this, the courage to undertake it and the perseverance to complete it will some day know something for himself, and not merely because somebody else has said it. He is now really ready to read the pages which follow and to get profit of them. But before he does this, let him make one more serious resolve. Let him determine to seek out and read for himself the references to other parts of the book, and to other parts of Scripture, for only so will he be able to judge for himself whether this writer has judged rightly, or has leaped hastily and unwisely to conclusions. The reader who does these things, and not merely dreams of them, has already become a student, and his reward is sure. Mastery up to the full measure of his native ability will be granted him in due season.

A Word for the Courageous. If you are a reader who will do and dare, then come, follow on to know, delve deeper, read through slowly and methodically what is here written. Let it now be confessed that you will still not know much about this great prophetic book. For it is an encompassing book, a book of wide horizons and of mighty deeps. You will only have begun, but even though, for the present, you go no further you will have your reward, and will be able to take any other prophetical book with far greater ease. But if you decline to wander straightway into other fields, you will need to be advised where fuller and better knowledge may be sought. Let me then here set down the names of the greater books on Isaiah, but not a mere skeleton list, but a list with such description or characterization as will give you real light upon the rich literature already made available for you. From such a list you will be able to select what you will next read, whither future studies may well lead you.

Literature. The greatest commentary yet written upon the *Book of Isaiah* was the work of Franz Delitzsch, professor in the theological faculty of the University of Leipzig, written in the German language, and first published in 1866, and its fourth greatly revised edition in 1889. This fourth edition was translated into English and published in 1890. Delitzsch was the first Hebraist of his day, but he was much more than that, great though that was. He was a man of genius, and his grasp of religion, the religion of Judaism and the religion of Jesus Christ, was as emotionally rich as his knowledge was profound. He could indeed think, but he could also feel. His life was noble and ennobling, and into this great commentary he poured his whole great soul. I was his pupil forty years ago, and, as did hundreds of others, owed him a great gratitude not for mere knowledge but for inspiration and enthusiasm. His book is now superseded in many parts, for other questions have arisen which were not visible above the horizon in his day, but much of it remains as valuable as ever. Next in importance after the commentary by Delitzsch I should place that of August Dillmann, who took a commentary on *Isaiah* first written by Knobel, and prepared its fifth edition (1890) after the death of its author. Without a trace of impiety in handling the work of another, Dillmann contrived not only to bring its discussions up to the requirements of that day but also to stamp upon it the impress of his own distinguished personality, his exact scholarship, his patient, toilsome disentangling of fact from hypothesis. It was a great commentary when it left his master hand, and I who have been his student in the University of Berlin find it still a model of learning, cold at times, seldom, indeed, so warm as the work of Delitzsch, yet well worth close study. The sixth edition of Knobel-Dillmann was admirably revised by Rudolph Kittel in 1898, and all serious students value it still and count it better than before. These are the monuments of modern learning available for those who can use the German language. If that fail, let us ask what may be directly and immediately available in English. The one that deserves first to be named, chronologically at any rate, is a book by Thomas K. Cheyne, *The Prophecies of Isaiah*, whose first edition appeared in 1870, and the fifth in 1889. The later editions are in many respects less sound than the earlier, for Cheyne passed into and through a period in which ingenuity supplanted sobriety of judgment, and all his work though suggestive and often brilliant requires caution in the using. Next to be named is the remarkable book, *The Book of Isaiah*, in two volumes, by George Adam Smith (first published in 1889–90; new and revised edition, 1927) in the Expositor's Bible, which is not a commentary, but an exposition, and a book beyond all ordinary praise. It has insight, literary and spiritual appreciation, and is solidly based on sound learning. Let him who has made his way through this present work on the prophet Isaiah turn next to George Adam Smith. Then the next move should be to read the learned and critical commentary on *Isaiah* by John Skinner in the Cambridge Bible for Schools (1896–98), with which might well be used for comparison in places, *The Book of the Prophet Isaiah*, with introduction and notes, by G. W. Wade (1911) in the Westminster Commentaries. This will seem a long road to travel for one who is but now beginning. But he who has traversed this whole road will not only know Isaiah but he will have laid a solid foundation for a much more adequate appreciation of the whole body of prophetical literature. He will know something definitely. He will be able to talk or even write sensibly on this great book and he will have such an insight into the whole O.T. progressive revelation of God as will make the N.T. also a new book for him. Perhaps also he will inspire some boy to become a master in this fascinating and romantic field of learning, and so will perpetuate in another his own knowledge and enthusiasm. He could do few services greater than that for the Church of Christ among us in America. It is much to be regretted that there has not yet been produced by our American scholarship any large, deep, learned, and comprehensive commentary on the whole book of Isaiah. There have been popular commentaries, some of them sound and good, and there have been contributions to portions, expositions and suggestions here and there, but in a large way we still trail far in the rear of Germany and England. Perhaps some boy who reads these words will at last take away our reproach!

The Historical Background. We shall later see reasons for the confident assertion that the book of Isaiah contains in its present form many words that did not come directly from the preaching of Isaiah himself, but, however numerous or important they may be, the book owes its origins to Isaiah of Jerusalem, who began his prophetic work about 740 B.C., and continued it for forty years. Years of fate were they to his people, and his words, to be clearly understood, should be read against the background of the history in which he lived, in which he was an actor, and for which he toiled and suffered. To behold the man as he was in the times in which he lived we need to reconstruct his times as well as we may, and, matching knowledge with a trained and restrained imagination, seek both to see him and hear him. But to secure the picture we must go behind the days of his activity and see what was going on in the days of his childhood and youth.

Isaiah was partly contemporaneous with Amos and Hosea, of whom there is much to be read elsewhere under appropriate heads in this Commentary. It will be sufficient now to remind ourselves that Amos preached in Bethel in the Northern Kingdom about 760 B.C. during the reign of Jeroboam II, who was by far the greatest king alike in effort and result that the kingdom of Israel produced during the whole of its separate existence. Hosea preached also in the Northern Kingdom, probably between 746 and 734 B.C. The message of Amos was concerned with righteousness, and righteousness was the character of the God whom he preached to a wicked and adulterous generation. A message of greater tenderness and of a deeper religious experience was that of Hosea, for his emphasis was upon God as a Being of love. The men being different, the message from God must be different, yet was there no conflict between the two messages. Each saw truly what he did see and gave forth truly what God gave him to see and to know. Righteousness and Love are both alike attributes of our God, and both attributes needed declaration and emphasis. If Israel were but able to take the divine love into human breasts, and work out the divine righteousness in human word and deed, a new and better world would be forming. But for messages of such moment, of consequence so far reaching, the times were ill fitted. Amos spoke to a people full of the glory of victory and suddenly enriched by successful war. Jeroboam II had defeated the Aramæans, plundered their chief cities of Damascus and of Hamath, and the fruit of victorious war was expressed in corruption in high places, and in a ritualistic but unmoralized religious worship. To these people Amos preached a declaration of doom. Against them Amos declared that a fearful war was in preparation sent by a God of righteousness. He declared that this war would come against Damascus and Gaza and Tyre and Edom and Ammon and Moab and Judah and Israel. For such a war as that a mighty power would be required, strong enough to assail these nations one by one, and beat them into pieces. Amos knew that such a power already existed, but he did not name it. What he does say is this, "Therefore thus saith the Lord God: An adversary!—even round about the land: and he shall bring down thy strength from thee, and thy palaces shall be plundered" (Amos 3[11]). Amos knew full well what power this was, which should thus execute judgment upon Israel, for there are hints enough in his book to show he meant the Assyrians. Hosea knew fully as well that disaster was in preparation and spared nothing in a passionate description of it. Not even the eloquence of Amos could excel words like these: "Samaria shall bear her guilt; for she hath rebelled against her God: they shall fall by the sword; their infants shall be dashed in pieces, and their women with child shall be ripped up" (Hos. 13[16]).

The Assyrian Empire had but small beginnings in a territory only about twenty-five square miles in extent between the Tigris and the Lower Zab rivers. But it early displayed a genius for war; and the conquest of neighboring peoples, the acquisition of territory for expansion, and a threat against all western Asia were soon to be seen. About 1120 B.C. the Assyrians produced a great king who took the name or style of Tiglathpileser I, who made raids westward and was even said to have reached the Mediterranean. That would be sufficient cause for apprehension among the several peoples who carried on their political and social existence along the Mediterranean littoral and its hinterlands. But the Assyrians were not able to produce another such king as he had been until 885 B.C., when Ashurnazirpal III began to reign over them, and even more violently shook the western lands with plundering raids. Still more dangerous were the threats of his successor Shalmaneser III (859–824 B.C.), who set systematically about the task of subduing the western peoples and of plundering their possessions. Eleven or twelve of the small nations of Western Asia had the foresight to oppose him and the courage to unite and face him in a decisive battle at Karkar in northern Syria (854 B.C.). The Assyrian king has left us boastful accounts of a great victory and a heavy slaughter of his opponents. But it was a victory without evident or extensive results, and he was compelled to return to Assyria and recruit. At Karkar, among the kings who sought to save the west was no less a person than Ahab, king of Israel, who contributed two thousand chariots and ten thousand men. For his sad matrimonial alliance, and his weakness in suffering the religion of Israel to come into danger of corruption, the prophets of Israel, with the mighty personality of Elijah at their head, have covered him with denunciation, but as a national hero in the defense of his land and people we may justly give him praise and honor. Very different was Jehu (842–814 B.C.), who sent costly tribute to the Assyrian king, and so gave him the first deadly grip on Israel, which should never be wholly relaxed until the end of the little kingdom in 722 B.C. But that day was yet a long way off, and the Assyrians were not able to produce another such king as Shalmaneser III had been for many a day. But however deferred his day of coming might be, a virile people like the Assyrians were sure to produce another great king at some time. He came in 745 B.C. in the person of a man whose name had probably been Pul, or Pulu (2 Kings 15^{19}), a man of determined energy and of immense resources alike in war and in peace. He was not likely to miss any favorable opportunity for fishing in troubled waters anywhere, and, as the outlook for Assyrian ambition had long been westward, Syria and Palestine would be most tempting. The Phœnicians held a strip of seacoast which their commercial genius had made into centers of world trade, as were the Aramæan cities centers of land commerce; the Lebanon and Anti-Lebanon ranges between these two produced cedar coveted beyond every other wood; the plains of Jezreel and of Samaria possessed fertile stretches much superior to anything that the homeland of Assyria could boast, and they with Phœnicia formed a bridge by which the untold wealth of Egypt might be reached. All of this part of western Asia was divided among small peoples, each too weak to make any determined opposition to Assyrian aggression. These little states had indeed once made common cause for a few glorious years, about 854 B.C., but were now severed, jealous of one another, blind to the signs of the times, incapable of any serious common enterprise. The Assyrians under Tiglathpileser III would be ready to strike at any favorable moment.

If there were space, it would be easily possible to show that every one of these petty commonwealths of the West was ripe for Assyrian plunder, but for our present purpose it is chiefly Israel and Judah that must claim our attention. The kingdom of Israel had received a new impetus from the conquests of Jeroboam II, and wealth had flowed in an enlarging stream into it, but social and religious weakness had come with it or in its train. There were swift changes in the royal dynasties, the kings were weak and vacillating in their external policies, and the political disorganization of the country went on apace. In the Southern Kingdom, the kingdom of Judah, there were interesting parallels to the experiences of Israel. Nearly contemporaneous with Jeroboam II of Israel, Judah had a strong king in Uzziah (782 (?)–740 or 737 B.C.). Edom was conquered and the Red Sea port of Elath restored (2 Kings 14^{22}) and these successful moves gave Judah control over the rich caravan trade with southern Arabia. The revenue thus secured developed the resources of the country and much increased its military efficiency (2 Chron. 26$^{1-15}$). Judah was now as rich as Israel, and quite rich enough to be an object of cupidity to its neighbors. "The land was full of silver and gold, and there was no end of its treasures; the land was full of horses and there was no end of their chariots" Isa. 2^{7}). But as in Israel so also in Judah, prosperity brought incalculable evils in its train, both social and religious. Luxury and debauchery spread widely among the upper classes (Isa. 3$^{16-23}$ 5$^{11, 12, 22}$ 28$^{1-8}$ 32$^{9f.}$). Capital increased in the hands of the few, and the old landowners were gradually deprived of their little farms, which were replaced by great landed estates (Isa. 5^{8} Mic. 2$^{2, 9}$) and a destitute and oppressed lower class was formed. When Uzziah died, about 740 B.C., the times called earnestly for a strong voice to be raised against these conditions.

It seems, as we look back upon these events, that the leaders both in Israel and in Judah ought to have had vision enough to recognize Assyria as the great and growing danger, but there was not enough foresight in either kingdom to have grasped the situation. So has it been over and over again in every succeeding age. Few indeed were they who foresaw the coming of the Great War in our own day, or made any wise provision for its dangers. Assyrian power seemed far away, and when Shalmaneser III was dead there seemed to western observers to be no successor to him. Even when Tiglathpileser III ascended the throne there were some years without much threat in them. If men of vision had ruled in

Samaria and in Jerusalem, there might have been a different story to tell, but Jeroboam II was busy with the aggrandizement of his kingdom at the cost of the Aramæans, and Uzziah with the enrichment of his people at the charge of Edom. But there was much worse in store. The only hope for the perpetuation of independent kingdoms in Syria and Palestine was in union for defense against Assyria instead of a move which seems to us so obvious. Rezin (the name should really be written "Rezon"), king of the Aramæans (the people of Damascus), and Pekah, king of Israel, conspired to attack and plunder Judah. The scheme, mad enough for the minds of lunatics, was apparently begun in the reign of Jotham but came to full force in the reign of Ahaz, king of Judah. The latter was a weak man, and ought to have taken the advice of Isaiah, whose vision of events present and approaching extended beyond the borders of Judah. Ahaz could see only the immediate present and the pressing danger. He appealed to Tiglathpileser III for help against this coalition, and received it promptly. Tiglathpileser invaded Israel in 734 B.C., plunging through Gilead, Galilee, and taking captive some of the inhabitants of Naphtali (2 Kings 15[29]) and later took Damascus, and slew Rezon (2 Kings 16[9]). The effect was immediate. Rezon and Pekah had approached Jerusalem but were compelled by this move of Tiglathpileser to withdraw. Judah was saved, but at fearful cost. Ahaz went off to Damascus to pay homage to his deliverer, and Judah as well as Israel had by this shortsighted folly of the Judæan king been placed in a position of tutelage to the great king from the Tigris Valley. The Assyrians would duly draw the proper conclusions from these situations, and arrange to take profit from them. Henceforth Judah had to pay a heavy annual tribute to the Assyrian overlord, and the Assyrian kings knew well how to make their annual collections from states which had accepted their overlordship. In 727 B.C. the great Assyrian king died and Shalmaneser V became his successor. He was far from equal to Tiglathpileser III, and, as happened so often in Oriental history at a change in kings, rebellions began in various parts of the empire. Hezekiah was now king in Jerusalem, though uncertainties in the chronological material make it doubtful whether Ahaz had died and Hezekiah had succeeded him, or was still alive with Hezekiah acting as regent. The Egyptians were doing their utmost to foment disturbances in western Asia, hoping to profit therefrom, but there is no evidence that Judah yielded to them. In the Northern Kingdom, however, the case was entirely different. Hoshea was now king in Samaria, having been appointed to office by Tiglathpileser as an Assyrian vassal. He was so mad as to yield to Egyptian intrigue, having entered into treasonable negotiations with a petty Delta king in Egypt, whose name is handed down in the Hebrew text in the form So, but named Sibe or Sabe by the Assyrians, which implies that the Hebrew form should be Seve. Hoshea refused the annual tribute and Shalmaneser moved against him, received shortly his personal surrender and began a siege of Samaria. The little city held out bravely against great odds for nearly three years, and surrendered to the Assyrian army in 722–721 B.C. In that very hour Shalmaneser died and one of the greatest kings ever produced in Assyria took his place, assuming the ancient name of Sargon, and fit for any enterprise, as his great Babylonian namesake had been. He incorporated the kingdom of the Ten Tribes into the Assyrian Empire (2 Kings 17[3-6]).

But the people of Israel were not so easily mastered, and the small neighboring peoples in Syria gained sufficient support and encouragement to begin a very promising revolt. Had the Assyrian monarch been a man of less force and character, the West might have won at least a fresh breath of independence. But there was no reason to hope for such a happy issue when Sargon was on the throne. He came west and opposition crumpled before him. The last gasp of Israel as a separate kingdom had come, and the whole of Syria went down with it. Sargon penetrated the coast to Ashdod, about thirty-three miles west of Jerusalem, and took it in 711 B.C. (Isa. 20[1]), and at Raphia defeated the allied forces to which the Egyptians had made a contribution. Judah had most wisely remained neutral, and so secured another breathing spell, or she also would have then and there vanished out of independent existence. Sargon's period of reign was now soon to end, for in 705 B.C. he was dead and his son Sennacherib ruled in his stead.

Sennacherib inherited a vast empire, but many perplexities and dangers came with it. Babylon was a dangerous problem, for a skillful and energetic Chaldean named Merodachbaladan seized the city for his people, and by this *coup* encouraged the western peoples to rebel while Sennacherib was detained by eastern problems. The advisers of Hezekiah thought the hour propitious for an attempt to cast off the Assyrian yoke altogether. Flattery of the king, of his wisdom and supposed prowess in war, may have had something to do with his decision to join in a rebellion against the Assyrian overlordship, and to cut off the annual tribute. The Assyrians regarded the people of Ekron as the real leaders of the uprising, for they had seized their Assyrian governor, Padi by name, expelled him from office, and handed him over to Hezekiah for imprisonment. All these western peoples were more or less obsessed with the greatness of Egypt, and were ever ready to believe that help against the Assyrians might thence be derived. There could seldom have been less justification for any such hope than at that hour. For Egypt had lost its national unity and the land was divided, as it had been more than once before, under the control of pretenders who sought each to rule in his own nome or district, hoping that some chance might make him ruler over all the land. There was at least one competent observer of events in Jerusalem who knew that Egypt was in grievous danger of internecine civil war and therefore helpless to give aid. Isaiah saw the whole situation with amazing clarity of view and soundness of judgment, saying in God's name:

> "I will spur on Egypt against Egypt,
> and they shall fight,
> Every man against his brother and
> every man against his neighbor,
> City against city, and kingdom against
> kingdom" (Isa. 19[2]).

These would be sorry helpers in an uprising against a power so united and so well directed as Assyria. But the die was cast and Judah must take the consequences of her king's folly.

Sennacherib set his troops on the march and in 701 B.C. invaded the West, striking the Mediterranean coast at or near Tyre. He did not, however, attempt the reduction of the city, which would not have been possible without a naval force. Sidon was taken without a blow, and Ethobal was set up as its king, receiving authority as far south as Mount Carmel. This spectacular success over the Phœnicians alarmed the faint-hearted members of small states who had joined the coalition, who now sent deputations with gifts and promises of fealty. But in spite of defections in Arvad, Gebal, Ashdod, Moab, Ammon, and Edom the rest of the little confederation stood fast. Sennacherib pushed on down the coast, and took Ashkelon, carrying its king off as a prisoner to Assyria. So suffered also the towns of Beth-Dagon, Bene-barqa, and Azuru. The way was now open to the chief culprits in Ekron unless help came speedily. Strangely enough, a force did come out of Egypt but was quickly defeated at Eltekeh. Ekron was now taken and severely handled.

Then came Judah's turn. Sennacherib marched from the coast up the fertile valleys toward Jerusalem, claiming in his own official story to have taken forty-six cities. Jerusalem was blockaded, but not taken, and the great king contented himself with the picturing of the taking of Lachish upon slabs of stone used as wainscotting of his palace walls. He was, however, not leaving this as the sole record of his triumph, for on his most beautiful inscribed prism he has caused to be inscribed a full account of his punishment of these foolish rebels. It is a most remarkable result of the discoveries and investigations of our times that we should possess a contemporaneous account of these tragic events from the Assyrian point of view. Let us here set down, in translation, a small portion of the king's boasts, that we may relate it to the biblical accounts and the better place Isaiah in his historical setting. Hear Sennacherib speaking:

"I drew near to Ekron, the governors and princes, who had committed sin [i.e., rebellion against him] I slew, and hung their bodies on poles around the city. The townsfolk who had committed wickedness and offense I counted as spoil; to the rest of them, who had not committed sin and wickedness, in whom no guilt was found, I proclaimed pardon. Padi, their king, I brought out from Jerusalem, and set him on the throne of dominion over them, and the tribute of my dominion I laid upon him. And of Hezekiah, the Judæan, who had not submitted to my yoke, forty-six strong cities, with walls, the smaller cities which were around them without number, by the battering of rams and the assault of engines, the attack of foot-soldiers, mines, breaches, and axes I besieged and captured them. Two hundred thousand one hundred and fifty men, young, old, male and female, horses, mules, asses, camels, oxen and sheep without number I brought out from them and counted as booty. [Hezekiah] himself I shut up like a caged bird within Jerusalem, his royal city. I cast up entrenchments against him, and whosoever came forth from the gate of his city I turned back. His cities, which I had plundered, I separated from his land, and gave them to Mitinti, king of Ashdod, Padi, king of Ekron, and Sillibel, king of Gaza, and diminished his land. Beside the former taxes, paid yearly, I added the tribute and presents of my dominion, and laid these upon him. As for Hezekiah, the fear of the majesty of my dominion overwhelmed him and the Arabs, and good troops whom he had brought in to strengthen Jerusalem, his royal city, deserted. With thirty talents of gold and eight hundred talents of silver, precious stones, antimony, lapis-lazuli, couches of ivory, seats of ivory, elephant-hide, ivory, boxwood and ebony, diverse objects, a heavy treasure, and his daughters, the women of his palace, male musicians, female musicians, he despatched after me to Nineveh, my capital city. He sent his ambassador to give tribute and make submission." (A translation of *The Taylor Cylinder*, col. iii, lines 1–41.)

Here, then, is Sennacherib's own version of these calamitous events. This campaign took place in 701 B.C., and is briefly characterized in 2 Kings 18[13]–19[8]. In this passage it is declared that Sennacherib withdrew because of some tidings which had come to him, for so do these words signify: "Behold, I will put a spirit in him, and he shall hear a rumor, and shall return to his own land; and I will cause him to fall by the sword in his own land" (2 Kings 19[7]). We shall perhaps come near the mark if we surmise that he was compelled to withdraw because tidings had reached him that arisings against his authority were occurring or threatening elsewhere in his kingdom. However that may be, certain it is that Jerusalem had not been taken, and the Assyrians withdrew without securing the chief prize of their enterprise. Yet had Judah suffered terribly for her madness in aiding the confederation, and Isaiah was not slow in reminding king and people of their losses, in words that both moan and sting:

"Your land is a desolation;
Your cities are burned with fire;
Your tilled land before you,
Foreigners are devouring it;
And the daughter of Zion (that is, Jerusalem) is left
Like a booth in a vineyard,
As a lodge in a garden of cucumbers,
As a city of watch" (Isa. 1[7, 8]).

But Sennacherib, at any rate, was gone, and king and people must pull themselves together as best they might, and they were soon as bold as before, and ready to take risks again. If, now, we correctly understand the rest of the narrative in Second Kings (19[91]), the events that followed were these: that Sennacherib did not give up the hope of ultimately taking Jerusalem, but sought and found another opportunity for the attempt. We know that Sennacherib was again in the West at some time between 688 and 682 B.C., for he has left us a tiny little text which may be translated thus:

"Telkhunu, the queen of Arabia, in the midst of the desert, from her I took away a thousand camels. The fear of my dominion cast her down and Hazael also. They left their tents and fled to Adummetu, whose location is in the desert, a thirsty place where there is neither provision nor places to drink."

This shows clearly enough that he was now near enough to threaten Jerusalem, and we may suppose that while on this expedition he sent messengers to Hezekiah. Tirhaka was now (689–663 B.C.) ruler in Egypt, and it was rumored that he might take sides against Sennacherib (2 Kings 19[9]), and Sennacherib took the first move and summoned Jerusalem to surrender. Isaiah stiffened the back of Hezekiah to refuse, assuring him that, "By the way that he came, by the same shall he return, and he shall not come unto this city, saith the Lord" (19[33]).

Following shortly upon this a great disaster befell the army of Sennacherib, for "it came to pass that night that the angel of the Lord went forth and smote in the camp of the Assyrians a hundred fourscore and five thousand: and when men arose early in the morning, behold, these were all dead bodies" (19[55] mg.). So was it the custom in Israel to describe and define all catastrophes, great or small, as the direct act of God. Perhaps we should describe this as a visitation of pestilence, sudden and relentless, and it may well have happened if Sennacherib's army was on the borders of Egypt, perhaps near Pelusium where the Nile flows in separated and sluggish channels and where pestilence has often begun even in modern times. A most curious and interesting parallel to this biblical story is probably to be found in a narrative preserved by Herodotus (ii, 141), to which it seems well worth while to give space here, and so to be able to compare all these accounts.

"The next king, I was told, was a priest of Vulcan, named Sethos. This monarch despised and neglected the warrior class of the Egyptians, as though he did not need their services. Among other indignities which he offered them, he took from them the lands which they had possessed under all the previous kings, consisting of twelve acres of choice land for each warrior. Afterward, therefore, when Sennacherib, king of the Arabians and Assyrians, marched his vast army into Egypt, the warriors one and all refused to come to his aid. On this the monarch, greatly distressed, entered into the inner sanctuary, and before the image of the god bewailed the fate which impended over him. As he wept he fell asleep, and dreamt that the god came and stood at his side, bidding him be of good cheer, and go boldly forth and meet the Arabian host, which would do him no hurt, as he himself would send those who should help him. Sethos, then, relying on the dream, collected such of the Egyptians as were willing to follow him, who were none of them warriors, but traders, artisans, and market people, and with these marched to Pelusium, which commands the entrance into Egypt, and there pitched his camp. As the two armies lay here opposite one another, there came in the night a multitude of field-mice, which devoured all the quivers and bow-strings of the enemy, and ate the thongs by which they managed their shields. Next morning they commenced their flight, and great multitudes fell, as they had no arms with which to defend themselves. There stands to this day in the temple of Vulcan, a stone statue of Sethos, with a mouse in his hand, and an inscription to this effect—'Look on me and learn to reverence the gods.'"

The explanation of this strange narrative is to be found in the consideration in ancient times of the mouse as the symbol of pestilence. Apollo Smintheus is known to the Greeks and is represented with a mouse in his hand. Here, then, we have a story, which Herodotus did not understand but which is apparently an echo of an actual historical occurrence, and may very well refer to the same event as that chronicled in Kings. The situation, then, would be, if we summarize all available information, that Sennacherib made two attempts to take Jerusalem and was called away from the first by troubles, political or military, at home, and from the second by pestilence in his army. (It should be noted, however, that many scholars interpret the evidence, biblical and otherwise, as implying only a single attack upon Judah and Jerusalem.) Home he went, and there soon afterward, in 681 B.C., he was assassinated either by one or by two of his own sons in a conspiracy.

So was Judah delivered providentially and spared for a season of hope and opportunity, which it was little able profitably to use.

We have now surveyed the whole historical situation in Israel and Judah during the life of Isaiah (cf. pp. 66–8). Let us turn now to the man himself and seek some picture of him as we see his noble and commanding figure against the background of his sadly troubled age.

Isaiah the Man. About the year 760 B.C. there was born, probably in the city of Jerusalem, a boy to whom was given the glorious name Isaiah, which means "Jehovah saves," or "Jehovah is salvation," which was a challenge to faith, to the belief that somehow at some time and in his own way Jehovah would save his people not only from political disaster, but from national wrongdoing, from evil of every kind. His father's name was Amoz (Isa. 1[1] and 2[1]) and there is a Jewish tradition which makes this father a brother of king Amaziah; and this, if true, would make Isaiah a cousin of king Uzziah. Though this is far from certain, there are indications enough to prove that Isaiah had social prestige, easy access to the kings of his day, and at least a hearing from the most prominent people of his time. Of his youth and the influences which molded it we have very little save conjecture to guide us. We know that he grew to manhood in the great and extraordinarily prosperous reign of Uzziah, and we might well expect him to be so much influenced by the material conditions as to take a very roseate view of the future. This was, however, not the case, and we must see, if we may, what were the influences which imparted a different color to mind and message. Three such influences spring at once to our thought. The first was the appalling earthquake which happened in this reign, though the exact year remains unknown to us. It made a tremendous impression both contemporary and later. The compiler or editor of the prophecies of Amos had heard of it (Amos 1[1]), and even so late as the days of Zechariah (14[5]) it was remembered. An impressionable boy such as Isaiah must have been could not have passed this over without serious thought. Next and more important were the influences exerted by the prophetic teaching of his distinguished predecessors Amos and Hosea, whose messages can be distinctly observed in his preaching. Third, and far the most important, was the influence of his vision of God, set down in glowing words, and representing vividly his *call* to the prophetic office (ch. 6). This came in the year that Uzziah died, about 740 B.C. The aged king, whose reign had been splendid, lay stricken with leprosy, and of his dreadful plight Isaiah must have heard much, and may, indeed, have with his own eyes seen the monarch almost in the jaws of death. He would be in any case sufficiently informed of the situation to be profoundly moved into an impressionable state.

He entered the Temple, quite probably to worship, and that he was admitted at all to a holy place intended only for priests, shows that he was linked in some way with priestly blood, or admitted as a man with royal family ties. There in that holy place he had a vision that changed his life. In a prophetic trance he saw Jehovah, God of Israel. The experience was actual, real, genuine, and not a fancy, not a vagary of a mind disturbed. It is described in prose, but the speeches are in verse. Nothing that even approaches it in grandeur of conception and beauty of expression appears elsewhere in the O.T., and this is equivalent to saying that it has no parallel in all the literature of all the Oriental peoples. (Let the reader go slowly and thoughtfully through the sixth chapter for himself.) There before the prophet's inner eye was Jehovah himself in grandeur, majesty, and holiness unapproachable. The prophet is overwhelmed at the sight, and feels himself by comparison a man of sin. Here, just here is a solemn difference between the prophet and ourselves. We belong to churches that *do* things. We are surrounded by clamors for service, for sacrifice, for work for God and for man. These are all well enough; they have an undoubted importance, but far too seldom have they any solid basis in an immediate personal knowledge of God. We do not *know* him in meditation and in prayer. We have not poured out our souls in adoration and praise and thanksgiving. Our prayer has been petition, and petition almost exclusively, and often very selfish, or at least self-centered. But Isaiah saw God, and from that day forward knew him. He had established a contact with the Divine, and was in a condition to receive inspiration from God and to represent him before man. But this came to him with no promise that men would accept him and hear his message and learn willingly from him the ways of God. Quite contrary is to be his experience. In the awful hour of God's revelation to him it is made clear that men will neither hear him nor make profitable use of his disclosure of God. It is revealed to him that the people of Judah have come to such unbelief because of sin, both national or social and personal, that they have entered into an incapacity for divine things, and are quite incapable of receiving the prophet's message. The more God is revealed the less will they be able to receive him. This principle appears again and again in the N.T. and often as a clear echo from the prophet: "This is the judgment, that the light is come into the world, and men loved the darkness rather than the light; for their works were evil" (Jn. 3^{19}), and see how the very words of Isaiah are quoted or referred to in other places (Mt. $13^{14, 15}$ Acts $26^{26, 27}$ Rom. 11^{8}). What a contrast does this present to the cheap optimism of our age! We keep looking for immediate results from the preaching of the gospel and the work of the church, and speak as though the reception depended on the preacher or teacher, forgetting that the receptive soil must be present, as well as the declared word. But too often neither the preacher nor the people have had any real vision of God and whatever is done must be done with mortal, and not immortal, tools or agents.

Yet, though Isaiah has been warned that the people of his day cannot accept him and his message, he is not left to hopeless despair for his people, for to the prophet there comes the promise of a *Remnant.* This doctrine, very characteristic of Isaiah, ought really to appear in the inaugural vision, and if the text, as it now stands, be correct, it does lie implicit in 6^{13}. There is, however, a doubt about the last clause of the verse, which does not appear in the LXX, and we shall therefore not insist upon it. But however that may be, we have the doctrine given plainly enough in the name of Isaiah's first son, called Shear-jashub, which means "Remnant—shall turn," i.e., "shall turn to Jehovah"; it does not mean "shall return," i.e., from captivity. Isaiah was probably already married when the vision came and called him to be a prophet, and the first son must have been born soon thereafter. His name is a promise. No matter how much Isaiah's own generation may refuse to forsake its sins and come to its true father, there will be another and a better day. A remnant shall remain and in due time turn to Jehovah.

The Three Periods of Isaiah's Activity. And now Isaiah has received his commission and his work for his people is to begin. Hard and sore will be the struggle, but Isaiah will be faithful to the end, and the issue will be in the hands of God. The prophetic career may well be divided into three main periods (so Robertson Smith) as follows: (1) From the death of Uzziah to the beginning of the reign of Ahaz. (2) The period of the Syro-Ephraimitic invasion, about 735 B.C. (3) The period of Assyrian domination, culminating in the fearful invasion of Sennacherib, 701 B.C., and the deliverance of Jerusalem.

At the end of the first period is a break in the prophet's activity more momentous and significant than any other. We have already heard of the coalition between Rezon, king of Damascus, and Pekah, king of Israel, with the purpose of attacking and plundering Judah and perhaps of utterly destroying her. Ahaz was in a serious position and knew it well. He consulted doubtless his best advisers, and decided that there was not strength in Judah sufficient to meet a threat so serious. "And his heart was moved, and the heart of his people, as the trees of the forest are moved with the wind" (7^{2}). Isaiah took his son Shear-jashub by the hand and went out to meet the king. He had probably learned that a decision had already been taken by Ahaz and his advisers to apply to Tiglathpileser for aid against the allies and to save Judah. Such a decision was madness in Isaiah's eyes, and he was determined to prevent its execution if it were possible. He felt nothing but contempt for Rezon and Pekah, *these two tails of smoking firebrands* (7^4), and he bade the king to be calm, trust in Jehovah, and rely on him and his resources and the resources of his people. But the king would not yield to him and was determined to carry out this fatal policy. Nor was he moved by the promise of a divinely given sign (for which see the commentary below on 7^{14}). Then Isaiah decided to carry the case to the populace, and seek over the head of king and counselors to prevent an alliance with Assyria, the real enemy of all the West. He was to set up a great tablet inscribed with the dreadful words "Maher-shalal-hash-baz"—a portentous combination word, the first two parts of which are Hebrew, the last two Aramaic and with the same meaning, the whole of which may be rendered in English as "Haste-spoil-speed-booty," and at the same time there was born to the prophet and his wife a second son, to whom was given this same name Maher-shalal-hash-baz. The people, as the king, refused the prophetic advice, and the fateful step was taken appealing to Tiglathpileser for help. The help, as we have seen already, was given.

Isaiah felt now that his present public service was at an end. He withdrew from all and every effort directly to reach either king or people and set himself to the service of his pupils. He would teach them in private and leave to them to work out in public, as best they might. He would write out his message, seal it up, and hand it over to them. "Bind thou up the testimony, seal the law among my disciples" (8^{16-18}). This was a most significant move. Many a time has it been shown in human history that great movements are best carried forward by a combination of some great teacher or leader with a company of disciples or followers. The greatest of all such examples is to be seen in the work of our Lord with his disciples. We do not know how much else Isaiah taught his disciples, but we shall not lose ourselves in empty speculation if we imagine that a man of his great and moving personality, his amazing gift of eloquence, his magical power over words, must have had an influence impossible to exaggerate. The influence of a great teacher lives long and powerfully after his little day is past. His pupils unconsciously take upon themselves not only the content but even the form of his teaching. They often imitate even his tones of voice and his gestures, sometimes the very expression of his countenance. These external imitations would tend to die out when the first generation was gone, but literary and spiritual reminiscences continue and are perpetuated through long periods. This may afford us a clue to some ideas and principles of value in the understanding of the book of Isaiah. It is now thoroughly well known that large parts of the book of Isaiah are not by the prophet at all but belong in some cases to considerably later periods. Some of these are so much like the portions of the book known to be by Isaiah that some students long held out that he had written them, because their points of view were similar or their language closely alike. These may indeed have been added to the book bearing Isaiah's name by editors who felt this resemblance, but in the first instance they may have been so produced under the projected influence of his glowing and potent personality.

But whether we attach much or little importance to this conjecture we shall do well to observe the prophet's method in this critical situation. He had tried to move both king and people from their mad resolve, and having failed was content to withdraw from public protestation and give himself to private teaching of such disciples as were willing to cleave to him.

With the accession of Hezekiah to the throne a new period of activity came to the prophet, and one more acceptable to him. Hezekiah was a different personality from his lame and weak predecessor, and Isaiah would find encouragement in him to come out boldly with his message. He gained also a valuable ally in the person of Micah, the prophet from the insignificant village of Moresheth-Gath, and so a prophet from the country-side as Isaiah was a city prophet. Micah spoke out boldly in defense of the common peasants and formed therefore an aide of importance to the social message of prophecy. But Isaiah continued to emphasize the political side, having a wider world-view than his contemporary.

Isaiah had his mind's eye on a dangerous situation in the state. The annual tribute payable to Assyria was naturally unpopular, and hot heads might at any moment wish to try a rebellion against it. Isaiah believed and taught that this Assyrian domination was providential, and that the divine will must be accepted. He was opposed to any leaning upon Egypt. He was sure that the future would show not a shrinking but an increase of Assyrian power, and that Judah must suffer from it. His only concern was to seek among his people such spiritual gains from Assyrian oppression as might be won. He felt assured that when the inevitable Assyrian invasion of the West began again Jerusalem would be spared. To this period belongs the tremendous passage 10^{5-34} in which Isaiah boldly faces the whole difficult problem of explaining how God could use the immoral Assyrian power for moral ends. It is "one of the longest and most characteristic of Isaiah's utterances and perhaps the grandest exposition of the religious interpretation of history that ever was written" (Skinner). And now there comes swiftly the climax in the prophetic activity of Isaiah. The Assyrian invasion begins and Isaiah speaks out boldly and continuously. Judah must be sorely punished, but he is equally confident that the destruction of Assyria must ensue, and then would come a glorious era for God's people. The two thoughts of Jerusalem's punishment and of Assyrian downfall interlace, sometimes one and at other times the other is predominant. At times as we read the menacing words addressed to Jerusalem we seem to feel her case hopeless, but then there follows emphasis on the other side, nor is it easy always to follow the intricacies of the prophetic thought. We must see how we shall find our way as we come to study the chapters and verses later. The prophet had to oppose the insensate folly of the war party plunging madly into intrigues with Egypt, which would certainly bring down the full might of Sennacherib upon them. He failed again as he had done in the days of Ahaz. The fatal step was taken, and Egypt was solicited for help. And now, as he had done then, he decides to make a record of his effort to save his people from this folly. Thus in 30[8]:

"Now go, write it before them on a tablet
And note it in a book
That it may be as a testimony for ever."

The invasion came, as Isaiah expected. Jerusalem was spared, as we have seen in our historical survey, and even in a second attempt Sennacherib, for all his great strength, could not work his will.

And now soon after 701 Isaiah slips quietly out of our sight. Some of his greatest prophecies that concern the glorious Messianic age may indeed have come from him during the retirement which followed the events of Sennacherib's invasion, but we have no proof of it and must content ourselves with the long and brilliant story of his life. Nor do we know how or when his exit from life came. A late Jewish tradition asserts that he perished in the heathen reaction under Manasseh, but Scripture is silent and we do well not to attempt to fill in the gap. Isaiah had done enough for his refractory people; he was entitled to a well-earned rest.

The Messiah and His Age. The contribution which Isaiah made to religious thought has many sides. Were we to attempt a picture of it all, in all its ramifications, we should fill a volume with description, quotation, and characterization. We should be required to take his doctrine of God and to ask what he had therein to declare, and we should find him an uncompromising monotheist, not conceding one single word to the existence of any minor deities anywhere in the world. Idols are nothing, heathen deities are naught. There is no God but Jehovah. Then he fills out the picture, portraying Jehovah not as a cold abstraction, not as a force, but as a Person rich in all goodness, of infinite power and of infinite capacity for the care of mankind. Then we should come to his doctrine of man and of his salvation, and to his doctrine of the social life and of the state. But there is neither need nor space here for all this. We must narrow our search and fasten attention upon one thought only, asking ourselves what doctrine of the prophet has had the greatest significance for later ages and the greatest influence upon them. The answer to this must be that it is his teaching concerning the Messiah. He does not use this word in the sense that we now attach to it. He portrays an ideal king, whom we call Messiah, and this word is a convenient term to apply here. The passages in which Isaiah describes this King, this Messiah, are 9[1-7] 11[1-9] 32[1-8] and 33[17]. Doubts have been often expressed, and still are, by very many of the best scholars as to whether all of these passages in their entirety are really the utterances of Isaiah, and we must say a word about that on these verses when we meet them later. For the present let it suffice to say that whether every word does really come from the prophet's own lips or not does not seriously affect the question in the main. There is enough material as surely his as any literary material out of so distant a past can be shown to belong to any writer. To these we ought and must add also 7[14-16], the Immanuel passage, even though it be difficult to range it chronologically with the others. (Many recent writers deny a Messianic import to 7[14].) The entire picture presented by these passages is of a figure so wonderful in his powers, so far above all former kings in wisdom that it is no wonder that the most diligent search by Jewish defenders of their faith, and modern critical students of all faiths or of none, has not been able to point to any historical character who measures up to this ideal. Some have thought of Hezekiah, or of some unknown son of Isaiah, but it remains still an insoluble mystery. The simplest explanation is that which is older than any of the others. Reduced to its simplest form it is this: that the prophet foresaw an ideal king and that no such king arose worthy for a moment to be compared with the picture, but that at long last Jesus came and did satisfy not only this picture but many more predicted elsewhere in the prophetical books. Of course it will be said that the prophet's hope was that the ideal king would come at a *time* which would enable him to deliver Judah, but that this was not the case and that therefore it is idle to bring the passages into any relation with the Christ. The answer to this is that the prophets seldom saw future events in perspective, and were therefore often wrong in their time relations. They expected the great problems to be solved quickly and the sublime issue to result quickly. In this they were mistaken. But with that exception marvelous indeed was the outreach of their hopes, and curiously well suited to the plans, as our day has shown them to be. When we come further on to search out these prophetic delineations of the Messiah word by word in the following commentary we shall be not less but more amazed at the prophetic teaching. (See *Excursus* at close of ch. 53, p. 664.)

Other Prophecies. Thus far all that has been here set down relates only to the life and work of Isaiah of Jerusalem, who was born probably about 760 B.C., and vanished out of our sight sometime later than 701 B.C., though he may well have still been living as late as 680 B.C. But the book of Isaiah contains many and long prophecies which cannot have been written by him. The whole body of prophecy which fills chs. 40–66 belongs to another age and to an entirely different environment. To it there will be devoted a special introduction in the proper place, and even as we traverse the first part of the book we shall find evidence that the editors who compiled this great book have inserted materials not by Isaiah. These must have mention as we meet them. But as we go forward all the way we must not lose sight or touch with the original Isaiah, the true founder of the book, a man whose outgivings were so great, so noble in utterance, so stately and beautiful in language, so profound in thought, that no matter how much of others' teaching might be set in with his or added to it he would still serenely dominate the whole.

Analysis of the Contents of Isaiah 1–39. The first part of the book of Isaiah falls naturally into four main divisions: (1) chs. 1–12; (2) chs. 13–27; (3) chs. 28–35; and (4) chs. 36–39. The last named is a historical booklet mostly excerpted from 2 Kings, while the other three may quite probably have been originally circulated as separate booklets. Let us now take up the study of these divisions in turn, interpreting them briefly and seeking for explanations of words and phrases whose meaning may not be at once clear to the mind. In the limits here properly imposed it will not be possible to attempt an elaborate and detailed exposition, still less a discussion of all the difficulties or of the solutions sought or found by scholars during hundreds of years of investigation. They who would penetrate thus deeply must have recourse to the large commentaries whose names have already been given. In order to follow even so much as here may be given it is imperatively necessary that one have the O.T. in the Revised Version always at hand, reading it steadily and consecutively while seeking now and again some attempted explanation of difficulties or obscurities.

Chapters 1 to 12: Volume of Discourses Centering Around Judah and Jerusalem

CHAPTER I

The Great Arraignment. The entire chapter is a fearful indictment of existing conditions.

1. Superscription. This applies only to chs. 1–12, for from ch. 13 onward there are many prophecies relating to other nations and peoples than Judah and Jerusalem. This first chapter is introductory only, and was probably uttered by the prophet later than chs. 2–12, perhaps much later. It cannot well be earlier than the troubled period after the Syro-Ephraimitic war, and much of it would fit even better the terrible situation after Sennacherib's invasion. The editor found it and thinking it would serve the purpose well—as, indeed, it does—placed it as an introduction.

2–9. Rebellion and Punishment of Israel. *Hear, O heavens.* The prophets regard the whole universe as a unity, and often appeal to heaven and earth as witnesses against man. *Rebelled*—the people have sinned against their God by idolatry and by refusal to hear the prophets Amos, Hosea, and Isaiah, and by many breaches of the moral law. *Holy One of Israel.* This was the view of God which Isaiah received at his call in the great vision, and God's holiness is ever before him. This phrase he probably coined, for we do not find it before his time. *Overthrown by strangers.* This is a tame conclusion, and we should probably read "like the overthrow of Sodom" (so Ewald). *Daughter of Zion.* A personification. It means Jerusalem. *Booth . . . lodge.* To keep off thieves it was customary to erect in the fields a frail structure on poles, and there sat the farmer, in most uncomfortable pose, watching all night long over his cabbages. It is surely a picturesque comparison for Jerusalem, watching over her desolated environment, but it is not unlike Isaiah to have struck out such a phrase as that.

10–17. "The False and the True Way of Seeking God's Favor" (Dillmann). The prophet enumerates all the regular forms of worship and their seasons, sacrifices, oblations, i.e., meal offerings, incense, the observance of New Moon and Sabbath, and boldly declares that God will not hear them. But what God does demand and must receive is righteousness of life and the fulfillment of the social obligations of taking care of the fatherless and the widow, who may readily otherwise fall under wrong treatment. It is a noble passage, and reminds one of Amos.

18–31. A Series of Miscellaneous Utterances. Vv. 18–20 contain a familiar and very rich passage. Men may be saved from their sins without the sacrifices. In vv. 21–23 the sins of all Judah are set forth in a severe castigation of Jerusalem, but there is a prospect of reform in vv. 24–28, for Jehovah has adversaries among his people; but they are dross and will be purged away, and good judges and counselors, as in earlier days, will take their place. It is a political change that the prophet foresees, and it is a restoration of former things. In his later teaching the prophet expects something far better than all the past has to offer. Then the chapter concludes in vv. 29–31 with a condemnation of tree and garden worship, which was common among the Canaanites, was adopted in Israel, and some forms of which continue in Syria in our day. Isaiah will have none of it. Men must worship Jehovah only.

Chapters 2 to 4: The Glories of the Messianic Age After a Period of Severe Judgment

CHAPTER II

1–4. A Messianic Prophecy. Chs. 2–4 formed probably a separate book originally. The section following the title begins with a Messianic prophecy in vv. 2–4; the occurrence of the same prophecy in Mic. 4[1-4] raises an interesting literary problem. Did Micah quote from Isaiah, or Isaiah from Micah, or both from an earlier prophet? The evidence is too slight for us to feel confident, but, on the whole, it seems the more probable that it comes originally from some later prophet, and was here and in Micah inserted by the editors of these books. It is a precious bit and we may well be glad that it has been so well preserved by insertion in two books. It is a picture of the Messianic age, and to the prophet's vision Zion is to be the world's religious capital, and thence Jehovah shall judge all peoples. (In v. 4 we should translate "arbitrate for" rather than "rebuke" as in the A.V., or *decide concerning* in the R.V. mg.) When that age comes, and the Messiah is really ruling, then wars will cease. There seems not to be much hope that this great boon will come earlier. Men must first be brought everywhere to accept their king.

5–22. A Judgment of Jehovah. V. 5 is a transition verse. Vv. 6–22 describe a great judgment of Jehovah, for Judah has been taking up many heathen customs, and in the great prosperity of Uzziah's reign has grown rich and learned too much of easy ways of life and of foreign ideas. All these evils must be purged out and man's pride humbled.

CHAPTER III

Three Oracles. (Including also 4[1].) These oracles follow naturally enough on the denunciation of idolatry and national pride in ch. 2, for they deal with social injustice and private luxury. In vv. 1–4 the prophet predicts a time of anarchy, for Jehovah will take away all rulers, all who might guide the people, and, according to vv. 5–7, men will seek everywhere to find someone to lead them, to heal them, only to meet with refusal and failure. The reason for all this is the guilt of the court and the nobles (vv. 8–12), *children are their oppressors, and women rule over them,* i.e., their rulers behave weakly and foolishly like children, and the queen mother and the ladies of the court rule over them. Then Jehovah rises and calls them to account for the mismanagement of the country and the oppression of the poor (vv. 13–15). Upon this there follows, 3[16]–4[1], a fearful castigation of the women of Jerusalem, and a threat of the degradation which awaits them. When the men of the nation have fallen in war, then the women will seek a husband in vain.

CHAPTER IV

1. See under ch. 3.

2–6. A Picture of a Glorious Messianic Age. This is to follow upon the day of the Lord. It begins with a picture of the Holy Land clad in a rich vegetable growth given by Jehovah. The translation *branch* is unfortunate. Either "shoot" or "sprout" would be better (mg.). It is not the same word as that translated branch in 11[1]. This runs parallel with *fruit of the earth* (mg.) in the next clause, and the prophecy is not of the personal Messiah but of his age. It is an idea frequently appearing in the prophets that great fertility will come to the land after the Messiah has appeared. Then those who have escaped the day of the Lord shall be holy, and shall be *written for life*, that is, predestined to life (v. 3). Then Jehovah will be revealed by means of *a cloud* *by day and the smoke of a flaming fire by night;* so should v. 5 be translated following the LXX. The imagery is derived from the wilderness wandering (Ex. $13^{21f.}$ 40^{34-38}).

CHAPTER V

1–7. The Parable of the Vineyard. A passage of singular beauty and grace, and with many echoes elsewhere in Scripture, e.g., Jer. 2^{21} $12^{10f.}$ Psa. $80^{8f.}$ Mt. $20^{1f.}$ $21^{33f.}$ The prophet assembles a company about him and in light, popular musical verse recites his parable, and then suddenly changes the rhythm in v. 7 and makes a severe application of the moral. The *choicest vine* was the *Sorek,* which produced red grapes; *winepress* should be "wine vat," a place to ferment and store the wine. In v. 6 the prophet begins to let out the secret, when he says *I will command the clouds,* for only Jehovah could do that. Then follows easily the application in v. 7. Observe how our Lord adapts this parable to the people of his day (Mt. 21^{33-41}).

8–24. Denunciation of the Guilty, and Declaring of Woes. Six woes are described. (1) *The first woe,* vv. 8–10, is directed against rich landowners who gradually absorb small holdings and crowd out the small holders, a process that seems often to have resulted in the deprival of civil rights, and a reduction to a sort of slavery. As a punishment the land shall be made barren. The word "acre" means so much as could be plowed by a yoke of oxen in a day. In our terms *ten acres* so interpreted would mean about five acres. Five acres of vineyard would produce only one bath of wine, i.e., about eight gallons; a homer is about eighty-three gallons, and an ephah about eight gallons; that is, only about one tenth as much as had been sown of seed (p. 79).

(2) *The second woe,* vv. 11–17, is directed against dissipation, and the dullness arising from it *early in the morning.* There was much intemperance in Israel and in Judah (Amos 2^8 4^1 6^6 Hos. 4^{11} 7^5 Isa. 22^{13} $28^{1, 7}$), but it was especially deemed an excess to drink early in the day, or before the ninth hour, reckoning twelve hours from sunrise to sunset. The instruments used at the feasting should be translated, "guitar and harp, tambourine and flute." With these instruments and benumbed by wine they are unable to think about God's works, or to pay attention to the warnings which he sent. And now, because the rulers or other prominent people so behave, the people go into captivity; *are gone* (v. 13) is the prophetic perfect. It would convey the sense more clearly to us if translated "go" or "goeth." This is the only explicit reference to captivity in Isaiah. In vv. 14–17 there is a threat of the destruction of Jerusalem. *Hell hath enlarged her desire,* i.e., Sheol, the underworld, the place of the dead, represented in a sort of personification as an insatiable monster. God sanctifies himself by these judgments which he has imposed, and the land shall be depopulated and turned into pasture.

(3) *The third woe,* vv. 18, 19, is directed against a sort of skepticism which doubts whether God will really punish, and they challenge God to do anything. For *cart rope,* a slight change would give us "rope of wickedness" (Knobel), which is much better.

(4) *The fourth woe,* v. 20, is against those who practice sophistry and confound moral distinctions.

(5) *The fifth woe,* v. 21, is against the self-confident, and is probably aimed at the politicians who suggest policies which the prophet thinks bad for the kingdom.

(6) *The sixth woe,* vv. 22–24, is against dissolute and unjust judges. To mingle strong drink means to re-enforce the alcoholic strength of wine by adding to it spices (Songs 8^2) or aromatic herbs, and so set up a secondary fermentation which would make the wine more heady, and so a strong drink. Distillation was then unknown. Judges who were thus befuddled with drink might readily be induced by bribery to declare the wicked acquitted or, on the other hand, *to take away the righteousness,* that is, to declare guilty the innocent. For this they are to be punished, because they have rejected the "instruction" or the "teaching" (so render *law;* see mg.) of the Lord.

25–30. An Avenging Nation. This passage, though possible of some interpretation where it stands, makes better sense placed after 10^4. Isaiah neither collected nor arranged his prophecies, and there is, therefore, no difficulty in supposing that the editor of the book may have misplaced these verses. It must, however, be admitted that they do not seem perfectly to unite with 10^4. We feel the need of a link, and another supposition suggests itself that something which would have joined them better may have been lost. These verses depict a nation whom Jehovah will bring to put vengeance on his people. In v. 26 *the nations* should be "a nation," so Amos 6^{14}; *will hiss*—summon them as a beekeeper does a swarm, with a sort of hissing whistle; in the rest of the passage *they* should be "he"; i.e., the Assyrian individualized. *Horses' hoofs . . . flint;* hard hoofs were valuable, as horses were not shod in antiquity; *their roaring*—their battle cry is compared first to the growls of lions and then to the voice of the sea. (See notes on 9^8–10^4.)

CHAPTER VI

Isaiah's Call. Now we come to the glowing chapter which portrays Isaiah's call to the office of prophet. If the book had been arranged with more strict attention to chronological order, this chapter would certainly be placed at the very beginning of the book, and not as the sixth.

1–4. The Vision of Jehovah on His Throne. *I saw.* There is no other way of describing such an experience than by using figures of speech drawn from experiences of the physical senses. So were called Moses (Ex. 3[3, 4]), Ezekiel (Ezek. 1[1f.]) and the apostle Paul (Acts 9[1-9]). God revealed himself to the inner spirit, but man must tell of it in words of the body. It was just as real as though the human eye had seen it. *His train filled the temple:* His skirts sweep outward and upward and fill all the space, and the awe-stricken prophet looks at them, rather than at the divine form and face. *The seraphim*—probably winged human figures, for they have hands, feet, and voice, and they somewhat resemble the cherubim (Ezek. 1[5-14]). *Holy, holy, holy,* the words thrice repeated for emphasis; to Isaiah the word "holy" has come to have a great moral meaning which it did not have in earlier times, and for him God, Jehovah, is the Holy One of Israel. So does the progressive revelation move onward. *Smoke*—here means the "cloud" that often accompanies theophanies (Ex. 14[19] 40[34] Ezek. 10[4]).

5–8. Effect of the Vision on Isaiah. Isaiah feels himself to be a sinful man, member of a sinful nation. He feels that he dare not address God to pray for his people. Then one of the seraphim touches his lips with a glowing coal and he is cleansed by fire. Immediately he hears God's voice, and for the first time. God has work to be done, and at once after his purification Isaiah is ready to undertake it. He receives his message, and it is his duty to declare it to the sinful people.

9–13. Effects of the Message. The message is a dreadful one. They are not to be healed. They are to hear and see. They are to listen to God's message as Isaiah declares it, but they will not be moved by it. They will be blinder than ever; hardened, not softened. The nation is to be exterminated as a terebinth, as an oak. But when a tree is felled there remains a stump, and this may sprout again. The last clause—*so the holy seed is the stock thereof*—is wanting in the LXX, and most scholars regard it as a later addition. But there is this to be said for it, that it accords well with Isaiah's doctrine of the remnant. For the present at least, and unless and until more cogent reasons for its rejection are brought forward, we shall do well to retain it.

CHAPTER VII

1–9. Isaiah's Interview with Ahaz. The chapter belongs to the period of the Syro-Ephraimitic war, 735–734 B.C., concerning which there is a historical account in the introduction (p. 633a). The first verse comes from 2 Kings 16[5]. The meeting with Ahaz is also described there, and a hint is given concerning the contempt which Isaiah felt for Rezon and Pekah, *these two tails of smoking fire brands* (v. 4), which means that they were only firebrands now flickering out. They are planning to take Jerusalem, as Isaiah well knows, and he even understands the plan so completely as to be able to name the man whom they intend to make king of Judah. *The son of Tabeal* (v. 6), or, rather, Tabeel, is some obscure adventurer. The name is Syrian, i.e., as we should say, Aramæan, and this shows that the men of Rezon were the leaders over the men of Israel. They could dispose of the future of Judah, if the war was successful. *Sixty-five years* (v. 8); these words are most probably an annotation or gloss by some later writer. The prophets do not usually deal in such precisely dated predictions. *If ye will not believe,* etc. The words in Hebrew are a beautifully expressed play or paronomasia. ("Gläubet ihr nicht, so bleibet ihr nicht," so Luther; "if ye will not have faith, ye shall not have staith," so G. A. Smith.) The king must accept God's word as given through Isaiah. "By the soul only is the nation great and free."

10–17. The Sign of Immanuel. In confirmation of the truth of his revelation of God Isaiah offers any sign that Ahaz may desire. Ahaz refuses the sign, fearful of committing himself to some change of policy. But Isaiah goes straight on with the sign. The passage is immensely difficult to interpret, and no absolute certainty or generally accepted explanation has even yet been secured. There is not space here for a discussion pro and con. It is possible only to express a cautious opinion. First of all, it must be said that the Hebrew word *almâh* may mean "virgin," but does not necessarily mean anything more than a young woman of marriageable age. Had the prophet intended specifically and precisely to say "virgin," he must have used the word *bethûlâh,* though even then there would be a faint shade of uncertainty. Leaving this then, on one side, what remains means that a child will be born, with the great name *Immanuel,* i.e., "God with us." He shall have *butter and honey,* the best foods of the land, and will not know poverty. Then, before he is two or three years old, the joint land of Syria and Israel will be destroyed, and the danger of Judah will be past. But now who was this mysterious Immanuel? The present writer believes that he was the personal Messiah, and here is his first appearance in prophecy. He is the same person who reappears in chs. 9 and 11. Ahaz is a poor king; this one will be the true King. Isaiah, of course, has his chronology all wrong, but so do the prophets regularly. He expects the Messiah to come to meet the issue then present, or the Assyrian danger. That was wrong in time, but the thought is sound in principle. There will be no hope for Judah, or for any other people, until the true King comes. He did come, but not for seven hundred years, and he was far greater than Isaiah dreamed. Both Skinner and Gray, in commenting on ch. 7, give a number of different interpretations of 7^{14}, which the student should read.

18–25. Four Pictures. The pictures portray the devastation wrought by the hostile army: Flies and bees; the hired razor; reduction of the population to the pastoral life of the desert; thorns and thistles.

CHAPTER VIII

1–18. The Refusal of Isaiah's Counsel. The prophet failed to influence the king, and the mad policy of reliance on the Assyrians went forward. Isaiah took the case to the people. He prepared a great tablet and wrote plainly on it the enigmatic words, *Maher-shalal-hash-baz*, i.e., "haste-spoil, speed-booty," and then within a year Isaiah's wife bore him a son, to whom this was given as a name. There was therefore a twofold sign, and the prophet interpreted it by saying that before the child could speak its first words, "father," "mother," i.e., within a year, Damascus and Samaria would be taken by the Assyrians. And in due time Judah also shall likewise suffer. The words to Ahaz, the sign Immanuel, the mystical name of the son, all failed to convince either king or people, and it was as clear as noonday that in a really sharp test on a great occasion Isaiah had failed. Isaiah could do no other than declare solemnly that the issue was certain, the land would go down before the Assyrians. For the prophet himself it would be idle, under those conditions, to continue his public ministry. He therefore withdrew, and among a company of his pupils he put into their minds, hearts, and hands a statement of his message (vv. 16–18). This is extremely significant and important, and has been already discussed in the introduction (p. 638a).

19–22. Three Fragments of Prophetic Teaching. (Including also 9^{1}.) These are addressed to Isaiah's pupils, or through them to the people. Vv. 19, 20 are a sharp rebuke against "spiritism." There are not wanting other warnings against those who practiced, or believed in, the bringing of the dead back to earth, for these practices were common at many periods in Hebrew history. Isaiah would have the people turn for instruction rather to the Scriptures or to the prophetic teaching. Vv. 21, 22 picture a man traversing a lonely desert who loses hope, curses God and king, and so condemns himself to death. 9^{1} portrays the recovery of Zebulun and Naphtali which had their ravaging at the hands of Tiglathpileser in 734 B.C.

CHAPTER IX

1. See under 8^{19-22}.

2–7. The Ideal King. Here is one of the noblest and most beautiful, most moving passages in Holy Scripture. No criticism, however severe, has ever been able to diminish its luster, or lessen its appeal. The content is simple even in its grandeur of expression. It begins with an introduction calling on the people to rejoice over the happiness of a new day, and the reason is then given. The better day is coming in the person of an ideal King of Israel, who is described in verses poetical and beautiful. He will reign in peace, and the very implements of war will be destroyed. He will be royal indeed, possessing dominion, and that practical wisdom so highly esteemed in the Orient (*Wonderful Counsellor*, mg.). In some peculiar sense, not easy to define, he is called *Mighty God*, but the meaning and content must not be whittled down. It means much more than mighty in war. It implies some divine quality or character, and the person so defined is no mere man, as, indeed, the next clause implies, for he is there called *Everlasting Father*, and that means that he does not die or cease to care for his people as do mortal kings—a thought re-enforced in v. 7, which describes his peace as without end. The passage may thus be translated and arranged in verse form:

2. The people that were walking in darkness
 Have seen a great light;
They that dwell in deep darkness,
 On them hath light shone.

3. Thou hast multiplied the nation,
 Thou hast increased the joy;
They joy before thee as men joy at harvest,
 As they rejoice when they divide the spoil.

4. For the yoke of his burden,
 And the staff about his shoulder,
The rod of his oppressor,
 Hast thou broken as in the day of Midian.

5. For every boot worn in tumult [of battle]
And every garment rolled in blood
Shall be for burning,
For fuel of the fire.

6. For unto us a child is born,
Unto us a son is given,
And dominion is upon his shoulder;
And his name is called—
Wonderful Counsellor,
Mighty God,
A Father for ever,
Prince of Peace.

7. Great is his dominion,
And endless the peace
Upon the throne of David
And throughout his dominion,
To establish it and support it
In justice and righteousness
From henceforth and forever:
The zeal of Jehovah of Hosts will do this.

In all the literature of antiquity, whether Occident or Orient, there is nothing to match this. (See notes on 11^{1-9}.)

8–21. The Doom of Ephraim. (Including also 10^{1-4}.) Following sharply on this beautiful passage of peace is a long passage of doom for Ephraim, comprised in 9^{8}–10^{4} 5^{25-30}. It is highly poetical in arrangement, much more than in any other part of Isaiah, and is divided into sections ending at $9^{12, 17, 21}$ 10^{4} and 5^{25} with the repeated refrain, *For all this his anger is not turned away, but his hand is stretched out still.* There has been much difference of opinion as to whether the passage relates to events already past, or is a prediction of serious events yet to come. It is, on the whole, much better to think that it was delivered shortly before the Syro-Ephraimitic war and to be a looking forward down the heavy years toward a complete fulfillment in 721 B.C. in the destruction of Samaria by the Assyrians. The burden of it is a complaint that Israel has learned nothing from her past experience, whether in war or in the severities of nature as displayed, e.g., in a severe earthquake (v. 10, with which we may compare Amos 1^{1}). What is to happen to Israel for this obdurate refusal to learn her lesson and abandon her sins is not made very clear, but in vv. 18–21 we catch a hint of civil war, and in 10^{1-4} we see the oft repeated charge of maladministration of justice of which Amos and others of the prophets made serious complaint. Then follows very well the passage 5^{26-30} in which is pictured God as calling up the Assyrians *from the end of the earth* to punish his willful people. (See notes on 5^{25-30}.)

CHAPTER X

1–4. See notes on 9^{8-21}.

5–27. Oracles Against Assyria. Written somewhere between 717 and 701 B.C., these oracles form together a remarkable philosophy of history. Assyria has been used by God to punish his own people, as in the destruction of Samaria in 721, but has quite failed to understand her mission and its limitations. She has ascribed her victories to her own prowess, and looks upon her achievements as proof that her gods are superior to the God of Israel whose people she has humiliated and destroyed nationally. God is therefore compelled to vindicate himself by destroying this proud power, and Judah shall be spared. The Assyrians, under Sennacherib, will come, but Jehovah will break their power, and the splendid words are pronounced,

"His burden shall depart from upon thy shoulder,
And his yoke shall cease from upon thy neck" (v. 27).

28–34. A Description of the Invading Assyrian. In these verses is contained a rhythmical account of the progress of an invading Assyrian army, though it is not intended to represent the exact route which such a force would take, nor, indeed, that which Sennacherib did take. At the very end of v. 27 there are three words in Hebrew which should probably be read, *He is gone up from before Rimmon*, which is about ten miles north of Jerusalem. Thence he goes forward, as place after place is named and often with a play (paronomasia) on the village names, until *Geba* is reached, only six miles from the capital. Then follows the ominous inference that he will soon fall upon Jerusalem. In vv. 33, 34 there is a short oracle, which did not form part originally of the preceding, but is happily enough placed here by the editor. Jehovah smites down the invader, just when he is ready to spring at Jerusalem. The destruction of the Assyrian is likened most picturesquely to the fall of a forest.

CHAPTER XI

1–9. The Messiah: His Person; His Influence. The world power, Assyria, is destroyed, and the prophet now returns to the Messiah, and his kingdom, following up and linking it with 9^{2-7}. In that passage there is a sort of world-view first; and only then does the majestic figure of the Messiah appear, but in this passage the Messiah appears at the very beginning, standing out in the forefront. The Messiah comes forth from the house of Jesse, as a shoot, and as a branch bearing fruit. Then at once his supernatural qualities are portrayed, as the Spirit of Jehovah rests upon him.

"The spirit of wisdom and discernment,
The spirit of counsel and might,
The spirit of knowledge and of the fear of Jehovah" (v. 2).

With these endowments he will judge men as no earthly king has ever done. He shall have no need of earthly guidance by the sight of his eyes or the hearing of his ears, but as he is the "Wonderful Counsellor" (9^6) he will of himself know how to judge. In v. 4 the text should be corrected, not *he shall smite the earth*, but, rather, "he shall smite the oppressor." Then follows in vv. 6–8 a most beautiful idyllic picture of the restoration of paradise among the animals. The wild animals are not destroyed, but their nature is changed. Man is not a creature apart; he belongs to the creation and so do the animals both wild and tame. Here in these beautiful figures we have a serious effort to show that in the Messianic Age it will not merely be man who is redeemed but the whole creation. This same conception carries over beautifully into the N.T. (Rom. 8^{19-22}).

10–16. A Prophecy of the Return from Exile. There is to be formed a great new Messianic people, to whom shall come God's scattered people from distant lands, Assyria, Egypt, and others. No such dispersion appeared near to Isaiah's time, but it did occur after the fall of Jerusalem in 586 B.C. It is perhaps not impossible that Isaiah could have foreseen this, but if we judge by analogy of Isaiah himself and of the other early prophets, who were engaged with the near, not with the remote, there is a strong presumption amounting almost to a certainty that these verses come from some later prophet. They are, at any rate, more easily explained on that supposition. In vv. 15, 16 the allusions are plainly to Israel's deliverance from Egypt at the time of the Exodus. Then the forces of nature, e.g., *the wind* (read *east* for *scorching*), are used by Jehovah, but in this passage there is to be a miraculous change in even the earth's surface, and the returning exiles will march homeward as upon a great highway.

CHAPTER XII

This chapter contains two songs: (1) vv. 1, 2; and (2) vv. 3–6, which are to be sung by the ransomed people, even as did Israel in early days sing (Ex. 15) when delivered from Egypt.

Chapters 13 to 23: Prophecies Against Nations Hostile to Israel and Judah

The Fall of Babylon. The section, 13^1–14^{23}, consists of two pieces quite distinct in manner, namely 13^{2-22}, which predicts the capture and plundering of Babylon by the Medes, and 14^{4-21}, an ode of triumph to be sung by the Jews in celebration of the downfall of their enemy; and these two are rather loosely united by a few verses (14^{1-4a}) in a different rhythm. The background of the whole passage is very clearly Babylon, and so evidently the editor understood. As we have been seeing, the background of the labors of Isaiah is Assyria, and not Babylon. When Isaiah lived and preached, Babylon was a province of the Assyrian Empire, and was little in the mind of the peoples of western Asia. In these oracles, on the contrary, Babylon is at the center of the stage. It is as clear as anything can be in ancient literature that these are the words not of Isaiah but of some later prophet. They were presumably written about 550 B.C., and Babylon did not fall until 538 B.C.

CHAPTER XIII

Capture of Babylon. It is unfortunate that the old translation *burden* (v. 1) should be retained in the R.V. The Hebrew word is *Massa*, the root of which means "to lift up," and the application of the meaning of the root is to the lifting up of the voice. It were better translated "oracle," or even "address," or "speech," or "sermon." The passage begins with a highly poetical, even ornate description of the preparations for the attack, and soon passes into the very plain but still poetic description of Babylon, desolated and deserted, as was, indeed, the case after 538 B.C.; there to be left lying until revealed by modern excavations.

CHAPTER XIV

See introductory paragraph to chs. 13, 14.

1–4a. The opening verses to 4a constitute an editorial link which quite successfully introduces the great pæan of praise, which begins in v. 4b with the words, *How hath the oppressor ceased*.

4b–23. The Pæan of Praise for Babylon's Fall. What follows is finely done and full of music. Very interesting is v. 8, in which the very trees rejoice at their deliverance, as well they might, for it is a common boast of both Assyrian and Babylonian kings that they cut down trees, sometimes to be used in their own building operations, but at other times out of sheer wantonness, or to impoverish the conquered. In v. 12 the R.V. unnecessarily changes the translation "Lucifer" to *day star*. It means literally, "shining one," and the old word "Lucifer" fits it beautifully. The conclusion in vv. 22, 23 is scarcely worthy of the preceding; it is prosy and without color.

24–32. Two Poetic Fragments. These two fragments undoubtedly come from Isaiah himself, the first (vv. 24–27) portraying the destruction of Assyria, the second (vv. 28–32) Philistia. They have nothing to do with the Babylonian prophecies which have just passed before our eyes, and may well have been written by Isaiah in the early days of Sennacherib's reign.

CHAPTERS XV, XVI

Prophecies Against Moab. Here are two chapters of so many difficulties both in text and interpretation that it is impossible, and likewise unnecessary, to attempt to deal with them in a commentary like this. They have little religious importance and their study may, for the greater part, be left to students who have time and patience and opportunity to consult the larger critical commentaries. For present purposes it suffices to say that there are notes of prediction in 15⁹ and in 16¹², but all the rest reads like an elegy over destruction and desolation already accomplished, or still in progress. In 16¹³,¹⁴ there is an epilogue which sounds quite like Isaiah in tone and force and quality, but all that precedes is quite unlike his utterance. It is worth noting that much of this elegy has an interesting parallel in Jer. 48, whose subject is the same and in which much appears almost literally. To explain this there remains only the conjecture that Isaiah and Jeremiah may both be using some earlier prophet whose message concerned Moab. But our present knowledge does not permit us the right to any dogmatic assertion about the problem.

CHAPTER XVII

1–11. The Coming Overthrow of Damascus and of Israel. Here we return to the words of Isaiah. To appreciate this prophecy fully in its historic setting it should be read immediately after the prediction which ends at 10⁴ and before ch. 7. It must have been uttered about 735 B.C., or slightly before that date. The chapter is fairly clear as to meaning in the English version and for our purpose needs little annotation, a few words only requiring elucidation. *The fortress* (v. 3) means the kingdom of Damascus which served as a buffer state to hold the Assyrians from direct attack upon Ephraim; vv. 4–6 describe the destruction of Ephraim, under figures of the wasting of disease, the reaping of grain and the gathering of olives. *The valley of Rephaim* (v. 5), which means "valley of giants," lay south of Jerusalem. *The Asherim* (v. 8) were wooden poles, representing female deities and commonly set up near Canaanite altars. *Sun images* is a very dubious translation of the Hebrew *hammanim*, the exact meaning of which is not known. They may have been stone or metal images to honor or represent gods of some kind. *Pleasant plants* (v. 10) seems to be an allusion to a custom in Greece of setting out pots of earth sown with grain or flower seeds, which matured quickly but perished as quickly. The prophet uses this to declare that all the reliance on foreign gods will bring no harvest.

12–14. Overthrow of the Assyrian Army. A pretty little poem by Isaiah describing the onset by many peoples in the contingents of the Assyrian army come to attack Jerusalem, only to be suddenly overwhelmed by Jehovah. It probably was written about 701 B.C., at the time of Sennacherib.

CHAPTER XVIII

Prophecy Concerning Ethiopia. Here is another very difficult chapter, the general meaning of which seems to be that messengers have come to Judah from Ethiopia, whose mission probably was to induce Judah to unite with other states in a conspiracy to throw off the Assyrian yoke. They were sent away empty, for Judah relied upon Jehovah. The rustling or whirring *wings* (v. 1) means locusts or other insects.

CHAPTER XIX

An Oracle Concerning Egypt. This is another difficult chapter. Jehovah will ride upon a cloud into Egypt, and punish it sorely by bringing about civil war. The chapter divides into two parts, vv. 1–15 and vv. 18–25, with vv. 16, 17 as connecting verses. In the first section the wrath of Jehovah and his fearful judgments will desolate the land. The Egyptian religion will collapse, and the people deprived of its hopes and illusions will plunge into civil war, which will end in a despotism. Then physical calamities will ensue (vv. 5–10), for the Nile will dry up and with it will end all prosperity, or even tolerable existence. The traditional wisdom of the Egyptians will fail (vv. 11–15), and the whole land will tremble under its load of misfortunes. All this prepares the way for the Egyptians to turn trembling unto Jehovah, and in vv. 18–25 we have a succession of cases in which the Egyptians will turn completely to Jehovah, and then there will be a great highway from Assyria to Egypt, and with Israel these will form a sort of triple alliance which shall bring great blessings to mankind. The first fifteen verses are clearly enough by Isaiah. The second section is also very probably his, though it would appear to belong to a later day. It is, however, not possible to date either with any assurance.

CHAPTER XX

Egypt and Ethiopia Will be Conquered by Assyria. This chapter is different in at least one respect from anything else in the book. Isaiah went naked, that is half clad, like a beggar, hither and yon through Judah for three years to call attention to his message. His message was that no help could be derived from Egypt and Ethiopia to get rid of Assyrian domination. On the contrary, these would themselves be conquered by the Assyrians. The date of the chapter is certain from the mention in the first verse of *Sargon*, and his attack upon Ashdod. We have learned from Sargon's own inscriptions that this was 711 B.C. (see intro., p. 633b). Isaiah was perfectly right in his thesis that Egypt would be conquered by the Assyrians, but the event did not come as early as he apparently expected. Egypt was first conquered by Esarhaddon in 672 B.C. The prophets are often mistaken in locating great oncoming events too soon. (See notes on 7[10-17].) But the main contention of Isaiah was sound. No help for Judah in escaping from Assyrian rule could come from Egypt or Ethiopia.

CHAPTER XXI

1–10. Oracle Concerning Babylon. This probably refers to the capture of Babylon by Cyrus in 538 B.C., and is therefore from some prophet later than Isaiah. Whoever he may have been he has a visionary way of describing the events which his prophetic sense expects. He depicts *Elam* and *Media* as uniting in a siege of Babylon; both of these were already dominions of Cyrus when he took Babylon, and the prophet sees the fate of the city with anxious care and much sympathy, which is an attitude not common among prophets or people in Judah. In v. 7 he describes the onset of the Persians by mentioning *chariot, asses* and *camels*, all employed, as we know, by the Persians in war. The epithets in v. 10 apply to Israel trodden down by Babylon.

11, 12. Oracle Concerning Edom. *Dumah* was a place name, but is here only a play on the name of Edom. The oracle itself is a quaint and curious bit of prophetic teaching, probably from the same period as the preceding and perhaps by the same writer. Though so very brief, it yet seems to be complete. From Seir there comes a cry, whether imaginative or real, asking for news about the future. The Babylonians have oppressed Edom. What hope is there? Will there come a better morning? The answer is intentionally ambiguous. The morning comes. Aye, and so does the night. The questioner receives no assurance, but is told to come again and inquire later. Perhaps he will then get a more definite answer.

13–17. Oracle Concerning Arabia. There is first a vision (vv. 13–15); a caravan of merchant traders from Dedan, overtaken by war, are turned from their way and are helped with food by the people of Tema. Then comes (vv. 16, 17) the interpretation of the vision. *Kedar*, a tribe of Ishmaelites (Gen. 25[13]), and representative of the peoples south and east of the Jordan and in northern Arabia, are to be punished by Jehovah's will. This prophecy probably belongs to the same period as its two predecessors.

CHAPTER XXII

1–14. The Sin of Jerusalem. Here the prophet rises to a threatening scarcely anywhere else approached in all his ministry. It is Isaiah himself who is preaching. He sees Jerusalem gay and light-hearted rejoicing over an assumed deliverance. It is the day of Sennacherib. He has raised the siege of Jerusalem and the populace is mad with joy, and has no power to take thought of the disgrace of Judah, overrun by Sennacherib's army, and left in misery. But the prophet can only see the city once more besieged (vv. 5–7). Then there follows very abruptly (vv. 8–11) an account of a previous experience in which the people defended their city, but gave no thought to their God. The prophet takes the religious view of history. Without God, and the recognition of his hand, there can be no hope for the future. Then comes the dreadful threat (vv. 12–14). They are still full of unbelief. They are satisfied with the moment. They eat and drink and take no thought. Jehovah has made it known to Isaiah that there will be no forgiveness for these deeds. *Surely this iniquity shall not be forgiven you* (see mg.) *till ye die.*

15–25. Denunciation of Shebna and the Promotion of Eliakim. This is the only place in which Isaiah attacks an individual. *Shebna* was governor of the palace, a sort of major domo. He has been supposed by some moderns to have been a foreigner, but the evidence is insufficient, and he may have been only an upstart. Isaiah evidently disliked him intensely. It may be assumed that he represented the Egyptian party, and Isaiah would certainly have found in this an occasion against him. He denounces him in violent language. He will be deposed and banished (vv. 15–19). In his place *Eliakim* will be appointed (vv. 20–23) and unto great power and honor will he come. But now comes a difficulty, for it is predicted in unmistakable fashion that Eliakim will fall (vv. 24, 25). This appendix must surely have been delivered later, after Eliakim had been tried in office and found wanting.

CHAPTER XXIII

Oracle Concerning Tyre. This chapter divides naturally into two parts: (1) vv. 1–14, a poem in three strophes concerning the great Phœnician cities, especially Tyre and Sidon, describing their destruction as something that had already taken place; (2) vv. 15–18, an appendix in prose, except for a snatch of song in v. 16, announcing the restoration of Tyre after seventy years. In the poem the *ships* of Tyre, which have sailed the whole length of the Mediterranean Sea, and out upon the Atlantic to Tarshish at the mouth of the Guadalquivir River, and are returning homeward bound, have called at the land of *Chittim,* which is the island of Cyprus named for the people who lived in its chief city, Kition. After leaving there they learn of the desolation of their home city, Tyre. Then the prophet addresses the inhabitants of Phœnicia, and mentions her sources of prosperity. *Sihor* (Shihor) probably means Egypt, though this is not quite certain; but we do certainly know that Tyre carried on a trade in grain between Egypt and various Mediterranean ports. Egypt will be sorry for the news about Tyre, and so also will Tarshish, to which the peoples of Phœnicia are warned to flee. *Tyre* is indeed a glorious city, well called the crowning city, as she had founded cities like Kition, Carthage, and Tarshish, each with a king of its own. The following verses to the end of 12 are plain enough, but v. 13 is quite hopeless. The text is in disorder and no conjecture satisfactorily solves the problem. The ordinary reader will do well to skip over it and leave it to the disputes of scholars. The date of vv. 1–14 is very doubtful. It may refer to the attack upon Tyre by Shalmaneser (727–722 B.C.), who is said to have besieged the city five years, or to the siege by Sennacherib in the expedition of 701 B.C. This only is certain, that the destruction of the city did not take place on either occasion, but was long deferred. As has been said before (ch. 20), the prophets frequently went astray on "times and seasons," and it may also be added that they were not mechanically precise in their foresight. They saw many things clearly, but others obscurely. The first fourteen verses are probably by Isaiah, but the appendix, vv. 15–18, is by some later hand. In Ezek. 26–28 may be read the magnificent passage which that great prophet devotes to Tyre.

CHAPTERS 24 TO 27: AN APOCALYPSE OF JUDGMENT ON THE WORLD

In these brilliant chapters we come upon a message different from all that have preceded it. In the twenty-three chapters that precede, whose beginnings are Isaiah's, and also much of their contents, the preaching is concerning definite and limited areas of peoples and countries. It has been the Moabites, Philistines, Israel, Damascus, Judah, and others that the prophet names. Here, on the contrary, his subject is not thus restricted but embraces the whole world. It is not of judgment immediate, but of judgment remote, not of *a* day of Jehovah, but of *the* day of Jehovah. We have here, indeed, no longer prophecy as it was preached from Amos to Isaiah, but *Apocalypse*, a "revealing" of the distant, the remote; its related literary products are Daniel in the O.T. and Revelation in the N.T., though this is not quite the same as they; nevertheless it is moving in their direction, and is not the same as the work of the earlier prophets (see art., *Literature of the Intertestamental Period*, p. 189). To say this is, however, not to disparage these chapters, for they are in religious importance of high value. "Two great truths in particular, the universality of salvation, and the hope of immortality, stand out with a clearness and boldness of conception nowhere surpassed in the O.T." (Skinner). Enough has already been said to indicate that Isaiah cannot have been the author of these chapters, and it remains only that a swift word be given to the question of their date. The problem is so difficult, complicated by questions of unity also, that it is impossible to do it any justice in a popular commentary. It must suffice to say that chs. 24–27 are certainly later than the book of Job, and must surely go into the Persian period. How much later is ever more dubious. It has even been plausibly argued that they are later than the book of Daniel, that is, later than 165 B.C. The question for present purposes may best be left indefinite. Let us now sketch briefly the progress of the prophetic thought, and now and again try to explain some word that seems at once both difficult yet capable of some elucidation.

CHAPTER XXIV

An Approaching World-Judgment. The whole earth and every form of human society will be doomed (vv. 1-3). The earth is under a fearful curse because of the sins of men, and under this weight all the little pleasures and comforts of mankind vanish (vv. 4-9). Some great unnamed city is to be destroyed, and the whole human race, save for a small remnant, shall perish (10-13). Then suddenly there is a change in the note of despair, for in vv. 14-16 there is a chorus of praise, but it ceases and again (vv. 17-20) the main theme of destruction is resumed and the imagery in the form of floods is so terrible that it must seem as though nothing could survive. Then in vv. 21-23 comes the climax, for Jehovah himself will appear, will vanquish all the powers of evil and take his everlasting throne on Mount Zion.

CHAPTER XXV

A Psalm of Thanksgiving; The Messianic Age; The Destruction of Moab. This chapter is made of three clearly marked sections: (1) It begins with a beautiful psalm of thanksgiving (vv. 1-5), in which Israel celebrates Jehovah's victory over some unknown city. (2) Then vv. 6-8 resume the themes of ch. 24 with a prophecy of the Messianic dispensation under the figure of a feast, to which all nations, and not the Jews only, are invited. Then comes the startling declaration (v. 8) that death is to be swallowed up, or abolished forever. This is the clearest expression of immortality anywhere to be found in all the prophetic literature, and the music of it sounds on and on into the N. T. in 2 Tim. 1[10] 1 Cor. 15[54] and Rev. 21[4]. (3) After this there is another hymn of praise (vv. 9-12) over the destruction of Moab. This is an odd bit to follow close on the heels of a prophecy of good for all mankind, and the hope of the life to come, and it sounds like some other voice than that of vv. 6-8. At any rate we know of no historic episode which might be the occasion of this outburst against Moab. (See below 26[20, 21].)

CHAPTER XXVI

Prayer for Deliverance; Israel is Immortal. The whole Jewish nation now prays to Jehovah for Jerusalem (vv. 1, 2) to be a city of truth and peace, and for the destruction of some hostile city (vv. 5, 6) which is not named. Israel then waits longingly for all of Jehovah's judgments (vv. 8-10), for only so will men learn righteousness everywhere. But (vv. 16-18) Israel has suffered much, and moans her losses; then suddenly, without the slightest warning (v. 19), there bursts on us this thrilling declaration that the grave shall give up their dead, all Israel's dead, or at least the pious in Israel who died before this new day shall again come forth, awake and ready to sing. Then the chapter ends (vv. 20, 21) with two verses that would be better set with the beginning of ch. 27, and carry us back to 25[8]. In these the people are bidden to hide until all evils and punishments are past and the Messianic age has begun.

CHAPTER XXVII

Climax of the Apocalypse of Judgment. Ch. 27 marks the end of this great apocalyptic prophecy. In v. 1 we have Jehovah executing judgment upon all the ungodly nations, under the figure of slaying *leviathan.* This poetical figure comes out of ancient Babylonian mythology, whose figures swept widely over the world and were worked up as metaphors by the poets. After this there follows a song (vv. 2-6) of Jehovah concerning his *vineyard,* but it is vague and difficult, nor in any way easy to bring into relation with the context. The final note (vv. 12, 13) is of the restoration of God's people. The first of these verses may be partially paraphrased and partially translated thus: "Jehovah will thresh out the grain from the ears of grain from the River, that is, the Euphrates, to the brook of Egypt, that is, the Wady el Arish." These were the two ancient ideal limits of Palestine. The meaning is that over all that territory Jehovah will separate carefully the grain from the chaff and the straw, i.e., he will separate the true Israelites from apostates or from heathen neighbors. Then (v. 13) at the blast of a trumpet the exiles will come from all lands, and worship the Lord on Jerusalem's holy mount.

Chapters 28 to 32: Prophecies Dealing with the Relation of Judah to Egypt and Assyria

From the distant future we come back to historic days; from the vast universe and its problems to Israel and Judah; from the apocalypses of chs. 24-27 to the straightforward and limited prophecies of Isaiah himself. These prophecies range in point of time down as far as the invasion of Sennacherib, 701 B.C., but the first four verses in ch. 28 were delivered sometime between 725 and 722 B.C., i.e., before the fall of Samaria.

CHAPTER XXVIII

1-13. **Denunciation of the Drunkards of Ephraim and of Jerusalem.** Debauchery will destroy Samaria, the *crown of pride* of Ephraim. Then suddenly, in vv. 5, 6, the prophet turns from that gloomy picture to a gleam of light and joy, a brief Messianic prophecy. The fall of Samaria will come soon, but the coming of the Messiah's age is *in that day*, i.e., it is indefinite. In vv. 7–13 Isaiah turns to his own people of Judah to give a solemn warning. The dissipation once common in Samaria is now found also in Jerusalem. He denounces the stupid drunkards who are plotting a rebellion against Assyria, and in a sort of dialogue they respond scoffingly to him that they are sick of his dull preachments, *line upon line*. But he flings back the sarcasm into their teeth, declaring that Jehovah will soon speak to them.

14–22. A Solemn Warning. He warns against the irreligious temper of those who declare flippantly that they *have made a covenant with death* in their proposed or already perfected alliance with Egypt. But the prophet knows that the only sure foundation is in Jehovah's purpose toward his people, and that all other forms of refuge will be swept away.

23–29. A Parable. The figures are drawn from agricultural life. *Fitches* should be "vetches," or black cummin, *Nigella sativa*, whose seeds were used to flavor bread. The wisdom and skill of the farmer are a faint semblance of God's wisdom in his plans.

CHAPTER XXIX

The Imminent Danger of Jerusalem; The Peace of the Messianic Age. Jerusalem is addressed under the mystical name *Ariel*, which means "altar hearth," and is so addressed because there was the great altar of burnt sacrifice. But to the prophet this place of bloody sacrifice is only a symbol of the bloody sacrifice of the whole city. Yet in the very moment of the enemy's triumph Jehovah appears and the enemies disappear as a dream (vv. 1–8). But though thus spared the city is full of blindness and unbelief (vv. 9–14) and Jehovah will be compelled to adopt tremendous measures. Hereupon there follows (vv. 15–24) another Messianic prediction. The conspirators have concealed from the prophet their Egyptian plans, and this is a rebellion against God. He will work a transformation in nature and in society. The glorious age that will then begin will be free of scoffing and of injustice and the true religion will come into its own.

CHAPTER XXX

A Series of Oracles Against the Egyptian Policy. This policy has been foreshadowed in ch. 29 but now comes out fair and square. The embassy to Egypt is already on its way and the prophet knows that it is folly, for no reliance can be placed on Egypt. In vv. 8–17 the prophet carries out the injunction laid upon him to write down his message in permanent form that it may endure for ever and ever. There will come a fearful disaster upon the people through this bad policy. Gladly does the prophet turn from this to another Messianic prophecy (vv. 18–26), in which there is predicted a return of the people to their God, with the disappearance of idolatry and a great change even in the face of nature. This passage strongly reminds us of 29[15-24].

CHAPTER XXXI

A Return to the Problem of the Egyptian Alliance. There can be no real help from Egypt, for the Egyptians are only men; from God alone can come deliverance (vv. 1–4). And God will really save Jerusalem (vv. 5–9); it is only needful that Israel trust in him, and stand by while he also destroys Assyria.

CHAPTER XXXII

1–8. Another Prophecy of the Messianic Age. In this prophecy the emphasis is upon the ideal Commonwealth which will then be ushered in. Then there will be a just government, public opinion will be cleansed, and there will be a true aristocracy of character.

9–20. An Appeal to the Women of Jerusalem. Here are burning words addressed to the women of Jerusalem who have evidently shown themselves unmoved by former complaints and admonitions of the prophet. At first, he threatens them with the destruction of their city, and bids them give way to mourning over the desolation. Then there will ultimately arise a new world, even the same Messianic world of which he has spoken so often. This is somewhat spoiled in its effect by v. 19, which recurs to a threat of destruction. This verse comes in so awkwardly here that it may perhaps have come improperly from some other part of the prophet's teaching.

CHAPTER XXXIII

Jerusalem's Delivery Out of the Nation's Dire Extremity. The prophecy begins with a prediction of the city's ultimate safety (vv. 1–6) but passes thence to portray the terrible extremity to which it has been reduced (vv. 7–12) and concludes with a description (vv. 13–24) of the effect of Jehovah's interposition upon the sinful and the resultant felicity to the righteous. The situation to which the prophecy belongs seems to be that described in 2 Kings 18[14-17]. There Hezekiah seeks to gain deliverance for his capital by promising a heavy tribute to Sennacherib, who the rather insists upon the city's surrender. In a coming day all these miseries will be forgotten, for men will see the king in his beauty, the fierce invader will have vanished away. Even good health will come to the people, and their iniquity, for which all these miseries have been a punishment, will be forgiven. In spite of argument to the contrary *the king in his beauty* (v. 17) can be none other than the Messiah.

Chapters 34 to 35: Contrast Between the Destiny of Edom and that of Israel

When we begin to read chs. 34 and 35 we are carried once more out of Isaiah's view, for the editor of the book has here introduced prophecies uttered by some unknown messenger of God who was living certainly after the destruction of Jerusalem in 586 B.C., and perhaps even after the Return in 537. His whole tone is different from Isaiah's, as are also his language and his historical allusions.

CHAPTER XXXIV

1–4. A Vivid Description of the Last Judgment. Not only shall the earth utterly perish, but even the heavens shall be rolled together as a scroll. This is certainly apocalyptic and not prophetic in character.

5–17. The Doom of Edom. The rest of the chapter is devoted to Edom, which has always shown hostility to God's people and is therefore to be visited with appalling slaughter and desolation. The land will then be given over to wild beasts, venomous reptiles, and demonlike creatures. It is a horrible passage. In marvelous contrast stands out the next chapter.

CHAPTER XXXV

A Prediction of Happiness and Prosperity. Here is a chapter full of joy and gladness, of hope in fruition, of redemption beyond compare. The imagery is largely derived from Isa. 40[1f.], and the language also owes much to the same source. This is intended as a contrast to ch. 34, as a prediction of happiness and prosperity to Israel as against the utter desolation with which the historic enemy of Israel has been threatened. The first two verses describe the desert as blossoming so beautifully as to compare well with the finest and fairest portions of Palestine. The rose is probably the autumn crocus (*Colchicum autumnale*). The rest of the beautiful chapter is largely a call to the exiles in Babylonia to strengthen one another in faith, and to prepare for the recompense of God, and his salvation. It shall be for all exiles, even for the blind and the deaf who shall find sight and hearing again, while the lame shall leap and the dumb find unloosed tongues. There is in v. 7 a very interesting word translated *thirsty ground* which is in Hebrew *Sharab*, appearing again in 49[10] (see mg.), which is now generally supposed to be the same word as the Arabic *Serab* which means "mirage." On this interpretation, even the mirage shall turn to real water.

CHAPTERS XXXVI—XXXIX

Isaiah's Activity during the Reign of Hezekiah

We have come to the end of the first part of the book of Isaiah. Here follow chs. 36–39, which are a historical narrative taken from 2 Kings 18[13]–20[19], where they are discussed, except for 38[9-20], which is discussed below.

Chapter 38[9-20]

Hezekiah: His Song of Thanksgiving. This passage, which is not found in the book of Kings, and is not discussed in the commentary on that book, must be here the subject of a brief discussion. It is called *The Writing of Hezekiah*. Kuenen suggested that one letter be changed in the Hebrew, and that instead of reading *Writing* we should read "Michtam," a term found in the headings of Psa. 16, 56–60. This was accepted by Marti, and has lately been adopted by Wade. As we have no evidence which enables us to define the word "Michtam," this does not give us any help. Wade tries an explanation by suggesting that "Michtam" perhaps signifies "a golden (that is, choice) poem" (cf. on Psa. 16).

The poem divides naturally into two parts: (1) vv. 10–14, a description of the writer's anguish and despair in the near prospect of death (Skinner); and (2) vv. 15–20, an expression of gratitude for the extension of life. Wade divides at v. 17, calling the first half a prayer and the second a thanksgiving, while Duhm makes it a prayer as a whole. Skinner's solution is preferable. It fits the situation fairly well, but there are no sufficient reasons for supposing it to be an actual composition of Hezekiah. It is absent from Kings, and it has all the air of a liturgical composition of a date considerably or even much later. Its metrical form is irregular, for in vv. 10–12 it is in the *Kinah*, or elegiac measure, while the rest of it does not so conform. The text is in sad disorder, and this in itself would point to much complicated handling, in being transferred from place to place for liturgical purposes. This indicates a later date than that of Hezekiah, as does also the introduction of Aramaic words among the Hebrew.

In the noontide of my days (v. 10); literally, "the stillness," which the R.V. mg. gives as "tranquility." Hezekiah would now be about thirty-nine years old. *The residue of my years*, perhaps refers to the time until the age of seventy. *I shall not see the Lord* (v. 11), is a reflection based on the widespread idea of the O.T. that in this life, and not after death, is the true scene of communion with God. This is the reason for the horror of the O.T. saints for death and Sheol. There they could not know God as they knew him here. (See v. 18 below and cf. Psa. 88^5.) The beautiful figures (v. 12) of the shepherd's tent, so easily taken down, and of the weaver rolling up the carpet he has woven and so concealing its pattern or figures, well picture the transitory nature of human life. *From day even to night* means "within twenty-four hours." *I quieted myself* (v. 13), and the mg., *I thought*, are neither quite satisfactory; by a conjectural restoration we might translate "I cried out"; but it is doubtful. The *breaking of bones* is a figure for pain. Vv. 15, 16 as the text now stands are almost hopelessly difficult. Speculation is in this place idle and, on the whole, the best thing to do is boldly to follow Duhm's conjectural restoration, hazardous though conjectures always are, and read:

"What shall I speak and say to him—for he has done it;
I must toss to and fro all my sleeping hours because of bitterness of soul;
Lord, of this doth my heart make mention of thee,
Give rest to my spirit and recover me."

In v. 18 we come again upon the point noted above that Sheol spoke no hope to the ancient days of the Hebrews. In the end of the verse is the word *truth*, but the LXX reads *thy mercy*, or *thy loving kindness*, which seems preferable. V. 20 seems very clearly not to belong to the psalm but to be a liturgical appendix, intimating that the psalm was used in religious services, accompanied by instruments. The plural form *we will sing* supports this, and the instruments used are supposed to be stringed. This is, unfortunately, not quite certain. Our knowledge of the ancient Hebrew instruments is very limited. It may here be noted that vv. 21, 22 are misplaced. In the book of Kings they appear in their proper place, 2 Kings 20^7.

Chapters 40 to 55: The Second Part of the Book of Isaiah

When the reader of Isaiah has come to the end of ch. 35, if he passes over the historical chs. 36–39 without reading them and proceeds at once to read ch. 40, he must be impressed with a marked difference. He would feel this still more if he had wisely read aloud some of the first thirty-five chapters. This would be especially noticeable if he would read chs. 32 and 33 aloud and then pass at once to ch. 40. He might then read bravely on until the end of ch. 55 were reached. He would by this time know, if his mind were really alert as well as open to conviction, that chs. 40–55 are not like chs. 1–33, but belong to quite a different historical situation, present another message to meet it, and presumably contain the preaching of another man. Such, at any rate, is now the common view of those who have studied most deeply and have meditated longest over this noble and impressive portion of Holy Scripture.

The reasons for this conclusion are many, some of them technical in character and requiring for their understanding a knowledge of the Hebrew language; while others are subtle, delicate, and dependent upon a wide knowledge of prophecy and its ways, which could only be secured from long years of reading and weighing of the prophetic books of all the other prophets; and yet others grow out of historical situations whose complete understanding requires a knowledge of ancient history only possible to those who have access to that extensive literature made available within the last fifty or sixty years by the unearthing of ancient cities and the decipherment of the records buried within them. A popular book cannot present all these various sides with any semblance of completeness, with any approach to thoroughness. The merest outlines may here be cautiously set down. The reader who would satisfy an inquiring mind must be asked to betake him to the elaborate critical commentaries whose titles and authors have already been named.

The arguments may then be simply classified, not characterized or completely worked out, under the following heads:

Style and Language. This is a subtle and delicate matter, and too much should not be made of it. Even in the English translation, however, the thoughtful and observant reader will notice a difference which he might find difficult to define, but may easily feel. If he now also commanded the use of Hebrew and set himself to examine the vocabulary he would quickly perceive that he who wrote chs. 40–55 had certain words and phrases much in use which appear seldom or not at all in chs. 1–35. He would, e.g., find the word for "righteousness" about seventeen times in the second part and only four or five times in the first. He would note a word for "work, reward," five times in the second and not at all in the first. He would discover a peculiar word to express the negative eight times in the second and not at all in the first, and a word meaning "also" or something allied to that, no less than twenty-two times in the first and not at all in the second. Such examples as these might be almost indefinitely extended. But when all were enumerated we should still be left with many indications more important yet far less easy to evaluate. We should certainly, if we read often enough and with sustained attention, feel marked differences in tone and method. The tremendous energy of the first part contrasts with a certain solemn beauty often sinking down into a deep and moving pathos, and running away again into duplications of phrase and descriptive repetition.

Religious and Theological Ideas. Much greater weight is to be attached to these ideas than to the foregoing points. Here we are in two quite different ways of apprehending and describing God and his relations to man. In the first part, e.g., we have the Messianic King, but in the second his place is taken by the Suffering Servant. The first insists continually on the Remnant who shall return, and this fills a great rôle, only to be but faintly present in the second. The second rises to great heights of eloquence in portraying the incomparableness of God, the universal Creator, the omnipresent Ruler. Much of this is indeed implicit in the first part, but is not so plainly and explicitly declared. So might we go on as do the great commentators to display differences which clearly suggest—if, indeed, they do not absolutely prove—the hand of another and different writer.

The Historical Background. Here we come to the most potent argument of all. There is no dispute that the chs. 40–55 deal with the human figures and with the political situation which obtained among the Jews in Babylonia during the Captivity which extended from 586 to 537 B.C. The writer places himself among the exiles, associates himself with their hopes rather than their fears, and endeavors to bring them out of a dull despondency into a new and living faith. In ch. 41 he touches for the first time clearly upon that historical situation. But he is soon much more clearly indicating it. For he portrays Cyrus as a world figure—nay, a world conqueror—and in 44^{24}–45^{25} there is a whole series of oracles dealing with the mission and work of Cyrus. Now, it was at one time energetically argued that it was Isaiah of Jerusalem who wrote this, having foreseen nearly two hundred years earlier the rise of Cyrus, and the meaning of his work. This argument seems latterly to be but little brought forward, and great names in biblical learning are no longer attached to it. The reason is simple. There is nowhere else in the prophetic literature any parallel to this. The prophets did, indeed, predict future events, but not events anything like so remote from their own day. Their messages were to the men who were before them as they spoke, and the future events with which they had to do were those nearly at hand. Amos preaching about 760 B.C. can predict an Assyrian invasion which occurred within thirty years, for it might come and did come within the lifetime of those who heard him. Such in a general way was the method of all the early prophets. They did, indeed, predict a Messiah and his age, which was remote, but this is a wholly different matter and is related to their connection of his person and work with the need of their own day. If Isaiah foresaw Cyrus, it must be admitted that this is a unique case in prophecy; and once that is conceded the whole argument breaks down before the facts and characteristics of prophecy everywhere exhibited. There is no advantage for prophecy in maintaining a proposition so strange. Every principle of the work and influence of revelation can the better be attained by the admission of another prophet, to whom these chapters belong. We may call him the Second Isaiah if we will, or leave his name even thus undefined, and as completely unknown as time and conditions have demanded. On this conclusion the exposition which follows is based for chs. 45–55. As to chs. 56–66 there will be a word of comment when we reach these chapters.

CHAPTER XL

I–II. **The Prologue.** This introduces the great theme which in one way or another fills the whole field until ch. 55 is ended. The beginning is sublime. The eloquence of these chapters is wholly without parallel in the entire literature of the ancient Oriental world. A poet and prophet united in one person gave them utterance in an ecstasy of joy, in a glow of hope, in a certainty of conviction. For him the night, the black night of exile, is at its end. The morning dawns and Jerusalem looms clear and vivid before his eyes. There is little in these verses difficult to understand and comment upon them seems almost superfluous. *Jerusalem* means the people in captivity, it is an idealistic word, as is *Zion* (v. 9) so often. *The voice* (v. 3) is here an interjection, and were well translated "Hark! one crying." It is not God's voice or the prophet's but angelic. *Prepare ye* is taken from the Oriental custom of clearing a road before the king's visit to a city or province. And now we are prepared for the introduction of Jehovah himself.

12–31. Jehovah, God of Israel, the Incomparable. (Davidson.) The deliverance is to come by the intervention of Jehovah, whose greatness is more than equal to the task. He is shown in his greatness by his operations in creation (v. 12), and by the knowledge which he has displayed (vv. 13, 14), and by the insignificance of everything in comparison with him (vv. 15–17). All this is declared in order to rouse the people out of despondency and unfaith. In contrast with this great God are the idols (vv. 18–20). The people of Israel were in Babylonia, and everywhere about them were imposing temples, each with its statue or image representing its presiding deity, Marduk, Nabu, Shamash, to whom was paid the homage or the sacrifices of their worshipers. To the prophet all these images are only the work of men's hands and with them it is impossible to compare God. Contrasted also are the characteristics of Israel's God (vv. 21–26) who is manifest in the works which he has created, and is the disposer of the fortunes of men. In the peroration (vv. 25, 26), magnificently eloquent, God as creator is celebrated. "The word 'create' occurs fifteen times in chs. 45–55, and five times in the chapters which follow; perhaps not more than nine times in the whole of the *earlier* literature. No other language possesses a word so exclusively appropriated to the Divine activity" (Skinner). Israel may safely trust in such a God (vv. 27–31). He will not fail. They who are his people will be borne upon wings, and not any longer be toiling wearily.

CHAPTER XLI

Encouragement of Israel. In this great chapter there appears the figure of Cyrus, to whose sudden rise and amazing success there was no earlier parallel. He was born prince of a small province called Anshan. He conquered Media in 549 B.C., destroyed the Lydian Empire, then under the rule of the famous Crœsus, in 540, and took Babylon in 538. The date of this prophecy may be fixed within narrow limits. It comes after the conquest of the Medes and before the taking of Babylon, i.e., between 549 and 538 B.C., and perhaps about 540.

1–7. Jehovah's Debate with the Nations. The chapter contains two debates, the first between Jehovah and the nations (vv. 1–7), the second between Jehovah and the idols (vv. 21–29), with an intervening passage (vv. 8–20) in which Israel is bidden to view this great crisis in history. *The man* (better than *one*) *from the east* is Cyrus, and it is Jehovah who has given him his victories, for it is Jehovah who has guided all human history from the beginning. The nations are alarmed at the intervention of this great God, and prepare to meet him by making new gods (vv. 5–7). These verses, though somewhat difficult in this connection, are, on the whole, better left where they stand, though they would give an easier connection if they were transferred and inserted in ch. 40 between vv. 19 and 20.

8–20. Israel's Security. But however much the nations may fear, Israel has no need so to do, for hers is a special relation to Jehovah; from the days of Abraham, her progenitor, she has been Jehovah's servant. Jehovah will strengthen her, giving her victory over all her enemies and a supply for all her wants.

21–29. Jehovah's Debate with the Idols. The prophet had before represented Jehovah as addressing the makers of idols; now the idols themselves are addressed. They are asked to give some proof of their foreknowledge. Can they point to any past which they have correctly predicted, i.e., any *former things* which came out into the present as they had said, or can they predict any future things? If they can do this, they will be known as gods. If they have no foreknowledge or are unwilling to make that test, let them *do good or do evil, that we may look around on one another* (v. 23, mg.). In v. 25 the prophet returns to the figure already mentioned in vv. 2–4, and here it is declared that *he calleth upon my name*, or perhaps better, "will call." The meaning is that Cyrus will ultimately recognize that his victories are to be ascribed to Jehovah and not to his former gods of Anshan or Media. He shall *come upon* (read *tread upon*) *rulers*. The idols know nothing of all this, neither can they understand it or explain it (vv. 26–29).

CHAPTER XLII

The "Servant Passages" in Isaiah. These important passages are as follows: 42^{1-4} 49^{1-6} 50^{4-9} 52^{13}–53^{12}. They afford us many difficulties, but no amount of thought or care lavished upon them would be unworthily bestowed. There is nothing in all the O.T. so rich as they, so far-reaching in teaching, so profoundly allied to the N.T. They are indeed evangelical, and the prophet who gave them utterance is well named "The Evangelist of the O.T." The interpretation which follows aims to explain them as a whole and as parts of the work of the Second Isaiah. They are poetical in form, but so also is his work in general. The rhythm of the Servant passages is, however, different from the rest, and this has been one of the causes, or origins, of much debate. There are two solutions which have been suggested. The one is that these passages are the work of another prophet, perhaps of a somewhat earlier date, which has been taken up and used by the Second Isaiah. The other is that they are interpolations inserted by an editor or by some other later hand into the work of the Second Isaiah. Of these two the second seems to many to break upon the rock that some of the Servant passages seem clearly to be utilized, commented on, expanded or explained by the Second Isaiah and must therefore have been used by him and not inserted without his knowledge. The first hypothesis is the more probable, but if it be the correct solution, then the question becomes purely academic. It does not matter for their interpretation whether they are original or quoted; for, if quoted, the author made them his own, and our interpretation of them may proceed as though he had written them just as well as the context in which they stand. The next question in importance is the question, Who is this Servant? Great and grave problems are suspended upon this, and it seems best to let the answer develop, as we proceed, from the exegesis of the separate passages rather than to discuss it under a separate head (cf. p. 664). (For those who would know it more perfectly and the views of modern scholars concerning it, reference should be made to the commentaries whose titles and authors have already been named, and to such discussions as those of A. Guillaume in *Theology* for Nov. and Dec. 1925 and Jan. and Feb. 1926; H. Wheeler Robinson, *The Cross of the Servant;* and C. F. Burney, *The Gospel in the O.T.*)

1–4. The First Servant Passage. Here is a picture of a Servant whom Jehovah has *chosen* and in whom he takes delight. He is to have a great work to do, and for it is prepared by having the divine spirit put upon him. So also were the prophets prepared, and so be it noted was the Messiah to be (11[2f.]). His mission is to carry *judgment* to the Gentiles. The Hebrew word here used means the ordinances or judicial decisions of Jehovah, i.e., the practical side of Jehovah's requirements of men, namely, *religion.* Next we are told how the Servant is to do this. He is to do it in quietness, by the operation of gentle spiritual influences. Now this was not the way of the prophets usually. They spoke out in the streets and often clamorously. But it reminds us of the still small voice of Elijah (1 Kings 19[12f.]), and we must not overlook the use made of it in Mt. 12[17f]. He is to be very careful not to quench any little wavering burning light of religion among these Gentiles, nor, as later appears, among Israel. He is not to be discouraged, but wait patiently until this religion is set up in the earth, and the *isles,* i.e., the coastlands, wait for his "instruction," which is the meaning of the word *law.* Let us now inquire who is this Servant? The answer seems plain enough. The connections before and after show that it is Israel, not indeed that general mass of people in captivity as they then were, but that same people idealized as they should be, as God in the beginning meant that they should be. To be such a people—such a Servant—is and always was their divinely appointed mission. They are now called to fulfill it.

5–17. The Greatness of the God Who Calls Israel. The prophet goes forward to make promises to Israel, and in his writing takes up the chain which he left off when he inserted the Servant hymn. The great Creator is he who calls Israel to a great mission, namely, to be a *covenant* (v. 6), i.e., he is to bring the people into a new covenant with God, and to open their spiritual eyes, and release them from a spiritual bondage. There will be *a new song* then to sing (vv. 10–13) "such as has never been heard in the heathen world" (Delitzsch). In vv. 14–17 Jehovah speaks again, but continues the figure from v. 13. He has long held his peace during the captivity of Israel (586–540 B.C.), but will now cry aloud, *gasping and panting,* by which the deep passion of the Almighty is expressed in vivid terms of man's nature. God will reveal himself in nature and the lives of men. But idolaters shall *be turned back,* i.e., put to shame.

18–25. Israel Rebuked for Its Blindness. In these verses the people of Israel is rebuked for a failure to understand its vocation and the process of education which Jehovah has been carrying on to prepare it for its heaven-sent obligations. Very different is Israel as here depicted from the Israel of the first Servant passage in vv. 1–4. The difference is that this is Israel as it actually is, and the other is Israel as God meant it to be, as he was desiring even yet to make it. This is a sorry picture, in contrast with those beautiful verses. *Servant . . . messenger*—so was Israel to have been; God's servant and his messenger to all mankind. In v. 19 there is a very difficult phrase, which in A.V. is *he that is perfect* and in R.V. *at peace with me,* and in the margin *made perfect* or *recompensed.* The meaning is still uncertain after much modern debate. Skinner translates "the befriended one," and Wade partially follows with "admitted to friendship with me." In the last clause of v. 19, *blind* should probably be "deaf," and is so given in some MSS. In v. 23 the prophet seeks to rouse the people to prepare for the coming salvation, and then reminds them that all that has come to them is from the Lord, but they had hitherto not laid this chastisement to heart.

CHAPTER XLIII

1–13. Gracious Promises of Divine Help. The thought of the last verses in ch. 42 carries over into this chapter, which begins with gracious promises of God's great good will toward Israel, for he had chosen her for himself and will ransom her at the cost of the great nations by whom she was oppressed. Egypt, Ethiopia, and Seba are to go to Persia, as, indeed, they did during the reign of Cambyses, though not by the hand of Cyrus. The exiles of Israel will be gathered again and brought home. In vv. 8–13 the argument from prophecy is repeated, not as before with the idols, but with the nations. Their gods have not foretold the coming event, as Jehovah has done.

14–28. The Fall of Babylon Predicted; Another Arraignment of Israel. The prediction of the fall of Babylon is here for the first time announced. It will be an unparalleled display of God's working, exceeding even the Exodus from Egypt, for Israel will be led miraculously through the desert. Upon this there follows at once (vv. 22–28) an arraignment of Israel similar to 42[18-25], and the people are declared to have burdened their God with sins and iniquities and not with sacrifices and offerings, but they are thus reminded only that God will blot out their transgressions for his own sake. The *first father* who sinned was Jacob, who gave his name to the nation.

CHAPTER XLIV

1–23. Dependableness of God; The Helplessness of Idols. The reproof at the close of the last chapter is followed by a promise of a full restoration to the divine favor (vv. 1–5). Israel is now called *Jeshurun,* which means "Upright One," in contrast with *Jacob,* which signifies "Supplanter." In vv. 6–23 the prophet returns again to a theme already twice before discussed, and uses similar expressions in setting it forth. It begins with an uncompromising declaration of monotheism, and then plunges into an exposure of the utter folly of idol worship (vv. 9–20) more severe than any found elsewhere in the book. And upon it there follows at once a glorious declaration of complete pardon to Israel for all her transgressions. And as he thinks of all that this means the prophet bursts into a pæan of praise and calls upon all nature to unite with him in it. He concludes with the expression of faith that God having redeemed Jacob will glorify himself in Israel.

24–28. The Choice of Cyrus. This passage introduces the message of the next chapter. Here Jehovah describes himself in a series of attributes, beginning with his creation of Israel in the womb, and passing thence to the creation of the heavens, and then displaying his wisdom and power in overthrowing the heathen soothsayers, while confirming the voice of prophecy, and so leading on to his choice of Cyrus, who is mentioned by name. Of him it is said that he will order Jerusalem to be rebuilt, and the foundations of the Temple to be laid. It is a remarkable passage, and a fine introduction to the following.

CHAPTER XLV

1–8. Jehovah Speaks Directly to Cyrus. He has taken this new world hero by the hand and will endow him with power to subdue nations, whose doors shall not be successfully closed against him. The *doors of brass* such as those described by Herodotus at Babylon, of which he says extravagantly that they numbered one hundred, will be burst open and their hidden treasures be revealed. This career of unparalleled conquest is *that thou mayest know that I am the Lord;* so is Cyrus to learn, not by a special revelation, but by experience as we do. The hope of the prophet was that Cyrus would come to acknowledge Jehovah as the only Lord, but this was not fulfilled, for his inscriptions, now in our possession, show that he continued as a polytheist. Nevertheless, God will gird him even though he knows him not. But others shall see and know and understand that God makes all things and does all things. Then follows a beautiful lyric verse (v. 8) to describe the coming felicity.

9–13. Rebuke for Protesting Jehovah's Purpose. Here is a sharp rebuke to the Jews in captivity, who have evidently expressed displeasure at God's plan to deliver them from exile by the hand of a foreign conqueror, Cyrus. They who thus complain are only potsherds and not men. In v. 11 the translation, with a slight change in the text, should probably be "will ye question me concerning the things that are to come, and concerning the work of my hands, command me?" (Cheyne). God has raised up Cyrus, and Cyrus will rebuild Jerusalem, and set the exiles free. The city was not rebuilt by

Cyrus but by Nehemiah, 444 B.C. (See intro. to Ezra and Nehemiah, pp. 457–62.)

14–25. The Universal Acknowledgment of Israel's God. Then the wealthiest nations will confess Jehovah, and come in chains, i.e., like slaves to serve Israel, in order from Israel to learn of the true God. Hereupon follows a magnificent passage (vv.18–25). God, the great creator of the habitable earth, has not spoken in secret, his predictions have been open and clear. He now calls all nations to come to him. It is tacitly assumed that the victories of Cyrus are so sure that they have already taken place. Let the nations who have seen come on and acknowledge the Lord who has wrought such marvels. He who declared it and showed it from ancient time, he is the Lord and there is no God beside him. Let them all turn unto him and be saved. God hath sworn by himself that all, all mankind, shall surely worship him. This tremendous prediction is slowly but surely coming about in our time by the dissemination of the Jewish knowledge of God through the missionary enthusiasm of Christianity. (Cf. Phil. 2[10, 11].)

CHAPTER XLVI

Contrasts Between Idols and Jehovah. Cyrus now slips into the background and the prophet gives himself to describing the downfall of the gods of Babylon. The two great gods of Babylonia, *Bel*, i.e., Lord Marduk, the chief god of Babylon, and *Nebo*, i.e., Nabu, the chief god of Borsippa, are carried away, on the backs of weary beasts. When the people who worshiped them are conquered they can only lift up the images of their gods and carry them away. Such gods could not deliver their people, but go off into captivity with them. On the other hand Israel's God carries her, and has always so done, and ever will (vv. 3, 4). In the next verses (6, 7) there is another contemptuous description of helpless, useless idols. But (vv. 8–11) in contrast Jehovah appeals to history to prove his divinity. The phrase *show yourselves men* is more than doubtful in Hebrew. The best that we can do is to make a conjectural emendation and translate "be ye ashamed." (Let the reader take note that there are still many unexplained words and phrases in the O.T. It is not so plain and easy as our translations often make it.) In v. 11 Cyrus is called *a ravenous bird from the east* because of his great and sudden conquests. *Ye stouthearted* (v. 12) seems to mean those who are obstinate in disbelief. God will show them his righteousness and salvation will not tarry. (See what trouble the ancient prophets had to bring the exiles into confidence and trust in God. So it is in our day. They had their discouragements and so have we, but the end is sure.)

CHAPTER XLVII

A Taunt-Song Over the Coming Fall of Babylon. There are four strophes of unequal length. Certain difficulties in them strongly suggest possible or probable errors of copyists.

1–4. *The first strophe* portrays Babylon under the figure of a very grand and delicately protected lady seated in the dust in humiliation. She is a *daughter of the Chaldeans*, which means that at this time Babylon was under the rule of a Chaldean king, and not a native prince. This once elegant dame is now grinding at a mill, which is a mark of a woman's servitude, her veil is cast off, and the long skirts are gone, replaced by short ones such as captives who had to ford streams used to wear. The phrase *will accept no man* makes no sense, and many efforts to overcome the difficulty meet no general acceptance. Perhaps the best is to change the text and translate *I will not be entreated.* (So Oort and Duhm.) V. 4 interrupts the connection and is difficult. The best solution is to connect it, as does the LXX, with v. 3 and read *saith our redeemer, whose name is the Lord of hosts, the Holy One of Israel.*

5–7. *The second strophe.* This consists of a renewed apostrophe to Babylon, no more to be called the Lady of Kingdoms, because she has harshly treated God's people. She had thought she could do all as she wished because she would be *a lady for ever*, but it will not be so.

8–12. *The third strophe.* On the contrary she shall lose her people and be plunged suddenly into widowhood and her sorceries and enchantments will not save her. Her supposed security has been based upon her *wisdom*, i.e., upon her knowledge of all sorts of magic, but it will fail and sudden destruction will come upon her (vv. 10b–12).

13–15. *The last strophe.* The last strophe in this taunting ode declares that Babylon may call her *astrologers*, literally, "dividers of the heavens," as the Hebrew has it, and her star gazers, but all in vain. Babylonia was famous for astronomy, and for the turning of such facts as they could learn into astrological theories, to prognostications of the future by observations of signs in the heavens. These astrologers will perish in fire, and all who had dealings with them will depart, *every one to his quarter*, or, better, "each straight before him."

And now the prophet turns sharply to utter

rebukes to his own people whose deliverance is near at hand, but they are still a sinful people, led astray by the idolatries round about them in Babylonia. This coming chapter has afforded interpreters much difficulty, and possible interpolations by later hands are not as improbable as in many other suggested places.

CHAPTER XLVIII

1–11. The Disloyalty of Israel in Its Captivity. Israel is rebuked for disbelief and idolatrous practices, and the prophet reminds them that the Lord has declared *the former things,* i.e., has predicted them in advance, and now they should remember this and believe and trust. They are, however, obstinate, and some of them say that an *idol has done* this. Though we have little definite information concerning much that went on among the Jews in Babylon, there is no evident reason for doubting that many must have been attracted by the ceremonial of the great Babylonian gods and so slipped away from Jehovah's faith. God has chosen them in this furnace, as he had done in Egypt, and for his own sake he will now save them.

12–16. Sole Deity of Jehovah. Here is a renewed declaration that the only God is the Lord Jehovah and he will destroy Babylon. In v. 14 the margin, as often in the R.V., is much better than the text. The passage should read *he whom the Lord loveth* [that is, Cyrus] *shall perform his pleasure on Babylon and on the seed of the Chaldeans.* (This last clause following Duhm.) In v. 16, *from the beginning* probably means from the beginning of the declarations concerning Cyrus, which are now so near fulfillment.

17–19. Lament Over Israel's Indifference. This is very troublesome here, for we feel almost instinctively that v. 20 would follow admirably upon v. 16. For this reason it has been much suspected as an interpolation, and so it may be; but it is well to remember that interruptions in prophetic discourses are common enough, and much more natural to the Oriental mind than to the more logical but less emotional Occidental mind.

20–22. A Joyous Outburst of Praise. The exiles are bidden to flee from Babylon and to carry to the ends of the earth the news that God has redeemed his people. The prophet speaks as though the great journey were already accomplished. They have traversed the deserts, but God has given them water to drink out of a rock. The words in v. 22 do not belong here at all. They have been taken by some editor or copyist out of 57[21], where they have a proper context.

CHAPTER XLIX

Concentration on Two Main Themes: the Servant of Jehovah and the Future of Israel. When we pass from ch. 48 to ch. 49 we cross a great divide in this great prophetic book. The prophet makes an advance in his teaching more marked than in any preceding case. As Driver has well said: "The controversial tone, the repeated comparisons between Jehovah and the idols, with the arguments based upon them, disappear; the prophet feels that, as regards these points, he has made his position sufficiently secure. For the same reason, allusions to Cyrus and his conquest of Babylon cease also; that likewise is now taken for granted." The prophet now devotes himself increasingly to two subjects—the Servant of the Lord and the glorious future of Israel. The Servant of the Lord is a personification at first of the ideal Israel whose duty it is to unite the rest of Israel and carry all forward in prosperity and peace; and, not stopping there, to be the agent of Jehovah in bringing the knowledge of him to all peoples, all nations of the world. If, now, the reader will turn back and read again the first Servant passage (42[1-4]) he will see there the beginning of these noble and inspiring messages, and so be the better prepared to understand the one which now begins, a second carrying on and developing the teaching of the first.

1–6. The Servant of Jehovah Addresses the Nations. In this passage the Servant is dramatically introduced as speaking to the nations. He calls on all peoples to listen as he introduces himself, then explains his vocation, declares his sense of past failure, but also his assurance of future success. His mouth is a sharp sword, he has been hidden, i.e., secretly prepared for his mission, he is a sharp arrow, kept in God's quiver until the proper time should come, but now God has given him a name as *Servant,* and he is specifically identified with Israel. He has, however, labored in vain, but is still confident and leaves with God the future result. God has prepared him from the womb to bring Jacob, i.e., all Israel, again to him. Here, then, we see clearly that the Servant is not all Israel, but the ideal Israel, represented by the faithful nucleus within the larger Israel, and that his first duty is to bring all Israel, the larger Israel, more or less estranged from God, back to him, and in this vocation God will be his strength. But this mission is not great enough, for v. 6, as correctly translated, begins —*It is too light a thing* to be the Servant and merely raise up and restore Israel. His commission far exceeds this, for he is to be *a light to the Gentiles,* and so to carry salvation into the ends of the earth. But it is to be remembered that the religion of Judaism was not adapted for a world-wide use. Its form of worship embraced sacrifices only to be offered in Jerusalem. This alone would prevent its adoption as a universal religion. But the sacrifices were not the best expression of its spiritual life. They with some other temporary forms and uses must be stripped off. This was accomplished by Christianity, which became the Ideal Israel under the Ideal King, the Messiah as a Person whose portrait is soon to appear in another Servant passage.

7–13. Promises of Blessedness Because of the Servant. Israel has been despised and abhorred, but shall be exalted, so that kings and princes shall see that she is the Lord's choice. Then comes the picture of the exiles, redeemed from captivity and traversing in safety the long journey. This is all plain enough save for the last word in v. 12. *Sinim* is still hopeless, for nobody knows what is meant. The attempt to identify it as the name of the Chinese is impossible. It might mean "Syene," but it is doubtful.

14–26. More Assurances of Israel's Future Security. Here begins a passage extending from 49^{14} to 50^{3}, consisting of assurances beautifully and eloquently presented that Zion is still Jehovah's well beloved, that her restoration is sure, that her scattered peoples will be restored to her, and that she may well alter her slow acceptance of the Lord's appeals and promises. The passage is singularly beautiful even in a book so rich as this. Zion is still an exile in Babylonia, and her hopes have not come to fruition. She counts herself forgotten of God, but is met by Jehovah's promise that even though a mother might forget her sucking child *Jehovah can never forget his people.* God has Jerusalem's walls before him and will rebuild them. They that destroyed the walls shall disappear and returning Zion shall find her scattered peoples like a bride's ornaments restored to her. So numerous will they be that the place will be too small for them. (V. 19 is too difficult for interpretation here. It seems highly probable that a portion of it has been accidentally lost by some copyist, which leaves the remainder in the air.) In v. 21 Zion speaks with surprise of all those who come to her on the return. They have been born in foreign lands. Upon this there follows a brief oracle (vv. 22, 23) in which it is promised that the nations will spontaneously restore the exiles. Swift upon this follows (vv. 24–26) a different view of their restoration as an act effected by force. The Chaldeans shall destroy themselves by civil war, and shall be reduced to such straits that they will devour themselves, and be drunken with their own blood.

CHAPTER L

1–3. The Unbreakable Bond Between God and Israel. The exiles have doubted whether God would ever restore them. They have gone so far as to believe that the marriage begun at Sinai between God and Israel had been terminated. Perhaps God had divorced her. To that the prophet gives an emphatic negative. There is not in existence any such *bill of divorcement.* Nor has God sold his children to any creditors. Only their own individual iniquities have sold them; they are the children, and their mother, Israel, has gone into captivity because of them. But God can and will *redeem* them. He has the power, and as a proof of that, appeal is made to the exhibition of divine power during the exodus from Egypt, when God dried up the sea, stopped Jordan's flow, and covered the heavens with blackness (cf. Ex. 10^{21}).

4–9. The Third of the Servant Passages. Here once more is the Servant of the Lord. He is not mentioned by name, yet it is certainly he who here speaks, and this must be accounted the third of the Servant passages. It forms an indispensable link between the second and the fourth, for here for the first time we have the Servant represented as suffering, and without this we could not find our way through the mazes of the greater passage which follows later. Let us see what the Servant has to declare. The Servant is prepared for his mission by God, who has given him a tongue with which to speak, a *tongue of them that are taught,* i.e., a tongue of disciples. With this tongue he will be able to—and now comes a difficult bit. The R.V. translates *to sustain with words him that is weary.* This gives an attractive sense, but is not based upon the Hebrew word, but upon Greek and Latin translations of it, and is therefore a little uncertain. The preaching that the Servant is to give comes from God, who comes to him early, as also says Jeremiah (7^{13}), "rising up early and speaking"; so now to the Servant comes God to teach him as one of his disciples. As a true disciple he was *not rebellious,* or turned away from duty, but persecution awaited him, and to that he gave no resistance, but accepted persecution as a divinely appointed messenger ought to do. He is, however, sure that God has helped him and has not suffered him to be confounded. God will justify him in the end, and little does it signify who shall rise up to contend with him. He has no fear of condemnation (cf. Rom.

8[33f.]). They who attempt it shall vanish away like a moth-eaten garment.

10, 11. An encouragement to believers and a solemn warning to unbelievers. The verses are very unlike the messages of the Second Isaiah, and may be by some later hand.

CHAPTER LI

1–16. Encouragement for the True Israel in Babylonia. The thought which had been uppermost, but was broken by the third Servant passage, is now resumed. The purpose is to encourage all the true Israelites who in Babylonia are still lamenting their sad fate and desire to return to the land of their fathers. It is not surprising that many of them have grown old in hope as they have in years, and wonder whether there is really any reason to believe longer in a restoration. The encouragement which the prophet offers is based on history and experience. They are first bidden to remember *Abraham and Sarah* from whom they had sprung in the very beginning. Abraham was but one, but God made his seed into a great nation, and comforted them and gave them prosperity (vv. 1–3). A glorious future awaits those who endure, for an exhibition of God's righteousness is near. Let them look upward at the heavens above, and at the earth beneath. These may pass away but God's salvation and his righteousness will abide forever (vv. 4–6). Let them not give thought to the reproaches of men and their revilings, for they will soon pass away (vv. 7, 8). Upon this there follows a magnificent apostrophe to *the arm of the Lord*, whose ancient triumphs are described as a conquest of *Rahab*. This figure is borrowed from the old Babylonian stories which represented chaos under the figure of Tiamat who was destroyed by the god Marduk, and so cosmos was possible. (See notes on Gen. 1, and art., *O.T. and Archæology*, p. 120.) Here Jehovah destroys Rahab, who corresponds to Tiamat. This is the same God who at the time of the Exodus dried up the sea for Israel to pass over (vv. 9, 10). In the same way exiled Israel shall surely return by his hand (v. 11). This verse has apparently been borrowed from 25[10] and inserted here by an editor, who found it to be as appropriate as do we. Then God himself speaks, seeking to bring comfort to those who still doubt. They ought not be afraid of men, forgetting that He who made them is He who made heavens and earth. What can their oppressors do or be in comparison with him? (Vv. 12, 13.) The next three verses are a complex of difficulties, and the LXX offers no valuable help. The text must very early have been wrongly copied, and both the Hebrew and the Greek have been trying to mend it and extract a meaning, especially from v. 14. On the whole, the best that can be done, save for an elaborate conjectural emendation, is in the R.V. In v. 16 there is an echo of the Servant song in 49[2].

17–23. Further Encouragement for the Exiles. These verses, together with 52[1-6] and 52[7-12], contain three separate oracles, all of the same purpose, the encouragement of the exiles by an assurance that God will certainly turn the captivity of Zion. In 51[17-23] Jerusalem is presented under the figure of a woman prone on the ground, intoxicated by the cup of God's indignation which she has drunk to the dregs. Her people have been carried away into captivity, and none of her sons are left to take her by the hand and lift her up. Her fate has been desolation and destruction and famine and sword. Such of her sons as remain with her have fainted and can give no help. But the afflicted city is not *drunken with wine*, but with the cup of divine wrath (cf. Rev. 16, 17); now God has taken the cup from her hand, and will pass it to those who have afflicted her, i.e., the Babylonians (v. 23).

CHAPTER LII

1–6. Triumphant Announcement of the Return from Exile. The city is urged to rise, array herself as a bride, for no more shall *the uncircumcised and unclean*, i.e., the enemies such as the Babylonians, come to ravage and destroy. In vv. 3–6 the poetical form disappears into prose, and the subject is changed. It is very doubtful whether they belong here as a sequel to vv. 1 and 2, and they certainly do not prepare the way for the exquisitely beautiful lines in vv. 7–12. We may perhaps safely disregard vv. 3–6 altogether.

7–12. Establishment of the Kingdom of God. In these verses we are back again in the main stream of beauty. They begin with the figure of a messenger who comes over the hills crying aloud in jubilation. He is the herald of salvation to announce that God has become King, has begun to rule, has established a kingdom to last forever. Paul lifts the thrilling words and applies them to the gospel ministry (Rom. 10[15]). The first to see the herald is, of course, the *watchman* on Jerusalem's walls (v. 8), who joins voice with the herald, and bids all to join in celebrating God's work for Jerusalem. The whole world will witness Jehovah's deliverance of his people. He calls on the exiles to prepare to leave Babylon, and accompany Jehovah, who will both go before them and also guard their rear as they march homeward. They shall not go out in haste, as did their ancestors from Egypt, but deliberately, and in perfect security. This differs somewhat from the picture in 48^{20} where they are represented as leaving in haste.

13–15. Introduction to the Fourth Servant Passage. (The identity of the Servant is considered in the *Excursus* that follows ch. 53 below.) The fourth Servant passage extends from 52^{13} to 53^{12}. These verses furnish an introduction to the whole, intended to state the import of all that follows. The general meaning and intent is to present the coming exaltation of the Servant as a contrast to his former abasement. And now let us see it sometimes word by word, at other times by phrases or sentences. It begins, *Behold my servant shall prosper;* the translation *shall deal wisely* is certainly wrong. There is, indeed, in the Hebrew a primary idea of "wisdom," but the secondary meaning which supplants it is the "success" which follows wisdom, as in Josh. $1^{7f.}$ 1 Sam. 18^{5} Jer. 10^{21}. The last time we saw the Servant (50^{4-6}) he was in suffering, left there unexplained, but now his exaltation is predicated upon those sufferings. Upon this there follows immediately a parenthesis introduced by the words *as many were astonished at thee,* which means that the sufferings were so great that men looked on astonished; then comes the explanatory parenthesis to describe poignantly what they saw, to be rendered thus, *so marred from that of a man was his visage, and his form from the sons of men.* The meaning is that disease had marred his features, and disfigured his body so that he seemed scarcely human. There the parenthesis ends, and the next phrase resumes the broken thread with the words, *so shall he startle many nations,* the translation *sprinkle* cannot be justified on any account; as Davidson well said, "It is simply treason against the Hebrew language to render 'sprinkle.' The interpreter who will so translate will do anything." The meaning, of course, is that the exaltation of the Servant will *startle* into surprise, amazement, many nations, or, as the LXX puts it, *many nations shall marvel.* Then comes the clause, *kings shall shut their mouths at him,* unable even to speak as they look at this marvel of the triumph which has come out of suffering, the like of which they had never heard of before, yet now do actually see, and are called to consider. Here ends then the first strophe, the introduction to what is worked out in greater detail in the following.

CHAPTER LIII

1–3. The Appearance of the Suffering Servant. This is a survey of the former career of the Servant, and it begins with a complaint of the unbelief or disbelief which led to the complete misunderstanding of him. The complaint is a confession of penitence. They who speak had heard but believed not. They say, *Who believed that which was revealed to us, and the arm of Jehovah, to whom was it revealed?* The translation *our report* gives probably to most readers a wrong impression; it is not our report, the report which we made, but the report received or revealed to those who so confess. The reference, then, is to the revelation made in the earlier Servant passages, or through the experiences of the Servant. *The arm of the Lord* is a metaphor for God's operation in human history. It was Jehovah who raised up the Servant, and who made him, his work, and his destiny known by the prophet. This verse is used in the N.T. to express the rejection of the Gospel by the Jews (Jn. 12^{38}, and partly also in Rom. 10^{16}). V. 2 begins a survey of the Servant's former history. Read *for he grew up like a sapling before him* (perhaps, better, *before us*), *as a root out of the parched ground.* He came so simply, growing like a young tree; read *he had no form, nor beauty that we should regard him,* or, better, *when we saw him,* nor *aspect* (or *beauty*) *that we should desire him.* Worse than all this, he was not only not to be desired, he was even so repulsive in some way or ways that men were actually driven from him. *Despised and rejected of men,* or "man-forsaken"; this is explained in the next clause, where read *he was a man of pains and familiar with illness, and as one from whom there is a hiding of the face;* i.e., men instinctively cover their faces that they should not look upon one so afflicted. *He was despised and we esteemed him not;* rather, "we held him of no account."

The picture thus far represents one as so fearfully stricken of God that men could not endure the sight of him because of their uprising of pity, or because they feared some contamination, some contagion. When, however, they had come thus far in contemplation and in thought upon the situation, there arose within them a new suggestion. They had felt, as did Job's friends as they looked at him, convinced in their minds that God had so terribly afflicted him because of some sins of which he had been guilty. They had to be brought to see that this was not true. So in this case the people of Israel began to repent of the judgments already formed and now adopt the view that the suffering Servant was really innocent, that the punishment which he was enduring was not personal but national. He was, rather, suffering for the sins of others, the sins of his own people, and for these he was suffering vicariously.

4–9. The Servant's Sufferings Endured for Others. Realizing this, they burst forth into the words, *Surely he hath borne our griefs and carried our sorrows.* But even the R.V., though generally so much better than the A.V., fails us here, for *griefs* should be "sickness," and *sorrows* should be "pains." The next clause, *Yet we did esteem him stricken, smitten of God and afflicted,* would better be rendered, "while we accounted him stricken," etc. The word *stricken* is very significant. It is the word used when God plunges a man into sudden and severe sickness (Gen. 12[17] 1 Sam. 6[9]), and it is particularly applied in the case of leprosy, which is the stroke of God for sin (Job 19[21] 2 Kings 15[5] Lev. 13[3, 9, 20]). In the description of the Servant there are not wanting a number of other hints that the author is thinking of leprosy as the sickness of the Servant, but we have no need to stumble over this as we seek to understand the prophecy. The picture is an ideal creation, and as such we must not apply to it the laws of logic and mathematics. It is poetry and must so be interpreted. The poet-prophet wills to portray the Servant as suffering deeply for the sins of his people, and leprosy is but color added to the picture. It was the most cruel, most awful and awe-inspiring of human afflictions, and is here used to intensify the color in the picture.

In v. 5 the confessors dip still more deeply into the great mystery, as they emphasize their own share in it. It is better translated thus: *Yet he—he was pierced for our rebellions, he was crushed for our guilt.* This punishment which he bears is the punishment which should have come upon us. The next clause is even more interesting and significant, for it reads, *The chastisement of our peace was upon him, and with his stripes we are healed.* The meaning is plain. Chastisement was an act of God intended not for punishment but for moral healing. God chastises to make men better. In this case instead of the chastisement put upon them in order to work itself out in their peace it is laid upon the Servant. He bears that as well as the punishment already mentioned, but it is they who secure its benefits. In v. 6 we need to change *have* to "had," so that the verse reads, *All of us, like sheep, had gone astray, we had turned every one to his own way, and the Lord had made the guilt to light upon him.* The confessing people here admit in the clearest manner that his work was both vicarious and redemptive. He suffered in their place for their sins, and in their place assumed the chastisement which was to bring them peace. Ah, these are profound matters which this prophet laid so eloquently before his people, nor are their deeps even yet fully explored!

In vv. 7–9 the account of the sufferings of the Servant comes to a finality. He must die and be buried, but the emphasis is placed not on death and burial, but on his submission. He accepts it all willingly, and the comparison is with sheep, the meekest of domesticated animals. *He was oppressed,* i.e., harshly and cruelly treated by the men of his day, but he neither forbade it, nor complained of it. *He opened not his mouth* (cf. Psa. 38[13, 14] 39[9]). *He is led to the slaughter as a sheep,* and as a sheep (literally, "ewe") that before her shearers is dumb (cf. Jer. 11[19]). *Yea, he openeth not his mouth.* This repeats in Hebrew precisely the words of the second line and is probably an accidental repetition by some scribe in copying a manuscript. V. 8 is a very difficult verse, and many are the suggestions which have been offered for its solution, and many the suggested translations which have followed. A word-for-word analysis is impossible here, but some suggestion must be made. The R.V. has much reason for its translation, but better, perhaps, would be, *From oppression and from judgment he was taken away,* i.e., taken away by death. The next clause offers a still greater problem. The R.V. again gives a fair meaning, but a better would be to take one word as Aramaic and translate it "dwelling," as does Duhm. The clause would then read, *And who gave heed to his dwelling?*—and then follows *For he was cut off from the land of the living;* and the last, if we here boldly follow the LXX, would read, *Through the rebellion of my people was he smitten to death.* Skinner adopts this, and so also, though with some modification, which I have not accepted, does H. Wheeler Robinson. *And they made his grave with the wicked,* is plain enough, but the next clause is again doubtful. It is, of course, very tempting to take the translation of the R.V., *and with a rich man in his death,* but *rich man* is too good to be true. On the whole, though doubtfully, the best seems to be to use a conjecture of Cheyne, and translate, *And with evil doers when he died.*

10–12. The Promised Reward of the Suffering Servant. In these verses again difficulties arise for us, and the text is apparently in disorder. We can only do the best we may with it. The LXX translates (v. 10), *It pleased Jehovah to cleanse him from sickness,* and H. Wheeler Robinson accepts this, but it hardly seems satisfactory. Dillman finds better support in other passages, when he translates,

"It pleased Jehovah to crush him incurably." Then translate the next clause, *When his soul shall present a trespass offering, he shall see a seed, he shall prolong his days.* The whole meaning, then, would be that after his sufferings, which are an offering for the sin of others, he will have a long life, and the purpose of Jehovah in the establishment of a universal religion will be met. George Adam Smith translates thus:

"But Jehovah had purposed to bruise him,
Had laid on him sickness;
So if his life should offer guilt offering,
A seed he should see, he should lengthen his days
And the purpose of Jehovah by his hand should prosper."

The great difficulty of the passage finds abundant evidence in the multiplicity of proffered translations. V. 11 bears a repetition of the thought of v. 10. *By his knowledge* is meant the knowledge which the Servant possesses and imparts in his prophetic activity. For v. 11b read *My servant, the righteous one, shall justify many.* Therefore, because of this great service and this great success of his, he shall inherit *with the great,* or "I set him a share with the great" (G. A. Smith), *and he shall divide the spoil with the strong.* It was the victors in battle who divided the spoil, and the meaning, therefore, is that he will be a victor, or *the* victor at last. And this final victory comes to him because he did not fail, but was faithful even unto death. *He poured out his soul,* i.e., his life, *unto death,* and let himself be numbered with the rebellious; in reality, he bore their sins, and made intercession for the rebellious.

So concludes this tremendous, this overwhelming prophetic passage, the last of the Servant passages. It were idle to deny that its difficulties are great. Some of them are insoluble or at least offer problems for which no general or universal solution can be found. Let not the general reader feel discouragement. He should at least be able to win for himself instruction enough to follow the main drift of the message. Even so little as that will be an enrichment of knowledge, a quickening of the emotions, and an enlargement of the spiritual vision and consciousness.

Excursus on the Identification of the Suffering Servant

We have above the fourth, the last, and by far the greatest of the Servant passages. It is also by far the most difficult of the four, and in its interpretation both saints and scholars have differed widely and still do differ. Any reader of keen and inquiring mind would find both pleasure and instruction in hunting down in the great commentaries theories old and new concerning it. This is not the place in which to enumerate hypotheses, criticize them, and attempt analysis. Nothing more can here be done than to set down very modestly, and with no little hesitation, what seems to this writer the best solution. Something must be taken for granted, something must be allowed of unwillingness to be too dogmatic; yet, on the other hand, there must be something definite to propose, some conclusion reached, some effort to lay the ghosts of idle controversy, some solution to the problem. If the reader will have patience to turn back and read again the three former Servant passages, and such slight comment as time and circumstance permitted, he will see that the explanation already advanced was that in chs. 42, 49, and 50 the Servant in one way or another was identified with Israel. It was, however, the writer's intention to represent the prophet as dealing constructively with his problem, as advancing with his message. The interpretation thus advanced means that the prophet first spoke of Israel as God's servant to all the world, bearing his message concerning sin and salvation. But Israel, whether from thoughtlessness or carelessness or sinfulness, or from all three, refused the mission, and did not perform the duty. Then God's command was narrowed and laid upon the inner or spiritual Israel, whose obligation it was to win the larger Israel, the whole people, to God's service and also to convey the same promise of salvation to the nations outside Israel. But now we must take another step forward and upward. The Servant passage now before us portrays no longer all Israel, no longer even the inner or spiritual Israel, but an individual, a person from that spiritual Israel who takes up the work which Israel as a whole would not, which the spiritual Israel would not likely be able to do. There are, indeed, difficulties in this passage in interpreting it of any individual, but there are still greater difficulties in continuing its interpretation as applying to a large or even a small body of the spiritual Israel. In spite, then, of the difficulties let it be contended here that an individual is intended and described. (This interpretation is made with the full knowledge that the majority of modern interpreters deny an individual implication here.)

The next question to press for answer will be this—*Who was this individual?* Several suggestions have been advanced, each with some supporters and each with some support, at least for the identification. The chief among them are these: (1) Zerubbabel. He is called the Lord's servant in Hag. 2[23] and a distinguished name is his. He led the people back from captivity in 537 B.C., and he it was who under the spur of Haggai and Zechariah was chiefly responsible for the rebuilding of the Temple, begun in 520. His is, indeed, a great name. (2) Jehoiachin, king of Judah, carried into captivity, and released by Evil Merodach (2 Kings 25[27, 28]). It is worth while to notice that it was Professor Sellin, once of Vienna, now of Berlin, who first suggested Zerubbabel, and then, finding that solution inadequate, offered Jehoiachin, equally, if not more, improbable. (3) Some unknown and otherwise unnamed teacher of the law, who was disfigured by leprosy and despised and rejected by his generation. This was Duhm's suggestion, even more vague and useless than its predecessors. (4) The best and the latest is also the earliest of the proposed solutions, that it is the Messiah who is here meant. This was, in part at least, the view of the Targum of Jonathan, and of the Babylonian Talmud, and it was positively accepted and propagated by the Fathers of the Christian Church. There are, indeed, some lineaments not discernible in the person of the Messiah, Jesus the Christ, but they are but the color which the prophet added to his picture. There is so much that is perfectly apposite that we should not hesitate to make the application. Jesus was the conscious fulfillment, nor is there any need to seek another. "The whole conception here given of the Servant of the Lord makes the prophecy the most remarkable anticipation in the O.T. of the 'sufferings of Christ, and the glory that should follow' " (Skinner). I personally accept also and make my own a fine testimony of George Adam Smith, which is in these words: "It may relieve the air of that electricity, which is apt to charge it at the discussion of so classic a passage as this, and secure us calm weather in which to examine exegetical details, if we at once assert, what none but prejudiced Jews have ever denied, that this great prophecy, known as the fifty-third of Isaiah, was fulfilled in One Person, Jesus of Nazareth, and achieved in all its details by him alone."

CHAPTER LIV

We have passed from the amazing spell of the Servant Songs, and, if we have been in any adequate way moved by them, we must necessarily feel our spirits let down, the strings of music less taut, the waves of hope and joy, of expectation and of fulfillment, sinking into a great calm. As we begin to read ch. 54 we shall not feel the same throb as resounded in ch. 53. Nay, more. If we read a few verses in ch. 54 and begin to sense a note somewhat familiar, we may easily turn back and find that it sounds much like an even continuation of 52[11, 12]. It seems almost as though the great Servant passage 52[13]–53[12] formed a break in the continuity of the prophet's teaching and may be an insertion. So have thought not a few scholars, and so some still declare. They would even argue that the difference is so great that the portrayal of the suffering Servant must have come from some other hand. But there is ready an easy and sufficient answer to this. In every great work of literary art there must be meadow lands as well as mountain heights. It would be very easy to leave out passages and find an easy continuation without them. Whole choruses might be left out of Greek tragedies, and the story would flow on without appreciable loss of them. Speeches in Shakespeare are sometimes so grand that the simple dialogue that follows seems unworthy of the same hand. So it is here. There is no sufficient reason to doubt ch. 54 as the work of the same brain and hand as ch. 53. The great prophet has merely finished that part of his message, and is ready now to return to the main business of comforting the exiles. The chapter divides naturally into two main parts, vv. 1–10 and vv. 11–17.

1–10. The Constancy of Jehovah. Zion, in captivity far from the land which once was her own, in which Jehovah acknowledged her as his people, and cherished her under the figure of marriage, he as the husband, and she as the wife, this Zion is now comforted with the word that she has more children than ever before, and they shall be restored to her, when her separation from her husband Jehovah is ended. The separation was but temporary, to be succeeded by a union resting on a new and unchangeable covenant.

Barren in v. 1 is here used not of a woman who never bore, but of one who is separated but shall return. Let her sing and prepare to return under conditions greatly improved, all under the figure of a great tent stretched out in the homeland, both north and south, compassing not only the old land of Palestine but also the lands and cities of neighboring nations, even though now they be desolate and uninhabited. When that joyous return has been consummated she will remember none of these desolate days of exile, when she was filled with shame. She need not fear, for "her husband is her Maker" (so, not *her maker is her husband*). Her husband is He that made all that is, and has therefore dominion over the whole earth. She is now recalled not as some old wife, no longer a joy, but as a *wife of youth.* The time of exile may have seemed long to her, but it is really only a small *moment*, and she will now be gathered again with great mercies. His face was hidden in wrath only for a moment, to be succeeded by an everlasting kindness. This new covenant is sure, and it is compared with the permanence of the covenant with Noah, and also with the everlasting hills.

11–17. The Splendor of Jerusalem Restored. Here we come to a brilliant description of the glories of the restored city of Jerusalem, for it shall far exceed all that the ancient city was, the city from which the exiles were carried to Babylonia. The city is to be rebuilt of stone, and the stones are to be laid in *fair colors*, but the Hebrew seems rather to mean "in antimony." The salt of antimony was, and still is, used by Oriental women as a cosmetic. It was carried in a box or small horn, and was gray in color, a slight line of it was deftly run on the eyelids and there it turned black and at a little distance enlarged the appearance of the eye, and supposedly its dark fire of beauty. Here it is to be used as a costly mortar to set off the beauty of fine stones. The foundation stones are to be sapphires, and the pinnacles rubies, and the gates are "fiery stones" which means probably *carbuncles*, though the LXX renders *stones of crystal*, and all the border, i.e., the outer wall, of precious stones. To correspond to this external splendor there is to be an internal spiritual life of the inhabitants (v. 13). The people shall all be disciples of Jehovah, not dependent upon human teachers; so shall be fulfilled the wish of Moses (Num. 11[29]). *In righteousness*, or perhaps better "in triumph," shall the city be established, and need fear no oppression or terror, i.e., destruction. Both oppression and destruction had the city well known, much feared and greatly experienced. This is now over and done; no more shall enemies gather, as they had so often done even under Jehovah's own command, but he shall raise them up no more, and if they gather of their own will they shall fall.

V. 15 is a difficult verse (see R.V. mg.), but there is no need to reject it, as Duhm and Cheyne have done, and the sense extracted by the R.V. seems reasonable and satisfactory. God will protect his people from any further attack upon them. No enemy can invade without arms, and arms are made by the smith, but the smith was created by Jehovah, and cannot make weapons without his will, nor can the enemy, the *waster*, destroy without Jehovah's will (cf. Nah. 2[1f.]). No weapon that any one can fashion shall be able to work against them, nor any tongue condemn. All these things are the heritage of the servants of Jehovah; all these blessings which have been enumerated in this ringing chapter are for the saints of his. Note here that we have *the servants of the Lord* in the plural. Skinner suggests, and rightly, that this connects the chapter with the Servant of Jehovah in the preceding passages. "The ideal represented by *the* Servant of Jehovah is now reproduced in each individual member of the new Israel."

CHAPTER LV

This is a chapter of great beauty, of a melody so exquisite that its opening words have sung their way down the centuries and found place in Christian liturgies and in Christian lectionaries. Yet for all its beauty of words it is withal a solemn and earnest chapter.

1–5. "Come . . . Without Money and Without Price." Let us remember to whom the words were addressed in the first instance. The people had gone into exile with many heartburnings and with sharp cries against their captors, of which Psa. 137 is a vivid reminder. Then Jeremiah (chs. 29f.) wrote them an urgent letter desiring them to accept the situation as God-given national punishment, to be reconciled to the Babylonians, and pray for their peace, to give themselves diligently to the ordinary business of life and there win prosperity until God should will otherwise for them. Some accepted his advice and applied it with too great energy. The Hebrews had a gift for religion perhaps never completely paralleled among any other people. But the rudimentary possibilities of other kinds were in them, and in Babylonia these came very strongly to the fore. They developed immense capacity for business, and many rose to great heights of wealth and power. Of these, few retained the old religious fire. We need only to look about us—nay, even into our own hearts—to see how readily do religious emotions die when religious practices are abandoned, even temporarily. In Babylonia there were no Jewish temple services, and great were the efforts of the prophets like Ezekiel and the Second Isaiah to keep faith alive. To those who were absorbed in successful business in Babylonia are these words addressed, calling them back to God and to religious thought and meditation. The people are called by the prophet to come and seek spiritual nourishment, here figured under wine and milk. Let them give over the mad race for money, only to spend it for those things which can never satisfy the deep cravings of the human heart. Let them, rather, take the religious life freely offered without money and without price. Nowhere else in all the O.T. is the gospel invitation more wonderfully foreshadowed than in these words of the prophet. The only condition necessary is to *incline the ear and come.* There are no barriers between these people and their God. He is ready to impart a new life and to make with them an everlasting covenant, even the same mercies or lovingkindnesses promised long before to David (2 Sam. 7[8-16]). David in his day was a witness, leader, and commander to his people, but the complete fulfillment of all the promises to him will only come in the person of the great Prince of his house who is later to arise. This coming Prince is the Messiah, who is indeed not elsewhere made known by the Second Isaiah, who has only portrayed the ideal King, not the suffering Servant. In due time, however, the Messiah, the ideal King and the suffering Servant all were blended in one person, even the Lord Christ. (See *Excursus* following ch. 53 above, p. 664.)

6–9. Repentance the Condition to Restoration. But before the Messiah can come men must prepare for his coming, and the first step is that they be summoned to repentance, not to wails and tears as too often the modern man is disposed to define repentance, but to an entirely new life. The people are still in exile in Babylonia, but their release is coming soon; let them make preparation for it by seeking the Lord. He is now near, for he will be the leader of his people in their great march homeward, and he will be easily found. But upon men must come the burden of action, and the action required is to *forsake* the old sinful ways and the old sinful thoughts. This is true repentance, an anticipation of the N.T. doctrine. But man need not fear that the Lord will be harsh to the sinner on his return—nay, he will have mercy and will abundantly pardon. Let us read the words over again and taste their beauty and power. While the great peoples of Egypt or of Babylonia are wearied in the search for some escape from sin by magic, or incantations and wild cries for deliverance, the Jew is worshiping a God who needs no such appeal, requiring only that man change his life and seek his God, who will, without question or hesitation, have mercy and abundantly pardon. The ground for confidence that Jehovah will really do as the prophet promises is that he is a God far above all the weakness of men. His thoughts are not like man's, but transcend them in every way. His will for men is for their redemption; his purposes cannot be compared with man's. (Turn back and look at Isa. 40[27], and compare the beautiful words in Jer. 29[11] and see also Mic. 4[12].)

10–13. God's Word as a Fructifying Power. Jehovah's will to deliver his people from their sins is expressed in his word. This word will accomplish its mission, and the accomplishment is pictured very beautifully and poetically in the figure of rain and snow. God has given an energy to his word, an energy of its own, as he has to rain and snow, and it will fulfill its purpose as they do theirs. Once again does the prophet return to the glorious deliverance from Babylon. Jehovah will come, take his people out with joy and peace, not as they came out of Egypt, but in glory and honor. Even the natural world shall know the import and celebrate its occurrence. The mountains, so solid, so stolid as their wont has been, will unite with the hills in singing, while the trees clap their hands. Then when they are on the march the desert flora will be changed, and its repellent wild growths will be changed to the useful or the beautiful. In v. 13 these growths are enumerated, and the first mentioned, translated *thorn,* is a word which occurs elsewhere only in Isa. 7[19] and is, with probability, supposed to be the same fiercely growing wild bush which is found still in the Jordan valley and up through the wilderness even close to Jerusalem. It has acquired the illfitting popular name of "Christ-thorn," and forms impenetrable clumps of savage, tearing thorns. It is to disappear and in its place will grow the very useful "cypress," here wrongly translated *fir-tree.* The word translated *brier* is in Hebrew *sirpad,* which is apparently an Egyptian word, the name of a kind of papyrus plant used in part for food. In its stead shall come up the *myrtle,* one of the most highly prized and widely distributed growths of all Palestine. In poor soils it is a shrub, but in good it rises to considerable size as a bushy tree. It has dark-green scented leaves, starry white flowers, and dark berries which are still eaten. It is still used among the cheerful decorations of the feast of Tabernacles. These all shall remain growing in the desert after Israel has passed by on the way to its former home, and they shall be an everlasting sign of God's providence.

So ends this beautiful chapter, and with it concludes the prophecy of that great prophet whose work began with ch. 40. He is indeed the Evangelical Prophet of God's people. He that carried down to us and our day the unforgettable pictures of the suffering Servant has fulfilled his mission, his work ends and we turn now to the consideration of other voices in chs. 56–66.

Chapters 56 to 66: The Third Part of the Book of Isaiah

To any observant and unprejudiced reader there comes the impression as he begins to read ch. 56 of a great change in circumstance, tone, and color. The break from the high tone of ch. 55 is sudden and unmistakable. The first eight verses of ch. 56 make the break far more noticeable than any verses in the whole series. Their subject seems fussy and small when contrasted with the organlike tones of ch. 55. The eunuchs and proselytes seem so poor a subject after the redeemed of the Lord, a whole people invited to return to the Lord and take up the march over a transformed desert. The modern reader is almost ready to say that it does not matter at all what happens to the poor eunuchs, nor even to a small gleaning of folk out of the nations that knew not Jehovah. There is nothing else in the whole series of chapters so poor as these verses, yet they have done their useful literary work and set these chapters apart. Very different would have been the effect if chs. 60–62 had followed immediately upon ch. 55. They have melody and beauty not at all unworthy to compare with chs. 40–55 and would very likely have found a general, perhaps a very wide, acceptance as the work of the same mind (see pp. 653–4). Indeed, there are still some who would be disposed to hold that they really belong to him and have only been accidentally misplaced. There will be opportunity for another word about these chapters later, and we may pass them by for the moment, and speak yet a word more about the remaining chs., 56–59 and 63–66. The very first impression which they make is that they are not homogeneous. They change every little while, and one reads on, thinking as he does that the sound is not of one but of several prophetic voices. Some of these we should feel lack markedly a richness of vocabulary, a beauty of phrase, a colorful expression, but this would not appear in 63[1-6], which has fire and dash, is graphic and sustained in rhythm. And again there follows upon this (63[7]–64[12]), a long prayer and confession which is sad, yet has a tone not unworthy of association with great passages elsewhere in this book.

With diversities so great as these here very imperfectly indicated, the date of these prophecies is extremely difficult to determine and doubts must be widely held concerning any attempt even to approximate it. On the whole, however, it seems clear enough that the major portion, if not all, comes from a period not only after the return from exile, but even as to most of it considerably after that significant event. It seems, e.g., clear enough that the Temple has not only been rebuilt, but its services have been long enough in observance to provide opportunities for minor difficulties and differences of opinion or practice to have arisen which cause debate or even confusion. If we consider the import of the rebuilt Temple, and of its services, we are carried down lower than the period of Haggai and Zechariah, i.e., later than 515 B.C. If we range with this matter other little hints too delicate for discussion without the citation of Hebrew, we must come down still later even to the period of Nehemiah, about 450 B.C. Let us rest the matter there and without dogmatism, but, rather, with much diffidence say that, on the whole, these chapters may better be located there than at any other time. And now come we to a brief exposition of the chapters and verses.

CHAPTER LVI

1–8. A Prophecy Concerning Eunuchs and Proselytes. The point of immediate emphasis for both these classes is the keeping of the Sabbath. The Jews have long been reestablished in their own land, and many hearts were sad enough with disappointment, for the glories foreseen by the prophets have not appeared. Life was drab enough. The salvation of the Lord had been, so far as they could see, postponed, deferred; perhaps it would never come. They are creeping along, not bounding forward. They are busy with ritual and with matters small and poor when compared with the grandeur that had been promised. In these dull verses, the *eunuchs* come first. They can feel no inheritance in Jewry, for they cannot found a family and carry on its name. Let them keep the Sabbath, and do no evil. The prophet offers this as a duty, and makes the promise that somewhere within the Temple precincts a memorial or, better, a monument shall be set up for them, and that will be better than sons and daughters. The second class, who appear to have been anxious concerning their status under the new regime in Jerusalem after the return, was composed of the proselytes (v. 6, *strangers*) who were fearful lest they be somehow excluded, saying, *The Lord will surely separate me from his people.* To them reply is now made in vv. 6–8. They are advised that if they keep the Sabbath, and hold fast the covenant, they need neither doubt nor fear. Jehovah will surely bring them to the holy mountain, i.e., the sanctuary, and all their offerings and sacrifices will be accepted.

Then comes the splendid declaration that God's house shall be a house of prayer for all peoples, and not for the Jews only. This is cited by our Lord (Mt. 21[13] Mk. 11[17] Lk. 19[46]). Then to those already gathered God will gather others. It is the true note of universal diffusion of the knowledge of God and its world-wide acceptance which was later to characterize Christianity.

9–12. A Furious Arraignment of the Leaders of Israel (including also 57[1, 2], which see). The passage 56[9]–57[21], which describes the idolatrous conduct of the people, is separated in thought as well as in form from the preceding. It comprises a severe indictment of disorders and of idolatry within the restored community. This runs on to 57[13a], and is followed by good and gentle promises to the humble and the penitent (57[13b-21]). The evils are plainly ascribed to the Jewish authorities of the period (56[10, 11]), and the seats of the idolatry are clearly Palestinian and not Babylonian (57[5-7]). The evils condemned are the same as those described in chs. 58 and 59, while the idolatries are again condemned in 65[1-7] 66[1-4, 17], and this makes it clear that those passages are contemporaneous; and the whole situation finds its parallel in Mal. 2[11] 3[5] Neh. 5[2-5] and Ezra 9[1, 2]. With these, then, we are fairly safe in fixing this passage in point of time. It remains only that we examine it in details just enough to get the general view of it.

The incompetence or ignorance of the leaders leaves the whole nation defenseless. In verse order it runs so: In a figure the wild beasts are bidden to come and devour the people, because dogs, who are their natural protectors, are sleepy and dumb, and they are ever greedy (vv. 9–11). (The comparison between the rulers and dogs is interesting. The Jews, like the modern Arabs, were never lovers of dogs, and the comparison is quite naturally against the dog. It seems to have been the Indo-European who more largely and truly loved man's first friend among the animals.) The figure is dropped and the rulers are painted as having most pleasure in a great drunken carouse (vv. 11, 12). As a consequence the righteous perish and find their only rest and peace in the grave (57[1, 2]).

CHAPTER LVII

1, 2. See comments on 56[9-12].

3–13a. An Attack Upon an Idolatrous Party. It is not easy to make sure who composed this idolatrous party. Among many attempts in modern times to identify them, the two that most stand out are that they were either the Samaritans or the Jews who were left behind in Palestine when Nebuchadrezzar carried out the deportation in 586 B.C. To the view that it was the Samaritans, Skinner gives his approval, but to me it seems much more likely to be those who remained in the land in 586 B.C., and formed various ties and connections with the Samaritans in the north and with their still remaining Palestinian neighbors. When the introduction of the Law under Ezra and Nehemiah took place they refused compliance, or were so much entangled with heathen or half-heathen rites and ceremonies that they would not have been acceptable to the orthodox. Their attitude toward religion was not a complete rejection of Jehovah. It was not a pure idolatry; it was a mixture of the worship of their father's God with idolatrous rites, or beliefs. It was, indeed, a religious syncretism. It was representatives of these ideas and practices that Nehemiah drove out, and so unconsciously produced the Samaritan religious community of which a sorry fragment remains to this day in and about Nablous. The castigation of them in the verses which follow is fearfully severe. Their forms of worship, *under every green tree*, "child sacrifice," "stone worship," all come under the lash. The allusion to *bed* (v. 7) hints at the connection between idolatry and adultery, while the next reference (v. 8) is to some heathen figure or idol used in private house worship. In v. 9 the word for *king* is in Hebrew *Melek*, which is the name of a Canaanite deity, and to him and the use of oils and unguents in his worship is probably the allusion, while the reference in *Sheol* (mg.) is probably to the gods of the infernal regions widely known and worshiped among neighboring nations. The journey to heathen shrines was often long and wearisome, but they kept on (v. 10) and were in fear of these idols, and not of the living God, and this perhaps because he was silent (v. 11; cf. Psa. 50[21]). *I will declare thy righteousness*—this is spoken ironically, and is followed at once by *thy works*, i.e., either their lives, or their idols, and *they shall not profit* (v. 12). *Them which thou hast gathered* (v. 13) is one word in Hebrew; it occurs only here, so its meaning is doubtful. It probably means idols; the wind shall blow them away. The next clause is a promise to those that take refuge in Jehovah, and introduces the next section.

13b–21. "The Lofty One that Inhabiteth Eternity. In fine and ringing sentences the prophet makes splendid promises to those who follow the Lord and not the idols. The figure with which he begins is the highway of salvation taken from 40[3] (cf. also 62[10]) and Jehovah is speaking. In the earlier passage it is a description of the highway by which the returning exiles shall come home to Jerusalem; here it is only a figure of speech for the removal of everything which hinders the spiritual advance of the people of God. The God who will accomplish this is he who inhabits eternity and is not only on high but also holy, yet is he, on the other hand, willing to dwell with him who is crushed and abased in spirit, and these will he revive in spirit and heart. God will not *contend* (v. 16), i.e., punish forever, because man is so frail that he would break down under the strain. But God has seen the ways of man and will heal him, and restore him. God will create the *fruit of the lips*, (v. 19), which means "praise and thanksgiving," and will cry out peace to those afar off, i.e., those that are still in Babylonia; and those that are near, i.e., those that have already returned. In contrast to these who are thus made happy are the wicked who are described by the figure of the troubled sea which *casts up mire and dirt*. This is a description of the movements of conscience which will not let the wicked be at rest (vv. 20, 21). There is an even finer picture of the evil conscience in Job 15[20-25].

CHAPTER LVIII

A chapter devoted to fasting and to the observance of the Sabbath. It falls naturally into two parts—fasting, vv. 1–12, and the Sabbath, vv. 13, 14.

1–12. Fasting. The fault the prophet has to expose is formal fasting, which the people could and did carry on without interfering with evil practices in their daily lives. Fasting as a religious observance was common at all periods of Hebrew history, but the period of the Exile systematized it. In exile the ceremonies of the Temple ritual could not be carried through, and other religious forms were sought to take their place. During the last siege of Jerusalem disasters occurred (Zech. 7[3-5] 8[19]), and the memory of these was kept alive by a regular series of fasts held in the fourth, fifth, seventh, and tenth months on their anniversaries. When the people returned they brought these ceremonial fasts with them, and thought by them to attract the divine favor. So the prophet is bidden to cry out to them. They have complained that God paid no heed to their fastings and prostrations. To which the prophet in God's name makes answer, that even while they fast they find time to indulge their own *pleasure*, or, rather, to attend to their business and oppress their laborers (v. 3; cf. mg.). Their fasting is an external exercise, and makes them irritable *for strife and contention*, and fails to make their voice heard on high. Skinner aptly quotes,

"My words fly up, my thoughts remain below,
Words without thoughts never to heaven go." (*Hamlet*, Act III, Scene 3.)

But these are not the suitable expressions for such a fast as Jehovah would desire. The true fast is described in vv. 6 and 7. Its expression is both positive and negative. They must abstain from oppressing the weak, and instead make provision for the destitute. (Cf. Ezek. 18[7-9] Zech. 8[16, 17] Job 31[13, 14] Mt. 5[7], 6[12, 18]). When such ethical fasts and social duties take the place of the empty forms which they practice, then will come the glory of God's healing, then they may call and the Lord will answer. Then will come a true prosperity, and they shall be able to rebuild the waste places. This suggests strongly the period of Nehemiah.

13, 14. The Sabbath. Once more we come upon injunctions to keep the Sabbath. This also points toward the period of Nehemiah, when regulations were enforced to protect the day (Neh. 13[15]). One phrase in this passage is unusual. The Sabbath is called *the holy of the Lord;* the word rendered *pleasure* should be "business." If they fulfill these commands, then God will cause them *to ride upon the high places of the earth*—which is apparently a quotation from Deut. 32[13]. So is scripture tied up with scripture, and echo answers echo.

CHAPTER LIX

1–8. Sin a Barrier Between God and Men. This paragraph is closely connected with the last chapter and seems to be a part of the same prophetic message. We shall probably not go far astray if we so assume, and attempt the exposition of it on that basis. The prophet blames directly on the people the troubles that are upon them. His argument is that God is as able as ever to succor his people, and their troubles in the land of restoration are not due to his inability or unwillingness but to their sin. The arraignment is sharp, for blood guiltiness is charged, and they are litigious, and not in righteousness. Under a figure they are described as carrying on schemes which are profitable neither to themselves nor to others. This continues in v. 6 under an expansion of the figure, the point of which is that no good can possibly come from evil works.

9–21. God's Willingness to Destroy the Barrier. There are, however, good men among them who correctly discern the situation and lament the evil which they recognize is due not to God's remissness but to the sins of their fellows. This leads to a confession in vv. 12–15a. In the people's name the prophet confesses their sins, as shown in manifold transgressions and a denial of God. Righteousness, truth, and uprightness are unable to maintain themselves. But though the present is dark, some day Jehovah will interfere (vv. 15b–20). When Jehovah sees that there is *none to interpose* (v. 16, mg.) he concludes that he himself must rescue Israel. It seems possible, but hardly probable, that the evils from which he will bring deliverance are those already recounted, the social ills of the people themselves; however, more likely the reference is to external ills of some sort inflicted by the Persians who now ruled them. The prophet speaks in the prophetic perfect as though the intervention had already occurred. God is represented as a warrior putting on armor, and the figure carries over into the N.T. (Eph. 6[14ff.] 1 Thess. 5[8]). In v. 18 *according to* and *accordingly* are very awkward in Hebrew, but the meaning is not very obscure, and we need not resort to conjecture. The last clause, *to the islands* (read with mg. *coastlands*) *he will repay recompense*, is wanting in the LXX and is probably an insertion. The translation of v. 19 in the R.V. is based largely on the LXX and is, on the whole, preferable to any other yet suggested, but the text is not above suspicion. In v. 20 the translation should be *And as a Redeemer will he come to Zion;* and in the next clause the LXX offers a better text in the translation, *and shall turn away transgression from Jacob.* Cf. Rom. 12[20], where there is a Messianic application. The final verse of the chapter seems to lack all connection with the preceding. It looks much like an insertion from some other prophetic message.

Chapters 60 to 62: The Future Glory of the City of Jerusalem

We pass quickly from gloom and sin, from confession and manifold anxieties, to a prophecy of uncommon beauty and eloquence in chs. 60–62. They also belong to this later period, though they are so much like chs. 40–55 that one is tempted to think of them as a fragment which is misplaced here and belongs rather with those beautiful chapters of the Second Isaiah. On the whole, however, it accords best with such probabilities as there are to assign the chapters to the later age. The prophecy antedates, however, the days of Nehemiah, for the city walls are still not built (60[10]).

CHAPTER LX

1–9. The Nations Flock to a Restored Zion. It is Jehovah himself who is here speaking, bidding Jerusalem arise and shine in the reflected light of his glory. The picture is of a city gleaming in the light of the morning, while the rest of the world is in darkness, and so the nations must come out of their darkness to Zion's light. In vv. 4–9 is a prediction that the scattered sons of Israel shall come home to their own people. One of the greatest difficulties of the restoration period was that so many of the exiles still remained in Babylonia and in other lands to which they had scattered. With them shall come also the *abundance*, i.e., the wealth of sea-borne commerce, and the great land caravans as well, typified under numbers of camels. *Dromedaries* should be "young camels," i.e., less than nine years old. *Ephah* is a Midianite tribe (Gen. 25[4]), and the Midianites were famed for their numbers of camels. *Sheba* lies in the southern part of Arabia; *Kedar* and *Nebaioth* are sons of Ishmael, and are pastoral tribes in Northern Arabia. The latter are probably the ancestors of the Nabateans, who formed a powerful kingdom in the second century B.C. (1 Macc. 5[25] 9[35]).

10–14. Jerusalem to be Rebuilt by Its Destroyers. The city is to be rebuilt by the very foreigners who had destroyed it and carried off its people. The walls were still in ruin when Nehemiah came in 445 B.C., and it was he who took the lead in their reconstruction, receiving help from Artaxerxes, the Persian king (Neh. 2[7, 8]). But the city will not need these walls for defense against evil nations. Rather her gates will be open day and night to receive the offerings of nations and their kings. V. 12 interrupts both thought and meter and is probably an insertion made out of Zech. 14[17-19]. The Temple has been rebuilt but upon a small scale, and it is now promised that it will be adorned and beautified by the choicest woods; and to this Temple shall come the descendants of the people who had harassed and destroyed Israel.

15–22. "The Lord Shall be an Everlasting Light." Whereas they had been a despised people they will now be fairly overwhelmed with adulation from abroad, and all the finest and most beautiful metals will take the place of humbler ones; and in correspondence with this external magnificence there shall be internal peace and righteousness. In that glorious age even the ordinary means of lighting the city shall not be needed, neither sun nor moon, but God shall be its light. The passage perhaps owes its primary suggestion to

Ezek. 43², and in its turn becomes the foundation of the fine description of the New Jerusalem in Rev. 21²³. The sun and moon will not be destroyed, but rather shall never set, and God will be an everlasting light, and there shall be no more mourning. But the ethical side is not to be forgotten, for all shall be righteous, and they shall be so increased in number that there will be a great nation. All this will come to pass in due time; when the Lord is ready he will hasten it.

CHAPTER LXI

This chapter follows upon and carries out further the prediction of the future glories of Zion, as they are portrayed in ch. 60, but it has even closer ties with ch. 62.

1–3. The Prophet Anointed to Preach Good Tidings. The beginning is here quite different from both preceding and following. Here it is introduced by a speaker, and we must ask who he was. The answer, in spite of much debate, must be that it is the prophet himself; but the description of him is much colored by the imagery of the suffering Servant, and the prophet here becomes a sort of type of him in outline. He is here an ideal prophet, and thus becomes a type of the Christ as the suffering Servant. For this reason it is that our Lord identifies himself with this speaker (Lk. 4¹⁸ᶠ·). This herald comes under a divine anointing to preach good tidings to the *meek*, i.e., the poor, the distressed, the humble. He is also to *bind up*, i.e., "heal" *the broken-hearted*, set free the captives, and to proclaim the *acceptable*, i.e., the "favorable" *year of the Lord*. There is also to be vengeance on the oppressors of the people, and perhaps also upon their own sinners. Then they are to have a garland on their heads instead of ashes, which were a sign of mourning, and oil of joy instead of mourning (for Orientals did not anoint themselves with oil when they were in mourning), and a garment of praise instead of a failing or flickering spirit. The *trees* are the terebinths, which were evergreen, an emblem of the life of the righteous.

4–11. Israel's Destiny as a Kingdom of Priests. In v. 4 we have the old predictions of rebuilding as in 49⁸ 58¹² 60¹⁰; for the need of this and the joy its accomplishment would bring was much on their minds. Then follows a picture of Israel as a nation acting as priest for the nations and so receiving such honors from other nations as the lay folk of Israel were in the habit of offering their priests. Israel had been called in the beginning to be a nation of priests or a kingdom of priests (Ex. 19⁶), and now this glorious destiny is at last to be fulfilled. In the glory of the nations *shall ye boast yourselves* (v. 6). This is sustained by the ancient versions, but the reading in the margin of the R.V., *to their glory shall ye succeed*, is perhaps preferable. The positions shall be reversed. Israel, which had suffered such humiliation, will now be moved into the place of glory and dignity formerly occupied by the nations. The robbery and iniquity (v. 8) are of the nations who oppressed Israel, and Israel is now to find a recompence, and God will make with them a covenant never to be broken.

In v. 10 Jerusalem is speaking, and giving thanks; as it breaks the connection between vv. 9 and 11 it must probably be regarded as a misplaced fragment. *God will cause righteousness and praise to spring forth.*

CHAPTER LXII

A beautiful and eloquent chapter well worthy to close the little group of prophecies in chs. 60–62.

1–5. "The Forsaken" to Become "A Delight." The speaker is probably the prophet as in 61¹, but there are some phrases which would make it appropriate to consider the speaker as Jehovah himself (cf. 61⁸); the reference to the Lord in the third person in vv. 2–5, however, makes the prophet as speaker seem on the whole most probable. As we read on it becomes more and more clear that the prophet is putting forth herculean efforts to encourage a people who were sorely discouraged. Just as it was the chief business and duty of the Second Isaiah to encourage the exiles to believe that Jehovah had not forgotten them but would see them safely out of Babylonia and on the way homeward, so now it was the mission of the "Third Isaiah" to encourage the returned people. They were obviously unhappy, as has before been pointed out, and to many of them the glories of earlier predictions must have seemed a mockery. So now the prophet appears as an intercessor with Jehovah on their behalf, and for their sakes will not be silent. For *lamp* in v. 1 read *torch.* Again we have the emphatic note that the nations will know and mark Israel's glory. They also shall have a *crown;* the ancient custom was to surmount a city deity with a mural crown, but in this case Jehovah will hold it in his hand, and over them. No more shall Jerusalem be called *Forsaken*, i.e., in Hebrew, *Azubah*, but, rather, *Hephzibah* ("delight in her") and *Beulah* ("married"), for she is to be married to the Lord.

6–9. The Duty of the Watchmen on the Walls. Here the prophet describes himself as assisted in the supplication just mentioned by a corps of watchmen on the reconstructed walls, who join in reminding Jehovah of his promises and in beseeching him for their fulfillment. The usual business of watchers on city walls was to sound the alarm on the approach of enemies, but these have a different purpose. They are apparently angelic visitors who stand on the new walls and take up the prophet's supplication to carry it on. Yet there are dangers to the city at the hands of marauders like the Edomites (Mal. 1[2-5]), or because of the exactions of Persian governors (Neh. 5[15]). These are slight but useful hints in locating the date of the chapter as belonging to the restoration period. The watchers need not cry out that the invaders are coming, but need only remind the Lord of his promised protection.

10–12. Complete Restoration. Here is the encouraging announcement that the rest of the exiles are coming. Many had remained in Babylonia, while others were in Egypt, or even more widely dispersed. They will now enter the gates of Jerusalem, and preparations must be made to facilitate their journey. The prophet is clearly influenced by the description given by the Second Isaiah of the preparations for the first return. The salvation of Jerusalem comes and the fine phrase, *Behold, his reward is with him,* is quoted from 40[10]. And they are henceforth to be called a holy people, redeemed of the Lord, and the city is to be called, *Sought out,* i.e., sought after, or much sought after, in contrast to "Forsaken" as it had been. It is to be just the opposite of that which is suggested in an earlier description, "This is Zion, whom no man seeketh after" (Jer. 30[17]).

CHAPTER LXIII

1–6. Jehovah Approaching in Avenging Fury. Here is a poem of great but awful beauty, quite detached from all that precedes and follows. The prophet on some place of lookout perceives approaching from the southeast, from the direction of Edom, a majestic and lonely but awful figure; on him are crimsoned (better than *dyed,* but the word means literally "sharpened") garments, which are described in our translation as *glorious,* but the word really means "swelling," and the figure is not very clear. Duhm thinks it means they are blown out by the winds, and this, though uncertain, may be correct. He is *marching;* Delitzsch beautifully explains the action out of Arabic parallels as a "gesture of proud self consciousness." The awe-stricken prophet calls out to ask who this may be, and receives an answer that shows the person to be none other than the Lord himself. The Lord declares himself as true in speech, and as *mighty to save.* The Christian fathers made the lamentable blunder of thinking this to be Messianic, a picture in some way of Jesus the Christ in his capacity of Saviour by the outpouring of blood. But this was hopelessly wrong. It is the Lord Jehovah in his capacity not as a Saviour but as an Avenger. For centuries his people have been trodden down, plundered, slain, exiled. He has at long last come to avenge their wrongs. The Warrior-Avenger answers the prophet and tells who he is and what he has done. All this is future in reality, but it is expressed in perfect tenses to give it a sense of certainty. The A.V. translates much in future tense, but the R.V. does the original justice by representing the whole picture through perfects. The Lord usually commissions men or nations to execute his judgments, but in this instance he trod down Israel's oppressors and did it alone. The crimsoned garments were sprinkled with the blood of his victims. *I trod* is perfect, though the Hebrew has "I will tread"; the LXX supplies the necessary correction. *Stained* should be "defiled," a stronger word, and it is worth noting that it is an Aramaic and not a Hebrew form, and is so another slight indication of a late date. In v. 4 *was in mine heart,* should be "is in my heart"; heart means the seat of purpose, as in many other places, e.g., in Judg. 5[15], 2 Chr. 12[14]. *There was none to help.* Jehovah looked the whole world over to see what nation or what man might save his people, but there was none and he must himself bring their deliverance. The contrast between this situation and that presented in the Second Isaiah is striking, for in the latter case the Lord had a deliverer ready for the task in the person of Cyrus. In v. 6 Jehovah again declares that he *trod down the peoples,* but the verb is not the same as that used in v. 3. *Made them drunk;* to make drunk is to lay prostrate, make helpless. Notice that it is *the peoples,* not "a people" that the warrior avenger is trampling in his anger. It is not only the people of Edom, historic enemies of the Hebrews since the days of Moses, but all other of the ancient enemies of the Israelites, including the Egyptians, Assyrians, and Chaldeans, as well as minor peoples such as Moabites, Philistines, Tyrians and the Aramæans of Damascus.

7–19. Prayer for the Renewal of Jehovah's Lovingkindness. In 63[7]–64[12] is found a remarkable prayer of deep and humble piety, and readily recognizable as representative of a type of devotion which arose especially during the exile. Then a people brokenhearted and demoralized, stripped of the sense of victory which they had enjoyed under David and Jeroboam II, were turning to God in humility of soul to find a way of assured communion with him and happiness therein. At first blush one would wish to ascribe this prayer to that period, were it not that difficulties obtrude. It is indeed a very complex problem. The historical allusions are not only very explicit in one place and vague in another, but, worse still, are at times even contradictory. Thus, e.g., it is made clear that Jerusalem and its Temple lie desolate (64^{10}) and the Temple has been burned (63^{18} 64^{11}). These allusions would suit well the period between 586 and 537 B.C. But then we read that they had possessed the desolated sanctuary but a little while (63^{18}), and this surely does not well fit the three hundred and fifty years or so that they had worshiped in it from Solomon to Nebuchadrezzar. Furthermore, the general tone suits the depressing period soon after the return better than the period of exile, and so one would think of the period between 537 and 520 B.C. But the Temple rebuilding did not begin until then, and 63^{18} would seem to imply that it had been rebuilt and only occupied for a little while. Thus we come to the difficulty of supposing that it had again been laid low; but we do not know of any destruction during this period, though suppositions have been advanced that the Samaritans had destroyed it. The simple truth is that we do not know the historical background of the passage and have no right to be dogmatic about it. On the whole, balancing probabilities, it seems best to express the hesitant opinion that it may be located shortly after 520 B.C. and between then and 500, though gladly admitting that this does not meet every indication. This would make it the work of some unknown prophet who lived a little earlier than the Third Isaiah.

At v. 7 the prophet turns back to past history and reminds himself of God's wonderful care of his people. This was very characteristic of the attitude of the devotionally minded. The glorious book of Psalms has much of it (Psa. 77^{10-15} $79^{1f.}$ 106^{2}). It was in human history that God was manifested, and the Israelites always harked back in thought to the days when the divine manifestation was most readily discernible. God had confidence in their fathers, and believed that they would not be faithless, and for this he became their Saviour.

9. The verse is so beautiful that it were a pity to supplant or to change it, but difficulties in the text and the lack of complete parallels make the reading problematic. The ordinary Hebrew text reads, "In all their affliction he was no adversary." It is the margin of the Hebrew text which has found a wide acceptance and this is adopted in both of our versions in the form, *In all their affliction he was afflicted*, literally, "there was affliction to him." Nowhere else in the O.T. is there so strong an expression of the divine sympathy as this, though there are approaches to it in Judg. 10^{16} and Psa. 106^{44}. That there is no parallel is, of course, not a proof that it does not occur here, but it does make one a bit doubtful. The doubt increases when we see that the LXX has a quite different text. It reads, *In all their affliction it was not a messenger or an angel but his own self* (Hebrew, his face, his presence) *that saved them.* This attracts us at once, and it may be right. *He bare them* would be better translated "he took them up." But though their God had so cared for them they proved faithless, and rebelled against him, and many are the illustrations of this which are reported in Holy Writ, as, e.g., in Num. 20^{1-13} Psa. $78^{17, 40}$ 106^{33}; with these compare Acts 7^{51}.

11. Here is a difficulty for which two solutions are proposed. It should be either *Then he* (i.e., Israel) *remembered the days of old*, or, *Then his people remembered the ancient days of Moses* (which is not a good order of words in Hebrew); the former is preferable. The next clause is, as commonly translated, ungrammatical in Hebrew, and one of the best LXX manuscripts is probably right in reading, *Where is he that brought up from the sea the shepherd of his flock*? This would make it a reference to the deliverance of the child Moses from the Nile (Ex. 2), the word "sea" being elsewhere used as an expression for the Nile (18^{2} and 19^{5}). The last word in the verse, *them*, should probably be "him," referring to Moses, as is the Hebrew, and also the A.V. The Lord's *arm* is personified, and is the symbol of God's power placed at the command of Moses, to divide the waters of the Red Sea and permit Israel to cross. Then in vv. 13 and 14 Israel is represented as crossing the sea just as firmly and securely as a horse treading the wilderness or the cattle going quietly into the valley. Thence God brought them to rest, i.e., in the promised land.

15-19. Basing his prayer on the experience of the past, the prophet in his day of gloom and disappointment appeals to God for a new manifestation, a new Theophany. God is represented as withdrawn from his people far away into heaven. He is not with them on earth as he was in the days of Moses, and piteously is besought to remember the mighty acts which he formerly wrought, and the yearnings of compassion toward his people which he then felt. God is then reminded that he is really the true father of the people. It is not Abraham, or Israel (Jacob), but God only, and he was the redeemer of old. The following verse (17) is very striking. The prophet actually reproaches Jehovah, and lays some of the blame upon him for the sins and the remissness of the people. God had not noticed their faint outreaching toward him. They were discouraged, and turned away from God rather than toward him. He had in effect hardened their hearts as he did Pharaoh's. Let God return to his people. V. 18 is again difficult in syntax, and it would greatly ease the matter to follow the LXX again, and read *We have possessed but a little while thy holy mountain.* This is not easy to explain, as has been intimated above in the introduction to this chapter, but no way out of the difficulty has yet appeared. V. 19 is quite plain, the meaning being that there is no longer any advantage in being an Israelite; they are as those heathen folk who have never had Jehovah as their God.

CHAPTER LXIV

Continuation of the Prayer for the Renewal of Jehovah's Lovingkindness. See notes above on 63[7-19].

Jehovah is besought for another great Theophany. It is put in a series of perfect tenses; read *hadst* for *wouldst*: "O that thou hadst rent," "hadst come down," "hadst quaked." The imagery is drawn from descriptions of other mighty theophanies, when the earth quaked, and the mountains melted (Ex. 19[16-18] Judg. 5[4, 5] Hab. 3[3f.] Mic. 1[3, 4] Psa. 18[9]). These were the glorious days, for in them God did *terrible things which we looked not for*, and so surpassed all their expectations.

4–12. The prayer changes into a less exciting strain, and becomes more tender in its supplication. It is not an easy passage, and the difficulty is at least partly due to the state of the text. In v. 4 especially is this the case. The Hebrew text differs from the LXX, and Paul's use in 1 Cor. 2[9] is based neither on the Hebrew nor the Greek but upon some other version to us otherwise unknown. See the critical commentaries. The prayer ends in a varied supplication that God may forget his anger, and hold his peace.

Chapters 65 and 66: The Faithful and the Rebellious

Chs. 65 and 66 are apparently a continuous discourse, not easy to interpret in detail and still less easy to make popularly interesting. The situation with which they deal seems to be in the restoration period, in which we are elsewhere able, faintly at times, clearly at others, to recognize a division among the inhabitants of Palestine into two opposing parties. The one, consisting of diverse elements, was composed of the descendants of the Hebrews who were not carried away in 597 B.C., or 586 B.C., with some original Canaanite stocks and many Samaritans who had drifted down from the north. This ill-assorted group nevertheless wished to be considered Jews and observed after a fashion the ordinances of the law of Deuteronomy with many intermixtures. The other party was much more homogeneous, its basal constituent being the returned exiles. The latter received a valuable re-enforcement when Ezra came (Ezra 9[1-4]). These two parties were at loggerheads and swords' points, each trying to excommunicate the other. It is a sorry picture.

CHAPTER LXV

1–7. Doing Evil in the Name of Religion. God complains of a people who are rebellious and practice impure rites. *Sacrificing in gardens* refers to worship under trees, a survival of Canaanite practices, but we have no idea what is meant by *burning incense upon bricks. Sitting among graves* is for purposes of necromancy; *eating swine's flesh* means at heathen sacrifices; and *broth of abominable things* was perhaps used in libations. God will not endure any of these offenses at their hands, remembering what their fathers did.

8–25. God's Rejection of the Faithless; A New Heaven and a New Earth for the Faithful. God will find new inheritors of the land, who shall eschew these evils, and as men preserve grape clusters for the wine later to be produced, so will he not destroy them all, but will give the land to the good among them; while he will slaughter the apostates who gave him no heed; the idolaters shall be sharply set apart from his true servants, who shall be well nurtured and shall sing joyously (vv. 13–16). Then shall begin the glorious Messianic age (vv. 17–25) when all these sad and disappointing days shall be forgotten. Man restored in spirit will find himself in a world likewise transformed, and sorrow and weeping shall be done away. Even untimely death shall disappear, and the child shall live to be an hundred years old. They who work and achieve shall have the reward of their labors, nor will they ever have need to appeal to their heavenly Father, for he will be quick to anticipate their desires even before they can be formulated into petitions. The poet catches up out of 11$^{6-9}$ the prediction of a transformed animal world, which he partly abbreviates and partly expands and so brings to an end the chapter.

CHAPTER LXVI

A chapter of mixed difficulties, of sudden shifts of subjects which afterward reappear. It remains to the Western mind, more methodical than the Eastern, enigmatic in its transferences and descriptive elements. We can do little else than divide it into sections and deal with them more or less separately.

1–4. A Protest Against Rebuilding the Temple. It must be inadequate whatever they may accomplish; the main problem is not a building but a poor and contrite spirit. It is a spiritual religion that God desires, and in v. 3 the point seems to be that sacrifices offered by unspiritual worshipers are as unwelcome as heathen rites symbolized under the slaying of a man or the breaking of a dog's neck.

5–14. The Results of a True Religion. The manifestation of God's pleasure will be in the increase of Zion. There follows (vv. 10–14) a prediction of peace, prosperity, and joy in the new Jerusalem, to participation in which all those are invited who have felt friendliness to the old city. In v. 11 there is one very difficult word, that which is translated *abundance*, in Hebrew *ziz;* this word is now known to us in Assyrian, where it means "udder," "teat," and it may be presumed to have the same meaning in Hebrew; metaphorically, therefore, *abundance* is not a bad attempt at translation.

15–17. Apostates and Their Certain Punishment. There is one doubtful phrase translated in the R.V. *behind one in the midst.* The best solution yet offered is to translate "after one in the midst," i.e., imitating his actions; and then to suppose that the intent is to picture a priest of some heathen cultus, surrounded by neophytes who imitate his movements in carrying out the sacred offices.

18–24. Restoration of Those Nations Which Survive the Judgment. The surviving nations shall be gathered to behold the Lord's glory, and among them God will set some great *sign*, i.e., a miracle. Then from among the survivors there will be chosen messengers to go and carry Jehovah's glory to many distant peoples whose names are taken from the book of Ezekiel (*Pul* should be *Put*, which was a land related commercially to the Egyptians and by them commonly called Punt). All these peoples will respond by bringing as an offering to Jehovah the Israelites who have been exiled or are dispersed among them. Israel thus reborn and remade shall be as enduring as the new heavens and the new earth. Then year in and year out, month in and month out, shall men worship the Lord, while outside of the sacred precincts shall they go to see the carcasses of the transgressors.

So ends the book in a note of horror, which the Massoretes felt so strongly that they gave directions that when this chapter was read in the synagogue, v. 23 was to be repeated after v. 24 had been read, that the book might be closed with words of consolation.

JEREMIAH

By Professor ADAM C. WELCH

Introduction

Historical Background. The period when Jeremiah was called to be a prophet was one of profound significance for Israel, especially for its religion. During the long reign of Manasseh the nation had been subject to Assyria, and this political dependence had brought with it a recognition of the religion of the suzerain power. Manasseh, who judged it impossible to resist Assyria, had accepted the inevitable consequences, and introduced several elements of Assyrian worship into the Temple at Jerusalem. Further, a large number of Eastern colonists had been settled in North Israel, and, though a Jewish priest had been sent back and had restored the old cult at Bethel, making it the religious center for the remaining Jewish population (2 Kings 17[28]), the religion of the North was becoming an amalgam of the two faiths. There was grave danger that, if these conditions continued in the two parts of the country, Judaism, losing all its distinctive characteristics, might disappear as a vital force.

Reign of Josiah. Hence Josiah from his accession in 637 B.C. could count on all the best elements in the kingdom to join him in any effort promising a reformation. The conditions of the time gave the reformers their opportunity. So long as Assyria was strong, it was hopeless to throw off its control over the life of its subject states. But now Nineveh was engaged in a fight for life with Babylon and its allies. Needing all its strength to resist its enemies at home, it could not maintain its hold on the distant provinces of Syria, and a breath of liberty passed over all the West. Josiah purified the Temple from every emblem of Assyrian worship (2 Kings 23[4f.]). The act was a declaration of Judæan independence, and appealed to the two strongest instincts in the kingdom, its passion for liberty and its zeal for its distinctive religion.

But in the weakness of Assyria Josiah saw an opportunity for Judah to extend its power over the now derelict province of North Israel and to reconstitute the old kingdom of David. He assumed authority over Samaria (2 Kings 23[19]), and since religion had always been the strongest bond between the kingdoms, that bond was drawn closer. About this time the religious literature of North Israel was adopted as the possession of all Jewry. E, the Israelite story of the nation's origin, was incorporated with J, the Judæan account. The records of the two kingdoms were amalgamated into the present books of Kings. Psalms from northern sanctuaries were admitted into the official Psalter. The book of Hosea was adapted to fit it for general acceptance. In the judgment of the present writer, Deuteronomy, originally an Israelite lawbook, was given wider recognition. (See, however, intro. to Deuteronomy, p. 320b.) Jewry was to become one through the possession of a common religious literature and common ideals. Finally the Temple at Jerusalem was made the only legitimate center for the worship of the restored nation.

Centralization of Worship. The time made this radical change possible. In Judah the Temple was the only shrine which had not been wrecked by the invasion of Sennacherib under Hezekiah. In Israel the one remaining sanctuary was that which had been restored at Bethel. Josiah merely needed, as he did (2 Kings 23[15f.]), to destroy and desecrate this altar in order to leave the Temple in Jerusalem the sole center for sacrifice and pilgrimage. What had thus become the only sanctuary *de facto* was declared alone legitimate *de jure*.

The large plan obviously appealed both to patriotism and to religion. Standing for the restoration of united and independent Israel under a descendant of David, it appealed to every Jew who recalled the glory of the past. In the conditions of the time it stood also for purity of worship. Men were to be brought to the one sanctuary which had preserved unbroken the practices and traditions of the past; they were not to be left to drift into semiheathenism. Since also the Jerusalem priests were declared the only legitimate priests, the plan secured the support of an official body all of whose interests enlisted its members for its success. Further, it appealed strongly to that large and dangerous body of opinion in every community which recognizes that something needs to be done and which accepts any reforming action that promises to be immediately effective. Few would have patience to ask on what ultimate principles the reform was based, and what therefore must be its consequences for the national religion.

Legalism and Nationalism. The reform, based as it was on false principles, led to disastrous consequences: it turned Judaism definitely in the direction of nationalism and legalism. Since it made one sanctuary and one priesthood not merely useful, but essential to right worship, it limited the grace of God and restricted the people's power to reach him. Only at the Temple and through its ritual could men enter into the full relation to their God. The older world had believed in a God who was the god of a race, whose power was largely limited to the country in which his people lived and who therefore could only be worshiped where his altar stood. The influence of this conception of religion appears in the remark of David (1 Sam. 26[19]). Josiah's reform meant in principle a return to this primitive form beyond which the better thought of Israel under the influence of its prophets had long advanced. Jehovah could only be rightly worshiped on the soil of Palestine. Again, since the Temple service with sacrifice and festival was essential to the faith, the method in which this ritual was performed by the priests and the ceremonial law which prescribed the correct condition of the worshipers became of primary importance. The attention of priests and people was directed to an exact observance of the outward means by which the divine grace was to be secured. Such an attitude meant simply a turning back to lower conceptions of the relation between God and Israel than those which had been taught by the prophets. For all these had insisted that obedience was more than sacrifice: and the obedience they had demanded had been an obedience to the moral and spiritual demands of the Law, not to its ceremonial requirements. The reform movement embodied both the legalistic, the nationalistic and the prophetic elements; emphasis on the ceremonial law represented both the nationalistic and the legalistic point of view; on the other hand, its moral and spiritual demands formed its historical and universal element, that is, its prophetic element.

The Prophet Jeremiah. It is easy to-day, in the light of the consequences which followed on centralization, to recognize its retrograde character. It is the peculiar merit of Jeremiah that he from the beginning saw how it threatened to undo the work of the prophets. He was a member of a priestly family at Anathoth, a village in Benjamin, north of Jerusalem—a fact which gave him special advantages in thinking about religion. He belonged to North Israel, in whose condition and fate he always felt a deep interest (cf. Jer. 3[6f.] 30). Therefore he was saturated in the thought of Hosea, the most spiritual of the prophets (cf. 2[1f.], etc.). He was reared in religious traditions, which meant that he knew something about the Israelite faith men were seeking to reform. Yet he did not belong to the professional priesthood, and was accordingly free from the narrowness which is apt to creep over an official caste. And three years before the Josianic reform he became a prophet (see 1[2], notes). It was through this experience that he entered into personal relation to the Eternal and learned to judge the laws which govern life and religion, not by their immediate and practical usefulness, but by their agreement with the divine principles, and especially with those which had been revealed to his predecessors in Israel's historic faith.

Like all the prophets he recognized the need for reform alike in Israel and in the world. To him as to them the day of the Lord was at hand: since the world was ripe for judgment, the foe from the North, the divine agent in judgment, would speedily come (1[14]). In some of his early oracles (4[5f.]) he warned his fellow countrymen of the near advent of the great hour. What he asked from them was true repentance. The two essentials to a right reform were God and the penitent: everything else was secondary (3[1-5] 3[19]–4[4]). For he went on to declare that, while Israel was indeed apostate like its sister Judah, it had at least not rendered itself impenetrable to the demands of its God by adopting a reform which was false in principle, and which therefore served to shut out from men's thoughts that which constituted a true return (3[6-12]). His meaning was made clearer when he went up to Jerusalem in the time of Jehoiakim and, at a great festival in the center of the national reform, proclaimed Jehovah's purpose to destroy the Temple as completely as he had destroyed the sanctuary at Shiloh (chs. 7, 26). In the interests of religion it was better that the Temple should disappear, since it was being made a hindrance instead of a help. And, as religion had continued without Shiloh, it could continue without Jerusalem. Thereafter, when the court was inclined to rebel against Babylon, the prophet recognized and bade men recognize in the new world-power the instrument Jehovah was about to use for the destruction of the city (ch. 20). From that time through the succeeding reign of Zedekiah he never wavered in his conviction that Nebuchadrezzar should overrun Judah and destroy its capital. It was the divine will that this should be.

Denationalization of Religion. Jeremiah wrote to the exiles in Babylon that they must cease from all their efforts to return to Jerusalem (ch. 29). Their God had brought them into exile, and therefore in an exile which was of the divine appointment they could remain in relation to Jehovah and serve him with loyal contentment. Turning to men in Jerusalem, he told the priesthood, who counted their brethren in Babylon doubly exiled because they were outcasts from the divine grace, that those men were nearer God than themselves (ch. 24). For they were in no danger of turning a mere human institution into a substitute for faith. And, finally, he received for himself the needed and comfortable assurance that, though church and state must vanish in Judah, true religion could continue and should continue among the humble men who worshiped Jehovah in the fields and olive-yards of a Babylonian province (ch. 42).

Courage of Jeremiah. A man with such a religious message could expect only stout opposition in a community which had set its heart on a definite program of reform. The opposition that Jeremiah had been warned at his call to expect came soon and increased in bitterness to the end. The first to recognize the inevitable clash were the men who best knew what was at stake—the priests. From the hour when Jeremiah denied (ch. 26) that the Temple worship was essential, they rejected him, as their successors rejected Jesus. It took longer for the laymen to recognize what was involved. But when they, straining every nerve to defend the independence of their state, discovered that the prophet counted the national life quite secondary, they put him into a dungeon as the surest means to silence him (ch. 38). He seemed to them a traitor.

Nothing could be further from the truth than the common picture of Jeremiah as a plaintive sentimentalist. He was, as his call said he needed to be, like a brazen wall. Wherever principle entered he showed the almost inhuman austerity of every Puritan. He saw one thing, the religion which made men servants of Jehovah and which delivered them from haunting fear of success or failure. A Jew who could meet God in his day could meet anything; he walked the world a free man, free to expect God's coming and to serve him till he came. To Jeremiah this was a gospel. And it came as a shock to the single-minded enthusiast that his fellows counted him a traitor to the dearest hopes of Israel.

Spiritual Religion. Jeremiah envisaged a religion which was not national, but historical, since it had been revealed to Israel. It required no special institution like a local temple, and no peculiar organization like state or priesthood. It could be practised in every country where men, while giving allegiance to their rulers, retained their final allegiance to their God. Its demands were spiritual, for men must pray; and moral, for they must serve. Jeremiah was thinking in terms of a universal religion. From this sprang that feature which has always been recognized in his attitude, his individualism. It was the corollary of his position as a prophet to the nations: the individual is alone the universal. But the basis of universalism and individualism alike was his spiritual and moral relation to his God (cf. the promise of the new covenant, 31[31-34]).

His weakness was his failure to recognize the place of the institution in religion. Every prophet who presents a great principle in a time of controversy exaggerates it. The nation did not accept Jeremiah's teaching in its full scope, for the returning exiles came back for the sake of the Temple and its worship, and they speedily restored the institutions of altar and priesthood (see intro. to Ezra-Nehemiah, pp. 458f.). It is equally just to remember that the Jews of the Dispersion, who came to form the major part of Jewry, maintained themselves by the prophet's message. They paid their Temple tax to Jerusalem and recognized that the daily sacrifice was offered in their name and for their benefit. But they found God in the prayers of their synagogues and served him in their strongly ethical community life. These things they learned from Jeremiah.

Significance of Jeremiah. It is possible, therefore, to recognize how, at this particular period of his nation's history, Jeremiah contributed to maintain its life and history. But it also becomes possible to set him in a larger succession. At three crises of the national and religious life three voices came to guide it. Before Samaria fell in 722 B.C. Hosea came to gather up the life of the past and preserve what was of eternal remembrance in the thought and deed of Israel. Before the collapse of Judah in 586 B.C. Jeremiah handed on to a people now without a state the truths by which their souls might still live. And before the Temple finally disappeared in 70 A.D. a greater than both conserved for the world through His living church the enduring things which could not die. And these three are intimately associated. Jeremiah borrows continually from his predecessor, and there is no prophet in the old life of Israel from whom Jesus quotes more freely and more intimately than Hosea and Jeremiah. They all saw beyond the outward forms the free spirit which had given these their worth and vitality, which was itself eternal and which, after the breakdown of the old, could build new forms for its fresh and inexhaustible expression.

The Book of Jeremiah. The text of the book of Jeremiah has come down in what virtually amounts to two recensions, for the LXX version contains only seven eighths of the material found in the Hebrew Bible. On this question the student must be referred to Streane, *Double Text of Jeremiah;* Volz, *Studien;* Cornill, *Commentary,* the Introduction. But, further, the present book is better described as a collection of material bearing on the period of Jeremiah than as oracles from or a biography of the prophet. Thus it contains material which ranges in date from Jeremiah's call to the period of Cyrus (51^{11-14}), and even to that of the return ($17^{19f.}$), and presents historical matter (chs. 40–42, 52) which is only indirectly connected with Jeremiah. Again, the book clearly contains little collections which once existed separately (cf. chs. 30f.; 46–51). Each of these has its own history, especially its own place and date of collection. Some of these booklets may have consisted entirely of oracles. But there also appear a series of records which present an informal biography of the prophet. Yet even in these the incidents connected with Jeremiah's career are presented in order to convey oracles which he uttered in certain circumstances and under certain conditions. And in this biographical material Jeremiah is sometimes introduced in the third person, in other cases in the first person. It will thus be seen that the whole question of the composition of the book is extremely complicated and perplexing. No explanation yet offered seems entirely satisfactory. To take for granted that Baruch was either the first or the final compiler appears unwarranted in view merely of the statement in ch. 36 (see commentary).

Two things need to be said in connection with the study of the book here presented. Since oracles here ascribed to Jeremiah appear elsewhere under the names of Isaiah and Obadiah, and since Jeremianic material appears alongside sayings of later date, it is clear that the original oracles were much briefer and more disconnected than they appear in the long chapters of the English versions. In some respects they resemble the Sermon on the Mount, which contains collected "logia" (sayings). Anyone who studies them for the first time in this form will probably be annoyed by the abrupt breaks. But he may find it profitable to be freed from trying to connect verses which have no connection beyond the fact that the editor so arranged them. Again, all the material has passed through the hands of men who attempted to interpret it for the needs of their own time. But these men had come through the great experience of exile and had also, in obedience to the principle of centralization, returned to Jerusalem for the purpose of maintaining their Temple worship. The natural result was that, while they reverently retained the prophet's oracles, they at times softened and glossed his strong utterances. In a short commentary it is not possible to give all the evidence for distinguishing these glosses and setting them aside as secondary. Readers who may count the decisions arbitrary are asked to remember that all the evidence cannot be presented.

Literature: Peake, *Jeremiah* (Century Bible); Streane, *Jeremiah* (Cambridge Bible); Skinner, *Prophecy and Religion;* Driver, *Jeremiah;* Longacre, *A Prophet of the Spirit;* G. A. Smith, *Jeremiah;* Knudson, *Beacon Lights of Prophecy;* Eiselen, *The Prophetic Books of the O.T.*, vol. i; Cornill, *Das Buch Jeremia*; Duhm, *Jeremiah* (Kurzer Hand Kommentar).

CHAPTER I

1–3. Title. Jeremiah's father was not the Hilkiah of 2 Kings 22^{4}. V. 2 dates the prophet's call in 624 B.C., three years before the Josianic reform described in 2 Kings 23; v. 3 dates his activity from 624 to 586; but this covers the book only down to ch. 39.

4–10. Jeremiah's Call. A man's birth makes him an American or a Jew and so qualifies him to speak to his own people. It also limits him in his sympathies and his appeal. Jeremiah is set apart (so read in v. 5 instead of *sanctified*) before his birth, because he has to speak to all nations (cf. Isa. $49^{5f.}$). Amos (1^{1}) was summoned to speak concerning Israel: but, since he spoke in the name of a God of righteousness, he could not limit his message to his own people, for righteousness knows no frontiers. Jeremiah is commissioned to utter the divine words (v. 9). These, in the thought of the prophet, contain the absolute standards of all right conduct, and therefore determine the fate, not of Israel alone, but of all nations. The prophet utters the final standards and speaks by the authority of the Lord of the universe. *A child* (v. 6)—"but young." Abraham's fighting men (Gen. 14^{24}) are described by the same Hebrew word. *Set thee over* (v. 10) in full authority like one who acts for a superior. The word is used about Joseph in Egypt (Gen. 41^{41}).

11, 12. The First Vision. Jeremiah sees a dry twig. When he gives it its right name of *shākēdh*, an almond, he receives the assurance that God is *shōkēdh*, awake and watchful over his word. The Hebrew was fond of such puns (see on Amos 5^{5}). The divine word, announced by former prophets, may have been delayed in its coming. But the judgment cannot fail and is now on the way. The Lord is at hand.

13–19. The Second Vision. Jeremiah sees a boiling pot, the blower of which (so read instead of the impossible *face* of v. 13) is from the North. The first and inevitable result of the emergence of the divine word expressing the final standards in the world shall be judgment on Judah for its sins, especially for its false religion. Judah is the boiling pot, and the influence which causes it to boil is being blown (so read with LXX instead of *shall break forth* in v. 14) from the North. The North here is not a point of the compass, and Jeremiah is not expecting any historical invader. The North is the source of the divine wrath (cf. how Ebal, the mount of the curse, lies toward the North, Deut. $27^{12f.}$; and how Joel, 2^{20}, can speak in general about the destroyer as the Northerner). Jeremiah describes the divine judgment under the form of an invasion, which was one of the favorite forms with several of the early prophets (see further at chs. 4, 5). *Burned incense* (v. 16) = offered sacrifice, and so throughout the book. The description has had some turgid phrases added. Omit in v. 18 *an iron pillar* against which no one fights, and with LXX read "wall" for *walls*.

Chapters 2^1 to 4^4: The Religious Failure of the People

This section comprises a collection of oracles, some addressed to the whole nation, others specially to North Israel. The oracles deal chiefly with the religious failure of the people rather than its social and moral corruptions. They are all early and may be confidently referred to the time of Josiah. They offer a reason why the people are ripe for the judgment of their God (1^{16}). The thought is deeply influenced by that of Hosea.

CHAPTER II

1–3. Israel the Chosen of Jehovah. Jehovah remembers in Israel's favor (*for thee*, v. 2) its tender loyalty during the wilderness period. Being loyal, it was also secure under the protection of its God. For it was set apart (or *holiness*, v. 3) as the divine property, like the first fruits. Anyone who treated such sacred property as if it were his own incurred the guilt of sacrilege. Jeremiah shares with Hosea (9^{10}) the idea of the innocent happiness of the wilderness period.

4–12. Israel's Apostasy Means Bitter Ingratitude. The oracle is addressed to North Israel. The people have gone after useless gods (*things that do not profit*, v. 8) and false worship (*vanity*, v. 5) to become false like them. Yet God (v. 7) gave them their land: note the emphasis and the contrast in "I." Hence he has still his right to assert against them (so translate v. 9a). Let them go east and west (vv. 10f.), and they will not find the like. V. 7b refers to the sin at Baal-peor (cf. Hos. 9^{10} and see comment there; Num. 25^3 Deut. 4^3). *Kittim* is probably Kition in Cyprus, *Kedar* is located in Arabia.

13–19. Israel's Dependence on Foreigners. This dependence has tainted Israel with foreign ideals, ruined its self-dependence, and sapped its national religion. The nation is making itself a mere slave so that it becomes a prey, subject to another's will (v. 14). The result is that the people of Memphis and Pelusium are shaving it bare (v. 16). Egypt is using the little buffer-state between itself and Assyria as a tool for its own ends. It is unnecessary to seek an exact parallel to v. 15 in the events of Jeremiah's time. The prophet, who described in vv. 1–3 Israel's security in the time of its dependence on its God, may refer to the helpless condition to which disloyalty has not once but constantly brought it. In its own divinely given ideals it had a perennial spring of life, instead of which it has elected the stale water of heathen cisterns, which are so cracked that they cannot retain their flat contents (v. 13). But nothing will now teach it except bitter experience: the disaster resulting from this wickedness must correct thee and convince thee of backslidings (so paraphrase v. 19a). Here again Jeremiah is following the thought of Hosea (cf. 7^{8-11}, etc.). In v. 17 omit as untranslatable *when he led thee by the way.*

20–22. The Apostasy Is Not of Yesterday. *Of old thou hast* (not, *I have*, v. 20) *broken thy yoke*, the bands of religion (cf. Hos. 11^4) saying, "I am not going to be a slave to any." What a change from the early condition! (Read v. 21b as an exclamation.) Israel has rebelled against its God, because his religion involves a moral demand. *Lye*=soda.

23–29. Futility of False Gods in Time of Need. When things go well, the nation says, "There is no use of good advice, for I love strange gods (v. 25, the *stock* and *stone* of v. 27) and will follow them." But when it is disappointed in its hopes and finds out its mistake (v. 26) it says (not *will say*, v. 27) to Jehovah, *save us*. The only response to a religion of this type must be that God asks what right men have to complain against him (v. 29a) if he does not help. *The valley* (v. 23) refers to some public apostasy of which we have lost the clue. Translate vv. 23c–25a: *thou dromedary in heat, changing its mates. Thou desert wild-ass, snuffing up the wind in its lust, which any male that wants it need not weary itself to discover, since in its season anyone may find it. Do not run your feet sore and your throat dry.*

30–37. Condemnation of the People's Self-Confidence. This section has a very difficult text: v. 34b is untranslatable, and the sense of v. 30 can only be conjectured. There is also little connection between the successive verses. It may really consist of a number of fragments. Thus vv. 36f. refer to dependence on foreign powers (cf. vv. 13–19), now to one, again to another of which the people go gadding. Since Jehovah will have nothing to do with these sources of confidence, the people will be disappointed in them. (For the gesture of abandoned sorrow in v. 37, cf. Tamar, 2 Sam. 13[19].) The other verses deal with religious apostasy, charging the people (v. 31) with having broken away from the divine restraint (cf. v. 20). They are so abandoned that they could teach even the vilest women methods of seeking love (v. 33). On their *hands* (not *skirts*, v. 34) is found the proof of some guilt, which, however, the condition of the second half of the verse prevents us from defining. Yet they count themselves loyal servants of their God. For the very reason that they believe themselves innocent, God must judge them (v. 35). In v. 30, for *your own sword* the LXX reads *the sword*, namely, of Jehovah. This may be correct (cf. the preceding "I"), but it is impossible to define the reference in the allusion.

CHAPTER III

1–5. Sham Repentance. These verses with vv. 19, 20 form one oracle. Both passages describe a facile and empty repentance. In v. 1, omit *they say;* it is part of a last introductory phrase like that in 2[1]. The figure of Israel as bride and son of God is from Hos. 9[1] 11[1]. No man who has divorced his wife, *or* (not *and*) whose wife has left him for another man, takes her back at a word. Such a *woman* (not *land*) is defiled. Yet Israel disloyal, not with one, but with many, counts repentance a trivial thing (vv. 1f.). It has learned nothing from the punishment which followed, and showed how seriously God regarded its sin (v. 3). Even then did not you call Jehovah "my husband," "my companion from childhood," and say "He will not always be angry," "He does not keep up a quarrel for ever"? See, you talked thus, but acted vilely and were capable of combining the two—fine talk and vile deeds (vv. 4f.). But I intended (v. 19; note the emphatic "I" contrasted with *thou*, v. 4) to treat you as a son, and give you . . . the goodliest heritage of the nations (Palestine). I thought then, etc. (vv. 19, 20a.).

6–13. An Oracle on Repentance and Forgiveness. Jeremiah addresses an oracle to the North (v. 12), because Israel, for whom it was destined, was living there. Judah and Israel have both been faithless to their God. But Judah, appalled by Israel's punishment in the collapse of the state (722 B.C.), has carried through a national reform by which it hopes to escape the same fate. This reform, however, has been not merely inadequate, but false in principle: the Hebrew word in v. 10 is much stronger than *feignedly*. Its effect, therefore, has been to make Judah worse than Israel, which obviously no mere inadequate reform could do. The reference can only be to the Josianic reform, since the oracle is dated in the reign of Josiah, and there was no other national reform at that period. Even if the prophet be taken to refer to the earlier movement under Hezekiah, the conclusion remains the same, since Hezekiah merely initiated the movement for the centralization of worship at Jerusalem, which was later carried into full effect. What the prophet demands in the divine name, in vv. 12f., is a right repentance and a return "unto me"—so read with LXX. There are two essentials of religion to Jeremiah—the penitent soul and the forgiving God of Israel.

Read, in vv. 7c, 8, *her sister Judah the traitress saw this, saw too, how, when*, etc. Omit in v. 9, with LXX, *the land was polluted, and. Shown herself more righteous* (v. 11), i.e., put herself in the right better.

14–18. A Later Promise of a Reunited Israel. A later generation which took the return of v. 13 to mean, not repentance, but return from exile, added a promise of reunited Israel. But Jeremiah, who pronounced Judah worse than Israel, could not regard a restoration to Zion (v. 14) a blessing to Israel. The writer too does not expect a renewal of the nation living in its own land (v. 12), but the restoration to their own land of scattered individuals (v. 14) from the country where both peoples are in exile (v. 18). So great will be the concourse of the exiles returning to the holy city that the ark shall not be remade (so read for *shall that be done;* cf. A.S.V. mg., v. 16). Jerusalem itself shall take the place of the ark and shall alone be adequate for the multitudes who throng to the Temple worship (v. 17).

19, 20. See notes under vv. 1–5.

21–25. The Penalty of Apostasy. Apostasy has brought disappointment and moral impotence. The *voice* Jeremiah hears is that of the better elements of the people, who know that heathenism has never satisfied and never can. They wail on the heights, where the false worship was practiced. The riot and tumult there (so read v. 23) have always been vain. It is the voice every preacher must be able to hear if he is to continue with hope of effecting any good. God bids them repent, and they are able to reply *we are thine* (not, *we are come unto thee*, v. 22). But they sadly confess that the Baal-worship (*shameful thing*) has eaten out their moral vigor and left them impotent (vv. 24f.).

CHAPTER IV

1–4. The Cure for Moral Impotence. The cure is sincere repentance. "If it is in thy mind to turn back, to *me* thou must turn back; if thou wilt remove thy false gods, thou must not wander out of *my* presence" (v. 1). Acknowledge Jehovah alone, since in him the world finds blessing (v. 2). The verse describes, not what shall be, but why a repentance which is more than impotent remorse is so blessed a thing. It brings men into relation to the one source of all blessing. Only the people must make clean work in repentance (v. 3), and their circumcision must be that of the heart (v. 4).

Chapter 4$^{5-31}$: The Day of Jehovah

This series of oracles deals with the day of Jehovah. Since the day brings the self-revelation of the God of righteousness, its first result must be judgment on every form of evil. And judgment must begin at Judah, because the people had received and ignored the revelation of the divine will. But, since Jehovah is God of the world, and the word he put in Jeremiah's mouth contains the absolute standards, and since the prophet's commission is to all nations, the day must bring a world-judgment (cf. ch. 25).

5–8. Imminent Doom. In the *lion* from his lair in the North, Jeremiah personifies the divine instrument in the work of judgment; he is the destroyer of nations. The figure gave rise to Ezekiel's Gog and ultimately to Antichrist in Revelation. As the adversary who appears in Job as a mere messenger developed into Satan, the opponent of God, so Jeremiah's instrument for chastisement grew into much more. *Send a trumpet-blast through the land*, v. 5, says the prophet, using words employed by the prophets in announcing the divine advent. *Set up a rallying-flag, bring your goods into safety, make no delay* (v. 6); for the time is at hand. For *sackcloth* as a sign of mourning cf. Isa. 22^{12}.

9–12. A Picture of Wasted Judah. The courage of the king shall die in him and the bewildered prophets shall say, *Ah, Lord* (so read in v. 9 with LXX, making v. 10 the utterance of these prophets. For Jeremiah's attitude toward these men cf. 28$^{7f.}$). The civil and religious leaders are in equal dismay, for there is appointed for this people a blasting sirocco (v. 11), a wind too powerful for fanning or cleansing—a destroying wind (v. 12). Note how Jeremiah uses other figures than that of invasion for the coming disaster.

13–17. The Foe from the North. The foe comes by Dan and Ephraim (v. 15). Nations are enrolled and summoned against Jerusalem (v. 16); the verbs are not imperatives. Besiegers come from far and utter defiance against Judah. For evil purposes make their home in Jersualem (v. 14).

18–22. A Cry of Regret Over the Inevitable Ruin. *My tent and my curtains* (its hangings) of v. 20 is Jerusalem. The city's wickedness has brought it about that the ruin is bitter and mortal (v. 18b). The bowels to the Hebrews were the seat of the feelings, the heart the seat of thought. In v. 21 for *shall I see* read *must I see.*

23–26. Chaos Come Again. The world is waste and void (v. 23), it returns to the condition from which God brought it in the beginning (Gen. 1^{2}). The mountains, which, according to Hebrew thought, sustained the world, tremble (v. 24). The fertile earth becomes a wilderness (v. 26). The day of the Lord involves a change, not only in man, but in the world (cf. Amos 7^{4} Isa. 11$^{6f.}$, etc.). From this conception of judgment bringing chaos has come the idea of the new heavens and the new earth of the consummation in Rev. 21^{1}–22^{5}. Obviously, God alone, and no human invader, could produce such a change.

27–31. Ruin of the World and Especially of Jerusalem. The *land* of v. 27 is the world (cf. v. 28); *the whole* (not *every*) *city* of v. 29 is the whole world (with LXX). At the *rumor* (not *noise*) of the coming foe men go into hiding (v. 29), and the prophet *can hear* (not *have heard*) the distress of Zion (v. 31). Omit v. 27b; the clause has come from 30^{11}. The first clause of v. 30 is untranslatable. In what remains Jerusalem is represented as a prostitute. The *paint* is antimony, which is used by Eastern women to darken the eyelids, and so make the eyes appear larger and more luminous.

Chapters 5 and 6: The Sin and Doom of Judah

A series of oracles describing the sin and doom of Judah. Dealing with doom, they were naturally joined with the oracles of judgment in the day of the Lord. The sins denounced in them are in general anti-social in character, as contrasted with the religious failure of chs. 2, 3.

CHAPTER V

1–6. The Unrighteousness of Jerusalem: A Threat of Doom. Jeremiah is horrified by the absence of uprightness in Jerusalem; *truth* in v. 1 is practically honesty, a moral quality (cf.

Gen. 18[16-33]). If men employ the sacred name, it is to perjure themselves by using it in support of a lie (v. 2). Yet that on which Jehovah is intent is honesty (v. 3a). When he thinks that these are humble people who go wrong because they have never learned their own religion, he remembers that the well-to-do are no better (vv. 4f.). The remark gives a tantalizing glimpse into the social and educational conditions of old Jerusalem. The *yoke* and *bands* (v. 5) are the restraints of their religion (cf. 2[20]). For *wolf of the evenings* (v. 6) read *desert wolf* and cf. 4[7].

7–11. Two Oracles on the Corruption of Judah. Read in v. 7 *How can I pardon them, saith the Lord, since, forsaking me, they acknowledge gods that are no gods* (the guilt is not in the children) *and settle down to play the harlot from me.* In v. 8 omit *in the morning* (cf. mg.). The reference in vv. 7f. is to spiritual disloyalty, not to physical immorality, though the lewd practices connected with the nature-worship of Baal may have helped to suggest the figure to the prophet. In v. 10 read *vine-rows* for *walls* (cf. the following *branches*). The figure of Judah as the vineyard of the Lord was a favorite one with the prophets (cf. Isa. 5[1]).

12–17. Penalty for Spurning the Prophets. Because men say of Jehovah, "He does nothing" (so in v. 12; cf. Zeph. 1[12]), and the prophets are becoming mere wind with no word of revelation in them (v. 13, but the sense here is very uncertain), the divine standards in the prophet's mouth (cf. 1[9f.]) must bring doom (v. 14). The instrument of that doom is then described in v. 15 in terms which appear in several other prophets, but which are not peculiarly applicable to any one nation of Jeremiah's time. From *which thy* (v. 17) read *they shall eat up thy sons and thy daughters.*

18, 19. Disciplinary Purpose of the Exile. An addition, applying the oracle to the conditions of the exiles. In v. 19 read *ye are serving* for *shall ye serve.*

20–29. Terrible Manifestation of Jehovah. The condition of the nation described in this late passage resembles that which appears in several of the later psalms, and the appeal to the divine power over nature is strongly reminiscent of Deutero-Isaiah. The writer says the people *had* (not *hath*) the heart of a rebel (v. 23) and never thought rightly of God (v. 24a). Their sins upset the laws of ordered life (v. 25), since God, to punish them, withheld the rains. The *former rain* fell in October, the *latter* in March-April. *Deceit* means the proceeds of their fraud. For *that they should prosper* (v. 28) read *so they prosper.*

30, 31. Preference for Lenient Leaders. Judah prefers for its spiritual leaders men who make slight moral demands. The verses offer an interesting illustration of the relation between prophet and priest in Jeremiah's time. The prophets are appealed to in connection with difficult cases and novel circumstances where the ordinary law of the priest fails to give guidance. Then the priest issues decrees in accordance with this decision (v. 31). Evidently, the two bodies of spiritual guides are able to work together.

CHAPTER VI

1–8. The Sin of Jerusalem Leads to Certain Judgment. Jeremiah's fellow-countrymen are bidden to flee from the doomed city to Tekoa (Amos 1[1]), and Bethhakkerem (Neh. 3[14]), villages in the south of the capital, because their own towns are already occupied by the northern foe. The enemies are present *every one in his place*, i.e., as if the place belonged to them (v. 3). If it were legitimate to render *Woe unto us* by *Ha! for us*, vv. 4f. would describe their confident eagerness and their fury in attack. Neither midday heat nor darkness can check their ardor. They hew down Jerusalem's trees (v. 6, see mg.); the phrase emphasizes the pitiless character of the war (cf. Deut. 20[19f.]). For the Lord has declared *woe to the false city* (so read with LXX for *this is*, etc.). As a cistern keeps fresh its waters, she keeps fresh her sin (v. 7a). The following words, *violence and spoil*, were a cry used, like our cry of "Murder," by one who was assaulted in the street. That cry was constantly heard in Jerusalem. The Hebrew text of v. 2 is untranslatable.

9–15. A Picture of Complete Devastation. Under the figure of a vineyard from which every grape is stripped, doom is pronounced on Jerusalem, because of its greed, and because of the moral insensibility of its spiritual leaders. Glean like a vine what is left to Israel, examine with care every twig (so read v. 9). The *remnant* here is not, as in Isaiah, any particular part of the nation: it is what is left after the harvest is over. The sense is that even the gleanings are not to be spared. For is there anyone to whom God may speak in the hope that he will listen? The divine word has become to them a nagging weariness (v. 10). Read in v. 11, with LXX, *my fury* (wrath) for *the fury of the Lord*, and *I must pour:* God is still the speaker. *Assembly* means *groups*. For *wives* (v. 12) probably read *vineyards;* the women have been already mentioned. Vv. 13–15 reappear at 8[10-12]. The time to which they refer is the time of God's appearance in judgment.

16–21. Indifference to the Messages of the Prophets. God sent prophets, the *watchmen* of v. 17 (cf. Amos 2[11]), with the trumpet warning of the coming divine judgment, but in vain. Read in v. 16 *said* for *saith;* cf. *set* in v. 17; both verses refer to the divine guidance given to Israel in the past (cf. Amos 2[11f.]). For *your souls,* which suggests too exclusively spiritual rest, read *yourselves;* the sense is that of well-being and security. Therefore he now calls heaven and earth to witness that the end is at hand. Read v. 18 perhaps, noting the appeal to the earth in v. 19, *Hear, O heavens, and bear witness against them.* But the text is corrupt. *Frankincense* (v. 20), used in connection with certain offerings (cf. Lev. 2[1]), was brought from Sheba in South Arabia (cf. Isa. 60[6] 1 Kings 10[10]). It and the calamus were valued because brought from the far distance. But no offering, however costly, is a substitute for obedience.

22–26. Advance of the Foe from the North. The foe from the North, *set in array like one man* (so read in v. 23), is advancing against Jerusalem. Vv. 22–24 are applied in 50[41-43] to Babylon. Evidently, then, the northern foe was not interpreted as a historical invader and especially could not be the Babylonians themselves, since the same enemy could not be expected to attack Judah in Jeremiah's time and Babylon much later (cf. 5[15]). *By the way* (v. 25), i.e., in the open roads. *Make thee,* etc. (v. 26), i.e., mourn for thyself as men mourn for an only son.

27–30. Jeremiah's Function. The function of Jeremiah is that of a trier and examiner (not *tower and fortress*). The effect is described in v. 29, where we should probably read in clause b *the fire is piled up,* and in clause d *the slag is not separated out.* The text is uncertain, but the general sense is clear: the corruption has gone so far that there remains only judgment. But the prophet brings the divine standards (cf. 1[9] and Amos 7[7f.]). In v. 28 omit *they are brass and iron* as a gloss.

CHAPTER VII

1–15. The Temple Address. This section gives Jeremiah's words in full; ch. 26 deals with the effect produced by the address on the people, and especially with the resultant attitude of the religious leaders to him. Ch. 7 appears among the oracles, ch. 26 in the biography. Two matters deserve close attention. The prophet severely blames the men of Judah for some new and false confidence in the Temple, as though its very existence could guarantee them security. It is natural to conclude that this new attitude was the reflection of the Josianic reform, which, by making the Temple the sole legitimate center of worship, led men to believe that Jehovah must maintain it as essential to true religion. Note that the address is dated early in Jehoiakim's reign, i.e., very soon after the reform. Again Jeremiah declares, not that Jehovah will chastise the people for their false ideas, but that he will destroy the Temple as he once destroyed Shiloh. To declare that it is the divine will to destroy the Temple is to say that its disappearance is in the interests of real religion. True religion, according to Jeremiah, can continue in Judah without the Temple at Jerusalem, as it continued after the shrine at Shiloh was wrecked. Jeremiah appeared in a court (not *gate,* v. 2; cf. 26[2]), probably at a great festival (cf. Amos at Bethel, 7[10], and our Lord at Jerusalem, Mt. 24[1] Lk. 21[5]).

In v. 3, repointing two Hebrew words, read *so that I may dwell with you in this place* for *and I will cause,* etc. The people did not live in the Temple. Then vv. 5–7, since they take the *place* to be the country, and also break the close connection between v. 4 and v. 8, are a little exhortation which has been added later. *Called by my name* (v. 10), i.e., specially dedicated to me. In v. 11 join *in your eyes* to *the house.* The sense is: "Is this Temple, which even in your eyes is peculiarly mine?" etc. The reference in v. 12 is to the sanctuary at Shiloh, where, immediately after the conquest of Palestine, the early center of worship for the northern tribes was set up with the priesthood of Eli and the sacred emblem of the ark (1 Sam. 1–3). Apparently, the place was wrecked by the Philistines when they overran Benjamin, for it suddenly disappears from history (cf. Psa. 78[60f.]).

16–20. An Oracle Against the Worship of Astarte. Astarte was mother and virgin, *queen of heaven* (cf. 44[15f.]). In various forms this worship has always been prevalent throughout the East, and, in particular, it was practiced under the name of Ishtar by the Babylonians, and may have found its way from them into Judah. If the oracle is by Jeremiah, it must belong to a very different period from that of the Temple address.

21–23. Jeremiah's Judgment on Sacrifice. The judgment is closely connected, in subject at least, with the Temple address. The oracle does not imply that there was no developed ritual with a code which claimed divine authority. Indeed, it would have been idle in any prophet to protest against such a sacrificial system, unless it had not only existed but had been exerting a powerful influence on men's minds through the fact that it laid claim to such great authority. The prophet with vehement exaggeration declares that the essential factor in the revelation to Israel was its moral demand. The exact sense of v. 21 is uncertain. The verse may mean that men may eat even the burnt-offering, which was generally reserved in its entirety to Jehovah, as they eat their other offerings, after having devoted part of them to him. God is indifferent about these petty refinements.

24–28. A Little Sermon on the Sins of the Fathers. This was a favorite subject with the exiles, who believed they were expiating this guilt. Jeremiah's habit was to stir the conscience of the living. *Daily rising,* etc. (v. 25), means, *never failing to send. Truth,* etc. (v. 28), i.e., faithfulness is dead and never spoken about.

29–34. A Late Oracle on Topheth. The place is located (v. 31) in what may have been an actual valley near Jerusalem (cf. 2 Kings 23[10]), but its site has not been identified. The Hebrew name of this valley, *gē ben Hinnom,* has supplied the word "gehenna" (Mk. 9[43]). The meaning of "Topheth" is also uncertain, for the Hebrew consonants have been repointed with vowels taken from the word "bosheth," or "shame," in order to suggest the shameful character of everything connected with it. Deut. 18[10] forbids passing children through the fire, regarding it as a heathen rite, which was practiced for purposes of necromancy. The last clause of v. 31, however, seems to imply that at some period these sacrifices were offered to Jehovah (cf. Mic. 6[7]). It is puzzling to understand why it should be counted necessary, here and in 32[35], to say that God never commanded them. In v. 32 read the last clause as in margin: so terrible shall be the judgment that their sanctuary shall become a cemetery. *Thine hair* (v. 29), since the Hebrew reads "thy crown," may be the consecrated hair of the Nazirite; or it may merely be the hair shorn in sign of mourning (cf. Mic. 1[16]).

CHAPTER VIII

1–3. An Oracle Denouncing the Worship of the Heavenly Bodies (cf. Deut. 4[19] Ezek. 8[16]). It must be late, since the people are in exile. The treatment of the corpses is both a dishonor to the dead and an insult to the objects of their worship, which look helplessly down on them. *Sought* (v. 2), i.e., in order to consult.

4–7. The Incorrigible Heart. If a man falls does he not get up again; if he wanders (from the road) does he not find his way back? But Jerusalem holds fast a false thing, like the wrong road of v. 4. God hears men say nothing of return; they hold on in their course. The unintelligent birds (*turtle-dove*) keep their dates of migration; men use their gift of reason to ignore the higher guidance of conscience and religion. In v. 4 omit, with LXX, the opening clause.

8–13. Condemnation of False Teachers. Omit vv. 10–12, which have been repeated from 6[13-15]; they break the connection here. The last clause too of v. 13, omitted by LXX, is untranslatable. Clearly Jeremiah is bringing no general charge, but refers to some definite act on the part of these scribes. He also accuses them, not of any trifling mistake in a minor point, but of some deliberate deed which in his view has completely changed the intention of the Law—their false pen has turned it, the Law, into a lie (so read in v. 8). Opinion is much divided as to the precise meaning of this accusation. But many have seen in it an evidence that the prophet was condemning the conduct of the priesthood in connection with the Josianic reform. In the judgment of the present writer, Jeremiah refers to the change made in the code of Deuteronomy. When this North Israelite book, which originally contemplated a multiplicity of sanctuaries, was adopted and given authority in Judah, a little preface, Deut. 12[1-7], was added, which prescribed centralization at Jerusalem. Jeremiah, who belonged to North Israel and was familiar with its code, recognized that by this slight addition the scribes had changed the entire character of the legislation and introduced a novel principle into the religion of the nation.

14–17. Doom From the North. This doom is to fall on *the whole earth* (not *land,* v. 16). Probably read, v. 16a, *the destroyer is heard from Dan, the snorting of his horses.* A noun is needed to which the recurrent *his* may refer. His *strong ones* are his stallions. Then continue, *when he comes* (instead of *for they have come*) *he will devour. The water of gall* (v. 14)—the same word is rendered "hemlock" in Hos. 10[4] and means "poison." Hence read *die there* and *brought us to death* for *let us be silent* and *put us to silence.*

18–22. A Hymn of Pity Over the Nation's Condition. The hymn includes also 9[1], which in Hebrew forms the closing verse of ch. 8. This hymn of pity over the nation's condition —*the daughter of my people* is the people itself —may be by Jeremiah, who foresees what shall be. But, since it vividly represents the country as already ruined and apparently forsaken by its God, it may emanate from the time when Judah lay desolate before the return of the exiles. Since *from a land that is very far off* (v. 19) may mean from "a land far and wide," the phrase does not necessarily imply that the nation is already in exile. *Strange vanities* are foreign idols, and *black* (v. 21) means "clothed in mourning garments." V. 20 does not refer to spiritual conditions. The people, using the natural imagery of an agricultural population, describe their condition as being like that of a farmer, who sees his grain harvest and the later harvest of wine and oil pass without bringing any relief to his needs. *Balm* (v. 22) was one of the products for which Gilead was famous (cf. Gen. 37[25]). Evidently it was used for medicinal purposes.

CHAPTER IX

1. See under 8[18-22].

2–6. The Disappearance of Mutual Confidence. Mutual confidence, the cement of all human society, has disappeared in the nation. It were better to live in a mere caravanserai among casual travelers who own no intimate relations to one another than in a country where these relations are so shamelessly exploited (v. 2). *Falsehood*, not faithfulness, has power in the land (so read with LXX in v. 3). Every brother is a very Jacob at supplanting (v. 4); this rendering brings out the allusion to Gen. 27[36]. Men heap violence on violence, fraud on fraud, and refuse to acknowledge me (so v. 6).

7–9. The Imminent Judgment. God must test the people in his furnace of trial, *because of my people's vileness*—so read with LXX the last clause of v. 7. On v. 9 see 5[29].

10–16. A Lament Over Ruined Judah. With this lament goes a summons to all thoughtful men to recognize and lay to heart what has brought Judah to this condition. Probably it dates from the period when the country was lying waste after the capture of Jerusalem. Thus, while it retains the form of a prophetic oracle, it does this clumsily, for the prophet is the speaker in v. 10, and Jehovah in v. 11. The *wilderness* of v. 10 is not the barren desert, but the steppes on which at certain seasons rain produces a short-lived but excellent pasture. These pastures lie waste (not *are burned up*), without the familiar sound of sheep (not *cattle*). In v. 15 read *for thus said;* the speaker emphasizes that Judah's ruin is the direct outcome of the divine warning.

17–22. A Similar Lament. The writer bids men summon the professional mourners, women skilled (cunning) in the practices connected with mourning and especially trained to chant the funeral dirge. For the people are expelled from their land and homes (v. 19b). Death cuts off the children in the streets, the youths in the public places (v. 21). Omit in v. 17, with LXX, *consider ye.* Omit in v. 22, with LXX, *Speak, Thus saith the Lord,* and read *lie* for *shall fall.*

23, 24. Man's Chief Glory. God's perfect purpose is the one source of human confidence.

25, 26. Jew and Gentile Will Suffer Alike. As it stands, this oracle seems meaningless. Omitting one Hebrew word and a preposition, we might read in v. 25 simply, *I will punish all uncircumcision.* With this change the thought of v. 26 would be: The nations named are uncircumcised in the flesh, Israel is uncircumcised in spirit; both stand essentially on the same level; hence both will suffer. The polled *corners* or shaved temples refers to a practice prevalent among some of the Eastern desert tribes (cf. Herodotus iii, 8). Probably because the custom implied a reverence for some deity, it was forbidden in Israel (Lev. 19[27]).

CHAPTER X

1–16. A Series of Lessons on the Folly of Idolatry. These lessons are intended for the guidance of the Babylonian exiles. What the people are warned against is not the syncretistic worship of Palestine, but apostasy to the idolatrous customs of the nation among which they are living. The resemblance between vv. 1–10 and Isa. 40[19f.] 44[9f.] is very close; the three passages reveal the same situation and danger. V. 11, which is in Aramaic, is a formula intended for the use of humble Jews who are being invited by their neighbors to join in heathen worship. Vv. 12–16 reappear in 51[15-19] among the oracles on Babylon. The section forms an interesting illustration of the careful way in which the religious leaders helped their people to resist the seduction of their new surroundings.

They must not learn the heathen religion (for *way* cf. Acts 9[2]), nor revere the heavenly bodies, which bulked largely in Babylonian worship (v. 2). The religious rituals of the heathen are absurd: a man carves a log which another has felled (v. 3). The thing stands dumb, like a scarecrow in a kitchen garden (so v. 5a), and must be carried about—a reference to the religious processions of Babylon (cf. Isa. 46[7]). But in all their pantheons (for *royal estate*) there is none like Jehovah (v. 7). V. 8b is untranslatable. *Tarshish* (v. 9) was probably "Tartessus" in Spain. *Uphaz* = Ophir, from which came the best gold. *Artificer* is "joiner." Read v. 11a *thus must you say about them,* i.e., the idols. There follows a description of Jehovah's power. His voice is the thunder, and he sends lightnings flashing through the rain (v. 13). All men are struck dumb and senseless (at this proof of Jehovah's power), but especially every maker of idols (v. 14). When those are put to the proof, they fail (v. 15b).

17–22. Fragments of Oracles of Doom. Vv. 17, 18 are untranslatable. In vv. 19, 20 Jerusalem is the speaker; the *cords* support the tent; the *shepherds* are rulers.

23–25. The Nation in Exile Acknowledges That It Is in the Divine Hands. The people have come to know that a man's fate is not in his own power (v. 23). But they plead that, while they merit punishment, they merit it less than the heathen world which works its will on them. If they are not succored they may disappear as a people, being made very small (v. 24). And with them will disappear the divine purpose which is involved in their continuance. The truth in this plea deserves more attention than it generally receives.

CHAPTER XI

1–14. Results of Disobedience to the Mosaic Covenant. This section has often been taken to describe Jeremiah's attitude toward the Josianic reform. It has even been suggested that the prophet undertook or was commissioned by the priesthood and court to carry out a mission for spreading the principles of that reform in the country. But nothing is said here of that book which 2 Kings 22[8-13] states to have been one originating cause of the official action. What vv. 3f. refer to is a *covenant* which is definitely stated to be no novelty, i.e., the old covenant at Horeb, by which Jehovah constituted the nation and made it his peculiar people. The present distress in which the people are involved is regarded in v. 8 as the outcome of their disobedience to that Mosaic covenant, not to any new covenant under Josiah. The real content of the passage is that Jeremiah's activity and message have been in close agreement with the attitude of all the prophets in Israel, and that, in now prophesying disaster, he is taking no novel course, but is merely continuing the tradition of his predecessors. Thus it represents practically the position Jeremiah took (28[6f.]) when he found himself in clear opposition to certain prophets who promised the nation success and peace. For *shall cry* (vv. 11, 12) read *may*, and change *for their trouble* (v. 14) to *in the day of*.

15–17. Israel to be Banished for Unfaithfulness. The nation must be expelled from Palestine in spite of its sacrifices. Since the Josianic reform, with its new attitude toward the Temple, attached greater value to correct sacrifice, the oracle may have special reference to that movement. Read, with help of LXX, *what right has my beloved to live in my house, so long as she cherishes lewd thoughts? Can vows and holy flesh take away your sin, or can you thus be saved? The Lord called you a spreading olive of fair shape; at his thunder its leaf withered.* Jeremiah uses Hosea's figure of Israel, the bride of Jehovah, and Palestine, the home to which he brought her.

18–23. Hostility to Jeremiah for His Message. Jeremiah states how in practical experience he learned the bitter truth involved in his commission as prophet (1[6]). When he sought to present the divine standards he became at once the object of violent attack. Since, however, the cause he upholds is the divine purpose, he commits (*have revealed*, v. 20) himself and his opponents into the hands of God. The Lord will maintain his own cause in his own way. The saying is expressed in quite general terms. In v. 19 for *with the fruit thereof* read *in its full vigor*. Vv. 21–23 refer the general statement of vv. 18–20 to a particular period of the prophet's life, about which unfortunately we have no further information, when he suffered from persecution at the hands of the men of his native village. Along with them should be read 12[3b, 6], which have no real connection where they stand. In all probability the verses are a later explanatory comment. For *even* (v. 23) read *in*.

CHAPTER XII

1–6. Jeremiah's Complaint and Jehovah's Answer. On vv. 3b, 6 see 11[21-23]. Jeremiah acknowledges that God is always in the right when he enters a plea before him. Yet he would urge the apparent injustice of granting prosperity to bad men, who, it is true, acknowledge God in their talk but keep him far from their real thoughts and aims (vv. 2, 6). Indeed, they say about God, *He never sees what we do* (so, with LXX, last clause of v. 4). *Yet thou, O Lord, seest by testing that my heart is thine* (so v. 3a). He receives for answer that, if in a time of relative calm he is seeking cover (*secure*, v. 5), he will fail when the severer test comes. Men who live, like the prophet, by standards which are not of this world need not be surprised if the world, which tries to ignore these standards, makes obedience difficult for them. Will the day's journey take the whole long day? From morn to night, my friend. The *pride of Jordan* (v. 5) is the belt of thorny jungle along the river-bed, apt to become half swamp when the floods are out. Hence it always offers bad going for a pedestrian.

7–13. Jehovah Alone Cares for His Heritage. A voice from Palestine (*mine* house, v. 7; cf. Hos. 8[1] 9[15]), lying desolate after the Exile, declares that none but Jehovah cares for it.

Many owners (*shepherds*, v. 10) have wasted it: the reference is to the conquerors who have worked their will on Judah. Brigands (*spoilers*, v. 12) wander there. Men are ashamed of their harvest, the harvest of the fierce wrath of Jehovah (so v. 13b). V. 9a can be translated only by means of a serious and highly problematical emendation of the text.

14–17. A Proposal to the Foreigners. Another post-exilic oracle, which promises a future to *the* (not *mine*, v. 14) heathen neighbors who have ravaged Palestine, on condition that they cast in their lot with Judah and adopt the true religion.

CHAPTER XIII

1–11. Degeneration of the Exiles in Babylon. Under the figure of a girdle spoiled by damp this oracle speaks of the degeneration of the exiles through contact with Babylonian life. Since it is impossible to suppose that Jeremiah took four journeys across the desert in order to perform this symbolic act, the *Prath* (=Euphrates, v. 4) referred to has been explained as Parah in Benjamin (Josh. 18[23]). But Parah is a town, and *Prath* elsewhere is always Euphrates. More probably, therefore, this is the warning of an exilic prophet who saw that contact with heathen practices was threatening the life of his nation. They are *becoming* (not *shall even be*, v. 10) like the rotten girdle.

12–22. Four Oracles of Doom. The terms of the first oracle (vv. 12–14) are very obscure. The *wine*, with which the jars, i.e., the nation, are to be filled, might naturally be the wine of the divine wrath. But why these jars should be dashed together is far from clear, since no potter dashes his jars together, especially when they are filled with wine. Probably we have the effort to interpret a badly transmitted utterance of Jeremiah. The second oracle (vv. 15–17) contains a summons to attention, before it becomes too late. Otherwise, the eye of the prophet and *your eye also* (so v. 17) shall weep sore over the rejected nation. The message of doom in the third oracle (vv. 18–22), describing the result of reliance on the foreigner, is addressed to the king and queen-mother, because the latter had great influence in old Judah. They are told that from their heads is falling their glorious crown (v. 18b). They themselves have taught their neighbors to treat them with contempt (v. 21a). They shall be exposed to dishonor and their shame laid open to sight (v. 22b). The situation does not suit any known historical conditions, nor is any particular king named. To refer it to the situation after Carchemish does not account for the description of the South, the district which falls away from Hebron to the desert, as shut up. Jeremiah is speaking, like Hosea, in general terms. The fourth oracle (vv. 23–27) compares Jerusalem to a woman, resolute in her infamous ways; how long can this condition last? (So v. 27b.) There can be but one end, since Jehovah is righteous. The *stubble* of v. 24 is described as "whirling before the sirocco." The idea of v. 26 is that of exposing a woman's person.

CHAPTER XIV

1–9. A Picture of Drought, with an Appropriate Prayer. Men sit mourning in the towns (*gates*) of Judah. Jerusalem, which has always been greatly dependent on cisterns (*pits*) hewn in the limestone rock, laments. To these cisterns its nobles send their servants (*little ones*), but the men return with covered heads in sign of grief (cf. 2 Sam. 15[30]). Lying untilled, the land faints (so v. 4a). Though men merit nothing, let God act for his own sake. He is no passing stranger, no man asleep (so, with LXX, for *astonied*, v. 9): he is Israel's God. Omit in v. 6 *like jackals*, with LXX.

10. The fragment of an oracle, condemning the people's apostasy.

11–16. Jeremiah Persists in Interceding for His People. Jeremiah, forbidden to pray for his people, urges (v. 13) that the fault lies, not in the people, but in the prophets who mislead them by promising success (cf. ch. 28). These men are denounced, as uttering no more than empty superstitions and the fancies of their own minds (v. 14b). Their doom (not *wickedness*, v. 16c) is sure with that of their misled followers. It deserves notice that a leading function of the prophet in old Israel was evidently to intercede for his nation. Even Amos, a prophet of doom, does this (7[2, 5]). The prophet's prayers too were regarded as possessed of peculiar efficacy. Jeremiah needs to be forbidden to pray, because now Jehovah is resolved (cf. Amos 7[8]). As man of God, the prophet knew the divine mind, both in the temporary need to punish and in the ultimate desire for reconciliation.

17, 18. A Lament Over Ruined Judah. In v. 17 read *mine eyes run and do not cease;* and in v. 18 for *them that are sick with* read *the horrors of*, and probably for *go about in the land* read *are bowed to the ground.*

19–22. A Prayer of the Exiles. This has probably been inserted near the prayer in time of drought because of the mention of Jehovah's power to bring rain. The writer, however, appeals to Jehovah's power over nature, as contrasted with the helplessness of heathen gods (*vanities*, v. 22), in a way which is characteristic of Deutero-Isaiah. For his own sake, for the sake of Jerusalem, the throne of his glory (i.e., the Temple), for the covenant's sake, he must redeem. For *is it not thou on whom we rely because thou doest such things?* (So v. 22b.) The *things* are the rain.

CHAPTER XV

1–4. Judah's Fate. Judah is doomed to four fates (*kinds*, v. 3) because of Manasseh's sin. On Moses and Samuel, as prophets and intercessors, cf. 14^{11-16}.

5–9. Another Lament Over Jerusalem. Who *now* pities or bemoans (not *shall*, v. 5) Jerusalem, the once prolific mother? (V. 9a.) God has winnowed her people out in their towns (v. 7a), for his pity was at last worn out, because of the vileness of their ways (so read, with LXX, the last clause of v. 7). Omit in v. 8 *against the mother of the young men*.

10–14. Miscellaneous Fragments. Vv. 10, 11 are a fragment with very uncertain text; v. 12 is untranslatable; vv. 13, 14 recur in $17^{3f.}$, where they are more in place.

15–21. Jeremiah's Prayer. Jeremiah prays God in his long-suffering toward his opponents not to ignore his servant, whose very loyalty has brought him *reproach from men who despise thy words* (so read, with LXX, the first clause of v. 16), for he is wholly dedicated to his God (v. 16c). He has not sat among mockers or those who made merry with them (v. 17a). Why should God fail him, like a brook which runs dry when it is most needed? (V. 18b.) The inner voice replies: "If thou surrender wholly to me and I restore thee, thou shalt be my servant; if thou make clear the difference between good and evil, thou shalt be as my mouth. Men may fight against thee, but they shall not prevail." The thought is that of the divine word of 1^{9}, which contains the ultimate standards of eternal validity. Men may turn to this, but the prophet dare not turn to them. *Magna est veritas et praevalet.* The *hand* of v. 17 is that of 1^{9}; the verse has nothing to say about the ecstatic or other conditions in which this hand appeared. In v. 15 omit, with LXX, *thou knowest*.

CHAPTER XVI

1–9. Jeremiah to Remain a Man Apart. Because the end is at hand, Jeremiah must remain unmarried and take no share in the ordinary tasks of life. The cuttings and baldness of v. 6 were forms of mourning (cf. Lev. 19^{28} Deut. 14^{1}). For the mourners' bread and the cup of consolation at death cf. Ezek. 24^{17} Tobit 4^{17}.

10–21. Israel Making Atonement for Past Sins. A little sermon, to explain that Israel in exile is atoning for the sins of the past. The explanation served in the end to dull the consciences of the exiles, since it led them to say that the fathers had eaten sour grapes and the children's teeth were set on edge (Ezek. 18). But it is not Jeremianic teaching. The idea of a double recompense (v. 18) is also an exilic thought (cf. Isa. 40^{2}). The *hunters* and *fishers* of v. 16 are the heathen conquerors who have carried out the divine will in chastising Israel. The *carcasses* of their detestable things (v. 18) are their dead and corrupt gods, and *mine inheritance* is the land, not the nation. In v. 13c, for *I will* read *which shall*. Vv. 14, 15 recur in $23^{7f.}$ and suit the connection there better than here. In v. 21 for *this once* read *at this time*.

CHAPTER XVII

1–4. An Oracle Against the Popular Worship. Perhaps read for v. 2 merely *as a memorial against them*. A later generation, believing Jeremiah to be attacking the forms of heathen worship, added the details about the Asherim, etc. But the prophet was attacking Judah's whole worship. The *pen of iron*, which was used for writing on rock (Job 19^{24}), is intended to suggest the hardness of Judah's heart, which demands such an instrument. Vv. 3, 4 contain a passage with a bad text, which closely resembles $15^{13f.}$ and is probably not original here.

5–8. A Late Psalm. This is not an oracle, but a psalm, closely resembling Psa. 1. In v. 6 for *shall inhabit* read *living, as it does, in;* and for *he shall be* here and in v. 8 read *he is. Careful* (v. 8), i.e., need have no anxiety.

9–11. Two Gnomic Sentences. These sentences are like those in Proverbs. One speaks of man's heart as secretive and set on evil, which only God knows. The other, using a popular idea about the habits of the partridge, describes it as hatching out eggs which it has not laid, with the result that the brood forsake their foster-mother.

12, 13. The Song of a Pilgrim. The pious, glad utterance of many a pilgrim to the Temple. Himself loyal to the faith of his fathers, he says that all renegades, "all who rebel against thee in the earth," shall be brought to shame (so v. 13b).

14–18. Jeremiah Affirms His Sincerity. Jeremiah, taunted with the fact that his predicted doom does not arrive, disclaims any malicious pleasure in uttering only prophecies of disaster. "Yet," he says, "I have not urged thee to hasten the disaster . . . what I really did say is before thy face" (so read v. 16a, c). He then prays to be vindicated before his opponents (v. 18) in terms which resemble his prediction of the fate of Hananiah in 28^15f^. It may be noted (v. 16) that the Hebrew words for "shepherd" and "disaster" only differ in their vowels.

19–27. Sabbath Observance Legislation. This piece of legislation about Sabbath observance belongs to the period of the restored Temple (cf. Neh. 13^15-22^). Its promise (v. 25) that Davidic kings (omit *princes*, since these did not occupy thrones) shall be restored implies that they had ceased to reign in Jerusalem. And the picture (v. 26) of worshipers streaming from Judah and Benjamin, the maritime plain (*lowland*), the hill country south of the capital (*mountains*), and the steppe running down to the desert (*South*), shows that the Temple had become the center of the national life. The LXX reads in v. 19, *gate of thy people*, meaning the gate of Benjamin leading to Anathoth; cf. 37^13^. For the offerings in v. 26, where *oblations* mean cereal or meal offerings, cf. such passages as 6^20^ Ex. 20^24^ Lev. 2^1f.^ 7^12^. The threat in v. 27 is modeled on Amos 2^5^.

CHAPTER XVIII

1–12. The Potter's Wheel. Jeremiah compares Judah in the hand of God to a vessel on a potter's wheel (vv. 1–6). If the clay proves incapable of taking the shape first designed for it, "being marred, as it is apt to be, in a potter's hand," the potter does not throw it away, but tries it in a different shape. Thus no special shape, such as that of state or kingdom, is essential to the nation as the instrument of the divine will. The *wheels* (v. 3) are probably the upper stone which carried the clay and the lower stone which the potter turned with his feet in order to leave both hands free for his work. Vv. 7–12 contain a later comment on the oracle which misses the point, for they make the divine change of plan depend on a change of mind in the instrument which God is shaping. Now, clay cannot change its mind. For *at what instant* (v. 7) read *at one time I may decree.* In v. 9 *at what instant* =*at another time.* Cf. on ch. 19.

13–17. Israel's Incredible Folly. Does snow vanish from Lebanon's crest, or do the waters fail from the Mediterranean? Yet Israel has done an equally incredible thing in sacrificing to idols (*vanity;* A.S.V., "false gods"); hence they have *stumbled* (not, *caused to stumble*) in their ways, thus making their land desolate. Jehovah must turn his back instead of his face to them in the day of their calamity (so v. 17b). The text of v. 14 is uncertain, but the sense is clearly as rendered above. The distinction between *bypaths* and the *cast-up* way (v. 15) is that between a rough track across fields and a built public road.

18–23. A Plot Against Jeremiah. Certain men plot against Jeremiah, from the sense that the result of listening to the prophet must be to nullify the guidance of all their other spiritual leaders. The verbs in v. 18b should be read in the present, not in the future: priest, wise man and prophet have counsel to supply. The men say, "Let us pay close attention to his words," i.e., in order to trap him. So to read v. 18b and, with LXX, to omit the negative lends double force to Jeremiah's prayer (v. 19a) that God will give equally close attention to him. He pleads that he has prayed for these men that God should not pour out his fury on them. Vv. 21, 22a are probably an addition to heighten the effect. The sentences break the connection between vv. 20 and 22b and anticipate the conclusion in v. 23.

CHAPTER XIX

The Symbolism of the Broken Pottery. Jeremiah is directed to take some of the leading laymen and priests down to the "pottery gate," so called probably because outside it the people of Jerusalem were in the habit of throwing their broken pottery. There he is to break an earthenware jar in token of the way in which Jehovah means to deal with the nation. The meaning of his act, like that at 18^2^, is to be revealed to him on the spot (v. 2). Hence vv. 3–9, which introduce the oracle before the symbolic act and thus nullify the whole effect of the act, must be an addition. The date of the prophet's action is quite uncertain. Since, however, it is followed, ch. 20, by an account of Jeremiah being thrown into the stocks, it should probably be set later than the Temple address (chs. 7, 26). There the people interfered in his defense. This renewed public outburst led the priests to a renewed effort to silence him. And since he here attacked the national existence, there was no one to interfere. In v. 4 *estranged* means "desecrated." Read also, *and the kings of Judah have filled.* To *hiss* (v. 8) is to whistle with amazement. Omit, in v. 11, with LXX, the clause about burying in Topheth. For *Topheth* cf. 2 Kings 23^10^.

CHAPTER XX

1–6. Jeremiah in the Stocks; His Rebuke of Pashhur. Pashhur *arrests* (not *smote*, v. 2) Jeremiah. Evidently this priest was an officer charged with the duty of maintaining order in the Temple. And according to 29[26] one part of his function was to take action against irresponsible prophets. Contrast how the priest at Bethel appealed to the king and did no more than warn the prophet Amos (7[10]). The priest is now invested with full authority in the Temple. Jeremiah declares that God will hand over to terror Pashhur and his friends (so v. 4a). He also declares that this policy of stifling true prophecy must bring ruin on the city. Pashhur has allowed lies to be prophesied, not *has prophesied* (v. 6). The man was no prophet, but Jeremiah charges him with having permitted the false prophets of success to speak unchecked. *Which was* (in v. 2)="beside."

7–11. "A Burning Fire Shut Up in My Bones." Jeremiah in his loneliness recognizes afresh that he can have peace with the world only by forsaking the life-task intrusted to him by God. The words may reproduce the thoughts of the prophet when he sat in the stocks. If not, this was a fitting place to insert them. God has led him where he would, and he has let himself be led. Yet, whenever he prophesies in obedience to the divine will, he has reason to cry, *Violence and wrong* (v. 8), i.e., he is maltreated (cf. 6[7]). But if he tries to hold his peace, the message becomes an inward fire, and he is so weary of enduring this that he can bear no more—it must out. He hears the whisper of the crowd, "He and his terror on every side"; "Let us denounce him"; the whisper of those who were his friends, "Perhaps he may make a false step, then we shall get our revenge." But God is with him and his vindication is sure.

12, 13. Two Misplaced Fragments. V. 12 has been repeated from 11[20]; v. 13 is an intruded verse from a psalm.

14–18. A Cry of Bitter Distress. *Making him glad* (v. 15)=congratulating him. V. 16 refers to Sodom (Gen. 19[25]). *Shouting* is the battle-cry. In v. 17 LXX reads *in the womb;* and *her womb always great* means that she should go with her unborn child to the grave.

CHAPTER XXI

1–10. Jeremiah Announces to Zedekiah the Coming Doom. Near the beginning of the final siege of Jerusalem in 588 B.C., Jeremiah informs King Zedekiah that there is no hope of the Babylonian army retiring (*go up*, v. 2). It is the divine will that the city should fall; and only those who surrender ("passeth over," A.S.V., v. 9) to the enemy shall survive and so at least save their lives.

Two matters deserve close attention here. (1) This victory of the Babylonians is never brought into connection with the consummation which the prophet announced (4[5], etc.). He sees the Babylonians, as Isaiah (10[5, 15]) saw the Assyrians, to be an instrument in the divine hands for chastising Judah. But they do no more because they can do no more. They cannot bring the consummation, since that involves more than judgment. The judgment of the consummation is but the preparation for a new and better order. And, since it involves so great and, above all, so positive an end, only God can bring it in. (2) But, further, Jeremiah believed that in this he was delivering a religious message. He was consulted as a prophet and he answered in that capacity. To him it was the will of God, or, in our modern language, it was better for the religion of Israel that the capital with its Temple should be destroyed. To say that Jeremiah was more clear-sighted than the court in his recognition of the inevitable issues of the war, or, as Volz bluntly states it, spoke plain common sense about the hopelessness of resistance to a power like Babylon, is to ignore this clear fact. Old Israel did not believe that a special revelation was given or needed to utter common sense. Jeremiah saw his people through the influence of the Josianic reformation making city and Temple essential to their religion. It was better for true religion that the things in which they trusted should go. The section should be compared with 37[3-10] and ch. 38. *Gather them* (v. 4) means "bring the conquerors."

11, 12. A Call to Justice. Cf. 22[1-9]. Read v. 11—*To the courtiers of Judah: Hear the word of the Lord, ye of David's house.* The first clause is the heading (cf. "concerning the prophets," 23[9]) to the series of oracles in ch. 22, addressed to the kings and courtiers of Jeremiah's time. *In the morning* (v.12), i.e., diligently. The *spoiled* are the wronged. The court exists to bring justice to all men.

13, 14. Jehovah Cannot Be Escaped. An oracle of uncertain origin against some unknown town, addressed as "dweller in the ravine, rock of the table-land," which boasts that none can "reach" it. In v. 14, for *her forest* read *your*, and for *about her* read *it*.

CHAPTER XXII

1–9. "Execute Ye Justice and Righteousness." Cf. 21[11f]. Jeremiah is to go down from the Temple to the palace which was connected with the Temple at a slightly lower level. He is to declare that power in Judah exists for the protection of the weak. The stranger is mentioned because he had no rights in his adopted country and was therefore open to wrong. Cf. Nathan's parable to David and note that Uriah was such a stranger (2 Sam. 12^1-15^). In vv. 6, 7, Jeremiah, referring to the hall in Solomon's palace (1 Kings 7^2^), the cedar columns of which were like trees on Gilead or Lebanon, says, *Once thou wert* (not *art*, v. 6) a *very Gilead* to Jehovah, but now thou art rejected. Vv. 8, 9 are a prose comment taken from Deut. 29^24-26^.

10–12. An Oracle on Josiah and Shallum. Josiah is the dead king (cf. 2 Kings 23^29f.^), and Shallum (Jehoahaz) the exiled king (cf. 2 Kings 23^31f.^). The verses should be rearranged: *Thus saith the Lord concerning Shallum who succeeded his father Josiah, Mourn not for the dead: weep bitterly for him who is going away, for he shall never return to see his native land. Once he has left this place, he shall never return, but,* etc.

13–19. Jehoiakim Blamed. Jehoiakim is severely blamed for his passion for fine buildings and his meanness in paying his workmen. Is a king proved a king by worrying about cedar? (V. 15.) He shall receive at death neither such mourning as men offer their kin nor such as is given to a great lord (v. 18). His father, Josiah, proved himself royal, when he cared for justice. The emphasis, however, with which it is said that then it was well with Josiah suggests that there was a period in the king's life with which Jeremiah was not in sympathy.

20–23. An Oracle on Obduracy. The oracle is against some unknown town (cf. 21^13f.^) situated east of the Jordan. *Abarim* is in Moab (Deut. 32^49^). The wind drives at its will its leaders, its allies are exiled (v. 22a).

24–27. The Fate of Jehoiachin. Cf. mg. and 2 Kings 24^8f.^ 25^27f.^

28–30. Two Fragments on the Same King. According to 1 Chr. 3^17^ Jehoiachin had children. The sense, however, here may be that he shall have no successors of his own children.

CHAPTER XXIII

1–4. Unfaithful Leaders to be Replaced. Jeremiah speaks against the leaders who have not cared for (*visited*) their nation. Throughout these oracles the leading idea is that power means opportunity for service. Vv. 3, 4 present a post-exilic promise of restoration from the lands to which Jehovah *has* scattered Israel.

5–8. Two Oracles on the Restoration of the Nation. Both of these appear again in 33^15f.^ and 16^14f.^ The first predicts Messiah, who is a shoot out of the present stump of the Davidic house. Hence to the writer the royal house of Judah has already been cut off. He is conceived as a second David, ruling by divine authority over a reunited nation. His title, *The Lord is our Righteousness*, can also be applied to Jerusalem (33^16^; cf. Ezek. 48^35^). *Deal wisely* (v. 5) means "prosper." The second oracle declares that the future shall surpass the past.

A Series of Oracles on the Prophets (vv. 9–40). The series corresponds to the series on the kings (cf. 21^11^).

9–12. Jeremiah's Agitation Over the False Prophets. Jeremiah's bones become without strength (*shake*) when he sees the spiritual guides of Judah disloyal in spirit (*adulterers*) to the God whose religion they teach. Their conduct is bad and they are strong only for evil (v. 10b). The penalty shall be a judicial blindness which urges them on to their ruin when God visits his world. To men who have ignored the eternal standards (*holy words*) the day of the divine self-revelation brings nothing but judgment. Omit in v. 10 the clause from *for because* to *dried up*.

13–15. "Folly in the Prophets." Prophets, in whom disloyalty to the divine standards of right and hypocrisy (*lies*) are combined, can only bring it about that no man feels it necessary to repent.

16–22. True Prophets Distinguished from False. It is easy to speak soothing words to careless souls. But any man who has stood in the divine council must listen with awed attention: who has ever heard God's word to purpose otherwise? (So v. 18.) God's anger cannot calm down till it has done his work, and his work is after his holy heart. True prophecy must deal first with the conscience. In the consummation men shall find this true. Vv. 19, 20 reappear in 30^23f.^

23, 24. The Inescapable God. Here is offered an oracle of very uncertain sense. If it were legitimate to render *at hand* by *local*, i.e., with narrow outlook and correspondingly limited power, the sense would be clear. But it is difficult to justify that translation.

25–29. Revelation of God's Mind a Great Theme. And how long will it be in the thought of prophets who utter their own false fancies, till, with their dreams which men hawk about, they make my people forget my name and all it means? Tell your dreams by all means: but why mix chaff with wheat, i.e., dreams with prophecy? True prophecy does not amuse, it converts men.

30–32. Prophets Who Lack Conviction. This passage is directed against prophets without inner conviction. The men of v. 31 are those who copy God's language and are constantly saying, *Thus saith.*

33–40. A Pun on the Word "Burden." For *What burden!* (v. 33) read, with LXX, *ye are the burden.* Jeremiah's answer contains a Hebrew pun. *Massa* means a load, but also, like our "burden of a song," means a divine oracle. The divine burden or message to you is that you have become a burden to God. *This people* (v. 33) = any layman, as contrasted with prophet and priest.

The saying in v. 33 having been misunderstood, the following verses are efforts to explain it. Vv. 34, 35 forbid the use of the expression "massa (burden) of Jehovah," and prescribe two others for public and private use. Vv. 36, 37 order "Never again employ the phrase, 'massa of Jehovah,' for how can his word be a burden to anyone?" (so v. 36a) and omit, with LXX, v. 36b. Vv. 38–40 declare that if men use the phrase God will lift them up like a burden and cast them off.

CHAPTER XXIV

Two Baskets of Figs. Jeremiah, seeing two baskets of figs, one good and one bad, beside the Temple (probably brought there as first fruits), receives the revelation that the good figs represent the exiles carried away with Jehoiachin, the bad figs the remnant population of Jerusalem, and that the former are peculiarly approved (*regard for good*, v. 5) by their God. Now, the first exiles were the leading men of the nation, and in this has been sought the reason for the prophet's preference. But to make this distinction the ground of the divine preference is to make Jeremiah count God a respecter of persons, and, what is worse, a respecter of persons for reasons of outward dignity and position. For the conqueror did not select his hostages from among the most religious citizens: he chose the men of influence whose absence would most weaken the resistance of Judah. Jeremiah was bringing a religious message, not a confirmation of men's estimate of what makes men favored of God.

Evidently, also, his message ran counter to an opinion which was prevalent in Jerusalem. Now, the exiles, cut off from the Temple and its worship, were regarded by their fellows as *ipso facto* cut off from relation to their God. They were even apt to believe this themselves. Jeremiah teaches that these men are nearer their God than the men who were living under the shadow of the Temple. These last count their Temple worship essential to any relation to God. The exiles have the opportunity, if they believe that God regards them in their captivity, to learn a higher conception of the divine power and the divine grace. Hence there is a special appropriateness in the baskets being set before the Temple. Figs of the first crop (v. 2) were regarded as the best (cf. Isa. 28[4]). For *to be tossed to and fro for evil* (v. 9) read *an object of disgust.*

CHAPTER XXV

1–29. Jeremiah Predicts a Seventy Years' Captivity. The first task here is to sift out the original, for the section has been seriously overlaid with later material. Now, vv. 2–8, with their clumsy introduction and their conclusion, which doubles back to the beginning, form a little sermon which is out of place in this connection. Again, the clause in v. 9, *and I will send unto Nebuchadrezzar the king of Babylon, my servant* is an impossible grammatical construction as it stands, and is absent from the LXX. Further, in v. 11a, *this whole land* appears in the LXX as *the whole earth,* and v. 11b appears in so curiously variant a form in the LXX that it is clearly secondary. Vv. 12–14 refer to chs. 50f. and ascribe those chapters to Jeremiah, but no one now credits the oracles on Babylon to the prophet. Vv. 17–29 describe Jerusalem as desolate *at this day* (v. 18), and must therefore date from the time after the destruction of the capital. Their late origin is further proved by their ascribing to Jeremiah in v. 17 what was physically impossible to any man. The later generation, which had lost touch with the actual situation, interpreted in a somewhat bald and literal way the fine symbol of the prophet being intrusted with the cup of the divine anger. What remains after these excisions is an oracle on the day of the Lord: Jehovah is about to bring all the families of the North (v. 9, cf. 1[14]) against Jerusalem first, but also against all the nations round it. The world shall become a desolation, returning to the condition from which God brought it at first (cf. 4[23f.]). Jeremiah is repeating the revelation he received in the second vision after his call.

For *and I will do you no hurt* (v. 6) read *to do you hurt.* Read v. 10b, *the millstones are heard in every hamlet, the candle seen in every home.* In v. 14a read *because many nations . . . have enslaved them,* i.e., the Jews, *I will,* etc. The *mingled people* (v. 20), or Ereb, apparently some part of the population of Egypt. *The land of Uz* (cf. Job 1[1]) is unknown. *The isle which is beyond the sea* (v. 22) is the Mediterranean coastlands. In v. 23 the reference is to Bedouin of North Arabia. Omit, in v. 24, *and all the kings of the mingled people.* The lands named in v. 25 lie east of the Tigris. *Sheshach* (v. 26) is Babylon.

30–38. Three Minor Oracles. Three minor oracles on the day of the Lord have been added to the longer one. There is no reason for denying these to Jeremiah, except the *a priori* dictum that he wrote no apocalypse. Havoc reaches from end to end of the world, for the Lord asserts his right and vindicates his claim among all nations: he will destroy the wicked. This, which reproduces v. 31, is the theme of the whole. God's self-manifestation concerns the world, because he is its God; it involves judgment, because he is righteous.

Chapters 26 to 52: The Predominatingly Biographical Section of the Book

From this point on the chapters contain more narrative and, where they report oracles, report them in connection with the circumstances in which they were spoken. The division cannot be pressed too far, since certain biographical material is found also in chs. 20, 21, and among the later chapters dealing with the story of Jeremiah appears the booklet of consolation, chs. 30, 31, which contains nothing but oracular matter.

CHAPTER XXVI

A Plot Against Jeremiah. This chapter should be compared with 7[1-15]. The address here has been softened by the addition of vv. 3–5 and v. 13, which make the destruction of the Temple contingent on whether the people repent. But the message Jeremiah had to deliver was so perilous and unwelcome that he was specially ordered to deliver it in its entirety (v. 2). Now, a call to repentance was no unusual message for a prophet to deliver; but in vv. 7–9 the religious leaders, reproducing Jeremiah's message in the form of an unconditional destruction of the Temple, declare that such an oracle in the name of Jehovah is simply incredible. Again, when the royal officials took their seats to examine and decide the case (v. 10), the point of Jeremiah's appeal in vv. 12, 14 is that he has spoken in his capacity as prophet by the direct authority of Jehovah, not that the priests have reported his words incorrectly. The lay court passes no judgment on Jeremiah's sincerity or insincerity; the men recognize the right of a prophet to utter his message (v. 16).

The elders present from the country, to whom Micah's words were familiar, since that prophet belonged to the country, not to the capital, recall how Micah uttered a prophecy in similar terms. And it is they who introduce the possibility that the doom on Jerusalem may be averted. In v. 8 probably omit *and all the people,* since in vv. 16f. the laymen support Jeremiah against their religious leaders. Evidently, the message was peculiarly offensive to the priesthood. Temple and palace (v. 10) were contiguous. *The mountain of the house* (v. 18) is the Temple hill (cf. Mic. 3[12]). *Great evil* (closing words of v. 19) means a great crime. *Common people* (v. 23)=nameless men. A man who was *ben* so and so, i.e., son of so and so, was buried with his fathers in the family grave. *Ahikam* (v. 24) was the father of Gedaliah, the official into whose charge Jeremiah was committed after the destruction of Jerusalem (40[5f.]).

CHAPTER XXVII

Oracles on Submission to Nebuchadrezzar. The chapter should be studied along with ch. 28. Both belong to the early period of Zedekiah (not Jehoiakim, v. 1, mg.). But they do not come from the same source. For, while 27[1], a later heading, speaks of Jeremiah in the third person, the two oracles in the chapter introduce him in the first person. On the other hand, ch. 28 begins with Jeremiah in the first person, but continues in the third. Nevertheless, the three oracles in chs. 27, 28 seem to be connected with the same historical situation. Apparently, certain neighboring states were seeking to draw Judah into an alliance for a rebellion against Babylon, and the movement was supported by several of the prophets at Jerusalem. What prompted these men to take this attitude is quite unknown. Few things would have thrown more light on the situation of Jewish religion at this period than the preservation of oracles from men whom Jeremiah denounced as false prophets. The attempted rebellion came to nothing, probably because Nebuchadrezzar, hearing of the movement, took prompt action. At least there is mention of a messenger sent from Jerusalem to Babylon in the early period of Zedekiah's reign (51[59]). By this means Jeremiah may have sent his letter to the exiles (ch. 29). The purpose of the messenger may have been to deny or excuse Zedekiah's share in the attempted coalition.

1–11. The First Oracle. In the first oracle of ch. 27 Jeremiah is directed to put on thongs and a yoke, such as were employed for plow-cattle. These are symbols of submission. He is also to send a message (so, with LXX, for *them,* v. 3) to the allied kings rejecting their offers of alliance. For Babylon is an instrument in the divine hand, and to oppose it is to oppose God. (On this position see intro., p. 678b.) Since the prophet had no power to contract or reject alliances, this narrative may once have had a different setting which represented it, like vv. 12f., as advice given to Zedekiah.

V. 7 interrupts the connection and may be an addition. For *dreams* (v. 9) read *dreamers*.

12–22. The Second Oracle. In the second oracle, given to Zedekiah, Jeremiah declares it to be the divine will that Nebuchadrezzar should conquer Jerusalem and despoil the Temple. The section has been modified by the addition of sentences which predict the fall of Babylon and show special interest in the fate of the Temple vessels. It is reported in such different terms in the LXX that many scholars reject the entire chapter. The present writer counts this too skeptical, but, using the evidence of the LXX, he has attempted to disentangle the original. Thus v. 13 is probably an addition, and vv. 18–22 should read *If they do prophesy and there should be a message from the Lord with them, let them plead with the Lord. For thus speaks the Lord about the other vessels which Nebuchadrezzar king of Babylon did not take when he carried Jeconiah into exile from Jerusalem: They shall be taken to Babylon.* The vessels are those mentioned in 2 Kings 24[13]. Evidently the hope of their restoration was being used as a religious motive by the prophets to support their plans. What Jeremiah announces is that the devastation of the Temple shall be made complete. In v. 15, for *that I might* read *so that I must;* and for *might perish* read *shall perish.*

CHAPTER XXVIII

Jeremiah's Reply to Hananiah. This is the third oracle in this series. (See opening paragraph under ch. 27.) From v. 10 it would appear that Jeremiah was wearing the yoke and thus that Hananiah's act was later than the oracles of ch. 27 (see introductory remarks to ch. 27). The incident is of great interest as illustrating the attitude of Hebrew prophecy. Jeremiah, when confronted by Hananiah, was conscious of having no special revelation to meet this case. He had already exhausted the terms of his commission and uttered his message. Yet he is inclined to discredit his opponent on the general ground that Hananiah's oracle was not according to the tradition of the great prophets of the past. A prophecy of success needed confirmation as a prophecy of doom did not: *The Lord confirm thy words . . . by restoring the vessels* (v. 6). In the same way Deuteronomy is not content (18[21f.]) to appeal to the event happening as a prophet foretold it, but Deut. 13[1-5] requires every prophet to be in agreement with the traditional faith of Israel. There is something more than rank individualism: corporate experience must also be considered. For *thou shalt* (v. 13; A.S.V., *thou hast*) read *I will* (cf. v. 14). From *all these* (v. 14) omit the word *these*, with LXX.

CHAPTER XXIX

1–23. Jeremiah Sends Counsel to the Exiles. As religious motives were being employed to stir up rebellion at Jerusalem (cf. chs. 27f.), so prophets were fomenting political unrest among the exiles. The men were cut off from the Temple, and that, in the judgment of many, meant that they were cut off from the divine grace (cf. ch. 24). Jeremiah uses the mission of certain royal envoys to Nebuchadrezzar to send a message to the men in exile. If the envoys, as suggested in connection with ch. 27, were sent to clear Zedekiah from the charge of plotting rebellion, it was peculiarly suitable for the prophet to send with them a letter the purpose of which was to counteract rebellion among the exiles. He bids the men recognize that their exile is God's will (*I have caused,* v. 4), and must therefore mean more than loss. Jewish homes can be founded in Babylon (vv. 5f.). They must loyally work for the good of their new country (v. 7). Nor must they imagine themselves forgotten of God. They are on his heart and so have a future which offers hope (v. 11). Therefore let them try whether the relation between him and them has come to an end. They will find it cannot come to an end through an exile which he caused. *When you cry to me, I will answer; when you pray, I will listen* (so v. 12). As for their saying that their prophets are teaching otherwise (vv. 15, 16), the names of these prophets shall be used as a curse, so dreadful will be their fate (v. 22), for God did not fail to take heed of their conduct (v. 23). The exiles can worship Jehovah without a temple and a native state: they can be loyal citizens of Babylon and loyal Jews. The best comment on the letter is the glimpse given of the non-returning exiles, Daniel rising to high office in the service of Babylon and praying three times a day to Jehovah, the loyal servant with a double allegiance.

The section has been retouched by the later generation which believed their return to the Temple essential to the faith. Thus vv. 16–20 are intruded; they break the connection, are absent from the LXX, and speak about the nations to which God has scattered Israel. V. 14b is late; it is addressed, not to the Babylonian exiles, but to the whole Dispersion. Vv. 10, 11 offer two reasons why the exiles should refuse to be influenced by their prophets. According to v. 10 the men are to wait patiently for the proof of the divine good will, which is to appear after seventy years; according to v. 11 they need not wait and need not rebel, for the divine good will is toward them now and where they are. V. 10 is an addition by the same hand which introduced the seventy years at 25^{11}.

In v. 1 omit *the residue of*, with LXX. For *your dreams*, etc. (v. 8), read *their dreams*.

24–32. Jeremiah Criticized by Shemaiah the Priest. The text here is very confused, especially at the beginning. Thus v. 25 opens with the customary formula of an oracle, but the oracle really begins at v. 30. The LXX and Syriac present a very different text. With their help it is possible to reconstruct a text which would run to this effect: "Shemaiah sent a letter to Zephaniah the priest as follows: you were appointed a priest in succession to Jehoiada, that there might be officers in the Temple to restrain anyone who plays the part of a prophet. Why, then, have you not restrained Jeremiah?" Shemaiah is remonstrating with the Temple authorities at Jerusalem for not having prevented Jeremiah from upsetting the movement among the exiles by his letter. On this new authority given to a priest to control prophecy see 20^{1f}.

Chapters 30 and 31: The Book of Consolation

A booklet which once existed in a separate form before being incorporated in the larger roll.

CHAPTER XXX

1–4. Title. The heading belongs to this minor collection, not to the whole book of Jeremiah. V. 3 gives the general character of the oracles: they are all concerned with the restoration of the nation. Hence the collection is often called "the book of consolation."

5–11. The Day of Jehovah. In the day of the Lord (v. 7) the heathen shall be destroyed. Israel shall be punished, since Jehovah cannot hold it guiltless (v. 11b); but in the end church and state shall be restored (v. 9; cf. Hos. 3^5). The oracle dates from a time when the entire nation had gone into exile. For the description of the day in v. 7 cf. Isa. 13^{6f}. For *his yoke* (v. 8) read *the*. Vv. 10, 11, absent from the LXX, are practically identical with 46^{27f}.

12–17. Zion to be Renewed. Jehovah will renew Zion, for which no other cares (v. 17b). Vv. 12–14 describe the past: read, therefore, in vv. 12f., *was* for *is*.

18–24. A Promise of Restoration. (See also 31^1.) Omit vv. 23f., which reappear in 23^{19f}., and, with LXX, v. 22, a duplicate of 31^1. Jeremiah promises that Jehovah shall turn the fortune of Northern Israel. He shall restore to himself a people which has lost courage to seek him: in v. 21 read *them* and *they* for *him* and *he*, and cf. 3^{21-25}. Their towns shall be rebuilt on the ruins of the old ones, and their palaces inhabited on the old sites (v. 18). Instead of diminishing and degrading them he shall make them many and honored (v. 19b). Their ruler shall be of native stock (cf. Deut. 17^{15}), and they shall be Jehovah's people. Nothing is said of return from exile or a Davidic king.

CHAPTER XXXI

1. See under 30^{18-24}.

2–14. Two Additional Oracles Promising Restoration. The first oracle (vv. 2–6) is based directly on Hosea. That prophet believed that Jehovah would reduce Northern Israel to the condition from which he brought it into Palestine. In the wilderness, Israel, again dependent only on him (cf. 2^{1-3}), should return to its true allegiance. Jeremiah sees this hope fulfilled in the consummation. Once before Jehovah revealed himself to it in a distant land, i.e., Egypt or the wilderness, and maintained his loving-kindness toward it (so v. 3, with which cf. Hos. 11^1). In that happy day men shall keep the vintage feast (*enjoy*, v. 5) in Samaria, and Israel, like the girls at Shiloh (Judg. 21^{21}), dance with her timbrels. In that day there will be a reunited nation (v. 6). The text of v. 2b is uncertain. The watchmen of v. 6 are those in the vineyards.

The second oracle (vv. 7–14) is from the period of Deutero-Isaiah. Northern Israel, restored from exile (v. 8), shall say, *The Lord has saved his people* (so, with LXX, in v. 7). Coming to Zion, they shall find poured out over their land God's richest gifts, *corn, wine*, etc. (v. 12). In this day of their restored prosperity the people's offerings shall be so abundant that priests and people shall alike be satisfied (v. 14). Note the different emphasis laid here on the promised return to Zion. For *together* in v. 13 read with LXX *shall be merry*.

15–17. Benjamin's Exile. Benjamin's exile shall issue, not in death, but in renewal. *Ramah* is in Benjamin, and there, according to 1 Sam. 10^2, Rachel died at her son's birth (cf. Gen. 48^7). The mother's *work* is her weary toil.

18–20. Ephraim's Prayer. Ephraim prays for the divine help that he may be wholly restored (v. 18). Now, he adds, that I have grown gray (*was turned*, v. 19) and have gained experience (*was instructed*) I repent, and bear the disgrace due to my youthful folly. Then v. 20 should be read, with LXX, as a statement, not as an interrogation. It is the divine response to this confession of moral impotence (cf. 3^{21}–4^4). I cannot forget that he is still this, i.e., *my dear son*, and my affections are stirred. To Hosea and Jeremiah salvation is as sure as the divine love.

21, 22. A Later Summons to Return from Exile. *Go hither and thither* (v. 22) means "hesitate." The final cryptic clause the present writer regards as a grammatical note which has crept from the margin into the text.

23–30. A Series of Promises. V. 24 should be read, with LXX: *May he bless also Judah, its towns, husbandmen and shepherds, when I shall have satisfied the weary soul.* The section in vv. 23–26 is a prayer for Judah, when God turns his fortunes (v. 22). The last phrase does not necessarily imply a return from exile. The turning of fortune may mean the new condition when Judah (or Jerusalem) can really be called a habitation of justice. Then v. 26 says that the very thought of this is sweet. **27, 28.** The promise of a new day; cf. 1^{10}. **29, 30.** Against fatalistic despair. Cf. note on $18^{5f.}$ and Ezek. $18^{2f.}$

31–34. The New Covenant. The new covenant will be established in the consummation—*after those days* (v. 32). For a covenant to endure, the law which every such covenant brings with it must cease to be something imposed from without. It must be loved and accepted as the law of life. *Although I was an husband unto them* (v. 32) read, with LXX, *and so I rejected them.*

35–37. Two Oracles in the Manner of Deutero-Isaiah. *These ordinances* (v. 36), i.e., if this order of nature may be changed.

38–40. An Oracle in the Manner of Second Zechariah (cf. Zech. 14). The Lord's city, Jerusalem, shall be rebuilt (so v. 38a). The author is peculiarly interested in the ceremonial purity of the new city, as containing the Temple. The old Hinnom valley, which circled round into the neighborhood of the Temple and which had been used for the unclean purposes of burial and false worship, shall be consecrated. Every risk of pollution shall thus be removed from the sacred precincts. On the *tower* and *gate* (v. 38) cf. 2 Kings 14^{13} Neh. 3^{1} 12^{39} Zech. 14^{10}. For *it shall not* (v. 40) read *they*, i.e., the people (cf. v. 28).

CHAPTER XXXII

Jeremiah's Purchase of the Field at Anathoth. The long introduction, vv. 1–5, serves to bring the incident here narrated into close connection with the period in Jeremiah's life when he expressed his conviction that in the interest of religion Nebuchadrezzar should capture Jerusalem and bring to an end both the state of Judah and the Temple with its worship (cf. 21^{7} 37^{17}). What, then, was to be the future of Judah? And since Judah had received a special revelation of God's will and was the representative in the world of pure religion, what was to be the future of religion, if the Temple were destroyed? Through a divine instruction to purchase a field in his native village the prophet receives a promise for the future. As the exiles in Babylon (ch. 29) could worship without a temple, the religious life of Judah was to continue in the lives of humble men who continued their daily tasks in the ruined land and recognized that, though robbed of capital and altar, they were not beyond the grace of God. The situation can be compared with that when the site of Hannibal's tent was put up for auction in the Forum. Only, the Romans were confident about the future of their city; Jeremiah about the future of religion.

The account has been expanded by additional matter, which, however, can be easily distinguished. Thus vv. 17–23 are an expansion of Jeremiah's prayer, the terms of which have no connection with the special situation. The *Ah Lord God* with which v. 17 opens should then be carried to and repeated at the beginning of v. 24. Again, vv. 28–41 form an irrelevant expansion. Since Jeremiah has already said that the city was as good as captured, it was unnecessary to repeat that this was sure. Further, v. 37 shows that this passage was written after the dispersion of the nation, while vv. 42–44 speak merely of Jehovah turning Israel's fortune and promising the continuance of life and well-being, not its renewal after exile.

Jeremiah held the first right of purchase as next of kin over a certain field (v. 7b). His cousin came to him in the guarded court of the palace (v. 2; cf. $37^{20f.}$), asking him to exercise this right, so that the property might remain in the family (cf. Lev. 25^{25} Ruth $4^{3f.}$). From Hanamel's coming after he had been warned to expect it, the prophet recognized that the matter involved more than a mere coincidence, even a divine revelation for the nation (v. 8b). Some of the words employed about the transaction are probably technical terms, the exact sense of which is unknown; but read in v. 11 *I further took the purchase deed containing the full stipulations, both the outer copy and the inner.* The purpose of making a double copy, which was the practice with papyrus deeds and clay tablets, was to preserve a record, though the outer copy became worn and illegible. *Even unto this day* (v. 20), i.e., "dost continue to do them to this day." *Behold, the mounts or siege-works are close to the city* (v. 24). *And thou hast* (v. 25); better, *yet.* Instead of *Jeremiah* (v. 26) read *me*, with

LXX. *That I should* (v. 31); better, *so that I must. One heart and one way* (v. 39), i.e., in thought and conduct alike. *With my whole,* etc. (v. 41), i.e., with my entire good will.

CHAPTER XXXIII

Five Oracles. All center round the restoration of Jerusalem and the worship there. The little collection may have been made in Jerusalem itself between its overthrow and its restoration. If so, the emphasis on the *difficult things* (v. 3) may reflect the apparently hopeless situation in which the community was placed.

1–9. A Happy Future for Jerusalem. In v. 2, for *that doeth it* read, with LXX, *who made the world,* and *formed,* not *formeth.* The text in vv. 4, 5, from *to make* down to *but it is* (R.V.) is hopeless. For the thought of v. 3 cf. Isa. 48[6]. *Truth* (v. 6), rather *security. Do unto them* (v. 9), read *it.*

10–13. The Happiness in Store for Jerusalem and Judah. It culminates in v. 11 in the restoration of the Temple worship. Note the introduction of the common liturgical phrase, *Give thanks,* etc. (cf. Psa. 106[1]). Then vv. 12f. describe the folds for shepherds in charge of flocks (v. 12b) among the pastures of Judah, and the security of those who are able to count their flocks in peace (cf. Lev. 27[32]).

14–18. A Promise of the Continuance of the Davidic House and the Sacrificial Worship. With v. 14 cf. 29[10], which is also late. *A Branch* (v. 15), cf. 23[5f]. *The Lord,* etc. (v. 16), cf. note on 23[6]. *Oblations* (v. 18), cf. 17[26].

19–22. Another Prophecy of the Davidic House and the Levitical Priesthood. The stress laid on the Levites points to a date earlier than the limitation of the priesthood to the family of Aaron. With v. 20 cf. 31[35]. *Of the day, of the night,* i.e., concerning day and night.

23–26. A Prophecy of the Nation and the Davidic House. This, again, points to a time when it was possible for outsiders to regard Israel as having ceased to be a nation (v. 24b).

CHAPTER XXXIV

1–7. Zedekiah Warned that the City Must Fall. Jeremiah, declaring it to be the divine will that Nebuchadrezzar should burn down Jerusalem, assures Zedekiah *Thou needest* (*shalt,* v. 4) *not die by the sword: thou mayest* (*shalt,* v. 5) *die in peace.* He is advising the king to surrender. *Burnings* (v. 5); this does not refer to cremation, which was never a Jewish practice, but to the burning of spices in honor of the dead (cf. 2 Chr. 16[14]). For *Ah Lord!* read *alas! your Majesty*—the suitable lament over a king. *Lachish* (v. 7), the modern Tel el Hesy, west of Hebron, and *Azekah,* west of Bethlehem, were two fortresses on the Philistine frontier.

8–22. The Perfidy Toward the Released Slaves. Apparently, when the Babylonians were besieging Jerusalem, the city authorities proclaimed a general freedom to all Hebrew slaves, which they confirmed by a solemn ceremonial rite in the Temple. This action was probably taken in the hope of thereby stiffening the resistance in the capital. When, however, an Egyptian army advanced to support their ally and the Babylonian army was compelled temporarily to raise the siege in order to meet this new enemy, the leaders, thinking themselves secure, withdrew from their contract. Jeremiah entered a vehement protest against this cynical conduct. "You did," he says, "an upright thing in the proclamation of liberty" (v. 15), or, as it appears in v. 9b, "in resolving that no Jew should hold his brother Jew in slavery. But you have profaned the divine name (v. 16) in this act of perjury. Therefore Jehovah proclaims unto you a general release, like that which you have proclaimed to your slaves. You in turn shall serve new masters, sword, pestilence and famine, and shall become an object of horror in the world" (v. 17).

The text has been confused by a legally minded editor who misconstrued the situation and added vv. 13f. Misled by the technical word for liberation in v. 8, he thought the covenant of v. 8 referred to the Sinai covenant with the nation, and the proclamation of release referred to the permanent divine law of Ex. 21[2], etc. But the covenant of vv. 8, 15 was no more than a civil agreement made by the leaders of the state, though sanctified and made binding by a religious ceremony. And the liberation was not the regular liberation granted to every Hebrew slave after a seven years' service: it was a special decree issued to meet the peculiar conditions of the time. Hence in v. 8 omit *unto them* after *liberty* and cf. Lev. 25[10]. *When they cut,* etc. (v. 18), literally, *the calf which they cut,* etc. The clause is a marginal note which has crept into the text at a wrong place. It should follow v. 19, and was meant to describe the ritual which was observed in such cases. For its meaning and purpose consult Gen. 15[10]. *Which are gone up* (v. 21), i.e., retired from the siege.

CHAPTER XXXV

The Rechabites' Refusal to Drink Wine. The Rechabites were a Jewish sect whose members, maintaining the old nomadic customs, rejected the settled agricultural life.

In particular they continued to live in tents and refused to cultivate the vine. Their objection to the vine was based primarily on the fact that it only yields after some years' culture. Nomads may sow a crop in some temporary settlement, and after reaping it may move on, as Isaac is said to have done. But men who plant vines have taken root themselves. They have become *fellahin*, not nomads. (Cf. further 2 Kings 10[15].) Jeremiah brought "the whole house" into one of the side-rooms of the Temple (1 Kings 6[5])—evidently the sect was small in numbers—set a wine-jar and cups before them and bade them drink. They refused, appealing to the rule of their founder, and adding that the only reason for their living in the city instead of in tents was the invasion of the enemy (v. 11). Jeremiah uses the sect's strict obedience to a narrower ideal to point a moral to Jerusalem: take a reproof as to how you should obey (v. 13). *Sons of Hanan* (v. 4); since the person referred to is called a man of God, this must originally have been a proper name. *Wherein ye sojourn* (v. 7), i.e., in which you are mere passing guests, tent-dwellers. *Stand before* (v. 19) is used in the special sense of 15[19].

CHAPTER XXXVI

Jeremiah's Roll Read, Burned, Re-written. Following the Temple address of ch. 26, or the arrest of ch. 20, Jeremiah was forbidden (*shut up*, v. 5) to enter the Temple by the priests charged with maintaining order there (cf. 29[24]). Accordingly, he dictates (*from my mouth*, v. 6) a scroll which Baruch is to read on a fast day, when the citizens of Jerusalem and the country people are gathered in the Temple (v. 6). Perhaps their petition, offered at their fast, may then become acceptable (so v. 7a). The contents of this scroll cannot have been so long as it is represented in the introduction (v. 2), for it was read aloud three times in one day (vv. 10, 15, 21). Its tenor also must have been uniform, since Micaiah was able to give a summary of it after one hearing (v. 13); and it is certain from v. 29 that it contained a prediction of Nebuchadrezzar's capture of Jerusalem.

Micaiah, recognizing that such a message was a state affair, went down to the palace, where he found councilors in session (v. 12), and gave a general report. These men, realizing the matter to be grave, summoned Baruch and bade him *read it aloud again to us* (so with LXX, v. 15). Startled at the message, they consulted together (omit with LXX *unto Baruch*, v. 16) and decided that they must report to the king. First, however, they made sure who was ultimately responsible by asking Baruch, *How didst thou write all these words at his dictation?* (V. 17.) There was no need to mention Jeremiah's name to his secretary. Baruch replied that he had been a mere secretary, he had reported faithfully (not *with ink*, v. 18). Thereupon they went to the king's private room (*court*, cf. 1 Kings 1[15]) and related the whole matter—not *all the words*, for they had left the scroll behind (v. 20). The king was in his winter room, for it was the ninth month (December, 604 B.C.). The month is mentioned to explain the room and to show how there came to be a brazier at hand for Jehoiakim's burning of the scroll. From the fact that the king was peculiarly irritated by the prophet's attitude toward Babylon (v. 29) it may be concluded that Jehoiakim was already planning that rebellion against Babylon (cf. 2 Kings 24[1]) which led to the first captivity under Jehoiachin. Hence too arose the dismay of the councilors and their decision that the matter must go before the king.

On learning the fate of his first scroll, Jeremiah instructs Baruch to write a new one (vv. 27f.). By this act he was not laying up a record for the future, but giving a message to the present. The scroll is rewritten, because it contains a word of the Lord: and no penknife, even that of a king, can mar the divine purpose. The one result of such destruction is to add more. It is unwise to conclude too much from such an act in connection with the difficult questions which center around the book in its present form. It is interesting, however, to note the division of opinion about Jeremiah. Here certain courtiers venture on a protest to Jehoiakim; in ch. 26 elders successfully maintain "liberty of prophesying." In 26[20] appears a prophet whose message agreed with that of Jeremiah. It was these elements in Judah that preserved his oracles. *The king's son* (v. 26), i.e., of the blood royal, not necessarily a son of Jehoiakim. With v. 30 cf. 22[18]. If this prophecy was fulfilled, it must have been after the final capture of Jerusalem. There is, however, no record of such treatment of Jehoiakim's body.

CHAPTER XXXVII

1–10. Reply to a Request. In reply to a request for help and guidance from Zedekiah, Jeremiah declares that the retirement of the Babylonian army from the siege of Jerusalem on the approach of an Egyptian force will afford a mere temporary relief (cf. ch. 34). The conviction that the destruction of Jerusalem at the hands of the Babylonians was part of the divine purpose and therefore served a religious end could not be more strongly expressed than it is in v. 10. Nebuchadrezzar carried Jehoiachin away captive because of his father's rebellion (v. 1) and appointed Zedekiah king (cf. 2 Kings 24[17]). *Surely* (v. 9), better, *wholly*. The reference is to their temporary withdrawal.

11–21. Jeremiah Released but Again Imprisoned. Jeremiah seized the opportunity of the raising of the siege by the Babylonians to go to Anathoth. The meaning of one Hebrew word in v. 12 is so uncertain that it is impossible to be sure on what business he went. But that it was private business and may have been connected with the inheritance of 32[6f.] is clear from the mention of his kindred (*people*). The captain of the guard arrested him on a charge of desertion to the enemy; and after examination he was flung into an underground cell (so read in v. 16). In reply to a secret message from Zedekiah, the prophet repeated his reiterated assurance of the victory of Babylon. He also took occasion to ask why he should receive exceptionally harsh treatment. If the king flung a prophet of disaster into a cell where was he confining the prophets of success, whose promises had come to nothing? (Vv. 18f.) On this he was removed to the guarded court and given rations. *Bakers' street*, or bazaar (v. 21): it is the practice in the East for each trade to occupy a special quarter.

CHAPTER XXXVIII

Jeremiah in a Dungeon; His Release; Another Secret Interview with Zedekiah. This chapter may be a variant of 37[11-21]. Both report that Jeremiah was flung into a cistern (v. 6), and delivered by royal authority into the guarded court. They differ as to the method, not as to the ultimate cause of the arrest. According to this chapter, certain leaders complain that the language the prophet is in the habit of using (so v. 1) is damping down the courage of the defenders. Vv. 2, 3 offer samples of the kind of oracles to which the men object. And it is necessary to acknowledge that there was sufficient cause for the men to take some action. For a state to allow a prophet to say openly what is no travesty of Jeremiah's message, but a fair reproduction of its contents, was to encourage sedition. And the steps taken by the authorities in Jerusalem to silence him were in principle no worse than the action taken toward conscientious objectors in America or Great Britain during the Great War, and it is a just question whether a state, engaged in a life-and-death struggle for its existence, will or can ever do otherwise.

This raises at once a question as to the view which should be taken of Jeremiah's conduct. The only excuse which can be offered for the worthy conscientious objector is that he was animated by nothing petty, but by profound conviction. The prophet must have been driven on by the same conviction. No mere idea of the hopelessness of the struggle meets the case. He believed it was better for the religion of his people and the world that Jerusalem should go. To men who believed that it was of life-and-death interest for the city to stand, that was the worst kind of treason. No question of expediency, but one of principle, was involved.

Ebed-melech, a eunuch on duty in the palace (v. 7), received authority from the king to interfere. He took three men (so, with LXX, v. 10) and provided them with old and worn-out clothes from a palace-wardrobe (*treasury*, v. 11) to put between Jeremiah's armpits and the ropes and so hoist him out of the cistern.

When Zedekiah asked the prophet for an oracle, the latter demanded an assurance of safety and added *whenever I give counsel, you do not listen* (so v. 15b). When, however, the king swore by God *who made us living men* that he would be safe, he received the old response that only by surrender could his life be safe. The closing terms of this oracle in v. 22 are obscure; but probably the sense is, "I saw in a vision the women of the royal harem being led before the Babylonian officers, and they were repeating, 'Thy intimate friends have deceived and overcome thee, have plunged thy feet in the mire and forsaken thee.' " So sure is the ruin that the prophet has heard the royal harem intoning a funeral dirge over Jerusalem, addressed as *thy* and *thee*. V. 23 may be an effort to interpret this dirge with reference to Zedekiah's position. *Of Malchijah of the blood-royal* (so v. 6); probably a marginal note, which should be read after Ebed-melech (v. 7), to explain that the eunuch, whose name means "royal slave," belonged to Malchijah. *The third entry* (v. 14)—perhaps the entry of the bodyguard (cf. 2 Kings 11[6]). These *words* (v. 24), better, *matters*. *The matter was not perceived* (v. 27), i.e., the interview had not been overheard.

CHAPTER XXXIX

1–14. The Capture of Jerusalem; Jeremiah Spared. The LXX omits vv. 4–13; i.e., it relates merely how Jeremiah fared after the capture of Jerusalem. The Hebrew text consists of two parts: vv. 1–10, which describe the fate of the city; vv. 11–14, parallel to 40^{2-6}, which deal with Jeremiah. It seems probable that into vv. 1–10 have been inserted materials, such as vv. 1f. and 4–7, taken from ch. 52, and that the section was originally concerned with the prophet's fate. But it is not easy to decide how much is original. The names and titles of the foreigners who set themselves down to decide the fate of the city have been confused. Read in v. 3, *Nebo-Shazban the Rabsaris, Nergal-Sarezer the Rab-mag.* These, probably civil authorities, appear in v. 13 alongside the captain of the bodyguard or military leader. *The gate between the two walls* (v. 4) lay south of Jerusalem opposite the breach by which the besiegers entered. The fugitives were making for the Jordan Valley and East Palestine (cf. Jos. 3^{16}). *Houses of the people* (v. 8) is a curious expression. The text reads *house,* and possibly the original was *house of the Lord.* Then the sense will be that with the fall of palace and Temple church and state came to an end. The text of v. 9 must be faulty, for there is no difference between *the residue of the people in the city* and *the residue of the people.* Perhaps by the second *people* was meant the country as contrasted with the city population.

15–18. Jeremiah's Promise to Ebed-melech. The section dates before the capture of the city and finds its natural connection after 38^{28a}. It may have been displaced. For *in that day* (v. 16) read *at this time.*

Chapters 40 to 44: The Jewish Community in Judah After the Fall of Jerusalem

These chapters relate the fortunes of the Jewish community in Judah after the fall of the capital; Jeremiah appears as a prominent figure merely in connection with one incident, namely, the flight of a body of Jews to Egypt. In most of the narrative he does not appear at all. Apparently, therefore, the chapters were not written in connection with the life of the prophet, but to serve another purpose. When they were inserted in the larger book it was necessary to provide them with some link; and the heading, *the word which came to Jeremiah from the Lord* was added. But the somewhat incongruous character of the heading only serves to confirm the impression of the independent character of what is introduced.

CHAPTER XL

1–6. Jeremiah Entrusted to the Care of Gedaliah. The account is parallel to 39^{11-14}. In dating the prophet's release a month after the capture of the city, this account has the greater air of verisimilitude. The conquerors would have more serious matters to engage their attention immediately after their victory, and might well postpone decision of the fate of an individual until the prisoners and spoil were being examined at Ramah before the long journey to Babylon. Nor is it easy to suppose that Nebuchadrezzar was so intimately acquainted with the inner life of Judah as to give the orders of 39^{11f}. On the other hand, the language of the general here (vv. 2f.) cannot be the *ipsissima verba* of a Babylonian. The exact terms of the liberty allowed to Jeremiah cannot be determined, for the first clause of v. 5 is hopelessly corrupt. It is tempting to conjecture that the original contained a refusal to allow the prophet to settle in Jerusalem. One notes that Gedaliah is appointed over the towns of Judah and settled at Mizpah, as though the Jews were at first given no authority over their ruined capital. In v. 5b read *the captain of the guard supplied him with rations.*

7–16. The Country Stripped of Leading Citizens. The country was stripped of its leading citizens, but not of the crofters and farmers. In leaving these behind the victors looked to their own interest (cf. 39^{10}), since they alone could pay the tribute. And they appointed Gedaliah, a leading Jew, to act as mediary between the native population and the foreign officials who administered the new province. Gedaliah first attempted to get in contact with and win the confidence of the leaders of the guerrilla bands (*forces,* v. 7) who were wandering in the country. He assured them that they need have no fear of the new officials; he himself would be responsible to such as were sent from time to time. They might confidently gather in their harvest, store it and settle in the wrecked villages which they might choose to occupy. But at the instigation of the king of Ammon, Ishmael planned the murder of Gedaliah (vv. 13–16).

CHAPTER XLI

The Assassination of Gedaliah. Omit in v. 1, with LXX, *and one of the chief officers of the king.* The man had nothing to do with the Babylonians. *Even the men of war* (v. 3), i.e., Ishmael murdered all the fighting men, whether Jews or Babylonians. *The second day* (v. 4), i.e., the next day. It is significant (v. 5) to find these men from North Israel, after the destruction of their Bethel altar by Josiah, on their way to the Temple with their offerings. Also, though they must have known of the destruction of the Temple, they continue to come. From the first the site continued to be used for worship by the population that remained behind. According to the LXX, it was the pilgrims (v. 6) who were weeping. *Into the midst of the pit* (v. 7), read *into a cistern. By the side of Gedaliah* (v. 9), read, with LXX, *was a large one.* The cistern was dug by Asa to serve his garrison when he fortified Mizpah (1 Kings 15[22]). Omit in v. 10, with LXX, *and all the people that remained in Mizpah.* For *great waters* (v. 12) read *great pool*, the scene of the incident in 2 Sam. 2[13]. Gibeon is one mile distant from Mizpah. For *the men of war* (v. 16) read *men, women, and children.* Ishmael had butchered the fighting men (v. 3). On their way they halted (*dwelt*) at the khan or caravanserai of Chimham (v. 17). Some of these khans were large and could accommodate a considerable body of travelers with their animals. Yet it is clear that those who migrated to Egypt with Johanan were a comparatively small body. They were men who felt that they might be held responsible by the Babylonians for the conduct of Ishmael. It is singular that nothing is said about Jeremiah, though he must have been among the men rescued from Ishmael.

CHAPTER XLII

Jeremiah Opposes Flight to Egypt. The fugitives consult Jeremiah as to their future course, asking him to pray for oracular guidance. The prophet agrees, and the people invoke on themselves the divine curse should they disobey; read in v. 5, *the Lord be a witness against us.* After ten days he delivers a message to the effect that they need have no fear of the Babylonians, for Jehovah will protect them and cause them to settle in their own land—so read, with Syriac, for *return* in v. 12; cf. v. 13. If, however, they elect to go down to Egypt, the divine curse will rest upon them to destroy them.

The chapter is far from clear. Thus the sense of v. 20a seems to be that the people have wronged their own souls in asking for an oracle at all; and v. 21 represents them as having made up their minds before consulting the prophet. When one recognizes that the chapter does not come from the same source as chs. 40f., and notes that the natural time to consult Jeremiah was before they began their journey, this rouses the suspicion that the passage has received additions. It may originally have contained merely the oracle advising the men to remain in Judah. When the incident was placed at the khan, after the people had started on the road to Egypt, the narrative naturally assumed an appearance of insincerity on the part of the people. For *Jezaniah son of Hoshaiah* (v. 1) read, with LXX, *Azariah son of Maaseiah* (cf. 43[2]).

CHAPTER XLIII

1–7. A Band Decide to Go to Egypt; Jeremiah Accompanies Them. The company, consisting of the little band round Gedaliah (v. 6) and some refugees who had returned in the hope of settling in Judah under his authority (v. 5; cf. 40[11f.]), were evidently in a panic. Their accusation against Baruch shows the inclination of such men to find a scapegoat. They followed the headstrong party, opposed to Jeremiah, who were naturally the guerrilla leaders, since these men were already suspected by the Babylonians. They fled to Daphne (*Tahpanhes*, v. 8; cf. 2[16]), a fortified town on the northeast border of Egypt, where the Syrian road crossed the frontier. In v. 2 for *Hoshaiah* read with LXX, *Maaseiah.*

8–13. Jeremiah Predicts the Conquest of Egypt. Jeremiah sets great stones before an official building in Daphne: the meaning of the words translated "mortar" and "brickwork" is wholly uncertain. On these Nebuchadrezzar will erect his victor's throne. In v. 10 read with LXX, *he will set* and *you have hid.* He will overrun Egypt, and especially will burn its temples. In v. 12 read with LXX, *he will kindle.* He will deal with Egypt's gods with the same ease with which a shepherd deals with his coat, ridding it of its lice (v. 12b). V. 13, which predicts the destruction of the obelisks of Heliopolis, a town north of the present Cairo, is an addition. It is inappropriate after the announcement of the departure of Nebuchadrezzar, and Heliopolis is too far from Daphne to have meant anything to newcomers in Egypt. Nebuchadrezzar conquered Egypt in 568 B.C.

CHAPTER XLIV

Jeremiah's Difficulties with the Jews in Egypt. This chapter is very puzzling. Not only is the text confused and full of intolerable repetitions, but it represents Jeremiah addressing a convention of Jews gathered from all Egypt. Migdol, or Magdolos, is another frontier fortress east of Daphne; Noph is Memphis; Pathros is Southern Egypt (v. 1). The Papyri from Elephantine, near the southern boundary of Egypt, have revealed a Jewish colony settled there at this time. But they have also shown it to have been possessed of a temple and therefore little likely to come north for religious guidance. Such a convention round a fugitive prophet is scarcely probable at this period. What remains clear is that Jeremiah rebuked the practice of a heathen rite which was peculiarly prevalent among the Jewish women. The present writer suggests that the original nucleus was a rebuke to the Daphne colony for its toleration of this cult. Jeremiah declared that the result of disloyalty to the first principle of their religion, namely, the acknowledgment of Jehovah alone, must be that the people will melt away into the surrounding heathenism and be submerged in its coming doom. At the beginning this original oracle was increased by a threat of doom against the people, because, in direct disobedience to the divine word, they have come to Egypt in the first place. In the end it was expanded into a statement that, since the Egyptian Jews were everywhere practicing such mixed cults, they shall be punished through some great calamity. It is not possible, however, fully to justify the analysis here.

1–14. The People's Sin in Coming to Egypt. The sin of the people consists in their coming to Egypt (note especially v. 12). Their false worship is merely incidental to and the outcome of their having resolved to settle there (v. 8). Nothing is said about the special sin of the worship of Astarte. The doom also shifts between all the Egyptian Jews and the Daphne colony. The text in v. 9 is very confused; probably read with LXX, *Have you forgotten the sin of your fathers, the kings of Judah and your leaders which*, etc., *how they were never contrite*, etc. All of v. 10 describes the past. Jehovah has now resolved (not *will set*, v. 11) against them. None shall survive, except casual refugees (*such as shall escape*, v. 14).

15–26. The Women Protest Against Jeremiah. Here the situation is entirely changed. A number of women, with a few of their husbands who have approved the conduct of their wives, protest with a loud outcry (so read for *a great assembly*, v. 15) against Jeremiah having interfered with their worship of Astarte. They intend to maintain the definite decision they have made to continue the rite which is no novelty, but dates from their time in Jerusalem. The women whose husbands are not present add (insert, with LXX, at the beginning of v. 19, *the women further added*) that their worship has been carried on with the full approval of their husbands. The point of the remark is that, according to the law of Num. 30[6f.], a woman's vow was only valid if it had been approved by her husband. The prophet's attack must therefore have been directed, not only against one definite form of worship, but against the women practicing it. Jeremiah declares that this mixed worship has ruined Judah, and is the same thing as complete apostasy (v. 26). Jehovah must be everything or nothing. In v. 19 for *to worship her* read *stamped with her image*. In v. 25 for *ye and your wives* read with LXX, *you women*.

27–30. The Ruin of Egypt Again Predicted. According to Herodotus, ii, 169, *Hophra* was deposed by Amasis, who rebelled against Nebuchadrezzar in 570 B.C. and was defeated in 568.

CHAPTER XLV

Jeremiah's Oracle to Baruch. This is dated in 604 B.C. (cf. 36[1]). Accordingly, it is long prior to the Egyptian incidents; it belongs to the period when the prophet was predicting the coming of the end (25[1]); evidently *these words* in v. 1 must mean the oracles in the scroll Jehioakim burned (ch. 36). The text is in bad condition. The first clause of v. 4 should be omitted: Baruch is directly addressed. The last clause, as it stands, is untranslatable and is absent from LXX. V. 4 then declares: *It is I who built up, who also break down*, etc. In v. 5 it is possible to insert the last clause of v. 4 with the addition of a word, and to read *I will bring evil on all flesh and ruin on all the world.* The sense will then be that in the coming consummation Baruch may be secure as to his life and must be content with this.

CHAPTERS 46 TO 51: PROPHECIES CONCERNING FOREIGN NATIONS

These chapters form a collection of oracles dealing with the fate or the temper of the nations which influenced Judah about this period. The collection once existed in a separate form, since it was inserted by the LXX in the middle of ch. 25, a more suitable position for it than its place in the Hebrew text. The oracles may have been collected in Palestine, but some of them were clearly uttered in Babylon and others in Egypt. They are also of varied dates, since parts of chs. 50f. belong to the age of Cyrus, while 46[2-6] was probably uttered under the tremendous impression produced by the struggle at Carchemish between Egypt and Babylon for the empire of the world. Another significant feature of the oracles is that several of them appear elsewhere and are ascribed to other prophets than Jeremiah. They abound in names of cities and peoples. For their identification the student must be referred to the more detailed commentaries.

CHAPTER XLVI

1. A Heading to the Entire Collection. The oracles are arranged under the nations dealt with: on Egypt, 46^{2}; on Philistia, 47^{1}; on Moab, 48^{1}, etc.

2–28. Oracles on Egypt. The oracles are alike in predicting Egypt's fall. **2–6.** *Mount, ye horsemen, and fall into rank* (v. 4). *Why are these dismayed, turned in retreat?* (V. 5.) *The swiftest may not flee* (v. 6). So powerful and self-confident was the Egyptian army, so utter its rout. **7–12.** Egypt advanced like its own Nile. Let its horses rear: the old Hebrews had a peculiar dislike for horse and chariot. Let its allies be many and well equipped. These may serve for common needs, but this is a day of Jehovah; *his sword shall devour* (so read v. 10, with LXX; cf. Isa. $34^{5f.}$). The mighty hath clashed with the mighty to their common ruin (v. 12b). In v. 8 omit *the city and*, with LXX.

In vv. 13–26 we have a collection of fragments with a new heading, probably derived from the Jewish colony in Egypt (cf. $43^{8f.}$). **14–17.** The sword is devouring on all sides. Why is Egypt's *strong one* swept away? The reference may be to the leading god or the Pharaoh. Jehovah has smitten him (v. 15). He has tottered and fallen. One says to another, *Arise* (v. 16). The text of v. 17 is bad. Perhaps read *they give Pharaoh a new name, the boaster who is never up to time.* **18, 19.** The destroyer comes, like one of Israel's highest mountains. Lady Egypt, who sittest so quietly, get thee gone. *Noph* (Memphis) was the capital. **20.** A gadfly stings the fat heifer. **21–24.** Egypt's mercenaries before the conqueror are like calves fattened for the butcher. The text of vv. 22f. can be restored only by conjecture. **25, 26.** This passage contains also a promise of Egypt's restoration in curiously different terms (cf. Ezek. $29^{13f.}$). *Amon of No* was the chief god of Thebes. **27, 28.** Added from $30^{10f.}$, where they more properly belong.

CHAPTER XLVII

Oracle on the Philistines. It refers to an otherwise unknown Egyptian attack on Gaza: the LXX reads merely, "On the Philistines." The flood from the North is no historical invasion. Like Jeremiah's Northern invader (1^{13}) it overwhelms the world (*land*, v. 2) so that mankind wail. *The day* (v. 4) is the day of the Lord. In this universal catastrophe the ruin of the Philistines is merely one feature. In v. 5b read *How long must you, the remnant of the Anakim* (cf. Josh. 11^{22}), *make cuttings in your flesh;* i.e., in sign of mourning, like Gaza's baldness? *Caphtor* (v. 4) is Crete, from which, according to Amos 9^{7}, the Philistines came. For *thou* and *thee* (v. 7) read *it*.

CHAPTER XLVIII

A Collection of Oracles on Moab. This may once have existed separately, since it has a formal heading and conclusion. The text is often very bad, local allusions to which we do not possess the key abound, and several of the oracles appear in other prophetic books.

1–6. This oracle of doom bears a general resemblance to Isa. 15. The student, however, should be on his guard against concluding that this, because taken from the Isaiah passage, must be later. We have no definite criterion to decide which of the two is earlier. *Misgab* (v. 1), perhaps Ar Moab. For *in Heshbon they* (v. 2) read simply *men*, i.e., some foreign enemies. In v. 4b read with LXX, *its cry can be heard as far as Zoar;* in v. 5a, *men climb the pass to Luhith in tears;* in v. 6 for *like the heath* read *to Aroer*, i.e., flee thither, as a place of refuge. **7–10.** Moab's insolence is the cause of her fall. *Chemosh* (v. 7) was the local god. For *and no city* (v. 8) read *nor shall Ar Moab, the capital, escape.* The *plain*=plateau. The last clause is a marginal note, which quotes an otherwise unknown prophecy: *As Jehovah said, Give wings to Moab, for she would fain fly away.*

11–15. Moab is like a generous wine, the flavor of which has endured unaltered (v. 11b). But now the destroyer of Moab and its towns has advanced (so read v. 15a), and he will pour it into new jars, emptying and destroying the old ones (v. 12b). The country was famous for its vines. **16–25.** Noteworthy, because of the sympathy it shows with Moab. *Name* (v. 17)="renown." For *rod* read *scepter.* For *in thirst* (v. 18), probably read *on the ground. Stand by the way* (v. 19), i.e., on the highway, to learn what comes. *Arnon* (v. 20)—the news has reached across the frontier. *Plain country* (v. 21)=plateau (cf. v. 8).

26–34. Moab is drunken—with the cup of the divine anger (see Rev. 14^{10}). He clapped his hands in derision, but shall himself be derided (so read with LXX). Did he catch Israel among thieves that he mocked the nation? V. 28b is untranslatable. With vv. 29–31 cf. Isa. $16^{6f.}$ In v. 31 for *shall they* read *I mourn.* With vv. 32, 33 cf. Isa. $16^{9f.}$ *Passed* (v. 32), i.e., they once stretched over the sea, reaching as far as Jazer (so with LXX). In v. 33 omit *the shouting shall be no shouting.* It is probably a marginal correction which has crept into the text. V. 34 appears in more intelligible form in Isa. 15^{4-6}. **35, 36.** V. 36a is found in Isa. 16^{11} and v. 36b is practically the same as Isa. 15^{7}; *soundeth like pipes*, rather, *wails like a flute.* **37–39.** Vv. 37f. appear in a slightly different form in Isa. 15[2f]. The terms of v. 37 describe the land in mourning. In v. 39 read *How it is broken!—take up your lament—how has Moab!* etc. **40, 41.** V. 40 appears in 49[22] among the oracles on Edom. In v. 40, *he* = "the coming destroyer." For *Kerioth* (v. 41) read *the towns*. **43, 44.** Applied in Isa. 24[17], not to Moab, but to the inhabitants of the world. **45, 46.** These verses repeat Balaam's oracles against Moab (Num. 21[28f.]). These seem to have been inserted at the close of the little collection of Moab oracles in order to emphasize that the old doom, though long delayed, is none the less sure. In v. 45 for *they that fled* read *refugees;* for *for* read *but;* for *corner* read *brows;* and for *tumultuous* read *arrogant*.

CHAPTER XLIX

1–6. An Oracle Against "the Children of Ammon." This oracle against Ammon, Milkom its god (v. 1), Rabbath its capital on the Jabbok and its dependent towns (*daughters*, v. 2), evidently refers to some border warfare in which that people took possession of Israelite territory in Gad. But, whether the writer refers to incidents of his own time or to older wars, it is impossible to decide. Read v. 4, *Why dost thou boast of thy rich valley, and glory in thy wealth, saying, Who can rival me?* The text of v. 3 is corrupt: for *Ai is* read *you are*, and for *run to and fro*, etc., read *make cuttings in your flesh*. But the verse is clearly an intrusion, for Heshbon belonged to Moab, not to Ammon; and the last clause is taken from Amos 1[15].

7–22. An Oracle on Edom. The section consists largely of material which appears elsewhere, and which is frequently applied to nations other than Edom. The places mentioned are in that country. Edom's proverbial sagacity has perished (vv. 7–10). V. 7 should not be read as an interrogation. The people must seek a secure abode (*dwell deep*) for Jehovah has brought (not *will*) calamity (v. 8). The gleaners will leave nothing, the thieves destroy all they can (v. 9)—the verse reappears in Obad., v. 5. *There is none to help* (so for *he is not*, v. 10). The connection and purpose of v. 11 are alike enigmatic. Those who were not destined to drink the cup of the divine anger (v. 12), i.e., Israel, *are drinking* (not *shall drink*) *it, how much more must Edom!* With vv. 14–16 cf. Obad., vv. 1–4. "I have heard how a herald is being sent to summon the nations against Edom, for Jehovah makes (not *made*) Edom small." In v. 16 omit *as for thy terribleness*. V. 17 is applied in 19[8] to Jerusalem. Vv. 18–22 are applied in 50[40f.] to Babylon. The destroyer will attack Edom's fortress, *for suddenly I will expel them thence* (so read in v. 19). Who can equal me (*appoint me a time*)? Their shepherds shall drag them away and their fold be startled at their fate (so v. 20b). Their wail shall be like that of the drowning Egyptians at the Red Sea (v. 21b). V. 22 is applied in 48[40] to Moab.

23–27. Damascus. Conquered by Nebuchadrezzar in 605 B.C. The oracle *may* refer to this event. *Hamath* and *Arpad*, cities in Northern Syria, are described as disquieted (over its fall) like the troubled and restless sea (so read v. 23b). The glorious city itself is doomed. V. 26 is applied in 50[30] to Babylon. V. 27 is made up from Amos 1[4, 14].

28–33. Three Oracles Against Some Eastern Tribes (vv. 28–30; 31, 32; 33). Their isolation in the Arabian desert shall afford them no security. Let them collect tents and tent-coverings (*curtains*), baggage and camels. Let them cry, *Terror on every side* (v. 29). Jehovah has said to the enemy, Arise, attack (cf. Ezek. 38[11]). In v. 32 for *cattle* read *flocks*.

34–39. Elam. On the hills east and north-east of Babylon. *The chief of their might* (v. 35), i.e., the bow is Elam's mainstay.

CHAPTERS 50 AND 51: PROPHECIES CONCERNING BABYLON

Two features of this long collection of oracles, which may have once been separate from the rest, deserve special attention. They all presuppose the destruction of Jerusalem, and many of them are addressed to the captives who are already settled in Babylon. But these exiles are addressed as though they constituted the Jewish community, not as the little company of the period of Jeremiah. The oracles also take an entirely different attitude toward Babylon from that which was taken by Jeremiah. The prophet regarded that nation as a divine instrument the mission of which was to destroy Jerusalem. In these oracles, however, Babylon is not merely the enemy of Israel but is the opponent of Jehovah. So far from the exiles being encouraged to work for the prosperity of their own new home, they exult in its downfall and are summoned to leave it. Indeed, Babylon becomes here almost a symbol of that worldly pride in power which is always hostile to the kingdom of God.

CHAPTER L

Babylon to be Destroyed; Israel to be Delivered. See introductory notes above. **1–5.** In the consummation the Northern foe shall destroy Babylon, and shall especially discredit its gods, Bel and Merodach. *Escape then and go, both man and beast* (so read v.

3b); Israel is addressed. The reunited nation shall at once make its way to Jerusalem with a common purpose: let us join ourselves to Jehovah, the eternal covenant must not be forgotten (so v. 5b). The consummation involves a reunited nation and a restored Temple, since these are essential to the covenant relation to God. **6–10.** *Jehovah's people have long wandered* (for *turned them away*), forgetting their fold (v. 6). Their foes have said, *We shall not suffer for ill-treating them, since their sin has merited it* (v. 7). Now, Babylon's foes are at her gates; *they are like a keen, sure arrow which does not miss* (so read v. 9b). In the coming collapse Israel, being forewarned, shall be like the bellwethers that head a flock (v. 8), the first to escape. **11–13.** The verses are addressed to Babylon, which is *your mother* (v. 12). Behold the end of a nation—*a wilderness,* etc., instead of a wanton heifer at grass. **14–16.** A shout of triumph over Babylon's fall, which means (v. 16b) deliverance to all her captives. In v. 15 read *because this is the vengeance of the Lord, take vengeance upon her.* **17–20.** Instead of *scattered* (v. 17) read *stray.* For *his soul* (v. 19) read *he.* There is no special reference to spiritual satisfaction. For *shall* be sought (v. 20) read *may.*

21–28. *Merathaim* and *Pekod:* the writer substitutes for names of two Babylonian provinces Hebrew words, meaning "double defiance" and "visitation." The no-men is to be an omen. *Thee* (v. 21); in the LXX it is the sword which is addressed. In v. 26 for *from the utmost border* read *from every side. Cast her up,* i.e., the contents of the storehouses. *Bullocks* (v. 27), i.e., warriors. Zion always survives Babylon (v. 28). **29–32.** Three fragments, united by the tag of *proud.* V. 30 is applied in 49[26] to Damascus. **33, 34.** Israel represents an enslaved world. Read v. 34b, *that he may give the world peace, he must disquiet Babylon.* **35–40.** For *upon* read *against* throughout; for *boasters* (v. 36) read *soothsayers;* for *mingled people* (v. 37) read *vast population;* for *drought* (v. 38) read *sword.* With v. 40 cf. 49[18]. **41–43.** This oracle may have been deliberately transferred from 6[22-24] in order to say that the doom pronounced on Jerusalem shall overwhelm Babylon. **44–46.** Applied in 49[19-21] to Edom.

CHAPTER LI

1–58. Further Description of God's Judgment on Babylon. See introductory notes preceding ch. 50. **1–6.** The *destroyer,* not *wind* (v. 1), brings Israel's deliverance. "Lebkamai," an acrostic for Babylon, means, in Hebrew, "the mind of my antagonists" (cf. 50[21]). For *strangers* (v. 2) read *winnowers.* Read v. 2b, *Woe unto her on every side in the evil day.* In v. 3 (cf. A.S.V. mg.) omit the first two negatives. Read vv. 5b and 6a, *Because their,* i.e., Babylon's, *land is full of guilt,* etc., *flee out of the midst of Babylon.* **7–10.** *The Lord has made good Israel's cause* (so v. 10a) against Babylon, which was once his instrument in the world. For *are* (v. 7) read *were* and for *not healed* (v. 9) read *incurable.* **11–26.** These verses show the hopes stirred in Jewry by Cyrus' advance: LXX reads, v. 11, *king of the Medes.* For *hold firm,* etc. (v. 11), probably read *fill the quivers.* The central clause of v. 14 presents a hopeless text. With vv. 15–19 cf. 10[12-16]. Cyrus is an instrument in the hand of Jehovah (vv. 20–24). Vv. 25, 26 are not very suitable to the alluvial plain of Babylon, where men built, not with stone, but with bricks. *Burnt mountain* (v. 25), rather, *slag-heap.* **27–33.** *Cyrus, king of the Medes* (so LXX, cf. *his* dominion, v. 28) has enlisted his host. Babylon, like a threshing-floor, is stamped hard for the harvest: soon the harvester will arrive (v. 33). Ararat, Minni, Ashkenaz are parts of Armenia. The writer sees the issue. In vv. 27, 29 for *land* read *world.* For *as the rough cankerworm* (v. 27) read *in swarms like locusts. Do stand* (v. 29), i.e., are being realized. For *to meet* (v. 31) read *after. Passages* (v. 32), i.e., fords. *Reeds* is suggested for the impossible Hebrew "pools."

34–37. Zion's complaint has been heard. Read v. 35, *O Zion, cry, Havoc and ruin against Babylon. O Jerusalem, cry,* etc. And in v. 34 read *us* for *me.* **38–44a.** Babylon *used to* (not *shall*) *roar* like lions. *But I will poison their banquets and make them drunken to stupefaction, and they shall sleep,* etc. (so v. 39a). An end is set to Babylon's greed. Doom has overtaken *Sheshach* (vv. 41–44a), an acrostic for Babylon (cf. note on 50[21]) and its god *Bel.* **44b–53.** Let Israel escape, since Babylon's walls are fallen (not *shall,* v. 44b). And let them not fear the flying rumors through the world (*land*): every year will have its rumor of *havoc* in the world, and of tyrant set against tyrant. V. 50 is a summons to Israel; v. 51, its reply, and vv. 52, 53, its encouragement. In v. 49 perhaps read *Babylon is about to fall, ye slain of Israel; yea, Babylon is about to fall, ye slain of the world.* **54–58.** *The Lord spoileth Babylon and destroyeth its loud tumult, he roars against it like mighty waters and utters his voice with threatening* (so read v. 55). In v. 58 for *shall be* read *are.* The destruction is conceived as having taken place. So nations toil for nothing and peoples weary themselves to feed the flames. With this *vanitas vanitatum* the collection of oracles on Babylon is brought to a striking close.

59–64. Jeremiah Commands Seraiah to Sink the Roll in the Euphrates. Jeremiah is said to have written on a scroll the preceding oracles (*all these words*) against Babylon, and to have delivered them to Seraiah, quarter-master of Zedekiah, when he went to that country charged with a commission *from* (so LXX, for *with*, in v. 59) the king. Seraiah is to sink the scroll in the Euphrates as a sign of the doom impending over Babylon. The story is dated at a period in Zedekiah's life when he was being urged to rebel (cf. ch. 28). Hence an embassy to Babylon to explain and excuse his conduct is probable. But at this period Jeremiah was publicly declaring in Jerusalem that Nebuchadrezzar was destined by Jehovah to conquer the capital, and was bidding the exiles live peaceably in their new country (cf. ch. 29). It is difficult to believe that he instructed a high court official to carry out a symbolic action the only effect of which must have been to annul his other messages. Further, the oracles Seraiah was bidden to sink in the Euphrates cannot be ascribed to the prophet. The section must have been written after chs. 50f. were already formed into a collection. The last clauses of v. 64, *and they shall be weary. Thus far are the words of Jeremiah* are a marginal note which has crept into the text. An editor, who wished to separate the oracles proper from the historical chapter 52, added, The oracles of Jeremiah extend only as far as "they weary themselves," i.e., as far as the last Hebrew word in v. 58.

CHAPTER LII

The Rebellion and Overthrow of Zedekiah. Vv. 1–27, which describe the final captivity under Zedekiah, are parallel to 2 Kings 24[18]–25[21], while vv. 4–16 have already appeared as Jer. 39[1-10]. Again vv. 31–34, which deal with the ultimate fate of Jehoiachin, are parallel to 2 Kings 25[27-30]. Between these sections this chapter places three verses which give the number of the exiles deported by Nebuchadrezzar. In the same place Second Kings sets a very brief synopsis, summarizing chs. 40–43 in Jeremiah and relating events in Judah after the destruction of Jerusalem.

The sense of v. 3 is: Matters went so far toward the Lord casting them away that Zedekiah rebelled. It is hardly possible to date to a day the outbreak of famine in a city (v. 6). Probably the ninth day of the fourth month refers to the breach in the wall of v. 7. The second half of v. 10 and the last clause of v. 11 are absent from Second Kings. *Tenth* (v. 12)—Second Kings reads seventh. Read v. 13b *the houses of the leading men burned he with fire.* In v. 15 omit *of the poorest sort of the people and.* For *residue of the multitude* read *the surviving artisans.* In v. 20 omit with 2 Kings 25[16] the reference to the oxen; these had been removed by Ahaz (2 Kings 16[17]). *Without weight*, i.e., unweighed. In vv. 21, 22 *the one=each, chapiter=capital;* for *it* read *each. On the sides* (v. 23); something has fallen out of the text. *Out of the city* (v. 25), i.e., from the lay population, contrasted with the priests of v. 24. *Seven*—Second Kings has "five." *Mustered*, i.e., enrolled the common soldiers. There are difficulties connected with the numbers in vv. 28–30, for which the student must consult more detailed commentaries. *Lifted up the head* (v. 31), i.e., showed favor to. *Before him* (v. 33), i.e., at the royal table.

LAMENTATIONS

By Professor W. G. JORDAN

Introduction

Place in Canon and Authorship. In the Hebrew Bible the book of Lamentations is one of the books in the third division, the miscellaneous collection called "The Writings"; but in the LXX, the Syriac, and the Latin versions it follows the book of Jeremiah; from the latter the order Jeremiah, Lamentations has passed into the English O.T. There are other evidences that the tendency of keeping Jeremiah and Lamentations together, and the tradition that Jeremiah was the author of Lamentations, go back to early times. The LXX sets at the head of the first chapter these words: "And it came to pass after Israel was taken captive and Jerusalem made desolate, Jeremiah sat weeping and lamented with this lamentation and said"; in the Vulgate the closing words are given in this form: "and, in bitterness of heart sighing and crying, said." The passage in 2 Chr. 35[25], whatever may be its significance, shows that very early this form of literature was connected with the name of the great prophet. No wonder that as late as 1882 a commentator, after citing a number of objections to the Jeremianic authorship, could say, "On the whole, therefore, we conclude that Jeremiah was beyond question the writer of this book." Since these words were written scholarly opinion has moved steadily in the opposite direction until at present it is almost unanimously admitted that Jeremiah did not write these elegies. Moreover, it is generally doubted that the five poems constituting the book were written by one and the same author or at approximately the same date. (For a detailed discussion see Eiselen, *The Psalms and Other Sacred Writings*, pp. 202–208).

Date. If there is diversity of authorship, as is practically certain, the dates of the individual poems are not easily determined. In view of the vivid descriptions in chs. 2 and 4 these two poems might be assigned to about 573 B.C. They are probably the work of one, or, possibly, two men who passed through the distressing experiences of the siege and capture of Jerusalem. Ch. 3, on account of its highly artificial structure and its pronounced didactic tone, is generally considered the latest of the five poems, originating about 325 B.C., or even later. Opinions differ widely regarding the date of ch. 1; on the whole, however, a date shortly before the return under Cyrus seems best to satisfy the internal evidence. To the same general period may be assigned ch. 5.

Nothing is known regarding the time when the individual poems were brought together to form the present book. It has been suggested that at first, about the time of Nehemiah, a collection was formed, consisting of chs. 1, 2, and 4; and that subsequently, about 300 B.C., chs. 3 and 5 were added by the author of the poem in ch. 3.

Contents and Significance. The book consists of five independent poems, all centering, though in different ways, around one common theme: the calamities that befell the people of Judah, and especially of Jerusalem during the siege and subsequent capture of the holy city. Poems 1, 2, and 4 are in the nature of dirges over the death of the city and nation; poem 3 describes the sufferings endured by the poet and his compatriots in the course of the calamity—the sufferings are traced to the anger of Jehovah, aroused by the sins of the people; but the knowledge of Jehovah's lovingkindness inspires a hope that the sufferings will not continue forever. Poem 5 is a prayer for speedy deliverance.

The first four poems form alphabetic acrostics; (cf. p. 154); the fifth poem has the requisite number of stanzas, but no attempt at alphabetic arrangement is discernible. The first four poems are in the so-called *kinah* meter (see Eiselen, *The Psalms and Other Sacred Writings*, pp. 22, 23). The consistent use of this particular meter and the alphabetic arrangement make it evident that the poems were constructed with conscious art: they are not the unstudied effusions of natural emotion, they are carefully elaborated poems, in which every trait which might stir a chord of sorrow or regret is brought together, for the purpose of completing the picture of woe.

Lamentations is of interest and value because it furnishes a vivid and in some cases at least a contemporaneous picture of the thoughts and emotions aroused by the Fall of Jerusalem. No doubt, the faith of some was shattered; but there were many others who remained loyal to their God and were convinced that, in spite of all appearances to the contrary, Jehovah's compassion and lovingkindness would never cease. These faithful saints were also persuaded that heartfelt repentance must precede the return of the divine favor. This conviction inspired the confessions of guilt, exhortations to repentance, and prayers for mercy, which constitute such an important element in the book.

Literature: Streane, *Jeremiah and Lamentations* (Cambridge Bible); Peake, *Jeremiah and Lamentations* (New Century Bible); Adeney, *Lamentations* (Expositor's Bible); Loehr, *Klagelieder* (Nowack's Hand Kommentar); Eiselen, *The Psalms and Other Sacred Writings;* Hastings' Dictionary of the Bible, article, "Lamentations," by Selbie; Driver, *Introduction to the Literature of the O.T.*

CHAPTER I

The chapter begins with the exclamation "How!" often used in lamentations (cf. 2^1 4^1 and Isa. 1^{21}) and is in its nature a dirge. Like other alphabetical poems it is not easily arranged in consecutive sections. The subject is the desolate condition of Jerusalem and the dispersion of the Jews. It is usually divided into two parts, vv. 1–11a, in which the poet speaks; vv. 11b–22, in which the city is supposed to speak, but v. 17 must also be placed in the mouth of the poet. The three-line verse of unequal parts prevails throughout.

How doth the city sit solitary—that was full of people;
She is become as a widow—that was great among the nations;
The princess among the provinces—she has become a bond-slave.

1–11a. Solitariness and Desertion of Jerusalem. The opening verse marks the contrast between Zion's past prosperity and her present misery (Isa. $47^{8, 9}$ 54^5). No human help is available in her hour of need; all her friends have failed her; the night which should be given to rest is a time of weeping with no hope in the morning (v. 2; cf. Job 7^3). There is uncertainty about the word rendered in v. 3, *because* (from); whether the statement should be taken to mean that the people had gone into exile to endure toil in Babylon or gone from Judæa to escape the forced labor (4^{19} 5^5). In either case they were driven to an unclean land where the exercise of their religion was not possible; *within the straits*="in her distress" (pains, Psa. 116^3). Zion itself and the ways leading to it were once covered with joyful pilgrims, but now they are desolate; instead of sacrifices and songs there is the sighing of priests and maidens. The opposite of the splendid promise in Deut. 28^{13} is due to her sins; this charge and confession is repeated in vv. 8, 18, 20, 22. Like *harts* (v. 6)—"rams" seems more suitable for *princes*, but the poet may have meant to lay stress on weakness and timidity. *All her pleasant things that were from the days of old* makes a fourth line and may be a marginal note.

Vv. 8–11a repeat the fact of Jerusalem's sins and the gruesome details of her punishment. Those that see her shame despise her as forsaken by God, and his sanctuary, which was to be kept inviolate, is desecrated by the heathen, i.e., the Chaldeans (Deut. 23^3 Ezek. 44^9). This feeling that the Temple was profaned by the presence of Gentiles increased in intensity in later times. *Pleasant things* (v. 10), the material treasures; the same word in 2^4 seems to be applied to the strong young men; any valuables that are left must go to buy that which is more precious, namely, bread.

11b–22. Severity and Justice of the Affliction. These verses, except v. 17, are a direct complaint of the personified community. The well-known plaintive appeal of v. 12 is in the first line uncertain, but the English probably represents the sense. V. 14 also is doubtful as to its exact form; it may mean that the Lord, in consideration of their sins, has woven a yoke around their neck and left them without strength in the presence of their foes. With the striking phrase, *abroad the sword bereaveth —at home there is death* (v. 20), cf. Deut. 32^{25}. The conclusion brings a prayer that the enemies, who have been the instruments of Jehovah's vengeance and who have exulted in the misery they have caused, may meet a similar fate.

CHAPTER II

A pathetic lamentation over the sorrows of "the daughter of Zion," a phrase repeated six times in the poem (cf. "daughter of Judah," 1^{15} 2^5). Whether by actual experience or imagination, the poet makes clear the terrible conditions into which Judah and Jerusalem were plunged by the Babylonian conquest. Even if the author was somewhat hampered by his alphabetical scheme he has managed to maintain a certain continuity of thought and strength of feeling. The structure of the verses is best seen in the following form, though in some cases it is not perfectly preserved:

How hath the Lord covered with a cloud
The daughter of Zion!
He hath cast down from heaven to the earth
The beauty of Israel,
And hath not remembered his footstool
In the days of his anger.

1–10. Suffering and Affliction a Divine Judgment. It is uncertain from the context whether *beauty* refers to the Temple (Isa. 64[11]) or to the political splendor (Isa. 4[2]); *footstool* is used for the earth (Isa. 66[1]), the ark (1 Chr. 28[2]), the Temple (Ezek. 43[7]; cf. Psa. 99[5] 132[7]); the latter is most suitable here. V. 2 describes the devastation of the country places (*habitations*), the destruction of the cities (*strongholds*), and the profanation of kings and princes. The Lord's anointed and those of royal blood received shameful treatment instead of the reverence due to their rank. *The horn* (v. 3), a frequent symbol of power and pride, is cut off. *His right hand*—instead of being used in Israel's defense is drawn back (Psa. 74[11]), and the fire of God which should protect consumes (Zech. 2[5]).

The following verses amplify and strengthen this terrible description of Jehovah's angry activity. V. 4 seems to be imperfectly preserved. For the figure of Jehovah as a hostile archer see Job 16[13]. V. 5 ends on an assonance for which "moaning" and "bemoaning" have been suggested. The destruction of the sacred place and the rejection of king and priest are clearly stated in v. 6, but the first line is obscure:

He has broken through his hedge like a thief,
  Destroyed his sanctuary,

is a plausible suggestion. V. 7 clearly refers to the desecration of the Temple, the noise and confusion being more like a heathen assembly (Psa. 74[3f.]) than the sober, solemn worship tendered to Jehovah. The close of v. 7b, *the walls of her palaces*, has puzzled the commentators, as it is difficult to explain it as referring to the Temple. Along with material damage there goes spiritual deprivation (v. 9). The hope of false prophets (Jer. 17[18]) has perished and now the leaders have gone *where the law is not*. *Law* (*torah*), i.e., priestly instruction (Mal. 2[7]). *Her prophets find no vision from the Lord*—cf. Mic. 3[5, 6]. V. 10 presents a pitiful picture of the community mourning its God-forsaken condition.

11–17. Depth of Distress and Despair. The poet inquires where he can find anything to compare with this, and how he can give comfort in such a case. *Liver poured on the earth* is a peculiar expression; it is compared with *pour out thine heart*, etc. (v. 19). A similar form means "glory" in the sense of soul or life (Psa. 42[4]). Here the blame is laid upon the prophets who saw *visions of vanity and foolishness* (v. 14c; cf. mg.) which lead to disaster rather than to deliverance. This great sorrow is aggravated by the scorn of those that pass by and compare in sarcastic tones the present wretchedness with the former splendor. It is easy for those that are self-content to point out the judgments of God on other people.

18–22. Prayer for Deliverance. Zion is urged to plead her cause with persistent earnestness. The first part of v. 18 is not in good order. Comparison with the Versions suggests something like "Cry aloud to the Lord; Virgin daughter of Zion. Let thy tears run," etc. A bold rhetorical appeal closes the poem (vv. 20–22). Jehovah is called to look upon the terrible things that have come upon the community as the result of his anger. What hope is there for a nation if its babes are to be consumed by the mothers who carried and caressed them or by the ruthless conquerors?

CHAPTER III

In the third poem there is a more artificial arrangement producing a more complicated structure. The verses are numbered from 1 to 66; i.e., three times the number of the letters in the Hebrew alphabet, but there are only the same number of lines as in chs. 1, 2, and 4, the difference being caused by the fact that here each line is numbered as a verse, and begins with the corresponding letter of the Hebrew alphabet, i.e., the first stanza (vv. 1, 2, 3) has three clauses each beginning with *âleph*, the first letter of the Hebrew alphabet, and so on. There has been keen discussion on the question of the collective or individual interpretation of the poem. The fact that the feminine form is so often used to personify the community leads many to regard the "man" here as an individual sufferer. His personal experiences may be intended to represent the sentiment of the community. The attempt to analyze the poem into two psalms (vv. 1–24, vv. 52–66) which the author used as distinguished from his own contribution (vv. 25–51) is interesting but not convincing.

1–20. Lament of the People. The speaker, *the man* (cf. vv. 27, 35, 39)—representing the community—claims to have had experience of misery on account of *the rod of his wrath*. A certain impressiveness is produced by the avoidance of the direct mention of the divine name. With v. 4 begin the particulars of his ill-treatment. Many of the figures used may be found in Job and the Psalms; *gall and travail* (v. 5) is a peculiar combination; *gall and wormwood* seems to be a preferable reading. V. 6 is found also in Psa. 143[3], where it reads, "He hath made me to dwell in dark places, as those that have been long dead." Here, to suit the alphabetical scheme, the order of the first two words (in the Hebrew) had to be changed, *In darkness he made me to dwell*, etc. In

vv. 7–15 the poet pictures his sad condition in figures made familiar to us by the book of Job: God hedges him round about, fetters his movements, blocks his path, obstructs his progress, turns him aside into dangerous ways (cf. Job 19[7, 8, 12]). Reduced to this miserable condition he has forgotten what prosperity is like. In v. 17 read *he has removed*, etc. As the prayer form is not maintained in v. 19 it is suggested that the reading should be *the memory of my afflictions and wandering is wormwood and gall.*

21–39. Jehovah's Loving-kindness the Basis of Hope. This section is gentler in tone: it preaches patience and submission because God's mercies do not fail and *the Lord will not cast off for ever* (v. 31). *This* (v. 21) should, according to the alphabetic structure, refer to what has gone before, but there is a strong temptation to apply it to the beautiful consolatory words that follow. Vv. 25–27 have been compared to the noble passage in Rom. 5[3-5]; each of the three verses begins with *good*, laying emphasis on the moral discipline of suffering (cf. Heb. 12[5-11]). The thought of waiting patiently on Jehovah who is the *portion* (v. 24) and inheritance of the saints is characteristic of many psalms. Several scholars accept Budde's suggestion for v. 31: "Not for ever does the Lord cast off the children of men" (Mic. 7[18] Isa. 55[13]). There are linguistic difficulties in vv. 34–39, but it is difficult to improve on the English translation. The poet asks questions of those who are doubtful as to the righteousness of God's actions (vv. 37, 39). Possibly v. 36 should take the form "Doth not the Lord see?"

40–54. Prayer of Confession and Penitence. Instead of vain searching into the ways of God, it is better *to search and try our* own *ways.* Note the striking phrase *lift up our heart with our hands.* Vv. 43–54 contain a recapitulation, partly in the singular and partly in the plural, of the sufferings caused by Jehovah's relentless anger. He has clothed himself in such a cloud of anger that even earnest prayers cannot reach him. V. 46 is probably quoted from 2[16]. The transposition suggested by Loehr, vv. 51, 49, 50, does not interfere with the alphabetical scheme and gives a better order. The constant weeping of the poet wears away his strength (v. 51); his sorrow is on account of the women of Jerusalem (cf. 2[12]) or the desolated countryside (cf. Psa. 48[11]).

55–66. Prayer for Vengeance. The poet closes the previous paragraph by declaring *They have cut off my life in the dungeon;* now he begins a prayer *out of the lowest dungeon.* He acknowledges that Jehovah has saved his life and calls upon him to take vengeance on the enemies. *To hide the ear* (v. 56) is a peculiar expression found nowhere else in the O.T. The line is too long; perhaps *my cry* is a gloss explanatory of *my breathing. Under the heavens of the Lord* (v. 66) is another peculiar phrase. Metrical considerations favor "under thy heavens." The Versions give *under the heavens, O Lord!* (Cf. Deut. 9[14].)

CHAPTER IV

This alphabetical poem differs from the preceding in the fact that each verse consists of two lines (in ch. 3, one line, in chs. 1 and 2, three lines). It is probable that it is by the same author and of the same date as ch. 2, on account of the vivid, concrete pictures of the great catastrophe found in both, their similarity of literary quality, arrangement of subjects and their affinities with Ezekiel. The contrast between the former glory and the present misery of Zion's sons is ascribed to the sins of the people. The horrors of famine are again described, priests and prophets are denounced for leading the people astray. The bitter reference to Edom's exultation brings the sad lament to a close. There are a number of textual difficulties, for full discussion of which the critical commentaries should be studied.

1–11. Distress of the People. The exact rendering of certain lines in vv. 1, 2 is uncertain, but it is clear that the contrast between the former prosperity of the citizens of Judah and their present miserable condition is set forth under the figure of gold and precious stones that by some strange process have become worthless. Leadership has been lost and motherhood has been crushed under the stress of fierce famine (vv. 3–5). Hungry mothers are as cruel to their children as the ostrich (Job 39[13-17]), less kind than the jackals, in whom the maternal instinct is strong. V. 6 contains a very strong statement, whether we follow the rendering of the text or the margin. In the first case the poet infers the greater sin of Judah from the greater suffering. Sodom fell at one stroke; Judah's suffering is a continual and increasing agony (Ezek. 16[47f.]). The concluding phrase—*and no hands were laid upon her*—is peculiar and uncertain. Suggested explanations are that there was no time for "wringing of hands," it was all so sudden; or "no human hands fell upon her," it was purely a divine act of justice. In vv. 7–9 the thought of vv. 1 and 2 is repeated in different terms expressing the deterioration and degradation of the Nazirites (probably the *nobles* here), and the section closes with the bitter reflection *they that be slain with the sword are better than they that be slain with hunger.* With

v. 10 cf. v. 3 (where probably *daughters* should be read) and 2[20].

12–16. Faithlessness of the Religious Leaders. V. 12 does not connect closely with what goes before or follows after. It is regarded as saying that no one believed that Jehovah's anger would carry to the extent of destroying Jerusalem, and that even the poet shared the general belief in the inviolability of Zion, a belief supposed to have been based on the teaching of Isaiah (cf. Jer. 26[6, 18]). In the succeeding verses the poet declares that this terrible suffering has come on account of the *sins of her prophets and the iniquities of her priests* (v. 13; cf. Jer. 5[31] 6[13]). Though the text is uncertain in places (probably *prophets* should be read for *elders* in v. 16) these verses produce a vivid impression of the terrible punishment that has come upon the leaders; they are treated as outcasts (Lev. 13[45]), the curse of Cain is upon them as they are driven to wander and doomed to find no rest.

17–20. Utter Hopelessness of the Situation. These verses picture the feeling of depression and hopelessness as the end drew near, and probably contain references to the *vain* reliance upon Egypt for *help*, and the miserable end of Judah's last king Zedekiah.

21, 22. Doom of the Edomites. The poem closes with a declaration that the *punishment* of the *daughter of Zion is accomplished* (Isa. 40[1]) and that Edom's turn has come. There are many evidences of the bitter feeling between Edomites and Jews (Psa. 137[7] Isa. 34 Ezek. 35). Here a certain satisfaction seems to be gained by the author from the thought that if Israel has suffered severely, the justice of Jehovah must punish the arrogance of other nations.

CHAPTER V

This poem resembles the previous chapters in having twenty-two verses, according to the number of letters in the Hebrew alphabet, but it is not, like them, an alphabetic acrostic. Moreover, it is a prayer rather than a dirge. The poet does not use the *Kinah* meter, but the regular parallel lines with equal number of accents. It contains a plaintive description of the sad condition of the Jewish community at the time it was written. It cannot be arranged in clearly marked divisions according to a definite course of thought.

1. Theme of the Poem. V. 1 strikes the keynote, with its appeal to Israel's God:

> Remember, O Lord, what is come upon us;
> Behold, and see our reproach.

Then particular features of the fierce oppression and terrible distress are described in detail. While all classes are involved special prominence is given to the sufferings of women and children.

2–18. Miseries of the Exiles. Whether taken literally or figuratively vv. 2–6 describe the sad condition of the community, as in a strange territory they have to buy wood and water. There is textual difficulty in v. 5. Proposals are: *With the yoke on our necks we are pursued*, or *The yoke on our neck they have made heavy*. In v. 6, *given the hand*, i.e., *submitted* (see Jer. 50[15]), here perhaps "in supplication." V. 7 contains a distinct declaration that the present generation is suffering for the sins of its predecessors (cf., however, v. 16). This raises a question that was much discussed in the exilic period (see Jer. 31[29] Ezek. 18); the terrible punishment is then sketched, dishonorable servitude, severe privation, the shame of the women, the torture of the children; there is no reverence for age and no joy for youth. *Sword of the wilderness* (v. 9) is not found elsewhere; words of similar form would give "wilderness," "heat," or "Arabians." Though all this is a wretched heritage from the past it deepens the present sense of unworthiness and helplessness and so prepares for the final appeal with which the chapter closes.

19–22. Prayer for Speedy Deliverance. Over against the changeful fortunes of men the poet sets the strength and stability of God's throne (cf. Psa. 45[6] 102[12]). V. 22 as read in the R.V. brings the prayer to an end in a hopeless tone, and it was so regarded in the Jewish synagogue where the reader was directed to repeat v. 21 as a more cheerful conclusion. The margin "unless thou hast," etc., softens the hopelessness somewhat, but not sufficiently. Some scholars maintain that it is possible to regard v. 22 as a question; but whatever the grammar may decide, we, like the ancients, refuse to believe that anger and scorn are God's last words to his people.

EZEKIEL

BY PROFESSOR W. L. WARDLE

INTRODUCTION

The Prophet. Our knowledge of Ezekiel ("God is strong," or "God makes strong") is limited to the information derived from his writings. He was a priest, the son of Buzi (1[3]), and, though there is no direct evidence that he had officiated in the Temple, his familiarity with its structure and ritual strongly suggests this. He was evidently trained in the circle of those who were influenced by the Deuteronomic Code (see p. 146). As a member of the upper classes he was deported to Babylonia at the capture of Jerusalem in 597 B.C. At this time he was probably in the prime of life, rather than, as Josephus says, a youth. That he was married appears from 24[16-18]—the tenderest touch in his book. He was settled at Tel-abib, near the Chebar canal, occupied a house of his own, and was regarded as a leader by his fellow exiles; the elders of the Jews frequented his house to receive oracles (cf. 8[1] 14[1] 20[1]). Though his utterances were appreciated as works of art (cf. 33[32]), the message he proclaimed was not popular, and the failure of events to justify some of his predictions tended to discredit him. However, the fall of Jerusalem in 586 B.C. established his reputation (cf. 33[30]). The last date given in the book is 571 B.C. (29[17]). Nothing is known of the end of his life.

Call and Method of Work. Ezekiel received his call to the prophetic work in 593 B.C. by way of a vision. Though the theory that he was a cataleptic is now not generally accepted he was certainly psychic, subject to trance and ecstasy (cf. 8[1f.] 11[1f.] 24[1f.] 33[1f.] 37[1f.]) and gifted with second sight (cf. 8[16] 11[13] 24[1]). Many of his prophecies were given in the form of symbolic actions, and it seems to be certain that these were actually performed. Such actions in Semitic thought are more than mere symbols; they are "sympathetic magic," tending to produce the results of which they are symbolic.

Ezekiel's own conception of his work may be gathered from 33[1-9]. More than any other O.T. prophet Ezekiel is a writer. The careful system of dates in the book is clear evidence that he prepared a collection of his prophecies, and even scholars who suppose that generally the collections of prophecies under the names of other prophets were put together by later hands make an exception in the case of Ezekiel. The vision of the roll confirms this conclusion (cf. 2[8]–3[3], note). Ezekiel's style, abounding in symbol and allegory, and often burdened with repetition, seems at times grotesque. But many of the oracles, as, e.g., the dirges of ch. 19, the picture of Tyre as a ship (ch. 27), the prophecies concerning the shepherds (ch. 34), and the dry bones (ch. 37), have both beauty and vigor.

Teaching. The central idea of Ezekiel's theology is his conception of God as spiritual, powerful, but beyond everything as "holy." The crime of Israel throughout its history he finds in the profanation of this holiness, and to punish it God is compelled to destroy the state. But to the Oriental a god and his people are indissolubly connected, and the destruction of a people proves the impotence of its god. Such an aspersion upon God is for Ezekiel intolerable, so he protests that the punishment of Israel is the action of God himself, unable to endure the profanation of his holiness, and he proclaims that God will yet restore his people, after cleansing them. Thus he rebukes the taunt of Israel's enemies that her God has failed in his purposes. The nucleus of the restored people is to come from the exiles, among whom, and not among the survivors in Palestine, Ezekiel finds the true heirs of the promises. The restoration, however, is not for the sake of the nation, but for the sake of Jehovah's name. In interpreting this phrase we must be careful to remember that for the Oriental the "name" means much more than it does for us, it being equivalent almost to "personality" (cf. Psa. 23[3] 75[1], etc.).

The great contribution of Ezekiel to the development of religious thought is individualism. Earlier prophets were concerned primarily with the nation as a unit. The destruction of the state raised a new problem. A restored state could be formed only of cleansed individuals. In ch. 18 Ezekiel insists that the individual has a standing before God. He is not condemned because he is the descendant of guilty ancestors; and he can be redeemed from his own guilty past. God is just in his dealings. The individual is judged by his own present conduct. The prophet does not consider the further question whether suffering is always punishment for sin. With that a greater poet, the author of Job, wrestled.

As a priest Ezekiel conceives of righteousness as obedience to laws and statutes expressing the will of Jehovah. For him there is no sharp line between ritual and ethics. While the Christian may find him unduly concerned with correctness of ritual, it would be unfair to say that he had not a lively sense of the importance of morality.

The Father of Judaism. Ezekiel stands in a position of great significance in the history of religion, because in him we find the transition point from the Hebrew state to the Jewish Church. That the latter ever came into being is due very largely to the work of Ezekiel in a time of religious as well as political crisis. Ezekiel's emphasis of ritual, forms and institutions has led to the charge that he "transformed the ideals of the prophets into laws and dogmas, and destroyed spiritually free and moral religion." This sweeping charge is not warranted. (1) Ezekiel had every reason for believing that his age required the expression of religious ideals in external, concrete forms. The great mass of people still needed the Temple, the sacrificial system, and other institutions as means of communion with God, and it is exceedingly doubtful that the religion of Jehovah could have survived without them. That later generations exaggerated the importance of externals until finally the spirit was altogether lost sight of was not the fault of Ezekiel. (2) The ritual does by no means exhaust the religious interests of the prophet. Again and again he insists that a pure and righteous life is an essential part of true religion (chs. 3, 18, 33). Besides, it must be borne in mind that the provisions in chs. 40–48, outlining the ecclesiastical organization of the restored community, are intended for a regenerated people. They are intended to aid a regenerated community to give proper expression to its devotion to Jehovah.

Arrangement of Book. The text of the book has suffered considerably in transmission, and the Greek translation, which differs widely from the Hebrew, has often preserved the better reading. The material is arranged according to an orderly scheme. The first twenty-four chapters contain, after the opening vision, utterances of almost unrelieved doom. The following twenty-four chapters give the reverse of the shield, telling of the doom of the nations who had been, or might yet be, oppressors of the people, of the new day of salvation, and of the coming Utopia.

Authenticity. Opinion as to the integrity and authenticity of the book has varied. Whether it should be admitted into the Jewish canon was a question debated among the early rabbis. Chronologically Ezekiel occupies a position between the Deuteronomic Code and the Priestly Code (see art., *The Pentateuch*, pp. 142–3). Some nineteenth century writers denied that the book was in any sense the work of Ezekiel; and some writers, like Seinecke, assigned it to the Maccabæan age. The prevailing opinion, however, among scholars has been that the work is from the hand of Ezekiel, and, indeed, freer from addition and interpolation than any other of the prophetic writings. Hölscher, it is true, has lately suggested that all but a nucleus of poetry is the work of later hands, and Burrows, on the basis of literary affinities with other biblical writings, is inclined to date the whole as late as the third century B.C. But Hölscher's view is doubtless determined in some measure by his late dating of the Deuteronomic Code, and literary parallels are very difficult to assess. On the whole we may regard the first thirty-nine chapters, allowing for minor supplements, as coming from Ezekiel himself, but in the remaining chapters much of the matter may have been added by later hands.

Literature. Davidson and Streane, *Ezekiel* (Cambridge Bible); Lofthouse, *The Prophet of Reconstruction*, and *Ezekiel* (Century Bible); Skinner, *Ezekiel* (Expositor's Bible); Toy, *Ezekiel* (Polychrome Bible); Peake, *The Problem of Suffering in the O.T.*

CHAPTERS 1 TO 3: THE PROPHET'S CALL

CHAPTER I

1–3. Introduction. In these verses are combined two titles, possibly from two distinct recensions of the book. V. 1 joins more naturally to vv. 4f., since in vv. 2, 3 Ezekiel is spoken of in the third person. No satisfactory explanation of the *thirtieth year* has yet been found. The Hebrew cannot mean "when Ezekiel was thirty years old." Duhm suggested that the *thirtieth year* may have been calculated with a view to explaining the discrepancy between the forty years assigned to the Exile in 4[6] and the seventy years of Jer. 25[11]; if so, the figure will be due to a later hand. The *Chebar* is the *nâr Kabari*, a canal flowing southeast from the Euphrates at Babylon—not the Habor of 2 Kings 17[6]. The *fifth year* is 593 B.C., counting the year of exile, 597 B.C., the first. *Priest* (v. 3) may refer either to the prophet or to Buzi; Ezekiel probably belonged to the Zadokite priestly family of Jerusalem (40[46] 43[19] 44[15]).

4–14. Vision of Four Living Creatures. Ezekiel in a state of trance (the meaning of v. 3b) receives his call in vision form. The description is full of the splendors of flashing light, so brilliant that the details are minutely revealed, but so dazzling that they are not clearly seen. Textual corruptions, which do not seriously affect the general interpretation, have aggravated the obscurity in some points of detail. The reminiscences of Isaiah's vision (Isa. 6), and of the sapphire pavement (Ex. 24[10]), show that the Divine Spirit of inspiration employs the ideas already existing in the prophet's mind. Herrmann and Hölscher have recently argued that the detailed description of the chariot is a later elaboration inserted between vv. 4 and 28b; but even if their arguments are cogent, the elaboration may have been the work of Ezekiel himself.

From the north, for the Hebrews a region of mystery (Jer. 1[14]), borne by a fierce wind comes a dark cloud haloed with light. Lightning flashes in zigzags continuously through it; at its heart is a flame with the sparkle (not *color*) of electrum (not *amber*)—a mixture of gold and silver. As it approaches, Ezekiel sees the *likeness*—note how this vague word is used throughout the vision to describe the ineffable—of four living creatures. These—the models for the four living creatures of Rev. 4[6]—are in general form human, but each has four faces and four wings. Apparently, they have straight jointless legs ending in a circular foot: probably each has but one, and the suggestion of sex is thus avoided. Each seems to stand at the middle of one side of a square, its wings when outspread just touching those of the creature on either side of it. The four sides of the chariot face the several points of the compass. The creatures never turn; i.e., all motion is from north to south and from west to east, or *vice versa.* To reach a point lying southeast the chariot would travel due east until it was due north of the point, and then due south to the point. The human face is in front, and the eagle face "on the inside" (so read for *and their faces,* v. 11, and join to v. 10). Their movements are controlled by *the spirit* of the enthroned Deity. In the midst (so with LXX for *as for the likeness,* v. 13) of them is a glowing, flashing fire. Delete v. 14 with LXX.

15–28. Vision of the Divine Glory. Beside each living creature is a double wheel (delete *faces thereof,* v. 15, with some of the ancient versions, and *and their work* and *their appearance and,* v. 16, with LXX) sparkling like topaz (not *beryl*), constructed of two wheels set at right angles about a common diameter, one in the north-south plane, the other in the west-east plane. The *four sides* may mean the four half-circles thus formed. Like the creatures, the wheels do not *turn;* their motion too is always due north, south, east or west. This would be impossible as a matter of engineering, but we are dealing here with a supernatural machine. (V. 18 is incurably corrupt at the beginning.) The felloes of the wheels are *full of eyes,* so that they go on no blind path. This trait is less strange when we read that the Divine Spirit animates creatures and wheels alike, insuring harmony of motion. In *Enoch* the *Ophannim* (=wheels) appear as a class of angels, with the cherubim and seraphim.

Poised above the heads of the living creatures (read plurals, v. 22, with some MSS. and versions) is a platform (not *firmament*) sparkling like *crystal* (the word usually means "frost" or "ice," which give a blue sparkle like sapphire). In v. 23 each creature seems to have six wings, as in Isaiah's vision, but some MSS. and versions do not contain the reference to wings covering the body, which may be a gloss from Isa. 6. In any case the platform rests above, not upon, the outstretched wings. The beating of the wings as the chariot moves resounds like the noise of a heavy thunder-shower. (The comparisons after *waters,* v. 24, are later additions, and v. 25 should be deleted.) Upon the sapphire platform—*as the appearance of a sapphire stone,* v. 26, properly follows *heads,* and must qualify *firmament*—is a throne, seated on which is a human form. Note how the prophet modifies the anthropomorphism by the circumlocution *likeness of.* This human form is half concealed and half revealed by the glorious light that enfolds it, the sparkle of electrum about the upper part, and a less brilliant light below, like the flaming color of the rainbow (cf. Rev. 4[3]).

From the vision we learn some of the leading conceptions that dominate the prophet's ministry—the supreme transcendence of God, his glory, and the conception of God as Spirit, not limited to the Temple at Jerusalem, but able to visit his people wherever they may be, and able to control all things by his power. If we should be tempted to charge the prophet with anthropomorphism, let us remember the delicate reticence with which he portrays—despite the detailed description—the form of the Deity. If God is to be pictured in concrete form, the loftiest symbol man can use is the human form: after all, was not the supreme revelation of God made in the form of the Man Christ Jesus?

CHAPTER II

1–7. Ezekiel's Commission. The divine voice—note the reticence which avoids mentioning the name of Jehovah—bids Ezekiel, who has fallen prostrate before the glory of the vision, arise, addressing him as *son of man*, i.e., "mortal one." He is unable to rise himself, but *spirit* (delete *the*, v. 2), divine energy, infuses his paralyzed body and raises him to his feet. He receives his commission to Israel, *rebellious* now as ever—this adjective rings like a keynote through the passage. He is to proclaim the divine message fearlessly, and without regard to the attitude of his hearers, though he will be like one surrounded by scorpions. **3.** For *children* read *house* with LXX, and delete *to nations* with LXX and Old Latin. **6.** *Though briers and thorns be with thee* is very dubious, possibly read *though they contend with thee and despise thee.*

8–10. The Roll. (Continued in 3[1-3].) The prophet is given the substance of his message in the form of a written roll, which he receives from the divine hand (Rev. 5[1]), though, unlike Jeremiah (Jer. 1[9]), Ezekiel avoids using the name of Jehovah. The roll is full of sad utterances, so numerous that they cover the back as well as the front.

CHAPTER III

1–3. Eating of the Roll. (Continued from 2[10].) The prophet is commanded to eat the roll, and, bitter as its contents are, in his mouth it tastes sweet (Rev. 10[9]). The significance of this may be that the prophet finds joy in doing the will of God, however painful his task (Jer. 15[16]). Obviously, this experience is not a literal happening; presumably it took the form of a trance. That it is genuine is attested by the description of the roll as containing unrelieved woes; at a later stage Ezekiel has more comforting words to speak, which would have been mentioned in a later production. The roll hints at the fact that the prophet is a writer as well as a speaker.

4–9. The Prophet's Endowment with Hardness. So powerful are the divine words that even had Ezekiel been sent to foreigners whose language he could not speak, they must have taken heed. So obstinate, however, are his fellow countrymen that they will refuse to listen. Like Isaiah, Ezekiel is warned from the beginning that his work will fail. But Jehovah will make him harder even than his hardened listeners, so that he will not be shattered in the conflict (cf. Jer. 1[18]).

10–15. The Prophet's Return. Ezekiel is bidden to announce himself to the exiles as prophet, by using the prophetic formula, *Thus saith the Lord.* Spirit lifts him up, and as he leaves the scene of the vision he hears behind him the sound of the departing chariot, a noise like an earthquake (the word rendered *rushing*, v. 12, is that used for "earthquake," 1 Kings 19[11]). Perturbed in spirit, and still in a state of trance, he makes his way to the colony of exiles at Tel-abib, where for seven days he remains appalled and dumb. **12.** *The spirit*—delete *the.* Read for *saying, Blessed be*, changing one consonant, *in the rising of.* **14.** The last clause means "and I was in a trance" (cf. 1[3]). **15.** *Tel-abib* means "Cornhill"; the name should possibly be read *Tel-abub*, meaning "Hill of the storm flood."

16–21. The Prophet as Watchman. A space in the Hebrew text after *days*, v. 16, indicates that vv. 16b–21 have been inserted here later, either by Ezekiel or by an editor. The natural continuation of v. 16a is found in v. 22, where *there* refers to *Tel-abib*, v. 15. The commission of v. 11 is properly followed by the account of its being carried out, not by a further commission. The insertion contains important elements of the prophet's teaching which will be considered in connection with chs. 18, 33. The difficulty raised for the Christian by *I lay a stumbling-block*, v. 20, is mitigated, though not entirely removed, by the fact that the stumbling-block is laid subsequently to the sin of the righteous man. **19.** *Soul* means "self," not the spiritual part distinctively.

22–27. A Further Commission. This forms the continuation of v. 16a. In a renewed access of trance Ezekiel goes at the divine command to the *plain* (v. 23)—so called, perhaps, in contrast to Tel-abib, which name implies an eminence (cf. on v. 15). Once more he sees the theophany, and as before is prostrated, and raised again by an influx of divine energy. He is commanded to keep at home, and warned that his freedom of movement will be restricted by the exiles, and that God will restrain his utterance, suffering him to speak only when specially directed to do so. The phrases for binding and dumbness are metaphors only (cf. Job 29[10]). **25.** Perhaps we should read *I will lay bands . . .* and *will bind*, so that **vv.** 25f. both refer to divine action.

CHAPTER IV

In 4[1]–5[4] four symbolical actions are recorded. That these actions were actually carried out is clear from the use of *sign* (4[3]) and *in their sight* (4[12]). The actions recorded in ch. 4 center around two subjects; there are some verses referring to the siege of Jerusalem and other verses referring to the Exile, the two having been inexplicably interwoven. The former group contains vv. 1–3, 7, 10, 11, 16, 17; the latter, vv. 4–6, 9, 12–15 and probably 8, which seems to be connected with both groups; but for *siege*, not the same Hebrew word as in v. 2, read *restraint*. The entire chapter may be treated under two heads.

1–3, 7, 10, 11, 16, 17. **Symbols of the Siege.** Ezekiel is to engrave upon a brick the plan of a city, and surround it with all the works and apparatus of a besieging army. Glaring steadfastly at the city, with arm uplifted (Isa. 52[10]) to strike, he is to enact the part of Jehovah, whose agents the besiegers are. The flat iron sheet (v. 3., mg.) to be set up between Ezekiel and the city may symbolize the absolute estrangement between Jehovah and Jerusalem, which name a glossator has added in v. 1. The prophet is to ration his food and water to meager quantities, taken at fixed times daily. This symbolizes the scarcity of provisions in Jerusalem during the siege. (Cf. 12[17-20] Isa. 3[1] Jer. 19[9].) 16. *Staff*—cf. 5[16] Lev. 26[26] Isa. 3[1] Psa. 105[16]. 17. For *be astonished* read *languish*.

4–6, 8, 9, 12–15. **Symbols of the Exile.** Ezekiel is to lie on his left side one hundred and ninety (so LXX) days, as one bearing a burden. These days represent the number of years the Exile of the Northern Kingdom is to endure (? reckoning from the time of Pekah; cf. 2 Kings 15[29]). Similarly, forty days on his right side symbolize forty years for Judah's exile. The position was presumably maintained only for part of each day. The prophet is to eat cakes made of many materials, cooked in an offensive manner, to symbolize the impurity of the food eaten in exile (cf. Hos. 9[3]). Ezekiel's protest (v. 14) shows the essentially priestly character of his outlook, and is further proof that the actions were really performed.

CHAPTER V

1–4. **Symbols of the People's Doom.** Ezekiel is to shave hair and beard: this, in itself a sign of mourning, is made more ominous by the use of a sword for a razor (cf. Isa. 7[20]). The hair is to be weighed on an accurate balance (so *balances to weigh*, v. 1) into three equal parts. When the days of lying upon his side (rather than *of the siege*, v. 2) are over, Ezekiel is to light a fire in the city, burn one part of the hair, thrust with his sword-razor at the second part, round the city, and scatter the remaining third to the wind. A few of these scattered hairs are to be retrieved, and bound for safety in a fold of his garment. Even of these some are to be cast into the fire. 2. The last clause is an interpolation from v. 12. 4. Read simply *and thou shalt say unto all the house of Israel*, attaching these words to v. 5.

5–17. **Explanation of the Symbols.** The city is Jerusalem, regarded by the Hebrews, as other cities by other peoples, as the navel of the earth (38[12]). Her wickedness is made conspicuous, on this account, to the other nations. V. 7b, indeed, suggests that Jerusalem falls below the level of her neighbors, but possibly we should read with some MSS. and Syriac *but* for *neither have*. Her punishment shall be as conspicuous as her situation. Siege shall reduce her people to cannibalism (Lam. 4[10]). Her survivors shall be exiled. Note that for Ezekiel her supreme crime is the pollution of the sanctuary. Jehovah will shave (so for *diminish*, v. 11) her. The fire of v. 2 is interpreted of pestilence and famine which destroy a third of the inhabitants. Another third, attempting to escape, shall be slain by the sword near the city, the remainder exiled, and even then pursued by the sword of Jehovah, which will destroy some. Jehovah's purpose in all this is that men shall know that his righteous anger is appeased. No specific explanation is given of the retrieved hairs (vv. 3f.), which suggests that those verses may be a gloss. 16. *Staff*—cf. 4[16], note.

CHAPTER VI

1–7. **Doom on the Mountains of Israel.** The mountains of Palestine, standing sharply in contrast with the plains of Babylonia, were notorious because of their association with the *high places*, i.e., local sanctuaries, where idolatrous rites were practiced. Ezekiel is to glare toward these and announce that Jehovah is on the point of bringing a sword against their devotees. Idols, altars, and sun-pillars (so for *sun-images*, v. 6) shall be shattered, and the corpses of their worshipers shall defile the sacred places before the broken images so impotent to help them. The shrines in the wadies and valleys shall share the same fate.

8–10. **A Repentant Remnant.** Those who as exiles escape this terrible fate shall *remember* Jehovah, i.e., recognize this as his doing, when he has broken the hearts and eyes that love and regard idols, and shall hate the sight of their own faces. These verses may have been added later. 8. Read *Inasmuch as ye shall have refugees among the nations and shall be scattered through the countries*. 9. Read mg.

11–14. **Utter Desolation Inevitable.** Vv. 11, 12 read like an oracle that is out of its context; it is more closely associated with ch. 5. The gestures in v. 11 are all gestures of triumph (for *Alas!* read *Aha!*). The reference is clearly to the siege. In v. 12 delete *remaineth and*. Vv. 13, 14 resume the threat of vv. 1–7, adding to the sacred shrines the luxuriant trees and leafy terebinths (v. 13, mg.), where the scent of sacrifice (cf. Gen. 8[21]) and incense had ascended. Doom shall sweep the country from the southern wilderness to Riblah (so Michaelis, for the unmeaning *Diblah*, v. 14). All this is to teach the people that Jehovah will tolerate none of these offenses. Note the recurrent *and they shall know I am the Lord.*

CHAPTER VII

The text in this chapter is very corrupt, in several places defying translation; it also contains duplicate passages. The order in LXX varies greatly. Some passages seem to refer to the Day of Jehovah (cf. pp. 206–7), while others relate more naturally to a disaster about to befall Jerusalem. It is as though two stained-glass windows, one representing the day of Jehovah, the other the Fate of Jerusalem, had been shattered, and their fragments afterward pieced together in one restored window. It is hazardous to say whether any of the verses are Ezekiel's, and difficult to interpret details.

1–9. Doom Is at Hand! Jehovah will relentlessly requite (so render for *bring upon*, v. 4) his people according to their abominations and ways. In v. 2, after *man* insert "say," and after *an end*, "is come," both with LXX. For *land* render *earth*, the Hebrew word meaning either; "the four corners of the earth" is a Semitic idiom for the whole earth (cf. Isa. 11[12]). Vv. 5–9 are a parallel to vv. 1–4. The text of vv. 5–7 is much longer than in LXX. Of v. 7 no certain translation can be given.

10–13. Universal Humiliation and Destruction. Whether *the day*, v. 10, means the Day of Jehovah or the day of Judah's doom is uncertain; the latter is more probable, but vv. 10f. are corrupt. The *rod of wickedness* apparently means a wicked ruler. So terrible is the time that even men of business cease to take interest in their dealings.

14–27. Helpless Dismay Paralyzes the Inhabitants. The few who escape from the horrors of the siege to the hills shall be as mourning (so for *of the valleys*, v. 16, with Syriac; cf. Isa. 59[11]) doves, and shall die (so with Syriac for *all of them mourning*, v. 16). In their despair the inhabitants will cast out with contempt the idols of gold and silver in which they had vainly trusted. These shall become the spoil of the invaders, who will penetrate even into the Temple. The *worst of the heathen* (v. 24), the Babylonians, will be the instruments of punishment in Jehovah's hand. In this disaster prophet, priest, and wise man will be helpless to aid. In their common calamity rulers and people will recognize that Jehovah punishes iniquity. **20.** Read mg., and for *his* read *its*, referring to gold and silver. **23.** *Make the chain* is unintelligible. **27.** Delete *the king shall mourn*, with LXX.

CHAPTER VIII

1–6. The Image of Jealousy. While the elders of the exilic community, who seemingly had a measure of self-government, wait in his house, the prophet falls into an ecstasy, and sees dimly the form of Jehovah. The divine hand lifts him by the hair, and divine energy transports him, in vision, to the Temple at Jerusalem. There he beholds Jehovah (as in 3[22]), and sees an idolatrous image. This may have been a replacement of the Asherah erected by Manasseh (2 Kings 21[3]), destroyed later by Josiah (2 Kings 23[6]). **2.** Cf. 1[4, 27]. For *appearance of fire* read *of a man*, with LXX. **3.** LXX omits *which provoketh* (Jehovah) *to jealousy;* the words are a correct gloss on *image of jealousy.*

7–13. The Mystery Cult. Ezekiel is bidden to dig through a wall. Thus discovering a door, he enters a chamber, whose walls are adorned with animal pictures (cf. the pictures on the walls of the Ishtar gate at Babylon). Before these seventy of the leading citizens are burning incense; among them *Jaazaniah,* evidently a man of eminence, though we know nothing else about him. The cult is probably Babylonian rather than Egyptian. V. 7b should probably be deleted with LXX. No satisfactory explanation of *chambers of imagery* (v. 12) is known.

14, 15. The Tammuz Worship. Jehovah leads Ezekiel to another place—the details of the itinerary, doubtless easy to interpret for those familiar with the plan of the Temple, cannot be clearly discerned—where he sees the women *wailing for Tammuz,* seated on the ground in the attitude of mourning (Job 2[13]). Tammuz was a deity of the Sumerians, whose worship continued to flourish among the Babylonians, who succeeded them. He was a vegetation god, supposed to die each year and to be recalled from the underworld by the litanies of mourning recited by his worshipers.

16–18. The Sun Worship. In another place the prophet sees some twenty-five men with their backs to the Temple, worshiping the sun-god, a cult popular in Babylonia, which had been introduced into Jerusalem by Manasseh (see on 2 Kings 21[3] 23[5]). The one ethical note of the chapter occurs here, the charge that these idolaters have *filled the land with violence* (v. 17c). The phrase, *put the branch to the nose* (v. 17d), is obscure (cf. Isa. 17[10]). It has been supposed to refer to phallus worship, and compared to the Zoroastrian worshiper's custom of holding a bundle of myrtle-rods, or the barsom held to the face by Parsee priests before the sacred fire. An Assyrian letter in which subjects say, "The king has brought us to life again by laying the plant of life to our nose" may also be compared.

CHAPTER IX

The Purging of the City. In response to the loud summons of Jehovah appear those to whom he has committed the cleansing of the city, seven angels, six armed with clubs, and the seventh, garbed in white linen—a mark of high rank (Dan. 10^5 $12^{6f.}$ Rev. 15^6)—equipped with an inkhorn, carried, as is to-day customary in the Orient, in the girdle at the side. This angel is bidden to go through the city, inscribing upon the forehead of each man who had dissociated himself from idolatrous practices a *taw*, the last letter of the Hebrew alphabet, originally in form like a cross. The club-bearers, following in his wake, are to destroy all who are not marked with this sign of immunity. They are to begin with the idolaters who are even now practising their unholy rites before the Temple, sparing neither age nor sex (vv. 1–7; cf. Rev. $14^{9,\,11}$ 2^{17}).

Ezekiel, appalled at the doom pronounced, utters a pathetic plea for reconsideration. Jehovah, charging his people with wholesale murder and persistent perversion of justice—ethical faults, be it noted—refuses to relent (vv. 8–10). The angel returns to report that his duty is done. We should have expected a report from the executioners too: possibly that has been suppressed because of its horror. Observe that Ezekiel's doctrine of individual responsibility is prominent here; each man is judged according to his conduct. The linen-clad angel is probably the Angel of Jehovah (cf. p. 204), the guardian angel of Israel (Ex. $23^{20f.}$). The number seven may have been suggested by Babylonian analogies, and certainly suggested the seven of Rev. 15^6. **1.** Here read mg. Delete last clause as duplicate from v. 2. **3.** Delete as anticipation of 10^4, breaking the connection. **7.** This, which repeats the order whose execution has already begun, is a parallel to vv. 5f.

CHAPTER X

Jehovah's Departure from the Sanctuary. The analysis of this chapter presents almost insuperable difficulties. The narrative of ch. 9 is resumed in v. 2, v. 1 being obviously an intrusion breaking the connection. Again, vv. 3–6 seem to be an intrusion, for v. 6 repeats the command of v. 2 and its performance. The continuation of v. 2 may be v. 7, though the language of v. 2 implies that the linen-clad angel is to take the fire himself rather than receive it from a cherub. The original narrative must surely have had as its conclusion the burning of the city. V. 8 refers back to 1^8, recalling that the living creatures possessed hands, to explain v. 7.

The rest of the chapter repeats, with noteworthy variations, much of ch. 1, and tells of the chariot's departure from the Temple. From the narrative of chs. 8f. one would hardly have expected any reference to the chariot—9^{3a} is an interpolation, cf. note—and it has been argued that all these references to the chariot are later interpolations; but some reference to the chariot is needed to explain where the fire was obtained (cf. 1^{13}). Probably the chariot is supposed to be kept at the Temple when not on its journeys. The insertions may be due to Ezekiel himself, though he certainly did not leave the chapter in its present form. He may be responsible for the identification of the living creatures in ch. 1 with cherubim. Apparently, it was not seemly that Jehovah should remain upon the chariot while the linen-clad man approached it closely. Note that in contrast to the description of ch. 1 the wings when at rest make a noise like thunder—*the voice of God Almighty* (v. 5). V. 12, which extends the eyes in the wheels of ch. 1 to the cherubim also, is based on a misconception of the word rendered *rings* in 1^{18}, here rendered *backs*. The substitution of a cherub face (v. 14) for the ox face of ch. 1 is probably a mistake.

CHAPTER XI

1–13. The Caldron and the Flesh. This experience cannot well be the immediate sequel of the Temple vision, for, even in a trance, Ezekiel could hardly relate these happenings in the city immediately after describing the burning of the city and the slaughter of its evil doers. Note too that Ezekiel is taken up by *spirit* (cf. on 2^2), in contrast to the simple "he brought me" which is used in $8^{7,\,16}$ for change of position. There is no need, however, to doubt that it is a genuine experience of the prophet, or that he himself inserted the record at this point. The twenty-five men (v. 1) are evidently a party of leaders, but hardly, as often supposed, the anti-Babylonian faction, for the latter could not reasonably be reproached with fear of the sword (v. 8). Two are singled out as familiar to the exiles; the *Jaazaniah* is not the one mentioned in 8^{11}. They are accused of murderous violence. Their boast *we be the flesh*, v. 3, may mean that the city walls protect them from danger as the pot keeps fire from the flesh, or that they are the flesh in contrast to the exiles, who, as bones and offal, have been cast away.

Ezekiel is bidden to prophesy against these cruel boasters: Jehovah knows their misdeeds, and will fetch them out of their "caldron," in which the only flesh remaining shall be that of their victims. They shall be delivered to exile and death (vv. 9f.). As he utters this threat Ezekiel, in vision, sees Pelatiah fall dead, and the fear that Jehovah will utterly destroy his people wrings from him a cry of agony. **3a.** No satisfactory explanation or emendation has been made. **7c.** Read mg., with MSS. and versions. **10.** Cf. 6^{14}, where "Riblah" should be read; cf. 2 Kings $25^{6, 20, 21}$ Jer. 52^{9-11}. **11f.** Delete with LXX. The climax is reached in the last words of v. 10.

14–21. A Glint of Sunshine. Here we encounter the first hopeful utterance. The opening formula marks it as an independent oracle; like the preceding section it does not belong to the Temple vision, but is inserted here because it agrees with that section in rebuking the arrogance of those who remained in Jerusalem after the first deportation. These have boasted that they, not the distant exiles, are the inheritors of the national estate. Jehovah bids Ezekiel proclaim that the exiles—to whom he could be but little of a sanctuary because their remoteness from the Temple limited their possibilities of practicing the cultus (cf. ch. 48)—shall be brought back. They shall purge the city of idolatry, and for a stony heart shall be given a fleshy one ($36^{26f.}$ Jer. 24^{7} 31^{33}), upon which his ordinances would be easily impressed (vv. 19, 20). The idolaters shall reap the reward of their sins. **15.** For *kindred* perhaps read *captivity*, with versions; for *are they unto* read *concerning;* and for *Get you* read *They are.* **16.** For *yet will I be* read *and have been;* and for *a sanctuary for a little while* read *but little of a sanctuary.* **19.** For *one* read *another*, with versions; for *you* read *them*, with MSS. and versions.

22–25. The Departure of the Chariot. This passage should follow ch. 10. The chariot rests on the Mount of Olives ere it finally disappears from view. Ezekiel awakes from his trance and relates his vision to the exiles.

CHAPTER XII

1–16. An Acted Prophecy of Exile. As the exiles obstinately refuse to understand Ezekiel, Jehovah bids him prepare such utensils—e.g., staff and scrip—as an exile might carry on his march into captivity. At night he is to carry these out through a hole previously made in the soft brick wall of his house. All this is to be done ostentatiously before the exiles. Having done this, next morning he receives from Jehovah an explanation of the object lesson. When asked the meaning of this madness he is to say, "Thus shall those who remain in Jerusalem go into exile, and be scattered among the nations." A postscript (v. 16) explains that the remnant who thus survive sword, famine, and pestilence, survive merely that they may bear witness that their country's fate is due, not to Jehovah's inability to protect it, but to his wrath at its sin.

Whether the references to the fate of the king belong to this context is doubtful. Not because the references which seem to foretell the blinding of Zedekiah (vv. 6, 12–14) are suspected as prophecies after the event; in that case the correspondence would have been more exact. Zedekiah was not blinded until he reached Riblah (2 Kings $25^{6f.}$). Nor did he go forth through a breach (2 Kings 25^{4} Jer. 52^{7}). But v. 7 does not record the fulfillment of the command to cover the face, and therefore that command is probably not original in v. 6. **3.** Delete *and remove*, with LXX, and *and thou shalt . . . in their sight.* **5, 6.** For *carry* read *go*, with versions. **7.** Delete *with mine hand*, with LXX and Syriac. For *brought it* read *went*, with versions. **10.** The beginning is untranslatable; for *among whom they are* read *who are therein.*

17–20. An Acted Prophecy of Siege. With this symbolic representation cf. $4^{10f.}$ The mention of *violence* (v. 19) once again strikes the ethical note. *The people of the land* (v. 19) usually means the rural inhabitants in contrast to the dwellers in Jerusalem. Klamroth has proved, however, that it may mean the people in contrast to their rulers. Ezekiel's object lesson could, of course, become known to them only by report. For *from all* read *and all.*

21–28. Rebukes for the Skeptics. The first rebuke (vv. 21–25) is meant for those who yet remain in Palestine, between whom and the exiles there is evidently constant communication. They are wont to taunt the predicters of doom, such as Jeremiah, with the failure of their predictions. Ezekiel, as elsewhere (11^{3} 16^{44} 18^{2}), uses a popular saying as a text (v. 23). Not the predictions of Jehovah's prophets, but those of the prophets who are falsely optimistic, shall fail. Their flattering mouths will be made dumb when Jehovah's word comes true, as it will in this generation. Ezekiel's companions too skeptically say that even if he prophesies truly, the fulfillment will be long deferred, but Jehovah announces that fulfillment is imminent (vv. 26–28). With these passages it is instructive to compare Jer. $23^{16f.}$ 28^{1-17}.

CHAPTER XIII

1–16. Against the False Prophets. In the first part (vv. 1–7) the false prophets are accused of palming off their own inventions as the inspired words of Jehovah, who expressly disowns them. Moral, rather than intellectual, folly is implied in *foolish* (v. 3, the epithet is absent from LXX). Vv. 4f.—possibly interpolated—are difficult: apparently they mean that, as foxes by their burrowing make ruins more ruinous still, so the false prophets, far from helping, make the situation worse—the very opposite of what they should do, namely, repair the breach (so for *gaps*, v. 5), and make a secure wall of protection, enabling Israel to hold its own in the Day of Jehovah. Compare the instructive passage 1 Kings 22^{6-28}. **2.** Delete *that* after *Israel*. **3.** The latter part is corrupt and the translation uncertain. **6.** Read mg.

Vv. 8–16 announce the penalty, which is that Jehovah's hand shall be upon them—not for inspiration, but for punishment. They shall be excluded from the community (so for *council*, v. 9), their names erased from the book of life (Isa. 4^3), i.e., the register containing the list of Jerusalem's inhabitants. This suggests that the passage comes from the later period when the prophet was looking forward to a reorganized nation. It is characteristic of the false prophets to promise prosperity—the real meaning of *peace* (v. 10)—when no prosperity is likely. They are compared to men who build an unsound wall, camouflaging its defects by some deceitful covering. Jehovah will hurl against it a torrential storm, which will level it to the ground, crushing them in its fall. Then will Jehovah ironically ask, "Where is the wall, and where they who daubed it?" (So render v. 15b.) **10.** See mg.; the unique word used here for *wall* may mean a wall of stones loosely piled together, with no cementing material (Ehrlich); the rendering *mortar* is dubious. **11.** Delete *ye, O*.

17–23. Against the Sorcerers. The sorcerers were predominantly women (Ex. 22^{18}), who, like modern witches, were credited with power of life and death over their victims. V. 18 is wrongly translated: for *pillows* read *knots;* the word rendered *kerchiefs* is obscure. The symbolical tying and unloosing of knots as charms by which a person might be brought into their power was a common practice of Babylonian sorcerers. The snapping of such knots released the victim. Thus one exorcism text appeals to the fire-god to "break the cords" whereby a sorcerer has bewitched his victim, and so release the latter from the spell. The sorceresses whom Ezekiel attacks usurp by their charms the divine prerogative of life and death, adding insult to injury by doing this for trifling fees (v. 19). Jehovah will snap the knots they have tied, and loose their victims. **18.** For *souls* read *men* (cf. 3^{19}, note). **20.** The mg. is preferable, but uncertain. **22f.** These add little to the meaning, and may be a later expansion.

CHAPTER XIV

1–11. Idol-Worshipers and the Prophets Who Encourage Them Are Doomed. When certain leaders of the exiles come to Ezekiel—presumably seeking an oracle—Jehovah reveals to him that they have reverted (so, *taken into their heart*, v. 3) to idol-worship. Jehovah will answer them, not through the prophet, but in his own person (so, for *therein*, v. 4). Unless they repent he will make an example by destroying them. The concluding formula (v. 8) shows that vv. 9–11 are an appendix—possibly added later. The prophet who gives a false oracle is lured by Jehovah to do so. For he who panders to idolatrous inquirers is equally sinful with them, and both shall receive the reward of their sins. This purging is necessary, that the people may be cleansed and become truly Jehovah's people. **5.** *Take . . . in their own heart*—cf. Psa. 102^b. **7.** *Strangers;* i.e., resident aliens—not the word so rendered in 7^{21} 11^9. Ezekiel contemplates that such will exist in the reformed community (47^{22}). **8.** Delete *an astonishment, for*. **9–11.** Cf. 1 Kings $22^{19f.}$ Deut. 13^{1-5}. **10.** The mg. gives the true meaning.

12–23. Why the Remnant Survived. Ezekiel's utterances had suggested that none would survive the fate of doomed Jerusalem. Probably this oracle is intended to explain why, after the fall of the city in 586 B.C., a second deportation reached Babylonia. Jehovah once promised Abraham (Gen. 18) that could ten righteous men be found in Sodom, the city should be spared; but now when he sends upon a land one of his four plagues, famine, beasts of prey, sword, or pestilence, though preeminent saints such as Noah, Daniel and Job dwell therein, they shall save themselves alone. How much more, when he sends all four upon Jerusalem, we should expect the conclusion "shall none escape." Yet here is the exception that proves the rule—some shall survive, not to their own comfort, but that from their conduct the exiles may see that Jehovah was justified in destroying the city (cf. 12^{16}). The references to Daniel (cf. 28³) and Job are not to the books we know by those names, which are later than Ezekiel, but to traditions—one of which may possibly survive in the prologue and epilogue to our book of Job—concerning heroes of those names. **13.** For *committing a trespass* read *playing me false;* on *staff of bread* cf. 4¹⁶, note. **15.** For *they spoil* read *I bereave.* **19.** Delete *in blood.* **22.** Read *bring* for *be carried.*

CHAPTER XV

The Worthless Wild Vine. Jeremiah (2²¹) compared Israel to a good vine become degenerate; Hosea (10¹) to a luxuriant vine; Isaiah (5¹⁻⁷) to a choice vine that produced but wild fruit. Ezekiel likens Israel to the wild vine, producing no useful fruit, its wood too poor to serve any useful purpose, not substantial enough even to make a peg, fit only for fuel. Should a half-burnt piece be saved from the fire (Amos 4¹¹), what good can it be? It was useless even before it was burned! Even so Jerusalem, the remnant of an unworthy people, is worthless. Though a remnant be saved from the fire, it can but be cast into the fire again! **2.** *The vine branch*—delete, with LXX^B. **6.** *I have*—read probably *has been.* **8.** *Committed a trespass;* render *played me false.*

CHAPTER XVI

This chapter contains two separate allegories. In vv. 1–43 the prophet, by the allegory of the foundling child, who became the faithless wife of her benefactor, shows the inevitableness of Jerusalem's destruction. The second allegory, that of Jerusalem and her sisters, is in vv. 44–63.

1–14. Jehovah's Gracious Kindness to the Foundling. The parable likens Judah to a girl-child unwanted and exposed to die, so receiving none of the attention or care usually given to an infant. Jehovah, passing by, sees the frail infant kicking convulsively (so for *weltering,* v. 6). He bids her live and flourish. Later, when she has grown to ripe womanhood, he sees her again, and solemnly espouses her. He decks her with fine clothing and beautiful ornament. For food he assigns her luxuries. Her beauty, enhanced in all these ways, is superb and famed among the nations. The point is emphasized that Judah owes nothing to herself, but all to Jehovah.

3. Read mg. On *Amorite* and *Hittite* cf. p. 60a. Though it is a mistake to attempt an explanation of all the details by historic events, it seems not improbable that Ezekiel follows a tradition of Israel's ancestry not found elsewhere in the O.T.; certainly the Hebrews were composed of divergent stocks. **4.** *Navel*—rather, "navel-string"; *salted*—the ritual custom of rubbing an infant with salt still prevails in the East. Salt is a "giver of life." **6.** *Yea I . . . live*—delete with MSS., LXX, Syriac. **7.** For *I caused thee to multiply* read *and thou shalt flourish;* for *excellent ornament* read *puberty.* **8.** Cf. Ruth 3⁹ Deut. 22³⁰; *sware*—this feature of a marriage is unique in O.T.; *covenant*—cf. Mal. 2¹⁴. **9.** Cf. Ruth 3³ Esth. 2¹². The washing away of the blood, which here can be only menstrual blood, is strange, and perhaps Kraetzschmar is right in removing this verse to follow v. 6. **10.** *Sealskin, linen*—translations uncertain. **12.** For bridegroom's *crown* cf. Isa. 61¹⁰ Cant. 3¹¹; the bride too wore one. **13.** *Fine flour;* cf. Psa. 81¹⁶. Delete last seven words with LXX.

15–34. Her Shameful and Shameless Ingratitude. Isaiah, Amos, Hosea, Jeremiah, speak of an early period of happy relations between Jehovah and his bride. For Ezekiel her sin begins immediately after her espousal. Her beauty, which has become renowned, she uses to attract lovers from the chance passers-by (Gen. 38¹⁴ Jer. 3²). The fine raiment her husband gave her she uses to make gay her high places (cf. p. 166)—or possibly to make tent-shrines (2 Kings 23⁷)—her ornaments, to make images. These she clothes with her gay apparel (cf. Jer. 10⁹), and to them she makes over her dainty food. Her crowning infidelity is that to them she sacrifices her children, who are really Jehovah's children. Not one thought does she give to the misery from which Jehovah had rescued her! **15, 16.** The last clauses are unintelligible. **17.** *Images of men*—the reference may be to phallus-worship. **19.** *Honey*—this, though a common element in Semitic sacrifice, was forbidden in Israelite cultus (Lev. 2¹¹). **20f.** Child-sacrifice, though exceptional, was not unknown in early Israel. It became increasingly popular in the troubled times from the reign of Ahaz on. Note that the victims are slain before they are burned (cf. 2 Kings 3²⁷ 17³¹ Jer. 19⁵ Mic. 6⁷). **24.** *Eminent place*—uncertain, but better than mg.; cf. the Calvaries and Madonna shrines in Roman Catholic countries, and Jer. 11¹³.

The figure changes in v. 26 from the Baalim to foreign nations. Foreign alliances, which in Jehovah's eyes are adultery, entailed some recognition of the cult of the allies, hence there is a connection between the two ideas. The bride has had relations with Egypt, notoriously a sensual people (the meaning of *great of flesh,* v. 26). Her appetite is never sated; so to Egypt she had added Assyria and Chaldea. Her licentiousness exceeds that of the common harlot who receives pay, for she, on the contrary, bribes her lovers. The reference here is to the tribute she paid to those nations. **27.** This is possibly an addition; punishment is described in a later section of the chapter; *diminished*—cf. Ex. 21[10]; *daughters*—a common Semitic idiom for dependent cities. **29.** The mg. gives the right meaning. **30.** *How weak is thine heart* appears to be corrupt; *imperious*—render *unrestrained.* V. 32, and probably also v. 34, are interpolated.

35–43. The Punishment of the Adulteress. The faithless bride shall be exposed naked before her lovers—here the nations, not the Baalim. Evidently the siege and destruction of the city in 586 B.C. are in view. Her ruin will reduce her once more to the beggarly condition from which Jehovah had brought her (v. 39 echoes v. 7). Now the figure changes to that of a solemn assembly gathered to inflict upon a faithless wife the customary penalties (cf. 23[26] Lev. 20[10] Deut. 22[22] Jn. 7[53]–8[11]). So shall the righteous wrath of Jehovah be glutted. **37.** For *with whom thou hast taken pleasure* read *whom thou hast loved inordinately; with all them that thou hast hated* is difficult to interpret and may be a gloss. **43.** The last clause is unintelligible and should be deleted.

A new subject—Jerusalem and her sisters—is introduced in v. 44, and continues to be the main topic to the end of the chapter. This section is hardly the natural continuation of what precedes, and if by Ezekiel must have been added later. The general tone of the references to restoration harmonizes better with Isa. 40–66 than with the latter part of Ezekiel; and there is something to be said for Hölscher's attribution of the passage to a later hand. At the same time it has many affinities with Ezekiel's style, and we must not expect rigorous logical consistency in a prophet's oracles separated by intervals of time.

44–52. Jerusalem Worse than Sodom or Samaria. Jerusalem shall be a byword for her likeness to her Hittite mother and to her sisters Samaria and Sodom in their unnatural treatment of husband and children. Her sin, indeed, exceeds theirs (cf. Jer. 3[11]). Sodom's sin is defined as arrogant prosperity and callousness: that of Samaria is, rather strangely, not specified. Beside Jerusalem's black guilt her sisters seem relatively innocent (v. 51) and are accordingly acquitted (v. 52).

45. The parallel suggested here seems inexact, for though Jehovah might be regarded as the husband of Samaria, this cannot well apply to Sodom or the Hittites. *Children*—the reference is probably to child-sacrifice. **46.** *Left hand* and *right hand* are idiomatic Hebrew for north and south respectively. Samaria is called *elder* (Hebrew "greater") as being more important than Sodom. **47.** *But . . . thing*—text and meaning uncertain. **50.** For *as I saw good* read *thou sawest.*

53–58. Jehovah Will Restore the Fortunes (so render *turn again . . . captivity,* v. 53) of Sodom, Samaria, and their daughter-cities, and—a surprising turn—also of Jerusalem. Then Jerusalem will be ashamed that her sisters have been able to congratulate themselves upon her greater iniquity, though before her nakedness (so for *wickedness,* v. 57) was laid bare, exposing her to the scorn of the surrounding nations, she had been too proud to speak her sister's name. Her punishment has purged her sin (Isa. 40[2]). **53.** *The captivity of thy captives*—read, with versions, *I will restore thy fortunes.* **57.** For *Syria* read *Edom,* with MSS.

59–63. Jehovah Remembers His Covenant. Though Jehovah will punish Jerusalem for breaking her covenant, he will remember that earlier covenant and renew with her an everlasting covenant. She will blush for shame when he returns good for evil by bringing her sisters under her domination—not because she has merited this by keeping faith, but of his pure grace. So shall she learn, not, as the phrase has heretofore implied, because of his sternness, but because of his grace, that he is Jehovah, and she shall be speechless before the wonder of his magnanimity.

CHAPTER XVII

1–10. The Allegory of the Eagle, the Cedar, and the Vine. This is clear in general, and only a few details need be commented on. **3.** The reference in *which had divers colors* is probably to the colored representations of the eagle as a symbol of royalty (cf. Hos. 8[1] Jer. 48[40] 49[22]) found on Babylonian monuments. **4.** *Land of traffic*—the Canaanites, in contrast with the Hebrews, were a trading people, and "Canaanite" became a synonym for "trader"; mg., a literal rendering, refers to Babylon, called *Canaan,* i.e., "a land of shopkeepers." **5.** In the place of *land* some read, changing one consonant, *cedar; fruitful*—better, *cultivated;* cf. mg. Delete *he placed it.* A single unintelligible word in Hebrew is rendered *as a willow tree,* but willows do not become vines. **6.** In the place of *and it grew and became* read *that it might grow and become.* **7.** For *beds* read the singular; a garden terrace is meant. **9.** *He*—the first eagle. Delete all from *even without* to the end. The whole verse, which does not harmonize with v. 10, the natural continuation of v. 8, may be a gloss.

11–21. The Interpretation of the Parable. The first eagle is Nebuchadrezzar; the cedar, Jerusalem; its top, Jehoiachin and the princes whom Nebuchadrezzar carried off. The *seed* (cf. v. 5) is Jehoiachin's uncle Zedekiah, whom Nebuchadrezzar appointed king, exacting from him an oath of fealty, intending that Judah should remain a kingdom, though but a vassal state. But Zedekiah has plotted with Egypt against his overlord, seeking cavalry (cf. 1 Kings $10^{28f.}$) and soldiery thence to assist him. Shall not such an ingrate be punished? Verily he shall die in Babylon. Probably the oath of Zedekiah had been sworn "by Jehovah," so his breach of faith was (v. 19) treachery also to Jehovah, who will therefore bring him to book. **16.** *With him* should follow *covenant.* **17.** This may be a gloss, corresponding to the gloss in v. 9; *make for him*—the Hebrew more naturally means "act against him"; those who retain the verse consequently delete *Pharaoh* as incorrect gloss. **18.** The natural continuation of v. 16. **20.** *Plead with* (cf. A.S.V.) in the forensic sense = "convict by legal argument." **21.** (*And all his*) *fugitives;* some MSS. and versions read *chosen ones;* but probably delete the phrase. With the whole passage cf. 2 Kings 24^{8}–25^{7}. The probable date of the allegory is a year or so before the final siege: Zedekiah doubtless sought Egypt's aid some time before he "rebelled against the king of Babylon" (2 Kings 24^{20}). That the prophecy is "after the event" need not be assumed; had it been, Riblah rather than Babylon would have been named in v. 20.

22–24. A Messianic Prophecy. Nebuchadrezzar's attempt at planting may have failed, but, says Jehovah, I—emphatic in Hebrew—will plant a tender cedar twig on a high mountain. It shall become a mighty tree, and the birds shall shelter in it. The other trees shall realize that Jehovah can work his will, whatever it be, on the trees. *Bear fruit* (v. 23)—a slight change gives "make wood"—cedars have no fruit. Cornill introduces "beasts" as subject of *dwell*, transposing *fowl* as subject of the following clause. Mic. 4^{1-5} and Isa. 2^{2-4} should be compared. Seemingly, despite the flaw in metaphor, both birds and trees represent Gentile nations. Other personal Messianic prophecies are found in Ezekiel (21^{27} 34^{24} 37^{24}); to reject these as interpolations because his final vision of the future (chs. 40–48) does not find room for a Messiah is to deny that the prophet's doctrine may have developed in the light of his experience.

CHAPTER XVIII

1–20. A Man's Standing Before God Is Not Determined by His Ancestry. Suffering, as they suppose, for their fathers' sins, the people utter their complaint in a popular proverb (cf. Jer. $31^{29f.}$ Lam. 5^{7}). Ezekiel retorts that every man stands in personal relationship to God: none dies save for his own sins. He gives an example of three generations. The grandfather (vv. 5–9) is righteous, and escapes death. His son (vv. 10–13) is unrighteous, and, as penalty, dies. The grandson (vv. 14–17) takes this as a warning, is righteous, and lives.

It is important to remember that *soul* here means "person" or "self"—the whole man, and not any special part of him. The ideal of righteousness is illustrated by typical virtues. The priestly cast of mind is evident in the order of their mention. First, avoidance of ritual sins (v. 6); even the last two named here are regarded as offenses rather against the cultus than as ethical transgressions. Then come the ethical virtues. A difficulty arises in the word *die.* All men, righteous and unrighteous alike, die. Therefore ordinary physical death cannot be what is intended; unless the idea of an early death, before man has completed the normal span of life, is in the mind of the prophet. Another possible interpretation makes death, as the most striking of legal penalties, a general synonym for punishment. Still other interpreters assign to the term an eschatological meaning, threatening that the sinner will perish in an imminent judgment like the Day of Jehovah. Such a judgment, though it accords ill with other utterances in the book, may at times have been Ezekiel's expectation. A modification of this view connects the utterance with the O.T. hope of the "kingdom of God." "Live," then, would refer to entrance into the glories of the Kingdom, while "die" would mean exclusion from these glories. The chapter does not connect closely with its context, and may be of later date. **1.** For *land* LXX reads *children.* **6.** *Upon the mountains* refers to impure worship. Many emend "with the blood"; cf. 33^{25} Lev. 19^{26}; *in her separation*—menstruous. **7.** Cf. Ex. 22^{26} Amos 2^{8}. **8.** *Usury, increase*—synonyms for "interest"; cf. Ex. 22^{25}. **10f.** The text is disordered; LXX varies considerably. The sense is obtained by substituting "that" for all words between *son* (v. 10) and *hath eaten* (v. 11). **14.** *Feareth* (so versions) is better than mg., which can be only accidental repetition. **17.** For *the poor* read iniquity, with LXX. **18.** For *in* read mg.

21–29. A Man's Standing Before God Is Not Determined by His Own Past. At the time of the eschatological (?) judgment a reformed sinner will not have his past brought up against him, nor will a backslider be able to plead his former righteousness. God will judge each as he is. Men may act capriciously, but God acts in accordance with eternal principles. This section considers a problem more advanced than that arising out of the popular proverb. **22.** *In*—render *for*. **24.** Delete, with versions, *shall he live?* **26.** Delete *and dieth therein* with support in versions; *in*—render *for*. **27.** *His soul* = himself. **28.** Delete *considereth, and*, with LXX.

30–32. An Appeal. Here Ezekiel becomes the evangelist, appealing to the house of Israel to realize that their fate is determined neither by their guilty ancestors nor by their own guilty past. God is merciful, and will, if they repent, rejoice to pardon them. **31.** For *wherein* read *which against me* with LXX.

CHAPTER XIX

1–9. Allegory of the Lioness and Her Whelps. The allegory, with its pictures of lion-hunting, is clear. The *prince* (v. 1; read singular, with LXX) is Zedekiah: the *lioness* (though see note at end of chapter) his mother, Hamutal (2 Kings 24[18]). The first *young lion* is Jehoahaz, an older son of Hamutal (2 Kings 23[31]), who after a brief reign was made prisoner by Pharaoh-necoh (2 Kings 23[33]). To him succeeded Jehoiakim, son of Josiah by another wife than Hamutal, and he in turn was followed by his son Jehoiachin. When the last-named was carried captive to Babylon a second son of Hamutal, Zedekiah, the second *young lion*, was appointed by Nebuchadrezzar to succeed him. Possibly Hamutal used influence to achieve this end. Zedekiah, rebelling against Nebuchadrezzar, was captured and carried to Babylon (2 Kings 25[7]). **3.** For *she brought*, LXX reads *there grew*. **4.** For *heard of* read, with LXX, *raised the alarm about*. **5.** Delete *she had waited, and*. **7.** The text of v. 7a is hopelessly corrupt; delete. **8.** For *from the provinces* read *their traps*. **9.** Delete *with hooks . . . they brought him into strongholds*.

10–14. The Vine and Its Branch. The *vine* is Hamutal; the conspicuous branch—*strong rod*—of the vine, Zedekiah. Vine and branch are uprooted and withered. Fire has kindled the dry branch and consumed the vine also. In other words, Hamutal has been involved in the catastrophe brought about by Zedekiah's rebellion. The sense has been obscured because *rod*, singular in versions, has been treated as plural. All references to the rod should be emended accordingly (cf. mg.). **10.** *In thy blood*—corrupt; the correct text uncertain. The planting (v. 13) comes strangely after v. 12, which has its natural continuation in v. 14. The last sentence reads like a scribe's note; *shall be* is really *has been*.

These two beautiful dirges, the most finished poems in Ezekiel, need not imply sympathy with Hamutal and Zedekiah any more than the Song of Deborah implies sympathy with Sisera's mother. According to another—less probable—explanation, the lioness and the vine are the country, and the second young lion is Jehoiachin.

CHAPTER XX

1–31. Jehovah Refuses an Oracle to the Elders. Vv. 1–3 state that in 591 B.C. the elders seeking an oracle through Ezekiel are rebuffed (cf. 8[1] 14[1]); vv. 4–31 give the reason for the rebuff: Jehovah chose Israel, revealing himself to them in Egypt (cf. on Ex. 3). He swore to bring them into the promised land if they purged themselves from Egyptian idolatry. Because they did not, he was minded to reject them. For his own sake, not theirs, he refrained, bringing them out of Egypt into the wilderness. At Sinai he gave them statutes by obeying which they might escape his anger, and so live. Ezekiel singles out the Sabbath as a sign marking off Israel from other nations: this idea became prominent during the Exile, when circumcision and Sabbath-keeping distinguished the Jews from their neighbors. Had the Hebrew Sabbath been derived directly from the Babylonian *shabbattu*, this distinction would have been vague, and, though there is doubtless some connection between the words, direct derivation is unlikely. So intimately is the Sabbath connected with Jehovah that it must have been adopted as his festal day when he was adopted as Israel's God.

The people reject this second chance, and again Jehovah is minded to destroy them. But, lest he should seem to the nations to have been baffled, while he denies that generation entrance into Palestine, he gives its successors another opportunity. They are equally recalcitrant, and, though for his own sake he does not destroy them, he dooms them to dispersal among the nations. Moreover, he gives them statutes, the observance of which would incur his anger, so that they might die. The custom of child-sacrifice is an example of these. The story of Abraham and Isaac and the incident of Jephthah's daughter suggest that this rite was not unknown in early Israel (cf. p. 368a). No doubt those who practiced it supposed they were pleasing Jehovah (cf. 16[20]).

Statutes of death in contrast with statutes of life recall food and water of death which the Babylonian Adapa legend contrasts with food and water of life, as gifts of the gods. That Jehovah should give statutes luring Israel to disaster, however inconceivable to us, is quite in harmony with the O.T. idea of God as the creator alike of good and evil (Amos 3:6). The elders who seek an oracle have imitated the treacherous conduct of their ancestors; therefore Jehovah rebuffs them. 4. *Judge*—cf. 22:2 23:36. 6. *Lifted up my hand*=swore an oath; *espied*—better, *gave*, with Syriac and Targum (cf. v. 15). 7. *The abominations of his eyes*=the idols he regards. 11. *In*—read mg. 22. *Hand*, i.e., uplifted to punish. 25. Read mg. 26. *Desolate*—rather, *appalled;* what follows should probably be deleted with LXX. 29. The meaning here is obscure, and the connection with context precarious. The Hebrew contains a play on words which cannot be reproduced in English.

32–44. **An Eschatological Appendix.** These verses connect harshly with what precedes. What is meant by *that which cometh into your mind*? (V. 32) Schmidt suggests that it is a project for building a temple in Babylonia; cf. the Jewish temple at Elephantine (p. 703b). The section assumes that all Israel is in exile, and therefore implies a date subsequent to 586 B.C. It was probably added later to vv. 1–31.

Jehovah will demonstrate that no god of wood and stone, but he only, has power over the exiles. He will, in his anger, bring them into the Syro-Arabian desert, and convict them of their sins, as he had brought their ancestors from Egypt into the Egypto-Arabian desert for a like purpose. As a shepherd who separates goats from sheep with his rod, so will he separate from their midst the rebels, who shall not return to Palestine. Israel may serve idols now, but the time is coming when all Israel shall serve Jehovah in his holy mountain (cf. Isa. 2:3 Mic. 4:2). Then shall his chosen people be filled with shame for their past misdeeds. All this will he bring about, not because they deserve mercy, but to prove his might in their eyes and in the eyes of the nations. 36. *Pleaded*—cf. 17:20, note. 37. *Bond of the covenant*—text and meaning are doubtful: LXX has simply *number;* "refiner's crucible" has been suggested. 40. The word translated *serve* is used specifically of priestly functions (cf. Ex. 19:6).

45–49. **Prophecy Against the Forests of the South.** Closely connected with ch. 21; indeed, 20:45–21:32 in English constitute ch. 21 in Hebrew. The section contains five separate oracles, four of them being linked together by the use of the term "sword." The subject matter has affinities to that of ch. 7, and the text has suffered considerably. Ezekiel is told to set his face against (4:3) the forest of the south, and proclaim that Jehovah will kindle a fire in it. Beginning in the dry undergrowth, this will consume even the green trees (Judg. 9:15) and burn the whole forest. All faces will be scorched by its flames. (It would be natural to interpret this of the spectators' faces, but it may refer to the trees—metaphor within metaphor.) The world will recognize that none but Jehovah can have done this.

46. Delete *of the field*, with support in versions. Three different words are used for *south;* probably *Jerusalem, sanctuaries, of Israel* in 21:2 correspond to these; *drop*, literally, *dribble;* cf. Amos 7:16 Mic. 2:6, 11. 47. Delete *flaming*.

CHAPTER XXI

1–7. **Jehovah's Sharpened Sword.** In 20:49 Ezekiel interjects that the people call him a speaker of riddles; so Jehovah gives him the interpretation, explaining figure by figure as though to mock those who bring this complaint. The fire becomes the sword of Jehovah—possibly the change of image, so frequent a phenomenon in dreams, gives us the clue as to the way in which Ezekiel received the revelation. It will destroy good and bad alike—green tree and dry. The prophet is bidden to utter a heart-broken cry (this fairly paraphrases *with the breaking of thy loins*, v. 6), to symbolize the sorrow now on its way, which shall cause the bravest to faint with fear in face of the inevitable doom. This impending disaster is Nebuchadrezzar's advance against Jerusalem before its capture in 586. 2. For *the sanctuaries* read with LXX *their sanctuaries.* 3. Contrasts glaringly with the doctrine of ch. 18, as fact often does with theory. LXX feels this so strongly that it deliberately substitutes *unrighteous* for *righteous.*

8–17. **The Song of the Sword.** This passionate outburst may well have been uttered in a state of prophetic frenzy that caused it to be in part incoherent; much of the text is now unintelligible, through the misunderstandings of scribes and the intrusion of glosses. The main sense is, however, still discernible. Into the hand of the slayer Jehovah has given a sharp, glittering, sword, whose victims are to be Jerusalem and her princes. By crying and howling Ezekiel is to symbolize the imminence of the doom, clapping his hands in sardonic satisfaction. The sword is to be doubled and trebled, i.e., it is to do the work of three swords. Jehovah himself will clap his hands in glee. It has been suggested that in delivering the oracle Ezekiel himself brandished a sword symbolically. The historical situation is the time immediately preceding the final attack of Nebuchadrezzar (*the slayer*, v. 11) upon Jerusalem.

10. The expression *shall we . . . tree* is corrupt; *tree* suggests a gloss connecting this

oracle with the preceding one. **12.** Cf. *smite . . . thigh* with Jer. 31[19]. **13.** This is corrupt and unintelligible. **14.** To *smite . . . together* is a gesture of hostile exultation; for *the third time* read *and trebled*, with Vulgate. What follows is unintelligible; mg. *compasseth them about* is preferable. **15.** Possibly the original in v. 15a was "That all hearts may melt, and the fallen be many at their gates, I have appointed the slaughter of the sword." **16.** This is an exhortation to the sword to sweep on every side.

18–27. Which Road Will the Sword Take? Ezekiel is to trace on the ground a land (Babylon) from which two roads fork, setting at the fork a direction-mark indicating that one road leads to Jerusalem, the other to Rabbah, the capital of Ammon, at this time leagued with Judah against Nebuchadrezzar. Nebuchadrezzar, now definitely named, is pictured as halted at the fork, consulting the oracles to decide which road he shall take. Two arrows are shaken in a quiver; the one drawn out by the king will decide. He also consults the teraphim (cf. p. 372b), and inspects the liver of a sacrificial victim—the most common method of divination in Babylonia. He draws the arrow which indicates "Jerusalem," raises the battle-cry, and sets off to besiege the city. The citizens of Jerusalem (v. 23) discredit the divination, still hoping that Rabbah will be Nebuchadrezzar's objective, so that they may have time to obtain succor from Egypt. But vain is their hope, says Jehovah: their wickedness has sealed their fate.

The day of doom has dawned also for that profane rascal (Zedekiah) *the prince*. Turban—symbol of priestly functions—and crown are to be stripped from him. Everything shall be turned upside down; the city shall be ruined and so remain until the Messiah of Jehovah's appointing shall appear (vv. 24–27.)

19. After *one land* read *set up a mark showing the road to either city, to Rabbah . . .* **20.** For *the defenced* read *in her midst*, with LXX. **22.** Omit the first *to set battering rams*. **23.** The meaning of v. 23b is obscure; *he* is referred variously to Nebuchadrezzar, Jehovah, and Zedekiah. Kraetzschmar sees a reference to the incident of Jer. 34[8]. **27.** For *it; this also shall be no more* read, with LXX, *her; woe to her! thus shall she be* ("her" = Jerusalem). The end of the verse echoes Gen. 49[10].

28–32. For Ammon, too, the Sword! This short oracle is probably the work not of Ezekiel, who treats of Ammon in ch. 25, but of a redactor who wishes to see in this context a punishment for Ammon parallel to that of Judah. It is largely a mosaic of phrases from what precedes, and is in detail very obscure. In v. 28 *reproach* has in view Ammon's taunt (25[3]). V. 30 has been variously interpreted as Jehovah's sword or Ammon's. *Brutish men* (v. 31) probably refers to marauding Bedouin.

CHAPTER XXII

1–16. The Sins of the City. Ezekiel is to arraign Jerusalem, city of bloodshed (cf. 24[6, 9], and, of Nineveh, Nah. 3[1]), and pronounce her doom. Her conduct has been such as to procure her woeful end; she shall be the derision of nations far and near. The scions of the royal house have set the example of wickedness, which the rest of the inhabitants have copied. Reverence for parents, kindness to unprotected folk like the resident alien, the orphan and the widow—the old Hebrew virtues—have been discarded. Things sacred to Jehovah, such as the Sabbath, have been profaned. Slanderers have procured the deaths of their victims. Infractions of the cultus and sexual sins have abounded. Citizens have been the victims of bribery and usury. Jehovah claps his hands (21[17]) and taunts Jerusalem; even her effrontery will fail in the day of doom when he exiles her inhabitants and thus destroys the corruption which has profaned him among the nations.

3. *A city*—better, with LXX, *Woe to the city*. **4.** *Days*—better, *day*, on basis of Targum; *and art come . . . years*—rather, *and hast brought about the time* (=*limit*) *of thy years*, with some MSS, and versions. **5.** For *tumult* cf. Amos 3[9]. **7.** On this cf. Ex. 20[12] 21[17]. **8.** The verse apparently breaks the context and may be an insertion. **9.** Cf. Lev. 19[16, 26] Jer. 6[28] 9[3]; *upon the mountains*—cf. 18[6], note. With **10** cf. Lev. 12[2] 18[7, 19] 20[11]; with **11** cf. Lev. 18[15] 20[12]; with **12** cf. Ex. 22[25] 23[8]. **16.** For *and thou shalt be profaned in thyself* read, with support in versions, *through which I am profaned in thee*.

17–22. Oracle of the Furnace. As mixed metals are smelted in a furnace with a fierce heat, so shall the various classes of the inhabitants of Jerusalem and its environs suffer in the city under the fierce heat of Jehovah's wrath. The reference is to the siege. In v. 18 delete *of silver*, and insert *silver* before *brass;* cf. v. 20.

23–31. An Arraignment of the Several Classes in the Community of Jerusalem. This indictment arraigns ruling princes, priests—the position of these, next to the ruling house, shows Ezekiel's estimate of their importance—officers, prophets, and finally—like priest like people—the common folk. The latter part of the oracle suggests that the disaster may already have befallen the city, and the oracle may have been added later to the two preceding ones, which presumably date from before the end of the final siege.

24. For *cleansed* read *rained upon; rained upon* which follows is a stronger synonym of this. **25.** For *there is a conspiracy of her prophets* read, with LXX, *whose princes are;* the prophets are dealt with in v. 28; *souls* = *men.* **27.** *Princes*—a different word from that suggested for v. 25, and used of less exalted persons, almost = *officers;* wolves rather than lions. **28.** Cf. 13[10-16]. **30.** Cf. 13[5].

CHAPTER XXIII

Oholah and Oholibah. The main theme of this chapter, with which cf. ch. 16, is the political alliances of Samaria and Judah, who figure as two sisters, Oholah and Oholibah. These alliances are regarded as disloyalty to Jehovah, and in the figure become adultery. The clearness of the figure is blurred by a secondary theme, the acceptance of the religious practices of the allies, also regarded as adultery. The text contains numerous glosses and corruptions; the ancient versions differ considerably from the Massoretic text.

1–4. The Youthful Sins of the Two Sisters. Samaria and Judah are pictured as sisters in 16[45f.], where Sodom makes a third. It is noteworthy that v. 3 appears to regard them as existing separately during the Egyptian sojourn: this is in a sense true, for the division of the kingdoms was fundamentally due to a division between the Judah and Ephraim tribes which went back to earliest times. *The whoredoms in Egypt* (cf. 16[26] 20[8]) must be religious rather than political disloyalty, though either is difficult to reconcile with v. 4, according to which it is subsequently that Jehovah takes the two sisters to wife. This last is a surprising feature in the allegory, because Lev. 18[18] prohibits a man from marrying two sisters; but it was a custom in the patriarchal period (cf. the case of Jacob). The names *Oholah* and *Oholibah* probably mean exactly the same thing—"one who possesses tents for (idol) worship" (cf. 16[16]). Schmidt thinks the names come from a folk-story adapted by the prophet—a theory which might account for some of the discordances in the chapter—and that no stress should be laid on their meaning. The date of the earlier part of the chapter may be the same as that of 22[1-22]. **3.** A preferable reading here is *were bruised* for *they bruised.* **4.** *And as for . . . Oholibah* is probably a (correct) gloss.

5–10. The Further Sin and Punishment of Oholah. Samaria, fascinated by the military prowess of the Assyrians, enters into political relations with them, consequently contaminating the worship of Jehovah by adopting Assyrian religious practices. (Assyria entered into relations with Samaria in the reign of Menahem; cf. 2 Kings 15[19].) Jehovah punishes her by handing her over to the Assyrians, who besiege her—*discovered her nakedness,* v. 10, may refer to the razing of the walls—and deport her citizens. **5.** Delete *neighbors* or emend to *men of renown;* the Assyrians were not neighbors, but came *from far* (cf. v. 40). **6.** For *blue* read, rather, *violet-purple.* It is possible that the references to the Assyrians are (correct) glosses.

11–21. The Further Sins of Oholibah. The fate of Oholah did not deter her sister, who contracted alliances with Assyria (vv. 12f.), Babylon (vv. 14–18), and Egypt (vv. 19–21). Assyrian cults appear in Judah from the time of Ahaz (cf. 2 Kings 16[10f.]), and especially after the death of Hezekiah (cf. on 2 Kings 21[3-6]). The references to Babylon may have in view the incident in 2 Kings 20[12f]. Kraetzschmar thinks of an embassy after the defeat of Pharaoh-necoh at Carchemish, 605 B.C. Jerusalem remained faithful to Babylon but three years (cf. 2 Kings 24[1]), and then reverted to her Egyptian love. Our knowledge of the political history of the period is fragmentary.

12. On *neighbors* cf. note, v. 5; *most gorgeously*—rather *with violet-purple.* **14.** The reference here is to pictures in relief—probably upon walls—outlined in vermilion (cf. the pictures of gods, 8[10]). Foreign art is anathema to the prophet. **15.** Instead of *exceeding in dyed attire,* render *with swelling turbans;* possibly all after *look upon* is a gloss. **20.** *Asses* and *horses* were proverbially lustful (cf. 16[26] Jer. 2[24] 5[8] 13[27]). **21.** The change to second person is difficult; the verse is probably interpolated. In the place of *for* read *to press* (cf. v. 5.).

22–30. The Punishment of Oholibah. Oholibah, like her sister, is to be delivered into the power of the lovers she had learned to loathe. With a great army shall the Babylonians come up against Jerusalem, and execute Jehovah's judgment upon her; she shall suffer the atrocities usually inflicted upon defeated foes by the Babylonians. **23.** This is probably an interpolation; *Pekod, Shoa, Koa:* names of nations east of Babylonia, appearing in Assyrian as Pukûdu, Sutû, Kutû. **24.** *Weapons*—an unknown word; read *a multitude of;* LXX has "from the North." **25.** The first *residue* here would naturally mean "descendants." If so, the latter part of the verse must be deleted; the *sons* and *daughters* cannot be slain and then deported; the second *residue* seems to refer to the buildings destroyed by fire; the word is not likely to have been used in such different senses in one verse. **26.** Comes too late, and should be deleted, or removed to another context. Vv. 28–30 furnish a parallel to the preceding verses stating the punishment in more general terms. **28.** *Will*—better, *am about to.* **29.** *Labor*—render *earnings.* A full stop should be placed after *discovered;* then read, joining to v. 30, *Thy lewdness and thy whoredoms have done this for thee.*

31–35. The Cup of Bitterness. The punishment is now pictured as the drinking of a cup filled with bitterness, a favorite metaphor in the Bible (cf. Jer. 25[15] Psa. 75[8] Mt. 26[39] Rev. 16.) **32.** Here delete *thou shalt . . . derision,* with LXX and Old Latin. **33.** *Drunkenness* is an unnatural parallel for *sorrow;* many would emend to *destruction.* **34.** The meaning of *gnaw the sherds thereof* is uncertain; the text may be corrupt.

36–49. The Sins and Punishment of the Two Sisters. This section, largely a mosaic of fragments from earlier passages, is of later date, and not Ezekiel's. Judah and Samaria were not, as is here assumed, punished simultaneously. Hölscher even suggests that a writer who desired to obscure the harsh judgments on Samaria and Judah represented Oholah and Oholibah as real women, punished as an example to their fellows. In vv. 38f. probably delete (*in*) *the same day,* with LXX. **41.** *Stately*—LXX reads *spread with a coverlet* (cf. Prov. 7[16]). **42.** This is incurably corrupt in the middle. **45.** On the usual interpretation *righteous men* refers to Assyrians and Babylonians as executing the righteous decrees of Jehovah. But this seems forced.

CHAPTER XXIV

1–14. The Stew in the Rusty Caldron. In order to guarantee his having received the intimation in a supernatural way, before the news could have reached Babylonia, Ezekiel is directed to record a certain day as that upon which Nebuchadrezzar has invested Jerusalem (2 Kings 25[1]). He is also to speak a parable of a caldron in which choice pieces of meat and bones are stewing over a fierce heat (vv. 1–5). **2.** For *the day . . . selfsame day* read simply *this day.* **4.** For *the pieces thereof* read with LXX and Syriac *pieces.* **5.** For *pile* perhaps read *kindle;* for the first *bones* read *wood;* for *make it boil well* read *boil its pieces.*

In vv. 6–8 it is made clear that the caldron represents Jerusalem; the stains of blood shed in Jerusalem are represented by *rust* in the caldron. The choice pieces and bones are the leading citizens who, after suffering the pains of the siege, represented by the fire, are to be removed *en masse;* vv. 7f. may be inserted to explain that the blood shed is that of children sacrificed: it is an old Semitic idea that shed blood cries out to heaven for vengeance (Gen. 4[10]). Were the exiles after the first siege selected by *lot?* (V. 6.) Jehovah will cause Jerusalem to suffer the heat of his wrath (vv. 9–12), because she can in no other way be purged of her bloodstains, even as the rust of the caldron can be removed only by setting it empty upon the fire till it becomes a mass of molten metal. **10.** *Make thick the broth* is in Hebrew *spice the spicing.* A slight emendation, with some support from LXX, gives *empty out the broth;* LXX omits *and let the bones be burned.* **12.** LXX also omits *She hath wearied herself with toil.* The remainder of the verse is misplaced here. **13, 14.** These give a statement in general terms of Jehovah's unalterable intention to purge the city in the fury of his wrath.

The order of vv. 1–14 is illogical, the two themes of the stewing meat and the rust being entangled. Rearrangement of the verses has been proposed to improve the logical sequence. Some think that the stewing refers to the siege of 597 B.C., the melting of the empty pot to the final disaster in 586.

15–27. Ezekiel's Abstention From Mourning His Wife's Death—a Symbol. Jehovah announces that Ezekiel's wife is about to die suddenly, but forbids him to perform the customary mourning rites. Next morning he is to speak to the people (cf. v. 18, note). When they ask an explanation of his unnatural conduct, he says Jehovah is about to profane his sanctuary—as precious to them as Ezekiel's wife to him. They too must abstain from mourning. The day of the Temple's destruction will release him from his dumbness (cf. 3[26]). He will now be free to prophesy and not limited to special occasions when Jehovah definitely instructs him to open his mouth. **16.** *Stroke*—a word used of sudden death; we cannot suppose that Jehovah causes the death merely to use it as a symbol. **17.** *Not aloud,* i.e., gently, in contrast to the customary loud wailing; *headtire*—cf. Lev. 10[6]; *cover . . . lips*—it was customary in mourning to veil the lower part of the face and the beard; for *men* read *mourning,* with Syriac and Vulgate. **18.** For *so I spake* read *and thou shalt speak.* Probably instructions as to what the prophet should say have been lost from the text. **21.** For *will* read *am about to;* for *your soul pitieth* read *you are concerned for*—the meaning of *set their heart* (v. 25). **22.** *Men*—cf. v. 17, note. **22f.** These are a gloss on or parallel to v. 24. **25–27.** *The day* would naturally be that of the Temple's destruction. But 33[22] dates the termination of Ezekiel's dumbness to the later day when a fugitive from Jerusalem reaches him. Some would delete v. 26 and *to him which is escaped* (v. 27) as insertions to harmonize this discord. Ehrlich takes *that day* as *about that time*, which is unlikely.

CHAPTERS 25 TO 32: ORACLES AGAINST FOREIGN NATIONS

CHAPTER XXV

Oracles Against Four Neighboring Peoples. These follow a clockwise geographical order, beginning in the northeast and working round to west. Ammon, Moab, and Edom were closely allied by race and language with Judah; Philistia was a near neighbor in the southwest. The date of the oracles is later than the fall of Jerusalem.

1–7. Against Ammon. Ammon appears early as a foe of Israel, in the stories of Ehud and Jephthah. When Jehoiakim rebelled against Nebuchadrezzar, Ammon and Moab, presumably as Nebuchadrezzar's agents, attacked Judah (cf. 2 Kings 24[2]). On the other hand, Jer. 27[1f.] shows Ammon, Moab, and Edom seeking the alliance of Zedekiah (cf. Jer. 27[1], mg.). In Jer. 41[10] we find Ammon backing Ishmael, who murdered Gedaliah, and Jer. 49[1f.] tells us that Ammon profited by Judah's distress and succeeded in annexing some of her territory. Even Judas Maccabæus found Ammon still hostile. Ammon's crime is malicious joy at Judah's discomfiture (cf. Obad. v. 12). Her punishment is devastation by hordes of Bedouin. **3.** *Unto*—render *regarding. Aha*—an exclamation of hostile glee. **4.** For *will* read *am about to.* **5.** *Rabbah*—Ammon's chief city; for *children* read *cities;* for *ye shall* read *thou shalt.* Vv. 6f. form a separate oracle.

8–11. Against Moab. For early strife with Moab cf. Ehud (Judg. 3[12f.]). Moab's crime is scorn of Judah because the latter's misfortunes had disproved her claim to be a "peculiar people." Moab's territory is to be opened to the marauding Bedouin. **8.** Delete *and Seir*, with LXX. *Seir* = Edom, dealt with in the next oracle. **10.** *To go against*—render *as well as* (*the land of*); emend the second *the children of Ammon*, to read *they*, i.e., the Moabites.

12–14. Against Edom. Edom, more closely akin to Judah, is the more bitterly reproached for profiting at Judah's expense. *Teman, Dedan* (v. 13)—extreme north and south points; v. 14 may be interpolated; Ehrlich emends to make Jehovah, not Israel, the avenger, as in the preceding oracles.

15–17. Against Philistia. Our knowledge of Philistia is fragmentary; she was allied with Judah against Assyria. The charge against her is obscure, the penalty vague. *Cherethites* (v. 16) = Philistines; the synonym possibly hints at a Cretan origin.

CHAPTER XXVI

Tyre is the theme of 26[1]–28[19]. Tyre was at this time the chief Phœnician state. Her action in seeking alliance with Zedekiah (Jer. 27[1-3]) against Nebuchadrezzar would condemn her in Ezekiel's eyes; he regarded the enemies of Babylon as opposing the will of Jehovah. (No oracle against Babylon appears in Ezekiel.) Her luxurious civilization would also be an offense to the prophet. Her island situation made her almost impregnable. In 701–696 B.C. Sennacherib deprived her of her territory on the mainland, but failed to capture Tyre herself. In 585 B.C. Nebuchadrezzar began a siege of Tyre that lasted thirteen years, but failed to take the city, though he reduced its power. Alexander the Great in 332 B.C. at last took the city by making a dam from the mainland to the island.

1–6. Tyre's Mockery of Jerusalem to be Punished. Tyre has gloated over the fall of Jerusalem because an important trade rival has been removed (?). Therefore Jehovah will bring *many nations* (v. 3) against her; they are the peoples compelled to march in Nebuchadrezzar's army. Her buildings shall be destroyed, and even the dust of the debris swept into the sea that encircles her, so that her site will be bare enough for the spreading of fishermen's nets. The number of the month has been accidentally omitted in v. 1; the date must be subsequent to the fall of Jerusalem. **2.** *Gate*—this is plural in Hebrew; Rothstein emends to "trade," or "trafficker." The Hebrew word is not one likely to be used for "a channel of commerce," and evidence, on the whole, does not suggest that Jerusalem was an important commercial city. The interpretation given above is therefore dubious. *I shall . . . that she:* LXX and Targum, "she that was full." **6.** *Daughters . . . in the field*—the mainland towns belonging to Tyre.

7–14. Nebuchadrezzar and His Armies. The many nations (v. 3) are now definitely explained as Nebuchadrezzar's army, and the siege-warfare is described in detail. Ezekiel assumes that cavalry will be as terrifying to Tyre as to the Hebrews; how horses and siege-trains are to be brought to the island he does not say. There were two famous *pillars* (v. 11) at the entrance to the chief temple, similar to but more splendid than those of Solomon's Temple (1 Kings 7[15-22]). **7.** *Nebuchadrezzar*—this is the more correct form of the Babylonian king's name. After *horsemen* emend, with LXX, *and an assemblage of many nations.* 8. *Buckler*—a large wicker structure for protection against missiles hurled from walls. 9. *Axes*—cf. mg., *swords.* It seems (Ex. 20[25]) that "sword" may be used for "iron tool." 11. For *go* read *he cast.* 12. For *they* read *he* each time, with LXX; and for *waters* read *sea.*

15–21. **Universal Consternation and Lamentation.** The maritime peoples will tremble, seeing in the fate of the seemingly invincible city the forerunner of their own downfall; their rulers will perform appropriate mourning ceremonies. When Jehovah causes the army of Nebuchadrezzar to raze Tyre to the ground as clean as though the hungry waves surging round had devoured her, he will bring her (now personified) down into Sheol (cf. p. 173), the place of shades, and she shall vanish forever from the life of earth.

15. *The isles*—as in Deutero-Isaiah, the word includes the Mediterranean coastlands. 17. *Lamentation*—a *qinah*, or dirge (cf. p. 710a); delete *art thou destroyed* with LXX; for *that wast . . . men* read *art thou ceased from the sea,* with support from versions. 20. *And I will set glory* is corrupt; read (?) *so that thou remainest no more in thy place.*

CHAPTER XXVII

1–9a. **Splendor and Glory of Tyre.** Vv. 1–3 are introductory. Ezekiel is instructed by Jehovah to utter a dirge for Tyre, which prides herself on her incomparable beauty. Her boast is true! Bounded on all sides by the sea, she is like a fair ship built of the most costly materials. Her planks are of fir-tree from Hermon (cf. Deut. 3[9]), her mast of Lebanon cedar. Oak of Bashan (cf. Isa. 2[13]) are her oars. Her boards are of ivory and cypress from the far Mediterranean isles. Her sail is Egyptian linen of checkered colors, the awning of her cabin purple from Elishah. As her materials are most splendid, so are her mariners most skilled: Sidon and Arvad furnish rowers, Semer (for *Tyre,* v. 8) pilots; the ship's carpenters are the elders of Gebal.

3. *Entry*—Tyre's natural situation made her the gate through which the commerce of the Mediterranean flowed into Asia; *isles*—cf. 26[15], note. 4. *Borders*—rather strange of a ship: perhaps we should accept Bertholet's conjecture "they [the builders] made thee great." 6. *Boxwood*—the *teasshur tree* (= cypress?); *Kittim* is usually supposed to be Cyprus, but probably includes other territories. 7. Delete *that it might be to thee for an ensign;* flags were not used for ships at this time; *Elishah*=Carthage(?). Cf. Gen. 10[4]. 8. *Zidon,* or "Sidon," a neighboring Phœnician town, at this time overshadowed by Tyre; *Arvad,* the island Ruad, eighty miles north of Sidon; for *Tyre* probably read *Semer,* a town northeast of Tripolis.

9b–25. See below, following vv. 26–36.

26–36. **Destruction and Resulting Construction.** The majestic ship—Tyre—has been rowed into raging billows, and broken up by an easterly gale. Cargo and crew alike fall into the depths of the ocean. The drowning mariners' cries resound over the sea. The terrified sailors in other vessels, abandoning their ships, seek the shore and mourn bitterly for Tyre. They raise for her the death-dirge; she, the incomparable, is brought to doom! In her days of prosperity her wares had supplied the nations and enriched their kings, but now her wares have sunk with her sailors in the ocean depths! The portent fills peoples and kings with horror. But rival trading peoples exult triumphantly over her fate—she is become a legend of terror, and shall be seen no more. 26. *Great*=tempestuous; cf. Psa. 77[19]. 27. This verse is overloaded with details from vv. 9b–25. 28. *Suburbs*—the text is corrupt and unintelligible. 30f. On these cf. 7[18] 1 Sam. 4[12] Job 2[8, 12]. 32. For *brought to silence* read, with versions, *destroyed.*

9b–25. **Nations Trading with Tyre.** This catalogue of nations trading with Tyre, and their exports, breaks the figure of Tyre as a ship, and is evidently a later insertion. It may come from Ezekiel, who loves detailed minutiæ. It shows us the magnitude of Tyre's commercial activities, and that for luxury her civilization compared with that of Babylon. The text contains many rare—and some unintelligible—words, and has suffered in transmission.

9. In the place of *occupy* read mg. 10. *Persia*—the earliest mention of Persia in the O.T., and, if correct, strengthens the suspicion that the passage is not Ezekiel's. Herrmann argues that an African nation is intended, perhaps the Pharusii of classical writers; *Lud* is probably near Egypt (cf. Gen. 10[13]), rather than the Lud=Lydia of Gen. 10[22]; *Put* is Abyssinia. 11. *With thine army*—another proper name would be expected here; an easy emendation would give "and of Hilakh," a people named in cuneiform documents; for *the Gammadim* LXX reads *watchmen.* 12. *Tarshish*= Tartessus in Spain. 13. *Javan*=Ionia, or Greece; for Greeks as slave-traders cf. Joel 3[6]; *Tubal and Meshech*—the Tabali and Mushki of Assyrian records, the former dwelling southeast of the Black Sea, the latter, their Eastern neighbors. 14. *The house of Togarmah*—render

"Beth-Togarmah," a people dwelling in the Taurus, a noted horse country. **15.** *Dedan* appears again in v. 20; read here, with LXX, *Rodan*, but whether this is Rhodes is dubious. **16.** For *Syria* the name *Edom*, read by MSS., and supported by versions, should be substituted; *Damascus*—Syria appears in v. 18; *emeralds*—perhaps *malachite; purple, broidered work, and fine linen*—out of place between the precious stones. Nor would Tyre import purple, for which she herself was renowned. Therefore read *emeralds and topaz*, as suggested by LXX; for the erroneous *coral* read *ramoth-stone*.

17. *Minnith* is in Ammon, not Judah (cf. Judg. 11[33]). Read with Cornill (cf. mg.), *wheat and spice (tragacanth gum) and wax and honey* (cf. Gen. 37[25] 43[11].) **18.** For *and white wool* read *and of Zimmin*. Cornill notes that "wine of Helbon" is mentioned on an Assyrian wine list and on a cylinder of Nebuchadrezzar; "wine of Zimmin" also appears on the former. Helbon lies northwest of Damascus. **19.** For *Vedan and Javan* read *they traded for thy wares*, joining to v. 18, and continue, *From Uzal wrought iron* . . . (cf. Gen. 10[27]). **20.** *Dedan*, in northwest Arabia. **21.** *Kedar*, the Syro-Arabian Bedouin. **22.** *The traffickers of*—an obvious error for a place-name. Cornill proposes "Havilah" (Gen. 2[11]); *Sheba*, in southwest Arabia; *Raamah*, in Arabia (Gen. 10[7]). **23.** *Haran* in the middle Euphrates district; *Canneh*—a people called Kannu appears in cuneiform records; *Eden*—the district Bit-Adini in Babylonia; *the traffickers of Sheba*—an accidental repetition; read, with LXX, *thy traffickers they were*. For *Chilmad* read *all Media*. **24.** *Chests of . . . merchandise* perhaps should be "carpets woven in colors and strongly bound skeins." **25.** *Ships of Tarshish*, i.e., ships fit for long-distance voyages. Toy compares "argosies," derived from "Ragusa" (=going) ships (cf. Jonah 1[3]). This verse forms a transition to the following part of the oracle, which part may, indeed, include v. 25b.

26–36. See above, following vv. 1–9a.

CHAPTER XXVIII

1–10. Against the Ruler of Tyre. The king of Tyre at this time was Ithobaal II. How far the charge against him is personal, and how far it treats him as the symbol of the national pride we cannot say. His proud seat in his secure island dominion induces him to liken himself to a god sitting on an inaccessible throne. He thinks himself supreme in the wisdom which he has employed to the increase of the traffic of Tyre and his own enrichment. His wealth has made him arrogant. But God will bring against him the Babylonians, most terrible of nations in the ruthlessness of their military activities; they shall destroy the brilliant splendor of his city. Far from sitting upon the throne of a god, he shall be slain and thrust ignominiously down to Sheol. There let him boast his divinity before his executioners!

3. *Daniel*—cf. 14[14], note. The following words are obscure. Herrmann reads *and no wise men are thy equals*, with some support in LXX. **4.** *Treasures*—render rather *treasure-houses*. **7.** *Will*="am about to." **8.** *Pit*—a synonym for "Sheol"; *deaths*—an intensive plural. **9.** Instead of *him that woundeth* read *them that pierce through*. **10.** *Deaths of the uncircumcised*—cf. note, v. 8. Like the Hebrews, the Philistines were circumcised. The phrase is commonly thought to mean that after death the prince will be no better off than the scorned uncircumcised. But probably the Hebrew word (*'ărelîm*) is connected with "Arallu," the Babylonian equivalent to "Sheol," and the phrase is equivalant to "death(s) of the inhabitants of the underworld."

11–19. Against the King of Tyre. Behind this oracle lies a myth concerning the primeval man who dwelt in the garden of the gods, resembling in some features the story of the Garden of Eden, though its points of contrast are even more significant. It probably goes back to primitive Semitic lore, but the references are too vague to dogmatize on the subject. The king of Tyre is likened to the primeval man, made in the divine image and dwelling, together with the cherub, in the garden of God. But through sin he has lost his original likeness to God and is expelled from the holy mountain. Because of his pride and iniquity God has laid him low before conquering kings, who gloat over him. He profaned Jehovah's sanctuary; therefore Jehovah caused fire to come forth from it and consume him. His terrible and irrevocable fate makes him a byword.

12. *Sealest up the sum*—an obscure phrase. Herrmann interprets it as meaning "art made in the divine image"; cf. Gen. 1[27]; *full of wisdom*—omitted in LXX; perhaps a gloss on the preceding words. **13.** The list of precious stones here (cf. Ex. 28[17f.]) is probably interpolated. The remainder of the verse, save the last clause, is unintelligible. **14.** Read, on the basis of LXX, *with the cherub I set thee on the holy mountain . . .; the anointed* and *that covereth* are obscure words, possibly inserted to connect the cherub with the cherubim of 1 Kings 6[23f.]; *mountain of God*—in Semitic mythology the dwelling-place of the gods is a mountain in the far north; the garden will be on the mountain. *Stones of fire*—the meaning of this allusion is unknown, and likely to remain so until the underlying myth is recovered. **15.** The opening words probably mean "Thou retainedst thine original felicity unimpaired." **16.** Omit *by the multitude . . . violence* as an interpolation spoiling the figure; for *I have destroyed . . . cherub* read *and the cherub hath destroyed thee*, on the basis of LXX. **18.** *In the unrighteousness of thy traffic*—delete as gloss on the preceding words; for *thy sanctuaries* read *my sanctuary;* for *midst of the* read, with Ehrlich, *midst of it*.

20–24. Against Zidon. At an earlier date Zidon (=Sidon) had been more important than Tyre, but was at this date subordinate to the latter city. There is no record of any conflict between Sidon and the Hebrews. No reason is assigned in the oracle for Sidon's punishment; perhaps the mere fact that she was an opponent of Babylon would be sufficient to account for an oracle against her. The concluding verse of the oracle gives the reason for these oracles against Judah's neighbors: they must be reduced to impotence so that none of them may be able to trouble the restored Judah to which Ezekiel looks forward. For *they* (v. 22) read *thou*, with LXX; in vv. 22f. for *her* read *thee*, with LXX.

25, 26. A Prophecy of Restoration. When her ancient enemies have been rendered harmless God will restore Israel to Palestine, where her people will be so free from alarm that they may build and plant for permanent occupation. The oracle may be later than the series of denunciations which it interrupts; v. 24 may have led to its insertion.

CHAPTER XXIX

Chapters 29–32 are devoted to oracles against Egypt. Except 30[1-19] these oracles are all dated: 29[17-21], inserted later where it now stands, is dated 571 B.C.; the others range from 588 to 585 B.C., being uttered in the months immediately preceding and following the fall of Jerusalem. The position of the small Palestinian states, between the great empires of Assyria and Babylon on the one side and Egypt on the other, caused Egypt to regard them as a first line of defense against her powerful rivals. She constantly incited them to oppose Assyria and Babylon, and attempted to seduce them from allegiance to her rivals by promises of support. But her promises came to little. She failed to sustain her weaker allies against Sargon (Isa. 20[5f.]), Sennacherib (2 Kings 18[21]), and Nebuchadrezzar (Jer. 37[5-8]). For her persistent attempts to divert Judah from the path which the prophets believed to be chosen of Jehovah Egypt incurs their sustained hostility (cf. Isa. 30[1f.] 31[1f.] Jer. 2[36]).

1–16. Oracle Against the Pharaoh. Seven months before the fall of Jerusalem the prophet receives this oracle against the Pharaoh—the reigning Pharaoh was Hophra—and Egypt. The Pharaoh is likened to a huge crocodile, claiming to be the creator of the Nile in which he lives. Jehovah will catch him with hooks—a method practiced, according to Herodotus, by the Egyptians—and throw his body on the desert sands, where he will inevitably perish. There is probably looming before Ezekiel's vision a coming battle between Nebuchadrezzar and Hophra, to be fought in the desert. The Pharaoh's carcass shall lie unburied, to be consumed by vultures and wild beasts. Rather grotesquely, the Pharaoh's subjects are pictured as little fishes adhering to his scales and sharing his fate. Thus shall they learn the power of Jehovah, who is incensed at their treatment of his people. Egypt is like a walking-stick made of hollow cane, which—so far from sustaining—breaks and pierces the hand that leans upon it (cf. 32[1-10]).

Jehovah will bring an army against Egypt, and all living creatures therein shall be destroyed. For her arrogance she shall become a desolate untrodden wilderness, from the extreme northern to the extreme southern boundary. Her inhabitants are to be dispersed, like the Jews, among the nations; but after forty years Jehovah will bring back the descendants of the exiled Egyptians, and they shall establish a kingdom confined to the southern part of Egypt, a kingdom so insignificant that it will never more seduce Israel, or, by causing Israel to sin, call Jehovah's attention to that sin.

The change from Pharaoh to Egypt as subject is possible, on the ground that the king is the symbol for his country: but it must be admitted that the passage seems hardly to be a consistent unity. It is difficult to reconcile vv. 8 and 12. Herrmann feels that vv. 13–16 are so much out of keeping that he attributes them to Ezekiel's old age, and accordingly deletes *forty years* from vv. 11f. Whether they belong at all to Ezekiel is extremely doubtful.

1. LXX has a later date than is given here, probably supposing that the passage must be later than 26[1]. **3.** The crocodile was worshiped in Egypt, and appears as a symbol on late Egyptian coins; *rivers*—a peculiar word, used in singular and plural specifically of the Nile; delete *for myself*, with versions. Herrmann proposes to retain the suffix thus rendered, and translate *I have made myself*—a phrase used by the Egyptian god Ra. This would be very dubious Hebrew. **5.** For *gathered* read *buried*, with MSS. and Targum (cf. Jer. 25[33]). **6.** For *they have* versions read *thou hast.* **7.** For *thy* read *the*, with MSS. support; for *shoulders* read *hands*, with versions support; for *be at a stand* read mg. **9.** For *he hath* read *thou hast*, with versions. **10.** Read mg. Migdol is the northernmost town; Syene, the modern Assouan, the southernmost. **14.** *Pathros*—the southern part of Egypt, from which the Egyptians originally came; *base* = lowly; cf. 17[14].

17–21. Egypt Shall Be Nebuchadrezzar's Prey. Dated 571, the oracle must have been inserted here, possibly by Ezekiel himself, after the other oracles had been collected. Nebuchadrezzar failed in his thirteen years siege to capture Tyre, though his soldiers labored till their helmets had worn off their hair, and their burdens chafed away their skin. But in this campaign he was acting as Jehovah's agent: he must not be denied his wages. So the wealth of Egypt shall be looted by him in a victorious campaign (cf. Isa. 43[3]). Appended is a verse promising prosperity to Israel—the *horn*, v. 21, probably has no Messianic significance—in that day, when Ezekiel, who seemed discredited by the failure of his prophecy against Tyre, would be able to speak again, because this new prophecy was fulfilled. **19.** LXX omits *and he shall carry off her multitude.* If the words are retained, render *wealth* for *multitude.* **20.** Delete *because they wrought for me*, with support from versions. **21.** *Horn*—cf. Psa. 132[17]; *opening of the mouth*—cf. 16[63].

CHAPTER XXX

Vv. 1–19 consist of a series of five undated oracles. The passage probably embodies scattered material collected from various sources and inserted here.

1–5. A Day of Doom for Egypt Is at Hand. **3.** *Of clouds;* "cloudy" is a standing epithet of the "Day of Jehovah," but whether that idea is in view here is doubtful. By a simple emendation Ehrlich gets "of peoples"—an excellent parallel to what follows, where for *heathen* render *nations.* **4.** *And they shall take away her multitude*—probably delete; cf. 29[19], note. **5.** *Put, Lud*—cf. 27[10], note; for *mingled people* perhaps read *Arabians; Cub*—unknown; error (?) for Lub = Lybians; *land that is in league*—an unintelligible expression. Comparison with versions suggests "Cretans," but the whole verse is probably interpolated.

6–12. Egypt Shall Be Utterly Destroyed and Made Desolate. In v. 6 read mg.; in v. 7 for *they* read *she*, with LXX. **9.** *Ships*—LXX suggests "haste"; *careless*—delete, with LXX. According to vv. 10–12 Nebuchadrezzar shall be the instrument causing Egypt's doom. **12.** *Rivers*—render *Nile.* The drying up of the Nile would in itself suffice to make Egypt a desert.

13–19. The Cities of Egypt Shall Know the Vengeance of Jehovah. The cities are named without regard to geographical order; several of the names are corrupt, and it is improbable that the passage belongs to Ezekiel. **13.** For *idols* read with LXX *great ones*—a good parallel to what follows, where *prince* should be *princes* (so LXX); *Noph* = Memphis; *and I will put a fear in the land of Egypt*—delete, with LXX. **14.** *Pathros*—cf. 29[14], note; *Zoan* = Tanis; *No* = Thebes. **15.** *Sin* = Pelusium. **16.** The repetition of names here is suspicious: for *Sin* perhaps read *Syene*, with LXX; *and Noph shall have adversaries in the day-time*—undoubtedly corrupt; Cornill emends *and her walls shall be razed.* **17.** For *Aven* read *On* = Heliopolis; *Pi-beseth* = Bubastis. **18.** *Tehaphnehes* = Daphnæ (cf. Jer. 2[16]); for *withdraw itself* read mg.; for *yokes* read *scepters*, with LXX.

20–26. Oracles Against Pharaoh. The date is 587 B.C. The reference in v. 21 may be to the abortive attempt of Egypt to relieve Jerusalem from the grip of Nebuchadrezzar (cf. Jer. 37[5f.]; cf. 34[21f.]). With v. 22 begins another oracle based on a similar figure, but this time both Pharaoh's arms are to be broken, and the king of Babylon is named as his opponent. The words *the strong, and that which was broken*, v. 22, should be deleted as an infelicitous attempt to weave the two oracles together. **21.** *Roller* = bandage. **26.** This, save for its last clause, is a duplicate of v. 23; vv. 22–26 read like two parallel versions of one oracle interwoven.

CHAPTER XXXI

Warning Against Pharaoh. The strange blending of symbol and reality in this allegory is almost inconceivable if we regard the chapter as a literary production; it recalls the kaleidoscopic changes of a dream, and its incongruities may perhaps be explained on the ground that the oracle was received in vision. The past tenses of vv. 10–12 are "prophetic," representing, as often in Hebrew, an event certain to occur as having already happened.

1–9. Pharaoh's Exaltation. The oracle is dated just before the fall of Jerusalem. Ironically the question is put to Pharaoh—who is comparable in greatness with him? He is like a *teasshur* tree, so mighty in growth that his top pierces the clouds. The subterranean ocean waters his deep roots, whereas other trees must content themselves with mere rills.

His branches furnish nesting-places for the birds and shade for the beasts. He was more magnificent than the trees in God's garden, and the object of their envy.

3. *The Assyrian*—the force of this would be that as great Assyria had perished so would Egypt. Though Ehrlich defends the reading, it is generally agreed that we should emend to *a teasshur tree*. This tree, rendered "box," forms the climax to lists of trees, Isa. 41[19] 60[13], and in the latter passage is associated with Lebanon (cf. 27[6], note); *was a cedar in Lebanon*—probably a gloss on *teasshur; and with a shadowing shroud*—omitted in versions, dubious Hebrew; for *thick boughs* read mg., with LXX. **4.** *Deep*=the primeval subterranean ocean; for *her plantation* read *his plantation*, with LXX and Syriac. The point is that, whereas his roots run deep into the subterranean ocean, the other trees receive merely small channels of water: this explains the first statement in v. 5. In this verse (5) probably delete *when he shot them forth*, with LXX. **6.** *And under his shadow dwelt all great nations*—a (correct) gloss, explaining what is meant by the birds and beasts.

10–14. The Punishment of His Pride. His magnificence has made him arrogant. Now the figure is replaced by the reality for which it stands—the Pharaoh is delivered into the power of Babylon. In v. 12 the figure is resumed: the branches of the felled tree cover mountains and valleys—possibly the reality symbolized is the covering of the land by the corpses of Pharaoh's soldiers. The birds now rest, not on his branches, but on his fallen trunk—the meaning of *ruin*, v. 13—while the beasts crush his branches. Here is a lesson for all trees to avoid such arrogance! All trees alike, i.e., all nations, must come at last to the shades of Sheol. **10.** For *thou art* read *he is*, with Syriac and Vulgate; *thick boughs*—cf. v. 3, note. **11.** For *will even deliver* read *have delivered; he shall surely deal with him*—corrupt and unintelligible; *I have driven him out for his wickedness* seems misplaced here, and would be more suitable in 28[13f]. **12.** Here all that follows *land* should possibly be omitted (cf. v. 6, note). **14.** *Thick boughs*—cf. v. 3, note.

15–18. The Mourning and Dread of His Compeers. As the coastlands mourned for Tyre, so the waters and trees mourn for the fate of the mighty tree. In v. 16a the reality replaces the symbol—the nations tremble at Egypt's fate; v. 16b returns to symbol—the trees already in Sheol are consoled to think that their fate is no worse than that of the nation they envied. The oracle then returns to the ironic question of v. 2, and briefly recapitulates Pharaoh's doom. **15.** *I caused . . . deep for him*—delete *I covered*, with LXX, and read *I caused the deep to mourn for him.* **17.** The text is corrupt, and the latter part is probably a gloss connected with the glosses in vv. 6 and 12. **18.** *The uncircumcised*—render "the inhabitants of the underworld" (cf. 28[10], note). The final sentence reads like a scribe's comment.

CHAPTER XXXII

1–16. An Oracle of Pharaoh's Doom. Ezekiel is to utter a dirge for Pharaoh—though what follows is rather a threat than an elegy. Pharaoh is likened to a monstrous dragon—by which we are to understand a crocodile—spouting water through his nostrils, and trampling the mud of his river until it becomes turbid. But Jehovah will take him in a net and throw him upon the land, where, removed from his element, he will die. Birds and beasts will batten on his carcass. So huge is the monster that his flesh will cover the mountains and his blood fill the streams. This hardly fits the figure, but probably the poet has in mind the reality—the bodies of Pharaoh's army—for which the symbol stands. In the dread hour of doom darkness will cover Egypt as during the plagues. Nations and kings will be appalled at Pharaoh's terrible fall. When they behold Jehovah brandishing his terrible sword—the sword of Nebuchadrezzar—they will fear for themselves. Egypt shall be plundered by the Babylonians, and bereft of man and beast. No creature shall survive to make the waters turbid with trampling—the surface of the Nile shall be unbroken. By her fate shall Egypt be made to recognize the power of Jehovah. **1.** Some MSS. and versions read "eleventh year" for *twelfth*, which fits better into the sequence of dates: this would give 586 B.C. **2.** *Thou wast likened unto a young lion of the nations* seems out of harmony with the figure of the crocodile. Many emendations have been proposed, but none is convincing. The figure of the net (v. 3) suits a lion; crocodiles were caught with hooks (cf. 29[4], note); for *breakest forth with thy rivers* probably read *spurtest forth water from thy nostrils;* for *their* read *thy*, with LXX. **3.** Delete *with a company of many peoples* as gloss on *net;* for *they shall* read *I will*, with LXX. **5, 6.** Bertholet aptly compares with the boast of Tiglath-Pileser I—"The corpses of their warriors I heaped in heaps upon the mountains; the blood of their warriors I caused to flow over the clefts and heights of the mountains." *Height*—an unknown word; LXX has "blood." Perhaps read *worms*

(=carcass). *Wherein thou swimmest*—Hebrew, "thy outflow"; possibly *thy blood* is a gloss on this; for *thee* read *thy blood*. **7.** *Extinguish*—dubious. Possibly *and when I shall extinguish thee* should be deleted. **9.** For *destruction* read *captives*, with LXX. **12.** *The terrible of the nations*=the Babylonians. **16.** *Daughters of the nations*—professional wailing-women were employed to mourn (cf. Jer. $9^{17f.}$ Mt. 9^{23}). Each nation is a single person in the figure.

17–32. Pharaoh's Descent Into Sheol. Again Ezekiel is bidden to utter a dirge for Egypt and the nations, and such is the efficacy of the prophetic word that by his mere utterance he is said to thrust them down. The text that follows is so disordered and complicated with glosses that it is simpler to describe the main features of the picture than to explain it. In the gloomy underworld there are still distinctions: the heroes of old have a position of pre-eminence, resting with their swords as pillows, their shields as covering. Inferior to them are the "uncircumcised" (cf. 28^{10}, note)—the ordinary dwellers in Sheol. Pharaoh's humiliation is in being relegated to this latter class. Each nation is depicted as occupying a special region. The king—Asshur stands both for king and nation, as "Norway" in Hamlet—is in the midst, surrounded by the graves of his people. So Assyria, Elam, Meshech and Tubal, Edom, the Sidonians, are pictured. The great nations had been sources of dread in the land of the living; now they lie powerless and despised in the nethermost recesses of Sheol. Pharaoh's poor consolation is that they are as badly off as he is (cf. Isa. 14^{3-20}, which may be based on this passage).

17. Insert here "in the first month," with LXX. A mention of Pharaoh would be natural in **18,** since he is the main subject; but king and nation appear to interchange. Probably *even her . . . nations* is a gloss. **19.** This is inserted by LXX in the middle of v. 21, as the speech of the mighty ones to Pharaoh. **20.** V. 20b is corrupt. **22.** *Asshur*—Assyria fell to the Babylonians in 612 B.C. **23.** *Which*—means not *the sword*, but the Assyrians. **24.** *Elam*—conquered by Assyria *cir.* 650 B.C., though it became independent again at the fall of that empire; *shame*—the disgrace of being assigned to the inferior place in Sheol. **26.** *Meshech and Tubal*—cf. 27^{13}, note. **27.** For *that are fallen of the uncircumcised* read, with Cornill, *the giants of antiquity*, with support in versions; *iniquities . . . their bones* gives no meaning, the simple emendation "shield" for *iniquities* (Cornill) is almost certain. V. 28 seems to be the end of the oracle; vv. 29–32 look like a later supplement.

CHAPTER XXXIII

1–9. The Responsibility of a Prophet. The date of this oracle is uncertain; some think it was given during the ecstatic experience of v. 22, but that is improbable. The substitution of the mild *children of thy people* for the earlier form of address, "rebellious house," points to a time subsequent to the news of Jerusalem's fall reaching Ezekiel. The passage may be prefixed to the prophecies of salvation which follow, as a restatement of the prophet's responsibility, for even these are not without their warning note.

The inhabitants of a city appoint a watchman to sound the alarm when the foe approaches the city wall. If he blows the alarm signal, he has done his duty: the citizen who ignores it must pay the penalty of his slackness. If the watchman neglect his duty, the citizen may be slain, but in that case God will hold the watchman responsible. Thus Ezekiel will be responsible only for warning the wicked of the penalty that follows sin, and held guiltless, whatever the wicked may do, provided he has given the warning. The oracle would seem almost to be a message of comfort to the prophet, despondent because his warnings were so little heeded. **2.** For *among them* Ehrlich would render *their ablest man*. **3.** Cf. Amos 3^6. **5.** V. 5b should be emended *but he who has given the warning has saved himself* (*from penalty*). The word *soul* means "self," and is rightly rendered *person* in v. 6. **6.** Read mg. and similarly throughout. **7–9.** Cf. vv. 17–19. **8.** Delete *O wicked man*.

10–20. The Responsibility of the Individual. This oracle is closely connected with the preceding, and repeats the teaching of ch. 18. The exiles realize that they are suffering the penalty of their sins; they are rotting—the literal meaning of *pine away*, v. 10—and have no hope of renewed life. Ezekiel is bidden once again to speak to them the heartening message that no man is the helpless victim of his own past. Not an arithmetical calculation balancing the good and evil deeds of life will determine a man's destiny, but the actual religious condition of the man, as evidenced by his conduct, at the time of judgment. The judgment is, of course, one in this life: there is no conception of immortality involved. Conversely, no man must presume on past right-doing as giving him license to turn to evil ways. The sins specified are, be it noted, ethical. **12.** Delete here *neither shall . . . sinneth* as a parallel to the clause beginning, *The righteousness*. **13.** For *that he shall* read *thou shalt*, with support in versions; alternatively render "concerning the righteous," and "concerning" for *unto* in 14, there changing *thou shalt* to *he shall*, with Ehrlich. 15. *Of life*—i.e., the observance of which saves from the penalty of death.

21–29. **An Oracle Against the Survivors in Judah.** Some six months after the city's fall the news reaches Ezekiel. On the previous evening he had been in a prophetic trance. When he hears the news his dumbness passes. Some time later, as v. 23 implies, he utters this oracle. The Jews in Palestine flatter themselves that, as the only heirs of Abraham left on the estate, all that Jehovah had promised to him and his descendants is now theirs. But, says Jehovah, their ritual and ethical sins utterly disqualify them from possessing the inheritance. His three plagues—sword, wild beasts, and pestilence—shall devour them. The land of promise, flowing with milk and honey, shall be made an uninhabited desolation, and the survivors shall thus know that Jehovah is not to be trifled with. The oracle shows clearly that Ezekiel regarded the exiles as the true inheritors of the promises. 21. Read, with support in MSS. and versions, "eleventh" instead of *twelfth;* the news may have taken six (cf. Ezra 7[9]), but hardly eighteen months to reach Babylon; *one*—the Hebrew word may be collective, and may refer to the deported captives. Schmidt thinks of a messenger sent by Gedaliah at a later date. 22. *Until*—difficult; probably read *when* (cf. 24[27], note). 25. *With the blood*—cf. 18[6], note. 26. *Stand upon your sword*—obscure; the meaning may be "use methods of violence." 28, 29. *Astonishment*—render *devastation.*

30–33. **An Oracle Concerning the Exiles.** The fulfillment of Ezekiel's prediction of the fall of Jerusalem causes him to be talked about when men gather in the cool shade of the walls and porches, and they come in crowds to hear his oracles. Yet they are but hearers, not doers, of his words. His predictions of hope sound pleasant in their ears, but they are deaf to the demand for righteous conduct as a preliminary to the realization of those hopes. A purging judgment is in store for them, and when it comes they shall know that Ezekiel is in truth a prophet. 30. *One to another* and the following clause are doublets. 31. *As the people cometh*—an obscure phrase, possibly meaning "in crowds"; *shew much love*—render *speak flattering things;* LXX and Syriac read *lies; gain*—the Hebrew word always implies "got by injustice or violence." 32. *Very lovely song*—rather, *singer of love-songs.*

CHAPTER XXXIV

1–16. **Against the Rulers of Israel.** In Babylon and Assyria, as by Homer, a king was called the "shepherd of his people." The shepherds of this oracle are the pre-exilic rulers of Judah. They have used the flock to their own profit but have neglected all the duties of a shepherd to his flock: "the hungry sheep look up and are not fed," and now are partly devoured and partly scattered—a reference to the siege and Exile. Jehovah himself will now take the place of these unworthy shepherds. He will gather the dispersed flock and bring it back to his pasture in Palestine. In plain words, Jehovah will be the only king of the exiles, and will restore them to the promised land. The oracle is based on Jer. 23[1-4], and is an anticipation of the N.T. figure of the Good Shepherd. 2. *Even to the shepherds* is a gloss. 3. *Fat*—we may repoint the Hebrew word and render *milk,* with LXX and Vulgate. 4. *But with force and* read, with LXX, *and over the strong.* 12. *That he is among his sheep*—the text here is dubious. Cornill emends *of thunder-storm,* and deletes *that are scattered abroad:* this last is an impossible rendering of the Hebrew, which may, says Ehrlich, be rendered, on Arabic analogy, "wounded by wild beasts." 13. For *inhabited places* read, with Ehrlich, *best;* cf. Gen. 47[6]. 16. *Destroy*—most moderns emend *guard,* which has support in versions. The Hebrew is certainly out of harmony with the rest of the oracle, but possibly correct: for the verse may be a supplement linking the preceding with the following oracle, where the idea would be in place. If the emendation is accepted, render *in the proper way* for *in judgment;* if not, render *with judgment.*

17–22. **Against the Arrogant Aristocracy.** The flock suffers not only from wicked shepherds, but also from sturdy sheep who, not content with eating the best of the pasture and drinking the clearest water, trample and foul what remains. The good shepherd will save the weak sheep from their thrusting fellows. The reference is obviously to the wealthy citizens who oppressed their poor neighbors. Ehrlich's suggestion to connect the concluding words of v. 17 with v. 18—"To the rams and he-goats Jehovah saith 'Seemeth it . . .' "—is attractive.

23–31. **A Messianic Prophecy.** Jehovah will appoint as deputy-shepherd a prince such as David was. In v. 25 the figure is blended with the reality: Jehovah will make a new covenant with his people; evil beasts—which symbolize the marauding neighboring nations—shall be no more. Rains—the essential basis of prosperity in Palestine—shall be regular and abundant, and the country shall flourish. When Jehovah has delivered them from their captors they shall know—not through his fierce anger, but through his gracious kindness —that he is Jehovah. In Ezekiel's prediction the Messiah appears after the restoration, not as its instrument.

23. *David*—Ezekiel does not contemplate a resurrection of David, but the appearance of one who shall have the traditional qualities of David. It will be observed that he is to be *prince,* not king. In contrast to Jeremiah, Ezekiel has no room in his future theocratic state for a king. *One shepherd* may point to a reunited kingdom of Judah and Samaria. **26.** V. 26a should probably be emended *And I will send them abundance of rain;* the Hebrew is certainly corrupt. **27.** *Broken*—he will not stay to loosen the yoke, but suddenly break the bars which hold it together. **29.** *Plantation for renown*—emend, with Ehrlich, *a staff of bread* (cf. 4[16] 5[16] 14[13]).

CHAPTER XXXV

An Oracle against Edom. This is a fuller expression of the thought in 25[12-14]. At first sight it would seem to be more in place with the oracles against foreign nations than here. But it is placed here as foil to ch. 36—doom for Mount Seir in contrast to blessing for the mountains of Israel. That Edom had lent assistance to the Babylonians in their attack on Jerusalem and had profited by her pitiful plight was a crime never forgiven by the Jews (cf. Obad. v. 10 Psa. 137[7]). Here three charges are brought against Edom: (1) her assistance of the Babylonians (v. 5); (2) her attempts to add the territory of the conquered Judah and Samaria to her own (v. 10); (3) her malicious rejoicing over Judah (vv. 12f.). Her punishment is to be desolation.

2. *Mount Seir* = the land of Edom. **3.** *Astonishment*—render *devastation.* **5.** With this cf. Amos 1[11]: the *perpetual enmity* may be traced back to the respective ancestors, Jacob and Esau; *in the time of their calamity*—LXX omits; *iniquity of the end*—read mg.: the meaning is "the final punishment of Jerusalem." **6.** Delete here *I will prepare . . . and pursue thee,* on basis of LXX; for *hast not hated blood* read *art blood-guilty,* with LXX. **7.** *Astonishment and a desolation*—render *desolation and devastation;* the use of the third person suggests that the verse is interpolated. Hence the changes in persons in subsequent verses. **8.** Delete *his mountains,* with LXX; from *his slain* delete *his,* with LXX: *hills* and *valleys* are objects to *fill.* **9.** For *ye shall* read *thou shalt,* with LXX and Syriac. **10.** *Two* = Israel and Judah; for *we* read *I,* with versions; *whereas the Lord was there*—the countries were not ownerless, but still the property of Jehovah. Ehrlich, however, may be right in emending "but the Lord was listening" (cf. v. 13). **11.** *Do*—add *to thee,* with support in versions; for *among them* read *in thee,* with LXX. **12.** For *all* perhaps read *the noise of.* **13.** Read second person singular throughout; and for *have multiplied your words* read *have spoken impudently;* LXX omits these words. **14.** V. 14b is a duplication of v. 15a, and should be deleted. **15.** For *even all of it* possibly read *a destruction; desolate,* literally "a desolation"; for *they shall* read *thou shalt,* with LXX.

CHAPTER XXXVI

1–15. An Oracle for the Mountains of Israel. In contrast to the desolation foretold for Mount Seir (ch. 35) prosperity shall come to the mountains of Israel. Their foes—Edom is particularly in mind—have mocked at their fate and encroached upon them. But Jehovah, incensed at this conduct—especially on the part of Edom, which was left by the Babylonians in possession of its territory (*the residue,* v. 5)—proclaims that these foes shall themselves become objects of such jeering as they had used against Israel. The latter, on the other hand, he will restore to abnormal fertility, and its inhabitants will multiply until not only the recent prosperity of the kingdom but that of the earlier golden age will be exceeded. The frequent repetition of the formula, "Thus saith the Lord," suggests that a number of smaller oracles are here combined.

2. *Ancient high places*—LXX, "the ancient waste places." It is true that Ezekiel would be unlikely himself to use in this connection the abhorrent term "high places," but he might use it in the speech of Israel's detractors. **3.** For *made you desolate* read *snorted at you,* or, even closer to the Hebrew, *rejoiced* (Ehrlich). **5.** *To cast it out for a prey*—corrupt and unintelligible. Vv. 10, 12 are probably expansions of the text; vv. 13–15 change the address from the mountains (plural) to the land (singular), and may be a postscript. **13.** For *you* read *thee,* with LXX and Syriac; *thy nation* = thine own inhabitants. **15.** Delete *neither shalt thou cause . . . more,* with LXX.

16–32. A Promise of a New Heart and Renewed Prosperity. The oracle is a review of Jehovah's dealings with his people, and a philosophy of his ways. In their own country Israel, by bloodshed and idolatry, had polluted the land. So for penalty Jehovah exiled them among the nations. But their sorry plight was a scandal to him among the nations, who, believing that a god was inseparably bound up with his people and stood by them, right or wrong, saw in Jehovah's chastisement of his people only his defeat by more powerful gods. For his own sake, then, not for theirs, he must bring his people back. They must be cleansed from their impurities, and given a heart of flesh instead of a heart of stone: that is, they must be made tractable instead of stubborn. Then they will do his will. The consequence will be not only material prosperity but the awakening within them of a sense of shame for their past sins. We miss here the note of Jehovah's love for his errant people that is found in other prophets: all is done for the sake of Jehovah's name. The change of heart is brought about by Jehovah's own activity: his people are passive in his hands. While this may be a one-sided view, it yet emphasizes a very important truth: men may in one sense work out their own salvation, but in another sense salvation is always the gift of God. Ezekiel's teaching here approximates to that of Paul.

17. *Uncleanness*—cf. 18^{6}, note, Lev. 15^{19}, and, for the general idea, Jer. 2^{7}. 18. Some versions omit *for the blood . . . idols.* 20. *Profaned,* i.e., their disasters reflected, in the eyes of the nations, disgrace upon Jehovah. 23. *Sanctify*—the reverse of *profane* (v. 20). 25. *Sprinkle*—render *dash.* Lustration with water is a prominent feature in Babylonian cult. For Hebrew usage cf. Ex. 30^{17-21}. 26. Cf. 11^{19}. 29. Cf. Hos. $2^{8f., 21f.}$ 30. *Reproach*—famine is evidence of anger felt by a nation's god.

33–38. **Two Pendants to the Preceding Oracle.** Palestine, now desolate, shall again be tilled and be miraculously fertile, her cities rebuilt, walled anew, and repopulated. The nations will then recognize the power of Jehovah. The reduced numbers of the exiles shall, on their return, be so multiplied as to remind the prophet gratefully of the thronging crowds of sheep brought to Jerusalem for sacrifice on a great feast-day—a characteristically priestly thought. Isaiah loathed the reek of the many sacrifices (Isa. 1^{11-15}).

CHAPTER XXXVII

1–14. **The Valley of Dry Bones.** In ecstatic vision Ezekiel is transported to the valley where earlier he had seen (3^{22}) the glory of Jehovah, and is made to pass up and down in it that he may see how full it is of dry bones—the bleaching bones of a slaughtered army (cf. *slain,* v. 9). Jehovah asks "Can these become living men again?" The idea of resurrection had not yet dawned upon the vision of the Hebrews. That it was possible for a departed spirit to enter the body it had just left and near by which it was still hovering was conceivable—probably that was why Elisha shut the door (2 Kings 4^{33}) to prevent the spirit from going off. But that spirits should return to bodies from which they had departed so long that the very bones were bare and bleached—impossible! Ezekiel's *thou knowest* is really a way of avoiding the answer "No!"

Jehovah bids him prophesy to the bones: he will cause spirit to enter into them, they shall be clothed with human bodies, and live. The prophet—thus bidden to "launch out into the deep"—obeys. The dead bones stir with a rattling noise, each finding its fellow, and their bodies are re-formed. Yet they lack life. The prophet at Jehovah's bidding summons spirit from the four winds—the bodies pulsate again with life, the army stands once more in serried ranks as before its destruction. Then Jehovah explains the vision. The bones are Judah and Samaria. The exiles are wont to say, "We are as nations almost dead—so near to death, reduced almost to bleached bones, that we can never live again." But Jehovah will renew their life and establish them once more in Palestine. Very noteworthy in this splendid vision is that the miraculous result is achieved not by direct fiat of Jehovah but through the instrumentality of the prophetic word, so mighty that its utterance insures the result.

5. *Will* = "am about to"; *breath*—render as mg., and so throughout the passage (cf. Gen. 2^{7}); for *and ye shall live* read, with LXX, *of life,* attaching to *breath.* 7. *There was a noise*—probably delete; *earthquake*—render "rattling." 9. *Wind*—in Hebrew one word expresses the ideas of wind, breath, spirit. Render "spirit"; except after *four.* 11. *The whole house*—the Northern as well as the Southern Kingdom; *hope is lost*—cf. 19^{5}. 12. *Graves* = the exile—a flaw in the figure. LXX and Syriac omit *O my people,* which should probably be deleted here and in v. 13.

15–28. **The Symbol of the Two Sticks.** Ezekiel is to take two sticks—probably shaped like scepters, or (so Schmidt) the two pieces of a scepter-shaped stick previously broken—inscribing on one "Judah and the southern tribes," on the other "Joseph and the northern tribes." He is to join them together, and, when asked the meaning of this symbolic action, to say that it foreshows the reunion by Jehovah of Israel and Judah. They shall be one kingdom with one king, a new David. They shall be cleansed and righteous, and they and their descendants shall dwell forever in Palestine. Jehovah will make a new covenant with them, prosper them, and show the world that they are his chosen people, by establishing his sanctuary permanently within their borders. **16.** *The stick of Ephraim* should probably be deleted. **19.** For *mine hand* read, with LXX, *the hand of Judah.* **23.** Read mg. **25.** For *your* read *their*, with LXX and Syriac. **26.** For *place* read *plant* or, with Targum, *bless.* **28.** *Sanctify*=set apart as mine.

CHAPTER XXXVIII

Chs. 38 and 39 contain oracles against Gog. These very difficult and obscure chapters raise many problems too intricate for discussion here, a loss the less serious in that few of them have been solved. The general theme is that, after Israel's settlement in Palestine, when the neighboring peoples have been rendered harmless, Jehovah will entice the far-distant peoples of the North to invade the country, and will overwhelm them in a disaster so terrible that none shall remain to challenge the peace of Israel, and Jehovah's power shall be universally recognized. This theme may come from Ezekiel, but has been elaborated by later hands.

1–9. Attack Upon Israel by Gog. Jehovah will entice Gog with his mighty army, which includes subordinate nations, to prepare an invasion of the mountains of Israel, where the returned exiles are dwelling in peace. Gog will descend upon the land like a devastating storm. But the sinister intent of Jehovah is evident in the initial, *I am against thee.* No wholly satisfactory explanation of Gog has yet been found, though many have been attempted. Some assume that it is a mythical name, but v. 2 tells against that view. It is best to regard Gog as typifying the "foe from the north" associated with the eschatology of the Day of Jehovah (cf. p. 681a). **2.** Delete *of the land of Magog; Rosh*—unknown; many critics prefer mg.; *Meshech, Tubal*—cf. 27[13], note, 32[26]. **4.** *And put hooks in thy jaws*—cf. 29[4]; the phrase, out of harmony with the context, is probably a gloss on the preceding verb. **5.** Herrmann deletes this (cf. 27[10]) as interpolated. **6.** *Gomer*—cf. Gen. 10[2]; possibly a Cappadocian people; *house of*—render *Beth-*, cf. 27[14], note; *hordes*—render *bands* (12[14]); probably=divisions of an army. **7.** *Guard*—meaning dubious, perhaps "agent"; for *them* read *me*, with LXX. **8.** *Visited*—better, *summoned.*

10–16. Attack Upon the Mountains of Israel. A parallel to the foregoing. Here Gog is represented as himself planning the attack on the Israelites, who are so confident of their safety that they dwell in unwalled cities. This is not necessarily inconsistent with v. 4, because Jehovah might be regarded as causing these plans to arise in Gog's mind. Gog's motive is plunder, and, if v. 13 be part of the text, other nations watch the invasion with interest, hoping to trade for the spoil of goods and slaves. But Gog will take "no gain of money"; he is being lured on that Jehovah may be glorified in his destruction. **11.** *To*—render *against* (twice). **12.** For *thine* read *my*, with LXX; *middle*—Palestine is regarded as the center of the earth (cf. Mic. 4[1]). **13.** *Young lions*—corrupt; a parallel to *merchants* would be expected. **14.** For *know it* read *stir thyself up*, with LXX.

17–23. The Doom of Gog. Gog has been the subject of earlier prophecies—this may refer to "the foe from the north." When he comes into Palestine he will be confronted not by a peaceful people but by the wrath of Jehovah, manifested in physical convulsions, and reducing him to panic. Pestilence and slaughter will be Jehovah's weapons. He that descended as a devastating storm on the land shall be the victim of a storm of hail, fire, and brimstone. **17.** For *art thou* read *thou art*, with versions; instead of *for many years* read *and in those years*, with versions, or delete. **22.** For *plead* read *contend* (A.S.V., *enter into judgment*).

CHAPTER XXXIX

1–10. Defeat of Gog. This oracle opens (cf. 38[3f.]) with an announcement of Jehovah's purpose to allure Gog to invade Israel. But Jehovah will strike his weapons from his hand, and his soldiers shall lie unburied, a prey to vultures and wild beasts—most terrible of fates to the Semites, who believed that tolerable conditions after death were possible only to those whose bodies were properly interred (cf. Amos 2[1]). The threat, v. 6, that Jehovah will send fire on Magog (cf. Amos 1[4, 7, 10, 12, 14] 2[2, 5]) seems out of harmony with the context, and may be an interpolation. The discarded weapons of Gog—no longer of use to Israel, since the last enemy is vanquished—will furnish sufficient wood to kindle Israel's fires for seven years. This hyperbole is probably a later elaboration. **1.** Cf. 38[2], notes. **6.** *Magog*—the country of Gog.

11–16. The Multitude of the Slain. This is another elaboration, contradicting the previous threat that the bodies of Gog's soldiers shall remain unburied. The Israelites shall bury the corpses in a valley, because, in a ritual sense, a corpse defiles the land. So numerous are they that the task takes seven months. To make sure that not a single bone remains to pollute the sacred territory, definitely commissioned men shall then search the land and erect a mark by any bone they discover, so that the burial parties may remove it into the valley.

11. *Them that pass through*—repointing the Hebrew gives "Abarim" (cf. Num. 27[12]), the name of a mountain range in Moab, which may have been given to a neighboring valley. This would fit the following words, for *the sea* is the Dead Sea; *it shall stop them that pass through*—corrupt and unintelligible. **13.** *People of the land*—in contrast to the priests (cf. 44[25]). **14.** *Bury*—probably read *search for; that pass through*—delete, with LXX and Syriac. **16.** The first clause is an obscure gloss.

17–24. The Great Sacrifice. With v. 17 the figure changes, and the slaughtered army of Gog is represented as a great sacrifice. The victims of an ordinary sacrifice furnished a feast for those who offered it and their guests. The prophet is bidden to invite the birds and beasts as guests to partake of these victims, who are compared to the finest cattle used for sacrifice (cf. Isa. 34[6f.]). Israel shall recognize the power of Jehovah, and the nations shall learn that it was through no lack of might in Jehovah that Israel went into exile. He deliberately punished his people in that way for their treachery. **18.** *Bashan*—noted for fine pasture and fat cattle (cf. Deut. 32[14] Psa. 22[12] Amos 4[1]). **20.** For *chariots* read *horsemen.* **23.** *Trespassed against*—render *were treacherous unto.*

25–29. Promise of Restoration. This short oracle has no connection with the threats against Gog, but would fittingly follow ch. 37. It is a promise of restoration for all Israel, Samaria and Judah alike. **25.** *Bring again the captivity*—render *restore the fortunes.* **26.** Here *bear* may have the sense of *realize:* another possible rendering is *forget; trespasses, trespassed against*—render *treachery, were treacherous unto.* **29.** *Poured*—cf. Joel 2[28].

Chapters 40 to 48. The Ecclesiastical Organization of the Restored Territory

In the preceding chapters Ezekiel expresses a threefold hope: (1) the spiritual regeneration of a remnant; (2) the destruction of the nations hostile to Israel, including those now occupying the promised land; (3) the restoration of the regenerated people to Palestine. In chs. 40–48 the prophet describes the organization of the restored community, so that the intimate relations between the people and their God may be maintained. On the significance of this description, see the introduction, section on "The Father of Judaism," p. 715a.

CHAPTER XL

The first part of this "constitution" deals with the Temple and the Temple area (chs. 40–43).

1–4. The Prophetic Vision. On New Year's Day, 573 B.C., Ezekiel is thrown into ecstasy. In his trance-vision God leads him to Mount Zion—risen now above the mountains of the earth (cf. Isa. 2[2] Mic. 4[1]). There he beholds the Temple of the restored people, its buildings so extensive that they resemble the *frame of a city* (v. 2). An angel with a measuring-line for large measurements and a reed for smaller ones is waiting to conduct him over the Temple; he is to take careful note and tell what he has seen to the house of Israel. **1.** *Thither*—LXX and Syriac omit. **2.** *Brought he me*—LXX and Syriac omit; for *on the south* read *in front of me,* with support in versions.

What follows describes the details of the prophet's vision.

5. The Encircling Wall. The whole of the Temple buildings are included in *house.* The measuring unit is the longer cubit of Babylonia, a handbreadth more than the ordinary cubit (see p. 79).

6–16. The Outer Eastern Gate. **6.** Here delete the last seven words, with LXX. **7.** For *lodge* read mg. (throughout); for *space* read *pillar,* with LXX. **8.** Delete with MSS. and versions. **9.** Delete *and the porch . . . house,* with LXX; for *posts* read mg. **10.** For *eastward* read *chamber opposite chamber,* with LXX. **14.** This is very dubious. *He made* seems quite out of place. **16.** *Palm trees*—carved symbols, replacing the trees which anciently were objects of worship.

17–49. Courts, Tables, Gates, Chambers of Various Sorts. Every detail of the Temple arrangements passes before the eyes of the prophet: The great outer court, with thirty chambers, possibly provided for participators in festal meals (vv. 17–19); the outer northern gate (20–23); the outer southern gate (24–27); the inner southern gate (28–31); the inner eastern gate (32–34); the inner northern gate (35–37); tables for washing and slaying the sacrifices (38–43). The text here is very corrupt. The *chamber* (v. 38) is probably by the eastern gate. Two chambers (so, with LXX, for *chambers for the singers,* v. 44) for the priests (44–46); the court and altar (47); the porch, or entrance to the Temple proper (48, 49).

CHAPTER XLI

The text of ch. 41 is very corrupt, and in places admits of no certain translation. For the contents cf. 1 Kings 6f.

1, 2. The Entrance—to the main Temple building. Delete, in v. 1, *which was the breadth of the tabernacle,* with LXX.

3, 4. The Holy of Holies—a square chamber, empty. Note that Ezekiel does not enter this.

5–11. The Buildings at the Sides—in three stories, v. 6.

12–14. A Building—the use of which is not defined, to the west of the Temple.

15–26. The Interior of the Temple. This is covered with wood, both floor and ceiling. The walls and doors are decorated with alternate palms and cherubs, the latter having each two faces, one a lion face, one a human face, in contrast to the four faces of the "living creatures" of the divine chariot. The small *altar of wood* (v. 22) may be the shewbread table.

CHAPTER XLII

The text of ch. 42 also is corrupt, and in places unintelligible.

1–14. The Cells in the Inner Court. These serve as refectories in which the priests eat the holy food (v. 13), and as dressing rooms, where they doff their clothes, which acquire holiness by contagion, ere they leave the inner court (cf. 44[19], note). Vv. 13f. seem misplaced in a context which is concerned with measurements and may be a later addition.

15–20. The Measurements of the Sides of the Whole Inclosure. V. 20 apparently contradicts 48[12], according to which the land beyond the inclosure was holy: nor does the usual explanation that there were degrees of holiness help much.

CHAPTER XLIII

1–9. Jehovah's Solemn Entry Into the Temple. As before Ezekiel had in vision seen Jehovah depart from the defiled Temple by way of the east gate (cf. 10[18f.] 11[22f.]), so now he sees him return in glory through the same gate. In the days of the monarchy the Temple had been a royal chapel, almost an appurtenance to the palace. Kings had been buried near to it. Now Ezekiel hears the voice of Jehovah from the inmost shrine, promising that he will dwell forever in the Temple, but demanding that such encroachments shall no longer be permitted. **3.** Read v. 3a: *And the vision was like the vision which I saw when he came to destroy . . .* **5.** For *the spirit* read *spirit;* for *this is* read *thou hast seen,* with LXX. **6.** For *a man* read *the man,* with versions. **7.** Delete *in their high places.*

10–12. The Law of the House. Ezekiel is to show his plan to the people, and, if the sight of it bring repentance, to give them written instructions for regulating all concerning it. **10.** Read the last clause *and its measure and its pattern.*

13–27. The Altar. This section comes in abruptly, and may be a later insertion. Vv. 13–17 give the measurements. Some of the terms used are obscure, and detail is therefore uncertain. The altar appears to have been formed of four squared stones, one above another, in descending sizes, and approached by steps. **14.** For *settle* read *ledge.* **15.** *Upper altar* is the same word as that rendered *altar hearth,* and should be so rendered; *horns*—cf. Ex. 29[12] Lev. 4[7] 1 Kings 1[50f.] The horns of the altar may possibly be associated originally with the bull which appears as a symbol of Jehovah. Vv. 18–27 describe its consecration. **18.** For *sprinkle* read *dash.* **19.** *Levites*—cf. 44[10], note. **21.** For *he* read *one* (A.S.V., *it shall be burnt*). **25.** If *seven* is right, then *eighth,* in v. 27, should be "ninth." It is altogether unlikely that the *thou* of this passage (v. 25) means Ezekiel. Herrmann's suggestion that it is due to imitation of the legislation in which "thou" means Moses is plausible.

CHAPTER XLIV

Chapters 44–46 are devoted to instruction concerning Temple servants and festivals.

1–3. The Closed Gate. The gate through which Jehovah re-enters the Temple is never to be opened again; but the prince—there is no longer to be a king exercising priestly functions—may be suffered to eat a sacrificial meal in its porch. **2.** For *the Lord* (*Jehovah*) read *he,* i.e., the angel-guide. Jehovah is referred to in the third person (v. 2b).

4–9. Exclusion of Foreigners from the Temple. Foreigners, though such had been previously employed in subordinate offices in the Temple, are to be rigidly excluded. **5.** For *the Lord* read *he* (cf. v. 2, note). **7.** For *they* read *ye,* with versions. **8.** After *set* insert "them as."

10–16. Degradation of the Levites. The menial offices are to be discharged by Levites, who, because they had connived at idolatrous practices, are degraded from the priesthood. In earlier times "priest" and "Levite" are practically interchangeable terms. Deut. 18[6f.] directs that the Levites, whose functions at the local sanctuaries disappear when only the central sanctuary is recognized, shall be allowed to minister at the Temple; but 2 Kings 23[9] shows that the Jerusalem priests succeeded in excluding them from this privilege. Priestly functions in the restored Temple are to be restricted to the Zadokite priests (cf. 1 Kings 2[35] 4[4]).

17–31. Regulations as to the Conduct, Duties, and Rewards of the Priests. **19.** *Sanctify*—the priestly garments acquire holiness, which is contagious, and would infect laymen with holiness so that they too would be subject to various taboos (cf. p. 283a). Contact with a corpse defiles (v. 25). Note the omission of "wife"; the exceptions permitted all concern blood relations. Behind the regulations probably lies a protest against the worship of the dead. **28.** For *an* read *no*, with Vulgate. **31.** This restriction is in Ex. 22[31] universal.

CHAPTER XLV

1–8. Assignment of Territory to Priests, Levites, and Prince. A rectangle of 25,000 by 10,000 cubits, in the midst of which is the Temple, is reserved, as specially holy, for the priests. A similar rectangle north of this is to be reserved for the Levites. On the south a rectangle of 25,000 by 5,000 cubits is allowed for the city itself. These together make a square. The further territory included by prolonging the north and south sides of the square to the Jordan and the Mediterranean Sea is the portion of the prince. **1.** For *ten* read mg. **2.** *Suburbs*, i.e., common lands. **5.** Read mg.

9–12. The Currency Shall Not Be Depreciated. Coined money is not contemplated. Weight of metal is paid for weight or measure of goods. The prince and his successors shall not depreciate the currency by manipulating units of measurement. On the units see p. 78. **12.** The text here is corrupt. Perhaps read *five (shekels) shall be five, and ten shekels shall be ten, and fifty shekels shall be your maneh.*

13–17. Dues to Be Paid to the Prince. These enable him to provide the costly sacrifices.

18–25. Days of Atonement, etc. These shall be celebrated on the first day of the first and of the seventh months. They introduce feasts that correspond to the Passover (v. 21) and the Feast of Tabernacles (v. 25). No feast corresponding to the Feast of Weeks is recognized. The point of v. 20 (read mg.) is that in the restored community no one will sin deliberately.

CHAPTER XLVI

1–10. Regulations for Sabbath and New Moon. These feasts are so closely associated in O.T. that it is natural to think that the Sabbath is based on a lunar reckoning; it may have been originally the Full Moon festival. The New Moon seems to be more important even than the Sabbath to judge from the extra sacrifice of a bullock. Note that even the prince may not pass into the inner court. Vv. 4–7 break the connection between v. 3 and v. 8, and may be a later insertion. **10.** Possibly we should read, with Syriac, *As for the prince in their midst, by the gate through which he entered shall he depart.*

11–15. Further Regulations for Offerings. V. 11 is quite general, and seems misplaced here. For the prince's freewill offerings the gate (v. 1) is to be opened as on New Moon and Sabbath. Vv. 13–15, treating of the daily offering, have the same form as 45[18-20] (see note). Some versions, however, have "he" for *thou.*

16–18. Regulations as to the Land Reserved for the Prince. The prince may give to any of his sons—though doubtless in any case the estate was treated as a family possession rather than an individual holding—part of his reservation as a permanent possession, but any gift he may make from it to a courtier automatically reverts to the prince at the year of release—undoubtedly the seventh year (cf. Ex. 21[2] Deut. 15[12] Jer. 34[14]), rather than the fiftieth (cf. Lev. 25[10]). The prince may not take from private persons their property, as Ahab took Naboth's vineyard, in order to give it to a courtier.

19–24. The Temple Kitchens. These verses form part of the itinerary last mentioned in 44[4], and would fittingly follow 42[14]. On v. 20 cf. 44[19], note. In v. 22, for *inclosed* read *small*, with LXX and Syriac.

CHAPTER XLVII

1–12. The Life-Giving River. This beautiful description of the life-giving stream comes into the rather arid detail of these last chapters with almost as refreshing a power as the stream itself came to the waters of the Dead Sea. The meaning is clear, and needs little comment. Ezekiel is taken about a mile and a third before the miraculous river reaches an unfordable depth. Even to-day there are no fish in the Dead Sea (v. 9). Though the idea of a miraculous stream in connection with the dwelling-place of God is a recognized feature of description (cf. Psa. 46[4]), Ezekiel probably means this to be taken literally. **8.** *Arabah*—the depression below sea level through which the Jordan flows down into the Dead Sea; for *into the sea . . . made to issue forth* read simply *the bitter waters; healed*—cf. 2 Kings 2[22]. **9.** *Rivers*—read, with versions, *the river.* **10.** *En-gedi*—approximately in the middle of the west shore of the Dead Sea; *En-eglaim* is unknown; for *their fish* read *its fish*, i.e., the Dead Sea's fish; *great sea*, i.e., the Mediterranean. **11.** The one good feature of the Dead Sea—the production of salt—is not to be lost. This verse may be interpolated. **12.** *Meal*—render *food* (as in A.S.V.; cf. Rev. 22[2]).

13–23. The Boundaries of the Land. No territory east of the Jordan is included, though Israel had at times possessed considerable holdings there. The northern boundary is difficult to trace, as some of the places named are unknown. Roughly, it seems to run from some point north of Tyre to the Lebanon range. **19.** The *brook of Egypt* is the *Wady El-arish. Tamar* is presumably south of the Dead Sea. With the passage cf. Num. 34[1-12]. Resident aliens who settle and bring up families are to share in the allotment of the land (vv. 21–23). This is an advance upon any position accorded to them elsewhere in the O.T.

CHAPTER XLVIII

1–7, 23–29. The Location of the Tribes. North of the land reserved for sanctuary, priests, Levites, city, and prince (45[1-8]) are to dwell in parallel strips, reckoning from the north down, seven tribes—Dan, Asher, Naphtali, Manasseh, Ephraim, Reuben, Judah; south of it, five—Benjamin, Simeon, Issachar, Zebulon, Gad.

8–22. Details as to the Sacred Reservation. Given more fully than in 45[1-8]. The city's population is representative of all the tribes.

30–35. The Gates of the City. Each side of the city has three gates, these being named after the twelve tribes. Since Levi appears among the twelve, Manasseh and Ephraim are united under the name "Joseph." In the passage in Rev. 21, based on this passage, the Temple disappears and the glory of the gates is enhanced. A new *name* (v. 35) implies in Semitic thought a new corresponding character. (On the significance of the idealized city and temple of chs. 40–48, see intro., section on "The Father of Judaism," p. 715a.)

DANIEL

By Professor HERBERT L. WILLETT

Introduction

Name and Place in the Canon. The name of the book in the Hebrew Bible is the name of the hero of the book who, according to tradition, was also its author. In the English O.T. it is the last of the so-called Major Prophets; in the Hebrew Bible it is one of the Writings. In other words, in the Hebrew Bible it belongs to the third division rather than to the second, in which are found all the other prophetic books of the English Bible. Various explanations have been suggested to account for the separation of Daniel from other prophetic books. But, if the book was written subsequently to 170 B.C., as is now generally thought, this fact in itself is sufficient to explain its position among the "Writings," for the prophetic canon was fixed about 200 B.C. (see art., *The Formation of the O.T.*, pp. 93–7).

In the LXX there are several additions to Daniel as given in the O.T., such as "The Song of the Three Holy Children" (following 3^{23} of the Aramaic text), "The History of Susanna," and "The History of the Destruction of Bel and the Dragon" (the latter two recounting stories of which Daniel is the hero). These are ordinarily included among the apocryphal books (see art., *The Intertestamental Literature*, p. 194).

Purpose of the Book. Daniel appears to have been written in the days of the bitter persecution of the Jews by Antiochus Epiphanes, king of Syria, who reigned from 175 to 164 B.C. In his efforts to compel the faithful in Jerusalem to abandon their practice of the Mosaic precepts and their worship at the Temple, he partially destroyed the city, defiled the sanctuary, and rendered the maintenance of service impossible until it was cleansed. Many Jews gave up their religion and apostatized to the pagan religion of the king. The Maccabæan movement was a patriotic effort to save the national faith. (See art., *History of Hebrew People*, p. 71; cf. p. 192.) Another effort was made by the author or authors of the book of Daniel. It was their endeavor to keep their fellow Jews loyal to the traditions of their fathers, even at the cost of martyrdom. They believed firmly that within a brief time (referred to often as three years and a half) the trouble would be over, the tyrant dead, and the happy age of deliverance and triumph for the Jewish people would come. In setting forth this hope and making this appeal, they employed the venerable figure of Daniel, a Jew of ancient days, either the Babylonian Exile (586-538 B.C.) or the still earlier Assyrian deportation of the ten tribes (721 B.C.). The prophet Ezekiel mentions such a man, along with Noah and Job, among the worthies of the past (Ezek. 14^{14} 28^{3}).

Contents of the Book. The first half of the book, chs. 1–6, is devoted to the stories of Daniel and his three friends in the Babylonian exile, the latter, however, appearing only in chs. 1 and 3. In these narratives the courage, wisdom, and loyalty of Daniel and his fellow confessors are pointed out, as also the place of importance to which he was promoted as chief of the wise men of Babylon. He interprets King Nebuchadrezzar's dreams and predicts the destruction of the world powers, the four heathen kingdoms, and the establishment of the kingdom of the saints of the Most High, i.e., the Jewish nation.

The second section, chs. 7–12, is devoted to a series of visions witnessed and described by Daniel, in which the general ground of the dream of ch. 2 is several times traversed, and the four kingdoms—the Babylonian, the Median, the Persian, and the Macedonian or Grecian—are described in terms which leave no doubt of their object, the description and doom of the "little horn," Antiochus the tyrant. The author employs the device of having the hero of the book predict the events of the years from his own time in the past to the period in which the book was prepared, that device being explained by the sealing up of the revelation till the events predicted were about to be fulfilled. This plan of pseudepigraphic authorship and the employment of the form of prediction for the narration of history was common with the apocalyptic writers, and was a most effective means of accomplishing their purposes (see p. 188a).

Type of Literature. The book of Daniel belongs to the apocalyptic literature of the Bible, a type of writing that took form in the later periods of persecution of the Jews and Christians, from about 200 B.C. to 150 A.D. It was designed to uphold the courage of the people of God during dark days, and made use of striking forms of speech, symbolic figures and numbers, and descriptions of political events in the form of predictive language. The most distinctive examples of biblical apocalyptic are the books of Daniel and Revelation, though there is an extensive extra-biblical literature of the same nature, including Enoch, Fourth Esdras, Baruch, the Assumption of Moses, etc. Some of them were Jewish and some Christian. (For details see arts., *Intertestamental Literature*, pp. 197–9, and *Backgrounds*, p. 843; cf. intro. to Revelation, p. 1364.)

Authorship and Date. Perhaps no book in the O.T. contains more definite indications of its date than does the book of Daniel. In view of this fact it may appear strange that there has been the widest divergence of opinion with reference to the authorship and date of the book. On the one hand, there have been many who insisted that the book was written by Daniel, the hero of the book, who was carried away from Jerusalem during the reign of Jehoiakim, and who subsequently attained a position of prominence at the court of Nebuchadrezzar and of his successors on the throne of Babylon. (The arguments commonly used to prove that Daniel is the author are outlined and criticized in Eiselen, *The Psalms and Other Sacred Writings*, pp. 256-263.)

At the present time scholars are generally agreed that the arguments usually brought forward to establish the claim that Daniel wrote the book are in no sense conclusive. On the other hand, they have discovered evidence of various kinds to convince them that the book is a product of the Maccabæan crisis, during the reign of Antiochus Epiphanes, who, as has been pointed out, sought to stamp out Judaism. Among the many considerations that have led scholars to this conclusion the following may be mentioned:

(1) The book is not included among the "Prophets" in the Jewish canon of the O.T., but is placed with the later collection called the "Writings."

(2) The language of the book, both the Hebrew and the Aramaic, is of a much later date than the Exile.

(3) The use of Persian and Greek words in the book suggests a date much later than the Exile.

(4) The historical surveys given in chs. 2, 7, and 11 show only vague familiarity with events belonging to the period of the Exile and the early postexilic age; they increase in accuracy and definiteness as they approach the times of the author, and culminate, in each case, with the figure and fate of the Syrian ruler.

(5) The important theological ideals and conceptions expressed in the book resemble much more closely the teaching of the Jewish writings of the second and first centuries B.C. than they do the thought of other O.T. books.

Summing up the available evidence, it would seem that all of it, without a single exception, points to a date not earlier than 300 B.C., while most of it points to a date after 200 B.C., during the reign of Antiochus Epiphanes. The exact date during that reign can, perhaps, not be determined, but there are some indications that fix it within narrow limits. Evidently the cleansing of the Temple, which took place in December, 165 B.C., was still in the future (8^{14}), as also the death of Antiochus (11^{45}). A date between 167 and 165 B.C. would satisfy most completely all the facts in the case.

In passing, attention may be called to the fact that the book of Daniel as we have it is in two languages—the Hebrew from 1^{1} to 2^{4} and from 8^{1} to the end of the book; and Aramaic, a relatively late dialect of the Semitic tongue, in the middle section of the book, i.e., from the words "in Syriac" in 2^{4} (or "in Aramaic," Moffatt and Smith; cf. mg.) to 7^{28}. No wholly satisfactory reason has ever been discovered for the use of the two languages. Perhaps the author, familiar with both languages, began to work in Hebrew and changed to the more familiar Aramaic at the point where the speech of the "Chaldæans" begins, whose language was thought to have been Aramaic. (See notes on $1^{17\text{-}20}$.) In ch. 7 Aramaic is continued because of the similarity of the subject matter to that of ch. 2, and in the final visions the Hebrew is resumed as more suitable for prophetic themes. (For other explanations see Eiselen, *The Psalms and Other Sacred Writings*, pp. 283-288.)

Teaching and Permanent Value. The purpose of Daniel, like that of other apocalyptic books, is primarily didactic. The author seeks to impress upon his readers some great religious truths, in order thereby to sustain their faith in God and in the ultimate triumph of his kingdom in the face of present disasters and persecutions.

(1) The principal idea of the book is *the ultimate triumph of the kingdom of God.* Earlier prophets looked with equal assurance for the establishment of the divine rule; and, like these men, the author of Daniel expected the reign of righteousness to begin in the near future. But while the Kingdom in the earlier expectation was little "more than a continuance of the existing state of society, only purged by a judgment from sin and freed from trouble," the book of Daniel marks a transition from this

to the idea of a heavenly kingdom as it appears in more developed form in later apocalyptic and N.T. writings.

(2) The teaching concerning *angels* marks an advance in several details over the idea expressed in other parts of the O.T. (a) Here for the first time appears in definite form the doctrine of patron angels, determining the destinies of individual nations. (The angels or "princes" of Persia, Greece, and Judah are mentioned in 10[13, 20, 21] 12[1]). (b) For the first time names are given to angels (Michael, the guardian angel of the Jews, 10[13, 21] 12[1], and Gabriel, a heaven-sent interpreter, 8[16] 9[21]). (c) Distinctions in rank among angels also appear for the first time in Daniel (10[13] 12[1]).

(3) The most definite reference to *resurrection* is found in 12[2]. The general O.T. conception of life or existence after death is hazy and, on the whole, gloomy and full of despair. But here and there rays of hope appear (see Eiselen, *The Christian View of the O.T.*, pp. 184-187; art., *Religion of Israel*, p. 173; cf. pp. 210–3). Sometimes the hope is expressed that Jehovah may keep his saints from entering Sheol (e.g., Psa. 16[8-11]); at other times, that, though they may have to enter Sheol, they may be raised again to life (e.g., Isa. 26[19]). Dan. 12[2] adds two ideas to the earlier teaching: (a) the resurrection of the wicked, which is clearly taught here for the first time; (b) the doctrine of rewards and punishments in the after-life, though the nature of these rewards and punishments is not defined. But even with these additional elements certain limitations remain. The context makes it clear that the author does not include non-Israelites in the promise of the resurrection; and the expression "*many of them* that sleep in the dust" suggests that not even all the Israelites are to be raised.

The influence of Daniel has been widespread and profound. The fact that the faith of the Jewish community was kept alive through a time of deep distress was due to the combined effects of the Maccabæan revolution and the reading of this book. So much a classic did it become that even after the crisis of Syrian persecution had passed, it retained its popularity and served to prepare its readers for other emergencies in the later days, e.g., the Roman war of 68–70 A.D. Jesus quoted its familiar words in commenting on the approach of that time of fresh calamity (Mt. 24[15] Mk. 13[14]). It has remained through the centuries one of the favorite portions of holy Scripture.

Literature: Bevan, *The Book of Daniel;* Driver, *The Book of Daniel* (Cambridge Bible); Charles, *The Book of Daniel* (New Century Bible); Montgomery, *Daniel* (International Critical Commentary); Eiselen, ***The Psalms and the Other Sacred Writings;*** Farrar, ***Daniel*** (Expositor's Bible); Charles, ***Eschatology,*** 2nd edit.).

Chapters 1 to 6: Experiences of Daniel and of his Companions

The first six chapters of the book present narratives of the experiences of Daniel and three of his Hebrew friends at the court of Nebuchadrezzar and his successors, Belshazzar, Darius the Mede, and Cyrus the Persian. The loyalty to the law and customs of their race, the devotion and heroism shown by the four youths, were intended as an example to the Jewish people in a time of persecution, when they were being tempted to renounce their faith and embrace the heathenism of the Syrian king, Antiochus.

CHAPTER I

1, 2. Conquest of Judah by Nebuchadrezzar. Jehoiakim was a son of Josiah (639-609 B.C.) and was placed upon the throne by the king of Egypt after the brief reign of his brother, Jehoahaz (2 Kings 23[31-34]). There is no mention elsewhere of this siege of Jerusalem, and the statement is one of the historical perplexities of the book. In Jer. 25[1], it is said that Nebuchadrezzar became king in the fourth year of Jehoiakim, and in 2 Kings 23[36] it is stated that the latter reigned eleven years in Jerusalem. The words of the text may rest on a mistaken combination of 2 Kings 24[1, 2] with 2 Chr. 36[6, 7]. *Nebuchadnezzar*—an incorrect spelling of "Nebuchadrezzar," the form which appears generally in Jeremiah and Ezekiel, the prophets who were contemporaries of the king. The Babylonian form of the word is *Nabu-Kudurri-usur* ("Nebo protect the boundaries"). *Shinar* (Gen. 11[2]) is used in the O.T. as equivalent to Babylon.

3–5. The School of the Palace. Certain youths were selected from the best families of the various subject nations and given instruction in the branches of learning that would fit them to become members of the guild of wise men, soothsayers, and interpreters of mysteries. The word *Chaldeans* is used in the later literature to denote the members of the body of magicians, astrologers and diviners consulted by the king at need. (See on vv. 17–20.)

6, 7. The Four Hebrews. In accordance with custom the Hebrew names of the four Jewish youths were replaced by Babylonian names. *Belteshazzar* and *Abed-nego* (an evident error for *Abed-Nebo*, "servant of Nebo") contain the names of Bel and Nebo, leading gods of Babylonia (Isa. 46[1]).

8–13. Daniel's Request for Simple Food. The Hebrew laws restricted the diet of the people, and forbade much of the food that would be regarded as desirable among the heathen (Lev. 11, Deut. 14[3-21], notes). Daniel's request for *pulse* ("vegetables," v. 12, cf. mg.) instead of the king's dainties and wine, was not merely because the royal food was pleasant but because it might contain unclean ingredients (Bevan, *The Book of Daniel*, p. 57), or might have been offered in sacrifice to idols (Charles, *Daniel*, p. 10). The officers who had them in charge feared to disobey the royal order and were not sure the young men might not suffer by the use of the meager fare. But Daniel proposed a trial of ten days.

14, 15. The Successful Test. Daniel's opinion was completely justified by the experiment. There was no further difficulty in the use of vegetables. A narrative of this kind would make a strong appeal to Jews who were in danger of giving up their observance of the Mosaic law regarding food. That was the chief mark of loyalty to the customs of their fathers.

17–20. Masters of Chaldean Learning. As the result of their abstemious and devout conduct, God gave these four Hebrews unusual command of the subjects of their studies, and to Daniel in particular the mastery of the secrets of Babylonian lore, the interpretation of dreams, and the power of divination. These were the chief functions of the caste of wise men, or "Chaldeans," the title now applied to them. It had been formerly the designation of the people of Chaldea, or southeastern Babylonia, but had come to stand for the class that perpetuated the ancient mysteries of the land. At the end of their three years of training, the four were presented to the king along with the other graduates of the school, and on examination by the king, none were found so competent as they. So they became the personal attendants of Nebuchadrezzar.

21. The First Year of Cyrus. The conquest of Babylon by Cyrus the Persian occurred in 538 B.C. The actual succession of rulers in Babylon, as disclosed by records and monumental sources, was as follows: Nebuchadrezzar, 605-561 B.C.; Evil-Merodach (2 Kings 25[27]), 561-559 B.C.; Neriglissar, 559-556 B.C.; Labashi-Marduk, 556-555 B.C., who was assassinated after a reign of nine months; the conspirators placed on the throne Nabu-naid, or Nabonidus, one of their own number, a native Babylonian, and unrelated to the line of Nebuchadrezzar. He ruled from 555 to 538 B.C., when Cyrus conquered the land and took the sovereignty. The succession as recorded in the book of Daniel is somewhat different. It is as follows: Nebuchadrezzar (chs. 1–4), Belshazzar (chs. 5, 7[1] 8[1]), Darius the Mede (5[30, 31] 6[1-28] 9[1] 11[1]), Cyrus, king of Persia (6[28] 10[1]). The reason for these variations from the historical order is probably to be looked for in the lack of any regular chronological system among the Hebrews, and in the length of time that had elapsed between the days of these earlier kings (605-538 B.C.) and the time in which the book was written (about 165 B.C.) The problem will be discussed more fully at the appropriate places in the following chapters.

CHAPTER II

Nebuchadrezzar's Dream and Daniel's Interpretation. Dreams were believed to be portents, significant as conveying the will of the gods, and therefore not to be disregarded. The practice of employing astrologers and diviners, whose business was the interpretation of dreams and other omens, prevailed throughout antiquity, and was still in vogue until recent years in the courts of Oriental princes. The fact that the king could not recall his dream made all the more significant the service which Daniel was able to render him.

1–3. The Royal Diviners Summoned. These were the men who had been trained to interpret dreams and give auguries. From the statements of 1[19, 20] that Daniel and his friends were the most skillful of the number it seems surprising that they were not present when the king asked for counsel. It will be noted that the word "Chaldeans" is used in its later and technical sense of magician or sorcerer.

4–6. The Forgotten Dream. With v. 4 the Aramaic section of the book begins with the words *in the Syrian language* (Moffatt and Smith translate "in Aramaic"). Aramaic was a Semitic dialect similar to Hebrew and was the ordinary tongue of Palestine from the third century B.C. If the diviners really had power to interpret dreams, it was not unreasonable to suppose that they could also discover the dream itself.

7–13. The Wise Men Doomed. Of course the diviners were helpless. Their profession gave them cleverness in finding meanings for dreams that could be recalled, as with modern fortune tellers. But beyond this they could not go. Their only recourse was to put off the matter till it should be forgotten, or some method devised to satisfy the king. But the mood of Nebuchadrezzar was peremptory, and the edict went forth for their execution.

14–16. Daniel's Request. As with the chief eunuch (1[9]), so with the captain of the guard, Daniel was on good terms, and this proved the means of securing a personal interview with the king, and of gaining time for an attempt to solve the mystery.

17–24. The Secret Revealed. Daniel at once sought the help of his three friends in prayer for light, the only means of saving their own lives as well as those of the other wise men. Their petitions were heard, the king's dream was made known to Daniel, and in overflowing gratitude he poured out his soul to God, much as did Hannah in her hymn of praise (1 Sam 2[1-10]). It is a model prayer of thanksgiving. Prepared thus, Daniel informs Arioch that the king's decree of death is unnecessary, and that he is ready to make known the royal secret.

25–30. The Captive before the King. No time was lost. From among the humble exiles of Judah had come a master of the magicians. Instantly Daniel was taken before the king, who demanded of him, addressing him by his Babylonian name, whether he could tell him his dream and its meaning. The response of the Hebrew was that the thing asked is beyond the power of any man, even the most gifted diviner, but that there is a God who, unlike the impotent deities of Babylon, is able actually to reveal the deepest secrets; and from him had come the answer to the king's word. It had to do with the future, the long future, of the kingdom and its people, i.e., the times in which the writer of the book lived. The secret was not made known because of Daniel's superior wisdom, but through the power of God and for the comfort of the king.

31–35. The Dream. The king had seen a great figure in human form, gigantic, terrifying. The head was of *gold*, the breasts and arms of *silver*, the body of *bronze*, the legs of *iron*, and the feet of *iron* mixed with *clay*. The declining value of the materials is a token of the author's view of the growing evils in world affairs. A stone dislodged from a neighboring mountain (see v. 45) struck the image on the feet and ground it to dust, which was blown away. The stone then became a mighty rock that filled the earth.

36–45. The Interpretation. Daniel informed the king that he, Nebuchadrezzar, was represented by the head of gold. Three kingdoms would follow, presumably the Median, the Persian, and the Macedonian or Greek. This last—under the rule of Alexander the Great—would be formidable, crushing, but of variable strength, and like the legs of the image, *divided*, referring apparently to the two states, Syria and Egypt, nearest to Palestine, that followed the break up of Alexander's empire. They were ruled by a succession of kings, some weak, some strong (ch. 11). Alliances formed by marriage and otherwise would be futile (v. 43). At that time God, the God of the Jews, would establish his own kingdom (represented by the *stone*, v. 45; cf. v. 35), the rule of his people in the earth, which would supersede and destroy all these world empires and endure forever. It would not rest on military strength, but on divine power.

46–49. God Acknowledged and Daniel Honored. The king, convinced of the correctness of Daniel's disclosure and interpretation of the dream, adored the prophet, confessed that his God was supreme among the gods, and promoted Daniel to the double position of viceroy of the provinces and master of the royal astrologers. At his request the three other Hebrews were given important offices under him.

CHAPTER III

Tried by Fire. Another lesson of fidelity and courage was taught by the story of the three Hebrew friends of Daniel, who, confronted with the king's command to worship the image of gold he had set up, refused, and braved the fiery death, from which they were miraculously delivered.

1–7. The Image, the Assembly and the Mandate. It was not unusual for monarchs to set up *images* of themselves or their gods as tokens of their power or as objects of worship. The remarkable proportions of this image are evident. A crowd of officials of every rank, and of the mixed population of the province, was assembled for the dedication of the statue. The signal for worship announced by the herald was the blast of music from the many instruments, including the *horn*, *pipe*, *lyre*, *trigon* (a four-stringed harp), *psaltery* (a triangular shaped harp) and *bagpipe*. Three of these words are Greek—an added reason for a date long subsequent to the Exile. The threat of death by flame brought the multitude to its knees at the signal.

8–12. The Three Jews Denounced. Daniel is not mentioned in this narrative, for what reason is not stated. The *Chaldeans*, or members of the guild of astrologers, would naturally be jealous of the unusual honors bestowed on the four Jewish youths. They were quick to see that the king's mandate was disregarded by Shadrach, Meshach, and Abed-nego.

13–18. Before the Angry King. Nebuchadrezzar was furious at the slight put by the three men upon his idol and his command. He would give them one more chance, since they were high officers of his realm. But they needed no further time, and they made no apology. Their answer was bold and to the point. They said: "We need not waste any words in discussing this matter with you" (Smith's version). If the God they worshiped were able or willing to deliver them from the fire, he would do so. But even if not, they were resolved neither to serve the gods of Babylon nor prostrate themselves before the king's image. This is one of the noblest defiances ever uttered to a false faith (cf. Jer. 26[8-15] Acts 4[18-20] 5[27-29]).

19–23. Cast into the Furnace. The king's fury was heightened by the bold words of the three confessors. He ordered them thrown into the furnace, heated to a tremendous degree. Bound just as they were, they were seized by strong men and thrown into the flames, which were so hot the executioners themselves were overcome and perished.

24–27. The Jews Uninjured, the King Alarmed. Nebuchadrezzar, looking into the furnace, saw a portent. Four men were walking unbound and unharmed in the fire. Rising in haste and alarm, the king demanded the reason of the fourth figure in the flame, who resembled *a son of the gods*, i.e., a godlike being (the A.V. rendering, "the Son of God," is incorrect). Approaching the door of the furnace, he called to the martyrs to come out. When they emerged from the fire the king and his officers saw that they had suffered no injury of any sort.

28–30. The Royal Doxology and Decree. Astonished and thrilled by the miracle, the king praised the God of the Jews, affirming that the fourth figure in the furnace was *an angel*, sent for the deliverance of the faithful three. Further, an order was issued that no disrespectful word be spoken against this God, on pain of dire penalties. Still higher honors (cf. 2[49]) were then conferred on the delivered confessors. Such a narrative of heroism must have done much to strengthen the spirits of the Jews who were passing through a period of dire persecution at the hands of their Syrian oppressor, Antiochus. For the nature of these persecutions, see First and Second Maccabees, *passim*, and Heb. 11[33-38] (consult art., *Intertestamental Literature*, p. 192b).

CHAPTER IV

The Dream of the Great Tree. This narrative is given in the form of a public document issued by King Nebuchadrezzar, reciting a dream of his and its interpretation by Daniel, much after the manner of ch. 2. The dream signified the malady that was to befall the king, reducing him to the state of a beast and depriving him of his throne for seven years. At the end of that period his reason was restored, and he was reestablished on his throne, whereupon he honored the King of heaven, the Most High.

1–3. The King's Proclamation. It is assumed in the narrative that Nebuchadrezzar was ruler of the whole earth, to whose people he made his declaration, praising the God of the Jews for the lesson taught him by the dream and its fulfillment, which are described in the rest of the chapter.

4–9. Impotent Diviners; a Confident King. As in the former case (2[1, 2]), the king, terrified by his dream, summoned his wise men, whose function it was to interpret such omens. When they failed, Nebuchadrezzar turned with confidence to the man who had on that former occasion given him the answer he sought (2[25-45]). He had named him *Belteshazzar*, honoring thus both his god Bel and the Jewish youth (1[7]).

10–18. The Royal Dream. The king beheld a gigantic *tree*, reaching to heaven, and visible from all parts of the earth. It was beautiful and it fed and sheltered all *beasts, birds*, and *men*. (A similar representation of the Assyrian king is given in Ezek. 31[3-9].) Suddenly an angel descended from heaven and ordered the tree hewn down, leaving only its stump and roots in the ground. In the middle of v. 15 the figure changes abruptly (*let it . . . let his*) from a tree to a man—the king—confined with a metal band like a maniac, living with the beasts and like a beast, for seven years. It was to be a lesson to the ruler who thought himself the equal of God.

19–27. Daniel's Interpretation. It was not easy to make known to an autocrat like Nebuchadrezzar the sinister meaning of his dream. But encouraged by the king the prophet began by wishing its meaning might be to the royal enemies. The tree, of course, represented Nebuchadrezzar himself. On him was pronounced the doom of a seven-years' exile from his throne and from sanity, until he learned the lesson of becoming humility. The seer closed with an appeal to the king to repent and redress the wrongs he had wrought.

28–33. The Sentence Executed. The doom fell upon the king as predicted, after a year's time. In the midst of his pride he was stricken; a voice repeated his sentence, he was banished from his royal estate, and became like a beast in body and behavior. The narrative of this chapter is one of the historical perplexities of the book of Daniel. There is no record in the inscriptions or in the history of Babylonia regarding such a malady as is here described. It is probable that some popular tradition regarding Nebuchadrezzar and the conquest of his kingdom by Cyrus forms the basis of the account (Farrar, *Daniel*, pp. 198f.) Whatever its historical value may be, the purpose is clear. It was to teach the futility of human pride and of opposition to the will of God. He will humble those who exalt themselves in pride and oppress his people.

34–37. **The King Restored.** Among the most difficult features of the book of Daniel are the accounts of the acknowledgment of belief in Jehovah, the God of the Jews, by heathen kings like Nebuchadrezzar (2^{47} $3^{28, 29}$ 4^{37}) and Darius (6^{25-27}). Even if there be little in the way of historical evidence for such representations, the motive is clear, and the desire of a Jewish writer to include such confessions by the worshipers of other gods can easily be understood.

CHAPTER V

The Feast of Belshazzar. At a banquet given to a thousand of his lords and his harem, Belshazzar, here represented as the son and successor of Nebuchadrezzar, ordered the golden vessels, taken from the Temple at Jerusalem, to be brought and used. A hand appeared, writing upon the wall words which the wise men could not interpret. Daniel was summoned and read their meaning—that the days of Belshazzar's kingdom were numbered, and it was to be divided and given to the Medes and Persians. Daniel was rewarded, and the same night Belshazzar was slain.

1–4. **Belshazzar's Impiety.** The reference to this man as king is one of the historical difficulties of the book. Nebuchadrezzar had no son Belshazzar, nor was there such a king of Babylon. (See notes on 1^{21}.) Three kings related to the ruling family followed Nebuchadrezzar. Then came Nabunaid, or Nabonidus, unrelated to the royal family, and his reign was brought to an end by the conquest of the land by Cyrus the Persian in 538 B.C. Nabunaid had a son named Belshazzar, who never came to the throne, but is referred to in the inscriptions as "the king's son." Babylon surrendered to one of Cyrus' lieutenants, Gubaru (Gobryas), and the Persian soldiers entered the city without fighting. Nabunaid was taken prisoner. Later on, Cyrus entered Babylon and proclaimed peace to the city. Belshazzar, the king's son, still held out in some fortified place. But in a night assault by Gubaru he was slain. These statements are contained in the "Annalistic Tablet," the writing of a contemporary. (See Driver, *Daniel*, p. xxviii.) The rule passed directly from the Babylonians under Nabunaid to the Persians under Cyrus. (For dates, etc., see art., *Chronology of O.T.*, p. 111.) But the writer of Daniel understood that the succession was from Babylonians to Medes, and from Medes to Persians. It is with his outline of history that we have to do in the book. The gold, silver, and bronze dishes and implements of the Temple were carried to Babylon after the capture of Jerusalem in 586 B.C. (2 Kings 25^{13-17}), and were impiously used by Belshazzar in his feast.

5–9. **The Mystic Hand and its Message.** At the height of the revelry a hand appeared, writing words on the wall opposite the king. He was terrified, and summoned his diviners to make known the meaning of the portent. As in the earlier instances (2^{10} 4^{7}), the wise men were unable to interpret the mystery. This left the king and his guests deeply troubled.

10–12. **The Queen's Wise Counsel.** In this crisis the queen mother advised the king to call in Daniel, now an old man, who had served Nebuchadrezzar years before in such emergencies ($2^{25f.}$ 4^{18}).

13–17. **Daniel Before the King.** When brought in the seer was questioned as to his ability to read the writing, and was promised a third part of the authority in the kingdom, with the appropriate symbols of his rank, as a reward. He declined these honors, but promised to give the interpretation of the writing.

18–24. **The Lesson Unheeded.** Fearlessly Daniel took the opportunity to remind Belshazzar of his father's experience (4^{4-26}), his pride, his fall, and his exile to the estate of a beast until he was ready to acknowledge the authority of the Most High. He then pointed out the arrogance and impiety of the king, and the reason for the sending of the mysterious hand.

25–28. **The Writing and its Meaning.** The words *mene, mene, tekel, upharsin* would seem to refer to three weights in common use, the "mina," the "shekel" and the "half mina." There would be little satisfaction to the diviners in such an inscription, but the words might suggest a more significant meaning, i.e., "numbered," "weighed," "divided." The two forms of the writing (vv. 25, 28) really mean the same (mg.). The Medes and the Persians were the two peoples who joined in the conquest of the Babylonian Empire, the Median soldiers having deserted Astyages their king in 549 B.C. and joined Cyrus.

29–31. **Daniel Rewarded; Belshazzar Slain.** The king kept his promise (see v. 16), and conferred on the seer the honors offered if he should interpret the writing. That night of revelry saw the king slain by the invaders. Of a *Darius the Mede* nothing is known. It would seem that the writer understood that the rule passed from the Babylonians to the Medes, and that Darius was the first king of the new dynasty. No Median kingdom is known to the historians as intervening between the Babylonian and the Persian. As for Darius, it may be that the writer had in mind Darius Hystaspes (521-486 B.C.), the father (not the son, 9^1) of Xerxes (Ahasuerus).

CHAPTER VI

Daniel Delivered from the Lions. In the organization of the kingdom by Darius, Daniel was made one of three chiefs, and was about to be promoted to the leading place in the realm, when the other princes, jealous of his honors, conspired to destroy him. Unwillingly, the king was compelled to sanction their evil design. But by a miracle Daniel was saved, his enemies were destroyed, and his God received the reverence of the king.

1–3. Daniel's Promotion. Already it has been recorded that the three friends of the seer were given high offices in the province (2^{49} 3^{30}) and that Daniel himself was held in special honor by Nebuchadrezzar (2^{49}), and made one of three chiefs by Belshazzar (5^{29}). Darius now planned to make him supreme. It may be that the idea of 120 satrapies, of which nothing else is known, was suggested by the 127 provinces mentioned in Esth. 1^1 8^9.

4–9. The Conspiracy Against Daniel. Filled with jealousy against the man whom the king planned to place over them, the other officials schemed to take advantage of Daniel's well-known habit of prayer, and rushed into the royal presence with their petition. This was flattering to the king's vanity, and without suspicion he signed the decree.

10–15. The Praying Prophet and the Plotting Princes. Daniel soon learned of the cabal against him, but undisturbed he continued his practice of praying thrice daily (Psa. 55^{17}) before his open window, that faced west toward Jerusalem, the city of his God. In the same way cathedrals are built with their altars at the eastern end so that the worshiper faces Jerusalem (Psa. 5^7), and the Mohammedan prays with his face toward Mecca. Finding themselves baffled, the plotters rushed again to the king with their accusation, and demanded that the penalty be enforced. Though alarmed for Daniel's safety, the king was bound by the edict.

16–27. Thrown to the Lions, but Saved. The sentence was carried out, to the grief of Darius, who passed the night in deep anxiety. Early in the morning he hurried to the lion pit, and called to Daniel in a distressed voice to know if he was safe. The prophet answered that he was. So he was taken unhurt from the den and the conspirators were punished with the same fate they had prepared for him.

25–28. The King's Decree. As in the former instances (3^{29} 4^1), the royal reverence for the God of Daniel is registered in an edict to all the people of the realm. Cyrus the Persian (see on 1^{21}) is understood by the writer to have followed the Median Darius.

CHAPTERS 7 TO 12: VISIONS OF DANIEL

The second half of the book (chs. 7–12) is of much greater importance in the thought of the author than the first (chs. 1–6). The first part narrated the experiences of Daniel and his three friends as a series of exhortations to constancy and courage. The second half relates a series of visions in which Daniel is made to predict the events of the period from his own day to that of the writer of the book, nearly four hundred years. The purpose was to teach that God has a program of history which cannot be thwarted and which he can make known to his servants. The recital of past events, familiar to the readers, would give them confidence that the short future regarding which actual predictions are made could likewise be trusted. The two sections of the book are held together by the striking similarity—indeed, the practical identity—of chs. 2 and 7, the story of the four world kingdoms, ending in the triumph of the kingdom of God.

CHAPTER VII

1–8. Daniel's Vision of the Four Beasts. The first year of Belshazzar takes the reader back to a time earlier than the events described in ch. 5. Out of the sea, symbol of the agitated world of mankind, four different beasts came up. The first was a *lion* with vulture wings, strong and swift, but soon changed to a human form and character. This referred, of course, to the Babylonian kingdom and its great ruler Nebuchadrezzar, and corresponds to the gold head of $2^{32, 38}$. The second beast was like a *bear*, fierce but less swift, with three ribs in its mouth, denoting conquered nations. Like the breast and arms of silver of the image ($2^{32, 39}$), it represented probably the Median kingdom, which, as the author understood, followed the Babylonian (5^{31}). The third beast was like a *leopard*, with four wings and four heads, swift of movement, and facing all quarters in its victorious career. This would point to the Persian rule, symbolized by the bronze of the image (2^{32}), its first king being Cyrus the Great (1^{21} 6^{28}). But the fourth beast was far more terrible, hardly to be pictured save in imagination (cf. v. 19). It had *ten horns*, among which another came up, small, but uprooting three of the ten, and having eyes that saw and a mouth that spoke. This nondescript beast seems to represent the Macedonian or Greek kingdom of Alexander with the kings who succeeded him, culminating in Antiochus Epiphanes, the Syrian persecutor (175–164 B.C.). It corresponds to the iron legs of the image (2^{33}), the two kingdoms of Syria and Egypt. Of the governments into which Alexander's kingdom was broken up, these two were nearest to Palestine. The *little horn* of this vision and that of 8^{9} unmistakably signify Antiochus, whose impious and cruel deeds filled the Jews with terror in this period (see notes on 8^{9-12}).

9–12. The Judgment. Suddenly the scene changed. Seats for a court were placed, and an aged judge with white raiment and hair took his place. This was the divine court with God as the Judge. Multitudes attended and the books of record were opened. Judgment was pronounced upon the fourth beast, and it was destroyed by fire. The other beasts lost their dominion, though their people still survived. Thus the vision pointed out the divine condemnation of the rule from which arose the persecuting tyrant.

13, 14. The Human Figure. While the seer looked on, one came with clouds *like a son of man*, a human being, contrasted with the beasts. He was brought to the aged judge, and the power and authority that had formerly belonged to the various kingdoms represented by the beasts were given to him as an enduring and world-wide rule. This figure, as is clearly shown in vv. 18, 22, represents the saints of God, i.e., the ideal and purified Jewish race, with whose fortunes the author was alone concerned. For a later application of the term, see p. 846.

15–28. The Interpretation. Daniel was worried by his vision. Of an angel who stood near he asked the meaning of what he had seen. The answer was clear: The four beasts represented four kings, the heads of four kingdoms. But it is to the saints of God, the holy race, that the enduring power shall be given. As to the *fourth beast*, it is here described more fully as a ferocious and persecuting power, making war against the chosen people until God interfered and judgment was rendered in favor of the harassed people. The Babylonian, Median and Persian kingdoms would be followed by the Greek, which would thresh the nations and master all the earth. A succession of kings would arise, ten in number, either actual or symbolical of the Syrian dynasty. But one in particular, Antiochus Epiphanes, making his way to the throne at the expense of three others, would be the arch enemy of God and his people, ruling regardless of law or right, and succeeding for a brief time—three years and a half. Then would come the end of his arrogant and devastating rule. To the holy people the dominion would be given, for the kingdom belongs to God and his saints. With this the angel's explanation ceased. But naturally the seer was greatly disturbed. The device of the writer of the book is skillful and effective. By making Daniel, the ancient seer, predict a series of events which all knew to have taken place, he was able to encourage his readers to wait a little longer for the end of the tyrant's career, when the dark days would be over, and the time of peace and victory for the Jewish people would be ushered in. This is made still more evident in the next chapter.

The earlier commentaries of Daniel understood the fourth kingdom to be Rome, for the reason that the expression *son of man* (v. 13) was believed to refer to Jesus Christ. But it is evident from the repeated identifications of this human figure with the *saints of the Most High* (vv. 18, 22, 25, 27) that it is not the Messiah, but the new Jewish state which is meant. The apocalypse is a Jewish and not a Christian message.

CHAPTER VIII

The Ram and the Goat. In this chapter a shorter period of time is covered, the first or Babylonian section being omitted; but the same device of prediction is employed, animal figures are used, and the same objective is reached—the outrageous conduct of Antiochus Epiphanes, and his impending fall.

1–8. Daniel's Vision of the Ram and the Goat. This scene is placed in the third year of Belshazzar, two years after that of ch. 7. The prophet was at Susa (*Shushan*), the capital of Elam, one of the chief residences of the Persian kings (Neh. 1^{1} Esth. 1^{2}). He saw a *ram*, the symbol of the Medo-Persian power, standing beside the river. It had two horns, both high, but one higher than the other, and the higher came up last (or "behind the other," Smith's version). The shorter horn represented the Median king or kingdom and the longer one the Persian (see v. 20). While the ram was pushing his way resistlessly farther and farther, a *goat* with one horn suddenly appeared from the west, i.e., from Europe, and with incredible speed hurled himself upon the ram, overthrowing him and breaking his horns. This is the description of Alexander's rapid and victorious career, coming out of Greece, and overthrowing completely the Persian Empire (334-323 B.C.). But at the climax of his power the horn was broken and four horns came up in its place. Students of history recognize at once the meaning of this part of the vision. Alexander, having conquered the world of his day, died in his early manhood, sighing for other worlds to conquer. There being no son who could succeed him, his empire fell to four of his generals, Cassander (Macedonia), Lysimachus (Thrace), Seleucus (Syria and the East) and Ptolemy (Egypt).

9–12. The Little Horn. From one of these four, Seleucus of Syria (312–280 B.C.), arose at length Antiochus IV (175–164 B.C.), called Epiphanes, "the manifest," or "evident," i.e., the god, arrogating to himself, after the manner of Alexander, the attributes of deity. But so erratic and violent was his conduct at times that he was given, especially by the Jews, the nickname of Epimanes, the "madman," or "madcap." He was the eighth of the Syrian line. His ambitions were the conquest of Egypt, the rival kingdom to the south, and the submission of all the peoples of his realm to the Greek religion. In this plan he met resistance from the loyal Jews in Palestine, *the glorious land* (v. 9). The author writes that in his pride Antiochus thought himself capable of plucking the stars from their places, he defied God himself, he defiled the Temple at Jerusalem and caused the suspension of its services for more than three years (1 Macc. 1^{20-50} 4^{44-61}), i.e., from 168 to 165 B.C. During this unhappy time the faithful Jews were subjected to great hardships and their rights of worship were suppressed. The final sacrilege was the erection of a heathen altar, and probably also a statue of Zeus, upon the altar of burnt-offering (1 Macc. 1^{54}). This was the horrible thing that necessitated the cessation of all use of the shrine till it could be purified. It was the abomination that made desolate the holy place (v. 13; cf. 9^{27}).

13, 14. Length of the Evil Time. The seer heard two angels conversing. One asked the other how long the desecration of the sanctuary was to continue. The answer was twenty-three hundred evening-mornings, or eleven hundred and fifty days, a little less than the three years and a half (1,260 days) usually designated as the time of affliction (7^{25} 12^{7} Rev. 12^{14}).

15–27. The Interpretation. As in former instances (7^{16}), the meaning of the vision was made clear to Daniel by an angel. This proved to be the angel *Gabriel*, also named as a messenger of God in $9^{21, 22}$ and Luke 1^{19}. Roused from a swoon of terror, the seer was told that the vision referred to the end of the age, a long time in the future, i.e., the time of the persecution by Antiochus, and the triumph of the Jewish nation that was to follow. Then the various features of the vision were explained in language so explicit that no one could mistake it. Three of the four kingdoms of ch. 2 and ch. 7 were meant by the two horns of the ram and the he goat. They were Media-Persia and Greece or Macedonia. Alexander and his weaker successors were symbolized by the horns of vv. 21, 22. Much later, toward the end of this Greco-Syrian dynasty, would arise the king represented by the little horn (see v. 9; cf. $7^{8, 11, 20, 24-26}$). He is described as defiant, designing, crafty, destructive, boastful and prosperous, against the holy people and even their God. Up to this point the career of Antiochus, familiar to the author, has been sketched. The rest is prediction, based on unwavering confidence that God will deal with the persecutor as he deserves. His success was only for a time. Suddenly he was to be cut off by divine visitation (vv. 23–25). Antiochus died on an expedition in Persia in 164 B.C. The seer was told that the vision was not to be revealed. This would account for the fact that it had been unknown all the years since the life of Daniel, and had been only just disclosed in the author's day. This was a favorite device of apocalyptic writers (Enoch 1^{2} 104^{13} etc.; see further art., *Intertestamental Literature*, pp. 188–9). So alarming did the disclosure seem to the seer that he was ill for some days, and never quite understood it (vv. 26, 27).

CHAPTER IX

The Seventy Weeks. In the prophetic book of Jeremiah, who preached in the last days of Judah and into the Babylonian Exile (i.e., from about 625 to 575 B.C.), references are made to seventy years during which the Jews were to be in exile, at the end of which period they were to be restored to their land (Jer. $25^{11, 12}$ 29^{10} 30^{18} 31^{38-40}). The author of Daniel, living in the days of Antiochus Epiphanes (175–164 B.C.), was troubled by the fact that no such restoration had occurred as the prophet had predicted, though more than four centuries had passed. It was his purpose to show that it was not *seventy years* that were meant by Jeremiah, but *seventy weeks of years*, or 490 years. That would place the date of fulfillment in his own days or later, and safeguard the prediction of Jeremiah from the appearance of failure. The author's scheme of years is not very definite, for the Jews had no exact system of chronology till they came under the Syrian authority in the third century B.C. In fact, of the many that have been proposed, no explanation of the seventy weeks has ever fitted accurately the chronology of the period as it is known to historians. The writer was using the best information he had, but his figures are general rather than precise. His purpose is evident, however. It was to show that the fulfillment of Jeremiah's prophecy was to be expected in his own age, the age of Antiochus, and not in the past at the end of seventy years from the time when the prophet spoke. To do this he divides the seventy weeks of years into three sections, the first of seven weeks of years, or forty-nine years; the second of sixty-two weeks, or 434 years; the third of one week, seven years, half of which (three and one half) is already past; another like period (three and one half years) will see the end of persecution, the fall of Antiochus, and the beginning of the time of hope and happiness for the Jewish race.

1, 2. Daniel's Study of Jeremiah's Prophecy. This angelic communication to the seer is placed in the first year of Darius the Mede, whose reign is represented as following that of Belshazzar (5[30] 6[1, 28], notes). The *books* here referred to are the writings of the prophets, which together with the books of Moses (Genesis-Deuteronomy) already formed a collection, or canon of sacred writings, in the second century B.C. (Ecclus. 1[1], and cf. p. 95a; for the passages in Jeremiah, see introductory paragraphs to this chapter.) *Seventy* was less a specific than a general number among the Jews, much as a hundred is with us.

3–19. Daniel's Prayer of Confession and Entreaty. It was a prayer for light upon the perplexing problem of the nation's continued failure to achieve its destiny of restoration and service. The causes for this lay in the sins of the past, and of these sins Daniel makes humble confession on behalf of his people. They had merited the curse uttered long ago by Moses (Deut. 28[15-19]). Yet in spite of these offenses, the seer pleads for Judah, that God may restore his favor to Jerusalem and the sanctuary. With passionate and pathetic fervor he prays for the renewal of Zion's ancient glory.

20–23. The Angel's Comforting Words. Two angels are named in the book, *Gabriel*, the divine messenger (8[16], and evidently also the speaker in 10[5, 6]; see also Luke 1[26]), and *Michael*, the heavenly champion of Israel (10[13, 21] 12[1]). The former came close to the seer, charged with a message of comfort for him, as beloved of God and worthy of an answer to his perplexity.

24–27. Seventy Weeks of Years. Now comes the interpretation of Jeremiah's prophecy regarding the seventy years. *Seventy weeks of years*, i.e., 490 years, are assigned as the time for the ushering in of the new age of peace and the consecration of the holy place. From the day when Jeremiah announced the future restoration of Jerusalem, i.e., from 586 B.C., to an anointed one, a prince, i.e., Cyrus the Great (538 B.C.) would be *seven weeks*, i.e., forty-nine years. This was the date of the formal close of the Exile by the decree of Cyrus, forty-eight years from the destruction of the holy city. There would follow *sixty-two weeks* (434 years) during which Jerusalem was to be rebuilt with streets and open spaces, but not without experiencing many troubles. At the end of that time an *anointed one* is to be cut off and deprived of all he has. This seems to refer to the deposition and murder of the beloved and honored high priest, Onias III, an event not mentioned specifically in the O.T., but of very great significance to the Jews of the time (2 Macc. 3[1, 31-40] 4[7f.] [23f.]).

This is not a reference to the Messiah of the N.T., as some of the early translations would seem to imply. The application is not to our Lord, but to an O.T. crisis and a martyred priest. The *prince* that was to come with an armed force to devastate the city and pollute the Temple is Antiochus Epiphanes, but his end was inevitable. He would be swept away as with a flood. To the end of the final week, seven years, his warfare against the holy people would continue. With the help of apostate Jews he would work his will. Half way through that week he would cause the discontinuance of the Temple services. In the place of the holy sacrifices, i.e., on the altar of burnt-offering, would be set up the abominable pagan altar, so appalling to pious Jews that the place had to be abandoned until purified. At the end the destined doom would be poured out upon the desolator (i.e., Antiochus, or the heathen altar). Thus the vision reaches the same object as in the former chapters, namely, the detestable conduct of the Syrian king, and his providential overthrow.

It is easy to see that the numbers employed in the vision (i.e., sixty-two week-years, 434 years) do not fit the facts of history. Neither does any other scheme that has been proposed by the commentators. The writer's chronology is too uncertain to be squared with the events of those centuries as they are now known to the student of history. But the purpose is sufficiently clear, the certainty that the reign of terror instituted by Antiochus was soon to cease, and the blessed consummation was soon to be ushered in. The impression produced by these references to the persecution and these predictions of its end must have been profound. They were not forgotten in later crises, like the Roman siege of Jerusalem, in anticipation of which our Lord quoted the words of the book of Daniel, with their fresh application to the impending tragedy (Mt. 24[15] Mk. 13[14], notes).

CHAPTER X

The Struggle of the Kingdoms. The final vision is found in the last three chapters of the book. For three weeks the seer had been fasting. He was then confronted by a celestial being of transcendent brilliance, the sight of whom overwhelmed him. Roused from his stupor, he was told of angelic contests in which the fortunes of the holy people were at stake. Then there was given him a long and detailed recital of events from the times of Cyrus the Great to those of Antiochus Epiphanes, who is the objective in every one of the dreams and visions. This recital is given in the form of a supposed prediction, after the manner of all apocalypses. In the earlier portion it is rapid and general. As it approaches the author's own time, the period of Antiochus, it becomes more precise and vivid. But as it comes to the actual time when the book was written, and seeks to portray the last days and downfall of the oppressor, it takes on again a more vague and uncertain form. This is the actually predictive portion of the vision. The details are obscure because unknown to the seer, but the central fact, the divine judgment on the foe of the sacred people, is made perfectly clear. Then comes the end of the age, marked by portents, and the resurrection of the Jewish race, some of them good and some evil. The revelation thus made is to be kept secret till the end of the age—i.e., of Antiochus—approaches. That end was to come a little less than three years and a half (1,260 days) from the desecration of the Temple. Happy would they be who survived to the new age of Jewish triumph, the Messianic time beyond.

1–9. The Heavenly Messenger. This vision in the third year of Cyrus follows appropriately that of 9[1f.] in the reign of Darius, according to the author's understanding of the history (6[28]). It had to do with a period of difficulty and hardship that was to follow the days of Daniel. In his anxiety about his people and the coming time of trouble he fasted for three weeks. Then by the banks of the Tigris came the vision of the shining herald from heaven whose appearance and words struck down the seer in terror.

10–21. Celestial Struggles. Roused by the angel's friendly touch, Daniel was told that he was to be informed of the future, in accordance with his anxious desire. The angel guardian of Persia, one of the hostile nations, had sought to prevent the revelation to the seer, but Michael, the angel champion of the holy people, had come to assist the messenger, who was therefore no longer detained there, but had come to enlighten Daniel. The idea of angel guardians for the different nations is hinted in earlier portions of the O.T. (Psa. 82[1] Isa. 24[21]), and is plainly set forth in this book of Daniel (10[13, 20, 21] 11[1] 12[1]; see also intro., section on "Teaching and Permanent Value"). The vision to be disclosed by the angel pertained to events of the distant future, i.e., the times of Antiochus. Prostrated afresh by these experiences, Daniel is strengthened by another angel who seeks to reassure him, and thus encouraged, he waits for the revelation. The angel herald, before giving his message, adds a further word regarding the events mentioned in v. 13. He says that as soon as he has given his disclosure to Daniel he must return to his conflict with the hostile angels of Persia and Greece in which he and Michael are engaged. As far back as the first year of Darius the Mede he had come to Michael's aid in defense of the fortunes of Israel.

CHAPTER XI

1–4. Xerxes and Alexander. It is too bad that the chapter division and v. 1 interrupt the thought. In v. 2 the vision proceeds. Three Persian kings, Cambyses (529–522 B.C.), Gaumata (7 months), and Darius Hystaspis (522–485) are to follow Cyrus (538–529), the reigning king (10[1]). Then will come a fourth, Xerxes (485–465), whose great expedition against Greece ended in disaster at Salamis (480 B.C.). Next in this list comes Alexander (336–323), the conqueror of Persia, whose brief career is to be followed by the break-up of his empire and its division among his four generals and others (see notes on 8[1-8]).

5–20. Kings of Syria and Egypt. Attention is now fixed upon the two kingdoms nearest Palestine, namely Syria and Egypt, whose capitals were Antioch and Alexandria. The characters described but unnamed in these verses are easily identified by the student of history. The story is too long to be told here. but it is easy to understand that the fortunes of Palestine and the Jewish people were profoundly affected by the struggles between the two neighboring kingdoms to the north and the south, each of which claimed the right of sovereignty over them. These verses give in vivid form the leading features of the reigns of the seven kings of Syria, from Seleucus I

(312–280 B.C.) to Antiochus Epiphanes (175–164), and of the ten kings of Egypt, from Ptolemy Soter (322–285) to Ptolemy Philometer (164–146; for these kings, see art., *Chronology of O.T.*, p. 112). In a general way these rulers are symbolized by the ten toes of the image in 2[42, 43] and the ten horns of the beast in 7[7, 20, 24]. The facts were apparently well known to the writer of Daniel, and contrast in their dramatic character and detail with the less definite and exact features of the earlier period (vv. 2–4). For the historical facts forming the basis of this recital, see Farrar, *Book of Daniel*, pp. 299–318; Bevan, *Book of Daniel*, pp. 171–200; Driver, *Daniel*, pp. 163–199; Charles, *Daniel*, pp. 118–138; Montgomery, *Daniel*, pp. 420–467.

21–39. The Career of Antiochus Epiphanes. With these verses the author comes to his main subject, the tyrant who is in his very day carrying on his campaign of impiety and persecution. There are given at length the facts of his reign in the customary guise of prediction—his rise through intrigue, his success in war, his deposition and destruction of Onias III, the Jewish priest-prince, his treachery, his gigantic briberies, his first successful expedition against Egypt, his insincerity in dealing with his nephew, the defeated Ptolemy Philometer, and his return with great spoil from this first phase of his southern campaign. Already the hostile attitude of Antiochus had been shown toward the faithful Jews in Palestine, but after his mortifying treatment by the Roman legates who, arriving in ships from the west, ordered him to withdraw from Egypt which he had again invaded, he appears to have vented his rage on the Jews and their religion. In this he used such apostates as had yielded to his flatteries and bribes and abandoned their national faith. It was at this time that the forces sent by him attacked Jerusalem, defiled the Temple, set a Syrian garrison over it, and erected the crowning infamy, the heathen altar, which rendered the ritual sacrifice impossible. This was the devastating outrage, *the abomination that made desolate* the house of God. (The story is told in 1 Macc. 1; cf. ch. 6.)

In spite of the most violent acts of persecution, great numbers of the Jews gave evidence of their invincible faith, even to the point of martyrdom. Of these facts the books of Maccabees are the eloquent record. In this hour of need arose the romantic and successful revolution of the Maccabees, which for a brilliant moment rescued the nation from foreign oppression. Probably the author of Daniel did not expect much from this enterprise, for he speaks of it somewhat slightingly as *a little help* (v. 34). But it was the means at last of breaking the Syrian power in Palestine. The remainder of this paragraph sets forth still further the monstrous arrogance of the king, his self-exaltation to godhead, his disregard of all gods but Jupiter, the god of strongholds, and his assignment of honors and rewards to his partisans.

40–45. The Time of the End. The author now comes to the moment when he is to describe the final stage in the career of the Syrian king. Up to this time he has followed with measurable accuracy the facts of recent history. Now he undertakes to predict the end of the drama. Of one thing he is perfectly certain—the tyrant is soon to fall. In this his prophetic vision is not at fault. But the details are quite different from the closing events of Antiochus' reign. Of such events as are related here there is no record. The king died not in Palestine, but in Persia.

CHAPTER XII

Final Words. At the end of the age, the time of the downfall of the evil king, Michael, the angel who defends the holy people, will be needed, for a period of bitter trouble will come. But the faithful, whose names are written in the book (see 7[10]), shall be delivered. There shall be a resurrection of many (v. 2), presumably Jews, to an enduring experience either of joy or of sorrow. In all probability the resurrection experience is expected to come to only some of the Jews, the martyrs who had given their lives for the faith—these are to be rewarded in the after life; and the apostates who betrayed the faith—these will receive the punishment they deserve. (See intro., section on "Teaching and Permanent Value".) In that time the wise and the righteous shall shine like stars (v. 3). But the words of the prediction must not be disclosed till their fulfillment approaches. Two angels were standing by the river. One of them asked the angel clothed in white how long it would be until the time of the end. The answer was given with assurance that it would be three years and a half. As soon as the tyrant was destroyed, all would be over (vv. 5–7). Wishing to know more of the matter, Daniel made further inquiry. He was told to let the matter rest. It was enough to know that from the date of the desecration of the Temple to the expected end would be somewhat more than three and a half years (1,290 days). Happy would be the ones who lived through that time, and survived till the days of glory (1,335 days). But Daniel was to depart and rest in the grave till the time of the consummation (vv. 8–13).

HOSEA

By Principal H. Wheeler Robinson

Introduction

The Prophet. Hosea ranks with Jeremiah as the most human of the prophets, which explains why he, like his spiritual kinsman, knows so much of the divine secret—the deathless love of God for man. The tragedy of the prophet's home life was the spring of his prophetic message, and perhaps of his prophetic activity. Like Longfellow's "Gasper Becerra," he carved his masterpiece from the brand that burned in the fire on his domestic hearth:—

"O thou sculptor, painter, poet!
Take this lesson to thy heart:
That is best which lieth nearest;
Shape from that thy work of art."

His book forms a fitting sequel to that of Amos, following it in time-order, and enlarging its teaching; and the introduction to that book (p. 775) should be read for a picture of the social and religious background of Hosea's prophecies. The brief prophetic activity of Amos may have belonged to any one year of the decade 760–750 B.C.; that of Hosea began toward the close of the reign of Jeroboam II, i.e., some time before 743, and extended over the next decade or more of Israel's history.

Hosea and Amos. Like Amos, Hosea addressed the Northern Kingdom; unlike Amos, Hosea himself belongs to the people he addresses (7⁵); he is, in fact, the only prophet belonging to the Northern Kingdom whose ministry has left a clear literary monument. As we compare his testimony with that of his predecessor, we cannot miss its characteristic differences, even when Hosea is dealing with the same evils as Amos. There is a changed emphasis, springing not so much from changed conditions (though these were not wanting) as from a difference of temperament, character, and personal fortunes between the two men. Amos dwelt on social evils, and incidentally described the abuses of the religion practiced in Jehovah's name at the high places. Hosea also insists on right conduct toward other men as essential to the true worship of Jehovah (4^{1-6} 6^{6} 10^{12}), but he says far more about the immorality, actual and figurative, of the contemporary worship, and his chief emphasis falls on the idea of religion as a right inward relation to God.

We might say that Amos presents religion in terms of morality, while Hosea presents morality in terms of religion. There can be no question as to which is the higher conception. Schleiermacher, in a metaphor drawn from music, has finely suggested the true relation between morality and religion. "A man's special calling," he says, "is the melody of his life, and it remains a simple, meager series of notes unless religion, with its endlessly rich variety, accompany it with all notes, and raise the simple song to a full-voiced, glorious harmony." The melody of Amos was harmonized by Hosea. This must be our sufficient compensation for the undoubted fact that Hosea is the most difficult of all the prophets to understand, because of his wealth of allusive imagery, his swift emotional transitions, and the frequent and deep-seated corruption of the text.

The Historical Background. Hosea in the north, like Jeremiah (later) in the south, interprets and justifies the decline and fall of a kingdom. His allusions to contemporary events confirm the testimony of the Second Book of Kings (ch. 15) that the period after the death of Jeroboam II, 743 B.C., was one of anarchy and social disorder. Zechariah, his son, after reigning for six months, was killed through a conspiracy promoted by Shallum, who succeeded him. But Shallum's reign was even briefer than his victim's, for he was slain by another usurper, Menahem, after a single month's reign. Menahem managed to keep on the throne for ten years, probably because he secured the support of Assyria by a heavy tribute. His son, Pekahiah, after two years, was overthrown by one of his military underlings, Pekah. This man, being anti-Assyrian in his policy, speedily suffered the loss of the northern part of his kingdom, and the deportation of its inhabitants. He was killed by Hoshea, an Assyrian protégé, who was allowed to rule until his rebellion against Assyria ended in the overthrow of the Northern Kingdom (722 or 721 B.C.).

This bewildering succession of plots and murders, bringing six men to the throne within a score of years, is reflected in Hosea's prophecies (7^{7} 8^{4} $13^{10, 11}$). Hosea abhorred the political scheming and the unprincipled alliances which were being sought with Assyria on the one hand, and with Egypt on the other (7^{11} 10^{4} 12^{1}). In the noble confession outlined for a truly penitent Israel in the closing chapter, one line is significant of this; Israel will say at long last, "Assyria shall not save us." Such a renunciation of worldly policy is as vital, from the prophet's standpoint, as the words, "What have I to do any more with idols?"

Religious and Political Apostasy. Hosea's historical perspective is longer than that of Amos. Israel's political paralysis in both domestic and foreign relations is traced back to those deeds of blood in Jezreel through which the dynasty of Jehu, with the approval of Elisha, mounted the throne. Before Jeroboam's death, and the beginning of the times of anarchy, Hosea calls his first-born child "Jezreel," as a sign that Jehovah "will avenge the blood of Jezreel upon the house of Jehu, and will cause the kingdom of the house of Israel to cease . . . and will break the bow of Israel in the valley of Jezreel" ($1^{4,\ 5}$). With a similar instinct for dramatic symbolism, characteristic of Hebrew prophecy, he calls his second child "Uncompassionated," and his third, "Not my people." By these names he is expressing Israel's alienation from Jehovah, the result of its past and present history. In more extended form, he describes it under the metaphor of a wife's infidelity to her husband. This is, indeed, the dominating figure of his book, and it became the classical expression for the prophetic condemnation of the popular religion. Like the naming of Hosea's children, the figure is closely connected with his family life. We must not think that when Hosea married his wife, she was already dishonored. (The marriage of Hosea is discussed fully in Eiselen, *The Prophetic Books of the O.T.*, vol. ii, pp. 373–377.) The prophetic way of stating consequences is often to read them back into the events from which they issued, and to speak of the seed as if it were the flower. The seven years covered by the first chapter of the book began in a normal marriage. But when Hosea's wife became unfaithful to him he saw a divine significance in the whole course of events. (See introduction to Amos, p. 776).

The Divine Love. His undestroyed love for the woman who had left him not only inspired Hosea to seek her out and to reclaim her, but it enabled him to enter into the very heart of God. Did not Jehovah feel toward Israel as Hosea himself felt toward Gomer? Was there not the same commingling of righteous indignation and compassionate pity? Was not Jehovah's love for his bride, Israel, at once her condemnation and her ultimate ground of hope? Thus does Hosea enrich the old idea of a marriage between a god and his people with a profound moral content. This is the contribution to the theology of the O.T. which Hosea was enabled to make from his own bitter experience; it is this which creates the depth and atmosphere of the picture he paints. Through the conspiracies of the capital city, the immorality and externalism of the worship at the high places, the idolatry which he seems to be the first to attack, the unkindness and deceit and violence of common life, we catch glimpses of God, pleading and expostulating with all the warmth of that passionate human heart which the prophet lent to its Maker (cf. especially 6^{4} $11^{8,\ 9}$).

Punishment and Restoration. Thus Hosea conceived the relation between Jehovah and Israel to be much closer than did Amos, as the predominant figure of marriage itself suggests. Amos looks around the whole horizon, and sees the God of righteousness active among the surrounding peoples as well as in Israel. Hosea looks up and sees the God of love, Israel's Saviour from the beginning (13^{4}). This does not mean that Jehovah will not punish the infidelity of his people; the contemplated penalty is exile to Egypt or Assyria (9^{3} $11^{5,\ 6}$). But Hosea is much more definite than Amos in his hope, or rather, his confidence, of the outcome, which will be the victory of God's patient and persistent love, in a new and spiritual betrothal ($2^{19,\ 20}$). The too facile penitence of those who lightly said, "Come and let us return unto the Lord" (6^{1}) will be followed by that deeper repentance, when Israel shall ask for the removal of its sinful *spirit*, shall repudiate its worldly expediencies and confidence in the instruments of war, and shall have no more to do with the idols its hands have fashioned. In that day it will humbly confess, as the result of its discipline and chastisement, "In thee the fatherless findeth mercy" (14^{3}). The words recall that other great figure of Hosea's experience, for he was a father as well as a husband—the figure of the Fatherhood of the God who called his son Israel out of the captivity of Egypt, and taught the little feet to walk, until the wearied child had to be picked up in the strong arms of the father ($11^{1f.}$).

The primary evil in Israel's relation to Jehovah is the sinful spirit (4^{12} 5^{4}), not those external acts which are its result. This is what underlies the worship of Jehovah as a mere Baal, the local giver of fertility, and inspires all the evils which cluster round the worship of God on the Canaanite high places—the sexual immorality (4^{13}), the superstition (4^{12}), the futile formalism (5^{6} 8^{13}), the use of material images (8^{4} 10^{5} 13^{2}), the vested interests of unworthy priests (4^8). "Because Ephraim hath multiplied altars to sin, altars have been unto him to sin" (8^{11}). So Hosea anticipates the day when "the thorn and the thistle shall come up on their altars" (10^8), a visible token of penalty, but destined to open a new chapter of history in which that evil past is left behind. The only Baal or "lord" worshiped on and around these altars in Hosea's day was Jehovah; yet the worship was utterly alien from him, for it belonged to that religion of "nature" which is always and everywhere at issue with the religion of "spirit." In the new day all alien elements will disappear—worship will be restored to its pristine purity and will be inspired by a deep sense of the abiding presence of God.

The Book of Hosea. The book falls into two distinct, but closely related, parts. The first three chapters contain the life-story of the prophet, the second chapter being a sermon-poem on the metaphor it has suggested. The remaining eleven chapters contain detached oracle-poems, in which the same ideas of infidelity and penalty constantly recur, without sensible progress, except that the book culminates in a confession of sin and a promise of divine grace. In the brief commentary that follows, only a few of the evident corruptions of the text can be indicated, and none of them can be fully discussed.

Until very recent times the book in its present form was commonly ascribed to the prophet whose name it bears; few, if any, passages were questioned as later additions or interpolations. However, with the advance in critical scholarship an increasing number of passages have come to be questioned. The alleged secondary elements, apart from words and sentences of minor importance, may be grouped as follows: (1) References to Judah; (2) passages picturing the glories of the future; (3) "phrases and sentences of a technical archæological or historical character, inserted by way of expansion or explanation"; (4) miscellaneous glosses and interpolations for which no special motive may be discovered. The complexity of the problem makes it impossible to deal with it in the limited space available here (see for a detailed discussion, Eiselen, *The Prophetic Books*, vol. ii, pp. 357–365). Here it may be sufficient to say that while the book is not entirely free from later interpolations (see comments below), the later elements are by no means as numerous as some recent writers seem to think. Moreover, the later additions do not modify in any fundamental way the teaching of the prophet Hosea.

Literature: Cheyne, *Hosea* (Cambridge Bible;) W. R. Smith, *The Prophets of Israel;* G. A. Smith, *The Book of the Twelve,* vol. i (Expositor's Bible); Horton, *The Minor Prophets,* vol. i (New Century Bible); Harper, *Amos and Hosea* (International Critical Commentary); Eiselen, *The Minor Prophets;* Welch, *The Religion of Israel under the Kingdom;* Melville Scott, *The Message of Hosea;* T. H. Robinson, *Decline and Fall of the Hebrew Kingdoms* (The Clarendon Bible.)

CHAPTER I

1. Title. The heading, which is probably a late editorial addition, dates a northern prophecy by a northern prophet under (1) four southern kings, covering 789–693 B.C. as maximum, and 740–720 as minimum; (2) one northern king (782–746). The contents enable us to fix the date fairly accurately. The first three chapters suggest the latter part of Jeroboam's reign, while the rest of the book reflects the disorder of the next decade. There seems to be no reference to the Syro-Ephraimitic war and the capture of Gilead by the Assyrians in 734, so that we may take 750–735 B.C. as Hosea's prophetic period. Nothing is known of him beyond the facts that may be learned from the book.

2–9. Israel's Infidelity Like Gomer's. When Hosea looked back on the earlier years of his marriage, knowing that the wife he had married in love and trust had proved unfaithful to him, and when, further, he had seen how like his marriage was to the relation of Jehovah and Israel, he relates his experience as if it were all known and interpreted to him from the beginning, just as a traveler writes up his day-by-day record in the light of the whole journey when completed. Thus Hosea makes the prophetic impulse (in part perhaps a product of this experience) to begin with his marriage, when in fact those events did begin which he subsequently re-interpreted by "prophetic symbolism."

He calls his first-born "Jezreel" in memory of the scene of Jehu's bloody massacre (2 Kings 9, 10), in requital for which Jehu's dynasty, and with it the Northern Kingdom, will cease to be. As a matter of fact, the kingdom survived the dynasty, which ended with Zechariah, its fifth representative, the son of Jeroboam; but the six kings between 743 and 721 B.C. had a precarious tenure of the throne. The *bow* (v. 5), i.e., the power, of Israel is to be broken (by Assyria) in the place of the century-old massacre (as might well have happened, since the plain of Jezreel is a natural battlefield). The second child is called "Uncompassionated," to express Israel's position in the eyes of Jehovah. (A contrast with Judah, perhaps added after the escape from Sennacherib in 701 B.C., is drawn in v. 7). The third child is called "Not my people," to the same effect. *Weaning* (v. 8) might be deferred for three years (2 Macc. 7[27]), so that the events of this chapter would cover about seven years of Hosea's life. Its continuation is described in 3[1-3].

10, 11. The Reversal of the Judgment. (See also 2[1].) This is expressed by the change of the second and third names from negations into affirmations, and by the re-interpretation of the first; great will be the day of "God's plantation" (*Jezreel*, see on 2[22, 23]). The two kingdoms will be reunited, and shall "go up" from exile (Ezra 2[1] 7[6] Neh. 12[1]) in unnumbered hosts. This reads like an interpolation of later date; in any case, it would more naturally follow 2[23]. The *living God* means the real God, as in 1 Sam. 17[26] (cf. Num. 21[29] for the idea of a nation as the offspring of a god).

CHAPTER II

1. See under 1[10, 11].

2–13. Israel's Infidelity. The allegory discovered in the actual events of the prophet's life is here developed on its own account. The "children" of Israel are bidden to strive (not "plead") with their mother, whose harlotry, with its penalty, descends upon them. The stripping of the adulteress (as in Ezek. 16[39]) belongs to the figure; the destruction of Canaan's fertility is to be literal fact (v. 3). The harlotry with which Israel is charged is spiritual, not physical (except so far as religious prostitution might be involved, as in Amos 2[7]). Israel has forsaken Jehovah, her husband, not, indeed, in name, but in fact. She has worshiped him at the sanctuaries of the local *Baals* (the "lovers" of v. 5), the supposed givers of the land's fertility, and therefore according to the Canaanite cult. Hosea's protest concerns (as we should say) Israel's idea of God; the erroneous idea of Jehovah (who seeks the moral qualities of v. 19) is allegorized into an actual abandonment of him—as, of course, it is (Elijah raised a different issue a century earlier, when he called Israel to choose between the worship of the Tyrian Baal, Melkart, and that of Jehovah; 1 Kings 18[21]). The character and emphasis of our worship reflect our idea of God, and two inconsistent ideas of God may mean in reality two Gods. The corn and wine and oil were the typical products of Canaan (Deut. 7[13]); the silver and gold, made into an image (v. 8 mg.), would come from Spain, Egypt, India, Arabia, by way of commerce. With v. 11, cf. Amos 8[10]. The *hire* (v. 12) is that of the prostitute (9[1]; cf. Gen. 38[17]), here represented by the fertility of the land.

14–23. The New Betrothal. Adversity will banish these false ideas and practices (v. 14 mg.); then Jehovah's compassion will lead Israel to make a new beginning (v. 15), in which she shall enter Canaan for the second time far otherwise than by the ill-omened entrance through the valley of "Troubling" (due to Achan, mg.). That valley (leading down from the hill-country to the Jordan valley by Jericho) shall become an entrance of better omen—a door of hope this second time. Jehovah has been worshiped as "Baal," but in the new age the very name shall be banished (Zech. 13[2]) because of its heathen associations. In the new prosperity neither beast nor man will have the power or the desire to do hurt (v. 18); outer welfare will correspond with the inner betrothal of spirit. The best comment on vv. 21, 22 is Wordsworth's "The Primrose of the Rock," where flower, stem, root, rock and earth are shown as upheld at last by God; Jehovah responds to the cry of the heavens and releases the rain, which moistens the earth and makes the vegetation to grow; so that "Jezreel" ("God sows") now becomes a name of good omen (cf. 1[4]).

CHAPTER III

1–3. The Redemption of the Faithless Wife. This chapter continues the story of Hosea's life from a point somewhat later than that reached in 1[9]. In the intervening period, his unfaithful wife has openly left him, and has sunk to the level of a slave. Nevertheless, Hosea's love for Gomer inspires him to redeem her by the payment of a ransom, though he cannot yet restore her to her old position. The *friend* of v. 1 should be "paramour" (as in Jer. 3[1], where translated "lovers"). *Cakes of raisins* were an article of food (2 Sam. 6[19] Isa. 16[7] Songs 2[5]); they may have been some feature of the vintage festival in Canaanite cults (cf. Jer. 7[18]). The male or female slave was estimated at thirty shekels of silver; here the value of the barley (twelve bushels) may represent the other fifteen. Chinese girls were bought up at thirty shillings each by the Salvation Army in 1922, to save them from a life of shame.

4, 5. Israel to Return. The *pillar* denotes a common object at Canaanite sanctuaries, a survival of stone-worship; the *ephod* is usually thought to have been an image of deity (Judg. 8[26f.]), but there are grounds for thinking that the primitive form of it was a loin-cloth with pockets from which the oracular lot was drawn or shaken; the *teraphim* were the *penates*, or household gods, of the Israelite (1 Sam. 19[13, 16] Gen. 31[19, 34f.]). Apparently, Hosea shows no disapproval of any of these, since he regards deprivation of them as being part of the penalty for Israel's disloyalty.

CHAPTER IV

Immorality due to False Religion. Hosea pictures the moral corruption of the Northern Kingdom, which will be punished by drought (v. 3). The priests are primarily responsible for all this (vv. 4–10); they have failed to teach the true knowledge of God, and have encouraged a false externality of religion in their self-interests (v. 8). The people (vv. 11–19) stupidly resort to divination; their life is wrong because their inner spirit is wrong (v. 12). Their worship of Jehovah (patterned on the tree-worship of Canaan, v. 13) is no true religion; sacred prostitution encourages and condones immorality in ordinary life. They are devoted to their sanctuaries, where there is idolatrous worship of Jehovah (v. 17); but these shall not save them from punishment.

1–10. The People's Corruption Due to the Priests' Faithlessness. The *controversy* of v. 1 is forensic (Mic. 6[2] 7[9]). Note the characteristic depth of insight into causes, implied in the reference to the want of the knowledge of God (v. 1, cf. vv. 6, 10, 12). In v. 2, we get a glimpse of the disorder of the decade after the death of Jeroboam II. In v. 4, *as they that strive with the priest* should probably read (by a redivision of Hebrew consonants) *with you is my controversy, O priests.* In v. 5, *thy mother* may refer to the whole clan of priests, rather than to the nation (as in 2[2]); the *stumbling* (cf. 5[5]) means the overthrow of priest and prophet who have failed in their task (cf. Ezek. 44[23], for the function of the priests as teachers). The reference in v. 8 is not to the actual consumption of the (later) sin-offering by the priests, but to their vested interests in religiosity. The priest is no better than the people (v. 9).

11–19. Religious Practices Condemned. The lack of true guidance in religion drives the people to divination by wooden rods and diviner's wands (v. 12). *They themselves* (v. 14) is masculine, and refers to the fathers, not to the daughters. (All mgs. in vv. 13–19 are preferable to the text, as usual; one of the ablest revisers used to say that the margins contain the scholarship of the R.V.). *Beth-aven* (house of iniquity, v. 15) is a contemptuous play on "Bethel" (house of God); for this and Gilgal, see on Amos 4[4] 5[5]; for oaths by local cults, see Amos 8[14]. V. 16b is best taken as a question. Hosea constantly uses the name *Ephraim* (Gen. 41[52], etc.) for the northern kingdom (v. 17). The doubtful text of v. 18 must be taken to mean that after their carousal they give themselves to sexual indulgence.

CHAPTER V

1–7. Priests and Rulers Have Misled the People. In this oracle, the leaders are made responsible for the false worship at the sanctuaries, where the attraction of the cult has been like a hunter's snare to the people. These are zealous in worship, but in vain, because the inner spirit is wrong. We note again (v. 4) the characteristic emphasis on the inner spirit, anticipative of the Sermon on the Mount (see previous oracle). *Mizpah* ("outlook-point," v. 1) is probably that in Gilead (Judg. 10[17] Gen. 31[49]); *Tabor* (Judg. 4[6]) is in Galilee (see the Bible Dictionaries, under "Hunting," for the figures of snare, net, and pit; cf. Amos 3[5] 1 Sam. 26[20] Psa. 10[9] 11[2]). V. 2a is obscure and corrupt; it should perhaps read, "the pit of Shittim they have made deep," with reference to the seat of the immoral Moabite worship of Baal-peor (Num. 25[1]). Note the contrast, in vv. 3, 4, between "*I* know Ephraim" (pronoun emphatic) and "they know not Jehovah." In v. 5, the *pride of Israel* refers to the arrogance expressed in ritual, as a witness against him. With the readiness to offer sacrifice in v. 6 cf. Mic. 6[6f.]; with Jehovah's refusal to hear, Mic. 3[4]. In v. 7, the marriage figure is revived; the infidelity of the bride leads to the illegitimacy of the children; they are *strange,* in that they do not worship Jehovah truly. The result is (v. 7b) that they and their property will quickly be destroyed.

8–15a. Penalty Issuing in Penitence. The approaching (military) attack is signaled from central places; but the overthrow of Israel by the enemy is certain, because Jehovah has determined it. It is the penalty of false worship, seen in the rottenness of the state. Appeal to foreign aid is futile; the only useful appeal is to God who waits for his people's penitence. *Beth-aven* (v. 8) is Bethel, ten miles north of Jerusalem (see on 4[15]); *Gibeah* and *Ramah* are on heights midway between it and Jerusalem; R.V. text in v. 8b is a warning to Benjamin from the bordertown of Bethel; R.V. mg. refers to the ancient war-cry of the tribe. The *landmark* (v. 10) was often put under religious sanctions; cf. the Roman god Terminus (Warde Fowler, *The Religious Experience of the Roman People,* p. 82); Babylonian private boundary-stones bear dedications to gods (cf. Deut. 19[14]). Follow R.V. mg. (*vanity*) in v. 11. Nothing is known of *King Jareb* (v. 13; cf. 10[6]), but the name means "he who strives," so that it might mean "the fighting king" (i.e., of Assyria). With Jehovah as a lion attacking Israel (v. 14) cf. Isa. 5[29] (refers to the nations). Jehovah's *place* is heaven (Mic. 1[3]). V. 15b belongs to the next oracle, as in LXX and Syriac version. The most recent German commentary (Sellin's) would refer 5[8]–6[6] to the Syro-Ephraimite war of 735–4 B.C.

CHAPTER VI

1–3. Israel's Return to Jehovah. With these verses should be taken 5[15b]. Distress drives the people to a facile penitence; they are too sure that God is on their side. In *he hath torn*, the pronoun is emphatic. In v. 2 the *two days . . . the third day* is an idiomatic expression of "shortly" (cf. the "three-four" of Amos 1[3]). With the anticipated revival, contrast the "death" of 13[1]. To live before God is to be under his protection (Gen. 17[18] Jer. 30[20]). The *going forth* of Jehovah is from his heavenly "place" (5[15]; so of the sunrise, Psa. 19[6]). The *rain* is the heavy winter rain, December to February (Songs 2[11]); the *latter rain* is that of the spring (March and April), just before harvest. Israel counts on the passing of Jehovah's anger with the certainty of the phenomena of nature—i.e., it has not yet learned to interpret its disasters ethically, and therefore is not yet truly penitent.

4–11a. Shallow Penitence and Deep Sinfulness. Jehovah distrusts this transient temper; he asks for an inner loyalty rather than an outer observance. Violence and sexuality go ill with "religion." The *morning cloud* is a fitting figure of transiency, for it soon vanishes in the heat of Palestine, together with the *dew*, here probably the night-mist brought up from the sea. The word of the prophet has objective efficiency; it is instrumental to its idea (v. 5; cf. Jer. 23[29]). In v. 5b read as mg. *God's judgment shall be unmistakable, seen by all, like the light.* V. 6 is the keynote of the whole prophecy (cf. Mt. 9[13] 12[7]). The same word for "mercy" (but see A.S.V.) is rendered "goodness" in v. 4; it denotes "duteous love," the loyalty to God which springs from a genuine inner devotion, here parallel with that knowledge of God which is more than an intellectual possession, and implies a volitional response. In v. 7, Israel's disloyalty to this covenant-love is what might have been expected of (common) men (mg.) without Israel's advantages, but not of a people favored like Israel. *Gilead* (v. 8), "foot-tracked with blood," is perhaps Ramoth-gilead (Judg. 10[17]); *Shechem* was a sanctuary (Josh. 20[7] 21[21]), here apparently abused by the actual brigandage of depraved priests (the verse is corrupt). The second part of v. 11 belongs to 7[1] (LXX).

CHAPTER VII

1–7. The Wickedness and Internal Disorder of Ephraim. God's instinct of compassion is checked by the moral disorder of the Northern Kingdom revealed in the fall of one ruler after another (v. 7). The country is helpless, and ignorant of its true helper; it turns instead to foreign alliances, doomed to fail. The general sense is plain, but the text, especially vv. 4–6, is undoubtedly corrupt. *Samaria* (v. 1) is here the country, rather than the capital (1 Kings 16[24]). With v. 2b, cf. Psa. 90[8]. The *oven* in vv. 4–7 was and still is a large earthenware jar, with the fire at the bottom of it; thin cakes of bread are baked by spreading them on the heated surface, when the fire has burned down. The figure of the present text is best referred to the smoldering and revival of lust, but the details are obscure, and the original reference may have been to the long succession of conspiracies and assassinations (2 Kings 15[8f.]); e.g., v. 5 might refer to the (unknown) events of some festival or coronation. Originally, v. 6 may have read *For their inward part is like an oven,* their heart burneth in them, while the meaningless sentence about the sleeping baker may have been (cf. R.V. mg.) *their anger smokes all the night*, maintaining the figure of the oven.

8–16. The Futility of Ephraim's Foreign Policy. When we turn (v. 8) from internal tumult and plotting to external relations, Ephraim is described as "a half-baked cake" of bread, to express the ineffectiveness of its life and policy (cf. v. 11); for the round flat cake baked on hot stones, cf. 1 Kings 19[6]. Similarly, he is pictured as in the weakness of old age (and therefore needing the more such help as is described in Isa. 46[4]), though unconscious of his senility. With v. 10a cf. 5[5]. The last clause of v. 12 must be taken to refer to such prophecies as those of Hosea. In v. 13b, "I" and "they" are emphatically contrasted in the Hebrew. *Upon their beds* (v. 14) should probably be "beside their altars"; in v. 14b, read as mg. Downfall by the sword of Assyria will provoke the scorn of the Egyptians, whose aid they have sought (v. 16).

CHAPTER VIII

Israel's Statecraft and Worship Disowned and Punished. The Assyrian comes to execute divine vengeance on a people that claims to know God; but both its politics and its religion are foreign to him. He spurns the bull-image of Samaria as a representation of himself (vv. 5, 6), and the many altars that dishonor him (v. 11); Israel's buildings shall be destroyed, and the people banished. The chapter is again difficult, because often corrupt, and its poetry is interrupted by prose glosses. The *trumpet* (v. 1) is the "horn" (in 5[8] rendered "cornet") that gives the alarm signal of an enemy's approach; the *eagle*, or rather, vulture, represents Assyria (cf. Deut. 28[49]; in Jer. 48[40] 49[22], of the Babylonians). *The house of the Lord* is really the land, as in 9[15]. The *calf of Samaria* (v. 5; cf. 10[5] 13[2]) was a small bull-image (overlaid with gold) by which Baal was represented among the Canaanites, but which was taken over by Israel as a representation of Jehovah. For the poetic comparison of Jehovah with the wild-ox, see Num. 23[22] 24[8]. Such bull-images were set up at Dan and Bethel (1 Kings 12[28f.]) as a natural form of divine representation, prior to the higher prophetic teaching. Here the image is declared to be without divine warrant (v. 6, "from Israel is even this" calf).

The lonely *wild ass* (v. 9) represents the willfulness of Israel, since this creature usually goes in droves; its Hebrew name affords a play on "Ephraim." The "gathering" of v. 10 is a threat, not a promise; v. 10b would refer to the burden of the tribute paid by Menahem (2 Kings 15[20]), but LXX reads more naturally, "and they shall cease for a little from anointing kings and princes." For the range of meaning of *law* in v. 12, see on Amos 2[4]; the verse implies that there were written laws—e.g., the Book of the Covenant, Ex. 20[22]–23[19]—but proves nothing as to the existence of the "Torah" in the later sense, i.e., of the entire Pentateuch (see art., *Formation of O.T.*, p. 92; and cf. pp. 145f.); indeed, the present context contrasts prophetic teachings (LXX reads the plural) with the ceremonial observances (developed so fully in the later "Law") which find no acceptance with God (v. 13). With the threatened return to Egypt cf. 9[3, 6], and Deut. 28[68].

CHAPTER IX

1–8. The Sorrows of Desolation and Exile. False worship will bring not fertility but exile (vv. 1–3), when there will be no longer an opportunity for (true) worship (vv. 4, 5). The desolation of the land is the inevitable outcome of the attitude displayed toward the prophets sent by God (vv. 6–8). Israel's infidelity is of ancient date, as well as shown at contemporary sanctuaries; barrenness and exile is its portion (see vv. 9–17). Note the continuous use of the figure of sexual, to express religious, infidelity (v. 1), though the actual practice of religious prostitution at the sanctuaries gave a realistic color to the figure. Israel has sought agricultural fertility by zealous worship —of the wrong kind, and shall not find what she sought (v. 2). The generality of the prophecy of exile in v. 3 is seen by the parallelism of Egypt and Assyria; it is the certainty of the penalty, not its precise mode of exaction, that matters to the prophet (cf. 8[13], and for the *unclean food*, Amos 7[17]). *The bread of mourners* (v. 4) is ceremonially "unclean," because death is a strong taboo (Num. 19[14] Deut. 26[14]); there will be no means of consecrating food to Jehovah in a strange land (v. 4; read mg.). The *destruction* of v. 6 is that of the devastated land where weeds grow over the cast down and abandoned silver gods; *Memphis*, one of the oldest and most important cities of Egypt, ten miles south of the present Cairo. V. 7 shows us what the average man thought and said of such a prophet as Hosea.

9–17. Israel's Long History of Sin and Crime. The present corruption has its counterparts in Israel's early history. *Gibeah* (v. 9): see 10[9] and cf. Judg. 19. *Baal-peor* (v. 10): cf. Num. 25; the *shameful thing* is Baal, which it replaces for theological reasons. V. 13a yields no good sense as it stands; LXX is better, viz., "Ephraim—his children are destined to be a prey." The sanctuary of *Gilgal* (v. 15, cf. 4[15]) is named because the false cult there and elsewhere is the central point of Hosea's denunciation. In the Hebrew of these poems there are frequent plays on words, which cannot be reproduced; e.g., in v. 15, *all their princes are revolters* is *kol sarehem sorerim*.

CHAPTER X

1–8. Overthrow of Israel's Altars as the Harvest of Wickedness. There are many altars, as a result of prosperity; yet Jehovah has been slighted and his name dishonored in false swearing (vv. 1–4). Therefore the "golden calf" of Bethel will be carried as booty into Assyria, and men will seek death as escape from suffering (vv. 5–8). "Whatsoever a man soweth, that shall he also reap" (vv. 9–15). The *pillars* (v. 1) are part of the apparatus of worship at the sanctuaries (3[4]). That the heart (i.e., the mind and the will) is *smooth* (so mg. in v. 2) means that it is deceitful, insincere; there is no straight thinking, no true religious spirit to correspond with the outward observance. In v. 3, *we fear not Jehovah* looks like a gloss, for it contradicts the context about excessive though external religiosity. The verse appears to reflect the disturbed political conditions (cf. 7[1-7]). In v. 4a, the divine judgment is represented as the poisonous plant that grows from the seed of sin; cf. Emerson's essay on "Compensation." The calf (sing. with LXX and Syriac in v. 5) of Bethel (4[15]) is captured by the enemy; the temple treasure and adornment of the idol —its *glory*—are appropriated by him (cf. the tribute paid by Menahem, 2 Kings 15[19]). The sufferings of the invasion will be such that men will cry to the very hills on which they worshiped Jehovah falsely to end their lives (v. 8).

9–15. Israel's Sin Reaps Retribution. From v. 9 the text is specially corrupt and obscure. *Gibeah*, cf. 9[9]; there is possibly a reference to the resistance of the Benjamites (Judg. 20). The *two transgressions* of v. 10 are the "calves" of Dan and Bethel. The privilege of the *heifer* (v. 11) treading out the corn was to eat freely (Deut. 25[4]); she is now to be yoked to do harder work (*I have passed over* is better taken as "I have spared" hitherto). In vv. 12, 13, it is natural to regard the reaping as the recompense for the sowing, whether it be good or evil, but *reap according to mercy* might refer to God's mercy or man's "piety" (cf. 6[6]); the latter is more probable, in view of the parallel in v. 13, *ye have reaped iniquity*. The close of v. 12 should probably read with the LXX "to the end that the fruit of righteousness may come to you" (note parallel in v. 13, "the fruit of lies"). For the figure of the *fallow* ground cf. Jer. 4[3]. The historical reference in v. 14 is obscure (cf. Amos 6[2]). Nothing is known of a place Beth-arbel; Shalman might be Shalmaneser V, who besieged Samaria, 723–1 B.C. (the clause then being a later addition); with v. 14b, cf. Gen. 32[11] 2 Kings 8[12]. *At daybreak* (v. 15) means "suddenly" (cf. Psa. 49[14] 90[5f.]).

CHAPTER XI

The Divine Father Unable to Destroy Israel Utterly. Israel is the child of Jehovah, whom he has taught to walk, carrying the tired child in his arms (cf. Deut. 1[31]). But the child has ungratefully turned from his father to the deserved penalty of the "far country" (cf. Lk. 15[13]). Even so, the fatherly compassions of God are too deep to allow him to abandon his child, and he will gather the scattered Israelites as birds that fly to their homeland (v. 11). It is unfortunate that this fine passage is so marred by textual corruptions that some of it cannot be translated, e.g., v. 7, of which the literal Hebrew is "my people is hung up to my backsliding . . . and upward they call him . . . together he will not exalt. . . ." But the principal thought is clear, and no one who grasps the meaning of the chapter will deny to the O.T. the doctrine of a suffering God.

Israel is now gray-haired (7[9]), but Jehovah's love was active from the days of servitude in Egypt (v. 1). In v. 2, as it stands, the reference is to the prophets' calling, but LXX suggests, "when I called them, they went away from me"; *graven images*, see on 13[2]. In v. 4 the figure changes to that of the kindly driver, suiting the harness to human weakness and divine affection, the last clause being, rather, *I inclined* (*my ear*) *unto him to feed him.* The *not* of v. 5 is a corrupt fragment of v. 4, and should be omitted; they turn to Egypt and Assyria, instead of to me. The *bars* (v. 6) are those of city gates (Jer. 51[30], cf. Job 17[16]). In v. 8 *deliver* (in A.S.V. *cast off*) should be *surrender; Admah* and *Zeboim* were cities overthrown with Sodom and Gomorrah (Gen. 14[2] Deut. 29[23]). G. A. Smith describes vv. 8, 9 as "the greatest passage in Hosea," which is saying much, though not too much (read as A.S.V.). Jehovah as a lion (Amos 1[2] 3[8]) calls the young lions after him (v. 10); they hurry home with the speed of birds (v. 11). V. 12, see 12[1] below.

CHAPTER XII

Israel Contrasted With His Ancestor, Jacob. The accusation (cf. v. 2) which Jehovah brings against Israel is that of disloyalty, shown in seeking foreign alliances (v. 1). How different was the conduct of Israel's ancestor, who wrestled with God. Israel is confident in his commercial prosperity (v. 8), but that will not save him (v. 9). How much more care (through the prophets) has been lavished on Israel than on his ancestor (vv. 12, 13).

In 11[12] (=12[1] in Hebrew) read as mg. *Oil* (12[1]) was a natural product of Palestine (Deut. 8[8]), here sent as a present to Egypt (Isa. 57[9]), which lacked it. The point of the contrast with Jacob is the earnestness of *his* striving with God (mg. in v. 3); he strove from the very womb (Gen. 25[22, 26]). The root from which the name "Jacob" comes means to follow at the heel, to overreach; but originally it may have meant that God "follows" and rewards its bearer, as in the Assyrian name *Ya'kub-ilu.* In v. 4, read *he strove with the angel* (as in v. 3 mg.); the detail of weeping and supplication is not given in the extant story of Penuel (Gen. 32[22-32]). The incident of Bethel (Gen. 28[10f.]) here comes in a different order. In v. 7, read as mg.; the translation derives "trafficker" from the fact that the Canaanites (cf. the Phoenicians) were traders, just as "Chaldean" came to mean "astrologer"; to this level Israel has sunk. *Labors* (v. 8), i.e., "products"; the verse gives Israel's reply to the charge that he is a mere Canaanite.

The dwelling in tents (v. 9) is a threat, not a promise; it will be like—yet unlike—the Feast of Booths, when people joyfully camped out. The prophetic ministry is characterized in v. 10 as mediating Jehovah's voice, through visions and symbols. *Gilead* (v. 11), see 6[8]; the district was captured by Tiglath-Pileser III in 734 B.C. (2 Kings 15[29]). The *heaps* of stones are no more than those taken from a plowed field; once they were altars (there is a play on the Hebrew name for "heaps," namely *gallim*, with Gilgal, cf. 4[15]). Vv. 12, 13 seem a subsequent addition to the previous Jacob references, recalling Gen. 27[43] 29[18] 31[41]. Jacob was once but a wandering Aramean (Deut. 26[5]), yet how great he became! His descendants have been escorted by a prophet (Moses) and instead of "keeping" sheep have themselves been "kept" (v. 13 mg.)—yet how low they have fallen.

CHAPTER XIII

1–8. Jehovah's Anger Over Israel's Ingratitude. Israel's pride has gone before a fall (v. 1), and idolatry brings extinction (vv. 2, 3). In prosperity, Israel's benefactor is forgotten (vv. 4–6). So Jehovah prepares to attack, like a wild beast (vv. 7, 8), and Israel will be helpless before the Assyrian, who executes God's just vengeance (vv. 9–16). The glory of Ephraim's past is pictured through the anxious respect shown toward him (*trembling;* cf. Job 29[7, 8]); his decline and fall is due to the guilt (v. 1 mg.) of his false worship. The *molten images* (v. 2), alone prohibited (Ex. 34[17]), were cast in metal, and were doubtless derived from Canaanite art and usage; they are to be distinguished from the "graven images" (11[2]) carved from wood or stone. On the extent of Israelite idolatry at this time, see Isa. 2[8]; for the *kiss* as a sign of homage or adoration, see Psa. 2[12] 1 Kings 19[18] Job 31[27]. *Chimney* (v. 3) should be *lattice*, or window, by which escaped the smoke of the charcoal or wood burned in a brazier (Jer. 36[22]). Mg. is better in v. 4; in v. 5, the *I* is emphatic—it was I, and not another; with v. 6, cf. Deut. 32[15, 18]. *Caul* (v. 8), properly meaning "covering," here denotes the breast, as the "cage" or inclosure of the heart.

9–15. Inevitable Doom. The obscure v. 9 perhaps once read: *He hath destroyed thee, O Israel—then who shall help thee?* With v. 11, cf. the attitude toward the monarchy shown in the (later) story of Saul's election (1 Sam. 8, 10[17-24], 12); the statement here is collective ("I give thee kings . . . I take them away"). The iniquity (v. 12) is *bound up* and stored for punishment, as in Job 14[17]. In v. 13, Israel is both the travailing mother and the unborn child (Isa. 37[3]); read *for now he standeth not [ready] in the mouth of the womb.* The next verse (14) should be taken as rhetorical questions, implying a threat, not a promise: "From the hand of Sheol shall I ransom them? from death shall I redeem them?" The answer is an emphatic *No!* Note the quotation of v. 14b, with reversed meaning, in 1 Cor. 15[55]. The figure of v. 15 (*fruitful*) is suggested by the meaning of the name "Ephraim"; the destructive sirocco is the Assyrian army.

CHAPTER XIV

Israel's Penitence and Jehovah's Promises. The prophet frames a liturgy of confession for penitent Israel, acknowledging the past folly of seeking help from Assyria and of idolatry (vv. 1–3). God promises forgiveness and fertility (vv. 4–7). This fine chapter might be called a preacher's program, for it appeals to the discipline of experience, makes articulate the inarticulate, affirms the evangelical patience of God, and the gift of new life from God, culminating in a dialogue of the soul's fellowship with God (v. 8). The *words* of v. 2 are to be those that follow, truly and sincerely expressing a change of heart; v. 2b is meaningless; read with LXX, *and we will pay the fruit of our lips* (cf. Psa. 51[16f.] 69[30f.]). *Asshur* (v. 3) is simply the transliteration of the Hebrew word for "Assyria." Alliance with Egypt meant the provision of cavalry (1[7] 10[13] Isa. 30[16] 31[1]; cf. 1 Kings 10[28]); hence the reference to *horses.* In the discovery of its own self-willed orphanhood (v. 3) Israel discovers also the divine fatherhood. *Smell as Lebanon* (v. 6), because of the cedars and other aromatic trees (Songs 4[11]) of its forests. V. 7 is obscure and corrupt; *his shadow* most naturally refers to God, but cf. Ezek. 31[6] (nations under the shadow of Pharaoh); there is no ground for rendering *memorial* (mg.) as *scent.* In v. 8 we have a dialogue, in which it is not certain how we should distribute the parts, but it is perhaps best to assign *I am like a green fir tree* to Ephraim, and thus get four alternating utterances.

The closing expression (v. 9) of piety is due to a *wise man* among the readers of the roll, and falls outside these precious but tantalizing poem-oracles of Hosea. It is an exhortation addressed to anyone seeking the way of life to learn from the book of Hosea.

JOEL

By Professor W. GLADSTONE WATSON

Introduction

Author. Of the author we have no direct information beyond his name and that of his father, Pethuel (more probably "Bethuel," LXX). His prophecy is concerned only with Judah (2^{23} $3^{1, 6, 8, 20}$), and it seems clear that he was a native of Jerusalem. The Temple (2^{17}), the priests ($1^{9, 13}$) and the daily sacrifice ($1^{9, 13}$ 2^{14}) are the things with which he is familiar. He also speaks of the locusts climbing the wall and entering the houses, presumably of the city (2^{9}). He seems to have great respect for the priests, but it is unlikely that he was one himself (1^{13} 2^{17}). He was a literary man of religious and studious habits. His style is the poetical style of the earlier prophets, but lacks the originality and vigor of an Amos or an Isaiah. He had evidently studied the great literature of the past and had reflected deeply upon it, so that its imagery and ideas had left a deep impression upon him. In this short book of only seventy verses there are no less than twenty quotations from other O.T. writers.

Date. The question of date is of great importance in connection with the proper interpretation of the book. The older commentators regarded Joel as the earliest of the writing prophets and assigned him most generally to the ninth century, during the minority of Joash (836–796 B.C.), but the evidence for such an early date is altogether inconclusive, and more recent commentators are practically unanimous in agreeing that a post-exilic date satisfies the conditions better. There are no references to kings, high places, or idolatry, silence concerning which would be strange in a pre-exilic prophet; the interest of the book in sacrifice is entirely opposed to the attitude of all pre-exilic prophets (Isa. 1^{10-17} Amos 5^{21-24} Mic. 6^{6-8}). Moreover, it would be very difficult to explain the attitude of Amos (5^{18-20}) toward the day of Jehovah if Joel had preceded him. On the other hand the book fits admirably into the post-exilic age, and may be assigned with a fair degree of confidence to the Persian period about 400 B.C., or even later. During this period the Jewish community was confined to a small territory around Jerusalem; the rule of the Persians was not oppressive and the Jews were left free to manage their own affairs under the elders and priests; the people constituted a religious community, of which the Temple was the center, with the Law as the rule of faith and practice; priests, not prophets, were the leading religious figures; prophetic teaching was giving place to apocalyptic hopes (see intro. to Ezra-Nehemiah, pp. 458f.; cf. p. 70). Such a situation suits Joel very well. It accounts for the leadership which he gives to the priests, his interest in the Temple and his concern about the cessation of the daily sacrifices; the apocalyptic character of the book also suits this age, but is entirely out of place in pre-exilic thought. There are other features that clearly point to a post-exilic date: The reference to the scattering of Israel among the nations (3^{2}) finds no adequate explanation except in the destruction of Jerusalem in 586 B.C., and the Exile and Dispersion which followed; and the bringing again of the captivity of Judah (3^{1}) is most naturally explained as referring to the restoration from the Exile or from the Dispersion; the Greeks (3^{6}) are not mentioned in the Bible before Ezekiel and the Exile.

The numerous parallels with other books are easily explained if they are quotations. Ezekiel was the most influential of all the prophets during the Exile and later, and there are many features of Joel which seem to have their origin in Ezekiel: The gathering of the nations and their destruction before Jerusalem (3^{1-3}) is based upon the destruction of Gog and his hordes (Ezek. 38, 39); the fountain issuing from beneath the Temple hill (3^{18}) finds its explanation in Ezek. 47^{1-12}; similarly, the outpouring of the Spirit and Jehovah's jealousy for his land find their counterpart in Ezekiel. Other parallels are most naturally explained as quotations; the most instructive illustration is 2^{32}, which is presented in the usual formula of a quotation; the original appears to be in Obad. v. 17, a relatively late passage.

Occasion and Contents. A terrible scourge of locusts, in successive waves, had visited Judah and had brought an unprecedented famine upon the people. This was accompanied by drought and fiery heat. The vintage and harvest had been destroyed, cutting off the food of man and beast; and what seemed more terrible still, the daily offerings in the Temple. Joel, who had been deeply influenced by the apocalyptic side of Ezekiel's teaching, interpreted these disasters as the prelude to the day of Jehovah, which entirely occupies his thought in the latter half of the book.

The book falls into two parts. The first part (1^{2}–2^{27}) consists of a graphic description of the invasion of the locusts and the consequent suffering of the people. In the first chapter the description is that of a calamity which has already happened "before our eyes," a calamity which has affected all classes, and which may be regarded as a divine judgment. It can be met only by fasting and prayer. In the second chapter it seems that a still more terrible scourge of locusts is just at hand, which will be a veritable day of Jehovah. It pictures the irresistible advance of the army of locusts with Jehovah at their head. But even this calamity may be averted by a thoroughgoing repentance, so that the prophet urges the observance of a solemn day of national humiliation and supplication that Jehovah would "spare his people." This was observed and Jehovah's favor was restored. The prophet then goes on to announce the immediate return of prosperity, and the section closes with a description of a satisfied people rejoicing in Jehovah's presence and praising his name.

The second part (2^{28}–3^{21}) is apocalyptic in character and deals with what shall come *afterward.* Jehovah will pour out his Spirit upon all flesh (Jews only), giving to all ecstatic experience and illumination such as formerly only the prophets had. This will be accompanied by portents of the day of Jehovah—the final judgment. The pious Jews from the Dispersion will be joined with those already in Jerusalem, and more abundant blessings will be poured out upon them. The Gentiles will be gathered in the valley of Jehoshaphat where they will be annihilated.

The marked difference between the two sections of the book, one concerned with a scourge of locusts, the other with the final judgment, and yet both parts relating to the day of Jehovah, has created difficulty for interpreters. The early Fathers and some moderns sought to avoid the difficulty by treating the first part as allegory, the locusts representing an enemy, or, rather, four heathen empires, but this view has now been abandoned. A more recent way of getting over the difficulty is to attribute the book to two authors, or to regard all references to the day of Jehovah in the first part as interpolations (*ad loc.*, International Critical Commentary). However, the latter method of solving the difficulty is still on trial. The difficulty is avoided if it is assumed that the day of Jehovah manifests itself in successive stages (see Wade, *Joel*, pp. liv–lxi).

Teaching. The religious teaching of the prophecy gathers around the *day of Jehovah.* The first reference to the day of Jehovah in prophetic literature occurs in Amos 5^{18}, a passage which shows that the idea was not new. It was popularly assumed that, in virtue of Israel's election by Jehovah, it would be a day in which Jehovah would manifest his power in a decisive victory over the enemies of Israel, who because of their hostility to his people were also his enemies. Thus the day of Jehovah would be primarily a day of glory for Israel. Amos shattered this view and announced that it would be a day of judgment upon all sinners, including the chosen people; indeed, that it would fall first upon apostate Israel. In all pre-exilic prophecy the judgment upon the sinners in Israel was emphasized. The pre-exilic prophets also held that, after the execution of judgment upon Israel, there would be left a purified remnant, which would form the nucleus of the new kingdom of God, and that upon this remnant would be poured out great blessings both material and spiritual. However, from Isa. 10^{4-34} Zeph. 3^{8} and Jer. 25^{9} and other passages it becomes evident that the day of Jehovah included also a judgment upon other nations.

The destruction of Jerusalem and its attendant sufferings could not help but modify the outlook of the prophets. They felt that in these events the terror of the day of Jehovah had been visited upon Israel. They had received "double for all their sins" and might now look for the restoration of Jehovah's favor. On the other hand, the time was ripe for a judgment upon the nations which again and again had caused suffering and hardship to God's people. But the weary years after the Exile rolled on without noticeable change in the prosperity of Israel, and with the heathen nations still dominant. In consequence of this disappointment there settled upon the Jews a feeling of depression which found utterance in the cry, "How long, O Lord, how long?" Surely, the day of deliverance for Israel and of judgment upon the Gentiles could not long be delayed!

It was in such a religious and intellectual atmosphere that Joel lived. It is not strange, therefore, that he should interpret the visitation of the locusts as a divine judgment, a harbinger of a still more terrible judgment near at hand. The coming judgment would fall upon both Jews and Gentiles, but the effects would not be the same. The Jews had thought that the divine wrath against their sins had exhausted itself in the sufferings endured during the Exile; to Joel the locust plague showed that for some reason the displeasure of Jehovah still rested upon them; hence the first thought which arose in his mind was the necessity of repentance on the part of his people. It is remarkable that he does not mention the sins of which they were to repent, but on this point he himself may not have been clear; nevertheless, he could not doubt the fact of their sinning: (1) The suffering caused by the locusts was infallible proof of sin; for Joel shared the commonly accepted opinion that sin and suffering were inseparable. (2) The cutting off of material needed for the daily sacrifice was conclusive evidence that Jehovah had turned against his people. Such reasoning on first thought may appear strange; Joel seems to put mere ritual observance above human needs and a right heart (contrast Mic. 6^{6-8} Mk. 2^{27} Jas. 1^{27}). But for Joel the daily sacrifice was the means whereby fellowship with God was maintained, and this fellowship meant more to him than life itself. The withholding of the materials of sacrifice meant that God himself had broken off fellowship with his people, and was making it impossible for this fellowship to be restored.

The attitude of God could be explained only on the assumption that there was sin in the Jewish community; hence the urgent appeal for *repentance.* In language that has become classic he shows that no mere outward or formal signs of grief will suffice; repentance must spring from a broken and contrite heart; it must be a real inward change of heart, a turning with mind and will unto God. His faith that God will receive the penitent who turns to him in this spirit is based upon the unsurpassed description of God's gracious character, which was revealed to Moses on the Mount (Ex. 34^{6}). However, in harmony with current ideals, repentance finds outward expression in the observance of a day of national humiliation and prayer. In the *prayer* which Joel puts into the mouth of the priests, he again sounds the depths of religious insight. Like the Lord's prayer it puts the glory of God in the first place (2^{17}; cf. Mt. 6^{9}); the petition for deliverance and prosperity is secondary.

According to the thought of that day, Jehovah's sovereignty could not be seen apart from the blessedness of his people. Hence the answer to the prayer is the removal of the locusts; and from this the prophet goes on to promise rain and fruitful seasons. The return of Jehovah's favor will lead the people to praise God for his goodness and to rejoice in the presence of Jehovah in their midst. So far as the immediate future is concerned, this will be the happy ending of their troubles and it will vindicate both Jehovah's justice and his grace toward Israel.

Thus once more the day of Jehovah as a judgment upon Israel is past; surely now the day of Jehovah as a judgment upon the Gentiles may be expected, a judgment in its most terrible and final form. It will manifest itself in the annihilation of the Gentiles, while marvelous spiritual and material happiness will be the portion of the Jews. Both of these results will come by the direct action of Jehovah. Thus will ensue a new earth in which will dwell a purified and Spirit-filled people, and the transformation will constitute the complete vindication of Jehovah.

Permanent Values. When Joel thinks of this victory as the glorification of the Jews and the destruction of the Gentiles he shows that he is but a child of his age, sharing its limitations and prejudices. He has failed to grasp the universality of the grace of God. Joel's view was probably the prevailing one of his age, but it was not the only view. In Isa. 2^{2-4} it is anticipated that Gentiles may come up to share with the Jews in their religious privileges. Deutero-Isaiah and Jonah went further and thought of Israel as the missionary to the Gentiles. The universalism of these prophets is irreconcilable with Joel's narrow nationalism. His view is also opposed to that of Paul and the general attitude of the N.T. To-day the household of faith includes vastly more Gentiles than Jews. It may therefore be confidently affirmed that Joel's prediction of the day of Jehovah can never be fulfilled as he conceived it. But we cannot leave the matter here. Behind his narrow nationalism there is a great and permanent truth. Joel illustrates a profound faith both in the justice and mercy of God. There must ultimately be a complete victory of righteousness over unrighteousness; the righteous must be rewarded and the wicked must be punished. The sovereignty of God must be recognized and established.

Literature: Wade, *Joel* (Westminster Commentaries); Driver, *Joel and Amos* (Cambridge Bible); Hennessy, *Joel* (Cambridge R.V. for Schools); Eiselen, *The Minor Prophets;* G. A. Smith, *The Book of the Twelve* (The Expositor's Bible); Horton, *The Minor Prophets* (New Century Bible).

Chapters 1^{1} to 2^{27}: The Locusts, the Harbinger of the Day of Jehovah

CHAPTER I

1. The Title. The prophet is introduced in an ordinary prophetic formula.

2–12. The Invasion of the Locusts. Successive swarms of locusts have overrun the land and left it a waste. The destruction is of such an unprecedented character that even the oldest inhabitants can recall no parallel, and the memory of it will be handed on to future generations. All classes are called upon to mourn. The drunkards, who represent the luxurious classes, are called to weep and howl, because the destruction of the vines has cut off their supplies. The locusts, likened to an irresistible army with teeth like lions' teeth, have devoured all vegetation, even stripping off the bark from the fruit trees and leaving them bleached and bare.

The community, personified as a woman, is called to mourning because the daily sacrifice in the Temple has been interrupted. The corn, the wine and the oil, which were used in the offerings, have failed. The priests are heartbroken and the very land mourneth. The husbandmen are in despair. Their crops are ruined and the joy of harvest is withered away. Famine has dried up the means of living. The prophet's reference to the cessation of the daily sacrifice is worthy of note (v. 9). For him, influenced by post-exilic religious standards, it meant the cutting off of fellowship with God. In this high regard for sacrifice he stands in marked contrast with the pre-exilic prophets, who had little or no use for these outward observances; they placed the emphasis rather upon justice, mercy and a humble walk with God (Amos 5[21-24] Hos. 6[6] Mic. 6[6-8]).

13, 14. Call to Repentance. The situation calls for penitence, for the only conclusion to which Joel could come was that Jehovah was angry because of the people's sin. He, therefore, calls upon the priests, the religious leaders of the people, to proclaim a day of public fasting and prayer in the Temple for the entire community. The sins to be repented of are not mentioned (contrast Amos 2[6-8]); which is characteristic of the prophets of the post-exilic age.

15–20. Terrors of the Day of Jehovah. The scourge of the locusts is the precursor of a still more awful calamity. It is the beginning of the judgment day—*the day of Jehovah.* The famine has cut off the means of sustenance, but, worse than all else, it has cut off public worship, the surest indication that Jehovah is about to destroy the world. Drought and fiery sun have added to the calamity. The prophet cries out in prayer for mercy; even the beasts of the field, lowing in thirst and hunger, are represented as praying. (It will help the reader to appreciate the awfulness of the locust scourge to read the stories of them told in Driver, or Eiselen, or G. A. Smith.)

CHAPTER II

1–11. Vivid Description of the Coming Judgment. This section opens with a call to blow the trumpet, to give warning of the approaching judgment (cf. Amos 3[6]). In the first chapter the description was that of an actual calamity; in this chapter the prophet looks forward to a still more terrible visitation; hence the description of the locusts, while still referring to real locusts, assumes an apocalyptic coloring. It opens with a quotation from Zeph. 1[15]; the language, which is highly figurative and evidently had already become stereotyped as a description of the day of Jehovah (cf. Amos 5[18-20]), is intended to produce terror. The quotation ends with *darkness;* the next clause should be read: "as the dawn there is spread—a great people," the great mass of fluttering insects dimming the light of day. As they advance they leave as it were a trail of fire behind them, and the fruitful garden is turned into a desolate waste.

The advance of the locusts is like the oncoming of a mighty army—horsemen running, chariots rattling on the hills with noise like the crackling of a prairie fire. Nothing can resist them; the people are in panic and their faces pale with fear. Neither walls nor weapons are of any avail to check their advance; the city and its houses afford no protection. In vv. 10, 11 the description becomes even more idealized. The locusts are represented as accompanied by earthquake and storm, and Jehovah himself as advancing at the head of his locust army. Jehovah's voice breaks forth in thunder. Truly this calamity is no ordinary event; it is a supernatural visitation, the great and terrible day of Jehovah.

12–17. Exhortation to Repentance. But even yet it is not too late to avert the calamity. If the people will truly repent Jehovah may restore his favor; however, no mere formal repentance will do. There must be a genuine conversion, a turning with mind and will to God. Repentance is not mere outward expression of grief, but a breaking up of the hard and stony heart, making it responsive to the divine influence (cf. Psa. 51[17]). It is to be noted that the expressed hope is that Jehovah will restore *a blessing,* i.e., the fruits of the earth, so that again the daily sacrifice may be offered. This will re-establish fellowship with him and be the sure mark of his restored favor. Again Joel issues a call to observe a fast and hold a solemn religious service, to which all the people are to come, old men and babes, nursing mothers and the newly married. The priests are to stand in the inner court of the Temple, while the great multitude are assembled in the outer court. As representative of the people the priests are to offer the prayer which Joel formulates. The plea is to spare his people, lest his own name should be disparaged. The reproach (reading the mg. of v. 17, *use a byword*) was that the heathen should conclude that Jehovah was not able to save his people (cf. notes on vv. 25-27 below). The sovereignty of Jehovah was the great consideration. It is, in a way, parallel to the idea that the supreme disaster was the cutting off from fellowship with God, through the cessation of the daily sacrifice.

18-27. The Prayer Answered and the Restoration of Prosperity. In v. 18 it is assumed that the day of fasting and prayer has been observed and that Jehovah has given a gracious answer. Two motives are given for Jehovah's change of purpose: the first, his *jealousy*—the dishonor done to his name must be forever removed; the second, his *pity*, which has been stirred by the penitence of his afflicted people. As a result Jehovah promises to give the corn, the wine, and the oil in abundance; never again shall the Gentiles have an opportunity to dishonor his name because of the poverty of his people.

The reference to the *northern army* in v. 20 is obscure. Locusts do not come from the north, and yet the term must apply to them. Probably the best explanation is that "northerner" had become a fixed term describing the executioner of the divine judgment on the day of Jehovah. In Jer. 1[14] 10[22] (notes) the evil threatening Judah is said to come from the north, and in Ezek. 39[1, 2] Gog (though part of his hordes are from Africa) is represented as coming from the north. It would seem then that "the northerner" had come to be used as a symbol of the agency of judgment without any reference to geography (cf. in English the use of East-Indiaman for any ocean-going merchantman). The announcement of the destruction of the locusts in the Dead Sea (*eastern sea*, v. 20), the Mediterranean Sea (*western sea*) and the southern desert is not to be taken literally; it is due simply to the carrying out of the figure of "the northerner." Note the contrast between the last clause of v. 19 and the last clause of v. 20—the day of the locusts has passed away, the day of Jehovah has come.

In. v. 21 the prophet bursts into song as he calls upon the land, the beasts, and the people to rejoice in the restored favor of Jehovah. In faithfulness to his promise (v. 23, *in just measure*, R.V. text), literally, *in righteousness*, mg. Jehovah is giving the rain, which is the necessary condition of fertility. The former rain comes in October-November and opens the agricultural year, while the latter rain comes in March-April, when the grain is filling out in the ear. (The Hebrew text is in some confusion and v. 23 cannot be translated smoothly, but the general sense is clear). In vv. 25-27 the prophet speaks as if he were Jehovah. He promises a full compensation for all the ruin the locusts had wrought. The people will praise Jehovah for his wondrous bounty and will have assurance that he is with them, and that he will continue to be their helper and defender forever. The renewed prosperity gives renewed confidence in Jehovah's presence and is the best answer to the reproach of the Gentiles in v. 17.

Chapters 2[28] to 3[21]: The Day of Jehovah

28-32. The Outpouring of the Spirit. The bestowal of the material benefits having produced a spirit of gratitude, and having created a confidence that Jehovah's presence with his people will never again fail, the prophet goes on to announce the coming of a still greater blessing. The ecstatic spiritual experience and illumination which hitherto had been confined to exceptional individuals like the prophets is to be given to all Israelites, irrespective of age, sex or condition. The prayer of Moses that all Jehovah's people be prophets (Num. 11[29]) is to be realized. Dreaming dreams and seeing visions are the familiar channels through which revelations came to the prophets. While the prophets were the bearers of important moral messages, they were generally, if not always, the subjects of deep religious emotion and ecstasy, and in this passage the emphasis is on the latter. These spiritual gifts are to be accompanied by marvelous portents in the heavens and on the earth—blood, fire, and smoke. These may be due to eclipses, fiery meteors or a dust-filled sky; or they may be accompaniments of war—bloody slaughter and burning cities. The figures used had become stereotyped forms of expression descriptive of all kinds of phenomena that inspire fear and alarm. The thought is that God will usher in the greatly to be feared day of Jehovah with terror-inspiring signs.

Peter saw in the experience of Pentecost the fulfillment of Joel's prophecy (Acts 2[16-21]). The profound feelings and deep convictions of that day gave to the apostles great freedom of speech and enabled them to speak in the universal language of the human heart, so that their message came to the hearers with great converting power, and thousands were caught up into the same ecstatic experience. This may be regarded as a proper fulfillment of the prophecy; but the important point is that these profound religious emotions, which had formerly been confined to the few, have been poured out upon the whole body of disciples. Moreover, the most powerful proof that the early disciples were filled with the Spirit is not to be seen in these ecstatic outbursts, but in their changed character and spirit, their love, gentleness, and goodness. The fearful signs of vv. 30, 31 will have no terrors for the Jews. In spite of the *all flesh* of v. 28 and the *whosoever* of v. 32, only those in Jerusalem and the Jews of the Dispersion who shall be called to share with them in salvation are meant. For the Gentiles there is nothing but a fearful judgment.

CHAPTER III

This chapter describes the destruction of the Gentiles and the glorification of the Jews.

1–3. The Wrongs Done to the Jews to Be Avenged. This section follows immediately upon 2[28-32], and explains how the Jews being assembled in Jerusalem will escape the judgment which is to fall upon the Gentiles. *To bring again the captivity of Judah* may refer to the return of the Jews who were still scattered abroad in heathen lands; or it may mean, without reference to return from exile, a restoration of good fortune, material and spiritual; if so, the former might still include the restoration of the scattered people. At the same time the Gentiles are to be gathered for judgment in *the valley of Jehoshaphat.* The identification of the valley is of no importance, though it must have been thought of as near Jerusalem. The name means "Jehovah judges" and is used symbolically. The idea of the assembling of the nations for judgment is common in late prophecy (Isa. 66[16-18] Zeph. 3[8] Ezek. 38, 39; cf. Mt. 25[31-46] Rev. 20[11-15]). The judgment falls on the Gentiles because they had taken Judah, and scattered its people into exile or slavery. Probably the reference is to the destruction of Jerusalem in 586 B.C. by Nebuchadrezzar. Captives taken in war were divided by lot among the soldiers, and here it is charged that they were later cheaply disposed of to gratify the sensual passions of the conquerors. See also vv. 9–17 below.

4–8. Judgment Upon Phœnicia and Philistia. This passage is probably an insertion. It breaks the continuity of the argument and is written in prose, while both that which precedes and that which follows is in poetry. It also predicts a different punishment, namely, slavery, whereas in the rest of the chapter the entire heathen world is condemned to annihilation. It may have been written about the same time. There was no uniformity of opinion among post-exilic Jews as to the fate of the Gentiles, but we should at least expect uniformity in the work of one writer. Phœnicia and Philistia have apparently been guilty of some act of spoliation of the goods and persons of Judah, or it may be that they have received them from others. Jewish slaves had been sold to the *Grecians.* This implies a late date for the passage, for the Greeks are not mentioned in Jewish literature until the Exile. Jehovah promises to restore the Jews to freedom and to visit the deeds of the Philistines upon their own heads. The Philistines shall be sold into slavery by the Jews to the distant land of *Sheba*, the other end of the world from Greece.

9–17. The World Judgment. This is the continuance of vv. 1–3. The Gentiles are called upon to prepare for the struggle with Jehovah; but it will be of no avail, for they are to be exterminated. *Sanctify war* (v. 9, mg.): in ancient times war was a religious act, for the gods of the contending peoples were at war too, and were thought of as leading their people. Hence soldiers were prepared by religious rites. In v. 10 the Gentiles are urged to make the best possible preparation in words which are just the opposite of those in the famous passage Isa. 2[2-4], which was no doubt in the mind of the prophet. They are to come down to the valley of Jehoshaphat where Jehovah sits not only to judge but also to execute the judgment. In v. 13 the heavenly host is addressed and the slaughter is set forth under the figure of treading grapes. In v. 14 the prophet calls attention to the enormous multitude involved in the judgment. The terrifying character of the judgment is like that caused by eclipses. In v. 16 the significant words of Amos (1[2] 3[4, 8]) are quoted, Jehovah is likened to a lion just springing upon his prey. In contrast to the imminent destruction of the heathen world is the deliverance and protection of the Jews. Jehovah will continue to abide in Jerusalem forever. With the destruction of the heathen world Jerusalem can never again be polluted by their presence, and thus its holiness will be secured. *Holy* (v. 17) is used here, not in an ethical sense, but in the sense which it has in Ezekiel and other late prophets, namely, freedom from contact with heathenism in any form, and complete dedication to Jehovah. (See art., *Religion of Israel*, pp. 174–5.)

18–21. Great Fruitfulness for Judah. After the judgment upon the world and the salvation of the Jews, there will be remarkable fertility. Judah was deficient in water, but henceforth it is to be abundantly watered. The *fountain* is suggested by the Virgin's spring which bursts forth into the Kidron valley from the Temple hill. The idea first appears in Ezek. 47[1-12]; it became a favorite expectation in late prophecy, and is referred to again in Zech. 14[8] and in Rev. 22[1, 2]. The *valley of Acacias* (v. 18, mg.) is unknown, but is probably some arid wady in the wilderness of Judæa. Acacias grow in dry places. Even the wilderness is to be redeemed. In contrast with the fruitfulness of Judah, Egypt and Edom are to become desolate wildernesses. It is probable that the Hebrew text of v. 21 is corrupt and that we should read *I will avenge their blood, which I have not avenged* (cf. mg.); that, at least, is in accord with the general tenor of the passage.

AMOS

BY PRINCIPAL H. WHEELER ROBINSON

INTRODUCTION

The Prophet and His Call. What made Amos, a countryman of Tekoa, leave his sheep and his fig-mulberries and the solitary places of his home, to intone rhythmic oracles of Jehovah at some crowded pilgrimage-festival of Bethel, a score of miles north, and in another land? It was not his professional calling; he was a layman, not a "cleric." But the passion of a true prophet burned within him—the passion of social sympathy and keen resentment against social injustice, and the passion of faith in Jehovah as a God demanding the right relation of man to man as the beginning of a right relation to himself, and a God able to enforce his demand by the events of history. Something more, however, was needed to make a prophet in those days, and Amos had this also; the prophet must be a man of abnormal psychical experience, who could see visions and hear voices and feel strange physical compulsions which gave to his personal convictions a divine authority in his own eyes and in those of others.

Economic Background. Let us try to see the social and religious life of the people to whom he is speaking. They live in small towns and villages, their one-roomed houses clustered on the hillside. Below is the village well, to which the women come morning and evening; at the gate the men meet to talk over common business; above the houses, near the hilltop, would be the "high-place," the local sanctuary. Most of the people work on the land, though some are now beginning Israel's future world-career of trading, under the guidance of the Canaanites. On the hillside there are grapes and olives to tend, and rock-presses in which to trample out their juices; down in the valley grow the wheat and barley, to be carried in due season to the threshing-floor, up near the hilltop and the "high-place." In the little houses, the oil and meal are kept in earthen jars, and are supplemented by various fruits; flesh is eaten very rarely, on festival days. Their clothing is of the simplest—a close-fitting tunic and an outer cloak, used as a sleeping-cover.

Social Background. The social organization of these village groups was hardly more elaborate than their manner of life. It centered in the family, over which the father ruled, and in the local assembly of male citizens, under the leadership of the elders. The king counted for little, except in time of war, or when his agents collected a tax. The priest at the "high-place" was much more important, for he frequently gave oracles or advice on practical difficulties; the prophet was a more irregular and occasional factor. The community was controlled by customs, local and national, rather than by formal codes of law. The local group was at once judicial, military, and religious; a citizen might be called on to act in any one of these three capacities at any time.

Religious Background. The religious life of the town or village centered in the "high-place." There was the altar, somewhat developed from its more primitive form of a rough block of unhewn stone, and near it, perhaps, some ancient and sacred tree; at any rate, there would be the *Asherah*, a wooden post, and the *Mazzebah*, stone pillar, these being survivals of more primitive tree and stone worship. There may have been an image of Jehovah, the ox being the favorite symbol, because of its strength. To such a sanctuary people of the district came in great numbers at the agricultural festivals, to a less degree at new moons and Sabbaths, and also on private visits, when they brought some gift and asked some favor. If an animal sacrifice was offered, the oldest method was to drain its blood on the altar, as belonging to the deity, while the family and their friends feasted on the flesh, and so realized communion with their God. (See art., *The Religion of Israel*, pp. 166–7.)

Moral and Religious Corruption. What, then, did Amos find wrong in this simple life? Chiefly three things. First, it was not the simple life for everybody; luxury and extravagance among the wealthy had replaced the older simplicity—the reign of Jeroboam II brought much prosperity and wealth. There were houses of hewn stone, furniture inlaid with ivory, cushions of silk, costly and elaborate dress, the drinking of wine from bowls, the eating of flesh every day, drunkenness and gluttony. The rich had turned from the good old simple ways of nomad life which the Puritan Rechabites maintained for centuries (Amos was virtually a Rechabite in spirit). Second, it was difficult for those not effectively represented in the local tribunal to get justice. Women who were wives or daughters might get protection through husbands and brothers; but the widow, the orphan, and the alien had nobody to speak up for them. The wealthy man had an enormous "pull" in his power to bribe the judges of a case. It was a hard thing to be poor in the Israel of those days; you might have to sell, not only your land-holding, but also your own person or that of your child, to get food for the rest of the family. In this way the smaller land-holdings were being absorbed into larger estates, and a "proletariat" was replacing peasant-proprietors. Third, the conditions of religious life were such as to antagonize fresh eyes trained to a desert-vision of the stern moralities and the absolute convictions. The method of worshiping Jehovah practiced at the "high-places" had been taken over from the Canaanites, with all its furniture and all its accompaniments. The Baal, or "lord," of each district was worshiped as the giver of its fertility; he was honored accordingly by sexual immorality. As Israelites gradually dispossessed Canaanites, Jehovah became heir to the worship and the sanctuaries of the Baals, and was regarded as the local Baal, his people settling down to agricultural life and needing a God of agriculture. Thus the God of the desert came to be worshiped even through "sacred" prostitutes, and the religion of Jehovah was becoming a nature-cult. This, then, was the triple deterioration against which the oracles of Amos are directed—the growing luxury, the cruel injustice and dishonesty, the flagrant immorality of religion, or, at least, the divorce of its ritual from morality. (For the relation of Amos and other prophets to religious ritual see art., *The Religion of Israel*, p. 168; cf. also intro. to Jeremiah, pp. 677–9.)

Political Background. The deplorable moral, social, and religious conditions were in large part the result of the external prosperity prevailing in Israel in the days of Amos. According to 1[1] Amos prophesied in the days of Jeroboam II (see comment on 1[1]), one of the most successful rulers of the Northern Kingdom. The reigns of Jehu and Jehoahaz during the latter part of the ninth century had proved disastrous; but under Joash or Jehoash the fortunes of Israel began to turn (2 Kings 13[25]). In part the victories of Israel at this time were made possible by the advance of Assyria, which compelled Syria to withdraw her forces from the southwestern boundary and concentrate them against the powerful foe in the southeast.

The successes of Israel continued under Jeroboam II; he became a "saviour" of Israel (2 Kings 14[27]), recovered all the territory that had been lost, and added to it in every direction; he even captured Damascus (2 Kings 14[23-29]). These triumphs in war, issuing as they did in the revival of commerce and in the new development of internal resources, raised Israel to a pitch of power and prosperity greater than had been enjoyed since the days of Solomon.

Teaching of Amos. The marvelous prosperity of Israel brought great moral, social, and religious evils in its train. As a result the religion of Jehovah was endangered by two perils: (1) The moral and religious corruption described in the preceding paragraphs, which was due to a wrong conception of the character of Jehovah; (2) the successes of the Assyrians, which were to the great mass of people an evidence of the superior strength of the Assyrian deities, and might lead to apostasy from Jehovah. All four prophets of the eighth century—Amos and Hosea in Israel, Isaiah and Micah in Judah—were convinced that both dangers could best be met by a statement or restatement, on the one hand, of the true nature and character of Jehovah; on the other, of the proper relation between Jehovah and Israel, as also between Jehovah and the other nations. This need Amos and his contemporaries in the prophetic office sought to supply. With reference to Jehovah he teaches that he is the one and only true God. "No one," says Marti, "can fail to observe that in this belief of Amos monotheism is present in essence if not in name." Concerning this one God he holds: (1) He is a person; (2) he is all-powerful; (3) he is everywhere present; (4) he knows all things; (5) he is merciful; (6) above all else Amos insists that Jehovah is a righteous God, whose favor can be secured only by a life of righteousness.

These truths Amos does not discuss abstractly but in their practical bearing upon the past, present and future history of Israel; but while he deals primarily with the Israel of his own age, he gives expression to several religious and moral truths that are of permanent significance. Of these the more important are: (1) Justice between man and man is one of the divine foundations of society; (2) privilege implies responsibility; (3) failure to recognize responsibility will surely bring retribution; (4) nations and, by analogy, individuals are under obligation to live up to the measure of light and knowledge granted to them; (5) the most elaborate worship is but an insult to God when offered by those who have no mind to conform to his ethical demands.

The Book of Amos. The plan of the book is straightforward, and raises few literary or textual problems. There is an *Introduction*, (chs. 1 and 2) in which Amos surveys surrounding peoples and condemns some characteristic sin of theirs—that he may fulminate with more effect against the sins of Israel. There are *three Addresses* (chs. 3, 4 and 5–6), which start from Israel's privileges, to infer her special penalties, denounce the sins which have just been indicated, recall the warnings which have been neglected, and proclaim the mourning of that "Day of Jehovah" when the Assyrian invaders will execute the righteous indignation of God. There are *five Visions of Judgment*, symbolized by locusts (7^{1-3}), fire (7^{4-6}), plumb-line (7^{7-9}), summer-fruit (8^{1-3}, expanded in vv. 4–14), the smitten sanctuary (9^{1-8a}). They suggestively indicate how a prophet worked up into rhythmical poetry some initial impulse, such as the idea of locusts as the devouring agents of Jehovah. An interesting paragraph of narrative (7^{10-17}), which a modern editor would put first of all, tells us about Amos and his experiences at Bethel. Finally, there is an *Epilogue* (9^{8b-15}) of later date, promising the restoration of prosperity.

Literature: W. R. Smith, *The Prophets of Israel;* G. A. Smith, *The Book of the Twelve Prophets,* vol. i (Expositor's Bible); W. R. Harper, *Amos and Hosea* (International Critical Commentary); Horton, *The Minor Prophets* (New Century Bible); Eiselen, *The Minor Prophets;* Edghill, *Amos* (Westminster Commentaries); Driver, *Joel and Amos* (Cambridge Bible); McFadyen, *A Cry for Justice;* T. H. Robinson, *Decline and Fall of the Hebrew Kingdoms* (The Clarendon Bible, vol. iii); Welch, *The Religion of Israel under the Kingdom.*

CHAPTER I

1. Title. This (editorial) heading tells us that Amos (of whom nothing is known beyond what this book tells us; cf. $7^{10f.}$) was a native of the Southern Kingdom (Tekoa is twelve miles south of Jerusalem), and that he prophesied about the northern one. Uzziah (i.e., Azariah, 2 Kings $15^{1-7, 8, 13}$) dates about 789–740 B.C., and Jeroboam II (2 Kings 14^{23-29}) about 782–743. The Dead Sea region is volcanic, hence the *earthquake;* the disturbance here referred to must have been severe, for it was remembered centuries afterward (Zech. 14^{5}).

2. The Preface. This verse strikes the fundamental note of judgment (cf. Joel 3^{16}) characterizing the book. The effect of the divine sentence of judgment, terrible as a lion's roar and as thunder (cf. Psa. 29), will be the desolation of the land, the drying up of its most essential and most striking verdure (so prolific on Mount Carmel).

CHAPTERS 1^{3} TO 2^{16}: INDICTMENT AGAINST ISRAEL AND ITS NEIGHBORS

Amos in this section denounces, in an impressive and repeated formula, each of six surrounding nations, namely, the Aramæans of Damascus to the northeast (vv. 3–5), the Philistines of the southwest (vv. 6–8), the Phœnicians of the northwest (vv. 9, 10), the Edomites of the south (vv. 11, 12), the Ammonites (vv. 13–15) and the Moabites (2^{1-3}) of the east. He then directs the same formula against Judah ($2^{4, 5}$) and finally Israel (2^{6-16}), the surprising goal of his prophetic pilgrimage. He says in effect, "As God judges each of these nations for some typical sin, so he will judge you, his prosperous protégé" (3^{2}).

3–5. Damascus. Damascus was the capital of the most important Aramæan kingdom, and here represents the entire nation. It had dominated Israel in the ninth century, when *Hazael* had invaded *Gilead* (east of Jordan); he is said to have destroyed many Israelite prisoners, making them like dust of threshing (2 Kings 10^{32} 13^{7}). Benhadad III was his son and successor (2 Kings 13^{3}). The repeated phrase, "for three . . . for four" means in Hebrew idiom "for many," "for more than enough." The *punishment* is the devouring *fire* of war, the breaking of the bronze or iron *bar* that secured the city gate; this threat was amply fulfilled by the Assyrian Tighlath-Pileser III in 733–732 B.C. *Aven* (or *On*) may refer to the temple of Baalbek in the valley between Hermon and Lebanon; the *house of Eden* may be Bit-Adini on the Euphrates; for the site of *Kir*, the original home of the Aramæans, see 9^{7}.

6–8. Philistia. Four of the five Philistine cities are named, the fifth being Gath. Their position was favorable to slave raids, for which they are here denounced. From the time of Tiglath-Pileser they suffered in successive Assyrian campaigns.

9, 10. Tyre. Tyre, the most important Phœnician city (Isa. 23^{3}), is accused of similar deeds (Ezek. 27^{13}), and also of wronging its own (Phœnician) brethren. Tyre had to pay tribute to Tiglath-Pileser, but its chief disaster was the siege and capture by Alexander the Great (332 B.C.), when thirty thousand of its people were sold into slavery.

11, 12. Edom. Edom was the mountainous district on both sides of the Arabah, south of the Dead Sea; its people were traditionally regarded as the descendants of Esau (Gen. 36^{1}). Their unbrotherly conduct toward Israel ("Jacob") was chiefly exemplified long after the time of Amos, when Jerusalem was destroyed in 586 B.C. The Edomites subsequently occupied south Judæa, and were ultimately dispossessed of their former territory by the Nabatæan Arabs (cf. p. 785a). *Teman*, the north district of Edom (Ezek. 25^{13}); *Bozrah*, capital of Teman (Isa. 34^{6}), perhaps Busaireh, twenty miles southeast of the Dead Sea.

13–15. Ammon. Ammon, east of Jordan, south and west of the river Jabbok, and south of Gilead, was easily open to their invasion. For another example of their "methods of barbarism" see 1 Sam. 11^{2}. David conquered their capital, Rabbah, and put the inhabitants to hard labor (2 Sam. 12^{31}, mg.). The motive of their invasion—not specially connected with the barbarity named—was territorial gain (cf. Judg. 11$^{12, 13}$). The *shouting* of battle is that of the assailants; the attack is figuratively described as a *tempest*. The words *their king* (Hebrew *malcam*) should perhaps be read, with some versions, as a proper name, Malcam or Milcom being the God of the Ammonites (1 Kings 11^{5}).

CHAPTER II

1–3. Moab. Moab, east of the Dead Sea, is better known than the rest through the "Moabite Stone" (see p. 117b). Nothing is known of this particular tomb-desecration. Ancient peoples regarded dishonor to the dead as even more grievous than dishonor to the living, since it made the ghost or spirit to suffer and prevented rest in Sheol. Hence the maledictions on ancient tombs against their possible desecrators. *Kerioth* (site unknown) is named on the Moabite Stone. Moab was made tributary with the rest by Tiglath-Pileser.

4, 5. Judah. The only other references to Amos' own country are 1^{2} 6^{1} 7$^{12f.}$ 9^{11}. The important word rendered *law* has a variety of meanings; it may denote teaching in a general sense (Isa. 1^{10}), technical instruction given by a priest (Jer. 18^{18}), a written code of law (Ex. 24^{12} Deut. 1^{5} Neh. 8^{1}), and "the Law" as the first part of the Hebrew canon (Psa. 119). Here it must mean religious and moral teaching given in Jehovah's name by priest or prophet. *Lies* stands for lying gods, i.e., idols or idolatries.

6–16. Israel. In these verses Amos comes to his main work, the rebuke of Israel, with which the rest of his prophecies are concerned. The sins condemned in this paragraph are bribery, a characteristic fault in the Oriental administration of justice (v. 6), the tyrannical oppression of the poor by the rich (v. 7), sexual immorality practiced in the name of religion (v. 7), the self-indulgent use of what has been wrung from the helpless (v. 8). Yet Jehovah deserves the gratitude shown in obedience, for it was he who dispossessed the former inhabitants of Canaan in favor of Israel, whom he led up to possess it. Besides this material gift, there was a spiritual one, for it was Jehovah who raised up inspired men to lead Israel, though his gift was scorned. So they will no more escape from the deserved judgment than a heavily laden cart can move swiftly; they will be held down to it, where they are. The form of the judgment will be defeat in battle; the enemy (obviously the unnamed Assyrians), after overthrowing the surrounding peoples, will finish with the northern kingdom, Israel.

Righteous (v. 6) is a forensic term, meaning "innocent"; a judge will give an unjust verdict for so small a bribe as *a pair of sandals* (1 Sam. 12^{3}, mg.; there may be a reference to the symbolism of land-transfer, Ruth 4^{7} Psa. 60^{8}). The obscure phrase in v. 7 (*pant after*, etc.) probably once read *crush the head of the poor on the dust of the earth*. The same verse refers to the sacred prostitutes found in the worship of the Baals, as of other nature-deities (Hos. 4^{14}); the point of the reference is that this thing is done openly, as by father and son, not that both resort to the same prostitute. The *clothes taken in pledge* (v. 8) ought to have been returned to their owners before night (Ex. 22$^{26f.}$). The fines extorted by injustice are spent in self-indulgence (v. 8). The whole attitude of Amos suggests the Rechabite protest against the civilization of Canaan (Jer. 35$^{1f.}$ 2 Kings 10$^{15f.}$). In vv. 9, 10, the "I" is emphatic; while you have done that, *I* have done this. *Amorite* is used generally for the ancient inhabitants of Canaan (Gen. 15^{16} 48^{22}); aborigines are often pictured as giants (Num. 13^{22} Deut. 1^{28} 2$^{10, 20}$ 3^{11}).

With the figure of the tree (v. 9) cf. the curse on Eshmunazar's tomb, "May he have no root beneath or fruit above" and our phrase, "root and branch." The *Nazirites* (cf. Rechabites) originally, like Samson (Judg. 13$^{5, 7, 14}$ 16^{17}) and Samuel (1 Sam. 1^{11}), assumed the vow for life, perhaps as a protest against Canaanite innovations in Israel's life. In the later law, Num. 6$^{2-21}$, the obligation is temporary; at the close of it the hair was sacrificed. They were "total abstainers" not only from intoxicants, but also from hair-cutting and the touching of corpses. In v. 13 the text expresses the impossibility of Israel's escape from the penalty; it may have read originally, *I will make you creak* [*groan*] *as a heavily laden cart creaks*, or even *I will make you totter*, etc.

Chapters 3^{1} to 6^{14}: Discourses of Warning and Exhortation

CHAPTER III

1–8. Privilege and Penalty. A new utterance, belonging to some other occasion, now begins, the first of three addresses (chs. 3–6). Israel's punishment will be proportionate to its privilege (vv. 1, 2); the prophet makes an important moral revaluation of the doctrine of divine election. (The reference to "the whole family" or clan shows that Judah is included, though the center of gravity of the whole people was in the north.) Here we see clearly the great change wrought by the eighth-century prophets; they denationalized religion by ethicizing it, for the truly ethical is the universal. The six rhetorical questions (vv. 3f.) lead up to the seventh (v. 6), and also to v. 8. All of them are illustrations of what we should call "cause and effect": Nothing happens without a cause; therefore, when you suffer, it is because Jehovah is punishing you, and when a prophet interprets it to you, it is because he is under compulsion to speak. The illustrations at the same time artistically prepare for the reference to the doom, by suggesting peril, except possibly the first (v. 3 mg.); this may refer to the need for an appointment when two are to come together, to avoid traveling alone on the lonely, robber-infested roads of Palestine. With the reference in v. 8 to the prophetic compulsion, cf. Jer. 20^{9} $23^{18, 22}$.

9–15. The Judgment of Samaria. In view of this approaching judgment, the very heathen of Philistia and Egypt are bidden to come and look on the disorder and oppression of Samaria; even they, men of violence as they are, will be shocked at what they see. Here, as elsewhere, it is the conduct of the rulers and upper classes which the democratic Amos has in view. The city of Samaria was built on an isolated hill, three hundred feet high, surrounded and overlooked by the mountains on three sides, and with a valley view of the sea (twenty-three miles) on the west. The position was almost impregnable, hence the long siege of 723–721 B.C. The special character of the site is indicated also in the phraseology of Isa. 28^{1}, where the walls of the city on this hill are compared with a drunken man's garland at a festival. It is, of course, the gains of "violence and robbery" that are stored up (v. 10). The threat of the prophet is that few of the wealthy will escape the judgment of war.

Amos looks on the luxury of the upper classes from the standpoint of the "proletariat"; even apart from moral issues, he seems to show a certain satisfaction in the prospect of its destruction. So complete will this be that nothing worth saving will be left (v. 12); according to the Book of the Covenant (Ex. 22^{13}), a shepherd had to produce the remains of an animal torn by wild beasts in order to exonerate himself; thus the figure is drawn from the customs of the time. *The corner of a couch* is still regarded in the East as a place of honor; the *silken cushions* are expressed in the Hebrew by almost the same word as "Damascus" (mg.), of which city they are conjectured to be the product. In the coming judgment, of which the justice will be acknowledged by the onlookers, both the sanctuary and the palace will perish. *Bethel* was that important and royal sanctuary of the Northern Kingdom ten miles north of Jerusalem at which Amos uttered his message, and called down the wrath of the priest, Amaziah ($7^{10f.}$). *God of hosts* (v. 13) refers to the abundant agencies and servants of God, probably his heavenly hosts, the angels (1 Kings 22^{19}) and the stars (Deut. 4^{19}), which were conceived as quasi-animate (Job 38^{7}). Amos significantly refrains from ever calling Jehovah "the God of Israel."

The reference to *the horns of the altar* (v. 14) implies that the right of sanctuary (1 Kings 1^{50} 2^{28}) will be lost. Originally the skin of the sacrificial victim with horns attached may have been spread on the altar (literally, "place of sacrifice"). In later usage, there were four horns, i.e., artificial projections at the four corners of the altar (Ex. 27^{2}) on which the blood of the victim was smeared (Lev. 4^{7}). *The winter house with the summer house* seems to denote the (single) luxurious building which has an upper story or higher structure on the roof, for use in hot weather (Judg. 3^{20}, "upper chamber of cooling," R.V. mg.; in Jer. 36^{22}, Jehoiakim is said to have a brazier burning in his winter house). In an Aramaic inscription of Zinjirli of about this date a royal tomb is described as both a winter house and a summer house. The *houses of ivory* are those decorated with it (Psa. 45^{8} 1 Kings 22^{39}); similarly, in 6^{4} Amos inveighs against "beds of ivory."

CHAPTER IV

1–3. The Luxurious Women of Samaria. The women, addressed as *kine of Bashan*, next arouse the prophet's wrath. These women of the "smart set" oppress the poor through their husbands, who have to get the wealth, by hook or by crook, which their wives demand for their own self-indulgence. *Bashan* is the fertile and extensive district east and northeast of the Sea of Galilee, noted for its pastures (Mic. 7^{14}) and, therefore, for its flocks and herds (Ezek. 39^{18}: "rams, lambs, goats, bullocks, all of them fatlings of Bashan"). These fatted animals—the pampered ladies of Samaria—are to be dragged out of their luxurious palaces like fish out of the water. Through the breaches made by the besiegers in the city wall before they captured it, they will be driven out, a train of captives, allowed to turn neither right nor left.

(The Assyrians actually did lead captives by a ring through the upper lip.) *Residue* is meant to suggest how few will escape, even so. *Harmon* is unknown, and the whole clause is dubious. The *holiness* of God by which he swears has been insulted by Israel's sin; the note of majesty and inviolable separateness is always found in the term "holy," in addition to the moral content given to it by the prophets.

4–13. Neglected Warnings. The prophet now turns from the ruling classes to rebuke the futile religiosity of the common people, who flock to the sanctuaries. They have neglected the five warnings of famine (v. 6), drought (vv. 7, 8), blight and locusts (v. 9), pestilence and slaughter (v. 10), earthquake (v. 11), here described, with the identical refrain, "yet have ye not returned unto me." "Let Israel, therefore, now prepare for judgment." For *Bethel* see 3[14]; *Gilgal*, the "circle" of stones near Shechem (Deut. 11[30] 2 Kings 2[1] 4[38]). A glimpse of periodic (annual) visits to a sanctuary is given in 1 Sam. 1; the present reference may be purposely exaggerated sarcasm: sacrifice every morning instead of every year, pay tithes every three days instead of every three years (Deut. 14[28]). *Leaven* (v. 5) was forbidden in Hebrew sacrifice (Ex. 23[18] Lev. 2[11] 6[17]).

V. 7 means that the heavy rains of winter, normally beginning six months before harvest, i.e., in November, have been withheld until January or February; the local irregularity of the rainfall, such as it was, made the warning more significant. The fullest account of a locust-plague (v. 9b) is given by Joel (1[4f.]); *after the manner of Egypt* (v. 10), because Egypt was notorious for diseases and epidemics (Deut. 28[27]); *the stink of your camp* is due to the unburied corpses. The "overthrow" of v. 11 is that of earthquake, cf. 1[1] and Gen. 19[25] (same verb); *as a brand plucked out of the burning* (Zech. 3[2]) means that they barely escaped complete destruction. V. 12 is a threat of doom, *thus* referring to an undefined penalty in the future, though the mission of the prophet as a whole implies a call to repentance. For *high places*, i.e., mountains, as trodden by Jehovah, cf. Mic. 1[3].

CHAPTER V

1–17. Israel to be Punished; A Righteous Remnant. In v. 2 is the "dirge" of Israel, which is to be destroyed in battle (v. 3); not the sanctuaries but Jehovah alone can save (vv. 4–9). The fruits of oppression will not be enjoyed (vv. 11–13). Do justly, and Jehovah will be gracious (vv. 14, 15); as it is, the "dirge" shall be sung by Israel in mourning (vv. 16, 17). The "dirge" of v. 2, written in the regular *Kinah* rhythm of 3:2 beats, is the death-song of the nation; cf. Ezek. 28[12], and the two dirges of David over Saul and Jonathan (2 Sam. 1[17f.]) and Abner (3[33, 34]). The army of v. 3 is mustered by cities, every citizen having his military duty. For Bethel and Gilgal, see 4[4]. *Beersheba* (Gen. 21[31] 26[23f.]), twenty-eight miles southwest of Hebron, was regarded as the most southern point of Canaan, as in the phrase "from Dan to Beersheba." There is a play on names in the Hebrew of v. 5, somewhat as though we said, "Gilgal shall glide into gloom; the house of God shall be a house of gore" (this, however, is *not* a translation).

The *house of Joseph* (v. 6) is the Northern Kingdom, its central unit, Ephraim, being traditionally descended from Joseph's son. *Wormwood* (v. 7), a bitter herb (Prov. 5[4]) here used figuratively of bitter things. Vv. 8, 9 (which read like an interpolation) point to two conspicuous sights of the sky by night (Job 9[9] 38[31]) to illustrate Jehovah's creative power, also seen in the succession of day and night, and in rain floods (Job 36[27-30], mg.) drawn up from the sea. The *gate* (vv. 10, 12) is where justice is administered (Ruth 4[1f.] Prov. 31[23]). With v. 14, *as ye say*, cf. Mic. 3[11]. V. 15 anticipates Isaiah's characteristic doctrine of the righteous remnant. In the coming doom the unskilled and the skilled in the professional lament will join together (v. 16b), the vineyard songs of joy will become wails of sorrow (v. 17). For the professional mourners, still employed in Syria, see Jer. 9[17]. The passing through of Jehovah (v. 17) will be like his passing through Egypt (Ex. 12[12]) when he smote the first-born.

18–27. The Day of Jehovah. The first of two *Woes* (cf. ch. 6) is directed against those who desire the intervention of Jehovah in misplaced confidence that God is on their side (contrast Lincoln's anxiety to be on God's side). Amos is here ethicizing the current eschatology; the "day of Jehovah"—i.e., the day on which Jehovah will manifest himself in the destruction of his enemies and the exaltation of his friends—will enforce the demand for justice and social righteousness, in place of elaborate religiosity. In the doom that is coming escape from one peril will only reveal another, either without or within the house (v. 19). The *feasts* (v. 21; cf. 8[10]) are pilgrimage-festivals (Ex. 23[14]), such as that of Ingathering (1 Kings 12[32]) instituted by Jeroboam I; for a similar condemnation of assemblies in the Southern Kingdom, see Isa. 1[13]. The *burnt-offerings* (v. 22), wholly consumed on the altar, and the *peace-offerings*, forming the material for a communion feast, were the two chief forms of pre-exilic sacrifice; the third kind of sacrifice here was probably vegetable. The *viols* (v. 23) or harps were used both for sacred (Psa. 33[2]) and secular music (Amos 6[5]).

V. 24 is the key verse of the entire book: Justice, not sacrifice. The question in v. 25 is a rhetorical one, expecting the answer, "No." In the golden age of Israel's desert youth there were no such sacrifices as you now offer, yet I cared for you then (cf. 2[9, 10], and contrast Psa. 95[10]). This is the common prophetic view; cf. Jer. 7[22]: "For I spake not unto your fathers nor commanded them in the day that I brought them out of the land of Egypt, concerning burnt-offerings or sacrifices." It would be very hard to explain such passages, if the elaborate sacrificial law had really come by Moses. The obscure v. 26 appears to refer to Assyrian (Babylonian) star-worship, "Siccuth" and "Chium" both designating the planet-god, Saturn; Israel shall take its false gods with it into exile (mg.). The R.V. rendering gives the sense much better than A.S.V. (For a more detailed discussion of this difficult verse see larger commentaries.) But the verse is probably a gloss, as Amos nowhere else refers to worship of other gods, but only to the false worship of Jehovah. *Beyond Damascus*, i.e., into Assyria, lying to the northeast of it.

CHAPTER VI

1–6. Selfishness and Luxury. The selfish luxury of Samaria's rulers (vv. 1–6), described in the second "Woe," will be punished by exile, as the culmination of a siege of terrible suffering (vv. 7–11). The moral perversity of Israel (vv. 12, 13) has caused Jehovah to send this invasion. With the opening characterization of luxury (v. 1), cf. Isa. 32[7]; v. 2 gives historical examples of the might of Assyria, from which Israel can have no hope of escape. *Calneh* may be the Kulunu near Babylon conquered by the Assyrians in 738 B.C.; *Hamath*, one hundred and fifty miles north of Damascus on the Orontes, was taken by Sargon in 720; *Gath* was taken in 711 (cf. 2 Chr. 26[6], of an event about 760 B.C.). Either the reference is to earlier disasters to these cities of which we do not know, or, as is perhaps more likely, the verse is a later addition. Another less probable view regards these cities as examples of prosperity; Israel's is greater. *Beds of ivory* (v. 4; cf. 3[12]), i.e., decorated, inlaid, with it. Sennacherib in 701 B.C. took from Hezekiah as part of his tribute "couches of ivory." The reference to *David* certainly suggests that in the time of Amos he was famous for secular rather than for sacred music; they think themselves second Davids. They drink from *bowls*, because cups will not satisfy their greed. The *affliction* (literally, "wound") *of Joseph* (v. 6) is the evil of his present condition, presaging disaster.

7–14. Sufferings of Exile. Those who were foremost in luxury shall be foremost in going into exile (v. 7). The *pride of Jacob* (v. 8, mg.) is the material prosperity of which Israel was so proud (cf. the parallel, "palaces"). The pestilence that accompanies the siege will destroy the mere handful left in some palace. The enigmatic v. 10 means that when a man's *uncle*, as next of kin, comes to bury him, and burn spices in the funeral rites (2 Chr. 16[14] 21[19] Jer. 34[5]), only one survivor is found, lurking terror-stricken in the remote parts of the palace, who begs that Jehovah be not invoked (as in lament or prayer) lest further disasters from him be provoked. This coming ruin will fall alike on great and small (v. 11). V. 12 describes Israel's conduct as unnatural, as unnatural as the running of horses on crags, the plowing of the sea with oxen (so render by a re-division of the Hebrew letters). The reference in v. 13 to *a thing of naught* conceals the place-name "Lo-debar," and that to *horns* the place-name "Karnaim"; these insignificant places east of Jordan (2 Sam. 9[4f.] 17[27] Josh. 13[26] 1 Macc. 5[26, 43f.]) were perhaps captured by Jeroboam II; Amos here puns on their names. The entrance to *Hamath* (v. 14; cf. 6[2]) is the pass between the Lebanons; *the brook of the Arabah* may be the Wady el-Ahsa, flowing into the Arabah three miles south of the Dead Sea.

CHAPTERS 7[1] TO 9[8a]: FIVE VISIONS OF JUDGMENT

The "Visions" of Amos, forming the third part of the book, are not literary devices, though poetically developed; they come from the psychic experiences which the prophet regarded as "objective" or external fact. Psychologically, they are shaped by his own consciousness and experience; philosophically, they represent the mysterious point of contact between human and divine personality. The first vision relates to the springtime, and the locust plague already named (4[9]) as a warning. The second relates to the drought (also previously named, 4[7]) of the summer heat, so that Amos seems to be speaking in the autumn, perhaps at the autumnal festival. The third vision, on the other hand, refers to a coming judgment by the plumb-line, not to be checked, like its forerunners, by the divine mercy and the prophet's appeal, but final and complete. The two remaining visions show the end itself, first by a symbol that suggests the word "end," and also represents Israel as ripe for destruction, and second by the spectacle of Jehovah actually destroying the temple of Bethel.

CHAPTER VII

1–3. The Vision of Locusts. Jehovah is seen creating the larvæ of locusts, which become full-grown locusts (so LXX) by the time the spring crop (*latter growth*) has yielded the customary tribute of *the king's mowings* (cf. 1 Kings 4[7] 1 Sam. 8[15, 17], of tithe). Part of the spring herbage was collected to feed the royal horses (cf. 1 Kings 18[5]). The Romans taxed Syrian pasture ground in the spring for their cavalry (W. R. Smith, *Religion of the Semites*, p. 246).

4–6. The Vision of Fire. A forest and field fire, frequent and dangerous in Syria, especially after long drought (cf. Joel 1[19, 20]); here the fire is so intense that even the subterranean waters (*the great deep*, Gen. 7[11]), from which all springs and fountains are fed, are dried up. If the phrase *called to contend* is original, it uses the figure of a forensic controversy, Jehovah's representative being irresistible fire (Isa. 66[16] Hos. 4[1] Mic. 6[2]).

7–9. The Vision of the Plumb-line. This differs from the two preceding visions, which referred to the past, by its reference to a coming judgment, through Assyrian invasion (*the sword*, v. 9). The prophet has no longer an opportunity to intercede. The vertical wall, supposed to be built in true perpendicular by the aid of a plumb-line, is now tested, and found to be out of plumb (Isa. 28[17] Zech. 4[10]). God will no longer *pass by them* in forgiveness (Mic. 7[18]). *Isaac* (cf. v. 16) is used for Israel by Amos only, perhaps it points to a claim of the Northern Kingdom to go back beyond the Jacob-Edom stage of history. The *high places* and the *sanctuaries* are not denounced by Amos as illegitimate rivals of the one sanctuary in Jerusalem (cf. Deut. 7), but because the worship is either immoral or nonmoral; here, with *the house of Jeroboam* (cf. Hos. 1[4]), they are symbols of the nation's power and pride.

10–17. Amos at Bethel. This narrative interrupts the series of five visions, but at the most suitable point, since the prophet has just named the reigning king, so that the interruption may represent an historical fact. Amaziah (not elsewhere named), the priest of *this* sanctuary only, sends to the king (probably to the capital, Samaria, twenty-four miles north); but after sending a messenger he feels free to proceed on his own initiative. He addresses Amos by the old name for "prophet," namely "seer" (1 Sam. 9[9]; cf. 2 Sam. 24[11], here possibly=visionary), telling him to earn his living (*eat bread*) in his own land of Judah (cf. 1 Sam. 9[7, 8] Mic. 3[11]). Amos disclaims professional prophetic status, without any contempt for it (cf. 2[11, 12] 3[7, 8]). He does not belong to the professional guild (v. 14, mg.); he is a herdsman who also treated *sycamores* (properly the fig-mulberries, Psa. 78[47]), which grew below Tekoa, by puncturing or nipping the figlike fruit, so that insects infesting it might escape. *An harlot in the city* (v. 17) is a strong phrase describing capture and open abuse by the Assyrians, whose land is described as *unclean* from the standpoint of the worshipers of Jehovah; they thought of him as more or less bound to his own land (1 Sam. 26[19]).

CHAPTER VIII

1–3. The Vision of the Basket of Summer Fruit. The Hebrew word for *summer fruit* (*kaitz*) suggests the Hebrew word for "end" (*ketz*), while the ripeness of the fruit itself suggests that Israel is ripe for destruction (cf. the similar play on the word for "almond-tree" in Jer. 1[11f.] mg.). With the vision in general we may compare Jeremiah's vision of two baskets of figs (ch. 24), good and bad, representing the Jews of Babylon and Judæa respectively. The Hebrew consonants in v. 3a should be rendered "the singing women of the palace shall howl"; follow mg. for v. 3b.

4–14. The Day of Jehovah Again. There follows an address, in the manner of chs. 3–5, denouncing greed, dishonesty, and oppression (vv. 4–6), and portraying the terrors of the "Day of Jehovah" (vv. 7f.), for those who "crush" (rather than *swallow up*, v. 4) the poor (cf. 2[7] and versions). The day of the *new moon* was observed as a religious festival, probably with suspension of trade (2 Kings 4[23] 1 Sam. 20[5f.] Hos. 2[11]), and was originally more important than the *sabbath* (here first named in prophetic literature; cf. Ex. 20[8]). The *ephah* was a dry measure, estimated at about eight gallons (in Zech. 5[7] it is big enough for a woman to sit in it); the *shekel*, meaning "weight," is the weight of silver or gold to be given in exchange for the corn; the Hebrews had no coined money prior to the return from exile, though ingots of known weight circulated. The passage describes three ways of cheating—by short measure, by obtaining more gold or silver than was just through heavier weights, and by using untrue balances. V. 6a seems interpolated (cf. 2[6]); v. 6b names a fourth way of cheating, by depreciation of the quality of what is sold.

The excellency of Jacob (v. 7), that in which he has "pride" (abhorred by Jehovah in 6[8]). *For this* (v. 8), i.e., the wickedness of Israel. The land is pictured as convulsed, like the Nile in its annual inundation, when its waters become turbid and red. In regard to v. 9, it should be noted that an eclipse was visible from Jerusalem in 763 B.C. The *sackcloth* (v. 10) was coarse cloth of goats' or camels' hair, worn by prophets (Isa. 20²) and mourners (Isa. 15³)—perhaps as the retention of more primitive costume. The *baldness* is that artificially produced by mourners (Isa. 15² Deut. 14¹). The result of the helpless terror will be an unsatisfied longing for Jehovah (vv. 11, 12). *From sea to sea* might refer to the Mediterranean and Dead Seas, but is more likely to mean the sea which is supposed to surround the earth (Psa. 72⁸ Zech. 9¹⁰). *The sin* (guilt) *of Samaria* (v. 14) is the "calf," the bull-image of Bethel (Hos. 10⁸); at Dan there was another "calf" (1 Kings 12²⁹). *The way of Beersheba* is used in an oath like "by the pilgrimage" (to Mecca).

CHAPTER IX

1–8a. The Vision of the Smitten Sanctuary. The fifth and last vision shows Jehovah actually in the act of destroying the sanctuary, presumably that of Bethel. An angel is told to strike at the head of the pillars, bringing down the roof on the heads of the worshipers; any who are not so destroyed will be killed by the sword, without exception; no remotest spot will afford a refuge to any (vv. 1–4). The description of Jehovah's power in vv. 5, 6 may be an interpolation (cf. 4¹³ 5⁸). Israel can plead no prerogative; she shall be treated like other kingdoms whose movements Jehovah controls (vv. 7, 8a).

With the (unnamed) destroying angel of v. 1, cf. the angel of pestilence of 2 Sam. 24¹⁶. The *chapiters* are the capitals, the tops of the pillars enlarged to support the roof; the *thresholds* here represent the foundations. The reference to *Sheol* (v. 2, R.V. mg.) as a subterranean cavern in the center of the earth is to be taken literally. While Jehovah states that he will pursue the fugitives as far as Sheol and drag them back, the passage does not mean that Jehovah's rule is yet thought to extend normally to Sheol, as is implied in the late psalm, 139⁸⁻¹² (see p. 173). For the contrast of heaven and Sheol, as upper and lower limits, see Job 11⁸ Mt. 11²³. *The top of Carmel* (v. 3) is eighteen hundred feet above the sea, with innumerable caves in its limestone, and hiding places in its forests. *The bottom* ("floor") *of the sea* is the last refuge of despair, naturally suggested by the promontory of Carmel. The *serpent* is the mythical sea monster, the dragon of the deep, the Tiamat of Babylonian myth, described in an inscription of 1500 B.C. as "a raging serpent" (cf. Isa. 27¹). In v. 6 we have a summary of Hebrew cosmology; the ends of the solid sky-vault rest on the earth, while above it are built the store-chambers of rain, etc. (Psa. 104¹³ Job 38²²ᶠ·). The *Ethiopians* (v. 7) of Nubia were known for their dark skin (Jer. 13²³), and therefore were despised: "you are no more to me than those Negroes." *Caphtor* was probably Crete (Deut. 2²³); the Philistine invaders were a non-Semitic people. *Kir* (cf. 1⁵), named with Elam in Isa. 22⁶, possibly west of the Caspian Sea.

THE EPILOGUE

8b–15. Preservation and Exaltation of a Remnant. *I will not utterly destroy.* The careful reader will note the transition of thought here from menace to comfort. The reason for regarding the rest of this chapter as probably later than Amos is not that Amos might not have added comfort to his menace, at some later stage of his prophetic activity, but that *this* comfort is in terms of post-exilic thought and language (see Driver, *Joel and Amos*, pp. 119f.). The previous moral emphasis is changed into one of material prosperity. The booth (*tabernacle*) of David (v. 11), i.e., the Davidic monarchy, is described as "fallen," which was not true before 586 B.C. Amos might have prophesied its fall—but hardly its restoration when nobody believed that it would fall. The term "booth" itself suggests the low estate of the Davidic line; it denoted a rough shelter for cattle (Gen. 33¹⁷), for soldiers on campaign (2 Sam. 11¹¹), for watchers in vineyards (Isa. 1⁸). The figure of the *sieve* (v. 9) transforms Israel's Exile from penalty to discipline. In the sieve of captivity, Israel's true wheat is sifted from the chaff-dust (*the sinners of my people*, v. 10), which falls to the ground, without loss of a single grain. The reference to *Edom* (v. 12) brings out the post-exilic enmity to Edom, due to its actions in 586 B.C. (cf. Obadiah, Psa. 60⁸ 137⁷). The phrase *called by my name* should be *over whom my name is called*, in ownership (2 Sam. 12²⁸ Deut. 28¹⁰). The lands once conquered for Jehovah by David and subsequently lost shall be again possessed.

In those prosperous days (vv. 13–15), corn will ripen so quickly that there will be hardly any interval between ploughing and reaping; the treading out of the grapes from the September vintage will take so long, because of its abundance, that before it is over it will be necessary to start sowing seed for the next crops. Vines were planted on the mountain slopes (v. 13b); the *sweet* wine is the pressed-out juice, unfermented. The phrase *bring again the captivity* may mean simply "change the fortunes" (Hos. 6¹¹, etc.). With this general picture of the future, cf. Isa. 65²¹ᶠ· Ezek. 28²⁶.

OBADIAH

BY PROFESSOR W. GLADSTONE WATSON

INTRODUCTION

The Author and His Message. There are thirteen persons bearing the name Obadiah mentioned in the O.T. but we cannot identify the author of this book with any one of them. The name means "worshiper of Jehovah," and it is possible that the name is not a proper name at all, but simply an appellative noun. The book is the shortest in the O.T., containing only twenty-one verses. It is a prophecy of doom upon Edom, because of its overweening pride and bitter hatred of Judah (vv. 1–14); and of the restoration of Israel and the universal rule of Jehovah (vv. 15–21).

Unity and Date. These two questions must be considered together. In vv. 10–14 there is a reference to the hateful conduct of Edom on the occasion of the capture and spoliation of Jerusalem. There were four occasions on which Jerusalem fell before invaders, but the only one which satisfies the conditions reflected in the book is that of 586 B.C., when Nebuchadrezzar sacked the city and carried off its inhabitants. This would fix the date of the book later than that event. But the question is complicated by vv. 1b–5, which occur in almost identical language in Jer. 49[14-16, 9]. Which of these is the original? Or did Obadiah and Jeremiah both copy from some earlier prophecy? The presence of additions in each, and of other differences, has convinced many scholars that both passages are derived from some earlier prophecy. This earlier prophecy may be assigned to the reign of Ahaz, when Edom smote Judah and carried away captives (2 Chr. 28[17]; cf. 2 Kings 16[6]); but this date is by no means certain.

The difficulty does not end here. The latter part of the book, vv. 15–21, is apocalyptic in character, and its point of view calls for a rather late post-exilic date. The language and style also differ from that of the earlier part of the book. The probability, therefore, is that the present book of Obadiah contains material from three different periods. The original prophecy, vv. 1b–5, may belong to the eighth century; the middle portion, vv. 6–14, would be suitable anywhere in the century following the fall of Jerusalem; the apocalyptic portion, vv. 15–21, may be assigned to the latter part of the fifth century or even later. To which of these sections the name "Obadiah" attaches is purely a matter of conjecture.

Edom and the Edomites. The territory of Edom lay south of the Dead Sea on either side of the Arabah, and was about one hundred miles long by less than fifty wide. The eastern range, though consisting of high rocky ridges with deep defiles, contained considerable good land and was well watered. Its mountain fastnesses made it very difficult of invasion. The original inhabitants were called Horites, which probably means "cave dwellers." They were dispossessed and probably absorbed by the Edomites. According to the biblical story, Esau, the twin brother of Jacob, was the father of the latter. In the Egyptian records the Edomites and Israelites appear for the first time in the thirteenth century. Edom seems to have made a permanent settlement earlier than Israel, for she blocked the road for Israel, while on the way to Canaan. The hostility displayed at that time marked her history to the very end (see Num. 20[14-21] Psa. 60[8] 137[7] Jer. 25[12-14]; but cf. Deut. 23[7], notes).

David subdued Edom. Solomon continued to hold it and carried on a flourishing trade through the port of Elath on the Gulf of Akabah, but before the end of his reign Edom rebelled under Hadad (cf. 1 Kings 11[14-22]). This does not seem to have interfered with the trade route to the sea, and after the division of the kingdom Judah controlled it for a long time, with some interruptions. In the reign of Ahaz (about 734 B.C.) Edom seems to have taken advantage of Judah's struggle with Rezin of Damascus; it seized Elath, thus destroying Judah's sea trade, smote Judah and carried off captives (2 Chr. 28[17]; cf. 2 Kings 16[6]).

During the following years, when all the little kingdoms of western Asia were engaged in a life-and-death struggle with Assyria, the enmity between the two peoples did not cease, and when Jerusalem fell, in 586 B.C., the Edomites not only gloated over Judah's calamity, but apparently participated in the plunder of Jerusalem. Shortly afterward the Edomites seized southern Judah and extended their borders northward beyond Hebron. It is conjectured that this invasion was due in part to pressure from the Nabatæans, who in the fourth century were firmly established in Edom, with their capital at Petra. With the establishment of the Nabatæan kingdom the name of the country was changed to Arabia

Petræa. The Edomites, who had moved into Judah, became known as Idumæans; eventually, in 128 B.C., they were conquered by John Hyrcanus and forced to accept Judaism. The Herods of N.T. times were Idumæans. (See art., *History of Hebrew and Jewish People*, p. 71b.)

Teaching. The first impression made by the book of Obadiah is that it is a hymn of hate, devoid of any religious lesson. Its theme is the doom of Edom; its spirit is that of vengeful retaliation. No doubt there was some reason for this temper. Israel had many enemies, but there was none so persistent and implacable as Edom. Trade rivalry, especially the struggle for the road to the sea, was a constant source of irritation which kept alive the ancient grudge. That which especially embittered Israel against Edom was the latter's malicious spirit at the fall of Jerusalem. This was aggravated shortly after when Judah was invaded and a permanent settlement effected by the Edomites. Judah was thereby reduced almost to extinction. Nearly all the O.T. passages, which, like the book of Obadiah, are bitterly resentful toward Edom, belong to this period.

G. A. Smith has suggested a deeper cause for Israel's attitude. It lay in the temperament, character, and ideals of the two peoples. In the story of their ancestors, Jacob, in spite of his cunning, was the man of ideals, while Esau would "take the cash and let the credit go." In the history of the two peoples the same differences were perpetuated. Edom was self-satisfied, confident in her isolation and hidden wealth, without pity, and keeping her wrath hot forever (Amos 1^{11}). She was reputed to have wisdom, but her wisdom was merely shrewd worldliness, not the wisdom which has its beginning in the fear of Jehovah. She was the typically irreligious nation. Israel, on the other hand, was the supremely religious nation, cherishing her ideals and yearning after God and the establishment of his righteous rule on earth. She was the people of faith and never was her faith stronger than in the post-exilic age. Though her city and Temple were ruined, her people scattered like sheep among the nations, the name of her God dishonored, yet in her suffering and humiliation under the tyranny and insolence of the heathen she still believed in God and in the ultimate triumph of his kingdom. To her indignant and passionate heart, the whole heathen world in its opposition to God seemed to be summed up in Edom, and she could not think of its destruction except as the necessary step to the inauguration of God's kingdom. With the destruction of the heathen world there would come the restoration of Israel to her own land, and then the kingdom would be the Lord's. This was the great consummation, and Israel's function in the world was to bear witness to this faith.

Obadiah's eyes were too full of tears to see, his heart too bitter to feel, that the heathen must be included in God's purposes of mercy, but he did believe that, in spite of all appearances, God is sovereign and ultimately the kingdom must be the Lord's. What this prophet saw with such conviction, and yet so imperfectly, finds its fulfillment in Christ and his kingdom—a kingdom without geographical limits or racial distinctions, a kingdom to be won, not by the physical destruction of his enemies, but by the power of the cross, the power of love. Obadiah was a long way from the spirit which could pray, "Father, forgive them; for they know not what they do," but he was on the way, and hence this little book, in spite of its narrow nationalism, finds a place in the unfolding revelation of God.

Literature: Wade, *Obadiah* (Westminster Commentaries); Eiselen, *The Minor Prophets; The Prophetic Books of the O.T.;* Hennessy, *Obadiah* (Cambridge R.V. for Schools); G. A. Smith, *The Book of the Twelve*, vol. i (Expositor's Bible); Sanders and Kent, *The Messages of the Later Prophets;* Horton, *The Minor Prophets* (New Century Bible).

THE PROPHECY

The book falls naturally into three divisions, vv. 1–9, 10–14, 15–21.

1–9. Condemnation of Edom. The opening sentence is the introduction to the whole book, and implies a communication from God received in an ecstatic state. In vv. 1b–5 there is a prophecy concerning Edom quoted from some pre-exilic source. The prophet hears that a confederacy is being formed against Edom; its success is assured by a divine revelation. Edom's boasted security in her mountain fastnesses will not save her, for Jehovah accepts her proud challenge and declares that he will bring her down. The destruction will be worse than the devastation wrought by the harvesting of thieves or grape-gatherers, for they would leave something, but Edom's destruction will be complete.

Vv. 7–9 describe an overthrow of Edom which may be regarded as a fulfillment of the previous prediction. Her treasures hidden in caves have been searched out and carried away. Her former allies have turned against her, driven her from her land and left her utterly bewildered. This probably refers to the Nabatæan invasion (see intro.), which may have taken place in the fifth century. Vv. 8, 9 may be part of the pre-exilic oracle. It announces that the proverbial wise men of Edom shall fail to deliver their nation from disaster. Her mighty men shall fail just as completely. *Teman*, a district of Edom, stands for the whole land (Jer. 49[7]). The LXX and Vulgate transfer *by slaughter* to v. 10, "for the slaughter."

10–14. Cause of Edom's Downfall. Edom's hostility to Israel in the day of her calamity is given as the reason for her overthrow. The day when foreigners entered the gates of Jerusalem, carried away her goods and cast lots for her captives was in 586 B.C., when Nebuchadrezzar utterly destroyed it (see 2 Kings 24, 25; cf. Jer. 52). Edom shared in the spoliation (cf. Ezek. 25), as Jeremiah had predicted (Jer. 49[7-22]). The negative imperatives in vv. 12–14 are probably to be taken as representing in a very vivid way what Edom actually did at that time. She rejoiced over the fall of Jerusalem, and showed it either by insulting speech, or by making her mouth large with derisive laughter; she entered into the gates of Jerusalem, gazed with satisfaction upon its calamity and looted its goods; she cut off the escaping fugitives and delivered them into slavery. The latter half of v. 15 is the sequel of this passage, and announces that Edom shall be paid in kind.

15–21. Judgment Upon Edom—Exaltation of Zion. This section, which is from a later hand, is concerned with the day of judgment upon the nations, especially upon Edom. The day of Jehovah was thought of as a day in which his character would be vindicated; which in pre-exilic times meant chiefly the destruction of the sinners in Israel. With the fall of Jerusalem the situation was changed. Jehovah's judgment had fallen with crushing weight upon Israel; it must now fall upon the nations, while the purified remnant of Israel may look for restoration. During the Exile and long afterward, the faith of the Jews was sorely tried. Their enemies were triumphant, they were in much affliction. But faith did not die. Any disaster that fell upon an enemy was hailed as a sign that Jehovah was at last going to judge the nations and bring consolation to his people. (For fuller reference to the "Day of Jehovah," see commentary on Joel; cf. also pp. 206–7).

In v. 16 the Jews are addressed. They have drunk the cup of suffering; now the nations shall drink it to the dregs. *Mount Zion* (v. 17) designates Jerusalem as well as the surrounding country. *Those that escape*—the purified remnant of Israel, including those who return from exile to possess their old territory. To speak of Jerusalem as *holy* means that no foreigners shall be there (cf. Joel 3[17]). According to v. 18 the two kingdoms of Israel are thought of as reunited; together they are to participate in the destruction of Edom. The translation of v. 19 is uncertain, but the general sense is that Judah will expand in all directions. In the post-exilic age Judah was reduced to a mere parish, but in the day of Jehovah it will include Edom on the south, Philistia on the west, Ephraim on the north and Gilead across the Jordan. Cf. the universalism of Isa. 2[2-4] Mic. 4[1-5].

The text of v. 20 is very corrupt; following the LXX, Wade translates "and the captivity of this fortress (Samaria) of the children of Israel shall possess the land of the Canaanites even unto Zarephath." This means that the children of those deported at the fall of Samaria shall return and possess the country northward to Phœnicia. The latter part of the verse means that the exiles from Jerusalem shall repossess the South. Thus the nation once more united will possess practically the old kingdom of David. *Sepharad* is of uncertain locality. *Saviours* may refer to strong leaders like the old judges. *The kingdom shall be the Lord's*—the destruction of Edom, which represents the world hostile to Jehovah, shall establish Jehovah's supremacy. In spite of the narrow nationalism exhibited in this book, and its bitter hatred of Edom, the prophet is reaching out to the day when Jehovah shall be King of kings and Lord of lords.

JONAH

By Professor WILLIAM C. GRAHAM

The Literary Form and the Text. The book of Jonah is a story written in limpidly clear narrative prose. At only one point does it depart from this literary style, namely, 2[2-9], where there stands a poem purporting to be the prayer uttered by Jonah during his incarceration in the great fish. This poem, be it noted, may be lifted bodily from the text without in any way disturbing the unity of the narrative itself. We shall here follow the method suggested by this and consider the poem separately.

While the Hebrew text is singularly free from difficulties, a few textual notes are added to help the exposition.

Salient Points of the Narrative. The narrative is easily followed, but there are certain salient points which may be passed over if not drawn to the attention. They are here briefly suggested together with necessary historical and topographical notes. The text of the tale should now be read with special attention to these points.

There are in the narrative four crises. In the case of the first three of these relief is vouchsafed by a happy turn of events. In the last, or major crisis, or climax of the story, relief is denied, so that it ends on a note of tragedy. By these crises the tale falls into four phases as follows: (1) 1[16], where a tragic fate is averted from the fragile ship and its crew. (2) 2[10], where Jonah escapes by a miracle from what seems like certain, horrible death. (3) 3[10], where Nineveh escapes a terrible fate. (4) 4[11], where the unrepentant Jonah is left unmoved by the divine effort to save him from himself. Let us consider the salient points of the story phase by phase.

First Phase, 1[1-16]. Jonah is the recipient of a *commission, directly from Jehovah,* to warn Nineveh of the consequences of its evil ways (vv. 1, 2). The only other mention of a prophet by the name of Jonah is found in 2 Kings 14[25], from which we learn that one so named exercised his ministry in the Northern Kingdom (Israel) during the reign of Jeroboam II (783–742 B.C.). *Nineveh* was the capital of the Assyrian empire, located on the eastern bank of the Tigris opposite modern Mosul. It was made the capital of Assyria by Sennacherib and was destroyed by the Medes and Persians in 612 B.C. Its area was at most not more than three square miles and its population a good deal under two hundred thousand. Jonah seeks to escape from the authority of Jehovah by flight from Joppa, seaport of Jerusalem, to Tarshish, a Semitic mining colony in the southwest of Spain (v. 3). The storm is sent by Jehovah to frustrate Jonah's design (v. 4). Other events follow in rapid succession; note, especially, the contrast between Jonah's behavior and that of the crew during the storm (vv. 4, 5); the readiness of the captain to accept assistance from Jonah's God (v. 6); the selection of Jonah as the guilty party by what virtually amounted to the modern flipping of a coin (v. 7); Jonah's profession of religion (v. 9); his magnanimity in confessing his fault and readiness to bear the consequences (v. 12); the reluctance of the sailors to cast Jonah overboard in order to save themselves (v. 13); their final yielding to the demands of self-interest (v. 15); the immediate subsidence of the storm and the escape of the mariners (c. 15); the spontaneity and sincerity of their gratitude to Jonah's God (v. 16).

Second Phase, 1[17]–2[1, 10]. Jonah's rescue from certain death *by Jehovah's appointment* of a great fish to receive him into its belly; the brevity of his stay in these confining quarters (1[17]); Jonah's turning again for help to the God he had defied (2[1]); Jehovah's immediate release of Jonah (2[10]).

Third Phase, 3[1-10]. The inflexibility of Jehovah's will; Jonah's original commission is renewed (vv. 1, 2); Jonah's immediate obedience, though all unequipped, in undertaking the long, difficult journey to perform an unpopular mission in a strange land (vv. 3, 4); the amazing effect of his direful message. Note the *extravagance* and *universality* of the penance it provoked though it came from the lips of a *foreign prophet* (vv. 5–9). The mercy of Jehovah toward the Ninevites (v. 10).

Textual Note. 3. *Of three days' journey*—read *with a walking distance of three days.*

Fourth Phase, 4[1-11]. The basic incompatibility between the mind of Jehovah and that of Jonah, and the latter's declaration that this had been the cause of his earlier disobedience (vv. 1–3); Jehovah's demand that Jonah be sure that his chagrin is really great enough to lead him to prefer death to what his pride leads him to regard as humiliation. See textual note on 4[4]. The prophet's misunderstanding of

Jehovah's meaning as solicitude for his hurt vanity;—note that he again takes heart, removes himself from the danger of being involved in the destruction which he now again expects, constructs for himself a flimsy shelter outside the walls and settles down to await the fulfillment of his wishes (v. 5); Jonah's appreciation of Jehovah's concern for his comfort (v. 6); Jehovah's greater concern for Jonah's soul, manifested in the removal of the means of his comfort (v. 7). Jonah's touchiness where his own comfort was concerned, and his self-destructive and stubborn persistence in preferring death to concurrence in the manifestation of divine favor to anyone but himself (vv. 8, 9); Jehovah's final and, so far as the story goes, futile effort to reach the perverted mind of his messenger with the truth about the divine character (vv. 10, 11).

Textual Notes. 4. *Doest thou well to be angry?* —read *are you so very angry?* 9. *Doest thou well to be angry for the gourd?*—read *are you so very angry over the gourd?* For *I do well to be angry even unto death* read *I am enough to die.* 11. For *persons* read *infants.*

The Poem, 2^{2-9}. This poem has many points of contact with the book of Psalms. By consulting Psa. 5^{7} 18^{6} 31^{22} 42^{7} 120^{1} 142^{3} 143^{4} this will at once become evident. It celebrates the gratitude of one who has been rescued from drowning and who now affirms his determination to acknowledge his debt to Jehovah, his rescuer, by the rendering of appropriate sacrifices and the discharge of the vows he had made when in danger of his life.

As a thanksgiving for deliverance actually uttered by Jonah the poem may appropriately be placed after 2^{10} but not after 2^{1}. This misplacement, together with its literary dependence on the Psalms, and the fact that the unity of the narrative itself is not at all disturbed by the poem's complete omission, stamp it, in the opinion of many, as a later addition to the book.

The Method of Interpretation. There are before us two possible methods of interpreting this book. These are, first, to interpret it *literally*, as a historical record of events; or second, to interpret it as a *didactic* work designed to convey truth applicable to a wider situation than is presented in the story itself. Let us consider what is involved in these respective alternatives and what fruit each method is likely to yield.

(1) The literal method involves not credibility but credulity with regard to miracle. The average reader is prone to think of only one miracle in the story, namely, Jonah's voyage in the interior of the great fish. Yet, interpreted literally, it fairly bristles with the miraculous: the storm; the selection of Jonah by lot as the guilty party; the sudden subsidence of the sea; the great fish whose arrival so perfectly synchronizes with Jonah's plunge into the deep; his survival of his piscatorial sojourn; his ejection, safe and sound, on shore; the gourd, which grew into an effectual shade in a day and perished as suddenly on the morrow—these are all manifestations of the miraculous. There are also other points which place almost as great a strain upon the credulity. How did Jonah make his message intelligible to people who spoke a strange tongue? Why does such a rebellious and self-willed prophet succeed so marvelously where an Amos or an Isaiah or a Jeremiah meets with so little success? Truly the story's tax upon the credulity is very great. Let the reader decide for himself whether his is able to bear it.

(2) The literal method of interpretation involves indifference to the fact that the writer exhibits neither the interests nor the methods of the historian. He is utterly vague upon many points about which a historian would have been specific. Where did Jonah land when ejected from the fish? Who was the Assyrian king and when did he reign? Are we to understand that Jonah remained sulking outside of Nineveh until he died? If not, what became of him? These are some of the queries which the literalist must find it hard to answer.

But suppose one is ready to ignore all these and other unmentioned difficulties, what harvest will he reap? Very largely this: first, that there was once such a stiff-necked prophet as Jonah for whom the Lord did much more than he deserved; and, second, some rather doubtful ground for the belief that God once intervened in the affairs of men in a manner which in our time he has completely abandoned.

And now for the other alternative. What does it involve? Simply the acceptance of the fact that O.T. religious teachers sometimes, like the Great Teacher himself, made use of allegory or parable as a vehicle for the delineation of great social tendencies and the inculcation of truths applicable to them (cf. pp. 19–20).

And what fruit will such a method yield? Let us see!

The Interpretation of the Book as Primarily Didactic in Purpose. There are two stages to the task which now confronts us. First, we must discover what the writer aimed to teach; and second, we must endeavor to identify the situation which stimulated such teaching.

(1) *The Teaching of the Book.* It must be obvious, even to the casual reader, that the author has drawn a sharp contrast between Jonah, the central character of the story, and all the other persons mentioned. Jonah repre-

sents one characteristic attitude to life, while the sailors and the Ninevites represent another. The Jonah of this tale, be it noted, is a real "character." In depicting him the author has been at no little pains to achieve a genuine character study. The careless reader is apt to find little to admire in him, to hold him in contempt as a selfish, whining, religious snob. Yet a catalogue of his capacities and virtues will reveal that Jonah is, potentially, a good man who possesses some of the qualities which make for greatness.

The prophet's individual force is a quality which dominates the entire characterization. He is at least not a nonentity. Whatever his faults may be, he has a mind, a will, a personality which single him out as noteworthy and significant. He is a man of great spiritual capacity, possessing the delicate psychological equipment which enables him to apprehend eternal and universal truth. To him alone God gives commission and message. He is, too, a religious man, that is to say, he confesses, when challenged by the sailors, to an habitual attitude of reverence toward the one true God. Of course the episode here narrated finds him in a mood of defiant rebellion. But that is not his soul's true aspect. When he is himself he is one who at least aims to live his life under the sway of his religious convictions. Because of this religious discipline which has been the habit of his life he has achieved certain virtues. He is capable of self-control in moments of danger. He does not lack moral courage, for he confesses his faith and his fault when such confession threatens to cost him dearly. When put to the ultimate test he displays the altruism which faces death with fortitude rather than jeopardize, through cowardice, the safety of others.

Jonah's one devastating weakness is precisely that to which forceful and highly gifted individuals are, in the nature of the case, prone. His individualism has overbalanced him until he has developed an anti-social mind. The only self-expression which interests him is that which ends in self-gratification. To his fellow men, particularly to all that are not of the same mind and attainment as himself, he is cold, unsympathetic, arrogant, patronizing, proud and cruel. He is a big man tricked by his very bigness into smallness, a good man who consumes his own goodness and becomes a moral bankrupt in the eyes of the world. In him the habit of taking has all but destroyed the impulse to giving. He is one who has labored hard to achieve a colossal moral failure.

Jonah is the only professedly religious character in the story. The sailors and the Ninevites are pagans. It is true they owe allegiance to many gods. But their relationship to them is not a deep and controlling loyalty. It is entirely pragmatic, practical, utilitarian. They turn to their gods only when they are cornered and need help. And even then they are moved by no abiding faith in them. They are, for example, quite ready to turn to other sources of help which are more promising. So sailors and Ninevites alike do not scruple to seek and accept material succor from Jonah's God. The only religion they know is on the plane of materialism. Of communion with God for its own sake they know nothing.

And yet these pagans because, perhaps, of this very religious pragmatism, possess something which Jonah does not possess. They have the social mind. The sailors stand by one another, and even by their troublesome passenger, until the last moment. The Ninevites impose upon themselves most rigorous penances for the common weal. These pagans instinctively think in social terms. Thus Jonah typifies official religion and the Ninevites typify paganism. Or, let us say, Jonah typifies the church and these others the world. What the writer desires to teach is that *the church needs the world and the world needs the church.* Each has something to give to the other, not only something to give, but something which it dares refrain from giving only at the expense of the fullness of its life. The church has the oracles of God, the secret of self-discipline, the spiritual power which raises human life above the plane of mere existence. These things are not intended exclusively for the church. They belong also to the world. To withhold them is rebellion against God, against the soul of the universe. And the world, what has it to give? An opportunity for loving service. Though potentially great, humanity is frail and helpless; its aching, unsatisfied need of the Infinite ever challenges the compassion and love of those who know God and experience his power. Without that love which it can cultivate only by service to all humanity the church can never worship God in spirit and in truth; it must always be in rebellion against him.

(2) *The Historical Situation Which Stimulated the Teaching of the Book.* What sort of a situation would stimulate a man to an endeavor to teach these truths? A situation in which a fully developed, self-conscious, religious institution, exhibiting the strong characteristics of good and evil typified by Jonah, was found, in defiance of a universal God in which it professed to believe, denying to a needy, suppliant and tractable outside world the sympathetic mediation of truth which should be the heritage of all men. This, of course, is the

situation in which religious Israel, to some degree, found itself from the days of the great prophets on. The first known Israelite to raise the issue and pronounce upon it was Amos (cf. Amos 3[2]). Yet the religious forces of Israel were never integrated into a religious institution, fully conscious of itself as such, until the days of the Babylonian Exile. And this institution, this Jewish Church, originally built up by the exiles in Babylon, was never challenged to define and determine, in real life, its attitude to the pagan world until it essayed the long and difficult task of transplanting itself from Babylon to the home land and the Holy City (cf. pp. 169–70).

Then there arose a very difficult situation. The native population of Judah was composed of many heterogeneous elements. The descendants of those Judæans who had not been carried off into exile had been interpenetrated by people of many different races and religions—Moabites, Ammonites, Edomites, Phœnicians, Egyptians, Syrians, Greeks, and what not else besides. With these they had intermarried and otherwise lived in close contact. The result was a hybrid race with its own peculiar blend of culture and religion.

Meanwhile the Jewish community in Babylon, partly because of the considerable measure of local autonomy they always enjoyed, but more because of the presence among them of a succession of great religious leaders, had contrived to maintain their solidarity and to develop a distinctive ecclesiastical organization, dominated by a highly developed religious spirit. To bring together these now alien groups and make of them a unified community, centering in Jerusalem, was an extremely delicate and difficult task. The Babylonian Jews, by reason of the humiliating experience of the Exile, had developed a profound distrust of foreigners, a hard shell of suspicion and prejudice by which they sought to protect themselves from a cruel world. They naturally attributed the difficulties they encountered in their efforts to restore what *they* considered a true Jewish regime in Palestine, to the presence, in the native population, of those alien elements which they despised and feared. In the days of Nehemiah and Ezra, then, this question of the relation of the Jewish Church, the true and faithful seed of Jacob, as its members considered themselves, to the Gentile world, was brought to an issue. The church demanded that all ties with foreigners, even the marital relationship, be dissolved. It was such an extreme demand as this which provoked the writing of the book of Jonah with its keen and searching analysis of the play of motives. It is a protest hot from the heart of one who lived in the midst of the issue he dealt with and who felt in every fiber of his being the great principles which were involved (see intro. to Ezra-Nehemiah).

That the situation must be historically so placed is substantiated by the sequence of events in the narrative itself, which symbolize the political and religious history of Israel in broad outline: Let Jonah stand for the true Israel, Nineveh for paganism at its very worst, the sea for world politics, the vessel for diplomacy, the polyglot crew for the neighboring nations with which Israel and Judah, to the disgust of the great prophets, were constantly intriguing, and the storm for the disturbance which shook the Near East when Babylon succeeded Assyria as the dominating power, and you have the main movements of thought and trend of events down to the Exile. The pre-exilic prophets bear witness that their people constantly refused to trust and obey their own God, Jehovah, steadily turned away from their spiritual vocation, and stubbornly preferred to work out their own destiny by means of diplomatic intrigue. History likewise witnesses that the nations in which Judah trusted for safety threw her overboard at last just as the sailors did Jonah.

Let the great fish stand for Babylon, Jonah's sojourn within it for the Exile, his miraculous deliverance for the freedom to return granted the exiles by Cyrus, emperor of the Medes and Persians, and the chastened Jonah, who carried out his original commission to Nineveh, for the returning exiles who undertook the difficult task of transforming a paganized Palestine, and you have the main points of what actually happened in history down to the writer's own time.

From that point on the incidents of the story typify the situation of his own day. The extravagant penance of the Ninevites indicates the real desire of the native population to be counted good servants of Jehovah and their willingness to attempt ethical reforms. Jonah, sulking in his pitiful booth, grateful for the gourd, whining over its loss, stubbornly refusing to make God's merciful attitude to the heathen his own, is the Jewish Church, as the writer saw it, pining away in its shabby rebuilt Temple, looking for miraculous interventions on its own behalf, and stubbornly refusing to open its heart to the great heathen world outside through the salvation of which it could, alone, become great in the eyes of posterity and acceptable in the sight of God.

Literature: Bewer, *Jonah* (International Critical Commentary); Perowne, *Obadiah and Jonah* (Cambridge Bible); Horton, *Minor Prophets*, vol. i (Century Bible); Eiselen, *The Prophetic Books of the O.T.*, vol. i; Gordon, *The Prophets of the O.T.*

MICAH

By Professor J. E. McFADYEN

Introduction

The Prophet. Micah the peasant was a younger contemporary of Isaiah the statesman, as he delivered his message during the last quarter of the eighth century B.C. Quite apart from the superscription (1[1]) we know from a very interesting allusion in Jer. 26[18] to his threat against Jerusalem (3[12]) that he prophesied during the reign of Hezekiah, but as he also predicted the ruin of Samaria (1[6]), the capital of the Northern Kingdom, which fell in 721 B.C., he must have begun to prophesy before that date. It is perhaps significant of his rural affinities that he singles out the capitals of both kingdoms as the special objects of the divine wrath: in them the wickedness of the kingdoms seems to him concentrated (cf. 1[5]). As a Judæan, living in a little village on the borders of the Philistine country (cf. 1[1, 14]), he devotes his main strength to attacking the vices of Judah.

Historical Background. Micah gives a peculiarly vivid picture of moral and religious conditions in Judah. To him as to Amos (2[6] 5[11]) the most exasperating offense was the exploitation of the poor, and those who were guilty of it he fiercely denounced as cannibals, "who eat the flesh of my people, and flay their skin from off them, and break their bones, chopping them in pieces as for the pot" (3[3]). We may perhaps infer from 2[2] that he had himself been a victim of their rapacity; he may have had the bitter experience of seeing his own home and fields annexed by some greedy landlord (2[2]; cf. Isa. 5[8]), who thus helped to build "Zion with blood and Jerusalem with iniquity" (3[10]). Men like these had no scruple in stripping the coat from the back of unsuspecting travelers, or in ruthlessly driving women and children from their homes (2[8]).

These atrocities were inspired by greed of gain, and unhappily not only the civil but the religious leaders of those days were infected by this base passion, which is combated by Micah with an earnestness which reminds us of Jesus. The priests and prophets, to whom the people might well have looked for guidance, were deflected from their duty by mercenary motives (3[11]): the nature of their message was determined by the size of the bite that was put in their mouths (3[5]). Trade was conducted by means of false weights and measures (6[10f.]), the best were bad (7[4]), society was honeycombed with treachery, and dissension reigned in the home (7[5f.]). And all this low morality had its root in a low religion. Worship was conducted with heathen symbols (5[12-14]). The deadly earnestness which the worshipers could on occasion display was devoted only to the externals of religion (6[6f.]), and in keeping with this they fondly imagined that the great Temple at Jerusalem was the guarantee of Jehovah's presence in the midst of them and that he would preserve them from all possible disaster (3[11]). The universal corruption of society fully explains Micah's terrible threat (3[12]). (For a more detailed description of political, social, moral and religious conditions in Judæa in the days of Isaiah and Micah see introduction to Isaiah, pp. 631–6.)

Message of Micah. Over against this degraded religion and morality stands the prophet's own incomparable conception of the divine demand upon men, expressed in terms of elemental simplicity—justice and kindness between man and man, and a humble walk with God (6[8]). That was religion, as Micah understood it (cf. Jas. 1[27]); and well might the man who offered such a definition claim to be inspired. The function of the inspired prophet—and he knew himself to be one (cf. 3[8])—was, not to predict the distant future, but to stir the popular conscience by confronting it with the moral demands of God.

The teaching of Micah is simple and forceful. In many respects it resembles that of his predecessors; he insists on the holiness of Jehovah and the universality and righteousness of the divine government of the world. This righteous God deals with all nations, Israel included, on the basis of ethical principles. As long as his people do right they will enjoy the divine favor (2[7]), but if they turn against him they must suffer punishment. Jehovah's good will is secured, not by a careful observance of the ritual, or by the bringing of sacrifices, whatever may be their intrinsic value, but by a life in accord with the principles of righteousness, by the diligent practice of kindness and brotherliness, and by a living fellowship with God in the spirit of humility, which should ever govern the intercourse of weak and sinful man with a holy and perfect God (6[6-8]).

The prophet did not deceive himself into believing that his high religious and moral ideals would be sufficiently attractive to bring about a complete transformation in the whole nation. He foresaw that the majority would continue in rebellion and that, therefore, a destructive blow must fall which would make an end of the national existence of both Israel and Judah. But he was just as strongly convinced that a remnant would be saved and that under the Messianic king this remnant would enjoy a life of permanent peace and prosperity. In his description of the Messianic ruler he passes beyond Amos and Hosea, agreeing substantially with Isaiah, except that he adds the birthplace of the ideal ruler (5[2-6]). Through the moral influence going forth from the remnant the knowledge of Jehovah will spread to all nations, and many will flock to him for instruction (4[1-4]).

A comparison of Micah with his greater contemporary, Isaiah, is not without interest. Both prophets cherished lofty conceptions of the character of Jehovah and of the obligations resting upon his people, and both had firmly established convictions concerning the nature and ultimate triumph of the kingdom of God. A comparison of the utterances of the two men reveals resemblances in style, thought, topics and even phrases; but the contrasts between the two in origin, training and sphere of activity are equally marked. One was a city prophet, of high social standing and the counselor of kings; the other, a simple country man, born of obscure parents, and in close touch and sympathy with the peasant class.

The Book. The book of Micah falls naturally into three parts, as follows: chs. 1 and 2, chs. 3–5, and chs. 6 and 7, each part beginning with "Hear ye." Each division contains a description of the present corruption, an announcement of imminent judgment and one or more pictures of a bright future. Of course, the three parts do not represent three connected discourses, but, rather, three collections of the essential elements of the oral utterances of the prophet throughout his ministry. It may even be that in the editorial arrangement elements not coming from Micah were added. (The more important later additions are pointed out in the comments on specific passages.) The principle of arrangement is not chronological but in a sense logical; i.e., the collector or collectors kept in mind the general scheme—corruption, judgment, salvation of a remnant, exaltation—but within the general scheme the separate utterances were arranged with less care and without the introduction of connecting links. As a result abruptness in transition is frequent, and at times it is difficult, if not impossible, to trace the exact line of thought.

Literature: Cheyne, *Micah* (Cambridge Bible); Horton, *Minor Prophets* (New Century Bible); G. A. Smith, *The Book of the Twelve Prophets*, vol. i (Expositor's Bible); Eiselen, *The Minor Prophets;* Sanders and Kent, *Messages of the Earlier Prophets;* T. H. Robinson, *Prophecy and the Prophets;* Farrar, *The Minor Prophets.*

CHAPTER I

1. Superscription. Two facts about Micah's date are certain: (1) that he began to prophesy before the fall of Samaria in 721 B.C. (cf. 1[6]), and (2) that he prophesied during the reign of Hezekiah (cf. Jer. 26[18f.]), which began in 725 or 715 B.C., and ended in 696 or 686. It is significant that this peasant prophet from the little village of *Moresheth* near Gath (cf. 1[14]), and therefore near the Philistine border, should have singled out the two capitals, *Samaria and Jerusalem,* for special condemnation.

2–9. The Doom of Samaria and its Justification. Though a Judæan, Micah notes the sins and announces the fate of Israel, especially of its capital, Samaria. He is so indignant at what he sees there that he summons *all* the *peoples* of the world to listen to his indictment and to the doom which Jehovah *from his holy temple* in heaven may pronounce upon them as well (v. 2). The doom of Samaria is vividly portrayed in terms of an earthquake, which will *split the valleys and melt the mountains* on which she is built, *pouring down her stones, laying bare her foundations* (v. 6) and reducing her to a heap of ruins (v. 5); and this devastation is effected by the angry Jehovah, who no sooner descends from *his place* in heaven (v. 3) and touches the *high places of the earth* than the earthquake, with its awful havoc, commences. Why *all this* wreck and ruin (v. 5)? It is because of *sin* in *Jacob and Israel,* i.e., the Northern Kingdom—there is a side-glance at Judah—especially in the capitals Samaria and Jerusalem, where the sin is concentrated. The sin is the sin of idolatry, with its apparatus of *images* and *idols* (v. 7: for *hires* read *images*)—an idolatry which the prophets (cf. Hos. 2[5]) regard as adultery; these idols, impotent to save their worshipers, will be seized and carried off to an Assyrian temple. At the thought of this impending ruin, this *wound incurable* (v. 9), the prophet, *barefoot and naked* like a mourner (cf. 2 Sam. 15[30]) or a captive (cf. Isa. 20[2-4]), breaks into loud and bitter wailing, for he sees the same fate drawing near Judah and Jerusalem (vv. 8f.). These last words may be a later addition, reflecting the experience of Sennacherib's invasion of Judah in 701 B.C.; on the other hand, they may refer to the consternation in Jerusalem created by the fate, just described, of Samaria. In v. 5 for *the high places of Judah* read *the sin of the house of Judah.*

The God whom Micah worships is no petty national God, committed unconditionally to the support of his own people, but a God who can be so provoked by sin as to hurl them to destruction.

10–16. Lament Over Judah's Doom. The text of this passage, crowded with proper names, is one of the most difficult and desperate in the O.T. In places it is hopelessly obscure, and resort must be had to the precarious remedy of emendation. But two things are quite clear. (1) The proper nouns are nearly all names of Judæan towns within the Shephelah, the district of low hills and flat valley land west and southwest of Judah lying between the higher Judæan hills and the Philistine plain (for further details see art., *The Land of Palestine*, p. 54); and (2) on the names of each of these towns there is a word-play, quite unsuspected by the English or American reader and impossible to reproduce in translation; e.g., *Aphrah* (v. 10) would inevitably suggest to a Hebrew ear the word *aphar*, which means dust. The prophet means that the town is well named —its name suggests its destiny—and calls upon it to *roll itself in the dust:* and so with the others. *Achzib*, e.g. (v. 14), suggests *achzab* = deceptive: that town, true to its name, would prove *a deception* to the king of Israel. It is as if towns or villages of ours were called *Duston* (or *Dustville*) and *Decepton*, and we should attempt to draw a moral therefrom. We have to remember how much more significant names were to ancient men than to us: Jesus, e.g., played upon the word "Peter," which means "rock" (Mt. 16^{18}). It would scarcely be worth while to describe the location of all the places named—enough that they are in the Shephelah. Just as Isaiah (10^{28-32}) names town after town on the line of the Assyrian advance upon Jerusalem, so Micah here, whether the terror which inspires his lament is due to an imminent Assyrian invasion or is simply the panic spread by the earthquake. Micah's own home is within the region of the doom ($1^{1, 14}$), which creeps on to *the gate of Jerusalem* (v. 12); and, as in mourning, it is meet that the head and hair should be shorn bald as the *vulture's* head (v. 16). In v. 13 Lachish is described as *the beginning of sin*, probably because, as one of Solomon's chariot cities (1 Kings 9^{19} 10^{26}), it induced a false confidence in military resources.

It is scarcely possible to translate this section, but it is possible to feel it. Its very obscurities invest it with a weird power of its own, as we watch the inevitable doom creeping on from city to city, a doom sent by Jehovah himself (v. 12).

CHAPTER II

1–5. The Divine Judgment on the Brutalities of Men in Power. In ch. 1 the justification of the terrible doom to fall upon Israel and Judah was not elaborated; only the false worship (1^7) and the false confidence in things material (1^{13}) were touched upon. But no prophet is content to censure these things alone, and Micah now proceeds to his real task, which is to lay bare the moral and social abuses of his time. He pictures the magnates who carry out as soon as it is daylight the plans they had conceived in their beds for robbing the people, as Ahab did Naboth (cf. 1 Kings 21), of the property they covet (vv. 1f.). But Jehovah, too, has his plan; he will bring upon them a disaster, inescapable and crushing (v. 3), and the lament which follows shows that what is meant is the disaster of war, in which their lands will be seized by and divided among the foe. The lament in v. 4 should probably read as follows:

The portion of my people is measured,
  There is none to restore it.
Our fields are divided among our captors,
  We are utterly ruined.

There will be no more casting of the line to determine the lot, for all will have been seized by the foe (in v. 5 for *thou* read *ye*). There is poetic justice in this: they coveted the fields of those who could not defend themselves and took them by violence, now their own are taken from them by one mightier than they.

6, 7. The Scornful Reply to the Prophet's Threat. Such preaching is at once unwelcome and incredible (cf. Amos 2^{12} $7^{10f.}$). "Don't prate to us," his opponents reply, "of things like these. Shame shall never overtake us. Jehovah is not so impatient, he does not do things like these. Has he not promised to deal graciously with Israel, his people?" Through the obscurities of the text it is only too plain that, lawless and unscrupulous as these men were, they were yet nominal worshipers of Jehovah, trusting to his patience and counting on his blessing.

8–11. The Prophet's Stern Reply. The text of these verses is very uncertain, but they seem to contain allusions to certain acts of callous cruelty which would be readily understood by the prophet's contemporaries. "As for you," he retorts, "you are not my people, nay, you are actually enemies of my people. You strip the garment from peaceful unsuspecting wayfarers as if it were booty of war, you drive the women of my people away from their darling children, you tear the mother from her babe, saying, 'Arise, begone, here you must not stay.' For a tiny little thing you exact a cruel pledge" (vv. 8–10). Here we see that passionate challenge of cruelty and, by implication, that passionate demand for justice and kindness in human relations which was afterward to crystallize in the humane legislation of Deuteronomy. But to insist on these things is not the way to popularity as a prophet; it is the false and empty soul who would preach about wine and strong drink—message of lies!—that would be a welcome prophet to a people like this (v. 11).

This passage finely contrasts the true preacher with the false. The true preacher rebukes that rapacity and violence which would strip the coat from another man's back and tear the mother from the child: the false preacher speaks to the people of wine and drink and the things they love. Here the preacher with the low ideals is satirized for all time: such a man, Micah roundly says, is a liar.

12, 13. The Deliverance. Here is a gracious promise, expressed in terms of shepherd life, that Jehovah will gather together the scattered flocks of Israel *like sheep in the fold* (not *of Bozrah*), and everywhere shall be heard the sound of rejoicing men. Then the figure slightly changes, and Jehovah, no longer Shepherd, is likened to *the breaker*, i.e., the leading ram of the flock, who goes up and butts every door open, i.e., demolishes every obstacle so that the flock can follow. Again a change of figure—Jehovah is King who marches ahead of his people.

It is curious to find so gracious a promise following immediately upon denunciation and threat (vv. 8–11). This, however, is a not uncommon feature of prophecy (cf. Amos 9[8-15] Isa. 29[1-8]). Sometimes it is open to suppose the promise was appended by a later hand: here, the scattered sheep seem to suggest the Exile, more than a century after Micah's time. Sometimes, however, it may well be the prophet's own (cf. Hos. 14): here, e.g., the remnant may be those who survive the Assyrian invasion of 701 B.C. In any case, whoever added these and similar promises was inspired by the sound conviction that threat and disaster could never exhaust the whole purpose of God. There must be "good news," a "gospel."

CHAPTER III

The Doom of Jerusalem and Her Leaders. This is an artistically constructed chapter, falling into three sections of equal length (vv. 1–4, 5–8, 9–12), and issuing in a terrific climax. It is here that the real Micah is most evident, with his passionate interest in the poor and exploited (cf. 2[1f., 8f.]); and it is noteworthy that he, like the prophets generally (cf. Amos 6[4-6]), lays the chief blame at the door of the civil and religious leaders. The reference to *Jerusalem* in v. 12 shows that *Jacob* and *Israel* in vv. 1 and 8 mean, not the Northern Kingdom, but Judah, and to this the whole chapter refers.

1–4. The Sin and Doom of the Judges. It was the business of the judges *to know judgment*, i.e., to care for justice. Instead, however, they indulged in the most ruthless oppression of the poor—e.g., by accepting bribes (cf. Amos 5[12]). As with Amos (5[15]) *the good* is social justice, and in language of amazing vividness, which reveals the depths to which the prophet's soul is stirred, he describes the oppressors of the poor as cannibals, *who eat the flesh of my people:* notice that *my people* are pre-eminently the poor (cf. Isa. 3[15]). When their own hour of need comes, the oppressors will cry to God in vain. The fact that they do cry to him shows that they are nominally religious men (cf. 2[7]).

5–8. The Sin and Doom of the Prophets. Unhappily, the religious leaders are themselves leagued with this unjust social system. Already we have had a glimpse of the popular prophets, with their easy sensuous gospel (2[11]); here we see them again as men whose message depends not upon the eternal moral laws but upon the size of the *bite* put between *their teeth:* the bigger the bite, the fairer the prophecy. They proclaim *peace*, i.e., good luck, when they have a good bite between their teeth, while they declare a holy war against all who either cannot or will not give them a satisfactory bite. Here is satirized the preacher who makes the quality of his sermon depend upon the amount of his salary; and black will be his doom in the great day of the Lord—darkness and not light (cf. Amos 5[18]), shame and mourning, of which *the covering of the lips* was a sign (cf. Lev. 13[45]).

In magnificent contrast to these despicable creatures is the true prophet (cf. note on 2[11]), and Micah is not afraid to claim to be such a prophet. He draws his inspiration, not from the prospect of his salary, but from *Jehovah* his God, and in trenchant and profoundly significant words he defines the function of the true prophet, which is, not to predict the future, but *to declare unto Jacob his transgression and to Israel his sin*—in modern words, to touch and stir the popular conscience by the exposure of social wrong. This is precisely what Micah has been doing throughout chs. 2 and 3 and what he proceeds to do with equal vigor and solemnity in the next section.

9–12. The Doom of Jerusalem. Here the prophet returns to the attack on the civil and religious leaders, among whom he now includes the priests (v. 11), and the charge he hurls at them all is their love of money: all their professional service is inspired by this unholy passion, and the man of mercenary mind cannot truly serve either the Lord or the people (cf. Mt. 6[25f.]). Yet all the time they *lean upon Jehovah* and fondly imagine that, under his protection, no disaster can ever overtake them —nominally religious men (cf. v. 4), yet with souls corroded by the love of money and the guilt of oppressive brutalities, *building up Zion with* the *blood* of the poor, which was, as it were, the mortar that held its stones together, and blind to the fact that they were thus infallibly preparing the way for its destruction. For because of their conduct the city of *Jerusalem* and the very hill of *Zion* on which *the house*, i.e., the Temple, was built were doomed to be reduced to a jungle. This terrible threat was remembered more than one hundred years afterward (cf. Jer. 26[18]). It shows how courageous and heretical, from the point of view of commonplace contemporaries (v. 11), a prophet could be, and how little the prophets cherished the patriotism whose motto is, "My country, right or wrong." Were not they the truest patriots after all?

CHAPTER IV

1–5. Jerusalem the Religious Metropolis of the World and Dispenser of Peace. The scene changes. From a Jerusalem reduced to a jungle we turn to a vision of the city as the religious capital of the world, fountain of justice and peace. Doubtless this transformation is to be effected *in the latter days* or, rather, *in the after days;* but it is unmediated, and at this point in the book it comes as a great surprise. As the same oracle is repeated almost word for word in Isa. 2[2-4], the question has been raised which of the two prophets composed it; or whether in both cases it may not have been taken from a common original; or, what seems to be more probable, whether it may not be a later addition, a foil to offset the dark picture of Jerusalem which had preceded. Much may be said on the different sides of this question, but the answer to it does not affect the sublime message of the section, to which we now turn.

The true prophet, while fully conscious of the difficulties and wrongs of the present (ch. 3), always looks wistfully forward to *the after-days,* when some better thing shall be. The writer sees men from *all nations* streaming to the temple on Mount Zion which is *established at* (cf. mg.) *the head of the mountains*—a phrase to symbolize its spiritual elevation. What they want is *law,* i.e., instruction, guidance, and they are conscious that they will get this in Zion as nowhere else in the world (a fine tribute to the acknowledged religious supremacy of Israel). They need guidance because there has been some international dispute. The *swords* and *spears* are not there for nothing; it was by their means that this dispute would have been settled had the nations not been inspired by the wise and happy thought of carrying it to Zion for arbitration. Nor do they travel in vain; they get there the decision for which they had hoped; and then, acquiescing in that decision, they beat into *plowshares* and *pruning hooks* the *swords* and *spears* for which they have now no more use. Nations that have learned to accept arbitration need *learn war no more,* can live henceforth in peace the happy life of the country (v. 5, which says that whatever idols other nations may worship, Israel will be eternally true to her own God, is on a less ideal level than vv. 1–4 and is apparently a later addition).

The passage is not an idealist's dream, it is full of practical insight, suggesting as it does the way to world peace. To secure this, there must be (1) a hatred and horror of war—the nations recognize that arbitration is "a more excellent way" than war; (2) a tribunal (here Zion) which the nations can trust; (3) nations willing to submit their case to arbitration and to abide by the result; (4) unquenchable hope —"it *shall* come to pass." As in his blood-drenched and war-weary world the prophet dared to cherish this confident hope, so may we.

Jerusalem's Changing Fortunes and Ultimate Triumph. This is the theme of 4[6]–5[9]. The section is not continuous, the changes are too abrupt and the contents too conflicting for that. Restoration, e.g., is followed by exile (4[6, 10]); Jerusalem is now weak and in travail, now triumphant (4[10, 13] 5[8]); now victorious, now besieged (4[13] 5[1]). As exile is in some sections presupposed, the passage as a whole is relegated by many scholars to the exilic age: but if it be Micah's, the changing moods will reflect the kaleidoscopic changes in the fortunes of the city in his time, especially during the Assyrian invasion of 701 B.C. (rather than the later Babylonian assault and deportation in 586).

6–8. The Gathering of the Dispersed and the Restoration of the Monarchy. This section would come very naturally after vv. 9f., which threaten exile, but the verses are probably independent in time of origin. Jerusalem is addressed as *tower of the flock* (cf. Num. 32[16]), in which the shepherd kept a look-out against the enemies of his sheep (2 Chr. 26[10]): she has lost her *former dominion,* such as she enjoyed in the great days of David and Solomon, but it is to be restored (v. 8), and better still, Jehovah himself will be her king: he will gather again to Zion his widely scattered flocks, and *reign over them for ever.*

9–13. Siege, Exile, Restoration and Triumph of Jerusalem. The beleaguered city is in anguish, *king and counselors* are helpless, exile is certain, but *Jehovah shall redeem thee*—here again the inextinguishable Hebrew hope—and not only redeem thee, but endue thee with strength to *beat in pieces* every opponent and stamp upon them, as with brazen hoofs, like an ox treading out the grain.

CHAPTER V

See introductory note in ch. 4 above.

1–6. Judah's Defender, the Messiah. Jerusalem is besieged, her *judge,* i.e., king (perhaps Hezekiah, cf. 2 Kings 18[27]), insulted; she is *cutting herself* (rather than *gather in troops*) in the intensity of her mourning (cf. Deut. 14[1]). But deliverance will côme, not indeed from the capital itself, but from the little country town from which David sprang (1 Sam. 17[12]), though it was least among the clans (not *thousands*) of Judah. This Messianic king was to be descended from an ancient family—*from of old, from everlasting* imply no more (cf. 7[14, 20]; also discussion in art., *Israel's Messianic Hope,* pp. 181–3)—doubtless that of David. After the birth of this wonderful child whom Isaiah (7[14]) had also announced (see comment on Isa. 7[14]), the fortunes of the people will change, the exiles will return, and the Messiah will rule the world, not in his own strength but in the strength of his God (vv. 1–4), securing for his people *peace,* i.e., protection, against the Assyrians when they dare to *tread* on Hebrew *soil* (not *palaces,* v. 5); nay, ravaging *the land of Nimrod* itself, i.e., Assyria (cf. Gen. 10[8-11]) with *sword* and *spear* (not *in the entrances*). Other *shepherds* too, i.e., leaders, will be raised up, *seven, eight,* i.e., as many as are needed. The Messiah is to be a conquering King who will bring peace to Judah and whose dominion will be world-wide.

7–9. The Irresistible Might of the Returning Exiles. The exiles, scattered among the nations, depending upon God alone (v. 7b), will be numberless as the raindrops and terrible as the lion—victorious everywhere.

10–15. War and Idolatry will be Abolished. *In that* blessed *day* to which the prophet looks forward every instrument of war (including fortified *cities*) and all the accursed apparatus of idolatry (cf. Deut. 18[10-12])—stone *pillars* and *asherim* (i.e., wooden poles)—will disappear, and drastic punishment will be meted out to disobedient heathen nations. This passage is almost certainly Micah's and may have paved the way for the reformation of Hezekiah (cf. 2 Kings 18[4]).

CHAPTER VI

1–8. Jehovah's Indictment Against the Ingratitude of His People. The mountains and the earth, older than man and witnesses of Israel's history, so crowded with ingratitude, are summoned to listen to the indictment (cf. Isa. 1[2]). Israel's sin is a sin against love. For, instead of *wearying* her with burdensome demands, Jehovah had from the very beginning of her history showered upon her his redeeming love, blessing her with great personalities, delivering her from the bondage of Egypt, and from the powerful word of the sorcerer Balaam (cf. Num. 22–24), and bringing her over the Jordan *from Shittim* (Josh. 3[1]) *unto Gilgal* (Josh. 4[20]) in the promised land. All this Israel had forgotten (cf. v. 5).

She now acknowledges her guilt, but pleads that she does not know how to approach the great God she has offended, and she is willing to go to any extreme, even to the sacrifice, like Abraham (cf. Gen. 22), of her *first born,* to placate him—a practice occasionally resorted to both in and after Micah's time (2 Kings 16[3] 21[6] Jer. 7[21]). The prophet's immortal answer (v. 8) shows how the popular and the prophetic conceptions of religion were wide as the poles asunder. Not ritual but righteousness was what Jehovah required of men (cf. Deut. 10[12]), not costly gifts of *things* but the surrender of *themselves* in the service of one another. His answer is a marvelous summary of the teaching of his three great predecessors, Amos, Hosea, and Isaiah; the divine demand was for *justice* (Amos 5[24]), mercy or *kindness* (Hos. 6[6]) and a *humble walk with God* who alone is exalted (Isa. 2[11]). The combination suggests that social morality is inseparable from and rooted in religion, and that the true worship of God is the service of man. The O.T. has no greater word than this.

9–16. The Doom of Commercial Dishonesty. *Hark! Jehovah calleth to the city,* doubtless Jerusalem. Omitting the next clause, which is obscure, the text should read *Hear, ye tribe* (of Judah) *and assembly of the city. Can I forgive treasures of wickedness in the house of the wicked,* etc.? *Can I count as pure him with wicked balances?* It is here primarily the *rich men* (v. 12) whom Micah, like Amos, attacks, whose palatial houses are filled with *treasures* acquired by violence and robbery (Amos 3[10]), and who acquire their fortunes by selling underweight—an *abominable* practice (Deut. 25[13-16]) also scathingly denounced by Amos (8[5]). How closely the religion of the prophet touches the intimacies of commercial life! Not only the rich, however, but all *the inhabitants* (v. 12) are *liars* and *cheats;* all social life is honeycombed with *deceit*, and Jehovah will not tolerate this. *Therefore* (v. 13) *I will begin to smite thee* (so LXX), and the blow threatened is the blow of war. In their besieged city hunger (not *humiliation*) would do its deadly work, no goods could be *removed* to safety, children would be the prey of the *sword*, the fruits of their toil would be reaped by the foe (vv. 14f.)—a just judgment, which would earn for them *the scorn of the peoples* (so LXX, v. 15), because they had followed the cruel policy of *Omri* and of his better-known son *Ahab* (1 Kings 16[29]), who had connived at the murder of Naboth in order to secure his vineyard (1 Kings 21).

CHAPTER VII

1–7. Lament Over the Prevailing Corruption. These verses present a melancholy picture of society. The prophet looks in vain (v. 2) for one who fulfills Jehovah's fundamental demands (cf. 6[8]). He is like a *fruit-gatherer at the gleaning*, who finds neither grape nor fig (read last clause of v. 1 as in mg.). Brutal egoism everywhere prevails—justice perverted, bribery rampant, the best like *briars*, "rough and ugly to deal with" (J.M.P. Smith), and—saddest of all—family life is ruined by internal dissension and treachery: evil is the only thing they do well (v. 3). But he, like Isaiah (8[17]) in a similar case, *looks* in faith to *the God of his salvation* (v. 7), when *the day* of penal *visitation* comes, foretold by the *watchmen*, i.e., the prophets (v. 4).

8–20. The Victory of Zion Over the Heathen World. This theme is treated in three separate poems, which seem to imply a later situation and a broader stage than Micah's: **8–10.** Theme—*The downfall of Zion's enemies.* Now Zion is suffering and in *darkness* because of her *sins* (v. 9), but a day of light is coming, when her God will vindicate her, and bring down to the dust those who mocked her and him (v. 10). **11–13.** Theme—*Restoration and return. In that day her walls*, now ruined, would be rebuilt, and her boundaries (cf. mg.) extended far (cf. Zech. 2[4]), her widely scattered exiles would return, and the earth (not *the land*, v. 13), swarming with Zion's enemies, would be *desolated*—all but Palestine. **14–20.** Theme—*Prayer for Jehovah's help.* The people are *dwelling solitarily in the forest*, i.e., in the hill country of Judah; they are near but have no access to *Carmel*, i.e., the fruitful land (not the mountain). Hence the prayer to Jehovah to *shepherd* them with his staff and restore them to the pastures of *Bashan and Gilead* (v. 14) east of the Jordan, which had not been theirs since 734 B.C. (2 Kings 17[1-29]). In v. 15 read *show us*, i.e., repeat for us the ancient miracle by humiliating our foes (vv. 16f.). The great v. 18 represents Jehovah as a God whose glory is his readiness to forgive, and he may assuredly be counted on to fulfill his ancient promises to the patriarchs (v. 20; cf. Gen. 28[13f.]). The ages are linked together by his love.

NAHUM

BY PROFESSOR WILLIAM C. GRAHAM

INTRODUCTION

Theme and Literary Structure. The book of Nahum, like so many discourses of Israel's prophets, was inspired by the imminence of an important political event. This was the fall of Nineveh and the destruction of the great Assyrian Empire of which it was the capital. Here we have recorded the reaction of a member of the prophetic class in Jerusalem to the perplexing events of those days. Here we may learn how one loyal Judæan churchman felt about the approaching disaster to Assyria and what policy he advocated for his own country under the circumstances.

Small though the book is, it abounds in difficult literary problems. These are complicated by the corrupt condition of the Hebrew text, especially in 1^{9}–2^{13}. This textual corruption has been regarded by many interpreters as sufficient warrant for a practical rearrangement of the prophecy, although none of the ancient versions support the transpositions which are necessitated. In the following commentary an attempt is made to interpret the text without recourse to such a rearrangement.

The heart of the book of Nahum is the record of a public speech in which the prophet joined issue with persons of an opposing mind on the momentous events of the day. This speech is imperfectly recorded in 1^{9}–2^{13}, and the latter half of it, 2$^{3-13}$, is devoted to an exceedingly spirited, imaginative description of an expected successful attack upon Nineveh.

The original document contained only a second poem on the general theme which absorbed the prophet's interest, the fall of Nineveh. It now stands in ch. 3. There is no ground for doubting Nahum's authorship of this chapter. It may be regarded as a second oracle, delivered possibly a few days later, and aimed at confirming and deepening the impression made by 1^{9}–2^{13}.

The opening section, 1$^{1-8}$, may reasonably be regarded as a later editorial addition. Its form and content stand in some contrast with all that follows. In form it is an acrostic, or alphabetical psalm-poem. Its thought may not be connected definitely with any historical event. Its outlook is universal, indefinite, eschatological. Yet it stands fittingly here as a sort of text for Nahum's utterances, since the ideas to which it gives expression are Jehovah's vengefulness toward his enemies, his consideration for those who rely upon him and the infinity of the power which he wields. Nahum's own utterances were so concerned with politics that the religious and theological convictions underlying them do not plainly appear. This introductory poem was doubtless placed where it now stands to supplement the religious inadequacy in his utterances.

The Historical Situation in Nahum's Day. Our understanding of the historical situation in Nahum's day has been radically modified by the recent discovery of a portion of the annals of Nabopolassar, king of Babylon at that time (cf. Gadd, *The Fall of Nineveh*). The principal facts elicited from this record are as follows:

(1) Nabopolassar, a former vassal of Assyria, and Cyaxares, king of the Medes, were openly at war with Assyria as early as 616 B.C. (2) Nineveh fell before the assaults of these allies in 612 B.C. (3) Egypt was involved in these events, during the years covered by the chronicle, as the ally of Assyria. (4) The struggle between these great powers did not end with the fall of Nineveh. The Assyrians moved their capital to Harran, which in turn also was lost to the foe in 610 B.C.

At this point the record breaks off. We know from other sources, however, that the struggle was not finally concluded until 605 B.C., when Pharaoh Necho of Egypt, presumably with the last remnants of the Assyrian forces, was defeated at the battle of Carchemish by Nebuchadrezzar, crown prince of Babylon.

When, in the light of this knowledge, one considers 2 Kings 23^{29} and 2 Chron. 35$^{20-24}$, one is inclined, until other evidence is forthcoming, to reconstruct the historical situation which Nahum knew as follows: As early as 616 B.C. the civilized world was divided into two hostile camps, Medes and Babylonians on one side, Assyria, supported for sound considerations of policy by Egypt, on the other. The prize in dispute was the domination of the Near East. The struggle was stubbornly contested but began to go against Assyria. In Judah pro-Babylonian sentiment gained ground with Josiah and the court party, who hoped that Judæan independence might follow as a result of Assyria's downfall. In 608 this pro-Babylonian party came to grief when Necho, learning the truth about their attitude, paralyzed any action they might have taken against his interests.

This happened when he was on his way to the East for the prosecution of the campaign. He summoned Josiah to appear before him at Megiddo and then assassinated him. It is difficult to prove any collusive communication between Judah and Babylon when this movement was developing at the Judæan capital. But Jeremiah, shortly after 605 B.C., addressing Jerusalem, says: "What wilt thou say if he (Jehovah) shall set over thee those whom thou hast accustomed to thee as familiar friends, for a head?" (Read thus for Jer. 13[21].) If, as is possible, Jeremiah is here predicting Babylonian domination of his country, the terms which he uses would indicate that he knew of former friendly relationship between Judah and Babylon.

We can now understand the position taken by the prophet Nahum, speaking probably between 614–612 B.C., after the Medes and Babylonians began to close in on Nineveh. He was an Assyrophobe and his influence was cast on the side of those who proposed a policy of alliance with Babylon, the policy which cost Josiah his life. Holding such views he undoubtedly found himself in opposition to Jeremiah, for despite the latter's stand a few years later, he was never a pro-Babylonian but always held the true prophetic position that salvation must come not through fortuitous circumstance but by moral regeneration. Because this was his position Jeremiah would see at this time that the expected victory of Babylon would mean no more to Judah than a change of masters (cf. p. 679a).

The Teaching Values of the Book of Nahum. As has been maintained above, this book emanates from the dominant religious elements of Jerusalem in Josiah's later years. It is an expression of the religious and political mind of the court party which, a few years earlier, had sponsored Josiah's religious reforms. As such its religious values may not, as is sometimes done, be lightly passed over.

(1) *Positive Religious Values.* Underlying Nahum's attitude to Assyria are two clear religious conceptions which all prophetic thinking supports. The first is the *adequacy of God's sovereignty.* The second is the *existence of a moral order in the universe.* Nahum gives little prominence to these doctrines as such. With him they are axiomatic. What he does do is to assert vigorously, on the basis of these beliefs, that Assyria, which in its relations with other nations has ignored these conceptions, must pay the price demanded of all who run counter to the eternal verities. The moral indignation of Nahum against Assyria needs no condonation. The truth that nations may not transgress the great conceptions of ethical religion with impunity; the conviction that mere physical strength is impermanent and evanescent; the certainty of the existence of a "higher court" before which nations must ultimately answer for their policies—these are ideas which the world needs in every age. And the fate of Assyria, so picturesquely predicted by Nahum, is a classical illustration of their truth.

(2) *Negative Religious Values.* These are equally important. Nahum has grasped certain great truths. But from them he had been led by his emotions, prejudices, human interests, to arrive at certain unwarranted conclusions. Sympathy with his people led him to conclude that Assyria's downfall meant Judah's happiness. Nationalistic prejudice led him to assume in Jehovah a special, unmoral interest in his own people. Considerations of personal interest must have influenced him to ally himself with the popular party and so to refrain from all moral criticism of his own nation.

Consequently, Nahum provides an outstanding example of arrested religious development. He makes *particular* applications of *universal* truths, which is to say, he fails to apply to himself and his people the standards by which he measures others. He was all right as far as he went, but, morally and spiritually speaking, he did not go far enough. It was this inadequacy in himself that made him the foe instead of the ally of Jeremiah. The mistake which Nahum made is a timeless error. We all make it. Our religious development is constantly diverted and perverted by our emotions, prejudices, and consideration for personal interests. Perhaps no truth stands in more need of continuous emphasis than this, *that all moral and spiritual truth is applicable chiefly, and in the first instance, to ourselves.* For the inculcation of this truth Nahum's book has definite value.

Literature: J. M. P. Smith, *Nahum* (International Critical Commentary); Davidson, *Nahum, Habakkuk, and Zephaniah* (Cambridge Bible); Driver, *Minor Prophets,* vol. ii (Century Bible); Eiselen, *The Prophetic Books of the O.T.,* vol. ii; Gordon, *The Prophets of the O.T.*

CHAPTER I

1. Editorial Superscription. A statement of the theme of the book, described as *an oracle on Nineveh* (see mg.), and of its authorship. The name of the author, *Nahum,* signifies "Comforter." So appropriate is this name to one who declared to Judah the downfall of oppressive Assyria that it may have been specially bestowed by a later editor. Since nothing is indicated concerning the prophet's genealogy he was doubtless an obscure person until his participation in the discussions of the day. *Elkosh,* according to the least difficult tradition, was located near the southwest border of Judæa. The prophet's utterances, however, were in all probability made at Jerusalem, just as Amos traveled to Bethel to deliver his oracles at the great shrine of the Northern Kingdom.

2–8. Jehovah's Irresistibly Implacable Vengefulness Toward His Enemies. **2.** *Avengeth*—read *an avenger;* for *the Lord avengeth* read *an avenger is Jehovah, and is full of wrath;* literally, *a master of wrath.* Cf. Gen. 37[19], where Joseph is described as a *master of dreams* (see mg.), i.e., a dreamer *par excellence.* The expression here used of Jehovah emphasizes very strongly his propensity to wrath; for *the Lord taketh vengeance on his adversaries, and he reserveth* [*wrath*] *for his enemies* read *Jehovah is an avenger to his foes, and a gaoler is he to his enemies.* The point made here is that the divine wrath is inescapable. **3.** *And great in power, and will by no means clear* [*the guilty*]—read *but for greatness of power he will not at all acquit;* i.e., Jehovah, though patient, will not allow mere strength to nullify his moral sovereignty. The object of the verb must be understood to be "his enemies" (v. 2). **4.** *Bashan languisheth, and Carmel*—read *Bashan and Carmel wither.* **5.** *Is upheaved*—read *is laid waste*; omit *yea.* **7.** *The Lord is good*—read *Jehovah is good to those waiting for him;* for *and he knoweth* read *Jehovah knoweth.* **8.** *But with an overrunning flood*—read *and in an overflowing flood* (*he delivers them*), and join with the last clause of the preceding verse which requires this treatment for the maintenance of the parallelism. *He will make a full end of the place thereof*—read *a full end will he make of his adversaries.*

Literary Note. Contrary to many interpreters, the writer believes that the acrostic psalm-poem ends at 1[8], which carries it to the letter *Kâf*, the exact middle of the Hebrew alphabet. The first letter, *Âlef*, heads three lines; all others one only. In the case of the fourth, seventh, and tenth letters slight and allowable alterations in the text are necessary to restore the acrostic. There is no valid reason why the first letter should not carry three lines since it expresses the major idea of the poem, the implacable vengefulness of Jehovah toward his enemies; nor is there any reason why an acrostic poem, complete, for its purpose, in itself, should not end at the middle of the alphabet. Compare on these points the acrostic Psa. 9, which also ends at the letter *Kâf* and allots two lines to each letter except *Yôdh*, to which it gives only one, and *Kôf*, to which it gives three. The attempt to reconstruct the acrostic past v. 8 has resulted, in the writer's judgment, in obscuring the significance of 1[9f].

The most important idea of this poem is that it is Jehovah's nature to visit the full weight of his wrath *upon his enemies*, who can never, no matter what their power, escape it. The poem begins and ends with this idea. Conversely, those who are in right relationship to him will find him able and willing to extricate them from the direst calamity. The nature of the calamity which the poet has in mind, however, is cosmical and not political, to be inflicted by miraculous, divine intervention and not by armed human forces. Storm, tempest, cloud, drought, earthquake and fire are the word-colors which he uses to paint his picture of the day of wrath.

The emphasis which the poem places upon Jehovah's supernatural power also renders it peculiarly suitable to its position at the head of Nahum's prophecy. This prophet's judgments, in the crisis which he interpreted, were based upon religious and theological convictions rather than upon a canvass of the facts. He supposed that Jehovah would punish his enemies and rescue those who relied upon him. But his mistake lay in thinking that he and his people belonged to the latter class. As a matter of fact, as Jeremiah saw, Nahum and all who followed him were not relying upon Jehovah at all, but on the prowess of Babylonian armies. The poem serves admirably to conceal this fact from the casual reader.

9–15. Nahum Proclaims the Certainty of Nineveh's Fall and Attacks Those Who Differ With Him. (See also 2[1, 2].) **9.** Omit *he will make a full end;* cf. v. 8b. *Affliction shall not rise up the second time*—read *he will not take vengeance distressfully a second time.* **10.** Read *thorns cut and dried . . . they shall be consumed like dry stubble.* **11.** Read *out of thee hath one come forth scheming against Jehovah, a fellow citizen who counsels ruin.* **12.** *Even so shall they be cut down, and he shall pass away*—read *yet shall they vanish.* **14.** Read *Jehovah has commanded concerning thee: There shall be sown of thy name no longer. From the house of thy God will I cut thee off. I will make thy grave a dishonor.* **15.** *The wicked one*—read *the destroyer;* omit *he is utterly cut off.*

CHAPTER II

1, 2. (1[9-15] continued.) **1.** Read *a shatterer has come up in front of thee, keeping guard, watching the road, strengthening the rear, reinforcing with the utmost strength.* **2.** Read *surely Jehovah will restore the prestige of Jacob, likewise the prestige of Israel; for the wasters will waste them and their branches they will destroy.* The section 1[9]–2[2] is an imperfect report of a speech made by Nahum, in Jerusalem, between 614–612 B.C., when the Medes and Babylonians were closing in on Nineveh (cf. intro.). At some moment when feeling ran high, possibly after such an utterance as that found in Jer. 7[3-15], Nahum takes up the cudgels for the anti-Assyrian court party. His opponents attribute evil to Jehovah. But he will not inflict on his people a *second* punishment, such, e.g., as that when Samaria fell in 721 B.C. On the contrary, "they" (the Assyrians and Egyptians, 1[10, 12]) will be destroyed.

Next Nahum turns his attention to some leader of his opponents (might it not be Jeremiah?). From thee (i.e., Jerusalem) has come forth one who schemes against Jehovah and counsels ruin. But the enemy is not too strong for Jehovah, whose attitude toward his people has undergone a sudden change. Far from the possibility of disaster, the hour of freedom has struck.

Nahum now makes a personal attack upon his opponent. (For similar situations cf. Isa. 22[15-25], Amos 7[14-17].) The latter is to suffer all possible indignity. Having dealt thus adequately with him, Nahum turns to his audience at large to urge upon them his own views. Already messengers are at hand with glad tidings (the news of Assyria's defeat) which means peace for Judah. It is true that a "shatterer" (Necho, on his way up the coastal plain on one of his several expeditions in support of Assyria) has just passed before Judah's face (cf. 2[1]). But "the wasters" (a peculiarly appropriate name for the wild Scytho-Medean horsemen) will waste them (the Assyrians) and destroy their branches. The term here translated "branches" is also employed to designate the "suckers" which grow up out of the roots of a tree and divert to their own sustenance its sap. Nothing could better describe Egypt's relation to Assyria at this time, nor could there be more strikingly expressed Nahum's conviction that Egyptian power would end with Assyria's defeat. As a result of this victory of "the wasters" Jehovah will restore the former glory not only of Judah (Jacob, cf. Isa. 43[1] 44[1] 46[3] Obad.[18]) but also of Israel.

The Attack of "The Wasters" and the Fall of Nineveh. Immediately upon his prediction of the turn events will take, Nahum launches into a stimulating description of the attack of "the wasters" on Nineveh.

3–5. The Attack. 3. Read *the shield of his warriors is reddened and the fighting men are made scarlet by the flame of the torches. The chariots are prepared on that day, the chargers prancing the while.* **4.** *Streets*—read *fields; broad ways*—read *open spaces; run*—read *speed ahead.* **5.** *He remembereth his worthies; they stumble in their march*—read *his officers are summoned: they pull themselves up short;* for *is prepared* read *is placed in position.*

The prophet describes the swift, wild, but well disciplined approach of the attackers to the walls of Nineveh. While it is still dark, on the day appointed, their camp is a bustle of preparation, the bodies and shields of the warriors glowing redly in the flare of their torches. With day the prancing steeds are harnessed to the chariots. Then away they rage in what looks like wild confusion but is a well-directed, irresistible onslaught. As the walls are approached comes an order. The leaders check the wild charge, dismount, and proceed to place in position the great mantelet under cover of which the walls are to be breached.

6–9. The Fall and Sack of the City. 7. *And Huzzab is uncovered*—read *Belit is driven forth into captivity.* **8.** Read *and Nineveh—like a pool of waters are her defenders, and as they flee, "Stand fast! Stand fast!" (one cries), but no one turns.* **9.** Omit *the glory of all pleasant furniture.*

Nahum expects a swift and easy conquest of the city. Its weak point is "the gates of the rivers." The various possibilities offered by the features of Nineveh's topography are admirably discussed by J. M. P. Smith, *Commentary on Nahum*, pp. 318f. The city's most vulnerable point lay on the northeast quarter, where there entered the River Khusur, from which Nineveh derived its water supply. The text suggests treachery, sudden entry, and the collapse of the defense, the headquarters of which would be in the palace. The besiegers now carry away Belit, i.e., the female consort of the god Ashur, while her female devotees mourn for the shame which has descended upon her and upon them. The defenders break ranks with unmanageable, panic-stricken force. They can no more be held together than a pool which breaks its banks. It is hopeless to try to rally them. The victors, unhindered, spoil the world's greatest treasure house.

10–13. The Prophet's Taunt. 10. Read

as a series of exclamations, e.g., *Emptiness! And void! And waste!* etc. **11.** *Feeding place*—read *cave;* for *where the lion and the lioness walked* read *whither the lion went to enter.* **12.** Read *where the lion tore prey sufficient for his cubs and rended for his lionesses and filled his dens with prey and his lair with booty?* The question in v. 11 is continued in this verse.

The victors utterly ruin Nineveh. But the contemplation of that eventuality draws from Nahum's embittered soul only a taunt expressing his satisfaction. The infamous den of the lion among nations is emptied. Finally the prophet links up this event with his own religious faith. One cannot at the same time believe in the real existence and power of Jehovah and expect any other result. Assyria's fate is divinely decreed. So likewise is Judah's restoration to prosperity. To doubt either of these propositions would, in the eyes of a man like Nahum, be tantamount to blasphemy (cf. $1^{9, 11}$).

CHAPTER III

The Degradation of Nineveh the Harlot. In a later address Nahum expands the general theme of 2^{3-13}, laying emphasis upon the idea of the degradation of Assyria's great capital. The change of the figure under which Nineveh is characterized from rending lion (ch. 2) to harlot (ch. 3), suggests that this is a distinct composition.

1–4. The Fall of the Harlot. 1. *It is all full of lies and rapine*—read *wholly false, replete with plunder;* for *the prey departeth not* read *prey ceases not.* **2, 3.** Read as a series of exclamations, e.g., *Crack of whip! And rumble of wheel! And galloping horses!* etc. *The horseman mounting*—read *the rearing horseman.* Omit *they stumble upon their corpses.*

Nahum has the prophetic intuition for an arresting opening sentence. Vituperation was a weapon commanded by all the prophets. The very daring of such an utterance about the still powerful Assyria must have drawn an audience which would be well repaid by the bold, colorful, impressionistic word-picture of fallen Nineveh which followed. From a literary standpoint the prophet's power of compression is notable. In the twenty odd words of vv. 2, 3 he gives us a picture of the conquerors raging through the streets of Nineveh, leaving piles of dead in their wake. But v. 4 is by all means the most important. Nahum's conviction of Nineveh's doom has a moral basis. She is doomed because her harlot-like lust has wrought evil doom for many nations.

The appositeness of the figure of the harlot as applied to Nineveh may be called in question. Nineveh is, of course, representative of Assyria, and Assyria had worked the will of Nineveh upon the world by brute force rather than seductive charm. Nahum, perhaps, had particular reason for the choice of this figure. Jeremiah used it prominently (cf. Jer. 2^{20-24} $3^{1-3, 6-8}$, etc.). But in his case this odious characterization was applied to Judah and Jerusalem, where, indeed, the metaphor is more apt.

5–7. Jehovah Puts the Harlot to Shame Before Her Victims. 6. *And make thee vile*—read *and treat thee with contempt.* **7.** *And it shall come to pass that*—read *so that;* for *whence shall I seek comforters for thee?* read *whence can I seek comforters for her?*

Once again Nahum repeats the source of his authority. Nineveh's fall is one of those things which in a divinely ruled world are inevitable. Jeremiah would doubtless have agreed with this. But there was this difference between them: Jeremiah was acutely conscious of the sins of his own people, whereas Nahum was conscious, rather, of their sufferings. Jeremiah, therefore, was not particularly interested in the fate of Nineveh. He saw no hope for Judah save in a psychological transformation. But Nahum, the nationalist, could and did gloat over the prospect of the humiliation of his country's oppressor. He wishes to see Nineveh placed, figuratively, in the position in which a condemned harlot was placed under the customs of the day. The implacability of his vengefulness appears in v. 7. There is to be no pity in all the world for Nineveh in the hour of her shame.

8–10. The Fate of One of the Harlot's Victims. 8. *That was situated among the rivers*—read *that sat by the great Nile;* omit *that had the waters round about her.* For *and her wall was of the sea* read *whose wall was water?* **9.** *Ethiopia and Egypt were*—read *Ethiopia was;* omit *and it was infinite;* for *thy helpers* read *her helpers.*

As a most conspicuous example among Nineveh's many victims Nahum selects No-Amon (Thebes), situated on the east bank of the Nile about one hundred and forty miles north of the first cataract. From 2100–945 B.C. Thebes was the greatest city in the Near East. In 661 B.C. it was captured by Ashurbanipal of Assyria, who carried home from it prodigious plunder. At that time Egypt was ruled by an Ethiopian dynasty, which was on friendly terms with Libya. But, as Nahum points out, though behind Thebes lay the strength, not only of Egypt which it itself represents, but also of Libya and Put (a land whose location is not now known), these did not suffice to save her.

This strophe is an example of Nahum's daring irony. By selecting Thebes as an example, he was able, while ostensibly illustrating the possibility of Nineveh's fate, to direct a verbal shaft at Necho, who, by the strange vagaries of politics, found himself supporting the very nation which only half a century previously had laid in ruins the most magnificent city of his kingdom.

11–13. Nineveh's Fate Will Parallel That of Thebes. **11.** *Thou shalt be hid*—read *thou shalt be faint.* **12.** *Shall be* [*like*]—read *are;* for *with the first-ripe figs* read *thy people are first-ripe figs.* **13.** Read *behold thy people are as women in thy midst; they have altogether laid themselves open to their enemies.*

The meaning of the text is so obvious that no exposition is necessary. It is notable, however, that Nahum here again suggests a low valuation of the material and moral strength of the Assyrian people as a whole. Apparently, the Egyptians did not share his opinion, and Nahum's contemptuous attitude may be put down either to the effect of Babylonian propaganda or to that disposition which opinionated people usually exhibit to undervalue the odds against any theory or cause they espouse. Assyria was by no means an easy conquest, and the stubbornness of her struggle for existence indirectly cost king Josiah his life and Nahum's party its control of the Judæan government.

14–17. An Ironical Challenge to a Hopeless Defense. **14.** *Make strong the brick kiln*—read *lay hold of the brick mold.* **15.** Omit *it shall devour thee like the cankerworm.* **16.** *Thou hast multiplied*—read *increased.* Omit *the cankerworm spoileth, and flieth away.* **17.** *Crowned*—read *sacred officials.* For *marshals* read *scribes;* for *in the hedges in the cold day* read *in the walls in the cool of the day.* Omit *where they are.*

Ironically the prophet urges Nineveh to prepare for a hopeless defense. The picture he draws is of the feverish activity of a city preparing for siege. The water supply and the forts and towers along the walls must be made ready. The walls of Nineveh being one hundred feet high and fifty feet thick, great gangs of men are set to work to make sun-dried and burned brick, the chief material then in use in Assyria and Babylon for construction. Re-enforcements pour into the city, among them swarms of merchants come to take care of their interests. Temple officials and civil servants dash here and there in officious preoccupation. But it is all of no avail. Behind the thickest walls fire and sword will search them out. And the busy officiary will vanish into thin air when it suits their convenience as a swarm of locusts flits from the shelter of a protecting wall when the warmth of the sun makes it advisable.

18, 19. A Later Addition to the Text. Omit *O King of Assyria.* A dirge, with a prosaic addition (v. 19c), over the fallen city. It adds nothing to the thought of the poem which precedes. On the clause *all that hear the bruit* (mg. *report*) *of thee clap the hands over thee,* cf. Isa. 55[12] Ezek. 25[6] Psa. 47[1]. The strongest objections to the inclusion of these lines in Nahum's original poem are their lack of conformity to the apparent strophical plan and their decidedly retrospective tone.

HABAKKUK

BY PROFESSOR J. E. McFADYEN

INTRODUCTION

Origin and Purpose. Opinion with regard to the origin and background of this book has undergone a marked change within recent years.

(1) *A Prophecy against Babylon.* Before this change, which began with Duhm's epoch-making book in 1906, Habakkuk was universally recognized as a contemporary of Jeremiah, his prophecy falling roughly about 600 B.C. The perplexing sequence of its various sections was explained by different scholars in different ways, of which the following seemed on the whole the most reasonable. In 1:2-4 the prophet complains to God of the prevalent injustice and brutality within Judah, perpetrated perhaps, but not certainly, by the ruling classes of Judah, and asks how long this is to continue. For answer (1:5-11) he is told that the Chaldeans (i.e., the Babylonians) are being summoned to avenge this wrong, and a vivid description is given of their military equipment and their irresistible advance. But (1:12-17) as the prophet becomes better acquainted with their cruel and aggressive methods, the solution which he seemed to have found only heightens the horror of his problem. So (2:1-4) in his perplexity he climbs his tower (of faith), where he receives from God a deeper solution in the form of an assurance that, despite all seeming, the divine purpose is hastening on to its fulfillment, and that the moral constitution of the world is such as to spell the ultimate defeat of cruelty and pride, and the ultimate triumph of righteousness—an assurance which was justified in less than seventy years by the fall of the Babylonian Empire. Then follows a series of woes upon the haughty conqueror (2:5-20), detailing his crimes and confirming his doom. The brilliant poem which follows (ch. 3), descriptive of Jehovah's coming for the salvation of his people (3:13), was usually believed to be from a different hand than Habakkuk's. (For a fuller discussion of this view and others representing various modifications, see Eiselen, *The Prophetic Books of the O.T.*, vol. ii, pp. 510–514.)

(2) *A Prophecy against Greece.* The interest of this view of the book is that in it we see a prophet driven by the pressure of events from a simple to a more radical solution of his religious problem. But this view has lately been challenged by another which has already found considerable acceptance. For reasons which there is no space to detail, e.g., the inapplicability of the description in 1:5-11 to the Babylonian army, another historical background for the book has been sought and found by the substitution in 1:6 of *Kittim* for *Chaldeans*, which is supposed to have displaced it. The reference would in that case be, not to the *Babylonians* of the seventh century, but to the (Macedonian) *Greeks* of the fourth, and the world-conqueror denounced and doomed in 2:5-20 would be Alexander the Great. The advantage of this view is the unity with which it invests the book; all the havoc and perplexity reflected in its various sections—1:2-4 no less than the others—would be that created by Alexander's victorious army. Ch. 3 could also be authentic; it is the vision of the world-conqueror's defeat at the hands of a mightier than he, even the ancient Jehovah.

It may seem unfortunate for this view that it rests upon an emendation of the crucial word *Chaldeans*, the one definite historical allusion in the book; but there is much to be said for it, and it will be a fine exercise of the critical judgment for the reader to go through the book carefully, keeping both these possible interpretations in view. On the second view of the book, the sorrow which stirs Habakkuk's heart is not a national but a great world-sorrow; and on either view the book suggests that the secret of patience in perplexity is an indomitable faith in the purpose of God and in the ultimate defeat of evil and triumph of good. "Though it tarry, wait for it; for it is sure to come, it will not lag behind" (2:3f.).

The Prophet and the Significance of His Message. The question of Habakkuk's date, as already suggested, is closely bound up with that of interpretation. If the book is interpreted as a message against the Chaldeans the date would be around 600 B.C., and the historical background would be the same as that reflected in at least a part of Jeremiah (see intro. to that book, p. 677). If it is directed against Greece the O.T. contains only incidental references or allusions to the conditions inspiring it (e.g., Isa. 24–27; Zech. 9–14, in part, etc.), and most of the information would have to be secured from extra-biblical sources.

The book itself throws little light on the person and life of the prophet, and the rest of the O.T. is silent concerning him; numerous legends have grown up around his name, but all are of rather doubtful historical value. Internal evidence shows that Habakkuk, like the other prophets, was a keen observer of his environment, but the things he saw, instead of furnishing him a message to his contemporaries (except the woes in ch. 2), inspired him to challenge the righteousness and holiness of Jehovah. He, like many other pious souls, was troubled and perplexed by the apparent inequalities and inconsistencies of life, which he found difficult to harmonize with his lofty conception of Jehovah. Nevertheless, he did not sulk; boldly he presented his perplexity to his God, who pointed the way to a solution, so that the prophet came forth from the struggle with a more intense faith in Jehovah and the ultimate triumph of his people.

Two great and permanent truths expressed by the prophet deserve special mention. (1) The universality of the divine government of the world. The prophet accepts a special Divine Providence over Israel, but he insists with equal emphasis that the destinies of all nations are in his hands. Temporarily the foe may worship other gods and prosper; but Jehovah is from everlasting and will attest his supremacy by utterly destroying the boastful conqueror with his idols. (2) The righteous shall live by his faithfulness. In other words, righteousness, fidelity, steadfastness constitute elements of permanency which endure forever. The assertion of confidence and faith in 3[17-19], which, however, may be a later addition, is unsurpassed elsewhere in the O.T. But even without the support of this passage Habbakuk may well be called "the prophet of faith."

Literature: Davidson, *Nahum, Habakkuk, Zephaniah* (Cambridge Bible); Driver, *The Minor Prophets*, vol. ii (New Century Bible); G. A. Smith, *The Book of the Twelve*, vol. ii (Expositor's Bible); Eiselen, *The Minor Prophets;* Stonehouse, *The Book of Habakkuk;* Sanders and Kent, *The Messages of the Earlier Prophets;* Peake, *The Problem of Suffering in the O.T.*

CHAPTER I

1. The Superscription. This reminds us that Habakkuk was a *prophet* (*burden*= oracle), for the opening complaint (vv. 2–4) and also vv. 12–17 suggest the skeptic rather than the prophet. It is well to remember that even prophets were not always on the heights (cf. 2[1]) but that they could be tortured with doubts like other people.

2–4. The Prophet's Complaint. Wrong is on the throne, *law* is paralyzed, *justice* is *perverted* (v. 4), the wicked have it all their own way, and—worst of all—Jehovah looks on (v. 3) in silence and *will not hear* when Habakkuk *cries* to him for help (v. 2).

5–11. Jehovah's Answer. Assuming that the word *Chaldean* in v. 6 is correct, we have in this section Jehovah's answer to the complaint in vv. 2–4; it is that Jehovah is raising up that people (*Chaldeans* practically=Babylonians) to punish the wrongdoing (in Judah) just described, and the special reference may be to Nebuchadrezzar's defeat of the Egyptians at Carchemish in 605 B.C., which made him master of Western Asia (as Assyria had been till her capital, Nineveh, fell in 612). The appeal in v. 5 is to *the treacherous ones* in Judah (so LXX reads, instead of *among the nations;* cf. also the quotation in Acts 13[41]): the *work* they are invited to look upon is the deadly work that will be done by the Babylonian armies—so terrible as to be almost incredible.

Then follows (vv. 6–11) a vivid description of their irresistible power and military methods and the havoc they work wherever they go—read *that implacable and impetuous people* (v. 6), with their fierce swift horses (v. 8) that scour the earth on conquest bent (v. 6), that frightful imperious people (v. 7), to whom kings and castles are but a laughing stock, who capture cities with ease by throwing up a mound of earth against their walls and advancing along it (v. 11; cf. 2 Sam. 20[15]) and, *sweeping by like the wind* (v. 11), *gather* their *captives as the sand* (v. 9). With them might is right; the sum of their offense is that they make might their god (v. 11; for *pass over and be guilty* read *passes on and makes his might his god*).

A growing body of scholars, however, believing that the foregoing description is not strictly applicable to the Babylonians, and arguing that v. 9 can only mean "their faces are set eastward," emend the word *Chaldeans* in v. 6 to *Kittim,* which they then take to refer to the (Macedonian) Greeks and the Asiatic campaigns of Alexander the Great (336–323 B.C.). In that case this section would not be an answer to the preceding complaint, but another description of the wrong there complained of, which would then be, not a wrong within Judah, but a world-wide wrong (see intro.).

12–17. A New Riddle. Assuming the correctness of the traditional reading *Chaldeans* in v. 6, this section is one of peculiar interest. In vv. 5–11 Habakkuk had welcomed the Babylonians as the "rod" with which the "angry" Jehovah would punish Judah, exactly as in the previous century Isaiah (10[5f.]) had welcomed the Assyrians. Terrible as had been that answer to his complaint, it had brought with it a certain moral satisfaction; but the satisfaction was destined to be short-lived. It soon became only too clear that the instrument of Jehovah's purpose was not in sympathy with that purpose, for might, not right, was his god (cf. Isa. 10[12-19]). His zeal in executing the divine commission, of which he was unconscious (cf. Isa. 10[7]), was inspired only by a sense of ambition and self-aggrandizement. The remedy he brought was worse than the disease, and the prophet is again perplexed. His faith is staggered by the problem of the moral government of the world, and he appeals again, as he had appealed before (1[2]), to Jehovah the holy God of his own people.

His perplexity grows as he watches the cruel havoc wrought by the Babylonians. He sees the nations like a shoal of fishes—leaderless, unorganized (v. 14)—swept into their all-devouring net (v. 15). He sees them *dealing treacherously*, *swallowing* up a nation like Judah which, bad as it is (vv. 2–4), is relatively far *more righteous* than the Chaldeans. He believes indeed that God ordained them to execute *justice* upon Judah, and for her discipline (v. 12); but he sees them behaving without mercy or moderation, *drawing the sword* (rather than *net*, v. 17) *for ever*, *slaying nations mercilessly* evermore, and actually deifying the weapons which had won them their rich conquests (v. 16), making very literally their might their god (cf. v. 11). And—saddest of all—the *holy*, *everlasting*, *immortal* God (v. 12: for *we shall not die* read *who dieth not*) looks on in silence upon all this treachery and brutality; he says nothing, does nothing. The answer to the prophet's prayer has only raised a fresh perplexity and made faith in God and in the moral order harder than ever.

Those who, reading *Kittim* in v. 6, take the reference to be to Alexander and his Greeks, regard this section simply as a fresh description of the march of his irresistible all-conquering armies (see notes under vv. 5–11).

CHAPTER II

1–4. The View from the Watch-Tower. In his distress Habakkuk climbs his tower to listen for some other sounds than the stroke of cruel Babylonian swords and to win a wider view of the purpose of God which is fulfilling itself in history. The *watch-tower* (v. 1), which some take literally, may be only a figure for some spiritual vantage-point where, in communion with his God, his spirit may become calmer and his vision clearer; from this he *looks forth to see what God will say to him and what answer he will get to his complaint* (v. 1). Nor does he climb in vain, for there *Jehovah answered me* (v. 2), and the answer is so important to others as well as to himself that he is told to *engrave it on tablets, so that everyone may be able to read it fluently.* There was a time when the prophet expected the solution of his problem to come in his own day (cf. 1[5]), but now that he gets a more spacious view of God's purpose from his tower, he sees that the solution lies in the future. It has its *time appointed*, and it *hasteth* (or *panteth*) *toward the end*, but the end may be far away. Nevertheless, however far, it is certain; *it will not deceive*, and *it will not be late.* It will come, if not in Habakkuk's time, yet in God's time: therefore, *though it tarry, wait for it, for it will assuredly come, it will not lag behind* (v. 3). It is a magnificent counsel of patience and of faith, "By your patience ye shall win your souls" (Lk. 21[19]). God is patient, because he is eternal (cf. 1[12]), and man would be more patient could he see things in the light of the eternal purpose.

Unhappily, the meaning of the great verse which follows (v. 4), which seems to be the very heart and climax of the *vision* (v. 2), is far from clear. The second clause is fortunately plain enough, but the text of the first is obscure and uncertain. *His soul is puffed up;* whose soul? Clearly—in contrast with *the righteous*—the soul of the Babylonian; it is an inflated soul, *not upright*, or, rather, not straight and plain. But the context seems to demand something stronger than this; the promise in the second clause suggests some condemnation in the first clause; and with the help of LXX we may restore thus: *As for that inflated one, my soul has no pleasure in him, but the just shall live by his faithfulness* (rather than *faith*), i.e., by firmly trusting Jehovah, despite all experiences that evoke impatience and disappointment. This is assuredly a word worth writing on tablets, to be read and remembered forever. In history it is not the empire of might (cf. 1[11]) but of *right* that shall *live*: it is the just man and nation that lives, and he lives by his union, through faithfulness and faith, with God; he is immortal as God himself (cf. 1[12]). There is something wonderful in the collocation of these three words—*justice* or righteousness, *life*, *faithfulness*. In the end it is the just that live, not the Nebuchadrezzars or the Alexanders, and they live by virtue of their faithfulness. The whole secret of religion is there. "He that believeth hath eternal life" (Jn. 6[47]).

Woe to the Oppressor. (Vv. 5–20.) This section, describing the sins and the doom of the world-conqueror, is an expansion of v. 4a. The *woes* are dramatically represented as being pronounced by the nations whom he had crushed (v. 6).

5–8. Woe Upon His Lust of Land. The one thing certain about the difficult v. 5 is that *wine*, here utterly irrelevant, is wrong. It has been emended to mean *Woe* (to the treacherous dealer), but one hardly expects the *woe* till the *taunt*-song has been mentioned (v. 6a), and there is much to be said for the view that it conceals the word *Greek*, which is very like the word for *wine*. This tends to strengthen the view that the conqueror throughout the book is Alexander and his Greeks. *Keepeth not at home* should perhaps be *unsated;* and the verse would describe the *Greek* as imperious, insatiable, greedy as death and *hell*, i.e., the underworld (v. 5), loading himself with *pledges*, i.e., tribute, from every nation (v. 6), but doomed to the fate of spoliation (vv. 7, 8), which he had inflicted on others. There are significant word-plays here; *pledges* also means *thick mire* and *biters* (v. 7) means also *creditors*. The point is that the tables will be turned, there is a Nemesis in history; and songs of mockery will be sung when the spoiler has been spoiled.

9–11. Woe Upon His Palatial Buildings. He had built lofty palaces (cf. Jer. 22[13-17]) with ill-gotten gain (cf. Amos 3[10]) to preserve the treasures he had stolen from other countries (v. 9), he had shortened his life (Alexander died young) by this course of *sin* which could only end in *shame* (v. 10), for the very *stone and timber* would *cry out* against his rapacity. Their silent accusing voices would be everywhere. His would indeed be a haunted house.

12–14. Woe Upon the Cities He Has Built. His cities, like Jerusalem (cf. Mic. 3[10]), had been *built with blood* and *established by iniquity* —built perhaps by the appropriation of the property of those who had been judicially murdered, or (if *blood* is not to be pressed) by the labors of conquered peoples, and *established* by the *iniquitous* withholding of the wages of the workmen (cf. Jer. 22[13]). But such labors are destined to end in *vanity*, i.e., in nothing, and to be consumed *in the fire* (cf. Jer. 51[58]). How foolish and futile it all is! For in the end *the earth is to be filled with the knowledge of the glory of Jehovah:* over it all his kingdom is to come. That is the divine destiny of the world. The world-conqueror is not Nebuchadrezzar or Alexander, but Jehovah; the world-empire is to be not Babylonian or Greek, but divine.

With these verses (or with vv. 9–11) should possibly go v. 17, which shows where and by what cruelty the material for the building had been acquired. *Lebanon* had been ransacked, her glorious cedars had been destroyed and the *beasts* that roamed her forests had been slain. This was a *wrong* done to it and to them. The beasts and the land have their rights and those who wantonly assailed them to gratify their own ambition and vanity would be punished in kind.

15–17. Woe Upon His Unholy Banquets. If these verses are to be taken literally and not simply as a metaphor for contemptuous cruelty (cf. v. 17), the reference will be to the court-banquets of the world-conqueror, at which wine was offered and drunk immoderately and for immoral ends. *That addest thy venom thereto* (v. 15) should perhaps read *out of* large *bowls*, and *be as one uncircumcised* (v. 16) should be *reel* or *stagger*. The immoral conqueror (v. 15) is another Ham or Canaan (Gen. 9[21f.]); and the point is, as before (v. 8), that there is a Nemesis in history. Jehovah too has his cup from which the conqueror must *drink*, and whose contents will send him staggering to *shame*. (On v. 17 see under vv. 12–14.)

18–20. Woe Upon His Idolatry. Idolatry is at once the secret and the climax of the conqueror's folly. His absurd conception of God (cf. 1[11]) explains the monstrosity of his practice. Creed profoundly affects conduct. The Hebrews were tireless in their ridicule of the folly of idolatry (cf. Isa. 44[9-20] Psa. 135 [15-18]). The idols were *dumb*, could give no response, no *teaching* or direction, like Israel's God (cf. Isa. 2[3]); there was no *breath*, spirit, energy in them. In glorious contrast with them is the great God of Israel whose *palace* was the heavens and whose due it was to receive the homage of *all the earth*.

Such was the message (2[3-20]) that came to Habbakuk upon his watch-tower (2[1]) and that he carried with him into his individual and international perplexities.

CHAPTER III

The Day of Jehovah's Coming. This brilliant poem represents the vision from the tower (2[2]) —what Habakkuk *saw* as 2[4-20] represents what he *heard*. As the "Woes" of 2[5-20] expand the thought of the doom of the arrogant conqueror in 2[4a], so ch. 3 expands the thought of the preservation of the righteous in 2[4b]. Jehovah *goes forth for the salvation of his people* (v. 13) and the scene and manner of his action are described throughout in terms which recall his deliverance of Israel from Egypt in the olden time.

1, 2. Habakkuk's Prayer. V. 1 is simply the heading. The prayer is in poetic form; both in the heading and at the close liturgical notes are formed. *Shigionoth* is a word of uncertain meaning. LXX reads "on the stringed instruments": see comment on v. 17. He begins with the prayer that the ancient *work*, i.e., deliverance, be repeated, and that Jehovah would again make himself (not *it*) known, for the present crisis calls for divine interference.

3–11. The Splendor and the Terror of Jehovah's Coming. Habakkuk saw God, as of old (cf. Deut. 33[2] Judg. 5[4]), coming from *Teman* in the northwest of Edom, and *Paran*, between Sinai and Edom—with dazzling light about him and *rays* on either side (cf. mg.), attended by *Pestilence* and *fiery bolts*, i.e., Fever. The moment he touched the earth, it shook (not *measured*), nations trembled (not *drove asunder*, v. 6), i.e., neighboring peoples like *Midian* (v. 7 *curtains*="tent-hangings"). He comes as a warrior, riding his *chariot* of storm-cloud, with *bow* and arrows (i.e., the lightning) and spear (for *the oaths . . . word* read *thou didst fill thy quiver with shafts*).

12–16. He Comes to Deliver His People. Wherefore this angry (v. 12) advance? (V. 8.) It was to crush the foe, to *pierce the head of their warriors with his shafts* (v. 14) and thus to save his people (v. 13: for *neck* read *rock*). Well might the enemy be terrified, for the sight had terrified the prophet himself (v. 16). But with this divine Warrior on Israel's side he can look to the future with calm confidence, and on this note he concludes: in patience *I will wait for the coming of that day of distress upon the nation that* now *assaileth* us.

17–19. The Triumph of Faith. These beautiful verses probably formed no part of the prophet's vision, which ends with v. 16; but they helped to adapt this poem, *set to Shigionoth* (perhaps=dithyrambic poem; cf v. 1), for use as a prayer. They are, however, peculiarly appropriate, for they are inspired by the same spirit of patience and hope (cf. 2[3f.]) as the message and the vision from the tower. In fruitful fields and flocks men had been taught to look for the presence and blessing of God (cf. Deut. 7[12f.]); but here is a man who can dispense with all that, who can believe where he cannot see, who loves God not for his gifts but for himself, who can dispense with them if he has but him (cf. Psa. 73[25f.]), and who can not only be patient but glad with a joy which no man can take from him (v. 18), so glad that he can walk upon the *heights* nimble and sure and happy (v. 19). This writer has entered into the innermost secret of spiritual religion and has bequeathed to us one of the most precious words in the O.T.

ZEPHANIAH

By Professor WILLIAM C. GRAHAM

Introduction

Theme and Literary Structure. In the form in which the book of Zephaniah has come down to us it deals with the imminent approach of Jehovah's day of universal judgment and Israel's survival of that supreme test. Down to 3^{13} the prevailing spirit is that of pessimism. Where a more hopeful mood does break through it is yet subdued and always charged with ethical earnestness. From 3^{14} on the outlook is vigorously optimistic and breathes the spirit which accepts as axiomatic Jehovah's partisanship for Israel. The transition which occurs at 3^{14} is so marked that scholars are quite generally agreed that this concluding section is a later, post-exilic addition.

Setting aside $3^{14f.}$, it will be seen that the remainder of the book is dominated by recurring predictions of a great catastrophe which is to sweep away the existing world order. Woven into this major and dominant theme are two closely related, specific applications of it. The first applies the coming judgment to Judah and Jerusalem, the second to the international political order. The ideas most prominent in the prophet's treatment of his own nation are disloyalty to Jehovah and susceptibility to foreign influences. When this is grasped it is easy to see the relationship of his utterances on these subjects to his predictions concerning foreign nations. His thought is that Judah, careless of Jehovah's will, and entangled in the meshes of pagan influence, faces the inevitable fate of being swept away in the crash of a decadent civilization. This is a common theme of practically all the writing prophets.

Here and there, in the pessimistic portion of the prophecy, we encounter isolated verses or verse-groups which interject notes of optimism into the composition. Are we to conclude that like $3^{14f.}$ all these previously occurring optimistic verses are later additions? In other words, are we to believe that Zephaniah holds out no gleam of hope to his contemporaries? Or are we to conclude that the presence of such passages in 1^{1}–3^{13} justifies the view that not only they but also $3^{14f.}$ are authentic utterances of the prophet?

Original Utterances of Zephaniah. The truth of the matter probably does not lie in either of these extreme views. Some of these optimistic verses are beyond doubt by Zephaniah. Some, but not all. For others may be shown to be, like 3^{14-20}, later corrective additions.

This commentary attributes to Zephaniah $1^{2, 3, 7, 10a, 12a, 14-18}$, 2^{2} $3^{5ab, 8}$, which furnish the dominant theme; $1^{4-6, 8, 9, 10b, 11, 12b}$, 3^{1-4}, which apply the catastrophe to Judah; $2^{1, 4, 5, 12-14}$, which deal with the international order; and $2^{3(?), 6, 7b}$ 3^{11b-13}, which touch on the new order which is to follow the catastrophe. Later writers have developed the optimistic outlook in $2^{7a, 7c-11}$ $3^{9, 10, 11a, 14-20}$. Other later additions include 1^{13}(?) 2^{15} 3^{5c-7}.

Zephaniah's Outlook. To be able to understand the prophet Zephaniah or to be able to present him to a modern class one must gain a reasoned opinion on at least three points. (1) What did Zephaniah think? (2) Why did he so think? (3) How does his thought bear on modern life?

The first of these questions must be answered from the text of the prophecy itself. Zephaniah believed that the civilization of the world of his day was intolerably corrupt; that his own nation, as such, was hopelessly involved in it; that since things could not be better until they were first worse, Jehovah would shortly sweep away the whole existing order; and that there would succeed it a new era wherein what few good people remained in the world would live a life of simplicity and harmlessness as in the good old days of long ago before men entered upon a life of competitive nationalism.

Why Zephaniah thought such thoughts as these must be sought in the book and in the sources of contemporary history. The prophets are never ordinary men and Zephaniah, as his utterances show, is no exception. To read his book is to see that he was highly sensitive to his surroundings and that imagination and emotion played a large part in molding his judgments. Next in importance to these characteristics of his own nature is the fact that he was rooted and grounded in the religious outlook upon life. The greatest of all realities to him was Jehovah, and his ideas of the character of God had much to do with determining his reaction to life. What were his ideas of God? That is a question which should be carefully pondered.

Zephaniah, like all of us, was much influenced by the world in which he lived, particularly by the social and political tendencies of his times. It is desirable to supplement his imprcssions of these as they have come down to us in his book by knowledge drawn from other sources.

Historical Background. Zephaniah prophesied during the first half of the reign of Josiah. It must be remembered that the latter's father, Amon, and his grandfather, Manasseh, had fostered policies of expediency in the realm of both religion and politics. In these policies they were not without opposition from a puritanical, monotheistic, nationalistic element in society, in which, no doubt, the finer prophetic spirits were prominent. A most significant event was the assassination of King Amon. And it is of even more importance that a popular uprising against those who assassinated him was necessary to secure the succession of his young son, Josiah, then only eight years old. So far as the policies of the nation went there was no change for at least eighteen years after the young king was crowned. When, however, Josiah was about twenty-six (621 B.C.) we find him throwing in his lot wholeheartedly with the puritan party, and reversing the traditional policies of his immediate ancestors in a great attempt at religious reform which had also, however, political significance. It is allowable, therefore, to infer that during the early years of Josiah there went on an intense internal struggle in Judah between parties espousing radically different religious and political principles. Zephaniah's ministry must be placed in this period while the puritan party was still in opposition, because the conditions of which he complains are those which Josiah later endeavored, with some temporary success, to rectify. It makes Zephaniah's utterances more vivid if we understand them to be those of a member of the opposition party, a record of the emotions and judgments of a puritan, himself of royal birth, who had thrown in his lot with the opponents of the then dominant elements in his own house. An understanding of these conditions throws, too, a flood of light on the prophet's pessimism. It is the pessimism of a leader of the opposition party. For the most reliable biblical source bearing on all this, cf. 2 Kings 21^{1}–23^{30}.

The international situation is also important. Assyria was still the dominant world-power, but just about Zephaniah's time there began to happen a series of events which resulted at last in its downfall. A great horde of barbarians commonly known as the Scythians swept down from the steppes of central Asia and overran the civilized world to the very borders of Egypt, massacring, burning and looting as they went. Although Zephaniah never mentions them by name it is inconceivable that he did not know of this threat to civilization. It may be taken as certain that it had much to do with his assurance that the existing order was about to be swept away. As a matter of fact, these barbarians did so weaken the great empire that a combination of Medes and Babylonians was able at last to break Assyrian power and to capture Nineveh in 612 B.C. In its death struggle Assyria was assisted by Egypt, and it is altogether possible that king Josiah was assassinated by Pharaoh Necho in 608 B.C. on suspicion of intrigue with Babylon against the Assyro-Egyptian cause (cf. p. 69a).

Teaching of Zephaniah. The teaching closely resembles that of the earlier prophets: Jehovah is the God of the universe, a God of righteousness and holiness, who expects of his worshipers a life in accord with his will. Israel is his chosen people, but on account of its sins it must suffer severe punishment. Wholesale conversion seems out of the question but a remnant may escape. He adds little to earlier teaching but attempts, with much moral and spiritual fervor, to impress upon his contemporaries the fundamental truths of the religion of Jehovah. There is, however, one point that deserves special mention, namely, the prophet's emphasis on the *Day of Jehovah*. Earlier prophets had spoken of it; Amos had described it in language similar to that employed by Zephaniah; but the latter surpasses all his predecessors in the emphasis on this terrible manifestation of Jehovah. Indeed, his entire teaching centers around this day, and in his utterances are found the germs of apocalyptic visions which are so common in later utterances of an eschatological nature (see especially $1^{2, 3, 14, 15, 17}$ $2^{4, 15}$ 3^{11-13}). The promises of a bright future are further developed by later writers, whose world-outlook is even broader than that of the original sections and who give a sublime picture of the glories of the Messianic era (see especially 3^{14-20}).

Permanent Significance. In two respects especially Zephaniah is of significance for modern life. His ethical idealism which comes out in his reaction to the social phenomena of his time is timeless and eternal. His pictures of conditions in Jerusalem, making all due allowances for the exaggerations of partisanship, passion and strong emotion, are applicable to any society in any age. The tendencies which he combated are with us to-day. Wherever the spirit of infidelity, of pride, of oppression, of selfishness exists his book is entirely up to date.

The same can hardly be said of his pessimism

and his catastrophic expectations. A study of these will show that they proceed from imagination and emotion, stirred by the historical and religious background in which he lived. They constitute the only motivation which the prophet, with his view of God and of the world in which he lived, was able to suggest in his effort to make his contemporaries realize their situation and turn from their ways. His ideas of God in his relationship to man stand in just as sad contrast to the glorious gospel in the N.T. of divine Fatherhood and human brotherhood, as his conception of a natural order subject to sporadic interferences from an enraged Deity stands to the modern scientific view of the universe.

Literature: J. M. P. Smith, *Zephaniah* (International Critical Commentary); Davidson, *Nahum, Habakkuk and Zephaniah* (Cambridge Bible); Driver, *Minor Prophets*, vol. ii (Century Bible); Eiselen, *The Prophetic Books of the O.T.*, vol. ii; Gordon, *The Prophets of the O.T.*

CHAPTER I

1. Editorial Superscription. The historical reliability of this editorial note is generally admitted. *Zephaniah* means "Jehovah is protector." His lineage is the longest recorded of any prophet and is derived from a certain Hezekiah, probably the king of that name who reigned in Judah during the later years of Isaiah's ministry. Certain features of the prophet's outlook seem to indicate that he enjoyed a position of rank and privilege.

2, 3. Announcement of the Major Theme: Universal Catastrophe. For *and the stumblingblocks with the wicked*, read *yea, I will cause the wicked to stumble.* Opening with the announcement of the divine intention to sweep away *all things*, the scope of these words is defined in v. 3 to cover all orders of living creatures. In the last two clauses of the reconstructed text the verbs and their objects are, in effect, through parallelism, synonymous. The prophet thinks of mankind as a corrupt race very much as did the author of the Flood story in Genesis. Later on he modifies this estimate slightly. (Cf. $2^{6,\ 7b}$ and 1 Kings 19^{14-18}.)

4-12. First Application of the Major Theme: to Judah and Jerusalem. The text of these verses has suffered, and has undergone various expansions. The following emendations have been suggested: **4.** Omit *with the priests.* **5.** Omit *which swear to.* **8.** Omit *it shall come to pass in the day of the Lord's sacrifice. Princes . . . king's sons*—i.e., members of the royal house in all its branches. **9.** *Leap over the threshold*—read *dance attendance at the threshold.* **11.** *Howl, ye inhabitants of Maktesh*—read *and a howl from the Maktesh;* for *they that were laden with* read *they that weigh out.* **13.** Omit the whole.

This section comprises four pungently suggestive sketches of contemporary conditions in Judah and Jerusalem, each introduced by a recurring allusion to the day of doom. The effect produced by the interweaving of the major theme is that of involving Judah inextricably in the anticipated visitation of Jehovah's punitive wrath.

4-6. These verses present a sketch of the religious life of the Judæan people. The nation has failed to achieve that spiritual unity and moral solidarity which lie in unswerving devotion to one God only. Several types of religious infidelity are suggested: (1) Remnant of Baal. A heathenized cult resulting from the popular identification of the local Baals of the ancient Canaanitic fertility cults with Jehovah. Zephaniah satirically calls the priests of this impure rite *Chemarim*, or pagan priests. The prophets are the traditional enemies of this eclecticism (cf. 1 Kings 17f., Hos., Isa.), which nevertheless persisted down to the Exile (cf. Jer., Ezek.). (2) Worship of the heavenly bodies, a common Semitic nature cult. (3) The cult of Milcom, god of the Ammonites. (4) Open apostasy from Jehovah. (5) Divided allegiance to Jehovah. The mental and moral confusion resulting from this religious inebriety is graphically presented in the concrete suggestion of the devotees who bow down to Jehovah yet swear by Milcom, which is as though a confessing Christian were to solemnize an oath in the name of Thor or Odin.

7-9. The second sketch is introduced by an attempt to create the atmosphere of tense expectation which precedes the consummation of some great event. The event expected is, of course, Jehovah's great final day of judgment, which is described under the figure of a sacrifice for which the victims have been prepared and the guests assembled and ritually cleansed (cf. 1 Sam. 16^5). It is futile to attempt to determine from this figure of speech who are to be the guests and who the victims in the coming day of doom. All that can with certainty be said is that this verse makes it clear that the so-called "upper classes" of society are to be included as victims. The charge against this ruling caste is that of aping foreign fashions, a phenomenon symptomatic of a decline in loyalty to the national genius. These rich and powerful people are surrounded by a class of social parasites, whom the prophet satirizes as *dancing attendance at the threshold* of their patron while utterly unscrupulous about the methods they employ in serving him.

10, 11. Introduced again by a reference to the approaching catastrophe, we have here, in all probability, the specific inclusion of the commercial and financial classes in the disaster. Four topographical terms are introduced—*fish gate, second quarter, hills, Maktesh.* On the actual significance of these we can only speculate, but the poetic form suggests two sets of balancing antithetical terms which, taken together, are inclusive of the city's business life in its social as well as in its commercial aspects. That these terms were early connected with the business classes appears from v. 11bc, whether it be regarded as a gloss or not. For the use of the term *Canaanite* for "merchant" cf. Hos. 12[7] (see mg.) Isa. 23[8].

12. Now the prophet gives us a picture of Jehovah searching Jerusalem with a lamp for *men that are settled on their lees.* This metaphor is very striking. In the process of ripening, wine must be poured "from vessel to vessel" (cf. Jer. 48[11, 12]). Left too long it becomes fit only for wasting. This expresses the prophet's judgment on most of his contemporaries. If the reader will concentrate his attention on these sketches of Judæan life, he will find impressive evidence of the prophet's artistic ability to suggest, by concrete examples, the whole spiritual atmosphere of the society in which he lives.

13–18. Emphasis of the Major Theme: The Terrors of Jehovah's Day. For a better understanding of the prophet's thought the following textual notations may be made. **14.** Read *the great day of the Lord is near, it is near and hasteth greatly; near at hand is the bitter day of the Lord, hastening faster than a warrior.* **17.** Omit *because they have sinned against the Lord.* **18.** Omit *in . . . jealousy;* for *land* read *earth.*

Beginning with yet another reminder of the proximity of the great final catastrophe Zephaniah passes on to enlarge upon the unmanning horror of it. It is to be inflicted directly by Jehovah through (1) disturbances in the natural order, *wasteness, desolation, darkness, gloominess, clouds, thick darkness,* and (2) disturbances in the political order, *wrath, trouble, distress, trumpet, alarm.* If, as is probable (cf. intro., section on "Historical Background"), Zephaniah had the Scythians in mind, it seems clear from 2[3, 6, 7b] and 3[8], and from what is known of the nature of these people, that they would be included by him among the victims. What the prophet expects here is a day when a corrupt international order will dissolve in the confused self-destructive conflict of its various elements and be swept away by calamitous manifestations of natural forces. Cf. art., *Intertestamental Religion,* pp. 206–7.)

CHAPTER II

1–15. Second Application of the Major Theme: to the Existing International Order. **1.** For this verse, where the present text is insoluble, read *conspire together, O ye nations!* **2.** Read for this verse *before ye become like fine dust, like chaff which passes away* (cf. Psa. 2[1-3, 9] and Ezek. 38, 39). **3.** Deleted by most critics, but quite possible as a word of Zephaniah if the genuineness of vv. 6, 7b be admitted. **5.** *Cherethites* (cf. 1 Sam. 30[14] Ezek. 25[16]). Omit *the word of the Lord is against you;* omit *Canaan;* for *the land* read *O land.* **6.** Read for this verse, *And thou shalt become pastures for shepherds and folds for flocks.* **7.** For this verse read only *By the sea shall they feed, in the houses of Ashkelon shall they lie down in the evening.* **8.** On *reproach* and *revilings* cf. Ezek. 25[3, 6, 8] Jer. 48[26, 30] Obad.[12]. **9.** On *Sodom* and *Gomorrah* cf. Deut. 29[23] Isa. 1[9] Jer. 23[14] Amos 4[11] Mt. 10[15], etc. **11.** For similar visions of Jehovah's world-wide dominion cf. Mic. 4[1-4] Mal. 1[11] Zech. 14[6], all of which are post-exilic. Vv. 7a, 7c–11 are to be regarded as later insertions. **14.** *Herds*—i.e., of wild beasts, cf. *all the beasts of the nations,* for which read *all the beasts of the field.* For [*their*] *voice shall sing in the windows; desolation shall be in the thresholds; for he hath laid bare the cedar work*—read *the owl will hoot in the window, the raven on the threshold.* Cf. LXX. **15.** Omit; cf. Isa. 22[2] 23[7] 32[13] 47[8, 10]. This verse was possibly inserted to connect the preceding context more closely with 3[1f.] so that the latter might be referred to Nineveh instead of Jerusalem as 3[2b, 5] make evident it should be.

The full significance of Judah's worship of foreign deities and aping of foreign ways reaches expression in this section, the original text of which has been much mutilated. Having lost the free, independent mind which inspires a nation to seek the creative realization of a unique destiny, Judah must now go down with that civilization which it has preferred to a truer way of life. The whole world order, from remotest Ethiopia to the farthest hinterlands of Assyria, is about to fall to pieces like a gay and pretentious but moth-eaten garment.

1–7. The passage opens with a satirical challenge to the nations to conspire together in futile resistance before the divine wrath overwhelms them. From satire the prophet passes to a general and tentative invitation to the *meek of the earth* (v. 3), simple, humble, unambitious folk, to seek Jehovah in the hope that they may escape the coming judgment. The motivation for this turning to Jehovah is the certain collapse of all existing powers which are dealt with in detail in the remainder of the chapter. Philistia occupies the attention in vv. 4–7. Her four chief remaining cities are mentioned. The driving out of the *Ashdodites at noonday* suggests that Zephaniah's expectation here was of a sudden, irresistible military onslaught. Doubtless he had the Scythians in mind as the perpetrators; but if so, they are to him no more than a passing element in the great confusion, just as are the portents in nature. Certainly, he does not contemplate their permanent possession of Philistine territory after the storm passes. Cf. vv. 6, 7b, and note on 1[13-18].

8–11. A post-exile prediction of disaster for Moab and Ammon. No previous prophet betrays a similar feeling against these peoples on the ground of their attitude to Judah. Cf. Amos 1[11-15]. The conditions here assumed fit better the years of the latter's supreme discomfiture (586–582 B.C.) when such was the attitude of these trans-Jordanic nations that all later literature reflects the bitter enmity that was then engendered. It is, moreover, extremely difficult to reconcile the thoughtful care displayed here by Jehovah for his people with the unmitigated threats of his destroying wrath in ch. 1. In addition, the original passage itself has again been interpolated, for v. 10 is a prosaic enlargement of v. 8, while in v. 11 the attention passes from Moab and Ammon to a prediction of Jehovah's world-wide dominion. One has also but to compare the recrudescence of the spirit of international cupidity and ambition which is reflected in the words, *my people shall spoil them*, with the genuine hope of Zephaniah for the future, to conclude that this section was hardly written by him. Finally, the marked contrast between the heathen nations' acceptance of Jehovah and the destruction of them predicted in the surrounding context, shows also an entirely different outlook.

12. An oracle against the Ethiopians who, living to the south of Egypt proper, here stand for the southernmost limit of the prophet's known world. Up to a few years before Zephaniah an Ethiopian dynasty had, for nearly a century, ruled in Egypt. On the analogy of the space devoted to other peoples by Zephaniah this prophecy has been considerably abbreviated, which may be due to the fact that no serious calamity overtook Egypt until 525 B.C. when Cambyses annexed it to the Persian Empire.

13–15. Here disaster is predicted for Assyria, whose empire reached to the northernmost confines of the civilized world. In Zephaniah's day Assyria was still the dominant world-power. Again it becomes evident that the prophet contemplates, on the day of divine wrath, only the sweeping away of an effete civilization to the accompaniment of cosmical disturbances. Nineveh is to remain a heap of desolate ruins, from the gaping thresholds and windows of which owls hoot and ravens croak. The contrast between this and the future of Palestine is psychologically convincing. It would be natural for the prophet to locate his utopia in Palestine, equally natural for him to feel Assyria would remain in a state of perpetual desolation.

CHAPTER III

1–13. The Major Theme Again Applied to Judah: The Perfidy of Jerusalem and the Sure Righteousness of Jehovah. There has been much later addition to the text of this chapter. Many critics deny Zephaniah's authorship of any single verse in it. Others limit his authorship to vv. 1–5. As will be shown below, vv. 14–20 are a post-exilic addition. The view taken here is that vv. 1–5, 8, 11b, 12, 13 accord with the prophet's previous conceptions. The exposition takes account only of these verses.

4. *The sanctuary*—read *that which is holy; the law*—read *instruction.* **5.** For *bring his judgment to light, he faileth not* read *establish his justice; light fails not;* omit *but the unjust knoweth no shame.* **6, 7.** These two verses interrupt the natural sequence between vv. 5, 8. V. 6 may be a notation commemorating the accuracy of Zephaniah's forecast in some particulars at least, possibly written after the great political changes which resulted from the overthrow of the Assyrian power by the Babylonians and the Medes, 612 B.C. V. 7 is a defense of Jehovah's character, claiming that it was no part of his plan to inflict calamity upon Judah until forced to do so by its incorrigibility. It was possibly written during the Exile and is in accord with the ideas of Jeremiah, Ezekiel, and Isa. 40–55. For *so her dwelling should not be cut off* [*according to*] *all that I have appointed concerning her* read *and there will not be cut off from her sight anything that I have laid upon her.* The conception of a disappointed God is the interesting feature of this suggested translation (cf. Lk. 20[13-15]). **9–11a.** This conception of a day of universal Jehovah worship is too advanced for Zephaniah, nor could he conceive a time when Jehovah's people would not be put to shame for their transgressions against him. Cf. also v. 7. **11b.** *For then will I take away*—the antecedent of *then* cannot lie in vv. 9–11a, because the universal acknowledgment of Jehovah contemplated there would surely be conceived as the result rather than the cause of the social transformation suggested in 11b. **12.**

For *afflicted* read *humble;* cf. Isa. 3[15]; *poor*—cf. Amos 4[1]. **13.** *Remnant*—cf. Amos 1[8] Ezek. 25[16] 36[3, 4, 5] Isa. 44[17]. These and many other passages in exilic and early post-exilic literature make it permissible to allow both the use of this term and the conception behind it to Zephaniah.

1–4. The prophet once more returns to the arraignment of his native city. The key to these verses lies in the adjectives *rebellious, polluted, oppressing,* applied to Jerusalem in v. 1. She is rebellious against Jehovah in that she has refused to listen to the prophets or to receive correction from properly constituted authority. She is polluted in that she has not trusted in Jehovah her God but has yielded to the spirit of the age, becoming entangled in international politics, and contenting herself with merely mundane aspirations. Then follows an exposition of the term *oppressing.* Prey to the cruel, insatiable greed of a profligate aristocracy and a corrupt officiary; confused and misled by a class of professional "prophets" who have become so impregnated with the materialistic spirit of the times that the spirit of God no longer functions through them (cf. Mic. 2[11] 3[5f., 11]); exploited by conscienceless priests who have no innate respect for holy things and who manipulate the ancient social standards intrusted to them for their own gain (cf. Hos 4[6-9] 5[1] 6[9] Amos 7[10f.] Mic. 3[11] Isa. 28[7] Jer. 2[8] 5[31] 6[13] 14[18])—such is the condition into which Jerusalem has fallen.

5–13. But the prophet is not finished. Men are what they are. But God is also what he is—inexorably righteous. Such a state of affairs cannot go on without challenge from him. So surely as he orders the rising of the sun in the world of nature, so surely will the sun rise again in the realm of human relationships and the dark shadows of crime and oppression be annihilated, with all who walk in them, before his irresistible righteousness.

Therefore, Jehovah now challenges the wicked city, *wait ye for me* (v. 8). My righteousness is about to be vindicated. One final proof will I give of it in a gathering together for destruction of the corrupted peoples of an outword social order. My punishment will be comprehensive and final; *all the earth shall be devoured with the fire of my jealousy* against those who dispute my moral sovereignty. "Then, and then only," the divine judgment proceeds, "will I cleanse this wicked city, sweeping away its proud and haughty oppressors in the debris of the great debacle."

The oracle is not, however, to close on the discordant note of doom. *But,* says Jehovah, *I will leave in the midst of thee a people* humble and poor by the standards of perverted mankind, but rich and exalted by a higher standard because *they shall trust in the name of the Lord.*

14–20. The Conclusion of the Major Theme: Israel's Golden Age. 15. For *judgments* read *opponents;* omit *even the Lord.* **16.** Omit as an interpolation interrupting the logical connection between vv. 15, 17. **17.** *He will rest in his love*—read *he will renew them in his love;* omit *he will joy over thee with singing.* **18.** For this verse read *I will take away those smiting thee and those bringing reproach upon thee.* **19.** Omit *whose shame hath been.* **20.** Omit as an explanatory gloss definitely referring v. 19, of which it is practically a repetition, to the Babylonian Exile.

The reader who has appreciated the significance of the continuous recurrence of the prediction of disaster in 1[2]–3[13], and who has observed how consistently the prophet there includes his own land and city in it, can hardly fail to realize that at this point there is a complete reversal of the prevailing mood of the prophecy.

Leaving aside later interpolations, the thought of the original supplementer is as follows: Zion, Israel, Jerusalem are called to whole-hearted rejoicing because Jehovah has vanquished their enemies. This manifestation of his peculiar good will justifies the following promise that a new day of perpetual felicity, due to the active beneficence of Jehovah, is at hand. In that glorious day all Israel's oppressors will be dealt with by him, and his own people will be made a *praise* and a *renown* in all the earth.

That here the writer looks back upon disaster as a historical fact and forward to felicity appears evident in vv. 15, 18, 19. But perhaps the clearest indication that Zephaniah did not write the passage lies in the contrast between the conception of the future exhibited here and that which we have observed in the rest of the book.

HAGGAI

By Professor J. E. McFadyen

Introduction

The importance of Haggai is out of all proportion to the length of his book. His two short chapters contain a summary of only four addresses and a few verses of narrative matter (cf. 1^12-15); but the ideas he expressed and the impulses he stirred produced a situation which profoundly affected the whole subsequent history of Judasim.

Date and Historical Background. Haggai's addresses are accurately dated; they fall between September and December of the year 520 B.C. (cf. 1^1 2^20), and, like pre-exilic prophecy, they were intimately related to the historical situation. The accession of Darius to the Persian throne in 521 had been the occasion of insurrections all over his empire, and reverberations of these may be heard in the messages of Haggai to his own people (2^6f., 21f.). This "shaking of the nations" had stirred their hopes, political as well as religious, and Haggai had the genius to seize his opportunity, which was all the more tempting that Zerubbabel, grandson of Jehoiachin the last king of Judah, and thus in the direct Davidic line, was now governor of Judah (cf. 1^1). It is significant, however, that throughout the book the name of "Joshua the high priest" is always, except in the specific promise to Zerubbabel (2^20-23), coupled with that of Zerubbabel (1^1, 12, 14 2^2, 4). The religious leader is as prominent as the civil leader, because the disastrous experiences of the last seventy years or so—the Exile (586–538 B.C.) and the disillusionment consequent on the return (for the causes of this disillusionment see Eiselen, *The Prophetic Books of the O.T.*, vol. ii, pp. 546, 547), which meant for Judah nothing more than a change of masters—had gravely shattered though it had not quite extinguished the people's political hopes, and they had begun to concentrate their hope and effort upon their organization as a religious community.

Rebuilding of the Temple. This ecclesiastical emphasis explains the passionate interest of Haggai and Zechariah (cf. Ezra 5^1 6^14) in the rebuilding of the Temple. With this, indeed, the prophecy of Haggai is almost exclusively occupied: to initiate and stimulate this effort he devotes his energy and eloquence, and with its anticipated consummation he interweaves the highest hopes (2^7-9). Haggai is thus one of the founders of post-exilic Judaism: he had doubtless his predecessor in Ezekiel, who sketched the post-exilic program (chs. 40–48), and his successor in Ezra, who confirmed and developed it (see intro. to Ezra-Nehemiah, pp. 460–2; cf. pp. 714–7), but to this development the Temple was indispensable, and it was the insistent and reiterated appeals of Haggai that made it possible. It was completed within four years, in 516 B.C.

The Messianic Hope. In a negative way Haggai also contributed to the spiritualizing of the Messianic hope. He looked for the speedy coming of the day when treasures of silver and gold would pour into the Temple from the ends of the earth (2^7f.), but the later book of Malachi shows how beggarly the Temple service was in reality, and how utterly those brilliant hopes had been blasted. And to Zerubbabel he had eagerly looked as the coming Messianic King, Jehovah's servant and signet, reigning victorious in a world subdued by Jehovah (2^20-23); but this daring hope, too, remained unfulfilled. Thus by these failures and disappointments was Israel, at least the nobler minds of Israel, led to abandon their dream of an earthly kingdom. The King and the kingdom came in time, but in a way undreamed of by Haggai (see pp. 185–6).

The Prophet and His Book. Scarcely anything is known of the personal life of Haggai. He appears upon the scene suddenly in 520 B.C., and disappears just as suddenly. Chiefly on the basis of 2^3 it has been suggested that he was born in Judah before the catastrophe of 586 B.C., and, thus, that he was one of a small company among the exiles who had seen the former Temple in all its glory. If so, he must have been an old man when he prophesied; which supposition agrees with the brevity of his public activity, for a short time after 520 B.C. Zechariah appears as the leading prophet in Jerusalem.

In recent years some attempts have been made to prove that more than one author is responsible for the four brief messages in the book. These efforts, however, cannot be considered successful. All the available evidence supports the view that the four prophetic oracles come from one and the same man. The two chapters may be accepted as containing summaries of Haggai's utterances put in their present form by an editor—who is responsible also for the insertion of the historical section in 1^12-15—desirous of giving an account of the prophet's contribution to the building of the Temple.

Haggai's One Idea. While Haggai touches upon many topics, he has been rightly described as "a man of one idea"—namely, the speedy restoration of the Temple of Jehovah. (See above paragraph on "Rebuilding of the Temple.") A word should be added in explanation of this emphasis.

The attitude of Haggai toward the Temple was not that of the pre-exilic prophets. True, they too considered the Temple the dwelling place of Jehovah, but their teaching dwelt almost exclusively upon weightier spiritual and ethical matters. The point to remember is that the change in emphasis on the part of Haggai (and Zechariah) was due, not to inferior religious capacity and insight, but to a change in environment. Conditions in Jerusalem in 520 B.C. were far different from what they had been in the eighth century. As a true prophet Haggai must adapt himself and his message to the needs of the new age. The Jews of the latter part of the sixth century were not prepared for the lofty conception of the presence of Jehovah which could dispense with a house made with hands. The common people needed the Temple as an external symbol of the presence of Jehovah as much as earlier generations ever needed the ark. Moreover, with the central political government gone a new bond was needed to hold together the different elements in the local community as well as the exiles scattered among the nations. In a religious community, what institution could serve this purpose better than a common center of worship, a place to which the hearts of pious Jews everywhere might turn, assured that there they could meet their God and hold intercourse with him?

Is it, then, too much to say that undoubtedly the very existence of Jewish religion depended, in the days of Haggai, on the rebuilding of the Temple? If that was the supreme need of the hour, Haggai, by pleading so persistently for the restoration of the Temple, rendered a service of incalculable moment.

Literature: Perowne, *Haggai, Zechariah, Malachi* (Cambridge Bible); Driver, *The Minor Prophets*, vol. ii (New Century Bible); Farrar, *The Minor Prophets* (The Men of the Bible Series); Eiselen, *The Minor Prophets;* G. A. Smith, *The Book of the Twelve* (Expositor's Bible); Bennett, *The Postexilic Prophets;* Sanders and Kent, *The Messages of the Later Prophets.*

CHAPTER I

The exiles had returned in 537 B.C. (Ezra 2) to a dilapidated city and a ruined Temple (2 Kings 25[8f.]). Anxious to re-establish their worship, they erected an altar (Ezra 3[2]) and possibly made a beginning with the building of the Temple, but under the stress of many discouragements little or nothing had been done during the next sixteen years. (For a somewhat different view of the progress of events during the latter part of the sixth century B.C., see Eiselen, *The Prophetic Books of the O.T.*, vol. ii, p. 547 and references there given.) As the Messianic age could not dawn, however, until Jehovah had a home in the midst of his people, the thing of central importance to Haggai and Zechariah (cf. Ezra 5[1f.] 6[14]) was the rebuilding of the Temple. That was the immediate task and to this they urged the people to address themselves with energy and without delay.

I–II. **Exhortation to Build the Temple.** The exhortation was addressed to the civil governor, *Zerubbabel,* grandson of King Jehoiachin (cf. 1 Chr. 3[17-19]), and therefore in the direct Davidic line, and to the religious head of the community, *Joshua,* in early September 520 B.C., *the second year of Darius* the Persian king (521–486 B.C., the Persian empire succeeded the Babylonian, which had destroyed Judah). The people had been disheartened by bad harvests; they had *sown much and brought in little* (v. 6), a *drought* had been upon the land, withering everything (v. 11), and, worse still. there had been a drought upon their hearts, The brilliant promises of Deutero-Isaiah (Isa. 40–55) had not been fulfilled, and they were disillusioned men. Prices were high and wages low, it seemed as if their money just dropped through *holes* in their pockets (v. 6). Sincerely enough they may have argued that the *time* had not yet *come* to build the Temple (v. 2). Their resources were too pitifully inadequate, and their sad plight showed but too plainly that their God was still angry with them: it was unreasonable to expect them to emulate David (cf. 2 Sam. 7[2]) in his enthusiasm to build Jehovah a house.

Haggai meets this mood, as prophets always did (cf. Amos 4[6-12]), by putting a moral interpretation on the people's disasters. He invites them to *consider their ways* (v. 5)—what their conduct had been and what it had led to. He points out that though they had neglected God's house, they had been careful enough of their own (v. 4), living as they did in *ceiled,* or, rather, paneled houses, i.e., "wainscotted with costly woodwork" (Driver; cf. Jer. 22[14]). If they had, indeed, been disillusioned, *looking for much, and lo, it came to little* (v. 9), they had only themselves to blame: it was because of their apathy and negligence that *the heavens had withheld their dew and the earth her fruit*

(v. 10)—because they had let Jehovah's house *lie waste*, while *every man* was *running* about eagerly in the interests of *his own house* (v. 9).

Let them change their policy and make a start on the building. The drought in Elijah's time had been sent as the punishment for idolatry (1 Kings 17[1f.] cf. 16[32f.]) and had been removed when the idolatry was removed (1 Kings 18[45]): so it would be again. Let them *go up to the hill country* in the neighborhood of Jerusalem *and bring wood and build the house* (v. 8). The ruins of the old Temple would probably furnish them with all the stones they required—there is an incidental mention of stones in 2[15]; but all the woodwork would be burned in the terrible sack of the city in 586 B.C. (2 Kings 25[9]), consequently the immediate need was for wood. Then, when this practical proof of eager interest in the Temple had been shown, Haggai declares in the name of Jehovah, *I will take pleasure in it and I will be glorified* (v. 8) or, rather, *I will get me glory*. In other words, the glory of the Messianic age would begin when, but not until, the Temple was erected. That was to be the acid test of their sincerity. Part of what the prophet means here by *glory* is indicated by 2[7-9], where the same word is used of the magnificent offerings which will stream into the Temple from heathen nations. But blessings of every kind would be added (cf. Mt. 6[33]). Whereas Jehovah had formerly *blown upon* the produce of their fields (v. 9), ruining the crops by the breath of his terrible east wind (cf. Isa. 40[24]), now in field and vineyard there would be abounding prosperity (cf. 2[19]).

12–15. Result of the Appeal. The prophet's noble appeal was not without effect. In less than a month after it was delivered (v. 15), a genuine response was made and the work was started (v. 14). The point is twice made (vv. 12, 14) that everybody participated in the work—the civil and religious leaders and *all the remnant of the people*, i.e., all the returned exiles, and they did so under a real religious impulse; *they feared before Jehovah*, recognizing Haggai as divinely commissioned to declare this message (v. 13), and their new enthusiasm was the work of God himself (v. 14). Their response justified the prophet in his assurance that now God was with them—echo of many a similar assurance in Israel's long history, e.g., to Moses (Ex. 3[12]), to Joshua (Josh. 1[5]), to Jeremiah (Jer. 1[8]).

CHAPTER II

1–9. Renewed Exhortation to Go on With the Building. A day or two past the middle of October, 520 B.C., and after the people had been engaged on the work for about three and one half weeks, Haggai finds it necessary to address them again. The preliminary work of clearing away the rubbish had discouraged them. With the progress of the work the difficulties became more apparent and even the braver spirits were downhearted. To meet this despondency Haggai comes forward with a divine message of encouragement, probably taking advantage of the last day or the last but one of the Feast of Tabernacles (cf. Ezek. 45[25] Lev. 23[33-43]) to address the assembled people (v. 1). In 536 when they had erected the altar (Ezra 3[2f.]) there would be some present who had seen the glorious Temple which had been destroyed by the Babylonians fifty years before, but in 520 very few of them would be still alive. In any case the contrast between then and now was too pitiful (cf. Ezra 3[12]); its *former glory* had vanished (v. 3). At this point Haggai makes his brave appeal to them all, leaders and people alike, to keep up their courage and go on with the *work* (v. 4) —wholesome advice, for apathy and indolence can lead nowhere; and in their work they are sustained by the glorious promise of the presence of God. *I am with you, and my spirit* (cf. Zech. 4[6]), *abideth among you* (omit with LXX the rest of v. 5).

The promise expands into a vision of almost incredible audacity (vv. 6–9), which reveals the prophet's unconquerable faith. On the accession of Darius in 521, revolutions had broken out all over the Persian Empire; unlike his contemporaries, Haggai interprets these not as a fresh perplexity, but as the prelude to the Messianic age. This *shaking of all nations*, these political convulsions, are the sign of the *glory* that is coming in *a little while*. The glory as before (cf. 1[8]) is associated with the Temple. Into it would soon be streaming *the desirable things of all nations*, by which, as v. 8 makes clear, is meant their *silver* and *gold*, which would go to beautify Jehovah's house and render it even more glorious than the glorious Temple of Solomon. Blessing of every kind would follow, for the Hebrew word rendered *peace* (v. 9) means not only peace but prosperity and welfare in the widest sense. When we remember the meager material resources of this poor (1[6]) and down-hearted (2[3]) community, we are lost in admiration of the prophet's magnificent courage and faith. Verily, it was "the Lord *of hosts*" in whom he believed (vv. 7, 9).

10–14. Exhortation to Abandon the Unclean Thing. Exactly three months after the work had been begun (cf. 1[15]) the prophet makes another appeal. In imagery drawn from the ritual practice he reminds the people that while direct contact with *holy flesh*, i.e., the flesh of a sacrifice, infects the thing it touches with its own holiness (cf. Lev. 6[27]) indirect contact (e.g., through the *skirt* in which it is carried) does not so infect it. On the other hand, even indirect contact with a ritually unclean thing infects with its uncleanness the thing it touches: one who has touched a corpse, e.g., communicates his ritual uncleanness to whatever he touches (cf. Num. 19[22]). In other words, unholiness is more contagious than holiness.

Till lately this "uncleanness" has been uniformly taken to refer to the prevalent apathy in the work of building: their selfish indifference would go on polluting all their pretended holy endeavor until they quite abandoned it and turned with real zeal to the work of building the Temple. Let them cast out this pollution and do with their might what their hands found to do and all would be well. This interpretation is now recognized as inadequate. *This people* (v. 14), which is usually a contemptuous phrase (cf. Isa. 8[5]), almost certainly refers not to the returned exiles but to the Samaritans, "the people of the land" (cf. Ezra 4[4]), the half-heathen people who were anxious to take part in the building of the Temple (cf. Ezra 4[1-4]), and Haggai is here warning his own people against having anything to do with them. They can only infect the noble enterprise with their own uncleanness.

15–19. The New Era of Blessing is About to Begin. This brief, but somewhat involved and often misunderstood section, becomes clear if we put its opening and closing words together: *And now consider . . . from this day will I bless you.* The beginning *and now* indicates a day which is to mark the opening of a new era, and v. 18 leaves no doubt as to the day intended—it is *the day on which the foundation of Jehovah's temple was laid*, the ever-memorable *four and twentieth day of the ninth month.* With the new era then and thus inaugurated is contrasted the old bad era when they were indifferent to the Temple and punished for their indifference by the relative failure of their crops. The difficult word is the word misleadingly rendered in vv. 15, 18 by *upward* (in R.V., by *backward* in A.S.V.), which in this context should rather be *onward* or *forward. Consider from this day and onward* (v. 15); omit *from* and begin a new sentence. *Before a stone was laid upon a stone in the temple, how did ye fare?* (So LXX.) They fared by suffering disappointment in their crops. *When one came to a heap of twenty seahs* (so LXX: a seah=two and two-thirds gallons), *there were but ten; and when one came to the wine-vat* (the lower cavity hewn out in the rock into which the juice flowed through a connecting channel from an upper cavity known as the winepress), *to draw out fifty seahs from the winetrough* (i.e., the wine-vat: A.V. is substantially correct here as against R.V.), *there were but twenty.* In other words, field and vineyard disappointed expectations; and this was the penalty imposed upon them by Jehovah—*I smote you* (v. 17)—for their religious indifference. He had sent the *blasting* east wind and the blight of *mildew* and the *hail*—proof enough that *I was not with you* (as the last clause of v. 17 should probably read), in direct contrast to the assurance which Haggai can offer now, *I am with you* (1[13] 2[4]). Notice how often the word *consider* (Hebrew "set your hearts upon this") appears (vv. 15, 18, cf. 1[5, 7]); Haggai is anxious that they learn the inner meaning of their disasters and lay it to heart. Now that the foundation stone is laid, let them see whether *the vine*, etc., *will still refuse to yield their fruit.* Nay, on the contrary, *from this day I will bless you.*

20–23. Zerubbabel to be the Messianic King. Here the prophet touches the highest heights of daring hope, which now centers upon Zerubbabel. The earlier promise of the *shaking of all nations* (v. 7) is here sharpened into the definite prediction of their overthrow, despite their powerful military equipment. Nothing is here said of Joshua the high-priest; *in that day* Zerubbabel was to be the central figure, and epithets of the highest honor are showered upon him, which show the daring and the vastness of the hopes reposed in him (cf. notes on Zech. 6[11-13]). He is compared to the *signet*-ring upon Jehovah's finger (cf. Jer. 22[24]), sealing as it were his purposes and clothed with his authority. He is invested with the exalted titles of *my servant* and *my chosen one* (v. 23)—titles which have led some scholars to see in Zerubbabel the fulfillment of the prophecy in Isa. 42[1f.] Haggai, like Zechariah (6[12]), sees in this man the Messianic King. It was an amazing vision to set before the eyes of a poor and helpless people, and is another testimony (cf. 2[6-9]) to the prophet's unconquerable faith (cf. Zech. 4[7]).

ZECHARIAH

By Professor J. E. McFADYEN

Introduction

The book of Zechariah falls naturally into two parts, chs. 1–8 and chs. 9–14. The utterances contained in the first eight chapters are ascribed in their headings to Zechariah ($1^{1, 7}$ 7^{1}) the contemporary of Haggai; no statements to this effect are found in chs. 9–14. This in itself does not necessarily point to diversity of authorship; but for a variety of other reasons (see below) practically all O.T. scholars believe that chs. 9–14 do not come from the author of chs. 1–8. For simplicity's sake, therefore, the two sections may be considered separately.

I. Introduction to Chapters 1 to 8

Zechariah and Haggai. Haggai and Zechariah were contemporaries. They began their prophetic work in the same year (520 B.C.) and addressed themselves to the same task—that of encouraging the disheartened people (Zech. 1^{17}) to believe in the imminence of the Messianic age. The initial impulse given by Haggai to the building of the Temple, without which it was vain to look for the coming of that happy day, appears to have died down (Hag. 2^{3}), and the fact that Zechariah continued his prophetic work till 518 (cf. 7^{1}) suggests that he made it his business to revive and re-enforce that impulse: which he did not unsuccessfully, as the Temple was completed in 516 (cf. Ezra 6^{15}). Zechariah advances on Haggai (cf. Hag. 2^{20-23}) in making the civil and religious leaders, Zerubbabel and Joshua, of almost co-ordinate importance: Joshua is to share with Zerubbabel in the Messianic dignity (cf. 4^{14} 6^{13}). It would be interesting to know how Haggai and Zechariah felt after the glorious hopes that were centered upon Zerubbabel had been fatally and finally shattered. The collapse of these political hopes explains the post-exilic concentration upon the religious life of the community. (For the historical background of Zechariah's message, see intro. to Haggai, p. 815).

Zechariah and the Pre-exilic Prophets. Zechariah is conscious, as we are, of the gulf that separates him from the pre-exilic prophets. He looks back to them (cf. 1^{4} 7^{12}), he quotes them (cf. 7^{7-10}), and he differs from them in obvious ways, notably in his interest in the Temple and its worship (so unlike Amos; for an explanation see intro. to Haggai) and in the prominence of the visionary element in his prophecies. Indeed, most of his message (chs. 1–6) takes the form of visions, and though some real experience lies behind them, it is clear that in their present form they are the work of conscious art. Point by point (see the notes below) they forecast the removal of the obstacles that stand in the way of the coming of the Messianic King, and they reach their glorious climax in the installation of Zerubbabel and Joshua in their high office (6^{13}). God too seems further away from Zechariah than from the pre-exilic prophets; an angel is needed to interpret the visions (cf. $4^{5f.}$ and contrast Jer. 1^{9}).

But between Zechariah and his mighty predecessors there is real kinship of spirit. He knows, as they do, that the better day can never dawn until sin has been removed from the land (cf. 3^{9} 5). He too can envisage the day when all nations shall worship Jehovah (cf. 2^{11} 8^{21}); and, despite his interest in the Temple, he is no whit behind "the former prophets" in his emphasis upon the supremacy of ethical interests. He, like them, believes that Jehovah is not served by fasting (7^{6}) but by the suppression of malice and cruelty and by the practice of justice and kindness between man and man (cf. $8^{16f.}$).

Teaching and Significance. Though reference has already been made to some of the points emphasized by Zechariah, a brief summary of his teaching may enable the student to appreciate more fully the prophet's significance.

1. Zechariah differs from his predecessors in three points: (1) the emphasis on visions as a means of divine communication; (2) the apocalyptic symbolism entering into the visions; (3) the large place angelic mediation occupies in his intercourse with Jehovah. In the account of the visions appear in embryo some of the ideas which are found in a more developed stage in the angelology of the intertestamental period and of the N.T. (see art., *Intertestamental Religion*, pp. 204–5). Closely connected with the increasing emphasis on angels is the tendency to consider Jehovah too sacred for direct contact with men and to remove him so far away that direct communion with him came to be thought of as almost impossible. Even prophecy seems to

have lost in a measure its sense of immediate communion with God; at any rate, the prophet is represented as receiving his instructions through an angel, who acts as intermediary, interpreter and guide.

A somewhat different phase of the same development may be seen in the figure of "the adversary," or "Satan," who appears for the first time in the vision of the trial and acquittal of the high priest Joshua (3^{1-10}). With Zechariah the word is not yet a proper name; it becomes such only in 1 Chr. 21^{1}; but it is not difficult to trace the thought development from "the adversary" in Zechariah to the figure called by the same name and playing an important rôle in the prologue of the book of Job, to "Satan"—now a proper name—in Chronicles and to the "Satan" or "Devil" of the intertestamental and N.T. literature.

2. The Temple occupies a unique place in the thought and teaching of Zechariah (see opening paragraph of this introduction and on Haggai, p. 815).

3. Of much interest are the Messianic hopes of Zechariah. The Temple plays a prominent part, but only as an earnest of better things to come; the high priest and his fellows receive honor, but only as a sign of one greater than they, namely "Branch." It is around the person of this Branch that the hopes of Zechariah center: it is he who will complete the building of the Temple, have constant access to Jehovah and reign in peace forever. The prophet identifies Branch with Zerubbabel (cf. 3^{8} with 4^{7-10} 6^{9-13} Hag. 2^{20-23}). The blessings of the Messianic age will be both temporal and spiritual; they will be enjoyed primarily by the Jews, but not by them exclusively (8^{18-23}).

4. The accusation that Zechariah is a teacher of heartless and unspiritual formalism is not well founded; for he clearly and specifically teaches that forms and ceremonies are not essential elements of true religion; they are valuable only as means by the use of which men may be led into purer and nobler lives. His conception of the future includes the removal of sin—people, city, land, all must be holy.

5. Zechariah constantly emphasizes the truth that ultimate victory is dependent on divine co-operation (4^{6}). It is only as Jehovah gives his support that the people can be restored to their own land, there to live in joy and felicity forever.

Literature: Perowne, *Haggai, Zechariah, Malachi* (Cambridge Bible); Driver, *The Minor Prophets*, vol. ii (New Century Bible); G. A. Smith, *The Book of the Twelve*, vol. ii (Expositor's Bible); Eiselen, *The Minor Prophets;* Bennett, *The Postexilic Prophets;* Farrar, *The Minor Prophets;* Sanders and Kent, *The Messages of the Later Prophets;* H. G. Mitchell, *Zechariah* (International Critical Commentary.)

CHAPTER I

Zechariah is very conscious of addressing a disappointed and discouraged people, and he makes it his business to hearten them (cf. 8^{15}). This he does by relating a series of visions (1^{7}–6^{15}) which are in part the allegorical embodiment of his thought, and which carry the assurance that the obstacles to the coming of the Messianic age will be cleared away. But one of the greatest obstacles is the sinfulness of the people themselves, so to this he first addresses himself.

1–6. Call to Repentance. Though he is of priestly lineage (Neh. 12^{16}), Zechariah's message has all the ring of *the former*, i.e., the preexilic *prophets* (v. 4) in attributing the people's misfortunes to God's anger at their *evil ways* and in summoning them to repentance. The fathers were obstinate and suffered; let their children repent. Fathers and prophets die, but not the words of God; his promises and threats will be fulfilled. This warning, delivered toward the end of 520 B.C. (v. 1), is followed by visions of encouragement.

CHAPTERS 1^{7} TO 6^{15}: EIGHT VISIONS OF ENCOURAGEMENT

7–17. The First Vision: The Colored Horses. All eight visions seem to fall within one night (cf. 4^{1}), about the middle of February, 519 B.C. (1^{7}). On close study the first vision seems very confused, with its abrupt introduction of *the angel that talked with me* (v. 9) and *the angel of Jehovah* (v. 11), etc. This indistinctness has been explained as involved in the phantasmagoria of the vision, but most modern scholars think it is due to some later modification of the original text. On this assumption it will help to restore the original distinctness of the passage if, with them, we omit in v. 8 *riding upon a red horse*, and if we remember that the man who *stood among the myrtle trees* (v. 8) is really a supernatural man and is to be identified with *the angel that talked with me* (vv. 9, 14), who is also called *the angel of Jehovah* (vv. 11f.). But there are other difficulties. Omitting the rider with the red horse in v. 8, there are only three horses, but the LXX gives four (red, dappled, piebald, and white) and there are four in the corresponding passage $6^{1f.}$—which seems more natural, the four horses corresponding to the four quarters of the heaven. Again, the scenery of the vision is quite uncertain. According to v. 8 it seems to be in the shade of a *myrtle* grove near Jerusalem, and the horsemen are supposed to have been suggested to the prophet's mind by the sight of Persian cavalry scouts. But for *myrtles,* the LXX reads *mountains,* which agrees with 6[1] and is adopted by Sellin, who interprets the mountains as the two mythological mountains regarded as the entrance to and the exit from heaven. Whatever may have suggested the vision, it is clear that the figures that move across the scenery are supernatural: nothing less than visitants and voices from heaven could have given Zechariah and his people the assurance that they needed.

And what is that? It is the assurance that Jehovah passionately cares for their welfare, is *zealous* for them *with a great zeal* (for *jealous,* v. 14). It did not look as if he cared. Not long before, Haggai (2[6, 21]) had looked forward to a great upheaval among the nations, which would have proved that Jehovah was bestirring himself, no doubt on behalf of his beloved Judah and Jerusalem: but instead, *behold, all the earth sitteth still and is at rest* (v. 11). This is the report of the heavenly couriers who have *walked to and fro through the earth* (v. 11). After the *seventy years* or so (v. 12) since the fall of Jersualem (586–520 B.C.) this was more than disappointing: but now at last comes the *good* and *comforting* message (v. 13) that Jehovah cares after all (v. 14). Soon the cities of Judah would *overflow with prosperity* (v. 17, mg.), Jerusalem would be rebuilt (the *line,* v. 16, is the measuring line, cf. 2[1]), and—most convincing proof of all—the building of the Temple, which had just begun, would be completed (v. 16). It was indeed a comforting message to men who needed comfort sorely.

18–21. The Second Vision: The Four Horns and the Four Smiths. But meantime Judah is living in a world of enemies, and Jehovah's *indignation* at their *easy* sensuous lives (v. 15) must manifest itself in their destruction. This is the theme of the second vision. The hostile world which has *scattered* Judah (v. 19) is symbolized by *four* aggressive *horns.* These, however, are to be hurled to the ground by *four smiths,* symbols of the supernatural powers, who will sharpen (so LXX) their axes (read thus, instead of *fray* or *terrify them* in v. 21) and effect the destruction of the nations that had dared to invade Jehovah's land and scatter his people.

CHAPTER II

1–5. The Third Vision: The City Without a Wall. The rebuilding of Jerusalem had been assured by the first vision (1[16]); this third vision discloses the nature of the city which the prophet would like his rebuilt Jerusalem to be—a city not only populous but unwalled (v. 4). The young man of the vision, typical of the rising generation, more eager for city walls than for the Temple, more concerned for home defense than for religion, is seen *with a measuring line in his hand* (v. 1); he wishes to set limits to the city and to surround it with a wall. But a wall, designed for protection, ultimately means limitation and exclusion; and God will have neither the one nor the other. The divine ideal is expansion, not exclusion, and the great designs of God for his people cannot be measured with a tape-line. Jerusalem is to be open and unwalled like a great village; partly because *many nations shall join themselves to Jehovah in that day and shall be my people* (v. 11)—what a generous ideal!—and partly because a city is best protected not by her walls but by her God. He will be at once her defense, *a wall of fire round about* (v. 5), and her *glory.* Haggai (2[8f.]) had seen the glory in the sheen of tributary silver and gold; Zechariah, with a more spiritual eye, finds it in the Divine Presence.

It is altogether a most original, courageous, and alluring vision. A city without a wall was for centuries all but inconceivable: here is a prophet who can see the peril of the wall, its power to limit the life of the citizens within it, to obstruct the city's power of expansion, to block its future and stultify its progress. He also sees that, in the end, a nation is saved and protected not by its military defenses, but by its moral and religious character and ideals. A world of unwalled cities is a vastly safer and happier place than a world of cities walled. The prophet's ideal is not a fortress, but an unwalled city; he is an apostle of peace.

6–13. Two Lyrical Epilogues. These verses constitute two little lyrical epilogues (vv. 6–9; 10–13) springing out of the fair vision (vv. 1–5). Into the city (vv. 6–9) must be gathered the Jews who are scattered throughout the world, especially those still exiled in Babylon (v. 7), who are precious to Jehovah as *the apple of his eye* (v. 8); so they are dramatically summoned to *make their escape to Zion* (v. 7) from the nations who had despoiled and enslaved them. Zechariah is conscious of his commission to make this appeal: for *his majesty,* i.e., the glorious Jehovah, *hath sent me* (so v. 8b should read). More especially is Jerusalem herself, Jehovah's chosen city, summoned to rejoice at the prospect of his coming soon to dwell there in the Temple, where he will be worshiped not only by Judah but by *many* foreign *nations* too, though Judah remains pre-eminently *the holy land* (v. 12).

CHAPTER III

1–8, 10. The Fourth Vision: The High Priest and the Accuser. It is not enough for Zechariah that his Jerusalem be populous and unwalled: he is even more deeply interested in her spiritual quality. That is of a low order. Sin still clings to the people, as is evidenced (according to ancient views) by the misfortunes which dog them (cf. Hag. 1[11]); they are tainted with the idolatries of the fathers, and they must be purged and forgiven before they are fit to dwell in the fair city promised. All this, on the general view of the passage, is symbolized by Joshua, the high priest, who appears in the vision in *filthy garments*—emblem of the national sin—at the bar of heaven, where he is accused by *Satan*, one of God's angels who delights in exposing the weaknesses of men (cf. Job 1[6]). But Satan is solemnly rebuked, Joshua's filthy garments are exchanged for *rich apparel* (v. 4) in token that the sin is forgiven (vv. 4, 9); a clean *mitre* or turban, such as the high priest wore (Ex. 28[4]), is set upon his head, and he receives the promise that if he is faithful to his priestly charge, he shall have full authority over the Temple, and rank among Jehovah's attendant angels (v. 7). He and the priests who are under him will be a *sign* (v. 8) and pledge that the Messianic kingdom is very near. *My servant the Branch* (v. 8) or *Shoot*—a name which had been given by Jeremiah (23[5]) to the coming Messianic King—would soon appear, and the happy day would dawn when men would sit in peace and safety *under the vine and fig tree* (cf. Mic. 4[4]). By the Branch (cf. 6[12f.]) the prophet unquestionably means Zerubbabel, the civil head of the community, as Joshua was its sacerdotal head.

9. This summary has left v. 9 out of account, as much ambiguity attaches to the *stone*. This is sometimes taken as the jewel in Messiah's diadem, but it seems more reasonable to identify it with the stone in 4[7], where (as also probably in 4[10]) it unambiguously refers to the coping stone of the Temple. The *engraving* upon it will doubtless be something like "Holiness to Jehovah" (cf. 14[20] Ex. 28[36]).

It is possible, however, as Sellin suggests, that Joshua appears here, not in a representative, but in a personal capacity. He may have been accused of being tainted with the uncleanness of Babylon (Isa. 52[11]), from which he had come, and therefore incompetent to be high priest; in that case Zechariah would here be defending him as the man chosen by Jehovah himself to be the religious head of the community.

CHAPTER IV

The Fifth Vision: The Seven-Branched Candlestick With an Olive Tree on Either Side. This confusing chapter becomes clear the moment it is recognized (1) that vv. 6b–10a, which deal entirely with Zerubbabel and interrupt the closely connected vv. 6a, 10b, form an independent piece; and (2) that v. 12, which but repeats and modifies v. 11, should be omitted as a later addition.

1–6a, 10b–14. The Vision. Now that the religious community (or the high priest) has been completely restored to favor, symbolized by the exchange of soiled robes for clean ones, it is important that the community receive the assurance of the unceasing vigilance and protection of the God they worship, the assurance also of the divine authority of their leaders. These assurances are conveyed in the somewhat fantastic vision of the seven-branched candlestick with an olive tree on either side. As in the post-exilic Temple, but not as in that of Solomon, which had ten lamps (1 Kings 7[49]), the candlestick of Zechariah's vision had seven lamps, each of which was connected by a pipe (not *seven* pipes, v. 2) with a bowl of oil above.

The explanation which this curious vision undoubtedly requires is furnished by v. 10b. The shining lamps fed from the oil in the bowl above represent, not the church fed and illumined by the Divine Spirit, but the all-seeing eyes of Jehovah himself (cf. 2 Chr. 16[9] Psa. 121[3f.]), ever vigilant to watch and protect the interests of his people. The olive trees on either side represent the *two sons of oil* (*anointed ones*, A.S.V., v. 14), an unmistakable reference to Zerubbabel and Joshua as the (anointed) civil and religious heads of the community who, ranking as attendant angels (cf. 3[7]), *stand beside the Lord of the whole earth.* (V. 12 introduces the unwarranted thought that the oil in the lamps is ultimately fed from the oil in the trees. The measure of truth in this is that the Divine Spirit is in both—in the light and in the men—but the human figures at either side of the candlestick are detached from and essentially independent of it—see v. 3.)

6b–10a. The Promise to Zerubbabel. Zerubbabel, who may have been relying on his own political and building enterprises (cf. 2[2]), is here reminded in the great words of v. 6 that success depends not upon human *might* and *power*, but on the divine *spirit*. Trusting to it, the *great mountain* of difficulty that confronted him would become level as a *plain*. He would be given the honor of completing the Temple he had begun, and the final placing of its coping stone would be greeted with shouts of joy, *Grace, grace*, i.e., "How lovely! How lovely!" or "May all *favor* attend it." Those who had despised the slender and unpromising beginnings would look with joy upon this chosen stone (rather than *plummet*, v. 10; cf. Psa. 118[22]) being set in its place (perhaps with an appropriate inscription, cf. 3[9]) by the hands of Zerubbabel. Again we see how indispensable is the Temple as a preparation for the coming of the Messianic kingdom. (On vv. 10b–14 see under vv. 1–6a.)

CHAPTER V

1–4. The Sixth Vision: The Flying Roll. The next two visions emphasize the necessity for purity within the new community. The ever-wakeful protection of God furnishes no license to sin and no immunity from its consequences. There must be an entire elimination of every sinful thing and sinful person. The sixth vision deals with the persons. The prophet sees an immense *roll*, thirty feet by fifteen, *flying* down from heaven across the whole land, crowded with terrible curses and lighting with unerring certainty and destructive power upon the guilty—the crimes singled out for special reprobation (though they are typical of others) being theft and perjury, crimes which may have been specially prevalent in that poverty-stricken community, crimes against neighbors and against God. The heaven-sent curse is tragically effective (v. 4).

5–11. The Seventh Vision: The Woman in the Barrel. This vision is more searching still, for it is not so much the sinner as the very principle of sin that has to be eradicated. The prophet expresses this profound thought through the curious symbol of a small barrel (an ephah = about seven gallons) with a leaden lid (in v. 7 *talent* = "disk"), which is being pushed up by a *woman* inside trying to effect her escape. But the angel thrust her down and closed the heavy lid upon her: whereupon two demonic female figures appeared and bore the barrel away on their powerful wings to the land of *Shinar*, i.e., Babylon (cf. Gen. 11[2]), where a *house*, i.e., a temple, is to be erected to the woman, who, as v. 8 discloses (cf. v. 6, where *their resemblance* should, with LXX, read *their iniquity*), is *Wickedness* personified. Incidentally, this throws a lurid light on Zechariah's conception of Babylon—the fitting abode for the worship of Wickedness, whose temple is the counterpart of the Temple of Jehovah at Jerusalem.

Behind this fantastic picture lies the profoundest moral insight. The prophet sees that the real enemy of a community is Sin, and that it is not sinners, nor even sins only, but Sin itself that must be banished. The mechanism by which this banishment is effected must not blind us to the moral penetration of the idea it embodies.

CHAPTER VI

1–8, 15. The Eighth Vision: The Four Chariots. The visions from the third to the seventh have concentrated attention on the Jewish community and on the moral and spiritual quality which must characterize it; this eighth and last vision, like the first two, opens up the wide vista of the world, and its imagery reverts to that of the first vision. From between two *mountains of bronze* (see note on *myrtles*, 1[8]) emerge four *chariots* drawn by *horses* of different color (in vv. 3, 6 read *dappled for grisled*, and in v. 3 omit *bay* with A.S.V.; and for *the bay* in v. 7 read with mg. *the strong ones*, which refers to *all* the horses). These horses, after *presenting themselves before the Lord of all the earth* (v. 5, mg.), go out *through* all *the earth* (v. 7), north, south, east, and west (emended text of v. 6), to (as v. 5 properly reads) *the four winds of heaven.* All the horses are impatient to start (v. 7), but attention is specially directed to *the north country* (v. 8), i.e., Babylon, where the exiles are.

The meaning of the vision turns on the interpretation of v. 8b. The phrase rendered *they have quieted my spirit* is usually taken to mean "they have pacified my anger," and the chariots are supposed to be sent forth to execute Jehovah's anger upon any power which may threaten Judah, and more particularly Babylon. But spirit does not necessarily mean anger, and Sellin may be right in connecting v. 8 with v. 15a and in supposing that the Divine Spirit is the spirit which will bring back the scattered Jews to take their part in the building of the Temple. This would certainly round off the visions admirably.

9–14. The Proclamation of the Messiah. A deputation of Babylonian Jews reaches Jerusalem with gifts of *silver* and *gold* doubtless intended for the Temple, and Zechariah is commissioned to make of these gifts a crown to be set on the head of Zerubbabel, the *Branch* or Shoot (cf. 3[8])—an eloquent indication that he is the Messianic King. This, which is quite certainly the original meaning of the passage, has been obscured in the text, because the hopes reposed in Zerubbabel were falsified by history. The grammar of v. 14, where *shall be* is singular, not plural, puts it beyond any doubt that the original passage mentioned only one crown, not two, and that that crown must have been designed for Zerubbabel, the anticipated king. He, and not Joshua, must be the subject of the address in v. 11, as it is he (4[9]) who was building the Temple ($6^{12f.}$). The last clause of v. 13 (*them both*) certainly implies that Joshua as well as Zerubbabel was mentioned (and that probably there had not been complete harmony between them); but there are not two *thrones;* v. 13 should read *and there shall be a priest*, or, better, *and Joshua shall be the priest upon his right hand* (so LXX). The unfulfilled promise to Zerubbabel was simply transferred by later hands to Joshua, the high priest, who, as in later times, is here regarded as the civil no less than the religious head of the community. The crown is to be deposited in the Temple in memory of the donors. (On v. 15 see under vv. 1–8.)

Chapters 7 and 8: The Call to Civic Duty and Some Precious Promises

CHAPTER VII

The Call to Civic Duty. Already, even through the fantastic visions, we have seen the practical quality of Zechariah's mind: in chs. 7 and 8, where the imaginative expression of truth is discarded, that quality discloses itself in a still more eminent degree. The occasion of the message in ch. 7 was the arrival of a deputation, probably of Samaritans (cf. Ezra 4^{1-5}), from Bethel, in December, 518 B.C., to consult the Temple priests and prophets as to whether the fasts in the fifth and seventh months to commemorate the burning of city and Temple (2 Kings $25^{8f.}$) and the assassination of the Jewish governor Gedaliah (2 Kings 25^{25})—fasts which had been observed since the fall of the city in 586—should be continued. Zechariah's answer, which is intended to reach the ears of *all the people* (v. 5), is of special significance when we remember his profound interest in the Temple: it shows that he, like *the former*, i.e., the pre-exilic, *prophets* (1^4), cared infinitely more for righteousness than for ritual. Their fasting, he reminds them, like their eating and drinking, did not in any way affect God, but only themselves. His demand, voiced by those prophets, was for something very different—for true *justice* (cf. Amos 5^{24}), *kindness* (cf. Hos. 6^6) and *pity* in their social relationships, and for the temper which would scorn to exploit the defenseless members of society or to harbor malicious designs against them (vv. 9b–11). This prophetic *law* (v. 12), i.e., instruction, though it had been mediated by the divine *Spirit*, they had willfully rejected, *turning a stubborn shoulder* (v. 11) like an animal that refuses to bear the yoke, with the result that Jehovah was indignant (v. 12), scattered them among strange nations (v. 14a), and abandoned their lovely land to desolation (v. 14b).

The force of this answer is somewhat blunted by the intrusion of vv. 8, 9a, which should be omitted. The point, then, is that the words beginning *Execute true justice*, etc. (v. 9b), quote, in substance, the message of the former prophets: and v. 7 should read *Are not these* (so LXX) *the words of the former prophets*, etc., namely, *Execute true justice*, etc.—Zechariah is conscious that his own words are but a repetition of theirs. *The South* in v. 7 is the southern district of Judah and the Philistine plain.

CHAPTER VIII

This chapter continues Zechariah's answer to the deputation, and yields a vivid glimpse not only into Zechariah's hopes and ideals, but also into the forlorn condition of the people and the land.

1–17. The Precious Promises. Many of their compatriots were in exile (v. 7). They themselves were slack, timid, disheartened (vv. 9a, 13b). There were few old people to be seen in Jerusalem and few children (v. 4). Unemployment was widespread, the neighboring peoples were hostile, there was internal dissension (v. 10), a drought (Hag. 1^{11}) had ruined the crops (v. 12), their name was a byword for misery in the world (v. 13). The situation was so desperate that it seemed as if only a miracle could transform it (v. 6). Very well, says Zechariah, God is equal to the miracle, it is no miracle for him. The misery of the *former days* (v. 11) before the building of the Temple was begun in 520 would be turned into joy (v. 19) and abounding prosperity; and this assurance is conveyed in detail in a series of promises, each solemnly introduced by the words, *Thus saith Jehovah of hosts.* Jehovah would return and dwell in his Temple; then Jerusalem would be a loyal and holy city (v. 3); old folks would sit watching happy boys and girls play in its streets (vv. 4f.), the exiles would be brought home (vv. 7f.), crops would be abundant, the name of the people would be a synonym for blessing; therefore *don't be afraid* (v. 15). But the prophet takes care to emphasize the point he had so earnestly made before ($7^{9f.}$), that this happy state could come into being only if they practiced loyalty and justice to one another and abstained from all malice and breach of contract (vv. 16f.).

18–23. The Attractive Power of the Holy City. Here the prophet comes to the real climax of his answer to the deputation ($7^{2f.}$). Their fasts—to the two already mentioned (7^5) are added other two which commemorated the beginning of the siege of Jerusalem in the tenth month (2 Kings 25^1) and its capture in the fourth (2 Kings 25^{3-5})—should be turned into *joy and gladness and cheerful seasons.* So attractive would this holy happy city be that men from foreign lands would join the Jews in exile who were returning home and would hasten to it to worship the great God of the place. They had caught its secret, *for we have heard that God is with you* (v. 23).

II. Introduction to Chapters 9 to 14

Date. The one certain thing about this perplexing section is that it is not the work of the prophet who wrote the first eight chapters of the book of Zechariah. An exhaustive discussion of all the arguments which have led to this conclusion would require more space than is available here; hence all that the present writer can do is to point out the lines along which the investigation must proceed and the most probable results to which the inquiry seems to lead. (For a full discussion see Mitchell, *Zechariah*, pp. 232–259.) The evidence to be considered is threefold—linguistic, historical and theological.

1. *The Linguistic Argument.* It has been pointed out again and again that between the two sections there are marked differences in diction, style, and other features of composition, and long lists of these differences have been constructed. Over against such lists have been prepared others calling attention to linguistic features thought to favor unity of authorship. But when all is said and done, it cannot be denied that, whatever similarities the two sections may reveal, each section is marked by some striking linguistic and stylistic peculiarities. Moreover, while similarities and resemblances in language and style may easily be explained—in this case they may all be explained by the fact that both sections belong to the same general stage in the history of the Hebrew language—in the presence of numerous dissimilarities one cannot escape the question whether the differences in language and style which remain after all due allowance has been made for difference in subject matter can be harmonized with the theory that the entire book comes from the sixth century Zechariah. To the present writer it seems that, even admitting as a general principle that style and diction by themselves are unsafe criteria, in the present case the two parts differ so widely in broad and general linguistic features that it is exceedingly difficult to believe that they were written by one and the same author.

2. *The Historical Argument.* The historical situation described and presupposed in chs. 1–8 is not that of chs. 9–14. The prophecies in the early part of the book have an intimate connection with events in Judah and Jerusalem in the days of Darius: the Jews are encouraged to rebuild the Temple and the city, and as reward are promised speedy deliverance from their present distress, and success and prosperity for the immediate future. Are the pictures of the impending destruction of Jerusalem and other calamities, which are to befall the nation prior to the final triumph, as outlined in chs. 9–14, adapted to the needs of the same community in the same age? What is true of conditions within the Jewish community is equally true of conditions throughout the whole Eastern world. Chs. 9–14 reflect a world situation far different from that appearing in chs. 1–8.

3. *The Theological Argument.* It would be strange indeed if resemblances in ideas were not found in the two sections; but such resemblances do not necessarily establish common authorship. (Similar resemblances can be traced between other prophetic writings certainly coming from different authors; who would claim in such cases that they prove common authorship?) Again, the crucial question is, Can the differences in ideas be harmonized with belief in unity of authorship? For instance, in chs. 9–14 there is not the slightest concern for the rebuilding of the Temple, which is the main theme of chs. 1–8; there are marked differences in the Messianic ideas and ideals of the two sections (cf. 3[8] 6[12, 13] with 9[9, 10] and ch. 8 with ch. 14); there are striking differences in the hopes for the future of the Jewish community (cf. 1[21] 2[8-11] 8[7, 8] with 12[2f.]).

As in all investigations of this character a mathematical demonstration may not be possible, but the facts enumerated make it practically certain that chs. 9–14 do not come from "Zechariah, the son of Berechiah, the son of Iddo." It is much more difficult to fix an exact date for the chapters. Such proper names and incidents as occur do not enable us to reach with certainty any tangible historical situation. It is not even certain that the section is a unity. (For a detailed discussion of this question see Eiselen, *The Prophetic Books of the O.T.*, vol. ii, pp. 567f.)

The situations change kaleidoscopically (see the notes below). The section rings almost throughout with the clangor of war, and some of the scenes are gruesome enough (cf. 9[15] 12[4] 14[12, 15]). Sometimes Jerusalem is in distress (cf. 14[1-5]), sometimes triumphant; once Jehovah's people displays the basest ingratitude (cf. 11[12]), and again the profoundest penitence (cf. 12[10-14]). Some of the utterances are enigmatic in the extreme, notably 11[8]. The general impression made by the prophecy is that it comes as a whole from a relatively late period, perhaps the fourth or third century B.C., when the distinction between the Jewish people and the rest of the world had grown very sharp, and the hope was passionately cherished that the supremacy of Jerusalem would be signally marked by the defeat and destruction of all who were opposed to her. A confirmation of this later date may be seen in the manifest discredit into which prophecy has fallen (cf. 13[2-6]); the decadence already visible in Zechariah and Malachi has reached its climax.

Teaching and Significance. For all their obscurity, these chapters constitute one of the most revealing documents of Judaism. We see in them the characteristic hope of its final triumph over heathenism and its hordes—the hope, however, not only of its political, but still more of its religious triumph. The book closes with a vision of pilgrims from once hostile nations streaming from foreign lands to worship Jehovah in Jerusalem (cf. 14[16]). But that very vision marks the limitations as well as the breadth of contemporary Judaism. The nations must come *to Jerusalem* to worship, their worship must take the form of the celebration of the Jewish *feast of booths* (14[16]), and those who decline this homage are to be punished (14[17-19]). The universalism turns out to be, after all, a Levitical and legalistic universalism. The distinctive teaching of the six chapters may be summarized as follows:

1. *The Messianic King.* The person of the Messianic King appears only in 9[9, 10], but there very distinctly. The King is primarily the "Prince of Peace" and the general conception of him is in perfect accord with that expressed in other prophetic books. Two new features, however, are introduced: (1) "Having salvation," that is, the ideal king will at all times enjoy the divine help and favor, so that everything he undertakes will prosper; (2) "Lowly," that is, he will be of lowly estate and humble in spirit.

2. *The Rejected Shepherd.* For details of interpretation see comments on 11[4-14] and 11[15-17]+13[7-9]. As is pointed out in these comments, the meaning of some features in the passage describing the good and the foolish shepherd is uncertain, but its general significance is clear. Evidently, the allegory presents a solemn warning that the divine care and grace may be frustrated by human obstinacy. It has been done again and again in the past; it has been done in the immediate past to which the prophecy points; it may be done again, unless the prophet's contemporaries take heed. The promises in chs. 9 and 10 are glorious; will they be realized? All will depend upon the attitude of those for whom the blessings are intended.

3. *The Restored and Penitent People.* All the eschatological hopes of chs. 9–14 center around the restored Jewish community. Whatever the immediate future may have in store, ultimately the Jews will triumph over all their enemies and enjoy abundant external prosperity and rich spiritual gifts. Uncleanness, even the spirit of uncleanness, and everything else that in any wise might interfere with direct personal communion with Jehovah, will be taken away. Ceremonial holiness plays a prominent part in the expectation; but the emphasis which the author places on moral and spiritual regeneration and heartfelt repentance furnishes sufficient evidence to show that the author of these chapters, like the pre-exilic prophets, was not without proper appreciation of the essential elements of Jehovah religion.

4. *The Divine Sovereignty.* During the Messianic era Jehovah will be supreme over all the nations. True, Jerusalem and Judah will enjoy the divine favor in a special manner; true, the nations will suffer terrible disasters; but when the last conflict is over, a remnant of all the nations will "worship the king, Jehovah of hosts."

Literature: See the titles at the close of the introduction to chs. 1–8, p. 820.

CHAPTER IX

The Coming of the Messianic Kingdom. The post-exilic, like the pre-exilic prophets, followed the course of history with the keenest of eyes, because they regarded it as the arena on which Jehovah's purpose was being worked out (cf. Isa. 5[12] 14[26f.]). Nothing is more natural, then, than that the conquering career of Alexander the Great (336–323 B.C.) should have been watched with the intensest interest and should have stirred the most daring hopes. It is no accident that the prediction of the advent of the Messianic King (vv. 9f.) follows the prophecy which in all probability describes the anticipated victories of Alexander (vv. 1–8). In the eyes of the prophet that great warrior was preparing the way for the Hebrew King who was to usher in the glorious days to which the prophets as a whole look forward. In this anticipation the prophet read the future more truly than he at the time could have realized; for, through the spread of the Greek language which followed in the wake of his conquests, Alexander was all unconsciously preparing the way for the LXX and the N.T. in which the story of our Lord was told to all the world: so that in a sense little dreamed of either by

Alexander or Zechariah, Alexander was one of those who prepared the way for the coming of the Lord.

1–8. Overthrow of Hostile Nations. After Alexander's victory over the Persians at Issus in 333 B.C. the prophet sees him in imagination triumphantly marching on from Syria in the north through Phœnicia to Philistia in the south, subduing Israel's historic enemies and thus making possible the restoration of her ancient kingdom in all its ideal extent. The *burden* (or, rather, oracle) declares that the cities of Aram, i.e., Syria (instead of *the eye of man*, Hebrew *Adam*), no less than the tribes of Israel, belong to Jehovah—*Damascus* being specially singled out, and *Hamath*, one hundred and twenty miles north of it, and *Hadrach*, also in the north (v. 1). Next to fall would be *Tyre* and *Sidon*, the chief towns of Phœnicia, despite their *wisdom*, i.e., skill in war and commerce, and despite their wealth and far-flung commerce (vv. 2–4).

Then would come the turn of the Philistines, four of whose towns are mentioned as marked for destruction, and the surviving population of idolatrous half-breeds (rather than *bastards;* v. 6), after abandoning the heathen practice of eating sacrificial meat from which the blood had not been drained (cf. 1 Sam. 14[32f.]) and other customs regarded by Israel as unclean and *detestable*, would at length be incorporated as a clan (not *chieftain*) in Judah and regarded as on a level with the people of Jerusalem (vv. 5–7), whose ancient name was *Jebus* (Judg. 19[10]). Jehovah would himself protect his *house* (i.e., the Holy Land), and the foreign armies that had been seen only too often passing across Palestine would be seen no more (v. 8).

9, 10. The Messianic King. Now that the land from north to south has been won for Jehovah, the Messianic *King* appears upon the scene, whereat Jerusalem may well *rejoice*. The description of him shows how the ancient idea of kingship, with its military glory, has been transformed. This King is *just* and the *Saviour* (so LXX) of the poor: he comes riding not upon a war-horse but upon an *ass*, the beast of peace. From end to end of his kingdom military weapons will disappear. By his word of arbitration he will dispense peace to the nations of the world (cf. Isa. 2[3f.]), and because his throne is founded on justice, his reign will be universal.

11–17. Promise of Victory and Freedom. In contrast with the ideal presented in vv. 1–11 is the grim reality. The Jews are dispersed in foreign lands; but if *prisoners*, they are *expectant* prisoners (vv. 11f.), and in virtue of the ancient covenant sealed with sacrificial *blood*, they are urged to *return* (not *turn*) to their own land, and are encouraged with the promise that Jehovah himself would fight for them and use them as his weapons—bow, arrow, and lance—against the adversary. (*Greece* is specially singled out, but most scholars believe this to be a later intrusion.) The *sling-stones* (v. 15) would eat the flesh (so Sellin) and drink the blood of the foe, the Jews would be drenched with that blood *like the corners of the altar*, and victorious they would shine like the glittering jewels of a crown (cf. mg.). The fierce description ends upon a quiet note of praise to God for his goodness, which shines resplendent in the fertility of the land.

This wild battle scene stands in such curious contrast to the preceding description of the King of Peace that Sellin proposes to transfer those verses (9f.) to the end of the chapter. In any case they represent conflicting ideals. Of the savage temper reflected in v. 15 the world has seen enough, and we turn from it with relief to the lovely picture of the King who rules the world not with weapons of war but with words of peace. And we also rejoice at the noble large-heartedness which deliberately put the Philistines, ancient enemies, upon the level of Jerusalem, and welcomed them into the Jewish commonwealth (cf. Isa. 19[23-25]).

CHAPTER X

1, 2. The Folly of Superstition. This passage has only an external connection with the context: the idea of fertility connects it with 9[17], and the word *shepherd* with 10[3]. In a time of drought the people had sought in superstitious ways to secure rain, by consulting diviners and *teraphim* (household gods used in divination; cf. Ezek. 21[21]): the prophet urges them to ask it from Jehovah, who, as Lord of nature, is Lord of the rain, on which the food of man and beast depends. Superstition, i.e., a way of life divorced from God and his guidance, is the parent of restlessness and instability and reduces men to the level of *shepherdless sheep*.

The Destruction of the World-Powers and the Gathering of Dispersed Israel. (10[3]–11[3].) This passage is parallel in thought to ch. 9, only it emphasizes the annihilation of the hostile powers rather than the reign of peace which is the sequel to their destruction, and it dwells more elaborately on the return of Israel from the lands in which they are scattered. *Egypt* and *Assyria* are definitely mentioned as the hostile powers (vv. 10f.), by which we are to understand the Ptolemaic dynasty of Egypt and the Seleucid dynasty of Syria, which contended for the possession of Palestine during the latter part of the fourth and throughout the third century B.C. (See pp. 70–1.)

3–7. The Victory. The Jews had been crushed by *shepherds* and *he-goats* (cf. Isa. 14^{9} mg.), i.e., foreign rulers. The prophet here promises that Jehovah will punish these oppressors. They would have rulers of their own (all the nouns in v. 4, including the word rendered *exactor*, are pictorial terms for *rulers*), and under their rule the helpless sheep of Jehovah's flock would be transformed into glorious war-horses (v. 3)—a promise which was amply fulfilled in the Maccabean struggles of the second century. With Jehovah on their side, their victory would be so complete that they would trample their mighty enemy in the mire (v. 5), and their joy would be exuberant (v. 7).

8–12. The Restoration. From the distant lands in which they were scattered (v. 9: read *I scattered* instead of *I will sow*), especially from Syria and Egypt (v. 10), where for some centuries Jews had resided, Jehovah would summon them by a call like a *hiss* (v. 8; cf. Isa. 5^{26}) or whistle, as a beekeeper summons his bees (cf. Isa. 7^{18}), and they would return in throngs (v. 10c) to Palestine with the *children* whom they had reared (v. 9, LXX). No conceivable obstacle would bar their way. Ancient miracles would be repeated to facilitate their journey home (cf. Isa. $11^{15, 16}$). As of old (cf. Ex. 14) they would cross the Red Sea in safety (for *sea of affliction*, v. 11, read *sea of Egypt*), and the power of their enemies would be broken no less surely than the barriers of nature. Their strength would come from Jehovah and in his name would they make their boast (so LXX, v. 12).

CHAPTER XI

1–3. The Ruin of the Hostile Powers. (See also 10^{3-12}.) It is possible that these verses, with their allusions to Bashan and Jordan, may describe an invasion of Israel; but more probably, in the context, they repeat the threat of 10^{3-7} of the destruction of the powers hostile to Israel, the more so as great forests (particularly Lebanon; cf. Isa. 10^{34}) sometimes symbolize a mighty world-power. The shepherds (v. 3) are, as before (10^{3}), the rulers of these powers. The *devouring fire* (v. 1), symbol of irremediable destruction, would swiftly come upon those powers, whose rulers would then *howl* in despair like the lions when driven from their lairs in the *jungle of Jordan*.

The whole passage (10^{3}–11^{3}) is alive with the keen consciousness of the distinction between Israel and the world-powers which oppress her and glows with anticipation of the day when the tables would be turned and victorious Israel would recover her rightful place; and this could be only when she was restored to her own land. Here again is revealed her passionate love of the ancient land.

The Two Shepherds, the Faithful and the False. (11^{4-17} 13^{7-9}.) Driver truly remarks that this "prophecy is the most enigmatic in the O.T." It is quite certain that 13^{7-9} should follow 11^{4-17}, as the "shepherd" idea controls both sections: 13^{7-9}, which has no connection whatever with 13^{1-6}, makes an admirable sequel to 11^{15-17}. But scarcely any two critics are agreed as to the historical background or implications of the prophecy. The clause on which everything has been made to turn, *I cut off the three shepherds in one month* (11^{8a}), besides being capable of interpretation in a great variety of ways, is believed by Sellin and other scholars to be an interpolation, in which case it cannot be used as a key to the meaning of the passage. Some take the *month* literally, others as implying a short period, others as several years, even centuries. The three shepherds have been taken to represent kings, or even empires, but are most commonly believed to stand for three successive high priests of the Maccabean period (2d century B.C.). In this overwhelming uncertainty it will be enough to admit with Driver that the expression "does seem to point to three definite persons, though our knowledge of the history does not enable us to say who they are. We are equally unable to explain with certainty other historical allusions in the prophecy."

But our difficulties do not end here. Usually 11^{4-14} is regarded as describing the conduct and the destiny of the faithful shepherd, and 11^{15-17} 13^{7-9} as describing the conduct and fate of the false shepherd. But some scholars believe that 13^{7-9} describes the fate of the good shepherd (cf. Mt. 26^{31}), while Mitchell thinks that both shepherds are bad, the one he describes as "the careless shepherd" (11^{4-14}), and the other as "a foolish shepherd" (11^{15-17} 13^{7-9}). The terms of the prophecy may have been intentionally obscured: the initiated among the writer's contemporaries would understand. But we, who are not in his secret, are not in a position to dogmatize. It will be a good exercise of the critical judgment for the reader to note, as he studies the passage for himself, expressions which create the ambiguity by lending themselves to either interpretation; e.g., could a good shepherd as well as a bad say of his sheep, *my soul was weary of them?* (11^{8b}.) Could a bad shepherd as well as a good be described as *my* (i.e., Jehovah's) *shepherd and the man that is my fellow?* (13^{7}.)

Our view of the passage will be determined by our answers to these and similar questions. In any case it is clear that the prophet has an inward call to impersonate first one shepherd and then another ($11^{4, 15}$). The shepherd represents the ruler, and the flock the people; in this way the prophet brings vividly home the quality of the rulers and the nature of the popular response to them.

4-14. The Faithful Shepherd. The people are like sheep, heartlessly bought and sold by the very *shepherds*, i.e., rulers, who ought to protect them and who actually have the effrontery to thank *Jehovah* (they appear to be native, not foreign rulers) for their ill-gotten gain (v. 5). So the prophet is summoned to *feed*, or, rather, *shepherd* (i.e., act the *rôle* of shepherd to) this flock exposed to *slaughter* (v. 4)—especially in view of the anarchy that is coming upon the earth (v. 6, not the *land*). The prophet did as he was told and took upon himself the task of shepherding, which had been so heartlessly performed by *those who had trafficked in the flock* (as, with LXX, we should read in v. 7 for *verily the poor of the flock*). Like the Oriental shepherd (cf. Psa. 23^{4}) he equipped himself with two staffs, named *Grace* and *Union* (v. 7, mg.), to symbolize respectively the divine *favor* by which Jehovah had guaranteed Israel against invasion by the neighboring peoples (v. 10) and the *unity* that should subsist between the two great sections of the people (v. 14). But the flock rejected this good shepherd (v. 8a is probably a gloss); so, growing impatient with them, he decided to shepherd them no longer, but to abandon them to internecine strife (vv. 8f.). To symbolize this decision, he broke the staffs, first the one (v. 10) and then the other (v. 14)—an act which made it plain to those who had *trafficked in the flock* (v. 11, cf. v. 7) and who had been *watching* him, that he was indeed a messenger of Jehovah (v. 11).

The shepherd then asked for his wages (vv. 12, 13); and their contemptuous response —*thirty shekels of silver* (about $25), which was the compensation for an injured slave (cf. Ex. 21^{32})—showed how meanly they thought of him and his services. And not only of him, but of the God who had appointed him, for he deposits the money in the treasury of *Jehovah's house*, i.e., the Temple (for *potter* read *treasury*, which is very similar in Hebrew)—a symbol that Jehovah had been insulted in the person of his prophet.

15-17. The False Shepherd. (See also 13^{7-9}.) Next the prophet impersonates a *foolish, worthless* (v. 17), wicked shepherd who cares nothing for the sheep when lost, scattered, bruised or hungry (for *sound* in v. 16 read *hungry*)—symbol of the ruler who neglects his people. In the shock of war he will meet his doom—paralysis and blindness. The sword is summoned to execute the doom, and the fall of the shepherd will involve the dispersal of the flock (13^{7}), two thirds of which will perish; but the surviving third, purified by trial, will become the devoted people of their God. Here we come upon Isaiah's doctrine of the remnant (cf. Isa. 37^{32}), through whom the religious mission and testimony of Israel will be carried on.

It is impossible to read of the insulting response accorded by the people to the good shepherd (11^{12}) without feeling how prophetic the passage is. Israel had not had a superabundance of good shepherds in the course of her history (cf. Ezek. 34); but when the greatest Shepherd of all came, ready to lay down his life for the sheep (cf. Jn. 10^{15}), he was despised and rejected, sold for the price of a slave (Mt. 26^{15}) and nailed to a cross. "The guilty sacrifice the innocent, but in this execute their own doom. That is a summary of the history of Israel" (G. A. Smith).

CHAPTER XII

The Heathen Assault upon Jerusalem. Her Deliverance, Penitence, and Purification. (12^{1-14}; including also 13^{1-6}.) The Jews were keenly conscious of their religious pre-eminence among the nations; in later times this contrast assumed the form of *Judæa contra mundum.* The nations, first her neighbors (12^{2}), then all the nations (12^{9}), are conceived as organizing a stupendous assault upon Jerusalem, which is not only defended (12^{8}), but crowned with victory, by the power of her God. With this political transformation is allied the more attractive thought of her religious transformation (12^{10}–13^{6}).

This passage, like the last ($11^{4f.}$), is beset by difficulties, the chief of which is created by the mention of Judah. Certain verses (e.g., $12^{2, 7}$) suggest a rivalry and even a conflict between Judah and Jerusalem; but it seems best, on the whole, with Sellin, to regard Judah as practically synonymous with Jerusalem and its immediate environment (except in v. 7, which may be a Maccabean gloss).

1-9. The Assault and Deliverance. The prophet anticipates a *siege* of Jerusalem (v. 2: omit *upon Judah also*), which is compared to a *heavy stone* (v. 3) which will but tear the hands of the nations that seek to lift it; for all their efforts, she will remain firmly planted and prosperous on her own site (v. 6), supported as she is by the God of the universe (v. 1). In v. 2 she is compared to a *cup of reeling*, i.e., a huge bowl, from which her assailants will drink to intoxication and then *reel* to their ruin. Their destruction will be created by a panic (v. 4; cf. Deut. 28^{28}), of which Judah, enjoying the favor of God (v. 4b), will take advantage to consume the enemy, all of them (v. 9), like *devouring fire* (v. 6). The weakest Jew would prove as strong as David, and the descendants of David like God himself (v. 8)—inspired with supernatural *strength* by Jehovah of hosts (v. 5).

10–14. Penitential Mourning. But penitence is a greater quality than strength, and forgiveness is more than victory. So the outpouring of the divine *spirit* impels the people, high and low, to *supplicate* Jehovah's favor and forgiveness for some great crime in which they had all had a share (v. 14). Some noble representative of Jehovah had been martyred (*pierced*, v. 10; read *they shall look upon him*, not *me*), and they are now filled with shame and sorrow. Who this martyr was we have no means of knowing. Those who see in 13^{7} a reference to the fate of the good shepherd naturally connect this passage with that; in any case it is tempting to connect this martyr with the shepherd who in $11^{12f.}$ was treated with such cruel ingratitude. Every family in the land would *mourn*, or, rather, *wail*, for their share in this public crime (v. 14): the princely and the priestly families are perhaps singled out as specially guilty (vv. 12f. *Nathan* was a son of David, 2 Sam. 5^{14}, and *Shimei* a grandson of Levi, Num. 3^{21}.) The monotony of the repetition in vv. 12–14 suggests the mourning litanies, and the bitterness of the wailing (v. 10) is compared to the bitterness of the *wailing for Hadad-rimmon* (v. 11), a deity with a compound name whose worship may have been akin to or confused with Tammuz (i.e., Adonis), whom Ezekiel (8^{14}) represents the women of his time as bewailing. (This seems better than to regard Hadad-rimmon as a place in *the valley of Megiddo* where Josiah was slain, 2 Kings 23^{29}, cf. 2 Chr. 35^{25}, for in any case the wailing for Josiah would have taken place at Jerusalem, where he was buried, 2 Kings 23^{30}.)

CHAPTER XIII

1–6. Forgiveness and Reformation. (See also opening paragraphs under ch. 12 above.) Just as there were ceremonial lustrations to purify from physical uncleanness (Num. 19), so a fountain would be permanently opened to cleanse the stain of this crime and every stain upon the soul; in particular, the stain of *idolatry*, which in Ezek. 36^{25} is associated with uncleanness. But much more than idolatry does false *prophecy* receive prominence in this passage: indeed, whereas Jeremiah (ch. 23) and Ezekiel (ch. 13) condemn false prophecy, here all prophecy seems to be condemned—a fact which shows that the era of prophecy is passing away. A prophet is an impostor; and any man who poses as such must be put to death by his own parents (cf. Deut. $13^{6f.}$ $18^{20f.}$). The prophet will discard the insignia (cf. 2 Kings 1^{8}) of his disgraceful profession (v. 4), and will hasten to repudiate his professional status, claiming to be but a simple peasant (the last clause of v. 5 should read *the soil has been my possession from my youth*); and if anyone should point to the marks on his breast such as the Baal prophets inflicted on themselves (cf. 1 Kings 18^{28}) as evidence that he is a prophet after all, he will explain them as wounds he had received from his *friends*, possibly his parents, for attempting to play the prophet.

The finest thought in the passage (12^{1}–13^{6}) is that the deliverance of Jerusalem inspires her people not to transports of jubilation, but to profound penitence for the shepherd whom they had rejected and slain. In Rev. 1^{7} the passage receives a stern turn; it is with remorse that those who had pierced him will look upon him.

7–9. See notes under 11^{4-17}.

CHAPTER XIV

The Final Assault upon Jerusalem. The Issue in the Universal Recognition and Worship of Jehovah as King. In a general way this chapter duplicates ch. 12, but there are significant differences. There Jerusalem was inviolable (12^{8}), here she is captured (14^{2}). There her deliverance was followed by the penitence and inward transformation of the people (12^{10}), here by pilgrimages of the lately hostile nations to Jerusalem. This chapter is less profound and spiritual and moves upon a more legalistic level; the nations express their allegiance to Jehovah by taking part in the feast of Tabernacles.

1–5. Jehovah Fights Against the Heathen Assailants of Jerusalem. All the nations are conceived as assaulting Jerusalem and perpetrating within her all the horrors of war; but Jehovah works a miracle for her, splitting by an earthquake the Mount of Olives in two, half of it moving to the north and half to the south, leaving from west to east *a great valley* or gorge, through which the people remaining in the city might escape. (*The earthquake in the days of Uzziah* (Amos 1^{1}), which their flight recalls, must have made a stupendous impression, as it had occurred four hundred years before.) One effect of the cleaving of the Mount of Olives is that (the spring of) *Gihon* on the east of the city *shall be stopped, for the gorge of the mountains shall reach to the side of it*, as we should probably read with Mitchell in v. 5a. (Others emend "the valley of *Hinnom* shall be stopped"—less probably, as this was west and south of the city, not east.) The *holy ones* of v. 5 are the angels (cf. Job 5[1]).

6–11. Climate and Scenery Miraculously Transformed. This miraculous deliverance will have its physical counterpart in the transformation of nature. In that great day cold and frost would be no more (v. 6, LXX), nor would there be alternating day and night (v. 7), but only *one* continuous *day*, with evening clear as the morning; and running water, without which there could be no Paradise for the denizens of that dry and rugged region, would be there in abundance—one stream flowing into the Dead Sea, another into the Mediterranean, never drying up in summer, like many a Palestinian stream. The rugged mountain land of Judah from north to south (*Geba* six miles northeast of Jerusalem; *Rimmon*, about ten miles north of Beersheba) would become level like a plain (*the Arabah* is the Jordan Valley) above which Jerusalem would rise conspicuous with *Benjamin's gate* at the northeast corner, another unnamed *corner-gate* at the northwest, *the tower of Hananel* near the northeast corner, and the *king's winepresses* at the southeast. Best of all would be the universal recognition of Jehovah as the only God and *King over all the earth* (v. 9). Idolatry abolished; monotheism triumphant.

12–15. The Fate of the Hostile Heathen. This fair vision is followed by two appalling pictures of the fate of Jerusalem's foes. In vv. 13f. they are seized by a panic in which they slay one another, and, the tables now turned (v. 1), Jerusalem seizes the abundant spoil. More terrible is the other picture (vv. 12, 15) in which man and beast, smitten as by some supernaturally swift stroke of leprosy, *rot away while they stand on their feet.*

16–21. The Universal Worship of Jehovah. So fearful a judgment brings *all who are left of the nations* to their senses. They confess their allegiance to *the King* (v. 9), *Jehovah of Hosts*, by making an annual pilgrimage to Jerusalem *to keep* the greatest of the Hebrew feasts, *the feast of tabernacles* or Ingathering (Ex. 23[16]) at the end of the agricultural year, in honor of Jehovah who crowns the year with his goodness (Psa. 65[11]) by blessing the land with rain. Should any nation decline to come, Jehovah would punish it by withholding his rain (vv. 16f.). But as this threat could not terrify Egypt, whose fertility depended not upon rain but upon the Nile, a special punishment would be reserved for her (vv. 18f.). In that blessed day the distinction between the holy and the profane would be done away, for all Judah and everything in it would be holy. The *horses*, once shunned (cf. Hos. 14[3]) as symbolic of war (see note on 9[9]), now ridden not by warriors, but by pilgrims, are holy. Holy too are the *pots*—not the Temple pots alone, but *every pot in Jerusalem and Judah*, so that any one of them can be used for boiling the sacrificial flesh (cf. Lev. 6[28]).

The religious temper of this chapter has unattractive and unprophetic traits. The picture of the enemies rotting away as they stand upon their feet is repellent, and an allegiance to Jehovah expressed in terms of a pilgrimage to Jerusalem to keep the feast of Tabernacles is conceived in the priestly rather than in the prophetic spirit. But the passage is redeemed by its confidence in the ultimate triumph of monotheism and by its vision of a day when Jehovah would be King over all the earth.

MALACHI

By Professor J. E. McFadyen

Introduction

Date and Background. Malachi's prophecy may be set somewhere about 460 B.C. (For a full discussion of the date see Eiselen, *Prophetic Books of the O.T.*, vol. ii, pp. 596–602.) The Temple, on whose construction Haggai and Zechariah had set such high hopes, is standing (1^{10}), but the whole book pathetically shows how deeply those hopes had been disappointed. (See Eiselen, *Prophetic Books*, vol. ii, p. 605.) The intervening sixty years or so had been years of disillusion and misery, and the situation to which Malachi addresses himself is melancholy beyond words. (For a description of the general historical situation during this period see intro. to Ezra-Nehemiah, pp. 458–61.) A curse is lying upon the land (3^{9}). Translated into concrete terms, the curse may seem to be nothing more than the not unfamiliar experience of drought and locusts ($3^{10f.}$), but it goes far deeper than that. The blight is on men's hearts and on their faith.

Religious Indifference. As in pre-exilic times, popular religion is now largely a matter of ritual; but whereas in the days of Isaiah (cf. 1^{11}) and Micah (cf. $6^{6f.}$), the ritualists were in deadly earnest, willing and eager to render a service of extravagant devotion, in Malachi's time apathy and niggardliness prevailed. Priests and people alike were guilty. The laymen made vows which they did not keep, acting as if anything were good enough for God. They offered blemished and imperfect beasts for sacrifice (1^{14}). They robbed God, by keeping back the tithes and offerings ($3^{8f.}$). The priests appear, if possible, in a still more unlovely light. They had traveled pitifully far from the ancient ideals of their order (2^{5-9}). They offer blind, lame, and sick animals, which they would be ashamed and afraid to offer to the Persian governor, yet they say (1^{8-13}), "Where's the harm." They groan under their professional obligations, and mutter, as they conduct the service (1^{13}), "What a bore it is!" thus treating the holy name with a hardly disguised contempt.

Skepticism and Social Corruption. This low religious life had its counterpart, as was inevitable, in an equally low social life. Adultery and perjury and exploitation of the poor were rife (3^{5}). Families were torn with dissension (4^{6}), among the well-to-do divorce was the order of the day (2^{14}), and in many cases the motive to it was the desire to marry a younger foreign woman (2^{11}), though she was likely to be a menace to the purer faith of the Hebrews. A spirit of skepticism too was abroad. The word of the prophet was challenged at every turn; notice the frequency of the phrase "But ye say" (cf. $1^{2,\,6}$, etc.). Worse still, the ways of God were challenged. Belief in his love had vanished (1^{2}). The world was turned upside down (2^{17}) and it seemed idle to serve God. There was no "profit" in it (3^{14})—a phrase significant of the utilitarian quality of contemporary religion. And the sad thing was that these challenges were uttered, not by blasphemers, but by good and pious men, who, seeing no traces of a moral order, cried in the anguish of their doubt (2^{17}), "Where is the God of Justice?"

Message of Malachi. Such was the situation which Malachi, or, better, the anonymous author of the prophecy (see comment on 1^{1}), had to face. He met it, on the one hand, by reminding the people that God's seeming indifference to them was due to their real indifference to him (cf. $3^{9f.}$); and, on the other, by assuring them that a day of judgment was coming speedily ($3^{1,\,5}$), in which destiny would correspond to character (3^{18}–4^{3}), and that meantime God had not forgotten them—the names of the good were being faithfully recorded in his book (3^{16}).

Malachi is not one of the giants of prophecy. His interest in ritual, his attitude to Edom (1^{3}), and his restriction of the Fatherhood of God to the Jewish people (2^{10}) stamp him as sharing the conventional opinions of his contemporaries. But in two respects he soars far above them—in his detestations of divorce (2^{16}), which Deuteronomy (24^{1}) had permitted, and in his magnificent recognition of all sincere heathen worship as being in reality offered to and accepted by Jehovah, the one God of all the earth (1^{11}). In these great words we breathe the very atmosphere of the N.T. (cf. Eph. 5^{28-33} Acts 10^{35}).

The book has been aptly described as "Prophecy within the Law." On the one hand, it reaffirms the truths taught by the great pre-exilic prophets, such as Jehovah's fatherly and loving care for Israel, his holiness and righteousness, the terrible judgment awaiting the wicked, and the exaltation of the righteous. On the other hand, unlike the earlier prophets, it places great stress on the Law as a disciplinary rule of life, bitterly condemns its lax observance, and closes with the exhortation, "Remember ye the law of Moses, my servant."

In fairness to Malachi the second characteristic must not be allowed to overshadow the first. True, he shared with other religious leaders of the postexilic period a high regard for the forms and institutions of religion, including the Law; but this new emphasis was due, not to lower religious conceptions, but to a different interpretation of the religious need of the hour (see on Haggai). He saw, as many others must have seen, that, after all, prophecy, as represented by the pre-exilic prophets, had failed to produce the transformation for which they had toiled so persistently. Generation after generation they had sought to build up a pure and holy nation, but after the lapse of centuries the people appeared to be as far from the ideal as ever.

Consequently, the question must have arisen in the minds of many whether the prophetic method was the one best adapted to the needs of the time, whether the people could be trusted to apply the principles of prophetic religion to the daily life or whether it would not be wiser to lay down specific rules and urge the people to observe these, and thus avoid the lapses of the past. The last question was answered in the affirmative, and the postexilic legalism was the result. However, in the beginning it was permeated by a spirit of intense moral earnestness; the exaltation of the letter of the Law is a later development. Malachi was a prophet as truly as were Isaiah and Jeremiah; but, unlike them, he emphasized the embodiment of the prophetic spirit and principles in external law.

Literature: Perowne, *Haggai, Zechariah, Malachi* (Cambridge Bible); Driver, *The Minor Prophets*, vol. ii (New Century Bible); Eiselen, *The Minor Prophets;* G. A. Smith, *The Book of the Twelve*, vol. ii (Expositor's Bible); Bennett, *The Postexilic Prophets;* D. Macfadyen, *The Messenger of God;* Sanders and Kent, *The Messages of the Later Prophets.*

CHAPTER I

1. Title. This book (cf. Zech. 9[1] 12[1]) is anonymous. The name *Malachi*, which means *my servant* (or "my messenger," or, by contraction, *servant* [messenger] *of Jehovah*), was apparently borrowed by the editor from 3[1].

2–5. Jehovah's Love for Israel. Malachi begins well—by emphasizing Jehovah's *love* for Israel. But the people whom he addresses find it difficult to believe in that love, for they see no evidence of it. They are a disillusioned and disappointed people. The daring promises of Haggai (cf. 2[6-9, 20f.]) and Zechariah (ch. 8) remained, after sixty or seventy years, unfulfilled; and the whole book is darkened by the skepticism of the people. Everything the prophet says is challenged; *but ye say.* The proof he offers them of the love of God is as unlovely as could be; it is that *I hated Esau*, i.e., Edom (cf. Gen. 36[1]), and the proof of that again is that Edom's mountainous land has been recently *desolated*—apparently by an Arab invasion from the south. From time immemorial (cf. Gen. 25[23]) Israel and Edom had been deadly enemies (cf. Psa. 137[7]), and the desolation of Edom Malachi interpreted as Jehovah's *indignation* at and *hatred* of her, and as proof of his *love* for Israel, who, when they *see* the desolation, will be convinced that their own God is no petty national God, but is *great beyond the border of Israel*—is, indeed, the God of all the earth (cf. v. 11).

6–14. The Clergy with the Low Ideals. Israel had answered Jehovah's love with ingratitude—especially the *priests* (v. 6), who, though responsible for the worship, had acted as if anything were good enough for God. *Father* (cf. 2[10]) and *Master*, as Jehovah was, they had shown him neither *honor* nor *fear* (i.e., reverence), but *contempt*, evidenced by the *polluted bread*, i.e., sacrificial flesh, they offered him, polluted by the spirit of irreverence in which it was offered; for they said—not, indeed, in words, but in their hearts—*the table of Jehovah*, i.e., the altar, is *contemptible.* Note how the priests, like the people, challenged every word of the prophet—*ye say* (vv. 6, 7). There was a law against offering blemished animals (Deut. 17[1]), but they had coolly disregarded it by offering animals that were *blind, lame,* or *sick* (v. 8), which they would not have dared to offer to the Persian *governor* of Judah (v. 8). *It is no evil*, i.e., there is no harm in it, they said. The appeal to the priests—such priests—to *entreat the favor of God* (v. 9) is ironical rather than a call to repentance. If *this* is the sort of sacrifice you offer (see mg. *from your hand*), can you expect him to look upon you with favor? Better *close* the Temple *doors* and extinguish the *altar* fires—which are but kindled *in vain*—than have the worship conducted by such low-minded, half-hearted ministers (v. 10). The great God of hosts can accept no *offering* at the *hands* of men like these. Sincerity in public worship meant much to Malachi. He virtually says, "Give God the best you have, or bring the worship to an end and get out of his service altogether."

Then follows one of the greatest utterances in the O.T., which stamps Malachi as a prophet indeed (v. 11). He reminds the unworthy priests that *among the Gentiles,* i.e., the heathen nations whom Israel despised, from east to west Jehovah's *name* was *great*—twice over—and that in *every place* across the world *pure offerings,* i.e., offerings unstained by irreverence —unlike those presented by his own people at Jerusalem—were offered to his name. This noble word of Malachi virtually recognizes all sincere worship, wheresoever and by whomsoever offered, as in reality offered to Jehovah (cf. Jonah 1[16]), the God therefore not of the Jews only but of all the earth. In sorrowful contrast with this is the worship of the Jews who, despite Jehovah's love for them (1[2], Amos 3[2]), *profane* his name (v. 12) by their blemished offerings (v. 13; for *that which was taken by violence* read *the blind;* the *fruit* and *meat* of v. 12 are just the sacrificial offerings). We cannot wonder at Malachi's stern condemnation of ministers of religion (cf. 2[3]) who said of the worship they were conducting (v. 13), *What a bore it is!* And the laymen who brought these *blemished things* to be offered (v. 14) were as guilty as the priests; so *a curse* upon them too! The peculiar shame of it all was that the God to whom these disgraceful offerings were presented was *a great King,* whose name, thus dishonored by the Jews, was *reverenced* (not *terrible*) among the Gentiles.

CHAPTER II

1–9. The Doom of the Clergy. For their careless and contemptuous conduct of the worship (1[6-13]), for not giving *glory* to Jehovah's name (v. 2), the word of *doom* (rather than *commandment,* v. 1) is now pronounced. Their *blessings,* i.e., the prestige and privileges of the priesthood, would be turned into *curses* (v. 2; cf. Deut. 28[20]). The opening words of doom, (v. 3), *Behold, I will hew off your arm* (which should be read instead of *I will rebuke the seed for your sake*), are very vigorous, implying that they would be forcibly deprived of their power and authority; and insult would be added to injury, for they would be bespattered with *the dung of their sacrifices,* and dragged away to the dung-heap! Then they would realize—when for them it would be too late—on what terms alone the *covenant with Levi* (v. 8, or "the sons of Levi," 3[3], i.e., the priests) could stand.

Then follows a beautiful description of the ideal minister (vv. 5–7)—an ideal so grossly violated by the priests (v. 8). *Life* and all that makes life worth living, *peace,* i.e., not only quiet of soul but welfare of every kind—these were the things that Jehovah promised and *gave* in the *covenant;* to this the true priest responded with *fear,* i.e., reverence, and humble *awe* (v. 5). He faithfully expounded the will of God, and he could do this because *in peace and uprightness he walked with God,* and did not merely talk about him, which is the preacher's temptation. *Knowledge* and *law,* i.e., true direction, could be sought from him by the perplexed (v. 7), and by his earnest instruction of them in the will of God *he turned many away from iniquity* (v. 6), for he was nothing less than Jehovah's *messenger* (the same word as *angel*). What a glorious ideal! The true priest is a veritable angel of God.

To this noble ideal, however, the priests of Malachi's time had proved utterly recreant. They had *turned aside out of the way* of life, peace, and reverence (v. 5), the noble way in which they had walked with God (v. 6); blind leaders of the blind, they had *in the law,* i.e., by their direction, *caused many to stumble,* and had *corrupted* (or ruined) *the covenant* which it was theirs to maintain (v. 8). But such things cannot be done by religious leaders with impunity. *Therefore have I also* (v. 9)—God on his part will deal with these men as they deserve by bringing their prestige and popularity to an end. *I will* (for *have*) *assuredly make* (for *made*) *you contemptible and base before all the people. Noblesse oblige,* and in the long run even a trustful people will despise the clergy who fall too pitifully below their ideal.

10–16. The Prophet's Challenge of Divorce. Malachi now turns to the laymen, for with them—with the people as a whole—Jehovah had a *covenant* (v. 10) as well as with the priests (vv. 4, 8). This covenant was being *profaned* by the people, who *played the traitor against one another,* an offense all the more despicable that, as Jehovah was the *father* of them *all* (not of all men, but of all Israel—cf. Isa. 1[2]); they were brethren and should have behaved like brethren. But they had profaned the covenant and *the holiness of Jehovah* by marrying foreign women. Each of these women, as *the daughter of a strange god* (v. 11, just as the Israelites were sons of Jehovah, v. 10), was a menace to the *holiness,* the distinctive religious and ethical quality, of the Hebrew faith. These were probably wealthy women of the neighboring peoples, e.g., Philistia, Moab, Ammon; but they would bring their alien religion into the Hebrew home, with the result that the Hebrew faith would be contaminated and Hebrew distinctiveness so obliterated that the children could not even speak proper Hebrew (cf. Neh. 13[23f.]). The prophet's threats are that such traitors will in the end be deprived of all civil and religious rights (v. 12).

Worse still, these marriages with foreign women had led to the divorce of native Hebrew women. Therein lay the climax of the *treachery*, that *the wife of thy covenant*, i.e., pledged to thee in a marriage contract which has been solemnly *witnessed* before and by Jehovah himself, should be repudiated in favor of an alien (v. 14)—the *wife* too *of thy youth*, the faithful companion of many years, discarded, when she is old, for a young and handsome stranger. It was for treachery like this that Jehovah had refused to *regard* their *offerings* and had shown his displeasure by sending some disaster, such as drought (cf. 3^{10}), which had led the people, in the passion of their grief, to *cover the altar with their tears* (v. 13). This treachery of divorce must therefore be abandoned. Besides, did he, i.e., God, not make man and wife *one* (cf. Gen. 2^{24})—one flesh and one life (literally, breath)? "But what else," they reply, "does God want but *seed*, i.e., children? It is therefore no crime to divorce an older woman for an younger one." To which Malachi replies, "Beware, the life of the two is one, and it dies if sundered by divorce." This appears to be the meaning of the very difficult v. 15; and this great defense of the sanctity of the marriage-bond concludes with the glorious word, which definitely anticipates N.T. teaching and again stamps Malachi as a prophet indeed, *I hate divorce* (v. 16; the next clause may refer to violence done to the wife—that too is detestable).

17. See under 3^{1-5}.

CHAPTER III

1–5. The Prophet's Challenge of the Popular Skepticism. This section, which begins with 2^{17}, goes to the root of the matter. The real reason which explains, on the one hand, the unworthy conduct of priests and people and, on the other, the misery of the times and the withholding of the divine blessing (cf. v. 10) is that they have all alike lost faith in God. Even good men have grown skeptical, for it should be carefully noted that 2^{17} and $3^{14f.}$ are the words, not of blasphemers or of the indifferent, but of God-fearing men. It looks as if God favored and prospered the wicked, and the good ask in despair, *Where is the God of justice?* (2^{17}.) Malachi's answer is that he is *coming, suddenly* and soon (3^{1}). His *messenger* is already on the way, to clear away the obstacles created by the people's sin, and the messenger will be followed by *the Lord* himself. But *when he appears* only the purest will be able to *stand* his searching test; for he will come to cleanse in a *purifying* judgment, like the *fire* which separates the base metal from the true (v. 2). And this judgment will fall first upon *the sons of Levi* (cf. 2^{4}), i.e., the priests, as the most highly privileged (cf. 2^{5-7}), the most responsible, and the most guilty. When the judgment has done its purifying work upon them, then their offerings would be accepted *as in the days of old* (vv. 3, 4). But the people, as we have seen (cf. 1^{14} 2^{10-16}), are no less guilty than the priests; so to them too *I will come near in judgment* (v. 5). Their crimes are summarized as sorcery, adultery, perjury, exploitation of the poor and defenseless, crimes which have their root and explanation in the lack of religion, for *they fear not me* (v. 5)—a profound diagnosis. This verse is peculiarly welcome as showing that Malachi, interested in ritual as he was, yet breathes the true spirit of the pre-exilic prophets with their emphasis upon the moral life of society.

6–12. The Prophet's Challenge of the People's Failure to Pay the Sanctuary Dues. V. 6 should probably read *For I, Jehovah, change not; but as for you, ye have never ceased to be sons of Jacob*, veritable tricksters. They had *robbed God* (v. 8) from the beginning (v. 7); that was why they were cursed (v. 9) with drought (v. 10). They had robbed him by failing to bring in, as the Law demanded (cf. Deut. 14^{22-27} Lev. 27^{30-32}), the *tithes* and *offerings* into the *storehouse* or treasury of the Temple. Dishonesty had brought a curse in the form of drought and the devouring locust (v. 11); let them *return to Jehovah* (v. 7) and show their penitence by paying their dues, and Jehovah would, in return, send his blessed rain in abundance from heaven (v. 10). Their prosperity would be so conspicuous that they would be the envy of *all nations* (v. 12).

13–18. Comfort for the Disconsolate. Again the old challenge (cf. 2^{17} 3^{5}) of God's ways with men, uttered as before (2^{17}) by the pious (3^{14}) who *feared Jehovah* (v. 16; the *then* should be *thus*, and their speech is in vv. 14, 15), but whose religion had a utilitarian tinge. They looked for *profit* (v. 14) from their service of God, but their obedience seemed unrewarded, while it was the *wicked* who were *built up* in prosperity (v. 15). Malachi comforts them by assuring them that they were not forgotten; *a book of remembrance* was being written, i.e., a book in which their names were recorded (cf. Esth. 6) and which would keep Jehovah in mind of them (v 16). In the day of judgment, *the day when I act*, i.e., interpose (rather than *that I do make*, cf. 4^{3}), they would not only be *spared*, but they would be Jehovah's *peculiar treasure*, specially guarded and specially dear (v. 17); and then they would see the difference that they cannot now *discern between the righteous and the wicked.*

CHAPTER IV

1–3. The Differing Destinies of Righteous and Wicked. The difference in the destinies of the righteous and the wicked would be infinite —for the wicked, a fire would *burn them up, root and branch* (v. 1); while upon the righteous the *sun* would *arise* in whose light they would be vindicated, and from whose *wings*, i.e., rays, would stream *healing* for wounded hearts and minds perplexed (v. 2). In their joy they would *frisk like calves*, and part of that joy would be to *trample the wicked* like *ashes* under the soles of their feet. This ugly vindictive trait reminds us how fierce the temper even of the later time could be, and how far we still are from the Spirit of Jesus (cf. Zech. 14[12]).

4–6. Concluding Appeal and Promise. The book concludes with an appeal to *remember the law of Moses* (probably Deuteronomy, whose ritual and ethical demands had been violated), and with a promise of the return of Elijah, who had left the world about four hundred years before; a promise which suggests that the age of the prophets is now felt to be over; and when he comes his business will be to restore harmony in the homes which had been ruined (cf. Mic. 7[5f.]) by divorce (2[10-16]); otherwise the land would be smitten with destruction.

IV. ARTICLES
THE NEW TESTAMENT

THE HISTORICAL AND RELIGIOUS BACKGROUNDS OF THE EARLY CHRISTIAN MOVEMENT

THE FORMATION OF THE NEW TESTAMENT

THE TRANSMISSION OF THE NEW TESTAMENT

THE STRUCTURE OF THE SYNOPTIC GOSPELS

THE CHRONOLOGY OF THE NEW TESTAMENT

THE LANGUAGE OF THE NEW TESTAMENT

THE NEW TESTAMENT AND CRITICISM

THE LIFE OF JESUS CHRIST

THE TEACHING OF JESUS

THE PARABLES OF JESUS

THE MIRACLES OF THE NEW TESTAMENT

THE LIFE AND WORK OF PAUL

THE NEW TESTAMENT AND CHRISTIAN DOCTRINE

THE HISTORICAL AND RELIGIOUS BACKGROUNDS OF THE EARLY CHRISTIAN MOVEMENT

By Canon GEORGE H. BOX

I. Survey of Post-Exilic Judaism

The Christian movement began its development in Palestine, in a Jewish environment, and therefore can properly be understood only in the light of contemporary Palestinian Judaism. It is true there was a larger Judaism, extended over the Græco-Roman world, which exercised a profound influence over the Judaism of Palestine, and also played a great part in the expansion of Christianity in the apostolic age and later. And here we are brought into closer touch with the manifold foreign influences which streamed in from the pagan world. These factors it will be necessary to consider in the latter part of this article. Our immediate task is to attempt to reconstruct the salient features of this Palestinian environment.

Devotion to the Law. The Judaism which flourished at this time in Palestine was a much more variegated and complex thing than the purely rabbinical Judaism which succeeded it in the reorganization that followed the destruction of Jerusalem in 70 A.D. In order to realize this it is only necessary to remember the various sects and parties which were active down to 70 A.D. Then, too, while the Temple existed it constituted a rallying spot and a spiritual center for the whole Jewish world. Pilgrims were constantly streaming to Jerusalem at the great festivals, and in this way the Temple became a focus of the manifold influences which flowed in from the Dispersion (Diaspora). Throughout the world every Jew of mature years contributed to the upkeep of the Temple by the payment of the Temple tax, and in this way was made to feel a personal interest in the maintenance of the cultus. Nevertheless, perhaps the most striking development of Jewish piety that occurred in the period of late Judaism was the displacement of devotion to the cultus, as such, by devotion to the Law. Indications of this meet us in the Psalter. Whereas the earlier Psalms of the post-exilic period, such as Psa. 27, 84, 122, breathe the deepest affection for and joy in the religious activities of the Temple as a source of spiritual satisfaction, a different note is struck in Psa. 1, the second part of 19, and 119. Here every line breathes devotion to the Law. All this is but the expression of a profound conviction that God has chosen to make a supreme revelation of himself and his requirements in the divine Law; and that man is sanctified by the divine Law which is the very principle of his perfection. The Law thus came to occupy in Judaism exactly the same position as the Person of Christ and the Incarnation in the Christian religion. Jewish piety of this type exhausts and expresses itself in the minute and punctilious performance of the divine Law, especially as this was later elaborately codified and defined by the rabbis. The performance of these duties was regarded as exercising a sanctifying influence on the worshiper; he felt that by so doing he was obeying the divine voice; and in this utter obedience he found a real spiritual satisfaction. This devotion to the Law became firmly marked, as an indelible characteristic of orthodox Judaism, from the Maccabean period (see below and art., *Literature of the Intertestamental Period*, p. 199b). The persecution then endured made the practice and observance of the Law, for its own sake, a thing specially dear to pious Jews. Fidelity to the Law became the hallmark of Jewish piety; and though the stately ceremonial of the Temple went on in its full splendor for more than two centuries the real center of gravity in Judaism was no longer the Temple and its cultus but fidelity to the Law as such; so that when the ruin of the Temple came in 70 A.D., the reorganization of Judaism, on the basis of the Law, was effected without difficulty. Devotion to the Law, as such, determined the character of later Judaism.

Bousset points out in this connection certain indications of the process described above. These are: (1) The existence of the sect of the Essenes, who deliberately abstained from taking any part in the Temple animal-sacrifices, and yet were regarded by masses of the people as models of piety. (2) The general tendency of the preaching of Jesus. The features in popular piety which he attacked are the sins to which the legalistic type of religion is specially prone, namely, undue emphasis upon the external observance of the Sabbath, the importance attached to the distinction between clean and unclean, the hypocritical assumption of special holiness in prayer, almsgiving and fasting. On the other hand, of exaggerated estimation of the sacrifices of the cultus his invective takes little account. His opponents are the Pharisees and the teachers of the Law, not the Priests; the Law and not the cultus. Jesus, indeed, was possessed by a holy zeal for the Temple of Jehovah and its purity. (3) Another indication to which attention has already been called is to be seen in the ease with which rabbinical Judaism became the predominant factor after the destruction of the Temple in 70 A.D.

The Maccabean Revolt. The decisive dates of the period of Judaism with which we are primarily concerned are from the beginning of the Maccabean revolt to the final destruction of Jewish national independence in 70 A.D., and later in the Bar-Kokba revolt in 132–135 A.D. i.e., from about 166 B.C. to 135 A.D.—a period of about three centuries. During this fruitful epoch Jewish patriotism asserted itself through the Maccabean movement, and, for a time, won national independence. The effects of this development on Judaism as a whole were marked. The range of Jewish influence in Palestine was decisively extended. The community expanded on a large scale, and Judaism itself became intensely proud and self-conscious. These results were by no means destroyed when Judæa, her national independence finally lost, became a Roman province in 6 A.D. The national feeling flared up from time to time, and culminated finally in the disastrous rebellion against Rome, 66–70 A.D., which ended in the destruction of the Temple and the ruin of the Holy City. The party of peace, which had never approved of the rebellion, now for a time triumphed, and under Jochanan ben Zakkai, Judaism was reorganized at Jamnia. But the nationalist elements were by no means finally overcome, and rebellions broke out again, first in 117 A.D., and finally in the great revolt of 132–135, under Bar-Kokba, in which the most famous rabbi of the time, Akiba, took a prominent part, and, with other rabbis, suffered martydrom. After the suppression of the final rebellion, Judaism devoted its energies, without distraction, to the task of consolidating its life as a community primarily on a religious basis. The teachers of the Law were now supreme as leaders, and the Jews became "the People of the Book." This is the era of rabbinical Judaism or Talmudism.

Rise of Parties. During the three centuries already referred to, the great parties and sects of Judaism were developed into the form in which we meet with them in the N.T. period. By far the most important of these developments was the growth of the Pharisaic party, which first emerges distinctly in the reign of the Maccabean prince John Hyrcanus (135–105 B.C.), and of which it will be necessary to speak, in greater detail, later (see below).

An older party, which continued to play a prominent part as the opponents of the popular and nationalist Pharisees, was that of the Sadducees. This party was mainly recruited from the priests, and represented priestly tradition and privilege, as these had grown up in conjunction with the Temple and its cultus. Though the Sadducees embraced within their ranks the high-priestly families and their adherents (i.e., the priestly aristocracy), and though these often included a worldly element, Sadduceeism was by no means deficient in piety. It often represented the conservative type of Judaism at its best.

Apocalyptic Literature. This period also saw the remarkable development of the Apocalyptic literature, which is largely embodied in extra-canonical forms, such as the Book of Enoch. The oldest elements in the Enochic literature date from a time possibly slightly anterior to the book of Daniel (165 B.C.), and this literature culminates in the twin apocalypses of the Syriac Baruch and 4 Ezra (=2 Esdras, chs. 3-14), which may be dated in their final form about 120 A.D.

The importance of this literature lies, to a large extent, in the fact that it emanated from lay circles, outside the rabbinical schools. The Apocalyptists were not an organized party like the Pharisees, yet seem to represent a distinct tendency within Judaism. It is possible that circles of this kind may have flourished in Galilee. (Cf. p. 188.)

II. The Great Parties of Judaism

It will now be necessary to speak in greater detail of the parties and institutions of Judaism.

Pharisees and Sadducees. The *Pharisees*, as we have seen, emerge into prominence toward the end of the second century B.C. The movement was essentially a *lay* movement in its inception, and largely so remained. It is true that priests occasionally are found within its ranks, but this fact did not seriously modify its fundamentally lay character. The Pharisees, in fact, seem to have been originally a body of pious laymen who carried on the work of teaching the Scriptures to the people, which originally had been carried out by the priestly scribes, or *soferim*. The last great representative of this class seems to have been Simon the Just (died about 270 B.C.). The supply of priestly teachers had apparently broken down, and their places were taken by laymen, who afterward became the Pharisees.

As the present writer has said elsewhere: "The age-long conflict between the Sadducees and the Pharisees was the most important factor in the development of Judaism. The Pharisees were the champions of the oral Law which at first was quite independent of the written Tôrāh, and was deeply intrenched in old popular custom and usage. On the other hand, the Sadducees mainly represented the old conservative positions of the priesthood, and inherited the tradition of the older scribism. The 'scribe,' as he is depicted in Sirach (c. 190 B.C.), is a judge and man of affairs, a cultivated student of 'wisdom,' well acquainted, of course, with the contents of the written Law, and a frequenter of the courts of kings. He belongs to the leisured, aristocratic class and is poles asunder from the typical Pharisee and teacher of the Law, who was drawn from the ranks of the people. It was in the reaction against Hellenism that Tôrāh-study [study of the Law] was born. The public reading and exposition of it in the synagogue probably dates only from the Maccabean period. Both parties were compelled now to devote themselves to Tôrāh-study, in the new and exacting way demanded by the times, the Sadducees because, on their view, the Law was the only valid standard for fixing juristic and religious practice, and the Pharisees, because it was necessary for them to adjust their oral tradition, as far as possible, to the written word. The first result of Pharisaic activity in this direction was the development of a remarkably rich and subtle exegesis. A further result was the evolution of new laws by exegetical methods" (Hastings' *Encyc. of Religion and Ethics*, vol. ix, p. 833, art., "Pharisees").

The Pharisees exercised an enormous influence with the people, which was due to the fact that they spent their energies without stint in the work of instructing the people in the Tôrāh, and in bringing religion to bear upon the popular life. In marked contrast with those of the Sadducees, their judgments on questions of Law were, as is well known, of a mild and compassionate character. Their positive achievement in the domain of religious observance and institutions was enormous. They built up the synagogue service; they brought religion into the homes of the people; in particular, they invested the home with the sanctions of religion—the home service on Passover night, for example, became a solemn festival of joy, in which the head of the household acted as priest. Their religious ideals were essentially democratic in character. They championed popular religious customs against the rigid conservatism of the Sadducean priesthood. A good instance of this is the solemn procession in which water was transferred from the pool of Siloam and poured out at the base of the altar in the Temple on the feast of Tabernacles (cf. Jesus' words, Jn. 7[37f.]). This custom was opposed by the Sadducees on the ground that it had no sanction in the Law, but they were unable to resist the popular will. Then, again, the Pharisees boldly transferred the atoning power connected with the Day of Atonement from the high priest and the sacerdotal ceremonies in which he functioned to the day itself. Outside the Temple the influence of the Pharisees was supreme, and even within the Temple itself, which, of course, was under the control of the Sadducean priesthood, the influence of the Pharisees made itself felt in decisive fashion. This influence grew as time went on until, during the last ten or twenty years of the Temple's existence, the direction of its ceremonial was practically under the control of the Pharisees. In the Mishnah tractate, *Yoma*, which deals with the ceremonies of the Day of Atonement in the Temple, from the *Pharisaic point of view*, we are told that seven days before the Day of Atonement the high priest, who was, of course, a Sadducee, went into retreat surrounded by a sort of Pharisaic commission of teachers of the Law, who took care to see that this sacerdotal head should carry out the ceremonial of the day itself in accordance with Pharisaic ideas. The high priest was made to rehearse the various acts connected with the day, and was fully instructed in the meaning and rationale of the ceremonial as understood by Pharisees.

Pharisaic Schools. It is well known that in the time of our Lord the Pharisaic party was divided into two opposed schools—the school of *Hillel* and the school of *Shammai*. The former represented the more moderate elements while the latter was more aggressive. The Pharisees at this time were sharply divided into various sections which were not exhausted by the rival schools of Hillel and Shammai. It is probable that the school of Shammai at this period was in the ascendant, though later the milder school of the Hillelites secured the supremacy (after the destruction of Jerusalem). There appears to have been a section of the school of Shammai, consisting of extremists, who were bitter and exclusive and were open to the charge of formalism and hypocrisy. It is probable that our Lord's invective in the Gospels was primarily directed against this section. It is notorious that the Shammaites were rigorous to excess in their requirements, and were the champions of a narrow and exclusive form of legal piety. Their attitude to the outside world was also harsh and unsympathetic. The fanatical section of the Pharisees—the *Zealots*—were closely allied with them. It may plausibly be inferred, to take an example, that in the time of Christ the matter of ritual hand-washing before meals was a party issue, championed by the fanatical Shammaites, and that Jesus strongly opposed the Shammaite view (cf. Mk. 7). That the neglect by Jesus' disciples of the practice of ritual hand-washing was not a departure from general lay usage may be inferred from the Gospel account itself. No protest was raised against it, apparently, until a deputation of scribes from Jerusalem arrived on the scene; and what they objected to was that a teacher—a rabbi—should permit his disciples to neglect the rite. As has already been pointed out, the influence of the Shammaites, up to the catastrophe of 70 A.D., seems to have been in the ascendant; but later the peace-loving and milder party of Hillel triumphed, and the oral Law was revised to accord with Hillelite views.

It is impossible, owing to restrictions of space, to do more than refer to the *Essenes.* Though they are not referred to in the Bible, nor for certain in the rabbinical literature, they are mentioned quite explicitly by Josephus and Philo. From these sources they appear to have been formed of small communities leading a religious and communistic life on the shores of the Dead Sea. They were organized in several grades and formed a closely knit brotherhood. They attached great importance to purity of life, practiced daily lustration and rejected animal sacrifices. We may, to use Moffatt's words, see in this "little Jewish order of over four thousand souls a league of virtue, with their agricultural settlements, their quaint semi-ascetic practices, their strict novitiate, their silent meals, their white robes, their baths, their prayers, their simple but stringent socialism, their sacerdotal puritanism, their soothsaying, their passion for the mystical world of angels, their indifference to Messianic and nationalistic hopes, their esoteric beliefs, and their approximation to sacramental religion" (Hastings' *Encyc. of Religion and Ethics*, vol. v, p. 400, art., "Essenes"). In spite of assertions to the contrary there is little reason to believe that Esseneism influenced early Christianity in any appreciable degree.

III. Palestinian Languages

Before we come to importance of the apocalyptic literature and the apocalyptists, a word must be said on the question of the language or languages with which our Lord was familiar. It must be borne in mind that he spent his early life in Galilee, and that there were marked differences, in external conditions and in the general character of the population, between Galilee and Judæa.

Judæa was the central stronghold of everything Jewish, in the strict sense of the word. Galilee, on the other hand, as its original name "Galilee of the Gentiles" suggests, was more mixed in character. In the time of Jesus it was densely populated, and was full of bustling life. "There were settlers from the neighboring cities of Phœnicia, Greek colonists, Roman officers and soldiers; there were wanderers, too, from the wild deserts of the East, or travelers from Syria and Arabia, passing to and fro. Everywhere there was life, there was stir, there was energy; and Jesus, moving among these mingled elements, found a readier hearing for his word" (Carpenter, *Life in Palestine When Jesus Lived*, p. 19). The population was mixed, but at this time was predominantly Jewish. According to the Talmud, the Galilæans were quarrelsome, but they are said to have possessed certain good qualities. Widows were well treated. There were certain differences in marriage and funeral customs; the Galilæans are said to have been strict in their religious observances. They were not particularly fond of the dialectical methods which were so assiduously cultivated in Judæa.

On the other hand, they were adepts in the whole field of Haggadah, which included everything non-legalistic, such as tales, parables, sermons, etc. (For the meaning of the Talmudic terms Haggadah and Halakhah, see p. 456.) Indeed, according to the Jewish scholar Geiger, the origin of the Haggadah must be ascribed to the Galilæans. It is interesting to note that the Galilæan pronunciation, especially of the gutturals, is ridiculed in the Talmud, as it is noticed in the Gospels (cf. Mt. 26^{73}), and by rabbinical enactment no Galilæan could act as reader of public prayers. In Galilee it is not surprising to find that the population was bi-lingual. The mother tongue of the Jewish population was the Galilæan Aramaic, but Greek was also known as a second language. We are told that it was customary for Galilæans to have two names, one Aramaic, and one Greek (cf. Peter's names *Cephas*, 1 Cor. 3^{22}, and *Petros*, both meaning "rock"). Sometimes, apparently, as in the case of Bethsaida, the Galilæan town had two quarters, one in which Greek was regularly spoken, and the other, where the poorer population lived, in which Aramaic predominated. Both languages were understood more or less by everyone.

But the position of Greek as a second language was not peculiar to Galilee; it was also spoken and understood generally in Judæa, in the time of Jesus. It has already been pointed out that Jerusalem was the metropolis not merely of Judæa but of Jewry, scattered throughout the world. Pilgrims were constantly visiting the Holy City, especially at the great feasts, and this meant a large influx of Greek-speaking Jews. Further, the presence of Roman officials and soldiers in the land must be reckoned with. All these factors contributed to make the population bi-lingual.

An eloquent witness to the fact is the extent to which Greek words have penetrated the dialect of rabbinical Hebrew. Some eleven hundred Greek loan words have been enumerated in the Talmudical literature. It may be inferred that the educated classes among the Jews of Judæa would be able not merely to speak but to write Greek. The fourth Gospel, as recent discussion has made increasingly probable, may be regarded as a work of a Jew whose mother tongue was Aramaic and who wrote Greek as a second language. The Greek is profoundly affected by Semitic constructions and locutions, and this would apply even more to the spoken language.

That Jesus was able to converse in Greek is thus highly probable. The conversation reported in Jn. 19[11f.] between Jesus and Pilate must have been in Greek (cf. p. 928b).

It is not, of course, suggested that Jesus did not habitually employ his native Aramaic in speech, both public and private. Greek was a second language only, to be used on occasion when necessity arose. But it is necessary to emphasize the fact again that the Greek so used had been profoundly modified by the Aramaic mother tongue. In consequence the gulf between the two languages was not nearly so great as might, on *a priori* grounds, at first be supposed. This fact has an important bearing on the gospel tradition in which the words and discourses of Jesus have been preserved. The Greek medium in which this is embodied is not so entirely alien as to be an uncongenial means of expression for the Aramaic material. The Greek of the N.T. varies in this respect in different parts. The Greek of the second Gospel is strongly tinged with Aramaisms, and C. F. Burney has shown (in *The Poetry of Our Lord*) that the discourse material in the first and third Gospels readily retranslates into Aramaic. (For further discussion of this whole subject, see art., *Language of N.T.*, p. 880.)

IV. Jewish Apocalypses and Their Main Conceptions

By the end of the first Christian century, the idea represented by the apocalyptic literature of Judaism had come to its most complete expression. This literature (produced approximately between the years 165 B.C. and 120 A.D.) has come down to us mainly in translations which owe their survival to the fact that they circulated among Christian communities where the apocalyptic books for a time enjoyed great popularity; but, with the important exception of the book of Daniel, the Hebrew or Aramaic originals have been lost. The latter book owes its good fortune to the fact that it was ultimately—only, it would seem, with some reluctance—included in the canon of the Hebrew Scriptures. The loss of the Semitic originals is highly significant.

Daniel and the Apocalypses. All this literature is important, not only from the historical point of view as enabling us to trace the evolution of certain doctrines and views, but also as possessing a certain validity even for an age later than that for which some of these books were primarily written. The book of Daniel, for instance, though originally it was evoked by a particular historical crisis—the persecution of the Jewish religion by Antiochus Epiphanes in 168 B.C. and the following years—yet continued to be studied and to exercise a marked influence long after the time when the original crisis had passed away. In fact, it served to shape a tradition which persisted, and was adjusted from time to time to meet new situations. The same is true, in greater or less degree, of the other apocalypses that have survived, such as the *Books of Enoch*, *Assumption of Moses*, *Apocalypse of Abraham* and *Testaments of the Twelve Patriarchs*; they continued to be cherished in certain circles, as is shown by the fact that they have come down to us in translations which were in circulation for a long time after the original publication of the books. (For a detailed consideration of the history and character of these books, see art., *Literature of Intertestamental Period*, pp. 191–9.)

Supernatural Coloring. The writers of the apocalypses regarded the written Law and its oral interpretation in much the same way as the rabbis. Nevertheless, there is a certain difference between the rabbinic and the apocalyptic types of thought. They are preoccupied with different things. To the rabbis "the Law was the center round which Jewish life and thought revolved." To spread abroad the knowledge of the Law, to extend the range of its practical application to the routine of everyday life—in a word, to reduce the Law to practice, on the largest scale, as a rule of life for priests and people of the community of Israel, was the primary object of the rabbinical teachers. True, they hoped for a better future;

but they did not dwell unduly upon it. The best preparation for it, and the best means for bringing it about, would be to enlarge the area of the Law's loyal adherents. The rabbinic ideal is aptly expressed in the opening paragraph of the Mishnah tractate, *The Sayings of the Jewish Fathers,* in the *dictum* ascribed to "the men of the Great Synagogue." They said three things: "Be deliberate in judgment"; and "Raise up many disciples"; and "Make a fence to the Tôrāh" (Law), i.e., "Impose additional restrictions so as to keep at a safe distance from forbidden ground" (Taylor).

On the other hand, when we turn to the typical apocalyptic books we at once feel ourselves in a different atmosphere. Perhaps the most striking characteristic of these books is their *supernatural coloring.* The two poles of apocalyptic thought are not so much present and future, on the plane of earthly development, as *above* and *below.* Earth is but a shadow of heaven, the issues are really determined in the realm above. The future age is conceived as a sudden irruption of celestial forces from the other world. It is for this blinding but glorious catastrophe that the Apocalyptist longs and yearns with painful eagerness. The otherworldly spirit thus reaches, in these books, its most sublimated expression. This supernatural coloring is also reflected in the *form* of the apocalyptic books. They are full of strange and cryptic symbolism (e.g., the animal symbolism of Daniel and parts of Enoch); they employ the vision and the dream as regular vehicles for revelation; there is also a rich angelology and demonology. Doubtless the employment of cryptograms and mystic signs (such as the number 666, and the "beast" in the Revelation or Apocalypse of John, and the "little horn" in Daniel, as symbols for Nero and Antiochus respectively) was dictated partly by reasons of prudence. Nevertheless, the particular symbols chosen reflect the mysterious character so much loved by these writers. But the mystery is not mere literary mystification. The Apocalyptists were conscious that divine secrets must contain in them something incomprehensible by merely finite intelligence. This feeling often comes to expression.

A Philosophy of History. In contrast with the rabbis, the Apocalyptists, who were eager students of Scripture, devoted themselves to the study of the Prophets rather than the Law. In a sense they may be regarded as the successors of the prophets. It is noticeable that in the later developments of O.T. prophecy the apocalyptic element becomes more and more marked. In the book of Daniel, which is almost purely apocalyptic in character, this tendency reaches a climax in the O.T. The Apocalyptists, who were deeply religious men, were profoundly concerned with the problems incident to the divine government of the world. They ardently desired to vindicate God's providential ordering of events, and so they evolved a sort of philosophy of history. They were striving to frame a theory of the world which should account for all the facts of experience. Their scheme was conceived on the grandest scale. It embraced not only the earth but the celestial sphere. History is surveyed from the beginning to the end—for the Apocalyptists envisaged as an imminent fact the end of the present age. Thus, to take an instance, the Ezra-Apocalypse begins its survey with creation (4 Ezra 3[4f.]), not, as the prophets do, with the exodus from Egypt, which marked the birthday of Israel as a nation (cf. Jer. 2[2] Hos. 11[1]). The whole course of events is pictured dramatically; the actors include not only men but the angelic and dæmonic powers, all working under the control of God; and the drama moves onward to the inevitable dénouement. Thus the apocalyptic literature may be regarded as the assertion of a profound belief that the course of human affairs is not purposeless; what happens is not the mere result of the action and reaction of blind and uncontrolled forces. The sequence of events has a meaning. History is marching onward to a predestined goal. It is subservient to the will of a higher and moral power; and to this power the evil forces of the world—which are dread realities to the Apocalyptists—however victorious they may seem to be for a time, are in the end subordinated.

Divine Transcendence. A word must be said about some of the more important theological conceptions that emerge in this literature. (See also art., *Religious Development of the Intertestamental Period,* pp. 200–13.) The transcendental view of God that characterizes it has often been remarked and is obvious. God is pictured as supreme over the world. He dwells at an inaccessible height, and is surrounded with an impassable barrier of fiery glory. One need only read such passages as Dan. 7[9f.] which describes "the Ancient of Days" seated upon a throne in heaven—a throne of "fiery flames, and the wheels thereof burning fire"—and ministered to by myriads of attendant spirits, to realize this aspect of the conception. Such descriptions as "the Most High," "the Exalted One" are common paraphrases for "God" (cf. 4 Ezra 7[33, 52, 62,] Baruch 4[10, 14, 22] Dan. 4[31f.]), and we may compare with these the terms common in the rabbinic literature, "The Holy One, blessed be he," "The Omnipresent," and similar expressions. One effect of this conception was to stimulate the development of a rich angelology and demonology. As Professor Porter remarks: "One-sided stress on the transcendence of God, above and apart from the world, always involves the substitution for his presence in the world of some sort of intermediary agency." This again is a characteristic of popular Judaism, as it had developed in the apostolic age, and can be traced not only in apocalyptic, but also in the Targums and other late Jewish literature. The way had been prepared by the quasi-personification of Wisdom (cf. Prov. 8), and the tendency is illustrated in later literature in the way in which such agencies as the *Memra* ("Word"), the Holy Spirit, the Shekinah, and the figure of Metatron are spoken of. In the apocalyptic literature the rôle of Metatron is assumed by Enoch "the heavenly Scribe," while in the figure of the heavenly Son of man of the Similitudes of 1 Enoch 37–71, the idea of a supernatural being, second only to God himself, who shares God's throne ($62^{3, 5}$), possesses universal dominion (62^{6}), and to whom all judgment is committed (41^{9} 69^{27}), the conception attains its highest expression. To the whole idea of any intermediate agency between God and man later rabbinical Judaism was intensely hostile, and the rabbinical teachers strove as far as possible to eliminate it from the popular consciousness.

It is sometimes assumed that the ideas thus current about the divine transcendence must necessarily have tended to remove God entirely from all contact with his world and to make him inaccessibly remote to the pious worshiper. Doubtless the danger was present; but that it could be—and was—overcome is shown by such a passage as 4 Ezra $8^{20f.}$ where the seer, in a prayer addressed to God, after heaping up expressions emphasizing the divine majesty and transcendence—"whose throne is beyond imagination, whose glory inconceivable," etc.—makes a direct appeal to the divine compassion:

Hear the voice of thy servant,
Give ear to thy creature's petition, and attend to my words (v. 24).

The danger of "a one-sided stress on the transcendence of God" was present, but the religious instinct was strong and vital enough to overcome it, without sacrificing the truth underlying the transcendental idea.

Resurrection of the Dead. Transcendental conceptions also exercised a profound influence in other directions. The older Messianic hope was sublimated. The golden age promised by the older prophets was lifted up from the place of the present earth into the heavenly sphere. "The contrast between the present and the coming age became a contrast of two worlds." This comes to most complete expression in 4 Ezra 7. "The most High hath made not one age but two."

Perhaps the most distinctive advance in doctrine made in the apocalyptic literature is seen in the emergence of the belief—which became a dogma in later Judaism—in the resurrection of the dead. This is the most important contribution made by apocalyptic to doctrinal belief. It first comes to clear expression in the apocalyptic section of Isaiah (chs. 24–27), which almost certainly is older than the book of Daniel. Here the belief is expressed that death will be abolished in the Messianic Age, and that the righteous dead will be raised to share in the coming glory of the nation.

In Daniel the belief assumes a fixed form (cf. $12^{2, 3, 13}$). The author has in view more particularly those who have suffered martyrdom for the faith in the persecution by Antiochus Epiphanes (168 B.C., and following years). The older view which knows nothing of the resurrection still appears in the older apocalyptic literature. Thus in 1 Enoch 5^{7-9} what seems to be contemplated is not a resurrection to life, but a life on earth unusually prolonged. It is worth noting that the association of martyrdom with the resurrection persisted, and reappears in the N.T. apocalypse (Rev. $20^{4f.}$; cf. 2 Maccabees.). For some time belief fluctuated as to whether the resurrection should be confined to the righteous only, or should embrace righteous and sinners alike. According to Josephus (*Antiquities*, bk. xviii, ch. 1, parag. 3), the former view was that of the Pharisees, as it certainly was of the author of 2 Maccabees (6^{26} $7^{9, 14, 36}$ 12^{44} 14^{46}). It is also represented in the Gospels (cf. Lk. 14^{14} and 20^{36}). Both theories are contained in the Johannine Apocalypse, where the martyrs are raised first, at the beginning of the millennium, to reign with Christ "a thousand years"; then at the final consummation, after the thousand years have ended, all the dead are raised to be judged (Rev. $20^{4f., 11f.}$).

It was inevitable that the question should arise: What is the nature of the resurrection body? (Cf. 1 Cor. 15). As a matter of fact a long passage is devoted to this subject in Baruch. Here it is said that the dead will first of all be raised in their old bodily form, in such a way as to be recognizable: afterward they will be transformed, the aspect of the wicked changing for the worse, while the glory of the righteous becomes ever more splendid.

A Transcendental Messiah. Another important development in apocalyptic thinking is the conception of the transcendental Messiah. This idea was apparently confined to a limited circle, and seems at no time to have penetrated the popular Messianic belief. It seems to have grown out of Dan. 7^{13} ("one like unto a son of man"). The kinship between this mysterious figure and the heavenly "Son of man" of the Similitudes of 1 Enoch is fairly clear, and probably also extends to the "man" of 4 Ezra 13. The author of Daniel used the term "one like unto a son of man" in contrast with the beasts who represent the world-empires, as a symbol for the people of Israel. But it does not follow that the figure "like a man" (or "son of man") may not have an individual significance. On the contrary, it seems probable that the term is a descriptive one for an angelic being—presumably Michael in the thought of the writer of Daniel—who acts as Israel's representative and counterpart. The figure is thus both a symbol and a person. The author of Daniel may have been influenced, in using the term "son of man," by the figure of the Cosmic Man, who in apocalyptic tradition was gradually invested with Messianic attributes. Originally in apocalyptic tradition this "man" or "son of man" was conceived as a heavenly being or angel, and was invested with attributes proper only to Jehovah himself.

The idea of the heavenly being who thus comes to view as a feature in old apocalyptic tradition is the source of the conception of the heavenly Messiah—the Son of Man—of the Similitudes of the Book of Enoch (1 Enoch 37–71). We have already seen that the heavenly being "like unto a son of man" of Dan. 7 was probably identified by the author of Daniel with Israel's angel-prince Michael; this angelic being was later, it would seem, invested with Messianic attributes, and so became the pre-existent heavenly Messiah of the Book of Enoch, who is to judge both men and angels.

His standing designation in the Similitudes is "this (or that) Son of Man," seldom "the Son of Man." In other passages in the same section of the book he is called "the Righteous One" (38^{2} 53^{6}); "the Elect One" (39^{6} 40^{5}); "the Elect One of righteousness and of faith" (39^{6}), and God's "Anointed" (i.e., Christ) (48^{10} 52^{4}). Unlike the earthly Messiah of the national hope, who is born on earth of the seed of David, the angelic Son of Man of the Similitudes has his home in heaven "under the wings of the Lord of the Spirits" (39^{7}). He is pre-existent in heaven ($46^{1f.}$); his name was named "before the sun and the signs were created, and before the stars of the heaven were made" (48^{3}); he was "chosen and hidden" before the Lord of the Spirits, "before the creation of the world" (48^{6}). A real pre-existence of the heavenly Messiah is here taught. It is to be noticed that the heavenly Messiah, according to the original conception, is not "born" upon the earth at all. When he appears upon earth he is suddenly "revealed." The Son of man comes like a lightning flash "in his day" (Lk. 17^{24}, cf. Baruch 53^{8-11}). This is one of the fundamental differences between the representation of the heavenly Son of man and the national Messiah. The latter is born of human parentage at Bethlehem, and though he might be concealed for a time, and then suddenly be "revealed," so that it could be said "when the Christ cometh no one knoweth whence he is" (Jn. 7^{27}), this representation in no wise impugns his human birth. But how difficult it was to conceive of a being, who pre-existed in heaven, as being born at all, is shown by such a passage as Jn. 6^{41}, where the Jews are represented as saying: "Is not this Jesus, the son of Joseph, whose father and mother we know? How doth he now say, I am come down out of heaven?"

The Eschatological Scheme. A word must be added about the eschatological scheme of the later Apocalypses. These combined together the old national eschatology which envisaged a temporary period of felicity upon this earth, with the idea of the eternal heavenly bliss. Hence arose a curious compromise. The belief grew up that the present age would terminate with a *temporary* Messianic kingdom, the duration of which was variously estimated. In the Apocalypse of Ezra it is fixed at four hundred, and in the Johannine Apocalypse at one thousand years (the millennium). The currently received eschatology, as is well known, pictured the Messianic Age as being preceded by a time of "travail" called the "birth pangs" or sufferings of the Messiah (cf. Mt. 24^{8} Mk. 13^{8}), the idea being a deduction from certain passages in the prophets (cf. Hos. $13^{12f.}$ Joel $2^{10f.}$ Micah 5^{1-6}). Finally a word must be said about the anti-Christ idea. The conception arose of the battle of God (or his representative) with the devil at the end of the world. "It is very likely," says Bousset, "that anti-Christ is originally nothing else than the incarnate devil, and that the idea of a battle of God with a human opponent, in whom all devilish wickedness would become incarnate, arose under the influence of definite historical conditions."

Apocalyptic Ideas in Jesus and Paul. How far was the transcendental conception of the Messiah prevalent among Jews in the time of Jesus? It was undoubtedly known to and influenced the mind of our Lord himself, as is shown by his appropriation of the title "Son of man." But he profoundly modified its import by combining with the idea of the glorious heavenly Son of man that of the Suffering Servant of Isaiah 53—a combination which fused the ideas of humiliation and glory, and which could not have been invented by any disciple. In the idea so modified Jesus seems to have found the most adequate expression of his Messianic consciousness.

There is some reason to believe that the idea of the heavenly Messiah grew up outside Judæa—probably in apocalyptic circles in Galilee. In Judæa, where Pharisaism had its stronghold, the orthodox rabbinic conception of the national Messiah, who was to spring from the family of David, prevailed. The Son of man was certainly not a popular or well-understood name for the Messiah. It is significant that in Jn. 7[25-36] "the multitude" (in the neighborhood of Jerusalem) are represented as asking, "Who is this Son of man?"

Apocalyptic ideas also influenced Paul. This can be most clearly seen in 4 Ezra (2 Esdras). "It is nothing less than astonishing," says Schweitzer, "that the close affinities [of St. Paul's writings] with the Apocalypse of Ezra do not receive any recognition. In this work there are elaborate discussions of the problem of sin, the Fall of our first parents, Election, the wrath, long-suffering, and mercy of God, the prerogative of Israel, the significance of the Law, the temporal and eternal Jerusalem, of the prospect of dying or surviving to the Parousia, the tribulation of the times of the End and the Judgment" (*Paul and His Interpreters*, p. 51). It should, of course, be added that Paul's discussion of these ideas is carried on under the influence of his knowledge of the crucified and risen Christ, a fact which lifts Paul out of the class of mere Apocalyptists.

V. The Jewish Dispersion (Diaspora)

"The first and most remarkable phenomenon," says Reinach, "presented by Judaism during the Græco-Roman period is its dispersion along the shores of the Mediterranean" (*Jewish Encyc.*, art., "Diaspora," vol. iv, p. 560). By the time of the rise of Christianity by far the greater part of the Jewish people lived outside the boundaries of Palestine. Exact numbers can hardly be determined; but the number of Jews dispersed must have been at least four times as great as those living in Palestine. They were mainly concentrated in the cities of the Græco-Roman world; agriculture was no longer, as in Judæa, their almost exclusive occupation.

Propagandist Zeal of the Jews. Theoretically the intercourse of the Jews with the pagan world was confined to commercial relations. The Jews lived in their own quarters, separate from the rest of the population. The pious Jew could neither dine at the table of a pagan nor receive him at his own table. Attendance at the theaters, the circuses, and the gymnasia was forbidden. These rules were not always, however, by any means rigidly adhered to. The Jews were profoundly affected by their environment in many ways. The influence of Greek culture told heavily upon them—as the Judæo-Alexandrine literature eloquently attests. They used Greek even in their religious services; they read the Bible in Greek, and they adopted Greek names, and to some extent Greek organization in their communal institutions. Above all they were animated by an intense missionary zeal to win over the pagan population to the higher monotheistic religion of which they were the chosen representatives. The Jews of the Diaspora were possessed with the conviction that they were destined to realize the prophetic word, "I have set thee for a light of the nations" (Isa. 49[6]).

This propagandist zeal was probably no new thing in the Diaspora. Its beginnings go back to the beginnings of the Diaspora itself. In fact, the Greek translation of the Bible—the LXX—doubtless owes its existence to zeal in converting the heathen world. So Philo (*Vita Moysi*, ii, 136) expressly says: "Some held it unfitting that the Laws were known only to a part of the human race, and that a non-Hellenic part, the Greeks knowing nothing about it; therefore they bestirred themselves about a translation of it."

An eloquent witness, too, to the energy and success of this propaganda is to be seen also in the fierce opposition it provoked from heathen writers. Cf. Apollonius Molon of Rhodes, 90 B.C.; Posidonius of Apamea, 70 B.C.; the Alexandrine Charemon, 50 B.C.; Lysimachus, 30 B.C.; Apion, the contemporary of Josephus.

Thus we see the Diaspora Jew fired with unquenchable zeal to convert the heathen world to his own pure, ethically severe, and monotheistic faith. All the Græco-Roman world was his field of operations: and over this world a number of forces were at work to make the missionary's message at once timely and welcome. "It must be admitted," says Reinach, "that Judaism lacked certain of those attractive features which drew the multitude to the cult of Mithras and of the Egyptian deities. Its physical exactions repulsed those wanting in stout courage; its cult, devoid of imagery and sensuous rites, presented only an austere poesy separating its adepts from the world and cutting them off, to some extent, from communion with the cultured. But the practical and legal character of its doctrine, furnishing a rule of life for every occasion, could not but appeal to a disorganized society. The purity and simplicity of its theology captivated the high minded, while the mystery and quaintness of its customs, the welcome Sabbath rest, the privileges enjoyed at the hand of public authorities, recommended the Jewish faith to those more materialistically inclined" (*op. cit.*).

The Græco-Roman world was ripe for welcoming a monotheistic faith which could combine with a pure doctrine of God high ethical fervor. The old pagan religion had largely lost its vitality; and the higher souls had taken refuge in philosophy. The causes which produced the success of the Jewish propaganda were thus fundamentally moral.

Success of the Propaganda. That this propaganda was highly successful there cannot be a shadow of doubt. No doubt the statements of Josephus, Philo, and even Seneca, "who represent the whole world as rushing toward Jewish observances, are, in some degree, exaggerated." "At the same time it is indisputable that proselytes were found in large numbers in every country of the Diaspora. The pagan authors, struck by this phenomenon, carefully distinguish the Jews by race from the Jews by adoption." We are told by Josephus (*Wars*, bk. vii, ch. 3, parag. 3) that in his time a large portion of the Greek population in Antioch was Judaized. Later, as we know, they became Christians (see Acts 11[19-26]). According to the same authority also "almost all the women" in Damascus observed the Jewish customs. Paul met with proselytes in Pisidian Antioch (Acts 13[43]), in Thyatira (16[14]), Thessalonica (17[1, 11]) and Athens (17[34]). In Asia Minor numerous indications suggest that Jewish proselytes were to be met with in large numbers. In Rome, the success of the propaganda is attested by Horace, Persius, and Juvenal. We cannot account for the enormous growth of the Jewish population in Egypt, Cyprus, and Cyrene without assuming a large adhesion of Gentile proselytes. It is noteworthy that Aquila, whose Greek translation of the Bible (second century A.D.) superseded in the synagogues that of the LXX, and Bar Giora, chief of the insurgents in the siege of Jerusalem, were proselytes, or sons of proselytes.

The question of the admission of proselytes had stirred Judaism to its depths. It threatened, in fact, to separate Hellenistic from Palestinian Judaism. The former was willing to admit Gentiles after they had undergone the rite of baptism, and without circumcision. The story of the conversion of the royal family of Adiabene, narrated by Josephus (*Antiquities*, bk. xx, ch. 2), illustrates the controversy. According to the story a Jewish merchant, Ananias, converts the royal household and assures the Prince Izates that circumcision is not essential. Then the Galilæan zealot Eliezer intervenes, and insists on the necessity of circumcision. The former denied to the uncircumcised proselyte the status of a full member of the Jewish community; but non-Palestinian Judaism did not make such a distinction till the Roman Wars, when the more rigorous view became prevalent everywhere.

A Preparation for Christianity. As we have seen, the Judaism of the Diaspora down to the second Christian century was possessed with a glowing zeal to convert the heathen world surrounding it to the higher monotheistic religion. It knew how to commend itself to the Greek world by a very clever literature, largely apologetic, which was clothed in a Greek garb and assumed a classical form. The thought of Israel as the chosen nation received a lofty interpretation. Israel was chosen to be a priestly nation for the whole world. To Philo the Jewish people is "above all the nations beloved of God, one that has secured the priesthood for the whole human race" (*De Abraham*, ii, 15). This liberal propaganda prepared the way in the most effective manner for the coming of a broad universalistic religion, freed from the trammels of race connection. But the Pharisaic Judaism of Palestine succeeded only too well in imposing particularistic limitations on the whole of Judaism.

A Jewish writer, referring to the liberal propaganda of the Dispersion, says truly: "It would have found even more appreciation if it had divested itself of its purely ethnic spirit; had sacrificed the accessory element (the manifold and vexatious usages) to the essential element (the religious and moral instruction); and had consummated at the proper time the transformation from a race to a religion—a transformation which is at once the program of its history and the problem of its destiny."

The transformation here indicated was, in fact, accomplished by a Hellenistic Jew—Paul of Tarsus—who by removing the barrier of circumcision and by proclaiming the great principle that in Christ is neither Jew nor Gentile, Greek nor barbarian, bond nor free, male nor female, abolished all artificial distinctions regarding religious status, and enunciated a universalism which could form the foundation-principle of a world-religion. The great apostle's inspired intuition enabled Christianity to reap the harvest so nobly sown by the missionary zeal of Hellenistic Judaism. This new Judaism—whose gospel was the Greek Bible, and its goal the establishment of a world-religion—lacked only one element, the

Messiah, who could sanction this more or less denationalized type of Judaism, supersede Jerusalem, Temple, and cultus, abolish the burden of Pharisaic ordinances, and lighten the yoke, even of the Mosaic laws, for the Gentiles. This Messiah was found in the person of Jesus of Nazareth. As the Jewish scholar Moriz Friedländer remarks: "If Jesus was the Christ, then the religion of the Jewish Diaspora was Christendom."

Specific Instruments of the Preparation. The three great means employed by Diaspora Judaism to produce these remarkable results may be summed up under the heads: (a) the Synagogue, (b) the Greek Bible, and (c) the Sabbath-rest.

(a) The Synagogue. The enormous importance which the synagogue possessed in binding the Jews of the Dispersion together, on the one hand, and in drawing the heathen to the monotheistic faith, on the other, has not, perhaps, been sufficiently recognized. The origin of the institution is wrapped in obscurity, but it probably spread from the countries of the Diaspora to Palestine. By the first century A.D., it had become an established institution wherever Jews were settled (cf. Acts 15[21]). In the Græco-Roman world outside Palestine the synagogue services were conducted in Greek. Every town had its synagogue—"a teaching-place of all the virtues"—whose open doors every Sabbath proved a great attraction to the heathen. It may be in reference to the wide-spread influence exercised by the synagogues that the remark of Seneca quoted in a famous passage by Augustine was made: "To such an extent have the customs of that detestable race prevailed, that they have found acceptance in all countries: the conquered have dictated laws to the conquerors."

(b) The Greek Bible. It is clear that the language employed for the discourses in the public services in the synagogues of the Dispersion was Greek. This must have been the case because of the large numbers of proselytes and adherents of the Jews who frequented them. The use of the Greek Bible (the LXX) is also just as certain. When Philo says that the fame of the laws handed down by Moses has penetrated all inhabited lands and has been spread abroad to the ends of the earth, we are not left in any doubt as to whether he is referring to the Hebrew or the Greek Bible. For he goes on to remark: "Originally the laws were written in the Chaldee language, their beauty being unknown to the rest of mankind. . . . Some thinking it unfitting that the laws should be known to a portion of mankind only . . . brought about a translation of it. For this reason there is still held yearly a great festival in the land of Pharos, in which not only Jews, but also many others, take part, in honor of the place where the translation originated, and to thank God for the old yet ever new deeds of good will." (*Vita Moysi*, ii, 137f.) It is a significant fact that the LXX became the Bible of the Christian Church.

(c) The Sabbath-Rest. The Sabbath was the regular time for the assemblages of the Jewish community. The seventh day thus acquired great significance and importance not only in the Jewish community but also in the Gentile world generally. Philo says: "God singled out for special honor the Seventh Day, because it is the festival not merely of a town or district, but of the *world*, and is alone worthy of being called the birthday of creation." (*De mundi opif.*, I, 22). It made a great impression upon the heathen world, and was respected by the Roman authorities. Thus taxes falling due on the Sabbath could be paid by Jews the following day, and by decree of Augustus no Jew could be haled before a judge on the Sabbath day (Josephus, *Antiquities*, bk. xvi, 6. 2).

VI. Influence of Greek Culture

At the time Christianity came out into the world, the world that confronted it was a Hellenized world, and this was true not only of Europe but of Asia over a very wide area. Everywhere both in the East and the West, in the countries included within the Roman Empire, the Greek language was spoken and read by the educated classes. Over a large area, of course, it was the language of everyday life. Everywhere, too, Greek institutions like the gymnasium and the theater were in evidence. Bevan, in his vivid and arresting way, says:

"We are often told in popular books that 'the East never changes,' that Orientals have an invincible repugnance to Western ideas, and so forth. . . . Well, you would make a great mistake if you imagined, say, the Damascus of St. Paul's time like the Damascus of to-day. In St. Paul's time we should have found ourselves in a Greek city: Arabs from the desert in native dress would no doubt have appeared in the streets, and Jews with their fringes and phylacteries, but we should have seen the citizens of the upper class to all appearance Greek, we should continually have heard Greek talked around us, and the environment would be largely made up of Greek temples, halls and colonnades" (*Jerusalem Under the High Priests*, p. 39).

Greek civilization and Greek institutions had indeed transformed the world. Hellenism had filled life with new interests. There was something very alluring about Greek culture—

it captivated and enthralled. Among other achievements it created a new tradition of education. When Christianity emerged into the wider world it came face to face with an *educated* world. Everywhere in the towns grammar schools were to be found, while at certain centers were great seats of learning, rather like the mediæval universities to which students of all classes resorted. Tarsus in Paul's time was a center of this sort. Students then, as now, attended lectures, and sometimes showed by their manner that they were thinking of other things —"leaving their minds outside," says Philo.

Teachers and professors occupied positions of social distinction and were treated with special consideration by state and municipal authorities, both in the matter of endowment and exemption from taxation. The Hellenic world—or perhaps it would be more accurate to describe it as the "Hellenized world"—was thus permeated with cultural forces which were all-powerful and all-absorbing. On its nobler side this Greek culture quickened and enriched human life generally. But it sometimes assumed base and degraded forms. Bevan (*op. cit.*, p. 41f.) has noted how these effects were specially noticeable in the province of Syria, in the centuries both immediately before and after the opening of the Christian era.

Signs of Moral Disintegration. When we ask ourselves, What was the moral state of the Græco-Roman world in the first two centuries of our era? it is perhaps not quite so easy to generalize as is sometimes assumed. Hatch, indeed, attempts to discount the evidence that has come down to us. He says: "It has been common to construct pictures of the state of morals in the first centuries of the Christian era from the statements of satirists who, like all satirists, had a large element of caricature, and from the denunciations of the Christian apologists, which, like all denunciations, have a large element of exaggeration. The pictures so constructed are mosaics of singular vices, and they have led to the not unnatural impression that these centuries constituted an era of exceptional wickedness" (*Hibbert Lectures*, p. 139, Scribner). Hatch goes on: "It is no doubt difficult to gauge the average morality of any age. It is questionable whether the average morality of civilized ages has largely varied; it is possible that if the satirists of our own time were equally outspoken, the vices of ancient Rome might be found to have a parallel in modern London; and it is probable, not on merely *a priori* grounds, but from the nature of the evidence which remains, that there was in ancient Rome, as there is in modern London, a preponderating mass of those who loved their children and their homes, who were good neighbors and faithful friends, who conscientiously discharged their civil duties, and were in all the current senses of the word 'moral men'" (*ibid.*).

This statement puts the case in as persuasive a manner as is possible. Yet it seems to the writer not to allow for the fact that the age was one of disintegration—the old moral and religious sanctions had broken down; the best spirits of the time were acutely conscious of this, and this fact will explain the movements toward moral reformation that had grown up. The world was desperately in need of a religion that would be adequate to the new needs; there was a conflict of religions—and in the end Christianity emerged victorious as the world-religion; but the conflict had not become decisive till well on toward the end of the second century of our era; and in the interval there was, to a large extent, religious and moral chaos. How can we explain the moral energy of the Jewish (and later the Christian) missionary propaganda unless there was present the conviction on both sides that paganism lacked the moral fiber that only Judaism or Christianity could give?

VII. Religious Unrest

"The age in which Christianity grew was in reality an age of moral reformation" (Hatch, *op. cit.*, p. 149). This manifested itself especially in Stoicism and the growth of the religious guilds associated with "mystery" cults.

Stoicism. "In Stoicism"—to use Bevan's words—"the mind of antiquity had not only reached in some respects the highest expression, but that expression had become popular in a way unparalleled in the history of any later school. The Stoic missionary, preaching the self-sufficiency of virtue in a threadbare cloak at the street corners, had been one of the typical figures of a Greek town many generations before Paul" (*Hellenism and Christianity*, pp. 72, 73, Doran).

Through these cynic preachers of righteousness Stoicism had made a profound impression upon the public conscience. Perhaps the most striking evidence of this is the fact that it had created a new set of ethical terms. Lightfoot, commenting on this fact, says: "It is difficult to estimate, and perhaps not very easy to overrate the extent to which Stoic philosophy had leavened the moral vocabulary of the civilized world at the time of the Christian era. To take a single instance: the most important of moral terms, the crowning triumph of ethical nomenclature, *suneidēsis, conscientia*, the internal, absolute, supreme judge of individual action, if not struck in the mint of the Stoics, at all events became current coin through their influence. To a great extent, therefore, the general diffusion of Stoic language would lead to its adoption by the first teachers of Christianity" (*On Philippians*, p. 303).

Stoicism was thus a real preparation for Christianity. It was governed by a great ideal, it was marked by high ethical power, and it produced a few great men of noble character. It impressed the conscience of the Greek and Roman world. But its ethics were not Christian: it was a creed of despair and acquiescence, and it despised all the Christian virtues that depend upon the affirmation, "God is love." It had no belief in progress, and its outlook on the world was dark and forbidding —removed poles asunder from that of the Christian. It totally lacked the dynamic which carried Christianity forward and made it a religion of moving power for mankind. If Christianity largely absorbed the ethical terminology of Stoicism, it invested the terms with an entirely new content and with new values.

Mystery Religions. If we turn to the "mystery" cults we can see in these religious brotherhoods another indication of the pathetic yearning of the ancient world for regeneration and salvation. The vogue of the mystery cults in the imperial age is well known. One of the most influential, and one, moreover, that illustrates the syncretistic character of these later religious movements, is the cult of Isis, as described by Plutarch in his famous treatise. The Isis-Serapis worship was widely practiced in the Hellenistic world. It can be traced at Athens, Pompeii, and Rome, and it spread wherever Roman influence penetrated. The cult evidently made a wide appeal, with its splendid ceremonial and "contemplative devotion" ordered with all the precision characteristic of Egyptian liturgic tradition. It also embodied the elaborate precision of the ancient Egyptian eschatology.

No detailed evidence has come down to us as to the character of the rites connected with the mystery-cults earlier than the second century A.D. The fullest is the well-known description in Apuleius of the initiation of Lucius at Cenchreæ into the Isis mystery-cult. The preparation of the candidate lasted several days, during which he was instructed by the high priest as to the meaning of what was to follow. (See Kennedy, *St. Paul and the Mystery Religions*, pp. 100f.) He was informed that "the initiation itself is solemnized as the symbol of a voluntary death and a salvation given in answer to prayer . . . and after [the initiates] have been by [the goddess's] providence in a sense born again she places them again in the course of a new life in salvation" (*ibid.*, p. 101). The initiation itself culminated in an experience which is thus mystically described: "I penetrated to the boundaries of death," he says; "I trod the threshold of Proserpine, and after being borne through all the elements I returned to earth: at midnight I beheld the sun radiating white light. I came into the presence of the gods below and the gods above, and did them reverence close at hand" (quoted *ibid.*).

Fortunately, we have this sympathetic picture of some of the aspects of a typical Hellenistic Mystery Religion, the solemn external preparation in the prescribed abstinences, the solemn baptism, the communication of the mystic formulæ, culminating in the overpowering scenes which came at the last; there is also the inward experience, a genuinely religious one, in the heart preparation, the idea of cleansing, the conception of regeneration, and the final mystical rapture which unites the soul of the initiate with the deity.

Paul and the Mysteries. These and the religious brotherhoods which made purity of life a condition of membership are genuine manifestations of the religious spirit, and may be regarded as a real preparation for Christianity. But it is very doubtful whether these cults entered so closely and intimately into the organic life of Pauline Christianity as is sometimes suggested. That Paul was ever really influenced in his thought by the mystery-religions is very unlikely. His thought and that of the mysteries move in two different worlds.

Paul's mysticism is thoroughly ethical in character. The Cross is central. The mystic death to sin of which he speaks is wholly different in conception from the mystical identification of the initiate in the mystery-cult with the death of the divine personage whose restoration to life was celebrated and depicted in the mystery ceremonial.

Paul undoubtedly uses terms which are characteristic of the terminology of the mystery-religions, just as he uses occasionally Stoic technical terms. But in both cases the language is charged with a new meaning and a new content.

The truth is that behind Paul's language there is a fundamentally different conception of God. The Jewish conception of God could not make terms with the Greek idea at all. To the Jew, God was one unique and holy Being, supreme and transcendent, the Creator and Ruler of the world, whose majesty could not be shared. To the Jew, the very idea of the deification of a man was utterly abhorrent. Not so to the Greek. Apparently in the earlier period of Greek religion, heroic qualities or the possession of unusual powers might lead to apotheosis. The mortal, as in the mystery-cults, might achieve divinity. The extent to which this was carried in the Hellenistic world from the time of Alexander the Great and onward, when divine honors were paid to living rulers, and legends grew up about their supernatural origin, is well known. First the Seleucidæ and the Ptolemies adopted the cult, and finally it was transferred to the Roman world and culminated in the state worship of the emperors. It may be possible to regard all this as the perversion of a true instinct in humanity, which leads men to regard supreme powers and endowments as God-like, and therefore to be invested with the halo of divinity. But to carry the process to the lengths reached in the Hellenistic period inevitably meant the frittering away of all worthy conceptions of Deity. To the Jew the state worship of the emperor was the blasphemy of blasphemies.

When Christianity came face to face with this Hellenic world, it confronted it with a lofty conception of God which had its roots in the ethical monotheism of the Hebrew prophets. It was the God revealed in Jesus Christ whom it preached, a lofty and exclusive conception that would tolerate nothing in the nature of apotheosis in the Greek manner. Whatever use Christianity made of Greek philosophical terms like *Logos*, or other terms like "salvation," it never compromised its central conception of God, which, indeed, stamped its use of these terms with a new meaning. And this is true not only of Pauline Christianity, but also, fundamentally, of the later type of Christian thought and theology, when the church had really become deeply influenced by Hellenism in various ways. Though threatened in the third century with syncretistic tendencies, the church kept its recognized theology free from idolatrous taint, and this result was due primarily and ultimately to the conception of God which is its inalienable heritage from Judaism.

Literature: General: Schürer, *History of the Jewish People in the Time of Jesus Christ* (Eng. trans., 6 vols., 2nd ed.); Morrison, *The Jews under Roman Rule;* Bevan, *Jerusalem under the High Priests;* Shailer Mathews, *History of N.T. Times in Palestine, 175* B.C. *to 70* A.D.; Box, *Jewish Environment of Early Christianity* (*Expositor*, July, 1916). For part II: Hastings' *Encyc. of Religion and Ethics*, arts., "Pharisees," "Sadducees," "Essenes." For part III: see literature cited under art. on *Language of N.T.*, p. 884. For part IV: Porter, *Messages of the Apocalyptic Writers;* Charles, *Religious Development between the O.T. and N.T.;* Box, *Jewish Apocalyptic in the Apostolic Age* (*Expositor*, Nov. and Dec., 1922); the various Apocalypses in *Translations of Early Documents* (S.P.C.K.). For part V: *Jewish Encyc.*, art., "Diaspora." For parts VI and VII: Hatch, *Influence of Greek Ideas and Usages upon the Christian Church;* Kennedy, *St. Paul and the Mystery Religions;* Angus, *The Mystery Religions and Christianity;* Cumont, *Mysteries of Mithra* (Eng. trans.); Clemen, *Primitive Christianity and its Non-Jewish Sources* (Eng. trans.); Legge, *Forerunners and Rivals of Christianity* (2 vols.); H. C. Sheldon, *Mystery Religions and the N.T.;* Hastings, *op. cit.*, art. "Mysteries"; C. Anderson Scott, *Christianity According to St. Paul*, ch. 3; Box, *Early Christianity and the Hellenic World* (*Expositor*, Aug., 1924); Hayes, *Greek Culture and the Greek Testament.*

THE FORMATION OF THE NEW TESTAMENT

By Professor JAMES MOFFATT

Sacred Books. The function of the Sacred Book in the religions of the world has yet to be studied thoroughly. Most of the great religions have their scriptures, but their character differs, and the relation of the worshiper to the Sacred Book is by no means the same in the various faiths. Judaism and Islam perhaps make this relation stricter than any of the far Eastern faiths like Hinduism or Sikhism or Buddhism. Yet even in them the precise character of the Sacred Book is not exactly what it is in Christianity. What is common to all sacred books is the conviction that they contain revelations of divine truth which are vital to the worshiper. But how this vitality is realized is another matter.

The Christian Book a Historic Record. The outstanding feature of the Christian Book, or Bible, is that it consists of two parts, the O.T. and the N.T. All religious literature is determined, in shape and form, by the particular conditions of life in the special nation or race or community for which and within which it was produced. Now both the O.T. and the N.T. reflect a religious movement which was stirred by faith in a God who acted within history. His revelations are made to his people from time to time, as they pass through certain well-marked phases and periods. "Testament" echoes the Latin term for "covenant," and "covenant" denotes the gracious purpose of God entering history, a purpose whose initiative is with him and whose outcome is revealed in his relations and dealings with his people. In Islam the Koran is regarded as an inspired book of oracles, given to the prophet by Allah. It claims absolute authority, on the ground that the oracles are either immediately made to the prophet or that he is commissioned to speak in the name of Allah. But the Koran is not a book of history. Its contents are the disclosures made by Allah to the prophet at one time. Whereas the Christian Bible is literature covering centuries, during which the revelation of the divine purpose passed through phases, but pre-eminently through two: the first, the period of God's people known as Hebrews, Israelites, and Jews, and the second, the period of the people as the Christian Church in its initial and classical period. This was the period in which the church set out upon its mission as God's people, fulfilling the former hopes and destinies of the community under the Old Covenant, no longer in any national sense but as intrusted with his message for all nations. What is common to both parts of the Bible is therefore the consciousness that God reveals himself in history, manifesting his purpose and mind through actions and events.

Use of the Old Testament by Early Christians. Our task is to survey the formation of the second part of the Sacred Book of Christians. But it must be remembered that this literature arose within a community which had the O.T. in its hands, mainly in the Greek version. For a while the church had no idea of forming any other collection of sacred books. "From a babe thou hast known the sacred writings which are able to make thee wise unto salvation through faith which is in Christ Jesus" (2 Tim. 3^{15}). This might have been said to almost any early Christian of the first generation. The Scriptures here are the O.T. books, read in the light of the Christian faith. They were the Bible of the church during the period in which the N.T. writings were being prepared; and at first the people of God never dreamed of needing any other. They lived by faith in Christ Jesus as the Son of God and the Redeemer of his people. This was the core and center, the new, vital element of their life as the Community of God. But they found much about their Lord in the O.T.; to their eyes he seemed to shine out from the pages of the Law, the prophets, and the Psalter. They discovered a sort of biography of Jesus, by anticipation, in the literature of the Old Covenant which they read in the light of Christ. To them it appeared, as the apostle put it (2 Cor. 3^{13-16}), that a veil was removed from the O.T., once Christian faith approached it; as Christians, they saw in it for the first time what they believed to be its true meaning. It predicted Christ, and they read it for such predictions, as literature of revelation which pointed forward to the Lord.

Effects of this Use on the New Testament. This explains two things. First, it explains why the formation of the N.T. came so slowly. At the outset nothing was written about Jesus by the church, both because everything needful seemed to have been written already in the O.T., and because the original disciples were still living and could tell orally what they had seen and heard. Secondly, it explains why the N.T. writings, when they did come to be formed, were so occupied with the fulfillment of prophecy. The use of the O.T. by the primitive Christians generally took these lines. (1) It was studied as a book which was prophetic of Jesus Christ. The evidences of this are written all over the N.T. pages, but special reference may be made to passages like Lk. 24[27, 44f.] Acts 8[25f.] 17[1f., 11]. (2) It was also involved in the conflict over the Law, as may be seen from the Gospel of Matthew and the Epistles of Paul; this led to a discrimination, although the difficulties were usually solved by means of allegorizing. (3) Finally, it was precious on account of its ethical contents, as a moral code for the discipline of life. When the early church came to draw up rules for private and social life, the appeal was often made to the O.T.; it is significant that the moral sanctions in the Epistles are frequently biblicized (e.g., in Rom. 12[19] 1 Cor. 10[1-11] and Eph. 6[1-4]). In the Christian mission the O.T. was prized and employed as an invaluable witness against polytheism and immorality. Furthermore, the early Christians required to construct no cosmogony, for that was already supplied by the book of Genesis. Naturally they had to provide a fresh eschatology, for the belief about the end of things depended upon the new revelation of Jesus Christ, although it rested ultimately on principles implicit in the cosmogony, as is plain from the book of Revelation. But in the Genesis stories about the creation of the world there was already provided for the church an effective weapon against the fantastic pagan myths regarding the universe, myths which failed to rival the biblical story in its simplicity and intelligibility.

Factors Determining the Structure of the New Testament. It is not surprising, therefore, to find (1) quotations and reminiscences of the O.T. in the N.T., and also to discover that (2) the new literature of the people of God occasionally took forms similar to those of the earlier Scriptures; e.g., the epistle and the apocalypse, especially the latter. Nevertheless, the conditions of life in the primitive church were very different from those in which the O.T. literature had been produced, and this served to determine the structure and shape of the writings now called into existence. Round the Mediterranean basin lay scattered communities of Christians, some in Palestine and Syria and Asia Minor, some overseas in Greece and Italy. From time to time they were visited by the apostles who had founded them. But they required constant supervision and guidance, and this was provided in part by means of letters or epistles. A letter implies absence on the part of a friend or counselor. It is the substitute for oral advice or direction. Hence the apostles, in their enforced absence, sent letters to churches which were in difficulties. The earliest part of the N.T. literature consists of such letters, about a dozen in all, mainly sent by the apostle Paul to various communities founded by himself or by some of his coadjutors. Sometimes they would be copied out, in order to be circulated in the neighborhood (Col. 4[16]). They were designed for the immediate needs of the communities in question, for the practical instruction and inspiration of people engaged in the attempt to understand and carry out the Christian gospel in novel surroundings, beset by pagan and Jewish practices and beliefs. Their origin was occasional. What moved the writer to send his message was generally some emergency, and the result is that the Epistles do not profess to convey any explicit and systematic outline of the faith; the Epistle to the Romans is a partial exception, but, as a rule, the Epistles merely discuss such aspects and elements of the gospel as happened to be challenged at the time being in any given community. They presuppose the life and belief of the church at large, which may be often inferred from their incidental allusions. They were read at public worship, when the local Christians met. None of them is a private letter, except the note to Philemon, and even that includes more than the actual recipient in its address. The only apostle besides Paul who is known to have written in this way is Peter. The First Epistle of Peter falls with the Pauline letters inside the years 50–65 A.D. Some would, however, include the Epistle of James as one of the earliest in this group.

Between about 70 and 100 A.D. the other epistles came into being, though little is known about their origin. Hebrews was probably written from the East to some community in Rome, the Epistle of Judas (Jude) is apparently an Eastern production, and the two smaller notes of John are associated with the personality of a presbyter called John of the region about Ephesus toward the close of the century. (These and following questions are discussed more fully in the introductions to the various Epistles. The student will observe that in some cases different writers come to different conclusions on the date and authorship of a given book. Cf. art., *Chronology of N.T.*, p. 879).

Literary Problems of the Later Epistles. This second group raises two problems of a literary nature.

(1) The epistle was a widely used literary form in the ancient world, into which it was not uncommon to pour philosophical and even scientific material, and it has been sug-

gested that some of these later Epistles were really not letters so much as addresses put into the form of epistles. But it should be remembered that the church developed a special requirement of its own, which produced an analogous development in literature, namely, the pastoral address or homily. It seems likely that the Epistle of James, e.g., belongs to this class, as well as the First Epistle of John; they were not addressed to any specific circle but to the church at large. Hence they came to be regarded as catholic, or general, Epistles. How easy it was for even church-letters to be classified thus, and used for wider purposes, may be gathered from the letters to the Asiatic churches in Rev. 2, 3. If Ephesians be taken as a letter or homily by some disciple of Paul, it falls into the same category. In any case, its original circle was much wider than that of any single church such as that of Ephesus.

(2) This starts the second problem, namely, of authorship. Second Peter was composed in the beginning of the second century by a Christian who wrote in the name of the apostle; he used the earlier manifesto of Judas, applying it to the special conditions of his age and circle. The Epistles to Timothy and Titus similarly, in their present shape, seem to have been composed by a Paulinist who wrote later than the lifetime of his master, though he incorporated some material from notes by Paul (cf. intro. to Pastoral Epistles for a different view). Here we are faced by a literary method which composed epistles, just as a contemporary historian might compose speeches, in all good faith, under the name of some older hero or apostle, to whom the sentiments are ascribed. This was done with the honest and humble aim of edifying the faithful. The disciple would conceal his own name, as he sought to reproduce what he believed were or would have been the ideas and instructions of an honored master. There was no literary ambition in the practice, but, rather, the consciousness that through the pages of the disciple the apostle still spoke.

Place of the Epistles in the Early Church. These Epistles were never composed as literature, whether they were pseudonymous or anonymous or directly dictated by the man whose name they bear. Frequently they are great literature. But their original aim was to inspire and control groups of Christian people, many of whom could not read at all. "No one will get at my verses," said Walt Whitman, "who insists upon viewing them as a literary performance." The same may be said about the N.T. Epistles. In their style and composition, they present literary problems. So little reliable tradition has been preserved about them that we are thrown back, as a rule, upon internal evidence, and this discloses the fact that in some cases our canonical letters have been edited by a later generation —an awkward fact for "plenary inspiration." The phenomena of the Greek MSS., e.g., point to the fact that the last chapters of Romans were not always as they stand: Romans must have existed once, perhaps during the apostle's lifetime, in two editions (cf. p. 1136). Ephesians did not have "in Ephesus" in the original text of 1^1. The Corinthian Epistles represent a collection of letters written at different times to the church of Corinth, and the last four chapters of the Second Epistle, in particular, were composed prior to the first eight or nine chapters (see intro. to 1 and 2 Corinthians). Such problems engage the attention of the modern student. But his ultimate aim is to recover and reconstruct the state of things when the precious papyrus rolls containing these letters were circulating among the churches, first dictated by the apostle to a secretary, then conveyed by a messenger (like Silvanus, 1 Pet. 5^{12}), and finally treasured up in the church's archives or copied out for transmission. And all for purposes of edification! "Faith comes by hearing," said the apostle. It was as these homilies were heard by Christians that their faith was quickened and trained. We may sometimes wonder what they made of difficult Epistles like Romans and Hebrews. Did the early converts understand the arguments that baffle us to-day? How much did they take away from listening to passages like Rom. 5^{11}, for example? Perhaps, like a modern Christian congregation, they got good, even when they could not exactly follow the abstruse reasoning that fell upon their wondering ears. Still, they were accustomed to words and arguments that have long ceased to be familiar to ourselves. What sounds remote to us, in our altered conditions, was once clear and intelligible to men in the first century. For the apostles wrote with their minds upon their hearers. Doubtless Paul sometimes let himself go, as in some passages of Romans, where we have the feeling that for the moment he is developing a theme which has moved his own soul rather than pressing home a truth on the conscience of those who were to receive his words. But this was exceptional. If there is one thing plain in the Epistles it is this, that they were designed for a Fellowship, and that what is not plain to us must have once been plainer to those who heard it read aloud from the papyrus roll of the writer. It is the function of scholarship to throw light upon the social and religious life of the age, until such obscure allusions become clearer to our minds.

Origin of the Written Gospel. Alongside of the Epistles, however, there was growing up another class of literature. One of the most striking features in the N.T.—which would be remarkable, were it not that we read the books with eyes dulled by conventional familiarity—is that four books are specifically called "Gospels." The title is significant. In the Epistles "the gospel of God" or "the gospel of the Lord Jesus Christ" means the entire message of the Christian revelation. For Paul the gospel is the saving message of God in Christ, a devotional and dogmatic expression for the grace and kingdom of the Lord. Yet this term came to be applied to the books which described the life and teaching of Jesus. In literature, that is to say, the word acquired a special connotation. Not that the four Gospels call themselves Gospels, for their canonical headings are, of course, later additions. The original title was "The Gospel according to"—Matthew, etc. There was one gospel, and these books were simply different accounts of it. Still, the essence of the gospel was regarded as the personality and spirit of Jesus Christ, and this it was which served to concentrate the use of the word upon the literary Gospels. "Remember the words of the Lord Jesus" (Acts 20[35]) was a counsel which must have been often on the lips of the primitive Christians, a far more common cry than we realize. The structure of the Gospels points to this. The earliest confession of faith, "Jesus is Lord," involved some acquaintance with the historical Jesus, some knowledge of what he was and what he said and did, of his commands and promises as regulative of the Christian communities in their new life. The Epistles reflect a church which knew something about Jesus. They were not written to convey that knowledge; they presuppose information about the Lord transmitted by traditions from the disciples and apostles. These memories supplemented and ratified the O.T. Scriptures (see, e.g., 1 Cor. 15[1f.]). And it was out of them, circulating in oral form and perhaps in written form during the first three or four decades of the church's life, that the canonical Gospels eventually arose.

The "Gospel" is a new literary form. Nothing exactly corresponding to it is to be found in ancient literature, for even the edifying biographies of the age are only a very partial parallel. The Epistle had its prototype in Jewish and classical literature, but the "Gospel" is a fresh creation. It is a departure inspired by the same interests and needs as the Epistles. A Gospel was written to instruct Christians about Jesus, to justify them in calling him by the sacred title of "Lord." It provided the sanction for their habits and hopes by means of tales and traditions about him. It was not a biography, but designed, as we see from Lk. 1[1-4] and Jn. 20[31], to promote active and intelligent faith in the communities of the Lord. The supreme interest lay in Jesus. In the preaching of the church, as we overhear it in the Epistles, everything depended upon the significance and authority of his Person. So in the Gospels, though here the interest is concentrated upon his Person as it had once appeared in history. The interest worked along three lines, though the three cannot be always kept separate. There was the moral interest in his actions and sayings, as the norm of the Christian life. There was what may be termed the theological interest, to which we have already referred, namely, the interest which led Christians to think of him as occupying the commanding place in the redemptive purpose of God, in the light of ancient prophecy. Furthermore, there was the human interest, felt by many, in his personality, which loved to recall the memories of his actions and sayings as he lived and moved among men. All these interests throbbed in the pre-literary phase of the gospel traditions, when oral tradition in the main preserved anecdotes about him, and also in the later period, when such traditions began to be put together for catechetical purposes, in a more or less complete form, particularly traditions about his Passion, his miracles, and his teaching.

Mark, Matthew and Luke. The earliest attempts at preserving these memories in literary shape for teaching purposes have not survived, although one or two of them may be traced behind our extant Gospels. Of the latter the earliest is *Mark's*. Tradition connects it with information supplied by Peter, and may justify us in associating its composition with the Roman church about 70 A.D. *Matthew's* Gospel is arranged upon a more systematic plan, with plain traces of its origin in the catechetical education of the communities, and with an equally plain aim of explaining Christianity as the true fulfillment of O.T. prophecies. No Gospel is so suitable for the position of opening the N.T., as the crown and sequel of the O.T. Nor is any Gospel so marked by the church-consciousness. Mark's Gospel is one of its sources, but only one; the unknown author draws on special traditions, including a collection of Sayings, which, in some form or other, must also have lain before *Luke*. The third Gospel is the most literary of the four, with a preface in which the author explains his aim and method. He too had access to special traditions, besides the Gospel of Mark, but they were traditions unknown to his predecessors, possibly such as he learned at Antioch and Cæsarea as well as at Rome. The modern tendency is to note the literary quality of the Gospel (which, by the way, in its handling of earlier material, proves that no verbal accuracy was regarded as essential in the transmission of the evangelic traditions), and at the same time to recognize the historical value of much that is characteristic of Luke. Few doubts are felt that he was the physician and friend of the apostle Paul, although his work was written after the latter's death. The audience he has in mind belonged to Christians of the outside world, such as the Theophilus to whom he dedicates his work; they were not acquainted with the inner interests of Judaism, as the readers of Matthew are supposed to be. (For fuller discussion, see art., *Structure of the Synoptic Gospels*, p. 867; also the intro. to each of the four Gospels.)

Acts of the Apostles. Luke's Gospel is the only one of the four which has a sequel. His second volume, called The Acts of the Apostles, carries on the tale of the primitive disciples from the Ascension to the arrival of Paul at Rome about 60 (65) A.D. That is, it covers about thirty years. Apart from some details about John and Peter and James, in the early chapters, it recounts, however, the acts and adventures of only one apostle, his hero, Paul. Here again sources have been employed, including a diary of travel composed by himself, extracts from which are incorporated in the book. It is far from giving a complete record of even Paul's missions. The interior troubles of the Pauline churches, e.g., are ignored in his pages, and we do not learn that the apostle ever wrote an epistle at all. But Acts is the first contribution to church history (see p. 1094), and, together with the Epistles, enables us to make out dimly the primitive expansion and obstacles of the communities within the empire. The data supplied by Luke and the inferences which may be drawn from his pages permit us to reconstruct an outline of the apostle's movements down to his final journey to the capital. In this class of literature Luke has predecessors. The art of writing speeches in character, the use of material from journals, the effective employment of dialogue and letters, are all signs that the author was familiar with the literary methods of historiography in his age.

The Fourth Gospel. The fourth Gospel was intended to supplant or, rather, to supplement the earlier narratives. It is written out of some independent apostolic traditions about Jesus, but in no Gospel, indeed, in no book of the N.T., do the Hebrew and the Greek worlds meet so conspicuously. The presentation of the Lord's life and teaching is recast, in order to confront speculative difficulties of Hellenism in the contemporary Asiatic world (see p. 1066). The author seeks to interpret the Christian revelation afresh for believers who were no longer living in days when the primitive Messianic and apocalyptic beliefs formed the main categories of religious thought within the communities. Along with the contemporary pamphlet, called the First Epistle of John, it comes from a circle at Ephesus toward the close of the first century, and, whatever be its sources, its affinities are Greek, in thought and language. It is inspired by a breath of the Platonic idealism which has touched the Epistle to the Hebrews (see intro. to Hebrews). In its dialogues and descriptions we note the desire of naturalizing Christianity in a new world of thought and feeling, where conceptions of reality and truth were swaying the religious mind. This is the preoccupation which distinguishes the fourth Gospel from the other three. Jesus is still the center of the revelation. The mystical inwardness of the faith rests on history, but the story is recast until allegorical or symbolical methods make it a new thing. "The Word was made flesh." Only a Hebrew mind could have written that sentence, which is the keynote to the book. As it develops, the reader is shown a deep, divine significance in the history by means of an Hellenic symbolism which goes far beyond anything in the first three Gospels, and for which the only anticipations are to be found in the later Epistles of Paul and in Hebrews.

The present form of the book shows that it has undergone some editing. The last chapter was either an afterthought, or added later by another hand. Also, in the course of transmission, the text has been changed by the transportation of certain passages. Ch. 6, e.g., originally lay before ch. 5 (see notes there). Other alterations can be detected. But there is an impressive unity of style and thought which renders it next to impossible to suppose that any original source can be disentangled from the extant text. Tradition in the second century assigned the book to a certain John at Ephesus, and some still hold that it may be the work either of the apostle John or of one of his disciples (see intro. to John, p. 1062–6). But there was a Presbyter John also, at this period and in this quarter, to whom the second and third of the Johannine letters are due. The intricacy of the literary and the historical problems, however, ought not to blind us to the startling novelty of its teaching, and especially to the relegation of the apocalyptic eschatology to the background. It is this concentration on the present and lasting message of the Gospel, coupled with a limpid style in its higher reaches, and an arresting power of religious intuition, which have made the book a prized possession of the church.

The Revelation of John. If apocalyptic prophecy is subordinated to the new interpretation in the fourth Gospel, it is otherwise in its contemporary book, the Revelation of John. Here the prototype is the book of Daniel and Jewish apocalypses of that class (see art., *Literature of the Intertestamental Period,* p. 197). It is a tract for bad times, written at the end of Domitian's reign, about 95 or 96 A.D., when the prophet warned the faithful in Asia Minor, his diocese, against the perils of the persecution, and promised them immediate relief in the second advent of Jesus from heaven. Like most apocalyptic writers, he freely drew on earlier sources. With the glow and fantasy of the Oriental imagination he depicted the sudden, near end of all things,

"With hue like that when some great painter dips
His pencil in the gloom of earthquake and eclipse."

Many of the details are cryptic, the symbolism is weird, and the literary arrangement of the oracles, in the middle part, is perplexing; but the clear message is that through the crises of history a divine purpose runs, which is bound up with Jesus Christ, and that loyalty to his cause and kingdom at all costs is the one hope and safety of the community, even although the state may threaten and harry the loyalists. Victory is assured to the gospel, and victory soon. The author, a true prophet, is in touch with the Asiatic communities, but we know little more about his personality. His pages prove that he was a master of this literary method, which he employs with splendid and strange power to present his thrilling call to arms, the arms being faith and patience. It is as though he were endeavoring to make his readers hear what he had heard the Lord say to himself, "Hold the fort, for I am coming."

Gradual Assembling of the Writings. No writer of these books was conscious that he was contributing to a N.T. The books came into circulation gradually and locally, as books of the fellowship, intended to keep Christians faithful until the end arrived. The writers, however, had done more permanent work than they knew. As copies were exchanged, a collection of Paul's Epistles was formed, perhaps in Asia Minor or at Corinth; thus a nucleus of the canon arose, and by the middle of the second century the beginnings of an authoritative collection of what is now known as the N.T. writings were laid. The four Gospels were selected out of a number of others, as genuinely apostolic, and Acts was added as a connecting link between the Gospels and the Epistles. The earlier stages of this process are obscure. But in the course of it the writings were edited; titles were supplied, gaps were filled (as at the end of Mark's Gospel), and some textual changes were made, in order to emphasize the catholic bearing of the various books, which were now the sacred writings of a world-wide church.

The Literature of a Religious Fellowship. From the first these books had been writings of a community, for church use. The N.T., in its formation, reveals itself more and more as literature of a great fellowship, and that in two special aspects. One is worship and the other is the sense of a mission. The various books become more intelligible in the light of these considerations. Their genesis and their form are plain, as we recognize them under these aspects; they are the Sacred Books of a church which produced them for the dual functions of worship and mission service.

(1) The very form of the Epistles occasionally betrays *their use in worship.* They end with "Amen," and although this is now and then due to the canonical editing (for the object of the canon was to sanction the books which could be read at worship), the tone and style of these writings show that they were naturally employed in worship as homilies. Indeed, an Epistle like Hebrews reads like a series of Bible-readings from the O.T. by a trained Christian expositor. The Apocalypse of the prophet John, which we call the Book of Revelation, has a special blessing for the reader (1^3), i.e., for the Christian minister who reads this prophecy aloud at public worship (see Mt. 24^{15}). The hymns in Luke's Gospel and the songs in the Revelation are probably early specimens of hymnology in the churches. And, in this connection, it is worth noting that the earliest confession of faith falls into rhythmical form. The fragment of primitive hymnology in 1 Tim. 3^{16} served as a semi-liturgical confession of faith; its short cola were written to be chanted or sung. For the primitive Christians recognized that any confession of faith ought to be "sung rather than signed."

(2) The subject of this early confession was Christ, and this was the topic of the N.T. books as *literature of a mission.* The Gospels in particular reveal the working of this interest, as they bring out the significance of Jesus for the world. They present the distinctive fea-

tures which commended Christ. That he was a real historical person, for example; that he truly fulfilled the prophecies of the O.T.; that he was no mere mythical or dubious figure like some of the heroes of the Mystery-cults of the age. Above all, it was essential for the Christian mission that the differentia of his person and career should be brought out, in order to make it clear in what sense he marked an advance upon Judaism and filled a gap left by any pagan cult. Hence three elements are singled out in the evangelic tradition: he taught, he suffered, he forgave sins. No real precedent for these, as they were exemplified in the story of Jesus, existed in any Messianic expectation. It was the hold of such truths that gave the communities their power and chance in propaganda. Probably there is no N.T. book written directly for outsiders, but every book was written more or less for communities which were conscious of their responsibility for the great mission and of their interest in the enterprise. In many there is an apologetic element, and this is bound up with their function as literature of communities sensible of wider aims than self-preservation. It is as we keep in mind the mission-interest that we realize why the Gospels concentrate upon certain phases of the life of Jesus, and why these phases are handled thus, and not otherwise.

Why Written in Greek. Finally, it was due to this mission-interest that the literature was composed in Greek. The O.T. of the time was a Greek translation made for the purpose of instruction and of religious propaganda by the Jews, and the N.T. could go anywhere in the empire because it was written in the Hellenistic vernacular spoken by all educated people. (See art., *Language of N.T.*, p. 880.) A religion whose sacred books were written in this language had an unrivaled opportunity. It was not handicapped by provincial dialects like Hebrew or Aramaic. Possibly some of the sources of the N.T. writings were originally in these languages. But as the books come before us, they are written in what was the most widely circulated tongue of the day. The church went out upon its mission to the great world with a literature which could carry far beyond Judaism or any Oriental range; the fact of these sacred books being in Hellenistic Greek enabled the Christian mission to address itself to men far and wide, in what was the international vernacular of the age.

Literature: Goodspeed, *The Story of the N.T.;* Harnack, *The Origin of the N.T.* (Eng. trans.); Milligan, *The N.T. Documents;* J. A. Robertson, *The Hidden Romance of the N.T.;* Gregory, *Canon and Text of the N.T.;* Souter, *The Text and Canon of the N.T.;* H. R. and C. E. Purinton, *The Literature of the N.T.*

THE TRANSMISSION OF THE NEW TESTAMENT

By Professor A. T. ROBERTSON

Definitions and Explanations. It is impossible to discuss this subject without using certain terms and symbols which may confuse the ordinary reader. These terms and symbols will be explained in the proper places, but a brief reference to them here will perhaps serve to promote clarity. The term *manuscript* (MS., plural MSS.) refers to the handwritten documents which from the earliest Christian times to the invention of printing preserved to us, in whole or in part, the contents of the N.T. MSS. are divided into *uncials* and *minuscules* or *cursives*. Uncials are written in large block capitals, each letter separate. Minuscules, or cursives, are written in smaller letters, which are usually joined together as in ordinary handwriting—hence cursive, or running script. The earliest manuscripts were written on *papyrus*, a material obtained from a reed. When these were of any length, they were *rolled*, but papyri MSS. have survived to us only in fragments. Papyrus was replaced about the fourth century by *vellum* or *parchment* (skin), and this made possible the *codex* (plural, *codices*), separate leaves placed together in book form. A *version* was the translation of the N.T., or a part of it, into another language. The most important early versions were the Syriac, of which there were several, and the Latin Vulgate (symbol, vg.), which included the O.T., made by Jerome in the fourth century. The *Textus Receptus* (symbol T.R.) means the text now commonly received, and is due chiefly to the work of Erasmus. For more convenient reference, scholars have worked out a system of symbols to indicate the various MSS. and versions. Thus the symbols of the Old Latin MSS. are small roman letters, a, b, c, etc.; of papyri fragments, superior arabic figures, ^{1}, ^{2}, ^{3}, etc.; of the Syriac versions, the abbreviation syr. followed by a superior abbreviation, syr.$^{\text{sin.}}$, syr.$^{\text{cu.}}$, etc. the second abbreviation indicating which version is intended; and of the minuscules, or cursives, ordinary arabic figures, 1, 2, 3, etc. The use of these symbols, however, is not uniform—a fact which often causes confusion. The ordinary reader is most likely to meet the symbols of the six great primary uncial codices, the use of which is fortunately quite uniform. These symbols, with one exception, are capital roman letters. A is the Codex Alexandrinus (British Museum); B the Codex Vaticanus (the Vatican); C the Codex Ephræmi Rescriptus (Paris); D the Codex Bezæ (Cambridge, England); W the Washington Codex (Washington, D. C.). The exception is the great Codex Sinaiticus (Petrograd), of which the symbol is א (Aleph), the first letter of the Hebrew alphabet. These various matters are all explained at length below.

No New Testament Autographs. We are concerned with the problem of how the books of the N.T. have been handed down to us. If we had the autographs, there would be no problem. No one now expects the discovery of an autographed copy of any book of the N.T., though it is abstractly possible, since there are many specimens of papyrus writing from the first century and even earlier. The dry sand piles of Egypt may yet yield more surprises than have been discovered. But even if an original MS. of one of Paul's Epistles were to be found, it would probably be in another's handwriting, save in the little Epistle to Philemon, which Paul apparently wrote himself (Philm. 19). His habit was to dictate to an amanuensis as in the case of Tertius (Rom. 16^{22}), or as Peter used Silvanus (1 Pet. 5^{12}). Paul's method was to sign his name at the close (2 Thess. 3^{17}) as proof of the genuineness of the Epistle.

The Age of Printing. The Mazarin Bible (1455 A.D.) was the first book to be printed, but it was not till 1514 that the first printed Greek N.T. came, the edition of Ximenes, and this was not actually published till 1522. The first Greek N.T. to be published was that of Erasmus, in 1516. It was hurriedly done because the publisher, Frobenius of Basle, was anxious for Erasmus to get his edition out before Ximenes. He succeeded in doing that, but at great cost. At first Erasmus claimed that he had produced the work *ad Græcam veritatem*, but finally he admitted that it was not so carefully edited as it might have been. He had five minuscule (cursive) MSS. that were late. He had one fairly good minuscule, 1, a tenth century MS., but he based his edition mainly on 2, a poor minuscule of the twelfth century. For the Apocalypse he had only 1^{r}, which was deficient in the last six verses of the Apocalypse; these Erasmus put into Greek from the Latin Vulgate. Unfortunately this hurriedly printed edition of Erasmus is the basis of the *Textus Receptus* and the King James Version (A.V.). The text of Erasmus, with some changes effected by Stephens, Beza and the Elzevirs, became stereotyped and won absolute dominion over scholars and the public generally. When Erasmus published his first edition, he was chided by Stunica for having omitted the passage about the Trinity in 1 Jn. 5[7, 8]. In a rash moment Erasmus said that if the passage could be found in a single Greek MS., he would insert it. The passage was translated from the Latin Vulgate and forged into the Greek minuscule 61 of the sixteenth century (now in Dublin). Erasmus suspected the truth, but stood to his promise and put it in. When the R.V. properly left it out, a cry was raised that it was done in the interest of Unitarianism. It should never have been put into the Greek text at all.

The Battle for the Original Text. It has been a hard and long fight to get back of Erasmus' late and imperfect text to a text closer to that of the first century. Even Bengel in 1734 published the *Textus Receptus* because the publisher and the public would not accept a corrected text. It was not till the time of Griesbach (1744–1777) that the revolt against the work of Erasmus took shape in a way that counted. Griesbach published his Greek N.T. with a critical apparatus that gave scholars an instrument with which to work. He went back behind the printed Greek Testaments to the MSS., which he divided into three families: (1) the Byzantine or Constantinopolitan (the text of Erasmus); (2) the Western type found in D and the Latin Versions; and (3) the Alexandrian as seen in A, B, C, L. The tide began to turn. Lachmann (1842–50) was brave enough to publish his own text with variations of the *Textus Receptus* at the end. This great innovation bore fruit. His idea was to restore the text of the oldest MSS. Tregelles (1857–1879) carried on the work by showing what was the oldest type of text, not merely that of old MSS. Tischendorf (1864–1872) gave a fuller apparatus than Tregelles, but to the great loss of scholarship Caspar René Gregory, a famous German specialist in the Greek text, was killed in the Great War without bringing Tischendorf up to date. None of the important new discoveries since 1872 are noted in Tischendorf.

It is Westcott and Hort (1881) who have shown modern scholars how to find the best text. They worked out a reliable theory for using the vast mass of MS. evidence for the N.T. books. There are, they said, two lines of evidence, internal and external. The internal evidence of single readings consists of transcriptional and intrinsic evidence. Transcriptional looks at the problem of variations in a given passage or reading from the standpoint of the copyist or scribe. Intrinsic evidence looks at it from the standpoint of the author. By study and care one is able to weigh the evidence in each single reading and to draw a tentative conclusion. By a like process one may test a whole document when each single reading in the document has been duly weighed. Then a group of documents can likewise be weighed. Last and most important of all, the several families or classes of documents can be tested. Westcott and Hort find four families of documents or MSS. (1) The Syrian (like the Byzantine of Griesbach) is found in the late documents only, and when standing alone is wrong. (2) The Western (same term as that used by Griesbach) appears in early documents like D, Old Latin, and Old Syriac, and is not always geographically "Western." (3) The Neutral is represented by the oldest and best documents, like א, A, B, C, Bohairic and Sahidic. (4) The Alexandrian has no document always Alexandrian; it is often found in א, C, L, and represents scholarly corrections of limited range. Streeter in his *Four Gospels* prefers the term "Byzantine" to "Syrian"; he makes Alexandrian include Neutral, and he divides the Western into Eastern and Western, all of which is plausible. He argues, however, for a further division of Eastern into Antiochian and Cæsarean, which is less probable. Von Soden has his own way of reaching very much the same result as Westcott and Hort by a much more complicated system. The method of Westcott still holds the field as scholars endeavor to feel their way back to the first-century MSS. (For a full statement of Westcott and Hort's principles for arriving at the correct reading, see the Appendix to their Greek N.T.)

The Greek Minuscule Codices. These immediately precede the age of printing and exist in very large numbers. There are so many of them for different parts of the N.T. that one is at first bewildered. Over 2300 are known, though many of them have not been examined with great care. When one remembers that there is not a complete copy of Homer before the thirteenth century A.D., or of Herodotus before the tenth, or of the Hebrew Bible before the tenth, he can realize what a marvelous thing it is that over 4,000 Greek MSS. of the N.T. are at the service of modern scholars (Papyri, 32; Uncials, 170; Minuscules, 2,320; Lectionaries, 1561, as

Gregory counts them). The minuscules supplant the uncials in the tenth century A.D., though the minuscule codex has been pushing out the uncial codex for two centuries. The minuscule codices are written in a flowing or running hand in smaller letters with accents and breathings, some punctuation, and some space between the words. The later minuscules are usually copied from other minuscules, though some of them are copied from uncials, even from early and excellent uncials. When the minuscules are opposed by the early uncials the presumption is strong against them. The minuscules are denoted by Arabic figures, but there is no uniform system observed. The minuscule termed 582 for the Gospels is called 227 for the Acts and 279 for Paul. Some of the minuscules, like 1 (tenth century), 118 (thirteenth century), seem to be copied from the same uncial. Ferrar, of Dublin, has shown that 13, 69, 124, 346 (all of the twelfth century save 69, which is of the fourteenth) come from a common uncial, the so-called Ferrar Group. There are now eight others known to belong to this same Ferrar Group (230, 543, 788, 826, 828, 983, 1689, 1709), a dozen altogether. Paper was not in common use in the West until the thirteenth century. The ordinary material for minuscule writing was the vellum, or parchment, which could show the smaller letters to advantage. The invention of printing won the victory of paper over vellum. There are only 46 minuscule MSS., according to Kenyon, that contain all the N.T., but Von Soden counts 167. The use of vellum made the Codex, or book form, convenient. The combination of the codex form and the small cursive style of writing made it possible for the whole N.T. to be put upon one MS. The papyrus roll and the uncial style of writing made it too cumbersome and unwieldy. The cursive style of writing for private documents had existed for centuries. What was new was the use of it for literary purposes. There are specimens of non-literary papyri as late as the eighth century. Some of the minuscule MSS. are very elaborately ornamented with flourishes at the beginning and at the end. Some are written on purple vellum and are very handsome.

The Greek Uncial Codices. The minuscules were preceded by the uncial codices, which only gradually gave way to them. The uncial letters were larger and were formed separately, like the printing done by children when they are learning to write. The codex book forms suited the uncial style of writing much better than the papyrus roll which preceded it. The parchment codex displaced the papyrus roll for literary purposes in the fourth century. So, then, the uncial codex period runs from the fourth to the tenth century. The pages in the parchment (membrane) usually were square and had two to four columns to the page. Two was the common number, as in A, though B has three columns to the page and forty-two lines to the column. ℵ has four narrow columns to the page and forty-eight lines to the column. There is no separation between the words; the value of the vellum made it necessary to conserve space. Surely, one needed skill to pick up the words and to read aloud in public, as was often done (Rev. 1^{3}). Some of the scribes developed wonderfully fine handwriting. There were schools for publishing books; the reader would dictate and the scribes would copy rapidly. In such cases the spelling would vary greatly because of the similarity of sound in some vowels and diphthongs. The scribe of ℵ is fond of iota (i) while the scribe of B prefers *ei* to *i*. It is possible that ℵ and B are two of the fifty copies of the Greek Bible ordered to be published by Constantine, an order carried out under the direction of Eusebius of Cæsarea. There had been great destruction of the Greek MSS. in the Roman persecutions. It is a wonder that any were spared at all.

The first complete Bibles in one language were the Greek Bibles, as we see in ℵ, B, and A, except when portions are lost. ℵ is the only uncial that contains the entire N.T. B stops in the middle of Hebrews (9^{13}) while A lacks Mt. 1^{1}–25^{6} Jn. 6^{50}–8^{52} 2 Cor. 4^{13}–12^{7}. There are 170 uncials for different portions of the N.T. They vary greatly in value. For the Gospels there are six primary uncials (B, ℵ, A, C, D, W). Two of these (ℵ and B) belong to the fourth century, A.D., and are far and away the best in value. B, the Vatican MS., is in the Vatican Library in Rome, and is the best single Greek MS. for the N.T., and the best representative of the Neutral type of text for the Gospels and Acts. Two correctors have made alterations in it. A good photographic copy can now be had. The Codex Sinaiticus is in Petrograd. Tischendorf discovered it at the Monastery of Saint Catherine at Mount Sinai. Its symbol is ℵ. There have been seven correctors who have made changes in it. The discovery of this MS. led Tischendorf to get out the eighth edition of his *Novum Testamentum Graece*, which, because of ℵ, differs in three thousand places from the seventh edition. It has a mixed text, usually Neutral with B, but sometimes Western with D, or Alexandrian with CL. A (Codex Alexandrinus) is now in the British Museum, and it also has been photographed. This codex belongs to the first half of the fifth century. Enlarged capital letters appear at the beginning of new paragraphs. It shows four different hands in the N.T. and has a mixed text. In the Gospels it frequently has Syrian readings, while in the Acts, Epistles, and Apocalypse it is mainly Neutral. It is the best MS. known for the Apocalypse. C (Codex Ephræmi Rescriptus) is in Paris and also belongs to the fifth century. It has fragments of all the books save 2 Thessalonians and 2 John. The manuscript is a palimpsest (a parchment which has been written over a second time). In the twelfth century, sermons of Ephræm Syrus in Syriac were written over the Greek of the N.T. (One wonders if other sermons have not sometimes obscured the meaning of Scripture!) The Greek was in one column and the Syriac in two columns. New paragraphs begin with larger letters and the Eusebian or Ammonian sections appear in the margin. It has also a mixed text (Neutral, Alexandrian, even Syrian). D (Codex Bezæ) belongs to the sixth century and is in Cambridge, England. It is bilingual, Greek (left page) and Latin (right page), and has only the Gospels and Acts. It is the earliest Greek form of the pure Western Text. The relation between the Greek and the Latin Text is not clear. It was apparently made in the West, as the Old Latin was, though it shows affinities with the Old Syriac of the East (Syriac of Cureton and Syriac Sinaitic—see below). There are some remarkable readings found nowhere else, as in Lk. 6[4]. The MS. contains frequent lacunæ or gaps. At the end of the Gospel of Luke there are many omissions and in the Acts so many additions that Blass, to relieve the scribe of D from the responsibility for these vagaries, has suggested two editions of the Gospel and the Acts by Luke himself, but the theory has not won much following. It is possible that this scribe knew Latin better than he did Greek. The sixth primary uncial is W (Washington Codex) which may belong to the end of the fourth, not later than the early part of the sixth century. It is in Washington and contains only the Gospels. It was bought in Egypt by Mr. C. L. Freer, of Detroit. The chief readings have been published by H. A. Sanders and E. J. Goodspeed. There are no chapter or section titles, though the paragraphs show a little punctuation. Brief titles appear at the beginning and the end of each Gospel. The books appear in the Western order (Matthew, John, Luke, Mark). After Mk. 16[14] there is a peculiar addition, found in no other Greek MS. It has a mixed text (Neutral, Western, Alexandrian, even Syrian). Photographic copies may be obtained of all these codices. Besides these six primary uncials there are over 160 secondary uncials of varying worth and of later date. Some of them have not as much value as the best of the minuscules.

The Greek Lectionaries. There are over 1500 of these lectionaries. They give detached portions of the N.T. for public reading in worship. They show explanatory changes in the text at the beginning or close of the passage to make the paragraph understood by itself apart from the context. The body of the passage is usually unchanged. The earliest lectionary known belongs to the sixth century. Most of them are in the uncial style of writing, which lasts in the lectionaries till the eleventh century, a century longer than the uncial style in the continuous text. The type of text is usually Syrian or Western. Those for the Gospels are called *Evangeliaria* or *Evangelistaria*, while those for the Acts or the Epistles are termed *Apostoli* or *Praxapostoli.*

Papyri Fragments. Sometimes papyrus codices appear, but usually the form employed for the papyrus sheets was the roll. The papyrus codex is found in Asia Minor as early as the first century A.D., but by the fourth century the parchment (or vellum) displaced the use of papyrus for literary purposes. Gregory thinks that Christian scribes introduced the codex, or leaf-book form, into the MSS. of the N.T. in order to be able more easily to find a passage.

Papyrus was employed by the Greeks for books from the fifth century B.C., to the fourth century A.D. The papyrus reed grew mainly in Egypt, though it was found also in Sicily and in Syria in marshes or pools. The inner bark or pith was sliced and these slices were placed side by side, pressed, and moistened with sticky glue. Then like pieces were placed crosswise. If only one side was used, the writing would be on the horizontal lines. The separate sheets were glued together to make a roll of any desired length. Often both sides were used in writing, like the roll in Rev. 5[1]. One in Greek would begin on the left and make column after column to the right. Then the roll would be folded so that the outside sheet would be at the beginning. As the roll was read, it would be unrolled on the right and folded up on the left. Sometimes a stick would be put in to hold the roll in place. The roll of the prophet Isaiah (probably in the LXX) was handed to Jesus in the synagogue at Nazareth, and he opened it (unrolled it) and shut it (rolled it up) and gave it back to the attendant (Lk. 4[17, 19]). Sometimes writing tablets were used in school or in correspondence. Zacharias apparently employed one (Lk. 1[63]). They were small, although a tablet might contain as much as 2 John or even Philemon. A stilus was used to write on the wax tablet. The usual method of writing in the first century (and till 300 A.D.) was the papyrus roll. The longer literary works might be on parchment. It is possible (by no means certain) that the Gospels and the Acts were written on parchment, though it is clear that the Epistles were first written on papyrus. A soot ink (black) was used on the papyrus. The pen was made from a reed. Note ink (black) and pen (reed) in 3 Jn. v. 13 and the black ink referred to in 2 Cor. 3[3]. For the roll, papyrus was preferable; for the codex form, parchment. The papyrus was light and delicate, but the parchment allowed the use of larger letters which were more easily read.

The great papyri discoveries of Grenfell and Hunt in Egypt have turned a flood of light on the whole subject of ancient writing. The vast mass of material already printed from Oxyrhynchus, Fayum, Hibeh, and Tebtunis preserve some specimens of the old Greek writers that were lost. Most of the specimens run from the third century B.C. to the third century A.D. (some even later). The papyrus is very brittle and has survived in Egypt only because of preservation in the dry sand. Many specimens are mere scraps and are mainly odds and ends of things, bills, receipts, love letters, tax-bills, etc. But there are thousands of examples of the very material employed by the N.T. writers, written in the very kind of Greek found in the N.T., the current *koiné*, mostly vernacular, but partly literary. (See art., *Language of N.T.*, p. 880.) But do the papyri furnish any portions of the text of the Greek N.T.? They do, but no entire book has yet been found such as we have so abundantly in the uncial and minuscule codices. But thirty-four N.T. fragments have turned up and one is constantly hoping that others may be found. Some of these fragments are leaves of books. Some are from rolls. A dozen of them belong to the fourth century, and give the text of ℵ B (Neutral). Several others belong to the third or fourth and a half dozen others clearly belong to the third century. Two of these, Papyrus[1] and Papyrus[5] give the oldest scraps of the Greek N.T. yet found in MS., a century older than ℵ and B. They give the same type of text, and strongly confirm the Neutral type.

The Need for Versions. The Greek *Koiné* in which the N.T. books were written was the common language of the Græco-Roman world. It was not degenerate Greek by any means, but a language wonderfully adapted to the commercial and literary needs of the time. By this Greek *Koiné* men of all classes were reached in address, conversation, letters, official documents, books. In Rome itself Greek was a common medium of communication. The Emperor Marcus Aurelius wrote his *Meditations* in Greek. Paul wrote to the Roman church in Greek a letter that was meant to be read in public. But there were outlying districts where Greek was little known. When the gospel penetrated the mountain districts of Syria, there soon arose a demand for a Syriac translation. A like demand for Egyptian (Coptic) versions came as the gospel went up the Nile from Alexandria. In North Africa around the old Carthage region Latin still held its place against the Greek. In the course of time there arose a call for versions in Æthiopia, in Armenia, in Persia and even in Britain (Anglo-Saxon). These later and secondary versions have little value for the text of the N.T. The versions do not compare in worth with the older Greek MSS. Many of the finer and more precise shades of meaning cannot be put into any translation. But the versions do bear witness to the presence or absence of a sentence, clause, or paragraph. The versions of chief importance are the Syriac, the Egyptian (Coptic), and the Latin. These alone call for discussion. We should not forget that in the versions we are dealing with MSS. often differ among themselves in giving some particular reading. These MSS. differ in date and in value.

The Syriac Versions. Palestine was a bilingual country, and Jesus himself spoke either in Aramaic or in Greek, as was true of Paul. The Syriac of Syria (or Assyria) was not identical with the Aramaic of Palestine, though closely kin to it. We do not know when the first Syriac translation was made. The famous *Diatessaron* of Tatian appeared in Rome about 170 A.D. It was the first of the Gospel harmonies, of which so many have since been made. Tatian made a continuous narrative by combining the four Gospels. It can now be read in English from the Arabic version. We do not know whether Tatian made his harmony in Syriac or in Greek. The type of text is mainly the Western, though sometimes Neutral with ℵ and B. It is held by Von Soden that Tatian's *Diatessaron*, because of its continuous narrative, is the chief disturbing factor in the text of the Gospels.

We know the Old Syriac (apparently made about 200 A.D.) from two important MSS. (1) The oldest is the *Sinaitic Syriac* (Syr.$^{\text{sin.}}$) which seems to belong to the fourth century. Mrs. Lewis and Mrs. Gibson, two scholarly sisters of Cambridge, England, discovered this MS., a palimpsest, in the same Monastery of Saint Catherine on Mount Sinai where Tischendorf found ℵ. The MS. is still at Mount Sinai, but it has been photographed.

It is defective and contains only portions of the Gospels. In Mt. 1^{16} it has the famous reading, "Joseph begat Jesus," but it also contains the passage Mt. 1^{19-25}, the message of the angel to Joseph, showing that the copyist accepted the virgin birth of Jesus. The MS., though belonging to the East, is mainly Western in type. (2) *The Curetonian Syriac* (Syr.$^{cu.}$) is the other Old Syriac document. It belongs to the fifth century and gives only the Gospels. Much of it is lost and it often gives the Western text. It does not always agree with the Sinaitic Syriac. It gives the usual text in Mt. 1^{16} and contains also Mt. 16^{17-20} (absent in the Sinaitic Syriac) and has a short doxology in Mt. 6^{13}.

The *Peshitta Syriac* (Syr.$^{sch.}$) was once supposed to be the oldest Syriac version, but is now placed in the fifth century. It does not contain 2 and 3 John, 2 Peter, Jude, or the Apocalypse. There are 243 copies of this version. The word *Peshitta* means "simple," and this version came to be the current version, like the Latin Vulgate or the English A.V. The type of text is usually Syrian, though occasionally pre-Syrian readings are retained. In the year 508 Philoxenus had a new revision made by Polycarp, called the *Philoxenian* (Syr.$^{phil.}$). In 616 Thomas of Harkel revised this revision, the *Harklean Version* (Syr.$^{h.}$). There are 51 MSS. of this version. It contains marginal readings in Greek which give a different text. The translation is literal and rather rough. When Tischendorf first made his critical apparatus he knew only the Peshitta and the Harklean, which he called *posterior* (later). The *Jerusalem or Palestinian Syriac* (Syr.^{h}·) is an independent version made in the sixth century. The various MSS. of this version do not agree, but they give the Neutral or Western type of text. (Cf. pp. 103–5.)

The Egyptian Versions. The Egyptian (Coptic) Versions are mainly two. The Sahidic or Thebaic belongs to upper Egypt, where a version would be needed first as the gospel spread up the Nile. The Coptic language is a sort of bridge between the Greek and the old Egyptian. The translation was probably made about 200 A.D. or a little sooner. There are 751 fragments of this version. The type of text is Neutral or Western. It does not agree with D or the Old Latin in any additions. The Bohairic is called also Memphitic or Coptic and is probably to be dated 250 A.D. It contains the whole of the N.T. and is used to-day by Coptic Christians. The MSS. do not always agree. The better ones omit Jn. 5^{4} and Jn. 7^{53}–8^{11}. Two copies agree with L in giving both endings for Mark's Gospel. (See notes on Mk. $16^{9f.}$). The type of text is usually Neutral or Alexandrian. Very little is known about the Bashmuric or Middle Egyptian Version, though it is rather more like the Sahidic than the Bohairic.

The Latin Versions. Tischendorf knew only two, the Old Latin and the Vulgate, but the Old Latin MSS. (represented by single letters, a, b, etc.) differ so much that scholars now hold to three Latin Versions. The oldest is the African Latin, made in North Africa by the end of the second century or the beginning of the third. Tertullian and Cyprian seemed to know it. The MSS. of it are few, like k, e, r, m. The type of text is mainly Western. The European Latin probably came in the third century. The chief MSS. are a, b, d, g, p, gig. The type of text is now Western, now Neutral. The Latin translation of Irenæus was the European Latin text. The confusion over the Latin MSS. led Pope Damasus to ask Eusebius Hieronymus (Jerome) to make a new translation. This he did, completing the Gospels in 383 A.D., and the whole of the N.T. by 386. He used the best of the Old Latin MSS. (a, b, g, k) and some good Greek MSS. of the Neutral type. As a result the Latin Vulgate is more often Neutral than is the Old Latin (African or European). Some of the 30,000 Vulgate MSS. continued to make use of the Old Latin. The work of Jerome was bitterly fought by many. It won slowly, and finally came to be regarded (as it still is in Roman Catholicism) as the only correct text. It had a tremendous influence on the modern versions and the *Textus Receptus*. The modern critical text has been fought hard, but not so hard as Jerome's Vulgate text was by "the little asses," as he dubbed them. Wordsworth and White have issued a critical edition of the Latin Vulgate text.

The Fathers. The quotations from the early Greek, Syriac, and Latin writers are helpful especially because they give a date for the type of readings found in them. Most of the quotations are not carefully made and are of more value as proving the existence of a passage than as furnishing the exact language. Occasionally a man expressly says that he is quoting a document. As a rule, a commentator is more reliable because he has a MS. or several of them right before him as he writes. The codex book form was more easily used for quotations than the roll. The Greek writers include Marcion, Justin Martyr, Irenæus, Clement of Alexandria, Origen, Eusebius, Athanasius, Cyril of Jerusalem, Cyril of Alexandria, Gregory of Nyssa, Gregory of Nazianzus, Epiphanius, Chrysostom. The Latin writers include Tertullian, Cyprian, Ambrose, Jerome,

Augustine, Pelagius, Primasius, the Venerable Bede. The Syriac fathers embrace Aphraates, Ephræm Syrus, Ishodad of Merv. The N.T. could be reproduced in sense from these writers. When we consider all the copyings and translations, it is a marvel how accurately the text of the N.T. can be restored to-day free from any heresy or real error.

Literature: For a fairly exhaustive bibliography on the subject of the Textual Criticism of the N.T. the reader may be referred to the writer's *Introduction to the Textual Criticism of the N.T.*, pp. 265–278. Other books of importance not there mentioned are Pitollet and Batiffol, *The Oldest Text of The Gospels;* Streeter, *The Four Gospels;* Robertson, *Studies in the Text of the N.T.* See also the articles on the subject in the various Bible Dictionaries.

THE STRUCTURE OF THE SYNOPTIC GOSPELS

By Professor E. W. BURCH

The Problem. The first three Gospels form a group of N.T. books to be studied in their mutual relations. These works present the oldest known form of the gospel story. They do not, however, represent the earliest written account of the ministry and teaching of Jesus. For Luke (1^{1}) plainly states that he is indebted to earlier written works. "Many," he says, "took it in hand to write of these things." Tradition warrants the supposition that Mark depended upon information furnished him by others. Tradition also suggests that the writer of the first Gospel depended upon memoranda of sayings of Jesus, and comparison shows that both Luke and Matthew depended upon Mark, the oldest Gospel now in our possession. The fact of mutual relationship is apparent to any reader of these three Gospels. But the *explanation* of that relationship is another matter. The minute and patient study of the Gospels by expert scholars during the past decades has resulted in the accumulation of a wealth of facts, but these do not submit to the demands of any one explanation thus far offered. *Synoptic criticism* is the name given to the study and attempted solution of the critical question: How shall all these facts be explained so as to present a clear and convincing account of the rise and interrelations of the first three Gospels? The term "synoptic" (of Greek derivation) as applied to these three Gospels describes their parallelism and general agreement in outline. The three Gospels can be *looked at together*.

The synoptic question is more than a speculative matter, and its solution will be more than the satisfaction of men's curiosity. For the literary history of the Gospels is closely bound up with the history of Christianity and with the development of thought about Jesus and his message. While the interpretation of the Gospels does not have to wait on the final answer to the synoptic query, all progress toward its solution will serve to shed further light on Jesus' life and teachings and on their effect upon the thought life of the early church.

I. Facts That Constitute the Literary Problem of the Gospels

1. Narrative and Discourse Material. There are two different types of material in each of the Gospels, namely, narrative and discourse. The *narrative* is basic. This is the story as such. In narrative there will occur some spoken words, as dialogue, necessary to carry the story. But in the story proper no extended address or teaching material, as such, is included. In Mark the narrative predominates, only about four thousand words of teaching or discourse being found in a total of over eleven thousand (Greek) words. (For more precise figures on the basis of the original see Burch, *Ethical Teaching of the Gospels*, pp. 18, 76, 160). In round numbers, Matthew has 8,000 words of narrative, 10,500 of discourse, total 18,500; Luke has 11,750 of narrative, 9,250 of discourse, total 21,000. The narrative of Matthew (8,000) is thus not far from that of Mark (7,270) in extent. Such passages as Mk. $1^{16\text{-}20}$, the Call of the Four Disciples, and Mk. $5^{1\text{-}20}$, the Gerasene Demoniac, illustrate narrative material.

Serious address to any company, large or small, constitutes *discourse material*, the second type of composition found in the Gospels. In Mark, the parables in $4^{2\text{-}9,\ 26\text{-}32}$ and in $12^{1\text{-}11}$ as well as the long address in $13^{5\text{-}37}$ illustrate discourse. The narrative portions are used chiefly in the study of the life of Jesus, while discourse portions form the chief object of study when the teaching of Jesus is under consideration.

2. Comparative Scarcity of Incidents. Relatively few incidents are chosen for portrayal in the gospel narrative, when the great number of things that Jesus did are considered. This is an impressive fact. In the basic Gospel, Mark, not over thirty-one days can be identified, at least as far as definite content is concerned. This count of thirty-one days is based upon the following passages: $1^{9\text{-}13}$ $1^{14\text{-}20}$ $1^{21\text{-}34}$ $1^{35\text{-}38}$ $1^{39\text{-}45}$ $2^{1\text{-}22}$ 2^{23}–3^{6} $3^{7\text{-}19a}$ 3^{19b}–4^{41} $5^{1\text{-}20}$ $5^{21\text{-}43}$ $6^{1\text{-}6a}$ $6^{7\text{-}13}$ $6^{30\text{-}52}$ 6^{53}–7^{23} $7^{24\text{-}30}$ $7^{31\text{-}37}$ $8^{1\text{-}10}$ $8^{11\text{-}26}$ 8^{27}–9^{1} $9^{2\text{-}29}$ $9^{33\text{-}50}$ $10^{1\text{-}31}$ $10^{32\text{-}45}$ $10^{46\text{-}52}$ $11^{1\text{-}11}$ $11^{12\text{-}19}$ $11^{20\text{-}33}$ $14^{1\text{-}11}$ $14^{12\text{-}52}$ 14^{53}–15^{47}. It is stated that the temptation continued for *forty days*, but no definite event of any of these days is given. So also such statements as *six days* later (Mk. 9^{2}) occur without accounting for any event within that time. The ministry of Jesus lasted for at least five hundred and fifty days, and probably longer (see art., *Chronology* *of N.T.*, p. 875). Yet the narrative of the ministry confines itself to less than five weeks in all. When a comparative study of the Gospels reveals that for the most part the synoptic writers all refer to this relatively small part of Jesus' life, the total number of days accounted for in all three scarcely exceeding forty, the fact becomes even more impressive.

3. Use of Mark by Matthew and Luke. The outline of Mark is traceable in both Matthew and Luke. At the point where the narrative of Matthew joins that of Mark (Mk. 1^{1} Mt. 3^{1}), the common subject is that of John Baptist's ministry. With a *Harmony of the Gospels* in hand (such as Finney's translation of Huck's *Synopsis*) one can trace the same subjects in Mark and Matthew in the same order until Mt. 4^{22} (parallel to Mk. 1^{20}) is reached. Beginning again at the story of Herod and Jesus (Mt. 14^{1}) and continuing to the narrative of the Empty Grave (Mt. 28^{1-10} Mk. 16^{1-8}) the narratives of Mark and Matthew proceed in the same order. Between Mt. 4^{22}, parallel to Mk. 1^{20}, and Mt. 14^{1}, parallel to Mk. 6^{14} (the Death of John Baptist), Mark has seventeen incidents (narrative passages), of which Matthew reproduces all but one (Mk. 1^{35-38}), but here the *order* of the narratives in Matthew is not the same. As far as Mark's narrative is concerned, it is practically all found in the first Gospel.

From Mk. 6^{14} (parallel to Mt. 14^{1}) to Mk. 16^{8} (parallel to Mt. 28^{8}) there are at least thirty narrative sections (the number varying slightly with the arrangement of topics in the Harmonies). Of these Matthew has all but the Widow's Mite (Mk. 12^{41-44}) and *in the same order*, excepting that Matthew places the Cleansing of the Temple a day earlier than Mark (cf. Mt. 21^{10-17} and Mk. $11^{11,\ 15-19}$). Matthew *adds* the narratives of the Temple-tax (17^{24-27}) and of the Lament Over Jerusalem (23^{37-39}). Thus fully does Matthew reproduce the order of the narrative of Mark.

Luke also follows the order of Mark's narrative. From Lk. 3^{1}, parallel to Mk. 1^{1}, to Lk. 24^{11}, parallel to Mk. 16^{8}, there are about fifty narratives, corresponding to Mark's order, exceptions offering but slight changes. E.g., Luke has a different account of the call of the first disciples (5^{1-11}) which is placed *after* the day in Capernaum rather than before it (cf. Mk. 1^{16-20}), and in places, as in ch. 8, the introduction of discourse leads to a rearrangement of narrative. These are negligible variations on the order of Mark. Some *non-Markan narratives* are introduced by Luke. These are Jesus' Rejection at Nazareth (4^{16-30}), the Centurion of Capernaum (7^{1-10}), Raising of the Widow's Son at Nain (7^{11-17}), the Messengers from John Baptist (7^{18-23}), Jesus Anointed by a Sinful Woman (7^{36-50}), Preaching Tour with the Women and the Twelve (8^{1-3}), the Inhospitable Samaritans (9^{51-56}), the Mission of the Seventy (10^{1-20}), the Visit to Martha and Mary (10^{38-42}), Healing of the Rheumatic Woman (13^{10-17}), Jesus Warned Against Herod (13^{31-33}), Healing of the Dropsical Man (14^{1-6}), the Ten Lepers (17^{11-19}), the Visit to Zacchæus (19^{1-10}) and many circumstances of the Passion Story. The *omissions* of Luke (with respect to the narrative of Mark) involve chiefly that part of Mark between the Feeding of the Five Thousand (6^{46}) and Peter's Confession (8^{27}). This long omission includes the Walking on the Water, Healing of the Greek Woman's Daughter, Return to Galilee, Feeding the Four Thousand, and Healing the Blind Man at Bethsaida. Luke is notable for his additions to the gospel material, perhaps over fifty per cent of his work showing unique material, chiefly discourse. But compared with Mark's fifty-five narrative sections, Luke offers about fifty, exclusive of chs. 1, 2. Luke's omissions in the parts parallel with Mark are balanced by his introduction of new material.

The outline of Mark is traceable in both Matthew and Luke most plainly when only the narrative portions are observed.

Below, under the consideration in section II, 4 and 5, of the document called Q (German *Quelle*, meaning "Source"), particular attention will be paid to the discourse sections found in Matthew and Luke.

4. Similarities Between the Gospels. Remarkable similarities in phraseology between the three Gospels often occur, and more often between two, i.e., between Mark and Matthew and between Mark and Luke. Similarities in phraseology between Matthew and Luke, chiefly in discourse, constitute a problem in themselves.

No attempt is made here to marshal all the evidence, but a few characteristic examples follow. (For greater detail see Hawkins, *Horae Synopticae;* Sanday, *Oxford Studies in the Synoptic Problem;* and Streeter, *The Four Gospels.*)

(1) Similarities between the narratives of the three Gospels. The narrative of the Healing of the Leper, Mk. 1^{40-45}, and parallels, is couched in words often exactly the same. The variations are chiefly those of style or word-choice. Attention is called particularly to Mk. 1^{40-42} Mt. $8^{2,\ 3}$ Lk. $5^{12,\ 13}$. In this part of the threefold narrative, of Mark's 28 words (Greek) Matthew exactly reproduces 20 and Luke 22. In the entire narrative Mark uses 97 words, Matthew 62, Luke 98. Of Mark's 97

words Matthew exactly reproduces 39, while Luke offers 42.

The Healing of the Withered Hand, especially that part of the narrative in Mk. 3^{4-6} Mt. 12^{12-14} Lk 6^{9-11}, furnishes a typical illustration of threefold agreement.

It cannot be claimed that any threefold parallel of considerable length is given in the same language throughout. The verbal agreement in a large number of these narratives is not far different from the examples above cited. Other passages which will repay study are the Healing of the Demoniac in the Tombs, Mk. 5^{1-20} Mt. 8^{28-34} Lk. 8^{26-39}; the Unrest of Herod at the Appearance of Jesus, Mk. 6^{14-16} Mt. $14^{1,2}$ Lk. 9^{7-9}; and the Feeding of the Five Thousand, Mk. 6^{35-44} Mt. 14^{15-21} Lk. 9^{12-17}.

A study of all the gospel material indicates a somewhat closer verbal correspondence between sections of discourse than between narratives. In the passages above cited the closest verbal agreement is found in words spoken by Jesus and his disciples. This rule applies as well to longer passages of teaching found in the three Gospels. Note such places as the following: Jesus on Fasting, Mk. 2^{18-22} Mt. 9^{14-17} Lk. 5^{33-39}; on the Danger of Riches, a combination of narrative and teaching, Mk. 10^{17-31} Mt. 19^{16-30} Lk. 18^{18-30}; the Synoptic Apocalypse, Mk. 13 Mt. 24 Lk. 21.

(2) Similarities between narratives of two Gospels. Similarity or identity of phraseology is frequent between Mark and Matthew and between Mark and Luke. In many such places, the remaining Gospel (Matthew or Luke) offers a near-parallel, identified as the same story, yet cast into other words.

The narrative of Mk. 6^{45-52} Mt. 14^{22-33}, describing Jesus walking on the water, has no parallel in Luke (cf. above, Luke's long omission). The narrative of the Alien Exorcist, Mk. $9^{38f.}$ Lk. $9^{49f.}$, illustrates again the twofold agreement. For other examples of double agreement, with Mark the basic text, see Mk. 1^{23-28} Lk. 4^{33-37}; Mk. 12^{41-44} Lk. 21^{1-4}; Mk. $4^{33f.}$ Mt. $13^{34f.}$; Mk. $6^{17f.}$ Mt. $14^{3f.}$ (cf. Lk. $3^{19f.}$); Mk. 10^{35-45} Mt. 20^{20-28}; Mk. 11^{12-14} Mt. $21^{18f.}$ As the number of illustrations implies, such parallels are much more frequent between Mark and Matthew than between Mark and Luke.

The occurrence of the third near-parallel, but in different form, is noteworthy in such passages as the story of Jesus' Rejection at Nazareth, Mk. 6^{1-6} Mt. 13^{53-58}, cf. Lk. 4^{16-30}; and the Storm on the Lake, Mk. 4^{35-41} Lk. 8^{22-25}, cf. Mt. 8^{23-27}.

The parallelism between Luke and Matthew, mostly in discourse, involves gospel material that is absent from Mark in almost all instances. This material (termed *non-Markan*) is generally traced to the long-lost document called Q (see below, section II, 4 and 5). Particularly noteworthy passages, frequently involving word-for-word parallelism in the original, are John Baptist's words, Mt. 3^{7-10} Lk. 3^{7-9}; Words to the Disciples, Mt. 10^{26-33} Lk. 12^{2-9}; On Backsliding, Mt. 12^{43-45} Lk. 11^{24-26}; The Woe upon Tyre and Sidon, Mt. 11^{20-24} Lk. 10^{13-15}; and many other passages, long and short. Harnack, who prepared the most widely known reconstruction of Q, estimates that the parallel non-Markan material amounts to one sixth of Luke and two elevenths of Matthew. (See Harnack, *The Sayings of Jesus* [Eng. trans.]. A more recent study of Q appears in Streeter, *The Four Gospels*, pp. 273-292.)

5. Dissimilarities Between the Gospels. Remarkable dissimilarities appear in a comparative study of the first three Gospels. These dissimilarities consist of (1) changes in context for certain sayings or incidents, (2) differences in content, (3) omissions from or additions to a given saying or incident, and (4) the use of unique material.

(1) Some of these phenomena find illustration in passages cited above. The incident of the anointing of Jesus by a woman (Lk. 7^{36-50}; cf. Mk. 14^{3-9} and Mt. 26^{6-13}) serves admirably to illustrate a *changed context*. The Lord's Prayer serves as an illustration in the Sermon on the Mount (Mt. 6^{9-15}), but in Lk. 11^{1-4} the prayer is repeated to a disciple who asks Jesus to teach him to pray. The so-called Lament Over Jerusalem is uttered by Jesus when in sight of Jerusalem, according to Mt. 23^{37-39}, but in Lk. $13^{34f.}$ the context indicates that Jesus was far from the Holy City (cf. Lk. 19^{41-44}). Matthew and Luke seldom agree upon the context of discourse material.

A single Gospel frequently contains the same saying in two different contexts. These so-called "doublets" suggest that often the writer himself was not certain of the original context but felt competent to use the saying as appropriate to more than one occasion.

(2) The *difference in content* between gospel passages is shown in two of the Beatitudes. Matthew says (5^3): "Blessed are the poor in spirit." Luke, in the parallel passage (6^{20}), says: "Blessed are ye poor." In the other Beatitude (Mt. 5^6, cf. Lk. 6^{21}), "Blessed are they that hunger and thirst after righteousness" is set over against "Blessed are ye that hunger now." These are clearly parallel sayings, yet they do not say the same thing.

(3) *Omissions and additions* are of various kinds and degrees. In narrative it has ap-

peared that both Matthew and Luke reproduce most of Mark, yet each has felt at liberty to omit matter that collided with his aim or with any particular view of the subject that he held. The dissimilarity in the latter instance goes back of the narrative or saying and represents a fundamental difference between writers. Such a datum, naturally, would be seized upon by the so-called *Formgeschichtliche* School (see below) as an evidence of development of thought about Jesus or about the movement that centered in him. Mark offers without comment the narrative of the Blind Man of Bethsaida (8^{22-26}), whose healing is described by no later evangelist, whether in view of the fact that Jesus made a second attempt before the cure was completed, or for other reasons, cannot be known. On the other hand, Matthew adds to his form of the Golden Rule (7^{12}) the explanation, "for this is the law and the prophets" (cf. Lk. 6^{31}). Such additions to matter found in a discourse source are usually ascribed to the writer of the Gospel. For to a later generation than that to which Jesus spoke some of his words, in the view of the evangelists, had to be explained. If the fourth Gospel were to be adduced here for illustration, there would be no lack of instances in point.

When large blocks of discourse (e.g., Lk. 9^{51}–18^{14}) are inserted it is usually supposed that a special source was available. The infancy stories and much of the Passion story come under such a category. Where neither a special source seems likely nor any trace of a personal bias is suspected, differences between the Gospels are accounted for by supposing that the source available to the writer was itself composite. (See, in intro. to Luke in this volume, pp. 1022–3, the newer theory as to Proto-Luke, a document made up of several earlier sources of different dates and places of origin.)

(4) *Unique material* is included logically in additions to the tradition, but in view of the extent of such material it claims special mention in an exhibit of facts. Recent writers on Gospel origins have emphasized the existence of special sources, from which a writer drew material not available to any of the others. Streeter's document M, containing matter found only in Matthew, and his hypothetical L, containing the Lukan unique tradition, find abundant warrant in the mass of special contributions made by these evangelists respectively. No special source (unless it be the once popular Ur-Markus) is required for Mark. Not even Q seems to be needed to explain the relatively small amount of Markan material that overlaps the reconstructed non-Markan source. On the other hand, such matter in Matthew and Luke is so extensive as to forbid its presentation in this article. A glance at the beginning of Matthew as compared with that of Luke, and even a superficial study of their respective Passion stories, impresses one with the wealth of special information available to the two evangelists or at least used by each of them. The list of parables peculiar to each of the two later synoptists is instructive and impressive. In Matthew the Tares (13^{24-30}); the Hid Treasure, the Pearl and the Net (13^{44-50}); the Unmerciful Servant (18^{23-35}); the Vineyard Laborers (20^{1-16}); the Two Sons (21^{28-32}); and the Ten Virgins (25^{1-13}), stand over against fully sixteen parables found in Luke only, among them some of the most frequently quoted, even in colloquial speech. (See art., *Parables of Jesus*, p. 919,)

Summary. A few statements at this point will summarize the facts comprising the chief elements in the literary problem of the Gospels. 1. The first three Gospels are from different hands, yet they present in the main a unitary view of Jesus' works and words. In this fact the name "synoptic" finds its appropriateness. 2. Two of the Gospels make extensive use of the outline of Mark. Thus one of the sources of both Matthew and Luke, especially for their narrative, lies at hand. 3. A large proportion of Matthew and Luke is non-Markan and also in a high degree parallel. This argues for a single common source (or sources), the substance of which is discourse. The theory of interdependence between Matthew and Luke is not supported. 4. Remarkable similarities in wording between the Gospels are counterbalanced by striking differences. This fact operates as a check upon the finding that the outline of Mark is traceable in both Matthew and Luke. Freedom in the use of sources and the use of sources not available to other writers are suggested by this finding. 5. Change of context for incident or saying is a frequent phenomenon where parallel matter is used. This does not invalidate the view that the matter came from common sources, in view of the freedom generally exercised by each evangelist. 6. The composite nature of both Matthew and Luke is established by the foregoing facts. Mark appears to be unitary, although the author himself was not an eyewitness. The use of sources, then, or at least of one source, oral or written, must be ascribed to Mark.

II. Stages in the Solution of the Literary Problem of the Gospels

The foregoing facts are not easily harmonized under a single theory. It is precisely the mixture of agreement and disagreement, of parallelism and non-parallelism, that stands in the way of a complete understanding of the literary history of the first three Gospels. The very multitude of facts brought to light has made progress slow, although the development of better technique in scholarship and the collaboration of a large number of investigators have brought fairly dependable results in this field during the past few decades.

1. The Textual Situation. The Gospels are written in Greek, while Jesus probably spoke in Aramaic. The autographs (original gospel documents) were soon worn out through handling and were replaced by hand-written copies. An unknown number of such copyings intervened between the autographs and the oldest existing MS. of the Gospels (dated in the fourth century A.D.). Thus repeated stages of translation and copying stand between the oldest known Greek Gospel and the actual words spoken by Jesus. In existing MSS. many variations in phraseology exist, and editors differ even to-day as to which of these "various readings" in certain places are original. The Greek Testament used by scholars is not a copy of any one MS. but the result of comparative study of all MSS. Thus it may happen that scholarship in the future will find an increased or a lessened degree of correspondence between the Gospels. It is not likely that a radical change will be made by this means, yet the reconstruction of the Greek text is very important to synoptic criticism and must always be reckoned with. (See further on this the art., *Transmission of N.T.*, p. 861).

2. The Environment of the Gospel Writer. The approach to the study of the Gospels from a historical as well as from a literary point of view has led to a study of the circumstances under which each Gospel was written. (See intro. to commentaries on Matthew, Mark, and Luke.) Each Gospel was written with a limited circulation in view. A given church, be it in Rome, in Antioch, or in Corinth, wished its own "Gospel," or written account of the Lord's life and words. The recognition of a specific place and of a certain group, living and working under its own conditions, has been found to assist in the understanding of the gospel material and its arrangement. The newer school in Germany that approaches the problem from the point of view of the shaping of the message or the incidents (*Formgeschichte*) makes use of this historic element. In one Gospel a saying of Jesus may be in almost if not quite the form in which Jesus uttered it, while in another Gospel that saying may be adapted to use in the liturgy or in the teaching of catechumens. This manner of historical study of the problem is likely to yield excellent results not yet attained.

3. Priority and Originality of the Canonical Mark. The discovery, about a century ago, that Mark was the basis of Matthew and Luke did much to discredit the theory of oral transmission, to which theory some credence was given even down to recent times. An element of oral transmission must be insisted upon, for writing did not begin at once. But it is clearly seen at present that the canonical Gospels cannot be explained as the product of an existing oral Gospel. The documentary theory was really well established when the priority of Mark was discovered. There was needed only the determination of the type of documentary theory, which awaited the discovery of the number and nature of the documents involved.

The originality of Mark was not established as early as was its priority. The long omission of Luke (see section I, 3), it was supposed, argued for the existence of a shorter form of Mark. It is as easy to suppose that Luke had a defective copy or that he omitted the section involved for some reason not now known. Streeter argues plausibly for the "mutilated copy" theory (*op. cit.*, pp. 174f.). Advocates of an earlier form of Mark could not agree as to its length, whether shorter or longer than the canonical Mark. At present the view that the canonical Mark best answers all critical requirements is chiefly in vogue.

4. Studies of the Non-Markan Discourse Source. Whatever the document or documents designated by the symbols Q or L (Logia or "Sayings") may have been, the same disappeared from human knowledge before the end of the century in which such sources or source found favor with gospel writers. The non-Markan discourse is preserved only in Matthew and Luke. It is possible that such a saying as that in Acts 20[35], "It is more blessed to give than to receive," could be traced to one of the written documents which the evangelists used, and many of the so-called *agrapha* (unrecorded sayings) may bring to us from patristic or other writings (e.g., apocryphal Gospels) traces of this hypothetical literature. The Gospels, however, may be supposed to have drawn from Q (or the Logia) all that was significant.

Many scholars have sought, through the study of the parallel non-Markan sections in Matthew and Luke, to reconstruct one document from which these two writers drew (see "Literature" at close of this article). The net result of these studies has done more to stimulate than to conclude the work of solving the synoptic problem. The resultant document as reconstructed severally by A. Harnack, O. Holtzmann, J. Wellhausen, H. H. Wendt, J. C. Hawkins, B. Weiss, J. Weiss, and other eminent scholars, has been exhibited in convenient form in Moffatt, *Introduction to Literature of the N.T.*, pp. 197–202. With these may be compared a recent study in Streeter, *op. cit.*, pp. 273–292.

Practically all of these results are gained through manipulation of that content of Matthew and Luke which lies outside Mark, consisting of about two hundred verses. For the most part this critical process is skillfully carried out. The relatively high degree of agreement between these scholars indicates that the methods they use are sound. The various reconstructions are, however, only theoretical, as the scholars themselves are the first to admit, and the parts common to Matthew and Luke (lying outside of Mark) may or may not after all represent the contents of a single earlier document.

There is practical agreement that Q contained very little narrative, although the baptism and temptation, together with the story of the centurion at Capernaum are generally included. Some (notably Barth, Réville, and Moffatt) think that a fivefold or sevenfold arrangement of sayings can be traced in Q, but otherwise it appears to be a collection of sayings without the finished form of a purposive work.

Recent criticism shows some impatience with the supposition that a single document is entitled to perform the function of Q, and the symbols $Q^{Mt.}$ and $Q^{Lk.}$ have been devised to satisfy the demand for a plurality (at least a duality) of such sources.

It should always be recalled, in the interest of clear thought upon the subject, that, after all, Q is a symbol that somewhat disguises yet does not remove modern ignorance of the early stages in the transmission of the Aramaic gospel. It is the conviction of some N.T. students that the by-products of the study of Q have been fully as constructive and positive in their nature as the direct result sought has been.

Some writers upon the gospel origins have even suggested that the hypothesis of Q has stood in the way of more satisfactory results. He would be a pioneer indeed who took it upon himself to discard the shadowy source, believing it only a name that does not reveal the past of the Gospels. Yet it may be that such a pioneer would lead the students of the Gospels into a state of greater certainty. The abandonment of the Q hypothesis could not be taken as a denial of the existence of rich parallels between Matthew and Luke, in any case. These are facts. They present phases of Jesus' teaching which came by some line of tradition to each of the evangelists. Even if there were at any time a single document such as Q, it could hardly furnish modern students with anything worth while after two such gifted writers had culled from it what they most highly prized. Thus for some Q has become a term of no great significance, since at best it represents only a fragmentary work, and doubtless, if it ever existed, it has been edited into better form, given finer contexts and deeper meaning than it ever had in its own right.

It has been very shrewdly observed that if Mark no longer existed and scholars set out to reconstruct that Gospel, knowing that almost all of it had been incorporated in Matthew and Luke, the resultant document would but faintly resemble the present second Gospel. One can scarcely hope for better success in reconstruction when a document whose very existence is hypothetical submits to the operation.

5. The Two-Document Hypothesis. The prevailing documentary theory has centered about the two foci, Mark and Q (or the Logia). Some of the shortcomings of this hypothesis have already appeared, especially in the discussion of the hypothetical discourse source, or the "second source," as it is frequently called. The weakness of this hypothesis is found in the impossibility of covering the facts with two documents only. There is Mark, the basis of the narrative outline; at least one source containing teaching of Jesus; at least one narrative each of Jesus' birth and youth, for Matthew and Luke; at least one Passion story apiece; and at least one source for each to account for their "unique matter." Here are seven documents at least. If, in the interest of economy, it is supposed that the common discourse document contained the "unique material" as well, one has to explain why Matthew discarded so much that was adopted by Luke. Certainly that portion of Luke (9^{51}–18^{14}), mistakenly called the "Perean source," bears evidence of being an entirely distinct document. And what shall be said of the "synoptic apocalypse"? The two-document hypothesis is a good step but far from the final step on the way.

6. The Four-Document Hypothesis. Recently (1925, Streeter, *op. cit.*, pp. 227f.) a four-document hypothesis has been proposed in place of the two-document theory. This would provide for different treatments of Mark at the hands of Matthew and Luke, who probably used different copies of the Roman Gospel. To Matthew the chief authority was Mark, but for Luke there existed a preferred source, namely, an earlier edition of his own Gospel, itself based upon Q, and another document called "L," which contained matter now embodied in Luke as his "unique material." The pre-Lukan Gospel Streeter calls Proto-Luke. It is not considered one of the fundamental (four) documents, but a stage half way between Q plus L and the canonical Luke. Matthew, on the other hand, prized Mark most of all, yet had access to a document called M (containing material now known as the "unique material" of Matthew) and to Q as well. Thus the newer documentary hypothesis, in brief, contemplates the rise of Q first of all (about 50 A.D. at Antioch) as a collection of Jesus' words; of M, a Jerusalem document, dated about 65; which, with L (a creature of a Cæsarean environment about 60), and Mark (Rome, A.D. 60) completes the groundwork of the canonical synoptic structure.

For further discussion of these questions, see the introductions to Matthew, Mark, and Luke in the present volume.

7. The Nature and Authority of the Synoptic Gospels. It is apparent that the synoptic Gospels are composite works. Their purpose was to transmit to later generations what Jesus did and what he taught. Each Gospel as it was prepared fell into the hands of Christians who naturally knew more than modern men ever can know about the literary history of the work. The fact that these early Christians accepted and used the Gospels as they did is therefore sound evidence that they were satisfied that the substance of doctrine contained in them, and their representation of the teaching and mission of Jesus, were in keeping with a much larger body of unwritten but reliable tradition. (See art., *N.T. and Christian Doctrine*, pp. 946–8.)

For the modern Christian the Gospels do more than report the sayings and deeds of Jesus. These works have also a message from the times in which they were written. They assure the church through the ages that one, two, and three generations after Jesus died and arose from the dead the early church had faith in the living Christ. The authority of the Gospels lies close to the heart of the gospel. And the heart of the gospel is the message of the living Redeemer in his own church, living his life over in the lives of those who loved him and for whom he gave himself.

Literature: Burkitt, *The Gospel History and its Transmission;* Castor, *Matthew's Sayings of Jesus;* Hawkins, *Horae Synopticae;* Hayes, *The Synoptic Problem;* Streeter, *The Four Gospels: A Study in Origins.* Harmonies of the Gospels: Huck, *A Synopsis of the First Three Gospels* (Eng. trans. by Finney); Burton and Goodspeed, *A Harmony of the First Three Gospels.*

THE CHRONOLOGY OF THE NEW TESTAMENT

By Professor ISMAR J. PERITZ

Chronology Only Approximate. Luke, who of all N.T. writers gives most attention to chronology, in stating the age of Jesus, says, "he was about thirty years of age" (3^{23}). Luke's "about" might well be taken as the keynote of this discussion: approximation only is attainable. The reasons are that N.T. writers apparently did not seem to think that it was important to be specific; the Romans at this time possessed no uniform method of dating the accession of their rulers; and the Jews based their calculations of the festal calendar upon such ordinary observations of the phases of the moon as made exactness impossible. As elements of each of these three contingents often enter into the calculations of an event, it can be seen what difficulties confront the chronologist. These difficulties account for the rather disconcerting variety of dates met with in the chronological schemes from the time of Irenæus and Tertullian down to our own time, when competent authorities sometimes are as much as ten years apart in dating the same event. Nevertheless, encouraging signs are appearing that discoveries of archæological material and a more exact treatment of the subject will bring closer approximations.

Chronology of the Life of Jesus. The main events in the life of Jesus on which the Gospels furnish data are his birth and baptism, the length of his ministry, and his death. Below is a conspectus of some recent representative opinions on the dates of these events; the aim of the following discussion is to account for the divergencies.

Date of Jesus' Birth. The date of 1 A.D., fixed by the Roman monk Dionysius Exiguus in the sixth century, was based upon a miscalculation. Matthew furnishes four data: (1) 2^{1}, before Herod died, i.e., before 4 B.C.; (2) 2^{16}, "two years old and under," the age limit of the children ordered slain by Herod, which would make it 6 B.C.; (3) 2^{2}, "the star," in which some have seen a conjunction of Jupiter and Saturn, calculated by the astronomer Kepler as 7 B.C.; (4) 2^{19-23}, a residence in Egypt without indication of its length. Luke 2^{1-5} connects the birth of Jesus with a census ordered by the Roman emperor Augustus when Quirinius was governor of Syria; such a census took place 6 A.D., but that was ten years after Herod's death. It does not seem probable that Luke antedated this census, for he mentions it in Acts 5^{37}. According to Tertullian, a census took place under Saturninus, who was governor of Syria about 9–6 B.C.; did Luke confuse the names? New light on the question has come from recent discoveries in archæology to which Sir William M. Ramsay has called attention in his works, *Was Christ Born at Bethlehem?* and *The Bearing of Recent Discoveries on the Trustworthiness of the N.T.* There is evidence that Quirinius carried on a military expedition against the Homonadenses, a tribe in the Cilician Taurus country, while he held official position in Syria in the lifetime of Herod, between 9–6 B.C. This, according to Ramsay, would meet all the requirements of Luke's statement, and he chooses for the date 6 B.C. A glance at the conspectus will reveal how all the extremes and the shades between them are represented. Probably the most satisfactory date is 6 B.C.

For the month and the day of the birth there are no data available. The earliest source for December 25 is Hippolytus, about 200 A.D.

Date of the Baptism. The baptism of Jesus took place, it would seem, after the ministry of John the Baptist was well under way. Luke gives for the beginning of the Baptist's ministry "the fifteenth year of Tiberius Cæsar" (3^{1-3}). The detail with which Luke gives this date is

	Birth	Baptism	Ministry	Death
Turner, 1898	7–6 B.C.	26 A.D.	3 years	29 A.D.
v. Soden, 1899	4 B.C.?	c. 28/29 A.D.	1 year	30 A.D.
Moffatt, 1917	c. 6 B.C.	25/26 A.D.	4 years	29/30 A.D.
Headlam, 1923	8/7 B.C.	29/30 A.D.	3 years	33 A.D.
Streeter, 1925	before 4 B.C.	27 A.D.	2 1/2 years	29/30 A.D.

evidence not only of his careful investigation but also of the importance which he attaches to it in fixing the chronology of Jesus. But here we meet with the difficulty whether to count the reign of Tiberius from his accession as coregent of Augustus or from his accession as emperor: the former would make his fifteenth year 26/27 A.D., the latter 29/30 A.D., the difference reflected in the conspectus. Luke's statement (3[23]) that Jesus was "about thirty years" of age when he began his public ministry fits the earlier date; and in view of Luke's chronological interest should be allowed more meaning than a mere phrase stating that he had entered into manhood. This cannot be said of the chronological import of the question in Jn. 8[57], "Thou art not yet fifty years old, and hast thou seen Abraham?" although it led Irenæus to hold that Jesus lived to be fifty years old; and in later time yielded a symbolic meaning to the effect that the life of Jesus covered a jubilee (7x7) of years, the fiftieth or jubilee year being that of his "glorification." According to John (2[20]), "forty-six years was this temple in building," and this was said during Jesus' early ministry. Herod's undertaking of rebuilding the Temple appears to be, according to Josephus, 19–20 B.C., which would yield as the date of the beginning of the ministry 27 A.D., and would accord with the earlier date. Mk. 1[14] and Mt. 4[12] connect the beginning of Jesus' ministry with the imprisonment of the Baptist, but its exact date cannot be determined.

The Length of the Ministry. Omitting the extreme view of a ten or twenty years' length, a glance at the conspectus reveals views ranging from one year to four years. Champions of the former appeal to Luke and the authorities of the second century, except Irenæus. Luke's quotation (4[19]), "To proclaim the acceptable year of the Lord," and the absence of any other specific note of time—except an evidently intentional division of the ministry into two halves, a longer of a few months (9[51]–19[28]) and a shorter (4[14]–9[50]), and the mention of only the last Passover—were taken as pointing to a year or even less. Those who contend for a two years' ministry point to Mk. 2[23] Mt. 12[1] Lk. 6[1], where mention is made of standing barley or wheat, followed after a lapse of time by the mention of "green grass" (Mk. 6[39]), implying an early springtime, hence two summers, and suggesting, therefore, a two-years' ministry. It is the fourth Gospel which offers most detail. There are mentioned, 2[13], a Passover; 4[35], "four months to the harvest"; 5[1], "the feast" or "a feast" (cf. text and mg. in A.S.V.); 6[4], a Passover; 7[2], the feast of tabernacles; 10[22], the feast of dedication; 11[55], the Passover. In 5[1] is an unnamed feast: those who take it as a Passover find in John four Passovers and a three years' ministry; those who take it either as Pentecost or Tabernacles find in John only three Passovers, and consequently a two-years' ministry; but those who question the text in 6[4], for which there is not sufficient reason, disregard it, and find in John only two Passovers and consequently a one-year's ministry. Thus John is seen to be in harmony with the synoptic Gospels by both those who hold to a two-years' and those who hold to a one-year's ministry. But it has long ago been pointed out that Jn. 5 and 6 are apparently out of place and should be transposed (see p. 857): this would simplify the sequence of events, and it would also make the unnamed feast (which has evidently caused difficulty as the text variants indicate) identical with the Passover of 6[4]. (Cf. Streeter, *The Four Gospels*, p. 381.) The longer ministry of two or even three years is regarded as the more probable because it accounts more satisfactorily for the geographical movements of Jesus and for the influence which he exerted both upon his friends and foes, for which the element of time is essential.

The Date of the Crucifixion. This is evidently the most important date and the starting-point of N.T. chronology. It involves both the day and the year.

(1) *The Day.* The synoptists (Mk. 15[42] Mt. 27[62] Lk. 23[54]) place the crucifixion on Friday, Nisan 15th; John (19[14, 31, 42]) places it on Friday, Nisan 14th. According to John, Jesus ate with his disciples the Passover, or a meal that was not really the Passover, the night before the "Preparation," and died on the cross at the time of the "Preparation," when the Jews killed their Passover lambs, thus making his death to coincide with the death of the Passover lamb. The synoptists, on the other hand, identify the Last Supper with the Passover meal, and place the crucifixion on the first day of the Passover, which had begun, according to Jewish reckoning, at sunset of the previous evening when the Passover meal was eaten. The Johannine dating is to be preferred: it is historically the more probable, for the Jewish officials were not likely to break the sacred feast; it accords with the Pauline attitude which identifies the death of Jesus with the Passover lamb (1 Cor. 5[6-8]); and it accords with the practise of the Eastern church which, as the term "Quartodecimans" or "Fourteenthsters" indicates, prided itself on the exactness with which it commemorated the fourteenth day of Nisan as the day of Jesus' death. Further, attention has been called to the words in Luke (22[15f.]), "With desire I desired to

eat this passover with you . . . but I shall not eat it . . ." as indicating that even in the synoptics there is a hint that it was not the Passover meal that Jesus ate with his disciples. It is probable that John writes with his predecessors before him, and possesses data based upon early tradition by which he aims to correct and supplement the synoptists. (Cf. p. 1088.)

(2) *The Year.* The Gospels furnish three data: (1) Jesus died while Pontius Pilate was procurator, i.e., between 27–37 A.D.; (2) while Caiaphas was high priest, i.e., before 36 A.D.; and (3) when the Passover fell on a Friday, Nisan 14th, computed on the basis of the full moon. The possible dates are from 28 to 35 A.D. For the year 29 Turner is the stoutest champion. It has in its favor that it is the earliest date fixed by the church by use of the consular lists as "the year of the two Gemini," i.e., whose consuls for the year were L. Rubellius Geminus and C. Fufius (or Rufius) Geminus. This date has recently been called in question on astronomical grounds, it being alleged that it was the only one of the possible years when the astronomical conditions were not met. There are some who favor the year 33 A.D., made popular by Eusebius, the church historian of the first quarter of the fourth century. The date, however, most in favor is 30 A.D.; it meets approximately all the requirements as well as the year 29 A.D. and is free from the astronomical objection to the latter.

Chronology of the Apostolic Age. The study of the chronology of the Apostolic Age has in our century entered on a new phase which promises more satisfactory results. It began with the recognition by Turner that Acts is arranged upon a definite plan, namely, six periods, or "panels," each of them ending with a refrain or summary; that these divisions are chronological; and that each covers a period of approximately five years. Acts accordingly is divided into two main sections: (1) $1–12^{24}$, consisting of three periods in which the leadership is with Peter and the Twelve; and (2) $12^{25}–28^{31}$, also consisting of three periods in which the leadership is with Paul, the whole covering some thirty years, corresponding to Luke's chronology of "about thirty years" of his life of Jesus. Turner's contributions have been followed up by C. J. Cadoux (*Journal of Theological Studies*, vol. xix, pp. 333–341) and B. W. Bacon (*Harvard Theological Review*, vol. xiv, pp. 137–166). The result is what may be termed the newer chronology of the Apostolic Age, adopted in the remainder of this article, in justification of which it may be claimed that it gives due weight to Luke's interest in chronology, which furnishes the only first-hand data in our possession, and deserves to be the basis of all calculations, considered in the light of other N.T. writings, particularly the letters of Paul, and Jewish and Roman contemporaneous history.

As a further aid in the same direction must be counted the new discovery in the field of archæology, the Delphian inscription. Adolf Deissmann, who has edited it with a photographic reproduction and reconstructed text, fully discusses its chronological bearings (*Saint Paul*, Appendix I, first edit., pp. 255–260), which is to fix definitely the date of the proconsulship of Gallio in Achaia for 51–52 A.D. and to furnish a definite starting point for the chronology of Paul. Of similar assistance has been a reconsideration of the visits of Paul to Jerusalem. Acts mentions three visits: (1) 9^{26}, the introduction visit; (2) 11^{27-30} 12^{25}, the famine visit; and (3) 15^{2}, the council visit; Galatians mentions two, 1^{18} and 2^{1}. It is generally agreed that the visit mentioned as first in both sources is identical. Opinions differ as to the identity of the others: some holding that Paul failed to mention the famine visit, feeling it to be irrelevant, and that Gal. 2^{1} and Acts 15 relate to the council visit. The present writer agrees with those who more recently have come to hold that Gal. 2^{1} and Acts 11 are identical, and relate to the famine visit, during which there was a private conference on the Gentile question, and that Galatians was written before the Council of Acts 15 took place, and consequently is not mentioned by Paul. This has important bearings upon the date of the conversion of Paul, which the newer chronology places as late as 38 A.D. The number "fourteen" in Gal. 2^{1} has created difficulties on account of its indefiniteness and length. Does it include the three years of 1^{18} or not? In either case it involves fourteen or seventeen years' of comparative inactivity, which appears rather strange for the energetic and restless Paul with his passion for regions beyond. On the other hand, the older chronology is forced by this "fourteen" to crowd the events between the death of Jesus and the conversion of Paul "into the limits of two years, or possibly even of a single year." If the element of time has any claim to consideration in a movement which involves the struggles that go with giving up strong beliefs, and in the spread of the movement to Damascus in such proportions as to incite the fiery zeal of a Saul, this is too short a space of time. Out of all these difficulties there is deliverance in following the suggestion of Grotius, to read the number "four" (*diadeton*), instead of "fourteen" (*diaideton*), the difference of an *iota* making the difference of ten years. The newer chronology is inclined to accept the suggestion and adjust its data accordingly. In doing so it finds the glaring inconsistency in the career of Paul removed, and Paul's own biographical chronology brought into approximate accord with that of Luke in Acts. Anyone acquainted with the history of the transmission of the text of the N.T. (see p. 860) cannot but consider such a change admissible. It might be accounted for as a harmonizing attempt of a scribe who transferred the number fourteen from 2 Cor. 12[2], where it belongs, to the last months of Paul's stay in Ephesus, about 54–55 A.D., and where it refers either to Paul's stay in Arabia (Gal. 1[17]) or to Luke's account of the vision in the Temple (Acts 22[17-21]), and falls in with Luke's chronological scheme.

The Six Periods of Acts. With these preliminary considerations in view, we may now proceed with the articulation of the six periods or panels into which the chronology of Acts is divided, and add the approximate dates.

Period I. Founding of the church in Jerusalem to the death of Stephen, 29/30–34 A.D. (Acts 1[1]–6[7]). The events here recorded include the re-gathering of the disciples to Jerusalem and the period to Pentecost; the beginning of their evangelistic activity; the growth of the church membership to over five thousand, in spite of the repeated imprisonment of its leaders; the need of better oversight of its relief work; and the implied organization of the church with its apostles and sub-apostles. Five years appear a reasonable time for this development, and there is nothing known as standing in the way of its assumption.

Period II. The expansion of the church in Palestine to the conversion of Paul and his removal to Tarsus, 34–39 A.D. (Acts 6[8]–9[31]). During this period of five years the activity and death of Stephen most probably occupied the earlier part, and might be dated 34 A.D. The subsequent spread of the faith into the country around Jerusalem, Samaria, and even into Egypt, might easily take two years. The remainder of the period, from 37–39, would cover Paul's activity of persecution, conversion, first visit to Jerusalem, and removal to Tarsus; this would bring his conversion to about 37/38. This would approximately allow for Paul's first visit to Jerusalem, dated by him in Gal. 1[18] three years after his conversion, as fractions of inclusive years are counted as if they were wholes; and it would not be excessively out of accord with Acts 9[26], which apparently places it nearer to his conversion. The other datum relating to Paul's conversion and first visit to Jerusalem yields a similar result. According to Acts 9[23-25] and 2 Cor. 11[32], Paul's escape from Damascus took place while the city was being guarded by the ethnarch, "under Aretas the king." No earlier date than 37–38 A.D. is possible for the control of Damascus by Aretas; and Paul the Roman citizen would most probably not have had to escape through a window and in a basket down a wall, if the Romans had been in control.

Period III. The beginnings of Gentile evangelization to the death of Herod Agrippa, 39–44 A.D. (Acts 9[32]–12[24]). According to an ancient tradition found in the so-called *Preaching of Peter* quoted by Clement of Alexandria, held to be reliable, the Twelve were to remain in Jerusalem preaching to the Jews before going out to evangelize the Gentiles. The beginning of this five-year period approximately coincides with this twelve-year period, and may well be meant to mark its beginning. It is highly probable that the execution of James (12[2]) fell in the beginning of the reign of Herod Agrippa, an initial measure to curry the favor of the Jews. Herod's accession took place early in 41 A.D., and his death in 44 A.D. In this period falls the famine visit of Paul and Barnabas to Jerusalem. The time of this visit is but vaguely indicated in Acts as having been predicted by the prophet Agabus, and it is said to have occurred "in the days of Claudius." Some identify this famine with the one described by Josephus in which Queen Helena of Adiabenė brought relief to Jerusalem, and which is dated variously from 44 to 47 A.D. The writer of Acts relates it in collocation with the death of Herod Agrippa, 44 A.D. If we adopt the reading four instead of fourteen in Gal. 2[1], the date 44 A.D. is in accord with the date of Paul's first visit four years previously, with his conversion seven years previously, and with the chronology of Acts.

Period IV. From the beginning of the Antiochian missions to the distribution of the Jerusalem decrees, 44–49 A.D. (Acts 12[25]–16[5]). The period begins with the first missionary journey, or the evangelization of Galatia. According to Turner, it took over one year, according to Ramsay over two years. The remainder of the period can be accounted for by the references to shorter and longer stays in Antioch (Acts 14[28] 15[35f.]); the council visit to Jerusalem (15[1-29]); and the first part of the second missionary journey (15[36]–16[5]), which involved no doubt considerable delay on account of the break with Barnabas and the choice of another companion, the time needed for confirming the churches of Syria and Cilicia, and the visitation of the Galatian churches. Taken altogether it might well cover a period of approximately five years.

Period V. The evangelization of Macedonia,

Achaia, and Asia, 49–54 A.D. (Acts 16[6]–19[20]). This period covers what is substantially included in the second and third missionary journeys. It appears to have originated with the crisis in Jerusalem at the council, where it became evident that the Jewish Christianity of the mother church was too conservative for Paul, who ultimately broke with both Peter and Barnabas, and chose new companions and new fields, where he was his own master and could preach his free gospel. For this period of the founding of the Greek and Asiatic churches the chronological data are Acts 18[11], "a year and six months" in Corinth; 19[10], "two years" for Asia, rounded up to "three years" in 20[31]; allowing six months for the work in Philippi, Thessalonica, and Berœa (16[6]–17[34]), and adding the "three months" of 19[8], the interval between his first coming, 18[19], and his return from a journey to Syria, 18[21f.], it aggregates the five years required for this period or panel. The exact date of Paul's stay in Corinth can now be ascertained by the Delphian inscription, which yields 50–51 A.D., and meets even more than approximately the requirements of the five years of this period.

Period VI. From Paul's journey to Jerusalem to his witness at Rome, 54–59/60 A.D. (Acts 19[21]–28[31]). This sixth and last period of Acts includes: "a while" in Asia (19[22]), until after the riot in Ephesus (20[1]); a journey into Macedonia (20[2]); a three months' stay in Corinth; an overland journey to Philippi; a sea voyage of five days to Troas; a week at Troas (20[4-6]); a land trip to Assos; a sea voyage to Miletus (20[13-15]) and Cæsarea (21[1-14]); by land to Jerusalem (21[15]); the imprisonment in Jerusalem (21[27]–23[22]); imprisonment in Cæsarea of two years to the accession of Festus (23[23]–24[27]), whose date most probably was 57 A.D.; voyage to Rome, arriving 58 A.D.; two years at Rome, 60 A.D.; the whole occupying about five years. This is as far as Acts brings us. Paul had evidently planned a third missionary journey, beyond Rome, in the extreme west—Spain (Rom. 15[22-29]); but there is no convincing evidence that the wish was ever realized. The tradition that involves his release, visit to Asia Minor and Spain, and second imprisonment, is merely an inference from his expressed wish. (The inference, however, has some solid support. See p. 1275.) He died in Rome in the reign of Nero, the most generally accepted date being 64–65 A.D.

Other Dates. Among other dates of the Apostolic Age that can be ascertained is that of the death of Peter, which some think was contemporaneous with that of Paul, while others place it later, Ramsay as late as 80 A.D. The date of the death of James, the brother of Jesus, the later head of the church of Jerusalem, is taken to be 61 or 63.

COMPARATIVE TABLE OF EVENTS IN THE LIFE OF PAUL

	Turner	Harnack	Ramsay	Bacon
Crucifixion of Jesus	29	29 or 30	30	30
Conversion of Paul	35–36	30	33	38
Second Visit	46	44	46	44–45
First Journey	47	45	47	45–47
Jerusalem Council	49	47	50	48
Arrival at Corinth	50	48	51	50
Arrest in Jerusalem	56	54	57	55
Arrival in Rome	59	57	60	58
Death of Paul	64–65	64	65	

DATES IN THE LIFE OF PAUL ADOPTED IN THIS ARTICLE

(Based mainly upon Turner, Cadoux, and Bacon). Cf. art., *Life and Work of Paul*, pp. 939–43.

Crucifixion	29/30
Death of Stephen	34
Conversion	37/38
First Visit (Gal. 1, Acts 9)	39
In Syria, Galatia, and Antioch	39–44
Second Visit (Gal. 2, Acts 11[30])	44
First Journey	45–47
Jerusalem Council (Acts 15)	48
Second Journey	49–51
In Corinth	50–51
In "Asia"	51–54
Winter in Corinth	55
Arrest in Jerusalem	55
Imprisonment in Cæsarea	55–57
Recall of Felix	57
Voyage to Rome	57/58
Arrival in Rome	58
End of "two years"	60
Death	64/65

COMPARATIVE TABLE OF EVENTS IN ROMAN AND JEWISH HISTORY AND N.T. HISTORY AND LITERATURE

B.C.		
9–6	Quirinius' campaign against the Homonadenses	
6	Birth of Jesus	
4	Death of Herod I	
	Herod Antipas to 39	
A.D.		
6	Philip Tetrarch to 34	
	Census of Quirinius	
	Revolt of Zealots	
	Annas High-Priest to 15	
11 or 14	Accession of Tiberius to 37	
18	Caiaphas High-Priest to 36	
26	Pilate Procurator to 36	Preaching of the Baptist
27	....	Baptism of Jesus
29/30	....	Death of Jesus
37	Accession of Caligula to 41	
37/38	....	Conversion of Paul
41	Accession of Claudius to 44	
47	....	*Galatians*
49	....	*1 and 2 Thessalonians*
52	Felix Procurator to 57	
52–54	....	*1 and 2 Corinthians*
54	Accession of Nero to 68	
55	....	Arrest of Paul
	....	*Romans*
57	Festus Procurator to 62	Paul's voyage to Rome
58–60	....	Paul in Rome
		Colossians, Philemon, Ephesians, Philippians, James
61 or 63	....	Death of James of Jerusalem
		1 Peter
64/65	Burning of Rome	Death of Paul and Peter
66	Revolt of Jews in Palestine	
69	Accession of Vespasian to 79	
70	Fall of Jerusalem	*Mark*
79	Accession of Titus to 81	
80	....	*Matthew*
		Hebrews
81	Accession of Domitian to 96	*Jude*
93	....	John the Presbyter (Ephesus)
96	Accession of Nerva to 98	*Revelation*
		Luke and Acts
98	Accession of Trajan to 117	*Fourth Gospel*
		Epistles of John
		Pastoral Epistles (in present form) *2 Peter*

The dates given in the above table for the Gospels and for the Pauline and other Epistles are not uniformly accepted by scholars. The question of date is discussed in the introductions to these various writings in the present volume.

Literature: Hastings' *Dictionary of the Bible* (5 vols.), art. by Turner on "Chronology of the N.T." (exhaustive and epoch-making); Hastings' *One Volume Dictionary of the Bible*, art. by Maclean; art. by von Soden in the *Encyclopedia Biblica* (represents the scholarly German view); Bacon, *The Fourth Gospel in Research and Debate;* Moffatt, *Introduction to the Literature of the N.T.;* Headlam, *The Life and Teachings of Jesus the Christ.* See also the references to literature in the body of this article, and under "Life and Work of Paul," p. 943.

THE LANGUAGE OF THE NEW TESTAMENT

By Professor HENRY J. CADBURY

The New Testament a Greek Book. All the books of the N.T. were in Greek when they were made into a collection. They were quickly translated into Latin, Syriac, and the languages of Egypt, and later into other languages, including English. But the N.T. as such is a Greek library. Even the O.T. is quoted in it in a Greek translation except for a single sentence of the Psalms (22[1]) used by Jesus on the cross, where for special reasons the original Hebrew or Aramaic has been transliterated into the Greek alphabet (Mt. 27[46] Mk. 15[34]).

Aramaic Background. Paul's letters, the other Epistles, and probably most if not all of the other parts of the N.T. were written originally in Greek, though nothing prevents our supposing that some of the books or their sources were written in a Semitic language and then translated into their present form. Greek was not the earliest language of Christianity. Jesus almost certainly talked to his disciples and to other Jews in Aramaic. This is one of the Semitic languages like Hebrew. In Palestine and the East it had been used for some centuries by the Jews. Apparently, it was the usual language throughout the Persian Empire before the coming of Alexander the Great, and it kept its currency in Babylonia and among the Jews of Palestine while Greek was making headway nearly everywhere else in the ancient world. Both the sayings of Jesus, therefore, insofar as they are original with him, and also all the N.T. narrative, to the extent that sayings and narrative alike rest upon the oral tradition of the first Palestinian disciples, have been somehow transformed into Greek from Aramaic. The oldest Christian discussion of any Gospels, that by Papias, implies that Matthew wrote in Hebrew or Aramaic and that Mark translated what Peter preached (quoted in Eusebius, *Hist. Eccl.*, iii, 39). It has recently been claimed that most of the first five (narrative) books of the N.T. were first written in Aramaic. This theory has been worked out for the fourth Gospel by C. F. Burney and for the first half of Acts (1[1]–5[35]) by C. C. Torrey. But not even in these cases has general agreement with the hypothesis of written Semitic originals been reached by scholars. Our consideration of the language of the N.T. must therefore be directed to the idiom of their present Greek form.

Place of New Testament Greek in History of the Language. The language in which the N.T. books are written used to be designated N.T. Greek. When the N.T. was associated with the Greek O.T., or LXX, the term "biblical Greek" was used. The use of these names implied that this language was unique. It was, indeed, very different from the standard form of Greek language with which scholars have been most familiar. Even now certain phenomena in the diction of the N.T. bring its various parts into resemblance to each other and to the LXX, but the language is not really unparalleled. It represents as a whole a much larger phase in the development of the Greek language. The recognition of this setting has been one of the romantic discoveries of modern times.

The history of the Greek language from Homer to the modern colloquial Greek covers some three thousand years. During this period the language has undergone normal changes, though at various times efforts at artificial standardizing and archaizing have interfered with these natural processes. Prior to the rise of Athens many dialects existed, but the political and literary supremacy of Athens gave to her own Attic dialect a supremacy. When Alexander and his successors extended and transplanted Greek culture until it reached from India to Italy, the Attic dialect developed into a universal or common language (called *Koine*="common") which continued in wide use until the downfall of the Roman Empire. Because it endured through this so-called Hellenistic period it is also called Hellenistic Greek. The N.T., written about the middle of this period, is a representative of this *lingua franca.* (Cf. p. 849.)

The Greek writers of this period did not, however, mostly employ this ordinary speech. Reverence for the past and an artificial standard of archaism led all of them from Polybius on down, more or less to affect the older idiom of the classical writers like Thucydides, Plato, and Xenophon. Even Jewish litterateurs like Philo and Josephus wrote in a Greek idiom of a rhetorical and literary sort. The actual natural everyday Greek broke through the formal writers of the period only in spite of themselves. Our knowledge of the vernacular speech revealed in these lapses from pure ancient Attic is now supplemented by a large body of more unstudied and natural contemporary documents. These are the inscriptions, and still more fully and simply the thousands of papyri containing letters, contracts, and various other simple documents written in Egypt in the centuries before and after the beginning of our era, which disclose the common language as used in ordinary speech and writing.

Characteristics of the "Common" Language. The nature of the common language as shown by these and other sources is singularly uniform in the several places from which evidence has come. In Rome, Asia Minor, Egypt, Syria, and elsewhere the current Greek idiom was evidently much alike. New local dialects are not manifest and the older dialects like Ionic and Doric, having contributed their small or negligible share to the common Attic base of this later tongue, have disappeared. But the older language has changed in vocabulary, in forms, and in syntax. Some of the changes are these: reduction of the number of different inflectional forms by surrendering to other forms the uses of the optative mood and the dual number; the elimination of some of the more irregular words and forms by the use of more regular forms and synonyms; the introduction of new constructions, of new words, and of new meanings for words, with the consequent disuse of the old locutions. If the classical Greek is taken as a standard, Hellenistic Greek is a natural development, just as Modern Greek is a natural development from Hellenistic Greek. Purists ancient and modern regarded Hellenistic Greek as degenerate, but in normal linguistic changes to call any single stage perfect is arbitrary.

Hellenistic Greek when not thus invidiously compared shows eminent convenience for the spread of religion whether by spoken or by written word. In this language even Judaism with its over-literal Greek translation of the Hebrew Scriptures had made headway in nearly every center of population where Greek was spoken, and Christianity adding its more intelligible Gospels and Epistles followed after. In this language Paul could preach "from Jerusalem round about to Illyricum"; in this language he wrote to Rome. Of course other languages were often in use side by side with Greek. Paul of Tarsus himself knew Aramaic as well as Greek and so did Palestinian Jews. In Lycaonia the multitude still spoke to one another their local patois (Acts 14[11]). In Rome Latin was far from dead. But wherever bilingualism was found, Hellenistic Greek was one of the media of communication.

An Expressive Language. It was an expressive and elastic language, as much so as any modern speech and as much so as the Attic of Athens' Golden Age. It could be as simple and vivid as the Semitic tongues, but it had capacities for expression of abstract ideas, for exact distinction of tenses, and for the formation of new and compound words such as the O.T. writers did not find available. It was not a hybrid speech. Even the N.T., for all its Semitic backgrounds, has Greek words and constructions for nearly everything. A few special terms are taken over from the Hebrew or Aramaic like *abba, amen, rabbi, pascha* (=Passover). Also certain Latin words had invaded the official language of the empire, and some of them like *census, denarius,* and *legion* appear in the N.T., as they do in other contemporary speech. We find them in the Greek documents of Egyptian scribes or peasants, and in the Aramaic writings of Palestinian or Babylonian rabbis.

In such a natural and universal tongue the N.T. was first written and heard. Whatever we may think of the difficulties of thought in Paul's letters (2 Pet. 3[16]), in diction they were simple indeed (2 Cor. 11[6]). Of course, to men of books and literary culture, whether Christians or pagans, the N.T. language fell short of fine writing. The Christians sometimes gloried in this simplicity of their Scriptures and sometimes they apologized for it. In the second century Celsus ridiculed the "sailor style" of the Gospels, and his Christian opponents of that time wrote as good a style as he did. There is later evidence that when the N.T. was quoted by preachers or copied by scribes, its unliterary expressions were often quietly corrected. But it is worth knowing that the Christians had "no special dialect of their own" (*Epistle to Diognetus,* ch. v; see Ante-Nicene Fathers, Eng. trans., vol. i, p. 26) and that the gospel was distinguished "not in word but in power" (Paul in 1 Thess. 1[5]).

Contemporary Light on the Language. For an understanding of this language it is evident that the bodies of literature closest to it are most useful. Parts of Hellenistic Greek vocabulary and syntax agreed with the older language, as parts of it still are used in Modern Greek. But for the N.T. idioms contemporary Greek, especially its popular records, offer the best illustrations. Some words or meanings in the N.T. have indeed no parallel in the ancient literary Greek writers, but are sufficiently illustrated by inscriptions or papyri. Professors Adolf Deissmann and J. H. Moulton (see "Literature" below) have been the pioneers in collecting such evidence of a grammatical and lexical character. Unexpected testimony to the vernacular character of some N.T. expressions occurs in the rule books of rhetoricians, when they explicitly condemn as modern or common the very phrases that the Evangelists employ. Of course the original meaning of the N.T. was often well understood by the earliest translators, though they tended to translate it somewhat mechanically with purely verbal equivalents. The later Christian literature, especially the apostolic Fathers, also represent a similar use of the Hellenistic Greek and so extend our knowledge of it. Many an idiom in the N.T. finds its first and most natural illustration in parallel usages within the N.T., particularly those in the same author.

In this connection the Septuagint (LXX) should be especially mentioned (see art., *Transmission of O.T.*, p. 103). It is the largest extant representative of Hellenistic Greek. Furthermore, it was actually known at least in part to most of the N.T. writers. Though it is hardly natural Hellenistic Greek, the literalness of the translation, its wide variety of authorship, its range of vocabulary, its general kinship of subject matter and its kindred unliterary pretensions make it indispensable for an understanding of the N.T. (see Edwin Hatch, *Essays in Biblical Greek*, 1889).

Language of Principal Writers of New Testament. That N.T. language can no longer be regarded as unique has been proved by comparison with contemporary vernacular writings. It is also proved by comparisons between the N.T. writers, for the language is not even uniform among the writers themselves. Fully a dozen separate authors have contributed to the contents of our N.T., and they differ from each other in style as writers generally do and as they themselves differ in personal interest and religious viewpoint. In part the differences are due to the unconscious mannerisms and personal terms of speech. In some cases they are due to different degrees of culture, or to the varying effect of Semitic idiom upon the writings. A few of the outstanding traits of style of the more extensive N.T. writers may be described briefly below.

Mark has the most naïve language of any of the Evangelists. Matthew and Luke evidently appreciated this, for they remove many naïve expressions in their paraphrase of Mark. Among the traits of Mark's language are his vernacular vocabulary, his repetitious and picturesque style, and his use of the connective "and" in place of a variety of conjunctions and constructions. Latin words are somewhat numerous in his short Gospel. They have been sometimes regarded as evidence that the book was written in Rome, but they are usually the terms which Roman government would make familiar in all parts of the empire. Mark also retains and translates a few original Aramaic phrases used by Jesus in prayer (14[36] *abba*=father; cf. on 15[34] above), or in working cures (5[41] *taleitha coum*=maiden, arise; 7[34] *ephphatha* =be opened). But his style is not conspicuously Semitic; it is, rather, simple unpolished Greek. In quoting the O.T. he used the LXX.

Matthew, as already said, improves upon the style of Mark, especially in syntax, but Matthew's language also is simple and inconspicuous. He is given to a kind of natural rhetoric which shows in balanced sentences and stanzas, in closing refrains, and in the continuous presentation of the sayings of Jesus. Some of his O.T. quotations are not in agreement with the LXX as we know it. This fact makes it possible to suppose that either the Evangelist or one of his sources knew the Hebrew O.T. His narrative, however, has few marks of continuous direct translation from a Semitic original. In fact, he is usually believed to have combined Greek sources, among them Mark and Q. (See art., *Structure of the Synoptic Gospels*, p. 868).

Luke's style in the Gospel and Acts is one of the most polished in the N.T. Jerome called Luke "the most erudite of the Evangelists." Evidences of his greater literary taste are found in the changes he makes in paraphrasing Mark, such as the avoidance of repetition, the substitution of more cultivated words and of more grammatical construction; they are found in his apology for or omission of non-Hellenic words (even as proper names), and in his employment of the optative mood and of idiomatic Greek expressions unusual in the N.T. (See Cadbury, *The Making of Luke-Acts*, 1927, chs. ix and xvi.) Many of these expressions are of the sort used in the literary writers of the period like Lucian, Plutarch, and Josephus. Luke's language is therefore rightly called by Moffatt a "book language," as distinct from the spoken language. But this difference from other N.T. writers is only in a limited degree. Luke falls far short of the artificial Greek of contemporary rhetorical authors.

Luke's language has sometimes been called medical, and his agreement in vocabulary with Galen and other doctors has been utilized as an argument supporting the tradition that attributes Luke and Acts to the "beloved physician Luke" mentioned by Paul (Col. 4[14]; see W. K. Hobart, *The Medical Language of St. Luke*, 1882; Harnack, *Luke the Physician*, 1906). The uniqueness of such coincidence has been greatly overemphasized, since it is only natural that the cultivated Gentile Christian historian should use words and phrases found also in medical writers though not exclusively in them alone.

The writings of this author display a curious homogeneity of language in all their parts, coupled with a noticeable variety. The literary traits are most numerous in the later chapters of Acts; the style elsewhere (except in the preface, Luke 1[1-4]) is more simple and also more Semitic. The Semitic features constitute an interesting problem to explain. Reference has already been made to Torrey's theory that the first half of Acts is a translation of a continuous Aramaic source (*The Date and Composition of Acts*, 1916). Torrey appears to hold a like view for the bulk of Luke's Gospel, as, indeed, for all the Gospels, except that he maintains that the stories of the infancy (Luke 1[5]–2[52]) have been translated from a Hebrew document. Such theories of translation account well for the Semitic idiom in these parts of Luke and Acts and naturally meet with favor.

The most probable alternative explanation is that the author, though himself a Greek and writing from Greek sources alone, was affected by the Semitic idiom of the LXX. It is possible that he really knew no Semitic language, but was familiar with the Greek Bible and through it with such terms as "it came to pass," "he added to send" (=he sent again, Lk. 20[11, 12]), "by the mouth of," and "before the face of." In composing his books to Theophilus he consciously or unconsciously fell into this biblical style, as English writers sometimes do. If he is more Semitic in some parts than in others, this may be due to the Palestinian background of those parts, which called forth in a kind of dramatic way the appropriate style. Thus at one extreme the idyls of the birth of John and Jesus with their canticles have the aroma of the O.T., while at the other extreme the speeches of Paul at Athens and before Agrippa with the adjacent narratives have what is for the N.T. a strikingly secular flavor in their style. The Semitisms of Luke are according to this latter theory due rather to imitation than to translation. There is evidence even in the choice of religious terms that this writer has an acute sense of the appropriateness of language to the setting. Whichever explanation of their origin is adopted, the intermittent Semitisms of Luke are a notable feature of his style.

The language of *Paul* is neither so Semitic nor so literary as Luke. The absence of Semitism is at first sight the more strange since Paul is the only N.T. writer of whom we can say with certainty that he knew Aramaic (Acts 21[40]). Yet he quotes the LXX in preference to translating the Hebrew Bible, and besides the Aramaic form of Peter's name (Cephas, 1 Cor. 1[12], etc.; Gal. 1[18], etc.) he uses only three Aramaic expressions, all apparently derived from liturgical usage: *amen*, *abba* (Rom. 8[15] Gal. 4[6]), and *maran atha* (1 Cor. 16[22]). It may be recalled that neither Philo nor Josephus is Semitic in style.

The absence of the literary style from Paul is due to the fact that, unlike Luke and Josephus, he was not writing for publication. His letters, even the most general parts of them, were occasional and spontaneous missives (see art., *Life and Work of Paul*, p. 931). Their style is in all probability the spoken style of Paul's milieu. They have also the particular style of Paul's own oral preaching. In some respects the letters remind us of the "diatribe" or popular ethical and philosophical tract of his time. Correct enough in grammar, comparatively simple in vocabulary, they display a distinct individuality and an emphatic natural rhetoric. They are peculiarly personal and they show with what ease and variety a "vivid" person like Paul could use the common Greek for the expression of every thought and emotion. His language is given to natural antithesis. His connections are loose, his climaxes abundant. There is often a liturgical fullness about the close of his sentences. If Ephesians is a genuine Pauline writing, it represents these traits in a somewhat intensified degree. The Pastoral Epistles, while in parts they have a genuinely Pauline style, differ constantly nevertheless by employing a quite different religious terminology and even a new selection of particles (see intro. to Pastorals, p. 1275). Their religious and ethical language, like that of 2 Peter, finds its closest parallels in writings of the second century, both pagan and Christian. (See P. N. Harrison, *The Problem of the Pastoral Epistles*, 1921.)

The language of *Hebrews*, though, on account of its subject matter, it might be expected to conform to that of the LXX, outside of its actual quotations is strictly grammatical. It ranks with Luke-Acts and Second Maccabees as among the more cultivated styles in the Greek Bible. The alliteration and balance of its opening sentence, the anaphora "by faith" in the eleventh chapter, the idiomatic use of particles and a certain regard for emphasis and perhaps for rhythm in its word order are some of the concrete examples of this elevation of diction. Its difference of style from the style of Paul has been felt by all attentive readers of the original and would supply sufficient evidence, if evidence were needed, that Hebrews was not written or dictated by Paul.

In like manner criteria of style divide the *Johannine writings*. Readers as early as the acute critic Dionysius of Alexandria in the third century saw that the Gospel and Apocalypse are scarcely from the same author (see intro. to John, p. 1065, and Revelation, p. 1365).

The language of the fourth Gospel is simple and grammatical, with a certain individuality especially in its tendency to repetition and in its limited and somewhat intellectual sounding vocabulary for mystical religion. Among its characteristic words are believe, know, judge, witness, truth, light, life, eternal life, and others less frequent but perhaps equally familiar to readers of this Gospel, like only-begotten, Word, and Paraclete. The Aramaic *amen* it uses always double: "Verily, verily." Its particles of connection are few, notably "then" (=therefore) and "and." Such simplicity is entirely compatible with the view that John is translated from the Aramaic, and arguments to that effect have been independently issued. (C. F. Burney, *The Aramaic Origin of the Fourth Gospel*, 1922; J. A. Montgomery, *The Origin of the Gospel according to St. John*, 1923–24; C. C. Torrey, *Harvard Theological Review*, October, 1923.) The arguments do not coincide and have not convinced other scholars generally. In spite of its use in the prologue of a Greek philosophical term, the Logos, the Gospel is apparently in touch with Palestinian places and with some Hebrew terms. Possibly the Semitic element goes no further. The cultural and religious background of this book can scarcely be determined definitely.

The three Epistles of John agree in vocabulary with the Gospel of John. They all share some of its familiar terms; 1 John especially is as akin in style as in subject matter (see intro. to 1 John, p. 1352).

The Revelation of John deals with different subjects and in a different literary mode, namely, the apocalypse. It has a wider vocabulary than has John, but it is not strikingly literary. Without formal quotation of the O.T. it is everywhere strongly influenced by it. Sometimes this influence may be identified as coming through the LXX; at other times, in the view of R. H. Charles the Hebrew O.T. has come into play. This influence need not be directly from the Hebrew. It may imply the use of another and more literal Greek version like that attributed to Theodotion (see art., *Transmission of O.T.*, p. 104). But Charles finds independent evidence of Semitic sources in certain recurrent idioms of the book. It is not clear whether either his evidence or his interpretation must be accepted.

The most remarkable linguistic eccentricity of Revelation is its occasional habit of putting words in the wrong case or gender. The author knows that appositives should agree in case with the nouns they modify and that adjectives and participles should agree with their nouns in gender and case. His lapses (e.g., 1^{5} 11^{4} 14^{19} 21^{9}, etc.; they are, of course, evident only in the Greek) are therefore due either to extraordinary carelessness, or to indifference, or to deliberate intention.

Value of Studying the Original Language. The interest of the study of N.T. language is mainly its help in discovering as closely as possible the thought of the author. Naturally, the nuances of the Greek cannot now always be recovered exactly and still less be carried over into a translation. But a self-respecting student of the Bible will often gain much satisfaction and instruction from a mastery of the original tongue. Even scholars have misunderstood the nature of that language and have misused its phenomena, but that does not prevent the careful use of its evidence in connection with problems of identical authorship and of the use of sources, as well as for determining the meaning of particular passages. Furthermore, a knowledge outside the N.T. of the nature and development of the Greek language through a longer period and in a wider group of writers enables us to place the canonical writers both linguistically and humanly.

Literature: Articles in Bible Dictionaries; Thayer, *Greek-English Lexicon of the N.T.;* Simcox, *The Language of the N.T.; The Writers of the N.T.;* H. A. A. Kennedy, *The Sources of N.T. Greek;* Jamaris, *An Historical Greek Grammar;* Deissmann, *Bible Studies*; *Light from the Ancient East;* J. H. Moulton and Milligan, *The Vocabulary of the Greek Testament;* Milligan, *Here and There Among the Papyri;* A. T. Robertson, *A Grammar of the Greek N.T.;* Dalman, *The Words of Jesus;* Hayes, *Greek Culture and the Greek Testament.*

THE NEW TESTAMENT AND CRITICISM

By Professor ERNEST F. SCOTT

The New Testament a Result of Criticism. N.T. criticism received its name early last century, and is often viewed suspiciously as a modern innovation. But while the name is new, the thing itself goes back almost to the beginnings of Christian history. The N.T. as we now have it may be said, indeed, to owe its existence to criticism. In its earlier period the church possessed a large number of writings which all claimed to be fundamental to its teaching. Some of them were of quite inferior value; others had been fabricated, under revered apostolic names, in the interests of heretical doctrine. To this mass of documents the church applied various tests, in order to single out those which had a genuine right to acceptance, and in this manner our N.T. was formed. (See art., *Formation of N.T.*, pp. 853–9.)

It is a striking fact that the books finally approved were precisely those which would be selected by a modern scholar. Occasionally he might give different reasons for his choice, but he would proceed on the same general principles. The church at the very outset had struck the true path of criticism. It was not till the third century, however, that the work of examining the N.T. was placed on a methodical basis. By that time a number of highly educated men had identified themselves with the church, and devoted to the Christian records the scholarly care which had hitherto been reserved for the classics of Greek literature. The chief center of culture at that time was Alexandria, and it was here, under the shadow of the famous library, that the foundations of N.T. criticism were laid. We owe it to Alexandrian scholars that the manuscripts of the N.T. were compared and edited, with a view to recovering the original text. They also did notable work in exegesis and in the study of literary problems. In not a few of their judgments they anticipated the conclusions of criticism in our own day. This might be illustrated by a remarkable passage in which the bishop Dionysius (about 250 A.D.) examines the book of Revelation, and argues that it cannot be by the same author as the fourth Gospel. Alexandrian criticism, however, was fatally hampered by its adoption of the so-called allegorical method. Recognizing the difficulties presented by much in the N.T., it fell back on a theory that the obvious meaning of the text was only a veil for some profounder spiritual meaning. It is very clear that an artificial method of this kind could lead to no solid results.

The Reformation and Criticism. For more than a thousand years after the time of the great Alexandrian scholars the work of criticism almost stood still. This was partly due to the arrest of all intellectual progress which followed the decline and fall of the Roman Empire, and partly to the stereotyping of belief by the Catholic Church. It was laid down as the duty of all Christians to accept everything that concerned religion without inquiry. The N.T. was now set apart as a sacred book, and the manner in which it had to be interpreted was fixed in the official creeds. Any attempt to raise a question about it, or even to dispute the authorized Latin translation, was at once put down as heresy. This attitude was changed by the Reformation. The bonds of ecclesiastical tradition were now broken, and the Bible was studied from fresh points of view—all the more eagerly because the Bible had now taken the place of the church as the final authority. (See also art., *O.T. and Criticism*, pp. 132–3). Luther himself, with all his boundless reverence for the N.T., was one of its most fearless critics. The commentaries of Calvin, in their clear and sane judgments and honest recognition of difficulties, are models of the true critical temper. From the time of the Reformation onward we can trace a steady progress toward that development which took definite shape in the last century.

The Motives of Modern Criticism. Before considering the nature of modern criticism it will be well to note the principal motives which lie behind it. (1) It arose primarily out of that great awakening of the human spirit of which the French Revolution was partly the cause and partly the consequence. All authorities to which men had submitted themselves out of mere habit were called on to vindicate their right, and the searchlights which had already been applied to political and scientific dogmas were inevitably turned on the Bible. For ages it had been a divine, authoritative book. If it was still to remain so, what were its credentials? (2) A more specific motive may be found in the new sense for history which had begun to manifest itself toward the end of the eighteenth century. Men learned to view the past in its right perspective. They realized that amidst the succession of events there had been a development, each age growing out of the one before it and giving birth to the one which followed. The N.T., whatever might be its permanent value, was a work of the first century. It cannot be rightly explained until it is put back among its surroundings. The key to its difficulties must be sought in the modes of thinking, in the social and political conditions, of that particular time. (3) Once more, the last hundred years have brought not only a new feeling toward the past but a vast increase of our historical knowledge. A wonderful series of discoveries have changed our whole conception of the life of antiquity. Buried cities have come to light; lost books have been recovered; the customs and ideas and beliefs of the ancient peoples have been illuminated from many sides. With all this additional knowledge, which grows in volume every year, scholars have gained a fresh insight into the N.T. They can now illustrate the Gospels and the Epistles of Paul from contemporary documents of which their predecessors knew nothing. They can reconstruct, in all its details, that world in which the N.T. was written. The change produced in criticism by the new knowledge now at our disposal may fairly be compared to that which came about in science through the invention of the microscope. (Cf. art., *Backgrounds*, pp. 843–50; also art., *O.T. and Science*, pp. 122–8.)

Characteristics of Modern Criticism. When we speak, then, of N.T. criticism we think of that mode of inquiry which has only become possible in our own times. "Criticism" means simply "examination," and the modern study of the N.T. is not essentially different from that which was bestowed on it by the ancient Fathers. In the one case, as in the other, the aim is to determine the true nature and message of writings which are confessedly difficult. Yet there are certain characteristics which belong peculiarly to modern criticism.

1. It sets itself to examine the N.T. as it is, without any preconceived ideas of what it ought to be. The ancient critics were bound by various dogmas, to which they tried to adjust everything that they found in the N.T. The object now is simply to discover the facts, and to consider their significance with an open mind. This does not mean that the modern critic cares nothing for the supreme religious message of the N.T. *Its message is one of the facts, the grand fact, with which he is ultimately concerned.* But he seeks, as far as possible, to allow the book to speak for itself. The official creeds, when all is said, were drawn up long afterward, and may have failed at times to represent the true meaning of the N.T. teachers. What do these teachers say when you look away from all later interpretations and carefully study their own testimony?

2. The N.T. writings are viewed in strict relation to the time and the special purpose for which they were intended. Their date and occasion were formerly treated as accidental. It was assumed that Paul's letters to Corinth or Galatia must be taken in a universal sense; that the Gospel of John dealt solely with the eternal truths of religion; that the book of Revelation embraced all history till the end of time. Modern criticism insists that the writings had all some immediate object. They were composed at a given time, for a given circle of readers, whose definite circumstances are always kept in view. A whole group of questions to which the earlier criticism was quite indifferent have thus become of primary importance. Who was the author of each of the documents? What was its precise date and place of origin? To whom was it addressed? What was the occasion which called it forth? Is it all of a single piece or was it written at different times and perhaps by several hands? On the answers to such questions the interpretation of each of the writings must depend.

3. In a larger sense the N.T. is to be understood historically. The church has always taken its stand on the great principle that the Word was made flesh, the Divine Life identified itself with humanity. But the implications of this truth used never to be fully grasped. It was assumed that the revelation broke in suddenly, and had nothing in common with anything that had gone before. We now recognize that although it was new it wove itself naturally into the existing life of the world. The forms in which it found expression had been prepared for it by an age-long process of development. Criticism, in its effort to explain the N.T., now takes full account of this historical preparation. It seeks at every point for connections and antecedents. How far did the early Christian customs grow out of similar practices in Jewish or pagan religion? What analogies to Christian doctrine can be discovered in apocalyptic and rabbinical literature, in the philosophies which the church encountered in the course of its early mission? This historical mode of inquiry is the distinctive feature of modern criticism, and in the hands of many writers it has certainly been pushed too far. Intentionally or not, they create the impression that the N.T. contains nothing which was not borrowed or adapted from some alien source. This pedantry, which is blind to the

manifest originality of the gospel, has sometimes brought the historical method into disrepute, but the soundness of its main conception cannot reasonably be doubted. For centuries before Christ men had been "feeling after God if haply they might find him," and the new revelation attached itself to what was noblest and best in the world's earlier thought. At every step in our study of the N.T. we must estimate the influence of the prophets, of later Judaism, of the Greek philosophies, of contemporary religion. Only thus can we learn to appreciate what is distinctively new. (Cf. H. R. Mackintosh, *The Originality of the Christian Message.*)

4. Modern criticism has been strongly affected in its aims and methods by the example of the sciences. The chemists and physicists of our time have achieved marvelous results by patient and exact observation, by minute analysis, by the collection and comparison of all available facts. They deal, to be sure, with material data which are capable of this precise examination, and in things of the spirit no such exactitude is possible. Yet the N.T. critic tries to make use, as far as may be, of those processes which in other fields have proved so fruitful. He studies a Gospel or Epistle in every detail of its structure, as a botanist examines a plant. He is confident that every fact, however trivial, is worth attention, and may possibly afford a clue to far-reaching results. Some of the most notable of modern N.T. theories have been founded on the careful investigation of some single word or phrase. What is meant, for instance, by the title "Son of man"? Why is Christ called "the Lord"? What was implied in the baptismal formula "in the name of Jesus"? (Cf. pp. 840; 939a and 1093; 1098b.)

The Various Forms of Criticism. In our time, when all knowledge has become so highly specialized, N.T. criticism is a many-sided term. The problems which it deals with fall into a number of distinct classes, each of which requires a whole science for itself. A generation ago it was customary to make a twofold division into the "lower" and the "higher" criticism, i.e., the inquiry into matters of text and language, and the larger inquiry into the origin and meaning of the several books. Those terms "lower" and "higher" were unhappily chosen, and have led to much misunderstanding. They were also inappropriate, for the "lower" criticism often involves the wider questions, and vice versa. It is better to adopt a more natural division on some such lines as these. (See art., *O.T. and Criticism*, pp. 129–33.)

1. Textual criticism, which seeks to determine what the authors actually wrote. The N.T. has come down to us in more than two thousand manuscripts, all of them varying in greater or less degree from each other. Amidst this conflict of testimony how are we to restore the text to something like its original condition? (See art., *Transmission of N.T.*, pp. 860–66.)

2. Exegesis, which investigates the precise meaning of each verse and paragraph. This work of exposition must be based on linguistic study, and it has been greatly furthered in recent years by the discovery, chiefly in Egypt, of great numbers of letters and other private documents. Hitherto we have known only the literary Greek of the first century, and the apostles wrote in the current language of the people. Those living turns of speech have now been illustrated and explained. (See Milligan, *Here and There Among the Papyri.*)

3. Literary criticism, which is concerned with all questions affecting the composition of the books. Their date and authorship, their style and purpose and sources, fall to be considered under this head.

4. Theological criticism, which takes up the results of all the other lines of inquiry and attempts, on the basis of them, to trace out the nature and development of N.T. thought.

It cannot be claimed that this broad division is in any sense exhaustive. The history of the canon, for instance (i.e., of the process by which the writings were selected and set apart as scripture; see p. 855), is a great subject by itself. The study of the life of Christ is perhaps the most important task of criticism, and yet it cannot be brought under any of the ordinary divisions. The rise of the church and the development of institutions are also to be assigned to special departments. Moreover, some of the subjects most vital for the understanding of the N.T. do not fall strictly within the N.T. field at all. The need for intimate acquaintance with O.T. scripture has always been evident. We are now aware that early Christian thought was also profoundly influenced by the teachings of later Judaism, and by the philosophical and religious conceptions which had grown up in the Greco-Roman world. No scholars are doing more at the present day to elucidate the N.T. than the experts in apocalyptic, in rabbinical literature, in Hellenistic philosophy and the mystery religions (see art., *Backgrounds*, p. 843; also art., *Religious Development of the Intertestamental Period*, p. 209). The N.T. is a small book which might be read from end to end in a few hours, but the study of it has expanded into a vast science, involving the skill and lifelong labor of a host of learned men. No one can now pretend to have a fully competent knowledge of anything but a little portion of the whole domain of N.T. criticism.

Special Problems in Criticism. In whatever department his work may lie the critic is confronted with a great number of special problems. Their very existence was hardly suspected a century ago, but it is now recognized that issues of the first magnitude are bound up with their solution. The nature of these problems will be best understood if we look at several of the outstanding examples.

1. Perhaps the most important of all is that which concerns the synoptic Gospels (see intro. to each). These Gospels to a great extent repeat each other, while at the same time they present many striking differences. On what theory of their origin can we explain at once their agreements and their variations? At first sight the problem may seem to be one of merely literary interest, but its significance is apparent when we reflect that these three Gospels are our primary records of the life of Christ. How and when did they originate? How far can we accept them as historical? Our faith as Christians must depend, in large measure, on the answer that can be given to these questions. Criticism endeavors to solve them by means of a detailed comparison of the three Gospels with each other. Endless patience and ingenuity have been spent on the inquiry, and it is still in process. Several points, however, may now be regarded as fully established: (1) The Gospels as we now have them were written in the latter part of the first century but they were compiled from earlier documents. (2) The oldest of our present Gospels is Mark. (3) Along with Mark there was a work now lost, which consisted mainly of Sayings of Jesus. (4) Matthew and Luke, independently of each other, combined the narrative of Mark with this lost work, each of them adding a considerable amount of extra material. The principal aims of more recent criticism are to determine the sources (probably in the Aramaic language) which lie behind Mark, and to ascertain the nature and extent of the lost document. (See art., *The Structure of the Synoptic Gospels*, p. 868.)

2. Only second in importance to the synoptic is the Johannine problem. Until a hundred years ago the fourth Gospel was universally accepted as the work of John, the personal disciple of Jesus, but critical examination has thrown doubt on this authorship. It is maintained (1) that the ancient evidence on the subject is by no means conclusive; (2) that the evangelist depends on the other three Gospels, as a firsthand witness would not require to do; (3) that some of the pervading ideas of the Gospel became current in the church at a comparatively late time, when John can have been no longer living. Some critics would assign the Gospel to a disciple of John; others to a later John, commonly called the Elder, who was a prominent figure in the Asian church; others conclude that the name of the author is now hopelessly lost, while a further theory, which has found considerable favor in recent years, would divide the work among several authors. It may be doubted whether the Johannine problem will ever be solved. The most diverse views are all tenable, and unless some entirely new evidence comes to light it seems impossible to choose between them (see intro. to Fourth Gospel, pp. 1060–6).

3. Outside of the Gospels there are a number of literary problems which are less cardinal, but still of the highest interest. How many of the Epistles which have come down to us under the name of Paul were actually written by him? Are the last four chapters of 2 Corinthians and the closing chapter of Romans to be taken as separate letters? Who wrote the Epistle to the Hebrews and to whom was it addressed? What is the relation of the Epistles of John to the fourth Gospel? What were the sources of the book of Acts? What was the origin of the book of Revelation, and how is it to be interpreted? Every writing of the N.T. has its own problem or cluster of problems, and all of them are still unsettled. (See individual discussions of these questions in connection with the several books.)

4. The relation of the N.T. to the apocalyptic literature gives rise to many crucial questions of a different character. Within the last century a whole series of writings have been recovered which date from about 160 B.C. to 100 A.D. and deal with the approach of the "new age" when God will establish his kingdom. Two books in the Bible, Daniel and Revelation, are typical of this class of literature. It cannot be denied that many of the apocalyptic conceptions (e.g., those which concern the Messiah, the kingdom of God, the resurrection, the judgment, the heavenly world) passed over into early Christianity (see art., *The Religious Development of the Intertestamental Period*, pp. 206–13). To what extent did Jesus himself adopt these conceptions? How far did he impress them with a new meaning? Are they to be considered an essential part of his message or merely a framework or scaffolding which can be easily removed? It is chiefly in the Gospels that the apocalyptic ideas are prominent, but they meet us everywhere in the N.T. To determine their precise nature and influence

is one of the primary tasks of criticism. (See notes on Mk. 13.)

5. A still more important question has emerged within our own generation in consequence of our larger knowledge of the historical background of Christianity. We are now aware that the union of East and West under the Roman Empire had led to the wide diffusion of certain Oriental cults, which had customs and beliefs resembling, at least superficially, those of the church. They possessed sacraments not unlike baptism and the Lord's Supper. They turned on the worship of divinities who had died and been restored to life and whose experience was supposed to repeat itself in that of their votaries. How are these affinities to be explained? In what degree was the church influenced, in the expression of its beliefs, by the example of the rival cults? Many writers have undoubtedly made too much of the apparent similarities, but that there was some relation between Christian doctrine and the contemporary beliefs can hardly be questioned. A new and profoundly interesting field has been opened for N.T. investigation (see art., *Backgrounds*, pp. 851–2, and cf. notes on 1 Cor. 11).

These are only a few of the larger problems with which criticism has to deal at the present day. On all of them there is wide difference of opinion, and perhaps none of them will ever be completely settled. Criticism calls itself a science, but it must never be forgotten that the sifting of ideas and historical origins is not like the physical sciences, which work with tangible material. Any results that can be gained are tentative at the best, and are subject to constant modification. It is very noticeable that the tone of criticism is always becoming less dogmatic. The claim was often made a generation ago that certain theories had been definitely proved, but later research has in almost every instance thrown doubt on them or overturned them altogether. There is no reason to suppose that present-day conclusions will be any more stable. Competent scholars only adopt them provisionally. They are anxious, above all things, to preserve an open mind.

The Helpful Results of Criticism. What, then, has been the effect of criticism on our estimate of the N.T., and of the message contained in it? At first sight it might appear that the results have been largely negative. The N.T. was formerly accepted as a book which, being divinely inspired, imparted a revelation which in all its details was valid forever. In the light of criticism this view is no longer wholly tenable. We have learned to see the N.T. writers as men of their own time, working under many limitations. We realize that in the message they delivered there was an admixture of more or less transient elements. We are compelled to make distinctions between different books of the N.T., and sometimes between different portions of the same book. Later traditions or doctrines of secondary value are mingled with genuine history and with passages that breathe the authentic spirit of the gospel. In these respects and in others criticism has disturbed the traditional attitude to the N.T. Its work has appeared to many minds to be purely negative and destructive.

This judgment, however, is far from representing the whole truth. On a deeper view it can hardly be doubted that criticism, instead of destroying the N.T., has set it on a firmer foundation, and has given a new power and meaning to its message.

1. If it has broken down the older doctrine of inspiration, it has replaced it by a truer and more satisfying one. According to the old idea God employed the sacred writers as mere neutral vehicles for the expression of his will. They were often compared to the harp or lyre which answers mechanically to the touch of the musician. We now think of the message as coming to us through inspired personalities. The apostles, as Paul himself declared, were men of like passions with ourselves, but through their knowledge of Christ they had attained to a higher faith and insight. Limited as they were by the conditions of their time and their own shortcomings, they were striving to proclaim the truth which possessed them. We can feel as we read their words that they were led by the Spirit of God.

2. In like manner criticism has done a real service by teaching us to distinguish between the forms or accessories of the gospel and the substance. It followed from the old doctrine of inspiration that everything contained in the N.T. must stand on the same level. Church regulations or details of theology were to be regarded as no less vital than the parables or the Beatitudes. This attitude of mind could lead only to a confusion in religious thinking. The mischief wrought by it is abundantly illustrated by many dark chapters of Christian history. We now have learned to recognize that many things in the N.T. belong to the age in which it was written. Those traditions and philosophies which served as a clothing for the message must not be confounded with the message itself.

3. The very fact that the N.T. has been thrown open to the freest and most searching examination must be reckoned as a great gain. Out of motives of mistaken reverence it was

formerly taken on trust, and for this reason Christian faith was liable to insecurity. A hundred years ago the most powerful argument against religion was always that it rested on mere authority. What was the guarantee for this divine book? Who could tell when or how it came to be written? What was the proof that all its teachings were not an arbitrary invention? Such arguments carry weight no longer. The N.T. has been examined more strictly than any other book. The main facts as to its origin have been verified on the fullest available evidence. No one can say that anything is being withheld, for every possible doubt has been put forward and magnified. As a result of all this sifting many of our old conceptions of the N.T. have been changed, but its claim has been established more surely than ever. It stands out, not on any dogmatic grounds but by its own intrinsic worth, as the chief spiritual possession of mankind. (See W. N. Clarke, *Sixty Years with the Bible.*)

4. We owe it to criticism that the life of Christ has been set on a firm historical basis. Our Gospels, it was always acknowledged, were written comparatively late, and on this account their value was often challenged. How was it possible that these records, composed after such a long interval, could give us anything more than vague memories and legends? Might it not be that they were wholly the work of pious imagination? Modern criticism has indeed distinguished various strata in the Gospels, some of them more primitive and trustworthy than others; but one fact it has clearly demonstrated—the evangelists, although they were men of a later generation, worked with materials which had come to them from the early days. Their records are compilations of briefer documents, some of which must go back to the time immediately following our Lord's death. We can feel certain that the facts are set before us with essential fidelity.

5. It is now possible to reconstruct the N.T. history, and to judge the true significance of the various characters and events. All the conceptions of early Christianity have hitherto suffered from a certain unreality. One has only to think of the familiar Bible pictures, many of them beautiful as works of art but designed, apparently, to illustrate some fairy book rather than a history of things which actually happened. It cannot be anything but a gain that this atmosphere of illusion has now been dispelled. We can place the apostles in their true environment. We can make out the process by which the church came into being, and follow the development of its worship and institutions and doctrines. In the light of this historical knowledge we are able to appreciate those elements of the gospel which secured its final victory.

6. It is due to criticism (and this, perhaps, has been its most valuable result) that we can now read the N.T. as a living book. There may be some truth in the argument that the Bible is no longer sacred when it is laid open to free inquiry. Men accepted it formerly as the literal Word of God: we now study it in the making, and discover that its writers were human beings, expressing themselves in the language and the forms of thought which their time afforded them. Something may be lost, but in return the N.T. has been brought far closer to our hearts and lives. We can see that it has everywhere a bearing on real needs and difficulties. Its writers had passed through the common experiences; they declared their message to a world that was strangely like our own, in spite of the two thousand years which separate it. Much of the indifference to religion in our time has grown out of the feeling that the Bible is an outworn book, which never had much relation to actual life and has now entirely lost its meaning. The most urgent task of the Christian teacher is to make the book living, and in this task he will find his best assistance in modern criticism. In recovering the lost links between these ancient writings and man's daily life, it has disclosed to us one of the chief sources of their power.

Criticism and the Spirit of Christ. It is a significant fact that the great periods of criticism have been just those when the Christian spirit was most vital. Whenever men have grown aware that the N.T. was no mere repository of old tradition but the vehicle of a life-giving message they have ceased to accept it out of pious custom. They have examined it eagerly, under the most searching light they had, in order to discover its true purpose and meaning. It was so in the early centuries when the church was engaged in its great conflict. It was so again at the Reformation. We have a right to believe that the critical movement of our own day has its ultimate spring in a new sense of the value of the gospel, and that it is preparing the way for some fuller revelation of Christ.

Literature: Cobern, *The New Archæological Discoveries and Their Bearing on the N.T.;* Ramsay, *The Bearing of Recent Discoveries on the Trustworthiness of the N.T.;* McClymont, *History and Results of N.T. Criticism;* Robertson, *Studies in the Text of the N.T.;* Moffatt, *The Approach to the N.T.;* Deissmann, *New Light on the N.T.;* Bacon, *The Making of the N.T.;* Conybeare, *The History of N.T. Criticism;* Peake, *Critical Introduction to the N.T.*

THE LIFE OF JESUS CHRIST

By Professor JOSEPH F. McFADYEN

Sources. Practically all that we know of the earthly life of Jesus we learn from the four Gospels. All four Gospel writers agree that the movement of which the Baptist was the center formed the beginning of the story of Jesus as the Christ. Mark, indeed, draws a veil completely over all that precedes; but "Matthew" and Luke, writing later, narrate stories of the birth and infancy of Jesus. Those in Matthew seem to be intended to establish parallels between the infancy of Jesus and that of Israel, in particular of Moses. The child Jesus, "Matthew" tells us, under divine guidance was taken to Egypt, and only by the providence of God escaped premature destruction. The star that guided the Magi suggests to some the star prophesied in Num. 24[17], the star which was to come forth out of Jacob.

[In this article the name "Matthew" appears sometimes with quotation marks, and sometimes without. When the name refers to the first Gospel, the marks are not used; they are used when it refers to the individual, to indicate that the author of the article questions the tradition that the author of the first Gospel was an individual named Matthew.]

Birth and Infancy. The very beautiful introduction to Luke's Gospel narrates the story of the birth of the Baptist as well as of Jesus. In these two chapters Luke gives us a background against which the subsequent story has to be read. The new religion, he seems to say, was born in a burst of song; Jesus and his forerunner the Baptist were born and cradled in song. Many, indeed, believe that the prominence of sacred lyrics in these chapters (like the Magnificat, the Benedictus, and the Nunc Dimittis) indicates the spirit in which they are to be read. In his introduction Luke implicitly reminds us that the men who hounded Jesus to his death did not represent the whole of Judaism. From these chapters we get a very different impression of the Temple, the priesthood, and the Jewish piety of the time from that which we get from the subsequent history. In the birth and infancy sections both of Matthew and Luke, we are struck by the prominent part played by angels and visions as a means by which God made his will known to his servants. While the records ascribe to Jesus himself a belief in angels, they played practically no part in his religious life. His communion with the Father God was so unhindered and direct that he was conscious of no gulf between them, and so felt no need of angels to act as intermediaries.

At a very early period in the history of the church the title Son of God was applied to Jesus. In their Gospels "Matthew" and Luke teach that Jesus was Son of God, not only in the sense that his will was one with God's will and that in him God had become incarnate, but in a physical sense also; that in his case the Holy Spirit took the place of a human father. The doctrine of the virgin birth, as it is called, has been asserted, doubted, and denied by men who all equally claim to be loyal followers of Jesus.

Those who hesitate to make belief in the virginity of Mary an essential of the Christian faith bring support for their position from various quarters. The virgin birth, they say, is clearly taught in Matthew, not quite so clearly in Luke; but apart from the introductions to these two Gospels, it is nowhere mentioned in the N.T. It was obviously not a theme of the first Christian preachers. If John does not deny it, neither does he affirm it. "Matthew" misunderstood Isaiah's prophecy from which he quotes; in Isaiah there is no reference to a virgin. Luke's only reference to the virgin birth is in the prophecy to Mary of the angel Gabriel in 1[34f.] Mary's question in 1[34] is not very intelligible as coming from a betrothed maiden. When Luke comes to describe the actual birth, he seems to make no further reference to anything miraculous in its nature.

Not only is Joseph called the father of Jesus (2[33]), but he and Mary are represented as being astonished at the message of Simeon (2[33]) and failing to understand the saying of Jesus that he must be in his Father's house—facts difficult to reconcile with the story in the first chapter. The theory of Mary's virginity seems to attach too much importance to a physical basis for holiness. In the judgment of many the true miracle is not the virgin body of Mary but the virgin soul of Jesus. If the Holy Spirit can cleanse from all taint of impurity the son of a woman, could not his influence be equally effective with the son of a woman and a man? (The Roman Catholics have been logical enough to note this weakness of the theory of the virgin birth. They evade the difficulty, since 1854, by teaching that the conception of Mary herself was immaculate.) Moreover, if Jesus did not enter the world as we do, then it is said he cannot be our High Priest and out of his own experience sympathize with us in our temptations. In any case, the claim is made that the incarnation and the virgin birth are not inseparably linked together; the divine is not limited to any one way of entering the human.

Those who accept the fact of the virgin birth point to such evidences as the following: The birth of Jesus from a virgin is clearly taught both in Mt. 1 and Lk. 1; moreover, these accounts come from independent sources, the former being given from Joseph's point of view, the latter from Mary's. "Matthew" (1^{23}) points out that the virgin birth was prophesied in Isa. 7^{14}. With insignificant exceptions, the church since apostolic times has accepted the fact. The author of the fourth Gospel almost certainly knew the story of the virgin birth, and, at all events, he does not contradict it. Further, it is asked, If the story is not authentic, whence did it arise? Not on Jewish soil, for Jews honored marriage and attached no special sanctity to virginity. Nor yet on pagan soil, for the story of the birth of Jesus moves on an altogether different plane from the often gross pagan fables of children born of divine fathers and human mothers. Further, the incarnation seems to require a physical miracle; like the resurrection, the virgin birth is entirely consonant with all that we know of Jesus.

Both "Matthew" and Luke record that Jesus was born in Bethlehem, six miles south-southwest of Jerusalem. Luke thinks of Nazareth in Galilee as the home of Joseph and Mary (1^{26} 2^{4}). From the early life of Jesus, Luke alone lifts the veil for a moment. On a visit to the Temple, when he was twelve years old, he became so engrossed in discussion with the rabbis, who were astonished at his ripe intelligence, that he failed to join his family party on its return journey.

Connection with John the Baptist. All four Gospels describe a great crisis in the life of Jesus which took place during the Baptist movement. (The data in Lk. $3^{1f.}$ point to a date about 28 A.D. See art., *Chronology of N.T.*, p. 874.) A prophet of priestly descent, John son of Zacharias, was the leading figure in a great religious revival. John is represented in the Gospels as a second Elijah. Like Elijah he wore a leather girdle and made his home for a time in the wilderness by the banks of the Jordan. Jesus found in him the fulfillment of Malachi's prophecy of the coming of Elijah as the forerunner of King Messiah. John was a Nazirite and an ascetic (Num. 6^{1f}). The brackish waters of the sluggish Jordan were by Jewish theologians deemed unfit for purificatory purposes; but John called on the Jews to submit to baptism in the Jordan, hitherto used for sacramental purposes only by Elisha. His call was to individual repentance, not, as that of the prophets had so often been, to national and social repentance; nor, like the Essenes, did he invite men to leave their calling, but to practice moderation, justice, and mercy in their calling.

John's call to repentance, his proclamation that a crisis in the story of God's dealings with his people was at hand, and the baptismal symbol with which he accompanied his message, stirred the country profoundly. The influence of his movement was long-continued and widespread (Acts $18^{24f.}$ and $19^{1f.}$); yet John worked within the Judaic system, with no recorded protest against its outworn ritual. Moreover, the note of doom was so prominent in his message that it could hardly be called a gospel.

Among the throngs that came to be baptized by John was Jesus of Nazareth in Galilee, thus abruptly introduced in Mark, our earliest Gospel, and as yet, so far as we know, unknown outside of his native town. The absence of reference to Joseph in the Gospel story suggests that he was long since dead, and that Jesus had been left with the care of his younger brothers and sisters. It is a tempting suggestion that his marvelous power of story-telling had been developed in the home circle. Like Joseph, he followed the trade of a carpenter (perhaps "artisan" or "builder" is a better translation). Eulogies on manual labor, based on this fact, are modern interpretations which had no interest for the primitive church. The fact that Jesus had been a manual worker is mentioned only once in the Gospels, and then only by his critics in order to depreciate his ministry (Mk. 6^{3}).

Mark quite simply relates that Jesus was baptized by John in the Jordan. Writing later, "Matthew" explains that John demurred at baptizing Jesus, and was reassured by Jesus' explanation that he must fulfill all the claims of righteousness. Immediately after his baptism Jesus had a strange sense of divine approval and consecration to a God-given ministry, an assurance of unique Sonship. As Mark tells the story, it may indicate only an inward and spiritual experience, though the later accounts give a more concrete form to the dove that symbolized the Spirit and to the divine voice.

Temptation. Alone with God in the wilderness after his baptism, Jesus spent weeks of intense meditation on the nature of the task that he now knew lay before him. Various alluring plans for discharging the trust committed to him presented themselves to his mind; but one who enjoyed the unbroken fellowship with God that Jesus knew, recognized that those suggestions did not come from God. The first bypath down which he was tempted to turn was the plan of concentrating on the effort to make life smoother and more comfortable for himself and his followers. There are indications that Jesus regarded even his healing ministry as in a measure but supplementary to his other work. Again, he was tempted to offer the people a "sign," such as that of leaping safely from a pinnacle of the Temple. But in his thought every gift with which he was equipped was meant to help men, not to dazzle them. Moreover, almost till the last day of his life Jesus is represented as taking steps to evade any danger that threatened to bring his work to a premature close.

The fact that Jesus was speaking figuratively in describing his temptations is made especially clear in the third narrative, which represents him as being offered, at the price of homage to Satan, the lordship over all earthly kingdoms which he viewed from a high mountain. The peculiar subtlety of this suggestion lay in this: that it might easily be made to appear that a long life of popularity and earthly power would provide far greater opportunity for beneficent work and lofty teaching than a short life largely spent in controversy and ending in a violent death. Jesus met all three temptations with one of the great texts of Scripture with which his mind was stored (Deut. 8^{3} 6^{16} 6^{13}).

Beginning of Public Ministry. John has much to tell of work of Jesus in Judæa before the Galilæan ministry began; indeed, he pays little attention to Galilee throughout the story. This is only one of many points on which the fourth Gospel leaves a somewhat different impression from the first three. Apparently John knew more than the other Gospel writers about Jesus' activity in Judæa, but there is also a deeper explanation. Writing long after the story had passed into history, John was anxious not only to record events and sayings but to interpret them; to show their significance on which the intervening history had shed much light. Throughout the story he sees Jesus, as it were, transfigured, and he is more deeply interested in spiritual truth than in questions of chronology or geography.

According to Mark, the ministry of Jesus began in Galilee, where he had been brought up. In four phrases Mark sums up the central points in his proclamation (1^{15}): "The time of waiting is over; God's reign is at hand; prepare for this reign by repenting, changing your manner of life; have faith in the good news." Every Jew would understand the phrase, "the Kingdom," or "reign of God." It might be paraphrased as "the world as God meant it to be." It was customary for the religious teachers of the time to wander, each with a small band of followers. The intimacy with Jesus of two pairs of fishermen brothers, Peter and Andrew, James and John, dated from the beginning of the ministry. Jesus, playing on the word, called them to become fishers of men, by patient skill to win men to the new life that would fit them for citizenship in the Kingdom. In a story which has often been compared with the resurrection episode in Jn. $21^{1f.}$, Luke in 5^{1-11} gives a fuller account of the call of Peter.

Aspects of Early Ministry. Next, Jesus made a tour of the cities and villages of Galilee, finding in the service of the synagogue or village church an excellent opportunity for delivering his message. He was often invited to translate the scripture passage for the day from the ancient Hebrew into the spoken Aramaic, and to expound it. The people were astonished at the note of authority in his teaching. Unlike their usual teachers, he made them hear the voice of the living God from the pages of the Book. At the very beginning of the story Mark introduces one more activity of Jesus—a healing ministry. Various attitudes toward disease are possible and have been actually taken. It may be regarded as the punishment of sin, our own sin in this life or in a previous life, or the sin of our ancestors; as a chastening discipline from God; as a test of our loyalty to God; or even as a mark of God, a special favor. It was the judgment of Jesus that in the kingdom of God, in the world as God meant it to be, disease has no place. Pity for weakness and pain, the fight with disease, and the belief that in this fight we have God on our side, the church has inherited from Jesus. The healing ministry was not an addendum to his work of announcing the Kingdom, or simply a verification of his claims. It was an essential part of his message. To cure all kinds of physical disabilities was but one side of the Messiah's work, of which the other side was to preach the gospel to the poor (Mt. 11^{5}).

In his earlier chapters Mark has little explicit theology, but he clearly means to represent Jesus as always Master (or Lord, to use the title which the later church loved to give him). He begins by subduing Satan; when he calls men to follow him they come at his call; when he teaches he teaches with authority; at his word foul spirits come out, the bedridden resume their activities, the paralytic walks and the leper is restored to human fellowship. A form of disease which plays a prominent part in the story is that of demon possession. In the simple medical diagnosis of the time possession by a demon was the explanation given of many diseases, especially cases of mental aberration. Mark represents the demoniacs as knowing that Jesus was the Messiah. His conception is that the demons, who were believed to inspire the utterances of the demoniacs, being servants of Satan, recognized in Jesus their arch-enemy before men in general discovered in him the Messiah. Men of deranged mind readily adapt the outlook of any character with which in their delusion they identify themselves, and from the beginning these poor people must have heard all round them much speculation on the nature and mission of Jesus.

Jesus varied his methods according to the case. Demons he exorcised by a commanding word; Peter's mother-in-law he took by the hand and assisted to her feet. The most revealing instance is that of the leper, whom Jesus touched. A leper's touch brought defilement, and the consequent exclusion from human society must to the sufferers have been almost more terrible than the disease. (See art., *N.T. Miracles*, p. 925a.)

Antipathy of Jewish Leaders: Its Causes. The next question to which Mark turns his attention is one which, in the early days of the church, attracted great attention both among Jews and among Christians. Why was Jesus rejected by the leaders of his own people, and why were the followers of Jesus persecuted by them, as the early chapters of Acts tell us they were? For the Christians it was a problem to be explained, as we see from the way in which Paul deals with the question in Romans.

(1) *Claim to Forgive Sins.* Mark's answer is that the indignation of the rulers against Jesus was aroused, in the first place, by his claim to forgive sins. At the time Mark wrote, the church put in the forefront of her creed that through faith in the name of Jesus men may have their sins forgiven. In the story of the paralytic brought to Jesus by four friends, Mark (2$^{1-12}$) tells us that the claims the Christians made for Jesus, Jesus had first made for himself. Forgiveness, the story implies, includes not only the cleansing of the conscience and the sense of reconciliation with God, but also, it may be in some way we cannot now understand, the cancelling even of the consequences of sin.

(2) *Differing Views of Holiness.* The antipathy of the Jewish leaders to Jesus was due, in the second place, to the irreconcilable opposition between his view of holiness and theirs. They differed vitally as to what was meant by holy people, holy conduct, holy food, holy days. The authorities were scandalized because Jesus not only invited a customhouse officer called Levi (in the first Gospel 9^{9} identified with Matthew) to be one of his closest followers, but attended a reception given by Levi at which many of the guests were "publicans and sinners." These "publicans" were not the rich *publicani* who farmed out the taxes, but the actual collectors. They were social outcasts because in Judæa they were in the service of the hated Roman government and in Galilee in the service of Herod Antipas, who was the creature of Rome; also because by the nature of their occupation they were compelled to rub shoulders with Gentiles; while no doubt they would often find it difficult or impossible to observe the Sabbath or to visit Jerusalem at the time of the Passover.

Who were the "sinners"? A sinner was a transgressor of the Law; but the Jewish Law included much that we should now call ceremonial. Thieves and adulterers were "sinners"; but so also were Gentiles, however upright in character (Gal. 2^{15}) since they were altogether outside of the Law. So also would be Jews who, through indifference, neglected the requirements of the ceremonial Law, or, owing to the circumstances of their lives, could not fulfill them. Perhaps "non-churchgoer" is the nearest modern equivalent. The Pharisees were the Puritans among the Jews. Their movement began in a serious attempt to secure the purity of the Jewish race and the Jewish religion. But separation of any kind is apt to engender feelings of superiority, contempt and self-satisfaction. They were the popular party, nationalist within limits, representing the middle classes chiefly of the towns, as opposed to the aristocratic Sadducees on the one hand and the humble village folks on the other. In a sense they were liberals, who maintained that laws given for an earlier stage of civilization needed adaptation before being applied in a more complicated social environment. There were, however, two serious weaknesses in their position. They did not believe in allowing the people to use their own instructed common sense in solving their moral problems; and their goodness was of the kind that rubs off. The Pharisee thought the other man's impurity would infect him; Jesus hoped his purity would infect the other man (Mk. 2^{7}).

(3) *Fasting.* One of the disputes concerned

fasting (Mk. 2[18-22]). In his teaching Jesus did not discourage fasting, but only ostentatious fasting (Mt. 6[16-18]); but his own neglect of the fast-days observed by the strict Pharisees was made the subject of gibes (Mt. 11[19]). Fasting, he taught, a sign of mourning and humiliation, was out of place in the glad, new epoch that his mission was inaugurating; and the expansive power of a living religion can never be confined within the framework that sufficed for bygone days. New wine needs new wineskins.

(4) *The Sabbath Question.* Another frequent source of conflict between Jesus and the Pharisees was the Sabbath question. The subject must have occasioned great difficulty in the early church, since Gentile converts had never previously known a Sabbath day; and the question how far the Jewish Sabbath was binding on Christians was only part of the very difficult question of the relation of Christians to the Jewish Law. In justice to the Pharisees, we have to remember that in their eyes the very existence of their religion was bound up with the observance of the Sabbath. On more than one occasion the enemies of the Jews had successfully taken advantage of their known reluctance to fight on the Sabbath. (See notes on Neh. 10[31] 13[15-22].)

But they looked only to the letter of the Law. Jesus looked in a broad way at the meaning of the institution of the Sabbath rest. In defending his hungry disciples for plucking and rubbing wheat-ears on the Sabbath (technically threshing) Jesus quoted the precedent of David, who with his followers in time of need ate the sacred loaves (Mk. 2[26]). David put the claims of humanity before the claims of ritual. Churlishness is always objectionable; churlishness in the name of religion is doubly so. In particular, the Pharisees urged that, except in cases of desperate illness, medical attention should not be given on the Sabbath. Jesus laid down the principle on which the world, and even the church, have been so slow to act: that human beings, even our employees, deserve as much consideration as our livestock or our draught-animals (Lk. 13[10-17] 14[1-6]). In healing on the Sabbath the man with the withered arm, in the face of the silent hostility of the authorities, Jesus uttered the pregnant saying that the Sabbath is a day for saving life, not for destroying it. On this Mark has the illuminating comment that, on this same Sabbath, those defenders of the Sabbath law began to plot the destruction of Jesus (Mk. 3[6]).

In this plot they joined with the Herodians, who must have been supporters of Herod Antipas, tetrarch of Galilee; possibly a party that hoped to see Herod an independent monarch. This union of the political and the religious leaders foreshadowed the combination which finally brought Jesus to his death. So far as the records show, this marks practically the end of the synagogue ministry. In the next scene Jesus withdraws with his disciples to the Sea of Galilee. So great were the crowds that came to his ministrations from all parts of the country, even from Tyre and Sidon outside the limits of Palestine, that sometimes he had to take refuge in a small boat and address the multitudes from this strange pulpit. We note that Jesus' disputes with the Pharisees were not all concerned with the ritual side of the Law. In the beautiful story of the woman who anointed Jesus (Lk. 7[36f.]) and in the passage at the beginning of Jn. 8 that has somehow wandered from its original context, the Gospels show that Jesus was no more afraid of moral than of ceremonial infection. It has taken even the Christian world a long time to develop Jesus' sense of chivalry in dealing with sexual sin. Though little is said on the subject in the Gospels, we gather that the harlots received his message with as much joy as the outcast tax-collectors (Mt. 21[31]). On this point the accredited defenders of social morality would feel doubly sure that their opposition to Jesus was God-inspired.

Choosing the Twelve. Next comes an event of great importance in the history of the church—the choosing of the twelve (Mk. 3[13-19] and parallels). Mark indicates three objects which were in the mind of Jesus when he selected them: (1) personal and close association with himself, a theological education by personal contact with the greatest of all teachers; (2) when their course was complete, a missionary tour; (3) equipment with the power of exorcising evil spirits. In modern language this would be described as a medical mission by faith healing; but it was then conceived as a campaign against Satan. Some of "the twelve" did work of far-reaching significance. That some of the others are almost unknown to us does not necessarily mean that they accomplished nothing. Some fishermen, a tax-collector, a politician or two, and one or two others who left hardly even a name behind them, nearly all of them Galilæans, not one of them so far as we know with any pretensions to scholarship, formed a not very promising theological college. But Jesus had the same insight and the same disregard of convention in his selection of his assistants as he showed in the choice of an audience. They had the double advantage that they were not trained by a rabbi and that they were trained by Jesus. In addition to the men disciples, Luke (8[1-3]) tells us that a number of women who were indebted to Jesus for relief from ill health or nervous or mental trouble traveled with the disciples and ministered to their material wants. Among these women was Mary of Magdala, a wealthy city south of Capernaum. Luke's remark that seven devils had gone out of her is often interpreted to mean that Mary had been rescued by Jesus from a life of shame. For this theory there is no evidence worth the name. She had been cured of some acute nervous disorder, possibly at times amounting to actual mental derangement.

His Mighty Works. Wherever Jesus went the excitement continued to be intense. A rumor began to spread that he was insane (Mk. 3[21]). Jesus' relatives tried to seize and restrain him. They may have shared the common view that his mind was affected; and they may well have been afraid, both for themselves and for him, of the growing opposition of the authorities. For scribes now appear on the scene who have come all the way from Jerusalem (Mk. 3[22]). The official verdict is that Jesus' wonderful power over the bodies and the minds of men is the result of a bargain he has made with the lord of the demons; in modern language, the price he has obtained for selling himself to the devil. The earnestness, almost fierceness, of Jesus' answer to this subtle explanation of his spiritual domination is explained in part by his recollection of the struggle he had with the tempter on this very point. All sins, he said, in which men consciously or unconsciously do evil instead of good, can win God's forgiveness; but to ascribe the work of God to Satan is to confound the whole moral order of the universe (Mk. 3[28f.]).

After giving some specimens of Jesus' teaching, Mark records four examples of the overmastering impression which he made on the minds of his disciples, namely, the stilling of the storm on the Sea of Galilee; the healing of the Gadarene demoniac; the raising of Jairus' daughter; and the healing of the woman with the menstrual hemorrhage. Mark is still continuing to portray Jesus as "Lord," Lord of the storm-fiend, of demons, of disease and death. The episode of the storm was not meant to teach that Jesus could not die. Not long after this, he did die—a far more terrible death than drowning. His beneficent activities have been an undying inspiration to the world as well as to the church; but the picture of Jesus sleeping amid the storm brings no less reassurance to our faith. He saw nothing to be afraid of. In life or in death, in the storm as in the sunshine, he was safe in his Father's keeping.

The detail in which the incident of the Gadarene demoniac is told suggests that it was regarded as a test case: if Jesus could fail anywhere, he would fail here. Many religious workers will be reminded of cases in which they have been confronted with apparently helpless victims of some vile habit that, like a foul monster, held them in its grip. To such the story brings its message that though the name of the devils within the man be legion (a word that indicates the thousands of mail-clad warriors in the most powerful military engine of the time), yet when the voice of Jesus is heard, "Come out of the man, thou unclean spirit," it will be obeyed. The story of Jairus' daughter is one that leaves unanswered many questions we would fain ask: e.g., when Jesus said, "The girl is not dead but sleeping," did he wish to be understood literally or figuratively? In any case, throughout the tale shines his serene confidence that God will call him to no task that is beyond the strength that God will give him.

One of the most beautiful stories in the Gospels is that of the woman who waylaid Jesus as he was going to the home of Jairus. Her illness was one that made her ceremonially unclean (Lev. 15[25]). Worn out with long years of weakness, social ostracism, and shame, with a strange mixture of superstition and faith she touched the tassel of Jesus' robe and knew that she had touched the fountain of life. All who have worked for others will understand Mark's remark that Jesus realized there had been a drain on his healing power (5[30]), for the Master's work of saving others was a costly work. In this case, as in so many others, Jesus told the invalid that her salvation was due to her faith. By faith he meant the assurance that all around us rivers of healing, life-giving energy from God, are flowing, beating against the barriers that we erect round our lives, barriers of blindness and deafness, of want of hope and courage. To have faith is to throw down the barriers, to let the river of God flow over our souls and save us. (Cf. p. 922.)

Sending Forth the Twelve. Very possibly the Jewish authorities had not fully realized the consequences of Jesus' attaching to himself the twelve disciples. The potentialities of the band were revealed when he decided on what we should now call a whirlwind campaign in the villages of Galilee. As this was the beginning, in an organized form, of that missionary activity which, by the time the Gospels were written, had attained such dimensions and was raising difficult problems, the details of Jesus' instruction to the missionaries would be carefully remembered (Mt. 10; Lk. 10).

He evidently felt that a crisis was approaching; the evangelization of Galilee was a matter of extreme urgency. There was no time for salutations, nor would there be opportunity to enter Gentile or even Samaritan territory (Mt. $10^{5f.}$). We would gladly know more of this mission than the Gospels have told us.

It is at this point Mark records the death of the Baptist, whose fate foreshadowed that of Jesus. As the first Elijah had rebuked Ahab and Jezebel, so the second Elijah rebuked Antipas and his illegal wife, Herodias, and paid the penalty with his life (though there is reason to think that fear of political trouble through John's great influence with the people was one of Herod's motives for this judicial murder). When the missionaries returned from their tour Jesus sought a quiet spot to give them rest. But the crowds would not leave them alone, and, in the words of Micaiah to King Ahab, they seemed to Jesus as sheep not having a shepherd (1 Kings 22^{17}). Mark (6^{52}) speaks of the meal that followed Jesus' teaching as he speaks of the parables, i. e., as of a mystery with a hidden meaning that only the enlightened could understand. It is to this story that John attaches the sermon of Jesus on the Bread of Life (6^{26-58}). The very language in which the Gospel writers tell how Jesus "took," "blest," "brake," and "gave" the bread is the language of the sacrament. When men are hungry for the bread of life, problems about material things will somehow solve themselves.

Attitude Toward Ceremonial Cleanness. A serious breach with the Pharisees took place over the question of the ceremonial washing of hands before meals (which has no relation to the sanitary washing of hands, Mk. $7^{1f.}$). It was before the days of knives and forks, and any pollution that a man might even unconsciously contract in the course of a day's work was supposed to be conveyed through the stomach to the person. We know from Galatians and other N.T. references that the early church nearly split over the question whether Jewish Christians could sit at table with Gentile Christians who did not observe the Jewish food laws and other items in the Jewish Law. Jesus discussed various aspects of the matter, with the authorities, with the people, and in private with the disciples. The burden of his teaching was that, in the sight of God, cleanness means a clean life; uncleanness means a deceitful, proud or sensual character. His view of the supreme place of character in the religious life has triumphed so completely that in our day we have to go to Hinduism even to understand the conception of cleanness against which he was arguing. We note that while Jesus deepens and spiritualizes the Jewish Law, he nowhere denounces the Jewish Law as such, not even the ritual element in it; he does not formally abrogate even the sacrifices. It would have greatly simplified the task of the enemies of Jesus, and later of Paul, if it could have been proved that they were trying to undo the work of Moses. Apparently, both decided that this handle should not be given to their critics.

A Journey Beyond Palestine. About this time Jesus seems to have left Palestine for a period. Why he did so, and what exactly was the route he took, we are in large measure left to conjecture. Perhaps there was a real danger that a combination of influential Pharisees with the tetrarch Herod might bring his mission to a premature conclusion; but that does not seem to be the whole explanation. Is it irreverent to wonder whether Jesus himself had been disappointed? A visit to the synagogue in his home town of Nazareth had begun with rapt attention on the part of the people (Lk. $4^{16f.}$) as he read the beautiful opening verses of Isa. 61; but when the people remembered that he was one of themselves, and noted that he implied that Isaiah's prophecy was fulfilled in himself, there was a revulsion of feeling which ended in his narrowly escaping from an attempt to fling him over a precipice. From Mt. 11^{20-24} and Lk. 10^{13-15} we learn that he had been rejected in the Galilæan cities of Chorazin and Bethsaida, and even in Capernaum, which had been the scene of much of his work. It was not only the religious leaders but the whole generation that was described as turning a deaf ear to the message both of the Baptist and of Jesus (Mt. 11^{16-19}). May it be that the lightning mission was expected to presage some startling interposition of God? When, instead of some manifest evidence of the coming of the Kingdom, opposition deepened among all classes, Jesus sought an opportunity such as he could never get in Palestine for meditation, for waiting on the will of God. At all events it was not to carry on his work that he toured the districts north of Galilee and east of the Jordan (Mk. 7^{24}). This too would help to explain his apparently harsh answer to the woman of Syrian Phœnicia (Mk. 7^{27}). It may be that she was voicing what was to Jesus at the time a very real temptation: to leave the work he believed God had given him to do among the Jews and start a mission among the Gentiles. There are indications that they would have been far more responsive than his own people.

Change in Teaching Following Peter's Confession. With a visit to Cæsarea Philippi, far to the north, near Mount Hermon and the sources of the Jordan, we reach a new and all-important chapter in the history of Jesus. He began to speak about himself. This he does regularly in the fourth Gospel, but only to a minor extent in the earlier chapters of the first three. At this point also there enter the gospel story certain elements that became distinctive features of the early apostolic preaching. It is well known that the theology of the church as expressed in the creeds was reached only gradually, by stages that continued through centuries. It has been customary to think of Jesus as having from the beginning of his ministry that estimate of himself and his mission which the church afterward came to have. Students of our day have found it difficult to accept this mode of thought. It does not seem to be in accordance with God's way of working. Many Christians to-day see no irreverence in agreeing with the author of the Epistle to the Hebrews that even Jesus had to pass through a process of spiritual education (Heb. 5[8]). Moreover, the subsequent story, as recorded in the Gospels, is at least compatible with the theory that Jesus only gradually, sometimes by painful disillusionment, entered into the full understanding of his own relation to God, and of the task God had entrusted to him.

In the neighborhood of Cæsarea Jesus asked his disciples what were the popular theories about himself, and then what was their own theory. It was Peter who uttered the historic words, "Thou art the Christ" (Mk. 8[29]). The word "Christ," or "Anointed One," was associated in the mind of Jews with the king, with the high priest, and with a figure that appeared in some of the Jewish pictures of the coming Kingdom, one of the lineage of David who would restore the splendors of David's reign. But for his conception of God's Anointed, Jesus pointed to Isa. 61, to the One who was anointed to proclaim good tidings, to deliver, and to heal. Moreover, there are indications that from a very early period of the ministry he had premonitions of the fate that awaited him, felt that one day the bridegroom would be taken from the disciples (Mk. 2[20]). He knew, too, the prophecies of the Suffering Servant in the later chapters of Isaiah, and saw their significance as the Jews did not. Thus in the very moment of what seemed his triumph, Jesus began the new teaching: "I am the Christ indeed, anointed not to glory but to suffering; no second and greater David but a man of sorrows and acquainted with grief." (See *Excursus* on the identification of the Suffering Servant, following Isa. 53, p. 664.) From this point we hear the watchwords that must have meant so much to the Roman readers of Mark's Gospel in the dark days of Nero's persecution: "bearing the cross" and "following Jesus" to martyrdom, "losing one's life to save it," "for my sake and the gospel's," "the coming of the Son of man." "Matthew" alone records that when Simon made his memorable declaration, Jesus, who had already given him the nickname "Petros," "the Rock-man," by a play on the word declared that the foundation stone had now been laid on which he would build the edifice of the great and sacred company of his followers (Mt. 16[18]).

The Transfiguration. With his passion now full in view, the very appearance of Jesus was transfigured. For a little while the veil was lifted (Mk. 9[2f.]) and the three favored disciples —Peter, James, and John—saw him in the glory of his utter consecration to the will of God, that will that was leading him to Calvary. No hint is given us of the way to the Mount of Transfiguration, any more than to the Mount of Ambition (Mt. 4[8]). In several points the story recalls the transfiguration of Moses on the mount (Ex. 34[29-35]).

The disciples were enjoined to keep the transfiguration a secret (Mk. 9[9]), as they had been previously instructed to tell no man that he was the Christ (8[30]). This is in line with his frequent injunction of secrecy about his healing miracles, and his silencing of the demoniacs when they would proclaim him as Messiah. Moreover, Jesus is frequently represented as giving private instruction to his disciples about his coming death and resurrection, instruction which the disciples could not understand. This element in the story has caused much difficulty. Sometimes, as in the case of Jairus' daughter, it is not easy to see how the instructions about secrecy could be carried out. Sometimes, as in the case of the deaf stammerer (Mk. 7[36]), they were flagrantly disobeyed. Moreover, unless Mark means that it was some supernatural hardening of the heart that visited the apostles, it is not clear how they could so completely misunderstand the thrice-repeated predictions of the death and resurrection in Mk. 8[31] 9[31] and 10[33f.] Jesus was clearly anxious to avoid being regarded as a mere wonder-worker. Sometimes a superficial popularity seriously interfered with his true work (Mk. 1[45]). But there is another element in the explanation. In later times the disciples, looking back from the vantage ground of the resurrection and the history of the early church, could see much in the story to which at the time they had been blind. Some think that this fact has in some degree influenced the form in which the Gospel records have been preserved.

The story of the epileptic (Mk. $9^{14f.}$) is remarkable for the expression of Jesus' boundless faith (v. 23), and for the record of a failure of the disciples in an attempted healing (v. 18). Subsequently Jesus ascribed this failure to insufficient faith (Mt. 17^{20}), or, as Mark puts it, to want of prayer and fasting (9^{29}). Doubtless these explanations became traditional for any failures they experienced in their work of exorcism when their Master was taken from them.

Cost of Discipleship. Luke ($9^{57f.}$) gives three illustrations of the way in which Jesus selected and dealt with the men to whom his message was making its appeal. To offer them attractions or smooth the way for them was the last of his thoughts. The effervescing enthusiast was told to count the cost of following a nameless wanderer, as Jesus had now become. The man who wanted to wait till his father died was reminded that the king's business requires haste: there were enough men with dead souls to bury his father when he died. A third made the excuse that before joining the band he wished to pay a farewell visit to his people at home. Jesus remembered how his own home folks had tried to divert him from his God-given work (Mk. $3^{20f.}$). There had been sad parting scenes too during the recent farewell visit to Capernaum (Mk. 9^{33-37}), for not long after this we find Peter reminding Jesus of all they have given up to be with him (Mk. 10^{28}). So Jesus told the candidate that the plowman who would plow a straight furrow must plow with his eye on the mark.

Journey Toward Jerusalem, and Its Incidents. The direct road from Galilee to Jerusalem was through Samaria; but Jesus was turned aside from his intended route by Samaritan discourtesy (Lk. 9^{51-56}). No longer anxious to be hidden, he traveled to Jerusalem, partly through Peræa (east of the Jordan), partly through Judæa. Perhaps about this time, a reply of Jesus to a question about divorce did much to increase the hostility of the civil and religious authorities. It asserted that Moses' permission of divorce was only a temporary concession to the weakness of human nature; which must have seemed to the scribes a dangerous and far-reaching principle. Further, Jesus implicitly went beyond the Baptist in his condemnation of Herod, for his reply declared immoral Herod's divorce from his first wife that had given a semblance of legality to his marriage with Herodias, while it gave the ugly name of adulteress (Mk. 10^{12}) to Herodias who had, under Roman law (she had been living in Rome), divorced her first husband to marry Herod.

With that dramatic appropriateness that sometimes characterizes the arrangement of the Gospel material, Mark introduces at this point the beautiful story of the parents who brought their children that the great Rabbi might lay his hands upon them in blessing (10^{13-16}). Against the background of the unsophisticated children, Mark draws the picture of the rich man who came running to ask Jesus how to get eternal life. Jesus was strongly attracted to the earnest, upright man and would fain have added him to the disciple circle; but with his usual insight he imposed on him the condition of parting with his wealth. In a flash, for the first time the man saw himself and went crestfallen away.

As Jesus went on his way to Jerusalem—the Jerusalem that killed her prophets and stoned the messengers God sent her—he no longer walked with his disciples as of old in friendly intercourse. He walked in front of them, alone, the physical distance between them faintly shadowing forth the gulf that separated his thought from theirs (Mk. 10^{32}). Following after, the disciples were amazed and frightened at the changed mood of their Master. When he did speak to them, it was of the fate that awaited him in Jerusalem. So little did they picture it as he pictured it that, even on this last journey, James and John begged for the posts of honor on each side of the Messianic throne upon which already in imagination they saw Jesus seated. Could they have seen his throne upon Calvary, would they still have prayed this prayer?

In Jericho, Jesus gave further offense to the religious leaders by accepting hospitality from the rich little Jewish district superintendent of taxation, Zacchæus. Like the rich ruler he had come to Jesus running; but whereas the ruler could not, when asked, divest himself of his possessions, Zacchæus, unasked, disgorged his ill-gotten gains (Lk. 19^{8}). As they left Jericho a blind beggar, Bartimæus, one of the few among those that Jesus helped whose names were remembered in after years, a man of that determined character that always appealed to Jesus, addressed him by the Messianic title, "Son of David"; the only occasion in Mark or Luke on which he is addressed by this title.

The Triumphal Entry. Jesus had apparently resolved that at the approaching feast he would declare himself as Messiah. Following a suggestion in Zech. 9^{9} Jesus approached Jerusalem riding upon an ass, which by previous arrangement he had borrowed from the village of Bethphage on the outskirts of Jerusalem. He followed the road along the Mount of Olives, from which the Messiah was expected to appear. In this way he half revealed and half concealed his claim to be the Messiah, and at the same time made clear that his kingdom was not of this world.

Events of Passion Week. The triumphal entry took place on the Monday of the last week of Jesus' life. Following the custom of every pious Jew, he went at once to the Temple, but that night, and each succeeding night, was spent in Bethany or in its neighborhood. At Festival time, accommodation in the city would be at famine prices. In any case, in the darkness of the night, one who had offended so many powerful interests as Jesus had was safer outside the city. When the time came, he was ready to be offered up as a living sacrifice, but his death must be one that had significance for God and man.

(1) *The Barren Fig Tree.* On the return journey from Bethany on Tuesday morning took place the puzzling incident known as the cursing of the fig-tree. Those whose views on inspiration permit them to think so, believe that at this point the tradition is inexact. The beautiful teaching of Jesus on utter trust in God (Mk. 11[23f.]) hardly seems appropriate on such a text, and it is known that Jesus repeatedly took a tree, especially a fig-tree, as an illustration (Lk. 13[6-9] 17[6] Mk. 13[28]).

(2) *Cleansing the Temple.* Also on the Tuesday took place the cleansing of the Temple. (Jn. 2[13-17] puts this incident very early in the ministry, and some think it is more in keeping with the days of the first enthusiasm when Jesus still saw hope for Temple, priests, and people.) The priests had allowed the traffic in sacrificial animals and in the coins required to pay the Temple dues to invade the precincts of the Temple itself. Amid the varied sounds and smells of a cattle and bird market, and the chaffering and cheating of the dealers, prayer was impossible for Gentiles in the only court they were permitted to enter. When Jesus, by the sheer force of his personality, ended the traffic for the time, the chief priests, for the most part Sadducees, of whom hitherto we have heard little, became as zealous for the death of Jesus as the Pharisees. Not only had he struck a blow at their lucrative monopoly and humbled them in the eyes of the laity; he had endangered the public peace and so rendered insecure the authority which they held under Rome. (Cf. p. 1069.)

(3) *"God or Cæsar."* Wednesday finds Jesus again in the Temple. The chief priests, scribes, and elders (i.e., representatives of all three official classes) formally demanded from him a statement of the nature of the authority which justified him in his proceedings, especially for his temerity in usurping the functions of the Temple police. It was a demand the answer to which might have delivered him into their hands. The question is one of the most vital that men are asking to-day. In effect Jesus' answer was that his only authority lay in this, that, as in the case of the Baptist, men of clean sympathies and responsive heart recognized in him the bearer of a divine commission. Then a new trap was laid for him. Ever since Judæa was taken over by the Romans in 6 A.D. a poll tax had been imposed on adult Jews. The tax was intensely unpopular, partly as evidence of Jewish servitude to Rome, partly because the dinar (the tax coin) bore the head of Cæsar and so infringed the second commandment. Jesus' reply to the deputation that came for his opinion: "Cæsar's to Cæsar; God's to God," forms the basis of all Christian thought on the relation of church and state; but its immediate effect was to strengthen the position of his enemies. By hinting at the insignificance of the whole political question in comparison with the eternal issues that were hanging in the balance, he lost his last chance of winning the support of the loyalists. At the same time, as he was to find two days later, and as he doubtless knew at the time, his answer did nothing to win for him the protection of the Roman government.

(4) *The Anointing at Bethany.* As they were leaving the Temple his disciples called his attention to the magnificence of the Temple buildings, of which every Jew was justly proud. Jesus, however, knew that more of worldly policy and worldly wisdom than of piety had gone to the building of Herod's Temple, and saw that the whole system for which it stood was tottering to its fall (Mk. 13[1f.]). Two days before the Passover, i.e., apparently, still on the Wednesday of Holy Week, the chief priests and scribes decided that the time to strike had almost come. A gleam of light is shed on the dark story by the insertion, between the account of the plot of the officials and of the treachery of Judas, of the ever-fragrant tale of the anointing of Jesus by a woman in the house of Simon the leper in Bethany, which was perhaps Jesus' home during the last nights of his life (Mk. 14[3-7]). It was in an exquisite form the greeting of host to honored guest; it was balm for the spirit that she saw daily bruised by the buffetings of an inappreciative world. She was one of those who saw in Jesus the Lord's Anointed, and felt it shameful that the end should come with no visible anointing. But Jesus recognized in it an even deeper significance. There loomed before his mind the death that might deprive his body of that respectful attention of friends that helps to rob death of its terror; and, when the by-

standers grumbled at the woman's extravagance and forwardness, he told them she had prepared his body beforehand for its entombment. (Cf. p. 1039b.)

(5) *Judas and His Bargain.* At this time an unexpected stroke of luck befell the enemies of Jesus. Surrounded as he was by friendly crowds during the day and leaving the city each night, they did not see how to arrest him till one of the twelve came to them with a proposition—for a certain sum of money to lead them to his nightly resting place and point him out. The motive of Judas has been the subject of endless surmise. Apparently, he was bitterly disappointed in Jesus. He would have followed a "Son of David" Christ, but had no interest in a Messiah whose constant theme was suffering and death, who resisted every suggestion that he should put himself at the head of the loyalists, and who even advocated payment of the poll tax.

(6) *The Last Supper.* We have now reached Thursday. The Passover Feast had to be eaten within the city, and Jesus had looked forward with keen anticipation to the celebration with his disciples of this particular feast (Lk. 22[15]). The visit had to be made in secret. Jesus had previously arranged with a friend to lend a room for the occasion. When night fell they sat down to supper. As with so much else in the life of Jesus, the significance of that meal was only gradually revealed. Doubtless with Jesus present, every meal of the disciple band had become in some degree the festival of a brotherhood, just as with the early Christians every meal was a sacrament (Acts 2[42, 46]). Ever since the Master had set his face toward Jerusalem the disciples knew that he was marching on to some strange destiny. It is not quite clear whether the meal was the regular Passover Feast or not (cf. p. 1017a); in any case, the Passover was in the minds of all, with its remembrance of sacrifice and redemption from bondage. Jesus knew that the hour of his death had all but come: he knew also that his death would be the gateway of life, not only for himself but for his followers. He had found inspiration in Isaiah's prophecy of the Suffering Servant on whom Jehovah had laid the iniquity of us all. He had studied Jeremiah's prophecy of the New Covenant (31[31]) and was familiar, as was every Jew, with the idea of a covenant inaugurated with blood (Ex. 24[8]). Moreover, he felt assured that the parting was but for a season. In a little while he and his followers would share in the glad feast prepared by God for those who inherited the Kingdom (Lk. 22[16]). With some such thoughts in his mind Jesus blessed and gave to his disciples the bread that meant his body; offered thanks and gave to them the cup that meant his blood of the New Covenant.

(7) *Gethsemane and the Arrest.* Since Bethany was outside Jerusalem limits, and it was contrary to the Law (Deut. 16[1-7]) to leave Jerusalem on the feast night, he went only to the Mount of Olives, stopping at an olive orchard called Gethsemane, one of his favorite resorts. There he endured that experience which Luke calls his Agony, which we can share only as we share his purity of soul and his divine love for the humanity he was trying to save. In trying to find its theological significance we sometimes forget the immediate circumstances. With a part of the mob he had a certain popularity, but his native city had turned against him; Capernaum had rejected him; he had been hounded out of his own Galilee. The priests and leaders of his people were but waiting their chance to slay him; he could not fully trust even the twelve; the three disciples of the inner circle could not remain awake in his hour of peril and agony of soul; one of the twelve even then was bringing his enemies to arrest him. Nor were these men monsters of iniquity; this was life; it is thus that God's children deal with God's messengers. Can we wonder that his soul was exceedingly sorrowful unto death?

Judas, who had slipped away from the company at some time during the evening, now arrived with a detachment of the Temple police and gave the Judas kiss, the prearranged signal for the arrest. None of the twelve were present at the trial of Jesus, and the details are not clear. It looks as if the treachery of Judas caused the authorities to change their plans. They had not meant to proceed with the arrest till after the days of unleavened bread were over. Now they saw their chance of getting rid of him before the Passover; but there were only about eighteen hours left. Utmost haste was necessary and they were not ready either with their formal charges or their witnesses, and it almost looked for a time as if they were going to be beaten. Apparently about this time the right of imposing the death penalty, at least in political cases, was taken from the Jews, but they had the right and the duty of conducting a preliminary investigation. In this, of course, the lead was taken by the Sadducaic priests, who had the political power. Apparently, after an unofficial examination during the night by Annas, an ex-high priest who still had great influence, the official investigation before Caiaphas, the actual high priest, began at daybreak. The only charge that could be seriously supported was one to the effect that Jesus had said he would destroy the Temple made by hands and in three days erect another not made by hands. Throughout the investigation Jesus held his peace until he was formally asked by the high priest, "Are you the Christ?" He replied, "I am." It was the moment up to which his whole life had been leading. It gave the priests the opportunity for which they were waiting; it was only necessary to translate the word "Christ" into the word "king," and they had a plausible charge on which to arraign Jesus before the Roman proconsul.

(8) *The Trial and Crucifixion.* Accordingly, he was now bound and handed over for official trial to Pilate. Luke, who alone gives the indictment, mentions three charges (23[2]): (1) Jesus is an agitator; (2) he has urged Jews not to pay the imperial taxes; (3) he claims to be Christ, i.e., a king. The first two charges were only meant to lead up to the third, which contained the real accusation. Pilate realized that there was more behind the case than appeared on the surface. Learning that Jesus belonged to the province of Galilee, he remitted the prisoner for examination and report to Herod. The trial and death of Jesus provided the humorists of the day with an abundant supply of material. Herod caught the prevailing spirit and gave his report by sending Jesus back to Pilate, dressed in mock royal array. This decision from a co-religionist of Jesus and the official head of his province greatly strengthened the hands of Pilate. For a moment Pilate saw a way out when a crowd of citizens, who had learned to expect the release of a popular prisoner at each Passover, came surging up demanding that Jesus be set free. It soon transpired, however, that the Jesus they wanted was Jesus Barabbas, who had achieved great popularity among the Jews by taking part in a serious anti-Roman riot. Therefore, shouted the crowd, "For Jesus Barabbas, liberty! for Jesus Christ, the cross!" Pilate doubtless more than suspected that there was involved in the case some religious question that did not interest him, one on which the Jewish priests might be supposed to know their business. Early in his term of office he had learned to dread the inflexible determination of the Jews where their religion was concerned. Little dreaming that he was earning for himself a shameful immortality, he pronounced the death sentence.

It is difficult for a man with any spark of humanity even to read a detailed account of what crucifixion meant. Suffice it to say that the unhappy victims of the torture were spared no circumstance of pain or shame, and that a more awful death it would hardly be possible to imagine. We are not surprised to read that the crucified used to curse and spit at their executioners. All this we must remember when we judge Peter for denying Jesus and the others for deserting him. As at the trial, so on the cross, Jesus for the most part preserved an unbroken silence. The cry from the cross that has most deeply impressed the church is given in all the first three Gospels: "My God, my God, why hast thou forsaken me?" They are the opening words of Psa. 22, that psalm which begins as a despairing cry of dereliction and ends as a song of triumph. At three o'clock, unexpectedly, the end came.

Risen and Alive for Evermore. Thus ended Jesus of Nazareth; thus began Jesus, the Christ, the Lord of the Christian Church. To the resurrection of Jesus from the dead, the whole N.T., the Christian Church, the Christian Sabbath, and all Christian experience bear ample testimony. That the new faith of the disciples began with appearances of the risen Christ is certain; but when we begin to ask of what nature were these appearances, and when and where they took place, we raise questions to which the N.T. does not, in the judgment of many, return an unambiguous answer. Three questions in particular have been discussed. Did women see Jesus as well as men? Was it the physical body of Jesus that rose, leaving the grave empty? Did the appearances take place in Galilee or in Jerusalem, or in both?

In our earliest account of the resurrection (1 Cor. 15[3-8]) Paul says nothing of appearances to women, and gives no data of time or place. He seems to imply that the appearance of Jesus to himself was of the same nature as the others, and there is nothing to suggest that what appeared to Paul on the way to Damascus was the body of Jesus risen from the grave. On the other hand, Peter at Pentecost does seem to imply that the body of Jesus did not undergo corruption (Acts 2[31]). (We note he is practically quoting from Psa. 16[10].) Unfortunately, our earliest Gospel, Mark, fails us here, for it is generally agreed that, for some unexplained reason, the Gospel as Mark wrote it ends at 16[8]. It seems clear that Mark was going on to record an appearance in Galilee to the disciples, especially Peter. In Mark the women disciples did not themselves see Jesus. In Matthew, but not in Luke, the women did see the risen Jesus. Both "Matthew" and Mark stress the fact that Galilee was the scene of the resurrection activity of Jesus. Luke insists that all the resurrection appearances took place in Jerusalem or in its neighborhood. John has his own set of resurrection stories, partly Jerusalem, partly Galilæan, the most beautiful being that of the appearance to Mary of Magdala.

There are certain general considerations to be borne in mind. There is nothing astonishing in the difficulties we experience in trying to piece together a connected account of the resurrection history, when we remember the extraordinary nature of the occurrences, the deep emotions that were being stirred, and the absence of a distant future for the world from the contemplation of any Christian. If the evidence for appearances to women is less strong than might be desired, the reason may well be that the gospel tradition was shaped by men. As for the scene of the appearances, we need not suppose that all the disciples kept together in the days following the death of Jesus. Jesus had many followers in Galilee, who may well have had the same experience as those that remained in Jerusalem. The fact remains that it was not in Galilee but in Jerusalem that the church first came into being, and Galilee speedily all but drops out of the story.

The real difficulty is about the nature of the resurrection body. The N.T. accounts are not all written from the same point of view. In Paul's conversion vision, we hear only of a light and a voice. Luke's Gospel insists that the body of the risen Christ could be felt, had flesh and bones, and could enjoy a meal (24[39-43]). In the last chapter of John the Christ was evidently able to prepare a meal and to hold a prolonged conversation with the disciples. The attitude of Christians to these stories varies, and perhaps will always vary, according to their view of Scripture and of the meaning of immortality. Those who accept the verbal inerrancy of Scripture will resort to various contrivances for harmonizing the different accounts. Others, who believe that the later experiences of the church were to some extent read back into the gospel history, will believe that this influence has been at work on some of the later resurrection stories, and that the emphasis in Luke on the physical nature of the resurrection body is dictated by a desire to confute the "docetists," who denied the human reality of Jesus even during his ministry. All the Gospels speak of the empty grave, and evidently by the time the Gospels were written it was considered an important point in Christian tradition to maintain this. (See art., *N.T. Miracles*, p. 930.)

To many Christians it seems that an exaggerated importance has been attached to the question whether and in what sense the earthly body of Jesus rose from the grave. In any case the appearances continued for a few weeks at most. To all Christians ever since, the Lord Jesus has been not a body but a spirit. Even the risen body described in the Gospels—one that could pass through closed doors and appear or disappear at will—is so unlike any body we know that some consider it a misuse of language to call it the same body that the disciples had known. In 1 Cor. 15 (see notes there), in highly poetical language, Paul discusses the resurrection body. He says it is the same as the earthly body only in the sense in which the plant is the same as the seed. Yet by body he did not mean flesh; he knew that flesh and blood could not inherit the kingdom of God. He seems to have meant much what we mean to-day by personality. To Paul apparently the important question was not what happened to Jesus' flesh but what happened to Jesus. Jesus, he maintains, lives on, and the Christian lives on, not as a disembodied spirit, but as a spirit that can express itself, that can know and be known, that can enjoy fellowship with other spirits.

However this may be, it is the unanimous testimony of the N.T., a testimony the validity of which has been amply demonstrated in the subsequent history of the church, that after the death of Jesus his followers had with him a communion more continuous and more vital than they had had in the days of his flesh, that their personality, in all its powers and in all its aspects, was quickened to an unexampled vitality. Of this they had no explanation, they sought no explanation, save that the risen Christ had taken possession of them, and to know that was sufficient,.

Literature: Stalker, *The Life of Christ;* Sanday, *Outlines of the Life of Christ;* David Smith, *The Days of His Flesh;* J. Paterson Smyth, *A People's Life of Christ;* Headlam, *The Life and Teaching of Jesus the Christ;* Moffatt, *Everyman's Life of Jesus* (the narrative in the words of the Gospels); Bosworth, *The Life and Teaching of Jesus According to the First Three Gospels;* Rush Rhees, *The Life of Jesus of Nazareth;* J. A. Robertson, *The Spiritual Pilgrimage of Jesus;* T. H. Robinson, *St. Mark's Life of Jesus;* A. W. Robinson, *The Christ of the Gospels;* Rall, *The Life of Jesus.* Studies which are not strictly "Lives" are Seeley, *Ecce Homo* (an old book, but by no means antiquated), and Glover, *The Jesus of History.* Of the older "Lives," those by Farrar, Edersheim, B. Weiss, and Geikie are still of great value. Such popular "Lives" as those by Papini and Middleton Murry need to be read with discrimination, and the same is true of the much more scholarly studies by Klausner, *Jesus of Nazareth* (written by an able Jewish scholar), Warschauer, *The Historical Life of Christ,* and S. J. Case, *Jesus, a New Biography.*

THE TEACHING OF JESUS

By Professor HARRIS FRANKLIN RALL

The Sources. Our earliest information as to the life and teaching of Jesus comes from the letters of Paul, some of which were written less than a generation after the death of Jesus. But valuable as these references are, as, e.g., against those who would dispute the historicity of Jesus, they contribute little to our knowledge of Jesus' teaching. Paul was more interested in what Jesus did for men in his death than in what he said to them during his life. He is an interpreter of Jesus rather than a reporter. The same, on the whole, must be said of the fourth Gospel. The writer goes back constantly to the deeds of Jesus and his words, but the report and the interpretation are so merged one into the other that we cannot draw the line of division with any assurance. In common, therefore, with the custom of the great majority of scholars, this article will use the first three Gospels as its primary source. (See art., *The Structure of the Synoptic Gospels*, pp. 867–73.)

The first three Gospels, called the synoptic Gospels, may be accepted as substantially reliable sources for the teaching of Jesus. In their present form they may come from a period anywhere between 50 and 90 A.D. They go back, however, to sources earlier than themselves. Mark, perhaps in an earlier form, serves as a source for Matthew and Luke, and scholars are quite generally agreed that there is at least one other source common to the last two, known as Q, a collection of the teachings of Jesus just as Mark is primarily an account of Jesus' deeds. Both these sources take us back to the time when the generation that knew Jesus in the flesh was still living. But if there were no other reason, the impression which these teachings make would persuade us of their authenticity. Their beauty, their freshness, their insight and power, above all, their inner unity, indicate their source in one great teacher.

Yet this by no means justifies us in assuming that every word here reported is given as spoken by Jesus. The writers of these Gospels are not mere reporters; they are interpreters and teachers who are trying to present Jesus so that men may believe. They share a common faith while at the same time differing in interest and individual point of view. Back of them lies the early Christian community which did not always understand its Lord. We are not surprised, then, at occasional differences in the accounts given. These materials were used orally in preaching and teaching long before our Gospels were written, and the most honest effort to hand on Jesus' teaching would not prevent changes through the desire to make plain or interpret. Yet all this concerns the lesser matters after all. It warns us not to rest too much on a single word or passage, but it leaves unchanged the conviction that we have here the essential teaching of Jesus.

Jesus as Teacher. Jesus began his work as a teacher. That does not mean that he was a philosopher or a theologian with a system to give to people, or that his interest was primarily in ideas. His interest was in men and in life. His great task was to bring in the new day, the kingdom of God. But to that end he had to teach; he had to bring to men a new vision of God and God's purpose and man's life. The story of the temptation is significant here. Jesus knows himself as the Messiah, but he will not begin with claims to power, with wonderful deeds that will bring the people to his feet and prove his office, or with alliances with the great that will bring to him the kingdoms of the world (Mt. 4$^{1-11}$). He will follow the clear way of duty and trust the issue to God; and the clear way is to teach men and serve men. So he goes about in all Galilee, "teaching in their synagogues, and preaching the gospel of the kingdom."

His teaching must be studied in the light of its purpose and consequent method. Jesus was not a lecturer in a classroom giving a course on the doctrines of religion. He believed that a new day was at hand, that a new world was waiting for men, and that men were to live a new life with God and their fellows. It was his task to proclaim this good news and to summon men to prepare for it. His call was, "Repent, believe the good news." And this purpose explains his method. In the end he talked with men about all the great questions of life, about God and his coming kingdom, about man and sin, about being lost and being saved, about how to live here, and about things to come. But it was all occasional as special questions arose; and it was always incidental to his great purpose to summon men to get ready for the new day and to begin the new life. And that was why he left to one side questions about state and industry and society in general about which we are so greatly concerned to-day.

Where did Jesus get his message, and what was his relation to the sacred writings of his people (cf. p. 853b) and to the religious leaders? The O.T. was the Bible of Jesus and the faith of his people was his faith. So he had been nurtured as a boy. So he began as a man, proclaiming the God of Abraham and of Isaac and of Jacob. The words of this Bible are with him in his temptation as they are upon the cross. In the hour when he turned at last from Galilee to Jerusalem and to the certainty of suffering and death, he seems to have been pondering the great passage of Isa. 53 with its picture of one who suffers and bears the sins of men. And yet this is not the source of his teaching. Certainly, his source was not that of the Jewish teachers with their constant appeal to tradition, to the authority of the great rabbis. Men listened and said, "What is the wisdom that is given unto this man?" He teaches with authority and not as the scribes, they declared. The teaching of Jesus did not rest upon precedent or even appeal to the Scriptures; he spoke from within and with the note of inner and immediate certainty. And the source was his own experience of God and his life with God. Some scholars have questioned whether Jesus ever spoke the great words of Mt. 11^{25-30}. To the writer these words light up Jesus' method as a teacher and make plain the whole spirit of his life. He had a life that was one with God; in this life God had given him the knowledge of himself, and because he had that he could say in all humility and dependence upon his Father, "Come unto me; learn of me; I will give you rest." It was not a supernatural endowment of omniscience; it was a knowledge that came out of his life with the Father. But it gave him that independence, that insight, that quiet and sure confidence, that sense of authority, which he showed at all times.

Striking is this independence and insight of Jesus in relation to the O.T. He selects for his use with unerring insight the psalms, the prophets, Deuteronomy. He passes by Messianic passages like Psa. 2 and Isa. 11^{4}, and turns to Isa. 53. The O.T. knows nothing of a distinction between ceremonial and moral law, and the Jew thought of both as divine and eternal. Jesus strikes at the root of this whole ceremonial emphasis when he declares that only the spirit counts and mere things can never make a man unclean (Mk. 7^{14-23}; cf. Lev. 11–15). Again and again he revises or rejects (Mt. $5^{21, 22, 27, 28, 33, 39}$ Mk. 10^{2-12}). If he showed this independence over against the Scriptures which he so revered, we need not wonder that this humble teacher from Nazareth should maintain his position when it brought conflict with the acknowledged and authoritative religious leaders and teachers of his people, the scribes whose life was given to the study and interpretation of the Law. Here, again, we are led back to the inner life of Jesus as the source of this certainty.

The study of Jesus' teaching because of all this can never be separated from the study of Jesus' own spirit and life. Never was there one in whom so truly life and teaching were one. His teaching is fragmentary and yet there is a wonderful unity because of this inner source. We must not, therefore, study it as a matter of separate ideas on many subjects, but constantly and only in relation to what he was and what he was seeking to do. Our supreme task, if we are to understand the teaching, is to understand Jesus himself.

Jesus' Conception of Himself and His Work. We need, then, to begin with the question, How did Jesus think of himself and his work? The two significant words here are "Sonship" and "Messiahship," and "Sonship" comes first. Striking is the reticence of Jesus in his speech concerning himself, and here the first three Gospels are in sharp contrast with the fourth. Yet the deep sense of Sonship, and of a unique Sonship, is plain. We see it in the glimpse of boyhood life (Lk. 2^{41-52}). It appears in the words that sounded in his soul at the time of baptism, "Thou art my beloved Son." His whole prayer in the garden, with its loyalty and trust, is summed up in the words, "Abba, Father," and he cries out "Father" from the agony of the cross. The supreme expression of this relation is found in Mt. 11^{25-30}. Its lyric form matches the exaltation of spirit that is here manifest. Sonship here is not a definition in terms of substance and essence, as it became later in the creeds; it is a living relation, personal and ethical, in utter unity of spirit. He and the Father are one. He looks up in reverence to him, the Lord of heaven and earth. Yet humbly he rejoices in this union with his Father, and in what God has given to him. And that is why he can summon men to learn of him. Clearly, Jesus shows here that his sense of mission and of authority rests back upon this inner experience, this oneness of his life as a Son with the Father.

Out of this comes Jesus' sense of his calling. The early church expressed Jesus' meaning for its faith in various terms such as "Messiah" (Christ), "Saviour," and "Lord." These words are almost wholly absent from the speech of Jesus, but their substance is not wanting. Jesus thought of his work inevitably in terms of the great hope of his people which he shared. So soon as a man believes in a good God and sees the evil in the world, he will either lose his faith or gain a great hope. The Jews had that hope, the hope of deliverance from evil, of the coming of a new age. That hope Jesus shared and called it the kingdom of God. He saw the meaning of his life in the light of that hope: the new age was at hand and God had chosen him to bring it in. That meant that he was the Messiah.

In this work there were for Jesus a proximate task and an ultimate one. The Kingdom was near at hand, but it was not here. It would come in God's time and by his deed. How literally Jesus meant the picture we do not know, but to something like this he refers when he speaks of the Son of man sitting at the right hand of power and coming with the clouds of heaven (Mk. 14^{62}). That was the ultimate task of establishing the Kingdom, but the what and the how of that belonged to the future and to God; there was a definite work that lay for him near at hand. His own words indicate how he thought of this immediate task, his life still more. Men must get ready for this coming rule of God, for its privileges and its judgment. It was his to call them to repentance, to summon them to that life of sonship with God and good will toward fellow men which was to be the life of the Kingdom. So he came to preach and save. He calls sinners to repentance, and seeks out the lost (Mt. 9^{13} Lk. 19^{10}). He is here to preach the good news (Mk. 1^{38} Lk. 4^{18}). But he realized too that he was here to love and serve and live the life of a son for his brothers and before them (Mt. 11$^{28, 29}$ Mk. 10^{45} Lk. 22^{27} Jn. 13^{15}).

But there was something more than teaching and serving. He was to die for men. A great Jewish scholar has said of Jesus: "Service . . . is the special feature of his own conception of the Messiahship, and still more of that conception of it which has moved the world. His idea of Kingship was that of Plato; he only is the true King whose life is given for his people" (C. G. Montefiore, *The Teaching of Jesus*, p. 136). We cannot tell just when, but it became clear to Jesus that the service of men and loyalty to his Father were leading him to an inevitable end, death at the hand of his foes. The significant fact here is not that he saw that death as inevitable, but that he saw it as part of his work, indeed, as the crown of it. We find the references to his coming death in Mk. 8^{31} 9$^{12, 31}$ 10$^{33, 34}$, and parallel passages. But of special significance are Mk. 10^{45} and 14^{24}. He is "to give his life a ransom for many," and of the cup of wine at the Last Supper he says, "This is my blood of the covenant, which is poured out for many." The second passage refers clearly to the great word of Jer. 31^{31}. Through his death God is bringing in the new age, is establishing a new covenant with men that shall supersede the old. We have no warrant for reading later theories of the atonement into the first word, but this is plain: Jesus declares that he is dying for men, dying to ransom them, i.e., to redeem them from the power of evil. The death, then, that he faces is not an unmeaning tragedy; it is part of God's purpose and of his task as Messiah in establishing the Kingdom. Isa. 53, with its moving picture of the Servant of Jehovah, seems to be echoed in the speech and thought of most of these passages. The word from the cross given in Mk. 15^{34} suggests that Psa. 22 was also in Jesus' mind. The Gethsemane prayer shows with what a struggle Jesus held to this conviction; but in this conviction he died. (Cf. p. 664.)

The Idea of God. Central in Jesus' thought about himself and his work and the coming Kingdom, as about all else, was his idea of God. Just as his experience of God shaped his whole life, so his thought of God shaped his whole teaching. What he brought was at no point wholly new. Jewish thought as well as the O.T. knew of God's mercy as well as his justice, and spoke of God as Father. What was new with Jesus was his emphasis, and in religion that is the vital matter. New also was the depth and vividness of his experience of God.

God is infinite mercy and good will; that is Jesus' central word. He is no mere distant ruler or creator of long ago, or giver of laws and stern judge. He is the Father whose very nature it is to be good and merciful. His loving care reaches each swiftly fading flower, each unnoticed bird, much more each child of man (Mt. 6$^{25-30}$). Parents care for their children, God vastly more (Mt. 7$^{9-11}$). He is not the taskmaster, giving laborers just what they have earned; his rule is that of mercy. And he draws no lines; sunshine and showers go to good and evil alike, and not even their ingratitude or enmity changes his spirit (Mt. 5^{45}). Especially does the parable of the eleventh-hour laborers sweep away all religion of law and reward, of earning and getting (Mt. 20$^{1-16}$). And this loving regard for men is individual; each man is heard as he goes to God alone in prayer, each single life is watched over by God (Mt. 6$^{6-8}$ 10$^{29-31}$). New and notable is the fact that this good will of God is no mere general attitude of kindness. It takes the initiative; it is eager, active, redemptive. The woman looks for the lost coin; the shepherd cannot be content with the ninety and nine that are safe; the father goes out to meet his son; and heaven rejoices over one sinner that repents (Lk. 15). More eloquent even than these parables, in which he defended his own conduct in relation to sinners, are the attitude and action of Jesus himself. In the spirit of such a father he seeks those who are lost, poor folk and rich, Samaritan and sinner, woman of the street, thief on the cross. And so the very gift of the Kingdom itself will be "not the product of calculating justice and retribution" but "the outflow of God's free and exuberant love" (Montefiore, *Teaching of Jesus*, pp. 97, 98).

The emphasis of the good will of God must not shut our eyes to the other side of Jesus' conception. The love of God does not mean sentimentalism or moral indifference or lack of majesty and power. Fatherhood for Jesus and for his day meant authority as well as goodness. Jesus' thought is given clearly and compactly in the opening words of the Lord's Prayer. The Father is the God in heaven, i.e., the God of all power and rule, the God who is infinitely above man. And man's attitude is to be not simply trust but reverence and awe. He is to pray, "hallowed be thy name." Nor does Jesus hesitate to say, "I will warn you whom ye shall fear" (Lk. $12^{4, 5}$), the reference being clearly to that God who has all power over men. His own prayer is revealing, "I thank thee, O Father, Lord of heaven and earth" (Mt. 11^{25}). But it is not fear in the common sense that we have here. Rather is it a reverence that engenders faith. This faith brings confidence and peace. These can come as men not only simply trust the goodness of God, but believe in his power. Lack of faith in God's power is as serious as lack of trust in his love. The Father is King. Jesus believed utterly in the power of God. The difference was that with him power was not alone and not first; good will was supreme and was in control of power.

Above all, Jesus emphasized the moral supremacy of God. The mercy of God is for him not a refuge for men who wish to sin and yet to feel secure; it becomes rather a challenge, the summons to lead a like life of good will and the standard by which in the end their life will be judged (Mt. $5^{44, 45}$ 25^{31-46}). This love is through and through ethical; we can have it in full measure only as we share it in our life. There is no forgiveness possible except to those who themselves forgive (Mt. 6^{15}). Moral demand and moral judgment are not lessened here but heightened (Mt. 18^{21-35}).

The Nature of Religion. Jesus' conception of religion, or of the religious life, flows naturally and inevitably from his idea of God, for it is the idea of God which always determines the idea of religion. Most commonly men have thought of God as Ruler, and their idea of religion has been institutionalistic. The great Ruler has determined upon those things which men must accept and do: laws to be kept, sacrifices to be performed, ritual to be followed, sacraments observed, doctrines believed, authority to be obeyed. Temple or church, system of law or set of doctrine or sum of sacred rites, there was a definite and prescribed institution which man was to accept and to which he was to submit. In Jesus' day the synagogue with its law and the Temple with its sacrifices were central. The rules concerning the Sabbath and the feast days, clean and unclean, tithe and offering, alms and prayers, covered the whole of life. (See art., *Backgrounds of Early Christian Movement*, pp. 839, 841–2, 849.)

Jesus makes no formal declarations against Jewish law and ceremonial and announces no abrogation of them. He attends the synagogue (but was finally excluded), goes to the Temple, observes the feasts, and bids the leper observe the appropriate law (Mk. 1^{44}). In the light of his teaching elsewhere, however, it is hard to believe that the words of Mt. $5^{18, 19}$ came from Jesus. Jesus' attitude toward the Law was different from that of his fellows; the Jewish leaders clearly saw how deep that difference went, and we must believe they were as a group sincerely concerned with the defense of their faith whatever may have been the faults of individuals. For Jesus, forms and rules and institutions were here to serve men and to express life. Hence he put the law of the spirit above the law of the form in relation to fasting, e.g., and the Sabbath (Mk. 2^{18-28}). From this standpoint he criticizes the main forms of Jewish piety—prayer, fasting, almsgiving (Mt. 6). The form is so easily made an end instead of a means, and then the spirit suffers (Mt. 23^{23-26}). The inner spirit is supreme. His epoch-making word is that of Mk. 7^{14-23}: things can never defile, only the spirit is evil or good.

The position of Jesus is plain. He is in the line of the great prophets (see Isa. 1^{10-17} Mic. 6^{6-8} Hos. 6^{6}; the last quoted several times by him), and of all those who have seen in religion primarily that which is ethical and spiritual. He believed in a God of righteousness and utter good will, a personal God between whom and man there was kinship and therefore could be fellowship, whom men could call Father. With such a God religion was a personal relation of reverence and trust and obedience. At the same time it meant moral likeness with this God, the sharing of his spirit of good will and the showing of that spirit in the life with men. Father, son, brother, these are the three points that mark the perfect circle of religion which Jesus drew. This conception of religion is purely spiritual and utterly simple; but no conception has ever come to men that was so profound in its depth, so wide in its reach, so lofty in its ideal, so searching in its demand. Upon this simple way a child may enter, yet after all these years its goal lifts itself far above our human achievement. We may study this conception of religion more closely in three aspects, namely, religion as the life with God, as the life with men, and as the life from God.

The Life with God. At the heart of religion there is always the thought of God, the idea of some higher Power from whom we may get help, and to whom we owe something in turn. Temple and ritual, altars and sacrifices, endless rules and offerings—all these represent man's effort toward a right relation with God that will secure the divine aid. For Jesus, however, God is not first of all a Power to be propitiated or persuaded; he is the Spirit of righteousness and good will, the Father with whom men are to live as children. Sonship, then, will describe this life with God according to Jesus, and its nature is wholly determined by the nature of the Father.

The first mark of this life is a whole-hearted trust. In this Father there is absolute power and utter goodness. For him who really sees that as Jesus did there is no room for anxiety or fear. So we have his constant call to men: "Fear not . . . Be not anxious . . . Behold the birds . . . Your Father knoweth." And here, again, his own unshaken confidence in the midst of danger and defeat speaks more loudly than words. Such a trust demands, however, not only a lofty vision of God, but an utter surrender of self. The way of sonship is a very simple one; Jesus could say, "My burden is light." Yet his demand went beyond all the rules and sacrifices that others required. These asked for tithes of income and sacred days and hours of worship; he asked for the inmost life of a man and for all his life. It is true that we have no right to treat the individual sayings of Jesus to particular men as though they were general rules laid down by him. Such passages as Mk. 10^{17-22} and Lk. 9^{57-62} have to do with the special case of those whom Jesus summoned to join his intimate fellowship or who themselves sought this. Yet in these words and elsewhere Jesus makes plain his position. Religion is not a section of life; it is all of life and it demands all. It is the treasure in the field for which one sells all else. God does not represent one among many claims; he brings the supreme and sufficient good, he represents the absolute demand. So we hear the uncompromising words: "No man can serve two masters . . . Seek first his kingdom and his righteousness . . . Enter in by the narrow gate." With this devotion there go humility and reverence. That does not mean self-abasement or self-depreciation, as has so often been supposed. Jesus did not teach men to cringe and cower and call themselves worms of the dust. He summoned them, rather, to think of themselves as sons of the Father, and he had a wonderful way of infusing hope and confidence in the lowliest and most evil. The clue to the explanation of all this lies in the fact that he bade men look at God and not at themselves. It was God's mercy that summoned them to sonship and made this possible. And so men became wonderfully humble because they knew it was all from God, and deeply reverent in the thought of such a God of holiness and power, and joyously confident in the sense of his mercy. (Cf. notes on Jer. 31^{31-34}.)

Here too we must note how it is that the utter obedience and pure reverence which Jesus demands involve a religion of freedom and not of servitude. It is not bare submission that he asks for over against an inscrutable Power to which we bend because we cannot do otherwise. Nor is the devotion which he desires that of a subject to his Monarch, unquestioning and blind. It is rather the devotion of a son to his Father. It is the surrender of one who has found at last the meaning of his life and its highest good, and who finds life in that very surrender. The freedom of a son about which Paul writes is clearly apparent with Jesus. For Jesus the Father is not blind fate or the monarch with command; he is the Life to which we open our life, the Spirit that becomes our new self. In the last analysis, we are his children because we are like him (Mt. 5^{45}). Utter devotion and perfect freedom are here one in the religion of the spirit, and the life with God reaches its highest point—that of moral likeness.

If religion is fellowship with God, then we may say that prayer is this fellowship coming to conscious expression. The words of Jesus concerning prayer must be supplemented and illustrated by his own practice. It is the idea of God which again determines everything. If only you knew God better, Jesus said to men, then you would pray more and fear less and pray better. Is he not better than the best of fathers of earth? Why not go to him, then, in your need? And if he be such a Father, then why think it needful to clamor so loudly and so long? That goes with a pagan idea of God. It is God that counts, not our prayers.

Since prayer is the conscious expression of our fellowship with God, the nature of that fellowship will determine the nature of prayer. The heart of prayer, with Jesus, is therefore that pure trust and deep reverence and utter devotion which should mark our life with God. Because of this trust in God we will bring to him all our needs. Hence Jesus encourages us to ask (Mt. 7[7] Mk. 11[24]). But because of this trust and because of our reverence we will not prescribe to God but will leave all things with God. The focal point of prayer for Jesus is God and not man. Prayer is not a device for the easy securing of our ends. The hallowing of God's name, the coming of his rule, the doing of his will—these stand first in the "Lord's Prayer." Prayer with Jesus is neither clamorous petition nor passive submission, it has a pronounced moral aspect. It is man bringing all his life into the presence of God and then thinking first of the holiness of God and his will and his rule. In such praying man comes to see his life aright and to gain strength for it. All this is illustrated by the praying of Jesus. Luke marks the great crises in Jesus' life by special reference to his praying (Lk. 3[21] 5[16] 6[12] 9[18, 28] 22[41]). Add to these the temptation narrative and note that prayer was the means by which Jesus sought to know the way that he was to take and to gain strength for it.

The Life with Men. Religion, for Jesus, was a way of living with men as well as with God, and the one grew out of the other. With God men were to live as children, in trust, in devotion, in oneness of spirit. The mark of the child was the spirit of the Father in him. But this spirit of the Father must be shown and could only be shown by his children in relation to their brothers. So the dual command of love to God and man, to which Jesus had reduced all commands, becomes one rule, one spirit, by which man is to live.

To be a brother to men in the spirit of the common Father is a very simple rule of life, but its scope is wide and its standard is high. It includes all men, good and evil, black and white, near and far. At once the status of woman, of the child, of the slave, of the man of "inferior" race becomes altered. Jesus recognizes the differences between evil men and good, between Jew and Samaritan. Yet that is most significant which these have in common. Each is a man, with a value outweighing a whole world of things (Mk. 8[36, 37]). Not one but is the object of God's love and care. Heaven rejoices when one wandering child of God comes back. Anger, scorn, contempt, the hard and unforgiving spirit—these are sins that call forth his strongest condemnation.

The demand of Jesus relative to man's life with men is plain. First of all, it is reverence for humanity in the person of every human being. Second, there must be the spirit of forgiveness, or there can be no forgiveness expected by us (Mt. 6[15]). Then there must be good will, love not as a vague sentimentality but as the positive and active will desiring the good of others. And, finally, there is the demand of service and sacrifice. Here is the test of greatness in the kingdom of God, and Jesus offers himself as example (Mk. 10[35-45]).

Some questions call for answer here. Did not Jesus look for the speedy coming of a new and wholly different order, the kingdom of God, and was not his moral teaching therefore an ethic *ad interim*, a teaching for this short interval only? Leaving aside for the moment the doctrine of the Kingdom, it is plain that the principles of Jesus suggested above have no relation to changing conditions; they belong to all time because they rest back upon God himself. Moreover, Jesus was not a giver of rules which must always change with circumstance; his concern was with the inner spirit. Specific demands and applications, of course, would be affected by the immediate situation: the men whom he summons for permanent fellowship must leave their nets; the rich young ruler is faced with a special challenge that is not applied by Jesus to others.

What about non-resistance with Jesus (Mt. 5[38-48])? Again we must remember that Jesus is not a giver of rules but the prophet of a new spirit. He is dealing with a great principle here, though, as usual, put in concrete and vivid form. And here, as elsewhere, he is not negative or passive. He knows the evil of reliance upon brute force and of the spirit of retaliation and revenge, or of the mere hard give-and-take. And he proclaims not only the duty of forgiving good will, that, like the love of God, shall not draw back even from the evil; but he shows his faith in the power of this good will as a conquering force to overcome evil. That is God's answer to the sin of man; that shall be man's answer to evil in his fellows. In the end the cross, with its "Father, forgive them," is but another declaration of this same great faith. Here is something, not passive, but active, aggressive, conquering.

Is not Jesus' teaching deficient on the side of social ethics? The answer is, Yes, and No. Jesus has little to say about the social life of man on its institutional side, about state and industry, about family and divorce, about war and slavery. He has more to say about property, or wealth, but at no point is there any systematic discussion, and at every point the approach is from the side of the individual and the spiritual. Several considerations help to explain this. (See Moffatt, *Theology of Gospels*, pp. 49–62.) He was living in an order wholly different from ours, an autocratic order in which his disciples had to accept what was found as given. He himself expected a new order to come, but not through human revolution or reform. The immediate need was repentance, a new spirit; with that God would add all else. It was his special task to call men to repentance, to make clear what was this spirit.

Nevertheless, the teaching of Jesus is social in the deepest sense. He is considering how men are to live together in the new order. It is a social life that he constantly envisages. And the principles which he enunciates have the most direct and sweeping significance for all the associated life of men, including the institutions in which that life is bodied forth. His teaching has all the more of permanent significance just because he did not lay down rules for application. What was needed was simply that men should come to have his spirit and to see its implications. His teaching on divorce is not an effort to give rules for civil or ecclesiastical procedure, but to set forth a spiritual ideal. If he gives more time to the matter of wealth, it is because of the besetting peril that lies here, the peril of putting things above men. Sometimes covetousness appears as hardness and oppression toward one's fellows, sometimes as the folly which sells its own soul (Lk. 12[16-21] 16[19-21]); the error is the same. But one has only to think of autocracy in government, of bond slavery and wage slavery, of nationalism and race prejudice and war, of modern economic rivalry and its practices of exploitation, to realize the revolutionary significance of the principles of Jesus on the social side. Reverence for all humanity, the acceptance of one Father, the obligation of brotherhood, the spirit of good will and cooperation and service—these may be decried as impossible ideals but not as socially unmeaning.

The Life from God. It has often seemed to men that the passage from Jesus to Paul was like moving into a wholly different world of religious ideas, that with Jesus religion was the simple life with God which anyone could undertake, while Paul brought to us an elaborate doctrine of salvation, with its theories of sin and atonement and the rest. (See art., *Life and Work of Paul*, pp. 931–2.) There is some difference here, and yet Jesus too has his definite teaching about what sin is and how men are to be saved. The simple speech of Jesus must not hide from us this fact. Religion is life, a wonderful life with God, the life which the son lives in devotion and trust, in strength and peace, in the spirit of love. But this life is for Jesus the gift of God; it is not only a life with God, but a life from God. And that is salvation. And there is something that stands in the way of this life and that is sin.

Jesus has nothing to say about sin in the abstract; the word is used by him very little as compared with Paul. But how keen was his sense of sin as a spirit and a power in men! We see his conception of sin as we note what he demanded and what he condemned. Sin was a matter of the inner spirit, of the attitude toward God and men. In relation to God it was the lack of trust and obedience, the attitude of men who said, "Lord, Lord," but did not do the will of God, of the son who said, "I go, sir," but went not. In relation to men it was the lack of love and forgiveness, it was the spirit of selfishness and hardness and scorn. Of the sins which root in the passions of the flesh he had not much to say, but he never condoned sin of any kind. It was the terrible thing that divided men from God; it was that which made men a stumbling-block and a curse to their fellows. So it comes that his very love for men moves him at times to terrific words of judgment and condemnation (Mk. 12[38-40] Mt. 23[4-13]).

Salvation with Jesus was a very simple and personal matter. The lost man was the man out of place, out of right relations, like the coin in the dark corner, the sheep off in the hills, the son among strangers. He was in wrong relations with his world, with men, and with God. But the relation with God was fundamental; make that right and the rest would be right. To that end a man had first to see differently and feel differently; he had to come to himself, to repent (Lk. 15[17]). Repentance was more than feeling; it was a total change of mind and will. And there must be faith, the faith which trusted God and turned with heart and will toward him. When Jesus found these he said simply, "To-day is salvation come to this house" (Lk. 19[9]).

But all this was simply the response of man to God. The supreme matter was the "good news" with which Jesus called men to repentance and faith. The great fact was God with his loving purpose for men and his saving help. The good news was first of all that of the coming kingdom of God. But there was something more here, something personal and present. That was God's willingness to receive men who wished to get ready for this kingdom, to forgive them and take them into fellowship with himself, so that they too might be children with the spirit of their Father. The simplicity of this must not hide from us the elements of profound meaning and moral power. This is the way that God makes men over, not by some magic rite of sacramental nature, not by some mysterious and irresistible action of grace, but by this new personal fellowship, this life into which he lifts men.

The Kingdom of God. It is customary to begin the study of the teachings of Jesus with the subject of the kingdom of God. We have left that till the last. There are several reasons for this. It is true that this phrase was very often on the lips of Jesus. He was, like the Baptist, a proclaimer of the Kingdom that was at hand. But he was something more, and it is this more that is significant. What Jesus meant by the kingdom of God he nowhere systematically defines. That was his way; he took the words that everybody knew and he gave them gradually his own meaning. He did not define what was meant to him by Messiahship, but he transformed that concept. He accepted nominally the idea of the Law and its authority, but when he had finished, the old system was broken forever. So with the idea of the kingdom of God. The important matter is not his use of the term, nor any definitions of it, but what he put into it by his whole life and teaching, especially his teaching about God.

The idea of a new age, a new order, was an ancient one with Israel. They believed that Jehovah was Lord of all. Why, then, the victories of their enemies, and why this evil in the world? There was but one reply: all this is but for a time, and then the day of Jehovah will come; his enemies will be overcome and he will rule in all the earth. Such a hope would vary widely. It could be material and political, or moral and spiritual. It might be selfishly nationalistic and Jewish, or splendidly universal in its outlook. Usually, it had a measure of all these aspects. With many in Jesus' day it was fiercely national, joined with a deep hatred of Rome and the hope for the overthrow of the oppressor. (See pp. 188–9, 206–10; 768–74, 809–10.) It was the effort to force this end by human action that led at last to armed revolt against Rome and the terrible destruction of Jerusalem. Others in that day held this hope in what we call the apocalyptic form. Not by man's work was the end to come, they said, but by the glorious deed of God. World history was divided into two ages. The present was utterly evil, left by God, wholly hopeless. It could only grow worse as it neared a terrible end. Then God would come with his angels, evil men would be destroyed, the saints would be raised from the dead, a new heaven and a new earth would appear, and so the new age be ushered in.

How far did Jesus share these ideas? Certainly, his conception of the Kingdom was not political or national. In the Beatitudes and elsewhere he speaks of those to whom the kingdom of heaven will belong; but there is never a word to suggest that the Jew has an entrance which does not equally belong to any other. It is spirit and attitude that determine, never race. He turns away from the political, from all the old ideas of rule. The Jews thought that the Messiah's coming would turn the tables, making them rulers over their former masters. Jesus declared that this whole idea of rule was wrong. In his kingdom pre-eminence was to mean service (Mk. 10[42-45]).

In some ways he approached more the apocalyptic idea. He believed that the day of God's rule was near at hand. "This generation shall not pass away till all things be accomplished" (Lk. 21[32]). And the kingdom was to be God's deed, God's gift (Lk. 12[32]). But there are differences from apocalypticism that are even more significant. Jesus had none of the hopeless pessimism of the apocalyptists who could do nothing but bewail the evil of their age and wait for something to happen. True, it was God and not man that was to bring in the Kingdom; but man had something to do. He must repent. Here and now, without waiting for a future day, he was to become a child of God and live the new life of good will. And this age was not hopeless or God-deserted. The beginnings of the Kingdom were here. They were here in the healing deeds of Jesus, in the new life which he was already offering to men, in the forgiveness of sin; Satan's kingdom was already being overthrown (Lk. 11[20] 10[18] Mt. 11[4, 5, 25-30]). God was not far off, passive till some future time of action. God was here, caring for bird and flower, here as the power that ruled, here in help and forgiving love. It was by the finger of God that Jesus cast out demons, it was God that forgave sinners through him. And one other difference: the apocalyptists were always anxiously scanning the heavens for signs, and calculating times and periods. Jesus left this all with God, giving himself to his great task, summoning men to his aid, declaring that "of that day and hour" he had no knowledge. The so-called apocalyptic discourses (Mk. 13 and parallels: Mt. 24, Lk. 21) seem to point another way. It is plain, however, that there have been changes and additions here. The elaborate depiction of signs does not fit with Jesus' reticence elsewhere (Mk. 13[32]). References to different events are mingled in confusion: to the capture of Jerusalem, the destruction of the Temple, the persecution of the disciples, the coming of the Son of man. These passages represent the early church probably more than they do Jesus. (See art., *Literature of the Intertestamental Period*, pp. 188–9; art., *Backgrounds*, pp. 843–7; intro. to Revelation of John, pp. 1364a, 1366b.)

We may now note briefly Jesus' conception of the Kingdom, for what is significant in Jesus' teaching is not the matter of how the Kingdom is to come, about which we have very little, but what the Kingdom is. "Kingdom of God" means rule or reign of God; that is the common element in the many and diverse conceptions of the Kingdom. But our idea of the rule of God will naturally depend upon our idea of God. If one thinks primarily of God as a heavenly Potentate, a Monarch of the skies, after the manner of earthly rulers, then his kingdom will be political and external. So the coming kingdom was conceived in Jesus' day. Of course it was to be a rule of righteousness, but it was nevertheless to be an external rule. The God of Jesus is not lacking in majesty and power, but the emphasis of Jesus is upon the moral character of God. God's relations with men are primarily personal and ethical. Hence the rule with which Jesus is concerned is of another kind, the rule of the inner spirit. We do not read about the avenging God, therefore, destroying the enemies of Israel. There is no talk of thrones and scepters and armies. It is the overcoming of evil, the destruction of sin, the presence of faith and good will with which Jesus is concerned. This inner and ethical nature of the Kingdom is seen in what Jesus says about the children of the Kingdom, those to whom the Kingdom belongs. Here the Beatitudes are most suggestive. That men of peace and good will, of meekness and purity of spirit, should form the kingdom of heaven shows plainly the nature of that kingdom. So also the declaration that men must become as little children in order to enter, and that the humble and childlike will be greatest in the Kingdom (Mt. $18^{3, 4}$). What Jesus had in mind was a world in which the spirit of the Father God should rule the life of his children and in which all evil should be done away.

We shall understand Jesus' thought of the new age better if we realize that the phrase, kingdom of God, is a figure of speech, and that there is still another figure which Jesus employs, a figure more congenial to his thought, and better adapted to express his distinctive message. That is the figure not of king and subjects but of father and children. Fatherhood does not exclude authority, but it does express more adequately Jesus' thought of the character of God and of his relation to men. And the whole figure lends itself better to set forth Jesus' ideal of the new age. It is a new humanity to which he is looking forward. Men are to be children of their Father, i.e., they are to be like him in spirit. In his spirit they are to live with one another as brothers. And that will be the kingdom of God.

Did the kingdom of God, then, mean for Jesus simply something individual and subjective? That does not follow from the position taken above. True, the kingdom of God is the rule of the spirit of God in the life of men, but we must notice the nature of that spirit. The spirit is one of good will, expressed actively in service, and the final test of its presence is just this service (Mk. 9^{35} 10^{42-45} Mt. 25^{31-46}). We are dealing here, then, not with mere inner emotion or mystical experience, but pre-eminently with a social spirit that can be expressed only in human relations. Other considerations lead to the same conclusion. There is the idea of brotherhood as a rule of life. There is the fact made plain in the Lord's Prayer that *thy kingdom come* means "thy will be done." The kingdom of God will mean man's putting into expression the will of God in every phase of human life. And, of course, no line can be drawn here between individual and social, between the personal and the institutional. The rule to which Jesus looks forward cannot be less than a rule over all human life and activity.

A final question remains. The modern man speaks constantly of working for the kingdom of God, of building it up, of bringing it in. Is this not contrary to Jesus' teaching? Was not the kingdom of God to be for him the gift of God and the deed of God? To the latter question we must certainly answer Yes. Jesus did not differ here from others. That is always the word of faith, the message of religion, to expect everything from God. It is trust in God, confidence in God's power and goodness. "Fear not, little flock; for it is your Father's good pleasure to give you the kingdom" (Lk. 12^{32}). But this emphasis on the religious does not exclude the ethical. God's gift does not shut out our deed or our active response. The kingdom is God's gift, but everything depends upon the nature of that gift. If it be a matter of killing enemies and setting up thrones, then it can be done by irresistible divine power, and no response or aid of man is involved. But that is not what Jesus has in mind. The goods of the Kingdom which God gives are conquest of evil, forgiveness of sins, the vision of God, the gift of his Spirit—in a word, the gift of life (Lk. 11^{20} 24^{47} Mt. 5^{8} Mk. 10^{17f}). Such

gifts cannot be passively received. They make searching demand. And that demand Jesus makes plain. He calls men to repentance, to utter change of heart and devotion of life. If they want the kingdom of God they must put it absolutely first in desire and allegiance. They must give themselves utterly to the life of love and service. The will of God becomes not something passively accepted, but actively practiced. The kingdom of God means life, but it is a life which men can have only as they live it. The kingdom of God is the gift of God, but it can come only as men give themselves with minds and heart and will to see the will of God and to do it.

Literature: Wendt, *The Teaching of Jesus;* Moffatt, *The Theology of the Gospels;* Rall, *The Teachings of Jesus;* Dickey, *The Constructive Revolution of Jesus;* Mathews, *The Social Teachings of Jesus;* Scott, *The Ethical Teaching of Jesus;* Burch, *The Ethical Teaching of the Gospels.*

THE PARABLES OF JESUS

By Professor H. G. Wood

The Word "Parable" and Its Associations. The essential idea in the word "parable" is that of comparison. It means, literally, "placing something alongside something else," in order to throw light on the latter. "Parable" is, therefore, most properly applied to a story of some familiar or, at least, intelligible incident which serves by comparison or contrast to illustrate some truth less familiar or less readily understood and appreciated. But an effective comparison need not always be worked up into a story. A *simile* or a *metaphor* may be regarded as a parable. They are certainly parables in germ, and they are sometimes called "parables" in the Gospels. When Jesus rebutted the charge of casting out demons by Beelzebub with the similes that a house divided against itself cannot stand, and a strong man's goods cannot be plundered except the strong man be first bound, Mark says he was speaking in parables (Mk. 3[23f.]). Similarly, Luke regards the sayings about the new patch and the old garment, the new wine and the old skins, and the blind leaders of the blind, as parables (Lk. 5[36] 6[39]). These and other such sayings are used to illustrate different truths by suggestive comparisons. The main idea of the word "parable" is thus here retained. But similes may be compressed into metaphors; and metaphorical sayings, and even paradoxical and enigmatic sayings, may then be included in the term "parable," not because they teach by comparisons, but because, in the case of the metaphors at least, they rest on comparisons. The use of the term "parable" in this broader sense may be seen in such passages as Mk. 7[17] (Mt. 15[15]) and Lk. 4[23]. The fourth Gospel uses a different word (Greek *paroimia*) in the same sense of "enigma" or "riddle" in 16[29]. This wider reference may be due to the fact that in the LXX the two Greek words *parabolē, paroimia,* are used to translate the Hebrew *māshāl*, which has all the meanings we have so far discovered in the use of the word "parable" in the Gospels. The phrase from Psa. 78[2], "I will open my mouth in parables," which Matthew cites as fulfilled in our Lord's ministry (Mt. 13[35]), clearly contemplates proverbial sayings rather than stories. Perhaps it would be safe to say that the Hebrew word *māshāl* meant primarily "sayings," and secondarily "stories," while the Greek word *parabolē* came to mean primarily "stories," and secondarily "sayings."

Parable Distinguished from Fable and Allegory. As a story the parable needs to be distinguished from both *fable* and *allegory*. The first distinction is simple, for the parable allows no such departure from nature as is characteristic of fable where animals and even inanimate objects may be endowed with human feelings and human speech. The relation of parable to allegory is not so easily determined. The popular tendency used to be to treat all parables as allegories, and so to find each detail significant. It was the great merit of Jülicher that he challenged this tendency and demonstrated that while in an allegory the comparison is detailed, every element in the description both of actors and action having a special meaning, in a parable the comparison is usually confined to some central point, so that we have as it were two pictures with one main feature in common but with no elaborate coincidence in detail. Thus many particulars may be inserted to complete the picture which have no significance for the comparison which is the point of the parable. This principle of Jülicher's is vigorously summed up in the saying that in the parable of the wise and foolish virgins nothing is meant by the oil. While this principle is a wholesome corrective of fanciful interpretations, it is a mistake to separate parable and allegory too rigidly, for a parable may easily include an allegorical element or shade off into allegory. Some details in the gospel-parables may properly receive allegorical interpretation. Thus in the parable of the sower, which might better be called the parable of the soils, the details are certainly significant. In some other parables in the synoptic Gospels, e.g., the parable of the wicked husbandmen, an allegorical element may be detected. In the fourth Gospel the parables of the door of the sheepfold, the good shepherd, and the vine and its branches, approach the class of allegory more nearly than is usual in the synoptics. (Cf. pp. 20–1.)

In one or two instances stories which are usually classed as parables are better described as examples or illustrations than as parables, since they directly illustrate some truth rather than illuminate it by comparison. Thus the story of the good Samaritan does not compare neighborly conduct to something else. It is a particular example of loving one's neighbor.

Use of Parables Among the Jews. Teachers

of the East have long made use of the parable. A good modern example will be found in the similitudes in which Sadhu Sundar Singh abounds and delights. The Oriental mind, or, at any rate, the Jewish mind, prefers concrete illustration and suggestive parallel to abstract definition and logical argument. As a method of teaching, the use of parable has all the advantages of "truth embodied in a tale." The Jews both before and after Christ were familiar with it. There are well-known examples of the effective use of parables in the O.T. In this way the prophet Nathan convicted David of sin, and in this way also the wise woman from Tekoa induced the same king to recall Absalom (2 Sam. $12^{1f.}$ $14^{4f.}$). The parable of the vineyard in Isa. 5 underlies the parable of the wicked husbandmen in the Gospels. In our Lord's own time parables were probably often used in interpreting the lessons from the Law and the Prophets which were read each Sabbath in the synagogues. Many such stories are to be found in the literature of Rabbinic Judaism. It is here that we find the nearest parallels to the parables of the Gospels. Many of these rabbinic parables are singularly beautiful, but, in general, they are in poorer literary form than those in the Gospels, and they are apt to be more conventional in character. They are traditional classroom illustrations rather than the outcome of fresh observation. It is noteworthy that while they do not neglect nature and the life of the common people the rabbis drew constantly on the life and conduct of kings for their similitudes. It is possible that the description of the man who gives a feast as a king in Mt. 22^{2f} reflects the influence of Jewish usage. (Cf. also Mt. $18^{23f.}$)

Reference Table for the Parables and Other Important Similes of Jesus. The following table is given to simplify the student's use of the present article, and to permit readier reference to the more detailed consideration of the parables in the commentaries on the Gospels.

Peculiar to Matthew:

The tares, 13^{24-30}
The hidden treasure, 13^{44}
The pearl of great price, $13^{45, 46}$
The dragnet, 13^{47-50}
The unmerciful servant, 18^{23-34}
The laborers in the vineyard, 20^{1-16}
The father and two sons, 21^{28-32}
The marriage feast, 22^{1-14} (cf. Lk. 14^{15-24}).
The ten virgins, 25^{1-13}
The differing talents, 25^{14-30} (cf. Lk. 19^{12-27})
The division of sheep and goats, 25^{31-46}

Peculiar to Mark:

The growing seed, 4^{26-29}
The watchful porter, 13^{34-36} (cf. Lk. 12^{35-40})

Peculiar to Luke:

The two debtors, 7^{41-47}
The good Samaritan, 10^{25-37}
The friend at midnight, 11^{5-8}
The rich fool, 12^{16-21}
The watchful servants, 12^{35-40} (cf. Mk. 13^{34-36})
The diligent steward, 12^{42-48}
The barren fig tree, 13^{6-9}
The indifferent guests, 14^{15-24} (cf. Mt. 22^{1-14})
The unfinished tower, 14^{28-30}
The improvident king, $14^{31, 32}$
The lost coin, 15^{8-10}
The prodigal son, 15^{11-32}
The unjust but shrewd steward, 16^{1-13}
The rich man and Lazarus, 16^{19-31}
The condescending master, 17^{7-10}
The importunate widow, 18^{1-8}
The Pharisee and the publican, 18^{9-14}
The ten pounds, 19^{12-27} (cf. Mt. 25^{14-30})

Peculiar to John:

The bread of life, 6^{32-58}
The shepherd, fold, and door, 10^{1-16}
The vine and the branches, 15^{1-6}
(Not especially considered in the present article are the briefer similes in the fourth Gospel, such as—Christ's body as a temple, 2^{19-22}; "ye must be born again," 3^{3}; the serpent in the wilderness, $3^{14, 15}$; the bridegroom, 3^{29}; the water of life, $4^{13, 14}$; Jesus' "meat," 4^{34}; the fields white to harvest, 4^{35-38}; "rivers of living water," 7^{38}; the light of the world, 8^{12} $12^{35, 46}$; the grain, 12^{24}.)

Common to Matthew and Luke:

The foundations, Mt. 7^{24-27} Lk. 6^{47-49}
The leaven and meal, Mt. 13^{33} Lk. 13^{21}
The lost sheep, Mt. $18^{12, 13}$ Lk. 15^{3-7}
(Compare Mt. 25^{14-30} with Lk. 19^{12-27}; also Mt. 22^{1-14} with Lk. 14^{15-24}.)

Common to Matthew, Mark, and Luke:

The lamp on the stand, Mt. $5^{15, 16}$ Mk. 4^{21} Lk. 8^{16}
New cloth on old garments, Mt. 9^{16} Mk. 2^{21} Lk. 5^{36}
New wine in old skins, Mt. 9^{17} Mk. 2^{22} Lk. 5^{37-39}
The divided house, Mt. 12^{25-29} Mk. 3^{23-27} Lk. 11^{17-22}
The sower, Mt. 13^{1-23} Mk. 4^{1-20} Lk. 8^{4-15}
The mustard seed, Mt. $13^{31, 32}$ Mk. 4^{30-32} Lk. $13^{18, 19}$
The vineyard and the husbandmen, Mt. 21^{33-41} Mk. 12^{1-12} Lk. 20^{9-18}
The fig tree in tender leaf, Mt. 24^{32} Mk. 13^{28} Lk. $21^{29, 30}$.

Three questions concerning the parables fall to be considered here, namely, the general characteristics of the parables of Jesus, his motive and purpose in using the parables, and the various themes they were designed to illustrate.

General Characteristics of the Parables of Jesus. In the N.T. and in early Christian literature the parable is almost the monopoly of Jesus—as distinctively his own as the use of the term "Son of Man" as a self-designation. Paul, indeed, compares the Christian community with the body and its members—a similitude familiar to the ancient rhetoricians—and he essays one doubtful experiment in grafting (1 Cor. $12^{14f.}$ Rom. 11^{17}), but he is no artist in parable. We can see from the similitudes of the Shepherd of Hermas, a Christian writing of the second century, the kind of capacity which the sub-apostolic Christians possessed in this direction. The parables in the Gospels clearly come, in the main, not from the church but from her Master.

The *freshness* and *fidelity to nature* which characterize the parables have often been noted. There are, indeed, occasionally present elements of exaggeration or hyperbole which are intentional. The unforgiving servant in Mt. 18^{23} owes an impossibly large sum to his lord, six thousand talents being ten times the annual taxation of Judæa, Idumæa, and Samaria, while his fellow servant owes him one six hundred thousandth part of his own remitted debt. The contrast is designed and deliberately intensified, as in the somewhat parallel saying about the mote and the beam. The irony of Jesus is sometimes present in his parables. But the persuasiveness and cogency of the parables are due in part to their naturalness. The pictures are taken straight from nature and from life, and the details have not been strained or perverted to enforce a lesson. In consequence the lesson is the more effectively enforced. This characteristic of Christ's teaching, which is exemplified in the parables, is admirably brought out by T. T. Lynch:

"He spoke of grass and wind and rain,
And fig trees and fair weather;
And made it his delight to bring
Heaven and earth together.

"He spoke of lilies, corn, and vines,
The sparrow and the raven:
And words so natural yet so wise
Were on men's hearts engraven;

"And yeast and bread, and flax and cloth,
And eggs and fish and candles—
See how the whole familiar world
He most divinely handles."

The *social background* of the life of Jesus is wonderfully reflected in the parables. They take us back to Galilee, and to Galilee in the first century A.D. We enter the home and watch the housewife making the bread or patching the old garment or looking for the lost coin. We see the life of the market place and watch the travelers on the high road. We traverse the fields with the sower or climb the hills with the shepherd or stand by the lakeside and pull the net ashore with the fisherman. We come to know also the local magnate with his large house, his capital, his vineyards, and his barns. We learn how he deals with his steward, his hired laborers, and his slaves, and we understand "the cares that press on the heart of worldliness." Nothing of the life of the busy thriving province of Galilee seems to escape the Master. His greatest interest was in the common people. He stopped to speak to those whom other teachers had passed by. He did that because he saw them as with the eyes of God—who looks beyond the accidental to the essential. It is not an idle phrase, when a modern poet speaks of Jesus as "Dear intimate of little folk."

Jesus' Motive and Purpose in Teaching by Parables. Mark suggests that Jesus adopted the method of teaching by parable when the ministry in Galilee had been in progress for some time. He seems to associate it with the period when, partly owing to the suspicion of the religious leaders and partly owing to the pressure of the crowds, Jesus began to withdraw from the cities and the synagogues and teach in the open air and in desert places. In connection with the use of parables the evangelist cites the passage from Isaiah about the people seeing and not perceiving, hearing and not understanding, and seems to suggest that the parables were intended to conceal the secret of the Kingdom from those who were outside (Mk. $4^{11,\ 12}$). This suggestion conflicts apparently with the later passage (Mk. 4^{33}), where we read that Jesus taught the people with such parables as they were able to hear, and also with the normal purpose of a parable, which is to elucidate and not to obscure truth. This difficulty can be removed by recognizing that Mark, or that Jesus himself as reported in Mark, treats the actual consequence of the teaching by parables as the divinely intended result. This is in accord with Hebrew ways of thinking. The effect of the parables was to sift Christ's hearers. The story of the sower is the story of Christ himself. He spoke, and his words met with very different reception from different hearers. Some perceived and understood nothing of the deeper meaning of the stories to which they listened. In their case the prophecy of Isaiah was fulfilled, though Jesus taught them as long as they were willing and able to listen. Yet we can hardly doubt that Jesus adopted the method of parables in order to win a further hearing for truths about the Kingdom, which were not familiar or welcome to the common people. Just as Nathan brought home an unwelcome truth to David by means of a parable, so Jesus taught the people many things concerning the Kingdom which did not fit in with their preconceptions.

There would seem to be a good deal of force in the contention of A. B. Bruce that there is a parabolic mood—a state of mind in which one who is conscious of misunderstanding and opposition and "whose spirit is saddened by a sense of loneliness frames for his thoughts forms which half conceal, half reveal them—reveal them more perfectly to those who understand, hide them from those who do not."

Subject Matter and Grouping of the Parables. When Jesus began to teach in parables, the main theme was the kingdom of God. Only four parables are recorded as such by all the synoptic Gospels—the sower, the mustard-seed, the wicked husbandmen and the fig-tree—but these four suggest two subjects with which the parabolic teaching of Jesus was mainly concerned. The sower and the mustard-seed stand at the head of that group of stories which deal with the nature and growth of the kingdom of God. The story of the vineyard and the wicked husbandmen is the most searching of those warnings of judgment awaiting the nation which our Lord addressed to Israel particularly in the closing period of his ministry. The fig-tree represents the associated warnings addressed to the disciples. (The synoptic Gospels contain in common, however, other suggestive brief similes: see the reference table above.)

In the *first group* we must place all the material collected in Mt. 13, together with Mark's parable of the seed growing secretly (Mk. 4^{26-29}). If we examine the parables in this group, we shall find that they bear out the contention that by means of them Jesus was striving to instill into the minds of the people a different idea of the Kingdom from that commonly entertained. The people were looking for a deliverer who should repeat and surpass the exploits of Judas Maccabæus. Jesus spoke of the Kingdom as God's gift, and he also spoke of it as something that should grow from within. He used imagery drawn in the main from agriculture and natural processes, and such pictures were intended and adapted to draw men's thoughts away from dreams of military conquest and empire. The parable of the sower suggests that the coming of the Kingdom depends on the response men make to the teaching of Jesus himself. Then we have two pairs of parables—the mustard-seed and the leaven, the hid treasure and the pearl-merchant—which set forth certain truths about the growth of the Kingdom and about the individual's discovery of the Kingdom. In the mustard-seed there is the contrast between the small beginning and the later development of the Kingdom. This is a picture of outward visible extension. The leaven, on the other hand, illustrates the way in which the life of the Kingdom is destined to permeate society, working from within until everything is transformed by it. The second pair of parables sets forth the Kingdom as man's highest good for which it is worth while joyfully to give up everything. A man may stumble on this treasure by accident, as in the case of the man who finds the treasure hid in the field, or he may find it as the result of long and conscious search; but however the Kingdom comes into a man's life, he will find the world well lost to attain it. It is tempting to associate Mark's parable of the seed growing secretly with the parable of the tares as the members of another pair. The first, then, may be directed to encourage those morbid, over-anxious souls who are forever pulling up the plants of goodness sown in their own hearts to see whether they are growing or not. The second is probably a warning to those eager patriots and impatient reformers who always suppose that methods of violent repression are the best means of advancing God's kingdom upon earth. But as it stands, the parable of the tares seems to be associated even more closely with the parable of the drag-net, and the lesson of both would seem to be the lesson which Paul commended to the Corinthians when he urged them to judge nothing before the time (1 Cor. 4^{5}).

To the *second group*, the parables of warning and judgment, will belong the barren fig-tree (Lk. 13^{6-9}), the great supper (Lk. 14^{15-24}), together with Matthew's feast of the king's son (Mt. 22^{1-14}), the section of the parable in Lk. $19^{11f.}$ which deals with the nobleman and his subjects, the parable of the two sons, Mt. $21^{28f.}$, and the picture of the Last Judgment in Mt. $25^{31f.}$ Associated with this group are a number of parables addressed to disciples and impressing on them the duties of watchfulness, of preparedness, of diligence and faithfulness in the tasks assigned to them. To this class we shall assign the reference to the watchful slaves in Lk. 12^{35-46}, since the evangelist regards this as a parable (12^{41}), the parable of the talents (Mt. $25^{14f.}$) and the parallel story of the nobleman and his servants in Lk. ($19^{11f.}$), the wise and foolish virgins (Mt. $25^{1f.}$), and the lesson of the fig tree (Mk. $13^{28f.}$ Mt. $24^{32f.}$ Lk. $21^{29f.}$).

It is impossible to determine the exact chronological order of the parables, but manifestly of these two main groups the first is characteristic of the Galilæan ministry, while the second belongs to the closing period of our Lord's life and is most naturally associated with Jerusalem.

The remaining parables are for the most part connected with the first group rather than the second. They are concerned with the character of the citizens of God's kingdom and with the defense and interpretation of the life of the Kingdom. They may be roughly classified as follows:

There are first stories told by Jesus *in defense and explanation of his own conduct.* Here we may place the two debtors, the story told in the house of Simon the Pharisee (Lk. $7^{41, 42}$), and the parables of the lost sheep, the lost coin, and the lost son. In Luke all these stories are told to defend the action of Jesus in befriending sinners. The parable of the lost sheep is also related in Mt. 18^{12} to enforce the warning against despising little ones. But these parables are more than defenses: they are appeals intended to transform foes to friends and to turn critics into disciples; they constitute the parables of grace and set forth the wonder of God's love.

We have, next, stories told *to set forth the Christian character*, and to commend more particularly the love of one's neighbor—charity in action and the forgiving spirit, charity in the heart and the humility of those who know themselves to be God's servants and God's debtors. This group will include the stories of the good Samaritan (Lk. 10^{30-37}), and of the unforgiving servant (Mt. 18^{23-35}). It may also include the parable from which Ruskin derived the phrase "Unto This Last" (Mt. 20^{1-16}). The advice to take the lower seats at a wedding feast (Lk. $14^{7f.}$), and the reminder that when we have done all we are still servants who have but done what they ought to have done (Lk. $17^{7f.}$), also belong here if we follow Luke in regarding them as parables. The picture of the Pharisee and the publican praying in the Temple should be included in this group.

Beyond this there are Luke's stories dealing with the subjects of *prayer*, and of the *use and abuse of riches.* To the first we assign the parable of the importunate friend (Lk. 11^{5-9}) and the parable of the unjust judge and the widow (Lk. 18^{2-8}). Perhaps the latter was originally intended to enforce the lesson of faith in Christ's ultimate triumph rather than persistence in prayer. In that case it would belong to the group of warnings addressed to the disciples as to their duties while waiting for the Lord's return. In the second group will stand the parables of the rich fool (Lk. 12^{16-21}), the unjust steward (16^{1-12}), and Dives and Lazarus (16^{19-31}).

The Transmission of the Parables of Jesus. Seeing that the parables are so characteristic a feature of the teaching of Jesus, it is somewhat strange that the synoptic Gospels have so few parables in common. As we have seen, the sower, the mustard-seed, the wicked husbandmen and the fig-tree are the only actual parables recorded by all the first three evangelists. If, however, we consider sayings which are treated as parables by one or other of the evangelists and which may be regarded as parables in germ, we can extend this list (see the reference table above, p. 915) by adding the sayings with which Jesus defended his disciples for their failure to observe the practice of fasting and with which he refuted the charge that he himself was in league with Beelzebub (Mk. $2^{21, 22}$ 3^{25}). But the evidence of the Triple Tradition (i.e., the common record of the first three Gospels) is always limited by the fact that Mark does not apparently set out to give any full account of the teaching of Jesus. The first three Gospels do, however, agree both as to the important place which parables took in the teaching of Jesus and as to their main subjects.

The Parables of the Earliest Gospel Record. It is perhaps rather more strange that Matthew and Luke, who seem to have drawn on some earlier record of the teaching of Jesus, have, after all, so few parables in common. In addition to those they record along with Mark, both Matthew and Luke narrate the leaven, the lost sheep, the marriage feast and the talents or the pounds. So far as the marriage feast and the talents are concerned, there are considerable divergences between the two evangelists, and it is sometimes supposed that the parables are distinct. But probably these parables in some form or other belong to the common record of Christ's teaching on which Matthew and Luke drew. Then we have seen how often parables are associated in pairs, and the woman seeking her lost coin is so clearly a companion-picture to the shepherd seeking his lost sheep that we may fairly assume they come from the same source, though the former is found only in Luke. Moreover, Mark may also be indebted to this common source, and in that case the parables he records may belong to it, including the parable of the seed growing secretly. This would permit us to include in the earliest record of Christ's teaching probably eight and possibly ten parables, namely, the sower, the mustard-seed, the leaven (the seed growing secretly), the lost sheep (the lost coin), the marriage feast, the talents, the wicked husbandmen, the fig-tree. B. S. Easton in his commentary on Luke (1927) adds to this list the parables of the importunate friend (Lk. 11[5-8]) and the foolish rich man (Lk. 12[13-21]), and there is a great deal of force in his arguments. We might extend this list still further by adding the sayings about watchful servants (Lk. 12[39f.] Mt. 24[43f.]), and the similitude with which the Sermon on the Mount concludes. We know that besides several actual parables, this record of Christ's teaching was rich in shorter comparisons and parables in germ. Yet many of the most arresting parables are found either in Matthew alone or in Luke alone (see reference table, p. 915). The source which they used in common seems to have concentrated on the sayings of Jesus rather than on his parables.

The Parables Peculiar to Matthew and Luke. It is generally assumed that Matthew and Luke derived from separate sources the parables which each alone records. But not only may some of these parables peculiar to Matthew or Luke belong to the source they both used, but it is also possible that parables came to either evangelist as detached memories. These stories which Jesus told would easily become separated from any particular context, and yet the stories themselves would not easily be forgotten. It is natural to suppose that stories were remembered and repeated singly, and both the first and the third evangelists may be indebted to many informants. Yet there are certain features of the parables peculiar to each which support the general assumption that the evangelists drew on earlier and distinct collections.

The *parables peculiar to Matthew* will be found to fall mainly into the two great groups which we distinguished in an earlier section. He brought together parables concerning the Kingdom, and he was interested in parables of judgment and warning. The note of moral responsibility is underlined in Matthew. It sounds in the picture of the last judgment, in the wise and foolish virgins, in the unforgiving servant, and in the incident of the man without the wedding garment at the wedding feast. The parables of the two sons and of the laborers in the vineyard would seem to be directed to warning the Jews that in the kingdom of heaven they were being surpassed by the Gentiles. These parables anticipate or reenforce the lesson taught in the parable of the wicked husbandmen.

The *parables peculiar to Luke*, on the other hand, are more varied in character. If the parables of judgment belong to Matthew, the parables of mercy and hope belong to Luke. Yet he too has parables which warn men of dangers and punishments here and hereafter. Many of Luke's parables may be traced to his special source, which Canon Streeter and others now contend must be as early as Mark and the record of the teaching of Jesus which Matthew and Luke used. First among these we must note the prodigal son. This story, though only in Luke, we now trace to one of the earliest sources of our knowledge of the life of Christ. To this parable Easton would add the two debtors (Lk. 7[41-42]), the good Samaritan, Dives and Lazarus, the Pharisee and the publican, and perhaps the unrighteous steward, the unjust judge, and the barren fig-tree.

We may here note two or three features of these parables peculiar to Luke. In the first place they illustrate many different sides of the teaching of Jesus, e.g., prayer, the need of persistence in prayer, the readiness of God to answer prayer, the need of sincere humility in prayer; riches, the poverty of the life which is taken up with the abundance of possessions (the rich fool), the sin of the selfishness which makes wealthy men ignore misery at their very doors (Dives and Lazarus), and the possibility of so using temporal wealth as to gain life eternal (if, indeed, that be the lesson of the original parable of the unrighteous steward); the love of one's neighbor overriding racial antagonisms (the good Samaritan); and the mercy of God in welcoming the penitent (the prodigal son) and postponing judgment on the barren fig-tree. Secondly, some of these parables in Luke strike the note of humor. This is manifest both in the story of the man who disturbs his neighbor at night with his ill-timed request for bread, and also in the story of the guests who made excuses for failing to come to the feast when it was ready. It must be remembered that this parable, according to Luke, was drawn from Jesus by the pious exclamation, "Blessed is he that shall eat bread in the kingdom of God!" Jesus answers, that when the time comes, the invited guests will make any excuse to stay away! Third, it is in Luke's narrative that Jesus appeals to the action of bad men—the unjust judge and the unrighteous steward—to illustrate a truth about God or to point advice to disciples. These examples make quite clear the danger of treating the parables as allegories. God is not like the unjust judge, and Christians are not to be dishonest stewards, though they might well be as farsighted as the man whose shrewdness the Lord commends.

Literature: Of the older books, Bruce, *The Parabolic Teaching of Jesus*, and Trench, *Notes on the Parables*, are worth consulting. Jülicher's great book on *Die Gleichnisreden Jesu* has not been translated into English. It gave the deathblow to the older type of allegorical interpretation. (A good popular book along Jülicher's lines for readers of German is that by Weinel, *Die Gleichnisse Jesu*. Fiebig's two books on the Jewish Rabbinic material, *Altjüdische Gleichnisse und die Gleichnisse Jesu*, and *Die Gleichnisreden Jesu im Lichte der Rabbinischen Gleichnisse des N.T. Zeitalters*, broke new ground and established important qualifications to Jülicher's main thesis.) For English readers, the note on the Parables in Abraham's *Studies in Pharisaism and the Gospels*, First Series, pp. 90–107, gives an admirable account of the Jewish parallels to the gospel-parables. Levison, *The Parables, their Background and Local Setting*, was written by one who was born and brought up in Palestine. A paper by Allen Menzies on *The Art of the Parables*, which appeared in the *Expositor*, July, 1915, and was reprinted in *The Study of Calvin and Other Papers*, is worth reading in this connection. Luccock, *Studies in the Parables of Jesus*, is a fresh and suggestive treatment. For the rest, good commentaries like McNeile or Allen or T. H. Robinson on *Matthew* and Easton or Plummer on *Luke* are as valuable as special works on the parables, and great sermons like those of F. W. Robertson on the Parable of the Sower should not be neglected.

THE MIRACLES OF THE NEW TESTAMENT

By Professor EDWIN LEWIS

The Approach to the Subject. The common custom of approaching the study of the N.T. miracles from the standpoint of a definition of the term "miracle" has not produced very satisfactory results. If it be defined in the popular way as "a violation or suspension of the laws of nature"—a definition not countenanced by any responsible Christian thinker to-day, and having no support in the great theologians of the past, such as Augustine, Anselm, and Thomas Aquinas—then those who believe that such violation or suspension is impossible will necessarily reject all the N.T. miracles. No evidence can substantiate what is already regarded as impossible. On the other hand, those who accept the definition will have no difficulty with the N.T. accounts, for they will regard the separate miracles as simply so many illustrations of the definition. They will, however, be in the unfortunate position of working with a definition which the modern view of the world has rendered utterly untenable. If there is not a "law" of miracle as there is of every other event then miracle will be surrendered by thinking men. This is why a convinced Christian like J. M. Thompson (in his *Miracles of the N.T.*) would entirely exscind from the N.T. the miraculous element while still claiming to retain the supernatural: he considers the evidence in the light of the supposition that the alleged event, being "lawless," could not have happened. Wendland, however, having a much truer philosophical conception of the relation of God and the world, claims that miracle has its own proper law. (See his *Miracles and Christianity*, pp. 3–12.)

As a matter of fact, the definition of "miracle" is not particularly important for a N.T. study. The real question is, "Did Jesus do any or all of the unusual things he is said to have done?" If he did, then miracle, however we define the term, is clearly not impossible. What is at stake, therefore, fundamentally is the substantial accuracy of the record, and that cannot be settled by a philosophical definition of a term.

Miracles as Signs. The "mighty works" of Jesus were regarded both by himself (Mt. 11^{2-6}) and by others (Lk. 7^{16}) as "signs." In his sermon on the Day of Pentecost, Peter stated the case as follows: "Jesus of Nazareth, a man approved of God unto you by mighty works and wonders and signs, which God did by him in the midst of you, even as ye yourselves know" (Acts 2^{22}). The Greek word translated "mighty works" is literally "powers," and in other connections could be rendered "capacities." Jesus—so we might paraphrase it—possessed a divinely given capacity whereby he wrought striking deeds, which were to be taken as signs. Wonders and signs are not separate events: the word "wonders" in the plural is never found in the N.T. except in association with the word "signs" in the plural, although "sign" and "signs" often stand alone. The wonders were in themselves signs.

The central feature of the miracle is therefore to be sought in its *signification.* Jesus "did many signs," as even his enemies admitted (Jn. 11^{47}). But a sign does not stand by itself: it is always a sign *of* something. The miracles of Jesus signified his possession of capacities; they signified that these capacities were of such a character that they must be God-given in a peculiar sense; and they signified that one who possessed these God-given capacities was in himself different from all other men.

As we shall see later, the whole question of N.T. miracle and its credibility depends upon this element of "difference" in Christ himself. (See Garvie, *Handbook of Apologetics*, ch. 3, pt. iii; Illingworth, *The Gospel Miracles*, pp. 40, 41.) The miracles are a "sign" of that difference. *But that very difference is also itself a sign.* It is a sign of the God who sent him, of the God who indwelt him, of the God of whom his whole life was an increasing revelation. Thus he always made the testimony of his miracles secondary to the testimony of his own person. It was, he said, a greater thing to believe in him for his own sake than it was to believe in him because of his "works" (Jn. 12^{44-50} $14^{10, 11}$). When the Pharisees asked for "a sign from heaven," he refused it, and in his ensuing conversation with his disciples he made it plain that neither they nor the Pharisees yet "understood" the truth of himself (Mk. 8^{11-21}). There is a similar allusion to himself and what he signifies in his statement that "a greater than Solomon" and "a greater than Jonah" is here (Lk. 11^{29-32}). His great discourse on the Bread of Life grew out of his realizing how little the people or the disciples understood "the miracle of the loaves." We do not evade the force of the words, "I am the living bread which came down out of heaven: if any man eat of this bread he shall live forever," by simply saying that the words are put into Jesus' mouth by the fourth Evangelist at a late date, for the reason that the words "fit" all that we learn about Jesus in the earlier Gospels. Jesus Christ is the world's greatest miracle because he is the world's greatest "sign," and if we believe in the greatest sign, the lesser signs become at least credible. (See Lewis, *Manual of Christian Beliefs*, pp. 74–76.) The lesser finds its rationale in the fact of the greater. There have always been men who could do things that others could not. We do not minimize their deeds: instead, we call them "gifted" men, meaning that God has done something in them that he has not done in the rest of us. If, then, God was in Jesus Christ as he was in no other human life, then the deeds of Christ were as "natural" to him—he being as he was—as our deeds are to us—we being as we are.

Place of Miracle in the Gospel Records. Miracles filled a much larger place in the ministry of Jesus than the records at first sight suggest. The four Gospels give an account of some thirty-five miracles performed by Jesus. Some of these are described at length, e.g., the relief of the Gadarene demoniacs (Mt. 8^{28-34}; parallel references here and elsewhere are omitted, except when there are important differences in the account); the raising of Jairus' daughter (Mt. $9^{18, 19, 23-26}$ Mk. $5^{21-24, 35-43}$); the feeding of the five thousand (Mt. 14^{13-21}); and especially the four miracles peculiar to the fourth Gospel, namely, the miracle of the wine at Cana (2^{1-11}), the healing of the impotent man at the pool of Bethesda (5^{1-18}), the healing of the blind man at Jerusalem (9^{1-41}), and the raising of Lazarus (11^{17-44}). In the case of other miracles there is often little more than the bare mention of the fact, e.g., the cure of Peter's mother-in-law (Mt. $8^{14, 15}$), of the dumb man (Mt. $9^{32, 33}$), of "certain women" (Lk. 8^{2}), and of one possessed, blind, and dumb (Mt. 12^{22}).

But there were also a great number of miracles of which we have no description at all. The significance of this fact may very easily be overlooked. Time and time again we meet a merely general statement that Jesus healed "all manner of disease and sickness," and that the people brought to him "all that were sick, holden with divers diseases and torments, possessed with devils, and epileptic, and palsied, and he healed them" (Mt. $4^{23, 24}$); and that those who "had plagues pressed upon him" because already "he had healed many" (Mk. 3^{10}); and that, at Peter's house, "they brought unto him many possessed of devils; and he cast out the spirits with a word, and healed all that were sick" (Mt. 8^{16} Mk. 1^{32-34} Lk. $4^{40, 41}$); and that "Jesus went about all the cities and villages teaching . . . and preaching . . . and healing all manner of disease and all manner of sickness" (Mt. 9^{35}); and that at Gennesaret they brought unto him "all that were sick" to be "made whole" (Mt. $14^{35, 36}$ Mk. 6^{53-56}); and that he healed "the lame, blind, dumb, and many others" (Mt. 15^{30}); and that "a great number" came from Judæa and Jerusalem, and Tyre and Sidon, "to be healed of their diseases" (Lk. $6^{17, 18}$). When two of John's disciples came to interview Jesus, we are told that "in that hour he cured many of diseases and plagues and evil spirits, and on many that were blind he bestowed sight" (Lk. 7^{21}); and a little later Luke tells us again that "them that had need of healing he healed" (9^{11}). John refers to "the signs which Jesus did on them that were sick" (6^{2}), and toward the end of his record declares that he has left untold "many other signs" (20^{30}).

Such a wealth of allusion would seem to make clear three facts, namely, that Jesus must have exercised himself in his healing ministry far more than a mere surface reading of the records would suggest; that the Evangelists practiced a remarkable reserve in their reports of the mighty works; and that the case for at least the miraculous cures does not rest upon the comparatively small number which are described, but upon what must have been literally hundreds wrought on people in all parts of Palestine.

This manifest reserve of the Evangelists indicates that they were not nearly the credulous men that rationalistic critics have been wont to allege. (See Strauss, *Life of Jesus*, and Renan, *Life of Jesus*, both in Eng. trans., and cf. notes in Hurst, *History of Rationalism*, pp. 259–267, 404–407.) Confronted as they were with an overwhelming abundance of material, they selected for description only the most meager amount. So far from letting their imagination run wild, they appear to have exercised a most remarkable restraint. Striking deeds naturally make a deeper impression on the mind than sayings and teachings, and are more easily remembered, yet the Evangelists give much less space to the former than to the latter. Think of all the possibilities of graphic description that lie latent in the bare statement, "He healed all that were sick" (Mt. 8^{16}). No wonder that John says that "the world itself would not contain the books" if all had been written that might have been (21^{25}).

A Record of Typical Cases. What the Evangelists have done for the most part is simply to record typical cases. The healing of the demoniac in the synagogue at Capernaum (Mk. 1[23-27]) is but a specific example of the numerous deeds only alluded to in Mt. 8[16]. According to Matthew, Jesus on his return from Tyre and Sidon "healed many" (15[29-31]), but he gives no details. Out of all that number Mark selects for description the cure of "one that was deaf, and had an impediment in his speech" (7[31-35]). The Evangelists are fond of saying that healing came to many as they "touched" Jesus (see Mt. 14[36] Mk. 6[56] Lk. 6[19]). Yet there is only one detailed example of healing power going forth from Jesus as he was touched, namely, the woman with the hemorrhage (Mt. 9[20-23]). He healed many who were blind, but there are described for us only the recovery of the two blind men in the neighborhood of Capernaum (Mt. 9[27-30]), of the two blind men of Jericho (Mt. 20[29-34], given as of one man, Bartimæus, in Mk. 10[46-52] and Lk. 18[35-43]), of the blind man of Bethsaida (Mk. 8[22-26]), and of the blind man of Jerusalem who was sent to wash in Siloam (Jn. 9[1-41]). The Evangelists could easily be shown to have followed the same method with regard to the record of the cure of other forms of disease.

Some of the miracles of Jesus, however, were either unique or performed only rarely. Only once is he said to have walked on the sea (Mt. 14[22-33] and parallels), and only once to have stilled the tempest (Mt. 8[23-27] and parallels). Only twice is he said to have fed the multitude in a miraculous way, first the five thousand, "besides women and children" (Mt. 14[13-21] and parallels, this being the only miracle recorded in all four Gospels), and later the four thousand (Mk. 8[1-8]; the addition, "besides women and children," being made in Mt. 15[38]). Some suppose that these are two different accounts of the same event, but Matthew and Mark could not have thought so, as each narrates them both, and each quotes Jesus as referring to them as two separate events (Mt. 16[9, 10] Mk. 8[19, 20]). Only three times is Jesus reported to have raised the dead, namely, the daughter of Jairus (Mt. 9[18, 19, 23-26]), the son of the widow of Nain (Lk. 7[11-16]), and Lazarus (Jn. 11). It is true that he is said to have instructed his disciples to "raise the dead" (Mt. 10[8]), and that he spoke of the raising of the dead to John's disciples (Mt. 11[4, 5]), but the latter allusion may very well have been to Jairus' daughter or to the young man of Nain, both of which events are given as preceding the time of the visit from John's disciples.

Rationalistic Explanation and Its Limitations. The work of J. M. Thompson (*op. cit.*) is a good example of an attempt to find a rationalistic explanation of the record of each alleged miracle. But such attempts still leave us with the problem of the miracle that is left undescribed. Suppose that a given mighty work did not take place in exactly the way described, or suppose that the account involves an exaggeration or a misunderstanding of an event not unusual in itself (Thompson, *op. cit.*, pp. 207–209; Pfleiderer, *Early Christian Conception of Christ*, ch. 3), that does not necessarily mean that the entire miraculous element in the gospel record is discredited. If Jesus performed mighty works at all, then exaggeration and misunderstanding here and there would be perfectly natural. To say, however, that *everything* is exaggerated or misunderstood when, as shown above, we are dealing with many hundreds of cases, is simply dogmatism.

It is undoubtedly possible to put an interrogation point after some of the accounts. Even scholars regarded as conservative feel compelled to do this. (Cf. Sanday, *Outlines of the Life of Christ*, §§39–44, and *Life of Christ in Recent Research*, pp. 102–104; Nolloth, *Rise of the Christian Religion*, p. 142, where he speaks of "disparities of evidence"; Denney, *Jesus and the Gospel*, second edit., pp. 144–146, who writes "there does seem something which is not only incongruous but repellent in the idea of the risen Lord eating"; Garvie, *Christian Doctrine of the Godhead*, pp. 69, 70; and Tillett, *Paths That Lead to God*, pp. 354, 355.) E.g., considering how suddenly storms arise and subside on the Sea of Galilee, the alleged stilling of the tempest may have been a mere coincidence. The walking *on* the water may have been in reality walking *by* the water or *through* the shoals. The recovery of the centurion's servant ("son" according to Jn. 4[46]), Jesus being at a distance and not even seeing him, may have been due to a favorable crisis which would have occurred in any case. The story of the coin in the fish's mouth whereby Jesus paid the temple tax (Mt. 17[24-27]) may very easily have originated in a command (Garvie says "a playful command," *op. cit.*, p. 69) to Peter to catch and sell some fish to obtain the necessary money. Many feel that the blasting of the fig-tree (Mt. 21[18–22]) is so out of keeping with Jesus' character and so irrelevant to the lesson he was said to teach thereby, that they are inclined to regard it either as originally a parable (cf. Lk. 13[6-9]; David Smith says "an acted parable," *Days of His Flesh*, p. 395), or as the result of confusion with some other event (the view of Deissmann in *The Religion of Jesus and the*

Faith of Paul, pp. 98–100). On the other hand, it may be said that Jesus, in keeping with his principle that a man was better than swine (Mk. 5^{1-17}) or sheep (Mt. 12^{12}) or institutions (Mt. 12^{1-8}), may have felt that the destruction of a fig-tree was a small price to pay for making dramatic to his disciples the nature and the conditions of the fruitful life. (Cf. Dougall and Emmet, *The Lord of Thought*, ch. 11; Lewis, *Jesus Christ and the Human Quest*, pp. 111, 112; Glover, *Jesus in the Experience of Men*, pp. 217–220.) No miraculous element is needed in the case of the great draughts of fish, either when Jesus first called his disciples (Lk. 5^{4-10}) or at the time of the closing interview (Jn. 21^{4-11}).

Some would like to feel that there was a "natural" explanation of the three stories of *the raising of the dead*. That neither of the persons concerned was actually dead is, of course, a possibility. Thus E. R. Micklem writes: "In the eyes of a twentieth-century practitioner a person who has been 'restored to life' *eo ipso* can never have died, and, however assured prior to the re-animation a doctor may have been that death had taken place, after that re-animation he would indubitably claim that he had been mistaken in his previous diagnosis" (*Miracles and the New Psychology*, pp. 128, 129, published by the Oxford University Press). In spite of Jairus' own fear (Mt. 9^{18}) and the message of the servants (Mk. 5^{35} Lk. 8^{49}), it may be that Jesus' words, "She is not dead, but sleepeth," are to be taken literally. In considering the case of Lazarus, we have to remember, first, that only John narrates the incident—as against three narrators for the incident of Jairus' daughter—and it is hard to see why the other Evangelists should have ignored so stupendous a deed; second, that John is writing some three quarters of a century at least after the event—an event of which we have no intimation in the intervening period; and third, that the fourth Gospel is admittedly highly symbolical and allegorical (see intro. there), which makes it not impossible that the terms "death" and "life" and "resurrection" in the account are to be understood in the spiritual sense so characteristic of the fourth Gospel. But even if this should be so, we still have the case of the young man of Nain, and there is nothing at all here to suggest any other than the obvious interpretation. If either of the three accounts is to be taken literally, then there is no reason why all should not be.

But the frankest recognition of all these facts and possibilities may be made and still the conviction remain that the evidence is overwhelming that Jesus wrought miracles. It can hardly be said that Christian scholarship has definitely abandoned the miracles of the N.T. when they are more or less accepted by such outstanding scholars and thinkers as Sanday, Gore, Garvie, Tennant, Headlam, Wendland, Griffith-Jones, H. R. Mackintosh, Henry Bett, Herrmann, J. A. Faulkner, Bowne, Peake, Von Hügel, Ramsay, Ménégoz, Sabatier, Streeter, R. Seeberg, W. R. Matthews, Galloway, Wobbermin, and Inge—and one could go on lengthening the list almost indefinitely. Few of these men would accept them all just as they stand, but it is the poorest kind of reasoning to say that if Jesus did not do *all* the mighty works he is said to have done therefore he did not do *any* of them. With much greater logical right we could say that if one single incident is authentic, then the *miracle-principle* is established, and we are justified in approaching all the other incidents at least without a bias against them. If we raise a question here and there, it will be either because of the uncertainty of the evidence, or because of some intrinsic difficulty felt to be in the alleged fact itself.

The Technique of the Miracles. Any discussion of the question of what might be called the technique of the miracles of Jesus must bear in mind that details of description are not to be pressed too hard; that the records of the same miracle sometimes differ as to its method; and that in such an event as that of the feeding of the five thousand the method throws no light whatever on the event itself.

The records show considerable variety in the technique or method of the miracles. Sometimes Jesus merely speaks the word, as when he "rebuked the winds and the sea" (Mt. 8^{26} Lk. 8^{24}), saying, as Mark alone reports, "Peace, be still" (4^{39}); or, as when he said to the fig-tree (but cf. the discussion above), "No man eat fruit from thee henceforward forever" (Mk. 11^{14}). Once he is reported simply to have touched the sufferer without addressing him at all, namely, the servant of the high-priest whose ear Peter cut off (Lk. 22^{51}). The healing, however, is not reported by Matthew ($26^{51f.}$) or John ($18^{10, 11}$), only the attack. Sometimes it suffices that he be simply touched, as with the woman with the hemorrhage, who would but "touch the hem of his garment" (Mk. 5^{28}); and there were other occasions when "as many as touched him were made whole" (Mk. 6^{56}), and when "all the multitude sought to touch him: for power came forth from him, and healed them all" (Lk. 6^{19}). Sometimes he both touches the sufferer and speaks some words—this, indeed, is quite common. Thus he "touched the hand" of Peter's mother-in-law, Luke alone adding that "he rebuked the fever" (4:39); Jairus' daughter he both touched and addressed (Mk. 5:41 Lk. 8:54; but cf. Mt. 9:25 where there is no mention of any words), and this was his method on both occasions with two blind men (Mt. 9:29 20:32-34), as it was with the woman who was "bowed together" (Lk. 13:11-13). In the case of the leper the touching was no doubt as deliberate as it was impressive. A leper was "untouchable," not only legally (Lev. 13:46), but by a natural human revulsion. The leper upon whom Jesus laid his hands (Mt. 8:3) probably felt at that moment the first friendly human touch he had known in many years, and the effect on him must have been overwhelming. One feels here the force of the closing words in Micklem's little book on miracles: "In conclusion it should be observed that the performance of the most amazing marvels is not to be compared spiritually and morally with the act of one who, in a land where ritual uncleanness was held the direst of crimes, voluntarily touches a 'leper' and speaks with kindness in the presence of a crowd to an 'unclean' woman who publicly confesses to have touched him" (*op. cit.*, p. 136). Again, there is sometimes a careful preparation of the sufferer for what is to come. This is so in the case of the man sick with the palsy (Lk. 5:18-26), blind Bartimæus near Jericho (Mk. 10:46-52), and the impotent man at the pool of Bethesda (Jn. 5:2-9).

The most striking example of this latter method, however, is where Jesus makes a concession to popular belief as to how disease may be cured, apparently for the sake of arousing the expectation of the sufferer, and even of the bystander. Thus he "anointed" the eyes of one blind with clay made from spittle (Jn. 9:6); for another blind man he used spittle only, and "laid his hands upon him," and later "laid his hands upon his eyes" (Mk. 8:22-25); and when he cured one who was both deaf and a stutterer, "he took him aside privately, and put his fingers into his ears, and he spat, and touched his tongue; and looking up to heaven, he sighed, and saith unto him, Ephphatha, that is, Be opened. And his ears were opened, and the bond of his tongue was loosed, and he spake plain" (Mk. 7:33-35). There was a popular belief that spittle had curative power (Edersheim, *Life and Times of Jesus*, bk. iii, ch. 34, parag. 2). It is not likely that Jesus shared the belief, but he utilized it for his own purposes. In the same way he went through an elaborate process of exorcising demons, as when, at Capernaum, he directly addressed the "spirit of an unclean demon" with the words, "Hold thy peace, and come out of him" (Lk. 4:33-35); or as when he carried on a conversation with the "Legion" of demons and then sent them into the herd of swine (Mk. 5:5-13); or as when, after the Transfiguration, he "rebuked" (Mt. 17:18) the demon in the epileptic boy, using, according to Mark, the words, "Thou dumb and deaf spirit, I command thee, come out of him, and enter no more into him" (9:25). The common phrase, "casting out demons," suggests the apparent use of effort. We need not inquire whether Jesus shared the popular belief in demon-possession: whether he did or not, the method had ample psychological justification, since the poor victim himself had no doubt at all that he was "possessed" and needed deliverance. (Cf. the chapter on "The War With the Demons," in Glover, *Jesus in the Experience of Men.*) This attempt to win the confidence and co-operation of the sufferer is, indeed, a general characteristic of Jesus' method. It is illustrated again when he said to the man with the withered hand, "Stretch forth thy hand" (Mt. 12:13), Mark and Luke adding that he first of all told the man to "stand forth"; and when he pronounced forgiveness for the palsied man before healing him (Mt. 9:2); and when he asked the impotent man if he would be made whole, before saying to him, "Arise, take up thy bed, and walk" (Jn. 5:2-9); and when he told the ten lepers to go and show themselves to the priests, although the leprosy was still on them when they started (Lk. 17:14).

Faith a Usual but not Invariable Condition. What Jesus was evidently trying to do in such cases as the foregoing was to induce an appropriate psychic state. This is usually called "faith," and the lack of it in the people of Nazareth is given as a reason why he could do there "no mighty work" (Mk. 6:5; see also Micklem, *op. cit.*, pp. 132–134.) Power was with him to heal (Lk. 5:17), but he required both faith and expectancy in the sufferer: "According to your faith be it done unto you" (Mt. 9:29). But faith is not invariably present as a subjective condition. It was obviously impossible in the case of those who were raised from the dead (and this would still be true even though they were only "as dead"), or in the case of those who were healed at a distance, i.e., the centurion's servant, and the little daughter of the Syrophœnician woman (Mk. 7:30). The healing was, indeed, a response to the centurion's faith and to the mother's faith, but that only complicates the problem psychologically: how can the faith of one avail for another?

Miracle not Explainable by Faith Alone. What has just been said about the place of faith has no bearing on the so-called nature-miracles. For this reason, some, like Arnold and Harnack, reject the nature-miracles entirely, although they are willing to accept the accounts of some of the healings. Even J. M. Thompson writes: "The evidence for works of healing is good evidence, but it is not evidence for miracles" (*op. cit.*, p. 41). No hypothesis of the power of faith suffices to explain the feeding of the five thousand, or the restorations to life, or the walking on the water. Such incidents become intelligible to us only on the condition that we assign a unique character to Christ's own person. And when we do that, the healings also cease to be a problem.

For the supposition that we can reduce Jesus to a purely human figure and still retain the healing miracles because they are psychologically explainable, cannot be maintained. Nothing that we know *yet* about psychology justifies us in explaining by its help the cure of leprosy, or the granting of sight to one born blind, or the sudden straightening of a woman who had been "bowed together" for eighteen years. And even if some of the healing miracles are being duplicated to-day by the application of psychological laws, we have still to remember that Jesus lived some two thousand years ago, among a people simple and superstitious, and that his anticipation of modern psychic therapeutics—supposing it to be that—is itself a "miracle" needing to be explained.

But why, instead of so much theorizing about the matter, are we not willing to fall back upon the simple expedient of adopting Jesus' own explanation of his mighty works, namely, *that he did them by virtue of a delegated power?* He nowhere appears as merely a skilled psychiatrist. As we saw above, he occasionally "staged" a cure, but the general characteristic of his healing ministry is its perfect *spontaneity.* His miracles, one might say, were "natural" to him. There is nowhere the least hint of the long-drawn-out processes of the modern psychic healer. "He spake, and it was done." Luke says that "the power of the Lord was with him to heal" (5[17]). When critics intimated that the power was from "Beelzebub," Jesus refuted them by the very nature of the case. How could good be done by evil? He declared it was blasphemy to ascribe to Satan what so manifestly was done "by the Spirit of God" (Mt. 12[28]; Luke in 11[20] says, "by the finger of God"). We do well not to fall into a like condemnation by our sedulous efforts to bring all that Jesus did under our own limited naturalistic categories! We admit the force of the naïve logic of the man born blind—that he who had restored his sight must have come "from God" (Jn. 9[33]; cf. 3[2]).

Miracles of the Disciples. The Evangelists report Jesus as having given to his disciples a like power to that which he himself possessed —"authority over unclean spirits, to cast them out, and to heal all manner of disease, and all manner of sickness" (Mt. 10[1]; and in 10[8] "Heal the sick, raise the dead, cleanse the lepers, cast out demons"). Mark, however, limits the power of the disciples to casting out demons (3[15] 6[7], but cf. the commission in the appendix, 16[17, 18]). Both Mark (6[13]) and Luke (10[17]) report the *success* of the disciples in casting out demons and healing the sick. There is, however, no statement in the *Gospels* that the disciples raised the dead. That Jesus gave them power for this is, in fact, reported only by Matthew.

Yet there is ample evidence that Jesus did not regard the power to work miracles as the most important part of the disciples' commission. "Howbeit in this rejoice not, that the spirits are subject unto you; but rejoice that your names are written in heaven" (Lk. 10[20]). When the disciples would have called down fire from heaven upon the inhospitable Samaritans, Jesus "rebuked" them for mistaken zeal (Lk. 9[51-55]). It is suggestive that in the three accounts we have of the Last Commission, only the least authentic of them—that in the appendix to Mark (16[17, 18])—says anything about performing miracles, and this may be an echo of Lk. 10[19]. In both Matthew and Luke the emphasis is on "teaching" and "witnessing." Luke, however, gives a significant addition: the disciples are to tarry in Jerusalem until they are "clothed with power from on high" (24[49]). This is hardly the power they possessed already, but a new power, moral and spiritual, greater than was given them when they first went forth to preach (Mt. 10[1]). It is suggestive that in his list of desirable "gifts," Paul puts miracles and healings in respectively the fourth and fifth places (1 Cor. 12[28]; cf. 14[18, 19]).

This implication of the incidental place of miracle in the future work of the disciples is supported by the fourth Gospel, with its great theme of "the abiding presence" (Mt. 28[20]). Of the thirty-five or more miracles described in the Gospels, John reports only seven. Three of these—walking on the water, feeding the multitude, and healing the centurion's son—are told by others. Four are peculiar to John, namely, the wine at Cana, the impotent man at Bethesda, the man born blind, and the raising of Lazarus (see above), and it is a striking fact that each of these four is susceptible of a symbolic and spiritualistic interpretation. However that may be, John, although he knows that there were plenty of "signs" (see 6[2] 20[30]), does not emphasize the miracle feature of Christ's ministry. The clue to his attitude is in the reference to "greater works" (14^{12}) to be done by the disciples than had been done even by their Lord. This can hardly mean "greater miracles," if we take miracle in the accustomed sense. It must mean, rather, all those triumphs of the disciples in the coming years which would be possible because of the new power that was to recompense the loss of their Lord's bodily presence (Jn. 14, 15, 16).

Miracles in the Acts of the Apostles. Taking as they stand the miracles recorded in Acts, we may classify them as follows: (1) Those which are obviously a continuation of the miracles ascribed to the disciples in the Gospels. (2) Those of which the apostles are themselves the subjects. (3) Those which belong purely in the realm of "spiritual experience"—the "greater works" of Jn. 14^{12}.

In *the first group* we include the healing of the lame man at the Gate Beautiful (3^{1-10}); the deaths of Ananias and Sapphira (5^{1-11}); the healing of the palsied Æneas (9^{32-35}); the raising of Dorcas (9^{36-42}); the infliction of blindness on Elymas the sorcerer (13^{6-12}); the healing of the cripple at Lystra (14^{8-10}); the change wrought in the divining maid at Philippi (16^{16-18}); and the healing of the father of Publius (28^{8}). It should be observed that of the original Twelve only Peter is described as having wrought any of these miracles. James did nothing in Acts 3; Paul was not one of the Twelve; and the Philip of $8^{6,\ 7}$ is not the disciple chosen by Jesus, but Philip the "deacon" (6^{5}). Another of the deacons also "wrought signs" (6^{8}). The miracles just referred to, however, are by no means exhaustive. We may count out the apparent raising of Eutychus on the ground that the fall had not actually killed him—"his life is in him," said Paul (20^{7-12})—as we may Paul's escape of ill effects from the viper on the ground that there is no clear evidence that the creature was venomous (28^{3-6}). But we have in Acts what we have in the Gospels—references to a great many miracles of which we have no detailed description. Thus we read that "many wonders and signs were done by the apostles" (2^{43} 5^{12}). "Sick folk and them that were vexed with unclean spirits" were brought to Peter, that "at least his shadow" might fall on them, and "they were healed every one" ($6^{15,\ 16}$). In the city of Samaria, Philip released the possessed and "healed many that were palsied and that were lame" ($8^{6,\ 7}$). At Corinth, "God wrought special miracles by the hand of Paul: insomuch that unto the sick were carried away from his body handkerchiefs or aprons, and the diseases departed from them, and the evil spirits went out" ($19^{11,\ 12}$). It may be to this that Paul alludes in 2 Cor. 12^{12}. And after the healing of the father of Publius, "the rest also which had diseases in the island came, and were cured" (28^{9}).

Undoubtedly, many of the apostolic miracles are susceptible of a "psychological" explanation, especially those involving the "shadow" and "handkerchiefs." The problem with the lame man at the Gate Beautiful may have been to induce him to do what already he was able to do, except that he either would not do it or did not believe it to be possible. But why should the man's sudden release from the domination of a "fixed idea" not be regarded as "a sign and wonder"? Many find a real difficulty in the story of Ananias and Sapphira. The narrative seems to imply on someone's part an almost brutal severity (cf. pp, 132b, 890). That the guilty pair should be excluded from the Christian community is credible, but not that they should have been "struck dead." For this was a community of brotherly love, and it is hard to believe that a member of it should suddenly have died and forthwith been buried, and that his wife, when she appeared, instead of being gently told of her husband's tragic death, should have been questioned, and so severely rebuked that she also died. This is not in keeping with Christ's counsel for such a case in Mt. 18^{15-17}, or Paul's in Gal. 6^{1}. One would like to believe that what we have in this case was originally a moral discipline such as Christ commanded—"Let him be unto thee as a heathen man and a publican"—which through continued retelling underwent exaggeration. (On the Jewish custom of excommunication, or "casting out of the synagogue," which in severe cases took the form of treating the guilty person "like one dead," see Edersheim, *Life and Times of Jesus*, bk. iv, ch. 9, pp. 183, 184.) The raising of Dorcas also presents a problem for many. It is the only detailed description in the N.T. of a *disciple* performing such a miracle (see above as to Paul and Eutychus). The narrative itself is, however, perfectly explicit. The real difficulty, of course, is with *the nature of the fact itself*, complicated as it is by being assigned to a purely human instrument. A person might feel that he could believe that Christ raised Lazarus without having to believe that Peter raised Dorcas. It must be largely a question of individual attitude, determined as that will be partly by the philosophical outlook and partly by the evaluation of the evidence. One may render an adverse judgment here, and still be convinced that "wonders and signs" characterized apostolic Christianity.

The second group of apostolic miracles comprise the deliverances from prison—incidents, that is, of which the apostles were themselves the subjects. We have no details as to the first deliverance, not even the names of those who were imprisoned (5^{17-23}). We are simply told that "an angel of the Lord by night opened the prison doors, and brought them out." The second imprisonment was of Peter alone, and there is a detailed account of his escape (12^{5-11}). In both cases, the instrument of deliverance is said to be an "angel." An angel is ordinarily supposed to be a supernatural being. The original of the word, however, in both Hebrew and Greek, means "messenger," and the supernatural connotation, while ordinarily present, is not invariably so. Thus, in the story of Abraham, the messengers who declared to him God's purpose concerning Sodom are called "men" (Gen. $18^{2, 16}$) and also "angels" ($19^{1, 15}$), but all their actions are clearly those of human beings. So also in the accounts of the resurrection, Matthew and John say "angels" were there; Mark and Luke say men. It is, therefore, not impossible that the "angel" of the deliverances was a friend of the apostles, connected with the prisons, who was willing to risk his life for their sake. We are to remember that the source of the second account must have been Peter himself, and he was so dazed by what was going on that it was not until he was outside the prison, and alone, that he "came to himself" and *then* exclaimed, "It must have been an angel" (12^{11}). The escape would be just as much a "sign" to Peter if it were made possible by human means as it would be if the instruments were purely supernatural—perhaps more so, considering the possibilities of detection and failure. Certainly it would be so on Wendland's principle that "striking events, of religious significance for our whole life, we may call miracles" (*Miracles and Christianity*, p. 163), and that "divine providences" may be likewise designated (p. 170). As to the experience of the apostles at Philippi, there is no suggestion in the record that "the great earthquake" which shook the prison and loosed the chains of Paul and Silas is to be regarded as of supernatural origin ($16^{25f.}$). All the prisoners were similarly affected (v. 26), and there was no attempt on the part of Paul and Silas to escape. The experience did, indeed, result in the conversion of the jailer and "all his." In that sense it may be included, with the two earlier deliverances, in those "providential happenings" which, to quote Wendland again, befall the believer who has the "assured feeling that round about him are the everlasting arms" (p. 178).

In *the third group* of apostolic miracles are those "greater works" which involve unusual religious experience. Here we include such events as the descent of the Spirit on the Day of Pentecost (2^{1-21}); the coincident visions of Cornelius and Peter (10^{1}–11^{18}); the appearance of Christ to Saul of Tarsus (9^{1-22}); and all those other indications that the life of the young church was the special organ of the Spirit of God.

There are two phases to the Pentecost experience—the coming of the Spirit, and the gift of new speech. From the standpoint of the needs of the Christian cause, the first was much the more important, and it is certainly the more intelligible to us. As it now stands, the account of the differing tongues spoken simultaneously by unlettered men is utterly inexplicable to us. Any attempted explanation of what happened is, of course, open to the charge of rationalism. But we may at least surmise that the foreign-born Jews who were at Jerusalem for the Feast of Pentecost were all familiar with the Greek language, which was then practically universal (see art., *Language of N.T.*, p. 881a); that Peter and the others spoke in Greek in their first outburst of enthusiasm; and that what amazed the listeners was just this fact that men who seemed to be unlettered Galilæan fishermen should discourse eloquently in Greek. The language of Palestine was Aramaic, and Angus, discussing this fact, infers from Acts 21^{40} and 22^{2} that "even in Jerusalem the people understood Aramaic better than Greek" (*Environment of Early Christianity*, section in ch. 8 on "Greek in Palestine"), and he quotes Schürer to the effect that "the lower classes in Palestine had only a scant acquaintance with Greek" (p. 217). Inasmuch, however, as Palestine was, after all, though only to a limited extent, bilingual, it was not impossible that the disciples should know Greek. Certainly what happened was not "the gift of tongues" of which we read elsewhere in the N.T., for "tongues" required an interpretation, which was one reason for Paul's low estimate of the gift (1 Cor. 14^{1-19}), whereas those who heard the apostles at Pentecost *understood what was said.* In any event, it remains that the significant aspect of the experience was *the empowerment of the apostles.* This was "the promise of the Father." This is what made them into flaming evangels. This is what added the final touch to their conviction, first engendered by the Resurrection, that "this Jesus, whom ye crucified, God hath made both Lord and Christ" (2^{36}). And this is the "sign" which may be duplicated in every age, and by which men may be made to hear and understand "the wonderful works of God."

There can be no good reason for not regarding the visions of Cornelius and Peter as true examples of divine leading, not to be brought under a purely naturalistic category, but "due to directly creative divine action" (Wendland, *op. cit.*, p. 15). There was a real danger that Christianity would become a mere sect of Judaism. Cornelius the Gentile was made ready by his vision to become a Christian, and Peter the Jew was made ready by his to receive him. The preparation of both was equally necessary, and their common feeling that it was due to the Divine Spirit is one that any Christian ought to be glad to share. One of the vital tests of modern Christianity is whether it can carry out the spirit of these visions, especially of Peter's.

Similar reflections are justified by the conversion of Paul (Saul of Tarsus), and the method of it. The variations in the four or five accounts are incidental. What is important is that Paul's opposition to Christ was broken down, and Paul attributed this collapse to the direct action of Christ himself. Undoubtedly Paul's conversion had been prepared for. His fiery zeal against "this way" may have been but a cloak for a conviction which first seized him at the martyrdom of Stephen (see Stalker, *Life of Paul*, ch. 2, closing paragraphs). But Paul never doubted that Christ laid his hand upon him in a supernatural way at Damascus. It was a "sign" wrought by the risen and glorified Lord, and when one considers all that issued from it, no "sign" of the earthly Jesus is more impressive, or more truly illustrative of the action of the divine.

These are simply examples of the presence and activity in the world of a new power, the historical bases of which were the life and work of Jesus of Nazareth. "The Acts of the Apostles" is the story of how Christ through the Spirit entered more and more fully into the life of men. The breaking of the divine into the human is here set forth as historical fact, and the ongoing life of the church is but confirmatory evidence thereof. This fact has still to be faced by those who repudiate the thought of a "transcendent" God who can do a "new" thing in an "orderly" way. It is a "greater work" to remake human characters than to restore withered limbs, and the indubitable fact that Christ does the first makes it credible that he did the second.

The Miracle of Christ Himself. It was said before that Christ is himself a "sign" as much as any of his mighty works. The problem of the miracles of the N.T. is in the end the problem of who and what he was. If one sees in Jesus Christ simply a Galilæan peasant of unusual religious insight, then one will naturally question the accounts of his miraculous deeds, except, perhaps, a few of the healings. It will be useless for those who accept this view of Christ to plead that they reject the miracles because of the inadequacy of the evidence—which was Hume's position. It is *the thing itself*, and not the evidence, which is the real stumbling-block of the skeptic. Miracles simply "do not happen," and that settles it. But if miracles do not happen, then there could not be such a person as Christ is represented to be, for he is himself the supreme miracle, beside which the greatest of his works appears as insignificant. The Christ of the N.T. cannot be explained on a purely naturalistic basis without doing violence not alone to the records but to historical Christian experience. Admit *him*, and the works ascribed to him take on verisimilitude, for they are just the kind of works that such a person may be expected to accomplish. (See Illingworth, *Gospel Miracles*, ch. 3.) If in Jesus Christ God made a manifestation of himself such as he has made nowhere else, then we may expect uniqueness of action to go with the uniqueness of personality. "For if," says Illingworth, "a new force entered human nature with the advent of Jesus Christ, we should antecedently expect that it would manifest itself in unfamiliar ways, ways which could not be judged by any criterion drawn merely from our experience of ordinary life" (p. 41). It is difficult to see anything unreasonable in such a statement.

Have we, then, this uniqueness of personality? The question whether we have or not is largely a question of his total significance for mankind's religious needs. That is something not to be settled merely by documentary assertions. It is true that we need the documents to begin with, but in the end they must be supported by personal experience. Did Jesus Christ bring into the world a new sense of God? Did there stream forth from him a new moral power? Did he teach men the secret of a transformed life? Did he make possible a faith in God's love which nothing could disturb? Did he act as a mediator between God and man to bring about their reconciliation? The N.T. says that to do this was why he came, and we have the confirmatory testimony of the intervening ages. He actually does what he is said to have come to do. The fact establishes him as the world's Saviour. The conclusion is irresistible that there is a divine quality to him such as we find in no other man. Granting that divine quality, and all we need for the miracles is sufficient evidence. The deeds of Christ are congruous with his character, his mission, and his religious significance. One who takes this position does not thereby surrender the right of documentary criticism, but his criticism will not be divorced from the main fact, namely, that "God was in Christ."

The Resurrection of Christ. The modern critical theory of the structure of the Gospels makes it impossible to settle the question of the Resurrection solely by the documentary evidence (see art., *Structure of the Synoptic Gospels,* p. 867). Precisely what happened during the days that followed the Crucifixion we shall probably never know. The one certain thing is the change—the radical change—that took place in the attitude of the disciples. They account for it by declaring that the Lord whom they had seen crucified and buried had since "appeared" to them, and convinced them that he was victor over even the grave. Is that credible? It is easy enough to make out a case against it by pointing out the discrepancies and inconsistencies in the narratives. In Matthew, Jesus appears to the two Marys near the tomb, and then later to the eleven in Galilee (28$^{8-10, 16}$). In Mark, he appears to Mary Magdalene, to two disciples walking in the country, and to the eleven, and neither appearance is located (16$^{9, 12, 14}$). In Luke he appears to the two disciples on the way to Emmaus, to Peter, and to the eleven, the second and third appearances being in Jerusalem (24$^{13-36}$). In John he appears to Mary Magdalene near the tomb, to the disciples (excepting Thomas) the same day in, apparently, Jerusalem, to the eleven (including Thomas) eight days later at an unnamed place, and to seven by the Sea of Tiberias (20$^{11-29}$ 21). There are other differences, e.g., the earthquake (given in Matthew only), the number of angels (Matthew one, John two; Mark one young man, Luke two men), and the number of women who were first at the tomb; and there is the "crudity" (Denney, see above) of the Risen Christ eating. Just what happened, and how, is largely a matter of inference, but unless something *had* happened, unusual, dramatic, overpowering, it is certain there would have been no Christian religion. "With what body he came"—where the line is which divides the "literal" from the "spiritual" in the narratives—in what sense there were conversations between disciples and Master—by what psychological processes the disciples "saw" the Lord—who shall say? We are moving here in the realm of the supernatural, and human language, forged out of contact with the natural, goes haltingly.

Perhaps we shall find our best clue in Paul. After stating the historic evidence of the Resurrection, Paul adds the significant words: "Last of all, as unto one born out of due time, he appeared to me also" (1 Cor. 15^{8}). How did Christ appear to Paul near Damascus? Certainly not under a physical form, yet in such a way as to leave the erstwhile persecutor absolutely certain of the fact that Jesus was Risen and Glorified Lord. In respect of *result,* the appearance to Paul and to the earlier disciples was identical. It is therefore not impossible that it was also identical in respect of *method.* And it is still true that the significant thing for Christians at this point is not agreement as to the method, but *certainty concerning the fact that Christ was not "holden of death," but still lives and works and forever shall.* Such certainty properly involves the supernatural element.

Light on the Apostolic Miracles. This faith in Christ as Risen and Glorified Lord throws some light on the miracles in the Acts. The mighty works of the gospel accounts are made credible by being looked at in the light of Christ's own unique character. The apostolic mighty works may be made credible on the same basis. It is often objected to their authenticity, that they ceased with the apostles. That is true only as we greatly restrict the connotation of the term "miracle." Anyone who knows how quickly the sub-apostolic church settled down into a well-regulated organization is not surprised at the limitations on its power, but even then "the miracles of grace" at least did not cease. And there is more than a suspicion among certain earnest Christians to-day that the loss of the full power of the apostolic commission may yet be remedied. No one will question that it is the business of the church to encourage social and medical and psychological science to the utmost extent. But it is more than possible that its obligation goes even beyond this to the point of demonstrating afresh that there are aspects to reality that cannot be reduced to science, and reserves of power that cannot be tapped by bare reason. It is such aspects to which religion answers, and it is such reserves of power of which prayer and faith are the keys.

Literature: Wendland, *Miracles and Christianity;* Micklem, *Miracles and the New Psychology;* Illingworth, *The Gospel Miracles;* Bruce, *The Miraculous Element in the Gospels;* Tennant, *Miracle and Its Philosophical Presuppositions;* Abbot, *The Kernel and the Husk;* Thompson, *Miracles in the N.T.* (The last two titles are attempts to eliminate the miraculous and still retain Christianity.) On the Person of Christ, Lewis, *Jesus Christ and the Human Quest.* On the Resurrection, Shaw, *The Resurrection of Christ;* Sparrow, *Resurrection and Modern Thought;* Denney, *Jesus and the Gospel,* bk. ii, sect. 1.

THE LIFE AND WORK OF PAUL

By Professor J. Vernon Bartlet

The Possibility of Discovering the Real Paul. There is, it has been observed, no one in the far past who can be so fully known as Paul; and none, save his Master himself, who is so well worth knowing. Both these assertions will sound strange to many to-day. For the real Paul has been so long overlaid by a conventional and artificial view of him that he has lost for most that vivid and intense quality, that closeness to the very heart of human life, which marked him as he moved among his contemporaries. Paul the theologian, difficult to understand and to appreciate, has come to replace Paul the missionary, the daring pioneer of the Christian mission beyond its native Palestine, without whom Christendom would certainly have been other in its history, and less distinctively Christian in its religion than it has been and is to-day. This does not mean that the actual effect of his writings has been in all ways to the good. They were written for the immediate needs of groups of early mission converts, in terms of their own place and time, and they were thereby apt to be misread in later times and other lands, when the original conditions were forgotten. Further, the distinction between their letter and their spirit—a distinction which their author himself thought vital to the religion of Christ—came to be ignored, largely as a result of a certain theory of verbal inspiration, which, as applied to his own letters (wrung from him as they were by special occasions and often written in haste), would have surprised no one more than himself.

This very fact, however, that Paul is known to us mainly through occasional and profoundly personal letters, justifies our statement that he is so knowable only if we read his letters as letters, and not as something else. For letters are the least artificial, the most self-revealing form of writing; they are in terms of the writer's personality; and where that personality is a powerful one, with a wide range of conditions and sensibilities, letters form an unrivaled medium of vivid expression, through which heart can speak to heart across the centuries. So it has been with Paul and countless myriads of readers, in spite of all difficulties; and so it may be again, and more than ever, once we get the right point of view as readers of letters which embody "the life-blood of a noble spirit." Thus read, they reveal for the most part his deepest personal experience and convictions about what matters most for life, as consisting first and last in personal relations, divine and human, and in the values of things seen in that light. Indeed, Paul is now for the first time becoming fully known, and we owe the discovery to the historic sense, and to the ensuing method of approach to all past persons and events which is the great acquisition of the last century, and which enables us to see them as they were seen by contemporaries. Such research has replaced Paul in the light of his actual setting, both in the outward world and in that world of the soul which was, we now find, so different in many of its thought-forms from our own. It is when we realize and allow for this that we can get behind the letter to the abiding spirit of what he taught and was, and may then transpose the essential theme of his message into the setting of our own times and conditions. This is what these pages aim at assisting the reader to do.

I. The Antecedents of Paul's Gospel

The Gospel of an Historic Jesus. Paul calls himself a bond-servant and missionary (apostle) of Jesus Christ, and ever points beyond himself to Him who has called him and given him his message. And while it is true that he says nothing explicitly about the gospel his Master had proclaimed any more than about the life he had lived in Galilee, this was not because he was unaware of or indifferent to either. He simply saw both in a fresh perspective, as compared with any other witness and missionary of God's Messiah. He looked at them always in the light of their issues, namely, the *cross*, as that in which their essential meaning was summed up, and the *resurrection*, which showed God's mind in contrast to man's, touching the work and person of Jesus as Israel's true Messiah, God's regal son, the vicegerent of his own Lordship over men. This meant that the outer, bodily, or merely human aspects of Christ's ministry—his past deeds and words as of a Jew among Jews—profited none save insofar as their inner and spiritual meaning, the very spirit of Christ's personality, reached the soul through the historic facts as media.

But while knowledge "after the flesh" apart

from spiritual insight was to him religiously of no value, even touching Christ (cf. 2 Cor. 5[16]), there is good evidence that he prized alike the words of Jesus and the stories of his actions, such as are preserved in our synoptic Gospels, but were then current only as oral tradition. For latent in them lay authentic means of insight into the mind of Christ, upon which depended that divine life which for the Christian made all things new (cf. 1 Cor. 7[25] 11[23] 2 Cor. 10[1]—"the meekness and gentleness of Christ"). None the less, the primary and all-inclusive manifestation of God "in the face of Jesus Christ" was the great act of the cross, where the inmost heart of God as gracious to the uttermost, transcending even human sin at its darkest, shone forth with incomparable splendor of self-sacrifice (1 Cor. 1[18, 23-25] 15[3] 2 Cor. 4[6] 5[14, 15]). This was the "piercing-point" of the gospel as Paul himself had experience of it and as he was wont to set it forth. Why this was so we shall yet see. But this must not blind us to the fact that it did not appear to him, nor was it proclaimed by him, in isolation from the historic "fact of Christ" as presented in the synoptic Gospels; for the very value of the act on the cross lay in the character and spirit of the Actor who achieved it; and this could not be realized apart from the life he had lived among men and the message touching God which he had himself delivered as his "Good News" in the name of God. But Paul felt "the word of the cross" to be especially *his* message, as regards emphasis and insight into its full implications, in comparison to that intrusted to his fellow apostles. For it was that which had been directly revealed to him by God, as the means of his own conversion after being his "stumblingblock" (or scandal), lying in the way to faith in Jesus as the Christ of God.

Another reason why Paul, with all his regard for the historic life and teaching of Jesus, makes so little reference to either lies in the very nature of his writings. They are addressed to those who, being already "in Christ," are conversant with the main facts of his ministry and moral teaching, which formed the tradition handed on to converts in close connection with baptism "into Christ." Hence, in letters dealing with special difficulties of theory or practice in this or that local church, it was needful to make only incidental allusion to such part of the tradition as bore on the point in question. And this is just what Paul does. In all things, however, he assumes that his own way of preaching the gospel is in continuity with his Lord's during the earthly ministry, and also in harmony with the form in which the other apostles, who were in Christ before himself, preached what had been intrusted to them by the Spirit of the self-same Lord.

The Gospel of the Older Apostles. Jewish religion in the time of Christ, as in the O.T. generally, rested on the idea of a covenant between God and his people (see art., *Religion of Israel*, p. 175). This special relation had its origin in a free, unmerited act of God, by which first Abraham and then his seed were chosen from among all mankind. Israel was "holy" or "devoted" to God's will and service in a unique sense; and it was only through his presence with it that "the nations" (the Gentiles) were destined to share the "blessing" which the covenant secured for Abraham's seed. That covenant had been further defined and made more explicit than in Abraham's day, assuming the shape of a code of God-given Law, "the Law of Moses." Under this the Jews now lived as a theocracy, their whole life, both corporate and individual, being regulated and made "holy," or devoted to God's will, by its prescriptions alike of worship and moral conduct; for there was no distinction in theory between ritual and moral "righteousness." Both meant conformity to the Law of the covenant or fundamental religious relation.

Further, for more than a century ere Christ came, a supplementary body of oral "traditions" of "the wise," or professional exponents of the Mosaic Law, had been current and more or less observed as giving fuller security for perfect rightness before God by obedience to his revealed will. Those who especially devoted themselves wholly to such piety, understood as loyalty to the Law, both written and oral (Torah or Divine Instruction generally), were the sect of the Pharisees. By such zeal they believed not only that they were securing for themselves special acceptance with God through personal merits, but also that they were bringing nearer God's final manifestation of his full presence and reign amid his holy People, with enhanced blessings for soul and body—in a word, the Messianic kingdom of God. For Moses himself had foretold that God would raise up a prophet comparable to himself, only greater, through whom the Law of God should become perfectly fulfilled in God's People. This hope had become blended with another, namely, the advent of a perfect King as God's vicegerent in Israel, and, through it, in the whole earth. With this latter conception was associated the promise of God's Messiah or Anointed One. This divinely given Deliverer would bring to an end that alien domination of Rome over God's holy People. This domination was a paradox shocking to Jewish sensibilities, one explicable only as divine judgment on imperfect fidelity to God's Law (see art., *Backgrounds*, p. 846a).

All these ideas were common to the whole Jewish people when Jesus came into Galilee proclaiming the "Good News" of God in the words, "The time is ripe; the kingdom of God has drawn near; repent and believe in the Good News." The "Good News" was none other than the nearness of God's real kingdom in and through his People, as redeemed by his more manifestly effective power from all its evils, both inward and outward. But the way in which this message was understood was different according to the relative stress laid in various circles upon different elements in the religion just described. The two greatest differences lay in the emphasis laid upon nationalism and on material rather than spiritual welfare, and on the Pharisaic conception of the Law as a means of acquiring religious merit, rather than on the covenant idea of God's attitude of gracious good will toward his People, and of trustful loyalty of heart in response thereto. There were various combinations of these several tendencies; and the coming of Jesus acted as a touchstone between them. Pure nationalists and legalists alike rejected him, fulfilling as he did the prophetic type of religion, a patriotism that was deeply spiritual, and so went down below the level of national exclusiveness to the essential humanity common to men of all races. For it, God and all moral goodness are causally related, and the idea of Heaven's favoritism gave place to that of the universality of divine grace.

Now, not only did Jesus himself proclaim the gospel as God's gracious fulfillment of his covenant relation with Israel, as pictured in Isa. 40–66, in contrast to a nationalism of vengeful and forcible domination over the Gentiles, and to the current Pharisaic ideal of legalism in religion. His personal disciples also, under the lead of the twelve apostles, had since his death caught the essential spirit of that gospel, and embodied it in their corporate life as his new Israel or church, called out from the People as a whole. The degree, however, to which they consciously realized what was involved was at first relatively small, even after the deeper insight into Jesus' fulfillment of the type of righteousness or holiness depicted as marking the Servant of the Lord in Isa. 40–66—above all through suffering, as in Isa. 53, which came to them with the coming of the Spirit at Pentecost. That experience not only meant confirmation of their faith in Jesus; it also brought their thoughts into closer touch with the real thought of Christ than had been the case in the days of his bodily presence with them (cf. Jn. 16[7]).

Yet they were still thinking on traditional lines as regards two points of prime importance, namely, the relation of Messiah's gospel to the Mosaic Law, and the Jewish nation conceived as the exclusive sphere of the kingdom of God. Their Jewish faith, while teaching them to expect Messiah to enable his People to share his own perfect righteousness, had said nothing about his changing its relation to the Law of Moses, either in its ritual or moral form. Nor had Jesus taught anything explicitly about that Law being superseded. True, he had given them a new idea of the divine character, one more like that of a perfect Father than of a just Judge, so that behind all thought of God's justice was seen the purpose of love; and this had made Jesus free to interpret God's will differently in practice from the way in which the Pharisees did when its precepts clashed, as those of any law must, in the letter. Particularly was it so where ritual requirements competed with the law of mercy toward human need, as when he laid it down that the Sabbath was made for man, not man for the Sabbath—a principle of far-reaching application. In so doing Jesus was acting as a prophet (such as Moses himself had foretold) superior to Moses in authority, with deeper knowledge of the inner purpose and so of the character of God. This, unlike the Pharisees, Jesus' personal disciples had recognized, and largely on that account had come to believe on him as Messiah. But that there was any need to carry further such a process of revision of the Mosaic Law and customs they did not imagine. Hence the beautiful picture of their life in Acts 2–5 is all in terms of devout Judaism, only with a new spirit of joy and love for God and each other, inspired by faith in God's love revealed in the Messiah and his patient love toward God's stiff-necked People, even to the death on the cross.

Thus the original apostolic gospel of God's reconciling love to his sinful People, even after Israel had made clear its unreadiness for his true Kingdom, included no new view of the Mosaic Law as a way of righteousness, or rightness with God. Israel had but to repent of its wrong attitude to God, implied in scornfully rejecting Him who was the incarnation of the Father's very Spirit, and then it would share in the new spirit of loving devotion and power for Christlike beneficence, due to the "Holy Spirit" or inspiration shed forth upon God's "chosen" ones, the true Israel within Israel, the heir of the yet greater blessings soon to be manifested in the fully consummated kingdom of "the coming age." But thus far there was no thought of the Law being superseded by the Person who had become its final interpretation and meaning in spirit, rather than letter, and therefore in truth or inner reality. And yet that Person had in their experience really replaced the Law itself as the medium of revealed relations between God and his People. In other words, Israel, so far as redeemed by Christ from its sins, and by him raised to a new level of covenant relations with God as holy Father, owed its salvation to Christ, a life-saving Person, rather than to the Law of Moses: so that Law could not henceforth be for Christ's People what it had been, especially for Pharisaic Judaism.

All this, however, had come about for the older apostles only in an instinctive and unreflective way, not as a matter of theoretic conviction, applicable to fresh cases of difficulty in practice. Such cases soon arose through the very vitality of the missionary impulse in the soul of the primitive fellowship, the Church of Jesus the Christ. So was it when the Samaritans, whose relation to Israel and its Law was an ambiguous one, began to believe on Jesus as the Prophet to whom Moses—whose five Law books they too acknowledged, as well as Abraham's covenant of circumcision—had pointed forward. Still more was it so when, as Peter preached about Christ to Cornelius and his friends—men who were in no sense incorporated into the People of the covenant by circumcision—the "holy inspiration" by which God's acceptance of men into the Messianic Community was recognized became visible in the case of even such men: "on the Gentiles also was poured out the gift of the Holy Spirit" (Acts 10[45]). Such a fact, for which even Peter had no explanation but God's sheer good pleasure, was an anomaly on the existing principles of the Jerusalem church. To the mind of one Christian only, thus far, was it obvious: that was Paul, the convert from Pharisaism. It was the manner of his approach to the gospel, through his experience as a Pharisee, which made him thus differ from his fellow Christians, and, indeed, in other features of the gospel as he viewed it.

Paul's Conversion. To Jesus, the Law of Moses was only a special form of God's covenant with Abraham on the basis of faith or confiding trust, a form not expressing God's full purpose of grace, but only so much of it as Israel was morally ready to receive at the time it was given through Moses (see Mt. 5[21] and cf. 19[8]). He read it ever in its spirit, in the light of its most general principles, which he saw in the great precept, "Thou shalt love the Lord thy God, . . . and thy neighbor as thyself": on these given principles "hang all the Law and the Prophets." Such discrimination of relative values in the Law struck at the legal principle in its use, which assumed that each clause was binding in itself. On this principle Pharisaism rested; and it was a true instinct which had led its sons to feel that it and the prophet of Nazareth could not live side by side. Hence the cross was a judgment between two radically contrasted principles and spirits in religion. For the moment it seemed that Jesus and his gospel of God's character and inner purpose of love, as the standard by which his Law was to be read, were condemned as blasphemous by God's own verdict through the highest authority in his holy People. But when it appeared that God's judgment had really vindicated Jesus, on the apostolic testimony to him as risen; and when the quality of the new life visible in the fellowship based on faith in him seemed to confirm that testimony, the problem of gospel versus Law, in the sense of Pharisaic legalism, pressed urgently for solution.

The simple minds of the disciples of Jesus, who had never been legalists at heart, though deferential to "the wise" or teachers of the Law, and whose consciences had responded instinctively to their Master's attitude toward it in practice, did not feel the problem acutely at first as a matter of theory. It was only when they were confronted by the cases already referred to, when the spirit of the Messianic kingdom was conferred apart from formal acceptance of the Law by circumcision—men being brought by divine act within the covenant simply by faith in Jesus as God's Messiah—that it came home to them practically, and demanded action which meant Yea or Nay to the divine leading manifest in such facts. "Who are we that we should resist God?" were the words in which they yielded to the logic of divine fact; though, as this course of events proved, with tacit reservations greater or less, according to degrees of prior sympathy with legalism in theory.

But it was otherwise with Paul, or Saul, as he is first called in the narrative of Acts. Though born outside Palestine, at Tarsus in Cilicia (northwest of Antioch, the great capital of the Roman province of Syria and Cilicia), and actually a Roman citizen by inheritance from his father, he had been reared in a Pharisaic home, and later was trained as a rabbi at the feet of the famous Gamaliel in Jerusalem. "As touching the righteousness (rectitude) which is in the Law, found blameless," is his own verdict on his life at that time.

But while such was the outer aspect of his state, his inner experience was one of profound dissatisfaction and unrest, owing to conflict between desire and outward conduct. The moving record of this division of soul, impulse, and conscience being at war stands written in Rom. 7 (see the commentary on this passage), a psychological picture not surpassed in power and insight by the similar and longer self-analysis in Augustine's *Confessions.* The gist of it is this: the divine Law, sounding "Thou shalt not" in his heart when desire prompted him toward indulgence of "the flesh" or sensual principle, in some form or other, brought "sin in the flesh" to conscious light; nay, more, it also aggravated it psychologically, by making more self-conscious sin's rebellion to the Law of God, which the reason of "the inner man" itself recognized and rejoiced in, as "holy" and "good." That was a terrible paradox; but its full misery lay in this, that the Law thereby proved in the sinner's experience not the means of deliverance or salvation which Pharisaism assumed it to be, but, rather, the means of deeper condemnation for his complicity with "the law of sin" in the flesh. That is, the holy Law, which ideally was given by God to be "unto life," did in fact, owing to the pathological condition of man as he is, work unto death. The result, then, of Saul's passionate effort to reach this peace of conscious harmony with God's will by the aid of God's Law was summed up in the despairing cry, "Who shall deliver me" out of this dreadful impasse due to the power of sin in the flesh? And the one answer he found in the end was this: "Thank God, Jesus Christ our Lord." But the struggle through which this was reached was a tragically acute one, both for himself and for the People or Church of Christ.

For Paul was not the sort of man to yield easily, even when he felt the inherited belief on which he stood giving way beneath him. He had leaned the whole weight of his soul's concern for acceptance with God upon the Law; and once he realized it was failing him he no doubt struggled hard to save the situation. It was probably at this point that the church's testimony to Jesus as "Saviour of his people from their sins" struck into the course of his soul's experience. We cannot be sure whether he had himself seen and heard Jesus in the flesh, though there is some reason to think that he had (2 Cor. 5[16] may well imply this, and several modern critical scholars favor the view, e.g., C. A. Scott, in *Christianity According to Paul,* pp. 11f.). As a Pharisee he would in any case fiercely resent Jesus' attitude toward the Law; and he must have accepted Jesus' condemnation by its guardians as God's judgment on him as a blasphemer. The very form of his death would be to Saul a confirmation of this; for did not the Law declare, "Cursed is every one that hangeth on a tree"? Hence when the bold argument of Stephen, the cultured Hellenistic Jew, against his fellow Hellenists—some from Saul's synagogue (Acts 6[9]), if not Saul himself—brought him to martyrdom, Saul indirectly participated. Indeed, we can well imagine him finding vent to his own restlessness, due to the Law's effect on himself, in such zeal against one who treated it as only a transient phase of God's progressive dealings with his People—one who declared the time to be near when God should dwell with his People in another and more real way than in the Temple made with men's hands, with which much of the Law was bound up.

But if so, his zeal brought the young Pharisee no relief: rather, the memory of Stephen's peaceful death in the spirit of his Master did but add to the impression produced on his subconsciousness by the joyous and loving life of the fellowship of Jesus' disciples. Hence he plunged yet deeper into repressive acts against those who impugned the immutability of the Law given through Moses; for how could divine Law be other than absolute and final to the last jot and tittle? This assumption, that no relative element can exist in anything that has had divine sanction, excluding though it does room for the progressive revealing action by the Holy Spirit, as Stephen urged once for all, must be duly noted as that which underlay Paul's action. Paul's error, as he found it to be on this point, and an abiding problem in the philosophy of religion, may remind us from the first of the universal interest of his religious development. On the road to Damascus he was in fact agitated by the problem touching Jesus and the Law, as alternative forms of God's self-revelation. This was involved in Jesus' claim to be, after all, in spite of the cross, God's Messianic Son. Certain elements in Jesus' teaching and character as forced on Saul's attention by the confirmatory fact of the life of his followers, based on faith in him as approved of God by restoration to personal activity after death, kept plying his soul with pricks of conscience. This seems implied by the words, "Saul, Saul, why persecutest thou me? It is hard for thee to kick against the goad"—like an ox against the guiding hand of its master (Acts 26[14]).

With Paul too, as with the older apostles, the solution came by the logic of facts in the first instance: the knot was cut by the sword of the Spirit, rather than untied. The Lordship of Jesus as verily God's Messiah was brought home to his immediate spiritual intuition in a way that virtually settled this issue between two alternative forms of God's self-revelation, along with other vital issues then preoccupying his soul. By an experience, the outer and temporary form of which cannot and need not be defined, "it pleased God to reveal his Son" in the earnest and sincere Pharisee, with a self-evidence which he could never thereafter doubt. Jesus was seen *on his own merits* as "Son of God," the image with human form of the invisible God, and for that reason as possessed of an absolute spiritual authority over the conscience. So his filial type of devotion to the heavenly Father was the very essence of real obedience—that of the undivided will of the inner man—and became the standard by which the legal type of obedience, which did not unite the heart in complete loyalty, must be judged, not *vice versa.* In a word, Jesus' holiness was one in the spirit, even when not in the letter also; and he himself was the inspirer of the similar free loyalty in others, as a "life-giving spirit" (2 Cor. $3^{6,\ 17}$ 1 Cor. 15^{45}).

II. Paul's Gospel

The Law and Christ Crucified. Such being Paul's line of approach to Jesus as the Christ, two things from the first marked his special apprehension of the gospel: a clear sense that it superseded the Law in principle, and, as bound up with this, a new emphasis on the cross. Hitherto, the cross had been regarded simply as due to Israel's sinful unreadiness to accept such a Messiah as Jesus, and as the means of bringing it to heartfelt repentance on this issue, and so to forgiveness of sins. But Paul saw it to have also a deeper meaning in relation to the kind of righteousness which was truly well-pleasing to God. Such righteousness was non-legal in quality, resting on a right attitude of soul toward God—the filial one—and not on merit acquired by human effort or "works," i.e., obedience to specific precepts. It was "the righteousness of God" as provided by God's grace in the gift of his Son and appropriated by the pure receptivity of faith, as personal trust or reliance upon God's grace in him. Such faith was akin to that of Abraham. By it he became "friend of God" and the recipient of the covenant of faith, to which the Law was added only later, in consequence of Israel's unreadiness to live on the level of its forefathers' more personal type of religion. "The righteousness in Christ" (i.e., union with Christ), as distinct from that in the Law of Moses, was thus continuous in principle with that enjoyed by Abraham.

What, then, of the authority of the Law? And how was transition from its jurisdiction, now seen to be an episode in the divine dispensation or plan for training the People of God, to come about without the Law seeming to be set aside arbitrarily or to be belittled even in its divine aspect? That the Law in its Mosaic or legal form as "letter" commanding from outside, rather than as "spirit" or internal inspiration to the will, had in fact proved unable to "make righteous," Paul himself had proved by his own experience. Only spiritual union with Christ had availed to free him "from the law of sin" working "in the flesh." "For what the Law could not do, in that it was weak (ineffective) through the flesh, God, sending his own Son in the likeness of sinful flesh, and as an offering for sin (or to deal with sin), condemned sin in the flesh: that the ordinance (or righteous intent) of the law might be fulfilled in us, who walk . . . after the Spirit" (Rom. $8^{3,\ 4}$). Such was Paul's joyous experience of the fact that Christ had proved strong where the Law had proved weak, namely, in bringing sin's usurping power to the judgment of death in his own person, in that he on the cross "died once for all to sin," and so proved its sway to be an illegitimate one (Rom. $6^{7,\ 10}$). As a result, it was possible for those united with Christ as Lord to share his death to sin, which was practically one with *its* death as lord over the human will (Rom. 6^{11}).

But Paul goes further than this. He relates Christ's cross to the Law, not only along this line of profound religious experience, or moral mysticism, but also along another, in which it has been and is harder for most to follow his thought. To him, however, there was a link between the two, in the fact that the Law in one aspect, namely, its human or psychological effect, is closely bound up with the very quality of sin *as conscious*, and so the more sinful, being now rebellion against the will of God (Rom. $7^{7f.}$). That being so, it is needful in a sense to "die unto the Law" also—as having legal claims on one—by union with Christ, in order to be joined to him in his new life not only of freedom from sin's power to tempt into further sin toward God (Rom. 7^{4-6}; cf. $6^{10f.}$), but also of emancipation from the realm of Law altogether, as the form in which God's will is done. "For I through the Law," writes Paul (Gal. $2^{19f.}$), "died unto the Law, that I might live unto God"—on a new plane of motive and with a new type of obedience, i.e., the filial. "I have been crucified with Christ [unto the

Law]; yet I live [unto God]; and yet no longer I, but Christ liveth in me: and that life which I now live in the flesh [here on earth] I live in faith, the faith which is in the Son of God, who loved me, and gave himself up for me"—and in so doing has inspired the believers with a new principle of obedience, namely, love as the motive power by which faith takes effect (Gal. 5^{6}). "For the whole Law is fulfilled in one word (or end), even in this: Thou shalt love thy neighbor as thyself" (Gal. 5^{14}).

The Christian Salvation and the Saviour. Here we have in germ Paul's whole gospel, which in emphasis and idea is a message of *salvation*, i.e., the making of life what it has in it, according to God's creative intention, to become ("life that is life indeed"). To this full positive idea, redemption and reconciliation are relative (see C. A. Scott, *Christianity According to St. Paul*, ch. 2); of these two, redemption is the more comprehensive, expressing the process by which all that stands between the soul and its inheritance of joint life with God, "eternal life," is done away with. Its first stage, sometimes called broadly and prophetically "redemption," is on its objective side Christ's worth *par excellence*. It roots in the cross, for redemption is "by his blood" (life poured forth in sacrifice for others). On its subjective side, it is reconciliation. Reconciliation is primarily of men to God, since God himself takes the initiative in giving his Son to produce this effect in men (2 Cor. $5^{19f.}$ Rom. 5^{10}); yet, of course, there is a sense in which this actual relation of God to a man is affected for the time by the man's attitude toward him. A synonym for this first stage, in terms of righteousness as "rightness" with God, is justification, or God's own declaration that a man is in a right relation or attitude to himself by faith (of the type of Abraham's). This for Paul is fundamental and contains in germ, in promise, and potency all that follows in the unfolding experiences of redemption, to wit, sanctification and redemption (i.e., of the body; see 1 Cor. 1^{30} Rom. 8^{23}; cf. 8^{11}). Thus, justification contains sanctification implicitly; and sanctification means the progressively full realization in moral act and habit of the religious relation once for all assumed in justification, namely, the filial and Christ-centered, instead of the self-centered attitude, to which corresponds adoption on the part of God.

The Sphere of Salvation: the Church. We have seen how intimately related to his experience of the need and fact of salvation was Paul's view of Jesus as God's appointed Saviour. How, then, did he interpret to himself, and set forth for others, the nature of Christ's saving personality? Acts tells us that after his conversion Paul forthwith proclaimed in the synagogues at Damascus Jesus' divine Sonship, as revealed in his own experience (Gal. 1^{16}). Jesus had done for the ex-Pharisee what bitter failure had taught him that no thing—not even God's Law—could do, but only the personal intervention of God in revealed form, namely, in one who could manifest God's grace in saving power, because he himself shared God's very nature. Jesus, then, the absolutely Spirit-anointed of God, was God's Son in the fullest and most absolute sense possible, consistently with the unity and ultimate sovereignty of God—which Paul, as a loyal Hebrew, always reserved for God the Father (see C. A. Scott, *op. cit.*, pp. 270–279) as distinct even from the "one Lord" of men, Jesus Christ (1 Cor. $8^{5f.}$). "All that God had been expected or could be expected to do for man in the field of man's spiritual or moral experience had been done by Christ" (*ibid.*, p. 278). Thus he was in the sphere of salvation, the specifically religious sphere, practically equivalent to God. It was in Jesus, as his vicegerent, that "God had wrought salvation for his People" in the absolute and final sense, and so had completely revealed himself "in the face of Jesus Christ." This was the personal form of "the Glory" (*Shekinah*), whereby in the O.T. theophanies God had appeared to men. All this Paul meant to express by calling Jesus the Son of God, one who stood to God in a uniquely close relation, as of a perfect Son to a Father whose nature and will he shared: and this relation Paul carried back into the pre-temporal order, ere the creation of the world.

In so thinking, Paul probably used certain conceptions in the rabbinic theology in which he had been trained, conceptions in which it was natural that he should see a new meaning in the light of his fresh experience in Christ. It is thus that we can best account for the fact that he nowhere explains or tries to establish such categories as he applies to Jesus, but takes them for granted, arguing that it is to him alone that they of right belong on his own merits, as he had lived and worked among men. Among such categories was the "Wisdom" of God, already described in personalized fashion in Prov. 8, which seems by Paul's day to have been identified with "the Image," or the self-expression in a form apprehensible to finite beings, of the invisible God, according to the largely symbolic story of man's creation in Gen. 1 (cf. Col. 1^{15-17}). Such is surely the general impression produced by the passage in Phil. 2^{5-11} (see notes), where

Paul sets forth Christ as one who had originally stooped from a state in which he was "in the form of God"—a being to be classed with God as divine—to assume man's estate as one of relative self-humbling. But it was just because he had so acted, instead of ambitiously grasping by direct means at "equality with God" in outward glory, that God has "yet further exalted him" (i.e., beyond the former state) so as to give him as a free gift the Name that is above every name, that of universal Lordship, such as belongs to God the Father himself by his very nature. Yet this enhancement of the Son's pre-incarnate glory, gained as it was through such filial devotion to the sovereign Father's will, redounded also to that Father's greater glory (Phil. 2^9-11^). This is a soaring speculation, but one rooted in profound insight into the nature of moral greatness, the glory of service in love, or the principle of *noblesse oblige;* it involves a distinctively Christian conception of greatness, which has changed the human moral standard for the noblest members of our race (see Mk. 10^35-45^). We have yet to see how in his own person and subsequent career Paul, the bond-servant, exemplified the supreme principle of self-forgetful love and service which had shone so bright in the Lord who had won his passionate allegiance. But before turning to this topic, we must describe yet another aspect of Paul's gospel which largely inspired his untiring ministry.

Thus far we have viewed Paul's gospel of salvation chiefly in its individual aspect, because that was the side on which it first found him and transformed him from foe to apostle. But while intensely individual in experience, as befitted this apostle of personality in contrast to law, his gospel was, in fact, nobly universal and corporate in its range, a message of fellowship in love. This comes out strikingly in the glorious psalm of love in 1 Cor. 13, which is strangely overlooked by those who regard Paul as the partisan of faith as compared with love. There is little doubt that Paul, who speaks with such contrition for having blindly persecuted the Church of God, had from the first been deeply impressed by the life of the church, the temple of God's Messiah, with its intense fellowship in brotherly love. Once, then, he had tasted its life within, as the very grace of Christ, as well as the love of God, and the fellowship of the Holy Spirit of adoption shed abroad in it, it was he above all others who expounded the idea of the church in all its fullness of meaning, as the fulfillment of God's purpose of boundless good will toward mankind, brought out on a plan or "mystery" of surpassing wisdom. In so doing he sketches the first real philosophy of history, in virtue of his experience of standing at the very heart of things. He is united to God, the Creator of all, in Christ, his revealed mind (cf. 1 Cor. 1, 2, espec. 2^6, 11, 16^ Rom. 11^33^ Eph. 1^3-14^ 3^1^). It was he who conceived and developed with great richness of application the idea of the church as the body of Christ, i.e., a social organism of persons unified by one animating spirit and directing mind, pictured as centered in its head, Christ its Lord. This unity of life he speaks of with wondering awe as the supreme "mystery," of which the unity of human marriage is another type (Eph. 5^23-32^). And the unity is so intimate and reciprocal that the whole organism, made up of head and members, he even terms "the Christ" (1 Cor. 12^12^). It has, i.e., one principle of life, the divine Spirit, concentrated in the Head and flowing from him to all his members. "For in one Spirit were we all baptized into one body . . . and were all made to drink of one Spirit." It is, we observe, in closest connection with the church and its supernatural or truly divine life that Paul develops his thought about the Spirit of God, now revealed in new and fuller form as the Spirit of Christ. It is the source of the fresh grace—(gifts or charisms)—which mark the Church of Christ, as distinct from that of Moses "in the wilderness," and which was the basis of the organization of those ministerial functions, in the widest sense, by which it edifies or builds itself up in love under the headship of Christ. It is that Spirit which constitutes the spiritual body one in a more marvelous way than even the animal body, which is its visible analogy. Nay the personal Head, Jesus Christ, is himself not complete in his Christship, his life-giving function, until his potential fullness has found realized expression in the corporate life of the new humanity, the church, which is thus the complement alike of his nature and his historical experiences, particularly his saving sufferings (Eph. 1^22f.^ 3^20f.^ Col. 1^24^ Phil. 3^10^). In this noble and profoundly ethical mysticism —for it is the basis of his most practical exhortations to Christ-like living—we have the explanation of Paul's teaching on Christ as the Spirit or life-saving principle of the new form of the covenant, as distinct from the old form as Law or "letters," and of the new form of God's People as Christ's church or body. Jesus as the second Adam, "heavenly" or spiritual in nature, causes men to share his own Spirit-nature; and in the power of that dynamic inspiration enables them to will and to do after God's good-pleasure (Phil. 2^12f.^). In "working out" or realizing the potential energy of the germ of salvation, as the Christ-life implanted in them by faith, or union with him as Head, they are but giving free course to the "mind" or Spirit of Christ (Phil. 2[5]), which is "working in" the body and its members to ever fuller unfolding of its transforming possibilities of Christly character—"the fruit of the Spirit" (2 Cor. 3[17f.] Rom. 12[1f.] Gal. 5[16-24] Phil. 4[8f.]). Here we have too the ground of Paul's wonderful hopefulness touching moral transformation in all those once really united to Christ in the Spirit. When actual persistence of habits and "fruits of the flesh" confronted him in his converts, as they often did in ways which to-day, amid standards of a Christian tradition of living, would awaken doubt as to those indulging them ever having been in Christ, Paul simply calls on them to awake to the inconsistency of their actions with the underlying impulse and trend of their soul as united to the Head, made "one spirit" with the Lord (1 Cor. 6[9-11] 17[19f.] Gal. 5[13] 6[6f.]). He never doubts but that, with the aid of the other members of the Body (Gal. 6[1f.]), the ailing member will be made whole again, or "saved" into healthful life by the power of Christ.

III. Paul's Missionary Activities and His Writings

Early Preparation. After the first days of enthusiastic proclamation to his Jewish compatriots at Damascus of the new light from heaven that had smitten so suddenly and transformingly on his spiritual vision, it seems that Paul—like his Master himself after his baptismal experience—felt the need of retirement into solitude, in order to ponder and assimilate more deeply the full meaning and practical implications of that divinely given vision. Christ had laid hold on him; but Paul had not yet adequately apprehended "the fact of Christ" and the range of the gospel. Indeed, Paul's whole life was to be a moral and mental "growing up in him" (Phil. 3[12] Eph. 1[17f.] 3[16-21] 4[15]). So he "went away into Arabia" for meditation, and he returned to Damascus to resume his public testimony to Christ and his salvation (Gal. 1[17]), with added power (Acts 9[22]). This stirred up such resentment among the Jews that he had to flee for his life; and thereupon he seized the chance of going to Jerusalem to visit Peter, doubtless to learn more of the historic facts of Jesus' life and teaching. But again Jewish resentment, this time on the part of "Hellenists" like himself, as formerly in the case of Stephen, drove him ere long from the hearth alike of Judaism and the church (Gal. 1[18] Acts 9[26]). And now he sought his native Tarsus. There, and in the northern part of the Roman province of Syria-Cilicia, he carried on an apostolate of some ten years, a period often forgotten, but one which no doubt had a great influence in shaping and confirming his distinctive gospel by the lessons of experience, to which Paul, like the other apostles, gave due heed as to the leading of the Spirit working in and through them. Hence when Barnabas, who had already befriended him in Jerusalem (Acts 9[27]), came to seek his assistance in the new mission which had arisen at Antioch, beyond the Holy Land altogether, through the spontaneous preaching of certain Hellenists of Stephen's type, and was now under Barnabas' supervision, Paul was fully mature in his principles and practice and prepared to co-operate (Acts 13[1f.]).

First Missionary Journey: Admission of Gentiles. Into the exact sequence of Paul's activities, and of his relations with the older apostles in connection with his liberal views as regards the admission of non-Jews into the Church of Christ on equal terms with Jews, apart from circumcision—hitherto regarded as the condition of full standing within God's covenant—it is hardly needful here to enter. (See Hort, *Judaistic Christianity*, for an account of each of Paul's Epistles in its historic setting, particularly as regards Jewish Law and Christian gospel.) But the opinion may be expressed in passing, that Paul had already taken steps to safeguard his distinctive gospel against misunderstanding in the apostolic circle itself; and so against any danger of hindrance from that quarter (Gal. 2[11]), even before he and Barnabas went on their great pioneering journey beyond Syria-Cilicia, first to Cyprus and then to the cities of South Galatia. But the agreement reached in private between them and the "pillars" of the mother church—Peter and John, along with James the Lord's brother, the permanent head of the local community—which meant a division of spheres of work, "the circumcision" and the Gentiles respectively (Gal. 2[2-10])—this agreement was not as yet publicly recognized by the generally conservative Jerusalem church. Thus even before the first missionary journey of Paul and Barnabas, as it seems, a difficulty arose in the relations of the two branches of the church, the Jewish and the Gentile, on the border-line question of intercourse at meals. This was an issue akin to that raised by caste in India, between those ritually "clean" and "unclean" or "untouchable," and became a burning one, owing to the coming to Antioch of certain "from James" (Gal. 2[12]). These brought the public opinion of the Jerusalem church to bear on the consciences of the local

Jewish Christians and caused even Peter, then on a visit to Antioch, and after him Barnabas too, to change their more liberal practices of teaching Gentile believers as full brethren in Christ in the matter of table fellowship. It was a matter on which Jewish tradition and feeling were strong; and no doubt Peter and Barnabas felt it expedient to defer to Jerusalem feeling when the issue of habitual practice (in contrast to such an exceptional case as that in Acts 10^{1}–11^{17}) was thus raised. But Paul stood firm as a rock and exposed the inconsistency of the line taken (Gal. $2^{11\text{-}21}$). Most scholars, indeed, think this happened after the public concordat at Jerusalem in Acts 15, after the issues of the Gentiles' standing in the church and their intercourse with Jewish Christians had been explicitly dealt with. But this seems less likely, especially in view of Barnabas' action.

Second Missionary Journey. After that concordat, which referred primarily to Antioch and Syria-Cilicia, had been reached, Paul began his second missionary journey. He seems to have had Ephesus, the capital of the Roman province of Syria, already in view as a new advanced base for yet more world-wide missionary work. But after revisiting his converts in South Galatia, and in his zeal for unity in Christ's one church between those whom "the middle wall of partition," "the law of ordinances," had once divided, he was diverted by divine intimation to the road leading northwest toward Europe (Acts $16^{6\text{-}10}$). This was the foundation of churches in Philippi and Thessalonica in Macedonia; and his relations to the latter gave rise to the earliest of his extant pastoral letters, written from Corinth in the winter following (51–52 A.D). These letters are simple applications of his gospel to certain practical problems which had arisen for his inexperienced converts in his own enforced absence, due partly to their belief that their Lord might return at any moment, so that some even neglected working for their daily bread; and partly to unenlightened views of conduct, especially in sexual purity, not befitting love to a holy heavenly Father and to men and women as his children.

Epistle to Galatians. To this same stay of eighteen months at Corinth may be assigned the circular letter to the Galatian churches. Judaizing Christians from outside, probably from Jerusalem, were undermining the loyalty of these churches to Paul's gospel of spiritual freedom from the Law through all-inclusive faith and obedience directed to Christ and his new law of love, under the inspiration of his Spirit in their hearts. The ostensible plea seems to have been that such was well enough to begin with, but that obedience to the Law, and the rite of circumcision as sign of incorporation into the People of the Law, were needful to a mature and normal Christianity (Gal. 3^{3}). This virtually challenged Paul's form of gospel and so his apostolic authority, which the interlopers represented as derived from the older apostles, not co-ordinate with theirs. What added to Paul's indignation at this challenge was its speciousness, and its using against him his very magnanimity in commending the concordat—as though it meant his owning to a human authority over his gospel—and in circumcising Timothy, a half-Jew by birth; whereas, in fact, he had done it for the sake of the Jews whom his mission might bring him, lest they should say that Paul forbade the national covenant sign even to born Jews (Acts $16^{1\text{-}3}$). Such disingenuous features of the attack explain the vehemence of his tone in this burning apology for his apostolate and sincerity all along. In it we have alike typical Jewish lines of argument to meet Jewish minds (Gal. $3^{10\text{-}22}$ $4^{21\text{-}31}$), hammer-like blows of appeal to sheer spiritual facts ($3^{1\text{-}5}$), and solemn asseverations of the authority of his gospel and his consistency in applying it in different circumstances ($1^{1\text{-}10}$ $5^{1\text{-}4,}$ $11^{f.}$). Running through all, too, is an affectionate, fatherly tone of yearning concern for the loyalty of his children to the gospel and to him as its direct witness. The appeal covers the whole gamut of human emotions. It shows the rich humanity of Paul, when we take the pains to read between the lines of the allusive, broken, and often ejaculatory pleading of what is emphatically a letter, in its changing but always personal modes of address. It reveals its writer, on certain sides, more than aught else.

Epistles to Corinthians. In Paul's next extant letters, those to the church at Corinth some four years later (56 A.D.), we meet, besides challenge of Paul's full apostolic authority stirred up by Judaizing interlopers, a whole range of new problems due to the non-Jewish and typically Greek mentality of a large section of the local converts. "The Greeks," says Paul, "seek after wisdom," in the sense of philosophy as the rationally understood; such was the main source of dissatisfaction with and deviation from Paul's own way of presenting the gospel at Corinth. Some who so felt contrasted with it the more idealistic way in which even Apollos, whom Paul generously recognizes as fellow worker, had followed in Paul's footsteps in the interval, using his Alexandrine culture of the Philonic type in his exposition of the same message which Paul had put more bluntly to the conscience, with its sense of moral failure and guilt, in terms of "Christ and him crucified" as the sum of personal salvation. Others, however, prided themselves on having struck out a fresh line of "wisdom" or superior insight (*gnosis*) into the true doctrine of Christ, which cut it away altogether from the moral genius of biblical religion. Stressing its intellectual suggestions, they threw it into a different perspective altogether, making it an ideology with little or no reference to the realism of the will and moral personality, in a world where the intimate relations of body and spirit must be harmonized and not ignored. This attitude led to egoistic individualism, divorced from love as the ruling principle of the gospel. Against it, as well as other abuses of the experiences and doctrine of the free Spirit of God, as the source of all spiritual gifts, Paul uttered his sublime prophetic outburst on love as the supreme spiritual reality, gathering up with itself its sister graces of faith and hope, and abiding throughout all partial and passing forms of human "knowledge" of things divine. "Knowledge puffeth up; love buildeth up," in the sphere of moral personality —the final reality in God or man.

Paul's Use of Terms. In expounding his thought to converts wont to use a terminology rather different from his own in its association and shades of meaning, Paul, with the tact of a great missionary, adopted certain words and phrases current among those to whom he wrote; and there are some who think that he took over also the special religious conceptions which they expressed in Hellenistic religion, particularly in the realm of sacramental ideas. Others, on the other hand, believe with the present writer that Paul, who held firmly that biblical religion had nothing to learn from the worship of "demons," adopted no positive conceptions, as distinct from illustrations, from such a source. (See C. A. Scott, *op. cit.*, pp. 122–135, for a careful discussion of this whole matter.) Be this as it may, we shall find in his letters henceforth constant reminders of the problems of adaptation to the forms of a new and largely non-Jewish world of thought and training— problems which every missionary to-day, especially amid ancient civilizations like those of India and China, has to face and solve.

Epistle to Romans. The second of Paul's letters to Corinth is full of passages revealing the very heart of the man, in his profound and sensitive humanity, and of his personal religion. But we must hasten on to the last of the letters of his first period of missionary work as known to us, that in which he was engaged mainly in vindicating the gospel as God's final message for man as man, against all who would make it an appanage of Judaism and of religion as divine law. The Epistle to the Romans, written to a church with which he had had no personal relations, is not so much a letter as a comprehensive manifesto of his gospel in various relations. It is meant at once for Jew and Gentile, setting forth Paul's thought in broad outline, and striving particularly to justify God's providential dealings with both in history, on the basis of the sovereign freedom of divine grace, in his successive dispensations or methods of treating man in bulk rather than individually. Overlooking this fact has led to much misreading of its teaching on predestination and election, with grievous results for Christian doctrine. It embraces, however, almost every aspect of Paul's theology and religion in a wonderful synthesis, throwing light both backward and forward over the whole of his teaching. It illustrates too, by its very structure, the way in which he was wont to apply his theology to daily conduct, and to root even the most practical details of the latter in the former as inspiration and source of motive power. We have already noted how he deals with moral inconsistency in the daily "walk" of Christians, not by falling back on the legal principle for help, but by calling upon them to think again and realize their essential standing as united by faith with Christ himself, in the holy freedom from sin's thraldom, achieved by virtue of his Spirit's power working within. But in a central section of this Epistle (chs. 6–8), he sets forth the theory of this experience of personal unity between Christ and his members, in a way which shows that his profound moral mysticism had not been grasped in certain quarters, and that his doctrine of justification and sanctification as alike by faith (in Paul's sense of the word) had been travestied into a condoning of moral laxity, later known as antinomianism.

IV. Last Things

Closing Experiences. Between this Epistle written to Rome and the second main group, written from Rome after an interval of some three years, came a series of dramatic experiences, illustrative of Paul's greatness of soul. His last visit to Jerusalem (57 A.D.), in the interests especially of cementing the unity in the one Church of Christ between Jew and Gentile by practical proof of love on the part of the latter in the form of relief for "the poor saints" at Jerusalem; his arrest through the enmity of Jews from Asia; his trials before Roman courts and detention in prison at Cæsarea; his appeal to the Supreme Court at

Rome, and his heroic bearing on the voyage thither (all described in Acts 21^{15}–27^{44})—all these had no little effect upon the perspective in which he now looked out upon the world, and upon the gospel as God's plan of salvation for meeting its needs, alike in their diversity and essential oneness.

Epistles to Colossians and Philemon. As illustrating the sort of mental diversity through which men of varying traditions interpreted the salvation of which they had tasted in Christ, we have the letter to the Colossians, who lived on the border of the province of Asia, where ascetic scruples as to foods in relation to religious purity, and also belief in a hierarchy of angels able to obstruct free access to God even through Christ, possessed certain souls with nervous fears alien to the "liberty of the children of God." This gave occasion to Paul to unfold his high theory of the person of Christ and of his all-sufficiency more fully than before; while the beautiful personal note to a member of this church, Philemon, illustrates alike its writer's Christian courtesy and his wise handling of a pressing point in Christian ethics, namely, the all-pervasive fact of slavery, viewed in terms of actual conditions. For the lot of the church was obviously a difficult one. It found itself in the midst of social institutions which could not abruptly be denounced without precipitating a conflict on what was, after all, only a secondary issue—secondary because the world was not expected to continue in its existing order, but was to be suddenly transformed by the return of Christ.

Epistle to Ephesians. Closely related, in time and outlook, to Colossians was the second of Paul's great manifestos on his gospel generally, an open letter to all his churches in the province of Asia, known to us as Ephesians (named from the copy preserved in the church of Ephesus; see notes on Eph. 1^{1}; cf. p. 855b), and referred to in Col. 4^{16} as that which was to be passed on to them after being read by the neighboring church of Laodicea. Its theme is the universality in idea of the church as the body of Christ, and its transcendent destiny, namely, humanity as made new and filled with the divine fullness of God latent in its Head, Jesus Christ (1^{1-10} 3^{14-21}). In it all artificial barriers of race and condition of sex are in principle done away, though the fruits of this can be realized only by a moral process of growing up into the Head in all things, as provided by divine gifts of ministry and self-edification through the Spirit (4^{1-16}); and this forms the incentive for zealous pressing on in the path of a Christly "walk" (4^{17}).

Pastoral Epistles: 1 and 2 Timothy and Titus. And now we are nearing the end alike of Paul's earthly life and his vision of human salvation. The so-called Pastoral Epistles to Timothy and Titus add little to our impression of Paul's personality and work. The present writer still inclines to the view expressed by him elsewhere (see the art., "Paul," in the eleventh edition of *The Encyclopedia Britannica*), that they are genuine as a whole, and not only in a few fragments (incorporated from minor personal notes to Timothy, in 2 Tim. 4 in particular; see intro. to the Pastorals, p. 1275). On that assumption they show Paul continuing the correction of erroneous semi-Jewish, semi-ascetic fancies (as in Colossians), especially the denial of any kind of resurrection body, a denial due to a dualistic prejudice against matter as such. Against such claims to superior "knowledge" he sets a truly religious life of love, on the lines of the pattern of "wholesome" moral instruction already given in his own teaching and example.

Epistle to Philippians. But whatever view we take of Paul's relation to the Pastoral Epistles, the swan-song of his spirit is the intensely personal and spiritually gallant letter to his loved church at Philippi, the first fruits of his mission to Europe. "Rejoice in the Lord always": such is its note. He has but slight hope, humanly speaking, apart from what he feels may be best for his converts (1^{22-24}) of escaping "the lion's mouth" for long, so far as concerns his earthly life (cf. 2 Tim. $4^{6-8, 16-18}$): but what of that? He will only be the sooner with Christ, in more immediate fellowship, which is "far better." He feels himself in the act of being "offered as a libation" (2^{17}; see mg. for the Greek) upon the sacrifice and service of his converts' faith; and the thought gives him joy, which he calls on them to share and not to cast down (2^{18}; cf. 2 Tim. 4^{6}). And so he passes from our view, a victim of Jewish enmity using Nero's appeal court as its tool. He died probably by beheading, as was his right as a Roman citizen, rather than by a more ignominious death such as befell Peter and many more a year or so later in 64 A.D., when they were made scapegoats for the public suspicions as to the source of a great fire in Rome that summer. Truly a triumphant end to a career of constant triumph in the train of Christ his Lord (2 Cor. 2^{14}).

And what was the end of human history as Paul saw it stretching away into the mists that envelop all human knowledge of things in space and time? Sooner or later this: the kingdom of God fully realized among men, when the divine life, eternal in quality in the redeemed as in the Redeemer and his Father, shall have cast out death and replaced it in all its forms. Then shall the vice-regency of

Christ, the Son, be merged in the sole all-inclusive sway of the sovereign Father, "that God may be all in all" (1 Cor. 15[24-28]).

(For further discussion of Paul and his work and teaching, see the commentary on Acts and the introductions to the various letters of Paul in the present volume.)

Literature: Stalker, *Life of St. Paul;* Sabatier, *The Apostle Paul* (Eng. trans., 1891); A. B. Bruce, *St. Paul's Conception of Christianity;* G. B. Stevens, *The Pauline Theology;* Ramsay, *St. Paul the Traveler and the Roman Citizen* (1896; marking a new epoch of historic realism in the study of Paul as a man in his actual environment); Deissmann, *Paul* (Eng. trans., 1912; new edition, 1927); Schweitzer, *Paul and His Interpreters* (Eng. trans.); Peabody, *The Apostle Paul and the Modern World;* C. H. Dodd, *The Meaning of Paul for To-day* (1923; one of the best of the recent brief studies); D. M. Ross, *The Spiritual Genius of St. Paul;* Glover, *Paul of Tarsus;* C. Anderson Scott, *Christianity According to St. Paul* (1927; exceedingly valuable); D. A. Hayes, *Paul and His Writings;* Foakes-Jackson, *The Life of St. Paul.*

THE NEW TESTAMENT AND CHRISTIAN DOCTRINE

By Professor EDWIN LEWIS

Doctrine and Dogma, and Their Use. Christian doctrine may be defined as that body of truth concerning God and man and their relations in Jesus Christ by the acceptance of which men make possible for themselves the life and experience recorded in the N.T. Christian dogma is the form in which a real or an alleged Christian doctrine is cast by a given ecclesiastical organization, which then requires the membership to accept the form. Some dogmas grow obviously out of doctrine, and are practically universal among Christian men, e.g., the Nicene and Chalcedonian dogma of the twofold nature of Christ. Other dogmas are indirect and inferential, and are not of universal acceptance, e.g., the Roman Catholic dogma of transubstantiation of the bread and wine in the mass, and the Calvinistic dogma of predestination by God's sovereign will.

The precondition of Christian experience is a knowledge of certain truths. That is why doctrine is necessary. A non-doctrinal Christianity is an impossibility. But Christianity is committed to a world-wide conquest; and that is why dogma is necessary. Truths must be spread in order that life may be engendered, and truth is spread more effectively in the degree in which it can be cast into precise forms (laying aside, for the time being, the power of personal testimony). Moreover, Christianity involves a certain view of the world and a certain philosophy of life, and it finds itself in conflict with other world-views of a radically different character. In opposing such views it must clearly state its own, and such statements must necessarily be, to some extent at least, dogmatic in character. But it is evident that *the doctrine is more fundamental than the dogma.* Doctrine—in the sense defined—may be regarded as something fixed and unchangeable, whereas dogma has a more purely relative character. It takes its color from its time and circumstances. It may undergo radical change. The dogma of one age may be surrendered by another age. The purpose of dogma is to spread that doctrine whence may issue the Christian life and experience, and it is to be judged entirely by its success in doing this. Dogma ceases to be justifiable the moment it obscures or hinders or perverts saving doctrine.

The Bible-Principle in Protestantism. The average Protestant takes it for granted that the Bible is "the sole and sufficient rule of Christian faith and practice," and that it was this principle which gave birth to the Reformation. As a matter of fact, however, the Lutheran Confessions say very little about the *formal* principle of Scripture, although they make plain enough the scriptural basis of Lutheranism. Thus the *Augsburg Confession,* one of the earliest Lutheran statements, drawn up in 1530, asserts in the preface that the doctrine of the Confession is "derived from the Holy Scriptures and pure Word of God." (See Schaff's *Creeds of Christendom,* vol. iii, p. 4. The citations from the various creeds in the present article may be confirmed from this great work of Schaff, published in three volumes, which will henceforth be referred to as *C.C.*). The fifth article contains a long criticism of those "traditions" which Romanism had fastened on the church. The *Articles of Smalcald* (1537), also Lutheran, declare that "the Word of God, and no one else, not even an angel, can establish articles of faith" (*C.C.*, i, pp. 253–257; cf. Hagenbach, *History of Doctrines,* ii, p. 232). The *Formula of Concord,* the last of the Lutheran Confessions (1580), was the result of an attempt to bring doctrinal unity to the Lutheran church. It begins thus: "We believe, confess, and teach that the only rule and norm, according to which all doctrines and all teachers ought to be esteemed and judged, is no other whatever than the prophetic and apostolic writings both of the O.T. and the N.T." It further asserts that "other writings, whether of the fathers or of the moderns, with whatever name they come, are in nowise to be equaled to the Holy Scriptures." (*C.C.*, iii, pp. 93–97).

The *Reformed Churches*—those in which the influence of Calvin and Zwingli prevailed—show a more rigid adherence to the letter of Scripture than characterized Lutheranism, and a more radical departure from ecclesiastical tradition. The Reformed Churches "start from the absolute sovereignty of God and the supreme authority of his holy Word," whereas Lutheranism "starts from the wants of sinful men and the personal experience of justification by faith alone" (*C.C.*, i, p. 216). Thus, as Hagenbach puts it, Luther himself reached his *formal* principle (the Scriptures as the only rule of faith) by means of his *material* principle (justification is by faith alone), and so argued at the Leipsic Disputation (*op. cit.*, ii, pp. 229f.).

Zwingli made free use of the principle that Scripture and faith were co-operants: to understand Scripture one must have faith, and Scripture in its turn confirms faith. In his *Sixty-seven Articles* (1523) he affirms that the gospel does not depend upon the approbation of the church; that the gospel sets forth all necessary saving truth; and that the gospel makes the doctrines and traditions of men useless as respects salvation (*C.C.*, iii, pp. 197f.; cf. i, p. 364). The *Second Helvetic Confession* (1566), which ranks next in importance to the Heidelberg Catechism among Continental Reformed symbols, holds that the Scriptures, being God-given, are their own sufficient authority, and contain all that is necessary to a saving faith and a holy life. Traditions which contradict Scripture, even though they claim to be apostolical, are to be rejected (*C.C.*, iii, pp. 237f.; cf. i, pp. 396–397).

Calvin wrote in his *Institutes* as follows: "This, then, must be considered as a fixed principle, that, in order to enjoy the light of true religion, we ought to begin with the doctrine of heaven; and that no man can have the least knowledge of true and sound doctrine without having been a disciple of the Scripture" (vol. i., ch. 6, §2, p. 73). He further argues that since the church was built "upon the foundation of the prophets and apostles," of whose teaching Scripture is the record, it is impossible for the church to have authority over that teaching (ch. 8, §§1, 2). And he also argues that only as the reader is guided by the same Spirit as that which produced the books in the first place can their true meaning be known (ch. 8, §13).

The *English Reformation* was a slow process, beginning in 1527 with Henry VIII's abolition of the authority of Rome over England, and the dissolution of the monasteries; making real advance under Edward VI, Henry's only son; suffering a reaction under Mary Tudor, Henry's oldest daughter; and attaining permanence as the Established Church of England under Elizabeth (d. 1603). Its reaction from certain Roman extremes was not so violent as in the case of Lutheranism and Calvinism, but it held the characteristic Protestant position on the sufficiency and supremacy of Scripture. Indeed, one of the richest fruits of the English Reformation was the translations of the Bible, culminating in the King James Version, 1611 (see art., *English Translations of the Bible*, pp. 80–7). The sixth article of the 1571 edition of the *Thirty-nine Articles* reads: "Holy Scripture containeth all things necessary to salvation; so that whatsoever is not read therein, nor may be proved thereby, is not to be required of any man that it should be believed as an article of the faith, or be thought requisite [as] necessary to salvation." The O.T. apocryphal books (see pp. 191–2) are affirmed to be useful, "but yet doth it not apply to them to establish any doctrine." The eighth article accepts the three historic creeds; the twentieth denies the power of the church "to ordain anything that is contrary to God's written Word"; the twenty-first denies the authority of the pronouncements of General Councils except in so far as these agree with Scripture; and the thirty-fourth allows a certain authority to tradition, but makes tradition changeable according to the necessities of time and place (*C.C.*, iii, pp. 487–516). The *American Revision of the Thirty-nine Articles*, made in 1801 for the Protestant Episcopal Church in America, leaves untouched the articles bearing on Scripture, except that it omits the twenty-first. The *Twenty-five Articles of the Methodist Episcopal Church* were prepared by John Wesley on the basis of the Thirty-nine. He left practically unchanged as to their sense articles six and thirty-four (respectively five and twenty-two in the Methodist articles).

The *Westminster Confession* (1647) opens with a vigorous assertion of the usual Protestant position. The Canonical Scriptures "are given by inspiration of God to be the rule of faith and life." One must be moved by the Holy Spirit if one would understand the word aright. "The whole council of God concerning all things necessary for his own glory, man's salvation, faith, and life, is either expressly set down in Scripture, or by good and necessary consequence may be deduced from Scripture: unto which nothing at any time is to be added, whether by new revelations of the Spirit, or traditions of men" (*C.C.*, iii, pp. 600–606). Discussing this Confession, Schaff says: "No other Protestant symbol has such a clear, judicious, concise, and exhaustive statement of this fundamental article of Protestantism. . . . The Confession plants itself exclusively on the Bible platform, without in the least depreciating the valuable aid of human learning . . . in its own proper place, as an aid in ascertaining the true sense of the mind of the Holy Spirit. . . . It is clear that Protestantism must sink or swim with this principle" (*C.C.*, i, p. 781). The various other churches organized on a presbyterian or independent basis accept this general Protestant position.

The position of the *Quakers*, or the *Society of Friends*, is unique. In the Established Church of England we have an example of Protestantism which *supplements* the Bible-principle with the principle of tradition. In the Friends, we have an example of Protestantism which makes the Bible-principle *secondary*, and gives the supreme place to the inward testimony of the Spirit. The Friends reject all outward authority in religion—including the Bible itself—and all the "ordinances of man." They therefore have no creed, as such, but they endeavor to exemplify the simplicity and devotion of the primitive Christians, and they hold the essentials of the evangelical faith. Their great theologian was Robert Barclay, who drew up in 1675 the *Confession of the Society of Friends.* Its main points for our purpose are as follows: (1) To know God in Christ is the height of human happiness. (2) The foundation of this knowledge is in the leading of the Spirit. He to whom God thus makes himself known is *certain* of the truth thereby learned, and will subject it for confirmation to nothing else, not even the written Word itself. (3) The Scriptures being a record of like revelations to other men, it follows that they are but "a declaration of the fountain, and not the fountain itself." The Spirit is first. To receive the Scriptures because they proceed from the Spirit is necessarily to make the Spirit supreme (*C.C.*, iii, pp. 789–791; cf. i, pp. 866–871). This is really the carrying to an extreme of the principle, present in all the Reformers, and, indeed, in the mystics of all ages, of the "testimony of the Spirit."

The Sources of Doctrine in Catholic Bodies. The affirmation of the Protestant principle gave rise to counter-affirmations on the part of the two great Catholic bodies, the Roman and the Greek. There was nothing new in what they said, however; they simply restated their historic positions.

The *Council of Trent*, originally assembled in 1545 and continued off and on during the next twenty years, represented the effort of the Roman Catholic Church to grapple with the problems created by the rise and spread of Protestantism. The Council decreed that the divinely given saving truth and the associated moral discipline are contained in the books and unwritten traditions which were "received by the Apostles from the mouth of Christ himself, or from the Apostles themselves, the Holy Ghost dictating." Hence both the books and the traditions are to be received and equally venerated. The Latin Vulgate (see p. 865b), which includes the O.T. Apocrypha, was declared to be the authentic translation (a pronouncement which greatly troubles modern Roman Catholic scholars). The decree denounces any interpretation "contrary to that sense which holy mother church—whose it is to judge of the true sense and interpretation of the Holy Scriptures—hath held and doth hold; or even contrary to the unanimous consent of the Fathers" (*C.C.*, ii, pp. 79–83). This position was reaffirmed in practically the same language in the Dogmatic Decrees of the Vatican Council of 1870 (*C.C.*, ii, pp. 240–242).

The position of the *Greek Catholic* or *Orthodox Church* was stated by Dositheus, Patriarch of Jerusalem and Palestine, as part of the *Confession of the Synod of Jerusalem*, 1672. The statement forbids private interpretation. It puts tradition on a level with the authority of the church itself. The church interpretation of Scripture and tradition is authoritative and infallible. (The Greek Catholic Church denies that there is a visible head of the church, a Pope, whose *ex cathedra* pronouncements on all questions of doctrine are infallible.) General and indiscriminate reading of Scripture is forbidden as tending to lead to error, since there are many things therein hard to be understood and only the authorized interpreter can make them plain. The position of Dositheus was reaffirmed in the *Larger Catechism of the Orthodox, Catholic, Eastern Church*, published at Moscow, 1839—"the most authoritative doctrinal standard of the orthodox Græco-Russian Church." It puts Scripture and tradition on a level, although it also emphasizes the fact that there was apostolic tradition before there was apostolic writing.

The Procedure in the Primitive Church. Christianity did not begin with a body of writings. The writings which make up our N.T. were a late *product* of the Christian movement. There were Christian men, and therefore the Christian life and experience, long before there were *written statements* held to be authoritative. Christianity began in certain historic facts associated with the life and work of Jesus Christ, and in the testimony to those facts and their meaning offered by a small group of men—the "apostles"—whose testimony was based on first-hand experience. The characteristic of the early church was freedom and spontaneity. Those who composed it accepted the authority of "the words of the Lord" as these were repeated by the apostles, and in this same "Lord" they saw One whom they regarded as a divinely given Saviour from sin, but there was as yet no elaborate and closely articulated body of theological belief. To live a holy life in the Spirit through faith in Christ, and to bear themselves in love toward their brethren—this was the central demand. They were concerned rather to cultivate for themselves and to awaken in others a certain life and experience than to formulate intellectual beliefs. (See art., *Formation of the N.T.*, p. 858b.)

But such life and experience necessarily implied a belief of some kind. To accept the apostolic testimony to Christ meant to believe something about him. This belief, in its simplest form, was expressed in the baptismal confession, i.e., the words required to be repeated by the candidate at his baptism. The original confession was probably a simple statement of belief in Jesus Christ as Messiah and risen Lord (Rom. 10[9]) but it was soon elaborated into belief in God the Father and in Jesus Christ his Son and in the Holy Spirit (see Mt. 28[19]). But even in the primitive church the range of belief was much wider than that, as is intimated in the details of "the mystery of godliness" given in 1 Tim. 3[16] and in the statement of "the first principles of Christ" given in Heb. 6[1, 2]. Among the "first things" which Paul said he had "received" were the death and resurrection of Christ (1 Cor. 15[3]), and he exhorts Timothy to "hold fast the form of sound words" which had been "committed" unto him (2 Tim. 1[13, 14]). In a similar way Jude exhorts his readers to contend earnestly for "the faith once delivered" (v. 3).

The baptismal confession soon became longer. This was due, first, to the necessity of guarding against errors; and second, to the spread of Christianity among Gentiles, many of whom were quite ignorant not only of the Christian facts but also of the underlying O.T. teaching. The baptismal confession took its most widely used and authoritative form at Rome. Before the middle of the second century, the confession there had taken the following form: "I believe in God, Father Almighty, and in Jesus Christ his Son, our Lord, born of the Holy Spirit and of Mary the virgin, crucified under Pontius Pilate and buried, on the third day rose from the dead, ascended into heaven, sitteth at the right hand of the Father, from whence he cometh to judge both quick and dead. And I believe in the Holy Spirit, the Holy Church, the remission of sins, and the resurrection of the flesh." The student must be referred to the authorities for the story of how this confession was developed, clause by clause, as the necessity arose of combating heresy, especially that of Marcion and the Gnostics, and of how it eventually became "The Apostles' Creed." (Cf. Harnack, *History of Dogma*, English translation, vol. i; Sabatier, *Religions of Authority*, English translation, pp. 44–55; McGiffert, *Apostles' Creed.*)

This confession, then, was held to be authoritative. But why authoritative? Because it had apostolic sanction. The answer calls attention to another feature of the early church, namely, the tendency gradually to centralize authority in the bishops, regarded as the divinely appointed successors of the apostles. This authority extended not only to ecclesiastical matters but also to questions of belief, until eventually obedience to the bishop was made a fundamental requirement of orthodoxy (cf. Harnack, *op. cit.*, vol. ii, p. 85). It was only a step from this to the contention, first stated clearly and explicitly by Cyprian, that "outside the church was no salvation." His theory was that the apostles were ordained of God; that the bishops were their successors in both office and power; that the church having been originally dependent on the apostles was therefore permanently dependent on their episcopal successors; and that therefore the bishops, on whom the church was founded, and by whom it was represented, and in whom was its bond of unity, had all authority in both faith and practice. (Cf. Sabatier, *op. cit.*, pp. 98–100; Harnack, *op. cit.*, ii, pp. 70–90.)

The bishops, then, before the middle of the third century, were the authoritative interpreters of the faith. But where was this faith (more strictly, body of belief) found? It was found in apostolic *tradition* and in apostolic *writings*, and these had already become, of course, integral parts of the life of the church. What was fluid and elastic in the common mind, and what was officially crystallized in the various baptismal confessions and other statements, was regarded as identical with the original apostolic faith. But by the middle of the second century there was also going on in the church a good deal of theological activity. Men like Clement of Rome, and Papias, and Hermas, and Irenæus, and Justin, and Tertullian, and Origen were passing through the crucible of their mind the apostolic inheritance and attempting to ally it with a prevailing philosophy—in the case of some of them, especially the Greek "Apologists," the so-called Logos-philosophy. The result was that there entered into the increasing body of "tradition" a certain amount of theological speculation. Not only so, but there was also an increasing stress on matters ecclesiastical. What Harnack calls the "secularizing" of Christianity arose not simply from the tendency to transform the original gospel of reconciliation into an imposing philosophy of religion, but also from the gradual surrender by the church of its "other-worldly" character as the kingdom of heaven temporarily on earth, and the conscious adoption of a purpose to make itself at home in the present world. All that went with this in the way of externalities of the life of the church conceived now as a visible organization of world-wide scope likewise entered into the body of "tradition" held to be apostolic. Cyprian's third-century conception of the function of the bishops, therefore (see above), seemed likely to fasten on the church, as essentials of Christianity and conditions of salvation, both a non-apostolic sytem of theology, and a non-apostolic system of ecclesiastical procedure—non-apostolic, that is, in the sense that it could not be *directly* traced to the original Christian brotherhood.

For our purpose, the ecclesiastical procedure is less important than the theology, although historically the two belonged together. It is impossible to give a complete statement here of the theological development of the second and early part of the third centuries. But such statements as those of Irenæus (*Against Heresies*, bk. i, ch. 10, §1), of Tertullian (*On the Præscription of Heretics*, ch. 13) and of Origen (*On First Principles*, bk. i, preface, §§4–6) show a general conformity to the long Roman baptismal confession given above. (All may be read at length in Schaff, *C.C.*, ii, pp. 13–23 or in the translations in various volumes of *The Ante-Nicene Fathers.*) There are, indeed, radical departures from this, as when Tertullian includes, as part of original Christianity, the belief that the world was created out of nothing, and that the creative agent of the world, the "Logos," was "made flesh" in the womb of Mary; or as when Origen includes in it the belief that the devil is a fallen angel, and that the writings of prophets and apostles have a secret meaning open only to those who are especially illuminated. Even with such debatable additions as these, however, it is still possible to claim that the statements by these men of "the rule of faith" are comparatively simple and primitive, and if this were all we had to deal with the problem would be easy. But in actual fact, a great deal more than this was held by these men to be of the essence of Christianity. They have left us a very considerable body of literature, and it reveals how great was the theological activity of the second and third centuries. Much that was written was in the nature of a defense of the apostolic faith, but much of it was also a theological elaboration of that faith, and the tendency was *to transfer the authority of the apostolic faith to the later theological elaboration.* With the corresponding theory of episcopal authority already strongly developed, and with the bishops inclined to regard *all* tradition as binding, it is easy to see that Christianity was in danger of traveling further and further away from the simplicity of the original gospel.

The Saving Influence of the New Testament in the Early Church. That danger was by no means altogether escaped, but that it was escaped to some extent was due to the fact that there had come to be included in the total apostolic tradition *that part of the tradition which was in writing.* What was written necessarily shared the authority of the total tradition, but just because it was written, and therefore in a sense static, it served as a check upon the unwritten tradition with its tendency to go on increasing. The story of how these writings were gradually collected and given their commanding position must be read elsewhere. (See art., *Formation of the N.T.*, pp. 853–8.) To read that story in connection with the changing emphases that were characterizing the church of the time, and not to see in the story the hand of God, is to be blind indeed. It is no exaggeration, but sober historical truth, to say that the collecting of a few documents from the first century and assigning to them a position of authority respecting Christian faith and practice *saved Christianity.* There was, it is true, a certain loss due to the fact that the faith became more or less standardized. Men ceased to look for new revelations, and more and more emphasized the revelation that had already been given. The recognition of the authority of the unwritten tradition also tended to obscure certain things in what was written. The rite of baptism, e.g., is hardly a conspicuous feature of the N.T., yet it had become so in the practice of the church, and continued to be so even after the settling of the N.T. canon. The N.T. nowhere makes assent to propositions more important than a man's being "a new creation in Christ Jesus," but it was just this assent to propositions rather than a life of love in the Spirit which the church—due, it must be said, to certain historical conditions—had more and more come to emphasize, and which Harnack calls "the most fatal turning-point in the history of Christianity" (*op. cit.*, ii, p. 31). Yet although Harnack gives this adverse judgment on the exaltation of mere belief, he agrees with the majority of scholars in regarding the formation of the N.T. canon as the greatest creative act in the history of the church (*ibid.*, p. 62, footnote). Among its beneficial results he specifies the following: (1) By modifying many prevailing views, it prevented the total secularization of Christianity; (2) it kept before the church the early Christian ideal; (3) on matters that were specifically Christian, it forced the O.T. somewhat into the background; and (4) by assigning so much importance to the writings of Paul, it kept before the church his keen redemptional consciousness.

Dangers of the Protestant Principle. This brief historical survey makes it evident that the Protestant principle has convincing support in early Christian history. The support is admittedly indirect, but it is not the less valuable on that account. It was the wholesome influence of the N.T. which held in check the dangerous principles of tradition and of episcopal authority in the third and fourth centuries. As time went on, however, that influence grew weaker, and the practically unlimited application of the opposing principles issued in that depraved state of the church which it required the Protestant Reformation, with its uncompromising appeal to Scripture, to remedy.

In the extreme form, however, which the Protestant principle came to have in the seventeenth century and later, it produced a brood of ills just as serious in their way as those which resulted from the more complex Roman Catholic principle. The authority of Scripture was made just as tyrannical in Protestantism as the authority of the church itself had ever been in Romanism. The sound principle of the original reformers, that "the Holy Scriptures contain all things necessary to salvation; so that whatsoever is not read therein, nor may be proved thereby, is not to be required of any man that it should be believed as an article of faith, or be thought requisite or necessary to salvation" (see above, article six of the Church of England, article five of the Methodist Episcopal Church, etc.), was transformed—more exactly was perverted—into the principle that *the belief of the whole of Scripture was necessary to salvation.* It has taken a century of devoted scholarship to save Protestantism from this perversion of its own principle.

This danger of perversion, however, should only make us the more determined to hold fast to the Protestant principle in its true form. We shall still listen with respect to tradition; we shall still be willing to listen to the collective judgment of Christian men according to the rule of Vincent of Lerins (d. 450), namely, that truth is established by the tests of antiquity, universality, and unanimity (*quod ubique, quod semper, quod ab omnibus creditum est*); but we shall still retain the privilege of appeal to the N.T. under the illumination of that same Spirit which produced the N.T. in the first place.

The Rule of What Faith? The claim that the N.T. is the rule of faith and the main source of Christian doctrine is, however, a claim that has its own problems, and these have been frankly faced by modern Protestant scholars, e.g., Ritschl, A. Sabatier, Sanday, W. N. Clarke, and W. P. Paterson. Thus Paterson (whose *Rule of Faith*, the Baird Lecture for 1905, published in 1912, is one of the best discussions of the subject) shows with great clarity that we cannot use the Scriptures as a rule of faith until we have discovered *what that faith is* of which they are to be the rule. We are confronted with a twofold fact: there is, first, what might be called the essence of Christianity, and this is the real subject of revelation and is verifiable in experience; and there is, second, a body of theological utterance which radiates from that living essence and is intended to explain and defend it. Now, if recent study has made one thing more clear than another, it is that *this distinction between living essence, revealed and experiential, and theological expansion, relative and instrumental, characterizes the N.T. itself.* It follows that not all things in the N.T. are of equal value for the purposes of the Christian life and experience, and therefore not all things are of equal authority.

Then have we no certainty at all? Is the lament of John Henry Newman justifiable—that certainty was to be found only in Rome? This is by no means the conclusion. It ought to be apparent that Jesus Christ came into the world to make Christian people, and that what sufficed to make Christian people in the first place will suffice to make them still. Our historical survey has shown that the more complicated the requirements the church of the early centuries laid upon its members, the more the original meaning of the Christian gospel became submerged. The virtue of the Protestant Reformation was that it called the church—or a part of it—back to the central fact. That central fact was that the church originated in a life and an experience. That life and experience grew out of the attitude of faith and love directed toward Jesus Christ conceived as the divinely sent Saviour from sin. The earliest Christian community was a group of men and women who had that faith and love. There has never been a more profoundly Christian group since, or a group that more nearly approximated the mind of Christ. By them Christianity began its conquest of the world. By them the N.T. was produced. But that of which the N.T. was the product existed before the product itself. What was that? A faith and a love, a life and an experience, centering around Jesus Christ as Lord and Saviour. The final significance of the N.T., therefore, is *not in the book itself, but in that to which it bears testimony.* It is there that we find the authority and the certainty, because it is there that we find something which may be validated in our own experience. What lies beyond the range of that experience, e.g., speculations on the relation of Christ to God, on the precise nature of the Holy Spirit, on the logical steps in the order of salvation, on the method of resurrection and judgment—these speculations, both within and without the N.T., will still have their proper place and value, but they will be secondary and not primary. On such questions Christian men will continue to differ. But in the nature of the case they cannot differ on that out of which such questions naturally arise, namely, utter surrender to the control of the Spirit of Jesus Christ, both in one's relations to God and in one's relations to others. It is through the N.T. that we learn best of all what that Spirit is and what it means to submit to its control. That is why the N.T. is indispensable for Christian doctrine as defined at the beginning of this article; but the authority resides less in the book itself than in the life and experience and associated facts which existed prior to the N.T. and of which the N.T. is both a product and a witness. (Cf. pp. 889–90, 1092–3.)

Literature: W. P. Paterson, *The Rule of Faith;* A. Sabatier, *Outlines of a Philosophy of Religion*, pts. ii and iii, and *Religions of Authority and of the Spirit* (both in Eng. trans.); Sanday, *Form and Content of the Christian Tradition;* Harnack, *History of Dogma*, vol. ii, chs. 1, 2, 3 (Eng. trans.); W. N. Clarke, *The Use of the Scriptures in Theology;* Deissmann, *The Religion of Jesus and the Faith of Paul;* H. R. Mackintosh, *Originality of the Christian Message;* Gore, *The Holy Spirit and the Church;* Scott, *The First Age of Christianity.*

V. COMMENTARY ON THE BOOKS OF THE NEW TESTAMENT

MATTHEW

BY PROFESSOR J. NEWTON DAVIES

INTRODUCTION

The Charm of Matthew's Gospel. The author of this most widely read Gospel in the early church, and one which has had such a profound influence in determining men's ideas of Christ, has been appropriately styled the architect among the Gospel writers. His finished work resembles a massive cathedral, representing the toil of various periods and hands, but withal so deftly harmonized and unified that it gives the impression of a living whole over the portals of which one could fittingly write the words "to the glory of the Most High God and the praise of his Son Jesus Christ." Within the sacred precincts of this building we meet with all sorts and conditions of men, shepherds, magi, centurions, fishermen, taxgatherers, farmers, vinedressers, blind beggars, generous women, scribes and Pharisees, children and aged men, representatives of every class in the social order and of every type conceivable in the moral order, suggestive of the wide appeal which the personality of Jesus made to men. The all-commanding figure that arrests our attention, however, and captures our imagination wherever we look is that of Jesus of Nazareth, the incomparable teacher of divine truth, the wonderful healer of disease and sickness, whose radiant life was completely dedicated to the service of men, whom the common people heard with gladness but whom the religious leaders, with tragic blindness, crucified. No one can walk in the sacred precincts of this Gospel without being moved to praise and prompted to worship in spirit and in truth.

Divisions of the Gospel. Like many Jewish books, e.g., the Psalms, this Gospel is divided into five sections, the dividing line being clearly discernible in the formula "and it came to pass when he had ended these sayings," which is found in 7^{28} 11^{1} 13^{53} 19^{1} 26^{1}. Each of the five sections again is divided into two parts, one consisting of narrative and the other of discourse, as follows: (1) Narrative, chs. 3, 4; discourse, chs. 5–7. (2) Narrative, chs. 8, 9; discourse, ch. 10. (3) Narrative, chs. 11, 12; discourse, ch. 13. (4) Narrative, chs. 14–17; discourse, ch. 18. (5) Narrative, chs. 19–22; discourse, chs. 23–25. To these five sections the author provides a prologue (chs. 1, 2) and an epilogue (chs. 26–28), the former heralding the coming of the King, the latter proclaiming his passing, and his entrance into glory. This architectonic tendency of the author is shown also in his love of arranging incidents and sayings in groups of three, five and seven (see Allen, *Matthew*, p. 65).

Structure of the Gospel: Relation of Narrative Sections to Mark. One of the assured results of devout criticism is that almost the whole of Mark is incorporated in "Matthew" (see art., *Structure of the Synoptic Gospels*, p. 868). This conclusion can be verified by any student who cares to examine in a synopsis a parable or incident which is found in both Matthew and Mark. This discovery indicates that the author was not one of the twelve, for one who had been an eyewitness himself would not resort to the work of a secondary witness. The incorporation of the material by the compiler of Matthew has not been done in a slavish, mechanical way but in a manner which reveals distinctly the compiler's own individual prepossessions and ideas; he does not hesitate to change, omit, tone down, and otherwise adapt the material in his source for his purpose, showing clearly that he did not consider that Mark's account was complete. (For a full survey of this whole question see the introduction to Allen's commentary on Matthew.)

Matthew's Omissions of Marcan Material. These are of several kinds: (1) Complete parables or incidents like the parable in Mk. 4^{26-29}; the healings in 7^{32-37}; the widow and her alms, 12^{41-44}. (2) Mark's references to the strong human emotions of Jesus are invariably left out. Cf. Mk. 3^{5} Mt. 12^{1-3}; Mk. $1^{41-43,}$ Mt. $8^{3,\ 4}$; Mk. 10^{14} Mt. 19^{14}. (3) Statements of inability on the part of Jesus, e.g., Mk. 1^{45} 6^{5} 7^{24} 14^{58} are omitted in Matthew. (4) The asking of questions on the part of Jesus is omitted. Mk. $5^{9,\ 30}$ 6^{38} $8^{12,\ 23}$ 9^{12}. These omissions are due to the growing feeling that anything which might be interpreted as disparaging to Jesus must be toned down or ignored.

Differences from Mark. The *changes* which Matthew has made vary in character. (1) Mark's uncommon words, like *skizomenos* ("rent asunder") in 1^{10} and *enankalizo* ("taking into the arms") in 9^{36} are changed to more ordinary ones. Many of Mark's vivid historic presents are converted into past tenses; repetitions and redundancies are condensed. (2) Perhaps with a desire to prevent possible misunderstanding of the character of Jesus, the question in Mk. 10^{18}, "Why callest thou me good?" is given in Mt. 19^{17} as "Why askest thou me concerning that which is good?" and the statement in Mk. 6^{3}, "Is not this the carpenter?" becomes in Mt. 13^{55}, "Is not this the carpenter's son?" (3) Matthew makes several changes also in matters affecting the disciples. Cf. Mk. 4^{13} Mt. $13^{16, 17}$; Mk. 4^{40} Mt. 8^{26}; Mk. 6^{52} Mt. 14^{33}. In Mk. 10^{35} James and John make the request to sit at the right hand and the left in the Kingdom; in Mt. 20^{20} it is *their mother* who does it for them. (4) In reference to the miraculous, Matthew's tendency is to dwell more fully on its striking features (cf. Mk. $1^{32, 33}$ and Mt. 8^{16}). The numbers in both the feeding miracles are increased by the natural addition of women and children, 14^{21} 15^{38}. Cures are by physical means and gradual in Mk. 7^{31} 8^{22}; in Mt. $8^{3\text{-}16}$ a word suffices. The difference, of course, is simply in the account, without implying any misunderstanding of the event itself. See also the description of the convulsive struggle of the epileptic boy, Mk. $9^{20\text{-}26}$ Mt. $17^{14\text{-}18}$. In the parable of the cursing of the fig tree the withering takes place *immediately* in Matthew (21^{19}; but cf. Mk. $11^{14, 20}$). (5) Another group of changes is in the form of additions, e.g., to Mark's story of the walking on the water by Jesus, Matthew adds the incident of Peter doing the same until fear possesses him. In the passion narrative, Matthew adds the statement about the earthquake and the rending of the rocks and the opening of the tombs of a number of saints, who then appeared in the city. Here again it must be said that the changes (more strictly, the differences) do not involve contradictions. There are also interesting examples of changes in which Matthew adds qualifying and explanatory statements; e.g., he adds in 16^{4} the words "but the sign of Jonah" to Mark's words in $8^{11, 12}$. Mt. 12^{40} has all the appearance of a piece of scribal ingenuity. The words about divorce in Mk. 10^{11} and Mt. 19^{9} show interesting differences. Mk. 1^{11}, "Thou art my beloved Son," becomes in Mt. 3^{17} "This is my beloved Son."

All these examples indicate that Mark may be regarded as the primary source, and that as far as the *narrative* sections are concerned Matthew represents a later stage in the evolution of the Gospel tradition. As to the real significance of this fact, see section below on "The Historical Value of Matthew."

Relation of Discourse Sections to the Source Q. When the contents of Mark are abstracted from Matthew we find large sections of discourse like the Sermon on the Mount (chs. 5–7), the preaching of the Baptist ($3^{1\text{-}12}$), the denunciation of the Pharisees (ch. 23), a long missionary charge (ch. 10), some of which is found in Mark, a discourse about the Baptist (ch. 11), and several parables (chs. 13, 22, 25). A great deal of this material is found in Luke. Varying views are held concerning the nature and origin of this extensive teaching material which forms so very important a part of this Gospel. Many think that Luke and Matthew have drawn from a common Aramaic source and that the variations in the two are due to the different ways in which the document has been translated. Others, and they represent by far the larger group, think that Matthew and Luke have derived their material from two different Greek sources of the sayings of Jesus current possibly at Antioch and Cæsarea, while there are some who think that both depended on oral tradition, there being considerable evidence that the Jews of the time could retain large masses of teachings in their memories. Josephus, e.g., in his *Apion* says, "If anybody asks our people about our laws he will more readily tell them all than he will tell his own name." A few have thought that Luke in compiling his Gospel borrowed directly from Matthew.

The second conjecture, that of a common source, is the most probable. The four great centers of the early church, Jerusalem, Antioch, Cæsarea, Ephesus, had each its own compilation of the sayings of Jesus, which would account for the variations in some of the sayings of the Master as we find them in our Gospels. Scholars usually refer to this teaching source by the letter Q, the first letter of the German word *quelle*, which means source. (For further discussions of Q see art., *Structure of the Synoptic Gospels*, pp. 871–2, and the chapter on "The Reconstruction of Q" in Streeter, *The Four Gospels*.)

Streeter thinks that Luke has preserved Q in a purer form than Matthew because Luke as a rule did not conflate his sources as Matthew did. About 272 verses in Luke represent, in his considered judgment, the contents of this old Gospel of the pro-Gentile church in Antioch. In determining its contents he seems to have worked on the following principles: (1) When similarity in statement is very striking, as in Mt. $3^{1\text{-}12}$ and Lk. $3^{1\text{-}17}$, this points conclusively to a common written document. (2) If what is apparently the same saying is expressed in a very different form in Matthew and Luke, it shows that Matthew has found his material in another document, the M document, which we will refer to in our next paragraph, or else in some way he has blended the two accounts; the documents Q and M in some way overlapped. Q did not contain, in his judgment, the Lord's Prayer; for the account in Matthew is embedded in material drawn from M, and in Luke from a section of the L document—the document standing to Luke as M to Matthew. (3) The document contained occasional narrative to explain some piece of teaching, the emphasis on the Baptist being due to the fact that the document was composed in a place where the prestige of the Baptist was strong; it did not, however, contain the Passion narrative, on account of the fact that this could be taught in oral tradition. It is ethical teaching that sooner or later needs a written document. Q was written to supplement *oral* tradition. (4) Matthew omitted the two Q passages, Lk. 9[51-56] (the Samaritan village) and 17 [20, 21] ("The kingdom of God is within you"), perhaps because one involves a rebuke to the apostles, and because the other emphasizes a view of the Kingdom which does not stress the objective catastrophic aspect which in Matthew is so conspicuous.

The Judaistic Element in Matthew. When both Mark and the material which scholars think formed the contents of this missing document Q are deducted from Matthew, there is left some material which is very Judaistic and particularistic in tone and feeling, representing, in the view of Streeter, the material Matthew derived from the church at Jerusalem. The following are some of the sections which have emanated from this source: 10[5, 6], which contains our Lord's command to the disciples not to preach the gospel to the Gentiles but to the lost sheep of the house of Israel; 10[23], which contains the statement, "Ye shall not have gone through the cities of Israel, till the Son of man be come"; 5[17-20], the paragraph in the Sermon on the Mount which lays stress on the value and validity of every jot and tittle of the Law; 23[2, 3], which enjoins not only obedience to the Law but even to the scribal interpretations; 18[15-22], the passage in which the word "church" occurs, which in all probability refers to the Christian group in Jerusalem, and where we find the words "Let him be unto thee as the Gentile and the publican"—a statement not easy to harmonize with the portrayal of Jesus' spirit as a whole. Streeter is of the opinion that Matthew has supplemented the narrative on the problem of divorce in 19[3-12] from this source, as well as the narrative in 12[9-13]. When the story of the Syrophœnician woman in Mk. 7[24-30] is compared with the account in Mt. 15[21-28], the latter is seen to be much more Judaistic; one sometimes wonders whether even the account in Mark has not been somewhat colored by this Judaistic emphasis. Streeter thinks it is not difficult to suspect the influence of the desire of the followers of James (see Acts 15) to find a justification for their disapprobation of the followers of Paul by taking sayings of Jesus out of the context in which they were originally spoken, and thereby giving to them a different meaning. To this source belong too the apocalyptic discourse and the parables which are of an apocalyptic and eschatological character (e.g., chs. 24, 25).

Other Sources. There are other sources which have been employed in the Gospel; e.g., Peter, who gives his own reminiscences in Mark, is a little different in the sources in which he figures in Matthew—the halo which the early church placed about his head is beginning to appear. Matthew must have stood in the main stream of oral tradition, from which he derived many of the details in the Passion story and in the infancy and resurrection narrative. While this does not seem to have been critically sifted and valued, it does not follow that it is not on the whole historical, or that the large element of the symbolical and poetic which it contains is to be ruled out as of no value. There are other ways of conveying truth than by statements which are coldly exact. For the detailed discussion see the commentary.

The Problem of Authorship. The author of this Gospel must remain unknown. The reason why Matthew's name has been linked with it is because of a saying of Papias quoted in Eusebius: "So then Matthew composed the oracles (*logia*) in the Hebrew language and each one interpreted them as he could." This statement refers in all probability to a collection of proof texts for the use of the catechists of the Christian Church, or it may refer to a collection of the sayings of Jesus which the apostle Matthew was instrumental in gathering together. The compiler of the Gospel was evidently a Jew of the Dispersion who lived outside Palestine, probably in Antioch, a man well versed in the Hebrew Scriptures, and who was profoundly impressed by the correspondence between the incidents in the life of Christ and the prophecies and Psalms of the O.T. To what extent the O.T. has influenced his narrative in the N.T. is a question of very real significance; e.g., in the story of the triumphal entry Matthew introduces two beasts whereas in the other Gospels there is only one, and he quotes Zech. 9[9] accordingly.

But the inference sometimes drawn that there were *not* two beasts is not at all necessary. There is nothing improbable in an ass having a colt by her side. The incident may just as well have called Matthew's attention to the prophecy as that the prophecy determined his telling of the incident. (See below on "The Historical Value of Matthew.") The incident concerning Jonah is seriously considered to be a type of the resurrection (12[40]). So in the Passion narrative—details in the experience seem to have reminded Matthew of Psa. 22 and 69, and he took care to point these out. He may, indeed, have overdone this. Many feel that such a cry of despair as Mt. 27[46] sounds strange on Jesus' lips, and that the version of Mark, which represents Jesus as absolutely silent on the cross with the exception of the final cry, seems more in keeping with the perfect confidence in God which he taught and exemplified throughout his life.

The Historical Value of Matthew. These critical insights into the composition of the first Gospel may be and, indeed, have been used to discredit its historical value. But such a use of them shows a complete misapprehension of the significance of criticism. (See art., *N.T. and Criticism*, p. 885.) It is true that there are differences between Matthew and the other Gospels. If there were not these differences, we should have only one Gospel instead of four, and therefore only one witness instead of four. The differences indicate not unreliability in the accounts, but, rather, richness and variety in the total gospel tradition, the respect of the guiding Divine Spirit for the individuality and especial purpose of the respective writers and compilers, and the place which experience necessarily came to have in the understanding of certain events in the life of Jesus and of the relation he bore to human salvation. Because Mark stands nearer in point of time to the historical Jesus than do those parts of Matthew which are not found in Mark does not mean that Matthew's additions are without value. We want to know not merely how Jesus appeared to his contemporaries, or to his disciples in the first days of their acquaintance, but how he appeared to a sympathetic observer of a later day who had grasped his connection with the O.T. and the Jewish religion, and wrote of him from that standpoint. This need is supplied by Matthew, just as Luke and John supply our need to see Jesus under still other aspects and in still other relations. No one Gospel tells us everything. Indeed, even the four Gospels together do not do that (see Jn. 20[30, 31]), and we supplement their testimony to the historical Jesus by other N.T. writings which are more especially concerned with the activity of the glorified Christ and his gradual embodiment in the life of the church. Something of this interpretative significance attaches to the parts peculiar to Matthew's Gospel. That he reports some things differently from the other writers is unquestionable. Equally unquestionable is his purpose to link up the life and work of Jesus Christ with the O.T. But far more important than the degree to which here and there a verse from a prophet may have influenced the telling of an event is the fact that Matthew is absolutely right in the conviction that controls his entire account, namely, that Jesus of Nazareth is the long-expected Messiah of his people, at once David's son and David's Lord (Mt. 1[1, 6, 16] 22[41-45]), in whom alone the Israel of flesh and blood can become the true "Israel of God" (cf. Paul in Rom. 9[6-8] Gal. 6[16]). Our critical study of the first Gospel would be so much waste of time if it did not, both directly and indirectly, reveal more clearly these divine-human features in the portrait of the Central Figure.

Literature: Commentaries by Box (Century Bible), Micklem (Westminster Commentary), T. H. Robinson (Moffatt N.T. Commentary), Allen (International Critical Commentary), McNeile (the last two use the Greek). Montefiore, *The Synoptic Gospels;* Streeter, *The Four Gospels.*

CHAPTER I

I–17. The Genealogy of Jesus. (Lk. 3[23-38].) Two important questions are dealt with in this opening chapter—the descent of Jesus from David and his fatherless birth. To the Jews, no Messianic claims could be considered valid unless they included descent from David, hence the emphasis on this in such N.T. passages as Acts 2[30f.] 13[23] Rom. 1[3] 2 Tim. 2[8] Rev. 22[16]. Jesus himself, as we see from Mt. 22[43-45], lays no stress at all on the question of his Davidic descent. It is strange that the genealogy and the virgin birth should occur in the same chapter, for many argue that they cancel one another. If Jesus is descended from David—so the argument runs—it must be through Joseph, for this is Joseph's genealogy. It must follow therefore that if the claims of Davidic descent are to have any validity, the blood of these ancestors must flow in the veins of Jesus, which was not the case in view of the story of vv. 18–25. The Sinaitic Syriac version of v. 16 reads as follows: "And Joseph, to whom was betrothed the virgin Mary, begat Jesus called the Christ." According to that ancient version (see art., *Transmission of N.T.*, p. 864b), the purpose of the genealogy was to demonstrate the Davidic descent of Jesus and that he was born of human parents. Jesus' own indifference to Davidic descent, however (22^{43-45}), may weigh on the other side.

The genealogy. (1) It is divided artificially into three divisions—Abraham to David (vv. 2–6a), David to the Babylonian captivity (vv. 6b–11), the Babylonian captivity to Joseph the husband of Mary (vv. 11–16). Each section has fourteen names, Mary and Joseph being counted as two generations. In order to make this mechanical division of an equal number of names (due, according to Canon Box, to the desire to make an acrostic on the numerical equivalents of the Hebrew letters of the name "David"), the names of many generations have had to be omitted. (2) A large number of the names is to be found in Ruth $4^{13, 17, 18-22}$, and in 1 Chr. 3^{10-16}. (3) The genealogy contains the names of women (an unusual factor in Jewish genealogies), to show perhaps that Jesus was to minister to women on whose lives there rested a moral stain, as on the women of the genealogy. (4) This genealogy strikingly suggests that all history prior to Jesus converges on him; the fallen fortunes of his own nation are to be restored through him; the dreams and hopes of the checkered story of the past are to be realized through his life and ministry; he is to usher in a new kingdom in which all that is noblest and finest in men will come to fruition. (5) It is impossible to reconcile this genealogy with that of Luke. Many attempts have been made to do so, but modern scholars tend to the opinion that both tables are incomplete, and that in the absence of fuller knowledge we can do nothing but let them stand as they are.

16. On *begat*, see note below.

18–25. The Fatherless Birth of Jesus. (Lk. 1^{26-56} 2^{1-20}.) This story is told with great delicacy and is free from that coarseness so often characteristic of the myths and sagas that tell of the birth of great heroes from gods and goddesses. It is told also in the terms of a lofty monotheism and not in those of a crass polytheism. To give the story a greater degree of credence the evangelist reports that Joseph received a communication from God in a dream by means of an angel. He was told to take Mary as his wife and that the miraculous birth of the Child to be was a fulfillment of the prophetic statement in Isa. 7^{14}. The value and point of this quotation were perceptible only to those who read the LXX, for the Hebrew word translated "virgin" in the LXX means a young woman of marriageable age, whether virgin or not, and there is no evidence that Isa. 7^{14} was ever understood in the sense given to it by Matthew till it was so applied by Christians. The evangelist must have been writing to Jewish Christians who lived in the Hellenistic world. Hence many scholars suggest that the expectation prevalent in that world that saviours and great deliverers must be born in a miraculous way has influenced the evangelist in the telling of this story. (See Pfleiderer, *Early Christian Conception of Christ*, ch. 1.) Others contend that the story has been influenced by the statement of Isaiah. (See further, art., *Life of Christ*, p. 892a.) The congruity of the idea, however, with the whole character and significance of Jesus is an undeniable fact, and this, for many, gives Matthew's story the required verisimilitude.

In the N.T., three presentations of the unique personality of Jesus are to be found: the *Marcan*, which sets forth the conception that it was at the baptism that the manhood of Jesus became a vehicle for the full expression of the Spirit of God; the *Matthean*, propounded here, which claims that Jesus was born of a virgin by direct interposition of the Spirit of God; the *Johannine* and *Pauline*, which emphasize the pre-existence of Jesus (Jn. 1^{1-18} Phil. 2^{5-8}). Perhaps it is because of the difficulty of reconciling the idea of pre-existence and that of a virgin birth that John and Paul have left out of their writings all reference to the latter (but cf. R. J. Cooke, *Did Paul Know of the Virgin Birth?*). It is admitted by all that the story of the miraculous birth appeared late in the preaching of Christianity.

Begat. It is often claimed that the Greek verb rendered *beget* denotes legal but not necessarily physical descent. The evidence for this, however, is of a very meager kind. In the other passages of the N.T. where the word occurs it means "to give being to," "to beget" or "to procreate."

18. In Jewish law not only an actual *betrothal*, but the mere possibility that one party believed himself or herself to be betrothed prevented marriage to any other party. A betrothed girl became a widow if her *fiancé* died. After betrothal therefore, but before marriage, the man was legally husband—an informal canceling of betrothal was impossible. Strack and Billerbeck claim that cohabitation was customary in Galilee but not in Judæa during betrothal (but cf. Edersheim, *Jewish Social Life in the Days of Christ*, pp. 148f.).—*Holy Spirit.* The narrative breathes the atmosphere of the O.T. and the word "Spirit" here is used in its O.T. sense, i.e.,

the power of God in active exercise (see Swete, *Holy Spirit in the N.T.*, pp. 27-31).

CHAPTER II

In this chapter the curtain is lifted for us on five moving scenes: the coming of the Wise Men to Jerusalem; their arrival at Bethlehem; the massacre of the innocents; the flight to Egypt; and the return of Joseph and Mary to Nazareth.

1-12. The Wise Men. Burne Jones, the artist, said that this story was too beautiful not to be true, and he has depicted the scene in a lovely tapestry. It really amounts to sacrilege to apply the cold implements of historical criticism to a narrative which breathes the spirit of such pure poetry. *Wise men* is the rendering of the word *Magoi* (Magi), a technical term for a Persian priest versed in magic and astrology. The Jews through their exile may very well have influenced Babylonian and Persian thought, and there are evidences that the people of the East were expecting a world deliverer to appear in the West who would usher in a golden era of world peace. We know also that a deputation from Parthia came to pay homage to Nero in 66 A.D. as Mithras incarnate; that deputation returned by a different route from the one by which it came. It is true also that the Parsees believed that the coming of a great hero was heralded by the appearance of a striking star, as was the birth of Alexander the Great. Whatever may have been the nature of the original event here described, the narrative has an abiding value which we must not overlook. It suggests the truth that the Babe of Bethlehem is to be a magnetic power to draw the Gentiles as well as the Jews, and that those men are deservedly called *wise* who in small beginnings see great possibilities, and who realize that life reaches its zenith in the adoration of Him who deserves the homage of our hearts and the choicest gifts that we can bestow. They also are wise who shun that spirit of worldliness whose purpose it is, as illustrated in the spirit of Herod, to destroy all that Bethlehem represents in life.

13-15. The Flight to Egypt. There is no mention of the flight to Egypt in the Lucan narrative, for there we gather that about two months or so after the birth the parents of Jesus left for Nazareth to settle there. The O.T. quotation (Hos. 11[1]) is not very apt, for the prophet in his statement refers to the past history of the nation and of how God called it out of bondage, and there is really nothing at all prophetic there. However, it is not impossible that the journey was made, and that, as so often in Matthew, it is narrated just because it can be connected with an O.T. passage.

16-18. The Massacre of the Innocents. Herod was quite capable of this act of cruelty, but no mention of it is made by any contemporary historian nor can we fit the incident very well into the Lucan chronology. The story of the infancy of Moses contains an interesting parallel to it.

17. Jer. 31[15]. *Ramah* was some distance to the north of Jerusalem while Bethlehem was to the south. Not *Rachel* but Leah was the ancestral mother of Judah. The purport of the quotation is hard to explain unless it be to create a mood and atmosphere appropriate to the present story.

19-23. The Return to Nazareth. Herod's realm was divided into four parts after his death. *Archelaus* was tetrarch of Judæa and Antipas was ruler in Galilee. The parents, according to the story, choose Nazareth because of their fear of Archelaus, and this may very well be the case, but we must also remember that they are going back to a town of which they have been long residents.

23. *Nazarene.* The Greek word is *Nazōraios,* which is a quite different word from *Nazarenos.* Some derive the word from the Hebrew word *Nezer* in Isa. 11[1], which means a "branch" or "shoot," and later came to have a Messianic significance. Others connect it with the Hebrew word *Nezorai* used in Isa. 49[6] to describe Him who shall both restore Israel and be a light to the Gentiles. Canon Box thinks that the word "Nazarene" was an early designation applied to Jesus and his disciples which in time acquired a contemptuous meaning (cf. Jn. 1[46]). Jewish Christians changed it to Nazaraean, a title of honor, which suggested that he was the "branch" of Messianic prophecy (cf. Isa. 11[1]). For a similar play on a word, see the note on Isa. 62[4].

CHAPTER III

1-12. The Forerunner of Jesus. See notes on Mk. 1[2-8], and cf. Lk. 3[1-20] Jn. 1[6-36]. There is a long interval of time between chs. 2 and 3. Without a preamble of any kind we are ushered into the wilderness of Judæa and are introduced to the ascetic, austere figure of the Baptist clad in his rude robe of camel's hair, bound with a leathern girdle. The description of the movement inaugurated by him and of the message he proclaimed has probably been colored by later Christian influences. The evangelists (especially the fourth) see John in the light of what happened afterward. If he held the Christian views attributed to him in the fourth Gospel (see 1[27]), it is impossible to understand why he did not identify himself with the disciples of Jesus (cf. 11[3]).

In this paragraph we learn several important things about John. (1) His *message* (v. 2) is exactly the same as that of Jesus in Mk. 1[14, 15]. The Greek word translated *repent* must not be interpreted exclusively from its etymological meaning, "change of mind." It includes also sorrow for sins and failures as well as moral conversion. (2) John is essentially a *pathfinder* (Isa. 40[3]). His special task it is to awaken in men the slumbering moral and religious emotions preparatory to the coming of Christ. (3) *He challenges Pharisees and Sadducees*—the former for choking religion with the bonds of ceremonialism, the latter for starving religion with the husks of materialism and worldly conduct. Both are compared by him to *vipers* (v. 7) because of their subtle poisonous influence on society and their tempting of men to evil courses. One of their worst faults (v. 9) was that of relying on good done by others in the past to excuse their own present sins. (4) He proclaims *an imminent judgment* (v. 10). The Jews believed in a judgment, but not on themselves; the heathen only were to experience its severity. The judgment announced by the Baptist will include those who lead lives that are useless and without fruit. (5) He employs *apocalyptic imagery*. The ministry of the coming Messiah is conceived of in terms of strength and fire; to this is added the emphasis on "Spirit" (*in the Holy Ghost*), for the ministry of the new Messiah is to be creative, soul-renewing and constructive. The figure of the *winnowing fan* means that Jesus will be concerned only with reality, and with those things that will sustain life. There is much that we regard as important which from Jesus' standpoint is nothing but "chaff for the burning."

13–17. The Baptism of Jesus. See notes on Mk. 1[9-11] and cf. Lk. 3[21, 22]. We now arrive at one of the great impressive moments in the career of Jesus. Luke informs us that at the baptism Jesus was engaged in prayer, and those prayer experiences of the Master were often the occasions of mystic visions. The Transfiguration, e.g., came upon Jesus "as he was praying" (Lk. 9[29]). It is while in the midst of this exalted spiritual mood that he receives a deep conviction of the transcendent majesty and power of God expressed symbolically in the words, *the heavens were opened;* to this there is added a new sense of the immanent working of God in the soul, expressed as *the Spirit of God descending as a dove.* The dove to the Jews was a symbol of gentleness, peace, and new-creating life: so the Spirit quietly broods (cf. Gen. 1[2]).

The question is often asked why Jesus came to a baptism which is described as a baptism for the remission of sins. The answer given in two recent popular lives of Jesus is because he was conscious of sin, a reason which the context does not justify. John's words to Jesus imply that he was previously aware of the moral ascendancy of Christ, and the important statement of Jesus to the Baptist implies that he felt that baptism was not necessary as far as he was concerned, but he submits to the rite because, in his words, *it becometh us to fulfill all righteousness.* By the word "us" he means all the people, and by "righteousness," their duty and obligation to God. In the thought of Jesus, baptism was a symbolical way of dedicating oneself to the ideals and demands of a new life of righteousness. He availed himself of this significant moment in the history of his nation to identify himself with its aspirations for a better and holier life, and to dedicate himself publicly to his great life task. In doing this he felt that he was fulfilling a divine demand and obligation.

CHAPTER IV

1–11. The Temptation of Jesus. See notes on Mk. 1[12, 13], and cf. Lk. 4[1-13]. The Greek word translated "temptation" in the LXX and N.T. denotes all those experiences in life such as pain, sorrow, disappointment, solicitation to sin, and conflict of duties, by which a man is tried or proved; the idea of solicitation to sin in the modern sense of temptation is found only in a very few passages in the N.T. This wilderness experience of Jesus, occurring as it does immediately after the baptism, and prior to the public ministry, is essentially a testing of him to ascertain what methods he is going to adopt to realize his ideals. To reach the real meaning of this incident we must get behind its symbolic phraseology. All the early Christians believed in a personal devil whose chief business it was to accuse and slander men: hence the name Diabolos, "the slanderer." The evangelist himself conceived of this incident as objectively enacted, but we must regard it as a profound spiritual experience of Jesus expressed in symbolic language. What was essentially inward is described as being outward as well. Incitement to evil may come from without, but the real struggle always takes place within. The narrative clearly shows that Jesus could not conform to the current Messianic ideals of the Jews, for it was just these Messianic ideals which constituted his temptation (cf. pp. 209–10).

The first temptation (vv. 3, 4) consists in the attempt to induce Jesus to give a prominent place to purely material ends. There is borne in on him the suggestion that the world's crying need is a new social and economic order. If only he would dedicate his God-given powers to this end, the world would be at his feet in a very short time. The answer of Jesus shows how well he knows that the heart of man is made for God. Bread alone will never satisfy the deep hunger pangs of the soul. He himself is sustained by that assuring word of God spoken to him at the baptism. The supreme task of Jesus is so to influence the hearts of men that they too will be able to hear the sustaining voice of God, not only as it speaks out of the pages of the ancient records, but as it speaks out of the transforming experiences of life. His great errand is a religious one in the widest meaning of the word.

The second temptation (vv. 5–7) takes us in imagination to the high roof of the Temple house where Roman soldiers were posted to overlook the crowds at the feast. The suggestion is made to Jesus that though he fling himself from this great height to the pavement below angels would bear him up in their hands according to the psalmist's promise, and in consequence men would flock to his banners and enthusiastically embrace his cause. By his answer Jesus shows that we are not to put God to the test by resorting to expediencies and ways that are direct violations of his laws. Jesus shows very conclusively that he is not going to resort to spectacular methods in his ministry among men. The fact gives us a criterion for judging certain events in the record.

The third temptation (vv. 7–9) is a very real one. The Jews expected their Messiah to be a great political leader leading his people to war against the oppressors and enemies of their race. Jesus absolutely repudiates the use of force to advance his cause; his help comes from God, and it is only as he conforms to his will that he can carry out his spiritual purposes among men.

12–17. Jesus Begins His Ministry at Capernaum. See notes on Mk. 1^14, 15^. Matthew sees in the Galilæan ministry of Jesus a striking fulfillment of the two prophecies in Isa. 9^1, 2^.

16. The symbol of *darkness* fittingly hits off the moral plight and confusion of the society of Jesus' day, while the figure of *light* which we meet here for the first time in the N.T. admirably sets forth the essential character of the ministry of our Lord. The ministry of Jesus was a veritable dayspring from on high whose aim it was to bring beauty and loveliness to the gray, drab lives of men, to call forth the latent powers of the soul, to inspire in the hearts of men the psalm of praise and to prompt men with a desire to minister to others.

18–22. The Call of the Four Disciples. See notes on Mk. 1^16-20^ Lk. 5^1-11^.

23–25. Early Ministry of Jesus. See notes on Mk. 1^21-39^ Lk. 4^31-44^. A resumé of the ministry of Jesus, the main elements of which were *teaching*, *preaching*, and *healing*. Its popular far-reaching character is emphasized in v. 25. The new movement influenced the whole of Palestine.

CHAPTER V

The Sermon on the Mount (chs. 5–7). Scholars differ among themselves as to whether Matthew or Luke gives us the sermon in its more original form. Wellhausen and J. Weiss think that the briefer, terser forms in Lk. 6^17-49^ preserve for us more accurately than Matthew the actual words of Jesus, while Harnack argues strongly for the early character of the Matthean account. It is not improbable that Luke is the earlier, but when we remember that our Lord spoke these words in Aramaic and that in translating them explanatory phrases are often necessary to make plain the true significance of his words, the longer forms in Matthew may be supposed to bring us often nearer to the mind of our Lord. In the work of interpreting this great sermon three things must be determined: (a) its significance for the disciples to whom it was first spoken; (b) its meaning for the church to whom the Gospel was written; (c) its application to the complex needs of modern life. (See further the notes on Luke's report).

1–12. The Beatitudes. The sermon opens with the moving lyrical strains of the beatitudes, which have inspired the hearts of multitudes through the ages, a sure sign of their genuineness and originality. Moffatt and others rearrange their order by bringing the third into second place.

3. *Blessed.* Some modern translators prefer the word "happy." The Semitic word does convey more the idea of happiness: it suggests success or prosperity, and is a formula of congratulation meaning "Oh the happiness of"; but to Greek-speaking Christians this did not exhaust the meaning of the word. Ignatius and Polycarp give the word a deep religious meaning when they use it to describe outstanding Christians, especially martyrs. *Poor in spirit.* Moffatt translates "who feel poor in spirit." To understand aright the type of character represented by this phrase we must remember that the term "poor" in the O.T. (Isa. 61^1mg.^ Psa. 9^12mg.^ 10^2mg.^) was frequently applied to those men and women who, often wanting in worldly goods and persecuted for their loyalty to God, still remained stanch and true. Such men had learned to place complete confidence in God as the only true source of strength. There were such people in the days of Jesus, often disdained and despised by the official classes (cf. Jn. 7[49]), who called them the *am-haaretz*—the people of the land. It is difficult to realize how venomous and bitter was the hate of the rabbis toward this ostracized and outcast class of people. Paul admirably described the poor in spirit in 2 Cor. 6[10] (where read *a pauper, yet a means of blessing to many; without a penny, yet possessing all things*). *Kingdom of heaven.* Matthew prefers this expression to "kingdom of God" because Jews preferred not to use the sacred name. *Realm* (as in Moffatt) or *Sovereignty* is better than kingdom, being less static and local, and expresses better the idea of the present manifestation of God's power as well as its full climactic manifestation in the future. The poor in spirit are the people whom God desires as his subjects and loyal followers; through such men he will manifest his authority and extend his power in the world.

4. *Mourn.* J. Weiss claims that the word includes the thought of loud lament such as is common in Oriental lands. This lays too much stress on the external signs of grief. The beatitude could be paraphrased in these words, "Oh the happiness of those who are peculiarly sensitive to sin in themselves and in society, and who feel deeply all the distress caused by the greed and covetousness, the selfish ambitions and cruelty of men." *Comforted.* The N.T. lays special emphasis on the ministry of comfort. The Greek word literally means "to call to the side of." Jesus comforts men by bringing them through his gospel to the presence of a God of compassion and a friend of sinners, and into a kingdom whose foundations are justice and truth, and to a life that is immortal.

5. *The meek.* The modern associations of the word "meek" unfit it to translate the Greek here (*praüs*). The word (an adjective) occurs only twice more in the N.T., in Mt. 11[29] 1 Pet. 3[4]; but the corresponding noun (*praütes*) is frequent in the Pauline Epistles (2 Cor. 10[1] Gal. 6[1] Col. 3[12]). In Mt. 11[29] Jesus emphasizes this beautiful grace as one that is outstanding in his own character, associating it with lowliness of heart; while Paul in 2 Cor. 10[1] appeals to the Corinthians by the gentleness and consideration of Christ. The word "gentle" conveys much better the idea underlying the Greek word, though it does not bring out the thought which is present in the O.T. idea of meekness, of reverence and humility before God. *Inherit the earth.* In the O.T. this expression is a symbolic expression for the good things which were to come with the Messianic kingdom. Here it conveys the daring thought of the Master that the world will be ultimately peopled by men and women who exemplify his Spirit in their lives. The possession of the earth by any other spirit leads to war, hate, and oppression. Since pride is considered by Jesus as one of the cardinal sins, it is no wonder that in his ethical teaching he enthrones its opposite.

6. *Hunger and thirst* is in the O.T. (Isa. 49[10] 55[1, 2]) an expression for intense spiritual longing. The compiler of the first Gospel is surely correct when he adds the words *after righteousness;* which are not in Lk. 6[21]. The word "righteousness" is found only ten times in the Gospels. Mark does not have it at all; Luke uses it once (1[75]); the fourth Gospel twice (Jn. 16[8-10]); the remaining occurrences are in Matthew's Gospel, and in all these occurrences Moffatt prefers to translate it by the word "goodness." The word has something of the O.T. meaning of *the pervading of life by the principles of equity and humanity* which is the immediate effect of the true religion of Jehovah. J. Weiss thinks that since this Gospel was written after Paul, the Pauline use of the word—righteousness before God as a ground of acceptance with him—is decisive for its meaning here. It has been well observed that blessedness is pronounced in this beatitude on unfulfilled aspiration. It is the intent and aim of our lives that is the all-important thing in the sight of God.

7. *Merciful.* The adjective is found again in Heb. 2[17] only, where Christ is termed "a merciful and faithful high priest," but the verb, *to obtain mercy,* is quite common in the N.T. The merciful are the men and women who banish all feelings of revenge and ill will out of their hearts and who seek to cultivate an attitude of love and sympathy toward all mankind, especially toward the disfranchised and dispossessed. To Aristotle the emotion of pity was a troublesome one, and the function of tragedy, he said, was to evoke pity so that an outlet might be found for the perilous stuff. To Jesus, on the contrary, it is a divinely beneficial emotion which must be harnessed to practical and redemptive actions. What a contrast there was between the attitude of Jesus and Buddha in the presence of misery and wretchedness! The latter sought to escape from them while the former enters the haunts of wretchedness and woe to grapple with them and alleviate the sufferings of those who are their victims.

8. *Pure in heart.* H. Wheeler Robinson points out that out of eight hundred and fifty-one occurrences of the word *heart* in the O.T. one third denote personality as a whole—the inner life, character. A proportion of the remaining two thirds denote the emotional aspects of personality, but in a very large number the intellectual and volitional functions of conscious life are stressed. The word "heart" in this beatitude is *the equivalent of personality.* The idea of purity in Psa. 51 is coupled with a right spirit, and the purity of the N.T. always includes the ideas of integrity, singleness of purpose, the absence of low aims. To such is given Heaven's richest reward—the capacity to see God wherever he reveals himself.

9. *Peacemakers.* This beatitude is placed last because the qualities described in the first seven are the essential prerequisites of the peacemaker. Its presence in the list shows the importance Christ placed on the ideals of peace, for he is pre-eminently God's ambassador of reconciliation among men. The establishing of good will and harmony in home and in church, in community and in international relations calls for peace *makers*—men who can organize and carry into practice the ideals which they hold. To such is given open access to the glorious privileges of sonship in the blameless family of God. For the N.T. conditions of sonship, cf. the following: 2 Cor. 6^16-18 Gal. 3^26 4^7 1 Jn. 3^10 Mt. 25^34-40.

10–12. Some commentators regard these verses as additions of the compiler because they reflect a later period when the followers of Jesus suffered a great deal of persecution for their faith (cf. 1 Pet. 3^14-17). On the other hand, Jesus may have anticipated the persecution of his followers; for he would well know that the man who in a pagan, worldly, materialistic society incorporated in his life the graces of the beatitudes would surely have to face scorn, obloquy, and severe persecution. The experience of the church when the Gospel was written may have led the compiler to see deeper meanings in the original language of Jesus. Luke (6^22) in his account of these verses carries the interpretative principle still further, and applies it to include excommunication.

12. *Reward.* To the O.T. and Jewish ideas of reward Jesus adds new elements. See especially Mt. 20^1-16 25^21-23, where the reward becomes a free undeserved grace and is out of all proportion to the character and extent of the service rendered.

13–16. **Four Sayings.** Four distinct sayings are grouped together here to illustrate the Christian character. Four metaphors are used—salt, light, a city on a hill, a lamp on a lamp-stand.

13. See notes on Mk. 9^49 Lk. 14^34. *Salt* was used in Palestine for many purposes, such as to give brightness to lamps by sprinkling it in the oil, to purify and preserve from decay, and to sprinkle with the sacrifices. The metaphor stresses the distinctive elements of Christian character, the prime function of which is to give brightness to life, to preserve society from the forces of putrefaction and decay, and to give to the routine of life, which often becomes insipid and dull, zest and vital interest. Christian character bleached of its distinctive qualities is an utterly worthless thing.

14a. *Light of the world.* The distinctive graces illustrated in the beatitudes are for world service. Jesus with an ever-increasing wonder must often have watched the slow breaking of the light of dawn on the lovely hills of Palestine, awaking the flowers from their sleep, evoking the morning song of the birds, calling man from his home to enter the fields of labor. In the same way he sees the bright influence of his gospel, as it spreads over the world, helping to unfold the beauty latent in all human hearts, to call forth the song of praise and gladness, and to lead men forth to deeds of service and usefulness. (Jn. 8^12.)

14b. *A city on a hill.* The character of the Christian must stand out in prominence and give to men who behold it the impression that it is built on firm rocklike foundations, inspiring confidence in others and providing them with a shelter and a refuge.

15. Some interpreters compare Jesus to the *lamp* and the Christian to the *stand,* whose chief duty it is to reveal Christ as the light of men. Paul in his letters re-echoes the light metaphors of Jesus, as when he speaks of the armor of light (Rom. 13^12), sons of light (1 Thess. 5^5), fruit of light (Eph. 5^9). In John we have light of the world (8^12), and sons of light, 12^36 (cf. 1 Jn. 1^5-8).

16. *Good works.* This expression in the N.T. as used in Rev. 2^2, 19 includes not only practical deeds of kindness but also sterling qualities of character.

17–20. **The Relation of Jesus to the Law.** If vv. 18, 19 are genuine sayings of Jesus he definitely asserts that every minute requirement of the Law is valid and will be fulfilled, and that any violation of any one of the most insignificant of these requirements involves the infringement of the whole Law. Such teaching does not represent the mind of Jesus as it is revealed for us in the Gospels as a whole. Some of the sources used by the compiler of the Gospel were evidently influenced by the controversy between Paul and the Jewish-Christian section of the church in

Jerusalem (see intro., p. 995a). This source Streeter designates by the letter M, and he thinks that in the heat of the controversy certain sayings of Jesus were interpreted by one or other of the contending parties, especially the Judaistic. The following verses are illustrative of the influence of this section of the church on Matthew's record: 10^{5-23} 18^{15-17} $23^{2,\ 3,\ 8}$ 24^{20}.

17. *Fulfill.* Jesus fulfilled the Law by showing that religion in its essence was a different thing from law, and that a man who has been inwardly changed becomes a law to himself, seeing that he is guided by the Spirit of the Lord—for where the Spirit of the Lord is there is liberty (2 Cor. 3^{17}). In his fulfillment of the Law Jesus distinguished between the moral and the ceremonial, and at the same time summarized the moral law in the two great commands of love to God and love to man (see 22^{34-40}).

18. *Verily.* The Hebrews used the equivalent of this word, namely, *Amen,* after prayer and praise to corroborate and indorse, while Jesus gives the word a new use by *prefixing it* to his statements to give them weight and solemnity. This does not seem to have been done by the rabbis. *Jot* represents probably the Greek name for the letter *i*, which is similar in sound to the Hebrew letter *yodh*, which was also very small in size. *Tittle* (a little horn) represents probably the point or extremity which distinguishes some Hebrew letters from others.

20. The *Pharisees* and *Scribes* were preeminently the two classes who claimed to be models in their exemplification of the Law and tradition of their nation. (See art., *Backgrounds*, pp. 840–2.) J. Weiss, commenting on the phrase "kingdom of God," claims that the Sermon provides no program for the improvement of the world and its affairs: it is only concerned with the question, What must I do to be a blessed one? This verse alone would suffice to show how very one-sided this judgment of Weiss is.

21–26. **Concerning Murder.** By inserting the second half of v. 22 after v. 21 we have a much more natural sequence. V. 22b will then represent a rabbinic comment on v. 21 and not the words of Jesus. This penetration beneath the overt act into the hidden springs of action reveals the true greatness and originality of Jesus as a teacher. Jesus here utters his protest against the whole spirit of the Judaism of his day, with its overemphasis on law and comformity to external codes. Since all improvement of character must begin from within, Jesus turns his searchlight upon the heart and shows men what are the lurking forces within that arrest all growth and possibility of reform. Mastery over anger is only possible to those who feel themselves responsible to God. An ethic without religion cannot do this.

21, 22. *The judgment.* It is best to take the word in both clauses as referring to the tribunal of God. *Raca* is an Aramaic word meaning "empty" and was an expression of contempt. *Council*—probably meaning the local Jewish "Sanhedrin" which existed in every small town. *Hell of fire.* A valley west and south of the city of Jerusalem, called Gehenna (see mg.), was the dumping ground for the refuse of the city; it became the symbol for the place of future punishment.—Zahn thinks that the whole of v. 22 is an utterance of Jesus, and that by it he is really satirizing the scribal methods of exegesis; but it is much better to regard it as a sample of current scribal interpretation which in course of tradition was without good reason attributed to Jesus.

23–26. Two illustrations are added to the comment of Jesus on the law concerning murder, both stressing the all-importance of good will and the fostering of right relations with men. In the first (vv. 23, 24) harmonious relations between ourselves and our fellows are emphasized; otherwise worship and communion with God are nullified. In the second (vv. 25, 26) the importance of paying one's debts at the right time is stressed to secure the welfare of society. Everything that occasions ill will, anger, misunderstanding, must be avoided because they are inimical to the best interests of the religious and social life as well as to the highest development of our own personality. *Farthing* (Greek *kodrantes*) was one fourth of an *as*, and an *as* was one sixteenth of a *denarius*, which was equal to about twenty cents (see art., *Time, Money*, p. 79).

27–30. **Adultery.** (Ex. 20^{14} Deut. 5^{18}.) Jesus combines the seventh commandment and the tenth. This moral law was enacted to secure the peace and the purity of the home. Jesus goes beyond the O.T. Law by condemning all wrong thoughts and desires. Impurity is one of the great evils against which the followers of Christ must make truceless war. Purity is an equal obligation on men and women, married and unmarried. The relation of vv. 29, 30 and the preceding verses is not very close. They are quoted again in Mt. $18^{8,\ 9}$ Mk. 9^{43-48} (see notes) to show that the costliest sacrifice is essential to enter into life, while the words are quoted here to stress the fact that no sacrifice is too great to attain the priceless gift of purity.

31, 32. **Divorce.** The N.T. teaching on

divorce is to be found in the following passages: Mk. 10[11, 12] Mt. 19[3-9] Lk. 16[18] 1 Cor. 7 (see notes). The exceptive clause *except for fornication* is found only in the Matthew version of the saying (cf. 19[9]). Among the Jews there were two schools, one led by Shammai, which granted divorce on the ground of adultery alone, and the more lax school of Hillel, which permitted divorce on any pretext which the husband might offer (p. 841). So in the early church there were two schools, one which made the words of Jesus absolute and the other which permitted the exception. Mark and Luke represent the first, while Matthew supports the second. A similar division is found among modern scholars. Wellhausen, R. H. Charles, and H. G. Wood, while they regard the exceptive clause as an interpolation, claim that it nevertheless interprets our Lord's meaning because he was addressing himself to the question of divorce on inadequate grounds. Gore and Box, on the other hand, claim that the exceptive clause was introduced by the early Palestinian church to secure divorce for proved adultery and the remarriage of the innocent party. There seems no doubt that the original words of Jesus expressed the prohibition of divorce in its absolute form, but whether this high ideal can be embodied in the civil codes of nations is a matter of debate. (Streeter, *Adventure*, ch. 3.)

33–37. **Truthfulness in Speech.** (Cf. on 23[16].) In the judgment of Jesus, truthfulness and the ability to depend on the simple assertions of men were indispensable for the maintenance of communal life. Pre-eminently was it essential when men appeared before God that language should be stripped bare of all unreality and pretense. V. 37 is found in purer form in Jas. 5[12], "Let your yea be yea, and your nay, nay." Jesus has in mind the casuistical distinctions made by the Jews between different formulas and especially of the way in which they abused the Corban oath (see on Mk. 7[11]). To *swear by the head* (v. 36) means to set one's life in pawn. Jesus is not thinking of the use of oaths in civil courts—a procedure which civilized communities have found useful in the administration of justice.

38–42. **The Law of Revenge.** (Ex. 21[24] Lev. 24[20] Deut. 19[1-11] Lk. 6[29].) J. Weiss thinks that Jesus is here laying down a principle for a particular period in the life of the church, and that in consequence the command is only of temporary educative value. The phrase *non-resistance* or *passive resistance* which is often applied to this passage is decidedly a misnomer. Jesus is giving illustrations of the principle, "Overcome evil with good," and in so doing is registering his firm belief in the victorious power of goodness and benevolence. To meet by a revengeful spirit injury or insult done to oneself is only to multiply the evil and increase it a hundredfold. (Cf. the discussion in art., *Bible Manners and Customs*, p. 75a.)

39. *Evil.* The Greek word can mean the devil or any maliciously disposed person. *Right cheek.* To strike a person on the right cheek one must ordinarily use the back of the right hand: such a blow was considered among the Jews a very real insult.

40. The picture here is that of a law court where a cruel client exacts the severest penalty of the law by taking a man's shirt. The defendant is urged to part with his upper garment as well, and so make his adversary feel utterly embarrassed. The language is hyperbolical.

41. *Compel.* The Greek word is of Persian origin and was originally used of compelling men to undertake postal services for the government.

43–48. **Love of Enemies.** This law is surely one of the highest and most difficult which Jesus has given to us. He himself perfectly and beautifully fulfilled it in his own triumphant life. The measure in which we carry it out in our daily life depends on the degree in which we possess his Spirit. In true *love* there are three elements: admiration, the desire to possess, and the will to benefit; but all three are not emphasized wherever we find the word. In *love to one's enemies* it is the third element that is stressed. The follower of Jesus who can attain to this high ideal of loving his enemies will discover as his reward that he is approximating to the character of God, since one of the most glorious features in his character is his impartial kindness. He will also gain an entrance into the ranks of the sons of God (v. 45); his conduct will have the hall-mark of what in Lk. 6[32] is called *charis* (*gracious adornment*) and here in Matthew *perisson* (*worthy of note*), a word which Loisy translates by the French word *extraordinaire;* lastly, he will find himself on the road to moral perfection.

48. *Perfect.* Luke (6[36]) has "merciful," which shows that the special aspect of perfection in this verse is not moral perfection so much as perfection in kindness, sympathy, and generosity. The other must not be excluded, however, for the *teleios* or perfect man, according to Epictetus, was the man who had set his feet on the true path and was still advancing—"going on unto perfection."

CHAPTER VI

The religious life must express itself in benevolence, devotion and worship, self-discipline and self-examination, and in self-possession and calmness of spirit. Jesus in this chapter sharply criticizes the outward forms in which the religious people of his day gave expression to their piety.

True Righteousness Illustrated. This is the theme of the chapter, and the illustrations concern almsgiving (vv. 1–4), prayer (vv. 5–15), fasting (vv. 16–18), and quiet trust and confidence (vv. 19–34).

1–4. Almsgiving. V.1 is the text; the rest of the chapter supplies illustrations. The Greek word ordinarily translated *righteousness*, Moffatt renders by the word "charity"; J. Weiss uses the German word which means "piety" the *Twentieth Century N.T.* has "religious duties." No one English word can convey the full meaning of this Greek word, which embraces the idea of piety as it expresses itself in various religious duties. Our Lord puts his finger on the weak place in the religion of his day in the phrase *to be seen of men.* As with so many Oriental cults, Judaism in his day lacked greatly the elements of inwardness and conscience. The Pharisee considered that he had been amply rewarded when he had gained a reputation among the people for devoutness of spirit. The men who aspire in religion after reputation and popularity miss altogether the highest rewards of the religious life—fellowship with God and the consciousness of his favor (cf. note on 5[6]).

2, 3. The giving of *alms* was not a religious duty required by the Law; for that reason special merit was attached to it. Ample opportunities presented themselves for ostentatious giving, for, as we read in Acts 3[3-10], beggars posted themselves near the Temple precincts, and during the great pilgrimages near the city gateways. What a contrast there was between the unostentatious almsgiving of a Cornelius and that of the Pharisees! His alms, we are told, went up as a memorial before God (Acts 10[4, 31]). His almsgiving illustrates perfectly that striking expression of Jesus, *let not thy left hand know what thy right hand doeth. Sound a trumpet* is a figurative expression for noisy ostentatious giving. Usually the sounding of trumpets was only resorted to on the occasions of public fasting and in times of drought. *Hypocrites.* This is the first instance of this word in the Gospel, where it occurs no less than ten times. In the Greek of the period the word denoted an *actor* or *stage player;* hence its use in the N.T. of a pretender or dissembler whose religion is a mask behind which there hides a great deal of unreality and treachery. *They have received their reward.* The Greek word *to receive* (*apecho*) is frequently found on the Egyptian ostraca used as receipts for money paid. Jesus intimates that the Pharisees have in the plaudits and approval of men received all the reward they are likely to get. They can now even give a receipt for the same.

4. The A.V. adds the word *openly*, which is not found in the best MSS. Its omission gives a meaning in complete harmony with the message of Jesus.

5–8. Prayer. Prayer formed a very important element in the religious life of the Jew; wherever he chanced to be the true Israelite lifted up his heart to God at dawn, noon, and sunset. It formed an important element in the life of the home and in the services of the synagogue and the Temple. At the great feast days special prayers appropriate for the season were offered by the people. Jesus singles out three elements for criticism in the prayer life of his day: (1) *Its ostentatiousness.* The Pharisees contrived to be in the most crowded thoroughfares at the appointed hours so that they might gain an audience. (2) *Its formality.* The Greek word translated *vain repetitions* (*battalogia*) means to babble or speak words without thought or meaning. A senseless heaping together of words and phrases was characteristic of many cults and of certain religious circles in Palestine. The well-known prayer of eighteen petitions which every Israelite prayed three times daily is ten times longer than the Lord's prayer. (3) *Its lack of filial trust and confidence.* This long, tedious repetition of all one's needs and desires showed, in the judgment of Jesus, a lack of trust in their heavenly Father who knew all their needs.

9–15. The Lord's Prayer. (See Lk. 11[2-4].) A comparison of this prayer in Matthew and Luke shows that the form in Matthew is longer. Most scholars are of the opinion that the prayer in Luke is the original one and that the additions in Matthew were made for liturgical purposes in the early church. The prayer is conspicuous for its brevity and for the revelation it gives us of the dominant concerns of Jesus in his earthly life.

9. *After this manner pray ye.* The Greek says literally "*so* pray ye," and the *so*—used in the emphatic sense—governs every petition of the prayer and indicates the fact that it is a model and type of what a liturgical prayer should be, for Jesus by giving this model prayer is showing how the church should imitate his method and *fashion new prayers* for the changing and growing needs of life. The compilers of the collects in the Common Prayer book learned their lesson admirably. Many church services would be greatly enriched by the use of some modern collects.

Our Father which [*who*] *art in heaven.* Luke has simply the word "Father," but we find Matthew's phrase in Mk. 11[25, 26], so it is quite possible that Jesus was accustomed to address God by this longer expression. The word *our* emphasizes the intimate loving relationship between father and son, while the words *in heaven* serve to bring out the majesty and power of God. *Thy name* is a periphrasis for God. *To hallow* is to regard a person or thing with reverence; the opposite of hallowing in the O.T. is "profaning," and men were guilty of that when they gave to God a divided allegiance and persisted in holding imperfect conceptions of him. We reverence him when our devotion to him is pure and when our thoughts of him are high.

10. *Thy kingdom come.* Modern translators prefer the word "rule" or "dominion" to the word "kingdom," the latter being too local and giving the idea that it was used by the Master in an exclusively eschatological sense—which is not the case, since Jesus referred to the exercise of God's power in nature and in the affairs of men, while in Mt. 21[43] he speaks of the Kingdom being taken from the Jews and given to some other people. Jesus appreciated to the full the manifestations in the life of his day of the beginnings of a lordship of God, but his followers are to pray constantly for a fuller manifestation of the sovereignty of God in the affairs of men. *Thy will be done.* This petition is a further unfolding of the preceding request, for it is only when the will of God is done by all in every section of society and when all that opposes that will is removed that the kingdom of God will come in all its power and influence.

11. *As in heaven.* Heaven is the place of perfection. There all is ideal because all embodies and expresses the will of God. The kingdom of God is therefore the kingdom of heaven realized on earth, i.e., the will of God expressed in all human life. *Daily bread.* The Greek word translated *daily* (*epiousios*) is a very rare word and is in consequence variously rendered. Origen and Jerome suggested "necessary for existence"; Loisy prefers "sufficient for the day"; Moffatt and many others think that the word means "for the following day." We can pray for the morrow but we are not to worry about it. Marcion's reading, *Thy bread give unto us,* was very widespread in the early church and may have reference to Mt. 4[4] and Jn. 4[32].

12. *Forgive us our debts.* For *debt* Luke has "sins"; the word "transgression" (*trespass*) has come into the prayer from the Common Prayer book. "Debt" is more comprehensive than "sin": it includes sins of omission and commission. We are to ask God to forgive us the non-fulfillment of our obligations to him and to society and to the moral discipline of our own personality. In order to receive his forgiveness we must continually exercise a forgiving spirit to those who have wronged us (cf. Mk. 11[25]).

13. *Bring us not into temptation.* The preceding petition pleaded for the forgiveness of sins that were past; this petition pleads for protection from sins in the future. Without our Lord's original words it is impossible for us to explain the real significance of this difficult request. The best light upon it is to be found in our Lord's experience in the garden of Gethsemane, when he enjoins his disciples to pray that they enter not into temptation. *Cause us not to be led unto temptation* would perhaps better convey the meaning of this prayer, for Jesus knew that in hours of great trial the soul was exposed to very insidious perils and moral dangers. *Deliver us from* [*the*] *evil* [*one*]. The word *evil* in the N.T. refers sometimes to Satan, in whose power the world lay, according to the belief of some in the days of Jesus (see art., *Backgrounds,* p. 846b; cf. p. 206a); but in other places the word means evil in the abstract. Here the first meaning is the probable one, for to the early Christians the sovereignty of the devil was opposed to that of God (see Rev. 12, note). From this malign influence the disciples are to pray for deliverance.

Thine is the kingdom, etc. The familiar doxology with which the Lord's Prayer usually concludes does not have the best MS. support. See v. 13 mg.

14, 15. Matthew adds to the prayer a further statement on the importance of forgiving one another as a pre-condition for receiving divine forgiveness.

16–18. Fasting. Jesus takes for granted the prevailing custom of fasting. It is not forbidden by him (Mk. 2[18-22], note), but he does severely condemn the practice of some in his time who wore the hair long and disfigured the face to make themselves unrecognizable. Jesus would have men anoint their heads and wash their faces and live normal lives and yet at the same time practice the most rigid self-discipline and self-control (cf. 23[23], note).

19–34. Piety as it Expresses Itself in a Life of Complete Trust and Freedom from Care. In this beautiful paragraph Jesus gives his answer to the all-important question of how a man can live a life free from distracting care and worry. The answer may be classified by verses as follows: 19, 20; 21–23; 24; 25–32; 33–34. Cf. notes on Lk. 12[13-34].

19, 20. We are to realize the uncertain

character of material possessions—expensive clothes easily spoiled by moths and worms, and silver and gold which thieves could steal in spite of the strongest barriers.

21–23. Cf. notes on 12[38-42] Lk. 11[29-36]. The heart is made for the light of divine knowledge which alone can illumine it and prevent sin from gaining possession of our lives. *Single eye* (v. 22). The Greek word translated *single* (*haplous*), according to Souter, means directing the eye to one definite object, and is a symbolic expression for singleness of purpose; others conjecture that since the word single is contrasted with *evil eye*, and as the latter is used in Proverbs for niggardliness, so the single eye is a metaphorical expression for generosity. In Mk. 7[22] the expression "evil eye" means envy, so possibly the single eye is one that is trustful and entirely free from envy.

24. Personality is incapable of a dual allegiance; it is so richly and wonderfully made that only God can fill the deep voids of the heart. If earthly treasures are made the chief ends of our human quest, we are doomed to failure and bitter disappointment, for the heavenly Maker of souls has so made us that we cannot find abiding peace outside himself. *Mammon.* The word occurs elsewhere in the N.T. three times, namely, Lk. 16[9, 11, 13]. The Aramaic word *mammon* is the equivalent of money, riches, worldly goods, and is derived by Dalman from *aman*, meaning "that on which one puts one's trust."

25–32. We are to realize the insignificance of things like food and clothing and to remember that there are some things beyond our control. To the Jew, man was a unity made up of a number of parts, all drawing their life from a breath soul which has no existence apart from the body. The body contains heart, liver, kidneys, eyes, ears, hands, and mouth, each capable not only of physical activity, but also of psychical functions (see art., *Intertestamental Religion*, pp. 202–4). Is the body consisting of such wonderful capacities to be occupied merely with questions of food and clothing? *Stature* (Greek *helikia*, v. 27). The word is sometimes rendered "age," but stature better fits the context. Jesus shows the futility of anxious care concerning one's physical size or the span of one's years.

33, 34. We are to overcome the evil of care by filling the mind and heart with the concerns of the kingdom of God, a great soul-filling and mind-absorbing end; and we are to struggle after his righteousness—the victory of good in the world, and also personal perfection. We do this by taking each day as it comes from the hands of a gracious God, permitting only the duties of the day to claim our thought. Such a frame of mind is an inexhaustible source of strength for a successful struggle for existence.

CHAPTER VII

1–5. Warning Against Censorious Criticism. (Lk. 6[37f.]) To arrogate to oneself the function of a censor of other people's conduct, especially when one's own life is far from blameless, has a demoralizing influence on character. It breeds arrogance and a sense of superiority —the deadly enemies of humility and self-examination and the sworn foes of tolerance and kindly sympathy. This perversity of character was far too widespread to be confined to the Pharisees: all classes provided examples of it. While the words must not be interpreted as meaning that we must close our eyes to the moral faults of our age, yet the beautiful example of Jesus, who said to those who brought the woman taken in adultery, "He that is without sin among you, let him first cast a stone at her" (Jn. 8[7], notes), should be our guide. Inability to realize one's own weaknesses leads to an unsympathetic judgment of others.

1, 2. In exercising the sacred function of *judgment* we must ever remember that we are to appear before the august and holy tribunal of God. This saying is expanded in Lk. 6[37, 38] by a beautiful statement illustrative of God's generous treatment of men. The *measuring* is a further illustration of the judgment, but in Luke it refers more to the exercise of good will and kindness, while in Mk. 4[24] it applies to the degree of moral and intellectual application given to the parables of Jesus.

3–5. This hyperbolical saying may have been an Oriental proverb of the time; the *mote* is any small piece of straw or splinter of wood, and the *beam* a large plank, figurative for a conspicuous moral fault. Even a small fault makes it hard for us to arrive at a true knowledge of others.

6. Guarding the Holy from Profane Use. F. Perles has tried to reconstruct the Aramaic of this expression, and he makes the claim that the saying originally ran, "Hang no rings on dogs and put no pearls on the snouts of pigs," which was probably a proverbial saying of the time, meaning that one should not present beautiful and noble things to those who have no capacity to appreciate them. In the form in which we have it, it is doubtful whether it correctly reports Jesus, since it seems to contradict violently the injunction of vv. 1–5. The words are probably the reflection of the Christian church in Jerusalem, which was much concerned that the word of God and especially the sacraments should not be given to unworthy men.

7–11. Importunity in Prayer. See notes on Lk. 11:9-13. The imperatives used in this paragraph could be translated, *Keep on asking; make a regular practice of seeking; continue knocking.* Perseverance in prayer is greatly emphasized in the teaching of Jesus and in the N.T. generally. It is the inwrought or heartfelt prayer that availeth much (Jas. 5:16). Importunity implies that the thing desired is a deeply felt want which we consider indispensable for our moral development. The other element in prayer which is stressed in these verses is that of *trust in a heavenly Father.* Jesus is probably giving us here a glimpse into his home life at Nazareth: he still carries the memory of the kindness of Joseph, who loved to give the boy an egg or fish for his morning meal. The Jews were fond of arguing from a lesser example to a greater. What were the *good things* (v. 11) that Jesus was thinking God would give us? Was he thinking of the precious gifts of aspiration, reverence, hope, love, and humility, which God freely grants to his loved ones? Luke (11:13) has "Holy Spirit," which reveals a later stage in the history of Christ's words.

12. The Golden Rule. The positive form of this noble rule, admirably described as golden, was first expressed by Jesus. Hillel gave expression to it in its negative form: "What is hateful to thee, do not to thy neighbor: this is the whole law, all else is comment." Israel Abrahams vainly tries to prove that the rule in its negative form is of deeper significance and wider application than the positive form of Jesus.

A Series of Practical Applications. (Vv. 13–27.) The discourse closes with a number of exhortations drawn from several sources, in which the contrast is drawn between the narrow and the broad way, the good and the worthless tree, and the sensible and the foolish builder.

13, 14. The Narrow Door and the Confined Way. Was this the pessimistic estimate of Jesus, or do the words reflect the insularity of the church in Jerusalem? In the saying in Luke (13:23, 24), the contrast between the narrow and the broad way is not made. The truth that Jesus stated there is that many will lack the moral stamina of the prophets to press on in the way of righteousness with all its hindrances.

15–20. Warning Against False Prophets and the Unfruitful Life. (Mk. 13:5, 6, 22, note.) Luke omits the saying about the false prophets, and as false Christian prophets did not appear till after the Lord's death, when the struggles with Judaizing Christians began (cf. Jn. 4:1), this saying probably reflects the judgment of the early church against those who made loud profession of their faith, but whose lives were completely out of harmony with it. *By their fruits.* Actions betray the condition of the soul. "By their fruits ye shall know them" is surely one of the most distinctive and oft-quoted sayings of the Master. The manner of the everyday life of the followers of Jesus should be one of the infallible tests by which they can be distinguished from others. Christian character is very fittingly compared to fruit: (a) Fruit is that for which the whole tree exerts itself and in which it finds its end. (b) Fruit distinguishes the tree. The infinite variety of fruits is one of the most wonderful provisions of a bountiful nature. Christian character need not be uniform and stereotyped but must express itself in ever fresh and varying forms. (c) Fruit has its own beauty. In the Greek of v. 17, two different words are used for *good.* The tree is *agathon;* the fruit is *kalos.* Hort defines *kalos* as that kind of goodness which is at once seen to be good, goodness as a definite object of contemplation, beauty being the obvious characteristic of such goodness. (d) Fruit takes time to mature and ripen. So the higher reaches of character are not attained except by long patience and resolute perseverance.

21–23. Warning Against Self-deception. When we compare these words, especially the reference to prophecy, casting out devils, and doing mighty works, with Lk. 6:46 13:25, it looks as if the form in Matthew has been developed from the simpler one in Luke. Miracle workers and exorcists, as we know from Acts, did their work in the name of Jesus, using it as a successful means of exorcism (cf. Mk. 9:38 Acts 19:13-19). Though the saying has suffered in Matthew yet it preserves a solemn warning of the Master—that it is possible to be engaged in the outward forms of Christian service, and even to gain apparently reliable results, without doing the will of God and truly serving his kingdom. Some commentators think that the words contain the condemnation of the early church against the overemphasis on exorcism and ecstatic gifts, to the neglect of the more inward and spiritual graces of Christianity (cf. notes on 1 Cor. 14:1-19).

24–27. The Parables of the Builders. It is very instructive that the Sermon on the Mount, a great architect's blue print for the building of the house of character, should close with these two contrasting parables. Jesus as a village carpenter would often be employed to do the wood work of synagogues, barns, and houses of varying kinds. From his experience he derives some most helpful counsel on the all-important business of building the house of life. Note especially the additions in Lk. 6[47-49]. (1) *The choice of architect.* According to Luke, the parable begins with the words "Everyone that cometh unto me." Christ is the peerless architect of character. His knowledge of the essential harmony between the beautiful and the useful, his understanding of the laws of strain and stress to which the building must be subjected, the unique building he himself has raised, the applicability of his designs for all classes and races, make him unequaled as a designer of the house of character. (2) The house must have *a permanent and dependable foundation.* If one can secure a rock foundation, the building can be lofty and spacious. The only worthy foundation for the house of life is the teaching of Jesus (1 Cor. 3[10f.] note). To reach its permanent principles three things are necessary: We must hear the words, dig deep into their abiding significance, and carry them out into practical life. (3) Luke tells that the house withstood the tempest because it had been *well builded* (6[48]). In the sermon Jesus shows us the lovely stones which we must build into the structure of our character—purity, gentleness, courage, sincerity, benevolence, trust, a passion for righteousness. The plan of Jesus makes special provision for two rooms—the inner chamber of prayer, which is the soul's sanctuary; and the living room, with its lamps of good works and its windows looking out on the glories of nature, and on life with all its sins and problems.

28, 29. The Impression Made by Jesus' Words. Even if it be true that Matthew has collected into one long discourse the teachings that were scattered throughout the ministry, this does not weaken the force of this closing tribute. The "common people," who "heard Jesus gladly" (Mk. 12[37], note), recognized in his words an *authority* which they did not find in the professional teachers. Those teachers were forever concerned with tradition and its interpretation. In what Jesus said there was a freshness and a power, enforced by his own personality, which even the most unlettered could appreciate.

CHAPTER VIII

Just as in chs. 5–7 Matthew collects the sayings of Jesus, so in chs. 8, 9 he describes for us ten typical mighty works. Nine of them are "healing" miracles, and one is a "nature" miracle. This is about the proportion in which the two kinds of miracle stand to each other throughout the Gospel record. (See further the art., *N.T. Miracles*, pp. 923–4).

1–4. The Healing of a Leper. See notes on Mk. 1[40-45] Lk. 5[12-16]. This miracle is reproduced by Matthew almost verbatim from Mark, with the characteristic omission (intro. p. 953b) of Mark's strongly emotional words "moved with compassion" (v. 41) and the words "strictly charged" (v. 43). Matthew also omits v. 45.

5–13. The Nobleman of Capernaum. See notes on Lk. 7[1-10]. Mark does not tell this incident in his narrative. It is one of the few incidents related in the Q document (intro., p. 954). This centurion was probably in the service of Herod Antipas. As Jews were exempt from military service he would be a Gentile, though there is no reason to infer that he was a proselyte. For a Jew to enter the house of a Gentile was pollution; consequently, some scholars make v. 7 read as a question, *Am I to come and heal him?* But surely Jesus had shaken off entirely the incubus of the law of ceremonial cleanness, and it is much more in harmony with his character to take the words as a direct statement. It is interesting to observe that the only two miracles in which the healing occurs without Jesus seeing the patient are in the cases of two Gentiles—here and in the story of the daughter of the Syrophœnician woman. According to Matthew the nobleman comes himself; in Luke elders of the Jews act as envoys. It is not improbable that the extreme Judaism of certain early evangelists sought to place a barrier between Jesus and the Gentiles. Some think that this incident teaches symbolically that Jesus helped the heathen without entering into their world, and that the centurion is the first fruit of the gathering of the Gentiles into the kingdom of God.

6. *Lord* here is simply a respectful form of address.

9. The contrast is with *under authority*, for Jesus was under no human authority in his work.

10. Jesus often spoke of the *faith* of those who appealed to him (cf. 9[22-29] 15[28]). This incident is important to the evangelist because in its revelation of faith it forms a notable exception in the ministry of Jesus.

11, 12. Matthew regards this as a fitting place to insert two significant sayings of Jesus. They occur in Lk. 13[29] in a different context, and later in the ministry of our Lord, after he had become convinced that those who were so peculiarly fitted by training and tradition for the kingdom of God would be rejected and the Gentiles from east and west would be drawn by the splendor of its ideals and the unusual magnetic power of the Lord of the Kingdom. This *universalism of Jesus* is wonderfully anticipated in Isa. 2$^{2-4}$ 49^{12}. Jesus is fond of comparing the Kingdom to a banquet hall (Mt. 22$^{1-13}$, note, Lk. 22^{30}). The graphic description of those in *outer darkness* (v. 12) must not be taken as a description of hell, for nothing is said definitely about the final fate of those who are thrust out.

14–17. Peter's Wife's Mother. See notes on Mk. 1$^{29-31}$ Lk. 4$^{31-44}$. Matthew sees in the healing ministry of Jesus a striking fulfillment of Isa. 53^{4}, one of his happiest O.T. quotations. Matthew does not quote the LXX here but translates freely from the original text. The Greek writer Galen uses Matthew's word *bastazo* (*to carry*) of bearing away sickness. Cf. 1 Pet. 2^{24}, where a different Greek word is used, but still in the sense of bearing away.

18–22. Two Candidates for Discipleship. See notes on Lk. 9$^{57-62}$. Both are followers of Jesus, though Matthew describes the first as a scribe who impulsively offers himself for permanent companionship, and the second delays to accept a call that has already been given.

20. *Son of man.* This is the first occurrence of the phrase in Matthew. There seems to be no doubt that Jesus used the title of himself, because it best expressed what he was, not only as a periphrasis for "I" but as a periphrasis for Messiah, and because it gave such little support to the political and nationalistic hopes which the Jews attached to the person of the Messiah. There is quite a distinct group of passages in the Gospels where the title *Son of man* is used in reference to the anticipated sufferings and death of Jesus (cf. Mk. 8^{31} 9$^{9, 12, 31}$ 14^{21}; also p. 846).

22. This saying of Jesus has perplexed many, because it was probably an Aramaic proverb which has been spoiled in translation. Some interpret the proverb to mean *Let the dead past bury its dead;* others reconstruct the Aramaic to read *Leave the dead to him who buries dead bodies.* Wendt thinks that the man's father was alive and that his request is only an excuse for delay. The first *dead* in the sentence can be interpreted as spiritually dead, for as such Jesus considers all those who have not responded to his appeal and who remain outside his circle. The saying may have been occasioned by some peculiar circumstance of the disciple unknown to us. Perhaps it was uttered by Jesus in a moment of tense emotion, after his experiencing in the example of others how the ties of family and home were proving an insuperable obstacle to the highest and best form of discipleship.

23–27. The Storm on the Lake. See notes on Mk. 4$^{35-41}$ Lk. 8$^{22-25}$. Matthew abbreviates by omitting several of the picturesque details of the narrative in Mark and by toning down the distressed cry of the disciples when they realize their plight (see art., *N.T. Miracles*, p. 923b).

28–34. The Gadarene Demoniac. See notes on Mk. 5$^{1-20}$ Lk. 8$^{26-37}$.

CHAPTER IX

See note at beginning of ch. 8.

1–8. Healing of the Paralytic. See notes on Mk. 2$^{1-12}$ Lk. 5$^{18-26}$.

9–13. Call of Matthew and Intercourse with Taxgatherers. See notes on Mk. 2$^{13-17}$ Lk. 5$^{27-38}$. Jesus quoted the saying in v. 13 from Hos. 6^{6}, *I desire goodness* [*kindness*, mg.] *and not sacrifice,* because it expressed so concisely his own mind concerning the elaborate ceremonial and ritual observances of the religion of his day which so often blinded the people to the paramount claims of social service and benevolent ministry.

14–17. See notes on Mk. 2$^{18-22}$ Lk. 5$^{33-39}$.

18–26. Healing of Jairus' Daughter and the Woman with the Flow of Blood. See notes on Mk. 5$^{21-43}$ Lk. 8$^{40f.}$

27–31. Healing of Two Blind Men. This incident looks uncommonly like a duplicate of Mt. 20$^{29-34}$, which corresponds to Mark's account of the healing of Bartimæus, the blind beggar at Jericho (10$^{46-52}$, notes). In the tradition as it reached Matthew there were two blind beggars, which might easily have been the case; though it is interesting to see how Matthew often increases the numbers of Mark (cf. Mk. 6^{44} Mt. 14^{21}).

32–34. Healing of a Dumb Demoniac. Dumbness, like other physical maladies, was in the popular mind attributed to demon possession, and could be healed by exorcism on the part of Jesus. Here, as in Mt. 12$^{22f.}$ Mk. 3$^{22f.}$ Lk. 11$^{14f.}$, the power possessed by Jesus over demons is said to be due to his alliance with the ruler of the demons. Such a charge, which in Mk. 3$^{20f.}$ (see notes) Jesus very effectively deals with, was, we may rest assured, made more than once during the ministry of Jesus.

35–38. Jesus Prepares to Appoint the Twelve. (Cf. Mk. 6$^{6f.}$ Lk. 10$^{1f.}$ and see notes on 10$^{1-16}$.) The commission of Jesus to his disciples is prefaced by a general statement of how he went through cities and villages preaching the gospel of the Kingdom in the synagogues and healing all manner of sickness and disease, and how the sight of the crowd stirred in him the deepest emotions of pity and compassion. The sight of the crowd called forth two very different pictures in his mind. (1) The first is that of a flock of *sheep* (v. 36) which is described as *distressed and scattered*. The word *distressed* is used of a hunted stag. It suggests that the flock was harried by dogs and wolves, and that to add to its plight it had *no shepherd* to act as its protector (Acts 20^{28-30}). The masses, Jesus knows, are harried by false hopes and darkening superstitions and are preyed upon by vain fears and anxieties; they are at the same time leaderless—without a strong dominating personality to lead them to safety. Christ confidently regards himself as the Shepherd of his people. (2) The other picture is of a more hopeful character and represents an earlier stage of his ministry. It is that of a ripening golden *harvest* (v. 37). The grain is only waiting for the sickle of the harvester. Work among men promises rich results, Jesus claims, and for that reason prayer should be continually made to *the Lord of the harvest* (what a beautiful description of God!) that he thrust forth workers.

CHAPTER X

The Commission of the Twelve. (Vv. 1–16.) See notes on 9^{35-38} Lk. 9^{1-6}.

1. General Injunction. The disciples are to be specially endowed with authority to cast out evil spirits and to heal every kind of infirmity. The omission of any reference to teaching and preaching is very singular. The gift of exorcism and physical healing was possessed by the disciples in an extraordinary degree (see art., *N.T. Miracles*, pp. 926–7).

2–4. The Names of the Twelve. See notes on Mk. 3^{13-19} and cf. Lk. 6^{13-16}. Matthew and Luke agree against Mark and Acts in making Peter and Andrew brothers; Andrew occupies fourth place in Mark. Matthew omits the word *Boanerges* as a description of James and John, and for Mark's Thaddæus he has Lebbæus.

5, 6. Their Parish. (Lk. 10^{3-16}.) The disciples are to avoid going to any Gentile or Samaritan town and are to confine themselves to the lost sheep of the house of Israel. To Jesus, a person is lost who either separates himself from God, and by so doing fails to realize the best that is in him, or who isolates himself from the service of his fellows, or who lives a life of aimless drift. This severe limitation of the sphere of the disciples' ministry is in complete opposition to the command of 28^{19} (note) and many question whether it really represents the mind of the Master. He may well have emphasized the great need of ministering to the abandoned of his own race, but the prohibition not to enter Samaritan or Gentile territory—which Jesus himself certainly did not observe (cf. Mk. $7^{24f.}$ Jn. $4^{4f.}$)—seems to be due to the influence of the Jewish Christian church (see intro., p. 955a).

7, 8. Their Task. They are to do everything which the Master himself did—proclaim the near approach of the Kingdom, heal the sick, raise the dead, cleanse lepers, cast out demons. Matthew has understood the words literally, and Paul in 1 Cor. 12^{28-30} has emphasized the gifts of healing, but it is not unlikely that Jesus meant these words (in part at least) metaphorically of the weak-willed, the impure, and those who were insensible to spiritual influence. The spirit in which this task should be carried on was to be one of glad devotion—*freely*—since they themselves had been the recipents of the free grace of God. Cf. notes on Mk. 1^{14-34}.

9–16. Rules of the Road. Cf. Mk. 6^{7-13}. (1) They are not to take any *money* in their girdles, nor must they do anything for gain—a precaution of Jesus lest they might be tempted to take gold for any exorcism or act of healing. The principle that missionaries had a claim to support from the churches prevailed in apostolic times (cf. 1 Cor. 9^{6-14}). Possibly the experiences of the early church with certain evangelists led to an even greater strictness than the original words of Jesus implied. (2) They are not to have a wallet or provide themselves with two coats or with sandals, and are even to dispense with a staff. The word translated *wallet* (Greek *pēra*) was used of a priest's begging basket. Mark permits *sandals* and a *staff* ($6^{8, 9}$), both of which were indispensable for long journeys. Every true workman is deserving of his support. Jesus' rules emphasize the importance of extreme simplicity, and while the details will doubtless differ according to circumstances, time and place, the *principle* is of universal application. (3) On entering a village and inquiring who is worthy, they are to salute (or greet) the house. By *saluting* is meant presenting their claims for aid, and a person's *worthiness* consists in his willingness to show hospitality. They are not to change their quarters in a city by showing preference for the homes of the better classes (v. 11). On all hospitable homes the blessing of *peace* is to be invoked (v. 13), for apostolic blessings have potent power. (4) They are to retire from all inhospitable towns by *shaking the dust from off their feet*—a truly Oriental way of expressing disapproval. Some would question whether the severe words of v. 15 are the words of the Master, for they are not in harmony with his large and patient heart of love. (5) Since they are to be *as sheep in the midst of wolves,* i.e., in a world full of antipathy to their ideals, facing constantly the fierce cruelty of heartless men, they are to be *wise as serpents* and *harmless as doves*. The Greek word translated *wise* is used in 7[24] (note) and means sensible, exercising common sense, having sound judgment. In thinking of the serpent Jesus forgets all its bad qualities and singles out the one good one which the disciples are to cultivate (Lk. 16[1-13], note). They are also to cultivate perfect sincerity and simplicity of spirit, like the dove—which is a symbol of the Spirit of God (3[16], note) in contrast to the spirit of evil, which tempts to sin.

17–23. Persecution. See notes on Mk. 13[9-13], where the words form a section of the "Little Apocalypse." V. 23 is found only in Matthew and should form part of the great speech, vv. 1–16. Here for the first time the title *Son of man* is used of the Messiah as one to come down from heaven (Dan. 7[13]; see also art., *Backgrounds*, p. 846, and cf. p. 209). The words express the thoughts of Mt. 24. See notes on Mk. 13 Lk. 12[1-12].

24, 25. The Disciple as the Teacher. (Cf. Lk. 6[40].) One cannot claim more from a pupil than his teacher can give to him—but one can claim as much. Hence we may read here a gracious promise of Jesus to his disciples that as they pass through the various stages of the school of life they shall become more and more like him. But the words also mean that what the Master encounters in the form of suffering, obloquy, and shame shall be the fate of his followers. The basest motives will be attributed to them, even to the extent of accusing them of being in league with the chief leader of the forces of darkness. *Beelzebub* (see mg.), originally "lord of flies," but by this time meant Satan, as lord of the house of demons. See notes on Mk. 3[20-30].

26–33. Jesus Demands Fearless Confession. See notes on Lk. 12[2-9]. These words anticipate trials of the severest order for the disciples; even martyrdom itself is hinted at. The thrice repeated *Fear not* (vv. 26, 28, 31) shows us that Jesus would have his followers composed and calm in the presence of the most heartrending ordeals. He states what are to be the *grounds for their confidence*, as follows: (1) The words of vv. 26, 27 may be taken to mean—in addition to their obvious sense—that those who are to deliver the message of Christ in the glare of publicity or in prominent places will be prepared for their task according as they commune much with God in the silence of the quiet places to hear his faintest whispers. (2) There is in the possession of all of Jesus' disciples something eternal and inviolable which only God can destroy (v. 28). Loyalty to the interests of the soul is to be the chief consideration. (3) They should be courageous in their confession because God takes cognizance of their lives (vv. 29–31). Should they fall in the fight, he who takes note of the fallen sparrow will surely be aware of them and will care for them. (4) Loyalty to Christ in word and deed secures for us his advocacy and mediatorship (vv. 32, 33).

34–37. Division in Homes. In Lk. 12[51] instead of *sword* is the word "division." Jesus intimates that what he had experienced in his own home would be a common experience wherever his message was proclaimed (Mk. 3[21, 31-35] 6[1-6], notes). Acceptance of Christianity will often involve bitter, implacable enmity on the part of parents and loved ones. Jesus quotes a saying from Mic. 7[6] where the prophet anticipates a condition of things similar to those Jesus discloses will be the fate of many of his followers See under vv. 38–42.

38–40. Some Further Conditions of Discipleship. Matthew in v. 37, by changing the word "hate" to *love*, has moderated what seems to us so harsh in this saying as contained in Lk. 14[26]. In cases, Jesus asserts, where the ties of home enter into conflict with the claims of the Kingdom, then the true disciple should not be in doubt. The absoluteness of his claims upon all our powers is strongly set forth in the saying in v. 38. *To take up the cross and follow after* has the technical meaning of undergoing martyrdom, the fate of countless numbers of brave followers of Christ in the closing decades of the first century. Some have thought that v. 39 has been worked over for the use of the later Christian Church. Self-denial and self-sacrifice are the only ways to self-discovery. Cf. 17[24-26] Lk. 9[23].

40. As Lk. 10[16] shows, this verse should come at the close of the commission given to the Twelve at their sending out. In going among men they were to feel that they were ambassadors of Christ and of God; their persons were sacred, and as ambassadors they must be true to their sender, love the people to whom they are sent, and seek in every possible way to effect a reconciliation between them and God.

41, 42. The Duty of Hospitable Reception. Three types of Christians are referred to in these verses. By the *prophet* is meant probably the apostolic missionary; the *righteous* is the Christian who is outstanding in piety; and the *little ones* refer to the ordinary rank and file Christians. To receive *in the name of* means in the full conviction that they are unusual personalities and should receive honor accordingly, for the most insignificant act of charity and kindness will be amply compensated by God. The whole chapter gives a very definite impression of the fearful struggle which had begun before the death of Jesus, as well as the conflict which the evangelist experienced during his residence either at Cæsarea or at Antioch (see intro., p. 955b).

CHAPTER XI

The first verse indicates a break in Matthew's record. In the words *and it came to pass*, etc., we have the technical formula with which the compiler of the Gospel concludes the five long teaching sections (see intro., section on "Divisions," p. 953a).

1–6. The Questions of the Baptist. Josephus says that John was confined in the fastness of Machærus, east of the Dead Sea. For the death of the Baptist and its causes see notes on 14[3-12]. Lk. 9[7-9] omits any reference to John's captivity but the tenses employed show that he considered the activity of John had ceased. (See notes on Luke's long section on John in 7[18-35].) The imprisonment shows that John had lost none of his moral courage. He had not become a follower of Jesus because he was not completely satisfied with his Messianic claims. Origen and others sought to explain this by saying that John himself knew the truth but sent his disciples in order that they might be convinced.

2, 3. Except in Mt. 1[17] none of the evangelists employs the title "Christ" by itself in his narrative. The phrase in v. 2 expresses the conviction of the evangelist and not of John.

For *he that cometh* read *The Coming One* (cf. Jn. 1[15, 23, 30]). So far as is known this was not a Messianic title. It refers to a Personality who might be considered either as Messiah or as forerunner of the Kingdom. Some regard it, however, as a Messianic title from Psa. 118[26].

4, 5. The answer of Jesus recalls Isa. 29[18f.] 35[5f.] 61[1f.] Many commentators claim that these words must be spiritually interpreted. If we interpret them so, it is hard to explain how the report of them could have reached the distant prison of Machærus (14[1-12], notes). Preaching to the poor was a sign of the Messianic age (Lk. 4[16f.], notes) and the enumeration follows the record of the miracles of Jesus in chs. 8, 9. To the early church the resurrection of Jesus was the conclusive proof of his Messiahship; for that reason John—who died before Jesus—is not said to have accepted the Messiahship of Jesus.

6. Is Jesus thinking of the Baptist when he gives expression to these words? What the *stumbling-block* was in the case of John we are not told. To others the attitude of Jesus toward the Law and tradition of the elders, the story of his descent, and the absence of any political and nationalistic elements in his Messianic claims, proved a real hindrance. Blessed is the man who has found the fulfillment of all his most cherished ideals and hopes in the Saviour of men and who can say with Paul, "In him is Yea" (2 Cor. 1[19]).

7–15. Jesus' Estimate of John the Baptist. (Cf. Lk. 7[18-35].) In these words of Jesus we see that the character of John had made a profound impression on him. He was deeply impressed by his rugged, fearless moral strength and his perfect self-discipline and love of simplicity. It is possible to interpret v. 9 as implying that when disciples went to see John they really expected to see one who was *more than a prophet*, i.e., the Messiah himself; but while Jesus concedes that John was a prophet, he qualifies his estimate by applying an O.T. quotation (Mal. 3[1]). Or this may be the work of the evangelist, to show that John was only a forerunner of the Messiah, whose special task it was to prepare the way. Jesus concedes (v. 11) that among the noblest men of his race John in virtue of the momentous character of his announcement is without peer, and he grants him a place in the Kingdom; nevertheless, because of the superior insight into the significance of the personality of Jesus and the greater loyalty and steadfastness shown by others, John's place will be only a minor and unimportant one.

12. This has been variously explained: some assert that the verse means that the Kingdom is violently treated in the person of its members; others that there is a reference here to those who thought of the Messianic blessings as political, which must be reached by rebellion and war; while there are some, and possibly the evangelist among them, who think that the portals of the Kingdom will be opened only to the enthusiastic souls like the reclaimed taxgatherers and harlots whom the orthodox excluded from it. The second explanation seems to be the probable one. Was this the cause, one wonders, of the doubt assailing John, and the cause of the obstacles he found in Jesus? The Kingdom will be brought in by those who, like Jesus, have the self-discipline, patience, and piety to wait on God.

13–15. It was part of the popular belief that Messiah's coming should be heralded by the return of *Elijah*. The early church held tenaciously that John had fulfilled the rôle of Elijah, and this Jesus believes also. Jesus infers (v. 15) that this fulfillment of prophecy was not accepted by some, and that for its full acceptance appeal is to be made not only to the events of history but to the faith and insight of men. (See further notes on 14$^{1-12}$.)

16–19. A Parable Drawn from Children at Play. In this beautiful and apt illustration drawn from his own experience as a child, Jesus compares his own generation to a group of willful, capricious children, who, when asked by their companions to play "a game of wedding," refuse to do so, as later they refuse to go to the other extreme and play at "a funeral game." Jesus compares himself to the group in whom the element of joy and gladness is uppermost, in contrast to John, who is by nature ascetic and aloof, yet both of them are found fault with by the same persons. This parable has varied applications: (1) It emphasizes the confused and bewildered state of mind of the contemporaries of Jesus, and especially their willful, mulish, stubborn character, blinding them to the true values of life. (2) It illustrates that fatal tendency in human nature to dislike the unusual and unconventional, and so to drag down all men to a mediocre average uniform level. The only liberty allowed is the liberty to fall in line with the majority. (3) It reveals a fatal tendency also to besmirch the character of distinguished public men. (4) It shows finally that what the contemporaries of Jesus considered to be a flaw in Jesus—his love of humanity and his befriending of the outcast and hated—posterity has considered to be his crowning glory.

The parable fittingly closes with a saying which has been best preserved in Luke, "Wisdom is justified of all her children" (7^{35}). *Wisdom* has been defined as the power to see the world, ourselves, and our concerns as God sees them and to order our lives in the light of that vision. Jesus, supremely, and John, to a measure, were real children of wisdom, and admirably demonstrated their parentage to one who had eyes to see. Wisdom loves manifoldness (cf. Eph. 3^{10}). It sets itself against the conventional in food and dress. It teaches that the Son of man would not exclude anything human from the sphere of his saving and soul-renewing activity.

20–24. The Doomed Cities. (Lk. 10$^{13-15}$.) The parable illustrating the rejecting of both John and Jesus leads the evangelist to introduce into this context a group of stern sayings against the cities of Chorazin, Bethsaida, and Capernaum, which also rejected the mighty words of Jesus. The sayings indicate how fragmentary are our records of the ministry of Jesus, for we know nothing of his visits to *Chorazin*, a town situated on a steep hill a few miles northwest of Capernaum, nor do we know much of his activity at *Bethsaida*, i.e., Bethsaida Julias, situated at the point where the Jordan enters the lake. *Capernaum* is singled out because it was the headquarters of the Galilæan ministry (Mk. 1^{21}, note), and in consequence was so privileged that it ought to have been elevated to the topmost peak of blessedness. *Heaven* in v. 23 expresses the highest renown and *Hades* the lowest shame. Even Tyre, and Sidon, and Sodom itself, those great centers of wealth, license, pride, and idolatry, would have been more deeply moved to repentance and righteous living.

23. The first clause should be a question and the second a direct statement (as in R.V.; cf. A.V.), to show that the city had already been covered with disgrace and ignominy. The passage suggests Jesus' familiarity with the language of Isa. 14$^{12-15}$, where the thrusting of the king of Babylon into the realm of the dead is described.

25–30. The Great Invitation. This unique paragraph, which reveals Jesus in an unusually exalted mood, is built up of two sections. The first, vv. 25–27, occurs in Luke also (10$^{21, 22}$); the second, vv. 28–30, is found here alone. Some conclude from this that they belong to separate occasions. However that may be, it shows unique insight and understanding on the part of the evangelist that he should have welded them together, for the worth and glory of the invitation in vv. 28–30 depend on the position and character of the person who gives it. The familiar invitation contains three main elements, as follows:

(1) *A Self-delineation of the Master who Invites.* Two features are singled out—the elements of *authority*, since he stands in a unique relation to God and possesses a unique revelation of him, and the element of *gentleness* and *lowliness of heart*. These two outstanding elements are always found in every portrait of Jesus in the N.T.—the Petrine, Pauline, and Johannine (see Coffin, *Portraits of Jesus in N.T.*). Ritschl claims that the word translated "gentle" means in Aramaic "pious." In this self-portraiture of the Master, the following elements are stressed: (a) The content of his message and the truth he declares are all *from God*. The Scribes prided themselves on the tradition of the elders and human teaching. Jesus claims that his message comes from the true source of all wisdom and light. (b) The full understanding of this revelation is *given by the Spirit of God* to those who are open-minded, humble, and expectant; minds marked by intellectual arrogance and blinded by pride cannot receive these things. (c) The

chief element in this revelation is *the unique relationship of Jesus to God.* He is his Son and in consequence his gospel is a gospel of God. To unveil before men the ineffable glory of the Divine Fatherhood is the glad and holy privilege intrusted to Jesus. (d) Though rejected in Capernaum and Chorazin, doubted by the Baptist, and misinterpreted by the Pharisees, he is *known of God,* who alone perceives the true inner wealth that is in Christ.

(2) *A Description of the Invited.* The wise and prudent are excluded. Such are the Pharisees and their like, who think that all revelation of God is complete in the Law and the Prophets, and in consequence no new light can be expected. This incapacity is attributed in true Hebrew fashion to divine interposition. Ultimately it is due to God, but more directly the incapacity is due to our willfulness and the disregard of his laws which determine the nature of our receptivity. The Greek word *nēpioi* means literally *babes,* but it may be taken here in the metaphorical sense of "simple" or "open-minded." To such Jesus unfolds the treasures of his mind and heart. All commentators without exception say that the words *labor and heavy-laden* describe those who are crushed in spirit because of the weighty burdens imposed on them by Pharisaic demands. The *am-haaretz,* "the people of the land" who knew not the Law, were despised by the Pharisees; they cared little for the Law and its interpretations. Aristotle applies to the common people, the proletariat of his day, the adjective *phortikos,* a word much like the Greek participle translated "heavy-laden." It is interesting to note that the word translated "weary" is always used in the N.T. either of those who are tired and spent because of hard manual work, or of those who labor and toil in spiritual ministry. The appeal of Jesus is therefore general and universal; he is calling to him all who need encouragement, sympathy, quickening of spirit, whatever be the nature and cause of the depression and weariness.

(3) *The Character of the Invitation.* Here we are to emphasize the yoke-bearing; the learning; and the ensuing rest. (a) *Take my yoke upon you.* The symbol of the yoke was used, e.g., of the Law. Thus if one takes upon him the yoke of the Torah, the yoke of civil government and of worldly care will fall from him. Jesus probably means by yoke the cardinal elements of his message, the adoption of which by men will enable them to perform useful services; for while the yoke is a symbol of slavery, more often it is a symbol of work and duty. The word translated *easy* (Greek *chrēstos*) means "benevolent," "kind," "useful." "Useful" would be a better rendering here than "easy." Sustained by faith, love, hope and patience, every burden becomes really light. One may wonder whether the original translators have conveyed correctly the Aramaic words of Jesus; for just as "easy" gives an erroneous interpretation of *chrēstos,* so the word translated *light* may not be a real equivalent of the word used by Jesus. The words "easy" and "light" seem to be incongruous in the N.T., and this is the only passage in the Gospels where they occur. (b) *Learn of me.* The Greek preposition shows that we are to learn not simply from the words of Jesus, but from his whole life and conduct among men. (c) *I will give you rest.* "Refreshment" is a better translation. Paul used the word of the inspiring influence upon him of noble personalities (Rom. 15^{32} 2 Tim. 1^{16}). In the school of Christ hearts are encouraged because there they enter into intimate fellowship with Him who is the peerless Teacher of men.

CHAPTER XII

1–8. **Jesus and the Sabbath.** See notes on Mk. 2^{23-28} Lk. 6^{1-5}.

9–14. **Healing on the Sabbath.** See notes on Mk. 3^{1-6} Lk. 6^{6-11}.

15–21. **Summary of Jesus' Activity.** See notes on Mk. 3^{7-12}. Mark does not give the long quotation from Isa. 42^{1-4}. The quotation is characteristic of Matthew's desire to link up the work of Jesus with the O.T. Its wonderful aptitude, however, is more clearly seen when the words are viewed in relation to the passage in Mark, which is more detailed than Matthew's.

22–24. **The Charge of Alliance with Beelzebub.** See notes on 9^{32-34} Mk. 3^{20-22} Lk. 11^{14-16}.

25–32. **Jesus' Reply to the Charge.** See notes on Mk. 3^{23-30} Lk. 11^{17-23}.

33. **The Tree and Its Fruit.** See notes on 7^{16}, and cf. Lk. $6^{43, 44}$.

34–37. **Words a Revelation of Character.** (Lk. 6^{45}.) The words a man habitually uses are an important key to his character. By the use of the metaphors of a fruit tree (v. 33) and of treasure, Jesus clearly teaches that the quality of our inward life determines the character of our speech and the worth of our actions. From a tree of inferior quality one cannot expect a high-grade fruit, and out of a treasury into which counterfeit base coins are being continually deposited one can only withdraw currency of a like nature. The great significance of "the subconscious self" is anticipated by Jesus. The reader should carefully study the passage in Jas. 3[1-12] on the same subject. Cf. notes on Mt. 7[15-20].

37. *Idle.* The Greek word ordinarily means "useless" or "worthless." O. Holtzmann thinks that here it has the meaning of bad or evil.

38-42. The Demand for a Sign. (Cf. 16[1-4] Lk. 11[29-36] 12[54-56] and see notes on 16[1-4] Mk. 8[11-13].) The early church naturally saw in the story of Jonah a prophecy of the resurrection of Jesus. According to Mark, Jesus refuses to grant any sign, while Luke states that the only sign will be "the sign of Jonah." It is quite evident from the two illustrations of the repentant Ninevites and the queen of Sheba that the significance of the answer of Jesus to his contemporaries is that his prophetic words of wisdom are the real proof and guarantee of his divine mission. If men fail to appreciate and to respond to that great message, no other sign will be given. Though Jesus surpasses Jonah in every way as a prophet, and though his wisdom is infinitely superior to that of Solomon, what a striking contrast there is between the attitude of the Ninevites and of the queen and the stubborn obstinacy and blindness of his own generation!

40. Probably a gloss. It is absent from both Mark and Luke. The statement made is inaccurate, for Jesus was in the grave only from Friday evening to Sunday dawn.

43-45. The Parable of a Great Relapse. (Lk. 11[24-26].) By means of the symbolism of this sad little parable drawn from the demonology of his day, Jesus teaches the great truth of the persistence of evil, and the possibility of increasing degeneration. Some words of Mark Rutherford in *Catherine Furze* are suggestive here: "If soldiers be slain on the battlefield there is an end of them. New armies may be raised, but the enemy is weaker at any rate by those who are killed. It is not the same with our ghostly foes, for they rise into life after we think they are buried and often with greater strength; day after day, night after night, and perhaps year after year, the wretched citadel is environed and the pressure of the attack is unremitting, while the force that resists has to be summoned by a direct effort of the will; and the moment that effort relaxes the force fails and the besiegers swarm upon the fortifications." To meet the persistent power of evil a neutral passivity will not suffice. A life *swept and garnished* and yet *empty* of resolute courage and force of character cannot hope to defeat the evil that continually besieges it. The ideals of the kingdom of God must take full possession of the house of life if the powers of darkness are to be kept under control.

46-50. Jesus' New Family. See notes on Mk. 3[31-35].

CHAPTER XIII

A Group of Parables. (See note at beginning of ch. 8.) The evangelist in this chapter groups together seven typical parables of Jesus, or eight if the saying about the householder in v. 52 is reckoned as a parable. In addition we have here the interpretations of two parables—the soils and the tares, and a statement of the reason for teaching by parables. All modern scholars seem agreed that the interpretation of the tares is not Jesus' own. There are many also who hold that the interpretation of the sower has not been handed down as Jesus originally gave it (see notes on vv. 18–23), but that during its oral transmission it has been considerably changed and adapted to different circumstances. (Cf. p. 916b.)

1-9. The Parable of the Sower and the Soils. (Mk. 4[1-12], notes on Lk. 8[4-18].) Many think that this parable reflects the experience of Jesus as a preacher, and that he delivered it especially to his disciples so that they might be prepared to know what to expect as missionaries of the gospel. Among their hearers, as there were among his, would be those for whom the gospel would prove utterly futile to produce any changes in life and character. On the other hand, he assures them, for their encouragement, that they would meet with receptive souls in whom the truths of the gospel would be appropriated and result in remarkable changes. The teaching of the parable may be itemized as follows: (1) Jesus and his followers have in the gospel that which is able to produce surprising and unexpected results in character. Jeremiah compares the word of God to wheat (23[28]); so Jesus here regards the truths of the gospel as necessary elements for the sustaining and building up of the moral life and character. (2) Just as in the seed, small as it is, there are locked up vital energies and living forces which given a receptive soil produce striking transformations, so the words of Jesus, his ideas and thoughts, are "living words," compact of dynamic energy, and capable when assimilated by men of producing incalculable results. (3) The followers of Jesus must sow the seed wherever they go. It is impossible for them to judge the nature of the soil entirely, but for the best results there must be complete co-operation between seed and soil. Our hearts and minds must appropriate the living word if there is to be fruitfulness. (4) Different types of soil are enumerated. There is the soil of the *wayside* that is trampled on, and which has become a path on which every passer-by walks, typifying the character that has lost all sensitiveness and sympathy with spiritual things; in this the seed cannot find lodgment of any kind. There is the *shallow* soil—the superficial nature that lives on the surface of things. Because there is no depth of scil the seed cannot produce adequate roots to sustain the life of the plant in the face of the hot sun. This shallow soil is typical of large numbers—the "temporary Christians" (v. 6) as they are styled in the interpretation. Then we have the *unclean* soil, typical of the men and women in whose hearts the multitudinous interests of life crowd out the ideals of the gospel and prevent them from growing. Lastly, there are the *good* soils, which vary in their yielding capacity. Jesus recognizes distinctions in men; just as there are men of five, two, and one talents respectively, so in the quality of the good soils all are not exactly alike, but each one produces according to the native capacity. (See Jesus' interpretation, vv. 18–23.)

10–17. The Aim of Teaching by Parables. (See discussion in art., *Parables of Jesus*, p. 916.) Many of the followers of Jesus were greatly perplexed by his apparent failure to win men, and in the question, *Why speakest thou unto them in parables?* there seems to be implied, judging by the answer, a perplexity on the part of his followers why the parable teaching was not completely successful. In his answer Jesus implies (vv. 11, 12) that the reason why men have not attained unto the knowledge of the *mysteries*, i.e., the revealed truths of the gospel, is because they themselves have not brought to the gospel the indispensable elements of reverence and receptiveness. The quotation from Isa. 6[9, 10] seems to have been made to show that, just as worldliness and materialism blinded the minds of the people of the prophet's day to his great spiritual message, so Jesus is face to face with a generation dull of hearing, and blinded by worldly ambitions. Cf. on Mk. 4[10-12].

16, 17. (Lk. 10[23, 24].) Taken with the passage from Isaiah these words can be nothing but the plainest revelation of Jesus' Messianic consciousness, as in 12[41, 42].

18–23. The Interpretation of the Parable of the Sower. (Lk. 8[9-15].) The arguments brought forward against the authenticity of this interpretation are (1) that it treats the parable as an allegory, whereas Jesus confined himself to parables and illustrations whose meaning was apparent on the surface; (2) that the meaning is so plain that an explanation is not necessary; and (3) that a later period in the life of the church is reflected in the interpretation. It must be remembered, however, that nearly all explanations of the parables involve treating them as allegories, though, of course, it is foolish to find meanings for all details. It would be entirely natural for Jesus to give a model interpretation which would later serve as a guide for the disciples. On the other hand, it is not like Jesus to make the birds, which he loved so much, typify the devil. For the most part, however, the interpretations of the shallow soil in vv. 20, 21 and the unclean soil in v. 22 are consonant with the mind of Jesus and have all the marks of being genuine sayings of his.

24–30. The Parable of the Wheat and Tares. (See also vv. 36–43.) This parable and its interpretation are found only in Matthew. All scholars reject the genuineness of the explanation in vv. 36–43 on the ground of its stilted style, and because the interpretations of successive details are mechanical; moreover, the presence of popular and conventional apocalyptic expressions, and the title *Son of man*, used of the earthly life of Jesus in v. 37 and then of his Messianic glory in v. 41, stamp it as secondary in character. Many cannot accept the parable itself as a genuine utterance, on the ground that it is entirely unlike Jesus to allow sins to go on unchecked and unchallenged. Would it not have been better to uproot the tares rather than have permitted them to grow as fodder for the furnaces of Gehenna? It is probable that the parable reflects a certain condition in the life of the early church when it was too timid to tackle various definite evils that had revealed themselves in its midst, and this interpretation represents an effort to justify the acquiescence. Those who accept the parable as genuine interpret it as meaning that we should exercise tolerance toward men and leave God to act as Judge; while others interpret it as meaning that we should not hold ourselves aloof from sinners.

31, 32. The Parable of the Mustard Seed. (Mk. 4[30-32].) In this simple parable Jesus is encouraging his disciples with the thought that from very insignificant beginnings great results are to be expected in the sphere of the kingdom. Who would have dreamed as they saw Jesus and his disciples on the highways of Palestine that from that small band of men would have issued the Christian Church with all its world-wide activities? The great difference between cause and consequence suggests also that there are other forces at work besides those we observe—forces which take our small human efforts and through them attain results for which those efforts alone are unable to account.

33. The Parable of the Leaven teaches the same lesson as vv. 31, 32. It emphasizes the fact that the ideals of the Kingdom work from within as a dynamic potent force. When placed under the microscope the working of leaven in the meal looks like a veritable battlefield: there is assault and penetration in the face of determined resistance until peace descends after the whole has been conquered.

34, 35. Teaching in Parables. The first statement is hyperbole, as is seen from chs. 5-7. The quotation in v. 35 is not from any prophet but is from Psa. 78². The evangelist finds support for the use of the parable in teaching in some of the methods used by the teachers of O.T. times. Cf. vv. 10–17, notes.

36–43. Interpretation of the Parable of the Wheat and the Tares. See notes on vv. 24–30.

44–46. Parables of the Treasure and the Pearl. Both these parables emphasize the fact that the kingdom of heaven stands for the highest values and ideals, to obtain and secure which absolute devotion and dedication are demanded. If a distinction is to be found, it is not, as some suggest, that in the one case the Kingdom is reached by accident and in the other only after a long search; but rather that the word *treasure* (money, in all probability) suggests that the ideals of the Kingdom must serve practical ends, while the *pearl*, being a thing of beauty, suggests that the possession of the Kingdom ideals contributes to the glory and the adornment of personality (cf. Job 28¹⁵⁻¹⁹ Prov. 3¹³⁻¹⁶ 8¹¹ Rev. 21¹⁹⁻²¹). In these parables the morality of the transaction is not taken into account.

47–50. Parable of the Fish Net. Here again we have parable and interpretation. The original parable probably ended at v. 48 and has been given a questionable interpretation by the same hand that is responsible for the interpretation of the tares. The fish caught by the dragnet do not represent *men* but, rather, *ideals and ways of life*. The church has to sit down and carefully consider what are those things in life which are noble and lofty. The Greek word used for *good* is *kalos*, an unusual word to use to describe fish (see notes on 7¹⁵⁻²⁰). The followers of Jesus must always approve the things that are excellent (cf. Jer. 15¹⁹ Phil. 4⁸).

51, 52. Preaching New and Old Truth. A beautiful saying of Jesus in which he emphasizes the importance and value of Christian learning and in which he gives sanction to the disciples to bring new things from their treasuries as well as old. The Greek word translated *old* (*palaios*) can mean "timehonored," and many think that Jesus refers to the permanent truths of the O.T. and the great principles of his own message, but that each disciplined apostle must also bring forth from the treasury of his own vital experience fresh living truths for men.

53–58. Jesus at Nazareth. See notes on Mk. 6¹⁻⁶.

CHAPTER XIV

1–12. Herod's Judgment of Jesus; Death of John Baptist. (Mk. 6¹⁴⁻²⁹; notes on 11¹⁻¹⁵ Lk. 7¹⁸⁻³⁵ 9⁷⁻⁹.) It is not strange that reports of the ministry of Jesus should have reached Herod (cf. 3¹⁶⁻²²) and that he, stung by remorse, should have thought that the Baptist had come to life again. The narrative presents us with a very interesting psychological study of the workings of conscience. Herod is not all black, for he was much perplexed after his conversations with John and used to hear him gladly. John apparently recognized in him a man of considerable religious feeling. But Herod was a man with a questionable past: he had recently married the wife of his brother Philip, who was still living, and this brought upon him severe moral censure from the Baptist —a censure deeply resented by Herodias, who plotted for John's life. With the determined will of a Jezebel, she ultimately prevailed upon Herod to give orders for the imprisonment of John at the remote fortress of Machærus (11²ᶠ·, note), and finally for his beheading. The reports of the noble work of Jesus and the impressions made by him on the multitude stirred into activity the almost moribund conscience of the Tetrarch and created in him, according to the account in Lk. 9⁷⁻⁹, a desire to see Jesus. The historical character of vv. 3–12 has been challenged by some interpreters on the ground that it would be unlikely for a princess to perform in the presence of a group of courtiers an Oriental solo dance to which her mother was forbidden to come. According to Josephus, John was imprisoned at Machærus, a fortress four days distant from Tiberias (*Antiquities*, bk. xviii, ch. 5: 1). How could the head have been brought so quickly? it is asked. Again it is considered unlikely that the head of a murdered man should have been brought in during a banquet. Salome, Herodias' daughter by her first husband Herod Boethos, married Philip the Tetrarch, who died in 33 or 34 A.D.; she was, therefore, hardly a young girl when this incident took place. Possibly the court was in residence at Machærus, and anyone who knows anything about Oriental courts of the time knows that they were capable of any infamous deeds. Beneath the literary freedom and embellishments of the narrative, we note the outraged public conscience at the adulterous marriage of Herod and the resentment caused by his execution of the great ascetic prophet John, as well as the interest roused in the ministry of Jesus in court circles.

13–21. **Feeding the Multitudes.** (Includes 15³²⁻³⁹; cf. Mk. 6³⁰ᶠ. and notes on Mk. 8¹⁻¹⁰ Jn. 6¹⁻¹⁴.) Many interpreters suppose that the second miracle (that of the four thousand) is only a variant version of the first (but see art., *N.T. Miracles*, p. 923a). This incident presents us with admitted difficulties and the exact historical situation can be recovered, if at all, only by conjecture. The fact that in v. 19 we have the words *took, looked up, blessed, brake, gave*—words which we find again in the account of the institution of the Lord's Supper in Lk. 22^{17-20} and 1 Cor. 11^{23-25} as well as in the Emmaus story (Lk. 24^{30})—would suggest that the incident had a sacramental, symbolical significance for the evangelist. This is confirmed by the fact that the incident as recorded in Jn. 6 is made the text for a discourse on the spiritual significance of the body and blood of Christ (but see notes there). Most modern interpreters call attention to the story in 2 Kings 4^{42-44}, where the prophet is said to have fed a hundred men with twenty loaves of barley. Not only were they all satisfied but a quantity of food was left over. So far, therefore, the miracle recorded here of Jesus means only that he possessed power similar to that of the prophet, but in an enhanced degree. Again we have to remember that the breaking of bread or of a loaf into small pieces before the meal proper was an essential part of the simple ritual of table worship at a social meal among God's covenant people. This could hardly have been done for five thousand with five loaves and two fishes; possibly an original round number has been exaggerated. It is astonishing to find in the *Synoptic* record no reference to the impression the incident made on the people; and very soon afterward, when short of bread, the disciples act as though in complete ignorance of what has happened (16^{5-12}). The gravest objection that can be urged against the historicity of the story is not any inherent incredibility but the fact that it runs counter to the fundamental principle of the ministry of Jesus, who persistently refused to give a sign of an astounding character ($12^{38f.}$ note) and who sought to bring home *gradually* to men the conviction of his divine commission and Messiahship. Even that objection, however, cannot be regarded as insuperable by one who admits the miracle-principle.

The view set forth by Menzies and Bartlet, that others besides the disciples had brought their provisions with them, and that what Jesus achieved was to get a mixed multitude to pool its resources and those who had food to share with those who lacked, is a naturalistic view that appeals to many. The converting of a self-regarding mass of men into an altruistic other-regarding group was, after all, a miracle of no mean order. In any event, the incident has great value in the light it throws on the belief of the early church in Jesus. It reveals (1) his deep compassion and sympathy with the multitude, whose shepherd and leader he yearned to be; (2) his ability to satisfy the deepest needs of men—although for this work he needs helpers; (3) the place of fellowship, orderliness and thrift in the work of the kingdom; (4) the ability of Jesus to kindle in men's hearts altruistic impulses; and (5) the duty of the church to concern itself about the economic and material needs of humanity if its ministry is to be a full-orbed one. Attempts to "explain" the miracles, however, by surmising what the "historical nucleus" must have been are necessarily only tentative. Due weight should be given to the fact that this is the only miracle described in all four Gospels. Cf. art., *N.T. Miracles*, p. 923b.

22–33. **Walking on the Sea.** Matthew and Mark (6^{45}, note) assert that Jesus compelled his disciples to enter a boat while he was dismissing the crowd, after which he went up into the mountain to pray (cf. Jn. 6^{15}). This compulsion on Jesus' part was prompted by the fact that he did not want his disciples to share the worldly views of the crowd about his Messiahship. The fourth Gospel states that they wished to make him king (6^{15}). During the night a storm arose and the wind became very contrary, so that the disciples made little progress. In the *fourth watch* (between 3 and 6 A.M.), when the light must have been very dim, Jesus saw they were in difficulties. The fourth Gospel account would seem to mean that Jesus walked over four miles on the lake. The explanation suggested by the rationalists of the last century was that Jesus was really walking by the edge of the lake (the Greek for *upon* could be rendered *by*) but seemed to the men in the boat to be walking on the sea; the storm drove the boat almost to the shore, so that Jesus waded to them through the water and calmed their fears. Like the miracle that precedes, this one had a great fascination for the early church. The church at Rome, passing through the Neronic persecution (cf. intro. to Revelation, p. 1365), must have derived great comfort from the story. Behind its symbolism we see these great facts: (1) that without Christ his church is in danger of being overwhelmed by the dark and stormy experiences through which she passes; (2) that in the hour of deepest need and distress Christ will come; (3) that his presence is a *real* presence, not a phantom; and (4) that his presence brings peace and composure; courage returns, and a forward movement is possible.

The story about *Peter,* which is found only in Matthew, is possibly a Christian *midrash* or an acted parable, in which the apostle's character is illustrated—his proud impulsiveness, full repentance, and restoration. It illustrates also the important truth that trust and valor accomplish great things, while lack of faith and cowardice result in downfall.

33. *Son of God* should not be taken here in its late theological sense, but, rather, as a Messianic title (Psa. 27.8).

34–36. Acts of Healing. *Gennesaret* ("harp-shaped")—another name for the Sea of Galilee, but occurring in the N.T. only here and in the parallels. The *land* referred to was west of the Sea, since the miracle of the loaves had taken place, apparently, on the east side (cf. v. 13). The phrases, *all that were sick* and *as many as touched,* suggest how much more extensive the healing ministry of Jesus was than would be supposed from the small numbers of miracles described in detail (see art., *N.T. Miracles,* p. 922).

CHAPTER XV

1–20. Tradition That Destroys the Law of God. See notes on Mk. 7:1-23.

21–28. The Greek Woman of Syro-Phœnicia. See notes on Mk. 7:24-30.

29–31. A Period of Healing Activity. See notes on 14:34-36 Mk. 7:31-37.

32–39. Feeding the Multitudes. See notes on 14:13-21 Mk. 8:1-10.

CHAPTER XVI

1–4. The Demand for a Sign. See notes on 12:38-42 Mk. 8:11-13.

5–12. Lessons from the Miracles of the Loaves. See notes on 14:13-21 Mk. 8:14-21.

13–20. Peter's Great Confession. See notes on Mk. 8:27-30 and cf. Lk. 9:18-21. This paragraph has presented unusual difficulties to scholars and widely divergent views are held both concerning its genuineness and its real meaning. The crux of the passage, vv. 17–19, is not included in the reports of the incident in Mark and Luke; in consequence there are many who regard it as a later addition inserted by the evangelist to give sanction to the claim of priority made for Peter by the early church; others regard it as a section taken from the document Q (intro., p. 954). McNeile is of the opinion that vv. 16–18 contain the nucleus of a genuine saying of Jesus because the language is so natural, intimate, and original, but that v. 19 is certainly a later addition. This judgment appears to be sound, for if the words *bind* and *loose* mean "to give moral and intellectual judgments based on the knowledge of the teaching of Jesus," there is nothing in the life and ministry of Peter to show that this important function was exercised in any unusual degree. Moreover, such a sanction would be in strange conflict with the special ministry of the Spirit of God, whose prerogative it is to inspire men in every age with a knowledge of the message of Jesus, so that they may interpret it according to the growing needs of life.

This scene takes place at a critical turning point in the life of Jesus. The disciples are taken by him to the region of Cæsarea Philippi. While there they are asked by the Master the important question, Who do men say that I am? (so Mark, Luke) or *Who do men say that the Son of man is?* (so Matthew). In answer they affirm that popular estimates lean toward John, Elijah, and Jeremiah as the prophets to whom he is most like. This shows in an interesting way the impression made by Jesus on his contemporaries, for the three stalwarts mentioned above were men of fearless courage, singular devotion, unflinching loyalty to high ideals, and men of great simplicity and stern self-discipline. Dissatisfied with the answers, Jesus asks a further question, *Who say ye that I am?* All three synoptists throw strong emphasis on the *You,* and Peter, as the representative of the group, in a moment of real divine illumination, answers, *Thou art the Christ, the Son of the living God.* This reply affirms two great truths concerning Jesus—his divine Sonship and his Messiahship. Even Peter, however, did not realize the full import of this confession, as is evidenced by the severe rebuke of v. 23; but the answer of Jesus, with the play on the word *petros* (*rock*), implies that he regarded this confession of his divine Sonship and Messiahship as the foundation on which the new Israel of God was to be built. The moral and spiritual content of the confession is more important than the intellectual. The second may change; the first is permanent.

21–28. Jesus Foretells His Sufferings, Death, and Glory. This is the first definite intimation Jesus makes to his disciples that he will seem to be a Victim rather than a Victor—or if a Victor, then only in a quite unusual sense. He had, indeed, told them before that discipleship would be a costly thing (10:9f.), and they had already seen him rejected in his own village (13:53-58), but his mighty works and his affirmations about his kingdom had kept alive their hopes of worldly power. The recent confession of Peter and its approval by Jesus (vv. 16, 17) must have greatly strengthened those hopes. Perhaps he realized that fact and desired to set them right. More likely, however, he felt that the confession provided an appropriate background for announcing what he had himself long known to be the truth—that he was, indeed, the Christ, but the *Suffering Christ* (cf. Isa. 53). In any case, *from this time* Jesus never lets the disciples lose sight of the fact that he is to suffer a violent death (17[9, 12, 22, 23] 20[17-19], and cf. Mk. 9[9-13, 30-32] Lk. 17[25] 18[31-34]). One who until now has been to them a teacher and wonder-worker endeavors from henceforth to have them see in him a Redeemer—one who must suffer to save. How little *Peter* understood v. 18 is evident from vv. 22, 23. He who had just been called a *rock to build on* is now a *stone to stumble over!*

24–26. See notes on 10[34-39]. The solemn words properly follow on Jesus' announcement of his Passion. The paradox of his own life must be the paradox of the life of his followers. *Self-discovery through self-surrender*—this was the law he laid upon them because he had himself learned its everlasting validity. It is not impossible to live selfishly—but what an impossible life it is. To give up life is only to lose a lower and find a higher.

27, 28. The verses belong to the "apocalyptic" features of the Gospel record. To take the words literally is to make them meaningless. To regard them as current language which Jesus employed as a vehicle of his self-consciousness as Messiah is to make them intelligible. See on chs. 24, 25.

CHAPTER XVII

1–13. The Transfiguration. See notes on Mk. 9[2-13]. Schweitzer (in *The Quest for the Historical Jesus*) suggests that this incident may be out of its chronological order. He would have it *precede* Peter's confession at Cæsarea-Philippi. This alone, he says, makes intelligible the confession and Jesus' reply that the truth was revealed to Peter not by flesh and blood, but by God. That is, it was revealed to him at the transfiguration. Coming from the mountain, Jesus charged the three to keep silence; but Peter, with characteristic impulsiveness, blurted out the truth in answer to Jesus' general question to the Twelve. Schweitzer's suggestion has some attractiveness, but it requires a forced interpretation of Jesus' response to the confession. As the record reads now, Jesus was *trying* to evoke a confession; on Schweitzer's theory, Jesus was *embarrassed* by his very success.

14–21. Healing of the Epileptic Boy. See notes on Mk. 9[14-29], and cf. art., *N.T. Miracles*, p. 925b.

22, 23. Jesus' Announcement of His Violent Death. See notes on 16[21-23] Mk. 9[30-32].

24–27. The Temple Tax and the Fish with the Stater. This incident is narrated by Matthew only. According to Ex. 30[13] every adult Israelite had to pay a half-shekel annually toward the upkeep of the Temple. After the fall of the Temple, the Romans continued to levy this tax for the support of the temple Jupiter Capitolanus in Rome. Whether Christians were required to pay it is uncertain, but it was a burning question at the time the first Gospel was written. McNeile claims that the argument underlying the words of Jesus (vv. 25, 26) is that, as earthly kings do not tax their own families or kin, so neither does God; hence the Jews are aliens and pay taxes to Cæsar, but Jesus and his disciples are sons who have a right to exemption. But if that is what the words mean, then they are so anti-Jewish that great doubt must be felt as to their genuineness. The more probable interpretation is that Jesus believed that the cause he and his disciples represented was so much greater than any temple that he felt no moral obligation to pay the annual tax; but, as no vital principle of conduct was involved, it would be best for him and his followers to conform to the custom of the time (cf. 3[15] 22[15-22], notes).

27. The story of the finding of the *shekel* (Greek *stater;* see art., *Time, Money*, etc., p. 78b) has been made unnecessarily difficult by the evangelist's literal-mindedness. As the record stands, it has a touch of magic for which there is elsewhere no warrant in anything Jesus did. It is highly probable that what was originally nothing but playful humor on Jesus' part, as he bade Peter get the money by fishing, gradually lost its true character, and was given the form appearing in the text. (See art., *N.T. Miracles*, p. 923b.)

CHAPTER XVIII

1–14. The Little Child as Object Lesson in Christian Character. See notes on Mk. 9[33-37] and cf. Lk. 9[46-48]. We have here an "acted parable," the use of which marks Jesus as the skillful teacher. He drew from it the following lessons: (1) To obtain the child spirit involves a very radical and complete change of attitude and life, which shows itself in freshness of outlook, responsiveness to truth, the spirit of eagerness and wonder (vv. 1–4). Such are some of the open sesames into the kingdom of God. (2) The followers of Jesus must ever welcome into their ranks the children of their people (v. 5); or possibly the phrase *one of these little ones* may mean men and women of humble and lowly station in life; to all such the hand of welcome must be outstretched and the welcome must always be *in his name*, i.e., either offered by them as his representatives or his blessing invoked as the act is performed. (3) Jesus lays down a stringent rule to govern the attitude of his disciples toward the lowly of his followers (v. 6). The arrogance of the Pharisees toward the *Amhaaretz*—"the people of the land," or the peasant classes—was one of the reasons why they were so disliked. On no account must the followers of Jesus offend (*cause to stumble*), i.e., present any impediment or obstacle which makes it hard for others to live an upright life. Such obstacles as pride, arrogance, intolerance, coldness of demeanor, inconsistency in conduct, are insurmountable barriers preventing the weak from entering the Kingdom. It would be far better for a privileged, gifted man to meet a violent death than for him to lead a life that made it hard for others to find purity and goodness. (4) The disciple of Jesus must exercise rigid self-discipline and self-denial (vv. 8, 9). Similar words occur in the Sermon on the Mount in a paragraph in which Jesus deals with the question of purity (5[27-30]). Low and unworthy ideals and practices present a real hindrance to conduct of the highest and worthiest kind. The appeal is strengthened by the reference to *angels* and their function (v. 10). The belief in angels was very prevalent in the days of Jesus; sometimes they acted as God's ambassadors (Lk. 1[19, 26]), sometimes as simple messengers (Lk. 2[8-13]). Nations and churches had their angels (Rev. 1[20]). The Persians believed that every person had his counterpart in heaven, traces of which belief seem to appear here (cf. p. 757b). J. Weiss thinks that if the *little ones* include all who are little in age, worldly importance, or religious development, the access of their angels to the presence of God is a beautiful expression of his unceasing knowledge and care. (5) The disciple must in the Spirit of God seek earnestly for those who have wandered from the fold (vv. 11–14; cf. mg.). The parable of the *sheep* is put in another context in Lk. 15[3f.] (note). In the sight of God, every individual, however obscure and lowly, is of value. He does not desire any man to live an aimless, lonely, purposeless life; in the judgment of Jesus to do that is to be lost. Men must dwell together in a community of believing souls, all possessed by common aims and ideals (see notes on Eph. 2[11f.]).

15–20. Some Further Brotherly Duties. In this section we have expansions of original sayings of Jesus when the church had already become an organized body. It is the most distinctly ecclesiastical passage in Matthew. Jesus dealt in the Sermon on the Mount (5[38-48], notes) with the question of reconciliation and the forgiving spirit as it affected the *individual;* here it is dealt with in its importance as affecting the life of the *brotherhood.* Some think that the word *church* is used here in a local sense equivalent to synagogue. Wellhausen takes it (as also in 16[18]) as a reference to the mother congregation of Jerusalem. The word, he thinks, denotes a small body of the Lord's followers.

17. Klausner, the Jewish scholar, in his estimate of the character of Jesus (in his *Jesus of Nazareth*) considers the words *as the Gentile and the publican* exceedingly strong terms of contempt. They are certainly out of harmony with all we know of Jesus and probably reflect a period when Jewish hostility was met by Christians in a spirit entirely unlike that of the Master.

18. Billerbeck and Strack claim that in Aramaic the expression *to bind and loose* was used of the verdict of a teacher of the Law who, on the strength of his expert knowledge of the oral tradition, declared some action "bound," i.e., forbidden, some "loosed," i.e., permitted; later the expression was employed to describe the function of the church in excommunicating members from its midst. It is not likely that the words describe an authority to absolve from sins.

19, 20. Harmony and good will are indispensable in the life of the church, because a church united in prayer accomplishes great things and continually receives new gifts from God's hands. This is true even when the group is very small. Jesus did not suffer from the illusion of numbers. The "little" church is as much his as is the "big" church. Frederick Heiler (in his *Spirit of Worship*) claims that all Christian forms of worship are based upon and dominated by the belief in the living Christ. This saying, however, could not mean to those who first heard it all that it meant to Christians at a later time—the Universal Presence of Jesus expressing itself in the church.

21–35. Forgiveness and the Parable of the Unfaithful Servant. The duty of forgiveness occupied a large place in the teaching of Jesus. The spirit of revenge had cast a dark shadow upon the life of his own race and upon that of primitive society in general. Unlimited forgiveness was to be the dominant spirit of the New Society. Evil of every kind, personal, social, international, was to be "overcome by good," especially in the form of good will and a conciliatory spirit. *Seventy times seven* (cf. mg.) is a hyperbolical way of expressing an unlimited number. Among the Jews the number of times one should exercise forgiveness varied, three being the fixed number in one statement in the *Mishnah*, in other statements seven.

This parable, as Jülicher notes, is one of the simplest and clearest we have from the lips of Jesus. The one truth which it illustrates is expressed in the final verse (35). To foster the spirit of pity and forgiveness in our hearts we must ever realize what God has had to pardon in us. Sins against God are symbolized by *talents* (v. 24, mg.), sins against men by *denarii* (v. 28, mg.). Jesus here emphasizes the great truth that mercy is enthroned in the heart of God and that forgiveness should shine like a jewel on the breasts of his followers. To forgive is to be Godlike. Ill-will and a revengeful, grudging spirit involve others in the consequences of our sins. The parable beautifully illustrates 5[7], and presents in a new light a truth proclaimed in the apocryphal book of Ecclesiasticus, "Forgive thy neighbor the hurt that he hath done thee; and then thy sins shall be pardoned when thou prayest" (28[1]).

24. *Talent*—six thousand denarii, about twelve hundred dollars (see art., *Time, Money*, etc., p. 78b). Judæa, Samaria, and Idumæa paid to the Imperial treasury six hundred talents a year; Galilee and Peræa paid two hundred.

25. Canaanitish slaves were sold by written contract as though they had been goods or cattle. They were often marked by a seal or stamp, or bells were hung round their necks. Their subjugation was complete and their treatment cruel in the extreme. The system in Israel as in every other land was a horrible plague corrupting the national life. A creditor could take the debtor forcibly before the authorities.

35. The fact that it is the *heavenly Father* who at the close is represented as punishing shows that the doctrine of God's Fatherhood does not mean that men can impose on his good nature. A father may be stern in the very interests of his fatherhood. Jesus nowhere says that God treats lightly the unfilial and unfraternal spirit—which, in the gospel, is the essence of sinfulness.

CHAPTER XIX

1, 2. Jesus Begins His Journey to Jerusalem. These verses mark an important break in the ministry of Jesus. He is beginning to fulfill his own prediction as to his fate (16[21] 17[22]). He turns his back on Galilee, the home of all his disciples except Judas Iscariot, where he could have been sure of a measure of popularity and even of safety, and "sets his face" toward Jerusalem. His journey thither is a leisurely one, and it is not direct. He goes by way of Peræa, the territory east of Jordan, and thereby avoids Samaria (cf. Lk. 9[51f.] Jn. 4[1-4]). John intimates that he visited Jerusalem twice (7[2, 3] 10[22f.]) before the final visit, which according to the Synoptic record falls some six months after this final leaving of Galilee. Luke devotes considerable attention to this ministry in Peræa, and to him we owe our knowledge of many of its incidents (see Lk. 9[51]–19[28]).

3–12. The Question of Divorce. (Mk. 10[2-12]; cf. Mt. 5[31, 32] Lk. 16[18] 1 Cor. 7.) It seems beyond doubt that Matthew derived his account from Mark, but that he reflects the mind of the early church at a later period than Mark. The order in Mark is (1) the question; (2) quotations from Deut. 24[1-3]; (3) the answer of Jesus, in which he quotes freely Gen. 2[24]; (4) the argument clinched by v. 9. The order in Matthew is (1) the question, with the significant addition of the words *for every cause;* (2) the quotation from Genesis; (3) the retort by listeners quoting Deut. 24[1]; (4) the reply of Jesus, stating that the Mosaic command was a concession to the people. (Note that in Matthew the questioners appeal to Deuteronomy against Genesis, in Mark, Jesus appeals to Genesis against Deuteronomy.) Then (5) the argument is clinched by a saying in which Matthew introduces the exceptive clause (v. 9; he also introduces it in 5[32]). It is only in the first Gospel that we find the exceptive clause, and the whole context shows that it is contrary to the spirit of the passage and was made when divorce for adultery had already grown up. Mark in v. 12 has what looks like a later addition, since the statement about a woman being able to divorce her husband was a Greek and Roman, not a Jewish custom. Many modern scholars (e.g., H. G. Wood and Klostermann), though they regard the exceptive clauses in Matthew as an interpolation, yet claim that it reflects the mind of Jesus, since the case of adultery would be dealt with as in Deut. 22[13f.] by the death penalty. It is very doubtful, however, if this penalty was inflicted in the days of Jesus (but cf. Jn. 8[1-11]). It is clear that Jesus is laying down an ideal for his followers. To what extent this ideal, which, like many others, we owe to Jesus, is applicable for modern society is a problem. (See Streeter, *Adventure*, ch. 3; Temple, *Essays in Christian Politics*, pp. 105f.)

Before the ideal can be reached it is very evident not only that modifications must be introduced into the legislation of nations, but also that a drastic change must take place in the attitude of many individuals. V. 12 seems to be an interpolation by the evangelist. The deliberate choice of celibacy for the Kingdom's sake has sometimes been justified, but many ills have gone with it also.

13–15. Jesus Blesses the Children. (Mk. 10$^{13-16}$, and see notes on 18$^{1-14}$.) Matthew characteristically omits the strong word "indignation" which Mark has in v. 14 as well as Mark's lovely word (Greek *enankalizo*) which means "to place a little one's head to rest on the bend of one's arm." The child nature is presented by Jesus as the ideal for his kingdom, not because it is either humble or innocent, but because of its dependence on others, its receptiveness, its capacity to develop, and its freedom from self-consciousness and worry. As the child rests its head on the strong arm of the Lord, so the soul of man must learn to lean and rest on the strength of the strong Son of God. Some scholars think that the phrase *kingdom of heaven* is here a synonym for Christian salvation in a general sense, hence they read *to such belongeth salvation.*

16–22. The Great Refusal. (Mk. 10$^{17-22}$ Lk. 18$^{18-23}$.) The rich man's salute of Jesus as *good* (see mg.) is not in any way ironical nor is it a meaningless compliment, nor is it a recognition of the perfect teaching capacity of Jesus or of his moral perfection. The Greek word translated "good" (*agathos*) on the lips of this suppliant is used more in the sense of gracious, benevolent, kindly disposed. The answer of Jesus as reported in Mark (10^{18}) occasioned difficulty to the author of the first Gospel, who changed it to *why askest thou me concerning that which is good?* (Cf. mg.) The statement seems most incongruous on the lips of Jesus, who was the very one to consult on all questions of moral goodness. The answer of Jesus, whether Mark or Matthew is correct, is nevertheless a mark of his profound humility and in harmony with such statements as Jn. 14^{28}, "My Father is greater than I." The source of all benevolence is in God himself. Some recent writers on the life of Jesus have fastened on these words and have tried to prove that they indicate on Jesus' part a consciousness of sin, an interpretation which only goes to show to what straits men are put to discover a flaw in the character of Jesus.

The inquirer is a Jew, in whose heart riches are slowly dethroning God, and the words of Jesus may have been purposely spoken to bring him to think of his relations to God. The *commandments* enumerated by Jesus are those of the second table, which emphasize social obligations and human responsibilities. The apocryphal Gospel to the Nazarenes asserts that to the young man's claim the Lord replied: "How sayest thou, 'I have kept the law and the prophets'? How does it stand written in the Law? 'Thou shalt love thy neighbor as thyself'; and see, many of thy brethren are covered with filth and dying of hunger while thy house is full of good things, and nothing at all goes out from it to them." This rich man makes an astounding claim when he asserts that he has fulfilled all these moral obligations, but despite such palpable self-righteousness, Jesus sees in his nature some lovable qualities, so much so that he endeavors to get him to join the inner circle. But the way is hard; in his case it must be for him to cut himself entirely free from his great wealth and live the simple life of a humble follower of Jesus. Great crises call for drastic demands. But the demand here was too great, and the young man sorrowfully turns away and misses the great opportunity of his life. It does not follow from this that Jesus meant that no Christian could hold property. Cf. Joseph of Arimathea. The law of the Kingdom is undivided allegiance: what hinders that must be given up.

23–26. Riches a Soul Peril. (Mk. 10$^{23-27}$ Lk. 18$^{24, 25}$.) Jesus, by his contacts with men in Capernaum, Jericho, the Decapolis, and Jerusalem, was made to realize how wealth influenced the character of certain publicans, courtiers, and Roman officials. Then as now it often deadened spiritual aspirations and desires and acted as a great deterrent to discipleship. By means of a popular hyperbolical proverbial expression about *a camel and a needle's eye,* he boldly states that from a human standpoint for a rich man to enter the Kingdom is well-nigh impossible. According to some important MSS., Mk. 10^{24} should read *how difficult a thing it is to enter the kingdom of God,* implying that entrance into the Kingdom is difficult not only for the rich but for all. To the consternation and questioning of the disciples Jesus gives the reassuring word that the salvation of men and the bringing of men into the kingdom of God is something that only the grace and power of God himself can accomplish, and this is always at the disposal of men.

27–30. Reward for Self-renunciation. (Mk. 10$^{28-31}$ Lk. 18$^{28-30}$.) Peter is anxious to know what compensations the disciples are to receive for having left all. The answer of Jesus seems to be best preserved in Matthew and Luke, who represent Jesus as saying simply that the compensations shall be *manifold* (v. 29, mg.), and who leave out the detailed enumerations of Mk. 10^{30}, a passage which we may suppose was added later when the communistic experiment was made in the church and the disciples held all things in common (Acts $2^{43f.}$). But the rich compensations of service in the Kingdom are attended by *persecutions* (Mk. 10^{30}), and when the Gospel was written these were of a very severe order. (See intro. to Revelation, p. 1365, a book reflecting the persecutions of this same period.)

CHAPTER XX

1–16. The Parable of Equal Pay for Unequal Work. We should be as grateful to Matthew for preserving this matchless parable as to Luke (15^{11-32}) for treasuring its twin companion, that of the prodigal son, with which it has the closest affinities, and which is, in fact, the best commentary on this parable. In both parables it is the grace and loving-kindness of God toward those who enter the Kingdom late that are extolled and magnified. The germ ideas from which have flowered the teaching of Paul, the apostle to the Gentiles, on the grace of God are found embedded in these two parables, Jesus presenting the ideas in a highly imaginative and colorful way and Paul presenting them more abstractly. The originality of Jesus is seen when we compare this parable with similar ones recorded in the Talmud. One such parable tells of a man entering the vineyard late, but because of his industry receiving much more than those who began earlier; in the same way, a certain rabbi did more for the Law in twenty-eight years than many other scholars in one hundred years. The grace of God strives to make men equal as regards what they receive in the kingdom of God from the Father. The blessings of the Kingdom are spiritual and intangible; the joy of the Lord is the same for all; but the parable does not mean that the man who has borne the heat and burden of the day may not be able to appreciate and use more fully an identical gift. While the main emphasis of the parable is on the grace of God, his justice and righteousness in dealing fairly with those who came first are also stressed.

Day (v. 2) was reckoned from dawn to sunset, roughly speaking from 6 A.M. to 6 P.M., and it was divided into four equal parts. *The eleventh hour* (v. 6) is chosen to make the apparent injustice as conspicuous as possible. The expression *evil eye* (v. 15) is found in the O.T. as the equivalent of a mean and niggardly spirit (cf. Deut. 28^{54}), and *good* is used here in the sense of kind, bountiful. We may paraphrase: "Does my friendliness produce in thee the unfriendly feeling of a disgruntled man?" The verse is important for the interpretation of the parable. (Cf. on 6^{21-23}.)

16. J. Weiss interprets the verse as meaning that every distinction between first and last vanishes in the kingdom of God. The words themselves, however, are either misplaced or they show that Matthew has misunderstood the meaning of the parable. The *first,* who have borne the heat and burden of the day, are not disparaged. That those hired *last* receive pay first is only part of the furnishing of the parable. *It is not the reversal of positions that is stressed but the equalizing of privileges.*

17–19. The Third Prediction of Suffering. See notes on Mk. 10^{32-34}. These words should be linked with $16^{21f.}$ $17^{22, 23}$ $19^{1, 2}$, notes. The shadow of the cross falls consistently across the path of the Saviour.

20–28. The Ambition of the Sons of Zebedee. See notes on Mk. 10^{35-45}. On v. 28, cf. 18^{11} A.V., and 18^{10} R.V. mg.

29–34. Healing Two Blind Men. See notes on Mk. 10^{46-52}.

CHAPTER XXI

1–11. The Triumphal Entry. (Mk. 11^{1-10} Lk. 19^{29-38}.) Rawlinson thinks the purpose of the story is clearly to represent Jesus' entry into Jerusalem as the coming of Zion's king. Matthew narrates the incident as though it were a direct fulfillment of the prophecy in Zech. 9^{9} and he bears the O.T. passage in mind in narrating the details of the story, for he mentions two animals (but cf. intro., p. 955b). Only Matthew of the three evangelists quotes the prophecy. Scholars like Weiss, Bacon, and others think that the Messianic coloring was an after-thought and that the multitudes greeted Jesus simply as a prophet. But may not Jesus have chosen to manifest his Messiahship at this juncture in his ministry in a way that would show that it was a spiritual and non-political one? (Cf. Jn. 12^{16}.) The authorities surely could not charge anyone entering in this lowly fashion with having political aspirations.

1. The *Mount of Olives,* a hill of moderate height, was a Sabbath journey westward from Jerusalem. Popular belief expected the Messiah to appear on Olivet. *Bethphage* ("house of unripe figs") was probably an estate on the western slope of the hill.

2, 3. The indications are that Jesus had already made a private arrangement with the owner of the ass. *The Lord* here, Allen thinks, is the equivalent of God. Zahn suggests that the owner was of the inner circle. In Greek-speaking usage "Lord" is the normal title for Jesus as Divine Head of the Christian Community (cf. Acts 19[5, 10, 13, 17, 20] 2 Cor. 3[17]).

9. *Hosanna* reminds us of the Hallel Psalms sung at the Passover (Psa. 113—118). The original Hebrew verb expresses a cry for help; it is addressed to a king (2 Kings 16[7]), and also to God in favor of the king (Psa. 20[9]) and of the people as a whole (Psa. 118[25]). In Christian liturgy it is simply a cry for help. The phrase *he who cometh* refers in the psalm quoted (118[26]) to any pilgrim, but is used here perhaps in a special Messianic sense of Jesus. *Hosanna in the highest* is probably an abbreviated form of expression meaning, "Give salvation, O Thou who dwellest in the height," or "Hosanna is called to Thee who dwellest on the height."

12–17. Jesus Cleanses the Temple. (Mk. 11[15-18] Lk. 19[45, 46]; cf. Jn. 2[13-16].) Some scholars prefer the Johannine position of this incident in the ministry of Jesus (but on the possibility that there were two cleansings, see notes on Jn. 2[13-16]). Matthew gives the account of the cleansing of the Temple before the cursing of the fig-tree; Mark reverses this order. The selling of doves and the exchanging of money was permissible in the outer courts of the Temple; the reason why Jesus protested was because the traders were in the habit of defrauding the pilgrims who came to the city from all lands. *A den of robbers* aptly describes the methods of these men. Just as the pilgrims at Mecca to-day are outrageously fleeced, so they were in Jerusalem in the days of Jesus. Israel Abrahams, referring to the stalls of vendors outside the Christian Church of the Holy Sepulcher in Jerusalem to-day, where sacred relics, painted beads, colored candles, gilded crucifixes, and bottles of Jordan water are sold, exclaims: "Would that Jesus were come again to overthrow these false servants of his as he overthrew those false servants of his in Israel long ago." Nothing so lowers Christianity in the thoughts of men like using it as a cloak for corruption in business.

13. There are two quotations from the O.T. here, Isa. 56[7] and Jer. 7[11]. The first is cited fully only by Mark; Matthew and Luke omit *for all the nations*, possibly because the Temple had been destroyed when they wrote. The emphasis on *prayer* shows that Jesus thinks of the Temple as a place for worship and not as a place for sacrifices.

14–17. Matthew alone adds this statement about Jesus healing blind men and cripples in the Temple precincts and the children crying out "Hosanna." The cry of the children may very well belong to the story of the triumphal entry, but v. 14 suggests the hand of an editor who has transposed this statement from another place.

18–22. The Cursing of the Fig Tree. (Mk. 11[12-14, 19-26].) Figs ripe enough to eat could not possibly be found on a fig tree before June in either Galilee or Jerusalem. The tree bears two crops; in Palestine, the real fruit is not ripe till August; but fruit of a sort ripens much earlier. Lagrange thinks we have here a symbolic miracle to teach the insufficiency of religious profession without fruitfulness. J. Weiss regards it as a legend whose origin we cannot explain. It has been suggested that there was a withered fig-tree on the road from Bethlehem to Jerusalem with which popular fancy busied itself, the withering of which was in course of time attributed to a curse by Jesus. Deissmann has treated the incident in a touching and convincing way in his *Religion of Jesus and Faith of Paul*, pp. 98–100.

The most probable interpretation is that the parable of the fig-tree in Lk. 13[6-9], which is a parable dealing with the faithlessness of the Jews, has in course of time developed into this miracle which, suggestively enough, is recorded for us in Matthew and Mark but not in Luke. Klausner and Middleton Murry lay stress on the historicity of the incident and deduce from it that Jesus really lost his temper and was afterward sorry for it! (See art., *N.T. Miracles*, p. 923b.)

Whatever the real nature of the incident, it provided the basis for a conversation between Jesus and the disciples on the question of prayer and what marvelous things can be wrought by its aid. Pointing to the old withered fig-tree, and to the mountain on whose slopes they are sitting, Jesus used the former as a symbol of a small, trifling thing and the latter as a symbol of a difficult thing. Not only is prayer a real help to accomplish the hard, big things of life, but its inspiration is essential also to fulfill the smaller, lesser duties. Jesus was facing the greatest task of his career in the full confidence that this great weapon of prayer would not fail him. Matthew stresses only the need of faith, while Mark elaborates the conversation and emphasizes the importance of persistence as well as the need of forgiving others, if our prayers are to be all-availing.

23–27. The Source of Jesus' Authority. (Mk. 11[27-33], notes on Lk. 20[1-8].) The words and deeds of Jesus in Jerusalem impress the rulers with his moral and intellectual authority (cf. 7[29]). Some of their number had once gone so far as to accuse him of being in collusion with

Beelzebub (12[24]). Jesus loved to answer his opponents by a counter question (22[15-21]), so he asked them to state their opinion about the authority of the Baptist. To give it a purely human origin would have displeased the people, but to attribute it to God would have been foolish, for they never acknowledged John as a divinely sent messenger. Though Jesus does not answer directly, the answer is self-evident. His conviction that he is the divinely appointed Messiah attains the clearness and distinctness of noon, and well do his opponents know it in their heart of hearts. Throughout these scenes at Jerusalem the Messianic claim is steadily maintained and put forward by implication, though it is not until the actual trial scene, in answer to the high priest's question, that the claim becomes explicit (26[63, 64]).

28–32. **Parable of the Two Sons.** The Greek MSS. vary in the order of the two sons. The R.V. gives the right order. The first son represents the publicans and sinners who refused the offer of the gospel but afterward repented and accepted, while the second son typifies the scribes who pretend to concur with the claims of the gospel but whose life clearly shows their concurrence to be but lip-service. Montefiore regards this parable as a deadly but most accurate satire on the morality of the scribes, who keep the letter and neglect the spirit of the law.

32. Some scholars reverse v. 32 and v. 31b, which gives greater clearness to the parable. While the parable speaks of relations with God, this verse deals with attitudes toward the Baptist; in consequence many regard the verse as not a part of the parable proper.

33–46. **The Parable of the Wicked Vinedressers.** (Mk. 12[1-12], notes on Lk. 20[9-19].) This parable contains a philosophy of the history of Jesus' people. The meaning is so clear that he who runs may read. It should be compared with Isa. 5[1-7]. The Jews as a whole represent the tenant farmers. It is clear that Jesus anticipated his death and regarded himself as occupying a position higher than the prophets. Burkitt defends the authenticity of the parable, affirming that an allegory would have contained some allusion to the resurrection. Lagrange thinks that it would have been a reflection on our Lord's moral character if he had not set clearly before his adversaries the blackness of the crime which they were plotting against him. The parable is his attempt to save them from their own folly. Jesus is careful not to involve the crowd in the crime.

34. The vine bore in the third year; the fourth year produce was sacred; that of the fifth year became the possession of the owners.

37. *Sent his son.* The words represent Jesus in his twofold relation of servant and Son. 41. The *other husbandmen* are, Lagrange thinks, the Twelve, as the new judges of the spiritual Israel (cf. v. 43). 42. Psa. 118[22, 23]. This was a favorite proof text of early Christian apologetic (cf. Acts 4[11] 1 Pet. 2[4-7] Rom. 9[32, 33] Eph. 2[20]). Some think the quotation is an afterthought of early Christian exegesis, while others are of the opinion that the application goes back to our Lord himself. This is the more probable in view of the evident purpose of the parable to express Jesus' conviction of his own significance. 44. See mg. If genuine, the verse expresses the dreadful cost of rejecting God's truth. 46. *A prophet.* Cf. 21[11]. The word suggests that the triumphal entry, though Messianic for Jesus, was not so for the people. Schweitzer, e.g., thinks that the people regarded Jesus as "Elijah," the forerunner of Messiah, and that the later popular demand for Jesus' death was due to a revulsion of feeling when they were told of his Messianic claim.

CHAPTER XXII

1–14. **The Parable of the Wedding Feast.** The parable occurs in Lk. 14[16-24] (notes) in what appears a purer and more original form. Its main lesson is to teach that those for whom the Kingdom was intended would lose their high privileges because they did not value them and the privileges which they had scorned would be granted to the despised outsider. The parable also stresses the truth that God's purpose would not know final defeat—guests would be found for the supper of the King. The deep universal note of the gospel sounds forth clearly in this parable. Note *the character of the excuses;* they are the normal, everyday concerns of life, things not sinful in themselves but when allowed to absorb all our thoughts and energy they can very effectively stand between us and the full acceptance of the joys of the Kingdom. The comparison with a wedding banquet serves to emphasize the joy and gladness of the Kingdom's life.

6, 7. These verses are not in Luke. While they show that Matthew had grasped the point that the Jews were to lose the privileges of the Kingdom, the representation of God as venting his anger on Jerusalem is not due to Jesus, but is probably a later addition to the parable.

8. The rejection of God by the people necessarily leads to the rejection of the people by God. This principle is embedded in the origin of Christianity, which was originally

intended as the consummation of Judaism, but finally became a separate movement (cf. Acts 18[6]).

11–13. *The man without the wedding garment.* People brought in from the byways and streets would have neither time nor means to procure a wedding garment. The little parable nevertheless may properly emphasize the fact that one must appear at the kingly feast with that pure garment which means *righteousness*, and that the day will come when the King will appear to sift the worthy from the unworthy. The note of divine severity appears often in the teaching of Jesus (5[20] 7[23] 11[20f.] 18[34, 35], note).

14. This is a detached saying. By it Jesus could only have meant that while many hear the word calling to repentance it is only a few who respond to the call. Matthew represents Jesus in places as entertaining a very pessimistic outlook for the future, such as is not the case in the other Gospels. This emphasis may be due to the fact that the persecution and difficulty which characterized the period when Matthew was compiled naturally led the author to select from the total available tradition those elements which seemed to bear on the immediate situation.

15–22. The Question of Tribute. (Mk. 12[13-17], notes on Lk. 20[20-26].) Rome, since 6 A.D., had imposed a head tax of about twenty-five cents a person on the population of Judæa. It was regarded as a badge of servitude to Rome. Jesus was no political revolutionary (cf. 17[24f.]), and by his own example he showed his countrymen that the way to change the oppression and tyranny of Rome was by gentleness, good will, and religious leadership. The disaster that befell the Jews (see it described in Josephus, *Wars of the Jews*, especially bks. v and vi, and ch. 1 of bk. vii) was ultimately due to their ignoring of this solution offered by Jesus. In ancient times the authority of a ruler was co-extensive with the circulation of his coinage, and coins bearing his image were ultimately regarded as his private property. Jesus' words in v. 21, as Lord Acton said, gave to the civil power, under the protection of conscience, a sacredness it had never enjoyed and bounds it had never acknowledged; they were the repudiation of absolutism and the inauguration of freedom.

16. A beautiful tribute to Christ, though given in flattery, emphasizing his perfect freedom from deference to the great and powerful. *Way of God* here means religion.

23–33. The Sadducees' Question Concerning Resurrection. (Mk. 12[18-27] Lk. 20[27-40] cf. Acts 23[6-8].) The Sadducees were the ecclesiastical political party, who sought the well-being of the people through political means and the appropriation of the culture of the Roman Empire. They were not in sympathy with the Messianic hopes of the nation. By this facetious question arising from the practice of the Levirate marriage among the Jews (see Deut. 25[5-10]), the Sadducees wished to throw ridicule upon the truth of the resurrection, in which they did not believe. The popular belief was that he who died without offspring had no one to care for the ancestor cult of the family, and this serves to explain the question (see notes on Ruth, p. 378b). Jesus intimates that the conditions of the resurrection life will be totally different from this. All will be *as the angels*, for whom, as an old saying has it, God has created no wives. This use of Scripture is rabbinic in character. Because God is styled *God of Abraham*, etc., long after the death of the patriarchs, it follows that the patriarchs still live. For defensive purposes Matthew and his readers considered this argument convincing; whether Jesus intended exactly this deduction may be questioned.

34–40. The Greatest Commandment. See notes on Mk. 12[28-34] Lk. 10[25-37]. The glory of Jesus is that he welded indissolubly together these two great fundamental commands which had long been held apart. The first is found in Deut. 6[4] (notes) and is known by the Jews as the Shema (Hebrew for the first word, *Hear*), which every Jew repeats at his prayers daily; the second is found in Lev. 19[18] (notes), but it was not given a place of much prominence. To Jesus they are the pivotal points of the new religion. He stands unique among men not only as the one who linked the two together, but as the first who incorporated them into his life, making them the primal laws of his every action. When *love* is analyzed we find it contains the elements of admiration, reverence, the desire to possess, and the will to benefit. These elements are not always present in the same degree or at the same time. But in all genuine love to God there is true reverence and awe, in which all the faculties of personality unite together; there is also a yearning to possess more of the Spirit of God, and a strong desire to be at his service. To the Jew the word *neighbor* usually meant fellow Jew. Jesus, as in the parable of the good Samaritan, expanded the word and lifted its portals so that it came to include any child of the human race, however lowly and despised. For him, neighbor is anyone who needs our help. Likewise, he who renders the help is "neighborly."

[The so-called *pericope* (Jn. 7[53]–8[11], notes) follows here—the story of the woman taken in adultery. The later church thought that

Jesus' intense love for sinners would injure his reputation. It therefore cut out this story, which fortunately has been treasured for us in some of the MSS. of the fourth Gospel.]

41–46. Son of David. See notes on Mk. 12³⁵⁻³⁷ Lk. 20⁴¹⁻⁴⁴. Jesus here seems to disparage his Davidic descent, the fact which his followers make so much of. He is far greater than a son of David—he is the *Lord* from above. Middleton Murry characteristically thinks (*Jesus, Man of Genius*, p. 300) that Jesus by this manifestly authentic saying "shatters the legend of his birth in Bethlehem." He was not of David's house. This paragraph, however, may very easily be explained as preserved by the early church just because of its value as a protest against the all too earthly Jewish interpretation of the Messiah. If so, the effort had no very striking success, for the belief in the Davidic descent of Jesus continued to be very persistent, as evidenced in the early chapters of Matthew and Luke (cf. Rom. 1^{3}).

44. Psa. 110, quoted here, of which David was regarded as the author, played a large part in early Christian theology (see Acts $2^{34, 35}$ 1 Cor. 15^{25} Heb. 1^{13}). The glorious music of Psa. 110 and 118—songs of victory out of defeat—echoed in Jesus' soul as he stood in the midst of his enemies. He felt that they had been sung of him centuries ago.

46. *Questions.* The chapter which concludes with this word describes three questions put to Jesus, and his answers. It is probable that we have here a characteristic Matthean grouping of material illustrative of a certain aspect of Jesus' teaching. But Jesus also could ask questions, and vv. 41–45 show how effectively he did it. Note that Mark (12^{34}) and Luke (20^{40}) have both put this verse in what seems to be a more logical position.

CHAPTER XXIII

Chs. 23–25 represent the fifth block of teaching in Matthew's Gospel (intro., section on "Division," p. 953). In ch. 23 we have a large collection of the utterances of Jesus directed against the scribes and Pharisees, the one word occurring like a fugue through the chapter being *hypocrisy* (see 6^{2}, note), a word which hit off to perfection the outstanding characteristic of many of these religious leaders. Even when we take into consideration that the massing of many sayings uttered on different occasions unduly darkens the picture, and when, further, we remember that the sayings, as they passed through minds in the early church filled with bitter animus toward the Jews and the part they had in the crucifixion of Jesus took on harsher tones, it nevertheless remains that we have in this chapter a very dark but, on the whole, a true picture of many Pharisees of the day (but cf. p. 841). Against this somber background the sincerity and truthfulness of Jesus stand out in striking contrast.

1–12. Warnings Against Pride of Place and Power. (Mk. 12^{38-40}, notes on Lk. 20^{45-47}.) Many feel that vv. 2, 3 present a genuine difficulty. As they stand, Jesus seems to say that the disciples are to pay heed to the Pharisaic interpretations of the Mosaic Law but are on no account to copy the Pharisees in the way they translate those interpretations into practice, whereas he is elsewhere represented as regarding the Pharisaic interpretations as "burdens." It is not impossible that a saying of Jesus that bore upon Pharisaism in a less friendly fashion has been manipulated by aggressive members of the anti-Pauline section of the Jewish Christian church in Jerusalem from whence the compiler of this Gospel derived a large part of the material that is peculiar to him (intro., section on "The Judaistic Element," p. 955a). Jesus certainly did not himself comply with the Pharisaic interpretations of the Law.

4, 5. Instead of interpreting the Law and helping the ordinary man to fulfill its requirements, the Pharisees added to the Law a number of interpretations which only increased the difficulty of fulfilling it. They themselves were meticulous in keeping those parts of the Law which served to bring them into prominence, such as *making broad the phylacteries.* Phylactery is the transliteration of a Greek word meaning "safe-guard." According to the Pharisaic interpretation every true Jew was to wear at the morning prayer, fastened on his wrist and bound round his forehead, a small leathern case—the phylactery—with four compartments containing four portions of Scriptures, Ex. 13^{1-10} 13^{11-16} Deut. 6^{4-9} 11^{13-21}. It was possible by enlarging the bands to make these look very imposing. In addition the Law required that four blue tassels—the *borders*—should be worn at the four corners of the outer robe. Jesus seems to have worn them (cf. Mt. 9^{20}), but evidently some Pharisees wore them large and long in conformity with that strong craving of theirs to do everything with a view to winning self-glory.

8–12. In contrast to the Pharisees, the followers of Jesus are not to be governed by the passion for popularity and love of place and power, since true brotherhood cannot live in such an atmosphere, and the service of humanity alone is the true pathway to greatness and real enlargement of personality. The titles *father*, and *master* (or leader), and *Christ* are sometimes regarded as showing the influence of a later time in adapting the words of Jesus to the existing situation (cf. Jn. 14[26] 16[13]). To search for honor for honor's sake is to lower one's position in the kingdom of God.

13–32. **The Seven Great Woes.** (Cf. Lk. 11[37-52].) Some MSS. add v. 14 (see mg.), but most modern editors leave it out; it is introduced from Mk. 12[40]. Luke has six woes, three against the Pharisees and three against the scribes (lawyers).

13. *The first woe.* Luke (11[52]) expresses this saying in more original form; it is placed last by him as though he deemed it of surpassing importance. The "power of the key" is symbolic of the teaching power of the Pharisees—a wonderfully precious instrument to be kept bright and oiled and well used in unlocking the gateways leading into the broad expanses of the kingdom of God (see Lk. 11[52]). But they are so preoccupied with outward appearances and are so lost in the unimportant things of the Law that they are now in the deplorable position of not being able either to enter in themselves or to help others.

15. *The second woe.* While the proselytizing zeal of the Jews waned somewhat before and after the fall of Jersualem, the letters of Paul (cf. Rom. 2[17f.]), the Acts of the Apostles, and the writings of Josephus (see *Antiquities*, bk. xxii, ch. 2: 3, 4, 5) bear testimony to the missionary zeal of the Jews of the Diaspora in the first half of the first century. This woe is not in Luke, and many scholars think that when originally uttered it was not so harsh, and that the latter part ran thus—*doubly worse than he was.* Jesus is not condemning the missionary movement so much as the missionary who leads it. (Cf. pp. 847–9.)

16–22. *The third woe.* Because the word "hypocrisy" is left out of the address, some think that this woe deals more with a religious and moral error than with a definite act of hypocrisy; and yet what worse form of hypocrisy could we think of than the endeavor to free oneself from some solemn oath by resorting to casuistry and evasion such as we find illustrated here (see notes on Corban, Mk. 7[8-13]). The Pharisees wanted to claim that an oath by the Temple and altar should include reference to the gold in the Temple and the sacrifice at the altar, otherwise the oath is not complete (cf. 5[34]).

23, 24. *The fourth woe.* (Lk. 11[42].) Tithing according to Lev. 27[30] was confined to the fruits of seed and tree. According to Deut. 14[23] it included corn, new wine, and oil. Rabbis extended it to all cooking vegetables, while the Talmud claimed that everything one eats and drinks and which has its growth from the earth—even the herbs from the kitchen garden—is tithable. The Pharisees were careful to observe these requirements, but the great moral demands of (a) *justice*, a passion to establish righteousness in all the relationships of life, involving as it does a constant crusade against wrong, oppression and injustice; (b) *mercy*, that great quality which is mightiest in the mightiest, which reveals itself in loving sympathy and a helpful ministry of the needy; and (c) *faith*, which here means fidelity, stanch devotion to principle at all costs, loyalty to truth and to one's friends—these were ignored by them. The last clause of v. 23 may not be part of the original saying; it is omitted from Lk. 11[42] in the Codex Bezae (see p. 863a). An illustration of the happy half-whimsical way Jesus possessed of expressing truth occurs in v. 24; the *gnat* corresponds to the mint and dill, and the *camel* corresponds to the weightier matters. Note the *strain out* of R.V. for the erroneous *strain at* of A.V.

25, 26. *The fifth woe.* The cleansing of cups and of hands before eating was an important ceremonial with the Jews, not on grounds of hygiene or physical cleanliness, but because of the danger of Levitical (ceremonial) impurity. If you were only as careful, Jesus suggests, to see that the *contents* of the vessels are derived in honorable and just ways you would not have to worry very much about the ceremonial cleanliness of the outside of your cups (cf. 15[1-20], notes on Mk. 7[1-8, 14-23]).

27, 28. *The sixth woe.* To walk over a grave caused pollution, and in order to enter the Temple this must be avoided; hence before Passover graves were chalked off lest pilgrims to the city might inadvertently walk over them. Lk. 11[44] is perhaps the original form of the saying. McNeile rightly thinks that whitewashed graves do not form a good simile of hypocrisy, since they proclaim to all the inward pollution instead of concealing the contrast as between the outward appearance and the bones and uncleanliness concealed within. The reference, however, may be to the ornamental plastering of the walls of sepulchers, for the purpose of making them look attractive. Jesus claims that the Pharisees—judged by the standard of inwardness—are as bad as the lawless libertines and heathen whom they so severely condemn.

29–32. *The seventh woe.* (Lk. 11[47, 48].) This deals with the spirit of self-righteousness. "How much better are we than our fathers," men were saying; "they slew the special messengers of God, we honor those messengers by raising memorials to their greatness." The Pharisees are the *sons of their fathers*, because this spirit of self-righteousness is the sworn enemy of all that is great and noble; those who have it are like those whom they denounce; indeed, before many days shall have elapsed these model sons will be howling, "Crucify him," "Crucify him," at the greatest prophet of their race. They are engaged in filling to the brim the measure which their fathers began (cf. 1 Thess. 2[16]). Jesus may also be suggesting in these words that tomb-raising is a very superficial way of showing respect. True honor is shown by living in the spirit of the prophets and carrying into practice their precepts.

33. This is reminiscent of the words of the Baptist and may have strayed here inadvertently. *Judgment of hell* (mg. *Gehenna;* see note on 5[22]) means the judgment which can inflict Gehenna, the place of punishment, upon one.

34–36. A Solemn Warning. (Lk. 11[49-51].) The neglect of privileges proffered by God ends in utter desolation and ruin. The words are in Luke attributed to "the wisdom of God." Some have thought that Jesus was here quoting from an apocryphal book; others have thought that if the wisdom of God is God in action, then the expression is the equivalent of "Thus saith the Lord"; in that case, the passage refers to the whole of God's gracious dealings with his people, who, however, have spurned and insulted God's prophets, killing and crucifying them. His knowledge that Jesus was himself crucified must have given this saying a poignant meaning for Matthew. *Abel* was not strictly a Jew, yet from a religious standpoint all early O.T. generations are ancestors of the Jews. *Zachariah* is in all probability the Zechariah mentioned in 2 Chr. 24[20-22]; the added statement that he was slain between the Temple and altar is due to popular tradition, not to the O.T.

37–39. The Lament Over Jerusalem. (Lk. 13[34, 35].) Schmiedel and Harnack regard the lament as part of some quotation, but the words are too personal and intimate to be only that. Jesus is deeply moved as he thinks of the impending doom coming swiftly on his nation. To the last he is ready to help at any personal cost the people whom he loves. In this tense moment, the simple figure of a hen in some farmyard protecting her brood from an unexpected peril is taken by him as a sublime and fitting symbol of all he desires to be to men.

39. The words have an eschatological significance, and they form a fitting prelude to the solemn discourses that follow in chs. 24–26. Jesus is anticipating his return to earth as the heavenly Messiah, and he clearly says that on his return he will be accepted. Taking the words in that sense, they have not yet been fulfilled. Taking them in a less rigid sense, namely, that when men, even the Jews, properly *understand* Jesus they will recognize him as their Lord, their progressive fulfillment is being seen in all Christian history and experience (cf. note on 21[9]).

CHAPTER XXIV

The parallels are Mk. 13 Lk. 21 (cf. Lk. 17[20-37]). For the nature of the discourse, see the introductory statement to Mk. 13. The notes on Mk. 13 cover the various sections of the discourse as given here in Matthew. On the general nature of apocalyptic discourse, see the articles on that subject, pp. 187, 200, the article on *Backgrounds*, pp. 843–7, and the introduction to Revelation.

The important differences between Matthew and Mark are as follows: (1) Mt. 24[7-14]; cf. Mk. 13[9-13]. Matthew writes from the standpoint of actual experience of persecution, and therefore adds some features, but he modifies in v. 10 the tragic note in Mark, v. 12. (2) In v. 22, Matthew has a future tense, which is past tense in v. 20 in Mark. (3) In Matthew, vv. 26–28 are an elaboration which is wanting in Mark. The elaboration is important for its emphatic denial of the supposition, still held by some, that Christ is to appear at some definitely located spot on the earth. Rather is his coming like the *lightning*—appearing everywhere at once. (4) The simple warning to *watch* in Mark, v. 33, is in Matthew the climax of a series of graphic illustrations (vv. 37–42) which appear to be Matthean expansions of various phrases in Mark. (5) In Matthew, vv. 43–51, the short parable and warning of Mark, vv. 34–36, are more fully worked out, the one important change being that in Mark the porter is *sleeping* on his lord's return, in Matthew he is *rioting*. Or v. 43 of Matthew may be regarded as the parallel to Mark, and vv. 45f. of Matthew as a second parable with a similar theme, a suggestion which seems to be supported by Lk. 12[35-40, 41-48].

CHAPTER XXV

1–13. Parable of the Ten Virgins. See notes on Lk. 12[35] 13[25-28]. One can well see how this parable would be cherished by the early church for its bearing on the prolonged delay of the return of Christ—a question which was keenly discussed in the church in the period between 45–65 B.C. (cf. 2 Pet. 3[8f.], notes). The implication of the parable is that the Lord taught his disciples about the Second Coming —the *Parousia*—but it has a permanent lesson apart from that. One of the supreme needs of his followers—so Jesus is saying—is foresight; the word translated *wise* (Greek *phronimos;* used in Mt. 7[24]) implies that prudence and that acute insight into life which prompt men and women to build up reserves so that periods of delay which put hope and loyalty to the test will be tided over. In the parable of the foundations in 7[24] this quality of character was displayed by the man who, knowing that life would present periods of storm and stress, took the precaution of building on the rock; the hurricane, therefore, left him unshaken. In the life of the Kingdom there will be inevitable delays when men long for the visible manifestation of the Spirit of Christ; how invaluable in the church at such crises are the men whose cruses are full to the brim with the oil of patience, hope, and truth, and whose lamps on the darkest night are bright and incandescent! The all-important lesson is inculcated that the Christian must learn to build up reserves of strength and fortitude, so that in all circumstances, favorable or unfavorable, he may cause his light to shine, and thus find the joy of the Lord (cf. Mk. 13[34-37]). According to the judgment of many scholars, the parable in its original form ended with v. 10.

14–30. Parable of the Talents. See notes on Lk. 19[11-27]. The eschatological element in this parable may be regarded as secondary. Its main purpose is clearly enough to impress on the followers of Jesus the importance of the consecration of the gifts God has intrusted to us, and to show that though we vary in our several capacities the spirit of faithfulness and dependability in the performance of our trust is equally required of all. Such a quality of character enriches our endowments and qualifies us for larger trusts, while neglect and laziness result in loss and deterioration of our original endowments. Modern psychology has amply verified this teaching. The unused capacity, mental and moral as well as physical, becomes the lost capacity. The sluggard loses *even that which he hath.* The parable seems also to lay emphasis on the truth that in the church it is the indifference of the moderately endowed men, who form the majority, that is to be deplored.

31–46. The Judgment of the Son of Man. This is less a parable than a prophetic description of a future Judgment. It is found only in Matthew (cf. Lk. 21[27]). Burney has called attention to the artistic construction of this moving portrayal by pointing out the Hebrew parallelisms. The details of the picture must not be pressed; the main purpose of the description is to give men counsel for the direction of their lives in the present rather than to emphasize what is to take place in the future. The real dividing line between men is whether or not they have the spirit of humanity expressing itself in kindly helpfulness wherever there is need and distress. The presence of Jewish apocalyptic elements, whether they come from Jesus or the evangelist, only serves to heighten the dramatic power of the description. Christian kindness is to know no limits of race or class but is to flow out unceasingly and naturally from a heart in complete harmony with the will of God. The bearing of the parable on the various accidental elements that divide men from each other—race, caste, creed—is obvious. Equally obvious is its teaching that salvation is finally "of the heart," not "of the head." Montefiore's comment on the parable is interesting. He says in effect that it would be foolish not to recognize the force and grandeur of the motive, "for his sake," in a religion, because as the religion is not one's own one cannot be stimulated by a personal motive. In v. 45 there is a wonderful anticipation of Paul's doctrine in Ephesians and Colossians of the mystical oneness of an immanent Christ with humanity.

CHAPTER XXVI

The Beginning of the End. The parallels are Mk. 14 and Lk. 22, on which see notes. The resemblances with Mark are exceedingly close. In some cases, Matthew has elaborated on Mark, e.g., cf. vv. 1–5 of Matthew with vv. 1, 2 of Mark; vv. 24, 25 of Matthew with v. 21 of Mark; v. 42 of Matthew with v. 39 of Mark; vv. 51–54 of Matthew with v. 47 of Mark. In a few cases, Matthew has shortened Mark, e.g., cf. v. 9 of Matthew with v. 5 of Mark; vv. 17–19 of Matthew with vv. 12–16 of Mark; vv. 60, 61 of Matthew with vv. 57–59 of Mark. Two striking omissions from Matthew are vv. 51, 52 of Mark, the story of "a certain young man" who escaped capture by leaving his garment in the soldiers' hands and fleeing (the presence of the story in Mark has led to the suggestion that the young man was Mark himself); and v. 67 of Mark, the line on Peter's "warming himself" (the presence of the line in Mark is one of those little touches which supports the tradition that the reminiscences of Peter were a main source for Mark's Gospel).

The differences in Luke are more considerable. A notable omission is the anointing in the house of Simon (but cf. Lk. 7[37-50]); the description of the experience in Gethsemane is shorter, and there is a difference in the process of the trial. Peculiar to Luke is the difficult passage, vv. 35–38, in which, in what purports to be a final instruction to the disciples, Jesus radically changes some of the instructions he gave when he sent them out the first time (Mt. 10^{9, 10}). Vv. 24–30 of Luke are evidently Jesus' comments—here out of their setting—on the request of the sons of Zebedee for a high place in the Kingdom (cf. Mt. 20^{20-28} 19^{28} Mk. 10^{35-45}).

CHAPTER XXVII

The Trial, Crucifixion, and Burial of Jesus. The parallels are Mk. 15 and Lk. 23 (cf. Jn. 18, 19); see notes. As in the case of ch. 26, the resemblances are closer with Mark than with Luke. A notable omission by Mark and Luke is the account of the death of Judas and the purchase of the field of blood (Mt. 27^{3-10}). Mark and Luke also omit the incident of Pilate's wife's dream and of the handwashing as a sign of innocency (Mt. 27^{19, 24, 25}). Matthew alone describes the earthquake.

Luke alone tells of the trial before Herod (23^{6-16}), of Jesus' words to the women who followed him to Golgotha (vv. 28–31), and of the conversion of one of the two thieves (vv. 40–43). He gives a much shorter account of the Barabbas incident (vv. 18, 19), omits the description of the mocking and scourging of Jesus by the soldiers, and shortens the account of the crucifixion, a notable omission here being that of the cry, "Why hast thou forsaken me?"

1, 2. Jesus Taken to Pilate. See notes on Mk. 15^{1-15}.

3–10. Judas and the Field of Blood. Herein is fulfilled Jesus' saying about Judas in 26^{24}. Judas, the only Judæan of the Twelve, may have joined the group in the first place from political motives, and the betrayal may have been due to personal disappointment. But this in nowise excuses Judas. For weeks and months he lived in the presence of Jesus and had the greatest opportunity ever offered to any man to come to a proper understanding of the true nature of the kingdom of God. So far was Judas from being a victim of divine predestination that the utmost God could do to save a man—show him Jesus Christ—was done for him. Judas destroyed himself physically because he came to realize that he had already destroyed himself morally. His *real* betrayal was less the betrayal of Jesus than the betrayal of his own soul. The idea that he was a necessary step in God's plan to save the world is utterly false. Jesus was not crucified because Judas betrayed him. He went to Jerusalem expressly to suffer death, and he made no effort to escape it once he was convinced it was the Father's will. Had Judas remained loyal, Jesus would still have died for the sins of the world.

The use by the priests of the returned money is a striking illustration of moral subterfuge. It was not—so they argued—wrong to take from the Temple treasury the money for corrupting Judas, but it was wrong *to put it back!* They did not see that no inherent "taint" attaches to money. The "taint" is in the user—in his motives and purposes. The action of the priests strikingly resembles Pilate's handwashing.

9, 10. This way of using the O.T. is characteristic of Matthew. The words quoted are from Zech. 11^{12, 13}, not from Jeremiah (although cf. Jer. 32^{6-15}). The original words had no such meaning as is here ascribed to them. The change of name from *the potter's field* to *the field of blood*, a name still in use when Matthew wrote, serves to prove the historicity of the transaction between Judas and the priests.

11–31. The Trial of Jesus. See notes on Mk. 15^{1-20} Lk. 23^{1-25}. Pilate tried to evade the responsibility of condemning Jesus. His first effort was the offer to release Barabbas—an offer that takes on a certain dramatic character from the tradition that the name of Barabbas was also Jesus. The choice was between Jesus the Robber and Jesus the Redeemer. Then, as now, right and wrong were balanced against each other; men were asked to choose between them; and the choice, once made, involved irrevocable results.

Pilate's second effort to evade responsibility was much less commendable than the first. The offer to release a prisoner was an attempt to prevent the doing of a wrong. The handwashing (v. 24) was an attempt to disclaim responsibility for a wrong which, although demanded by others, could not have been done without his consent. The clause in the Apostles' Creed perpetuates forever the Roman governor's moral weakness—"Crucified under Pontius Pilate." The dream of his wife may be construed as a divine effort to strengthen his will to do the right. Here again, as with Judas (see on vv. 3–10), there was no question of God's purpose to save men being conditioned on Pilate's doing wrong. The death of Christ had its final ground and reason not in the will of men but in the will of God.

32. Simon of Cyrene. See notes on Mk. 15^{21}.

33–44. The Crucifixion. See notes on Mk. 15^{22-32}.

45–56. The Death and Its Accompanying Signs. See notes on Mk. 15[33-41]. The assertion that earthquake and resurrection accompanied the death of Jesus may best be understood as a later interpretation as literal of what in the original tradition was symbolic. Lk. 23[44, 45] seems to represent the process of change from Mark to Matthew. It is evident that a violent storm took place during the crucifixion, and this storm came to be understood as nature's sympathetic travail with her suffering Lord. Symbolically the description is entirely true. *The meaning of the past,* as represented in the Temple with its "holy of holies" and in the great religious leaders, *became clear in the light of the suffering Christ.* This, indeed, is the burden of the Epistle to the Hebrews.

57–61. The Burial. See notes on Mk. 15[42-47].

62–66. The Sealed Tomb. This account of the care of the authorities to guard against the removal of Jesus' body is peculiar to Matthew. Some connect it with 28[11-15], as an attempt on the part of Matthew to make the resurrection both more wonderful and more credible. But there is nothing essentially improbable about such precautions being taken. It is certain that Jesus had foretold his resurrection, and it is apparent that the disappearance of his body, by whatever means, would be regarded by many as a fulfillment of the prediction. What the enemies of Christianity did not realize was that the resurrection of Jesus was a much bigger question than the disappearance of his body (cf. 1 Cor. 15 and notes there). As a matter of fact, it was not the discovery that the tomb was empty that convinced the disciples that their Lord had conquered death, for the discovery dismayed them (Lk. 24[3, 4, 11, 12]); rather it was their actual experience of his living presence.

CHAPTER XXVIII

1–10. The Visit of the Women to the Tomb. See notes on Mk. 16[1-8] Lk. 24[1-12] Jn. 20[1-18]. Burial in artificial tombs, many of which have been found near centers of population in Palestine, was reserved for the rich; the poor were buried in the ground or in natural caves. The rock-hewn tombs in natural caves were so close to one another that identification of the bodies was very difficult, especially when inscriptions were lacking. Isolated rocks often had a tomb chamber quarried in them. A very common plan for single cave tombs was to have nine shaft tombs running horizontally into the walls of the chamber, three in each wall (excluding the wall which contained the entrance). The bones after decay were placed in an ossuary, so that many more than nine bodies could be buried in one tomb.

This story of the visit of the women to the tomb in Matthew is evidently derived from the account in Mk. 16[1-8], but Matthew has added new elements to the story. According to him, the purpose of the visit was to see the tomb, while Mark states that it was to anoint the body of Jesus. The "young man" in Mark has become an *angel,* who assists in the resurrection by rolling away the stone. Matthew informs us also that an earthquake took place (cf. 27[51]) and that the tomb was specially guarded. The message of the angel is practically the same in both Gospels, but Mark adds that the women went out from the tomb because astonishment had come upon them, and they said nothing to anyone, for they were afraid. Matthew, on the contrary, says that they ran to make known the news to the disciples (v. 8). Gardner Smith, in his recent study of the resurrection narratives, suggests that the words in v. 6, *He is risen,* were not originally part of the story, and that v. 7 has been subsequently added. This verse, he claims, is inconsistent with the statement in Mk. 15[8]. If the young man had spoken, as Mark reports, the fear of the women would have been turned to joy. It is incredible that any women possessed of the greatest news ever intrusted to human beings would keep silence for any length of time. Smith further suggests that the women came to the wrong place and mistook an empty tomb for the one they were seeking, and that a young man, of whose identity we know nothing, sought to correct the mistake, pointing to another tomb as the place where they laid him. Terrified at the unexpected apparition and covered with confusion at the failure of their plans, the women ran away and told not a word of their adventure to any man. This story—so the suggestion runs—was quickly expanded and interpreted and has assumed different forms in our synoptic Gospels. The difficulty with the suggestion is that it overemphasizes the importance of the empty tomb (see note on 27[62-66]; cf. p. 930).

For if, as is probable, the disciples had left for Galilee before the return of the women from the tomb, then it follows that they became convinced of the reality of the resurrection on account of the appearance of the risen Christ and not because of any report of an empty tomb. As Montefiore puts it, no story of the empty tomb had reached the disciples when the resurrection faith was born in them. Belief in the risen Jesus on the part of the disciples was independent of a belief in an empty tomb, and care must be taken not to confuse the fact of the resurrection with the stories to which it naturally gave rise in an unscientific and uncritical age.

9, 10. *An appearance of Jesus to the women* is recorded only in Matthew, and many modern interpreters regard it as a late addition, since the narrative seems to be a doublet; cf. vv. 5–7, which considered the "young man" as the Lord himself. Matthew represents the first appearance of Jesus as made to the women on the morning of the third day. The Jews identified personal survival with bodily life, which accounts for the presence of many materialistic elements in the resurrection narratives. Today, we can think of life surviving independently of the physical organism. (See art., *Religion of Israel*, p. 173; art., *Intertestamental Religion*, p. 210; cf. note following 1 Cor. 15.)

11–15. **Bribery of the Soldiers.** This is found in Matthew only, but this does not mean that it has no historical value, since it is exactly what we should expect in the circumstances. The extreme critical view, that it is a late tradition introduced into the gospel narrative in support of the teaching of the early church about the empty tomb, is based on pure subjectivism (see note on 27[62-66]).

16, 17. **The Appearance to the Eleven in Galilee.** (Cf. 1 Cor. 15[5].) This incident seems to rest on stronger historical foundations than any of the resurrection appearances of Jesus. There are some who think that those who *doubted* were not of the eleven but belonged to the larger group of people who were with them on the mountain. On the other hand, the doubt may not mean more than that they were uncertain about the identity of the Lord (Denney, *Jesus and the Gospel*, bk. ii, sect. 1).

18–20. **The Last Words of Jesus.** Similar farewell words, although with differences, are reported by both Mark (16[15f.]) and Luke (24[44f.]). They are in perfect keeping with the cherished convictions of the early church. The divine claims of Christ in vv. 18b and 20b need cause no difficulty. Many feel, however, that v. 19 forms a real crux, and they prefer to regard it as an expression of a truth which the church had learned as a result of the resurrection and on which it still rests its faith. Even if this be allowed, it must still be insisted that there is nothing in the words as they stand which is inconsistent with the gospel portrayal of the self-consciousness of Jesus.

18. *Authority.* Cf. 7[29] 11[27] 21[23] Phil. 2[9-11].

19. *Make disciples.* This describes a comprehensive duty of which baptizing and teaching form a part. *All the nations* (cf. 24[14]). In the light of this last command of Jesus, the action of the disciples as described in Gal. 2[1-9] and Acts 11[1-3] is inexplicable. The universality of the Christian message is inherent in all the teaching of Jesus, but it was due largely to the spiritual experiences of Paul that this universality received definite expression. It is impossible to maintain that everything which goes to constitute even the essentials of Christianity must necessarily be traceable to explicit words of Jesus. There is a progressive element in the Christian revelation. *Baptizing into the name of* means baptizing them so that they are entered as the possession of the Father. Eusebius quotes this verse with the words "into my name," instead of the Trinitarian formula, which represents the earliest baptismal formula. The baptismal rite of the early church must ultimately rest on an explicit command of Christ.

MARK

BY PROFESSOR J. NEWTON DAVIES

INTRODUCTION

The Earliest Gospel. One of the assured results of gospel criticism is that Mark is the earliest of our four Gospels. Many scholars like Allen, Rawlinson, Bartlet, and Stanton date the Gospel sometime before the fall of Jerusalem in 70 A.D. Bacon and J. Weiss date it after 70 A.D. on the ground that the references to wars and rumors of wars in ch. 13 are to the clash between the Romans and the Jews. In any case, the use made of Mark by Matthew, Luke, and the author of the fourth Gospel points conclusively to the fact that it must have been written before 80 A.D.

The Place of Origin. Most interpreters of this Gospel regard it as a Roman Gospel written to the church in that city not long after the terrible Neronic persecution so vividly described in the Annals of Tacitus. When it is read with that bloody catastrophe as a background we begin to understand the reasons for the great emphasis laid upon the heroic bravery of Jesus in the face of all his sufferings and the important place given to the story of the Passion in this Gospel. (See p. 1365,)

The latinisms, the allusion to Rufus (15^{21}, cf. Rom. 16^{13}), the translation of Aramaic words, the explanation of Jewish customs and practices, the persistent tradition that links Mark with Paul and Peter during their stay in Rome, all point to the imperial city as the place where the Gospel was written.

Authorship. John Mark's name has long been associated with the authorship of this Gospel. The oft-quoted testimony of Papias, as well as the many references in the early Fathers, makes the association a very probable one (cf. art., *Formation of N.T.*, p. 856b). Zahn and Bartlet are of the opinion that Mark's signature to his Gospel is to be found in the story of the young man who was so nearly arrested in the garden of Gethsemane (told only in this Gospel), for the story seems to be purposeless except to identify the young man with Mark, the author. The references to Mark and his home in the N.T. show how favorably placed he was to be a recorder of gospel narrative. His home in Jerusalem was probably the place where Jesus and his disciples met for their Last Supper together, and the early Christian community must often have gathered there for prayer and fellowship (Acts 12^{12}). Paul, Peter, and Barnabas were friends of the family. Some of the stirring scenes associated with Pentecost perhaps took place within this home (Acts $1^{13f.}$). All this supports tradition and makes the testimony of Mark peculiarly valuable in reference to the Jerusalem ministry of Jesus.

Characteristics of the Author. The characteristics of the evangelist are suggested or implied in his Gospel.

(1) It is very evident that he was *a bi-lingual speaker*. His narrative reminds us of a palimpsest, the upper writing of which is Greek and the lower Aramaic. He is not translating, but his mind is so steeped in Semitic modes of thought that the structure of his sentences and the idioms that he employs clearly reveal his Hebrew origin. On the other hand, though he is deficient in culture and his vocabulary is small, yet he is not without some feeling for the niceties of the Greek language, as evidenced in his striking use of the colorful imperfect tense and of some arrresting Greek words.

(2) As a writer he is *little concerned with either chronological or psychological development*, though he seems to have been careful to confine the ministry of Jesus in Jerusalem to a week and to have divided the last day of our Lord's life into four periods corresponding to the Roman watches. Mark makes it quite clear also that Jesus gradually restricted his teaching, as it became more advanced, to a limited number of followers, i.e., to the Twelve. There is inevitably a simple natural development impressed on his record. He begins with the story of the baptism, which is followed by that of the temptation. Then we have the record of a specimen day in the life of Jesus, which reveals his popularity with the masses as a teacher and healer. After that comes a series of incidents in which Jesus clashes with the authorities; this opposition gradually grows in intensity till we come to the arrest in Gethsemane and the crucifixion. This simple story is crowned by a resurrection narrative. Mark's narrative is therefore seen to be made up of a series of episodes loosely linked together and chosen especially for their moral and spiritual value. They are selected with the express purpose of confirming the loyalty and strengthening the endurance of the much-tried Christians in Rome. As a

Christian himself of long standing, the author knows that following Christ is attended by many hardships and sufferings, and that it calls for rigid self-discipline and self-denial and a willingness to take up the cross in a very literal sense.

(3) His narrative shows that he was *peculiarly fond of numbers* (for detailed statement see Stanton's art., *Journal of Theo. Studies*, April, 1925). This was in contrast to the custom of ancient educated rhetoricians, who avoided as far as possible the names of places and persons and the giving of exact numbers. Mark, on the contrary, tells us that the Temptation lasted forty days (1^{13}), and that the woman had suffered with an issue of blood for twelve years (5^{25}); his favorite expression for the disciples is "the twelve"; the disciples are sent out two by two (6^{7}); in the parable of the sower we note the parallelism between the three classes of seed that germinated and the three that did not (4$^{1f.}$); in the story of the feeding of the five thousand the disciples have two hundred denaria worth of bread (6^{37}); while the ointment in Mary's cruse cost three hundred pence (14^{5}).

(4) The evangelist was *a man of decided opinions*, one might even call them prejudices. For example, he seems to have thought that the purpose of Jesus in teaching by parables was to confuse the minds of the unbelieving masses and to prevent them from understanding the message of the Master (4$^{11, 12}$). In this he is clearly wrong and has done Jesus a grave disservice. Another prejudice which he has superimposed on his narrative is the thought that the demons possessed a knowledge of the Messiahship of Jesus and of his divine Sonship denied in the beginning even to the immediate followers of Jesus (3^{11}). On the other hand his *love of symbolism* is shown when he informs us that when Jesus was crucified the veil of the Temple was rent from top to bottom and that from the hours between twelve and three darkness covered the whole land (15$^{33, 38}$).

Dependence on Peter. Papias makes the following statement: "And the presbyter said this: Mark, having become the interpreter of Peter, wrote down accurately whatsoever he remembered. It was not, however, in exact order that he related the sayings or deeds of Christ. For he neither heard the Lord nor accompanied him. But afterward, as I said, he accompanied Peter, who accommodated his instructions to the necessities [of his hearers], but with no intention of giving a regular narrative of the Lord's sayings. Wherefore Mark made no mistake in thus writing some things as he remembered them. For of one thing he took especial care, not to omit anything he had heard, and not to put anything fictitious into the statements" (Fragment VI, *Ante-Nicene Fathers*, vol. i., pp. 154, 155, Edinburgh edition. Preserved in Eusebius, *Eccles. Hist.*, iii, 39). According to this, Mark was dependent on the reminiscences of Peter. A careful study of his Gospel confirms this, for after a very cursory introduction the ministry of Jesus begins with a series of incidents in Capernaum, Peter's home town, and it is in his house that Jesus stays while in the city. Peter appears in this Gospel nearly always in an unfavorable light (8^{33} 14$^{37, 66-72}$); none of the halo that later writers painted about his head, which is plainly visible in Luke and Matthew, is to be seen. Peter was in nowise injured by this frankness, since the church at Rome knew how fully he had atoned for any lack of loyalty which he may once have shown in his following Jesus. The relative prominence given to the Twelve in the Gospel, and the fact, as Stanton points out, that the evangelist tells his story in the plural, though not himself one of the company who went about with Jesus, indicate that in many places in his narrative Mark is dependent on the personal recollections of one of the inner circle. For much of the teaching of Jesus in his Gospel, Mark would have recourse to a collection of the sayings preserved in the church, which corresponded in a large measure to that document which scholars designate by the letter Q (see art., *Structure of the Synoptic Gospels*, pp. 871–2).

Purpose of the Gospel. The chief purpose of the Gospel is to portray the personality of Jesus in such a way that the church in the hour of its severe trial would receive power to endure and to remain faithful. The words, "Consider him that hath endured such gainsaying of sinners against himself (mg.), that ye wax not weary, fainting in your souls" (Heb. 12^{3}), would form a very appropriate headline for this virile Gospel.

The Portrait of Jesus. The following are some of the outstanding features in the character of Jesus emphasized in the Gospel.

(1) The *many-sidedness and wealth of Jesus' personality* are brought out in the varying estimates that we have of him in ch. 1. In v. 1 we have first of all Mark's own estimate (but see mg.) in the words "Son of God"; in v. 7 the Baptist's "mightier than I"; in v. 11 the judgment of God, "Thou art my beloved Son"; in v. 22 that of the people in the synagogue, that he "taught as having authority"; and in v. 24 the opinion of the demons, "the Holy One of God." In the same chapter Jesus is presented in the following rôles: He is One whose

coming is anticipated by the prophets (vv. 2, 3); a baptizer of men with the Holy Spirit (v. 7); a recipient of wonderful visions (vv. 9–11); One ministered to by angels (v. 13); a preacher of the gospel of the Kingdom (v. 15); a maker of evangelists (vv. 16–20); an authoritative teacher of new truths (v. 22); One who could cast demons from men (v. 25); a healer of the sick and of lepers (vv. 31, 40–45); a man of prayer (v. 35); and One whose soul is aflame with missionary passion (vv. 38, 39).

(2) The *courage and moral heroism* of the Master are apparent on every page. There is no trace of fear on the part of Jesus in the presence of wild demoniacs and lepers; he is perfectly calm and self-possessed when scribes and Pharisees try to defame his character with their scornful insults; in the presence of high priests, Roman soldiers, and procurators he is every inch a king; and while the storm is raging on the lake he is asleep on the cushion. In this brief Gospel we have presented before us the sublime figure of One who, though he is fully conscious that a terrible end awaits him in Jerusalem, yet remains undismayed, pursuing his road with fearless tread.

(3) Another beautiful feature in the life of Jesus emphasized by Mark is his *unfailing kindness and willingness to help*. The physician's duty is ever to be at the disposal of the most needy cases. The reply to the scribes in Lk. 13[32], "I cast out devils and perform cures to-day and to-morrow, and the third day I am perfected," exactly expresses the character of Jesus as outlined in this Gospel. No one appeals to him in vain; the little children receive a blessing from his hands; distracted suffering women find in him a real friend; and the ostracised of the community find in him One who truly understands their case and has for them a real sympathy.

Abiding Value of the Gospel. Just as the first readers in Rome of this vivid portrayal of the Son of man were encouraged to face cruel tortures and punishments of unheard-of severity, and above all to maintain their loyalty and missionary zeal in the face of colossal obstacles and continuous disappointments, so the Christian Church to-day, in reading afresh the story of the life of Jesus as written by Mark, will be greatly strengthened and encouraged in its task of presenting the claims of Christ to an age bewildered by many conflicting emotions, torn by faction, burdened by many sorrows, weighed down by the spirit of materialism, and yet in its heart of hearts yearning for one who will be its guide and shepherd through the perplexing mazes of its day. The road to the future, it has been well said, is the road back to the N.T. We cannot more effectively begin to walk that road than by reading and rereading this striking presentation of the Lord of life by John Mark.

Literature: Commentaries by Allen (Oxford Church Commentary), Bacon, Bartlet (Century Bible), Rawlinson (Westminster Commentary), Gould (International Critical Commentary—uses the Greek). Menzies, *The Earliest Gospel;* Montefiore, *The Synoptic Gospels;* T. H. Robinson, *Mark's Life of Jesus;* Streeter, *The Four Gospels.*

CHAPTER I

1. **The Beginning of the Gospel of Jesus Christ the Son of God.** This phrase, according to some interpreters, is a title for the complete gospel, and not merely for this record. By it the author wanted to suggest that a written gospel could only be a mere beginning of the spiritual movement which it helped to make possible. It was necessary for redeemed lives to take up the story and complete the tale of the cross in every generation. Others think that what is meant is that the story of the Baptist is the starting point of the gospel. The probabilities are that the expression refers to the opening chapter as a whole, which aims at giving the record of a typical day in the ministry of Jesus. The various incidents have been chosen to show the many-sided character of his work. (For the various ways in which, in this single chapter, Jesus is presented, see intro., section on "The Portrait of Jesus.") This typical introductory chapter fittingly closes with the statement "they came [or, kept on coming] to him from every quarter."

The word *gospel* is found far more frequently in Mark than in any other of the Gospels. Usually, as in 1[15] 8[35] 10[29], it stands alone without further definition, showing that when this Gospel was written it had become a technical term for the message of salvation proclaimed by the early evangelists. In 1[14] it is defined as a "gospel *of God*"—a message whose special aim it is to inform men of the character and grace of God; here it is described as *the gospel of Jesus Christ*, indicating that Christ is the sum and substance of the gospel. The expression *Jesus Christ*, when this Gospel was written, had become a proper name; henceforth there was no need to say "the Christ." One important MS., the Sinaiticus, omits the words *Son of God*, but the witnesses for their insertion are weighty and there does not seem to be sufficient reason for their omission. The expression occurs again in 3[11] 5[7] 15[39]. In the Book of Wisdom the righteous man is called "a son of God"; Plato and Alexander the Great were given this title by their contemporaries; and the expression is found in the Emperor cults of the Græco-Roman world. When used of Christ the words signify his possession of a unique moral and religious quality.

2–8. John the Baptist. See notes on Mt. 3:1-12 Lk. 3:2-16. Mark gives a graphic picture of the forerunner of Jesus, as follows:

(1) *His coming was foretold by the prophet Isaiah.* The first part of the quotation in vv. 2, 3 is from Mal. 3:1. It is omitted in Matthew and Luke and is probably a gloss. The words in v. 3 are from Isa. 40:3 and originally referred to Cyrus, who was to deliver the Israelites from captivity; so John was to herald the coming of Jesus the great Emancipator of men.

(2) *He was a man with a message* (v. 4). While it is true that the etymology of the Greek word translated *repentance* means change of mind and attitude, the fact that the word was chosen in the Greek Bible (LXX) to translate the Hebrew word meaning "to be sorry" shows that the emotional elements should not be entirely eliminated. The Greek word translated *remission,* employed by the Greeks of unfastening a boat tied to a post by the shore to launch it into the water, was taken over by the early Christians to indicate that act of God whereby he releases men from all forms of bondage to send them forth into a life of honorable service. John's message produced a religious awakening which touched even the capital itself (v. 5).

(3) *His diet consisted of locusts and wild honey* (v. 6). Both are a common diet in Palestine to-day. They reveal John's simple ascetic mode of living. His only garment, made of camel's hair, was well adapted for inclement weather. It probably reminded his contemporaries of his likeness to the great Elijah, whom he resembled also in prophetic power and directness.

(4) *His confidence in Jesus is complete* (vv. 7, 8). He recognizes in Jesus a greater moral dynamic power than he possesses himself. He expects him to baptize not in water but *in spirit.* Mark omits the words "with fire" found in Matthew and Luke. The man who is fully baptized in the Spirit of Jesus has moral enthusiasm. The Hebrews thought of the Divine Spirit as a quasi-physical substance which could be "poured out" like water (cf. Isa. 44:3 Joel 2:28). John (14:16, 17, 26) and Paul (Eph. 2:1-22) later spiritualized the conception.

9–11. The Baptism of Jesus. (Mt. 3:13-17 Lk. 3:21, 22.) The news of the religious revival in the Jordan Valley quickly reached the quiet town of Nazareth. Jesus, who had long been pondering over the great purpose of his life, felt in his inmost soul that for him an important hour had struck. The conviction was slowly borne in upon him that the Baptist was none other than his Elijah preparing his way, so that he might have access to the hearts of the people. The dawning consciousness of being his people's Messiah reached its meridian in a remarkable vision at Jordan, whither he had come to show his complete sympathy with this new religious awakening. This vision, the account of which is expressed in highly symbolic language, was a profound personal spiritual experience. The symbolism used is such as was natural to the time.

He saw the heavens rent. The Jews believed in a plurality of heavens, in the remotest of which dwelt the Most High. By this symbolic language the idea is conveyed that Jesus at his baptism was given a unique vision of God and came into living vital fellowship with him. The later evangelists in reporting this scene have converted the poetical symbolical representation of Jesus into one of actual fact (cf. Luke's "in a bodily form, as a dove"). In rabbinic literature the dove is sometimes a symbol for the Spirit of God: sometimes it is compared to the hovering of a bird over the young in its nest (cf. Gen. 1:2, mg.). The dove is also a symbol of moral purity, guilelessness, gentleness, and peace. Mark thinks of the *voice* (v. 11) as audible. The words originally conveyed the idea of a profound subjective experience by which Jesus was assured of his heavenly Father's love and of his call to undertake a great divine mission. One important MS. gives as the words heard at the baptism, "This is my beloved Son, to-day have I begotten thee." The Greek word translated "well-beloved" has been found in certain contexts with the meaning of "only," and such may be its meaning here (cf. Jn. 1:33f.).

12, 13. Jesus' Temptation. See notes on Mt. 4:1-11 Lk. 4:1-13. The round number *forty days* was used in the O.T. for the fast of Moses and Elijah. It was a favorite number with Jewish historians. Mark alone mentions the *wild beasts;* for him they serve either to intensify the loneliness of the wilderness or to typify the strong merciless character of the forces of evil. The *angels* may very well symbolize the forces of righteousness and purity that are ever present in the arena of the soul's struggle; the word *ministering* in the N.T. means often to nourish or support with food. The evangelists probably think of the Lord as being sustained, like the Israelites in the wilderness (Neh. 9:15) or like Elijah (1 Kings 19:5), by supernatural supplies. On the other hand, since "angel" may also mean "messenger," it is possible that the sustenance was brought by human hands.

A Typical Day. Vv. 14–45. The incidents recorded in this section are grouped together in the framework of a single day in Capernaum, and to the evangelist they represent a typical day's activity in the life of our Lord.

14, 15. Jesus the Preacher. (Mt. 4^{12-17}.) Mark says nothing of a contemporary ministry of John the Baptist. This statement may have been determined by ideal considerations. The work of the forerunner must be completed before that of the new preacher of righteousness begins. Mark is giving us here his own summary of the ministry of Jesus, who hardly went about Galilee repeating this same stereotyped phrase. The description stresses the following points:

(1) *Jesus proclaimed a gospel (good tidings) of God.* The message he preached brought new light on the character and nature of God, enriching the spiritual conceptions of the prophets by making love and mercy central in his character. To the church of Rome, for whom this Gospel was written (see intro.), Christianity set forth the unity, sovereignty, grace, and holiness of God, and withal his accessibility to and personal interest in every child of the race. What a contrast all this was to the polytheism prevailing in the Græco-Roman world!

(2) *The time is fulfilled.* This may be an echo of Paul (Gal. 4^4). The coming of Christ was exceedingly timely. Rome had established its marvelous organization from the British Isles in the west to Persia in the east; Greece had made her matchless language a universal medium of intercourse and thought; and the Jews had planted synagogues all over the Roman Empire and had preached a noble conception of God and a lofty morality. Throughout the world there was a feeling of ennui and dissatisfaction and a yearning for a more deeply spiritual salvation (see art., *Backgrounds*, pp. 850–2).

(3) *The realm of God is at hand.* A new day is about to dawn when the will and sovereignty of God will sway the hearts and thoughts of men. Those who would have the experience must *repent.* Like John the Baptist, Jesus stressed the importance of a complete break with the past. For the meaning of repentance, see note on v. 4. The penitent must also *believe in the gospel.* The demand for a complete trust in his message was a primary element in the ministry of Jesus.

16–20. Jesus the Leader. (Mt. 4^{18-22}, notes on Lk. 5^{1-11} Jn. 1^{35-42}.) Jesus realizes that he must gather around him those whom he could train for the great task of winning men to God. The first four of this small group are Peter, Andrew, James, and John; they must have come into contact with Jesus before this and must have heard him preaching and teaching in Galilee (cf. Jn. $1^{35f.}$). Whether the resolve to follow Jesus involved a complete abandoning of their daily work there and then is doubtful. It certainly involved this later on, but Mark gives the impression that the four never returned to the task of fishing as a means of livelihood. It is said that men in India to-day will sometimes with equal abruptness leave home and occupation to become disciples of a wandering teacher.

17. They are first called to discipleship, and while following Jesus they are to be *made* into evangelists, or fishers of men, moral and spiritual net-menders.

19. The net was the small cast-net, in the throwing of which great skillfulness was required. It is even to-day a specialty of fishermen on the sea of Gennesaret. The Greek word used for *mending* (Greek *katartizō*) is used in Lk. 6^{40} of the perfecting of a pupil. Paul employs the word (1 Cor. 1^{10}) of mending the net of the church torn by faction and division, and (Gal. 6^1) of restoring a soul spoiled and marred by a moral lapse. In 1 Thess. 3^{10} the church's faith is the net; it is full of defects, and consequently needs restoration.

21–34. Jesus the Teacher and Healer. (Mt. 8^{14-17} Lk. 4^{31-41}.) Capernaum is chosen by Jesus as the chief center of his early ministry. It was on the great trade route to Damascus and was a center of customs. The Roman garrison was quartered in the town; in consequence, it was an admirable place for Jesus to minister in. On the Sabbath, Jesus enters the synagogue for worship. He embraces the opportunity to address the congregation. Mark says nothing of the content of his teaching (cf. Lk. $4^{14, 15, 23}$) but emphasizes his manner and the influence it exerted on the crowd. The teaching was new (*kainē*); it was vital, spiritual, and authoritative, wholly unlike that of the scribes, who were always quoting what this or that rabbi had said or had contended for. The teaching of Jesus was not sophistical; it did not emphasize minute points; on the contrary, it stressed general principles of importance for life and religion (cf. Mt. 5–7).

Jesus' first act of healing (vv. 23–26). The patient is a worshiper in the synagogue and is described as a man possessed with an *unclean spirit.* It is strange that such a man should be found within the synagogue precincts. Belief in demons was widespread in the days of Jesus and he himself does not seem to have disputed this popular belief. The demons formed under the devil a kingdom of their own and were responsible for inflicting on men and women all kinds of extreme abnormal sicknesses (see Glover, *Jesus in the Experience of Men*, ch. 1). The person possessed became the abject slave of the demons, and acted as their mouthpiece. The passionate preaching of Jesus stirs this man to the deeps of his soul and in the quiet of the synagogue he utters a shrill cry. Jesus delivers him—to use psychological terms—by the power of his strong personality and through the influence of suggestion. The main difficulty of the narrative is the acknowledgment on the part of a man possessed by demons that Jesus is *the Holy One of God*. Many commentators think that Mark has worked over this incident and has introduced into it a theory of his own that demons possessed supernatural knowledge and consequently knew things denied to ordinary mortals. It is certainly a real difficulty if we are to believe that men in the power of evil spirits had knowledge which was not possessed even by the followers of Christ. To the church at Rome this incident would serve to emphasize the truth that the kingdom of evil could not stand before the kingdom of God.

For *hold thy peace* (v. 25) read *be quiet*. The Greek word was technically used in hellenistic magic to express the binding of a person by means of a powerful spell so as to make him impotent to do harm.

Jesus' second act of healing (vv. 29–31). Simon and Andrew had a house in Capernaum which was Jesus' headquarters while in the city. Simon's mother-in-law is laid aside with a fever. What the nature of the complaint was we are not told, but Jesus simply grasps her hand, and there is healing power in his touch (see art., *Miracles of N.T.*, p. 924b). The influence exerted by the strong will and sympathy of Jesus is sufficient to explain what happened: the term "miracle" hardly needs to be used here. That Jesus was able to effect remarkable cures on people, however, the Gospel tradition makes quite evident.

A general healing (vv. 32–34). There were in Capernaum many sick folk and persons possessed by demons. It is not surprising then that their friends at sundown, when the Sabbath was over, brought them on stretchers to this wonderful Physician. Mark carefully distinguishes between demon-possession and sickness. Perhaps his statement that they brought *all* who were sick and only *many* were healed implies that there were some cases which even Jesus could not cure (cf. 6[5]). On the other hand, Matthew says that all were brought and all were healed (4[24]), perhaps because he thought that Mark was liable to misinterpretation.

35–39. **Jesus Seeks Retreat.** (Mt. 4[23-25] Lk. 4[42-44].) Many reasons are given for Jesus leaving Capernaum. His seeking a place of quiet at dawn may have been a life-long habit. Successful ministering to men, Jesus realized, could be accomplished only by constant communion with God. To meet the tests and challenges of Jerusalem one must have a Bethany and a Mount of Olives. To live nobly in the living room of life depends on our having an inner chamber whose doors we can close and in whose silence we can hear the words of God by which alone man can live (see notes on Mt. 7[24-27]). Can we imagine the chagrin and dismay of the four disciples when they opened the door in the morning and saw the expectant multitude but discovered that there was no Christ within? Will the multitudes to-day when they come to the house of the Lord find there the Spirit of the Christ to heal and bless?—Others think that the work of healing was interfering with the task of preaching and teaching, and that that was the reason why Jesus fled. His answer to the eager disciples in v. 38 suggests that a consuming missionary passion had something to do with the sudden departure.

40–45. **The Healing of the Leper.** (Mt. 8[1-4] Lk. 5[12-16].) The variant readings of this story show that it is one that has occasioned difficulty. In v. 40 some MSS. omit *and kneeling down to him*. In v. 41 instead of *being moved with compassion* some authorities read *being angry*. Leprosy was of many kinds, curable and incurable. Elaborate rules are laid down in the O.T. (see Lev. 13[45, 46]) to regulate the conduct of lepers. The fact that priests could pronounce a leper clean (v. 44) shows that some forms of the complaint would yield to treatment. Some interpreters suggest that the man simply came to Jesus to ask him to pronounce him clean. The suggestion robs the story of its greatest significance, which is less in the healing than in the fact that Jesus *touched an untouchable*. Therein lies a real test of his followers. Mark relates the incident, in part, to illustrate our Lord's fidelity to the Law. In matters relating to hygiene, we can well imagine how careful Jesus would be to support the religious authorities in their endeavor to prevent the spread of this terrible disease. (Cf, p. 925a.)

45. Some prefer to make *he* refer to Jesus, and to regard *the matter* as the word of the Gospel, the preaching of which caused two very dissimilar results—enmity on the part of the religious and political leaders, and increased popularity and influence with the people.

CHAPTER II

The Rising Tide of Opposition. Just as in ch. 1 we have the description of a typical day in the ministry of Jesus, so here we have a series of incidents arranged by Mark to show the rising tide of opposition.

1–12. **Enmity Because of the Claim to Forgive Sins.** (Mt. 9:1-8 Lk. 5:17-26.) Certain difficulties arise here as to the manner in which four men could have brought the paralytic to the roof and let him down where Jesus was. External staircases were common in many houses, and there may have been one here. Wellhausen thinks that the expression *they uncovered the roof* (v. 4) is a mistranslation of an Aramaic expression meaning, "they brought him to the roof."

The great crux in this incident, however, is the phrase *The Son of man hath power on earth to forgive sins* (or, *power to forgive sins on earth*). This is the first occurrence of the expression "Son of man" in the Gospel. In the days of Jesus the phrase was used to denote man as distinct from beasts and angels. There are examples (and some claim this to be one) where Jesus uses the expression of man in general (cf. Mt. 8:20). Ezekiel frequently uses the title to describe himself as a prophet (2:1, 3, 8 3:1, 3, 4, 10, 17, 25), and there are some who deduce from this that Jesus employs it here and in other passages in a prophetic sense. The title is found in Dan. 10:5, 16, 18 12:6, 7 and in the Book of Enoch in a decidedly Messianic sense. In what sense is it used here? Does it mean "man," or is it the equivalent of "I," or has it prophetic meaning, or does the title here and elsewhere in the Gospels have its full Messianic sense? It is not likely that Jesus would have adopted the title to set forth his Messiahship thus early in his ministry; but in the days when the Gospel was written it was a generally accepted Messianic designation and would therefore be naturally employed by Mark for describing this early incident. There is no passage in Jewish writings where the Messiah is said to be endowed with the power to forgive sins: forgiveness was always the exclusive prerogative of God, hence the plain inference here concerning the nature of Christ himself. The claim that to forgive is a prerogative delegated to men by God cannot be maintained, not even with the help of Mt. 9:8. Jesus claims here the unique power of assuring men that their sins have been forgiven and are no longer a barrier to their fellowship with God.

13–17. **Enmity Because Jesus Calls a Tax Gatherer.** (Mt. 9:9-13 Lk. 5:27-32.) The Romans exacted taxes of various kinds from the inhabitants of Palestine. Water, meat, salt were all subject to taxation; there was also a road tax, a city tax, a house tax, as well as a poll tax. Judæa, Peræa and Idumæa were required to contribute 600 talents (about $720,000; see art., *Time, Money*, etc., p. 78b) in taxes. From this we can surmise that the publicans, the collectors of these dues, were far from being popular men; they were ranked as robbers, brigands, ruffians, murderers and reprobate, whose evidence in courts of law was invalid and whose money could not be accepted as alms. To register his protest against such an attitude of intolerance and aloofness, Jesus called one of this class to his inner circle and invited others of them to a feast. He would remind his scornful critics that the place of the true physician was among those who needed him most, however outcast or obscure. If Mt. 9:9 is a parallel, then *Levi* is probably "Matthew the publican" in the list of disciples in Mt. 10:3, although Matthew is nowhere called "son of Alphæus."

18–22. **Enmity Because Jesus and His Disciples do not Fast.** (Mt. 9:14-17 Lk. 5:33-39.) Fasting was of two kinds—a general fast obligatory on every man, and a private fast which was voluntary. The *general* fasts were held on the ninth of Ab (the fifth month), the anniversary of the burning of the Temple; in time of great national need such as drought, crop failure, and pestilence; and on the day of reconciliation. They were usually held on Mondays and Fridays. *Voluntary* fasting is referred to in 2 Sam. 12:16 Psa. 35:13 Mt. 6:16. It was an indispensable mark of true piety—to make good a wrong, to atone for a fault, to fulfill a wish, and to secure a hearing for a prayer. The fasting of v. 18 must be the fast ordained as an expression of mourning for a beloved leader and the supererogatory fasts of the Pharisees referred to in Lk. 18:12.

The *sons of the bride-chamber* (v. 19) were the intimate friends who waited on the groom, who rejoice while their friend is with them, but are sad when he goes away (see note on Lk. 5:34). Jesus here hints that the day is coming when his disciples will have ample occasion for being sad—a hint, undoubtedly, of his impending death.

20, 21. By the use of these two homely yet radical allegories, Jesus shows very clearly (as an additional reason for not fasting) that the new religion which he has come to establish cannot be harmonized with the old customs and practices of Judaism. It must create its own forms and practices, which will best express its genius and preserve its purity and power. The *new cloth* of Christianity is not to be used for patchwork purposes, but to provide the sons of the Kingdom with new garments for the needs of the new day. The *new wine* of the gospel which is to satisfy the aspirations of men and women is to be enshrined in appropriate forms. The Eastern bottle was a goat-skin, which weakened with age, and which the fermenting of new wine might burst. Christian truth must be given clear, full, and adequate expression. This requires that it change its "thought-forms" according to the age in which it lives and in harmony with the development of other branches of knowledge. The *content* of the gospel is "the same, yesterday, to-day, and forever": what needs to change with changing experience is the *method* of presenting it.

23–28. Enmity Because of Alleged Sabbath Violation. (Mt. 12:1-8 Lk. 6:1-5.) Jesus and his disciples in passing through the field plucked grain and rubbed out the kernels in the hands. This was regarded as a violation of the law which prohibited reaping and threshing on the Sabbath. Jesus justifies his conduct by quoting the example of David, who once ate the shew-bread (1 Sam. 21:1-6). It must be remembered that when this Gospel was written the Sabbath was not observed by Gentile Christians, and no doubt this incident and the following one were regarded as justifying their freedom. The obligation of the Sabbath is admitted, but the question of exceptions is raised, and in case of exceptional needs the Sabbath law must be subordinate. This is the Christian principle: human need, not mere caprice, is determinative.

25. The practice of setting twelve loaves of unleavened bread—*the shew bread*—every Sabbath in the Temple was a very ancient one. The flour had to be of the finest, and the loaves were large in size. This rite goes back to the pre-Mosaic stage of Hebrew religion, and its origin is no doubt due to the naïve conception that the god needed physical nourishment. The number twelve may have had originally an astronomical significance (the twelve signs of the Zodiac), but in later times it would naturally be associated with the twelve tribes. The rite in the later period also acquired a new and higher significance. It was a concrete expression of the fact that Jehovah was the source of every material blessing, and it became (Num. 4:7) the standing expression of the nation's gratitude for the bounties of his providence.

27, 28. Neither Matthew nor Luke has v. 27, which probably comes from another context. In v. 28 we have either an independent saying or a Christian comment. The rabbis had a similar law, "To you the Sabbath is given over but not you to the Sabbath." Jesus enunciates here a principle of far-reaching significance: the Sabbath is a gift of God to be utilized for spiritual and moral equipment, so that men may render their highest and best service to their fellows. For the creation and maintenance of the Christian ideal of life, worship and praise are absolutely indispensable to the Christian himself, and provision must be made for them for others. If the expression *Son of man* is interpreted messianically the verse is best taken as the conclusion of the evangelist; the alternatives are to take it as the equivalent either of Christ himself or of man (see note on 2:1-12).

CHAPTER III

1–6. Climax of the Opposition to Jesus. (Mt. 12:9-14, notes on Lk. 6:6-11; cf. Jn. 9:13-34.) As was his custom (Lk. 4:16), Jesus came to the synagogue for the service on the Sabbath. One of the worshipers was a man with a withered hand—a stonemason, according to the Gospel to the Hebrews. Friends and foes alike take Jesus' power of healing for granted and the latter watched to see if he would heal on the Sabbath. The word used here for *watch* always implies in the N.T. an evil intent. He divines their thoughts immediately, and with his customary fearlessness he bids the man stretch out his hand. Healing on the Sabbath was only permissible among the Pharisees in case of danger to life; where there was no danger healing was unconditionally forbidden. No medicines or special foods could be taken on the Sabbath, no fractures could be set, nor could a hand or foot out of joint be immersed in hot water. Such rules must have been extremely obnoxious to Jesus, and by this action he cancels the whole array of merely legal requirements of this character. His deed illustrates the principle set forth in 2:27.

The question of Jesus in v. 4 refers not merely to what he knows he is about to do, but also to the plotting against his own life, which he knows his enemies are on that same Sabbath day contemplating! Who is the best observer of the Sabbath, he is asking, the man who uses the day for another's good, or the group of people who use it to devise another's hurt? They remain silent under the evident reproof, and Jesus proceeds with the man's cure.

5. Mark is especially fond of drawing attention to the *looking* of Jesus (cf. 3:34 5:32 10:23 11:11). Matthew and Luke omit this attribution of *anger* to Jesus (cf. intro. to Matthew, p. 953b). His righteous indignation is called forth by the emphasis of these men on what he considers to be unimportant things, but his anger is tempered by pity—he is *grieved at the hardening of their heart.* The Greek word used here for "hardening" (*pōrōsis*) was also used of the process by which the extremities of fractured bones are reunited by a callous; here it is a metaphorical term for obtuseness or moral blindness. Some MSS. read *deadness.*

6. The *Herodians* were not a special party but were some of the supporters of the Herodian court. The consent of Herod would be needed for the trial of any of his subjects for breaking the Sabbath.

7–12. The Popularity of Jesus. As a contrast to the opposition of the leaders, Mark in a few rapid sentences shows in what enthusiastic esteem Jesus is held by the common people. The summary shows us clearly that a new phase in the ministry of Jesus has begun; the synagogue is forsaken and the open places and the seashore are sought. Jesus, in a word, begins an open-air ministry. One is reminded of the way in which the great pioneers of the modern evangelical movement were forced out of the churches of their day, and of how in consequence that great open-air crusade was begun which had such far-reaching results on the life of England and America. The many places mentioned in vv. 7, 8 serve to emphasize the far-reaching character of Jesus' ministry.

9. The Greek word (*proskartareō*) translated *wait on* (or *to be in attendance*) occurs only in this verse in the Gospels; in all its other occurrences (Acts 1^{14} 2$^{42, 46}$ 6^{4} 8^{13} 10^{7} Rom. 12^{13} 13^{6} Col. 4^{2}) the word denotes diligence in prayer. It looks as though the writers of the N.T. wanted to suggest to other readers that prayer should be to them in their busy lives what the little boat was to Jesus—a refuge from the pressure of the crowd, a means to seek places of rest, an agency to secure food for the daily supplies, and a pulpit from whence to deliver the oracles of God.

11. *Son of God.* For Mark this title given to Jesus by the unclean spirits means more than "Son of David." As Rawlinson puts it, Mark proclaims a Christ whose person suggests already the supernatural mystery of the Incarnation—a Christ who is the Divine-human Lord of the Christian society, stronger than demons, able to rebuke the storm, to open blind eyes, and to overcome death.

13–19. The Call of the Twelve. (Mt. 10$^{2-4}$, notes on Lk. 6$^{12-16}$). Jesus during his brief ministry gathered around him many followers. These varied considerably in the strength of their loyalty and attachment. Luke informs us (8^{3}) that certain women ministered to him of their substance. Such men as Joseph of Arimathæa (15^{43}), Simon the leper (14^{3}), and the owner of the house where the Passover was held (14$^{12-16}$), were some of his Jerusalemite followers. The tradition, however, is very early and strong that Jesus called twelve men to be in specially close contact with him. Mark suggestively states that they were called to be with him so that he might send them forth *to preach and to cast out devils.* The success and value of all ministry rendered in the name of Jesus is entirely dependent on the constancy and sincerity of our fellowship with him.

The list of names here varies from the list in Lk. 6$^{13f.}$ and Acts 1^{13}, but is identical except in order with Mt. 10^{2f}. Mark knows nothing of the identification of Levi with Matthew. Thaddæus in Mark becomes in Luke and Acts Judas the son of James. Some have concluded from this that the inner circle was larger than twelve. Most of the men in the list are only shadowy names, of whom we know next to nothing. Some have epithets or surnames, e.g., *Simon called Peter,* or in Aramaic, *Kephas,* the name by which he was known to Paul (1 Cor. 1^{12}). It is interesting to note that a man so voluble and changeable should have borne the name meaning *rock.* Did Jesus give it to him (Mt. 16^{18}) because he foresaw his stanchness and martyr end; or was it given in the hope that the name would have a steadying influence upon him? James and John are given the epithet *sons of thunder.* Only Mark records this. The epithet may indicate an inflammatory disposition, or may have been given because the two were twins. Simon is described as the *Canaanite,* a word which Luke explains as meaning Zealot, a party opposed to the domination of Rome. *Iscariot* means *the man of Kerioth.* Kerioth was in southern Judæa. Judas was the only one of the Twelve not a Galilæan.

20–22. A Twofold Charge Against Jesus: Fanaticism and Alliance with Satan. (Mt. 9$^{32-34}$ 12$^{22-24}$, notes on Lk. 11$^{14-16}$.) This paragraph reveals the extreme judgments formed about Jesus, by his own family and by the officials. The former assert that he is a religious fanatic for whom they must care; the latter maintain that he is in collusion with the forces of darkness and evil, in the employ and pay of Beelzebub. These judgments show how wide was the gulf that separated Jesus from those who should have known him best and from the religious circles whose training and life should have prepared them for the understanding and appreciation of his true character. Such erroneous declarations must have deeply wounded his sensitive nature, and they serve to show how lonely and isolated must have been his life.—For *Beelzebub* some MSS. read Beelzebul; the former means "lord of the dwelling," the latter "the lord of flies" (cf. 2 Kings 1[2] and see note on Mt. 10[25]). From the word-play in v. 27 and Mt. 10[25] Beelzebub is probably correct. The epithet came to be attached to the devil, perhaps as lord of the house of evil spirits.

23–30. Jesus' Reply to These Charges. (Mt. 12[25-37], notes on Lk. 11[17-23].) Jesus replies first to the Pharisees in two parables. In the first parable he shows how utterly ridiculous and senseless the charge is, for the kingdom of darkness knows full well that it cannot achieve its ends without co-operation and unity. That anyone whose avowed purpose it was to storm and overthrow the world of evil spirits should be aided by their leader is the height of folly. To relieve the distressed is a good deed; Satan is concerned to oppose the good and spread the evil; how, then, can Jesus in his good deed be in league with Satan? Opposition to the good is always supported by illogical reasoning. In the nature of the case, the good cannot be found fault with: if it is, the reasons are fallacious. The second parable (v. 27) is but loosely connected with the first. In it Jesus shows that instead of acting under the control of Beelzebub he is engaged in the endeavor to overthrow and fetter him so that he may *spoil his house*—i.e., may rescue all those who have been brought under his subjection. It is implied in Mt. 12[28] that Jesus is deeply conscious that the Spirit of God is helping him in this struggle against the forces of darkness.

28, 29. The saying of Jesus with regard to "the unpardonable sin" has occasioned perplexity to scholars and anxiety and unnecessary pain to many devout believers. No true believer could ever claim that Jesus was possessed by Beelzebub. The sin referred to—*blasphemy against the Holy Spirit*—is that callous attributing of evil motives to what is clearly the result of the working of the Spirit of God—a sin which is the slow outcome of years of worldly living. One important MS. has *no forgiveness* for *never forgiveness.* If we may adopt this reading, it would seem to imply that although the sin is essentially unforgivable while this state of mind exists, nevertheless a change may take place and repentance ensue.

31–35. Jesus' New Family. (Mt. 12[46-50] Lk. 8[19-21].) Jesus next replies to his relatives. The gist of the reply is in the words contained in vv. 34, 35. The charge of insanity brought against Jesus by his own loved ones showed that they had virtually thrust him for the time out of their lives (but cf. Gal. 1[19]). The home circle at Nazareth was no longer his for solace and love, but a new circle of brothers and sisters was being created to which he would now increasingly turn for consolation and friendship. We are introduced here to the formation of that great family of God, the elder brother of which is Jesus, and the members of which are drawn from all races and lands. The experience of Jesus must have been repeated a thousand times in his own age, and these words would bring a wealth of comfort to many in Rome whose initiation into the Christian family had involved the severing of warm ties of love. Jesus also enunciates here a cardinal principle when he states that the condition on which men and women are brought into vital relationship with him is that they *shall do the will of God.* He includes in this the demand for repentance, renunciation, sacrifice and self-discipline, and all that is contained in the Sermon on the Mount.

CHAPTER IV

Parabolic Teaching and Its Reasons. Still following his method of grouping together typical examples of Jesus' activity and experience, Mark in this chapter gives us a number of illustrations (see vv. 33, 34) of Jesus' parabolic teaching. The chapter is largely parallel to Mt. 13 (cf. also Lk. 8).

1–9. The Parable of the Sower and the Soils. See notes on Mt. 13[1-9].

10–12. The Aim of Teaching by Parables. See notes on Mt. 13[10-15]. Matthew has clearly elaborated Mark at this point. Perhaps this is because he writes from the standpoint of the later experience of the church, when it had become evident that so many *did not* understand *the mystery of the kingdom of God.*

13–20. The Interpretation of the Parable of the Sower. See notes on Mt. 13[18-23].

21–25. Sayings Concerning the Right Use of Parables. Mark has here grouped a series of passages which are scattered in various parts of Matthew and Luke (cf. 8[16-18]). Out of their context it is hard to state their exact meaning. In the first group (vv. 21–23) Mark seems to emphasize the fact that the disciples of Jesus must publish far and wide the message of the gospel. Mark erroneously held that the function of parabolic teaching was to veil the truth. Even so, the time has now come for the veil to be removed, so that the ordinary man—for *he that hath ears to hear* means everybody—may understand the full glory of the gospel. In the second group (vv. 24, 25) is emphasized the importance of cultivating a right attitude to the truth. The man who comes with reverence, insight, application, and a sincere desire to learn will be amply rewarded by continued discoveries in the rich fields of truth; while inattention and indifference will result in a serious impoverishment of those divine capacities by which truth is apprehended (cf. Mt. 25[29]).

26–29. The Mystery of Growth. Mark alone records this parable of the seed growing apparently of itself (but cf. Mt. 13[24-30]). Jesus here seeks to point out, first, that there is a mysterious divine element working in spiritual growth as well as in natural growth; and second, that in the spiritual realm one must wait on God's time. The preacher's duty is to prepare and clean the soil and sow the right kind of seed; like the farmer he must exercise patience and hope in the full conviction that in the spiritual universe as in the natural there are divine forces which promote the growth of good impulses and produce great fruitfulness in human lives. This parable records the optimism and hopefulness of Jesus, and must have been of great inspiration to the persecuted church of Rome as it may be to us to-day. For v. 29 see Joel 3[14]; it probably is a reference by Jesus to the impending Judgment (cf. 13[4f.]).

30–32. The Parable of the Mustard Seed. See notes on Mt. 13[31, 32] Lk. 13[18, 19].

33, 34. Unrecorded Parables. Mark here intimates that he is reporting only a selected number of Jesus' parables. The four Gospels give us a *reliable* account of Jesus' work, but not a *complete* account (see Jn. 21[25]). Mark also intimates that Jesus' teaching was *progressive:* he taught *according as they were able to hear.* His private exposition to his disciples was due to his purpose to have them adequately prepared for the work they were later to do (cf. v. 10; Mt. 13[18, 51, 52] 16[5-12]).

35–41. The Storm on the Lake. See notes on Mt. 8[23-27] Lk. 8[22-25]; also *N.T. Miracles,* p. 923b. The storm which overtook the boat in which Jesus was, overtook also the *other boats,* and the ensuing calm meant safety as much for them as for his own boat. The incident has, therefore, value as an acted parable: Jesus entered into the severest experiences of men, but he also brought with him a power to utilize them for good. He shares our lot, and we share his victory.

CHAPTER V

1–20. The Gerasene Demoniac. (Mt. 8[28-34] Lk. 8[16-39].) We have set before us here very clearly certain popular conceptions of antiquity in reference to demons. Since they were *unclean* (v. 2) they preferred to make their dwelling in unclean places such as tombs, or in unclean animals like pigs. Knowledge of a demon's name (v. 9, cf. 9[38] Acts 19[13f.]) gave to the exorcist power over the possessed person. Some claim that in the present case the name was withheld and that only the number—*Legion*—was given. The demons were believed to be very averse to changing their abode and were terrified to be without an abiding place. Mark has superimposed on the narrative a preconception of his own that demon-possessed persons, though they had never seen or heard Christ, had the power immediately to recognize his Messiahship. To us to-day it is incredible that a raving lunatic should possess a knowledge which even those who lived closest to Jesus were slow in obtaining.

To reconstruct the historical nucleus of this story is impossible at this distance of time. It would seem that Jesus on this first visit of his to the Decapolis, or ten cities, a district peopled chiefly by Gentiles, met a man suffering from the delusion that he was possessed of a legion of evil spirits. After some conversation with him Jesus was able to deliver him from the delusion and restore him to mental health. The most satisfactory explanation of the story of the swine is that they were stampeded by the ravings of the maniac (see art., *N.T. Miracles,* p. 925). The church in Rome would find in the incident evidence that Jesus could do mighty works outside the borders of Palestine—Decapolis being non-Jewish territory—and that no man, however sinful and depraved, was beyond the pale of Christ's redeeming grace. The incident seems to show also that one of the great obstacles to work in heathen centers was the material losses which a community suffered when Christianity was adopted in place of a pagan cult. But that discipleship may involve loss is true anywhere. "The world" has never been friendly to Christianity and its purposes.

1. *Gerasenes.* Some MSS. read Gadarenes (Mt. 8[28]), others Gergesenes. Gadara is too far south. There was a Gerasa a long distance from the lake but this incident occurred at the shore. Sanday identifies the spot with Khersa or Kersa, near Magdalan.

21–24, 35–43. The Healing of Jairus' Daughter. Mark, like Matthew (9[18f.]) and Luke (8[40f.]), dovetails this story with that of the woman with the flow of blood (see notes below on vv. 25-34). The duties of Jairus, as a synagogue ruler, would be to arrange the synagogue services. He seeks the help of Jesus to restore his child to health. Messengers come to say that since the child is dead the presence of the Master is no longer needed. Jesus overhears the remark but nevertheless proceeds with the father to the house of the sick child. The professional mourners have gathered by the time he arrives, but after seeing the child Jesus is aware that she is *not dead but asleep.* Suspended animation must often in those days have been mistaken for death; hence the "four days" test of Jn. 11[39]. The diagnosis is received with mocking laughter. Jesus both touches the child and addresses her, seeking to reach her mind through two bodily senses. He speaks in his own Aramaic idiom. The words, *Little girl, get up,* may have been the very words with which the weeping mother had been wont to call her in the morning. To the amazement of all, the child responds.

Rawlinson thinks that the evangelist is describing a resurrection and not a recovery from a swoon, and he uses the narrative to show that death is not an "eternal repose" but a sleep looking forward to an eternal awakening. It is not at all unlikely that in the course of tradition the incident served this purpose, as it may continue to serve it still, but Jesus' own words, that the child was not actually dead, should be taken at their face value. (Cf. p. 924a.)

23. To *make whole* and to *live* are Semitic expressions meaning to restore to health and to heal. **36.** *Not heeding.* The Greek word can also mean *overhearing* (see mg.) and this is preferred by many in this context. **39.** There is a story that an ancient physician, Asclepiades, meeting one day a funeral procession, examined the body and found that it still had life in it. Tradition magnified the incident, so that in later accounts it is said that he had restored the dead body to life.

25–34. The Woman with the Flow of Blood. (On the time of the incident, see above under vv. 21–24.) Mark describes the serious nature of the complaint by dwelling on its long duration and on the fact that medical treatment instead of helping only resulted in aggravating the disease. It was the belief of the time that even the garments of eminent personalities had power to heal (cf. Acts 5[15] 19[12]), and this woman believes that by touching the tassel of Jesus' flowing robe she would find immediate remedy. From a psychological standpoint, the power of autosuggestion and the intense emotional disturbance caused by coming into the crowd played a very great part in the cure. Jesus, sensitively aware that something unusual has happened, addressed the woman—*Who touched my garments?*—evidently with a view of transforming her confidence in him, mingled as it was with elements of superstition, into something higher and purer. In his final words to her Jesus implies that the woman has the beginnings of a faith that shall also be *morally* effective—a faith which, like a grain of mustard seed, can effect great transformations. Matthew modifies the story. He makes the healing the result not of the woman's touch of faith but of the direct pronouncement of Jesus (see art., *N.T. Miracles,* p. 925a).

35–43. See above under vv. 21–24.

CHAPTER VI

1–6. Jesus at Nazareth. See also notes on Lk. 4[14-30]. This paragraph reveals several things concerning Jesus. (1) He had evidently been satisfied to spend his early life in the little town of Nazareth. (2) He was a member of a large family. There were four brothers, one of whom, James, played a prominent part in the life of the early church (Gal. 1[19] Acts 12[17]). There were also two, if not more, sisters. The father's name is not given, presumably because he is not living. There is a tradition that Joseph died before Jesus grew up. Rawlinson suggests that to describe a man as the son of his mother was to convey the insinuation that his paternity was unknown, and he infers from this that Mark may have been acquainted both with the Christian tradition of the virgin birth and with the Jewish insinuation of illegitimacy. The inference seems hardly to be sound in view of the fact that Mark nowhere makes an explicit affirmation on this important question. (3) Jesus toiled as a carpenter. Matthew characteristically changes this to "the carpenter's son" (13[55]). The word used here, *tektōn,* means a man who did the wood work of any building; hence Jesus would go from place to place as need arose and thus gain much invaluable experience from contact with men. (4) Jesus was spurned by his kinsfolk and old friends. Rumor had reached them of the outstanding works performed by him (Lk. 4[23]); his teaching in the synagogue revealed his unusual insight and wisdom; and yet his experience illustrated perfectly the old saying that men of unusual gifts are rarely honored by those among whom they spend their early years. In the Oxyrhynchus Logia, v. 4 is quoted as follows: "No prophet is popular in his native town and no physician effects cures among his friends." (5) The result of the rejection was to check the exercise of Jesus' power. Then as now he needed the co-operation of faith and love. Even the divine Lord is impotent in an atmosphere that is cold, critical, and unappreciative.

7–13. The Commission of the Twelve. See notes on 3[13-19] Mt. 10[1-16] 9[35-38] Lk. 9[1-6] 10[1-12] 13[22].

14–29. Herod's Judgment of Jesus and the

Death of John the Baptist. See notes on Mt. 14^{1-12} Lk. 9^{6-9}. Matthew has no equivalent of Mk. 6^{15}. These various opinions concerning Jesus were well known to the disciples, who repeated them to him (8^{28}).

30–44. Feeding the Multitudes. See notes on Mt. 14^{13-21} Mk. 8^{1-21} Lk. 9^{10-17}, and cf. Mt. 15^{32-39}.

45–52. Walking on the Sea. See notes on Mt. 14^{22-33}. In view of the tradition that Peter is Mark's source, and that in this Gospel Peter usually appears in an unfavorable light (see intro., p. 997b), it is curious that Matthew and not Mark should tell of Peter's failure to walk to Jesus.

53–56. Jesus' Popularity. See notes on Mt. 14^{34-36} Mk. 3^{7-12}.

CHAPTER VII

Tradition that Destroys the Law of God. Vv. 1–23. (Mt. 15^{1-20}.) This paragraph, in which, as Montefiore admits, Jesus aims a tremendous blow at the ceremonial laws of the Jews, is composite in character. Attempts to discover the original nucleus are, however, unsatisfactory. The historical occasion is clear enough, namely, the questions of prying critics (vv. 1, 2, 5) to which Jesus made an unanswerable reply. The gist of the reply is in vv. 14, 15, regarded by the disciples as a parable, which he thereupon proceeds to explain (vv. 18–23). The illustration from the oath or vow Corban (vv. 8–13) is in perfect keeping with Jesus' attitude (see Mt. 23), and there is no reason for regarding it as a later addition. The explanations in vv. 3, 4 are, of course, Mark's own. The quotation in vv. 6, 7 is from the LXX of Isa. 29^{13}.

1–8. Ceremonial Cleanness. The Jews were scrupulously careful to cleanse the hands before partaking of food to avoid ritual uncleanness, and very definite regulations were laid down as to the manner in which this should be done. It was necessary to pour a certain minimum quantity of water over the hands up to the wrist twice, care being taken that none of this water should flow beyond the wrist, lest it flow back and render unclean the hand again. If one's hands are washed by another, the hand must be held with the fingers pointing upward. The word translated *diligently*, in v. 3 (Greek *pugmē*), means literally "with the fist," but it may also be rendered "up to the elbow" or "up to the wrist." Such punctiliousness on the part of the Pharisees recalls to the evangelist the very appropriate words of Isa. 29^{13}. The Hebrew text does not yield this meaning, wherefore some conclude that the quotation, being from the LXX, is due to the evangelist.

Plea is made here for the inwardness of religion, the consecration of the whole personality to the moral demands of God, devotion to the law written in the inward parts. In his noble answer (vv. 14, 15) Jesus shows very clearly that the things that defile the soul and poison the wellsprings of life are moral and spiritual in character, such as mean motives, arrogance and self-righteousness, intolerance and envy, impurity and uncleanness: these are the insidious forces which corrupt human life, not failure to wash the hands in the prescribed way.

9–13. The Oath "Corban." Mark has translated this Semitic word by the Greek word meaning *gift* or *given*. Josephus translates the word by the phrase "gift of God." By *corban* was meant that something was declared taboo and so withdrawn from use for another, except that the thing so dedicated should be brought to the Temple as a sacred gift. Jesus seems to have known of cases in his day in which sons made use of the oath to avoid the sacred duty of helping their parents. Rules were later enacted to soften the severity of this vow and still later its use was condemned altogether. It was too obviously a mere device for evading obligations. A money-lender in the days of Origen informs us that debtors used to love to delay paying their debts by the use of this Corban formula.

14–23. The Inwardness of True Religion. Rawlinson suggests that the principles of Jesus are here applied to the life of the church at Rome under the literary device of a private conversation between Jesus and the disciples. The preservation of the purity of motive and impulse is imperative, because therein lie the springs of human action. The catalogue of sins in v. 22 is typical of the prevailing sins in the Empire (cf. Mt. 15^{19}). *Evil thoughts* is a general expression. It stands first as the prolific fount of the black brood of the eleven evils that follow. Three of the sins, *fornications*, *adulteries*, and *lasciviousness*, are sins of passion and impurity: they leave their defiling touch on every age; three—*theft*, *murder* and *covetings*—are sins against property and the persons of others; three—the *evil eye* (or envy), *deceit* (or guile), *pride* (or arrogance)—are sinful tempers of mind; the remaining two describe attitudes of the heart toward the spiritual—*railing*, meaning irreverence, ridicule of the sacred, even blasphemy, and *foolishness*, meaning here moral obtuseness and religious indifference.

The word *wickedness* both summarizes the sins already mentioned and includes others not mentioned, as though the writer intended to stop at this point. Instead of stopping, however, he goes on to specify still other forms of wickednesses that have their real origin in evil thoughts.

24–30. The Greek Woman of Syro-Phœnicia. (Mt. 15[21-28].) Jesus may have crossed the borders of Galilee for Tyre either to secure a period of rest or because he was driven from Galilee by the authorities. It is not likely that he penetrated very far into the country. Luke omits this incident, presumably because he feels that the words of Jesus were liable to be misunderstood by the Gentiles. Matthew so narrates the story (especially if we adopt the reading of several MSS. of v. 26, *it is not lawful* for *it is not meet* or *good*) as to show that Jesus' mission was solely to the lost sheep of the house of Israel. Mark, on the other hand, introduces the word *first* into the saying of Jesus in v. 27, implying that the turn of the *little dogs* (for such is the meaning of *kunarion* as distinct from the pariah dog of the streets) would come in due time. Jesus must have spoken the words in a half-whimsical way and with a smile, for there was that in his manner which encouraged the woman to persist. He knew full well that the provisions of his Father's table would suffice for Jew and Gentile alike. The incident is a fine revelation of Jesus' gracious attitude to women. It is of interest also because the conversation was carried on in Greek. This is the only miracle in Mark where Jesus heals a patient whom he has not seen (see art., *N.T. Miracles*, p. 925b).

31–37. A Period of Healing Activity: the Miracle at Decapolis. (See Mt. 15[29-31] and cf. Mk. 5[1-20].) Mark gives here a typical miracle from the healing activity of Jesus following his return from the country of Tyre. He relates only one incident of the Tyre ministry (vv. 24–30), and only one incident of the present Decapolis ministry. A reference to Matthew, however, will show how extensive the latter ministry was. Among those who, Matthew says, were brought to Jesus in this non-Jewish district (*Decapolis* means "the Ten Cities," a Greek-speaking league in the territory southeast of the Sea of Galilee) were the dumb. This man—who was also deaf—was one of these, and Mark describes the cure in detail. The fact that the man could apparently talk a little, although unintelligibly, would suggest that he was not born deaf. What Jesus did was to restore faculties that had become impaired.

We have here a striking account of what might be called Jesus' psychological procedure. He aroused the man's confidence and expectancy. Everything he did was designed to break down any possible psychic barrier. Taking him aside, examining his ears, using spittle, manipulating his tongue, looking heavenward, exhibiting emotion (the *sigh*), and then the sudden command, "Hear, speak!" —all these have the appearance of being steps deliberately chosen to lead up to the desired result (see art., *N.T. Miracles*, p. 925a).—*He spat.* It was a common belief of the time that spittle had curative power, especially for diseases of the eye (cf. 8[23]).—In *ephphatha* Mark has preserved the Aramaic, which he also translates (cf. 5[41]). Since the man himself may have been a Greek the representation of Jesus as using his own native Aramaic is a sign of Mark's historical accuracy—since the man was deaf, and Jesus would normally use the Aramaic, and only Greek when speaking to Greeks.

CHAPTER VIII

1–10. Feeding the Four Thousand. See notes on Mt. 14[13-21] and cf. 6[30-44] Mt. 15[32-39]. In distinction from the feeding of the five thousand, Jesus is here presented as one who is able to satisfy not only the Jews but the Gentiles as well, for the location is changed to Gentile soil. Jesus is apparently still in the region of the Greek Decapolis on the east side of the lake, since the *Dalmanutha* for which he took boat (v. 10) is on the west side. As in the other feeding miracle, the words of v. 6 suggest the procedure at the Eucharist. The statement in v. 2—that the crowd had now been with Jesus three days—implies that they were accustomed to take food with them when they accompanied him and that the supply was now exhausted. Abbot sees a symbolic significance in the five loaves and twelve baskets of the one miracle and the seven loaves and the seven baskets of the other, as well as in the fact that in the one case the basket is a Jewish basket (Greek *cophinos*) and in the other a Gentile basket (Greek *spuris* or *sphuris*). That is, the twelve baskets suggest that he is ministering to the twelve tribes of Israel; the two sevens suggest respectively the seven spirits of God and the seven churches mentioned in the book of Revelation as representing the Gentiles. (On the relation of the two miracles to each other, and other questions, see the art., *N.T. Miracles*, p. 923a.)

11–13. Demand for a Sign. See notes on Mt. 12[38-42] 16[1-4]. It is deeply significant that the demand for a sign should have been given immediately following one of the most spectacular events in the ministry of Jesus. The refusal of Jesus is absolute and unqualified (but cf. Mt.). It is evident that the mighty works already accomplished are not enough to authenticate the divine mission of Jesus, yet the demand for signs is evidence of his increasing influence. He grieves deeply over the request because it reveals superficiality and an extreme emphasis on external things. He refuses the request because he knows that loyalty and faith that are a product of the miraculous are defective in depth and power. He who is not convinced of the value of unseen things from a knowledge of the personality and spiritual message of Jesus will be unmoved by the most spectacular miracle (cf. Lk. 16^{31}). Jesus' supreme evidence is himself, not his miracles.

14–21. Lessons from the Miracles of the Loaves. (Mt. 16^{5-12} Lk. 11^{53}–12^{1}.) The disciples are perturbed at discovering that they have only one loaf, and they apparently discuss with one another what they shall do. They are rebuked by the Master for their spiritual density (vv. 17, 18), to which Matthew (v. 8) adds lack of faith. The language of the rebuke shows very clearly that Jesus intended the two miracles of feeding to have spiritual significance, and it is the inability of the disciples to understand what this is that he blames so severely. The message which Mark wished this conversation to teach to the church in Rome was that the resources of Jesus were amply sufficient to meet all their needs. The paragraph reveals the radical difference in outlook as between Jesus and the disciples: they are immersed in the material, while he rises from the material to the spiritual.

15. The verse is probably out of place. Mark interprets it as referring to the teaching of the Pharisees and Herodians, while Luke (who puts it in a different context, 12^{1}) suggests that the word *leaven* refers to the "hypocrisy" of the Pharisees, a poison against which the disciples must ever be on their guard. Others suggest that the leaven of the Pharisees and Herodians means the determined opposition of these two groups. Interpreters with sacramentarian sympathies are inclined to regard the miracles of feeding as veiled parables of the death of Jesus and its vicarious character.

16–21. If we interpret literally these verses recording the rebuke to the disciples, Jesus must mean by them that there was no need for the disciples to worry about bread; what he had done for the five thousand and the four thousand he could repeat whenever occasion arose. Such teaching would be fatal: it would rob the disciples of all foresight and care for their physical needs. The words must be interpreted to mean that Jesus is blaming the disciples for their inability to see the significance of the symbolical feeding. Or we may have here an echo of the rebuke by the early church of certain groups who were unable to see the deeper meaning of the Eucharist.

22–26. Healing of the Blind Man at Bethsaida. (Jn. 9^{1-12}, notes.) Omitted by Luke and Matthew either because they have other healings of the blind (Mt. $9^{27f.}$ Lk. $18^{35f.}$) or else because the cure is a gradual one and lacks a certain dramatic element. Spittle was frequently thought by the ancients to have medicinal value (cf. 7^{33}). This miracle would serve the evangelists in their ministry to the church at Rome to emphasize the truth that while some are ushered into the Kingdom by sudden and almost instantaneous conversion, others find the entrance is slow, gradual, and painful. For them, the perception of the glories of the Kingdom comes only by degrees (see art., *N.T. Miracles*, p. 925a). Some important MSS. read in v. 26, *Tell no one in the village*, which is a much more natural reading.

The Preparation for the Passion (8^{27}–10^{45}). The parallels are, roughly, Mt. 16^{13}–20^{28} Lk. 9^{18-62} 18^{15}–19^{28}. This section—so Wellhausen thought—is as solemn and sacred as the story of the Passion itself. The thrice-repeated predictions of the Passion which it contains (8^{31} 9^{31} $10^{33,\ 34}$) are like the solemn tones of some muffled bell. Jesus now leaves the crowd and concentrates his attention on the disciples with the purpose of giving them clearer and more definite views of himself and his work. The section is full of significant and semi-technical terms, such as the gospel, the name of Jesus, present and future age, kingdom of God, glory, life, ransom, discipleship. The words of Jesus concerning his sufferings must have made a profound appeal to a martyr church passing through the dark experiences of persecution. As Jesus was not taken by surprise but foresaw what would happen, so they must realize the end awaiting many of them.

27–30. Peter's Great Confession. See notes on Mt. 16^{13-20} and cf. Lk. 9^{18-21}. The name *Cæsarea Philippi* was given by Philip the tetrarch to the city which he had built in honor of the Emperor, on the site of the ancient Paneas, at the source of the Jordan on the southwest slopes of the Hermon range. In the vicinity Herod the Great had built a large temple to Augustus. It was here, where the forces of nature and the incarnation of political power were worshiped, that Jesus gave to the disciples definite teaching concerning his character as the Messiah. The Marcan account, which is virtually reproduced by Luke, has in Matthew important additions which have given rise to much controversy. According to Mark, Jesus, after he had received from his disciples the popular estimate, turns to them to ask what they themselves think. Peter quickly answers for the group, *Thou art the Christ.* Jesus thereupon warns them to keep silence. The Greek word translated *charged* is exceedingly strong. It means to address angrily, to blame, to speak solemnly or to make remonstrance, to bring something to an end or to prevent something from being done. It would seem from this that Jesus was dissatisfied with Peter's confession. If he were, it would be not because of the words themselves—which were true—but because Peter showed by the tones of his voice that he was not yet free from the old popular notions of Messiahship. That this was the case was very quickly discovered (v. 8[32]).

31–33. **Jesus Foretells His Sufferings and Death.** See notes on Mt. 16[21-23] and cf. Lk. 9[22].

34–38. See notes on Mt. 16[24-28] Lk. 9[23-27].

CHAPTER IX

1. See notes on Mt. 16[27, 28] Lk. 9[27].

2–8. **The Transfiguration.** See notes on Mt. 17[1-13] and cf. Lk. 9[28-36]. Historical facts most certainly underlie this incident, although just what they are it is difficult to say. The early church attached very great evidential value to it, and it is not impossible that in the course of time the incident was somewhat colored by the desire to make this evidence more emphatic. Some have seen in the incident an expression of the faith of the church represented as a symbolic vision; others like Wellhausen and Loisy suppose that the story is based on a post-resurrection appearance of Jesus to Peter; still others explain it as a subjective vision granted to Jesus and the disciples in a sort of mystic trance like Paul's when he was caught into the third heaven—a trance induced by intense absorption in prayer, which Luke informs us was the original purpose of Jesus in going up the mountain. The prophets received divine intimations through similar channels (Isa. 6[1f.] Ezek. 1[28] 2[1]; cf. Rev. 1[10]). The statement in Luke concerning the subject of the conversation of Jesus with Moses and Elijah, namely, his "decease," shows that his mind was preoccupied with the thought of the suffering and death that awaited him in Jerusalem. What he needed was reassurance of the Father's favor, and strength to face the coming encounter with death, and in this experience the need was met.

The value of the incident for us is in its illustration of the fact that prayer exercises a transfiguring influence on life and character, and that moments of high exaltation must be converted into a means of serving one's fellows. It means also that Jesus is the culmination of revelation. The Law and the prophets—represented by Moses and Elijah—are fulfilled in him; henceforward men are to concentrate their thought on the message which he has given. The transfiguration is first and foremost an individual experience in the life of Jesus, the exact nature of which must have been communicated by him to the disciples. That they did not understand the full meaning of his announcement of his impending death (v. 10) is only what we should expect. Here, as so often, the meaning of Jesus' words and deeds had to wait for the illumination of later experience.

2. The exact statement of time—*after six days*—serves to link the transfiguration very closely with the incidents that precede. The eight days of Lk. 9[28] may be due to a system of reckoning like that which puts the resurrection of Jesus three days after his burial. The Greek word here translated *transfigure* is a technical term in Hellenistic Greek for magical metamorphosis. Luke omits it, perhaps because of its association with such processes.

5. Peter's words are natural to one in a half-hypnotic state of mind. Some take his words to mean that he feels it is a fortunate thing for the disciples to be present to show honor to these strange visitors by providing shelter for them and the Master.

7. The *cloud* symbolized the divine glory (cf. Ex. 16[10] 1 Kings 8[10, 11]): the Shekinah was to appear again in the Messianic period. Where the cloud of glory was there was the Divine Presence. The word *beloved*, as in 1[11], is used in the LXX, and in other Greek writings, in the sense of "only," so that the phrase is equivalent to "only-begotten" (Jn. 1[18]).

9–13. **Conversation with the Disciples.** (Mt. 17[9-13].) Jesus' conversation with the disciples serves to show very clearly what had been occupying his mind on the mountain. Turner would transpose the second half of v. 12 to follow v. 10, which certainly removes some difficulties. It is clear that the identification of the Baptist goes back to a genuine saying of Jesus (cf. Mt. 11[14]). The conversation seems to show that for Jesus the experience of the transfiguration impressed on his mind that suffering was inevitable but that it would be an "exodus," a departure (cf. Lk. 9[31], mg.), and a means whereby the people would be led from the servitude and bondage of sin into a life of liberty and freedom. The preparatory work, which the Jews said would be accomplished by a return of Elijah, Jesus states had already been done by John the Baptist.

14–29. The Healing of the Epileptic Boy. (Mt. 17^{14-21}, notes on Lk. 9^{37-48}.) The contrast between the effulgent glory of the mountain scene and the confusion in the plain below has been strikingly depicted in Raphael's great masterpiece. The recurrent convulsions with their attendant dangers, the fits, the temporary aphasia, foaming and rigidity, all show very clearly that the boy is epileptic. According to the belief of the day the disease was due to the presence of a malicious demon. The incident brings out also the contrast between the all-conquering faith of Jesus and the impotence of the disciples, due to their unbelief (v. 19). Jesus appears to resent the element of uncertainty in the father's expression, *if thou canst*, but the father's words in reply to Jesus, *I believe; help thou mine unbelief*, show what was the actual fact of the case, namely, that a struggle was going on in his soul for certainty against the ever-present forces of doubt and unbelief. He not only expresses his own feelings but that of multitudes of men in every age who are confronted with the harrassing problem of suffering. (Cf. Lk. $17^{5, 6}$.)

19. By these words Jesus may have implied that his end would come soon.

24. Several MSS. add after *said* the words *with tears.*

28, 29. These verses may be later additions and reflect the judgment that certain demons cannot be exorcised except by those who live a life of asceticism and prayer. Several MSS. add after *prayer* the words *with fasting.*

30–32. The Second Announcement of the Passion. (Mt. $17^{22, 23}$, notes on Lk. 9^{43-45}.) This is more general and less definite than the first announcement. The disciples are still completely mystified and act as though they had not heard the first at all, which only serves to show how tenaciously they clung to the old conceptions of the Messiah.

33–37. Childlikeness and True Greatness. This is one of a group of sayings and incidents (vv. 33–50) which serve to illustrate the sacrificial principle which Jesus is now applying so persistently to himself. See notes on Mt. 18^{1-14} 20^{20-28}; cf. Lk. 9^{46-48}. The disciples, clinging to the old conception of an earthly kingdom, are disputing with one another as to which one of them would receive the positions of greatest honor and renown in it. The altercation had been audible to Jesus, who was walking ahead. He detested overweening pride and love of power, because they fomented the spirit of rivalry and cruelty in the hearts of men. He tells the disciples very definitely that the two elements in greatness are humility and willingness to serve others. He enforces his teaching by taking a child, and putting his arm around his neck in a protective way (for so the Greek word means) he affirms that there is no diviner service than the service of boys and girls—helping them to form right habits and ideals and sheltering them from the pitfalls of life.

38–40. The Strange Exorcist. (Lk. $9^{49, 50}$.) Jesus had shown himself to have such unusual power in casting out demons that it is not surprising that some person should use his name for exorcising. The Master's answer as given here is preserved in the opposite form in Mt. 12^{30} and Lk. 11^{23}. It is a great saying on the importance of cultivating the spirit of tolerance. There are plenty of real enemies without creating new ones out of those who are already engaged in doing good in the world.

41–48. Concerning Hindrances. See notes on Mt. 18^{1-14} Lk. $17^{1, 2}$. These verses follow more naturally vv. 33-37. Rather than live so as to make it difficult for the innocent and immature to follow the path of honor and purity, it would be much better never to have lived at all. No sacrifice is too great (vv. 43–47) in life to reach that strength and purity of character which will enable us to be of greatest service to the youth of our community. What a splendid revelation we have in these words of Jesus' enthusiastic interest in and love for young life! And, on the other hand, what a revelation of the danger which attends that selfish use of our faculties—*hands, feet, eyes*—whereby wrong is made easy and right is made difficult for those whom we should help!

47, 48. The Greek word for *hell* is Gehenna, a name originally given to the ravine outside Jerusalem where human sacrifices were offered to Moloch (Jer. $7^{31f.}$). Later, because the name was of evil omen, it became a metaphorical expression for the place where the wicked were punished (2 Esdras 7^{36}). The imagery of the second part of v. 48 is taken from Isa. 66^{24}. As Rawlinson suggests, it calls to mind maggots preying on offal and fires perpetually burning for the destruction of refuse. It typifies the destruction of waste products in God's creation rather than the prolonged torture of human beings. This teaching about hell, J. Weiss thinks, fits in well with the Jewish belief in revenge, but not with a gospel of God, whose character is love.

49, 50. The Metaphor of Salt. See notes on Mt. 5^{13} Lk. 14^{34f}. Some MSS. add to v. 49 *and every sacrifice shall be salted with salt.* This is a gloss suggested by Lev. 2^{13} to make clearer the thought of the first part of the verse. Just as salt purified the flesh, the sacrifices of Judaism, and so made them acceptable to God, in like manner suffering and sorrow make life clean and pure. A saying like this would be a source of great inspiration to the members of the church of Rome, facing as they were daily the possibility of martyrdom.

Pure salt cannot lose its saltiness (v. 50a), but when mingled with other foreign ingredients as was the salt of the Dead Sea this loss was possible. *Salt* in this saying is a metaphor to signify all that was most distinctive in Christian character—those qualities of love, hope, faith, self-discipline, and humility which make a Christian man a vital force in a community to preserve the things by which its life is sustained. Salt in v. 50b is a symbol of peace and friendship. To eat bread and salt with one another was in the East a sign of covenant relationship. So among Christians concord and co-operation are indispensable qualities.

CHAPTER X

1. See notes on Mt. $19^{1, 2}$.

2–12. The Question of Divorce. See notes on Mt. $5^{31, 32}$ 19^{3-12}.

13–16. Jesus Blesses the Children. See notes on Mt. 19^{13-15} Mk. 9^{33-37} Lk. 18^{15-17}.

17–22. The Great Refusal. See notes on Mt. 19^{16-22} Lk. 18^{18-23}.

23–27. Riches a Soul Peril. See notes on Mt. 19^{23-26} Lk. 18^{24-27}.

28–31. Reward for Self-renunciation. See notes on Mt. 19^{27-30} Lk. 18^{28-30}.

32–34. The Third Prediction of Suffering. See notes on Mt. 20^{17-19} Lk. 18^{31-34}. Jesus' anticipation of suffering and ultimate death at the hands of the religious and political authorities grew more definite as he drew near to the city. The evangelist, of course, wrote these words long after the Passion took place. It is therefore not unlikely that the words are colored by his knowledge of the actual event. For all that, it is only in the light of Jesus' anticipation of a necessary suffering that we can understand his procedure during these closing months.

35–45. The Ambition of the Sons of Zebedee. (Mt. 20^{20-28} Lk. 22^{24-27}.) According to Matthew, this request for pre-eminence in the coming kingdom is made by Salome the mother, and not by James and John. If, as some think, she was a sister of the mother of Jesus, she may have thought that family relationship should give her sons some claim to priority. The two brothers, according to Mark, think of the coming kingdom in terms of grandeur and outward pomp, and they consider that Jesus has it in his power to confer on them the chief places in that kingdom. The request reveals how slowly "the training of the Twelve" had proceeded. In his moving answer Jesus shows clearly that to attain power and pre-eminence cups of bitterness must be drunk and baptisms must be undergone, and instead of lordship over men there must be self-devotion to their service and a purpose to free them from all forms of bondage (v. 39). Willingness to suffer and to engage in sacrificial service, not ambition for high place, are the essentials for the sons of the Kingdom. Jesus illustrates his meaning by contrasting the ideals of his kingdom with those of the great empire in which he lived, where autocratic power was wielded and where men of the type of Cæsar and Alexander held sway (v. 42). He also points to his own life dedicated to the good of others as the ideal to which they must attain. In his own case, all self-interest was entirely consumed by his burning passion to be of help to sin-stricken humanity.

38. The *cup* is a common scriptural symbol for both happy and bitter experiences (cf. Psa. 11^{6} 16^{5} 23^{5} 73^{10} Jer. 16^{7} 25^{15} Mt. 26^{39}). *Baptism* (cf. Lk. 12^{50}) is a symbol for suffering of an overwhelming character. It is as though one were plunged into troubled waters (cf. Psa. 18^{16} 42^{7} 69^{1} 124^{4}). There is no need to infer that these words are a prophetic anticipation of the martyrdom of these two disciples. James we know was a victim of the Herodian persecution (Acts 12^{2}), but tradition is uncertain as to the manner of John's death.

40. Jesus here touches on one of the paradoxes of the life of the kingdom of God. God chooses men for great service, but men so chosen must show themselves fit to be chosen.

45. This is the only place in the Gospels where the Greek word translated *ransom* occurs. It means, literally, a price paid for the deliverance of a person or thing. In the LXX it is used for the redemption of a slave (Lev. 19^{20}) and of a life (Ex. 21^{30}). The language of this great saying is reminiscent of Isa. 53, in which the sufferings of the Ideal Servant are described. Indeed this chapter in Isaiah may have helped Jesus to arrive at the conviction that his sacrificial life was destined to exercise a redemptive influence on multitudes in all lands shackled by sin. We are not to infer, however, from this use by the Master of the metaphor of ransom that he considered his life and death as an exact penal equivalent for all sin. His thought moves from result to cause. The *result* is the deliverance of mankind from sin. The *cause* is himself—the way in which he *gives his life*. Hence his self-giving is as a ransom because it does what any literal ransom does—*it delivers.*

46–52. The Healing of Blind Bartimæus (cf. Mt. 20:29-34 Lk. 18:35-43). Matthew relates that there were two blind men. Jericho was only fifteen miles from Jerusalem. It was a busy commercial and religious center. The retinue of Jesus has been considerably increased by the pilgrims going to the feast. Blindness was very common in Palestine and its wretched victims often posted themselves at the city gateways, especially at the Passover seasons. The cry of help calls from the disciples a severe rebuke, but Jesus, deeply touched, commands the blind man to be brought to him, and restores his sight. The Sinaitic Syriac version of the man's reply in v. 51 is *that I may see thee.* According to Matthew, Jesus touched the eyes of the two men before their sight was restored (see art., *N. T. Miracles*, p. 925a).

47. Only here in Mark and the parallel in Luke is Jesus directly addressed as *Son of David* (cf. 12:35). Because of its Messianic significance the title is frequent in Matthew. The blind man may have heard it applied to Jesus by some of the crowd. This would indicate a growing consciousness on the part of the people of Jesus' real character.

CHAPTER XI

1–10. The Triumphal Entry. See notes on Mt. 21:1-11 Lk. 19:29-38 Jn. 12:12-19.

11. This verse may really parallel Mt. 21:10, 11. In that case, it would seem that Jesus did not actually enter the city on the day of the public acclaim, but turned aside to spend the night in Bethany (cf. v. 19). Luke puts the lament immediately after the acclaim (19:41).

12–14. The Cursing of the Fig Tree. See vv. 19–26 and notes on Mt. 21:18-22 Lk. 13:6-9.

15–18. Jesus Cleanses the Temple. See notes on Mt. 21:12-17 Lk. 19:45-48.

19–26. See also vv. 12–14 and notes on Mt. 21:18-22. For v. 26 see R.V. mg.

27–33. The Source of Jesus' Authority. See notes on Mt. 21:23-27 Lk. 20:1-8.

CHAPTER XII

1–12. The Parable of the Wicked Vinedressers. See notes on Mt. 21:33-46 Lk. 20:9-19.

13–17. The Question of Tribute. See notes on Mt. 22:15-22 Lk. 20:20-26.

18–27. The Sadducees' Question Concerning Resurrection. See notes on Mt. 22:23-33 Lk. 20:27-40.

28–34. The Greatest Commandment. See notes on Mt. 22:34-40. Matthew omits the beautiful and far-seeing comment of the scribe and Jesus' answer to it (vv. 32–34). Luke makes the incident, with the scribe's question, "Who is my neighbor?" the basis of the parable of the good Samaritan (10:25f.). The parable fits the setting perfectly. Why Matthew omits both the scribe's comment and Jesus' parable we cannot say, unless it was that he disliked the slight on ceremonialism implied in the first (but cf. ch. 23), and a similar slight together with a fine universalism in the second.

35–37. Son of David. See notes on Mt. 22:41-46. The remark about *the common people* is not found in Matthew. Mark contrasts their interest with the suspicion of the religious leaders. To the people, the argument about David's Son seemed reasonable enough. To the scribes it was less convincing. Perhaps this explains what Jesus went on to say.

38–40. Condemnation of the Scribes. See notes on Mt. 23, especially vv. 1–7. Mark gives here a brief example of denunciations which Matthew records in similar circumstances at great length (cf. Lk. 20:45-47).

41–44. True Sacrifice: the Widow's Mite. See notes on Lk. 21:1-4. The money brought was for the support of the Temple. The rich gave ostentatiously. This widow was not ashamed of her small gift, for she made no effort to conceal the amount. Jesus, looking on, saw into the hearts of the various givers, and he was not deceived by the differences of value. He found three lessons in what he saw: first, that the sacrifice is real only when the giving is costly; second, that gifts are not acceptable to God which were obtained in the first place by unjust means (see v. 40); and third, that where there is sorrow and loneliness, surcease for it may be found in the house of God.

CHAPTER XIII

The Apocalyptic Discourse. (See introductory note on Mt. 24 and cf. Lk. 21:5-36.) This chapter, which contains the only long discourse in Mark's Gospel, and one entirely different in character from our Lord's usual discourses as recorded in Matthew and Luke, presents many perplexing problems. Few modern interpreters believe that the whole discourse can be attributed to Jesus. The lack of unity, the presence of so many stereotyped apocalyptic formulæ, the complete contrast which it presents to our Lord's declaration in Lk. 17:20f. (note), all go to support the theory that the chapter is a composite structure made up of genuine sayings of Jesus and a Jewish or Jewish-Christian apocalypse. Even the genuine sayings of Jesus seem to be colored by the prevailing eschatological hopes and expectations of the early church. On the one hand, we have the declaration which exhibits the Kingdom as imminent, with no other sign of its nearness than the Gospel itself; and, on the other hand, the declaration which exhibits the Kingdom as being delayed till after a series of spectacular events shall have been accomplished, and we must choose between them. Scholars have long agreed that vv. 7, 8, 14–20, 24–27 form part of a short Jewish or Jewish-Christian apocalypse. (See art., *Intertestamental Literature*, pp. 188–9.) Three events are depicted in these verses, namely, the woes or birthpangs of the new age, the revelation of the antichrist or the abomination of desolation, and the manifestation of the Son of man (see Dan. 8[13] 10[5, 6] 11[31] 12[11], notes). The discourse should be carefully compared with the parallel accounts in Matthew and Luke. The variations in the forms of additions and omissions form another clear proof of composite character.

1–4. The Occasion of the Speech. Jesus foretells the inevitable doom which is awaiting the city of Jerusalem. The four disciples want to know both the *time* of the event and its *sign*. Their questions relate to the fall of Jerusalem, but the rest of the chapter and the form of the question in Matthew (24[3]; cf. mg.), "What shall be the sign of thy coming, and of the end of the world?" show that the evangelist is thinking of much more than that. Indeed, the questions are for him but the point of departure for the entire following discourse.

5, 6. False Messiahs. Three of these are referred to in Acts, namely, Theudas (5[36]), Judas of Galilee (5[37]), and "the Egyptian" (21[38]). All may be read about in Josephus (*Antiquities*, xviii, 1: 6; xx, 5; xx, 8: 6).

7, 8. The Beginning of Travail. The woes and labor pangs of the Messiah was a technical rabbinic expression for the national calamities which were to usher in the advent of the Messiah (cf. Isa. 66[7-9]).

9. Persecution. A typical saying of Jesus in which he anticipates the persecution of his followers (see Mt. 10[17]).

10. The Universality of the Gospel. This statement seems quite out of harmony with the Jewish character of the whole apocalypse. Luke omits it; it was probably not in the tradition known to him. The saying has all the marks of a genuine utterance of Jesus which may have been spoken by him on another occasion.

11–13. Help from God; the Division of Families. This promise of the help of the Spirit of God in times of emergency and the prediction of the inevitable division in families owing to the reception of the gospel by some of the members are both repeated from the instructions in Mt. 10[17-22]; cf. Lk. 21[12-17]. The word *end* (v. 13) may refer either to the death of Jesus or to the end of the world.

14–20. The Reign of Terror. The phrase *abomination of desolation* (or *abomination which causes desolation*) is derived from Dan. 9[27]. There it refers to the altar of Zeus erected by Antiochus on the site of the altar of burnt-offering, to the great horror of the Jews. Jesus' use of the phrase on this occasion probably refers to the predicted desecration of the Temple in Jerusalem by the Roman armies. He emphasizes (vv. 15–19) the unexpected and sudden nature of the calamity before which all must flee. *The tribulation* is a technical apocalyptic term for the period of distress which is to precede the manifestation of the Messiah. If Jesus is referring to the destruction of Jerusalem under the Romans in the near future, then what he says in v. 20 is literally true. The populace was almost annihilated (see Josephus, *Wars of the Jews*, v, vi.).

21–23. False Messiahs Again. These verses seem to reflect the apostolic age and probably represent the admonitions of the evangelist to the church to guard against all pretenders. The warning holds good for every age: there is always the possibility of a false or imaginary Christ being put in the place of the true Christ.

24–27. The Coming of the Son of Man. The early church took the vision found in Dan. 7[9-14] of the coming of the Son of man on the clouds of heaven and applied it to the return of Jesus. Since we know that Jesus made free use of apocalyptic language, there is no reason why he should not have made this identification. Nature's sympathy with the great events in the life of Jesus is often stressed in the N.T. (cf. Mt. 27[50f.]) and the thought is reflected in much Christian art and poetry. The early church undoubtedly thought of the second coming of Jesus as a visible event, but the evident delay of it brought about a gradual change in the point of view (1 Thess. 4[13-18], and cf. notes on 2 Pet. 3[3-7]).

28–37. Two Parables: the Fig-Tree and the Householder. The fig-tree, one of the commonest trees in Palestine, has already been used in Mark to give warning (11[12-14, 20], and see notes on Mt. 21[18-22]). Here it serves as a simple analogy. Just as leaves in spring herald the coming of summer so the things described in vv. 9–13 will show that the destruction of the Temple is near and the coming of the kingdom of heaven following closely upon it. For us the teaching means that periods of stress—personal or national—may herald spiritual advance.

30. If this verse refers to the fall of Jerusalem, it shows that Jesus thought of it as impending and to take place in the lifetime of those listening to him. This would dispose of the supposition, often made, that "the coming of the Son of man" is identical with "the end of the world." At the same time, his coming, whatever form it may take, involves change: "the old order changeth, giving place to new."

32. This was regarded by Schmiedel as one of the nine "foundation pillars" for an authentic life of Jesus. The principle he went on was that any statement that implied a limitation on Jesus' knowledge or power must be true: otherwise it would not have found a place in the record. Some suppose that Jesus, as Son of God incarnate, voluntarily assumed ignorance, but it is difficult to make that psychologically intelligible.

33–37. The result of all the teaching is an appeal for vigilance illustrated by the parable of the householder. This idea of the necessity of watchfulness appears in various parabolic forms elsewhere (Mt. 7[24-27] 12[35-48] 25[1-30]).

CHAPTER XIV

The Story of the Passion. We come now to "the beginning of the end." The synoptic parallels are Mt. 26 and Lk. 22, on which see notes.

1, 2. The Plot to Kill Jesus. (Jn. 11[45f.]) Mark and Matthew assert that two days before the Passover the chief priests and scribes held a meeting to devise means to arrest Jesus before the crowds gathered together for the feast. The word *passover* is used (a) for the Passover lamb slain on the afternoon of Nisan 14 and eaten after sunset Nisan 15, (b) for the appointments needed for the paschal supper (cf. v. 16), and (c) for the great festival itself, lasting from Nisan 14 to 21. It is used in v. 1 in this third sense. The Jews reckoned a day from sunset to sunset; the Romans from dawn to dawn. Wednesday, Nisan 13, remained such to the Romans (as to us) even after sunset, while to the Jews Nisan 14 began with sunset on Wednesday. This difference in the calculation of time is responsible for the variation in the Gospels on the date of the crucifixion and of the Last Supper (see notes on Jn. 19[31] and cf. art., *Chronology of N.T.*, p. 875). *Unleavened bread* (called *Azuma*) was the food of the Jews at the Passover feast. It was to be entirely free from leaven. The word was also a technical term for the feast itself. It is used metaphorically in 1 Cor. 5[6-8] of a pure and true way of life and of men in whom sin has been conquered.

3–9. The Anointing at Bethany. Luke omits this story because he has recorded a similar one (7[36-50]). The fourth Gospel tells us that Mary the sister of Martha anointed the feet of Jesus (12[1-8], notes). Matthew and Mark here say, his head. It would be easier to anoint the feet, for Jews in their ordinary meals reclined on carpets strewn on the floor, and rested the elbow on cushions. The story serves to bring out, on the one hand, the mercenary character of Judas, who wanted to put a money value on what was priceless; and on the other hand the insight and understanding of Mary, who seemed to divine the fate of Jesus. Mary in the N.T. is always found at the feet of our Lord (Lk. 10[39]). Only one utterance of hers is recorded, and that is a repetition of her sister's (see Jn. 11[21, 32]); but her actions are like great works of art whose value lies in what they suggest. The words Jesus applies to her act (Greek *kalon ergon*, v. 6) could be translated *a beautiful deed.* His commendation shows the high valuation he placed on the symbolic and the sacramental. Art and beauty have a proper place in the Kingdom: to be indifferent to them is to lessen the worth of life. When the good is adorned with beauty its appeal is made stronger. To eliminate the adornment is only justifiable when it is absolutely necessary. In this case it was not necessary: that is why Jesus rebuked Judas (v. 6, cf. Jn. 12[4]). True love gives its all. There is an abandon about it which makes questions of mere economy look small indeed.

3, 4. *Nard* was a fragrant oil derived from an Indian plant. There is much discussion as to the propriety of the first syllable in the R.V. name *spikenard.* See R.V. mg. for alternative readings, such as genuine nard, pure nard, and liquid nard. The complaint of *wastefulness* may well have been made (as John says) by Judas, who in Jn. 17[12] is called "the son of waste" (or "perdition"), i.e., one in whom the forces of moral decay had almost finished their deadly work.

8, 9. Jesus here suggests the truth we so often forget—that deeds of love done for the living are of greater worth than deeds done for the dead. Such deeds of love are imperishable. Every act of self-forgetting service is an everlasting *memorial*—"music sent up to heaven by the lover and the bard; enough that he heard it once—we shall hear it by and by."

10, 11. The Bargain of Judas. Luke (22[3-6]) adds two significant details: that Judas fell under the control of Satan, and that the arrest was to take place privately. Only Matthew mentions the thirty pieces of silver (see notes on 27[3-10]).

12–16. Preparation for the Passover. (See notes on Lk. 22[1-13] Jn. 13[1, 2] 19[31].) According to the fourth Gospel, Jesus was crucified when the Passover lambs were slain in the Temple on Nisan 13 and before the actual Passover festival began. If that was so, the meal which Jesus had with his disciples was not a true Passover meal. Nevertheless, he may have intended it to have all the spiritual significance of the Passover rite. The probabilities are strongly in favor of the suggestion that the house where the Last Supper took place was the house of John Mark, which seems to have been the rendezvous of the early disciples. This was perhaps the house to which the disciples fled after the crucifixion (cf. Lk. 24[8-12]) and where the stirring events of Pentecost took place (Acts 1[13f.]). It was certainly to this house that Peter came after his release from prison (Acts 12[12]). For the Passover there were required unleavened cakes, wine, water, bitter herbs, a sauce called charosheth, and lamb brought from the Temple to be roasted. Jesus had probably made previous arrangements with certain members of this household so that the statement in v. 13 need not imply supernatural knowledge on his part.

17–25. Jesus at the Last Supper. According to Matthew and Mark (Jn. 13[21-30], notes; but cf. Lk. 22[14-23]), one of the first things which Jesus does after the disciples have reclined for the meal is to announce the presence of a betrayer. The emphasis on *he that eateth with me* is made because table fellowship involved certain sacred obligations. The phrase *he that dippeth with me in the dish* is its equivalent. From this one would gather that Judas was not pointed out at the outset of the meal and that he partook of the Last Supper. The accounts in Matthew and Mark of the institution of the Eucharist are practically identical. Luke in his narrative approximates to that of Paul in 1 Cor. 11[23-25]. The important addition in the latter is the command to perpetuate the rite as a memorial of the death of Christ. Matthew and Mark when they wrote knew the important place the rite already had in the services of the church and so perhaps did not think it necessary to record it. To the simple statement in Mark, *this is my body*, Paul adds "which is for you," and Luke adds "given for you," and the *blood . . . shed for many* in Mark is in Luke "poured out for you." In every case what is emphasized is the sacrificial character of Christ's suffering, and the bread and wine as symbols of that fact. In commemorating the Eucharist today, the Christian may be confident that he is doing that which goes back to a specific command of his Lord.

25. The Greek word used here for *new* is *kainos*—a different word from that used for "new wine" in 2[22]. The latter means "newly made," whereas the present word means that Jesus would enjoy with the disciples fellowship of a spiritual order under entirely new conditions.

26–31. Peter's Denial Foretold. (Mt. 26[31-35], notes on Lk. 22[31-34].) It was customary at the Passover celebration to sing the so-called Hallel Psalms (115–118). The *hymn* sung by Jesus and his disciples may have been one of these. On the way to Olivet Jesus intimated that all would be *offended*. The meaning of "offend" in this case was that they would come under such severe testing that their loyalty would weaken and they would fail. Jesus substantiates this by a verse from Zech. 13[7] which reveals to us the intimate relationship—*shepherd*—he holds toward his disciples. He himself, however, is confident of an immediate triumph and in the very face of death he promises to meet his disciples in Galilee. Peter characteristically asserts that, whatever the rest may do, he will prove himself stanch and loyal. But Jesus knows Peter better than Peter knows himself, and he tells him that before the cock has crowed twice he will have denied him thrice. Oscar Holtzmann quaintly remarks that the cock could not keep up with Peter. Matthew and many MSS. of Mark omit *twice*.

32–42. Jesus in Gethsemane. (Mt. 26[36-46], notes on Lk. 22[39-53].) Jesus was wont to resort to Gethsemane for rest and meditation, but on this visit momentous issues are impending; far-reaching decisions have to be taken; the cross and all its shame are clearly revealed; and for a moment he shrinks and hesitates. It is only by earnest prayer that his will is brought into complete harmony with the Father's; but once that is achieved, he leaves the garden without fear or hesitation.

The moving record is full of suggestiveness for the reverent mind. (1) We find there the *loneliness of Jesus*. Judas was already in league with the authorities; eight of the disciples are outside the garden; the three who are permitted to enter are a stone's throw away (according to Luke) and even they are drowsy after the excitement of the day and quickly fall asleep. (2) We observe the contrast between the tremendous *moral resolution* of Jesus and the apathy and indifference of the disciples. (3) We observe, too, the intensity of Jesus' emotions. For *greatly amazed and sore troubled* in v. 33 Moffatt reads *appalled and agitated*. If v. 34 is a quotation from Psa. 6[3] ("my soul also is sore troubled"), it is significant that Jesus should add the words *unto death*. The sweating of blood is mentioned by Luke alone. (4) Finally, we observe that the petitions are reminiscent of the Lord's Prayer; e.g., *Abba, Father; what thou wilt* (v. 36); and that this reminiscence continues into the words spoken to the disciples, *that ye enter not into temptation* (v. 38). It is as though during his agony he had been staying his mind with the very Prayer which he had given to others as a model.

Whence came the evangelist's knowledge of this experience? Jesus was too far away for the disciples to have heard him, and in any case they were asleep. H. G. Wood suggests that if they were not physically close enough to have heard him, they were afterward spiritually near enough to interpret the scene aright. If Mark was the young man of v. 51 who had followed Jesus and his disciples, he may be depending here on his own experiences. If he was not the young man himself, he may have known him. There is, however, something very attractive about the suggestion that the youthful Mark was an unsuspected observer of the events in Gethsemane, and that his experience that night definitely won him for Christ's cause.

41. It has been suggested that the Greek word translated *It is enough* really refers to Judas, and might be rendered *He has it*, i.e., "Judas has his price, and the hour is here." This would supply a vivid touch to the narrative, but it involves a forced translation of the word.

43–50. The Arrest of Jesus. (Mt. 26^{47-56}, notes on Lk. 22^{47-53} Jn. 18^{3-11}.) The arrest was carried out by the orders of the Sanhedrin, who despatched a number of Temple police to do the work under the guidance of Judas. Judas hides his purpose under a greeting and an effusive kiss. The intensive form used here for the verb *kiss* is the same as describes the father's greeting of the prodigal and the kiss of the woman who anointed Jesus' feet in the Pharisee's house (Lk. 15^{20} 7^{38}). It means kissed much or passionately, and therefore suggests the depths of shame to which Judas had fallen. The synoptists vary in their reports concerning the attitude of Jesus to Judas. In Luke, Jesus says, "Judas, betrayest thou the Son of man with a kiss?" In Matthew he says that which is almost unintelligible, "Friend, do that for which thou art come." Some prefer to translate it, "Friend, what are you doing?" The disciple who draws his sword and cuts off the ear of the high priest's servant is identified in the fourth Gospel as Peter; the servant's name is Malchus (18^{10}). Luke alone states that the ear was healed. Only Mark is silent on Jesus' disapproval of Peter's action. His words about the futility of drawing the sword in such circumstances are found only in Matthew. All the synoptists, however, agree in reporting Jesus' astonishment at the manner of the arrest; it implied he was wont to hide himself instead of appearing openly in the Temple. The words in Matthew about the legion of angels Jesus could have called upon are the more striking in view of the recent prayer. The story of the arrest closes with the statement that it was all in fulfillment of Scripture. When Mark was written it was already an accepted belief of the church that all events in the life of Jesus happened according to Scripture, although Matthew makes much more use of the formula than Mark.

51, 52. The Young Man with the Linen Sheet. Many scholars, e.g., Zahn and Bartlet, are of the opinion that Mark is describing a personal experience of his own and that here we have in a hidden corner of his Gospel his own signature (see closing notes under vv. 32–42). If it could be definitely proven that the passion narrative was written by a Jerusalemite, the fact would be an effective reply to those who feel that the Gentile character of the Gospel makes it difficult to believe that it has come from the hands of one who was in such close touch as Mark with the actual events.

53–65. Jesus Before the High Council. (Mt. 26^{57-68}, notes on Lk. 22^{66-71}.) Mark has probably antedated this preliminary trial of Jesus before the Sanhedrin. Luke ($22^{54, 66}$) correctly places it in the early hours of the morning of the next day. The court found it difficult to discover a charge upon which witnesses could agree. Some swore—falsely, says Mark—that Jesus had declared he would destroy the Temple made with hands and build in its place in three days one not made with hands. Jesus could hardly have meant literally the first part of this statement; the second part contains the nucleus of a great truth, namely, that though the earthly temple would one day be destroyed, in its place there would arise a new spiritual temple in the form of his church (cf. Eph. 2^{19-22}). The fourth Gospel (2^{19-22}) "spiritualizes" these words by referring them to the crucifixion and resurrection of Jesus—a questionable interpretation. Some think that the words contain a reference to the apocalyptic expectation of a new Temple coming down from heaven at the end of time (cf. Ezek. 40–43). Unable to find unanimous testimony on the accusation (v. 59), the high priests shift their ground. Is he the Christ? they ask. Jesus had remained silent on the first charge; this question, however, he answers in a bold affirmation. The high priest used the phrase *Son of the Blessed* to avoid using the sacred name God. "Son of God" does not seem to have been in Judaism a widely recognized title of the Messiah, although it could claim the sanction of Psa. 2[7]. This is the first time the question of the Messiahship of Jesus comes to open expression between him and his opponents, but the very fact that the question is now raised shows that it was already openly discussed by people. The words in v. 62 about the future may be an addition of the evangelist in which he asserts in apocalyptic terms the faith of the early church in the return of the Messiah. Yet since it is certain that Jesus predicted his return, there is no reason why he should not sometimes have used apocalyptic language for the purpose as well as the more spiritual language of Jn. 14[3, 18, 19, 28] 16[16-24]. The high priest is satisfied that the case against Jesus is fully proved by his affirmative *I am.* The affirmation is declared blasphemous, and blasphemy was punishable by death. The servants and court officials begin the cruel mishandling of their victim, although their mocking invitation to him to prophesy was unintentional evidence to the fact that in the popular opinion Jesus was regarded as a prophet (cf. Mt. 21[46]).

66–72. Peter's Denial. (See also v. 54, Mt. 26[69-75], notes on Lk. 22[54-65] Jn. 18[16-18, 25-27].) While Jesus was undergoing a supposedly legal trial, Peter was undergoing a moral trial. The night was chilly, and the fire was attractive to one who was cold, and hungry, and sleepy. To the accusation of the maid and the bystanders, Peter makes a bold denial—even with curses—of any connection with the prisoner. Luke in 23[61] graphically reports that it was a look from Jesus after the third denial that reminded Peter of the recent warning about the danger he was in (Mk. 14[30]). Drawing his mantle over his face (for so we may render the Greek word translated *when he thought thereon*), Peter went out weeping bitterly. The placing of the two trials side by side very forcibly brings out the contrast between the strong moral resolution of Jesus and the vacillating weakness of the erstwhile bold spokesman of the apostolic circle.

CHAPTER XV

The Last Day of Jesus' Life on Earth. This is the theme of the present chapter. The parallels are Mt. 27 Lk. 23 and Jn. 18[28-40] 19[1-30], on which see notes.

1–15. The Trial Before Pilate. See notes on Mt. 27[11-31] Lk. 23[1-25]. The Roman procurator was in residence at Jerusalem during the Passover, and as the Sanhedrin had no power to impose the death penalty, the case of Jesus had to be brought before him. It is probable that Jesus knew enough Greek to be able to dispense with an interpreter (cf. notes on 7[24-30] 7[31-37]). The charge brought against him is that he claimed to be the king of the Jews. This expression he himself would interpret in a spiritual sense, but Pilate and the authorities regarded it as treasonable in its implications. Pilate is wise enough to see that the religious leaders are actuated by envy and malice, and for a moment he refuses to pass sentence. He even suggests a way out of the difficulty. The demands of the crowd, however, become so clamorous and insistent that, partly out of fear, and partly out of desire to win popular favor, Pilate yields.

16–20. The Scourging and Mocking. To scourge before crucifying was the customary procedure. Josephus speaks of men whom the procurator Florus "whipped, and nailed to the cross" (*Wars of the Jews*, ii, 14: 9). The mockery was the crude and gruesome humor of rough men who failed to comprehend the real character of their victim. They should be judged accordingly—not as we should judge those whose eyes were enlightened. Did not Jesus himself pray for them? (Lk. 23[34].)

21. Simon of Cyrene. Cyrene was a Jewish colony in north Africa. Simon was probably on his way to keep the Passover. This is a more reasonable supposition than that of those who would translate the phrase *from the country* by *from a field*, as though he were coming home from work. For in that case he would be living in the neighborhood, and the very reason for mentioning him as from Cyrene seems to be to connect him with Africa, just as the reason for mentioning his two sons is to establish a connection with the church in Rome of which they were members (Rom. 16[13]), and for which Mark wrote his Gospel. It is as though Mark were saying that the one kindly act done for Jesus that day was done by a non-Jerusalemite, the father of Roman Christians. Both Matthew (27[32]) and Luke (23[26]), however, record the incident.

22–32. The Crucifixion. (Mt. 27[33-44], notes on Lk. 23[26-49] Jn. 19[17-37].) The Greek word *crucify* can mean impalement on a single stake as well as fastening on a cross. The fact of the superscription over his head, however, would indicate that Jesus was crucified. The place of crucifixion was usually barricaded, and according to the report of Mark only Roman soldiers and Jewish officials were near the cross. This cruel form of punishment was usually inflicted only on slaves and the worst criminals. Plutarch mentions the custom of criminals carrying the cross to the place of execution. Not one of the synoptic writers tells us whether Jesus was bound or nailed to the cross. The former was the less immediately painful method, but it really prolonged the suffering, for the victim slowly died of starvation. The belief that Jesus was nailed is due partly to Jn. 20[25] and partly to the fact that his death took place within a few hours; the exact number cannot be decided, but probably it was not more than six. Mark has the crucifixion begin at the *third* hour (9 A.M.; v. 25), the darkness come on at the *sixth* hour, and death occur just after the *ninth* hour (vv. 33–37; but cf. Jn. 19[14]). Death was due to overstrained nerves, exhaustion, and heartbreak. The Marcan account emphasizes the utter loneliness of Jesus, who during three hours—"dark" in more senses than one—was without a friend of any description to show sympathy. The *myrrh* was a narcotic (v. 23). Jesus' resolute refusal of it reveals his purpose to "tread the wine-press alone." The raillery gets its point from the fact that Jesus had indeed spoken of *destroying the Temple* and of having come *to save others*. Had the mockers been able to take the long look they would have seen how profoundly true his claims were. The future was his, not theirs.

33–41. The Death of Jesus. See notes on Mt. 27[45-56] Lk. 23[44-49]. Mingled with the historical statements are statements of a symbolical significance. The *darkness* referred to is probably due to the desire of the author to emphasize the sympathy of nature with the suffering Christ. An eclipse is known to have been impossible, and it is unlikely that clouds alone would have caused a dense darkness. The rending of the Temple veil must also be taken as symbolical. The Holy of holies, where the glory of God dwelt, entrance to which was denied to ordinary men, is now open to all by the cross of Christ.

34. This cry of Jesus has caused great perplexity to many. A common supposition is that it was introduced into the narrative from Psa. 22, of which it is the first verse. It is not at all impossible that details from that psalm, which in so striking a way depicts the emotion of Jesus on the cross, have crept into the narrative (but see note on Matthew's account). On the other hand, the psalm as a whole is not a cry of despair, and the quoting of the first verse only may have been to show that although Jesus had in his suffering recalled that psalm, nevertheless, as with the psalmist so with him, the feeling of despair is only momentary. Mt. 27[51-53] supplies additional material which may be supposed to be more or less legendary in character (see notes there). The account of the influence of the crucifixion on the centurion in charge bears the marks of verisimilitude, but we should not read into his words a confession of the full deity of Christ as that was defined in the later creeds (v. 39, mg.). To the evangelist he is the first fruits of that great band of Gentiles who gladly owe allegiance to the *Son of God* (cf. Acts 10). While the disciples are nowhere to be seen, the loyal women keep anxious vigil at a distance. The cause of the Cross will never lack loyal women. They feel the emotional appeal of all that is connected with it. Its great need is for more men of the caliber of the centurion—*convinced* men.

42–47. The Burial of Jesus by Joseph of Arimathæa. (Mt. 27[57-61] Lk. 23[50-56] Jn. 19[38-42].) The character of Joseph, who immortalized himself by this noble act of love, is drawn in a few strokes. He is of good social standing and a distinguished member of the Sanhedrin. It is probably from him that the evangelist derived certain information as to what took place in the court at the trial of Jesus. He is a man of real moral courage, for, though a member of the Sanhedrin, he is a follower of Jesus and eagerly awaits the immediate coming of the kingdom of God. Only John says that he was a disciple "secretly, for fear of the Jews" (19[38]). In approaching Pilate to request the body he was running the serious risk of incurring social and political ostracism. He was willing to pay the cost of discipleship in another way, for he spared nothing to give the body of Jesus an honorable burial. The tomb was newly hewn, says Matthew, and one in which no man had yet lain, says Luke. Again the symbolism is suggestive. Jesus was to give death a new meaning, and it was fitting that the tomb he was to immortalize should be new and unpolluted.

CHAPTER XVI

1–8. The Resurrection. The parallels are Mt. 28[1-10] Lk. 24[1-12], on which see notes, and cf. Jn. 20[1-10]. Mark's Gospel broke off suddenly at v. 8, or it may be that the original ending became lost. At a later period, efforts were made to complete or restore it.

9–18. The Appearances. See the parallels, Mt. 28[16-20] Lk. 24[13-49] Jn. 20[11]–21[23]. This is the "longer ending" of Mark. It is absent from the Old Syriac and the Old Latin MSS., as well as from the two great codices, the Sinaiticus and Vaticanus. This longer ending is a mosaic made up of materials drawn chiefly from Luke's Gospel and non-canonical sources. It tells of an appearance to Mary Magdalene, and gives a condensed account of the visit to Emmaus (vv. 12, 13; cf. Lk. 24[13-35]). The appearance of Jesus to the eleven is not on a mountain as in Mt. 28^{16}, but at a simple evening meal, perhaps as in Lk. 24^{36f}. The style of this ending is in striking contrast to Mark's own style, for the whole appendix is characterized by an emphasis on the *disbelief* of the disciples (cf. vv. 11, 13, 14), and the didactic aim is very conspicuous throughout. In the margin of an ancient Armenian MS. this appendix is ascribed to one Ariston. Papias speaks of an Aristion who was a disciple of the Lord (quoted in Eusebius, *Eccles. Hist.*, iii, 39). This first appendix was added to the Gospel about the end of the first century. The codex Washington adds after v. 14 a rather crude paragraph which has been taken from some early second-century Christian writing. In some MSS. of the Gospel another shorter ending has been added as well: "But all that had been enjoined they reported concisely to Peter and his companions; and after these things, Jesus appeared to them, and from east to west sent forth through them the sacred and incorruptible proclamation of eternal salvation." This ending is probably Alexandrian in origin and was taken from an apocryphal writing of the second century.

19, 20. The Ascension. Neither Matthew nor John says anything of an ascension. It is mentioned in Lk. 24^{51}, and in Acts 1^{9-11}. The words must not be taken too literally. The real meaning of Jesus being *at the right hand of God* is that Jesus and what he represents is the determining influence in God's governance of the lives of men. The outlook of the later apostolic age is clearly reflected in v. 20. The verse has value in indicating what has actually been accomplished. The best commentary on it is the Acts of the Apostles.

LUKE

By Professor J. A. FINDLAY

Introduction

The Dedication. This Gospel, like the Acts, is dedicated to "Theophilus," addressed as "most excellent," which is equivalent to the English "Right Honorable," and indicates that, like Felix and Festus, who bear the same title, he was a Roman official. We do not know whether he was a Christian, but Christians did not use such titles in their intercourse with one another, and we may infer that he was simply a distinguished outsider who was inclined to be sympathetic. Perhaps the Gospel converted him, for he is no longer addressed as "most excellent" in the Acts.

Why the Gospel Was Written. As Theophilus was a Roman official—Theophilus may not have been his real name; it would have been unwise to give him a name that the world would recognize—Luke probably wished to show that the empire had nothing to fear from the church. The author emphasizes the fact that Roman officials acquitted first Jesus and then Paul of political crime. If Jesus was crucified and Paul sent in chains to Rome, if Peter was imprisoned, it was done to please the Jews. Everywhere the Jews are described as the instigators of persecution, and Paul feels sure of justice when he appeals to the emperor's tribunal. He himself is a Roman citizen; Felix, a notoriously corrupt official, married to a Jewess, only keeps him in prison at Cæsarea to oblige the Jews.

Dr. Plooij has lately suggested that the Gospel and the Acts were both, in whole or in part, intended to brief Theophilus for the defense of Paul before Nero, Theophilus being a member of the court which was to try his case. If the whole of the two books were written for that purpose, it would involve a very early date for them, for Paul arrived in Rome in 59 A.D. Perhaps we may modify the theory, while retaining its essential features, if we say that the author, who seems to describe himself as traveling to Palestine in 56–57 A.D., but was not imprisoned at Cæsarea with Paul, though he set out for Rome in his company two years later, spent the interval in collecting materials. He tells us in 1[3] that he had taken pains to make personal inquiry into the facts, his purpose being to prepare a defense of his friend in the trial he knew was impending, and to send to Theophilus an outline gospel along with his record of Paul's missionary journeys. This would account for the fact that the story (in Acts) breaks off in a most tantalizing way with Paul enjoying a considerable degree of personal freedom in his own hired house in Rome, no hint being given us of the tragic end of his career. (But cf. pp. 942–3.) Luke apparently did not make Mark's acquaintance till he reached Rome (Philm. [24] Col. 4[10, 14]). Then he discovered that Mark also was projecting a Gospel; as the result of consultation with him he later on—perhaps after the death of Paul—combined his own collections with information derived from Mark and published the combined work for the general benefit. In this commentary the view is taken that Luke's own material formed an outline-Gospel based on the collection of sayings of Jesus known as Q. The scheme on which the Gospel is built up will then be Q plus Luke's own material (here referred to as L), plus material from Mark's Gospel afterward worked in, plus a birth-story and an account of the Passion and resurrection, both of which may or may not have been part of L. (Cf. art., *Structure of the Synoptic Gospels*, p. 868.)

Authorship. Luke is mentioned by name three times in the N.T., unless, as Deissmann thinks, "Lucius of Cyrene" (Acts 13[1]) is another way of writing his name. The three places are Philm. v. 24 Col. 4[14]—here he is called Paul's doctor, for that is what "the beloved physician" means—and 2 Tim. 4[11]. Is this Luke the author of the third Gospel as well as the Acts? In Acts 16[10-18] 20[5]–21[18] 27[1]–28[16], the writer apparently speaks of himself as one of the company; "they" and "them" become "we" and "us." This means either that the author of the whole book has joined the party, or that he is using a diary kept by a companion of Paul, without warning us that he is doing so (cf. p. 1095). As ancient writers do not acknowledge authorities, we cannot take it for granted that the author of the travel-diary is the author of the whole book, and other tests must be applied. Before we pass on to consider them, however, we should notice that, if the Western text (cf. p. 861b) can be trusted, we must add one more to these "we-passages," for in Acts 11[27, 28] that text adds, "And there was great rejoicing, and, when *we* were gathered together." This locates the diarist at the Syrian Antioch. Even if "Lucius of Cyrene" is not Luke, there are good reasons in favor of the view that he was at one time a member of the church there. Ramsay pleads for Philippi as his home, on the ground that the first generally recognized "we-passage" is connected with Paul's visit to Philippi, and that Paul leaves the diarist there (17^1) and picks him up again in Macedonia (20^4). But if he lived at Philippi why did he stay at Lydia's house? (16^5.)

Luke was a doctor, Paul tells us. Some years ago Hobart discovered medical terms on every page both of the Gospel and the Acts and Harnack has re-enforced his conclusions. H. J. Cadbury has shown that Hobart's argument has been carried too far; by the same method it could be proved that more than one other contemporary writer (e.g., Lucian) was also a doctor. It is clear that we cannot overpress the "medical" argument; however, a residuum of instances remains to make it reasonably certain that the diarist, as well as the evangelist and the author of the Acts, uses words in the description of disease which were confined (in that sense) to medical writers. *We may infer that they were all three the same person, and that he was Luke, Paul's doctor and companion in Rome.* At Lk. 8^{43} our evangelist is following Mark; he has got as far as Mk. 5^{26}. There he reads "had suffered many things of many physicians, and had spent all that she had, and was nothing bettered, but rather grew worse"—a sweeping hit at the faculty! The best texts of Lk. 8^{43} read simply "who had not strength to be healed by any" (see R.V. mg.). The word "doctor" is omitted, and the blame is put, not upon medical incompetence, but upon the woman's inability to respond to treatment. Surely, we can infer that the writer is a doctor himself.

General Characteristics of the Gospel. Luke is keenly interested in social reform, and is inclined to think of the contemporary social order as fundamentally bad. He is intensely sympathetic with the poor and hungry, is a townsman not habitually resident in Palestine, for he tends to be hazy about the details of Palestinian topography. A man of the larger world, he is yet able to assimilate the point of view of the old-fashioned Jewish quietists who welcome Jesus into the world, and even to reproduce their language. The birth-story is a triumphant and sympathetic reproduction of the ideas of people who lived an entirely different life from his own. His personal interests, however, are all with Samaritans and Gentiles, but he is no anti-Semite, and is eager to record instances of friendship between Jews and Gentiles (cf. Lk. 7^5) and to show that Paul, Peter, and James were all in fundamental agreement. He has his likes and dislikes. He tells with gusto and twice over the story of the experiment in voluntary communism in the church at Jerusalem, and in 12^{33} extends to all believers the suggestion made to the young ruler. He dislikes crowds, and shows a bias in favor of asceticism and against married life. His most endearing characteristic is his chivalrous attitude toward women.

Luke's Accuracy. Luke is certainly not a scientific historian in the modern sense of the word. Attacks have been made upon his accuracy in recent years, but most of them can be repelled with the help of evidence from inscriptions. The most serious question is that of the census which is used to date the birth of Jesus in 2^1. It is alleged (1) that there is no evidence for any census of Palestine earlier than the one mentioned in Acts 5^{37}, and this took place in 8–9 A.D.; and (2) that Quirinius was not governor of Syria till that date. Tertullian, himself a Christian Father, seems to contradict Luke on this point; he tells us that Saturninus was governor of Syria when Jesus was born. To these objections Ramsay (in *Was Christ born at Bethlehem?*) replies: (1) After 8–9 A.D. a census was taken every fourteen years; correspondence passed between Herod the Great (who died 4 B.C.) and the Emperor Augustus on the desirability or otherwise of holding such a census in Palestine; hence it is probable that a census was attempted fourteen years before 8–9 A.D., and that the direction that people should go to the place of their family's origin to register was intended to make the census palatable to the Jews. (2) We have inscriptional evidence, dealing with Quirinius' career, to the effect that about 8–6 B.C. he held a military commission in Syria. We may infer that Luke is right, and that Jesus was born about 6 B.C., if not earlier. (Cf. art., *Chronology of N.T.*, pp. 874–5.)

A Theory of the Composition of Luke-Acts. The treatment in this commentary assumes some such reconstruction as follows of the course of events leading up to the composition of Luke-Acts.

In 59 A.D., Luke comes to Palestine with Paul (Acts $21^{15f.}$), bringing with him Q, the collection of the sayings of Jesus (see p. 872). He knows that Paul intends to appeal to Cæsar (Acts 23^{11}), and so spends the two years of Paul's imprisonment in South Palestine collecting materials for the trial, intending to send them to Theophilus. The result is an outline-gospel (called L in this commentary) based on Q, and this he combines with a birth-story (learned in Jerusalem) and a

Passion and resurrection narrative. In his second volume (the Acts) he combines stories —learned in Jerusalem and Samaria—of the ascension of Jesus and the early days of the church with a diary of his own travels in Paul's company, and with information derived from Paul of his adventures when the author was not with him. When Paul sails for Rome he goes with him, after adding to his book a history of Paul's imprisonment and speeches at Cæsarea. In Rome he completes his book with an account of their shipwreck and arrival in Rome. The so-called Proto-Luke or original Luke (L) had been already despatched to Theophilus, perhaps from Palestine; now Luke sends or hands him his second volume. All this has happened before Luke has met Mark; his meeting with Mark leads to the reconstruction of the Gospel already written (L), for Luke discovers that he had a very inadequate record of the Galilæan ministry; perhaps he had not been to Galilee during his residence in Palestine. At the same time he rewrites the early chapters of the Acts, including in his narrative an alternative account of the beginnings of the church at Jerusalem on the basis of information about Peter given him by Mark (Acts $3^{1-5,\ 16}$ 9^{32}–12^{24}). The completed books were afterward published for the benefit of the church at large.

The contents of the original gospel written by Luke in Palestine and sent to Theophilus will then be: birth-stories of John the Baptist and Jesus; John's preaching; the baptism and the voice from heaven ("Thou art my Son; this day I have begotten thee"); genealogy of Jesus; temptation; sermon at Nazareth; call of Simon Peter; list of the Twelve; sermon on the level place; healing of the centurion's servant (from Q); raising of the widow's son at Nain; John the Baptist's message and a discourse thereon; an anointing by a woman in Galilee; names of the women who supported Jesus; transfiguration; journey to Jerusalem; charge to seventy and sayings on their return; parable of the good Samaritan; teaching about prayer and the parable of the friend at midnight; casting out of a dumb demon (from Q) and discourse on Satan casting out Satan, with parable of the haunted house; the woman in the crowd; invective against Pharisees at dinner; discourse about "the leaven of the Pharisees" and what his followers must fear; the preciousness of little things and people in God's sight and the unforgiven sin; the appeal for arbitration and the parable of the rich fool; "consider the lilies and the birds"; the privileges and the duties of would-be followers, and the parable of the wicked slave; the impatience of Jesus and the consequences of his coming in the sphere of domestic relationships; the need for getting rid of entanglements and of instant repentance, individual and social; the parable of the fig-tree spared one year longer; the cure of the woman bent double; parables of the mustard-seed and the leaven; sayings about the narrow door and the danger of exclusion; Herod's murderous intentions and the refusal to be intimidated by them; a last appeal to Jerusalem; healing of the man with the dropsy and specimens of the table-talk of Jesus; parable of the rich man's supper; a demand for absolute devotion; parables of the tower-builder and the king going into action; a saying about saltless salt; parables of the lost sheep, the lost coin, and the lost son; the unjust steward and "Dives" and Lazarus, with sayings on the sanctity of the law and divorce, about repeated forgiveness, and faith like a grain of mustard-seed; the parable of the dutiful slave; the story of the ten lepers; sayings about Lot and Lot's wife and about making one's soul one's own; "one shall be taken and one left"; the body and the eagles; parables of the importunate widow and the Pharisee and the publican; the story of Zacchæus; parables of the nobleman and the pounds; the triumphal entry; prophecies of the fall of Jerusalem and weeping over it; a further description of the siege, and various warnings and encouragements; the story of the woman taken in adultery (?); the Last Supper and sayings at the table and afterward; the agony in Gethsemane and the arrest of Jesus; trials before the Sanhedrin, Pilate, and Herod, and Peter's denial; the story of the cross, with two otherwise unrecorded sayings, and the story of Dysmas (see the notes on 23^{39}); the weeping of the woman, and the saying about the green tree and the dry; the resurrection appearances, with the story of the Emmaus road; last discourse, and parting at Bethany.

The only *additional sayings* found in this Gospel in Marcan connections are in 5^{39} ("old and new wine") and (in the "Western" text) the saying to the man working on the Sabbath (after 6^{5}). It will be observed that it is precisely in regard to the ministry by the lakeside that Luke's knowledge was defective before he met Mark, and that all the incoherencies in the Gospel as finally published are due to Luke's attempts to fill up gaps in L. The same somewhat patchy effect is noticeable in Acts 1–12. So much stress is laid upon L in this commentary, because Streeter's theory (in *The Four Gospels;* for fuller discussion of Streeter's theories, see intro. to Matthew, Mark, and John respectively), reinforced as it has been by Vincent Taylor in

Behind the Third Gospel, is much the most important and reassuring contribution that has been made to gospel-study in recent years; it has added a new and very early witness to synoptic tradition.

Special Significance of This Gospel for Our Interpretation of the Person and Work of Jesus Christ

In attempting a summary exposition of Luke's Gospel we must lay chief emphasis upon the three sections in which most of our evangelist's own contributions are embedded, namely, 1^{1}–4^{30}—the birth-story, and the beginning of the Galilæan ministry of Jesus; 9^{51}–18^{14}—the so-called Travel-Document; and 22^{14}–24^{53}—the story of the Passion and resurrection. In the detailed commentary which follows, we shall perhaps fail to see the wood for the trees; that is why it has been thought well to bring out here in outline the purpose of the Gospel taken as a whole.

The Key Passage. We look, then, for some one passage which may be regarded as summarizing the message of the book, as Mt. 28^{20} summarizes that of the first Gospel, or Mk. 3^{14} that of the second. Our Lord's own text and sermon at Nazareth (Lk. 4^{13-27}) suggests itself. Jesus has come, first, to bring the good news of salvation to poor people (the birth-story); second, to preach release to the captives, and sight to the blind (his ministry in Galilee); and third, to proclaim one year of the Lord which men must accept. To do his work he must not delay, but "set his face like a flint to go to Jerusalem," and those who would avail themselves of "the day of salvation" must not dally or even look back, but leave all else behind to follow him. These three points are all contained in his text ($4^{18, 19}$). A fourth point is developed in the sermon. It is that the reason why Jesus cannot stay at Nazareth or among his own people is that he has a world to redeem ($4^{26, 27}$), and so must *go out* from Nazareth to Capernaum, from Galilee to Jerusalem, from the few who loved him and would keep him to themselves to the many; and to win the many it is not enough that he should go about doing good in Palestine. Time is short, and he cannot cover the ground. He must die, must shed his blood "for many." It is for us to cover the ground (24^{47}), but what we have to carry is not simply the story of "the words of grace which proceeded out of his mouth" or of his wonderful deeds of power in Palestine (19^{37}), but the Gospel of a crucified and risen Saviour, who is alive for evermore. So this book gives us the history only of "the things which Jesus *began* both to do and to teach" (Acts 1^{1}).

The Stories and Songs in Chapters 1 and 2. In these chapters are a number of stories and songs which Luke collected in Jerusalem and its neighborhood during his two years' residence in Palestine (57–59 A.D.). They have considerable historical value, for barely thirty years have elapsed since the Passion, and Mary the mother of Jesus may well have been alive still. If she had removed to Ephesus by that time—tradition has it that she did so in her old age—Luke would probably have met her already; he is at Miletus with Paul in Acts 20, and there meets the elders of the Ephesian church. The story here is throughout told from Mary's point of view, and Mary is a peasant girl of Nazareth. The key-words of these early chapters are "salvation" and "Saviour" ($1^{47, 68, 69, 71, 77}$ $2^{11, 30}$), not only salvation "from their sins" (cf. Mt. 1^{21}), but from all their "enemies" ($1^{71, 74}$). Jesus is to "redeem *his people*" (1^{68} 2^{38}); by this is meant the removal of tyrants from their thrones and the exaltation of the lowly (1^{52}). The poor are to be filled with good things, and the rich sent empty away. The coming of Jesus is "good news for the poor." This deliverance is not to be brought about by war but by the act of God which will inaugurate the reign of *peace* on earth and good will among men (2^{14}); "the day spring from on high" is to guide men's feet into the way of *peace* ($1^{78, 79}$). It is clear that Luke has brought out with skill and sympathy the feelings of the poor and lowly "people of the land" who first welcome Jesus into their arms. He is aware of the narrowness of their outlook (2^{35}), and one of his purposes is to show how narrow this outlook is. He is careful to make it plain, too, that even after the resurrection some of them at least still clung to it (24^{21} Acts 1^{6}). For a little time, however, Luke is content to sun himself and us in the radiance of that morning, and reproduce the simple melody of the songs sung by these old-fashioned people who had so long been waiting for it.

Zacharias and Elizabeth, Simeon and Anna, and to some extent even Joseph and Mary, are representatives of a type of piety that had survived into a new age, and was out of touch with the times. With John (the Baptist) we catch for the first time a sterner and deeper note. God's ancient people have no prior claim to a place in the new Israel, for an entirely fresh beginning is to be made. Descent from Abraham will have nothing directly to do with their position in the new Israel; repentance alone, with the change of life that follows true repentance, will be of any value. Luke deliberately continues the quotation from Isa. 40 (made also in Mk. 1:2 Mt. 11:10, but not given at such length) till he comes to the words "and *all* flesh shall see the salvation of God" (3:4-6). Not merely the aristocracy of church or state, "the Pharisees and Sadducees" (Mt. 3:7), but the crowds as a whole (Lk. 3:7) are called "generation of vipers," i.e., "children of the devil"; neither Jewish blood nor poverty is to provide a passport into the new Israel: even the poor must learn to share the necessaries of life with each other, and to be content with their wages, while the richer publicans are to refrain from extortion and profiteering on the taxes (3:10-14). There is no reference now to "salvation from our enemies," or to any distinction between God's people and the Gentiles. Indeed, the change from the atmosphere of ch. 2 to that of ch. 3 is as sudden as any in the N.T., and there can surely be no doubt that the contrast is intentional. We are in a new age indeed; much of chs. 1 and 2 might belong to the O.T.; in ch. 3 we have been carried violently past the old landmarks, and find ourselves in a new world. Only in the book of Amos have we anything approaching the bluntness with which this other prophet of the wilderness sets on one side all national prerogatives.

The Sermon at Nazareth. The breach between the parochialism of his own people and the universalism of the Kingdom, proclaimed by John and realized in Jesus, becomes complete in ch. 4. "No prophet is acceptable in his own country," because his own people know, or think they know, so much about him. It is characteristic of Jesus that he refuses to be monopolized by anybody. It is the same after the resurrection: "He made as though he would go further" (24:28; cf. Mk. 6:48), and when they recognized him, "he vanished out of their sight" (24:31). "But he, passing through the midst of them, went [or was going on] his way" (4:30); so far as we know, he never went back to the village of his boyhood. This detachment, the refusal to be managed or dictated to by anyone, however dear, had been characteristic of Jesus as a boy. When Mary claims him in the Temple (2:48), he admits the justice of her claim by going back with her, and becoming subject to his parents, but at the same time hints that their right in him is not unqualified. He will go back with them and stay a long while, but not forever; his final loyalty must be to his "Father's business."

The Call of Peter. We can detect the same suggestion in the story of Peter's call. "Put out into the deep" (5:4), says Jesus to Simon; the words might be a motto for the Gospel and the Acts as well. Peter, like Jesus himself, and all those who follow him, is to be a "come-outer"; his fisherman's net is already too small for his catch (5:6). As Nazareth has become too small for Jesus, so Peter is to come away from the fishing, and angle for a less manageable prey—live men (5:10). Jesus leaves Nazareth, Peter leaves Bethsaida, and they go on trek together; the happy ending of the great adventure can be found in Jn. 21:19.

The Call of Levi (Matthew). In 5:28 Levi the publican falls in, and his call leads to our Lord's declaration of a radical program (5:38). Yet he does not leave friends and home and the dear, familiar customs of the past through any itch for novelty; he is no revolutionist by preference. Luke alone (5:39) tells us that, at the very moment when he detached himself most completely from the religious and social conventions of the past, he expressed his sympathy with the people who liked the old ways best. He understood and perhaps shared their preference, but one thing was dearer to him than all dear familiar things and people, and that was to do his Father's will.

The Anointing of Jesus in Simon's House. We may pass over ch. 6 and the greater part of ch. 7, for apart from the story of the raising of the widow's son at Nain, and one or two other details—dealt with in the commentary—the material this section contains may also be found in Matthew or Mark. But at 7:36 we come to one of Luke's loveliest stories. Both Simon and the woman are described as lovers, and all lovers are adventurers. Simon's love for Jesus was not heroic, but perhaps it was an adventure for him to ask this peasant-prophet to dinner at all. True, he did not go to seek him, but, staying timidly at home, invited certain acquaintances of his who could be trusted not to talk too much outside about the low company he was entertaining to meet Jesus. And his entertainment was half-hearted too. After all, prophet as he had become, Jesus had been brought up, he thought, in a peasant home, and would not expect water for his feet, scent for his head, or the salutation suitable to a social equal. Simon's love was indeed so little, so much more like patronizing curiosity than anything worthy the name of love, that it needed the magnanimity of Jesus to call it "love" at all; that was because Simon did not feel that he had any special reason for gratitude. The sinful woman, on the other hand, "would have inclosed herself in alabaster had she dreamed that he was sweet enough to keep." She made a great venture, for she was risking a public rebuff, because she loved so well. Jesus too is out on the road; he is leaving behind him the safe friendships of Nazareth, and becoming notorious as the boon companion of publicans and sinners; he has launched out "into the deep," and is quickly losing the confidence of most of the good people of his day; the cross is already visible at the end of the road.

Jesus' New Family. So he goes on his way with his motley company (8[2, 3]), Joanna the aristocrat and Mary of Magdala, Simon the fisherman and Levi the publican together. The issue of his choice of friends is seen in 8[19-21]; his mother and brothers make one last attempt to save him from himself, but he declares that he will not go home again; he will find mother and brothers among his new companions. What this severance must have cost Jesus we can only guess. Surely, he did not *prefer* the company of these publicans to that of his mother! When he sat at Matthew's table the conversation must have jarred upon him, for these people would not change their habits of speech in a moment. The difference was that they followed *his* way, while the others would lead him *their* way; so he bore with it all. We may be sure that he would not spare the vices of the company when he sat at the publican's table any more than in a Pharisee's house he refrained from denouncing the abuses characteristic of Pharisaism (11[39f.]).

Anticipating the Cross. We next come to 9[51-62] (vv. 57–60 only are found also in Matthew). We notice the phrase in v. 51, "the days of his taking up" (as the Greek says literally). This cannot refer to the ascension, for no one could say that the ascension was yet drawing near. It is suggested in the commentary that the story of Elijah is in the mind of the evangelist here; there is a clear reference to him in v. 54, and to the call of Elisha in v. 61. This may account for the phrase "his taking up." It means his exaltation to the cross, what the fourth Gospel calls his "lifting up." As Elijah left his companions, the "sons of the prophets," behind, as stage by stage he descended to the Jordan (2 Kings 2[1-12]), till only one was left to see him carried away, so Jesus is to leave his disciples behind as he marches on to the exalted desolation of the cross. Like Abraham, he goes out, but, unlike him, knows where he is going, and his face is set like a flint to go to Jerusalem (the phrase appears to be taken from 2 Kings 12[17], where Hazael set his face to go to Jerusalem, to destroy, as Jesus did so to save; there is another parallel in Isa. 50[7]). The hardening of his purpose is brought out more and more clearly as these chapters go on; the shadow cast by the cross has now begun to fall between Jesus and his disciples. Earlier in the chapter Jesus has challenged them "to take up their cross daily" (see the notes on 9[18-27] for this phrase) and share his supreme adventure; already it is clear that none of them will really do so.

The Transfiguration. The same idea is present in the transfiguration scene (9[28-36]). Jesus is talking with Moses and *Elijah* about "the departure (mg.), which he was about to accomplish at Jerusalem," and as he does so the look of his face becomes different ("was altered"), while a cloud parts him from his three friends, "and they feared as they entered into the cloud." The reference to the events of Passion night is unmistakable. Those who will follow him now must expect no settled home, as Jesus could never "lay his head" to rest till he bent it on the cross (9[58]; cf. Jn. 19[30]—"he bent his head," the same words); they must not go back, even on the most necessary business; they must not even *look* back (v. 62). Over the whole section there broods the sense of urgency. As a matter of fact, Jesus does not go straight to Jerusalem; one's conclusion must be that these passages come from someone who had left all to follow Jesus, upon whose mind the challenge had made an indelible impression.

The Charge to the Seventy. Much of the charge to the seventy missionaries in ch. 10 follows lines suggested by other gospel material, but we may notice "salute no man on the way" (v. 4). Salutations in the East take a long time, and the king's business requires haste. If the suggestion made in the commentary (at v. 18) is right, the words of Jesus on their return deepen our sense of his growing isolation. While they had been enjoying their easy successes over "all the power of the enemy" (v. 19) he, whose powers had made such victories possible, had been watching Satan "fallen like [destructive] lightning from heaven." Their immunity from hurt by "all the power of the enemy" was to be won by his surrender to it, for "he saved others; he could not save himself." But he soon forgets his own sorrow in contemplation of the triumph he was winning for these "baby-minds" (v. 21), in rejoicing that things hidden from men of wise and quick perception were now to be revealed to these simple friends of his, who, little knowing what it would cost, were embarked with him in his great adventure.

The Parable of the Good Samaritan. This parable (10[25-37]) further defines the nature of the campaign which Jesus is undertaking in his journey to Jerusalem. He, like the good Samaritan, is shortly to undertake "a business-journey" (see commentary on the word translated "as he journeyed" in 10[33]) along the road from Jericho to Jerusalem which had earned the name "the ascent of blood" from its sinister associations. Again, like the good Samaritan, he was in haste to fulfill his mission (cf. 12[50]). But he too was delayed on the road by his compassion for the lost, the victims of the world's carelessness or cruelty. Neither priest nor Levite could stop to succor the publican and sinner—they were so busy with their engagements or so careful of their security—but he could not pass, and, while he lingered, was himself overtaken. This is the Gospel of the road to the cross.

We are to carry on his work of rescue; he was the stranger—"a Samaritan" was one of the names they gave him (Jn. 8[48])—who proved himself our "neighbor" at such a cost; we must prove ourselves neighbors in a world rapidly becoming as hostile to our faith as it was to him, and prove it in the same way.

The Parable of the Friend at Midnight. The next considerable block of Lucan material is to be found in 11[5-8], the parable of the friend at midnight. If this "acceptable year of the Lord" is rapidly drawing to a close, if the sands are running out, all the more need that those who are to share with Jesus this business of redemption should put forth all their powers. If they could not themselves rescue the fallen, they must pray with the persistence of the man who will not stop knocking at his neighbor's door, in his impatience to supply his friend's wants. Our pity for the lost and broken should make us "shameless" in the instancy of our prayer.

11[27, 28]. Here a woman in the crowd sentimentalizes over Jesus. He keeps sternly to the point; this is no time for personalities, good or bad; his only real friends are those who hear and vigilantly treasure God's command and are heart and soul with him in this business.

11[29-54]. The rest of the chapter, most of which is common to Matthew and Luke, emphasizes the responsibility of the generation who were fated to live at such a time of crisis, and the need for an instant and complete surrender to his own claim. Those who are not energetically with him are against him. They can do only one of two things with such a one as he: either follow him, or crucify him. Scribes who taught the people that the whole duty of man consisted in a meticulous attention to ritual, in superficial purifications, were hindering, not helping; they were taking away "the key of knowledge" (v. 52), for they at least might have known better.

The Dangers of Wealth and Self-centered Ease. Ch. 12 follows in the same strain. The parable of the rich fool (vv. 14–21) is directed against all those whose ideal in life is to secure some kind of property and then settle down to enjoy it alone, letting the tiresome world go by. Jesus will not be a divider of property; the whole question of the rights or wrongs of property-owning is brushed impatiently aside as irrelevant to the real business of men in times like those. "They are asking for *you*" (v. 20), God, by the lips of Jesus, said to that generation, and he still says it to this. The only question that matters is not "How much do you own?" but "How much will you give?" Seek first his kingdom, and necessaries at least will come your way; seek first to keep yourself alive, and your soul will die. Sooner or later, *you* will be wanted, and, if you have locked yourself up, the summons will find you dead amid all your plenty; even the things you have stored up for yourself will then go back into the common stock. Whether it be health of mind and body or the salvation of your soul, you can only secure it by risking it in the business you were made for, the service of the age you live in. "The little flock," the few who had thrown in their lot with Jesus, had no reason to fear the future (v. 33); if the possession of material goods made them unwilling or afraid to venture, better get rid of them; the only strong rooms that could not be broken into, the only purses that would never wear into holes were in God's treasure house; the only coins banked there were deeds and prayers of brotherly compassion. So, with loins girt and lanterns burning, they were to be "like men looking for their Lord," who prove their readiness for his coming and earn promotion by providing for the needs of the other members of his household (v. 42); their reward will be that he will provide for their needs himself (v. 37). After the parable of the slave who exploited his position of trust and tyrannized over the domestic staff (vv. 45f., found also in Mt. 24[45-51]) Jesus points out that the greater the responsibility—and what responsibility could be greater than that of the men who lived with and listened to him?—the more exacting would be God's requisition (vv. 47, 48). Then the impatience of Jesus to set the world on fire with his own passion of love to God and pity for men sweeps over him again. The early dreams of peace and good will (2[14]) have faded now; there can be no peace so long as the times are what they are, and he is what he is. Men and women must take sides; families will be divided. Cannot they read the signs of the time? The best, the only thing for discerning men to do is to cut themselves away from all entanglements, to cut their losses and settle their feuds; otherwise they will be caught in the toils of a justice which will exact the last penny of loss and suffering from those who dally with minor issues on such a day of grace and of danger as this.

A Call to Repentance and Deeper Insight. In ch. 13 the same challenging appeal is continued. Catastrophes were happening here and there, it was true, but this did not prove their victims specially guilty; unless they all repented, they would all be destroyed. This sweeping prophecy was literally fulfilled less than forty years later. The fig-tree (Jerusalem—see notes on 13[1-9]) might be spared one year longer; Jesus himself would make one last and yet more moving appeal to his Jewish contemporaries; and, if that failed, there was an end of the world as they had known it. While they are making up their minds, however, he can still fulfill his mission. A woman in his congregation has a nervous disorder, and cannot lift herself up (vv. 11f.); she is a "daughter of Abraham" (cf. 19[9]), and therefore has a double claim upon him. She has been bound by Satan for eighteen years, and he cannot wait till the Sabbath is over to set her free. That is what he has come for, to break into the strong man's house, and distribute his spoils (that means, "release his victims"—see 11[22]), and "the better the day, the better the deed." But the message he has come to deliver is no mild and amiable doctrine of universal benevolence; it has the potency of the mustard-seed, the buoyancy and penetrative power of the yeast in the dough (vv. 18–21). In any case, things can never again be as they had been in a country and a world in which such words as his had been spoken, and such deeds as his done.

A Call for Instant Decision. In the next section (13[22-35]), the note of passionate urgency is heard even more resoundingly. We have a picture (v. 24) of men waiting at a closed door and a hand waving them away from the window, of people left out who felt sure of reserved seats, while others who had never had a chance before and come from most unlikely places crowd in. Some of the Pharisees, either with good intentions or because they want to move this uncomfortable prophet on, warn him that Herod, who ruled in Perea as well as in Galilee, is intending to kill him (v. 31). Jesus has no fears of that crafty "fox," and refuses to be hustled (cf. Jn. 7[6]) to suit anyone's convenience. "On the third day"—i.e., very soon—Jesus must take the road again, for Jerusalem is calling him. He cannot rest now till his work is done.

The Table-Talk of Jesus. In 14[1-24] we have an example of the table-talk of Jesus, but the same note, in more subdued tones, can be heard. The people who will not fulfill their engagement to supper have other business and domestic engagements. That was the tragedy of it; the men of that generation were so busy (cf. 17[26-30]). Well, if they would not come in, others would; if the banqueting-hall cannot be filled from the streets and lanes of Judaism, he will go further afield, out into the highways and byways of the great world's life; he is not to be beaten by the obstinacy or preoccupation of any one set of people.

Counting the Cost. In 14[25-35] we are told that in these days Jesus was still being followed by great crowds of people. Passion like his is certain to gain some response, even if the response is only that of easily impressed curiosity. In Perea, as in Galilee, Jesus has a kind of popular success. But he is under no delusion; he warns his crowds of admirers that he cannot now enlist them unless they mean business. He is building a tower of refuge, undertaking a campaign against an enemy numerically stronger than himself (see commentary for a more detailed exposition of vv. 28–32); let those alone follow him now who are prepared to stake everything and bid farewell to all they possess (v. 33).

Three Parables of Losing and Finding. Ch. 15 begins by noting that the audacity of Jesus' claim repels all but "the publicans and sinners," but them it draws the closer; they are not afraid of his demands, because their daily experience had forced home upon them the desperateness of their own condition. Jesus goes on to vindicate his behavior to such people. Some of them were lost outside the fold, others inside the house, but all of them had a place in the family; and, if they were brought back home (the lost sheep), or, in the home, yet not of the home, they were found in the home (the lost coin), all the more if they came back of their own accord (the lost son), the Father would not, could not, refuse to have them in, no matter how many others of the happier children stayed out because they could not endure such disreputable company. Nor can he spend much more time arguing with their critics; they must make up their minds quickly whether they would come in or not, for by and by "the acceptable year" would be over.

The Unjust Steward. Like the unjust steward, people with a place in society are now in a more secure position (ch. 16). Very soon there will be a reversal; there had been signs of such a change for some time (7[29, 30]), but now the tide has turned. From henceforth the first are to be last and the last first (13[30]). The men who had been in possession had mismanaged the estate, and were already under notice of dismissal. What could they do? Let them hasten to make friends of these publicans and sinners. Just for the moment the position which they held so insecurely enabled them, if they would, to earn their gratitude. Like the steward's tenants, for a little while the outcast and the fallen were dependent on their social and religious superiors, but it would not be so for long. Let them use their more fortunate position to make friends (v. 9), so that, if they cannot gain an entrance on their own merits, they may at least have friends in the new world who will be kinder to them than they themselves had ever been in the old days.

"Dives" and Lazarus. The parable of "Dives" and Lazarus (16[19-31]) makes the same suggestion, but much more forcibly. Here were these two living side by side, seeing one another and each hearing the other's voice every day of their lives, "Dives" representing the rich middle and upper-class Jew, rich in possession of "Moses and the prophets" if not in material goods, and Lazarus the poor outcast. The publican was not poor in this world's goods, but his condition was no less pitiful; he was on the threshold of the Jewish Church, yet always just outside. But it would not be so for long; the time would come when Lazarus would be in "Abraham's bosom" (cf. 19[9]), and "Dives" turn would come to be outside. Then, when it was too late, he would claim acquaintance with Lazarus, would realize that he needed the man with whom he would have nothing to do in happier days. And he might have known better; "Moses and the prophets" bade him care for "the stranger within his gates," not to turn away from his own flesh. These publicans and sinners were "his own flesh," children of Abraham like himself, though he would not own them.

A Parable of Service. The first part of ch. 17 is more or less closely parallel to material in the first Gospel, and need not detain us here. However, in vv. 7–10 we have another fragment from Luke's own collections. This little parable is obviously connected by deliberate contrast with 12[37, 38], a contrast brought out in the commentary. Those who are to be the friends of Jesus must be ready to do something more than their bare duty; the emphasis is on the word "commanded" (v. 10); to enter into real fellowship with him it is not enough to be exemplary in conduct, as some of the Pharisees were (18[12]); the self-forgetting or self-abasing surrender of passionate love must permeate the whole relationship if it is to be anything better than that subsisting between slave and master (v. 10, and cf. Jn. 15[14]).

The Grateful Samaritan. The story of the grateful Samaritan further illustrates this point (17[11-19]). The nine Jewish lepers took Jesus literally, punctiliously obeying his command to "show themselves to the priests." The "foreigner" (v. 18, mg.) could not even do what he was told to do until his gratitude had found some vent. So his "faith" saved him (v. 19), and faith is more than mechanical obedience; it is love in action (Gal. 5[6]).

Prophecies of the Fall of Jerusalem. Through the remainder of ch. 17 the note of warning is intensified. Rejecting his last appeal, Jerusalem would soon become a veritable city of destruction. They must escape for their lives, must not return home to secure their most necessary goods, must not even look back, "in that day." Whatever Jesus meant by "the day when the Son of man is revealed" (v. 30), Luke takes him to mean the day of the capture of Jerusalem by the Romans; notice the reference to the "eagles" in v. 37. "That day" was the logical outcome of Passion week.

Two Parables of Prayer. In ch. 18 we have another appeal for persistent prayer. If you cannot be moved to such "shamelessness" by desire to help a needy friend (cf. 11[5-8]), at least for your own soul's sake, now you have been warned of what is coming, storm the gates of heaven with all the instancy of prayer, as a shrewish woman would pester a comfort-loving magistrate because she thinks herself wronged. Why God's own elect should have to suffer with and for their times is a mystery, and God's apparent inability to find an easier way out than such world-catastrophes, as the men of the age to which Jesus came, and such as we have lived through, is a deeper mystery still. All the more, because you cannot fathom the depths of his purpose, you should "pray without ceasing." In v. 8 Jesus seems to be as near despairing of the issue as he ever was before he uttered his cry of desolation on the cross. Was there no one who would hazard all with him in the great adventure? It is a comfort to us to know that he too felt the oppression of our fears for civilization, that his prophecies of doom were not of the "take-it-or-leave-it" type. He bore the burden of our fears for the world as well as all our other burdens.

The one thing which he could not understand was complacency, and so we have, in yet another parable (vv. 9–14), the picture of the Pharisee and the publican at prayer together, yet so far apart; one imprisoned in his own immaculate record—there is no reason to suppose that the claim the Pharisee made for himself was not justified—the other redeemed by nothing but his penitence; the one secure but unreachable, the other with the barriers all down, wide open to redeeming grace.

In the rest of the chapter Luke rejoins the Marcan outline again, and we need only notice the contrast between the children, with whom Jesus was happy because their minds were open still, and the rich ruler or magistrate who, though he professes to want the one thing more, has a mind too rigidly made up to face the ultimate demand.

The Story of Zacchæus. Zacchæus (19^{1-10}), on the other hand, is carried out of himself so completely by the honor done to him by the prophet that he is ready, like Abraham (v. 9), to "go out, not knowing whither he went." Still is the path to the cross lit up for Jesus by his discoveries of the few, lost in the crowd if he had not singled them out, who are ready to hazard all with him.

The Parable of the Pounds. This parable (19^{11-27}) contains yet one more protest against those who, in face of the challenge of a great responsibility, hold fast to what they already have, and will take no kind of risk for fear of losing it (cf. 17^{33}). It contains also a prediction of the fate of the appeal he is about to make to Jerusalem. Though Luke has an independent account (see commentary) of the triumphal entry, his story does not add very much that is relevant to our line of study, nor in the next two chapters (20 and 21) is there much that is not included in the first and second Gospels.

Prophecies of the City's Fall. In 21^{20-36} we have an even more detailed prophecy of the fall of the city; its most important feature is to be found in v. 28, where the word translated "redemption" appears for the first time. Here the Jewish Messianic hope is no longer meant (cf. 2^{38} 24^{21}), but the deliverance of believers from approaching world-catastrophes. By the suffering of the present time only can the Kingdom come. The hope of bringing about a nation-wide act of repentance by preaching the word has passed altogether out of sight; only through struggle and calamity can the new order be brought in (for the same idea in Paul, cf. 2 Cor. 4^{17} and the phrase "fill up what is lacking in the sufferings of Christ," Col. 1^{24}).

The Last Supper. In the first part of ch. 22, Luke is following Mark still, and, especially if vv. 19, 20 are not part of the original text of the Gospel (see commentary), we have nothing distinctively Lucan till we come to v. 21. The reason why Jesus cannot share the loving-cup (vv. 17, 18) is that "the traitor's hand"—as we may read v. 21—is with him on the table. Much as he had looked forward to that evening (v. 15) he was preoccupied, unable to throw himself whole-heartedly into the fellowship. Nor had the Twelve ever been further from understanding him, for they are still disputing as to who was greatest among them. Perhaps Judas was responsible for this unhappy development; he had started the old controversy to cover his own embarrassment, and the others became involved in it without realizing what they were doing. Everything suggests that there were times during the meal when Jesus was unlike himself, silent and remote. There is pathos in the words of v. 28, "ye are they which have continued with me in my temptations (or trials)"; they were not to be with him any longer; his consolation is to think that his loneliness will soon be over now, and to look forward to the consummation when misunderstandings will be forgotten (vv. 28–30). He is the servant, waiting upon the others (v. 27; cf. Mk. 10^{45}); they should be waiting upon him (17^{7-10}), strengthening him against the dark hour so soon to come, but he cannot make them understand, and, if he could, he would not now, for he will not let them see more of his sorrow than they can bear. He finds momentary relief in thinking of them, in praying for Peter through the trial coming to him, in his knowledge that Peter will not fail, and that his recovery will mean that the others will come round too. The Peter who is so soon to deny him is still the rock on which the church is to be built (cf. Mt. 16^{18}); "the gates of hell shall not prevail against it." Meanwhile Jesus must go on his way alone (v. 22); *his* destiny has reached its climax (v. 37). Friend of outcasts as he had been, he is now to be himself an outcast. While his disciples, whom he had striven for so long to win over to share his thoughts, are childishly quarreling about precedence or foolishly planning to defend him with their puny swords (see commentary for the detailed exposition of vv. 35f.), he must meet his darkest hour alone.

The Agony in the Garden. He had come to rouse the sleeping beauty in the men whose love he had given up everything to win, and he has only succeeded in making them all the worse for his coming (Jn. 15^{22}). Hitherto he has been sustained by the certainty of ultimate triumph, but that does not comfort him now, for he cannot forget the people of his own times and nation. Even if one go to them from the dead, they will not be persuaded (16^{31}). Jesus was a true patriot; in Gethsemane he is agonizing in pain and deadly fear for "those who were his own" (cf. Jn. 1^{11} Lk. $23^{28f.}$). As his pain and fear grew to a crisis he prayed yet more desperately, and his sweat became like great clots of blood falling to the ground (v. 44). That it should come to this! The people of his own nation were no worse than those of other times and places—indeed, in some respects they were better—but that *this* people, so laboriously trained, should seal their own doom by murdering Him who had come "to save his people from their sins"! Nor was it merely with the tragedy of tomorrow that Jesus was laboring, for the sorrow of all the ages is being forced through the channels of his soul. He knew how many times it would be repeated! He had warned them, poured out unavailingly his burning compassion and flaming wrath, but it was too late for works of mercy now, too late for anger. There was nothing to do but feel it and be sorry. To the end he will seek to hold despair at arm's length by thinking of the few whom he had won. They are not ready, but he will pray for them when they are too weary and bewildered to pray for themselves (cf. v. 46 and v. 32). Soon it is too late even for this, for Judas is here; there is but time for one last cure (v. 51), one last protest against the stupidity of it all (vv. 52, 53).. It is their "hour indeed, and the triumph of the dark."

Peter's Denial. Peter is in the dark, too; what he was doing between the arrest and his appearance before the fire in Caiaphas' courtyard (22^{54}) we do not know, but we can imagine him stumbling about among the stones of the Kedron ravine with the devil wrestling for his soul. Surely, he had been loyal, but all through these demoralizing months, since Jesus had begun to talk about failure and death, he had lost touch with him, and the surrender in the garden had been the last straw. What could Peter do anyhow? When he did try to defend his Master he was only rebuked for his pains. Loyalty and resentment are fighting a life-and-death battle in his mind, and by the time he reaches the high priest's house he is in no fit state to be seen. The challenge of the serving maid provokes the explosion. Sick of the humiliation into which his association with Jesus has landed him, his one desire is to get back to Galilee away from those mocking townspeople, to do a man's work again in the sun and the air, and try to pretend that he had always been Simon the fisherman. But he cannot get away, for the prayer of Jesus holds him fast. The searching glance (v. 61—the same word is used of our Lord's first sight of Peter in Jn. 1^{42}) does the rest, and Peter's heart is broken.

In the morning we watch the Sanhedrin at cross-purposes with Jesus in the hall of Caiaphas' house. The exact meaning of vv. 67–70 is discussed in the commentary, but, verse by verse, our impression of the widening gulf between Jesus and all the others is deepened. The chief impression we get from Luke's story is that of the futility of it all. Only Jesus is master of himself, for the storm of violent emotion has passed.

The Trial and Crucifixion. The one idea of all the others is to hurry Jesus away; he is sent from Pilate to Herod, and back again to Pilate, mocked and browbeaten, and finally given up to the mob in sheer desperation, because there seemed no other way of getting rid of him (ch. 23). On the way to Calvary Jesus is still thinking of his people's sorrows rather than his own; he is quietly coming to a conclusion, which he expresses in his redeeming prayer (23^{34}). It was too bad to be true; this monstrous delusion could not last forever. If they crucified him, it was only because "they know not what they do." This is his verdict on the tragical history of man. "Hypocrisy"—that men would not be true to themselves—had been his greatest hindrance; in the fact that his murderers were all consciously or unconsciously playing a part he now finds his ground for hope in the dark hour of his fate. Men are not altogether bad when they crucify the Christ, for "an enemy hath done this." His own suffering will break the strong man's power, for he is stronger to endure than Satan is to attack him. He will distribute his spoils, he will set the strong man's captives free ($11^{21, 22}$). True, he could not save his people from the doom that must follow such a deed, for if such things could be done in springtime, what will be the issue when winter comes? (23^{31}.) But the destruction of the Jewish state is not to be the end; these people are more to be pitied than blamed, for they were only doing as they did because they were captives, and his prayer will at long last set them free (cf. Heb. 12^{2}). The dying thief's cry was, we may be sure, a welcome assurance that in their despair his people would turn to him. We are still waiting for the answer to our Saviour's prayer; at least we can be sure that he was not mistaken.

Meanwhile the Gentile soldiers divide between them his garments, while the Jews look on (vv. 34, 35); here is another promise for the future. If the Jews of that generation, spectators then, were fated to be spectators of the world's history for long centuries, that would only mean that he would thus become the Saviour of the Gentiles (cf. Rom. 11^{25} and the same idea in Lk. 21^{24}). Luke omits the cry of despair (Mt. 27^{46} Mk. 15^{34}), and passes on to Jesus' self-committal to his Father; content to leave the problem with him, he falls asleep at last.

The Resurrection. Luke's account of the resurrection is chiefly distinguished by the story of the walk to Emmaus. Jesus is still the stranger (24^{18}) staying "all by himself in Jerusalem," but he is master of every situation and spends the few hours he has with his disciples in tracing out God's age-long purpose, of which his suffering was but a part (vv. 26, 46). Even now, when they would fain appropriate him, he vanishes "out of their sight." Set free from three and thirty years, from a narrow land, from the limitations of space and time, he is setting out upon his conquest of the world. No longer the monopoly of the few, he will only continue to be theirs as they share him with all the others. Even now he does not forget his people; the disciples are to begin at Jerusalem (v. 47). His Holy Spirit their possession, they will be safe, for he has faced and fought through the worst fears that come to men who risk failure and heartbreak for the world's redemption. So, with a last blessing, he is parted from them; as he left Nazareth and Galilee behind, going out and out and out until he is left alone in a region where we cannot follow him even in thought, so now he leaves our little world of time and space behind, "from henceforth serenely waiting till all his enemies fall beneath his feet." His security, so hardly won through a travail we could not share, is ours, for he has given to us his Holy Spirit (v. 49), the power "from on high"—i.e., power won by a victorious, ascended Christ. We are to go out and out and out, as he did (Acts 1^{8}), until, lifted up out of the earth, he draws all men to him. So he who was alone shall become "the firstborn of many brethren."

Literature: On the English text alone, Commentary by Ragg (Westminster Commentaries); Ramsay, *Luke the Physician;* Stanton, *The Gospels as Historical Documents,* pt. 2; Sanday, *The Life of Christ in Recent Research;* M. Jones, *The Four Gospels;* J. A. Findlay, *Jesus as They Saw Him,* pt. 2; Burkitt, *The Gospel History and Its Transmission;* Hayes, *The Most Beautiful Book Ever Written;* Cadbury, *The Making of Luke-Acts.* For students who use Greek, the Commentary on Luke by B.S. Easton will prove of great value.

CHAPTER I

For special interpretative notes on ch. 1 see the introduction, pp. 1025–6.

1–4. The Writer's Aim and Method. In these verses Luke gives us a carefully written preface summarizing his sources of information. With Paul's arrival in Rome, a period of gospel-writing has begun. There have been many attempts in that direction, but Luke is satisfied neither with their completeness nor their accuracy. A Gospel bearing the name of Matthew cannot have been included among the "many," but "eyewitnesses from the beginning" means that Luke had consulted disciples of Jesus. In the Acts he mentions "Mnason, an original disciple," whom he met when traveling from Cæsarea to Jerusalem in Paul's company (21^{16}), and we may think also of Manaen, Herod Antipas' foster-brother (Acts 13^{1}); Joanna, the wife of Chuza, Herod's steward (Lk. 8^{3}); Mary, the mother of Jesus; and John, the son of Zebedee, who is prominent in both the books. Mark is called "the minister of Peter" in early patristic writings, and "those who became ministers of the word" may refer to him. Luke's criticism of earlier writings lays stress upon the fact that they did not tell the story "in order from the beginning"; neither Q nor Mark had a birth-story, whereas Matthew's Gospel has (cf. notes on Mt. 1^{18-25}).

5–25. The Annunciation to Zacharias and Its Consequences. This story must have come from the inner circle in Jerusalem, for it is steeped in Semitic thought and language. Luke is specially interested in John the Baptist, because when he wrote followers of John were common in the East. In the Acts ($18^{24, 25}$) he describes Apollos as "understanding only the baptism of John." The fourth evangelist shows signs of the same concern (Jn. 3^{30}). Apostolic preaching, like Mark's Gospel, began with the baptism of John (Mk. $1^{1, 2}$ Acts 1^{22}); Luke will tell us what led up to his birth.

There were twenty-four *courses* (v. 8) of priests, and they took turns in coming up to Jerusalem for a week's duty in the Temple. The parts individual priests played was decided by lot, and it fell to Zacharias that morning to carry the fire from the altar of burnt-offering, which was outside the Temple proper, to the golden altar of incense in the Holy Place. V. 17 foreshadows our Lord's identification of John with the *Elijah* who was to be at once herald of Messiah's coming and his attendant when he came. The idea that Zacharias was afterward martyred by the Jews is probably due to a mistaken identification of this Zacharias with the Zachariah of Mt. 23^{35}. Along with Jesus and John the Baptist he is venerated by the Mohammedans as an ascetic and holy man.

26–38. The Annunciation to Mary. This intimate account of her experiences may well have come from Mary herself. Luke's interest in the birth-story centers round Mary; in Matthew (1^{18-25}, note) the story is told rather from Joseph's point of view. *The Most High* (vv. 32, 35) is a reverent evasion of the name of God, which was too sacred to be uttered when it could be avoided. So "in the presence of the angels" (15^{10}), "Heaven" (15^{21}), "who art in heaven" (Mt. 6^{9}), "the Power" (Mk. 14^{62}), all stand for "God." The picture of Mary's innocent and serene submission is as beautiful as it is convincing. (See further p. 957; and on the question of the virgin birth, see art., *The Life of Jesus Christ*, p. 891.)

39–56. **The Magnificat.** One of the characteristic marks of Luke's Gospel is its emphasis on *praise*, and this note pervades the birth-story. In addition to the Magnificat and the Benedictus, we have the angel's song, while the shepherds (2^{20}), Simeon (2^{28}) and Anna join in the chorus (cf. also 4^{15} $5^{25, 26}$ 7^{16} 8^{56} 9^{43} $11^{27f.}$ $13^{13, 17}$ 17^{18} 19^{37} 24^{53} Acts 4^{21}, etc.). The Magnificat should be ascribed to Elizabeth, not Mary, for the best reading in v. 46 is "and *she* said," not "and Mary said." It was Elizabeth whose "reproach"—that of childlessness—was taken away. Her hymn is modeled on Hannah's song (1 Sam. $2^{1f.}$); she also had been a childless wife. Like Hannah, Elizabeth shows a certain animus against the rich and well-fed. Luke himself shared this feeling; it was the one thing he had in common with the simple people who welcomed the new-born Jesus into their arms. Jesus did not long for the overthrow of the rich; he was sorry for them rather than resentful against them. But the old-fashioned folk among whom he was born longed for the redress of social inequalities as well as for the redemption of Israel (see also p. 1025, and cf. Jas. $5^{1f.}$).

57–80. **The Birth of John the Baptist.** The name "John" means "Jehovah's gift." He is to be the morning star—this is what is meant by *the dayspring from on high* (v. 78). Cf. Jn. 5^{35} where he is described as "the lamp that burns itself out in giving light," and is put away when the sun rises. In Rev. 22^{16} Jesus is himself the morning star. We may refer here to the fact that Luke lays continual emphasis upon the person and work of the Holy Spirit ($1^{41, 67}$ $2^{26, 27}$ 3^{22} $4^{1, 14, 18}$ 11^{13} 12^{12} 24^{49}). With the exception of 11^{13} 12^{12} these references cease altogether when the ministry of Jesus has well begun until after the resurrection. If we compare 12^{12} with 21^{15}, it would seem that, as the Passion draws near, Jesus himself has taken the place of the Holy Spirit. (Cf. Edwin Lewis, *Manual of Christian Beliefs*, ch. 10.) This fact should be studied in connection with Jn. 7^{39}; there "glorified" means "crucified." Luke never uses the phrase "the Spirit of God" (cf. Mt. 12^{28} Lk. 11^{20}).

CHAPTER II

For special interpretative notes on ch. 2, see the introduction, pp. 1025–6.

1–7. **The Birth of Jesus.** Jn. 7^{42} suggests that our Lord's descent from David and his birth at Bethlehem were not generally known at Jerusalem. There is no hint in Matthew or Luke that Mary also was descended from David, unless the fact that she went up to Bethlehem to be enrolled may be thought to suggest this. Jesus was not son of Joseph in any but a legal sense, so that his descent from David might be regarded as doubtful if it were not for the unanimous testimony of N.T. writers (cf. Mt. 1^{1} Lk. 2^{4} Rom. 1^{3} Heb. 7^{14} Rev. 22^{16}). Jesus seems not to have been enthusiastic about it, if we may judge from Mk. 12^{37}, even if he did not repudiate it.

"There was no room for them in the living-room" (v. 7) is a better translation than "inn." It was a foretaste of the Lord's experience throughout his earthly ministry (cf. 9^{58}). Nothing is said about an *inn*-stable; by the "stable" is meant the entrance to one of the village houses, in which the animals are tethered in rough weather. On each side of the steps leading up to the living-room, which is on a higher level and further inside, a pit dug in the floor contains the animal's food. These are the *mangers;* we must think of Mary as giving birth to Jesus in a narrow space near the cottage door, while up the steps the people to whom the house belonged were living as usual. The very early tradition that the birth of Jesus took place in a cave may be correct, for many Syrian peasants still live in mere holes in the rock.

8–20. **The Shepherds and the Angels' Song.** Jesus cannot have been born at Christmas; Bethlehem is generally intensely cold at the end of December, and no shepherds could have been "watching over their flocks by night" then. In the winter the flocks are taken into sheepfolds or caves at night, but in late summer sheep are too languid to feed in the daytime, so the shepherds take them out at night. Everything points to the late summer or early autumn of 7 or 6 B.C. as the date of the birth (see p. 874). In spite of the R.V., the best reading of the angels' song is "Glory to God in the highest, and on earth peace, good will among men." To translate "Among men of his good will" upsets the rhythmical balance of the hymn. The angels' hymn of peace should be compared with the shouts of the disciples at the triumphal entry, "Peace in heaven, and glory in the highest" (19^{38}); and with the words of Jesus, "I came *not* to bring peace on the earth." (See pp. 891–2.)

21–39. The Circumcision of Jesus: Simeon and Anna. Simeon was a Pharisaic quietist who had long been waiting for the *consolation of Israel* (v. 25). Side by side with the man stands the woman, as so often in Luke. We think of the Queen of Sheba and the Ninevites, of Dionysius the Areopagite and Damaris, of Aquila and Priscilla. We also notice Luke's emphasis upon fasting; it is characteristic. *A sign spoken against* (v. 34) recalls the "sign of Jonah" (11^{29}). The clouds are already creeping over the sky (cf. Isa. $8^{14, 15}$). *A sword* (v. 35) is to pass through the heart of Mary too; it is the sword of separation, for by and by she will be tragically sundered from her son (8^{19}). The "Lewis" Syriac version, the oldest translation of the Gospels in any language (see p. 864b), has "Thou shalt cause a sword to pass through thy heart," suggesting that Mary herself was partly responsible. The words "ransom (redemption) of Jerusalem" (v. 38) remind us of a phrase at the other end of the Gospel (24^{21}). For the broader Christian hope of world-redemption Luke uses another word from the same root, best translated "redemption" (21^{28})—see note on that passage.

40. Whereas John grows in strength (1^{80}) Jesus grows in "wisdom and charm," for *charm* is what Luke means here by the word translated "grace." Cf. 2^{40} 2^{52} 4^{22} ("charming words"); 6^{33} 7^{42} ("he charmingly forgave them both").

41–52. The Visit to the Temple. His first visit to the Temple was for Jesus an exhilarating adventure. When he entered the city as an adult his impressions were less favorable, and found issue in a whip of small cords (Jn. 2^{15}). His words in v. 49 may be translated "engaged in my Father's business," or "in my Father's house," or "among my Father's people." The company of the men who spent their leisure in Bible-study must have been delightful to the eager boy, who had perhaps found visiting preachers at Nazareth disappointing. The rabbis too were pleased with him; what was disturbing in a grown man was amusing in a boy. Josephus tells us a similar story about himself! The tone of Mary's expostulation suggests that she was already finding her Son beyond her; Luke sympathizes intensely with her, as in that sadder scene when she comes to fetch him home (8^{19}). Jesus understands, and goes back to Nazareth until his time should come; Joseph has fallen into the background. This narrative must have come from Mary herself, like that of the visit of Gabriel ($1^{28f.}$) and of the shepherds (2^{19}); in two of the three cases Luke adds, "she kept all these things in her mind." Already Jesus speaks of God as his Father; all the same, he goes back to Nazareth, and all we are told of his life in his teens is that he was more popular than ever.

CHAPTER III

1–20. The Ministry and Imprisonment of John Baptist. See notes on Mt. 3^{1-12} 14^{1-12} Mk. 1^{1-8} 6^{17-29}. Peculiar to Luke in this section are vv. 1, 2, 5, 6, 10–15, 19, 20—vv. 10–15 evidently coming from L (see intro., p. 1023). Luke puts the ministry of Jesus in its world-setting, and continues the quotation from Isa. 40 until he gets the universalistic note (v. 6). As he tells of the experiment in voluntary communism made by the first Christians in Jerusalem (Acts $2^{43f.}$), he is glad to recall the fact that John bade his converts share the necessaries of life (v. 11). *Publicans and soldiers* (vv. 12, 14) were associated in daily life, for the taxgatherer was so unpopular that a military guard was needed for his protection. Jesus and John alike were successful with publicans and soldiers.

Other points to be noticed are: (1) Luke makes John call not merely the Pharisees and Sadducees (Mt. 3^{7}) "generation of vipers" (v. 7), i.e., "children of the devil," but the "crowds"; his dislike of crowds peeps out here; (2) he puts the blame for the imprisonment of John, as for his murder (9^{9}), on Herod, not Herodias (v. 19). The almost unanimous conclusion of critics is that the original reading of v. 16 in Q was, "I baptize you in water . . . he shall baptize you in fire." Mark interpreted "fire" as "Holy Spirit," and Matthew and Luke combine Mark and Q.

21–38. The Baptism and Genealogy of Jesus. See notes on Mt. 1^{1-17} Mk. 1^{9-11}. Luke says it was when Jesus *was praying* that heaven was opened; he brings out the fact that Jesus prayed at all the crises of his life (cf. 5^{16} 6^{12} $9^{18, 28, 29}$ 11^{1} $22^{31f.}$). The three parables on prayer are all peculiar to Luke ($11^{5f.}$ $18^{1f.}$ $18^{9f.}$) and so are the two prayers on the cross ($23^{34, 46}$). The words "in bodily form" (v. 22) are found in Luke alone, and informed opinion seems to favor the Western reading of the voice from heaven: "Thou art my Son; this day have I begotten thee." This reading was altered to harmonize with the other Gospels, and also because it encouraged the Adoptionist heretics, i.e., the men who thought of his baptism as the birthday of the divine in Jesus.

The *genealogy*, which is tacked on rather

awkwardly to the story of the baptism, is chiefly remarkable because, unlike Matthew, Luke traces the pedigree of Jesus back, not merely to Abraham, but to Adam and to God. *Beginning to be about thirty years old* (v. 23) is a strange phrase, suggesting, if the reading is correct, that Luke was not quite sure how old Jesus was. He must have been over thirty, if he was born in 6 B.C., and the Baptism is to be dated 26 A.D. Luke has evidently an independent story of the Baptism of Jesus (L), to which a genealogy was attached.

CHAPTER IV

1–13. The Temptation. See notes on Mt. 4:1-11 Mk. 1:12, 13. Here Matthew and Luke are keeping step, the order of the last two temptations being reversed, Luke following the order of Q, and Matthew improving the dramatic sequence of the story. Jesus is tempted to use his divine power to maintain himself in comfort (the first temptation) or to advertise his mission (the third in Luke's order). He rejects both suggestions in words taken from Deuteronomy, words which apply to all God's children. Then, the tempter suggests, if he will not overbear men by divine power, the only course left open is that of human compromise. Jesus will accept neither alternative, and so chooses the way of the cross. The last words of v. 13 should be rendered "until his opportunity." Satan returned to the charge in Peter's well-meant protest (omitted by Luke), in the taunting cries of enemies, when Jesus was crucified (23:35). His claims to world-empire are stated more strongly in Luke than in Matthew (cf. Lk. 4:6 Mt. 4:9); we cannot be sure that he has not an independent account of the temptation, as of the baptism.

14–30. The Sermon at Nazareth. (Mt. 13:53-58, notes on Mk. 6:1-6.) Here a story from L gives a very appropriate setting to a saying from Q: "No prophet is acceptable in his own country." Rendel Harris thinks that the "Targum"—an Aramaic translation of the Hebrew O.T.—was read in the synagogue at Nazareth. The extant Targum reads: "The spirit of *prophecy* is upon me, because *it has brought me* up to preach the gospel to poor people." If that was the text of Isa. 61:1 which Jesus read, we can understand the sequence of the narrative better. "He says," the people of Nazareth would be thinking, "the spirit of prophecy has brought him up. We know where he was brought up—at the carpenter's along the road!" One of the "unwritten" sayings of Jesus (sayings, i.e., not found in the Gospels) discovered at Oxyrhyncus reads, "A doctor does not work cures on those who know him well"; it sounds genuine, and fits in here. "Doubtless," says Jesus, "you will be saying to me: 'Prophet, preach at home! Doctor, heal yourself'. . . . But no prophet gets a hearing among his own people; no doctor can cure the people who know him well!" After his barren visit to Nazareth, Jesus most reluctantly, we may be sure, cut his connections with the village of his boyhood; so far as we know, he never returned. Mary apparently was not at the service which ended so tragically; she held aloof, and we can only imagine what her thoughts were.

See further on vv. 18–27, the introduction, p. 1025b,

31–44. The Ministry in Galilee. See notes on Mt. 8:14-17 4:23-25 Mk. 1:21-39. Luke here inserts from Mark an account of the lakeside ministry of Jesus. (See Mk. 1:21f.) The doctor's hand is visible in the more accurate description of Peter's mother-in-law's complaint—it was malaria. In v. 44 we read in the best MSS., "in the synagogues of Judæa" (not "Galilee"—see R.V., mg.). *Judæa* here stands for the whole of Palestine (cf. 7:17 23:5). Luke comes from Syria, and does not divide up Palestine as Palestinians did and still do.

CHAPTER V

1–11. The Call of Peter and of the Sons of Zebedee. See also notes on Mt. 4:18-22 Mk. 1:16–20; intro., p. 1026. Here Luke leaves Mark to give an alternative version (from L) of the call of the first disciples, his custom being to give us layers of information from his different sources. The order of L was baptism, temptation, sermon at Nazareth, call of Peter. But into this scheme he has fitted rather awkwardly an account of preaching by the lakeside taken from Mark. In Mark, the call of Peter comes before the account of ministry by the lake (1:16f.) and long before the visit to Nazareth (6:1f.); whereas in Luke the people at Nazareth talk about the mighty works he has been doing in Capernaum, before his first visit to Capernaum has been mentioned! (4:23, 31.) It is impossible to reconcile Luke's account of Peter's call with Mark's much simpler narrative. In Mk. 1:16f. Peter is fishing by himself; in Lk. 5:3f. he has been fishing all night from a boat with the others. The similarity of Luke's story with the post-resurrection narrative of Peter's second call, in Jn. 21:15f. (notes), tempts a conjecture that Luke has heard of the later incident, but was not aware that it took place *after the resurrection.* Mark has the right of way here, for he gives us Peter's own account, and the latter's

"Depart from me, for I am a sinful man, Lord" (5[8]), is more probable after the denial than long before it. *Launch out into the deep* (5[4]) reminds us of "Follow me" (Jn. 21[19]), and *the nets were breaking* (5[6]) of "the nets were not broken" (Jn. 21[11]); but there is a transition from *catching men alive* (5[10]) to feeding lambs and sheep (Jn. 21[15-17]) which makes one hesitate.

12–39. The Ministry in Galilee Continued. See notes on 4[31-44] Mt. 8[1-4] 9[1-17] Mk. 1[40-45] 2[1-22]. Luke is here following Mark again (see Mk. 1[35-39]). Notice his emphasis on our Lord's habit of solitary prayer (v. 16) and his description of Peter's one-roomed peasant's cottage as having tiles in the roof, like a Roman villa (v. 19). He is not familiar with housing conditions in the cottages of the poor by the lake of Galilee (cf. Mk. 2[4]). Luke alone is our authority for the statement that Levi *left all* (v. 28), and the words "to repentance" (v. 32) are peculiar to him (see also intro., p. 1026). For other instances of Luke's emphasis upon *the need for repentance* see 6[48] ("he dug and went deep"); 9[62] 13[1f., 8, 24] ("agonize"); 14[26] ("yes, and himself too") [30, 33] 15[7, 10, 18, 21] 16[30] 17[4, 32] 18[13] (cf. 7[38] 5[8]); 19[8, 9] Acts 3[19] 9[35] 15[19], etc.—all found in this form in Luke only. Other points at which Luke breaks away from Mark are as follows; for "in that day" (Mk. 2[20]) he has "in those days" (v. 35)—the institution of Lent is based on this Gospel; and for Mark's "fast" (2[19]) he has "make them fast" (v. 34). But the most important variation comes in v. 39. Jesus understood the prejudices of old-fashioned people; he was a radical and a conservative in one.

CHAPTER VI

1–11. The Ministry in Galilee Continued. (Mt. 12[1-14], notes on Mk. 2[23-28] 3[1-6].) The correct reading in v. 1 is *a sabbath*, not the obscure "second sabbath after the first" of A.V. A scribe wrote in the margin of an early copy "first" before "sabbath"; then another scribe corrected "first" to "second," and later copyists, unable to discover which was right, wrote "second-first." Between vv. 5 and 6 the Western MSS. read: "On the same day he saw a man working on the sabbath, and said to him, 'Man, if thou knowest what thou art doing, blessed art thou; but, if thou knowest not, thou art accursed and a transgressor of the law.'" This fragment shows signs of Luke's style, and may have been left out as offending the susceptibilities of sabbatarians. It is in accordance with the spirit of Jesus (cf. Rom. 14[5, 6]).

12–16. Choosing the Twelve. See notes on Mt. 10[1-4] Mk. 3[13-19]. For the list of the Twelve, Luke may have had an independent authority, for he differs somewhat from Matthew-Mark. Jesus spends the night in prayer before choosing them. When we come to the list itself we notice the name of "Judas of James" (i.e., "the brother of James") between Simon the Zealot (Matthew-Mark "Cananean") and Judas Iscariot. As the apostle whom the MSS. of Matthew-Mark variously call "Thaddæus" or "Lebbæus" is not in Luke's list, we may take it that "Judas of James" is the same person. The "Judas, not Iscariot" of Jn. 14[22] helps to support Luke's accuracy here. Judas was probably his name and Lebbæus (which reminds us of Levi), or Thaddæus, his nickname. "Zealot" means political extremist; zealots as a party are not mentioned till the eve of the fall of Jerusalem, but the tendency to direct action against the government appears much earlier, and the second Simon's nickname labels him as of that way of thinking. Possibly the name "Iscariotes" (Western text, "Scariotes") is to be explained in the same way, for "sicarii" (translated "assassins") are mentioned in Acts 21[38] and they also were active during the last agonies of the siege. The names "Simon," "Judas," and "James" also occur (Mk. 6[3]) among the brothers of Jesus; they may have been so, and this would account for certain jealousies, if comparative outsiders, like Peter, James, and John, seemed to be favored at their expense.

17–49. The Sermon on the Level Place. See notes on Mt. 5[1-12, 38-48] 7[1-5, 12, 16-27]. Here we leave Mark again for Q and L. Luke follows Mark as far as v. 19, except for the mention of the "level place," but in v. 20 we come to *beatitudes* corresponding to those found in Mt. 5[1f]. Three points of difference should be noticed: (1) In Matthew, the sermon is delivered on the mountain, whereas Luke says that Jesus came down to the level place; (2) in Matthew, Jesus goes *up* to get away from the crowds; in Luke he comes *down* to meet them; (3) in Matthew, there are eight beatitudes, in Luke four beatitudes and four woes. Under the first and second headings there is no serious discrepancy. The "mountain" is the hill that rises behind the site of Capernaum; there is a level place about two thirds of the way up; Jesus went up to the top for privacy with his disciples, then came down to meet the crowds. The sermon on the level place is a kind of manifesto, that on the mountain-top a confidential talk to his Twelve. We may accept the general scheme just outlined and yet be doubtful whether the whole of Mt. 5–7 was delivered on the mountain, or the whole of Lk. 6[20-49] on the level place.

Comparison with Mt. 5–7. If the main body of Mt. 5–7 and Lk. 6^{20-49} comes from Q, we must pick out from Luke what does not occur in Matthew. (1) First come *the four woes* (vv. 24–26); they must come from L, and, if so, have an early tradition behind them. (2) Whereas Matthew has "*the* poor *in spirit*," "*they* that are hungry *and thirsty for righteousness*," Luke has "*ye* that are poor *now*," "*ye* that are hungry *now*," "*ye that weep now*" (Matthew "*they that mourn*"), "*for the Son of man's sake*" (Matthew "for *righteousness'* sake")—the words peculiar to each Gospel are in italics. Q probably had "blessed are the poor, the hungry, the mourners," etc.; Matthew's additions are meant as explanations of the words "the poor," etc., whereas Luke takes them literally. The woes are inspired by pity rather than indignation (cf. the parable of Dives and Lazarus, which also comes from L). (3) V. 34, part of v. 35 ("lend, hoping for nothing again," or "despairing of no one") and v. 38 come from L. (4) In v. 29 the picture is that of forcible seizure of a garment on the road; in Mt. 5^{40}, on the other hand, the action takes place in a law-court; hence in Luke the upper garment is snatched away, and the undergarment is to be surrendered voluntarily, while in Matthew the undergarment, the absence of which would not be so much noticed as the unfortunate man left the court, is sacrificed first, and the upper garment is to follow. (5) In Mt. $5^{46, 47}$ we have "What reward have you?" and "What do ye extra?" in Luke, twice over, "What grace have ye?" In v. 35c comes Luke's characteristic "graceless" (not in Matthew), and in v. 40 "everyone who is perfected" (also Luke only); in Mt. 10^{25} we are led to think of patience under hard conditions, in Luke of positive achievement. (6) Again in vv. 47–49 (cf. Mt. 7^{24-27}) Luke has in mind North Syrian conditions (great rivers and river floods), Matthew the Palestinian wadi, dry for the greater part of the year, but in the rainy season the bed of a raging torrent. Matthew is much more racy of Palestinian soil. (7) In the whole passage Luke has consistently emphasized differences in social conditions and their promised redress; Matthew thinks that Jesus refers to the humble and dissatisfied, as contrasted with the proud and complacent, Luke thinks that he refers to the poor and hungry, as compared with the rich and well-fed. (8) The Jesus depicted by Luke has no animus against laughter (v. 25) for no Gospel so charmingly expresses his happy humor. But in the sunniest parables, tears are never far away; there is more laughter, but there is also more weeping in this Gospel than in the others. For hilarious joy, see 1^{44} 6^{23} ("leap," Luke only); 10^{21} ("exulted," Luke only); $15^{7, 10, 24, 25}$. Notice the contrast between the right (15^{24}) and the wrong kind of revelry (12^{19} 16^{19}); for tears, cf. $6^{21, 25}$ $7^{13, 38, 44}$ 19^{41} 23^{27}. (9) In 6^{20-49} we have a picture of abounding generosity abundantly rewarded (v. 38) not only by God, but in the long run by men as well. "Ask, and it shall be given you" (Matthew); "*give, and it shall be given you, pressed down, shaken together, and running over*" (Luke only; cf. Acts 20^{35}).

Matter found in Mt. 5–7 in one solid block lies scattered in Luke, not only here, but in 8^{16} $11^{2-4, 9-13, 33-36}$ $12^{22-34, 58, 59}$ 13^{24-27} $14^{34, 35}$ $16^{13, 16-18}$; the presence of the pointless "but" in 6^{27} means that Luke has omitted from Q the contrast with the law of Moses developed in Mt. $5^{21f.}$, but has forgotten to drop the "but" which depends for its force upon that contrast; the omission is due to the fact that it would not be interesting to Theophilus.

CHAPTER VII

1–10. The Centurion's Servant. See notes on Mt. 8^{5-13} Jn. 4^{46-54}. In v. 1 is the only occurrence in Luke of a formula five times repeated in Mt. 7^{28} 11^{1} 13^{53} 19^{1} 26^{1}. It came from Q and separated the sermon from the story of the centurion. This was one of the only two narratives found in Q, if we do not count the temptation (see p. 872a), the other being the healing of a man possessed by a dumb demon (11^{14}; cf. Mt. 12^{22}). The centurion would be in the police service of Herod Antipas; his synagogue is now being reconstructed out of its ruins at Tell-Hum, the most likely site of Capernaum. The stones, some of which weigh five tons, are so elaborately carved that they cannot be dated later than the first century (A.D.), for after that the rabbinic schools at Tiberias insisted that no new synagogues should be built with figures of animals carved in stone. The appearance of the Roman eagle over the porch suggests that a Roman was the builder. He must have been a wealthy man, for the synagogue was large and most elaborately decorated; in police administration opportunities for the acquisition of wealth were many; then as now Matthew makes the man approach Jesus himself; in Luke he appeals by deputies, and, after sending them, is seized with further scruples, and sends more emissaries. The servant knew of the appeal to Jesus, and his faith helped the cure (but cf. p. 925–6).

11–17. The Widow of Nain. This story, unlike the last, comes from L. "Soon afterward" (v. 11) hints that Luke is not quite sure when it happened. Nain was not in Galilee proper; its modern equivalent, Nein, lies on one of the hills which border the plain of Esdrælon to the southeast, and overlook its narrow outlet toward Jezreel and the Jordan Valley. The death of a widow's grown-up son was regarded as the greatest possible misfortune, and the "whole city" was expressing its sympathy. Nain would be a tiny village, but all Luke's villages are "cities." A bier was "unclean," but Jesus ignores this, and touches it, as he touched the leper (5^{13}). The miracle rouses the same difficulty as the raising of Jairus' daughter; it is possible that the young man was not really dead, but to suggest such an easy explanation in each case when a dead person is said to have been raised does not settle anything. It is clear that it was believed that Jesus could and did raise the dead. (See art., *Miracles of N.T.*, p. 924a.)

18–35. The Message of John the Baptist, and the Discourse to Which it Gave Occasion. See notes on Mt. 11^{2-19}. Here we are back again in Q, for Matthew and Luke are closely parallel. Typically Lucan touches are to be found in v. 21, "he graced with sight," and the addition of "luxury" to the "glorious apparel" of v. 25. Luke alone tells us that Jesus himself was once clothed in glorious apparel in a king's palace, but then it was in mockery (23^{11}). V. 29 looks like Mt. 21^{32}, but is strangely different. According to Matthew, "publicans and harlots go into the Kingdom before the Pharisees"; in Luke "the publicans justified God, being baptized with the baptism of John, but the Pharisees and the lawyers" (i.e., "scribes" of Matthew-Mark; Theophilus would have taken "scribes" to mean "clerks") "set at naught the counsel of God as regards themselves, not being baptized by him." Luke is here in a difficulty with his sources. The Old Syriac reading, "justified themselves in God's sight," appears to harmonize better with 10^{29} ("wishing to justify himself"; cf. also 16^{15} 18^{14}). Luke uses Pauline expressions, like "grace" and "justify," not quite in the Pauline sense. In v. 32, "weep" for the "beat your breasts" of Mt. 11^{17} (mg.) is Lucan and Greek. In v. 35 Luke has "children," Matthew (11^{19}) "works"; again we have a variant translation of a common Aramaic original, for in Semitic language the ideas of works and children lie very close together.

36–50. The Anointing of Jesus in Simon's House. See also intro., p. 1026. This story is distinct from that of the Bethany anointing in Passion-week (Mt. 26^{6-16}, notes on Mk. 14^{3-9} Jn. 12^{1-11}; not given in Luke). It is inserted here to illustrate the saying from Q about Jesus as the friend of publicans and sinners. We must, of course, ascribe it to L. In this Gospel only are we told that Jesus went to dinner not only with publicans, but also with Pharisees (cf. 11^{37} 14^{1}). There is no valid reason for the identification of this woman either with Mary Magdalene (8^{2}) or with Mary of Bethany. The phrase "out of whom seven demons had gone" (8^{2}) does not imply that Mary Magdalene had lived a specially sinful life, and the traditional use of her name to denote a "fallen" woman is a libel upon her. The fact that the host in Galilee was Simon the Pharisee, and at Bethany the host was, according to Mark-Matthew (not John), "Simon the leper" has led to the suggestion that the two stories are different versions of the same incident, or that this Galilæan woman was Mary of Bethany, who repeated her act twice. Probably Mark had heard parts of both stories, but did not know that there were two; from the Galilæan story of the anointing he got the host's name, from the Judæan that it took place at Bethany. He knew of a Simon who had been a leper at Bethany, and of his relations with Jesus, and jumped to the conclusion that he was the host in question. (Jn. 12^{2} says nothing about Simon.) Luke takes this Galilæan story from L; when he gets to the place in Mark where the anointing at Bethany comes he quite naturally omits it because he has already told a similar story.

Jesus was reclining in the lowest place, nearest to the door; there was no back to his couch and anyone looking in through the open door would see the feet of its occupant tucked up underneath him. The woman had been looking for Jesus; he had been her best friend, and she had something for him. So she slips in, bends over his dusty feet, washes them with her tears, and dries them with her unbound hair, afterward drenching them in scent which she had brought in a flask hidden under her cloak. By this time Simon has noticed what is going on at the other end of the room and calls his neighbor's attention to it. Jesus then gives him a lesson in courtesy, using the poor woman as his example. At first the parable does not seem to fit. We should have expected "she is forgiven, because she loved." But that misses the point. Both Simon and the woman are forgiven, for "he charmingly forgave them both" if v. 42 may be so applied. But the value of God's forgiveness depends upon the reception it receives. Jesus is not comparing Simon's sins with the woman's but Simon's ingratitude with her abandon of grateful love. Simon appreciated neither his own sin nor God's free grace.

CHAPTER VIII

1–3. The Women Who Supported Jesus. (See also intro., p. 1027.) This fragment (from L) informs us how Jesus and his disciples were maintained. Mary Magdalene had been possessed by *seven demons.* J. Weiss thinks that the phrase means that she had had six relapses; perhaps we should think of recurrent attacks of hysteria. *Chuza* was a highly placed official; we know nothing about him from other sources. One other prominent figure at Herod's court became a Christian (Manaen—Acts 13[1]); perhaps Chuza was himself sympathetic, as were several other aristocrats (cf. Jn. 18[16]). In any case, women brought up in official circles enjoyed as much liberty as American women do to-day. Joanna was probably one of Luke's informants (see 24[10] with note).

4–18. The Parable of the Sower and Other Sayings. See notes on Mt. 13[1-23]. The entire section is found in Mk. 4[1-25] (notes); the fact that 8[16] is a "doublet" of 11[33f.], which comes from Q, shows that Luke sometimes gives the same saying from two sources, as Matthew commonly does. The setting by the lakeside, common to Matthew-Mark, is omitted, and in v. 10 a quotation from Isa. 6[9, 10], again common to Matthew-Mark, is cut short. Luke is too conscientious to drop it altogether, but he does not care for it, though he gives it at full length in Acts 28[26f]. There it is directed against the Jews in general, and sums up the history of their rejection and the entrance of the Gentiles into the Kingdom. *With patience* (or "in endurance," v. 15) is a typically Lucan addition, and in the phrase *an honest* (or "perfect") and *good heart* we have the Greek expression for a perfect gentleman. We notice also "*how* you hear" (v. 18) for "*what* you hear" (Mk. 4[24]); Luke lays great stress on the ways in which different people respond to the responsibility of hearing; some hear with the ear, others listen with the mind (cf. 16[6] 9[44] 7[1]—"in the ears of the people"; 2[19, 51] Acts 2[14], etc.).

19–56. The Galilæan Ministry Continued. See notes on Mt. 12[46-50] 8[23-34] 9[18-26] Mk. 3[31-35] 4[35-41] 5[21-43]; cf. p. 1024a. From Mk. 4 Luke now goes back to Mk. 3[31f.], but the difference between v. 21 and Mk. 3[35] makes one suspect that he has an independent source, especially as he goes to Mk. 4[35] for the next detail in the narrative. He has omitted the parable of the seed growing secretly (Mk. 4[26]) as well as that of the leaven and the mustard-seed, which he inserts from Q at 13[18f]. In v. 24 we have "Master, Master, we perish!" for Mark's "Teacher, carest thou not that we perish?" (in Matthew, "Lord, save! we perish!") and in v. 25 "Where is your faith?" for Mark's "Have ye not yet faith?" In the next story of *the Gerasene demoniac* (vv. 26f.) Luke interprets Mark's "out of the country" (5[10]) as meaning "out of the inhabited earth," and so he has "into the abyss" (i.e., "back into the underworld," v. 31). "In the whole city" (v. 39) is a strange rendering of Mark's "in Decapolis," for Decapolis is a large district held by ten Greek cities; perhaps he means by "the city" the lakeside Gerasa (modern *Khersa*). To the story of *Jairus' daughter* Luke adds the fact that she was an "only" daughter (v. 42)—so "only" son in 9[38]. "Before all the people" (Luke only, v. 47) emphasizes the courage of the woman. In v. 50 Mark's "Fear not, only go on believing" (5[36]) becomes "One act of faith, and she shall be saved" (such a rendering brings out the change of tense in the Greek). His language has been influenced by the doctrine of salvation by faith (cf. Acts 16[31]). In Luke the formula, "Thy faith hath saved thee," is applied not only to the healing of the body (Mk. 5[34] 10[52]), but also to the forgiveness of sin.

CHAPTER IX

1–6. The Mission-Tours of the Twelve. See notes on 10[1-12] 13[22] Mt. 9[35-38] 10[5-16] Mk. 6[7-13]. Luke has two accounts of mission-tours and two ordination-charges, one addressed to twelve, the other (ch. 10) to seventy. Both narrative and discourse are in ch. 9 based on Mark, in ch. 10 on Q. Luke emends Mark's colloquial "brass" (see the Greek) to "silver" (Mk. 6[8]), tidies up his grammar, and for his "do not wear two undergarments" has "do not possess a change of undergarments" (cf. 3[11]). He did not know that Galilæan peasants wear two undergarments in cold weather. Moreover, in Luke the disciples are *not* to take a staff; here Luke and Matthew agree against Mk. 6[8]; this detail must come from Q. The "wallet" mentioned in all three Gospels is the religious mendicant's collecting-box; they were *not* to take collections at their services. Nor were they to "affect the gentleman"; sandals were worn on the road, slippers carried to be put on in the house. For "shake off the dust from your feet" cf. Acts 13[51].

7–17. Herod Hears of Jesus, Who Retires to Bethsaida and Feeds Five Thousand Men. See notes on Mt. 14[1, 2, 13-21] Mk. 6[14-16, 30-44]. At this point Mark tells of Salome's dancing. Luke gives us no information as to how John the Baptist met his death except that Herod was responsible. He also alters Mark's "John whom I beheaded is risen" (Mk. 6[16]) to "John I beheaded, but who is this?"

In regard to the feeding of the five thousand,

there are two points to notice: (1) The incident is located at Bethsaida. There were perhaps two Bethsaidas; one Bethsaida Julias, a Græco-Roman city on the right bank of the Jordan above the lake of Galilee, the other on the western lakeside between Magdala and Capernaum. The latter site would accord well with Mark's narrative, for he says—and Peter was not likely to be mistaken here—that the crowds went on foot, and got to the scene of the supper *first*. This would be possible if Jesus did not cross the lake, but only the bay between Capernaum and this Bethsaida. The modern road between the two places is very rough, but is less than three miles long. Bethsaida Julias is out of the question; it could not be described as "a desert place." (2) The Western text makes it clear that Jesus was praying (v. 16) when the loaves were multiplied; that is exactly the sort of detail that Luke usually brings out.

18–27. Peter's Confession. See notes on Mt. 16^{13-20} Mk. 8^{27}–9^{1}. We come now to what is called "the great omission." It has been thought that Luke has jumped, so to say, from Mk. 6^{45} to 8^{26}. More probably he returns to L; although this is doubtful in the case of vv. 18–27, for 14^{25-34} looks more like corresponding material from L. On the whole, it is best to accept the view that Luke had no version of Peter's confession in L (it was not in Q), and so took that important narrative from Mark before giving his alternative version (from L) of the transfiguration. He has abbreviated Mark rather drastically, leaving out the reproach addressed to Peter. Matthew includes *both* the praise and the reproach of Peter; Mark leaves out the praise and keeps the blame; Luke leaves out both praise and blame. Peter comes out worst precisely in Peter's own account!

J. L. Bryan has recently made a strong plea for the rendering of "take up his cross" (v. 23) as "take up his tent-peg." He argues that carrying the cross would at that time mean to the disciples "die a revolutionist's death," for crucifixion was the death meted out to *political* prisoners, and the last thing that Jesus desired was to suggest to his disciples that they should court such a fate; they were only too ready to dream of revolution. Moreover, though Jesus had foretold his death at that time, he had not mentioned that it was to be by crucifixion. It is important to remember that he was himself crucified as a revolutionary leader, not as a blasphemer; the penalty for blasphemy was death by stoning. The original meaning of the word translated "cross" is "something that sticks up," and the Arabs still use a word very like it when they bid their women take up the tent-pegs before they set out on their day's march. The fact that Luke adds to the phrase the word "daily" helps Mr. Bryan's argument. "Daily" is characteristically Lucan (cf. 11^{3}, where Mt. 6^{11} has "to-day").

In v. 24 Luke omits Mark's "and the gospel's"; as Mt. 16^{25} does the same, we may suggest either that Luke has Q in his mind, if not before his eyes, or that the words are a later addition in Mark. In v. 26 Luke modifies the sharpness of Mk. 8^{36} (cf. Mt. 16^{26}); he has "lose" or "forfeit," whereas Matthew has "forfeit." Doctor Field suggested that the former word implies total, the latter partial, or temporary, loss. Luke also omits the words "come with power" from Mk. 9^{1}, thus generalizing the saying. He consistently interprets Mark's eschatology in a less definite fashion whenever possible. Matthew is more precise even than Mark, for he has "the Son of man coming in his kingdom."

In vv. 20 and 21 we might render, "What do you say about me when you are away preaching," or, "in answer to inquiries?" Peter says, "We say you are God's Messiah." But "Jesus reproved them, and bade them never say it to anyone in future." Though Jesus did not in so many words repudiate the title "Messiah" or "Christ," he seemed to avoid it as much as possible (but see note on 10^{1-24}). It is curious that from the very beginning Christians have called him by a name which with one doubtful exception (Mk. 14^{62}, see note) he never used of himself!

28–36. The Transfiguration. See notes on Mt. 17^{1-13} Mk. 9^{2-13}; intro., p. 1027. Luke differs from Matthew-Mark in dating the ascent of "the mountain" (Matthew "a high mountain") *eight* instead of *six* days after the first prophecy of the Passion. Instead of "was transfigured before them" (Matthew-Mark)—in its strict sense the words involve a radical transformation (cf. Rom. 12^{2})—he has the more cautious phrase "the look of his face became different." Moses and Elijah are talking of "his exodus which he was going to accomplish in Jerusalem" (v. 31, cf. mg.); no hint of this is given in the other Gospels. The disciples are "laden with sleep" (v. 32); this detail too is found in Luke only. The words rendered "When they were fully awake" might be translated "having managed to keep awake." Luke tells us that "they feared as they entered into the cloud" (v. 34); Matthew-Mark have simply "and they were sore afraid," while Matthew adds that Jesus touched them and dispelled their fear. Instead of "This is my beloved Son; hear him" (Mark-Matthew), Luke has "This is my Son, my chosen" (v. 35; cf. 23[35], "the elect," again Luke only). For Mark's "he did not know what to answer" (9[6]) Luke has "he did not know what he was saying" (v. 33)—an intentional change, to avoid the suggestion that Peter said something because he did not know what to say. Luke has not altogether discarded Mark, but his version as a whole is based on L. The drowsiness of the three reminds us of Gethsemane, where once again the disciples "do not know what to answer" (Mk. 14[40]). In both cases Jesus is thinking about his death; in one case Moses and Elijah, in the other "an angel from heaven" (Lk. 22[43]) are in attendance; in both cases the disciples are heavy with sleep, but the scene of one incident is a mountain in Galilee, of the other a garden in Jerusalem. At the transfiguration the face of Jesus is shining; in Gethsemane his sweat is "like great clots of blood."

Moses and Elijah had each had their exodus from the range of hills to the east of the Jordan which form the background to every picture of the land. Neither had come down again, and it was thought that their spirits still haunted those hills. No wonder then that Peter and the others saw them with Jesus there, and that Peter wondered whether Jesus was not going to forsake his humble friends for his new-found companions, and leave them to go sadly home alone, like Elisha. Every time Peter tries to push away the thought of his Master's death he is separated from him; so it is with the modern disciple. "They feared as they entered into the cloud" suggests that the chill shadow of the Passion was already creeping over their spirits. Luke leaves out the conversation about Elijah which took place on the way down as not interesting to Theophilus.

37–48. The Healing of the Epileptic, and Another Prophecy of the Passion. (Mt. 17[14-23]; notes on 18[1-5] Mk. 9[14-37].) The healing of the epileptic boy is told briefly, for Luke has nothing to add except that the boy was an "only" son (cf. 7[12] 8[42]). The typically Lucan expressions, "they were all struck aback at the magnanimity of God" (v. 43) and "put into your ears these words" (v. 44; cf. 1[44]) should, however, be noticed. Luke says three times over in different ways that the disciples did not understand this second prophecy of the Passion, in spite of the fact that in this Gospel there is here no reference to actual death. He insists that his nearest and dearest did not understand Jesus (cf. 2[50] 18[34] 24[16]). In Mt. 17[23] grief rather than bewilderment is suggested. Mark paints a sorry picture of the behavior of the disciples in 9[33f.]; they quarrel behind the back of Jesus, and when challenged are silent and embarrassed. Mt. 18[1] makes them bring a straightforward request for information to Jesus, while Lk. 9[46] mentions simply that a dispute had "come in" without saying how it began.

49, 50. Jesus States the Law of Toleration. V. 50 (cf. Mk. 9[40]) gives us a striking contrast with 11[23]; the former states the law of toleration, the latter that of self-examination, the one the point of view from which we are to criticize others, the other that from which we are to criticise ourselves. In neither case is neutrality possible.

51–62. Jesus Starts for Jerusalem. (Mt. 17[22, 23] 19[1], cf. 8[19-22]; see also intro., p. 1027.) Here Luke leaves Mark once again and does not return to it till we get to 18[15]. If it was at this point that Jesus "set his face like a flint to go to Jerusalem" (v. 51), we can only say that he was a long while getting there, for at 17[11] he is still "between Samaria and Galilee." All that takes place between 9[51] and 18[15] cannot be assigned to this one journey, unless it was a very circuitous one! Perhaps Luke associated the stories and sayings he gathered together in L during his residence in Palestine with the country he went through himself, and the people he met with, between Cæsarea and Jerusalem (cf. Acts 21[16]). Luke is quite clearly almost hypnotized by this last journey of Jesus, for he keeps on referring to it (9[51, 53, 57] 10[1, 38] 13[22, 33] 17[11] 18[31, 35] 19[28]). "The days of his taking up" (v. 51) is a difficult phrase; we cannot say that the days of his ascension were coming on; we can only conclude that Luke is giving us *verbatim* a phrase used by his informant. This section is permeated by suggestions of the story of Elijah and his last journey (vv. 54, 61); this may account for the use of the word translated "taking-up" here. In v. 54 the A.V. reading is preferable; the words, "as Elijah did," and "the Son of man is not come to destroy men's lives, but to save them," were omitted from some MSS. because they seemed to favor the Marcionite heresy, which laid great stress on the contrast between the O.T. and N.T. Over the whole passage there broods the atmosphere of an urgency that brooks no delay. Elisha was allowed to "kiss his father and his mother," but this man must not even look back. The Syrian plow has only one handle; we read "put his hand"—not "hands"—"to the plow." In this section, vv. 51–56 and 61, 62 come from L, the rest from Q (cf. Mt. 8[19-22]).

CHAPTER X

1–24. The Mission of the Seventy and Its Results. (Cf. on 9[1-5] 13[22] Mt. 9[35-38] 10[5-16]

11^{20-27} $13^{16, 17}$ Mk. $6^{6-11, 30}$; see also intro., p. 1027.) Luke had evidently heard in Palestine, perhaps from one of them, that seventy disciples were sent to prepare the way for Jesus on his journey south. Both Q and Mark contained a charge to missionaries, and Luke has already given us his version of Mark's ordination-charge (9^{1-5}); now he applies his similar Q material to the sending of the seventy, using his own information to illustrate Q.

Lk. 10^{3-16} is parallel to Mt. 10^{5b-16}, but there are striking differences. (1) Mt. $10^{5b, 6}$ are absent; they were out of place in a charge given to men who were to travel through Samaria; they are probably a Matthean addition to Q. (2) To the words in Mt. 10^{7} Luke in v. 9 adds "to you"—i.e., "to you Samaritans." (3) "Greet no one by the way" is absent from Matthew, who is all for friendliness; Oriental salutations take a long time. Again the note of urgency, as everywhere in Luke. (4) Mt. 10^{10} has "the workman is worthy of his food," Lk. 10^{7}, "the workman is worthy of his *hire*"; in 1 Tim. 5^{18}—the only place in the N.T. where the words of Jesus are cited as "Scripture"—we have the saying in its Lucan form. Matthew is thinking of allowances, Luke of wages. The words "freely ye have received, freely give" are also wanting in Luke. (5) V. 2 is found in Mt. $9^{37, 38}$, vv. 13–15 in Mt. 11^{21-24}.

With the return of the seventy we come back to L. Whether *I was watching Satan fallen like lightning from heaven* (v. 18) is meant to suggest triumph or foreboding is not clear. The words sound like exultation in the coming defeat of Satan, but the casting out of Satan from heaven, according to Jewish ideas, meant "woe for the earth and the sea" (Rev. 12^{10-12}). Perhaps we should think of a mingling of exultation in ultimate victory with a foreboding of the trouble which must be endured before that consummation. Meanwhile, successful preachers must not be elated by results; they will have sufficient reason to rejoice, if, after a lifetime of preaching to others, their names are found *written in the book of life* at the end (v. 20). At the gate of an ancient city was posted a list of burgesses, and so the idea had grown up that God kept a roll (cf. Ex. $32^{32, 33}$ Ezra 2^{62} Neh. 12^{22} Ezek. 13^{9} Psa. 139^{16}).

With vv. 21f. we come back to Q again (cf. Mt. $11^{25f.}$). "Jesus exulted in the Holy Spirit" (Matthew "Jesus answered and said") because, *not the learned and the wise, but baby-minds* like those of his followers were first to be intrusted with the broadcasting of his unique knowledge of God. It is important to notice that this passage undoubtedly comes from Q, for Matthew and Luke are closely parallel here. Q is our earliest source for the teaching of Jesus, and yet *its Christology is as high as anything in the fourth Gospel;* our earliest and latest authorities agree in asserting that Jesus claimed to be in a class by himself with God the Father, over against all created beings in heaven and earth (cf. Mk. 13^{32} Jn. 14^{6}). He is the "Only Son," for none of us can hope to be a second Christ; all the same, though we cannot share his experience with the Father, all the knowledge that he has gained through that experience he will share with us. Baby-minds find it easier to understand than the "wise and prudent," because they have less to unlearn. But they are not to be elated, but humbly to acknowledge that better men than they have longed to catch a glimpse of the truths that are being lived out before their eyes, and died without the sight. We are not worthier than other men, only more fortunate.

25–37. The Parable of the Good Samaritan. See notes on Mt. 22^{34-40} Mk. 12^{28-34} and intro., p. 1027b. The conversation with the scribe—Luke calls the "scribes" of the other Gospels "lawyers," because Theophilus would understand "scribes" to mean "clerks"—reminds us of Mk. $12^{28f.}$, and is perhaps a reminiscence of the same incident from another source. That source is not Q, but L; if it had been Q, Matthew would have given us both the Marcan and the Q versions. The Samaritan was a commercial traveler with two mules, one to carry his samples, while he rode on the other. On the other hand, priest and Levite had no pressing business; they came that way *by chance.* The priest was going *down* away from the Temple, and so was not in danger of incurring ceremonial defilement. The main point of the parable is to be found in its concluding words: "Who of the three proved himself a neighbor?" The question is not "Who is my neighbor?" but "To whom can I show myself a neighbor?" In the next chapter (11^{5-8}) we meet a man who was a neighbor, but was not neighborly; here we have one who was not a neighbor, but was neighborly. Jesus was himself nicknamed a "Samaritan" (Jn. 8^{48}); perhaps the fathers were not far wrong when they suggested that he was thinking of his own journey along that dangerous road, though to identify the innkeeper with the church, the two pence with the sacraments, and "when I come again" with the Second Coming seems artificial.

38–42. The Home at Bethany. Luke knows Bethany, for he refers to it elsewhere (19^{29}); his calling it "a certain village" is in line with the reserve practiced by the other Synoptic Gospels about this family; Mark-

Matthew suppress the name of the sisters, calling Mary a "woman"; Luke suppresses the name of the village where they lived. It is a perversion of the story to call Martha the "practical" sister. She had allowed herself to get hustled; not understanding Jesus, she thought that he would appreciate fussy and elaborate preparations. What he really wanted was quiet and sympathetic listening, and this Mary gave him. Vv. 41, 42 should be rendered: "Martha, Martha"—Jesus often repeated his friends' names twice (cf. 22[31])—"you are worrying and working yourself up over getting a big supper ready; one course will be enough. Mary has chosen the menu that suits her and me, and she is not to be dragged away from it."

CHAPTER XI

1–13. How to Pray, with an Illustration. See notes on Mt. 6[9-15] 7[7-11]. Only Luke says Jesus was himself praying, when his disciples asked him to teach them to pray like that; also that John the Baptist gave similar instructions to his converts. *The Lord's prayer*, as it stands in the best MSS. of Luke, runs as follows: "Father, hallowed be thy name; thy kingdom come; give us day by day our bread for the coming day; and forgive us our sins, as we ourselves forgive everyone who is in debt to us, and bring us not into temptation." Luke's version is in prose; Matthew's (6[9-13]) is rhythmical, and its form is probably that of the primitive church liturgy. Luke gives us the original form of the prayer, as it stood in Q, though Marcion had an additional clause in place of Matthew's "Thy will be done," etc., namely, "Let thy Holy Spirit come upon us and cleanse us." This is not specially Marcionite, so may be genuine. *Abba* might mean "Father" or "our Father," and *which art in Heaven* means simply "God."

The parable which follows (L) may contain a reminiscence of the boyhood of Jesus (see also intro., p. 1023). We can see the peasant-family asleep on the floor of their one-roomed dwelling round the fire with its embers still glowing, and the lamp, an old slipper filled with oil, burning on its stand. Visitors after the door is shut are unusual, for the Syrian village is silent after nightfall. The *friend who had come on a journey* might be only a casual wanderer; hospitality is rarely refused to a stranger. When an unexpected guest arrives the host's first precaution is to share bread and salt with him; those who have partaken of bread and salt together are fast friends and will keep faith. The man inside was not a churl; his reluctance to get up was due to the inconvenience of disturbing the whole family, as he would have to do, when they were all herded together in the little dark room! But would anyone but Jesus have dared to use an illustration like this when speaking of prayer? Another of his three prayer-parables (all three we owe to Luke) is equally audacious; a shrewish widow bullies a cynical magistrate into doing the right thing for once by making herself a nuisance! There was no danger of serious misunderstanding; if a peasant who does not want to get up out of bed can be made to do so by sheer unashamed persistence, how much more will your heavenly Father, who welcomes the knock at his door, be quick to listen and reply! He has difficulties greater than we dream of in answering our prayers, and needs our perseverance.

Jesus does not tell us that we shall get what we want when we ask; when we seek, that we shall find what we expect; when we knock at the door, that what waits for us on the other side will be altogether to our taste. It will at least be the best possible. God does not play practical jokes on his children, as the heathen gods do with their worshipers, leading them on, and then cheating them with *snakes* that look like *fish* till they sting. The *egg* and the *scorpion* come in Luke only; Mt. 7[9, 10] has loaf and stone, fish and snake; Luke fish and snake, egg and scorpion. As this passage comes from Q, it is difficult to believe that Matthew and Luke's editions of Q can have been identical. In v. 13 Luke has "the Holy Spirit"; Mt. 7[11] "good things."

14–28. A Miracle, Followed by a Slander and a Compliment. See notes on Mt. 9[32-34] 12[22-32, 43-45] Mk. 3[20-30]. The story of exorcism must come from Q, for it occurs in the parallel passage in Mt. 12[22f.]; where, however, we read that the possessed man was both blind and deaf (see note on 7[2f.]). In the Q passage which follows Luke has perhaps inserted one verse from Mk. 8[11] (v. 16); further on he takes the Q passage about seeking a sign (vv. 29f.). Luke has in v. 20 *finger of God*, where Mt. 12[28] has "Spirit of God"; for some reason he always avoids the phrase "Spirit of God." Vv. 21, 22 are very full; they give us a parable on false confidence in material treasure. In vv. 27, 28 a sentimental woman intervenes (this from L), wishing in very audible tones she were the mother of Jesus (see intro., p. 1028). Jesus has said before (8[21]) that "those who hear the word of God and keep it" will be mother and brothers to him; now he replies that "those who hear the word of God and keep it" have a happiness greater than his mother ever knew. Our aspiration should be, not to bear a relationship to Jesus that no one else can share, but "to hear and do" his "every word"; if, however, we do so, we shall, without having sought it, enter into intimate relations with him.

29–36. The Reply to the Demand for a Sign. See notes on Mt. 12:38-42 6:22, 23. The sign desired was a voice from heaven, supposed to guarantee prophetic inspiration. The Queen of Sheba comes in (v. 31) before the Ninevites (cf. the reverse order in Mt. 12:41, 42). Vv. 33–36 form a doublet with 8:16; that comes from Mark, this from Q. The word translated *light* at the end of v. 33 means a light reflected through a window or seen through a door; as in 8:16, Luke is thinking of the effect of a lighted room *seen from the road;* Mt. 5:15 of its effect on the inmates of the room. This is characteristic of the difference in outlook between the two Gospels.

37–54. Woes Upon the Pharisees and a Dirge Upon His Contemporaries. (Cf. 20:45, 46 Mt. 16:5-12 23:1-31, notes; Mk. 12:38-40; see also intro., p. 1028.) Luke had heard that the woes upon the Pharisees contained in Q (cf. Mt. 23) were uttered when Jesus was at dinner in a Pharisee's house; some, thinking of the requirements of courtesy, will question if this was really so. The phrase "the Lord said" (v. 39) implies oral tradition, for members of the inner circle called Jesus "the Lord" to outsiders (cf. Mk. 11:3). The same expression (in narrative) is found in Lk. 7:13 10:1, 41, (cf. Jn. 4:1); in all its Lucan instances, the passage in which it occurs comes from L. V. 41 is peculiar to Luke, and should be emended—by a slight change in the suggested Aramaic original—to *only purify what is within, and behold all is pure to you*—i.e., "to the pure all things are pure." In v. 44 we have *unseen tombs,* where Mt. 23:27 has "whitewashed tombs"; there were whitewashed tombs in the Temple, sepulchers of idolatrous kings who had been buried there; Matthew has the topical reference right (cf. Acts 23:3). *They killed, and you build* (v. 48) seems awkward; it appears to mean that the fathers killed the prophets, the sons completed their work by burying the prophet's memory under a mountain of insincere flattery. *Therefore the wisdom of God said* (v. 49) suggests that Jesus is quoting here from a Wisdom book; Harnack thinks that the phrase comes from Q, and that the quotation went on to "Jerusalem, Jerusalem," etc., which follows in Mt. 23:36f. In that case Matthew has given us the quotation complete, Luke has broken it up into two parts, for he does not give us the lament over Jerusalem till we come to 13:34f. For "you shut the kingdom of heaven" in Mt. 23:13 Luke has *you have taken away the key of knowledge* (v. 52); and in vv. 53, 54 we should render "began to be very angry and, extending the scope of debate, to snatch at his words, lying in ambush for him to catch him in some unguarded answer"—three alternative translations of a difficult Aramaic phrase (cf. "bed" in 5:18, "mattress" in 5:24, "that on which he was laid" in 5:25, and in 14:12 "dinner," "supper," or "reception"). All three passages suggest the conscientious use of variant translations in a dictionary.

CHAPTER XII

1–12. Warnings and Encouragements. See notes on Mt. 10:17-33 Mk. 3:23-30. V. 1 (L) contains a note from the memory of one of Luke's informants. Then follows another passage from Q, containing a warning against the men who had so lately been guilty of malignant slander. Vv. 4, 5 correspond to Mt. 10:28; in both Gospels it seems more consonant with the teaching of Jesus to interpret *him who has authority to cast into hell* of Satan, not of God. *Five sparrows for twopence* (v. 6) is an interesting variation of the "two a penny" in Mt. 10:29; the suggestion of the odd one thrown in as a makeweight cannot have been an invention by Luke, but must have come from the memory of a hearer of Jesus. The extra sparrow casually thrown in by the salesman counts full value with God; *is not forgotten before God* (v. 6) is a reverent way of saying, "God does not forget." Mt. 10:29 has "not one of them falls to the ground without your Father."

13–34. On the Dangers of Wealth and Self-centered Ease, and How to Escape Them. (See notes on Mt. 6:19-21, 24-34 and intro., p. 1028.) In this section, vv. 14–21, 32 and part of 33 come from L, the rest from Q (cf. Mt. 6:19f.). *The parable of the rich fool* is one of the raciest of the stories told by Jesus. When people said *soul* to themselves, they meant what in England is meant by "old man," and *take thine ease, eat, drink, and be merry* means literally, "you ought to be retiring from business; have a good meal and a drink and try to be merry." But the liveliest touch comes at the end; *this night thy soul is required of thee* should be rendered, "this night they are asking for your soul." The man was a fool because he tried to be merry by himself; as if anybody but a curmudgeon would try, and even he could succeed! Into his carefully secluded dining room there came a visitor, as there always does sooner or later, however jealously the door is barricaded. It was God, and the man looks up to see his Maker, who bids him join "the great majority," and be a democrat at last. There was everything in the room, a well-spread table, splendid appointments, everything but a man, for men and nations wither when they shut themselves up. Nor can they shut themselves up for long; sooner or later the door blows open, and reality must be faced; men and nations must ultimately take their chance with the rest, and, if they wrap themselves up in self-centered ease, they will presently have no soul left to face reality with. *To be rich toward God* (v. 21) means to be rich in experience of communion with God and fellowship with men, and this only comes from a life of self-denying adventure.

In v. 29 we notice the phrase translated *Be not of a doubtful mind.* It is unique in the N.T., and is connected with wind and weather; indeed, it is equivalent to the colloquial, "Don't get the wind up." V. 32 gives us a precious fragment from L; it has the hall-mark of authenticity upon it. *Sell your goods* (v. 33) extends to all disciples the advice given to the rich young ruler (18[22]). There is nothing so sweeping anywhere else in the N.T., but it is probably genuine reminiscence, for it seems reasonable to suppose that all who joined the inner circle of disciples disposed of their property before doing so; Peter and the others had "left all." Such membership was voluntary, like the communism of the early church. Some of the friends of Jesus did not leave home (e.g., Martha and Mary), but those who traveled about with him had a common purse (8[3]), and critics of the experiment described twice over in Acts (2[44, 45] 4[34, 35]) must realize that it was *not* a new experiment; it was an attempt to go on as before.

35–48. The Lord's Coming; Its Conditions and Demands. (Cf. 17[7-10] Mt. 25[1-13] 24[42-51]; see also intro., p. 1028.) Vv. 35, 36 are Luke only, and should be ascribed to L. They remind us of Mt. 25[1f.], but, whereas there the Master is the bridegroom coming suddenly to claim his bride, here he is the bridegroom bringing his bride home, unless the "wedding" is not his own. The Syrian bridegroom feasts with his bachelor friends for an unspecified time, then suddenly leaves them to fetch his bride home, while his friends depart (5[34, 35]). Servants wait up to admit him when he returns. We are to be *like men who wait for their Lord* (v. 36), who comes when he is least expected. The last part of v. 37 also comes from L, and provides us with an interesting contrast with 17[7f.]; there the servant of Jesus is told that he must not dream of his Master thanking him, much less waiting on him; here the promise is given that, if he is faithful, his master will thank him.

We should observe a delicate point in vv. 42–44 which we render ". . . whom his Lord will set in *temporary* charge of his catering. . . . Truly I tell you, he will set him in *permanent* control of all he possesses"; and also that where Mt. 24[45] has *slave*, Luke has *steward* (cf. 16[1]), where Matthew has *food*, Luke has *rations;* both changes are characteristic. Vv. 47, 48 come from L, and suggest that, whatever may be the doom of the unregenerate, it will at least be capable of comparative alleviation.

49–59. The King's Business Requires Haste. (See notes on Mt. 10[34-36] 16[1-4] 5[25f.] and intro., p. 1028.) In vv. 49–51 we have one of the few passages which suggest impatience in Jesus; vv. 49, 50 come from L, v. 51 from Q, but, whereas Mt. 10[34] has *a sword*, Luke has *division;* Theophilus might take "a sword" too literally. In v. 53 Luke has "five in one house divided, three against two, and two against three," all of these words being absent from Mt. 10[35]. Again, as in the saying about five sparrows (v. 6), we infer that Jesus is repeating the sentence in an improved version. *Three against two, and two against three* reproduces the domestic situation; the husband's mother is the tyrant of the house, and with the casting vote ranges herself with her son and his daughter against her daughter-in-law and her son! Moreover, according to the Greek, the women are at daggers drawn, while the men merely have a difference! Subtleties like these could not be expressed in Aramaic, but in Greek-speaking districts Jesus probably could and would talk Greek; he was bilingual (see p. 880).

The passage about "the signs of this time" is not found in the best texts of Matthew (16[2, 3]), and so must come from L. In this Gospel we see Jesus as the messenger of God, not only to individuals but to the life of his day and of all times, with an appeal to be forced home quickly and a mission to be accomplished within a given time, and, as for the Master, so for his followers, there can be no rest till the work is done. They must be off and away, getting rid of the adversary quickly; by *the adversary* (v. 58) here is meant anyone or anything that stands in the way. Mt. 5[25, 26] gives a different color to this saying; he has "Be friendly with your adversary"; Luke's version should be translated, "Take pains to be rid of your adversary." The setting in Matthew is that of a Jewish, in Luke that of a Roman court.

CHAPTER XIII

1–9. Except Ye Repent. (See also intro., p. 1029.) The whole of this section comes from

L, and its note is still that of urgent appeal. Pilate's massacre of Galilæans, of which we have a fuller account in Josephus (*Antiquities*, bk. xviii, ch. 3, and footnote in Eng. trans.), exasperated Galilæan opinion to the last degree; it was a factor in the growing alienation of the populace from Jesus, who steadily refused to countenance direct action. In v. 4 Jesus transfers the subject of discourse from Galilee to Jerusalem, on which his thoughts tend to rest more and more. *The parable of the fig-tree* spared one year suggests the parable found in Isa. 5[1f.], and looks forward to the triumphal entry. The "fig-tree" stands for Jerusalem, planted in the "vineyard" of Palestine; the "three years" implies that Jesus had, as the fourth Gospel says, carried on a prolonged ministry already in that city. This parable should be read along with the cursing of the fig-tree (Mk. 11[13] Mt. 21[19], notes; not in Luke). The first of the two stories—both are really parables (see p. 924a)—betrays the hopes of Jesus as he approached the city, the second betrays his despair, when his supreme appeal had failed.

10–21. Another Cure, and Two Parables. (Mt. 13[31-33], notes; Mk. 4[30-32]; intro., p. 1029.) In this passage the phrase *the Lord* (v. 15) comes in again; we infer that it comes from L. Healing was allowed on the Sabbath, if it were a matter of life or death; in this matter practice was better than theory, for animals were watered on the day of rest. With the phrase *daughter of Abraham* (v. 16) compare "son of Abraham" (19[9]) and "Abraham's bosom" (16[22f.]), all found in Luke alone. It is curious that this Gentile appreciates so keenly the patriotism of Jesus. The tone of the story is that of Mt. 12[12]—"it is right to do good on the sabbath." The Sabbath is not designed merely for rest or even for worship, but for humanitarian service. In vv. 18–21 Luke is closely parallel with Mt. 13[31-33], so we are back in Q.

22–35. A Call for Instant Decision. See notes on 9[1-5] 10[1-12] Mt. 7[13, 14, 21-23] 8[5-13] 23[37-39] and intro., p. 1029. This section comes from L. V. 22 reminds us once again that we are on the road to Jerusalem. In v. 24 we are on Q ground (cf. Mt. 7[13]), but, whereas Matthew has "Enter through the narrow *gate*," Luke has *Agonize to enter through the narrow door*. We should probably omit the period at the end of v. 24, and read straight on to v. 25: *shall not be able* (Matthew has "few there be that *find* it") *when once the Master of the house*, etc. The note of urgency is unmistakable; we have a picture of latecomers waved away from a window. For Mt. 7[23] "I never knew you," Luke has *I know you not whence you are* (v. 25), in other words "I don't remember where you come from"—once more the universalistic note. According to Matthew, the unadmitted plead all they have done in the name of Jesus (7[22]), according to Luke all he had done for them (v. 26); we can scarcely believe that Matthew and Luke are here working at a common document.

In vv. 31–33 we are still with L. Whether the Pharisees who warn Jesus of Herod's design mean to be friendly or not is not clear; in any case he is not going to move on before his time to please either them or Herod. V. 33 should be translated (with early Greek commentators) "only I must cast out demons and accomplish cures to-day and to-morrow, and on the day after that take to the road again." "Two or three days" is a phrase corresponding to our "day or two" (cf. Hos. 6[2]).

34, 35. *The plaint over Jerusalem* comes in Luke before the triumphal entry, in Matthew after it (23[35f.]); the consequence is that in Luke *until the time comes when ye shall say* (v. 35), etc., refers to the entry itself, in Matthew to the Second Coming. The cry of the hen-bird is the cry of the Heavenly Wisdom (cf. 11[49] and note); no inferences can safely be drawn from this passage as to earlier visits to the city.

CHAPTER XIV

1–24. The Table-Talk of Jesus. (Cf. on Mt. 22[1-14]; see also intro., p. 1029.) For the third time in this Gospel (cf. 7[36] 11[37]) Jesus is asked to dinner by a Pharisee. The story of the healing of *the man with the dropsy* comes from L, but the ironical advice to guests is found also in the Western text of Matthew between 20[28, 29]. Evidently, Jesus is the guest of the evening, and as such sat in the highest place (at the right hand of the host), was expected to start the ball of conversation rolling, and was allowed considerable license in teasing his fellow guests. Perhaps Jesus had taken the lowest place (cf. 7[36f.]) and had been called up to the top table. If this was a so-called charity-feast, as some authorities suggest, v. 12 would contain a shrewd thrust at the host; the poor, the maimed, the halt, and the blind ought to have been there.

The interrupter in v. 15 seeks to relieve the tension by a platitude, and *the parable of the great supper* that follows exposes the hollowness of pious patter. Mt. 22[1f.] is a partial parallel, but the parable in Matthew has a different introduction and a different dénouement, being colored by the tragedy of Passion week. In Matthew, "both bad and good" come in to the prince's wedding feast, in Luke *the poor, the maimed, the halt and the blind* partake of the supper; in Matthew the main point of the story is the fate of one man who came in, and was turned out, in Luke the main point is the behavior of the invited guests who were *too busy to come.* The story in Luke is gayer than its counterpart in Matthew, and is told in a most humorous way. Notice the politeness of the farmer and the cattle-dealer ("I pray thee, have me excused") as contrasted with the downright refusal of the married man ("I am married to a wife, and therefore I cannot come").

25–35. Counting the Cost. (Cf. 11^{33} Mt. 5$^{13-16}$ 10$^{37, 38}$; see also intro., p. 1029.) At this stage Jesus appears again to be threatened with popularity. Not only does he get invitations to dinner, but large crowds are following him. But he is not encouraging, and his sternest words to would-be disciples follow immediately upon this Indian summer of popular favor. The *hate* of v. 26 goes back to an Aramaic word which means "love less," so that Mt. 10$^{37, 38}$ is an accurate rendering of the meaning, if not of the actual words, of Jesus (cf. Mt. 5^{43}: "Thou shalt love thy neighbor more, and thine enemy less"). Luke slips in the wife (v. 26) among the people we are to love less (cf. v. 20); the evangelist's bias is unmistakable (cf. 18^{29} where again "wife" is in Luke only). *Yes, and himself too,* is also peculiar to Luke. In Mt. 10^{39} we hear of "losing" self, here of *loving self less.* Three times over Luke has *cannot be my disciple* (vv. 26, 27, 33), three times over Mt. 10$^{37, 38}$ has "is not worthy of me."

The two parables from L inserted here (vv. 28–32) should be understood as meaning that Jesus will count the cost before he takes all and sundry into his service. He is the man building the tower, the king going into action with a numerically superior adversary. The Kingdom has two aspects; it is to be a tower of defense for the distressed, and will involve an agelong crusade against the powers of evil. V. 33 reminds us of 12^{33}, calling, as it does, for an entire surrender of *all* material possessions (cf. notes on 12^{33} and 5^{28}): *whoever does not say good-bye to all he possesses* (cf. Mk. 6^{46} for the word translated "say good-bye"). V. 35 is nearer to Mk. 9^{50} than to Mt. 5^{13} but probably comes from Q.

CHAPTER XV

Three Parables of Losing and Finding. (Mt. 18$^{10-14}$; see also intro., p. 1029.) In spite of, or perhaps because of, the relentlessness of Jesus, the publicans are still attracted to him, and three parables follow, one from Q, the other two from L.

The parable of the lost sheep has a different application in Matthew (18$^{12-14}$, note); there we read that the Father's face is set against one of these "little ones" being *lost,* here that there is "joy in heaven over one repentant sinner *found.*" Luke's is the gospel of *penitence* (cf. 5$^{8, 32}$ 7$^{29, 38}$ 13$^{3, 5}$ 15$^{7, 10, 18}$ 16^{30} 18^{13} 19^{8} 22^{32} 23^{41} 24^{47}). Through this chapter there runs a rising note of *joy;* "joy in heaven" (v. 7), "joy in the presence of the angels"—a reverent way of saying "joy in God's heart" (v. 10)—and merriment, joy in which God and man share. This is in perfect harmony with Jesus' fundamental thought of God as a Father. Only a fatherly God could be a rejoicing God.

Characteristically, Jesus adds a woman's parable (cf. 13$^{18-21}$), appealing to each section of his audience in turn (cf. also 17$^{34, 35}$), but *the parable of the lost coin* is no mere replica of that of the lost sheep. The coin is lost *inside* the house, the sheep *outside* the fold. The publicans belonged to God's family; like Zacchæus, they were "children of Abraham." Memory of days at Nazareth may have suggested this parable; the peasant-woman would miss her coin, and her recovery of it would provide a topic of conversation at the well for many days.

In *the story of the lost son* the characters are sketched to the life. The casual youngster who never realizes how badly he has treated his father till he swoons away with hunger, the puritanical elder brother who has no use for him, but calls him "thy son," the father who smothers his son's remorse with a welcoming kiss, and sets everyone in the house feasting and dancing because the ne'er-do-well has at last deigned to come home, all are alive. At the beginning of the story the father is on the point of retiring from the management of the farm, and vests profits and responsibilities equally in his two grown-up sons. When the younger of them disappoints him he would have to go back to work again. *The husks that the swine did eat* (v. 16) were carob-pods, still counted a delicacy in the East, and known to schoolboys as "locust-beans" or "honey-beans." But there are sweet and bitter carobs; Tatian's *Gospel-Harmony* (second century, A.D.) has "carobs of the sea" (salt carobs); the nicely brought-up youth could not stomach bitter carobs, which are still given to cattle. *Came to himself* (v. 17) is a medical term, and means "came to his senses after fainting." The *hired servants* were poor relations, taken into the house and paid for menial service, members of the family, though not on a level with the children. Notice the contrast between the prodigal's limping walk and his father's *running*, and that the father does not allow him to say, "Make me as one of thy hired servants," but smothers the odious suggestion with a *kiss* (R.V.). He wants everything at once, ring (to show that he is still heir of what is left of the property), clothes, shoes, and *fatted calf*. This calf was taken from its mother and forcibly fattened for the table (only being given a rest on the Sabbath); it was kept for some great occasion. The *music* provided was the bag-pipes (in Old English, "symphony"—cf. Wycliffe's translation—now called "sampoon" in the Near East). The *elder son* is disgusted when he finds the house all lighted up and the proceedings in full blast; he has come from his work and is tired. The servant from whom he demands an explanation is glad that the young master has come home, but his ardor is soon damped when the elder brother refuses to come in. Then the father tries his hand, but does not know how to deal with the son who had stayed at home. While he is hesitating the young man airs his grievance: "I have been a perfect slave to you all these years." Jesus makes us sympathize with all his characters in turn; we know that the child who stays at home does sometimes get taken for granted. But even if he had cause for complaint, that of all days was not the day to bring it out! Only of another Elder Brother was it true that he never disobeyed one of the Father's commands, and that all that the Father had was his (cf. Jn. 17^{10}); he did not grudge his brethren their welcome home, but went into the far country (cf. 19^{12}) to live with them and die for them, to show them what home was like.

CHAPTER XVI

1–18. The Unjust Steward, and Some Sayings. (For vv. 14–18, cf. Mt. $5^{31, 32}$ 6^{24} 11^{7-19}; see also intro., p. 1029b.) This story from L has caused difficulty to Bible students, because it seems to involve an approval of dishonesty. Jesus is not holding the steward's conduct up to admiration, *except in one particular*. He is using a corrupt social order as an illustration, not setting his seal upon it. The steward is a "steward of injustice," not because he was dishonest, but because he was involved in a way of life which Jesus condemns without argument. He worked on commission, as all agents, including tax-collectors, did in the Levant until recent times. In other words, he was not paid a wage, but was expected to maintain himself out of the rent, part of which went into his own pocket, and part to the landlord. He was *accused* (v. 1), not of fraud, but mismanagement; sending for the books meant notice of dismissal. He was not robust enough to go on to the land, yet wished to retain his self-respect. So he called a meeting of tenants, two of whom were in arrears with their rent, which was paid in kind. Remitting his own share of the rent they owed, he knew he would earn their gratitude, not at the master's, *but at his own expense*. They, he calculated, would find him work, or hospitality, until he could get work for himself. He was a shrewd business man, who knew that friends go further than money.

We are all stewards, for the only independent capitalist in the universe is God. We are concerned, not with the ownership of material goods, such as money, health, time, etc., but with their circulation. Like the steward, we work on commission, being allowed to use a proportion of these good things for ourselves in return for service to the community. We are all set under authority, some people above us, others below us; we are not better than those who have less money, health, time, than we. We are unjust stewards; if our accounts were required for audit, they would not bear strict examination. In any case, we are all under notice of dismissal, as the steward was. What can we do? Jesus says, *make friends* with the people dependent upon us for the time being; before long we shall be dependent upon them. *They will receive you into the eternal tents* (v. 9) means that the friendship of those we have helped will be our lasting possession, while the money, health, time we give up to secure their friendship will not be ours for long anyhow. Life, as ordered by God, depends on giving and taking, and it is not selfishness, but humility, to be willing to make use of one another.

The Pharisees are charged by Luke, not by Jesus, with being *lovers of money* in v. 14; it does not appear that they were specially open to that accusation, whatever "devouring widows' houses" (Mk. 12^{40}) may mean. *You are they who justify yourselves* (v. 15) reminds us of 7^{29} 10^{29} 18^{14}. The saying in v. 16 is found in a very different form in Mt. 11^{12}; there it seems to mean, "John was the last of the prophets, and with him the days of violent preaching are over." Here, on the other hand, John is thought of as inaugurating a new era of pressure in which men must do violence upon themselves in order to enter the Kingdom. V. 17 is certainly from Q, corresponding closely to Mt. 5^{19}. The other saying—about *divorce*—is nearer to Mk. $10^{11, 12}$ than to either Mt. 5^{32} or 19^{9}.

19–31. "Dives" and Lazarus. (See also intro., p. 1030.) This parable is connected with that of the unjust steward; both illustrate our dependence upon one another, the unjust steward in this life, "Dives" and Lazarus in the world beyond the grave. Here are two men traveling along the same road from birth to death, neither knowing how the other lives. What did "Dives" think about Lazarus? Perhaps he was sorry for him, and would have made a donation in support of some institution in which such poor creatures could be looked after; but why should he be planted on his doorstep? Lazarus was too far gone to think about "Dives" at all; he was there because guests at the rich man's table would use pieces of bread to wipe their fingers on and then toss them over their shoulders out of the open window into the road, where Lazarus would be waiting to catch them. So they pass their lives, daily within sight and sound of each other, but in different worlds. In course of time both men die, and the rich man is buried. Soon the undertaker's trappings are put away, and meanwhile Lazarus has disappeared. There is no one to bury him, so he is taken by the angels, who care for this world's unfortunates, to *Abraham's bosom.*

Paradise, according to contemporary belief, was situated in the third of the seven heavens (cf. 2 Cor. 12[4]), on the south side. There were Abraham and the patriarchs, but on the north side, parted from Paradise by a deep ravine, was the abode of the rich who had neglected their poor brethren. All this is figurative, but there must be truth behind it, or Jesus would not have used such imagery. "Dives" and Lazarus are still within sight and sound of each other, but Lazarus is in now and "Dives" is out. Like many rich people, "Dives" thinks that everyone is at his beck and call, and he remembers having seen Lazarus before, so he tries to claim acquaintance with him. But the gulf between the two has deepened; "Dives" *would not* cross then, now Lazarus *cannot.* Here is a state of affairs the commonness of which blinds us to its absurdity; two men living close together, but with a great gulf between them, and never a human word passing from one side to the other. Such barriers, easily surmounted at first, strengthen as time goes on. Vague dislikes become antipathies, antipathies harden into hatred. Yet God would not throw us continually together unless he meant us to make overtures to one another; he gives us a hint that we shall want a certan man some day by obtruding him upon our notice.

But Jesus never leaves us with a warning without opening a window of hope somewhere in the story. The name "Lazarus" (Eleazar) means the same thing as "Jesus"; the former may be translated "God has delivered," the latter, "Jehovah has saved." Do not the words, *If one go to them from the dead* make us think of One who did? Mohammedan writers tell us that there was no name which Jesus loved better than to be called "the poor man." Lazarus was a "poor man," while "Dives" and his brethren stand for the Jewish nation, who *have Moses and the prophets.* Like Lazarus, Jesus had not where to lay his head, and his friends were "poor outcasts of men, whose souls are despised." He accepted the patronizing invitations of the rich (7[36] 11[37] 14[1]), willing to be fed with the scraps from the rich man's table. Soon he knows he is to die; the angels are waiting to take him home (Mt. 26[53]), but what of the people he has come to save? The months are slipping by, their hearts are hardening, the great gulf is deepening. Can he reach them from that other side? *Father Abraham,* who represents orthodox Jewish eschatology, says, "No; when men die, their fates are fixed." *Now* they will not, *then* they cannot. But does this dogma settle the question when one of the two is Jesus? The early church had no doubt that, when Jesus died on the cross, he passed the barrier, broke into the prison where those who died in sin and unbelief lay, and preached the gospel to them (but cf. note on 1 Pet. 3[19]). We must leave it there; we can almost hear Jesus talking to himself, and can only state our faith that *the cross must have a meaning for all men wherever they may be,* that there is no part of his universe cut off from the saving ministry of Him who has "the keys of death and Hades" (Rev. 1[18]).

CHAPTER XVII

1–10. Some Sayings and a Parable of Service. See notes on 12[47, 48, 35, 36] 13[25] Mt. 25[1-13] 18[6-9, 15-22] Mk. 9[42-48] and intro., p. 1030. Vv. 1, 2 must come from Q (cf. Mt. 18[6, 7], though Matthew is there following Mark). V. 3. is puzzling; it looks a little like Mt. 18[21, 22], but is differently turned. In Matthew, Peter is bidden to forgive his brother up to "seventy-seven times" (the best reading); here the disciple is bidden to forgive his brother "seven times in a day," *if* he professes repentance: there is no mention of penitence in Matthew. We must surely refer v. 3 to L. In the next verse we have the unusual phrase in narrative *the apostles* (v. 5); and the occurrence of the phrase *the Lord* (v. 6; see the note on 11[39]) confirms our view that we are concerned here with oral tradition (in other words, with L). There follows the saying about *faith as a grain of mustard-seed,* but in a curious form. Mt. 17[20] 21[21] has "say to this mountain," like Mk. 11[23] from which Mt. 21[21] comes. Where has

Luke got his *say to this sycamine tree* from? As Mt. 17[20] comes from Q, we should infer that Q had "say to this mountain." Luke found the saying both in Q and in Mark connected in Mark with the cursing of the fig-tree; he omits the latter, but has worked the fig-tree into the saying! The little parable (from L) in vv. 7f. is almost the exact opposite of 12[37] (see note). We should drop out the word *unprofitable* (v. 10), and read "we are slaves; we have only done our duty."

11–19. The Grateful Samaritan. (See also intro., p. 1030.) Jesus is still going to Jerusalem, but is farther away than ever! This story comes from L, and appeals to Luke, who is interested in the Samaritans (cf. 9[52f.] 10[33] Acts 8[5f.]). Some excuse may be found for the nine; they would hurry off to obey the command to show themselves to the priests; the Samaritan would not go to Jerusalem at all. The sympathy of the foreigner Luke with *this foreigner* (v. 18) is unmistakable.

20–37. Prophecies of the Fall of Jerusalem. (Mt. 24[26-28, 37-41] Mk. 13[1f.]; see also intro., p. 1030.) Luke tends to apply (see on 13[34]) sayings which in Matthew refer to the consummation of history at the Second Coming rather to historical events such as the fall of Jerusalem; here is a signal instance of his method. V. 20 comes from L: *with observation* means "when you are looking for it"; the first half of v. 21 is from Q (cf. Mt. 24[23]), the second from L again. One of the sayings of Jesus found by Drs. Grenfell and Hunt at Oxyrhynchus in Egypt confirms the meaning *within you.* V. 22 also comes from L; the title *Son of man* is thus attested for all our Gospel-sources, Q, Mark, L, Proto-Matthew, and John (on these sources, see art., *Structure of Synoptic Gospels*, pp. 872–3). As this saying is addressed to the disciples, one is inclined to think that it refers to a regretful longing they will experience for the days of "the Jesus of history" rather than to disappointed expectation of the Second Coming. In vv. 23f. we are back again in Q; Luke uses *in his day* instead of "the coming of the Son of man" (Mt. 24[27]); he deliberately avoids the word for "Second Coming." Vv. 25, 28, 29, 30, 32 come from L; they are not in Matthew. In Mk. 13[14-16] ("the little apocalypse") as in Mt. 24[17, 18] we have the same warning to flee from the doomed city, but Luke omits the passage about "the abomination of desolation" and "let him that readeth understand" (Mt. 24[15] Mk. 13[14]). In v. 33 we have another version of a saying found six times in the Gospels (Mt. 10[39] 16[25] Mk. 8[35] Lk. 9[24] 17[33] Jn. 12[25])—each time in a slightly different form. Here we should translate: "Whoever wants to make his life his own shall lose it, and whoever loses it shall bring it to life again."

CHAPTER XVIII

1–14. Two Parables of Prayer. (See also intro., p. 1030.) The story of *the unjust judge* reminds us of that of the friend at midnight (11[5f.]), the difference being that in the latter case the persistent neighbor was anxious to help a friend, while the widow insists on justice *for herself.* Here again we have an unforgetable picture: the termagant who will not be snubbed, patronized, or bullied by the cynical magistrate, whose only concern is for the maintenance of his dignity. Every day she gets more violent, until the old worldling says to himself, "Even though I don't care for God or man, yet because this widow keeps on bothering me, I shall have to redress her grievance, for I am afraid that in the end she will give me a black eye!" (Cf. v. 5 mg.) The last phrase is slang, used by Paul when he says, "I buffet my body" (1 Cor. 9[27]). The magistrate is not seriously afraid of assault and battery in open court, but was afraid of a scene, by which his dignity would be so badly compromised that, whenever he sat there, people would remember how he was bearded by a widow! The A.V. "weary me" (v. 5) is due to the desire of the translators to avoid a colloquial phrase, and was suggested by the fact that when people are tired they have dark shadows under their eyes.

The verses (6–8) that follow are difficult Their meaning seems to be that if a cynical magistrate can be forced to do the right thing by a woman who will not be put in her place, how much more will God listen to the prayers of his children? He is *long-suffering* in their case (v. 7); that is only because wrongs are not easily righted. In v. 8 Jesus seems to despair for a moment, not of the justice of God, but of the persistence of men. *The faith* (mg.) means "the right kind of faith." How swiftly light and shadow follow one another as we read this brightly colored and various Gospel! At one moment we are listening to a story bubbling over with humor, the next we are plunged into the dark, and Jesus is almost in despair!

The other story—that of *the Pharisee and the publican* (vv. 9–14)—gives us a picture of the *wrong* kind of shamelessness in prayer. What the Pharisee was saying aloud would be the prayer which every Jewish boy was taught, "My God, I thank thee I was not born a Gentile, but a Jew, not a slave, but a free man, not a woman, but a man"—cf. Gal. 3[28], where Paul contradicts the first prayer, clause by clause. What the Pharisee was saying *to himself* (v. 11—"within himself") Jesus lets us overhear. Here are two men at prayer together; the Pharisee separates himself from his fellow worshiper, the publican feels himself desperately alone: "God," he says, "you might be friends with me, the outcast!" The man who holds himself aloof goes home unblessed, the man who longs for fellowship is *justified rather than the other*.

In these parables *all the people who keep away from their fellows come out badly:* the rich fool who tried to be merry all by himself, the elder brother who would not come in, "Dives" who did not want Lazarus on his doorstep. On the other hand, Lazarus wants to be fed with the crumbs that fall from the rich man's table, the prodigal son, ne'er-do-well as he is, comes to himself and longs to get back home to the others, the unjust steward is eager to make friends, the publican mourns his loneliness, and these get the best of it. In nearly all these parables the same phrase recurs in different forms; the rich fool "reasoned *within himself*," the prodigal son "came *to himself*," the unjust steward "said *within* himself," the unjust judge "said *within himself*," and the Pharisee "prayed *to himself*."

15–30. The Coming of the Children and the Rich Young Ruler. (Cf. 22[28-30] Mt. 19[13-30], notes; Mk. 10[13-31]; intro., p. 1031.) In v. 15 Luke takes up Mark again, but the children are *infants*, the *needle* is a surgeon's needle (v. 25); both are medical terms. Luke also puts in *wife* among the possessions left behind by those who follow Jesus (v. 29; cf. note on 14[20]), and has *for the sake of the kingdom of God*, where Mt. 19[29] has "for my name's sake," and Mk. 10[29] has "for my sake and the gospel's sake."

31–43. Another Prophecy of the Passion and the Healing of a Blind Beggar. (Mt. 20[17-19, 29-34]; notes on Mt. 9[27-31] Mk. 10[32-34, 46, 52].) In vv. 31–34 we have an abbreviated version of Mk. 10[32f.]; like Matthew, Luke alters the "after three days" of Mark—a colloquial expression for "in a day or two" (cf. Hos. 6[2] Lk. 13[33])—to the more precise phrase *on the third day*. Mark tells us that the blind man's name was Bartimæus, and that he received his sight when Jesus was leaving Jericho (10[46]); Luke seems to be deliberately correcting him. He has also omitted the story of James' and John's request and its sequel (see Mk. 10[35f.]).

CHAPTER XIX

1–10. The Story of Zacchæus. (See also intro., p. 1031.) In this section Luke deserts Mark again, giving us another story from L. Who was the man *little of stature*—Zacchæus or Jesus? The last alternative is possible, as the text does not clearly say; if Jesus was little, it would be natural to get up into a tree over the road to get a sight of him in the crowd. Here and there in the Fathers there are hints that Jesus was of insignificant stature, but they may only involve an inference from "when we see him, there is no beauty that we should desire him" (Isa. 53[2]). When Jesus went to the house of Zacchæus, for one new friend he made, he would lose many; we can hear the murmurs of the crowd: "Do you see with whom he has gone to stay? the richest profiteer in the town!" Jericho was the pantry of Judæa, and is still exceedingly fruitful; the chief publican there would be a very rich man. But, like many other wealthy men, he had a soft spot somewhere, and Jesus touched it. He would know what it would cost Jesus to be seen going home with him, and would be immensely proud to have such a guest. Like the publican in the parable he felt his position acutely, and his repentance was as thoroughgoing as we should expect. Jesus rewards him by calling him *a son of Abraham* (cf. 13[16]), one of the "lost sheep" (Mt. 10[6]) whom Jesus had come to seek and save (Mt. 18[11]—omitted in R.V.—is not part of the true text of that Gospel, so v. 10 must be assigned to L).

11–27. The Parable of the Pounds. (Mt. 25[14-30]; see also intro., p. 1031.) In this section two parables from L appear to be combined; there is a double plot. One is concerned with a nobleman who went to a far country to claim a kingdom, while his fellow-citizens intrigued against him; the other with a master who left his slaves in charge of sums of money, and came back to settle up accounts with them. The latter of the two parables reminds us of the parable of the talents in Mt. 25[14f.], but it can hardly come from the same source. In Matthew the slaves start with *unequal* opportunities (one has five talents, another two) and the successful slaves end with an *equal* reward, for the same words of commendation are bestowed upon both; in Luke they start with *equal* opportunities (each has a pound) and end with *unequal* rewards (one gets ten cities, another five). *The reward of faithful service is greater responsibility* (cf. 12[48]). This parable is intertwined with another (vv. 12, 14, 27) referring to the fate of the Jews. One of the Herods, Archelaus, went to Rome in pursuance of his claim to Judæa, Samaria, and Idumæa; he succeeded in getting the title of ethnarch, not of king, and exacted vengeance on the citizens of Antipatris, who had intrigued against him. Jesus is leaving the Jews to found a world kingdom, and the Jews will suffer for their rejection of his claim, as, indeed, they did.

28–48. The Triumphal Entry and Its Sequel. (Mt. 21[1-17] Mk. 11[1-11, 15-19].) In this section we come back at first to Mark again. In v. 37 Luke makes it plain that it was the *disciples* who shouted; he omits "Hosanna" (unintelligible to Theophilus); if he knew what it meant (it is equivalent to "God save the king"), he might have taken it as implying that, after all, Jesus did claim an earthly kingdom, the very thing Luke wished to avoid! He also leaves out (Mk. 11[10]), "Blessed is the coming kingdom of our father David." He has *Peace in heaven, and glory in the highest* (cf. 2[14] "Glory in the highest, and peace on earth"). The words are a reproduction from the memory of an eyewitness of the confused cries of the disciples, for "peace," "heaven," "glory," and "the highest" are all ways of addressing God without using the sacred name. The impression grows upon us as we read that Luke is not solely reliant on Mark here; he has an independent account of the entry in L.

Vv. 39–44 are peculiar to Luke, though we have in Mt. 21[16] a complaint about the shouts of the children. V. 40 contains a reminiscence of Hab. 2[11], "the stone will cry out of the wall" (cf. Lk. 3[8]). *The very stones* (v. 40) of this city of blood will protest if no one acclaims the coming of its king! *Weeping over the city* follows naturally, and this detail must have come from an eyewitness. The mind of Jesus is burdened not so much with his own sorrow as with the city's doom; his patriot heart is breaking. The fall of Jerusalem occupies a more prominent place in this Gospel than in the others (cf. also 21[24-26, 28, 35, 36] 23[28-31]). In the hurried description of *the cleansing of the Temple*, Luke is dependent on Mark (11[15-18]).

CHAPTER XX

1–26. Disputation in the Temple and a Parable. See notes on Mt. 21[23-27, 33-46] 22[15-22] Mk. 11[27-33] 12[1-17]. Here too Luke closely follows Mark. In v. 15 the wicked husbandmen cast the Son out of the vineyard, *before* they slay him; Mark has "slew him, and cast him out of the vineyard" (12[8]). According to the best modern critical opinion, Matthew followed Mark in this detail; in our text he agrees with Luke (Mt. 21[39]). If by the *vineyard* (cf. Isa. 5[1f.]) is meant Palestine (Mt. 20[1f.]), it would not be true to say that Jesus was cast out of the vineyard, and then slain. Luke thinks of the "vineyard" as Jerusalem, and so has altered the order, for Jesus suffered "*outside* the gate" (Heb. 13[12]). In v. 16 we have, in Luke only, the exclamation translated *God forbid!* ascribed to the opponents of Jesus. Dr. J. H. Moulton pointed out that this is one of Paul's characteristic formulas (cf. Gal. 2[17] 6[14], etc.) and inferred that his friend Luke wished to suggest that Saul of Tarsus was the leader of the chorus of protest on this occasion. He afterward became the chief expounder of the text, the quotation of which, if Moulton is right, roused his fierce resentment (cf. Rom. 9[33]). In the rest of the section (except v. 18) Luke follows Mark closely.

27–47. More Discussions. (Mt. 22[23-46] 23[1-12], notes; Mk. 12[18-40].) The most important difference from Mark to be found in this section comes in vv. 34, 35, and here Luke's preference for the celibate life betrays itself. Mk. 12[25] (cf. Mt. 22[30]) has "when they rise from the dead" (Matthew, "in the resurrection" only); Lk. 20[34f.] has "the sons of this world marry and are given in marriage, but those who are counted worthy to attain that age and the resurrection from the dead do not marry": this could be interpreted as "do not marry *in this life*." No doubt this was not meant, but Luke does not trouble to avoid the ambiguity. The words as found in Luke suggest also *conditional immortality*, i.e., immortality dependent upon fellowship with God (cf. 1 Cor. 15[50-58]). Jesus refutes the Sadducees out of the Pentateuch (v. 37), their doctrine being that only the first five books of the Bible were in the fullest sense inspired.

CHAPTER XXI

1–38. The Widow's Mite and Prophecies of the City's Fall. See notes on Mt. 24[4-22, 29-36] 25[31-46] Mk. 12[41-44] 13[1-37]. In the story of the widow's mite there is no change from Mark except that Luke heightens a little the pathos of the widow's poverty by a stronger word for *poor*. Then Luke follows Mark closely as far as v. 11, though for "not yet is the end" (Mk. 13[7]) he has *the end is not immediately* (v. 9), and he adds *epidemic diseases* in v. 11 to the list of the coming woes. He also abbreviates the long description of portents in the sky (Mk. 13[24-26]) to "there shall be frightful and great signs from heaven" (v. 11). Vv. 12–17 roughly correspond to Mk. 13[9-13], though the order is different, and for "he that speaks is not you but the Holy Spirit" (Mk. 13[11]) Luke has *I will give you a mouth and wisdom*, etc. (v. 15). This is a doublet in Luke (cf. 12[11, 12]), but 12[12] is nearer than 21[15] to Mk. 13[11]. As Mt. 10[19] is more general than either, it is possible that Lk. 12[12] comes from Mark, and that here Luke has turned from Mark to Q; vv. 18–22 which follow come from L. In v. 24 we have the phrase *until the times of the Gentiles are fulfilled*, which reminds us of Rom. 11[25] ("until the full complement of the Gentiles has come in"). The great mass of the Jews were to be left out of the Kingdom to make room for the Gentiles, but only for a time. Neither Jesus nor Paul could rest content with anything less than the salvation of his own people, for both were patriots. Vv. 25 and 26 are quite different from Mk. 13[24, 25], but in v. 27 we are back in Mark again (13[26]) while v. 28 is peculiar to Luke. The word *redemption* (v. 28; see also intro., p. 1031) is not the same as that used in 2[38] 24[21]; there the narrower Jewish hope is meant; here the thought is nearer Rom. 8[23] ("the redemption of our body," i.e., "of society"). In Jewish eschatology the idea that the darkest hour must come before the dawn was deeply rooted; before the Messianic age must come "the Messianic woes" (see arts., *Intertestamental Literature*, pp. 188, 210; *Backgrounds*, p. 846). In vv. 29–33 we find Marcan material again, only the phrases *and all the trees* (v. 29) and *the kingdom of God* (v. 31) being peculiar to Luke. On the other hand vv. 34–36 are distinctive. After v. 36 it is generally agreed that Jn. 7[53]–8[11] should come in, as they actually do in one important group of Greek MSS. (the "Ferrar" group; see p. 862a). They bear the marks of Luke's authorship, and certainly do not belong to the fourth Gospel at all. The story was also found in the "Gospel of the Hebrews," of which only a few fragments remain. Its right place is in Passion week; in v. 36 we read *and to stand fast before the Son of man;* in this story (Jn. 8[1-11]) we hear of a sinful woman who *did* stand before the Son of man, while her critics were shamed away.

CHAPTER XXII

1–13. Preparations for the Last Supper. (Mt. 26[1-5, 14-20], notes on Mk. 14[1, 2, 10-16].) Luke omits the story of the anointing at Bethany, because he has already told us another story of the same kind from L (7[36f.]), but he follows Mark in his insertion of the betrayal by Judas at this point. He follows Mark too in what looks like a mistake in v. 7 (Mk. 14[12], note). The paschal lamb was normally killed on the afternoon of 14th Nisan, which would last that year (probably 29 A.D.) till 6 P.M. on Friday (i.e., on Friday afternoon). The fourth Gospel makes it clear that the paschal lamb had not been eaten when Jesus was being tried (Jn. 18[28]). That must have been so, for it is incredible that the crucifixion could have taken place on Saturday. Both Paul (1 Cor. 5[7]) and John (19[36]) think of Jesus as himself the Paschal Lamb; in that case his death would have taken place on Friday afternoon, as all Christendom has always believed. It has been said that in special circumstances it was regarded as permissible to eat the paschal lamb on the evening before, and that this was the case here. But the suggestion is beset with difficulties, and it is more likely that the association of the Last Supper with the passover meal itself was a mistake, and that the fourth Gospel has deliberately and rightly corrected Mark on this question (see art., *Chronology of N.T.*, p. 875, for these various points). Canon Box has told us lately that it was customary for rabbis and their pupils to meet on the eve of great feast-days, and greet the coming of 6 P.M. with a simple meal of bread and wine and the passing round of the loving-cup; this pre-Christian lovefeast (the "Qiddush") was the meal of which Jesus partook on Thursday evening; there is no mention of a lamb or of bitter herbs in our accounts. Luke alone tells us that Peter and John were the two disciples sent to make preparations; otherwise he follows Mark closely here.

14–38. The Last Supper. (Mt. 26[21-35], notes on Mk. 14[17-31]; see also intro., p. 1031.) In the account of the Supper itself Luke is divergent from Mark; his informant must have been one of the Twelve, or perhaps the host of the evening; here, as in Gethsemane, we probably have John the son of Zebedee's account. Vv. 15, 16 are peculiar to Luke, and possibly support Box's theory (see under vv. 1–13): "I longed earnestly to eat this Passover with you before I suffer, but I have been disappointed, and I will not eat of it till it finds its fulfillment in the kingdom of God." Mark (14[25]) tells us that Jesus said he would not drink of the fruit of the vine, but says nothing about not eating the Passover. Some editors print v. 15 as a question, "Have I earnestly desired?" etc., the answer expected being "No." In our text as it stands there are two cups (vv. 17, 20). but it is practically certain that vv. 19, 20 (see R.V., mg.) should be excised from this Gospel. They are absent from many of our earliest authorities, and their presence in later texts is due to the fact that the actual words of institution were wanting in Luke, and they were inserted from 1 Cor. 11[23f]. This reduces the number of our authorities for the institution of the Eucharist from four to three (Mark, Matthew, Paul) but weakens little, if at all, the evidence for its historicity. V. 21 certainly follows v. 18 admirably: "I will not drink of the fruit of the vine [the loving-cup] . . . because the hand of the traitor is with me at the table."

In the verses which follow there are many

details which remind us of Mark-Matthew, but Luke is clearly independent. It is strange that the Twelve should have been disputing about precedence at the Last Supper itself; one can only think that Judas covered his retreat by starting again the old question, "Who is the first?" In Mark-Matthew, much of the material found here comes in connection with the request of James and John, which is dropped altogether by Luke (Mk. 10[42f.] Mt. 20[25f.]). There is an obvious connection between the words in v. 27 and the story of the feet-washing (Jn. 13[1f.]), which perhaps comes from the host of the evening. After *I am among you as the one that waits on table* (v. 27) the Western text beautifully adds, "and you have grown while I waited upon you to be like the servant."

Vv. 28–30 are peculiar to Luke, except the last clause, which comes from Q (cf. Mt. 19[28]). It is like Jesus to tell them, at the last moment at which it was true, that they had been with him in his trials; in Gethsemane they could not stay with him any longer, or "watch with him one hour."

Vv. 31, 32 also come from L; Jesus begins by addressing Simon, his name being twice repeated (cf. 10[41]), but goes on to speak of all of them ("Satan has desired to have *you*"), then comes back to Simon ("I have prayed for *thee*"), and passes on to the others ("strengthen thy brethren"). They were all to go astray; it was enough that he should pray for Peter, for, when Peter turned, they would all turn. Peter would turn by and by, but Jesus "turned" first (22[61]); just as we are to pray to escape from all that is coming (21[36] 22[40]), but Jesus prays for us (22[32, 40]); we are to "dig and go deep" (6[48]), and Jesus digs about us (13[8]); we are to "agonize" (13[24]), and he is in agony for us (22[44]).

Vv. 35–38 are also peculiar to Luke. When they went out on their earlier missionary tours (9[1f.]) they did not need to provide for or defend themselves; every door was open to them, because they were his. Now every door would be shut in their faces precisely for the same reason. Jesus is now "numbered among outcasts" (Isa. 53[12]). This passage may be taken in one of two ways: (1) It may be taken literally. Jesus is telling his disciples that they must be prepared to defend *themselves* if necessary, though not to defend him (cf. Mt. 26[52]). They were not ready for martyrdom yet, and had not done their work. In any case he would have them leave him, and keep out of danger. (2) The other explanation is profounder. If they decide to defend themselves by force, the time will come when they will have to sell the very clothes off their backs to buy weapons. They do not understand him—how could they?—and think he is appealing to them for protection. *Lord, here are two swords*, they say, and he replies, *Let it go at that.* The second explanation is more convincing.

39–53. The Agony in the Garden and the Arrest. (Mt. 26[36-56], notes on Mk. 14[32-52]; intro., p. 1031.) Luke is here quite independent; did this story in L come from John the son of Zebedee, like that of the transfiguration? It must have come from one of the three, and it was not Peter, for Peter's story is in Mark. Luke emphasizes, as we should expect, the command of Jesus to pray (vv. 40, 46): Mark-Matthew have "watch and pray"; Luke has simply *pray.* He does not tell us that only Peter, James, and John were allowed to enter the garden. Vv. 43, 44 do not appear in some early MSS. (see R.V., mg.) and their authenticity has been questioned. But we can more easily understand their being omitted than their being inserted, for many early Christians would be disturbed by the idea that the Son of God could be in such agony at the prospect of death. If we can find any good reason why early readers should question the genuineness of a passage we ought to retain it in our text, for the probabilities are that it would be deleted as needlessly disturbing in the days before the text was settled. Moreover, the medical language of v. 44 confirms us in the view that it was written by Luke; we should translate, not *drops of blood*, but "clots of blood." *Sleeping after sorrow* (v. 45) hints at a kindly excuse for the three, quite in Luke's manner; he makes Jesus *kneel* in Gethsemane (v. 41), whereas in Mark-Matthew he "falls" (Mt. 26[39] says "on his face," Mk. 14[35] says "on the ground"). Kneeling was the Greek mode in prayer; Jews stood, or, in deep emotion, prostrated themselves in prayer. Stephen (Acts 7[60]) kneels; cf. Eph. 3[14], where Paul is writing to Gentile Christians.

V. 48 is in Luke only; according to Mt. 26[50] Jesus said to Judas, "Comrade, why are you here?" The healing of the servant of the high priest's ear is also recorded by Luke alone (v. 51), and the same is true of his last sad words as Jesus is being led away (v. 53); they are strangely in the Johannine manner.

54–65. Peter's Denial. (Mt. 26[57-75], notes on Mk. 14[66-72]; see also intro., p. 1032.) Here again Luke is quite independent of Mark. In Mk. 14[67, 69] the same girl challenges Peter twice, while Mt. 26[71] tells us that his second assailant was "another girl." In Luke, on the other hand, first a girl, then two men in turn attack him, nor are we told that his dialect betrayed him; Theophilus would not be interested in the Galilæan dialect. It is more important that in Luke alone Jesus, here called *the Lord* (v. 61), turns and looks at Peter, casting upon him the searching glance which made his first meeting with the Master of his soul memorable (Jn. 1⁴²); in these two looks is written the history of Peter.

66–71. The Trial Before the Sanhedrin. (Mt. 26^{57-68}, notes on Mk. 14^{53-65}; see also intro., p. 1032.) V. 67 is found in Luke alone, again strangely in the Johannine manner. What does *If I ask* (v. 68) mean? What was he to ask? Luke omits the Marcan, "I am," in reply to the high priest's challenge (Mk. 14^{62}), but in v. 70 he has "*you say* that I am." Mt. 26^{64} has "Thou hast said"; Mk. 14^{62} "I am"; Lk. 22^{70} "you say that I am," a combination of Mark and Matthew. At any rate, we have strong evidence that Jesus did not say simply "I am," for it must be remembered that here Matthew and Luke are independent authorities; there is no question of Q. This is important, for nowhere but in Mk. 14^{62} does Jesus in so many words call himself "the Christ" (see, however, Mk. 9^{41}, which also is altered by Matthew and Luke). It is difficult to believe that he would have done so on this single occasion. Doctor Abrahams has argued that "Thou sayest," "Thou hast said," "You say" do not mean "Yes" or "No," but something between the two. The idiom, which is purely Semitic, is found also in Mt. 26^{25} Jn. 18^{37} Lk. 23^{3}; in all three cases for one reason or another Jesus wishes to avoid giving a direct answer. In the first of them he repeats the words of Judas' question, "Rabbi, surely it is not I?" and answers, "Surely not, Judas!" and in the second "The 'King of the Jews,' you say; I have been born for this . . . to bear witness to the truth." We may then understand Lk. 22^{67-69} to mean, "You say, 'the Christ': I say, 'the Son of man.'"

CHAPTER XXIII

1–25. Trials Before Pilate and Herod. See notes on Mt. 27^{11-26} Mk. 15^{1-15} and intro., p. 1032. We have an interesting various reading in v. 2. Marcion's edition of this Gospel adds two clauses to the list of charges against Jesus; they are, "and destroying the law and the prophets . . . and leading astray the women and the children." For the first of these clauses, cf. Mt. 5^{17}, a repudiation of the charge; the second looks as if it might be authentic, for the influence of Jesus over women is often emphasized by Luke. In v. 3 we notice the formula *Thou sayest,* again; at this point Luke confirms Jn. 18^{37}. Luke is evidently independent of Mark through the whole of this section. In v. 5 (cf. 4^{44} 7^{17}) *Judæa* stands for the whole of Palestine, including Galilee. The trial before *Herod* (v. 7) is recorded by Luke alone; he had special information about Herod and his court (cf. 8^{3} Acts 13^{1}). The only time that Jesus was "clothed in a glorious robe" came when he was in a king's palace (cf. 7^{25}), just as the only time he was with the rich was when he was buried (Isa. 53^{9}). Luke transfers the mockery of Jesus from the Roman soldiers (Mk. 15^{17}) to Herod's court: this may be a correction with knowledge. He also makes the people of their own motion declare for Barabbas; Mark says that "the chief priests stirred them up" (15^{11}). According to Luke, three times over did Pilate assert his belief in the innocence of the prisoner; in the same way three officials in succession pronounced Paul guiltless of any offense against public order (Acts 23^{29} $26^{31, 32}$). Throughout his Passion story the evangelist is concerned to throw the chief blame for the murder of Jesus upon the Jews; notice the phrases in v. 25, "him that for sedition and murder had been cast into prison, whom *they* were asking for," and cf. Acts 2^{36} ("*ye* crucified") and Acts 3^{14} ("*ye* denied . . . *ye* asked for a murderer").

26–49. The Crucifixion. (Mt. 27^{32-56}, notes on Mk. 15^{22-41} and intro., p. 1032.) One is tempted to look for Luke's chief authority for his wonderful story of the cross to Simon of Cyrene, who afterward, apparently, became a Christian (Mk. 15^{21}; cf. Rom. 16^{13}). If "Simeon who was called Niger" (Acts 13^{1}) was the same person (his nickname, "Niger," or, as we should say, "colored," suggests Africa, and we have "Lucius *of Cyrene*" as the next name in the list of "prophets and teachers" at the Syrian Antioch), he must have been thrown into close contact with Luke, who was once (see p. 1023a) a member of that church, and afterward moved to Philippi. Another suggestion that has found some favor is that Luke's authority was Saul of Tarsus himself; he was a pupil of Gamaliel (Acts 22^{3}), who was teaching in Jerusalem at that time; his interest in Pharisaism and in Jesus' attacks upon it would naturally bring him to Calvary, if he was in Jerusalem then, and he might well have been present at the trial before Pilate (cf. also note on 20^{16}). The parallels between the Lucan story of the Passion and that of the martyrdom of Stephen are striking (cf. Lk. 23^{34} and Acts 7^{60}; Lk. 23^{46} and Acts 7^{59}—in both cases Jesus is to Stephen what "the Father" is to Jesus), and we know that Saul was present at Stephen's martyrdom. May he not have drawn his friend's attention to the parallel? Moreover, in 1 Tim. 1[13] Paul applies the words of Lk. 23[34] to his own case; he, like the dying robber, had been "crucified with Christ" (Gal. 2[20]), and caught up to Paradise (2 Cor. 12[4]), and Luke alone tells us the story of the penitent robber!

The seven words from the cross are as follows: (1) "Father, forgive them; they know not what they do" (Lk. 23[34]); (2) "Woman, behold thy son . . . behold thy mother" (Jn. 19[26, 27]); (3) "To-day thou shalt be with me in Paradise" (Lk. 23[43]); (4) "My God, my God, why hast thou forsaken me?" (Mk. 15[34] Mt. 27[46]); (5) "I thirst" (Jn. 19[28]); (6) "It is finished" (Jn. 19[30]); (7) "Father, into thy hands I commit my spirit" (Lk. 23[46]). The only one of the seven sayings reported by Mark-Matthew is (4), the cry of despair, which, we are told, was uttered in a loud voice. Galilæan friends and followers of Jesus were standing at some distance (Lk. 23[49]), and so would only hear what was said in a loud voice. Mark-Matthew report another loud cry, but their authorities could not make out what was said then (Mk. 15[37] Mt. 27[50]). This is just what we should have expected, for the first and second Gospels come from the Galilæan circle.

The omission of the cry of despair from Luke and John sets us a more difficult problem. In John it may be accounted for by the absence of the "disciple whom Jesus loved," who would be engaged in taking Mary home (Jn. 19[27]). Luke perhaps could not bring himself to believe that Jesus had felt himself forsaken in the hour of his direst need.

Other details peculiar to Luke are the wailing of the women on the way up the hill, and the words of Jesus to them (vv. 27f.), with the saying about the green and the dry tree (v. 31). It is characteristic of Luke to find a redeeming feature in the behavior of women, and of Jesus even then to be thinking of other people's future troubles rather than his own present sorrows. As he moved up the hill the trees were all in leaf; if this could be done in the spring, what will happen when winter comes? The reference to that terrible last winter before the city fell is obvious (vv. 28f.).

The great saying, *Father, forgive them* (v. 34), faces us with a more difficult problem, for it is absent from some of the oldest MSS., like 22, 44 (see art., *Transmission of N.T.*, p. 860). Evidence for its authenticity may be found in Acts 3[17], but an even stronger argument has been based upon the fact that the words were always taken in antiquity as applying to the *Jewish* murderers of Jesus, not specially to the Roman soldiers who carried out the crucifixion. In that case we can understand how the words came to be dropped, for it would be argued that the fall of Jerusalem proved that the Jews had not been forgiven; it followed that Jesus could not have prayed for them, for the prayers of Jesus must have been answered. Like 22[43, 44] (see note) these verses can confidently be kept in the text, for it is far easier to account for their omission than for their insertion after the doom of the Jews had come upon them. Jesus had found in "hypocrisy," which in the Gospels means not so much conscious insincerity as self-delusion, the most insuperable obstacle in his way. Now, so to speak, he turns it inside out, and sees it as his ground of hope for humanity. Men are not all bad, even when they crucify Christ; they are tragically mistaken, and delusions cannot last forever.

In the rest of v. 34 there is another dramatic touch; the Jews stand *beholding*, while Gentile soldiers divide between them the garments of Jesus. Looking on then, as they had got into the habit of doing (Zech. 12[10]), the Jews have been fated to be spectators of the world's history ever since. In v. 35 we have a word which, as used of Jesus, is peculiar to this Gospel; it is *the chosen one* (cf. 9[35]).

The story of the dying *malefactor* (v. 39)—or, rather, as we ought to render the word, "revolutionist" (cf. Jn. 10[8] 18[40], where the word "robber" has the same meaning)—is Luke's greatest contribution to the Passion story, whether his informant was Simon of Cyrene, the centurion, or Paul. His traditional name was Dysmas, and he probably came from Galilee; we can reconstruct the outline of his biography from the records of that distressful time, when bands of irregulars harassed the Roman legions as they marched along the defiles of Galilee, swooping down from the hills on their rear, doing as much damage as they could, and then taking to their heels. In the company of an older and more callous companion, Dysmas had sunk lower and lower, until he had been caught red-handed in an act of brigandage and condemned, as all political prisoners were, to the cross. How did he come to think of Jesus as a king? Perhaps he had been present at the trial, awaiting his turn; in any case, he would have seen the superscription, "This is Jesus *the king* of the Jews," over the cross. When they are near death, men's minds work rapidly, and possibly he had heard in his boyhood that the king when he came would be rejected and killed by the wicked rich, and afterwards come again in glory (cf. Isa. 53 Zech. 12[10]). We cannot be sure of this, however, for it is not certain, though it may be regarded as likely, that the idea of a suffering Messiah is older in

Judaism than the second century A.D., when it first explicitly appears in its literature. However the dying man reached his conclusion, Jesus welcomed it, and was ready with one last effort to lift the lost sheep out of his despair to Paradise before he sank himself. With what delight he must have greeted the prospect of having a man with him on the other side, for he had not fallen out of love with human nature yet! Like every other unprejudiced person in the Gospel, Dysmas acquits Jesus of any crime against the civil power.

In v. 44 Luke's language seems to suggest an eclipse of the sun; this, of course, would be impossible at full moon. The other Gospels use more guarded language, and their testimony is to be preferred here. Luke passes over the forsaken cry during the hours of darkness, a cry which, following so soon after the rescue of Dysmas, poignantly illustrates the words "He saved others; himself he cannot save." For *the rending of the veil* (v. 45) there is an interesting parallel in rabbinical writings, where we read that forty years before the destruction of the Temple, at *the passover*, the doors of the Temple swung open of their own accord. Evidently, some unusual event at this Passover was long remembered (see notes on Mk. 15[33-41]).

After his despair Jesus rallies again to *commit his spirit* to his Father's keeping in the words of Psa. 31[5]. Mt. 27[50] ("let his spirit go") and Jn. 19[30] ("gave up his spirit") suggest the same idea, though the thought in Matthew is that he gave up his spirit to men, in John that he gave it up to God; once again Luke and John are associated together (cf. Lk. 22[53, 67]). The centurion's confession (v. 47) tallies with Mt. 27[54] Mk. 15[39], for a "son of God" (Matthew-Mark) and "a righteous man" were synonymous terms in current Jewish language (the theological interpretation was to come later); but the belated repentance of the crowds who came to see *this sight* (v. 48) is recorded by Luke alone.

50–56. The Burial of Jesus. (Mt. 27[57-61], notes on Mk. 15[42-47].) Here Luke comes back to Mark for a little while. The only difference is that in Luke the women prepare the spices before 6 P.M., while in Mk. 16[1] they wait till the Sabbath is over (Saturday 6 P.M.) before they buy them. Luke also tells us that *no one had ever yet been laid* in the tomb in which Jesus was buried (Jn. 19[41] confirms this detail). Evidently, Joseph buried Jesus very hurriedly.

CHAPTER XXIV

For special interpretative notes on ch. 24, see the introduction, p. 1033a.

1–12. Resurrection Day: Morning. See notes on Mt. 28[1-10] Mk. 16[1-8]. Discrepancies between the resurrection-narratives are serious, but not greater than we should expect, for, at a time of such wild excitement, there would be a happy incoherence, and everybody would be talking at once, as fresh witnesses to the truth of the amazing news came pouring in. We should have been properly suspicious of connivance in a made-up tale if everybody had agreed as to the detail of what actually happened. (See art., *Miracles of N.T.*, p. 930.) According to Mark, the women saw "a young man clothed in white"; according to Matthew, they saw an angel; according to Luke, "two men in gleaming robes" (Mk. 16[5] Mt. 28[2] Lk. 24[4]); the simplest account is probably nearest the truth. *Why seek the living among the dead?* (v. 5) and the inclusion of Joanna—probably Luke's informant—among the witnesses are peculiar to Luke; from Joanna perhaps comes the lifelike touch of resentment at the skepticism of the men (v. 11; the "Lewis" Syriac version has "as if they had spoken out of their wonder"—an unmistakable suggestion of hysteria). V. 12 is to be excluded on textual grounds (like 22[19, 20]); it probably comes from Jn. 20[3f].

13–35. Resurrection Day: Afternoon. The traditional site of Emmaus is a long way from Jerusalem, and can only be reached by road nowadays by a long twenty-five mile detour. But there is a rough and difficult path which provides a much shorter route, longer, however, than the sixty furlongs (v. 13) mentioned by Luke. The two friends (some traditions say they were a man and his wife) were arguing hotly, and were "throwing words at one another" when the stranger overtook them, for they are still unconvinced by the story of the women. In v. 18 we should render their surprised question, "Have you no friends in Jerusalem?" or "Do you lodge all by yourself in Jerusalem?" V. 21 reveals in a flash how little the rank and file of his disciples understood Jesus even now; they are still harping on their hopes of a national Redeemer; that was perhaps why *their eyes were holden.* When they get to Emmaus they press the stranger to come in; like the Jesus of Galilee (Mk. 6[48]), he will never force himself upon anyone, but waits for an invitation. Only when he takes the head of the table, breaks the bread, and repeats his familiar blessing over it do they recognize him. Perhaps they had not caught sight of the nailprints on his hands before, or perhaps no one else did the honors of the table in quite the same way. Directly they recognized him *he vanished out of their sight* (v. 31). It is still the same with us; when we try to keep him to ourselves we lose him. They had to go back and join the others before they could see him again (for the same idea cf. Jn. 20[17] Mt. 28[10]). Forgetting their weariness, they return over the rough, dark path to Jerusalem, and find the others still up. But before they can tell their great news the others break out with, *The Lord is really risen; he has appeared to Simon* (v. 34, and cf. 1 Cor. 15[5]). It was just like him to find time to visit broken-hearted Peter. For another suggestion of the risen Lord's special regard for Peter, cf. the mention of his name separately in Mk. 16[7]. In v. 32 there are three beautiful readings: "burning," "veiled," and "burdened." The subject of the unknown traveler's discourse on the road is the same as it was in Jerusalem later on in the evening—the doctrine of the suffering Messiah, illustrated from the O.T.

36–53. Resurrection Day: Evening. V. 40, like v. 12, does not belong to the best text; like v. 12, it comes from the fourth Gospel (Jn. 20[20]). It is surprising that even now the disciples need so much convincing, but this very fact tells strongly in favor of the authenticity of the story, for, in a manufactured narrative, recognition would have been instantaneous. Just as on the road earlier in the day, Jesus preaches a sermon to them from the O.T. Before the publication of any of our N.T. books, someone (perhaps Matthew the publican) made an anthology of O.T. texts, interpreted as referring to Jesus, for the benefit of Christian preachers and teachers, and for many years this collection of "Testimonies against the Jews," as it was called, provided an armory for the defense and propagation of the gospel; it was used by all N.T. writers, including Paul himself, and so must have been written very soon after the resurrection. This idea must surely have originated with Jesus; Jn. 2[22] states in so many words that the disciples did not understand "the Scriptures" (i.e., the O.T.) till Jesus was risen, and Paul's first line of defense (cf. 1 Cor. 15[3, 4]) was the O.T. Probably, then, Luke is substantially right when he tells us that this was what Jesus busied himself with on Resurrection day—he explained the O.T. The O.T. will always keep its place in our Bible if only for the reason that it meant so much to Jesus (Mk. 14[49] Mt. 26[54] 5[18]); indeed, we cannot understand him fully without its help; only, *we must read it through his eyes.*

The words *and was carried up into heaven* (v. 51) cannot have been part of the original Gospel, for they not only flatly contradict Matthew and John—both describe subsequent appearances—but also Acts 1[3]. The ascension cannot have taken place on the evening of Resurrection day, and the Western text saves Luke from very serious self-contradiction by omitting these words, together with "he was taken up" in Acts 1[2]. In the second part of his work, not in his first, Luke described the ascension.

(For a note on the theory of the composition of Luke-Acts suggested by the treatment in this commentary, see intro., pp. 1023–5; and for a note on the special significance of this Gospel for our interpretation of Jesus Christ, see intro., pp. 1025–33.)

JOHN

By Principal ALFRED E. GARVIE

Introduction

Comparison with Other Gospels. Any careful reader of the Gospels will at once be struck by the likeness to one another of Matthew, Mark, and Luke on the one hand, and the unlikeness to them of John on the other, and a closer scrutiny only confirms the impression. These three Gospels are called the *Synoptic*, because they give *a common view* of the ministry of Jesus, almost entirely different from that of the fourth. In those, the ministry is placed in Galilee and surrounding regions, except in the last week in Jerusalem; in this, with the exception of a few incidents, the ministry is exercised at Jerusalem at the great feasts. In those, the ministry might be confined to one year; in this, it must have extended over at least three Passovers. In those, Jesus calls his disciples from their fishings at the Sea of Galilee; in this, he calls them from following John to join him beside the Jordan. In those, the cleansing of the Temple is at the end; in this, at the beginning of the ministry. In those, the Last Supper takes place at the time when the Passover is being celebrated; in this, on the evening before, and Jesus is on the cross when the Passover lamb is being slain. In those, most of Jesus' teaching is in short sayings of—as Wendt describes them—"popular intelligibility and impressive pregnancy" (*The Teaching of Jesus*, vol. i, p. 109), in proverbs and parables; in this, the teaching is generally in long discourses, and sustained argument, sometimes of perplexing subtlety. In those, the tone of controversy is subordinate; in this, predominant. In those, the kingdom of God (Mark and Luke) or the kingdom of heaven (Matthew) is the principal theme; in this, the person of Jesus as not only the Christ, but as even the Son of God. Matthew and Luke begin with the stories of the infancy; Mark with the baptism of John; John with what is generally known as the Prologue, the description of the eternal Word of God and his manifestation in time. Those three begin on the plane of human history; this one begins on the heights of divine reality. Luke in his preface indicates the purpose of his careful research in his address to the most excellent Theophilus, "that thou mightest know the certainty concerning the things wherein thou wast instructed" (1^4). John in his conclusion states regarding his selection of the signs done by Jesus, "These are written that ye may believe that Jesus is the Christ, the Son of God; and that believing ye may have life in his name" (20^{31}). The one has a historical, the other a doctrinal purpose, although common to both are the religious interest and motive. Can such diverse representations of the same life be both accurate? If we accept the Synoptics as historical, must we reject the fourth Gospel as unhistorical?

The Historical Value of the Fourth Gospel. The complex character of the fourth Gospel excludes the two extreme solutions of the problems of its historicity, namely, that on the one hand this Gospel can be regarded as accurate historical narrative to the same extent as the Synoptics, and that, on the other hand, history is so manipulated in the interest of doctrine that we must set it aside as mainly if not altogether unhistorical. Westcott's *The Gospel of St. John* may be mentioned as an instance of the one extreme; and Ernest F. Scott's *The Fourth Gospel* as illustrating the other. An intermediate position is possible which assigns to this Gospel a greater historical value than most scholars have in recent years allowed to it, and seeks to do justice to all the evidence which can be offered of the subordination of history to doctrine in the purpose of the author. A writing has a double reference in time, the time *about which* it is written, and the time *in which* it is written, and so also of place. Even a modern historian cannot so completely transport himself to another age and another land as to conceal altogether when and where he writes. An ancient historian never regarded it to be his duty so to transport himself. In regard to this Gospel, the one reference is to Jerusalem in the fourth decade, the other to Ephesus in the last decade of the first century. The question to which divergent answers are being given is this: Which of these two references is the more important for our interpretation and valuation of the Gospel? Has the author more to tell us about the Judæan past or the Ephesian present of his writing? It is conceded that the author shows, or at least appears to show, a familiarity with Jerusalem in the time of the ministry of Jesus; is the explanation offered by Scott adequate, when he states that "apart from its allegorical value, the picturesque detail in John's narrative can be set down, not to the accurate memory of the eyewitness, but to the fine instinct of the literary artist"? (*Op. cit.*, p. 19.) Is it not preferable to find here a confirmation of the belief that much in the Gospel goes back to an eyewitness? It may be admitted that there is much in the doctrinal development of the Gospel which finds its more probable setting in the Ephesus of the last decade than in the Jerusalem of the fourth; but does that justify the assumption of the one setting when the other is at least as probable? Is it not more reasonable to treat as historical what there is not convincing reason to regard otherwise? Some considerations can be advanced to justify an unprejudiced inquiry regarding the historical value of the Gospel.

1. *The Account of the Ministry of Jesus Incomplete.* Without depreciating the historical value of the Synoptic Gospels it may be urged that they give an incomplete account of the ministry of Jesus. The historical framework of Matthew and Luke is supplied by Mark; and according to a trustworthy tradition he reported what Peter had preached about Jesus (see p. 997). Peter's interest as a Galilæan would be in the Galilæan ministry. That he makes no mention of a Judæan ministry prior to Passion Week is no evidence that such a ministry did not take place, as we are not compelled to assume that he was always with Jesus when he passed beyond Galilee and the neighboring regions. The sources from which the other material used in Matthew and Luke comes carry no guarantee of adequacy or completeness. The character of the Synoptic Gospels does not exclude the possibility of words and works which they do not record, and a longer ministry. "The chronology of the life of Christ," says Canon Streeter, "is simply a question of Mark against John" (*The Four Gospels*, p. 424, The Macmillan Company), and "the Johannine chronology solves more difficulties than it raises" (*ibid.*, p. 421).

2. *Evidence that the Account is Incomplete.* This possibility seems to be turned into a probability, if not a certainty, by this consideration. We think of Christ as World Saviour and Lord: he came and offered himself to the Jewish people as the Messiah. Would the offer have been adequate if made for many months in the province of Galilee, despised by the Judæans, and only for at most three weeks in Jerusalem? Is it not in the highest degree probable that he made his appeal to the nation, when the largest number could be reached from all parts of the world, as at the great feasts, just as the fourth Gospel records? This consideration should have decisive weight for the historicity of the chronological framework and local setting of the fourth Gospel.

3. *Further Evidence from the Synoptic Record.* The Synoptic record of Passion Week (or weeks) lends confirmation to this conclusion. Would a previous ministry exercised in Galilee have provided an adequate cause for the extreme hostility of the Jewish rulers, and their reckless determination to rid themselves of Jesus? Does not their conduct become more intelligible if it were preceded by a series of controversies of increasing acuteness, such as the fourth Gospel presents to us? Is not Jesus' lament over Jerusalem robbed of all its pathos if he had not made any more effort to gather "her children together, even as a hen gathereth her chickens under her wings" (Mt. 23^{37}) than the Synoptics record? Do not the words "how often" suggest more than one visit? This evidence in favor of the representation of the fourth Gospel cannot be lightly set aside.

4. *Historicity of the Supplementary Material.* If, as has just been shown, the fourth Gospel can be regarded, even on Synoptic evidence, as supplementing the historical testimony of the other Gospels, although the recording of biography or history is not its primary intention, we need not assume that in "the signs" reported the Gospel is very freely handling, modifying for its own purpose at will, Synoptic material. The narrative in Jn. $4^{46\text{-}54}$ need not be regarded as a variant of Lk. $7^{2\text{-}10}$; nor that of Jn. $5^{2\text{-}9}$ of Mk. $2^{1\text{-}12}$. A convincing proof of identity in the second instance is not supplied by the use in both records of the words, "Arise, take up thy bed," and of the vulgar word *Krabatton*, which Matthew and Luke both avoid. (See Estlin Carpenter, *The Johannine Writings*, pp. 381, 382.) Whether literary dependence is involved is another matter. So we may further ask, Is it certain that there can have been only one cleansing of the Temple, or may not the one have been a prophetic challenge at the beginning, the other a Messianic claim at the end of the ministry? Is it incredible that there were two anointings—the one Luke records ($7^{36\text{-}50}$) and the other reported in Mt. $26^{6\text{-}13}$ Mk. $14^{3\text{-}9}$ and Jn. $12^{1\text{-}8}$, even if, as Canon Streeter maintains, John's report of the one incident was influenced by Luke's record of the other? (*Op. cit.*, p. 402.) Even if John had access to and was familiar with the Synoptic Gospels, any literary dependence which can be proved does not exclude the probability of his having other sources of information which he regarded as equally trustworthy. And, if there were a Judæan as well as a Galilæan ministry, similar events may have taken place, similar cures have been wrought, and similar words spoken.

5. *The Author's Influence on His Own Ma-*

terial. Canon Streeter, after a careful scrutiny, reaches the conclusion that John did not use Matthew and that, even if he knew the Gospel, he refused to accept it as apostolic because of its apocalyptical and Judaistic sayings. He is certain that John used Mark, because, although only one fifth of the words are the same, yet "he often reproduces some of the more out-of-the-way phrases of Mark." He bases his argument for the literary dependence of John on Luke on those instances in which John supplements Luke in supplying particulars of persons and places mentioned less definitely in Luke. Not so certain, but probable in his view, is the dependence, not on a Proto-Luke only, but on our Luke also (*op. cit.*, pp. 395–426). It is difficult not to regard such an argument as Canon Streeter here presents as finally conclusive. But one difficulty must be stated. If these written Gospels were known and used by John, the differences between the fourth Gospel and the Synoptics show a very free handling by the evangelist of the material he had before him. Two considerations do partially relieve the difficulty. The one is that, if the author (or source) was himself a witness of the life of Jesus, or was directly dependent on a witness, these Gospels, neither of which claimed an apostle as author, would not have the authority for him which they possessed for a later generation. The other consideration is in the fact that the writer of the fourth Gospel is not mechanically piecing together materials found on a written page, but is rather presenting us with a picture resulting from the fusing of his own materials, as Canon Streeter puts it, "in the crucible of his creative imagination." Again one seems justified in raising this further question. If "the disciple whom Jesus loved" was either the evangelist or the source of his independent material, he is represented as after the resurrection in close association with Peter (20^2), from whom Mark, according to tradition, derived his material. May he not accordingly have absorbed much of this tradition, even in verbal details, before Mark's Gospel was written? A similar question may be raised regarding the dependence on Luke. Canon Streeter postulates an earlier work than our Luke which he calls Proto-Luke, which was independent of Mark. If Luke gathered this material when he came as Paul's companion on Paul's last visit to Jerusalem, would he not be moving in circles in which the beloved disciple also moved, and thus would not both be gathering their material from the same sources? It would betray rashness to challenge the conclusions of a scholar so competent as Canon Streeter; but may not a scholar, just because he is always handling documents, assume literary dependence as the only possible source of a resemblance which may better be accounted for by personal contacts?

6. *The Fourth Gospel at once Parable and Fact.* Although Canon Streeter, feeling that the fourth Gospel belongs rather to the literature of devotion than to history or biography, describes John as mystic and prophet, and speaks of his "creative memory," he yet separates himself from many more recent writings on the fourth Gospel in insisting that John was not indifferent to historical facts, and concerned only about the eternal truths which the facts symbolized. "John may have been mistaken about his facts," he says, "but to him it is as important to emphasize the historical as to see in the historical a symbol of the Eternal" (*op. cit.*, p. 389). John sees in the historic fact of the Word made flesh "an acted parable." There was a real coming of the Eternal into time, a real life, a real death, a real resurrection. For him, the taking of flesh, i.e., the incarnation, was a real event involving sacrifice, limitation, and suffering, and not merely, as certain Gnostics held, a piece of unreal phantasy. If the evangelist himself was not indifferent to fact, we are justified in looking for *fact* in his narrative.

The Literary Character of the Fourth Gospel. While at the first glance the fourth Gospel shows a literary unity which has led to the comparison of it to "the seamless robe" (Jn. 19^{23}), yet on closer scrutiny it is discovered to be a complex composition. The Gospel seems to have had a checkered career after it appeared in its original form. Of this the first indication may be found in the R.V. mg. of 7^{53}. "Most of the ancient authorities omit Jn. 7^{53}–8^{11}. Those which contain it vary much from each other." A close examination of the language shows it to be not Johannine but Lucan; and it is probable that if this passage never had a place in our Luke, it belongs to the same source that much of the Lucan material has been derived from. If such an insertion was possible in a sixth century MS. (Codex Bezae; see p. 863a), it being absent from MSS. of the fourth and fifth centuries, it is not rash to assume the probability of insertions in the centuries before our oldest MSS., if the internal evidence justifies such an assumption. Another indication may be given. Moffatt in his *New Translation* inserts $7^{15\text{-}24}$ after 5^{47} with the note, "Restoring $7^{15\text{-}24}$ to this its original position in the Gospel" (pp. 120, 121); and in other places a similar rearrangement will be found. Many scholars now agree that in many parts there has been displacement. Still another indication may be offered. So conservative a scholar as Westcott describes ch. 21 as an Epilogue, and states that "this chapter is evidently an Appendix to the Gospel, which is completed by chapter 20" (*Gospel of St. John*, p. 299). His argument that this Appendix was written by the author of the Gospel is not convincing. Even if "there is no evidence to show that the Gospel was published before that appendix was added to it," i.e., evidence of a textual character, the two facts mentioned above forbid our assumption that even our oldest MS. of the fourth century preserves the Gospel in its original form. Lastly, any careful reader of the Gospel must realize what may be described as a change of mental scene, when he passes from John 1[1-18] to what follows. A theological exposition of the truth regarding the Word of God gives place to a historical narrative, in which the Word is not again mentioned, but much is said about the Son of God. Scholars agree in describing 1[1-18] as the Prologue, but are not agreed whether, like the Epilogue or Appendix, it is to be regarded as part of the original work. These three facts—the possibility of later insertions, the probability of displacements, the detachment on account of their distinctive character of the Prologue and the Epilogue from the main body—afford a starting point for our investigation.

1. *Character and Significance of the Appendix.* We may begin with the Appendix, as there is here most general agreement that it is an addition to the original Gospel. Our view of it will be affected by our conclusion regarding the last two verses (vv. 24, 25). Even Westcott regards these verses as "separate notes attached to the Gospel before its publication" (*op. cit.*, p. 306) and ascribes v. 24 to the Ephesian elders. The hyperbole of v. 25 would itself make it suspect, and the oldest MS., Codex Sinaiticus (p. 862b), omits it; it is probably an addition by a very early scribe. The intention of v. 24 is to identify the author of the Gospel with the apostle John, since the sons of Zebedee are mentioned in v. 2, although there is not a word in the Gospel to support such a contention, and even the Appendix does not make the identification inevitable, since "two other of his disciples" are also mentioned. The tradition of authorship, which afterward became common, was evidently still challenged when this attestation of quite unknown authority was added, affording us unintentioned evidence that the authorship was in doubt. If v. 24 is not an added note, but belonged to the Appendix as originally written, then this attempt to settle a disputed question must be regarded as one of the reasons for the Appendix. Two other reasons for the Appendix may be suggested, the one concerned with "the disciple whom Jesus loved" (v. 20), and the other with Peter (vv. 15–17). Jesus' words in Mk. 9[1], "Verily I say unto you, there be some here of them that stand by, which shall in no wise taste of death, till they see the kingdom of God come with power," were evidently understood as a promise that one of the disciples would survive to the Second Advent. If the beloved disciple was identified with John the son of Zebedee, and was thus reckoned as the last survivor of the apostolic company, to whom the words were addressed, his death would cause widespread bewilderment. Had the Lord been slack in the fulfillment of his promise? The explanation of the promise in vv. 22, 23 was intended to relieve that bewilderment. The apostle's death seems the more natural occasion for such an explanation; but Canon Streeter, who expresses a far higher estimate of the character of the Appendix than most scholars, holds that the Appendix comes from the author himself, or one of his pupils, who "desires to forestall the dangerous disillusionment which he foresees will inevitably result from the non-fulfillment of this hope" (*op. cit.*, p. 464). In that case the Elder or his pupil must have accepted without challenge the identification of him with the disciple whom Jesus loved.

The reason why Peter is mentioned is this: In the greater part of the Gospel, Peter and the other disciples with whose names the Synoptics make us familiar fall into the background, and only the beloved disciple and unnamed disciples come into view. The author of the Appendix seeks by the record of his restoration after his fall to recover for him his place of prominence and authority. If v. 24 is part of the Appendix, then the Appendix seeks to claim the authorship of the Gospel for one of the Twelve. Canon Streeter points out another consideration which throws light on the intention of the writer of the Appendix. In the Gospel itself only appearances in Jerusalem are recorded. Probably the edition of Mark current in Ephesus recorded as does Matthew an appearance in Galilee. The Appendix both confirms and corrects Mark. There was an appearance in Galilee, but it was the third, being preceded by the appearances in Jerusalem recorded in the Gospel (*op. cit.*, p. 473). This interest in the Galilæan group of disciples, and the Synoptic representation of the ministry, runs through other passages, which in several cases interrupt the context, and may probably be later insertions of the author of the Appendix, *whom we may call the redactor.* Attention will be called to these passages in the commentary following; and a list of them need not be given here.

2. *Character and Significance of the Prologue.* Turning now to the Prologue, it may be affirmed that it does not dominate the representation of the person and work of Christ to the degree in which Scott in the work already mentioned assumes that it does, nor does it stand apart to the extent which Harnack asserts, for its influence can be traced in some passages which may be briefly described as of a more *metaphysical* character, showing a tendency to emphasize the supernaturalness of the person of Jesus more than the rest of the record itself warrants, and as betraying an interest in the current eschatology, which the theology of the Gospel generally has left behind, but which reappears in the First Epistle. Canon Streeter, who very vigorously combats attempts at source-criticism, admits "a very large number of disarrangements," leaving the door open for such insertions as are suggested in the paragraph above, "and also a few editorial additions—5[28, 29], for example, which reflects the apocalyptic conceptions of an external judgment, thus directly contradicting the lesson of the previous verses" (*op. cit.*, p. 382). Other passages there are which seem to indicate the standpoint of the Evangelist, who in the respects mentioned was not in entire agreement with the "disciple whom Jesus loved," whose witness he is for the most part reproducing, and to whom he seems to have stood in a relation similar to that of Mark to Peter. The designation, the "disciple whom Jesus loved" (20[2]), is his tribute to the teacher to whom he owed his knowledge of the life and teaching of Jesus, although 1[14] and 1 John 1[1-4], if they must be taken as referring to sensible and not only to spiritual contact, might indicate that he, as a boy or youth, may also himself have had some personal acquaintance with Jesus. As the Epistles go with the Gospel, we need not hesitate about naming the Evangelist "John the Elder," to whose presence in Ephesus at the end of the first century tradition bears testimony. To the Evangelist is due the Ephesian standpoint of the Prologue and other passages. The commentary will indicate where his distinctive thought appears clearly, although there must be many other places where he has modified the contribution of the Witness.

3. *The Nature of the Contribution of "the Witness."* Before any attempt is made to identify the Witness, the nature of his contribution must be examined. In that contribution we must distinguish two strata. About half a century must have elapsed between the events reported and the report of them by the Witness to his disciple, the Evangelist. That report need not have been a private communication; it may have been given in public discourse to the Christian community. We need not assume that the Evangelist reported *verbatim* what he heard; but his own thought and style may have been so influenced by his teacher's, that even when he was not reproducing accurately the resemblance would be maintained. Characteristics of the Gospel, such as the Prologue and other passages, make it necessary to distinguish three persons, namely, the Evangelist, the Witness, "the beloved disciple" of Jesus, who in preaching told what he had seen and heard, and the disciple of this beloved disciple who recorded in the Gospel that teaching. In distinction from the positions set forth in the present discussion, Canon Streeter's view is that the beloved disciple is the apostle John idealized, whom he credits with some slight connection with the contents of the Gospel; and that the writer of the Gospel is a disciple of the apostle, himself responsible for the contents of the Gospel in its present form. What he says of the Evangelist as mystic and prophet (p. 365f.) *would on the view here taken apply rather to the Witness.* "The mysticism of John," he says, "like that of Paul, is a mysticism centered, not on Absolute Being, but on the Divine Christ." He lived in intimate contact and intimate communion with his living Lord. Not only so; there was a "revival of prophecy" as "the conspicuous feature of the early church." The mystic regarded himself, and was regarded by the church, as an inspired prophet, guided in his reminiscences and reflections alike by the Holy Spirit; and for him accordingly it was not necessary to distinguish the one from the other, as from the point of view of historical interest we could wish he had done. We can imagine what took place in his preaching. Even if experiences of the past, words heard, and deeds done are vividly remembered, they are affected and cannot but be affected by the experiences of the intervening years; a thoughtful man especially will color his reminiscences by his reflections; and the more thoughtful he is the less likely is he to reproduce what he has seen or heard without his own comment. Still less will a mystic in communion with Christ, a prophet filled with the Spirit, be only a *verbatim* reporter of past memories. When this mystic and prophet preached, past history and present experience were blended in the eternal reality of the present Christ and present Spirit. No separation of what was remembered from the interpretation now given to it would seem necessary, or even be possible either for the preacher or his hearers. Remi-

niscence and reflection are so blended that only here and there in the Gospel can we venture to detect the transition; and wherever this is possible it will be indicated in the commentary; but no complete analysis can be attempted.

Summary Statement of the Theory of Composition. The theory of the composition of the fourth Gospel which the writer has endeavored to maintain in the preceding section may be stated briefly as follows: (1) The foundation of the Gospel is in the personal reminiscences, supplemented by reflection, which constituted the preaching of the *Witness*, identified with the unnamed "beloved disciple," a Jerusalemite. (2) This preaching was reported with reasonable fidelity by the *Evangelist*, identified with John the Elder, of Ephesus, who added such comments, e.g., the Prologue, as seemed necessary to make the book intelligible for his environment. (3) At a considerably later date the *Redactor*, who cannot be identified, desirous of removing what might be a hindrance to the acceptance of the Gospel in the churches generally now familiar with the Synoptic tradition, if not accurately acquainted with the Synoptic writings, made such additions, e.g., passages dealing with the Galilæan ministry, and, in part at least, the Appendix, as he was honestly convinced were necessary to supplement the Gospel in regard to matters of interest and importance to him. Various points in this theory still wait to be considered.

The Authorship of the Gospel. Tradition in the church in the latter half of the second century connects the Gospel with the apostle John, the son of Zebedee. After a very thorough survey of all the earlier evidenee, Canon Streeter comes to the conclusion that all the conditions are fulfilled by John the Elder, who was afterward on insufficient grounds identified with the apostle John. The Second and Third Epistles claim to be written by the Elder. This identification of the Evangelist with the Elder may be accepted without further discussion. But Canon Streeter assumes that the Elder had some personal connection with the apostle John. He says that only on this assumption can we make psychologically explicable the attitude toward the beloved disciple expressed in the Gospel (*op. cit.*, p. 433). Since it is assumed by the present writer that the beloved disciple was the Witness to the words and works of Jesus, which form the main content of the Gospel, so slight a connection would not suffice, and so we must press the questions: Are there reasons against identifying the Witness with the apostle John; and what does the Gospel itself reveal to us about "the disciple whom Jesus loved"? (Cf. p. 857b.)

1. *The Author's Interest in the Judæan Ministry.* It has already been pointed out that the passages dealing with the Galilæan ministry are probably later insertions by the redactor; as will be shown in discussing them, they seem less accurate than we should expect them to be if they came from an eyewitness, such as the son of Zebedee was. The dominant interest of the Gospel is, not in the Galilæan, but in the Judæan ministry. Is this what we should expect from a Galilæan disciple? In the Gospel there is evidence of such a familiarity with things Judæan—places, persons, customs, changes of feeling in the multitude, and of policy in the rulers—as points to a Judæan rather than a Galilæan source. At the proper places indications will be given of an intimate knowledge of the ruling circles in Jerusalem, such as a Galilæan fisherman, even if he sometimes came to Jerusalem to sell fish, was not likely to gain. The Synoptic records show that John, the son of Zebedee, was indeed in the inner circle of the disciples, but not that he had either the moral character or the spiritual capacity to become the confidant of Jesus about his inner life, as the fourth Gospel represents the beloved disciple as having been. When it is argued that the Son of Thunder was changed into the apostle of love by the lapse of many years, what is ignored is that the fitness for such intimacy with Jesus must have been shown during the earthly ministry. Again, would the Galilæan fisherman have had the interest in the controversies between Jesus and the Jewish teachers and leaders which fill so large a place in the Gospel? A Jerusalemite disciple, closely associated with these Jewish circles, would much more certainly have such an interest. Much is lost and nothing gained for the value of the Gospel by attempting to restore the tradition of the authorship by John the son of Zebedee.

2. *Theories Concerning the Identity of the Witness.* The identification of the Witness with "the rich young ruler," Lazarus, or Nicodemus, cannot be proved, even if a plausible case can be made out. Without attempting any such identification the writer is content with bringing together such evidence about the position and the character of the Witness as the Gospel itself suggests. The description of him as "the disciple whom Jesus loved" (13^{23} 21^{20}) is not a self-designation, but was given him by the Evangelist as the grateful tribute of a disciple who had been led by him into intimacy with the Lord. He may have been "the other disciple" who accompanied Peter to the tomb (20^{3-8}), as he may have been Peter's host in Jerusalem. If a wealthy citizen of influential position, he too may have provided the ass

for the triumphal entry by previous arrangement with Jesus (Mk. $11^{5, 6}$) and also the upper room for the Supper ($14^{13, 14}$), at which as host he was present. It is not unlikely that it was he who was known unto the high priest, and entered in with Jesus into the court of the high priest, and "went out and spake unto her that kept the door, and brought in Peter" (Jn. $18^{15, 16}$). These indications lead us to the assumption that he belonged to one of the priestly (or even high-priestly) families. In the attitude of the Gospel to demonic possession, angels, and the resurrection, in these parts which can be ascribed to the Witness, some scholars find an indication that he belonged to the Sadducees. If his discipleship began at the Jordan, he being the other of the two disciples of John who followed Jesus (1^{40}), that discipleship was not a constant companionship in Galilee, but was renewed at Jesus' visits to Jerusalem, and was probably kept secret for family reasons. There may be a personal confession in $12^{42, 43}$, "Nevertheless even of the rulers many believed on him; but because of the Pharisees they did not confess it, lest they should be put out of the synagogue; for they loved the glory of men more than the glory of God," although the statement itself seems to reflect the conditions of a later time. This would adequately explain why this disciple does not appear at all in the record in Acts. Was his testimony and influence in distant Ephesus at the close of his long life the atonement that he sought to make for the years of secret and silent discipleship? But did the same reasons as had constrained him to so long secrecy and silence lead him to withhold his name, and was this disciple respecting his Master's feeling in these indirect indications of his personality? We are here in the region of conjecture, to which a high degree of probability can be given only by the cumulative impression of a number of minute details, which will be noticed at their proper places in the commentary.

The Religious Significance of the Gospel. It has been necessary in this introduction to deal with these critical problems, as there is no other N.T. writing about which there is so great a diversity of opinion as about the fourth Gospel. But great as may be the divergence on these matters, the agreement is general as to the religious significance of the fourth Gospel. It bridges the gulf between the Jerusalem of the fourth decade and the Ephesus of the last decade of the first century. It presents to us the Jesus of history transfigured by the light of the Christ of faith. It links history with philosophy; sets the events of time on the background of eternity; makes explicit what is implicit with the other Gospels, and roots the Christian experience in the Christian history. It so discloses the glory of the Son of God in truth and grace as to evoke the faith which in him lays hold on eternal life.

Scientific Criticism and Appreciation of Spiritual Values. For the relation between a scientific criticism of the fourth Gospel and the discernment of its teaching and the appreciation of its profoundly spiritual character, see the discussion and summary with which the commentary concludes, pp. 1092–3.

Literature: Westcott, *The Gospel According to St. John;* Sanday, *The Criticism of the Fourth Gospel;* E. F. Scott, *The Fourth Gospel: Its Purpose and Theology;* Stanton, *The Gospels as Historical Documents*, pt. iii; Marcus Dods, *The Gospel of St. John*, 2 vols.; Burney, *The Aramaic Origin of the Fourth Gospel;* Garvie, *The Beloved Disciple;* Hayes, *John and His Writings;* Manson, *The Incarnate Glory;* Strachan, *The Fourth Evangelist, Dramatist or Historian?* Lord Charnwood, *According to St. John;* Streeter, *The Four Gospels*, pt. iii.

CHAPTER I

1–18. The Prologue: The Word Become Flesh. This is by some scholars regarded as giving the key to the Gospel, and as an integral part of it; others regard it as an introduction added to commend the Gospel to readers interested in current philosophical thought. Scott sees every part of the Gospel in the light of the doctrine of the Word (Greek *Logos*, meaning "reason" as well as "word"). Harnack denies any influence of the doctrine on the presentation in the Gospel. In the exposition here it is assumed that the Prologue is due to the Evangelist, that several passages in the Gospel show its influence, but that what is due to the Witness presents the conception of Christ as Son of God, and not as Logos (on the identity of the Evangelist and the Witness see intro., pp. 1064–6). The Prologue is regarded by Rendel Harris as "a hymn in honor of *Sophia*" (Wisdom), in which the term *Logos* has been substituted for that of *Sophia*, and in his view it need not be ascribed to the same author as the Gospel. Burney (*The Aramaic Origin of the Fourth Gospel*), who ascribes an Aramaic origin to the Gospel, derives the doctrine of the Logos from a Palestinian source in the Targums; the *Logos* is the *Mēmrā*, the *tabernacled among us* is the *Shᵉkīntā* (Shekinah) and the *glory* is the *Yᵉḳārā* (p. 39). Stanton and most scholars, however, maintain that the doctrine depends on Philo, who combined by the allegorical method of interpretation Greek philosophy with the Hebrew

Scriptures. While there are many resemblances, the crucial difference is this: that Philo had not reached the conception of the full personality of the Logos, because the fact of the incarnation was not within his ken. That *the Word became flesh,* fully man, necessarily modified the conception of the Word.

The idea of the Logos is common to both sources of Philo's theology. In the O.T., God's relation to the world is mediated by such conceptions as Angel, Spirit, Wisdom, Word, which are all personalized, but not presented as fully personal or as distinct from God himself. The associations of the Hebrew conception of the *Word* are carried over into the term *Logos,* while in Greek philosophy the emphasis lay on the meaning "Reason." The Prologue has more kinship with Hebrew than Greek thought. The Word is God's self-revealing activity within God himself before the world was, distinguished but not separated from God (vv. 1, 2) within the creation of all things (v. 3), and within the animation and illumination of man (v. 4), an illumination which men because of their spiritual incapacity failed to receive (R.V. mg. of v. 5, *overcame* for *apprehended*). Here is sounded the tragic note of the Gospel; rejection where reception should have been (cf. v. 11).

Vv. 6–8 are clearly an insertion, or at least a digression, the purpose of which is to deny that this divine illumination was to be found in John the Baptist, and to assert that his function was solely to testify; and this subject is taken up again in v. 15, in which the Baptist asserts the superiority of the Christ because of his priority (an evident reference to his *preexistence*). This reference to the Baptist is probably to be explained by the existence of a sect in or near Ephesus, which claimed for the Baptist a position superior to that of Christ, and which may even have identified him with the Logos. (Cf. Acts 18^{24}–19^{7}. Apollos came from Alexandria, to which Philo belonged, and he knew only the baptism of John; the twelve men in Ephesus, whose baptism is mentioned in immediate connection with the account of Apollos, were also adherents of the Baptist.) It may be that the Evangelist belonged to this same sect, until the Witness unfolded to him the truth about Jesus.

Vv. 9–13 revert to the doctrine of the Word, and describe his activity prior to the incarnation. This illumination was constant (always *coming into the world*) and universal (*every man*). The R.V. mg. refers the coming to each man. The *world* here means, not the physical universe, but humanity, estranged from and asserting its independence of God. Thus it ignored the creative presence in this illumination; for although it was his possession the men who belonged to him rejected him (the Greek of the first *his own* is neuter, of the second is masculine). The primary reference here is to the Jews, who had the advantage of the special revelation of God. The rejection, however, was not complete, as those who received, because regenerated by God himself, acquired the status and enjoyed the privileges of the children of God. V. 13 in the present reading contrasts spiritual with natural birth, possibly with reference to the Jewish boast of descent from Abraham (cf. 8^{39}); there is patristic evidence for the singular (*who was born*); with this reading there would be clearly a reference to the virgin birth.

In v. 14 the fact of the incarnation is stated. Humanity under all its conditions and limitations—for this is what *flesh* here means, not the body only—was assumed by the Logos. The Incarnate Word *tabernacled* (R.V. mg.) among men, and on him, as on the tent of old, rested the Shekinah, or God-presence. What distinguished this God-presence, however, was that in it divine sonship was revealed (*an only begotten from a father,* R.V. mg.). This links the Prologue with the rest of the Gospel, where not the Word, but the Son is the predominant notion. This revelation in the Son combined attractiveness and reality (the meaning which *truth* has throughout the Gospel). V. 15 breaks the continuity. In v. 16 the Evangelist reckons himself among those who shared the increasing benefits of this revelation; if he was John the Elder, he may as a boy have come into contact with Jesus, but any impression then made may have been deepened by his intercourse with the Witness. V. 17 contrasts this revelation in its attractiveness and reality with the legal system associated with the name of Moses. For all previous revelations of God suffered from necessary imperfection; only through the Son in intimate relation to the Father could the Fatherhood be fully revealed (v. 18).

19–34. The Baptist's Testimony: the Contrast Between Himself and the Christ. The first part of the Gospel (chs. 1–4) deals with testimony. The Baptist here, in his first testimony (cf. 3^{22-30}), disclaims his being the Messiah, or Elijah (Mal. 4^{5}), or the prophet (Deut. 18^{15}), and is content to describe himself in the words of Isa. 40^{3}. Challenged as to his right to baptize, he declares that his rite is only a purification preparatory to the manifestation of One so much greater than himself that he feels himself unworthy to perform for him the most menial offices (v. 26 suggests that the Baptist was aware of Jesus' presence).

The scene of this event is not known, and at an early date Bethabarah, or Betharabah, was suggested (R.V. mg.). This disclaimer was made to a commission, instigated by the party of the Pharisees (v. 24), but consisting of priests and Levites (v. 19). Is this a confusion, for the priests and Levites were mostly Sadducees? These religious leaders desired to look into this new religious movement, just as Nicodemus came, on behalf of his party, to interview Jesus himself (3^{1-10}).

Next day, probably after the commission had left, on the approach of Jesus, the Baptist bore witness (v. 29) to the atoning death, which, in view of his teaching as reported in the Synoptics, and his later doubt about the mission of Jesus (Mt. 11^{3}), is perplexing. If, however, Jesus was with John some days (v. 26), it is probable that they had some conversation, and that Jesus imparted his conception of his vocation, as in Isa. 53 (see p. 664). John may have been for a time at least lifted above his own habitual mode of thinking about the Messiah. The message sent to him through his disciples in this time of doubt would be a reminder of this conversation (Mt. 11^{5}). If this explanation is correct, the *lamb* is neither the paschal lamb, with which Paul identifies Jesus (1 Cor. 5^{7}), nor the lamb of the morning and evening sacrifice, but the lamb to whom the Suffering Servant is compared in Isa. 53^{4}. V. 30 repeats v. 15 and each verse breaks the continuity. As Jesus and John were related (Lk. 1^{36}), v. 31 cannot disclaim personal acquaintance but only recognition of function as Messiah. Vv. 32–34 present a serious difficulty. Mark's account of the Baptism indicates that it was Jesus only who saw *the dove as a symbol of the Spirit* descending (Mk. $1^{10, 11}$; cf. Mt. $3^{16, 17}$). Did the Baptist share that vision? Or did Jesus tell him of it, and of his consciousness of his calling as Messiah; and do these verses record an imperfect reminiscence, changed in the lapse of time with a heightening of the supernatural, which is characteristic of other passages in the Gospel? The second view seems the more probable. Even although the term *Son of God* in v. 34 is used as a title of the Messiah, and not in the sense the Gospel itself gives to it, so open a declaration of Messiahship by the Baptist is not at all probable; and we must recognize here, as in the next passage (vv. 41, 45, 49), that a more developed phase of the Christian faith is thrown back to this early stage. All through the Gospel, the time *about which* the Evangelist is writing is seen in the light of the time *at which* he is writing, and the perspective is foreshortened. It is difficult, unless by a conscious effort which the Evangelist never made, to see the past just as it was, and not as the present makes it appear.

35–51. The Call of the First Disciples. In Mk. 1^{16-20} (notes) the call is recorded of Simon and Andrew, and the two sons of Zebedee. This call to constant companionship in the public ministry in Galilee is not inconsistent with this account of an earlier intercourse with Simon (Peter) and Andrew. It has been sometimes assumed that *the unnamed disciple of John* (cf. vv. 35 and 40) was John the son of Zebedee, and that he also brought his brother to Jesus. But if this disciple was "the disciple whom Jesus loved" he was not, according to the view of authorship here taken, John the son of Zebedee (see intro., p. 1065). The account of the two days may come from an eyewitness; but his reminiscences are colored by reflections in two respects. So definite a confession of the Messiahship (vv. 41–45, 49) at so early a date would rob of its significance the confession of the Messiahship at Cæsarea Philippi (Mt. 8^{29}; cf. Mt. 16^{16}). The words spoken to Peter (v. 42) also seem antedated, and to belong to a period when Jesus had gained a more intimate knowledge of his character. In v. 42, as in v. 48, appears the tendency of the Evangelist to assign to Jesus a supernatural knowledge of the secrets of human hearts in addition to the spiritual and moral insight the Synoptics also recognize. Jesus may have seen *Nathanael* with the bodily eye at his devotions; how did he gain such intimate knowledge as the commendation implies? It is Peter, not Jesus (v. 43), who desires to go to Galilee. As Bartholomew is usually the companion of Philip in the Synoptic lists, Nathanael (v. 45) is usually identified with him. Although the Evangelist lays stress on the supernatural knowledge of Jesus, he records words of Jesus which depreciate a faith so based (v. 50). In a symbolic saying with evident reference to Gen. 28^{12}, Jesus declares that the disciples will be the witnesses of a constant and intimate communion of God and man in him, the Son of man, a title used by himself alone (except Acts 7^{56}) to express both his dignity and his humility; he was above and yet with man.

CHAPTER II

1–12. The Marriage of Cana of Galilee. This incident is often regarded as an allegory of the transformation of religion which Jesus was to bring about; the water of Judaism is changed into the wine of Christianity. The story itself offers no hint of any such meaning. It is evidently intended to be the record of a miracle, less difficult to imagine than the multiplication of the loaves and fishes (6^{1-13}), but more difficult to understand because the occasion does not seem adequate for such a display of supernatural power. Some suppose that a natural occurrence, which was afterwards misunderstood, may lie behind the narrative, the more so if the disciple who was the witness of the Judæan ministry was not present. As the incident had a personal interest for the mother of Jesus (v. 4), she may have been his informant, as she was committed to his care (19[26, 27]). Jesus' answer to her is not discourteous or disrespectful, according to the usage of the term "woman" at the time; but it is an assertion that in the use of his supernatural power he could follow no human prompting, not even his mother's (cf. Mk. 3[33-35]), but only God's. The mother's words to the servants show that she did not feel rebuffed, but remained expectant. When the divine indication came, her hopes were fulfilled. The six jars would hold about one hundred gallons. The jest of the chief servant (vv. 9, 10) need not be taken seriously as an indication that there was any excess. V. 11 seems to be a comment of the Evangelist's not consistent with Jesus' estimate of the value of faith based on miracles (cf. 2[23] 4[48]).

13–22. The Cleansing of the Temple. As a similar action is placed at the end of the ministry by the Synoptists (Mt. 21[12-17], notes), it is held by many scholars that the Evangelist for his own didactic aims displaced the incident. Two other possibilities, however, remain: (1) As the Synoptics record only one visit to Jerusalem, they may have brought together in their record incidents of several visits. (2) More probable is it that there were two cleansings; the first here recorded an outburst of prophetic enthusiasm, as the quotation in v. 17 suggests; the second a more definite assertion of authority as the Messiah. The account here seems accurate in its details and fuller than the Synoptic. The rebuke (v. 16) is less severe than that in the second record (Mk. 11[17]). Devout Jews visited the Temple at the three great feasts as often as possible; and Jesus, according to this Gospel, made a practice of going up at the feasts, when the city was full of pilgrims, and he could reach a larger multitude of his people than at any other time. When the hostility of the Jewish rulers became more marked, the presence of so many of his fellow countrymen from Galilee was a protection to him (cf. Mk. 14[2]). Challenged to give some proof of his authority, Jesus uses a symbolic saying (v. 19), which clearly means, "Destroy religion as you are doing, and I can quickly restore it." The rulers with prosaic literalness recall that the second Temple was begun by Zerubbabel in 559, and completed in 513, in the ninth year of Darius. The rulers, however, may have been referring to the Temple restoration begun by Herod in 20 B.C. In that case, the *forty and six years* would cover 20 B.C.–26 A.D., the latter year, if Jesus was born 5 or 4 B.C., being the year in which Jesus began his ministry (see p. 874). We could then paraphrase: "This Temple was begun forty-six years ago, and still it is not completed"—for the work on it continued until 63 A.D. The Evangelist, looking back after the resurrection, finds in these words a reference to it. It is possible that Jesus himself foresaw what the outcome of Jewish hostility would be (cf. Mk. 2[20-22]), and yet was sure of his triumph. It is this saying of Jesus which was recalled at his trial as a charge against him, but in a distorted form (Mk. 14[58]).

23–25. Jesus' Distrust of Belief Resting on "Signs." In Jesus' distrust of a belief resting on miracles the Evangelist again finds a proof of his supernatural knowledge (although the Greek word used for *knew* in v. 25 means not intuitive, but acquired knowledge). *The struggle between truth and error, unbelief and faith, which is the recurrent theme in the Gospel, is thus begun* (cf. 1[10, 11]). It may be that this discovery of the hostility he would encounter led Jesus to greater reserve of utterance and restraint of action regarding his Messiahship, so that the breach should not be forced before the hour had come.

CHAPTER III

1–21. The Interview with Nicodemus. Nicodemus is often described as the "anxious inquirer," but against this view are the following considerations: his address to Jesus is patronizing; Jesus' answer conveys a rebuke of the patronage and indication of the speaker's inability to form a judgment; and v. 7 (the plural *ye*) suggests that he came as representative of the Pharisees as a class, who, anxious to keep their leadership in religion, desired to discover whether they could come to an understanding with this new teacher. It is this view of the incident that the severity of the tone and the uncompromising demand of Jesus suggest. The whole passage is one of the best instances of *reminiscence being supplemented by reflection* which the Gospel offers. Probably definite reminiscence ends at v. 10, with a curt dismissal of one who, claiming to be a teacher, was not willing to learn. What follows is largely reflection, into which sayings from another setting may have been attracted, as, for instance, vv. 13, 14, which have similar content to 12[31, 32]. The Ephesian environment of the Witness is reflected in v. 11. It is a mistake to assume, however, that the record has no relation to the Jerusalem situation. The teaching about *the new birth* is not solely a reference to Christian baptism, but has in view the baptism of John, and the baptism of the Spirit, which John foretold of the Messiah (Mt. 3[11]), and which Jesus himself experienced at his baptism (v. 16). The truth of the new birth is paralleled in the Synoptic teaching (Mt. 18[3]).

The substance of the teaching in vv. 1–10 is consistent with the occasion assigned, even if the form may have been affected by the later environment of the Evangelist. Even as the Baptist had demanded a thorough change (Mt. 3[7]), so does Jesus, as a condition of having any understanding of or share in the *kingdom of God* (vv. 3–5); a phrase common in the Synoptics for the good that had come from God in Jesus and would still more fully come, but used in this Gospel only here (cf. 18[36]—"my kingdom"), *eternal life* being the corresponding Johannine phrase. In the Synoptic report of the rich young ruler, the counterpart of Nicodemus, this Johannine phrase is used (Mk. 10[17-22]). Nicodemus' objection to the doctrine does not show that he understood Jesus too literally; but that he wished to show how ridiculous was such a demand for change as addressed to his party. Hence Jesus does not correct a misapprehension, but repeats the demand with more direct reference to the actual situation. On John's baptism of repentance must follow the baptism of the Spirit's illumination. V. 6 may be a comment from the Evangelist's standpoint, *flesh* meaning here not necessarily the sensual, or even the sinful nature generally, as in Paul, but nature apart from God's renewing Spirit. In v. 8 there is a play on the word *pneuma*, which may mean "wind" as well as "spirit," as does the Hebrew *ruach*. The persistent incredulity of Nicodemus proved that nothing could be gained by continuing the conversation, and led the Witness, or the Evangelist, to rebuke the similar unbelief of those to whom the Gospel was addressed regarding the truth taught (v. 11). Incapacity to understand teaching about man's need of inward change proves unfitness to receive the higher truths about the incarnation (v. 12). Only the Incarnate, who comes from heaven (cf. 1[18]), can bring down such a revelation (v. 13; cf. Deut. 30[12]). Although the Jews in their unbelief reject him, lifting him upon the cross, God will also exalt him to be the Saviour of all who believe (this double sense is implied).

From v. 16 onward we have *reflections of the Witness*, and not record. God gives his *only begotten* Son (literally, unique, one who is like no other) as Saviour, not as Judge, as the Jews expected the Messiah to be (cf. Mt. 3[12]); but the offer of salvation is a test of character, and so inevitably judgment; acceptance shows the true or right disposition, rejection the false or wrong disposition (cf. 9[39]; the analogy of light and darkness is used in many religions). While these verses suggest an inherent dualism of character, a moral determinism, the Evangelist elsewhere recognizes man's liberty and responsibility (vv. 16–21; see following paragraphs).

22–30. The Second Testimony of the Baptist. (Cf. 1[19-34]). The Evangelist's comment seems to be given in vv. 31–36. Accordingly, vv. 22–30 are generally regarded as displaced, and as properly following 2[11]. The brief Judæan ministry on the lines of the Baptist's probably followed the visit to Cana, and came before the visit to Capernaum (2[12]). The Judæan ministry, although similar to the Baptist's, proved more attractive than his. The jealousy of those disciples of John who had not followed Jesus was due probably to a taunt from the Jewish disputants (v. 25). The Baptist himself rose above any such feeling, and as before confessed and accepted his inferiority, and even rejoiced in it. Some of the ideas here seem antedated and belong to the theology of the Gospel rather than the thought of the Baptist; even if he recognized Jesus as Messiah, it is not likely that he spoke without any reserve. This *figure of the marriage* is used by Jesus himself in regard to his relation to his disciples (Mk. 2[19-20]).

31–36. The Evangelist's Comments. This passage does not seem to be reflections of the Witness, as is 3[16-21]; but, rather, comments of the Evangelist, either on these reflections, if v. 31 follows v. 21, or on the Baptist's testimony, if it is also displaced. If the second connection is preferred, then the contrast is specially between John as of the earth and Christ as from heaven; if the first, it has a more general reference. One whose origin is heavenly can alone disclose the heavenly realities; if many reject this testimony, those who receive it can confirm that here is the truth of God. God's messenger delivers God's own words, either because he is himself fully inspired (A.V.), or because he fully inspires those to whom his words come (R.V.). As loved of God, and endowed with universal authority by God, the attitude of men to him of faith or unbelief determines their destiny of life or death, God's approval or displeasure.

CHAPTER IV

1–26. Christ and the Samaritan Woman. If this story is not a record of fact, it is a triumph of literary realism. While the subsequent experience of the church may have affected the language at some points, it may be accepted as substantially historical. As no disciple was present, the conversation must have been reported either by Jesus or the woman. It is more probable that the woman told the story with some exaggeration of details. In v. 29 she claims that her whole past life had been disclosed; and this suggests that in v. 18 she is confusing what Jesus had actually said and what her own conscience recalled in his presence. It is suggested by the allegorists that the number "five" (five husbands) refers to the five senses, or the five books of the Law, or the five gods worshiped by the Samaritans (2 Kings 17[30-34]). Great as was Jesus' moral and spiritual insight, it is improbable that it would extend to complete knowledge of the woman's life, although something must have been said which impressed her with his insight. While vv. 21–23 follow naturally on the woman's inquiry, so general a statement as v. 24 may be a reflection of the Witness, or comment of the Evangelist. (Cf. 1 John 1[5] and 4[8].)

The title *Lord* (v. 1) belongs to the post-resurrection period (cf. 6[23] 11[2] 20[20] 21[7] Lk. 18[6]). The motive of the *withdrawal to Galilee* (v. 2) was an avoidance of even an appearance of competition between Jesus and John, of which the Pharisees would have been ready to make use, or a desire to prevent any premature Messianic movement, which would provoke opposition. The journey through *Samaria* as the shorter was preferred to that through Peræa, even though the strict Jew shunned the defilement it might involve. Jerome identified *Sychar* with Shechem (Nablus), but it is now usually identified with 'Askar, eastward of Mount Ebal. As the disciples had taken the rope and bucket with them, Jesus was not able to draw water for himself, and had to ask the woman. Her curt refusal, prompted by the hatred of Jew and Samaritan, which Jesus rebuked in the parable of the good Samaritan (Lk. 10[33]), gave Jesus an opportunity for a talk in which he offered, and she welcomed, a still higher boon than he craved and she withheld. Water is here used not as a symbol of cleansing, as in the conversation with Nicodemus (3[5]), but of *the satisfaction of the soul's deepest need.* That the gift might be desired, conscience had to be aroused. The attempt to evade the question by an inquiry about ritual led to (*a*) a demand for sincere worship, (*b*) an assurance that such worship would not be localized, and (*c*) an assertion that the Jewish worship was more intelligent, and God's purpose to save would come from this people. A spiritual worship of God as Father will supersede all local rituals. The woman defers the solution of this and all other problems to *the Messiah,* whom the Samaritans, who used the Pentateuch at least, were expecting no less than the Jews. The announcement of his Messiahship by Jesus is in accord with the Evangelist's view that he made the claim from the beginning, but is inconsistent with the Synoptic record, unless we may assume that less reserve was necessary in Samaria than Galilee, as there was less danger there of precipitating the crisis.

27–38. The Return of the Disciples. The surprise of the disciples on their return to find Jesus talking to a woman illustrates the difference he has made in the position of woman. A Jewish rabbi would have avoided such conversation. The disciples' request that Jesus should take food was met by the assurance that he had found a deeper satisfaction in fulfilling his calling, for in the multitude whom the woman was bringing to him from the town he saw *the speedy harvest of the seed he had sown.* (The words in v. 35 mean either that four months usually separated seedtime and harvest, or that it was still four months to harvest. The second explanation would fix this incident in December, or January.) The disciples might share the joy of a spiritual harvest, of which they had not sowed the seed, even as, in accord with a popular proverb (v. 37), in the bread they had brought they were reaping where they had not sowed.

39–45. The Testimony of the Samaritans and the Return to Galilee. Responsive as the Samaritans were, Jesus, recognizing the prior claim of "the lost sheep of the house of Israel," or not desiring to encourage any Messianic movement in Samaria, spent only two days among them. The title *Saviour of the World* (v. 42) represents the Evangelist's own theology. Two thoughts are suggested in this passage: (*a*) the greater readiness of non-Jewish people to believe; and (*b*) the greater value of a faith resting on personal experience than of one based on the testimony of others. The motive of the return to Galilee stated in v. 44 recalls the use of the saying by Jesus at Nazareth (Mt. 13[57]). Here it is doubtful whether the words are a statement by Jesus of his motive or by the Evangelist. If the former, Galilee is the country; if the latter, Judæa, which in the Evangelist's judgment was the proper home of the Messiah. If Galilee is referred to, what the words mean is that Jesus expected less ready response there than he had found in Samaria; if Judæa, the Evangelist means that Jesus expected a better reception in Galilee than in

Judæa. In the first case, Jesus' expectations were not fulfilled; in the second, they were.

46–54. The Healing of the Son of the King's Officer. The story need not be regarded as a variant of the Synoptic story of the healing of the centurion's servant at Capernaum (Mt. 8[5-13], notes). If the Witness did not accompany Jesus on this visit to Cana, he may have had the story from his mother Mary (cf. 2[1, 2]). Nor need we assume a heightening of the supernatural features in the greater distance of Cana from Capernaum, than that in the Synoptic story. If Jesus' miracles were answers to prayer (cf. 11[42]), distance would make no difference: but only if the healing depended on his personal presence (see art., *Miracles of N.T.*, p. 925b). Jesus' reply to the request (v. 48) indicates his unwillingness to begin in Galilee the kind of ministry that had disappointed him in Judæa (2[23-25]). A cry of need, however, he could not resist; but faith was tested in the response given. As the Jews reckoned the day from sunset to sunset, the *seventh hour* (one o'clock afternoon) would fall in the previous day if the father returned after sunset. If Mk. 1[14] continues the story after v. 54, it was Jesus' intention to avoid the working of the miracles as far as possible, and to carry out a preaching tour in the synagogues of Galilee.

CHAPTER V

As *Testimony* is the theme of chs. 1–4, so *Controversy* is the theme of chs. 5–11. It is the view of many scholars that ch. 5 should follow ch. 6, in which an account is given of the ministry in Galilee, and that 7[15-24] is the sequel of ch. 5.

1–9a. The Cure at the Pool of Bethesda. If the feeding of the five thousand took place shortly before the Passover (6[4]), *a feast* (5[1]) or *the feast* (R.V. mg.) might possibly be Passover, but was more probably the next great feast, Pentecost. The Witness here shows his intimate knowledge of locality in describing the place; the present tense need not mean that the sheepgate and pool had remained despite the ruin of the city to his own day. The MSS. vary as to the name, Bethzatha being probably the original (R.V. mg.); for Bezetha, Josephus tells us, was the name of the northern quarter of the city. As R.V. mg. shows, the last clause of v. 3b and v. 4 are omitted in the best MSS., and are a later insertion. The resemblance of this story to that of the palsied man, even to the use of the same word for "bed" (v. 8; cf. Mk. 2[11]), does not prove that this narrative is a free handling by the Evangelist of Synoptic material.

9b–18. The Controversy Regarding the Sabbath. As the Synoptic records show, Jesus' healing on the Sabbath soon led to controversy (Mk. 3[1-6]). Although himself a Judæan, the Witness uses the term "Jews" in a depreciatory sense for the enemies of Jesus. The man's ignorance of his healer is a token that the story is not invented; and to find a reference to the thirty-eight years of wandering in the wilderness (Deut. 2[14]) in v. 5b is hypercritical ingenuity. The man's report to the Jews in v. 15 does not necessarily prove treachery, although Jesus' warning in v. 14 shows his unfavorable view of his character. Jesus' defense in v. 17 does not bear the meaning the Jews put on the words. As Son he claims to be doing as his Father does, whose activity for man is not interrupted by the Sabbath. (Cf. Gen. 2[3].) The estimate of the intentions of the opponents seems premature (v. 18); their hostility probably took time to develop fully.

19–29. The Relation of Father and Son. There seems little doubt that this passage (except v. 24, which might be an authentic saying, and might fittingly follow v. 40 or v. 47) is neither reminiscence nor reflection of the Witness, but a *theological exposition* added by the Evangelist (see intro., p. 1062). In the following passage (vv. 30–47) Jesus uses the first person, here (except in v. 24) the third person is used throughout; and a doctrine of the relation of Father and Son is developed which it is altogether improbable that Jesus would present to his opponents; it is the Christology of the end of the century. The *eschatology* of this passage (vv. 25–29) is also in contradiction to the teaching of Jesus as reported elsewhere in this Gospel—a present judgment, a spiritual resurrection, and an eternal life here and now (v. 24). V. 29 is, indeed, the only passage in the Gospels in which *a resurrection of judgment*, in accordance with the solitary passage in Dan. 12[2], as well as a resurrection of life, is taught (cf. Acts 24[15]). With this teaching vv. 19–23 stand in contradiction, for they refer to *a present inward experience*. The Son is so intimate with the Father that he imitates him; and this he can do because the Father has given the Son power to do what he himself does, a greater work than physical healing, even spiritual quickening, namely, the exercise of a present judgment on men, in order that equal honor may be given to the Son as to the Father. The warning is added, that disrespect of the Son is disrespect of the Father. It is difficult for us to understand how in one mind two such disparate conceptions could rest; but we find the old eschatological conception of the Second Advent returning in Paul's letters (Phil. 1[21] 3[21]), even when he had reached the experience of constant present communion with Christ.

30–47. The Witness to the Son, and Jewish Unbelief. V. 30 resumes the thought of v. 17, and while we cannot assume that we have a *verbatim* report of the controversy, and we must admit that the Ephesian environment has colored the record, it is not improbable that Jesus had such a controversy with his Jewish opponents. Jesus' appeal in v. 17, that he was doing as God does, is now justified. He perfectly knows God because he is entirely dependent on and obedient to God. Should his witness be challenged, he can appeal to *the witness of John*, so highly regarded by the people, and to even a greater witness—*his own works*—as proofs of his divine mission (vv. 30–37a). Their unbelief is due to their ignorance of God, so that they cannot even understand the Scriptures, of which they are so diligent students. *Their mental incapacity is due to a moral defect.* They lack love for God, and are concerned about their own reputation among their fellows. They would be deceived by a self-assertive teacher. Their rejection of him he need not charge against them, as the very Scriptures would bring the accusation, since they too bore witness of him (vv. 37b–47). His appeal to the Scriptures calls forth the taunt, "How can this uneducated fellow manage to read?" (7[15]; Moffatt's *N.T.*, p. 120); for 7[15-24] is undoubtedly the continuation of this controversy.

CHAPTER VI

Ch. 6 is the proper sequel to 4[54]; Jesus having just come from Judæa to Galilee would not be likely to return again. If, however, there had been a crisis in Galilee, such as ch. 6 records, there was reason for his withdrawal from Galilee, unaccompanied by any disciples (5[1]) and for a time unknown (vv. 13–15). The description of his movements in 6[1], *the other side of the Sea of Galilee*, is more appropriate if he were in Cana (4[46]) than if he were in Jerusalem (5[47]). In the introduction (see p. 1061b) it has been shown that this chapter is probably due to the redactor, and offers a summary of the Galilæan ministry, into which records of the Judæan controversy have been mingled. To disentangle the intertwined threads is "a forlorn hope" for any scholar.

1–14. The Feeding of the Five Thousand. It is much less probable that Jesus became concerned about the feeding of the crowd as soon as they gathered (v. 5) than that at the close of the day (Mk. 6[35, 36]) his disciples should express their concern. Again, while it is not improbable that Jesus addressed such a question to Philip, it is improbable that the motive was as v. 6 states it. Both these details illustrate a characteristic of the Christology of the Gospel, namely, *Jesus' independence of human counsel or help;* he is always represented as taking the initiative. Other details peculiar to this record show no such theological tendency, and may be historical. The Passover may be mentioned in v. 4 to account for such a crowd, composed of pilgrims on their way to Jerusalem, or to prepare for the Eucharistic teaching of the following discourse (vv. 52–59). That the miracle precipitated a crisis (vv. 14, 15) is not improbable in itself and gains support from Mk. 6[45], which tells of the constraint on the disciples to leave him alone to deal with the multitude. Such a miracle as this, even as the other nature miracles, presents a greater difficulty than the healing ministry; and while there was more adequate occasion here than at the marriage in Cana it is more difficult to imagine the *mode.* At what point did the supernatural increase take place? To answer such a question lies beyond the province of a commentator. There is, indeed, a naturalistic explanation which may be mentioned, although many will regard it as far-fetched, namely, that the generosity of Jesus and his disciples, in sharing their scanty store with others, so stimulated the generosity of those who had any food with them that the needs of all were met (cf. art., *Miracles of N.T.*, p. 923a).

15–25. The Walking on the Sea. The narratives here and in the Synoptic record (Mt. 14[22-33] and Mk. 6[45-52]) do not differ substantially. The Greek preposition *epi* in v. 19 may mean "by" as well as "on." It is not impossible that Jesus was walking on the shore; and that the disciples in their excited condition believed him to be literally "on" the sea; as v. 21 shows they were nearer the shore than they thought (see p. 923b). While Mark states that Jesus entered the boat, John records that, reassured by his words of cheer, *they were willing to receive him into the boat* (v. 21). This naturalistic explanation, however, obviously destroys that very feature of the event which inspired the disciples' fear. It is not at all unlikely that a conversation on the lakeside did take place next morning (vv. 22–25); neither Matthew nor Mark has any record, but the summary in Mk. 6[53-56] in its lack of details suggests that some of the disciples, in their disappointment that he had not made use of the popular enthusiasm, had for a time gone home, or that to allay their excitement Jesus had sent them home. In view of the mention of the synagogue in Capernaum in v. 59 it should be noted that the crowd found Jesus not in Capernaum, where at first they sought him, but "on the other side" of the sea, perhaps between Bethsaida and Capernaum.

26–40. The Teaching on the True Bread. It is certain, as far as in so difficult a matter we can be certain, that there was both a *conversation* with "a great multitude" (v. 2; cf. vv. 14, 22) at the seashore on the True Bread—theme appropriate to the occasion—and a *controversy*, arising out of this teaching, with the Jews (v. 41 and v. 52) in the synagogue in Capernaum (v. 59). It is not so certain, however, that the conversation ended at v. 40, and the controversy began at v. 41; for in the report it would seem that the redactor has woven in the contents of another discourse on the bread of life, which, since it is probable that 7^{15-24} should follow 5^{47}, belongs to that empty place between 7^{14} and 7^{25}. As the Feast of Tabernacles was associated with the wanderings in the wilderness, the demand of $6^{30, 31}$ would be at that feast much more probable than in the present setting, just after a miracle which had excited such enthusiasm. Since Mk. 7^{1} reports that certain scribes had come from Jerusalem to Galilee, probably to assist the local Pharisees in contests with Jesus, the Jews here mentioned may not be Galilæans, but Judæans, controversialists whom he had to meet in Jerusalem. This would make it more easy to explain why here in Galilee the teaching is so unlike the Synoptic reports, and so like the teaching reported by this Gospel as given in Jerusalem. (For a critical analysis, see A. E. Garvie, *The Beloved Disciple*, pp. 46–50.)

The content of the conversation may briefly be indicated. The summons of Jesus to care more for the spiritual good than material goods elicits the question from the people regarding their duty. Jesus' claim to faith as God's messenger is challenged on the ground that he has not yet given ground for their faith. Will he give again the new manna from heaven, as, according to the Apocalypse of Baruch 29^{8}, the Messiah was expected to do? Jesus offers the assurance that, as the manna of old came not from Moses, but God, so now in himself God is giving them the soul's true nourishment. (V. 33 is a reflection of the Evangelist, which breaks the continuity.) The request for this gift is met by the assurance of complete satisfaction; and followed by the reproach that faith is lacking. It is suggested that $3^{11, 12}$ would find a more appropriate context between v. 36 and v. 37 than in its present setting. The thought of the bread of life is not carried on in vv. 37–40; but the teaching is not unrelated to the occasion. Jesus' refusal of the homage (v. 15) which had been offered was due to his entire submission to the will of God, and his purpose to accept only such as were led to him by the Father (cf. Mt. 16^{17}), i.e., yielded to him the right kind of faith, not such as a miracle might excite. Those so accepted were assured as to their final destiny. (The last clauses of v. 39 and v. 40 seem to be an intrusion of the current eschatology, inappropriate to the context.)

41–51a. The Controversy with the Jews. Another ground of objection to the claim just made was found in the knowledge the opponents had of the earthly descent, as contrasted with the heavenly claim (v. 42; cf. Mk. 6^{3}). The reply of Jesus reiterates the teaching of vv. 37–40. Those alone can exercise faith whom God enables, according to the prophetic promise of divine instruction (Isa. 54^{13}), not by direct vision, but through the divine messenger; and to them eternal life is assured (the last clause of v. 44 is another intrusion). The repetition of the teaching about the bread of life seems to take us back to the seashore; unlike the manna, the partakers of which died, this bread gives eternal life. As to the claim of descent from heaven (v. 51) it is likely, in view of what the Synoptics represent as Jesus' method, that the later Christology has here colored the reproduction of whatever teaching may on this occasion have been given.

51b–59. The Eucharistic Teaching. While v. 58 is a reflection of the Evangelist on the teaching of vv. 32–35, 48, 49, 51a, and corresponds closely to the reflection in v. 50, the teaching of the flesh and blood as the soul's nourishment, here introduced as a development of the teaching about the bread of life, probably did not belong to this occasion. It is difficult to suppose that Jesus would freely talk to his opponents about his Passion before he had made any announcement of it to his disciples. While it is possible that Jesus may in the upper room have expounded to some of the disciples the truth implicit in the words of institution of the Supper, it is more probable that a controversy of later days is here reflected. The last clause of v. 51 attaches this teaching to the discourse on the bread. The spiritual bread, which is contrasted with the material in the preceding discourse, now becomes his flesh, his atoning sacrifice. It is Jewish objections to Eucharistic teaching in Ephesus that are here being dealt with, and not anything that Jesus said, or that his hearers heard, in Capernaum. Jesus made eternal life depend on personal faith; here it is made to depend on participation in the Sacrament. *This doctrine is neither the Witness' nor the Evangelist's but is due to the redactor* (cf. intro., p. 1065a).

60–71. The Galilæan Crisis. This passage describes the crisis in Galilee, which took place soon after the feeding of the five thousand, when Jesus, according to Mt. 15[21], found it expedient to withdraw "into the parts of Tyre and Sidon." Although the redactor regards *the hard saying* (v. 60) as referring to the previous discourse, yet the more probable reference is to the teaching about clean and unclean, which the disciples reported to Jesus had offended the Pharisees (v. 12). To this objection v. 63 would offer some sort of a reply; but v. 62 seems to have no relevance to the situation, and connects itself with the circle of sayings in 3[13-15] and 12[20-36], which deal with the necessity of the exaltation of Jesus for the fulfillment of his vocation. The comment of v. 64 on Jesus' reference to the unbelief of some of his hearers restricts it unduly, and introduces a theological interpretation which the occasion does not justify. If the phrase *from the beginning* (v. 64) is intended to express a dateless knowledge, namely, that Jesus always knew who should betray him, then it contradicts the limitation of knowledge, which other evidence justifies us as ascribing to Jesus as a necessary condition of the reality of the incarnation. If it means that Jesus by his insight was quick to discover when the first thoughts of treachery entered the mind of Judas, then we may suppose that it was after the first announcement of the Passion (Mt. 16[21]) that Judas began to harbor the evil thought, and Jesus detected the change, for the second announcement (Mt. 17[22]) includes as a new detail a reference to betrayal (here A.V. is to be preferred to R.V.). V. 65 simply repeats the thought of v. 44.

Vv. 66–71 may be regarded as the counterpart of the scene at Cæsarea Philippi (Mt. 16[13-20]) only cast by the redactor into the mold of the rest of the Gospel. V. 65 recalls Mt. 16[17]. As the Gospel ascribes to the disciples a confession of the Messiahship at their first interview (1[41, 45, 49]), and thus has antedated it, the situation here is represented not as an advance to a new conception, but as a danger of relapse from existing allegiance. Further, as the interest of the Gospel is in the truth taught, Peter's answer, *Thou hast the words of eternal life,* is a Johannine paraphrase of "Thou art the Christ." The words following, *Thou art the Holy One of God,* have more of a Synoptic ring. Again the announcement of the betrayal is antedated, as betrayal is mentioned only in the second announcement; and the change of feeling in Judas would be due to the first announcement of the Passion. The words themselves recall the rebuke of Peter, "Get thee behind me, Satan." If the view here presented, that the redactor is giving a confused account of the ministry in Galilee, of which he had imperfect knowledge, is rejected, then the alternative is that the Evangelist used Synoptic material in an arbitrary way.

CHAPTER VII

The *first visit* to Jerusalem was marked by the cleansing of the Temple (2[13-25]); the *second* by the cure of the impotent man, and the controversy about the Sabbath (5[1-47] 7 [15-24]); on the *third visit* (now to be described) the controversy regarding the authority of Jesus was continued.

1–14. The Feast of Tabernacles. When the brethren who clearly shared the disappointment of the multitude (cf. Mk. 3[21, 31-35]) taunted Jesus to go to Jerusalem to declare himself openly as Messiah in the capital of the nation, the sacred city, he refused, as he knew his danger, and ran no risk unless at the Father's bidding, whose plan he must follow (cf. 2[4]). The *yet* in v. 8 was probably added in later MSS. to avoid the appearance of contradiction with what follows. After their departure the divine indication must have come, and he went up, but for a time did not openly show himself. There was divided opinion about him, although fear of the rulers, known to be hostile, restrained open speech. Jesus must have been sufficiently assured of safety to justify his public appearance; the sequel to which is given in v. 25, as vv. 15–24 belong to the record of the previous feast in ch. 5.

15–24. The Close of the Controversy at the Previous Feast. (See also notes under 6[26-40].) There are three reasons for attaching this passage to ch. 5. (1) Jesus' appeal to the Scriptures (5[45-47]) evokes the surprise at his learning, he not being a rabbi (v. 15). (2) Vv. 16–18 repeat the argument of 5[30-44]. (3) V. 19 shows an apprehension of the hostile intention of the rulers, which explains Jesus' reluctance to go up at the next feast (vv. 7, 8); and the angry retort of the crowd (v. 20) shows that they were not aware of the rulers' intentions, as they afterward became (v. 13). (4) The cure on the Sabbath was the occasion of the hostility, and Jesus reverts to the cure and justifies his action (vv. 21–24). If the Sabbath law can be set aside that the rite of circumcision may be performed—much more may it that the whole man may be restored. A judgment which went beneath the appearance would not justify the intention to transgress in their anger the law against murder.

25–36. The Controversy at the Feast of Tabernacles. In this report we are able to trace the hand of an eyewitness. Note the knowledge that is shown of the varied and varying currents of opinion and attitudes toward Jesus. The multitudes (v. 12) consist of the pilgrims and those with whom they consorted in Jerusalem. The Jews are the hostile party (vv. 11, 13), and include the *rulers* (v. 26), the *chief priests and Pharisees* (v. 32; cf. Mt. 21[45] 27[62], probably a description of the Sanhedrin, or supreme Jewish court). As the Pharisees were the democratic party, they could discover what the people were thinking more easily than could the Sadducees, the aristocratic. *Some of them of Jerusalem* (v. 25) refers to citizens who, though not themselves hostile, were aware of the plans of the rulers; the Witness himself may have been in contact with them. In 8[31] Jews are mentioned, whose hostility had so far been overcome that they recognized his Messianic claim, but resented the suggestion that they had not yet found the truth that would make them free from the prejudices they still cherished regarding the nature of the Messiahship (v. 33). They are distinguished from those who fully believed in him (v. 30). These citizens of Jerusalem can explain the inaction of the rulers only on the assumption that those believe him to be the Messiah. They themselves have the difficulty that the Messiah is to appear suddenly (see Enoch and 4 Esdras), and this man's antecedents they know. Acknowledging that they know him, Jesus explains their continued unbelief by their ignorance of God, and his mission from God. This apparent blasphemy provokes an attempt to arrest, prevented only by the friendliness of the crowd, which is persuaded that even the Messiah could not do greater works. The growing popularity determines his opponents to carry out the arrest. Conscious of his danger, Jesus foretells his departure, soon, when he will be beyond reach. While he is thinking of his return to God through death, the people are so bewildered that the only conjecture they can make is that he may be intending a mission to the Jews scattered among the Gentiles, and even to the Gentiles.

37–53. **The Last Day of the Feast.** Here also there is proof of the trustworthiness of the record in the appropriateness of the imagery used. Jesus offers himself as the *living water* (v. 37), and later as the *light of the world* (8[12]). While in early times the Feast of Tabernacles or Ingathering at the end of summer lasted seven days (Deut. 16[13]), later an eighth day was added (Lev. 23[36]). Water was brought from Shiloah, and poured out before the altar, to recall the gift of water in the wilderness (Ex. 17[6]); as this was being done Isa. 12[3] was recited. On the eighth day this custom was discontinued, as that day celebrated the entrance into a "land of springs of water." Jesus uses this symbolic act *to turn attention from the physical thirst to the spiritual thirst of man*, and to give assurance of its satisfaction in himself to those who believe (the proper rendering of vv. 37 and 38 seems to be, "and let him that believeth on me drink"). No words of *scripture* correspond to the citation in v. 38, but Ex. 17[6] tells of the water flowing from the rock, and Ezek. 47[1] promises a flow of water from the Temple as symbol of the Spirit given. There was a tradition that the Messiah or his forerunner would restore the gift of water as well as of manna (cf. 6[31]). The comment of v. 39, referring to Pentecost, is appropriate, even though it hardly expresses what Jesus was thinking. Only when Christ had risen was the fullness of life in him possessed. This assurance of Jesus led the people to discuss whether he were the prophet of Deut. 18[15], or Jeremiah (cf. Mt. 16[14]), or even the Messiah. The Galilæan origin was a difficulty, since the Messiah was expected to be of Davidic descent and born at Bethlehem (Mic. 5[2]). Divided as was opinion, the feeling was favorable enough to make arrest dangerous. V. 49 exposes the attitude of the rulers to the people, and can be illustrated from other sources. The plea of Nicodemus for a fair trial is met by a contemptuous reference to Galilee as an unlikely home of a prophet, although Nahum and Jonah (2 Kings 14[25]) both came from this district. V. 53 belongs to the next passage.

CHAPTER VIII

1–11. **The Woman Taken in Adultery.** It is certain that this story does not belong to this Gospel. It breaks the continuity of 7[52] and 8[12]; the style and language are Synoptic and not Johannine. The textual evidence is against its authenticity as part of the Gospel (see R.V. mg.). It nevertheless seems to retain a true tradition; for the incident is congruous with Jesus' attitude toward sinners, and in view of its character was certainly not an invention of the early church. The purpose was to put Jesus in a difficulty; if he set aside the Law, he would lose favor with the people; if he decided for carrying it out, he would challenge the Roman authority, which had withdrawn from the Jews the right of inflicting death. His action did not decide this issue, but raised the question to a higher level; it challenged the accusers' right to condemn, and claimed for himself the right not to condemn. Why did Jesus stoop down and *write upon the ground?* (V. 6.) To show his disregard for his questioners, or to hide his own embarrassment, or to spare the woman? All are possible motives. An ancient MS. reads for *when they heard it*, "when they read it"; and this change is probably due to the legendary explanation that, when each man read what had been written by Jesus, he read his own sin. The sin of the woman is not condoned, as the last words show, although not condemned; but neither is it forgiven, as it would have been had penitence been shown.

12–20. The Light of the World: Discourse in the Treasury. The record of the last day of the feast is here continued. The second figure Jesus uses, *I am the light of the world*, is as fit as the first (cf. 7[37]); during the Feast the Court of the Women, where was the treasury (v. 20), was very brightly lighted. The claim to be the Light, however, would fitly follow the miracle of giving sight (ch. 9). It must be admitted that these chapters show a lack of continuity; but in this they may be reproducing the historical situation, the ebb and flow of opinion and feeling in the varied groups brought into contact with Jesus. Challenged by the Pharisees that this witness of himself is not true, Jesus asserts his own knowledge of himself as contrasted with his opponents' ignorance. His judgment is not according to human prudence (*flesh*), but according to divine insight, and is confirmed by the witness of his Father. Their taunt that he has not produced his witness is rebuked by a declaration of their incapacity to know him or his Father. Restrained by the public feeling, his opponents do not venture his arrest; the Evangelist expresses the situation in his own way: the appointed time had not yet arrived (v. 20).

21–30. Warnings of the Near Judgment. On a later day Jesus uttered *a solemn warning* that the day of grace would soon be closed by his departure. A more sinister suggestion than on the previous occasion (7[35]) is made —even that he would commit suicide. This taunt makes him assert the contrast between their nature and his, involving their rejection of him, and consequent doom. The attempt by a question to force an open declaration of his Messiahship, which might be used as an accusation before the Roman authorities, is foiled by an answer about which there is much difference of opinion (v. 25). The R.V. mg. (cf. A.S.V. mg.) gives a rendering which has behind it the authority of the Greek fathers: "How is it that I even speak to you at all?"—a contemptuous gesture. Another suggestion is this: "I am nothing else than what I am saying to you," in other words, "Judge who I am from what I say." He does not fall into the trap set for him; but throws the responsibility on his hearers to show whether they can respond to the truth he speaks. The comment of v. 27 does not seem relevant. As such a response is not given, Jesus again solemnly declares that at his exaltation even those who do not believe now will confess him as Messiah, the Son dependent on, sustained by, and approved of the Father. These warnings elicited in some of his hearers a faith which was soon shown to be inadequate.

31–59. Controversy with "those Jews which had Believed." While it is difficult to discriminate, the severer tone of vv. 37–50 suggests that here Jesus turned from those who had a partial faith to his irreconcilable opponents. The assurance that the truth he taught would bring *freedom* was resented by the Jews, who prided themselves on their descent from Abraham. Jesus explains that it is not political freedom but freedom from sin's bondage that he as Son can offer. Turning to his opponents, he admits their physical descent from Abraham; but their intention to kill him and their opposition to his revelation prove that they cannot really be Abraham's children in showing a moral likeness to him. Their deeds point to another moral ancestry. The reference to *fornication* in v. 41 is probably not due to any of the current slanders about Jesus' birth, which were of later date, but *fornication* is used, as is also *adultery*, for any departure from God as in idolatry. Their claim of God as Father Jesus challenges without qualification, and he boldly charges them with *descent from the devil*, whom as murderer and liar they imitate. (The last clause of v. 44 may also be rendered "For a liar is also his father," a reference to the devil's father. By substituting *Cain* for *devil* in the first clause—cf. 1 Jn. 3[12]—the difficulty of assigning a father to the devil is evaded, and the devil is represented as Cain's father. Neither suggestion commends itself.) The challenge in v. 46, *Which of you convicteth me of sin?* may mean either that no moral offense could be proved against him, or that he could not be proved in error in what he had been teaching about sin. Pressing home his charge against them, that their unbelief proves that God is not their father, he provokes them to retort that he is a Samaritan (a deadly taunt) and even is *possessed.* Repudiating the charge, Jesus asserts his disinterestedness, and rebukes their attitude toward him. Turning (v. 51) again to those whose budding faith might be brought to bloom, he offers deliverance from death as a reward of discipleship. The opponents, however, again intervene. Such a claim proves demonic possession. Since the great men of the past are dead, does he claim to be superior to them? He disclaims any vain ambition; and if he claim any dignity, it is from fidelity to God.

This opposition inspires his confidence, and he declares that the prospect of his coming *brought joy to Abraham* (v. 56). In the apocalyptic literature such joy in the Messianic glories is ascribed to Abraham, even in his earthly life; even if Jesus knew this tradition he was probably thinking of Abraham in Paradise (cf. Lk. 16[22] Mt. 22[32]). The Jews, taking the words literally, dismiss the claim as absurd. (From the reference to *fifty years*, Irenæus inferred that Jesus taught till he was forty or fifty.) Jesus asserts his priority in time to Abraham; he claims *eternal existence* (v. 58). The Evangelist understands the words as meaning pre-existence, such as is claimed for the Logos in the Prologue. We must not interpret the words as meaning a continuity of consciousness from the former state through birth into the present; that would make the incarnation unreal. What we may assume is that in a swift intuition Jesus recognized that his relation to God, so certain and so intimate, was not temporal, but eternal. The opposition of men threw him back on God, and God gave him this assurance, when he most needed it. Such a claim so enraged the Jews that they sought to put him to death without any trial. The reading of the R.V. mg. and A.V. suggests an escape similar to that at Nazareth (Lk. 4[30]), when his presence overawed. The less hostile multitude may have helped his escape.

In this controversy not only is the hostility of the Jews intensified, but Jesus is himself represented as assuming an attitude of ruthless severity, which for many reasons appears incredible. If he assailed his opponents as he is here represented as doing, it is no wonder that he aroused their hate. Severe he could be, as the woes on the Pharisees show, but the conclusion is inevitable that at this point *the vehement devotion of a disciple has imported into the vindication of the Master's claims against contemporary opponents a polemic tone which was not characteristic of Jesus himself.* The substance of the controversies we may regard as historical; but in the development of the themes the influence of the Evangelist's environment must be recognized.

CHAPTER IX

The teaching of ch. 10 is closely linked to the foregoing incident, and that teaching is assigned to the Feast of Dedication (10[22]). The passage 10[19-29] attaches itself most closely to 9[41], and leads up to the teaching in 10[1-18]; while 10[30] follows more fittingly 10[17, 18] than 10[29]. These transpositions give us a greater continuity. Throughout the Gospels we are often confronted with evidence of disarrangement. The narrative in ch. 9 makes a convincing impression of historical reality.

1–12. The Healing of the Man Born Blind. (Mk. 8[22-26].) The disciples (v. 2) need not be the Galilæan, but may be Judæan; would the fishermen be interested in the theological question asked? The *sin before birth* which is assumed as possible might have been committed in a previous existence, as some Greek thinkers held (Wisdom 8[19f.]), or in the womb, as some rabbis taught. The problem was not resolved, but the truth was taught that man's need gives God's grace its opportunity, and Jesus as God's agent seizes the opportunity, as for him it will now be brief. While life remains, he sheds God's light on the world (the physical miracle serves as symbol of the more constant spiritual work). The use of means of cure recalls the mode in Mk. 7[33] 8[23], and points to an early tradition. Did too weak a faith in the recipient need thus to be encouraged? (See art., *Miracles of N.T.*, p. 925a.) *Siloam* is the form used in the LXX; Shelah in Neh. 3[15]; Shiloah in Isa. 8[6]; the original meaning is *sending forth*, not *sent* (v. 7). The rest of the story is vivid realism.

13–34. The Trial of the Blind Man Now Seeing. The multitude first addressed themselves to the Pharisees, more accessible than the Sadducees, who probably were afterward called in, as the term *Jews* (v. 18) would include both parties. At first they try to shake the evidence for the cure, since a Sabbath-breaker could not have such power from God. The man asserts the fact, and confesses his faith in his healer as a prophet. Next, possibly at an informal meeting of the Sanhedrin, the parents are questioned, to get from them some contradiction of the fact that their son was born blind. That fact they testify, but from prudence decline to explain the cure; and throw back the questioners on their son. V. 22 is held by some scholars to be an anachronism, as in the time of Jesus not the synagogue but only the Sanhedrin could excommunicate; in Ephesus, however, at the time the Gospel was written the synagogue could pronounce the extreme sentence. A slip of memory, if there be such, on the part of the Evangelist, does not discredit the whole story. Once more the man is recalled, and adjured to tell the truth in the words *Give glory to God* (cf. Josh. 7[19] Ezra 10[11]). They assert their own conviction that Jesus is a sinner; this involves that the cure must have been wrought by Satan's help (Mk. 3[22]). The man lets "courage rise with danger." He will not be drawn into discussions about matters regarding which the questioners are more competent than he, but of the fact of his cure he is sure. He refuses to be entrapped into a second recital, and asks if they desire fuller knowledge to justify belief. Abuse is their only argument, and growing bolder, he expresses his surprise at their inability to solve the problem, as it has been solved for him in the certainty that Jesus is God's agent, and not a sinner. With reviling he is driven out.

35–41. Faith and Unbelief. Jesus, having heard of this treatment, either seeks out the man, or by chance meets him, and tries to win him as a disciple by the testing question: *Dost thou believe in the Son of man?* (R.V. mg., the more probable reading). Ignorant of the meaning of the title, he is won when Jesus claims the title for himself. Jesus' judgment of the whole incident is: the man spiritually blind, but willing to be taught, has gained spiritual vision; the Pharisees claiming to know, hence unwilling to be taught, have become blind spiritually (cf. 3[17-21]). Thus his Presence has here also proved to be judgment.

CHAPTER X

The rearrangement suggested in the first paragraph under ch. 9 above makes the sequence of events to be as follows. Violent difference of opinion was the result of the miracle (vv. 19–21). The opponents vehemently demand a confession of the Messiahship. Why they desired it, and why Jesus refused it, has already been shown. The reply is that he has in word and deed given sufficient grounds for faith, and that unbelief shows alienation of spirit. They do not belong to his flock (vv. 22–26); but he has a flock (the disciples, including this man) obedient to him, having security in him, because the divine omnipotence is its guarantee (vv. 27–29).

1–18. The Good Shepherd. How fittingly this leads up to the teaching about the Good Shepherd, which does not conform to the type of parable (v. 6) found in the Synoptics, but tends to become an *allegory*, although it may have had the strictly parabolical form; reflection may thus have transformed reminiscence. It appears as if two parables, one in which Jesus compares himself to the door of the sheepfold (vv. 7, 9), and another in which he describes himself as the Shepherd (vv. 1–5, 8, 10–16), are woven together. We may even distinguish within the second parable two, one dealing with the relation of the sheep to the Shepherd (vv. 1–5) and the other with the relation of the Shepherd to the sheep (vv. 8 10–18). As the door, Jesus declares himself to be the only Mediator of salvation and satisfaction for men. The sheep (the true disciples) know, hear, and follow the Shepherd, but shun the stranger (thief or robber). A transition from the one parable to the other is made at v. 8 (omitting v. 9), and the two parables about the sheep and the Shepherd are linked by the thought of the sheepfold with that of the door in vv. 1, 3. Only the true Shepherd enters, and is admitted by the porter; the thieves and robbers climb in another way. The thieves and robbers are the teachers and leaders of the people, whom true disciples will not follow, as the new-won disciple had just shown (9[27, 28, 31-33]), and who seek only their own ends and their own glory (cf. 5[44]). With them Jesus contrasts himself as the Good Shepherd, who is devoted to the interests of his flock even unto death. In v. 15, the relation of the Shepherd to the sheep is likened to that of the Father and the Son (it is his intimacy with God that is the motive of the sacrifice no less than his care for his disciples; cf. v. 18). As Jesus contemplates that sacrifice, a larger flock than these Judæan disciples presents itself as the object of his solicitude. The sacrifice is voluntary, even though God desires it, and he approves it because it is freely made. It is thus that the unity of purpose of Father and Son is manifested (see v. 30, which follows v. 18 much more fittingly than it follows v. 29).

19–42. The Feast of the Dedication. The sequence of thought in vv. 19–29 has been indicated above; only some details need comment. The Feast of Dedication kept in remembrance the restoration of the services in the Temple in 165 B.C. by the Maccabees after three years' desecration under the Syrian king, Antiochus Epiphanes (pp. 755–7). It began on December 25 and lasted eight days. Peter spoke to the crowd in Solomon's porch (v. 23) after the cure of the lame beggar (Acts 3[11]). The better attested reading in v. 29 in R.V. mg. seems exegetically impossible, unless the meaning is that in the disciples greater works than even those which he is doing will be done by the Father (cf. 14[28]). V. 30 does not affirm a metaphysical unity, but a moral, and we must not read the later creeds into the words. As the claim to do as the Father did was by the Jews regarded as blasphemy (5[17]), so was this claim, and another attempt at stoning is made. The argument Jesus advances in self-defense (vv. 34–36) puts his claim to speak of his relation to God as he does on a less metaphysical basis. If men whom God has appointed as his agents can be addressed as *gods* (Psa. 82[6]) much more can one whom God set apart and sent into the world call himself without blasphemy the Son of God. He makes a last appeal for faith on the ground that his works confirm his claim. Escaping from their hands, Jesus retires for safety to Peræa, the scene of the Baptist's ministry. The ministry in this region is confirmed by Mk. 10[1] and Lk. 13[31]. The familiar scene recalled to some of his followers the witness of John, and faith was confirmed.

CHAPTER XI

1–44. The Raising of Lazarus. This narrative raises greater difficulty than any other portion of the Gospel; the problem of miracle is here presented in its acutest form; but that problem confronts us in the Synoptics no less than in the fourth Gospel (see art., *Miracles of N.T.*, p. 924a). The feeding of the five thousand and the walking on the water are in the Synoptic tradition also; the turning of the water into wine is not more incredible than these nature miracles. The miracles of healing in this Gospel do not assume a more supernatural power than those in the Synoptic record. The restoration of Lazarus is not the only instance of the raising of the dead. The three Synoptics record the case of the daughter of Jairus (Mt. 9[18-26] Mk. 5[35-43] Lk. 8[49-56]). Luke alone records the raising of the widow's son of Nain (7[11-17]). The scholar betrays his modern naturalistic standpoint when he charges Luke with outbidding the common Synoptic tradition, since the daughter of Jairus had just died, and the widow's son was on the way to burial. Would the difference of time for the Evangelist enhance the wonder of the miracle? While v. 39 in this chapter does suggest a desire to magnify the greatness of the miracle, does a longer lapse of time, unless corruption has set in, make it more difficult to believe this miracle than those—if, indeed, we are dealing with miracles? To the explanation of v. 39 we must return; but meanwhile we may ask the question: Do we know enough about what death involves as regards the relation of soul and body to be able to say when, if restoration be at all possible, it becomes impossible? The record about Lazarus does not challenge the trustworthiness of the fourth Gospel more than the records of restoration from the dead in the Synoptics do theirs. Whether the Son of God incarnate, who was himself raised from the dead, could or could not work such a miracle is a problem which a commentary cannot attempt to solve, but the solution of which will depend on the Christology which any writer feels justified on all the evidence in holding. Speaking for himself, the present writer will not deny the credibility of this narrative.

Another difficulty in addition to that inherent in the nature of the miracle itself is the silence of the Synoptics. A miracle which according to the Gospel made such an impression on the Jews (v. 45), and which led the rulers to take counsel to put Jesus to death (v. 53), must, it is said, have been recorded by the Synoptists. But it has already been shown that the Synoptic record is almost exclusively concerned with the Galilæan ministry. Peter, whose preaching was the basis of the Synoptic tradition, is not mentioned as present in Bethany, or even when the news of Lazarus' illness came to Jesus. Had he been, would he not have spoken, as he was always ready to do? Thomas is the only one of the Twelve mentioned by name. The Synoptics, it is said, connect the decision of the rulers with the cleansing of the Temple, and the author of the fourth Gospel, having used that incident at the beginning, substitutes for it the story of this miracle. The Synoptics do not show that intimate knowledge of the Jerusalem situation which this Gospel shows (11[53]); and in their ignorance of the other grounds of provocation of the rulers they fixed on the one which alone was known to them. Much more probable, however, is John's representation that the resolve to get Jesus out of the way had *many* grounds.

A careful examination of the narrative justifies these conclusions: (1) that the Witness was not present throughout, although he may have been at the grave, or in close touch with the sisters; (2) that his report was worked over by the Evangelist, who elsewhere shows a tendency to exaggerate the supernaturalness of Jesus' knowledge and power; and (3) that the redactor with his interest in the Galilæan disciples may have inserted the name "Thomas." Some of the grounds for this conclusion may be mentioned in examining the narrative in detail.

V. 2 points forward to 12[1-8] (cf. Lk. 10[38-42]). V. 3, *Lord*, anticipates the post-resurrection title as in other places. V. 4 may mean either that Jesus did not anticipate death, or was confident that he could restore from the dead; while the first is the more probable, the second seems to be what the narrative intends. Compared with 9[3, 4] the emphasis on the glorifying of the Son of man seems improbable. The Witness reads the result back into the intention. Would one who loved as v. 5 assures us think at such a time of the credit the issue of the illness might bring to himself? While v. 6 gives the impression that the delay was due to the intention that death should take place, and so a greater miracle should be performed, it need not mean more than that Jesus was waiting now as always for the divine indication (cf. 2[4] 7[6]). When that came he obeyed, despite the danger pointed out by the disciples, because he is certain that as long as duty guides safety is assured until the appointed hour comes (cf. 9[4, 5]). How Jesus knew of Lazarus' death we know not, unless in his waiting upon God the intuition needed at the moment came; what his intimacy with God made possible to him our psychology cannot explore; he conveys the knowledge to his disciples in figurative language, which shows his confidence in what God will do by him; he can speak of restoration from death as awakening from sleep. The declaration in v. 15 as in v. 4 cannot have fallen from the lips of Jesus. The opportunity of working a miracle which would confirm the faith of his disciples cannot have been so great a compensation to him for the sorrow of the two sisters as to justify gladness. Submission to God's will in the death of his friend, assurance that God's power would be so used through him as to turn sorrow into joy there may have been, but not so as to overcome his natural grief. Surely this Stoic pose which lāter theological thought assigned to him is inconsistent with what is recorded in vv. 33, 35, 38, and is much less attractive and impressive. The references to *Thomas* in 14[5] and 20[25] are not inconsistent with the brave summons: a feeble faith can, when proved, be faithful (v. 16).

As burial followed death quickly, the *four days* (v. 17) indicate the time since the death. This is mentioned here to indicate (as Martha's words in v. 39) that corruption had set in; and thus to enhance the greatness of the miracle, as the restoration would involve that either the process of decay had been prevented, or was reversed. That the one or the other is impossible with God we cannot affirm, unless our point of view is wholly naturalistic. One way out of the difficulty may be mentioned, although with no assurance that we are justified in taking it. In v. 39, *dead* is printed in italics to show that the word is not in the Greek text; what stands there is, "he is in the fourth day," and this may have referred originally to the duration of the illness, and not the time of death. In that event, a misunderstanding of the expression could have started the tradition which ended in the words ascribed to Martha. If these words are authentic, at the most they express her *surmise*, and do not necessarily record a fact.

It is a relief to turn from all these difficulties which a commentary cannot honestly shirk to a narrative that *for the most part can claim historical probability in its main features.* Martha as the older is probably told first, and so goes out to meet Jesus. Her natural regret at his absence is compensated for by the confidence his presence inspires. The assurance of Jesus does not itself indicate restoration of bodily life, but recalls her to the higher life which death cannot affect. The current Jewish hope of *resurrection* (see arts., *Intertestamental Religion*, p. 210; *Religion of Israel*, p. 173; *Backgrounds*, p. 846b), to which she thinks Jesus is alluding, does not offer her the comfort she craves. The assurance of vv. 25, 26 is in entire accord with the teaching of the Gospel. Through faith in Jesus men are brought into such a relation to God as assures eternal life (cf. the argument in Mk. 12[26, 27] that relation to God assures immortality); for them physical death does not involve spiritual. Not able to understand, she is content to confess her faith in him as Messiah. Jesus' desire for a private conversation with Mary, who would have proved more understanding (cf. Lk. 10[42]), was defeated by the number accompanying her (the Jews were the opponents of Jesus). Her complaint, which showed her faith, moves Jesus deeply, but he severely restrains himself, and is distressed lest he should break down (see v. 33, R.V. mg.). When he reaches the tomb his emotions overcome him (his sorrow for his friend and his sympathy with the sisters explain the tears). The bystanders are variously affected; some even mock; the grief, they think, must be feigned, since the occasion of it might have been prevented. In the renewed emotion, indignation at this unbelief may have had a part. Martha's remonstrance in v. 39 has already been discussed; it is met by the assurance that the issue will be for God's glory. The *thanksgiving of Jesus* for answered prayer (v. 41) suggests that not only had Jesus been waiting upon God since the news of Lazarus' illness reached him, but that probably all the miracles were answers to prayers (see Mk. 9[29] and cf. art., *Miracles of N.T.*, p. 926b). As he required faith in the recipients of the healing, so he exercised faith as the agent of God in healing. V. 42 introduces the same discordant element as vv. 4 and 15. Was Jesus always, even in his intimacy with God, thinking of the impression to be made on men, the assertion of his claims? Rather, was not the cry *Lazarus, come forth!* a confession of triumphant faith that God had raised the dead, even as the cry "Peace, be still" (Mk. 4[39]) that he had allayed the tempest?

45–57. The Consequent Decision of the Jews. Apprehending the danger of a Messianic movement as a result of the growing popularity of Jesus, and of a loss in consequence of such privileges as a nation as the Romans had left them, the rulers resolved that some decisive measures were necessary.

Caiaphas, "a worldly ecclesiastic," demands the death of one man rather than the ruin of the nation (v. 50). In this the Witness sees *an unconscious prophecy of the universal salvation which should be secured by the death of Jesus;* to him it seems fitting that, however unworthy, the high priest should be used by God for such an oracle. His minute knowledge of things Jewish forbids the inference that he regarded the high priesthood as an annual appointment. *That year* means the year so significant, because of the death. Jesus, aware of his danger, withdrew to Ephraim, a place thirteen miles north of Jerusalem in the wilderness of Bethaven. The people who came up earlier to prepare for the feast were wondering whether he would run the risk of coming to it himself.

CHAPTER XII

The last section of the Gospel, which begins with this act of homage, may be described as *the Glory*. Here the Gospel is often on common ground with the Synoptics.

1–11. The Anointing in Bethany. This passage is parallel to Mt. 26^{6-16} and Mk. 14^{3-9} (note); but not to Lk. 7^{36-50} (note), which refers to another incident, and is not a variant of the same (even though in John's record there is agreement in one detail as against Mark and Matthew, namely, that Mary anointed the feet, and not the head) since, as has already been indicated, the Witness and Luke derived their material from the same circles in or near Jerusalem (see intro., p. 1061). Mark (14^{3}) places this incident in the house of Simon the leper; he may have been a neighbor of the sisters or, as Luke (10^{38}) speaks of Martha's house, she may have been his widow. Mark dates the incident only two days before the Passion if Mk. 14^{1} is a note of time for this incident also; but possibly the devotion of Mary is recorded just before the treachery of Judas (Mk. $14^{10, 11}$) to throw the contrast into bolder relief. It is probable that John is right; and that the feast was held on the Sabbath evening.

The *spikenard* in v. 3 is explained in R.V. mg. of Mk. 14^{3} as follows: "Gr. *pistic nard,* 'pistic' being perhaps a local name. Others take it to mean 'genuine,' others 'liquid' " (cf. A.S.V. mg.). Here the murmuring is ascribed to Judas (in Mk. 14^{4} to "some"), and in this complaint a selfish motive is assigned to him: the Witness may have had independent knowledge of Judas, or in his hatred of the traitor may have been ready to believe any evil of him. In Mk. 14^{6-8} the defense of Mary is fuller, and its meaning clearer; what she had done was done in anticipation of his burial. Here the meaning is: "Let her keep what remains of the ointment to be used at my burial" —a word of warning to his disciples of the impending tragedy. The hatred of the chief priests toward Jesus may have been extended to Lazarus, the cause of Jesus' increased popularity (vv. 10, 11). The fourth Gospel, being written so long after the event, can give the names more fully than could the Synoptic tradition.

12–19. The Triumphal Entry. This incident is told with less detail than by the Synoptists (Mt. 21^{1-11}, notes). As it was for the most part a demonstration by the Galilæan pilgrims, it may not have had the same interest for the Witness, a Jerusalemite. The greeting from Psa. 118^{26} may have been addressed to all pilgrims; but it is made a Messianic declaration by the words *even the King of Israel.* How the ass was found is not told, as in Mk. 11^{1-6}; it may be because the Witness himself furnished it; but the quotation from Zech. 9^{9} is given (v. 15). Jesus accepted the homage as Messiah, and in riding on an ass indicated that he came not as a warrior King but as the prophet expected—"lowly". V. 16 is a characteristic comment of the Evangelist's; in the light of later days, events disclosed their meaning. Vv. 17, 18 show the importance which for the Witness the raising of Lazarus had; but the motive here assigned would affect only the Judæans; and v. 19 is another sign of how clearly he followed the development of the hostility to Jesus. The cleansing of the Temple is omitted because a similar act was recorded at the beginning of the ministry, and because the significance attached to it in the Synoptics is replaced by other considerations.

20–36. The Request of the Greeks. This narrative combines the interest in the Galilæan disciples and the imperfect reproduction of Synoptic material, which characterizes the redactor's insertions (cf. intro., p. 1062a). The occasion of the group of sayings here brought together would be more probable in Galilee than in Jerusalem. After the request is made the Greeks are not mentioned, and Jesus declares the necessity of his death for the fulfillment of his purpose. While v. 24 recalls 1 Cor. $15^{36, 37}$, it is a saying which is fitting on the lips of Jesus, who spoke the parable of the sower (Mt. 13^{1-9}). Vv. 25, 26 recall Mk. 8^{34-38}. Only by sacrifice could he, or his disciples, fulfill their calling. Vv. 27, 28 seem to reproduce the import of Gethsemane, and the Voice experienced at the baptism (Mk. 1^{11}) and the transfiguration (Mk. 9^{7}). But is it credible that before an indifferent or even hostile crowd, such a sacred scene of intimate communion with God can have been enacted?

Some manifestation, variously interpreted by the people, there may have been (v. 29); and to this the words of Jesus (vv. 30–32) may refer. In his exaltation by death there would be judgment on the world's unbelief, and overthrow of the power of evil in *this world* (on *Satan*, cf. Lk. 10[18] Col. 2[15]); and the sphere of his influence would be extended (cf. 3[13, 14] 6[62]). The Evangelist's comment in v. 33 narrows the reference unduly; both resurrection and ascension are included. Such a declaration perplexes the multitude, as contrary to popular expectations of the Messiah based on the apocalyptic teaching (cf. p. 1015). With a final appeal to use the fast receding opportunity, Jesus withdraws. It is probable that vv. 44–50, a summary of the teaching that had been given, preceded vv. 37–43, the Witness' or the Evangelist's estimate, justified by prophecy.

37–43. The Results of the Ministry. The failure, despite the miracles as signs of a divine mission, is explained by prophecy, Isa. 53[1], the Messiah being regarded as *the arm of the Lord;* and also its deeper cause in spiritual insensibility (Isa. 6[9 10]). V. 41 expresses the current view of prophecy, as anticipation of future events. The failure was not total, but self-interest prevented some from an open confession.

44–50. The Summary of the Teaching. Belief in Christ is belief in God. While his coming is for salvation, to unbelief it proves condemnation; for the revelation rejected is divine, and its acceptance brings eternal life.

CHAPTER XIII

1–20. The Washing of the Disciples' Feet. The story bears the signs of the eyewitness; possibly the beloved disciple was himself the host; and his telling of the tale is a confession of failure to fulfill one of the demands of hospitality—the provision of a slave to wash the feet of the guests, necessary to comfort in a hot and dusty country, in which sandals were worn (cf. Lk. 7[44]). The failure may have been passed over in Peter's record (Mk. 14 12-26) out of consideration for a fellow disciple. The interpretation of Jesus' consciousness in vv. 1 and 3 is cast in more theological terms than would be the thoughts of Jesus; but he was conscious both of his own dignity and the humility of the act as a last service of love, rebuking the ambitions and rivalries of the disciples, which were a danger to the cause he was intrusting to them. V. 2 is inserted to show that *even treachery could not quench his love.* Peter's characteristic first remonstrance is met by a summons to present trust, an assurance of future understanding; the second by an indication of the symbolic character of the act; only as cleansed by him could the disciples remain one. The deed was *sacramental* as well as *exemplary.* Peter as usual rushes from one extreme to another, and is answered with a homely proverb, *He that is bathed, needeth not to wash* (v. 10, R.V. mg.). The thought of the traitor weighs heavily on the mind of Jesus. V. 11 seems an unnecessary explanation. Asserting his dignity as acknowledged by the disciples, Jesus points to the humility of his act as exemplary; setting an example often involves a moral pose; but here there was a moral necessity to bring about the change in the disciples, without which they would be unfit to carry on his work. The way to happiness for them is not that which they are now taking, but that of acknowledging and following him as Master, not deeming too servile what he by his own act has commended. Again his mind reverts to the traitor. From his insight no character or motive was concealed. In this treachery he recognizes the fulfillment of prophecy (Psa. 41[9]). The explanation of the reference to future events (v. 19) as a means of confirming faith seems unnatural on the lips of Jesus at such a moment of tense feeling. If it belongs to this context at all, v. 20 should follow v. 17 as carrying on the thought, that such service rendered to a fellow disciple is rendered to Jesus, and through him to God; but it recalls Mk. 9[37], where it is in an entirely appropriate setting.

21–30. The Traitor Unmasked. Some scholars would insert chs. 15 and 16 between v. 20 and v. 21. The failure of Judas was grief to Jesus (cf. 12[27]); and, unable to be silent longer, he speaks plainly. Instead of the looks of amazement and inward doubts, the Synoptists record a question from each to Jesus (Mk. 14[19], notes). Jesus' answer conveys no more than that the traitor is at the table. The fourth Gospel records a more definite intimation to one of those present—the host, who occupied the place of honor next Jesus, and whose presence there may have excited the jealousy, which the lowly service rebuked. Peter by a gesture induced him to ask the question. The position described is not one of special endearment, but the normal, where the guests reclined on couches round the table. By leaning back, this disciple could hear the answer as others did not. The giving of the sop, or handling of a choice morsel, was common at a meal. In itself, therefore, it did not serve as a sign, although the fact that it was given to Judas first was significant for the host, but probably for no other; would Peter or even John, the son of Zebedee (cf. Lk. 9[54]), have allowed the traitor to depart? V. 27 presents a difficulty: did Jesus' action provoke the resolve, as the strong symbolic language suggests, or was a purpose long maturing at last made final? Jesus' dismissal is not an approval or command, as though he were using Judas as a tool that the divine purpose might be fulfilled; it is an acquiescence in a resolve which his insight showed was *so fixed as morally to be the equivalent of the deed.* The act produced a reaction (Mt. 27^3), while a resolve hindered of fulfillment would have bred inward corruption; even for the traitor the love of Jesus acted for the best. Jesus' words were not understood; that some "business" was still possible shows that the feast had not begun. *The night* into which Judas passed from the lighted upper room was symbolic of his state.

31–38. The Parting Command and the Warning to Peter. Moffatt in his translation of the N.T. places chs. 15 and 16 after v. 31a, and it must be admitted that 13^{31b}–14^{31} is a more appropriate close of the talk; 14^{31} indicates that Jesus rose from the table, and that the prayer (ch. 17) was uttered as all stood, ready to go forth to Gethsemane; other indications, too minute to mention here, point to some such sequence. Other arrangements have been suggested: the only one which need be mentioned is that chs. 15 and 16 should follow 13^{35}. In this arrangement Jesus, relieved in spirit by the withdrawal of the traitor, rose from depression to exaltation of spirit; in his passion, now so near, he anticipated his triumph, in which he would be honored, and God in him. But his triumph meant separation from his disciples. Using the term of endearment *little children,* he warned them how short their time together would be. They must compensate for his absence from among them by their love to one another, which will be a constant witness to the world of their relation to him.

The fourth Gospel is silent in regard to the Last Supper; the silence may be due to the absence of the Witness, who may have followed Judas to discover what he and also the opponents of Jesus were doing; or he may have disapproved of superstitious ideas that by the end of the century were attaching themselves to the ordinance (cf. 6^{63}), of which the insertion in 6^{52-58} (see notes there) gives an indication; or he may not have attached such importance to the ordinance as the church at an early date did. It is suggested that the *new commandment* (v. 34) refers to the institution, the purpose of which is to promote mutual love of the disciples. Peter's remonstrance against any separation leads to the warning of his betrayal. It is placed on the way to Gethsemane in Mk. 14^{29}, another indication that the present arrangement of the record is not the original and historical.

CHAPTER XIV

1–31. The Last Talk. In the talk and prayer (ch. 17) we have not and cannot expect to have a *verbatim* report. The characteristic vocabulary of the Witness and the Evangelist appears; reminiscence passes over into reflection, and comment is added. Pregnant sayings of Jesus were developed in the meditation of the Witness; and sayings from other contexts were attracted by association of ideas into this context. But that the *substance of the teaching* fell from the lips of Jesus we need not doubt. Could even a spiritual genius have developed these truths in his meditations, unless there were utterances of Jesus which served as the starting-point? The Jesus of these chapters satisfies religious aspiration fully.

The main current of the thought must be briefly traced. The sorrow of separation could be comforted by faith in him, and in God through him (the disciples began with trusting in their Master, and through that trust gained faith in God). There is room for them in the Father's house (heaven and earth are not distinguished, but as Jesus was himself departing from this world, he is probably thinking of the world unseen). Had they any doubts, he would have removed them by the assurance that the object of his departure is to prepare for the disciples. Yet the departure will be followed by a return (either at the Second Advent, according to the current eschatology, or at death; cf. 2 Cor. 5^{6-8}). They surely understand now that his death is the only way for such preparation for them, and return to them. Thomas' protest of ignorance is met by Jesus' assurance that he himself, as truth revealing God and as life renewing them, is the mediator with the Father, bringing men to God and God to men; since the revelation of God as Father was so certain in him, that knowledge should be inevitable for those who knew him as they did. Misunderstanding the words *have seen* (v. 7) as referring to physical and not spiritual vision, Philip asks for a theophany such as Moses and the prophets experienced. Such a request shows failure to perceive that the union of the Father and Son had been such that the words spoken were God's, and the deeds done God's, so as to command faith. Great as had been the revelation in him, his departure to the Father would enable his disciples to accomplish a still *greater work* (v. 12; the limitation of the ministry in time and place is what is referred to here). But the relation to him of his disciples must be one of dependence in prayer, and obedience in love, if this greater work is to be done by them.

In v. 16 a theme is introduced which, present in the Synoptics, has a larger place in this Gospel, especially in these discourses, *the gift of the Holy Spirit*. The Baptist foretold that the Messiah would baptize with the Holy Ghost and fire (Mt. 3[11]). Jesus recognized the working of the Spirit in his own ministry (Mt. 12[28]), and promised it to the disciples (Mt. 10[20]). After the resurrection, the descent of the Spirit as power from God was expected (Lk. 24[49] Acts 1[4, 5]). In the Synoptics and Acts the Spirit is conceived as source of supernatural powers; in these discourses as cleansing, enlightening, and renewing grace, as also in Paul; but while in Paul sanctification is stressed, here it is illumination: God will give, in answer to Jesus' prayer, this invisible Divine Presence to be to the disciples what he has been, *one called to the side of another* to counsel and to help. As Christ is also called *Paraclete* (or *Advocate*) in 1 Jn. 2[1], it is evident that the Spirit's presence is not a *substitute* for Christ's but only makes that presence, and the Father's presence in him, *more real*. A condition of the realization of the presence, however, is love's obedience. Judas' inability (v. 22) to understand how a presence invisible to the world can be real to the disciples leads to a repetition of the condition—love's obedience. In relation to the present teaching the Spirit, who will continue the revelation (i.e., will be sent in the name), will recall it, and supplement it. V. 29 is one of those comments which betray the Evangelist's mind. The parting is close at hand, the Hebrew *Shalom* (*peace*) is given; but invested with what fullness of meaning! It is his very own peace, unlike any the world can give. With such an assurance, there should be not sorrow, but joy in his departure, the return of the Son to the Father, the *greater*. The hour of the final struggle with evil is at hand, and will not end in defeat; but the Father's summons to meet it is accepted.

There are here two thoughts for Christology: (1) the earthly life was a relative separation compared to the heavenly; and (2) the Son regards himself as dependent on and subordinate to the Father.

CHAPTER XV

1–17. The Vine. There may have been a parable of the care of the vinedresser for the vineyard (cf. Isa. 5[1-7]), as of the shepherd for the sheep (10[1-18]); but that has been allegorized, and the dominant thought is the dependence of the branches on the stem. The allegory is not carried out consistently, but literal and figurative sayings are interwoven. V. 2 seems to refer to Judas, who had cut himself off, as we should say; but whom God had taken away, as Jesus, ascribing all to the Father's will, thought. Ability for Christian service depends on communion with Jesus, as the source of truth and life. Assurance in prayer is also a result of such communion. The disciples will prove their discipleship, and bring glory to God by faithfulness. This communion is the reception and the response of love, a love like that of Father and Son, and shown, as is the Son's, by obedience. In such loving obedience the disciples can come to share the Master's joy. This loving obedience will be shown in the mutual love of the disciples for one another. He is giving the greatest proof of his love for them in his sacrifice. Although in v. 16 the thoughts of vv. 4, 5, and 7 recur, in vv. 13–16 another illustration emerges—that of *friendship*. He shows his friendship in his sacrifice; they in their *obedience*. No longer incompletely as to servants, but wholly as to friends, he fully discloses to them all he knows from the Father. The initiative in this friendship was not theirs, but his. V. 17 repeats v. 12. Throughout these discourses we have this constant movement around one central thought, suggesting that the Witness' mind kept revolving around certain sayings of Jesus which he remembered.

18–27. The World's Hatred. In contrast to the relation of the disciples to their Master and one another will be their relation to the world. As he is hated so will they be, because they do not follow the world's ways, but are walking in his way; they as servants can only expect what he has experienced. This persecution of disciples and Master shows ignorance of God, a culpable ignorance, as the persecutors have hated God's messenger, rejected his words, and the witness of his works. Here (vv. 21–24) recur thoughts often repeated in the controversies. This unjustified hostility too had been foretold (Psa. 35[19]). V. 25 seems to belong to the current Christian apologetic in Ephesus rather than to Jesus in the upper room; 16[1-4] follows on vv. 18–25, and vv. 26, 27 seem to break the continuity. The connection of thought, however, might be as follows: Despite all persecution, truth will prevail over error, since through the Spirit, whose function it is to impart the truth, and who comes from the source of truth himself, God will bear witness to Jesus; and as the channels of that

Spirit, so will the disciples also bear witness, to whom his whole ministry has been known. The words used in v. 26, *which proceedeth from the Father*, have been made the basis of the doctrine of the procession of the Spirit. The Son is begotten, the Spirit proceeds; in the Greek view, the proceeding is from the Father only; in the Latin view, from the Son also; in a mediating view, from the Father through the Son.

CHAPTER XVI

1–4. The Warnings of Persecution. The chapter division here is a blunder, as these verses continue the theme of 15[18-27]: a plain warning is given of the persecution which the disciples may expect, so that, forewarned, their faith may not fail. The reserve that had hitherto been employed must now cease, as the departure is near. This persecution will be regarded as a service acceptable unto God, because the revelation of God in the Son has been refused.

5–24. The Sorrow of the Disciples at the Departure. The reproach of v. 5 sounds strange after Peter's question (13[36]), and Thomas' bewilderment (14[5]), an indication of the displacement of these two chs. 15 and 16. Their sorrow is offered the comfort that *the departure will be for their advantage*, as it is the condition of the fulfillment of the promise of the Spirit. Two reasons for this condition can be suggested: (1) the disciples could not experience the invisible presence till the visible had been withdrawn; and (2) the work of Christ in death and rising again had to be accomplished before the new life in the Spirit could become the possession of believers.

In the exposition here (vv. 7–15) the work of the Spirit is related to the world, to the disciples, and to Jesus himself. *The relation to the world*, i.e., mankind, indifferent and even hostile to God, is threefold: the Spirit exposes sin as shown in unbelief toward Christ, vindicates righteousness in witnessing to the triumph of the Son, and executes judgment in Satan's overthrow by Christ. *The relation to the disciples* is this: the Spirit will give the teaching which owing to their incapacity they cannot receive from Jesus himself; but the teaching will always be subordinate to that of the Son. The words in v. 13 give expression to the current appreciation of prophecy as prediction. *The relation to Christ* is one of subordination, as the Son's relation to the Father is primary. As the thought of v. 16 links up closely with the thought of v. 6, the conclusion forces itself upon one that this passage—as also the others dealing with the Spirit, which can even in the same way be shown to break the continuity—does not belong to the present context; and that it should be regarded rather as *an exposition of Christian experience* than a prediction of Christ's, one of the things the disciples could not bear, but into which the Spirit would lead them.

The reference of Jesus to his approaching departure (vv. 16, 17) bewildered the disciples, and he, aware of this, sought to relieve them by the assurance that, just as a woman's sorrow is turned into joy when the child is born, so will their sorrow at his departure be turned to joy on his return in a communion, in which they will have no perplexity to be removed, and in which all requests in his name will be met.

25–33. The Disciples Profess to Understand Jesus. The time comes, says Jesus, when there will be no need of figurative language (v. 25; *parables*, R.V. mg.; *dark sayings*, A.S.V.); but the Father will be plainly revealed. No need of his intercession, as the Father's love will be made manifest in response to their love and faith in him as God's messenger, who comes from and goes back to God. The avowal by the disciples of their clear understanding and full faith in him is followed by his warning that they will all forsake him, but the Father will still be with him. What he has taught has been necessary to give them peace in himself amid all the distresses they will meet in the world. In his conquest they may find the inspiration of courage.

CHAPTER XVII

The High-Priestly Prayer. In dealing with so sacred a theme the voice of criticism may appear an unwelcome intrusion; but for the understanding of the passage it must be pointed out that, even if the substance of the prayer was spoken by Jesus as he and his disciples stood ready to go forth to Gethsemane, the *language* is that of Witness or Evangelist. This prayer is in form more of a soliloquy than petition. On this occasion, the disciples were privileged to overhear his converse with his Father. While throughout reminiscence has been transformed by reflection, yet only in two places does the recorder obtrude himself. V. 3 is quite obviously a theological reflection, the term "Jesus Christ" distinctly points to a later date. So also vv. 12, 13 seem incongruous, especially the reference to the fulfillment of prophecy in v. 12. (The phrase *son of perdition* illustrates a Hebrew usage: it means one closely related to destruction, "a lost soul." Cf. 2 Thess. 2[3] "the man of sin"; Mt. 23[15] "a son of Hell.") The first part of the prayer refers to Christ himself (vv. 1–8);

the second to the disciples (vv. 9–19); and the third to the wider circle of believers (vv. 20–26).

1–8. The Prayer of Christ on His Own Behalf. Conscious that the appointed time for the fulfillment of his calling has come, he prays that God may so honor him in becoming the bearer of life to all men (*flesh*—man as natural and mortal) that by him God himself may be honored. The finished task warrants the reward of the recovery of all that as Son he had eternally enjoyed. (Is this reference to pre-existence in v. 5 due to the theology of the Gospel, or does it express Jesus' self-consciousness? Cf. 8^{58}, and the note there.) For this Gospel the resurrection meant a recovery of what had been already possessed; for Paul it meant a gain of a further exaltation as reward for the humiliation (cf. Rom. 1^{4} Phil. 2$^{9-11}$). Those whom God had given him (guided to him by the Spirit, cf. Mt. 16^{17}) had received from him and had accepted the revelation of the relation of the Father and the Son.

9–19. The Prayer of Christ for His Present Disciples. Confining his regard to the disciples as his and God's peculiar possession, in view of his departure and their continuance in the world, he intercedes on their behalf for God's preservation of them in the revelation which has come through him, so that their unity may be even as that of Father and Son. His guardianship, now ending, has availed for all except the one disciple, doomed by his character to ruin. His intercourse with them has completed their joy; although it has brought on them the world's hostility. He prays not for their removal from, but their preservation amid, the evil of the world (probably *the evil* is thought of as personal, v. 15). Their separation from the world, like his, because of their relation to him will be completed by God's making them holy as he himself is by means of the truth in his revelation. Himself God's missionary, he makes them his missionaries. His consecration of himself is in view of their consecration of themselves to their mission.

20–26. The Prayer of Christ for His Future Disciples. From the messengers the prayer turns to those who receive their message, that their unity in the Father and Son, as pattern of theirs with one another, may be extended, so as to convince the world of his divine mission. As the Father honors the Son, so has he, the Son, honored believers with a mutual indwelling for the completion of their unity as evidence of his mission, as the channel to them of the same love as the Father gives the Son. For these believers, the Father's gift, he desires that they may share with him the honor, which his return to the Father will bring, a token of God's eternal love to him (cf. v. 5). The appeal is to God as righteous to reward those who in an unbelieving world did believe, so that God's love to the Son might be theirs in the presence of the Son in them.

It is possible only to trace the course of thought in this chapter without attempting to explain every detail, for here also meditation revolves around a few centers.

CHAPTER XVIII

1–11. The Arrest. Here, to the end of the Gospel, John follows the Synoptics (Mk. 14$^{43-50}$, notes). A minute comparison of the varying narratives need not be attempted, but attention may be called to the important *differences.* In this passage we are at once confronted with the question, Why does not John record the agony in Gethsemane? We need not rashly offer the explanation that the fact was inconsistent with his doctrine of the person, as he does recognize that Jesus was fully subject to emotion (11$^{33, 35, 38}$ 12^{27}). If, as is here maintained, the source of most of the material is the report of an eyewitness, the simpler explanation is that he was absent, having hastened from the upper room to discover what steps were being taken by the authorities, and that he returned with the company sent to arrest Jesus. This company included a *cohort* (v. 3, R.V. mg.) of Roman soldiers as well as the Temple guards; and Judas served as guide to the place of retirement familiar to him. In this record Jesus does not wait for the traitor's kiss, the sign of identification given to the captors (Mk. 14$^{44, 45}$), but freely offers himself (this is in accordance with the characteristic of the Gospel to insist on Jesus' initiative; 1^{43} 2^{4} 4^{7} 5^{6}). There was no further need of the services of Judas. In some confusion at the boldness displayed, the soldiers drew back, and some may have fallen. As at Nazareth (Lk. 4^{30}), so here, the presence of Jesus may for a moment have overawed. Jesus' solicitude about his disciples gives the Evangelist occasion for pointing out a fulfillment of prophecy (v. 9). The name of the servant is not added as a bit of literary realism, but may have been known to the Witness. The words of Jesus in v. 11 recall the prayer in the garden (Mk. 14^{36}); and the Witness, having heard of the agony from some disciple present, may have misplaced them here.

12–27. The Jewish Trial. It is not easy to follow the course of events. If Annas, although no longer high priest, was an instigator of the arrest, it is not at all improbable that there was a private preliminary inquiry in his house, although no mention is made of it in the Synoptic tradition. The Witness, at home in Jerusalem, having free access to the priestly homes (v. 15), may have been present in the house of Annas, while Peter knew only of the public trial before Caiaphas. But conceding this possibility, there still remain these difficulties: (1) Why is the account of Peter's denial broken in two (vv. 15–18, 25–27), whereas the Synoptics give a continuous narrative? (See Mk. 14[66-72].) (2) If the *high priest* of vv. 15 and 19 be Caiaphas, as v. 13 states, how does v. 24 assert that he was sent from Annas to Caiaphas? (3) If, however, the high priest of these verses be Annas, not only is there an inaccuracy in the description, but Peter must have known of this inquiry before Annas, and the silence of Mark remains unexplained. The *solution of the problem* seems to be this: that the redactor has inserted the story of Peter's denial, and has done so unskillfully, bringing about a displacement, and that v. 24 should follow v. 14. The record in vv. 19–23 is not of this private inquiry in the house of Annas, but of the public trial before Caiaphas. If the Witness was *another disciple* (v. 15), as is here assumed, after obtaining admission for Peter, he entered the high priest's court himself, and was present at the time. The story of Peter's denial does not come from him, and the minor differences between the report here and the Synoptic record are easily explained by variant tradition or by the redactor's imperfect knowledge. Jesus' answer to the high priest in v. 20 agrees substantially with his remonstrance to his captors in Mk. 14[49]. Sayings were remembered, not always their setting. The detail in v. 22 may be more accurate than the more general statement of Mk. 14[65]. This last denial (v. 25) may have taken place just as Jesus passed through the court yard, and there may have been given the look which brought penitence (Lk. 22[61]).

28–32. The Transfer of the Trial to Pilate. The scene of the trial before Pilate was the palace (mg. *praetorium*), either Herod's palace in the western part of the city, or Antonia, at the northwestern corner of the Temple precinct (see Acts 21[31-37] 22[24]—"the castle"). The reason given for the avoidance of defilement by entering a heathen's dwelling shows that the Passover was not passed, as the Synoptic records assume in regarding the Last Supper as the paschal meal; but that Jesus died when the paschal lambs were being slain. It is probable that the fourth Gospel is right. (See art., *Chronology of N.T.*, p. 875b.) Avoiding a definite charge, the accusers are curtly dismissed; if it is a matter falling under their jurisdiction, let them attend to it. Determined on the capital sentence, which they are not at liberty to inflict, they insist that the charge is of sufficient gravity for the governor's notice. Here again the Evangelist sees a fulfillment of Jesus' prediction of crucifixion, since the Jewish method of execution was stoning (cf. Acts 7[59]).

33–38a. The Private Examination by Pilate. This account is peculiar to the fourth Gospel, and the explanation is the same: the Witness had access to the governor as to the high priest. The interest of this Gospel in *the truth* may have colored the language in vv. 37, 38. Pilate's first question suggests that the Jews had made some more definite charge of sedition. Jesus in turn asks in what sense the term "King" is used, and assures Pilate that any Kingship he claims is no danger to Rome, since his supporters have taken no action to justify any suspicion. Asserting his Kingship in the realm of truth, he only provokes Pilate's scornful skepticism.

38b–40. The Attempt at Compromise. Deeming Jesus a harmless dreamer, and convinced of his innocence, Pilate tries to placate the Jewish fury by a compromise; having condemned Jesus he will release him in accordance with a custom at the feast. Luke (23[7-12]) records the previous attempt to transfer the trial to Herod. Mark (15[8]) represents the demand for the release of a prisoner as first coming from the people. While there is no direct evidence of such a custom, it agrees with the way Rome governed subject peoples. A papyrus of 85 A.D. contains the words, "Thou art worthy of scourging . . . but I give thee to the people." The people demand the release of Barabbas, probably a bandit patriot.

CHAPTER XIX

1–7. The Scourging and Mockery. Though acknowledged innocent, Jesus is scourged, usually the preliminary to crucifixion, and mocked by the soldiers, doubtless with a view to please the governor. Presenting him in his seemingly helpless misery, Pilate appeals to the compassion of the crowd. Whatever his offense, will not this content them? Instigated by the rulers the ominous cry is heard: *Crucify him!* Again trying to shirk responsibility, Pilate bids them wreak their own vengeance. Then the charge of blasphemy is made. Moved by his own superstition, or dreading Jewish fanaticism, he fears. (The message from his wife, Mt. 27[19], may have added to his distress.)

8–11. The Second Private Examination. This second interview with Jesus within the palace is also peculiar to the fourth Gospel. Jesus' silence, a silence of judgment on the judge afraid to deal justly, irritates Pilate into an assertion of his authority, which Jesus meets with the reminder that all authority, as delegated, carries responsibility. Nevertheless, Pilate's sin is not so great as that of him by whom Jesus had been delivered (v. 11). It is uncertain whether Judas, Caiaphas, or Satan as instigator of all evil, is meant.

12–16. The Sentence Pronounced. Still more convinced of Jesus' innocence, and protesting his freedom from responsibility in the symbolic act of hand-washing (Mt. 27[24]), Pilate is at last cowed into submission by the threat that, if he does not condemn Jesus, and passes over this charge of sedition, he may be accused of treason against the emperor. Preferring the counsels of prudence to the dictates of conscience, he passes formal sentence of crucifixion. (The derivation of the name *Gabbatha* is uncertain.) According to Mk. 15[25], Jesus was crucified at *the third hour* (9 A.M.). The *sixth* hour of v. 14 would be noon. The discrepancy has not been satisfactorily explained, either by ascribing to this Gospel another than the current reckoning of time or by appealing to the elastic notions of time in the East. (See art., *Chronology of N.T.*, p. 874a.) A final despairing appeal to their patriotism is vain; as, to compass their end, they bow their heads to Cæsar's yoke. In their rage they even invoke God's judgment on themselves and their children (Mt. 27[25]).

17–37. The Crucifixion. The statement that Jesus was *bearing the cross for himself* is characteristic; the independence of Jesus in action and passion is in this Gospel emphasized. It is unnecessary, however, to regard the statement, as some do, as a deliberate correction of the story of Simon of Cyrene (Mk. 15[21]). The omission of this story of Simon may also be due to the fact that some of the Gnostics asserted that Simon was crucified instead of Jesus. The *Hebrew* of v. 20 is probably Aramaic, the current language of the Jews, akin to the Hebrew. (See art., *Backgrounds*, pp. 842–3, and cf. p. 880a.) Pilate's refusal to amend the title illustrates the petulance of the feeble man. A coward in the great matter, he asserts himself in the small. It is conjectured that it was either when the nails were being driven into the hands and feet, or when the cross was being lifted up, that Jesus uttered the prayer for the forgiveness of his foes recorded by Luke (23[34]), who also records (23[43]) the assurance to the penitent thief of continued companionship through and after death. There is no ground for suspecting the fact in vv. 23, 24, even though there is this close correspondence with the words of the Psalm (22[18]). If *his mother's sister* (v. 25) was "the mother of Zebedee's children" (Mt. 27[56]) and Salome (Mk. 15[40]), it was fitting that the mother of Jesus should be intrusted to a nephew; but this assumes that the disciple whom Jesus loved was the son of Zebedee, an assumption against which reason has been shown (see p. 1065). If the Witness was the host in the Upper Room, and one who had a closer intimacy with Jesus, and if the mother of Jesus did not desire to return to Galilee, and especially to Nazareth to be exposed to mockery, and wished to linger in Jerusalem, it was fitting that such a charge was given to him and her. Even in dying, love was unforgetting. If the disciple led away the mother at that moment, his silence regarding the cry of desolation (Mt. 27[46] Mk. 15[34]) does not prove his theological bias, but was due to the absence. So touching an incident need not be allegorized, as in the older commentaries, as referring to the relation of the Gentile churches to the Jewish church. *Thirst* was one of the aggravations of crucifixion; but the Evangelist invests an utterance, natural in the circumstances, with an artificial theological significance (v. 28). For *hyssop* we should probably substitute *javelin.* The Greek of the two words is closely similar. The last words here recorded (v. 30) express relief from suffering, confidence in a task accomplished. Luke (23[46]) adds the prayer of self-committal to God as Father (cf. Psa. 31[5]). The demand of the Jews (v. 31) was based on Deut. 21[23]; defilement especially at such a time must be avoided. The breaking of the legs was an act of mercy to hasten death. A spear thrust as an alternative to ensure death is quite a credible act. The physical result is declared by some medical testimony as also credible. The Evangelist's asseveration (v. 35) that *the witness is true* may have been made either to prove the reality of the death against a current heresy, Docetism (the heresy that Jesus' life in the flesh was all mere appearance, not reality), or in view of the symbolic significance afterward given to the fact (1 Jn. 5[6]). The facts being in themselves credible, there is no justification for regarding the statement as invented to prove the fulfillment of prophecy (Psa. 34[20] Zech. 12[10]). The record is, however, in contradiction with the words in the account of the institution of the Last Supper (1 Cor. 11[24]), according to many ancient authorities. "This is my body which is broken for you" (A.V.), but R.V. reads "which is for you," following other MSS.

38–42. The Burial. Had Joseph not intervened, the body of Jesus would have been cast with the others into a pit (cf. Josh. 8[29] Isa. 66[24]). He was a rich man (cf. Isa. 53[9]), and a member of the Sanhedrin (Mt. 27[57] Mk. 15[43]). His act and that of Nicodemus showed how faith inspired courage. The details of the burial mark its temporary character.

CHAPTER XX

1–10. The Empty Tomb. (Mt. 28[1-10], notes.) John agrees with Luke in placing the appearances in Jerusalem, not in Galilee (as in Matthew, Mark and the Appendix to John—ch. 21). Mary Magdalene alone is mentioned; in the Synoptics "other women"; but the *we* of v. 2 implies their presence. Luke (24[12]) mentions Peter alone. Peter as always is swift in action; but the other disciple, probably younger in years, can be speedier of foot. The orderly arrangement of the grave clothes indicates that the body had not been stolen or removed, but that "the mortal had put on immortality," and had passed from the sensible to the supersensible sphere, leaving these behind in their former place. The comment in v. 9 indicates that there was no expectation, and that it was the appearance that first awakened the faith. (For further discussion, see art., *Miracles of N.T.*, p. 930a.)

11–18. The Appearance to Mary Magdalene. Renan uses the fact that the appearance was first to Mary Magdalene as the basis of his explanation of the resurrection as due to subjective vision; a woman "out of whom went seven devils" (Lk. 8[2]) would be a violent demoniac, and in his judgment a fit subject for hallucinations. The phrase does not necessarily mean, however, that Mary had been insane. Moreover, the narrative itself carries the evidence of historical reality. The statement in vv. 11–18 is not in contradiction with that of vv. 1–10, as some scholars assume. For Mary may have returned alone to the tomb after, along with the other women, telling the disciples that it was empty; the word *standing* in v. 11 does not deny a possible departure and return; and the vision of angels in v. 12 may be accounted for by her highly wrought condition of feeling on account of the empty tomb (Lk. 24[4] lends some confirmation to this trait in the story). The failure to recognize Jesus (cf. Lk. 24[16]) may indicate the change from the natural to the spiritual body (1 Cor. 15[44]); but the familiar tone of the voice here (v. 16), the familiar gesture of the hands there (Lk. 24[30, 31]), indicate a *continuity despite change*. The prohibition of the act of worship by touch (v. 17; cf. Mt. 28[9]) may mean that the old relation of sensible contact was over (yet Lk. 24[39] is a call to "handling" in relief of doubt); and the new spiritual relation must await the Ascension. The difference of the relation of Jesus to God, and that of his disciples, is emphasized in v. 17; would Jesus himself at such a time have emphasized it? Has not a later theological development here colored the record?

19–23. First Appearance to the Disciples. The record here calls attention to the fulfillment of the promises given in chs. 14, 15, 16. They are not left *orphaned* (14[18]); his bequest of peace is theirs (14[27]); their sorrow is turned into joy (16[22]); they are his missionaries as he is God's (17[18]); the Spirit for which he prayed he now imparts (16[7]). Lk. 24[36, 39, 40] offers a parallel to vv. 19, 20, although in Luke the reality of the body for sense is emphasized. The *authority to remit or retain sin* (i.e. the penalty) is similar to the promise in Mt. 16[19], although the reference there is to the declaration of what is allowed and what is forbidden, the exposition of the Law. How is this endowment with the Spirit related to Pentecost? Were the action and words here only symbolic prophecy, or were the apostles endowed with a privilege and authority peculiar to themselves, unshared by others? The second interpretation is maintained by those who hold the theory of apostolic succession. There is no proof, however, that only the Eleven were present, and such an action would not accord with Jesus' attitude generally. Here as elsewhere the Witness may have antedated.

24–29. Second Appearance to the Disciples. Despondency may have kept Thomas away; his doubt was not peculiar to him (Mt. 28[17] Mk. 16[11-13] Lk. 24[11-25, 38]), only it was harder to remove. The story is told to enforce the truth that the faith which springs from spiritual insight is superior to the faith which rests on sensible evidence, even although to overcome doubt that evidence is given (Lk. 24[40]). The detail in vv. 19 and 26 is probably mentioned as an indication that the body was not subject to normal physical conditions, and yet could be made sensibly manifest. One cannot but feel that in Luke especially there is the tendency of a later time to emphasize this sensible evidence, an emphasis which Jesus' words (v. 29) rebuke. The questioning disposition here assigned to Thomas is quite in accord with what is elsewhere recorded of him (11[16] 14[5]); although his exclamation in v. 28, if it is to be regarded as a confession of faith, goes so far beyond the early apostolic preaching that we must suppose it reflects the theology of a later age. An interesting sidelight on the utterance is the fact that the emperor Domitian first advanced the claim, according to Suetonius, to be called "Our Lord and God."

30, 31. Conclusion. The Evangelist here states his method and his position. He has selected from a larger mass of available material; but he does not indulge in the hyperbole of the close of the Appendix (21[25]). Mark's interest is in the Messiahship of Jesus; and his narrative gathers around the confession by Peter (Mk. 8[29]). Here a higher claim is made; the divine Sonship is the dominating conception, not that of the Logos in the Prologue. This theological interest is, however, not theoretical but practical. Through faith in this divine Sonship of Jesus eternal life—the complete and permanent satisfaction of man's spiritual nature—can alone be obtained. The theologian is also the evangelist.

CHAPTER XXI

This chapter is commonly described as the Appendix, and even those who ascribe it to the same author as the rest of the Gospel regard it as an addition of a later date. In the introduction (p. 1063) reasons are given for assigning it with other passages to a redactor, who wished to give the impression (although he could not offer the proof) that the disciple whom Jesus loved was John, the son of Zebedee; to assert the authority of Peter in the church; to deal with a difficulty due to the death of the beloved disciple, in view of words spoken by Jesus; and generally to bring this record into closer accord with the Synoptic reports. The evidence of the language lends support to the contention that the Appendix is not due to the author of the rest of the Gospel. The exaggerated statement of v. 25, and the attestation of the trustworthiness of the Evangelist and of the value of his work (v. 24), cannot have come from him. Setting aside these two verses, the Appendix falls into three parts: (1) the appearance at the Sea of Galilee (vv. 1–14); (2) the conversation with Peter (vv. 15–19); and (3) the question about the beloved disciple (vv. 20–23).

1–14. The Appearance at the Sea of Galilee. The resemblance between this story and that of Peter's call in Lk. 5[1-11] (notes) is so close that, although direct literary dependence on Luke is excluded, the conclusion seems inevitable that we have variant traditions of the same event, less probable here than when it is placed at the beginning of the ministry. As to the *fishes*, the figurative saying at the call of Peter and Andrew about making them fishers of men (Mk. 1[17]) may by later tradition have been turned into the story of a miracle. The two sons of Zebedee are mentioned so that the identification of the beloved disciple with one of them may at least be suggested; but two other disciples are also mentioned, as the writer himself cannot be positive about that identification. There is no other evidence of a return of the disciples to their former calling after the resurrection; whereas it is probable that after the first intercourse with Jesus, as recorded in this Gospel (ch. 1), these earliest disciples did return till called to constant companionship. If a miracle did take place, it was one of supernatural knowledge, and not of power; the record does not demand the supposition that the multitude of fishes was created. (See art., *Miracles of N.T.*, p. 923b). The beloved disciple has the quick discernment, but Peter, the swift action (cf. 20[6-8]). As soon as he swims ashore he prepares the meal, unless the record is meant to indicate a supernatural provision by Jesus himself, for where could Peter get fish and bread? The number of fish has been very variously interpreted as symbolic—much learned trifling. V. 13 may be compared with 6[11]: in both there is a Eucharistic reference. The term *manifested* in v. 1 and v. 14 is not used elsewhere in this Gospel in connection with the resurrection, but it is probably our best clue to the nature of the resurrection appearances.

15–19. The Conversation With Peter. While the previous narrative may be of doubtful historical authenticity, the conversation with Peter is undoubtedly of much higher value. The occasion for this incident is indicated in Lk. 24[34] and 1 Cor. 15[5]. On one of the earliest of his appearances on the day of resurrection Jesus restored the penitent to his apostleship. To the redactor we can ascribe the words connective with the previous incident in v. 15a. In view of the denial it was necessary that a confession should be elicited. The difference (in the Greek) of the words for *love* used by Jesus and Peter should not be overemphasized, although the word used by Jesus (*agapein*) means the more discriminating affection, and that used by Peter (*philein*) the more emotional attachment. Peter is grieved not that Jesus uses this word (*philein*) in the third question, but that he should think it needful to ask the question thrice. In restoring him Jesus sets him his task; both lambs and sheep are to be cared for, and teaching and feeding are both needed. The figure of the fisherman at the call is replaced by the figure of the *shepherd;* the one points to the evangelizing, the other to the pastoral function of the ministry. Devotion to himself is the qualification Jesus requires in his ministers. V. 18 need not be suspected as prophecy after the event, if the words refer to martyrdom, and not to the growing dependence of old age; 13[36] indicates Jesus' confidence that Peter's cowardice would be turned into courage, and he would be ready to "follow" even unto death. V. 19 is the redactor's comment, although the words themselves are open to the other explanation.

20–23. The Question about the Beloved Disciple. This question and its answer belong to another context in the view of the previous incident here taken. The saying of Jesus in Mk. 9[1] was understood as a promise that one of his companions would survive to the Second Advent. The disciple whom Jesus loved was generally believed to be the last survivor of the company. When he died, the difficulty was felt that the promise had not been fulfilled. The redactor here tries to remove the difficulty. He assumes, although on the evidence he cannot assert, the identity of this disciple with John, the son of Zebedee, according to the current tradition. His solution of the problem is that the promise was conditional, and not positive, wholly dependent on the will of Christ. The other explanation, that the Greek word here translated *tarry*, which has the same root as the *mansions* of 14[2], refers to abode in the intermediate state is too farfetched. Again in v. 23 there is the redactor's comment.

24, 25. Conclusion. The first part of v. 24 asserts the redactor's belief that the beloved disciple was the author of the whole Gospel. In this commentary he is identified with the Witness, of whom the Evangelist was a disciple (see intro., p. 1064). The *we* in the attestation may refer to the circle to which the redactor belonged, or it may be used as in 1[14] to associate the other companions of Jesus with this eyewitness. The hyperbole of v. 25 compares unfavorably with the moderation of 20[30]; its purpose is to explain how so much of the Synoptic material is here omitted.

Conclusion

1. The Relation of Criticism to Interpretation. The writer of this commentary cannot part from his work without adding some words to correct a false impression. A commentary on a writing like the fourth Gospel, which presents so many literary and historical difficulties, must needs be critical; and it is only justice to the reader that these difficulties should not be glossed over, but should be fully and frankly dealt with, as there can be profit from the study of the Bible only as there is knowledge of the truth. This necessary criticism carries with it the danger, however, that it may obscure the appreciation which any writer on the fourth Gospel must desire to transfer from himself to his readers. Scholars have busied themselves so much with these problems because they are themselves convinced that to this Gospel must be given a foremost place among the N.T. writings. To explain the differences from the Synoptic records as due not to an arbitrary handling by the author of the fourth Gospel of Synoptic material, but to the well-intentioned, although not adequately informed activity of the redactor, whose insertions break the continuity and cause displacements, is to remove a difficulty. To recognize displacements, and to restore the original order, is to make the course of events and the development of the teaching more intelligible. To show that the philosophy of the Logos, or Word, presented in the Prologue and in a few other passages, and traceable in theological comments throughout the Gospel, may be ascribed to the Evangelist allows us to discover as the precious core of the Gospel the historical testimony of the Witness to the divine Sonship of Jesus Christ, and the relation of believers to him as the satisfaction of every spiritual need and desire. That in this historical testimony we may and must distinguish the reminiscences and the reflections of the Witness does not lower its religious value; for if in the one we recover much of the earthly life which the Synoptics do not record, in the other we capture the continued activity of the risen Christ by his Spirit in a personal development, similar to that of the apostle Paul, and even if influenced by his, no less due to the same heavenly source. To take the historical testimony of what Jesus was, and of what he spoke to his disciples in his ministry on earth, and of what by his Spirit he made of a spiritual genius such as was this Witness, and relieve this of the repetitions and the vehemence of the controversies with the Jews, by transferring to the Ephesus of the end of the century from the Jerusalem of the time of Jesus not the fact or subjects of controversy, but the presentation of it, in chs. 5, 6, 7, and 8 especially, is for the writer at least an incalculable gain. To be able to place alongside of the Synoptic another equally trustworthy tradition of a ministry at successive feasts during a period of two years in Judæa is to secure a broader historical basis for the significance and influence of the earthly life of Jesus more congruous with his function as Founder and Head of his church. The measure in which on the historical evidence we can give distinctness to the beloved disciple, who could receive, and preserve, and develop the distinctive teaching of Jesus regarding his relation to God, and to believers in him, which the other disciples were incapable of understanding, is the measure in which we can enrich our own spiritual life by another inspiring companion, who, like Paul and with Paul, can show to us the glory, beheld by them, "full of grace and truth, of the only-begotten of the Father," the Saviour of all who believe. It is from such a motive and with such a purpose that even the literary and historical criticism of this commentary has been written.

2. Fundamental Truths of the Fourth Gospel. In closing let us try to recall some of the truths, in the knowledge of which is eternal life, which this Gospel enshrines. The divine Sonship of Jesus is presented to us, not as a theological abstraction, but as the historical reality of the personal experience and character, no less human than divine, and of the constant dependence, intimate communion, and complete submission of the Son toward the Father. As the gift of God's love to the world his mission is not condemnation but salvation for men, and nevertheless unbelief brings doom and faith brings life. This life is eternal because in quality it is like, as in source it is from, the eternal God himself. Accordingly, death has lost not only its terror but even its reality for those who through faith in Christ share this life in God. The current eschatology is transformed. The presence of the Son of God, provoking unbelief, or evoking faith, is the present judgment. The change from unbelief to faith, which is the passing from death to life, is present resurrection. The possession of the salvation which faith in him secures is present eternal life. (In Paul we can trace a similar development.) What the Father is to the Son, that the Son is to believers. He meets all their wants, and satisfies all their aspirations as the Bread from Heaven, the Water of Life, the Door, the Good Shepherd, and the Vine. Their relation to him ought to be, and ideally is, what is his to the Father, constant dependence, intimate communion, and complete submission. The mutual activity of Father and Son is love; the Son expects love from believers, and requires their love for one another. And as the unity of Father and Son is constituted by love, so are all believers to be made a unity in him. While his presence and activity are continued as risen Lord, yet it is no longer in any sensible manifestation, but by his Spirit, the Spirit of God, who as God's gift in answer to his prayer will make believers receptive and responsive to God's presence and activity in him, will preserve the memory of what he was, spake, and did in his earthly life, and will disclose in that teaching truths that they could not then receive. Understanding and experience will increase side by side. Does any other writing, even in the N.T., contain profounder truth about God, or sublimer grace for man?

ACTS OF THE APOSTLES

By Professor ERNEST W. BURCH

Introduction

The Nature of the Book. The Acts, the fifth book in the N.T., offers the only extant account of the beginnings of the Christian Church. It is a historical work, based in part upon documents, in part upon oral tradition, and largely upon personal reminiscences of the author. (See below, *Sources.*) The position of Acts between the Gospels and the Pauline correspondence is well designed to explain how Paul came to prominence in the early church, although he was not one of the Twelve. The book is chiefly narrative in character, varied here and there by the introduction of speeches by important characters. A period of from thirty to thirty-two years is covered in twenty-eight chapters, thus necessitating omission of many facts that would be of interest to students of the early church. Some of these events are traceable in the letters of Paul, e.g., the mission to Illyricum (Rom. 15^{19}), the difficulties in the churches of Galatia and Corinth, and the great collection raised among the churches of Paul for the Jerusalem saints (Rom. $15^{25f.}$ 1 Cor. 16^{1} 2 Cor. $9^{1f.}$).

Acts is the oldest handbook of Christian missions. It opens to modern students the initial pages of the great volume of Christian progress throughout the world. While to its author the book had as its chief aim the explanation of the expansion of Christianity, Acts opens to the modern reader to some extent the inner life and thought of the parent church in Jerusalem and expounds the view of salvation held by its great men. Most important of all, no doubt, is the contribution of Acts toward an understanding of the type of religious experience current in the earliest church.

No reader of Acts can fail to note how closely knit together were the people of "the Way" and the people of Israel during the first few decades of the history of the Christian religion. The men of "the Way" still remained within Judaism (3^{1} 21^{20b} 22^{17} 23^{1} 24^{11-18}) and engaged in the old forms of religious worship, but in addition these saints became increasingly convinced that Jesus was the Messiah of God and that salvation was centered in him rather than in the institutions of Judaism. So Acts portrays the steps by which "the Way" at length separated from the parent religion and set out to conquer the world "in the name" of Jesus.

The Contents. Analyses of the contents of Acts incline either to a twofold or a threefold division. (See D. A. Hayes, *The Synoptic Gospels and the Book of Acts*, p. 304.) With some writers, the form of the Great Commission in 1^{8} is determinative of a threefold division, involving the successive stages of the church's development. A brief analysis follows:

Introduction. 1^{1-26}—The Risen Jesus and the Apostles

I. The Church in Jerusalem.

- 2^{1-47}—Outpouring of the Spirit.
- 3^{1}–4^{31}—Acts of Peter and John.
- 4^{32}–5^{11}—The Jerusalem Church.
- 5^{12}–6^{7}—Acts of the Twelve.
- 6^{8}–8^{3}—Acts of Stephen.

II. The Church in Syria and in Asia Minor.

- 8^{4}–11^{18}—Acts of Philip, Paul, and Peter.
- 11^{19-30}—Rise of the Gentile Question.
- 12^{1-24}—The Church and Herod.
- 12^{25}–15^{39}—Acts of Barnabas and Saul.

III. The Church in the Roman Empire.

- 15^{40}–18^{11}—Acts of Paul and Silas.
- 18^{12}–28^{31}—Acts of Paul.

The Author. Earlier criticism of Acts led to a doubt that Luke was author of the work, but painstaking and thorough study of the style and choice of words reveals good evidence (1) that the writer of the so-called *we-sections* (see below, *Sources*) is the same person who wrote the narrative in which they are imbedded, and (2) that the author of Acts is the author of the third Gospel. (See Harnack, *Date of the Acts and the Synoptic Gospels.*) The *we-sections* have been ascribed to a number of Paul's companions, but the evidence favors Luke himself as the eyewitness involved. The work as it stands is anonymous, like the Gospel, but the name of Luke was associated with both from an early date, and with this tradition the mass of evidence presented in the studies of Hawkins, Ramsay, and Harnack agrees. In the following commentary the name of Luke is freely used as that of the author.

The Sources. Much ingenuity has been expended upon the identification of different documents from which the author made up his work (by Spitta, Holtzmann, Wendt, J. Weiss, and others), and their able research has fully demonstrated the fact that written sources and possibly oral tradition were available for the work. Exact demarcation of these sources is made difficult precisely because, as shown in his use of sources for his Gospel, Luke puts the stamp of his own style upon the text of his source and engages in editorial abbreviation or expansion quite freely. (See art., *Structure of the Synoptic Gospels*, p. 868.) A relatively simple analysis of source material (which does not indeed reach the ultimate sources) is that offered by Professor Torrey, *Date and Composition of Acts* (1916), namely, the suggestion that in the first half of his book Luke translated into Greek a document written in Aramaic, while from 15[35] to the end of Acts the personal reminiscences of the writer (*we-sections*), supplemented by other eyewitness material, form the basis of the author's free composition.

The we-sections (16[10-17] 20[5-15] 21[1-18] 27[1]–28[16]) are thus named because the passages concerned are written in the first person plural (*we, us*) and so become differentiated from the surrounding text. It is quite generally believed that these passages formed parts of a diary kept by the traveler concerned, and that they were reproduced with little or no change. In all the portions of the journeys of Paul covered by these diary excerpts Luke was with the party. It has been suggested that other narratives are as intimately connected with the memory if not the observation of the writer, e.g., the scene in the jail at Philippi (16[25-40]), and the address of Paul at Miletus (20[16-38]), the absence of the pronoun in the first person plural being inappropriate in the recital as here given.

The speeches in Acts offer occasion for theories as to special sources, although it scarcely seems necessary thus to account for them. Details of the style of some of the speeches are noted in the commentary. In no case, unless the long speech of Stephen in ch. 7 be the exception, is a speech in Acts more than a summary or outline of the address in question. If Torrey's plausible theory be accepted, the synagogue speech in 13[16-41] goes back to another author than Luke. But Luke must have heard synagogue addresses which would in any case enable him to formulate the material transmitted to him. The Areopagus speech was not made in Luke's hearing, and it is to be assumed that Luke composed the summary in 17[22-31] from Paul's account of his adventures in Athens. No special *speech-source* is necessary for Acts.

The Date. It does not seem possible to fix an exact date for Acts. Its period is determined first of all by the date of the third Gospel. It must have been written after the Gospel (Acts 1[1]), for the Gospel is "the former treatise." It may, indeed, be supposed that the present Gospel of Luke is a revised work, later than Acts, and that Acts was written in the early sixties, being brought up to the very date of writing, when Paul was still awaiting trial at Rome. (See Torrey, *Date and Composition of Acts;* Harnack, *Date of Acts and the Synoptic Gospels;* Hayes, *The Synoptic Gospels and the Book of Acts.*) It has also been suggested that since no letter of Paul is mentioned in Acts, the book must have been written before the Pauline correspondence had more than local circulation. This consideration, joined to the fact that in Acts no indication appears that Jerusalem had fallen, weighs somewhat heavily in the scale in favor of a date in the seventh decade of the first Christian century. These points, however, are not conclusive. The third Gospel *does* betray a consciousness of the fall of Jerusalem (e.g., Lk. 21[20]), and since that Gospel is later than Mark (about 63 A.D.), and Acts is later than the third Gospel, Acts would fall somewhere in the eighth decade. The best position to assume, in view of all the facts, which prevent setting any hard and fast date, is to date Acts between 72 and 75 A.D. Much later dates have been proposed, in view of a possible use of Josephus by Luke. The tendency in N.T. criticism, however, is toward the earlier dates in cases like the present question, where both late and early dates have been proposed.

The Miracles in Acts. The narratives of the miracles in Acts are integral parts of the entire narrative and reflect, as do all the Bible miracles, certain tendencies of the time. Exorcism of demons and evil spirits plays an important part in these miracles (5[16] 8[7] 16[18] 19[13-18]). "Signs and wonders" is a frequent phrase. Typical miracles are those of healing of diseases, but instances of the "punitive miracle" are not absent (12[23] 13[11]; cf. 28[4f.] and possibly 9[8f.]). As in the Gospels, the narratives of miracles are offered to the reader as additional evidence of the power of the gospel, and at the same time chief emphasis is laid by the writer upon the message of the gospel and the personal ministry of Jesus through the apostles. To the writer of the book of Acts and to his first circle of readers the miracles need no explanation, no special plea. They were part and parcel of the early spread of Christianity. (See art., *N.T. Miracles*, p. 927.)

The Message of Acts. The book of Acts

is in a real sense the Magna Charta of the religion of Jesus Christ. We have here the story of the growth of the church from the little group of original disciples to an organization found in all parts of the Roman Empire. It brings us face to face with the gospel in action. It is a record of the actual incarnation of the teaching of Jesus. It is the Book of the Holy Ghost, whether it deals with the church in martyrdom, in conquest, in joy, in pain and toil, at home or abroad. It is the message of *the Way of God*.

Literature: Furneaux, *The Acts of the Apostles;* G. H. Gilbert, *Acts: The Second Volume of Luke's Work on the Beginnings of Christianity* (The Bible for Home and School Series); Rackham, *The Acts of the Apostles* (the foregoing are all commentaries). McGiffert, *A History of Christianity in the Apostolic Age*, revised edit.; Hayes, *The Synoptic Gospels and the Book of Acts;* Ramsay, *St. Paul the Traveler and the Roman Citizen;* B. W. Robinson, *The Life of Paul;* Hayes, *Paul and His Epistles.*

CHAPTER I

1–11. The Last Days of Jesus on Earth. The "former treatise" is the Gospel according to Luke, which ends, as Acts begins, with the great missionary commission and the ascension of Jesus. The Gospel tells what Jesus did and what he taught. Acts narrates how the apostles and their successors carried out the Lord's last command. In Acts is found a more detailed account of the interval between the resurrection and the ascension. In Luke (see 24[36-53]) the impression is given that Jesus ascended almost immediately after his resurrection. Acts 1[3] explains that Jesus remained forty days with his disciples. The period between ascension and Pentecost was thus ten days.

These forty days were made radiant by many appearances of the risen Lord, effectually proving the reality of his resurrection. As in the Gospel, *the Kingdom* formed the topic of his teaching (v. 3., see art., *The Teaching of Jesus*, pp. 911–3).

The place of the appearances was in or near Jerusalem. Nowhere does Luke record appearances of Jesus away from the Holy City. The apostles must await promised spiritual preparation. This would happen in Jerusalem (v. 4). Then only could the program of the apostles' mission be carried out.

The *Ascension of Jesus* is described (vv. 6–11) in greater detail than in Lk. 24[50f]. Jesus talked of a new order to be brought in (vv. 6–8), while the disciples were looking for an old order to be restored. The new order cannot happen of itself. It must be brought about by men upon whom the Spirit of the Lord has come (v. 8). These men can then become *witnesses with authority* in the whole world.

The apostolic charge (v. 8) is perhaps the original form of the great commission, which appears in Mt. 28[19] Mk. 16[15] Lk. 24[47] and here. The substance is the same in all forms. In Acts this solemn charge to the apostles forms the theme of the book.

Jesus' last words (v. 8) were scarcely spoken when he disappeared from the apostles' view. The *mode of the ascension* of Jesus is not definitely described, for the obvious reason that the disciples themselves were under great emotional stress when they found that Jesus was no longer with them. The accounts of the event given the other disciples upon the return to Jerusalem would vary as greatly as do the narratives of the resurrection appearances in their surviving literary form. (See under Mt. 28, Lk. 24, Jn. 20–21.) In the tradition about the ascension as Luke received it, a cloud obscured the disciples' view of the departure of the Lord (v. 9), and as they instinctively looked into the sky for some token, they were reminded that such a course was vain.

The literary account of the ascension draws upon a large fund of current Jewish religious thought and imagery, to which is added an expression of the hope of Jesus' return, which was warmly cherished by the church of Luke's period (see pp. 846, 1366–7).

The ascension of Jesus marks a real turning point in the religious experience of the apostles. The last words of Jesus (v. 8) placed upon them a vast responsibility and opportunity. They sought more earnestly and directly the promised spiritual endowment. The ascension thus proved to be the logical and almost immediate preparation for the baptism of the Holy Ghost ten days later.

12–14. The Apostolic Prayer Circle. Until *the women* and *Jesus' brothers* are named (v. 14), the Eleven only are in the mind of the writer. These were living in an *upper chamber*, perhaps the "large upper room" of Lk. 22[12]. This may have been the house of Mary, mother of John Mark (Acts 12[12]). Hither the eleven returned from Olivet (v. 12) and with the other disciples (v. 14b) engaged continuously in prayer. The brothers of Jesus are mentioned by Luke in the Gospel, 8[19f.] (see Mt. 12[46f.] 13[55] 28[10] Mk. 3[31f.] 6[3].) In N.T. literature there is no fixed order in which the apostles are named. Cf. v. 13 with Mt. 10[2f.] Mk. 3[16-19] and Lk. 6[14-16]. Peter always heads the list. A conspicuous feature of the Jerusalem prayer circle is its *unanimity*. This oneness of spirit goes far in the explanation of the following events.

15–26. Matthias Takes the Place of Judas Iscariot. A larger group emerges in v. 15. Including the apostles, the women and the brothers of Jesus, there were six score. Peter as spokesman took counsel with this larger group, proposing that the apostolic circle, broken by the defection of Judas Iscariot, should be restored (vv. 15f.). Peter reviewed the treachery of Judas in guiding the foes of Jesus out to Gethsemane that fateful night, and quoted Scripture to justify filling his place (vv. 16–20). On the manner of Judas' death cf. Mt. 27[3-10], where he is said to have hanged himself. The successor of Judas was chosen from among eyewitnesses of Jesus' ministry. The Eleven appear to have made the nominations, and the election was by lot, which fell upon the second nominee. Greater weight is put upon the prayer (v. 24) than upon the lot. The passage is no proof-text to justify a lottery.

I. Chapters 2[1] to 8[3]: The Church in Jerusalem

CHAPTER II

1–4. The Apostles Filled With the Holy Spirit. Pentecost, an established Jewish festival (the Feast of Weeks, see art., *The Religion of Israel*, p. 167a), proved to be the time when Jesus' promise (1[4f.]) to the apostles was fulfilled. In the morning of this day (v. 15), the Twelve (1[15-26]) were gathered together, perhaps in the "upper room," when a rushing sound was heard and seeming *tongues of fire* were seen, distributed among them. These are the lesser points in the experience. The important and abiding experience is that described by the words (v. 4) *they were all filled with the Holy Spirit*. Even the final statement about the speaking with tongues, spectacular as this was, does not have, in the mind of the writer, the importance of the baptism of the Holy Spirit. The promise (1[5, 8]) specified the gift of the Spirit but mentioned no gift of tongues. Luke uses the expression "filled with the Holy Spirit" or its equivalent more than twenty-five times, while only twice, outside ch. 2, does he mention speaking with tongues.

The meaning of the phrase *filled with the Holy Spirit* should not be confused with the present-day doctrine of the Holy Spirit. The writer of Acts is not a theologian. In this book the phrase represents Luke's thought about the type of religious experience enjoyed by the men in the apostolic church. This experience (1) was based upon the certainty of the resurrection, (2) assumed the actual presence of Jesus with them in their daily life, (3) identified in some tangible way the achievements of the church with a practical inspiration, and (4) was validated by the presence of an enthusiasm and fervor that was not of earth. Even if the manner of expression changes from time to time, this apostolic experience must be affirmed of all genuine Christianity in all times. (See art., *N.T. and Christian Doctrine*, pp. 949–50.)

The book of Acts should be called the Holy Spirit book, for more than any other book of the N.T. it exalts and glorifies the Spirit. In the following pages of the book of Acts, the Holy Spirit is often imparted to others *through the apostles*. It seems likely that here only the Twelve were concerned in the gift of the Spirit and of tongues.

5–13. Effects Upon the People. The scene changed. The apostles left the seclusion of the house (v. 2), for the *rushing noise* and the speaking in tongues were heard by others. Many came together. Luke thinks of the permanent inhabitants of Jerusalem, who had come from widely distant parts of the Diaspora to end their days in Judæa. Others, visitors to the feast, may have been in the company. The fact that they heard intelligible speech in other languages than that of the Galilæans (v. 7f.) aroused their curiosity. Differing explanations were given. Some ascribed the phenomenon to strong drink; others were plainly impressed, but were without an explanation. It remained for Peter to give the true reason for the astonishing event.

14–36. Peter's Sermon. (1) *The charge of drunkenness refuted.* The charge that the men were intoxicated fitted none of the facts. But the Oriental must have some explanation of an observed phenomenon. Peter did not dwell on this, for it was plain that the day was too young for such a degree of intoxication. Then, the *hearing* of the various languages could not be explained by any state of the speaker (vv. 14f.). (2) *The real explanation.* Peter argued that in the events of the hour the beholders were witnessing a fulfillment of the prophecy spoken by Joel (2[28-32]) which he quoted with slight change (vv. 17–21). The word of the prophet, Peter urged, was not here fulfilled for the first time. For in Jesus of Nazareth they saw the divine inspiration, having witnessed his miracles (v. 22), and on this day they saw the descent of the Holy Spirit upon his disciples (vv. 16–21). (3) *The awful accusation.* To crucify the Messiah, whom David celebrated in well-known words (Psa. 16[8f.]), was a terrible deed! God rebuked this blasphemy by raising up again the slain Messiah, to whose resurrection this company of Spirit-filled men were witnessing (vv. 22–28). (4) *The Crucified indeed the Messiah.* Jesus was proved Messiah both by the prophecy of

David (Psa. 16[8f.]) as to his resurrection, and by the testimony of men who recognized Jesus risen from the dead. Not David, but the Christ, is now at the right hand of power (vv. 29–36). A reference to Psa. 16[8f.] will show that Peter took considerable liberty with the meaning of the original.

37–41. **Many Convinced and Converted.** The hearers appeared to be reasonable men. They were impressed by the manner of the speaker, supported by his fellow witnesses. Their conviction was so deep that it demanded immediate counsel from the speaker. *What shall we do?* met its answer, *Repent, be baptized and receive the Holy Spirit in yourselves* (v. 37f.). These hearers were Jewish men, as were the apostles. They were entitled to the fulfillment of God's promise. The conditions laid down by Peter seemed to be, first, repentance, then baptism; i.e., they must take the right attitude toward Jesus Messiah and they must identify themselves with his movement, called, even thus early, *the Way*. About three thousand joined the movement that day. This may be taken to be the actual beginning of the Christian Church. Yet many stages of development awaited the infant community now just in its swaddling clothes.

42–47. **Rise of the Community of Believers.** Into six verses Luke compresses his account of the community of those who followed Jesus Messiah. The apostles were authoritative teachers, this authority being evidenced by many miracles. Although those of *the Way* frequented the Temple, in groups (v. 46), they also met at home for their own love feasts. There developed a very close fraternity, which involved a community of goods (vv. 44f.). The important and abiding elements of the life of these early believers were the apostolic teaching, unity in fellowship, and the observance of the Eucharist and prayer (v. 42). As an expedient for the relief of their needy brethren, property owners among them in some cases voluntarily sold their possessions and distributed the proceeds to the suffering. The superlatives (*all things . . . to all*) of vv. 44f. are modified by later references to this community of goods (see under 4[32-37] 5[1f.]). On the whole this communism is to be thought of as an experiment which did not last many years, yet which produced many examples of unselfish devotion and sacrifice. Even the experience of Pentecost was not designed to enlighten the leaders of *the Way* as to every detail of their organized church life. It became necessary at times to adopt new measures as problems arose (see under 6[1]). In the sixth decade of the first century, when the Gentile churches were waxing mighty, the Jerusalem church was reduced to dire poverty and need. In this emergency their distant brethren ministered to the Jerusalem saints. But information about this missionary help, aside from the special contribution mentioned in 11[29f.], must be gleaned from the letters of Paul (see 1 Cor. 16[1] 2 Cor. 9[1f.] Rom. 15[25f.]).

CHAPTER III

Luke cites deeds of certain groups of apostles. He takes here Peter and John, the two names occurring together six times (3[1]–4[31]), while the name of Peter occurs separately three times.

1–10. **A Lame Man at the Temple Door.** The first circumstantial narrative of a miracle of healing in Acts (cf. 2[22, 43]) illustrates the power of *the name* of the risen Jesus in this Jewish Christian group. The formula, *In the name of Jesus Christ of Nazareth* (v. 6), like that on the lips of Paul (16[18]), occupies the point of emphasis in the story. Contemporary religious men, non-Christians, used names of demons and deities as formulæ of exorcism or as instruments with which to inflict harm (see 19[13f.]). Here it is not the mere pronouncing of the name of Jesus but the invocation of his presence and power that heals the lame man. In Oriental thought the name stood for the authority and for the personality itself of him who bore the name. The name indicated the character of the person, as in Mt. 1[21], where the name describes Jesus' character as Saviour. Supposedly, the early Christians inherited the common views as to the intrinsic power of a pronounced name, but assuredly they also believed that the personal ministry of Jesus effected their salvation, the cure of their ills, the exorcism of evil spirits and all other notable works.

The miracle of healing in this case (3[1-10]) is wrought rather through the power of the spoken name (v. 10) than through contact with Peter, who expressly repudiates the thought that he had exercised any power upon the man (v. 12), although popular thought upon the subject often identified healing with such contact (even with the shadow of a person of authority, with handkerchiefs from his person, or with the edge of his garment; see 19[12]).

The writer of Acts writes his narrative in such a way as to convince his reader that he himself had no doubt that the restoration of the cripple was genuine. The cure was attested by popular identification of the man (v. 9) and by the tacit admission of the Sanhedrin that the miracle was irrefutable (4[14]). Luke does not attempt to explain what really happened, for, like the people, he could but be filled with amazement at that which had happened (v. 10). (See under 9:32-43 for further discussion as to explanation of miracles.)

11–26. Peter's Appeal to the People. As the people ran toward the apostles, impressed with the cure of the lame man, Peter made an appeal to them, first of all to correct their conclusion that the source of power was in him or his fellow worker (v. 12). In brief, he told them that their God, through his Servant Jesus, was showing his power before their eyes (v. 16) in the cure of the lame man. Peter reminded his hearers of the tragic mistake in the all too recent past, when Jesus was *delivered up and denied* (v. 13) by his own people. This accusation is softened by the fact that only since the death of Jesus and his resurrection had his Messiahship become plainly evident. The O.T. prophecies (Isa. 42:1 52:13 53:11) showed that the fate of the Servant was to suffer (vv. 17, 18). Moses himself, so Peter argued, announced the human nature of Messiah, "a prophet like unto me" (Deut. 18:15), and urged that this prophet be heard (v. 22). All the prophets from Samuel on (v. 24) had something to say about Him who should come. With this strong support from the past, Peter made his plea to his Jewish brothers: Repent! Co-operate with this new movement! Then God will bless you, his people, and bring in a new day! (Vv. 19, 20, 25, 26.)

In this appeal Peter showed his deep interest in the religion of his fathers and at the same time revealed a new and deep insight into the real meaning of the history of his people. The prophecies no longer represented to him words alone. Those prophecies were alive in the life of the Son of God, whom indeed the heavens had received for a time (v. 21), yet who was actually in touch with men who believed in him (vv. 19, 26).

CHAPTER IV

1–4. Peter and John Arrested. The response of the people to Peter's words was quite different from the reaction of the ecclesiastical authorities, for (v. 4) the former seemed convinced, as on Pentecost day. So many came into the Christian community that the total number reached five thousand (v. 4). But the group of leaders (vv. 1f.) who arrested Peter and John (v. 3) were chiefly concerned at the teaching of the resurrection, and in particular the case of Jesus. The party known as Sadducees (see art., *Backgrounds*, pp. 840–1; cf. pp. 210–3) did not accept the traditional teaching of the Pharisees as to the resurrection (see 23:6-8). The reader cannot fail to commend the practical faith of the thousands who cast themselves upon Jesus in a sublime trust, thus receiving the pardon of their sins, in contrast with the purely academic and technical attitude of the Sanhedrin members.

5–12. Peter's Defense at the Hearing. The Jewish leaders arrested the apostles chiefly because of the teaching about the resurrection. At the hearing (vv. 5–7) the next day the question concerned their authority. In the language of the time *the name* stood for the essential personality of the one concerned. (See Gray, art., "Name," in Hastings' *Dictionary of the Bible*, vol. iii, p. 480.)

Peter's answer was singularly direct. It was no less than an inspired statement, for he was filled with the Holy Ghost as he spoke. As for the lame man, who was present (v. 10), health came to him *through the name*, i.e., through the personal power of Jesus. But the power of this name cannot be limited to the physical healing, for above all names that are invoked, the name of Jesus avails for salvation, said Peter (v. 12). The courage of the chief apostle in this presence is explained only through the meaning of Luke's phrase, *filled with the Holy Ghost.* (See under 2:1-4.) As Peter recalled the power of the name to save, he thought with shame of the cruel fate to which this same court sent Jesus. A bold figure conveyed his accusation, again directed at those in power. Jesus, the Cornerstone, was set aside by ignorant builders, but is now restored through an overruling power. Twice before (2:23 3:15) had this accusation been voiced, but here for the first time (v. 10) Peter had the ear of the judges themselves. This bold directness itself produced the dilemma in which these leaders in Israel presently found themselves.

13–22. The Dilemma of the Sanhedrin. The facts assembled at the hearing were hard to reconcile. Peter and John were bold, when it was dangerous for them to be bold; they were not educated men; they had been Jesus' disciples; the healed man stood there before them; the people and the court knew the cure was genuine; but the influence of the Sanhedrin itself was in danger if the movement went on. The question was, What is the best policy?

The course pursued had all the weakness of the court's own position. They forbade the two apostles to speak openly *in the name of Jesus.* The stubbornness of the facts proved even less than the determination of the two apostles. Their words to the court were scripturally sound: *A man must obey God first of all! We shall witness to those things which we know from experience.* This, in effect, is what they said—and what thousands have said since. The dilemma remained. The cured man was of the people, who sided with the apostles. With wordy but empty threats the court dismissed the case.

23–31. The Followers of Jesus Encouraged. While Peter and John were before the court the brotherhood engaged in earnest prayer. This Luke believes to be a source of empowerment (13^3 16^{25}). Their prayer reads like a hymn, or like one of the psalms. Psa. 2 is in part quoted and the opening sentence has a verse from Psa. 146. Appropriately these Jewish Christians clothed their religious thought and feeling in O.T. terms.

The term *Servant* as applied to Jesus (vv. 27, 30) is chosen from the so-called "servant-songs" of Isa. 42^{1-4} 49^{1-6} 50^{4-9} 52^{13}–53^{12} and suggests that very soon after the resurrection of Jesus these passages in Isaiah were given Messianic meaning by the Christians. The former translation, *holy child* (see mg.) obscures this fact. (See p. 664.)

The high points in this passage are: the great unanimity of the company, their sublime faith in prayer, their confidence in the triumph of the Kingdom, and their restraint in the face of this striking victory for their leaders and their cause. In those meetings of the primitive church the emotional values in experience were subordinated to the practical forwarding of the message. But the emotional experiences were to them real evidence of the presence of God.

Practical Working of the Community. This is described in 4^{32}–5^{11}. A paragraph following the story of Pentecost (2^{42-47}) gives a glimpse into the life of the followers of Jesus. Luke seldom offers any definite statement of the passing of time, but between 2^{47} and 5^{11} at least some weeks, if not months, must have passed. That Luke selects only incidents here and there is seen from the known fact that between the beginning of his book and ch. 12, the story of James' martyrdom, at least fourteen or fifteen years must have elapsed.

32–37. The Community Described. The group of believers early developed a social conscience. Poverty was to be banished through an equable distribution of goods. The right to private property was voluntarily given up (v. 32) and provision for the comfort of all was made through the sale of real estate (v. 34) and the dedication of the proceeds to the common weal. It does not appear that all submitted to the rule, for Peter implied in his remark to Ananias (5^4) that it was proper to offer a part of the price received from a sale *provided the brother stated that he was offering a part.* The example of Joseph (vv. 36f.) is a case where the disciple chose to offer the whole amount. In 12^{12} it appears that John Mark's mother still owned her house in Jerusalem. The writer considers this community of goods as a means to an end, not as a cardinal element in the growing Christian Church. The emphasis here (vv. 32–37) is upon the unanimity, the unselfishness, the brotherly love of its members, and upon the public ministry carried on (v. 33), marked as it was by power and grace. For *Joseph* (vv. 36, 37) see following paragraphs.

CHAPTER V

1–11. The True Disciple and the False. Jesus himself realized that the less worthy and the unworthy would come into the fellowship of his followers, and so taught (Mt. $13^{47f.}$ 18^{17}). So the event proved. Even if the common fund was administered for all, this was no guarantee against unfairness (see 6^1). If members did sell their houses and lands and contribute the proceeds, this could not exclude cases of hypocrisy. The examples cited (4^{36}–5^{11}) teach that, however much evil might arise within the church, the church would not tolerate it. The contrasting examples are those of Joseph Barnabas and of Ananias and his wife. The true disciple is described in two verses, while eleven are devoted to the hypocrisy of the false disciples.

The narrative of Joseph (Barnabas) implies that he voluntarily sold his field and as voluntarily brought all the proceeds to the common store. Others had done as much (v. 34b); in fact, it seems to have been the prevailing practice (*as many as were possessors . . . sold them*). Luke does not make invidious comparisons by devoting words of special praise to Joseph. He was a good man and he did a good deed with a good will.

More space is given to the cases of *Ananias and Sapphira* because of the sinister significance of the incident in those early days of the church. If Judaism prided itself upon its high moral teaching, Christianity set itself at once to the practice of high morality. The teaching of Jesus emphasized high ethical principles and the apostles took up the strain. The deed of Ananias and his wife was destructive. The brotherhood of this early community could not be spoiled from without, as the book of Acts shows. The life of the church was more seriously endangered by hypocrisy or treachery within. The story of Ananias and Sapphira leaves the distinct impression that in the early days of the church there prevailed a high ideal of honesty and unselfishness among the disciples. But the impression is further that of an excellent discipline, no small part of which was due to the spiritual insight of the apostles. As in the Ananias case, the apostles were quick and certain in their moral judgments. This led to a commendable respect for the leaders and to a heightened morale among the members of the community.

It is best to take this story of the deaths of Ananias and Sapphira as an account of a real happening in these early days. As in the case of other narratives touching the unusual, attempts have been made to explain its meaning as symbolical or at least as figurative. Some students, e.g., suggest that what *really* happened was that the guilty pair were solemnly excommunicated, and thereupon became "dead" to the church, and that this "death" was later taken by others in a literal sense. (See art., *N.T. Miracles*, p. 927b.) The deaths of the two persons concerned, however, are given as real deaths, sudden, awe-inspiring, and undesigned by the apostle, as far as the narrative shows. Peter does not prophesy the death of either person. The context (2^{43} 5^{13}) teaches that men both outside and within the church were impressed, even fearful, at the many signs of power and authority vested in the apostles. This may have been a superstitious fear, but such an emotion has always a powerful effect upon the body. In view of this element in Luke's narrative it may be supposed that at Peter's stern rebuke (vv. 3, 9) these dishonest persons became so overcome by their emotional reaction that they died forthwith. The story of Ananias and his wife can be understood as that of a "punitive miracle" only on the supposition that Peter intended their deaths. This cannot be shown from the text.

12–16. Acts of the Twelve. Beginning with 5^{12} and continuing to 6^{7} we find described the "Acts of the Twelve." The Twelve as a group were, of course, active from the first, but here Luke turns his attention to the remarkable effects that followed a certain part of their public ministry. Not only the case of Ananias and Sapphira but the many miracles that accompanied the work of the apostles created a certain attitude of fear on the part of those outside the community (v. 13), although this did not in any way hinder the growth of the church itself (v. 14). It appeared to outsiders that a supernatural power was present in this group, and superstitious fear kept them aloof. Several things contributed to this attitude. The unusual boldness of these unlearned men (4^{13}), their actual victory over the Sanhedrin ($4^{23f.}$), and the whole train of events since Pentecost, narrated only in part, had created a wholesome awe for the infant but mighty church.

While the author does not say that the shadow of Peter as it touched a sufferer had healing efficacy, he does say (v. 16) that the sufferers brought to the apostles *were healed every one.* This may be taken to include those of v. 15, who were brought into the street through which Peter might pass.

17–25. The Arrest and the Angel. At first the apostles attracted the attention of the high priest and Sadducees, i.e., only a part of the Sanhedrin (vv. 17–21a), but later (v. 21b) these called the entire council together to consider the matter. The resulting efforts of the Sanhedrin to silence the witnesses of Jesus appeared in the sequel to be as futile as before.

The naming of the Sadducees as the party of the high priest, and the mention of their "jealousy," introduce into the story the question of motive in the imprisonment of the apostles. As the narrative stands of the escape of the apostles at the hands of an angel, fact and explanation are mingled. The facts are the arrest of the apostles, their imprisonment, their escape during the night and their summons before the council. The explanation involves an angel (v. 19) who was the medium of a deliverance accomplished so skillfully that the prison was intact and the keepers unaware of the flight of the prisoners. The large number of prisoners involved made the unnoticed escape of the men inexplicable, except through angelic intervention. (See 12^{7-10} for a narrative with even greater detail of explanation.) It is fair to surmise that during the night the apostles themselves discovered a way out of the prison and that their interest in their message led both to the desire to escape and to enter the Temple as soon as it was open, disregarding their own safety. Since they had been imprisoned under Jewish authority and guard, no such severe penalty was meted out to the custodians as in the case of Peter's escape (12^{19}; see art., *N.T. Miracles*, p. 928b.) The apostles themselves had the assurance of a divine guidance in their actions ($5^{20, 29, 41}$) and the modern reader cannot do less than believe their confidence was based on experience.

26–40. The Apostles Again Warned and Beaten. The displeasure of the Sanhedrin was justified in their own eyes, for the apostles were disobeying the command they laid upon Peter and John (4^{18}) only shortly before. The total defense of the Twelve here was that they were obeying a higher authority than that of the Sanhedrin (v. 29). It appears from the narrative that in reality the charge of responsibility for the death of Jesus weighed most heavily upon the Israelite Solons, for Peter solemnly repeated his awful accusation before the council (vv. 30–32).

The stoning of the apostles might have resulted, as later in the case of Stephen, had it not been for the counsel of the wise Rabban Gamaliel. Although the more zealous members no doubt labeled him an obstructionist and too conservative, the whole council accepted his policy. Gamaliel argued that whether the work was really of God or not they should await developments. If, as they supposed, the movement was one of enthusiasm only, it would soon be deflated. If, on the other hand, God were really speaking to these men, as they affirmed, it was not the place of the Sanhedrin to oppose it. Thus Sadducees led the opposition to the Messiah group and a noted Pharisee advised moderation. Presumably, the stripes (v. 40) were given as a punishment for disobeying the previous order of the council.

41, 42. The Ministry of the Word. It does not appear that the Twelve were again prosecuted by the Sanhedrin. They were popular in Jerusalem. Witness the caution shown by the men who arrested them in the Temple (v. 26) and the fact that later, during the persecution that arose upon the stoning of Stephen, the apostles remained in Jerusalem, although many of the Christians were scattered (8^{1}). The apostles did not compromise in the slightest degree. They continued to declare publicly that Jesus was Messiah (v. 42), and in private meetings they taught over and over the things about Jesus and the things that Jesus taught. These men, so unaccountable on all conventional standards, felt the thrill of martyrdom at its best (v. 41), for nothing counted with them except the glory of the Name Jesus.

CHAPTER VI

1–7. A Problem and its Solution: the Seven. A single verse (v. 7) points out the rich results of the ministry of the apostles ($5^{41f.}$) in that the influence of the Word spread, and even *a great company of the priests were obedient to the faith.* In the meantime certain adjustments had to be made in organization. The church could not become fully adapted to its enlarged membership all at once. Some of the members were not natives of Palestine, although they were all orthodox Jews. There appeared so much discrimination between the natives and the non-natives that the Twelve made an appeal to the church upon the matter, as follows (vv. 2–4): "The ministry of the word is the most important aspect of the work of the church, but unselfishness and brotherly love must continue to rule in the community. Now, it would be absurd for us to forsake our faithful public ministry, but it is also absurd that such differences should continue to exist. So elect seven well-qualified men to superintend the distribution of food and to see that unfairness is kept down." The Seven probably ministered to Hellenists alone. The ceremony referred to in the words, *laid their hands upon them,* is to be understood as a formal inauguration into office. The Seven received the Spirit long before (vv. 3, 6). Chief among them was Stephen. Usually, a man who is both good enough and able enough to control such a matter as this distribution of the common store is able also to deal in larger matters. No wonder, then, that Stephen both did his assigned work well, and took opportunity to support the apostles in their public ministry.

Acts of Stephen. These are described in 6^{8}–8^{3}. He is nowhere numbered among the apostles, but he was one of the "witnesses" (the original meaning of the English word "martyr") *to* Jesus as the Christ, or Messiah. His was the power that is traceable to the gift of the Holy Spirit (v. 8), and the violence with which he was assailed is strong testimony to the inability of his opponents to answer his logic. Resort to physical force is usually an indication that moral and intellectual defense is weak. Stephen was, as his name indicates, one of the Jewish men from outside Palestine. Luke introduces his story at this point to prepare for the appearance of Paul, the greatest of the Hellenistic Jews, and to forecast the victory of the cross in the Dispersion.

8–10. Stephen and the Synagogues. Stephen proved to be a man larger than his set task. The apostles could not leave their ministry to serve tables, yet Stephen found some time for the larger ministry after his steward's work was done. There were many synagogues in Jerusalem. The members of these congregations often represented places far away. For many had moved to Jerusalem from other parts, but unlike the Judæan Jews, did not use the Hebrew Scriptures. Stephen and the other Hellenists worshiped, even prayed, it is likely, in Greek. There were probably two of these Greek-speaking congregations with which Stephen came into contact: the synagogue made up of Jews who were descended from men of the first century before Christ, who had been taken prisoners, carried to Rome and later freed, hence called *Libertines.* With these were associated people from Cyrene and from Alexandria. The second synagogue in question was made up of people from the country surrounding Ephesus, and from Cilicia, whose city, Tarsus, was the early home of Paul. It is entirely possible that Paul himself was an occasional opponent of Stephen. The miracles wrought by Stephen are barely mentioned by Luke, for they are not as important as the wisdom with which Stephen spoke and the evident power of the Holy Spirit (v. 10).

11–15. **Before the Sanhedrin.** Failing in their rebuttal of Stephen's arguments, the injured Hellenists tried to bring about the defeat of that hero through false dealing. They persuaded men to perjure themselves before the court (v. 11) to which they dragged Stephen on a charge of blasphemy and insurrection, much as their Judæan countrymen did with Jesus, not long before. The charge that Stephen had said that Jesus would destroy the Temple (*this holy place*), and alter the customs of the fathers, was a result of malicious misunderstanding. The charge presented, Stephen is asked to plead "guilty" or "not guilty," but instead of the simple answer, he defended his course in an elaborate address to the Sanhedrin (ch. 7).

CHAPTER VII

1–53. **Stephen's Defense and Counter-Charge.** This address, the longest speech in Acts, is the more difficult to understand because its method is so Oriental. Western minds do not follow lines at all like those along which Stephen's hearers and Luke's readers traveled. Briefly, Stephen recited the following facts, upon which he built his charge of guilt, addressed to the Sanhedrin directly but at the Jewish people indirectly: God called our father Abraham from the East, and he came at length into this land, but it was not yet his (vv. 2–5) except in promise. The possession of the land had to wait upon weary centuries before it could be fulfilled (vv. 6–19), for the people languished in Egypt until Moses arrived as deliverer (vv. 20–36) and led them out into the wilderness. The promise to Abraham was even then unfulfilled, and Moses foretold that another prophet like himself should come (v. 37) to make good the promise. So the congregation in the wilderness came into this land and Solomon built the Temple (vv. 38–47) although God himself does not dwell in a man-made house (v. 50).

At the climax of this résumé of Israel's temporal and religious history Stephen seemed entirely overcome by his feeling of shame for his people. How blind they had been! How meanly had they treated the great deliverer! How often in the past had their fathers persecuted prophets who tried to do them good! Most shameful of all, how wickedly had this generation betrayed a Saviour! Thus he cried out to them his agony, not so much in anger as in sorrow, but with pitiless, clear, incisive words: *The Righteous One you have now betrayed and murdered* (v. 52).

54–60. **Stephen the Martyr.** A surge of hate drove the council to an elemental outburst. Rules of order did not bind their action. One passion ruled—This fellow must die! Thus they wrote with their deed their involuntary approving comment upon his words. There and then the Sanhedrin killed another prophet. But Stephen was no longer of their courtroom; he was no longer of this earth; for even before the cruel stones fell upon his body the heavens were opened for him and he beheld the martyred Son of God. Yet in his heavenly vision he did not forget his fellow men, however deeply they sinned. They were still the people for whom that glorified Saviour died. His last words were a prayer, asking God not to lay this sin to their charge (vv. 57–60).

The hour of Stephen's death saw a new name entered on the roll of heroes of the cross. But the name was at first that of an enemy of the cross. Saul of Tarsus (8^{1}) stood by and approved the stoning of the first Christian martyr. (For the names *Saul* and *Paul* see under 13^{9}.)

CHAPTER VIII

1–4. **First Mention of Saul of Tarsus.** Up to this point Luke has set forth the progress of the Christian community in and about Jerusalem. With the appearance of Paul on the scene of Stephen's death and his entrance upon a career of bitter persecution of the disciples, the field of the witnessing to Jesus is widened, for the believers, scattered, proclaimed their message everywhere. The story of Saul is begun (8^{1-4}), but is interrupted for a time (8^{4}–9^{1}) to permit of a recital of the activities of Philip, one of the Seven.

II. Chapters 8^{4} to 16^{5}: The Church in Syria and in Asia Minor

4–25. **Philip in Samaria.** The first movement in the widening of the circle of Christian influence arose through the activities of three men, Philip, Paul, and Peter, only one of them from the circle of the Twelve, no one of them like any other. They had this in common—that circumstances compelled each to take a chief part in the expansion of the Messiah movement. There is little reason to think that the persecution (8^{3} 9^{1}) carried on by Saul was a widespread influence. It was centered at Jerusalem and those who went so far only as Samaria were out of its power. Even the Twelve remained safely at Jerusalem ($8^{1, 14, 25}$ 9^{27}).

Philip went to the capital city of Samaria, the O.T. *Samaria*, but since the days of Herod the Great called *Sebaste* (Greek for *Augusta*). More emphasis is laid upon the miracles of healing that attended his teaching than in the case of Stephen (6^{8-10}). This emphasis is called for in contrast to the *sorceries* of Simon the magician (vv. 9-11). This Simon became a convert to Christianity, for the statement *Simon also himself believed* (v. 13) can be understood only thus. But Simon did not easily acquire the Christian point of view. Vv. 14–24 contain a most instructive narrative of the way in which the new teaching was sometimes misunderstood. The apostles at Jerusalem sent Peter and John to Samaria to investigate the work done by Philip. Their approval of the mission was so hearty that on their way back to Jerusalem Peter and John preached to other Samaritan communities (v. 25).

This venture of Philip at Samaria is so instructive as to call for a statement of the following conclusions: *First*, the religious experience of these early disciples of Jesus had tempered their race prejudices. Luke has not introduced into his narrative a single note of surprise that Philip, a Jew, should thus fellowship with the people of Samaria. *Second*, the apostles at Jerusalem at this time had begun to act with authority (cf. 6^{2}) in all that pertained to the propagation of the message of Jesus. While Philip could baptize converts, none of the Samaritans received the Holy Spirit until the apostles prayed for them and laid their hands upon them. *Third*, the presence of the Holy Spirit in the community was evidenced in some very conspicuous way, for Simon, in his regenerate but uninformed state, was willing to invest in a power so evident to the beholder. *Fourth*, the mission of Philip, seconded by Peter and John, constitutes the first page in the annals of world-wide Christianity. *My witnesses . . . in all Judæa and Samaria* (1^{8}).

Few of the essential details concerning Samaritan Christianity are handed down by Luke. Another incident in the ministry of Philip turns attention toward the vicinity of Gaza.

26–40. Philip and the Ethiopian Eunuch. The men of the early church were sensitive to spiritual guidance, a facility which followed naturally from their effective spiritual preparation. *An angel of the Lord* directed Philip to take the road toward *Gaza*, an old Philistine city, southwest of Jerusalem. Philip was not divinely directed when he went to Samaria, as far as narrated, but in this instance his spiritual direction is explicit. The road concerned ran through uninhabited country (a lonely road, *desert*), where ordinarily few people would be encountered. The situation, then, was quite the opposite of that in Samaria. In other respects also this narrative is a counterpart to that of the Samaria mission. The subject of the story is evidently a proselyte, a man who lived far from Jerusalem, who came to the Holy City at stated times to worship. But he was not a fully instructed proselyte, although a student of the Greek Bible. From this translation Luke draws the Isaiah quotation, vv. 32f., which formed the text of Philip's discussion of the Christ. In the Samaria mission, the Holy Spirit came upon the converts after their conversion through the laying on of hands by the apostles. Here the eunuch is baptized, but nothing is said of the coming of the Holy Spirit upon him. The Samaritans would not come to the Temple to worship, but this man came from afar. The eunuch was really closer than the Samaritans to Judaism.

In terms of the charge of Jesus (1^{8}) the witness to the Messiah was now reaching the wider world. A part of southern Egypt was to hear the gospel as this eunuch returned. And tradition has it that the queen of Ethiopia (whose title, like that of Pharaoh or Cæsar, was *Candace*) was baptized by this converted eunuch. Philip preached Jesus to the man, *beginning from this scripture*, which was Isa. 53^{7} in the widely used Greek translation. A chief element of confidence in the new movement thus arose from the assurance that it was not a different religion from the old faith, in which they had been instructed, but that *the Way* led men to higher levels of religious experience than the prophets before Jesus had been able to point out.

One of the aims before the writer of Acts is to show that Christianity developed directly out of the religion of Moses and the prophets, and was in reality a higher and truer phase of that ancient religion.

CHAPTER IX

1–19. Saul's Conversion. The conversion of Saul of Tarsus from persecutor to missionary is so important to the author of Acts that he offers three separate accounts of it (cf. 22^{3-21} and 26^{2-23} with 9^{1-19}). As appears from Paul's own words, in Acts and in his letters (Rom. 7^{19-25} 8^{1-4} Gal. 1^{14} Acts $22^{3f.}$), he was a religious man of high ideals, and withal, a man of high moral purpose. His *conversion* was not so much a transformation from an evil life to a good life as it was a transformation from one type of goodness to another. As a lover of the Law he had high ideals which he could not attain. Other men would have been satisfied where he fretted. Paul's was an active, restless, achieving nature. (For the change of name from Saul to Paul, see 13⁹). No one can tell what definite influence Stephen's discussions had upon the conversion of Saul, but directly or indirectly Stephen must be held to some degree responsible for the persecutor's awakening. Saul was empowered by the Jerusalem authorities to extend the persecution of Christians to the Damascus synagogues (vv. 1f.) and was on his way to carry out the plan. This journey to Damascus was the occasion to which Paul often referred afterward as the revelation of Christ to him (see 1 Cor. 9^{1} 15^{8} Gal. $1^{15f.}$ and cf. Acts 22^{9-11} 26^{14-19}). The actual experience of Saul on the Damascus road can be described in present-day terms as follows: As a result of reflection upon his errand, together with the occurrence of some striking physical event, the thought of the traveler was focused upon the person whom these men of *the Way* worshiped. Whatever the particular combination of events was, the apostle always thought of them as divinely arranged. Saul became so awakened to the living presence of Jesus in the world and before himself that he objectified that person when his own accusing conscience smote him for persecuting the followers of Jesus. This event on the road was not the conversion in fact. As in most cases, a human guide was needed, and Ananias, the disciple in Damascus, was that man (vv. 10f.). The first phase of the epochal experience was highly emotional (awakening, conviction, remorse). The second phase (*three days*, v.9) involved reflection and prayer (v. 11). The last phase (vv. 17–19) brought instruction, encouragement, fellowship, and baptism. There can be no doubt that the gift of the Holy Spirit crowned this work of grace (v. 17).

The story of Saul's conversion explains in large measure why it was that a man not one of the original apostles should supersede all or any of the Twelve in importance to the Christian religion. Note the importance of the words addressed to Ananias (vv. 15f.): *He is a chosen vessel . . . to bear my name before the Gentiles.* The *things he must suffer* for the sake of Jesus' name are partly described in their fulfillment in Paul's own words in 2 Cor. 11^{23-33}, concluding with an experience which he had in that very city of Damascus. (See art., *Life and Work of Paul*, pp. 934–5.)

20–31. Paul the Persecuted. Paul first appeared in Acts as a persecutor of *the Way.* He may even have belonged to one of the synagogues with whose members Stephen dealt so successfully. Immediately after his conversion Paul was found in the ranks of the persecuted, first in Damascus (vv. 20–25), then in Jerusalem (vv. 26–29), and perhaps even in Cæsarea (v. 30).

Luke here offers a vivid picture of a man of the highest type of moral courage. A stubborn character could not have taken such a position before both friends and enemies. Saul was in danger of making enemies of his friends and creating suspicion in the minds of the disciples (cf. v. 21). The converted Saul actually repudiated his past, confessed publicly that he had been wrong, and set at work to retrieve his former misdeeds. In this, Saul of Tarsus sets an example for all Christians since his day. How well he supported by this act of courage his appeal to the Corinthians: *Come out . . . be separate . . . and I will receive you!* (2 Cor. $6^{17,18}$.) Whether Saul's stay at Damascus was long or short (*certain days*, v. 19, *many days*, v. 23), Luke gives the impression that Saul wasted no time in raising his voice to defend the teachings that he had branded before as heresy. His message centered in the Messiahship of Jesus, *that he is the Son of God* (v. 20). At first his Jewish hearers found themselves more confused and astounded than outraged. Paul's coming as persecutor had been heralded, but now he defended *the Way* (v. 21). His method of proof from the Scriptures could not easily be attacked. Some of the Jews were convinced. If all had been so convinced, vv. 23–25 could not have been written. The unconvinced ceased wondering at Paul and took action. What logic could not do force might accomplish. Paul's friends sensed the danger and aided him in a night escape through the wall of the city, since the gates were being watched (cf. 2 Cor. $11^{32f.}$).

The return of Paul to Jerusalem brought new experiences. The disciples had not heard of his remarkable conversion and feared his pretense as a trick (v. 26) until the good offices of *Barnabas* prevailed. Possibly Barnabas (v. 27) had been in Damascus and returned with Paul, thus being able to certify the events in Damascus. Both the church at Jerusalem and at Antioch valued the services of Barnabas highly, sending him on various missions that demanded tact and judgment ($11^{22,\ 30}$ 12^{25} 13^{2}), and he may have been sent to Damascus by the apostles at the time Saul set out upon his journey to that city. It is certain that the disciples in Damascus had timely information about him (v. 13). This was, at all events, the beginning of a comradeship between Paul and Barnabas that lasted until the affair of John Mark (15^{39}). The Christians of Jerusalem came to some understanding of the new preacher, but not so his former companions, the Hellenists. With these Paul now debated, trying to convince them that Jesus was Messiah, but history repeated itself and they proposed to do with him as Paul had willingly seen them do with Stephen. But the Jewish Christians aided Paul in an escape to Cæsarea, from which city he later returned to his home in Cilicia (v. 30).

The concluding note of this section (v. 31), referring to the peaceful outcome of the persecution that had its rise at Stephen's death, closes *for the present* Luke's account of Paul. He turns to Peter's activities, especially in forwarding the spread of Christianity out to the uttermost part of the earth (1^{8}). In v. 31 Luke mentions the church in Galilee, although he has not written a word as to its rise.

32–35. Peter at Lydda. Hitherto in Acts the apostles have been at Jerusalem. Here the fact emerges that Peter made journeys *throughout all parts*, no doubt to supervise the growing work, just as he and John went to Samaria to aid Philip (8^{14}). A brief account of his visit to Lydda illustrates one way in which Christianity was forwarded, namely, through a miraculous cure. There was a church at Lydda (v. 32), yet none of those saints had healed Æneas. Peter called upon him to arise, and *straightway he arose* (v. 34). Throughout the region the impression was so deep that *all . . . turned to the Lord.* The statement is probably rhetorical, since some, of course, would remain unconvinced. For in the story of Tabitha which follows (vv. 36–43) the statement occurs that as a result of her restoration to life *many believed on the Lord* (v. 42). If merely the performance of miracles were to convince men, surely the raising of a dead woman would be more convincing than the cure of a palsied man, even though he had been bedridden for eight years!

36–43. Peter at Joppa. While Peter was at Lydda, the church at Joppa, about three hours' journey away, met with a severe loss in the death of a useful member, Tabitha. Peter was called to Joppa and came promptly (vv. 36–39). Luke does not say whether Tabitha was young or old, married, single, or widowed, but her ministries had been deeply appreciated by the widows of the congregation and they were the chief mourners in the upper chamber (v. 39). Like Jesus, when he raised Jairus' daughter from the dead (Mk. 5^{39-43}), Peter dismissed the mourners and addressed the woman: *Tabitha, arise* (v. 41), and she sat up. In the Master's case, no prayer is mentioned (Mk. 5), but Peter prayed (v. 40) before he bade the dead woman arise, thereby showing his sense of dependence upon the Lord in this time of need. The similarity between "Tabitha, arise" and "Talitha, cumi" (Mk. 5^{41}), often commented upon, is but accidental. A favorite method of interpreting such narratives as that of the restoration of Tabitha is to assume that the subject of the miracle as narrated was only seemingly dead. So in the present case, the easiest answer to the question, Was Tabitha really dead? is that the overworked disciple had fallen into a state of coma, from which Peter's voice aroused her. This would be in reality to raise her from the dead, for if left in this state she would no doubt soon be dead in fact. If, however, the attitude of the writer of Acts be sought, it must be sought through an understanding of the narrative as it reads. The conviction of the writer is that Tabitha actually died, that the disciples believed that Peter could do something in the emergency, and that through his prayer and faith God himself brought life again to her body. In the study of all such narratives it is well to bear in mind that when the author is not an eyewitness he is *dependent upon others for their understanding of an event*, thus perhaps does not himself know all the facts in the case as it occurred. (See art., *N.T. Miracles*, p. 924a.)

CHAPTER X

1–48. Peter and Cornelius. Cæsarea was more than forty miles north of Joppa. The former was an important city, often mentioned in Acts (8^{40} 9^{30} $10^{1, 24}$ 11^{11} 12^{19} 18^{22} $21^{8, 16}$ $23^{23, 33}$ 25^{1}) as important to early Christian history. In Cæsarea were at least five "bands" or cohorts of soldiers, and Cornelius, the captain of one of these, became the first Gentile convert through the influence of Peter.

Cornelius was doubtless a Roman citizen but was deeply impressed with the Jewish religion. His whole "house," i.e., his family and slaves, were believers in the one true God, and no doubt took part in synagogue worship. It appears from the sequel that Cornelius had not become a proselyte in fact (11^{3}; cf. $10^{28, 45}$), hence was considered as a pagan outsider. Even the Christian apostles at Jerusalem were at first in doubt as to whether Peter should have even gone into the house of Cornelius.

The simultaneous visions of Peter and Cornelius were not mere coincidences in the thought of Luke. Each vision emphasized and clarified the other. With Peter, religious scruples, well entrenched in his Jewish consciousness, had to give way. The entire episode is exceedingly instructive to one who seeks light upon problems of *internationalism and inter-racial contacts* in the present time.

In these early days precedents were continually being established. Not only did a chief apostle hold fellowship with a Gentile, but he saw men outside the Jewish church receiving the Holy Spirit (see under 2^{1-4}). The reader wonders whether Peter had any difficulty with his conscience when he conceded that these Gentiles should be baptized. The event was epochal in the history of *the Way* for three reasons: (1) The Christian belief that salvation was for Jews alone were modified. Here a chief apostle abandoned the exclusive attitude of his orthodox brothers. (2) The ceremonial distinctions between foods was seen to have no decisive analogy in the realm of persons. This passage does not annul the Jewish food laws, but it does make the brotherhood of men in the gospel actual. (3) A decisive precedent was established for the extension of Christianity into the Roman Empire.

CHAPTER XI

1–18. Peter's Fellowship with Gentiles Explained at Jerusalem. The rumor that reached Jerusalem produced among the apostles an unfavorable attitude toward Peter. It is not said that he was summoned, but when Peter came to Jerusalem he was asked to explain his irregular behavior (vv. 1–3). Peter had taken with him to Jerusalem the six men from Joppa who witnessed the events at Cæsarea, and appealed to them during his testimony before the apostles (v. 12). Peter did not deny that he ate with Gentiles. He had lodged the messengers of Cornelius (10^{23}) and he had entered a Gentile house ($10^{24f.}$), which violated the rules governing an orthodox Jew's life. Rather than deny the facts, Peter frankly admitted them and cited a higher authority than custom to justify him (v. 17).

In the interview, the apostles took no exception to evangelizing Gentiles; they raised no question as to the baptism of Cornelius; thus it is not fair to define the issue merely as a race question. If Cornelius had been a circumcised proselyte, and if all the scruples of the Jewish religious man had been observed, the occurrence might have attracted no attention. The issue was one of *religious particularism,* narrow to an outsider but protective to the insider. From the story of Peter's defense of his course with Cornelius the modern reader learns how reluctant the first Christians were to understand that the religion of Jesus was like new wine which could not be contained within the old wine skins.

Peter told his story in full and Luke repeats it quite at length (vv. 5–15) in much the same words as are found in 10^{9-32}. He omits the detail of lodging the messengers (10^{23}) but states explicitly that he *entered into the man's house* (v. 12). His appeal to the fact that the Holy Spirit fell upon the Gentile company was too powerful to refute. The apostles may not have been convinced, but they could not object. Not even the Sanhedrin wished to come into opposition with God (5^{39}). So the apostles here (v. 18) held their peace and confessed: *Then to the Gentiles also hath God granted repentance unto life.*

19–21. Gentiles Converted at Antioch. When Stephen was stoned and Saul began to persecute those of *the Way* (8^{1-3}), many followers of Jesus, like Philip, escaped to other parts. These fugitives kept on declaring in the synagogues their faith in Jesus Messiah (v. 19b) and carried their mission efforts beyond Samaria to the coast (Phœnicia) and to one island at least (Cyprus). They were heard of as far north as Antioch in Syria.

Whether all these missionaries were Hellenistic Jews or not cannot be known. Certain Hellenists (of Cyprus and Cyrene) were the first to vary from the practice of preaching to Jews only (v. 20b) when they came to Antioch. (On the church at Antioch see under 13^{1}.) The instant success of this movement was marked by large accessions of Gentiles to the church. The context implies that these converts were received into fellowship with Jewish Christians without submitting to the rite of circumcision. This fact definitely raised the Gentile question on a much larger scale than in the case of the individual Cornelius.

22–26. Barnabas and Saul at Antioch. In Jerusalem, up to this time, the admission of uncircumcised Gentiles into the church was regarded as irregular and, in fact, an impossible proceeding. The case of Cornelius and those with him was the only Gentile conversion on record, if it be admitted that his conversion occurred before the Antioch movement began. Hence when the saints at Jerusalem heard that large numbers of Gentiles were being received (v. 21) they sent a trusted man to inspect the work and report (v. 22).

Barnabas was chosen because of his long connection with the church ($4^{36f.}$) and perhaps because he was a native of Cyprus, who would have influence with the Jews of the Diaspora (see pp. 847–9). He had done well on other such missions. (See note under 9^{27}.) Luke speaks high words of praise for him, and briefly but positively hints in this section that this was by no means the least of his successes. Barnabas, convinced that the work was of the Lord, went to Tarsus and invited Saul to help him, and together they worked for a year in Antioch, building up that church remarkably. The name *Christians,* used to designate Jesus' disciples, probably originated outside the church, and its use may at first have been ironical.

Nothing is said of the report given by Barnabas to the Jerusalem church, but it must have been favorable. That it was not approved by all the Jewish Christians appears from succeeding events (15[1f.]), but it is most likely that the apostles accepted the Antioch movement as inevitable and right. (See notes on the conference at Jerusalem, ch. 15.)

27–30. Generosity of Antioch toward the Jerusalem Church. The words *in these days* (v. 27) mean that the visit of Agabus took place about the time of the revival of vv. 21–26. Agabus represented a group of men in the early church called *prophets*, often associated with apostles and teachers. The prophet was possessed of such gifts of the Spirit that he could interpret the Lord's will to others. Agabus was a well-known prophet of the time and appears again in 21[10]. His prophecy of an impending famine was fulfilled at least in part, although no famine that affected all the inhabited world in those times has left any trace in history. The Antioch saints recalled this prophecy of Agabus when the shortage of food came in Judæa (between 40 and 50 A.D.) and dispatched Barnabas and Saul with their offering. The contribution would be in the form of food rather than of money (v. 30).

CHAPTER XII

The Church and Herod. In Herod, the church met a new kind of opposition—the opposition of the purely political authority. The purpose of ch. 12 is to show how triumphantly *the Way* continued as a live movement in spite of difficulties, opposition, persecution, and even the death of some of its leaders. The Sanhedrin had tried repeatedly to stop the teaching of the Cross; the special groups within the Sanhedrin did their best to hinder the disciples; inner dissension scarcely showed its head before it was checked (5[1f.] 6[1f.]); at last Herod took a hand, with what fatal results to himself!

1–6. James Killed and Peter Imprisoned. Herod Agrippa I ruled over all Palestine from 41–44 A.D. The death of James took place near the end of Herod's reign. Compared with the detail found in Stephen's story, this account is brief. The chief interest of the writer lay in what pertained to the spread of the gospel into the Gentile world. Stephen had an important influence upon this movement. Peter, also, whose story here is recounted, had weight in the program of world-Christianity. As in the case of Jesus (Mk. 14[2]), it was felt to be inadvisable to execute Peter during the feast (vv. 3–6). But Herod took unusual precautions with his prisoner. Sixteen men were assigned, four for each watch of the night; two soldiers were in the cell with Peter constantly, the other two posted outside. To make assurance doubly sure, Peter was chained to his two cell-companions. In the meantime the entire Christian group of Jerusalem had assembled in a service of prayer for Peter. It is hardly probable that the church expected his release (v. 15), since James had paid with his life for his faith.

7–10. Peter Delivered from the Prison. An *angel of the Lord* is often mentioned in Acts (5[19] 8[26] 12[23] 27[23]) to express the Christian belief in God's active interest in his own.

The narrative of the escape of Peter from prison is an excellent example of the way in which literary accounts of unusual events use a large number of details to hold the interest of the reader and to intensify the supernatural element believed to reside in the occurrence. As the church had developed the narrative, Peter was sleeping soundly in his perilous situation. When summoned, he did not need to hurry. He could dress for the street. The chains falling off of themselves and the gate opening automatically are similarly impressive details. In an instance such as this, the actual facts do not lie on the surface of the narrative. But the narrative expresses the implicit faith of the church in Providence and in the power of God exercised in the interest of the growing community of believers. Through this miracle narrative one gets a glimpse of the strenuous prayer life of the early Christians (v. 5), of the tenacity with which the members of the church clung together in emergencies (v. 12), of the caution with which the disciples surrounded themselves when meeting (vv. 13–16), and, in general, of the developing consciousness of the Christian Church. An event to which others may have given a "natural" cause was properly regarded as "supernatural" by the intense religious consciousness of the church. (See art., *N.T. Miracles*, p. 928a.)

11–19. Peter at the Home of John Mark. While Peter was in prison the church was praying. Peter instinctively turned in the direction of this meeting-place, evidently a house of considerable size, accommodating a goodly number, fitted with an outer gate, where a maid, Rhoda, was stationed. The fact that Rhoda recognized the voice of Peter suggests that she was a disciple.

Jewish belief in a guardian angel attendant upon each person led the company to suppose that the maid saw only Peter's angelic shadow. But the loud and continuous knocking soon admitted the flesh-and-blood apostle. Peter stayed just long enough to tell his story, then went away, to what city or town is not known. Peter's message to James, the brother of Jesus (v. 17b; cf. 1[14]), implies the latter's leadership in the church. Later (15[13] 21[18]) James is found to be actually the head of the Jerusalem church. It is unpleasant to read that four soldiers paid with their lives for the disappearance of Peter (vv. 18f.), a penalty demanded by Roman discipline.

20–23. The End of Herod. Herod spent only the feast time at Jerusalem. His home was at Cæsarea. An event that occurred some time after his return from Jerusalem was closely connected with Herod's death, brought about, as the church believed, through a stroke divinely inflicted (v. 23), when he accepted the worshipful but hypocritical plaudits of the people. Herod had persecuted the Christians because he found that this gave him popular favor (v. 3). The author of Acts uses this event as a commentary upon the power of the church to resist its persecutors.

24. Continued Success of the Gospel. Luke frequently closes a section of his narrative with a brief paragraph as to the *state of the church* (2[42] 4[32-35] 6[7] 9[31] 16[5] and other similar places). Here the single statement is made that the church, persecuted by Herod, bereft of one of its apostles, still increased in power and numbers.

25. See under 13[1].

CHAPTER XIII

1. Leaders in Antioch. (See also 12[25]). The acts of Barnabas and Paul form the theme of 12[25]–15[39]. The story of the so-called first missionary journey of Paul, which begins with 13[4], is prefaced with a summary account of the *spiritual leadership at Antioch.* Among its members were *prophets* and *teachers*, but no apostles. The latter were, until the appearance of James as leader in Jerusalem, at the head of the mother church. The Twelve did not seem to impress Luke with their powers of leadership, for his account of the development of the Gentile church traces all the initiative and power of the movement to Antioch rather than to Jerusalem. Hence the importance of this list of names. Five men are mentioned, three of whom are unknown, apart from their mention here. Luke's omission of their stories does not show that they were inactive; e.g., no details of the tour of Barnabas with Mark in Cyprus (15[39]) have been handed down, notwithstanding its general importance. So, in the case of each of these three, Symeon, Lucius, and Manaen, heroic stories might probably have been told. Their exploits are omitted because at this particular time the divine choice fell upon Barnabas and Saul. Luke's story is of these two. The omission, however, is not without its own significance. These three men are types of that vast host of "unsung heroes of the Cross" upon whom, from that day to this, the spread of the gospel has so largely depended.

The church at Antioch in Syria may have been nearly as old as that in Jerusalem, but it was totally different in its type of Christianity and in world-outlook. Acts teaches that the Antioch church was the instrument used by the Lord in making Christianity a world religion. The men of the church at Antioch were less hampered by Jewish narrowness, partaking, as they did, of that liberality that characterized the Jews of the Dispersion. This church became the center of "foreign missions," as their movement would be called to-day. Yet it is instructive to note that the people of Antioch made no invidious distinction between work abroad and work at home. The Holy Spirit sponsored both (vv. 2, 4). The spirit of the Antioch church was liberal in every good sense of the word (11[27f.]). It showed throughout a fraternal attitude toward Jerusalem and other churches (15[2]), and readily received the brethren sent to Antioch for special work (11[22f.] 15[30-35]). In those days there was place for both the conservative and the liberal type of churches, and the modern reader learns through Acts that co-operation between the two types rather than selfish competition builds the Kingdom upon earth.

2, 3. The Call of Barnabas and Paul. In a few words these verses report a most important and decisive Christian meeting. The saints at Antioch devoted themselves to a prayerful inquiry as to whom the Lord would select to carry the gospel of Jesus abroad. A deep solemnity pervaded all. Fasting, prayer, laying on of hands, and all the religious devotion bound up in the phrase *ministered to the Lord* (v. 2), formed their religious exercises. In some unmistakable way, the choice fell on Barnabas and Saul, in that order. The principle followed here is one which the church can never afford to neglect, namely, that those who are set apart to lead its work shall have the manifest approval of the Spirit of God.

4–12. The Mission to Cyprus. The guidance of the Lord is emphasized in the phrase *sent forth by the Holy Ghost* (v. 4; cf. v. 2). Seleucia was the seaport of Antioch in Syria. Cyprus is an island of the Mediterranean, whose eastern end lies about sixty miles from the Syrian coast and whose northern shore is some forty-six miles south of Cilicia. The island at that time had a large Jewish population and a number of synagogues. Salamis (v. 5) was a city near the eastern end of the island, while Paphos (properly New Paphos) was about one hundred miles west of Salamis. The journey *through the whole island* (v. 6) surely involved much missionary effort in the synagogues on the way.

At Paphos the proconsul, Sergius Paulus, became a convert to Christianity (v. 12) not only through the victory of Paul over the magian, Bar-Jesus, but through the real worth of Paul's message. For Sergius Paulus was an intelligent man (vv. 7, 12), looking with open mind for new truth. His invitation to Barnabas and Paul to discuss their message with him led Bar-Jesus to antagonize the missionaries (v. 8). The English word *sorcerer* means to the present-day reader something other than the word "magian" (cf. Mt. 2[1], "magi," plural). The parenthesis in the text (v. 8) indicates that sorcerer or magian (see mg.) is the translation of Elymas, not that Elymas is the equivalent of Bar-Jesus (v. 6). Thus the proper name of the man was Bar-Jesus, while he claimed *magus*, or was given that name, as his title. The story of Bar-Jesus the magian is to be accepted at its face value, not as a figurative representation of Judaism as persecutor of Christianity, nor, again, as a picture of the apostle himself, "blinded" before his conversion. The narrative presents an excellent example of the *punitive miracle* (cf. 12[23] and the expectation implied in 28[4]). The theory underlying this form of miracle was that through his representatives on earth God visited punishment upon men, usually for evils done, but sometimes with a view to their repentance (as in 9[8f.]). The punitive miracle is not to be confused with such events as the visitation of dumbness upon Zacharias (Lk. 1[20]). In the case of Bar-Jesus the blindness was temporary (v. 11). During the period of darkness the magian might see the true light. The use of the narrative here is to show what salutary effect the incident had upon Sergius Paulus (v. 12). (See art., *N.T. Miracles*, p. 927a.)

This point in the story of Paul is selected by Luke as a fitting opportunity to explain the double name of his hero. He offers the explanatory note (v. 9) that *Saul is also Paul*, i.e., both names are truly his. Nothing in the text indicates that at this time Saul assumed the name of Paul, much less that he took the name of his distinguished convert, Sergius Paulus. As a Roman citizen and free-born (22[28]) Paul bore not only one Latin name but three. (See Ramsay, *Cities of St. Paul*, pp. 208–214; and Deissmann, *St. Paul*, first edit., p. 93.) Roman law or procedure would require Paul to use his Roman name, although usually his associates knew him by his Aramaic name, Saul.

13. Paul, Barnabas and Mark. The events in Paphos proved so significant for Paul that Luke from this point on prefers the order, *Paul and Barnabas.* A transition phrase is *Paul and his company* in v. 13. The name Barnabas is placed first in 14[12] 15[12, 25].

From Paphos to Perga of Pamphylia meant a sea voyage of about one hundred and seventy-five miles, in a direction a little west of north. John Mark left the party here (v. 13b) for reasons which are subject only to conjecture. 15[38] offers to some a ground for the opinion that Mark showed cowardice, but this seems a harsh verdict upon slender evidence. Perhaps Mark had undertaken the journey with a definite understanding that Cyprus only was to be visited. The estrangement between Paul and Mark was not permanent (2 Tim. 4[11]). It is not certain that no work was done in Perga. Luke's interest or his lack of information leads him directly to Pisidian Antioch, where occurred the first conspicuous instance of direct appeal to Gentiles (13[46b]).

14, 15. In the Synagogue at Antioch. It was the custom of Paul to address his fellow countrymen first whenever he entered a city. "To the Jew first" was with him a principle, but experience added to that "and also to the Greek" (Rom. 1[16]). No doubt Paul entered heartily into the synagogue service. After the Scripture reading, the rulers of the synagogue invited the visitors to address the people if they would. Paul took up the word. The only synagogue address of Paul reported in Acts follows.

16–41. Paul's Address to the Jews of Antioch. The first part of the address is somewhat similar to the speeches of Peter (2[14-40]) and Stephen (7[2-53]) in that the speaker calls to mind how God chose Israel and cared for them throughout the national troubles, down to the time of David (vv. 17–22). The introduction of Peter's Pentecost sermon appropriately quoted the prophecy of Joel about the outpouring of the Spirit (2[17-21] Joel 2[28f.]), but then Peter came to "the patriarch David" (2[29f.]), whose words forecast the coming of Messiah. Stephen began with Abraham (7[2f.]), and after showing that Moses foresaw a greater prophet than himself (7[37]) came down to the time of David and Solomon in his survey of Messianic prophecy (7[45-47]). Peter at Pentecost emphasized the "resurrection of Christ" (2[31]) in Davidic terms; Stephen, in his last words, accused his hearers of being the betrayers and murderers of the Righteous One (7[52]), whose coming all the prophets foretold; Paul, in the Antioch synagogue, reminded his hearers of the goodness of God in saving Israel from Egypt and in giving them the land of Canaan, then in leading them through the time of the judges to Saul the king and on to David, of whose seed God, in his goodness, *brought unto Israel a Saviour, Jesus* (vv. 16–23).

Like his predecessors in Acts, Paul preached Jesus from the text of the old Scriptures. The Jewish training of the apostle taught him to show that he preached a religion in no way alien to the religion of the fathers. In the course of time, he assured them, the old promises had been fulfilled and it was the duty of the Jewish man who prayed for the coming of Messiah to recognize that Messiah had come and his prayers were answered (v. 33). The Messiah was Jesus, raised from the dead (vv. 34–37). The coming of Messiah meant something to the old religion in that a personal redemption supplanted the function of the law. Heretofore justification had been sought through the law (v. 39), but now *through this man is proclaimed remission of sins* (v. 38).

Paul closed his sermon with a warning from the Scriptures. His hearers should not be like the despisers described by Habakkuk (Hab. 1^{5}) who shut their eyes to the work of the Lord in their midst (vv. 40f.).

42, 43. Antioch Impressed. The effect of this address was uniformly favorable. All wished to hear Paul speak the next Sabbath (v. 42). On the day of Pentecost the words of Peter produced a sincere conviction in the minds of the hearers ($2^{37f.}$), for the movement was then just launched. When Stephen spoke before the Sanhedrin his words precipitated his own death, but lodged unerringly in certain minds and later bore fruit. Here in Antioch, remote from the scenes of Jesus' death, Paul brought real news as well as good news to the Jewish people. It took a little time for persecution to start, following private discussion of the address in the synagogue. Barnabas was not the chief speaker, but both he and Paul spoke at length and more informally to the interested Jews and proselytes, urging them *to continue in the grace of God*, i.e., in the spirit of the foregoing, to seek the favor of God by falling in with his ways and by accepting Jesus as Messiah and Redeemer (v. 43).

44–52. The Mission Opposed by the Orthodox Jews. A different synagogue service was held in Antioch on the second Sabbath after the arrival of Paul and Barnabas. No report of an address is given, and it is doubtful if either missionary was offered a chance to expound the Scriptures.

The element of novelty brought an unusual number to the synagogue service (v. 44) while the augmented congregation provoked the regular leaders to jealousy. These leaders have something to be said for them, in that they were responsible for decorum and for sound teaching. They lacked the background which a knowledge of the Christian movement could give them. On the other hand, they cannot be justified in the method which they used to muzzle the two apostles. The phraseology implies a disorderly scene in the synagogue. Private discussion had brought out the unconventional elements in the teaching of these two men. In that the rulers of the synagogue *contradicted the things which were spoken by Paul* (v. 45) their statements were rightly called *blasphemy* by Luke, for they would thus deny the Messiahship and the resurrection of Jesus.

The two apostles felt some strict necessity upon them compelling them to offer their gospel first of all to Jews (v. 46). However, they felt released from that necessity after the Jewish people in Antioch had rejected them. They were free to preach directly to heathen men. This situation prevailed, of course, for the people in Antioch alone. In each place yet to be visited, the Jews must have first chance (see 14^{1} 16^{13} $17^{1-3,\ 10}$ 18^{4} 28^{17-28}). Paul supported his decision to turn to the Gentiles by a quotation from Isaiah, in which Messiah was addressed as *a light of the Gentiles . . . unto the uttermost part of the earth* (v. 47; cf. Isa. 49^{6}). Throughout the Acts the Christian preachers based their message soundly upon the words of Scripture, mostly upon the prophets. The response of the Gentile population was spontaneous (vv. 48–50), and the Church in Antioch very probably consisted chiefly of other than synagogue members. The *disciples* who were *filled with joy and with the Holy Ghost* (v. 52) were the residents of Antioch and vicinity (v. 49) who responded to the preaching of Paul and Barnabas.

A genuine element of the Jewish theology of these early missionaries appears in the phrase *as many as were ordained to eternal life* (v. 48), the writer having, perhaps, in mind the idea of a book of life, in which even names of Gentiles might be recorded. (See Fairweather, art., "Development of Doctrine," in Hastings' *Dictionary of the Bible*, vol. v., p. 293.) The fact of foreordination is assumed frequently in the N.T. (Rom. $8^{28f.}$ Eph. $1^{4f.,\ 11}$ 1 Pet. $1^{1f.}$). Several weeks of activity are represented in the statement that *the region* was evangelized (v. 49), yet all this time opposition was increasing toward the apostles' work. In this opposition even prominent women (v. 50) appeared in connection with the city authorities. These women were probably proselytes, whose social position gave them influence.

Luke does not specify the accusation against the apostles. Some form of political charge is probable. Whether formally tried or not, the two apostles found themselves compelled to leave Antioch and seek still other Gentile territory. In characteristic Jewish fashion Paul and Barnabas shook off even the dust of Antioch from their feet (Luke 9[5]), a witness against their adversaries, not against the disciples (v. 52), whom they left in full enjoyment of their Christian experience.

CHAPTER XIV

1–4. Iconium. (See also 13[51, 52].) The power of the apostles' preaching is witnessed in Iconium, as in many other places, by the large number of converts won within a short space of time (v. 1). Iconium was a city of importance about eighty or ninety miles southeast of Antioch. The synagogue was the first mission field and results similar to those in Antioch followed (v. 2). The opposition did not grow to decisive proportions for some time (v. 3), and in this interval a good work was accomplished. In Iconium the authorities did not play a prominent part in the expulsion of the apostles. Mob violence was threatened, apparently under the strong influence of the Jews, for the mob proposed to stone them.

5–21a. Lystra and Derbe. The work at Lystra began with a miracle, not with a synagogue service (v. 8; cf. 13[5, 14]). A cripple sat in some open public place, perhaps at the city gate (v. 13), or in a market-place, where the unfortunate begged for a living. No plea was made by the lame man, except the signs of wistful faith (v. 9), which Paul perceived. Most miracles of healing in the N.T. have as their condition faith on the part of the subject. (See art., *N.T. Miracles*, p. 925.) The population of Lystra were polytheists, following the gods of the Roman pantheon (vv. 11–13), hence it was obvious to them that some of their deities were appearing in human form. Paul, because he made the address (vv. 9, 12), was believed to be Hermes, the messenger and herald of the gods. The view that Paul's personal appearance was unattractive at that time cannot be supported by this incident, but is, rather, discredited, for Hermes (Mercury) was represented as of fine face and figure, e.g., the Hermes of Praxiteles (but cf. 2 Cor. 10[10]). Barnabas was doubtless older than Paul, perhaps appeared to be a leader, hence was designated Jupiter (Zeus). Yet no certainty as to the personal appearance of the apostles can be based upon a hasty (and erroneous) guess made by the Lystrans.

The Christian work done in Lystra, as far as reported (vv. 5–18), was slight enough. No conversions are indicated, but the mention of *the disciples* in v. 20 argues that Luke passed over the details of the evangelization of Lystra in the interest of his detailed story of the miracle wrought upon the lame man. On Paul's second visit to Lystra he found Timothy among the disciples of that city (16[1]), and there is reason to suppose that before the Jews of v. 19 came to interrupt the work Paul and Barnabas had built up a Christian community in Lystra. That this is not mere surmise is witnessed by vv. 21b, 22, where we read that the presence of *disciples* in Lystra, Iconium, and Antioch demanded the hazardous return over the route by which the apostles had come to Derbe.

The *Jews* who came *from Antioch and Iconium* were orthodox members of the synagogues in those places, and were among the opponents of Paul and Barnabas when they began their preaching among them (13[45] 14[5]). At Lystra, as at Iconium, these antagonists sought to stone the two missionaries, and here at Lystra succeeded in stoning Paul (v. 19). It is not known how Barnabas escaped. After his well-nigh miraculous return to life, Paul, with Barnabas, left for Derbe the next day. At least that interval was necessary for recuperation after the terrible ordeal of stoning (v. 20b). The work at Derbe was successful. Luke relates no miracles, describes no synagogue service, and gives no names of converts. Paul and Barnabas spent enough time there to make *many disciples* (v. 21). This general statement of success implies that Luke's sources offered no extended account of this part of the mission.

21b–24. The New Churches Revisited. Nothing speaks more eloquently for the character of these preachers of the cross than the accomplished plan to return from Derbe through Lystra and Iconium to Pisidian Antioch, in the face of acute danger to themselves. Their work had been too abruptly broken off, and if left to themselves the converts would be apt to fall away under stress of persecution. An important contribution to church history is found in the statement that *elders* were *appointed in every church* (v. 23). Paul himself does not use the term "elders" in his letters. Instead, he speaks of "them that are over you in the Lord" (1 Thess. 5[12]), "apostles, . . . prophets, . . . teachers" (1 Cor. 12[28]), "bishops and deacons" (Phil. 1[1]). The elders would be men chosen because of maturity, judgment, and Christian experience, to act as a sort of official board. In the absence of trustworthy information about the office it may be supposed that the term represents no standardized church official. We certainly ought not to read back into the names "deacons," "elders," and "bishops," the meaning they came to have in later ecclesiastical developments. (See discussion of this question in intro. to 1 and 2 Timothy, pp. 1277–8.) The substance of the apostles' message on this organizing tour was heroic (v. 22), for the disciples faced suffering as the price of loyalty to the kingdom of God. The N.T. witnesses throughout to this theme as a dominant note in early Christian preaching (Mt. 10[17-22, 34-39] Mk. 13[9-13] Heb. 10[32-36] Rev. 6–9). The *we* of v. 22 is not analogous to the pronoun in the so-called *we-sections.* (See under 16[10f.] 20[5f.] 21[1f.] 27[1f.]). The clause (v. 22b) represents a bit of vivid indirect discourse, and the *we* includes the apostles in all the hazards of *the Way.*

25–28. Gentile Mission Justified at Antioch in Syria. The journey of Paul and Barnabas through Cyprus and Asia Minor was an experiment which was the fruit of the spiritual impulse that seized the church at Antioch (13[2f.]) after many Gentiles had become members of that church. The Antioch church was therefore eagerly awaiting the report of the apostles. V. 24 adds some unnamed churches to the list of those established by Paul and Barnabas on this journey, for the expression *passed through* (v. 24a), so frequently used in Acts (8[40] 11[19] 13[6, 14] 16[6] 19[1]), connotes rather extensive missionary activity.

Attalia (v. 25), about twelve miles southwest of Perga, was a new point in the itinerary of the apostles. On arriving from Cyprus (13[13]) Paul's party had come directly to Perga, which was six or seven miles from the sea. On the return journey Attalia offered better possibility of transportation. The voyage back to Antioch in Syria did not include Cyprus.

The arrival of the party at Antioch occasioned a special assembly, at which meeting the report of the missionaries was given in full (v. 27). The *door of faith unto the Gentiles* which God had opened means that Gentiles were now to be admitted to the fellowship of the church without submitting to Jewish rites and without entering the Jewish church. This was one point in question when the tour was undertaken, and it became a policy in which all the Christian Church did not at once concur. To the church at Antioch the report of Paul and Barnabas offered proof that God himself approved the policy.

CHAPTER XV

1, 2. Circumcision of Gentile Converts Demanded by Some. A bitter and lengthy controversy is here summarized in two sentences. As a whole, the church at Jerusalem had from the first adhered closely to all Jewish services and beliefs, *adding to their Jewish faith their new faith in Jesus as Messiah.* From their point of view, the new departure of the church at Antioch was irregular, so with the best of motives some of the Jewish Christians from Judæa went to Antioch to correct the supposed error by urging that unless Gentile converts were circumcised they could not be saved. The resulting difference of opinion formed a real danger to the new Messiah movement (v. 2a) which could be warded off only through an understanding between the conservatives and the forward-looking parties. A conference on the question was therefore proposed.

3–12. The Question Taken to Jerusalem. At least two sessions are described, the first (vv. 4f.) being made up of the church generally, a rather large gathering. The apostles were present, but also the elders and other members, one group being particularly named (v. 5), the Christian Pharisees. Here stronger claims are made than at Antioch (cf. v. 1). No complete account of this meeting appears, for between vv. 5 and 6 the account of one meeting ends and that of the second begins. The second meeting (vv. 6–21) was smaller, consisting only of the apostles and elders (v. 6) with Barnabas and Paul. The *multitude* of v. 12 means the membership of that group, equivalent to "the rest of them." James, the Lord's brother, appears (v. 13) as an important official, whether as apostle or as elder is not stated. James voices the decision of the conference.

The outcome of the first meeting is not announced. The second meeting of the apostles and elders was called to decide the question (v. 6) after hearing the facts. At first (whether in the presence of Paul and Barnabas is not certain) there was a general discussion, which had no decided outcome (vv. 6, 7a). In view of this uncertainty, Peter rehearsed the story of his visit to Cornelius and the latter's conversion (vv. 7b–11), dwelling particularly on the outpouring of the Holy Spirit upon the Gentiles. As before (cf. 11[18]) the plain narrative of Peter formed an unanswerable argument (v. 12). Peter claimed that he was the mouthpiece of God to the Gentiles (v. 7); that God imparted the Holy Spirit in witness of his favor to the Gentiles (v. 8); that with Gentiles and Jews alike, the inner experience came *through faith* (v. 9); hence it would be *making a trial of God* (cf. 5[9]), i.e., laying one's own life liable to the wrath of God, to overlook the plainly expressed will of the Father in this matter. The words are strong, justified by a critical situation. It is significant that Peter adds: *but we believe that we shall be saved . . . in like manner as they* (v. 11), making the experience of the Gentiles the standard for that of the Jew. The conventional mind of Peter's brethren would not easily assent to this emphasis, but none of them had an argument in return (v. 12a). The contrast between grace and the burden of legalism (v. 10) was noticed again and again in early Christian circles (Gal. 2[4] 5[1]; cf. Mt. 23[4]).

13a. The Decision of James. The appeal of Peter was supported by Barnabas and Paul (v. 12), who gave a graphic account of their contact with the Jews and Gentiles of Cyprus and Asia Minor. The *signs and wonders* (v. 12) include all the evidence of God's presence with them, not merely such miracles as the healing of the lame man at Lystra. The meeting proceeded in an orderly way toward its close, the only evidence of violent debate being found in v. 7. After Peter, Paul, and Barnabas had spoken with such effect (*kept silence*, v. 12; *held their peace*, v. 13), James arose to pronounce the decision of the assembly. There is no record of a vote. James had the authority of a leader. Jesus was his brother (see under 1[12-14]), and had appeared to James after his resurrection, perhaps at his conversion (1 Cor. 15[7]). At this time (Acts 15) James had come to be the leader at Jerusalem, superseding even Peter, who before stood at the head of the list of apostles. (See under 1[15-26].) In v. 14 Peter is referred to under the name *Symeon*, the Aramaic form by which the apostle would best be known in that intimate circle. The experience of Peter is more impressive to James, for he does not mention Paul and Barnabas by name. Yet his decision touches chiefly the problem raised by the work of Paul and Barnabas rather than by Peter's experience with Cornelius. Strangely enough, the book of Acts reports no further activities of Peter among the Gentiles. (Cf. Gal. 2[11-14].) The explanation is to be found in the author's desire to focus attention upon Paul. The decision of James, in his own words (v. 28), is not a private opinion, but a conclusion supported in some definite way by indication of divine approval (cf. v. 19, *my judgment is*). James and the others of the assembly saw in the events certified by Peter, Paul and Barnabas clear evidence of God's will (cf. 11[18].)

13b–21. The Address of James. The mind of James could become reconciled to the new point of view only when he found a passage of Scripture to support it. The meaning of the passage was revealed to him by the events now taking place, an experience that is continually being repeated. The *new thing* was that God had made a people for himself from among Gentiles, as Peter had told. And, lo, in Amos *it is written* that Messiah will return and build up the fallen tabernacle of David, and the nations (Gentiles) shall seek the Lord (vv. 16–18). That the mind of James was in reality comforted by this statement of the prophet is reflected in his words (v. 19). As noted above, the whole proceeding cannot be explained as a private judgment of James. Yet James was the one whose voice was most decisive in the matter.

The text of the decision (vv. 23–29) is in substance, although not in order, the same as vv. 19–21, the words of James spoken to the council. As James presented it orally, his *judgment* was that converts from paganism ought not to be asked to submit to circumcision (v. 20), but that they should submit to certain other restrictions that partook of rather a moral view, although in part they seem to be food laws. These restrictions were: (1) urging the non-use of flesh that had been offered to idols and abstention from idolatry, corresponding to the second commandment; (2) freedom from sexual sins; (3) avoidance of flesh from animals or birds that were strangled; (4) omission of blood from the diet. The two latter prohibitions overlap yet are not identical. These words are addressed to pagans whose familiarity with blood in heathen ritual might lead them to offend Jewish Christians in their city unless warned that such practices were inadvisable. V. 21 explains this still further. The Mosaic law was familiar to synagogue attendants throughout the world. The restrictions, excepting that concerning fornication, were chiefly advisory in the interests of Christian harmony. This principle of voluntary abstinence for the sake of others is still valid.

22–29. A Conciliatory Document. The question arose as to how to carry out the results of the conference. Should Paul and Barnabas, with others (v. 2) who had brought the question to Jerusalem, take back the account of the decision of James and the other leaders at Jerusalem? A better plan was to select other delegates from Jerusalem to accompany the Antioch brethren (v. 22) and with them to acquaint the church at Antioch with the terms of the decision. Such a policy was not uncomplimentary to Paul and Barnabas, as appears from the high tribute paid them in v. 26 and from the report of high satisfaction at Antioch with the decision and with the policy of the Jerusalem church (v. 31).

The document containing the text of the decision bears the form of a typical letter, beginning with *Greeting* (v. 23) and ending with *Fare ye well* (v. 29). The specific address of the letter includes non-Jewish converts in Antioch and the surrounding parts, including all Syria and Cilicia. The points emphasized are: (1) the Judaizing Christians of 15[1] are in no way authorized by the Jerusalem church to insist on circumcision; (2) it is the unanimous view of the leaders at Jerusalem that Barnabas and Paul are notable heroes of the faith; (3) Judas and Silas, as our representatives, will assure you of our sincere views in this matter; (4) not only do we agree that circumcision is unnecessary for you Gentiles, but we declare that the following constitute the only restrictions that should be put upon you as you enter and continue in the church: (a) avoid the use of food that has been presented in heathen temples; (b) do not use blood, which represents the life; (c) likewise, do not use strangled things for food, another offensive use of blood; and (d) keep yourselves from sexual immorality.

In this formal letter, the items of restriction are grouped in such a manner as to put the food-rules together. The fourth item, *fornication*, is a strictly moral precept. In view of v. 21, it is clear that these four items do not constitute a system of moral procedure, but they form the basis of a program which will result in harmony between the Jewish and Gentile portions of the church, in particular between the Jewish Christians of Judæa and the increasing number of Gentile Christians.

30–35. Favorable Impression at Antioch. The letter, borne by the delegates from Jerusalem, was read publicly before the assembled Christians of Antioch. These would doubtless include Jewish Christians as well as Gentile converts. Judas and Silas (v. 32) confirmed the assurance of v. 27 and in addition to repeating the story of the apostolic council went on to preach and exhort the Antioch church, i.e., they exercised their gift as prophets (cf. 13[1]) in the church. The effect of the letter upon the Antioch church was favorable. The impression given by vv. 30–33 is that the victory was on the side of the Gentile Christians in the struggle for liberty from the yoke of ceremonial requirement, centering in the demand for circumcision. True, the letter expressly avoided the use of the term "circumcision," and the same is true of the report of the proceedings at Jerusalem (vv. 4–21). Both the debate and the letter emphasize the liberty of religious experience as the test of God's approval and the approval of the church. The restrictions within the letter protect the Christian group from inner conflict over relatively unimportant points.

As a witness to the significance of this decision at Jerusalem and the visit of Silas and Judas with Paul and Barnabas, the program of the church at Antioch went forward with renewed vigor (v. 35). Luke does not pause long upon the details of Christian life at Antioch, for his interest lies with the propagation of Christianity throughout the empire, especially by Paul, who was particularly responsible to this missionary church. (See 13[2f.] 14[27f.] 18[22f.])

The entire episode referred to as the conference at Jerusalem is instructive for all who seek progress in moral and spiritual reform, even to-day. No great achievement has been wrought except through reasonable compromise, for with the best of men truth does not dawn clearly all at once. As the Christian Church has gradually outlawed slavery and is now making serious efforts to outlaw war, along with the contemporary struggle in various countries to establish effective prohibition of alcohol as a beverage, the essential principles of the struggle for freedom on the part of the Gentile churches have been raised and used to good effect.

III. Chapters 15[40] to 28[31]: The Church in the Roman Empire

The so-called *second missionary journey of Paul* begins at 15[40] and merges into the *third journey* at 18[22]. Paul himself is not authority for this conventional arrangement of his travels, but the division is convenient and is generally followed. The analysis here preferred follows the hint given in the title of the book of Acts, thus entitling the sections of the narrative after its chief *dramatis personæ*. (See intro., "Contents.") The opening section of this third part of Acts deals with the acts of Paul and Silas (15[40]–18[11]).

40, 41. Barnabas Superseded by Silas. The last grand division of the book of Acts describes the expansion of Christianity out into the empire, even to Rome itself. In the first phase of this mission Silas takes the place of Barnabas beside Paul. As the text stands, v. 34 is omitted (see mg.). The time interval between vv. 33 and 40 is long enough to permit Silas to return to Antioch after being dismissed (v. 33) following the work of grace in which Judas and he ministered with the others. If v. 34 is accepted, Silas was not among those dismissed.

At some time following the events of vv. 32–35 Paul initiated the plan to revisit the churches *in every city*. Barnabas proposed to take John Mark with them, but here for the first time it appears that John's withdrawal from the party at Perga (13[13]) aroused Paul's displeasure. Upon John Mark the two apostles could not agree, and their disagreement decided the fate of the proposed tour. The itinerary was divided, Cyprus being the objective of Barnabas and Mark, Asia Minor being Paul's destination. Barnabas, who has been mentioned fully twenty-four times thus far in Acts, appears no more in the narrative. The silence of Luke is not to be construed as a denial that Barnabas carried on extensive missionary work thereafter. Luke's interest is in Paul almost solely from this point forward. The partial nature of Luke's account of the rise of Christianity in Anatolia is seen in v. 41. *The churches* which were confirmed, i.e., strengthened by further organization and teaching, are not mentioned by name, and accounts of none of these churches of Syria and Cilicia are found in Acts. They may have been established by Paul earlier, or by other Christians who had their first instruction in the faith at Jerusalem (cf. 8[1, 4]).

CHAPTER XVI

1–3. Timothy Chosen as Helper. Paul and Silas came to Derbe and Lystra, which had been the outermost places reached on his first journey with Barnabas as companion. The Christian groups there are meant by the term *the brethren* (v. 2; cf. 15[40]). Among the Christians of Lystra was one Timothy, a disciple of excellent reputation, son of a Jewess who was a disciple, Eunice by name (2 Tim. 1[5]), and of a Gentile father, who was probably not a disciple. His name is not known.

The Jewish Christians of Lystra demanded that Gentile converts be circumcised. Paul, to satisfy this demand, had Timothy submit to the rite before going out to the work. In this Paul exhibited a truly compromising attitude, complimentary to him and of noticeable aid in his missionary work. If Paul had been disappointed in John Mark, quite the reverse can be said for Timothy. He remained the loyal supporter of Paul to the end.

4–8. Roundabout Through Asia Minor. One duty of the apostles on this journey was to publish the letter containing the decision of the Jerusalem authorities as to the status of Gentile converts in the church. The letter was addressed to the Gentile Christians of Syria and Cilicia (15[23]) but naturally was of interest to all Gentile Christians. Although he delivered the apostolic letter to these churches, Paul had his own way of dealing with meats offered to idols and the diet question in general, as his letters show (Rom. 14[1-12] 1 Cor. 10[14] 11[1]). Paul does not refer to the decree from Jerusalem in any extant letter.

The passage (vv. 4–8) is greatly compressed. The activity of Paul on this itinerary was enormous and extended over some weeks. It is possible that the cities Ancyra, Pessinus, and Tavium, in the province of Galatia, were visited. If, as is likely, Luke himself joined the party of Paul at Troas (vv. 10f.; note *we, us*) this would explain the brevity of this section, compared with the story so rich in particulars that follows. (On the location of the Galatian churches see under 18[22, 23] and cf. introduction to Galatians, p. 1207b.)

The events that correspond to the expressions *the Spirit of Jesus suffered them not* and *forbidden of the Holy Ghost* (vv. 6f.) are personal experiences exceedingly vivid and real, clear and unmistakable in meaning, but not further explained for the reader. In this *Book of the Holy Ghost* it did not seem necessary to explain an experience which was fundamental in the life of the church that first read the book. The writer means to show that Paul was divinely directed through unmistakable indications to the city of Troas, there to receive further revelation which should lead the apostle across the sea to Macedonia. Or it is possible that we have here an example of the interpretation of an apparently incidental circumstance in the light of the results to which it led. Whatever prevented the apostles from going to Bithynia, it made possible their going to Macedonia. That involved the spread of the gospel to Europe. The original hindrance may therefore well be attributed to a special divine interference.

9, 10. The Call into Macedonia. The climax of the series of providential events that determined Paul's route is found in the dream, according to which a Macedonian stood before the apostle and urged him to come into Macedonia. The added words *and help us* identify the man of the vision with a needy company who did not know Paul by name yet who were earnestly desiring the spiritual life which he preached. Primarily, no doubt, the writer has in mind certain Greeks whose interest in Judaism was aroused but who had not found in it the satisfaction they craved. Such persons would be ready to hear and to respond to Paul's message, for it was his rule to speak first in the synagogues, where such interested Gentiles would be found.

11–15. Arrival in Philippi. The first of the *we-sections* begins with v. 10 (see intro.). Most of the journey from Troas was by water, across the Ægean Sea. Philippi (v. 12) was seven or eight miles from Neapolis, which served only as a way-station. Philippi became important in Paul's life and work. He returned to it again and again, and one of his finest letters was addressed to the church in that city. Philippi had been a Roman colony since 42 B.C. The size of the city is probably overestimated in the phrase (v. 12), *the first of that district.* Paul found no synagogue building, but instead a place by the river where the relatively few Jews and proselytes met for prayer, if not for more formal services (v. 13). The *we* frequently found in this paragraph indicates that Luke was in the company. *Lydia,* who became the first convert to Paul's Messianic gospel, was not a Macedonian at all, but was from Thyatira, a city of Asia Minor (Rev. $2^{18f.}$). Her family were all baptized with her (v. 15; cf. v. 33), and she urged Paul to accept her hospitality. (See H. J. Cadbury, *Luke's Interest in Lodgings,* Journal of Bib. Lit., 1926, pp. 305–322.)

16–18. The Rise of Opposition. Paul's early experiences in Philippi were with women. It is supposable that no men were at the riverside service. Not until Paul came into conflict with certain commercialized interests did the men take account of him. Just what effect this lack of masculine interest had upon Paul's faith in his *man of Macedonia* is not indicated. Perhaps it acted as a test of his faith. It is a characteristic of the Gospels and Acts to note that beings of the demonic world were sensitive to the presence of an inspired person. Mark notes repeatedly their response to the character of Jesus (Mk. 1^{24} 3^{11} 5^{7}). So here (v. 17) the possessed maid cried out that these men were God's servants. The description of the "gift" of this woman emphasizes her ability to prophesy, i.e., to forecast events. The actual ability possessed may have been ventriloquism, which, in the opinion of her contemporaries, carried with it uncanny powers. It was not that this person had insight enough to declare them servants of God that led Paul (v. 18) to exorcise the *spirit of divination,* but because she became a nuisance through her repeated attentions to him and Silas.

19–24. Imprisoned Without Trial. The group that controlled the ventriloquial maiden became aroused over their loss of profits (vv. 21f.) and forcibly brought the apostles before the *prætors,* or magistrates. Luke does not make it plain that a trial of any sort took place. If a fair examination of Paul and Silas had been made, the fact that Paul was a Roman citizen must have come out, especially in view of the charge that he was teaching *customs . . . not lawful . . . to observe, being Romans* (v. 21).

Philippi did not have a large Jewish population (note lack of a synagogue), hence the probable existence of anti-Jewish views which made the summary action more agreeable to the magistrates. It was as Jews, not as Christians, that Paul and Silas were persecuted. Popular indignation was invoked (v. 22) against Paul and Silas, who alone are concerned in the arrest and imprisonment. For some reason not known Luke and Timothy were not taken before the magistrates. Before being imprisoned Paul and Silas were beaten with rods (vv. 22f.), *many stripes,* not the thirty-nine of Jewish regulation, being inflicted. This instance is the only one described of three such punishments endured by Paul. (See 2 Cor. 11^{25}.) The imprisonment of the two followed. The stocks which held their feet was a means of torture as well as of confinement.

25–29. Midnight in the Philippian Jail. The apostles counted it a joy to suffer for the cross of Christ (cf. 5^{41}) and poured out their feelings in song and prayer (v. 25). The remark that the *prisoners were listening to them* implies, first of all, wonder, then belief that these men were no ordinary evildoers. Then the earthquake followed, accompanied by the loosening of the bonds of all. The failure of the other prisoners to escape may be ascribed to their interest in the two apostles (v. 26).

The *attitude of the jailer* himself changes rapidly between vv. 27 and 29. At first the jailer's natural conclusion was that the prisoners had escaped through the open doors (v. 26b), in which case his own life was the forfeit. (See 12^{19} and 27^{42}.) Upon hearing Paul's voice, assuring him that all were still there, the jailer was awe-struck. These men were being supernaturally protected and all his superstitious fears were aroused (see 5^{19} and $12^{1f.}$).

It is probable that the number of prisoners was small. The jail was dark, and Paul's knowledge of the situation is accepted by the author as an example of that insight which often showed itself in the apostle's life (as in $27^{10,\ 22f.,\ 31f.}$).

30–34. The Second Conversion in Philippi. It is probable that Paul's converts in Philippi numbered more than Lydia and her household together with the jailer and his family; but these two notable instances are all that Luke offers, notwithstanding he is here using a *we-source.* The mention of *the brethren* in v. 40 implies a Christian community already formed at the time of Paul's departure.

The conversion of the jailer is briefly but graphically narrated. His question, *What must I do to be saved?* (v. 30) must not be given too much religious meaning, nor must such meaning be wholly denied it. The man was greatly upset mentally, had within a few minutes seriously proposed suicide, had had all his fears of the supernatural aroused, and faced these men whose presence in the jail had clearly brought about the earthquake, for so he would believe. The content of the question (v. 30b) concerns first of all his rescue from mental distress, as shown by the words, *trembling for fear* (v. 29). Paul seized the opportunity to explain his message of salvation through faith in Jesus, the words of v. 32 indicating the more elaborate exposition of his text, *Believe . . . and thou shalt be saved* (v. 31). Paul took the man's own word, "saved," and deepened its content.

The baptism of the jailer and his family followed immediately after the jailer had washed the wounds of the two. This may have been one of the rare cases when Paul himself baptized (cf. 1 Cor. 1[14-17]), although Silas may have officiated. It is difficult to make out these baptisms as instances of immersion. Christian faith is here characterized as *believing in God* (v. 34).

35–40. A Conclusion Favorable to the Apostles. It is only fair to the prætors of Philippi to believe that overnight they reconsidered their hasty action, taken at the instance of prejudiced men (v. 22f.), and thus ordered the jailer not to detain Paul and Silas. A dramatic scene followed the announcement of their message to Paul. For up to this point the author of Acts has withheld the information that Paul was a Roman citizen, an honor and privilege shared also by Silas. At least two Roman laws, the *lex Valeria* and the *lex Porcia*, protected the dignity of a Roman citizen against even privately inflicted blows, and these Romans had been beaten publicly! To this was added the indignity of punishment without trial (v. 37). The action of Paul in requiring as much publicity in connection with their release as had attended their imprisonment was not egotistical. He had in mind the dignity of his cause as well as that of his Roman citizenship. The departure of Paul from Philippi followed the release from prison. He took only time to give some earnest instruction to *the brethren* (v. 40) who, perhaps, made Lydia's house their meeting-place.

CHAPTER XVII

1–9. In Thessalonica. The next city in which Paul and Silas paused was Thessalonica (modern Saloniki), a little over one hundred miles southwest of Philippi. The apostles could make the journey in about four days, unless they paused in Amphipolis and Apollonia, of which there is no record. Luke uses the same word translated here *passing through* in Luke 8[1], a passage which describes extensive preaching and teaching on the part of Jesus. An analogous situation is found in the statement of Paul (Rom. 15[19]) that he had preached as far as Illyricum, while no record of labors in that region (modern Albania) is found in Acts. The narrative of Luke often passes deliberately over items that have become known to modern scholars in other ways. An example is the Galatian controversy (see introduction to Galatians, (p. 1208), about which Luke is silent.

In Thessalonica there was a synagogue (v. 2), and Paul followed his custom of first declaring his message to his countrymen in their own place of worship. In Thessalonica it is probable that only Paul and Silas were together. Timothy is mentioned in connection with Berœa (v. 14), and in 1 Thess. 3[1] Paul speaks of sending Timothy back to Thessalonica to see how they prospered. This may imply that the Thessalonians had some previous knowledge of Timothy. (Cf. 1 Thess. 3[2].) The book of Acts does not offer full information about the movements of all the members of Paul's party on the way from Philippi to Corinth.

Thessalonica became an important Christian center, but few particulars are given in the story of the rise of this church. For *three Sabbaths* (v. 2) Paul used his synagogue privilege, after which he was doubtless excluded by *the Jews moved with jealousy* (v. 5), and, as in other places (18[7] 19[9]), found a separate place of meeting for the disciples of the Lord. The apostles lodged with Jason (vv. 5, 7), but it is not certain that his house was the meeting-place. Vv. 2f. indicate the substance of the synagogue preaching of Paul, but his message before the disciples was more elaborate, as reflected in the Epistles to the Thessalonians. In the synagogue Paul always began with the lesson from the Scriptures (O.T.) and identified Jesus of Nazareth with Messiah (vv. 3f.).

The method adopted by Paul's Jewish adversaries is noteworthy. The Jews were of the opinion that their influence with the authorities was limited. So they stirred up a number of common loafers of the city, Macedonians, to join them in raising a disturbance against the visiting apostles (v. 5). The aim was to bring these men, who, it was loudly charged, were upsetting things (v. 6), *to the people,* i.e., to the properly constituted court. In Corinth, later (18[12]), when the Jews tried to obtain a verdict from Gallio, they were not even heard. The plan in Thessalonica succeeded partly. These Jews did not find Paul and Silas, but they took Jason and some others (v. 6) before the court, where they found it expedient to give bonds (v. 9) to keep the peace, whereupon Jason and the others (*the brethren* of v. 10) advised Paul and Silas to leave town. The authorities may have made it a condition that the apostles should not remain, as the prætors at Philippi had done. The Christians of Thessalonica sent the apostles away by night, lest another scene should ensue.

10–14. In Berœa. Nothing indicates that Timothy was at Thessalonica (see vv. 1–9), but at Berœa (modern Verria), forty odd miles southwest of Thessalonica, the three were surely together (v. 14). Had Paul to deal only with the Jews of Berœa, open-minded as they were (v.11), his success might have been even greater. Paul's most serious hindrance lay in the Jews who followed him up after his expulsion from Thessalonica. In the synagogue of Berœa the apostle was having a successful work (v. 12) when there arrived from Thessalonica some of his Jewish foes. These adopted their old tactics of setting the town against Paul (v. 13). Taking advantage of his former experience, Paul left the city of Berœa, thus providing the brethren with the continued labors of Silas and Timothy until a message from Paul at Athens (v. 15) directed their further movements. In Berœa the attack of the Jews was centered upon Paul.

15–21. Athens Visited. From Berœa to Athens Paul traveled first by land, then by sea (v. 14). The *brethren* from Berœa probably accompanied Paul as far as the nearest port, thence he proceeded, not alone but with some unnamed escort, to Athens. He speaks of being at Athens alone when writing to the Thessalonians (1 Thess. 3[1]). In his epistle above referred to Paul shows that Timothy (and perhaps Silas, see v. 15) came to him in Athens, thence went to Thessalonica When Paul left Berœa none could tell just where he might go. His movements had to be secret and no doubt were uncertain even to himself. The mission in Athens, while it claims considerable space, was not successful. No church was established, as far as recorded. A few souls believed (v. 34), but the total atmosphere of Athens was such as to make its inhabitants immune to the message of Paul. The apostle never indicated a desire to revisit the city. The Athens visit, however, is notable in that Luke has preserved a record of the address made to some of the distinguished Athenians. This address is usually referred to as the address on Mars' Hill. It is more correctly described as the address before the *Council of the Areopagus*. This speech was delivered after Paul had been some time in the city, for he had preached in the synagogue on the Sabbath (v. 17a) and during the week had spoken with those whom he met in the market place (v. 17b). As Paul became better known, the philosophers encountered him and passed their criticisms (v. 18). Some took Paul's reference to *Jesus* (a masculine noun) and to the *resurrection* (in the Greek a feminine noun, *anastasis*) to mean that he was preaching a male and female deity respectively. Thus their surmise that he was *a setter forth of strange gods* (v. 18). All in all, it seemed well to give the visitor a more formal opportunity, hence the invitation to address the Council (v. 19). This proceeding was in no way a trial of Paul, although he spoke before a high court. The Stoics and Epicureans (v. 18) wished to discover whether the new doctrine that he taught was worthy of their consideration. For this reason the more formal session was provided (vv. 19–21).

22–34. The Areopagus Address. The idols in Athens stirred Paul's Semitic soul to its depth. It is not in contradiction to this feeling, but because of the proper control of it, that Paul began with a reference to a particular altar or monument that he had observed, with the inscription: *To an unknown god.* The example furnished Paul with an appropriate text from which to expound his message. The words in v. 23b do not reflect upon the intelligence of the worshipers in this case. The words *in ignorance* mean that the worshiper is not able to identify the god concerned. Deissmann (*St. Paul*, first edit., Appendix II, pp. 261f.) points out that under a regime of polytheism a worshiper could not be certain which of his protecting deities had been a chief aid. Hence the inscription upon the altar, erected in commemoration of a deliverance: *To the god whose name is not known.*

The Athenians wished an exposition of Paul's message. That message concerned the one true God, who made all the world and all men, and who called all to repent before the Day of Judgment. At the very close of the address a reference to the resurrection introduced a favorite Pauline theme. The tone of this address is remarkably conciliatory and winning, its content is closely condensed, its thought unitary. It has been objected by some that its style is not that of Paul, and this objection has weight. Doubtless all the speeches in Acts in their literary form owe something to the author of the book (see p. 1095a). The *substance* of what is here said could very well have been said by an educated Jew like Paul to cultured Athenians. The opinion here maintained is that the speech represents substantially an address actually delivered by Paul before the Court of the Areopagus, notwithstanding the phraseology is that of the author. The actual address must have been much longer. In condensing an address the reporter must use phraseology of his own. *The sense of the address* is as follows: Athenians, I observe that you pay great attention to matters of religion. You erect altars even to deities whose names you do not know. For myself, I am sure there is only one God, and he is the Creator of the world and of men. Such a God cannot live in builded temples, but he can be found anywhere by men who really seek him. This is the more true since he made us all of one blood. It is time for all to see this truth, to seek the one true God and to be saved in the Last Judgment. The crowning assurance of the truth of what I say is found in the fact of human resurrection.

The point to which his hearers took exception was the mention of the resurrection (v. 31). Many wanted to hear Paul further, either then or another day (v. 32b). The actual fruitage of souls was disappointing (v. 34). One of the converts was a member of the Court which Paul addressed (vv. 19, 22). The other convert named was a woman, of whom nothing further is known than her name, Damaris.

CHAPTER XVIII

A Year and a Half in Corinth (vv. 1–11). The two large cities in Achaia (Greece) visited by Paul, Athens and Corinth, were quite different in almost every respect. Corinth, with harbors both on the east and the west, invited and received the commerce of the world and well-nigh all sorts of men. It was a cosmopolitan city indeed. (For description see W. M. Ramsay, art., "Corinth," Hastings' *Dictionary of the Bible*, vol. i, pp. 479–483.

1–3. Paul, Aquila and Priscilla. Early in his stay at Corinth Paul found a devoted couple, *kinsmen*, as he would call them. These Jewish people had been recently (49–50 A.D.) expelled from Rome and had settled in Corinth. Later they were to become Paul's helpers in Ephesus (vv. 18f.). Like Paul, Aquila and Priscilla worked on tent cloth. Having a common trade and similar interests, Paul took lodgings with them, probably remaining with them during his stay in Corinth.

4. Paul in the Synagogue. Following his unvarying custom, Paul worshiped in the synagogue each Sabbath and proclaimed his message of the crucified Messiah. (See 1 Cor. 1[23] 2[2].) At first this activity of Paul was accompanied by less directness and force than usual. The rupture with the Jews did not occur until Paul was fired with enthusiasm by reassuring news from Macedonia (vv. 5f.).

5–11. The Church in Corinth. V. 5 is a striking commentary upon a certain trait of Paul, illustrated in his own words, 2 Cor. 2[12f.], where the apostle says that he could not do his best work while he was concerned so deeply about the Corinthian church and its troubles. Here Luke points out that only after the arrival of Silas and Timothy in Corinth with good news from Philippi and Thessalonica did Paul really have freedom in his preaching in the synagogue. Fire struck fire and the Jews contradicted Paul (v. 6) as they of Antioch had done (13[45]). The apostle then declared his mission to the Gentiles, meaning that he would preach the gospel to all men, whatever their race, and at once withdrew with those who believed in the Lord Jesus Christ to a separate meeting-place (v. 6). The movement carried with it the *ruler of the synagogue*, Crispus (see 1 Cor. 1[14]), who was succeeded by one Sosthenes (v. 17). The number who now made up the Christian Church in Corinth was not small (v. 8b), neither was the opposition light. At a time of discouragement Paul was reassured in a vision (v. 9) that he should keep boldly on, for the church must grow to still larger numbers. No further account of the work appears, but the promise of divine protection was made good during a year and a half of constructive activity. The experience has often been repeated since. Power to "see the invisible" is God's gift to his servants, to keep them resolute amidst difficult circumstances.

Acts of Paul. The other apostles now drop into the background, and the rest of the book is occupied entirely with the acts of Paul (18[12]–28[31]).

12–17. Paul's Enemies Repulsed by Gallio. The opposition against Paul developed slowly in Corinth. After the first outbreak in the synagogue (v. 6) the Christian group continued peaceably under Paul's direction. The change of proconsul, the Roman ruler of the province, some year and a half after Paul began his work in Corinth (vv. 11f.) gave the orthodox Jews, as they supposed, a good chance to obtain judgment against Paul. V. 12 describes the action taken by the synagogue under its leader, Sosthenes, whereby Paul was brought before Gallio, the new proconsul. Paul, it was charged, incited men to worship contrary to the Jewish Law. Literally Roman law permitted Jews to exercise their religion *according to Jewish law.* (See Josephus, *Antiquities*, bk. xiv, ch. 10: 20, 21.) Thus the religion taught by Paul, it was thought, could be shown to be *contrary to Roman law* for the reason that it was a non-Jewish religion. Gallio, however, took an unexpected course. He caught at once the note of theological discussion and positively refused even to entertain the charges against Paul. The case did not develop even as far as a plea of *Guilty* or *Not guilty* (v. 14), for Gallio expelled all from the courtroom before Paul was arraigned. In precise terms Gallio pointed out that the Jewish authorities themselves should pass upon such technical points. In this Gallio showed a certain regard for the Jews. The scene which occurred directly after the refusal of Gallio to hear both sides of the controversy was participated in by Gentile onlookers, who took their cue from the attitude of the proconsul (v. 17). The Sosthenes here mentioned cannot be identified with the person mentioned in 1 Cor. 1^{1}.

In Corinth Silas had doubtless been Paul's helper most of the time, but from 18^{5} on no further mention is made of him. It may be concluded that Luke is narrating the *acts of Paul and Silas* from 15^{36} to 18^{5}, where Silas is last mentioned. Paul alone figured as the intended victim of the Jews who haled him before Gallio. Certainly from this point forward to the close of his book (18^{12}–28^{31}) Luke has only the *acts of Paul* in mind. With 18^{23} begins the so-called *third missionary journey*, which had for its purpose not so much the founding of new churches as the further strengthening of those already founded. If Paul did enter new territory during this period, Luke does not indicate it.

18-21. From Corinth to Antioch by Way of Ephesus. The departure of Paul from Corinth did not occur until some time after the discomfiture of his opponents. He used his advantage in prosecuting the work in the Corinth church (v. 18a). When he left by vessel from Cenchræa, Priscilla and Aquila accompanied him. Either Paul or Aquila, presumably the latter, as the order of words indicates, had taken some sort of vow that involved the cutting of his hair (not a genuine Nazirite vow, which could be consummated only in Palestine). The purpose of Luke in offering this item of information, however ambiguously, may be to show that Paul was not, as his enemies averred, encouraging Jews to forsake all Jewish rites. In 21^{26} Paul himself undertakes a thoroughly Jewish ceremony. The first appearance of Paul at Ephesus (v. 19) evoked a favorable response on the part of the Jews of the synagogue (v. 20), who urged him to stay longer with them. But the apostle felt that it was now time to report in person at Antioch, to which church he was responsible for his work. So, promising to return to Ephesus (v. 21), he left on a vessel bound southward, made his way to Cæsarea, thence to Jerusalem (*went up and saluted the church*), then on to Antioch. (The expressions "went *up*" and "went *down*" refer to the altitude of Jerusalem as compared with that of the coast and of Antioch in Syria.)

22, 23. Preparing for a New Journey. The *some time* (v. 23) spent at Antioch in Syria was presumably given to a recital of his labors, to making plans for further visitation, and to the work at Antioch among the Gentiles. On leaving Antioch, Paul's route led him through a good part of Asia Minor (note *upper country* 19^{1}), most certainly involving visits to all the churches previously established. V. 23 is most compact, covering as it does months of time, inestimable effort on the part of the apostle, and many unspecified Christian triumphs. The expression *region of Galatia and Phrygia* (cf. 16^{6}) has given rise to extensive discussion, and the whole question as to the location of the *churches of Galatia* hangs upon the correct solution of the meaning. An opinion expressed above (under 16^{4-8}) is here reiterated, namely, that the Galatia in question is the province of that name, whose cities, Ancyra, Tavium, and Pessinus may have been visited by Paul and Silas during that part of the second missionary journey so inadequately reported in 16^{4-8}. An acceptance of this opinion carries with it an obligation to find the churches of Galatia farther north than Antioch, Iconium, Lystra, and Derbe. (On the Galatian question consult Moffatt, *Introduction to the Literature of the N.T.*, pp. 90–101. Also introduction to Galatians, p. 1208.)

24–28. Apollos at Ephesus and Corinth. In the meantime the work at Ephesus had been going forward, perhaps under the direction of Aquila and Priscilla (although Luke prefers to give the name of Priscilla first). Paul calls her Prisca (Rom. 16^{3} 2 Tim. 4^{19}). During Paul's absence there arrived at Ephesus a learned Jew named Apollos. Afterward he became a figure at Corinth (v. 27; 1 Cor. 1^{12} $3^{6, 22}$). The story of his Christian experience is of interest. The paragraph on Apollos (vv. 24–28) is too brief to be understood fully, yet certain outstanding facts are clear. Apollos was an orthodox Jew of the finest type, probably a disciple of Philo, a learned Jew of Greek sympathies in Alexandria, eloquent (his *learning* is indicated in the context) and effective in discourse, and well read in the Scriptures (v. 24). Apollos was familiar with some gospel material known to Luke himself, hence Luke's statement that Apollos *taught carefully the things concerning Jesus* (cf. Lk. 1^{3}). He had also been taught orally (v. 25 mg.). At this point the omission of information is puzzling. Apollos was baptized after the manner of John Baptist, Luke's own understanding of John's baptism being found in Lk. 3^{7-14}. In Lk. 3^{16} John Baptist says that the mightier One who follows him will baptize "with the Holy Ghost and with fire." It should follow in vv. 25f. that Apollos was baptized (as were the twelve men of 19^{5}) and that he received the Holy Spirit. But these statements are not made about Apollos. Luke does say that when Apollos began to speak publicly in the synagogue Priscilla and Aquila took him aside and *expounded unto him the way of God more carefully* (v. 26).

The *argument from silence* should not be used to discount the plain teaching of Acts that Christian experience was validated by the unmistakable presence of the Holy Spirit. (See under 2^{1-4}.) It seems best to hold that Apollos was rebaptized in the name of Jesus and that he received the Spirit. The expression in v. 25, *fervent in spirit*, refers to a personal characteristic, not to a spiritual gift or *charism*.

The brethren (v. 27) is an expression implying the presence already of a Christian community in Ephesus. (Cf. 1^{15} 9^{30} $15^{1, 3, 22, 32}$ 16^{40} and similar places.) The spiritual equipment of Apollos, together with his other gifts and graces, made him particularly effective in further work at Corinth (v. 28) to which city he had gone with the blessing and recommendation of the Ephesian saints.

CHAPTER XIX

1–7. Paul and Disciples of the Baptist. On his return from inner Asia Minor (*upper country*, v. 1) Paul came upon a dozen men who believed (v. 2) and were therefore reckoned as Christians, yet they did not possess the indispensable gift of the Holy Spirit. For they adhered to the John Baptist movement, which from the days described in Lk. $7^{16f.}$ had continued as a separate religious movement. John Baptist was in doubt as to whether Jesus was really He for whom they were looking, and probably his followers still looked for a different Messiah (see Lk. $7^{18f.}$).

Like Apollos, these men knew only the baptism of John, they had received no instruction about the Holy Spirit, by which they meant that they had not heard that the Holy Spirit was present in human experience. Their prophet, John Baptist, did not live to see his own prophecy (Lk. 3^{16}) fulfilled.

Paul showed these men that John baptized with repentance in mind, urging his hearers *to believe on him which should come* and that Jesus of Nazareth was the very one of whom John spoke. They had already believed (v. 2) on Jesus; now they were *baptized in his name* (v. 5). The Holy Spirit fell upon them only after Paul had laid his hands upon them (8^{17}; cf. 6^{6}). Their experience was similar to that of the men on whom the Spirit came at Pentecost (see under 2^{1-4}), in that they *spake with tongues* (cf. 10^{46}.) They also *prophesied*, i.e., in modern terms, they gave personal testimony. The coming of the Holy Spirit, therefore, meant a quickening of the spiritual life, which was attributed to divine agency.

This passage is to be regarded as a bit of history of the apostolic age which we are incapable of fully understanding precisely because of its fragmentary nature. In Luke's sources, no doubt, it had a context which has not been preserved with it. The passage was far more intelligible to the first readers of the book than it is to a modern reader.

8–12. Synagogue and Church in Ephesus. The friendly relations between Paul and the synagogue in Ephesus continued for three months after his return. The substance of Paul's teaching is described as *the things concerning the kingdom of God* (v. 8b) which is the equivalent of *the Way* (v. 9), more fully expressed above as *the way of God* (18^{26}). The exact cause of the rupture between Paul and the synagogue does not appear. There arose public contradiction that could not turn out at all helpful (v. 9); so Paul, no doubt reluctantly, took with him the followers of Jesus and withdrew to one of the schools of Ephesus. For two years he met the brethren daily in the School of Tyrannus, thus obtaining such an extensive hearing that it could be said, at least rhetorically, that all Asia was evangelized (v. 10). No extensive account of the work is rendered, although Luke says (v. 11) that miracles accompanied Paul's ministry, chiefly healing of diseases and exorcism of evil spirits. These wonders are described as out of the ordinary (v. 11f.), i.e., not such works as were wrought by men like Simon Magus (8^{9}) and Bar-Jesus (13^{6}), or by the *strolling Jews* of the context. Magic was universally practiced in the East, as the following context illustrates from Ephesus itself (vv. 19f. See intro., "The Miracles in Acts").

13–20. Christianity and Magic at Ephesus. These verses give a graphic account of the struggle between *the Way* and a prevailing system of magical incantation. The critical phase of the struggle appeared when the devotees of magic tried to appropriate a Christian formula (v. 13b). It is difficult for a modern citizen of the western hemisphere to understand how closely *the Way* seemed to the pagan to approach his own system and principles. Precisely when the Christian missionary appealed to the reality of the spiritual world (as Paul in 1 Cor. 2^{10-16}) it appeared to the pagan that he was invoking his own world of spirits (or dæmons). In the passage under consideration (vv. 13–20) Luke shows how even certain Jews who practiced the prevailing magical cult were shown conclusively that Christianity was not a new form of magic, but a spiritual power whose source was in the person Jesus. (See Mt. 12^{27} for Jesus' own reference to the exorcism of evil spirits by the Pharisees; also see Josephus, *Antiquities*, bk. vii, ch. 2: 5 for an interesting example of exorcism through the name of Solomon.) The point of the narrative lies in its significance for the growth and prestige of Christianity at Ephesus. The value of the magical books burned in testimony to the power of the gospel (v. 19) was almost ten thousand dollars, or two thousand pounds sterling, which in those days was a very large sum.

21, 22. The Plan to Visit Rome. A period of growth in comparative rest from conflict (vv. 20f.) gave Paul an opportunity to plan still wider conquests. He must visit Macedonia and Achaia on his way to Jerusalem, then go west to Rome. Part of this plan came to pass, although the manner of his journey to Rome was not foreseen. Paul spent more time in Ephesus than the two years mentioned in v. 19. (In 20^{31} the total stay of the apostle in Ephesus is named as three years.) In ch. 19 only two years and three months are accounted for. The indefiniteness of *after these things* (v. 21) and *about that time* (v. 23) easily provides additional time in Ephesus. Note also the period indicated in v. 22b, *stayed in Asia for a while.*

23–41. Christianity and Commercialized Religion in Ephesus. The conflict with magic was more easily decided than was the conflict of *the Way* with the commercial aspects of Diana worship in Ephesus. In his Gospel Luke shows a deep interest in the teaching of Jesus that touches upon the lure of material profit (see Lk. 12^{13-21} 14^{18-24} 16^{1-13}), and in Acts he includes available narratives that illustrate the antagonism of materialism to the spiritual aspects of the gospel. The story of Demetrius and his fellow-workers is characteristic.

The growth of Christianity in Ephesus had turned some of the worshipers in the great temple of Diana (Artemis) away from their devotion to that goddess, and the profits of Demetrius and his guild were endangered. These silversmiths made small models of the temple, which pilgrims bought to offer to the goddess and in some cases to carry home with them as keepsakes, or to use as amulets. After the sobering incident of the bonfire made with magical papyri, these artificers plotted to turn the leaders of the Christian movement out of town (v. 25). The chief accusation of Demetrius was laid against Paul (v. 26), and that too because he had well-nigh converted the province of Asia (cf. v. 10). Appealing to the instinct of self-preservation, Demetrius worked up a high degree of mob spirit (vv. 28, 29, 32, 34) which seized alike upon the religious sanction and upon race prejudice as its motives. Paul was not present at any time during the uproar. The friendship of the authorities and the plea of *the brethren* kept him out of the mob scene (vv. 30f.). An attempted speech of a certain Alexander (probably not the coppersmith of 1 Tim. 1^{20} and 2 Tim. 4^{14}) was drowned by the senseless roar of the crowd, and not until the town clerk himself (vv. 35f.) spoke with authority did the mob break up. This official denied that these men (v. 37, probably some of the Christians of Ephesus, here unnamed) were *temple-pilferers*, as the words of Demetrius implied. Neither had they said anything against the goddess. If any had complaint to bring, the courts were at hand. With these words and other admonitions the town clerk dismissed the assembly. Not long afterward Paul left for Macedonia (see v. 21).

CHAPTER XX

1–6. A Grand Circuit from Ephesus through Macedonia and Greece. After the tumult in the theater Paul made seemly haste to leave Ephesus. In sixteen verses (vv. 1–16) Luke describes months of labor and weary miles of travel by sea and land. In 2 Cor. $1^{8, 15f.}$ $2^{12f.}$ 7^{5-16} Paul so describes his travel plan that this journey can be traced first to Troas, thence to Philippi and Thessalonica and other Macedonian churches, where he spent some time, writing at least 2 Cor. 1–9 (see intro. to 1 and 2 Corinthians). Thence Paul went to Corinth for a stay of three months (v. 3), after which the change of plan was made (v. 3b) which took him back through Macedonia, across again to Troas, and thence by land and water to Miletus, very near to Ephesus (vv. 15f.), thence on to Tyre (21^{3}), whence he made his way to Jerusalem.

The book of Acts narrates none of the distressing circumstances in the Corinthian church which are reflected in Paul's Epistles to the Corinthians. The omission makes it possible for Luke to compress into this small space a journey of Paul's which was perhaps as filled with emotion as any of similar length in his career. The evangelization of Illyricum may have occurred during the time indicated in v. 2, *when he had gone through those parts.* In his sources Luke probably did not find any information about this part of Paul's work. (Another possibility for the Illyricum mission is between vv. 12 and 13 of ch. 17.)

The Jews of v. 3 are probably they who brought Paul before the bar of Gallio ($18^{12f.}$). Many surmises are possible at the size of the bodyguard of Paul as he went from Corinth through Macedonia to Asia Minor. The plot against Paul's life (v. 3) offers an adequate occasion for protection. Seven men, from Macedonia, Asia, and Lycaonia, accompanied him, probably from Corinth to Philippi.

While Paul remained there the seven went across the sea to Troas and there awaited him. Luke also accompanied Paul, at least from Troas on, for the second *we-section* begins at v. 5 and continues to v. 17. Of the seven mentioned in v. 4, Sopater and Secundus are named nowhere else; Gaius is not to be identified with others of that name in the N.T.; Timothy, Tychicus and Trophimus are mentioned by Paul himself as helpers; and Aristarchus is the same as in 19[29] and Philm. v. 24. The extra time spent in Philippi was due to the celebration of the Passover and Feast of Unleavened Bread (v. 6), which Paul wished to observe with his Jewish friends in Philippi. (See art., *Religion of Israel*, pp. 169–70.)

7–12. The Meeting at Troas. No account of the founding of the church at Troas has been preserved but the city is known to be important to early Christianity. (See 16[8] 2 Cor. 2[12] 2 Tim. 4[13].) The apostolic party numbered at least nine (vv. 4f.), and with the brethren at Troas, gathered for the Eucharist, no wonder the *upper chamber* was crowded. *Eutychus*, about whom nothing else is known except that he slept during an exceptionally long sermon (v. 9), fell from the window in which he was sitting and was supposed to be dead. Paul, however, on investigation (v. 10), assured the anxious friends that he was alive, and the meeting went on. The lad is "picked up for dead," as we should say. Luke is not narrating an instance of raising from the dead, or it would have been so stated in definite terms, as in the case of Tabitha, where (9[37, 41]) the author states first that "she fell sick and died," and that the apostle "presented her alive."

The important contribution of this story (vv. 7–12) is its glimpse into the community life of a primitive Christian church. The memorial Supper of the Lord was not yet made a formal sacrament. It was called *breaking bread.* It was the custom to meet on the Lord's Day, the first of the week. The *agape* (love feast) was accompanied by a discourse, in this case preceding the breaking of bread (v. 7) and also following it (v. 11b). Here the entire service was at night, no doubt because the day was a day of business and the Christian brethren met after their day's work was done.

13–16. Troas to Miletus. For some reason not now understood, Paul walked across the peninsula on which Troas is situated, and met the ship and his companions at Assos, on the southern side of the peninsula. The plan was made by Paul himself (v. 13) and may have been dictated by a natural desire to be alone for awhile.

Vv. 14f. indicate the route of the ship as it skirted the shore of Asia Minor. The plan of Paul to be in Jerusalem at Pentecost (seven weeks after leaving Philippi, v. 6) led to the choice of a vessel that did not touch at Ephesus, for to stop there would oblige him to lose time, thus endangering his plan (v. 16).

17. Paul at Miletus. From Miletus, south of Ephesus (see Ramsay, art., "Miletus," Hastings' *Dictionary of the Bible*, vol. iii, pp. 368f.), Paul sent for *the elders of the church* (cf. above, p. 1112b) to come to him. On their arrival, which must have been at least the second day after Paul reached Miletus, these officials were addressed by Paul. The substance of what he said is found in vv. 18b–35. He closed with a most beautiful and much quoted saying of Jesus which is not found in any of the Gospels.

18–35. The Address of Paul. The address here given while Pauline in substance is in the style of the author of the book of Acts. (See intro., "Sources.") In this respect, the report resembles in particular that of Paul's address to the Athenians at Mars' hill. See under 17[22-31], and cf. the long prayer of Christ in Jn. 17.

The address does not have such clear and logical sequence as, for instance, the address at Athens (17[22-31]), but, rather, presents fragments of more abundant material which Luke found in his sources. The address is intensely personal in tone. Superlatives abound, as *all lowliness of mind* (v. 19); *I shrank not . . .* (vv. 20, 27); *the whole counsel of God* (v. 27); *I ceased not . . . night and day* (v. 31); *I coveted no man's silver* (v. 33). These statements, strong but true, are presented in the words of a sympathetic friend and advocate, and from the point of view of the writer's time. In this address Paul refers to *plots of the Jews* (v. 19b), although the author has not given any account of such in Ephesus. It would be remarkable indeed if the Jews, orthodox or Christian, had not tried to interfere with the work among the Gentiles in Ephesus.

A few additional items appear about the type of work carried on. Not only in the school of Tyrannus (19[9]) but *from house to house* Paul had taught (v. 20). There is possibly a clear and primitive distinction between God and Jesus Messiah in v. 21. *Repentance* was exercised as *toward God; faith,* on the other hand, was directed *toward Christ.* Repentance and faith were the two notes in the initial message of Jesus himself (Mk. 1[15]. Note *gospel of God,* Mk. 1[14] and cf. Acts 20[24c]). The ministry of Paul had been without partiality, including Jews and Greeks (v. 21), and the whole message (v. 27) had, of course, been given to

all. Summing up (v. 25), Paul's message had been that of *the kingdom*, as that of Jesus had been during his last days on earth (1[3]).

At this time Paul had a clear conception of the dangers facing him, even to the point of foreboding death (vv. 22f.), and the brave note in his declaration that he did not prize life itself as the chief thing (v. 24) is quite in line with his words in Phil. 1[21-24] 3[10] and with Jesus' words in Mt. 10[28] addressed to the Twelve. The writer of Acts does not introduce into the speech any information as to the actual outcome of events. He reserves this for his concluding chapters, thus leaving, it is believed, the essential message of Paul to the Ephesian elders, with only changes in the style. Thus here, as elsewhere in Acts, is found a dependable report *in substance* of what was said.

Vv. 28–30 constitute a solemn charge to the *bishops* (or *overseers*) of the flock, declaring their responsibility to God and pointing out dangers from without and from within which would certainly arise. The *bishops* are the same as *elders*, i.e., the officials whom Paul is addressing. The term "elders" does not occur in this sense in the letters of Paul outside the pastoral Epistles, but the word "bishops" appears in Phil. 1[1]. The duties of bishops changed with time, and at a later date the office by that name was differently regarded. The meaning of the term in Paul's mind and in that of the author of Acts corresponds somewhat to the meaning of "class-leader" in the early days of Methodism, stressing *oversight* and *personal responsibility* for religious instruction (see intro. to 1 and 2 Timothy, pp. 1277–8).

The *grievous wolves* of v. 29 may be referred to in 1 Tim. 1[3, 20] 6[3f.] Deliberate and mischievous evil is indicated in the term. An invocation solemnizes this charge to the elders of Ephesus as Paul commends them all to *God and the word of his grace* (v. 32), and *to him who is able* (rather than "which is able"), thus emphasizing the personal presence of the gracious God with *the flock*.

36–38. The Tender Farewell of Paul. Oriental custom marks the manner of Paul's leave-taking, but the words of the passage leave no doubt that the emotion was real, not simulated. The greatest source of sorrow with the Ephesian disciples was the finality of the farewell.

CHAPTER XXI

1–6. From Miletus to Tyre. The entire passage 21[1-18] forms another *we-section* (see 16[10-18] 20[5-17] 27[1]–28[16]). This third *we-section* begins at Miletus (v. 1), where the second ended (20[15]). The indications are to the effect that the address of Paul was taken from another source than the diary. (See intro., "Sources.")

Vv. 1–6 contain an account of the route from Miletus to Tyre and a short, vivid story of a sincere but disregarded warning given to the apostle at Tyre.

Quite certainly the same vessel bore Paul and Luke from Miletus to Ptolemais. Change of cargo occasioned the stay of a week at Tyre, during which time warnings were sounded in Paul's ears repeatedly: *Do not go up to Jerusalem.* Notwithstanding inspired men thus spoke (v. 4, *through the Spirit*), Paul persisted in his plan. No small part of his persistence was due to his responsibility for the collection (Rom. 15[26] 1 Cor. 16[1] 2 Cor. 9[1f.]) about which, however, Acts is silent, except possibly for the one statement of Paul (24[17]). The motive of Paul's persistence is given (20[16]) as his determination to celebrate Pentecost that year at Jerusalem.

The church at Tyre is here first referred to, although the expression *the disciples* (v. 4) implies a well-known group. This church was probably established soon after the martyrdom of Stephen.

7–14. Paul at Cæsarea. The sea voyage ended at Ptolemais, the first port after Tyre. From Ptolemais to Cæsarea Paul and Luke doubtless went on foot. They remained but a day in Ptolemais, where another church already existed, with whose members Paul seems to have been acquainted. At Cæsarea familiar names reappear. Paul stayed with Philip, whose story in 8[4-40] reveals that he had been for years a resident there. The prophet Agabus (v. 10) was originally of Judæa (11[28]) and at Antioch in Syria foretold the famine in the reign of Claudius.

The events in Cæsarea might well have caused Paul to change his plan, but he proved to be unchangeable. It is not said that the four daughters of Philip made any definite prophecy at this time (v. 9). But Agabus came with certain information as to the attitude of the Jews in Jerusalem toward Paul. He acted out his prophecy in O.T. fashion (vv. 10f., and cf. Jer. 19 and Ezek. 4), prefacing his action with the solemn formula: *Thus saith the Holy Ghost*—an authentication which was as strong as could be offered. Paul did not deny the validity of the prophecy (v. 13) but declared that he was *willing even to die.* This Agabus had not foretold.

The passage gives the distinct impression that not alone the delivery of a sum of money, nor the fulfillment of a personal desire to celebrate a Jewish festival at Jerusalem drove Paul on in his course. It was nothing less than *a principle which must be defended* that led Paul to risk life itself in his attempt. Here is something closely akin to the determination of Jesus, some thirty years before, to go up to Jerusalem. Luke (9^{51}) says that Jesus "stedfastly set his face" to go to Jerusalem. Paul's sacrifice was just as real, even though he did not at that time lose his life. Paul literally *gave up his life* for the Gentile cause—for the principle involved in his empire-wide mission. It is motive and purpose that give a deed its moral significance. The Christian community at Cæsarea saw the sublime purpose in their hero. The author of the *we-source* identifies himself with the company who breathed that sacrificial prayer: *The will of the Lord be done!*

15–17. On to Jerusalem. Here is portrayed the loyalty of the brethren at Cæsarea to Paul. Some of them went with him for a part of the journey toward Jerusalem, a two-days' trip altogether (cf. 23^{31-33}). If it were certain that the author of Acts knew about the collection which Paul was bringing up to the Jerusalem saints, it could be supposed that these brethren formed a sort of bodyguard to protect him and the collection from thieves. Since we know from Paul himself that he gathered funds from the Gentile churches for the saints at Jerusalem, the assumption here that Paul needed protection is well warranted, whether Acts carries any account of the collection or not. The travelers were probably mounted. Paul's party lodged with Mnason, one of the early disciples, for the one night spent on the way to Jerusalem (v. 16), or (as others read it) the Cæsarean brethren accompanied Paul all the way to Jerusalem, and Mnason was his host while he was in the city. The presumption is, however, that a sister of Paul lived in Jerusalem (see 23^{16}) in which case Paul would lodge with her. This gives the preference to the former interpretation.

18–26. The Advice of James. The Christian church in Jerusalem gave Paul a welcoming hand, and the day after his arrival Paul sought out James, the head of the church there, to make his report. Paul had not been sent out by this church, but the apostle knew their interest would be excited by his account of the spread of the Christian movement. James regarded the movement from the conservative, Jewish side, but gloried in Paul's achievements (vv. 20f.). The church at Jerusalem, still composed of Jewish people, was in doubt as to the loyalty of Paul to the law (v. 21). It was desirable to convince them that they were misinformed. James did not doubt Paul, yet felt that the burden of proof rested upon Paul himself. Hence his proposal that Paul pay the expenses of four men who had undertaken a Nazirite vow. This would compel the presence of Paul in the Temple and also would require him to submit to the Mosaic ordinances in question (vv. 22f.).

The Jews whom James had in mind as opponents of Paul were Christian Jews (v. 20) and presumably resided at Jerusalem (v. 22). It turned out that certain Jews from Asia (v. 27) incited the mob against Paul, and these were probably *not* Christian Jews. The whole story of this peril which Paul survived teaches how loyal the Judæan Christian church remained to Judaism throughout at least the first generation. Men may have the Christian spirit, and still cling to some of the customs of their native "culture."

False information had been spread among the Jews concerning Paul. He was painted as a renegade who made it his business to turn people away from Moses and the Law (v. 21). The report, James halfway admits, may have arisen from the message sent to Gentile converts to Christianity ($15^{22f.}$), the import of which he repeats here (v. 25). The proposal of James involved no compromise on Paul's part, interfered with no principle, offended his conscience in no way, so he readily acceded to it. The *four men* were presumably members of the Christian church of Jerusalem (v. 23). Seven days of ceremony were involved in the discharge of the vows in question, and it began to appear that the advice of James was well given. The sequel proved the reverse.

27–36. Seized by the Jews: Rescued by the Romans. Paul was not known by face at Jerusalem even at this time, for he had been there infrequently and for only brief periods. Jews from Ephesus (Asia, v. 27) recognized both the apostle and Trophimus (v. 29) of Ephesus, the latter an uncircumcised Christian. It was charged that Paul had introduced Trophimus into the Temple unlawfully. This charge, no doubt false, yet loudly made (v. 28), was sufficient to arouse against Paul a strong feeling based on both racial and religious grounds. He would have been assassinated had not the guard of Roman soldiers in the neighboring Tower of Antonia, attached to the Temple, rescued him from the Jews.

The mob (v. 30) tried to get Paul outside the sacred area to carry out their murderous plan. It would be *illegal to lynch him in the Temple!* It was a large crowd that attacked Paul, although the report that *all Jerusalem* was in confusion was a rhetorical exaggeration. It was the duty of the Romans to keep the city clear of such uprisings. The captain of the guard supposed that he had to deal with a genuine insurrectionist, which accounts for the unusual precaution taken (*two chains*, v. 33). The mob had responded to the fanatical cries of the Asiatics without really understanding the case, thus no coherent account of the cause of the attack could be given (v. 34). This had its favorable aspect for Paul, since it became necessary to remove him to the Tower for examination. The Jews had ceased their beating of Paul on the arrival of the soldiers, but they did not cease their verbal abuse as he was being taken away (v. 36). The menace of the crowding mob was such that the soldiers actually carried Paul (v. 35).

37–40. A Favor Asked and Granted. Paul was by no means a passive prisoner. As soon as possible he addressed the captain in Greek: *May I speak?* The captain's reply shows his surprise that Paul did not address him in Aramæan, the language of the Judæan Jews. The situation invited further questions and favored the prisoner at least for the moment. Paul explained that he was a citizen of Tarsus (v. 39), but it does not appear why he withheld information about his Roman citizenship until later (22^{25}). Even in his earnest desire to speak to the people in his own defense Paul could not resist the impulse to speak well of his home city (v. 39). It was not agreeable to Paul to be mistaken for an Egyptian Jewish criminal whom the guard supposed he had arrested (v. 38). Josephus tells of this Jew, whose home was in Egypt, and who gathered many followers (Josephus says 30,000) in an abortive attempt to capture Jerusalem. The attempt occurred during the procuratorship of Felix, somewhere between 52 and 60 A.D., but, of course, before Paul's arrest, which occurred probably in 58. Paul asked leave to address his pursuers, and, his request granted, turned on the stairway (v. 40) and, using the familiar language of the Judæan Jews, began to speak.

CHAPTER XXII

1–21. Paul's Defense. No merely selfish motive led to the request of Paul. A few words might quiet the tumult. He might reassure them as to the new movement, about which they were so misinformed (21^{21}). All that Paul would have said is not known, for his address was rudely interrupted at the mention of the hated word *Gentiles* (v. 21) and no further opportunity to address the Jews of Jerusalem ever again offered itself. His address as here given contains the second account in Acts of the apostle's conversion (cf. 9$^{1-9}$ 26$^{12-23}$.)

The crowd obeyed his gesture for silence (21^{40}) and became attentive when they heard the Aramæan language. I am about to offer you my defense, Paul declared (vv. 1f.). This was quite necessary, for many of those present thought he was an enemy of all that was Jewish, perhaps that he himself had no right to be in the Temple. Their law threatened death to all who entered the holy place illegally. The address first established Paul's Jewish nationality and education (v. 3), then gave an account of his eager and zealous persecution of *the Way*, even in distant cities (vv. 4f.), and narrated vividly the vision on the road (v. 6) and the subsequent experiences (vv. 7–13), until Ananias of Damascus interpreted the experience as one granted by *the God of the fathers* (v. 14), whereupon Paul had returned to Jerusalem (v. 17) and was praying in this very Temple, when God spoke to him in a vision, declaring that he was to go to the Gentiles. Here the address broke off. Had he been allowed to go on, no doubt Paul would have recounted some of his conquests on heathen soil which had so stirred and convinced the more enlightened Jews (see 14^{27,} 21$^{19f.}$). His later words in 26$^{18-20,\ 22,\ 23}$ form the substance of such a sequel as might have appeared after v. 21 had Paul not been interrupted.

In detail, the address was admirably designed to conciliate the Jews. Paul's religious training had been at the hands of a great master, in the Holy City itself, in full accord with tradition. Paul was as fully in sympathy with the ancient Law as any of his assailants, and he knew it better than most of them (v. 3). He had felt as they did against the followers of Jesus and had persecuted them, to which the high priest himself could witness (vv. 4f.). True, the speaker was no longer a persecutor of *the Way*, because God himself had shown through an undoubted vision that he should become rather the apostle of the new movement (vv. 6–21). A comparison of this account of Paul's conversion with 9$^{3-9}$ shows no more than one discrepancy of note. In 9^{7} "the men . . . with him stood speechless, hearing the voice but beholding no man." Here (v. 9), Paul says: *They that were with me . . . heard not the voice of him that spake to me.* The verb "to hear" often bears the sense of "to understand," as in 1 Cor. 14^{2} Mk. 4^{33}, where the same verb is variously translated in R.V. Luke would see no real discrepancy between his accounts. He meant to say that Paul was the only man in the company who heard intelligible words. So also the statement (26^{14}) that all had "fallen to the earth" collides verbally with the expression, "the men . . . stood speechless" (9^{7}), yet the author is satisfied to let them stand unharmonized. It is fair to say that in all essentials the three accounts of Paul's conversion fully agree with one another.

22–29. Paul in the Tower of Antonia. At mention of the Gentiles the Jews uttered incoherent cries (v. 22a). Some who phrased their horror declared that Paul was not fit to live. In their frenzy they threw garments about and filled the air with dust (v. 23), typical Oriental expressions of rage and horror. If the Roman officer did not understand Paul's Aramæan speech, the outburst of the Jews convinced him that torture alone would elicit the facts (v. 24). Paul would surely have been beaten with the thongs (v. 25) had he not made known his Roman citizenship.

The centurion conferred a favor upon the tribune (*chief captain*) when he promptly reported Paul's question (v. 26). The tribune, who had already broken the law in ordering Paul to be bound, found to his surprise that Paul was *free born*, i.e., had the right of citizenship by virtue of his father's citizenship, while he, Claudius Lysias (23[6]), had *purchased* the privilege (v. 28). But the discovery that Paul was a Roman did not explain to Lysias why the Jews had so nearly killed him. To obtain the facts he decided to inquire of the highest court of the Jews.

CHAPTER XXIII

1. Paul Before the Sanhedrin. The Sanhedrin summoned (see 22[30]), Paul addressed them forthwith. The council was expected to explain to the Roman officer the nature of Paul's offense. The conclusion that the Jewish authorities themselves were none too clear about the charge against Paul is based on their desire to hear Paul before writing their decision. Such a decision would be an official document, which, if the situation required it, Lysias could forward to Rome. Not only here, but in chs. 24–26, the Romans appear in great doubt as to how to phrase the charge against Paul. At times they confess that he is technically guilty of no fault (25[25] 26[31f.]).

2–10. Paul Again Rescued. The council meeting was called by the Roman captain, who kept watch over the proceedings (v. 10). Paul's address was never completed as planned, for he no sooner affirmed that his conscience was clear (v. 1) than the high priest commanded attendants forcibly to silence him. This indignity Paul resented (v. 3) with such forceful words that he found himself in contempt of court (v. 4) from which situation an apology rescued him for the moment. But Paul still stood upon his rights to a fair trial (v. 3b). Why Paul did not know that the presiding officer was high priest is unaccountable (v. 5). The versatile apostle immediately changed his course and addressed the assembly again: *I am being tried because I believe in a resurrection!* (V. 6.) This threw the Pharisees and Sadducees into active discussion, and although the Pharisees in the council moved to exonerate Paul (v. 9), the Sadducees (the majority) so set upon the prisoner that he was forcibly rescued again by the Roman guard and carried to the Tower (v. 10). From this deliberative body Lysias saw he could expect no great light.

11. Encouraged by a Vision. To Paul, visions were real appearances of God or of his messengers. They revealed to him the will or purpose of God (see 16[9] 18[9f.] 27[23f.]). As in the present case, times of discouragement or of crisis were occasions for visions. The night after his second rescue from his would-be murderers the Lord (Jesus) reassured Paul that he should at length see Rome.

12–32. Paul Secretly Transferred to Cæsarea. A plot to assassinate the apostle was discovered by Paul's nephew and made known to Claudius Lysias (vv. 16–21), who had become friendly toward his prisoner. Lysias bound the lad to secrecy and at once made preparations to transfer his prisoner to the protection of the governor, Felix, at Cæsarea (vv. 22–24). The proposal of the council (vv. 14f.) was never actually made to Lysias.

A strong body-guard composed of four hundred foot-soldiers and seventy horsemen escorted Paul to Cæsarea. From Antipatris (about half-way to Cæsarea, at the foot of the Judæan hills, northeast of Joppa), the seventy horsemen went on with Paul while the infantry turned back to Jerusalem. The letter of Claudius Lysias to Felix is the second typical Greek letter given in Acts (see 15[23-29]). The conventional word *Greeting* opens the letter in each instance, but here the concluding formula, *Farewell*, does not appear in the best texts (but see mg.). The letter itself (vv. 26–30) is in direct and precise style. Lysias says that he rescued Paul *because he had learned that he was a Roman* (v. 27), which scarcely corresponds to fact. The text of the letter is an admirable summary of the events detailed in 21[27]–23[24]. The last statement in the letter (v. 30b) concerns directions given to Paul's accusers after his departure from Jerusalem.

33–35. Imprisoned at Cæsarea. The guard delivered Paul safely at Cæsarea and presented the letter of Lysias to Antonius Felix, the procurator. No ceremony marked the event. Formal inquiry was made as to Paul's residence, quarters were assigned him in the Prætorium, and the formal hearing was deferred until the arrival of the accusers. The citizenship of Paul was recognized, his rights were safeguarded, and Roman law was for the time satisfied.

Paul spent two years in Cæsarea under Felix (24[27]) and a further period, not well defined by Luke, under Festus (see 25[1-3, 21], 27[1]). The period of imprisonment in Cæsarea was probably much in excess of two years.

CHAPTER XXIV

1–9. The Judæan Jews at Cæsarea. The high priest, with selected members of the Sanhedrin, prepared to win the good graces of Felix through the offices of a professional orator, Tertullus (v. 1). The hearing began on the fourth day after Paul's arrival. The speech of Tertullus is conventional, too full of flattery for the reader but not for the particular hearer addressed. History does not agree with Tertullus that Felix was a good ruler. (See Josephus, *Antiquities*, bk. xx, ch. 8: 5–8; *Jewish Wars*, bk. ii, ch. 13: 2–6.) The charges of Tertullus against Paul were as extravagant and as general as his praise of Felix (vv. 5–8). The case for the accusers was closed by a general approval of the words of the orator (v. 9).

10–21. Paul's Defense. Using no compliments, but recognizing the experience of Felix in the law, Paul stated the points that proved his innocence. He left Cæsarea for Jerusalem less than a fortnight before (v. 11). The time was inadequate for such wrongs as were charged against him. The real accusers, those *Jews from Asia* (21[27]), Paul urged, did not come down to Cæsarea (v. 19), yet all they could testify to would be the fact that Paul was in the Temple, engaged in worship, and that, too, after bringing alms and offerings to the Jews (v. 17). Turning to the accusers present (v. 20) Paul demanded that they show evidence to support their charges. The only real cause for complaint was, Paul declared, that he said, in the presence of the council: *I am being tried because I believe in a resurrection!* (Cf. 23[6b].)

22, 23. Felix Delays a Decision. The legal reason for postponing a decision in Paul's case lay in the absence of Claudius Lysias (v. 22b), but a secondary reason is found in the fact that Felix knew about the movement called *the Way.* (See 9[2b] 19[9, 23] 22[4] 24[14]; cf. 18[25f.] *the way of the Lord.*) This insight enabled Felix to discern the injustice of the charges against Paul. Felix showed Paul favors, admitting his friends to visit him (v. 23) and permitting a degree of freedom. That other Roman officials treated Paul thus indulgently is shown in 28[16, 30f].

24–27. Two Years of Imprisonment. Felix did not forget Paul, yet in the two years that followed the hearing at Cæsarea (vv. 1–21) his decision was still undeclared. The first of a series of private hearings is detailed in vv. 24f. Paul took the opportunity to impress Felix with the ethical message of Christianity, emphasizing *righteousness*, or the right way of life, *self-control*, a cardinal Christian virtue, and *the judgment* or the great day of decision, when the Judge of all men would delay his decision no more (v. 25). The message made Felix tremble, but his cupidity overcame his fears. He still hoped for a bribe from Paul to hasten his favorable decision (v. 26). The expensive litigation in which Paul was engaged must have cast the apostle upon his own resources. If, as surmised, Paul worked his way during the two years in Rome (see under 28[30]), he may also have done this in Cæsarea. Or he may have inherited money.

The successor of Felix, Porcius Festus, found Paul after two years still a prisoner, officially neither guilty nor innocent (v. 27); Felix had left him thus to placate the Jews, having his own advantage in mind.

CHAPTER XXV

1–12. The Appeal to Cæsar. As the new procurator of Judæa, Festus promptly visited Jerusalem (v. 1) seeking the good will of the Jews. When Paul's old enemies requested a new trial at Jerusalem Festus diplomatically refused (v. 4), possibly suspecting their sincerity. A week or more later (v. 6) in the presence of his accusers (v. 7) Paul had his first hearing before Festus. The charges, as deduced from Paul's answer (v. 8), were that he had transgressed the Jewish law, that he had defiled the Temple, and that he was politically dangerous. When Festus showed a disposition to transfer him to Jerusalem for trial (v. 9) Paul took strong ground in his own defense, and demanded a decisive trial before Cæsar as his right (v. 11b). This demand was disconcerting both to Festus and the Jews, yet their course had made it necessary. The sequel shows with what difficulty Festus formulated a charge of sufficient definiteness and weight to justify his transfer of the prisoner to Rome. After conference with his legal counselors it appeared that the appeal was admissible (v. 12), and Festus acceded to Paul's demand.

13–22. Agrippa Hears About Paul. Somewhere near the beginning of the procuratorship of Festus, Marcus Julius Agrippa II made an official visit at Cæsarea. With him was Bernice, his sister (and also sister of Drusilla, the wife of Felix). During the visit Paul's case was discussed, perhaps because Agrippa had a deep interest in Jewish questions. Festus asked counsel of Agrippa, reviewing the details of the case as he knew it (vv. 14b–21), whereupon Agrippa professed a desire to hear him

(v. 22). Festus promptly arranged a hearing for the next day.

23–27. A New Hearing Opened. The hearing before Agrippa was not a trial, but an occasion of great pomp, which notables (v. 23b) attended to counsel with Festus as to how to frame the accusation against Paul. (See the opening words of Festus, vv. 24–27.)

CHAPTER XXVI

1–23. Paul Addresses Agrippa. Although Festus officially presided, Agrippa signaled Paul to speak. Agrippa alone was addressed. Paul expressed a genuine satisfaction at the prospect of declaring himself before a man who was familiar with Judaism (v. 2). For he was about to show that in his adherence to *the Way* he was not, after all, disloyal to the principles of his ancestral religion (vv. 3, 7). V. 5 in no way affirms that Paul's Pharisaism was of the past only. In 23[6] Paul said: "I am a Pharisee," which was as though he said: "Religiously, I am orthodox." (Vv. 6f.). In regard to the particular question of the resurrection (v. 8; cf. 25[19]), Paul affirmed the soundness of his position. His crusade as persecutor of *the Way* (vv. 10f.) furnished the occasion for the real appearance of the risen Jesus to him (vv. 12–15; cf. 9[3-5] 22[6-8]). Paul had persecuted Christians in other foreign cities than Damascus (v. 11), although Acts gives no account of these expeditions. Paul said of the Christians whom he persecuted to death that *he gave his vote against them* when they were condemned (v. 10). Practically, the same statement occurs in 8[1], "Saul was consenting to his death" (cf. 22[20]). No evidence appears here to show that Paul was at any time a member of the Sanhedrin. According to a reliable tradition, supported by the gospel narrative of Jesus' trial, the Jewish court was not allowed to affix the death penalty upon any criminal.

In vv. 12–18 is an expanded narrative of Paul's conversion experience, showing some verbal differences, yet with no essential discrepancy. Here no command to go into Damascus is expressed, but the words in vv. 17f. remind one of the words of Ananias (9[15f.]), spoken to Paul the third day after his vision. (See under 22[1-21].) The mention of the *Hebrew language* (v. 14) is peculiarly intimate. The deepest religious experiences are best expressed in one's mother tongue. So the revelation to Paul seemed to be expressed in Aramæan, the language especially dear to Jewish hearts (cf. 22[2]). Paul would naturally explain to Agrippa his motive for missionary work among the Gentiles, since his contact with Gentiles was a grievance to the Jews (see 21[21] 24[5]). Hence Paul briefly describes his loyalty to the vision in Damascus, at Jerusalem and in Judæa (v. 20) and among the nations (Gentiles), offering this course as the basis of the attack and the charges of the Jews (v. 21), notwithstanding which, affirmed Paul, *I am honestly declaring only that which the Jewish faith holds* (vv. 22f.). Here Paul quotes no O.T. text to support his statement that Moses foretold the resurrection of Messiah. He uses the term *Moses* for "the Scriptures" generally, and is thinking possibly of Isa. 53. The thought is that of v. 6 at the beginning of his speech.

24–29. Festus Interrupts the Prisoner. Although the belief of Paul in the resurrection was not new to Festus, the address (of which Luke has given a mere outline) seemed to move the governor, who interrupted the speaker to accuse him of raving (v. 24). The self-control of the apostle appeared adequate in his polite address to the *most excellent Festus* (v. 25) as he protested his complete sanity, pointing out the wealth of facts which must have convinced Festus himself. Then Paul appealed to King Agrippa, rightly assuming his loyalty to the Hebrew prophets (vv. 26f.), and would have pursued his advantage had not Agrippa in turn interrupted the apostle with that protest so difficult of interpretation: *Paul, with few words thou art indeed persuading me to be a Christian* (v. 28). This is the plainest sense of the text in the best MSS. The words may be ironical or they may have been spoken seriously. Surely, no one can doubt that Paul himself hoped for the conversion of Agrippa. With the insight into Judaism that Agrippa had it would not be impossible for him to become persuaded that Jesus was Messiah. The answer of Paul supports this plain interpretation. In substance the answer of Paul was: "Under any circumstances I earnestly wish that Agrippa and all others here were sharing my experience, excepting only my experience as prisoner."

30–32. A Private Judgment. Paul was not permitted further to speak. The evidence sufficed to enable Festus to formulate an official accusation, and the prisoner had directed his address too searchingly at King Agrippa. The latter fact caused the abrupt ending of the hearing. Agrippa did not become a Christian, but his words (v. 32) indicate a sympathetic attitude toward Paul. Both Festus and the king agreed (v. 31b) that only Paul's appeal to Cæsar warranted his being kept a prisoner. It is not certain that Paul would at this time have been liberated if he had not appealed, although it was apparent even to Felix, before the appeal, that Paul was no criminal (see 24[27]).

CHAPTER XXVII

1–12. Embarked for Rome. The last two chapters of Acts contain one of the most circumstantial accounts of travel on the Mediterranean Sea in the first Christian century known to modern readers. Although Luke has given no account of any other voyage of Paul, the apostle's own statement (2 Cor. 11^{25b}) accounts for much of his insight and experience shown during the dangerous moments of this voyage. The long section 27^{1}–28^{16} comprises the fourth and last *we-section.* Some weeks or even months after the hearing before Agrippa, arrangements were perfected to send Paul, with a number of other prisoners, on to Rome. The centurion, Julius, who with a detachment of soldiers (see v. 42), had the prisoners in charge, probably commanded one of the five cohorts stationed at Cæsarea. Since no vessel sailing directly for Italy was at hand, a convenient ship, hailing from Adramyttium, on the west coast of Asia Minor, and homeward bound, was used for part of the voyage. Paul had at least two companions, Luke, the author of the *we-narrative,* and Aristarchus of Thessalonica, who accompanied him voluntarily (v. 2). The course of the vessel was first north, along the coast to Sidon (v. 3), where Paul was allowed the privilege of disembarking to enjoy the hospitality of friends. This is the first mention of the church in Sidon, although in the neighboring city of Tyre ($21^{3f.}$) Paul had been entertained on his way to Jerusalem. A stay of several days may have been made at Sidon. From Sidon the course lay north of Cyprus, then west between Cyprus and Cilicia (v. 5) to obtain protection from opposing winds (v. 4), to Myra, on the coast of Lycia (see map). The ship of Adramyttium from this point could not be of further use. Her destination lay to the north. A ship from Alexandria, in Egypt, on the way to Italy, carrying passengers (v. 37) and grain (v. 38), was chosen by the centurion for the completion of the voyage (v. 6). Thus the party continued the voyage westward along the shore of Asia Minor, meeting unfavorable winds (v. 7) and suffering delay. From Cnidus, at the southwest corner of Asia, the course changed to the southwest, toward the island of Crete. The wind made impossible the desirable course directly westward. After a difficult time the ship reached the place called Fair Havens, near the city of Lasea, on the south coast of Crete (v. 8). A long stay in this harbor added to the delay already experienced, and October came, for *the Fast* (v. 9) was already gone by. (*Yom Kippur*, 10th of Tisri, Lev. 16^{29-31} 23^{26-32}.) The conditions always made navigation after this season dangerous. Between November and March shipping was at a standstill.

At this point (v. 9) Paul appeared as adviser to the ship's officers, probably through the friendly Roman centurion, Julius (v. 11). On the basis of his own experience on the sea Paul strongly advised that they remain for the winter in Fair Havens, at the same time criticizing the policy of delay that had prevailed (v. 9b). Not only the master of the vessel had to be consulted, but the owner himself, who was on board (v. 11). These both opposed Paul's advice, and the centurion, who was actually in command (cf. vv. 42f.), ordered the vessel put to sea. The objective was Phœnix, a port near the southwest corner of Crete (v. 12). Phœnix would offer a more comfortable harbor for the winter. The difficult expression *looking northeast and southeast* is believed to mean that the land inclosing the harbor sheltered vessels from winds blowing from those directions.

13–15. The Storm. The departure from Fair Havens was under favorable conditions. But the gentle south wind (v. 13) was only a "weather-breeder." The course toward Phoenix was toward the northwest, and although the high land would protect the vessel from the north wind for part of the way, some open water threatened them when crossing the Gulf of Messaria. (See Ramsay, art., "Phœnix," Hastings' *Dictionary of the Bible,* vol. iii, p. 862.) If Phoenix stood on the site of the modern Lutro, at least twelve hours would be required for the voyage, long enough to arouse apprehension in the mind of an experienced traveler. Phœnix was not reached. Soon after the ship left Fair Havens cautiously sailing along the shore (v. 13b), it encountered a severe windstorm (v. 14), probably a "northeaster," as the context shows. The force of the Mediterranean winds and waves was terrific. This large vessel (see under v. 37) was unable to face such a wind as *Euraquilo* and was driven before it (v. 15) until it came under the shelter of a small island, Cauda (or Clauda, mg.), which lies twenty miles south of Cape Matala, the southernmost promontory of Crete (v. 16), around which cape the vessel had sailed soon after leaving Fair Havens.

16, 17. The Ship Re-enforced. Under the lee (on the south side) of the island of Cauda two necessary precautions were taken. First of all, the small boat, usually lashed to the stern above the water level, was brought on board. The difficulty encountered (v. 16) was due to the fact that the boat was filled with water and also because, even in the more quiet water, this operation required strength and patience. This boat was later (v. 30) sacrificed when the sailors lowered it under false pretense. The second precaution involved strengthening the ship itself against the stress of wave action and shifting cargo, which would bring unusual pressure upon the keel. Ropes were bound around the vessel, under the keel and over the deck (v. 17), the ropes being lowered over the bow and carried back to the desired point, then lashed tight.

The direction of the wind was such that the ship's crew feared lest the gale should drive them upon the *Syrtes Major*, fearful sandbars along the north African coast (v. 17b), and to guard against this the spread of sail was reduced; i.e., only storm sails were used. The words *they lowered the gear* (v. 17b) may mean that a sort of drag was employed to retard the motion of the vessel.

18–26. The Peril and the Vision. Despite all precautions, the outlook for the people on the boat was dark. Much water was taken on board and the slow process of bailing had little effect. Pumps were then unknown to navigators. The second day of driving before the wind found the crew throwing overboard some of the cargo, to lighten the vessel (v. 18). On the third day *with their own hands* (v. 19), i.e., aided by the passengers, the ship's company threw out even things like utensils, perhaps baggage (see mg., *furniture*). Even the mariners were lost when neither sun, moon, nor stars appeared for days to determine their location (v. 20). As the storm still continued, all became despondent and even lost desire for food (v. 21a). If Paul had his despondent period, as is possible, he became full of hope when an angel of God appeared to him. Immediately (v. 23, *this night*) the apostle brought his message of cheer to his companions, but not without a note of triumph over those who had rejected his advice. Loss of property is inevitable, he said (v. 22), but no life will be the price of reckless adventure. An angel of my God appeared to me to-night assuring me that I shall yet appear before Cæsar (v. 24). We shall not be cast on the Syrtes, but upon an island (v. 26). The precise *method* in which this divine message came to Paul can only be conjectured, but the event proved the truth of his belief.

27–44. The Shipwreck. Two weeks after leaving Fair Havens, one night the lookout detected signs of land (v. 27) and hove the lead repeatedly to discover how rapidly the land was drawing near to them. The depth of water decreased so rapidly that they feared being cast upon the rocks in the darkness and cast out four anchors from the stern, hoping they would hold at least till daylight (vv. 28f). The anchors could not be cast from the bow, else the ship must have foundered in the trough of the sea as it swung around. Paul, alert as any on the vessel, intercepted the plot of the sailors to escape in the boat (v. 30). With the boat cut away (v. 32) nothing could be done until dawn. Here Paul again assumed the rôle of adviser and urged that food be prepared, since their fast had endured for the fortnight (v. 33). They had not gone without food entirely for that period, but it had been sparsely and irregularly served. With a word of cheer to the ship's company (v. 34b) and offering thanksgiving to God before them all (v. 35), Paul took food and they all followed his example. The number of people on the vessel is impressive—a total of two hundred seventy-six (v. 37). After the meal the desire to be active in some way was satisfied when they took part in the final lightening of the ship, throwing overboard the rest of the cargo (v. 38), a task begun twelve days before (v. 18). This was desirable since they must drive the ship as near as possible to land when the hawsers were cut. The outcome justified the measure. At early dawn, no one recognized the land before them. Noting a bay with a beach, the steering oars, which had been tightly lashed, were made ready, the foresail was hoisted, the hawsers at the stern were cut and the steersman directed the course toward the beach (vv. 39f.). Lightened as the ship was, still the prow struck upon a sand bar and held fast while the stern began to break up under the battering of the waves (v. 41). Nothing now remained but to make for the shore as each one could. Disorder did not prevail. The centurion gave orders which were obeyed by all; the prisoners with all others either swam or drifted on planks to the shore, and when the muster-roll was called all were found safely on land (vv. 42–44).

CHAPTER XXVIII

1–10. The Winter on Malta. The island proved to be Malta, an island about eighty miles south of Sicily. The inhabitants are here called *barbarians* because they did not use the Greek language. The English word "natives" is quite exact, without implying that the Maltese were uncultured. The expression *no common kindness* (v. 2) reveals the expectation of less hospitable treatment and records the gratitude of the rescued. Paul found himself gathering twigs for fuel, and, thus engaged, was bitten by a viper. The phrase *fastened on* means "thrust his fangs into." The sequel plainly shows that in the judgment of the onlookers the snake was of a poisonous variety, for (v. 4) they expected a fatal outcome. Paul did not share their fear; his demeanor was calm as he disposed of the snake, and his own expectation was fulfilled. The event emphasizes Paul's implicit trust in God, which cast out all fear. The quaint philosophy of the Maltese as expressed in their change of point of view, was not peculiar to them (vv. 4–6). Human experience testifies that justice does not always triumph promptly. Their later conclusion that Paul was a god resembled that of the inhabitants of Lystra (14^{12}). Here (v. 6) it is not said that Paul rebuked the people for their view. The sojourn of the apostle in Malta is sparingly described. The centurion, his soldiers, the crew, the master and the owner of the ill-fated vessel are all disregarded. Aside from Paul's remarkable escape from the serpent, another miracle is narrated (v. 8), and other miracles of healing are mentioned (vv. 7–10). (On these miracles, see art., *N.T. Miracles*, p. 926.) Publius, the ruler of the island (representing the Roman government), extended generous hospitality to Paul and Luke (*we*), and perhaps to Aristarchus. It would be strange thus to honor a prisoner, who must have been chained to a Roman soldier according to regulations. The incident of the snake may have given Paul this prestige. (See 24^{23} 27^{3} and note the manner in which Paul's advice, certainly not unasked, had been received by the Romans, 27^{10}.)

It is Luke's purpose, in narrating the wonders that accompanied Paul's activity in Malta, to exhibit the inherent power of the gospel even in a wholly un-Jewish environment. From Jesus' day the apostles had practiced the healing of diseases.

11–15. The Voyage to Rome Ended. For three months Paul and his companions enjoyed the hospitality of the people of Malta, awaiting the opportunity to make their way to Rome. Another vessel of Alexandria, which had made a more fortunate choice of a harbor in which to winter (v. 11), would transport at least the prisoners, for the centurion was bound to deliver them all safely at Rome. The *sign* of the vessel was, after the manner of that time, an image or painting on the bow. In this case it consisted of Castor and Pollux, "the twin," favorite deities of seamen (v. 11).

The first port out of Malta was Syracuse, on the southeast coast of Sicily (v. 12), where a stay of three days, for trade or waiting for a favorable wind, ensued. Thence the route lay between Sicily and the tip of Italy, with a stop overnight at Rhegium (*after one day*, v. 13). A favoring wind took them to Puteoli, somewhat over two hundred miles north of Rhegium. This was the destination of the vessel, and the rest of the journey to Rome was by land (v. 13b). At Puteoli they found *brethren* (v. 14), i.e., Christians, who wished to entertain Paul for a week. Whether this wish was fulfilled or not rested with the centurion. *And so we came to Rome* (v. 14). Thus briefly is the fulfillment of Paul's desire to see Rome expressed! The sentence is anticipatory, for Puteoli was one hundred and thirty miles from Rome and the *we-writer* yet describes the welcome offered to Paul by the Christians of Rome, some of whom came out forty miles to meet the apostolic party at the Market of Appius, while others waited at the Three Taverns, thirty miles out of the city. This tribute touched Paul very deeply. He had written an important letter to these Christians several years before, but had never seen them.

16–31. Paul in Rome Two Years. Acts gives no account of the trial of Paul at Rome. Certainly, the trial had not taken place after two years (v. 30), during which time Paul lived under relatively comfortable conditions, renting a house (v. 30), calling in various people whom he wished to see (vv. 17, 23, 30), but chained to a soldier guard (vv. 16, 20). The fact that Paul was able to hire his own dwelling indicates that he had means. It is possible he continued to work at his trade. The generous treatment accorded him arose possibly from the service that Paul had rendered during the voyage, but more likely from the nature of the report and accusation sent by Festus. In the light of the verdict at Cæsarea ($26^{31f.}$) there is no reason to suppose that Paul's trial resulted in his execution. Probably after the long delay to which almost all processes of law are subject, then as now, Paul was set at liberty for further activity (cf. p. 1275b). One incident of that two years, narrated by Luke (vv. 17–28), is weighty. Paul improved his earliest opportunity to meet the prominent non-Christian Jews of the city and present to them his gospel. He could not go to them, but they came to his dwelling. The edict of Claudius issued some ten years before (18^{2}) was no longer in force, and the Jewish synagogues as well as the Christian church in Rome were active as before. On the third day of his stay in Rome the leaders, probably the rulers of the synagogue, were thus addressed by the apostle (vv. 17b–20):

"I am a prisoner here through the accusation of my fellow countrymen, although I am fully innocent of any wrong to them, or of any violation of our law. I am in the custody of Rome in self-defense, for I was compelled to appeal in order to save my life, not that I accuse my own folk. For the Romans would have set me free, but the Jews objected." It will be noticed that here Paul placed the decision of Festus and Agrippa *before* his appeal. The narrative of Luke does not so place it (see 24^{24-27} 25^{9-12} 26^{30-32}).

The Jews answered: "You are, of course, a member of this sect against which we hear so much said. However, we have not had any report, oral or written, about you. We shall be glad to hear your views from your own lips" (vv. 21f).

A day was then set, upon which a much larger number of Jews came to hear Paul (v. 23a), who explained his view of the kingdom of God and quoted from the Law and the prophets to support his claim that Jesus is the Messiah. The session lasted all day (v. 23). This mission of Paul, carried on under such remarkable conditions, resulted in a division of his hearers. Some believed, others did not (v. 24). To the latter Paul delivered a parting shot as they withdrew, probably with some feeling: "You deserve to hear that rebuke administered by Isaiah to your fathers (see Isa. $6^{9f.}$). For the prophet knew that the people to whom he spoke would not really hear nor clearly understand. They were preoccupied with their own affairs. Their ears were deaf. It was as if they were afraid they would hear and profit by the inspired words. Since you will not believe the message," said Paul, "take comfort in the thought that the Gentiles will hear. And the Gentiles *shall* hear this word!" (Vv. 25–28.) The mg. of v. 29 records the statement that the Jews left Paul disagreeing among themselves.

The Conclusion. It has been thought by many that the closing paragraph of the book (vv. 30, 31) is abrupt and unfinished. Some argue from this that Luke carried his story as far as his material permitted, i.e., that he wrote Acts early in the 60's while Paul was still a prisoner at Rome. This is hardly in accord with what is known about the date of the Gospel, which must have been written earlier than Acts. (See art., *Formation of N.T.*, p. 857a; cf. also pp. 1022–3.) The closing paragraph of Acts is no more abrupt than the corresponding paragraph of Luke's Gospel. The style of the writer, not a shortage of material, dictates the form of the conclusion. (Cf. Lk. 24^{50-53}.)

Paul paid his own expenses while in Rome (see under 24^{26}), as had been his rule throughout his ministry. As he last appears in Acts the apostle was quite free to preach, teach, and receive visitors without hindrance from the Romans or from the Jews (vv. 30f.).

ROMANS

By Professor C. ANDERSON SCOTT

Introduction

Place of the Epistle Among Paul's Writings. This Epistle stands first among Paul's writings in our N.T., but that is not because it is the earliest of his letters which have come down to us. According to the generally accepted dates there are five earlier Epistles: two to the Thessalonians, two to the Corinthians, and one to the Galatians. This Epistle owes its position to the early recognition of its outstanding importance, and possibly to the importance of the church to which it was addressed. It is distinguished from the others by a comprehensiveness of treatment, a breadth of application, and a general objectivity of outlook which give it more the character of a treatise than of a letter (cf. p. 941). That it was the work of the apostle Paul there is no reason to doubt; any denial of his authorship which has been made may be reckoned an eccentricity of criticism. It was written from Corinth at a date which is variously estimated by different authorities between the years 54 and 58 A.D. Paul was by this time "in the late afternoon of his career." He had been for more than twenty years a missionary of the gospel, and had only some six (or ten) years of his course to run. Concerning the first fourteen years of his life and activities as a servant of Christ we know little or nothing. Then he suddenly emerges from obscurity (cf. Acts 11[25] 13[1f.]), and from that time onward, through the Acts and through his Epistles, we have an opportunity of knowing his career and his character, to which antiquity offers but few parallels.

The Church at Rome. In writing to the Romans Paul was writing to a church which he had never visited, one in whose founding he had had no part. And down to the end of ch. 14 the style and tone of the letter are in harmony with this fact. He writes as a stranger would write to strangers, making no allusion to anything particular in their history or circumstances. That he uses Greek in writing to a community at Rome need not surprise us in view of the fact that it was only at the end of the second century that the language of worship at Rome was changed from Greek to Latin. There has been much discussion as to the composition of the church at Rome, some having maintained that its members were wholly or predominantly of the Jewish race, others that they were wholly or predominantly of Gentile origin. It is now agreed that both Jews and Gentiles had contributed to its membership, and that neither section greatly predominated.

Purpose and Character of the Epistle. The discussion on the composition of the church at Rome had significance for its bearing on the purpose and character of the Epistle. So long as the impression prevailed that the letter was polemical in character it was important to ascertain which of the two sections of the community Paul was arguing with or against. But it was probably an initial mistake to regard the letter as polemical or even controversial. It is really *declaratory and persuasive.* Its purpose is to declare the great mercies of God in Jesus Christ, to show both the necessity and the validity of a salvation the sole conditions of which are the free grace of God and the response of faith in man, and then to draw practical inferences for the conduct of those who had accepted the unsearchable riches of Christ. And so far as persuasion enters into the apostle's purpose, it is not (in the first eight chapters) either Jewish Christians, or Gentile Christians whom he has in view, but the Jews, or a typical Jew, who had not yet believed. The Epistle is written under the strong consciousness of the wonderful work which God had wrought in providing for men, both Jews and Gentiles, a righteousness which was not their own, but with a subconsciousness that the Jews as a whole were still standing aloof. This leads him time and again to be diverted from the direct current of his thought to consider an objection which is raised or might conceivably be raised by the Jew. Such objections are, "But *we* do not need righteousness like the Gentiles." "But we have our own divinely appointed means of securing righteousness, through the Law." "But Abraham was only justified because he showed his faith by his works." "But are you not encouraging men to remain in sin?" Or, "Are you not coming perilously near to treating the Law itself as if it were sin?" With each of these objections Paul deals patiently and hopefully. It is so clear to him that since the death of Christ a new era has begun, that all the Jew had ever hoped for and more is now open to his acceptance on the sole condition of faith, the faith which becomes operative by love, uniting the believer to God in Jesus Christ, that he cannot conceive how men can be blind to it. From every such excursion he returns to his theme, *The Gospel as a Divine Force unto Salvation*, a message of free and emancipating forgiveness, the full contents of which he expands in ch. 8. But the sub-theme which has also been present to his mind again asserts itself, and the problem of *the Jew and his future* has to be faced and settled (chs. 9–11) before he can proceed finally to show how salvation finds expression in life, conduct, and character. The letter differs from some other Epistles, like those to Corinth or Galatia, in that it does not reflect or respond to anything specific in the circumstances or the internal life of the community which he is addressing. It differs also in that we find here a sustained and continuous treatment of one great theme, salvation, its root and its fruit. But it does not differ from any of the others, in that the motive of it is the positive exposition of the mercies of God in Christ (cf. pp. 855, 936–7, 941),

Problem of the Closing Chapters. The last two chapters raise problems of their own, which will be found clearly set out and authoritatively discussed in Lake's *Earlier Epistles of St. Paul*. There is a considerable amount of ancient evidence, and that of a varied character, that this Epistle circulated toward the end of the second century in two forms or recensions. One of these stopped at 14^{23}, with or without the doxology, 16^{25-27}; the other was in the form preserved in our N.T. There is also early evidence of the existence of a text which omitted the words "in Rome" in both places where they occur in ch. 1, thus leaving the Epistle without any indication of the church to which it was addressed. This textual evidence finds confirmation when the contents of chs. 15 and 16 are examined. In $15^{14f.}$ we feel for the first time that the apostle is addressing a definite group of people and his travel-plans, which are there explained, point to Rome as their probable abode. 16^{1-23} stands by itself. It has long been felt to be very unlikely that Paul should have in Rome so many acquaintances as those to whom he here sends greeting. And it is not only that he knows their names; with many of them he has evidently been in close personal contact. Two of them have shared with him in some imprisonment. Others have worked with him. The mother of Rufus has been "a mother to me also." The reference to Epænetus as the "first-fruits of Asia" would be more natural in a letter to Asia than to Rome. Moreover, vv. 17–20a strike a note of concern and warning for which the rest of the Epistle leaves us quite unprepared, and uses a tone of authority which is hardly to be expected if Paul were writing to Christians who had never seen him. It is highly probable that in this chapter (16^{1-23}) we have preserved a note sent by Paul to the church at Ephesus in order to commend Phœbe to its care, and reflecting in the many greetings it contains his affectionate interest in individuals whom he knew there, as well as (17–20a) his anxiety about certain dangers which he knew to be threatening that church.

There remains the problem of ch. 15. Bishop Lightfoot (though he still maintained that 16^{1-23} was part of the original letter) thought it probable that Paul, having written and sent the Epistle as we have it to Rome, subsequently adapted it as a letter suitable for sending to other churches by cutting out ch. 15 and 16^{1-23}, and also the words "to Rome" in ch. 1. It is a serious objection to this theory that there is such obvious continuity of thought between ch. 14 and the opening section of ch. 15 that it is hardly credible that the writer himself would make the division at 14^{23}. A much more natural point would be 15^{21}.

Granted that there were two recensions, a more probable theory is that put forward by Lake, namely, that the shorter one (chs. 1–14, with or without the doxology at the end of our Epistle) was the earlier, and that it was prepared as a general or circular letter for the benefit of several churches; and that at a later period Paul turned it into a letter particularly addressed to Rome by adding chs. 15 and 16^{1-23} and inserting the words "to Rome" in ch. 1. The continuity between chs. 14 and 15 would be simply explained if we supposed that having read, or having had read to him, the closing portion of the earlier recension, Paul felt moved to connect the new matter with the old by a few sentences recapitulating the argument of the preceding section.

Analysis of Contents. As to the analysis of the Epistle, the common division into two parts, Doctrinal (chs. 1–11) and Practical (chs. 12–16) is unfortunate if it is allowed to obscure the complete continuity between the two. Here, as always, Paul felt and showed the interlocking of theology and ethics, of doctrine and practice.

I. 1–7. Introduction and Salutation.
8–17. Thanksgiving for the conversion of the Christians at Rome, leading up to the theme of the Epistle, the provision and communication of a divine righteousness.
18–32. The divine wrath is already being experienced, as may be seen in the condition of the

ungodly world which has sunk deeper and deeper in moral degradation.

II. 1–16. But the same principle applies also to the Jew, and by the same principle he also falls under condemnation.

17–29. For the Jew, no less than the Gentile, has failed to keep the Law.

III. 1–8. Objections and difficulties which might be raised by the Jew.

9–20. Conclusion that guilt is universal, and so, therefore, the need for a divine righteousness.

21–31. How this righteousness has been secured and conveyed, "from faith to faith."

IV. 1–25. Does not the case of Abraham point the other way? No, for his faith was manifested before he was circumcised.

V. 1–11. Justification is to lead to peace with God, to life upon a new plane, upon which the process of salvation is to advance to completion.

12–21. The effects claimed for the obedience of Christ illustrated from the admitted effects of Adam's disobedience.

VI. 1–14. Sin is incompatible with the new life; its dominion has been broken.

15–23. Subjection to sin is unreasonable for men who have been emancipated by Christ.

VII. 1–6. An illustration from the obligations of marriage.

7–13. The true purpose and function of the Law.

14–25. The discord within himself, as well as between him and the Law.

VIII. 1–11. The supremacy of the spiritual over the material.

12–17. The privileges of the Christian, Sonship and Heirship.

18–27. Even present suffering is but the condition of future glory.

28–39. The contents and certainty of the Christian hope.

Excursus: The Problem of the Jew, chs. 9–11.

IX. 1–13. Within Abraham's stock itself there has been selection.

14–33. Objections which might be raised by the Jew.

X. 1–13. The simplicity and directness of the Gospel.

14–21. Israel cannot excuse itself as not having heard the Gospel.

XI. 1–12. Israel's rejection neither complete nor final.

13–24. The Gentiles are seriously warned against self-complacency.

25–36. God's purpose of mercy toward all men.

XII. 1–2. The ethical principles of salvation: general introduction.

3–21. The natural attitude of Christians to one another.

XIII. 1–7. Christians and the State.

8–14. Love the fulfilling of the Law.

XIV. 1–14. The duty of toleration for those of a too scrupulous conscience.

15–23. Further duty of those who are strong to abstain for love's sake, even from things permitted.

XV. 1–7. General precepts and encouragements.

8–13. The work of Christ first for the Jew, then for the Gentile.

14–21. Direct address to the Romans; Paul's activities and success in the Gospel.

22–33. Paul's plans for the future.

XVI. 1–2. A note commending Phœbe.

3–16. Greetings.

17–20. Sudden introduction of serious warnings.

21–23. Greetings from Paul's companions.

24–27. Doxology.

The exposition of the Epistle in the following pages follows this analysis section by section.

Literature: Useful commentaries on the English text are those by Handley Moule (in the Expositor's Bible and in the Cambridge Bible for Schools and Colleges), by A. E. Garvie (in the Century Bible) and by Bishop Gore. The last is specially to be recommended. For those who read Greek, Sanday's commentary in the International Critical Commentary is of great value. For expositions of Romans in books not strictly commentaries, see the relevant sections in Bruce, *St. Paul's Conception of Christianity;* Sabatier, *The Apostle Paul* (Eng. trans.); D. Smith, *The Life and Letters of Paul;* Hayes, *Paul and His Epistles;* C. Anderson Scott, *Christianity According to St. Paul.*

CHAPTER I

1–7. The Writer and Those to Whom He Writes; His Qualifications; and His Subject, the Gospel of God and Jesus Christ. "Paul

. . . to those [in Rome] who are beloved by God, grace be unto you and peace from God our Father and from the Lord Jesus Christ." So runs the salutation proper. But it is expanded into a long paragraph by several additional clauses. Paul begins by presenting, as it were, his credentials to people to whom he is not personally known. He is *a thrall of Christ Jesus*, as Moses had been "a servant of God" (Psa. 105[26]) and as John also calls himself (Rev. 1[1]); the word describes an abiding inward relation of dependence and obligation. He is *an apostle by calling*, set apart like Jeremiah of old (Jer. 1[5]), but set apart unto the gospel of God (15[16]), having had bestowed upon him the grace for apostleship, that he might bring the nations into the obedience that belongs to faith (cf. Eph. 5[26], "holiness which springs from truth"). He reminds those to whom he writes of their standing as Christians. They are "Christ's by calling," "beloved of God," and "God's people by calling." He prays that theirs may be the grace and the truth which have their source alike in the Father and in the Lord Jesus Christ.

The emphasis upon *calling* is to be observed. In all cases it is "effectual calling," not merely an invitation, but one which has taken effect. Not, however, that these Christians are already *saints* in the modern sense of the word. Paul uses the word here, as almost always, in the sense which it has in the O.T., where it means "set apart for," or "belonging to God," "having this seal, the Lord knoweth them that are his." It is part of the message of the gospel that those who are "saints" in this sense will ultimately become saints in the other sense (cf. 1 Pet. 1[16]).

The *gospel of God* to which he has been set apart is something the promise of which has been revealed of old through the prophets and is found in the Scriptures of the O.T. This refers not so much to particular texts and passages as to the whole trend of prophecy in the O.T. revealing the character of God as One who will indubitably redeem his people (cf. 3[21]). The gospel of God is concerning his Son, who according to his physical constitution was descended from David, but who in accordance with the Spirit of holiness, which was his, had been instated as Son of God with power. The emphasis is upon *with power* (v. 4). The Son of God (8[3, 32]) had lived on earth in weakness and humiliation; since the resurrection he had been manifested in power. This is in accordance with the apostle's belief that there had come to Christ at the resurrection a great accession of glory and power (Phil. 2[9-11]). He is from henceforth Jesus Christ *our Lord*, bearing the name that is above every name, and receiving the homage and obedience which men otherwise owe to God alone.

In Rome (v. 7). See intro., p. 1135a,

8–17. Thanksgiving for the Conversion of the Christians at Rome; Paul's Eager Desire to Preach the Gospel at Rome also, the Gospel being Something which, so far from being Ashamed of, He is Eager to Proclaim Everywhere; for It is a Divine Force, Producing Salvation.

As in nearly all his Epistles Paul follows up the Salutation with Thanksgiving (Galatians is an exception). By *the whole world* he means, of course, the world as then known; but even so there is an obvious rhetorical exaggeration. (Cf. 1 Thess. 1[8].) At the outside it was in the lands fringing the Mediterranean that the news had spread that there were Christians in Rome. Still, the report of their "faith," their acceptance of the gospel, has gone far and wide, and fills Paul's heart with thanksgiving. This finds constant expression in his prayers. He takes God to witness of this, and also of his anxious desire to visit Rome and see them face to face. Could that take place, he might be able to bestow on them some spiritual gift, and certainly he and they would be encouraged by recognizing the true Christian character, each of the other (v. 12), and the apostle might be able to gather some harvest of souls at Rome, as he had already done in other Gentile cities.

The closing words of v. 13 make it clear that there was in the Christian Church at Rome a considerable element drawn from Gentile or heathen sources as well as Jews (see intro., p. 1135a).

Paul's debt to Christ makes him a *debtor* (v. 14) to men of all types, of all races. It did not matter whether they were cultured Greeks, or rough barbarians, learned or ignorant, he was ready to preach to all. Neither in the presence of high culture nor before great learning was he ashamed of the gospel. For to all alike it was a Divine Force producing salvation. There he strikes the keynote of this section of the Epistle, *divine righteousness*, a righteousness which is characteristic of God and is by God bestowed on men.

"For therein a divine righteousness is being revealed, on the ground of faith, to faith" (v. 17). Paul here announces the theme which is to be explained and defended in 1[18]–7[25], and developed in all its fullness in ch. 8. He strikes the keynote which is heard again at 3[21], "But now apart from law a divine righteousness has been revealed," and again at 5[1], "Therefore being justified on the ground of faith, we have peace with God," and once more at 8[1], "There is now therefore no condemnation to those who are in Christ Jesus." These sentences, all referring to the same fact of experience, mutually illuminate one another, and taken together leave no doubt as to what the apostle meant by "the righteousness of God."

Taken by itself this very important phrase is capable of *several diverse meanings*, due to the versatility of the genitive in Greek. The best supported of these are (a) the righteousness of God as an abstract quality of the divine nature; (b) a righteousness valid before God, one with which God is satisfied; and (c) a righteousness which comes from God. The probability is that no one of these by itself does justice to Paul's meaning. The third, however, finds support in 10^3, where Paul contrasts the righteousness of God with man's "own righteousness," and even more expressly in Phil. 3^9, "not having my own righteousness, the righteousness which is on the ground of law, but that which is through faith in Christ, the righteousness that comes from God, resting upon faith."

What Paul has in mind, therefore, is a righteousness which is characteristic of God, which is valid before God, but which is emphatically *a righteousness now being conveyed to men by God* (v. 17). This is borne out by several considerations. (1) In the first place, it harmonizes with a notable usage of certain writers in the O.T., according to which the righteousness of God is brought into close connection and parallelism with the salvation of men. Thus we have in Psa. 98^2, "The Lord hath made known his salvation; his righteousness hath he openly shewed in the sight of the nations"; Isa. 56^1, "My salvation is near to come, and my righteousness to be revealed" (cf. also Psa. $35^{24, 28}$ Isa. 62^1). The Jews looked on the righteousness of God in a very practical way. It was something that was to be shown, displayed, vindicated, in the deliverance or salvation of his people. It was conceived as something bound up in his faithfulness to his promises, and so with the salvation he had promised. (2) Secondly, this accords with the true meaning of the words which follow. This divine righteousness "is being revealed" in the sense that God's righteousness is being demonstrated in the salvation of his people, but it is being so revealed because it is reaching his people in the form of salvation. That which had formed a principal element in the Jewish hope of the future was already, in a far higher form, being manifested in the experience of those who believed on Christ. For this interpretation of the phrase alone admits of a satisfactory explanation of the words *from faith to faith* (A.V.). Other explanations, such as "starting from a smaller quantity of faith to produce a larger," or "everything is of faith from first to last," are obviously inadequate. The words mean "on the ground of faith and to faith," the verb ("is revealed," A.V.) involving the idea of conveying or communicating. (3) Finally, no other interpretation makes the quotation from Habakkuk relevant to the foregoing statement. As spoken by the prophet the words had meant that the just should escape, save his life, by his faith or faithfulness. For Paul *to live* meant to be saved in a higher sense. But the quotation loses all point unless what it illustrates is a statement to the effect that a man is or can be saved. We may paraphrase v. 17, therefore, thus: "For therein [in the Gospel] a Divine righteousness, no merely human one, is being communicated to faith on the ground of faith."

18–32. The Coming of a Divine Righteousness Illustrated by the Present Manifestation of the Divine Wrath. The paragraph falls into three sections dealing successively with the responsibility of men for their refusal to recognize the being and the demands of God (vv. 18–23), and with the progressive judgments by which they had in consequence been visited (vv. 24–27; 28–32).

The proof of the arrival of divine righteousness must of necessity be mainly internal and spiritual. It is otherwise with the operation of the divine wrath, the effects of which are only too open to observation. By the Wrath (3^5 5^9 12^{19} Eph. 5^6, etc.) Paul does not mean anger as the continuous reaction of God against sin so much as the expected letting loose of that anger at the Judgment. The Jewish expectation of the future included not only righteousness—salvation—for some, but the manifestation of the Wrath, a day of judgment, for others. And Paul, who in v. 17 has proclaimed that the one is already, through Christ, within reach of men, claims as a proof of it that the Wrath also has moved forward so as to come within the range of present experience, as may be seen from the punishments which godless men are undergoing (see p. 846b).

For they are *responsible for their godlessness.* Even apart from revelation, such as has been enjoyed by the Jews, men can have a sufficient knowledge of God to act upon it. Paul here claims—indeed, asserts—the possibility of a natural religion. Men, however (he is thinking of the Gentiles), have been willfully blind to the evidences of God, and have refused to render him either glory or thanks. They have suppressed living truth with iniquity, so that, baffled in their speculations and darkened in their understanding, they have sunk into idolatry and substituted for the spiritual glory of God images of men or beasts or reptiles.

Wherefore (v. 24). It is important to observe that what follows is asserted to be the working of the divine judgment, the punishment of folly and sin. And the punishment takes, as so often, the form of men's being allowed to plunge deeper and ever deeper into sin. God *handed them over* (vv. 24, 26, 28; cf. Acts 7[42]).

The threefold repetition of the words introduces increasingly detailed descriptions of the degradation which had fallen upon an idolatrous world. Paul is keenly aware of the close connection of religion and morality, of idolatry and immorality. Having emphasized their connection in vv. 25, 26, he proceeds to show how the immorality takes concrete form in *sexual enormities*, such as are condemned not only by the revealed religion of the Jews but by the common judgment of mankind (26, 27); and in the last section (vv. 28–32), pursuing the analysis still further, he gives an appalling catalogue of the types of conduct and character which have resulted from this denial of God and reckless indulgence in disgraceful passions. There has been deliberate rejection of God (v. 28), and now behold its consequences in a society in which these are the ruling dispositions, and these the prevailing types of character. The catalogue is remarkable, like similar catalogues in the N.T. (Mk. 7[20-22] Gal. 5[19-21]), for the way in which it condemns, along with conduct which is condemned in common by any and every moral code, dispositions, or conduct which non-Christian codes treat with indifference or altogether ignore. Of such are "envy," "feuds," "slanderers," "insolent," "supercilious," "callous," "ruthless."

When these are studied (along with the parallels above mentioned) *two inferences* occur. The one is that Christianity involves a positive, comprehensive and high ideal of character very different from that which results from the mere avoidance of that which is forbidden; and the other that by laying a ban on these and such-like tempers and dispositions God has taken the human personality in all its aspects and in all its relations under his protection. "They that behave in such ways are worthy of death."

CHAPTER II

1–16. The Application of the Principle to the Jew, and His Condemnation Thereby. The Jew may be supposed to have been listening with much complacency to this indictment of the heathen society in the midst of which he dwelt, its idolatries and its immoralities. Paul now turns suddenly round upon him (cf. Amos 2[6]), and (without naming him, until v. 9) declares that he also has no defense.

The Jew is misled by two things. (1) One is the very *kindness and forbearance of God* who "is not swift to mark iniquity," to visit unrighteous men with final retribution. The Jew failed to read the purpose of that forbearance, which was intended to lead him to repentance (v. 4). He was apt to trace it to some good qualities in himself. It is true that the Jew does enjoy special privileges (3[1, 2]). But these do not release him from moral obligation. On the contrary, the Jew no less than the heathen has to face the Day of Judgment, and, so far as the goodness of God is not leading him to repentance, he is actually accumulating against himself the divine wrath which will then burst forth (v. 5). Every man will then be *judged according to his deeds*. The classification will then be not Jew and Gentile, but those who have done evil and those who have done good. Eternal life will be the portion of those who have shown steadfastness in well-doing, wrath and indignation that of those who, acting in a hireling spirit, have yielded themselves to iniquity (vv. 7, 8). The hireling spirit is the spirit of those who serve God for wages, for reward, taking a mean view of their relation to God (cf. 6[23]). The same thought is repeated with yet greater emphasis in the two following verses.

(2) Paul next touches on the second mistake which the Jews are making. "There is *no favoritism with God*" (v. 11). It is true that he has "loved Jacob," chosen Israel, bestowed special privileges on the Jews. But to infer from that that they or their forefathers deserved this favor of God, or that they were in any sense free from the moral requirements which God laid upon the heathen, was to make a fatal mistake. There is no such distinction as the Jew imagines. The Law, though it is a mark of his privilege, is at the same time that by which he will be judged, as certainly as the heathen will be judged to whose case the written Law cannot be applied, because to him it has not been revealed. Even Gentiles, who are assumed to be without law, do in some measure recognize what God requires of men, and so "are a law unto themselves," or, as Paul puts it in v. 26, "they observe the just requirements of the law" (cf. 9[30]). They do to some extent conform to what is demanded by the written Law. This they do *by nature*, which does not mean "by their own unassisted powers, without the help of God," but "without the help of any special revelation."

Such Gentiles have the witness of their own consciences to the fact that they do obey an unwritten law (v. 15) when their thoughts coming to light in mutual discussion pronounce either a favorable or an unfavorable verdict on their conduct. These verses (14, 15) either represent a long parenthesis, or v. 16 has become displaced (so Moffatt), and should be read after v. 13. In any case, it carries on the thought of that verse, and its reference to the Judgment. It was no novelty in Paul's Christian message that God would judge the secret conduct of men, for that was understood by the Jews. What was new in his message was that the Judgment would be carried out by Christ, acting as the Representative of God (2 Cor. 5[10]; cf. Mt. 25[31f.]).

It is interesting to compare the apostle's opinion of the non-Jewish world and the possibility of Gentiles either doing right or receiving credit for it with *the opinions which were current in orthodox Jewish circles.* There even good works and a good life were pronounced valueless in one who was uncircumcised. If such an one prays to Jehovah, his prayer is not answered. If he commits sin and repents, that does not help him. No virtue is of value in the sight of God unless the man who practices it is a Jew by circumcision. Compared with such opinions which prevailed in his time, Paul's view is much more liberal. He predicts "glory and honor and peace" for everyone who does good, no matter whether he be Jew or Gentile (v. 10). How far he would carry the same principle in reference to Christians and non-Christians is difficult to say. "Between 1[18] and 3[20] Paul has nothing to say about Christians." His attention throughout this passage is concentrated upon the Jew, his difficulty in understanding his own need of a divine righteousness, his objections based upon the privileges of the chosen people and on the classical case of Abraham. What the apostle has to say about the fate of the Gentiles is drawn from him by the necessity of insisting that *Jews and Gentiles will be judged on the same principles.* It does not follow, however, that he would regard these principles as invalid when the heathen came to be contrasted with Christians. He is quite definite in asserting that "all of us [Christians] must appear before the judgment seat of Christ, that each may receive the things he has done with his body . . . whether good or evil" (2 Cor. 5[10]). And no doubt he would hold that the heathen also are to be recompensed according to the good they have done as well as according to the evil, having, in varying degrees, the light of conscience for their use of which they may fairly be judged.

17–29. The Inconsistency and Danger of the Jew. Paul now presses home upon the Jew (who is now directly addressed for the first time) the inconsistency between his religious claims and the breaches of divine law of which he is guilty, and shows that these claims lose all validity when they are not connected with righteous living.

He begins by setting out in a long list the grounds on which the Jew bases his confidence in God (vv. 17–20). He relies on the Law; he prides himself in God; he flatters himself that he "distinguishes the things that matter" in religion. Some of the phrases which follow ("a light to those who are in the dark," "the trainer of those without wisdom," "the instructor of infants") may echo the actual language of complacent Judaism proclaiming its superiority to the Gentiles.

The long sentence breaks off unfinished (v. 20). The charge has developed on lines which are too general. It is to be made as personal as may be. The irony becomes scathing. Glaring types of inconsistency are pilloried, theft and adultery by men who actually teach the Ten Commandments. The reference to the robbing of heathen temples is not uncalled for. There is an allusion to the practice in Acts 19[37], and also in Josephus. Here, however, it seems unnecessary, being covered by the general reference to theft; it has, moreover, the appearance of an anticlimax. That appearance is removed, however, when we recognize that this particular type of offense reveals something more than readiness to flout a written law. When he who *loathes idols* (v. 22) enriches himself by robbing their temples, he displays a want of religious good feeling, a flippant recklessness, which is an even truer index of character than the actual breach of written law. Compare the charge laid by Amos against Moab that he "burned the bones of the king of Edom to lime" (2[1]). Such action belongs to a type which Paul stigmatizes as what is "unseemly," "not fitting"; and it is covered by the word translated *foolishness* in the list of things which, according to our Lord, "defile a man," i.e., disqualify him for fellowship with God. The quotation from Isaiah (52[5]) in v. 24 is taken not from the Hebrew but from the LXX, which by inserting "because of you" changes a charge against the oppressor of Israel into one against Israel itself.

V. 25 is important for our estimate of Paul and his teaching. "Circumcision has its value," if it is accompanied by obedience; on the other hand, willful transgression actually cancels it. Paul is no violent revolutionary. He recognizes value even in the ceremonial Law, at least for the Jew, as well as validity for the contents of the moral law (Rom. 7[12]). This must be borne in mind when we find him proclaiming that Christ is "the end of the law" (10[4]). By that he meant that the legal system had been superseded as a means of obtaining righteousness. But the contents of the moral law remained as a guide to those who through faith in Christ had exchanged a legal for a filial relation to God. And, for a Jew, even circumcision was not without value, provided he held it in due subordination to moral effort and achievement—a position which is not without its bearing on the apostle's estimate of the sacraments, and particularly of baptism. That also had its value; but it was an ancillary one (v. 27). So far was the absence of circumcision in a good-living Gentile from disqualifying him from religious privileges, that he would actually sit as judge over him who in spite of having both a written code and circumcision showed himself a transgressor of the Law.

The closing verses (28, 29) sum up the thought of the paragraph in terms of a metaphor which had been current since the time of Deuteronomy (10[16]; cf. Jer. 4[4] 9[26] Ezek. 44[9]), when the people had been called on to *circumcise their heart;* i.e., no longer to be content with outward circumcision, but to cleanse their hearts and purify their wills. It is the first appearance in the Epistle of the idea of a spiritual Israel, one whose qualifications are not racial or ritual but moral and religious.

CHAPTER III

1–8. Possible Objections and Difficulties. Here, as not infrequently, Paul shows himself singularly sensitive to what may be going on in the minds of those whom he is seeking to convince. It is possible, of course, that some of the objections with which he proceeds to deal had actually occurred to his own mind when he was facing the implications of salvation by faith. The arguments and counter-arguments are best brought out by a paraphrase. If all this is true, says the Jew, then *what advantage has the Jew* over the Gentile? "Much advantage in every way," replies Paul; "first of all, the Jew has been intrusted with the utterances of God, including the promises to Israel." "Exactly," answers the Jew (v. 3), "but are you not arguing that because some Jews have been guilty of bad faith, their bad faith *overturns the faithfulness of God*, causing him to depart from his promises?" "By no means," says Paul (v. 4). "If it comes to a question of the truthfulness of God, that would not be affected though every man were false. What does the Psalm say?" "Well, then," replies the Jew, "that means that our want of righteousness serves to throw into relief the righteousness of God. Is it not, then, unjust in God to punish us for that, by bringing on the Judgment?" To which Paul answers: "I was speaking as a man may. Of course not; God cannot be unjust, for, if so, how is he to judge the world?" (V. 6.) "Nevertheless," persists the Jew (v. 7), "as you say the effect of my falsity is to enhance the truthfulness of God and so promote his glory, why am I to be haled to judgment as a sinner? And is it not a natural inference that we may *do evil that good may come?*" (v. 8)—"as, indeed," so Paul adds here on his own account, "we are insultingly accused of saying. People whose reasoning leads to a conclusion like that deserve the condemnation which falls upon them."

It may be felt that not all the apostle's arguments are as conclusive as we could wish, and the closing words of the paragraph may strike us as almost the abandonment of argument. But it is not so. Paul, whether he was arguing with himself or with some imagined opponent, felt that the case put up for the defense of the Jew had led step by step to a *reductio ad absurdum.* "If that be the issue to which your argument brings you, the suggestion that we may do evil that good may come, then the verdict of conscience is swiftly and inevitably pronounced against you, and inferentially against the whole string of arguments on which your immoral conclusion is based." Men may play with intellectual doubts and difficulties about God and his government of the world, but these questions are not to be solved by pure intellect alone. When reasoning on these subjects brings men within measurable distance of a conclusion which conscience unhesitatingly condemns, it is good evidence that the reasoning has been wrong.

9–20. Guilt is Universal, and so also the Need for a Divine Righteousness. Paul now summarizes the conclusion from the discussion which began at 1[18]. Confronted by the Judge who calls every man to account for the deeds done in the flesh, the Jew is not in any better position than any other man. All, whether Jew or Gentile, are under the dominion of sin, as, indeed, can be abundantly shown from the O.T. Some of the quotations are *verbatim* from the original; some have been slightly shortened and altered. In v. 19 *the Law,* as occasionally elsewhere (cf. 1 Cor. 14[21]), refers to the O.T. as a whole, including here the Psalms and Isaiah. The Jews being obviously within the ambit of the Law must accept as a description of themselves what is the judgment of the older revelation generally. In fact, the real purpose of the Law is to bring about the recognition of sin (4[15] 5[20]; cf. Gal. 3[19]). The conclusion of the whole matter therefore is that no human being can expect acquittal at the bar of God on the ground that he has merited it by observance of law.

21–31. How the Divine Righteousness is

Secured and Conveyed. The ground is now cleared. The necessity for the coming of a divine righteousness has been shown. Paul can now return to the exposition of the theme announced in 1[17], namely, that, in fact, such a righteousness is being revealed. He begins by repeating it; *now*, as things are, under the new dispensation of Christ, the very thing which is universally required by human nature has been displayed. And it is a righteousness which has nothing to do with law; it reaches all those who believe, through their faith in Christ. It is a righteousness to which the Law and the Prophets bear witness; that is to say, it is in accordance with the whole trend of the earlier revelation, and in particular with God's repeated promise of salvation. This righteousness reaches *all* who have faith in Christ, for (emphasizing once more the all-important fact) all have sinned and both lack and feel the lack of the glory of God. The *glory of God* (v. 23) embodies a conception which, like not a few others, we find in the N.T. at the point of transition from a material to an ethical significance. In the O.T. and in the post-canonical writings it stands for the physical radiance radiating from the presence of God. It is seen resting on Sinai (Ex. 24[16]), over the tabernacle (Ex. 40[34]) or the lid of the ark (Psa. 80[1]). A reflection of this glory was traditionally believed to have shone on the face of Adam before the Fall, but to have been lost by him after it. And post-canonical writers predicted as part of the privileges awaiting the righteous in the New Age that they would again be clothed in the glory of God. But as increasing emphasis came to be placed on the character and the ethical attributes of God his glory was interpreted in terms of his majesty and goodness. And ultimately it came to connote moral splendor of character, "full of grace and truth" (Jn. 1[14]; cf. Eph. 1[6] 3[16]). It is best to regard these sentences (vv. 22b, 23) as parenthetic, and to recognize that in v. 24 Paul picks up the thread from v. 22a, and declares concerning all those who believe that they are *justified freely;* the righteousness which is not their own but God's is theirs, and that without price. It is theirs by the free bounty of God, through the *redemption* that is in Christ Jesus. That redemption, as we learn from other references in Paul, was deliverance from all the shifting servitudes to which man had become subject, from the domination and fear of evil spirit-forces (Gal. 4[3] Heb. 2[14]), from the bondage of the Law (Gal. 4[5]) and from the tyrannous domination of sin (Rom. 8[3]).

So far the paragraph has dealt with the fact that a divine righteousness has been displayed and conveyed to men, so as to justify all who believe, in entire independence of the Law, and apart from any other condition except faith on the part of man and the undeserved mercy of God. This is important for the interpretation of the pregnant passage which follows.

Whom God (publicly) set forth (v. 25). It is clear that the apostle was profoundly impressed by the crucifixion as a spectacle. A description of it seems to have formed part of his proclamation of the gospel (cf. Gal. 3[1] 1 Cor. 2[2]). There is, indeed, something in the manner of his references to the blood of Christ which would be explained if he had been an actual witness of the scene, a mingling of horror at the fact with wonder at its meaning. Note, however, the comma which in R.V. (cf. mg.) now separates the words *by faith* from *in his blood.* It is all that a translation can do to mark the important fact that Paul does not, as the A.V. would lead us to suppose, connect the reconciling efficacy of Christ's death with "faith in his blood." There is, indeed, no case in the N.T. where "faith in" or "believe in" stands for faith in a concrete object (not even Mk. 1[15]). It always refers to faith in a person. The words "in his blood" must therefore be connected either with *propitiation,* or more probably with *set forth;* and their meaning may be represented by such a phrase as "suffering unto blood" or "as a blood-stained victim." Christ, who is thus publicly set forth by God upon the cross, is described as one who is or who becomes *through faith a propitiation.* The word Paul used is itself an adjective, and the substantive "propitiation" is arrived at by supplying what seems the most natural word (if any word is to be supplied at all) namely, "sacrifice." It is, however, possible and on the whole more natural to take Paul's word as an adjective qualifying the relative "whom" (for such a combination we may compare Philm. v. 15). It would then be translated "as one having propitiatory power" (so Denney), or, if we keep close to the etymological meaning of the word, "one with power to restore friendly relations."

The traditional interpretation of v. 25 is not obscurely indicated in R.V., which substitutes *because of the passing over of sins done aforetime* for the A.V. "for the remission of sins that are past." And it comes out even more clearly in the rendering of Moffatt's translation, "in view of the fact that sins formerly committed during the time of God's forbearance had been passed over." It is further emphasized by the use of the word *shew* (Moffatt, "demonstrate") in place of the word "declare." The meaning of the verse according to this interpretation is that in order to demonstrate his own righteousness, which had been impugned in consequence of his overlooking sins in the past, God set forth his Son as a propitiatory sacrifice to satisfy his justice, and so to manifest his righteousness even when he treated as righteous those who were sinners.

The traditional interpretation is, however, not the only one which is possible, and it is doubtful whether it is the right one. The chief reasons are as follows. (1) It involves the assumption that hitherto God had conspicuously failed to punish sin, and so to manifest his righteousness. For this there is only very inadequate support in Scripture, and, on the contrary, there is much evidence that in all periods God was understood to punish the sins both of the Jews and of the Gentiles. (2) It involves the assumption that God's righteousness had in consequence been challenged or impugned. Of this there is no evidence. (3) It involves a sudden change in this verse of the meaning attached to the "righteousness of God," and the introduction of a meaning different from that in which the apostle has been employing it from 1[17] onward. It is righteousness as an abstract quality of the divine nature which is understood to have been challenged, and now to be demonstrated, whereas Paul is interested in it, mainly if not wholly, as a quality of the divine nature which reaches men in the form of justification or salvation. (4) The "propitiation" provided by the sacrifice of Christ must be understood to be absolute, something independent of any condition provided by man. Yet the words "by faith" clearly suggest that it is something conditioned by faith on man's side. To explain that it was something absolute in reference to God though conditioned in the experience of man would be to read into the simple words more than they will bear. (5) The word "display" ranges with "is being revealed" (1[17]) and "has been manifested" (3[21]) as referring to a manifestation of divine righteousness which makes its arrival in the experience of men. It is a "display" which has for its result what is experience in 8[1], "there is now no condemnation to those that are in Christ Jesus." (6) The words translated "because of the passing over of sins done aforetime" do not necessarily refer to a passing over aforetime; they may equally well mean "with a view to the passing over now" (so Lietzmann).

A survey of the whole verse in its context suggests that the O.T. analogue which was before Paul's mind was not any of the Levitical sacrifices but *the brazen serpent* (Num. 21[4f.]). Moses at the command of God lifted up the serpent on a pole. So was the Son of man lifted up, set forth upon the cross by God. The serpent was itself a visible likeness of the evil from which Israel was suffering. So Christ was made "in the likeness of sin's flesh," "was made sin for us," identified (short of consent to it) with the root-evil of human experience. The children of Israel were called on to gaze upon the symbol of their enemy, to see it vanquished. Men were called on to behold Christ crucified, to see in his death the doom of sin, and the demonstration of the love and mercy of God, and, when they accepted the message of the cross with the hearing of faith, to find the healing of their hurt and reconciliation to God.

We may then translate or paraphrase the verse thus: "Whom God set forth a victim unto blood as one able to effect reconciliation through faith, unto the bestowal of God's righteousness, with a view to the passing over of former sins in the forbearance of God, unto the bestowal of his righteousness in this present time, that he may be himself righteous and also pronounce righteous him who founds on faith in Christ." The last words sound like a conscious echo of Isa. 45[21] (cf. 5[8] 2 Cor. 5[19]).

All human claim to merit righteousness, any claim of the kind which the Jew was in the habit of making, is then finally excluded. That Paul proceeds to speak of *the law of faith* (v. 27) does not mean that faith involves or imposes a law of its own. Far from it. He uses the word "law" here (as in 8[2] Gal 6[2]) in the sense of a governing principle, somewhat as we speak of the laws of nature. A man may be pronounced righteous altogether apart from the performance of any legal obligation (v. 28). That does not mean that there is no moral obligation imposed upon the Christian or to be fulfilled by him. Paul would have had no difficulty in agreeing with James that "faith without works is dead." The question for him was, and it was one of tremendous importance, *Which comes first?* The Jew at his best thought of himself as obeying in order to be saved. Paul's contention was, You must be saved in order to obey. So he can meet the question, whether by his doctrine of salvation by faith he is not overturning the Law, with the firm assurance that he is actually establishing the Law, not as a system for securing righteousness but as to its abiding contents. As there is only one God, he must be the God of Jews and Gentiles alike, and can deal with them only on one and the same principle; and the single principle which applies to both of them alike can be faith only (vv. 29, 30a).

CHAPTER IV

1–12. The Case of Abraham. It might be supposed that Paul had now made his point, proved the universal need of righteousness, the impossibility of man providing that righteousness for himself, and the revelation through the gospel of what alone can meet the need, a righteousness bestowed by God. He might now proceed to the triumphant exposition of "all the good things that are ours in Christ" as we find it in ch. 8, the chapter which, with the possible addition of ch. 12, represents the crowning purpose of his writing. But again his sensitiveness to the point of view of others leads to a digression. What about Abraham? Abraham was indeed, on the surface at least, a strong case for the Jew to appeal to. He was the Founder of the People, the Friend of God; and his life had been marked on more than one occasion by conspicuous obedience to the will of God. "When he was called, . . . he went out not knowing whither he went"; "when he was tried, he offered up Isaac" (Heb. $11^{8, 17}$). And the fact that the writer to the Hebrews traces his obedience on both occasions to "faith" (though he uses the word in a different sense from that peculiar to Paul) is evidence that these works of obedience were regarded as proofs of his faith. On this it would not be difficult to found an argument that in this classical instance justification had followed on a combination of faith and works or on works alone, as, indeed, we find it in the First Book of Maccabees: "Was not Abraham found faithful in temptation, and it was reckoned unto him for righteousness?" (Cf. Jas. $2^{21, 22}$.) Paul faces the possibility of such an argument, and admits, If Abraham was, as perhaps you say, justified on the ground of merit, then, of course, he had a ground of claim (contradicting 3^{27}). But it cannot be really so from the point of view of God; for Scripture itself connects his justification with his faith, and says nothing about his works. Indeed, the text tacitly excludes any question of merit. For if justification was granted in answer to faith, it was granted out of grace and not as something which had been earned. The text in Genesis could in fact apply only to a case where all idea of earning righteousness by merit had been abandoned (v. 5). The verses quoted from Psa. 32 are relevant in so far as their silence as to any condition on the side of man suggests that the divine forgiveness was unconditioned, in other words, *of grace*.

Paul now takes a further point (v. 10). He raises the question, At what period in Abraham's history was he thus *reckoned or acknowledged to be righteous?* Was it before or after his being circumcised? This was of crucial importance because the typical illustration of "works of the law" at least on its ceremonial side was circumcision. It was the ceremony of ritual purification by submitting to which the Jew became "a debtor to do the whole law" (Gal. 5^{3}); he placed himself upon a footing of compact with God. Had the acknowledgment of Abraham's righteousness been made *after* his circumcision, it would have been possible to argue that the keeping of the Law was at least included in the conditions of his justification. But exactly the reverse was the case. It was while he was as yet uncircumcised that he was acknowledged to be righteous. And, in fact, his circumcision was a sign or seal placed upon that righteousness which was already his by faith. He is therefore the prototype ("father") of those Gentiles who believe though not circumcised, and are therefore justified; as he is also the prototype of those (Jews) who do not rest on their circumcision (cf. 2^{17}) but imitate the faith which he displayed while still uncircumcised.

These verses have an important bearing on a theory which has often been advanced in some quarters with great confidence. The theory is that Paul taught a "sacramental religion" in the sense that for him the sacraments were not merely "efficacious signs," granted to and strengthening faith which had already provided the sufficient condition of salvation, but did actually and in themselves (*ex opere operato*) secure and convey the bestowal of the new birth or of immortality. In this way Paul is understood to have metamorphosed the Christianity of Jesus and given it the character of the Greco-Oriental mystery-cults (see p. 851). There are many reasons for regarding this theory as unproven and unsound; but these verses in themselves are sufficient to show the unsoundness. The Christian analogue to circumcision is, of course, baptism as a rite symbolizing purification and admission to the redeemed community. And there can be no doubt that all Paul had to say about circumcision he would say equally about baptism. Like circumcision, baptism "had its value" (2^{25}), but, like circumcision, it had no value except for a new creature.

13–17. A Third Point: Abraham's Stock Universal and Spiritual. The argument here becomes difficult to follow. The clue to it is at the end (vv. 16, 17), where Paul quotes Gen. 17^{5}, "a father of many nations have I made thee," and draws the inference that Abraham is "the father of us *all*," i.e., of all of us believers, whether Jews or Gentiles. It followed that some (the Gentiles) must be his "descendants" not in the physical sense but in a spiritual; and the inheritance which was to be shared by all alike must devolve on the principle of grace (not "compact"), on the ground of faith (not the keeping of the Law), if the promise was to be fulfilled as it was made "to all his stock" (v. 16). This repeats only more clearly what has been said in v. 13, where the emphasis is on *to his stock*. If it were to be such as founded on the Law who were to be heirs of the world, then faith would have been nullified and the promise rendered valueless. For the Gentiles, part of Abraham's stock (v. 17) were obviously unable to fulfill the condition. We find here again the idea of *a second Israel*, Israel according to the spirit contrasted with Israel according to the flesh. V. 15 is a parenthesis pointing out how different is the function of the law from that of faith. Its ultimate effect is to produce wrath; for only when there is law is there also contravention of law or transgression, such as produces wrath in God ($5^{13, 20}$ Gal 3^{19}).

18–25. How Abraham Manifested His Faith. At the close of the last paragraph Paul has touched upon the particular circumstances in which Abraham displayed his faith, his acceptance of God's word in connection with the promise that he should have a son even in his old age. God in whom he believed has been described as one who both restores the dead to life and calls non-existent things into being. And Abraham's confidence in such a God had been conspicuously manifested when he accepted the promise that his descendants would be as numerous as the stars in the sky, setting against the hope or natural expectation of man the hope which rested on the word of God. In view of the advanced age both of himself and of his wife such a prospect appeared quite hopeless. Nevertheless, his faith in God showed no weakening. When confronted by that promise he did not waver (v. 20; cf. Jas. 1^{6}), but glorified God by his confidence that he would perform what he had promised. And the fact that on this occasion *his faith was reckoned to him for righteousness* was recorded not for his sake alone but for ours. For exactly the same principle applies now. Abraham's faith was in a God who calls non-existent things into being; ours is in a God who raised our Lord from the dead. But in our case no less than in his, faith in the same God is reckoned as a ground for being accounted righteous.

V. 25 stands somewhat apart from the line of argument which has been developed in the paragraph, rounding it off with a slightly rhetorical touch. It would be a mistake to suppose that Paul is drawing any significant distinction between the death of Christ and his resurrection in respect of the reasons for the one or the results of the other. That death and that resurrection are for him but two moments in one tremendous event.

Point of View of This Chapter. It must be remembered that throughout this chapter Paul is dealing expressly with the Jew and from the Jewish point of view. The faith of which he has been speaking is faith as the Jew understands it, faith in the sense in which it meets us in the O.T., a taking of God at his word, which involves trust in him as he is known. Now, faith in that sense is an element in Christian faith, but it is not the whole, even as the justification of which Paul speaks is not the whole consequence of faith in God as he is known to us in Christ. For he is now known not only as one who restores the dead to life, but as one who "so loved the world that he gave his only begotten Son." And faith in consequence takes on an added quality and a new meaning. In its restricted sense it might lead to a justification which was no more than a sterile acquittal. In its expanded sense—the faith which "is made operative through love" (Gal. 5^{6})—it becomes something the effect of which does not stop short of reconciliation to God.

CHAPTER V

1–11. Justification Completed by Reconciliation. Once more Paul strikes the keynote which we have heard in 1^{17} and 3^{21}; but now he feels himself at liberty to develop his theme. *Being justified by faith*, as he has shown so fully and so persuasively in the preceding chapters, let us not omit the next step; *let us have peace with God*. Let the effect of Christ's sacrificial death have full scope, not stopping at justification or remission of sins, but including in our experience peace with God, forgiveness in the deep sense of restoration to fellowship, reconciliation. For Christ and our faith in him are to bring us on to a new footing with God, a new platform or plane. We are to be lifted above the old level of legal compact and of servile obedience to the written code that killeth and are to rejoice in the hope of that same *glory of God*, the lack of which we have so deeply felt (3^{23}).

Vv. 3–5 are parenthetical. The full glory of God is not yet ours, for we are not yet fully conformed to the image of his Son. And on the other hand, tribulation is still the portion of the Christian no less than of other men (Jn. 16^{33} Rev. 1^{9}); but in that also we can proudly rejoice. For we have in the love of God the secret of an alchemy by which *tribulation is transmitted into a sure and certain hope*. The steps of that process are plain to see. Tribulation produces endurance, endurance testedness, the consciousness of having been tried and having stood the test; and testedness produces hope. By *hope* Paul again means something other than an inclination to expect the best; it approaches very nearly to "conviction," or "faith" in the sense of the writer to the Hebrews. The fact that this hope shall not be disappointed is guaranteed by the love of God by which, through the action of the Spirit, our hearts have been flooded. Everything that happens to the Christian happens within the atmosphere of the divine love, or upon the plane of the divine grace; so that even tribulation becomes something in which we can proudly rejoice.

In v. 6 Paul picks up the thread from v. 2, and in words which speak for themselves reminds his readers of the central fact of the gospel. As Christ came "not to call the righteous but sinners to repentance," so he died for men who made no claim to righteousness. It was just conceivable that one man might be willing to die for the sake of another who was good and lovable. The wonder of divine love was that Christ *died for the ungodly and the unlovable.* And precisely because it was so incredible for one who knew himself to be ungodly that he should be the object of love to a holy God, the purpose of Christ's death was to confirm beyond all doubt this unbelievable fact, and not only to confirm it but to press it home upon his heart (v. 8).

Justification (v. 9) and *reconciliation* (v. 11) are not for Paul interchangeable terms, neither do they describe the same factors in Christian experience. They are connected with and describe different ways of regarding man's wrong relation to God. "Justification" looks at that wrong relation from a forensic point of view. Sin is transgression, violation of law. The sinner is under condemnation. He can be justified or receive "remission of sins" by the working of the sovereign will of God. He is then acquitted, pronounced not guilty or righteous. And it is conceivable that the process should stop there with the removal of guilt and condemnation. But Paul also saw more deeply into the true meaning of sin. He saw it not merely as a transgression, which could be overlooked or pardoned, but as something which vitally affected the personal relation between God's children and himself, which "estranged them from the life of God" (Eph. 4[18]), made them suspicious of his goodness, unbelieving of his promises, hostile to his purposes and even to himself. This was a situation which could not be dealt with even by a sovereign act of God, or by any arrangement external to the sinner himself. It called for the operation of some mighty force, whereby the sinner could be induced to throw away his hostility, his suspicion, his shrinking from God, whereby he could be not only justified but reconciled.

And Paul saw this force also in *the cross.* In two successive verses (8, 9) he touches on these two aspects of Christ's work in relation to sin, and emphatically connects that work in both its aspects with the death of Christ. We have been *justified by his blood,* or (as the preposition ought probably to be given the local sense) "in the conditions created by his death." The phrase is a highly condensed summary of what we have already had expounded in 3[25]. God had set forth Christ as a victim unto blood, and the result to which that led was that God now justified those who founded upon faith in Christ. Much more, then, argues Paul, we shall be saved from the Wrath through him. The insertion by R.V. of the words *of God,* which are not in the text, obscures Paul's point, and also not unnaturally raises the question whether that is not already included in the justification. The phrase is eschatological in its outlook, and expresses the assurance that those who are justified will through Christ be saved in the Day of Judgment. But, more than that, those who, equally through his death, have been reconciled, will be *saved by his life,* his life as a risen and glorified Saviour. Once more Paul passes from the forensic to the ethical and the personal. Those who have been reconciled have "Christ in them the hope of glory" (Col. 1[27]; cf. Gal. 2[20]). He is their life (Col. 3[4]). By the power of the living Christ who dwells in them they shall be saved as they progressively approximate to the knowing and the doing of the will of God (Phil. 2[13] Jn. 15[5]). Nay, more; not only have we this double confidence as those who have been justified and reconciled, but we *pride ourselves in God* (v. 11) through Jesus Christ, through whom we have received and accepted the reconciliation. The Christian "rejoices or prides himself in God" even as the Jew does (2[17]), but with new and far better reason.

12–21. Effect of Christ's Obedience Illustrated by the Effect of Adam's Disobedience. Once more the clue to a somewhat complicated argument is found in a clear summary of it toward the end of the paragraph. There v. 18 may be rendered, "so then, as one man's transgression resulted in condemnation passed upon all men, so did the righteous act of one result for all men in a righteousness which leads to life." The first of these statements Paul takes for granted; it embodies an opinion which had come to prevail among the Jews as to the consequences entailed upon all his descendants by the disobedience of Adam. Upon that accepted proposition Paul bases his inference as to the participation by all who are by faith united to Christ in the consequences of his obedience. But the working out of the argument suffers in clearness, *first*, from the necessity he feels to distinguish between those who lived before and those who lived after the giving of the Law as to the nature of their responsibility; *secondly*, by his desire to show that the effect of Christ's obedience is not only parallel to that of Adam's disobedience but vastly greater (vv. 15–17), and, *thirdly*, by his failure to complete the opening sentence.

In v. 12 Paul is thinking of sin as an external force, quasi-personal and active prior to any lodgment it acquires in human nature. The disobedience of Adam has opened the door for the entrance of this hostile force into humanity. And through the door thus opened has passed Death, also conceived as an external force, one of the spirit-forces of evil (cf. 1 Cor. 15^{56}, where death is represented as using sin as a sting wherewith to stab men). And so *death passed upon all men*, all men became subject to it. It is true, as is commonly said, that Paul has not before his mind the distinction we commonly draw between physical death and spiritual death. He is thinking of death in all its forms and manifestations. But the emphasis here at least is upon death as the cutting off of human life from God. This is seen when we come to vv. 17 and 21, and find that the condition introduced by Christ which counteracts this death, and operates on the same principle, is a condition of *life*, meaning not physical life, but life that is "eternal." It is further borne out by the passage in 7^{7-11}, where the parallelism of thought, though not exact, is sufficiently clear. "Sin sprang to life, and I died," obviously not in the sense of natural death. Compare also, "ye who were dead in your trespasses and sins" (Eph. 2^{1}). Death in every sense had imposed itself upon all men, *for that all sinned* (v. 12). This is the right translation, the rendering in the Latin Vulgate ("in whom, *scil.* in Adam, all sinned") being one which has had unfortunate results in Christian theology. But the phrase is not adducing the reason why death passed upon all men; that has already been given earlier in the verse. "Inasmuch as all sinned" calls attention to the fact as proof of the statement that moral death had seized mankind. Sin was thus in the world, lodged in human nature prior to the giving of the Law; but it was not *reckoned* (cf. 7^{8b}); men were held responsible for conforming to such moral principles as were within their knowledge (2^{12}); but they were not condemned as violators of a written code. Nevertheless, they were *under the rule of death*, even though they had not, like Adam, broken an express command. Their universal experience of being under the dominion of death was due to their connections with Adam; and in that he was a type of the Christ who was to come. For the bond with him which it was for faith to establish would secure for them, apart from any personal deserts, the reversal of the condition of death and the righteousness which leads to life.

But the case of Adam and the consequences entailed upon his descendants by his act of disobedience, though a good illustration, is, after all, an inadequate one (vv. 15f.). The gift which comes to men through Christ's supreme act of obedience is of transcendent scope. (Moffatt's translation should be consulted here.) It counterbalances not only the single transgression of the one man Adam but all the transgressions of all individual men since Adam. If it was due to the transgression of one man that death reigned over human nature, how much more certain was it, not merely that life should now reign, but (with a striking breach of the parallelism) those who accepted the free and abounding gift of righteousness should themselves *reign in life*. Having summed up the argument of the paragraph in v. 18, Paul repeats it in a slightly different form, one which further illuminates his point of view. The transgression of Adam is now clearly defined as his *disobedience*, and the righteous act of Christ as his *obedience;* and the results in both cases are that the rest of men receive a certain status, in the one case the status of *sinners*, in the other the status of *righteous*. The imagery is wholly forensic. If we may not say that the ideas of personal moral guilt and of personal moral righteousness are absent, they are at least far in the background. Paul is thinking of the relation of men to God in terms of a status into which they had been introduced, in the one case by the transgression of Adam, in the other by Christ's great act of obedience, but in both cases the status is something to be voluntarily accepted. Once more (v. 20) he touches on the function of the Law (cf. 3^{20} 4^{15} $7^{8, 10, 12}$ Gal. 3^{19}); it is to bring transgressions to light in all their copiousness, to show that men have not only the status of sinners but the *habit of sinning*, in order that for the reign of sin in death might be substituted the rule of grace which leads to eternal life through Jesus Christ (v. 21).

CHAPTER VI

1–14. Sin Incompatible with the New Life. A new question, though one of the same class as 3^{5a}. If the result of sin is to give opportunity for the manifestation of God's abundant grace, does it not follow that we should continue in the practice of sin? It is a captious question, yet Paul deals with it seriously, for it gives him the opportunity of showing the indissoluble connection between the experience of the believer in Christ and a life of purity and high moral endeavor. There is, indeed, he suggests, something irrational in the idea that Christians should live under the power of sin, because they have already *died to sin* (v. 2). The significance of this important phrase is to be learned from v. 10. Christ when he died, died to sin. The thought springs out of Paul's conviction as to the reality and the completeness of the resurrection. Christ came "in the flesh," "born of a woman," truly and completely man. And the flesh in which he came was *sin's flesh* (cf. v. 6, 8[3]); that is to say, it was the human constitution of man, as that had come to be since Adam's trangression, an appanage of sin. This "flesh" or physical constitution of man, like everything else that God made, had originally been "good." But historically it had come to belong to sin (5[12]), to be under sin's dominion (7[14]). And Christ, being truly in the flesh as it had then come to be, felt the full force of sin's power, the full brunt of its attack. His experience of sin was in all respects identical with that of man, save in one respect, namely, that he never consented to it (2 Cor. 5[21]). Among the things which happened at his death upon the cross was this, that he stripped the flesh from off himself (Col. 2[15]) and in so doing escaped from the power of sin; in fact, "died to it." And the faith by which men were united to Christ was of such a character that *they too died to sin*, died from under its authority, were henceforth free from its dominion. But Christ not only died but rose again, rose to live unto God (v. 10). And, once more, faith-union with him had a similar result for those who believed. They were made alive "together with Christ" (Col. 2[13]). They had passed through an experience which made it simply irrational to continue under the power of sin.

Now, of this experience Paul saw a vivid picture in *baptism*. Those who had gone down beneath the waters of some pool had in their memories an acted picture of having died, even been buried with Christ; and the emergence from the water which followed was an unforgettable witness to the fact that they had become partakers of the higher life; they were *alive unto God*. *For* (v. 5) introduces further confirmation of what has gone before. What follows is an attempt to bring out the same double truth by means of another metaphor, one which we find more fully developed in Jn. 15[1f]. It is *a vital union* in which Christians are united to Christ, a union like that of the branches with the vine; and if they have shared in his experience of dying to sin they must share in his experience of new life. "If we have grown into him by a death like his, we shall grow into him by a resurrection like his" (Moffatt). "Union with Christ at one point (his death) is union with him altogether (and therefore in his resurrection)" (Denney). But (this metaphor not proving plastic in his hands) Paul goes on to add a third, *our old man was crucified with him* (v. 6; cf. Gal. 2[20] Eph. 4[22]). The experience into which we have entered corresponds to that of Christ upon the cross; there he died to the dominion of sin, inasmuch as the body which belonged to sin was destroyed; and that also is the result of our being crucified with him. To have carried through this metaphor consistently Paul should have pointed out that for us also as well as for Christ this "crucifixion" was followed by entrance into a higher life. But he changes the form of the thought and expresses the ultimate consequence of the faith-union in terms of *freedom from servitude to sin*. In v. 7 he is probably quoting a proverbial Jewish saying, one which corresponds to our "death clears all scores." It is hardly to be supposed that he means that death itself procures the remission of sins, as R.V. would suggest. Both words, "sins" and "justified," must be understood in a rigidly concrete and forensic sense. He that is dead has received a quittance from Sin; he has escaped from Sin's jurisdiction. In v. 6, *body of sin* means body that belongs to Sin; cf. 7[24], "body that belongs to Death," and 8[3], "flesh that belongs to Sin." V. 8 repeats in plain language the truth which is illustrated by these metaphors, at the same time throwing the emphasis of the life-experience into the future; we *believe that we shall live with him*. This does not throw any doubt on the conviction hitherto expressed that the life will continue and be perfected in eternity. Deliverance from the power of Sin implies deliverance from the rule of Death. It is for Christians to hold firmly to the lesson of their experience that they are now dead to sin and alive unto God through Jesus Christ (v. 11).

We should note in this paragraph the *variety of metaphors* which Paul employs to illustrate the double experience of dying to sin and living again to God: (a) baptism, in which they pictorially die and are buried with Christ; (b) the vital union of the parts of a tree; and (c) crucifixion itself. Under each of these figures Paul attempts to visualize the completeness of the union with Christ which faith effects, and that not only in general but in the particular aspects of union with him in his death to sin and his living to God. It was possible to visualize all these illustrations, and to convey them by the use of metaphorical language. But only one of them,. namely, baptism, was it possible to pictorialize in action. The symbolism of the others was necessarily confined to words. But the way in which Paul brings them together in this passage illustrates the fact that baptism also was a *symbol.* It was a symbol in action, but did not otherwise differ from the rest. That is to say, there is no indication here that Paul understood that the rite of baptism in itself conferred any new status, or the new life. It was a word made visible, a seal and symbol of the fact that the believers had already through faith been united to Christ in his death and in his life.

In v. 12 Paul turns from argument to precept. He has refuted the objection raised in v. 1. It is for the Christians to whom he writes to put in action the conclusion he has established, to refuse any authority over themselves to Sin, to avoid any yielding to the passions of the lower nature. They are to cease *using their members* as instruments of wrongdoing, and to make them over to God as instruments of righteousness; Sin is no longer to lord it over them. The word *righteousness* (v. 13) appears to be used here (possibly for the first time) to describe not status before God but righteousness of conduct and character. These closing verses also introduce us to the paradox which Paul neither fails to perceive nor shrinks from stating, the paradox of a salvation which is real and complete at the moment of believing and yet requires to be worked out with fear and trembling. However real may be the experience of having died with Christ, *the old man* is not wholly dead. Christians are still in the flesh, "in the world" though not "of the world." Those who are dead to Sin have to guard against the revival of Sin's tyranny. What makes all the difference is that they start by being reconciled to God.

15–23. Subjection to Sin is Unreasonable for Men Who are Free in Christ. Paul now urges the same argument from a slightly different angle. It is contrary to reason that those who have been made free by Christ should be subjects of Sin; alternatively, there has been a change of masters, and the very subjection to Sin which Christians have known in the past is to be from henceforth the measure of their subjection to Christ now.

The thought that Sin is no longer to lord it over them has led him at the end of the last paragraph to proclaim: "Ye are no longer under law, but under grace. But"—to paraphrase the fuller explanation of this in vv. 15–23—"the Law forbade sin. Are Christians, therefore, to sin because they are no longer under the dominion of the Law? Not at all. Remember that to whomsoever you yield yourselves as submissive thralls, whether it be Sin or whether it be God to whom you yield obedience, the submission is complete. And there can be no doubt in your case. For God be praised that when you were thralls of Sin you gave heart-felt allegiance to the form of teaching to which you were committed. I am using human language because of the weakness of your human nature. For just as you had yielded your members to serve impurity and lawlessness, so now you have yielded them to serve righteousness that you might become holy. At the time when you were thralls of Sin, righteousness had no control over you. Now, what kind of harvest did you reap then? Nothing but what now fills you with shame. For what these things lead to is death. But now that you have been freed from the dominion of Sin and made thralls of God, you are finding your harvest in holiness, and what lies before you is eternal life. For the wage paid by Sin is death, whereas the free gift of God is eternal life."

The three-fold contrast in v. 23 is very impressive. There is the contrast between the two masters, Sin and God; the contrast between the two terms of engagement, contract issuing in wages paid and grace issuing in a gift freely bestowed; and the contrast between the things a man ultimately receives, death and eternal life.

CHAPTER VII

1–6. An Illustration From the Obligations of Marriage. "It is only when a man is alive that he is subject to law. You, to whom I write, know this, for you are familiar with the Law. So, for example, a married woman is bound by law to her husband so long as he is alive. But if the husband die, she is released from the husband-law (the law concerning husband and wife). So long, therefore, as he is alive, she will be reckoned an adulteress if she passes over to another man. But should he die, she is exempted from that law, so that she does not become an adulteress by belonging to another man."

Up to this point (v. 4) it is the wife who being released by the death of her husband provides an illustration of the Christian's emancipation. Here, however, the illustration becomes somewhat confused. We should expect Paul to draw the inference that the Law being dead, Christians are exempt from its authority. But for that he substitutes the idea that Christians have *died to the law.* It is *by the body of Christ* that they have so died, i.e., by the death of Christ and their participation in it; for he died to the Law in the same way as he died unto sin. But if the Christian thus owes his release from the Law to the death of Christ, the result of that release is to bring him into a new relation with the risen and living Christ.

Thus we may paraphrase: "In the same manner you also through the death of Christ have been released from the Law; you have been made dead to it, so that you now belong to another, to him who was raised from the dead, in order that the harvest of our lives might be for God. For when we lived on the material plane, the passions which lead to sinful acts, being stimulated by the Law (v. 7), were active in our members, so that the harvest of our lives was a harvest for death. But now we have been released from the Law, having died to that wherein we were once imprisoned, so that our service is rendered now within the sphere of spirit and not of a written code."

7–13. The Purpose and Function of the Law. Paul has already touched more than once the question, What was the function of the Law? It "produces wrath" (4^{15}). It has been introduced in order that transgressions may abound (5^{20}; cf. Gal. 3^{19}). But what he has just written, proclaiming triumphantly that Christians are dead to the Law, raises the question in an acute form, especially as he has already shown that they are dead to Sin. He seems, therefore, to have brought the Law into the same category as Sin itself, inviting the question, *Is the Law Sin?* To which he answers: "Not at all. It was only through the Law that I came to a knowledge of Sin. If it were not that the Law said, 'Thou shalt not covet,' I would not have known wrong desire. But Sin (personified as before) seized the opportunity which the Law offered, and produced all manner of evil desire in me. So long as there is no law, sin is dead or dormant (cf. 4^{15} 5^{13}). So I lived at one time independent of law, innocent in a sense but only because ignorant of God's will. But when I became acquainted with the commandment, Sin sprang to life and I died (cf. 5^{12}). And so the commandment which was intended to lead to the higher life, actually led in my case to death. For Sin, seizing the opportunity offered by the commandment, deceived me (as the Serpent deceived Eve), and slew me. But this was no part of the original purpose of the Law. And in spite of the use which Sin has made of it, it remains true that the Law is holy, that is, belongs to God; and the commandment is holy and just and good."

Note on Paul and the Law

Paul has been accused of glaring inconsistency in his language about the Law and in his practical relation to it. On the one hand he asserts its divine origin and character, its high ethical quality, as in v. 12, and its function as a tutor to bring men to Christ (Gal. 3^{24}), and he sometimes practices some of those ceremonial requirements which we should expect to be the first to be abrogated (Acts 16^{3} 18^{18} $21^{18f.}$). On the other hand he appears to reckon the Law among the spiritual foes of man; it is something to which Christians have to die as they die unto Sin; and "Christ is the end of law for righteousness to everyone that believes" (10^{4}). *The inconsistency is, however, more apparent than real.* It disappears when we recognize the distinction which was clearly present to the apostle's mind. That is the distinction between the Law as a system whereby the Jews had learned to expect that they could establish a claim upon God's favor, could earn his forgiveness and secure a righteousness of their own, and the Law as the expression of the moral ideals which God set before his people. We must remember also that in recent generations the Law as a whole had been exalted into a kind of palladium of the Jewish race, having an intrinsic supernatural quality which almost led to its replacing God. It was the Law in this aspect, and especially as a system in which men trusted to establish a righteousness of their own, that Paul dreaded, criticized, and proclaimed to have come to an end in Christ. Yet he saw it as something which had been perverted from its original purpose, though something which had not lost its original character. And even for the ceremonial law or some parts of it he retained a genuine respect ("circumcision has its value" 2^{25}), even as he continued to regard the moral ideals of the Law as valid, provided always the observance of neither the one nor the other was understood to establish a claim upon God. The Jew thought that if he kept the Law he would be saved. Paul taught that man must be saved in order to keep the Law (see above, notes on 3^{27-30}).

14–25. The Discord within Himself as Well as the Discord Between Himself and the Divine Law. Was it possible that this thing so good in itself had produced this result, that Paul found himself "dead in trespasses and sins"? Not at all. Once more it was Sin that was responsible. Sin had made use of this good thing to produce that death, so that its sinful character might be abundantly manifest through the commandment. "For we know that the Law belongs to the world of spirit; but I am a creature of flesh, and one who has been sold to be a subject of Sin. I do not know my conduct for my own. For it is not what I want but what I hate that I do. And as things are, it is not I who do the deed, but Sin which has taken up its abode within me. For I know that there dwells in me (I mean, of course, in my corrupt nature) nothing good. I have the longing for high things, but when it comes to doing them, No! For I do not do the good thing I wish to do; rather do I do the evil thing I do not wish to do. But if this be so, then it is no longer I that do the deed, but Sin which has taken up its abode in me. This, then, is the rule that I find working, that *when I wish to do right, the wrong thing lies ready to my hand.* My inner man consents cordially to the law of God; but I perceive another rule in my members which is not the law of my mind but holds me captive to the law of Sin which prevails in my members. So, then, with my mind I am subject to the law of God, but with my flesh to the law of Sin. [This last sentence, v. 25b, appears to have got displaced, and should probably be placed here after v. 23.] Unhappy man that I am! who shall deliver me from this body which belongs to death? God can; thanks be to him through Jesus Christ our Lord."

It is not necessary, even if it were possible, to decide whether Paul is describing his experience before his conversion or after it; or, again, whether all the features of the description are drawn from his own experience or some of them from observation. At the same time Paul was under no illusion that the struggle was over even for one who had believed on Christ. What we have here, made for the first time in human history, is *the penetrating analysis of moral struggle*, the struggle between the higher and the lower natures in man, and the acknowledgment of its hopelessness apart from the redeeming power of God. Paul writes in the present tense, but he is really projecting his mind back to the period before his conversion, when he had found the promise held out by the Law or on behalf of the Law a hopeless deception. It was not able "to make alive" (Gal. 3[21]). For it was overruled by the indwelling power of Sin. The *flesh*, which was the seat and organ of Sin, was too strong for the mind, even though that was convinced of the beauty of goodness. And though it was true that the situation was changed from one of despair to one of hope through faith in Christ and its consequences, the old antinomy had not wholly disappeared. It was still necessary to "slay the deeds of the body" (8[13]), "the members that are upon the earth" (Col. 3[5]), to put off the old man, and put on the new (Eph. 4[22f.]). And if we hear throughout the greater part of the paragraph the cry of every man who has found himself confronted by conscience with the moral demands of God and discovered his inability to meet them while he is cut off from the life of God, we hear in the last verse the triumphant assurance of victory to those who are in Christ.

CHAPTER VIII

1–11. The Supremacy of the Spiritual Over the Material. Once more, and for the last time, Paul returns to the theme with which he set out in 1[17] (cf. 3[21] 5[1]), *There is therefore now no condemnation to them that are in Christ Jesus.* This expresses in a negative form the result of the divine righteousness which is being revealed, the meaning of the justification which the coming of the righteousness implies. But now Paul, having dealt with successive difficulties and criticisms which presented themselves to his mind, is free to expand his theme without any further digression. And the first thing is to connect the experience of acquittal with the further experience of life by the Spirit and on the spiritual plane. He begins by exhibiting the antithesis between the material and the spiritual, and the supremacy of the spiritual over the material. There is *no condemnation* to those who are in Christ Jesus (see below), because they have been emancipated from the Law which procures condemnation, the law which leads to sin and death (cf. 2 Cor. 3[7, 9]); and what has secured their freedom is the spirit-principle that leads to life in Christ Jesus. We note that the word *law* is used in two different senses in the same verse (v. 2). In the first case it refers not to any positive or external law, similar to the Law of Moses, but to an internal regulative principle, the influence of the Spirit exercised along definite lines. When the Law had proved itself a failure, as Paul has shown, especially in the previous chapter, God had intervened and introduced a new method whereby the righteous requirements of the Law might after all be fulfilled (v. 4). And what he had done was nothing less than the *sending of his own Son*, in the likeness of Sin's flesh (i.e., of the flesh that had come to belong to Sin) and in connection with Sin (i.e., to deal with Sin).

These last words introduce us to a new way of conceiving salvation, in terms of *the antithesis between flesh and spirit*, and the experience of being lifted from the lower to the higher. This Paul now proceeds to develop in vv. 5f. Those that are wholly material take the material point of view, but those that are spiritual the spiritual. The material point of view is death; but the spiritual point of view is life and peace. For the material point of view is enmity against God, because it neither is nor can be submitted to the law of God, and those who are wholly material cannot be pleasing to God.

Those who are in Christ Jesus (v. 1). This

very significant phrase meets us here for the first time. The possibility of Paul's using it, and the significance he attaches to it, depend upon two considerations. In the first place, he conceives of Christ in glory in terms of spirit, exempt from all conditions of space and time, and therefore as a sphere or atmosphere within which men may dwell, one in whom they may "live and move and have their being" (Acts 17^{28}). Secondly, Paul equates the spiritual fellowship, the Body of Christ, the church in that sense, with Christ himself (cf. 1 Cor. 12^{12}), in such a way that the idea of members of the fellowship being also "in Christ" became easy and natural for him.

Sinful flesh (v. 3) in R.V. conveys a wrong impression. The words mean "Sin's flesh," and Paul is not referring to any quality or disposition in the physical constitution of Christ, but to the fact that it was like the physical constitution of mankind in general, in that it had come to be under the dominion of Sin. *Condemned sin* (v. 3) is not strong enough. It might mean no more than the expression of strong disapproval. Better "pronounced the doom of Sin." Sin was thenceforth deposed from its autocratic power. *The ordinances of the law* (v. 4), i.e., the Law's just requirements. For though the Law as a system has come to an end, its moral requirements are still to guide the conduct of the Christians.

The distinction between the flesh and the spirit is best expressed for us in terms of the distinction between the material and the spiritual; and when Paul here asserts the incommensurable superiority of the spiritual he is reproducing the teaching of his Master, when he insisted repeatedly on the incommensurable value of the soul and also of the kingdom of God, that is to say, the spiritual side of life in its individual and its corporate aspects.

Christians have their being on the plane of spirit; in this sense they are "spiritual" (v. 9). The new life which was due to faith in Christ, a participation in his spiritual life, was a life no longer on the material, but on the spiritual plane, and was guaranteed by the fact that the Spirit of God made his abode in the believer. No one can claim to belong to Christ unless he has the Spirit of Christ. But if Christ has made his abode in you, then the body or lower nature is *dead because of sin*, but your *spirit is alive* (v. 10) to bring forth the harvest of righteousness. Sin may not have wholly died out from the body, but the body has lost its controlling power; that has passed to the spirit now quickened and re-enforced by the Spirit of Christ. And if the Spirit of Him who raised Jesus from the dead dwells in you, then He who raised up Jesus shall also bring to life your bodies which are marked for death through his Spirit that dwells in you (cf. 6^5 1 Cor. 15^{44} 2 Cor. 4^{10}).

Note on Paul's Conception of the Spirit

Paul's conception of the Spirit found here and elsewhere shows marked development from that which we find in the O.T. and even in the earlier parts of the N.T. There the Spirit of God is looked on, along with the Word of God and the Wisdom of God, as a Divine Force, belonging to God, proceeding from God, and carrying out the purposes of God. To the Spirit are specially assigned, though not exclusively, the quickening of life, the enhancement of natural human powers, and the bestowal of prophetic inspiration; but it is always as a *non-personal* organ of God's will. The same conception meets us in the synoptic Gospels, and even in the narrative of Pentecost. But in the case of Paul something has happened, which can best be described by saying that as Jesus had revealed the Father, so also he revealed the Spirit. *The Spirit is now understood to have the same character and qualities as Jesus,* to act and influence in the same way as Jesus had acted and influenced men. We find now ascribed to him self-consciousness and self-direction, qualities which we recognize as connoting personality. He is spoken of as a person. And while it cannot be said that Paul ever ignores the distinction between the Spirit and Christ, even the spiritual Christ in glory, it is equally true that he treats them as *interchangeable* in the practical experience of men. He traces various aspects of Christian experience now to the one and now to the other (cf. v. 26 with v. 34). Of this we have striking illustration in these verses where the indwelling of the Spirit, of the Spirit of Christ or the Spirit of God, evidently refer to one and the same experience. (For a fuller discussion, see Lewis, *Manual of Christian Beliefs*, ch. 10.)

12–17. The Privileges of the Christian, Sonship and Heirship. Such experiences as have just been described carry their own imperative. Those who have been raised to the plane of spirit are bound to live on it. What has in one sense been accomplished (cf. 6^6) in another has still to be worked out. It is those who are governed by the Spirit of God who are really sons of God. The spirit you have received is not a spirit of servitude, renewing your old dread of spirit-forces of evil, but a spirit of sonship which leads us to address God as Father. And to our own conviction is added the witness of God's own Spirit that we are indeed the sons of God (1 Jn. 3^1 Jn. 1^{12}). In this quiet way Paul introduces what is probably the highest conception of Christian experience and of Christian privilege. *An overwhelming sense of sonship together with an overwhelming sense of brotherhood which the Spirit creates within the fellowship*—in these two experiences we have the heart of Christianity. And the new relation of sonship is so genuine that it carries with it the privileges of inheritance (Gal. 4[7]). It involves a partaking in the heritage of God (cf. 1 Cor. 2[9f.]), a partaking which we share with Christ, on the one condition that we share also in his suffering.

18–27. Even Present Suffering is but a Condition of Future Glory. "The suffering of the present life is not to be compared with the glory that is to be revealed in us. For that glory is not for ourselves alone, but will involve something for which all created being is waiting on tiptoe, the revelation of the sons of God. For creation indeed has been subjected to hopeless futility, not of its own will, but because of him, namely, God, who so subjected it in hope; for not merely humanity but the world of created being shall be set free from the bondage of corruption, and brought into the liberty of the children of God, whereas, as we know, it sighs and throbs with pain up till this present time. And that is true also of ourselves, even though we have the Spirit of God as a first-fruits of our glory. We also sigh within ourselves waiting for the perfect realization of sonship, when our body also is delivered. For that is the hope unto which we have been saved. Hope, we must remember, is always for something not yet realized; and if we continue to hope for that, then we wait for it with patience. And, besides, we have the Spirit helping to sustain our weakness. We know not what to pray for as we ought; but the Spirit himself pleads for us with sighs that are beyond words. For God, the searcher of hearts, knows what is the mind of the Spirit, that he pleads for us in accordance with the purpose of God."

Sons of God (v. 19). We should naturally expect "the revelation of the Son of God." But the phrase is in harmony with Paul's doctrine of a redeemed humanity as the perfected self-realization of Christ (Eph. 1[23]), whose manifestation would be part of and equivalent to his own (Eph. 4[13]). *The whole creation* (v. 22). The phrase suggests to us pre-eminently though not exclusively the world of nature and of inanimate being; to Paul it probably stood mainly though not exclusively for the world of sentient being, including the spiritual forces in the unseen (cf. Eph. 3[10]). *Redemption of our body* (v. 23), i.e., through the transforming of the natural body of flesh into the spiritual body of the life to come (1 Cor. 15[44]). *The Spirit himself maketh intercession* (v. 26). The same function is predicated of the Spirit here as is predicated of Christ in v. 34.

28–39. The Contents and the Ground of Christian Hope. Paul assumes that the man who accepts the love of God which is commended to us through the death of Christ, will love God in return, and proclaims that with all such God co-operates for their good. He then further defines these in view not of man's response to God, which might be fluctuating, but of God's choice and calling, on which he does not go back (cf. 11[29]). The goal toward which *the Divine purpose* (v. 28) moves is variously described as bringing them into conformity to the image or character of Christ, and as causing them to participate in the glory, the moral splendor, of God. And the certainty of this result rests ultimately not on any human choice or action, but on the timeless knowledge and will of God, which had found its first expression in the divine calling (cf. 1[6, 7]), and then in the bestowal of the divine righteousness (2 Tim. 2[19] Jn. 15[16]). From this fact alone the Christian is to draw the strongest possible comfort and encouragement. With God upon our side, it does not matter who is against us. And of that we have the conclusive proof in that he was willing to sacrifice his own Son (cf. Gen. 22[16]). After that we may well believe that there is nothing which is truly for our good that he will not give us. Who has the right to challenge those whom God has chosen? (Cf. 14[4].) Our business is with God; and he is the one who pronounces acquittal. Who has the right to condemn? We have to do with Christ, and he is the one in whose death, resurrection, and ascension we see the "power of God unto salvation." Planted on such a foundation the Christian can securely face everything that menaces either happiness or life. For none of these things can separate us from *the love of Christ* (v. 35).

Some authorities read here "the love of God"; and this is what we should expect from the context, as it is also what we find in v. 39. But, as Chrysostom put it, "it is so much a matter of indifference to Paul whether he mentions Christ or God." The quotation from Psa. 44[22] in v. 36 is a parenthetic illustration of the danger which God's people may incur from the sword of the enemy. The thought now moves on to the climax. None of the things which menace happiness or life can separate us from the love of Christ. But there were believed to be worse foes of man than these, namely, *the Forces which were understood to rule human life from the start,* "elemental spirits of the world" (Gal. 4[3]), "spirit-forces of evil in the unseen" (Eph. 6[12]). Fear of these was poisoning human happiness and destroying human freedom, creating a real bondage of dread (cf. v. 15). (See Glover, *Jesus in the Experience of Men*, ch. 1.) Paul looks round the whole world of ghostly enemies of man, including even angels (for they too might be foes of God and man), and proclaims their helplessness to destroy the Christian's relation with God.

I am persuaded that neither Death nor Life, not Angels or Principalities or Powers, not the Powers of the Empyrean or the Powers of the Abyss, shall be able to separate us from the love of God which is in Christ Jesus our Lord.

This is the culminating point of the Epistle. We feel that in a real sense it was for this it was written, to pass on to Christians conscious of being faced by many hostile forces the triumphant assurance which for Paul was rooted and grounded in the fact of the gospel: "We are more than conquerors through Christ who loved us."

Chapters 9 to 11: Excursus on the Problem of the Jew

Paul has brought to a most impressive conclusion his account of "the good things that are ours in Christ." He is now ready, we should suppose, for the exposition of the ethical implication of salvation which we are to find in chs. 12–14. But the very wonder of all that has been passing through his mind recalls this sad and perplexing fact, that his own nation the Jews, as a whole, have failed to respond to the message of the gospel, have ruled themselves out of its privileges. And he turns aside to devote the next three chapters to the discussion of this problem, *Why does it appear as though God had rejected Israel?*

General Considerations Bearing on the Problem. In studying these chapters in detail it is well to bear in mind certain general considerations which emerge in the course of the argument and must affect our understanding of the details. (1) There is, first of all, the general conclusion to which the whole argument moves; "so all Israel shall be saved" (11^{26}), and "God hath shut up all unto disobedience, that he might have mercy upon all" (11^{32}). (2) Paul lays the foundation for his answer to the main question by pointing to the fact that a principle of selection has been at work from the beginning of Israel's history. It began, indeed (though Paul does not mention this), when Abraham was chosen and called out of a world that knew not God. It was illustrated in the choice of Isaac and the passing over of Ishmael; and even more strikingly in the choice of Jacob and the passing over of Esau. (3) This selection depended on the sovereign will of God; it was something against which no human protest or cavil could be admitted. (4) The selection was to privilege and responsibility in this world; and it was not (as the Jews thought) absolute and unconditional. (5) The purpose of the selection was that through those selected blessing should ultimately come upon those who were passed over (cf. Gen. 18^{18}). (6) The position of those who were passed over was that of the Gentiles, which he dealt with in 2^{6f}. They did not participate in the privileges, but they had open to them the alternatives described in 2^{8-11}.

It should be added that the question which at once occurs to us, *What was the ultimate fate of those who passed away before the saving purpose of God was accomplished?* does not appear to be touched on by the apostle. It is, indeed, to this fact that our difficulty in appreciating his argument is largely due. (See also p. 1159b.)

CHAPTER IX

1–13. Within Abraham's Stock Itself There Has Been Selection. (Cf. preceding paragraphs on the problem of the Jew.) Paul begins by emphasizing the poignancy of the situation, his own insistent grief, and the manifold privileges which the Jews have enjoyed. After the most solemn asseveration of his sincerity he says in effect: The wish was in my heart that I myself might be banned from Christ for my brethren's sake. What privileges have been theirs! Adoption, the Shechinah, the Covenants, the Legislation, the Worship and the Promises; the Father too, and the Messiah, at least on the human side. And it is no true explanation of Israel's position now to say that God's word of promise has failed. The fact is that all along there has been a principle of selection at work. Not all who belonged to Israel according to the flesh have belonged to the true Israel. Not all the descendants of Abraham have been his "children," and so *heirs of the promise.* For example, the promise was limited to the descendants of Isaac; the descendants of Ishmael were passed over. It follows that the privilege of being God's children does not depend on physical descent (cf. Mt. 3^9), but on God's promise. Jacob and Esau provide an even clearer case of selection; for even before they were born God had chosen Jacob and passed over Esau, when he said that Esau the elder should serve his younger brother (Gen. 25^{23}).

Who is over all (v. 5). According to the punctuation of R.V. and most authorities, these closing words of v. 5 refer to Christ, and involve the ascription to him of the divine name. It is, nevertheless, more probable that we should put a full stop after "flesh" (cf. mg.), and see in the words that follow a benediction upon God such as was very common in Jewish writings and is actually found in 1[25] and 2 Cor. 11[31].

Jacob have I loved (v. 13). The sentence is from Mal. 1[2, 3], and a careful examination of the passage shows that the prophet is speaking not merely of the individuals Jacob and Esau but of the nations to which they had severally given rise (Israel and Edom). He traces back the present condition of these peoples to the original choice of Jacob and passing over of Esau. The original selection of Jacob had approved itself in the divine favor which Israel continued to enjoy. The original passing over of Esau, whereby he and his descendants were left in the position of "Gentiles," had issued in a condition which could only be interpreted as due to the disfavor, anger, hatred, of God. For the use of the word *hate* in the sense of "treat as if he hated" cf. Lk. 14[26].

14–33. Two Objections Which Might Be Raised by a Jew. If God thus chooses one and passes over another in entire indifference to character or qualification, *does he not act unfairly?* To this objection Paul replies by referring the Jew to familiar passages in the O.T. He cannot call God unjust if he acts in accordance with the principle there revealed. Speaking to *Moses* God had declared that his mercy followed his sovereign choice (Ex. 33[19]), so that it does not depend on human will or effort but solely on the divine will. Conversely, *Pharaoh* was one on whom in the exercise of the same divine sovereignty God had brought hardening of heart. Paul states this in uncompromising terms, being concerned only at the moment to assert *the irrefragable independence of the divine will.* Nevertheless, it would appear from what follows that had he been asked whether Pharaoh was responsible for the conduct which is described as due to the hardening of his heart (cf. Ex. 8[32] with Ex. 9[12]), he would have replied in the affirmative. His position on the question of predestination and free will was probably that common to the Pharisees, which is thus described by Josephus: "All things are governed by fate, yet they do not take away from men the freedom of acting as they see fit; for their idea is that it has pleased God to mix up the ideas of Fate and man's will, so that man can act viciously or virtuously" (*Antiquities*, bk. xiii, ch. 5: 9).

This leads to a second objection: *Why, then, does God continue to hold man responsible, seeing that no one can resist his will?* It cannot be said that Paul refutes this objection. He is content to repel it as one which the creature has no right to raise against the Creator. And he illustrates this by referring the objector to familiar passages in the O.T. (Isa. 45[9] Jer. 18[6]). "When the chosen material (i.e., the Jews) would not mold to the high purpose for which the Potter was fashioning it, who shall complain if he diverted it to lower uses or threw it away to destruction, and produced out of his stores other vessels which he had already prepared and destined for glorious functions (that is to say, the Gentile Christians)?" (Gore.) The truth is that "to this objection there is no answer, and it ought to be frankly recognized that the apostle does not answer it. The attempt to understand the relation between the divine will and the human seems to lead of necessity to an antinomy which thought has not yet succeeded in transcending" (Denney).

But what if God, though desirous to display his wrath, has tolerated most patiently the objects of his wrath, ripe and ready to be destroyed? (Moffatt.) And what if his purpose has been to make known the wealth of his glory (v. 23) in the case of the objects of his mercy, that is to say, ourselves whom he has called, Gentiles as well as Jews? Had not *Hosea* predicted the calling to be God's people of those who were not his people (Hos. 2[23] 1[10]). And had not *Isaiah* with his doctrine of the remnant, which was at once the heir and the agent of salvation (Isa. 10[22] 1[9]), recognized the working of the principle of selection in the later history of Israel?

30. Drawing a provisional conclusion, Paul falls back upon facts, the facts of observation. Gentiles, some of them, had accepted what Israel had refused. It was not an answer to the problem, but it opened the door to one (11[30, 31]). Gentiles who had not consciously pursued righteousness had laid hold of it, while Israel, always in pursuit of a law which was to produce righteousness, had never caught it up. And the reason was that what Israel sought to earn by merit the Gentiles were ready to accept on the ground of faith. Then even the Messiah himself had proved nothing better for Israel than *a stone on which they stumbled* (Isa. 8[14]), and not one on whom to believe would, as Isaiah had foretold in another passage (28[16]), put a man beyond the reach of shame.

CHAPTER X

1–13. The Simplicity and Directness of the Gospel. We see here the dawning of hope for Israel in the apostle's heart. He could not have expressed his heart's desire and prayer for Israel's salvation had he looked on its rejection as due to an immutable decree. And he proceeds to explain more fully than elsewhere the fundamental mistake of the Jews. Failing to recognize the righteousness that comes from God, and still seeking to establish a righteousness of their own, they had refused to bow their wills to the divine righteousness. Yet it was a mistake, *for* (v. 2), on the one hand, Christ had put an end to law, to any legal system as a means for obtaining salvation, by securing righteousness for everyone who believes; and, on the other hand, the condition for securing *life* (v. 5) which Moses had laid down in Lev. 18[5] is one not possible to be fulfilled (cf. Gal. 3[12]). What, however, is the testimony of the righteousness that rests on faith? Paul boldly personifies that righteousness, and makes it say in effect: "There is no need to ask these despairing questions, Who will go up to heaven for us?—namely, adds Paul in parenthesis, *to bring Christ down;* or, Who will descend into the abyss? namely, *to bring Christ up.* For the message that matters is close beside you; nay, it is in your mouth, and in your heart. And that," adds Paul, "is the message that leads to faith, the message that we proclaim. For if you confess with your mouth Jesus as Lord, and believe in your heart that God raised him from the dead, you shall be saved. Does not the Scripture itself say, No one who believes on him shall be put to shame? (Isa. 28[16].) And that holds good of all; for there is no difference between Jew and Gentile, for the same Lord is Lord of them all."

6–8. Three phrases in these verses are echoes rather than quotations from Deut. 30[12, 13], which appears to have been a favorite passage with the Jews. Moses had applied them to the Law; Paul applies them to the gospel. The main idea is that the gospel is within immediate reach of men; but Paul works in with this the thought that it is needless to seek for Christ either above or below; for Christ has already come from above, and he has already been brought up from the dead.

9. The open acknowledgment of Jesus as "Lord" appears to have been the one necessary condition for baptism and admission to the sacred society. *Believe in thine heart.* Faith is something that goes beyond intellectual assent; it is "a specific state of emotional nature" (cf. Lk. 24[25]).

13. To *call on the name of the Lord* is commonly used in the O.T. as a synonym for worshiping Jehovah, the word "name" describing a person as he is known. The sentence in Joel 2[32] predicates deliverance for the true worshiper of Almighty God. It is highly significant that Paul evidently predicates the same for those who call upon the name of Christ, i.e., accept him as Lord in the same way as men under the old dispensation had accepted God.

14–21. Israel Cannot Excuse Itself as Not Having Heard the Gospel. The paragraph begins with a series of rapid questions which are supposed to be put by a Jew seeking to make excuse for his people not having yielded to the gospel. And to these questions Paul gives a summary answer, but what he evidently feels to be a sufficient one, in the sentence quoted from Isa. 52[7]. That is to say, he contents himself for the moment with drawing attention to the wide dispersion of missionaries of the gospel into all the countries which come into consideration. It is not true, he would say, that the Jews have not had opportunity to hear the message of Christ. What is true is suggested by another sentence from Isaiah (53[1]). They have heard, but have refused to believe. But the fact remains that faith follows upon hearing, and hearing upon the proclamation of the message about Christ. In v. 18 Paul harks back to the main question, *Is it true that Israel has not heard?* Why, the whole world has heard; so great has been the number of the preachers. Only the familiar language of Psa. 19[4] can do justice to the situation; "their voice has gone out to the ends of the earth."

Having dealt with the question, Have they not heard? Paul raises a further one—*Is it true that Israel did not know?* (V. 19.) And he answers it with three quotations from the O.T. to the effect that if it were so, it could not be for lack of warning. As far back as Moses it had been announced that God would give Israel cause for jealousy against a nation that was not his people, stirring them to anger against those who could not be credited with religious sensitiveness (Deut. 32[21]). And Isaiah had declared even more boldly that God would manifest himself to peoples who did not inquire after him (Isa. 65[1]); whereas the situation in regard to Israel was that God was continuously stretching out his hands toward a people who were disobedient and contentious (Isa. 62[2]). God had all along been pleading with Israel, but in vain.

CHAPTER XI

1–12. Israel's Rejection Neither Complete nor Final. In this paragraph we see the light of Paul's hope for Israel growing stronger and clearer. Has God, he asks, altogether thrust away his people? Not at all. He, Paul, is himself a case to the contrary, a Jew of pure descent, who has found salvation in Christ. The situation is, indeed, like to the one recorded in that passage of the O.T. known as "Elijah" (v. 2, cf. mg.). There we learn how the despairing prophet laid before God his complaint against Israel (1 Kings 19[10]), and added "and

I only am left," only to receive the divine assurance that it was not so, that there were actually seven thousand who had not "bowed the knee to Baal." In like manner there is even at the present time *a remnant of those who are selected by grace* (v. 5); and if by grace, then obviously not on the ground of merit, for in that case grace or unmerited favor would have lost its character. It follows (v. 7) that though Israel as a whole has failed to attain the object of its quest, a remnant or section of the people has attained it. As for the rest, they have forfeited their sensitiveness to the message of God. It was not that God had rejected his people (cf. v. 1); but Israel as a whole had rejected itself by proving unworthy of the destiny to which it was called, to be a blessing to all peoples. And so it had incurred judgment, not only by seeing the opportunity pass over to the Gentiles, but by being allowed to sink to the moral level of those who knew not God.

This explains the quotations which follow, where the language which in Isa. 29^{10} and Deut. 29^{4} is used of the heathen is now applied to the Jews, and the even fiercer denunciation in Psa. $69^{22,\ 23}$ is given a similar direction. Israel, no less than the Gentiles, must undergo the utter judgment of God (cf. 1 Thess. 2^{16}). The question in v. 11, *Did they stumble so as to fall* (irrevocably)? is, however, at once vigorously repelled; and then follows an explanation of their stumbling which connects its results with the gracious purposes of God. The failure of Israel has opened a door to salvation for the Gentiles, whereby the Jews themselves may be stimulated to follow their example. And if wealth has come to the world through their failure, and to the Gentiles through their grievous loss, how much greater will be the gain when they too are replenished with the grace of God.

The horizon is clearing. Israel cannot escape the penalties of its obstinacy and culpable refusal. It has lost its status, and punishment must fall upon its sin. But the casting off of Israel has not been complete. Neither is it final. God's calling, the offer of salvation, has passed over to the Gentiles. But their joyful acceptance of the gift of God in Jesus Christ will be an example and a stimulus to the Jews. So that there is new ground of hope of their coming into the Kingdom, to the further enrichment of the Gentiles and even of mankind itself.

13–24. The Gentiles Are Seriously Warned Against Self-complacency. Attentive consideration of Paul's argument up to this point might have the effect of giving the Gentiles a sense of superiority to the Jews, as they might draw the inference that they had taken the place of the Jews in God's favor, and then proceed to make the same mistake as the Jews had done. Conscious of this, Paul turns now to address the Gentiles. To begin with, they must not think, for all his eagerness to be the Apostle of the Gentiles, and to make good their claim, that he had ceased to magnify his wider ministry which included Jews as well as Gentiles; that still moved him to seek to stir up his flesh and blood, his own countrymen, with a view to *saving some* of them (v. 14). For if, as he has just shown, their temporary rejection is a step toward the reconciliation of mankind, their being received back into God's favor would be nothing less than a veritable *resurrection* (v. 15). There is already a nucleus of believing Jews, and as the heave-offering of old was understood to consecrate the whole mass from which it was taken (cf. Num. 15^{20}), as the branches of a consecrated stem themselves became consecrated, so the mass of the Jews, Paul trusted, would be drawn into the circle of grace.

The reference to the stem or root and the branches (v. 17) introduces the famous *simile of the olive trees*, the garden olive and the wild olive, symbolizing the Jews and the Gentiles. The apostle recalls passages in the prophets in which Israel was spoken of as God's olive tree (Jer. 11^{16} Hos. 14^{6}). Some of the branches have been broken off. The Gentile who was originally no other than a wild olive, has been grafted into God's olive, and become partaker of its rich sap. But "beware of scorning those branches which have been cut off. If thou dost congratulate thyself, remember that it is not thou that supportest the root, but the root that supports thee. The Gentiles might plume themselves, saying, 'These branches have been broken off in order that I might be grafted in.' Quite true. They were broken off because of faithlessness, and you owe your position to faith. Be not uplifted in your mind, but be careful. God will not spare you any more than he spared the branches which belong naturally to the olive. Mark well the kindness and the severity of God. Those who fell have felt his severity; you experience his kindness, but only if you continue to dwell in that kindness; otherwise, you also will be cut off. Moreover, those old branches, if they depart from their faithlessness, shall again be grafted in. For God is able to do that (cf. Mk. 10^{27}). And, indeed, it is all the more probable that those who naturally belong to the tree should be again grafted into their own olive, in view of the fact that you were cut out from the naturally wild olive and grafted into the fine quality olive in a way contrary to nature" (v. 24).

Paul's unconquerable love for his nation and his conviction that God's gracious purpose toward it remains unchanged nowhere find stronger expression than here. So far is "Israel" from being finally rejected that it is into Israel that the Gentiles are to be ingrafted. Even the Gentile-containing church for whose establishment and upbuilding Paul is giving his life, is not to be any new or independent creation; it is to be a spiritual Israel, continuous with the "church in the wilderness" of which Stephen had spoken (Acts 7[38]), which had now been baptized with the Spirit of Christ, and was now the new people of God, united to him in the new covenant.

25–36. Conclusion: God's Purpose of Mercy Toward all Men. As a further argument against self-complacency on the part of the Gentiles Paul reminds them again of "this open secret" (*mystery*, v. 25), that the insensibility which has overtaken Israel is only partial and that it has a limit of time. It is to last until *the fulness of the Gentiles be come*, or, better, until the appointed number of Gentiles have entered in (cf. Mt. 7[13] Lk. 13[24]), and so Israel as a whole shall be saved. Paul now illustrates this conclusion by a series of phrases from Isa. 59[20] 27[9] Jer. 31[33] and again Isa. 27[9]. The first phrase he boldly adapts to suit his purpose by writing *shall come out of Zion*, where the Hebrew has "shall come to Zion" (the LXX differs from both). The Jews are from the point of view of the gospel treated by God as enemies for the sake of the Gentiles; from the point of view of the original selection they are still beloved of God for the sake of their forefathers. They are still beloved of God, for God does not go back on his gifts or his calling. And that will be seen when Paul's hope is fulfilled. For just as the Gentiles were at one time disobedient to God, but have now had mercy shown to them in consequence of the disobedience of the Jews, so the Jews have now fallen into disobedience because of the mercy which they saw the Gentiles enjoying, in order that they in their turn might have mercy shown to them. For God has *concluded them all alike under disobedience* (cf. Gal. 3[22]), Gentiles (v. 30) and Jews (v. 11), in order that he might have mercy upon all. The contemplation of this conclusion of the whole matter fills the apostle's heart with the amazement and thankfulness which find expression in v. 33. The thought that God's ways are *past finding out* is illustrated by another composite quotation from Isa. 40[13] and Job 41[11] (though for the latter Paul appears to follow a text unknown to us). For, he concludes, throwing back his thought to v. 32, all things have in him their *Source*, their *Sustainment* and their *Goal*.

26. *All Israel shall be saved.* The phrase is neither to be expanded to include every Israelite, nor limited to the spiritual remnant. The situation contemplated is when that remnant or first-fruits shall have consecrated "the whole lump," the fullness of the Gentiles, the number which corresponds to the purpose of God.

Retrospect of Chapters 9, 10, and 11. As we look back over these chapters one thing becomes clear, namely, that the process of thought which they embody has brought peace to the soul of the apostle. The agonizing anxiety with which he had contemplated the position of Israel (9[2, 3]) has given way to rejoicing confidence in God and in his purpose of mercy. In working out the process for ourselves we see as the essential thing the moving of the apostle's mind from the purely intellectual to the religious standpoint. The problem which is insoluble when looked at as a problem for the mind alone comes to be, not solved, but soluble, when studied in the atmosphere of faith. Paul does not provide any satisfactory solution of the antinomy between divine foreknowledge and human responsibility, between divine sovereignty and the moral freedom of men. But if he does nothing to reconcile these intellectual contradictories, he does much to *reconcile us to the acceptance of them as bound to find a synthesis in the revealed character of God.* For that character as revealed in Jesus Christ leaves no uncertainty as to the purpose of God, namely, to have mercy upon all men. Human history, says Paul in effect, must be read in the light of that purpose. And so reading it, Paul sees the outline of the divine method. It is a method of selection, selection of individuals, of groups and of nations, to be agents of his gracious purpose toward mankind. It is therefore *a selection for duty as well as for privilege.* And persistent refusal to recognize the duty while resting in the privilege leads to the suspension though not the canceling of the selection. It was this suspension which had befallen the Jews, and the selection had passed over to the Gentiles. But it is theirs on the same conditions. It may be forfeited for the same reasons. *Man's moral freedom works within the ambit of the divine will.* That will neither crushes the human will nor destroys its responsibility. We may not derive from Paul's teaching here any authorization for saying that every man is to be saved; but only that it is the will of God to have mercy upon all. Neither may we derive any authorization for saying that any man is already finally rejected. Paul has singularly little to say that bears directly on the case of individuals. There is little beyond the reference to Pharaoh. He throws his thought into the form of generalization, studying the divine method on a large scale. But his main concern is with the passing over of the Jews and the admitting of the Gentiles to favor. And when he has recognized how these things also are part of the gracious purpose of God toward all men he is lost in admiration and wonder. (See p. 1155.)

CHAPTER XII

1, 2. The Ethical Implication of Salvation; General Introduction. It is only for convenience that we describe this as the second main division of the Epistle. It forms an integral part of Paul's purpose in writing. He had no use for religion or theology which did not translate itself in terms of character and conduct. So the word *therefore* has great significance here. In the three chapters immediately preceding Paul has dealt with a subject in which his own personal interest is keener even than that of those to whom he writes. Now that he passes on to expound the ethical implications of salvation, the principles of Christian motive and Christian conduct, he recalls the contents of chs. 1–8, in which he has analyzed and exhibited *the mercies of God.* And it is in view of these that he now appeals to his readers to *present their bodies a living sacrifice.* "Therefore" forges the link between the doctrinal and the ethical teaching of the Epistle. By "bodies" Paul suggests all the activities of the earthly life; and the consecration of these he describes as *a living sacrifice,* and "your spiritual or immaterial worship." Henceforth, God neither seeks nor requires material sacrifice of any kind. That has been completely replaced by the joyful surrender to him of human hearts and wills. Christians, therefore, are not to pattern themselves on the present order of things, but to accept such a change in themselves, a change of mental outlook, that they will be able to discern the will of God—what is good and well-pleasing and ideal.

3–21. The Natural Attitude of Christians in Their Relations to One Another. Paul is about to describe the kind of temper and the forms of conduct which are natural and becoming in a Christian. He throws his teaching into the form of precepts, and the precepts become useful guides to the individual; but they are addressed to the community as a whole, and to the individual in his relation to the fellowship or sacred society of which he is a member. It is seldom indeed that Paul contemplates the individual as an isolated unit. Nearly always he thinks of him as a member of the Christian Community. For the faith-union by which he is united to Christ is also a love-union by which he is united to his fellow believers, and it is in this fellowship that he is to find the full opportunity for the realization of his new personality. That is why in vv. 4, 5, after laying down the first requirement of *modesty,* Paul emphasizes as a motive for that modesty *the common life of the Body of Christ,* a common life shared by many members, each of whom has his own function, each of whom is related to every part as well as to the whole. On every such member he urges, in the first place, modesty in his estimate of himself, taking for his standard no human qualifications he may possess but the degree of faith which God has granted to him. There is something individual in the quality of each man's faith; and corresponding to that is the particular grace-gift which is assigned to him. To that also is to correspond the use he makes of it (v. 6), whether it be public speech (*prophecy*) or personal service (*ministry*) or teaching or comforting or giving. *He that ruleth* (v. 8) should probably be rendered "he that hath a concern for the church"; as in 1 Thess. 5^{12} and 1 Tim. $3^{2f.}$, let one who attends to the general interests do so with diligence. And in general let the love upon which the whole structure is rooted and grounded be free from insincerity.

In vv. 9–21 Paul passes from the spiritual grace-gifts and the proper use of them to recount *the general characteristics of the Christian's attitude,* specially toward those "of the household of faith." And here we have to observe not only the specific echoes of our Lord's own teaching in the Sermon on the Mount (vv. 14, 19), but how closely Paul reproduces the spirit of that teaching, while throwing it into many various forms. We have to register this phenomenon, explain it how we may, that although Paul was not himself a disciple of Jesus, and although the record of Christ's teaching was not yet available in the Gospels, *the Christian man as Paul describes him is not distinguishable from the portrait of the ideal man as we should construct it from what we know of our Lord's teaching.* The ultimate basis of this harmony is the common recognition that "love is the fulfilling of the law"; but even then there is something very striking in the harmonious application of the principle.

There is little in these verses that calls for interpretation. The following *alternative renderings* of some phrases are offered as either clearer or more exact than R.V.: **12.** Read *let your hope be a joy to you* (Moffatt). **13.** Read *sharing in the necessities of God's people; chasing opportunities for hospitality.* **16b.** Read *drawn into fellowship with humble folk.* **17.**

Observe the admission of the opinion of others as at least a subordinate standard for the conduct of the Christian (cf. Mt. 17^{27}). **19.** Read *make room for the Wrath*, i.e., allow the judgment of God to take its course. **20.** Quoted from Prov. $25^{21, 22}$; the closing words may be paraphrased as by Moffatt, "in this way you make him feel a burning sense of shame." **21.** "Evil is all around the Christian, and it is a strong man armed. But the Christian has with him the forces of good, which are yet stronger; and by no partial withdrawal, but by the active exercise of good, he is to win the victory over evil" (Gore).

CHAPTER XIII

1–7. Christians and the State. The question of the relation of God's people or the church to the state was an important one, though not so difficult in Paul's time as it afterward became. It had already been laid before Jesus by the Pharisees, who framed what seemed to them a dilemma by which he could not fail to be caught. "Is it lawful to pay tribute to Cæsar or not?" And Paul's handling of the subject is in close correspondence with the purport of our Lord's reply, "Render unto Cæsar the things that are Cæsar's, and to God the things that are God's." The claims of the state are to be recognized within its proper sphere. But Paul proceeds to assign reasons for this which are not included in our Lord's reply. "The existing authorities have been *ordained by God*" (v. 1).

The principle is a true one, and yet not absolute in its application. Paul's experience of the state, and the experience of the church, had been up to this time only favorable. Nominally a republic, the Roman state was now governed under republican forms by an emperor. And so far as subject peoples were concerned, the Roman administration was marked by wisdom and tolerance. The Jews in particular enjoyed great internal freedom and certain special privileges. Paul's natural instinct, therefore, was to credit the state with good intentions, and also with a wise administration of justice. And the state had not hitherto displayed hostility to the Christians; still less had it indulged in any organized persecutions. On the contrary, it had on more than one occasion interfered to protect the Christians from the Jews by whom they were frequently attacked and rabbled. It was in full confidence in Roman justice that Paul appealed to Cæsar. And in 2 Thess. 2^{5-7} he acknowledges the function fulfilled by the Roman state in restraining for the time being the activities of Antichrist.

In these circumstances it was not difficult for Paul to acknowledge the civil authorities of his time as *ordained of God.* Only a few years had passed, however, before the situation was entirely changed. The cruel persecution under Nero marked the beginning of an alteration of the attitude of the state to the church. That strange amalgam of religion and politics, the cult of the Roman emperor, suddenly acquired great importance; and Christians who refused to worship a man as god were branded as enemies of the state (cf. intro. to Revelation, p. 1365). Rome was already "drunken with the blood of the saints" (Rev. 17^{6}); Antipas had perished at Pergamum (Rev. 2^{13}); and every considerable town in Asia Minor was a place where Satan had his throne, the Temple of Rome and the emperor, who was hailed as "our Lord and our God" (see Jn. 20^{24-29}, note).

In this changed situation the Christians were compelled to revise their judgment of the state. And Paul leaves room for such revision. His words are to be understood of the civil authorities as he knew them, and the functions of justice which he saw them to be discharging. His teaching here is *wrongly applied* when it is taken to mean that all existing authorities of any kind and character are divinely appointed. Paul himself suggests the test. When they are a terror not to the worker of good but to the evildoer, when they administer even-handed justice, they are ministers of God within civil life, and Christians are bound to show them all due respect and provide them with all reasonable support.

8–14. Love the Fulfilling of the Law. Leave no debt unpaid, saving, of course, the debt of love, which is one that never can be fully paid. Christian love has been defined as "the identification of self with God's interest in others"; and where it is present, it puts it beyond possibility that we should inflict injury on our neighbors of any form or kind. So the second table of the Law is summed up in "Thou shalt love thy neighbor as thyself." This was one of the two commandments of which Jesus had said that on them hang the law and the prophets (Mt. 22^{40}); and once more the apostle reproduces his Master's teaching. He proceeds (v. 11) to enforce it by calling attention to the brevity of the opportunity in view of *the expected early return of Christ.* "Remember the character of the time. The day which is to see the completion of our salvation is nearer than when we believed. The light of that great day is even now dawning. It behoves us, therefore, to comport ourselves with dignity, not in reckless or riotous living, not in factious or envious bickerings. On the contrary, see that you enrobe yourselves in the Lord Jesus

Christ, and pay no attention to the demands of the lower nature."

Again, it is seen to be part of the Christian standard of conduct to *behave with dignity and self-respect.* Many things which cannot be classed as sins, things which are not forbidden by any law, are nevertheless to be shunned by the Christian as inconsistent with this ideal.

CHAPTER XIV

1–12. The Duty of Toleration for Those of a too Scrupulous Conscience. Paul now proceeds to examine the application of the universal law of love to certain special problems which arose in the intercourse of Christians with one another. It was not difficult when the fellowship was met together for worship to realize the unity of the Spirit in the bond of peace, to feel the throb of mutual affection between the brethren. But when the worship came to an end, when the brethren separated to meet again in ordinary social intercourse, personal idiosyncrasies made their appearance on one side or on both, which tended to destroy the fellowship, producing discussion, discomfort, and even disunion. It is with this in view that Paul in 1 Cor. 13[13] prays that the love which is characteristic of God may continue with members of the community. Here the special case which he singles out is that of those who are *weak in the faith* (v. 1). The "faith" to which Paul now refers is not religious faith, the faith in God through Christ whereby men are saved, but the fruit of such faith in clear vision and firm conviction as to the mind and will of God. And by those who are "weak" in the faith he means those who have not a sufficiently strong grasp upon spiritual realities to claim their complete freedom in Christ and to cease, because of their assurance on other grounds, the practice of asceticism or the observance of lucky and unlucky days.

Paul takes his *first* illustration from food and the distinction between *foods which were ritually clean and unclean.* In the law of Moses much attention had been given to this subject; and much of the religious observance of a pious Jew consisted in punctilious avoidance of such kinds of food as Moses had forbidden. The Essenes, as it would appear, had gone a step further, and regarded it as a religious duty to abstain from all kinds of flesh food. In this they followed the example of the Pythagoreans in the Greek world. Indeed, religious vegetarianism was, as it still is, quite common in the East. The watchword of these schools of thought was "Touch not, taste not, handle not" (cf. Col. 2[21]). Now, our Lord in his teaching as to the true character of sin had started from a destructive criticism of this whole point of view. Nothing, he said, absolutely nothing that reaches a man from without can "defile" him, that is to say, render him unfit for public worship, disqualify him for communion with God. With this teaching he "cleansed all meats" (Mk. 7[19]), i.e., abrogated the distinction between what was clean and unclean. And this teaching had been confirmed to Peter in the vision which he had on the roof of the house at Joppa (Acts 10[9f.]).

Nevertheless, there were evidently those in the primitive church who could not shake off the idea that it was wrong to eat certain kinds of food, or, at any rate, that there was merit in abstaining. There is always a type of mind to which asceticism makes a strong appeal. But this raised a very practical question in connection with the daily social life of the Christians. How were those whose grasp on spiritual realities was strong enough to enable them to treat all such matters as unimportant to behave to those scruplers whose "faith" was not so strong? The answer, in the first place, is that the strong are to *welcome the weak*, but not to contentious discussions (v. 1). The one who feels free to eat anything is not to despise the one who abstains; neither is he who abstains to criticise the one who claims freedom in such matters. The important fact is that both alike have received the welcome of God. Moreover, the weak or overscrupulous man must remember that it is *the servant of another* that he is criticising (v. 4). He is Christ's servant, and it is to the judgment of his Master alone that he is amenable. Paul's own opinion is clear enough from 14[14] (cf. 1 Tim. 4[4]). He ranges himself along with those who are strong in the faith.

The *second* illustration of such unnecessary scruples is taken from *the superstitious observance of special days* (v. 5). The reference may be to Jewish festivals, or Paul may have in mind Gentile forms of superstition according to which certain days or dates were connected with certain of the planets, or the elemental forces which ruled the world (Gal. 4[9, 10]), and men shaped their conduct on these days accordingly. In this case the same rule applied. Each man was to be held responsible for his own conviction and for acting upon it. These were not matters on which it was necessary that the community should think or act alike.

From this Paul passes back, as he so often does, to general considerations (v. 7), his conviction being that if men could but realize clearly and continuously their relation to Christ, these problems of conduct would solve themselves. The truth is that no one of us Christians is an isolated individual (v. 8). In life and in death alike *each one of us belongs to the Lord.* It was, indeed, to this end that he both died and came to life again, that he might be the Lord of the dead and of the living. For Christians to criticize one another in matters such as these is to take up an attitude of independence toward one another which is incompatible with their common life in and for Christ. And, further, it is inconsistent with the humility which becomes those who must all alike appear before *the judgment seat of God* (v. 10). Elsewhere (2 Cor. 5[10]) Paul speaks of "the judgment seat of Christ," even as in Phil. 2[10, 11] he applies to Christ the language of Isaiah (49[18] 45[23]) which the latter here uses of God. It is in this way that Paul gives the clearest indication of the place which he assigns to Christ, and also shows that the soil in which his thought is rooted is not any Hellenistic speculation or the Oriental mystery-cults, but the O.T.

The sum of the matter is that those whose faith makes them independent of ritual prohibitions and superstitious precautions should not give the cold shoulder to the weak, but welcome them to the fellowship, showing patience and toleration. To the weak and scrupulous Paul appeals with much more elaboration of argument that they should refrain from criticizing those who claim to exercise freedom in matters of external observance.

13–23. Further Duty of Those Who Are Strong, to Abstain for Love's Sake. After giving general application to the principle that Christians ought not to criticize each other's conduct in such matters, Paul turns again to those whose faith is strong enough to set them free from scruples and from self-imposed asceticism and urges them not only to welcome these weaker brethren, but for love's sake to waive the exercise of their own freedom. For the weaker brother to see his fellow Christian indulging in food or drink which he, the weaker, thinks wrong, is to cause him real distress, and even, it may be, to expose him to temptation. It is quite true, as the strong would argue (and Paul will have no mistake about it), that all such practices have ceased to have meaning or obligation. Christ has said so (Mk. 7[19]). The enlightened Christian conscience says so. Still, there are those who are not enlightened. And if they still look on such things as meat or wine as causing defilement, then these things act so in their case. If by your ostentatious enjoyment of food which he thinks to be forbidden you cause your brother pain, then it is not love that guides your conduct.

Paul appears here (vv. 15, 16) to direct his attention to food of a special kind, such as meat that had first been offered in sacrifice to idols, and his teaching here finds an instructive parallel in 1 Cor. 8[7-13]. He that is strong in his faith knows that no idol is anything and he can eat any kind of meat without raising any question as to where it came from. But the weak brother, when he sees him do so, may not only be shocked; he may be tempted to do the same, even though it be against his conscience; for he is not so sure that "the idol is nothing"; and so he may be ruined in his Christian life. Do nothing, says Paul (v. 15), to bring disaster on your brother, *for whom Christ died* (see discussion of this phrase below). And, in general, "do not let what is right for you get a bad name." After all, the kingdom of God has not to do with either enjoying or refraining from certain meat and drink; it has to do with righteousness and peace and joy in the Holy Spirit. And he who in this way shows himself to be a true servant of Jesus Christ is well-pleasing to God, and also approves himself to human opinion. So, then, we set our ambition on what makes for peace and mutual upbuilding. Do not, merely to gratify your own taste or appetite, undermine *the work of God.*

It is true, he repeats, that *all things are clean* (v. 20); nevertheless, it is bad for a man to eat with offense to his conscience. It is fine, on the other hand, neither to eat meat, nor to drink wine, nor to do anything that causes your brother to stumble. You are rightly thankful for your greater enlightenment; but keep it as something between you and God. He is a fortunate man who does not expose himself to criticism by what he approves. The freedom of the Christian man is to be used with caution; it does not mean license. On the other hand, he who eats, though he is not sure that it is right, has been condemned already.

Once more Paul has shown how thoroughly he has apprehended the mind of Christ. "Judge not that ye be not judged"; "whatsoever thing from without goeth into a man, it cannot defile him"; "but lest we should cause them to stumble" (Mt. 7[1] Mk. 7[18] Mt. 17[27])—it is of these principles that Paul gives an exposition and an application.

For whom Christ died (v. 15). There is something striking in the simple and unpremeditated way in which Paul, here and in 1 Cor. 8[11], brings in this allusion. It is for him an incontrovertible fact and one of immeasurable importance. It is a fact which has changed life for everyone who has accepted its message, and one which should govern the attitude of every Christian to every other Christian, and, in a wider sense, to every other man. The phrase is one which caught the imagination of the past in a way we should do well to recover.

To give one example: When there was a rebellion in Norfolk, England, in the sixteenth century, led by a man called Kett, and a government official alluded to Kett's followers as "these villeins," Kett answered, "Call not them villeins for whom Christ died."

Special attention should be given to the changes in R.V. of certain words in vv. 20, 23, which as they stand in A.V. have caused no little difficulty and misunderstanding. Paul does not say "all things are pure" (A.V.), but "all things are *clean*," meaning that the ritual distinction between clean and unclean has disappeared. And he does not say, "he that doubteth is damned" (A.V.), though his words have often been quoted in that form. He says that he who is in two minds (cf. Jas. 1[6]) as to whether it is right or wrong to eat some particular food, comes under condemnation by the act of partaking. He is *condemned by his own conscience.*

CHAPTER XV

1–7. General Precepts and Encouragements. The new paragraph opens with a summary of what has just been said (cf. 13[8]). We who are strong in the faith ought to bear with the weaknesses of those who are not strong. *Noblesse oblige.* To please ourselves is not our duty. Let each one of us seek to please his neighbor. But that does not mean just to do whatever that neighbor likes. It is assumed that the same ideal is accepted on both sides. For such conduct we have a supreme example in Jesus himself. He was conspicuous as one who *did not please himself.* This does not refer mainly, if at all, to the fact that Jesus was unselfish, not seeking personal satisfaction, or honor or wealth or power, the things which men commonly seek. It refers, rather, to the example of Jesus in its bearing on the matter in hand. He was not self-centered. He did not open his fellowship and his friendship only to those who agreed with him. Rather was he perpetually breaking through barriers which were erected between him and other men by differences of taste, feeling, disposition, outlook, or character. Had he been one who pleased himself, he could have found excuse in nearly every case for holding aloof, but the question of liking, of harmony of opinion, never occurred to him as conditioning his relation to men. He pleased not himself.

On the contrary, there might be applied to him the words which a psalmist had spoken of himself (Psa. 69[9]): "For all words which have been so written were *written for our instruction*" (cf. 2 Tim. 3[16]). These ancient scriptures did not fulfill their purpose in their own time or for the old covenant. God intended them for Christians, who need their teaching. The burdens of life are so many, its requirements on their patience so constant, that they find it hard to maintain their hope. Yet what is the O.T. full of? Lessons of endurance and encouragement (Gore).

In v. 5 the words *according to Christ Jesus* are emphatic. They suggest at once the standard for the common mind for which Paul prays and the direction of its purpose. The words might be rendered, "May the God from whom come the endurance and the comfort grant unto you minds at harmony with one another and with Christ Jesus." If this be granted, they will in a body and with one voice glorify the God and Father of our Lord Jesus Christ.

To the glory of God (v. 7). This is commonly taken to mean "for the greater glory of God," and connected (note the comma in R.V.) with both the foregoing clauses. And, of course, the greater glory of God is the ultimate issue both of the life of Christians and of the work of Christ in any of its aspects. But the rest of the verse seems hardly to give sufficient motive for the introduction of this idea; and while it is quite legitimate, it may be preferable to take the words as describing the admission of Christians by Christ "into the glory of God," the moral splendor of the divine character which men had forfeited through sin (cf. 3[23]).

8–13. The Work of Christ first for the Jews, then for the Gentiles. It is difficult (though it is attempted by most commentators) to fit vv. 8–12 into the context in which we find them. It has been said that "in what follows we have the expansion and proof of the idea that God's glory (the glory of his faithfulness and mercy) is the end contemplated by Christ's reception alike of the Jews and of the Gentiles" (Weiss); that "we have here the conclusion of the argument begun in 14[1]; probably the relations of the Jews and Gentiles were involved directly or indirectly in the relations of the weak and the strong" (Hort); that Paul "writes to remind the Gentiles that it is through the Jews that they are called, [and to remind] the Jews that the aim and purpose of their existence is the calling of the Gentiles" (Sanday and Headlam). None of these interpretations would seem to emerge naturally from Paul's words. But a paraphrase which would do justice to them would be as follows: "Welcome one another, for though the ministry of Christ was to the people of the circumcision because God would keep his promise, yet it led to the Gentiles glorifying God."

It is not easy to perceive the relevancy of the O.T. quotations which follow; only that the second (Deut. 32[43]) brings the Gentiles into combination with the Jews, and the third (Psa. 117[1]) summons the Gentiles to take their share in the praises of the Lord, and so anticipates their being brought to "call upon his name" or worship him. If, however, the purpose of these verses is to enforce the unity of Jews and Gentiles, so justifying the summons to "receive one another," it does seem to fulfill that purpose in a very obscure way; and while the introduction (v. 8) is very abrupt, and difficult to connect with v. 7, there is an equally abrupt transition between v. 12 and v. 13. Moreover, Dr. Rendel Harris has pointed out how Paul here suddenly returns to the use of a Book of Testimonies, a collection of texts from the O.T. arranged under headings, of which he appears to have made free use in chs. 9–11. And there is much to be said for Harris's suggestion that those verses really belong to the discussion carried on in these chapters, and have somehow fallen out of place. In that case v. 13 would form the natural conclusion to v. 7, and possibly the conclusion, so far as it has come down to us, of the Epistle in its original form (see intro.).

14–21. Direct Address to the Romans; Paul's Activity and Success. On the connection between the rest of this chapter and the Epistle as a whole see intro. (p. 1136). At this point the appearance of a personal touch is unmistakable. Paul is persuaded, he as well as others who have better acquaintance with the church at Rome, that the Roman Christians, as well as others better known to himself, are fully supplied with goodness and provided with spiritual knowledge of every kind, so that they are well able to give advice to one another. He has used a certain freedom in writing to them, desiring to refresh their memory, because of the function graciously intrusted to him by God. And that is "that I should be *the minister of Christ Jesus to the Gentiles*, fulfilling a priestly duty in respect of the gospel of God, that the offering up of the Gentiles might prove acceptable, being consecrated by the Holy Spirit" (v. 16).

This verse (16) contains three striking illustrations of the figure of speech which the Greeks called "the unexpected." Three times does Paul give a startlingly unexpected turn to the thought, and in each case the turn is suggested by a single word. Two of the three words (*ministering* and *offering*) have definite association with the sacrificial system, and the third to which such an association may attach may be said to acquire it here from the context. That word is *minister*, which may mean no more than "public servant" or even "servant," but in connection with worship has a definitely technical sense. It is "exactly the word that would be used of the discharge of the priest's office in the Temple" (Sanday); and it is used here, says Thayer, of Paul likening himself to a priest. But his is a priesthood of an extraordinary kind. He is conscious of being a priest but—a priest *of the Gentiles*. The word *ministering* definitely means "ministering in sacrifice" (so R.V. mg.). But again the contents of this ministry in Paul's case is something hitherto unheard of; it is nothing else than *the gospel of Christ* (strictly here *of God*, but for their identity cf. Mk. 1[1] 1[14]); it is that which Paul handles in his priestly ministry. The word *offering* leaves even less room for variation in meaning; it refers to *the offering up*, the culmination of the sacrifice. But once more the unexpected falls like a blow. The matter of the offering is not anything of the kind used under the old dispensation. It is not even the "praise and thanksgiving" in which later writers of the O.T. had seen a sufficient and superior form of sacrifice. The matter of this sacrifice is nothing else than the Gentiles themselves (cf. 12[1]), who having been united into a living body of Christ have further been consecrated by his Spirit.

The evidence of a priestly consciousness in the apostle cannot be gainsaid. *But it is a priesthood of an entirely new order, dealing with a sacrifice of an entirely new kind.* Paul was probably thinking of occasions when it was his privilege to preside at a celebration of the Lord's Supper, when, after he had been the instrument of the Holy Spirit in leading the brethren to realize their oneness in Christ, to realize themselves as forming a true body of Christ, and to participate in the cleansing of the Word and the consecration of the Spirit, he had led them to the solemn offering up of themselves to God as the climax of their worship. It is to this genuine though immaterial ("spiritual") sacrifice that we probably find further allusion in 1 Pet. 2[5].

What we call *Sacerdotalism* has been the result of the perversion and materializing of this wholly spiritual and ethical conception, in which all the passages in early Christian literature which appear to connect the idea of sacrifice with the Lord's Supper find their true explanation. All such allusions have in view this self-presentation to God of the living Body of Christ, the church. The idea is found persisting down to the time of Augustine, who says, "The sacrifice itself is the body of Christ, which is not offered to them, for they themselves are it." And, again, "This is the Christian sacrifice, the many become one body in Christ"—material sacrifice of every kind had been utterly abolished. Even the personal body of Christ was offered, and could be offered, only once. But his living body, of which he was a part, could offer itself continually. It was thus, in presenting themselves to God as a living sacrifice, that Christians fulfilled the condition of spiritual worship. And the clue to all the early allusions to sacrifice in connection with the Lord's Supper is found in this phrase, "the offering up of the Gentiles."

"I have therefore in things pertaining to God my proud satisfaction in Christ Jesus. For I will not venture to tell of anything except what Christ has wrought through me to bring about the submission of the Gentiles both in word and in deed, what he has wrought in the power of signs and wonders, and of the Holy Spirit" (vv. 17–19). The power of the Holy Spirit had been manifested in connection with Paul's preaching, and in forms which could only be described as *signs and wonders*. Paul's claim that God worked miracles through him cannot be overlooked. It is confirmed in 2 Cor. 12[12], where he appeals to such things as proofs of his apostleship, and reminds the Corinthians that they had taken place within their observation. If, according to Headlam's definition, "a miracle means really the supremacy of the spiritual forces of the world to an extraordinarily marked degree over the merely material," the religious mind will have no difficulty in believing that such things took place. (See art., *N.T. Miracles*, pp. 927–9.)

V. 20 introduces us to a self-imposed rule to which Paul evidently attached great importance. So free was he from personal ambition and from sectarian narrowness (cf. Phil. 1[18]) that he studiously refrained from intruding upon ground where the work of evangelizing had already been done by others. Here he illustrates by two lines from Isaiah (52[15]) his method of going only to those who have not yet heard the gospel.

22–33. Paul's Plans for the Future. He announces that his ultimate purpose is to journey to Spain; and he looks forward to visiting Rome in passing. But meanwhile he has to complete a very important task. Many of the churches under his care have been busy for a long time past (cf. 2 Cor. 9[2]) making collections for the benefit of the poorer Christians at Jerusalem. And now that the collection is complete, Paul must first go thither in order to hand over their bounty.

Wherefore in v. 22 refers back to v. 19. It is because of the many openings and calls he has had in the East that he has been hindered these many times from visiting Rome. But now he sees no longer any opening in these countries for the pioneer work to which he is resolved to confine himself, and he casts his eye on the furthest west. His projected visit to Spain will give him the opportunity he has desired these many years of visiting Rome on the way. (As to whether the journey was ever made, see p. 1275.) He will see them and they will speed him on his way, after he has satisfied at least in part his longing to see them. The sentence in v. 24 should have closed with a repetition of his intention to visit Spain; but it remains unfinished, and he breaks in with a reference to the task immediately before him. "But at the present moment I am bound for Jerusalem to bring help to God's people there."

The collection (v. 26), the proceeds of which Paul was to take with him, was something in which he was greatly interested. He had given careful instructions concerning it to the Corinthians (1 Cor. 16[1f.] 2 Cor. 8[1-4] 9[2, 12]) as he had done previously to the churches in Galatia. He attached great importance to it not only because of the need of the church at Jerusalem but as the expression of the common brotherhood in which all the churches were bound together, and particularly as a possible means of healing the soreness between the Gentile and the Jewish sections of the church. Moreover, it was the *payment of a debt*. The Gentiles had been made partakers in the spiritual privileges of the Jewish Christians; they were bound, therefore, to minister to them in material things. When Paul had accomplished that duty the way would be open to Spain. But he seems to have felt some nervousness or anxiety about this visit to Jerusalem and what might await him there at the hands of unbelieving Jews. And he makes earnest entreaty that he may have the prayers of Christians at Rome not only for his personal safety, but that the help he is carrying may be appreciated by the Christians there, that they may accept it in the spirit in which it is bestowed. So will his coming to Rome be a joyful one. He concludes with the prayer that God the Author of peace may be with them.

By the love of the Spirit (v. 30), i.e., the love which the Spirit inspires (cf. 1 Thess. 1[6] 2 Thess. 2[13]).

CHAPTER XVI

This chapter consists of five sections which are but loosely connected with one another; (1) a commendation of Phœbe; (2) an unprecedentedly long list of greetings; (3) a serious warning against party spirit and false teaching; (4) a short list of greetings from Paul's companions; and (5) a doxology. Apart from the last of these there is no reason to doubt that any one of them is from the pen of Paul; but there is reason to doubt whether they, all or any, belong to the Epistle in its original form. (On the questions thus raised, see intro., section on "Closing Chapters.")

1, 2. Commendation of Phœbe. Such letters of introduction given to Christians who were passing from one church to another were of great importance and very common in the early church. Paul commends Phœbe, a deaconess of the church at Cenchreæ (the port of Corinth on the eastern side of the Isthmus) very warmly to those to whom she brought the letter. He invites them to stand by her in *whatever matter* she may have need of them, for she herself has been found a good patron and helper of many, including the apostle himself.

3–16. Greetings to Numerous Individuals. To this letter of commendation Paul may have attached this long list of greetings, which serves to reveal his strong personal attachments and his appreciation of the character and services of many men and women. *Prisca* (or Priscilla) and *Aquila* had been his fellow workers in Christ; nay, for his life they had risked their own; not only Paul but all the churches of the Gentiles had reason to be thankful to them and to the church which gathered at their house for worship. Observe how Paul emphasizes the thanks due from the Gentiles to Prisca and Aquila, who were Jews by birth. Paul had met them first in Corinth (Acts 18^{2}), whither they had migrated from Rome when the Jews were expelled by Claudius, and they had subsequently accompanied Paul to Ephesus (Acts $18^{18\text{-}26}$). The mention of *the church in their house* reminds us that not before the end of the second century do we find clear evidence of buildings specially set apart for Christian worship. Doubtless they came into use before we have evidence of their existence; but there was a long period during which the Christians were dependent upon the hospitality of those of their number who had houses large enough to accommodate them (cf. 1 Cor. 16^{19} Col. 4^{15} Philm. v. 2). The names which follow have all been found in ancient inscriptions, not only in Rome but in many parts of the empire, though some of them are rare. Nearly all of them appear to have been names which were commonly borne by slaves. *Epœnetus* had been the first convert of the gospel in the province of Asia, as Stephanas had been in Greece (1 Cor. 16^{15}). *Andronicus* and *Junias* were Paul's fellow countrymen who had also shared in one of his imprisonments. It is uncertain whether Junias was a woman (Junia). Chrysostom took that view, remarking on the fact that a woman was found worthy to be "one of note among the apostles." Beyond what Paul tells us about some of them nothing further is known about the persons mentioned here. It is probable that those *which are of the household of Aristobulus* were the dependents of the grandson of Herod the Great, who lived and died at Rome. They would doubtless include many Jews who had become Christians. *Herodion* naturally suggests the same origin. *Rufus* may have been the same who is mentioned in Mk. 15^{21}, the son of Simon of Cyrene; his mother had been also as a mother to Paul. The closing sentence is remarkable for its reference to *the churches of Christ*, a phrase found only here in all the N.T. Elsewhere we read of the church, or churches, of God.

17–20. Sudden Introduction of Serious Warnings. The sudden change both of subject and of tone is not easy to account for. There is nothing in the foregoing chapters to account for his sharp warning against party spirit and false teachers. The discussion hitherto has been conducted without any direct reference to special circumstances in the community addressed. Those who think that this paragraph belongs to the Epistle suggest that "now at the end of his writing the apostle with a sudden impulse breaks through the reserve he has hitherto practised, clearly indicates his opponents, warns the Romans while praising them, and expresses his confidence in the ultimate victory of the right" (Lietzmann). The fact remains, however, that there is no reason to presume any such previous "reserve," neither has there been anything to suggest the presence or activity of definite opponents or propagators of false teaching. It seems more probable that Paul is here addressing a community which was better known to him than that at Rome, and one where the circumstances were different.

V. 19 guards against any suggestion that he is criticizing the community as a whole; it is only the mischief-makers he has in view, "I would have you experts in good, innocents in evil" (Moffatt). Ancient authorities differ as to the position of the benediction (v. 20b), some placing it here and others after v. 23.

21–23. Greetings from Paul's Companions—Timothy and Sosipater (cf. Acts 20^{4}), Lucius, who may be the Lucius of Cyrene mentioned in Acts 13^{1}, and Jason, who appears as Paul's host in Acts 17^{5}. Tertius, who has acted as Paul's amanuensis, puts in a greeting of his own. Finally, Erastus, the city treasurer, a man of importance, adds his greeting, and Quartus, whose only claim to recognition is that he also is a member of the Christian Church.

24–27. Concluding Doxology. V. 24 is now omitted by R.V. (see on v. 20). The appearance of a doxology at this point is contrary to the usual practice of Paul, who generally concludes his letter with a benediction. And its contents present a somewhat mechanical combination of phrases which have played their part at the beginning of the Epistle (e.g., "stablish you," cf. 1[11]; "my gospel," cf. 2[16]; "obedience of faith," cf. 1[5]) with others which are specially characteristic of the Pastoral Epistles. "It is very difficult to believe that such mosaic work is the original composition of Paul" (Denney). When it is further remembered that the position of this doxology is uncertain, some ancient authorities placing it after 14[23], it will appear as most probable that it was provided by some later hand for an Epistle which was felt to lack a suitable ending.

FIRST AND SECOND CORINTHIANS

By Professor W. F. HOWARD

Introduction

Paul's Relations with Corinth. The story of Paul's arrival at Corinth in the course of his Second Missionary Journey, of his breach with the synagogue, of the founding of the church, and of his successful proclamation of the gospel during a residence of eighteen months is told in Acts 18^{1-18}. Luke also records a later visit, when Paul, after his long stay in Asia, left Ephesus, journeyed through Macedonia and spent three months in Greece (Acts 20^{3}). Between these two visits we must find room for a vigorous correspondence between Paul and his Corinthian converts, the dispatch of two trusty messengers, a hurried and unsuccessful visit by Paul himself, and a crisis unparalleled in Paul's missionary career, when this important church flouted his authority and was nearly lost to the apostolic obedience (cf. p. 940b).

The following outline represents the probable sequence of events.

(1) Paul, after eighteen months at Corinth (Acts 18^{11} 1 Cor. 1^{14-16} 2^{1} 3^{6}, etc.), left with Aquila and Priscilla, and settled at Ephesus, where later on he was joined by Apollos, who had continued his work at Corinth (cf. Acts $18^{18, 19, 27, 28}$ 19^{1} 1 Cor. 16^{2}).

(2) Paul wrote his first letter (A) to Corinth, alluded to in 1 Cor. 5^{9}. Almost certainly part of this is embedded in 2 Cor. 6^{14}–7^{1}. Some scholars suspect other fragments in 1 Cor. 6^{12-20} 10^{1-22}.

(3) The Corinthian church replied in a letter (probably brought by Stephanas, Fortunatus, and Achaicus, 1 Cor. 16^{17}) asking a number of questions. Meanwhile Chloe's people (1^{11}) brought Paul news of factions in the church. Paul's reply to all that he had been asked and had learned forms the Epistle (B), known as First Corinthians. In it he rebukes party spirit and every lapse from the highest Christian standards, answers certain specific questions (7^{1} 8^{1} 12^{1}), announces that Timothy will come as his representative (4^{17} 16^{10}), and that he will himself follow as soon as possible (4^{19} $16^{2, 5-7}$).

(4) Timothy left for Corinth with Erastus, via Macedonia (Acts 19^{22}). Either he did not reach Corinth, or, more probably, he proved unequal to the emergency. Hearing that the situation was getting out of hand, Paul paid a hurried visit (unrecorded in Acts but implied in 2 Cor. 2^{1} 12^{14} 13^{1}). This was evidently an unhappy visit, when Paul suffered insult and defiance from some recalcitrant member of the Corinthian church. We infer from 2 Cor. 2^{5-8} that ultimately the offender was disciplined by a majority of the church, and Paul was able to plead for his reinstatement. Possibly a sudden attack of Paul's recurrent malady prostrated him at the moment when he needed all his energy to cope with the revolt (2 Cor. 10^{10}).

(5) On his return to Ephesus, Paul wrote (C), a severe letter (cf. 2 Cor. $2^{3, 9}$ 7^{8-12}), which he sent by the hand of Titus, who was to return by way of Macedonia and Troas. It is widely, but not universally, believed that part of this letter is preserved in 2 Cor. 10–13. (It has been suggested with less cogency that to (C) also belong 2 Cor. 2^{14}–6^{13} and 7^{2-4}).

(6) After a grave illness in Asia (2 Cor. $1^{8, 9}$) Paul set out for Macedonia, abandoning a project of a direct visit to Corinth in the present state of the church ($1^{15, 16, 23}$). At Troas, in spite of evangelistic opportunities, he pressed on to Macedonia in utmost concern about the result of his admonitory letter (2^{13}). Here his anxiety was relieved by the arrival of Titus with excellent tidings of the restored discipline within the church, and the affectionate regard of the members for Paul (7^{5-16}).

(7) Thereupon Paul wrote (D), a letter of warm affection, contained in 2 Cor. 1–9, sending it by Titus and two other honored brothers, who were to complete the collection of the gift for the Jerusalem Christians before Paul's arrival (2 Cor. 8).

(8) Paul's last visit to Corinth (Acts $20^{2, 3}$).

Corinth: The City and the Church. The largest and most prosperous city in Greece was destroyed by Lucius Mummius, the Roman general, when crushing the Achæan League, 146 B.C. Just a hundred years later Julius Cæsar refounded Corinth as a Roman colony. Its commanding position on the isthmus separating the Saronic and the Corinthian gulfs gave it high commercial importance as a center of trade between the eastern and western Mediterranean. As the political capital of the Roman province of Achaia it was the seat of the proconsular government (cf. Acts 18^{12}). Its large population was made up of native Greeks, Roman colonists, Jewish settlers, and a mixed crowd of sailors, and traders from the east. A few men of standing and wealth joined the church, but for the most part the gospel won its recruits from the artisans and dock-laborers, the petty tradesmen, the slaves and freedmen, who formed a large proportion of the populace. The two deities held in special honor at Corinth were Poseidon, patron of the famous Isthmian games (cf. 1 Cor. 9^{24-27}), and Aphrodite, whose temple, with its thousand dedicated prostitutes, towered above the city on the lofty summit of the Acrocorinthus. Thus the foulest immorality flourished under the sanction of religion, and Corinth became proverbial for its vice through all the Greek world. Temples in honor of Serapis and Isis bore witness to the prevalence of the mystery religions. Wandering exponents of Oriental mysteries, sophists and rhetoricians found a ready hearing in this cosmopolitan vortex. It is not to be wondered at that Paul's main troubles in this church arose from the low moral standards of pagan converts, the factiousness traditional in Greek democracy, a superficial intellectualism, and a tendency to exalt impressive accomplishments at the expense of ethical values.

The Message and the Value of These Letters. For the curious minds and corrupt lives of the people at Corinth Paul proclaimed one supreme message, "the word of the cross." The wisdom of God and the power of God shown forth in a crucified Christ are the theme of the early chapters of First Corinthians. In all that follows we see how Paul applies that message to the problems of personal and social life. In Second Corinthians he goes further in the argumentative exposition of this message ($5^{14f.}$). Most of the questions discussed in the light of the cross are due to the human failings in an undisciplined and imperfectly instructed society, or to the perplexities inevitable when a new ethical standard is applied to complex relationships that are only partially adjusted to a fresh way of life. The Christian thinker here reveals himself as a practical administrator. Theology leads to statesmanship. But there is one matter of speculative interest which arises directly from the word of the cross. The cross is the symbol not only of the death but of its sequel, the resurrection. In 1 Cor. 15 and 2 Cor. 4^{16}–5^{10} we have Paul's first clear treatment of the Christian's reasoned hope in victory over death. His interpretation here of the resurrection of the body still commends itself to the Christian mind.

Each letter has a value of its own. First Corinthians of all Paul's letters shows most fully the peculiar perils and problems of a missionary church in the first century. It is of priceless worth for the incidental evidence that it supplies regarding the primitive Christian tradition about the institution of the Lord's Supper and the appearances of the risen Lord. It proves that in that early age before a single written Gospel was in existence the Christian Church was guided by the memory and tradition not only of what Jesus both said and did, but also by what he was. Second Corinthians is the most vehemently personal of all Paul's letters, and is more autobiographical even than Galatians. It both sustains and supplements the narrative of Acts, and at the same time reminds us how many chapters in the life of the great apostle must forever remain unwritten (see $11^{23f.}$). Nowhere else does the rich human nature of the man reveal itself so openly. Paul himself stands before us in its pages with his fiery energy, his indomitable zeal, his mystic raptures, his abysmal despondency, his mordant irony, his scorching indignation, his tender affectionateness, his pride and his humility, his uttermost love and wonder at the grace and glory of the Lord Jesus. This letter alone is enough to show how great Paul was, both as a man and as a Christian.

Main Divisions of the First Letter. These divisions are as follows:

I. Greeting and Thanksgiving, 1^{1-9}.
II. Parties in the Church, 1^{10}–4^{21}.
III. Moral Disorders in the Church, 5^{1}–6^{20}.
IV. Reply to Questions that Have Perplexed the Church:
 (1) Sex, 7^{1-40}.
 (2) Sacrificial Food and Social Life, 8^{1}–11^{1}.
V. Disorders in Church Assemblies, 11^{2}–14^{40}.
 (1) Spiritual Gifts, 12^{1}–14^{40}.
VI. The Resurrection of the Dead, 15^{1-58}.
VII. Administrative and Personal, 16^{1-24}.

Main Divisions of Second Letter. For these, see pp. 1194–5.

Literature: Dobschütz, *Christian Life in the Primitive Church;* Deissmann, *Paul;* Lake, *The Earlier Epistles of St. Paul;* David Smith, *The Life and Letters of St. Paul;* E. D. Burton, *Letters and Records of the Apostolic Age;* D. A. Hayes, *Paul and His Epistles;* also, as condensed commentaries (especially of the very difficult Second Epistle), A. S. Way's translation, *The Letters of St. Paul*, and Moffatt, *A New Translation of the N.T.*

FIRST CORINTHIANS

CHAPTER I

1–3. Address and Greeting. Paul emphasizes his direct missionary vocation, couples with his own name that of a brother known at Corinth (probably not Sosthenes the synagogue ruler of Acts 18[17]), reminds his readers of their call to lead a dedicated life, and includes in his appeal the members of all the churches in Achaia. They are to be united in reverent worship of Jesus as Lord, and in the brotherhood of the church. Greetings characteristic of the Greek and Hebrew worlds of thought (*grace, peace*) receive a new meaning when God is revealed in Christ.

4–9. Thanksgiving for the Corinthian Church. A comparison with his other letters shows that Paul's prayers for his churches are not stereotyped forms, but reveal a just sense of the spiritual state of the local community. In natural endowments this church was rich; but observe Paul's silence here upon those less showy gifts which endeared the Philippian church to him. Yet their hope in the Parousia (the *revelation* of v. 7) is evidence of a faith which God will not disappoint. In the fellowship of God's Son they will be sustained and prepared for the ordeal of the day of Judgment.

Chapters 1[10] to 4[21]: Parties in the Church

10–17. Their Unhappy Divisions: Paul not Responsible. The fellowship has been broken and the church prevented from declaring the mind of Christ to the world (cf. 2[16] Eph. 4[20-32]) by the spirit of faction. Recent visitors have reported that the names of three renowned missionaries are being debased into sectarian watchwords. Paul protests that sectarianism is a mutilation of Christ—horrible thought! Grateful as the converts may well feel to those who led them to the light, Christ alone has died for them, and into his name alone have they been baptized. Happily, Paul cannot be charged with attempting to gain a personal ascendancy, for he remembers with thankfulness that only a few of his converts were baptized at his hands. His supreme concern had been the proclamation of the good news with such simplicity that neither the intellectual sublety nor the rhetorical splendor of the form of the message should conceal its substance—the paradox of a gibbeted Messiah.

12. The verse is difficult, for it seems to presuppose four parties in the church, one of which was the self-styled Christ-party. The words *I* [*am*] *of Christ* have been variously explained. (a) As a protest against party spirit by a section of the church which was scandalized by the glorification of human leaders. In that case Paul would hardly have included this among the party cries. (b) As an arrogant attempt to claim a monopoly of Christian loyalty. But Paul would surely have added some word in condemnation of such a pretension. (c) As a claim of a small number to have been personal disciples of Jesus (cf. 2 Cor. 10[7]) and therefore that they are superior to their fellows. This is improbable at Corinth, though 2 Cor. 5[16] might be so interpreted. (d) As the watchword of a Jewish Messianic party of which there is no further trace in either Epistle. (e) As Paul's vehement counter-assertion to the sectarian shibboleths (cf. 3[23], *ye are Christ's*): "I am Christ's bond-servant and can be no party leader." (f) As a gloss, originally written in the margin by a scribe and brought later into the text. This was the view of J. Weiss, the greatest commentator on this Epistle, but it is an explanation to be entertained only when a passage will otherwise yield no sense. We must not infer from 4[6] that there were no such parties in Corinth as those which professed special allegiance to Paul and Apollos. It is significant that no heresiarch gave his name to a party. It is *not false teaching but factious hero worship* which Paul deprecates. Jewish Christians would cling to the name of *Cephas* (the Aramaic form for Peter), "advanced" adherents would favor the rhetorical exuberance and the philosophical terminology of *Apollos* the Alexandrian Jew (cf. Acts 18[24]–19[1]), while some who owed their souls to the gospel preached by *Paul* would defend his name with defiant loyalty.

14. No disparagement is intended of baptism, which is assumed by Paul as the normal rite of initiation into the Christian community (12[13] Rom. 6[3f.] Gal. 3[27] Col. 2[12]). Gentile converts knew that in the mystery religions a special relationship was observed between the initiate and the mystagogue. Jews were familiar with the title "the disciples of John the Baptist." Paul's custom of leaving the baptism of most of his converts to his colleagues has secured him from the reproach of aiming at the personal attachment of devotees. For *Crispus* see Acts 18[8]; *Gaius*, Rom. 16[23] (not the Macedonian of Acts 19[29]); the household of *Stephanas*, 16[15].

18–25. The Reproach of the Cross. The central message of the Christian revelation is the cross. This is the touchstone of character.

Those who can see in it only the crowning absurdity of the apostolic tale seal their own doom. They lack the moral discernment to recognize their need and God's response to it. Those who are on the way to life eternal are those who discover in the very shame and weakness of the cross the way by which God's power is saving the world. It is no new thing for the worldly wise to perish in their blind self-confidence. Isaiah had warned the politicians of Jerusalem that by their statecraft they were heading for disaster (Isa. 29^{14}). Their successors can be found in Greek sophists, Jewish rabbis, nimble dialecticians. Which of these has a message commensurate with the impending crisis? Their horizon is limited to the present age, and their boasted wisdom is proved bankrupt. It was part of an all-wise dispensation that the quest of human wisdom after God should fail. Man's extremity is God's opportunity. Intellectual pride is staggered by the nature of the proclamation. Yet

"Where reason fails, with all her powers,
There faith prevails and love adores."

It is this believing response to the preaching of a *foolish* theme that saves a soul alive. This is the paradox of the divine wisdom. God falsifies the expectation of mankind. The Jew demands a *sign* or guarantee (cf. Mk. $8^{11f.}$), which is a moral impossibility in the region of faith (Lk. 16^{31}). The Greek relies exclusively upon *wisdom* or the speculative reason, and insists upon a philosophy of life. Our one reply to both is the challenging declaration of a crucified Messiah (v. 23). The Jew stumbles at this emblem of servitude, this badge of failure. The Greek is repelled by the futility of such a manifesto. But those of us, whatever our nationality or temperament, who have heard and answered God's call have found in that very aspect of the Christian story which to the world seems the tragic climax of ineffectiveness the sure evidence of God's power and God's wisdom. His *wisdom,* because God's apparent foolishness has revealed to us his nature as the wisest of men never discovered it; his *power,* for what seemed contemptible weakness in the defeat of Calvary has proved to be the force that raises us into newness of life.

20. The language has echoes of Isa. $19^{11, 12}$ 33^{18} 44^{25}.

21. R.V. mg. is better. It is the foolishness of *the thing preached,* the preacher's theme, i.e., a crucified Christ, which brings deliverance. Observe that all through this paragraph it is not Paul's design to disparage philosophy as such, but, rather, the arrogant self-sufficiency of mere intellectualism—"Every high aspiring thought, that would not stoop to thee."

For the thought in v. 18 (*us which are being saved*) and v. 24 (*them that are called*), cf. Browning's "Abt Vogler," stanza 11:

"But God has a few of us whom he whispers in the ear;
The rest may reason and welcome: 'tis we musicians know."

26–31. Christ the Wisdom of God. Paul now turns the tables upon the self-satisfied Corinthians by reminding them that their own call into the church was proof of God's resourceful wisdom. Few of them had any title to worldly respect by reason of knowledge, influence, or birth, yet they had been selected that God might carry out his sovereign plan. Apostolic tact brings in the saving phrase *not many.* A few men of distinction were to be found among the artisans, dock-laborers, slaves and freedmen who formed the bulk of the membership of this church. True to his age-long method, God to achieve his ends chose out of all the wealth of the world those who were deemed of no account. The reason for this is stated in a sentence which sounds the knell of Pharisaism—*that no flesh should glory before God* (v. 29). This is central to Paul's theology (Rom. 3^{27} Eph. 2^{9}). It is an echo of the teaching of Jesus (Lk. 18^{9-14}). Status and merit are irrelevant considerations when man stands before God. Cf. Tennyson, "In Memoriam," lines 35, 36:

"For merit lives from man to man,
And not from man, O Lord, to thee."

It is in the heart purged of pride that God's power operates most effectually (cf. 2 Cor. $12^{9, 10}$). It is altogether of God's grace that these despised nobodies have found a place and status in the fellowship of Jesus the Messiah. Paul has reminded them of their lowly origin that he may magnify their new estate. To him, as well as to them, Jesus the Messiah has become the revelation of the true Wisdom. The doctrine of a gibbeted Messiah has been derided as "sheer folly." But it has passed the practical test; for this crucified Christ has brought Paul and his converts into a new religious status by making them morally righteous, ethically pure, spiritually free. Such a vitalizing and regenerating energy, far more than mere knowledge, deserves to be called *wisdom,* for it manifestly comes from God. Thus we can give a new meaning to the prophetic word that boasting or glorifying is to be in the Lord alone.

30. Note how the ironical harping on the *foolishness* or "folly" of the cross is now dropped as the supreme *wisdom* of Christ crucified is enforced and vindicated by reference to his threefold gift of righteousness, sanctification, and redemption.

31. The citation is from Jer. 9[23, 24]. It is noteworthy for the transference in meaning of *the Lord* from God to Christ. This frequent N.T. adaptation of O.T. allusions to Jehovah is deeply significant (cf. 2[16]).

It is possible, though not certain, that the phrase *Christ the wisdom of God* (v. 24) and the statement *Who was made unto us wisdom from God* (v. 30) refer to the identification of Jesus with the personified Wisdom of Prov. 8[12, 22, 23, 30] Ecclesiasticus 1[1-20] Wisdom 7[22]–8[21]. That Paul does apply to Jesus language originally used of Wisdom is clear from Col. 1[15f]. The resemblance between Heb. 1[3] and Wisdom 7[26] is closer still. The Wisdom of Solomon (an apocryphal book) was a product of Alexandrian Judaism (see p. 197a) and it is not unlikely that the Alexandrian Jew Apollos had given in Corinth an impulse to this Christian appropriation of the Wisdom passages. There is reason, however, to think that the equation of Wisdom and Christ goes back to Jesus himself (cf. Lk. 11[49] Mt. 23[34]). Notice the resemblances between 1 Cor. 1[19-27] and Mt. 11[25-27], where the words of Jesus which follow are based upon the language of Wisdom (cf. Ecclesiasticus 6[26-28] 51[26, 27]). It may well be that in the present chapter we have the germ of the thought which reappears in the developed Christology of Col. 1 (cf. pp. 1066–7).

CHAPTER II

1–5. Paul's Way of Preaching Christ. The apostle has not spared the Corinthians in exposing their vain pretensions to superior wisdom and standing. But the sting of sarcasm is removed when he places himself on the same lowly level. They are reminded of his own first arrival in their city, a preacher of God's testimony who dispensed with the arts of the rhetorician and the sophist. He had already resolved to know nothing while in their midst but Jesus as Messiah, and that a crucified Messiah. The messenger was as unpretentious as his message. He came to them in a state of bodily weakness and nervous anxiety. The style and the substance of his preaching were marked by no graces of oratory, no philosophic subtlety. Yet it wrought conviction in his hearers by means of a spiritual force which came from God. Thus Paul's purpose and method matched the very nature of the gospel. The faith that was evoked depended on no human cleverness but on the power of God.

1. Perhaps the better reading (so R.V. mg.) is *the testimony of God*. Simplicity and directness of statement befit one who is giving evidence.

3. From Acts 17[14]–18[11] and 1 Thess. 3[1-10] we may supply the interpretation of this poignant sentence. Jewish intrigue and mob violence had interrupted the successful mission, first at Thessalonica and then at Berœa. Paul arrived at Athens alone, Silas and Timothy being left to confirm the harassed disciples in these Macedonian cities. Challenged to give an account of his teaching before the Areopagus (the court which licensed public lecturers in that university center, see Ramsay, *Paul the Traveler*, pp. 246f.), Paul in a skillful exordium prepared the way for a sympathetic hearing of his message. But the mention of Jesus and the resurrection was misunderstood as the proclamation of two fresh divinities, and the audience broke up. The speech was not a failure, for one member of that court was won for the faith. A few other converts were gained at Athens, but Paul was depressed by the superficial religiosity of the city, and saw no hope of making a deep impression. Moreover, he was burdened with anxiety about the newly founded churches in the north, and was restless for the arrival of his colleagues with the latest tidings. This condition of mental depression in which he arrived at Corinth probably induced a return of his recurrent malady (cf. Gal. 4[13] 2 Cor. 1[8-11] 11[30] 12[5, 9, 10]). The style of address quite properly suited to the Areopagus was not congenial to Paul's temperament, and it was discarded with relief at Corinth. Here Paul was cheered by the return of his colleagues with good news from Macedonia, and a successful synagogue ministry was followed up by a vigorous assertion of the Messiahship of Jesus.

6–16. God's Wisdom in a Mystery. Paraphrase: "Yet simply as the divine message in Christ has been presented at Corinth, let no one imagine that simplicity precludes profundity. To men of ripe understanding we impart wisdom: not indeed as this passing world understands that term, nor the dark powers who are in control of this world, though their days are numbered. To men of mature experience we utter as an open secret God's hidden purpose which he cherished before the worlds were formed with a view to our sharing in his glorious life. Had the dark powers who influence human destiny been aware of this divine purpose they would never have committed the monstrous folly of putting the Lord of glory to the shameful death of a slave. They did not fathom the bold magnificence of the method of God's wisdom—the cross the path to glory—so in their craft and force they overreached themselves. It is otherwise with us. The wisdom that we impart consists of 'Things which eye never saw, and ear never heard, Things which never entered into the heart of man, All that God prepared for those that love him' (thus read v. 9). To us who have this discerning love God has unveiled his secrets through that Spirit who searches and discloses the deep designs of God. For as a man's secret thoughts are hidden from his fellow men and are known only to his own spirit, so only the Spirit of God perceives the thoughts of God. But it is that Spirit which issues from God himself that we have received, not the spirit which animates and blinds worldly-minded men. This has God added to all his other lavish gifts, so that we might know what is ours in Christ. The language in which we make this revelation known is not that acquired from human philosophy but that learned in the school of the Spirit, for we need a spiritual medium to convey spiritual truth (v. 13). Now the unspiritual man does not welcome the teachings of the Spirit of God, for they seem mere folly to him. He cannot understand them, for they are appraised only by spiritual tests. But the spiritual man can put all things to the test, and is himself subjected to no human test. For we Christians, by virtue of our spiritual fellowship, become the organ through which the mind of Christ finds expression. He lives in us; we share his thoughts. While this relationship holds good we may confidently quote the prophet's challenge: 'For who hath known the mind of the Lord, that he should instruct him?'" (Isa. 40[13] in LXX.)

6. *The perfect.* It has been urged by some recent writers that Paul is here using a technical term from the mystery religions, in the sense of "those who have been initiated into the Christian mystery." The evidence for such a contemporary use of the Greek word is not convincing, and every occurrence in Paul's writings is covered by the rendering "mature." In view, however, of the probability that some members of the Corinthian church had been formerly in close touch with these cults, and bearing in mind Paul's ironical allusion to such an initiate in Col. 2[18], we must allow for the possibility that the language here is two-edged. For the anticipatory sense in which Paul uses the term of comparative novices in the Christian life, see Phil. 3[12, 15]; cf. his use of "saints" in 1[1], also the appeal in Rom. 6[11]. *The rulers of this world* (see also v. 8) are not the Roman authorities or the Jewish chief priests, who were the historical instruments in the crucifixion of Jesus, nor yet the moral rulers of the world, the philosophers. The reference is to "the rulers of this dark world, the spiritual hosts of evil in the heavenly regions" (thus read Eph. 6[12]). See also Col. 2[15] and mg., and read "When he despoiled the principalities and the authorities and made an open parade of them, leading them in his triumphal procession by means of the cross." They are *coming to nought* because they belong to *this age*, which (15[24]) is fast hastening to an end. (For this survival of later Jewish angelology and demonology in the Christian thought of Paul, cf. pp. 204–6; see Glover, *Jesus in the Experience of Men*, ch. 1.)

7. *In a mystery* goes with *we speak* rather than with *wisdom.* The proclamation of this wonderful purpose of God is conditioned by the spiritual fitness of the hearer. But there is no solemnly guarded secret which the Christian initiate is sworn never to divulge. Apostolic reserve follows the counsel of Mt. 7[6]. To the ordinary mind the redemptive purpose of God working through the tragedy of the cross is a thing incredible. The mystic secret is open to all who do not shrink from the means by which God "brings many sons to glory" (Heb. 2[10]). Cf. J. H. Newman's "O loving wisdom of our God," "O wisest love"; and Charles Wesley's "Wisdom in a mystery of bleeding love unfold." The end of all the travail of the Lord of glory is that we should share in the unimaginable bliss of the divine life.

9. The rhythmic lines are given as though they were cited from the O.T. The first and third lines are a reminiscence of Isa. 64[4] and the second line of Isa. 65[17]. But the resemblance is far from exact. Origen attributes the quotation to the *Secrets of Elias*, and Jerome found it in this apocalypse, as also in the *Ascension of Isaiah*, but denies Paul's debt to these later apocryphal sources. It is of interest to notice that the words are quoted (from 1 Corinthians?) in ch. 34 of the letter from Clement of Rome to the Corinthians, exactly as here, but with "them that wait for him" (as in Isa. 64[4]) instead of *them that love him* (see Ante-Nicene Fathers, Edinburgh edition, vol. i, p. 14).

13. The paraphrase given above brings out the meaning generally given to the text followed by the R.V. The translation *comparing spiritual things with spiritual* hardly yields an intelligible meaning. It is, rather, "combining spiritual truth with spiritual expression." R.V. mg. *interpreting spiritual truth* (or *things*, A.S.V. mg.) *to spiritual men* better agrees with the context. Some scholars think that *words* has crept into the text from v. 4, "in words of wisdom." With this omission read the whole verse thus: "Of which we speak also

—not amongst men who are instructed by human wisdom, but amongst men who are taught by the Spirit, explaining (literally, *bringing together*) spiritual revelations to spiritual men." This suits the argument of the whole paragraph, that the deep counsels of God can only be appreciated by spiritually minded men.

14. *The natural man.* The word so translated stands in classical Greek for the man who is under the control of the reason. With Paul it has a slightly disparaging flavor. Such a man is far removed from the sensualist, and represents unregenerate human nature at the highest. "Humanist" gives the meaning approximately.

15. The man whose mind is illumined by the Spirit of God, and shares the thoughts of Christ, has a criterion by which he can test every principle of conduct. Insofar as he conforms to the mind of Christ he is beyond the range of the natural man's assessment. The mere humanist is no more competent in that sphere than is one who is tone-deaf to criticize music, or a man who is color-blind to discuss a painting. Cf. *Letters of James Denney to Robertson Nicoll*, p. 216: "Nothing in [Mark Rutherford's] story seems to explain adequately his antipathy to evangelicalism; it seems to me pretty much another proof that literature is the work of the natural man, and that non-conforming self-conscious virtue is essentially repugnant to it. Of course, such virtue is very liable to Pharisaism, and can be criticized by inspiration, but it is much more frequently caricatured from a lower level than corrected from a higher."

CHAPTER III

1–9. Sectarian Rivalry Blind to Divine Use of Complementary Service. By an adroit transition Paul returns to the theme of 2[1-5], explaining why, with all their boasted gifts of utterance and knowledge, he could preach the gospel only in its simplest form to them. When first he visited them, they were in a rudimentary stage of Christian experience—so we may paraphrase—Christ's little ones who needed spiritual milk, and could not assimilate food appropriate for the full grown. Even now, when time has brought development, they are still unfit for what only the spiritually-minded can receive. Their ethical relationships disclose a state of mind in no way different from that which might be looked for in ordinary men. Jealousy and faction can have nothing in common with the mind of Christ. How could those in tune with the divine will raise these party watch words? (V. 4.) Apollos and Paul are nothing in themselves. Rather are they servants, each with his own peculiar gift, through whom the Corinthians were brought into the Christian life by a decisive act of faith. What though Paul planted the seed which has grown into this church, and Apollos watered the growing plant? All the processes of growth, all the elements that contribute to its life, are from God alone. The planter and the waterer are one in aim and service, though each is responsible for his separate duty. Paul and Apollos are fellow servants in God's service. The Corinthian church is God's tilth, or, to change the figure, God's building.

1–3. Three words of great importance in the Pauline psychology occur in these verses. That rendered *spiritual* means "having a nature in which spirit predominates," i.e., in which the human spirit is united with the Spirit of God. *Carnal* in v. 1 renders a Greek word (*sarkinos*) meaning "made of flesh," "having a nature in which the fleshly qualities still predominate." The same word in v. 3 (twice) is used to translate a term (Greek *sarkikos*) which is more distinctly ethical, "having the characteristics of flesh," "carnally minded." The former carries no reproach when applied to those who are still in their spiritual infancy. The latter marks a low standard of worldly behavior.

8. For the idea of *reward*, cf. v. 14, 4[5] 9[17] 15[58] Gal. 6[4, 5] 2 Jn. v. 8. It is used to emphasize the reality of moral responsibility, as in Mt. 16[27] Rom. 2[6] and the two parables Mt. 25[14-30] Lk. 19[12-27]. Some writers affect to despise it as a survival of the commercialized ethic of Judaism. But the reward is regarded as internal rather than external, and it represents the principle that no good is ineffectual in a morally ordered universe.

10–15. The Foundation and the Superstructure; Ordeal by Fire. Here the metaphor is changed from a tended field to a building. Paraphrase: "It was by God's grace—so Paul writes—that, like a sound master-mason, I laid a foundation which will endure. It is upon Jesus Christ whom I preached that all who are building will base their work. There is no question about the foundation; but let the builders be sure of their material and build only what will endure. Does one man use precious metals and costly marbles, while another makes use of wood and thatch? The difference will be disclosed in the testing day when fire will be the instrument of God's ordeal (v. 13). The quality of each man's work will then be clearly shown, for one will have the reward of seeing his life-work stand, while the other will suffer the penalty of seeing his life-work perish in flames. Singed and scarred he shall escape from the burning pile. He is not doomed to death, for he has at least built upon the true foundation. It is his work that suffers destruction."

16, 17. The Church the Temple of God. Paraphrase: "You are God's building, as I said. Need I explain to men of knowledge the character of that building? It is a sacred shrine in which God's very presence dwells. You are the church of the living God. Woe to him who desecrates by foul conduct the temple consecrated by the habitation of the Holy Spirit. Woe to him who brings this hallowed structure down in ruins by his divisive efforts."

16. *Ye are a temple of God.* Here, as in 2 Cor. 6^{16}, the reference is to the Christian society as the home of the Spirit. For the same metaphor, cf. Eph. 2^{20-22} Col. 2^{7} 1 Pet. 2^{5}. For the individual as a temple of the Spirit, see under 6^{19}.

18–23. The Folly of Worldly Wisdom; The Unlimited Wealth of the Christian. As happens so often in Paul's letters (cf. 12^{31}–13^{13} 2 Cor. 8^{9} Phil. 2^{5-11}—all roads lead to Christ!), a trifling occasion, or some failure in conduct, starts an argument in which the writer is borne far beyond the expected goal to assert an abiding truth of religion. Logic here passes into inspired appeal, and we are swept onward from party strife at Corinth, through realms of experience and worlds unknown, to the throne of the universe.

"Be on your guard"—so we may paraphrase—"against the self-deception of worldly wisdom. The only wisdom worth gaining is that which brings us to God. This he gives only to those who have taken the first step toward wisdom by acknowledging their simplicity. Scripture has given us many warnings that disaster overtakes the strategy of the clever who will not stoop to learn from God. Put not your trust in mere man. Yours is a vast inheritance in which all human agents are your ministers through whom God bestows his gifts on you. The world with all its wealth is yours, in life and death, in the present age and in the age to come. You are lords of creation, just because you are owned by Christ, who himself bows to the sovereign sway of the Father."

18. *Wise in this world*, literally, *in this age* (R.V. mg.), implying the passing fashion of worldly wisdom.

CHAPTER IV

1–5. The True Standard of Judgment. Paraphrase: "Let there be then no more of this excessive valuation of mere men, who are but servants of Christ, and stewards of the secret truths of God. Are we stewards? In that case the chief qualification is fidelity (cf. Lk. 16^{10}). So it is a matter of indifference to me what inquiries into my fitness may be conducted by you or any human tribunal. I am not even concerned to search my own heart, for my conscience is not uneasy. Not that this acquits me, but the one judge to whom I am accountable is the Lord. Therefore withhold your criticism until the Lord comes. He it is who will bring all dark secrets to light, and expose men's real motives. Then, and not till then, every man will get his due praise, and it will come from God."

6–13. The Corinthian Disciples Superior to Their Teachers! Paraphrase: "Now I have used these illustrations from farm life and building (3^{5-10}), and have brought in my name and that of Apollos to show you that you have no warrant from us for this vain party rivalry. What claim has any one of you to superiority? Have you any spiritual possession which has not come to you as a free gift? Then is there any ground for boasting? The trouble is that the disciples have grown too big to acknowledge their teachers! You Corinthians have all you want; you have made your fortune; you have come into your kingdom, and we are left outside! Would that you had really come into your kingdom, for then we might share in your royal bounty! How far away we are from that dream! It seems rather as though God had made a public spectacle of us missionaries, for all the world, angels as well as men, to gaze at (v. 9.) We are the doomed captives at the end of the triumphal procession. While we preach the sheer folly of the crucified Messiah, you secure a reputation for an 'intellectual faith.' Mark the contrast between your strength and influence and our weakness and low repute. We know what it is to go without the bare necessities of life, to suffer violence, to roam as homeless vagrants (cf. Mt. 8^{20}), to toil at manual labor. We have learned to submit with gentle dignity to insult, persecution, slander. To this day we are accustomed to be treated as the scum of society, the refuse of the world."

6. The five Greek words translated *not to go beyond the things which are written* are almost certainly a marginal gloss which originally called attention to a copyist's error in the manuscript. (See *Expository Times*, xxxiii, p. 479, where they are shown to make excellent sense as a marginal note.) Their intrusion reduces the text to nonsense, from which no expository ingenuity has ever drawn a satisfactory meaning. Without these words the text states, "I have used these metaphors in writing of Apollos and myself on your account, to show how absurd it is for any of you to pride himself on his party loyalty to one of us by disparaging the other."

7. The meaning is difficult. It may be "God has given you any spiritual endowment you possess, therefore boasting is excluded." Or, connecting with the preceding verse, "For who has authorized you to pose as a party leader? Certainly neither Paul nor Apollos." A third possibility is, "To whom do you owe the discovery that you are spiritually rich but to these despised missionaries who brought you the gospel!"

12, 13. Where did the erstwhile proud Pharisee learn this secret? See notes on ch. 13, and cf. 1 Pet. 2^{21-24}.

14–21. The Ground of Apostolic Authority. Paraphrase: "Why do I write in this strain? Not to reduce you to abject self-reproach, but to remind you that I am your father in the faith. You may have any number of spiritual guides, but one man alone brought you into living fellowship with Jesus Christ. This gives me the right to appeal to you to model your way of life upon mine. You may have forgotten some of those unstudied lessons once learned from my example, so I am sending Timothy, another of my spiritual sons, to remind you of these principles of practical Christianity which I am responsible for making known wherever I preach Christ (v. 17). As for those braggarts who are so confident that I am never going to visit you again, they will soon have an opportunity of showing whether their high-sounding boast is anything but wind. The presence of the kingdom of God is proved by spiritual influence, by moral strength, not by mere talk. As soon as God opens the way I shall visit you. It is for you to determine whether I am then to vindicate my apostolic authority as founder of the church at Corinth by disciplining the offenders, or to appear among you in self-effacing love as your spiritual father."

15. The Greek word translated *tutor* here and in Gal. 3^{24} signified the trusty slave to whom the father committed his son. He was responsible for the boy's care out of school.

16, 17. Cf. 11^{1} Phil. 3^{17} 1 Thess. 1^{6}. The missionary's bearing and behavior would be a practical object lesson for pagan converts. The Christian way of life is *caught* as well as *taught.*

Chapters 5^{1} to 6^{20}: Moral Disorders In the Church

This was one of the most serious questions that Paul had to deal with in the Corinthian church.

CHAPTER V

1–8. The Moral Scandal and the Responsibility of the Church. A flagrant case of immorality—a man's incestuous union with his step-mother—has not even disturbed the indulgent complacency of the Corinthian church. To preserve the church from corruption, and to save the soul of the sinner, Paul has resolved on drastic action. He directs that the local church shall meet in full session, conscious of the presence in all his power of the Lord in whose name they meet, remembering too that the apostle is with them in thought. Acting upon his counsel they shall excommunicate the gross offender with every solemn circumstance.

5. The sound recommendation of the missionary pastor and statesman is obscured for modern readers by the language of v. 5. The sentence is *to deliver* the obdurate sinner *to Satan.* The immediate result will be *the destruction of the flesh;* the ultimate aim, *that the spirit may be saved* (or *preserved*) *in the day of the Lord Jesus.* This is a striking instance of Paul's use of current Jewish ideas. The synagogue elders exercised the ban (cf. Ezra 10^{8} Jn. 9^{22} 12^{42} 16^{2} Lk. 6^{22}). Outside the beneficent influences of the Christian community the condemned reprobate would be unprotected from the authority of Satan. Numerous bodily ills were attributed to demonic influence, and death itself was regarded as under the dominion of Satan (15^{26} Jn. 8^{44} Heb. 2^{14} Wisdom 2^{14}). This man's punishment will be wrought in the sphere of his sinful practice—he sinned in the flesh, and it is the flesh that must be destroyed (cf. the cognate idea, $11^{29f.}$). But the body (the *flesh*), the organ of the personality, is to be destroyed, so that the spirit may be saved in the day when the Lord passes judgment. If Paul's language sounds harsh, we must remember (1) that Jesus allowed (Mt. 18^{15-18}) for extreme discipline in the case of a man who persists in flouting the moral authority of the Christian brotherhood; (2) that it would have been fatal to the purity of a church largely recruited from paganism to tolerate lax moral standards in the community; (3) that physical sufferings were regarded as the inevitable result of alienation from the society that enjoyed protection from demonic assault; and (4) that this chastisement of the flesh was expected to work out godly repentance and ultimate spiritual salvation.

6–8. Turning from the doom of the sinner to the danger of the acquiescent church, Paul rebukes the pride that can suffer such a stain, quotes a proverb (cf. Gal. 5^{9}) in reminder of the extent to which this foul infection will spread, and finds a happy application of the Christian symbolism of the Paschal feast. For the ancient custom of removing all yeast from the house on the 14th of Nisan, see Ex. 12^{15} 13^{3} (notes). If, as the fourth Gospel seems to declare, Jesus was crucified on the 14th of Nisan (see art., *Chronology of N.T.*, p. 875b, and notes on Mt. 26^{17-19} Jn. 18^{28}), and if (cf. 16^{8}) this letter was written shortly before Easter, this figurative language becomes the more effective.

9–13. The Internal Discipline of the Church. An earlier letter, with its warning against tolerating men of immoral life in the Christian community, has been misunderstood as forbidding intercourse of any kind with the heathen world. In view of the indulgent attitude to the gross offender in their own midst, it seems less likely that the Corinthian Christians had made a brave attempt at social isolation than that they urged the impracticability of this policy as an excuse for ignoring Paul's high demand for internal discipline. Paul concedes the obvious necessity for all but anchorites to have business dealings with men of the world who fall below the Christian standard of monotheism, sexual purity, disinterestedness, and honesty. It is not the missionary's duty to pronounce sentence upon those who have not accepted the Christian yoke. That would surely be to usurp the divine function. But it is the duty of the church to maintain its high moral standard among its own members. Christian fellowship must be withheld from anyone bearing the name of brother not only if he lapse into idolatry or sexual sin, but also if he discredit the Christian standard of life by losing control of appetite or tongue, or by inordinate desire for gain, leading to unfair exactions. Tolerance has gone too far. The scoundrel must be expelled.

9. For the possibility that part of that earlier letter has been preserved in Second Corinthians, see introduction, section on "Paul's Relations with Corinth," (5), p. 1169.

11. The condemnation of *covetousness* (cf. Col. 3^{5}) recalls the teaching of Jesus (Lk. 12^{15} 16^{13}), but the word is often used by Paul in a wider sense than greed for gold, and covers all selfish disregard of the just claims of brotherhood.

CHAPTER VI

1–11. Christians in Dispute before Heathen Tribunals. Paul describes the judicial prerogative and responsibility of the Christian society. This function may be exercised in simpler fashion to save the scandal that has arisen from the spectacle of fellow Christians suing one another before heathen courts (v. 7). Four reasons are given why the church should provide for arbitration in all such disputes: (1) *The saints shall judge the world* (v. 2)—a mingling of the Jewish belief that the righteous will share in the divine judgment of the heathen nations (Wisdom $3^{7, 8}$ Dan. 7^{22}, and cf. Rev. 20^{4}) with the promise of Jesus to his disciples (Mt. 19^{28} Lk. 22^{30}). Much more easily then can they settle these trifling disputes. (2) The saints are also to *judge angels* (v. 3)—an allusion to the popular Jewish belief contained in the apocryphal Book of Enoch (see 91^{15} and cf. Jude v. 6, 2 Pet. 2^{4}) that angels will be involved in the Judgment (cf. p. 204). (3) Those accounted fit for such exalted offices will surely not submit *things that pertain to this life* (v. 3) to the judgment of the despised heathen! Yet a church that boasts of its "wisdom" cannot find one member wise enough to arbitrate between fellow members! (4) Even apart from the unsuitable character of the tribunal, a defeat is sustained by the mere fact of going to law against a fellow Christian (v. 5). How much better to suffer injustice and fraud than to incur this reproach! On the contrary, they are inflicting such treatment on their brothers! This conduct excludes them from the kingdom of God (v. 9). Membership in that redeemed society is impossible for those who practice idolatry or the shameful vices of the Gentile world. But self-indulgence of appetite and speech can exclude, as also will any kind of dishonesty. The greed, then, which leads to these squabbles must be suppressed. All these repellent vices have found representatives in the Corinthian church. But when they offered themselves for baptism they came under the purifying influences of the Christian fellowship, and found pardon in virtue of the name of Christ and by means of the Spirit of God (v. 11). The apostle humbles their pride that he may extol the effective grace of God.

Two questions emerge from this discussion. (1) Does Paul advocate a complete divorce between members of the church and state institutions? (2) Is Paul interpreting the teaching of Jesus as passive submission to evil? In answer to (1) we must refer to Paul's teaching in Rom. 13^{1-7}, his appeal to the imperial tribunal, Acts $25^{10, 11}$, and his insistence upon respect for Roman law when its forms and privileges were lightly ignored by officials, Acts 16^{37} 23^{25-30}. The Roman power secured impartial administration of justice, and gave protection from mob violence. Paul was too wise and experienced a traveler to disparage these benefits in an ordered society. The answer to (2) must be determined accordingly.

It is evident that passive endurance of all evil was not regarded as essentially Christian. Moreover, the question is not raised how far the vindication of one's good name, or the determination of the right ownership of property may compel a Christian man in the interests of others to appeal to the properly constituted courts of his country. Paul is concerned to rebuke the litigious habit of his converts, who do not scruple to expose disputes of fellow Christians to the public scorn. He also probes to the root of the trouble and declares it to be desire for gain that warps the sense of justice. Notice again the prominence of covetousness and extortion in a catalogue of vices (vv. 9, 10). So Jesus replied, "Keep yourselves from all covetousness," when appealed to on a question of property division (Lk. 12[15]). The teaching of Jesus (Mt. 5[39,40]) in setting a higher value on good will and friendly relations than on the successful assertion of rights is further echoed in v. 7b.

9, 10. There is suggested here the raw material upon which the gospel worked at Corinth, the city in which Paul wrote his terrible description of the pagan world (Rom. 1[24-32]). Yet by the alchemy of grace (v. 11) this dross has been refined.

12–20. The Sanctity of the Body. In this section (possibly a fragment from an earlier letter—see intro., section on "Paul's Relations with Corinth," (2), p. 1169), Paul takes up some of the watchwords of the antinomians, and argues with those who cannot recognize the deadly nature of sexual vice.

Paraphrase: "Do you quote the formula, 'All things are lawful for me'? But Christian freedom has its limits, and everything is not to my highest advantage. Nor on the strength of this liberty will I allow anything to tyrannize over me. You quote the saying, 'Food is for the belly, and the belly for food.' True, but these belong to the temporary phase of our earthly life. Eating and drinking are legitimate functions of our present physical organism, but fornication is an abuse of bodily functions, and inflicts a permanent injury upon the personality. Remember that our bodies are to be transformed, and are to become fit raiment for the soul in the eternal realm where the risen Christ reigns. Indeed, our bodily powers are organs of that spiritual body whose head is Christ. Sexual union involves one bodily life. This applies to immoral intercourse (v. 16) as well as to the primal bliss of Eden (Gen. 2[24]), whereas a spiritual union with the Lord is the Christian's privilege. You must therefore avoid immorality, for while other sins may not leave a stamp upon your bodily life, this is a sin which desecrates the shrine of the Holy Spirit, who cannot take up his abode in so dishonored a home. One thought more: You have been liberated from a cruel servitude to become the slaves of Christ in that service which is perfect freedom. Remember the cost at which you were ransomed. Your gratitude to God must be shown in the pure service of your bodily powers."

The reasoning of the libertines (not infrequently reproduced in our own time) was that the use of bodily functions is natural and therefore permissible. Paul replies: (1) Your illustration touches only the instinctive requirements of that body which perishes (v. 13a). There are bodily reactions upon the soul which are of lasting effect. This is the bodily life which is raised to immortality (vv. 14, 18; cf. 15[44, 50]). (2) Your illustration ignores the distinction between the designed use and the abuse of instinctive functions (v. 13b). (3) The union of man and woman is not only physical, it is psychological. The two lives grow incorporate into one another. The spasmodic union with a prostitute is injurious to that growth of the higher self which depends on spiritual fellowship with Christ (vv. 15–17). (4) The body is designed to fit us for union with God. This privilege is forfeited by debasement of the body (v. 19a). Libertinism claims a freedom to follow its own will, which a ransomed servant of Christ can never assert (vv. 19b, 20). The main difficulty arises from Paul's conception of the body as something more than the perishable tenement of the soul. To him it is the outward and visible form of the entire personality. (See Anderson Scott, *Christianity According to St. Paul*, pp. 208f.) We must also allow for Paul's mysticism, in which the metaphor of union becomes almost a physical relationship. The modern Christian may wonder that Paul is silent about the shameful wrong to womanhood that underlies prostitution, and that he does not urge the ennobling influence of marriage and the Christian home. He will do well at the same time to contrast with the prevailing attitude to sensuality in the contemporary Greek world the strong emphasis which Paul constantly lays upon chastity.

20. *Ye were bought with a price.* See Deissmann's *Light from the Ancient East*, ch. 4, for a vivid exposition of this technical term in the process of manumission. By a legal fiction the slave's savings were handed over to the priest in the temple, who then bought him from his master and freed him by transferring the ownership to the divinity in whose shrine they were. Even so Christ has bought us for himself, not with our hard-won earnings, but with his own life blood. Hence he has a claim upon our souls and bodies (see pp. 1190–3).

Chapter 7: Paul's Reply to Questions Concerning Sex

As explained in the introduction (section on "Paul's Relations with Corinth," (3), p. 1169), Paul received from the Corinthian church a number of questions, which he proceeds to answer in 7[1]–11[1].

CHAPTER VII

1–7. Marriage and its Obligations. Consulted by the Corinthian church on the general question of marriage, Paul declares celibacy to be preferable, but will not make this an unconditional counsel. In view of the danger of sensuality Christian marriage is recommended. There is no trace of asceticism, for mutual marital obligation is recognized in the intimacy of wedded life, with the self-control demanded by seasons of special prayer. Such separation should be temporary and by consent. The dangers arising from the ill-disciplined Corinthian character, and the sensuality of life in that city, influence this counsel, which Paul would not have them regard as a command. His own wish is that they might all share his gift and remain unmarried, but each man's state must be determined by God's gift of temperament.

6, 7. In the phrase, *this I say*, it is impossible to decide whether *this* refers to the abstinence, or to the resumption. Read v. 7a thus: *But I am quite willing that all should be as myself*, i.e., undisturbed by the dominance of desire.

8–24. Moral Safeguards; Mixed Marriages; Outward Conditions Unchanged by Christian Call. The unmarried and widowed do well to remain so, but marriage is better than incontinence or an inflamed imagination. With regard to divorce, the actual prohibition of Jesus is quoted (cf. Mk. 10[11, 12]). If separation has actually taken place, let the woman remain single or else be reconciled to her husband. This rule of the indissoluble bond of Christian marriage applies equally to both partners. For the grave problem of mixed marriages Paul has no dictum of the Lord to cite, but gives his own judgment (vv. 12–16). The Christian husband or wife whose heathen partner is willing to share the home is not to sever the tie, for the believer consecrates the partner, whether husband or wife, just as children of Christian parents are not unholy, but consecrated to God. If, on the other hand, the heathen husband or wife dissolves the union, this situation is to be accepted, for in such conditions the Christian wife or husband is in no slavish subjection to marriage; for God called us to a life of peace. It would be dangerous presumption to hold that the heathen partner must inevitably be saved by the forced attachment of the other.

The Christian's call does not involve a change in external conditions (vv. 17–24). This is a universal requirement in the churches of Paul's foundation. This applies alike to the status of Jew and Gentile. No operation is to be attempted to acquire or remove the mark of circumcision (v. 17). Loyalty to the moral code is what matters, not mere externals. A man should be content to remain in that status which is his at the time of his conversion. A slave need not trouble about his position when called by God (though if an opportunity of gaining freedom is given he should take it—v. 21), for the Christian slave is the Lord's freedman, just as the Christian freeman is the slave of Christ. All alike are slaves of Christ (by whom they were bought for a great price —cf. 6[20]); in the Christian Church no artificial distinctions are to be observed (cf. Gal. 3[28]), and no servant of Christ is to stand in slavish fear of human opinion. So then, seeing that we are brothers, let every man remain in that state in which he was called of God, for God is with him there.

14. *Is sanctified in the wife*, i.e., has been consecrated to God by means of his wife's consecration. The meaning is not that her influence will gradually change his character, for the perfect, not the future tense is used. The conception belongs to a group of ideas inherited from Judaism, according to which family relationship involves a share in ritual consecration. The word is used in its technical religious, not in its moral sense. Similarly *unclean* and *holy* are used in this ritual sense of the children of a Christian parent.

17. Uniformity of teaching in local churches. Cf. 11[16] for uniformity of practice.

19. This fundamental distinction between the external and the spiritual is found also in Gal. 5[6] 6[15]. There the vital requirement is "faith working by love," or "a new creation" (mg.). Here we see that faith, the moral dynamic of the new creation, inspired by love, results in the observance of God's commands (cf. Jn. 14[15] 15[10]).

21. *Use it rather* is an ambiguity to cover the deep division among commentators. Some supply the word "slavery," others "opportunity." The former hold that the context favors the interpretation, "Remain in slavery even if you have a chance of winning your freedom. Use that state as a sphere for glorifying God." In view of the tense of the imperative Paul probably meant, "Don't let your position as a slave weigh upon your mind. But if, as a matter of fact, you can get your freedom, the rather seize the chance."

25–40. The Marriage of "Virgins." Here again the apostle can give no direct answer from a definite saying of the Lord. He can only express a judgment as one whose special treatment by God marks him as trustworthy. The general trend is that, while marriage is honorable, it is unwise to incur fresh responsibilities in view of the near approach of the Advent, and the tribulations that will herald its dawn (vv. 29–31). The cares of the home encroach upon a single-minded devotion to the Lord. An attitude of detachment to the claims of this rapidly passing world is necessary for concentration upon the Lord's affairs. This counsel is offered with no desire to restrict freedom, but in the interests of seemly and efficient Christian service.

The specific case, however, on which Paul's advice was sought presents unusual difficulties. According to the older interpretation (followed in the R.V.), vv. 26–35 resume the general teaching regarding marriage already given, explaining more fully the apostle's preference for the unmarried state, with merely a passing reference to virgins in vv. 28 and 33. The special case is first introduced in v. 36, and is concerned with the duty of a father or guardian to a virgin who is under his control. But the word *daughter* is not in the Greek (see mg.), the phrase *his own virgin* (v. 37) hardly bears this interpretation, and in v. 36 the sentence *let them marry* must refer to *any man* and *his virgin*. There is strong reason for accepting the theory that Paul is here dealing with a case of what came to be known as "spiritual marriage." In recoil from the prevalent sensuality of Corinthian life asceticism was highly favored in some quarters. One manifestation of this tendency may well have been (as we know it was in the second and third centuries) an agreement by which an unmarried man and a maid pledged themselves to one another in a spiritual union. (See art., "Agapetæ," in Hastings *Encyc. of Religion and Ethics;* Lake, *Earlier Epistles of St. Paul*, pp. 184–191; D. Smith, *Life and Letters of St. Paul*, pp. 266f.) With this clue to guide us, Paul seems to have two possibilities before him. In vv. 26–28 he is considering those who have been betrothed with this understanding that they will never unite in wedlock. "My opinion is that as a general principle, in view of the impending distress, it is honorable for a man to remain in this state. If you are pledged to a woman, do not look for release from this pledge. If you are free from any such pledge, do not look for a woman. But if either you or your betrothed maid has taken the step of becoming married, that is no sin. I only want to spare you the outward trouble which will be the portion of all who take that step."

Here it appears that one of the parties to the agreement wishes for an ordinary marriage, the other is unwilling, and so the betrothal has yielded to marriage with a third person. Paul refuses to denounce the termination of such an agreement as sinful. But in vv. 36–38 he seems to be considering a case in which the conditions they have imposed upon themselves prove too strong a trial of endurance. In that case, says the apostle, let them marry. "But if any man thinks that he is not behaving properly to his spiritual bride, if his instincts are vehement and necessity urges, let them marry. He is not sinning in carrying out this wish. But the man who is steadfast in his resolve, who has control where his will is concerned and is not driven by necessity, and has resolved to keep his spiritual bride as such, will do well. So then he who marries his spiritual bride acts honorably, and he who does not marry follows the better course of action."

In vv. 39, 40 Paul rounds off his principal counsels. He has already dealt with the marriage of a Christian couple (vv. 10, 11), and of mixed marriages where the heathen partner happily preserved (vv. 12–14) or else severed the bond (vv. 15, 16). It remains to settle the case where a wife is required to live with an uncongenial husband. The apostolic counsel is emphatic. Marriage is indissoluble during the husband's lifetime, but the widow is free to make a Christian marriage after his death. Paul adds once more his advice in favor of single blessedness, with a final reminder, aimed perhaps at some prominent leaders whose "spirituality" lifted them above such practical questions, *And I think that I also have the Spirit of God.*

36. *Past the flower of her age.* The rare Greek word may equally well mean "overpassionate," and is either masculine or feminine.

38. *Giveth in marriage.* There is good reason to render "marries."

Note on Paul's Teaching on Marriage

We observed with surprise that Paul's denunciation of immorality in ch. 6 fails to urge the true consecration of the sexual impulse in the home and family life. The disappointment deepens in ch. 7, where marriage is treated on sufferance as a refuge from grossness of thought and practice. There are, however, conditions of time and place which left a deep impress on this letter. When Paul wrote it he was eagerly anticipating the speedy return of the Lord, and looked for tribulations as its sure accompaniment (vv. 26, 29; cf. Lk. 21[23]). With this shortened perspective it was natural to view responsibilities in a changed relativity, and to give marriage a lower place in consulting the welfare of his converts (vv. 31b, 32a, 35). It must also be remembered that all this teaching is projected against the foul moral background of Corinth. Knowing their antecedents, and the polluted atmosphere of their city, Paul adopts a courageous realism in vv. 2, 5b, 9, when warning his correspondents of their peril. For it is probable that in such a place sensuality led to an ascetic reaction. The apostle holds the balance evenly, and, while stating his own preference in view of the world-crisis, he recognizes differences of temperament as varied gifts from God, refusing to impose his advice as an injunction. It is significant that the one dogmatic command is a word of Christ's, based upon the ideal permanence of the marriage bond. We must not overlook the mutuality of the marriage obligation in v. 4. The woman's right stands on the same footing as the man's. The curious situation disclosed in vv. 25–28, 36–38, arose in a city where grave perils may have led to strange safeguards. Paul is asked to advise in certain exceptional cases. As this experiment has not survived, Paul's advice is only of historical interest. Whatever the conditions, it is clear that he recognizes as the only possible alternative to a life of consistent celibacy honorable Christian marriage, just as the former is the only alternative to the latter. This is the last letter dominated by the imminent expectation of the Advent. The teaching about marriage in Eph. 5[22-33] reveals a steadier outlook upon society and a higher conception of the Christian home.

Chapters 8[1] to 11[1]: Paul's Reply to Questions Concerning Sacrificial Food and Social Life

On the origin of these questions, see the introductory note to ch. 7.

CHAPTER VIII

1–13. Meat Offered to Idols; Christian Freedom and the Restraint of Love. The first group of questions related to the various *problems of sex* (see ch. 7) which perplexed the church. The second group arose out of the *social relationships* of Corinthian life, and consisted of two questions raised through the pervasive influence of heathen religion. Most of the meat sold in the market had been offered first to some idol. Social and business relationships often involved participation in a common meal that was either held in a temple or attended by some recognition of the divinity. Paul was asked, (1) Can a Christian eat such meat? (2) Can he share in such a meal? The discussion ranges over the next three chapters. In ch. 8 Paul takes up some of the catchwords of the "advanced" party who pride themselves on their "knowledge" (vv. 1–3) that idols are nonentities and who, therefore, see no reason to avoid the alleged contamination which the "weaker" (vv. 7f.) members fear.

Paraphrase of vv. 1–13: "Beware of the conceit that is bred by superior 'knowledge,' for it is love which alone admits us to the friendship of God. Of course I know as well as you that 'idols don't exist,' and that 'there is no God but one.' There are plenty of so-called gods and lords, but for us there is one God, the Father, source of all things, and end of our existence, one Lord Jesus Christ, agent of the creation and of our redemption (v. 6). But this higher knowledge is not understood by all. Some who were reared in idolatry cannot even now eat food that has been sacrificed to an idol without recalling the old associations, and their conscience, morbid as you consider it, tells them they are defiled. Now, food is not an important factor in religion. Abstinence does not separate us from God, nor does eating bring us nearer (v. 8). The main thing is to take care that the exercise of your right does not trip up the man who is not yet established. There is a risk that a weak man of this kind may see you taking part in a meal at an idol temple. The sight of one with your superior knowledge sitting there, so far from establishing his feeble conscience, will encourage him to act against his scruples and thereby come to grief. So his ruin will lie at your door (v. 11), all because of your superior 'knowledge.' Yet he is a brother for whom Christ has laid down his life. The injury that some of you are doing to others when their conscience is in that morbid state is a sin against the brotherhood, and therefore against Christ. Rather than trip up my brother, if meat is a stumbling-block in his case, I will be a vegetarian all my life!"

3. Cf. 13[12] Gal. 4[9] 1 Jn. 4[7, 8].

7. Rendel Harris conjectures a change in the order of two Greek words, with this result: *But some eat the sacrifice from long habit as if they were eating the idol.*

The *weak conscience* in this chapter (v. 7b, etc.) is the morbid conscience which cannot see things in their right proportion. It is a symptom of immaturity. The *weak* brother is not yet so established in the faith as to rid himself of false but powerful fancies. The danger is so real to him that he must be handled sympathetically.

CHAPTER IX

1–27. The Apostle's Example of Self-Surrendered Liberty. The twofold question regarding sacrificial meat, and common meals under the auspices of a heathen divinity, is answered with a double reference. In ch. 8 Paul has considered the Christian's action in relation to others, returning to this in 10[23f.] In 10[1-22] he discusses such action as it affects the character of the man himself. Ch. 9 connects the two by a frank expression of his own attitude toward the assertion of rights. At first, the eager assertion of apostleship seems irrelevant to the main discussion, but v. 22 picks up the thread apparently dropped at 8[13], and v. 27 effects with remarkable skill the transition to 10[1-13]. What at first seems to the superficial reader egotism is seen at last to be consummate tact.

Paraphrase of vv. 1–27: "I have said what I should do. But the policy of my whole career warrants this appeal. My apostleship began with my vision of Jesus at Damascus. For you it has been sealed by God's use of me in your conversion. Apostleship entitles me to maintenance, just as though I were a soldier, a vinedresser, or a shepherd. Peter and the Lord's brothers, and the other apostles, even take their wives with them on their missions. Barnabas and I alone claim no support. This is not strictly just, for the Law recognizes in analogous cases (Deut. 25[4] Lev. 6[16, 26] 7[6, 31-34] 10[12-15]) a principle which is applied to our case by the Lord himself, when he said that those who proclaim the gospel should live by the gospel (v. 14). Now, at Corinth I have waived this right to avoid injuring the cause of Christ. I am not claiming it now, for I would rather starve than feel that I have hindered the good work by accepting grudging support. Preaching the gospel in itself is no ground for satisfaction, for I do that under a sense of moral compulsion. If I act thus on my own initiative, I am entitled to my hire; but if otherwise, my position is that of a slave intrusted with a stewardship (v. 17). My reward, then, is that in preaching I lay no burden of cost on the gospel, so as not to make full use of the right which is mine as a preacher. My voluntary renunciation of privilege, I say, amounts to resignation of absolute freedom, becoming the slave of all in order to win as many as possible. I have adapted myself to all sorts and conditions of men in the hope of saving some (v. 22). All this I do for the sake of the gospel, that others may share it with me. Now, efficiency depends upon steadfastness of purpose and rigorous self-discipline. Like a trained athlete I keep my body in fit condition, lest after preaching to others I should myself be disqualified."

1–3. Paul's apostleship rests on two claims: (1) His vision of the risen Jesus (15[8] Acts 9[3f.]) who commissioned him (Acts 22[18f.] Gal. 1[15f.]). (2) There was fruit to his ministry (2 Cor. 3[2]). **5.** *The Lord's brothers,* cf. Mk. 6[3] Gal. 1[19]. **6.** On Paul's financial independence of the Corinthian church, cf. 2 Cor. 11[9] Phil. 4[15] Acts 18[3]. **9, 10.** A glaring instance of rabbinical exegesis. The injunction was purely humanitarian. **14.** Cf. Mt. 10[10] Lk. 10[7]. Note, as in 7[10], the reliance upon authentic sayings of the Lord (cf. Acts 20[35]). **17.** *Stewardship.* Often a slave's appointment, thus giving meaning to v. 19. **20.** At what point of his missionary career did Paul conduct himself as a Jewish legalist? The unrecorded period of Gal. 1[21]–2[1]? **22.** The adaptability of self-renouncing love is not to be confounded with pliable opportunism. When vital principle was at stake, Paul proved adamant (Gal. 2[5]).

CHAPTER X

1–13. No Sacramental Guarantee of Salvation; Temptation and Trust. Paul now urges the need of vigilance upon the self-confident intellectuals of Corinth. Perhaps they imagine that they are secured by sacramental grace from the moral perils of heathen society and social customs that bring them into a pagan atmosphere. By a bold application of the story of the wilderness experience of the Israelites he reminds them that baptism in the cloud and enjoyment of miraculous food did not save these favored Israelites from the consequences of their sins (v. 5). They stumbled into grave moral perils. Idolatry and its attendant immorality brought death to thousands. Others were brought low by a reckless pride that challenged God, or a discontented spirit that resented the restrictions of their lot. The church in the wilderness was a type of the church at Corinth. These experiences stand on record for the special warning (v. 11) of those who live in these momentous days in which all the lines of history are converging toward the climax. Then let the self-confident man be most of all on his guard. Yet severe as are the trials, the powers of darkness have not proved invincible. God may be relied upon not to allow his servants to be subjected to an impossible strain. He is responsible for the moral order, and has not only set us in the midst of so many and great dangers, but will always provide the means of victorious endurance (v. 13).

4. An allusion to a Jewish legend based upon

the double narrative of the water which gushed from the rock at Horeb (Ex. 17:1-7) and at Kadesh (Num. 20:1-13). Rabbinical fancy identified the rocks and thus accounted for the water supply of the Israelites in their wanderings. Cf. the Song of the Well (Num. 21:16-18). Paul uses this as an illustration. There was a spiritual source which never failed the needy Israelites, which source he identifies with the Messiah.

5–10. The historical references are to Num. 11 (for v. 6), Ex. 32 (for v. 7), Num. 25 (for v. 8), Num. 21 (for v. 9), Num. 14 (for v. 10).

11. The usual translation (R.V., A.S.V.) means: These events had a deeper significance than contemporaries understood. They illustrated a principle of religious life which is seen most clearly in this last period of human history—the meeting point of the age now ending and the new age that will shortly begin. The last clause of the verse contains two words which admit of a different translation: "to whom the tolls of the ages have come down as an inheritance." We are spiritual heirs of all the ages.

14–22. The Incompatibility of Fellowship in the Eucharist and in Idol Feasts. The Corinthian converts must not lose heart because of the moral dangers which surround them. But any deliberate participation in idolatrous rites is a wanton risk, and an act of disloyalty to the entire Christian relationship. The argument in this section is based on an ancient conception which is remote from modern thought. Participation with any person (see on 7:14) or institution that is consecrated to a God involves the participator in a permanent relationship. (See Anderson Scott, *Christianity According to St. Paul*, pp. 181f.) In the Jewish temple those who eat the sacrifices become partners of the altar. Some of its sacredness passes over to them. In the same way those who share in the cup and the bread at the Lord's Supper become partners in the sacred Christian fellowship of the church, which is the body of Christ, whose members are bound to one another and to their Lord by the covenant of his blood (v. 17). There is a sense in which participation in an idol feast brings the guest into definite relationship to the idol. Paul repudiates the thought that the idol has any real existence, but he regards all pagan rites as closely bound up with demonic influences. This, then, makes it a moral impossibility for a comrade in the fellowship of Christ to enter into a fellowship with demons (v. 21). The metaphysical conception belongs to another age than ours, but the logic and the underlying ethical principle are irresistible. Such a conflict of loyalties is intolerable. The closing note is an ironical inquiry whether the self-styled *strong* are stronger than the Lord, whom they are *provoking to jealousy* (in the language of Deut. 32:21) by such flagrant disloyalty.

23–33. Meat Sacrificed to Idols; The Principle of Edification. (See also 11:1.) Returning to sacrificial meat, Paul finds here no question of lawfulness, but, rather, of expediency and edification. "Your neighbor's good is the criterion," so we may paraphrase. "Eat any meat from the market without raising conscientious scruples, for all that the earth produces is the Lord's. If you accept an invitation to an unbeliever's table, eat without scruple the food before you (v. 27). But refrain if told that the meat is sacrificial, for your informant's sake. Your own conscience is unchallengeably free (v. 29); but put no difficulties in the way of Jew, or Gentile, or the church. I follow Christ's example by sacrificing my own advantage to that of the many for their salvation. Copy me in this."

Chapters 11:2 to 14:40: Disorders in Church Assemblies

This section is marked by Paul's characteristic ethical passion and deep concern for order. (Cf. notes on Eph. 4:25–6:9 Col. 3:5–4:6.)

CHAPTER XI

1. See under 10:23-33.

2–16. The Veiling of Women in Church. The advice of Paul here is an outstanding example of a missionary's treatment of a question of the hour which is not permanently binding. His requirement that women should be veiled in public assemblies was wise in view of Greek custom. The reasons he gives are rabbinical, and as such invalidate his judgment for modern readers. In Greek city life, if a Christian woman went about with head unveiled she might be classed with the *hetairæ;* i.e., women who contracted irregular marriages and entered into public life, while the matrons kept to the privacy of the home. To avoid scandal it was imperative that members of the church should refrain from exposing themselves to misrepresentation.

Paul had before given information about the general Christian practice with special reference to local conditions. This has been accepted (v. 2), but on one point further explanation is required. The veiling of women who take public share in church services is desirable for the following reasons. (1) Vv. 3–6. In the economy of the Christian life woman is subordinate to her husband, as every man is subordinate to Christ. Subordination does not detract from equality of honor, for in the same way Christ is subordinate to God. For a man to pray or prophesy with covered head is to dishonor his Head (i.e., Christ); for a woman to do this with uncovered head is to dishonor her head (i.e., her husband). For she might as well go a step further, and have her hair shorn—the sign of marital infidelity! (2) Vv. 8, 9, 11, 12. This custom is based upon the traditional origin of woman (Gen. 2[21-23]), for Eve was created out of Adam, and for the sake of Adam. Yet here again remember that subordination does not mean inferiority, for every man owes his birth to woman in the creative wisdom of God, and both man and woman are mutually dependent in the Christian conception of the home. (3) Vv. 13–15. Nature itself shows the seemliness of this custom by providing woman with abundant covering of hair. (4) V. 16. If anyone wants to quibble about this matter, my final argument is that we missionaries do not sanction the usage you write of, nor is it customary in any of the other churches. (See on 7[17].)

There are several baffling difficulties in this curious passage:

4. *Dishonoreth his head.* As above, or "does shame to his head" by implying that some superior is present. There is a further difficulty about the practice referred to. The custom with Greeks of both sexes was to offer sacrifice bareheaded; with Romans of both sexes to do so with head covered; whereas it is often said that among the Jews men were required to wear the *tallith* or veil during prayer. But praying and prophesying in a Christian assembly has no connection with sacrificing, and probably a saying of Plutarch's applies to the Græco-Roman world in general: "It is more customary for women to come forward in a public building covered, and for men, uncovered." As for Judaism, Strack and Billerbeck in their Rabbinical Parallels to the N.T. show that in the N.T. period there was no obligation for men to pray with covered head, except when under some kind of curse or affliction.

6. "For if a woman makes a practice of going about unveiled, let her get shorn once for all." An ironical rebuke for what might well be regarded as immodesty.

7. That man is *the image and glory of God* is an interpretation of Gen. 1[26] and Psa. 8[5]. There is a late rabbinical comment which interprets Isa. 44[13], "according to the beauty of a man," as meaning "woman, because she is her husband's glory." Another passage, in the Talmud, says, "In the disgrace of his wife lies the disgrace of the husband." Perhaps it is straining the meaning of "glory," which in the Bible so often means "self-expression," to find here the thought that the best (or worst) in the man is brought out by the woman.

10. Exceedingly difficult. R.V. and A.S.V. insert *sign of* before *authority.* This may be taken in two ways. (1) It may be the sign of the husband's authority. So Strack-Billerbeck show from rabbinical sources that the bride walked in the wedding procession with uncovered head as a token of her free maidenhood. Then, as a sign that the husband's authority was upon her, Jewish usage required that the married woman should always appear abroad with covered head. (2) Ramsay, *Cities of St. Paul*, pp. 202f., shows from Dion Chrysostom that Tarsus was a most Oriental city, especially in this, that the women went about deeply veiled. With this fact he combines the evidence of Thomson, *The Land and the Book*, p. 31, that in Oriental lands the veil is the power and dignity of the woman. It protects her from insult. Without it her authority is lost. He demands that the ordinary meaning of "authority" (active not passive) be retained. "Her authority"—that which secures respect for her—ought to be upon her head, seeing that she is her husband's glory, owing it to him to preserve dignity and to command the respect of men.

Because of the angels (v. 10b). Two interpretations out of many deserve notice. (1) Some find an allusion to evil angels, who figure largely in later Jewish speculation. Gen. 6[1f.], and the elaborations of that story in the book of Enoch, show that it was not impossible for Jews to think of women as in danger from the lust of fallen angels. Tertullian understood the passage in this sense. Bousset therefore takes *authority* as possibly meaning a charm. The veil will serve as an amulet to protect the woman from the evil influence of the angels who are present. (2) It is urged against this view that *the angels* (with the definite article) in the N.T. always means good angels, who, in early Christian thought, were regarded as specially interested in the welfare of men (Lk. 12[8] 15[10] 1 Tim. 5[21] Heb. 1[14] 1 Pet. 1[12] Rev. 3[5].) For late Jewish belief in the angels' concern in human prayer, as also for the conception in (1), consult index to Charles' *Apocrypha and Pseudepigrapha of the O.T.* (See also art., *Intertestamental Religion*, p. 204.) Unseemly behavior in Christian worship is distressing to the ministering spirits who encompass us (cf. Heb. 1[13, 14] 12[1]).

17–34. The Abuse of the Lord's Supper; Its Institution and Meaning Recalled. Praise for the wholesome observance of apostolic tradition (v. 2) must be qualified in one respect. Cliques are evident in their church gatherings. Paul adds with grim irony that one good result of this is that men of character stand out in bold relief. The deplorable consequence is seen at the Lord's Supper, which ceases to deserve that name (v. 20). "Instead of Christian fellowship there is a shameful display of greed and ostentation. The rich man does not wait for the poor man to arrive (on his return from work), but indulges too freely in the sumptuous fare that he has provided, so that his poor neighbor has to go without. What an exhibition of uncontrolled appetite! What contempt for the church of God! What humiliating treatment of the poorer brother! Contrast this with the precious tradition of the Last Supper in the upper room (vv. 23–26). Unworthy participation is to be guilty of profaning the sanctity of the passion of the Lord. It is an occasion for self-examination, for the man whose light irreverence blinds him to the meaning of the sacred symbols brings doom upon himself (vv. 27–29). This accounts for the enfeebled health of many in the church, and even the death of some. How different our condition would be if we practiced self-examination! But if we are suffering the Lord's judgment, it is a beneficent discipline to save us from being involved in the doom of the world. The practical issue may be summed up in a word: *Wait,* to begin the supper together (v. 33). He whose appetite is not under control must have a meal at home. The remaining instructions must stand over till the next visit."

Note on the Eucharist at Corinth and in the Teaching of Paul

From the allusions in this Epistle it is evident that the Eucharist in no way resembled the impressive dramatic representations to which initiates were admitted in the mystery religions. (For the mysteries, see art., *Backgrounds*, p. 851.) As was usual at Greek dinner parties, each person brought his own provisions. At some point in the supper one loaf was broken, a symbol of the unity of the body of Christ (cf. 10^{17}, which may be translated thus: "Many as we are, we are one loaf, one body, for we all partake of the one loaf"). At the close of the meal they all drank from the cup. Paul's complaint is that at Corinth the supper of the assembled church is not sacramental. Some of the members by their unsocial behavior displayed a spirit which contradicted the meaning and purpose of the Lord's Supper. They stand condemned by the very fact that they could join in the sacrament of fellowship, without having a true sense of the body of Christ, the church of which their poor brothers were fellow-members with them (v. 29).

In vv. 23–26 we have the earliest record of the institution of the Eucharist. In some particulars it differs from the accounts in the Synoptic Gospels. The closest resemblance is found in Luke, but in all probability Lk. $22^{19,\ 20}$ is a harmonistic addition based on 1 Cor. $11^{24,\ 25}$, as the words are not found in some very early authorities. There is no ground, however, for disputing the authenticity of Paul's account. It is improbable that he attributes this knowledge to a vision. The actual words indicate the "tradition" which has reached him, to be handed on to the Corinthians in their turn. The ultimate source is the Lord himself on the last night of his earthly life. Remote from any connection with the mysteries is the double emphasis on the historical and the eschatological. Cf. with vv. 23, 26, George Rawson's eucharistic hymn,

> "And thus that dark betrayal night
> With the last advent we unite,
> By one blest chain of loving rite,
> Until He come."

The historical origin of the sacrament is not invalidated by Gal. $1^{11,\ 12}$. Paul distinguishes between the historical facts of the Christian religion (cf. $15^{3\text{-}11}$) and his gospel, the interpretation which his illumined heart has given to them. The worthy celebration of the Lord's Supper is a proclamation of the Lord's death. Every Eucharist is, or should be, a sermon on the central text of the Christian revelation, the cross. The very purpose of Jesus (v. 24) was that he should be recalled to our minds as the one who had brought the faithful together in the fellowship of love, sealed by a covenant ratified by his own blood. That sacrificial death was symbolized in the cup. Can we drink that cup of blessing ($10^{14\text{f.}}$) which represents our fellowship with the Jesus who gave himself utterly for others, and at the same time flout the demands of human fellowship in the society of the Lord Jesus? The same thought is brought out in Phil. $2^{5\text{f.}}$ which we may read: "Let your thoughts in fellowship with one another be the same as your thoughts in fellowship with Christ Jesus," who stooped in lowly obedience to the utmost limit of the cross.

Chapters 12^{1} to 14^{40}: Spiritual Gifts

This is properly a part of the section 11^{2}–14^{40}. See the introductory note to ch. 11.

CHAPTER XII

The next three chapters deal with the same great central theme—spiritual gifts. These vary in character and worth, but supreme among them is love (12^{31} 13^{13}).

1–3. The Criterion of Spiritual Gifts. Paraphrase: "Your pagan experience tells you how at one time you used to be swept away by frenzied impulses under the control of idols that only spoke by those whom they possessed. Even so, the man who breaks out into ecstatic language in your assemblies will reveal the quality of his inspiration. If he curses Jesus, you know the source. If he acclaims Jesus as Lord, it is indeed a power of the Holy Spirit which possesses him."

4–11. Variety of Gifts but the Same Spirit. Paraphrase: "The rich variety of special gifts displayed in your church is but a manifestation of the resourcefulness of the one Spirit, who considers the profit of every member. So he gives to one philosophic speech, to another the language of insight into truth, to another faith, to another healing gifts, to another miraculous energies, to another prophecy, to another the faculty of distinguishing good from evil spirits, to another varieties of 'tongues,' to another the interpretation of 'tongues.' But all these spring from the energy of one and the same Spirit, distributing to each according to his will."

8–10. See below on vv. 28–30, and cf. Rom. 12[6-8] Eph. 4[11].

12–31. The Body and the Members. This diversity in unity is no arbitrary dispersal of gifts, but inheres in God's design of an organism to fulfill his will on earth. "The Christ that is to be" (cf. Tennyson's "In Memoriam," end of stanza cvi) is the thought which Paul here introduces. We are not merely the body of which Christ is head. We are all united in the Christ, by the Spirit which we received when faith enabled us to make the public confession which was symbolized in baptism. Imbued with one Spirit we rose above all national and social distinctions. This idea is then illustrated by a parable which Paul had no doubt often met with in Stoic diatribes. It was a favorite story with the political philosophers of that period, and is best known to us from Shakespeare's use in *Coriolanus* of the fable of Menenius Agrippa, which is borrowed from Plutarch's *Lives*. Paul lifts the parable to the highest application in v. 27 (cf. Rom. 12[5] Eph. 5[30]). If then the church is the body of Christ, it follows that its members will be endowed with a wide variety of gifts for spiritual ministration.

28–30. Cf. vv. 8–10, Rom. 12[6-8] Eph. 4[11]. *Apostles* come first, partly on chronological grounds as first-hand witnesses, partly as those who gave the first impulse to the local Christian communities. The *prophets* come next, including not only those who have the gift of "prophecy" in the narrower sense (cf. Acts 11[27f.] 21[10f.]), but also the "word of wisdom" and the "word of knowledge" (vv. 10, 8). In the third place come the *teachers*, who probably took regular part in the instructions at public worship, as well as in the special work of training candidates for baptism. Then follow a group of functions, in contrast to the personal titles, "apostles," "prophets," "teachers." *Powers* (see mg.) would include both "faith" (v. 9) and "workings of powers" (v. 10); *gifts of healings* are regarded as distinct from these. *Helps* may well have covered such functions as "ministry," "distribution," "deeds of compassion" named in Rom. 12[7, 8]. *Governments* will represent all administrative and judicial offices, and it is significant that at this stage in ecclesiastical development this kind of gift ranks low in the list. Last of all comes the gift upon which so many of the Corinthians prided themselves. The meaning of *kinds of tongues* will appear in ch. 14. A necessary complement to this gift of uncertain value is that of *interpretation* (v. 30). It is obvious that all cannot exercise all these gifts. The health of the whole body depends upon the faithfulness with which each makes use of his special endowment. Yet it becomes every man to exert himself to possess the qualities of highest value to the church. It is of more importance to the Christian society that there should be prophets and teachers than that there should be many "speaking with tongues." Yet even this worthy ambition may be followed in an unworthy spirit. Envy, rivalry, ungenerous depreciation of another's gift will not bring us to our goal of highest spiritual attainment. There is a super-excellent way, which the apostle now points out in the noblest lines he ever wrote.

CHAPTER XIII

The Most Excellent Way of Love. Nowhere does Paul show more clearly how entirely his thought is ruled by the Spirit of the Lord Jesus. This hymn is a lyrical interpretation of the Sermon on the Mount—the Beatitudes set to music. The translations by A. S. Way (*Letters of St. Paul*) and by Moffatt are valuable, and out of the vast literature of exposition Henry Drummond's *The Greatest Thing in the World*, and Percy Ainsworth's *St. Paul's Hymn to Love* are classics of the devotional life.

1–3. The Worthlessness of Spiritual Endowments Apart from Love. Without love, the most exalted speech ever heard on earth or possible in heaven is a senseless sound, like the clashing cymbals of the frenzied priests of Cybele (v. 1); a mastery of every field of knowledge joined with inspired insight into hidden truth will not raise a man above a cipher (*nothing*); the mountain-moving energy of faith of which Jesus spoke (Mt. 17[20]) will leave him of no account (v. 2); even the dutiful doling away of every possession, even self-immolating devotion, wins no advantage (v. 3).

3. *To be burned* (mg. reads *that I may glory*) may mean "Though I surrender my body as a living sacrifice (cf. Rom. 12[1]) so as to have 'whereof to glory in the day of Christ'" (cf. Phil. 2[16]).

4–7. **Love Described.** Love takes long views and acts with kindness; is free from jealous thoughts, from boastful words, from self-conceit, from discourtesy; it is not self-seeking nor passionate, keeps no reckoning of wrong, takes no delight in injustice, but finds its joy in that which rejoices Truth also. It sets no limit to tolerance, trustfulness, hopefulness, endurance. It is easy to find in all these verses a tacit rebuke of the besetting sins of the religious at Corinth. Is there not also more than one stab of self-reproach? In Jesus, Paul had learned that love saves enthusiasm from passing into fanaticism (cf. v. 3).

5. *Is not provoked.* The translation conceals the sharp edge of the Greek word (*paroxusmos*) which Luke uses twice of Paul (Acts 15[39] 17[16]), and our word "paroxysm" preserves. The quick temper and the incisive tongue survived the crucifixion of the old Adam and may have served a disciplinary use in puncturing complacent conceit (4[18-21]) and exposing flagrant injustice (Acts 23[3]). But Paul had learned that as love is the first of the fruits of the Spirit, so is self-control the last and crowning gift (cf. "temperance" and see mg. in Gal. 5[22, 23]).—*Taketh not account of evil.* Cf. Mt. 18[21, 22].

6. *Rejoiceth not in unrighteousness*, etc. Is not this a bitter memory of the time when Paul found it "hard to kick against the goad"? He who consented to the judicial murder of Stephen could only persecute him who is the Truth. Cf. the close of Francis Thompson's *Hound of Heaven*, "Thou dravest love from thee, who dravest Me."

7. *Beareth all things* (R.V. mg., *covereth*). Cf. 1 Pet. 4[8]. *Hopeth all things.* Cf. Lk. 6[35]. For the whole verse, cf. the thought in Shakespeare's Sonnet 116:

"Love alters not with his brief hours and weeks,
But bears it out even to the edge of doom."

8–13. **The Imperishable Quality of Love.** Love is contrasted with *prophecy* and *knowledge.* See the noble paraphrase of this verse in F. W. H. Myers, *St. Paul.* These gifts are transitory because fragmentary, just as the language, disposition and mental processes of childhood are superseded by those of adult life. Now we try to guess at truth as we see its blurred and distorted outlines in the mirror of burnished metal. Prophecy (or Scripture) and knowledge (or Theology) (as G. G. Findlay happily suggested) serve our needs now, but of necessity leave much unexplained. These gifts belong to the present order, but will have had their day when immediate communion brings us into the presence of Him who knows us perfectly. There are three gifts of God which we shall exercise even in the world to come. For *faith* will still find scope in the ever-deepening mysteries of the unfathomable wisdom of God, and *hope* will still look onward with assurance to some fresh fulfillment of God's redemptive purpose. *Love* too abides forever, but is greatest of these, for it is of the very character of God.

CHAPTER XIV

1–19. **"Tongues" and Their Tests: Intelligibility.** Provided that love is in the foreground, the Corinthians are exhorted to cultivate these spiritual gifts; but prophecy rather than "tongues." Paul does not dispute the reality of this experience, or deny its spiritual origin; he even claims a pre-eminence in this endowment (v. 18). But he counts it inferior to prophecy, which is also inspired utterance, for the latter edifies, comforts, consoles, while the exercise of "tongues," though it may edify the performer himself, brings no revelation of truth, nor insight into spiritual values, nor inspiration, nor instruction to the assembled church (vv. 9–11). "Unless musical intervals are properly observed"—so we may paraphrase —"how can any air be recognized when a player is breathing into the flute or twanging the harp? Or what citizen will arm himself and rush to the walls for defense against the enemy unless the bugler sounds the alarm in notes that can be recognized? This is not only true of inanimate instruments. There are many human languages on earth, all foreign and unintelligible except to the man who can speak them. Let edification determine your desire for some spiritual endowment. If you want to speak with a 'tongue,' pray for the gift of interpretation, or you are merely wasting your breath (v. 13). The spirit may be speaking, but the intelligence has no share in the utterance. You may be mouthing sounds with superb impressiveness, but when you have finished how is the uninstructed novice to join in the 'Amen,' and make your thanksgiving his own? I prefer to leave my own gift in abeyance and speak a few intelligible words to explain the Christian message to others rather than make a long and meaningless oration."

20–25. The Test of Convincing Power. Paul next suggests that this undue respect for "tongues" is childish (cf. 13[11]). The childlike heart is to be preserved unembittered through life, but the intellect must reach maturity. Words are quoted from Isa. 28[11, 12] to show that "tongues" are intended to impress unbelievers, whereas prophecy is for those who believe. A picture is then drawn of a full church meeting when all are exercising the gift. In the midst of this babel some novices and unbelievers come in, and conclude that they are among madmen. If, however, a series of prophecies is heard, the stranger, whether an unbeliever or a mere novice, will feel that his secret thoughts are being read and examined. Deeply convinced of his unworthiness he will abase himself before God and recognize the divine presence in the Christian Church.

21, 22. The use made of Isa. 28[11, 12] is another instance of Paul's rabbinical handling of scripture. When Isaiah's simple message of warning was derided by the tipsy priests and prophets of Ephraim he declared that if he was taunted as a stammerer, a time would indeed come when God's message of judgment would sound at their gates in the uncouth tongues of barbarian invaders, and then their bitterness would lie in the memory of the rest and refreshing which they had once refused. "Nay, but by *men of* strange lips and with another tongue will he speak to this people; to whom he said, This is the rest, give ye rest to him that is weary; and this is the refreshing: yet they would not hear." There is, of course, no connection between the divine judgment inflicted by a foreign nation and the gift of "tongues." The past tense of "hear" has been changed into the future. Paul has drawn the inference that "tongues" are intended for unbelievers and not for believers, and by contrast infers that the opposite must be true of prophecy.

23–25. It is strange that in these verses prophecy is shown to be a far more powerful sign to unbelievers than "tongues." The connection of thought is logical only if we may understand by "sign" in v. 22a, as in Lk. 2[34] ("a sign to be spoken against"), a means for confirming the unbelieving in their unbelief.

26–33. The Test of Control. The principle of edification, as already shown, demands intelligibility on the part of those who speak. They must also exercise self-control, and submit to the restraint of others. There is room for each to contribute his gift, whether it be a hymn of praise, a spiritual exposition, an immediate perception of the will or thought of God (cf. Acts 13[2] Gal. 2[2] Rev. 17[9-18]), an ecstatic utterance, or an interpretation. "Let two or at most three who have the gift of tongues speak in succession, with an interpreter. In the absence of an interpreter let him indulge his gift in silence. In the same way let two or three prophets speak in turn, while the others use the gift of discrimination (cf. 12[10] 1 Jn. 4[1]). If while one prophet is speaking a neighbor is inspired to speak, let the first speaker stop, so that all may have an opportunity of doing and receiving good. Prophetic self-control is possible, since the inspiring spirit comes from God, who rules in ordered peace."

34–40. The Test of Decency and Order. There are strong reasons for believing that vv. 34, 35, are a later marginal gloss, or an addition to the text by a later writer. For (1) these verses are placed differently in a number of important MSS.; (2) the sequence of thought is interrupted; and (3) the prohibition contradicts 11[5, 13], where no objection is offered to a woman's public share in the service of the church, but only to her speaking with head uncovered. It is quite possible that these words were based on 1 Tim. 2[11f.], and inserted here at a time when this letter was used as a standard to regulate worship. The belief that First Timothy was entirely from Paul's hand would give warrant for such editorial expansion. V. 36 then follows closely after v. 33b (v. 33a being part of a parenthesis), and we may paraphrase thus: "As is the case in all the churches of the saints. Do you resent this as an encroachment on your liberty? Are you the original church, or do you suppose that you are the only church to receive the gospel?" (Cf. 7[17].) Paul believes that the man of real spiritual discernment will recognize that these counsels accord with the Lord's command (v. 37).

To sum up (vv. 39, 40)—prophecy is a gift to be cultivated; speaking with "tongues" is not to be suppressed. The guiding principle is that all things be done in a seemly and orderly fashion.

Note on the Gift of Tongues

The gift of ecstatic utterance referred to above was one of the most remarkable phenomena in the life of the early church. The narrative of Luke shows that it often accompanied some special sense of spiritual quickening (Acts 2[4] 10[46] 19[6]). It is often assumed that Luke understood the phenomenon as a miraculously conferred facility in the use of foreign languages (cf. Acts 2[11], which is capable of another explanation; see Latham, *Risen Master*, pp. 439f., and art., *N.T. Miracles*, p. 928b). In view of the widespread use of the Common Greek, which was a *lingua franca* throughout the empire (p. 881), there is no need to postulate a special endowment to equip the apostles for missionary preaching. But whatever may be thought of the data in Acts, there is no room for doubt in the case of Corinth. The problem here is psychological, not linguistic. From time to time in the history of the Christian Church similar manifestations have appeared in times of spiritual awakening. The best-known parallel was associated with the preaching of Edward Irving, but even more significant is the account written by Thomas Erskine, of Linlathen, of some remarkable occurrences in the homes of simple pious folk at two places on Clydeside, Scotland, in 1830–32. (See his *Letters*, edited by Hanna, pp. 129–167.) Two or three facts are well attested: (1) these persons while "speaking in the Spirit," whether in their own language or in the unknown sounds, had every appearance of being under direction; (2) they declared that their organs of speech were used by the Spirit of God, and their utterances did not convey their own conceptions; (3) the sounds corresponded to those of normal human speech, though no known language was heard; (4) the speakers themselves could not interpret, except on rare occasions, when this gift was added in answer to urgent prayer. The correspondence to the situation at Corinth is remarkably close except in two particulars: for there was a complete absence of ostentation and unseemliness on the part of these Scottish peasants, and it is clear that the experience was induced by much earnest desire for a revival of the gifts possessed in the early church.

CHAPTER XV

The Resurrection of the Dead

This section does not, like chs. 7, 8, 12, open with the formula "Now concerning," which marks Paul's detailed reply to a question. Information had reached Paul that a bodily resurrection was denied by some in the Corinthian church. The thought was not congenial to the Greek mind (as he had found at Athens; cf. Acts 17^{32}), which found satisfaction rather in speculations about the immortality of the soul. But Paul determines to treat the matter in considerable detail, for contempt of the body has already led to immorality. See 6^{12-20}, with the appeal to Christ's resurrection and our future rising as a refutation of the reasoning of the libertines (6^{14}).

1–11. Paul and the Christian Tradition. Gospel and tradition are blended: the facts that were central to the Christian message have their significance for the faith of the church. Truth embodied in a narrative is the essence of the gospel. This is the foundation of their life as Christians, the means by which they entered into a saving relationship with God, unless, that is, their grip on truth has relaxed, or they never have believed firmly.

Among the things of primary importance which Paul had himself received in the apostolic tradition, and then handed on to his converts at Corinth, were statements affirming the death, burial, and resurrection on the third day of Jesus, and a series of appearances to individual disciples and to groups of varying number. As an addendum to this list, Paul declares his own vision of Jesus near Damascus, for that had convinced him of the truth of the primitive Christian testimony, and gave him a place in the apostolate, in spite of his earlier career as a persecutor of the church. Indeed, though he started late (v. 8), God's grace had been so abundantly bestowed on him that he had by now outstripped all the other apostles in missionary labors. So whatever different views might be held about apostolic rank and authority, there was common ground in this tradition, which was shared alike by the Twelve, by Paul, and by the Corinthian believers.

The main difficulties in these verses must be treated.

3. That Christ's death was in some way related to human sin, and conformed to a spiritual principle taught in the O.T., was undoubtedly a conviction of the primitive church. See Acts 2^{23} 3^{18} $8^{32f.}$ $13^{27f.}$ In the Gospels see Mk. 9^{12} $14^{21, 49}$ Lk. $24^{26, 27}$. Cf. 1 Thess. 5^{10} Gal. 1^{4} Rom. 4^{25} 1 Pet. 2^{24}. Such passages as Psa. $22^{7, 8, 16, 18}$ $69^{9, 29}$ must have been in the thought of the early believers, but most important of all was the great song of the Suffering Servant of Jehovah in Isa. 52^{13-15} 53. It must have been Jesus himself who first made the daring identification of the Messiah with this mysterious figure in Hebrew prophecy (see the *Excursus*, p. 664.) The use of the title "Servant" for "Jesus" (see R.V. Acts $3^{13, 26}$ $4^{27, 30}$) is another witness.

4. *Raised on the third day according to the scriptures* is still more difficult. Prediction of the resurrection would be discovered in Psa. 16^{8-11} (cited in Acts 2^{25-28} 13^{35}) and, by the Greek-speaking readers of the LXX, in Isa. 33^{10}, which there reads, "Now I shall rise up, saith the Lord, now shall I be glorified, now shall I be lifted up." Hos. $6^{1f.}$ could not be regarded as in any way a prediction. The true solution seems to have been offered by B. W.

Bacon (*Expositor*, VIII, xxvi, pp. 426f.). He suggests Lev. $23^{4f.}$, and compares 1 Cor. $5^{7f.}$ 16^{8} 15^{20}. In the year of the crucifixion the Passover fell on Friday, Nisan 14, so that it was on Sunday, Nisan 16, that Jesus rose (see art., *Chronology of N.T.*). The symbolism was unmistakable to the early Jewish Christian. Just as Paul alludes to the ceremony of preparing for the Passover by purging the house of leaven, so he refers to the law for the offering up of the sheaf of firstfruits on Nisan 16, "the morrow after the Sabbath" (Lev. 23^{11}). So also "hath Christ been raised from the dead, the first-fruits of them that are asleep" (v. 20). Thus as the Scriptures have been fulfilled in the offering up of the true Paschal Lamb on the Passover, so they have been fulfilled in the new meaning which henceforth belongs to the ceremony of "lifting up" (cf. (Jn. 12^{32}) to God the new sheaf of firstfruits on the third day from the Passover.

5–7. For the problems raised by the divergent accounts of the first Eastertide see J. M. Shaw, *The Resurrection of Christ*, or his article in Hastings' *Dictionary of the Apostolic Church*, vol. ii. It must not be forgotten that our earliest testimony is this obviously primitive tradition repeated as from a catechism by Paul. The difficulty of harmonizing this terse summary with the gospel narratives is due to a difference in aim. The evangelists are concerned principally with the empty tomb. Paul is here concerned with the actual appearances of Jesus to his friends after the resurrection. He cites five appearances. (1) That to *Peter* (Cephas) is simply referred to in Lk. 24^{34}. (2) *The twelve:* cf. Lk. 24^{36} Jn. $20^{19, 26}$, also Acts $10^{40f.}$ (3) The *five hundred* together, probably in Galilee, possibly disciples not at the feast, or, with such, some who had gone up to Jerusalem (cf. Jn. 11^{55} $12^{12f.}$). (4) *James:* cf. Jerome, *Of Illustrious Men*, 2, who quotes from the Gospel according to the Hebrews: "Now the Lord, when he had given the linen cloth unto the servant of the priest, went unto James and appeared to him (for James had sworn that he would not eat bread from that hour wherein he had drunk the Lord's cup until he should see him risen again from among them that sleep)"; and again after a little, "Bring ye, saith the Lord, a table and bread," and immediately it is added, "He took bread and blessed and brake and gave it unto James the Just and said unto him: My brother, eat thy bread, for the Son of man is risen from among them that sleep." Whatever degree of truth there may be in this story, we know that the brothers of our Lord are represented in the Gospels as not believing in him (Jn. 7^{5} Mk. $3^{21, 32f.}$ 6^{3}), whereas James soon took a leading place in the church at Jerusalem (Acts 12^{17} 15^{13} 21^{18} Gal. 1^{19} $2^{9, 12}$). The reference in the present passage helps to an understanding of the apostolic rank which was evidently accorded to this brother of our Lord. (5) *To all the apostles.* Perhaps this refers to the final appearance recorded in Lk. 24^{50} Acts 1^{4-9}. To this primitive tradition, officially certified, Paul adds his own testimony to the appearance of the glorified Lord. It is of a different order from the others, but inasmuch as apostolic status depended partly upon witness of the resurrection (Acts 1^{22}), Paul always insists upon his first-hand assurance of this fact (cf. 9^{1}).

8. *One born out of due time.* Paul actually wrote "the abortion" (see mg.), and the reference is doubtless to the contrast between the maturity of preparation with the other apostles, and his own abrupt conversion to faith and immediate service.

10. Boasting is excluded; all is of the grace of God (cf. Gal. 2^{20}).

12–19. The Logic of the Empty Tomb. Although this witness to the risen Christ had never been challenged at Corinth, the cognate belief in the resurrection of believers was assailed under the form of a universal negative, *There is no resurrection of the dead.* Paul shows that under that proposition the Christian testimony about Christ is nullified, and the whole structure of Christian faith and character is undermined.

19. This is not clear. The order of the Greek words favors R.V. mg. rather than the text. There is no point in attaching *only* to *in this life*, for hope in this special sense belongs essentially to this life and not to the future state. The difficulty of the other rendering is that *hope* seems to be emptied of its virile and victorious meaning, elsewhere in the N.T. inseparable from its use. Probably Paul's meaning has best been brought out in the rendering, "If we are men that have had our hope in Christ in this life, and nothing more," then we are most to be pitied of all men, because our hope in Christ has raised us to such a height of confident expectation only in the end to be dashed ruthlessly to the ground.

20–28. The Significance of Christ's Resurrection. Paul has provided a *reductio ad absurdum.* By assuming that the assertion of resurrection is false, he has followed out the consequences of that assumption to the point of logical absurdity. Now he reasserts the undeniable conviction of the witnesses that Christ has actually been raised from the dead, and claims that this is the test and pledge of the revival of all that die. Just as Adam is natural head of the race and all men share in his death, so Christ is spiritual representative of the race and all mankind must be raised from death through him. (For these racial acts and their results see notes on Rom. 5^{12-21}; also Peake, *The Quintessence of Paulinism*, pp. 23f.) But though a universal resurrection must follow from Christ's representative act, it will take place by stages. First Christ has risen (for *firstfruits* see on v. 4); then Christ's followers will rise at his Advent. A third stage seems to be required, but the sequence *then cometh the end* is inappropriate, for we are immediately told that *he must reign till he hath put all his enemies under his feet.* There is good reason to follow several recent commentators in taking v. 24a as meaning, "Then the rest, when he shall deliver up the kingdom to God." This idea of a general resurrection appears in Jn. $5^{28f.}$ Acts 24^{15} Rev. 20^{11-15}. Meanwhile the reign of Christ must continue until every foe has been vanquished. Language is borrowed from Psa. 8^{6} 110^{1} (with striking adaptations) to emphasize the completeness of the Messianic victory. The ultimate enemy is death. Then, after gaining that final triumph, Christ will hand over this universal dominion to Him who is God and Father. Paul's belief of the subordination of the Son to the Father is as clear here as in 3^{23} 11^{3}. *That God may be all in all* is the

" . . . one far-off divine event,
To which the whole creation moves."

29–34. The Dreadful Alternative. Paraphrase: "We can scarcely bring ourselves to imagine what is involved in denying the resurrection. Even some who deny the doctrine prove that they really believe it by their otherwise meaningless custom of undergoing vicarious baptism for their relatives who have died before being received by baptism into the Christian fellowship. If I had not the confidence inspired by this blessed hope how could I run into deadly peril as I do every hour of my life? If I seem to be exaggerating, I can only appeal to your generous appreciation of my toils and sufferings in Christ's service, and declare that 'my daily life is a daily dying.' There was that desperate peril in which I was involved at Ephesus. If I had actually been flung into the arena, as might well have happened, to fight in vain for my life with beasts, what gain would there have been for me in death? (Cf. Phil. 1^{21}.) It is fatally easy for some of you in your loss of all hope to say, like the men in Isaiah's day (Isa. 22^{13}), 'Let us eat and drink, for to-morrow we die.' Do not let your old associations lead you astray. There is truth in the line, 'Bad company spoils good morals.' Start up from your slumber as you ought to do. Cease from sinning. There are those whose superior knowledge is mere ignorance of God. This I say to rebuke you."

29. The interpretation followed above presupposes a local usage—namely, baptism in behalf of the dead—which Paul neither commends nor condemns, for which parallels can be supplied from later custom in some heretical sects as well as in certain mystery cults. Paul merely uses this as an illustration of the principle that "the Heart has its reasons that Reason does not know" (Pascal, *Thoughts*, Art. xvi, 3). "Someone's death" disturbs the skeptic's unbelief, and "the grand Perhaps" is "on his base again" (see Browning, *Bishop Blougram's Apology*). Life is continually challenging logic.

32. Read *If men had wrought their will and I had been thrown to the lions.* It is best to take this in the literal sense, and to recognize that Paul passed through some terrible peril during his stay at Ephesus, when such a doom seemed imminent. Did Aquila and Priscilla make some great sacrifice to spare him this fate? See Rom. 16^{4}.

33. A line from the *Thais* of Menander, chief representative of the New Comedy at Athens, whose sententious moralizing made his plays a quarry for quotation. For other traces of Greek literature in Paul compare lines from Epimenides and Aratus in Acts 17^{28}, from the same context in Epimenides in Tit. 1^{12}, the sentence from Aristotle in Gal. 5^{23}, and the possible allusions to lines of Euripides in Acts 21^{39} 1 Tim. 6^{12}.

35–49. The Natural Body and the Spiritual Body. Paul now turns to the doctrine of bodily resurrection, to remove difficulties by explaining its true meaning. The main obstacle is a materialistic view of resurrection. By the parable of the grain of wheat we are reminded of the difference in outward form of the present and the future body. The present body must perish (v. 36); God gives a new body according to his own creative decree (v. 38). Even in this world there are generic differences in types of fleshly bodies. There is also a vast difference between the kind of body suited for this region, and that suited for the higher region of life. In the same way, in that higher region there are differences in outer appearance, just as the "heavenly bodies" shine in the firmament with varying splendor. All this illustrates the resurrection of the dead (v. 42). Our present life is the seed-time, marked by perishableness, dishonor, weakness (cf. Rom. $8^{10, 21}$ Phil. 3^{21} 2 Cor. 13^{4}). Through death we pass to the state of incorruption, glory, power (cf. Rom. 8^18-23). Corresponding to these two conditions are two different kinds of body, one natural, the other spiritual. The first corresponds to the needs of the soul in this order of physical existence, fulfilling the requirements of thought, feeling, will, and is thus in process of adaptation for the higher service of the life above the realm of the senses (cf. Gal. 6^8). In that spiritual sphere a suitable vehicle of self-expression will be needed. The type of the first is the first man, who, in the words of Scripture, "became a living soul" (Gen. 2^7). As the first Adam was thus made of the earthly substance which fitted him for life on this earth, so there is a last Adam, who by his entrance into the realm above has assumed a form that accords with the spiritual realm, and has also become a life-giving spirit. It is the resurrection of Christ which assures us that as we have hitherto borne the image of the man of earth, so hereafter we shall wear the likeness of the man of heaven. The new humanity united in Christ has a solidarity no less than that of mankind on earth.

50–58. Death Swallowed up in Victory. The central principle of the foregoing argument is summed up in v. 50. In speaking of bodily resurrection Paul has no material body in mind. The perishing cannot inherit the imperishable. So self-evident is this that Paul discloses the secret purpose of God. At the advent of Christ we shall all be changed, whether dead or alive at the moment when the trumpet blast announces his arrival. For the conditions of that new order of life demand that this corruptible nature of ours should be clad in an immortal vesture (cf. 2 Cor. 5^4). When our mortality has been replaced by immortality the full meaning of Isaiah's mighty affirmation will be seen (the quotation in v. 54 is from Isa. 25^8). In the form of the Greek translation known to Paul the words "for ever" in that citation are superseded by *in victory.* That word provides the keynote for the rest of the chapter. Hos. 13^14 (quoted, although with a considerably adapted meaning, in v. 55) is flung down in triumphant challenge to death. But even in this moment of exultation at the thought of Christ's victory over death, Paul cannot separate the empty tomb from the cross. It is *sin* that has invested death with terror, that has brought desolation to the heart of man by alienating him from God (Rom. 5^12 7^9f.). It is the *law* that gave power to sin (Rom. 4^15 5^20 6^14 7^1-25 Gal. 2^16 3^10, 13, 21 5^1-3). So then "the word of the cross" is made complete in the risen Saviour. God be thanked, who offers us (read thus for *giveth us*) the victory over both sin and death through our Lord Jesus Christ. To the careless reader the closing words (v. 58) form an anti-climax. To Paul the only justification for this inspired speculation and argument is the glory of the Lord made known by the victorious advance of his gospel and kingdom. He therefore finds a wagon to hitch to the star of the Christian hope. Apostolic preaching, the Christian's faith, is *not vain* (v. 14), neither is the toil of those steadfast heroes who share the travail that gradually brings in the kingdom of God.

Note on Paul's Doctrine of the Resurrection of the Body

We have been so deeply influenced by the Greek doctrine of the immortality of the soul that Paul's teaching sounds remote from modern thought. Later Judaism in working out a belief in a future life adopted the idea of a resurrection of the material body of flesh and blood. The dead sleep beneath the earth (Dan. 12^2) until the day of judgment (Jn. 5^28), which is also the day of resurrection. The future life was generally conceived in material terms, but our Lord's rebuke of the Sadducees (Mk. 12^18-25) is evidence of a spiritual interpretation with which his interrogators should have been familiar. To the Jew of the first century the Greek doctrine was no more than a faint hope of a shadowy survival. He craved for the preservation of the entire personality, and this could be secured, according to Jewish psychology, only by the restoration and reanimation of the body (see H. Wheeler Robinson, *Religious Ideas of the O.T.*, ch. 4, sec. 4). Now Paul shared the Jewish belief in a general resurrection at the end of the age, and he carried over into his Christian thought much of the apocalyptic imagery in which the hope of Judaism found expression (see p. 846b). This is very evident in First and Second Thessalonians and First Corinthians, though it fades away from this time on. But the notable feature of Paul's teaching is his insistence on the spiritual nature of the future life, and the spiritual character of the resurrection body. The body that decays in the tomb does not rise again. "Flesh and blood cannot inherit the kingdom of God." The body which is "raised" is a medium of expression and communication fitted to the spiritual conditions of the new life of the persistent self. Paul takes up the question again in 2 Cor. 5^1-10 (see notes). Compare Spenser, *An Hymne in Honour of Beautie:*

"For of the soule the bodie forme doth take;
For soule is forme, and doth the bodie make."

CHAPTER XVI

Administrative and Personal

The chapter is concerned with certain administrative problems, and contains as well many interesting *personalia*.

1–9. The Collection. This favorite project of Paul's later missionary career is very prominent in the letters of this period. Support of it was to be the visible sign of the loving loyalty of the Gentile churches to the mother church at Jerusalem. Begun in Galatia (v. 1; cf. Gal. 2[10] 6[10]), it was carried on in Macedonia (2 Cor. 8, 9) as in Achaia. See also Rom. 15[25-28]. In the three letters named Paul refers to it under seven different Greek words, meaning "collection," "grace," "fellowship," "bounty," "blessing," "service," "ministry." In Acts 24[17] he is reported to have described his mission to Jerusalem: "I came to bring alms to my nation, and offerings." Vv. 2–4 incidentally tell us much about early church usage. *The first day of the week* (cf. Rev. 1[10], "the Lord's day") was evidently already honored in Christian worship (cf. Acts 20[7]). On that day each was to put aside at home something from his weekly earnings, forming a little hoard, so that there might be no hasty effort to raise funds on Paul's arrival. The local church was to appoint its own representatives, who would carry the gift to Jerusalem, with credentials from Paul. If the amount was worthy of the occasion, Paul would take these representatives with him. In Acts 20[4] we find the names of the delegates from the other three provinces (three from Macedonia, two each from Galatia and Asia). No names represent Achaia. Does this mean that in spite of all his pleading the total raised was trifling, or that the Achaian representatives went in advance of Paul and his friends? Paul's plans are given that they may know when the money should be raised. For the present, great evangelistic opportunities, combined with formidable opposition, keep him at Ephesus. But after Pentecost he intends to take the overland route through Macedonia, reaching Corinth in time to spend the winter months among them. To reverse the route, and take Corinth first on his way to the Macedonian churches in the north, would mean only a passing glimpse.

10–12. The Visits of Timothy and Apollos. For the former cf. Acts 19[21, 22], and note the silence in Second Corinthians about Timothy's visit. Vv. 10, 11 accord with the impression of Timothy's character made by 1 Tim. 5[21-23] 2 Tim. 1[6-8] 2[1, 3, 15] 4[1, 2]. (For Timothy's proposed visit to Corinth, see intro., section on "Paul's Relations with Corinth," (3) and (4), p. 1169.) Paul takes care to make it clear that no jealousy of Apollos is in his own heart. He has urged him to visit them, but the popular Alexandrian rhetorician declines to go just now. Probably he knew the danger of the party feuds, and feared that his coming might be exploited by the Apollos faction, and this he would desire to avoid.

13–24. Closing Messages and Greetings. Four brisk imperatives give a martial warning against external perils, followed by an appeal for love as the solvent of divisions within their camp. *Stephanas* and his household deserve respect on two grounds: they were the first family in the province to embrace the Christian obedience, and their self-dedication to the humble service of the brotherhood gave them a primacy in the church. Willingness to work hard and ability to work in harness form the true hall-mark of ecclesiastical rank. This man and his two friends have brought joy to Paul by bringing Corinth to him. A personal visit supplies what no letter or gift can confer (cf. Phil. 2[30]).

Greetings are sent from the churches of the province of *Asia*, for Ephesus is now the center of a group of churches (cf. Rev. 1[11] Col. 4[16]). For *Aquila and Prisca* see Acts 18[2, 3, 18, 26] Rom. 16[3] 2 Tim. 4[19]. The lecture hall of Tyrannus was the scene of Paul's public preaching (Acts 19[9]); the home of this devoted pair was the rallying center of the members. Vv. 21–24 are the Pauline autograph to the dictated letter (cf. 2 Thess. 3[17] Gal. 6[11]). *Marana tha:* the original Aramaic prayer of the Palestinian church, meaning, "Our Lord, come!" (Cf. Rev. 22[20].)

SECOND CORINTHIANS

Introduction. See Introduction to First and Second Corinthians, p. 1169, especially for discussion of the view that chs. 10–13 belong to the intermediate letter referred to in 2 Cor. 2[3, 9] 7[8], a question also considered in notes to ch. 10 below.

Main Divisions of the Second Letter. These divisions are as follows:

I. Greeting and Thanksgiving, 1[1-11].

II. Paul's Relations with the Corinthians, 1[12]–7[16].

(1) Defense against the Charge of Untrustworthiness and Harshness, 1[12]–2[17].

(2) The Glory of the Apostolic Office, 3[1]–6[10].

(3) Paul's Reconciliation with the Corinthian Church, 6^{11}–7^{16}.

III. The Collection for the Church at Jerusalem, 8^{1}–9^{15}.

IV. Paul's Defense of His Character and of His Work, 10^{1}–13^{10}.

V. Farewell and Benediction, 13^{10-14}.

CHAPTER I

1, 2. Address and Greeting. Cf. 1 Cor. 1^{1-3}. Timothy (Acts 18^{5} 1 Cor. 4^{17} $16^{10f.}$) now replaces Sosthenes, and the indirect reference to Achaia now becomes explicit. These churches would include Athens (Acts 17^{34}) and Cenchreæ (Rom. 16^{1}).

3–11. Thanksgiving and Hope. The silence about the state of the Corinthians is significant. Paul gives thanks for God's comfort of him in his tribulations, which will work out to their salvation. The exact nature of the apostle's terrible ordeal is uncertain. Not the experience of 1 Cor. 15^{32}, for it must have happened after that letter was dispatched. Conceivably the formidable opposition described in Acts $19^{23f.}$ involved Paul in perils unrecorded by Luke. Probably his keen anxiety about Corinthian loyalty, together with the daily risks of work in Ephesus, brought on a dangerous illness after he had left the city but was still within the province of Asia. From the very brink of death God had rescued him, teaching him the dependence of faith and the confidence of hope. Let the Corinthians join their prayers with his, that God's continued deliverance of his apostle may give many of them ground for thanksgiving that their prayers have been answered.

CHAPTERS 1^{12} TO 2^{17}: DEFENSE AGAINST THE CHARGE OF UNTRUSTWORTHINESS AND HARSHNESS

Paul's moving statement of this defense is the first part of the general section, 1^{12}–7^{16}, on Paul's relations with the Corinthians.

12–22. The God of the Amen, and His Apostle. Among the complaints murmured against the apostle at Corinth were his self-confidence and his failure to act straightforwardly. Paul repudiates the suggestion of any worldly-minded diplomacy. His own conscience assures him that in all his public conduct, not least in his intercourse with the Corinthians, God has enabled him to behave as a consecrated and sincere man. They are surely intelligent enough to read that in his letters! As for his confidence, is there not mutual boasting? Some of them know him well enough to be proud of him, as he confidently expects to be proud of them in the judgment day ($3^{2, 3}$ 5^{12} 1 Cor. $1^{7, 8}$). It was this confidence in them that led Paul to propose a double visit to Corinth, one on his way to Macedonia, another on his return before sailing for Judæa. His failure to carry out the proposal was not due to the mundane policy of saying "yes" and "no" in one breath (vv. 17, 18). He had not so learned Christ (the Jesus whom he and his colleagues had proclaimed on his first visit to Corinth), the eternal warrant of the faithfulness of God. The entire gospel gives the lie to such moral inconsistency. This same God is continually confirming those whom he has called to his service, both apostles and converts, to whom he has given an installment of his own Spirit.

15, 16. This does not refer to the proposal of 1 Cor. 16^{5-7}, for the itinerary is quite reversed. On the whole, the best explanation is that at the close of his short intermediate visit (see on 2^{1}) Paul promised another, and even hoped to make it a double visit. Further information convinced him that the time was not opportune, and he sent the sharp letter described as (C) in the introduction (section on "Paul's Relations with Corinth," (5), p. 1169). This has led to misunderstanding which Paul here removes. The visit is only postponed.

20. An excrescence in a Pauline argument generally yields a goodly pearl to the expositor. Many as are the promises of God in the Scriptures, or in the heart of man

> "August anticipations, symbols, types,
> Of a dim splendor ever on before,"

all find their authentication in Christ. In himself, his life, death, and resurrection, he proves that God is as good as his word. He does more. Jesus, as made known by his missionaries, kindles the desire to appropriate these promises and claim their fulfillment, thus proving the faithfulness of the divine character.

23, 24. See notes on 2^{1-4}.

CHAPTER II

1–4. An Alteration Due to the Forbearance of Love (including $1^{23, 24}$). The postponement of the promised visit has left his friends sore. Let them know that he forebore to inflict and suffer further pain. The severity of his rebuke and the authority he had been compelled to exercise (1 Cor. 4^{21}) exposed him to the charge of spiritual tyranny. How unfair to one who rejoiced in the freedom of their faith, and shared with them in the joy of service! One return visit had indeed been paid. But so unhappy was this that Paul had resolved not to repeat the experience. Where was he to look for happiness if he inflicted pain on those from whom he looked for cheer? This was the burden of his last letter, that it was better not to visit them if that would bring grief to him instead of happiness, for he was confident that their happiness depended on his. That letter had been wrung from his heart with anguish and tears. His purpose was not to grieve them, but to let them know his overflowing love for them.

1. The order of words in the Greek text favors the interpretation which implies a previous visit, though some commentators take the verse to mean, "My first visit was happy; I determined that my second visit should not be painful." For the second visit and the painful letter, see the introduction (section on "Paul's Relations with Corinth," (4), p. 1169).

4. Against the theory that chs. 10–13 are part of this preceding letter, it has been urged (1) that the vehemence and mordant irony of those chapters do not fit the description of v. 4. See, however, Newman's account of the writing of the *Apologia*, or that part of the self-revelation which followed the biting sarcasm of the polemic against Kingsley: "I have been constantly in tears and constantly crying out with distress" (Wilfrid Ward, *Life*, vol. ii, p. 25). It has also been urged (2) that the sternness of those chapters is inconsistent with the "abundant love" of this verse. But see Francis Paget, *The Hallowing of Work*, p. 53, for the note of severity in true love.

5–11. **Discipline and Reinstatement.** This section, supplemented by 7[12], throws further light upon the obscure "intermediate visit." The personal tone of the language precludes any reference to the incestuous person of 1 Cor. 5[1]. When last at Corinth, Paul had been wronged (vv. 5, 10) by some member of the church. The injury (probably an insult which flouted his apostolic authority) was condoned by a section. News now reaches Paul that the loyal majority have insisted upon the severe punishment of the offender. Now that the principle for which he had contended is established, Paul pleads that the culprit has undergone enough discipline and may be restored. After all, it was not Paul himself but the whole church, or, rather, the loyal majority, that had suffered by the offense. The purpose of the severe letter had been answered (cf. 10[6]); the Corinthians had shown their readiness to comply with apostolic requirement even when compliance was difficult. As they had been willing to exercise discipline at his request, so he would gladly forgive anything there might be in the way of personal injury if they saw their way to forgive (v. 10). There is a twofold reason for this. He thought of their own interest as he called to mind the presence of Christ. He thought also of the offender, who might become the victim of remorse and fall into the clutches of Satan. Mischief enough had been wrought through this unhappy incident. Satan was defeated by the restored harmony. Let them not give this wily adversary a chance of wresting from them this trophy of a penitent soul.

5. R.V. (cf. A.S.V.) is preferable to A.V. *In part* is ambiguous. It probably limits *you all*—a delicate reminder of the minority who had not supported Paul—and means "in some degree," modifying *he hath caused sorrow.* The parenthesis *that I press not too heavily* may mean "that I be not too severe," or simply "not to overstate the case."

10. *If I have forgiven anything*, i.e., if I had anything to forgive. Compare the delicate tact of the same "if" in v. 5. Paul wishes to minimize the personal affront. Yet forgiveness by Paul (thus, he hints, by the church also) is not a careless oblivion, but a solemn act in *the presence of Christ* (A.S.V.; cf. R.V. mg.). For the discipline and restoration of the offender cf. 2 Thess. 3[14, 15].

12–17. **Paul's Tribulation, and the Triumph of the Gospel.** This is a striking instance of Paul's broken method of narrative. The story begun at 1[8], broken off at 1[10a], is resumed at 2[12, 13], only to give way at once to a doxology which expands into a glowing exposition of the apostolic ministry. The thread of narrative is picked up once more at 7[5]. It seems that Titus had been sent with the severe letter and was to return by the overland route to rejoin Paul at Troas with news of the effect produced at Corinth. Recovered from his grave illness in Asia, Paul carried out his purpose of a missionary campaign through Troas and Macedonia. Great success and fresh evangelistic opportunities met him at Troas, but growing anxiety about Corinth due to the delay in the arrival of Titus robbed him of the power to work, and he pressed on into Macedonia. At this point in the story he was to describe his joy at meeting Titus and hearing the good news of reconciliation with the church at Corinth, but the memory of that vast relief overwhelms him with thanksgiving. "The word of God has won the day at Corinth," so in effect he writes. "There, as elsewhere, Christ makes his way as conqueror, and we are led in his procession of triumph, captives of his grace. By means of us he wafts abroad in every land the incense of the triumph, which is the knowledge of Christ. It is Christ whom we preach, and our message is well pleasing to God, though it produces opposite results upon the hearers. Those who are doomed to destruction find it a deadly fragrance that leads them on to death, while those who are on the way to salvation find it a life-giving fragrance that leads them on to life (vv. 15, 16). Who is fit for such a ministry? By God's grace we are; for unlike many we are not reducing the divine message to make profit. As men of sincerity, commissioned by God, we proclaim the Christian message as in the sight of God."

14. The A.V. "causeth us to triumph" misses the point. Paul has no thought of his personal victory over opponents. With supreme humility he regards himself as merely a captive in Christ's triumphal train. For the thought cf. 1. Cor. 4[9]; for the Greek word Col. 2[15c].

17. The first reference in this Epistle to rival teachers. Cf. 3[1] 4[2] 5[12] 10[1]–13[10]. The R.V. text and mg. (cf. A.S.V.) represent attempts to bring out the depreciatory meaning of a verb derived from a Greek noun for "huckster."

Chapters 3[1] to 6[10]: The Glory of the Apostolic Office: The Weakness of an Apostle

Paul now leaves his consideration of the charge of unworthiness and sets forth the glory of the apostolic office, even though the apostle himself be weak. This is the second part of the general section, 1[12]–7[16], on Paul's relations with the Corinthians.

CHAPTER III

1–11. The Old Ministration Surpassed by the New. Part of the opposition at Corinth seems to have arisen from some Judaistic Christians, who, without denying Paul's apostleship to the Gentiles, regarded this mission as inferior to Judaic Christianity, and hinted that his credentials were not of the highest. They appear also to have wanted a commendatory letter from the Corinthian church to present elsewhere. Paul meets this double disparagement by showing how unnecessary such certificates of character are in his case, and by proving the superiority of the ministry of the new covenant to that of the old. Self-recommendation indeed is no praise, but God has ratified his work. The lives of the Corinthian disciples are letters written by Paul at God's dictation. How much better is a letter written with the Spirit of the living God than one written in ink! And how much inferior is a covenant engraved on stone tablets, as was that given on Sinai (Ex. 24[12] 31[18] 34[1]), to such a covenant as that which Jeremiah (31[33]) and Ezekiel (11[19] 36[26]) dreamed of! But that is the nature of the covenant of which God had made Paul fit to be a minister; no lifeless code, but a spiritual covenant (v. 6). It is the thought that God has deemed him fit for this ministry, not any confidence in his own fitness for judging the effectiveness of his own work, that makes him write in this strain. What a glorious ministry is this! Even the old covenant with its legal system that brought condemnation and death to the sinner was inaugurated with such dazzling brightness that the Israelites could not gaze on the fading reflection of the divine glory which still shone from the face of Moses. Then that vanishing splendor pales in comparison with the overwhelming and abiding glory which must accompany the ministry of the Spirit, under a covenant which brings the sinner into a state of righteousness and inspires him with newness of life.

12–18. The Liberating and Transforming Spirit of the Lord. Paraphrase: "This hope that the divine splendor of the new covenant will endure gives us confidence to speak with candor. We have nothing to hide, as had Moses, who veiled his face that the people should not see that the glory was fading away from his face. But the frankness of our message makes no impression on the dulled perceptions of the Jews, who have not yet learned the meaning of that veil on the face of Moses. Indeed, to this day when the Scriptures of that old covenant are read in the synagogue their meaning is veiled—that is, the hearts of the hearers are obscured by a veil of ignorance concerning the waning validity of the Law given through Moses (v. 15). Just as Moses removed the veil when he 'went in before the Lord to speak with him' (Ex. 34[34]), so now any man who turns to the Lord finds the veil lifted from his heart. That is why we use such boldness of speech. For the Lord to whom we turn, Jesus Christ, represents the Spirit, not the letter, and where the Spirit of the Lord is, there is freedom from legal bondage (v. 17). But all we who bear the Christian name gaze with unveiled face at the glory of the Lord until we reflect its brightness, and from that reflected glory we are being gradually transformed into the same likeness as himself. This change is wrought by the Lord, who is Spirit."

17, 18. *The Lord and the Spirit.* These verses are further evidence of the equation of Jesus with the Lord (i.e., Jehovah) of the O.T. in the mind of Paul (cf. 1 Cor. 1[31]; it is, however, not impossible that Paul uses "Lord" as it is used in Jn. 20[2, 13, 18, 20] of the risen Christ). The identification of Jesus Christ with the Spirit of God must not be inferred from this passage (cf. 13[14]), for the context demands a reference to v. 6, where the contrast between letter and spirit is the key to interpretation. Nevertheless, in the region of Christian experience Paul writes as though there were equivalence of function on the part of the exalted Christ and the Holy Spirit. Theological precision is not to be looked for in Paul's letters (cf. Rom. 8[9-11] and see Anderson Scott, *Christianity According to St. Paul*, pp. 257f.; H. A. A. Kennedy, *Theology of Epistles*, pp. 88f.). Both the A.V. mg. and the R.V. mg. (cf. A.S.V.) interpret a difficult Greek verb as meaning that we gaze at the glory of God as it is reflected in the face of Christ (v. 18). The R.V. takes it as meaning that as we gaze upon Christ his glory shines reflected in our character. For this thought cf. 1 Jn. 3[2, 3].

CHAPTER IV

1–6. The Light of the Gospel. Such is the ministry of the new covenant. It is only of God's mercy that we are called to this privilege (cf. 3[6] 1 Cor. 15[10]), and we owe it to him not to tire in his service (cf. 2 Thess. 3[13] Gal. 6[8, 9]). There is no place in such a ministry for dishonorable secret practices (cf. 1 Cor. 4[5]), for unscrupulous methods (12[17] Eph. 4[14]), nor for any falsification of the gospel message (2[17]). Our confidence is that the self-evidencing truth of our message will illuminate the conscience of every man (Eph. 5[8-14]). "If any find our gospel dark, it is because Satan has blinded their minds to prevent the illumination of the gospel of Christ's glory from shining upon them. Self-commendation is thus no part of our message (v. 5). We proclaim Christ Jesus as Lord (1 Cor. 12[3] Phil. 2[11]) and ourselves as your bond-servants for the sake of Jesus. The God whose creative fiat called light out of darkness (Gen. 1[3]) is he who shone into our hearts so that we might flash back to men the truth of the divine character as it is disclosed in the face of Christ."

4. *The god of this world.* For this conception of Satan, cf. Eph. 2[2] 2 Thess. 2[11] 1 Jn. 5[19] Jn. 12[31] 14[30] 16[11] 1 Cor. 2[6]. *Christ, who is the image of God.* For this term, pregnant with theological import, cf. Col. 1[15] Heb. 1[3] Jn. 1[14] 14[9]. The word is actually used in the descriptive personification of Wisdom (see Wisdom of Solomon, 7[24-27]). *The face of Jesus Christ* (see 5[16]).

7–15. The Paradox of Apostolic Service. The contrast between the priceless treasure and its humble, fragile casket emphasizes the relation between the divine power and the human messenger. The apostle survives humiliations and sufferings by the life of Jesus within him. "We are one with Christ, delivered up to death as he was, so that the power of his resurrection may give life to our mortal bodies (v. 12). Our physical sufferings in the ministry of Jesus are a living death, but the inner secret that sustains us is a dying life (Gal. 2[19, 20]). A further paradox—the ministry which means self-mortification for us brings life to you. Faith produces hope. Therefore in the same confidence as the psalmist (Psa. 116[10]) we speak out, assured that the power which raised Jesus from the dead will enable us who share the death of Jesus to be presented with you, who are spared our mortal sufferings, before the throne of God (v. 14). For all our service and suffering is in your interest, so that the grace which equips us for our ministry may overflow into an increasing number of lives, and so bring forth a richer chorus of thanksgiving to the glory of God."

16–18. The Transient and the Eternal. "Once more, we yield to no languor or despair. Not only does the memory of God's converting grace (v. 1) prevent that; there is also in our fellowship with the risen Christ (Col. 3[3]) a secret source of inward renewal (Eph. 3[16-19]) which counteracts the wastage of physical exhaustion. We have also the liberating grace of hope, which calls in the new world to redress the balance of the old! What is the light trouble of the fleeting age that now is compared with the incalculable weight of glory in the eternal realm which it secures us (Rom. 8[18-25]) if we will but fix our gaze on the world unseen? (Col. 3[1, 2] Heb. 11[26, 27] 12[2].) For the visible is transient, the invisible is eternal."

CHAPTER V

1–10. The Eternal Habitation of the Soul. This very difficult section is closely related to Paul's doctrine of the resurrection body already discussed under 1 Cor. 15[35-58]. We saw there that Paul was concerned with the body as an integral part of the personality, the organ of the soul. Discarding the thought of the resurrection of the physical body, he taught (1 Cor. 15[50-52]) that at the trumpet blast heralding Christ's Advent, a new body shall be formed by resurrection or transformation from the old, incorruptible instead of corruptible, a spiritual body fitted for the high uses of the heavenly realm. An advance in thought meets us in the present passage. Meanwhile Paul has trembled on the brink of the grave (1[8, 9]). He no longer assumes his own survival till the Advent. But if God gives to each man his new body on that day, is the soul to shiver in nakedness from the hour of death until the day of the Lord? He has now found an answer to that alarming thought. There awaits him in heaven a spiritual and enduring body.

The language is obscure because of the change of metaphor. First Paul speaks of the present body as a *tabernacle* (tent) to be superseded by a *building*. The insecurity and temporary nature of the one is contrasted with the durability and permanence of the other. Substituting "the earthly body" for "earth," Paul's thought is well paraphrased in the hymn,

"Earth's but a sorry tent,
Pitched but a few frail days."

Then Paul alternates between the metaphor of *habitation* and that of *clothing*. Discontent with the present burdensome vestment of the soul is not a desire to be unclothed, but a longing for investiture with the raiment of immortality. This new raiment is put on above the old, which then perishes without leaving us naked (v. 3). The idea is akin to that of 1 Cor. 15[54], "when this corruptible shall have put on incorruption, and this mortal shall have put on immortality." Read the phrase here as *that what is mortal may be absorbed by life*. In 1 Cor. 15[54] it was "death is swallowed up (or absorbed) in victory." The certainty of this expectation (v. 1) is based on the inner renewal (4[16]), which is evidence of God's creative design, and finds a guarantee in the gift of the Spirit, a pledge and foretaste of the powers and processes of the spiritual realm (v. 5). "With such a confidence, and knowing that presence here in the body means exile from our home in the Lord, we prefer to go into exile from the body and to enter upon our life at home with the Lord. But it is not for us to choose. Our one concern must be to give satisfaction to our Master, whether here in the body or in the spiritual realm. For our confidence in the certainty of the abiding home that awaits us hereafter brings no exemption from the ordeal of judgment." This paragraph follows closely on the last. The toils and troubles of the present time cannot daunt one who has no reason to dread the sequel to death. Nevertheless, this assurance of future bliss does not diminish the ethical alertness of one who lives with the judgment throne before his eyes.

Two points call for further treatment. (1) Paul's thought of life in the body as exile from the Lord does not deny his cardinal doctrine of the mystical union with Christ. The apparent denial is qualified by the parenthesis in v. 7, where read *We lead our life in faith, without seeing him*, i.e., in the present order a veil of the senses hides Jesus from our vision. That barrier will have vanished after death. (2) Paul shares the Jewish doctrine of the final Judgment of all. But for the Christian Christ is the judge, and, inasmuch as the new body is in readiness for him in the hour and article of death, his judgment takes place then. He does not dread that ordeal (Rom. 8[1]), for faith has brought him the power of the Spirit, with immeasurable moral reinforcement.

An arresting feature of this section is the virtual discarding of traditional Jewish eschatology for the personal and ethical trust in Jesus. The future life for the Christian means a fuller enjoyment of fellowship with Christ, guaranteed by our present experience of this union. (See Phil. 1[21, 23] Jn. 14[19], and cf. art., *Intertestamental Religion*, pp. 210–3.)

11–19. The Ministry of Reconciliation. Remembrance of the Judgment insures for Paul's ministry honorable methods, transparent to God and to the readers' honest scrutiny. Not another instance of "self-commendation"! (3[1].) This is rather a weapon for his champions (1[14]) when defending him from those who lay stress on outward advantage. Do his critics charge him with "madness"? (V. 13.) His ecstatic gifts are reserved for private intercourse with God (1 Cor. 12[1] 14[18]). He is severely "sane" in his dealings with the church (1 Cor. 14[19, 40]). All selfish considerations are impossible in a ministry ruled by the love of Christ. The central doctrine of the cross, "Christ for all: all in Christ," is the negation of selfishness (Gal. 2[20] Rom. 14[7-9]). There is, therefore, no place for pride of privilege in the Christian ministry, even though it be based on knowledge of the human life of Jesus (v. 16). Fellowship with the living Christ brings a man into a new world, in which old advantages no longer count. God is the author of this new creation—God, who reconciled these sinners who are now his missionaries, and then sent them forth on the ministry of reconciliation, to tell mankind that in Christ God was reconciling the world to himself—by forgiving men their sins.

12c. The reference is to those who pride themselves on acquaintance with some of the Jerusalem apostles (cf. Gal. 2[6]) but do not bear the hall-mark of genuine Christian experience.

16. The most probable of many explanations of this difficult verse follows the Greek text by keeping *after the flesh* in close adverbial relation to *know*. From the time when his spiritual apprehension of Jesus wrought a revolution in Paul's life, he no longer stood in the same relations to his kinsfolk and friends (cf. Mk. 3[33] 10[29f.]). All his outward relationships changed when he began to live "in Christ." In the same way, there was a time when as a zealous Pharisee he had seen Jesus and known his outward way of life (cf. Phil. 2[7]), but had possessed only the kind of knowledge possible to the flesh (cf. Mt. 16[17]). The true discernment of Christ first came when God revealed his Son to him (Gal. 1[15, 16]). The words contain no disparagement of the original disciples of Jesus. So far as they have a polemical reference they are directed against those who pride themselves on closer relations with the Palestinian disciples (v. 12c). Paul never discounts the value of the historical basis of the faith. God has revealed his redemptive purpose in history, but the revelation must be spiritually discerned. For the probability that Paul saw Jesus during the last week in Jerusalem, and the possibility that he was an *agent provocateur* in gathering evidence for the trial, see J. Weiss, *Paul and Jesus*, pp. 17–56; J. H. Moulton, *Expositor*, VIII, ii, pp. 16–28.

20, 21. See notes on 6[1-10].

CHAPTER VI

1–10. The Christian Embassy; Pains and Consolations (including also 5[20, 21]). The supreme dignity of the apostolic office is that the minister is God's ambassador, the actual representative of Christ, delivering his message, *Be reconciled to God* (5[20]). As always in Paul, it is man, not God, whose antagonism is the barrier. The urgency of the appeal is marked by the cost at which this reconciliation is announced to the world. Elsewhere Paul has set forth the significance of the death of Christ in relation to human sin in bold language. He is a "propitiation" (Rom. 3[25]), a "curse" (Gal. 3[13]). Nowhere else is paradox carried so far as here in 5[20, 21] in the attempt to express the complete self-identification of Jesus with the sinful race he came to save. The Sinless One was identified in some mysterious way with our sin, that by that same union with him we might become righteous, not according to the human but the divine standard of character.

Paraphrase of vv. 1–10: "As fellow workers with God in this embassy our appeal to you is to make effective use of this gracious message. Now is 'the favorable opportunity,' 'the day of salvation' spoken of by the prophet (Isa. 49[8]). Our aim as ambassadors is to put no sort of obstacle in your way, so that no blame may attach to our ministry if you reject God's overtures. What are the marks of a genuine ministry? Unflinching endurance (vv. 4, 5) of such sufferings as befell our Master (cf. 4[10] Gal. 6[17]); a blameless character after the pattern of Jesus himself (v. 6); effectiveness in attack and defense in the righteous cause of Christ (v. 7), repelling every slander and triumphing over every adversity by the spirit of disinterested love."

Chapters 6[11] to 7[16]: Paul's Reconciliation with the Corinthian Church

We saw that in 1[12]–2[17] Paul was defending himself against false charges, and that in 3[1]–6[10] he was setting forth the apostolic office. He now rejoices in the reconciliation which has been accomplished. This is the third part of the general section, 1[12]–7[16], on Paul's relations with the Corinthians.

11–13. Paul's Large-Hearted Appeal. Paul's personal relations with the Corinthian church are once more the theme. Reconciliation has been effected, and he has written with the frankness of their spiritual father. Will they not respond with the same unrestrained affection? (An interpolation interrupts the appeal, which is resumed at 7[2].)

14–18. Warning Against Pagan Entanglements (including also 7[1]). This passage so obviously breaks into the sequence of thought which would otherwise flow smoothly from 6[13] to 7[2-4], that it is generally taken to be a fragment of another letter, probably the letter (see letter (A) in intro., section on "Paul's Relations with Corinth," (2), p. 1169) referred to in 1 Cor. 5[9]. (For the possibility that loose papyrus sheets became detached, and were wrongly replaced when the Pauline correspondence was collected and edited at a later stage, see G. Milligan, *The N.T. Documents*, pp. 181f.) Mixed marriages and all compromising entanglements with pagans are deprecated on the ground of moral incompatibility. Some of his readers seem to have taken the prohibition too stringently, and to have understood it as forbidding any kind of social or business connections with their pagan neighbors. This misunderstanding was corrected by Paul, 1 Cor. 5[10].

15. *Belial* (R.V. mg. Beliar) in later Judaism (e.g., *Book of Jubilees*, and *Testaments of Twelve Patriarchs*) was often used for Satan, or some personal power of evil. (See art., *Intertestamental Religion*, p. 205, and cf. p. 846b.) The word itself was Hebrew, meaning "worthlessness," and commonly occurs in the O.T. phrase "man of Belial," i.e., "worthless fellow." An elaborate demonology (as well as angelology) was a marked feature of post-exilic Jewish thought. It is possible that, as the word "Belial" is sometimes rendered "transgressor" in the LXX, Paul here uses the name for Antichrist, for the term "Man of Lawlessness" is used in that connection in 2 Thess. 2[3], mg.

16. No greater contrast could be imagined

than the Jewish Temple, in which no image was allowed, and a heathen temple with its statuary. But Paul immediately turns to the favorite Christian conception of the "temple not made with hands" (Acts 7:48 17:24) and claims that the Christian Church (so 1 Cor. 3:16f. Eph. 2:21) is the shrine of the living God. The mosaic of O.T. phrases is made up from Ex. 29:45 Lev. 26:12 Jer. 31:33 Isa. 52:11 Ezek. 20:41 2 Sam. 7:14 Jer. 31:9 Isa. 43:6. The entire course of religious development through the O.T. leads up to the new society created in Christ, which is called to purification, not from ritual but from ethical defilement, and to the positive achievement of all that the holy will of God demands.

CHAPTER VII

1. See notes on 6:14-18.

2–4. The Appeal Continued. In resuming the affectionate plea interrupted at 6:13, Paul protests his innocence against three reproaches that seem to have been thrown at him, or else hints that in this respect some of his critics compare unfavorably with him. He has wronged no one, ruined no one, taken advantage of no one. Cf. 4:2 1 Thess. 2:3 Acts 20:26f., and the challenge in 12:17f.

5–16. The Successful Mission of Titus; the Discipline of Godly Sorrow. At last Paul picks up the thread of narrative dropped at 2:13. From Troas he had pressed on to Macedonia in deepest depression. The churches of Galatia and Corinth were in revolt, his work in Asia was endangered by Jewish and heathen fanaticism, his own mind was tormented by restless fears. Had the sharp letter (described in intro. as (C); section on "Paul's Relations with Corinth," (5), p. 1169) done harm rather than good? At this crisis of his fortunes Titus arrived with the news that the Corinthian church was loyally and affectionately disposed toward the apostle. Not only was Paul relieved of the intolerable strain; the mind of Titus, that trusty ambassador whose wisdom and firmness had saved the situation, was also set at rest. Nowhere does Paul's tact and tenderness show better than in the words in which he confides to his readers that Titus now shares his pride in the Corinthian church, which Paul had preserved all through the painful controversy. The vindication of this confidence was to be found in the joy with which Titus gave his report (v. 7).

There was still the memory of the painful letter. Even this, however, is now a source of satisfaction (v. 9). It was written primarily, not for the punishment of the offender, nor yet to secure redress for the victim, but to bring home to the Corinthians a keen sense both of their fault and of their love for him (v. 12).

8–10. These verses distinguish between a morbid sorrow which leads to despair and death, and the God-given pain which leads to repentance and life. We may contrast the remorse of Judas and the penitence of Peter. For *the sorrow of the world* see F. Paget, *The Spirit of Discipline*, in which the essay on Accidie and the sermon on these words together form a classic of the devotional life. For *godly sorrow* cf. R. L. Stevenson's lines in *The Celestial Surgeon*, and the closing sections of Tennyson's *Guinevere*.

12. He *that did the wrong;* not the incestuous person of 1 Cor. 5:1-5, for Paul could not have written so lightly of this appalling sin. He *that suffered the wrong;* probably Paul himself (see on 2:5-11). Some think the reference is to Timothy (so Findlay, art., "Paul," Hastings' *Dictionary of the Bible*, vol. iii, p. 711). It is quite possible that the ringleader of the opposition to Paul had first insulted Paul's emissary, Timothy, and then refused any apology on Paul's hurried visit to assert authority in his own person.

CHAPTERS 8:1 TO 9:15: THE COLLECTION FOR THE CHURCH AT JERUSALEM

This collection forms the theme of the next main division of the letter.

CHAPTER VIII

1–15. The Macedonian Example an Encouragement to Corinth. This perfect confidence in the love and loyalty of the Corinthians enables Paul to refer to the collection (see 1 Cor. 16:1-9). The extraordinary generosity of the Macedonian churches is quoted as an example. Unasked, these poverty-stricken communities begged to share in the privilege of relieving their poor brethren at Jerusalem, and had given beyond all expectation, dedicating first themselves and then their scanty savings to the Lord, and through him to his apostles. Moved by this abounding liberality Paul has asked Titus, who had started the arrangements for this fund at Corinth, to visit the church to see the scheme through to a successful result (v. 6). There can be no doubt that a church rich in every endowment (cf. 1 Cor. 1:4-8), and united to Paul by ardent love, will contribute on a scale worthy of its spiritual wealth. Not that Paul would put any pressure on them. He cites the zeal of the Macedonians to give the Corinthians an opportunity of showing that their love is no less sincere (v. 8). Not that he would use rivalry as a motive. The supreme motive must be gratitude to the Lord Jesus for his transcendent grace (cf. Mt. 10[8]). Nevertheless, the Corinthians were first in the field, both in their desire to help and in their organization a year ago. They are ready to give, and are not expected to give beyond their means, or to relieve the responsibility of others. At present it is within their power to help the Christians at Jerusalem. Later on the position may be reversed (v. 14). The principle of equalized supply is taught in the story of the manna in the wilderness (Ex. 16[18]).

9. Here, as in Phil. 2[5-11], Paul indoctrinates his ethics, as elsewhere (e.g., 1 Cor. 15[58] Gal. 5[22f.] Eph. 4, 5 Col. 3, 4, notes) he moralizes his theology.

16–24. Titus and Two Others Commended for this Mission. The first named, as Paul's intimate colleague, was already well known at Corinth. He needed no pressing to go on this mission, but had volunteered. The two companions of Titus are unnamed here. One was appointed by the Macedonian churches to share Paul's responsibility in collecting and conveying this benevolence to Jerusalem. His zeal in spreading the gospel has already won him wide renown. The appointment of such co-treasurers is part of Paul's deliberate policy to prevent suspicion and scandal where detractors are busy (v. 21). It is more than probable that Luke was the delegate. We know that he accompanied Paul to Palestine, and we read (Acts 20[4]) of two Thessalonians and one Berœan among the delegates, but no Philippian. Ramsay's argument that Luke's home was Philippi gives point to this suggestion. A. Souter (*Expository Times*, vol. xviii, pp. 285, 335f.) argues from the use of the Greek article that the words here used mean that Luke was Titus' brother, which would explain the otherwise inexplicable omission of the name of Titus in Acts. Speculation is less fruitful with regard to the third name, but he may well have been one of the three Macedonian representatives named in Acts 20[4].

CHAPTER IX

1–5. The Reason for this Mission. With delicate tact Paul hints that, though he has no anxiety about the readiness of the Corinthians to do their utmost for this fund, he does not want his Macedonian friends to suspect him of overestimating their zeal. After stimulating them with the cry, "Achaia hath been prepared for a *year past*," it would be humiliating to arrive at Corinth in the company of Macedonian delegates only to find the Corinthian church unprepared. For the credit of the apostle (not to say of Corinth), he was sending the three brethren in advance, so that in due course their reputation for foresight and for generosity would stand secure.

6–15. The Ground of the Apostolic Appeal for Liberality. Paraphrase: "Remember that the sparing sower reaps a sparing harvest, and the lavish sower a lavish harvest (cf. Prov. 11[24f.] 19[17] 22[9]). Let no man give on impulse, or yet under compulsion, but as the cheerful giver whom God loves (Prov. 22[8, 9]). God, on the scale of the divine bounty (Phil. 4[19]), will make this possible by supplying all your actual needs and giving you also enough to meet every claim on your generosity (v. 8). You will be like the man of whom the psalmist (Psa. 112[9]) sings, 'He hath scattered abroad, he hath given to the poor; his righteousness abideth for ever.' The same Lord who multiplies the farmer's seeds will make all your good deeds fruitful. While you are being enriched in every way so as to become generous in every direction, your generosity administered through me will evoke thanksgiving to God. For the distribution of this fund will at the same time supply the wants of the poor Christians at Jerusalem and inspire a chorus of thanksgiving to God (cf. 1[11] 4[15]). Men will recognize the true meaning of your service, and will praise God as they see the outcome of your creed in your conduct, and the generosity of your contribution to them and to the whole church. They will also pray for you, and will be drawn into a closer fellowship with you as they think of the overwhelming grace of God which he has poured upon you. Thanks be to God for his inestimable gift."

7. Cf. Wordsworth's sonnet, *King's College Chapel*,

"Give all thou canst; high Heaven rejects the lore
Of nicely calculated less or more."

8, 10. In later Judaism *righteousness* was often a synonym for "almsgiving." Cf. Mt. 6[1, 2].

10. Language borrowed from Isa. 55[10] and Hos. 10[12].

Chapters 10[1] to 13[10]: Paul's Defense of His Character and of His Work

A sudden change of tone strikes harshly on our ears as we pass from the tender-hearted, conciliatory appeal of the preceding chapters to the vehement self-assertion of this closing section. Most of the weapons in Paul's polemical armory are brought into vigorous use. This fighting temper seems the more ill-timed as an immediate sequel to the doxology of

9[15]. Those who stand by the integrity of Second Corinthians have to assume that, after addressing the loyal majority, Paul now turns to the disloyal minority. The calumnies and innuendos of his detractors are now disposed of with withering scorn and sarcasm. It is said that a letter which was dictated at intervals during the course of several days would reflect different moods of Paul's mercurial temperament. Psychological probability, however, favors the view that these four chapters are part of the severe letter to which Paul definitely refers (2[3, 9] 7[8]). There are, indeed, passages in chs. 10–13 which seem to be alluded to in chs. 1–9. Cf. 10[6] with 2[9]; 13[2] with 1[23]; 13[10] with 2[3]. The protest in 3[1] and 5[12] that "we are not again commending ourselves" may well be a reply to criticisms provoked by 10[7] 11[5, 23]; and "whether we are beside ourselves, it is unto God," 5[13], becomes significant if 12[2] had been twisted into a confession of an unbalanced mind. Eager self-defense and relentless exposure of his slanderers were not only permissible but obligatory for one who was struggling to save the Corinthian church from the mischievous propaganda that threatened the peace and loyalty of communities in the Christian mission. It is less easy to justify this personal polemic after the complete victory signalized in 7[11-16]. For these reasons the priority of chs. 10–13 to chs. 1–9 is here accepted.

CHAPTER X

1–6. The Charge of Cowardice Repelled. Paraphrase: "I make my personal appeal to you in the name of the gentle and gracious Christ. Do not put me to the necessity of drastic dealing with insubordinate agitators when I visit you. I know the slander, 'He cringes when present, but can be bold enough at a distance.' I shall have to show those people that we conduct our campaign on no worldly policy. Our weapons are invincible for the demolition of strongholds—all sophistries and every rampart raised to oppose the knowledge of God. I shall capture every plan and bring it into the obedient service of Christ, and I am ready, once your submission is complete, to exact a penalty for every mutinous act."

1. *Meekness* in modern English is inadequate for this fine ethical quality. It is the velvet glove that encases the hand of iron. It saves the giant from the tyranny of using his strength as a giant. Cf. Psa. 18[35] Mt. 5[5] 11[29]. The word translated *gentleness* in A.V. and R.V., and "sweet reasonableness" by M. Arnold, is cognate with that rendered "forbearance" in Phil. 4[5].

4–6. These verses are full of martial metaphors well brought out in Moffatt's translation.

7–11. The Charge of Weakness Repelled. Paraphrase: "Then there is the sneer, 'He is powerful with the pen, but a weakling to look at, and a poor speaker' (v. 10). Have you eyes for outward appearance only? (V. 7.) I have as good a claim to the authority of Christ as any other man, and though I may seem to exaggerate my authority now, it will prove no empty boast when I arrive among you. This authority was given me to build up the church, not to pull it down (as is the case with my rivals!), so I do not want to overawe you by my letters. But let the man who sneers at me make sure of this, that however strong may be the language of my letters I shall prove just as strong when I stand in your midst."

10. This may preserve a malicious jibe at Paul's personal appearance (cf. the traditional description in the *Acts of Paul and Thecla*, 3). On the other hand it may refer to Paul's failure to make his presence felt on his last unfortunate visit. If this was due to physical prostration, we may compare the language of Gal. 4[13, 14].

12–18. The Charge of Trespass Repelled. Paraphrase: "I cannot bring myself to emulate those self-praisers whom you know so well, or to compare myself with them. In their folly they set themselves up as a standard of self-measurement! But I will not glory beyond my legitimate province, but will keep within that province which God measured out to me, which embraced our mission to you. By this I mean that in bringing Corinth within our sphere of operations I was not straining my commission. We were the first to come to you (v. 14, R.V. and A.S.V. mg.) as missionaries of the gospel. I make no illegitimate boast as the result of other men's labors, but hope that as your faith grows our range of influence may be enlarged through you, so that my legitimate province may be extended, enabling me to preach the gospel in districts beyond Achaia. But in doing this I shall not (as some whom you know) trespass on another man's province, and then boast of work that he has already brought within sight of success. In any case we must remember Jeremiah's maxim (Jer. 9[24]), 'Let him who boasts, boast in the Lord.' For there is one decisive test, which is not self-commendation, but commendation by the Lord."

12b, 13a. The interpretation of this very difficult passage is complicated by a variation in the text. Some ancient authorities omit four words (for the change thus produced see Moffatt's translation). The paraphrase given above represents the R.V. text. With the shortened form of text the meaning will be: "These self-praisers poach on other men's preserves and then boast of their success. I keep my own province, compare myself with my own standard, which is limited for me by the province God has appointed me."

CHAPTER XI

1–15. Counter-Attack on Spurious Apostles. We have already met with several allusions to some opponents who disparaged Paul's status, and trespassed on his apostolic sphere of influence. They are not the overzealous partisans of Peter or Apollos (1 Cor. 1^{12}), but some wandering propagandists whose motives and methods arouse Paul's deepest resentment and concern. In this painful section he warns the Corinthian church, and exposes the character of his opponents. This personal statement of his own position will, of course, seem "folly." His defense is his earnest desire to present the Corinthian church to Christ with a stainless reputation. After all, they put up with folly enough from these interlopers, who are asking them to accept another Jesus, a different Spirit, a different gospel. Is Paul really inferior to these superlative missionaries! He may be less glib, but he has spiritual insight, and he can make his meaning clear (v. 6). The cruel wrong is that his scrupulous care to avoid being a burden to them has been twisted into a confession of defective title. He has supported himself, has even accepted help from the Macedonian churches so that his gospel should cost the Corinthians nothing. Now he will persist in this course, not that he loves them too little to receive gifts from them, but in order to expose the contrast between his method and that of his rivals in the eyes of all Achaia (v. 10). So far from taking advantage of his forbearance they will now have to meet him on equal terms, and they will be found out as sham missionaries, masquerading as ministers of righteousness, just as Satan, their master, masquerades as an angel of light.

2. This is the first appearance of the figure of *espousal* representing the mystical relationship between Christ and his church, which is developed in Eph. 5^{26-32}. It is based on O.T. language regarding Israel's relations with Jehovah (Ezek. 23 Hos. 1–3).

5. The R.V. mg., *Those pre-eminent apostles,* is preferable. There is no reference to the Twelve. Cf. 12^{11}.

16–33. The Fool Answered According to His Folly. Paraphrase: "I am driven to the necessity of meeting my detractors on their own ground. It sounds boastful and foolish, and you must not think that I am speaking as the Lord's mouthpiece, or in my own character. You must not complain, for you fall a ready victim, in spite of your boasted shrewdness, to any charlatan who domineers and fleeces you, who hoodwinks you, who lords it over you with arrogance and insult (v. 20). It is a shameful confession to make, but really I was not man enough to adopt that course! For all that, if I must play their foolish game of self-advertisement, I can make claims as big as theirs. What is their vaunt on grounds of language, nationality, ancestral privilege? I am at least their equal. Do they claim to be ministers of Christ? It is sheer madness to talk like this, but how does their record of service compare with mine! (V. 23.) What do they know of all my toils, and imprisonments, and scourgings, and deadly perils! Think of the catalogue of adventures! Five times the Jews have inflicted on me the severest legal flogging, three times I have suffered the Roman lictors' rods, once I suffered the sentence of stoning, three times I have been wrecked at sea, and once for a whole night and day I was adrift on the deep. Think of all I have suffered in my travels: dangers from swollen torrents, from brigands, from hostile Jews and fanatical Gentiles, dangers from city mobs and from unpeopled deserts and from the uncertain sea; worse still, dangers from the treachery of men who bear the Christian name. Think of all my toils and hardships, sleepless nights, hunger and thirst, shortage of food and fuel and clothing (v. 27). These are the bodily sufferings, but in addition to them I have the care which haunts me every day—my anxiety for all the churches. Whenever some poor weakling stumbles and falls, virtue goes out of me as I share his weakness and shame. If there is to be any boasting, that alone shall be my boast—the toils and troubles that drain my strength."

18. *Glory after the flesh,* i.e., rely boastfully on the accidental privileges of birth and nationality. Cf. Phil. $3^{4f.}$

23–27. Cf. 6^{4-10}.

24. *Five times.* See Deut. 25^{3}. Not one of these judicial acts of the Synagogue against Paul is recorded in Acts. They may belong to an earlier period of his ministry. In any event, the reference shows how much of Paul's Christian labor is unrecorded (cf. Jn. 21^{25}).

25. *With rods.* Roman magistrates alone could sentence to this punishment. Paul as a Roman citizen could claim exemption from corporal punishment (cf. Acts 22^{25}). The one instance recorded in Acts $16^{22f.}$ suggests that Paul may have endured this illegal outrage on each occasion because his comrade could not demand exemption. At Philippi his endurance of this illegality may have enabled him to secure his friends from official molestation by the threat of exposure (cf. Acts 16^{37-39}). The stoning was that at Lystra (Acts 14^{19}). The only *shipwreck* reported in Acts (see ch. 27) belongs to a later period than this letter. Must we allow for an active ministry before Paul was sent out with Barnabas from Antioch? (Acts 9^{30} 11^{25}.) Or must we recognize that Luke's narrative is but an outline of journeys far more adventurous than even his pen could describe?

29. *And I burn not* may mean to burn with sympathetic shame, or to blaze with indignation at the tempter (cf. Mt. 18^{6}).

32, 33. The verses have the appearance of a postscript. Cf. Acts $9^{24, 25}$.

CHAPTER XII

1–10. Visions and Revelations of the Lord. Paraphrase: "This hateful necessity brings me to another subject for boasting—mystical experiences which the Lord has granted me. It is fourteen years since this ineffable privilege was mine. I only know that I was transported to the dwelling-place of God and heard unutterable secrets. I could boast of the Paul who enjoyed that ecstasy, but of the Paul whom you know my only boasting must be of his weaknesses (v. 5). For, to save me from undue elation because of the visions, God gave me a painful affliction, like a stake in the flesh, to keep me humble. Three times I have made earnest prayer to be delivered from this affliction, and this is his reply: 'Enough for you is my grace, for my power is perfected in weakness.' For this reason my proudest boast shall be in the things that make me weak, so that I may find protection under the power of Christ. Therefore I delight in all I suffer for Christ's sake, for in him I find my strength when I myself am weak."

2–4. Paul naturally describes this ecstatic experience in the language of his Jewish contemporaries. According to post-exilic ideas, the Jews spoke sometimes of a series of seven heavens, at other times of three. Here Paul seems to identify the *third heaven* with Paradise (cf. Lk. 23^{43} Rev. 2^{7}), the dwelling place of God. (For a discussion of these terms and the varying conceptions in the Jewish apocalypses, see arts., *Intertestamental Literature*, pp. 188–9; *Intertestamental Religion*, pp. 210–3; *Backgrounds*, p. 845–7.) The date, *fourteen years* before (i.e., as we reckon, thirteen), emphasizes the actuality of the experience. The "unutterable utterances" (v. 4) are not the "voiceless groanings" of Rom. 8^{26}, but transcendent and incommunicable revelations which left on Paul's mind a sense of assurance. In accordance with all ancient mysticism it was regarded as irreverent to report such sacred sensations to the unsympathetic.

7. Paul's *thorn in the flesh* has been a theme for endless discussion. The phrase *a messenger of Satan* recalls Job 2^{1-7}. The most likely meaning is some physical malady, intermittent or chronic, which not only tried the apostle's endurance, but sometimes reduced him to abject helplessness.

10. Cf. 13^{4}, also Phil. 4^{13} Eph. 3^{16} 6^{10} Col. 1^{11}.

Note on the Mysticism of Paul

Recent studies in the psychology of religion have given this description of the mystic trance considerable importance in the treatment of the mysticism of Paul. Reference may be made to Inge's essay on the psychology of mysticism in *Studies of the English Mystics*, ch. i; Inge, *Christian Mysticism*, pp. 60–72; R. H. Strachan, *The Individuality of St. Paul*, ch. xiv. Deissmann, who offers an illuminating study of Paul as a reacting (as opposed to an acting) mystic (*Paul*, 2nd edit., ch. vi), remarks, "Paul himself subordinated ecstasy to ethos." For a parallel to this Pauline memory of a special revelation granted years before, cf. Principal Shairp's record of words spoken to him by Thomas Erskine of Linlathen (*Letters of Thomas Erskine*, p. 539). On the alleged dependence of Paul's mysticism on the mysteries, see Morgan, *Religion and Theology of Paul*, pt. ii, ch. 1, and for a contrary opinion see H. A. A. Kennedy, *Paul and the Mystery Religions*. Cf. art., *Backgrounds*, p. 851.

11–18. Apostolic Credentials. Paraphrase: "You drove me to all this foolish self-commendation, for you ought to have been as quick to defend my reputation as you were to give letters of commendation (3^{1}) to those superlative apostles (11^{5}) whose superiority I am not prepared to acknowledge, though they affect to regard me as a nonentity. While we were in your midst none of the signs were missing that mark an apostolic ministry. Without grudging the cost (cf. Mk. 5^{30} 9^{29}) we so labored and prayed that God's marvelous powers were at work among you. In what way do you suffer in comparison with churches founded by other apostles, except that I have refused to be a financial burden to you? You must forgive me for this omission! I am ready to visit you for the third time, without burdening you; since it is you and not your money that I want (v. 14). For, after all, I am your father, and it is only fitting that instead of drawing on your savings I should gladly spend what I have and be utterly spent myself for your souls. Do you love me less because I love you all too much? But the charge is that, though I was not a burden to you on the claim of personal maintenance, I was cunning enough to trick you into paying in another way. Is that true? Did I fleece you by means of any of my emissaries? I asked Titus to visit you, and his brother (cf. 8[18]) with him. Did Titus fleece you? Of course not! Yet, as you well know, he and I are guided by the same principles and follow the same course."

16–18. These spurious missionaries, who were themselves drawing supplies from the Corinthian church, first tried to score off Paul by hinting that he did not take maintenance because he knew he was not entitled to do so (11[7]; cf. 1 Cor. 9[3-18]). When that line of attack failed, they whispered that the fund which his agents were organizing at Corinth and elsewhere was an instrument of Paul's craft and cupidity. Hence Paul's honorable safeguards. See 8[20f].

19–21. Paul's Hopes and Fears for the Corinthian Church. Paraphrase: "Do not imagine that in all this I am standing on my defense before you. It is at God's tribunal that I stand as a servant of Christ, and my motive is that the church at Corinth may be built up. For I have misgivings, unless things change, that my next visit may bring mutual disappointment. You will find me helpless in the face of a church divided, and demoralized by every un-Christlike temper. I, on the other hand, shall be heartbroken by finding some who have in the past practiced heathen vice flaunting themselves unabashed in the ranks of the church" (cf. 1 Cor. 6[11]).

CHAPTER XIII

1–14. Final Warnings and Appeal. Paul continues on the same note. Paraphrase: "If such there be, they must repudiate any unlawful associations before my approaching visit, when there will be a thorough investigation. This is but to repeat the warning given during my second visit. I shall exercise my disciplinary powers to the full, and thus prove that I am the representative of Christ, who is not weak but full of power in his dealings with you. In human weakness he died upon the cross, but he is alive for evermore in the power of God. My weakness brings me into fellowship with him whose boundless power will give me strength to deal with you (v. 4). The urgent question, however, is not whether Christ is in me, but whether he is in you. Put this to the test and discover whether you have that faith in Christ which saves from sin. I cannot believe that you shrink from this test. I hope that you will have reason to know that I have not failed in the test applied to my mission (cf. 1 Cor. 3[12-15]). For the apostle is responsible for the purity of life of the churches under his control. Therefore I pray that you at Corinth may reach a high moral standard. This is not that I may get the credit of a spiritually prosperous church. Indeed, from one standpoint I should have failed, as the test of my moral authority is effective disciplinary action, which in this case would not have been put to the proof. But I am not influenced by the thought of personal prestige, but of what is right and true (v. 8). What if my detractors call me a 'weakling' once more for not justifying my promise of bold action? If the true reason for my inactivity is that you have proved the strength of your faith in Christ, I shall rejoice in the lost opportunity of showing my strength. So I pray that God may supply all that is at present lacking in your Christian character, and I send this warning to avoid the necessity of displaying my apostolic authority, which was given me for the one purpose of building you up in the Christian life (v. 10). Farewell, brothers, make good your defects, attend to my exhortations, live in harmony and peace, so that you may claim the presence of the God of love and peace."

1. *Third time.* Cf. 12[14], and see introduction, section on "Paul's Relations with Corinth," p. 1169. *At the mouth,* etc., is a quotation from Deut. 19[15]. The original words may simply indicate a formal inquiry with judicial results, or it may be an instance of rabbinic "preciousness" in the use of scripture. Remote as such citations are from our modern conceptions of sound scripture exegesis, there are undeniable instances in the letters of Paul (cf. Gal. 3[16] 4[25]) of survivals of his rabbinical days.

4. Cf. Phil. 2[7, 8] 1 Pet. 3[18] Rom. 6[4]. **4b.** Cf. 12[10] Gal. 2[20]. **10.** Cf. 10[8].

14. The triple benediction contains in solution the Christian doctrine of God which was crystallized later in the trinitarian dogma of the creeds. Here, as in Eph. 2[18], the theology of experience prepares the way for the definitions of a metaphysical age (see Garvie, *Christian Doctrine of the Godhead,* pp. 24–26).

GALATIANS

By Professor JOHN DOW

Introduction

To Whom Addressed? When Paul on his first missionary journey passed from Cyprus into Pamphylia a rift appeared in the company and John Mark broke off (Acts 13:13). It is natural to suspect here a change of plan due to untoward circumstances. In the lowlying coastlands Paul may have contracted malaria (cf. 1 Cor. 2:3 2 Cor. 12:7; Ramsay's *Galatians*, p. 422). Consequently, he headed for the highlands of the interior, entering territory less hospitable and civilized, which may well have seemed a foolhardy experiment for a sick man. Here, however, in Pisidian Antioch, Derbe, Lystra, and Iconium, the apostle made friends and founded churches. The Galatians here addressed may be the people of this region. They had received him generously in spite of something repulsive in his ailment (cf. 4:13). Steeped as they were in pagan superstition, they even took Paul for a god (cf. 4:14). To such people, believers in multitudinous evil spirits and astral divinities and the magical efficacy of ceremonial rites, he preached faith in the one living God—who made the heaven and the earth and the sea, and all that in them is (cf. 4:9 Acts 14:15f.). A volatile people, they were quick to hear, as later they were quick to change again (1:6 3:1).

In Pisidian Antioch Paul pursued his regular method of appealing first in the synagogue to the Jews, and some of his fellow countrymen doubtless adhered to him. Other converts were Gentiles who had previously attached themselves to the synagogue and had gained the moral discipline of the Jewish ethic. But probably the majority of the converts would pass straight out of paganism into Christianity. Thus came into being a new phenomenon, a predominantly Gentile church, and with it arose new problems. Judaism in particular had reason to regard the movement with alarm. The synagogue leaders saw their own ranks thinned and their Gentile adherents drawn elsewhere. They were jealous of a cause far more successful than their own and they resented the non-enforcement of their traditional laws and practices—a cheapening of religion in their eyes (1:10). Small wonder that in this region the apostle found himself pursued by the fanatic hate of his compatriots. They drove him from city to city, pelting him with stones, covering him probably with those scars which he proudly calls the "marks of the Lord Jesus" (6:17; cf. Acts 13:51 14:5,6,19,20).

The deepest national prejudice was stirred by this admission of Gentiles to equality with Jews in the Pauline churches with the consequent social intermingling. It meant a national disintegration, and startled even Christian Jews. On his return from this journey Paul found himself faced with a crisis in the church at Antioch on this very question (Acts 15). Those who forced the issue before the church were not likely to leave unvisited with their propaganda the district in Galatia through which Paul had passed. Emissaries traversed the region, insinuating (1) that Paul was no true apostle, but only a secondary authority dependent on the Jerusalem apostles; (2) that he had made the way into Christianity too broad by removing the barriers of circumcision and the Jewish Law, simply to curry favor with men (1:10). Before this propaganda—with its specious appeal to the authority of those who had been actually with Jesus and to the pagan reverence for ascetic and ritual practices—the Galatian converts lapsed into doubt and fell away from the simple gospel. Paul writes this letter (1) to vindicate the divine right and authority of his own apostleship as derived immediately from the risen Christ, and (2) to affirm faith in Jesus Christ as the essential gospel independent of the Jewish Law. He courses on in burning hot haste, the quick nervous sentences tumbling from his pen so fast that grammar is defied and the sense frequently clouded. (The questions raised here are discussed at length in the art., *Life and Work of Paul*, pp. 936–7, and in the commentaries on Acts and Second Corinthians.)

Location of the Galatian Churches. This account assumes the destination of the letter to be the churches of South Galatia (Derbe, etc.). The Romans had taken the name of the small kingdom of Galatia and applied it to a large province including part of Lycaonia, Pisidia, and Phrygia. Paul's habit was to use the Roman provincial titles (Asia, 1 Cor. 16:19 2 Cor. 1:8; Achaia, 1 Cor. 16:15 2 Cor. 1:1; cf. Rom. 15:19 1 Thess. 1:7 4:10). The one name comprehending all the churches of that region was "Galatia." They were the fruits of his first missionary journey and very precious to him, and allusions in the letter fit his experiences there at many points. Some, however, still assign the letter to the ethnic kingdom of Galatia, the region about Ancyra, in northeast Asia Minor. The question will be found discussed at length in the larger commentaries on this Epistle. (See also pp. 940, 1112b.)

Date. The Galatians had lapsed from Paul's teaching soon after he had left them (1^6). He had already paid them two visits—if we take "the first time" (4^{13}) to mean *the former of two* (visits). These two visits might be on the outward and return journey of Acts 13, 14. Thus the letter can be dated any time after the first journey (Acts 13, 14). The Jerusalem Decree was pertinent to the subject of the letter and would have been quoted surely to strengthen Paul's case had it been issued. Probably then we should date the letter as soon as possible after the first missionary journey.

If the visits going and returning in Acts 13, 14 are counted as one, the second visit would be that which Paul paid with Silas (Acts 16). The letter would then be written from Corinth.

The North Galatian theory requires a later date. The two visits would be those of Acts 16, 18 on the second and third journeys. This would place the letter about the Ephesus period during the three-years' sojourn. As far as doctrine is concerned Galatians could have been written any time after Paul's conversion.

Importance. Galatians has a fourfold interest, as follows:

(1) It shows Christianity in the first hard bout of its lifelong struggle to maintain its freedom and spirituality. What is passing, what permanent, is an issue ever with us. Indeed, in the very beginning, beneath the practical grievance that led to the appointment of the Seven (Acts 6) may have been a difference of interpretation: a Stephen who preached that God needed no temple made with hands (Acts 7) was following a different line from the older disciples with their close concentration on the old Temple worship. Conflict was inevitable. The Hebrew trained in law and precept tended to literalism; the Greek trained in philosophy sensed the ideal and spiritual. The challenge raised in Galatia was really whether or no Christianity was to carry too much lumber: was she to be free, or bound by Jewish legalism? Paul was the first church statesman to have courage to cut away dead wood. He was true to Jesus in maintaining that the children are free (Mt. 17^{26}). Christians are under no obligation to the Temple tax or to any modern form of imposition that conscience may not approve. Through Christ we enter into gracious spiritual relationship to the Father and in the strength of that we regulate life.

(2) It shows that the testing of Christianity is not in her doctrine but in the application of her doctrine to life. The issue was more than a dispute about the rite of circumcision: it involved the whole question of whether Christianity was to follow Judaism in segregating itself from the rest of mankind. The test of true brotherhood is the common table, the ability to eat and live together. The food laws and Sabbath laws of the Jews made concrete their claim to be a separate people. By the discipline of legalism Judaism had hedged itself off from contaminating paganism. Jesus by his contact with publicans and sinners had broken through that hedge, and the problem of Christianity now was whether it could maintain that gap and continue fraternal intercourse. The difficulties were human and social. Meat offered to idols appeared on the tables of one's friends. An invitation to dinner might be coupled with the name of a pagan god. (J. H. Moulton, *From Egyptian Rubbish Heaps*, p. 41.) To keep up the Jewish Law and racial prejudice inside the Christian Church meant a policy of separation from the world, which had no redemptive power. It is precisely on this field of social intercourse that Christianity is still in the testing. Is there yet fellowship between white, black, and yellow races?

(3) It is invaluable as a study of the human factor in the history of Christianity. This marks the first great deliverance of the faith from the danger of being smothered by nonessentials, and it was because Paul's own experience was so direct and personal a contact with the living Christ that he could thus so clearly distinguish the essential gospel. Again and again the good news is reborn.

(4) It is of incomparable historic value as a piece of autobiography and a document of church history. The opening of Christianity to the Gentiles was a crucial episode, and upon this struggle the Epistle casts light. It reminds us how great are the walls of prejudice that must be beaten down and how terrible the toll of pain and tears that the task demands of chosen souls before victory is won for the forces of progress. Progress is not automatic: it comes by the repetition of the fact of the cross, the reincarnation of Christ in the Pauls of history.

Literature: Commentaries: Bacon (Bible for Home and School); Burton (International Critical); Emmet (Readers'); Findlay (Expositor's Bible); Lightfoot; McFadyen (Interpreter's); Ramsay. Also Luther *On Galatians;* Macgregor, *Christian Freedom.*

CHAPTER 1

1–5. Paul States His Theme. Paul states at once what is to be the burden of his letter, namely, the divine source of the salvation that is in Christ, and the utter adequacy of this salvation to all human need. These deep convictions of Paul were being challenged by the men who could see in the gospel of Christ nothing but a means of increasing the influence of Judaism. (See art., *Life and Work of Paul,* p. 936.) He vindicates his apostolic authority by deriving it directly from Christ. It was the risen Christ who commissioned Paul (Acts 26^{16}). Christ, however, did not raise himself: God raised him, that through him he might work his will. Already, in his life and suffering, Christ had given himself up to that will to open the way to salvation, and the divine raising had to do with the salvation being carried out (Acts 2^{22-24} Phil. 2^{5-11}). Hence both Paul's commission and his message, equally with the saving grace that he proclaims, are derived ultimately from God through Christ.

There is a certain pessimism about Paul, revealed in his description of the *present world* (or age) as evil (v. 4). The pessimism is not, however, hopeless. The divine grace in Christ makes a transformation possible. The age of evil does not have to pass before the age of good can appear. A person leaves one age and enters the other accordingly as he passes from the control of the "flesh" to the control of the "spirit." Flesh and spirit are principles, each with its appropriate expression (5^{16-24}).

6–9. One Gospel Only. In the nature of the case, there cannot be two gospels. The contrast between salvation by faith in divine grace and salvation by observance of law and personal self-righteousness is fundamental and absolute. Either men can save themselves by perfect obedience or they cannot. If they can, divine grace is unnecessary, and Christ's sacrifice becomes meaningless. If they cannot, then their reliance must be placed on something other than themselves. A gospel is a piece of good news. How can that be good news, Paul is asking, which increases men's moral burden, when what they need is to have the burden lightened?

The gospel may be susceptible of various interpretations, but an interpretation which takes Christ from the place of supremacy is a *perversion* (v. 7). How strong Paul's feeling is when he says he would not give way even to an *angel* (v. 8) becomes evident when we remember the large place occupied by angelic mediation in Jewish belief (3^{19} Gen. 22^{11} Judg. 6^{11} Zech. $1^{9, 12, 14}$ Lk. $1^{11, 26}$). The *anathema* (v. 8), or curse, is not uttered upon the person of the man or angel who might bring a perverted gospel. Paul's meaning is that one must turn from such a message and messenger as from an unholy thing. They are to be taboo, fled from in horror as incredible impieties.

10. One who utters such severe rebukes as this is on the face of it concerned only to please God. To incur human enmity, or to endanger personal friendship, in duty's name, is a severe test.

11–17. Events Following Paul's Conversion. Paul has in mind the charge that he is not a real apostle, because, unlike the Twelve, he had not personally known the Lord. He meets the charge by showing that no man was his teacher in respect of the gospel. If an apostle is one who received the truth directly from Christ himself, then Paul is an apostle.

Paul's language in vv. 15, 16 may echo the claims of the Judaizers. They had professed reverence for the traditions of the fathers, prided themselves on their name as Pharisees ("separated ones"), insisted that God had *separated* the Jews from the beginning and revealed his law in Israel, to which Paul retorts that God *separated* him also from his mother's womb like the prophets (cf. Jer. 1^5 Isa. 49^1) and had revealed *in him* something better than the Law, namely, *his Son,* and that too for preaching *among the Gentiles* (v. 16).

There are certain difficulties connected with Paul's vigorous assertion that he had no human instructor in Christian things. A comparison of this passage, and the ensuing one, with Acts reveals some apparent inconsistencies (see Acts 9^{10-30}). He proclaimed Christ immediately after his conversion, but he had heard Stephen's defense (Acts $7^{57, 58}$), and had doubtless been instructed by Ananias. The visit to Jerusalem with Barnabas (Acts 9^{27}) seems to have been soon after his conversion, notwithstanding v. 17. The writer of Acts, however, is not giving a complete biography of Paul. He says nothing, e.g., of Paul's visit to Arabia, which evidently marked a significant period in the young convert's life. Moreover, when we get the drift of Paul's present contention, we see that his assertion of independence is correct. What he is insisting on is that his gospel came to him *by revelation* (v. 12). When he was first converted, nobody had yet grasped the full meaning of the gospel. Certainly, Paul himself had not; he simply proclaimed Jesus "the Son of God" and "the Christ" (Acts 9:20-22). But he later saw in him the universal Saviour of men from sin. Whence came that conviction? From others? No, but from the guidance of the Spirit. Hence Paul can speak of "*my* gospel" (2 Tim. 2:8). **17.** *Arabia* was probably the neighborhood of Damascus.

18–24. Paul Asserts His Independence of Jerusalem (cf. also 2:1, 2). Paul had been represented as a second-rate apostle completely dependent on the real apostles at Jerusalem. This he refutes by stressing the scantiness of his intercourse with them, the fewness and brevity of his visits.

(1) He went to Jerusalem indeed, but not to *consult* Peter, only to *visit* him, the Greek word implying a visit of curiosity to a famous person or place. He was there only fifteen days—too short a time for any course of teaching. He had been hunted out of Damascus by plots against his life, and so marked a man dared not long remain in Jerusalem, where he was most hated and bitterly remembered as a turncoat. These may have been dangerous days, which would explain why so few apostles—only James and Peter—were in the city. Paul dared not appear in public and therefore could not make himself personally known to the churches of Judæa (i.e., Jerusalem and district). He was merely known by reputation as a converted ex-persecutor for whose changed life they "kept praising" God (v. 24).

(2) Immediately thereafter (v. 21) Paul went right away north, far from any conceivable intercourse with Jerusalem, and there for fourteen years in absolute independence he pursued his way, teaching his gospel without reference to any authority but the witness of the Spirit within. This stay in Syria and Cilicia almost casually mentioned took up half of his missionary career. How little we know of formative periods even in the lives of the great! But Paul had arrested attention and, when the hour struck, Barnabas sought him out (Acts 11:25,26).

CHAPTER II

1, 2. Paul Admits a Relation to Jerusalem. Paul now approaches an apparently vulnerable point in his story. He had to confess one visit paid fourteen years after—dating either from the last visit or from his conversion—distinctly for conference with the older apostles. It had been represented as a quest for credentials, a sign of Paul's utter dependence on higher authority. In answer he maintains that the visit would stand examination; it was made in the company of Barnabas and Titus. The mention of *Titus* is intended to confound the opposition. He was an uncircumcised Greek, and yet Paul dared to take him right in among the pillars of the circumcision party—the lamb in the presence of the lions. What had the Judaizers to say about the fact that the pillar apostles had suffered this Gentile in the Holy City and in their own company? This visit, moreover, was not by command from headquarters; it was prompted *by revelation*, i.e., by the Spirit, the form of guidance on which the early church laid greatest emphasis. Paul was frequently guided by revelation. Some equate this visit with that of Acts 11:30, when Agabus "by the Spirit" foretold a famine, in relief of which Paul and Barnabas went to Jerusalem. Others take the visit as that of Acts 15, when the same two men went up by appointment of the church, but only after seeking the guidance of the Spirit. The atmosphere was one of crisis. The church decided to appeal to Jerusalem, Paul and Barnabas to be delegates. They were officially welcomed and the conference was public. The occasion was thus a formal charge laid before the church by the circumcisionists. The decision was likewise formal—a church decree, duly signed and sponsored, allowing the liberty of the Gentiles in the matter of circumcision, but making certain reservations, and addressed only to the local centers of agitation in the Antioch district, where Jewish and Gentile civilizations met and clashed on equal terms. (For a fuller discussion, see notes on Acts 15.) On the other hand, Paul insists here that the conference was unofficial and *private*, a consultation simply with the "would-be authorities," as he calls them, with a touch of irony perhaps, taking up the catchword of the Judaizers who had made out Paul an insignificant nobody in comparison. Paul wanted simply to have, not authorization, but influential assurance that he was not on a false track (metaphor from the race course). For that purpose Paul laid before them the "gospel." Not that he would have surrendered it had they disagreed. Only he set value on their indorsement for the good of the work in future. That "gospel" meant the admission of Gentiles without circumcision. Paul's *private conference* may have preceded the public discussion.

3–5. Titus and the False Brethren. Paul now runs into an obscurity, not in the confusion of a bad case, but through excitement and haste. The facts are known to his readers and only allusions are needed. There are two possible interpretations: (1) Titus was not circumcised albeit he was a Gentile. The much-quoted people of consequence did not demand circumcision in this glaring case before their eyes. In that view Paul is triumphant here. (2) Titus was circumcised—*not because of any compulsion*, but simply as a concession which it was thought wise policy to make. In that case Paul is claiming credit for large-mindedness. The former makes the stronger and likelier case for Paul. If this one Greek was suffered uncircumcised in the very citadel of Judaism by the pillars of orthodoxy, then Paul's case was proved up to the hilt. On the other hand, the apostle's failing was toward compromise.

Every syllable rings with indignation against the *false brethren*. These were not Jews who pretended to be Christians to gather evidence of disloyalty to Jewish customs, but more piquantly actual Christians who posed as brotherly and yet played the traitor. They had had themselves introduced by a side door to *spy* upon the new-found liberty of the Christian fellowship; they would fain have dragged their victims back into utter enslavement to the legal system. Crafty scheming has ever been the method of ecclesiastical reactionaries. But there was no craven yielding, not for a moment, to these plotters. There are times when a Christian cannot bend. The freedom of life and conscience under the gospel had to be made good for all time for these Galatians and so for all Christians in general.

6–10. The Verdict of Jerusalem: Not Command, but Approval. This historic verdict decided that Christianity was to be a world religion, not a sect, a gospel of personal faith in God through Christ, and not a bondage to legalism.

6. The "authorities" (quoting the Judaizers, and possibly ironical), "whatever status they held, or whatever they once were (i.e., disciples of Jesus in the flesh)," left Paul indifferent. Human standing does not count with God (an O.T. phrase). They had no addition to make, i.e., no limiting stipulation —not quite consistent with the decree in Acts 15[20, 29], which has a modifying clause.

7. They recognized two commissions equally divine: Paul's to the Gentiles, Peter's to the Jews—a momentous decision, as Pauline Christianity without the Law was thus put on the same rank nominally as Petrine with the Law. Really they avoided a definition of the essential gospel by simply delimiting spheres of influence. The issue was shelved, not decided. Gentile Christianity was "suffered." The simple ex-pagan saw Jews with all their prestige as kinsmen of the Lord still adhering to the old forms, and he doubted his liberty. Was his Christianity not being simply tolerated? Good enough for Gentiles, it was not good enough for Jews evidently. Open disapproval is often more welcome than toleration. You can fight the one but only gnash the teeth at the other.

8, 9. The leaders saw that Paul's work, like Peter's, was certified by "signs" of the Spirit, e.g., miracles of healing, the supreme practical authentication of an apostle. Hence they gave the right hand in formal fashion before the church. These leaders were James, brother of Jesus, Peter, and John, son of Zebedee. James had taken first place as a kinsman of Jesus or because of his ascetic piety or organizing gifts. The phrase *reputed to be pillars* seems to drop out as if it rankled in Paul's mind. He is sensitive about his authority derived from Christ. Surely, he himself had been selected as pivotal—by the fact that Christ had apprehended him.

10. The only request made was a matter Paul had already on his conscience—to collect for the poor in Jerusalem, where under enthusiastic apocalyptic hopes they had burned up their capital; or they had suffered social and business ostracism (cf. 1 Cor. 16[1-4] 2 Cor. 8, 9 Acts 9[30], 11[25]). Amid all the confusions and upheavals of ages Christians have always found this common service.

11–18. The Antioch Affair. This incident, not mentioned in Acts, evidently happened after the Jerusalem concordat. Antioch was a place where the division into Gentile and Jewish spheres as defined by the Jerusalem Decree could not work. It was a mixed community with inevitable interflow between Jew and Gentile in social life. Table fellowship was the testing point (see intro., p. 1208b).

Peter had lived in free intercourse with his Gentile Christian brethren unhampered by scruples. Then *certain came from James*—delegates from Jerusalem, self-appointed guardians of James' conscience or his real emissaries. Peter, from fear or policy or pressure, withdrew from his free intercourse with Gentile Christians, especially refusing them fellowship in the love feast. The man who had quailed before a serving maid quailed again. It was a crucial issue: it was disrupting the body of Christ.

Paul broke out on Peter openly. This was not Peter's innermost conviction: he was playing an unreal part and others joined him in this inconsistent conduct. Even Barnabas, companion of Paul for so many years in propagating a liberal view of the faith, succumbed to the atmosphere (v. 13)—his Levitical training being still in his blood (Acts 4[36]). This probably marks the first break in the friendship with Barnabas which afterward led to separation. (See Acts 15[37-40].)

This exposure of Peter was in public (v. 14).

As his action had affected the community in general, there was call for public rebuke. Peter might claim that he was going his own way and not legislating for others, but such action as his undermined the confidence of immature converts. They felt they were reckoned on a lower plane. "Why this right-about turn?" asks Paul. "You used to eat with Gentiles; that is, you accepted Gentile standards of living, showing that you really felt no obligation to maintain Jewish practices. How utterly inconsistent, then, that you should now want Gentiles to accept those Jewish standards you used to discard!" Here the public rebuke may end (v. 14), but Paul continues the argument. "We who are true-born Jews, and not 'Gentile sinners,' as you disdainfully call them, are aware that our 'justification' is not won on the basis of keeping the Law. Jews though we were and proud of it, we yet became disciples of Jesus simply because we could be set in the right relation to God only in that way—through faith in Christ. That was a practical confession of the valuelessness of the Law. No man's salvation can be achieved by it. Yet here you are reviving it as a standard and essential!" (Cf. Romans for the idea of justification.)

Faith in Christ (v. 16) was to Paul a personal reaching out to the love and peace of God that discovers itself in Jesus. *Justification* is a formal legal word, but it signifies simply our acceptance before God, admission to standing as members of his household, recognition as sons with all the potentialities of sons, that restoration to status which the prodigal received from his father's grace when all he sought was rank as a servant. Note how Paul clinches his argument by a quotation from the O.T. (Psa. 143[2]). Scripture was to the Jew the final court of appeal.

17. Peter's conduct is still in Paul's mind. By withdrawal from table fellowship with Gentiles he in effect condemned it as sinful. But he had done it himself once, led thereto by his Christian faith. It was sin, then, that he had perpetrated under Christ's leadership. Christ was the inspirer of his former intercourse with Gentiles and therefore responsible for sin. How absurd! **18.** It is the man who goes back to the Law who is the sinner. Peter in reverting to his legalistic scruples was re-establishing what his Christian conscience had outgrown. That was sin, and it was his own doing.

19–21. Paul's Religion: His Self-identification with the Crucified but Still Living Christ. Paul now has definitely "drifted away from a mere narrative of the Antiochian crisis into the memory of that crisis in his own life, which was ever present to his mind" (Ramsay, *Galatians*, p. 330). Whatever Peter and these like-minded may do or think, Paul for his part has ceased to live in the same universe as the Law. For him it does not exist, and that renunciation came *through the Law* itself, i.e., (1) it set up impossible demands so that man could not live under it; or (2) it provoked to sin and compelled man to find deliverance elsewhere (Rom. 7[7]); or (3) it piled up the score against man so that Christ had to die to satisfy its claims and end its rule.

20. Paul's life has now one drive, one urge —toward God, not like Peter's which wavered between the rule of Law and the way of grace. The heart of his religion is a faith-attitude ethical and spiritual. (1) It is primarily a warm personal bond, faith in the Son of God who loved *me* and gave himself for *me*. (2) It deepens into mystical union whereby he feels himself a sharer in the experiences of Christ in his attitude to God and to sin. (3) In particular the old bad man in him perished with the other powers that Christ vanquished on the cross. When Christ rose there took place a fresh creative act; a new power began to animate personality, and that power was Christ. Thus Christ lives in him, exercising sway through the vital moral nexus of faith. *Flesh* to Paul is the seat of sin, the poisoned constitution of man, not the body only, but the whole human organization of thought, will, etc. (Rom. 7[14-25]; cf. Mk. 8[33]).

21. This Christian reliance on faith was not, as the Jewish party urged, a nullification of the gracious revelation of God in the O.T. and the Law. On the contrary, that revelation was carried to completion, for men's salvation, in Christ—and it was for that he died. His death would be an act of futile waste, empty of purpose, if redemption could be achieved by the legal system.

Paul forgets to tell us the issue of the Antioch incident. It raised the crucial issue of faith or the Law, the good news of grace or the tyranny of legalism, and the defense of that drives lesser issues from his mind. If religion has first place, the lesser things need not trouble us.

CHAPTER III

1–6. Does the Spirit Come by Faith or by Law? Affectionate yearning here mingles with rebuke. This relapse into Jewish legalism is foolish, and more: people of intelligence would not act so; there is something uncanny about such a quick change—it must be the work of the evil eye. To think that Jesus Christ painted so vividly as the Crucified before their eyes should fade out of sight! One question: How had the Spirit come? Gifts of healing, tongues, etc., were the work of the Spirit and were supremely valued. Did that new power descend with the keeping of the Jewish Law or with the receiving of the message of the cross by faith?

1. Ramsay thinks Christianity drew largely from the progressive class desirous of education. The sense is, "O you who plume yourselves on your intelligence—how foolish!" *Openly set forth,* i.e., placarded like an advertisement. Paul had preached not with cold argument but in appealing graphic pictures.

3. The Judaizers had either patronizingly allowed that the Christianity of the Galatians was a *beginning* or simply pooh-poohed it as "elementary," "crude"; the highest form required obedience to Law. How absurd! To begin with moving spiritual experiences and end up with external trivialities like circumcision. Christianity to-day often begins in simple faith and ends in ritual and denominational refinements. *Begin* and *perfect* may be technical terms from the mysteries (see p. 851), but are more apt if taken as catchwords of Paul's opponents.

4. Had they experienced all these things in vain, i.e., experiences of the spirit, not necessarily persecutions, though that was the lot of Christians generally, through social ostracism if not from governments? (Cf. Acts 14[5, 22].)

5, 6. God's lavish supply of spiritual gifts was not the outcome of law-keeping, but of dynamic faith—the quality which God approved in the spiritual father of the race, Abraham. The Greek word for *supply,* used of providing the chorus for dramatic performances, suggests unstinted lavish expense: the Spirit is given without measure.

7–14. Faith Brings the Blessing, Law a Curse. Paul has cited the evidence of experience, "gifts": now he appeals to Scripture. To claim for his case Abraham, the pattern of righteousness, was to steal a march on the traditionalists. The opposition, being Jews, were readily impressed by subtle exegesis. Rabbinism apart—there is a real point here—the great souls of the O.T. had a relationship with God deeper than the legalistic bond, a spiritual converse with God. Thus faith under the original regime was the principle of acceptance with God. Christians by their faith-relation to God are Abraham's real descendants—truer to his type than circumcised Jews. Scripture which to the pious Jew is inspired of God had foretold this in Gen. 12[3] 18[18]. The Hebrew really means that Abraham was to be a famous example of bliss—"all the nations of the world are to seek bliss like his" (Moffatt). But to Paul this is a prediction of Christianity. Abraham was the pioneer of the faith-relation and all men of faith come under that blessing.

10–14. Paul next attacks the Law. So far from being the instrument of salvation that the Judaizers claimed, it was actually the source of a curse. Deut. 27[26] implies that the whole Law must be kept or else we are under a curse, and no man can possibly keep the whole Law. Thus the curse falls on all men. Obviously, then, on that basis of law, no man can stand right with God. Salvation must come on a different basis—by faith. Hab. 2[4] is quoted, but the sense there really is that during the Chaldean upheaval the prophet had urged that by faithfulness, i.e., steadfastness, the just would live (see note there). The Law is based, not on faith, but on a radically different principle, as in Lev. 18[5]. "So keep my rules and regulations: if a man obeys them, it means life for him" (Moffatt). A promise of life, no doubt, but *on condition that* a man keep the whole Law! A specious and illusory promise! Really, the effect is to cast us all under a curse, i.e., the Law brings condemnation, not salvation. There would be no help for us but for Christ. It is by his intervention that the curse is removed. He hung on the cross and thereby took the Law's curse on himself and *bought us out* of its power (*redeemed us*). Deut. 21[23] says that an impaled man is under a curse ("of God" is the complete text from which Paul shrinks). As our representative he took the Law's curse on himself for our sakes and rendered it null and void. That opened up the way for the rule of faith again: now the Gentiles inherit the blessing foretold to Abraham, in Christianity through Jesus Christ, and we receive the promised endowment of the spirit through the moral nexus of faith.

Paul is not thinking of Christ's death as achieving some quantitative transaction, nor has he any idea of a ransom paid to the devil. In that age a slave purchased his liberty by payments deposited on the altar: he really *bought himself out* of his master's keeping into the God's service, i.e., into freedom. So Christ *bought us out* of the Law's bondage into liberty: the personal intimate faith-relation to God could now be resumed. The free man enters into a new set of relationships, and so does the Christian. Christ is somehow representative of us and his deeds achieve results, not within us psychologically merely, as modern thinkers hold, but in a formal objective way. Taking on himself the Law's curse, he canceled it, broke its efficacy. So he was made sin for us (cf. 2 Cor. 5[21]).

15–22. The Law's Function: Not to Cancel the Promise, but to Expose Sin. The true lineage of Abraham is spiritual: his blessing descends to those who like him are men of faith. But the Jew might ask: "What, then, was the function of the Law?" Paul answers that it did not come in to cancel the promise, but simply as a supplement.

Paul grows more tender as his indignation works off. "Brethren"—and it is as if he draws them closer for a confidential word—"though I am speaking of a divine promise, I am to take an illustration from human affairs. Take the case of a man's will. Once it is properly ratified, the legal forms duly observed, it stands as final: no man can annul it or add to it. If that holds of a mere human agreement, how much more of God's agreement! A duly authenticated word of God must stand. Such was the promise to Abraham: it is final and could not be canceled or admit any addition." Now, what was this promise? The bequest was to a single recipient, not to many. It was to Abraham's *seed* (singular), not *seeds* (plural). The reference is to Christ (and by implication to all in Christ). The Law was a later affair, four hundred and thirty years after, and does not cancel or make invalid the earlier agreement, the promise. The blessing we inherit cannot come both ways: if it is determined by law-keeping, the promise would cease to be operative; but God chose the method of its operation—it was to be a gracious gift freely bestowed in fulfillment of his promise. Law and promise are different in principle, the one pivoting on recompense for conduct, the other on acceptance of an unconditional gift. The Judaizers in combining Christianity and legalism were trying to unite two irreconcilable principles.

15. The Greek word for *covenant* means an "arrangement." The most common "arrangement" was a will, and Paul's Greek readers in the first century would so understand it. For readers of the LXX, however, it had also a different association, being applied there to God's covenant. The Galatians could see in it both shades of meaning. Thus they could pass rapidly in thought from the analogy of "will" to the "covenant" of God. The "covenant" was God's "will" or "bequest." According to a Roman-Syrian lawbook, which may preserve the practice contemporary with Paul, whereas a man cannot disown his real son without good reason, he *never* can put away an adopted son. Christians were adopted into God's family (which was originally the Jews) and so were in a stronger position than the natural born sons, the Jews.

16. The thing promised in Genesis is actually the land of Canaan which the Jews *had* actually inherited. "In other words the original passage has the very meaning which Paul denies to it" (McFadyen). Here the promise is interpreted to apply to the kingdom of God. The *seed* in both Greek and Hebrew is expressed by a singular (Gen. 12^{7} 13^{15} 17^{7} 22^{18} 24^{7}). The rabbinic mind readily seized on such a fine point. Paul tends to interpret the covenant as a will with formal bequests. It is quite in legal style to quibble over exact phrasing. In Rom. 4^{16}, where it suits him, Paul takes this same word in a collective sense. Legalists were well met with legalistic weapons. But finally the issue is decided by Paul's principles of freedom and spirituality.

17. For the number four hundred and thirty cf. Ex. 12^{40}: according to the Hebrew text this period covers only Israel's sojourn in Egypt, but according to the LXX and Samaritan Pentateuch it includes also the time in Canaan, i.e., the whole period from Abraham to Moses. Paul often uses the LXX.

19–22. By his sharp antithesis Paul appeared to have allowed no place for the Law. But as a pious Hebrew he had reverence for it as Scripture and divinely ordained. It must, therefore, have some distinctive function in God's redemptive process. It was not an instrument of salvation, as the Judaizers said, nor had it any permanent binding force: it was a temporary expedient, introduced because of sin, and valid only till Christ came. The Jews prided themselves on the Law and gloried in the tradition that it came *through angels by the hand of a mediator.* To Paul that was no distinction, but a mark of inferiority. The promise had real distinction: it was communicated by God in person, without any mediation. It was no contract between two parties, but a promise in which God, the Promiser, is everything. The Law is not antagonistic to the promise. Far from it! But the Law has no power to create new life; if it could have done that, it might have stood to rival the promise. But Scripture consigned all men without exception to the same pen of sin (v. 22)—to leave but one way out: only by way of faith in Jesus Christ could men come by the promise: it was restricted to those who had faith.

19. The Jewish legend that the Law was given by angels is based on the LXX version of Deut. 33^{2} (cf. Acts 7^{53} Heb. 2^{2}). It was considered to add dignity to the Law and that was enhanced by the prestige of the mediator, Moses, the high priest of legalism. Moses had actually *handled* the tables. But God spake with Abraham face to face (cf. 2 Cor. 3^{12-18}). It is curious how reverence wrongly applied—as here in the introduction of angels to give the Law—really removed God further off. Devotion can over-refine even beautiful ritual and worship with the same result.

20, 21. The Law was essentially a contract between two parties. Such a contract calls for a *mediator* to adjust relations between the two partners. The Law laid obligations on both sides, men to keep the Law and God to give the recompense. It was, therefore, a highly conditioned contingent affair. The *promise*, on the other hand, had not contractual element. It was the affair of one, absolute and unconditional. God spake and it stands. No mediation is needed. God is everything in the promise relationship.

The great truth Paul is probably trying to express is that under the faith dispensation there are no disturbing "ifs," no dubieties as to our salvation. It is the glory of the Christian faith that its promises are sure—they are God's affair and he never fails. *God forbid* is a strong term. Paul strongly resents the idea that the Law is hostile to the promise. It simply could not supply the moral energy that men needed: it could not quicken the new higher life and therefore could never save men.

22. *Scripture* may mean (1) O.T. in general, which included the Law; (2) definite O.T. passages, e.g., those quoted in Rom. 3 to establish universal depravity; (3) Psa. 143[2] or Deut. 27[26] (cf. v. 10). The Law that the Judaizers exalted as essential to salvation was the inexorable force rounding them all up into the same pit of despair and the one way out was by faith in Christ.

23–29. Under the Law, Subjection; under Faith, Sonship. "The Law was a regime of supervision. Before Christianity came we were under jurisdiction, confined like prisoners, with only one prospect of escape, the faith that was due for revelation. The Law has been a kind of guardian-tutor exercising a preparatory oversight only: the ultimate purpose was that by faith we should find acceptance with God. That faith is ours now: we are done with tutors; we have reached our spiritual majority, recognized in virtue of faith as sons in God's house, in the fellowship of Christ. All of you, Jews and Gentiles alike, are God's children in the fellowship of Christ by faith. All of you who were baptized into Christ adopt the Christ attitudes. There are no distinctions in Christianity—of race or class or sex. You are all one-and-the-same in Christ, and, as you are Christ's, you are already acknowledged as the true descendants of Abraham, his heirs as the promise specified, under no obligation to establish that claim by observing the Law as those Judaizers insist."

23. *The faith* as used here means almost "Christianity," the dispensation which required simply faith.

24–26. The *paidagogos* (tutor) was a male slave who took general charge over growing boys between the ages of six and sixteen. He did not merely bring the boy to school but kept him from evil courses. He was the symbol of minority age and immaturity. The Law, then, was not what finished off religious development as the Judaizers had claimed; on the contrary it covered our undeveloped stage: it was a moral caretaker that we outgrew. The point of the comparison is not that the Law brought us to the school of Christ: Christ the schoolmaster is an utterly inappropriate image; rules and regulations hold in school, but the mark of the Christian life is the freedom of a son in the house. The analogy lies in the temporary character of the tutor's rule, the irksome supervision he imposed like the Law. Confinement and restriction make a boy long for freedom. Christianity with its faith-relationship marks the real stage of maturity, that perfection of religion that had been wrongly identified with Jewish legalism.

27. At baptism we are "invested" with Christ. In the mystery faiths a robe was donned by the initiate, but here the reference is, rather, to the putting on of some garment on reaching maturity. The actor *put on* a robe. The robe at least signifies a new character and set of relationships, a higher form of manhood. It brings with it a more liberal outlook, an ability to transcend distinctions of race and class and sex. This linking of higher human qualities with the rite of baptism shows that Paul has no magical conception of baptism. Faith is the kernel of religious life to him, and that means the inward ethical spiritual urge is everything (cf. 1 Cor. 10[1-12]).

28. This loftier humanity to which we attain through Christ does not abolish distinctions but, rather, enables us to rise above them. The effect of Christianity has been to undermine the distinctions and work toward their abolition, e.g., slavery. Its method is not to overturn the constitution of society but to leaven humanity with this new spirit so that society changes itself. Paul saw Christianity drawing together into one fellowship all sorts and conditions of men. In Christ Jesus all racial differences and class prejudices dropped out of view. Men found something in common in Christ—a single higher level of personality.

29. We are Christ's in the sense that we are members of his: he is our representative. And in virtue of this membership in him we come to inherit the blessing that was promised, the kingdom of God. Christ's people enjoy his status. This determination of Paul to retain Abraham for Christianity reminds us how much Christianity drew from the O.T. It thus linked itself with the faith of the saints and sought not to destroy but to fulfill. Its policy in the mission field is still the same—to carry forward the earlier strivings of men to the higher and richer revelation in Christ. It has a right to inherit all religions because it has the kernel truth beneath all religion, the faith attitude that accepts the Father and the Father's purposes with childlike trust.

CHAPTER IV

1–7. The Fulness of the Time. The analogy suggests another point. "An heir is legally an infant, without rights, till he enters on his inheritance. We too had our time of religious tutelage under the elemental world-powers. But God's time matured for establishing a more liberal regime through his Son and the Spirit. (1) Jesus was born into the world-order under the reign of the Law to 'buy out' (*redeem*) those who lived under that slavery and secure for them the status of sons. (2) In view of your position as sons he endowed you with the spirit of his Son: it is that that teaches you to acknowledge God as Father. You rank now as sons, not as slaves any more, and heirs—all by God's doing."

It is not clear to what legal practice Paul refers. "We have no knowledge of a guardianship the period of which is fixed by the father" (Burton, *Galatians*, p. 214). The time of coming of age was usually fixed legally but some latitude may have been given the father about details. The tutor, or *guardian* (*epitropos*), had general charge of the child; the curator, or *steward* (*oikonomos*), looked after property and business affairs. Under Roman law the minor was under his tutor till the fourteenth year, and thereafter under the curator till the twenty-fifth. The father could appoint only the tutor, not the curator.

3. Under *we* Paul must include the Jews who had traduced him as well as the Gentiles. It was cutting them to the quick first to describe as slavery the Law on which they so plumed themselves and then to include them together with the Gentiles as equally under tutelage—babes in religion.

Rudiments was applied to (1) the letters of the alphabet, (2) elementary principles, (3) primary elements of the physical world of earth, air, water, (4) angelic beings who were believed to preside over the elements.

Under (2) "the undeveloped principles of religion" would be an apt description of the Law, and this same phrase is linked in Col. 2[8, 20-22] (notes) with "traditions and commandments," also apt definition of the Law. Rudiments *of the world*, however, is a clumsy expression for the Law. Under (3) the meaning would be "enslaved under the material things of the world," i.e., outward ceremonies, etc. Under (4) the most satisfactory sense is obtainable. There was positive fear of the stars and star-spirits as uncanny influences. It was, as the word here suggests, a real enslavement to be under them. In v. 9 there is the hint that these Galatians had taken specially to days and seasons, festivals which were fixed according to the movement of the heavenly bodies. Angel-worship was also a feature of the Colossian heresy (Col. 2[18]), and in 3[20] Paul quotes the idea that the Law was given by angels. These, then, would be *the guardians and stewards* (or overseers) of Jews and Gentiles alike. It must have wounded Jewish vanity to have their usages and feasts lumped together with the pagan rites and festivals that they despised.

4. According to Paul's view, Christ was uniquely related to God in that he inaugurated this new regime. He divided the old order from the new creation. Clearly, he is here regarded as a divine figure, sent forth into humanity, born of woman, subjected to a life of earthly conditions such as the Law, and specially associated with the gift of the Spirit. His function was to redeem us out of the bondage of the Law—which he achieved by accepting its conditions and completing its demand and canceling it. In Roman law, in adopting a son a man made a fictitious purchase from the child's own father.

The fulness of the time, i.e., the world's history was all articulated and predestined stage by stage according to the hidden counsels of God. (Cf. Paul's speech at Pisidian Antioch, Acts 13[16f.]; Ramsay, *Galatians*, p. 399.)

5. Jews require adoption as well as pagans. The characteristic note of the Christian faith is to know God as Father—the supremely intimate name that Jesus made his own. (Cf. C. G. Montefiore, *The O.T. and After*, pp. 204, 205.) The form of address *Abba* (=*Father*) was evidently established in the early church.

8–11. A Pitiful Relapse. To think that the Galatians should lapse from a faith so high and spiritual, and turn back to the poor flabby stuff of paganism! More in sorrow than in anger Paul makes his reproach. These old gods of theirs were not real gods. He does not deny their existence, but he denies their divine nature: they were demons, not gods. It is incomprehensible in those who had once come to know the true God, or, rather—for it was presumptuous to ascribe initiative or achievement in such knowledge to men—in those of whom God had graciously taken cognizance and to whom he had communicated his saving truth. It was fundamental to Paul's faith that God did everything: religion was his gift. God broke in upon his life, simply arrested him, on the Damascus road, and he interprets all religious experience in the light of his own (cf. Phil. 3^{12} 1 Cor. 8^{3} 1 Cor. 13). How can converts of his continue to lapse back to a superstitious worship of the uncanny powers of the elements? These deities had nothing of the might and grace of God, no strength to give, no power to save, no rich depth of nature to satisfy religious men. Actually to want to return to such bondage!—to a slavish round of sacred and festival days.

The external observances of Judaism—the Sabbath laws, festivals, etc.—had been introduced to the Galatians. The circumcision party regarded these as the ornaments of their faith. Paul here classes them with the pagan celebrations which the Jew scorned as orgies and superstitious rites. Back in Jewish legalistic ritual, they are back again at the level of their old paganism. Actually Paul was not far wrong. While these Jewish feasts had been ethicized and associated with great religious events in the history of Israel, they originated in pagan nature-worship; e.g., the Passover ran into the Feast of Unleavened Bread which marked the return of spring and the new crops, the Feast of Tabernacles retains features of the Feast of Ingathering as shown by the harvest decorations of the synagogue. (Cf. Oesterley and Box, *Religion and Worship of the Synagogue*, pp. 384f.) In the same way our saints' days take over ancient pagan ritual; e.g., casting pennies into a sacred well and hanging rags on neighboring bushes, as is done in the Highlands of Scotland to-day.

10. *Days* would refer to Sabbath; *months*, to the Passover, etc.; *seasons* (*times*), to festive seasons; and some take *years* of the Sabbatical year which fell 54–55 A.D., and certainly it would be piquant if Paul is writing the letter in this very year.

12–20. A Pathetic Appeal. The very thought of that pitiful relapse stirs emotion in Paul and he breaks away from theological argument into personal appeal. "Free yourselves," he urges, "(from bondage) as I have done, for I also was like you (enslaved). I have no personal complaint to make against you: you have never been anything but kind to me. You remember I came to you a sick man, forced your way for health's sake." This was "on the former of two visits," but perhaps we should simply interpret "at first" (cf. intro., p. 1208a.)

Paul had a physical ailment—perhaps disfiguring—which might have tempted them to despise or shun him (literally, "spit out," mg., v. 14)—as the ancients did on meeting a man with disease, to avoid the influence of the evil spirit in the man. This malady is variously interpreted as (1) ophthalmia (cf. v. 15), (2) malaria (intro., p. 1207a), (3) epilepsy, common in men of ecstatic experience and highstrung temperament like Paul, and regarded with peculiar horror in ancient times as suits the case here (but cf. Woods, *Was the Apostle Paul Epileptic?* and 1 Cor. 12^{7}).

They had received Paul as an angel (cf. Acts 14^{12}), nay, with greater respect still, as if he were Christ himself. Paul puts Christ in the supreme place, above angels. They had congratulated themselves on their privilege in having Paul. They would have plucked out their very eyes for him—a proverbial phrase, or, literally, to replace his own weak eyes. Now everything is changed—inexplicably. The Galatians seem to look on the apostle as their enemy. Why? Because he could not keep from insisting on the true gospel and challenging the false!

17. The Judaizers had gone about with specious propaganda, protesting the while that they were merely solicitous for the good of the Galatians. Paul answers that pretense. While he is out for the truth only, these Judaizers are not disinterested: they are partisan. "They are making much of you," says Paul, "but it is for no good end: their policy lands you on their doorstep, outside the pale of God's chosen, and that means you have to make much of them to gain admission to the elect. It is a nice thing to be made much of, provided it is for a good end. I don't mind others (like the Judaizers) making much of you—I don't want that to be restricted to when I'm with you—only, I say it must be for a good end." Solicitude is a fine thing when it is for a high object—such as salvation or liberty, not when it is the cloak to gain sectarian advantage. Ecclesiastical schemers have always been strong in unctuous ways.

19. Maternal tenderness bursts forth—*My little children*—more in John's style. Paul had been their spiritual mother and now he would fain see them "born over again." They are only babes, Christians in the making yet. Christ has to be *formed in* them, i.e., reembodied in each man. Conversion means that Christ reincarnates himself in us (cf. $1^{15,16}$).

20. Paul longs for a personal talk. Face to face they would understand one another better. His anxiety, love, hunger for their good, and all his emotions would become clear in the tones of his voice as they could not in a letter.

21–31. Bond Slaves and Free Men. (Cf. also 5^1.) Paul's subtle mind flashes to another point: he will confute the enthusiasts for the Law from the Law itself, and that too from the case of Abraham, their spiritual father. He had two sons—Ishmael, the slave-woman's child, born in the ordinary course of nature; Isaac, the freewoman's child, born when Sarah was past the normal age, in vindication of God's promise. Following the ingenious exegesis of his time, he sees therein an allegory. These sons adumbrate and correspond to the two covenants, the one given on Mount Sinai responsible for the enslaved legalists, the other issuing in the freedom of the Christian regime. Hagar would appear to be the Arabic name for Mount Sinai. The Hagarenes were an Arabic tribe (Psa. 83^6) who had shared in a conspiracy against Israel (cf. v. 29), and in Arabic legend Hagar was represented as Abraham's legal wife. The word "hagar" (meaning "stone" or "rock") would aptly describe rocky Mount Sinai, and Paul would know something of the language (cf. 1^{17}). Hence there was a specious reason for linking Hagar and Sinai. The Jerusalem of the time, under Roman rule, represented that old lineage of bondage, while the new Jerusalem—the ideal which according to Jewish ideas existed in heaven (cf. Rev. 21^2 Heb. 12^{22})—corresponded to the Christian Church.

29. According to ancient story (Gen. 21^9), Ishmael had mocked at Isaac, and legend had magnified that probably into persecution. Here was another correspondence—a foreshadowing of the persecution of the Christians by the Jews. And what did Scripture enjoin? The casting out and disinheriting of Hagar and her child, i.e., the Jewish people would lose its place in the Kingdom. They were utterly different in spirit from Christians and could not be copartners. Christians had secured freedom through Christ, and it was theirs now to stand fast in that privilege and not be caught again in a system of slavery.

CHAPTER V

1–6. An Appeal: Stand by Christian Liberty. Paul has established his case. Experience of the spirit within us and the testimony of O.T. revelation behind us combine to make clear that salvation is by faith, by the response of free moral personality to the gracious approach of God. Christ has canceled any claim that the old dispensation had upon us and he has done it to secure freedom for us. That means freedom from Mosaic regulation and from all external authority whatsoever. Man has spiritual autonomy; conscience is free to regulate its own life. Paul had caught the full significance of Jesus' teaching (Mt. 18^{18}). Men even yet are so inured to external ordering of their spiritual life that they refuse to take the air though the prison doors are open.

Exultant himself in the exhilarating air of freedom, Paul is amazed that his converts should want again to be confined by constricting observances. The Jewish Law from this standpoint is no better than their old pagan rites. Whatever others may teach, he, Paul, has his testimony to give (cf. 2 Cor. 10^{1f}). He challenges them to face the dilemma: Christ or circumcision. Circumcision was not an extra safeguard which could be added without injuring their Christianity; it was the acceptance of a principle radically different; it put a man outside the gracious relationship of faith and outside the sphere in which Christ could help him. To be granted status among the righteous and so be enabled to gain eternal life in the Kingdom is the objective of our Christian hope. This salvation comes through a spiritual attitude, a responsiveness to the working of God's Spirit upon us, and not through the following of outward fleshly observances. So Paul, having established the theory of his gospel, goes on to urge its practice.

7–12. A Pause for Expostulation. On the edge of practical exhortation Paul breaks off to recall how well they had borne themselves in the Christian life before this interruption of the Judaizers: "It was a fine pace you were keeping. But who cut in on you and kept you from following on the right way (literally, obeying the truth)?" The metaphor is that of running a race (cf. 1 Cor. 9^{24}), and some one or some impediment gets in the way as one blocks a road in war. "It is God who is calling you, but that was not his sort of counsel." It was an exhortation from some evil source to which they had listened. The evil was acting like an insidious leaven. Paul quotes a proverb (cf. 1 Cor. 5^6) significantly. They know to what or to whom he refers: (1) this false teaching about circumcision is poisoning the whole Christian life, or (2) the small Judaistic section are spreading their evil influence through the whole church. "As for myself I have confidence in you. I am Christ's and so are you, and that is my ground for confidence. I'm sure you will not do other than the right thing." They will take Paul's view of what constitutes true religion, the gospel of faith, and have nothing to do with this Judaizing influence. "The man responsible for confusing you will yet have his judgment to bear, no matter who he be." The reference may be to some one agitator who does not need to be named, as they all know him; or, less likely, to Peter or James; or to anyone who in the future may happen to upset them, as the construction suggests.

"And as for myself, if I am really an advocate of circumcision, why am I an object of persecution? Then the stumbling-block of the cross would be done away" (ironical). Paul had been accused of really standing for circumcision though he had pretended otherwise. Perhaps they quoted some of his actions against him (Acts 18^{18} 21^{26}) or his having Timothy circumcised (Acts 16^{3}), or even Titus (cf. 2^{3}). These actions looked like acceptance of the Law as binding after all. Paul, then, was a legalist. But if that were true, he would be popular with Jews, not persecuted as he was. The objection to him was that he preached a gospel of the Cross that did away with the Law. If he were a legalist, and not a preacher of the Cross, they would see nothing offensive in him.

"Would that those who are upsetting you would have themselves mutilated!" Paul utters a bitter, scathing word. They talk, talk about this cutting process—circumcision. Why don't they go further and go in for regular self-mutilation like the worshipers of Cybele? (Cybele was a popular deity in Asia Minor.)

13–26. Liberty Implies the Practice of Love and the Moral Life. Paul returns from his digression to state the implications of the Christian liberty to which the Galatians are called. Paul's letters, even the most theological, lead up to practical exhortation. He is no theorist, but knows well the welter of paganism and the stern problem of maintaining a Christian life in that environment. Converts have every temptation to slackness; so he must be always urging and encouraging. The call of Christ is to a life of freedom, but that did not mean, as some might welcome, the abandoning of the moral restraints. Liberty is not to be made an excuse (starting-point) for indulging the lower instincts. Service to legal prescription is gone, but service of another kind begins, loving service of one another. Christians do not strain over the minutiæ of the Law but they fulfill it in spirit. The whole idea behind the Law is carried out in one precept—"Thou shalt love thy neighbor as thyself" (Lev. 19^{18}). Jesus had found the whole essence of Law and prophecy in that command (Mt. $22^{36f.}$), and Paul here shows that he knew more of the Master's teaching than his few quotations suggest. An original mind does not repeat the letter but captures the spirit of his teacher as in 1 Cor. 13. The significance of *neighbor* has also been silently enlarged in Christianity (cf. Lk. $10^{29f.}$). Once meaning "fellow Jew," it now takes in mankind.

15. This law of love means that bickering in the Galatian church must cease. Nagging and snapping at one another, like wild beasts, they must take care and not prove one another's complete undoing.

16. There is no doubt a tug-of-war going on in human nature—flesh and spirit straining against one another: it is inherent in the constitution of things that we are not free to do as we wish. But if the spirit is the driving force in our Christian life, we will not be under the dictation of Law. There are two forces that may control human life: (1) the *flesh*, man's baser nature with all the evil lusts; (2) the *spirit*, the higher power, not native to man but given by God. Ideally, man gives himself over to the leading of the spirit and is spiritual. But the fleshly element struggles to keep the mastery, as Paul knew in his own experience (cf. Rom. 7).

19–21. These lists, which mirror pagan society, fall into four groups: (1) sexual vices: *fornication, moral impurity* (in its grossness, sins of the flesh), and *wantonness* (unrestrained indecency); (2) vices associated with heathen worships: *idolatry* (which might carry with it immorality practiced in pagan temples) and *sorcery* (literally, the drugs used for enchantment); (3) sins of faction: *enmity* (in general), *wrangling, jealousy* (of another's goods or fortune), *passionate outbursts* (of bad feeling), *self-seeking* (or party spirit), *dissensions, differences* (of opinion or sentiment rather than *heresies*), *envying* (preferable to the other reading *murders*); (4) sins of appetite: *drunken debauches, carousings* (as in honor of Bacchus). Cf. Rom. 1^{29} 13^{13} 1 Cor. 5^{10} $6^{6\text{-}10}$ Eph. 4^{31}.

22. The Law issues in painful toil and effort, i.e., "works"; but Christian virtues are *fruit* springing effortless and spontaneous from the inner principle of life. The catalogue corresponds significantly with vv. 19–21. (1) There are no sexual vices, the flesh is crucified; (2) for idolatry there is the enlightened ethical service of a righteous God—*love*, and for fear of demons is a *happy confidence in salvation;* (3) for enmity is *peace* with all men (rather than with God), *patience*, etc., *faithfulness* (i.e., fidelity rather than faith, which is the root, not the fruit of Christian life). Those who follow this way of life are in another atmosphere, beyond the artificial jurisdiction of legalism. There is no need to define these Christian graces further: they are a spirit, not a system to be catalogued like the Law.

In an age which valued the ecstatic, Paul here linked the Spirit indissolubly with wholesome ethical conduct and so set Christianity on the way toward right values (cf. 1 Cor. 12, 13).

24, 25. Christ in the flesh overcame and ended the power of the fleshly principle, and so all in mystical union with him died to sin in his death and are finished with the flesh, even with its inner disposition and desires. Yet there is no automatic attainment of goodness: we must strive to make our lives keep in line with the ideal within.

26. The reference is to the Judaizers who wanted to be fussed over (cf. 4[17]), or to the two parties, Jewish and Pauline, who each were parading their form of Christianity as superior, with an offensive note of challenge.

CHAPTER VI

1–10. Christian Social Obligation. *Brethren* strikes the keynote of the last chapter—an affectionate plea for Christian considerateness. News may have reached Paul of some case of harsh judgment, perhaps inspired by the fanatical spirit of these Judaizing Christians, and here he urges that if any man is detected in wrong conduct, or caught unaware by some temptation, the attitude of Christians—as possessors of the Spirit, one of the fruits of which is meekness—is not to cut him off, as one cuts off a broken limb, but to "mend" or "set" the limb (*restore* it—a medical term). Christian policy is constructive, not destructive. We must recognize that "to err is human, to forgive divine." If we bear one another's burdens, we shall find we are fulfilling the real law, higher than that of Moses, the law of Christ. What the Judaizers did was as Jesus protested of the Pharisees, to bind *artificial* burdens on men's shoulders—legal restrictions—a yoke unbearable (Lk. 11[46] Acts 15[10] 15[28]). The Christian was, rather, to lighten the real burdens of sorrow, sin, hardship, by sympathy and so fulfill the royal law (cf. 5[14] Mt. 8[17]).

3. *Thinking oneself to be "something"* is the tendency of a man who does not rely wholly on faith but on "works." The whole thing rests on a radical self-deception. To pride himself on a superior righteousness to his neighbor's and crow over him (as, e.g., circumcisionists might over the uncircumcised) is wrong: a man must put himself over against an absolute standard and test his actions in the light of the ideal. That would yield joy from one's own real achievement and not false satisfaction out of another's demerit.

5. Every man has his own pack to carry (here *burden* is a different word from v. 2, used of a ship's cargo, soldier's kit); i.e., his own responsibility, stewardship of which he must give an account—irrespective of his neighbors. Each Christian life has its own contribution to make and has its own possibility of weakness or failure. Let us see to that and not cast a comparative glance at others (cf. Mt. 7[1f.]).

6. The word here used, *taught, teacheth,* is specially applied to oral instruction: hence "catechetical," "catechumens." (1) Probably the reference is to paid teachers who gave full time and required *a share in all good things,* i.e., including material support (so Burton; cf. 1 Thess. 5[12] 1 Cor. 12[28] Eph. 4[11] 1 Tim. 5[17]). This is to assume that conditions of the second century existed in Paul's time. Some kind of instruction in doctrine and ethic must have been given, and Paul approved the principle of support for teachers though he himself preferred to earn his living (cf. 1 Cor. 9[11]). (2) The reference may be a delicate hint that the Galatians might have maintained closer spiritual relations with Paul, their teacher, instead of flying off after false teachers and neglecting to share this wonderful new teaching with him.

7, 8. It is weak to take this as a detached moral precept. It must be knit up with v. 6. Liberality toward spiritual teachers is sowing to the Spirit and would bring the spiritual man's reward—life on the higher level of the Kingdom. What is spent on spiritual teachers should come back to us in spiritual momentum. Those who, rather, spent their substance on carnal satisfaction were ministering to what was destined to decay and death. The materialistic sensualist need not look for resurrection. In 2 Cor. 9[6-10] this same simile is applied in reference to the collection for the saints. Others take *sowing to the flesh* of circumcision and legalism. *Eternal life* refers to moral quality of life, not temporal extension (cf. Rom. 2[7] 5[21] 6[22]), the blessedness enjoyed by spiritual beings who realize sonship with the Divine. *Mock* means literally "turn up the nose at"—probably a proverb.

9, 10. Some may have grown faint-hearted and lapsed as the Lord's coming was delayed. Paul was still sure of it. But to him it was no reason for slacking: time is a limited season in which we can seize our chances (cf. Lk. 16[1]). The reference to the *household of faith* seems to support the financial view of v. 6. Believers are a family (cf. Mk. 3[33-35]), hence the communistic movement, the collection for the poor saints, etc.

11–18. Conclusion: the Complete Sufficiency of the Crucified Christ. Paul regularly dictated to an amanuensis (cf. Rom. 16[22] 2 Thess. 3[17]

1 Cor. 16^{21} Col. 4^{18}). At this point he takes the stylus himself and adds a few words in bold characters, equivalent to underlining, intended for emphasis and to certify the genuineness of the letter. These words read aloud would add a touch of personal appeal and draw attention to the essential lesson which Paul wanted to teach.

12–16. Paul's personal word is very blunt: he imputes a motive to the Judaizers. They want to show up well before their fellow Jews by inculcating a Christianity that keeps up the old Jewish Law and so avoid persecution. In the very earliest days the Christians did not offend Judaism: they merely added to the praxis of good Jews the dogma that Jesus was Messiah. Paul discarded the Law and also linked the sacred Messianic office to the hated cross of a criminal (1 Cor. 1^{23}): he placarded the cross. The Judaizers suppressed the cross and made a show of zeal for the Law and, as nine-tenths-orthodox Jews, were unharmed. They gloried in the fact that the Christians were being circumcised—a worldly success for their policy. Paul had no pride in such worldly success: his glory is in an eternal truth—salvation through the cross. On the cross the fleshly principle was overcome for all time, and so Paul's old self was crucified there too. The present world meant nothing to him after that: it had no appeal. Externals like circumcision do not matter: one thing matters—the new inner life of the Spirit that transforms the whole being (cf. John 3^{3}). On those who conduct their life on that principle the apostle feels he can pray for blessing—the peace of God (in a world of factious strife though they be) and mercy (in the end at the Judgment). These followers of the spiritual life are, in spite of the Judaizers and the Mosaic Law, the real Israel, the faithful remnant who, according to Isaiah, were to be counted worthy to inherit the promised kingdom of God. Christianity proudly claimed the spiritual ancestry of Israel and thus linked itself with all the pious strivings of the best in the past. This was in line with Jesus' claim that he came to fulfill the law.

17. The Judaizers have troubled Paul much: for the future he wants no more mischief-making, no more cause for having to defend his right to apostolic authority: his authority is printed on his body: he has brands that stamp him as Christ's. Persecution had left marks on him (cf. 2 Cor. 4^{10} 11^{23} Phil. 3^{10} Col. 1^{24}). There may be a special reference: (1) he had received wounds in south Galatia (Acts 14^{19}); (2) he was a slave of Christ, and slaves were branded with the owner's mark; (3) Herodotus speaks of a slave who took refuge in a temple and there received on his body the marks of the god, after which *he could not be touched;* (4) Paul may have in mind the custom of carrying amulets. A papyrus (third century) has a charm in very similar language, but there it is a miniature coffin of Osiris that is carried. Paul was proud to fill up the sufferings of Christ (Col. 1^{24}). The marks he bore authenticated him and raised him beyond the slanders of such people as the Judaizers. He does not resent trouble. But what was the use of attacking a man with such a hallmark?

18. The strong Epistle ends in tenderness—*Brethren.* He prays that the gracious kindness that marked Jesus in the flesh, and is his characteristic gift always, may be theirs. That gift comes to the *spirit* that Paul has just vindicated over against the flesh.

EPHESIANS

By Professor C. H. DODD

Introduction

The Two Halves of the Epistle: Theological and Ethical. The Epistle falls naturally into two halves, the one mainly theological, speculative and mystical, the other mainly practical and ethical. Its structure may be compared with that of Romans. Just as the theological section of Romans culminates in the apostrophe of 11^{33} and the doxology of 11^{36}, and the ethical section opens with the "I beseech you therefore, brethren" of 12^{1}, so the theological section of Ephesians ends with the prayer of 3^{14-19} and the doxology of $3^{20, 21}$, and the ethical section opens with the "I beseech you therefore" of 4^{1}. In no other Epistle is the transition so clearly marked as in these two, though Galatians and Colossians also display the same broad division into two parts. The theological section of Ephesians, however, differs profoundly from that of Romans. The latter is closely argued, with a logical process from point to point, complicated, indeed, in Paul's manner by subtle cross-references, digressions and resumptions, but nevertheless constituting a continuous reasoned proof of a thesis. The tone of Eph. 1–3, on the other hand, may perhaps best be described as *liturgical.* It opens with a long passage in which a statement of God's reconciling purpose in Christ is put in the form of a sustained thanksgiving (1^{3-14}). Next follows a prayer which passes insensibly into a stately recitation of the dignities of Christ, the Head of the church (1^{15-23}). Next, in the same elevated tone, we have in ch. 2 a description of the work of Christ in the experience of the readers, passing into a proclamation of the unity and universality of the church—all this, not as a reasoned statement meant to convince, but as a prophetic declaration of incontrovertible, patent facts, in a new and lofty setting of eternal principles. Ch. 3 sets out once more to be a prayer, but pauses long upon a note of awed wonder at the part assigned to the apostle himself in a scheme involving all the universe and both eternities, before it reaches at last the intercession, in which the whole thought of the first part is lifted into the region of prayer, and the doxology, in which it is finally absorbed in praise. The whole section is a sustained piece of slow-moving, stately eloquence, never rising into the passionate poetry of Rom. 8^{28-39} or 1 Cor. 13, but never falling below the dignity of rhythmical liturgical prose.

The style of the second part of Ephesians is more varied. It starts (4^{1}) with an exhortation to keep the unity of the church, powerfully enforced by a fresh recitation of the divine basis and destiny of that unity. Then follows a series of paragraphs exemplifying in various connections and applications the fundamental moral principles which are embodied in Christ and so are of the essential being of his church, the whole forming perhaps the widest and fullest practical survey of the field of social relations to be found in any one continuous passage of the N.T. The section culminates in a picture of the Christian warrior arrayed in the armor of God for the conflict with evil (6^{10-20}). All that remains is a very brief epistolary conclusion without news or greetings.

Theme of the Epistle. The general theme of the Epistle may be said to be the glory of the church, as the society which embodies in history the eternal purpose of God revealed in Christ. This purpose is the ultimate unity of all being in him. While in the universe at large there are still unreconciled powers affronting the sovereignty of God, the ultimate issue is certain. God has determined to "sum up all things in Christ" (1^{10}). That might be pure speculation, but for the fact that history and experience witness to the reconciling power of Christ in the creation of that supernatural society in which warring sections of the human race are perfectly reconciled into a whole of harmoniously functioning parts—the church. That Jews and Gentiles should have found their place in the unity of the church seems to the writer the most signal manifestation of reconciling grace. And it is worth while recalling that the enmity of Jew and Gentile was one of the fiercest in the ancient world, and that in the third quarter of the first century it reached its climax in a conflict whose desperate ferocity shocked all beholders. Well might the author, writing about that time, see in the unity of Jewish and Gentile Christians in the one church *a mystery and a miracle.* He saw that the reconciliation was not accomplished by any kind of compromise between the diverse parties, but by a divine act creating out of both one new humanity. This new humanity is mediated by Christ. He sums up in himself the whole meaning of God, and communicates himself to men, so that humanity may come to realize and express that meaning. The church is "in Christ"; it is his Body, and its members have "put on" the new humanity which is Christ in them (2:11-22). Thus the corporate life of the church is a perpetual manifestation of Christ as the Fulfiller of the purpose of God. Its ethical practice, down to details, is a working out of that purpose on the level of human experience. The divine purpose which is thus being accomplished is a cosmic purpose. In the great universe, too, there is movement toward unity and completeness: Christ's work will not be done till the whole universe is one in him, to the glory of God. The living and growing unity of the church is, so to speak, a sacrament of the ultimate unity of all things.

Relation to Colossians and Philemon, and the Question of Authorship. The three Epistles, Ephesians, Colossians and Philemon, form a closely related group over against the other Pauline Epistles. Philemon and Colossians are linked by greetings from the same group of friends, and by the allusions to Archippus and Onesimus. Ephesians and Colossians are linked by the reference to Tychicus as the messenger by whom personal news omitted from the letters is to be communicated to the recipients. But beyond this formal link these two Epistles have very close connections of *thought and language*, which extend to whole sections similarly arranged in both. As Philemon does not deal with any of the doctrinal topics with which the other two are concerned, we cannot expect to find any of these contacts of thought; nevertheless there are subtle echoes of the language both of Colossians and of Ephesians. Further, the situation of the writer as a prisoner seems to be the same in all three. It is clear that we are dealing with an interrelated group of writings, and the critical questions they raise can best be discussed as one problem.

Denial of Pauline Authorship. The authenticity of all three as the work of Paul has been doubted, on grounds of divergences in thought and language from the undoubted Pauline Epistles. These divergences must be at once admitted, at least as regards Ephesians and Colossians, and in the case of each it is easy to make out a plausible motive for the production of the writing under the name of Paul. The teaching they put forth is new and important, and Paul's authority might well be used to commend it.

The case of Philemon is different. If it is not a genuine letter of Paul, then someone has been to extraordinary pains to produce complete verisimilitude. What is there in the letter which would make it worth anyone's while to take such pains? It puts forth no doctrine, touches no controversy, serves no ecclesiastical interest. It has, indeed, been suggested that it was intended as a *polemical tract on slavery*. The suggestion shows a complete misunderstanding of the letter. It may fairly be said that this is one of the cases where, at the risk of seeming to be "subjective," one has the right to say that the writing carries its authentication on its face. Nowadays, in fact, to reject it is a mere eccentricity of criticism. But its acceptance has a bearing on the more difficult question of the authenticity of Colossians and Ephesians. For Philemon shares, though in a lesser degree, in their peculiarities, and at least forms a bridge between them and the admitted Pauline Epistles.

The Argument from Style and Vocabulary. Ephesians and Colossians both show certain peculiarities of language as compared with other Pauline writings. Nor are these such as can be readily accounted for by lapse of time. The linguistic question cannot profitably be discussed in detail in a commentary not addressed to readers of Greek. Even the English reader, however, must be aware of a certain difference of style in reading, say, 1 Corinthians and Ephesians. An attempt has been made to reduce the vague feeling of style to precise terms by a measurement of Pauline rhythms (see H. J. Rose, *Journal of Theol. Studies*, Oct., 1923).

Then there is the difference of vocabulary. Both Colossians and Ephesians contain many terms not elsewhere used by Paul. Here again a statistical computation has been made (P. N. Harrison, in *The Problem of the Pastoral Epistles*). From a count of the new words appearing in Epistles undoubtedly written by Paul, and a comparison with the number of new words appearing in Colossians and Ephesians, Harrison finds that the proportion is about the same in each case. What is true is that the fresh vocabulary of these Epistles, especially of Ephesians, tends to be of a certain marked type. This, however, may perhaps be accounted for by the subject matter and the new lines of thought.

The Argument from Content: Colossians. To the subject matter and the new lines of thought we must now turn; for, indeed, the purely linguistic and stylistic arguments are not conclusive. That the Christology of Colossians is in some respects different from that put forth in any of the admitted Pauline Epistles is certainly true. For those who cannot think that Paul is likely to have made any serious new departure in his theological thinking during the comparatively short period covered by his Epistles—a period, too, falling fairly late in his life—this will seem a very weighty count against Pauline authorship. Yet Paul's thought can be proved to have developed within his earlier epistolary period, and countless instances could be cited of men, certainly no more free or versatile in their thinking than Paul, who made much more profound changes in their philosophy at an even more advanced age.

But it has been supposed that the type of thought attacked in this Epistle belongs to a later age than Paul's lifetime. This, which to a former generation of scholars seemed a formidable objection, has lost its force through the more adequate study of the early history of Gnosticism (cf. art., *Backgrounds*, pp. 849f.), which has shown it to be in its main outlines actually pre-Christian. There is, in fact, no difficulty in supposing that the type of "heresy" attacked in Colossians may have confronted Paul in the later stages of his ministry. The question is whether he is likely to have replied to it in just this way. The commentary will show that there is nothing in the Christology of Colossians which could not have developed, along lines of argument strictly analogous to those employed by Paul in undoubted Epistles, from positions assumed by him at an early stage.

More striking than the new Christology is the new attitude to existing social institutions as compared with 1 Corinthians. If Paul wrote Colossians, certainly he had greatly changed his mind since writing to Corinth. But was Paul incapable of learning from experience? As a matter of fact, already in the ethical teaching of Romans there is some foreshadowing of the change from eschatological fanaticism to the positive valuation of the social order in Colossians. If it be urged again that certain characteristic doctrines of "Paulinism," such as original sin, imputed righteousness, or justification by faith, are absent or unimportant in Colossians, the answer is that we do wrong to define "Paulinism" narrowly on the basis of Romans and Galatians alone, and that the central ideas of Paul's gospel (apart from the over-emphasis of certain aspects called forth by controversy) are as clearly and forcibly expressed here as in any other Epistle The supposed objections to Pauline authorship from the character of the thought do not, on examination, prove to be insuperable, or, indeed, if it be once conceded that Paul did continue to develop in thought after writing Romans, very cogent. We may therefore permit ourselves to be influenced by the strong impression which the letter makes of having been written at the same time as Philemon, by the same person, and in the same general situation.

The Argument from Content: Ephesians. The case of Ephesians is more difficult. On the one hand the recognition of Colossians as genuine might seem to help to establish Ephesians, which shares with it so many peculiarities. But since this Epistle, if genuine, must have been written practically simultaneously with Colossians, every smallest difference in style and thought is more difficult to account for than if the two could be regarded as separated by an interval. And the differences are actually by no means small. Even where the characteristic vocabulary of the two Epistles is the same, it is sometimes used with varying shades of meaning, surprising in letters written at one time. Again, though many of the ideas of Colossians, notably its "cosmic" Christology, reappear in Ephesians, yet the general emphasis and direction of the thought are often appreciably different. Then there is a difficulty in the reference to "apostles" (of whom Paul counted himself one) as the "foundation of the church," as though the writer were living in a period when the apostles were no longer living. There is also, apart from the reference to Tychicus, no evidence that the writer had personal knowledge of his correspondents or any interest in their particular concerns, whereas Paul had the deepest interest in Ephesus. It is therefore often held that the Epistle is the work of a disciple of Paul, writing after his death, and using Colossians as the basis of a new work in which he sought to set forth some fresh developments of Paulinism, true, as he believed, to the general spirit of his master, though never explicitly thought out by him.

This is a hypothesis which cannot be lightly dismissed in face of the undeniable difficulties of the theory of Pauline authorship. It is, however, itself not without difficulties. When Ephesians is compared closely with Colossians, it is by no means clear that Colossians is always prior to Ephesians. There are places where it would seem that if one is borrowing from the other the borrower is Colossians and not Ephesians.

The greatest difficulty, however, of the negative view is a *psychological* one. Suppose that the real author of Ephesians is someone other than Paul. Then he is at once a powerful and original thinker, and one who has entered into the very heart of Paul's own thought in such a way as to bring the whole course of his theological development to its predestined climax. For whether the Epistle is by Paul or not, certainly *its thought is the crown of Paulinism.* This supposed author, then, must have been a man of exceptional intellectual vigor. Yet he must be held to have modeled his great work slavishly on Colossians, certainly a less powerful composition, to the extent of imitating its arrangement and borrowing its phrases. Does one find such faithful dependence and such daring originality in one and the same person? Or is it more likely that the freedom and power of Ephesians, combined with such close similarity to Colossians, is the result of a more sustained and concentrated intellectual effort on the part of the same mind which had just produced the lesser work?

If this argument be felt to carry any weight, then the reader will be disposed to allow full force to the attempt made in the commentary to show that at several points the thought of the Epistle, rightly understood, has a deeper unity both with the specific thought of Colossians and with Pauline thought as a whole than sometimes at first appears; and that even those passages which seem least reconcilable with Pauline authorship are perhaps capable of being understood in a way consistent with it.

The difficulty of the un-Pauline style still remains. Yet there are passages which by their very roughnesses and imperfections recall the characteristic style of earlier Epistles. It is not easy to imagine such being produced by an imitator. If, however, Paul is the author, then we can say with something approaching certainty that *Ephesus was not the destination.* The objections to such an Epistle being sent to the Ephesians from the hand of Paul are, indeed, insuperable. But the name of Ephesus is not very securely attested in the address (see notes on 1^1), and it remains possible that the writing was something like an encyclical —a document intended to be read by a larger circle of Christian communities, some known, others unknown to the apostle. There are, indeed, difficulties in this hypothesis, but there are difficulties about any solution yet proposed to this perplexing problem.

Literature: Hort, *Prolegomena* to Romans and Ephesians; Westcott, *The Epistle to the Ephesians;* Dale, *Lectures on Ephesians;* Armitage Robinson, *St. Paul's Epistle to the Ephesians;* Abbott, *Ephesians and Colossians* (International Critical Commentary); Barry, *St. Paul and Social Psychology: An Introduction to the Epistle to the Ephesians.*

CHAPTER I

1, 2. Epistolary Address. The form of address is one of the various modifications of current convention found in the Pauline Epistles, and is closely similar to that in Colossians.

The words *at Ephesus* are absent in some of the best MSS. Similarly in Rom. 1^7 there is authority—though less strong authority—for the omission of the words "in Rome." The absence of the words might be accounted for in two ways: either (a) a letter originally addressed to a single church may have been later adapted to general reading by the omission of the name, or (b) a letter originally written either for general publication or to be sent to many churches may have been addressed in one particular copy—the ancestor of most of our MSS.—to the particular church mentioned. The former is generally thought to be the explanation in the case of Romans. In the case of Ephesians, the question is complicated by the fact that Marcion in the second century knew this Epistle as *The Epistle to the Laodicæans.* It is possible, therefore, that both Ephesus and Laodicæa may have possessed copies of the original letter, each naturally addressed to the particular church by name. Without the words *in Ephesus* the address might be rendered *to the saints who are also believers in Christ Jesus.*

3–14. Ascription of Praise to God for His Redeeming Purpose. Paraphrase: "Blessed be God who has given us all blessings of the heavenly life in Christ! From eternity he chose us for his own, and predestined us to be his sons through Christ, and this has come to pass by his grace toward us in the Beloved—to his praise and glory. For in Christ we have freedom, forgiveness, and (by his grace) knowledge of his secret purpose to bring the whole universe into unity in Christ—the same in whom we, who cherish this great hope, have been made God's own people, with a destiny before us that will redound to his praise and glory. In him *you*, my friends, who heard and believed the gospel, have received, in receiving the Divine Spirit, a present guarantee of the final consummation when the people of God will be wholly free—to his praise and glory."

It was a convention of the period to commence even ordinary letters with thanksgiving and prayer. Paul adopted this convention and used it to set what he had to say from the very outset in its true religious context. Usually he employed the ordinary phrase, "I thank God," in various settings; in 2 Corinthians he used the more Hebraic formula, "Blessed be God." This is the form here (which is not, therefore, either un-Pauline or unsuitable to a genuine letter). The ascription of praise is virtually complete in v. 3; but the thought of the blessings enjoyed in Christ branches out in various directions, and leads to the long chain of clauses, which formally are but one sentence, down to v. 14. It is a kind of hymn of the grace of God, in rhythmic prose. The sound and rhythm are the best guide to the articulation of the thought. We may take the recurrent phrase, *to the praise of his glory*, as a refrain rounding off the several strophes, which are introduced by the words *in whom.* We then have, first, an outburst of praise to God for all he has done *in Christ*, and then a meditation on those last two words, in three stages.

3. *Spiritual blessing* means more than blessing belonging to the non-material sphere; it is explained by v. 13. Blessings mediated by the Divine Spirit are enjoyed by Christians *in the heavenly places.* Christ, having left this mortal sphere, is alive on a higher plane of existence (1[20])—the plane on which discarnate intelligences live, evil as well as good (1[21] 3[10] 6[12]). But insofar as we are "risen with Christ" we too are denizens of this immortal sphere (2[6]; cf. Col. 1[12] 3[1-4] and notes there). The most real life of the Christian is not that ostensible existence which is still involved with material conditions, but the life in which he communes with eternal realities, which is the same life essentially that he will live beyond the grave.

In Christ (a phrase which governs the whole of this passage, and, indeed, in some sort the whole Epistle) is an expression apparently coined by Paul on the model of the common expression "in the Spirit." The underlying metaphor is derived from space-relations: Christ is thought of as the encompassing atmosphere (as it were) of the true life of the Christian community (which according to another metaphor is his "body"). It stands for the idea that Christians are in such inconceivably intimate spiritual relations with their Lord (cf. 1 Cor. 6[17]) that he may be regarded as in some sort an "inclusive personality," embracing the whole of the real life of his church, each member of which can therefore ideally use the words, "I live, and yet no longer I, but Christ liveth in me" (Gal. 2[20]). The content of this idea is greatly enriched and illuminated from various points of view by the argument of this Epistle (see intro.).

4. With this verse is introduced the thought (which runs through the passage) of the divine *choice*, expressed elsewhere as *predestination, good pleasure, will* (v. 5), *counsel*, or *purpose* (v. 11), conceived as prior to history and human experience. Philosophically the idea raises difficult problems of free-will and determinism. But here (and in the N.T. in general) it is not, primarily at least, a philosophical conception but a religious one. The more deep and powerful religious experience is, the more strongly is it colored by a sense of awe before that in God which utterly transcends our intelligence (cf. Rom. 11[33]). For Paul (and for the author of this Epistle, whether Paul or not) the deepest and most powerful religious experience is that of the grace of God, with all its riches of "spiritual blessing." It is all felt as utterly miraculous and mysterious, and at the same time as so urgently real that it is referred at every point to the direct working of God himself (see Col. 1[12], note). The sense of awe with which this experience is consequently suffused expresses itself in such language as this. As a contribution to theology it may be regarded as establishing the fact that in religious experience we are in touch with a free originating act of the mighty will of God, unconditioned by anything in the world or out of it. Where this fact is firmly held in view, religious thought is safeguarded alike from a mechanical determinism and from a mechanical legalism.

Holy and without blemish. The holiness and blamelessness spoken of in v. 4 are primarily (as in Col. 1[22], note) the marks of our present religious standing before God, not of our ultimate moral attainment; though this is not excluded from view in so wide-ranging an utterance as this. There is some doubt whether *in love* should be connected with what precedes (as generally in this Epistle); if it should, then it would most probably stand for the inclusive moral quality of the life which in a religious sense is holy and blameless. If it should be connected with what follows, it means the love of God as the foundation of his purpose for us. Either would give a good sense; the former is favored by the rhythm.

7. Cf. Col. 1[13], note.

8, 9. Insight into the *will* of God is part of "salvation" (cf. Col. 1[9, 10, 27]; and notes). Such insight involves the recognition of something which is not knowable in the ordinary ways of knowledge, but revealed as a *mystery* to faith, namely, the ultimate goal of the divine purpose. When the process of history is completed—*the fullness of the times*—all diverse and often conflicting elements in the universe will be brought into unity in Christ. *To sum up* means, in logic, to bring a multiplicity of concepts under one inclusive idea (Rom. 13[9]); in mathematics, to express in one quantity the value of many separate quantities. A cognate word is used of a corporation so completely organized that a single individual can fully represent the whole body and all its members (so in Xenephon, *Cyropædia,* viii, 1:15). In 1 Cor. 15[24-28] all powers in the universe are subjected to Christ, who then surrenders the sovereignty to God. In Col. 1[20] (see note) Christ reconciles all warring powers among themselves and to God. The thought here is similar (and therefore thoroughly Pauline).

11. The church is "the Israel of God" (Gal. 6[16]); and therefore God's *heritage* or lot, like ancient Israel (Deut. 9[29] 32[9]; cf. Rom. 9[25]). The sense is illustrated by comparison with 2[1-22] 3[6].

12. At this point it becomes important to determine what is meant by the *we* of this verse, as distinguished from the "ye" of the next. The same question arises at other points in the Epistle. Some hold that here and throughout *we* means Jews (Jewish Christians), and "ye" Gentiles. On this view the closing words of the present verse would refer specifically to Jewish believers, to whom the gospel first came (cf. Rom. 1[16]). The general sense would then be, "In the inscrutable providence of God it came about that we Jews were the first to hope in Christ, but you Gentiles (v. 13) none the less have been made a part of his people." The thought of the union of Jews and Gentiles in one church is one of the principal themes of the Epistle. Nevertheless, the distinction does not seem in place here, in a passage where *we* has consistently stood for the *whole* Christian community, and no indication is given that it changes its meaning at this point. Take the last words of v. 12, then, as meaning, not "hoped before others," but "hoped before the event" (cf. Rom. 8[24, 25]). Some day the unification of the universe in Christ will be manifest to all, but we, who have cherished this hope before the issue became plain, will be God's greatest glory. V. 13 then applies to the readers in particular ("you") what has been said of the church in general (cf. Col. 1[21]).

13, 14. The possession of the Spirit of God is appealed to as a matter of experience, a fact from which inferences can be drawn (cf. Gal. 3[2f.]). This experience of life in the Spirit is the *earnest* or "first installment" of full salvation (cf. 2 Cor. 1[22] Rom. 8[23]). Though the church has already been "redeemed" or "emancipated" (v. 7), yet in another sense this "emancipation" is future (cf. Rom. 7[24] 8[23]), and the present experience of the Spirit is "a first installment of our inheritance, pending the full emancipation of God's people." This conception of salvation as a state of blessedness which cannot be fully realized within the present order of things, and yet can be authentically enjoyed here and now in religious experiences, runs through the whole N.T., and may be traced back to the teaching of Jesus Christ about a "kingdom of God" for whose coming we are to pray, and which has already come (Mt. 12[28]).

15–23. Intercession for the Readers of the Epistle, Passing into Contemplation of the Glory of Christ in His Church. Paraphrase: "That is why I thank God for your faith, and pray constantly that you may have a clearer vision and a fuller apprehension of the infinite grandeur of all that is destined for you, and of the divine power that lies behind it—the power that raised Christ from death to the place of universal sovereignty. This sovereign Christ is the Head of the holy Community, which embodies in itself the totality of what he is."

The beginning of this section corresponds pretty closely with the normal epistolary opening of thanksgiving and prayer as we find it in most Pauline Epistles (and notably in Colossians); but the theme of thanksgiving having already expanded to great length in the preceding section, the writer passes quickly to prayer. Both thanksgiving and prayer are similar in content to those found in Col. 1[3-5, 9] (notes). The prayer, beginning in v. 17, passes insensibly at v. 20 into a statement of the dignity and work of Christ. There is no break grammatically at this point, but there is a break in the sense, and the prayer is not fully resumed until 3[14].

18. *Hope*, here as in Col. 1[5], is the thing hoped for, not the hopeful state of mind. It depends on God's *calling*, which is correlative to his "choice" (1[4]) and "good pleasure" (1[5]; see Rom. 8[29, 30] Gal. 1[15, 16a.]). The thing hoped for is otherwise described as the *inheritance* (so best here, not of the church as God's "heritage"). It is the state of full salvation with all that it involves. This spiritual estate (to carry on the metaphor) is God's (hence *his* inheritance) before it is "ours" (1[14]), and it is he who has delivered to us the "first installment," which makes it quite sure that ultimately the whole will be ours. We "inherit" not individually but as members of a "holy" community (the form of expression rests upon such passages as Num. 32[19] Judg. 11[2]; cf. Acts 20[32] 26[18]).

19, 20. The thought passes from the knowledge of God to the experience of his power as in Col. 1[9-11]; and this is associated with the resurrection of Christ, as in Col. 2[12]. For a writer who (like Paul and most Jewish thinkers; see p. 845b) did not hold the Platonic (and modern) conception of the natural immortality of man, all life from the dead is miracle, i.e., direct manifestation of divine power (and every true conversion is life from the dead; see below, 2[5]). Thus the resurrection of Christ after death is a standing proof of the reality and greatness of divine power, to which nothing is impossible.

21, 22. Christ is not merely alive from the dead, but is raised to the supreme place in the universe (cf. Phil. 2:9-11 Col. 1:16-18 2:10 3:3; and see notes on Col. 1:16-18 for the theology underlying this). The traditional names of the superhuman orders of being are used here, as frequently by Paul, with a certain carelessness, as of contempt, and the list is left incomplete with a kind of "et cetera." The word *name* is used because these titles of mythical beings were taken with great solemnity and used as "names to conjure with" in the literal sense. The pronunciation of the appropriate names was held to call forth immeasurable powers, and such invocation was very frequent in magical practices (cf. Acts 19:19 for such practices at Ephesus). Paul says, in effect, "name all the names of power you know, and still there is a Power supreme over them." For the two worlds or ages, cf. Col. 1:13, note.

22. The transition from Christ's sovereignty in the universe (which is a matter of faith) to his sovereignty in the church (which is a matter of experience) is made exactly as in Col. 1:17. The full significance of this connection of ideas comes out more fully later in this Epistle (especially 3:9-11). The church is here, as in Colossians, the body of which Christ is the head; a figure closely similar to that found in earlier Pauline Epistles, where the church is "the body of Christ," or "one body in Christ" (1 Cor. 12:12, 27 Rom. 12:4, 5). In both cases the underlying idea is the same, namely, that the unity of the church is grounded in an inconceivably intimate connection with Christ, as well as a complete subordination to him.

23. The church is the *fullness* (*pleroma*) of Christ. The precise meaning of this statement is not clear. The technical sense of *pleroma* is explained in Col. 1:19, note. We may not, however, assume that this precise technical meaning is in place here. Yet the root meaning, "full content," "totality," which underlies the technical use, must be maintained here and throughout the Epistle. Thus in 1:10 "the fullness of the times" means the time-process as complete. In 3:19 we have the expression "the *pleroma* of God," closely similar to "the *pleroma* of deity" (i.e., the totality of the divine attributes) in Col. 2:9. Now, according to Colossians the *pleroma* of deity resides in Christ. Thus in Eph. 4:13 we read of "the *pleroma* of Christ," which we may take to mean the full content of the divine nature and character as embodied in Christ. This, further, is something to which the church, according to 4:13, is to attain. It is therefore the less surprising to learn in the present passage that the church is itself ideally the *pleroma* of Christ, in the sense that it embodies in its own life and experience the whole meaning, value, and power of the life of its Head. Accordingly, we can understand the prayer of 3:19 that the church may be completed until it becomes a *pleroma* of God, i.e., until its perfected life expresses the whole of the life of God as revealed in Christ. The thought is difficult, but not unintelligible in the light of Paul's deep mysticism. Its governing assumption may be put in the form that Christ is to the church as God is to Christ (cf. 1 Cor. 11:3).

We now turn to the second part of the verse. Here it is doubtful whether the verb *to fill* is to be understood as active or passive. In 3:19 it is the church which is filled, or completed, and in 4:10 it is Christ who fills. We should therefore expect here the sense given by the R.V. *who filleth all in all;* and this, indeed, may be the sense (except that the implied meaning would be more accurately—"who is gradually filling"). But if so, the grammatical form of the verb is very exceptional. It should naturally mean "Christ who is being filled, or completed." If Christ is thought of as an "inclusive personality," *in* whom the church lives and grows (2:21) and *in* whom the whole universe is ultimately to be "summed up," then there is a sense in which he is not complete until this process is finished. Thus it would be possible to understand the whole verse as meaning "the church, as being his body, expresses the totality of Him who is everywhere and in all respects growing complete."

CHAPTER II

1–10. New Life in Christ: The Witness of Experience to the Grace of God. Paraphrase: "Of that holy community you are members. Once you were no better than dead—so deeply were you implicated in the wickedness of an evil world-order, whose governing principle is active to-day in pagan society. We were *all* implicated in it, for we were at the mercy of our evil impulses and ideas, destined to a terrible retribution. But God was so infinitely loving and pitiful that even when we were dead in our wickedness he raised us from death to a heavenly life with Christ. This establishes for all succeeding ages the wonderful wealth of his graciousness in Jesus Christ. For it is by his grace that you have been delivered, through trusting him; and even that trust itself was his gift and no merit of yours. We are his handiwork, created by him in

Jesus Christ to do good according to his purpose from of old."

The passage of thought from the universal dignity of Christ, through a reference to his lordship in the church, to a direct appeal to experience in verification, is parallel to the movement of thought in Colossians from 1^15-20^ to 1^21-23^ (cf. also Col. 2^13-15^; and notes on both these passages). There is no real break in sense or grammar at Eph. 1^13^. The theme—continued in the present passage—is still the power of God as witnessed by the resurrection of Christ, and now by our resurrection with him. Parenthetically the writer dwells on the condition out of which Christ raised us (2^2, 3^). He then returns and completes what he started to say. This line of thought reaches its natural conclusion in v. 6. But in developing it the writer has been led, through contemplating the terrible and hopeless condition in which man lies apart from God, to feel acutely that nothing but sheer grace could meet such a situation. So the thought passes from the power of God to his love, pity, grace, kindness. It is these qualities which form the subject of vv. 7–10. Yet they are, after all, another manifestation of the power; for they too are creative (v. 10).

2. Non-Christians are living still in *this world* (or *age*), while Christians live in "the age to come" (see Col. 1^13^, notes). This age is thought of as under the domination of spiritual powers hostile to man's true life (cf. 1 Cor. 2^12^ 2 Cor. 4^4^ Gal. 1^4^).

3. That which in experience bears witness to that domination is the inward power of evil instincts (*the desires of the flesh*) and false ideas (*the desires of the mind*). The writer associates himself with his readers as having known what it was to be under this dominance of evil (if he is Paul we may aptly compare Rom. 7^7-24^). In that condition all were *children of wrath*, i.e., according to a common Hebraic idiom, "within the sphere of wrath." *Wrath*, as in Paul regularly, is not an emotion of anger in the mind of God, but a process of retribution in history (cf. Rom. 1^18f.^ 1 Thess. 2^16^). The meaning is not that an originally corrupt nature made us children of wrath; Paul uses *nature* either in a neutral sense (e.g., Rom. 2^27^ 11^21-24^ Gal. 2^15^ 4^8^) or in a definitely good sense (e.g., Rom. 2^14^ 1 Cor. 11^14^; cf. Rom. 1^26, 27^, where that which is "against nature" is therefore wrong); the sense is that within a natural order itself good, evil character and conduct necessarily bring disaster. It is just the fact that in a universe of God's making man has nevertheless brought destruction on himself that makes the tragic knot Christ came to unravel.

6. *Raised us up*, and *made us sit* simply repeat the verbs used about Christ in 1^20^. The underlying thought is the intimate "mystical" union of Christ and his people (cf. Col. 2^20^, note). Here, however, the "death" out of which we rise is not the fellowship of Christ's death to sin (as in Rom. 6^2-4^), but the moral and spiritual condition which is the exact opposite of "eternal life" (as in Col. 2^13^, cf. Rom. 7^10, 11^). Note that here as in Col. 1^13^ salvation is regarded as an accomplished fact, though in Eph. 1^14^ (see note) it is an object of hope.

8, 9. A most precise formulation of the central Pauline idea: we are saved—not *by* faith, but—*by grace, through faith:* the efficient cause is God's grace alone, and our faith (not our works—the familiar Pauline antithesis) is the condition of its exercise (cf. Rom. 4^2, 16^). A parenthesis makes it clear that "saving faith" must not be regarded as a meritorious activity of the human will, but as itself God's gift. To press this into a theory leads to great difficulties, but it is vital to religion as Paul conceived it (see notes on 1^3-14^ Col. 1^12^).

10. *Good works.* They are a result, not a cause of salvation (Jas. 2, notes).

11–22. The New Unity of Mankind in Christ. Paraphrase: "Remember that there was a time when you, as pagans, were entirely outside the divine society (as represented by the Jewish people), and had no part in the purpose of God. But Christ has by the sacrifice of himself brought the outsiders in. It was the institutions of the Jewish Law that kept us apart and made us enemies one of another. This Law Christ has abolished: he has broken down the barrier and made peace between the hostile sections of the human race. In doing so he has brought into being a new type of humanity. And so we are now one body, animated by one Spirit, and reconciled to God. The consequence is that you, formerly outsiders, are now members of the family and commonwealth of God. That commonwealth is like a great building, which, with the prophets and apostles for its foundations and Christ for its coping-stone, is growing into a temple of God. Into this temple you are being built, and in it God dwells."

In this section we have the first express exposition of what is the specific central idea of this Epistle. The writer has just reminded his readers of their experience of the life-giving grace of God. That experience is the "first installment" (1^14^) of God's ultimate purpose; so far he is recapitulating what must have been familiar to all Pauline Christians. He now calls their attention to one special aspect of Christian experience, namely, *the experience of unity in a true commonwealth*, which for him is the "first installment" of the unity of all being spoken of in 1^{10}. This is more definitely new teaching, and it is set forth with some elaboration. There are points of close contact with Col. $1^{20, 21}$ 2^{14}.

11. Here for the first time the readers are identified, for purposes of argument, with Gentile Christians in general; but note how carefully the writer avoids identifying himself with Jewish Christians over against them ("*you* that were far . . . *them* that were nigh" [v. 17; cf. v. 13]; while *we* [v. 18] stands for the Christian community as a whole). With the attitude to circumcision cf. Col. 2^{11}, note.

12. *The commonwealth of Israel* is an ideal community, continuous in history (cf. Rom. 9–11, where the whole philosophy of the matter is expounded); temporarily embodied before Christ in the Jewish nation, to which the *covenants* historically appertained (cf. Rom. $9^{4, 5}$). Consequently, before Christ non-Jews were alien from the divine commonwealth, and belonged to "the world," under the dominion of the "world-rulers" (6^{12}).

13. Here already Isa. 57^{19}, quoted in v. 17, is present to the writer's mind. The reference to this prophecy determines the course of the argument, which, formally regarded, is a demonstration that Isaiah is speaking of Christ and his reconciling work. Cf. Rom. 10^{5-15}, where the argument is similarly based on the continuous exegesis of an O.T. passage. The method is thoroughly Pauline. On the *blood of Christ* see Col. 1^{20}, note.

14, 15. The *enmity* and *peace* spoken of in these verses are primarily between sections of the human race, though, as the hostility of man to man is bound up with alienation from God, so reconciliation among men involves reconciliation to God (vv. 16, 18). It is best to take *the enmity* in apposition to *the middle wall of partition* (as the reality of which that is the figure), instead of in apposition to *the Law* as in R.V. We may render, "He made both one and destroyed the dividing barrier of enmity, by abolishing the Law with its statutes and precepts." The words *in his flesh* might be connected with either clause, signifying that it was through his human life and death that Christ effected this. It is an important point that the abolition of the Law was necessary if Jews and Gentiles were ever to meet on equal terms in one society; for the Law was essentially a national institution, and it was valued precisely for its effectiveness in maintaining the separateness of the Jewish people. The new unity is not simply a reconciliation of Jew and Gentile as such; it is a creative act (cf. v. 10)—the creation of a new human type, which is neither Jewish nor Gentile, but Christian. In fact the *new man* is Christ living in his church (cf. 4^{13-16} Col. 3^{11} Gal. 3^{28}).

16–18. Note the close parallelism of the clauses *to reconcile both* | *in one body* | *unto God* | *through the cross: we both have access* | *in one Spirit* | *unto the Father* | (through him). The one body and the one Spirit are correlative ideas (cf. 4^{4} 1 Cor. 12^{13}). The *body* is that mystical body of Christ, the organ of his personality, which had a temporary manifestation in his body of flesh destroyed on the cross, but a more permanent manifestation in the church, which is constituted his body because his indwelling Spirit creates its common life.

19. Gentile Christians are thus no longer foreign to the divine commonwealth; nor are they mere "resident aliens" in it. (The term translated *sojourners* was used to denote residents in a Greek city without full civic rights, and the corresponding term in the O.T. to denote Gentiles resident in Israelite territory.) This was, in fact, the status to which the old Judaizing party, Paul's lifelong adversaries, had wished to confine Gentiles in the church. They are full members of the holy community. Thus is signalized the success of Paul's long championship of Gentile rights.

20, 21a. The figure of the body is suddenly changed (the change being mediated by the reference in v. 19 to the "household" of God) into the figure of a building (cf. 1 Cor. 3^{10-17}). O.T. passages lie behind this figure, especially Isa. 28^{16} Psa. 118^{22}. (Cf. also 1 Pet. $2^{4f.}$ Mk. $12^{10, 11}$, with expanded parallels in Matthew and Luke.) The foundation of the building here (unlike 1 Cor. 3^{11}) consists of the apostles and the (Christian) prophets (cf. 3^{5} Mt. 16^{18}); and Christ is the *chief corner stone*, i.e., probably the stone forming the angle of a pediment or gable, and so completing the whole building. Thus the "chief corner stone" is to the building what the head is to the body, and the two figures are kept parallel. Yet it is impossible to make the analogy adequate to describe the relation of Christ to his church, for it is "in him" (see note on 1^{3}) that the whole process of its growth or upbuilding takes place. The phrase *each several building* is required by the strict grammatical rules of classical Greek; but it gives no good sense; for the idea of a great church composed of federated churches is entirely alien, and if Jews and Gentiles were meant, we should have had "both" and not "every." But the looser grammar of Hellenistic Greek allows the

A.V. rendering "the whole building," which is appropriate.

21b, 22. Note again the close parallelism: *in whom* | *the whole building* | *fitly framed together groweth* | *into a holy temple* | *in the Lord: in whom* | *ye* | *are builded together* | *into* (mg.) *a habitation of God* | *in the Spirit*. What is said of the whole church is applied with precision to the special case of the readers. And observe that *in the Lord* and *in the Spirit* are closely related expressions.

CHAPTER III

1–13. The Revelation of the Mystery. Paraphrase: "For this reason I am praying for you here in my prison. You know what God has done for me—how he has given me insight into his deepest truths. I can only refer you to what I have already written for proof of this. In former generations no one suspected the truth which has now been revealed to the apostles and prophets of God, namely, that the non-Jewish peoples stand on the same footing as Jews in the purpose of God—partners in the great inheritance, members of the same body, sharers in our high destiny in Christ. This is the glorious secret that I have been divinely commissioned to proclaim. The very existence of the Christian society is a plain demonstration to all discarnate intelligences in the universe of the many-sided wisdom of God in his age-long purpose embodied in Christ, our sole and sufficient Ground of assurance. Since this is the truth for which I am imprisoned, there is nothing in my imprisonment to cause you either discouragement or shame."

The words *for this cause* clearly begin the sentence which is completed in v. 14; i.e., the writer is intending to hark back to his interrupted prayer (1^{17-19}). The sentence, however, is scarcely begun when a fresh interruption occurs. Paul feels the need to say something about his own standing in relation to the readers and in relation to the remarkable ideas which he is communicating. He is a person intrusted with a special revelation which he dare not keep to himself. He therefore states first briefly and decisively the content of this revelation (vv. 5, 6), and then passes on to speak of the task in consequence laid upon himself (vv. 7–13), with a fresh parenthesis (vv. 10–12) further developing the idea of the revelation of an ancient secret. The section has an intricate parallelism with Col. $1^{23, 29}$ (notes). For further Pauline parallels cf. Rom. 1^{11-16} 15^{15-19} (with some remarkable echoes of language) and 16^{25-27}.

2, 3. This conviction of having, through the sheer *grace of God* and through no merit of his own, received a direct *revelation* is thoroughly characteristic of Paul (cf. 1 Cor. 3^{10} 4^{1} Gal. $1^{12, 16}$ 2^{2} 2 Cor. 2^{10-14} $12^{1f.}$). This is for him nothing to boast of (2 Cor. 12^{5}), for it not only leaves him no scope for the display of intellectual distinction (1 Cor. 2^{3-5}), but even leaves him no free choice in the matter of his life-work (1 Cor. 9^{15-18}). Hence the combination of this lofty sense of a divine mission and authority with a humility which is not mock-modesty (v. 8). The reference to something he *wrote before* is to vv. 11–22 (not to a previous letter). If the readers will attentively consider what they have just read they will see that, brief as it is, it contains something that could only have come to a man through divine illumination, and therefore understand why the author takes such an authoritative tone.

5. The revelation comes *in* (by) *the Spirit*, and therefore to "spiritual" or inspired men, and especially to *apostles* and *prophets*, the first in the various orders of inspired ministries (4^{11} 1 Cor. 12^{28}). If, therefore, Paul is the writer, he is claiming no more than we know him to have claimed. Yet in Col. $1^{25, 26}$ the mystery is revealed to the "saints" or members of the holy community in general.

6–9. A precise definition is given in v. 6 of the content of the "mystery" (v. 4; cf. v. 9). In Col. 1^{27} it is otherwise stated (but see note there). In 1 Cor. 2^{6-10} the "mystery" is (as in v. 10 below) the mode in which the divine "wisdom" exists, and it refers especially to future glory. So in Col. 1^{27} it concerns "the hope of glory," and in Eph. $1^{9, 10}$ it refers to the ultimate "summing-up" of all things in Christ. In Rom. 11^{25} one particular aspect of the "mystery" is touched upon, namely, temporary "hardening" of Israel with a view to the ultimate gathering-in of the Gentiles. In Col. 1^{27} the reference to the conversion of the Gentiles is present in the context, and here it is made the central feature of the "mystery." Thus there is a real coherence in all references to the "mystery" in the Pauline Epistles, only that different aspects of it are emphasized in different places, and if we compare the earlier Epistles with the later we observe on the whole a tendency to give increasing emphasis to present experience in the church as a part of the revelation of the "mystery."

10. In 1 Cor. $2^{7, 8}$ the "mystery" of the divine wisdom was concealed from "the rulers of this age" (i.e., the superhuman orders of being, the "world-rulers" of Eph. 6^{12}), when they brought about the crucifixion of Christ. Now the existence of the Christian Church, uniting the hostile sections of the human race in one body, is a plain proof which these "world-rulers" cannot ignore, that God is, in fact, summing up all things in Christ. Note here (1) the idea that the final cause of man's salvation lies outside man; it is the manifestation of God's *manifold* (many-sided) *wisdom* (as in 2^{7} it is the demonstration of his grace); and (2) the cosmic interest, present also in 1^{10}, as it is dominant in Colossians. This harmonizes the points of view of the two Epistles; in both the ultimate destination of the divine purpose is cosmic; but in Ephesians attention is in general fixed upon the critical stage of that purpose represented by the creation of the church.

13. The note of prayer returns; but it is probably to be understood as a prayer of Paul for himself (whether penned by him or put into his mouth). In 2 Cor. 4^{7-18} Paul describes the terrible "afflictions" attending his work, but adds (v. 16) "we do not give in (or faint)." Now, an older man, and in prison, he prays (using the same terms) that he may not give in or *faint* in the face of greater afflictions.

14–21. Renewed Prayer and Adoration. Paraphrase: "And so I am praying for you to the Father of all, from whom all family life in heaven and earth derives its name and nature, that by the strength of the Divine Spirit and the indwelling of Christ you may be so deeply rooted in the love which binds his family together that you will apprehend the full scope of his love, and come to embody in your corporate life the full content of the divine nature. God can do for us things beyond all our imagining through his power working in us. To him be all praise in and through Christ, in and through the Christian society, for all generations!"

Having worked back through devious ways to his original point of departure ("prisoner for you Gentiles," v. 1, "tribulations [afflictions] for you," v. 13), the writer continues with the originally intended sequel to v. 1, his prayer for his readers. The R.V. somewhat obscures the articulation of the prayer. There are, first, three petitions: (a) for spiritual strength, (b) for the indwelling of Christ, (c) for moral stability (*rooted and grounded in love*, v. 17). Cf. the threefold prayer of Col. 1^{9-11}. On this follows (v. 18) the prayer for knowledge (life precedes knowledge and is its condition). This is the prayer to which he has been working up since 1^{16} (cf. 1^{17-19}). Lastly comes the final issue of it all—a consummation which cannot be confined to any one range of experience, whether moral or intellectual, but can only be defined in terms of God himself, the religious Absolute.

15. There is here a significant play upon words, for the Greek word used for *family* (*patria*) is derived from the word for *father* (*pater*). The etymological kinship of the words suggests a real kinship in idea: each family-group on earth is called by a name which recalls the one universal Father, and rightly recalls him, for he is the source of all true family relations.

18, 19. The four dimensions, with the word *fullness* (*pleroma*, on which see 1^{23}, note), are echoes of current religious language of the period in Gnostic or mystical circles (cf. the mystery-language of Col. 1^{19} $2^{8,\ 9,\ 18}$, and notes there). Originally the dimensions seem to have been thought of as those of the heavenly "house of Almighty God." Here, in association with *pleroma*, they convey the suggestion of absolute completeness and finality in religious experience, without inviting further definition. Such language is appropriate to the revelation of a "mystery," and yet it is used, in the spirit of Col. 1^{26-29} (notes), of experience accessible to the simple believer in Christ. The important word is *love*. The kind of knowledge which is of ultimate worth is not intellectual apprehension of abstract principles, but personal apprehension of the love of Christ (i.e., the love that Christ has for us; cf. Rom. 8^{35}). This love *passeth* (or transcends) *knowledge*, probably not in the sense that love is a greater thing than knowledge (as in 1 Cor. 13^{2}), but in the sense that it is too great to be fully known. We have, then, a paradox—a prayer for knowledge of that which is unknowable. But ultimate religious truth is often paradox to the logician. Note that the true knowledge is only to be enjoyed *with all the saints*, i.e., in the fellowship of the Christian society.

CHAPTER IV

1–16. The Christian Society: Unity Through Diversity of Function. Paraphrase: "I urge you therefore to live a life worthy of this great destiny; and above all to preserve the unity of the Christian society by love to one another. For the church is one, as being the organ of the one Spirit of God. God is one, the Source of all being; Christ is one, the Lord of our society; and we have a common faith and hope expressed in the common rite of baptism. The endowments we possess individually are derived from Christ—for, indeed, the very purpose of his incarnation and exaltation was that he might communicate the content of his own nature to man and the universe. Our endowments, therefore, are directly related to function within the society, as apostle, prophet, preacher of the gospel, or leader and teacher. The object of all such ministries is the consolidation of the society which is the body of Christ, and its growth to social maturity, i.e., to the point at which it fully expresses the whole of what Christ is. We must not be like helpless children, the sport of any chance external influence; we must grow up by affirming the truth in the practice of love. The standard and goal of our growth is, in fact, Christ, the Head of the society; and the body grows to maturity through the contribution made by every individual member in dependence on him."

From this point onward the Epistle is concerned with the presentation of Christianity as *social ethics*. The general form is hortatory, though there is much exposition of principles by the way. The present section deals with the conception of the Christian society as such, calling attention to its religious basis, and emphasizing the importance of individual endowment for function as contributing to the progress of the community.

3, 4. *Unity of the Spirit* is more than "unity of spirit" in our reduced sense of the phrase. It is a unity produced by the power of the Spirit of God in the lives of all its members. The best commentary is 1 Cor. 12[4-14, 27, 28]. "Inspiration," or possession by a spirit, was a common feature of religion at the time quite apart from Christianity. The Christian standpoint is that monotheism implies necessarily that all inspiration having religious value is produced by the *one Spirit*, the Spirit of God or of Christ. Thus the principle of social unity in the church is given in religious experience (cf. 2[16, 18], notes).

7–10. A fresh stage in the argument begins with v. 7. Hitherto the emphasis has fallen on the unity of the social organism. Now it is to pass to the diversity of function by which this unity is made real. But the argument is complicated by the introduction (v. 8) of a piece of exegesis of the O.T. (Psa. 68[18], quoted in a form different from our Hebrew text and from the LXX; the chief variation, from "received" to "gave," is known to follow a Jewish exegetical tradition). The parenthesis (vv. 9, 10) has the purpose of identifying what is spoken of in the psalm with the work of Christ. The descent *into the lower parts of the earth* is probably not the "descent into hell" of the Creed, but the incarnation itself regarded as a descent from "the heavenly places" to the earth as the lower plane of being (the form of words in the original would admit of such a rendering). *That he might fill all things* probably means more than that the purpose of the incarnation and ascension was to bring all things to completion. The suggestion is that by passing through all planes of being Christ is able to become immanent, as it were, in every part of the universe, and to fill it with the content of his own being (cf. Jer. 23[24]). It is another aspect of the "summing-up" of 1[10].

11–14. Paul returns after the parenthesis to the thought of v. 7, but with the ideas of vv. 9, 10 as a background. In furtherance of his purpose to "fill the universe" with himself, Christ endowed the church with ministries for its *building up* (v. 12), until it reaches the standard of the *fullness* (*pleroma*) of Christ (v. 13); i.e., until it perfectly realizes and expresses all that Christ is (as ultimately the universe will realize and express his fullness). This idea is set forth under the figure (already introduced in 1[23] 2[16] 4[4]) of a body (which crosses the figure of a building introduced in 2[20]). A *full-grown* human body is a "mature" man—for such is the meaning of the word *perfect* (v. 12), which is, however, chosen with a side glance at its use in the sense of "fully initiated" (cf. Col. 1[28], note). The *stature* of the full-grown man is measured by the standard of all that Christ is (his *fullness*). It is thus suggested that "perfection" in the full sense is not anything to be attained by an isolated individual, but the goal of the Christian society (though in another sense each Christian is to be perfect: Col. 1[28]).

15. The reference here is not to the duty of veracity in ordinary intercourse (which is introduced in v. 25), but to the affirmation of *the truth* (as opposed to the "wiles of error" in v. 14).

16. The basal idea is the same as in Col. 2[19], but Ephesians brings into prominence the thought of individual function as a contribution to the growth of the whole. We thus get a very fine and full statement of the conception of a social organism.

17–24. The Christian Society the Moral Antipodes of Paganism. Paraphrase: "There must, therefore, be a clear and substantial distinction between the morals of the Christian society and those of paganism. *There* you have darkness, ignorance, alienation from the life of God, with consequent outrageous vices. That, as you know, is the exact reverse of all Christian teaching, which calls for a radical moral change—the abandonment of evil desires, a transformation of moral values, and the assumption of a new character exhibiting the divine ideal of righteousness, holiness, and truth."

As the account just given of the "social organism" provides the positive basis of Christian ethics, so the present section serves to define them negatively *by contrast with the prevailing practice of the pagan world.*

18, 19. Cf. Col. 1[21]. But the best commentary is Rom. 1[21-32]. There we are told that because men willfully rejected the knowledge of God (cf. *ignorance,* v. 18) and gave themselves over to futility (the *vanity* of v. 17) God abandoned them in their lusts (cf. v. 22) to "impurity" (the *lasciviousness* and *uncleanness* of v. 19) and to the anti-social sins (the *greediness* of v. 19, and cf. note on v. 3). As in Romans the "senseless heart" is "darkened," the "reasonings" are "vain," and the "reason" is "reprobate," so it is here. The phrase, *hardening of their heart,* does not mean quite what that phrase means to us; for the "heart" is for a Jewish thinker the seat of the intelligence even more than of the emotions (see p. 1156a). The degradation of the reasoning faculties goes hand in hand with moral corruption.

20, 21. Cf. Col. 2[6]. *In Jesus* as distinct from "in Christ" (if it is more than a stylistic variation) may carry an implicit reference to "the Jesus of History," in accordance with Paul's general usage of the names.

22–24. Cf. Col. 3[9] Rom. 12[2]. In Paul's psychology the *mind,* or "reason," is the higher part of man in his natural state (=the "inner man," Rom. 7[22-25]). It is capable of knowing God, but becomes "reprobate" through sin (Rom. 1[28]). In order that it may be a sure guide to truth and right, it must be *renewed* or "transformed" by the infusion of the Spirit. For the *new man,* and his "creation," cf. 2[15], note.

25–32. Ethics of the Christian Society. See also 5[1-20]. Paraphrase: "In actual practice the distinctive Christian ethic will work out in such ways as the following: Speak the truth. Do not let anger lead you into sin. Do not enrich yourselves by dishonest means, but by hard work at honorable trades earn enough to contribute to the needs of others. Avoid all foul speech; it is offensive to the Divine Spirit. Let what you say be helpful to others. Get rid of all bitter, abusive, and malicious talk. Be kind and pitiful, and forgive as God forgave you."

From 4[25] to 6[9] we have the application of the broad principles of Christian ethics already laid down, namely, the principle of the social organism and the revolt against pagan immorality. These principles are applied in reverse order, the former finding its place in 5[21]–6[9]. We begin here with the opposition of Christian virtues to certain flagrant sins of paganism. In 4[25-32] (see also 5[1, 2]), truth of intercourse, placability, honest industry, purity and propriety of speech, and the social virtues of compassion and forgiveness are set against their contrary vices.

A good deal of the same material is present in a less ordered form in Col. 3[5-17], but this (with 5[1-21]) is a more sustained attempt to set forth a plan of Christian ethics as applied to social life, and as such may be compared to Rom. 12, 13. The style of all such passages (cf. 1 Thess. 4[1-12] 5[12-24] Gal. 5[13]–6[10]) has a certain uniform character, unlike Paul's usual manner. It is probable that this was the recognized form of ethical instruction in the early church. It recalls the Wisdom literature of the O.T., the Epistle of James, the Teaching of the Twelve Apostles, and in some respects the sayings of Jesus as we have them in the Synoptic Gospels. The present passage is the most elaborate expansion of the common form, and contains important original elements contributed by the writer, particularly in the assignment of definitely Christian motives. But even here the treatment is exemplary rather than systematic or complete.

26. Cf. Psa. 4[4]. The first half of the clause is concessive, in accordance with Hebrew idiom. Therefore read *Though you be angry, do not sin.* The meaning is that an instinctive impulse to anger is natural and not necessarily sinful; to brood over it is to "give the devil his chance." This is true psychology, and only a pedantic interpretation would find a contradiction to 4[31] or Col. 3[8] or Mt. 5[22]. The advice not to cherish anger after sunset goes back to the Pythagoreans. It is excellent practical psychology.

28. Note the motive for *labor.* There is here an advance on 2 Thess. 3[6-12]. Throughout the N.T. it is assumed that all Christians have a claim upon the economic resources of the community according to their need (cf. Rom. 15[27]). This was the basis of the "communism" of the early days (Acts 2[44-47] 4[32-35]). The writer is perhaps taking warning from the fate of the Jerusalem church (for which Paul had to collect alms among the churches of Asia and Greece) in impressing upon his readers the necessity of honest labor to replenish the common stock.

32. Connect with 5[1, 2].

CHAPTER V

1–20. The Ethics of the Christian Society. (4[25-32] continued.) Paraphrase: "Love, as Christ loved you—to the point of sacrifice. Sexual immorality, with all that accompanies it, is of course unthinkable in a holy community. There is no place in the ultimate divine Society either for sexual vice or for grasping self-assertion, which is no better than idolatry.

Let no specious arguments lead you astray on this point. There is an ultimate difference between darkness and light: you belong to the light; you must exercise your moral discernment. Have nothing to do with the dark ways of paganism, but bring everything out into the light. You remember the hymn:

'Sleeper awake!
Rise from the dead!
And Christ will dawn upon you.'

Use discretion and common sense, and make the best use of your time. Avoid the false excitement of intoxication; drink your fill of the Divine Spirit; and when you want to sing, sing praise to God."

In vv. 3–14 the two root-sins of paganism, impurity and grasping self-assertion, are explicitly condemned in all their forms. Vv. 15–20 inculcate conscientious sobriety of judgment and the right sublimation of those instinctive impulses which when perverted lead to intemperance.

1, 2. There is no break at 4[32], which demands these two verses for the completion of the sense. Here the full Christian motive comes to noblest expression.

3. This verse seems clearly to allude to a classification of vices widely current among pagan and Jewish moralists of the period. The classification is in two groups: (1) *sins of the flesh*, under the head of "intemperance" (or, as here, *uncleanness*); and (2) *anti-social sins*, under the head of *covetousness* (as here, *pleonexia* in the Greek), grasping self-assertion regardless of the rights of others (the "greediness" of 4[19]). Paul follows this classification in a general way when he has occasion to give anything like a catalogue of sins (see Rom. 1[24-32] 1 Cor. 5[10, 11] 2 Cor. 12[20, 21] Gal. 5[19-21] Col. 3[5, 8]). In 4[19], however, *pleonexia* (covetousness) is brought into such close connection with "impurity" as almost to lead to the suggestion that the two great typical sins have, after all, one common root (cf. 1 Thess. 4[4-6]). That *pleonexia* is a form of idolatry (v. 5; cf. Col. 3[5]) is in harmony with known teaching of the Jewish rabbis (cf. also Mt. 6[24]).

5. For the implications of *inheritance* see Col. 1[12, 13], note.

6. For the significance of *wrath* see 2[2, 3], note.

8–14. *Light* is a natural and universal religious symbol. In the thought of Paul it is specially associated with the idea of "the coming age" (see Col. 1[12, 13], note). Christians are *children of light* (cf. 1 Thess. 5[5]) as belonging to the new order of the kingdom of God. In what follows there is a varying play on other senses of the word "light," especially as signifying that which makes things *manifest* or visible, and so as the symbol of divine revelation of truth (so v. 10, with which cf. Col. 1[9] Rom. 12[2] Phil. 1[9]).

11. Not *reprove*, but "expose," "show up"; not necessarily in word, but by the whole attitude to life.

13. The last sentence is difficult. We should expect, "Whatever makes manifest is light"; but it is doubtful if the verb in the original could possibly have that sense, and, in any case, the statement would not be very pointed. But the word "light" is used not only of that which illumines, but of that which is illumined (as the "light and shade" of a picture; cf. Shakespeare's "How soft the moonlight sleeps upon this bank"). Sin itself is *darkness*, but the recognition of sin is a part of the light of the kingdom of God; and in this sense it might be said that whatever is made manifest belongs to the realm of light (cf. 1 Jn. 1[5-7], note).

14. Probably a quotation from an early Christian hymn, of the kind alluded to in v. 19.

15. Cf. Col. 4[5].

18. In many forms of religion (particularly in orgiastic cults of this period associated with Dionysus) intoxication is regarded as a means of communion with the Divine. Hence it is here opposed to the condition of true inspiration. (Cf. Lk. 1[15]; *Odes of Solomon* 11[7]: "I drank and was inebriated with the living water that doth not die; and my inebriation was not without knowledge; but I forsook vanity and I turned to the Most High my God.") Inspiration, or possession by the Divine Spirit, finds natural expression in poetry and song. How little the writer thinks of religion as an unemotional matter of pure reason or pedestrian morals!—This passage and the parallel in Col. 3[16] afford interesting evidence of the production of a poetical literature in early Christianity.

21–33. Christian Ethics in the Home. (See also 6[1-9].) Paraphrase: "Mutual subordination is the rule of the Christian society. Thus, wives should subordinate themselves to their husbands, and husbands should love their wives to the point of sacrifice. Marriage is a sacrament of the love of Christ for the holy community."

The treatment of household duties here (and in 6[1-9]) is closely parallel to Col. 3[18]–4[1]. See notes there.

21–24. The participle *subjecting* should be translated as an imperative. (This grammatical usage of late Greek, unknown to the Revisers, but revealed by recent discovery, clears up many places where Paul's grammar looked odd.) When this is realized, then it becomes clear that in grammar no less than in sense this verse makes a fresh departure. The dominant motive of the last sections has been the contrast of Christian morality with pagan immorality. This motive now disappears, and we recur to the positive conception of a Christian society developed in 4[1-16]. One mark of it will be mutual subordination. In v. 22 the author brings under this general head the subordination of women, which is stated absolutely in Col. 3[18]. It cannot, however, be said that he carries the idea through consistently. Really, the attitude of wife to husband is simple subjection, as absolute as the subjection of the church to Christ (cf. 1 Cor. 11[3, 7]), who is her Saviour. (We are probably not intended to find a parallel to this in the marital relation.)

25–33. *The doctrine of Christian marriage*, as set forth here, is based on a far-reaching application of the quasi-mystical idea that the relation of husband and wife represents that of Christ and the church. As regards the attitude of wife to husband, the application has already been made. Here follows a fuller exposition, having for its purpose the definition of the relation of a husband to his wife.

26. The sacrament of baptism is described as *washing of water with the word* (read *a water-bath accompanied by a word*). There is the act of immersion and there is utterance which gives it meaning—probably either the baptismal formula or the confession of faith (cf. 1 Pet. 1[25] 1 Cor. 6[11]). This constitutes the sacrament of sanctification, for in it the believer is dedicated to God. For the connection of baptism with the death of Christ see Rom. 6[1-11].

27. The ideal and final perfection of the church is regarded as given in the initial act of sanctification. In pursuance of the figure of marriage, the motive of Christ in giving himself is represented as the counterpart of the lover's desire to enjoy the beauty of his beloved (cf. 2 Cor. 11[2]).

28–31. The comparison is complicated by the introduction at v. 28 of a fresh element. We now have three relations which are treated as analogous or identical: (a) Husband—Wife; (b) Christ—Church; (c) Person—Body. We have already learned that (a) = (b); we are now to be shown (vv. 28, 29a) that (a) = (c); then we learn (v. 29b) that (b) = (c); fortified by the recognition of this identity, we are prepared to see a deeper meaning in (a) = (c), which is now restated. It might have been enough for Paul's purpose to show that marriage, according to nature and Scripture (Gen. 2[24], cited in v. 31), is so intimate a union that any default of love is at once unnatural and impious; but this would be for him a bald abstraction, lacking the cogency of the Christian motive; hence he brings in that mystical relation which makes us *members of Christ's body*, the church, which is also his bride.

32. *Mystery*, according to Greek usage, implies an ineffable truth and its symbolic manifestation. In any particular case it is doubtful whether the word is applied specifically to the symbol or the truth symbolized. Here the subject-matter is the marriage relation described in the words of Gen. 2[24]. Either Paul says that marriage is itself a sublime symbol, or he says that the truth symbolized in it is sublime. His probable meaning is: "This marriage relation is a sublime symbol; and I interpret it in reference to Christ and his church. However, putting that aside for the moment, it is clear that the individual Christian must love his wife as he loves himself." The passage is made the scriptural basis of the Catholic doctrine of marriage as a sacrament.

CHAPTER VI

1–9. Christian Ethics in the Home. (5[21-33] continued.) Paraphrase: "Children should obey their parents as they would obey Christ. Parents must not exasperate their children by scolding, but give them a really Christian training. Slaves must obey their masters as they would obey Christ, and do their work with a sense of direct personal responsibility to him. Masters must treat their slaves in exactly the same spirit, for they too are slaves of Christ."

See note on household duties immediately following the paraphrase of 5[21-33].

1–4. *Children—parents.* See on Col. 3[20, 21].

5–9. *Servants—masters.* See on Col. 3[22]–4[1].

10–18. The Christian Warfare. Paraphrase: "For the rest, be armed and well prepared for the fight against the spiritual forces of evil. Put on the divine armor—truth for belt, righteousness for breastplate, readiness to affirm the gospel for shoes, faith for shield, and the inspired word of God for sword. Watch and pray."

Behind this passage lies the idea, so constant in Jewish eschatology, of the Last War, in which the powers of good should finally vanquish the powers of evil (often referred to in the revived eschatology of to-day as "Armageddon," after Rev. 16[16], which see). This war is depicted in crude colors in 2 Thess. 1[6-9] 2[3-12]. In 1 Cor. 15[24-26] the conception is more spiritual. Here it is fully "sublimated." The enemy is no "man of sin"—no human adversary at all, but the spiritual powers called (after Jewish usage) "Princedoms" and "Powers," or (after pagan usage) "World-rulers," but, in any case, only half-personified in the writer's thought, since the comprehensive term used is the neuter expression *spiritual hosts of wickedness* (read *spiritual forces of evil*, v. 12). The belief in a period of final warfare in history survives in the phrase *the evil day* (v. 13); but with scarcely more than a shadow of its old realism. In effect the writer is speaking of that perpetual struggle with evil which in its various phases always lies before the Christian. It is the "substitute for war in the moral sphere." (Cf. pp. 206–7, 846b.)

In the imaginative description of the spiritual armor which follows, the writer is expanding a figure already found in Rom. 13[12] 1 Thess. 5[8], with the aid of reminiscences of Isa. 11[4, 5] 59[17] Wisdom 5[18]. In all these passages God is the Warrior, and *the armor of God* (vv. 11, 13) here probably starts from the meaning of the armor worn by God, and so also by those who have "put on Christ." The *shoes* (v. 15) are suggested by Isa. 52[7]; *gospel of peace* is peculiarly appropriate to this Epistle. For the *word* (not, of course, the canon of Scripture) as *sword*, cf. Isa. 11[4] Heb. 4[12]; a cruder form of the same idea is in 2 Thess. 2[8] Rev. 2[16]. Finally, the ceaseless *watching* (v. 18) to which the soldier is bound is associated with prayer (*supplication*) as in Mk. 14[38] (cf. Col. 4[2]).

19–24. Personal Matters and Conclusion. Paraphrase: "In your prayers pray for me, that, prisoner as I am, I may declare the secret of God with complete frankness. Tychicus will give you news of me. Farewell."

The *personalia* are scanty and perfunctory. Greetings are entirely lacking. For news of the writer the readers are referred, as in Colossians, to Tychicus, the bearer of the letter (v. 21).

20. Paul speaks of himself as an *ambassador* for Christ in 2 Cor. 5[20]. Now he is in prison, but an ambassador still (cf. Philemon, v. 9).

24. *Uncorruptness* is for Paul elsewhere the antithesis to "corruption" in the sense of mortality or perishableness (cf. Rom. 2[7] 1 Cor. 15[42, 50-54]). It is difficult to give the word here the ethical sense of "sincerity," which, in fact, does not seem to be anywhere found. Paul holds that the Christian is "risen with Christ" into a life already essentially immortal. Thus his love for Christ is no mere feeling of the natural, mortal human soul, but a spiritual affection "in the heavenly places."

PHILIPPIANS

By Professor JAMES ALEX. ROBERTSON

Introduction

The City of Philippi. The tenderest of all Paul's letters is addressed to the church in Philippi. Philippi was the first European town to be evangelized by the great apostle. It was situated on the Via Egnatia—the great Roman road which stretched from Dyrhachium on the Adriatic to Byzantium on the Hellespont. Krēnidēs was its original name, derived from the springs which abounded in the neighborhood; but the great Philip of Macedon renamed it after himself. Gold was found in the adjoining mountains and Philip coveted it. An important battle was fought in the plains of Philippi in 42 B.C., when the Emperor Octavianus defeated the republican forces. Octavianus established a military colony there, with special privileges. Philippi was also a great religious center; the chief shrine of Dionysos was in the neighboring mountain Pangæus. At the time of the apostle the religious activities there were part of the world-wide yearning for redemption from the futility of life. Aratos the poet wrote his poem *Concerning Nature* in Macedonia. And in it he sang,

"All the ways are full of God,
All the gathering-places of men, the sea, and harbors;
And at every turn we are all in need of God,
For we are all of kin to him."

The last line Paul quoted once in Athens (Acts 17[28]).

Paul and Philippi. Paul was drawn to Philippi in the course of what is known as his second missionary journey. All along his way through Asia something—perhaps it was already the call of the distant field of Europe, through some representative—hindered him from turning aside to other near-hand centers. And at Troas at length he saw the vision of the man from Macedonia calling, "Come over and help us." The conjecture has been made by Ramsay that Luke was the instigator in all this. For (1) it is here in the course of this narrative in Acts (ch. 16) that the "we" passages most clearly emerge; which means that Luke was now in Paul's company. (2) The description of Philippi, here in Acts, suggests that Luke or his family originally belonged to this city. Luke calls it "Philippi, which is a city of Macedonia, the first of the district, a colony." Of no other town has he so full a description. Now, we know that Philippi was not universally regarded as "the first city" of the district. Luke, therefore, is taking sides in a dispute here. Who more likely to do so than a former citizen, jealous for his city's status? (3) Luke is familiar also with certain details about the place. He knows that the Roman governors there were called *strategoi*, or prætors. Particularly he seems to know that there was a small group of Jews and proselytes who used to worship in the open air in the vicinity of the town. "On the Sabbath day we went forth without the gate by a river side, where we supposed there was a place of prayer." That well attested reading, "*we* supposed," suggests that Luke had been aware from early recollections of these religious ongoings. (4) Further, in the narrative of Acts, when Paul passed on from Philippi to other towns, the "we" passages cease for the time being. Luke had been left behind to consolidate the work there, and perhaps became the leader of the little Christian community. At least, we do not find him in Paul's company again until five years have elapsed. (On the "we" passages, see intro. to Acts, p. 1095a.)

All this suggests a possible solution of one of the difficulties in the letter to Philippi. When, toward the end, Paul pleads for the reconciliation of two women who had differed in the congregation, he adds, "Yea, I beseech thee also, true yokefellow, help these women." Who was this yokefellow? Many conjectures have been made. (a) Clement of Alexandria, Erasmus, Zwingli, etc., think Paul refers to his own wife, whom Renan conjectures to have been Lydia, the Asiatic proselyte who was the first to be won there for Christ by Paul—a very improbable conjecture, since the word is masculine in form, and Paul himself claims to have been unmarried (1 Cor. 7[7]). (b) Others suppose it to be the husband of one of the women referred to. But the word obviously means that it was a yoke shared with the apostle. (c) This colleague in labor with the apostle seems to have been a pastor or teacher in Philippi. It can hardly have been Epaphroditus, for he was with Paul at the moment of writing. It cannot have been Timothy, who was also with Paul at the time; nor Barnabas, who was never associated with Paul in Philippi. Silas, who was with Paul on his first visit to Philippi, is a possible conjecture, only we have no hint that he was near Philippi at this time. (d) Luke, however, was apparently not with Paul at this time. And we know from the letter that the Philippians probably had some previous communication from Paul. Was the messenger Luke? There is no more likely place to which Luke could have gone than this town with which he had had such a long and honorable connection. (e) Lastly, the word "yokefellow" indicates a closer connection with the apostle than "fellow worker." There is none of Paul's immediate circle whom it fits so well as Luke.

The only hypothesis that seriously stands in the way of this identification is that *syzygos*, the word translated "yokefellow," may be a proper name. In favor of it is the use with the word of the adjective "true" or "genuine," as if the apostle were saying, "Syzygos, for you are genuinely worthy of your name." But that interpretation is not inevitable, the more so as no such proper name is found in Greek.

The Genuineness of the Letter. It was Baur of Tübingen who first seriously challenged its genuineness, and as he has said most that can be said against it, we may first summarize his arguments, and then consider their validity. (1) The mention of bishops and deacons is said to be an anachronism in a letter of Paul. (2) The Clement referred to in the letter is held by Baur to be Clement of Rome, who belongs to a later period than Paul. (3) The letter is said to misunderstand Paul's monetary transactions with Philippi. (4) The style is held to be un-Pauline, especially in its marked subjectivity of feeling. (5) Certain doctrinal objections are adduced. The great passage about the incarnation (2^{5-11}) is held to be Gnostic.

None of these objections are really serious. As to (1), Haupt, following Chrysostom, suggests that the two words stand for the same persons—those who had had the oversight of the arrangements in collecting and sending the gift to Paul which this letter speaks of. That is probably making too little of the terms. But the opposite extreme must be avoided. The fact that "bishops" is plural shows that there was more than one holding this position in the community. "Bishops" were practically equivalent to "presbyters" in the earliest days of the church; both terms were applied to those who because of their long standing as Christians were looked up to as grave and reverend seniors. As for the deacons, even women sometimes held that office in Paul's day. It must be remembered that the words are plastic and indefinite, implying little of their later signification (see discussion, pp. 1277–8). (2) There is no real reason for identifying the Clement mentioned with Clement of Rome. It is said that when the writer speaks of Paul's bonds being manifest in Christ throughout the prætorium, and sends a salutation from them of Cæsar's household, he is probably thinking, among others, of Flavius Clemens, a kinsman of Domitian, who was put to death as an atheist, a charge often levelled at Christians. But the ground for identifying Flavius Clemens with Clemens Romanus is very flimsy. Nor can either be identified with the Clement of Philippians, for the greetings from members of Cæsar's household could not include Clement's, seeing he was already in Philippi. (3) The supposed contradiction about monetary matters is got by pitting $4^{15f.}$ against 1 Cor. 9^{15}. But in the letter to Corinth Paul is not asserting that he received no help from any church; he only says he waived his right for good reasons with regard to the Corinthian church. In 2 Cor. $11^{7, 9}$ he admits receiving help from others, and from Macedonia. (4) With regard to the question of style, the subjectivity of Philippians is explained by the very nature and circumstances of the letter. With no other church were Paul's relations so personal: this letter has sometimes been called the love letter of Paul. It has also been called "the Epistle of Humility," for he is writing to urge upon them, by word and example, that humility which leads to unity, as well as to express his thanks brimming over with love for help received. True, it is not one of the great doctrinal epistles, and yet it contains the important passage about the incarnation and self-emptying of Christ (2^{5-11}). The letter is the spontaneous outflow of a heart of grateful love. (5) The supposed traces of Gnosticism are easily explained. It is not a case of this writer borrowing from the Gnostics, but of the Gnostics borrowing from Paul; and it is absurd to find in the word "prize" or "thing to be grasped," which Paul uses in the incarnation passage, a kinship with the wild theories of such a Gnostic as Valentinus, who taught that the power Sophia (wisdom) sought to penetrate the essence of the All-Father; and to find in the phrase "in the likeness of men" a docetic meaning (i.e., a denial of the reality of Jesus' human body), or to parallel "He emptied himself" with the Gnostic phrase, "to be in the Kenoma" (the empty Void). On the other hand, Gnostics would not call Jesus "Lord"; nor would they assign a body to the exalted Christ or to glorified believers.

The external evidence for the genuineness of the letter is strong. Clement of Rome (95

A.D.), and Ignatius and Polycarp, early in the second century, all echo its phraseology.

Integrity and Unity of the Letter. Is the letter a single whole, or does it consist of fragments of separate letters? When Paul says, "To write the same things to you, to me indeed is not irksome but for you it is safe," we do have a hint of more than one letter to the Philippians, but no proof that we have fragments of two letters here joined together. What follows is not a repetition of anything in the earlier part of the letter. It is probably a previous letter to which Paul is referring. Nor does the phrase translated "finally" (3^{1}) necessarily imply that Paul is here ending one letter and that what follows is part of another. The phrase does mark a transition from a general to a special part of the letter perhaps. The letter is so artless and natural that the apostle may have intended to draw to a conclusion at this point, when another train of thought started in his mind, and set him off writing at considerable length again. Lightfoot conjectures an interruption in the process of writing; and that when Paul resumed he found he had something more to say.

Where was the Letter Written? This question has given rise to various conjectures. Corinth has been suggested, but without any adequate reason. Ephesus has more recently been thought of. But while there may be certain grounds for suggesting that Paul was once imprisoned in Ephesus, it can scarcely have been for any lengthy period. The main dispute is still between the claims of Rome and Cæsarea. The letter indicates that Paul was imprisoned in close confinement, and waiting an impending trial. Both Rome and Cæsarea answer to these requirements. The reference to the prætorium (1^{13}) might be said to hold good of either place, for the dwelling of Herod in Cæsarea was sometimes called the prætorium. In Rome the word was not applied to the emperor's palace; it would be either the judgment hall of the prætor, or the barracks of the imperial lifeguards, or a collective name for these soldiers who kept watch and ward over the apostle.

A more decisive phrase is the phrase "Cæsar's household," near the end of the letter. That cannot refer to Herod's retinue, and it is unlikely that it should be applied to slave-groups outside Rome. But the most decisive argument is the situation in which the apostle finds himself at the time of the writing of the letter. The decision of the law court which Paul was awaiting was evidently a life or death decision. This points to the final issue of his appeal to Cæsar. Again, he has a certain freedom in his present situation, such as he scarcely possessed in Cæsarea. He is in contact with a large and active church (1^{14-17}). There was not such a church in Cæsarea. He is receiving visitors (4^{18}), dispatching messengers (2^{19-30}), and entertaining friends ($4^{21f.}$). All the evidence therefore seems to point to Rome.

Date of the Letter. It is one of the Imprisonment Epistles. Colossians, Ephesians, and Philemon were also written from Rome. Is Philippians to be placed before or after these? Lightfoot admits that several communications must have passed between Paul in Rome and the church at Philippi: (1) One from Rome to Philippi announcing Paul's arrival in Rome. (2) One from Philippi to Rome accompanying the gift sent at the hands of Epaphroditus. (3) One from Rome to Philippi—word of Epaphroditus' illness. (4) A letter of inquiries from Philippi—a letter which seems to have asked (a) about Paul's prospects (1^{12}), in a prayerful spirit (1^{19}); whether he was likely soon to visit them ($1^{25f.}$), if Epaphroditus was better (2^{26}); and it may have apologized for not sending help sooner ($4^{10f.}$). All this implies a considerable stay in Rome before the sending of this letter. But the main argument for a later date than the other imprisonment epistles, in spite of the letter's affinity with earlier letters, is that obviously Paul is on the verge of a great crisis in his affairs. His trial is imminently impending. No doubt he is still hopeful for his release (1^{25} 2^{24}), but he is far from buoyant about it. His hope is fixed not on earthly helpers. He argues that the Disposer of all events will recognize his indispensableness to the Philippians. But that argument would not have any weight in a law court. Indeed, Paul also prepares his friends in this letter for the possibility of the other alternative being fulfilled—his execution. It was written therefore somewhere between 62–64 A.D.

Condition of the Philippian Church. (1) The Philippian Christians were able once more to show their love for the apostle by a generous gift. Paul recognizes their constant thoughtfulness, but for a time they lacked opportunity (4^{19}). The fact that Paul, so jealous about his independence, was willing to receive bounty at their hands shows the close personal bond of affection that existed between him and this church. (2) There were possibilities of persecution in their environment. Paul had offended a certain section of the community by interfering with their means of livelihood and for this he had suffered imprisonment at Philippi (Acts $16^{11f.}$). They had sought to kindle pagan prejudice against him by calling him a Jew. So the Gentile environment had become hostile. We can see this fact influencing the course of the letter, when Paul exhorts the Christians to show a united front to their adversaries (1^{27-30}). Suffering must not daunt nor disintegrate them. (3) But we see, already mingling with this, another feature of the church life at Philippi. There is a certain disunity or disharmony among them which Paul is anxious should be healed (1^{27} $2^{1-11, 14}$ $4^{3, 8, 9}$). He urges the duties of harmony and fellow feeling. Perhaps it was due to spiritual pride or vain-glory, for Paul in a noble passage urges the imitation of the humility of Christ. The danger of internal friction is still present in his mind at 3^{15f}. And in the end of the letter he urges two prominent women to be reconciled. (See p. 942b.)

Analysis of the Letter. (1) The letter opens with the usual salutation, thanksgiving and prayer, characteristic of Paul's writings, but considerably prolonged in this letter (1^{1-11}).

(2) Then, probably in answer to inquiries, he explains his personal situation, and the progress of the gospel in spite of rivalry and opposition (1^{12-26}).

(3) Apparently in response to information received, he goes on to urge them to manifest harmony by an absence of self-seeking (1^{27}–2^{4}).

(4) And there follows the noblest passage in the letter in which he puts forward the example of Christ, urging them to copy it (2^{5-16}).

(5) He returns to personalia, speaking of plans for his own freedom, if God will; his intention to send Timothy; the illness and return of Epaphroditus (2^{17-30}).

(6) Then he seems to begin his final injunctions (3^{1}), but either an interruption occurred, or a new train of thought is started in his mind, and he inserts some warnings (a) against formalism (the Judaizers) (3^{3-11}), (b) against spiritual pride (3^{12-16}), passing into antinomianism or lawlessness (3^{17}–4^{1}), the extreme dangers to which Paul found Christianity prone.

(7) Resuming final injunctions, he makes his personal appeal to Euodia and Syntyche ($4^{2, 3}$).

(8) There follows an exhortation to joy, carefreeness, and lofty moral endeavor (4^{4-9}).

(9) He concludes by thanking them for their gift (4^{10-20}).

(10) And with salutations the letter ends (4^{21-23}).

Bibliography: Commentaries: Lightfoot; Vincent (International Critical Commentary); M. Jones (Westminster Commentary); Kennedy, in Expositor's Greek Testament; Moule, *Philippian Studies.* Christological: Bruce, *Humiliation of Christ;* Gore, Bampton Lectures *On the Incarnation;* Forsyth, *Person and Place of Jesus Christ.* General: Moffatt, *Introduction to Literature of N.T.;* Peake, *Introduction to N.T.;* Ramsay, *Paul the Traveller;* Deissmann, *St. Paul;* Weinel, *St. Paul, the Man and his Work.*

CHAPTER I

1, 2. Salutation. Timothy was probably the amanuensis. He had been associated with Paul in his earlier contacts with Philippi (see intro.). Paul does not call himself here by the more usual designation, apostle; the letter is artless and affectionate; he describes his vocation as the *slave* of Christ, in whose service is perfect freedom. He addresses the *saints* in Philippi in Christ Jesus, the consecrated ones, God's chosen people. There is a contrast between earthly location and spiritual status. Many social advantages may depend on location in a particular community, but the supreme spiritual privilege of being in Christ does not. And how often he uses that word *all* in the letter ($1^{4, 7, 8, 25}$, $2^{17, 26}$ 4^{21}). He is anxious to show he is not going to discriminate between any possible sects or factions in the church at Philippi. For the phrase *with the bishops and deacons*, see introduction.

In v. 2 the Greek and Hebrew forms of greeting are combined, fine examples of how Christ makes all things new. It must have been Christ who restored new life to the worn-out coin *grace*, and to *peace*—colorless and gray like a hillside after sunset. It was God saying, "My favor to you," as he renewed his glad tidings every morning through the Master; God saying, "Peace to you"—the middle wall of enmity broken down in Jesus. God is the ultimate source of spiritual blessing, and Christ the channel. The two names are set side by side without incongruity.

3–11. Thanksgiving and Prayer. Paul reverts to the first person singular. Though Timothy writes, the letter is in no sense a joint production, but a purely personal outpouring of love and gratitude. *My God*—God "whose I am and whom I serve" (Acts 27^{23}). "The suppliant thanks while he asks, and blesses as he petitions." Thankfulness with joy runs like an undertone through the whole letter. Bengel says the sum and substance of the Epistle is "I rejoice: do ye rejoice." The occasion of his thanksgiving is not "your fellowship with each other in the gospel": he could hardly praise them for their unity; nor yet "your participation in the blessing of the gospel": that would be too obvious; but it is *your fellowship* [with me] *in furtherance of the gospel* (v. 5). There is perhaps a hint of their monetary contribution —the "now" suggests that; but it was more: it was their community of interest and sympathy with him in the gospel. God is described as *He which began a good work in you* (v. 6). "Began" is a technical term from Greek religion, used of initiating a ritual. If it is a sacrificial metaphor, then "a good work" is the Philippians' self-sacrificing conduct in relation to Paul; but it may be more general—the production of spiritual life in them. *Will perfect it* continues the ritual metaphor: he who initiated the process will complete the initiation (cf. Gal. 3[3]). *The day of Jesus Christ* (v. 10) is a Christianized O.T. expression. "The day of the Lord" is in the O.T. the day of God's visitation of the earth in judgment and redemption. Christ, in the N.T., is to be the Judge. The Second Advent is prominent in Paul's earliest letters, and it is not absent, as we see here, from his latest. Paul regarded it as imminent (1 Thess. 4[17]; but cf. 1 Cor. 15[51] Phil. 1[23]).

7. The thought of the Philippians for Paul (manifested in their gift) is answered by Paul's thought for them, his hopes of their religious prospects. *In my bonds* describes Paul's immediate situation; *in my defense* refers to his impending trial. This is the great crisis in his affairs which hangs like a shadow over all the letter. *Confirmation* stands for the guarantee of the value of the gospel which such a defense would afford. The *grace* here is the entire grace of God.

8. The last phrase is an intensified form of Paul's favorite phrase "in Christ"; "in the heart of Christ" it might be rendered. "In the breast of Paul," says Bengel, "it was not so much his own as Christ's heart that beat." Paul believed that his affection for the Philippians was just a pulse-beat of a mightier love than his.

9–11. Paul's prayer for the Philippians. *Your love* is to be taken either as love absolute—love to God and men—or more probably as love to one another, for that was somewhat lacking in Philippi. There was about the Philippians a certain eager enthusiasm which was apt to carry them just a little beyond the bounds of spiritual common sense. I pray that your love may get cleared eyes, he says.

The cause of Christ occasionally suffers from the impetuous enthusiast. The cure for this is not less love and more sense, but a truer love, says Paul. It is the highest and holiest love that has clearest eyes. As our love grows we become more and more sensitive to the wise and searching eyes of God, and therefore more and more alive to the things that matter. Knowledge is clear insight into the heart and mind of God, a grasp of the great principles of religion, ability to read the thoughts of the Eternal. And judgment, or sense, or moral discernment is power to apply those thoughts of eternity to the facts of life, to know how to *approve the things that are excellent* or to "prove the things that differ." This last is perhaps the better rendering, for discrimination is the function of discernment (cf. Rom. 2[18]). The two words *sincere* and *offenseless* correspond exactly to knowledge and discernment. Sincerity is transparency, perfect openness toward God. According to one derivation the word for "sincere" means "suntested." You turn up a stone, and the insects beneath scuttle away into the dark again, unable to endure the strong sunlight. Sincerity is sensitiveness to the awful holiness and besetting inexorable love of God. Only so do our lives become less of a stumbling-block to men.

Righteousness in the phrase *the fruits of righteousness* (v. 11) is again a right relation between God and the soul. It is something that God gives in (or through) Christ. "Only so far as the life of the believer is absorbed in the life of Christ, does the righteousness of Christ become his own" (Lightfoot). See the parable of the vine and the branches (Jn. 15[1f.]).

12–26. Messages Concerning Paul's Personal Situation. *I would have you know* is a frequent formula in ancient letters, and betokens probably that Paul is writing in answer to inquiries. *Rather* contains a hint that the Philippians were expecting different news—"rather than what you suppose." The gospel has been furthered by Paul's fetters in Christ, i.e., fetters incurred on account of his relation to Christ. For *prætorian guard* see introduction. Probably it refers to the body of men rather than to any building. That conforms best with the phrase which follows, *to all the rest*—i.e., to the wider circle of the city itself, in particular to the Christians in Rome. Though the R.V. takes *in the Lord* with *the brethren,* (v. 14), it is perhaps better to take it with *being confident.* "The brethren" already means "the Christians," and "the Christians in Christ" would be tautological. *In Christ* (v. 13): Christ is the region or landscape in which they now move and think. *Through my bonds* is a strange reason for men's daring to give utterance to the word of God. The very fact that Paul was in chains for the gospel's sake was a testimony to its power.

15. *Some* can scarcely refer to the minority already indicated, for this party also preached the gospel. They were not the Judaizers; Paul always utterly repudiates the Judaizers and all their works. On their view Christ had died in vain; but this party preaches Christ. Because of Paul's success the influence of this party which had hitherto enjoyed a special prominence had faded: this was their grievance. They resented his presence in Rome, even in fetters. The word for *strife* means "rivalry." They imagined Paul would feel bitterly the activities of rivals. The gospel had come to Rome before Paul, and some of its first promulgators were making claims to priority.

16–18. Notice that in R.V. vv. 16, 17 stand in reversed order to that of A.V. *I am set* (v. 16) like a soldier posted on guard by his captain. *Defense* does not refer to his defense before Nero's tribunal, but his whole propaganda on behalf of Christ. *Faction* is worthless self-seeking—ambition. There is, says Lightfoot, a moral contradiction between "ambition" and "Christ." Yet even if his opponents increase his sufferings by adding gall to his wounds (the meaning of v. 17b), no matter, so Christ is proclaimed. *In pretense or in truth* (v. 18) represents not difference in substance but in purpose of preaching. *Therein I rejoice*, says Paul. This verse was quoted in the early church in favor of heretics. It raises the question, Are unconverted men warranted or qualified to preach the gospel? We cannot argue a general rule from such an exceptional case. Undoubtedly, the correct principle is that the best preparation for preaching Christ is to have his Spirit.

19, 20. *My salvation* is not to be taken narrowly as Paul's release from prison. *The supply of the Spirit* has nothing to do with his liberation, only with his soul's health. The supply of Christ's Spirit is in answer to their prayer: a noble indication of the humility of Paul: he expresses himself here as dependent on the prayers of others. The reference is not to the spirit of unshakable steadfastness which possessed Jesus when he walked the earth in the midst of his sufferings, but to the Holy Spirit. The Spirit is both giver and gift. Paul often practically identifies the Holy Spirit with Christ (cf. 1 Cor. $12^{4,5}$ 2 Cor. 3^{17}). The bestowal of salvation is an act of the exalted Christ who works in the Spirit. *Earnest expectation* (v. 20) is literally a desire with head stretched out and away from other things, and *hope* is expectation combined with assurance. There is probably a looking forward here to his comportment in the hour of his trial. *Boldness*, i.e., of speech: again he is thinking of his conduct at his impending trial.

21–26. The contrast between bodily life and death or what follows death runs through this passage. *To live* therefore means "to live in this present world." "The presence of Christ is the cheer of my life . . . the Spirit of Christ the life of my life, the love of Christ the power of my life, the will of Christ the law of my life, the glory of Christ the end of my life" (Eadie). *To die is gain*—this is very different from the world-weariness of the pagan poet who said "to die is better than to live in wretchedness." To Paul it was the life which follows death that would be gain. He is torn between conflicting emotions. He would fain continue to labor for Christ in this life, yet he longs for the closer union with Christ which death would give. *What I shall choose I wot* (know) *not* (v. 22). As Lightfoot points out, the sublime guess of Euripides, "Who knows if to live be death, and to die be life?" which was greeted with ignoble ridicule by the comic poets, has become an assured truth in Christ. *To depart* (v. 23) is a metaphor used of breaking camp, or weighing anchor, or the departure of guests. *To be with Christ* seems different from Paul's former view of death as a sleep. This new thought cannot be limited to those who suffer a martyr death. Those who had a similar relation to Christ as Paul had in life can look forward to being with Christ after death. Paul comes down finally on the side of remaining. And he is so sure that the Philippians need him still that he feels assured that God thinks so too. Joy, the characteristic note of the Epistle, is repeated here.

27–30. Exhortations to Unity in Fellowship. (See also 2^{1-4}.) If I am to remain in the flesh, Paul seems to say, do you make it worth my while by behaving in the right spirit. And writing out of the heart of the imperial city to a Roman colony he uses a word which would appeal to him and to them, for he says (v. 27), *Behave as citizens*, put in practice your duties as burgesses of the Kingdom. Their conduct is to be (1) outwardly, a fellowship in contending, (2) inwardly, a fellowship in lowly love. The metaphor in *striving* is apparently drawn from the combats in the Roman amphitheater. *In one Spirit* is a hint that there were differences among the Philippians. Paul uses "Spirit" in a religious, not a psychological sense. It is the Spirit of God which creates unity of purpose, stirs up sympathy and will to cooperate ("with one soul"). "*For* the faith" (cf. mg.) gives the better meaning here. "Faith" leans toward its later sense here—the body of truth which is the gospel. Not being *affrighted* (v. 28)—stampeded, a word used of scared horses. The *adversaries* were not the Judaizers. The danger from them would not be intimidation but seduction. It is the idol-worshipers of Philippi who would look menacingly on any new faith that sought to undermine their worship. Paul gives three grounds for encouragement in a brave endurance: (1) The opponents themselves have inwardly the feeling of defeat. (2) Suffering for Christ is a high honor. "Adversity is the blessing of the N.T." (see Mt. 5^{1-10}). (3) They may have the feeling of sharing a common fate with Paul. "The Christian gladiator," says Lightfoot, "does not anxiously await the signal of life or death from the fickle crowd." It is God who sets the contest, and he gives the warrior the "sure token of deliverance."

CHAPTER II

1–4. Exhortations to Unity Continued. (See also 1[27-30].) As Paul continues his exhortations, his words take on a more earnest tone. He heaps up his reasons for summoning his readers to unity. He gives four grounds of appeal: (1) If there be any incentive in the fact that you are in Christ, (2) if there be any tender appeal originating in your feelings of love, (3) if there be any reality in your fellowship of the Spirit, (4) if there be in you any heart of mercy and sympathy. Then Paul multiplies phrases about unity in a "tautology of earnestness" (Vaughan). *Faction* and *vainglory* (v. 3): exaltation of party and exaltation of self are the two enemies to a real love-unity. "It is a strange phenomenon in religious history that intense earnestness so frequently breeds a spirit mingled of censoriousness and conceit" (Kennedy). *Lowliness of mind* is a word practically of Christian coinage. The adjective "humble" in common Greek usage meant abject, groveling. Through the influence of Christ's life and character humility was raised to its true level. Ruskin makes it "the first test of a truly great man." In v. 4 Paul is not encouraging any inquisitiveness, only a gentle regard for each other. Unselfishness is the real road to harmony.

5–11. The Example of the Incarnate Christ. Not the self-sacrifice but the self-humiliation of Christ is emphasized in this great passage. Paul has just been dealing with the Christian's practical relation to his brethren; here he is dealing with the state of mind which lies at the basis of this relation. But the section goes far beyond the particular occasion: it has a high Christological value. Do these verses speak of a pre-existent Christ or merely of the attitude of Christ when he became man? The first is the interpretation of almost all the early Christian Fathers; the second is a more modern view; but the majority of the modern expositors still hold to the first. In the second interpretation, *the form of God* is regarded as the divine glory or power which Jesus inwardly possessed on earth but for the most part did not display. Against this, however, stands the fact that the words *He emptied himself* speak not of an abeyance or concealment but of a genuine putting off. *Being originally* (Greek) *in the form of God* expresses something about the pre-existent Christ; yet the subject of the sentence, *who,* refers not merely to the pre-existent Christ but to the single Personality who in his pre-existence and in his earthly existence is one and the same. "Form" signifies the inward being or essence, the native constitution of the reality, irrespective of the conditions under which it may appear. The point of emphasis in the whole passage is the unspeakable contrast between the heavenly and the earthly states, between being in the form of God and taking the form of a slave. Paul is gripped and governed by the profound ethical significance of the humiliation.

Counted it not a prize [or *a thing to be grasped*] *to be on an equality with God.* This does not mean that Christ might have considered his equality with God a possession to be clung to; or that he would have retained his equality with God as a robber grasps his prey, if he had not undergone the incarnation. The "prize" is something *to be* seized or clutched at, i.e., it is something still in the future. We get a glimpse of what it means in the episode of the Temptation. Christ was tempted by a dazzling display of power on earth to lay claim to the divine glory which really belonged to him; tempted by using illicit worldly means to raise himself to a political Messiahship, lording it over the kingdoms of the world. That would have been making his lordship a *res rapienda,* a thing to be clutched at. On the contrary, he chose the long, bitter, sorrowful way of humiliation, suffering, and death. So *he emptied himself,* divested himself of the divine glory which he had when in the form of God, and assumed the form of a slave. To the being or essence of God there was added the being or essence of a slave. Not that he became the slave of men, but that as a man he bore the nature of a slave. Whose slave he became is not stated. Servitude belonged to the essential nature of his humanity, as the next phrase, *being made in the likeness of men,* indicates. This likeness was no shadowy insubstantial thing. Nor does *being found in fashion as a man* (v. 8) mean that his humanity was less real than his previous form of Godhead had been. The word "fashion" merely emphasizes "the transitory quality of our materiality" (Gore). *Found,* i.e., by men. It was as a man that men reckoned him. *He humbled himself* really repeats "He emptied himself" in a more ethical way. To whom Christ became *obedient* is not mentioned. But as a fact, his death was undertaken not in obedience to men but to God. In his earthly life he willed to surrender his own will to the Father's. He learned obedience through suffering. *Unto death* expresses not the duration but the highest degree of his obedience. Death seems to men unnatural. Horror of death is a human emotion. And it was intensified in the case of Christ by being the *death of a cross.* Not "*the* cross"; the atoning significance of Christ's death is absent from the context. It was the fate of a slave he suffered, the uttermost degree of shame (cf. Heb. 12[2]), in contrast to the honor and glory which the pre-existent Christ had. Death on a cross meant for a Jew not merely loss of citizenship but being outcast from the divine community. This stands in deepest contrast to being in the form of God. He was reckoned with the transgressors. In this was completed his obedience. It was the utmost point of his humiliation, the fullest contradiction of the form of God, the absolute giving up of his own will.

The consequence was his *exaltation* (v. 9). This is a principle of divine action which Christ himself laid down (Lk. 14^{11}). *The name above every name.* God is the giver of the name. Paul considered Jesus as in some sense subordinate to the Father (cf. Jn. 14^{28} Rom. $1^{3, 4}$ 1 Cor. 15^{28}). "The name" denotes office, rank, dignity, and is undoubtedly the title "Lord." "Jesus is Lord" is the shortest, simplest and most common creed in the N.T. It is a name given to God alone in the O.T. Paul is thinking, in the first place, most probably of the O.T. usage, though he is aware that it is the name given in the mystery religions to the supreme mediator of the mystery. In "the name which is above every name" he appears to compare and contrast the lordship of Jesus with that of all the lords of the mystery religions (cf. Eph. 1^{21}). *Things in heaven*, etc., is perhaps better rendered "beings in heaven," etc. Though Lightfoot says, "The personification of universal nature offering its praise and homage to its creator in Psa. 148 will serve to illustrate Paul's meaning here," we are inclined to agree with Theodoret, who says, "He calls the invisible powers beings in heaven, and men still living beings on earth, and those who are dead beings of the world below."

In v. 11 the title given to Jesus is clearly indicated. The confession that Jesus is Lord might be called the N.T. creed (cf. Acts 2^{36} Rom. 10^{9} 1 Cor. 8^{6} 12^{3} Eph. 4^{5} 6^{24} Col. 2^{6} 1 Pet. 1^{3} Jude v. 4). And this acknowledgment of Jesus' exaltation tends to or issues in the glory of God the Father. Christ has carried his manhood—the manhood that has redeemed humanity—into the Godhead, and as such now receives the homage of creation.

12–18. Work Out Your Salvation. *So then* —"having the example of Christ's humility to guide you, the example of Christ's exaltation to encourage you" (Lightfoot). The obedience here recalled is not obedience to Paul, but to God: that is brought out by *with fear and trembling,* i.e., with a nervous anxiety to do right before a Supreme Master (cf. Eph. 6^{5}). "For there is nothing which ought to make us incline more to humility and fear than when we hear that we stand by the grace of God alone" (Calvin). It is God that works both the *willing*—the very original impulse to right action; and the *doing*—the carrying out of that will in action. God's grace is at once "prevenient" and "co-operant" (cf. Eph. 2^{8}). Yet they are called to work out their own salvation themselves. Free will coincides with grace in the working out of God's purpose. There is no doctrine of irrevocable election here: the divine purpose does not reduce man to a machine.

The *murmurings* and *disputings* (v. 14) are either against God, or more probably friction among the Philippians. Murmurings, as Lightfoot suggests, may be a word of moral import—smoldering discontent; and disputings of intellectual import—rebellion against God. It is obvious that Paul has an O.T. reference in mind (Deut. 32^{5}). But it is more a memory-echo than a quotation, and must not be pressed as giving a clue to the meaning here. *Are seen* (v. 15) might be rendered "shine," and *in the world* is either in the human world of good and evil (Lightfoot), or in the cosmos of created things (Kennedy)—carrying out the metaphor of *lights*, or luminaries (Greek). Not "holding fast" but *holding forth* the word of life fulfills the metaphor best (cf. 1 Jn. 1^{1-3}). Paul wants to win some credit from Christ in the Philippians, hence the use of metaphors from the race course and the athletic games. In v. 17 he introduces a new metaphor. He thinks of the Philippians as the priests, their Christian achievements as their sacrifice, his own possible martyr death as the accompanying libation.

19–30. Personalia. *I hope in the Lord.* All Paul's activity now takes place in Christ; his emotions, thoughts, boasts are those of Christ: his very hopes, even the slightest, are a throb of the hopes of his Lord (cf. v. 24). The steadfastness and reliability of *Timothy* are in contrast to the way some in his own immediate circle have apparently treated Paul. In the sudden vehement expression of feeling, however, in v. 24, he may have only one man in his mind's eye. Was it Demas? (2 Tim. 4^{10}.) Who *Epaphroditus* (v. 25) was is not otherwise known. Hardly Epaphras (Col. 1^{7} 4^{12} Philm. v. 23), for he was a native of Colossæ, and this man is closely associated with the life of Philippi. Paul describes him finely here, as brother and fellow worker and fellow soldier. Anselm paraphrases: my brother in the faith, my co-operator in preaching, my comrade in adversity. He is further their *apostle* (mg.), i.e., delegate or messenger; and minister to Paul's need. Epaphroditus had been ill and homesick in Rome, unhappy because the Philippians had heard he was ill. Note that Paul does not expect to cease from sadness, but only to be *less sorrowful:* the sadness of his present situation remains. *Hazarding* (v. 30)—staking, adventuring—a metaphor from gambling; cf. the *parabolani*, the brotherhood who at the risk of their lives nursed the sick and buried the dead.

CHAPTER III

1–11. Against the Judaizers and Spiritual Pride. *Finally* may mean that Paul intended to end his letter here, but a new train of thought set him off again (see p. 1240a); or it may simply mean "in continuance." *Rejoice:* an exhortation from one who is himself in prison. But even in the prison he has his Lord. V. 1 suggests that Paul had already been in communication with the Philippians. Probably he had already warned them about the Judaizers (see notes on Acts 15[1f.] Gal. 2[4]), a warning which he is now to repeat. Some have attempted to find three different classes indicated in v. 2—Gentiles (*dogs*), self-seeking Christian teachers (*evil workers*), unbelieving Jews (*the concision*). But it is more natural to take these as three descriptions of the same class. "Evil workers" implies that they were within the Christian community, and since they were advocates of circumcision the Judaizers are suggested. The first word describes their character—roaming and insolent, dogs that barked and bit at Paul, a word used possibly by way of retort to what the Judaizers said of those who were without the pale of circumcision. The second phrase describes their conduct—they sought to seduce Paul's converts from the true freedom that is in Christ (Gal. 3). The third word describes their destructive creed—that circumcision was necessary for a complete Christian. By the ironic word "concision" Paul suggests that they were insisting on mere manual mutilation. It is those who render to God a spiritual obedience who are the true circumcision.

Note the contrast between *in Christ Jesus* and *in the flesh* (v. 3). The flesh is the soil where the plant of the soul's life roots and grows at first; it is the sphere in which forces of evil lay ghostly fingers on the soul and drag it down. "In Christ" means in the clear, serene region or atmosphere into which the soul springs by faith, and in which it blossoms and blooms: it is the region of freedom and power to overcome, in which the soul can exult with a victorious Christian gladness. Paul goes on to describe (1) his fleshly or hereditary privileges, as if they were a staff he possessed but did not lean on. (a) No proselyte circumcision his: a Jew from infancy. (b) His parents were not proselytes either. "Israel" expresses the spiritual nobility of the race—of the true covenant stock. (c) He was of no renegade tribe, but a tribe which remained faithful to Judah at the disruption of the kingdom (see 2 Chr. 10[1]–11[12]). (d) A Hebrew of the Hebrews—different in language and manners from the Hellenists. (2) His privileges from personal choice: (a) a Pharisee—strict in observance of ritual law; (b) "as touching zeal, persecuting the church"—a phrase of deep and concentrated irony: he talks of it in the present, as if the memory of it were still shudderingly upon him; (c) omitting no legal observance however trivial: nothing that was supposed to make a man accepted with God. Cf. the Rich Young Ruler; only he failed to take the step which Paul next relates.

7–9. *Gains*—plural, as though he were in the habit of counting them one by one as a miser; *loss*—singular, as though he now threw them all together. *For Christ*—"the lamp is superfluous when the sun is shining" (Theodoret). *The knowledge* (v. 8) is the highest degree of faith, "the reflection of faith in our reason" (Beyschlag), illumination, the stage reached by the complete initiate into the Christian mystery. It is knowledge of *Christ*, the Anointed One, in his exalted power and glory; knowledge of *Jesus*, who in the days of his flesh shared our trials and sorrows and whose heart still throbs with ours; knowledge of the *Lord*, through whom we enter into spiritual victory over the world; and "*my* Lord" in contrast with all other lords or mediators of mysteries. (See art., *Backgrounds*, pp. 851–2, and cf. pp. 1253–5.) To know Christ is "to have the key which will unlock all the secrets of existence." *Suffered loss:* perhaps Paul was excommunicated from the synagogue at Tarsus when he returned there after his first visit as a Christian to Jerusalem—lost all his Jewish privileges. *Win Christ*—Paul speaks here as though it were something he had not yet attained. To win him is to possess him, to have him within; and to be *found* in him is the other side of this truth. It involves the complete identification of the believer with Christ, becoming a member of his body—a union close, tender, vital and constant. For the meaning of *a righteousness of mine own, even that which is of the law* (v. 9), cf. Gal. 2[16-21] 3[10-12] Rom. 3[21-31] 4[13, 14] 9[30-32] 10[4, 5]. The sphere of the Law, which might be said to lie between those of the flesh and of the Spirit (in Christ), was like a house of mirrors to conscience, demanding obedience to every jot and tittle, but impotent, unable to give power to fulfill. It was the propitiation wrought out by Christ which gave one power, living in Christ, in the life of the Spirit, to fulfill the Law. The only condition required for attaining this righteousness is faith. Faith in this deed of God means union with Christ. To be righteous or to have righteousness is to make a divinely empowered response to this forgiveness of God.

10, 11. Paul goes on again to speak of *knowing Christ*—the apotheosis of faith; not mere intellectual recognition, but communion, appropriation; not historical insight nor theoretical information, mere acquaintanceship with facts and dates, but the highest reach of Christian experience, a living intimacy with the living Christ. The *power of his resurrection* is not the power which brought about his resurrection, but the power which his risen life gives to those that are in him, victory over the flesh (Rom. $7^{24f.}$), the assurance of immortality (Rom. 8^{11} 1 Cor. 15^{14}), a quickening and stimulating of the whole moral and spiritual being. *The fellowship of his sufferings* may mean either the prior experience of being conformed to the death of Jesus, or fellowship with the sufferings which the exalted Christ still endures in his Body, the church. *Attaining unto the resurrection from the dead* means to the resurrection of the righteous into a new and glorious life.

12–16. **Laying Hold on Christ.** Paul here launches into a description of the deficiency of all Christian experience, but it is couched still in the first person: his gentle way of rebuking some in Philippi who were inclined to pride themselves in having attained great heights in spirituality. I have not yet attained perfect Christian experience, he says, I am not yet fully initiate. As Luther said, paradoxically, "He who is a Christian is no Christian." The verb *press on* expresses the intense action of a runner in the stadium. Some Greek Fathers introduce the idea that Paul was fleeing from Christ when he was apprehended. Cf. Francis Thompson's *Hound of Heaven:* "Fear wist not to evade as Love wist to pursue." Spiritual self-satisfaction, Paul is saying here, is a deterrent to any real advance. When he speaks of forgetting *the things that are behind*, he means not merely all his Jewish privileges and Jewish attainments, but also that part of the Christian race which he had already run. Paul did not repose on memories. One of the best gifts a man can have is the faculty of knowing how and what to forget. If the past is to live anywhere it is in our consciences rather than in our imaginations. Men are prone to revive amiable non-essentials for the satisfaction of pride. The man who is buried in the complacent contemplation of his past, who goes about trying to recall what he did yesterday, is apt to become narrow-minded. Spiritual growth is stopped. No room is left for the countless treasures of God's grace. Does the duty of life consist merely in honoring the memory of old ties, or does it not also include listening to the divine claim of new ones? Certain it is that when the supreme love of our life comes to us, and Jesus Christ enters the heart, there is nothing that can oppose its claim to his.

In what follows Paul is quite clearly using the metaphor of the chariot races. It is perhaps not necessary to distinguish between the *goal* and the *prize* (v. 14). They were one—the purified life which results in unbroken and complete fellowship with Christ. *Perfect* (v. 15) means mature or initiated. Augustine says, "perfect pilgrims, not yet perfect possessors." Chrysostom says the apostle is speaking not about dogmas, or matters of belief, but about perfection of life. Still there may be just a hint of reproachful irony here, a reference to some in Philippi who thought themselves versed in the higher mysteries of the Christian faith. As initiates, Paul says, think of yourselves rather as entrants on a race the goal of which is not yet attained. Let them utilize their experience. What has been helpful in the past will still be helpful. And Paul pleads for unity in conduct and faith. In the spirit of the metaphor of the race, they are urged to keep step with one another.

17–21. **The Danger of Antinomianism or Lawlessness.** (See also 4^1.) Paul feels compelled to set himself and his associates up as a standard. For if the Philippians are not to follow the Judaizers, they are not to swing away to the opposite extreme of lawlessness. By *many* he means professing Christians: Paul's tears would have little meaning otherwise. *Enemies of the cross* would have been a mere platitude had he meant heathen. The cross of Christ is the complete contradiction of all that the natural man esteems highly (cf. Rom. 16^{18}). The true Christian is crucified with Christ. (See Gal. 2^{20}.) Paul attacks here (v. 19) the self-indulgence which wounds the tender conscience of others and turns liberty into license. These lawless ones make a boast of what is really a shame and a disgrace to them. And Paul urges that *our citizenship*, or rather commonwealth, "is in heaven" (see note on 1^{27}). "We are a colony of heaven" (Moffatt). Just as the Roman colonists might expect a protector in the Roman magistrate or emperor (to whom the term "Saviour" was sometimes applied), so "our" Deliverer is to come from the divine commonwealth—heaven. Paul still kept his expectation of the Lord's return. In what he says about the body (not "vile" as in A.V.), Paul is not endorsing the Platonic and Stoic suggestion of the body as a clog to the soul. Contempt for the body is not Christian teaching. The body is to be changed—*fashioned anew*—not destroyed. The connection of thought here is this. The Antinomians reckoned the soul's bliss as the only thing that counted. The body with all its passions could be abused or indulged, for it was to pass away into the oblivion of death, Paul therefore has to remind his readers that some sort of body persists after death, and though it is not the body we bury in the grave, it is in some way related to it. For Paul's doctrine of the heavenly body, cf. 2 Cor. 5[1-5] 1 Cor. 15[35-58]. It is Christ, the life-giving Spirit, who effects this transformation. And the body which he now inhabits as a Spirit in glory is the standard according to which our spiritual bodies will be fashioned; and he is to do it by virtue of the fact that there belongs to him the power to subdue all things to himself.

CHAPTER IV

1. Exhortation to Steadfastness. After all this warning (3[17-21]) the apostle's love finds expression for itself in an accumulation and repetition of words of endearment. His *crown* is his garland of victory and joy, something of achievement he will be able to show Christ at the last day. He counsels them to maintain their ground within the sphere of Christ's living Spirit.

2–7. Exhortations to Christian Virtues. The disunion in Philippi, which Paul has been hinting at in the course of the letter, comes out into the open here. He repeats the word *I exhort* with each name to show that he is not blaming one side more than the other. The women may have been deaconesses, each with her own little coterie of followers. They are to be of *one mind:* in the sphere of the life of the risen Christ there is no room for dissension. For the *yokefellow* see p. 1238b. Their laboring with Paul in the gospel indicates that these two women occupied a high and honorable position in the Philippian church. Probably they belonged to the band of women with whom Paul had conversed by the river bank when he came to Philippi (Acts 16[11f.]), and who had thenceforward taken an active part in bringing others to hear Paul preaching. *Clement* was evidently a prominent Christian in Philippi (see intro.). As for the rest, their names are in the *book of life.* The book of life was originally an O.T. expression for the register of the covenant people. To be blotted from that book was to forfeit the privileges of the theocracy. But it came to refer to immortality (Dan. 12[1] Psa. 69[28]). In Revelation it is constantly so used. There are many members of the Christian Church whose names count for little in the eyes of men, but who nevertheless are all remembered before God. The figure suggests the minuteness and infallibility of the divine knowledge.

The dominant mood of the Epistle—*rejoice* —recurs with v. 4. It seems to resume 3[1]. Paul repeats the word, as Herbert says, "to take away the scruples of those that might say, 'What, shall we rejoice in afflictions?' " "The 'new people' are always happy, always in the full bloom of thought, always at springtime" (Clement of Alexandria). *Forbearance* means readiness to be reasoned with. It implies gentleness, the opposite of a spirit of contention and self-seeking; a quality needed in Philippi. Forbearance produces an undisturbed heart, the true atmosphere in which one can rejoice. *The Lord is at hand* was evidently a kind of password (*Maran atha*) among Christians of the early church. The Lord who is to be the final Judge of all actions is coming soon. Have done with censoriousness. Let him do the judging.

The following sermon divisions of v. 6 are familiar: (1) careful for nothing (i.e., not careless but carefree); (2) prayerful for everything; (3) thankful for anything. *Thanksgiving,* a rare word in secular Greek, is used twelve times by Paul. Thanksgivings are the wings of prayer. *The peace of God* is a rich phrase: not the peace in a man's soul which has God for its object, but the peace in God's soul (subjective genitive) which he bequeaths to man (genitive of origin) in the reconciliation wrought out by Christ. "Peace I leave with you, my peace I give unto you," said Jesus. Such a legacy of peace is found through reconciliation. It is the carefree man that can share God's peace. This is a peace which transcends all power of conception (Eph. 3[19, 20]). *Guard* (v. 7) is suggestive. Paul thinks of Christ as a citadel; the peace of God as its bulwarks, or sentinel at the gate; and the heart as a regiment of thoughts and purposes—the inhabitants of the citadel. It is union with Christ which secures this peace.

8, 9. Things to Think On. Paul specifies at length the kind of thoughts his readers ought to make the subject of meditation. They are not specifically Christian virtues: they belong to pagan morality also. *True*—truth exists apart from the gospel: the gospel sheds light on its nature and obligation. *Honorable*—having "a noble seriousness" (Matthew Arnold). *Just* or righteous. This word with "true" forms the foundation of all morality. *Pure*—untainted, free from all debasing elements. *Lovely*—things whose grace attracts, having "the grace of graciousness" (Walter Pater). This is one of the terms of moral approbation. The other is *of good report*—high-toned. *Virtue* sums up the first four qualities named: a word of Greek ethics used by Paul only here. Beza says, "It is too lowly a word if compared with the gifts of the Holy Spirit." Christian virtues have a special fragrance of their own; and here doubtless Paul would signify "all that becomes a man redeemed by the blood of Christ and tenanted by the Holy Spirit." *Praise* sums up the last two qualities named. Erasmus says, "Praise is the companion of virtue." These then are the kind of thoughts the Philippians are to harbor if the peace of God is to be their guardian.

From considering their proper line of meditation Paul turns to consider their true line of action (v. 9). "Meditation precedes, then work follows" (Calvin). They are to obey his precepts and to imitate his example. The first two verbs refer to his conduct as an instructor, the last two to his private demeanor.

10–20. Paul Returns Thanks for the Gift. Paul has now practically closed his letter. "The God of peace shall be with you" sounds like a farewell. The *But* at the beginning of v. 10 "arrests a subject which is in danger of escaping" (Lightfoot). Paul's thanks—one of the motives for his letter—are reserved almost for a postscript. There is noticeable a certain hesitancy to speak of his indebtedness. The sensitiveness of his language, which he veils in financial terms used in a semi-playful way (see below), reflects his resentment at the slander—that he was a mountebank living off the gospel—which had been leveled at him in Thessalonica and Corinth (cf. 1 Thess. 2^9 2 Cor. 10). There is a metaphor in the word for "revived" (v. 10). It means "put forth new shoots." The Philippians had flourished green again, not in their care for the apostle, which had never withered, but either in their own temporal circumstances or in opportunities. He adds, however, "My gratitude is not a beggar's thanks for charity" (Beet). He is *content* (v. 11). This is a frequent word in Stoic philosophy, but whereas Paul's self-sufficiency was due to his faith, that of the Stoics was due to their pride. *I have learned the secret* (v. 12) means "I am initiated. I possess the mystery." Initiation into the mystery cults was a slow and laborious process. Not without toil and pains had Paul reached this stage of perfection. Perhaps he also suggests that the final result was a divine revelation to him.

In v. 13 the apostle rises from knowledge to power: Knowledge *is* power. Then he praises them. *Ye did well* is like an echo of the Master's "Well done." Their sympathy with the apostle in prison is the very trait which the Judge selects for eulogy at the last. It was no new thing on their part, this sympathy. The beginning or introduction of the gospel is when the gospel was first preached to them. *In the matter of giving and receiving* (v. 15) is a figure borrowed from pecuniary transactions. Paul had bestowed on them priceless spiritual gifts: it was only right that he should receive material blessings from them. Still he is anxious to remind them that he allowed no other church to have such dealings. And he is anxious to impress on them that it was not the gift but the giving which gave him joy. *I have* (v. 18) is the regular expression found on the papyri to indicate the receipt of what is due. "He indicates that the transaction is a debt" (Chrysostom). Their giving had, however, overflowed the account. For *an odor of a sweet smell* cf. Gen. 8^{21} Ex. 29^{18} Ezek. 20^{41}. Paul reveals here again his fondness for the metaphor of sacrifice (cf. 2^{17} Rom. 12^1 15^{16}).

The *my* in v. 19 is emphatic. "The apostle uses the simple future as if he pledged himself for God" (Eadie). He is assured of this because of the riches which are in the glory—the manifested divine character—which is yours through your union with Christ. Then he breaks into doxology. "Doxology flows from the joy of the whole epistle" (Bengel). To God, who is for the Christian community *Father*, in that he has set them in the sphere of his life, belongs the praise which magnifies him in the æons of æons. A German hymn says, "We need Eternities since times are too short to offer thanks to him."

21–23. Final Salutations and Benediction. The phrase *every saint* suggests that the greeting is to be conveyed to each member individually. This paragraph may have been written, according to Paul's custom, in his own hand. Paul's own immediate circle join in the salutations, then all the Roman Christians, especially the slaves and freedmen who had become Christians in the imperial residence. It used to be assumed that this phrase, *they that are of Cæsar's household*, designated persons of high rank, and extreme critics used it to attack the genuineness of the letter, thinking that it referred to Clemens and Domitilla, relatives of the Emperor Domitian, who suffered for the faith at the close of the century. But of this there is no shadow of proof. The closing benediction is almost certainly an autograph.

COLOSSIANS

By Professor C. H. DODD

Introduction

The Divisions of the Epistle: Theological and Ethical. The Epistle falls (if we exclude the formal epistolary address and the personal matter at the close) into two main sections, like Romans, Galatians and Ephesians—one chiefly theological (1^{3}–3^{4}) and one chiefly practical and ethical (3^{5}–4^{6}). The division, however, is not so clear-cut as in these other Epistles. The theological section has two principal passages, the one (1^{12-23}) growing imperceptibly out of the thanksgiving and prayer with which the letter begins, and containing a condensed statement of a doctrine of the person of Christ, with its verification in Christian experience; the other (2^{8-19}) consisting of a polemic against certain false presentations of Christianity, both theological and ethical, and leading up to a restatement of the fundamental Christian experience (2^{20}–3^{4}). These two passages are connected by a passage in which the writer makes a personal appeal to his readers (1^{24}–2^{7}). The transition from theology to ethics is already made in the passage (2^{20}–3^{4}) describing the Christian experience of "dying" and "rising again" with Christ, and this is made the basis for the practical precepts which follow in the latter main section of the Epistle, which is, in fact, a very concise survey of Christian ethics in principle and practice, with some examples (3^{5}–4^{6}).

Purpose of the Epistle. The primary purpose of the Epistle is clearly indicated by the polemical passages, particularly 2^{8-23}. The Colossian church had been troubled by teaching of a type which Paul considered dangerous to the faith. It claimed to represent a "Higher Thought" ($2^{8,\ 18}$), offered initiations (2^{18}), enjoined the observance of holy days such as the Jewish Sabbath and New Moon (2^{16}), and of ascetic practices ($2^{16,\ 21}$), and set forth as objects of worship beings variously described as "Elements of the Universe," and "Thrones, Dominations, Princedoms, Powers," in such a way that Christ ceased to be the Supreme Head of the religious society. It is not difficult to recognize by these signs a type of religious thought widespread in the world into which Christianity came. It is a type of thought to which the term "Gnosticism" is in a general sense applied. Gnosticism has been regarded as a Christian "heresy or group of heresies." Really the Christian "heresies" comprised under that name were only aspects of a much wider movement of thought. It arose from a mixture, or syncretism, of Greek and Oriental religions, supported by a kind of philosophy or pseudo-philosophy borrowing largely from Platonism and Stoicism. Like modern Theosophy, which sometimes claims, not without justice, to be the lineal successor of Gnosticism, it often sought to interpret the meaning of all religions within a highly speculative theory of the universe. Beings corresponding to the gods of polytheism were ranged in a hierarchy of spiritual essences—or "discarnate intelligences" (to borrow an apt phrase of Thomas Hardy)—mediating between the Absolute and the world of men. Under the auspices of this imposing "philosophy" the practice of religion was built up from materials derived from all manner of sources—Oriental, Jewish, Anatolian, Egyptian, Greek, and even farther afield. There were mysteries and initiations, and a great variety of ceremonial and ascetic practices. In a world where the older paganism had largely lost its hold on thinking men, Gnosticism seemed to offer something like a universal religion resting on a philosophical basis, and capable of endless adaptation. (See further, art., *Backgrounds*, pp. 847–52.)

It is apparent that "Gnostic" thought at Colossæ had a strongly Jewish tinge, and it was ready to "adopt" Christianity, and to find a place for Christ within its hierarchy of spiritual beings. Paul saw that this would mean that what was distinctive in Christianity would be swamped in a vague and unprofitable syncretism, while in the ritual and ascetic practices recommended he saw a relapse into a position indistinguishable in principle from the Jewish legalism against which he had fought.

Paul's Reply to the Challenge of Gnosticism. His method of dealing with the problem thus presented is to develop a new and more adequate statement of the position and dignity which Christian experience necessarily assigns to Christ. (For the details of his new Christology, see notes on the relevant passages of the Epistle.) The outcome of it is to set forth the person and work of Christ as having a cosmic significance. If Christ, known as

Saviour, were but one among a host of unknowable Powers, the Christian would still be a stranger in a universe which might at last prove to be hostile. If, however, what we find in Christ is the ultimate Meaning of the universe, then the salvation he brings is absolute and final. This is the faith that Paul seeks to safeguard by identifying Christ with that divine Wisdom by which the world and all powers controlling it were brought into being, and through which at last God will fulfill his purpose in it all.

It is thus that Paul takes up the challenge of the "new thought," by placing his teaching about salvation in Christ upon a more philosophical basis. But in doing so he reasserts with remarkable force and clarity what had always been the core and center of his gospel: Christ died to reconcile men—to reconcile all beings—to the will and purpose of God. Through faith in him we become reconciled by sharing mystically in his death and resurrection. Nowhere else in the Pauline writings is the whole of the Christian life more clearly exhibited as the working out of what it means to die and rise again with Christ. In particular, it is made plain past all possibility of misunderstanding that this dying and rising again is an actual moral experience, manifesting itself in character and conduct. Gnostic speculation was morally barren. As Paul saw, its asceticism was a mere playing at morality. The Christian way is above all *radically ethical*, and the "emancipation" it brings is the one sure beginning of a free, progressive, and positive morality for men individually and in society. Thus the careful outline of Christian ethics is no less relevant to the main purpose of the Epistle than the Christology.

Relation to Ephesians and Philemon, and the Question of Authorship. See introduction to Ephesians, pp. 1223–4.

Destination of the Epistle. The Epistle is addressed to the Christians of Colossæ, an ancient but declining Phrygian city, situated with Laodicæa and Hierapolis (cf. Col. 4[13]) in the Lycus Valley, in the Roman Province of Asia. Though Paul had not himself visited the city, the introduction of Christianity there was no doubt one of the indirect fruits of his residence in that province (Acts 19[10]). The time of writing was one at which Paul was in prison—probably the Roman imprisonment recorded at the end of Acts.

Literature: Lightfoot, *Colossians and Philemon;* Maclaren, *Colossians and Philemon* (Expositor's Bible); Peake, *Colossians* (Expositor's Greek Testament); Abbott, *Ephesians and Colossians* (International Critical Commentary); Kennedy, *St. Paul and the Mystery Religions;* C. Anderson Scott, *Christianity According to St. Paul.*

CHAPTER I

1, 2. Epistolary Introduction. This follows Paul's customary form, a slight individual modification of the epistolary convention of the period. He associates *Timothy* with himself as joint author, though it does not appear that Timothy's authorship was more than nominal.

3–8. Thanksgiving. Paraphrase: "I thank God for your Christian life of faith and love, based on the hope which is the content of the gospel as it is known to you—and not only known to you, but known everywhere, as a growing and fructifying principle. You learned it from my loyal comrade Epaphras, to whom I owe my news of you."

For thanksgiving and prayer at the opening of an epistle, see Eph. 1[3-14], note.

4, 5. The triad of *faith, love* and *hope*—the three permanent things, according to 1 Cor. 13[13]—is for Paul the least inadequate brief summary of what the Christian life is (cf. also 1 Thess. 1[2, 3]). Elsewhere the combination of faith and love ("faith working [operating] through love," Gal. 5[6]) suffices; so here faith and love form a pair within the triad. *Faith* describes the Christian life on its religious side, *love* on its ethical side, and these two sides can no more be separated than the two sides of a coin. The life of faith and love is represented as being based on *hope;* hope being here not so much the act of hoping as the object hoped for. The quality of a life depends on the idea of its goal, because by this idea the dominant force of desire (the "libido" of the psychologists) is directed. Thus the idea of a divine purpose for human life revealed in Christ gives a fresh orientation to personality. Its life is then marked by faith and love. This divine purpose for human life is the "hope" which Paul describes as the content of the gospel.

6. The readers are now reminded that this gospel of hope is a universal gospel—*all the world*. There were in the first century, as to-day, many little local esoteric sects, with "fancy religions" of their own. If the "heretics" had their way, the Colossian church might well become such an eccentric local cult. But Christianity, as Paul conceived it, is a faith that lives in the open, making a universal appeal, and ready to prove itself in contact with the varying conditions and outlook of men in all parts of the world. In a word, it is a catholic, or world-wide religion.

To say that in the sixties of the first century it had actually been preached in all the world is something of an exaggeration. But in principle it appealed to the whole world, and in actual fact the geographical area it had already covered is astonishing. Moreover, as Paul goes on to observe, it had proved effective as a working faith in the most diverse parts of the world—it was *bearing fruit and increasing* (cf. Mk. 4[8-20]) everywhere, just as it did at Colossæ.

9–14. Intercession, Passing into a Statement of the Facts of Salvation. Paraphrase: "I pray that you may clearly discern the will of God, and be wise, so that you may lead a life worthy of Christ and pleasing to God—a life of moral fruitfulness, of strength to endure, and of joyful thankfulness for God's gift of salvation. For he *has* saved us; we are no longer dominated by the Dark Powers, but we are under the rule of God's Son, and are therefore emancipated from sin."

The Colossians were great devotees of what they called *wisdom*—meaning thereby pretentious speculations. Paul prays that they may have that kind of wisdom which will enable them to live a morally sound life after Christ's pattern. The sarcasms of 1 Cor. 1, 2 are sufficient to show how Paul judged the empty rhetorical "philosophy" which was too popular then and in the following centuries. Rom. 12[2] Phil. 1[9, 10], and other passages show how fully he assumed that the conscience of ordinary lay Christians was competent to form true judgments of the will of God. That was what it meant to be guided by the Spirit; hence he prays here for *spiritual understanding.* In what follows, put a stop at . . . *knowledge of God;* another at . . . *longsuffering;* and a third at . . . *light* (vv. 10–12). We then have in three finely balanced rhythmical clauses three characteristics of the morally sound life of a Christian, namely, (a) ethically effective action; (b) growing power to endure; and, (c) underlying both, a spirit of joyful thankfulness to God. The theme of thankfulness deserves all the emphasis that Paul puts on it here and everywhere in his Epistles; and the connection here suggested between thankfulness and moral strength, both active and passive, is actually of the closest. Be sorry for yourself, and your strength to do and endure is sapped (that is good psychology, because it is plain experience); feel joy in what life brings you, and inhibitions are removed. That is something never understood by Stoics and by a certain type of Puritan. Paul's gospel was in a certain real sense "salvation by joy." But it was joy of a particular kind, founded on nothing less secure than what God has willed and done.

12, 13. We have here an important definition of what Christian salvation means. First, we observe the fundamental fact that however the blessings which make up the "saved" state be described, it is by God's act alone that we are capable of them. For *made us meet* read *made us capable;* the same word as in 2 Cor. 3[5, 6]—"who also made us sufficient as ministers," i.e., made us capable of acting as ministers. This "sole causality of God in matters of salvation" is central to Paul's whole conception of religion.

Next we observe that salvation itself is conceived under the aspect of a transition—*translated us*—from a realm of *darkness* to a realm of *light.* In Jewish thought of this time (in which Paul was brought up) a sharp distinction was made between "This Age" and "The Age to Come." Long experience of the evils of oppression, injustice, and every kind of misery and corruption had convinced Jewish thinkers that the present age was under the sway of the powers of darkness, and could never offer to men a life worthy of the name. That God rules they did not doubt, but all the benefits of his rule they postponed to the future. Then at last all evil would be done away, and all the promises of their religion would be fulfilled for the "holy" people of God. As the present age is the age of darkness, so the age to come will be the age of light. In God's eternal purpose his "holy ones" (*saints,* but that word has misleading implications for us) have *an inheritance* (read *lot*) *in the light*—when it comes. In the apocryphal 2 Esdras (which throws much light on Paul's pre-Christian outlook; see p. 199b), there is a gloomy presentation of the doctrine of the two ages, with the doctrine of predestination that accompanied it. "Esdras" finds it difficult to see how any man at all, or at best more than a mere handful, can possibly inherit the age to come, under the stringent conditions laid down in the Law. The same distressing problem was evidently present to the mind of Paul the Jew. But now he has found a sufficient answer to his questionings. What the Law could not do, God has done (cf. Rom. 8[3])—he has made us capable of sharing the lot of the holy in light.

But, further, for Jewish thinkers the age of light was wholly future. It is Paul's constant postulate (ever since he "saw the Lord," and knew that life was triumphant over death and sin) that the "age to come" *has* come. What was future has begun to be present. The two ages, so to speak, overlap. While the world apart from Christ is still under the sway of the powers of darkness, for those who are "in Christ" the new age is already here (cf. Gal. 1^{1-5}, note). The night is past and dawn has come. (See pp. 206–7.)

14. What has happened may further be described as an "emancipation" (for this is the effective sense of *redemption*). This is a great Pauline word. The crucial instance of a divinely wrought emancipation in history was the escape of the Hebrew clans from Egyptian servitude—the "redemption of Israel." By act of God the serfs were freed and became a people. So once again by act of God a free people had come into existence—the Christian Church, which is "the Israel of God" (Gal. 6^{16}). That there may be no mistake about the kind of "emancipation" of which he is speaking, Paul adds the further definition—*the forgiveness of our sins.* The enslaving power was moral evil, fixing the chains of guilt about the conscience—chains now broken (cf. Rom. 6^{15-23}).

15–20. The Cosmical Significance of Christ. For Paul, the finality and absoluteness of this salvation correspond to the absoluteness and finality of the Saviour. Paraphrase: "Christ is the divine Agent both of the original creation of the universe and of its ultimate unification under the rule of God. In the former aspect, he is the 'image' of God (spoken of in Gen. 1^{27}); he is prior in time and therefore in dignity to all created beings; by his energy not only the visible world, but its unseen rulers were brought into being; and as he existed before the universe so he maintains it in being. In the latter aspect, the totality of Godhead resides in him, so as (through his sacrificial death) to reconcile all warring elements in the universe, including the warring powers of the unseen world."

Here Paul comes to grips with the matter which primarily moved him to write this letter (see p. 1250). It is not without significance that he has approached it by way of the consideration of salvation as a glorious experience. We observe here *the practical religious interest which his speculative theology serves.* The important question is, whether the Christian can be sure that the Christ in whom he believes can do, and has done, *all* that needs to be done for his final salvation, so that nothing in the world or out of it can ever alter the fact. To be a saved man you must be able to be sure of that; for if you are still worrying about possible factors outside yourself which conceivably might interfere with your salvation, then it is no salvation at all. It is therefore not the theoretical finality of Christianity as a religious system that is at stake, but the practical finality of Christian salvation as a personal experience.

It is therefore a practical religious interest to know what is *the relation in which Christ stands to God and to the whole order of reality* within which our present and future existence lies. In vv. 15–18 Paul gives the answer, in effect, that this relation is that which Jewish theology attributed to Wisdom. Behind the present passage lies a piece of Scripture exegesis by rabbinic methods (which Paul had doubtless learned from Gamaliel in early days). What is said of Wisdom in Proverbs and in the apocryphal Wisdom of Solomon (a comparatively new book when Paul was a young student and evidently one that he had eagerly read) is combined with the creation story in Gen. 1. "The Lord possessed me in the beginning [or, as the beginning] of his ways, before all his works." So speaks Wisdom in Prov. 8^{22}. Wisdom, therefore, is the "beginning" spoken of in Gen. 1^{1}. But the same Hebrew word (which etymologically suggests the meaning "head") can also be rendered "chief," as a close cognate is actually rendered in Prov. 4^{7}, "Wisdom is the principal thing." Further, the word used for "beginning" in Genesis and Proverbs, in the Greek translation can mean not only that which is temporarily prior, but that which is logically prior, or the "first principle"; and, in fact, the first two words of Genesis were understood by some ancient commentators to mean not "in the beginning" (i.e., before anything else happened), but "by means of a first principle," which first principle was then identified with Wisdom on the basis of Psa. 104^{24}, "in (or by) wisdom hast thou made them all." Once more, the Wisdom of Solomon in a noble passage ($7^{22f.}$) describes Wisdom as "an image of his goodness." It was therefore not difficult to find Wisdom in that passage of Genesis which declares that man was made in the "image" of God. Thus the theological vocabulary of the present passage—*image, firstborn, in him were all things created, before all, head, pre-eminence*—can all be found in the context of these speculations about the divine Wisdom. All these terms, applied by Jewish thinkers to Wisdom, are here applied to Christ, whom Paul had years before declared to be "the Power of God and the Wisdom of God" (1 Cor. 1^{24}; cf. notes on Jn. 1^{1-18}).

15. Christ is *the image of the invisible God*—like Wisdom. But Paul knew him to be such because he had seen "the glory of God in the face of Jesus Christ" (2 Cor. 4^{6}). It is a religious postulate of the Bible, from Moses to Paul and John, that man cannot "see God"—that God in his essence is not an object of human experience. Always our knowledge of God is mediated through something belonging to our own experience. For Paul it was mediated by his experience of a divine-human Person. If we would be true to the central thought of Christianity, we must always find the form of our experience of God in Christ, his image.

The word *firstborn* most naturally implies priority in time; but so closely was primogeniture associated with superior dignity that it is often used simply in the sense of "chief" (and as such is actually used sometimes to translate the same Hebrew word used in Gen. 1[1] for "beginning"). Possibly, therefore, Paul means simply "the chief of creation"; but as he uses just below the phrase "firstborn from the dead" (v. 18) in the sense of one who rose from the dead before anyone else, i.e., in the sense of temporal priority (cf. Rom. 8[29] 1 Cor. 15[20, 23]), it is probable that temporal priority is implied here also. But in that case the meaning cannot be "the One created before all other created things," for this is ruled out by the context. The meaning must be "One who was in being before the creation" (like Wisdom in Prov. 8[22]).

16a. To Christ, as Wisdom, the *visible* and *invisible* worlds owe their being; and Paul adds, to be explicit, that this includes all orders of discarnate intelligences (see p. 1250b). The Colossian "heretics" were setting them in a position of rivalry to Christ. But if it be true that Christ stands to God and the world in the relation of creative Wisdom, then the Powers which control parts of the universe must owe their being to him and, therefore, as derivative beings, must be subordinate to him. The names *Thrones, Dominations, Princedoms, Powers* (as Milton renders them) are borrowed from the angelology of Jewish apocalyptic.

16b, 17. All orders of being, then, were created "in" Christ (v. 16a). The choice of the preposition is probably dictated by the phrase of Genesis "in the Beginning," which Paul took to mean "in Wisdom" and therefore "in Christ." It is not, however, in itself a very perspicuous phrase, and so Paul proceeds to say in unambiguous language just what he conceives the relation of Christ to creation to be. First, it was *through him* that the universe came into being; i.e., the divine energies which brought the universe into existence were exercised by Christ. Secondly, the universe was created *unto him,* i.e., he was not only its "instrumental" but its "final" cause; the purpose of its being is inherent in him. Thus, not only is he prior to the world, and so transcendent, but he is also immanent in it, and by his energies all is maintained in being. On the theological and philosophical significance of this see the introduction.

18. There is here a transition in thought, *from the significance of Christ in creation to his significance in relation to the destiny of the universe.* We must recall that although Paul held that the universe has fundamentally the character of a divine creation "in Christ," yet he recognized that in the present phase of things powers alien from Christ bear wide sway—as is, indeed, undeniable for any honest thinker. Yet it must be that the titles which belong to Wisdom, and therefore to Christ—"Head," "Chief"—must ultimately have their full meaning in relation to the whole of reality. On this he has the following things to say. Here and now there is a *body* to which Christ is really in the fullest sense *head,* namely, the church. (Recall what was said above on v. 13.) The church lives already in the "Age to Come," under the kingdom of Christ, within the sphere of the direct and unimpeded exercise of divine power. Of this new age Christ was most truly the *beginning,* in that he was the first who ever passed from death to life. It is important to bear in mind that Paul, like Jewish thinkers in general, did not believe in the natural "immortality of the soul," in the Greek (Platonic) sense which colors our own thought. For him a dead man was really dead and done for unless and until it should please God to raise him from the dead. Thus for Paul all the great and good of ancient time "were not" (for the shadowy half-existence of Sheol did not count) until the "Age to Come" should bring the resurrection. Jesus, and Jesus alone, had already risen from the dead, and thereby initiated the new age, in which, "each in his own order" (1 Cor. 15[23]), the holy dead should rise. As the new age advanced, his present primacy in the church would become a universal primacy (cf. 1 Cor. 15[23-27] Phil. 2[9-11]).

19. This verse contains the first of the theological terms in this passage which has not a scriptural (O.T.) basis—*the Fullness.* Its meaning here obviously cannot be essentially different from "the Fullness of the Godhead" in 2[9]. The term so translated (Greek *pleroma*) originally meant the "full content" of a vessel or the like (e.g., the "full strength" of a military unit or a ship's crew), or the "totality" of a series (e.g., the "sum total" of monetary items). It had a considerable variety of usage, but what concerns us here is the fact that it was used by both Christian and non-Christian Gnostics as a technical term for the totality of "powers," "emanations," "æons," or whatever term was used for superhuman orders of beings supposed to intervene between man and the Absolute. Paul takes over from the Colossian "heretics" their quasi-philosophical term—not precisely in the same sense, since his philosophy was not theirs, but in a sense which they would readily understand. For him it means the sum of the divine attributes and powers not as distributed through a hierarchy of spiritual beings, but as concentrated in the One God. Gnostics too could speak of the "*pleroma* of good" as "God" (so *Corpus Hermeticum*, vi, 4; ix, 7), but in a sort of pantheistic sense, whereas Paul thought of God in personal, not pantheistic terms. Thus for him "the Totality" (*the Fullness*) or "the Totality of Godhead" would mean God himself regarded in his attributes rather than in his personal identity. We should probably take "the Totality," so interpreted, as the subject of the sentence, which might then be rendered *in him the Totality chose to make Its dwelling.* "The Totality" (=God) is, then, also the subject of the following verbs. It is he, acting in and through Christ, who will finally bring the entire universe into the unity of his own rule (cf. Job 25^{2}).

20. The question has been much discussed, what are the parties to this *reconciliation* or "peace-making"? The view that the parties are men on the one hand and the heavenly beings on the other seems to be excluded by the very form of words (*whether . . . or*). We have a reconciliation either between men and God, and between the heavenly beings and God; or else a reconciliation *among* men and *among* the heavenly beings. The simplest would seem to be a reconciliation of men and heavenly beings respectively to God (cf. Rom. 5^{10} 2 Cor. $5^{18, 19}$, where the "world" at least does not exclude beings other than men). On the other hand, the grammatical construction here is not quite the same as in the passages cited, and may perhaps suggest that created beings are reconciled among themselves and, in being reconciled, brought into subjection to God (or Christ—for it is not quite clear, nor does it make much difference, whether we are to read *to him*, i.e., to Christ, or *to himself*, i.e., to God). In the thought of the time, both Jewish and non-Jewish, there was a strange longing for an assurance that the warring powers of the universe (whose conflicts, it was thought, embroiled men) would ultimately be harmonized (see p. 1250b); and as the thought-atmosphere in which Paul's controversy with the Colossian "heretics" moves is very closely in touch with ideas of this sort, it seems on the whole best to regard him as meaning that *through Christ God has chosen to put an end to all the distressing disharmonies within his universe, and bring all under one effective rule.* This certainly gives the best sense to the words *having made peace*, and it is the teaching of Ephesians.

The reconciliation is effected by means of *the blood of his cross.* No hint is given here of the way in which this is to be understood. The meaning is certainly not that the shedding of Christ's blood propitiates God. Such a thought would be wholly foreign to the context. It is probable that any reference to *blood* in such a thinker as Paul would suggest a reference to sacrifice in a general way. But the idea of sacrifice itself has a very wide range. Underlying it all is the quasi-mystical identification of blood with life (see Gen. 9^{4}). The very fact that Paul has here in view chiefly the discarnate intelligences shows that the *blood of his cross* can only be regarded as the symbol, or projection upon the material sphere, of something in its essence spiritual and so applicable to spiritual beings. We are in a realm of ideas which defy exact analysis; but the august conception moves in the background, that the utter consecration of the life of Christ in self-sacrifice has about it something so absolute and final that it establishes once and for all a supremacy of good in the presence of which all evil is powerless.

21–23. The Verification in Christian Experience. Paraphrase: "What I have said of the universe in general applies to you; for you were alienated, and God has reconciled you through the death of Christ, so as to give you an unimpeachable standing in his presence. In saying so, I assume that you are maintaining your faith, and not moving away from the hope which the gospel brought you when you heard it. Remember, it is a world-wide gospel."

The above exposition has appeared rather speculative. Paul now *appeals to the evangelical experience* which for him is always the real foundation of theology. At bottom, his belief in the cosmical significance of Christ is grounded on an inward sense of the absoluteness and finality of Christ's work in saving the Christian people—in saving Paul himself and the people he knew. The reconciliation of which they are conscious is primarily a reconciliation to God. They had been alienated from God: their mental attitude to him was a hostile one, for their deeds were evil. Now they are reconciled to him by his own act. (This is Paul's constant teaching—not that God, having been hostile to men, was reconciled to them, as he is sometimes misrepresented.) It was, as they know, through the death of Christ that this was done; and so the reconciliation, like the death, was the work of a concrete personality, incarnate among men (*the body of his flesh*—probably in contradistinction to any "discarnate intelligences" that might be supposed to have a part in the work of salvation).—Once again Paul does not explain how the death of Christ reconciled. Behind the single clause lies a whole process of thought common to him and his readers, which could be assumed without argument.

Another aspect, rather than merely a consequence, of the reconciliation is the good standing before God which the reconciled enjoy. It is probably wrong to take the words *to present you holy*, etc. (v. 22) as referring to the ultimate issue of the divine purpose, in the final moral perfection of Christ's people. It is "justification by faith" of which Paul is speaking. It is not that the Colossians have attained, or are to attain in some remote future, a moral perfection which will secure their acceptance at the Last Judgment. It is that here and now, by grace of God, who "justifieth the ungodly," they stand before him as his consecrated people, to whom he "imputes" no fault. How they must make good this justified status by practical moral effort, Paul sets forth in the latter part of the Epistle. Here it is the divine act of grace that is in view.

23. *If so be* . . . If the preceding clause had been taken to refer to the ultimate moral perfection of Christians, then this sentence would naturally have been referred to the future perseverance of the Colossians, as a condition of their ultimate acceptance in the Judgment. But the actual grammatical form of the clause as well as the context is strongly against any such interpretation. The idea is that faith is that which keeps us in such a condition that at any moment it may be said that God presents us *holy and without blemish* (*blameless*) *before him*, i.e., that we are justified by grace. Thus what Paul has just said about the Colossians being reconciled and so justified is true *on the assumption* that at this present moment they are maintaining their faith. This is exactly what in strict grammar the clause would naturally imply, and it suits the context. The qualification is pointed by the fear Paul felt that by listening to the "heretics" the Colossians might actually be *moving away from the Christian hope* in its full scope.—In the close of the verse the Colossians are again reminded of the catholicity of the gospel, as in 1^{6}, and for a similar reason.

24–29. Paul as Missionary to the Gentiles. Paraphrase: "I am suffering on your account, and I am glad of it because it is helping the church, which is Christ's body, to make up the tale of sufferings which must befall it in communion with him. I am a servant of the church by God's commission, my task being to bring into full effect the fiat of God. It was long a secret; but now he has chosen to make known to his own the full wealth of that secret as it affects the Gentiles. The secret is this: CHRIST IN YOU THE HOPE OF GLORY. I want *every* man to know that secret, so that every man may be a full initiate into Christ. I labor for that end with all the energy God gives me."

The controlling idea here is that of *the mystical union of Christians with and in their Lord*. This union is thought of by Paul as the closest possible, both for the individual (as in Gal. 2^{20}) and for the church, which is the body of Christ, as the organism through which his Spirit lives and works in the world. The sufferings of Christ are not the sufferings endured by Jesus on earth (as though these were not sufficient for the redemption of the world, and must be supplemented), but all the sufferings which the Church of Christ must endure before the consummation (of which the historic Passion of Jesus was, so to speak, the focal point). These sufferings are sufferings of Christ because Christ is the true Subject of every experience of the church in fulfilling the will of God. According to that will there is a tale of sufferings yet to be made up. Paul is glad that so much of it falls to his lot. In bearing it he is most directly serving the church.

26, 27. The age was one of "mystery-Religions," i.e., cults in which ineffable secrets were imparted to the initiated in carefully guarded ritual forms (see art., *Backgrounds*, pp. 851–2). The "heretics" of Colossæ, like the Gnostics in general, doubtless felt the influence of this type of religion. Well, Paul has a *mystery* into which he initiates men (cf. 1 Cor. 2^{6-16}). There is a divine secret which for ages no man guessed. Much of the counsel of God was made known to the Jews, but behind that old dispensation lay a fuller purpose of God, undreamed of by generations of faithful Jews, embracing the Gentiles also. Now, it has pleased God to make known this secret, and Paul has been intrusted with its revelation. It may be summed up in the words, *Christ in you the hope of glory*. There are three main elements. First, there is the whole glorious content of the Christian hope (which is the principal purport of the "mystery" in 1 Cor. 2). This is, indeed, something which in one sense is inconceivable to the human mind; yet for the Christian it is of a piece with present experience, which is the "earnest" or the "firstfruits" of his coming inheritance. Thus, secondly, there is the nature of the experience which gives a present foretaste of that which eye cannot see nor ear hear nor heart conceive. It is in a word the experience of the indwelling Christ. Thirdly, there is the universal scope of this hope and experience. This is not expressly contained in the formula (except insofar as the *you* means primarily Gentiles, for such the Colossian Christians were), but is explicit in the immediately preceding words.

28. Paul has spoken of this as a "mystery" into which men must be initiated. The purpose of initiation, according to current phraseology, was to make a man *perfect.* Paul hastens to make it clear that he is not contemplating any esoteric initiation, confined to a selected few: no, it is his commission to instruct *every* man in the *whole* of Christian philosophy, so that *every* man may be a *perfect* initiate—this doubtless against an esoteric tendency present among the Colossian "heretics," as generally among Gnostics.

CHAPTER II

1–7. Paul and His Unknown Correspondents. Paraphrase: "I write thus because I want you to realize how deep is my concern for you and your neighbors of Laodicæa, although we have never met—a concern that you should be consolidated in love and have a full understanding of that divine secret to which I have alluded. The secret is, in one word, CHRIST; for in him all wealth of wisdom and knowledge are comprised. If you have once grasped the secret, you will never be misled by any specious arguments. Although I am absent, I am watching with satisfaction the disciplined order and the solid front of your faith in Christ. So firmly maintain your Christian life and faith in the purity in which you received it; and be very thankful."

These verses apply what Paul has said of his commission to declare the "mystery" (1^{26}) to the Gentiles, to the particular case of the two churches of the Lycus Valley. Though he did not found these churches, and has never visited them, he yet feels responsibility for them, and wishes them to recognize the fact. Thus he passes from the general exposition of the fundamentals of Christian theology to a direct appeal to his correspondents to resist the allurements of the "heretics."

5. The words *order* and *stedfastness* are both military terms, and are doubtless used here with full intent of the Christian warfare (Eph. 6^{10-17}).

8–15. The Central Christian Experience as Security Against False Speculations. Paraphrase: "Do not be misled by any attempt to found religion on the 'Elemental Powers' instead of on Christ. For he is superior to all powers; the Totality of Godhead is in him; and in him you have all you need for full salvation. The only 'circumcision' worth the name is that which he gives, namely, the discarding of the lower nature through union with him (by baptism) in his death and resurrection. Yes; dead as you were in sin, God gave you new life when he forgave you and released you from all claims of the Law; in fact, abolished it by virtue of the cross of Christ. Thereby he triumphed over all Powers and reduced them to impotence."

8. *Rudiments*—read *elements* (R.V. mg.). The reference, however, is not to elementary knowledge, superseded by the fuller knowledge in Christ. The word was used technically in current religious philosophy of the time for spiritual beings supposed to animate and preside over the elements of the physical universe, and generally conceived as resident in the heavenly bodies. In syncretistic circles they were identified with the Princedoms and Powers of Jewish angelology (cf. 1^{16}).

9. For the *fullness* or totality, see above on 1^{19}. *Bodily* is "corporately" rather than "corporally." The totality of divine attributes is present as a whole in one "Body" or concrete individual personality, not distributed through a hierarchy of beings.

10. As the fullness of Godhead is in Christ, so he mediates a *full* religious experience; i.e., all that the religious life can require is to be found in Christ, and need not be looked for elsewhere. This is particularized in what follows.

11–13. *Circumcision* is for Paul the Jew a fundamental religious idea. The outward rite he cannot believe to have any worth (Rom. $2^{28, 29}$), and when an attempt was made by Jewish Christians to force it upon Gentile converts, he strenuously resisted (see Galatians). Yet he could not abandon the thought that it symbolized something ultimately true. While, therefore, in dealing with early Jewish propaganda in Galatia he contented himself with a purely negative attitude to the rite, here he takes the view that the real circumcision is nothing less than the *putting off*—the cutting away (as it were)—of *the body of the flesh,* i.e., the whole organization of the lower instincts in man (or, as it might be put in psychological terms, the dissolution of "sentiments" organized about wrong centers); and this, he holds, takes place effectively only in a Christian conversion (v. 13; cf. Phil. 3^{3}). For that involves being united with Christ in his death (the decisive break with the bad past) and in his resurrection (the beginning of a new life). Such a conversion he held to be a true miracle, exhibiting the same power of God which was manifested in Christ's resurrection (cf. on 1^{18}). The mystical union with Christ which is the condition of this "death" and "resurrection" (*raised,* v. 12, *quicken* or *make alive,* v. 13) took the form of incorporation into the church, the "body" of Christ; and the incorporation took place by baptism, the symbolism of which was admirably adapted to represent dying and rising again (*buried with him,* v. 12). Paul cannot be thought to hold that baptism "in the flesh made with hands" would have any more virtue than circumcision with the like limitations. Only if baptism is in the given case a *real* moral death and resurrection is it "valid" (see Rom. 6[1-11]). But Paul knew of no being "in Christ" which was not also being in the fellowship of the church, and so mediated by baptism.

14, 15. What was accomplished on the cross was a defeat of the *princedoms* and *powers* (=the "Elemental Spirits"; cf. 1[16]). The Law was the sign and the medium of their rule over men (see Gal. 3[19] 4[9, 10]). Hence the abolishing of the Law—*bond*—*ordinances*—means their defeat: the rendering *having put off from himself* is probably wrong. The meaning is "having stripped" or "despoiled," as a triumphant warrior stripped his defeated foe of his arms. This word, therefore, as well as *triumphing,* is a military metaphor.

16–23. True Religion not Ascetic and Ritual Practices but New Life. (See also 3[1-4].) Paraphrase (including 3[1-4]): "Let no one impose upon you food-regulations or the observance of holy seasons. These are shadows: Christ is the reality. Again, do not accept the censure of any one who lays stress upon asceticism and the worship of angels. With all his pretentious claims he is not loyal to our Head, who alone gives unity and power of growth to the body. The twofold Christian experience of death and resurrection should save you from all this: (a) By dying with Christ you have passed beyond the sway of the Elemental Powers; then why pay heed to ritual prohibitions which belong to their sphere? Such schemes of behavior, with all their show of philosophy, are really quite futile. (b) You are risen with Christ (3[1-4]), and so you should be governed by motives arising in the unseen world where Christ is—for there your real life is, hidden now, but to be brought to light when Christ is manifested."

16, 17. The "heretics" passed judgment on members of the church who were careless about certain ritual regulations which they laid down. These appear to have been borrowed from Judaism. They consisted (1) of rules for clean and unclean food (*meat*) and (2) of the observance of special holy *days,* such as *new moon* and *Sabbath,* both Jewish festivals. Both food and divisions of time, as belonging to the material world, would for Paul and his adversaries alike come within the sphere of the Elemental Powers (the latter in particular because new moon and Sabbath mark the revolutions of the heavenly bodies, supposed to be intimately associated with these Powers; cf. Gal. 4[8-10]). For *them,* it was religiously important to keep on good terms with the Powers; hence one must scrupulously observe all forms of taboo associated with material and temporal things. For Paul all that had become irrelevant (cf. Rom. 14[2-6, 14] 1 Cor. 8[8] 10[23-26]). He had fought against the imposition of rules of this kind when they had been associated with the attempt to force the observance of the Jewish Law upon Christians. Now they cropped up again under the guise of "enlightenment" to bring men to a greater degree of "perfection," and he deals with them even more sternly. What would he have thought of the rigorous Sabbatarianism of later ages?

18. To borrowing from Judaism the "heretics" added definitely ascetic practices (for this is the meaning of the words translated *humility* here, and "will-worship," "humility" and "severity to the body" in v. 23). These were associated with the cult of angels (=the Elemental Powers). The phrase rendered *dwelling in the things which he hath seen* has long been a puzzle to commentators, and attempts have been made in ancient and in modern times to emend the text. It is now known that the verb was a technical expression in the mystery-religions for entering upon a certain stage of initiation. Paul is not careful to use it with precision; he adopts the grandiose style of the mystery-mongers in a tone of mockery. We might render the phrase "entering the portals of vision." The pretentiousness of all this kind of thing he thinks simply silly (cf. 1 Cor. 8[1]), with its claim to the exercise of pure "reason" (or, as we might say, "higher thought"). It is, after all, he says, only a *fleshly reason* (*mind*), since it exalts the material to a place in religion which does not rightly belong to it.

19. The fundamental error is that this type of religion does not hold fast by Christ as the supreme Head of the body; and a body without a head has neither organic unity nor power of growth. In other words, the new tendencies in the Colossian Church are toward social disintegration within the Christian community.

20–22. On *rudiments,* see 2[8]. Union with Christ in his death means that we have passed from under the domination of the material, and therefore owe nothing more to the Elemental Powers. Prohibitions affecting not imperishable moral principles but things that *perish* *with the using* are irrelevant to one who has *died to the world.*

23. This sentence as it stands in the original is scarcely intelligible, and some primitive corruption of the text is suspected. The words might be rendered "which commandments, though they make a profession of wisdom which rests rather on gratuitous asceticism than on any element of real worth, only serve to indulge the lower nature." If this is right, Paul is commenting on the often observed fact that asceticism in certain directions frequently provokes unrestrained self-indulgence in others.

CHAPTER III

1–4. New Life in Christ. (2^{16-23} continued. See paraphrase of that passage.) The other side of "dying with Christ" is union with him in his resurrection. Morally that means the dominance of new motives and new energies which lift the conduct of life to a higher level. It is lived for and by eternal, not temporal values (v. 2; cf. 2 Cor. 4^{18}). Yet this does not mean a vague "spirituality," indifferent to the practical issues of daily life on earth (as Paul sufficiently shows in the following ethical section). For the eternal values are defined for us by Christ, as the unseen world is for us the world where Christ is supreme. If we are "in Christ," then our real life is in that world (v. 3). It is *a hidden life*, its meaning half frustrated at present by the intractability of our material environment; but it is real, and one day, when all that is material has passed away, it will be revealed—*manifested*—as the only real life there is. Meanwhile, we live most truly our own life when we refer everything to motives which are centered in Christ. For in the deepest sense he *is* our life (cf. Gal. 2^{20}).—The immediate relevance of this is to show that thoroughgoing Christianity emancipates the conscience from the trivialities of such ritual and ascetic disciplines as the "heretics" advocated. Religion always tends to fall back into that kind of thing; for many people in all Christian denominations that is what religion mainly means. But real Christianity goes deep beyond all such mere fussiness. In rebutting a false ideal Paul has at the same time laid the foundation for a positive construction of Christian ethics with which the following section of the Epistle is concerned.

5–17. General Principles of Christian Ethics. For Paul, Christian morality has a negative and a positive aspect. Paraphrase: "Certain things must be got rid of: these are not any ritual uncleanness, but lusts of the flesh and grasping self-assertion (you know what I mean from experience of your pagan days)—all sins of this kind, including anger, malice, and untruth. Such things as these constitute the bad self which you must put off as you would put off an outworn garment. Then you must put on a new self, divinely formed, functioning on a level where distinctions of race, culture, and social standing are irrelevant. The qualities of this new self are such as kindness, tolerance, forgiveness, and love, the bond that makes all perfect. Peace must be the governing principle of your inner life, as peace is the end of your organization in one body. The Christian message should be thoroughly familiar to you, and you may find much mutual instruction in poetry and song through which you express your thankfulness to God. And as you thank God through Christ, so all your conduct should have the mark of Christ upon it."

We have here a very brief outline of Christian ethics—no doubt a summary of the kind of moral instruction Paul was accustomed to give his converts. It is based upon the twofold religious experience just described, and set in contrast with the morally irrelevant asceticism which has been rejected. The Christian has died with Christ; and that means, ethically interpreted, *the abandonment of evil ways;* and he has risen with Christ, and that means *the acquisition of virtuous ways.* The evil and the virtuous life are characterized concisely but with sufficient detail to give definiteness and concreteness to the moral ideal, positively and negatively. (Cf. the greatly expanded ethical outline in Eph. 4^{25}–5^{20}, and notes there.)

5a. In principle the "body of flesh," or the system of sinful dispositions, has been killed and buried, in baptism ($2^{12,\ 13}$). The ethical life demands that the surviving *members* or organs of this body should be actually suppressed. Then we have a curious transition from organ to function, made easier for Paul by the fact that in Hebrew psychology each member is thought of as individually responsible for its acts. (This survives in some popular ways of thought. Did not Cranmer say "This *hand* hath offended"? Cf. Mk. 9^{43-48}.)

5b–7. Cf. Eph. 5^{3-8}, and notes there, for the implied classification of vices. The words, *upon the sons of disobedience*, are not authentic here (see R.V. mg.); they seem to have crept in from the parallel passage in Eph. 5^{6}.

8. A further list of vices, falling under the general head of "grasping self-assertion" (on which see Eph. $5^{3,\ 4}$, notes).

9–11. In Gal. 3^{27} Christians are said to have "put on" Christ. To *put on the new man* is not very different in meaning (cf. Eph. 2^{15}

4[24]). In both those places, as here, the new man is a creation of God; and here it is added that he is created *after the image* of God (cf. Gen. 1[27]). For Paul, Christ is the image of God (1[15]). Thus the new humanity is humanity "in Christ." That it is thought of corporately rather than individually is indicated by v. 11: in this new man (or new humanity) all accidental distinctions are transcended (cf. Gal. 3[27, 28]—"ye are all one [person] in Christ Jesus"). Paul's mystical way of thought makes it possible for him to speak of Christ as a "corporate personality."

12. As the sin to which the Christian has died has been sufficiently characterized by a short list of typical vices, so here the life of virtue to which he is risen is characterized by a brief allusion to certain typical virtues. As on the negative side special stress was laid on anti-social sins, so here the most prominent virtues are those which have a direct *social* value (cf. Eph. 4[32]–5[2]).

14. *Love*, or charity (for which Paul, like other Christian writers, uses a word practically unknown to pre-biblical pagan Greek), is presented as the principle of perfection in the moral world. For the meaning which Paul attached to the term, see especially Rom. 12 and 1 Cor. 13. It is not love as "tender emotion," but love as an organizing "sentiment" (to use the psychological terms).

15. The best commentary is Eph. 2[11-22] 4[1-6] on which see notes.

16. Cf. Eph. 5[19].

17. Christians are baptized *in the name of the Lord Jesus* (1 Cor. 6[11]; cf. 1 Cor. 1[13]) with the confession "Jesus is Lord" (Rom. 10[9]). The rite and the language used implied that the baptized person is the property of Christ. Paul here urges that his property-rights should be asserted in every *word* and *deed* of a Christian.

18–25. Christian Ethics in the Home. (See also 4[1].) Paraphrase: "Thus, it is a Christian thing for wives to show deference to their husbands and for husbands to love their wives; for children to obey their parents and for parents to show respect for the personalities of their children. Slaves should pay strict obedience to their masters, not to curry favor, but because all service is rendered to Christ, our Master and Judge. Similarly, masters (4[1]) must treat their slaves fairly, for Christ is their Master too."

The only social area in which Paul applies his constructive principles with any particularity is the household, involving the three reciprocal relations of husband and wife, parent and child, master and slave. The slavery with which he deals is domestic slavery; industrial slavery, which has provided most of the worst horrors of the system, does not fall within his view. For men of the ancient world the domestic slave was as much a member of the household, or *familia*, as the child. The treatment is very meager, and it must be confessed that we have no more than a slight and tentative beginning toward a Christian ethic of family life. But we must not miss the significance of the fact that there is any such section in the Epistle at all. In Paul's earlier thought, as set forth in 1 Cor. 7, the whole of family life belongs to the category of "the things of the world," and distinct from "the things of the Lord" (1 Cor. 7[32, 33]), and the only Christian attitude to it is a detachment as complete as possible. At that time Paul was under the dominance of the belief that the end of all things was very close at hand (1 Cor. 7[29]). His gradual emancipation from that belief now made it possible for him to recognize a positive value in existing social institutions. When Paul is criticized for apparently giving a Christian sanction to slavery and the subjection of women, we may well bear in mind that at least he came to see that marriage and domestic service must be somehow Christianized. As long as thought remained at the level of 1 Cor. 7, completely indifferent to family life, it could not begin to deal effectively with its problems. To admit that family relationships could be *in the Lord* (vv. 18, 20) was an advance that necessarily challenged further advance. In making this admission, Paul could hardly do other than start from social institutions—including slavery—fundamental to the civilization of his time, to the duties of which institutions he would give a Christian character.

18, 19. *Wives and husbands.* The naïve treatment here is expanded in Eph. 5[21b-33], which see.

20, 21. *Parents and children.* That obedience is the duty of children is good O.T. doctrine (hence the precept is in Eph. 6[1, 2] buttressed by a quotation of Deut. 5[16]). The injunction to fathers, repeated in similar terms, Eph. 6[4], is more striking, and may be regarded as the first step in giving weight in ethics to the new valuation of the child-personality in the teaching of Jesus.

22–25. (See also 4[1].) *Slaves and masters.* The treatment is here fuller, possibly because Paul was at the moment dealing with a particular case of the master-slave relation (Philemon and Onesimus). To define the Christian position in this matter, he goes to root-principles. Essentially, there is no distinction of bond and free within the Christian Community (3[11]). The Christian, whether bond or free, is the "slave" of his heavenly "Lord"—*ye serve the Lord Christ.* Masters, too, *have a Master in heaven.* For the slave, this means that he acquires a full moral personality, responsible ultimately to Christ alone. Slaves, therefore, must make of their earthly service a service of Christ, by conscientious sincerity in all they do. If they *do wrong,* it is Christ they have offended and he judges impartially (v. 25). This verse is to be referred to slaves, not, as the corresponding Eph. 6^{9}, to masters; Paul had just dealt with a defaulting slave (cf. Philemon, v. 18). Similarly in Eph. 6^{5-8} the slave is to render service to Christ by obeying his earthly master in sincerity, with good will and singleness of mind. Masters are to "do the same," i.e., show the same "good will and singleness of mind," in relation to their slaves. So here, the master is to treat his slave with justice and equity (4^{1}).—The outcome of all this is to make the slave no longer a chattel but a spiritually free agent, whose dignity as a person is not to be outraged because he is allotted subordinate functions in society. This does not solve the problem of slavery, but it is a definitely Christian contribution to the solution of one of the cardinal problems of ancient society, though its full implications were not worked out in ancient times.

CHAPTER IV

1. See 3^{22-25}, and notes.

2–6. Christian Ethics; Concluding Precepts. Paraphrase: "Be watchful and pray persistently (for me too, that I may have opportunity of telling the secret of Christ, though I am in prison). Show discretion in your dealings with non-Christians. Use every opportunity to the full. Cultivate grace and tact in speech."

2. "Watch and pray" is a precept derived from the highest authority (Mk. 14^{38}), introduced here as in Eph. 6^{18} to clinch all the moral exhortations.

3, 4. Paul claims a place in his correspondents' prayers, because of the special difficulty and the special opportunities of his present position. So also Eph. $6^{19, 20}$. Here the request for prayer makes a parenthesis, for the writer has still some general precepts (corresponding to those in Eph. $5^{15f.}$).

5. Religious enthusiasm is no substitute for common sense, especially when the religion is that of a minority. *Outsiders* deserve consideration (cf. Rom. 12^{17}). *Buying up the opportunity* (R.V. mg.) rightly renders an expression borrowed from commercial language, where the verb means to "make a corner" in a commodity. Eph. 5^{16} assigns the motive, "because these are bad times." Just because all the powers of evil are abroad (cf. Eph. 6^{12}), mustered for the last fight, every effort must be made to turn every opportunity to the best account in the good cause.

6. *Seasoned.* Paul employs a culinary metaphor. Tastes differ, and so the seasoning must differ. A form of address that would be acceptable to one person might offend another. Speech is *with grace* when it is considerate of the person addressed. Courtesy is thoughtfulness.

7–18. News and Greetings. Paraphrase: "Tychicus and Onesimus (a good Christian and one of yourselves) will tell you all my news. I am to give you greetings from Aristarchus, Mark (who may be coming to you; make him welcome), Jesus Justus—my only Jewish fellow workers; from Epaphras, who is one of yourselves (I can testify how deep an interest he takes in you and the other churches of the Lycus Valley); from Luke, our dear physician, and from Demas. Greetings to friends at Laodicæa, especially Nymphas and the congregation in his household. After you have had this letter read, send it on to Laodicæa, and do you read the letter from Laodicæa. Tell Archippus to be thorough in his work for the Lord.

"And now a greeting in my own hand—PAUL. Remember that I am a prisoner. Grace be with you!"

7–9. The letter ends with personal matters. No detailed news is given, because Tychicus, the bearer of the letter, will be able to tell all that is necessary. He is accompanied by Onesimus, who is given a not unnecessary note of commendation.

10, 11. There follow *greetings from Paul's companions.* First *Aristarchus* (cf. Acts 27^{2}), *Mark* (known to us from Acts as a companion of Paul and Barnabas, and here introduced to the Colossians, whom he intends to visit, as Barnabas' first cousin), and *Jesus Justus* (not otherwise known), who are described as Paul's only Jewish helpers; so understand v. 11, punctuating and translating as follows— . . . *and Jesus Justus, who—and these alone of the circumcision—are my fellow-workers for the kingdom of God.* The current translation commits Paul to an absurd exaggeration, and one contradicted by the next words. The other Jewish Christians of the locality must be supposed to have been of the Judaistic or anti-Pauline party.

12–14. Next, *Ephaphras,* himself a Colossian, and one who stands in a special relation of responsibility to the three churches of the Lycus Valley (cf. $1^{7, 8}$), *Luke,* Paul's physician, and one *Demas* (neither otherwise known to us, except from Philemon, v. 24 and 2 Tim.

4[10], which add nothing to the present passage). Luke is very likely the author of the travel-diary contained in the latter part of Acts, and according to persistent tradition the author of Acts and of the third Gospel. These three, therefore, were Gentile Christians co-operating with Paul.

15. Greetings to Christians of the neighboring city of Laodicæa, especially one *Nymphas* (or possibly the feminine Nympha) and a group of Christians belonging to his (her) household (either actually or for ecclesiastical purposes).

16. Paul has written at the same time to Laodicæa, and he gives instructions that there shall be an interchange of letters. The Laodicæan letter has almost certainly perished. Certainly, the Epistle which passes under that name in some MSS. is a forgery.

17. For *Archippus*, cf. Philemon, v. 2.

18. Paul has dictated the letter, as was his practice (cf. Rom 16[22]); but he now adds a greeting in his *own hand* (cf. Gal. 6[11] 2 Thess. 3[17]). Such autographs at the end of dictated letters are known to us in many papyri of the period.

FIRST AND SECOND THESSALONIANS

By Professor C. C. McCown

FIRST THESSALONIANS

Introduction

Paul's Previous Activities. In all probability the first letter to the Thessalonians is the earliest preserved writing of Paul as well as the oldest N.T. book. It is not, of course, Paul's first letter, nor is it the work of a tyro in missionary preaching or theological thinking. For fifteen years or more now he had been a Christian missionary engaged in vigorous labors in a wide variety of fields. He had been compelled to defend his faith against every type of national religion, mystery cult, and school of philosophy.

The Nature of Paul's Letters. Yet Paul was not a philosopher, and his letters were not deeply learned and carefully prepared theological treatises. Though not written to individuals, they partake of the nature of the private letter. Each was occasioned by certain definite conditions and problems in the church addressed. Particularly is this true in the case of the two short Thessalonian letters. Their difficulties are largely due to their personal and occasional character. Their interpretation depends upon a correct reconstruction of the circumstances of their origin.

Thessalonica. The date of 1 Thessalonians and the circumstances under which it was writtten are to be discovered from the letter itself and the relevant section of Acts (17^{1}–18^{17}). Thessalonica, modern Saloniki, had a most favorable location. Lying at the head of the Thermaic Gulf, it had a good harbor and a hinterland of rich and well-watered plains. In Paul's day it stood at the center of that great artery of traffic, the Ignatian Way. Cicero, who went there during his exile a century before Paul's time, speaks of it as "placed in the lap of the empire." Its size, commercial importance, and trade connections explain the seemingly exaggerated language of Paul when he boasts of the large part which the Thessalonian church had had in the spread of the gospel (1 Thess. 1^{8}). It was, moreover, a free Greek city ruled by its own officials (politarchs, Acts 17^{6}), not a Roman military colony like Philippi or Corinth. It was sufficiently large to have a Jewish synagogue, which Philippi, apparently, did not possess (Acts 16^{13}).

The Founding of the Church. Paul, Silas, and Timothy had been driven to this thriving metropolis by persecution at Philippi. When, after three Sabbaths of Christian preaching in the synagogue, the majority of his fellow Jews had rejected the new faith, Paul had founded a Christian synagogue consisting of a few Jews, many "devout (i.e., God-fearing) Greeks," and "chief (or honorable) women not a few." How long he was allowed to continue preaching to the new congregation we cannot know, but probably only for a few weeks, when the recalcitrant Jews had appealed to the prejudices of the mob and the loyalty of the politarchs and had driven him out of the city. Soon after they followed him to Berœa and, though the Jewish colony there had received his message with favor, they compelled him to flee to Athens, whence he had gone to Corinth (Acts 17^{1-15} 1 Thess. $2^{2,\ 17}$ $3^{2,\ 6}$).

The Occasion of the Letter. Paul had spent so short a time with his Macedonian converts and they had been so quickly subjected to severe persecution that he was most anxious as to their steadfastness. Circumstances had for some time prevented him from communicating with them. Apparently Luke, if he was the author of the *we-sections* of Acts (see intro. to Acts, p. 1095a) has been left at Philippi, and Silas perhaps at Berœa. From Athens Paul sent Timothy back to bring him news of the churches in Macedonia (1 Thess. $3^{1f.}$). Shortly afterward he and Silas came to Paul at Corinth with most encouraging tidings. At Corinth, then, in the winter or spring of 51 A.D., relieved of anxiety, full of joy, and engaged in an intense and successful missionary activity, Paul wrote this letter. At no other place in the narrative of Acts do we find the three missionaries together as called for by the proper sequence of events (Acts 18^{5} 1 Thess. 1^{1} 3^{6}).

The expressed reasons for writing were three, as follows:

(1) The church at Thessalonica was mainly Gentile according to the testimony of Acts (17^{4}) and 1 Thessalonians (1^{9} 2^{14}). It was natural—indeed, almost inevitable—that such a church should have difficulties with doctrines so novel as the Second Advent of Christ and the resurrection of the body, ideas utterly foreign to Greek thinking. To answer a question which had arisen in the minds of members

of the church on these matters was one of the reasons for writing (4^{13}).

(2) Another of his purposes was to put the new converts on a firmer moral foundation. He wished to strengthen their hearts so that they might be blameless in holiness before God when Christ should appear for the Last Judgment (3^{13}). Coming, as they largely did, from the lower classes, being small tradesmen, freedmen, and slaves, some of Paul's converts were poorly instructed as to right standards of living, and the apostle gives a considerable proportion of every letter, as of this one, to instruction on questions, often most elementary questions, of moral conduct.

(3) The third expressed desire of the apostle was to encourage the Thessalonians to bear their persecutions and troubles without wavering (3^{3-5}).

Two other reasons for writing are not expressly stated but plainly implied.

(1) Apparently Paul had learned from Timothy and Silas that their absence and failure to communicate with the Thessalonians had suggested to the minds of some of these converts suspicions as to the apostles' motives. Such doubts were not wanting in plausibility. One of the most familiar figures in the cities of the early Roman Empire was the traveling philosophic lecturer. The literature of the period is full of jibes at him. Sometimes he was but a showy rhetorician, dealing in startling antitheses and moving climaxes. Others were rough and brutal curbstone orators, who affected the philosophic robe and staff and begging scrip and the manners and methods of Diogenes. But there were some who were sincere and earnest preachers of morality—real shepherds of souls. Such were Dio Chrysostom, Epictetus, and probably Apollonius of Tyana. If there had been no genuine, high-minded preachers of righteousness, the false imitators would not have been able to thrive. Among the Greeks and Romans the early Christian missionaries must often have been classed as philosophers. So Paul was rated at Athens (Acts 17^{18}), and at Ephesus he actually lectured in the school of a no doubt converted rhetorician daily from eleven to four (Acts 19^{9}, etc.; see Moffatt). When he and his companions disappeared from Thessalonica and their converts heard nothing from them, questions naturally arose in their minds. Had he forgotten them for new and richer friends? Was he in the business of preaching, like so many of these traveling lecturers, just for what he could get out of it? It was a charge which his enemies again and again made against him (2 Cor. 7^{2} 12^{17}), and evidently it had already cropped up at Thessalonica (1 Thess. $2^{3f.}$). Wisely Paul does not explicitly mention it, but he tries to counteract it in several trenchant verses (2^{3}–3^{13}).

(2) From Timothy Paul had also learned that there were divisions and jealousies in the church. Some were "walking disorderly," refusing to follow the leadership of the officers of the church and also spending their time, not in productive industry but in fomenting dissensions. For these the letter contains a few pointed sentences ($5^{12f.}$).

The Teachings of the Epistle. As a summary of *Paul's missionary message* 1 Thessalonians is especially valuable. The writer felt called upon to recapitulate the gospel that he had preached at Thessalonica. Therefore we may secure from the letter some idea of what his missionary message to a Gentile congregation must have been. No doubt he fed them, as he did the Corinthians, with milk, not with solid food (1 Cor. $3^{1f.}$). An ethical monotheism, with emphasis on the wrath to come and Christ as the Saviour from that wrath, the present gift of the Spirit, a demand for moral living, the future coming of Christ—these seem to have been the burden of his preaching.

There are numerous Pauline ideas that are not emphasized in this letter. There is here no attempt to discuss such problems as the rejection of Israel, which occupies the space of three valuable chapters in Romans (9–11), the person and place of Christ, and the relations of the Law, works, and faith. Indeed, if one may judge by the context, "faith" in the letter to the Thessalonians (see especially 1^{8} $3^{2, 5, 6, 7}$) means faithfulness rather than that combination of mystical trust in God and communion with him, which elsewhere seems to suit the Pauline usage.

Yet *Paul's characteristic mysticism* is everywhere implied. The peculiar phrases which express his "faith" occur frequently enough and in such connections as to prove that he had long used them. "In Christ," or some equivalent is found seven times (1^{1} 2^{14} 3^{8} $4^{1, 16}$ $5^{12, 18}$); "through Christ," three times ($4^{2, 14mg.}$ 5^{9}); "in God," twice (1^{1} 2^{2}); "in the Holy Ghost," once (1^{5}). When Paul speaks of the churches of God that are in Judæa "in Christ Jesus" (2^{14}), or of those individuals who are set over the congregation "in the Lord" (5^{12}), there is implied a long development of the idea that all the Christian's life is fundamentally a fellowship with the exalted Christ. Allusions to the Spirit and to prophesying ($1^{5, 6}$ 4^{8} 5^{19}) imply the same phenomena of miracles (note "in power," 1^{5}) and vigorous religious emotionalism which the Corinthian church enjoyed (1 Cor. 12, 14).

Though Paul does not discuss *the nature of God,* incidental allusions show that he must have made a special point of preaching an emphatic ethical monotheism to the idol-worshiping Thessalonians (1^{9}), a "gospel of God" (2$^{2, 8, 9, 13}$). In contrast to their formerly accepted deities he had preached a "living and true God" (1^{9} 4^{5}). They are beloved by God and chosen by him (1^{4}). He has given them the Spirit (4^{8}) and their confidence rests upon God (1^{8}), to whom they turned from their idols (1^{9}). It is he who tries men's hearts (2^{4}), and before him they must be approved (1^{3} 2$^{12, 15}$ 3^{13} 4$^{1, 3, 6f.}$ 5^{18}). It is he who raised Jesus from the dead and will likewise raise believers (4^{14}). They live "in God" as they do in Christ (1^{1} 2^{2}).

The *large place of Christ* in Paul's thinking is clearly implied. He is God's Son (1^{10}). Paul prays to him as he does to God (3^{11}) and mentions him on equal terms with God (1^{1}), although in some matters he is subordinate to God (1^{10} 4^{14}). Their calling and election are from God (1^{4} 2^{12}), but it is Christ upon whom their hope of salvation depends (1^{10} 5^{9}), a salvation that was wrought by his death (5^{10}; cf. 2^{15}).

There is the customary Pauline emphasis on *the Christian virtues.* In two passages faith, love, and hope appear together (1^{3} 5^{8}), as in the famous hymn of 1 Cor. 13^{13}, and faith and love together in one (3^{6}). Intended as it is to encourage steadfastness, this letter lays repeated emphasis on the Christian's joy (1^{6} 5^{16}), endurance (1$^{3, 10}$), and hope. Hope, not love, is here the climax of the trinity of virtues and the distinguishing mark of the believer (4^{13}; cf. 3^{13}).

Paul, however, is as little concerned to maintain a mere emotionalism as a merely formal adherence to Christ. Faith must bear fruit in *strict morality.* Spirit, soul, and body must be blameless (5^{23}). Fundamental to a vigorous and united church are peaceableness (4^{11} 5^{13}), mutual kindliness (5^{14}), and, above all, love (3^{12} 5^{13}), i.e., brotherly love (4^{9}). Love is to be shown by doing good, not only to members of the local church and to Christians living elsewhere, but unto all men (4^{10} 3^{12} 5^{15}). Paul is much concerned that the Christian make a favorable impression upon those outside the church (4^{12}). Righteous living, therefore, is fundamental. Paul urges a high standard of purity and rigorous self-control in sex relations, but there is no hint of asceticism (4$^{1-8}$). The letter is unique in its emphasis on industry as a necessary element in Christian morality. Paul himself has worked with his own hands (2^{9}) and expects all Christians to do the same (4$^{11f.}$; cf. 2 Thess. 3$^{8-12}$). How much is to be read into the concise exhortations with which the letter closes (5$^{21f.}$) his longer writings can inform us.

All these exhortations are given especial urgency in view of *the imminence of the Second Advent.* This item of Paul's faith receives its fullest exposition in the Thessalonian letters. Twice in the first letter he prays that the new converts may be found blameless at the appearance of the Lord Jesus Christ (3^{13} 5^{23}), when he expects his own final triumph (2^{19}). They had turned from idols to serve God and wait for his Son from heaven (1$^{9f.}$). It is Christ who rescues believers from the wrath that is coming (1^{10}), a wrath that is already beginning to fall upon the disbelieving Jews (2^{16}) and is soon to come upon others who reject the gospel. But Christians, being called to God's kingdom and glory, will be saved from this wrath (2^{12} 1^{10}). How large the idea of the "Advent" bulks in Paul's thought at this time is indicated by the half-parenthetical reference to it in 2^{19}. The apostle expects at any moment to be compelled to give account of his ministry before his glorified Lord (cf. 5$^{1-4}$). His discussion and description of the Second Coming in 4^{13}–5^{10} are sufficient evidence that it must have constituted an important element in his missionary message to the Thessalonians. (Cf. Rom. 1$^{18-32}$, notes.)

Paul's views on this subject seem to have undergone *a modification of emphasis, but no radical change.* In no other letters does he have so much to say regarding the Second Advent as in the two to the Thessalonians. It may be that the difficulties which his preaching of that doctrine had raised in this case rendered the apostle somewhat more cautious in his future missionary activities. He may have sensed the dangerous excesses to which undue emphasis upon the subject might lead. That he entirely abandoned this hope, however, can hardly be proved. Allusions to the Second Coming in later letters even down to Philippians clearly imply a continued expectation of that event, even though at the last Paul himself may no longer have hoped to be among those living to see it. See 1 Cor. 7$^{29-32}$ 15$^{51f.}$ Rom. 8$^{18-24}$ Phil. 3$^{20f.}$ These passages fit perfectly into the scheme of 1 Thess. 4^{13}–5^{11} and 2 Thess. 2$^{1-12}$. (See McCown, *The Promise of his Coming,* pp. 170–177.)

Genuineness of the Epistle. In spite, then, of the admitted peculiarities, there is no reason to suspect the genuineness of the letter. The characteristic ideas of Paul are practically all implied, if not explicitly stated. The allusions to his missionary activity in Macedonia and to his movements fit so admirably into the framework of the book of Acts that the trustworthiness of both documents is plainly indicated. The one apparent discrepancy, the statements in Acts (17^{15} 18^{5}) which imply that Timothy had not been with Paul at Athens (cf. 1 Thess. $3^{1f., 5f.}$), only serves to strengthen the evidence by showing that neither is dependent upon the other. The fathers at the end of the second century, Origen, Clement of Alexandria, Tertullian, and Irenæus, accept the letter without hesitation.

Textual Problems. Textual difficulties of importance are few. In 2^{7} the word *ēpioi*, "gentle" (A.V. and R.V. text), is to be preferred to *nēpioi*, "babes" (R.V. mg.). It is clearly better suited to the context though the latter is the better attested. The previous (Greek) word ends in *n*, which might easily be repeated to change the unfamiliar *ēpioi* (elsewhere in the N.T. only 2 Tim. 2^{24}) to the familiar *nēpioi*. In 3^{2} the reading "God's fellow worker" (for "God's minister") found in some western MSS. is attractive as a basis for explaining the variants (cf. A.V. and R.V.). In 3^{3} the change of *sainesthai*, "shake like a dog's tail," to *siainesthai*, "be unnerved," has much to commend it, though it is found in only two uncial MSS. In 5^{4} "as thieves," found in the codices Alexandrinus and Vaticanus, is to be preferred to "as a thief."

Analysis of Contents. The main divisions of the Epistle are as follows:

I. Superscription, Thanksgiving, and Prayer, 1^{1}–3^{13}.
II. The Two Chief Problems: Morality and the Resurrection, 4^{1}–5^{11}.
III. Suggestions as to Church Discipline, 5^{12-24}.
IV. Conclusion, 5^{25-28}.

Literature: Ellicott, *St. Paul's Epistles to the Thessalonians;* Milligan, *St. Paul's Epistles to the Thessalonians;* Moffatt, *The First and Second Epistles to the Thessalonians* (Expositor's Greek Testament, vol. iv); Frame, *The Epistles of St. Paul to the Thessalonians* (International Critical Commentary); Plummer, *A Commentary on St. Paul's First Epistle to the Thessalonians; A Commentary on St. Paul's Second Epistle to the Thessalonians;* Hayes, *Paul and His Epistles.*

CHAPTER I

1. The Superscription. In his adaptation of the formal epistolary greeting Paul associates with himself Silvanus (doubtless Silas, Acts 18^{5} 2 Cor. 1^{19} 1 Pet. 5^{12}) and Timothy ($3^{2, 6}$ Acts 18^{5} 2 Cor. 1^{19}), in a fashion unusual but not unknown in Greek letters between intimate friends and relatives. Almost the entire letter seems to have been written with this plural authorship in mind, much more clearly so than in the case of 1 and 2 Corinthians and Colossians. With the originality of genius Paul turns the word employed in the Greek letter for "greeting" (*chairein*) into "grace" (*charis*), using a noun derived from the same root, but of vastly fuller meaning, and to it he adds the Semitic salutation, *peace.* The formal address is turned into a genuine expression of Christian good will.

The greeting here is the shortest found in Paul's letters; the following thanksgiving (see above, "Analysis") is the longest. The character of this section as a thanksgiving and prayer (cf. 1^{2} 2^{13} $3^{9f.}$) allows Paul to remind his readers of much that will serve to encourage them and bind them in affection to their apostle and his Master. It is the warm outpouring of an affectionate nature, guided and controlled by keen insight and practical good sense.

2–10. A Model Church. Paul emphasizes his continued personal interest and encourages them by praising their Christian character (vv. 2f.), and by recounting the happiness and enthusiasm of their conversion (vv. 4f.) and their steadfast and exemplary conduct (vv. 6f.), putting them on their mettle also by mentioning their widespread reputation as exemplary Christians (vv. 8–10).

3–7. In v. 3 is an even fuller and richer exposition of the rounded Christian character than the more familiar 1 Cor. 13^{13}, for it indicates the value of the fundamental traits of the Christian. Faith produces practical activity, love undertakes toilsome labor, hope supports endurance in view of the imminent return of Christ (cf. Col. $1^{4,5}$ Gal. 5^{5} 2 Thess. 1^{4}). All their labor is performed under the watchful eye of God, who will not fail to take note of it, for he has loved them and chosen them. Of this they can have no doubt if they remember the circumstances of their conversion. Not without a touch of pride Paul recalls the miraculous manifestations, the sense of the Spirit's presence, and the full conviction on the part of the new converts which had accompanied the preaching of the gospel. In the persecutions they had been compelled to bear they were only imitating their leaders (cf. 2^{14} and Acts 17^{5-9}), but their spirit had been such that they had become the model church of Greece and Macedonia.

8–10. *The reverberation of the word of the Lord in Macedonia and Achaia* (the latter is the Roman province of Greece) seems to imply an extensive missionary activity with Thessalonica as its center. Moreover, if everywhere—the exaggeration is pardonable—

people are prepared for the gospel message by the story of their enthusiastic reception of it, how can they become discouraged and turn back? Three of the chief elements of the missionary preaching of those early days seem to be indicated in this passage. For the phrase *wrath to come* (v. 10) see below, 2[16]

CHAPTER II

1–12. The Apostles' Conduct Defended. The allusion to the Thessalonians' experience of salvation easily and naturally paves the way for a paragraph describing the apostles' conduct among them and indirectly defending it against possible suspicions. The missionaries had not really resembled the mercenary charlatans who posed as philosophers and preachers of morality (see p. 1264a).

1, 2. Their entrance to the hearts of the Thessalonians (cf. 1[9]) had not been with an inane message but one which, in spite of the sufferings of the apostles at Philippi (Acts 16 22-40), had been bold and powerful, even in the midst of renewed conflicts with persecutors. These verses take up 1[5]. Endurance of opposition and persecution also served to prove their sincerity.

3–6. For the appeal of the Christian missionaries did not have its source in *delusion* (or *error*), like many rival philosophies and religions; nor in *uncleanness*, such as was exemplified in the worship of Aphrodite at Corinth, where Paul was writing; nor in *deceit* (or *guile*), as seen in wandering philosophers and strolling priests of cults such as those of *Dea Syria* (described by Apuleius, *The Golden Ass*, viii, 24–ix, 10). Since God had tried their inner motives and had approved them and intrusted them with the gospel, they were concerned to please him and not men. Therefore, unlike the popular preachers of the time, they had presented no flattering message, they had come with no fine pretext to cover their greed, they had no desire for fame, though, as apostles of Christ, they had the right to be held in honor and be a (financial) burden to their converts. (There may be an intentional play upon this double meaning in the phrase of which the translations *claim honor* (*use authority*, A.V.) and *be burdensome* exchange places in the text and mg. of the English versions.)

7, 8. Instead of conducting themselves like proud and grasping rhetoricians, the apostles had been *gentle* (see p. 1266a), treating their converts as a nurse does her own children, with self-sacrificing tenderness. The word translated *affectionately desirous*, hitherto unexampled elsewhere in Greek, has been discovered by Ramsay in a fourth-century inscription, used by heathen parents of a deceased son (Milligan, *Expositor*, ix, 9, Sept., 1925, pp. 226f.).

9–12. Paul appeals to the conduct of the apostles in Thessalonica as evidence of the sincerity of their purposes. The toil and weariness which they had seen the missionaries undergo as they worked night and day so as not to be a burden to their converts (v. 9) and their blameless conduct (v. 10) as well as the fatherly love they had shown (v. 11) and the high moral standards they had insisted upon (v. 12) should convince the Thessalonians of the purity of their aims. The application to a certain type of modern popular preacher is evident.

13–16. Renewed Thanksgiving at the Recollection of Their Former Relations. Quite naturally the account of the apostles' conduct in Thessalonica leads to another reminder of the heartiness of the new converts' reception of them as true messengers of God. Then they were convinced that the gospel was not merely a human concoction but a message from God, who had attested its genuineness by working in the hearts and lives of the believers. If, now, they were tempted to doubt its divine origin because God had failed to protect them from persecution, they should remember that they had then unhesitatingly accepted persecution as the lot of believers, thinking of themselves as walking in the footsteps of the first Christians in Judæa, who had suffered persecution from the Jews as the Thessalonians had at the hands of their heathen fellow countrymen. Persecution need not disturb their faith, for the Lord himself as well as the ancient prophets and the present missionaries of the gospel had been compelled to endure it. The thought of the Jews' responsibility for all this stirs the apostle. They were displeasing God and showing their animosity toward all men (a suggestion of anti-Semitism) in hindering the apostles' preaching of salvation to the Gentiles. They were thus rapidly adding to the weight of their sins in the scales of God's justice, and the *wrath of God*, i.e., the woes of the last days and the punishment to follow the final Judgment, was hanging over them. The last clause (v. 16c) is found in the *Testaments of the Twelve Patriarchs*, *Levi*, vi, 11.

17–20. The Apostles' Continued Personal Interest in the Thessalonian Christians. (See also 3[1-13].) Having thus reconstructed the atmosphere of hopefulness and mutual confidence which existed when he was with them, Paul proceeds to show that he and his companions had not forgotten them as soon as they had gone elsewhere.

The keenness of his personal feeling for the Thessalonians is emphasized by the terms he uses in v. 17. More than once he especially had tried to return. Satan himself was back of the circumstances that had prevented. Why should he not wish to see them? They are his *hope*, his *joy*, his *crown of glorying* (or *pride*). The last phrase comes into his mind along with the thought of the expected *parousia*, the visit of the Lord, and reminds him that they are the crown with which he will honor the Lord when he comes, just as cities or princes honor the emperor with a crown at his official "visit" (cf. Milligan's Commentary, pp. 145f.).

CHAPTER III

Additional Evidence of Paul's Interest. Evidence to this interest, begun in 2[17], is continued throughout ch. 3.

1–5. The Sending of Timothy. Paul's deep personal interest in the Thessalonians was further demonstrated by his continuing alone his missionary labors in Athens, and later in Corinth, that he might send Timothy back to Thessalonica. Silas had probably remained in Macedonia (Acts 17[14f.] 18[5]). The emphatic "I Paul" of 2[18] supports the view that the *we* of this section is entirely editorial, but does not prove it. The purpose of Timothy's visit was twofold: (1) to establish and encourage the Thessalonian Christians, and (2) to relieve the apostle's anxiety as to their steadfastness. The mention of their tribulations leads to another assertion of the inevitableness of these sufferings, even as he had told them in advance.

6–8. Paul's Joy at News from Thessalonica. The relief to the apostle's mind when Timothy returned is vividly expressed by the expression he uses: Timothy *brought us glad tidings* is, literally, *preached the gospel to us*. They had desired to see him as he did them—a delicate hint that he had had as good reason to doubt them as they him. Vv. 7f. refer to the discouragements and difficulties he had faced alone at Athens and Corinth (Acts 18[5f.] 1 Cor. 2[3]).

9–13. His Thanksgiving and Prayer. Paul again returns to the epistolary framework of thanksgiving and prayer. What adequate thanksgiving could he render to God for the joy they occasioned him? In these verses he expresses in heartfelt fashion his longing to visit them and complete their instruction in the Christian way of life and his desire that they may increase and abound in the Christian graces and be morally blameless, so that they may be ready for the imminent "visit" (*coming*) of their Lord with its ensuing divine judgment. The word translated *saints* in v. 13 and in 2 Thess. 1[10] means "holy ones," and is often applied to the angels (see Zech. 14[5] Deut. 33[2] Jude v. 14, 1 Enoch 1[9]). Since Paul usually employs the word for "Christians," its meaning here is uncertain.

CHAPTER IV

With 4[1] begins the second main division of the Epistle (see intro., "Analysis").

1–12. Exhortations as to Christian Conduct. Having thus allayed suspicions of ulterior motives and callous forgetfulness on his part, Paul is ready to attack directly the two chief difficulties of the Thessalonian church. For the first section, which urges strict morality (vv. 1–8) and brotherly conduct (vv. 9–12), he had prepared by his prayer that they might be found blameless. Even a model church might improve. The purpose of God for them is that they be devoted to a holy life. The clauses which follow plainly define this *sanctification* as sexual purity. (1) Christians must avoid *fornication*, which means all manner of sexual impurity. (2) Each must *possess himself of his own vessel* in all purity of thought. This may mean either *control his own body* or *secure for himself a wife*. The latter meaning for the expression seems preferable in view of ancient usage (cf. 1 Pet. 3[7]). The clause may be translated: *that each of you respect his wife and keep her to himself in all purity* (Frame). (3) Above all *in this matter*, i.e., in regard to sins of the flesh (not in *any* matter, i.e., *business*, A.V.), one must be especially careful not to invade the rights of another Christian home, perhaps a reference to some actual case at Thessalonica.

9–12. On the positive side he urges brotherly love, which includes almsgiving, for thus mainly, no doubt, they showed their love for Christians in other places. In this fundamental virtue (cf. Gal. 5[14] Rom. 13[8f.]) again the model church could grow in grace. Apparently, Paul's exhortations to quietness, minding one's own business, and working with the hands bore small fruit (see 2 Thess. 3[6-15]). The exhortation to consider the impression their conduct makes upon non-Christians is characteristic (cf. 5[15f.] Rom. 12[17, 18] 13[7f.] Col. 4[5]).

13–18. The Resurrection and the Second Coming (see also 5[1-11]). This section evidently grows out of a report from Timothy or other information to the effect that some of the Thessalonian Christians were in doubt as to the fate of those of their number who had died since their conversion. How could the dead share in the glory of the Second Advent?

To Greeks, who had never heard of the resurrection of the body, this was a natural question. The "farewell" frequently found upon tombstones of this period is indicative of the *sorrow without hope* that prevailed widely in the ancient world. Passages in the O.T. and the Jewish apocalypses, as well as heathen inscriptions, speak of death as an "eternal sleep." "There is hope among the living, but hopeless are the dead" (Theocritus, *Idyls*, iv, 42). Paul tells the Thessalonians that *those who are asleep*—a characteristic but not original Christian designation of the dead—were to share in the joyful welcome to the returning Saviour. He does not answer the fundamental question as to the nature of the resurrection. That he attempts in 1 Cor. 15. Here he merely seeks to dispose of the Thessalonians' anxieties as to their friends who were "asleep." They should rise even as Jesus had, and that before the "rapture" of the living. The Lord will appear with a command for them to rise, with an archangel's shout, and the sounding of a divine trumpet. The Christian dead will be raised first; then the living, among whom Paul expected to be numbered, will be *snatched in clouds into the air to meet the Lord* (so read v. 17), and thereafter they should be always with him—a most comforting assurance for these harassed and persecuted Christians.

CHAPTER V

1–11. Reticence Concerning Times and Seasons. (Cf. 4[13-18].) Paul here sounds a warning which later millenarians would have done well to heed. No one could know the times and proper seasons when these things should take place, for, as Jesus had repeatedly assured his disciples (Mk. 13[32]=Mt. 24[36]; Mk. 13[33-37] Mt. 24[42f.]=Lk. 12[39f.]; Mt. 24[50]=Lk. 12[46] Mt. 25[13]) and Paul had taught the Thessalonians, the *day of the Lord* (the O.T. phrase is applied to Christ's Advent for the purpose of judging the world and vindicating his own) was to come as unexpectedly as *a thief in the night*. The inescapable punishment would fall when least anticipated. But the Christian, prepared for the Judgment by righteous living, need not fear. The phrase *thief in the night* suggests to the apostle an interesting and apposite figure. The Christian is living in the light of day. He not only need not fear the thief in the night but he must live in the light of day. He must be neither drunken nor asleep, as people are at night, but awake and sober. Clad in the Christian's armor (cf. Eph. 6[13-17]), he is sure of his rescue from sin and punishment, for God has chosen him and Christ died for him. The *waking* and *sleeping* of v. 10 mean life and death. (For a fuller discussion of Paul's views on the Second Coming see p. 1265b and below on 2 Thess. 2[1-12]).

12–24. Suggestions as to Church Discipline. The practical turn which Paul so characteristically gives his discussion of the Second Coming prepares for a concluding section of detached exhortations tactfully addressed to all the church but intended, no doubt, for a particular group. There probably was friction between the leaders and some whom they had admonished, and the latter are urged to *know*, i.e., respect and appreciate (cf. 4[4]), and love their leaders who labor to weariness for the church. V. 14 is intended to support the leaders in their efforts to discipline the disorderly and also to suggest the variety of needs with which they must deal. The *disorderly*, i.e., idle busybodies, the *easily discouraged* (or *fainthearted*), and the *weak* must be treated each according to his disposition and all must be regarded with magnanimity. No spirit of revenge can be tolerated either within the group or toward those without it (v. 15). Joy, prayer, and thanksgiving mark the normal Christian spirit (vv. 16f.). Vv. 19–22 are a condensed summary of the more explicit instructions given later to the Corinthians (1 Cor. 14). While the ecstatic gifts of the Spirit and prophesyings are to be given legitimate range and not despised, they are to be tested by their fruits. Vv. 23f. put into a brief prayer the ideals which are uppermost in the writer's mind: peace, that complete purity of life and spirit which makes ready for the coming of the Lord, and finally the certainty of that Advent and its rescue of the faithful from the sins and sufferings of life, a certainty based on the faithfulness of God.

25–28. Conclusion and Benediction. The closing sentences are probably autobiographic (cf. 2 Thess. 3[17]). Like those found in many letters, ancient and modern, they are disconnected injunctions and greetings. The earnestness of the adjuration that the letter be *read unto all the brethren* suggests more of division and quarreling in the church than one would otherwise suspect.

The benediction takes the place of the customary good wish of the ordinary Greek letter, "I hope that you are in good health." Paul's chief desire for his converts was spiritual *grace*, not mere bodily health. It is a final illustration and confirmation of von Wilamowitz-Moellendorff's description of Paul's letter style as being "Paul, nothing but Paul, inimitable though often copied."

SECOND THESSALONIANS

Introduction

The Occasion and Purpose of the Letter. The circumstances under which 2 Thessalonians was written are more difficult to determine with certainty than those of 1 Thessalonians, since the letter is less personal in its tone and less detailed in its references to its occasion. Apparently, the first letter had soon been answered by the leaders of the church. The Thessalonian elders had deprecated Paul's praise of the church (see on 1^{3}). They were praying that they might be found ready when Christ should appear, but many at least were disturbed, fearing that it would be impossible for them to develop the necessary graces and purity of life if, as they understood Paul's letter to imply, the day of the Lord was already upon the world ($1^{10, 11}$ 2^{2}). Some of the disorderly whom the first letter had rebuked had refused to accept reproof ($3^{11, 14}$) and had possibly rejected that letter as a forgery (3^{17}), while others had been excited to greater fanaticism by the supposed imminence of the Second Advent. In general, the situation had not greatly changed—for but a short time, perhaps a few weeks or months, may be supposed to have intervened—but what change there was was for the worse. The mood of the apostle also had altered. The happy relief from anxiety over the Thessalonians which marks the first letter is replaced by disappointment at the new difficulties which had arisen. Moreover, unrighteous and evil men (2^{2}), probably the unbelieving Jews of Corinth, were disturbing the apostle. The tone of the second letter is, therefore, less buoyant, affectionate, and intimate, and somewhat more official and severe than that of the first. Its thought centers around two classes—those who are disturbed or discouraged by the dreadful imminence of the day of the Lord, and those who are disorderly.

Evidence Against Its Authenticity. The argument against the letter receives its strongest support from the peculiar combination of similarities in language and alleged differences of thought to be discovered by comparing 1 and 2 Thessalonians. Many sentences in 2 Thessalonians sound almost as if they had been copied, somewhat laboriously and clumsily, from 1 Thessalonians (cf. 1 Thess. $1^{2f.}$=2 Thess. 1^{3}; 2^{13}=2^{13}; $3^{11f.}$=$2^{16f.}$; $4^{1f.}$=$3^{1f.}$; 5^{24}=3^{3}; 5^{23}=3^{16}), while one whole section which is new is largely a canto of O.T. phrases (1^{8-12}). Yet there are some words and turns of expression which are not elsewhere found in Paul (*eternal destruction*, 1^{9}, the parenthesis in 1^{10}, *manifestation*, or appearing, 2^{8}; cf. 1 Tim. 6^{14} 2 Tim. 1^{10} $4^{1, 8}$ Tit. 2^{13}). The difficult phrase *by epistle as from us* (2^{2}) raises a question, and the undisguised attempt to guarantee the letter's genuineness might easily be a forger's device. The purpose of such a literary forgery (to use a modern ethical judgment too harsh for ancient custom) would probably have been to gain the support of the apostle's name for the views as to the Second Advent expounded in 2^{1-12} and for the disciplinary measures advocated in 3^{6-16}. (See p. 188a.)

Evidence for Its Authenticity. The difficulties which this theory seeks to explain cannot be denied, and the problem cannot be said to have been definitely solved. But the case against the authenticity of the letter is not so strong as has been thought by some. It must be especially noted that the passage on the Second Coming does not embody the current Jewish-Christian ideas as to the signs of the end. It says nothing of earthquakes and wars, of falling stars and darkened suns. It merely insists that the time is not yet. Paul may not elsewhere state this view as here, but it is not inconsistent with 1 Thessalonians, and, for all that we read in his other letters, he may have held it until his death (see intro. to 1 Thessalonians, "Teachings"). The change in Paul's views during the ten or twelve years covered by his letters has often been overemphasized. The letter was known and accepted as genuine by Origen, Clement of Alexandria, Irenæus, Tertullian, the Muratorian Canon, and Marcion. It seems to have been used by Justin Martyr, Polycarp, and probably the Epistle of Barnabas. It is impossible, therefore, to suppose that it was written after 100 A.D. The external evidence is even stronger than that for 1 Thessalonians.

Textual Criticism. There are but three words of importance about which there is noteworthy difference of textual attestation. On 1^{10}, *was believed*, see commentary. In 2^{3}, *anomias*, "of lawlessness," the reading of the Sinaitic and Vatican MSS., the Coptic Version, several Fathers, including Tertullian, and the R.V.mg, is preferred by the majority of modern scholars to *hamartias*, "of sin," of the R.V. text. In 2^{13} the R.V.mg., *as first fruits*, suits the context better than *from the beginning*, though the latter has the better attestation.

Analysis of Contents. The main divisions of the Epistle are as follows:

I. Superscription, Thanksgiving and Prayer, 1¹–2¹⁷.
II. Injunctions as to Conduct and Church Discipline, 3¹⁻¹⁵, and Conclusion, 3¹⁷, ¹⁸.

Literature: See literature under introduction to 1 Thessalonians, p. 1266.

CHAPTER I

1, 2. Superscription. The *superscription* of 2 Thessalonians differs but slightly from that of 1 Thessalonians, but the change to *our* Father adds a sense of intimacy to the Christian fellowship, and the addition specifying the divine source of *grace and peace* decidedly strengthens the sense.

3–12. Encouragement. The section really constitutes one sentence. It is grammatically involved, but clear as to meaning.

(1) Paul insists (vv. 3f.) that their faith, love, and patience have deserved high praise. The emphatic *we are under obligation to give thanks . . . as is fitting* (so read v. 3), which is peculiar to this letter (cf. 2[13]), was doubtless occasioned by deprecatory remarks in the letter from the Thessalonian leaders to Paul. It is this disclaimer and the discouragement which it revealed that led to the partial repetition of 1 Thess. 1[2-4] in 2 Thess. 1[3f]. Their discouragement calls forth the emphatic reiteration of the claim that the apostles have a right to be proud of the Thessalonian church.

(2) They need not be discouraged, their ultimate vindication is sure (vv. 5–10). The writer adroitly represents their very persecutions, along with their patient endurance of them, as a proof that God's judgments are righteous. Otherwise, how could God justly reward them and punish those who do not believe? The Advent and judgment are for the author something promised in sacred Scripture. But the prophecy is impossible of fulfillment unless there be persecutors to be punished and suffering saints to be saved and vindicated. The cross must precede the crown. Because they are bearing the cross they may feel sure of the crown. The same idea of certain necessary preliminaries to the day of the Lord is seen in 2[1-12]. *If so be* in v. 6 is, of course, ironical. A large part of vv. 8–10 is made up of quotations from the O.T., and the rhythmic structure of the passage suggests that it may be an adaptation of a Christian hymn. The parenthetical phrase of v. 10 as usually translated implies that the Thessalonians are to share in the promised glory because they had believed in the apostles' testimony. The Greek, however, is difficult, and such eminent scholars as Markland, Hort, and Moffatt accept a slightly attested reading which gives the meaning, *our testimony* (i.e., that Christians must suffer) *has found confirmation in your case,* a sense that does not so well fit the context. On *saints* see 1 Thess. 3[13].

(3) Vv. 11f. may be paraphrased thus: "In order that this glorious experience may be yours we continually pray that God may consider you worthy to receive the heavenly rest to which he called you, and so may mightily bring to fruition every good intention and every work that springs from faith, in order that our Lord Jesus may be glorified in you and you in him."

CHAPTER II

1–12. The Delay of the Second Advent. This section, turning away from material strictly consonant with thanksgiving, was probably written in direct answer to reports which had come from Thessalonica to the apostles, perhaps in the letter from the church. Some members, at least, had been greatly disturbed over the supposed imminence of the *parousia,* the expected Advent of Christ, which Paul had so vividly described in his first letter. It would appear, however, that it was not merely his letter that had unsettled them. He tells them (vv. 1f.) that they were to be disturbed neither *by spirit,* i.e., ecstatic prophecy, nor *by word,* i.e., oral teaching, nor *by letter, as if by* (not *from*) the apostles. The last phrase, *as if by us,* may apply to all the three preceding; i.e., either a misunderstanding or a misinterpretation of something the apostles had said or written had caused the difficulty. Unfortunately, the explanation intended to set them right is couched in such involved and intentionally mysterious language that, though its meaning was doubtless clear to the Thessalonians, we are at a loss to understand it.

In the interpretation of apocalyptic terminology three points must be borne in mind: (1) The ancients used it with reference to persons and events of the present and immediate future. There was no thought of long ages to come. Paul believed, as his language plainly implies, that the *parousia* of Christ, the Second Advent, would come before his death (see intro. to 1 Thessalonians.) The powers or persons to whom he alludes are, therefore, to be sought in his own time and environment. (2) The technical apocalyptic terms, such as "apostasy," "man of lawlessness," the "restrainer" (Satan), and *parousia,* had long been in use. They had been handed down from previous writers and in their Greek form often represent attempts to reproduce the peculiar ideas of one language (Hebrew or Aramaic) in another of an entirely different genius. (3) The ultimate origin of many apocalyptic ideas and phrases is to be sought in ancient polytheistic mythology. Back of this passage, it seems certain, is the old myth of the primæval dragon which revolted against the gods. In the beginning this monster had been conquered and chained but not destroyed, and it would, in the last days, reappear and make a final, desperate attempt to regain the mastery of the world. (See Bousset, *The Antichrist Legend;* Oesterley, *The Evolution of the Messianic Idea*, pp. 83–107; McCown, *The Promise of His Coming*, pp. 47–51; also arts., this Commentary, pp. 188, 206, 843.) It is to this expected embodiment of evil that Paul is referring, though we must beware of reading into Paul's language all the ideas either of previous Jewish writers or of later Christian works such as Revelation.

Paul had instructed the Thessalonian Christians in his beliefs on this subject. Here he is merely reminding them of what they were supposed to know well. Unfortunately, we have no means of ascertaining what his views were in detail, and we shall never be able to interpret all of his language with certainty. In its general purport, however, his meaning is clear. The Advent of Christ was not immediately to be expected. The outline of future events as Paul anticipated them is perhaps as follows: (1) a preaching of the gospel to the whole inhabited world, while some power held the forces of evil in leash; (2) the removal of the *restraining power* (v. 7) and the development of unbelief and opposition until it culminated in the great *falling away* (or "apostasy") led by *the lawless one;* (3) the appearance of Christ on the clouds to visit summary punishment upon the wicked and to reward the righteous by transforming their bodies into a form suitable to the kingdom of God which was to be inaugurated upon a transformed earth.

3, 4. Paul and his circle evidently accepted the common idea that the end with its terrible judgment could not come upon the earth until the wicked had filled up the measure of their sins, and God was thus fully justified in punishing them (cf. 1^{5-10} and 1 Thess. 2^{16}). A great *apostasy* must first occur, led by a human embodiment of lawlessness, who is, therefore, peculiarly marked out for *perdition*, or *destruction*, and who is the exact opposite of the divine but claims a place of superiority to every divine being or object of worship. He will go so far as to enthrone himself in the Temple and proclaim himself as God (cf. Mk. 13^{14} Dan. 11^{36}). These traits may be an allusion to the deification of Oriental monarchs and of the Roman emperors, possibly to Caligula's attempt to set up his statue in the Temple.

5–7. The time for the "mock" Advent is not yet come. Paul had foretold it but had also explained that some restraining power was preventing the lawless one from revealing himself, in spite of the fact that the energy which was behind him, though hidden, was already at work. Some have supposed that Paul regarded Claudius as the *one that restraineth now.* More likely, the restraining power and person is the Holy Spirit (see especially v. 6). Only Paul's converts, whom he had personally instructed, could know to whom he referred. If he were alluding to the Roman Empire, he might well be cautious about committing to papyrus his ideas as to its overthrow. If v. 7b refers to the emperor, it might be thought highly seditious.

8–12. The *restrainer* gone, the false messiah would have every opportunity to deceive the multitudes by spurious miracles, signs, and wonders (cf. R.V.mg., and Mk. 13^{22}=Mt. 24^{24} Rev. $13^{13f.}$), which were to authenticate his *coming* (*parousia*), just as real miracles accompanied the first Advent of Christ and were supposed to guarantee the genuineness of every divine manifestation (cf. Deut. 13^{1-3}). Because men had refused to believe the truth, God would give them up (cf. Rom. $1^{24, 26, 28}$) to belief in falsehood, and they with their deceiver would be justly and terribly punished for their sins.

13–17. Renewed Thanksgiving and Prayer. The thought of the fate of unbelievers suggests to Paul the contrasted happy future of believers, and he turns again to thanksgiving, which, he insists, is justified. Having been *beloved, chosen*, and *called* by God as *firstfruits* (mg.) of Europe, the Thessalonian Christians needed only to *stand firm and hold* (*fast*) *the traditions* which he had given them both *orally* and *by letter.* May they be comforted by the certainty of their hope and be active in well doing!

CHAPTER III

1–5. Observations and Admonitions. Vv. 1f. appear to refer to the missionary labors of Paul and his companions at Corinth and the opposition which they were encountering from unbelieving Jews. But if men are faithless, the *Lord is faithful* and he will save them, not only from *evil men*, but from the evil inclination (cf. R.V.mg.) which would lead to disaster, for Paul is convinced that they will remain faithful to his instructions (vv. 3f.). *Love for God* and the *patience* which fellowship with Christ produces are necessary (v. 5).

6–16. Directions for the Discipline of the Disorderly. It would appear that Paul's brief and general admonitions to the disorderly in

1 Thess. 5[12-15] had not been heeded. It is often assumed that the disorders mentioned in this section, especially the refusal to work, were due to expectations of the imminent Advent which, it was thought, would render labor unnecessary. This can neither be proved nor disproved. The meaning to be assigned to *walking disorderly* is to be gathered from the following verses. It involved living in idleness at others' expense and being *busybodies* instead of *busy* (v. 11). Both in word (v. 10) and by example (vv. 7f.) Paul had handed down to them the Jewish tradition of the value and necessity of *manual labor.* The importance of the matter in Paul's view is shown by the measures of excommunication which he urged against the disobedient. His personal interest in the individual comes beautifully to the surface in the final injunction not to treat such as if they were beyond reformation.

17, 18. Conclusion. Paul probably availed himself of the services of some friend who wielded a ready pen, or of a slave trained to the task. His own handwriting was large and angular (Gal. 6[11] "large letters"). This specific mention of the authenticating subscription along with the phrase *by letter as if by us* (2[2]) may point to a forgery in his name. But it seems more natural to suppose that it was noted because the disorderly at Thessalonica had refused to accept as genuine his former letter.

THE PASTORAL EPISTLES: FIRST AND SECOND TIMOTHY AND TITUS

By Professor W. J. LOWSTUTER

Introduction

The Term "Pastorals." The term "Pastoral Letters" is so commonly applied to 1 Timothy, 2 Timothy, and Titus that it is natural enough to suppose that they have been so known "from the most ancient times." As a matter of fact, the term is comparatively modern; for while Thomas Aquinas (1274) applied to them the term "pastoralis," it was Paul Anton (1726) who introduced the habit of referring to these letters as "the Pastorals"; other scholars took up the classification, among them the great English scholar, Alford (1849), with the result that the term has passed into universal currency.

Appropriateness of the Term. In some ways the title is appropriate. It fastens attention at once upon the fact that the letters were written from the pastoral point of view. It was no essayist who wrote these letters but a man of affairs whose concern was not to air views or discuss theories for the sake of doing so, but to provide for actual situations. There is the air of life about them; they suggest the parish, not the cloister. While they have become world-literature, known and appealed to wherever Christian leaders have organized converts or believers into Christian churches, they clearly give the impression that they were written for specific times and particular parties. They belong to their own age and setting, however valuable they may be for all ages. We find ourselves reading here so many pages from the daily record of a great pastor, part of whose work was to train pastors and provide leadership for the churches he had helped to found. We see him facing the possibility that perhaps he was soon to leave his whole parish to the care of others, and his heart was concerned about a successor. The writer knew the situation in Ephesus, Crete, and elsewhere, the need of leaders who, equipped by personal attainment in Christian experience and by training for Christian service, would confirm converts, build up believers into a Christian community, exercise wise discipline and see to it that new recruits should ever be in training for the propagation of the glorious faith of Christ. He believed thoroughly in pastoral efficiency, the efficiency that comes only through discipline and training. Both the prophet and the propagandist in him discerned the need of trained leadership for the gospel. In these little letters to two of his younger friends the great apostle published to all ages his conviction that the church must ever have a trained ministry.

Limitations of the Term. On the other hand, the term "pastoral" is somewhat unfortunate, mainly because it raises expectations and gives presumptions which are not realized. The letters cannot be described as a compendium of church management, ministerial discipline or parish methods. It is misleading to refer to them as a "manual of church life," because there are so many phases of pastoral and parish work not touched upon (Harrison, *The Problem of the Pastoral Epistles*, p. 15). The term is especially not happily applied to 2 Timothy. While it fits 1 Timothy and Titus much more truly, even they are too incomplete as to pastoral instructions, duties, and methods to qualify as a handbook on practical theology. The modern worker will find all too many of his problems untouched, but he will find here many valuable suggestions for the oversight of a modern church. Better, he will find here ideals and inspiration to furnish him new zeal and devotion for his task; better still, he will find opportunity here to keep fellowship with a Great Pastor, contact with whose spirit must make any man a truer son of God and a better minister of Jesus Christ.

Did Paul Write the Pastorals? On this point there has been great difference of scholarly opinion and persistent controversy. There have been those who have enthusiastically and ably defended the Pauline authorship, including among many others, Adeney, Barth, Findlay, Hort, Knowling, Lightfoot, Plummer, Ramsay, Sanday, Weiss and Zahn. Among those who have challenged it are men like Davidson, Holtzmann, Jülicher, Meyer, Weizsacker, and others, who credit the pastorals to a later hand. Then, there are a large and growing class of critics like Bacon, Harnack, Deissmann, Harrison, McGiffert, Moffatt, Lock, Peake, and others, who have found embedded in these letters certain genuine Pauline fragments, such as Tit. 3:12-15 2 Tim. 1:16-18 4:6-8, etc., small unpublished notes, historical paragraphs from the pen of the apostle, incorporated in these larger documents and issued later by some Paulinist who wished to exercise the apostle's influence and authority in administering the situation to which they were directed. In doing this he thought he was expressing accurately the apostle's mind. He was evidently quite familiar with Pauline thought and usage and, consciously or unconsciously, imitated or reproduced in striking measure the characteristics of the apostle. The practice and precedents of his age would fully account for his so writing and justify him in doing it. (Cf. pp. 855a, 942.)

Alleged Objections to the Pauline Authorship. Those who deny the Pauline authorship do so on four main grounds.

(1) There are marked divergences from the Pauline writings in *vocabulary* and in other linguistic features. For a detailed study of these divergences, see Harrison, *The Problem of the Pastoral Epistles.* Most of these divergences could be accounted for by the character of the subject matter and by Paul's increasing years.

(2) The *personal attitude of the writer* is held to be incompatible with Pauline authorship. Timothy and Titus are old and tried friends of Paul, yet they are addressed here in an almost patronizing way, and are given advice which seems to imply a doubt as to their dependability. It is difficult to see, however, why a man of Paul's years and experience should not write in this style to those who, after all, were much younger than he, and for whose activities he felt himself responsible.

(3) The Pastorals mention visits to Ephesus (1 Tim. 1:3), Miletus (2 Tim. 4:20), Troas (2 Tim. 4:13); a mission in Crete, and possible missions in Gaul and Dalmatia (2 Tim. 4:10); also other activities which it is *difficult to fit into the story of Paul's life* in Acts.

This difficulty is a real one. The only way it can be met is by assuming (a) that Paul was released from the Roman imprisonment of Acts, and returned to the East to visit Ephesus, Troas, Miletus, Corinth, Crete, etc.; (b) that during this time he wrote 1 Timothy and Titus; and (c) that later he was again arrested, and from this second imprisonment wrote 2 Timothy.

The crucial question is whether Paul was actually released from the first imprisonment at Rome. There are good reasons for believing that he was. It is incredible that he should have been put to death on such indefinite and insufficient charges as those preferred at his first arrest (see Acts 25:27). Upon a second arrest the charges could be more specific and dangerous. Paul evidently anticipated release from his first imprisonment; he wrote hopefully about a favorable outcome of his trial to both Philemon (v. 22) and the Philippians (2:19-24) and arranged for another visit with them. A difficulty is found in the fact that he told the elders of Ephesus they should not see his face again (Acts 20:25), but, according to the Pastorals, they did see his face again. When Paul so spoke to those elders he was closing his ministry in the east with a definite plan to turn west through Rome to Spain; he did not expect to see them again; a return seemed utterly improbable. But after four years in prison he found it necessary, upon his release, to look after affairs in the eastern churches before he could follow up his plans to go to the West, to Spain. It is simply the case of where a man in the light of developing circumstances felt compelled to change his plans, as many another good man since has done. There is nothing in the letters from the first imprisonment that indicates decisively that his first imprisonment ended fatally. Church tradition has preserved certain references, variously estimated, in support of a release and of labors in Spain (Clement of Rome, Acta Pauli, the Muratorian Fragment, etc.). Weiss, Lock, and others rightfully emphasize that no valid reason can be given for denying a release and no proof can be cited that actually disproves it. The Pastorals presuppose a release. This allows very reasonably for the various historical references which otherwise prove so hard to manage. Upon release, he could revisit his old churches, renew contact with old work, open new work in Crete, Dalmatia, and Gaul, plan for a winter at Nicopolis, leave a cloak and books at Troas to be sent for in a short time after he had again been thrown into prison, and from a second imprisonment write that his course was finished, his case without hope in imperial courts. (Cf. art., *Life and Work of Paul*, pp. 941–3.)

(4) The Pastorals presuppose a high degree of church organization which many claim appeared at a later time than Paul. Yet there is plenty of evidence in the N.T. to such organization as is here implied. When Paul and Barnabas were returning from their first campaign in the Gentile missions, they (Acts 13, 14) organized their new converts, appointed elders, provided for discipline and thus planned for the establishment of these churches. In Thessalonica and Corinth (1 Thess. 5:12 1 Cor. 5:1-5) similar arrangements were made for organization and discipline; brethren were called to official leadership who exercised every

function implied in the Pastorals. As the congregations grew and became more permanent, very naturally the necessity for better organization would increase; official distinctions, discrimination of duties, division of labors, provision for discipline and proper control and other features of organization that are incident to the attempt to teach men and women to live together in a group, would develop and receive more emphasis. The Pastorals, written near the end of Paul's life, fit naturally into both this expectation and the known facts of church organization.

Altogether, therefore, the evidence is favorable to the Pauline authorship. After all, the problem of the Pastorals is not primarily one of Pauline dictation but of Pauline mind and spirit. Other hands may have been upon these writings in the transmission, but their touch has not affected the portrait of the great apostle himself. In the Pastorals, we find still the man who kept fellowship with Jesus Christ, and who counted all things loss for the excellency of Christ; only, where we meet elsewhere the Enthusiast for Christ we meet here the Statesman for Christ, providing with care for "the church which is his body."

Paul Revealed in the Pastorals. We assume, then, that Paul was released from his first imprisonment and that he afterward wrote these letters. Ramsay says he was released in February, 62 A.D.; Deissmann and Turner argue for a year later. The constant tradition that eventually he sealed his ministry with a martyr's death during the Neronic persecutions places his death before the close of 68. Hence these letters may be dated between 62 and 68. Their order is disputed; we would place 1 Timothy first, followed by Titus and 2 Timothy; but many put Titus as the earliest, followed by 1 and 2 Timothy; others put Titus last. Paul was still campaigning when he wrote 1 Timothy and Titus; it is hopeless to determine his activities accurately, as Zahn and Ramsay have tried to do. He commissioned Timothy and Titus to take his place in supervising the work in Ephesus and Crete and presumably elsewhere. They were to rejoin him shortly, but both letters imply in their content and in the attitude of the writer that the commission was to be permanent. The apostle was turning over his work to these men. His emphasis upon the technical and external grew naturally out of the situation. This was the kind of coaching they needed; these were the things that could not be disregarded if they were to prove good ministers of Jesus Christ. The church must have the Spirit; it must also be trained, taught, and disciplined if the Spirit is to bring forth its rightful fruits. The apostle saw that this could best be accomplished by proper organization, by trained leadership and by effective administration. He was not substituting these things for faith and the things of the Spirit so prominent in the other letters; he was insisting that orderly, disciplined, consistent conduct in church, home, and the individual is essential to spiritual attainment. Character and Christian excellence thrive best under discipline and come to richest, surest fruition under orderly care. 2 Timothy was written from prison; Paul felt the end was near and wanted his beloved Timothy with him. This letter is exceedingly personal, yet even here the apostle's anxiety that Timothy should be efficient in church administration, a workman approved unto God, crowds to the front and shows his concern in behalf of his successor.

The Commission of Timothy and Titus. The great statesman of the church who dictated the Pastorals wrote from the personal point of view. His problem is the equipment and training of those upon whom is to devolve so shortly the care of his churches. What were some of the duties he was most concerned to have these delegates fulfill?

(1) They were to *teach*. Religion always has a message. God has something to tell people. The prophet's work never ceases. Where there is no knowledge, no vision, the people perish. Other things the church should have; intelligence about God and his Word they must have. More important than his methods or technique is the teacher's message. It is his first duty to learn the things of God, to be initiated in the life of the Spirit, to know the secret and power of righteous living. Paul was a master builder when he stressed as he did the teaching function of the church leader. In his judgment, Timothy and Titus were primarily the religious experts of the community and whatever else they wrought for the churches they were to inform their people and make them intelligent about religion. The phrase "sound teachings" (mg.) or "sound words" occurs some half dozen times in the Pastorals (1 Tim. 1:10 6:3 2 Tim. 1:13 4:3 Tit. 1:9 2:1) but it can hardly be construed as meaning a standardized body of doctrine. What Paul was asking was the kind of simple, straightforward, wholesome instruction that called for clean, moral, self-controlled living, that insisted upon outward as well as inward holiness, that demanded that Christian conduct should exemplify Christian doctrine, that set up Jesus' type of living as the standard and pattern for Christian discipleship, and that asked for renewed character as the gospel's best apology. A glance over the repeated demands

for the simple requirements of a healthy, normal Christian life will confirm our interpretation and show that the aim and end of the teaching was holy living, not doctrinal correctness. Paul's helpers were building men, and doctrines were of importance only as they contributed vitally to that work.

(2) They were to *select and train others* to teach and to supervise the work of other teachers. They were to guard the faith as others transmitted it, see that emphasis was properly placed and that idle speculation or pretentious learning was not substituted for the moral and spiritual requirements of the gospel. Part of their task was the correction of false teachings to which believers were exposed either from pagan contact on the outside or from misguided teachers within the church. All this work, the attention both to teachers and teachings, received the emphasis it did because of the important part it played in determining the character of believers.

(3) They were to *oversee the organization and administration* of the church. This was largely provided for by the selection of proper officials and leaders. It was the finest kind of statesmanship that regarded leadership in this strategic way and sought to provide leaders worthy of the faith. In choosing them great weight was laid upon personal qualifications, as though the first requirements for true leadership were genuine Christian character and experience. The influence and power of the official, his usefulness in edifying believers or in making converts, was measured more by what he was than by what he knew or what he said.

(4) These delegates were to *exercise discipline*, always a delicate, difficult, thankless duty, though often a salutary and a needful one. The peddler of dangerous teachings or of unseemly tales, the man who neglected his own needy kin, the pretender who traded the form of righteousness for its power, the offender against the common decencies of life, the official who misused or abused his office, the brother who would continue practices discountenanced even by pagan standards, all called for correction and discipline. The discipline was wholesome, administered for the sake of the offender in the hope that he might be reclaimed, and for the benefit of the church to provide against the contagion of bad example and the influence of harmful precedent. The prophet can come with gentleness (1 Cor. 4^{21}) or he can come with sternness and a rod. Paul stood sponsor for that neighbor love which seeks another's good with an intensity of devotion which both suffers for that other and allows that other himself to suffer that he may attain his best. These letters prescribed disciplined life both for individual and church in pursuit of holiness.

The False Teachers. The trouble-makers described in the Pastorals as false teachers were within the church. Otherwise Timothy and Titus could have exercised no jurisdiction over them. Just what they were teaching is indeterminate and for that reason doctrines and speculations have been ascribed to them which belong to a later period in church life. They were regarded as false teachers because they were disloyal to the great trunk lines of ethical and spiritual requirements along which Paul built his missions. They liked to hear themselves talk, they were addicted to vain words, they affected scholarship, resorted to display, and appealed to traditional precedents. They were self-seeking, coveting reputation and influence, and possibly they had financial gain in mind. Their work was dangerous in that it shifted emphasis from essentials, encouraged careless living, broke down ethical distinctions, removed moral restraints, and overthrew discipline. By teaching and by personal attitude they threatened the morale of the whole church. References to myths, genealogies, law and circumcision indicate that some of these false teachers were Jewish converts who had not learned the true character of the gospel. It is possible that there was also an element of asceticism on the part of some extremists who forbade marriage, restricted the eating of meat and prescribed certain physical exercises as essentials of religion. These teachings needed the censor's blue pencil, not because of their esoteric, speculative character but because they perverted the ordinary truths of Christian living and misrepresented the faith even in regard to ordinary sins. They subverted the simple requirements of Christian character; their words did not befit sound, wholesome teaching; they engendered strife; led foolish souls away from Christlike conduct; wrecked the faith of those who could be persuaded that religion according to the gospel is something else than obedience to the law of Christ and a personal likeness unto him in all the activities of life. It was the moral results of their work, the unwholesome type of living and thinking they invited, the demoralization of Christian character they encouraged, that made these teachers false and called for their discipline.

The Ministry and its Orders. What is the evidence as to the development of ministerial orders? (1) Bishops—overseers—are mentioned in 1 Tim. 3^{2-7} and in Tit. 1^{7-9}. (2) Elders—presbyters—are mentioned in 1 Tim. 5^{17-19} and Tit. $1^{5,6}$. (3) Deacons are mentioned in

1 Tim. 3^{8-10, 12}. And the following are also frequently recognized as official orders: (4) Deaconesses, 1 Tim. 3^{11}; and (5) Widows, 1 Tim. 5^{9, 10}. Bishops also find mention in Paul's address to the Ephesian elders at Miletus, Acts 20^{28}, and in Phil. 1^{1}; presbyters or elders, in Acts 14^{23} 15^{2, 22, 23} 20^{17}, etc. Timothy and Titus were admonished to use great deliberation and discretion in the selection of these officials. Every precaution was to be taken to prevent the calling or ordination of unworthy candidates. Strange to say, the thing we should most naturally expect in this connection, the thing we have a right to expect, is missing, namely, a list of the duties pertaining to these officials and their relations one to the other. In place of this what we have is a list of the personal qualifications to be required in candidates for office with emphasis almost entirely upon moral considerations. Academic and ecclesiastical requirements are practically ignored. The several lists of qualifications are so similar, so nearly identical, that discrimination of the several terms is exceedingly precarious. The complicated development of ecclesiastical offices and distinctions in the later church naturally gave rise to the need of precedent and authority. Appeal was made to the Pastorals to this end, and the custom grew up of justifying this later ecclesiastical development by the Pastorals. This has given these terms an official significance and imputed to them a refinement of distinctions which the letters themselves do not guarantee. How many separate offices were referred to by the terms "bishop," "presbyter," and "deacon"? Did they refer to different orders of the ministry or were they synonymous or were there only two officers indicated, one being referred to in two ways? Or did these terms confuse office, order, and the functions of office? On such questions Christian thought has long been divided. The early Christians invented none of these terms; they found all coined and in common currency and appropriated them to their own use. The term "elder"—presbyter—was thoroughly familiar in Jewish usage and, no doubt, throughout the empire; among the Jews it held a certain degree of official significance but nothing at all to correspond with or justify the dignity and authority accorded it in later Christian usage. So the term "bishop"—*episcopos*—was equally familiar in Greek usage to describe one who was called to preside at meetings and exercise oversight of varying degree and dignity in any organization; it enjoyed no such implication of exalted place and authority as the Christian bishop soon came to have. "Deacon" was a term found everywhere and indicated a servant or employee whose duties were various and indiscriminate, with no suggestion of official dignity; he was to serve, to minister to the will of some master. There is nothing in the Pastorals to show plainly that these terms had as yet acquired clear distinctions of meaning. They seem to be used without discrimination so far as bishops and elders are concerned. While duties are not enumerated, certain ones are implied, but no duty or dignity is implied for a bishop that is not just as clearly implied for an elder; qualifications for both are without distinction. There is reason for believing (1 Tim. 3^{13}) that the deacon was a less significant official, who could hope to attain higher office through good service.

Critical opinion still differs most widely over this matter. The distinction between bishop and elder is the point at issue. Some contend the terms were simply synonymous and identical while others make them quite distinct, designating separate offices and orders; and these raise the bishop to the more exalted order. There are those who insist that the term "bishop" referred not to an office but to a function of an office; the term "elder," or "presbyter," designated an office; the term "bishop" designated the function of oversight; in which case the bishop and elder were the same person; as elder he was an official; the function of his office was episcopacy or oversight. Others reverse this with the explanation that there was no office of elder; the elders were simply the older and more experienced members of the church from whom an overseer or bishop was chosen. Again we are informed that both terms primarily designated function; and bishops were elders with special prerogatives. The normal deduction from the records would recognize the term "deacon" as describing a minor official or office and the terms "bishop" and "elder" as interchangeable designations for officials of the same rank, with the possibility that "elder" was the more general term for the superintendents or leaders from whose number the one asked to preside was more and more generally spoken of as the bishop or overseer. (For fuller discussion, see Hort, *The Christian Ecclesia;* Allen, *Christian Institutions;* Vincent, *Commentary on Philippians;* Parry, *The Pastoral Epistles.*)

Some Great Teachings from the Pastorals. The character of these writings makes exact analysis difficult, but certain teachings stand out prominently.

(1) God's work will be best served and advanced by orderly, careful methods.

(2) The disciplined life and the disciplined church furnish the finest medium for transmitting the power of the Spirit.

(3) The supreme qualification for any Christian worker is character.

(4) The greatest service one can render the cause of Christ is personal influence and holy example.

(5) The sins that break down the cause and shipwreck faith are the ordinary sins.

(6) Pagans or outsiders will never respect a faith with lower standards of living than their own.

(7) The church may rightly be described as a school for character.

(8) The one all-inclusive work of the church is to build lives after the pattern of Christ. Living is the final test of all religion.

These Epistles are therefore not merely ecclesiastical, but share the N.T. ethical emphasis.

Literature: Moffatt, *An Introduction to the Literature of the N.T.;* Lock, *A Critical and Exegetical Commentary on The Pastoral Epistles* (International Critical Commentary); St. John Parry, *The Pastoral Epistles, with Introduction, Text and Commentary;* Harrison, *The Problem of the Pastoral Epistles.*

FIRST TIMOTHY

Introduction

For the general introduction, see the preceding discussion.

Timothy the Man. Timothy had been associated with Paul long before he received this letter. He was of Jewish heritage on his mother's side, with a Greek father, who along with his grandmother and mother became converted to the gospel on the occasion of Paul's first visit to his home-town, Lystra (Acts 14). When Paul returned for a second visit (Acts 16[1]), he claimed the young convert as a helper in his gospel campaigning. From the frequent mention of his name both in Acts and the letters, it is evident that he has been in constant fellowship with Paul ever since. This letter suggests they had lately been together in Ephesus, and when Paul left he committed the work there to Timothy. Parry (*The Pastoral Epistles*) makes the very interesting and probable suggestion that before Paul's departure Timothy had been consecrated or ordained as Paul's special delegate or successor, to have supervision of the churches and to exercise authority over them such as he had not had before. This together with Paul's knowledge of Timothy and of the situation will account for the character of much of the advice given. The letter is very personal and betrays the apostle's concern for the younger man whom he regards as a son, but it also vibrates with the writer's ceaseless interest in the churches. "Ye are in our hearts to die together and to live together" (2 Cor. 7[3]). The letter was the outcome of his desire to help Timothy administer the churches so well that he would prove himself a good minister of Jesus Christ and enable the churches to fulfill their proper function in the rearing of godly men.

CHAPTER I

1, 2. Greeting. Paul writes to Timothy as a friend; he also writes him as an apostle, one who is under orders from his Lord. It is the King's business on which he addresses him. The word *mercy* is added here to the usual greeting of the apostle. The phrase *God our Saviour* is one of the new phrases of the Pastorals, where it appears six times. The idea, however, is basic in Pauline thinking; all his gospel rests back ultimately upon the fact that the God revealed in Jesus Christ is a saving-God. The great discovery Paul made upon the Damascus road was that Jesus was right in telling men that God is friendly and forgiving. He gloried in being the servant of One who would save.

3–11. The Teacher's Stewardship. Paul and Timothy have previously discussed the problem occasioned by certain members at Ephesus —purposely left unnamed—who want to teach. Their work is having disastrous results. Forgetting or ignoring the fact that teaching is a stewardship (dispensation) from God and that the end or goal of the teacher's charge is to instruct and train in that kind of living which is marked by love, clean thinking, pure conscience and loyal obedience to God, they are raising all kinds of questions and discussing subjects that are irrelevant and have nothing to do with restraining men from sin and helping them to learn righteousness. Their interest is their own personal ambition rather than the good of their hearers. It is possible that their chief fault lies in insisting upon teaching when they are not prepared to do so; such teachers can do sad damage. Evidently, they bolster up their pronouncements by citation of law and appeal to fear (v. 7). The Christian is the last man who needs to fear the law. The law is not made for a man who is striving to live honorably and righteously as is the follower of Christ. The chief criticism of these teachers in Ephesus is their failure to give their hearers *sound doctrine* (v. 10), i.e., teaching morally wholesome and conducive to spiritual health (see pp. 1276–7). Timothy's problem is how to persuade them to give up their unprofitable teaching and devote themselves to that kind of instruction which produces wholesome life and conduct, a real stewardship of faith.

12–17. A Gospel That Saves. In a paragraph that seems disconnected Paul gives thanks to God for his personal knowledge of a gospel that saves; though he had once been a blasphemer, a disputer and destroyer of the faith—possibly a false teacher—the gospel had brought him wholesomeness of spirit. *It is a faithful saying* (v. 15)—a phrase he employs repeatedly in the Pastorals to emphasize some truth that is wholly reliable—it is the gospel's most blessed truth, that Jesus came into the world for that very purpose of saving sinful men. Paul offers himself as a proof of his saving power and argues that if the gospel could save him, the chief of sinners, it can save any sinful man who will believe on him who hath been sent by the King Eternal. Is Paul here telling Timothy that the gospel which was strong enough to show him the error of his way and save him unto the truth in Christ is also strong enough to help him correct the false teachers and make them wholesome?

18–20. Passing on the Trust. The *charge* Paul is passing on to Timothy is simply that which has been intrusted to him. Timothy is to be even as Paul has been, a propagandist for Jesus, a teacher of the wholesome doctrine of the gospel and supervisor or overseer of all the interests of the work of Christ. The instructions that follow in 2^1–6^2 may be taken as illustrating what he means by the charge. Judging from this, Paul is not writing to give a finished statement of the faith nor to compile a complete manual of church duties and church government. The trust committed to him is his ministry in the gospel with all that that involves. Paul is writing to strengthen Timothy's personal morale for the many duties confronting him. The *prophecies which led the way to thee* (mg.) were probably the indications and advices which convinced Paul that he should ordain Timothy as a minister and possibly appoint him as his successor in the care of the churches. Timothy can hope to succeed in his work only by keeping faith with Christ in his own life; to do otherwise means *shipwreck* as in case of Hymenæus and Alexander, whom Paul disciplined in the hope of saving them.

CHAPTER II

1–7. The Ministry of Intercession. The universal character of the gospel inspires an interest in all men. Let the Christian worker pray for all and labor in behalf of all. A prayerful attitude toward kings and those in authority will disarm suspicion against the Christians and leave them quiet and unmolested to pursue their work. There is but one God, and the gospel worker should have the same attitude toward all men and the same interest in saving them that God manifested in sending Jesus to show his compassion for men and his longing to win them to himself. In his timely coming Jesus revealed the friendly will of God and gave himself, as unreservedly as one ransoms a friend, to make every provision necessary for the saving of men (v. 5). This Christlike attitude toward others, this passion for the saving of all men, lies at the heart of the Christian ministry. With a vehemence that is unexpected here, Paul recalls his own appointment as teacher and apostle of this universal gospel which intercedes for all men.

8–15. Living and Praying; Place of Women. Believers are to pray often, *in every place*, whenever they come together. Timothy is to teach them that prayer has its conditions. If it is to be effective and prevail, it must be re-enforced by consistent conduct. Let men remember that we lift our prayers to God with *holy hands*, by clean and holy living; that we pray better by conduct and character than by words alone, however fine; that ill will and unfriendly disposition toward others will defeat any verbal praying in their behalf (cf. Psa. $24^{3f.}$). "He prayeth best who loveth best." Women are reminded that a Christian woman's best adorning, her finest testimony to the gospel and her best way of making religion attractive, is not costly apparel, precious jewels or modish appearance, but good works, winsome womanliness and godliness of character. Paul shares the thought of his age in relation to women. They are not to aspire to leadership, to preach or teach nor to take precedence over men (v. 12). This is *prudential advice* dictated by the needs of the age for the good of the cause, and to be revised when the good of that same cause justifies it. It is to be remembered that Paul employed and commended Priscilla, Phœbe and other women helpers. In this letter, he sanctions the employment of deaconesses (3^{11}) and official-widows (5^9). While he recognizes woman's limitations and supports it by appeal to the Eden story, he points out that she has a wonderful ministry to fulfill; she is to find her greatest ministry as mother and home-maker. God has no greater work to offer. She shall help save the world by the children she bears and rears; in bearing and rearing children her religion shall be her strength. Some see here a reference to the incarnation, reminding us that through the Son one woman bore we are saved.

CHAPTER III

1–13. Choosing Church Leaders. In this paragraph attention turns from advices for the whole church to a discussion of its officials, namely, the bishop, the deacons, and the deaconesses. No mention is made of their duties, how they are chosen nor of their ordination. It is injudicious to make these records say what they do not say in regard to these officials. Whatever technical development may have taken place in such matters, evidently Paul does not attach as much importance to them as he does to the character of the officials, the kind of men who are going into the ministry and becoming leaders in the church. His whole interest here is upon personal equipment; the requirements dwelt upon pertain almost exclusively to matters of conduct and character (see intro., p. 1277b). Their teaching and "ruling over the church" will be influenced most of all by daily living, by consistent illustration of the faith. In preaching to outsiders, in maintaining the betterness of the gospel, in winning converts and establishing believers, it will be conduct, not creed, character, not controversy, practice, not precept, that will play the weightier part. Christlikeness is wondrously attractive and contagious. If some of the advices seem needlessly simple and elemental in regard to the most ordinary moral virtues and practices, it is to be replied that a minister can nowhere else fail so disastrously as in these essentials of holy living. The man from mission lands is telling us to-day that our failure there is not due to our teachings but solely to the way supposed Christians have behaved themselves.

1–7. The Bishop. Whatever his other qualifications—and we take it for granted that the rigid insistence upon moral excellence implies a like rigid scrutiny of his other qualifications and a similar demand for high standards of excellence in other respects—he is to be a man whose personal life will be an asset to the church, whose living will "give no handle for criticism." The requirements were written for first-century Christians living in contact with a civilization for which these requirements might seem very high and exacting. The church was bold to oppose old standards and to expose the sinful character of so many popular practices. It still takes fine courage to insist that religion must be clean and straight-going both ethically and morally.

The bishop is to be *the husband of one wife*, a specification that finds its most probable explanation as an instance of the gospel's conflict with the current practices in forbidding or protesting against polygamy, a legal custom of the empire. This was part of the attempt to combat the loose sexual life of the age and raise all life to a level of holiness. Again the bishop is not to be a tippler, a slave to wine or other excess, nor a contentious man too ready to settle difficulties with violence or his fists, arbitrary and hard to live with. Neither is he to have an itching palm for money. On the contrary, he is to be abstemious, self-controlled, hospitable, and courteous, both personally and socially. Other marks in one who would be a bishop are aptness in teaching, attentiveness to the business of his office and ability to preside, take charge, and rule; the discipline he maintains in his own home will indicate how he would rule in the church, for the church is truly only one great family, the household of faith. The work of the bishop is too serious to be intrusted to a novice, or new convert or one without the maturity of experience. Such a man should command the respect of outsiders for himself and the faith.

8–10. Deacons. Deacons may be lower in office but the demand for moral refinement, holy living, and consistent character on their part is not one whit lower. Let the deacon show a worthy dignity, let him control his tongue, his appetites, and his desire for gain; let him maintain the faith by conscientious living. A man is to be made a deacon only after he has been properly tested; the office is too important to be trusted to the untried. When he has served well as a deacon he may hope to be qualified for higher service. If women are received for service, they too are expected to qualify for office by the same blamelessness of conduct and holiness of character. Note the high assumption through all this discussion that elevation to office is justified solely by thought of service. Office means service. To serve well one must attend on the school of discipline. He who will lead well must first learn to follow. The disciplined life promises the richest service.

14–16. The Mystery of Godliness. It is not easy to understand why, if Paul hopes soon to rejoin Timothy, he should write him so elaborately about the oversight of the church. It must be that Timothy is making an experiment new to him, in superintending the churches, and Paul's eagerness to have him succeed manifests itself in writing these many instructions with which he hopes to aid him in persuading men to conduct themselves as members of the church. The necessity for all this instruction, all this discipline of the members, all this guarding of tuition, all this enforced care over the qualifications of officials, is to be found in the character of the church. It justifies all this care and concern because the church is the household of God, his family, to whom he has committed his truth and through whom he will establish it in the world. And beyond controversy it is a great revelation which the church should embody and express in the lives of its members. It is nothing less than finding the secret of godliness, how to live godly lives, how to become like God. This marvelous secret the church has learned through her great Lord Jesus Christ who revealed it to men by living it himself in the days of his flesh, who was vindicated by the spirit he revealed and by his victory over sin and death, who was the marvel of angels, heralded among the nations, accounted worthy of trust in the world and exalted high in heavenly glory. This truth that God through his incarnate, glorified Son offers men salvation from sin and the power unto godly life and character is the heart of the gospel. The church exists solely to bring this power to men and to help them attain it. The magnitude and importance of her task justifies every effort to make her indeed God's household, the place where men will find and meet God and learn to become like him in Christ.

16. This is believed by many to be part of an early Christian hymn.

CHAPTER IV

1–5. Warning of Dangers. Heroic zeal and unflagging watchfulness are called for in the care of the church. She is and is still to be beset by many dangers. Timothy is reminded of an old "prophecy about a later crisis which is now being fulfilled." The reference is indefinite; many words prophetic of doom or danger, either from the O.T. or from Christian tradition, could be pressed into service here. There is no necessity for limiting this warning to some particular crisis; the references are very general, such as may be anticipated repeatedly; as a matter of fact, Paul had time and again encountered troublous times involving every evil here mentioned and worse. Timothy and every other minister must anticipate the same. Paul knew defection of some converts in Galatia, for instance. False teachers were a constant menace to the N.T. church. Paul was ceaselessly vigilant to curtail their work. He has lately met some of them at Ephesus and knows they are misguided spirits who profess inspiration but teach doctrines that could come only from demons, never from Christ. They dabble in hypocrisy and lies until their consciences are seared and they no longer realize that they are hypocrites and liars. They say, for instance, that the way to please God is to refrain from marriage and to refuse to eat meats. The truth is God himself gave men these gifts. What men need to be taught is how to use them, thankfully and prayerfully, in the spirit of Him who bestowed them, and to fulfill his will.

6–16. Counselling a Good Minister. The counsels here become exceedingly personal. Timothy is a delegate from Paul; first and foremost he is a minister from Jesus Christ. As a good minister, he will keep reminding the brethren of the things of Christ; he will hold Christian ideals before them constantly. The art of repeating, of saying the same thing over and over again from some new angle, of keeping a desired truth before his hearers, of making a proper "time exposure," is an essential part of the good minister's equipment; it is to be most earnestly coveted and sought after. To this end, Timothy is admonished to nourish his own soul with the truth that keeps faith fresh and strong; let him look carefully after his own life; let him diligently continue in that wholesome teaching to which he has been so loyal and let him avoid discussions which often are as foolish and worthless as the tales a grandmother tells the children (v. 7).

The good minister disciplines his own soul and keeps it "fit" by exercising it in the practice of godliness. *Bodily discipline,* perhaps athletic exercise, but more probably ascetic practices recommended by false teachers, has its profit, but it is the discipline of the soul, the training and exercising of the spirit in the practice of godliness, that enriches all life, both the present and that which is to come. So true is this that to this end, the achievement of godliness, all our labor and effort are devoted; this is the end of all our quest, to find God and become like him. The minister does his finest preaching and teaching by his example, by his own gospel-disciplined life (vv. 7–12).

Even a young man can give a demonstration in this way that will compel respect and make others forget his lack of years. He can be *an example* of what gospel power and gospel living are. Such teaching cannot be refuted. He is to instruct his people and guide them in their reading. Let him be diligent about *his own reading* and study. It is refreshing to hear the apostle advise his son to keep up his work as a student, to find time in his busy days for study and reading. 2 Tim. 4[13] intimates that Paul himself had the practice of carrying books around with him and, amid all his pastoral cares, of keeping up his studies.

The teacher, however, does not qualify as a good minister of Jesus Christ until the training of the school in logic, rhetoric, and similar arts, is re-enforced with the matchless power of a life that constantly shows forth the spirit of Jesus in word, in manner of living, in good will and in purity. *The gift* he is not to neglect is his authority as a recognized official leader to exercise these various functions Paul has mentioned, which was conferred upon him by the elders, who felt they were led of God to choose him and appoint him to such work as they did, when they laid their hands upon him. This *laying on of hands* (v. 14) was an old custom, without thought of any magical transmission of right or power, a symbol on the part of the elders of their good will and blessing and also of their prayer that God was acting through them. Whether this refers to his appointment and ordination at Lystra (Acts 16[1-3]) when first he joined Paul and Silas, or to a recent ordination, we may not say. The trust of the brethren bestowed on him is to be honored and confirmed by the faithful discharge of his duties and steadfast loyalty to his task. Diligent heed both to his example, his own salvation and to his teachings will be rewarded in seeing his hearers saved unto Christian life and living. This is the final evidence that he is a good minister.

CHAPTER V

Handling Special Cases. These cases constitute the theme of ch. 5 and of 6[1, 2]. Upon Timothy will also devolve pastoral cares and the administration of discipline. Here follow a number of special cases where the personal preparation spoken of above will be most fortunate and most needed. In the household of the Lord there can be no harsh discrimination, no censoriousness, no vindictiveness or personal bias. If brotherly love, the spirit of Jesus, self-control and purity of motive are ever needed by the church leader, it is when he is called upon to discipline a brother, to decide between brethren or pass judgment upon an offending member. Happy the pastor who is gifted with tact, discretion, and power bestowed of God to sense the values involved and the real issues at stake. His strength will needs be tempered with tenderness and his firmness with the gentleness that seeks but to serve the offender's good.

1, 2. Discipline Adapted to the Offender. Be considerate of a brother well advanced in years, older than yourself; treat him as you would your own father, try exhortation and encouragement before rebuke. Deal with older women and with younger men and women in the same considerate way; the personal element transcends the official; the purpose is to uplift and help, not to mar or brand.

3–16. Widows. It is of the very genius of the gospel to care for the poor and needy. The first mention recorded in the annals of the church to do this systematically was in the case of widows (Acts 6), and this had fine precedent in the solicitude with which Jewish piety supervised the care of its orphans and widows. (See Edersheim, *Sketches of Jewish Social Life*, p. 167.) There is division of opinion whether provision made here was for one class or more than one class. It is quite clearly the duty of any Christian who has a widow in his family connection to provide for her and not allow her to become dependent upon the charity of the church. A refusal to do so proves one worse than an unbeliever. Pagans often evinced a high quality of humanity in their charitable care of their needy ones. Christians cannot do less—particularly if they are to describe the church as a family, God their Father, and other believers their brethren. They must honor that name of brother or change it (v. 8).

There has been no little dispute concerning instructions in regard to the widows who were dependent upon the church. It would be harsh discrimination to refuse aid to any widow under sixty years of age. A rearrangement of the text as follows, vv. 3, 4, 8, 7, 5, 6, 9 (see Parry) simplifies the matter by indicating that an official list was first to be compiled of all dependent widows who were entitled to receive alms from the church; from this list a certain number, all over sixty, were selected for various duties or services for which they received some recognition from the church. The arrangement was somewhat precarious; it was to be guarded most carefully, lest it bring the church into disrepute. The qualifications for candidacy to this class are rather well-defined and severe. The younger widows are advised to remarry (cf. 1 Cor. 7), as though the normal field for a woman's activity is in the home, playing the unrivaled part of wife, mother, and good neighbor.

17–25. To Discipline an Elder, etc. The word *elder* was used in 5[1] merely in the sense of an older brother; here that meaning scarcely satisfies the context, and the term is better understood as having official significance. Such an official may both preside and teach, and when he renders this double service he is to be regarded by the church as worthy of double honor, esteem, and possibly also larger remuneration or support. This very reasonable advice is verified by two citations referred to as Scripture, one from the O.T. (Deut. 25[4]) and the other the words of Jesus (Mt. 10[10] Lk. 10[7]). This reference shows how Jesus became supreme authority with his followers; here is evidence how the authority accorded him naturally came to be attached to his words;

the church was unconsciously building a new canon (see p. 948b). An accusation against an elder has no hearing unless it is presented scripturally, by two or three witnesses. An elder found guilty deserves public reproof, that others may be restrained from imitating him. Timothy is most impressively admonished to use the greatest discretion in such cases, avoiding all influences that might prejudice his interest or distort his judgment (v. 21).

22. *Lay hands hastily on no man,* could be an injunction against ordaining any man as an elder hastily, without due deliberation; "carelessness in appointment involves responsibility for sin." In the present connection, however, the more likely interpretation is to construe it as an exhortation not to lay hands in acquittal too readily upon one under trial or not to be too hasty to restore to office one adjudged guilty. Such readiness to overlook guilt may breed guilt. It is a grave offense to palliate sin or treat wrongdoing lightly. An official who lets an offender off too lightly may really embolden him or encourage him to further wrongdoing and so become responsible for this new sin, a partaker in the offender's guilt. Let Timothy be so judicious as to avoid having any share in or responsibility for the sins of others. Paul adds (vv. 24, 25) that some cases for discipline will be easy and almost decide themselves, so evident their merits; in other instances longer and more careful investigation will be necessary before a decision can be rendered. And so it is with works; some are obviously worthy; others, though not so obvious, will eventually reveal their true character.

23. This verse has often been seriously abused. It is hard to fit it into the discussion, unless it may be that with this thought of avoiding responsibility for sins of others Timothy had refrained from all use of wine, and Paul, knowing his friend's physical condition, indigestion or weak stomach, advised a sparing use of wine as a medical remedy.

CHAPTER VI

1, 2. Advice for Christian Slaves. (Continuing the "special cases" discussed in ch. 5.) Believers who are slaves of pagan masters are enjoined to show respect to those masters and render them good service; poor service will reproach them and the God they confess. Those in service to Christian masters or employers are not to presume upon the fact of Christian brotherhood; rather let them serve all the more diligently because the master who receives the benefits of their service is a believer and beloved.

3–10. Godliness and Gain. The apostle resumes his warnings against the teacher of unsound doctrines. The unwholesomeness of the teachings of one such manifests itself in his own character, in his egotism, presumption, tiresome wranglings, suspicion, and low thinking. His teaching makes him utterly unloving and unlovable. He reveals his mercenary spirit and wrong motive by his constant talk about profit. He would give one the idea that he is godly simply as a matter of good and gainful business. There is great gain in godliness, though not the kind he prates about. According to Paul, gain consists of material wealth, while the gain that godliness brings lies in the enrichment of personality, in the content and possession of spirit that only those can have who are at peace, on good terms with God. Religion does not neglect normal physical needs and a rightful provision for the same, but it does apply a very ugly name to the man who thinks that the end of life is building bigger barns; for we came into the world without things and without things pass we into the next world. Jesus talked much about the danger of riches. When the desire of the heart is to become rich, to possess many things, the needs of the higher life are apt to be crowded out and forgotten. *Root of all evil* is this covetousness after money, after possessions, as can be all too freely illustrated by those who, in going in search of riches, lose the way to life, to abiding contentment and to God.

11–16. Lay Hold on Eternal Life. Paul has drawn many shafts of criticism for writing Timothy as he does in this paragraph, exhorting him to fight the good fight of faith, to avoid the temptations of riches, to keep his eye and heart on eternal values and strive persistently to attain them. Why not an exhortation like this even to Timothy? When does the leader or any other Christian become immune to danger from the desire for things and other temptations just as ordinary? The apostle confesses "I have not attained; I press on" (Phil. 3[13]). Let Timothy *flee all that is false,* loyally remembering his call to be God's man and the good start he made before many witnesses. It is still his charge to maintain faith with God and Jesus Christ in *fulfilling the trust* committed to him, the attainment of eternal life for himself and others, even until the day when Christ shall come again in honor and power eternal.

17–19. The Rightful Use of Riches. This paragraph concerning riches and their proper employment seems quite awkward and is apparently misplaced. Those who have riches suffer temptation to trust in what they have rather than in God. There is an echo here of

the words of Jesus admonishing that those who would be wise lay up their treasures in heaven by investing in his work here and now.

20, 21. Entreaty to Guard the Treasure. The apostle's closing word to his son Timothy is an entreaty, voicing the desire of his heart, that he guard as the treasure of his life the opportunity given him to serve the Church of Jesus Christ, whose minister he is and whose grace is with him.

SECOND TIMOTHY

Introduction

For the general introduction see the discussion preceding 1 Timothy.

The Deep Personal Note of the Letter. Paul is a prisoner in the city of Rome and is alone save for his beloved physician Luke. He speaks touchingly of the attention he received from an Ephesian friend, Onesiphorus, who sought him out apparently with difficulty and ministered unto him. His conditions are such as to leave no doubt as to his fate; the letter is dominated by the thought that his end is near and his campaigning closed. (See p. 1275; cf. p. 942.) He summons Timothy in the hope that they may have a farewell visit together before the end. The letter contributes but little doctrinally or ecclesiastically. It is the most favorably estimated of the Pastorals; many critics who do not receive the whole as genuine find authentic Pauline sections in it. It is intensely personal, not in the sense that it was written to Timothy alone but in view of the note of close friendship and paternal concern. It is almost like a father writing a son to bequeath him his business, the great interests of his life. How natural under the circumstance for memory to flood in as he writes, with thought of their days together and of the experiences that have bound them with the ties of deep affection and with passion for a common cause! There is fine spiritual value in listening while the old apostle, filled with years and labors devoted to the Lord whom he adores, commits his work to the younger man and sketches for him the kind of leader he would have him be; and there is high inspiration also in learning with what spirit of trust and fearlessness this follower of Christ faces the crossing of the bar. He hopes to see his Pilot face to face.

CHAPTER I

1, 2. To Timothy the Beloved. Whatever other distinction Paul may have been able to claim, the one for which he counted all others as loss was the privilege of knowing himself called and sent of God to preach the gospel of Jesus Christ. To Timothy he was the representative of Christ who had claimed his devoted allegiance and affection through many a year of service. Paul struck the keynote of the letter when he greeted Timothy as his *beloved child.*

3–14. Thanksgiving for Timothy. The lines here are very personal and winsomely frank. The heart and the mind both speak; memory and emotion mingle and blend with instruction and encouragement until in the rush of suggestions one may find oneself confused. Paul thanks the God of his fathers whom he serves with a clear conscience for Timothy, for his past life, his character, his friendship, his service; mentions him regularly in his prayers by day and by night, and longs eagerly to see him once more as he recalls the tears the tenderhearted Timothy shed at their parting. It may be Timothy was apprehensive for his beloved apostle; parting was a serious matter for the campaigners in those days.

Some readers find a hint in v. 5 that Paul has had a late reminder of his friend's devotion, a letter, a gift, or some other token which reminded him anew of Timothy's sincere and unreserved loyalty to the faith, that faith which both his grandmother Lois and his mother Eunice owned, loved, and bequeathed to him as a precious heritage. It is great joy to the apostle to remember how the faith came to this household; how those good women accepted it so wholeheartedly and earnestly that, when the young son of the home, their fond hope, confessed the Christ and would go out in his service they hesitated not, but offered him willingly, that Paul might lay his hands upon him to consecrate him to the task.

The apostle, however, does not lose himself in memory; he appeals to Timothy to stir up, "to keep at white heat," that gift of grace, that endowment of the spirit, which God bestowed upon him when the apostle consecrated him for service (v. 6). That gift included no fearfulness, no cowardice, no reluctance to suffer or endure, but strength to serve, power to care for others and a spirit to discipline and train himself for his ministry. Let him never be ashamed of his faith that he is a Christian nor of his friend who is in prison for the faith, but let him, like his friend, be ready to suffer shame and share any hardship that must be incurred in preaching the gospel. Strength for this God will supply, and an earnest of this we have already had in the power with which he saved us and called us to holiness of life and service. For we were neither saved nor called by reason of our merits or our strength but by virtue of that saving purpose and generous grace of God which, though true of him from all eternity, has been but lately fully manifested in the coming of Jesus, who had power to release us from our fear of death and make us sure of life and immortality (vv. 9, 10). The writer of that is a prisoner facing death! Paul was called to spread this gospel throughout the world and it is because he has done so he is now in prison. For all that he is not ashamed, neither has he any doubt about his gospel; he knows Him whom the gospel has taught him to trust and is peacefully confident that he has power to honor and fulfill the gospel's every promise even unto death.

12c. Parry translates to read "he is able to help me maintain my trust, to be true to the gospel intrusted to me until the day when I shall have completed my work." The apostle is convinced that he knows Jesus Christ; that is the dynamic secret of his ministry; his whole Christian life has been built on the conviction that he has not been alone; that Jesus has been with him; his passion has been not so much devotion to a cause as to a great personality. Jesus was an abiding reality.

13. Timothy is earnestly entreated to hold in the same way to the gospel, to that type or pattern of wholesome teaching which Paul has told him was the truth of Christ; he is to hold it with firm faith and love that can be known only in union with Christ. This precious gospel has been committed to Timothy and he is to guard it with the help of God's Spirit which dwells in men.

15–18. One Who Was Not Ashamed. The appeal to Timothy not to be ashamed of his friend in bonds is not mere sentiment. Paul refers to an experience when, either in Asia or in Rome, he needed friends, and some of his friends from Asia who were at hand were ashamed of his bonds and forsook him. On the other hand, the good *Onesiphorus* had been generously loyal; when he came to Rome he diligently sought out Paul and ministered unto him. It is inferred by many that Onesiphorus had since died and Paul's benediction is accordingly cited as proof that he sanctioned prayers for the dead. Both are inferences only, and are equally precarious.

CHAPTER II

1–13. A Good Fellow Soldier. The old campaigner for the gospel, convinced his campaigning days are over, appeals to Timothy to see to it that the campaigning shall not cease. He is to recruit and train helpers who will pass on the things learned from Paul and proved in so many testing experiences. Any good soldier will suffer hardship for his cause! The service of Christ calls for the same kind of fidelity and rigorous devotion which prompts a soldier to free himself from all distracting interests and give himself with undivided zeal to the leader whose approval he seeks, which prompts an athlete to keep himself in training and to keep all the hard rules of the game, that he may win his laurel, or a gardener to toil slavishly, that he may reap a harvest (vv. 4–6). Every worthy end demands its toll in labor, hardship, devotion, and loyalty. The Lord enable thee to see how the tremendous responsibility of taking the gospel of Christ to others justifies every hardship and all devotion! This is increasingly clear to one who keeps thinking about Jesus Christ, of David's royal line, raised from the dead, according to that gospel for which Paul has been imprisoned like a common criminal; but stopping him or binding him will not stop or bind the gospel; that must go on (v. 9). He endures everything gladly, that he may aid others, all God's chosen ones, to share the saving power and fellowship of Jesus Christ. It is a faithful word that promises rich reward for all we suffer or endure. In suffering or dying for the gospel we suffer and die with Christ, and he will see to it that our reward is sure.

14–26. The Workman Approved. Paul proceeds in this paragraph to give Timothy further counsel as to how he may become the kind of workman that God will approve. He begins with advice about training others who are to become Christian teachers; the great central truths of the gospel are to be kept clearly before them while they are warned against mere word-wars, against contentious preaching which antagonizes the hearers and neither wins nor profits converts (v. 16). Then he changes to direct appeal and urges Timothy to win God's approval by living the truth, and exemplifying his words. Let him give exposition of the gospel both in his teaching and in his character so true to the spirit of Christ that his work may never cause God to blush. The *babblings* decried in v. 16 are empty, irreligious discussions always current, which distract attention from the true issues of godliness, break down the spiritual life and in their demoralizing activity spread like cancer. An illustration of this is the case of Hymenæus and Philetus, who by their hapless speculations about the resurrection already being past, got away from the truth and unsettled some in the faith. Despite all such foolish teachers, God's truth stands firm, and the true teacher of his truth must pass two tests: first, he must in some way show that God is with him—*The Lord knoweth his own*—and, second, his life must correspond to his teaching—*Let every one that nameth the name of the Lord depart from unrighteousness.* As in any household there are many kinds of vessels and furnishings, of varied value, rank, honor, and grades of service, so in the church, the household of God, the members are vessels to be used of the Master, some for higher, some for humbler service. Let the teacher keep himself clean and free from the contaminations of the false teachers so that he may be a vessel of honorable rank, set apart, fitted and equipped for good work in his Master's service (vv. 20, 21). That Timothy may be such a vessel of honor, let him flee every sin, great or small, which unfits a man, young or old, for Christian service; let him pursue the virtues that mark Christian character and keep company with others of like pursuit who will aid him in attaining the same.

Again, he is cautioned against taking part in senseless debates, aimless discussions whose only outcome will be strife, bad temper, and hostility (v. 23). Men are never shown the error of their way and won to righteousness by such means. The Lord's servant will, like his Lord, be patient with those who err, hoping with more courteous, tolerant, tactful methods to disarm opposition and lead to repentance and a knowledge of the truth that shall mean their escape from evil and their saving. So will he show himself approved of God.

CHAPTER III

1–17. Equipped for Crisis. This chapter, like the preceding, deals with the task of equipping Timothy for the work which is to devolve upon him as he takes over the leadership which Paul realizes he has already laid down. To impress upon him more strenuously the need of the qualifications advised, undivided devotion to Christ, loyalty to gospel truth, courage to suffer for the cause and consistent Christian character, he is warned that the worst has not yet passed. *The last days* may describe the days preceding the Lord's return, but there is no need so to limit them; they are really quite general and have been fulfilled over and over again, days "when the patience of the Lord will be tried to the uttermost and his servants will find the times hard." The picture (vv. 1–8) is revolting; sin will run rampant; religion will be perverted; men will maintain a show of godliness but know nothing of religion as a power that turns them from sin and makes them new men in Christ; there will be those who will win their way into homes and impose upon sin-laden souls who cannot discern the truth. As Moses had his Jannes and Jambres, men who tried to discredit him and to compete for his leadership, so may the Christian leader expect similar opponents, conscienceless reprobates, who also must be exposed and restrained, as they will be when their true character is shown. How shall Timothy equip himself to meet and deal with such situations? Let him follow and maintain the training he has had under Paul, what he has learned from him, his teaching, his conduct, his faithfulness, his readiness to suffer and endure (v. 14). For Paul took it for granted that every follower of Christ can count on suffering for the cause; it was part of the program; yet out of all these hardships Paul was delivered; i.e., God was with him to enable him to endure them and remain faithful. Even if things should get worse and more critical situations arise, Timothy will still prove steadfast, remembering what he has learned and who his teachers have been, namely, those Scriptures which he learned even as a babe and which when interpreted in the light of Christ are able to make one wise unto salvation. So personal Christian experience, training under Christian leaders such as he has had under Paul, and a wise use of the sacred writings will prove sufficient equipment with which to meet great difficulties and strong opponents.

8. The two men named here are otherwise unknown. There may have been an apocryphal book which told about them (so Origen); or a purely oral tradition. Some suggest the reference may be to Ex. 7[11].

16. These sacred writings, *scriptures inspired of God*, i.e., breathing the spirit and character of God (see art., *The Divine Element in the Bible*, pp. 26–31), are an instrument of great power, whether for discipline, for instruction in the right way of living, for revealing the mind of God, wherewith the man of God, the teacher, apostle, preacher may be completely and thoroughly equipped for service. A comparison of translations by various authors of vv. 16, 17 will show at once the uselessness of being dogmatic about an exact translation. A better approach will be to recall Paul's attitude toward and use of his O.T., which, of course, "scriptures" here means. Now, Paul undoubtedly believed firmly that the Scriptures were given of God and very valuable to the Christian. However, he did not find salvation in or through the O.T., as is evidenced by his own repeated confession in the letters. The O.T. had permanent value for him only as he learned to find in it confirmation for his experience in and interpretation of Christ. (See art., *Formation of N.T.*, p. 853, for early Christian use of O.T.). His authority was Christ, and for him the authority of Christ superseded that of the O.T. and all else besides. Perhaps he is intimating here that the best test for writing that is to be called sacred is its inherent power to inspire and equip a man for Christian life and service.

CHAPTER IV

1–8. The Campaigner Closes His Work. With the earnestness of a man who is looking at things as though he were standing in the presence of God and the eternal Judge, the old apostle once more charges Timothy to be incessant, tireless in his labors to spread the gospel and fulfill the many duties involved in ministering to the churches. The times will test him; the days will come when men will be impatient of the real teachings of the gospel; its ideals will seem too high and exacting and men will want an easier way (v. 3). Against such times let Timothy be prepared to keep his balance, to face hardship and to work uncompromisingly as an evangelist should unto whom have been committed the interests of Jesus and his gospel in the lives of men. Now comes a statement accounting for all the eager pleading of the whole letter. The apostle's urgency and anxiety to have Timothy be a good minister, a workman approved, is explained in the old campaigner's word that his days are numbered, his ministry in behalf of the churches and the beloved gospel has closed. All through the lines he has been committing his work to his son in the faith, challenging the younger man to take up the torch he flings him and carry on for Christ. In words of rarest beauty and the greatest spiritual charm, he goes on to speak of his present situation and the outlook for to-morrow—a veritable swan song. His life-blood is about to be poured out and he thinks of it as an offering to God (v. 6). He has long been on campaign for his Lord, now he awaits orders for the last march. With all its hardships, his service with Christ has been a glorious struggle and brings no regrets; he has kept faith with his Lord and is perfectly confident that his Lord will keep faith with him; there is for him laurel greater than victor-athlete ever won, a crown of life itself which the Lord in the days when conflict is over will confer on every faithful campaigner for his cause. He is not alone; the Christ who has dwelt in him (Gal. 2[20]) is present now; not even death can separate him from the love of God in Christ Jesus.

9–22. Last Instructions. His message to Timothy, his challenge and charge, are finished; ere he closes, Paul adds a few bits of personal information and instruction, asking Timothy to find Mark and come to him, bringing with him certain reading matter and a cloak from Troas. Warning is given about one Alexander who is hostile to the cause. Paul's severity toward him is more likely to have a moral rather than a merely personal or doctrinal basis. See on *anathema*, Gal. 1[6-9]. It was an injury to the cause of Christ that aroused Paul. The allusion to *Mark* (v. 11) is interesting. It shows that whatever misunderstanding there may have been over his "defection" (Acts 12[12, 25] 13[13] 15[37-40]) was now past.

16–18. The reference here to a *first defense*, when the apostle was deserted by all who should have stood by him, is very indefinite. The usual supposition is that it is out of place. The reference may be to a preliminary trial, or to his trial at the close of the first imprisonment, or to some other experience unknown to us. On the one hand, he seems to be telling us that he was delivered from the first trial so as to go on with his preaching, and he expresses the hope that the Lord is to grant him a similar deliverance now; yet, on the other hand, he has just written (vv. 7, 8) his conviction that his work is finished. Perhaps we should say that Paul remains hopeful in the face of a hopeless outlook.

The mention of so many names here shows how wide was Paul's acquaintance, and their connection with so many different places shows how intimately he knew the life of the church. Some of the persons mentioned are otherwise quite unknown to us, a fact suggestive of the extent to which the work of the church depends upon the quiet fidelity of obscure people. There has been many a faithful soul whose record, like that of Paul's unknown friends, is written only in heaven.

TITUS

INTRODUCTION

Titus the Man; Reasons for the Letter. (For a fuller discussion see intro. to Pastoral Epistles, p. 1274.) The time when Paul had been in Crete to found the churches there and to leave Titus in charge of them is a matter of conjecture: we have suggested (see p. 1275a) some time during his release from the first imprisonment. The work has prospered and requires more careful organization and supervision. Our information about Titus is limited. Tradition has it that he was a Gentile convert of Paul. No mention is made of him in Acts. He first appears when Paul took him as a test case in the question of circumcising Gentile believers (Gal. 2³); later he was Paul's delegate to consider misunderstandings between the apostle and the church at Corinth; evidently, Paul regarded him as very capable and trustworthy —a genuine son in the faith. The personal bond between them was not, however, so close as that between Paul and Timothy. This letter savors much more of the official than the letters to Timothy. The lack of the personal in Titus is decidedly noticeable in comparison, though the few personal references that do appear are suggestive of high regard and confidence as though Titus were older, more efficient, and a stronger personality than Timothy. One feels that there was less need for personal guidance and advice in his case than with the younger and more timid Timothy. As to how Paul came to write and from what point we can only guess; with him at the time were Artemas, Tychicus, Zenas and Apollos, who were to visit Titus, and who may have carried the letter. The advices and instructions are very similar to those in 1 Timothy. They are written to aid, guide, and encourage Titus in his endeavor to raise the Cretan converts from their low current standards to the higher levels of Christian living. In doing this much will depend upon careful selection and training of leaders and rightful discipline. Hence the attention in the letter to such matters.

CHAPTER I

1–4. Greeting. This is unusually long. Paul explains that he is writing as one who has been called into the service of God and of Jesus Christ and has come to know what real godliness is. The godliness he knows holds the promise of eternal life, which God who cannot lie promised long ages ago, and has now confirmed and proclaimed in the gospel. This gospel God had commanded him to publish. He feels he can write Titus as to a son, since he too knows this wondrous faith in which they share the peace and grace God only can bestow in Jesus Christ.

5–9. Concerning Officials. In setting things in order in the Cretan congregations, as he has been left there to do, Titus will find it necessary to give attention to matters of organization and to provide proper officials to assist in the supervision and conduct of the work. In every place elders must be appointed, men whose personal qualifications will justify their appointment to leadership, against whom no charge can be sustained, free from polygamy, training their families in the Christian faith, whose conduct is a credit to the church. Likewise in every place a bishop, or overseer, must be sought out and placed in charge. (For discussion of officers, their duties, order and relation, see pp. 1276–8, and also notes on 1 Tim. 3.) Even very ordinary judgment would dictate that these appointees should possess the gifts and graces necessary to the duties of their office. But Paul's emphasis is upon their moral and spiritual fitness. Let them be men who subscribe to the gospel both in doctrine and in practice, who exercise such graces as tolerance and self-control, who do not resort to violence, nor serve God for gold, but whose lives are above reproach, who are hospitable, who make religion attractive, who sanely put emphasis upon things truly essential to the faith. Such men have double power when they preach the gospel, either to win converts or to withstand opposition; they have the power inherent in wholesome truth and the power that comes from truth exemplified in consistent Christian living.

10–16. Silencing the Disturbers. Among the many things that call for officials who can properly guide and guard the interests of the church is the case of certain members of questionable and unruly character, who are assuming leadership and seriously troubling and interfering with the churches. They are, in part at least, Jewish converts cleverly dispensing erroneous ideas that unsettle the faith of entire Christian families. For the sake of money they are indulging in discussion that propriety forbids and saying things that will demoralize the crowd they may attract. (See discussion on p. 1264a.) They must be summarily dealt with, officially silenced. Current standards of morals and decency were proverbially low among the Cretans, whom one of their own poets caustically and truthfully described as "liars always." What the Cretans need is not encouragement in their natural disposition, but help in raising their standards to Christian levels. Titus is a man of action, an able disciplinarian, and Paul advises him to call the trouble makers to a sharp halt (v. 13) and make an end of their pratings about Jewish fables and perverted distinctions about defilement, about what is clean and unclean. Such distinctions create false ideas, for defilement, cleanness and uncleanness, is a matter of the inward man. To the pure in mind and heart all things are pure; to the defiled heart and mind nothing is pure; no ceremonial can cleanse the sources of action. Professing to know God, these false leaders show by the lives they live that it is impossible for them to be regarded as acquainted with God. God could not fellowship with their unholy conduct.

CHAPTER II

1–15. Applying the Wholesome Gospel. The proper correction for this unsettling and demoralizing work of the unprincipled or misguided teachers in Crete will be a clean, clear-cut, honest setting forth of the health-giving ideals and the power-giving spirit of the gospel. Let the gospel be applied among the Cretans. Let all classes practice it, the *aged* and the *young*, both *men* and *women*, and even those who are but *bondservants* of others. Let the older men see what the gospel can do toward making them steadfast, sober, tolerant, friendly, and patient under hardship or persecution; Christ has power to make old age beautiful. Likewise the older women should learn the sane manners and practice the simple graces inculcated by the spirit of the gospel. Nothing makes a woman quite so beautiful as simple goodness. And the older Cretan mothers will do well to pass this word on to their younger sisters in the faith, training them to be faithful and loyal to husband, home, and children; chaste, wholesome, an honor to God. And the younger men can do their part in this work of applying the gospel. Think of charging young men to make religion respectable! Titus is to live a Christian life before them, an example in good works and Christian manhood. The finest way to answer, silence and disarm a scoffer or opponent is to live a better and a more blameless life and show a higher quality of spirit. How clear it is to the apostle, and how persistently he keeps it before others, that the gospel is come to bring life and make new in Christ! Even slaves and servants may adorn the doctrine of their Lord by an honorable and trustworthy discharge of duties and a courteous attitude toward their masters. Let it be said that if you want a good, honest servant or workman get a Christian!

This insistence upon *applied Christianity* is the only true way to teach the gospel. It is entirely practicable, for the gospel promises the grace of God to help men obey its teachings. Christianity bestows the power of fulfilling its own ideal. The gospel is a school for character, instructing men to renounce all impiety, to curb all lustful impulses and to learn the discipline of self-control and the beauty of righteousness; it is also a training place where men acquire the strength and power to fulfill these instructions in this present world. And it inspires with the hope that some day we may see at closer range that great saving Friend who has made all this possible, who was so interested in us that he invested himself, with all his life and power, in the great endeavor to save us from sinful selfish living and make us people like himself, peculiar in our devotion to good works and beautiful living. Titus has the task to set and hold these ideals before the Cretans and to have no tolerance with any who would allow that being a Christian can mean anything less than a living likeness unto Christ.

CHAPTER III

1–11. Maintaining Christian Attitudes. Paul exhorts the Cretan believers to be law-abiding, loyal citizens, ready to support every good cause and deserving the respect and protection of the authorities. Let them also show their appreciation of what God has done for them by the attitude they maintain toward others, particularly outsiders; for time was when all of us, believers now, were living much as these unbelievers are. But when God came with saving power into our lives, not by reason of our merit but purely because of his great grace, we were made like new men by the power of God's Holy Spirit; our lives were cleansed, and we were given the promise of eternal life. Surely, it is incumbent upon those who have received such wondrous favor to maintain that attitude which will be helpful and profitable unto the saving of others, to practice good works, and to refuse part in any activity that is not animated by the Spirit of Christ. Any convert who is persistently factious and refuses to conform to plain Christian standards cannot be "regarded as a colleague or a friend"; his own actions classify and condemn him.

The *kindness* (v. 4) of God means his grace, and in the Scriptures the grace of God means the undeserved favor with which he regards mankind. Our salvation has its real ground in that favor. *Regeneration* and *renewing* (v. 5) are not acts of man but acts of God. We are saved, not by what we do—*works of righteousness*—but by something that is done for us—*poured out upon us richly* (v. 6). There is danger, however, that the meaning of this shall be misunderstood: hence the exhortation to honesty and goodness of life (v. 8). This is characteristic Pauline teaching, such as we have in both Romans and Galatians. A *factious* man (v. 10) is one who would divide the church over such unimportant questions as those mentioned in v. 9.

12–15. Conclusion. Paul is considerate of

Titus, and would provide for his being temporarily relieved of his responsibilities. Concern for his subordinates is a true sign of greatness in a leader. A similar interest is shown in Zenas and Apollos as they travel: Titus is to see to their wants. Whether this is the Apollos of Acts $18^{24f.}$ and 1 Cor. 3^6 we cannot say, but it is not unlikely.

14. This verse suggests that the inherent Cretan idleness (1^{12}) still needed to be watched: even with divine help it is no easy matter to destroy deep-seated habit.

PHILEMON

By Professor C. H. DODD

Introduction

Character of the Epistle. The Epistle to Philemon is a simple letter to a friend on a personal matter, with no doctrinal or ecclesiastical purpose. In language and form it resembles the typical private correspondence of the period, of which we possess numerous examples among Egyptian papyri.

Reason for the Epistle. The circumstances can be gathered from the letter itself. Philemon was a well-to-do resident at Colossæ. At some period (probably during the apostle's residence at Ephesus) he had come under the influence of Paul, and been converted to Christianity (v. 19). He became a leading and active member of the church at Colossæ. Some time afterward one of his slaves, Onesimus, ran away. He was not, like some members of the household of Philemon, a Christian. The runaway somehow or other came into touch with Paul, then in prison. It is idle to speculate what led to the meeting. Under Paul's influence he became a Christian, and made himself so useful to the prisoner that he would have liked to retain him in his service. Mindful, however, of Philemon's rights, and unwilling to presume on friendship, he sent Onesimus back, bearing the letter which we have before us, in which he requests the master, on the highest Christian grounds, to take back and forgive his erring slave, undertaking at the same time to indemnify him out of his own pocket for any pecuniary loss he may have suffered (vv. 18, 19).

It was a good deal to ask of an injured master under the conditions of the time, but Paul believes that the Christian sentiments of Philemon, particularly toward one who is now a fellow Christian, will override the natural resentment and class feeling of the employer and lead him to regard Onesimus in a wholly new relation. This is all that he expressly asks. He does not request Onesimus' emancipation; but, on the other hand, he does hint (v. 14) that if it were to occur to Philemon to send Onesimus back to him, it would be greatly appreciated. Philemon would doubtless like to be of use to his friend. He cannot be with him in prison; perhaps he would like Onesimus to act as his deputy.

An Expression of a Christian Principle. Such is the purport of the letter. Its chief interest is in the light it throws on Paul himself at a moment when he is neither the preacher, the controversialist, the theologian, nor the ecclesiastical authority, but simply a man writing to a friend in the interests of another friend. It has sometimes been quite wrongly treated as a tract on slavery. It is hardly necessary to point out that no question of principle regarding that institution is even raised. What Paul had to say on slavery in theory is to be found in Colossians (see 3^{22}–4^{1} and notes), and even there he does not raise the question whether or no the institution as such should or should not exist. In the present letter he simply accepts the situation in which the law and custom of the time had placed Philemon and Onesimus, and asks what, in that situation, is the Christian duty of Philemon. His answer is in effect that the relation between them is to be wholly ruled by the Christian principle of love or charity. All that he says is steeped in obviously genuine affection for the runaway, and he expects that the Christian master will treat the slave as a "brother beloved" (vv. 12, 15, 16). What will ultimately become of slavery on that basis he does not stop to ask. But it is worth while to observe that it was at this point that Christianity first tackled the matter, and not by way of any theorizing about the "rights of man."

A Historical Contrast. The actual situation in which Paul, Philemon, and Onesimus stood at the moment when the runaway met the apostle may be illustrated from a document published in the Oxyrhynchus Papyri, Vol. 14 (1920), No. 1643 (dated 298 A.D.). Here one Aurelius Sarapammon writes to a friend, whose name has perished, as follows: "I commission you by this writ to journey to the famous city of Alexandria and search for my slave, by name . . . , about 35 years old, known to you. When you have found him you shall place him in custody, with authority to shut him up and whip him, and to lay a complaint before the proper authorities against any persons who have harbored him, with a demand for satisfaction."

See further the introductions to Ephesians and Colossians.

Literature: Oesterley, *Philemon* (Expositor's Greek Testament); Vincent, *Philippians and Philemon* (International Critical Commentary); and literature under Ephesians and Colossians.

THE EPISTLE

1–3. Epistolary Address. It is a little surprising to find Timothy's name at the head of a purely private letter; no doubt there were good reasons of which we can know nothing. With Philemon as recipient are associated *Apphia*, whom we may confidently assume to have been his wife, and *Archippus*, possibly a brother or son, but in any case doubtless a leading member of the *church in his house*. That phrase probably meant originally the Christian members of the *familia* (the family, slaves, and dependents; cf. Acts 16[15, 33] 18[8] 1 Cor. 1[16] 7[14] 16[15] 2 Tim. 4[19]); but at a very early date Christian "brothers" who met for worship and fellowship at the house of a wealthy fellow-Christian were regarded as members of his household and so of the *ecclesia* (church or congregation) which that household constituted from a religious point of view (cf. Col. 4[15] 1 Cor. 16[19] Rom. 16[5]). Early Christianity was a family affair to an extent not always realized.

4–6. Thanksgiving and Intercession. Paraphrase: "I thank God, in all my prayers, for your Christian life of faith and love, displayed both toward Christ our Lord and toward all Christians, and pray that the faith which you hold in common with us all may work out in a clear intuition of every good thing that brings us into union with Christ. I was especially glad to hear of the act of Christian charity by which you have [recently] brought such contentment to your fellow-Christians."

4. Thanksgiving and intercession belong to the epistolary convention of the time. Paul, however, regularly gives to it a more than conventional significance (see Eph. 1[3-14], note 1[15, 16]).—*Love* and *faith* here as in Col. 1[4, 5] (where see note) stand for the Christian life in its integrity, as religious and ethical both. Paul passes, with some obscurity of expression, but without any real obscurity of sense, from thanksgiving to petition, the purport of which is much the same as in Col. 1[9], though more succinctly expressed.

7. Paul has a special ground for thanksgiving. The reference must be to some particular manifestation of love or charity on Philemon's part. Paul was quick to mark, and tenacious in remembering, such acts of grace (cf. 2 Tim. 1[15-18]).

8–21. A Request on Behalf of Onesimus. Paraphrase: "Because I know you are such a good Christian I will not tell you what your duty is in the matter I am about to mention —though I might have done so without presumption—but I will make a request for your charity's sake. It is a request of Paul, Christ's ambassador and prisoner. My request is on behalf of a son of mine, born while I was in prison—Onesimus. A worthless fellow, you say! Yes, once worthless to you, but now of much worth to you and me. I am sending him back to you, and it is as if I sent my own heart. I should have liked to keep him here to do me the service you would have wished to do me in my imprisonment for the gospel. But I would not do so without your consent, that any kindness you show me may be of your own free will. I think the reason why [in God's Providence] he was separated from you for a time was that he might come back as something more than a slave—a dear brother —dear to me, surely dearer to you, with whom he has both earthly and spiritual ties. If, therefore, you think of me as a comrade, welcome him as you would welcome me. If he has done you any wrong, or if he is in your debt, put it to my account. I will make it good. This is a formal undertaking, and I sign it with my own hand—Paul.—Not to mention the fact that you owe all that you are to me! —My dear friend, do me this satisfaction; content my heart 'in Christ.' I write in the certainty that you will do even more than I ask."

9. There is a difficulty about the word rendered *the aged* (in mg. *an ambassador*). Properly there is no doubt that the Greek word *presbutes* means "an old man." Though Paul can scarcely have passed sixty or so, he may have been feeling very old. But the word is easily confused with another word, differing from it by one letter, *presbeutes*, and meaning "ambassador." It is noteworthy that this confusion does actually occur several times in the Greek O.T. (which was Paul's Bible). Now in Eph. 6[20] we have the verb *presbeuo* in the expression, "I am an ambassador in bonds." If Paul wrote Ephesians, this would seem to settle the meaning here. If he did not, then the disciple who wrote Ephesians in his name (see p. 1223) must have understood the Philemon passage to mean "an ambassador and prisoner of Jesus Christ." In any case this is the more probable meaning, whether Paul misspelled the word, or whether the error arose in MS. transmission. He will not command Philemon, on his apostolic authority, but in making his request he will remind his correspondent that it is the request of one who being dedicated to Christ's service makes no such request lightly, and may claim the more deference because he is in a position of impotence—which increases his moral authority in the eyes of any Christian.

11. The words rendered *profitable* and *unprofitable* suggest by sense though not by sound the etymological meaning of the name "Onesimus." Paul may have intended the play upon words. But the epithet "unprofitable" is probably chosen as the one which would be at once suggested to Philemon by the name Onesimus, "the wastrel!"

16. There is no formal request that Onesimus shall be emancipated, nor is it clear that Paul contemplated that in becoming *a brother beloved* (read a *dear brother*) he would cease to have the legal status of a slave. Rather he would appear to imply that the original relation of master and slave provided a basis, in an intimate relation *in the flesh*, for a still more intimate relation *in the Lord.*

18, 19. Paul offers to guarantee Philemon against any loss incurred through Onesimus. To give his guarantee legal validity he signs it in proper form. At the same time he would obviously have been bitterly disappointed if Philemon had accepted this offer from the man who had brought him to Christ.

20. Paul repeats the expression he had used in v. 7 about Philemon's service to the church. Let him show himself again the man he was! The word translated *let me have joy of thee* is actually the verb from which the name "Onesimus" is derived; Paul was hardly unconscious of the word-play (cf. v. 11). *In the Lord, in Christ,* are the distinctively Pauline terms for the central Christian experience of a "mystical" union with Christ (see Eph. 1[3], note). Here they indicate that the service Paul is asking from Philemon is something which falls within the sphere of the common religious life whose characteristic manifestation is love or charity.

21. Paul feels confident that Philemon will do as he asks—and not only this, but something *beyond*—surely meaning that he will take the hint of v. 14 and send Onesimus back to make himself useful to Paul in prison.

22–25. Paul Closes in His Usual Way, with Personal Matters, Greetings, and Benediction. This is no doubt one item in the news that Tychicus was to tell to the church (Col. 4[7]). Paul expects shortly to be set at liberty —on what grounds we cannot say. If the letter is from Rome, then evidently things looked definitely brighter than when he wrote to Philippi (cf. Phil. 1[20, 30] 2[17]). He means to use the opportunity of his expected release to visit Colossæ. Whether the release and the journey ever took place is one of the unsolved problems of N.T. history. (See art., *Life and Work of Paul*, p. 942b, and cf. intro. to Pastoral Epistles, p. 1275.)

23. Greetings from the same group of friends as in Colossians, except Jesus Justus.

HEBREWS

By Professor H. T. ANDREWS

Introduction

To understand a N.T. epistle we must first of all seek to discover the circumstances under which it was written and the purpose the author had in view.

Occasion of the Epistle. There is no difficulty in discovering the *occasion* which led to the writing of the Epistle to the Hebrews. It was composed during one of the great persecutions—probably the Domitianic. The writer describes it as a "word of exhortation" (13[22]). It was intended to encourage and inspire the Christians to meet the challenge of the enemy with fortitude and heroism. They had "endured a great conflict of sufferings." They had been held up to public scorn. Reproaches and taunts had been heaped upon their heads. Many of them had been imprisoned. Others had their property confiscated. They were ostracized from society. They were not allowed, as we are told in the book of Revelation (18[11]), to buy or sell in the market places. Every effort was taken to make the boycott as complete as possible. A systematic attempt was being made to establish Cæsar worship on an extensive scale—and the clash between Christianity and Cæsar worship entailed untold sufferings upon the followers of Christ. To profess the Christian faith meant the risk of martyrdom and the certainty of petty persecution in the ordinary vocations of life. The First Epistle of Peter describes the sufferings of the church as a fiery trial sent to test the faith (4[12]). Under the strangle hold of persecution, the strain upon the loyalty of the members of the Christian Church became well-nigh intolerable, and it is not surprising that large numbers of men and women were tempted to renounce the faith.

The supreme peril of the church under the stress of persecution was the peril of relapse, and the primary object of the Epistle to the Hebrews is to face this peril and stem the tide of desertion. There is hardly a chapter in the Epistle which does not contain an appeal or a warning to those whose faith was faltering. The writer continually points to the sufferings of Christ as an example to be followed and urges his fellow Christians to be steadfast, that they too may be perfected through suffering. Even Jesus had to learn obedience "by the things which he suffered," and his followers must be scholars in the same stern school. Suffering is always hard and cruel, but out of its soil there springs up the harvest of righteousness. Nor does the writer hesitate to warn his readers in the harshest terms about the danger that comes from the compromise of faith. The faith once lost can never be regained. If we part with our birthright, it can never be restored to us. It is impossible to renew unto repentance those who crucify the Son of God afresh (6[6]). "If we sin wilfully after that we have received the knowledge of the truth, there remaineth no more a sacrifice for sins, but a certain fearful expectation of judgment" (10[26, 27a]).

Intellectual Problems. But though the dominant note of the Epistle lies undoubtedly in its practical appeal for loyalty and its warning against the danger of relapse, it has also a strong interest in the *intellectual problems* of the time. It was never an easy thing in the first century to reconcile Christianity with the old Jewish faith. To the mind of the Jews, it was a fundamental belief that the O.T. contained the final revelation of God and that in the Law of Moses God had made known completely his will and purpose. If that is so, what need is there of any further revelation? Does not Christianity become superfluous? What room is left for Jesus Christ? Questions such as these were of intense interest in the debates that took place in the apostolic age between Christianity and Judaism. Paul had to face the problem in one of its aspects in the Epistle to the Galatians—and the Epistle to the Hebrews deals with another phase of the same issue. The Epistle denies that the O.T. contains a complete and final revelation of the will of God—God spoke to the prophets "in broken fragments" (1[1]) only. It is only in Christianity—in the revelation through his Son, that there has been a complete manifestation of his will.

Philosophical Background. In order to understand the strength and force of the argument of Hebrews it is necessary for us to realize the *philosophical background* of the Epistle. Hebrews appears on the surface to be one of the most Jewish writings we possess. The argument seems to move entirely within the circle of Jewish ideas. From its commencement to its close—from the string of quotations in the first chapter to the appeal to the altar and the sacrifice of beasts whose bodies were burned outside the camp in the last—the thought of the Epistle seems to be "cribb'd, cabin'd, and confin'd" within the narrow precincts of Jewish thought. In reality, however, when we look beneath the surface, we find that there is no book in the N.T. which is so tinged with Greek ideas. The nerve of the argument of Hebrews is Greek and not Jewish. *Hebrews is the first great attempt that was made to explain Christianity in terms of the Platonic philosophy.* The characteristic feature of Plato's philosophy is what is known as his "Doctrine of Ideas"—a theory by which he maintained that everything on earth has a heavenly counterpart which is the true reality and of which the earthly thing is only a shadow and imperfect copy. The heavenly archetypes are the supreme facts. They are not mere abstractions of thought. They actually exist in the heavens, the perfect types of their imperfect representations upon earth. This theory is taken up by the author of Hebrews in the contrast which he draws between the earthly and the heavenly tabernacles. The true sanctuary "which the Lord pitched and not man" is in heaven (8^{2}). The earthly tabernacle is but a shadow and a copy of the heavenly reality (8^{5} 9^{23} 10^{1}). The difference between the O.T. and Christianity is, therefore, this: in the O.T. we have only the earthly shadows of the heavenly realities: in the N.T. the heavenly realities themselves have broken into the world of time and space. (Cf. pp. 1066–7, 1253–5.)

A Philosophy of the Christian Religion. The Epistle to the Hebrews therefore is the first attempt to create a philosophy of the Christian religion. It defends and expounds its Christian faith in terms of current philosophical thought. Its main theme may be condensed into a single phrase: *Jesus Christ is the ideal High Priest who offered the ideal sacrifice in the ideal sanctuary.* The writer does not make any attempt to prove the need of the priest or the sacrifice or the sanctuary. He assumes that they are the three essential elements of religion and that no religion can exist without them. Like all the other facts of life, they have their heavenly counterparts. In their ideal forms they exist only in the heavenly sphere. As earthly institutions they are but imperfect representations of the true realities. The priesthood is defective. The priests are imperfect men. They are constantly changing. There is no permanence about them. The sacrifices are defective. They cannot cleanse the guilty conscience. They can make no real atonement for sin. Even the Temple is defective since it represents merely a copy of the heavenly original. The religion of the O.T., therefore, only provides an imperfect sacrifice offered by imperfect priests in an earthly sanctuary.

In contrast to this defective system, Christianity provides a perfect sacrifice offered by a perfect High Priest in a perfect sanctuary. The heavenly realities have been brought down to earth in the transcendent person and work of Jesus Christ, who as the Son of God has made the perfect revelation of the divine will and purpose, and by his sacrifice has wrought out the perfect redemption for mankind.

The Plan of the Epistle. These two main lines of thought in the Epistle—the practical and the intellectual—are so interwoven that it is not easy to disentangle them. The march of the argument is often side-tracked by the digressions. The practical interests of the writer and his earnest moral appeals often override and obscure the elucidation of his theological thesis. It is therefore necessary for the student to study carefully the map of the plan of the book. If we omit the digressions and the paragraphs of practical appeal, it will be found that the development of the line of argument proceeds along the following course: (1) The writer begins in 1^{1-14} by proving the supremacy of Christ over the Angels. (2) After a digression in ch. 2 he demonstrates in a short paragraph, 3^{1-6}, the superiority of Christ to Moses. (3) Then after a long digression in the latter part of ch. 3 and ch. 4 he indicates in 5^{1-10} the defects of the priestly system of Judaism and suggests that Christ is the supreme High Priest after the order of Melchizedek. (4) More digressions follow, and it is only when we come to ch. 7 that the line of thought adumbrated in 5^{1-10} is worked out in detail and the supremacy of the high-priestly work of Christ demonstrated. (5) In ch. 8 the writer shows that Christ is not only the ideal High Priest but that he ministers in an ideal sanctuary, and his ministry constitutes the establishment of a new covenant between man and God. (6) In ch. 9 the writer demonstrates that Christ as the supreme High Priest offered the supreme sacrifice for the sins of the world. (7) The argument culminates in ch. 10^{1-18}, where the writer again demonstrates the futility of the Jewish sacrifices, and the finality and completeness of the redemption wrought by Christ. Thus the main argument of the book is found in the following passages: 1^{1-14} 3^{1-6} 5^{1-10} 7^{1}–10^{18}. It is in the last section, 7^{1}–10^{18}, that the largest and most sustained and most subtle piece of reasoning in the Epistle is found.

The chief digressions from the main argument may be summarized as follows: (1) In ch. 2 the writer turns aside to discuss the significance of the sufferings of Christ. (2) From 3^{7} to 4^{16} there is a long digression on the promise of rest—a promise which has never yet been realized—and which, therefore, is a great inheritance into which the writer summons the Christians of his own time to enter. (3) From 5^{11} to 6^{20} there is a long warning against relapse, in which the writer describes the supreme peril involved in forsaking the faith. (4) 10^{18-39} contains another great appeal and a further warning of the fate which awaits those who fall away from the Christian faith. (5) Chs. 11 and 12 contain a final challenge based on the heroic story of the saints and martyrs of the past, a further discussion of the meaning of suffering (12^{7-13}), and a very powerful description of the contrast between the Old Covenant and the New. (6) Ch. 13 gives some final injunctions and personal messages.

No student should attempt to read the Epistle through until he has, first of all, constructed a map of its contents on the basis of the facts which have just been given. To understand Hebrews it is necessary to have a very clear idea of the writer's objective in each section of the Epistle.

The Question of Authorship. It is quite impossible to determine with anything like certainty who was the author of the Epistle to the Hebrews. Origen, writing about the year 225 A.D., said, "Who wrote the Epistle to the Hebrews God only knows," and modern scholarship to-day is equally incompetent to arrive at a sure decision. The traditional view—which was preserved in the title given to the Epistle in the A.V. ascribing the Epistle to the apostle Paul—has now been entirely abandoned. It was challenged in ancient times. Its style is quite different from Paul's manner of writing. And though at first sight there seems to be on the surface a community of ideas between Hebrews and the epistles of Paul, when we come to make a detailed examination it becomes apparent that the differences between the two writers are far more extensive than the resemblances. The thought of the writer of Hebrews moves almost entirely in the region of the Jewish sacrificial system, which is very rarely referred to at all in the Pauline epistles. The great mystical conception of union with the risen Christ which is so characteristic of Pauline thought is entirely absent from Hebrews. Theologically speaking, at any rate in matters of detail, the two writers seem to stand almost in antithesis to each other.

Probably the name which has won most support among modern scholars is that of *Barnabas*. Among the ancients Tertullian certainly thought that he was the author of the Epistle. And Origen in one of his moods, as we know from his recently discovered *Tractatus*, held the same view. There are many points about Barnabas which render his claim reasonable. He was a Levite and so would naturally be interested in the details of the sacrificial system. He seems to have lived in Cyprus (Acts 4^{36}), where it would be possible for him to come into contact with the thought of Alexandria. But the arguments do not amount to proof; and it is not easy to see why, if he were the author, the book should have been published without his name attached to it.

Luther made the brilliant suggestion that *Apollos* was the real writer of the book. From the description of Apollos in Acts 18^{24-28} it is clear that he is the type of man who might have written the Epistle—but, in the absence of any tangible evidence, the theory can never be more than pure hypothesis. *Luke*, *Clement of Rome*, *Silas*, and *Philip* have all at different times found their supporters, but the arguments which have been put forward to prove the case have failed to carry conviction.

The most interesting modern theory (which has secured the championship of such outstanding scholars as Harnack and Rendel Harris and Peake) is that the book was written by *Priscilla* with the help of her husband *Aquila*. Quite a romance has been built up around the name of Priscilla. On the evidence of certain inscriptions which have been found on the catacombs and elsewhere, it is supposed that Priscilla originally belonged to a distinguished family of high social standing in the city of Rome. She lost caste, however, through her marriage with the Jew Aquila and was disowned by her family. When she and her husband became Christians she won a position in the Christian Church which more than atoned for the sacrifice she made at the time of her marriage. She is supposed to have written the Epistle to the Hebrews anonymously, because in that age it would seriously have detracted from the value of the book if it had been known that it was the work of a woman.

The theory is attractive and certainly does help to explain some of the characteristics of the Epistle, but it is only guesswork and does not rest upon any substantial foundation of fact. There is one point that militates against it rather strongly. In 11^{32} the writer uses the phrase, "Time would fail me telling," etc.

The participle translated "telling" is in the masculine gender in Greek. Priscilla, of course, might have concealed the fact of her authorship by using a masculine participle, but the sentence might have been written in a dozen different ways, and it is scarcely credible to suppose that she would have selected a phrase which made it necessary for her to suggest to the world that the book was written by a man.

Characteristics of the Author. But though we cannot determine the name of the author of Hebrews we can form a fairly clear conception of his personality. (1) He was first of all pre-eminently a preacher. He speaks of the Epistle as a "word of exhortation" (13[22]). Time after time he abandons the main line of argument in order to preach. His digression on the "rest of God" in chs. 3 and 4 is one of the best specimens we possess of an early Christian sermon. (2) He was a man of great literary ability. There is no book in the N.T. written in better Greek than the Epistle to the Hebrews. If there is any truth in the dictum, "The style is the man," we are bound to admit that the author of Hebrews was a literary genius. (3) He was a man of wide philosophical knowledge. He was intimately acquainted, as we have seen, with the whole system of Platonic philosophy. A phrase which he uses in 11[3] shows that he was equally familiar with the Epicurean theory of the universe, and some technical terms which he employs in 5[14] make it plain that he was conversant with Aristotelianism. In the most skillful way he brings his wide range of knowledge to the interpretation of the Christian faith. (4) If he was a Jew, as he probably was (though this is incapable of absolute proof), he belonged to the more liberal school known as the Hellenists. The Bible which he used and from which he constantly quotes, is the Greek translation known as the Septuagint (LXX), and not the original Hebrew text, with which he does not seem to have been acquainted. (5) In interpreting the O.T., like all the scholars of Alexandria, he used the allegorical method. There is more restraint, however, in his application of the method than there is in the case of Philo, with whose writings he was certainly familiar and from whom he derived many of his ideas. The best illustration of the use of allegory in Hebrews is the treatment of Melchizedek in 7[1-10]. (6) He was passionately devoted to the Christian faith. To him it was the only adequate and final philosophy. A knowledge of philosophy often blunts the edge of faith, but in the case of the author of Hebrews it served to strengthen and intensify it. He was an enthusiast, and his enthusiasm was based on knowledge and insight. It was a great boon to Christianity in early times that it possessed so convinced and so well-informed an advocate as the unknown author of the Epistle to the Hebrews.

The Recipients of the Epistle. The title of the Epistle, which is found in all the ancient manuscripts, tells us that it was written "to the Hebrews." The word "Hebrew" had a specific meaning in N.T. times. It is used in antithesis to the term "Hellenist." The Hebrew was a conservative type of Jew who maintained the use of the Hebrew tongue, used a Hebrew Bible, and carried out strictly the injunctions of the Jewish law even though he might be living in a foreign land. The Hellenist, on the other hand, was much less rigid. He conformed to the customs of the people among whom he was living, used the Greek language, and read the Greek version of the Bible. The title suggests that the Epistle was written for Hebrews in general, in whatever part of the world they might happen to be living. There are, however, certain specific references in Hebrews which make it clear that the writer has a particular group or fellowship of Hebrew Christians in mind. He tells us, for instance, in 13[19] that he intends to visit them. He praises the services which they had rendered to the saints (6[10,11]). He bemoans their dullness and the slowness of their development in the Christian life (5[11,12]). It seems, therefore, perfectly obvious that he is writing to a particular community and not to Hebrews at large.

But where did this particular community live? That is a question which it is not so easy to answer. There has been a great diversity of opinion upon the point among modern scholars. Jerusalem, Alexandria, and Rome have all had their advocates. On the whole, opinion to-day seems to preponderate in favor of Rome. We know that the Epistle was known and used in Rome earlier than in any other place, for it is quoted at considerable length by Clement of Rome—the earliest Christian writer outside the N.T., who wrote an epistle to the Corinthians about the year 95 A.D. A further point in favor of this theory is to be found in the phrase in 13[24], "They of Italy salute you," which seems to refer to Italian friends of the members of the church who were at that time in contact with the author of the Epistle, possibly at Alexandria. The best modern theory, therefore, is that the Epistle was written for a community of Jewish Christians living in the city of Rome.

The Date of the Epistle. The limits within which it is possible for the Epistle to have been written lie between the years 60 and 96 A.D. The latter date is determined by the fact that it was quoted by Clement of Rome about that time. The earlier date is settled by the implications in 2:3 and 13:7 that a generation of Christians had already passed away. Within these limits there are two dates which have been warmly advocated by different scholars of repute. The earlier, which puts the Epistle between 64 and 67, connects it with the period immediately following the Neronian persecution. The main argument upon which this theory rests is the absence of any reference in the Epistle to the destruction of Jerusalem, which occurred in the year 70 A.D. It is maintained that if the book had been written after 70 A.D., there must have been some allusion to that event. An argument which is based upon silence is always precarious. It is almost equivalent to the assumption that no book could be published to-day without some reference to the European war. The other date suggested for the Epistle falls in the reign of Domitian (somewhere between 80 and 90). This date seems the more probable of the two. The church is face to face with an organized form of persecution. In the time of Nero persecution was spasmodic and irregular, and it was not till Domitian that it became a settled and permanent policy of the empire. Moreover, though there is no allusion to the destruction of Jerusalem, the arguments of the Epistle seem to be intended to comfort Jewish Christians who were smarting under the destruction of the Temple and the overthrow of the Levitical system.

The Form of the Epistle. The Epistle to the Hebrews lacks the marks of an ordinary letter. It was an invariable rule in ancient times that a letter should begin, as all the epistles of Paul do, for instance, by stating the name of the writer and giving a message of greeting to the recipients. There is nothing of this kind in Hebrews. The writer plunges at once *in medias res* without the slightest reference to himself or the people to whom he is writing. How is this strange opening to be explained? Some scholars think that the writer had some special reason for wishing to conceal his identity. Others, again, suppose that the book is not an epistle at all but a theological treatise. The latter theory seems unlikely in view of the personal references and appeals in the book, especially in ch. 13. It seems probable that the writer of Hebrews constructed his book, as many modern preachers do, out of sermons and addresses which he had delivered on different occasions, weaving them, of course, into a unity, and making them all serve his main argument. It was originally intended probably as "a tract for the times." The author had in mind not merely the particular church to which it was finally sent but the whole body of Jewish (and probably Gentile) Christians of his time. The last chapter may have been added when the author despatched his book to the church at Rome.

The Place of the Epistle in the New Testament Canon. It is rather surprising to find that an epistle of such value as Hebrews had some difficulty in securing its place in the N.T. and that it was a long time before it won general acceptance. Eusebius, writing about 325 A.D., tells us that even in his day "some rejected the Epistle to the Hebrews on the ground that it was controverted by the Roman Church as not being Paul's." Speaking generally it may be said that the Epistle at the end of the second century A.D. was accepted in the Eastern division of Christendom and rejected in the West. It is omitted from the Muratorian canon (about 200 AD.), and little importance was attached to it by the Latin Fathers. The ground for its rejection seems to have been the conviction that it was not written by Paul. The Alexandrian Fathers, on the other hand—Pantænus, Clement and Origen—were unanimous in accepting the Epistle on the ground of its intrinsic merit, though some of them questioned the Pauline authorship. This cleavage of opinion between the East and the West is best explained by Westcott: "The Easterns, attracted by the intrinsic value of the work, accepted it, and because of its intrinsic value tried to connect it with Paul. The Westerns, feeling sure that it was not the work of Paul, rejected it solely on this ground —their rule being not to admit anything into the canon which could not be definitely traced back to an Apostle." "Experience," Westcott adds, "has shown us how to unite the conclusions on both sides. We have been enabled to acknowledge that the apostolic authority of the Epistle is independent of the Pauline authorship. The spiritual insight of the East can be joined with the historic witness of the West."

Literature: The best critical commentaries on Hebrews are those of Moffatt (International Critical Commentary) and Westcott, but both these are based upon the Greek text and their value is restricted to scholars. The best commentaries for ordinary readers are Peake (Century Bible), and A. B. Davidson (Handbooks for Bible Classes). Among the books which deal with the general teaching of the Epistle, the most useful are Dale, *The Jewish Temple and the Christian Faith;* Bruce, *The Epistle to the Hebrews;* Milligan, *The Theology of the Epistle to the Hebrews;* Nairne, *The Epistle of the Priesthood.*

CHAPTER I

1–3. Introduction: God's Self-Revelation Consummated in the Person and Work of a Son. The most remarkable feature about the commencement of the Epistle is that none of the marks of an ordinary letter are to be found at all. The writer plunges at once into his great theme without any personal references or salutations. Some scholars think this proves that the so-called epistle is not a letter at all but a theological treatise. Others (e.g., Harnack and Peake) maintain that the absence of the usual personalia is due to the fact that the Epistle is very largely the work of Priscilla, and that, being a woman, she countered the prejudice that would otherwise have arisen by omitting any reference to herself (see p. 1297).

The introductory paragraph states the *theme* of the whole book. The writer boldly states the position which he intends to maintain in face of the two problems which faced the church in his day: (1) What is the relation between the Christian faith and the O.T.? If the O.T. contains a final revelation of the will of God, as every Jew considered that it did, what need is there of any further revelation? Is not Christianity therefore superfluous? (2) What is the true interpretation of the Person and work of Christ? How are we to explain his relation to God and the value of his sacrifice? The first sentence deals with the first problem and the remaining verse of the introduction with the second. The R.V. translation rather blurs the contrast which the writer draws between the O.T. and the Christian faith. *God having spoken of old time . . . by divers portions and in divers manners.* It makes the point clearer if we translate the last two clauses *in many fragments and by many methods.* The contrasts which the writer tries to bring out are: (1) The O.T. revelation was fragmentary and piecemeal; the Christian faith is final and complete. (2) In the O.T. many methods were adopted as the vehicle of the divine communications. God made use of historians and prophets and psalmists at different times; the Christian faith is revealed in one way and one way only, i.e., through Christ. (3) In the O.T. God used human agencies, e.g., the prophets; the Christian faith has been brought to the world by God's own Son.

At this point the statement passes to the second problem. Who was the Son? How does he stand related to God? What was his achievement? The writer replies to these questions: (1) The Son had been appointed by God heir of all things. The order of the words proves that the reference here is to a pretemporal and therefore eternal act of God. (2) He was the agent of God in the creation of the world—a statement which reminds us of the great passage in Colossians (1^{15-18}) in which the apostle Paul describes the cosmic activity of Christ in the work of creation. (3) The next phrases, *the effulgence of his glory and the very image of his substance,* describe the relationship between Christ and God. Both are metaphors. The first is borrowed from a passage in the Book of Wisdom (7^{26}), which describes Wisdom as "an effulgence from everlasting light." The Greek word may mean either "reflection" or "radiance," and the phrase therefore may signify either (a) that the glory of God was reflected in the person Jesus Christ and mirrored in his work, or (b)—and this seems the more probable explanation—that as the light streams from the sun the radiance of the glory of God streams from Christ. The metaphor in the second phrase is different. The word translated *very image* means, literally, the stamp cut by a die, and so the impress made upon a seal: thus the phrase signifies that the essence of the divine nature was stamped on the Person of Christ. He was the impress of God's essence. (4) The fourth statement, *upholding all things by the word of his power,* means that Christ is the center of the life of the universe. Compare the statement in Col. 1^{17}, "in him all things consist" (or cohere). (5) The next statement defines the work of Christ during his earthly life. *He made purification for sins.* This phrase emphasizes the redemptive work of Christ, which is to be the main theme of the book. (6) Finally he ascended to heaven and *sat down on the right hand of the Majesty on high.*

Such is the summary of the writer's conception of Christ, and it becomes all the more remarkable when we remember that these words must have been written within fifty years of the crucifixion.

4–14. The Superiority of Christ to the Angels. (See also ch. 2.) At this point the introduction slides off into the first great argument of the Epistle, which sets out to prove the superiority of Christ to the angels. This occupies the remainder of ch. 1 and the whole of ch. 2. The course of the argument falls into the following divisions: (1) The statement of the theme (v. 4). (2) The first set of proofs (vv. 5–14). (3) The practical application (2^{1-4}). (4) The second proof (2^{5-8}). (5) The reply to the objection that the humiliation and death of Christ prove that he is of lower rank than the angels (2^{9-18}).

The *theme* is found in the concluding words of the introduction which form the transition to the new line of argument—*Having become so much better than the angels.* The *more excellent name* is the name of Son. The *first set of proofs* is composed of quotations from the O.T. We must remember that the fulfillment of prophecy was the first line of defense for Christians in the apostolic age, and there was no argument that appealed more cogently to the Jewish mind. The relevance of the whole discussion can be best appreciated by referring again to the Epistle to the Colossians, in which Paul finds himself compelled to deal with a theory which identified Jesus with one of the lowest of the angels. It is quite possible that this theory still survived and that in the opening chapters of Hebrews we have the second great attempt to give it a death blow. (Cf. pp. 1253–5.)

The proof-texts which the writer cites from the O.T. are seven in number: (1) The first two are taken respectively from Psa. 2[7] and 2 Sam. 7[14] and are intended to prove that O.T. prophecy bestowed the title *Son* on Christ. (2) The next quotation does not occur in the Hebrew Bible but is an addition which the LXX makes to the Hebrew text of Deut. 32[43]. It is interesting to note that the writer does not scruple to use a text which is not found in the O.T. proper.

There is a difficulty about the phrase which is used to introduce the third quotation (v. 6). The word *again* may be connected with the main verb as in the R.V. or it may be used separately to indicate the use of another quotation as in the R.V. mg. The reference in the phrase *when he bringeth . . . into the world* seems to be the second advent of Christ. (3) Of the next two contrasted proof-texts the first (v. 7) is taken from Psa. 104[4]. In the Hebrew there is no reference to angels. The psalmist is referring to the forces of nature which God uses as his agents. "Who maketh winds his messengers; his ministers a flaming fire." The LXX, however, modified the translation of the Hebrew and the writer of the Epistle adopted its renderings. The second quotation (vv. 8, 9) is from Psa. 45[6, 7]. In contrast to the humbler position of the angels the Son is accorded divine rank and his throne is described as eternal. He has been anointed by God and set in a higher position than all his fellows. (4) The quotation in vv. 10–12 is taken from Psa. 102[25-27]. It describes the Son as the creator of heaven and earth and says that though they are transitory and will pass away, the Son abideth forever. (5) The last proof-text, in which the writer reaches the climax of his argument in v. 13, is the famous passage in Psa. 110[1]. It represents the final return of the Son to heaven in triumph—and the argument is that such words as these cannot be applied to angels.

CHAPTER II

1–4. The Practical Application of the Preceding Argument. This paragraph illustrates the interest taken by the writer of Hebrews in the practical bearing of theology upon life. His purpose is not merely to demonstrate the truth of a theological proposition but to show also how that truth has a meaning for life and conduct. "If I have made out my case," he argues, "if I have proved the superiority of Christ to the angels, then it follows that we ought to pay greater heed to his teaching than to the Law which was given through the medium of angels—for how shall we escape if we neglect the great salvation?" This salvation was first of all proclaimed by the Lord himself and was passed on by the original disciples to the next generation of believers, and all the way through it has been confirmed by miracles and the outpouring of the Holy Spirit.

The phrase in v. 1, *lest we drift away*, is very significant. One of the problems with which the church was confronted at this time was the drift of its members back to the world under stress of persecution. The *word spoken through angels* (v. 2) contains a reference to the later Jewish belief, which is not found in the O.T. itself but occurs in an addition which the LXX makes to the text of Deut. 33[2], that angels were used as intermediaries in the giving of the Law. The same idea is also found in other passages of the N.T., e.g., Acts 7[53] Gal. 3[19]. It is interesting to note that miracles are regarded in v. 4 as confirming the truth of the Christian gospel. The reference is not merely to the miracles of Christ; it includes also the miracles wrought by the apostles. (Cf. the claim of Paul in Rom. 15[19] and 2 Cor. 12[12] that his work had been attended by miracles.) *The gifts of the Holy Ghost* refer to Pentecost primarily and also to the later bestowal of spiritual gifts (as in 1 Cor. 12–14).

5–8. Additional Proof that Christ is Superior to the Angels. The writer now turns back again to the argument from which he had departed at the end of ch. 1. The new point is made with the utmost brevity. Christ (and not the angels) is to be Lord of the future. *The world to come* is the new era which is to be established on earth at the return of Christ. The quotation which is used to prove the argument is taken from Psa. 8[4-6]. The term *Son of man*, which was originally in the mind of the psalmist simply a synonym for man (the two opening clauses being strictly parallel), is here taken as a Messianic reference to Christ, and the significant words of the quotation are to be found in the last two sentences, which predict the final triumphant reign of Christ over the earth. The first part of v. 8 clinches the argument and states that nothing will finally be uncontrolled by Christ. (Cf. p. 846.)

9–18. The Reply to Objections and the Significance of the Death of Christ. The relation of the remaining part of ch. 2 to the writer's main line of argument is not easy at first sight to detect. The connection appears to be this: There is one clause in the quotation which has just been cited which seems to give away the writer's case, namely, the phrase, *Thou makest him a little lower than the angels.* These words are evidently supposed to refer to the humiliation of Jesus during his earthly life. Why was this humiliation necessary? What is the explanation of the sufferings of Jesus? It is to questions such as these that our attention is directed in the last part of this chapter. Jesus was made lower than the angels that he might taste death for every man and become the author of their salvation (v. 10). In order to do this it was necessary for Christ to be perfected through suffering (v. 10). He had to share our human nature and be made like unto his brethren (v. 14), that he might overcome the power of death and of the devil (v. 15). He must identify himself with us and endure our temptations that he might be able to come to our rescue (v. 18).

9. There are many interesting points in this statement, but before we can discuss them there is to be faced in v. 9 a serious difficulty, one which has given rise to much debate. The question turns on the meaning of the clause *Crowned with glory and honor.* We should naturally expect that the coronation would follow and not precede the words *that he should taste death for every man.* The triumph of Christ naturally follows the cross and does not come before it. The difficulty probably arises from the congestion of ideas involved in the statement, and the fact that the rush of these ideas has probably interfered with the logical exposition of the writer's thought.

The writer begins the sentence by drawing the contrast between Jesus in his earthly humiliation and his subsequent glory. We see Jesus made a little (or for a little while) lower than the angels and afterward crowned with glory and honor. And then, as an afterthought, to make the purpose of the humiliation more explicit, he adds the phrase *that by the grace of God he* [*may*] *taste death for every man.* The latter phrase is not dependent on the words *crowned with glory and honor* but is the conclusion of the whole statement. It should be mentioned, however, that there are some scholars who take a different view and think that the earthly life of Jesus may be described as a coronation, because the choice of the cross as a supreme act of self-sacrifice may be said to have crowned him with glory and honor. But this idea is too modern to be likely to contain the true solution of the problem. There is a curious reading found in some of the ancient Fathers which substitutes for the phrase *by the grace of God* the words "apart from God," and the reference is supposed to be to the sense of dereliction which led Jesus to cry out as he was dying upon the cross, "My God, my God, why hast thou forsaken me?"

16. This has also been a matter of dispute. *For verily not of angels does he take hold, but he taketh hold of the seed of Abraham.* Two interpretations have been given of these words. One is found in the translation of the A.V. *For verily he took not on him the nature of angels;* i.e., he did not become incarnate in the form of an angel, but he took upon himself our *human* nature. The second and probably the correct explanation of the text is, "He did not come to the help of angels, but he comes to the help of men."

This paragraph contains some of the most characteristic ideas of the Epistle. (1) The purpose of the humiliation of Jesus was the salvation of the race (v. 9). (2) As the author or pioneer of salvation it was fitting that Jesus should be made *perfect through suffering* (v. 10). The problem of suffering is felt very acutely in the Bible (cf. the book of Job), and was aggravated for the Christian by the sufferings of Christ. It is here suggested that one element in the purpose of suffering is the perfection of character. There is nothing, however, in this statement which conflicts with the view that Jesus "was holy, guileless, undefiled, separated from sinners" (7[26]). The meaning is, rather, that Jesus could not be a perfect mediator between man and God unless he shared in the sorrows and tribulations of his brethren (see also 5[8,9]). (3) Though Christ has been described in the first chapter as the radiance of the glory of God and the impress of his essence, yet on the manward side he is one with the human race (vv. 11–14). The Saviour and the saved are alike of one origin and therefore he is not ashamed to call them brethren. Three passages are quoted from the O.T. to prove the bond of union that exists between Christ and men. The first (v. 12) is taken from Psa. 22[22]. Here God is represented as saying, *I will declare thy name* [i.e., the Messiah's] *unto my brethren.* The other two (v. 13) come from Isa. 8[17, 18]. (4) The motive of the incarnation now becomes apparent. *Since then the children are sharers in flesh and blood, he also himself in like manner partook of the same* (v. 14). It was only by taking our human nature that Jesus could identify himself with the race. To the writer of Hebrews the doctrine of the incarnation is of supreme importance, since it is only through the incarnation and all that it involves, that the cross gains significance and validity. (5) Vv. 14 and 15 are a surprise. We expect the writer to speak of the redemptive work of Christ and its power to save men from sin. But suddenly he goes off on another line—and describes the result of Christ's work in terms of deliverance from the fear of death. Death is here regarded as the work of the devil. This idea is common in Jewish thought. The writer is probably thinking of a famous passage in the Book of Wisdom (2[23, 24]): "God created man for incorruption, and made him an image of his own proper being. But by the envy of the devil death entered into the world, and they that are of his portion make trial thereof." The statement of Hebrews reminds us of the words in 2 Tim. 1[10], "Our Saviour Christ Jesus, who abolished death, and brought life and immortality to light." The problem of the future life was very acute in the first century. The quest for some token of immortality was keenly pursued, especially in the Greek mystery cults. Not the least thing that Jesus did was to give men a complete assurance of a future life and so lift the burden of fear that weighed so heavily upon their spirits. (See art., *Backgrounds*, p. 850.)

16–18. The whole line of argument is summed up in the concluding verses of the chapter. It was necessary for Christ to be made like unto his brethren *in all things.* The last phrase is emphatic. It excludes all forms of the Doketic heresy, which maintained that the humanity of Jesus was unreal and only formed a kind of mask (cf. 1 John 4[2]). The idea is repeated in 4[15], "one that hath been in all points tempted like as we are, yet without sin." The motive for the complete incarnation was twofold: (1) That Christ might be a merciful and faithful High Priest to make propitiation for the sins of the people. Here for the first time the writer reaches the idea which is to be the keynote of the Epistle—the high-priestly work of Christ—but he reaches it only to leave it again, for the next reference to it (except for a brief allusion in 3[1]) is in 4[14]. (2) But there is another motive given in v. 18 which is also an important characteristic of the Epistle. *In that he suffered . . . he is able to succor them that are tempted.* It is because Christ lived our human life and passed through all its experience, that we can be sure that he understands the sorrow and suffering of life and can sympathize with us. The word translated *tempted* may refer either (a) to inner temptation or (b) to outward trial or persecution. Probably both ideas are included here. Jesus had to face both inner temptation, as in the wilderness, and outward persecution, as in the death upon the cross and all that preceded it, and therefore he is able to succor us and sympathize with our troubles from whatever source they may come.

CHAPTER III

With 3[1] begins the second section of the Epistle. This section is composed of two main parts: (1) A short argument to prove the superiority of Christ to Moses (3[1-6]). (2) A long digression of practical appeal (3[7]–4[13]).

1–6. The Superiority of Christ to Moses. Though the paragraph which deals with this point consists of only six verses, it is extremely important. The Jews believed that in the Law Moses had given to the Jewish race a complete and final revelation of the will of God. He had spoken the last word and there was nothing more to be said. It was essential, therefore, that a Christian apologist should prove that the authority of Christ was greater than that of Moses. The writer tries to demonstrate his point by two arguments. (1) The first is given in v. 3 in the phrase *he that built the house hath more honor than the house.* Moses belongs to the created world, Christ is the Creator (cf. 1[2]). The creator is greater than the thing created, therefore Christ is greater than Moses. (2) The second argument is in v. 5. Moses is described in Num. 12[7,8] as a servant of God "faithful in all mine house: with him will I speak mouth to mouth." The latter clause refers to the words in v. 5, *for a testimony of those things which were afterward to be spoken,* i.e., the Law. Moses is, therefore, a servant in the house while Christ is a Son with a position of authority over it. Such is the main thread of the argument.

There are some interesting phrases in these verses. In v. 1 Christ is called *the Apostle and High Priest of our confession.* The early church cannot be said to have possessed a creed in any formal sense of the term, but it had a confession of belief, and its content is summarized in the words, "Jesus, Apostle and High Priest." There is a further reference to this confession in 4[14]. It is interesting to note that the word *Apostle* is here applied to Christ. The word means in this connection "the delegate" or "envoy" of God, and when it is used of men it is generally equivalent in meaning to our word "missionary." What is involved in the term *High Priest* as it is used of Christ will become apparent in the later chapters of the Epistle. The words of v. 6, *if we hold fast . . . unto the end,* indicate one of the main warnings of the Epistle. The danger of relapse was great. Many men who started well on the Christian race fell away. It is not so much the start as the finish of the race that counts (cf. also v. 14 and the words of Jesus in Mt. 10^{22}).

7–19. Digression: A Practical Appeal (continued in 4^{1-13}). At this point the writer digresses from the main argument. The digression contains a very fine specimen of a sermon or homily. It is complete in itself and is one of the most perfect examples we possess of the method of preaching in the apostolic age. The author takes a text, expounds its meaning, draws out the ideas involved in it, and then makes a practical appeal to his hearers.

There has been much discussion as to the connection between the digression, or sermon, and the previous argument. We saw that at the commencement of ch. 2 the writer clinches one of his arguments by making a great practical appeal, and many scholars think that this apparent digression is a similar kind of appeal though of much greater length. Others—and this seems to be the most natural view—think that throughout this section there runs a sort of latent contrast between the failure of the work of Moses and the success of the work of Christ. It was because Moses failed in bringing the nation into "the rest of God" that the work of Christ was rendered necessary.

The digression, or sermon, is composed of the following parts: (1) The text and the statement of the theme (vv. 7–14). (2) The explanation of the text (vv. 15–19). (3) The theological idea and promise involved in the text (4^{1-10}). (4) The final application and appeal (4^{11-13}).

7–14. The Text of the Theme. The text is taken from Psa. 95^{7-11}. The main theme is concerned with the failure of the people of Israel during their sojourn in the wilderness to hear the voice of God through the hardness of their hearts and their rebellion against him. As a consequence of this revolt God kept them in the wilderness for forty years and would not allow them to enter into a peaceful life in the land of promise. This text is used by the author of the Epistle as a warning to the people of his own day. "Be careful," he urges, "that history does not repeat itself in your own case. Hardness and rebellion against God will be as fatal for you as for the Israelites of old. See that an evil heart of unbelief does not lead you to revolt against God. It is only those who keep their faith and courage firm to the end who can be said to belong to Christ."

15–19. The Explanation of the Text. The author or preacher now proceeds to explain the historical references in the text, "Who were these people with whom God was angry?" he asks. They were the people of Israel whom Moses had led out of the Egyptian captivity. Their carcasses are bleaching in the wilderness as a proof of their unbelief.

CHAPTER IV

1–10. The Theological Idea Involved in the Above Text. It is this section that contains the interesting and original part of the sermon. Taking up the last clause of the text, *They shall not enter into my rest,* the writer argues that these words imply a divine promise of eternal value. Throughout history God had held out to the world the vision and ideal of rest and peace, but up to the present the great promise of God had not been appropriated by humanity. The people of Israel might have inherited it, but their obstinacy and blindness led them to revolt. The psalmist repeated the promise in his day and generation, but once again the people refused to grasp it. The unrealized promise is still available for Christians, if only they will seize the opportunity of making it their own.

When we think of the circumstances amid which these early Christians lived—the persecutions they had to endure, the dangers that threatened them, the sense of insecurity that always oppressed them, the fear of imprisonment or the confiscation of their property—we can understand how this section of the sermon, with its promise of peace and rest, must have appealed to them. God's ideal not only for these primitive Christians but for the world is the ideal of peace. The prophet Isaiah had proclaimed the Messiah as the "Prince of Peace" (Isa. 9^{6}), and had foretold the coming of a time when "nation shall not lift up sword against nation, neither shall they learn war any more." When Christ came, it actually looked as if the promise would be realized. His advent seemed to usher in the era of peace. As Milton puts it in his "Ode to the Nativity":

"No war or battle's sound
Was heard the world around,
The idle spear and shield were high uphung;
The hooked chariot stood
Unstained with hostile blood,
The trumpet spake not to the armed throng.
The kings sat still with awful eye
As if they surely knew their sovran Lord
was by."

But it was only a fitful gleam of the vision of peace that came to the world. Another chance was missed. War, strife, and persecution broke out again with new intensity. And yet the promise of God stood firm and still stands firm to-day.

The argument which is worked out in this section of the sermon may be paraphrased thus: "The promise of peace which has never yet been realized still holds good for us (v. 1). We must see to it that we too do not miss the opportunity of obtaining it. The good news has been proclaimed to us as it was to our forefathers. It was unbelief that made them fail (v. 2). We who believe may lay hold upon that promise and make it our own. The promise has existed from the first. It is one of the works of God that were finished at the creation of the world (v. 3). The proof of this may be seen in the statement of Scripture which declares that, after the making of the world, God rested on the seventh day. Rest, therefore, is an attribute of God. It is divine. It is God's ideal for mankind (vv. 4, 5). The promise still remains to be realized. The Israelites failed through disobedience (v. 6). Joshua failed too to lead the nation into rest (v. 8). The psalmist offered the promise to the men of his day (v. 7): they did not accept it, and so it was postponed for future generations." The climax of the argument is reached in v. 9. "There still remains a rest like the peace of a Sabbath day for the people of God to realize, and this rest will be like that which came to God himself when, after the creation, he rested from his works."

11–13. The Final Appeal. The last words of the sermon are an earnest appeal to the Christians of the first century to give diligence to secure for themselves the promise of rest and not to lose their opportunity through disobedience like their forefathers. The ground for the urgency of the writer's appeal is given in vv. 12, 13. Though the word of God (and by this phrase the writer means the revelation of God as it is given in the O.T. and the teaching of Jesus) contains great and inalienable promises, there is another side to it as well. It contains the threat of judgment. It is no dead letter, no antiquated theory. It is alive and active. It is like a sword with a double edge—one the edge of promise and hope, the other the edge of reproof and retribution. And this sword of judgment does not merely make a flesh wound; it penetrates to the very core of our being, and touches the vital spot where body and soul are united together. And, moreover, its verdict is passed not merely upon outward acts of sin and of disloyalty—it judges the thoughts and the intentions of the heart. A man does not need to commit open apostasy in order to come under its condemnation. The apostasy of the mind is equally a matter that falls under its jurisdiction. There is no possibility of concealing our inner disloyalties from God. There is no man whose life is not like an open book to him. Everything we do or think is naked and open to God. We may try to cloak our deeds and hide away our thoughts in the secret recesses of our souls, but the eyes of God penetrate through all the masks and guises in which we have sought concealment and our souls are stripped bare before their gaze. It is to be noticed that in these verses the writer follows the teaching of Jesus in the stress which he lays upon the motives and intentions which lie behind conduct and give it its moral value. Compare the statements of Jesus in Mt. 5^{21-48}.

The whole passage about the word of God resembles a statement in the writings of Philo and was probably suggested to the writer by that statement. Philo speaks of the word "which cuts through everything, which being sharpened to the finest possible edge never ceases dividing all the objects of the outward senses, and when it has gone through them all and arrived at the things which are called atoms, then again this divider begins to separate from them the things which may be contemplated by the speculations of reason." Philo, however, confines its action to the intellectual sphere, while the author of Hebrews applies the idea to the moral realm.

In the phrase *naked and open*, the last word represents the translation of a very interesting Greek word, and the exact meaning of it is not very certain. The word means "to bend back the neck," and the reference is probably to a wrestler catching his opponent by the neck and pressing his head back so that it is exposed to the view of the heavens.

14–16. Main Theme of the Epistle Broached. (Continued in 5^{1-10}.) The writer now approaches the main theme of the Epistle, which has already been hinted at in 2^{17} and 3^{1}, the highpriesthood of Christ Jesus; 4^{14-16} is a transition paragraph linking the sermon on "the rest of God" to the commencement of the comparison between the work of an ordinary high priest to that of Christ which forms the theme of the opening section of ch. 5.

The transition paragraph describes Jesus as *a great high priest who hath passed through the heavens.* By this phrase the writer indicates that the distance which separated the ordinary high priest from God has been transcended by Christ. He has passed through the heavens into the immediate presence of God. All barriers have been broken down. The gulf between heaven and earth has been bridged and complete communion with God established. But this is not the only characteristic of the highpriesthood of Christ. If, on the one hand, there is perfect communion with God, there is, on the other hand, equally complete identity with the human race. Our High Priest is not one who is incapable of sympathizing with our frailty, since he has lived our life and has been tempted in all points as we are, though there is this difference between him and us: under pressure of temptation we often fall; he never fell. It is interesting to observe how the writer of Hebrews keeps the balance even between the human and the divine elements in the Person of Christ. No N.T. writer has a higher conception of the divinity of Christ and no N.T. writer attaches so much importance to the reality of his humanity. As in 2^{17} the writer says that Christ ought in all points to be made like unto his brethren (see note), so here he emphasizes the fact that *he was in all points tempted like as we are.* The phrase *in all points* is of vital importance in both statements. The conflict with temptation was as acute in the experience of Jesus as it is in that of his followers. Jesus, to use Milton's fine phrase, "was no carpet knight who never sallied out and saw the foe." And if the victory over temptation from the start reduced the strain of the conflict for Jesus in some of its aspects, yet there are temptations connected with his high vocation which always, as in the wilderness, occasioned him anxiety and conflict. It is no meaningless phrase when Jesus says in Jn. 17^{19}, "For their sakes I consecrate (mg.) myself."

The paragraph ends with an appeal (v. 16). Seeing that we have a High Priest who is one with God and one with man, we must approach the throne of grace with confidence. The metaphor which the writer uses suggests the right of admission to a royal presence or the court of a supreme judge. Jesus has obtained for us the privilege of direct access to the Father, and this privilege is one which Christians ought to use to the full. The object of the approach is defined in a twofold way. First, that we may *obtain mercy*—which is the fundamental and primary need of the human soul; and, secondly, that we may obtain *grace to help* us in our time of need. The latter phrase must be interpreted in the light of the circumstances and conditions under which these Christians were living at the time, e.g., the persecutions, and the temptations to drift back to the life of the world.

CHAPTER V

1–10. The Qualifications and Characteristics of the Work of the High Priest. (See also 4^{14-16}.) In later chapters the writer develops at some length the points of contrast between the work of the ordinary high priest and the work of Christ (cf. ch. 10), but in this paragraph, which opens the discussion, he dwells upon the points of similarity rather than the points of difference. Stress is laid upon two main qualifications which are necessary in every high priest. (1) The high priest must be sympathetic and humane (vv. 2 and 3). (2) He must be divinely appointed (v. 4). It is then proved that Jesus possessed both these qualifications in a supreme degree (vv. 7–10).

1–3. The First Qualification. The first qualification for the office of high priest is described in vv. 1–3. The significant clause is found in v. 2, *who can bear gently with the ignorant and erring, for that he himself also is compassed with infirmity.* It is this clause which forms the link between this paragraph and the preceding. Christ was tempted in all points, and so was able to sympathize with our frailty. The high priest is compassed with infirmity and so is able to bear gently with the ignorant and erring. There is a point, of course, at which the resemblance breaks down. Christ is *without sin.* The high priest is bound *as for the people, so also for himself, to offer for sins.* Forbearance, therefore, is a quality common to both Christ and the earthly high priest. But, as is plainly implied in the phrasing, the forbearance is not extended to flagrant and willful sin but is shown, rather, to the *ignorant and the erring,* i.e., to those who fall into sin through ignorance. The Epistle shows infinite sympathy with the tempted soul and with the sin of ignorance, but it denounces in unmeasured terms flagrant and willful transgression. For the former it has unstinted sympathy, for the latter the most fiery denunciation.

5, 6. The Second Qualification. The high priest is not self-appointed. He derives his authority and his office from God. Even Aaron owed his appointment to a direct divine call. The highpriesthood of Christ is equally divine in its origin. Two proof-texts are cited to establish the argument. The first is from Psa. 2^7 and has already been used by the writer in 1^5. The second is of much greater importance, and plays a very significant part in the later argument of the Epistle (cf. ch. 7). It is taken from Psa. 110^4: *Thou art a priest for ever after the order of Melchizedek.* For the writer's interpretation of these words see note on 7^1.

7–10. The Manner in Which Christ Fulfilled These Qualifications. Once more the writer returns to one of his favorite themes and points out again how the experiences and suffering of Jesus during his earthly life fitted him for his highpriestly work. In the days of his flesh (i.e., during his earthly life) Jesus offered up prayers and supplications with bitter cries and tears to Him who was able to save him from death, and was heard because of his godly piety. The reference here is undoubtedly to the agony in the garden of Gethsemane (Mt. 26^{36-46} and parallels). The intensity of the struggle in the mind of Jesus is revealed in the phrase, *with strong crying and tears.* The statement that the prayer of Jesus was heard is difficult in view of the fact that it remained unanswered. Some scholars translate the phrase, "He was heard so as to be delivered from fear," though this is not the most natural meaning of the Greek words. It is better to assume that the real answer to the prayer consisted in the endowment of Jesus with strength to meet his fate. The crisis of Gethsemane is cited as a new illustration of the manner in which Jesus identified himself with the life of humanity.

Vv. 8 and 9 indicate the function of the sufferings which Jesus endured in his being equipped for the work of salvation. Though he was Son, yet he learned obedience from the things he suffered, and having been perfected by them, he became the author of salvation (see note on 2^{10}). Finally, in v. 10 the writer restates what he has already said in v. 6, that the claim of Jesus to be the true High Priest rests upon the fact that he belongs to the order of Melchizedek.

Another Digression: A Warning and an Encouragement. At this point the writer breaks away from the main line of his argument and enters upon another digression—an admonition which extends from 5^{11} to 6^{20}. This *great admonition,* as it may be called, falls into the following divisions: (1) The peril of stagnation, 5^{11}–6^{3}. (2) The peril of lapsing from the faith, 6^{4-8}. (3) A message of encouragement and hope, 6^{9-12}. (4) The faithfulness of God illustrated from his dealings with Abraham, 6^{13-20}.

11–14. The Peril of Stagnation. (See also 6^{1-3}.) The writer begins by stating the motive for the digression. He has much to say about Melchizedek and he admits that his argument will be difficult to follow. He is afraid that the people to whom he is writing will not be able to appreciate his line of reasoning because they have become stagnant in thought and life. They are dull of hearing. They ought by this time themselves to have become teachers, whereas they still need someone to teach them the rudimentary principles of the Christian faith. They require a diet fit for infants; they cannot assimilate the food of full-grown men. They are still babes and have not yet been sufficiently disciplined to be able to distinguish instinctively between good and evil. The writer then proceeds at the beginning of ch. 6 to describe these elementary principles which formed the basis of Christian faith and practice in the first century. They consisted in: (1) Repentance and faith in God. These represented the moral demands made upon the believer. (2) Teaching about baptisms and the laying on of hands, i.e., about Christian rites and ceremonies. The plural *baptisms* (6^{2}) is meant to cover other kinds of baptism besides that practiced by the Christian Church—e.g., Jewish and pagan, and the phrase, *teaching about baptisms,* means instruction in the difference between the Christian form of baptism and other types. (3) The doctrine of the resurrection and eternal judgment. These three groups give us the characteristic features of the minimum demands made by the Christian Church on its members.

The writer appeals to his readers to develop out of the minimum into the maximum stage of Christianity. *Let us press on to perfection.* His protest in this passage is mainly against the intellectual stagnation which prevented Christians from a full appreciation and understanding of Christian truth.

CHAPTER VI

1–3. See under 5^{11-14}.

4–8. The Peril of Lapsing From the Faith. This is one of the most difficult and perplexing paragraphs in the Epistle. The writer seems to state in the most categorical way that the condition of those who have lapsed from the Christian faith is hopeless and there is no possibility of their restoration. When men have once been enlightened, it is argued, and have tasted of the heavenly gift and have become partakers of the Spirit, and have tasted the good word of God and the powers of the world to come, and then have fallen away, it is impossible to renew them again unto repentance, since they crucify the Son of God afresh and put him to open shame.

Many attempts have been made to soften the harshness of the passage. (1) Some scholars, observing that the Greek word translated *to renew them* is in a different tense from the other verbs in the passage, have sought to find relief by giving it the meaning "to keep on renewing." It is impossible to keep up the process of renewing those who have fallen away. A single lapse may admit of recovery, but repeated lapses make it impossible. (2) Another method is to apply the same principle to the participial phrase, *crucifying the Son of God afresh,* and to argue that the use of the present tense in the Greek denotes continuous action. "It is impossible to renew those who have fallen away *while they continue to crucify* the Son of God afresh."

There is some justification on linguistic grounds for each of these suggestions; and if this passage stood alone, it would be possible to find a way out of the difficulty by adopting one or the other of them. But in 10[26] the doctrine is restated in a form which admits of neither of these methods of escape: "If we sin willfully after that we have received the knowledge of the truth, there remaineth no more a sacrifice for sins, but a certain fearful expectation of judgment."

Nor can we evade the difficulty of stressing with Westcott the word *repentance* and arguing that as repentance involves "a complete change of mind consequent upon the apprehension of the true moral nature of things," it follows necessarily "that in this large sense there can be no 'second' repentance."

We must look in another direction for the real explanation of the severity of the passage. It appears to be an exaggeration of a very common psychological experience. Everybody knows that cases of relapse are very difficult to deal with. When the religious emotion has once been aroused and then has died down, it is very difficult—often it seems quite impossible—to kindle it afresh. John Wesley says in his *Journal*, "From the terrible instances I have met with in all parts of England, I am more and more convinced the devil himself desires nothing more than this, that the people of any place should be half awakened and then left to themselves to go to sleep again." And on another occasion he writes: "I was more than ever convinced that the preaching like an apostle, without joining together those that are awakened and training them in the ways of God, is only begetting children for the murderer. . . . The consequence is that nine in ten of the once awakened are faster asleep than ever."

The experience of John Wesley must have been common in the apostolic age. The problem of the lapsed baffled the heart and the intellect of the church. What wonder is it that the writer of the Epistle drew from his own bitter experience the theological inference that the restoration of the lapsed was an impossibility! His statement is a generalization —perhaps a too absolute generalization—from the experience of the church. Psychologically the statement is in accordance with almost universal experience, but whether the author of Hebrews was justified in hardening a psychological fact into a theological proposition may be regarded as, at any rate, open to question.

The writer concludes the paragraph by an illustration taken from nature (vv. 7 and 8). Fertile land which absorbs the rain and produces fruit receives a blessing from God; but if it only produces thorns and thistles, it is rejected and comes nigh to being cursed—its doom is to be burned. Compare with this the words of Jesus in Mt. 7[17-19].

9–12. A Message of Encouragement and Hope. Lest the terrible words of the preceding paragraph should discourage and dismay his readers, the writer now proceeds to reassure and comfort them. Though we have found it necessary, he argues, to describe the doom of the lapsed, we are confident that such a fate as that will never befall you. God will never forget your service and the love you have shown and are still showing in ministering to the needs of his saints. It is our keen desire that you will show equal eagerness in realizing the full meaning of the Christian hope and follow the example of those who through their steadfast faith inherit the promises of God. For a further explanation of the record of the service rendered by these Christians, see 10[32-34].

13–20. The Faithfulness of God and the Promises Which He Made to Abraham. The word *promise* is the link which connects this paragraph with what goes before. The phrase in v. 12, "those who inherit the promises," suggests the idea of the inviolability of the promises of God. We have not merely our own steadfastness and resolution to rely upon as the guarantee of victory: behind all this stands the promise of God which cannot be broken.

The particular promise referred to is contained in Gen. 22[16, 17]. There are two points in these words which the writer emphasizes; first the *promise* itself and then the *oath* by which it is assured. Among men it is customary in making a promise to call upon some higher power to bear witness that they have sworn to carry out their bond. The oath sets its seal upon the promise and makes it binding and secure. When once the oath has been taken, it means that God has been called in as a party to the transaction, and that assurance has been made doubly sure, since any breach of the contract would now involve despite against God. Now, God in making this promise to Abraham had no higher power that he could call in as witness. He therefore *interposed with an oath* (v. 17), and swore by himself. The Christian hope, therefore, is doubly attested. It is attested, in the first place, by the solemn promise itself, and then by the oath which God himself added to the promise to make it still more secure. Both promise and oath alike are immutable and inviolable, and these *two immutable things* (v. 18) guarantee the hope and make it absolutely secure (cf. the argument in 7[21]). Christians, like refugees from a hostile world, have laid hold of this hope —and it has become *an anchor* (v. 19) which keeps them unmoved amid all the storms that sweep down upon them. But the anchor of hope has not merely value for the life that now is. Christians stand as it were between two worlds—the present world and the world that is to come. Over the world that is to come there hangs a veil which hides it from our eyes. But the anchor of the Christian hope penetrates the veil and is fastened sure and firm upon the other side. We are anchored not in time but in eternity. But even that does not cover all that we possess in the other world. Jesus too has passed beyond the veil and entered into the life beyond, and where he has gone we shall follow, since he is but the forerunner.

We have therefore two pledges to guarantee our inheritance: (1) The anchor of hope based upon the immutable promise of God; (2) the presence of Christ, "the firstborn among many brethren," in the land behind the veil. At this point with a skillful turn of the sentence the writer steers our thought out of the backwater into the main stream of the argument of the Epistle by adding the words *having become a high priest for ever after the order of Melchizedek.*

CHAPTER VII

Christ the Ideal High Priest After the Order of Melchizedek. The writer now resumes the argument which he had dropped in 5[10], and it is at this point that the line of thought becomes involved and complicated for the modern student. What is the point in the comparison which the writer makes between Christ and Melchizedek? The question can only be answered by recalling to mind the main problem which the Epistle is facing. If we have in the Jewish Law a divine revelation and a divinely appointed priesthood to act as a mediator between man and God, what need is there of anything more? Why do we require another high priest? What room is there left for the highpriestly office of Christ? It is exactly the same problem which in a different aspect Paul found himself compelled to grapple with in Romans and Galatians. The common belief in the finality of the Jewish Law as the expression of the will of God was a serious difficulty for his doctrine of justification by faith. In meeting this fundamental objection to the Christian position Paul and the author of Hebrews adopt the same method of reply. They both attempt to go back behind the Law to the religion of the patriarchal age. Paul appeals to the faith of Abraham, the author of Hebrews to the priesthood of Melchizedek. The assumption of both is that the ideal religion is to be found in the age of the patriarchs and that the Mosaic law represented a declension from that ideal. The golden age of Israel lies in the most primitive period and subsequent history involved a gradual falling away from that high standard. Christianity represented the recovery of the faith of the golden age which had been submerged under the legalism of later times. The task of Paul, however, was far easier than that of the author of Hebrews. He could take his stand on the faith of Abraham, who was universally recognized as the father of the Jewish race, and whose religion might easily be regarded as the prototype of the Christian doctrine of justification by faith. The author of Hebrews could find only one example of a priest in the golden age, and that was Melchizedek. He was not the first, however, to make the discovery. The author of Psa. 110 had already discovered Melchizedek and had spoken of him as the representative of the ideal priesthood, and had said that the Messiah when he came would belong to the type of Melchizedek and not to the type of the ordinary Levitical priests.

But the author of Psa. 110 and the writer of Hebrews had very little basis in fact for the ideal portrait which they draw of Melchizedek. Melchizedek appears on the stage of history for only one brief moment and plays what seems to be a minor part in the record of the life of Abraham. All that is known about him is told in three verses (Gen. 14[18-20]): "And Melchizedek king of Salem brought forth bread and wine: and he was priest of God Most High. And he blessed him, and said, Blessed be Abram of God Most High, possessor of heaven and earth: and blessed be God Most High, which hath delivered thine enemies into thy hand. And he [i.e., Abram] gave him a tenth of all." Such are the scanty facts which underlie the ideal picture of Melchizedek in Psa. 110 and in Hebrews. The argument in both is that Melchizedek represents the heavenly ideal of the priesthood which degenerated in the Aaronic system and was recovered by Christ.

The analysis of the argument of ch. 7 falls into the following divisions: (1) The portrait of Melchizedek and its significance for religion (vv. 1–3). (2) The relation between Melchizedek and Abraham, proving the superiority of the former (vv. 4–10). (3) The inferiority of the Levitical priesthood (v. 11–17). (4) The superseding of the Levitical priesthood by Christ (vv. 18–25). (5) Christ as the ideal High Priest (vv. 26–28).

1–3. The Portrait of Melchizedek and Its Significance for Religion. The writer begins by stating the facts derived from Gen. 14, and then he proceeds to develop and expand the facts by means of etymology and allegory. First of all he takes the name "Melchizedek" itself and points out that the word means *king of righteousness*, and then he takes the word "Salem" and says that it means *peace*. In this way he clothes the figure of Melchizedek with the great and divine attributes of peace and righteousness. Then, in v. 3, he makes a very remarkable use of the argument from silence. Nothing is said in Genesis about the parentage of Melchizedek. We are not told anything about his father or his mother. There is no reference to the beginning of his life or to its end—to his birth or to his death. Since, therefore, in the view of the writer the silences of Scripture are as significant as its statements, he concludes that Melchizedek is a kind of divine figure (like unto the Son of God) without human origin and existing eternally. And here we must not forget the Platonic background that lies behind the writer's thought (see p. 1296). Melchizedek represents the divine archetype of the idea of priesthood, which broke into human history in his person in the patriarchal age, was eclipsed by the Levitical system, and finally was recovered by Christ. In Christ there is a return to the ideal.

The allegorical method which the writer employs in his interpretation of scripture, and the unrestrained use he makes of it in the deductions which he draws from its silences and omissions, leave the modern mind unconvinced. But we must remember that the Epistle was written in the first century and not in the twentieth, and the writer is only doing what many of his contemporaries, pagan as well as Christian, did in their treatment of sacred literature. Paul uses a similar form of allegory in making Hagar and Sarah types of the Law and of the gospel in Gal. 4^{21-31}. As a matter of fact, the N.T. is much more restrained in its use of allegory than Philo or the later Alexandrian Fathers.

4–10. The Relations Between Melchizedek and Abraham. The writer now proceeds to demonstrate the superiority of Melchizedek to Abraham. Abraham was universally regarded as the founder of the Jewish race. The Jews looked back to him as the father and fountainhead of their national greatness. It was a daring argument to attempt to prove that he had any superior in the patriarchal period, but our author does not hesitate in making the assumption. He fixes upon the phrase in Genesis, "And he [i.e., Abraham] gave him a tenth of all," and argues that these words imply that Abraham recognized his own inferiority to Melchizedek. *Consider*, he says, *how great this man was, unto whom Abraham, the patriarch, gave a tenth out of the chief spoils* (v. 4). "It is quite true," he proceeds to argue, "that the sons of Levi who hold the priestly office have the right under the Law to exact tithes from the rest of the people, though they, like themselves, are also the children of Abraham." But this man Melchizedek, who did not belong to the Levitical order of priests and who therefore had no such right in law, exacted tithes from Abraham and pronounced a benediction on the great patriarch who was the possessor of the divine promise. Now, a benediction is always pronounced by a superior over an inferior. Hence it follows that Melchizedek must have been greater than Abraham. But there is another difference between Melchizedek and the priests of the Levitical order. They are mortal men, but Melchizedek is one of the immortals, since the statement is made about him that "he lives." There is no record of this in the Genesis narrative, but the writer is referring to the deduction which he has drawn in v. 3 from the silence of Genesis, *having neither beginning of days nor end of life*.

Then follows, in v. 9, a very subtle line of reasoning. Melchizedek exacted tithes from Abraham: but Abraham is the father of the tribes of Israel and among them of the tribe of Levi. It may be argued, therefore, that in the person of Abraham their forefather the Levitical priests paid tribute and tithe to Melchizedek. Because Melchizedek is superior to Abraham, he is superior also to his descendants and for the same reason. Hence it follows that the type of priesthood represented by Melchizedek is of a higher order than that represented by the sons of Levi.

11–17. The Inferiority of the Levitical Priesthood. There is yet another argument which proves the inferiority of the Levitical system. It has shown itself to be a failure. It did not secure perfection for men. If it had been adequate, there would have been no need for the psalmist to proclaim the rise of a new order. The words which the 110th psalm applies to the Messiah, "Thou art a priest for ever after the order of Melchizedek," are a proof that there existed a deep-seated conviction that the Levitical priesthood had never achieved the purpose for which it had been established. It had proved itself incapable of securing victory over sin and the sense of a full communion with God. And the failure of the priesthood meant the failure of the entire legal system, for the Levitical priesthood was the heart and core of the Jewish Law. *Under it hath the people received the law;* i.e., the Jewish code as a whole had grown up around the central fact of the priesthood. The need, therefore, of a new order of priesthood involved a revolutionary change in the whole legal system. The Law depended for its validity and efficacy upon the success of its priesthood, and when the priesthood failed, the whole system became obsolete and useless.

In vv. 13, 14 the writer seems to be replying to a criticism that might be brought against his line of reasoning. "Granted," the objector seems to say, "that your argument is sound and that the failure of the existing Levitical system is proved, why on that account should the whole of the Law be discredited? Why should there not be a reformation in the Levitical system? Why should not a new and better order of priests arise under the legal system?" In reply to this challenge the writer asserts that the facts are against such a theory. The psalmist does not speak of a reformed Levitical system but of the rise of an ideal priest who did not spring from the tribe of Levi at all but belonged to *the order of Melchizedek*. And Christ himself, who in his own person has fulfilled the prophecy of the psalmist, came out of the tribe of Judah, and the tribe of Judah, according to the Law, has no connection whatever with the priesthood. The credentials of the Levitical priest are based simply upon genealogy. He must be in the true tribal succession. His official rank depends entirely upon his fulfillment of the demands of an external (this is what the word *carnal* in v. 16 really means in this connection) commandment. The credentials of Jesus are very different. They are displayed in his *power of an indissoluble* (*or endless*) *life*. It is upon the fact of his resurrection, and the proof which it afforded that his life was indestructible, that the claim of Jesus to be the real fulfillment of the psalmist's prophecy really rests. The psalmist had declared that the ideal high priest would be *forever*—and only one whose life could not be destroyed by death could be said to answer to the psalmist's ideal.

18–25. The Superseding of the Levitical System by Christ. It follows from the argument of the previous paragraph that since the whole Law is involved in the failure of the priesthood, it is now repealed and canceled. It has proved itself futile and so there has been *a disannulling of a foregoing commandment* (v. 18). It has been shown by experience to be weak and profitless. It could not achieve the purpose for which it was set up. It could not produce moral perfection. Therefore it has now been superseded, and a new era has been opened for us. In contrast to the sense of despair which the Law created in the minds of men, the new era is described as the era of hope; and its supreme characteristic is to be found in the fact that it does what the Law could never do—it enables men to *draw nigh unto God*. There are two points in which the superiority of the Priesthood of Christ to the Levitical system can be demonstrated: (1) By means of an argument similar to that which he has used in 6:13-18, the writer shows by elaborating the statement of Psa. 110 that the priesthood of Christ rests upon the solemn oath of God. *The Lord sware and will not repent.* There is no such basis to be found for the Levitical system (v. 21). The reason why the divine asseveration was made in the case of Christ is to be found in the fact that he is *the surety of a better covenant*. This is the first introduction of the idea of the *new covenant* which is subsequently developed in ch. 8. (2) The second argument (v. 23, 24) is an expansion of the phrase, *the power of an endless life*, which the writer has already used in v. 16. The argument has two phases. (a) The Levitical priests are an innumerable host. They are always changing. There is no permanence about them. We Christians have a single Mediator. (b) The Levitical priests are mortal men. They are subject to death. They do not abide and consequently their office and work are transitory. Christ, on the other hand, is immortal, and his work is therefore permanent and uninterrupted. He is able, therefore, to provide the most complete salvation for us, since he is alive for evermore and is able to make continual intercession for us. The phrase translated *to the uttermost* is of uncertain meaning. It may have a temporal significance and mean "for all time," but probably the R.V. mg. is right in translating the phrase *completely*. The saving power of Christ covers the whole range of human life and no sphere of conduct is outside the scope of its influence. The means by which this salvation is secured is the continuous intercession of Christ. A similar idea is found in Rom. 8:26, where Paul, speaking of the Holy Spirit, says, "He maketh intercession for us with groanings which cannot be uttered."

26–28. Christ as the Ideal High Priest. In the final section of the chapter the writer summarizes the arguments by which he has sought to prove that Christ is the ideal High Priest. His credentials are thus described: (1) The perfection of his character. He is *holy, guileless, undefiled*. The Levitical priests hold their office by right of descent; Christ by right of his own innate purity. Compare with this statement of the sinlessness of Christ the words of 1 Pet. 2[22]. (2) He is free from all contact with sinful men. The Levitical high priest spent the week before the Day of Atonement in isolation in the Temple, that he might be untainted by contact with sin when he offered the sacrifice. It is in this sense that the phrase is here used of Christ. (3) He has been made higher than the heavens. This phrase explains the words *separated from sinners.* Jesus has entered into the highest heaven and so his separation from sinners is complete. According to the common belief of the time, there was a series of seven heavens, each higher than the one below it. It was in the highest heaven of all that God had his dwelling place, so the phrase *made higher than the heavens* means that Christ had passed through the lower heavens into the very presence of God himself.

Then the writer proceeds in vv. 27 and 28 to recapitulate the points of contrast between Christ and the Levitical priests. The high priests needed to offer a daily sacrifice both for their own sins and those of the people. Christ offered a single sacrifice *once for all,* and it possesses eternal efficiency. There is a difficulty in the first half of the statement. According to the O.T., the high priest sacrificed a sin-offering for the people only once a year and, judging from the references in other parts of the Epistle (9[7-25] 10[1]), the writer was perfectly familiar with the fact. Why then does he state here that there was a daily offering? It is true, according to Lev. 6[19-23], that there was a daily offering, but this is a cereal offering and was not intended to be an offering for sin. Possibly the writer had this enactment in his mind and put a larger interpretation upon it than the words of Leviticus warrant. Philo also assumes that there was a daily offering made by the high priest, and this may be one of the cases in which the writer agrees with Philo (with whose writings he was undoubtedly familiar) against the text of the O.T. Another suggestion is that the word *daily* means "yearly on a definite day," but this seems too farfetched to be a true interpretation. Westcott thinks that the word *daily* applies not to the high priests but to Jesus and his continuous intercession. But this idea seems to be in flagrant contradiction to the phrase, *this he did once for all, when he offered up himself.* It is perhaps best to say with Moffatt that "the writer blends loosely in his description the annual sacrifice of the high priest on Atonement-day and the daily sacrifice offered by the high priests." In the last phrase in v. 27 the writer, as is his wont, introduces for the first time a new idea, that Christ offered sacrifice *once for all,* which he develops later in ch. 10. In v. 28 he emphasizes again the superiority of the prophecy in Psa. 110 to the Levitical system.

CHAPTER VIII

The writer has proved in ch. 7 that Christ is the ideal High Priest, and he now proceeds to argue that the sphere in which he exercises his office is an ideal and heavenly sanctuary. And thus he becomes the Mediator of a new and better covenant. The chapter, therefore, falls into two divisions: (1) The heavenly sanctuary (vv. 1–5). (2) The new covenant (vv. 6–13).

1–5. The Heavenly Sanctuary. There is a difficulty in the opening statement. *Now in the things which we are saying the chief point is this.* This sentence as it is translated seems to imply that the writer is about to recapitulate the main points in his previous arguments. As a matter of fact, however, he proceeds to develop an entirely new idea. It is probable that the true interpretation of the opening clause is this: "The climax of what we have already said is as follows." The reference is to the clause in 7[26], "made higher than the heavens." The expansion of the idea involved in the statement is made in vv. 1, 2, where it is stated that Christ as the ideal High Priest took his appointed seat on the right hand of the throne of God and became the minister of the ideal sanctuary in heaven. Here we have the emergence of a new movement in the thought of the Epistle. Christ is not only the ideal High Priest, but he exercises his office not in any earthly sanctuary but in the ideal sanctuary in the heavens. The argument throughout this paragraph is based on the Platonic conception that everything on earth has its heavenly counterpart (see p. 1296a).

The true tabernacle, which the Lord pitched, not man, refers to the ideal sanctuary in heaven, which is the counterpart of the earthly tabernacle (v. 2). The ministry which Jesus exercised in the heavenly temple is higher than that of the Levitical order. Even in the heavenly sanctuary some kind of an offering is needed to establish communion between God and man. *Every high priest is appointed to offer both gifts and sacrifices* (v. 3)—the ideal high priest must therefore have an offering to make. Here the writer drops a preliminary hint of the great theme which he develops in ch. 9, where he describes the ideal sacrifice which the ideal high priest offers in the ideal sanctuary. But in the present passage the idea is introduced merely as part of the general argument. Assuming that sacrifice is essential to the work of a high priest, the offering that Christ made is different from the sacrifices offered under the Levitical system. Christ does not belong to the Levitical system at all, and would not have any right at all to exercise a Levitical ministry on earth, since he is not a member of the Levitical order. But this does not in the least degree detract from the value of the sacrifice which he actually made. The Levitical priests minister in an earthly tabernacle which is only a *copy and shadow of the heavenly things* (v. 5). The derivative and inferior nature of the earthly tabernacle is proved by an appeal to the words of Ex. 25[40]: "See that thou make them after their pattern, which hath been shewed thee in the mount." God is here represented as showing Moses in a vision the ideal sanctuary in the heavens and telling him to use it as a model for the construction of the earthly tabernacle. The same line of thought is found in the Book of Wisdom (9[8]). "Thou gavest command to build a sanctuary in thy holy mountain, and an altar in the city of thy habitation, a copy of the holy tabernacle which thou preparedst aforehand from the beginning."

The metaphor of the *shadow* goes back in its origin to Plato's famous parable of the cave-dwellers in the seventh book of the *Republic.* In this parable Plato pictures mankind shut up in a kind of dungeon or cave with their faces turned to the wall at the back and so fixed that they are unable to move them round. Across the front of the cave figures are continually passing but all the prisoners can see are the shadows which their forms cast upon the wall on which their gaze is set. If the prisoners were released and taken out of the cave, their eyes would be blinded with excess of light. The parable is easy to read. Mankind dwells in the prison-house of sense, and sees only the shadows and reflections of the true realities under conditions of time and space. Plato's parable represents exactly the position taken up by the writer of Hebrews.

Under the covenant of the O.T. men lived in the land of shadows, seeing only the inferior earthly copies of the heavenly realities. Christ has brought them out of the cave of shadows and given them the great realities. A similar argument is used in 9[23] and 10[1].

6–13. The New Covenant. It follows from what has been said that there is a radical difference between the Levitical system of the O.T. and the work of Jesus Christ. In the work of Christ we pass from the realm of shadows into the world of reality, and he may be said, therefore, to have established a new covenant between God and man. This new covenant is superior to the old because the divine promises upon which it rests are superior to those which formed the basis of the Levitical system. The *better promises* are described in the quotation from Jeremiah which follows. But what right have we to speak about the institution of a new relationship between God and man? What right have we to pass judgment upon the divine revelation contained in the Jewish Law? What right have we to speak of it as superseding? In reply to questions such as these, the writer advances one of the most adroit and skillful arguments in the Epistle. The O.T. itself bears witness to the failure of the Jewish Law. God himself pronounced judgment upon it when he gave Jeremiah the promise of a new covenant. If the first covenant had been above all criticism, there would have been no room for a second. All through the divine promise to Jeremiah there runs the note of criticism on the old order. In passing judgment upon the Jewish Law, therefore, and challenging its finality, we are only doing what God himself has done. We claim that the new covenant prophesied by Jeremiah has been fulfilled in the new relationship established between God and man by Jesus Christ.

The quotation is taken from Jer. 31[31-34] and follows the LXX version, though, except in one clause, this is in substantial agreement with the Hebrew. The one difference occurs in the clause in v. 9, *And I regarded them not, saith the Lord,* where the Hebrew reads, "although I was a husband to them, saith the Lord." Some question has been raised by modern scholars as to whether the quotation forms an authentic part of the prophecy of Jeremiah (the issue is discussed by Peake in the Century Bible edition of *Jeremiah,* vol. ii, pp. 101–103), but this is quite irrelevant to our present purpose, as the passage formed undoubtedly an integral part of Jeremiah at the time when this Epistle was written.

The main points in the quotation are: (1) The introductory words in which the writer describes the reproach of God against the people of Israel (v. 8). (2) The divine promise to establish a new covenant with the nation (v. 8). (3) The new covenant will differ in character from the old covenant established after the release of the Israelites from Egypt (v. 9). (4) The character of the new covenant (vv. 10, 11). The old covenant was external. It was written on tables of stone. The new covenant will be inscribed on the heart. Moreover, the old covenant was made with the nation as a whole: the new covenant will embrace individuals. The result will be that the knowledge of God will become universal. *All shall know me, from the least to the greatest of them.* (5) In consequence of this new attitude to God on the part of the people, he will blot out their transgressions (v. 12.)

The concluding verse of the chapter (v. 13) summarizes the argument. The fact that God speaks of the covenant as *new* implies that the former covenant is out of date and antiquated. And because it is out of date and antiquated it is now on the verge of decay. The O.T., therefore, contains within itself a prophecy that it is to be superseded by something higher and greater.

CHAPTER IX

The writer now proceeds to demonstrate the third point in his main theme. He has already shown that Christ is the ideal High Priest exercising his ministry in an ideal sanctuary. He now sets out to prove that he offered the ideal or perfect sacrifice. The chapter falls naturally into the following sections: (1) A description of the earthly tabernacle (vv. 1–5). (2) The fatal defects of its worship (vv. 6–10). (3) The ideal sacrifice offered by Christ (vv. 11–14). (4) The necessity and value of that sacrifice (vv. 15–22). (5) The relation between the ideal sacrifice and the ideal sanctuary (vv. 23–28).

1–5. The Description of the Earthly Tabernacle. The contrast between the old and new covenants is developed in the account which is now given of the tabernacle which is called *a sanctuary of this world* in contrast to the heavenly sanctuary which was the scene of the ministry of Christ.

It was not because it lacked the means of worship that the old covenant failed. On the contrary, the tabernacle was magnificently equipped with the most exquisite and ornate furnishings. It contained (1) the candlestick, i.e., a golden lamp-stand with seven lamps (Ex. 25[31-40]), which stood in front of the sacred table. (2) The table itself (Ex. 25[23-30]). It was made of acacia wood overlaid with pure gold and with a golden crown around it. (3) The shewbread, literally, bread of the setting forth (Ex. 25[30] Lev. 24[5-9]). The shewbread consisted of twelve cakes which were set out in two rows on the table of the Lord. Only Aaron and his sons were allowed to eat these sacred cakes, though on one occasion (1 Sam. 21[4-6]), which is referred to by Jesus (Mk. 2[26]), David, when he and his men were hungry, ate "the shewbread, which it is not lawful to eat save for the priests, and gave also to them that were with him." Such was the furniture of the first division of the tabernacle known as the holy place.

The holy place was separated by a veil (Ex. 26[31-33]) from the more sacred part of the tabernacle, which is called "the Holy of Holies" and is the innermost sanctuary. The contents of the holy of holies are enumerated as follows: (1) The golden censer. There is some doubt, however, whether this is an accurate translation of the Greek word, which may also mean "the altar of incense." As there is no reference to a golden censer in the O.T. most modern scholars think that the marginal reading of the R.V., "altar of incense," is to be preferred. There is a difficulty, however, in this theory because the altar of incense belonged to the holy place and not to the holy of holies (Ex. 37[25-29]). To minimize the difficulty which thus arises some scholars argue that the phrasing of Hebrews, *the holy of holies having a golden altar of incense,* need not imply that the altar was placed in the holy of holies, but may simply mean that the altar was the means of approach to the inner sanctuary. It is interesting to note that the author of Hebrews is not the only writer who connects the altar with the holy of holies. It is definitely placed in the holy of holies by the Apocalypse of Baruch. Very possibly there were two distinct traditions with regard to the location of the altar. (2) The ark of the covenant (Ex. 25[10-12]) was a box made of acacia wood and covered with gold both outside and inside. (3) A golden pot holding manna (Ex. 16[32-35]). This was a memorial of the gift of manna in the wilderness, "that they may see the bread wherewith I fed you in the wilderness, when I brought you forth from the land of Egypt." (4) Aaron's rod that budded (Num. 17[1-10]), which was a symbol that the priesthood belonged to the tribe of Levi. (5) The tables of the covenant (Deut. 10[2-8]), i.e., the tables of stone on which the commandments were written. (6) The cherubim of glory over the mercy-seat (Ex. 25[17-22]). The mercy-seat was the lid of the ark, and was a square slab made of wood. It was sprinkled with blood on the day of atonement, and hence it obtained its name "means of propitiation" (this is the literal interpretation of the Greek word), or mercy-seat. The cherubim were two winged figures placed on each side of the ark. They symbolized the presence of God, and the mercy-seat indicated his compassion and readiness to forgive sin.

The contents of the tabernacle were, therefore, rich in meaning, but the writer of Hebrews says that it is impossible for him to discuss the significance of the symbolism.

6–10. The Defects of the Tabernacle from a Religious Point of View. But in spite of the wealth of its equipment and the rich symbolism connected with it, the tabernacle was seriously defective. It failed to establish a real communion between man and God. This becomes evident when we consider the arrangements which were made for worship. There were two types: (1) the worship connected with the holy place, (2) the worship connected with the holy of holies. The holy place is the scene of ordinary worship. The priests enter it regularly day by day to offer the ordinary sacrifices. But the inner shrine—the holy of holies—is only entered once a year by the high priest who makes blood offerings both for his own personal sins and for those of the people. The word translated *errors* (v. 7) is a special term and denotes sins of ignorance—sins which have been committed unwittingly. This arrangement was ordained by the Holy Spirit (v. 8) to show that there was no free access into the presence of God under the order of worship connected with the tabernacle. The right of approach was confined to the high priest on one solitary occasion in the year. Moreover, the arrangement is a kind of parable which is intended to teach us a lesson (v. 9), and the lesson is this: The gifts and sacrifices offered by the priests cannot possibly make the conscience of the worshipers perfect, since they are external ordinances and do not therefore affect the inner spirit of men, because they only deal with questions of food and drink and actual washings. They have, therefore, only a temporary value and have been imposed *until a time of reformation*, i.e., until the new covenant with its new order is established.

The point of the paragraph is this: The Jewish Law broke down on two fundamental issues. One purpose of religion is to secure access to God, and Judaism failed in achieving this end, since it only provided for a rare and occasional communion on the part of the high priest alone. Another purpose of religion is to discover the means of moral regeneration. And here too Judaism failed, since its regulations and ordinances were little more than external acts of ritual and never touched the conscience and the inner life. Judaism, therefore, is a temporary makeshift, not a final religion.

11–14. The Ideal Sacrifice Offered by Christ. The writer now proceeds to show how Christ has made good the defects in the Jewish Law. As Moffatt puts it, "Christ came on the scene and all was changed." He became the High Priest of the happier age (*the good things*) that was to be. It is a little uncertain (since the MSS. vary) whether the writer means "the happier age that was to be" or "the happier age which has now been realized." The same phrase occurs in 10[1], where the reference is unmistakably to the future, but that does not necessarily imply that the writer must have said the same thing here, as the words are used in a different context. Many scholars think that "the happier age which has now been realized" is what he wrote here. From the writer's standpoint the realization of the *good things* was no longer a future dream. It had already come to pass, and was the inheritance into which every Christian entered.

The writer now produces the facts which constitute his argument to prove that where Judaism failed, Christ had succeeded. His success was due to two things: (1) He entered into the heavenly sanctuary—not into the holy of holies of the tabernacle like an ordinary high priest, but into the ideal sanctuary in the heavens—a sanctuary not made with hands and not belonging to the world of created things. Many of the Christian Fathers took the phrase *through the greater and more perfect tabernacle* (v. 11) to refer to the perfection of the human nature of Christ (cf. 10[20]), but it is very difficult to get this interpretation out of the text. The explanation given above is much more in line with the writer's general argument in this section of the Epistle. (2) He offered the perfect sacrifice—*his own blood*—and not an imperfect sacrifice like that of goats and calves. Moreover, this sacrifice which Christ offered needed no repetition like the sacrifices of the Jewish Law. It was offered once for all and wrought an eternal redemption. The effect produced by the sacrifice of Christ, therefore, transcended in value the sacrifices of the Jewish Law.

The writer of Hebrews does not deny that the ordinary sacrifices had a value of a kind. They *sanctify unto the cleanness of the flesh* (v. 13). In this phrase he refers to the type of sacrifice described in Num. 19. There were certain things, e.g., contact with a dead body, which rendered a man ceremonially unclean. The law of purification required that a red heifer should be slain and its blood sprinkled seven times toward the sanctuary. The body and blood of the beast were then burned with cedar wood, hyssop, and scarlet wool. The ashes were mixed with water, and this was sprinkled on the body of the man who had been contaminated. But this rite affected only ceremonial uncleanness and merely cleansed the body. The sacrifice of Christ, however, was much more potent in its efficacy. It *cleansed the conscience* from dead works to serve the living God.

In v. 14 the writer gives the grounds upon which he attaches supreme value to the sacrifice offered by Christ. He assumes that sacrifice is an eternal necessity. He assumes also that the shedding of blood is essential to sacrifice. (Cf. the statement in v. 22, "apart from shedding of blood there is no remission.") These are the two postulates upon which his argument is built up. On the assumption that these postulates are true the writer argues as follows: (1) The value of the sacrifice of Christ rests upon the fact that he offered himself and not an external sacrifice. It was the surrender of his own life that counted. (2) This sacrifice fulfilled the condition that the offering must be without blemish since he was "holy, guileless, undefiled, separated from sinners." (3) It was *offered through the eternal Spirit.* There is some doubt as to the exact meaning of this phrase. The translation of the R.V. seems to suggest that by eternal Spirit the Holy Spirit is meant, but this is improbable owing to the phrasing of the words in the original Greek. It is generally assumed that the meaning of the phrase is identical with that of the words in 7^{16}, "after the power of an endless life." The efficacy of the sacrifice of Christ depended on the fact that he was not mortal, like an earthly priest, but possessed a spirit which was eternal. He belonged to an eternal order and his sacrifice therefore had eternal value.

15–22. The Necessity and Value of the Sacrifice of Christ. The argument in this paragraph is difficult to follow because there is a play on the Greek word translated *covenant* which it is not easy for an English reader to understand. The Greek word may mean either a covenant or a will or testament, and the writer passes from one to the other and bases his argument on both. He begins by emphasizing again the idea which is the theme of 8^{6-13}, that Christ is the Mediator of a new covenant.

But the making of a covenant does not necessitate a death. There is no mention of a sacrificial death, for instance, in Jeremiah's prophecy of the new covenant quoted in 8^{8-12}. And yet the writer of Hebrews regards the death of Christ as essential to the new covenant which he has established: *A death having taken place for the redemption of the transgressions that were under the first covenant* (v. 15). How can the necessity for this be proved? In two ways, argues the writer. (1) The word *covenant* also signifies a "will" or "testament," and a will only comes into force when the testator is dead (vv. 15–18). While the testator is still alive the will does not operate. So the death of Christ was necessary, in order that his testament might come into effect. (2) By a swift transition to the other meaning of the word (vv. 19–22), the writer argues that even the first covenant was dedicated by the shedding of blood. The reference is to the statement in Ex. 24^{3-11}. After sacrificing burnt-offerings of oxen unto the Lord, "Moses took half of the blood, and put it in basons; and half of the blood he sprinkled on the altar. And he took the book of the covenant, and read in the audience of the people: and they said, All that the Lord hath spoken will we do, and be obedient. And Moses took the blood, and sprinkled it on the people, and said, Behold the blood of the covenant, which the Lord hath made with you." The writer seems to be quoting from memory, for he makes several additions to the narrative in Exodus. (1) He speaks of the sacrifice of goats, which are not mentioned in Exodus. (2) There is no reference in Exodus to *water, scarlet wool, and hyssop.* (3) It is not stated in Exodus that the book was sprinkled. But in spite of the variance in the details, the main point of the contention of Hebrews is fully proved—sacrifice was certainly used in the establishment of the first covenant. It is strange that the writer does not quote the words used by Jesus in the institution of the Lord's Supper, "This cup is the new covenant in my blood" (1 Cor. 11^{25}), but it is in keeping with the absence of any distinct reference to the Eucharist in the Epistle.

The paragraph ends with a general statement. *I may almost say, all things are cleansed with blood, and apart from shedding of blood there is no remission* (v. 22). The writer qualifies his general statement by the phrase, *I may almost say,* because under the Jewish Law those who were too poor to offer animal sacrifice might be assured that their sins were remitted without it. With this qualification, however, the writer regards it as a fundamental axiom of religion that sacrifice is essential to the remission of sin.

23–28. The Relation Between the Ideal Sacrifice and the Ideal Sanctuary. The writer now returns to the Platonic argument which he has used with such cogency in $8^{1,2}$ (note, and see p. 1296a). The earthly sanctuary which is a copy of the heavenly had necessarily to be cleansed by the sacrifices offered under the Jewish Law. But the heavenly sanctuary needed better sacrifices than these, because an ideal sanctuary demands an ideal form of sacrifice. The sanctuary of Christ is not like the earthly tabernacle which was made by human hands and was only a shadow and reflection of the heavenly reality. It was the heavenly sanctuary itself, and when he entered it he came into the very presence of God. But now another question emerges: What right have we to assume that the sacrifice of Christ was final and will never be repeated? Wherein does it differ in this respect from the sacrifice offered by the high priest which needed to be repeated every year? In this paragraph the writer attempts to answer the question, and he uses two arguments to prove that the sacrifice of Christ was final and complete. (1) It has been already stated in v. 15 that the sacrifice availed for the redemption of the transgressions that were under the first covenant. It covered, therefore, all the past, or else Christ must *often have suffered since the foundation of the world.* And if it covered all the past, it may be assumed that it will cover the future too. (2) Death comes only once to men. It is always the final issue of life. Christ too was subject to the same law. He could be subject to death only once. In the case of men death is followed by judgment; in the case of Christ by his reappearance on earth in triumph. Moreover, there is no time left for the repetition of the sacrifice in the future. Christ died *at the end of the ages* (v. 26), and the final consummation is near at hand. Like practically all the other N.T. writers, our author firmly believes in the speedy return of Christ (cf. 10[37,38]).

CHAPTER X

The discussion of ch. 9 is continued in ch. 10. The chapter contains the following divisions: (1) The failure of the Jewish sacrifices and the finality of the sacrifice of Christ proved by the prophecy in Psa. 40 (vv. 1–10). (2) Further proof from the O.T. (vv. 11–18). (3) The moral appeal to the readers of the Epistle (vv. 19–25). (4) Words of warning (vv. 26–31). (5) Words of encouragement and hope (vv. 32–39).

1–10. The Failure of the Jewish Sacrifices and the Finality of the Sacrifice of Christ. In this paragraph the writer emphasizes again the futility of the sacrifices of the Levitical order and shows how they have been superseded by the perfect sacrifice of Christ. He uses five arguments (some of which are a repetition of the previous discussion) culminating in an appeal to the great statement in Psa. 40. (1) He begins by reiterating the argument based upon the Platonic philosophy which he has already used in 8[1, 2] (see notes). The Law is only the shadow and not the reality of the revelation which was to come in Jesus Christ. The O.T. was the shadow cast by the Christian faith before its advent. In Christianity the heavenly reality—the very truth of God—broke into human history (v. 1). (2) The facts themselves prove the inefficiency of the Jewish sacrifices (vv. 1, 2). There was no finality about them. They had to be constantly repeated. They never took away the sense of sin from the hearts of the worshipers. If they had been effectual, there would have been no need for their constant repetition. (3) All that the sacrifices could produce was an annual *remembrance of sins* (v. 3). Instead of removing sin, the Law only intensified the sense of sin. This is exactly the position taken by Paul. "Through the law cometh knowledge of sin" (Rom. 3[20]). "The law came in beside, that the trespass might abound" (Rom. 5[20]; cf. Rom. 4[15] 7[8] Gal. 3[19]). (4) The very nature of the sacrifices proves that they are invalid (v. 4). It is impossible that the blood of animal victims should be able to cleanse a guilty conscience. The sacrifices are external. There is no bond of communion between the offerer and the sacrifice, and consequently there is no moral element in it. (5) The new and most powerful argument in the passage is based upon the quotation from Psa. 40[6-8]. The writer follows the LXX version as usual, and it is the translation in this version which really gives him his argument. The first two lines in the original Hebrew differ substantially from the rendering in the Greek version. "Sacrifice and offering thou hast no delight in; mine ears hast thou opened." For the latter phrase the LXX reads, "But a body didst thou prepare for me"; and it is this line which constitutes the basis of the argument. The writer holds that the words of the psalmist represent the utterance of the Messiah when he comes into the world. The Messiah is depicted as asking the question, "What is the function for which I have been sent to the earth? What is the *rationale* of my mission?" And the answer comes: "God took no pleasure in the old sacrifices and offerings. His remedy for human need lay in a divine incarnation ('a body hast thou prepared for me'). Burnt-offerings and sacrifices for sin were not the object of God's desire. What God needed was entire obedience and consecration of spirit." And so the Messiah adds, "*I am come* in fulfillment of prophecy, for the whole of the Old Testament speaks of my Advent. 'In the roll of the book it is written of me'—I am come to consecrate a life of complete obedience to thee, O God." The whole passage, as interpreted by this writer, contains a striking contrast between the Jewish Law and the divine ideal of religion as it has been realized in Christianity. The former consisted of external sacrifices, the latter of an incarnate life of complete obedience to the will of God. Granted the accuracy of the LXX rendering of the passage (and this was admitted by all Greek-speaking Christians at the time), the argument is very powerful, especially for the first-century mind. The quotation contains a condemnation by the O.T. itself of the sacrificial system and a prophecy of the incarnation and the life of supreme obedience which are destined to supersede the Law in the new era of the Christian faith. The O.T. by the mouth of the psalmist abolishes the system of sacrifices and establishes the new type of religion introduced by Christ. The paragraph ends with the triumphant assertion that because Christ has fulfilled the will of God and offered a sacrifice which met the divine requirements as the Jewish sacrifice could not do, we *have been sanctified through the offering of the body of Jesus Christ once for all* (v. 10).

11–18. Further Proof from the Statements of the Old Testament. The writer introduces further arguments to prove the finality of the offering of Christ. The ordinary priests stand day by day in the Temple offering their sacrifices. "Their mighty labor," as Peake says, "like that of Sisyphus, ends always in nothing. The pathetic inefficiency of all the elaborate apparatus, this daily addition of naught to naught which at the end of the long centuries have mounted up to zero, is all the more striking in the light of Christ's sacrifice offered once only but effective forever." The finality of his sacrifice is proved by the fact that after it had been offered he triumphantly *sat down on the right hand of God*, thus showing that the whole purpose had been achieved and nothing more now remained to be done. The point is demonstrated by a fresh appeal to one of the writer's favorite psalms, which has already been cited in 1^{13} 5^{6} $7^{17, 21}$. The psalm (110^{1}) represents God as saying to the Messiah, "Sit thou at my right hand, until I make thine enemies thy footstool." The work is complete; all that remains is to wait for the final victory. The writer then clinches his argument by a reference to Jeremiah's prophecy of the new covenant previously cited in 8^{8-12}. On this occasion, however, the important fact lies not in the general prediction of the establishment of a new covenant but in the last phrase, *Their sins and their iniquities will I remember no more*. These words imply that the power of sin has been finally destroyed and that there is no further need of another offering. Therefore the sacrifice of Christ is final and complete and there is no need for any further offering for sin.

19–25. The Moral and Spiritual Appeal. Our faith should give us confidence for two reasons: (1) We are no longer like the Jewish people who had the right in the person of their high priest to enter the holy of holies only once a year. Christ has opened for us by his sacrifice a new and living way into the immediate presence of God (v. 20). He has passed through the veil which no longer now hides God from our eyes. *The veil was his flesh.* It is not easy to see exactly what the writer means by the last phrase. Some scholars have taken it to mean "through the incarnate life," and have argued that it was the fact that Christ took upon himself our human nature that broke down the barrier between God and man. The difficulty about this interpretation is that it is out of harmony with the whole purpose of the writer's argument, namely, to show that it is the *offered* life that opens the new way for men. It is better, therefore, to assume that the phrase refers not to the incarnate life of Christ but to his death. At death Christ passed through the veil of flesh into the immediate presence of God. (2) In Christ we have a great High Priest (v. 21) who has now been set in authority over the house of God, and to him we can come without dismay. But there are certain conditions which must be fulfilled before the approach is possible. We must come (a) with sincere hearts, (b) with the full assurance of faith, (c) with our conscience purged and cleansed, (d) with our bodies washed in pure water (v. 22). The allusion in the last clause is probably to Christian baptism. And faith should lead on to hope (v. 23), and, relying on the sure promise of God, we should cling with tenacity to the Christian hope which is part of our creed. Moreover, faith and hope should result in charity (v. 24). We should challenge one another to a life of love and service. We must not leave the Christian fellowship, for it is in fellowship that we gain the greatest stimulus to Christian service. It is obvious from the phrase, *as the custom of some is*, that there was a tendency in some quarters for Christians to drift away from the common life of the church. It may be that under stress of threatened persecution some of them thought they would avoid danger by ceasing to identify themselves with the Christian community: or possibly the writer is referring to people who left a small and struggling cause in the lurch (for that is what the word *forsaking* really means) in order to join a more flourishing church; or it may be that the reference is to men who, like many of the devotees of the Greek cults, thought when once they had been initiated that there was no further need for fellowship. But whatever may have been the type of people the writer has in mind, his words are a strong protest against individualism in religion. The church is as necessary for the individual as the individual is for the church.

26–31. The Penalty of Apostasy. Once more, as in 6^{4-8} (see notes), the writer pronounces the terrible doom which will fall on those who lapse from the faith. To the writer willful apostasy is a fatal and unforgivable sin. He justifies his position (1) by an appeal to the Law of Moses, which in Deut. 17^{2-7} definitely laid it down that in the case of willful transgression of the commandments of the Law, "thou shalt bring forth that man or that woman, which have done this evil thing . . . and thou shalt stone them with stones, that they die." How much more terrible will be the fate of the apostate, since he has trampled the Son of God under his feet, profaned the covenant sacrifice, and done despite to the gracious Spirit of God! (2) By an appeal to two O.T. texts which speak of God's punishment of sin. One of these is from Deut. 32[35], "Vengeance is mine, and recompence"—a text which is quoted by Paul in Rom. 12[19] with a different application. The second quotation occurs in two O.T. books, Deut. 32[36] and Psa. 135[14], "The Lord shall judge his people." The severity of the writer of Hebrews is due to the fact that apostasy was one of the greatest perils of the church in his time. This passage should be read in the light of the discussion of the problem in the notes on ch. 6.

32–39. Words of Encouragement and Hope. As in ch. 6, the writer follows his description of the fate of the apostates with a message of assurance and confidence (see 6[9]). The splendid history of the church in the past will be the guarantee of its final victory. It has already passed triumphantly through a severe testing time. It has endured a great conflict. It has been held up, as a public spectacle, to reproach. It has stood firm through the crisis. When some of its members were thrown into prison, it did not abandon them to their fate but had compassion on them. It took joyfully the confiscation of property. The translation of the next clause, which gives the reason for the readiness to endure the spoiling of goods, is uncertain. The rendering of the R.V., *knowing that ye yourselves have a better possession* (v. 34), seems to be weak and inadequate. The marginal translation is preferable, *ye have your own selves for a better possession.* The soul is the highest human possession and is far more valuable than property. The persecuted Christians rejoiced in confiscation because they felt that spoliation of property made for the welfare of the soul.

Such heroic endurance in the past ought to nerve the church to meet the trials of the present. You must not through cowardice now lose the reward of your earlier sacrifices. It will not be a long struggle. For, as the prophet Habakkuk said of the appointed time, "Though it tarry, wait for it; because it will surely come, it will not delay" (2[3]). The interpretation which the writer puts on the words of the prophet is of course, "The coming of the Lord is at hand, and we must wait with courage till he comes."

The following words of the prophetic oracle are still more appropriate to the situation: *My righteous one shall live by faith.* This is the text upon which Paul lays such stress in Rom. 1[17] and which he makes the basis of his doctrine of justification by faith. In Habakkuk faith meant loyalty or steadfastness—and this meaning of the word is more appropriate in Hebrews. Then follows a note of warning: *If he shrink back, my soul hath no pleasure in him.* The whole quotation is taken from the LXX, which differs considerably from the Hebrew. The writer reverses the order of the last two clauses. The paragraph concludes with the reassuring statement: "We are not like the men of whom the prophet speaks. We do not shrink back from the faith into destruction. We are men of faith and our faith will save our souls."

CHAPTER XI

The main argument of the Epistle is now concluded. The writer has proved his theme that Christ is the ideal High Priest who offered the ideal sacrifice in the ideal sanctuary. He now proceeds to the more practical part of the Epistle, and in ch. 11 he takes up the word *faith* with which he concluded his appeal in ch. 10 and proceeds to define and illustrate its working in the history of the past.

1, 2. The Definition of Faith. Faith is defined as the confidence that our hopes will be realized and the conviction of the reality of the unseen world. This definition differs from the conception of faith which we find in the epistles of Paul. To Paul faith is the surrender of the soul to Christ. To the writer of Hebrews it means (1) the full assurance that the Christian hope and the promises of God will be fulfilled, and (2) the belief that the unseen world is the supreme reality. Cf. the statement in v. 27, "He endured as seeing him who is invisible." The writer in the remainder of the chapter illustrates his interpretation of the meaning of the faith by appealing to history.

3. Faith and the Creation. We believe that the world was created by the fiat of God. We reject all other theories of its origin. The visible universe was not, as the Epicureans maintain, made out of the fortuitous concourse of atoms. No materialistic explanation of the origin of the world is adequate. Nature cannot explain itself. This is the meaning of the difficult phrase, *so that what is seen hath not been made out of things which do appear.* God, and not mere matter, is the source of everything.

4. The Faith of Abel. It was faith that enabled Abel to offer a better sacrifice than Cain. The writer does not explain in what the superiority of Abel's offering consisted. He probably, however, means to imply that faith created in the mind of Abel an instinct that God required not merely cereal offerings but a blood-sacrifice (Gen. 4[4]). Otherwise we must assume that the value of Abel's offering lay in the fact that it was more costly than that of Cain and so involved greater self-denial.

5, 6. The Faith of Enoch. The writer accepts the common tradition based on Gen. 5[24] that Enoch was translated into heaven without passing through death, and says that this miracle was the reward for his faith and piety. There was another tradition, however, which is preserved by Philo, that the translation was simply the conversion of Enoch from a life of vice to a life of virtue. The reference to Enoch ends with a further analysis of the conception of faith. Faith involves two convictions: one, that God exists, the other, that he recompenses all who are in quest of him.

7. The Faith of Noah. The essential point of Noah's faith is described in the phrase, *warned of God concerning things not seen as yet.* This is the first real illustration of that part of the definition in v. 1 which describes faith as the realization of things not seen.

8–19. The Faith of Abraham. Abraham is the supreme example of faith. His faith is illustrated (1) by his journey to the promised land (vv. 8–10); (2) by his confidence that God would give him sons in accordance with his promise (vv. 11, 12); (3) by his sacrifice of Isaac (17–19). The first illustration, as the writer develops it, is a magnificent example of faith. The call of God comes to Abraham in Ur of the Chaldees to leave home and kindred and go forth as a pioneer in quest of the promised land and the city of God—the city which has the true foundations, whose architect and builder is God.

The writer elaborates the story of Genesis, which contains no account of the vision of the ideal city. According to a later tradition, however, which has been preserved in the Apocalypse of Baruch, Abraham was shown a vision of the celestial city during the incident described in Gen. 15.

The second illustration is concerned with the faith which resulted in the miraculous birth of Isaac (cf. Gen. 15[2-21]). It is significant, and in keeping with the general tone of Hebrews, that stress is laid on the faith of Sarah and not merely on that of Abraham. In the reference to the same subject in the epistles of Paul (Rom. 4[19]) though the faith of Abraham is strongly accentuated, there is no reference to the faith of Sarah.

The next paragraph (vv. 13–16) is an interlude in the argument. It contains a general reflection by the writer on the faith of the patriarchs. The vision that came to them was a vision far too great to be realized in their day. In obedience to faith they went out on their quest but they never realized the divine promises, though they saw them dimly hovering in the distance and hailed them from afar. They acknowledged that they were only strangers and wanderers seeking the promised city. They might have given up the search and returned to their old country. But to do that would have been to abandon their ideal. It is plain, therefore, that their quest was for a city which would not be found on earth but could only be realized in heaven. God recognized their faith and bestowed on them a celestial city.

The final illustration of the faith of Abraham (vv. 17–19) is found in the sacrifice of Isaac (Gen. 22[1-18]). Though Isaac was Abraham's only son (Ishmael is excluded because he was not included in the divine promises), and though the future depended upon him, yet when he was put to the test (R.V. *being tried*) Abraham did not shrink from obeying what he took to be the call of God to offer him as the supreme sacrifice. He was confident that as God had given Isaac in the first instance by a miracle, he would, rather than break his promises, restore him to life again by another miracle. The last phrase of v. 19 may be paraphrased thus: "Abraham, figuratively speaking, received Isaac back from death, though he did not actually die." There may also be a hidden reference to the resurrection of Christ in the words, which may be translated, "Abraham received him back by what was a parable of the resurrection of Christ," though the explanation seems to read into the text more than it actually contains.

20–22. The Faith of the Patriarchs. The writer passes very lightly over the faith of the other patriarchs. He cites two illustrations of blessings pronounced by Isaac and Jacob respectively on their descendants assuring them that the promises of God to Abraham would be fulfilled for them and their children. The last phrase in v. 21, *He worshipped, leaning upon the top of his staff*, differs from the Hebrew narrative in Gen. 47[31] which reads, "And Israel bowed himself upon the bed's head," and follows the LXX, which substitutes the word "staff" for "bed's head." The faith of Joseph consisted in the conviction that the Israelites would be delivered from the thraldom of Egypt and that his body would be laid to rest in the Holy Land (Gen. 50[24-26]).

23–29. The Faith of Moses. The writer finds many more illustrations of faith in the career of Moses. (1) There is the faith of his parents who saved his life in infancy (v. 23). (2) There is his act of self-renunciation by which he declined the royal position and prerogatives and identified himself with his own outcast race (vv. 24, 25). The motive which actuated him is given in v. 26, *accounting the reproach of Christ* (or the Messiah) *greater riches than the treasures of Egypt*—a phrase which seems to assume that it was faith in the Messiah which was the guiding principle of Moses. The writer by using these words makes Moses an example to the men of his own generation, who in the persecutions were called upon to suffer *the reproach of Christ.* (3) The third illustration of the faith of Moses consists in his flight to Midian (Ex. 2[14f.]). The point of this illustration is more difficult to explain, especially as the phrase, *not fearing the wrath of the king,* seems to contradict the statements of Exodus, where it is stated: "When Pharaoh heard this thing he sought to slay Moses. But Moses fled from the face of Pharaoh." In view of the difficulty of finding a real example of faith in the retreat to Midian and also in view of the apparent discrepancy between the statements of Hebrews and Exodus, many scholars have attempted to find in the phrase, *he forsook Egypt,* an allusion to the Exodus itself. There is, however, an overwhelming objection to this view because the order of the verses compels us to find in v. 27 an event prior to the keeping of the Passover in v. 28, and the retreat to Midian is the only incident which meets the requirement. The real explanation seems to be this: Moses at the moment was smarting under a sense of failure. His own people had turned against him. He had incurred the enmity of the king. He was forced to abandon the enterprise upon which he had set his heart. It looked as if the opportunity of emancipating his people had gone. And yet he did not lose heart. In spite of disappointment and disillusionment he kept his faith. He knew that Pharaoh could not finally thwart the divine purpose and so *he endured as seeing him who is invisible* (v. 27). As Peake says: "He rose above the realm of sight and his steadfast courage grew strong in contemplation of the unseen. For the courage to abandon work on which the whole heart is set and accept inaction cheerfully as the will of God is of the rarest and highest kind, and can be created and sustained only by the clearest spiritual vision." (4) The next act of faith (v. 28) is seen in Moses' obedience to commands of God (Ex. 12[12-48]) in connection with the instructions to keep the Passover and sprinkle blood on the lintels and doorposts *that the destroyer of the firstborn might not touch them.* (5) The fifth and last illustration of the faith of Moses (v. 29) consists in the passage of the Red Sea.

30, 31. Two further illustrations of faith are given in these verses: (1) The collapse of the walls of Jericho (Josh. 6[1-20]). Here it is the faith of a whole people that secures the victory. (2) The faith of Rahab—the faith of an individual.

32–38. A Summary Statement of Later Illustrations of Faith. The writer now abandons the attempt to compile a further list of particular illustrations of faith and contents himself with a general statement. He alludes first of all to the exploits of the four great judges—Gideon, Barak, Samson, and Jephthah—and then to the achievements of David, Samuel, and the prophets; and then in a series of telling phrases, he gives a list of their mighty acts of faith. Some of these phrases, e.g., *wrought righteousness, obtained promises, from weakness were made strong, waxed mighty in war, turned to flight armies of aliens* are quite general, and apply to many of the heroes of whom the writer is thinking. Others, however, are far more specific, and contain a reference to some definite event in the history of Israel. *Stopped the mouths of lions* refers to Daniel (ch. 6); *quenched the power of fire,* to Shadrach, Meshach, and Abed-nego (Dan. 3); *women received their dead by a resurrection,* to the widow of Zarephath (1 Kings 18[8-24]) and the Shunammite (2 Kings 4[18-37]); *others were tortured* (literally, "beaten to death," or "broken on the wheel"), to the martyrdom of Eleazar and the seven brothers recorded in 2 Macc. 6 and 7; *they were stoned,* to Zechariah (2 Chron. 24[20-22]) and to the tradition that this fate befell Jeremiah in Egypt; *were sawn asunder,* to the tradition mentioned in the Ascension of Isaiah (5[1-14]) that Isaiah was sawn in two with a wooden saw during the reign of Manasseh; vv. 36–38 contain a general reference to the sufferings of the faithful Jews during the persecution of Antiochus Epiphanes (see intro. to Daniel) when they were harried and hunted into the mountains and forced to take refuge in holes and caves.

39, 40. The Epilogue. All these heroes of the past won a reputation for faith and realized some of the divine promises. But the final promise—the realization of the Messianic kingdom—was not granted to them. The writer frankly admits that their faith did not obtain the supreme reward, and in that respect, at any rate, it failed. But the failure was not due to any defect in them; it was simply a necessary condition in the working out of the divine purpose. The reward was only deferred till it was possible for Christ to come. We have entered into the great inheritance of faith, and through us, and the revelation that has been vouchsafed to us, the faith of the heroes of the past has been perfected. The realization of the hopes of the faithful in Israel's history depends upon our loyalty and steadfastness, since *they without us cannot be made perfect.*

CHAPTER XII

Ch. 12 opens with an urgent appeal based upon the record of the achievements of faith in ch. 11 (vv. 1, 2) and then proceeds to discuss the meaning and significance of suffering (vv. 3–11). This is followed by an appeal to the church to strive to attain the Christian ideal (vv. 12–17); and, finally, Christians are warned of the great responsibility which the establishment of the new covenant throws upon them and the terrible doom which will fall upon those who are disloyal and unfaithful (vv. 18–29).

1, 2. The Urgent Appeal to Run the Christian Race. The writer in this paragraph depicts the Christian life as a race in the amphitheater. The metaphor is borrowed from the Greek games. There is the arena surrounded by tiers of seats which are thronged by spectators who watch the various contests and cheer on their chosen champions. The conditions of success are described. The runners throw off all their superfluous garments, that they may be free to exert their maximum strength and gain their maximum speed. Their footsteps never flag and their efforts are never relaxed. Their eyes are fixed steadily upon the goal and they strain every nerve to win the prize. The use of this metaphor seems to have been very popular and there are frequent references to it in the N.T. Cf. 1 Cor. 9^{24-27}, where Paul draws lessons both from the footrace and the boxing match.

Every phrase in vv. 1, 2, is based on the metaphor, and every phrase is used with telling effect. As the amphitheater is surrounded by tiers of seats from which the spectators watch the game, so the arena of life is surrounded by a *great cloud of witnesses.* The allusion, of course, is to the list of heroes enumerated in the previous chapter who are represented as being intensely interested in the struggle of the early church, since they without us cannot be made perfect. To succeed in the Christian race we *must lay aside every weight, and the sin which doth so easily beset us.* The meaning of the last phrase has been much disputed, as the Greek word is never found elsewhere and its significance is uncertain. The best suggestion is that it means "close fitting," or "clinging closely round," and refers to the hampering effect of sin, which, like a clinging robe, impedes the steps of the runner of the heavenly race. *Let us run with patience. Patience* here means "steadfastness," or "loyalty," and the phrase should be translated, therefore, "Let us run with unflinching purpose." *Looking unto Jesus.* As the eyes of the runner in the race are fixed upon its goal, so the eyes of the Christian must be fixed upon Christ. *The author and perfecter of our faith.* The word translated *author* is found also in 2^{10}, where Christ is described as the author of salvation. The phrase used here is very significant. Christ is not only the author or founder of the Christian faith. He is the completer or finisher as well. He can never, therefore, be superseded. He has spoken not only the first word but the last word too. Christianity, therefore, is final in a sense in which the O.T. revelation could never be. Hence the Christian life must be an *Imitatio Christi.* But what is it in Christ that ought to dominate the vision of the Christian? The answer to this question is given in the following phrase, *who for the joy that was set before him endured the cross, despising shame.* We should interpret the word *joy* by giving it the sense which Bergson ascribes to it. "Nature," says Bergson, "has set up a sign which apprises us every time our activity is in full expansion. That sign is joy. True joy is always an emphatic signal of the triumph of life. Wherever joy is, creation has been, and the richer the creation the greater the joy. True joy is always the symbol of creative work." It was because the work of redemption was the greatest creative act ever wrought that the joy of Jesus was supreme, and it was this sense of joy that enabled him to despise the shame and endure the cross.

3–11. The Meaning of Suffering. The reference to the suffering of Christ in v. 2 leads the writer on to discuss the meaning of the sufferings of the Christians of his day. He has already in 2^{10} and $5^{8,9}$ dealt with some aspects of the problem and shown how Christ himself was made perfect through suffering and learned obedience by the things which he suffered. He now proceeds to apply this principle to the sufferings which befell the Christians of his time under stress of persecution. "Take Christ as your example," he urges. "Think of all the sufferings which he endured at the hands of his enemies, and it will keep your hearts from fainting and failing (v. 3). His sufferings were far greater than yours, for you have not yet had to shed your blood, as he did, in resistance to evil (v. 4). You must not forget the appeal which God makes to you in the words of the book of Proverbs, where suffering is described as the chastening or discipline of the Lord. The Lord disciplines the man he loves and scourges everyone upon whom he bestows the name of son (vv. 5, 6). It is therefore for the sake of discipline that you have to endure these sufferings. God is treating you as sons, and discipline is a necessary element in such a relationship. If you were not sons, there would have been no ground for this remedial discipline; but the very conception of the Fatherhood of God implies the necessity of discipline (vv. 7, 8). If discipline were absent, it would mean that God did not regard you as sons. We recognize the right of earthly parents to punish their children for their good; ought we not to submit to the Father of our spirits when he disciplines us for our advantage that we may attain eternal life? (V. 9.) Our fathers exercised discipline over us during our youth for their own ends and according to their own standards and ideas (which may sometimes have been erroneous), but God never makes mistakes; his discipline is perfect and the end which he has in view is to make us partakers of his own holiness (v. 10). Discipline always seems at the time to be irksome and painful, but when it is divine discipline it produces in its final issue a life of peace and righteousness."

12–17. An Exhortation to Pursue the Christian Ideal. "Since suffering is a discipline, we must not allow ourselves to be dismayed by it. We must not let our hands hang listlessly down or our knees grow weak. We must encourage the flagging energies of fainting souls and try to smooth the path of life for them, that the road may be made easier for them, so that those who are lame may not have their feet dislocated by the rough places in the way (vv. 12, 13). We must always set before ourselves the two supreme elements in the Christian ideal—peace and consecration (v. 14)—and we must watch carefully lest any of us may miss the grace of God. And we must strive after these virtues not only for our own personal lives but for the life of the Christian community as well. We must always be on our guard lest the poisonous root of bitterness spring up and contaminate the church. We must see to it that no member of the church is guilty of immorality or lives a profane life like Esau. Esau should be a warning to us. For a single plate of food he sold his birthright (v. 16). He lost his blessing forever though he afterward made the most strenuous efforts to regain it. He found no place of repentance" (v. 17).

Three interpretations of the last phrase are possible. The words, *though he sought it diligently with tears,* may be connected with the first clause of the verse. In this case it is the blessing which he seeks to regain in vain. Or they may be connected with the clause which the R.V. puts in brackets. *He found no place of repentance, though he sought it diligently with tears.* In this case we must suppose that Esau had committed the unpardonable sin for which no forgiveness was possible, and he becomes an illustration of the terrible words of 6^{4-6} and $10^{26, 27}$. Another alternative is suggested in the rendering in the A.S.V., which makes a change of mind in Isaac the thing that Esau sought in vain (see R.V. mg.).

18–29. The Old Covenant and the New. The warning words of the previous paragraph are now driven home by a contrast between the responsibilities involved in the two covenants, the old and the new. The character of the old covenant is first described in sensuous images. "You Christians," says the writer, "have not come, as Moses and your forefathers did, to an earthly mountain like Mount Sinai, that blazed with fire and had its head shrouded in mist and darkness, while a terrible storm raged all about it. Out of the tempest came the blare of a trumpet and a Voice so awful that men prayed that it might never be repeated. Such sanctity was attached to the mountain that no one was allowed to approach it. If even a beast committed unconscious trespass upon it, it was immediately stoned to death. So full of dread was the scene that even Moses, to whom the law of God was to be revealed, trembled with fear and said, 'I am terrified and afraid.' " Such is the picture which the writer draws of the circumstances under which the old covenant was given to Israel. The unapproachable mountain stands as the symbol of an unapproachable God (vv. 18–21).

The writer now turns to the other picture. "You Christians have not come to a mount of terror like Sinai, but to Mount Zion and the eternal city of the living God—the New Jerusalem in heaven. It is no scene of dread that meets your eyes. The vision you see is the vision of a festal assembly of angels and a great concourse of the first-born sons of God whose names are inscribed in the register of heaven. Amid this great assembly stands God the Judge of all men, and with him are the spirits of just men who have been made perfect, and Christ himself the mediator of the new covenant, who has offered the perfect sacrifice, the sacrifice which is far superior to that which Abel offered in the patriarchal age" (vv. 22–24).

Such is the contrast which the writer draws between the two pictures—the picture of the horrors of Mount Sinai and the picture of the bliss and joy of heaven. In the latter vision there are some difficulties of exegesis. In the R.V. the phrase, *to the general assembly and church of the first-born*, suggests that the writer links with the *innumerable hosts of angels* a vast company of the redeemed gathered together in a heavenly church. There are difficulties, however, about the interpretation. (1) There is no connecting article before the second phrase, and it looks, therefore, as if the second clause stood in apposition to the first. For this reason it seems probable that *the general assembly and church of the first-born* further describes and defines *the innumerable hosts of angels*. The word translated *church* need not be taken in its technical sense and may simply mean "gathering." (2) The human elements in the heavenly throng are subsequently described as *the spirits of just men made perfect*, and it seems improbable that the redeemed saints would be mentioned twice in the picture. For these reasons it seems better to translate the clauses thus: "to innumerable hosts of angels in festive gathering, the assembly of the first-born whose names are registered as citizens of heaven."

The next paragraph contains an appeal based on the two visions which have just been described (vv. 25–29): "See that ye refuse not to listen to the divine voice. Remember the fate of those who spurned the commands which God uttered at Sinai. How much greater will be the penalty that will fall on those of us who despise the voice that comes to us from heaven! At Sinai God's voice shook the earth (Ex. 19^{18}), and the prophet Haggai ($2^{6, 21}$) has told us that another earthquake will shake the world at the end of time: 'Once more I will make the earth and the heavens tremble.' That prophecy has yet to be fulfilled—as the phrase *once more* clearly denotes, and this shaking will be final. In this final shock all material things will perish; only the spiritual realities will remain unshaken. We belong to a kingdom which cannot be affected by the convulsion which will destroy the material universe. Let us be thankful that when the kingdoms of this world perish in the last catastrophe, the realm to which we belong will come scathless out of the fires. Let us serve God faithfully, and let us do it with fear and awe, for our God is a consuming fire and in this fire all that is unworthy and impure will be destroyed."

In this last phrase the writer emphasizes the moral severity and sternness of God who never fails to inflict punishment on the sinner. Some scholars see in the phrase *consuming fire* an allusion to the cleansing and purifying influence of fire, and they suggest the inference that the final end of punishment is always remedial—but there is nothing in the phrase itself or in the context to warrant the interpretation, which seems quite foreign to the general teaching of the Epistle.

CHAPTER XIII

Ch. 13 is a postscript to the Epistle. It may be divided as follows: (1) Sundry counsels to the members of the Christian Church (vv. 1–6). (2) An exhortation on the respect which is due to the leaders of the church (vv. 7–9a). (3) A paragraph of warning in view of the perils of the times (vv. 9b–16). (4) Personal messages and a great doxology (vv. 17–25).

1–6. Counsels to the Members of the Church. The writer gives the following injunctions bearing upon the life of the church. (1) *Let love of the brethren continue.* The phrase "brotherly love" always denotes in the N.T. "love of your fellow church member." One of the earliest names given to Christians to describe their relations to each other was the term "brethren." In fact, the word "brother," except in the few cases where it is used of natural relationship, always means "fellow church member." (Cf. 1 Jn. 4^{20}: "He that loveth not his brother [i.e., fellow church member] whom he hath seen, cannot love God whom he hath not seen.") (2) Cultivate hospitality. Hospitality is regarded in the N.T. as one of the Christian virtues. (Cf. Rom. 12^{13} 1 Tim. 3^{2} 1 Pet. 4^{9}.) Hospitality often brings unexpected blessing: *Some have entertained angels unawares.* The allusion is to Gen. 18^{2}–19^{3}. (3) Remember those who are in prison for conscience sake; and those who are suffering persecution (v. 3). (4) An exhortation to chastity (v. 4). The marriage bond must be kept intact. Immorality and adultery will be severely punished by God. (5) The Christian must be free from avarice (v. 5)—another injunction which is often emphasized in the N.T. Cf. Col. 3^{5}, where avarice is described as idolatry. The Christian need not fear that by obeying this precept he is running the risk of poverty, for God has given us the most explicit promise that he will never desert us in our hour of need.

7–9a. The Right Attitude Toward the Leaders of the Church. The leaders of the church are entitled to honor and respect. We are not told what exact position it was that these leaders held in the church, or whether they corresponded to the bishops who are mentioned in Phil. 1^{1}, or to the elders who are found in many apostolic churches, or the deacons who are frequently alluded to in the N.T. (see discussion on pp. 1277–8). The use of the general term "leader" seems to suggest that no technical titles had as yet come into use in the church to which Hebrews is addressed, though, of course, it is possible that it may be employed to cover all the different types of men who held offices of any kind in the church.

The special function of the leaders referred to here was preaching. *They spake unto you the word of God.* Some of them seem to have suffered martyrdom, and their glorious death ought to be an example to the rest of the flock. The paragraph ends with the fine phrase, *Jesus Christ is the same yesterday and to-day, yea, and forever.* Leaders may come and go. They are with us for a time and then depart. But Jesus remains unchangeably the same. What he has been proven to be yesterday he is still to-day, and what he has been yesterday and is to-day he will continue to be forever.

9b–16. A Warning Against False Sacramental Ideas. The concluding phrase of the last section forms the introduction to that which follows. As Christ remains the same and his teaching is therefore the permanent test of truth, we must be careful not to become the victims of false teaching. Against whom is the warning directed? It does not seem, as some suggest, to be uttered against an ascetic Jewish sect which taught that the spiritual life can be maintained only by complete abstinence from certain kinds of food. The definite statement of the writer seems to point in another direction. Some maintain that the spiritual life is nourished not by abstinence but by eating certain kinds of food. It is against this theory that the writer protests when he asserts that *it is good that the heart be established by grace; not by meats, wherein they that occupied themselves were not profited.* It is probable that the reference is to the sacrificial meals which were common both among Jews and pagans and which were supposed to strengthen and intensify the religious life. There may even be a suggestion that the writer intends to make a protest against the sacramentarian theories which were creeping into the Christian Church and beginning to transform the Lord's Supper into a sacrificial meal. If this is so (and a strong case can be made out in defense of the theory), the Epistle to the Hebrews is the first challenge to the introduction of the sacramental doctrines which afterward corrupted the church. Whether the sacramentarianism which the writer has in mind is Jewish, pagan, or Christian cannot be determined with absolute certainty, but we may be sure that in some form it constituted the *strange teachings* against which the Epistle fulminates in this very difficult paragraph.

The argument which is used to demolish sacramentarianism is very intricate, and scholars are by no means agreed about all the details of its interpretation. The writer draws a contrast between two types of sacrifice. (1) There were some sacrifices, i.e., those which were offered for minor offenses, when the flesh was eaten by the priests and Levites (Lev. 6^{25-29}). (2) But in the case of the important sin-offerings—and especially the sacrifice on the Day of Atonement—the flesh was never eaten but was burned in the fire (Lev. 6^{30}).

The point of the argument seems to be this: We Christians have an altar and a sacrifice, but it is not a sacrifice which can be eaten. It belongs to the type of the most sacred sin-offerings, the blood of which was brought by the high priest into the holy place, and the bodies could not be eaten even by the members of the priestly caste but were consumed by fire outside the camp. The supreme element in the sacrifice which Christ offered is the blood which as supreme High Priest he offered in the ideal sanctuary in heaven. His body was afterward destroyed, and it is entirely a mistake to suppose that there is any possibility for the Christian to partake of that body in the communion service. In that service, Christ is received "after a spiritual manner."

The paragraph ends with an appeal (vv. 13–16). Jesus suffered *without the gate.* He was expelled from the city. We too must welcome persecution and exile, that we may follow him. We must not set store upon our earthly status and our social ties; we must be prepared to abandon everything and share the reproach of Christ. There is nothing permanent in the state of the earthly city in which we live. Our quest is for the eternal city—the city not made with hands, whose architect and maker is God (cf. 9^{11} 11^{10}). And though we have no sacrifices such as are offered by Jews and pagans in their temples, there is a spiritual sacrifice which we can make to God, and that sacrifice is the sacrifice of praise that proceeds from lips that make public confession of Christ. Moreover, there is a further form of sacrifice which is well-pleasing to God—the sacrifice of charity and beneficence.

17–19. Another Reference to the Leaders of the Church and a Request for Prayer. In a previous paragraph (vv. 7–9) the writer has referred to the leaders of the church in the past. He now claims obedience for the actual leaders who presided over the church at the time when he was writing. "Give obedience," he says, "to your leaders and yield to their counsels, for they have your spiritual welfare at heart and are like watchmen standing guard over your souls. They bear a heavy weight of responsibility and will have to give an account of their stewardship to God. Do not make their task heavier than it already is. Let their work be a joy to them rather than a burden. The greater the burden you throw upon them, the greater will be your own loss."

In vv. 18, 19 occurs the first personal note in the Epistle. Hitherto the writer has kept his personality in the background. Now he pleads for the readers' prayers. The people to whom he is writing may not always have agreed with him, but his own conscience is quite clear. He has done his best for them and has always striven to live for the highest ends. One result of their prayers may be that he will be able to return to them more speedily.

20, 21. A Great Doxology. Having asked his readers for their prayers the writer now prays for them, and the prayer takes the form of a magnificent doxology. The prayer is a canto of phrases culled from the O.T. and every phrase is used with telling effect. God is called *the God of peace*—the God who amidst the distractions of life and the storms of persecution brings peace to the soul. Jesus is described as the *great shepherd*, a phrase which seems reminiscent of the allegory in which Jesus describes himself as the Good Shepherd in Jn. 10^{11-17}.

The first and only direct reference to the resurrection of Jesus in the Epistle occurs in the phrase, *who brought again from the dead.* The words, *with the blood of the eternal covenant,* indicate the purpose and end of the resurrection. Jesus was raised from the dead that he might offer his blood—which effected a new covenant—in the heavenly sanctuary. It is a noteworthy element in the teaching of Hebrews that the actual work of atonement follows and does not precede the resurrection. Then comes the actual prayer itself—that God may make these Christians perfect in every good work, that they may be enabled to do his will and what is well-pleasing in his sight. Whether the concluding phrase, *to whom be the glory for ever and ever,* refers to God or to Christ is uncertain. The doxologies of the N.T. are generally ascribed to God, and the construction of the sentence seems to suggest that the ascription is here also made to him. But the fact that the final doxology is immediately preceded by the phrase, *through Jesus Christ,* has led many scholars to think that in this particular case the words are intended to apply to him.

22–25. Final Messages. In the final paragraph the writer appeals to his readers to bear with the appeal which he had made to them. He describes the Epistle as a *word of exhortation,* showing that he regards the practical appeal rather than the intellectual argument as the essential part of the letter. The stress which he lays upon the last request seems to suggest that he was conscious that his advice might be resented and criticized by some member or members of the church.

The reference to Timothy in v. 23 suggests that Timothy and the writer of the Epistle were colleagues in the work of the Christian ministry. What is meant by the phrase, *hath been set at liberty,* cannot be precisely determined. On the face of it, it seems to indicate that Timothy had been imprisoned and had now regained his freedom. But the words might also mean "set free from other tasks."

The salutation proves that the letter is addressed to the community of Christians, who are asked to convey a message from the writer to their leaders.

It is difficult to determine exactly the meaning of the phrase, *They of Italy salute you. They of Italy* may simply signify Italians; and if that is the case, the writer is obviously in Italy when he is writing the letter. But the words may also mean "those who have come from Italy," and in that case would seem to indicate that the Epistle is addressed to some church in Italy.

JAMES

By Principal EDWARD H. SUGDEN

Introduction

The Title. This is the first of the seven Epistles known as the General or Catholic Epistles, because they are not addressed to particular churches, like those of Paul. The Second and Third Epistles of John, though addressed to individuals, are included, since they are naturally connected with his First Epistle. In the oldest MSS. the Catholic Epistles follow Acts; but Jerome, in the Vulgate, put them after Hebrews; the English versions have followed his order.

Canonicity of the Epistle. It was formally admitted into the canon by the third Council of Carthage, 397 A.D. Eusebius (314 A.D.) includes it in his list, but classes it among the Antilegomena, i.e., books about which there was some dispute. He himself, however, accepts it and quotes it as Scripture. Origen (c. 200 A.D.) quotes it frequently as the work of James, and expresses no doubt as to its canonicity; and it was definitely recognized as canonical by Jerome and Augustine. On the other hand, it is not in the Muratorian Canon (toward the end of the second century), nor in the Old Latin version used by Tertullian (*cir.* 200 A.D.). The Peshitta Syriac version contains it, but the date of that version is not quite certain. The doubt felt about it was due (1) to its lack of apostolic authority; (2) to its Jewish cast of thought; (3) to the supposed opposition of its teaching on faith and works to that of Paul. It is now included in the canon by all the churches, though Luther spoke of it as "a right strawy Epistle," because he thought (quite wrongly) that it disagreed with Paul's doctrine of justification by faith.

The Author. In 1^{1} the author describes himself as "James, a servant of God and of the Lord Jesus Christ." "James" is the English form of "Jacob," derived from it through the old French *James*, which again is an abbreviation of the Italian *Giacomo* from the late Latin *Jacomus*. It is unfortunate that our English translators have not retained Jacob as the name of the author, as the average reader does not connect *James* with *Jacob*, and so misses the fact that the author was named after the great forefather of Israel. From his name, as well as from the contents of the Epistle, it may be inferred: (1) that the author was a Jew, both by race and by religion, who had been converted to Christianity (1^{1} 2^{1} 5$^{8, 9}$); (2) that he was not an apostle, or he would surely have claimed that position in the heading of his Epistle, as Paul and Peter expressly, and John inferentially, do in their letters; (3) that he held a position of authority in the church; and (4) that he was so well known that his name alone was sufficient to enable his readers to identify him without any further description.

There are four Jacobs (or Jameses) mentioned in the N.T.: (1) James the son of Zebedee and brother of John, one of the apostles; (2) James the apostle, the son of Alphæus, who is almost certainly to be identified with James the Little, the son of Clopas (Mk. 15^{40}); (3) James the father of the apostle Judas (not Iscariot—Lk. 6^{16}); (4) James the brother of our Lord (Mt. 13^{55} Gal 1^{19}), and of Jude (Jude 1^{1}). Can any of these be identified with the author of the Epistle? James the son of Zebedee is out of the question, as he was beheaded by Herod, 44 A.D. (Acts 12^{2}). Of the second and third Jameses nothing is known beyond their name. But about the fourth we have a good deal of information. Along with Joseph, Simon, and Judas he was a brother of Jesus (Mt. 13^{55} Mk. 6^{3}). Whether he was the son of Joseph and Mary (the Helvidian view), or of Joseph by a former wife (the Epiphanian view) or a cousin of our Lord (the Hieronymian view), is a question not relevant to our present inquiry. (See art., "James," in Hastings' *Dict. of the Bible.*) His father, Joseph, was "a just man" (Mt. 1^{19}), i.e., a strict observer of the Law; the names of his children are those of the forefather of his race, and of three of the patriarchs; and they were doubtless brought up in the atmosphere of rigorous Judaism. Along with Mary they regarded the early ministry of Jesus with suspicion and sought to restrain him (Mt. 12^{47} Mk. 3$^{20-33}$). They did not believe in him (Jn. 7^{5}), and therefore cannot have been among his apostles. Hence on the cross Jesus committed the care of his mother, not to them, but to the apostle John (Jn. 19^{26}). After his resurrection our Lord appeared to James (1 Cor. 15^{7}), and this resulted in his conversion; so that he and his brothers immediately associated themselves with the apostles (Acts 1^{14}). His character and his relationship to our Lord secured for him the leadership of the church in Jerusalem. On his release from prison Peter at once sends word to him (Acts 12:17); Paul visited him on his first visit to Jerusalem after his conversion (Gal. 1:19) and later refers to him as one of the reputed "pillars" of the church (Gal. 2:9). He was regarded by the Judaizing members of the church as their leader (Gal. 2:12); but his real attitude is made clear by the action he took as chairman of the Synod of Jerusalem (Acts 15:13-21). When Paul visited Jerusalem in 58 A.D., he consulted James and the elders, and they advised him to conciliate the Christians who were zealots for the Law by joining with four men who had taken the Nazirite vow, and paying their charges (Acts 21:18-26). From 1 Cor. 9:5 it is inferred that he was married—which is antecedently probable. He is mentioned no more in the N.T. but Josephus (*Antiquities*, xx, 9: 1) relates that he was stoned to death about 62 A.D., by the high priest Ananus; and Hegesippus (quoted by Eusebius in his *Ecclesiastical History*, ii, 23: 4–18) gives us many traditions about him; such as that he was a Nazirite from his birth; that he prayed so continuously that his knees became hard like a camel's; that he was called "The Just" and "Oblias," i.e., "the bulwark of the people"; that the Pharisees flung him from the roof of the Temple; and that he was killed by a blow from a fuller's club (see also *Ante-Nicene Fathers*, Eng. trans., vol. viii, pp. 762–3).

All this agrees so well with what we may infer about him from the Epistle that there can be little hesitation in claiming him as its author. Of course it is possible that the James of the Epistle may be some otherwise unknown Christian; or that it was originally anonymous and that the first verse was prefixed later as a likely guess. But such theories are quite needless, and the majority of scholars hold that the author was the brother of the Lord (but see note below). In harmony with this conclusion are these facts: (1) that the author's style is based on that of the Wisdom Literature of the O.T. and Apocrypha; and that he refers in many passages to the O.T. and to the Jewish apocryphal books, Ecclesiasticus and Wisdom; (2) that he knows and quotes from the Sermon on the Mount, for it was not the ethical teaching of Jesus that he disapproved but his Messianic claim; and one can easily understand how hard it was for him to believe that his own brother was the Messiah; (3) that in the circular addressed to the Gentile converts by the Synod of Jerusalem under the presidency of James (Acts 15:23) the form of the greeting is the same as that in the Epistle, and is not used elsewhere in the N.T. except in the letter of Claudius Lysias to Felix (Acts 23:26). Moreover, of the two hundred and thirty words used in the circular and in the address of James, eight occur also in the Epistle, and nowhere else in the N.T. in the same sense.

Date of the Epistle. Assuming that it was written by James, the brother of the Lord, it must have been written before his death, 62 or 63 A.D. This is confirmed by the absence of any reference to the destruction of Jerusalem, 70 A.D. The coincidences between this Epistle and Romans and 1 Peter are best explained by the assumption that Paul and Peter had read it and were referring to it. The date of Romans is 58 A.D. and of 1 Peter 64 A.D. (cf. intro. to each epistle). The silence of the author in regard to the decision of the Synod of Jerusalem, 51 A.D., indicates that it was written before that date. With this agrees the unorganized condition of the churches addressed; they still met in the synagogue; there is no mention of bishops or deacons; the only officers are the elders of the synagogue; and any member of the congregation could act as a teacher as the Spirit moved him. The theology of the Epistle is undeveloped; there is no mention of the incarnation or the atonement, and the author's attitude is much the same as that of Peter and Stephen as indicated in their addresses in the early chapters of Acts. The great majority of modern scholars therefore fix the date as somewhere between 40 and 50 A.D., and so make it the earliest book in the N.T.

There are, however, contrary opinions as to both authorship and date. J. H. Ropes (in *James*, International Critical Commentary) denies both the early date and the Jacobean authorship, and finds that the writer was "a Christian teacher in some half-hellenistic city of Palestine" somewhere between 70 and 125 A.D. B. W. Bacon supports him, in *The Apostolic Message*, especially pp. 177–180.

Destination of the Epistle. It is addressed to *the twelve tribes which are of the Dispersion*, or Diaspora. In the first century A.D. Jews were to be found in every city of importance throughout the civilized world. In almost all the cities visited by Paul on his missionary journeys he found Jewish synagogues, where Moses was read every Sabbath day. The Jews of the Dispersion were expected to pay their yearly Temple tax, and to visit Jerusalem at least once during their lives. An instructive list of those who were present on the Day of Pentecost is given in Acts 2:9, 10, and they undoubtedly carried back home with them the substance of Peter's teaching, and especially the good news that the Messiah had come in the person of Jesus of Nazareth. In this way it is probable that many Jewish-Christian communities were founded all over the empire. Later, in their annual visits to Jerusalem, they would become acquainted with James, and would recognize his official position as the head of the church there; and he would feel himself to be in a pastoral relation with them, which would suggest the sending to them such a communication as this Epistle. They were still Jews, proud of their descent from "Abraham our father" (2^{21}), familiar with the O.T. ($5^{4, 11, 17}$), and zealous for the Law (2^{12} 4^{11}); but they had accepted Jesus as the Messiah (2^{1}) and were looking for his second coming (5^{7}). They attended the synagogue (2^{2}), and their relation to it was much the same as that of the early English Methodists to the Established Church. For fifty years the members of Wesley's societies were regarded by him as members of the Church of England; they attended service and took the sacraments at their parish churches; and their own meetings were not held in church hours. Their position was thus curiously parallel to that of these Jewish Christians, and their characteristics were much the same. The early Methodists were persecuted by the rich and influential members of the church, and were tempted to show undue subservience to them; they were mostly men "of low degree"; there were serious outbreaks of antinomianism among them, owing to the emphasis laid by Wesley on salvation by faith alone; ignorant but zealous brethren were ready to set themselves up as teachers; and Wesley had frequently to correct them for quarreling and strife among themselves. These are just the faults which James notes and against which he warns his readers. Peter, in his first Epistle, addresses the members of the Dispersion, but limits his scope to those in Asia Minor; and some have thought that James was specially thinking of the Eastern Dispersion in Mesopotamia; but of this there is no proof, and there is no ground for supposing that he was not addressing all the Jewish-Christians throughout the Roman world. It has been suggested that by "the twelve tribes" he means the whole Christian Church, as being the true Israel; but this is to credit him with the idea to which Paul later gave currency (Gal. $3^{7, 29}$ Phil. 3^{3}) and to ignore the obviously Jewish tone of the Epistle. From Gal. 2^{9} we learn that James regarded himself as being called to "go to the circumcision," and he would not be likely to travel beyond his commission. (Cf. pp. 847–9.)

Style and Contents of the Epistle. The style of the Epistle is influenced by the Wisdom books of the O.T. and Apocrypha, with which the author was obviously well acquainted; but he did not set himself to imitate them; their influence was not present to his consciousness, though he naturally threw his thoughts into the form familiar to him. He had certain things to say and he said them without any attempt to express them in this or that literary style. In his case it is emphatically true that "the style is the man." We recognize his intense earnestness, his hatred of all shams, his practical temper, and his indignation at all forms of evildoing; which finds expression in an ironical scorn hardly paralleled anywhere else in the N.T. The epistolary form is merely conventional; the letter is really a continuous exhortation, and in its one hundred and eight verses there are no fewer than fifty-four imperatives. He has no time to elaborate his terse, vivid apothegms; though he has a happy gift of striking illustration, which he uses most effectively. He makes no attempt to link his various subjects together on any logical system; he deals with each as it occurs to him, and often the only reason one can see for their order is some verbal suggestion which leads from one to another. Ropes (see "Literature") has pointed out the similarity existing between this Epistle and the popular Greek ethical addresses known as Diatribes; but the likeness is due to their common practical aim, and certainly not to any deliberate imitation of them by James; probably he had never heard of them. His Greek is, on the whole, pure and idiomatic; but not more so than would be quite possible to the inhabitant of a bilingual country, such as Palestine was in the first century (cf. p. 881). That the Epistle was written in Greek and not, as some have thought, in Aramaic, is shown by the frequent use of plays upon words, and alliteration; and by the author's familiarity with the LXX version of the O.T. and Apocrypha.

Teaching of the Epistle: Religion and Human Behavior. This Epistle is notable for its strong practical emphasis. It is characterized by an ethical passion which reminds us of the Hebrew prophets, the teaching of Jesus, and such great Pauline writings as Romans 12 and 1 Cor. 5–11. It is not especially concerned with questions of doctrine. One might almost say that the entire teaching of the Epistle is an elaboration of 1^{22}: "Be ye doers of the word, and not hearers only, deluding your own selves."

The ordinary supposition that James decries "justification by faith" is mistaken (see notes on $2^{14f.}$). He simply undertakes to correct false inferences from that great doctrine, which we must therefore assume was being generally taught. As R. W. Dale points out, unless the doctrine were being taught in the church, James would hardly have engaged in this polemic against its misapplication. For Paul, the works that do not justify are legal and ceremonial acts, and it is not such works that James proposes to exhibit as proof of his faith (2^{18}), but works such as those that Paul glorifies in Rom. 12 and 1 Cor. 13 (cf. Jas. 1^{27}). For James, it is not mere intellectual belief that justifies, but utter self-commitment to the service of the Lord Jesus Christ (1^{1} 4^{15}), and this is in substance what Paul means by the "faith" that "justifies" (Rom. 4, 5).

James makes one of the supreme tests of the religious life the attitude to others (2^{1-12}). For him, the Christian Community is essentially a democracy, more exactly a brotherhood, in which all superficial differences as between rich and poor drop away. Hence his injunction against "respect of persons," and especially against the unjust treatment of the poor by the rich (5^{4}). He is concerned also that there shall be gentleness of speech within the brotherhood. He had evidently had experience of "the railing tongue," or had heard of churches disrupted by it (cf. 1 Cor. 6^{1-7}), and much that he has to say bears upon the necessity of being "swift to hear, slow to speak" (1^{19} 3^{2-12} $4^{11, 12}$ 5^{9}). The unkindly tongue is the expression of an unkindly temper, and an unkindly temper is alien to the name of Christ and to the perfect law ($1^{25, 26}$).

James also recognizes that consistent discipleship of Jesus will bring persecutions and testings (1^{2}; see notes on 4^{4} 5^{7-11}). It necessarily involves enmity with the world (4^{4}). He does not mean that Christians are to wrap themselves in a robe of righteous "superiority" (see 2^{1}), but that there are some things that, as Christians, it is not possible for them to do (cf. Mt. 6^{24} 1 Cor. 10^{21}). The refusal to do them cannot be made without cost, but the cost is itself intended as a disciplining and refining influence (1^{2-4} $5^{10, 11}$).

There are two passages denouncing religious inconsistency (4^{1-10} 5^{1-6}) which might well have been lifted right out of the pages of Isaiah (1^{2-17}) or of Amos ($5^{10-15, 21-24}$). They reveal James as the prophet of social righteousness, but also as one who recognizes that the way in which Christians shall behave in the wider relationships of life will depend upon their possession of moral inwardness. "Cleanse your hands . . . purify your hearts . . . humble yourselves" ($4^{8, 10}$)—these are the indispensable conditions to the "good life" (3^{13}), and to the just treatment of the poor by the rich (2^{6}). Where there is not this inwardness, expressing itself in the just deed and the serviceable life, nothing can prevent a final collapse (5^{3}). To know the good and not do it, this is sin indeed (4^{17}).

In a word, James is concerned with exalting that true wisdom which consists in submission to the perfect law. His repeated use of the word "wisdom" (1^{5} $3^{13, 15, 17}$) indicates that he felt himself to be in line with the "wise men" to whose writings he so often alludes (see the many references in the commentary to Proverbs, Wisdom, and Ecclesiasticus). But it is wisdom in respect to a law—the perfect law of liberty (1^{25}), more fully defined in 2^{8} as the "royal" law, "Thou shalt love thy neighbor as thyself," and obedience to which—the true wisdom—works out in a life "full of mercy and good fruits, without partiality, and without hypocrisy" (3^{17}).

Summary of Contents. Owing to its unsystematic structure it is difficult to give a summary of the contents of the Epistle as a whole. All that can be here attempted is a list of the topics dealt with; any suggestions as to their interconnection will be best left to the detailed commentary.

1^{1}. The Salutation.

1^{2-19}. Trial; its object and the way to secure wisdom to endure it. Its benefit both to poor and rich. The temptation arising from trial is not to be attributed to God, but to our own desires.

1^{20-27}. Preparation for and subsequent conduct to the hearing of the word. The test of true religious service.

2^{1-13}. Warning against subservience to the rich.

2^{14-26}. Faith and Works.

3^{1-12}. Warning against ambition to be teachers; the dangers of speech.

3^{13}–4^{12}. Warning against strife, and its origin in rivalry and in pleasure-loving.

4^{13-17}. In laying plans for our life, God is not to be left out of account.

5^{1-6}. Denunciation of those who abuse riches and oppress the poor.

5^{7-11}. Exhortation to patience.

5^{12-20}. Miscellaneous exhortations in regard to (1) oaths, (2) prayer for the sick, (3) restoration of a fallen brother.

Literature: Mayor, *The Epistle of James;* Knowling, *The Epistle of James;* Ropes, *The Epistle of James* (International Critical Commentary); Plummer, *James* (Expositor's Bible); Oesterley, *James* (Expositor's Greek Testament); Articles on "James" in the Bible Dictionaries.

CHAPTER I

1. Epistolary Greeting. On James and on *Dispersion* see introduction. *Servant*—the

Greek means "a bond-servant" (R.V. mg.). Cf. Rom. 1[1] Phil. 1[1] Tit. 1[1] Jude v. 1. The same word is used in LXX of Moses (Mal. 4[4]) and of the prophets (Amos 3[7] Jer. 7[25]), and frequently by our Lord of his disciples, e.g., Lk. 17[7-10]; but cf. Jn. 15[15]. It is hard to translate, as "slave" suggests to the English reader the enslaved Negro; and "servant," a hired domestic or farm help; whereas the slaves in the Roman Empire at this time were not of a different race from their masters, and were, on the whole, kindly treated; on the other hand they were the property of their owners, and could not leave their service when they liked. R.V. mg. gives uniformly *bond-servant*, an unfamiliar word. The Christian is "bought with a price" and so is not his own, but the Lord's. James and Jude by using the word imply that, though brothers of the Lord, they are in no way privileged above their fellow Christians. The phrase *of God and of the Lord Jesus Christ* implies the belief of James in the divinity and the Messiahship of Jesus. *The twelve tribes*—see Acts 26[7] Mt. 19[28]. *Greeting* might better be rendered "wishes joy," so as to show the connection with the next verse.

2–4. The Place of Trial in Perfecting the Life. James wishes his readers joy; he is not unmindful of the trials they are suffering, but he reminds them that trials are matter for joy, not for mere resignation, because trial is at once the test and the school of endurance. The athlete enjoys the race, the student enjoys the examination, for they both prove and strengthen his power (cf. Mt. 5[10-12] Rom. 5[3] 1 Pet. 1[6, 7] 4[12-14] Heb. 12[11] Ecclus. 2[1f.]). *All joy*—supreme joy. *My brethren*—James uses this word nineteen times; he is the brother of the Lord, but all the more he emphasizes the thought that he is the brother of all Christian people, however humble. *Temptations* (mg., *trials*)—we discriminate between trials and temptations, but the Greek has only one word for the two. All trials are temptations to murmuring and distrust, as well as to hatred of those who cause them; and all temptations are trials and are bitterly painful to the sensitive soul. In this clause James is thinking of suffering; in vv. 13f. he deals with allurements to sin—temptations in the narrower English sense. *Proof* (testing)—cf. Wisdom 3[4-6] Prov. 27[21] 2 Cor. 8[2]. *Faith*—James agrees with Paul in regarding faith as the foundation of the Christian life. *Patience*, i.e., endurance, steadfastness (cf. Mt. 24[13] Rom. 12[12]). *Perfect*—realizing its full purpose; a favorite word with James (cf. Mt. 5[48] 19[21] Heb. 2[10]). *Entire*—complete in all its parts (cf. Acts 3[16] 1 Thess. 5[23] Wisdom 15[3]). It is explained by the next phrase, *lacking in nothing*.

5–8. Digression on Wisdom and the Way to Attain It. The word *lacking* suggests to the writer that which is the most fatal lack of all—the lack of *wisdom*. To him wisdom is what faith is to Paul, hope to Peter, and love to John—the essence of the Christian life. And the four are essentially one. Faith is union with God, and this involves wisdom, which means estimating the values of life from God's standpoint; hope, which is the vision of the future as God intends it; and love, which is the consummation of fellowship with God and through him with his children. In order to rejoice in tribulations, it is necessary to have the wisdom which enables a man to form a true valuation of life from the divine point of view. This view of wisdom as "the principal thing" was no doubt largely due to the author's familiarity with the ideas set out in Proverbs, Wisdom, and Ecclesiasticus (see in particular Prov. 8). This wisdom is the gift of God, not a mere philosophical inference from the facts of life. Hence it is given in answer to prayer. (See pp. 157b, 171–2, 606–8.)

For God as the giver of wisdom see 1 Kings 3[9-12] Wisdom 7[7] Ecclus. 1[10]; cf. Mt. 7[7]. *Liberally*—better, unconditionally, without bargaining. *Upbraideth not*—cf. Ecclus. 20[13] 41[22]. *In faith*, i.e., in such close fellowship with God that the believer knows what the will of God is and can be sure that he is asking in accordance with it (1 Jn. 5[14, 15]). *Nothing doubting*, or, rather, not at variance with oneself (cf. Mt. 21[21]). This is not a repetition of *in faith*, but adds another condition—that there must be no division of aim, no double purpose, no failure in whole-hearted and single-minded devotion. In contrast to this is the *double-minded man* of v. 8 (cf. Ecclus. 1[29] 2[12-14]). Such a man is like the surge or froth by the seashore—now coming in, now going out, as the waves and the winds drive it hither and thither; a very natural figure for a man who had spent his youth near the sea of Galilee, and perhaps had gone fishing there with his cousins John and James (cf. Eph. 4[14] Ecclus. 1[28]).

8. The entire verse is in apposition to *that man* (R.V.); not as a new sentence (A.V.), or as the subject of *shall receive* (R.V., mg.). The Greek word for *double-minded* appears to have been invented by James, but is often used by later Christian writers, and occurs forty times in the *Shepherd of Hermas*.

9–12. The Author Returns to the Question of Joy in Trial. The majority of the Jewish-Christians were poor and of inferior social position (1 Cor. 1[26]). They are to exult in the spiritual dignity which Christianity has brought to them (Jer. 9[23] Lk. 6[20] 1 Cor. 7[22] and cf. 2[5]). There were some rich men among them, who probably suffered in social prestige and in their business through their connection with the Christian community. They are to exult in these humiliations, because they are thus reminded of the transitoriness of riches, and so are saved from setting their hearts on earthly things (Jer. 9[23] Mt. 18[4] 1 Tim. 6[17]). Poor and rich alike, if they endure trial, will receive the crown of life.

The rich, i.e., the rich brother, not the rich non-Christian, who is denounced in 5[1-6]. *The flower of the grass*—quoted from Isa. 40[6], which is also quoted more fully in 1 Pet. 1[24] (cf. Psa. 102[4, 11]). *He shall pass away,* i.e., as a rich man. *The scorching wind*—the sirocco, or southeast wind, common in Palestine (cf. Job 21[18] 27[21]). *In his goings*—perhaps the words mean "in his business journeyings." *The crown of life*—in Paul this means the wreath of victory (1 Cor. 9[25] 2 Tim. 2[5] 4[8]), given as a prize in the Greek games; but James would not be likely to refer to these games, which the Jews regarded with abhorrence; he is, rather, thinking of the O.T. use of the word, meaning "a mark of dignity" (Ecclus. 15[6] Wisdom 2[8] Prov. 4[9] Isa. 28[5] Zech. 6[11]). The crown is eternal life, begun here and to be continued hereafter (1 Pet. 5[4] Rev. 2[10d] Jn. 10[10]). *The Lord*—(Greek, *which he hath promised*); the implied subject may be *God* or *the Lord*—probably the latter; the reference may be to some word of our Lord's not recorded elsewhere. For the form of the clause cf. Psa. 1[1] Mt. 5[3-11].

13–18. The Source of Temptation. The author now turns to what in English we mean by temptation, as distinguished from trial; though in Greek, there is only one word for the two meanings. The man who yields to temptation must not excuse himself on the plea that the temptation is from God; or, in more modern phrase, that his sin is due to heredity or environment. It is unthinkable that God should either himself be tempted or should tempt men (Ecclus. 15[11-20]). Temptation comes from the lower desires of the flesh and the mind (Gen. 3[6] Eph. 2[3] Rom. 8[5-8]) which overcome the higher and more recently developed moral and spiritual instincts, and so generate sin, which in its turn generates death. From God only good can come; in contrast to the monstrous birth of sin from desire, and death from sin, is the Christian's birth to righteousness, wrought by God through the preaching of the gospel; and it is impossible that God should counterwork his own purpose by tempting his children. Of course we are here face to face with the fundamental problem of divine sovereignty and human free will. James attempts no solution of it; he takes his stand on the moral conviction that God cannot have anything to do with sin, much as Paul meets a very similar difficulty in Rom. 3[4] 7[7, 13] 9[14] with an indignant "God forbid!"

The R.V. translation of vv. 13, 14 (cf. Psa. 7[14]) is preferable to that in the mg. *Lust* (v. 15) —this word has become so limited to sexual passion that it is better to substitute for it a more general word, "desire" or "impulse." *The Father of lights* (v. 17), rather, of *the* lights, i.e., the sun and moon (Gen. 1[14] Psa. 136[7-9] Jer. 31[35] Ecclus. 43[1-10]); but unlike the sun, which rises and sets, and the moon which waxes and wanes, there is no variation in his changeless goodness (Ecclus. 17[26] 27[11] 1 Jn. 1[5]). *Shadow cast by turning*—i.e., the shadow cast on the face of the moon by the revolution of the heavens. *He brought us forth*—cf. 1 Pet. 1[3] Jn. 1[13] 3[3]. *The word of truth*—as in the next paragraph, James means the perfect law of liberty, i.e., the gospel; cf. 1 Pet. 1[23] Rom. 10[17] Eph. 1[13] Jn. 8[31]. *Firstfruits*—which were sacred to God. The early Christians were the firstfruits of the harvest of the world (2 Thess. 2[13] R.V., mg.). *Creatures*—a wider word than "men"; it seems to suggest the same thought as Rom. 8[19, 20].

19–27. Hearing and Doing. The mention of the word of truth suggests the subject of the next paragraph, which deals with *the right way of hearing and practicing the word.* It must be remembered that there was no N.T. in existence yet; so that the Christians were dependent upon the preaching of traveling missionaries such as are mentioned often in the second-century document known as *The Teaching of the Twelve,* and of local teachers (Acts 13[1]) for their knowledge of the gospel. To get profit from this they must be ready to hear, slow to obtrude themselves (3[1]), and slow to lose their temper when what is said does not agree with their prejudices (Acts 22[22]). They must prepare themselves by cleansing their hearts from impurity and malice. And, having heard the word, they must practice it. As to the form of service, they must not be content with outward rites and ceremonies, for the ritual acceptable to God is the practice of kindly help toward orphans and widows and of personal purity and single-mindedness.

Ye know, or, *Know ye*—probably the indicative is intended (cf. Eph. 5[5] Heb. 12[17]). *Swift to hear*—supply "the word of truth" (Ecclus. 5[11]). *Wrath* (Ecclus. 1[19-24])—fanatical opposition to the teacher's message—a fault not unknown to-day. *The righteousness of God*—not used in Paul's technical sense, but of right conduct such as God approves. (Cf. Mt. 5[20] 6[33].) *Putting away*—literally, "stripping off," as a filthy garment, unfit for wearing in the service of God's house; a common figure (1 Pet. 2[1]

Rom. 13[12] Eph. 4[22] Col. 3[8]); the filthy garment is defined by the following words: *the overflowing of malice* (mg., v. 21). *Receive*—not simply hear (Jn. 1[12] Acts 17[11]). *The implanted word* (Jn. 6[63])—the word rooted in the heart, which is the indwelling Christ; he saves the soul from those evil desires, which are the origin of sin (see v. 14).

The figure of the *mirror* (v. 23) is not so easy for us to understand as it was for the readers of the Epistle. We have mirrors on every dressing-table, and photographs of ourselves in every album; in the older days there were no photographs, and mirrors were rare and costly. An occasional passing glance at their reflection would be all that most of these people got. *The law of liberty* (v. 25) is the teaching of our Lord, especially as contained in the Sermon on the Mount, which there is abundant evidence in the Epistle that James had heard and remembered; into it we must stoop down (cf. 1 Pet. 1[12]) and look minutely; and in it we shall see reflected our own best ideals, the image of what we ought to be; and by continuing to study it, and trying to conform ourselves to its ideals, we shall grow into the same image. The law of liberty is contrasted with the law of commandments contained in ordinances (Psa. 119[43] Mt. 5[17] Acts 15[10] Rom. 8[2] 2 Cor. 3[16]; cf. Jer. 31[33]). It is the *perfect law*, i.e., attaining its end in enabling men to be righteous; which the old Law could not do (Rom. 8[3] Heb. 7[19]). *Religious* (v. 26)—exact in religious observances, such as attendance at the synagogue, fasting, carrying out the ritual of the Law, etc. *Religion* (v. 27)—religious observance. In modern language, going to church and taking the sacrament are of no use, unless a man controls his speech (cf. 3[2-12]). The ritual most acceptable to God is care for widows and orphans (Deut. 27[19] Ecclus. 4[10]) and purity from the sins of the godless world (5[4, 5] 2 Pet. 2[20] 1 Jn. 2[15-17]).

CHAPTER II

1–13. Warning Against Subservience to the Rich. The mention of the right way of hearing the word suggests to the author an abuse that he has noted in the public services. The rich man who comes in is shown to a good place, while the poor man is made to stand or sit on the ground. This indicates worldly motives still operating in the conduct of the Christians. They have forgotten the dignity which faith in Christ gives to the poor, and the persecutions which they have suffered from the rich. True, we must love the rich man as being our neighbor; but we must equally love the poor. Neglect of this duty cannot be atoned for by even the most complete obedience to the law in other points. The law we have to observe is a law of liberty; of the spirit, not of the letter; and its spirit is the spirit of mercy. If we treat the poor without mercy, we ourselves shall be judged without mercy; but if we show mercy, God will show mercy to us, even though we have deserved condemnation. How many of our modern churches come under this condemnation! What of pew-rents, seats sold by auction to the highest bidder, free seats in the worst part of the building?

Hold not, or, *do ye hold?* Both renderings are possible, but the first is the better. *Of glory*—it is better to take these words as in apposition to *our Lord Jesus Christ*, i.e., our Lord Jesus Christ who is the Glory. The Glory is used for the Shekinah, the visible glory of God in the Temple, where he sits between the Cherubim (Isa. 4[5] Rom. 9[4]). So Christ is the manifested Glory of God (Jn. 1[14] Heb. 1[3] Col. 1[27]). In Eph. 1[17] God is called "The Father of the Glory." A possible, but much tamer rendering, is "our glorious Lord Jesus Christ." To one who has through faith seen the glory of God in the face of Jesus Christ (2 Cor. 4[6])

> "The glories of our blood and state
> Are shadows, not substantial things,"

and he cannot be dazzled by gold rings and raiment of purple and fine linen. *Respect of persons*—regard for the outward appearance, the mask (*persona*) of the actor (Lev. 19[15] Acts 10[34] Rom. 2[11] Eph. 6[9] Col. 3[25] 1 Pet. 1[17]).

Synagogue (v. 2)—the gathering of the Jews for worship. (See intro., "Destination.") Strangers were admitted to the synagogue (1 Cor. 14[23]), and both the persons referred to here were probably casual visitors. *In a good place* (v. 3)—cf. Mt. 23[6]. But perhaps the translation should be *Please sit down here. Under my footstool*—on the ground at my feet. *Divided in your own mind* (v. 4)—actuated sometimes by pure motives, at others, as in this case, by worldly considerations, evil thoughts. *Rich in faith* (v. 5)—cf. 1[10] and note. *Heirs of the kingdom* (Lk. 6[20] Rom. 8[17])—the poor are heirs, not because they are poor, but because they are sons of God, and love him (cf. 1[12]). *Drag you* (v. 6)—the early persecutions of the Christian Jews came from their rich and influential countrymen (Jn. 16[2] Acts 4[1] 8[1-3] 13[50] 1 Thess. 2[14-16]).

Blaspheme (v. 7)—properly "slander"; but often used in N.T. in the modern sense (Acts 13[45] 18[6] 26[11] 1 Tim. 1[13]). *The honorable name*—Jesus; *which* (R.V., mg.) *was called upon you*, i.e., in baptism (Acts 2[38] 5[41] Phil. 2[9-11]). As blasphemy is associated with the divine name, this passage implies that James accepted the divinity of Jesus. Cf. Amos 9^{12} and Acts 15^{17}, where James uses the same phrase. *The royal law* (v. 8)—the supreme law (Mt. $22^{39, 40}$ Rom. 13^{8}), or, better, the law given, not to slaves, but to those who are kings (2^{5}), and, therefore, a law of liberty (1^{25}). *The scripture* —Lev. 19^{18}. *Ye do well*—James uses a similar expression in Acts 15^{29}. *Convicted by the laws* (v. 9)—Lev. $19^{15\text{-}18}$. *Guilty of all* (v. 10) —so R. Jochanan in *Sabbath* 70^{2} says, "If a man does all things, but omits one, he is guilty of each and all." *The law of liberty* (v. 12)—cf. 1^{25}. The law of the spirit, the law of love, not of specific ordinances. To transgress against love is to transgress the whole law. *Judgment is without mercy* (Mt. 5^{7} 7^{2} 18^{34})—but if the law of love is observed, mercy will pardon the sins which otherwise would incur judgment (Tobit 4^{9} Heb. 6^{10}).

14–26. Faith and Works. The mention of faith in v. 1 above, and the demonstration that faith must involve the observance of the law of love, lead to this discussion of the general relation between faith and works. But there is a change in the meaning of faith, which has given rise to much misunderstanding. Faith means sometimes assent to a proposition, sometimes a trust in Christ which results in union with him (faith *into* Christ), and reliance upon him for salvation (faith *upon* Christ). This second meaning is the usual one in the writings of Paul and John; and this is the faith of 1^{6} $2^{1, 5}$. But in this passage it is plain from v. 19 that James is thinking of acceptance of a creed; and it is this sort of faith that is shared by the demons, and cannot save them or anyone else; in other words, what James means is that orthodoxy is of no use at all unless it leads to and is manifested by good works. A creed can no more save a man's soul than a fine speech can feed the hungry or clothe the naked. It may perhaps be suggested that faith and works are separate gifts of co-ordinate value, like, e.g., the gifts of tongues and of healing; one man has one, another the other. James replies that they are inseparable; faith cannot be proved except by works, and a faith like that of the demons, which does not result in good works, produces nothing but terror. Abraham and Rahab were justified; i.e., their faith was proved to be genuine, by the acts that accompanied it. Faith and works can no more exist apart than the body and the spirit.

Paul is as emphatic as James on this point (see Gal. $5^{6, 22}$). His contrast is not between good works and faith but between the works of the Law (the observance of the old Jewish Law), and the righteousness which results from faith in Christ (Rom. $3^{21, 22}$ 6^{12} 8^{12}). The theology of James is not as fully developed as that of Paul, but there is no real contradiction between them. (See pp. 936–7.)

Works—good deeds, not what Paul calls "works of the law" (Mt. 5^{16} 2 Esdras 9^{7}). *Naked*—insufficiently clothed (Isa. 20^{2} Jn. 21^{7} Mt. 25^{36}). *Go in peace*—the ordinary salutation, "Good-bye!" *In itself* (v. 17)—inwardly. *Yea, a man will say*, or (R.V., mg., v. 18), *But some one will say.* Two questions arise: (1) Who is this man? an objector or an ally? (2) Where does his speech end? The sentence "But some one will say" usually introduces an objection (Rom. 9^{19} 11^{19} and especially 1 Cor. 15^{35}), and it is best to take it so here, as has been done in the summary above. James's answer then begins "Shew me thy faith," etc. *Thou* and *I* are used in the sense of *one* and *another*. If the speaker is an ally, he must be supposed to be addressing the person censured by James—"Thou hast faith, while I (the ally of James) have works; but since thy faith cannot be demonstrated by works it is practically dead, whereas my works prove that I have faith as well." Or we may take the first phrase as a question—"Hast thou faith?" to which James answers, *I have works*, etc.

God is one (v. 19)—the primary article of the Jewish creed, expressed in the Shema (Deut. 6^{4}); cf. the opening of the Nicene Creed. *Demons*—evil spirits; for their faith and terror see Mt. 8^{29} Mk. 1^{24} Acts 19^{15}. *Wilt thou know*—art thou willing to accept a decisive proof? The proof is given from the history of Abraham and of Rahab. For Abraham's faith see 1 Macc. 2^{52} Wisdom 10^{5} Ecclus. 44^{20} Rom. 4^{3} Gal. 3^{6} Heb. 11^{8}. Here it is the sacrifice of Isaac (Gen. $22^{1\text{-}18}$) that proves Abraham's faith; in Rom. 4 it is his faith in the promise of a son; in Heb. 11^{8} it is his leaving his own land for an unknown country. *Justified* (v. 21)—not in the technical Pauline sense, but as in Mt. 11^{19} Lk. 7^{29}, "shown to be just." *Made perfect*—by the production of its proper fruit. *The Scripture*—Gen. 15^{6} (LXX) Rom. 4^{3}. *Friend of God* (v. 23)—the words do not occur in O.T. (cf. Gen. 18^{17}) but the designation was a common one among the Jews; cf. the Arab name for "Abraham," *El Khalil*, i.e., "the friend." *Rahab* (Josh. 2, Heb. 11^{31})—she is selected as being a woman, an alien, and a harlot—at the furthest remove from Abraham. *Spirit*—James uses "spirit" (*pneuma*) for the non-material part of man; not in the Pauline sense of the higher moral nature, as opposed to the soul (*psyche*). Cf. Gen. 2^{7}. It might be translated *breath.* The point is not that faith is the body and works the soul, but that the two are inseparable, and must concur in all human activities.

CHAPTER III

1–12. Warning Against the Ambition to Become Teachers. In young and isolated churches there is always a danger that zealous but ignorant men may set themselves up as teachers. Many religious leaders have had to meet this tendency among their followers. There is the same danger to be guarded against in the churches to-day. Zeal and piety are not sufficient qualifications for a teacher without due study and preparation. (See pp. 1276–7.)

James points out that teachers will be judged with greater severity than others. Sins of speech are only too easily committed. The tongue is like a horse's bridle or the rudder of a ship—small in size, but able to control the direction of the movement of the whole body. It is like the tiny spark which sets a whole forest aflame. So a trifling word may set on fire the whole round of mortal life; and the devil is ever on the lookout to kindle that fire. Savage and venomous animals may be tamed; but the tongue is more active and venomous than any of them, and cannot be tamed. It has, further, the monstrous and unnatural power to combine the blessing of God with the cursing of our fellowmen; like a spring at once salt and fresh, or a tree which bears two opposite kinds of fruit.

Teachers—we find teachers in the church at Antioch (Acts 13[1]), and the title, equivalent to the Aramaic "Rabbi," was given to the itinerant teachers mentioned in *The Teaching of the Twelve.* For the danger from unauthorized teachers, cf. Mt. 23[8] Acts 15[24] 1 Tim. 1[6, 7] Heb. 5[12]. *We* (v. 1)—i.e., we who are teachers. *Perfect*—because one who can bridle his tongue can *a fortiori* control all his actions. *Bridle* (v. 2)—cf. 1[26] Prov. 10[19] Ecclus. 5[13] 19[16] Mt. 12[36] 15[4]. *Now if*—another, and in some ways preferable, reading is *Behold. Rudder* (v. 4)—the same comparison is made by Pseudo-Aristotle, *Mechan.* 5, and other Greek moralists. *Impulse*—or pressure of the hand on the tiller. *Boasteth great things* (v. 5)—plumes itself on its great power. *How much wood*—or, *How great a forest.* Bush fires were common in Palestine. Cf. Psa. 83[14] Isa. 9[18] 10[17]. We in Australia know too well how hundreds of square miles of bush may be consumed by a spark from a locomotive engine, or a match thrown into the grass before it has quite gone out.

The tongue is a fire (Prov. 16[13] Ecclus. 28[13-26])—R.V. text (v. 6) puts the stop after *fire*; R.V. mg. puts it after *iniquity.* Either rendering is possible; but the one in the text seems better. *The world of iniquity*—i.e., the wicked world; cf. Lk. 16[9]; the meaning is "In our little world of man the tongue represents the unrighteous world, for it is through the tongue that we come into relation with the wicked world, both by hearing what others say, and conversing with them, and so become defiled" (cf. 1[27] 4[4] 1 Jn. 5[19]). *The wheel of nature*—the whole round of life. *Hell*—Gehenna; as "Heaven" is used for "God," so "hell" is used for "the devil." The tongue is the world (in the bad sense in which James always uses that word); our members are the flesh, and hell is the devil; so that we have here the three sources of evil—the world, the flesh, and the devil. *Poison* (v. 8)—cf. Psa. 58[4] 140[3] Rom. 3[13]. *In the likeness of God* (Gen. 1[26] Wisdom 2[23]). *Ought not so to be*—because such inconsistency is unnatural, as is shown by the examples of the spring and the tree (cf. Mt. 7[16] 12[33]). *Sweet*—fresh.

13–18. Warning Against Strife and Party Spirit. True wisdom is shown by meekness and the absence of jealousy and faction. Strife arises from evil desires, and from worldliness. Our spirit covets the goods of others, and so leads to envy. But the grace of God can overcome our natural disposition; therefore submit to God and resist the devil. Draw near to God in humble penitence and sorrow, and he will exalt you.

Wise—in the sense of 1[5]; the possessor of the wisdom which in James's thought is equivalent to religion. *Life*—conduct; conversation in the old English sense (1 Pet. 1[15, 18] 3[2, 16] Gal. 1[13]). *Meekness*—cf. 1[21] 1 Pet. 3[16] 2 Tim. 2[24] Ecclus. 3[17]. *Faction* (v. 14)—party spirit (cf. Phil. 1[17]). *Lie not*—by making a profession of wisdom which is proved false by your conduct. *Wisdom* (v. 15)—the same contrast between earthly and heavenly wisdom is drawn in 1 Cor. 2[6]. *Earthly*—derived from the finite world of human life (Jn. 8[23] Phil. 3[19] 1 Cor. 15[47]). *Sensual*—arising from the *Psyche*, or animal soul, which man shares with the lower creatures (1 Cor. 2[14] 15[44-46] Jude v. 19). Cf. Gen. 2[6], where the temptation appeals to the lower psychic motives; and Eph. 2[2, 3], where the desires of the flesh and of the mind correspond to the psychic motives, and are, as here, connected with the devil. *Confusion*—anarchy (1[8] 3[8] 2 Cor. 12[20]). *Pure* (v. 17)—Wisdom 7[25]. *Peaceable*—Mt. 5[9] Rom. 8[6]. *Gentle*—considerate, sweetly reasonable (2 Cor. 10[1]). *Easy to be entreated*—rather, "ready to obey," submissive to discipline. *Without variance*—undivided, whole-hearted (1[6] 2[4]). *Without hypocrisy*—unfeigned (1 Pet. 1[22] 2 Cor. 6[6]). *The fruit of righteousness*—the reward which righteousness brings (Prov. 11[30] Heb. 12[11] Phil. 1[11]). *Them that make peace* (Mt. 5[9]).

CHAPTER IV

1–10. The Warnings Continued. In this paragraph, already summarized above, James describes the cause and cure of the strife and quarrelsomeness he has just rebuked. The cause of strife is the selfish love of pleasure, which produces inward conflict between the various pleasures that crave for indulgence, and outward conflict with others who stand in the way of their satisfaction (1 Pet. 2[11]).

Lust—desire; lust is limited in modern usage to sexual desire, while the word here is quite general and includes all desires for self-gratification (cf. 1[14]); v. 2 in R.V. puts a colon after *have not;* it is better to put the colon after *kill.* The translation will then be, "Ye desire and have not; and so ye murder. Yea, ye covet and cannot obtain; and so ye fight and war." It seems unlikely that even these factious Christians would commit murder to gain their desires. But possibly James had in mind the teaching of Jesus in Mt. 5[21]; (cf. 1 Jn. 3[15].) Hate is potential murder. The change of one letter in the Greek word translated "murder" would give a word that might be translated "envy." With this change, the verse might be rendered, "Ye desire and have not and this gives rise to envy; ye covet and can not obtain, and then ye fight and war." Many commentators adopt this emendation. *Ask not* (Mt. 7[7])—the promise is not fulfilled, because you ask wrongly (1 Jn. 5[14]). *Adulteresses*—the idea that God is the husband of his people is common in the O.T. (Jer. 3[20] Ezek. 16 Hos. 2); and in the N.T. the church is the Lamb's wife (2 Cor. 11[2] Eph. 5[23] Rev. 19[7]). Hence faithlessness to God is adultery; and those who are faithless are adulteresses (Mt. 12[39]).

Vv. 5, 6 have received many interpretations, which cannot be discussed in detail in our limited space. The one which involves fewest difficulties is as follows: "Do ye think that the Scripture speaks idly in denouncing friendship with the world? The spirit, i.e., the immaterial part of man, which God made to dwell in us at the creation(Gen. 2[7]) has desires which lead to envy (v. 2). But God will add to his original gift the gift of greater grace, by which these desires can be controlled." James does not use the word *spirit* in relation to the Holy Spirit but to the human soul, as in 2[26]. *He saith,* i.e., God saith (Prov. 3[34]; quoted also in 1 Pet. 5[5]). *The devil*—cf. 3[15] where the devil is the instigator of evil in us (see note, 3[6]). *Draw nigh* (v. 8)—used specially of the priestly office (Ex. 19[22]). Hence the need for purity. *Double-minded*—cf. 1[8] Mt. 6[22]. *Be afflicted*—endure hardship by giving up the pleasures that lead to strife (1 Cor. 9[27]). *Humble yourselves*—cf. 1 Pet. 5[6].

11, 12. Charity in Judgment. Evil speaking must not be indulged in, as it is contrary to the law of love, and implies criticism of that law. This is a detached section, which some think should come after 2[13]. *Speak against*—Wisdom 1[11] Psa. 101[5] Mt. 7[1] Rom. 14[10-13] 2 Cor. 12[20] 1 Pet. 2[1] 3[16]. *The law*—i.e., the law of love (cf. 1[25] 2[8]). To break the law is to condemn at once the law and the lawgiver. *Who art thou?*—cf. Rom. 14[4].

13–17. Recognition of God. God must not be shut out from our plans for carrying on our business. Religion and business must not be kept in separate water-tight compartments. The Jews of the Dispersion were mostly engaged in commerce, and traveled from town to town in the pursuit of their occupation.

Go to—a call to attention; only used here and in 5[1] in N.T. *Vapor*—cf. Job. 7[7] Wisdom 2[4] 5[8-14]. The meaning is "mist," rather than "smoke." *If the Lord will*—a common formula among the ancient Greeks; cf. the modern Arabic *Inshallah,* and the Latin *Deo volente* (D.V.). The sin is, however, in the thought, and is not avoided by the perfunctory use of a "D.V." or "God willing" in our announcements. *Vauntings*—insolent presumptions (cf. Prov. 27[1] Mt. 6[34]).

V. 17 is a general maxim, applying to all the warnings and advices hitherto given in the Epistle. Sins of omission are just as culpable as sins of commission (cf. Mt. 7[26] Lk. 12[47]). Moffatt would transfer this verse to the end of ch. 2.

CHAPTER V.

1–6. Wealthy Tyrants. Denunciation of the rich not for the possession of wealth, but for the way in which, like some of their modern representatives, they have made their money by withholding their wages from their employees, and for spending it in luxury (cf. Amos 5[11] 8[4] Wisdom 2 Lk. 6[24] 18[24] 1 Tim. 6[9, 10]). These rich men were Jews who attended the synagogue, but not necessarily Christians, though some of them may have been so by profession.

Miseries that are coming upon you, i.e., in the days of the Messiah (cf. v. 8). *Moth-eaten*—Mt. 6[19]. *In the last days*—it is better to put a full stop after "flesh" (v. 3) and to translate, "You have treasured up fire in the last days," i.e., in the days immediately preceding the coming of the Lord. Their accumulated wealth is a fire that will destroy them. *Hire*—cf. Deut. 24[15] Mal. 3[5] Ecclus. 34[21, 22]. *Lord of Sabaoth*—Lord of the hosts of heaven; a common title of Jehovah in O.T.; quoted here from Isa. 5[9]. *In a day of slaughter*—cf. v. 3, Jer. 12[3] 25[34]. The day of slaughter is the day of divine vengeance which precedes the coming of the Messiah, which James thought of as now imminent. *The righteous one*—the rich Jews may have caused some of the poorer brethren to be put to death by false accusations. Some take *the righteous one* to mean our Lord, but this is not likely. James himself was called "The Just," and it is possible that this verse is a later insertion referring to his murder by the Jews.

7–11. The Need of Patience. By the example of the farmer, and in the expectation of the speedy coming of the Lord, James exhorts his readers to patience. The sufferers must not murmur, even against their oppressors, but endure like the prophets and Job, whose patience was richly recompensed in the end.

The coming of the Lord—the "Parousia," which, like all the early Christians, James expected to take place in a very short time (v. 8; cf. 1 Pet. 4[7]). *Early and latter rain*—in October and April (Deut. 11[14] Jer. 5[24]). *That ye be not judged* (Mt. 7[1])—the judge, the Messiah, who will judge both the poor and their oppressors, is at hand (Mt. 24[33]). *The prophets* (v. 10)—cf. Mt. 5[12] 23[34-39] Acts 7[52] Heb. 11[32f.] *Job* was a stock example of patient endurance under trial. *The end of the Lord*—his final treatment of Job (Job 42[10]). Some have imagined a reference to the death of Christ, but this is highly improbable.

12. This is practically quoted from Mt. 5[33f.]; cf. Ecclus. 23[9].

13–18. Prayer and Praise. In trouble, pray; in cheerfulness, sing. Special directions are given for the treatment of the sick.

Sing praise—properly, sing to the accompaniment of the lyre; but used generally for singing praise (Eph. 5[19] 1 Cor. 14[15]). *The elders*, i.e., of the synagogue, which James assumes to be in this case a Jewish-Christian assembly. At first the Christian churches followed the precedent of the synagogues in their organization, and the elders were the official leaders (Acts 20[17]). *Anointing him with oil*—oil was the commonest of remedies (cf. Isa. 1[6] Lk. 10[34]). The modern equivalent would be "Giving him his medicine in the name of the Lord." Ordinary remedies are not to be omitted, but reinforced by prayer. There is no justification here for extreme unction, which is given, not to cure the sick, but to prepare them for death. *Confess your sins one to another* (v. 16)—not to a priest. Confession of sin is the best method of curing many diseases, and is the foundation of modern treatment by psychoanalysis. *In its working*—probably the word is passive and means "when energized by the Holy Spirit"; prayer can be successful only when it is according to the will of God (1 Jn. 5[14]); and this we can know only through the guidance of the Spirit (1 Cor. 2[11]). *Elijah*—1 Kings 17[1] 18[42, 43]. It is to be noted that Elijah knew the will of God before he prayed.

19, 20. By turning a sinner from the error of his ways, the converter saves the sinner's soul from death, and secures the forgiveness of his (the sinner's) sins. It is possible that the last clause refers to the sins of the converter (cf. Prov. 10[12] Dan. 12[3] 1 Tim. 4[16] 1 Pet. 4[8]). It was a common Jewish belief that almsgiving and prayer for others brought forgiveness to the man who so helped another.

FIRST PETER

By Professor BENJAMIN W. ROBINSON

Introduction

The Purpose of the Epistle: A Plea for Fortitude. This Epistle, originally written to hearten and encourage early Christians in a time of special affliction, has become one of the world's greatest expressions of the glory of fortitude in enduring the hardships of life. As the key word to the understanding of the Epistle of Jude is "antinomianism" (lawlessness), and as Second Peter centers in the "promise of Jesus' coming" (3^{4}), so First Peter unlocks its spiritual treasures to one who holds constantly in mind the word "persecution" (1^{7} 4^{12}).

There is no more rewarding study in all the field of religion than that of the problem of suffering. The book of Job offers one solution, namely, that God lets his children be afflicted to prove their loyalty. In the Suffering Servant of Isa. 53 the problem is solved by the expression of the conviction that suffering finds its glorification in service to others. There were many attempts among early Christians to explain the sufferings of Jesus. Chief among them was the idea that he suffered because of the sins and shortcomings of others.

Later comments will indicate that First Peter has many different ways of stating Peter's solution of the problem of suffering. Foremost among them is his positive and convincing way of saying that suffering is *a means of purifying and ennobling the soul* (1^{7}). It brings us into closer fellowship with Jesus, and so helps us to attain that higher life which Jesus imparts (2^{1-11}). "One who really suffers ceases from sin and lives the rest of his life in harmony with God's will" ($4^{1, 2}$).

The Background of Persecution. Christians in Pontus, Galatia, and other provinces of Asia Minor were undergoing a time of testing. "You have now been put to grief in manifold trials in order that your faith may be found more precious than gold when tested with fire" ($1^{6, 7}$). "Do not think it strange that a fiery test is being put upon you" (4^{12}). Among the countless papyrus sheets discovered in recent years containing letters and records from the early centuries, are many little pieces called *libelli.* They are the signed statements of individuals who made affidavit in the time of the Decian persecution that they were not worshipers of Jesus or of the Christian God. One of these signed statements, mentioned by Milligan (*Here and There Among the Papyri,* p. 142), reads in part as follows: "To the Sacrifice Officials: Aurelia Demos, wife of Aurelius Irenæus, makes affidavit that it has always been my custom to offer sacrifices to the gods, and I have now in your presence, according to your command, offered sacrifice and libation, and have partaken of the offering." It is not likely that people who were not associating with Christians would be suspected. The probability is that many who had been Christians in name did in a cowardly fear obey the command to offer incense. (See intro. to Revelation, p. 1365, and cf. pp. 755, 846b.)

It so happens that we have a letter written by the governor of Bithynia, the province mentioned in 1^{1}, written in the year 110 A.D. to the Roman emperor, about the Christians: "With those who have been brought before me as Christians, I have pursued the following course: I have asked them if they were Christians, and if they have confessed, I have asked them a second and a third time, threatening them with punishment: If they have persisted, I have commanded them to be led away to punishment." (For further discussion, see B. W. Robinson, *The Life of Paul,* p. 160.)

Who shall say how many were saved from a cowardly surrender by the triumphant faith and conviction conveyed in such an epistle as this of Peter? If many fell away, the church was purified and made stronger. This Epistle and the spirit pervading it made the victory sure. In every age, the Spirit of Jesus expressing itself through his followers assures the triumph of the higher kind of life and more and more ennobles human experience.

First Peter is best understood as a revelation of a great historical situation in which the purer and higher triumphed over the baser and the worse. The Epistle is no longer viewed merely as a statement of doctrine by a single author. History proves that the Epistle found response in the hearts of a great multitude. This is shown not merely by the fact that Christianity triumphed over all persecution, but also by the fact that the Epistle was preserved and taken into the canon of Scripture. In a very real sense it may be said that First Peter is the triumphant song of countless heroes who saved the world from militarism and materialism, setting up an ideal of spiritual fellowship and brotherhood which is still marching toward the great victory.

The Author of the Epistle. First Peter was in use in the churches in the first half of the second century. Polycarp makes several quotations from it (see his *Ep. to Philippians*, chs. 1, 2, 8, 10, Ante-Nicene Fathers, Eng. trans., vol. i). According to Eusebius (*Hist. Eccles.*, iii, 39) it was used by Papias. There are two difficulties with the view that Peter was the author of the Epistle. (1) Peter probably died in the time of Nero, about 64 A.D. But there was no official persecution of Christians in Asia Minor until the time of Domitian in the last decade of the first century. (2) The Epistle is written in a very pure and fine Greek style. It is not easy to think of the Galilæan fisherman becoming such a master of a language which was not his mother tongue.

The first of these difficulties may be answered by the statement that there is no reference in the Epistle to a systematic persecution, or to shedding of blood. The references to persecution may be understood as referring to such a situation as may have developed under Nero, or even earlier. Paul himself as early as the year 50 makes definite reference to persecution and suffering in Thessalonica (1 Thess. 2[14, 15]).

The second item, regarding the Greek style, is easily explained by the part which Silvanus had in the writing of the Epistle. The statement is plainly made in 5[12] that it is Silvanus who is doing the actual writing.

The modern reader of the Epistle has no difficulty in the matter of authorship. Anything in it which does not sound like a direct word of the apostle Peter may be regarded as due to the work of Silvanus. He was Greek, as his name shows. He may have been the same Silvanus (called Silas in Acts) who accompanied Paul on his second missionary journey.

Silvanus may either have written at Peter's dictation, or have been told by Peter to write the Epistle. It is even conceivable (as suggested by von Soden) that Silvanus may have written after the death of Peter. In any case, the Epistle stands forth in all its glory as an expression of that remarkable fortitude which Peter manifested in his imprisonment and endurance of every kind of persecution, even to his death by crucifixion.

Date and Destination. The date of the letter is somewhat uncertain. If it is thought that the persecution was that of Domitian, it must have been written near the end of the first century. But as great an historian as Mommsen has said that the situation revealed in the letter may be as early as the time of Nero (64 A.D.). Most scholars find no serious difficulty with the date of 64 A.D., within the lifetime of Peter (cf. Bigg, *St. Peter and St. Jude*).

The provinces to which the Epistle is addressed should not be understood in too limited a way. The list does not mean that the bearer of the letter went first to Pontus and when it had been read there, went on to Galatia and then to the other provinces mentioned. The Epistle is rather a general one for the use of all Christians wherever found, who were subjected to trials.

The Content of the Epistle. The Epistle is best understood when read as a whole. It is not so much a collection of individual texts as it is the following of a lofty line of thought. The spirit of the letter is hope and triumph. There is no effort to deny the reality of the persecution. The author had known the sufferings of Christ and had, through his own experience, become a partaker in the Christian triumph. There was in his mind that promise to the sons of Zebedee that they should drink the cup which Jesus drank (Mt. 20[20f.]). There was perhaps also in his mind that word in Jn. 21[18]: "When thou shalt be old, thou shalt stretch forth thy hands, and another shall gird thee, and carry thee whither thou wouldest not." The fiery trial makes those who experience it partakers of Christ's sufferings, so that they may rejoice and may share in the revelation of his glory (cf. Fowler, *History and Literature of N.T.*, p. 264).

The general content, stated in unconventional terms, is somewhat as follows:

Peter, a messenger of Jesus, sends greetings to the Christians in the provinces of Asia (1[1, 2]).

We offer thanks to God for the everlasting blessings which we have inherited from Jesus, and for the reward and glory which are soon to be ours. Your persecutions and trials, though manifold, are but temporary. Their purpose is to purify, as fire purifies gold. Jesus, whom you love without having seen, sheds a joy in your hearts and through him your souls are saved. Prophets have long foreseen that, after a time of suffering, there comes a time of glory when the Spirit of Jesus triumphs (1[3-12]).

Keep your minds and hearts upon the higher level, obeying the commands of Jesus. Do not give way to your former temptations and weaknesses, but live like Jesus in the holiness of the Father. Remember that Jesus shed his lifeblood for you. As he triumphed over death, so shall you with him rise above your inherited desires and your sufferings (1[13-21]).

To your purity of soul, add a deep spirit of

love and service one for another and remember that you are living a higher kind of life that is above the realm of the flesh (1^{21-25}). You have been born into a new life. Feed on the spiritual milk which is not adulterated, that you may grow rapidly and become healthy. You are stones in a new building, a living temple, of which Jesus is the corner stone. You are a holy priesthood offering spiritual sacrifices. You are God's chosen people called out of darkness into his marvelous light (2^{1-10}).

Be sure that you honor the name of Christ in all your living. Do your duty in public and private. If persecuted, endure it with fortitude. Jesus is your example. When he was reviled he reviled not again. He died that we might live. By his stripes you are healed (2^{11-25}).

Let wives and husbands live in peace with each other. Be sympathetic toward all, do not return evil for evil, keep your lips from unclean or violent words (3^{1-12}).

Who will harm you if you do what is right? And if you do suffer for uprightness, do not be afraid, but reverence Jesus. Make your defense respectfully as he did and keep your conscience clear. It is better to suffer for doing right than for doing wrong. That is the way Jesus suffered, and he is now in heaven at the right hand of God (3^{13-22}).

You have spent time enough in the past in unchristian dissipation. Men are surprised that you no longer consort with them in these things. That is the reason they speak evil of you (4^{1-6}).

But the end is not far away. Be serious and take time for prayer. Keep your spirit of love vigorous. Love covers a host of shortcomings. Serve each other with all the power of God's Spirit (4^{7-11}).

Do not think it strange that a fiery test is upon you. It makes you partners of Christ's sufferings. Punishment for murder or theft is a disgrace, but suffering as a Christian glorifies Christ and God and him who suffers (4^{12-19}).

As a fellow elder I exhort the elders among you to tend the flock of God, not for money but in the spirit of the Great Shepherd. To the rest of you, I appeal to be loyal to your elders. Put your worry and anxiety in God's hand, and he, after your brief suffering, will make you perfect (5^{1-11}).

Written by the hand of Silvanus. The church in Babylon sends greetings.

Literature: (The simpler books are listed first; the more critical and those based upon the Greek text are put last.) Goodspeed, *The New Testament*, An American Translation; Hastings, *Dictionary of the Apostolic Church*, article, "First Peter"; Fowler, *History and Literature of N.T.*, pp. 259–266; Kent, *Work and Teachings of the Apostles*, pp. 248–250; Cone, *International Hand Books to N.T.*, vol. iii,pp. 297f.; Mitchell, *First Peter* (Westminster N.T.); Moffatt, *Introduction to Literature of N.T.*, pp. 315–344; Hort, *Commentary on First Peter;* Hart, *First Peter*, in Expositor's Greek Testament, vol. iv; Bigg, *St. Peter and St. Jude* (International Critical Commentary).

CHAPTER I

1, 2. The Writer Sends Greetings. The Epistle is addressed to the "elect who are sojourners of the Dispersion." The word *elect* means chosen by God, and should be understood in the particularly personal sense of "invited ones." *Sojourners* recalls Gen. 23^4 and Psa. 39^{12}. As Abraham was a sojourner, so Christians are pilgrims who have been "invited" to the land of promise.

The *Dispersion* would literally refer to Jews who had become Christians. But the term here plainly refers to all Christians, Gentile or Jew (cf. p. 847). It became the favorite custom among early Christians to carry over such terms from Judaism into a spiritual application to Christianity (cf. Jas. 1^1). *Pontus:* The provinces named cover practically the whole of Asia Minor.

Peter here understands the Christian salvation to include (a) God's plan of the work, (b) the Spirit, and (c) the ministry of Jesus. *Sanctification* is a word of long and rich history (see Bible Dictionary). It indicates that the Spirit not only cleanses, but imbues with a sort of divine antisepsis which renders the soul immune to the contamination of the world. *Blood:* Westcott has well said that the blood represents the energy of the physical, earthly life. This means that Christians are saved not alone through an atonement, but through receiving the life and Spirit of Jesus into their souls (Rom. 5^{10}).

3–12. Trial and Suffering Bring Spiritual Blessing. The second birth into a new life through the resurrection of Jesus is also portrayed in Jn. 3, in the story of Jesus' talk with Nicodemus. There is also a close relation here to Paul's teaching that Christians rise with Jesus in newness of life (Rom. 6^4). Fowler has pointed out that the words of vv. 3 and 4 are a graphic reminder of Peter's own experience. Peter had denied his Lord and had gone out into the darkness and wept bitterly. With all his hope gone, he had returned to Galilee to resume his former life of fishing. Then it was to Peter first that the risen Jesus came (1 Cor. 15^5), with his message of life and hope.

The paragraph goes on to describe the inheritance incorruptible which Christians receive through the power of God, the pure and eternal fellowship with Jesus which is God's gift out of heaven (vv. 4, 5). The greatness of this gift is not to be weighed against sufferings; rather our various trials are to be undergone as a means of purifying and thus making more precious the spiritual inheritance which is ours (vv. 6, 7).

Whom not having seen, ye love (v. 8). This has become one of the watchwords of Christianity. It is a remarkable expression of a purely spiritual love and a spiritual religion. *Salvation* (v. 9). This is a word which has a long history in Greek and Roman as well as Christian thought. Here, "salvation" is both present and future, both personal and social. The higher spiritual life upon which Christians enter here and now comes to its perfection in the future revelation of Jesus (v. 7). *The prophets* (v. 10). God does not change his mind, nor subject his children to whims of his will. Prophets of old have revealed the heart of God, have told of the relation of suffering to glory. Now the Holy Spirit (v. 12) has brought the good news with a plainness and clearness never before known.

13–25. Jesus as the Great Example. In these verses, the author gives his central message. Jesus suffered even to his death upon the cross, and has become the Saviour of the world. If Christians can be holy (v. 13), if they will lead lives of devotion and faith and hope, if they will purify their souls in a sincere love of the brethren (v. 22), God will grant them to share in the glory of Jesus.

13–16. The practical nature of the author's meaning is clear. His purpose is to win his readers away from their lower and physical desires and bring them to the higher manner of living.

17–21. These verses, and especially the words *redeemed with blood*, convey one of the most precious doctrines of the Christian religion. "Redeemed" means emancipated. The redemption of a slave out of his bondage was a common occurrence among the Greeks and the Romans. It was indeed a joyous occasion on which some slave, after years of servitude, came to the day when, through the generosity of a friend, or as a reward for unusual service, he found himself officially set free. This is a picture of what Jesus can do for anyone who enters into fellowship with him. It is Jesus' life, his life of holiness and service, which emancipates our souls. He poured out his life with utter unselfishness, even to the cross. "Blood" is a word filled with life and meaning (see v. 2, note). It is Jesus' self-sacrifice which saves. His followers, in union with him, receive his spirit of unselfish service and, as they attain the higher life, God wipes away their shortcomings. (See Hastings, *Encyc. of Religion and Ethics*, art., "Blood.")

22–25. The emphasis upon love of the brethren is again united to the conception of the second birth. Compare the word of Jesus to Nicodemus: "That which is born of the flesh, is flesh" (Jn. 3^{6}). Flesh perishes, but the higher Christian spirit and life are imperishable. This is the Christian "gospel" (v. 25), which endures forever because it is the word of the ever-enduring God.

CHAPTER II

1–10. You are God's New Spiritual Temple. In these verses, Peter describes the Christian life in three successive figures: (1) second birth, (2) a living temple, and (3) a royal priesthood. *Spiritual milk* (v. 2). The idea of regeneration is a very frequent thought, not only in this Epistle (1^{3} 1^{23}) and in other parts of the N.T., but also in other religions of the Roman Empire. For example, in the Mysteries of Attis, the ancestral religion of central Asia Minor, the district to which this Epistle was addressed, milk was taken during the regular religious service, as a sort of sacrament. The purpose of the sacrament was to impress upon the hearts and minds of the worshipers the thought that they had entered upon a new life, in which they would find nourishment and growth. (See art., *Backgrounds*, p. 851.) *Without guile.* This is one of the expressions which has received light and meaning from the study of the papyri (Deissmann, *Bible Studies*, p. 256). The word is found in the simple sense of *unadulterated.* It should be so taken in this passage—"unadulterated milk" (but cf. A.S.V. mg.).

Judaism had its magnificent Temple at Jerusalem, in the early days of the Christian religion. Christianity had no temple. One of Paul's favorite figures (v. 4) is that of the Christian spiritual temple. 1 Cor. 3^{10-17}: "Ye are God's temple"; Eph. 2^{20}: "Jesus is the chief cornerstone" (cf. Mt. 21^{42} Mk. 12^{10} Lk. $20^{17f.}$). It is noticeable that the language expresses a fulfillment of the prophecy of Jn. 2^{19}, "Destroy this temple, and in three days I will raise it up" (cf. Mk. 14^{58}). *A living stone.* This phrase is to be taken with *whom* and refers to Jesus. The meaning of the rather involved sentence is: Come to Jesus, the living stone, and you also as living stones will build with him a living temple.

Spiritual sacrifices (v. 5). The verse would indicate that the author had read Rom. 12^{1}. The words "living," "spiritual sacrifice" are found both there and here. It is the word "spiritual" of v. 2 which seems to be an echo of the same word in the Romans passage. There are many such echoes of Pauline expressions in 1 Peter. Peter builds up his picture of the spiritual temple in a vigorous and vivid way. His readers cannot but feel the responsibility and the honor which God had laid upon these simple people of Asia Minor, through whom was to be carried on and fully realized the purpose which had been frustrated by the disobedience of others.

11–25. Live as Citizens of a Higher Heavenly Community. The author here turns to a long series of practical precepts for Christian living. These have been often misunderstood and much abused. The key of the approach to these verses is to be found in the expression, *sojourners and pilgrims* (v. 11). As the Jews of the Dispersion were "sojourners" (1[1]) in various lands, so Christians have their loyalty to their spiritual temple, and are but pilgrims, so far as these other matters are concerned. Physical desires (v. 11) are but strangers, among whom Christian souls dwell for a brief while. Likewise *civil ordinances* are but secondary (vv. 13–17). Christians should be willing to die, if necessary, rather than obey a governor's order to offer sacrifice to the emperor. But this superior citizenship and responsibility should not be used as a *cloak* to wickedness. They must show by purity of life that their opposition to certain ordinances is based on conscience, not on a desire to be lawless. (See notes on Rom. 13, and cf. intro. to Revelation, p. 1365.)

18–25. *In subjection to your masters* (v. 18). Peter urges that this subjection be shown not only to good masters but also to severe ones. H. G. Wells, in his *Outline of History* (p. 512), states that the N.T. has condoned the institution of slavery. If Wells were right, we should expect to find a definite description of the institution of slavery as a part of the expected kingdom of God on earth. Paul and others, to the contrary, state repeatedly that in the Christian commonwealth there is no such distinction as that of master and slave (Gal. 3[28] Eph. 6[8] Col. 3[11] 1 Cor. 12[13]). What the present passage advises is self-control and patience even in the service of severe masters. When you are reviled, do not use the same base language which has hurt you. Jesus bore in his body the sins of others, and through it all gave to humanity its greatest healing pattern of brotherhood and fellowship. To meet violence with violence is simply to increase the confusion. But to meet violence with meekness is to introduce a principle which promises that, sooner or later, violence will be overcome. It is in this indirect way that we are *healed by Christ's stripes*, and that the way is prepared for the destruction of all those social institutions which involve injustice between man and man. (See intro. to Philemon, p. 1292; Brace, *Gesta Christi, passim.*)

CHAPTER III

1–12. Love, Peace and Brotherhood. What has been said regarding the Christian attitude toward slavery applies to the much-quoted injunction, "Wives, be in subjection to your husbands." According to the point of view of Judaism, a woman's religion was that of her husband. If he is a Jew, she is, by that fact, a Jew. The Christian gospel, as preached by Jesus and Paul, gave women their independence in religion. Paul has much to say (cf. 1 Cor. 7[14]) concerning the woman who is a Christian, though her husband is not. He even goes so far as to say that if the non-Christian husband leaves her, she is not bound to follow him. There is no doubt that the Christian religion did more in the first century—and has done more in modern times—for the education and liberation of woman than any other influence. (See Brace, *op. cit.*, chs. 3, 11, 24.) Such new-found freedom was naturally often abused among uneducated people. Peace and brotherhood and patience are the keynote and harmony of these verses. The husband should show respect and tenderness to the wife (v. 7). All should have the sympathetic attitude (v. 8), and above all things, refrain from using words and language which are not truly Christian.

13–22. Jesus was Victorious through Persecution, Suffering, and Death. The secret of high living is to enthrone Jesus as Lord in the heart (v. 15). Keep your conscience clear. Then if you suffer, it will bring you closer to God, as Jesus suffered and brought us all to God (v. 18).

Preached to the spirits in prison (vv. 19, 20). These verses have been called the most difficult in the N.T. The meaning of the text as it stands is that Jesus, in the spirit, went down into Hades and preached to the spirits imprisoned there. The reference is to the tradition based on Gen. 6[1-4], "The sons of God saw the daughters of men, that they were fair." The story of the Flood as a punishment for the wickedness of (apparently) the offspring, immediately follows. The tradition is elaborated in the Book of Enoch: The children of this unlawful union taught men evil arts and were sentenced to condemnation. They were bound and imprisoned in Sheol, or Hades. Peter then is here stating the universality of Christ's salvation, that he went even to the world of the dead and saved even those superhuman spirits condemned in the days of Noah. This agrees also with 4[6].

Rendel Harris and many other scholars (cf. Goodspeed's *N.T.*) have noted that in the Greek the first words of v. 19, "in which also" contain the letters *e n o k*, and they have suggested that v. 19 should be translated "Enoch (*enok*) went and preached." This saves the passage from the peculiar statement concerning Jesus which is not found in the N.T., outside of 1 Peter. But Peter also says (4[6]) that the gospel was preached to the dead, and that the supernatural world is subject to Jesus (3[22]), which would seem to bear out the first interpretation given above. In any case, the heroic challenge of the passage is clear. Jesus was persecuted, he suffered and died; but his spirit marched triumphantly on, saving and healing, until he now dwells at the right hand of God.

CHAPTER IV

1–11. Suffering Purifies the Heart. The first verse contains one of the deepest principles of the Epistle. The thought connects with that of the preceding paragraph in which Jesus is portrayed as the great example. Be loyal to Jesus; follow his example. He who suffers for the right, rather than yield to the wrong, is delivering himself from the power of sin. The principle, stated in modern terms, is that the experience of suffering for the right strengthens the character and gives spiritual power. V. 2 continues, "Such a person no longer lives in accord with the physical desires of men, but in harmony with the will of God."

3, 4. Peter gives an explanation of the fact that worldly men speak evil of you. Such men feel that you have turned away from them; they cannot understand your higher ideals; they try in every way to induce you to come back; when unsuccessful, they resort to abuse. A good illustration of this may be read in Augustine's *Confessions* (v, 8). He tells how a young friend of his, Alypius, having resolved to lead a virtuous life, was induced by his former boon companions to attend a gladiatorial show, at the sight of which he forgot all his good intentions, "and was delighted with that guilty fight, and intoxicated with the bloody pastime." Cf. also the experience of Bunyan's Christian, when he ran from the City of Destruction, and his former friends, Pliable and Obstinate, pursued him to bring him back (*Pilgrim's Progress*, opening section).

5, 6. Even those who have died will not escape the great judgment upon those who live lives of sensuality, drunkenness, and dissipation. This is the reason that the gospel was preached even to the dead. The meaning evidently is that Jesus, after his earthly ministry, descended into Hades and preached to the departed souls; hence even they must stand in the divine judgment. No one, dead or alive, can set up any other standard, or have any excuse for not living according to God, in the spirit. This is the meaning of Jesus' description of the Judgment in Mt. 25[31f].

7–11. *The end is near.* Earnest Christian souls in all ages have felt the urgency of preparation for meeting the great Judge and Maker. Peter does not claim any specific knowledge as to the time and manner of the great Coming. So spiritual are Peter's words that he might be understood as referring to the "end" of each individual life, when every man closes his earthly career. But we are probably closer to Peter's thought when we say, in the twentieth century, "the kingdom of God is at hand" (Mk. 1[15]), just as Jesus said it in the first century. The Kingdom is already among us spiritually (cf. Lk. 17[21]), but we all look forward to an outward realization of universal human brotherhood. A thousand years in God's sight is as one day (2 Pet. 3[8]). The great consummation is always just ahead of us as something toward which we are to strive eagerly (cf. Rom. 8[18]). No trial and no suffering are to be compared to the glory that shall be revealed. Be therefore earnest and serious. The expectation of Christ's Coming is not to make men negligent of present duties. The list of virtues which Peter enumerates is comparable to the passage in Gal. 5[22] (notes) on the fruits of the spirit. Peter mentions *prayer*, and, above all things, *love* for one another. He also urges *hospitality* and the use of whatever talent each one has in *ministering* to others.

12–19. Persecution Gives You a Share in Christ's Glory. To suffer as Jesus did gives you a closer fellowship with him. At his revelation, you will rejoice to have been his comrades in suffering.

In these verses are several echoes of ideas mentioned earlier in the Epistle. Chief among them are: (1) "You should not be surprised at the coming of persecution, for, as followers of Jesus, you should expect to follow his example" (cf. 2[21]). (2) "It is better to suffer because of doing what is right, than to suffer because of doing what is wrong" (cf. 3[17] Rom. 13[3, 4]). To suffer for murder or theft is a disgrace; but to suffer for Christ leads to glory and honor.

Fiery trial (v. 12). For the character of the persecution being endured, see introduction. The use of the word "fiery" indicates how terrible the trial was. But there seems also to be a subtle allusion to the fact that fire purifies.

Trial bravely endured purifies the soul—"proves" it. *Partakers of Christ's sufferings* (v. 13). Cf. Paul's "fellowship of his sufferings" in Phil. 3^{10}. It is by suffering that the world is to be saved: that is why Christ suffered. To suffer for Christ's sake is to suffer *with* him, to make his own sufferings more effective, and to share with him in his redeeming work.

17–19. Peter draws a contrast here between the end of the wicked and the salvation of the righteous (cf. Psa. 1, notes). If a man has any doubt as to the value of right living, he can in any case certainly see the end of the ungodly and the sinners. Let those who suffer climb to the glorious spiritual heights to commit their souls to the great Creator who will not be found unfaithful. *Scarcely saved* (v. 18). Perhaps an echo of Jesus' words about the "strait" gate and "narrow" way. Salvation is never something to be taken for granted. There is always the possibility of a falling away. "Sin coucheth at the door" (Gen. 4^7), waiting to spring upon the unwary. Hence the need to "watch and pray." See Jesus' parables of watchfulness, Mt. 24^{32}–25^{30}. How much greater is the danger of the careless and unconcerned!

CHAPTER V

1–11. Stand Together in Your Fight Against Evil. The author refers to himself as an elder, writing to his fellow elders. This note of fellowship is characteristic of the Epistle. See note on v. 13 below. *Elder* is probably not used in a very technical sense, but is to be understood in contrast to the word "younger" in v. 5 (but cf. intro. to 1 and 2 Timothy, pp. 1277–8).

Tend the flock (v. 2) recalls the scene of Jn. 21. Though the John passage was perhaps written later, either that passage or the oral version of it is probably behind the present passage. As Jesus told Peter to "tend" his sheep (Jn. 21^{16}), so Peter enjoins the elders to "tend" the flock. Not for *filthy lucre*. Peter draws a contrast between the hired shepherd and one who shepherds because he loves his sheep. Jn. 10^{12} pictures the hireling who in time of persecution leaves his sheep and runs away; Jn. 10^{11} tells of the good shepherd who lays down his life for the sheep. Peter applies this to the shepherds of the Asia Minor flocks (cf. Acts 20 $^{28-31}$). The phrase *neither lording it* (v. 3) also suggests Jesus' words about lordship and service (Lk. $22^{24f.}$) and his own example in his washing the disciples' feet (Jn. $13^{2f.}$).

Gird yourself (v. 5). It is again reminiscent of Jn. 13^4 and 21^{18}. Jesus girded himself with the towel at the supper. It was a symbol of humility, for to carry a towel was a servant's task. Peter too girded himself with humility after his return from his denial, and now he, in the great chain of Christian fellowship, urges upon his readers that they likewise gird themselves with humility, to serve one another.

The devil as a roaring lion (vv. 8–11). Peter's reason for advising unity and discipline is the danger from the common adversary. He shares the belief of his time in the reality of the devil and other evil spirits. (See Glover, *Jesus in the Experience of Men*, ch. 1.) The hungry lion roars as he seeks his prey. The devil is hunting for human souls, and he must be *steadfastly withstood*. "Our wrestling is not against flesh and blood, but against . . . the world-rulers of this darkness" (Eph. 6^{12}).

12–14. Conclusion. *By Silvanus.* Silvanus was a "faithful" follower of Peter. It is he who writes the Epistle. (See introductory remarks on authorship.) He may be the same Silvanus (Silas) who, with Paul, wrote the letters to the Thessalonians, and whose history we know to a considerable extent from Paul's letters and from the book of Acts. *She that is in Babylon* (v. 13). Babylon is mentioned repeatedly in Revelation (cf. 14^8, notes) with reference to Rome. In all probability that is the meaning here. The reference then is to the church at Rome, which sends greetings. *Elect together.* See note on 1^1 above. As the elders are exhorted by their fellow elder (5^1), so the elect(1^1) are here greeted by one who is a fellow elect with them. On the word "elect" see 1^1, note. The early Christian was so keenly aware of the dangers from which Christ had saved him that he could never feel otherwise than that divine grace had "sought him out." Seeing the evil man he could, with all humility, say, "But for the grace of God, there am I."

With a Christian salutation, a kiss of love, and a wish for peace, the Epistle ends. When the reader has patience to penetrate behind the veil of words, he feels the heroic spirit of its author and understands one of the secret springs of the river of Christian power and persistence which has flowed down through the centuries in ever-increasing achievement.

SECOND PETER

BY PROFESSOR SHIRLEY JACKSON CASE

INTRODUCTION

Purpose. Happily there have been preserved for us in the N.T. several short books which when first issued were essentially "tracts for the times." A devout Christian had sensed some crisis threatening the welfare of one or another congregation. By issuing a vigorous warning he sought to rectify the situation and avert further disaster. Following a custom of the day, he cast his message into the form of a letter. Sometimes he addressed a particular church, but often he had in mind the needs of all Christians who might be menaced by the danger in question. His epistle, he hoped, would correct the trouble. Such was the little treatise now known as 2 Peter.

Occasion. The danger that loomed on the author's horizon was a threatened lowering of Christianity's moral standards. As the new religion spread to Gentile lands it had drawn into its membership persons whose ethical ideals were quite different from those cherished by its earlier adherents. From the Jewish point of view the moral life of Greeks and Romans seemed frightfully low. As a rule, Gentile converts lacked the discipline in virtuous living that had been furnished Jews through attendance upon the services of the synagogue and study of the O.T. Paul had said some very uncomplimentary things about the character of the Corinthians prior to their conversion (1 Cor. 6[9-11]; cf. Rom. 1[18-32]). Even after the adoption of Christianity they were slow in making their conduct conform to the ethical requirements of the new religion. The apostle Paul was constantly confronted by the problem of teaching Gentile Christians the necessity for proper morality. A large section of almost every letter that he wrote was given over to the task of inculcating the most elementary virtues (see 1 Cor. 5, 6, 7, 10, 11). On the other hand, Paul had very emphatically asserted that no one could hope to be saved simply by performing good works. In his controversy with the Christians of Judæa over the question whether Gentiles could enter the church without submitting to circumcision, Paul had made it plain that, in his opinion, salvation was not to be secured by mere obedience to the Law. Through faith in Christ and endowment by the Holy Spirit one became a new creation in Christ Jesus (Gal. 6[15] 2 Cor. 5[17]). The Christian lived entirely under the guidance of the Spirit, which furnished authoritative direction for all conduct. Only by walking in the Spirit could one be insured against yielding to the lusts of the flesh (Gal. 5[16] Rom. 8[1-14]).

The ideal of spiritual direction in Christian living as expounded by Paul contained both a challenge and a menace. In stressing liberty from law he increased the necessity for moral stamina on the part of the individual who now must possess a keenly sensitive conscience if he would strive toward the highest attainments in moral excellence. The guidance of the Spirit would then beckon him on to new endeavors. But if he were a man whose conscience had been less well disciplined, he might then fall back upon the principle of freedom from the law as an excuse for inferior attainments. He might say that he was now free to follow his personal inclinations. Since he was under the guidance of the Spirit only, a line of conduct that his inner conscience did not condemn might not seem reprehensible even though it did vary from the standards that would have been prescribed by the law. In the second century Christianity embraced in its membership persons who were disposed thus to pervert the Pauline principle of spiritual liberty. At first these individuals were to be found scattered among different churches. They affirmed that, as persons who possessed the Spirit and who had superior knowledge of the way of salvation, they were free from the legalistic restraints that had characterized Judaism. For them salvation was an affair of mental comprehension and not a matter of morality. It is this type of Christian whose presence in the communities worries the author of 2 Peter, and he writes his tract in order to warn the churches against the activities of these liberalists whom he regards as gross falsifiers of Christian truth. (Cf. p. 1277.)

Destination. Although this document is cast in the form of a letter, it is not addressed to any particular congregation. The danger which it seeks to check is not confined to one or two churches, but is felt by the writer to be more widespread. Hence he addresses himself generally to all who have espoused the precious faith of Christendom. We cannot now determine the specific congregations that he had in mind, but he makes very clear the type of error that he would like to rectify. Any Christian group into whose hands the letter might fall would have no difficulty in discovering that his words of reprimand could be fittingly applied to its situation if there were any persons among its members representing the attitude he so fiercely condemns.

Date. The rise of libertine Christian sects came about through the adoption of Christianity by Gentiles who were less sensitive to moral purity than Jews had been. These sects had become sharply differentiated from the main body of Christendom by the year 200 A.D. The situation which the author of 2 Peter confronts seems to represent an early stage in the course of this development. In his day people of the libertine tendency were still within the church. They were present at the gatherings of the community where they slyly carried on their evil designs. But the exact date at which our author wrote is very difficult if not impossible to determine. He assumes that his readers are familiar with a collection of Pauline letters which have already come to be regarded as sacred Scripture within Christianity (3^{16}). Also he seems to assume that they know of the prediction about Peter's death recorded in the last chapter of the Gospel of John (1^{14}). Likewise he refers to the incident of the Transfiguration reported in the ninth chapter of Mark (1^{16-18}). By the author's day the Christian movement seems to have crystallized into an institution which had not only an O.T. Scripture but also a N.T. canon including the letters of Paul and the four Gospels. Among other Christian writers we find no such general acquaintance with the early Christian books before the middle of the second century. And the type of false teacher whom our author seeks to suppress is, judging from other Christian references, just beginning to appear toward the close of the first century (cf. Col. $2^{8,\ 18f.}$ 1 Tim. 1^{6-11} 2 Tim. 3^{1-8} Rev. 2^{14}). Not until a generation or more later do these trouble-makers seem to have attained the prominence given them in 2 Peter.

Author. The allusions of the author to contemporary Christian history would lead us to place the composition of the letter at about the year 150 A.D. The fact that the document itself is not mentioned by any Christian writer before the year 200, and even then is not generallly recognized as having a place in the N.T. canon of Scripture, would still further confirm the probability of its relatively late origin. But the writer explicitly calls himself the apostle Peter, and if this book is a work of Peter's pen, it can hardly have been later than the seventh decade of the first century. On the other hand, the character of the document's content and its references to contemporary conditions in the churches are thought by the majority of modern interpreters to compel a much later date for the composition. The unknown author's use of the revered name of Peter is a literary device employed to give greater weight to the very important and timely message of the Epistle. This practice of pseudonymity is a familiar one both in late Jewish and early Christian religious literature. (See art., *Intertestamental Literature*, p. 188a; art., *Backgrounds*, p. 840b; intro. to Revelation, p. 1364a.) From the point of view of that age the procedure was entirely justifiable, and of very great practical value. If the message to be delivered was regarded as worthy of the ancient spokesman whose honored name it bore, the real author had no more hesitation in speaking for the ancient worthy than a present-day preacher has in delivering from a N.T. text a message to his congregation in the name of Paul or of Jesus. Pseudonymity was a recognized and acceptable literary method in ancient times. The church in the second century knew other documents, which were often highly prized, that had been issued in the revered name of Peter. There were an Apocalypse of Peter, a Preaching of Peter, and a Gospel of Peter which apparently were of about the same date as 2 Peter. The later writers assumed that their cause was entirely worthy to be served by the use of an apostolic name. They adopted this device, not to deceive their readers but to give authority to an important message and thus to preserve a genuine and worthy type of Christianity.

Summary of Teaching. Briefly outlined, the teaching is as follows: After the usual words of formal epistolary introduction ($1^{1f.}$) the writer affirms the divine character of the Christian life ($1^{3f.}$). But even though the Christian salvation imparts to men a divine nature, the struggle for moral perfection must be strenuous and persistent (1^{5-11}). This fact gives the author his task, which is to impress upon his readers the authority of his message. Back of his words stand the revelation made by Christ and the predictions of ancient prophecy (1^{12-21}). Next, he turns upon those persons who by their misdemeanors are perverting the Christian ideals by introducing lower standards of morality (ch. 2). He warns them that the failure of Christ in instituting an early judgment is no sign that they will not ultimately be called to account (3^{1-13}). The homily is brought to a close with an admonition to remain steadfast to the true faith (3^{14-18}).

Literature: The most elaborate critical commentary is Mayor, *The Epistle of Jude and the Second Epistle of Peter*. For contemporary eschatological thinking, see Case, *The Millennial Hope;* also R. H. Charles, *The Book of Enoch*, and *A Critical History of the Doctrine of a Future Life*, second edition, pp. 412–416.

CHAPTER I

1, 2. Salutation. Dignity is added to the apostle Peter by prefixing his original Jewish name in an ancient form of spelling, *Symeon* (mg.; cf. Acts 15[14]). Also the use of the two epithets *servant* and *apostle* serves to heighten the impressiveness of the address. Peter's attachment to Jesus Christ is thus made doubly clear. He is totally enslaved to the will of his Master. At the same time he is a fully authorized apostolic representative who speaks on behalf of the priceless possession which he and all other Christians share in common through their membership in the new religion that has been established by Christ, who is hailed as both God and Saviour. After Christianity had become distinctly a Gentile religious movement it gradually lost its former hesitation, natural enough while it was still composed mainly of Jewish members, in calling Jesus *God*. In the second century this terminology became fairly common (cf. Jn. 20[28] Tit. 2[13]). *Lord* and *Saviour* are, however, most frequently used by this author to designate the dignity of Christ (1[11] 2[20] 3[2, 18]). "Saviour" as a title for Christ first became popular in Gentile circles. These were effective epithets to employ for the purpose of impressing upon the Gentile world in particular the dignity and power of Christianity's founder. *Righteousness* and *knowledge* indicate two essential aspects of the new religion. It owes its origin to a course of procedure on the part of God and Christ by which forgiveness and reinstatement in the divine favor have been made possible for mankind. Also the religious life of the redeemed man is distinguished by experience of continuous growth in the comprehension and fellowship of both God and Christ. One thus has an especially intimate knowledge of things divine, and may expect to possess an ever-increasing measure of God's favor and truth.

3, 4. The Divine Nature of Christians. Those who have true knowledge of God and of Christ, in contrast with the false knowledge paraded by those whom the author opposes, have been completely endowed with the capacity to live a truly godly life. This gift has been obtained only through the kindness and efficacy of divine power itself. Not by their own virtue or right, but through the favor of heaven, have believers acquired this privilege. It insures escape from condemnation for past sins and also a genuine transformation of the human being so that he now possesses a truly divine nature. This change has made possible escape from the corrupting life of the flesh and an elevation of experience to a new and higher plane where worldly lusts no longer have power over the Christian. The idea that membership in the Christian community carried with it a divinizing of human nature is, perhaps, only an extension of the Pauline conception that the believer is a new creation, or of the Johannine idea of the new birth. But in the church of the second century this notion had become a generally accepted belief. One who had received baptism and had partaken of the body and blood of Christ in the Eucharist not only shared in the triumph of the Christian Saviour figuratively or spiritually, but partook also of his own divine nature.

5–11. The Necessity of Moral Endeavor. Just because the Christian possessed a divine nature it was necessary for him to engage in a strenuous struggle to maintain his purity and increase the wealth and effectiveness of his piety. He could not have been saved without exercising faith in the Saviour, but the cultivation of virtue in his own personal living was a binding obligation upon him ever afterward. He must also seek to grow in the knowledge of things divine and go on to the attainment of every true virtue. Escape from former sins was only the starting point for the Christian life. If one fell back into the evil ways of former living, forgiveness for past sins would not save one from the terrors of the Judgment Day. To effect this result one must go on to positive growth in new knowledge of things divine, day by day experiencing new visions of truth and reaching new attainments in virtuous living. At least the first status of new purity acquired on entering the church must be preserved untarnished throughout one's career. Only by this course of action could one be sure of attaining unto final salvation through admission into the kingdom of the Lord and Saviour Jesus Christ when he would come to judge the wicked and reward the righteous.

12–21. The Divine Authority of Christian Tradition. The writer spoke in the authority of the past. God, Jesus, and ancient prophecy were behind the words of a Christian apostle. It was the latter's duty to deliver instructions that would be serviceable for admonition and guidance in a later day. This was only another way of reminding the church at the moment of the necessity of turning back to apostolic tradition as a means of refuting the novel ideas more recently brought forward by the disturbers in the Christian gatherings. The readers were told that Christianity did not rest on those mythical fabrications that were characteristic of the various pagan religions, but depended, rather, upon well-attested historical facts of which apostles had themselves been eyewitnesses (v. 16). Here the writer assumed that his readers were familiar with the Gospel account of the Transfiguration (Mk. 9[2f.] and parallels). But the Christian congregations have as a guide not only their N.T. Scriptures, telling the story of Jesus' life. They also hark back to the O.T., which had been taken over from the Jews. These older Scriptures were a source of light to illumine the darkness of man's ignorance, since prophecy—so it was believed —was an infallible forecasting by God of events to transpire in the future. But, of course, prophecy was subject to interpretation. On the principle that Satan can always quote Scripture to his own advantage, the false teachers themselves undoubtedly were indulging in their own expositions of prophecy that were at variance with the more usual opinions of older Christian teachers. These were *private* readings of prophecy, which our author declares to be illegitimate.

CHAPTER II

1-9. A Sure Judgment Awaits the Errorists. The whole of the second chapter is a vigorous arraignment of the false teachers. Speaking of prophecy, the writer sees in the false prophets of ancient times the prototype of the disturbers now active in the church. They are stealthily introducing into what should be a perfectly united body the divisive influences of their novel opinions, particularly with respect to a proper type of moral conduct. Before giving the readers a detailed account of these evil persons' activities, the author dwells on the certainty of the judgment which is to overtake them (vv. 4f.). Since he is writing in the name of Peter, who had lived before these troubles had actually arisen, the present message is cast in the form of prophecy. The apostle, it is assumed, had anticipated the events that were now transpiring. He had foreseen that pernicious sects would appear in the church, and that their teachings would be a denial of the Saviour who had died on behalf of even these evildoers. Their perverse conduct would bring disgrace upon the church, as their doings were noised abroad among outsiders. But their ultimate destruction was sure. One had only to remember how severely God had punished the angels who had sinned in ancient times. Not even these supernatural beings, much less mere men like the false teachers, could hope to disobey God with impunity. Here the reference is not only to the O.T. account of the Flood and its occasion (Gen. 6[1-7]), but also to tradition about the punishment of sinning angels mentioned in later Jewish books (see comments on Jude, v. 6).

The use of the word "Tartarus" for *hell* (v. 4, mg.) as the place where the degraded angels were in bonds would impress Gentile readers all the more forcibly because they would recall the fate that had overtaken the Titans who had incurred the displeasure of the mighty Greek deity, Zeus. For the comfort of the faithful it is to be noted also that in punishing the wicked God is not unmindful of the rewards due the righteous. He knows how to save godly persons from temptation (v. 9). Only those who give way to their fleshly desires and who despise the admonition of the older Christian teacher are in danger of punishment. The righteous Noah and his like-minded companions had not been engulfed in the Flood, nor had the pure Lot been left to perish in the destruction of Sodom and Gomorrah.

10-22. The Evil Doings of the False Teachers. The principal accusation brought against these evil persons concerns their grossly immoral conduct. They allow themselves to be dominated by the lusts of the flesh. Then, also, they are defiant in their attitude. Just what *dominion* it is that they despise, or against what *dignities* they rail, is not perfectly clear (cf. Jude, vv. 9f.). Perhaps they flout the control of Christ by rejecting those ideals of Christian living which the older teachers in the church advocated, and perhaps they speak lightly of such things as happened to dignitaries like the fallen angels. Whatever may be the nature of their preposterous reviling, they assume for themselves a freedom which not even the angels ventured to claim. All of this proves their utter senselessness, and is in line with their disposition to follow the impulses of their animal nature. They are no better than beasts. They are sure to receive, as the wages of their wrongdoing, divine punishment. Their evil deeds are performed even in the open (v. 13). Within the very sanctity of the Christian gatherings they ply their nefarious trade, endeavoring to lead the righteous astray. Their lustful desires are always uppermost. Instead of walking in the way of righteousness, they, like Balaam of old, turn aside to ways of wickedness. Covetousness for gold had tempted Balaam to pervert his prophetic gift, but apparently these later offenders were coveting what the author calls *unsteadfast souls* (v. 14) who could be drawn away from loyalty to the regular teachers and persuaded to side with the new agitators. But what blind guides they will be found to be! They are wholly unsubstantial and worthless. They are like waterless fountains that betray the thirsty soul, or like wind-driven storm clouds that drop no moisture on the parched fields. They are destined for eternal doom. They speak *great words* (v. 18), promising their hearers a new liberty of action, but this freedom is only an invitation to a lustful life to which more recent converts are especially susceptible. The principle of freedom is thus being used as a means of bringing men into bondage to fleshly appetites. One who has accepted Christianity, having thereby escaped the defilements of the world, would on the advice of these teachers presently find himself in a more evil state than that from which he had originally been rescued.

CHAPTER III

1-13. Certainty of Christ's Return in Judgment. Whether or not the persons accused were actually guilty of all the charges brought against them, undoubtedly they were sharply opposed to the older views regarding an early end of the present world to be effected through the return of Christ. This expectation of a catastrophic end had held a prominent place in first-century Christianity (see 1 Thess. 4[13]–5[11]), but as time passed without bringing the hope to fulfillment some Christians began to abandon the idea and to live as though present society would continue indefinitely under existing conditions. With the expectation of an early Judgment abandoned, the older leaders feared an immediate slackening of moral endeavor. They believed that one who cast off the fear of judgment would plunge into unrestrained immoral activities. In fact this skepticism seemed to them motivated by a desire to pursue without restraint a line of conduct dominated by the appetites of the flesh. With this thought in mind the author now returns to the subject of the impending Judgment, which had been his theme before he entered upon his tirade against the false teachers. His description of these evildoers, given in ch. 2, had been borrowed in large part from an older and briefer pamphlet, the Epistle of Jude. Now the author resumes the earlier theme. The validity of traditional Christian teaching about an early end of the world and a sure judgment of sinners is reaffirmed. Its certainty is divinely assured. Readers are called on to remember that Christian teaching had been foreshadowed in the ancient prophets and that this wisdom had also been communicated by Christ to his apostles. In particular, the day of the Lord had been announced by the prophets, had been preached by Jesus, and had been reaffirmed by the apostles (v. 2). It was preposterous, therefore, for moderns to deny the expectation of Christ's return. When they said that all things had been going on for a hundred years or more since his death just as before, they were failing to recognize that God does not count time as do men. With him even a *thousand years* might be as a single day. They who imagine that the end of the world is still far off are deceiving themselves. Its dissolution is sure (vv. 8f.; cf. pp. 206–7, 846b).

In his vivid portrayal of the end our author combines eschatological imagery from both Jewish and Gentile areas of thinking. The idea of a Judgment in the last times was a distinctly Jewish concept, but Stoic teachers were proclaiming a dissolution of the world by a conflagration very similar to that used in this picture. Eschatological speculation, however, is not this author's primary interest. His chief concern is for the maintenance of high standards of Christian morality. The great lesson that he tries to drive home is the absolute necessity for holy living and the cultivation of genuine godliness on the part of all persons within the church.

14-18. Final Exhortation to Righteous Living. In view of the certainty of coming judgment readers are exhorted to live a blameless life. They should remember what Jesus had suffered for the very purpose of making salvation possible. This fact was an unmistakable indication of the divine favor for man, as had been so emphatically stressed by the famous apostle to the Gentiles in all of his letters. Mention of Paul raises a delicate problem for our author (v. 16). Doubtless his opponents were themselves using the Pauline Epistles, and especially the ideal of freedom for the spiritual man, to justify their own liberty of conduct. Admittedly, there are some things in Paul *hard to understand*, but certainly the false teachers have been perverting this new Christian Scripture when they used it to justify disbelief in judgment and immoral conduct. Their followers will surely meet misfortune. The only safe course is to maintain the traditional knowledge of Christ as Lord and Saviour which has been mediated through the apostolic teaching and which constitutes the generally accepted tradition of the church.

THE EPISTLES OF JOHN

BY PROFESSOR BURTON SCOTT EASTON

FIRST JOHN

INTRODUCTION

Theme of the Letter. If any man asks, "What is God like?" the answer is, "Look at Jesus Christ and see!"

This, John's universal theme, is the sole topic of our Epistle, stated and restated in every conceivable form and with all manner of applications. John would not have denied in principle that a knowledge of God might be gained by other means—in 3^{12} he speaks of Abel as righteous—but his own experience had been so overwhelmed by the person of Jesus that he could not think other methods worth discussion. "No man hath beheld God at any time" (4^{12} Jn. 1^{18}); the Divine in its essence is beyond our reach unless revealed, and the only perfect revelation is in Jesus: the character of Jesus is the character of God. Two conclusions follow, which to John were simply contrasted sides of the same truth: (1) the historic fact of Jesus' life is the basis of all religion, and (2) a religion is self condemned which teaches a righteousness other than that taught by Jesus; or, in modern terms: At the supreme moment—from the birth of Jesus until his return to the Father—history and the philosophy of religion were not two but one.

The Gnostic Denial of the Theme. Toward the end of the first century, however, both these basic facts were denied by men who professed and called themselves Christians. The fashion of the day was to combine Hellenistic philosophy with Oriental religious traditions, and such a combination we term Gnosticism. The term, consequently, is vague, as it describes a method rather than a result, and covers all sorts of systems. Gnostics might be ascetic and puritanical to the last degree, or they might be debased libertines who quite literally gloried in their shame. They might be men of high mental attainments—some of the second-century Gnostics were able speculative thinkers—or they might be intellectually beneath contempt. And when Gnosticism was combined with Christianity the result might be so nearly orthodox as to cause no trouble, or it might be utterly subversive of the church's faith and life. With the milder forms N.T. writers were not greatly concerned; such were only "profane and old wives' fables" (1 Tim. 4^{7}), a foolish waste of time, no doubt, but not seriously dangerous. But the more vicious types of Gnosticism could receive no quarter, and it was with those that John had to deal. (See intro. to Colossians, p. 1250.)

Tradition gives as his chief antagonist a certain Cerinthus, who taught in Ephesus around 95 A.D., and what early Christian writers tell us about this man agrees with what we can deduce from the Epistle itself. The name "Gnostic" ("one who knows") is derived from the boast, "We know God" (2^{4}). Such knowledge, derived in part from ecstatic experiences (4^{1}), was quite different from that taught in Christian tradition, so that anti-Gnostic writers urge the novelty of the doctrine as one reason for rejecting it (2^{24}).

Almost universal among the Gnostics was a philosophical dualism, which identified spirit with good and matter with evil. This made the incarnation unthinkable, since the divine could not come into contact with matter, and thereby presented Christian Gnostics with a puzzling problem. They generally agreed that the incarnation was in appearance only (a heresy technically described as "docetism," derived from the Greek word meaning "to seem"), but Cerinthus added a peculiar theory of his own, teaching (2^{22}) that Jesus and Christ were different beings. On the former, a mere man, at the time of his baptism the celestial Christ descended—"he came by water" (5^{6})—and used him as a medium for his revelations; although the words were Christ's the voice was that of Jesus, so no one could really hear Christ speak, while he certainly could not be seen or touched (1^{1-3}). When Christ concluded his message, he left Jesus and the latter was crucified, an event that had no religious significance, as Christ was not involved; "he did not come by blood," according to Cerinthus (see 5^{6}).

Acceptance of such tenets made a man a Gnostic, a spiritual being who could boast, "I am in the Light" (2^{9}) and "I have fellowship with God" (1^{6}). Being himself "beyond good and evil," he had no longer to concern himself with sin ($1^{8,\ 10}$) and his sole concern was to keep the rules in the Gnostic law (3^{4}). A superman, he had no feeling of responsibility toward ordinary "psychic" men (i.e., men who had not attained to the "spiritual" or "pneumatic" stage); they were as far below him as the lower animals and he was no more bound to love them than he was to love beasts or reptiles (3[10, 15] 4[8, 20]). Yet it is only fair to note that John does not accuse his particular adversaries of a licentiousness which appears in other Gnostic groups (2 Pet. 2[14]).

In John's day the more thoroughgoing Christian Gnostics had left the church (2[19]) and had founded communities of their own, into which they were endeavoring to entice others by all sorts of arguments and promises. And even among those who remained there were those who found Gnostic tenets attractive, a class that must have included many who were only lax and thoughtless. This was the situation that John wrote to meet.

John's Reply to the Gnostics. "Jesus Christ is come in the flesh" (4[2]) is the formula which lays the axe to the root of the tree. All that Jesus said and did is the revelation of God, not merely certain parts of his teaching and life which alone the Gnostics attributed to "Christ." And what Jesus said and did is no secret, to be learned from these new teachers, but has been preached without reserve ever since Christianity began. It can all be summed up in the single word "love": this is God, this is Jesus, this is Christianity. And so John, in replying to a teaching that bewilders modern readers with its fantastic absurdity, raises his answer to the utmost religious heights.

Against the Gnostic dualism of spirit and matter he sets the Christian dualism of good and evil; however evil may have originated—and John does not waste time in puzzling over the problem—the important fact is that it exists and must be fought. And in this war there is no compromise. Whoever hopes for God's approval thinks of sin as exceeding sinful, "purifieth himself even as he is pure" (3[3]), and displays his purity in moral activity. "This is his commandment, that we should believe in the name of his Son Jesus Christ, and love one another" (3[23]); such belief and such love are inseparable.

The Christian and the Church. Since Christianity manifests itself in love, it demands social relationships, and, therefore, it demands a special, consecrated society in which these relationships may be practiced to the full; this was as axiomatic to John as it was to the O.T. writers, who think of "God" and "Israel" as well-nigh correlative terms. We have fellowship with God because "we have fellowship one with another" (1[3,6, 7]). And so John's doctrine of the church is the most pronounced of the whole N.T., even though he does not use the word (in 3 John it describes only the local congregation). In large part this doctrine is simply the result of his observation of facts as they were. Writing near the end of the first century, he saw the degradation of the Hellenistic world with the eyes of a pastor who had labored in it for years. And the church, which took as its charter God's demand for utter righteousness, was the sole visible alternative. So John extended his dualism to cover the practical facts of his experience; the church is on God's side while the rest of the world—or *the world* directly—is on the devil's. This may be called "ecclesiasticism," but it is the ecclesiasticism of a passionately earnest man face to face with overwhelming problems and unconcerned with anything except the immediate practical issue.

Hence, to all intents and purposes, church membership was to John the necessary and sufficient condition for salvation. "We are of God and the whole world lieth in the evil one" (5[19]). To be sure, "not all are of us," (2[19]) but the nature of these will be made clear by their departure, either of their own accord or by excommunication (4[4]). For those who remain faithful John has only the highest and most unconditional praise: "Your sins are forgiven you" (2[12]), "ye have overcome the evil one" (2[13]), "ye are strong" (2[14]), "ye know all things" (2[20]), "ye need not that any one teach you" (2[27]), "we have passed out of death into life" (3[14]), "ye have eternal life" (5[13]). No Gnostic could use more realistic language to describe the certainty of his converts' salvation.

Security still Requires Watchfulness. And without doubt the extreme assurance of the Gnostics supplied John with one motive in his use of such phrases; he wished to make his readers feel that they were already in possession of all that Gnostics might promise. Another factor was pastoral tact; John knew that more men suffer from diffidence and despondency than from presumption, that encouragement and judicious praise are more helpful than denunciation. But, besides this, he was once more speaking from experience: The band of men and women who, on the one hand, had made the very real sacrifices involved in embracing Christianity, and who, on the other hand, had resisted the Gnostic seductions, had a right to be taken seriously as moral persons. The basic reason, however, for John's confidence was his faith in God and in Jesus Christ. "Herein is love, not that we loved God, but that he loved us" (4[10]); the way to God is not a human quest with endless opportunities for error. The power comes from on high, and man, once in the right way, has only to yield himself to that power.

Not that the process is merely automatic, for throughout the Epistle there is an undercurrent of warning, various significant "if's," and a frank recognition that (grave) sin is an ever-present possibility (1^{8}-2^{12} 5^{16}). But John does not let himself dwell on these things; instead he sets before his readers an ideal sinlessness so extreme as to seem out of the reach of flesh and blood (3^{5-9}). Many commentators consequently explain his words as expressing *only* an ideal to remind us that the more we progress the less we shall sin. But John means precisely what he says, and thinks of sinlessness as something not only attainable but frequently attained; God's demands on us are so simple and his commandments so much the reverse of grievous (5^{3}) as to be well within our power. So, if we are making a real effort in the important matters, we can safely dismiss worry about minor imperfections, for these things, inevitable as long as we are in the body, do not cloud our relation to God. Even though a scrupulous conscience condemns us, God takes our *whole* nature into consideration; when we remember this we may reassure our heart ($3^{19f.}$). This is what Paul means, in part, by justification by faith. (See notes on Rom. 3^{21-31}.) Such counsel comes from a very wise and experienced pastor, who knows the harm that anxious scrupulosity and dread may work (4^{18}).

Form and Style of the Letter. As to *form*, 1 John is rather a tractate than an epistle in the strict sense of the term, for the conventional opening and closing formulæ are lacking. But the traditional designation is accurate enough, for the work was evidently written for a concrete audience (4^{4}), who are addressed throughout in the second person.

More important is the question of the *style*. This, which is unique but the perfect expression of John's thought, is determined by his intense feeling for the unity of the Christian message; as he sees it, there is only a single revealed truth, whose various aspects are so interdependent that they blend at every point into one another. So all Christian terms are practically synonymous and any one of them may be replaced at will by almost any other. This conception produces a perfectly smooth stylistic flow, in which practically every sentence is linked with the preceding and the following, but at the same time it is fatal to logical development in the ordinary sense of the word; since everything Christian is more or less the same in essence, any of John's paragraphs may contain almost anything. And he sees no reason to avoid repetitions, for to him nothing after his first sentence can escape being a repetition in some sense. The Epistle is accordingly the despair of the formal analyst, and even the traditional paragraphs of the printed editions are little more than inherited conventions; other groupings of the verses are often urged by modern commentators.

Summary of the Letter. John opens with four verses that state his theme (1^{1-4}), and his development then seems to be controlled by the three words "fellowship," "sin," and "commandments," which appear in varying uses (1^{5}–2^{11}). A succinct, really independent paragraph (2^{12-17}) forms a resting place, with a direct appeal to the readers. Then the discussion is resumed around "Antichrist," "abiding," "begotten of God," and "love" (2^{18}–3^{24}), with no pronounced breaks anywhere. A second resting place is offered by another independent paragraph (4^{1-6}) on true and false inspiration, and then John sums up in the magnificent section 4^{7-21}, after which the futilities of Gnosticism (5^{1-13}) appear grotesque by contrast; 5^{13} concludes the Epistle proper; 5^{14-17} deals with a painful but necessary question, while the epilogue (5^{18-21}) provides a worthy conclusion to the whole, with its superb triple declaration and its two crisp final sentences.

Authorship. The writer of the Epistle was evidently a man of great authority; on the title "elder," which he uses in 2 and 3 John, cf. on 2 Jn. 1. And much the most natural interpretation of 1 Jn. 1^{1-3} is to understand him as claiming membership in the authoritative band of eyewitnesses of Jesus' earthly life.

The thought and the style of the fourth Gospel and 1 John agree so closely as to make a common author more than probable (on the further questions involved see intro. to the fourth Gospel). But there are certain real differences of emphasis—e.g., the insistence on the nearness of the end in 1 Jn. 2^{18} is lacking in the Gospel—that make it impossible to bring the two works too close together; certainly they were not meant to be mutually supplementary.

Tradition points unanimously to Ephesus as the place of writing. The date cannot be very far from the year 100 A.D.

Literature: The "classical" English commentary on John's Epistles is Westcott, *The Epistles of St. John*, first published in 1883. It is learned and deeply spiritual. Brooke, *The Johannine Epistles*, in the International Critical Commentary, is expository rather than exegetical. An excellent popular commentary is Pakenham-Walsh, *The Epistles of St. John.* More purely expository works: Robert Law, *The Tests of Life*, brilliantly written; Watson, *The First Epistle General of St. John*, the work of a skilled pastor; and Gore, *The Epistles of St. John*, written with deep spiritual insight.

CHAPTER I

1–4. The Place of Personal Experience. In a single sentence (vv. 1–3) packed with implications John sets forth not only the theme of his Epistle but the essence of his argument as well. Gnostics were usually docetics, teaching that the manifestation of Christ on earth was only in appearance, that either his form was a physical illusion or else what was visible was not Christ at all (see intro.). John contradicts such teaching at every point. Jesus Christ's voice could be heard, his form could be seen—a fact so important that John repeats it three times, varying the verb for emphasis—and human hands could handle him. Conversely, the person of whom this was true was no mere instrument of a higher power. He *was* that higher power, he came from the Father, he is eternal, and he is so completely the source of all life that he may be spoken of simply as "life" itself. All this is completely attested and (v. 4) the joy the Christian message brings must not be clouded by plausibly suggested doubts.

The *we* throughout, particularly in its contrast to *you* in vv. 2f., is most simply taken to mean those who were "eyewitnesses and ministers of the word" (Lk. 1^{2}), whose testimony was still active even though most of the group were dead. The fellowship of this group with God and Jesus Christ was so intense that their teaching is normative for all Christians—a common theme in anti-Gnostic writings, but the present passage is unique in its vivid sense of personal experience. In v. 1 the *word of life* is presumably the Gospel message, but the exact force is debated.

5–10. Sin Excludes from God. Since God by his very nature is perfect righteousness (=*light*), any religion that treats evil lightly is self-condemned. And so the Gnostics are self-condemned, despite their boasts, *We have fellowship with him* (v. 6), *We have no sin* (v. 8), and *We have not sinned* (v. 10). The last two of these sentences stir John's anger to a special degree: people who say such things show that they do not know what evil is. Sinners who acknowledge their fault can be pardoned, for their very acknowledgment proves they retain a true ideal, but nothing whatever can be done for the man who refuses to admit even the existence of his errors. Note how in v. 6 to *lie* is to *do not the truth;* to John a word *is* an act, and this particular act he regards as conscious and deliberate.

This passage displays John's dualism (cf. intro.). God is *light* and evil is *darkness*—and there is no third term. Note, moreover, how in vv. 6f. *have fellowship with him* in the negative statement is replaced by *have fellowship with one another* in the positive, as if the phrases were exact synonyms: to be outside the proper Christian social relationships is to be cut off from God. Consequently, it is only within the community that sins can be cleansed. This cleansing, however, is not effected simply by a right moral attitude; although such an attitude is an indispensable prerequisite, the cleansing is God's act—and by *the blood of Jesus his Son* (v. 7). This last phrase, which is worded in the most anti-Gnostic terminology possible (cf. 5^{6}), John treats as so familiar as to need no explanation.

CHAPTER II

1–6. Keeping His Commandment. This paragraph is chiefly an emphatic reiteration of the teaching of 1^{5-10}, now with the Gnostic phrases *I know him* (v. 4) and *I abide in him* (v. 6). But sin in a Christian is something which John is not eager to discuss; after repeating his promise of cleansing (v. 2) he drops the subject and does not touch on it again until 5^{16} (apart from the passing allusion in 4^{10}). Christians should live a life above sin and should "walk in the light as he is in the light" (1^{7}); God's readiness to pardon the penitent is no excuse for relaxing effort (v. 1).

For *Advocate* ("Interpreter"?) cf. especially on Jn. 14^{16}, where the Spirit is called "another Advocate" (in addition to Christ). For *propitiation* in v. 2 cf. on Rom. 3^{25}; neither John nor Paul, however, means all possible implications in the word to be stressed—such implications, e.g., as that God is not already gracious to men, but must be made gracious by an offering; and that the offering is accepted in place of something else. The second clause of v. 2 attacks the Gnostic dogma of a salvation offered only to a small band of *illuminati*, but, of course, neither John nor anyone else in the first century held a pure universalism (5^{19}).

The word *commandment* is now introduced and is used six times in vv. 3–8; it is taken from the O.T., but John ignores the O.T. meaning. In his vocabulary the *commandment* is to *walk even as he walked*, to imitate Jesus, and no other commandment has any Christian importance. This is the *word* which is to be kept, the sole means for perfecting man's love of God (v. 5). The concluding words of v. 5, *in him*, belong to the language of mysticism and have, strictly speaking, almost a local force. In a pure mysticism this would lead to the thought of the final absorption of the soul in the Divinity, but Christianity, with its unvarying emphasis on the reality and dignity of human personality, avoids such a conclusion; the righteous soul is completely surrounded by God but always remains itself. The whole discussion thus far is summarized in v. 6.

7–11. The Commandment is Love. The crucial point lies in v. 9. The Gnostic, who proclaimed *I am in the light*, believed that he belonged to an order of beings so high as to be above obligations to ordinary, "psychic" men (see intro.). Such teaching is in utter conflict with the fundamental Christian principle of love, and this principle John now prepares to state, emphasizing its wholly basic character by prefacing it with two verses (7f.) of description. To Christians the commandment is *old*, for they learned it at their conversion (*the beginning*) and their whole experience ever since has been simply its continual application. But to the world the same commandment is *new* (*which thing* is this novelty), realized for the first time in Christ and in his church (*in you*). To John, evidently, all pre-Christian and non-Christian love is so inadequate by comparison as to be negligible.

Finally John comes to his own summary (v. 10): The true Gnostic—he who is truly in the light—is *he that loveth his brother;* such a man, thanks to the illumination of his road, *never stumbles* (the correct translation of v. 10b). And so (v. 11) John's adversaries, despite their boasting, are of all men the most pitiable. It may be observed that v. 10 can be used to commend the best O.T. and Gentile ethics as thoroughly as v. 8 can be used to discredit them, but John does not take such problems into consideration.

12–17. Love is Possible to All. This paragraph marks a pause in the argument and John passes to a direct appeal to his readers. In their relation to him they are all *little children*, with the universal Christian privileges of forgiveness (v. 12) and knowledge of the Father (v. 13). But they may be divided into *fathers*, the more mature who are rich in meditation and wisdom, and *young men*, the comparative neophytes who have still to progress in the spiritual life and are appropriately pictured as strong warriors, engaged in victorious warfare with Satan. The change from *I write* in vv. 12f. to *I have written* in vv. 13f. is formal only, *I have written* referring simply to the Epistle thus far, without any reference to some earlier (lost) letter or to the fourth Gospel.

The full Christian experience (vv. 12–14) includes a joyous certainty; John's readers are already in a state of salvation, they are already abundantly taught by God, and so they need no assistance from anyone—least of all from the Gnostics. And yet (vv. 15–17) no Christian has progressed so far that he can afford to be careless; the *world*—the aggregate of a humanity lost in sin and under the rule of the powers of evil—is very near and, despite its wickedness, may only too easily be found attractive. John sums up its allurements in a triple phrase, where the word translated *life* is used in the special sense of "money." So *fleshly desires, tempting glitter and the parade of luxury.*

V. 17, while summing up, links to the next paragraph by means of its mention of the impending dissolution.

18, 19. The Threat of Antichrist. Like all Christians of the apostolic age, John believed that the end of the world was at hand, and he was ready to find corroboration in every "sign" he thought he could identify; the same tendency has reappeared constantly throughout Christian history and is familiar even to-day. Now, Jewish apocalyptic commonly taught that just before the end the growing evil in the world would find its supreme embodiment in a single diabolic being, in all regards the antithesis of the Messiah. (See art., *Backgrounds*, p. 846b.) Hence the name *Antichrist*, although this title is not found in works earlier than 1 John. As to details, however, there was little agreement among apocalyptists and each drew freely on his own fancy; 2 Thess. 2:3–12 is a fairly typical prediction but there were many other forms; and this vagueness left John free to make his own identification, which is stated in the present passage; as to him nothing could be worse than this perverse wickedness appearing from within the church, the Gnostics seemed to be the most poignant fulfillment conceivable of the expectation. To be sure, they were only human beings, but—as John took for granted—they were so suffused with the diabolic spirit (vv. 21, 22) that each of them individually *was* an antichrist.

John could not give us a better picture of his horror at this evil that raised its head in the community supposedly dedicated to perfect righteousness. It was with relief that he saw the Gnostics depart (v. 19); at least they proved that *not all are of us*, that not all who claim to be Christians are so in reality. And no one trained in the historical interpretation of the N.T. will be troubled at John's identification of the impending crisis with apocalyptic expectations; to blame John for thinking in such terms would be to blame him because he lived in the first century. But attempts to use John's language in support of modern apocalyptics are discredited in advance; the purpose of religion is not to minister to curiosity.

20–25. An Anointing from the Anointed One.

Returning to the specific Gnostic errors, John emphasizes once more the maturity and understanding of his readers but now introduces a new word, *anointing*, which is to reappear in v. 27. It is a play (in Greek) on *Christ;* he, "the Anointed One," has given his own character to his disciples, so that they *all know* (mg.). They know the truth—no simple one!—contained in vv. 18f. But they know also the more vital truth of v. 22. To claim that Jesus and Christ are not one but two is to deny the completeness and the reality of the revelation of God in Jesus, and this last conclusion is the sum of all possible religious errors. To deny the Son is to deny the Father; criticism of Jesus manifests ignorance of the nature of God. So important is this theme to John—it is one of the most common in his Gospel—that he repeats it in v. 23 in strict formal parallelism in order to give it all possible emphasis. That this truth should be denied by so-called Christians is monstrous, for the Gnostic teaching contradicts the universal apostolic preaching (v. 24; cf. 1^{3} 2^{7}); the faithful, who are certain of the validity of their religious experience and of its final realization in the life eternal (v. 25), have not so learned Christ.

In v. 20 *the Holy One* is Christ, not the Father; cf. Acts 2^{33}, etc.

26–29. The Discovery of New Truth. These verses summarize and reiterate vv. 18–25, much as vv. 1–6 reiterate 1^{5-10}; such cumulative repetition is characteristic of John's style. While v. 21 has affirmed that the readers are already in possession of all fundamental truth, v. 27 promises that the same anointing will enable them to solve each new problem as it arises. By this teaching (cf. Jn. 14^{26} $16^{12f.}$) John takes a line of his own in the Gnostic controversy. In opposition to the novelty of the Gnostic doctrines, "orthodox" writers were inclined to deprecate questionings of any sort on the part of Christians and to set up an ideal of rigid adherence to the received tradition, without seeking to inquire further (e.g., Jude v. 3). But John holds that the answer to Gnostic inquiries is to be found in more far-reaching inquiries; if these are conducted in the proper spirit, they will be rewarded by the discovery of fresh truth. To be noted throughout this paragraph is the insistence on the doctrine of Christian religious democracy; John himself has the right to teach other Christians only as a fellow expounder of the truth which in essence they all share.

The slight variant possibilities (indicated in the mg.) of the translation of vv. 27–29 do not affect the general sense.

In v. 29, which returns to the moral emphasis of the earlier sections, John prepares also for ch. 3 by introducing the phrase *begotten of God*, around which the next paragraph is to turn. This phrase reappears in 4^{7}, $5^{1, 4, 18}$; and is consequently characteristic of the Epistle. In the O.T. it is found only in Psa. 2^{7}, and elsewhere in the N.T. only (in all essentials) in Jn. 1^{13} and 3^{3-9}. It is derived partly from the fundamental Christian conception of God's Fatherhood, partly from transferring a characteristic of Christ to his followers (5^{1}), and partly, no doubt, from the language of the Hellenistic religions. In them it is extremely common and it is presumably a favorite Gnostic phrase, which John turns against its users.

CHAPTER III

1–12. Perfect Life Through Perfect Love. John resumes his development of the moral argument, now, in so triumphant a tone that he dispenses with exhortation and takes Christian salvation completely for granted. How can we fail? We are God's children, not only in name but in fact, with a character so supernatural that the world cannot understand it (v. 1). Already we are God's children, even in our present imperfect state, and are destined to be transformed wholly into his likeness (v. 2). John's proof (v. 2b) of this last promise uses a mystical argument; we know that we shall see God (Mt. 5^{8} may be specifically in mind), and this proves that we shall be transformed into complete likeness to the Divine, since inferior beings cannot gaze at God. But again (cf. on 2^{5}) John's mysticism always preserves human identity.

No one with the glorious hope of vv. 1f. can fail to prepare himself in advance to the utmost of his ability (v. 3). Not (v. 4), of course, with the artificial purifications of the Gnostics, who laid all stress on obeying the laws of their eccentric codes and paid no attention to sin. On the contrary, *sin is lawlessness*—the only lawlessness that matters—and Christ (v. 5) is the antithesis of sin in all its forms, not only atoning for it but *taking it away*. And so (v. 6) *whoever sinneth hath not seen him, neither knoweth him*. By *sin* here John means primarily the deliberate choice and defense of sin, but he also means more than this; he is setting before his readers an ideal of sinlessness which he is convinced lies wholly within their power (cf. intro.).

Consequently (v. 7), the Gnostics are to be ignored, for words without deeds are nothing. The dualism that exists in our universe (v. 8) is moral, with the hosts of God arrayed against the hosts of the devil—and in this warfare neutrality is impossible. John's language grows more and more unqualified until it becomes almost physical (v. 9); God's *seed*—probably the Spirit—so transforms a man that he cannot sin. Once more John is talking about actualities, not about an impossible ideal. Such men and women exist and in sufficient numbers to be a real factor in the universe.

In v. 10 we have an amplification of Mt. 7[20], with a concrete application at the end which looks back to 2[10] and also links forward to the next section. At the same time it suggests Gen. 4[3-5] as an obvious illustration; here only in the Epistle does John commend a non-Christian (v. 12).

13–24. Love Within the Brotherhood. The principles of vv. 1–12 are summarized for the supreme test, "Does love prove itself in action?" Now, while Christian love is universal and unrestricted, its existence in practice must be demonstrated concretely within the circle to which the individual belongs. And for first-century Christians this circle was primarily the church—*"the" brethren*—whose claims were imperative. This fact, coupled with the extreme sense of personal consecration and an equally extreme dread of the corruption and idolatry of the "world," made Christians a race apart from other men. And these other men not unnaturally resented the Christians' attitude, so that all sorts of stories were in circulation, accusing them of the vilest practices. Such hatred, replies John, comes from the fact that we belong to a different world, which such men cannot understand (vv. 13f.; cf. v. 1b.); *we have passed out of death into life* (cf. on Jn. 5[24]). That the transformation has really taken place is demonstrated by the presence of love—note that this love is the effect, not the cause, of salvation—for love and life are the same thing and both are from Christ (v. 16; cf. Mk. 10[45], etc., and the abundant parallels in John's Gospel).

The existence of such love (vv. 17f.) is seen in the common incidents of everyday life (cf. Mt. 5[42]) and (v. 19) its presence should free men from all despondency or scrupulosity. Spiritual depression is, no doubt, a common occurrence (v. 20), but it is needless, for God is actually more merciful than a spiritual man's own conscience, because God takes everything into consideration. The proper attitude, therefore, is a joyous confidence (v. 21), trusting so deeply in God as never to question his full response to every need of ours. For John's doctrine of prayer see more fully on Jn. 14[13], etc., his underlying thought being that, if we are in the right relation with God, our requests will be such as can always be granted.

In vv. 22–24a John sums up in familiar terms; it is interesting to compare v. 23 with Mt. 22[36-40] and to observe how axiomatic it was in Christian experience to replace "love the Lord thy God" with *believe in the name of his Son Jesus Christ.* V. 24b connects with the next section.

In the above paragraph there is a constant anti-Gnostic warning, for spiritual depression frequently leads men to change their faith, in the hope that the new system will prove more potent. And the Gnostics, with their boasts of knowledge and sinlessness, knew how to take advantage of such moments.

CHAPTER IV

1–6. A True Test for Prophetic Utterance. Here is a second resting place (cf. 2[12-17]), which deals with an important practical problem. In the apostolic church all were convinced that prophecy was revived and that men spoke through the inspiration of the Spirit to declare hidden truths. But Christians soon realized that ecstatic utterances are not always edifying, an experience that led them to interpret some "inspiration" as the work of evil spirits; cf. especially 1 Cor. 12, 14, and with the present passage cf. particularly 1 Cor. 12[1-3]. Both Paul and John declare that the content of a prophecy is the test of its inspiration, and both apostles give a summary formula for practical use. In Paul (1 Cor. 12[3]) this is the primitive Christian watchword, "Jesus is Lord," in John (v. 2) it is slightly elaborated, *Jesus Christ is come in the flesh,* in order to meet the more complicated denials of the Gnostics; this is the beginning of a process that was to issue in the creeds of later Christianity.

V. 4 indicates that excommunications had taken place. On the serene confidence of v. 6 cf. intro.

6–21. Love Central and Supreme. After the short digression in vv. 1–6 John returns to 3[23] for his theme, *love,* which he uses (noun and verb) no less than twenty-five times in the present fifteen verses, besides two instances of *beloved.* With such a theme the primary appeal is emotional and so John, with consummate literary tact, avoids raising new questions and writes in language that no one can fail to understand; the result is a passage whose beauty is rivaled only in 1 Cor. 13. God is love—has made his love known to man through his Son—awakening man's echoing response—demonstrated in visible acts of service to others. In these acts religion culminates, and if such acts do not appear, the whole structure is futile. God has set our brother where we can see him in order to give our love an object; if we neglect this object which stands before us, there is no profit in proclaiming our affection for an invisible God (v. 20), for without love of man love of God cannot exist. Here John, himself a mystic, parts company from the "pure" mystics; they find man's highest destiny on earth in contemplation; John finds it in practical activity.

For v. 12 cf. on Jn. 1^{18} and note how it prepares for v. 20.

John's insistence that love must come from God before it can be practiced by men (vv. 10, 19) has no anti-Gnostic point, but is to him a mere statement of a religious axiom; the Shepherd seeks the sheep, not the sheep the Shepherd. On v. 12a cf. intro.; *beheld* in this clause is balanced by the same verb in v. 14 (cf. Jn. 1^{18}) and the saying helps prepare for v. 20. V. 14 (cf. 1^{1-3}) is the perfect summary of the apostolic message; here *world* does not have the usual evil sense. With v. 17b cf. 3^{14}, but now the self-consciousness is even more extreme; apparently, *although in this world, we, by sharing the divine life, are far above it, even as Christ is.* And in v. 18—a verse comparable only to Jn. $15^{14, 15}$—this self-consciousness reaches its supremest exaltation.

CHAPTER V

1–13. The Spirit and the Victorious Life. As the last paragraph expounds the Christian ideal as it is in itself, so the present section expounds it in contrast to Gnosticism. But John avoids any sharp transition; vv. 1–4 summarize once more, although in so doing the intellectual element is brought to the front in v. 1 and is repeated at the end of v. 4 in *faith.* This all-important Christian noun occurs nowhere else in John's Gospel or Epistles, apparently because John's experience was so vivid as to carry his convictions into the realm of certainty; even in the present instance his emphasis is on faith's true correspondence to its object rather than on its trustful quality. (The same is true about his frequent use of the verb *believe.*) On v. 3b cf. intro., p. 1352a.

Vv. 5–13 open with a restatement of a basic Johannine doctrine; cf. 2^{22}, $4^{2f., 15}$, 5^{1}. On v. 6 cf. intro. The verse is directed specifically against Cerinthus, who taught that "Christ" descended on Jesus at his baptism but left him before his Passion, thereby emptying the death of Jesus of all religious meaning and making, e.g., the appeal in 3^{16} a sheer absurdity. So much is clear enough, but John's development in vv. 7, 8 shows that he had in mind a further meaning, which we cannot reconstruct with certainty. The Voice from heaven at Jesus' baptism (Mk. 1^{11}) and the miracle at the crucifixion (Jn. $19^{34f.}$; even if the Gospel were published after 1 John, this tradition must have been familiar in Johannine circles) are often invoked to explain the passage. And they may really be relevant—the Spirit (v. 8) explaining their inner significance—but, even if this is true, the exact force is obscure to us. Quite possible also is a sacramental reference to Christian experience in baptism (Jn. 3^{5}) and the Lord's Supper (Jn. $6^{58, 63}$), or this explanation may be combined with the preceding. But John's choice of mysterious terms is evidently deliberate; he knew that his (initiated) readers would understand his allusions, but his meaning was too deeply mystical to be stated baldly.

At any rate, John's invocation of the witness of the Spirit is—at least in part—an appeal to the witness of religious experience. *The witness of men* (v. 9) unquestionably helps toward belief (1^{1-3}), but belief itself rests on something deeper and more enduring. And also (v. 10a) on something more personal and inward, for *he that believeth on the Son of God hath the witness in him*, even though (v. 10b) assent may be refused.

And finally (vv. 11–13) John sums up his whole Epistle around the word *life*, balancing his use of the same word in his opening verses (1^{1-3}). The paragraph division in the English versions is unfortunate, for v. 13 is the solemn conclusion (cf. Jn. 20^{31}) and all that follows is epilogue (cf. Jn. 21).

8. *The Threefold Witness.* This mention of the threefold witness suggested to Christian students of a later day the Three Persons of the Trinity. And so, some time in the fourth century or toward the end of the third, a Spanish Christian (probably), who wrote in Latin, formed a corresponding sentence: "There are three who bear witness in heaven, the Father, the Word and the Holy Spirit, and these three are one." Perhaps he wrote this on the margin of his copy of 1 John and some later copyist thought it part of the text, but in any case these words were quoted as part of the Latin Bible in Spain at least as early as 380 A.D., *on earth* being added to v. 8 to balance the insertion. This "gloss" (as such insertions are called) spread, and finally became so universal in Latin-speaking Christianity that it was even translated into Greek and was added to a few late Greek MSS. (see p. 861a). From these it found its way into printed editions, and so into the first English versions. But R.V. and A.S.V. rightly omit all mention of it, as it has no claim to be considered John's words.

14–17. Forgivable and Unforgivable Sin. It would almost seem that John, on rereading what he had written, was a little disturbed by his uncompromising teaching of the necessity of sinlessness, and so he qualifies by returning to 1^{7}–2^{2}, reintroducing his theme there with two verses (14f.) on his doctrine of prayer. These repeat something of 3[21f.], although now with the explicit addition of *according to his will.* But in what follows (vv. 16f.) this addition is less a restriction than a reassurance, for nothing can be more according to God's will than the restoration of a sinner who can be brought to repentance. (Whether or not *God* is read in v. 16a does not affect the sense.) Yet, unfortunately, as John knows only too well, some men have let themselves go beyond the possibility of repentance (v. 16b). Tragic though the truth may be, *there is a sin unto death;* evil may be followed so persistently that the moral sense is at last destroyed. Specifically in John's mind—although his language and the fact described are quite general—are the Gnostics, men who by denying the reality of sin have made repentance a meaningless term. It is hardly worth while even to pray for such, since the chances of a good result are next to hopeless; such prayer is, of course, not forbidden, but there are better objects for the exercise of spiritual energy. And (v. 17) the existence of such a class is a warning against taking sin lightly, for *all unrighteousness is sin.* And yet no one need despair, for *there is a sin not unto death;* if repentance can be awakened, then there is life in the soul.

This passage corresponds to the teaching in the Synoptic Gospels concerning blasphemy against the Holy Spirit (Lk. 12[10] is the most primitive form), the sense being the same in both places. Unfortunately, these sayings have been made the basis of heartless deductions that have caused untold mental distress, and the natural result has been a violent reaction in modern times against any such doctrines. But when all allowance has been made, the truth remains that men *can* lose the power of distinguishing between right and wrong, whether by persistent gross sin or (more fatally) by refined and vicious self-deception. We may decline to speculate about the final spiritual result of such a condition, but its existence cannot be denied.

Morbid souls, however, who may torment themselves over the possibility of such sin, should be instructed that their very anxiety proves their innocence of it.

18–21. The Threefold "We Know." The addition of vv. 14–17 necessitates a new conclusion, which John frames in conscious contrast to the Gnostics' formulæ, with their favorite *we know* three times repeated in a Christian sense; the result is intensely impressive. V. 18 qualifies vv. 16f.; even though sin can be forgiven, it should be transcended (cf. 2[1]). In the second half of this verse the text (not the mg.) of R.V. should be followed (A.S.V. reverses), for the change from *whosoever is begotten* (the Christian) to *he that was begotten* (Christ) is in John's most perfect manner. The meaning then is that Christ, the once-begotten, "keeps" all those who through him are likewise born of God. V. 19 could be—and perhaps was—used unchanged by the Gnostics. And in v. 20 there is only one word that they would certainly have avoided, but that one word—*Jesus*—changes the whole sense.

The Epistle ends with an affirmation and an exhortation, both of which grow naturally out of what has been written. The affirmation: *This is the true God, and eternal life.* The exhortation: *My little children, guard yourselves from idols*—from everything, physical or mental, that distorts or falsifies God.

SECOND JOHN

Introduction

Relation to First John. This little Epistle may be described as a miniature edition of 1 John, for almost every phrase in it occurs in the larger work as well. See therefore the introduction to 1 John. It is, however, a true epistle in strict form, with the conventional opening and closing formulas.

To Whom Written. The *lady* of v. 1 is naturally not an individual but a church, as is seen from the plurals in vv. 6, 8, 10, 12, as well as by the general tenor of the whole. *Certain children* of this lady—i.e., certain members of the congregation—have recently visited John and have pleased him deeply by the sincerity of their faith (v. 4), and he perhaps sent this little greeting in their care as they returned home; he explains (v. 12) that a longer letter would not have been worth while, as he expects to visit them soon. The close connection with 1 John shows that the two Epistles are certainly by the same author, and that they must belong to approximately the same period. But there is no way of determining their relative priority.

THE EPISTLE

1–3. The Christian Truth. John describes himself simply as *The elder,* a term that has occasioned much discussion, as, according to traditional theories of the authorship, *The* *apostle* might be expected. Without entering into this question (cf. the intro. to John's Gospel), 1 Pet. 5[1] may perhaps be compared, while it may be observed that Papias, a writer of the next generation, calls all the apostles simply "elders." For the title cf. further on Acts 11[30], etc., and on 1 Tim. 5[17] Tit. 1[5].

Why John does not name himself we do not know, nor do we know why he addresses the church as *lady*, but the double anonymity gives a graceful turn to the Epistle that would be lacking if it opened with (say) "John to the church of Smyrna." *Elect* does not occur in 1 John and here does not convey more than the fact of God's choice, without further implications.

The first four verses are dominated by the word *truth*, which varies its force characteristically, *in truth* in vv. 1 and 3 meaning only "truly," while otherwise the noun describes the Christian message. In v. 3 John rather curiously includes himself with his readers in the benediction. And the unique phrase, *Jesus Christ the Son of the Father*, points John's emphasis on the identity of Christ's gifts with the Father's.

4–11. The Sign of a False Teacher. John must have met these *certain children* while they were away from home, as otherwise only a small part of their congregation would have held the true faith. With v. 5 cf. 1 Jn. 2[7] 3[11], etc. V. 6 reverses 1 Jn. 3[23] in typical Johannine fashion. With v. 7 cf. 1 Jn. 4[2, 3], although here "is come" is replaced by *cometh*, perhaps to indicate timelessness. The warning in v. 8 is a little sharper than anything in 1 John, possibly because of local conditions; for *we* (not *ye*) in this verse cf. 1 Jn. 1[1-3]. In v. 9 *goeth onward* carries with it the implication *in the (supposed) pursuit of knowledge*, and the reference to "having" God refers no doubt to a Gnostic boast; with the verse as a whole cf. 1 Jn. 2[23f].

V. 10 describes itinerant preachers, familiar figures of the post-apostolic age. Many of them, of course, were devoted missionaries (3 Jn. v. 7), but this, unfortunately, could be so little taken for granted that Christians were warned (cf. p. 1264a) to examine them carefully before extending official hospitality. The *house* is, of course, the congregation, and the *greeting* formal acceptance in the community; the principle involved here makes irrelevant the contrary teaching in Mt. 5[47].

12, 13. Cf. 3 Jn. vv. 13, 14a; this must have been a favorite salutation of the elder's, and its style corresponds to that of the introductory greeting. John was not yet too old to travel. The *sister* is naturally the church from which he was writing.

THIRD JOHN

Introduction

1 and 2 John have to do with doctrinal disputes, but of these there is no trace in 3 John, which rebukes the insubordination of a church leader, Diotrephes (v. 9), not his theology. And the situation is clear, when set in a wider historical environment.

The Changing Ecclesiastical Situation. From 1 Timothy we learn that when the Pastoral Epistles were written, the churches in the neighborhood of Ephesus were organized—or were being organized—according to the plan of Acts 11[30]; i.e., under the control of a council of elders, who were responsible as a body. But around the year 110 A.D. the letters of Ignatius of Antioch prove that in the same locality a different system was now accepted; the elders were no longer rulers of the church, but had become simply the advisers of a single individual, the bishop, whose powers are justly described as "monarchical." Consequently, as Ignatius wrote only a decade or so after John, the new system must have been emerging in the latter's day. Now, in 3 Jn. vv. 9f. a certain Diotrephes is described as possessing certain powers: He has *the pre-eminence*, he controls the church's correspondence, he receives or rejects Christians from other localities, and he can excommunicate. But these powers, taken together, are precisely those of a "bishop" in the Ignatian sense.

Diotrephes, then, was such a bishop, who claimed exclusive jurisdiction over the church in his own city, and he was supported in his claim by a majority of his congregation. On the other hand, John had exercised a traditional authority over the entire district, so that a clash had resulted.

One source of the difficulty, no doubt, was the somewhat vague nature of John's power, as his exact rank in the Christendom of western Asia Minor could not have been closely defined. He was not the founder of the churches there —this had been Paul's work—and even apostolic authority hardly extended to another man's foundation (Rom. 15[20]). A congregation, consequently, might think itself justified in refusing to obey his orders, especially since aged saints, despite all their wisdom and holiness, are not infrequently "difficult."

One thing at least is clear; the new method of organization—or something like it—was inevitable. The churches were growing enormously and their problems were growing with them, particularly in view of the Gnostic dangers. And the unwieldy boards of elders were not adapted to cope with the situation; the time had come for single executives with undivided responsibility. This "polity," which originated in Jerusalem (Acts 21^{18}), had by the time of 3 John spread well throughout Palestine and to the north at least as far as Antioch, so that its adoption in Asia Minor was easy and natural. [This is a correct account of the origin of the "episcopacy," but it also shows that the episcopacy was not so much something inherent in the very nature of Christianity as it was a natural development of the life of the church in the circumstances in which it found itself. See further the intro. to 1 and 2 Timothy, pp. 1277–8.]

John's Fear of the New Polity. Our little Epistle shows, however, that, even apart from the personal difficulties with Diotrephes, there was no enthusiasm for the plan on John's part. He does not seem to have fought it determinedly, for Polycarp, who knew John personally and idolized him, accepted the bishopric of Smyrna. None the less, there is contempt in John's *who loveth to have the pre-eminence among them* (v. 9), and other Christians certainly shared his reluctance to accept the novel organization. Even by Ignatius' day objections in Asia Minor had not died down, while churches in other parts of the Empire adhered tenaciously to the older system. But episcopacy proved efficient, so efficient that by the year 300 A.D. other forms of church government were all but forgotten, with the result that Diotrephes, had he lived, might have claimed the victory.

And yet the conduct of which John complains in v. 10 was inexcusable; however good a case Diotrephes may have had at the start—and we do not know the precise difficulty—he managed to put himself permanently in the wrong by his unfeeling behavior. 3 John is consequently an intensely human document, illustrating the difficulties caused by the age-old problem of efficient organization in conflict with personality, while the Epistle incidentally gives us an important side-light on a very obscure period.

A Personal Letter. In form 3 John is a highly confidential note from a leader to his lieutenant, the very reverse of an "epistle" meant for public reading. Its preservation must have been accidental, and it was made part of the N.T. at a relatively late date, when anything by John was felt to be inherently sacred. (See art., *Formation of N.T.*, p. 857b.)

THE EPISTLE

1. Salutation. The greeting is brief, as befits a private and informal note. *Gaius* occurs also in Acts 19^{29} 20^{4} Rom. 16^{23} 1 Cor. 1^{14}, but the name was extremely common and no identification is possible. This particular Gaius seems to have been the minority leader (v. 14) in "*the*" *church* of v. 9; in any event he was well known in the district and was probably one of John's converts (v. 4).

2–8. Kindness to Strangers. Some missionaries (cf. 2 Jn. v. 10) had been entertained by Gaius (v. 5), perhaps after Diotrephes had refused to receive them (v. 9). When they made their public report after reaching home (v. 6), they praised Gaius' hospitality in the highest terms—to the special joy of John, who (v. 3) had been in doubt about his disciple's loyalty. His satisfaction is voiced in the charming turn he gives to the conventional wish (v. 2) for Gaius' good health: "May your physical well-being correspond to your spiritual achievements!" (Much in need of fresh emphasis to-day is the underlying thought that the soul-life is the true measure of prosperity.)

Now, the same missionaries were to return, carrying the present letter to Gaius, who is asked (v. 6) to care for them once more. No doubt such repeated visits were burdensome (v. 8), but the duty of Christians was clear, all the more because scruples existed about receiving hospitality from even friendly non-Christians (v. 7). Paul's example (1 Cor. 9^{18}, etc.) may be responsible for this last custom; contrast Lk. 10^{8}.

9–12. The Evil of Christian Division. (Cf. intro.) It is interesting to note that John, like Paul (2 Cor. 13^{1-4}), was convinced that his personal presence would bear down all opposition. The letter mentioned in v. 9 is lost, for it cannot be 1 or 2 John. Gaius would, of course, be familiar with the events described in vv. 9f., but John wished to make his own position plain. V. 11, with an inimitably Johannine turn of thought and language, takes up v. 6; John was afraid that Gaius might resent this new burden. About Demetrius we know nothing.

13, 14. Cf. on 2 Jn. v. 12. The *friends* in the final clause were the local members of John's party.

JUDE

By Professor SHIRLEY JACKSON CASE

Introduction

Occasion. Like 2 Peter, Jude was called forth by the presence of certain persons in the church who were thought to be perverting the purity of Christianity. They were teaching a liberty of conduct that seemed a menace to Christian virtue. It had been the author's intention to write a treatise on the general character of the Christian salvation (v. 3), but on learning of the danger that threatened certain congregations who were being led into improper ways of conduct by false teachers he hastily composed this brief tract urging his readers to strive with all their might to preserve the traditional ideals that had been set up by a previous generation of Christian leaders. The occasion was essentially the same as that which had prompted the writing of 2 Peter (see pp. 1345–6.)

Date. The close parallelism between Jude as a whole and the second chapter of 2 Peter in particular is apparent at a glance when the two documents are placed side by side. It is now generally agreed among scholars that the shorter letter of Jude was the older and was largely reproduced by the author of 2 Peter. The former is more spontaneous, is less studied in its style, and shows other evidences of priority. It is easier to understand why a writer should elaborate a briefer treatise than to suppose that a longer work such as 2 Peter should have been abbreviated. But even assuming the priority of Jude, its exact date of composition is still very doubtful. The type of trouble which it seeks to correct was already beginning to show itself in Christianity toward the close of the first century. In some of the later N.T. books there are vague references to these troubles (cf. Col. 2[8, 18f.] 1 Tim. 6[1-11] 2 Tim. 3[1-8] Rev. 2[14]). But apart from Jude and 2 Peter, the danger is not thought to be so serious as to call for a special treatise on the subject. Probably this critical stage was not reached before the early part of the second century.

Destination and Author. The location of the communities addressed is as uncertain as is the case with 2 Peter. But the more informal style of Jude readily leads one to believe that the author had more definitely in mind specific congregations than did the writer of 2 Peter. Nor is it so clear that Jude is pseudonymous. The name "Jude" (literally, "Judas"), though no doubt common enough, was not particularly distinguished, and it is difficult to imagine that a writer who wanted to claim for his message the authority of some famous personage of the past would have chosen one that was so inconspicuous. Other N.T. books mention a Judas who had been one of Joseph's ancestors (Lk. 3[30]), a Judas among the brothers of Jesus (Mt. 13[55] Mk. 6[3]), a Judas Iscariot (e.g., Mk. 3[19] 14[10, 43] Acts 1[16, 25]), a Judas who was son of James and one of the apostolic company (Lk. 6[16] Acts 1[13]), a Judas of Galilee (Acts 5[37]), a Judas with whom Saul lodged in Damascus (Acts 9[11]), and a Judas surnamed Barsabbas who was a companion of Paul (Acts 15[22-34]). The name was very common among Jews, and that some Christian Judas should have written this timely tract to groups of believers with whom he was in close touch is not at all improbable. Yet it would have been quite unlikely that in the first quarter of the second century a brother of Jesus, or even a companion of Paul, would have been still alive. But perhaps when later Christendom was in process of forming its canon of N.T. Scripture this little document was felt to be so useful for resisting the libertine sects of the later times that the document was further accredited by making its author a "brother of James," now famous as a leader in the ancient church.

Summary of the Teaching of the Epistle. It is the author's message, and not his name, to which he would attract attention. After a very brief form of greeting he passes immediately to his central theme. He writes to place Christians on their guard against the activities of certain despicable persons who are slyly undermining the godly character of the Christian community (vv. 3f.). First he emphasizes the certainty of the divine judgment (vv. 5–11), and then follows a vivid characterization of the wickedness of the trouble-makers (vv. 12–18). The true Christians are to fall back upon the authority of the apostles and to continue steadfast in perpetuating the original customs of the new religion (vv. 19–23). A characteristic exhortation ends this brief communication (vv. 24f.).

Literature: Same as for 2 Peter; also Ferrar, *The Assumption of Moses.*

THE EPISTLE

1, 2. Salutation. Christian teachers sometimes called themselves the servants of Christ (Rom. 1:1 Phil. 1:1 Jas. 1:1 2 Pet. 1:1). They wished it understood that they spoke on behalf of their master and not primarily for themselves. Also they employed language that would remind the readers of the high status of privilege enjoyed by every Christian. The church is the object of God's love and is preserved for Christ, probably meaning particularly for his future coming when he would institute judgment and establish his kingdom. An increase of mercy, peace, and divine love may fitly be wished for the faithful.

3, 4. Danger to the Faith. Christians as privileged people, who share in common the hope of salvation that has been insured to them through the work of Christ, was a theme upon which the author had been meditating and planning the production of a composition. But suddenly he had been impelled to write a less finished treatise in a more strenuous vein. He had learned that the pure Christian heritage was in danger of perversion. He is not thinking so much of a perversion of dogma or creed as he is of an erroneous type of conduct. Certain base persons have insinuated themselves into the respect of the congregations and their presence is a serious menace to the standards of Christian morality. These individuals refuse to follow the content of religious teaching as it has been passed on from Jesus Christ by successive generations of Christian leaders. This is the threatening danger against which the author raises his voice of protest. Christians are to contend strenuously for the maintenance of their purity.

5–11. Certainty of Judgment. Before describing more particularly the character of the evildoers, the author dwells on the certainty of judgment awaiting all those who deviate from the right path. Examples from history are cited to prove that divine punishment will surely overtake sinners, even though they belong to the chosen people of God once so highly favored as to have been conducted out of bondage in Egypt (cf. Num. 14:29, 37 26:64f.). But the writer does not restrict himself to the O.T. for examples of God's dealings with the Jews. His readers are supposed to know the story of the rebellious *angels* as described in certain Jewish apocryphal writings, particularly the Book of Enoch. (See art., *Intertestamental Religion*, pp. 204–5; cf. also pp. 197–8.) There a vivid picture was painted of the manner in which the sinning angels had been ejected from heaven and cast down to the abyss, where they were enchained until the Day of Judgment (see Enoch, chs. 5–16, 21f., 54, 64, 67f.). If even angels had been unable to escape the displeasure of God, how much less likely would these men who were sinning against God in the church be able to avoid punishment. The fate that overcame *Sodom* and *Gomorrah* because of the people's sin is a further reminder of God's vengeance (Gen. 19:24). The sinners in the church are not unlike the wicked people of the ancient cities in their vice. In their very dreams they defile themselves with their evil minds, and in their waking moments they brazenly throw off the restraint which Christ would impose upon them. They despise the instruction of the older Christian teachers, even as they ignore the lessons to be learned from the fate of such dignified beings as angels. Again the author turns to an apocryphal Jewish book, the Assumption of Moses, for a further illustration of proper respect for authority, a trait so conspicuously absent from the false teachers. (See art., *Intertestamental Literature*, p. 198b; cf. p. 1277b.) Even the archangel, Michael, when disputing with Satan for possession of the body of Moses, did not presume to usurp the authority of God by pronouncing judgment on the devil, but left the rebuke to be given by the Lord himself (v. 9). On the other hand, the present offenders lift up their voice against all authority. They show themselves to be senseless animals utterly devoid of reason. By their conduct they are bringing down upon their own heads ultimate destruction. *Cain* and *Balaam* and *Korah* are other prototypes from whose punishments faithful Christians may deduce the certainty of judgment that threatens these more recent sinners. Cain's crime had been murder (Gen. 4), but probably it is his godlessness in general that constitutes his likeness to the wicked persons in the church. They are also guilty of the desire for gain that characterized Balaam (Num. 22–24), while in their rebellious attitude toward Christian leaders they are guilty of Korah's sin of disobedience (Num. 16). But the same sad fate awaits them that overtook their predecessors in sin.

12–18. Character of the Evildoers. Having emphasized the certainty of judgment, the author now undertakes to describe more particularly the character of their offenses. They set themselves up for leaders of the Christian communities and are to be found at the common meal of the society where, however, they feed themselves rather than the needy flock (see 1 Cor. 11:17-34). There is no life or substance in their teaching. They are likened to *clouds* which yield no rain for a parched soil, or are like *trees* that cumber up the ground while they are thoroughly dead and have no sign of life left even in their roots. They are noisy like the waters of the sea, but by their talking they merely display their own shameful characters and do not contribute to the building up of true religion. They would like to shine as *stars* in the heavens, but they are like shooting meteors that are destined to burn themselves out in eternal darkness. But Christians are not to be astounded at the presence of such persons in their midst. The coming of this sad day had been revealed beforehand in prophecy. Again it is the Book of Enoch, from which one learns that it would be necessary for God to send an angelic host to execute judgment upon just such sinners (Enoch 1^9 27^2).

The troublers seem to have been chronic fault-finders who complained about others but who followed their own lustful desires regardless of consequences, except as they were willing to act in a deferential manner toward anyone from whom they hoped to receive an advantage. Even more recently God had indicated that such persons were to appear within Christianity. The apostles themselves were believed to have foretold the present situation (v. 17). Where this prediction was found in apostolic tradition we do not now know, but the author would not have the readers think that these present unhappy conditions had not been anticipated by God and had not been provided for through apostolic instruction. The activity of persons who followed the impulses of their fleshly desires was but one of the many signs that the last days were at hand.

19–22. Correct Procedure for Christians. In contrast with Christians who walked by the Spirit, the false teachers were without the Spirit and lived under the domination of sensual appetites. Those who wished to continue in a way pleasing to God are to give themselves to prayer and a course of conduct dictated wholly by the promptings of the Holy Spirit. Thus will they continue to be the objects of divine love and in the Day of Judgment they will not feel the punishment of God's wrath but will share the joyous rewards of eternal life through the kindness of the Lord Jesus Christ. In their conduct toward the sinners in their midst they are also to show kindness and self-restraint (v. 22). Some of the offenders are as yet not utterly perverse, but are only wavering and may still be drawn back into the right way. The doubts that have been stirred up by the trouble-makers may be allayed. Others who have drifted further from the right course may be rescued by a more strenuous effort to snatch them from the fire of judgment before it is too late. But some of the sinners are so far gone in their pursuit of error that the most merciful procedure on the part of the faithful Christian is to look upon them with fear and to guard himself carefully from contamination by contact with their besmirched personalities.

24, 25. Benediction. Even this brief letter does not lack the typical farewell paragraph. The persons addressed are committed to the care of their own powerful God and Saviour. Their gaze is directed forward to the Judgment Day, when those Christians who have lived blamelessly will rejoice in the reward that is to be theirs who remain faithful to the Lord Jesus Christ.

REVELATION

By Professor F. BERTRAM CLOGG

Introduction

The Character of the Book. From about the third century B.C. the Law was established in Israel as the complete embodiment of God's revelation. No place was left, therefore, for men in whom the spirit of prophecy lived to give expression to fresh and independent messages of divine truth. Because of this, Jewish writers, who believed they had a message from God for their own time, used some great name of the past, such as Enoch or Moses, in order to hide their own identity and to win for their writings that respect which they would not otherwise have won. These apocalyptic writers, as they are called, used the forms of visions, by which the messages of the prophets had sometimes been disclosed; but they were concerned not so much with the present as with the future. They were in despair over the present, and they looked to the future to vindicate their hopes. They relied upon terrible revelations of supernatural powers in catastrophes of nature and in national upheavals to purge out the sins of humanity and lead men to God. This was because they believed that God was supreme over the world of nature and over all the political movements among the nations, as well as over the spiritual and ethical world. Moreover, their reliance upon a supernatural Messiah as the only hope of humanity was a witness to the fact that man cannot be saved by precept but only by example. The theme of the apocalyptists was the "Day of the Lord," and all the questions and problems which were connected with it. In the O.T. the book of Daniel belongs to this type of literature, in the N.T. the book of Revelation. This book differs from the others in some important respects. In the opinion of the present writer, it is not pseudonymous, but is written by the author under his own name. He writes in reference to a present crisis with a message for those in the churches which he mentions by name. Further, while the other apocalyptic writers foretell the coming of the Messiah, he reveals the coming again of a Messiah who has already triumphed over sin and death; who bears the marks now of his suffering; but who is on the throne of the universe. (See further, *Intertestamental Literature*, pp. 187–90; *Intertestamental Religion*, pp. 206–10; *Backgrounds*, pp. 843–7; cf. also on Jude.)

Methods of Interpretation. (1) *Mystical.* Origen, Augustine, and others have interpreted the book allegorically, each vision being symbolical of some principle or institution. The white horse, e.g., which descends through the open heaven (19[11f.]) represents the pure light of knowledge which reveals heaven to believers. Such a method may be edifying, but tends to be merely fanciful. (2) *Historical.* The "futurists" say that it all refers to the end of the world. Others that it is a plan of history, some of which has been fulfilled, some is still to be. Others maintain that the writer wrote of his own century and had no other age in view. The vivid imagery, the mysterious predictions and the apparent references to events and persons in history have led to innumerable attempts to identify the Beast, etc., and to date the final struggle of good and evil. In the twelfth century the Beast was identified with Mohammedanism; in the sixteenth with the Papacy; in the eighteenth in England with Napoleon; and in the twentieth with the ex-emperor of Germany. The diversity of these interpretations has discredited the method, and no two attempts agree in the explanation of the book as the diagram of history. Moreover, the writer makes it clear that his prophecies will shortly be fulfilled, so that the reference to the end of the world, as it is commonly understood, is impossible.

There is no doubt, however, that the true method of interpretation is the historical. The visions clearly relate to events contemporary with John and his readers, and to future events insofar as they arise out of the others. The book refers to things that have happened, to definite kingdoms and powers and expectations. It is not an allegory, but the visions are not restricted to contemporary events. The last sixteen chapters describe a series of events which affect earth and heaven, which John expected would take place immediately, and which would bring human history to a definite end. The fulfillment of his prophecy has not taken place as John anticipated. There is a sense in which many crises in history have been a fulfillment, for no one single event or series of events can be a full and complete fulfillment. It is so with the expression of every great moral and spiritual truth made by the God-inspired men of all ages. Again and again history illustrates and vindicates their words in ways of which they never dreamed.

The Historical Situation. The Roman province of Asia in which the seven churches were situated was one of the most prosperous parts of the empire. The wealth of its cities was seen in the splendor of their public buildings and in their religious worship, where, amid magnificent architecture, stately *public and private sacrifices* were performed with lavish munificence, which not only made such occasions a splendid spectacle but a scene of luxurious feasting and every kind of sensual indulgence. The Christian who did not partake of such sacrificial feasts socially ostracized himself, and yet to partake meant grave moral temptation. It was no wonder that some were willing to compromise—the Nicolaitans, whom the writer censures in no measured terms (cf. 2[14f.]).

But that form of heathenism which no Christian could avoid, however he might keep himself aloof from the social and commercial life of his fellow citizens, was *the worship of the emperors*, which was increasingly imposed upon all the inhabitants of the empire, whatever their race or religion. It was at Pergamum that a temple had first been built in honor of Augustus, and all his successors were in their turn deified, and similar temples were built in their honor. Domitian, in whose reign this book was in all probability written, was called, even in Rome, "Our Lord and our God." This Cæsar-worship became the unifying religion of the empire; and in the provinces, where the benefits of Roman justice and peace were independent of the vices of particular emperors, it was sedulously encouraged by officials and priests as a matter of policy. Just because this religion was universal in its scope it clashed inevitably with the Christian faith. Rome was tolerant of all religions; all her subject races might worship their own gods, for each of whom a place was found in the Pantheon; but the deified emperor demanded the worship of all his subjects. An edict had been issued under Vespasian which condemned to death all who would not worship the image of the Beast (13[15]). The magistrates had orders to treat the Christians as criminals, and this they did.

Paul had found the Roman power friendly. More than once it protected him from the Jews, who were the persecutors of the church in his day (Acts 21[31-34] 23[12-24]; cf. 27[42, 43]). He writes favorably of this power as that which restrains "the mystery of lawlessness" (2 Thess. 2[6, 7]), but the author of Revelation identifies it with the Beast, following the precedent set by the author of Daniel, who had pictured the world empires in the forms of a lion, a leopard, and so on. The readers of this book well understood that the Beast was Rome. The first time Rome became the persecutor of the Christians was in Nero's reign, when, in 64 A.D., to escape the opprobrium of having himself set the city on fire, Nero made the Christians the scapegoat and had his gardens lighted with Christians impaled on crosses smeared with pitch and set on fire. But that enormity was confined to those living in Rome. It was left for Domitian, morose, suspicious, cruel in the extreme, making war in his last mad years against almost all his subjects, to vent his worst fury on the Christians. In 93 A.D. the persecution raged not only in Rome but in Asia also, and the Christian blood poured out in the last four years of his reign seemed to John, the writer of this book, to presage a universal martyrdom for all who were loyal to their faith, and to cry aloud to God for vengeance (6[9]). It was to encourage men to resist even unto blood the blasphemous claims of the Roman emperor that this "Tract for the Times" was written.

Authorship. The author of the book is John (1[4]), who saw the visions in the island of Patmos, where he was suffering for his Christian faith. Patmos was a penal settlement, and it seems likely that John was condemned to work in the quarries there—a form of punishment which many of his fellow Christians had also suffered (1[9]). Tradition associates him with Ephesus, and this is supported by his evident first-hand knowledge of the seven churches of the Roman province of Asia to which he writes, and of which Ephesus was the most famous. Almost certainly John was a Jew. In this too tradition and the internal evidence of the book agree. The Greek in which he writes has long been a puzzle to scholars, for it is not like any other Greek we know. The words are Greek, but the grammar and idiom are largely Semitic, and the most probable explanation is that the writer thought in Hebrew, often consciously or unconsciously framing his sentences after the manner of the prophets, and then translated them into Greek without strict regard for Greek idiom and style. A Jew who had lived in Asia all his life would have known Greek better than Hebrew or Aramaic (see p. 842). The author of Revelation probably lived in Palestine in his early years and did not go to Ephesus until middle life. This seems to support the tradition that he was John, the son of Zebedee, who is supposed to have settled at Ephesus, where he wrote the fourth Gospel and the three Epistles, and, as some think, wrote to the church there this book of visions.

But there are some serious difficulties in the way of this view. (1) The author of Revelation never calls himself an apostle, though the title, if he were the son of Zebedee, would have been natural, and would have supported his authority. He calls himself a prophet, an inferior position to an apostle (cf. 1 Cor. 12^{28}). (2) Grammar, diction, style, and theological outlook make it almost impossible to believe that the author of the fourth Gospel was the author of Revelation, though both may well have been members of the same religious circle in Ephesus. The author of this book mentions his name; the author of the Gospel does not. The former does not identify himself with the beloved disciple, or with the disciple who leaned on the breast of the Master at the Last Supper, or with the brother of James. When Revelation and the fourth Gospel use similar phrases the meaning is generally different; e.g., the *Word* in the Gospel is a metaphysical conception, in Rev. 19^{13} it is the name of Christ as the Warrior King. Again the conception of God in Revelation is much more like that of the O.T. than like that of the Gospel, where the love and Fatherhood are so much emphasized. The Gospel lays stress on the coming of the Spirit, and on a judgment which is spiritual; in Revelation the conception of the Second Coming and of the Judgment is in concrete symbolism. (3) There is another tradition mentioned by Papias that John and James were both martyred in Jerusalem. If true, then the son of Zebedee was the author neither of the fourth Gospel nor of Revelation. (4) At least two ancient authorities did not believe that the son of Zebedee was the author of Revelation but another John, called by Papias, the Elder. If, however, as many scholars hold, John the Elder was the author of the Gospel, then he was not the author of Revelation (see "2" above). The John who wrote the two shorter Epistles calls himself "the Elder," and these have much closer affinities with the First Epistle and the Gospel than with Revelation. (See further intro. to fourth Gospel, p. 1065, and intro. to Epistles of John, p. 1352.)

It is enough for us to know that the author was a Jew, probably of Palestine, who lived at Ephesus and was exiled to Patmos. Though his Greek was full of solecisms, and was evidently not the language in which he thought, he was far from being illiterate. He was steeped in the O.T., especially in the books of Isaiah and Ezekiel, as well as in the earlier apocalyptic literature, especially Daniel and Enoch, so that about one quarter of his book is either quotation from or allusion to some of these. Just as Bunyan wrote his allegory in the language of the English Bible, so John found it most natural to express his visions in the language of the prophets and apocalyptists who were before him.

The Purpose and Message of the Book. John wrote to encourage his fellow sufferers to be faithful unto death. His message is summed up in 1^{7}, "Behold, he cometh with the clouds," and in the testimony of Christ himself, "Behold, I come quickly" (22^{7}). Antipas was probably typical of many who had died for the testimony of Jesus (2^{13}). Rome was already intoxicated with the blood of the martyrs (17^{6}). This book is an answer to the cry of the martyred, "How long, O Master . . . dost thou not . . . . avenge our blood?" (6^{10}). The answer is that the time is at hand for God's final judgment upon the world and the vindication of the saints. Life was an intense struggle for the Christians in Asia, when any day might bring the ordeal Cæsar or Christ, and there was reason to fear that many would not be able to stand the strain. John by his searching exhortations and reassuring promises seeks to nerve the trembling faith of those who were dreading the future, to warn the faithful, and, by a proclamation of God's wrath upon the world, to summon the churches to endure, because the coming conflict will issue in the vindication and blessedness of the redeemed. Before that final consummation there is a series of events which he describes in the main section of his book. In these the struggle between good and evil grows continuously more intense because of the interposition of God himself on the one side and of the spiritual powers of darkness on the other. The preliminary judgments of God only harden men's hearts. But the issue is not uncertain, for it has been already decided in heaven ($12^{7, 8}$). Satan has been defeated and cast out of heaven. That means the struggle is about to reach its climax on earth. But the armies of God are already moving against them. The victory has been already won in heaven; it will soon be finally accomplished on earth.

It is clear that these prophecies are related to Nero and Rome and have had no literal fulfillment. The truth which the book contains is not the truth of history. It is clear also that the moral and ethical standards of the author in reference to the non-Christian world and the purpose of God in letting loose almost indescribable horrors upon men are below the Christian level. But the permanent message of the book is its witness to the belief, which history has again and again proved to be true, *that spiritual and not material forces are in the end the strongest.* On the one side are the kings of the earth and all the powers of evil and on the other the Lamb that had been slain. The victory is not to the big battalions but to sacrificial love. The Beast and his armies stand for those forces of corruption which tyrannize over mankind: the Son of man on his white horse with the armies of heaven represents the spiritual powers which in the end will prevail, the power of truth, love, justice, and peace.

True to the spiritual insight of his race, John saw the Golden Age in the future, not in the past. But he does not expect this age to be reached gradually but through gathering crisis, and as the issue of an awful struggle. He was too conscious of the evil elements in humanity to have any easy dreams. He knew that the nearer evil was to its defeat the more violently it would resist. So though he wrote when the outlook for the church was at its blackest, he was no pessimist. The very menace of universal martyrdom he makes the basis of hope, and, when little could be heard from the church but the cry of suffering, he heard the Hallelujahs of a triumphant host in heaven and saw a blessedness which even he is unable to describe.

The Unity of the Book and the Method of the Revelations. The difficulties of explaining the book as a whole and of reconciling the internal indications of authorship and date, as well as the strong Jewish tone which pervades much of it, have led many scholars to suggest that the book is not the work of one author. These suggestions have taken many forms, some maintaining that this is a Jewish work to which some Christian has added an Introduction (chs. 1–3), and an Epilogue (ch. 22), and a few interpolations here and there. Others suppose several sources, some Jewish and some Christian, loosely put together by an editor. But more and more the unity of the book is being accepted, although John almost certainly used apocalyptic material taken from many sources. As the prophet of the O.T. said, "Thus saith Jehovah," so John wrote "I saw." The one heard the voice of God, the other saw the vision. But similar psychical experiences are common to both prophet and seer. Dreams and visions, in sleep and waking moments, are familiar in the experience of O.T. prophets and Jewish apocalyptists as means for conveying the revelation of God. Modern psychology does not deny the reality of such experiences, but their value is to be judged by the source from which they come and the influence they have on character. That which distinguishes the visions of the Bible from most of those known in other religions is the sort of religious faith they express and their power to uplift moral standards. The elaborate nature of the visions of Revelation shows that John had seen things which he only partly understood and which he could not express except by symbols. The symbols he used belonged to his conscious experience and to the apocalyptic traditions he had inherited. Naturally, he expressed what he had heard and seen in the thought forms peculiar to him and his age. He is trying to describe things beyond the range of his readers' experience, things he had seen in his ecstasies: the images he uses have to be symbolic and cannot be literal. But his description of his psychical experiences is arranged by the reason. The visionary in this book is a literary artist. It may well be that the visions extended over several years, but they are woven together into one book, in which can be seen a steady development of movement and thought. John has arranged and adapted his material into an ordered whole which is a dramatic unity. He not infrequently uses allegory, as in the visions of the seven seals and of the seven bowls, and he freely uses traditional material (e.g., 11^{1-13}) which passing through his thought becomes in whole or in part transformed. In recounting his visions he has woven in fragments of O.T. prophecy and Jewish apocalypse, as well as his own thoughts upon his ecstatic experiences, and we cannot distinguish what he had seen from these reminiscences and thoughts and prophecies which are all worked into his book.

The Date. That the book belongs to a later than the Pauline era is evident from the condition of the churches, the presence of Nicolaitanism (2^{6}), and the widespread persecution. Ancient tradition was almost unanimous in assigning the book to the later years of Domitian's reign, when the emperor's demand for divine honors, his widespread use of informers, and his special enmity against the Christian Church established a reign of terror from which there was no relief till his death in 96 A.D. With this most modern scholars agree. The Cæsar-worship against which John wrote so vehemently was not stringently enforced until Domitian's reign. Nor did the persecution of Nero's reign extend beyond Rome. It was not till Domitian's edict that Asia became the scene of persecution against the Christians. Some scholars have suggested an earlier date, the time of Nero, because in $11^{1, 2}$ the Temple is spoken of as if still standing, and that was not true after 70 A.D. Others suggest the time of Vespasian, because of the allusions in 17^{10} to the death of Nero, and the identification of the reigning emperor with Vespasian. This view is held by those who attribute this book and the fourth Gospel to the son of Zebedee, and who feel that considerations of style demand that there should be some interval between the writing of this and the writing of the Gospel, which is generally thought to belong to the last decade of the first century. But these difficulties are adequately met by the suggestion that in these passages John is using material which belongs to an earlier time, and he has not in all points adapted it to the time when he was writing.

The Problem of the Rearrangement of Chapters 20–22. The problem is created by the following facts: (1) In 20^{4}–21^{8} are related events from the imprisonment of Satan until all things are made new. Heaven and earth have passed away; the Last Judgment has settled the destiny of all sinners and the powers of evil, while the saints are reigning in the new Jerusalem. (2) In 21^{9}–22^{2} is described the heavenly Jerusalem which stands on the old earth and is surrounded by heathen nations and their kings, who bring their glory into it. (3) In 22^{15} evil in every form exists outside this city, though in $20^{11\text{-}15}$ it appears that all who are not redeemed are destroyed.

These contradictions have puzzled all commentators. Some suppose that John is using material derived from different sources, and has not formed it into a consistent whole. But there is no evidence of different sources in these chapters. Others explain the apparent confusions on psychological grounds; consistency is not to be expected in mystic visions; but there has been up to this point a wonderful consistency in this book. Only here in the *dénouement* the orderly development of the drama fails. R. H. Charles' solution is drastic but illuminating. The key to it is that there are two cities described; the first, the seat of the millennial reign of Christ on earth, 21^{9}–22^{2}, and the second, $21^{1\text{-}4a}$ $22^{3\text{-}5}$, the new, i.e., transformed Jerusalem which appears after the heaven and earth have vanished away, and is the abode of the blessed forever. Charles thinks that John died when he had written as far as 20^{3}, and that the rest was left in a series of independent documents which a disciple not very intelligently put together. Whether or not that is the source of the confusion in these chapters, the rearrangement removes many of the difficulties and provides a fitting climax to the visions of the book. The order is thus restored: $20^{1\text{-}3}$ 21^{9}–$22^{2,\ 14,\ 15,\ 17}$ $20^{4\text{-}15}$ $21^{5a,\ 4d,\ 5b,\ 1\text{-}4abc}$ $22^{3\text{-}5}$ $21^{5a,\ 6b\text{-}8}$ $22^{6,\ 7}$ $22^{18a,\ 16,\ 13,\ 12,\ 10}$ $22^{8,\ 9,\ 20,\ 21}$. If this order in the main is followed, $21^{9f.}$ is meant to supplement $19^{6\text{-}9}$ as $17^{1f.}$ supplements 14^{8}. The portrait of the Bride is in contrast with the picture of Satan imprisoned. Planted on the same site as the Jerusalem which Roman armies razed to the ground a new city appears, where the martyrs are to dwell for one thousand years. It is to be the center from which the gospel is preached to the surrounding nations, and many will be converted and enter into it, but all that is unclean must remain outside ($22^{14,\ 15}$). When the one thousand years are ended Satan is unloosed and gathers the forces of the heathen and attacks the city, but is defeated, and with the Beast and the False Prophet is cast into the lake of fire ($20^{7\text{-}10}$) to be tormented forever. The general resurrection and the Last Judgment follow. Those who were outside the heavenly Jerusalem during its existence on earth (22^{15}) are condemned to this lake of fire, which is the second death (20^{14}). The old heaven and earth pass away, and a new heaven and earth, such as suit the new conditions of life, appear. From this new heaven comes the new Jerusalem, where God and his saints are to dwell forever. There is no elaborate description of this city, but it is expressly said that there shall be no death or sorrow or anything accursed in it ($21^{1\text{-}8}$). John could not describe this transformed Jerusalem in terms of material measurements or fabrics. Though he had seen it in his vision, its description belonged to those unspeakable things of which Paul writes in 2 Cor. 12^{4}. It may be noted that this conception closely agrees with 1 Thess. $4^{13\text{-}17}$ 1 Cor. $15^{23\text{-}28,\ 35\text{-}49}$. Paul there says that the last trumpet shall sound, and Christ will appear, and the righteous dead will rise to meet him with their spiritual bodies, together with the righteous living, who will be similarly and suddenly transformed. Then begins the reign of Christ, which is to continue until he has put all enemies under his feet. The last enemy is death: the climax of his victory is the destruction of death (Rev. 20^{14}). The Messianic kingdom comes to an end when Christ is triumphant. Then he delivers up the kingdom to God, who is all in all. Though there are important differences, the two conceptions agree in general.

Outline and Analysis. Many attempts have been made to analyze the book into acts and scenes. While it is helpful to liken the main part to a drama, it is pressing it too far to try to fit the whole into some dramatic scheme. Indeed, the appropriateness of the term "drama" in any sense is doubted by some scholars, who deny that there is any movement in the plot but only a repetition. In the analysis that follows, it will be seen that there certainly is a climax to the series of visions, and the word "drama" is the most fitting term to apply to the whole. The rearrangement of the last three chapters follows in the main that of Archdeacon Charles, to whose monumental work all students of this book are indebted. (See commentary on ch. 20–22.)

OUTLINE

Preface and Salutation, 1[1-8].

I. Prologue on earth, 1[9-20].
II. Letters to the Seven Churches, chs. 2, 3.
III. Prologue in heaven, chs. 4, 5.
IV. A Series of Judgments.
   (a) First Series of Judgments—the Seals, ch. 6.
   (b) Second Series of Judgments—the Trumpets, chs. 8, 9, 12, 13.
   (c) Third Series of Judgments—the Bowls, followed by the doom of Rome, the victory of Christ and the chaining of Satan for a thousand years, 15[1]–20[3].
   (d) Three Parentheses, chs. 7; 10, 11; 14.
V. The Millennial Kingdom, 20[4-10] 21[9]–22[2].
VI. The Last Judgment, 20[11-15].
VII. The New Jerusalem, 21[1-5] 22[6-12, 16, 18-20].

Benediction, 22[21].

ANALYSIS

1. Preface and salutation, rising into an address of praise to the Almighty. 1[1-8].
2. Prologue on earth. The Seer, and the vision of the things which are and which shall be hereafter. 1[9-20].
3. The letters to the seven churches, which set out the problem of the book—the apparent failure of the cause of God on earth. Chs. 2, 3.
4. Prologue in heaven. The vision of God to whom the world owes its origin and of the Lamb to whom it owes its redemption. The Lamb takes the book of fate sealed with seven seals, the loosing of which represent judgments. Chs. 4, 5.
5. (a) The seven seals—the first series of judgments, which affect all men. Ch. 6.

   The first parenthesis. Before the seventh seal is opened the saints are marked with the seal of God to prevent them from being affected by the next judgment. Then is seen a vision of the sealed and martyred host in heaven. Ch. 7.

   (b) The seven trumpets (chs. 8, 9)—the second series of judgments making manifest the servants of God and of Satan. The seventh seal is opened and there is silence in heaven for half an hour to mark the change from history to prophecy. Then seven angels sound their trumpets and the last three sound three woes. The third of these is the reign of anti-Christ on earth; but before this is described there is

   The second parenthesis. Ch. 10 shows that the hour prayed for by the martyrs has come. God's purpose will be fulfilled. The Seer is given a little book to eat. Before the third woe he then inserts two songs in heaven, which show that though what follows is apparently the triumph of Satan the real result is the coming of Christ and his kingdom. Chs. 10, 11.

   The third woe—the reign of anti-Christ. Chs. 12, 13.

   The third parenthesis. Two visions of the church triumphant on earth and of the judgment of Rome. Ch. 14.

   (c) The third series of judgments, which affect the heathen—the seven bowls—and the powers of evil. Beginning with the song of the martyrs, this act describes the judgment of the great Harlot and of the Beast, the vision of the victorious Christ, and the binding of Satan for a thousand years. 15[1]–20[3].
6. The millennial kingdom. 21[9]–22[2, 14, 15, 17] 20[4-10].
7. The last Judgment, in which Satan who has been loosed at the end of the thousand years and his allies are cast into the lake of fire. Heaven and earth have vanished and there is a great white throne before which the dead appear for judgment. 20[11-15].
8. The new Jerusalem, where the saints reign for ever. 21[1-5a] 22[3-5].
9. Epilogue. 21[5b-8] 22[6-12, 16, 18-21].

Literature: C. Anderson Scott, *Revelation* (Century Bible), and *The Book of the Revelation* (Devotional and Practical Commentary); Alexander Ramsay, *Revelation* (Westminster N.T.); W. M. Ramsay, *The Letters to the Seven Churches of Asia;* Peake, *The Revelation of John;* Charles, *Schweich Lectures on the Apocalypse;* Dean, *Visions and Revelations;* Thorn, *Visions of Hope and Fear;* Workman, *Persecution in the Early Church.*

CHAPTER I

1-3. The Source, Contents, and Blessed Significance of the Book. God gave the revelation to Christ who sent and signified it by his angel to John. John bare witness. The book contains the word of God, the word attested by Jesus Christ, seen by John in a vision. Similarly the blessing of the book is threefold: upon him who reads it in the public services of the church; upon the worshipers who hear it read; upon those who observe its teaching.

Our Lord's words about his Advent were interpreted in the light of current apocalyptic ideas, and to the expectation of the glory of that time the hope of the primitive church added the thought that *the time is at hand* (cf. 22[20]). The end was near and would come with catastrophic suddenness, thought the early Christians. We have learned to think of agelong processes of development, continuous progress. But has not history records of crises of judgment as well as of years of steady growth? Progress does not move with uniform acceleration and in one unbroken line. In biology and in history life has developed in certain directions and then come to a dead end.

4-8. Greeting of John to the Seven Churches. This is the introduction to his letter to the seven churches: the rest of the book is the letter. He uses the apostolic salutation such as is found in many of the N.T. Epistles—a combination of the Greek *grace* and the Hebrew *peace.* "Grace and peace from God and from Christ Jesus: glory be to him—lo! he comes." The last is the motto of the book.

The writer uses no pseudonym, as is the custom of apocalyptic writers (intro., p. 1364). It is significant that he calls himself John only, without adding "apostle."

4. By *Asia* is meant the Roman province formed about 130 B.C. *Seven* was a sacred number. For the significance of these seven churches see v. 11. *From him which is,* etc. John breaks the rules of grammar here in order not to decline, as the rules of grammar require, the Greek translation of the sacred name for God, which the A.S.V. renders Jehovah. The rabbis paraphrased Ex. 3[14] as "Who was and who is and who shall be." For the third phrase John uses *who is coming,* for "the Coming" is the theme of his book. *And from the seven Spirits which are before his throne.* This is generally understood as a reference to the Holy Spirit, the number seven expressing the perfection of God's energy and perhaps referring to the churches in which the Spirit works (cf. Isa. 11[2, 3]). Others see a reference to the seven archangels, who may have been derived from the Babylonian cult of the star deities. But this, though Jewish, is foreign to John's thought. The order, in which the Holy Spirit—if that is the meaning—is put second, and the difficulty of the phrase, support Charles in regarding the words as an interpolation.

5. *The first born of the dead* (cf. Col. 1[18]). Foremost among the dead, sovereign among the living is the meaning. *Unto him that loveth us and loosed us from our sins by his blood and hath made us to be a kingdom*—not as R.V. The peculiar Greek is due to John's dependence upon a Hebrew idiom (intro., p. 1365b). The A.V. has *washed* for *loosed*—a weakly attested reading.

6. *A kingdom, priests*—based upon Ex. 19[6] (cf. Isa. 61[5, 6] 66[21]). Those whom Christ has loosed from their sins are the true Israel, a society in which his will is realized. In the Messianic kingdom the glorified martyrs will be kings and priests to the nations as the true Israel was to be. But apart from that, there is an eternal kingship and priesthood of all the faithful. Corporately they are a kingdom, a holy nation, a theocracy. Individually they are priests having access through his blood into the Holy of Holies, offering living, reasonable, and spiritual sacrifices, making intercession for all men (Rom. 12[1] Heb. 13[15]).

7. John combines Dan. 7[13] with Zech. 12[10] (cf. Mt. 24[30], where the two passages are also combined in reference to the Advent). Jn. 19[37] quotes Zech. 12[10] in reference to the crucifixion. John writes with prophetic certainty as though his eye already sees him coming. *Every eye shall see him* and all those who by their attitude to him share the guilt of those who crucified him, *and all the tribes of the earth shall mourn* [*because of*] *him.* Then follows the double asseveration, *It is so, Amen.* That event, which causes the faithful to lift up their hearts because their redemption is drawing nigh, causes consternation to those who have not been able to read the signs of the times.

8. This word from God himself is the climax. The *Almighty* is better rendered the All-ruler. It is the word used by the LXX to translate *Lord of Hosts.* There is some ground for supposing the verse is misplaced here, for it is not expected after the double asseveration of v. 7, and it seems to imply that John is already in a trance, whereas that follows. For the meaning of the verse see note on 22[13].

9-20. The Prologue on Earth. The Call of John and the Vision of the Son of Man. The writer uses his name again, a sign of personal relationship to his readers. But he claims no title of authority, only he is a sharer with them in their trials, and he has seen a vision of the Son of man risen and glorified, and has been charged to tell of what he has seen. *Fellowship in the tribulation and kingdom and endurance which is in Jesus* (note the order) is characteristic of early Christian experience (cf. Lk. 12[32] Rom. 5[3] 2 Cor. 1[7]). Endurance (*patience*) is put last because the struggle still remains, though the ultimate triumph is assured. It seems that John was not in *Patmos* now but had found himself there in consequence (not for the sake) of *the word of God and the testimony of Jesus*. Patmos was a small island off the southwest coast of Asia Minor used as a penal settlement.

10. John fell into a trance *on the Lord's day*. This is the first place in Christian literature where *the Lord's day* is named. The first day in each month was called Sebaste, the emperor's day, and Deissmann thinks a day of the week was so called. It was natural for Christians to call that day when they gathered for worship in the name of Him who died and rose again on the first day of the week the Lord's day. To do so was, moreover, a direct challenge to the emperor worship to which John refers so often in this book.

11. Ramsay points out that these churches all stand on the great circular road in the west central part of the province, so that they would serve as good centers of communication for the surrounding districts. But doubtless the number *seven* was chosen because of its symbolism for sanctity and completeness. These seven represent the universal church.

12. The thought of the *golden candlesticks* is based on Ex. 25[31] and Zech. 4[2]. But here there are seven candlesticks, which symbolize the churches whose function it is to embody and give forth God's light upon earth (v. 20).

13. Among the candlesticks is *one like unto the Son of man* (R.V. mg.). The reference is to Dan. 7[13] and is to be understood here as a title of Messiah. In immediate relationship to the churches John perceives the churches' Lord. He moves among them as if he were the priest tending the lights, but he is no human priest. His *robe* down to his feet symbolizes his dignity, possibly his priesthood. The *golden girdle* suggests royalty.

14. The description of the Ancient of Days in Dan. 7[9f.] is quite naturally transferred to the risen and glorified Christ, but the *white hair*, appropriate in Daniel, may perhaps have no special significance here, unless the ancient commentators are right in finding in it a reference to pre-existence. In the days of his flesh men noted the penetrating glance of Jesus and the indignation that sometimes burned in his eyes (cf. Mk. 3[5, 34]). So here the glowing eyes represent the all-penetrating insight and consuming wrath of holiness against sin.

15. Read *feet of burnished brass when it is smelted in the furnace*. Strength and stability are suggested, power to trample down all enemies (Ezek. 1[7]). Perhaps the roar of the Ægean around seagirt Patmos was in his mind when he wrote *his voice* [*is*] *as the voice of many waters* (cf. Ezek. 43[2]).

16. *The seven stars* representing the heavenly bodies are subject to him. *The two-edged sword* is the symbol of judicial authority (cf. "the word of God," 19[13-15]). Once on earth at the Transfiguration his face shone as the sun (Mt. 17[2]).

17, 18. The seer is overwhelmed at the vision. *Fear not*, says the one like unto a Son of man—a word of good cheer so often on the lips of Jesus. And he who held the seven stars in his hand laid that same hand upon his bewildered disciple. *I am the first and the last*—an O.T. title (see note on 22[13])—*and he that liveth and was dead*—so the verse should read, the Greek translating a Hebrew idiom. *He that liveth* recalls many passages in the O.T. where Jehovah is contrasted with the dead gods of the Gentiles. Here the emphasis is on the living Christ whom death could not hold, for he has the keys of death and of Hades, the intermediate abode of the wicked in this book. He who has conquered death can rescue from its grasp all who trust him.

20. *The secret meaning*—that is the sense in which *mystery* is used here—of the stars and the candlesticks is the angels of the churches and the churches. The *angels of the churches* have been understood as (1) the messengers who take the letters; (2) the bishops of the churches—but angels must represent superhuman beings; so (3) their guardian angels: but the best interpretation is (4) the heavenly counterparts or representatives of the churches and the candlesticks are the actual churches. The one represents an ideal, the other the reality. Christ holds in his hand the stars, which are the angels of the churches, and the candlesticks. He has the ideals in his power: in him alone they can be realized. By the angels is personified the essential spirit of the churches.

The significance of this vision is that among these churches which were typical in their weakness and their strength of the universal church there moves the risen Christ. They were surrounded by paganism, but their Lord held them in his hand. Persecution, however severe, can be borne if it is seen against the background of the eternal order. Material power and physical force are not the dominant factors. The Lord who became dead and who is alive for evermore, he is the Lord of life, he is the arbiter of human history.

CHAPTER II

The Letters to the Seven Churches (chs. 2, 3). Theories that these letters are from another hand and do not belong to the book are not proven. The whole book is cast in the form of a letter which, as the N.T. shows, had proved itself a useful form of literary composition (cf. p. 854). It is true that in some passages it is expected that the church will survive until the last Advent (2^{25} 3^{3}), whereas the expectation of the rest of the book is that a universal martyrdom will take place before that event (cf. 13^{15}). Therefore Charles thinks that John wrote these specific letters some time before he wrote Revelation, and that he himself edited them, adapting them as messages to the universal church when he wrote the book of which they are now an integral part. This is doubtful, but it is clear that in each letter he is writing with an intimate knowledge of the individual church, and it is equally clear that the message is to the church universal. In the geographical features and political history of each city, John, writing for Jesus, the true Lord of the churches, sees forces that mold the character of men. The church is in a sense the city with distinct characteristics and in each case with a distinct destiny.

1–7. The Message to the Church in Ephesus. Ephesus was the capital of the province of Asia. Situated at the western terminus of the great system of Roman roads in Asia it was foremost in commerce, and as Temple-warden (cf. Acts 19^{35}) it played a great part in the religious life of the province. This title was given for the city's devotion to Artemis, whose temple was one of the seven wonders of the ancient world. But the title meant also that the city was warden of the imperial cult. We have a coin on which are represented a shrine and altar to Augustus within the sacred precinct of Artemis. A temple had been erected in the city to Claudius or Nero, and later other temples were erected to other emperors. The city was a hotbed of every kind of superstition. The Ephesian books were notorious (cf. Acts 19^{19}). After the destruction of Jerusalem it became the chief center of the Christian faith in the East. Those who were traveling from the East to Rome and back mostly passed through Asia. Perhaps as the result of the persecution threatening when John was writing, the city is called by Ignatius "the passage way of those who are slain unto God," i.e., the place through which passed so many on their way to martyrdom in the amphitheater at Rome.

The church in Ephesus has a record of *labor* and of *patience*, especially of the labor of resisting false teachers, and of the brave patience with which the Christian faces the hindrances and trials which beset him. John emphasizes this patience and steadfastness and describes their motive as *for my name's sake* (v. 3). But the controversies with those who *called themselves apostles and were not* had apparently caused faction and division in the church (cf. Acts $20^{29, 30}$), and the Ephesians had lost the enthusiastic love they had shown in the days of Paul (Acts 20^{37}). The first glow of the awakened spiritual life had passed. Perhaps their concern for orthodoxy had made them censorious. The writer of the fourth Gospel and the first Epistle lays much emphasis on "love of one another," and he also writes to Ephesus. John recalls the three stages of their conversion—*remember, repent, do* (v. 5). Then follows a threat as to the fate of Ephesus, if it does not heed the warning, *her lampstand shall be moved out of its place.* The lampstand means the church, and most commentators read this as a threat of destruction and point to the fulfillment of the prophecy in that all that remains on the site of the once famous city is a railway station and a few huts; the rest has been buried by the dust of the ages. Ramsay sees in these words a threat not to destroy but to uproot the city and its church and to move it to a new spot. For he emphasizes change as the characteristic of its history. The site and scenery of the city constantly varied; what was land at one time was water at another; where once was a teeming population was a bare hillside again; the great harbor where Paul landed is a marsh to-day. But the message does not end with a threat. In the matter of the *Nicolaitans* (v. 6) and their pernicious teaching the Ephesian church was true and sound (cf. $2^{14, 15}$). Then follows the promise that to the Ephesian who in the persecution wins the crown of martyrdom—*overcometh*—it shall be given *to eat of the tree of life* (v. 7). The Christian life is constantly described as a warfare in the N.T. There is no discharge from that warfare, but he who becomes a victor in it wins the right to *eat of the tree of life which is in the paradise of God,* the street of the heavenly Jerusalem (22^{2}). That tree is the symbol of immortality.

1. The cities may be likened to a circlet of jewels which Christ *holds in his hand.*

There is the contrast between the ideal light of the star and the actual light of the lamp.

2. There were many itinerant preachers and the Christian Church had to test them. The *Teaching of the Twelve Apostles*, a recently discovered document of the sub-apostolic age, gives careful warning about this. Ignatius bears witness to the discrimination of the Ephesian church in respect to those who brought evil doctrine.

6. The *Nicolaitans* have been interpreted as (1) the followers of Nicolas (Nicolaüs) the deacon (Acts 6[5]), an early guess which has little or no justification; (2) the Balaamites. "Nicolaos" is probably a translation of "Balaam," meaning "he has consumed the people." The followers of Jezebel were a part of this sect (2[14, 15, 20]). They converted the liberty of the gospel into license, carrying to an extreme the doctrine of those whom Paul had to rebuke at Corinth for trying to carry over into Christianity the pagan divorce between religion and morality (1 Cor. 5). The Nicolaitans were idolaters and fornicators.

8–11. The Message to the Church at Smyrna. Smyrna was some fifty miles north of Ephesus and disputed with the latter the title of chief city of Asia. Its loyalty to Rome had been conspicuous: a temple to Tiberius had been built there, so that Smyrna, like Ephesus, had the honor of being called Temple-warden.

The description of Christ as *he who was dead and came to life* is specially appropriate for this city, which in the sixth century B.C. was destroyed by the Lydians and after four hundred years was refounded. John is aware of the suffering of the church; but, as he knows the city triumphed over death, so he sees it is rich in reality despite its material poverty. He knows that the hatred of the Jews, i.e., of those of them who claim to be Jews but really are no *synagogue* of Jehovah but *of Satan*, has been violent against the church. An illuminating example of this hatred is in the way the Jews of the city, even violating the Sabbath, brought faggots into the stadium to burn Polycarp in 155 A.D. Further suffering will come upon them: *the devil will cast some of them into prison* (v. 10), the usual prelude to martyrdom. But loyalty was characteristic of Smyrna. John does not disdain this appeal to civic patriotism to remind them that loyalty to Christ will win the crown of life. "The hill Pagos, with the stately public buildings on its rounded top, and the city spreading out down its rounded slopes," had made the *crown* of Smyrna a familiar phrase. On coins the city is represented as a figure with a mural crown upon her head. But the Christian martyr will receive no crown of towers, no garland of an athlete, destined to fade (Smyrna was famous for its games), but a crown which belongs to the eternal life. Neither the death which he suffers as a martyr nor the death which follows the final Judgment can harm him (cf. 20[6]).

12–17. The Message to the Church at Pergamum. Pergamum was some fifty miles from Smyrna and fifteen from the coast. Commercially it was falling behind Ephesus and Smyrna, which were better situated for trade, but it was superior to both in official and religious importance. Behind the town was a hill, one thousand feet high, crowned with temples to Zeus, Soter, Athena, Dionysus, Æsculapius. The last was the most famous, and because of it the city had a great school of medicine. But the most significant thing about the city to John was that here the first temple in Asia was dedicated to the emperor worship. Prior to Ephesus and to Smyrna, Pergamum was a Temple-warden. She was the center of the imperial cult—*where the throne of Satan is*—which menaced the very existence of the Christian Church.

It is fitting that, in this message to the church in the city where official authority resided, Christ should be described as *he that hath the two-edged sharp sword* (cf. 1[16]), i.e., as possessing absolute and universal authority, that power of life and death symbolized by the sword, which was vested in the proconsul of the province. John bears witness to the loyalty of the church to the *Name* in the city where men were confronted with the alternative of worshiping Cæsar or receiving sentence of death. *Antipas my faithful witness* (the word here is probably equivalent to "mårtyr," its common meaning in the next century) is mentioned as representative of many who had proved their loyalty thus in Pergamum. But there was a minority in the church of Pergamum that held the teaching of Balaam, the prototype of all false teachers (see note on v. 6). It was the Nicolaitans that troubled the Christians of Pergamum as well as those of Ephesus. The danger was of compromise between Christianity and the state religion. What harm was there in burning incense to the emperor? Why make life so intolerably difficult by refusing to take any part in the social and civic life of Pergamum because there were immoral practices associated with it? They were under grace, not under Law. But John, like Paul, saw that this argument belonged to the deep things of Satan. The church must not lower the standard; either it must conquer the imperial idolatry or be itself destroyed.

17. To him who refused to compromise the promise is that he shall have of the *hidden manna.* According to 2 Baruch 29[8] the treasury of manna which was in the ark, which Jeremiah was thought to have hidden in a cave on Mount Sinai, was to descend from heaven during the Messianic kingdom and the blessed were to eat of it. The meaning here is that he who abstains from forbidden meats will be fed by bread from heaven. Further than that, the victor in this fight will receive *a white stone* and *a new name written upon it.* Probably this is to be explained as an amulet with some magical name by which the possessor could secure entrance into heaven. Popular superstition in the power of a secret name to open closed portals and to give the user supernatural powers was widespread. *He who has kept the Name* in the Christian warfare shall receive a symbol of transcendent powers: upon it is inscribed the name that is above every name, the name that marks the recreation of his personality as son of God and heir of heaven.

18–29. The Message to the Church in Thyatira. Thyatira was about forty miles southwest of Pergamum, a Lydian city on the borders of Mysia. This and Philadelphia were the least famous of the seven cities, but the message to Thyatira is the longest of all. Inscriptions show that Thyatira was remarkable for the number of its trade-guilds. It is these which are the danger to the church.

Christ is here called *the Son of God*, a challenge to the title which the imperial cult applied to Cæsar. The further description of *the eyes* that flash with indignation, and *the feet* that can tread down his enemies, is specially appropriate in view of the severity of the message. The works of the church are praised: *love and faith, service and endurance.* And unlike the Ephesians the Thyatirans were progressing in good works. But there was a *Jezebel* calling herself *a prophetess* who was corrupting members of the church and teaching them immorality and idolatry (v. 20). The common meal of the trade-guilds, such as that of the workers in bronze (cf. v. 18), involved participation in eating food offered to idols. It was not possible to belong to such a guild and not participate in banquets at which acknowledgment of heathen deities was made, and at which there might be orgies of licentious revelry. Perhaps it was argued the worship was a mere form, and the Christian need not deny his Christian faith by it, as he need not participate in the obscene practices. Perhaps some claimed that the Christian ought to know the deep things, evil as well as good. "All things are lawful," they may have asserted (cf. 1 Cor. 2[10]). At any rate both in his social and business life this trade-guild was most important for the artisan and workman. What was the Christian to do? In Ephesus the lax doctrine of the Nicolaitans, who allowed Christians to participate in all the practices of such guilds, was rejected (2[6]), but at Thyatira the church was silent, because of the presence of an influential woman, who had long and notoriously advocated the principles of the Nicolaitans. She cloaked her activities under the name of prophetess and her teaching under the title of broad-mindedness, liberalism, but she was really a modern *Jezebel* (see below on v. 20).

The problem of the Thyatirans is always before the church. Life in an old-established and highly organized society involves contact with practices of which the Christian cannot approve. To live up to the Christian ideals is inevitably to clash with many customs of the world, though that world is nominally Christian to-day instead of wholly pagan, as in Thyatira. How far ought one to overlook things of which he did not approve? Did not Paul agree (1 Cor. 5) that it was not necessary to leave the world severely alone? To John the issue is clear. Should the church conform with the ordinary customs of society or be at war with them? To have conformed would have reduced Christianity to a cult. The religion that was to win the victory over the empire was made of sterner stuff; and it was due to the insight of the author of this book that the issue was so clearly presented. The specious prophetess of Thyatira had been warned how superficial and wrong were her pleas. Now her punishment is announced (v. 22). She is to be *cast on a bed* of suffering, and with her those who, misled by her influence, had tried to combine Christianity with paganism: those who were her spiritual progeny were to perish by plague. And so when the news spread through the province all the churches would know that Christ searcheth the will and affections and thoughts (*the reins and the heart*) and renders to each his due (v. 23).

But not all in Thyatira were thus misled, not all knew the depths of knowledge, as these called them, depths not of God but of Satan. Upon the faithful the two commands of the apostolic decrees were imposed: abstain from food offered to idols and from fornication (Acts 15[28]). Let them keep these rules until the Lord come. Their reward shall be to share in the Messianic kingdom (vv. 25, 26). V. 27 read *and he shall break them with a rod of iron, as the potter's vessels shall they be dashed in pieces.* The prophecy has been fulfilled in the social and national systems which have been destroyed by the influence of the church, and at the same time in the influence upon national life and character which the church has exercised. The promise ends with the difficult words *I will give him the morning star*. In 22[16] this is a title of Christ (see note). After the tribulation, when he has won through, the reward is Christ, or, as Moffatt interprets it, eternal life. Perhaps the meaning is less definite—the future belongs to the Christian who has proved himself more than conqueror.

20. Other interpretations of *Jezebel* are (1) the wife of the bishop, because of the variant reading *thy wife* for *the woman Jezebel*. This rests probably on a wrong reading and certainly on a wrong interpretation of the angels of the churches. (2) The Chaldee Sibyl: but Jezebel is obviously a member of the church.

24. *The deep things of Satan* is otherwise interpreted as a boast of the libertines, who claimed that the spiritual man should know the deep things of Satan, i.e., should take part in heathen practices but remain unaffected by them.

CHAPTER III

See introductory paragraph to ch. 2.

1–6. The Message to the Church in Sardis. Sardis was the old capital of Lydia, a third-rate city in Roman times notorious for its licentiousness. Its characteristics here are degradation, false pretension, and death.

The description of Christ—*he who has the seven Spirits of God and the seven stars*—emphasizes him as wielding his divine power in the seven churches, perhaps in contrast with the deadness of a church which was only nominally alive. But in spite of the spiritual death there is made this final appeal. *Be watchful*—a word the church of Sardis would find specially appropriate. For twice the supposedly impregnable city, high in a rocky plateau, had fallen into the hands of the enemy through lack of vigilance. The steep rock was unguarded and by that unguarded way the soldiers of Cyrus *like a thief* captured the city, ruled by Crœsus, in 549 B.C. And in similar way Antiochus the Great took the city in 218 B.C., because the garrison did not watch the side they thought could not be scaled. John bids them to be watchful and to reconstruct on a firm basis whatever remained out of the wreck of the city but was now ready to die. For the works of Sardis have been deficient in God's sight, however complacent the church is about them. *Remember, keep, repent:* that is the message (v. 3). It is noteworthy that Sardis and Philadelphia are not attacked from within by heresy nor from without by persecution, yet they are the least satisfactory of the churches. Perhaps they would have been regarded as flourishing and successful churches, yet they are most to be criticized of the seven. Sardis appeared to be a live church full of various activities, but moral contamination had sapped her spiritual vitality. Yet Sardis, though in a critical, is not in a hopeless condition. There are a few persons even in Sardis who have not besmirched the professions made in baptism (v. 4). For them is spoken the gracious and tender promise that they shall continue to the end white and pure as they had continued amid the notorious impurities of their city. Those who are victorious shall receive *white garments*, i.e., spiritual bodies represented as robes of light and glory in the resurrection life. Those who resist the spiritual death which is characteristic of many in the church shall have their names enrolled forever among the citizens of the city of God, and their names shall be acknowledged before God.

5. *The book of life* (cf. 20[12]) is derived from the O.T., where a divine register of men is mentioned in Ex. 32[32] (cf. Psa. 69[28] Isa. 4[3]). The idea is developed in apocalyptic literature. To have one's name erased from the book of life meant exclusion from the heavenly kingdom: to have one's name retained was the symbol of eternal fellowship with God and his people.

7–13. The Message to the Church in Philadelphia. Philadelphia was about twenty-eight miles southeast of Sardis—an ancient city, which in the first century A.D. had suffered much from earthquake shocks. The chief pagan cult was that of Dionysus, the god of wine, as was natural in a vine-growing district: but the Christian Church suffered more from Jewish than from pagan opponents. The Christianity of Philadelphia was of a high character. This missionary church was neither vexed by heresy nor shamed by heathen practices.

Christ is described as *the Holy* par excellence, the true, the genuine Messiah, who has complete authority to admit or to exclude from the city of David. As the prophet (Isa. 45[14]) anticipated the submission of the Gentiles to Israel, so the Philadelphians are bidden to anticipate that these Jews—who have belied their name and its privileges—will submit to the church, the true Israel of God. Philadelphia had *kept* (v. 8) the gospel of patient endurance which Christ exemplified, and Philadelphia shall be kept when the testing time for the whole world which was imminent came. The time is short before the Second Advent (v. 11), and because Philadelphia is to be kept in the hour of trial she is to guard (*hold fast*) the prize which might otherwise be taken from her and given to one who is more faithful (Mt. 25[28]). After the great earthquake of 17 A.D. few people ventured to live in the city owing to the continuance of minor shocks. The record of that experience, a little more than half a century earlier, made the promise to the Philadelphian victor more appropriate that he should *go out from the city no more* (v. 12). The Philadelphians knew what it was to live in expectation of the hour of trial. But the victor in the Christian contest shall be firm as a *pillar* upon which the Temple rests: he shall be shaken by no disaster in the great day of trial. After the great earthquake, because of the kindness the city received from Tiberius, Philadelphia received another name, Neo-Cæsarea, meaning the city of the young Cæsar, either Tiberius or Germanicus. So the name of the imperial God was written on this city. That explains the significance of *new name* in v. 12. The Christian martyr shall have written on his forehead the *name of God*, for he is his possession; the name of the *city of God*, for he has the right of citizenship; and the *new name of Christ*, which will be revealed when he comes. It is significant that Philadelphia, living in constant danger of earthquakes, was the city that in subsequent history, long after all the surrounding cities had passed under Turkish domination, alone held up the banner of Christianity.

7. *He that hath the key of David.* Perhaps the synagogue that claimed to be the synagogue of Jehovah but was really the *synagogue of Satan* (v. 9; cf. 2[9]) had excommunicated the Philadelphian Christians. But they had no authority to open or shut the door into the Kingdom. Christ who had the key had set before the Philadelphians an open door which none could shut. One day the contemptuous Jews would learn their mistake and seek to be taught by the Christians whom they had thought to shut out of the privileges of the true Israel.

8. *A door opened.* This is generally understood as an opportunity for missionary effort (cf. 1 Cor. 16[9]). Moffatt refers it to Christ, the door of the sheep; but Bousset renders it the door of entrance into the Messianic glory. The *door of spiritual privilege* seems not inappropriate here.

12. It is not clear whether it is to be rendered *I will write upon him the name of my God* or *upon it*, i.e., upon the pillar. If the latter, the reference is probably to the fact that the priest of the cult of the emperors after his year of office erected his statue in the temple with his and his father's names upon it, his place of birth and year of office. The statue was a perpetual memorial to his priesthood. So should the faithful stand in the temple of God. And upon him would be written God's name, the name of the city and the sacred name which gives power to the user.

14–22. The Message to the Church in Laodicea. Laodicea was only a few miles from Colossæ (Col. 4[15, 16]), and the church there was probably founded by Epaphras of Colossæ (Col. 1[7] 4[12]). The city was great and rich, so much so that it disdained the help of the emperor when it was destroyed by the earthquake in 60 A.D. It was a banking center, famous for the manufacture of black wool, carpets, and cloths, and had a flourishing medical school. There are several points of resemblance between this message and the Epistle to the Colossians which was to be read in Laodicea (cf. Col. 4[16] and especially Col. 1[18] 1[27] 2[2, 3] 3[1]). Most likely the writer knew this letter of Paul and the letter to Laodicea (Col. 4[18]).

The title of Christ emphasizes his authority: he is *Amen, the true one* who keeps covenant: his counsel and rebuke are authoritative; he is the supreme moral critic, the primary source of God's creation (Col. 1[18]). The indictment of the church that follows is uncompromising. Success in moneymaking is not the best proof of the higher qualities of citizenship. The wealth of the city, the energy that had made it a center of trade, did not conceal from the eye of *the faithful and true witness* the *lukewarmness* that was fatal to the highest side of human nature. What was true of the city was true of the church. There was money enough to support its enterprises: it was popular and well supported, for it did not set too high a standard of social or commercial life. Religious enthusiasm was characteristic of the natives of Phrygia, but Laodicea was a Greek city and was above all that. The church adopted a spirit of accommodation and of broad toleration, and was entirely self-satisfied. Proud of its prestige in the city, of its apostolic traditions, of its generosity and wealth, it *had need of nothing* (v. 17) in its own eyes.

The absolute rejection of religion is preferable to the half-hearted Laodicean expression of it. There is hope for the outsider, but for the Christian who is so only in name, who is content with the comparative warmth of a religion which is neither hot nor cold, there is expressed the divine disgust. Dante at the gate of Hell heard "sighs with lamentations and loud moans." Vergil explains that this was the fate of "those who lived without or praise or blame," that these Laodicean, neutral souls were driven forth from heaven and the depth of hell does not receive them. In this message it is made clear that the wealth and self-sufficiency of Laodicea are of no avail, though by them the city was rebuilt after the earthquake. There is *a gold refined by fire* (v. 18), but it is not paid to the man who compromises with his soul. The church that is rich toward God does not boast about it. Let Laodicea buy (but "without money and without price") the golden gift of a new heart of fellowship with Christ, for that means *the white garments* of the spiritual bodies, wherewith the righteous shall be clothed when the wicked remain disembodied (cf. 3[5]), and that gift brings with it the vision of the things that are unseen and eternal. Of how much more value are these than the boasted riches or the glossy black cloths or the *eye-salve* which in the fame of men made the city renowned. But though the rebuke is so severe, it is from one whose love inflicts the discipline of suffering to win them back (cf. Prov. 3[12] Heb. 12[6]). So let them *be zealous* (v. 19; the tense implies that fervent enthusiasm must be a permanent element in their Christian character) and change their mind. This appeal is made more intimate by the picture of Christ *knocking at the door* of the individual heart (v. 20). How courteous for the Lord of the world to *stand at the door* not presuming to enter until he is invited. "God is always courteous," said Francis of Assisi, "and does not invade the privacy of the human soul." He who hearkens and opens will find Christ both guest and host, yes, and the feast too (Jn. 6[54]). The common meal is the symbol to the Oriental for confidence and affection (Jn. 14[23] Lk. 24[29, 30]).

21. The verse is eschatological—the Christian martyr shall reign with Christ—and is fulfilled in 20[4]. This is the conclusion to the messages to all the churches rather than to Laodicea only. The Christian is one in his experience with Christ in his struggle and in his victory (cf. Jn. 17[24]).

CHAPTER IV

The Prologue in Heaven. With dramatic suddenness the scene changes from earth to heaven, from the churches with their imperfect works, their disloyalties, and their fears of martrydom, to the heavenly hosts worshiping around the throne: from the restlessness and distractions of this world to the perfect peace and assurance of heaven (cf. Isa. 6[1-4] Ezek. 1[24-28] Dan. 7[9, 10]).

1–11. The Vision of the Sovereignty of Creative Power and of Redemptive Love. (See also ch. 5.) There stands a door in heaven already open. The seer in his vision hears the former voice, i.e., of the Son of man, bidding him come to see *what must come to pass hereafter.* He has seen the vision of things as they are on earth in chs. 2 and 3. He sees now a vision of things as they are in heaven. This is necessary for him in order that he may understand the future. Human history is to be rightly conceived only if seen *sub specie eternitatis*—against the background of the eternal order. In heaven stood a throne from under which came lightnings and thunders; before it were *seven lamps of fire* (v. 5) and *a sea of glass* (v. 6; cf. Ezek. 1[27, 28]). Immediately surrounding the throne were *four living creatures* (v. 6) and in a wider circle outside them were *twenty-four thrones* and *twenty-four elders* upon them (v. 4). The living creatures and the elders join in songs of praise to God who sits upon the central throne. No form is visible, only the luster of the *sardius* (v. 3; perhaps a green translucent stone) and the blood-red *jasper* flashing through a nimbus of *emerald* green which concealed Him who sat upon the throne. The lightnings and the thunders recall the theophany in Ex. 19[16] (cf. Heb. 12[19]). These with the seven lamps symbolize the purity and the energy in its perfection of the Divine Being. The sea is to be explained from Gen. 1[7], "the waters above the firmament," and in the *Testimony of the Twelve Patriarchs* a sea is described as hanging between the first and second heavens. Only a part of this is visible *as it were a sea of glass like unto crystal* (v. 6). The four living creatures are the *cherubim:* the description is derived from Isa. 6 and Ezek. 1. They are generally thought to represent the whole animate creation in the thought that the unresting activity of nature under its Creator is a ceaseless offering of praise to him. But in the Jewish hierarchy the angels of service are appointed over the world of nature and they are an inferior order. The cherubim in this book stand for the highest order of angels. In Ezekiel the cherubim have four faces each in the likeness of a lion, an ox, a man and an eagle, and have four wings. The description is similar but not the same here (v. 7). Beneath their wings they are *full of eyes* suggesting the unresting vigilance with which they guard the throne. Both the cherubim and the elders unite in a hymn of praise, the words of which interpret the significance of the scene. On earth men bowed in fear before Domitian, who claimed to be "Our Lord and our God" (*Dominus et Deus noster*). He had power of life and death over all his subjects. Only the Christians refused to bow the knee to him. For them there was only One who could claim worship and he was on the throne of the universe (v. 11). Creator, sovereign Lord of all—who should make them afraid?

3. Perhaps *the emerald rainbow* was understood as a protection for human eyes against the dazzling splendor of the glory of the Divine Presence. Anderson Scott suggests that it may refer to the freshness which follows rain and so to the seasons of refreshing from the presence of the Lord.

4. The twenty-four elders are variously interpreted: (1) as the twelve O.T. patriarchs and the twelve N.T. apostles—but that idea of the church is mediæval; (2) as a group of angelic beings—originally Babylonian star-gods whom the Jews transformed into angels—but though they sit on thrones these elders do not act as judges; (3) as the angelic counterpart of the heads of the twenty-four priestly orders (cf. 1 Chr. 24$^{7-18}$), for they later perform the priestly ministry of offering the golden bowls of incense. This is the best explanation. Charles suggests that they may be intended here to represent the faithful, all of whom are kings and priests.

9. According to a Hebrew idiom the translation should probably be *and whenever the living creatures give*—a description of the regular order of divine worship in heaven.

11. *They were and were created;* i.e., by thy will they first existed in the world of thought, and then by one definite act they were created.

CHAPTER V

1–14. **The Vision Continued.** (See ch. 4.) This chapter shows the relation between the scene of worship in heaven just described and the world. John sees a book *in the right hand of him that sat on the throne* (cf. Ezek. 2^{10}), a book roll, so full that it was written on both sides, and he could see the writing on the reverse side as the book was held up. This he feels convinced is the book of destiny containing the things that shall be. But the divine counsels are a profound secret, the book is sealed with seven seals. A strong angel challenged anyone to open this fateful book and the seer was distressed because there was no response. He wept because he feared the revelations could not be disclosed. Then he was told that *the strong scion of Judah's tribe, David's offspring* (Isa. 11$^{1-10}$), would open the book (v. 5). He looked to see a conqueror; he expected power and strength, and he saw *a Lamb;* he looked to see one who should slay his foes, and he saw a Lamb as though slain in sacrifice, with all the appearance of wounds (cf. Jn. 20$^{25, 27}$), yet not dead but alive. But the Lamb does not lack power—he has *seven horns,* symbolical of power and kingly dignity, and he has *seven eyes* betokening his active insight and intelligence (v. 6). He is portrayed under figures that represent him as the supreme ruler with fullness of power and of knowledge, and at the same time as the supreme example of self-sacrifice and self-surrender; and that has been the avenue to his power. The Lamb is *in the midst of the throne, and of the four living creatures, and in the midst of the elders* (v. 6). The meaning is that the Lamb is the central figure upon whom the attention of all is fixed. The Lamb takes the book from the hand of Him that sits upon the throne, and his action is the signal for another burst of praise—*a new song* (v. 9)—from the four living creatures and the twenty-four elders. Again the song interprets the scene. It was because the Lamb had been slain and *had purchased unto God with his blood men of every tribe* (cf. 14$^{3, 4}$ Mt. 20^{28} Acts 20^{28} 1 Cor. 6^{20} 7^{23} 1 Pet. 2^{9}) that he was worthy to open the book. This song is taken up by innumerable angels around the throne; and finally all created things from every part of the universe swell the great chorus, to which the four living creatures say *Amen* (v. 14; cf. 1 Cor. 14^{16}), while the elders bow in adoration.

So ends *the introduction to the book:* it tells of the two principles of (1) the creative power, and (2) the redemptive purpose of God, which are the moving forces in history. It has thus a special message to people who were entangled in the circumstances of the time. There is a picture of the church on earth, its temptations, failures, triumphs, rewards. There is an interpretation of the facts of history—God made the world and is redeeming man in terms of eternity. But God has been seen not only as the sovereign Creator but also as the Love which bears all the sin of the world. At the heart of God's sovereignty is redemptive, sacrificial love: in the midst of the throne is *a Lamb standing as though it had been slain.* In the vision of John it was such a God who alone was able to strengthen the seer's fellow Christians to bear the storm which was about to break over them (cf. Paul's triumphant conclusion in Rom. 8$^{31-39}$).

"Love is and was my King and Lord,
　　And will be, though as yet I keep
　　Within his court on earth, and sleep
Encompass'd by his faithful guard,
And hear at times a sentinel,
　　Who moves about from place to place,
　　And whispers to the worlds of space
In the deep night, that all is well."

1. With the loosing of each seal a part of the contents of the book is disclosed, and that is the theme of the following chapters. Others think the book is a will, which according to Roman law bore the seven seals of seven witnesses and could not be executed until all the seven seals were loosed. It is more likely that the book is conceived as a roll than as a codex.

8. Read *having each of them a harp and golden bowls full of incense.* The words *which are the prayers of the saints* are a gloss and incompatible with 8^{3-5}, where prayers and incense are not identical. Even if the words are retained, there would be no justification for interpreting the prayers of the saints as intercessions for the church in the mediæval sense. The "saints" in the N.T. are the faithful, and more often the reference is to the church militant than to the church triumphant.

9, 10. "Heaven is revealed to earth as the homeland of music," says Rossetti. The *song* here is to the Lamb for his redemptive work: he was slain, but at the cost of his blood he bought for God men of all nations, and they whom he has bought (not the Cæsars) are the true kings of the earth and the true priests. *And they shall reign*—probably the future tense is right here in accordance with Hebrew idiom, whether the present or future is read in the Greek.

12. The first four parts of the ascription—*power, riches, wisdom, and might*—are those which the Lamb assumes; the last three—*honor, glory, blessing*—mark the recognition of the Lamb by mankind. It is to be noted how John, a Jewish monotheist, equates, without hesitation, these two figures, God and the Lamb, with the highest worship—a suggestion looking in the direction of the later doctrine of the Trinity.

CHAPTER VI

The Opening of the First Six Seals. Not unlike a drama in three acts are described the visions of the Seals (ch. 6), the Trumpets (chs. 8, 9), and the Bowls (chs. 15–20^{3}), but the orderly sequence is more than once interrupted (the so-called parentheses). The seals are the signs of the destruction of the present world. This world is the training ground for the children of God; when the training is finished the world will be destroyed. This destruction will be heralded by the disintegrating disasters such as war and pestilence (vv. 1–8). Then will follow disorders in the universe (vv. 12–17). The best interpretation is that John is following the eschatological scheme of Mk. 13 (cf. Mt. 24 Lk. 21), where, combining the three accounts, are recorded seven signs that will be seen when these things are about to be accomplished (Mk. 13^{4}), wars, civil strife, famines, earthquakes, persecutions, pestilence, signs in the sun, etc. John has combined earthquakes and eclipses into the sixth woe and has changed the character of the seventh. He has changed the order, because he personifies four of the woes under the four riders, and because of the dramatic fitness by which the social disasters come first (vv. 1–4) until a certain proportion of the martyrs is obtained (vv. 9–11—the fifth seal). After that follow the disorders in the universe (the sixth seal). But the writer is not merely using this familiar apocalyptic material in a traditional way; he interprets some of the signs in reference to contemporary events. The four horsemen are suggested by Zechariah's vision (Zech. 1^{8} 6^{1-8}), but the significance has little in common with the O.T. prophet. The whole is cast in dramatic form. The visions are not read from a book but the judgments are translated into action as each seal is broken.

1–17. The Judgment of the World Through the Opening of the Seals by Christ. The imagery here is all designed to emphasize one theme—Christ the Judge of men.

1, 2. As Christ opened *the first seal* in response to the *Come* of one of the living creatures, a rider on a *white horse* armed with a bow to whom was given a crown went forth. *Victorious War* is meant, and the bow makes clear the reference to the Parthian Empire, always a nightmare to the inhabitants of the Eastern provinces of the Græco-Roman world after Crassus' defeat in 53 B.C. The cleverness of the Parthian horsemen with the bow was a byword in Roman literature after that defeat, and any thought of invasion of the empire was associated with that frontier. In v. 1 it is not certain whether the *Come* is addressed to the Seer, to Christ or to the rider on the white horse. The *rider on the white horse* has been interpreted as Christ coming forth to conquer in answer to the summons *Come*. In 19^{11} he is rightly thus portrayed. Here Christ is the Lamb who sends forth the rider by opening the seal and he cannot be the rider. Besides, the woes are the precursors of the coming of Christ.

3, 4. *The second seal* lets loose a rider on a *red horse* symbolizing revolution, civil strife. Some have understood it of Rome as the destroyer of order and life, but this is less likely. This rider will take away the peace of the earth, which is not the peace of Christ.

5, 6. *The third seal* lets loose a rider on a *black horse* with a balance in his hand; and a voice, perhaps of the Lamb, speaks of the price of wheat and barley as in a time of famine, and forbids harming the olive and the vines. A ration of wheat will cost a day's wages—twelve times its normal price; the same sum will not buy enough barley for a man and his family. But the famine will not affect the luxuries, the oil and wine. Perhaps there is a reference to Domitian's edict in 92 A.D. to cut down vineyards in the provinces because of the shortage of cereals, an edict which was rescinded because of the protests against it from the cities of Asia.

7, 8. From *the fourth seal* issued a *pale horse* and its rider and his name was *Death*, i.e., Pestilence. The word "Death" is used as Europeans speak of the "Black Death." Authority was given to him over one quarter of the earth. Nearly always pestilence followed famine in olden times. Hades is often associated with Death in this book (cf. 20[13], note).

9–11. *The fifth seal* stands for *persecution*. John could not follow out the symbolism of the horses and their riders by making God send forth a horse to martyr the saints. So he uses another figure to represent the persecution to which they are subject. The souls of the martyrs are represented as the blood of sacrifices flowing under the altar in heaven on which they have been offered. These pray for vengeance. Their cry goes up *How long?* (Cf. Psa. 7[8] 36[1] Lk. 18[7].) When will the righteousness of God be vindicated? They are told they are to enjoy quiet for a time, until the completion of their number, till the roll of the martyrs is finished. The time will not be long. It is for John and those to whom he writes that the souls of the martyrs are waiting (cf. Heb. 11[40]), but the reference here is probably not as there to the O.T. saints, but to the Christians (v. 9) whose story we read in Acts, to Antipas (2[13]), and to those massacred under Nero. But the meaning is the same, that the church militant and the church triumphant are so much one that the blessedness of the church triumphant lacks something until the church militant has become the church triumphant. These martyrs are clothed with a white robe, their spiritual resurrection body (cf. 3[5]), which John conceives as given to the righteous only (cf. 2 Cor. 5[2, 3]).

12–17. The woes thus far described are in the past. The *sixth seal* reveals woes not yet fulfilled. The continuance of the world depends on the stability of the heavenly bodies; when they forsake their order the end is at hand. The O.T. descriptions of the Day of Jehovah supply the imagery (cf. Joel 2[30, 31] Isa. 50[3] 34[4] 2[19] Hos. 10[8] Ezek. 32[7] Lk. 23[30]). Not only the sun and moon and stars are affected, but heaven itself is described as rent in two, whereupon the divided portions curl into a roll on either side. Mankind in *seven classes* is described as panic-stricken. First, those who might think themselves secure by position, the kings, i.e., the heads of the heathen nations; the princes (the word means the chief men of Parthia); the captains, i.e., the Roman military tribunes; then those who trust in wealth or strength to protect them; and lastly the two classes which embrace all, every bondman and freeman. The conscience-stricken question of men, *Who is able to stand?* (v. 17) is answered in 7[9]—a great multitude which no man can number standing before God.

Apart from the sixth seal the judgments let loose under the others were all familiar enough in the ancient world. Wars, revolutions, famine, pestilence, persecution—these have been known in most centuries. If they are the precursors of disasters in the universe, earthquakes and the like, which were long ago foretold as the last signs of the end, men might well be utterly terrified, unless they can see a meaning in it all. This chapter shows that *it is the Lamb that was slain who unlooses these forces of destruction.* They must then be under his control, and even these forces must ultimately be to his glory.

CHAPTER VII

1–17. The Vision of the Triumphant Host. (The first parenthesis.) At this point there is an interlude in the unfolding drama. The first six seals have predicted judgments which increase in intensity and range. Before the seventh is revealed there is this vision which is intended to reassure the redeemed that they cannot be harmed by the plagues and disasters which are to befall the world. Always before some specially critical revelation of judgment John interposes a vision of consolation and hope. In this chapter he perceives four angels who are set over the four corners of the earth holding the winds from blowing. (The Jews considered the winds from the four corners harmful.) Here the angels represent the forces which are to bring destruction on the world. The seer is conscious of another angel rising from the east, whence the life-giving sun rises (Ezek. 43[2]), bidding the four angels, who are to let loose demonic woes, to hurt nothing until the servants of God have been sealed (v. 3). Hitherto the hosts of evil have been invisible, mysterious: now they are to make open war on God, who puts his mark upon his servants as temple-slaves bore the brand of the god (cf. Gal. 6[17]). By this they are known as the property of Jesus and no spiritual powers of darkness can hurt them (cf. Ezek. 9[4]).

Later baptism was called "a sealing," a sure protection against alien powers. Those who were thus protected were the spiritual Israel, and John uses a traditional Jewish apocalyptic number, 144,000, to signify the completeness of Israel (v. 4). It is clear they were protected from spiritual harm in the coming reign of Anti-Christ but they are not protected from martyrdom by this sealing. For in vv. 9–17 there is a second pause in the drama. The seer anticipates a later development by inserting a vision of these same sealed and now martyred Christians in heaven. The reason of this is to encourage them in their suffering by the contemplation of coming blessedness. The great host of v. 9 is the same as the 144,000 of v. 4. In vv. 1–8 the writer is influenced by his remembrance of some Jewish apocalypse, but as the vision unfolds it is no limited or racial redemption which is revealed. The representatives of the Jewish tribes have become a great multitude from all nations and tribes and peoples and tongues. These chant together a hymn of praise ascribing salvation to God and to the Lamb. The inhabitants of heaven confirm with *Amen* the praise of the redeemed. *Who are these?* One of the elders anticipates John's question and in v. 13 says that these are they who have passed through *the tribulation* and the fires of martyrdom. The tribulation is probably that referred to in Mk. 13^{19} Mt. 24^{21}. It is that which is caused by the appearance of Satan on earth and the woes that arise therefrom.

2. *Having the seal of the living God.* Sealing is used (1) to authenticate a message, as in Jn. 6^{27}; (2) to claim ownership in the branding of slaves, as in 2 Cor. 1^{22} Eph. 1^{13} 4^{30}; (3) to protect on the ground of this ownership (Ex. 12^{23} Ezek. 9^{4-6}). It is this meaning combined with (2) which is characteristic of this book (cf. 9^4 13^{16} 14^{1-5}; cf. also 2^{17} 3^{12}). The branding of slaves with the mark of the owner was familiar everywhere in the Græco-Roman world. The wearing of Tephillin—phylacteries—on the forehead as protective amulets was Jewish (cf. Deut. 6^8). In the last resort this sealing means the outward manifestation of character (13^{17}, note; cf. Rom. 8 and Paul's expectation of the revealing of the sons of God). This manifestation of character is completed in the spiritual body which the righteous receive after death. Every Christian has this body potential and actual: he can defile it (3^4); he can cleanse it and make it white (7^{14}). Actually God or Christ gives him the white garment, but in the sense that he co-operates with God it can be said *they wash their garments and make them white in the blood of the Lamb* (v. 14). Because the Lamb had been slain for them they had been able to endure martyrdom. In vv. 15–17 is described in simple language reminiscent of the O.T. the blessedness of these martyrs. The Christian Church has rightly seen in these verses the most comfortable assurance for all those who amid struggle and disappointment and sorrow hold fast to "the word of God and to the testimony of Jesus" (1^9).

5–8. The order of the tribes is inexplicable. It is suggested to rearrange vv. 5ab, 7, 8, 5c, 6: Leah's sons, Rachel's sons, Leah's handmaid's sons, Rachel's handmaid's sons. Judah is placed first, because from him is to spring Messiah. Dan is omitted because Anti-Christ is to spring from him (cf. Gen. 49^{17}). Manasseh is substituted for Dan, though he is already included under Joseph. Another suggestion is that a scribe mistakenly wrote "Man" for "Dan," and the error was understood as an abbreviation for Manasseh.

CHAPTER VIII

1–13. The Sounding of the Seven Trumpets. (See also ch. 9.) With *the seventh seal* we expect the judgments to reach a climax. Instead a new series begins with the sounding of the seven trumpets. It is as if all is working up to a definite culmination but the crisis comes and passes and it is not the end. So it always is with the divine judgments; they mark an end, but they also prove a beginning. But a solemn point is here reached, for at the opening of the seventh seal the psalmody of heaven is hushed for the space of half an hour. There is tense silence that the prayers of the suffering saints on earth may be heard before God's throne. To the Seer in his vision the events of the six seals were future; to the Seer recording his vision they were of what had already happened. Now the host of heaven are aware of a vision of crises, which shall come, some of which are without any precedent. The pause in heaven is appropriate to mark the point where *history ends and prophecy begins.*

J. Weiss and Charles find reason to believe that vv. 7–12 are an interpolation because they are colorless repetitions of the seals and the bowls upon which they are modeled. Their diction and style are not that of John, and they conflict with the expectation created by 7^{4-8}, and there are some inconsistencies in them, e.g., 8^7, 9^4. If this be so, there are three angels with three trumpets who herald three woes recorded in chs. 9, 12, 13. Charles reads the verses thus—1, 3–5, 2, 6, 13, etc., and translates vv. 2, 6 *And I saw three angels . . . and there were given to them three trumpets . . .*

and the three angels who had the three trumpets made ready to sound them. Then v. 13 simply introduces the three trumpets that follow.

3–5. The reason of the silence in heaven (v. 1) is explained. These verses give another pledge that the cause of the suffering saints is counted of supreme value in heaven. There was a belief in Judaism in the angels of heaven who sing by night only and not by day, in order that the praises of Israel may be heard by day. Here heaven is silent for *another angel*—Michael perhaps—to cense the prayers of the saints; i.e., to make them acceptable by offering them upon the golden altar before the throne of God. There is only one way into heaven, and it is through self-sacrifice. The souls of the martyrs are under the altar in 6[9]; the prayers of the saints are here laid upon the altar so that the last taint of self may be cleansed and they may be made acceptable to God (cf. Enoch 9[3f.]). But the angel takes up the censer for another purpose; he fills it with fire and casts it forth upon the earth. The prayers of the saints are accepted, and upon the earth are lightnings and earthquakes, a fitting prelude to v. 13, the announcements of the judgments which are to come upon the impenitent.

"Never a sigh of passion or of pity,
 Never a wail for weakness or for wrong
Has not its archive in the angel's city,
 Finds not its echo in the endless song."

6–12. The first four angels sound and in response four terrible calamities occur in the world of nature, but their effect is only partial. V. 7 describes a rain of hail and of fire mingled with blood. In 1901 in Italy blood-red rain fell, caused by the air being full of particles of fine red sand from the Sahara. Volcanic eruptions have produced similar phenomena elsewhere. There is a resemblance between these woes and the plagues of Egypt (cf. Ex. 9[24] Psa. 18[12, 13]). In vv. 8, 9 a burning mountain falls into the sea, and one third of it becomes blood (cf. 16[3] Ex. 7[17-21]). In vv. 9–11 a star burning as a torch falls upon the rivers and poisons one third of them, so that men die who drink of the bitter wormwood waters. Zoroastrianism has a story of the great star Gocihar falling on the earth. In v. 12 the light of the sun and moon and stars is diminished by one third (cf. Ex. 10[21-23]). The destruction of one third of the sun would not shorten the day by one third. Probably with one MS. we should read for the last phrase of v. 12 *and the third part of them did not shine by day nor likewise by night.*

13. An eagle is seen flying in mid heaven, i.e., where he can be seen and heard by all. An eagle was a familiar messenger of doom. This is a last warning to the world before the angels sound the other trumpets. The three-times repeated woe corresponds to the threefold judgment to follow, two parts of which are referred to in 9[12] and 11[14].

CHAPTER IX

1–12. The Fifth Trumpet: The First Woe, the Locusts. The star which John sees fallen to the earth is an angel, who had descended with authority to open the abyss (cf. Enoch 86[1] 88[1]). The *abyss* is the place of punishment for fallen angels and the Beast during the Messianic kingdom. The final place of punishment is the lake of fire and brimstone (20[15]). Originally the abyss was the ocean, which was shut up in a subterranean depth: but in later thought it stood for the chasm in the earth where the wicked are punished (cf. Enoch 88[1]). The angel opens the pit, and a cloud of smoke issues from it, darkening the sun. Then out of the smoke *locusts* came forth. Perhaps the meaning is that what looked like smoke proved to be a cloud of locusts. The description of the locusts begins with a phrase from Joel 2[2-11], but these are not the destructive pest with which he was familiar. The description shows them to be infernal locusts, which hurt not the grass or the trees but men. Locusts commonly live for five months, and these are to torment men for that period. Their time is defined; they do not come independently of the divine plan. They come as an army under a king who is called in Hebrew *Abaddon*, i.e., destruction (v. 11). The Greek equivalent, it is said here, is *Apollyon.* There may be a reference to the Greek god Apollo, of whose cult the locust was a symbol. These locusts were allowed to hurt only the men who were unsealed (cf. 7[4f.]). The mark which God set upon the faithful will therefore be manifest—they will be revealed in their true form as the sons of God; their character will be clearly seen over against the assaults of evil. The locusts do not kill; they torment. Really they are demonic powers, which resemble locusts, though they have human faces, women's hair, lions' teeth and scorpions' tails (vv. 7–10). This is described as *the First Woe.*

13–21. The Sixth Trumpet: The Second Woe, the Demonic Horsemen. The Seer hears the command to loose the four angels at the Euphrates. This voice comes from *the horns of the altar* where the prayers of the martyrs were censed (8[3]), and is in answer to those prayers. The angels are not the four mentioned in 7[1], for they are at the four corners of the earth. But these are the agents of the wrath of God and their mission is to destroy one third of mankind (v. 15). In the description two ideas are blended. They are *fire breathing monsters*, a trait of mythology; and they are *squadrons of cavalry*, twice ten thousand times ten thousand. This is due to the fact that on the Euphrates lay the border provinces between Parthia and the Romans, and from there Rome always feared some destructive agency. As in the case of the locusts it is some calamity which men had learned to dread, which is heightened by the conversion of the locusts into demonic agencies, so here the picture of an invasion by a Parthian army is developed into one of demonic horsemen breathing fire and smoke and brimstone. These awful demon hosts destroy one third of mankind. Both the locusts and the horsemen are messengers of punishment upon the heathen world, but the survivors of that world did not repent (v. 20).

The two visions of the locusts and the demon horsemen can only be understood by reference to the universal belief in the ancient world that the very air men breathed was full of spiritual powers of darkness which were continually at war with God and with his people. The Jews believed in the existence of these evil spirits much as did the heathen. They were regarded as fallen angels or as demigods (cf. Gen. 6[1, 2] Secrets of Enoch 20[1]). For Paul's belief see 2 Cor. 4[4] Eph. 2[2] 6[12] Col. 2[20] Gal. 4[3, 9]. It was the glory of the gospel that Christ triumphed over these demon agencies, and set free those who were his, so that no demons any longer had power to harm them. The fact that this world of demonology is for us of merely mythological interest shows how true was the Christian claim for the victory of Christ. (See Glover, *Jesus in the Experience of Men*, pp. 1–17.) The two facts which are of most significance here are that these demons are under the authority of Christ, and that they have no power to hurt those who are sealed with his name on their foreheads. Every missionary who has seen men and women haunted by superstitious fears under the power of demon-worship testifies to the reality of the deliverance from these supernatural fears which Christ still brings. But the Seer knows that even these revelations of supernatural judgments will not cause men to repent (vv. 20, 21). Dire calamities are recognized as the judgment of God upon great moral evils by those who can read him upon every page of history. But those who know him not are terrified, but not unto repentance (cf. Rom. 1[20, 29]). It is to be noted that these judgments heralded by the trumpets fall upon the world. The faithful will suffer from the first four, which are physical, but against the fifth and sixth, which are demonic woes, they are protected. To the faithful these are a part of the discipline of life, discipline administered by their heavenly Father, but they are not sent in judgment (cf. Rom. 8[28]).

19. The reference to the *tails* may be a reference to the skill of the Parthian horsemen in shooting their arrows as they fled from the enemy.

CHAPTER X

1–11. The Vision of the Strong Angel with the Little Book. (This forms, with ch. 11, the second parenthesis.) As after the opening of the sixth seal, so here at the end of the sixth trumpet there is a pause; the climax is again postponed. Ch. 10 is designed (1) to show that the hour prayed for by the martyrs (6[9]) when God's purposes will be fulfilled has come; (2) to serve as an introduction to the little book (11[1-13]). The Seer is on earth and sees a *strong angel* descending from heaven—Gabriel, perhaps, whose name suggests strength. He is described in terms which recall 1[15], so that some scholars understand Christ himself to be meant. But it is far more likely that the angel is so described to represent the covenant mercy—*the rainbow upon his head* (cf. Gen. 9[14-17])—and the invincible power of the Lord whose messenger he is. When this angel spoke, *the seven thunders uttered their voice* (v. 4). The seven thunders mean another series of judgments similar to those connected with the seals and the trumpets. The Seer is bidden to *seal*, i.e., not to reveal the message which came to him in those seven thunders (cf. Paul's vision of the things he could not utter, 2 Cor. 12[4]). The strong angel, who stands partly on the sea and partly on the earth, has in his hand *a little book* (v. 2). He swears solemnly that there will be no more delay (v. 6, R.V. mg., not as text). That means that the hour for the reign of the Anti-Christ has all but struck. This is *the third Woe*, recounted in ch. 12. At the sound of the trumpet of the seventh angel *the mystery of God* (v. 7), i.e., the whole purpose of God in regard to the world, the purpose which was declared to the prophets (cf. Gal. 3[18]), is finished. The Seer hears again the voice from heaven bidding him take the little book which the angel has in his hand. He eats the little book (cf. Ezek. 2[9]-3[3]), finding it *sweet in his mouth and bitter in the belly* (v. 10). The taste of the book means that the contents were mercy and redemption, disappointment and destruction. The eating of it symbolizes the renewal of the inspiration to prophesy *concerning many* *peoples and nations and tongues and kings* (v. 11; cf. Acts 9[15]).

6. *That there shall be time no longer.* If this is correct, the meaning is that time shall be abolished and eternity begin (cf. Secrets of Enoch 33[2]). But more likely the marginal rendering *delay* (adopted in text of A.S.V.) is right, i.e., the time of waiting is at an end.

CHAPTER XI

Contents of the Little Book. In vv. 1–13 John has embodied one or probably two fragments of Jewish apocalypses and has adapted them to his own purpose, which is to emphasize his main theme, that loyalty to Christ insures security against the assaults of spiritual powers of darkness, and though that loyalty entails martyrdom, it brings ultimate victory in all things. The chief reasons for the supposition that he is here adapting earlier sources are (1) *literary*—the style and idiom are different from those of the rest of the book; (2) *historical*—the difficulty of date. These verses suppose the Temple is still standing; i.e., they were written before 70 A.D. Note that the Temple in these verses means the Temple in Jerusalem: elsewhere in this book it means the temple in heaven (cf. 7[15] 11[19]).

1, 2. The Temple to be Measured—Its Meaning. These verses describe the measuring of the Temple, the altar and the worshipers. But the outer court is left unmeasured: it is given over to the Gentiles; this and the Holy City are to be *trodden under foot* for three and a half years (cf. Lk. 21[24]). The Zealots occupied the inner court of the Temple when the Romans captured the outer court in the great siege in 70 A.D. John uses in these two verses a fragment from some Zealot's writing prophesying that the Temple would not be destroyed. The Zealot wrote of the Temple in Jerusalem; the measuring denoted in his writing the preservation of the sacred building. John understands all symbolically. The *outer court* represents to him the unbelievers given over to Anti-Christ, the conflict with whom is shortly described. The *measuring* denotes the preservation of the faithful from spiritual harm. *Temple, altar* and *worshipers* in John's interpretation stand for the Christian community of God. Elsewhere John uses the *holy city* only for the new Jerusalem (21[2], etc.); the earthly Jerusalem is Sodom (11[8]). Here he is using it in the sense in which the Zealot used it, in a prophecy of the destruction of the city and the safety of the Temple. The *forty-two months* are from Dan. 7[25] 12[7]—three and a half years. That was the actual duration of the persecution under Antiochus Epiphanes, 168–165 B.C., and is regarded as typical of the duration of the persecution under the Anti-Christ. Possibly the fact that it was half of seven, the perfect number, may have helped to make the number traditional.

3–13. The Prophecy of the Two Witnesses. This is a fragment from another apocalyptic writing adapted by John. It is based on Zech. 4[2, 3, 14]. During the same three and a half years that Jerusalem is to be trodden under foot, *two witnesses* (cf. Mal. 4[5]) are to prophesy, clothed in sackcloth. They are identified with the two olive trees and two candlesticks in Zechariah's vision (v. 4). But there the olive trees feed the lamps, and represent the heads of the church and state, Joshua and Zerubbabel. Here the olive trees represent Moses and Elijah, the Law and the Prophets. The testimony of these two witnesses will be authenticated by wonderful signs and miracles (v. 6), but when they shall have finished their testimony they will be overcome by the Beast from the abyss, and lie dead in the streets of Jerusalem (v. 7). Their enemies rejoice for three days and a half, but then the breath of life returns into the dead bodies (cf. Ezek. 37[10]) and they arise and are summoned to heaven, to the consternation of their enemies who see them (vv. 9–11). A great earthquake follows causing the tenth part of the city to fall and the death of seven thousand persons. The earthquake is common in apocalyptic (Joel 2[10] 3[16] Zech. 14[4]). The rest are afraid and glorify God (v. 13). According to Josephus, Siloam and other springs almost dried up before the coming of Titus against Jerusalem and after his coming flowed again abundantly.

These two fragments of Jewish apocalyptic, which clearly belong to the period before the fall of Jerusalem in 70 A.D., are used by John *to prepare his readers for the prophecy of the appearance of Anti-Christ.* Anti-Christ is traditionally associated with Jerusalem, and though John associates him with Rome, he here uses the earlier conception which relates to Jerusalem, though Jerusalem was no longer in existence when he was writing. As always, he adapts that which he borrows. The destruction of Jerusalem was a fulfillment of the earlier prophecy. God's witnesses had been killed, even the greatest of them all, for he adds his own description of Jerusalem as *the place where their Lord was crucified* (v. 8). If there is a more terrible manifestation of Anti-Christ threatening his readers, John would remind them that beyond death is resurrection and triumph. Note the tenses in vv. 11–13. They are past but they represent the future of prophetic certainty, for that which shall be is as sure as that which has been, because it has been determined by God.

14–19. The Prophecy of the Third Woe Heralded by the Seventh Trumpet. Here is resumed the unfolding of the drama from the point where the author digressed, 10^1. In the order of action 11^{14} follows 9^{21}. The final crisis is not yet ushered in, however; but, as in 8^1, this passage prepares the reader for a new cycle of visions. The third and last woe is heralded in by the trumpet of the seventh angel followed by two songs in heaven. No silence follows the sounding of the seventh trumpet as followed the opening of the seventh seal (8^1), but the sound of voices is raised in a pæan of victory. The Woe (chs. 12, 13) apparently results in the triumph of Satan and the overthrow of the church. But these two songs which precede it show that the real result is the coming of Christ and the establishment of his kingdom. The tense is that of *prophetic certainty*—the kingdom of the world has become the kingdom of our Lord (ch. 15), though all is in the future. But there is no more doubt about the future than about the past if God has determined it. The song of the elders (cf. 4^4) celebrates the coming of the Kingdom, the Last Judgment, and the final reward of the servants of God.

18. Charles rearranges the order of the clauses thus: *And the nations have waxed wroth, and thy wrath has come and the time to destroy them that destroy the earth* (i.e., the Beast, the False Prophet and their followers), *the small and the great, and the time for the dead to be judged, and [the time] for the giving of their reward to thy servants the prophets, and the saints and them that fear thy name.*

19. The temple of God in heaven is opened. As the first two Woes were connected with the heavenly altar (8^3 9^{13}), this third Woe is connected with the *ark*. The earthly ark was a witness of God's covenant with Israel. The ark is here revealed in the temple in heaven to witness to the covenant between God and the spiritual, the true Israel, i.e., the Christian Church. The showing of the ark of the covenant is associated with the revelation of God's presence in the midst of the convulsions in the natural world (cf. 8^5 16^{18}) such as happened on Sinai. Jewish tradition believed that the ark was carried to a place of safety by Jeremiah and would reappear when the Messiah came (2 Macc. 2^{1-8} 2 Baruch 67^{-10}).

CHAPTER XII

1–17. The Vision of the Woman, the Man-Child and the Dragon. To understand this chapter it must be recognized that every mystic uses in his visions theological material already familiar, which he shares in common with those who belong to his age and world of thought. This material is refashioned in his ecstatic vision, and the result may not always be self-consistent when he tries to put into words the truth of which he has been made aware when in the spirit. The theological material behind this vision is a primitive myth of the conflict between light and darkness, order and disorder, under the figure of a child, born of a sun-goddess, persecuted by a dragon, the latter being finally overthrown. This had been spiritualized into an allegory of the religious history of the Jews and their expectation of a Saviour. John freely uses this, allegorizing in his own way the mythological features.

1–6. A woman arrayed with the sun is about to give birth to a son. A red dragon stands ready to devour the child when he is born. The child is caught up to God and the woman flees to a place in the wilderness prepared by God for her.

In the original myth, which was pagan and has elements derived from the mythologies of Babylon, Egypt and Greece, the *woman* was a goddess, clothed with the sun, with her feet on the moon as a footstool, and her crown studded with the signs of the zodiac. This description John follows, but it has no special significance for him. In its Jewish form the story represented the expected birth of the Messiah from the Jewish Church. John has adapted this to the birth of Christ. The woman is therefore the true Israel. In the O.T. the spiritual Israel is the spouse of God; in this book elsewhere the Bride of Christ (cf. ch. 21).

3. The seven-headed *dragon* is familiar in Babylonian mythology, the chaos monster. We should expect seven horns. The ten may be a reference to Dan. $7^{7, 24}$. Perhaps the seven diadems are due to the fact that Christ has many diadems and his great foe likewise. Or the reference may be to the kings through whom the dragon's power is exercised. The tail of the dragon casting the stars to earth (v. 4) was originally the explanation of falling stars or other phenomena in the heavens, but in the Jewish form of the myth it refers to the war in heaven, by which Satan is cast down to earth where the woman is. The *child* is the Christ. The power of darkness cannot destroy him, for he is caught up to God (v. 5). Only his birth and ascension are mentioned—neither his life nor death. But the point is that the dragon is foiled in his attack upon the woman.

6. The church is to be protected during the reign of the Anti-Christ, the period of twelve hundred and sixty days (see notes on 11[2, 3]). This verse anticipates v. 14 and may be out of its true order.

7–12. An episode prior in time to vv. 1–6 and explanatory of them. There had been war in heaven, and Michael and his angels had prevailed, and hurled Satan down to earth (cf. Isa. 14[12] Lk. 10[18] Jn. 12[31]). But with this event in the past is blended a song of triumph in heaven, proclaiming the victory of the faithful over the dragon *through the blood of the Lamb and the witness of the faithful to it* (v. 11), and their readiness to lose their life in order to save it (cf. Lk. 14[26] Jn. 12[25]). Heaven may well rejoice; though the advent of the dragon means woe for the earth, it is only for the time.

7. The Greek here represents a Hebrew idiom. Read *there was war in heaven: Michael and his angels had to fight with the dragon.* Michael was the patron angel of Israel and so of the true Israel of God (cf. Dan. 10[13, 21] 12[1]). There were two traditions about Satan: one that he had been hurled from heaven at the beginning (cf. Secrets of Enoch 29[4, 5]), the other that he had his place in heaven in historic times (cf. Job 1[6, 7]). This led to the belief that Satan's overthrow from heaven is the first of the last great struggles between the kingdom of God and the kingdom of Satan. The fact that he has been cast down from heaven (v. 9) means that evil is already defeated, the most important and first stage in Satan's conquest has been already achieved (Lk. 10[18] Jn. 12[31]). The *dragon* and the *serpent* and *Satan* are all identical here. Originally the serpent was a dragon hostile to God and man—Satan was one of God's vice-regents whose duty it was to act the part of a public prosecutor (cf. Zech. 3[1, 2]) or of a heavenly detective (Job 1[6]–2[10]). Gradually the idea of the tempter and enemy of man developed, partly through Persian influence (1 Chr. 21[1]), and in the N.T. it is complete.

13–17. The myth of the dragon and the woman is resumed. The dragon persecutes the woman after her child is caught up to heaven. She is given *the two wings of an eagle* to escape into the wilderness, where she is nourished for three and a half years. The dragon casts a river of water out of his mouth to destroy her, but the earth swallows it, and the dragon goes away to war with *the rest of her children who are faithful to God* (v. 17). The reference to the eagle (v. 14) probably belongs to the original myth and has no special significance here. In vv. 14–16 the reference may be to the fact that some of the Jews fled to Jabneh and the Christians to Pella before the fall of Jerusalem in 70 A.D. (cf. Mt. 24[16]). But elsewhere John anticipates the universal martyrdom of the faithful before the final overthrow of Satan.

The "truth embodied in a tale" is that *the conflict between good and evil did not originate on earth but in heaven*—a very ancient belief. The disorder of this world is only a part of the disorder which affects the whole spiritual world. The final issue does not depend upon the result of the conflict on this earth. Already the battle has been won in heaven. God's sovereignty has been vindicated. Satan has been hurled to earth. That means an increase in the malignity of evil forces here, an apparent victory of Satan, which will involve the universal martyrdom of the saints. But in reality it is Satan's last struggle: he has been decisively beaten: his time of seeming triumph is short. Those who are faithful to the end will realize the victory on earth, which has been already won in heaven.

CHAPTER XIII

The Visions of Two Beasts. In this chapter John is making use of two earlier and probably Hebrew writings—one referring to the Roman Empire as Anti-Christ (vv. 1–10); and the other to some power which would claim the prerogative of Deity and require men to worship him (vv. 11–18), a conception of Anti-Christ akin to that in 2 Thess. 2[1-12]. John uses these sources freely and interprets them in his own way (see opening paragraph under ch. 12).

1–10. **The Vision of the Beast with the Ten Horns.** V. 1a need not be separated from the words that follow, as in R.V., nor is the variant reading, *and I stood upon the shore of the sea*, to be preferred. The dragon standing on the shore summons a beast from the *sea.* Doubtless the Mediterranean Sea is meant. The Jews always feared the sea, all the more in this century because to face the Mediterranean was to have the Roman Empire before one's eyes. The *beast* is a terrifying monster whom the whole earth worships (v. 4). He makes war upon the saints, and it is given to him to overcome them, so that all worship him except those whose names are inscribed *in the Lamb's book of life* (v. 8). The beast is the Roman Empire: the conception is based on Dan. 7[2-7], where the fourth kingdom, by which was meant the empire of Alexander and his successors, was in N.T. times universally interpreted of the Roman Empire (cf. Lk. 21[20]). The horns and heads correspond with Daniel's conception and doubtless represent Roman emperors. *The ten diadems* (v. 1) are peculiar to this vision. *The names of* *blasphemy* means the title of divine authority (Sebastos) which the emperors arrogated to themselves. The immediate cause of the persecution, which this foretells, is the refusal of the faithful to acknowledge such claims. For the *leopard*, the *bear*, and the *lion* in v. 2 cf. Dan. 7. The meaning is that the Roman Empire united in itself the qualities of the other empires. One of the heads of the beast is represented as *though it had been slain unto death*, but the death stroke was healed (v. 3). The same word *slain* is used of the Lamb in v. 5, and shows that the beast is the counterpart of Christ, i.e., the Anti-Christ. *Slain as it were unto death* means slain and restored to life. So the reference is to a Roman emperor, in whom the power of Satan was personified on earth, who was slain but came to life again. Nero is the emperor as understood in the Nero redivivus myth. In his death and in his return to life the Anti-Christ is a diabolical counterpart of Christ. So the worship offered to him is a mockery of the worship due to Christ. And his empire is to be universal (v. 7) for a time. Satan was the antagonist of Christ in heaven. Rome represents Satan on earth; Nero is the personification of the Roman power, i.e., of Satan. He is the devil's Messiah—the Anti-Christ. The power of Rome is the power of Satan (v. 4), *not moral power but brute force.* This power wins the allegiance of all whose names are not written in the Lamb's book of life (cf. 3^{5} 21^{27}). The world is amazed at the power of the beast and gives him the worship he claims. Worshiping the beast is worshiping the devil, whose representative he is. It is possible to take the words *from the foundation of the world* (v. 8) with *were written*—a reference to predestination (cf. 17^{8} Mt. 25^{34} Eph. 1^{4}), but they may be taken with *the Lamb that hath been slain* (cf. 5^{6}). As Moses had been ordained mediator of the covenant from the foundation of the world, so Christ was ordained as Redeemer from the beginning of things. *There was a cross in the heart of God before there was one on Calvary* (cf. 1 Pet. $1^{19, 20}$). Love and sacrifice are at the heart of God's sovereignty. The Seer concludes that loyal endurance will win through in the coming persecution (vv. 9, 10). But even those whose names are written in the Lamb's book of life must endure martyrdom. By recognizing even the pain of martyrdom as the will of God for them the saints show their patience and prove their faith.

5. *Forty-two months*, cf. 11^{2} note.

6. *His tabernacle* cannot mean the earthly Temple. Perhaps heaven is meant but more likely his Shekinah, his glory. *Them that dwell (tabernacle) in heaven* are the angels. Others see here a reference to the attempt of Caligula to set up his statue in the Temple, an attempt which was frustrated only by his death in 41 A.D.

10b. Read *if any man is to be slain with the sword, with the sword must he be slain.*

11–18. The Vision of the Second Beast. The second ally of Satan is the second beast, also called *the False Prophet* in 16^{13} 19^{20} 20^{10}. The devil is the symbol of material power divorced from morality, and as such he gives power to the beast, i.e., the Roman Empire (v. 4); he is also the father of lies (Jn. 8^{44}), and he appropriately calls the False Prophet to his aid. Christian thought had conceived of a False Prophet. Among the Jews the Anti-Christ was to be such. This explains the Seer's identification of the second beast with the Anti-Christ myth here. This beast has *two horns like a lamb:* he exercises the authority of the first beast, and does wonderful miracles, making an image of the first beast breathe and speak (vv. 14, 15). Those who will not worship the image he puts to death (cf. 2^{13}). Those who do worship it are marked with the number of the beast, and those who are not so marked are liable to a sort of commercial boycott (vv. 16, 17). In appearance this beast is less fearsome than the first, but that is in keeping with its identification with the False Prophet. Our Lord had spoken of "false prophets in sheep's clothing" who "within are ravening wolves" (Mt. 7^{15}). This second beast represents the imperial priesthood and Roman officials generally in the provinces, who compelled all men to worship the emperors, and who performed lying and magic wonders in that service, and who put to death all who refused such worship. The *two horns* (v. 1) may be a reference to the headdress worn by the priests. Pliny's famous letter to Trajan testifies that the alternatives were emperor worship or death.

The faithful who have the *mark* of the Lamb on their foreheads suffer martyrdom. Those who worship the beast are likewise marked on their right hand or forehead (v. 17). Probably the writer has in mind the custom of the orthodox Jew who wore Tephillin—phylacteries—on his left hand or head (7^{2}, note). What underlies the wearing of the mark here is belief in supernatural protection. In the broader sense the mark witnesses to *the finality of character.* Other interpretations of the marks relate them to (1) the branding of slaves; (2) the branding of soldiers with the name of their general; (3) seals stamped with the name of the emperor affixed to legal documents, or coins bearing his image. We know that in later times certificates were issued to those who fulfilled the regulations about the emperor-worship. Perhaps something of this sort is referred to here. The local authorities issue certificates of loyalty to the state religion. Those who were not openly Christians were by this means hunted out and prevented from earning a living (v. 17).

18. John here gives a further clue to the identity of the beast, by which men of understanding can perceive his meaning. The mark on the right hand or forehead of those who worship the beast is the *number of the beast*. It is the number of a man and it is *six hundred and sixty-six*. It is clear some individual, who would be recognized by his readers, is meant. Already reasons have been given for believing the beast represents Nero. If Neron Cæsar be written in Hebrew and the letters be given their numerical values, the total is six hundred and sixty-six. If the final N of the Greek spelling be dropped and the Latin form Nero be used, the total value is six hundred and sixteen. This is a variant reading found in some MSS. in this verse. This interpretation is therefore satisfactory from several points of view. Among other explanations one that was made at the end of the second century A.D. has been accepted by some modern scholars, that the threefold six suggests a continual falling short of the perfect number, seven. It is a summary of the apostasy that has taken place during the last six thousand years, according to Irenæus. In Marcus the Valentinian, and in the Sibylline Oracles, the number eight hundred and eighty-eight represents Christ. That is the total numerical value of *Jesus* in Greek letters, and suggests that he is beyond perfection. Perhaps the sea-dragon of mythology was in some way connected with the number six hundred and sixty-six, and John here asserts that this number fits a man also. The word "Cæsar" has to be written defectively in Hebrew to make the total correct, but this is not without parallel. John may mean that *the mythological beast has become incarnate in a man*. It is not unlikely that he had some older use of the cryptic number in mind, when he used it of Nero here, recognizing that whatever sinister associations it had were appropriately summed up in the conception of him as Anti-Christ.

The meaning is unmistakable. Rome and the cult of the emperor are the enemies of the church on earth. In them the heavenly war between Satan and Christ is palpable and incarnate. In one way or another, every Christian is faced with the challenge—emperor-worship or persecution, the service of Satan or of Christ. In the ordinary business of every day the implications of the choice are made clear (v. 17). There can be no hesitation or compromise. The application of his vision is appropriate to many other expressions of the blasphemous spirit, which was shown in the imperial cult of ancient Rome. We may legitimately see an application in events in history without supposing that John had these in his mind when he wrote. Whenever the church or the state has usurped the place of God, and claimed unquestioning authority over the consciences of men, the same spirit of Anti-Christ has been manifested, and the same duty of unhesitating opposition is demanded from the servants of Christ. In the mediæval church, with its encouragement of idolatry, its use of material power and the blasphemous claims of its Popes, the same spirit was at work. In our own time, without the claim of the unlimited authority of the state to obedience, the World War of 1914–1918 would hardly have been possible. More insidiously, but no less mischievously, the idols of the market place and of the forum, the tyranny of social and political customs claim obedience from men to-day, and in the blurring of the distinctions between the church and the world the warning of John to recognize that there can be no compromise is all the more necessary.

Perhaps 14[12, 13] should follow here as the end of this chapter. See notes thereon.

CHAPTER XIV

Two Visions of the Church Triumphant on Earth, and of the Judgment of Rome. (The third parenthesis.) The last chapter spoke of the universal martyrdom of the faithful; this chapter is *a third interlude* breaking the sequence of the visions with a picture of a later stage, in order to encourage the saints to be faithful. It describes the glory of the martyrs in the Messianic kingdom (cf. 7[9-17]); the doom of Rome and of the heathen nations. It forms a general introduction to 16[17]–20[10].

1–5. Vision of the Lamb on Mount Zion, and Round Him the 144,000. (Cf. 7[4-8].) The number 144,000 suggests that the writer is using a Jewish prophecy, which has been transformed in most respects in his Christian experience. In the details of the vision there are striking contrasts with some of the details in the visions of the dragon and the beasts (chs. 12, 13). The worshipers of the dragon were marked on the right hand and on the forehead with the number of the Beast. So the redeemed host has the name of the Father upon the forehead. The blasphemous song *Who is like unto the Beast?* of 13[4] is answered by the anthem from heaven of 14[2]. This heavenly anthem is like the thunder of waves breaking on the shore (cf. 1[15] 6[1] 19[6] 2 Esdras 6[17]); it is a song sung by angel choirs which *only the redeemed could learn* (v. 3). For it is a song of the spirit, and they only through the travail and tears of earth have won spiritual understanding. In v. 4 these 144,000 are called the *first-fruits*, but the Greek word is better translated *sacrifice*, as often in the LXX. Perhaps the editor who understood it as first-fruits added the phrase which describes them all as celibates. These words (v. 4a) should be excised. The number of the redeemed certainly includes men and women, and nowhere else does the writer emphasize the ascetic view of marriage as sin which v. 4a seems to imply. It is possible that by the word *virgins* (which is masculine here) he only intends to emphasize the purity of the redeemed (cf. 7[14]), following the figure of speech so common in the O.T., by which idolatry is described as fornication. But it is more likely that these words are a marginal comment added by some ascetic scribe and have wrongly crept into the text. This is the more probable because the purity of the redeemed is emphasized in v. 5 (cf. Psa. 32[2] Isa. 53[9]). It is because they were like a lamb *without blemish* that they were fit to be offered in sacrifice to God (cf. Col. 1[22] 1 Pet. 1[19] Jude v. 24). In 6[11] the martyrs, whose souls were beneath the altar, were seen as waiting there till their number was complete. Here the number is complete, and as in life they followed the Lamb to death, so now they follow him wherever he goes.

So once again John summons the faithful to withstand the temptation to give up the struggle by picturing the ultimate triumph of Christ and of all who are his. John thought the end would come before the generation to whom he was writing had passed away. It has not come yet, but still his vision of the assurance of ultimate victory never fails to encourage men to "hold fast that which is good" (1 Thess. 5[21]) despite the seeming contradiction of things.

6, 7. The Vision of the Angel with the Eternal Gospel. John sees another angel going forth to evangelize the world. The appeal is to the universal impulse of man to worship the Creator (cf. the urgent call of Paul to the men of Lystra, Acts 14[15]). This appeal is to be contrasted with the imperial decrees to worship the emperor.

8. The Vision of the Doom of Rome (Babylon the Great). (Cf. 16[17]–18[24].) Babylon is typical of the enemies of Israel, and John naturally uses the name to designate the foe of the true Israel, the Christian Church, finding in the prophet's words phrases which are most suitable for his present purpose (cf. Isa. 21[9] Jer. 51[7, 8]). *The wine of the wrath of her fornication* is to be explained as a combination of two ideas, the wine of her fornication, i.e., the intoxicating and corrupting influence of Rome, and the wine of God's wrath (cf. 18[6]).

9–11. Announcement of the Punishment for the Worshipers of the Beast. In 13[16, 17] there is a proclamation of the boycotting of those who have not the mark of the Beast. V. 9 is an answer to that, a proclamation of the doom of those that have that mark. The description of the punishment meted out is reminiscent of Isa. 34[8-10], which tells of the doom of Edom. Features from the description of the doom of Sodom, and the punishment of Edom, and the undying fires of the valley of Hinnom, are all blended here. If material and physical punishment was in the mind of John, his picture may remind us of the consuming terrors of remorse.

12, 13. The Patience of the Saints. The Blessedness of Those Who Die in the Lord. These verses seem out of place here; they fit admirably after 13[18]. While all men are capable of exhibitions of self-sacrifice, such as are seen on the battlefield in those from whom it is least expected, sustained, persistent faithfulness—*patience*—in face of unceasing persecution is that which marks out the saints. In such a conflict the saints need strong consolation; God in his mercy gives it (v. 13). Faithfulness demands something of the martyr's courage in all ages. There have been living martyrdoms which have not ended in either a quick or a violent death. In the O.T. salvation depends upon the number of good over evil works. Here the *good works* which accompany the righteous souls are rather the revelation of lives redeemed by Christ. The word *labors* suggests the weariness of toil. That will end for the redeemed at death. But their works, i.e., their acquired capacities, the results of all their labors, the characters which those labors have helped to form, these go on into fuller development (cf. Mt. 25[34-40]). So Milton writes:

"Thy works and alms and all thy good endeavor
Stayed not behind nor in the grave were trod,
But, as Faith pointed with her golden rod,
Followed thee up to joy and bliss for ever."

Heaven is freedom from the weariness of toil but work is there. Only all work is worship, because all will be undertaken for the glory of God and in his service in

". . . those great offices that suit
The full-grown energies of heaven."

Swete aptly says that this beatitude—*blessed are the dead which die in the Lord*—needed a voice from heaven to proclaim it.

14–20. A Vision of Judgment on the Heathen Nations. This is described fully in 19^{11-16}. The judgment here is represented as *the harvest and vintage of the world* (cf. Joel 3^{13}). The double picture of the reaping of the corn and the treading of the grapes is an example of Hebrew parallelism (but see below on vv. 15–17), and is not to be understood as the gathering of the saints and the destruction of the wicked (cf. Isa. 63^{1-6} Rev. $19^{13, 15}$). In Dan. 7^{13} *one like unto a son of man* means the saints of the Most High (but cf. notes there). In apocalypses men are symbolized by beasts; angels and supernatural beings by men. So in Daniel the passage means that the faithful remnant of Israel is to be transformed into supernatural beings. The author of the book of Enoch interprets *one like to a son of man* of an individual, the Messiah, and so it is used in the Gospels by our Lord himself. The supernatural claim he made was in the revelation of the Father which he showed in his sinless and redemptive life, death, and resurrection. Here *the one like unto the Son of man* must mean *an angel* unless the text is corrupt. Then the agents of judgment are all angels, though later the judgment is in the hands of Christ (19^{15}).

15–17. Charles excises these verses as a doublet of vv. 14, 18, 20. He thinks that the Son of man is Christ who has the sickle in his hand. The number of martyrs is complete, and their prayer from beneath the altar can be fulfilled, so the angel, who has to do with the souls of the martyrs beneath the altar, carries the command to the Son of man to thrust in the sickle and reap the vintage, i.e., to execute judgment. If Charles is right, the confusion in the text has caused *the angel* to be put for *the son of man* in v. 19.

20. *The city* is probably Jerusalem, for Jewish tradition associated the neighborhood of Jerusalem with the judgment of the Gentiles (cf. Zech. 14^{4}). The measure *sixteen hundred furlongs* may be meant to suggest the completeness of the slaughter.

CHAPTER XV

The Preparation for the Vision of the Bowls. The development of the drama was halted at 13^{18}, and John looked forward, anticipating the future in its final triumph of Christ (ch. 14). Now he resumes from the end of ch. 13. The entire description of the third series of judgments, now beginning, extends from 15^{1} to 20^{3}.

1. Seven Angels Having Seven Plagues. This is the subject of the new vision.

2–4. A Vision of the Redeemed; Their Song. John describes a vision of the entire martyr host praising God for his power and righteousness and kingship of the nations. It may be that the form of that vision owes something to some experience in Patmos, where John may have watched the sun set in the Ægean, and felt himself on the shore of *a glassy sea*, and seen a great host who had come out of great tribulation. Such a vision would remind him of the deliverance of the Israelites at the Red Sea and the Song of Moses (Ex. 15^{2-19}), though there is no reference to that song in what follows. The *theme of the song* here is the vision of God and his works in which thoughts of self are wholly forgotten. This scene, before the outpouring of the bowls, where the praises of the redeemed are offered to God, is similar to the scene in 8^{3-5}, where their praises are offered to God before the sounding of the trumpets.

5–8. The Vision of the Seven Angels. These came out from the temple, i.e., the tabernacle of the testimony in heaven, clothed in linen (R.V. mg.). They had *the seven bowls of God's wrath* in their hands. The temple is seen *filled with smoke* as Isaiah saw it in his vision of a thrice holy God (Isa. 6^{4}). The smoke does not here represent the incense of worship, but is the symbol of God's holiness in contact with man's sin. That holiness is about to blaze forth in fire to consume the wicked. This divine glory and power fill the temple, so that no one can enter the temple, i.e., avert by prayer the judgment before it is executed.

CHAPTER XVI

1–21. The Contents of the Seven Bowls—the Plagues. These plagues affect only the heathen world, for the Christians who had been sealed have already been martyred. This is the distinguishing feature of these plagues over against the woes heralded by the seven trumpets. These judgments have all to do with the Roman Empire as punishment for her emperor-worship and persecution of the Christians.

2. *The first plague*—grievous sores upon men—recalls the Egyptian plague (Ex. $9^{10, 11}$ Deut. 28^{35}). Its incidence is on the adherents of the Roman Empire, the men who had the mark of the Beast and worshiped his image.

3. *The second plague*—the sea turned into blood and the death of all animal life—recalls the first Egyptian plague (Ex. 7^{17-21}), but there the Nile only is smitten.

4–7. *The third plague* turns the rivers into

blood. This is regarded as peculiarly appropriate because Rome had poured out the blood of the martyrs.

8, 9. *The fourth plague* is scorching heat. But, as in the case of the sixth trumpet (9^{21}), the wicked do not recognize the hand of God in these torments.

10, 11. *The fifth plague* brings darkness upon the throne of the Beast, i.e., Rome (cf. Ex. 10^{21-23}). As only the faithful were the victims of the fifth seal (6^{9}), so only the followers of the Beast are affected by the fifth plague. Perhaps the darkness of the kingdom is to be interpreted from the Woe described in $9^{2f.}$, when the smoke from the abyss darkened the sun, and demonic locusts tormented men, so that they longed for death.

12–16. *The sixth plague.* In the Woe in 9^{13-21} monstrous horsemen who are really demons appear. Here the Euphrates, the natural barrier between East and West, is dried up, so that the Parthian kings under Nero redivivus may attack Rome, the throne of the Beast. Thus his kingdom is divided against itself. Rome calls to her help *three unclean spirits* (cf. 1 Tim. 4^{1} 1 Jn. 4^{3})—Satan, the Beast and the False Prophet, i.e., the second Beast. They are described as *like frogs*, which in the Zend religion are the cause of plagues and death. These unclean spirits gather the nations together to war. This war is the decisive conflict of God with Rome (v. 14). The scene is to be the battlefield of Israel. At Megiddo, Deborah and Barak had overthrown Sisera (Judg. 5^{19}), and there Necho had overthrown Josiah (2 Kings 23^{29}). But John makes not the plain of Megiddo but the mountain of Megiddo (the meaning of *Har-Magedon* in v. 16) the scene of this final battle.

15. The description is interrupted here to insert a warning to *watchfulness*. Charles thinks this to be an interpolation, and he restores it to the middle of 3^{3}, because there is no hint that these plagues affect the Christians at all, and the sixth bowl will hardly take the world by surprise since the preparations for it must be on a great scale. The first reason is important, but a warning to watchfulness is appropriate at all times. Those who lived through the first two decades of this century will remember how easy it is to live with all the preparations for a world-wide catastrophe before their eyes and yet to be unaware of them (cf. Mt. 24^{38-44} 1 Thess. 5^{2-4} 2 Pet. 3^{10}.)

17–21. *The seventh plague* is an earthquake. Rome (*Babylon the Great*—cf. 14^{8}) is described as split into three parts. This is not quite consistent with chs. 17, 18, where Rome is dealt with. The weight of the hail—*a talent* (see p. 78b)—is about one hundredweight (cf. Ex. 9^{18-26}). For v. 19 cf. 14^{8}.

The truth of these vivid and arresting descriptions of judgment is not to be found in any exact correspondence between events in history and the words of these prophecies, but in the holiness of God and the inevitable consequences of sin. Dante and others have emphasized the seeming exultation with which John tells of the destiny of the persecutors of the church. Such a spirit seems directly contrary to our Lord's injunction, "Love your enemies," and is most inconsistent with his example, "Father, forgive them, for they know not what they do." But the spirit of the O.T., with its law of retaliation, is strong in the writer of this book; he has not as yet come to realize all the implications of the love of God revealed in Christ Jesus. Compared with other and Jewish apocalypses and many Christian writings of a later date, his descriptions of the punishment of the wicked are far from extreme. He would emphasize the inevitable punishment that awaits sin because of the holy love of God. Against some of the vague sentimentalism of to-day in reference to God's attitude to sin, it is well to recall that those who have suffered in times of persecution have always been upheld by their belief in the justice of God, which would not allow the sin of their oppressors to go unpunished, and to recall too, that those who are most sure of the love of God are those who feel most keenly the awful penalty which sin entails.

CHAPTER XVII

1–6. The Vision of the Judgment of the Great Harlot and of the Beast. Already the fall of Rome has been proclaimed under the name "Babylon" (14^{8} 16^{19}). The identification of Babylon and Rome is made explicit, and the doom of the imperial city—the source of the persecution of the Christians—is described. Rome is *the great harlot.* In the O.T. the word "harlot" is used of Nineveh (Nah. 3^{4}), and of Tyre (Isa. 23^{17}) in respect of their intercourse with the heathen world, their idolatry and immorality. So Rome had made the nations one with herself and corrupted them with the wine of her fornication. In Jer. 51^{13} Babylon is described as *sitting on many waters*, and so the phrase is added here, though the description as applied to Rome is inappropriate. (That is the reason for the interpretative gloss in v. 15.) The Seer in an ecstasy is carried into a wilderness, where he sees *the woman sitting upon a scarlet-colored beast* (v. 3). This is the Roman Empire (cf. 13^{1-10}), the description indicating its luxury and magnificence. The woman is full of *names of blasphemy.* In 13[1] (note) that phrase refers to the deified emperors. Perhaps here it refers to the godless multitude of gods which Rome worshiped. The Beast has *seven heads and ten horns* which are explained in vv. 9–12. The woman holds in her hand *a golden cup* (cf. Jer. 51[7]), *full of the abominations* (v. 4) with which she has corrupted the nations. The harlots in Rome wore upon their brows labels bearing their names. The name of this woman written upon her forehead is a *Mystery* (v. 5), i.e., to be understood spiritually, not literally. And the name is *Babylon,* i.e., Babylon is the mystical name for Rome (cf. vv. 7f.). The description is not overdrawn. Tacitus describes Rome as "the place where all things hideous and shameful from every part of the world find their center and become popular." The woman herself *is drunken with the blood of the saints* (v. 6)—the Jewish martyrs who fell in 66–70 A.D.—*and of the martyrs of Jesus*—the Christians who died in the Neronic persecution.

7–18. The Interpretation of the Vision. The description of the Beast, the symbol of the Roman Empire, as that which *was and is not and is about to come* (v. 8) is a parody of the divine name "Jehovah," as written in 1[4] (see note). The heads and horns belong to the mythological tradition, and that makes it difficult to be sure of the historical facts which they symbolize. To understand these things requires *the intelligence which is wisdom.* The seven heads of the Beast are described as *seven hills* (v. 9). Really this is a description of the woman—Rome, the city of the seven hills. But then the geographical facts fade and are replaced by political facts. For in v. 10 the seven heads are further called *seven kings,* i.e., emperors. Which? Probably the series is meant to begin with Augustus. Omitting Galba, Otho, and Vitellius, who between them reigned only a few months, the seven would be Augustus, Tiberius, Caligula, Claudius, Nero, Vespasian, Titus. *Five are dead, the one is* (v. 10). If the list is correct this is written in Vespasian's reign. Titus *is to come,* but only to last for *a short time.* Perhaps the writer knew of the hopeless condition of Titus' health. He is therefore either using a literary convention, and assuming an earlier date than is the fact to give his words the force of a prophecy concerning Titus, or, more likely, he is using here material written in Vespasian's reign which partly suits his purpose and partly not; for there are very good reasons for thinking that this book was written, not in Vespasian's reign, but in Domitian's (see p. 1367b). Already John has identified the Beast with Nero redivivus, finding in the mysterious number of the Beast the letters of Nero's name (13[18], note). In v. 11 the Beast is said to be *of the seven and himself an eighth.* That has been interpreted as Domitian, who is regarded as an incarnation of Nero. But it can hardly be said of Domitian that *he was and is not,* nor is Domitian *one of the seven.* It is best interpreted as Nero redivivus, Anti-Christ. As the heads of the Beast symbolized emperors, so the *horns* (v. 12) symbolize kings, probably Parthian satraps. For popular superstition believed Nero to have escaped to the East and feared his return at the head of Parthian hosts. Three pretenders appeared between 69–88 A.D. under Nero's name, and claimed the imperial throne. The expectation here is that Nero will return in fury against the city which at the last rose against him. The Anti-Christ thinks he is accomplishing his own purposes, but he is really marching to his own destruction, which is God's purpose. The kings were unanimous in their purpose to destroy Rome (v. 13); God caused that unanimity, for he is all in all and works in all things. The forces which destroy Rome are themselves destroyed by the Lamb and the martyr host of warriors. The Lamb is called *Lord of lords* and *King of kings* (v. 14; cf. 19[16] Deut. 10[17] Dan. 2[47]), perhaps as a challenge to the title given to Domitian of "our Lord and our God." The significance of the title is also in the fact that, whatever the conflicts on earth between good and evil, the victory of goodness has already been won in heaven, and on that heavenly victory depends the ultimate victory on earth.

CHAPTER XVIII

The Doom of Rome. This was the vision promised to the Seer in 17[1].

1–3. A Great Angel. This angel comes down from heaven and announces the fall of Babylon, i.e., Rome, and tells how the ruins of the city have become *the dwelling place of unclean spirits and hateful birds.* The tense is the past tense of prophetic certainty; it represents that which was destined to be as though it had already happened.

4–20. Features That Will Accompany the Doom. Another voice from heaven summons the people of God to come forth out of the city (cf. Jer. 51[45] Mt. 24[16]) to escape the plagues by which she will be punished; and then in the style of prophetic passages from the O.T. chants a song of doom over her (cf. Isa. 13, 14, 34; Jer. 50, 51; Ezek. 26–28). Though Rome in her wantonness says *I will sit a queen, and am no widow, and shall in no wise see* *mourning* (v. 7; cf. Isa. 47⁸), double punishment will be her lot (Jer. 16¹⁸). Suddenly plagues will come upon her—pestilence, destruction, famine, and fire. If Nero and the Parthians are her destroyers, it would mean the cutting off of her food supplies, hence famine and pestilence (v. 8). The greatness of the calamity which shall overtake her is suggested by the dirges which those who have shared in her impurity shall sing. *The kings* shall stand at a distance and wail over her (v. 9), afraid lest they be themselves swallowed up in her destruction. *The merchants* (Ezek. 27³⁶) shall lament the loss of their trade (v. 11). The long list of imports into Rome closes dramatically as in Ezek. 27¹³ with *the souls of men* (v. 13). The reference is to the traffic in human life, in slavery or immorality or the shows of the amphitheater. The *shipowners* and sailors (Ezek. 27²⁷⁻³⁰) shall bewail the loss of their freights (v. 17). But *saints and apostles and prophets* are called upon to rejoice as in Jer. 51⁴⁸ because *the judgment of God* has been wrought over her (v. 20).

8. The word here translated *death* probably means "pestilence," and the word translated *mourning* may mean "destruction" (6⁸, note).

20. Charles puts this verse between vv. 23 and 24.

21–24. The Final Description of the Doom. This is preluded by a symbolic action on the part of another angel, who *throws a millstone into the sea* to represent the ruin of Rome (cf. Jer. 51⁶³, ⁶⁴). Then the description is resumed of the silence and desolation of the ruins. The familiar sounds of the household, of its work, its rejoicings, will be no more heard; the arts of civil life will cease; the light of the lamp will be extinguished (cf. Jer. 25¹⁰ Ezek. 26¹³). If Charles is right as to the position of v. 20 (see above), then the chapter ends with the summons to *the saints, apostles and prophets* to rejoice over the fate of the harlot city that was the cause of all the blood shed upon the earth (cf. Jer. 51⁴⁹). Rome could not be charged with all the martyrdoms which had occurred in the history of Israel, but as the mistress of the world Rome is held responsible for all that happened in the empire.

Was the Prophecy Fulfilled? Rome never was destroyed quite as this prophecy foretells, though the sack of the city by the Goths, the crumbling of her empire, and the decay of her power are facts of history. Gibbon quotes an Italian writer, Poggius, who in the fifteenth century described the ruins of the city as he had seen them. The last part of his description is apposite: "The Forum of the Roman people, where they assembled to enact their laws and elect their magistrates, is now inclosed for the cultivation of potherbs and thrown open for the reception of swine and buffaloes. The public and private edifices that were founded for eternity lie prostrate, naked and broken, like the limbs of a mighty giant: and the ruin is the more visible from the stupendous relics that have survived the injuries of time and fortune" (see *Decline and Fall of Roman Empire*, ch. 71). But the particular fulfillment of a prophecy like this is not its most important element. It had reference to a particular time and a particular city. But just as the Seer uses ancient prophecy about Babylon, Tyre, and Edom to describe the judgment of God on Rome, so the permanent value of his prophecy is in its message of *the victory of righteousness over evil*, even though evil arm itself with the strongest political, material and mechanical resources. In his commentary on Isa. 47, George Adam Smith reminds us that we must not choke our interest in such prophecies in the dust and ruins which were their first fulfillment, because Babylon never dies. John saw that this city of harlotries, of which the prophets had spoken, had come to life again in Rome. We may see the same spirit wherever there are *forgetfulness of God*, militarism, and the acquiescence in the existence of hideous and naked wrong because it has been long established, and because political and financial interests are supported by it. Perhaps the most common incarnation of this spirit is the *worship of wealth*. The description of the fate of such worship is found in vv. 11–16, which record the ruin of the commercial city, that lived only for success, and the loneliness of her mercenary life, for the merchants stood afar off from the city in her hour of destruction—the city that had only been to them a place of gain and pleasure. Babylon and Rome both stood for arrogance, hardness of heart, the worship of success, indifference to all the higher values of life. Against these things and their fate this vision is a memorable warning and John's words still have their personal summons—*Come forth, that ye have no fellowship with her sins* (v. 4).

CHAPTER XIX

1–10. The Heavenly Anthem Over the Doom of Rome. In 18²⁰ the Seer had appealed to the host of heaven. These verses are the response first by the angels, and then by the elders and the Cherubim (cf. 4¹¹ 5⁸⁻¹⁴ 11¹⁶), and then by the martyrs over the judgment on Rome. John's method is to set over against a vision of tribulation one of deliverance; and over against a proclamation of judgment on the enemies of Christ to set one of the ultimate blessedness of the redeemed. Actually the doom of Rome (ch. 18) is future; from the point of view of heaven it is past.

6. Read *Hallelujah! for the Lord God Almighty has become king.* There are two stages in the destruction of evil in the universe; the first was when Satan was cast out of heaven; the second is when Rome is destroyed and God becomes King of the earth. Again the writer has in mind Domitian's title, "Our Lord and our God."

7, 8. *The marriage of the Lamb.* The figure goes back to the O.T. representation of Jehovah married to Israel (Hos. 2^{19} Isa. 54^{1-8}). Here it denotes the indissoluble communion of Christ with the community of men and women whom he has purchased with his blood ($5^{6, 9}$ 7^{17} 14^{1}). This community is the martyrs, who reign with Christ for a thousand years; it is, indeed, the Holy City itself (21^{9} 22^{17}). It is the part of the church to make herself ready, and it is given her by God to clothe herself (cf. Phil. $2^{12, 13}$). The bright, pure raiment of the bride is in striking contrast with the harlot's vesture (17^{4} 18^{16}). This raiment is interpreted as *the righteous acts of the saints,* and refers to the spiritual bodies which the righteous have in accordance with their characters.

9. *They which are bidden.* All men are *called* by God, but when the time has come for the bride to become the wife of the Lamb the faithful are bidden, invited (Mt. 22^{3} Lk. 14^{8}), and upon those bidden this blessing is pronounced. There is a natural confusion in that the church is the bride and at the same time is the guests at the wedding supper.

10. This incident is repeated in $22^{8, 9}$, and may be an interpolation here. If not, what causes John to offer the homage is the overwhelming impression of the vision of heaven which he has seen. *The testimony of Jesus* may mean (1) the testimony which *men bear to Jesus;* if so, the angel is claiming that he is a fellow servant of all who have the prophetic spirit; or (2) the testimony *borne by Jesus,* i.e., the revelation made by him. Then the angel means that the spirit of prophecy is governed by the revelation of "the truth as it is in Jesus."

11–16. The Vision of a Divine Warrior on a White Horse Leading the Armies of Heaven. The subject of the marriage of the Lamb is not proceeded with until 21^{2}, but John recounts the judgments upon the Beast, the False Prophet and the Dragon. *The name no one knoweth but he himself* (v. 12) is variously interpreted. It may mean the Lord (Phil. 2^{11}); or Jehovah; or a name known only to Christ (cf. 3^{12}). The reference is to the belief that to know the name of a God gave one power over him. The name at least corresponds to his nature. It cannot be known to any on earth, for none can know the depths of his personality. *The Word of God* (v. 13) is the Messiah (cf. Jn. 1^{1}). But the conception of the Word is more akin to Heb. 4^{12} than to the prologue of the fourth Gospel. He is not here described as "the Word that tabernacled among men" giving them light and life, but as the Warrior-judge. *His flaming eyes* see through all deceit. Upon his head are the tokens of universal sovereignty. *The blood on his vesture* is not his own but of his foes (cf. Isa. 63^{1-3}). *The sharp sword* (v. 15) is the symbol of judicial condemnation (cf. 1^{16} 2^{12}). There follow him the white-clad armies of heaven on white horses—a symbol of victory. The two metaphors of the *winepress* and *the cup of wrath* (v. 15) are mixed (cf. $14^{10, 19}$, note). The meaning is that from the winepress trodden by the divine warrior (Isa. 63^{3}) flows the wine of the wrath of God, and his enemies are to be made to drink of it. Probably we should omit the words *on his garment* (v. 16) with some authorities. Then the reference is to the names of statues or to inscriptions which were often written on the thighs of statues. The picture is of the Divine Warrior leading his heavenly host and sweeping on against the armies of the Beast. So swift is the charge that their garments stream behind them and on the thigh of their Leader is disclosed the name *King of Kings, Lord of Lords* (cf. 17^{14}, note; 1 Tim. 6^{15}). Again a challenge to Domitian's title, "Our Lord and our God."

17, 18. The Vision of an Angel in Mid-Heaven Summoning the Birds of Prey to Feast on the Slain. (Cf. Ezek. 39^{17-20}.) There is a contrast between the great supper of God here and the marriage supper of the Lamb in v. 9. That the dead should be left unburied for the birds of prey to feast on added to the shame of defeat. In no way could the dishonor of these captains and mighty men be more forcefully described than in this.

19–21. The Final Battle of Armageddon. (See note on 16^{16}.) John describes the struggle of the Warrior on the white horse with the Beast, the False Prophet and the kings of the earth. The reason for the summoning of the birds of prey is now given. The battle has been fought between the heavenly Warrior and his foes. The *Beast* is Nero Anti-Christ, and his followers are the Parthian kings, whom Nero, when he returned, was expected to bring with him. The issue of the battle only is described. The Beast, i.e., the empire, and the False Prophet, i.e., the imperial priesthood, which practiced all kinds of magic to beguile men to worship Rome and her emperors (cf. $16^{13, 14}$ 13^{11}), are cast alive into *the lake of fire* (cf. $20^{10, 15}$ 21^{8}); and the rest of their army is slain and their corpses left to the birds to feed on.

CHAPTER XX

The Problem of the Rearrangement of Chapters 20–22. R. H. Charles' suggested rearrangement of these chapters, which in their present order seem to be confusing, is considered in the introduction, p. 1368.

1–3. The Binding of Satan for a Thousand Years. This is the climax of the divine judgments. Already Rome has fallen; the kings of the earth have been destroyed; the two Beasts have been cast into the lake of fire (19^{20}). As Satan's expulsion from heaven is connected with the birth and ascension of Christ (12^{1-11}), so his chaining here is connected with Christ's Second Coming.

2. *A thousand years.* Originally the Messianic kingdom was thought of as lasting forever (see pp. 208–9), but in the last century B.C. this earth came to be regarded as wholly evil and suitable for the manifestation of the Kingdom only temporarily. In the apocryphal apocalypse, the Secrets of Enoch (32^{2}–33^{2}), the history of the world is divided into days, each day representing 1,000 years (cf. Psa. 90^{4} 2 Pet. 3^{8}). Since, including the day of rest, there were seven days of creation (Gen. 1) the world was to last for 7,000 years, the last day, or 1,000 years, being a Sabbath-millennium. John identifies the 1,000 years of rest and blessedness in the world's history with the period of the reign of the Messiah on earth. The number 1,000 is symbolical, like most of the numbers which John uses. It is described as *for a little time* in v. 3. The idea behind it is that of perfection and completeness.

4–6. The Vision of the Glorified Martyrs Reigning With Christ for the Thousand Years. The apocalyptic writers generally in their conception of the Messianic kingdom pictured the saints as reigning with the Messiah. Jesus had used these thought forms to convey his spiritual message of the reality of judgment and reward (Mt. 19^{28}; cf. 1 Cor. $6^{2, 3}$). Here it is not those who are alive when the Lord comes who will reign with him (cf. 1 Thess. 4^{14-17}). John does not believe there will be any survivors of the faithful on earth; all will have suffered martyrdom before the Day of the Lord comes. And it is not all who have "died in the Lord" who are to share his reign with him. Only the martyrs will have this reward of loyalty. In 6^{11} the souls of the martyrs are given each *a white robe*. i.e., a spiritual resurrection body when they are waiting for their roll to be complete. In the present passage, the roll is complete and the host of the martyrs rise *in the first resurrection* (see v. 5 below), in which the rest of the dead take no part. This is peculiar to John and is due to the emphasis he lays on martyrdom. In his day that might well have been stressed as the only test of loyalty, although we know that there are other tests. He defines these martyrs as *priests of God and of Christ* (v. 6), perhaps as having special functions of evangelizing the nations during the reign of Christ on earth.

5. *The first resurrection* has been interpreted in a spiritual sense as a resurrection from the death of sin to the life of righteousness. But it is clearly the reward of martyrdom at the end of life on earth, and to allegorize it away is to introduce a method of interpretation which takes most of the significance out of language.

6. *The second death* is the death at the end of the Messianic kingdom after the Last Judgment, as distinguished from the physical death which is the lot of all humanity (cf. 20^{14} 21^{8} Mt. 10^{8}).

7–10. The Vision of the End of the Messianic Kingdom. At the end of the one thousand years Satan is loosed and with Gog and Magog attacks *the beloved city.* He is cast into the lake of fire where already the Beast and the False Prophet had been cast (19^{20}). *Gog* is from the land of Magog in Ezek. 38^{2}. In Gen. 10^{2} he is called Magog, son of Japheth. Elsewhere they are both leaders in battle against God and Messiah. Here they represent all the faithless upon earth.

11–15. The Last Judgment. *A great white throne* is set, in the light from which the secrets of all hearts are revealed. Its whiteness symbolizes the equity of the judgment. He who sits upon it is not named, and he is alone on the judgment seat, not accompanied by the martyrs as in v. 4. *The heaven and the earth disappear.* Jewish contemporary thought accepted this notion of the end of all things (cf. 2 Pet. 3^{10-12}) and the beginning anew (cf. 21^{1}); but perhaps here the thought is that in the presence of the Supreme Judge men lose consciousness of everything else. All are judged *according to their works* and for this *the books are opened* (v. 12). These (cf. Dan. 7^{10}) recorded the deeds done in the flesh, good or bad. And there is *another book* which had in it the names of the saved (cf. 3^{5} 13^{8} 17^{8}). The books of deeds were "vouchers for the Book of Life." Before the throne stand *the dead given up by Death and Hades* (v. 13; in this book Hades is the intermediate state where the souls of the righteous are). The sea too surrenders those whom it has swallowed up. Death and Hades are cast into the lake of fire (v. 14; cf. Mt. 25[41]). They are personified as two demons in 1 Cor. 15[26, 54].

13. *Sea.* Charles says that this reference to the sea involves an idea of bodily resurrection which was common in rabbinic tradition but is not taught elsewhere in this book or in the N.T. It would seem from v. 11 that the sea had already disappeared. So Charles reads—*and the treasuries gave up their dead*, i.e., the treasuries which contained the souls of the righteous.

CHAPTER XXI

1–8. The Vision of the New Universe and its Inhabitants. The Seer takes up again the theme of 19[7f.], the marriage of the Lamb. Earth and heaven having perished (20[11]) a new universe appears, new not in the time sense of being young and not old, but *new in quality*, transformed, like but unlike the other (cf. Isa. 65[17]). There is *no sea* in it (v. 1). This echoes the horror of the peoples of the ancient world, and especially of the Jews, of the sea, "the unplumb'd, salt, estranging sea," the great divider of men and lands. There could be no such devouring enemy of man in the world made perfect. John sees *the new Jerusalem coming down from heaven as a bride* (cf. Isa. 61[10]–62[5] Mt. 22[2] 25[10]). Before describing it he relates what he heard about the meaning of the vision. This *new Jerusalem* (cf. Gal. 4[26]) signifies the manifestation of the divine presence (v. 3); *God is to dwell with men*, and the inhabitants of the city are to be *his peoples*. The plural of this word *peoples* is sometimes used with the same meaning as the singular, but if the plural here has its full force, then the meaning is that there will be one kingdom but many peoples, as in Jn. 10[16] our Lord speaks of "one flock" but "many folds." By the presence of God himself all sorrow and even death are banished (v. 4). He himself proclaims that he makes all things new (Isa. 43[19] 2 Cor. 5[17]). All will have won in this Kingdom the "more life and fuller" which is beyond the pain and travail of this life. This glorious vision is related to the present distress of those for whom he writes, by the message from God himself, who holds out *hope to him that is athirst* (v. 6). There follows a list of those who have disfranchised themselves—*the fearful* and others, who in the struggle with the Beast have played the coward, denied the faith and worshiped the emperor. Not for them the divine sonship, but, rather, *the lake of fire* (cf. 19[20]), the dreadful death at the Last Judgment after their physical death (cf. 2[11] 20[6, 14, 15]).

6. *Alpha and Omega.* See note below on 22[13].

9–27. Description of the City. (Continued in 22[1-5].) One of the seven angels who had the bowls bids John come to see the bride. Perhaps it was the same angel who showed him the judgment of the great harlot (17[1]). The contrast is a stimulus to awe and hope. The description that follows is based upon the idealized conception of prophets and psalmists. Though, as they knew it, the city was cursed by the wickedness of its rulers, the idolatry of its people, and often despoiled by its enemies, it remained the city of God. It may well be that in the pagan idea of heaven as the city of the gods with the sun and moon and twelve signs of the zodiac is the germ of the Jewish conception. But into these words a new idealized meaning was implanted. The Jerusalem that now is was unworthy to be the center of the Messianic kingdom, but the hope arose that its heavenly counterpart (Gal. 4[26]), which had been prepared in heaven from the beginning, would come down to be the abode of God's Messiah on earth. This idea of the heavenly Jerusalem was not widely held before the destruction of the earthly city in 70 A.D., but the conception of an idealized city is found in Isa. 54[11] Ezek. 40. John has, however, remolded the older pictures "nearer to the heart's desire." The earthly Temple was the symbol of God's presence; the new Jerusalem has the Shekinah, the glory of his presence (cf. v. 3). It is surrounded by a wall, and it has twelve gates which bear the names of the tribes of Israel, and the foundations of the city have the names of the twelve apostles engraven on them (v. 12). This symbolizes the connection between the O.T. and the Christian Church. *The wall* marks the security of its citizens, a protection against the wicked and unclean (21[27]). *The twelve gates* each with a guardian angel denote that it can be entered from different sides and in different ways. It is not required of those who enter that they should be limited to one language or race or point of view. The angel *measures the city* to reveal the meaning of it to John (vv. 15–17). It is a *square*, the symbol of perfection to the Greeks. In v. 16 it is described as a *cube* following the analogy of the Holy of Holies. Each side or perhaps all the sides together measure *twelve thousand furlongs*, nearly fifteen hundred miles. The *foundations of the walls* are *pre-*

cious stones (vv. 19–21), which correspond on the whole with those on the high priest's breastplate (Ex. 28[17-20]). These were connected with the signs of the zodiac, but are given here in the reverse order from that which the sun follows through those signs. The impression which this description makes is of perfect beauty. Goodness, truth and beauty are the three eternal values which belong to the life of the spirit. All are characteristic of the city of God. Even the splendor of the sun is put to shame by *the glory of God* himself (v. 23). The *gates of the city* are always open to the nations (v. 25), and as cities of the earth are enriched by the gifts of kings and nations, so the glory and honor of the nations shall be brought into this city (v. 26; Isa. 60[19]). No unclean or false persons are allowed to enter but only those whose names are in the Book of Life (v. 27).

CHAPTER XXII

1–5. Description of the City Continued. (See 21[9-27].) In the midst of the heavenly way there runs a *river* like the river in Eden which watered the garden (cf. 7[16, 17] 21[6] Ezek. 47[1-12] Jer. 2[13] Zech. 14[8] Jn. 4[10]). On each side of the river are *trees of life* (the singular is generic), which bear twelve different kinds of fruit, one each month, and the leaves are for *the healing of the nations* (cf. Ezek. 47[12]). There shall be in this city *no accursed things* (cf. Zech. 14[11] Isa. 59[2]). God's servants having *his name on their foreheads* (7[3] 14[1]), i.e., his character stamped upon them, are qualified for the vision of himself (cf. Mt. 5[8]). *He shall give them light* (v. 5) is a shortened form of "He shall cause his face to shine upon them" (Psa. 67[1] 80[3, 7, 19]).

3. *His servants shall do him service* (A.S.V. *serve him*). There is a familiar story of a monk who in his early life, after having studied this book with some companions, was asked by the teacher which promise in the book seemed to him most attractive. He answered, "His servants shall serve him."

One naturally asks the question, *Is this kingdom present or future?* Is it an idealized representation of the Christian Church or a picture of a perfect state of society not yet realized on earth? The ideal city of the future is an ideal for the present. Socrates in Plato's *Republic* says that perhaps in heaven is laid up a pattern of the ideal city (which Glaucon, his interlocutor, says is not to be found anywhere on earth) for him who wishes to behold it and beholding to organize himself accordingly. And the question of its present or future existence on earth is quite unimportant. For in any case he will adopt the practices of such a city to the exclusion of those of any other (cf. Phil. 3[20]). No process of development or mechanical progress is here conceived as producing this city. It is not through an orderly evolution but after the crisis of judgment that it comes down from heaven. In this ideal city John sees *the bride of the Lamb* (21[2]), the society of the redeemed pure and spotless. In it Christ sees of the travail of his soul and is satisfied (Isa. 53[11]).

The Epilogue and Benediction. (Vv. 6–21.) These closing passages contain various testimonies, warnings, and invitations, an adjuration, and a benediction.

6, 7. Christ's Testimony to John's Book. The most significant part of the message is in v. 7, *Behold, I come quickly* (cf. 3[11] 1[7]).

8, 9. John's Own Testimony. A last warning against angel worship (cf. 19[9, 10] Col. 2[18]).

10–15. Final Injunctions and Warnings. John is forbidden to seal the book (cf. 10[4] Dan. 12[4] Isa. 8[16, 17]). The reference is to the sealing of apocalypses, i.e., the withholding of them until the actual time of the author. V. 11 suggests that the character that has been formed is fixed or that the present age is so near its conclusion that there is not time for change. *Christ is coming quickly* and each will be rewarded as he deserves (v. 12). He is *the Alpha and Omega* (v. 13), the first and last letters of the Greek alphabet (cf. 1[8, 11] 21[6]). This was an ancient saying even in Plato's time and originally seems to have been "Zeus is the beginning and the middle and the end of all things" (cf. Rom. 11[36]). God is the initial cause, the sustaining cause and the final cause of all things.

"Yea through life, death, through sorrow and
  through sinning
 Christ shall suffice me, for he hath sufficed;
Christ is the end, for Christ was the beginning,
 Christ the beginning, for the end is Christ."
—F. W. H. Myers, *St. Paul.*

Vv. 14, 15 show that character alone, not race, nor position, nor birth, decides men's fitness for the Kingdom. To enter the gates must precede the eating of the tree, but John may be thinking of Christ as the tree of life, and as the gate into the city; those who partake of him enter the city; those who find in him the way of life know him as the gate into the city. *Every one that loveth and maketh a lie*, i.e., makes falsehood his object and practices it. This is put as the climax to the list. Those who deny the truth cannot have part with Him who is the Way because he is the Truth, and the Truth because he is the Life (Jn. 14[6]).

16. Further Testimony of Jesus. Jesus

claims to be the root and branches, and so to combine in himself all the Messianic claims of David's family (cf. 5⁵ Isa. 11¹, ¹⁰ Mt. 1¹). He is *the morning star* (2²⁸), i.e., in him is all that Israel hoped for in the past; in him is the promise of all that is to come (cf. Num. 24¹⁷ Mt. 2² Lk. 1⁷⁸).

17. The Invitation of the Spirit and of the Bride. The Spirit is Christ himself (cf. 2⁷, ¹¹, ¹⁷), and the Bride (cf. 21²) is the inhabitants of the heavenly Jerusalem, and those who have heard and accepted the message are those who are *thirsting* for life and truth. It is not, as it is sometimes understood, a call to Christ to come. He has come already and is reigning in the city (20⁴).

18, 19. Solemn Adjuration Respecting Any Who Should Alter the Words of the Book. It was customary to append such among Jewish and Christian writers (Deut. 4² 12³²). The fact that the words happen to come at the end of the English Bible has led some to suppose that they applied to the whole Bible itself. This, of course, is not so. As a matter of fact, several N.T. books were written *after* Revelation (see p. 858a).

20, 21. Christ's Final Words, John's Prayer and Benediction. *Come, Lord Jesus* recalls *Marana tha* (1 Cor. 16²²), meaning "our Lord come," or, "our Lord has come." The benediction shows that the book was intended to be read in the church services (cf. 1³). *The saints* means the faithful. Paul uses the word for the whole body of the baptized (Rom. 16¹⁵ 1 Cor. 16¹ 2 Cor. 1¹ Eph. 1¹ Col. 1⁴).

The Real Value of the Revelation of John. The expectation of the immediate return of Christ has been with John all through. His final message is *it is at hand.* But the Lord did not come when John anticipated. The value of this book is not in its accuracy of prediction of the future but in its insight into the things that are unseen and in its power to kindle faith in those things. The O.T. prophets were true prophets, even if some of the things they predicted were never realized. They used the crises of national history to set forth the true ideals and destiny of their nation. It is because their words are a testimony to the moral order in the universe that they arouse the conscience and have a message for times quite other than those in which they were written. So John, dealing with the consummation of all things, bears witness that behind all the events of time is a moral order, and that moral order will be made clear in the revelation of Christ as Redeemer and Lord. In regard to the coming of Christ, Swete points out that, according to Paul, it takes place with the change from flesh and blood into the spiritual body, so that it is not likely to be apparent to our present organs of sense. It may be that the change in ourselves will be the appearing of Christ: Christ most truly appears according as he becomes enthroned in human hearts and his spirit becomes enthroned in social institutions.

Like the other apocalyptists, John felt sure that the kingdom of God under the conditions of this world could be only temporary. Only the spiritual could be permanent. Therefore he looked for a new order, a spiritual order, a Jerusalem that was to be transformed to the conditions of that spiritual order where the saints would dwell forever with God and with the Lamb. The value of these visions is that they have taught men to look forward, not backward, to strive toward an ideal which men recognize as that which ought to be, and that to which the whole creation moves. The ideal is a new state of society on earth, of which the foundations are peace and brotherhood, justice and mercy. That has been given a hundred different expressions among men, but no more fitting symbol has been found for it than that of the heavenly Jerusalem. But John did not regard this as the end. It was a means to a spiritual kingdom, in which alone man's true destiny and his eternal home could be realized. The heavenly Jerusalem answers to the earthly hopes of others besides Christians; the new Jerusalem is the completion of hopes which can never be realized on earth. And that "more life and fuller" which Christianity has inspired men to hope for has never been more adequately described than in 21³,⁴. On the one hand are the visions of the doom of the lost, which, though in some respects more Jewish than Christian, may remind us that persistent rebellion against God renders the soul liable to some measure of eternal disability and loss. On the other hand are his visions of the victory, peace, consolation, worship, knowledge and fullness of perfect being. Dante follows out these by his description of the redeemed shining like a great white rose unfolding itself petal by petal in the presence of the glory of God.

> "In fashion, as a snow white rose, lay then
> Before my view the saintly multitude,
> Which in his own blood Christ espoused."
> —*Paradise*, canto xxxi.

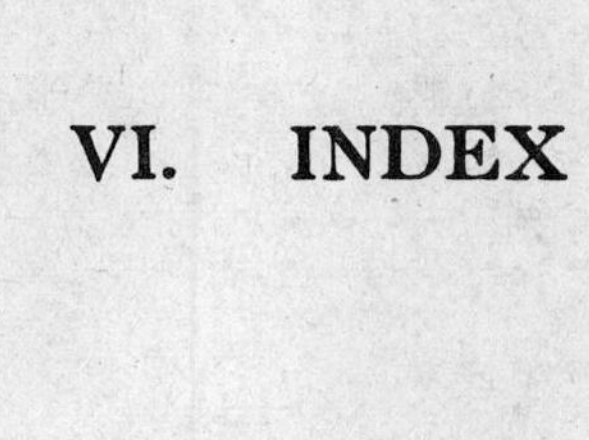

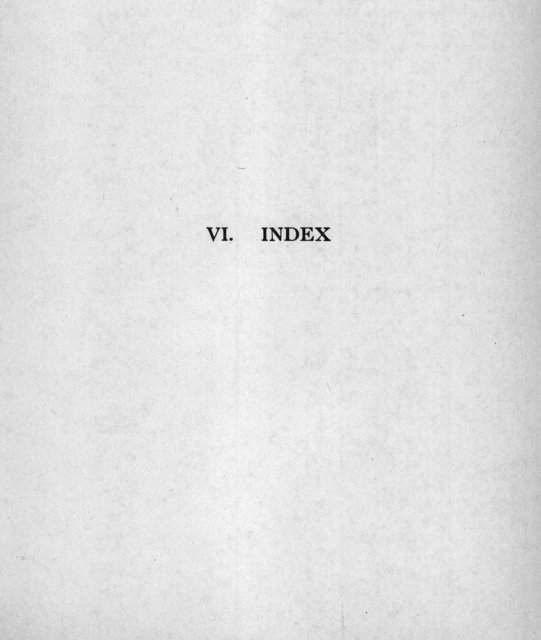

VI. INDEX

VI. INDEX

NOTE—While this Index is fairly extensive, it is in no sense exhaustive. The purpose has not been to provide a concordance. Names of individuals or of places are listed only when the reference contains some definite statement about them. If a reference is not found under a given word, it may frequently be found under a related word. The letters a and b following a number refer respectively to the left and right columns of the page. See also the Explanations on pages xv and xvi.

D

E

G

I

J

K

M

R

S